YEARBOOK OF THE UNITED NATIONS 1992

Volume 46

Yearbook of the United Nations, 1992

Volume 46   Sales No. E.93.I.1

Prepared by the Yearbook Section of the Department of Public Information, United Nations, New York. Although the *Yearbook* is based on official sources, it is not an official record.

Chief Editor: Yobert K. Shamapande.

Senior Editors: Kathryn Gordon, Christine B. Koerner.

Editors/Writers: Lynn Homa, Matthias Gueldner, Peter Jackson, Tamara Lee, Donald Paneth, Melody C. Pfeiffer.

Contributing Editors/Writers: Eugene Forson, Dmitri Marchenkov, Juanita J. B. Phelan.

Copy Editors: Alison M. Koppelman, Ian Steele.

Indexer: Elaine P. Adam.

Editorial Assistants: Lawri M. Moore, Nidia H. Morisset, Joyce B. Rosenblum, Leonard M. Simon, Elizabeth Tabert.

Typesetters: Andrew T. Angelopoulos, Sunita Chabra, Laura Frischeisen.

YEARBOOK
OF THE
UNITED
NATIONS
1992

Volume 46

Department of Public Information
United Nations, New York

Martinus Nijhoff Publishers
DORDRECHT / BOSTON / LONDON

Published by Martinus Nijhoff Publishers

P.O. Box 163, 3300 AD Dordrecht, The Netherlands

Kluwer Academic Publishers incorporates the
publishing programmes of Martinus Nijhoff Publishers

Sold and distributed in the U.S.A. and Canada
by Kluwer Academic Publishers,
101 Philip Drive, Norwell, MA 02061, U.S.A.

In all other countries, sold and distributed
by Kluwer Academic Publishers Group,
P.O. Box 322, 3300 AH Dordrecht, The Netherlands

Yearbook of the United Nations, 1992
Vol. 46
ISBN: 0-7923-2583-4
ISSN: 0082-8521

UNITED NATIONS PUBLICATION
SALES NO. E.93.I.1

Printed in the United States of America

Foreword

THE CHARTER OF THE UNITED NATIONS envisages an Organization actively working to achieve international peace and security, universally striving to advance justice and human rights, and strongly committed to promoting social progress and economic development.

Embarking upon a new era, the international community has grasped an exciting new challenge. The Security Council's historic meeting in January 1992, the first ever at the level of heads of State and Government, signalled a new international commitment to the purposes and principles of the Charter. The presence of the United Nations in an increasing number of areas in the world reflects this new level of determination and international commitment.

We see a new and unique opportunity for progress. Among the peoples of the world, a new global awareness is beginning to take hold. Among States, there is a new sense of purpose and a recognition that new and urgent challenges require a united and determined international response. Expectations remain high, even as the United Nations struggles to adapt old machinery to its newly expanding responsibilities.

The changed international outlook is reflected in all aspects of the work of the Organization. The new spirit of cooperation is reflected in issues of peace and security, in matters of economic and social development, in the provision of humanitarian assistance, in the field of human rights, and elsewhere. In 1992, at the "Earth Summit" in Rio de Janeiro, the largest ever gathering of world leaders adopted a new plan of action, known as "Agenda 21", for sustainable development in the twenty-first century.

The United Nations, which now comprises an international community of 184 Member States, embodies humanity's highest aspirations for peace, progress and development. As a record of United Nations activities, the 1992 *Yearbook of the United Nations* is an indispensable guide and resource. It provides a uniquely valuable vantage point from which to assess our collective progress towards the goals of the United Nations Charter and the horizons of the twenty-first century.

Boutros BOUTROS-GHALI
Secretary-General
New York
October 1993

Contents

FOREWORD, by SECRETARY-GENERAL BOUTROS BOUTROS-GHALI   v

ABOUT THE 1992 EDITION OF THE *YEARBOOK*   xiv

ABBREVIATIONS COMMONLY USED IN THE *YEARBOOK*   xv

EXPLANATORY NOTE ON DOCUMENTS   xvi

REPORT OF THE SECRETARY-GENERAL
ON THE WORK OF THE ORGANIZATION   3

Part One: *Political and security questions*

I.   INTERNATIONAL PEACE AND SECURITY   33

MAINTENANCE OF INTERNATIONAL SECURITY AND STRENGTHENING OF THE INTER-
NATIONAL SECURITY SYSTEM, 33: Heads of State and Government Security Council
summit, 33; "An agenda for peace": preventive diplomacy, peacemaking and peace-
keeping, 35; Maintenance of international security, 41; Implementation of the 1970
Declaration, 42; Science and peace, 43. REVIEW OF PEACE-KEEPING OPERATIONS, 44:
Protection of peace-keeping personnel, 48. REGIONAL ASPECTS OF INTERNATIONAL
PEACE AND SECURITY, 49: Strengthening of security in the Mediterranean region,
49; South Atlantic zone of peace, 51. AERIAL INCIDENTS AND THE LIBYAN ARAB JAMA-
HIRIYA, 52: Charges of air terrorism, 52; Incident at Venezuela's Embassy in Tripoli, 57.

II.   DISARMAMENT   59

UN ROLE IN DISARMAMENT, 59: United Nations machinery, 59. MAJOR TRENDS AND
DEVELOPMENTS, 63: Chemical weapons, 64; Non-proliferation, 67; Regional disarmament, 70; Transparency, confidence-building and the Arms Register, 75; Nuclear arms limitation and disarmament, 79; Conventional armaments and advanced
technology, 94; Prevention of an arms race in outer space, 97; Economic aspects of
disarmament, 100; Disarmament and the environment, 101. INFORMATION AND
STUDIES, 103: World Disarmament Campaign, 103; Disarmament Week, 106; Disarmament studies and research, 106.

III.   PEACEFUL USES OF OUTER SPACE   110

SCIENCE, TECHNOLOGY AND LAW, 110: Space science and technology, 110; Space law,
116. SPACECRAFT LAUNCHINGS, 122.

IV.   OTHER POLITICAL QUESTIONS   123

INFORMATION, 123: Mass communication, 123; UN public information, 125. RADI-
ATION EFFECTS, 129. ANTARCTICA, 130: Antarctica and the environment, 133; Participation of South Africa, 133. INSTITUTIONAL QUESTIONS, 133: Admission to UN
membership, 133; Institutional machinery, 140; Commemoration of the fiftieth anniversary of the United Nations in 1995, 142. COOPERATION WITH OTHER ORGANI-
ZATIONS, 142: League of Arab States, 142; Organization of the Islamic Conference,
144; Conference on Security and Cooperation in Europe, 146; Observer status for
the International Organization for Migration, 146; Other organizations, 147.

Part Two: *Regional questions*

I.   AFRICA 151

SOUTH AFRICA AND APARTHEID, 151: Other aspects, 165; Relations with South Africa, 168; Aid programmes and inter-agency cooperation, 174. OTHER STATES, 178: Angola, 178; Comorian island of Mayotte, 188; Eritrea, 189; Liberia, 191; Mozambique, 193; Somalia, 198. COOPERATION BETWEEN OAU AND THE UN SYSTEM, 214.

II.   AMERICAS 218

CENTRAL AMERICA SITUATION, 218: El Salvador situation, 222; Guatemala situation, 231; Nicaragua, 232. THE CARIBBEAN, 232. OTHER QUESTIONS RELATING TO THE AMERICAS, 238: Cooperation with OAS, 238.

III.   ASIA AND THE PACIFIC 240

EAST ASIA, 240: Korean question, 240. SOUTH-EAST ASIA, 241: Cambodia situation, 241. SOUTH ASIA, 262: Papua New Guinea–Solomon Islands, 262. SOUTHERN AND WESTERN ASIA, 262: Afghanistan situation, 262; Cyprus question, 265; Iran, 272; Iraq-Kuwait situation, 275.

IV.   EUROPE 326

YUGOSLAVIA SITUATION, 326: Croatia, 327; Bosnia and Herzegovina, 344; Implementation of the weapons embargo and sanctions, 381; UNPROFOR financing, 383; Former Yugoslav Republic of Macedonia, 386. BALTIC STATES, 387. OTHER STATES, 388: Armenia-Azerbaijan, 388; Georgia, 391; Tajikistan, 394.

V.   MIDDLE EAST 395

MIDDLE EAST SITUATION, 395: Proposed peace conference under UN auspices, 396; United Nations Truce Supervision Organization, 399. PALESTINE QUESTION, 399: Public information activities, 402; Jerusalem, 403; Assistance to Palestinians, 404. INCIDENTS AND DISPUTES INVOLVING ARAB COUNTRIES AND ISRAEL, 408: Iraq and Israel, 408; Lebanon, 408; Israel and the Syrian Arab Republic, 415. TERRITORIES OCCUPIED BY ISRAEL, 420: Fourth Geneva Convention, 426; Expulsion and deportation of Palestinians, 427; Palestinian detainees, 431; Israeli measures against educational institutions, 433; Golan Heights, 434; Israeli settlements, 435; Economic and social repercussions of Israeli settlements, 437. PALESTINE REFUGEES, 440: UN Agency for Palestine refugees, 440.

VI.   REGIONAL ECONOMIC AND SOCIAL ACTIVITIES 456

REGIONAL COOPERATION, 456. AFRICA, 459: Economic and social trends, 462; Activities in 1992, 465; Programme, administrative and organizational questions, 477. ASIA AND THE PACIFIC, 477: Economic and social trends, 479; Activities in 1992, 482; Organizational questions, 492. EUROPE, 493: Economic trends, 494; Activities in 1992, 496. LATIN AMERICA AND THE CARIBBEAN, 503: Economic trends, 504; Activities in 1992, 505; Cooperation between the United Nations and the Latin American Economic System, 513; Organizational questions, 515. WESTERN ASIA, 515: Economic trends, 516; Activities in 1992, 519; Organizational questions, 522.

Part Three: *Economic and social questions*

I.   DEVELOPMENT POLICY AND INTERNATIONAL ECONOMIC COOPERATION 525

INTERNATIONAL ECONOMIC RELATIONS, 525: Development and international economic cooperation, 525. ECONOMIC AND SOCIAL TRENDS AND POLICY, 539. DEVELOPMENT PLANNING AND PUBLIC ADMINISTRATION, 540. DEVELOPING COUNTRIES, 542.

II. OPERATIONAL ACTIVITIES FOR DEVELOPMENT   550

GENERAL ASPECTS, 550: Financing of operational activities, 556. TECHNICAL
COOPERATION THROUGH UNDP, 557: UNDP Governing Council, 558; UNDP operational activities, 558; Programme planning and management, 563; Financing, 566;
Organizational issues, 569. OTHER TECHNICAL COOPERATION, 570: UN programmes, 570; United Nations Volunteers, 571; Technical cooperation among developing countries, 572. UN CAPITAL DEVELOPMENT FUND, 574.

III. SPECIAL ECONOMIC, HUMANITARIAN AND
      DISASTER RELIEF ASSISTANCE   575

SPECIAL ECONOMIC ASSISTANCE, 575: Critical situation in Africa, 575; Other economic assistance, 581. HUMANITARIAN ASSISTANCE AND DISASTER RELIEF, 584: Coordination of humanitarian assistance and disaster relief, 584. HUMANITARIAN AS-
SISTANCE ACTIVITIES, 588: Africa, 588; Asia, 597; Europe, 600; Latin America and
the Caribbean, 601. DISASTERS, 603: Disaster relief activities, 603.

IV. INTERNATIONAL TRADE, FINANCE AND TRANSPORT   611

EIGHTH SESSION OF UNCTAD, 611. INTERNATIONAL TRADE, 615: Trade policy, 616;
Trade promotion and facilitation, 619; Trade facilitation, 620; Restrictive business
practices, 622; Commodities, 622; Environment and trade, 628; Consumer protection, 629; Services, 629. FINANCE, 630: Financial policy, 630. TRANSPORT, 639: Maritime transport, 639. UNCTAD STRUCTURE, PROGRAMME AND FINANCES, 640: Institutional matters, 640; UNCTAD programme, 641.

V. TRANSNATIONAL CORPORATIONS   644

DRAFT CODE OF CONDUCT, 644: Bilateral, regional and international arrangements,
645. STANDARDS OF ACCOUNTING AND REPORTING, 645. COMMISSION ON TNCs, 646:
TNCs in South Africa, 646; Contribution to UNCED, 647; TNCs and international economic relations, 648. CENTRE ON TNCs, 649.

VI. NATURAL RESOURCES, ENERGY AND CARTOGRAPHY   654

NATURAL RESOURCES, 654: Exploration, 654; Committee on Natural Resources, 654;
Coordination of UN activities, 655; Mineral resources, 655; Water resources, 655.
ENERGY, 657: Energy resources development, 657; New and renewable energy
resources, 658; Energy use and air emissions, 659; Nuclear energy, 660. CARTOG-
RAPHY, 661.

VII. SCIENCE AND TECHNOLOGY   663

SCIENCE AND TECHNOLOGY FOR DEVELOPMENT, 663: Implementation of the Vienna
Programme of Action, 663; Strengthening technological capacity in developing countries, 664; Science for sustainable development, 665; UN Fund for Science and Technology for Development, 665; Operational activities, 665. TECHNOLOGY TRANSFER,
666. ORGANIZATIONAL MATTERS, 668.

VIII. ENVIRONMENT   670

UN CONFERENCE ON ENVIRONMENT AND DEVELOPMENT, 670: Action taken by the
Conference, 670. GENERAL ASPECTS, 681: Sustainable development, 681; International conventions, 681; Global Environment Facility, 684. ENVIRONMENTAL ACTIVI-
TIES, 684: State of the environment, 684; Protection against harmful products and
wastes, 685; Ecosystems, 685. PROGRAMME AND FINANCES OF UNEP, 689: Finances,
689. ENVIRONMENTAL ASPECTS OF POLITICAL, ECONOMIC AND OTHER ISSUES, 690.

IX. POPULATION AND HUMAN SETTLEMENTS   693

POPULATION, 693: 1994 International Conference on Population and Development,
693; UN Population Fund, 696; Other population activities, 701. HUMAN SETTLE-
MENTS, 702: Conference on Human Settlements, 702; UN Centre for Human Settlements (Habitat), 704.

X. HUMAN RIGHTS 709

DISCRIMINATION, 709: Racial discrimination, 709; Other aspects of discrimination, 715. CIVIL AND POLITICAL RIGHTS, 726: Covenant on Civil and Political Rights and Optional Protocols, 726; Self-determination of peoples, 727; Rights of detained persons, 734; Disappearance of persons, 741; Other aspects of civil and political rights, 747. ECONOMIC, SOCIAL AND CULTURAL RIGHTS, 751: Covenant on Economic, Social and Cultural Rights, 752; Right to development, 753; Right to an adequate standard of living, 754; Extreme poverty, 754; Right to own property, 755; Right to adequate housing, 756. ADVANCEMENT OF HUMAN RIGHTS, 756: National institutions for human rights protection, 758; UN machinery, 758; 1993 World Conference on Human Rights, 763; Public information activities, 765; Advisory services, 766; International human rights instruments, 768; Electoral processes, 772; Regional arrangements, 775; Responsibility to promote and protect human rights, 776; Internally displaced persons and humanitarian assistance, 777. HUMAN RIGHTS VIOLATIONS, 778: Africa, 778; Asia and the Pacific, 784; Europe and the Mediterranean, 794; Latin America and the Caribbean, 801; Middle East, 808; Mass exoduses, 809; Genocide, 810; Other aspects of human rights violations, 810. OTHER HUMAN RIGHTS QUESTIONS, 812: Additional Protocols I and II to the 1949 Geneva Conventions, 812; Rights of the child, 812; Youth and human rights, 815; Women, 815; Human rights and science and technology, 816; Human rights of disabled persons, 816; Human rights and peace, 817; Trade union rights, 817.

XI. HEALTH, FOOD AND NUTRITION 818

HEALTH, 818. FOOD AND AGRICULTURE, 824: World food situation, 824; Food aid, 826; Food and agricultural development, 828. NUTRITION, 829.

XII. HUMAN RESOURCES, SOCIAL AND CULTURAL DEVELOPMENT 832

HUMAN RESOURCES, 832: UN research and training institutes, 832. SOCIAL AND CULTURAL DEVELOPMENT, 834: Social aspects of development, 834; Crime prevention and criminal justice, 841.

XIII. WOMEN 863

ADVANCEMENT OF WOMEN, 863: Implementation of the Nairobi Strategies, 863; Research and Training Institute for the Advancement of Women, 867. WOMEN AND DEVELOPMENT, 869: UN Development Fund for Women, 872. STATUS OF WOMEN, 873. ELIMINATION OF DISCRIMINATION AGAINST WOMEN, 877.

XIV. CHILDREN, YOUTH AND AGEING PERSONS 880

CHILDREN, 880: UN Children's Fund, 880. YOUTH, 887. AGEING PERSONS, 889.

XV. REFUGEES AND DISPLACED PERSONS 892

PROGRAMME AND FINANCES OF UNHCR, 892: Programme policy, 892; Continuation of UNCHR, 894; Financial and administrative questions, 895. REFUGEE ASSISTANCE AND PROTECTION, 896: Assistance, 896; Refugee protection, 904.

XVI. DRUGS OF ABUSE 906

Drug abuse and international control, 906; Supply and demand, 919; Conventions, 925; Organizational questions, 926.

XVII. STATISTICS 927

XVIII. INSTITUTIONAL ARRANGEMENTS 932

RESTRUCTURING QUESTIONS, 932: Revitalization of the Economic and Social Council, 934. ECONOMIC AND SOCIAL COUNCIL, 936: 1992 sessions, 936; Cooperation with other organizations, 938; Other organizational matters, 940. COORDINATION IN THE UN SYSTEM, 941: ACC activities, 941; CPC activities, 942. OTHER INSTITUTIONAL QUESTIONS, 942: Work programmes of the Second and Third Committees of the General Assembly, 942.

Part Four: *Trusteeship and decolonization*

I. QUESTIONS RELATING TO DECOLONIZATION 945
1960 DECLARATION ON COLONIAL COUNTRIES, 945. OTHER GENERAL QUESTIONS,
959. OTHER COLONIAL TERRITORIES, 961.

II. INTERNATIONAL TRUSTEESHIP SYSTEM 973
TRUST TERRITORY OF THE PACIFIC ISLANDS, 973. OTHER ASPECTS OF THE INTER-
NATIONAL TRUSTEESHIP SYSTEM, 975.

Part Five: *Legal questions*

I. INTERNATIONAL COURT OF JUSTICE 979
Judicial work of the Court, 979; Other questions, 986.

II. LEGAL ASPECTS OF INTERNATIONAL POLITICAL RELATIONS 987
INTERNATIONAL LAW COMMISSION, 987: International criminal jurisdiction, 988. IN-
TERNATIONAL STATE RELATIONS AND INTERNATIONAL LAW, 990. DIPLOMATIC RE-
LATIONS, 993. TREATIES AND AGREEMENTS, 995.

III. LAW OF THE SEA 996
UN Convention on the Law of the Sea, 996; Preparatory Commission, 999; Division
for Ocean Affairs and the Law of the Sea, 1002.

IV. OTHER LEGAL QUESTIONS 1004
INTERNATIONAL ORGANIZATIONS AND INTERNATIONAL LAW, 1004: Strengthening the
role of the United Nations, 1004; Host country relations, 1006; United Nations Decade of International Law, 1007; Observer status of national liberation movements, 1011;
Asian-African Legal Consultative Committee, 1011. INTERNATIONAL ECONOMIC LAW,
1012: International trade law, 1012.

Part Six: *Administrative and budgetary questions*

I. UNITED NATIONS FINANCING AND PROGRAMMING 1019
UNITED NATIONS FINANCING, 1019: Financial situation, 1019; Financing of peace-keeping
operations, 1023; Efficiency review, 1028. UN BUDGET, 1030: Budget for 1992-1993,
1030; 1990-1991 programme budget, 1038; 1994-1995 proposed programme budget,
1038. CONTRIBUTIONS, 1040: Scale of assessments, 1040; Budget contributions in 1992,
1041. ACCOUNTS AND AUDITING, 1041. UNITED NATIONS PROGRAMMES, 1044: Programme planning, 1044. ADMINISTRATIVE AND BUDGETARY COORDINATION, 1052.

II. UNITED NATIONS OFFICIALS 1053
RESTRUCTURING OF THE SECRETARIAT, 1053. INTERNATIONAL CIVIL SERVICE COM-
MISSION, 1055. PERSONNEL MANAGEMENT, 1059: Staff composition, 1060; Post clas-
sification system, 1063; Career development, 1063; Staff rules and regulations, 1064;
Staff representation, 1064; Level of secretaries of intergovernmental organs, 1064; Privileges
and immunities, 1065. STAFF COSTS, 1066: Emoluments of top-echelon officials, 1067;
Salaries and allowances, 1068; Pensions, 1070. TRAVEL, 1075: Standards of accom-
modation for air travel, 1075. ADMINISTRATION OF JUSTICE, 1076.

III. OTHER ADMINISTRATIVE AND MANAGEMENT QUESTIONS 1077
CONFERENCES AND MEETINGS, 1077: Mandate of the Committee on Conferences,
1077; Calendar of meetings, 1077. DOCUMENTS AND PUBLICATIONS, 1082. UN
PREMISES, 1084. INFORMATION SYSTEMS AND COMPUTERS, 1085: Technological in-
novations, 1085; Access of Member States to UN informatics systems, 1087. OTHER
ADMINISTRATIVE AND BUDGETARY ARRANGEMENTS, 1088: United Nations Scientific
Committee on the Effects of Atomic Radiation, 1088; UNITAR, 1088. UN POSTAL
ADMINISTRATION, 1089.

Part Seven: *Intergovernmental organizations related to the United Nations*

I. INTERNATIONAL ATOMIC ENERGY AGENCY (IAEA) — 1093

II. INTERNATIONAL LABOUR ORGANISATION (ILO) — 1099

III. FOOD AND AGRICULTURE ORGANIZATION OF THE UNITED NATIONS (FAO) — 1104

IV. UNITED NATIONS EDUCATIONAL, SCIENTIFIC AND CULTURAL ORGANIZATION (UNESCO) — 1111

V. WORLD HEALTH ORGANIZATION (WHO) — 1116

VI. INTERNATIONAL BANK FOR RECONSTRUCTION AND DEVELOPMENT (WORLD BANK) — 1123

VII. INTERNATIONAL FINANCE CORPORATION (IFC) — 1129

VIII. INTERNATIONAL DEVELOPMENT ASSOCIATION (IDA) — 1135

IX. INTERNATIONAL MONETARY FUND (IMF) — 1140

X. INTERNATIONAL CIVIL AVIATION ORGANIZATION (ICAO) — 1145

XI. UNIVERSAL POSTAL UNION (UPU) — 1149

XII. INTERNATIONAL TELECOMMUNICATION UNION (ITU) — 1152

XIII. WORLD METEOROLOGICAL ORGANIZATION (WMO) — 1156

XIV. INTERNATIONAL MARITIME ORGANIZATION (IMO) — 1162

XV. WORLD INTELLECTUAL PROPERTY ORGANIZATION (WIPO) — 1165

XVI. INTERNATIONAL FUND FOR AGRICULTURAL DEVELOPMENT (IFAD) — 1169

XVII. UNITED NATIONS INDUSTRIAL DEVELOPMENT ORGANIZATION (UNIDO) — 1172

XVIII. INTERIM COMMISSION FOR THE INTERNATIONAL TRADE ORGANIZATION (ICITO) AND THE GENERAL AGREEMENT ON TARIFFS AND TRADE (GATT) — 1178

Appendices

I. ROSTER OF THE UNITED NATIONS — 1185

II. CHARTER OF THE UNITED NATIONS AND STATUTE OF THE INTERNATIONAL COURT OF JUSTICE — 1187
Charter of the United Nations, 1187; Statute of the International Court of Justice, 1196.

III. STRUCTURE OF THE UNITED NATIONS — 1201
General Assembly, 1201; Security Council, 1212; Economic and Social Council, 1214; Trusteeship Council, 1221; International Court of Justice, 1221; Other United Nations–related bodies, 1222; Principal members of the United Nations Secretariat, 1224.

IV. AGENDAS OF UNITED NATIONS PRINCIPAL ORGANS IN 1992   1227

General Assembly, 1227; Security Council, 1233; Economic and Social Council, 1235; Trusteeship Council, 1237.

V. UNITED NATIONS INFORMATION CENTRES AND SERVICES   1238

Indexes

USING THE SUBJECT INDEX   1242

SUBJECT INDEX   1243

INDEX OF RESOLUTIONS AND DECISIONS   1274

HOW TO OBTAIN VOLUMES OF THE *YEARBOOK*   1277

About the 1992 edition of the *Yearbook*

This edition of the *YEARBOOK OF THE UNITED NATIONS*, like the previous volumes, is intended to provide the general public and research community with the most comprehensive and up-to-date reference tool on the activities of the United Nations. The timely publication of the 1992 edition within 1993 reflects the continuing commitment by the Department of Public Information of the United Nations to ensure that the "peoples of the United Nations" receive, within a single volume, current and detailed accounts of the dynamic political dramas and substantive work of their Organization. The efforts to restore the *Yearbook* to a timely annual publication imply having to rely on provisional documentation and other materials for the preparation of the required articles, as not all final documents were available at the time of writing.

Structure and scope of articles

The book is subject-oriented and the issues are treated under seven broad themes: political and security questions, regional questions, economic and social questions, trusteeship and decolonization, legal questions, administrative and budgetary questions, and intergovernmental organizations related to the United Nations.

Various chapters and topical headings present summaries of pertinent United Nations activities, including those of intergovernmental and expert bodies, major reports, Secretariat activities and, in selected cases, the views of States in written communications. At the end of each chapter or subchapter is a list of REFERENCES, linked by numerical indicators to the text and supplying additional sources of information on the issues concerned.

Activities of United Nations bodies. All resolutions, decisions and other major activities of the principal organs and, where applicable, those of subsidiary bodies are either reproduced or summarized in the respective articles. The texts of all resolutions and decisions of substantive nature adopted in 1992 by the General Assembly, the Security Council, the Economic and Social Council and the Trusteeship Council are reproduced or summarized under the relevant topic. These texts are followed by the procedural details giving date of adoption, meeting number and vote totals (in favour-against-abstaining); information on their approval by a sessional or subsidiary body prior to final adoption, approved amendments and committee reports; and a list of sponsors. Also given are the document symbols of any financial implications and relevant meeting numbers. Details of any recorded or roll-call vote on the resolution/decision as a whole also follow the text. The texts of resolutions and decisions of a purely procedural nature are not reproduced, but are summarized and their numbers highlighted in bold type.

Major reports. Most reports of the Secretary-General, in 1992, along with selected reports from other United Nations sources, such as seminars and working groups, are summarized briefly. The document symbols of all reports cited appear in the REFERENCES.

Secretariat activities. The operational activities of the United Nations for development and humanitarian assistance are described under the relevant topics. For major activities financed outside the United Nations regular budget, information is given, wherever available, on contributions and expenditures. Financial data are generally obtained from the audited accounts prepared for each fund and cover the 1992 calendar year unless otherwise specified.

Views of States. Written communications sent to the United Nations by Member States and circulated as documents of the principal organs have been summarized in selected cases, under the relevant topic. Substantive actions by the Security Council have been analysed and brief reviews of the Council's deliberations given, particularly in cases where an issue was taken up but no resolution was adopted.

Related organizations. The *Yearbook* also briefly describes the 1992 activities of the specialized agencies and other related organizations of the United Nations system.

Terminology

Formal titles of bodies, organizational units, conventions, declarations and officials are given in full on first mention in an article or sequence of articles. They are also used in resolution/decision texts, and in the SUBJECT INDEX under the key word of the title. Short titles may be used in subsequent references.

How to find information in the *Yearbook*

The 1992 edition has been designed to enable the user to locate information on United Nations activities by the use of the table of contents, which highlights the broad subjects and subheadings; the SUBJECT INDEX, which locates individual topics and specific references to the bodies dealing with each topic; and the INDEX OF RESOLUTIONS AND DECISIONS, which provides a numerical list of all resolutions and substantive decisions adopted in 1992 by the principal organs, with page numbers for their text. The *Yearbook* also contains five appendices. APPENDIX I comprises a list of Member States with dates of their admission to the United Nations; APPENDIX II reproduces the Charter of the United Nations, including the Statute of the International Court of Justice; APPENDIX III gives the structure of the principal organs of the United Nations, including the members, officers and date and place of sessions of each body; APPENDIX IV provides the agenda for each session of the principal organs in 1992; and APPENDIX V gives the addresses of the United Nations information centres and services worldwide.

ABBREVIATIONS COMMONLY USED IN THE *YEARBOOK*

ACABQ	Advisory Committee on Administrative and Budgetary Questions
ACC	Administrative Committee on Coordination
ACPAQ	Advisory Committee on Post Adjustment Questions
ANC	African National Congress of South Africa
ASEAN	Association of South-East Asian Nations
CCAQ	Consultative Committee on Administrative Questions
CCISUA	Coordinating Committee for Independent Staff Unions and Associations of the United Nations System
CCSQ	Consultative Committee on Substantive Questions
CDP	Committee for Development Planning
CEDAW	Committee on the Elimination of Discrimination against Women
CERD	Committee on the Elimination of Racial Discrimination
CFA	Committee on Food Aid Policies and Programmes (WFP)
CILSS	Permanent Inter-State Committee on Drought Control in the Sahel
CMEA	Council for Mutual Economic Assistance
COPA	cross-organizational programme analysis
CPC	Committee for Programme and Coordination
CSDHA	Centre for Social Development and Humanitarian Affairs
DESD	Department of Economic and Social Development
DHA	Department of Humanitarian Affairs
DIEC	Development and International Economic Cooperation
DPI	Department of Public Information
DTCD	Department of Technical Cooperation for Development
EC	European Community
ECA	Economic Commission for Africa
ECDC	economic cooperation among developing countries
ECE	Economic Commission for Europe
ECLAC	Economic Commission for Latin America and the Caribbean
ECOWAS	Economic Community of West African States
EEC	European Economic Community
ESC	Economic and Social Council
ESCAP	Economic and Social Commission for Asia and the Pacific
ESCWA	Economic and Social Commission for Western Asia
FAO	Food and Agriculture Organization of the United Nations
FICSA	Federation of International Civil Servants' Associations
GA	General Assembly
GATT	General Agreement on Tariffs and Trade
GDP	gross domestic product
GNP	gross national product
IAEA	International Atomic Energy Agency
ICAO	International Civil Aviation Organization
ICITO	Interim Commission for the International Trade Organization
ICJ	International Court of Justice
ICRC	International Committee of the Red Cross
ICSC	International Civil Service Commission
IDA	International Development Association
IDDA	Industrial Development Decade for Africa
IEFR	International Emergency Food Reserve
IFAD	International Fund for Agricultural Development
IFC	International Finance Corporation
ILC	International Law Commission
ILO	International Labour Organisation
IMF	International Monetary Fund
IMO	International Maritime Organization
INCB	International Narcotics Control Board
INSTRAW	International Research and Training Institute for the Advancement of Women
IPF	indicative planning figure (UNDP)
ITC	International Trade Centre (UNCTAD/GATT)
ITO	International Trade Organization
ITU	International Telecommunication Union
IUCN	International Union for Conservation of Nature and Natural Resources
IYY	International Youth Year
JAG	Joint Advisory Group on the International Trade Centre
JIU	Joint Inspection Unit
JUNIC	Joint United Nations Information Committee
LDC	least developed country
NATO	North Atlantic Treaty Organization
NGO	non-governmental organization
NPT	Treaty on the Non-Proliferation of Nuclear Weapons
NSGT	Non-Self-Governing Territory
OAS	Organization of American States
OAU	Organization of African Unity
ODA	official development assistance
OECD	Organisation for Economic Cooperation and Development
OPEC	Organization of Petroleum Exporting Countries
PAC	Pan Africanist Congress of Azania
PLO	Palestine Liberation Organization
SC	Security Council
SDR	special drawing right
S-G	Secretary-General
SPC	Special Political Committee
TC	Trusteeship Council
TCDC	technical cooperation among developing countries
TDB	Trade and Development Board (UNCTAD)
TNC	transnational corporation
UN	United Nations
UNCDF	United Nations Capital Development Fund
UNCED	United Nations Conference on Environment and Development
UNCHS	United Nations Centre for Human Settlements (Habitat)
UNCITRAL	United Nations Commission on International Trade Law
UNCTAD	United Nations Conference on Trade and Development
UNDCP	United Nations International Drug Control Programme
UNDOF	United Nations Disengagement Observer Force (Golan Heights)
UNDP	United Nations Development Programme
UNDRO	Office of the United Nations Disaster Relief Coordinator
UNEF	United Nations Emergency Force
UNEP	United Nations Environment Programme
UNESCO	United Nations Educational, Scientific and Cultural Organization
UNFICYP	United Nations Peace-keeping Force in Cyprus
UNFPA	United Nations Population Fund
UNHCR	Office of the United Nations High Commissioner for Refugees
UNIC	United Nations Information Centre
UNICEF	United Nations Children's Fund
UNIDIR	United Nations Institute for Disarmament Research
UNIDO	United Nations Industrial Development Organization
UNIFIL	United Nations Interim Force in Lebanon
UNITAR	United Nations Institute for Training and Research
UNPAAERD	United Nations Programme of Action for African Economic Recovery and Development 1986-1990
UNRFNRE	United Nations Revolving Fund for Natural Resources Exploration
UNRISD	United Nations Research Institute for Social Development
UNRWA	United Nations Relief and Works Agency for Palestine Refugees in the Near East
UNSO	United Nations Sudano-Sahelian Office
UNTSO	United Nations Truce Supervision Organization (Israel and neighbouring States)
UNU	United Nations University
UNV	United Nations Volunteers
UPU	Universal Postal Union
WFC	World Food Council
WFP	World Food Programme
WHO	World Health Organization
WIPO	World Intellectual Property Organization
WMO	World Meteorological Organization
WTO	World Tourism Organization
YUN	*Yearbook of the United Nations*

EXPLANATORY NOTE ON DOCUMENTS

References at the end of each article in Parts One to Six of this volume give the symbols of the main documents issued in 1992 on the topic, arranged in the order in which they are referred to in the text. The following is a guide to the principal document symbols:

A/- refers to documents of the General Assembly, numbered in separate series by session. Thus, A/47/- refers to documents issued for consideration at the forty-seventh session, beginning with A/47/1. Documents of special and emergency special sessions are identified as A/S- and A/ES-, followed by the session number.

A/C.- refers to documents of six of the Assembly's Main Committees, e.g. A/C.1/- is a document of the First Committee, A/C.6/-, a document of the Sixth Committee. The symbol for documents of the seventh Main Committee, the Special Political Committee, is A/SPC/-. A/BUR/- refers to documents of the General Committee. A/AC.- documents are those of the Assembly's ad hoc bodies and A/CN.-, of its commissions; e.g. A/AC.105/- identifies documents of the Assembly's Committee on the Peaceful Uses of Outer Space, A/CN.4/-, of its International Law Commission. Assembly resolutions and decisions since the thirty-first (1976) session have been identified by two arabic numerals: the first indicates the session of adoption; the second, the sequential number in the series. Resolutions are numbered consecutively from 1 at each session. Decisions of regular sessions are numbered consecutively, from 301 for those concerned with elections and appointments, and from 401 for all other decisions. Decisions of special and emergency special sessions are numbered consecutively, from 11 for those concerned with elections and appointments, and from 21 for all other decisions.

E/- refers to documents of the Economic and Social Council, numbered in separate series by year. Thus, E/1992/- refers to documents issued for consideration by the Council at its 1992 sessions, beginning with E/1992/1. E/AC.-, E/C.- and E/CN.-, followed by identifying numbers, refer to documents of the Council's subsidiary ad hoc bodies, committees and commissions. For example, E/C.1/- and E/C.2/- refer to documents of the Council's sessional committees, namely, its Economic and Social Committees; E/CN.5/- refers to documents of the Council's Commission for Social Development, E/C.7/-, to documents of its Committee on Natural Resources. E/ICEF/- documents are those of the United Nations Children's Fund (UNICEF). Symbols for the Council's resolutions and decisions, since 1978, consist of two arabic numerals: the first indicates the year of adoption and the second, the sequential number in the series. There are two series: one for resolutions, beginning with 1 (resolution 1992/1); and one for decisions, beginning with 200 (decision 1992/200).

S/- refers to documents of the Security Council. Its resolutions are identified by consecutive numbers followed by the year of adoption in parentheses, beginning with resolution 1(1946).

T/- refers to documents of the Trusteeship Council. Its resolutions are numbered consecutively, with the session at which they were adopted indicated by Roman numerals, e.g. resolution 2195(LIX) of the fifty-ninth session. The Council's decisions are not numbered.

ST/-, followed by symbols representing the issuing department or office, refers to documents of the United Nations Secretariat.

Documents of certain bodies bear special symbols, including the following:

ACC/-	Administrative Committee on Coordination
CD/-	Conference on Disarmament
CERD/-	Committee on the Elimination of Racial Discrimination
DC/-	Disarmament Commission
DP/-	United Nations Development Programme
HS/-	Commission on Human Settlements
ITC/-	International Trade Centre
LOS/PCN/-	Preparatory Commission for the International Seabed Authority and for the International Tribunal for the Law of the Sea
TD/-	United Nations Conference on Trade and Development
UNEP/-	United Nations Environment Programme

Many documents of the regional commissions bear special symbols. These are sometimes preceded by the following:

E/ECA/-	Economic Commission for Africa
E/ECE/-	Economic Commission for Europe
E/ECLAC/-	Economic Commission for Latin America and the Caribbean
E/ESCAP/-	Economic and Social Commission for Asia and the Pacific
E/ESCWA/-	Economic and Social Commission for Western Asia

"L" in a symbol refers to documents of limited distribution, such as draft resolutions; "CONF." to documents of a conference; "INF." to those of general information. Summary records are designated by "SR.", verbatim records by "PV.", each followed by the meeting number.

United Nations sales publications each carry a sales number with the following components separated by periods: a capital letter indicating the language(s) of the publication; two arabic numerals indicating the year; a Roman numeral indicating the subject category; a capital letter indicating a subdivision of the category, if any; and an arabic numeral indicating the number of the publication within the category. Examples: E.92.II.A.2; E/F/R.92.II.E.7; E.92.X.1.

Report of the Secretary-General

Report of the Secretary-General on the work of the Organization

*Following is the Secretary-General's report on the work of the Organization, submitted to the General Assembly and dated 11 September 1992. The Assembly took note of it on 27 October (**decision 47/407**).*

CONTENTS

		Paragraphs
I.	Introduction: An opportunity regained	1-9
II.	The United Nations as an institution	10-55
	A. Expanding responsibilities	10-22
	B. Streamlining the Secretariat	23-38
	C. Reinvigorating the International Civil Service	39-43
	D. Securing financial stability	44-55
III.	Global partnership for development	56-109
	A. An integrated approach to development	64-85
	B. Action undertaken for development	86-104
	C. An agenda for development	105-109
IV.	Peace endeavours	110-164
	A. An overview of United Nations activities	110-130
	B. An analysis of five conflicts	131-55
	C. Conflicts and humanitarian assistance	156-164
V.	Conclusion: Democratization and development	165-170

I. *Introduction: An opportunity regained*

1. As I came into the office of Secretary-General in January 1992, the first-ever meeting of the Security Council at the level of heads of State and Government took place.

2. The summit represented an unprecedented recommitment, at the highest political level, to the purposes and principles of the Charter of the United Nations. It represented the start of a new phase in the history of the Organization. The power struggle of the cold-war decades and its underlying assumption that history is the unfolding of a struggle between two competing systems permeated international relations and made the original promise of the Organization extremely difficult to fulfil. In that situation, the world envisioned in the Charter seemed to be an aspiration for a distant future. The success of the majority of Member States in keeping that vision alive throughout those difficult years merits praise and admiration.

3. With the end of the bipolar era and the opening of a new chapter in history, States see the United Nations once again as an instrument capable of maintaining international peace and security, of advancing justice and human rights, and of achieving, in the words of the Charter, "social progress and better standards of life in larger freedom". The summit was a symbol of the unique point that has been reached in world affairs and in the history of the United Nations.

4. Thus, at the outset of my tenure as Secretary-General, it is possible to sense a new stirring of hope among the nations of the world and a recognition that an immense opportunity is here to be seized. Not since the end of the Second World War have the expectations of the world's peoples depended so much upon the capacity of the United Nations for widely supported and effective action.

5. As I write this report, one great reality stands out: never before in its history has the United Nations been so action-oriented, so actively engaged and so widely expected to respond to needs both immediate and pervasive. Clearly, it is in our power to bring about a renaissance—to create a new United Nations for a new international era.

6. The transition from the old to the new United Nations is neither easy nor risk-free. We are still absorbing the lessons of the end of the cold war. The bipolar competition, which carried an ever-present threat of nuclear devastation, provided a tenuous framework for international relations. New and more enduring structures must now be built. As we look towards days filled with promise, we must also be prepared to deal with uncertainty. The departure of one set of global problems has been followed by the emergence of a multitude of others.

7. In my view, the United Nations has not confronted a time of such significance since the period of its founding in 1945. The years between 1992 and the fiftieth anniversary in 1995 may well determine the course and contribution of the Organization for the next generation or more. Improvement is a never-ending task. Yet there is an expectation, which I wish to see fulfilled, that a fundamental renewal of the United Nations will be complete by the time it marks its first half-century of existence.

8. It is in this setting that, in accordance with Article 98 of the Charter, and eight months into my tenure as Secretary-General, I submit my first annual report on the work of the Organization. In these pages I seek to give my sense of the Organization and its changing role at a time when

the world community is entering largely uncharted territory. We need a new spirit of commonality, commitment and intellectual creativity to transform a period of hope into an era of fulfilment.

9.   In the second section of my report, I discuss the process of change that the United Nations is undergoing as an institution; the third section deals with the challenge of international cooperation for development; and the fourth section looks at the United Nations peace-keeping operations throughout the world. Finally, I return to the dominant theme of my report, which is that the current international situation requires an Organization capable of dealing comprehensively with the economic, social, environmental and political dimensions of human development. This requires the full application of the principles of democracy within the family of nations and within our Organization. I take this as my central priority as Secretary-General.

II.   *The United Nations as an institution*

A.   *Expanding responsibilities*

10.   Each major turning-point in the course of this century has been reflected by changes in the community of States. The founding of the United Nations confirmed the centrality of the sovereign State as the primary entity of international relations. The end of the colonial era during the mid-century decades brought many new Member States into the United Nations. Today, the transition from one international era to another is symbolized by the wave of new Member States that have now taken their seats in the General Assembly: Armenia, Azerbaijan, Bosnia and Herzegovina, Croatia, Georgia, Kazakhstan, Kyrgyzstan, Republic of Moldova, San Marino, Slovenia, Tajikistan, Turkmenistan, Uzbekistan—all joining the Organization in the first eight months of 1992. Most of these new States represent people who have recently gained freedom. They embody a renewal of the fundamental concept of the State by which peoples find a unity and a voice in the international community.

11.   In many of these lands, cold-war constraints served to suppress deep-rooted antagonisms. Ethnic, cultural, religious and linguistic diversities were held in check by political suppression or by the threat of outside intervention and dangerous escalation. Far fewer reasons for restraint exist today. A resurgence of open rivalry and strife is now taking place. As many new States find themselves free to pursue more open forms of economic policy that promise progress, the very achievement of statehood often involves the breakdown of old and predictable patterns of economic interaction.

12.   Today, no State is immune to the revolutionary changes in the international system. Old assumptions, preconceptions and structures have been swept away in a torrent of change. While change brings renewal and a fresh dynamic, it can also bring disruption and violence. The task of adjusting the institutions of international relations will have to take place in a period of tumultuous upheaval. The process of adjustment will be painful and costly, yet we have an unrivalled opportunity to breathe new life into our vocabulary and institutions.

13.   Present demands on the United Nations have no precedent in its history. The presence of the Organization is being more intensely felt world wide as it helps people in danger, need or despair. The United Nations is constantly at work: from Security Council meetings and consultations on an almost continuous basis to peace-keeping operations in four continents; from good offices and quiet diplomacy to essential humanitarian missions and responses to emergencies all over the world; from major economic and social conferences, such as the Earth Summit, to technical cooperation activities in practically every developing country.

14.   The turning-point in the scale and scope of United Nations activities can be discerned after the year 1987. For the first time in many years, agreement on a wide range of issues became possible, effectively marking an end to the cold war. Yet this same point also can be seen to mark the beginning of shockwaves caused by the reawakening of old conflicts and the emergence of a number of new rivalries. A consequent increase in United Nations activities can be traced quite clearly after 1987.

15.   Graphic illustrations of the expanding role of the United Nations are depicted in charts at the end of section V. In reviewing the work of the Organization over the course of the past five years, one cannot avoid the feeling of looking at a qualitatively different body. Some figures speak volumes about the changing international scene.

Expanding activities of the Security Council

16.   The Security Council's workload today, when compared with that of the cold-war period, reveals a dramatic increase. The extent of change can be discerned in the sheer number of scheduled activities. In all of 1987, the Council met 49 times, whereas in the first seven months of 1992 alone there were 81 official meetings. The same drastically changed pattern is reflected in the number of consultations. In 1987, there were 360 bilateral consultations; in the first seven months of 1992, 598 took place. Similarly, in 1987 there were 43 consultations of the whole, yet the first seven months of 1992 produced 119. As a consequence of such expanded activity, 14 Security Council resolutions were adopted in all of 1987.

In the first seven months of 1992, there were 46. As for presidential statements, there were 9 in 1987, while in the first seven months of 1992 alone, 43 were issued (see figures 1 and 2).

Expanding role of peace-keeping

17. Between 1948 and 1987, the United Nations established 13 peace-keeping operations. Since 1988, 13 new peace-keeping operations have been organized in addition to 5 which have continued from the earlier period. Currently, the United Nations administers 12 peace-keeping operations in various regions of the world (see figures 5 and 6).

18. Nearly 40,000 authorized military personnel are serving under United Nations command in peace-keeping operations around the world. Peace-keeping operations approved at present are estimated to cost close to $3 billion in the current 12-month period, more than four times the previous highest annual figure—and this only if no new operations are required. The nature of peace-keeping operations is evolving rapidly and requires, in addition to military personnel, substantial numbers of civilians, including specialists in electoral procedures, health, finance, engineering and administration. Their work is crucial to post-conflict peace-building.

19. The reality of those remarkable increases is revealed in raw numbers. In 1987, there were 9,666 military personnel deployed. In mid-1992, the number deployed stood at 38,144. As for police personnel deployed, in 1987 there were 35; at present, 2,461 police are deployed; in 1987 there were 877 civilians employed in peace-keeping operations; as of August 1992, the number of international and local civilian personnel reached 9,461 (see figure 4).

Expanding mandates of the Secretariat

20. The responsibilities of the Organization's administrative body have expanded in a corresponding fashion, also vividly demonstrating the remarkable change from cold-war levels of activity to those at the present time. This year, to date, 75 diplomatic missions of fact-finding, representation and good offices have been undertaken on my behalf. In response to requests from the General Assembly, 189 reports have been submitted by the Secretary-General to the Assembly during its recent session. In 1987, the Secretary-General received only 87 such requests.

21. On the other hand, available resources have not paralleled the rapid expansion of United Nations activities. In 1987, the number of United Nations posts financed by the regular budget was 11,409. Today, in 1992, it has decreased to 10,100, despite the enormous increase in responsibilities entrusted to the Organization. The regular budget itself has not increased significantly, in real terms, since the mid-1980s (see figure 3).

22. I welcome those increased duties and responsibilities. They signal a recognition that the United Nations is the strongest hope for a better world. I welcome the added demands they place upon the Organization and accept the challenge they pose in requiring a search for greater efficiency in the conduct of its mandated activities. Under these circumstances, I have taken and will continue to take all reasonable measures to increase the efficiency, productivity and responsiveness of the Secretariat.

B. Streamlining the Secretariat

23. An effective response to the enormous responsibilities and opportunities inherent in this era will require the fullest possible cooperation between Member States, the Secretary-General and the staff of the Organization. For my part, to meet the new challenges and adapt the Organization to the evolving demands of the times, I have initiated the process of restructuring the Secretariat. My intention is to make the most effective use of resources at my disposal through a rationalization and streamlining of structures and procedures, as well as managerial improvements. A more effective and efficient Secretariat means clearer and more direct lines of responsibility, the capacity to deploy staff and resources where they are most needed and the ability to respond flexibly to new requests and changing mandates.

24. The General Assembly has before it the outcome of the first phase of that restructuring. A number of offices have been regrouped, related functions and activities have been consolidated and the redeployment of resources has been undertaken. Unnecessary bureaucratic layers have been reduced through the elimination of several high-level posts. Lines of responsibility have been more clearly defined by concentrating the decision-making process in seven key departments at Headquarters under eight Under-Secretaries-General. The needs of each component of the Secretariat are now being re-evaluated with a view, on the one hand, to eliminating any remaining duplication and redundancy and, on the other, to reinforcing those offices and departments with expanding mandates and responsibilities.

25. A greater integration of efforts in support of development was the main objective of the first phase of the restructuring in the economic and social area. This will be pursued and further refined in the second phase. The capacity of the Secretariat to provide a timely and coordinated response to complex emergencies and the delivery of humanitarian assistance has also been consolidated and strengthened.

26. In the political sector, the purpose is to strengthen the support provided to the Secretary-General in matters related to the maintenance of

international peace and security and to enable the Secretariat to respond swiftly and efficiently to the mandates of the Security Council and the General Assembly. My aim is to develop an enhanced capacity for good offices, preventive diplomacy, peacemaking, research and analysis and early warning, as well as to strengthen the planning and managerial capability of the Secretariat in peace-keeping.

27.   I believe that the Secretariat will be better able to provide more effective and integrated assistance to Member States with a streamlined structure comprising components with clearly delineated responsibilities and greater managerial accountability and better aware of the essential linkages among the various mandates of the Organization.

28.   While the first phase of the reorganization was focused on offices at Headquarters, I am now extending the process of reform to other parts of the Organization, with special attention to the economic and social sectors. A primary objective will be a more effective Organization-wide distribution of responsibilities and balance between functions performed at Headquarters and those carried out by the regional commissions and other United Nations organs and programmes, based on a clear understanding of our priorities and the comparable advantage of each component. I am seeking broadly representative high-level advice on these complex issues from an independent panel of experts to help me ensure that the Organization as a whole provides Governments with advice and support adapted to their changing needs.

29.   I firmly believe that the focus of the United Nations must remain in the "field", where economic, social and political decisions take effect. A unified United Nations presence at the country level, would, in my view, greatly enhance the impact of the Organization and facilitate inter-agency coordination in support of national action. I intend to work further towards that end. The experience of the United Nations Interim Offices, which I have asked the United Nations Development Programme and the Department of Public Information of the Secretariat to establish in six countries of the former Soviet Union, will be drawn upon to further this integrated approach.

30.   Strengthening linkages between global strategies and operational activities in the field is a major concern. Current intergovernmental discussions on the reform of operational activities and their governance can be of great significance in this regard. It is important that the restructuring should be supportive of this objective and lead not only to a more dynamic Organization, but also contribute to greater coherence and effectiveness for the entire United Nations system.

Administrative Committee on Coordination

31.   As the highest body bringing together the executive heads of all the specialized agencies and organizations of the United Nations system, the Administrative Committee on Coordination (ACC) must be the guiding force to promote coherence in the work of the system. The firmest foundation for effective coordination, I am convinced, is a strong commitment on the part of all concerned to an international civil service whose conditions are administered in a truly common system and which shares clear common objectives and goals.

32.   As we look towards the fiftieth anniversary of the United Nations, with various reforms under consideration, it is essential that the current system should be made to work to the full extent of its potential. In that respect, I am sure that the specialized agencies will want to ensure that their autonomy is consistent with the overall view which the world situation demands. Impressively, this was the attitude of the Directors-General of the specialized agencies and the heads of the Bretton Woods institutions and the General Agreement on Tariffs and Trade (GATT), who make up the membership of the Administrative Committee on Coordination, at the meeting of that Committee, held at Geneva from 8 to 10 April 1992.

33.   One reason why the problem of coordination has appeared intractable is the fact that the structure was devised in 1946 at San Francisco on the basis of a deliberate decision to organize international cooperation through the combined action of the United Nations, on the one hand, and a number of autonomously functioning specialized agencies, on the other. Functional autonomy is explicitly and implicitly recognized in the agreements concluded from that time onwards between the United Nations and the existing or future specialized agencies. The system with which we are operating has remained virtually unchanged over the last 46 years.

34.   The need to improve coordination has been a continuing theme in the General Assembly, the Economic and Social Council, and the governing bodies of the organizations which make up the United Nations system. The many efforts made so far have brought modest and partial improvements.

35.   The executive heads of the agencies of the United Nations family all believe that a fresh look is urgently required to enable the system to meet new challenges and objectives, including the ambitious goals recently set by the Rio de Janeiro Conference with respect to sustainable development and the environment. They are fully in agreement that, in the months to come, the problem of coordination must be tackled seriously at the level of both programmes and operational activities. The goal is to ensure that the services

which the system provides to Governments are coherent, that its component parts draw on one another's resources rather than duplicating them, and that there is selectivity and coordination in coverage.

36. Alongside current efforts to revitalize central intergovernmental bodies, particularly the Economic and Social Council, reforms in the functioning of the Administrative Committee on Coordination itself are in order. Intergovernmental bodies need an effective and responsive ACC in a position to bring to bear on their work the wealth of experience and the wide range of analytical and operational capabilities available throughout the system, and able to support it with well-grounded policy options. In turn, the effectiveness of ACC depends in many ways on a better coordination of national and group positions in the various governing bodies of the system and on the capacity of the United Nations intergovernmental machinery to build a strong international consensus, based on a comprehensive approach to global, regional and national security, which can guide and harness the work of the various organizations of the system.

37. As its Chairman, I intend to give close personal attention to the work of ACC. Our objectives should include: better focused inter-agency consultations; enhanced system-wide arrangements for data exchange; clear agendas for common action supported by strong analysis and wide consultations; active direct contacts among executive heads outside formal meetings; and a streamlining and continuous assessment of existing consultative mechanisms and constant adaptation of them to meet evolving needs.

38. In agreement with the members of ACC, I have commissioned a comprehensive study by a high-level consultant of the functioning of this key body with a view to developing new approaches to system-wide collaboration and ensuring that the structures of inter-agency coordination are well adapted to the challenges ahead. Further steps will be taken when I have received the report and its recommendations.

C. *Reinvigorating the International Civil Service*

39. The restructuring process I have initiated must be accompanied by a deeper appreciation of and respect for the International Civil Service. My efforts at organizational reform within the Secretariat will be successful only if they are accompanied by strong political support to preserve the integrity, international character and independence of the staff of the Organization. Of all the tangible and intangible resources available to the Organization and to the Secretary-General, nothing matches the worth of its staff. They must be provided conditions of employment which ensure

that the service will continue to attract the best qualified personnel from all parts of the world. At this time of unprecedented responsibilities and ever-expanding mandates, the Secretariat of the United Nations is stretched thinly across a widening range of activities. The confidence of the international community in the Organization's ability to respond swiftly, effectively and impartially rests largely on the performance of its staff.

40. Since I assumed office I have been repeatedly impressed by the dedication and versatility of the United Nations staff. In the course of less than a year they have responded to many hitherto unfamiliar tasks. Many have assumed new or additional functions or volunteered for mission service at short notice, often in hardship and dangerous situations—frequently compelled to leave their families behind for extended periods. They have done so willingly, in the interests of building a new society, ensuring the fairness of an electoral process or facilitating the delivery of humanitarian assistance. At Headquarters, staff members are responding on a 24-hour basis to the constant requirements of complex operations in many time zones, servicing double or triple the number of meetings, and producing increasing volumes of documentation with shorter and shorter deadlines. They are being called upon to undertake research and provide policy options in a rapidly changing world where long-established modes of thinking and acting are being constantly questioned or redefined. Others are managing, in a situation of financial uncertainty, complex operations involving tens of thousands of military and civilian personnel in the field.

41. In any institution restructuring and change are unsettling for the staff, and that is particularly so at a time when substantially increased demands are being made on them. I am fully aware of current concerns, and I am counting on the dedicated professionalism of my staff to cope with the demands of this period of transition. I want them to grasp the inherent possibilities of the expanding role of the Organization. I see here a unique opportunity to build a stronger, more self-reliant Secretariat, where the best traditions of public service are combined with modern management practices.

42. Once the current phases of restructuring have been completed, I intend to focus on the improvement of the conditions of service, including salaries, long-term recruitment policies, grade structure and career development opportunities. I should like to build an Organization based on competitive recruitment at all levels, with career development policies which will motivate and reward staff for creativity, versatility and mobility, and the comprehensive training necessary to adjust staff skills to changing requirements. It is to-

tally unacceptable that some staff members receive national subsidies to support their emoluments, while others are subjected to a salary freeze owing to considerations of financial restraint. I intend to avoid politicization of the Secretariat, to resist outside pressures which favour a few at the expense of the majority, and to give proper recognition to the contributions and talents of many who may not have received equal attention in the past, including women in all parts of the Organization.

43. As I have said, I am committed to eliminating unnecessary bureaucratic levels, abolishing duplication and using the human and financial resources at my disposal in the most efficient and responsible manner possible. I believe that the staff have demonstrated that they share my aspirations and are rising to the challenge to make the Organization the most effective instrument possible for peace and development.

D. *Securing financial stability*

44. The Organization is being restructured to serve its ends anew. Yet amid the tumult of demands placed upon it, the United Nations cannot afford to become a victim of its own popularity, suffering from a crisis of expectations rather than, as in the past, from a lack of credibility in its capacity to command consensus. In carrying out its added responsibilities, the institutional innovation and political resilience of the Organization have been as striking as its financial insecurity. To ensure that the Organization is fully prepared to respond to the new requirements of international action, the United Nations will need the unstinting financial support of its Members.

45. The programme budget of the United Nations for the current biennium was adopted by the General Assembly by consensus. The same consensus prevailed for the adoption of the previous programme budget, as well as for the acceptance of all major budgets of recent peace-keeping operations. Such broad agreement of all Member States—major and other contributors to the financing of the Organization—represents a significant and welcome change from the not too distant past. A major step forward in this regard was General Assembly resolution 41/213 of 19 December 1986, which established a new budgetary process for the United Nations.

46. A fundamental aspect of General Assembly resolution 41/213, calling for payment in full and on time by all Member States of their assessed contributions, however, has yet to be implemented. As of September 1992, only 52 Member States had paid in full their dues to the regular budget of the United Nations. Unpaid assessed contributions totalled $908.5 million. Unpaid contributions towards peace-keeping operations stood at $844.4 million. At the end of August 1992, I was able to

pay the salaries of the regular staff of this Organization only by borrowing from peace-keeping funds with available cash. Perennial shortages, the absence of reserves, and a debilitating uncertainty over the immediate future are the main characteristics of the financial situation of the United Nations.

47. When putting into effect Article 17 of the Charter, which states that the General Assembly considers and approves the budget of the Organization, Member States have an opportunity to examine in depth the budget proposals of the Secretary-General. At that time, it is their privilege and their duty to question, sometimes to criticize and, in all cases, to analyse both the basic orientation and the detailed provisions of the various budgets of the Organization. After adoption, especially when such adoption occurs by consensus, it is the obligation of Member States to pay in full and on time their assessed contributions in order to ensure the financing of all activities of the Organization which Member States themselves consider and approve. The simple reason for the present deplorable financial situation of the Organization remains the fact that a number of Member States do not meet their obligations. Figure 3 below illustrates the dimension of what has become the perennial financial plight of the United Nations.

48. There are two main areas of concern: the ability of the Organization to function over the longer term; and the immediate requirements to respond to a crisis.

49. A number of proposals are before the General Assembly to remedy the financial situation of the United Nations in all its aspects. I urge that they be acted upon.

50. To deal with the cash-flow problems caused by the exceptionally high level of unpaid contributions, as well as with the problem of inadequate working capital reserves, it is proposed that:

(*a*) Interest be charged on the amounts of assessed contributions that are not paid on time;

(*b*) Certain financial regulations of the United Nations to permit the retention of budgetary surpluses be suspended;

(*c*) The Working Capital Fund be increased to a level of $250 million, with endorsement of the principle that the level of the Fund should be approximately 25 per cent of the annual assessment under the regular budget;

(*d*) A temporary peace-keeping reserve fund be established at a level of $50 million, in order to meet initial expenses of peace-keeping operations, pending receipt of assessed contributions;

(*e*) The Secretary-General be authorized to borrow commercially, should other sources of cash be inadequate.

51. The establishment of a United Nations peace endowment fund, with an initial target of $1 billion, has also been proposed. The fund would be created by a combination of assessed and voluntary contributions, with the latter being sought from Governments and the private sector, as well as individuals. Once the fund reached its target level, the proceeds from the investments of its principal would be used to finance the initial costs of authorized peace-keeping operations, other conflict resolution measures and related activities.

52. In addition to those proposals, other ideas include: a levy on arms sales that could be related to maintaining an arms register by the United Nations; a levy on international air travel, which depends upon the maintenance of peace; authorization for the United Nations to borrow from the World Bank and the International Monetary Fund, for peace and development are interdependent; general tax exemption for contributions made to the United Nations by foundations, businesses and individuals; and changes in the formula for calculating the scale of assessments for peace-keeping operations.

53. As such ideas are debated, a stark fact remains: the financial foundations of the Organization daily grow weaker, debilitating its political will and practical capacity to undertake new and essential activities. This state of affairs must not continue. Whatever decisions are taken on financing the Organization, there is one inescapable necessity: Member States must pay their assessed contributions in full and on time. Failure to do so puts them in breach of their obligations under the Charter.

54. In those circumstances and on the assumption that Member States will be ready to finance operations for peace in a manner commensurate with their present and welcome readiness to establish them, I recommend the following:

(a) Immediate establishment of a revolving peace-keeping reserve fund of $50 million;

(b) Agreement that one third of the estimated cost of each new peace-keeping operation be appropriated by the General Assembly as soon as the Security Council decides to establish the operation; that would give the Secretary-General the necessary commitment authority and assure an adequate cash flow; the balance of the costs would be appropriated after the General Assembly approved the operation's budget;

(c) Acknowledgement by Member States that, under exceptional circumstances, political and operational considerations may make it necessary for the Secretary-General to employ his authority to place contracts without competitive bidding.

55. Member States wish the Organization to be managed with the utmost efficiency and care. I am in full accord. As the present report indicates, I have taken important steps to streamline the Secretariat in order to avoid duplication and overlap, while increasing its productivity. Additional changes and improvements will take place. As regards the United Nations system more widely, I continue to review the situation in consultation with my colleagues in the Administrative Committee on Coordination. The question of assuring financial security to the Organization over the long term is of such importance and complexity that public awareness and support must be heightened. I have therefore asked a select group of qualified persons of high international repute to examine this entire subject and to report thereon to me. I intend to present their advice, together with my comments, for the consideration of the General Assembly, in full recognition of the special responsibility that the Assembly has, under the Charter, for financial and budgetary matters.

III. *Global partnership for development*

56. The end of bipolarity has released vast political energies hitherto held mostly captive to ideological rivalry. The search is now on for institution building, less confrontational approaches to global issues and more productive outlets for the utilization of human, material and technological resources. The decades of cold war had imposed the pre-eminence of political over economic considerations. With the cold war behind us there is a distinct trend towards the economics of international relations shaping its politics.

57. In this context, the United Nations as an institution is uniquely placed to press for global solutions to global problems in the economic field, whether they pertain to aid, trade, technology transfer, commodity prices or debt relief. Collectively, the international community itself is better equipped today for dealing with the recurring man-made and natural disasters which demand compelling attention as the world comes to grips with the economic consequences of the end of the cold war. It is an opportune moment to evolve a set of global priorities in the short, intermediate and long term. It is also a propitious time to accelerate the implementation of economic targets agreed upon in a less conducive political climate.

58. Many hopeful areas of consensus are already visible to indicate an embryonic pattern of global partnership for development. Democratic structures, popular participation and observance of human rights are being widely recognized as sources of creativity in the process of development. Above all, a new vision of development is gradually emerging. Development is increasingly becoming a people-centred process whose ultimate goal must be the improvement of the human condition. Viewed thusly, development is a global goal, since the need to strike a balance between

social equity and economic growth is near universal—even more so now than earlier because both the industrialized and the developing countries are faced with equally demanding tasks: poverty alleviation for many among the former and recovery from economic stagnation for many among the latter.

59.   Most industrialized countries today need to sustain their levels of development and most developing countries need to attain higher levels of development. The ecological sustainability of development further strengthens the global linkages between the economic destinies of the developed and developing countries. As will be seen in paragraphs 75 to 79, the Earth Summit, held at Rio de Janeiro in June 1992, showed that this planet simply cannot be demarcated into separate zones of immunity from and vulnerability to ecological decay. The Rio spirit provided a vision of development that can be realized only through a global partnership.

60.   As in the past, the United Nations continues to be an important source for putting forward new approaches and promoting consensus. Many ideas originating at the United Nations, and considered too radical at the time, were eventually adopted as viable policy options by the international community. Examples include concessional lending through the International Development Association, "adjustment with a human face" of the United Nations Children's Fund, negative resource transfers and debt relief, where major conceptual advances were made at the United Nations. I believe that the current concerns for humanizing development will also become an accepted basis for infusing new life into the socio-economic sectors of the work of the Organization.

61.   The United Nations still has a continuing obligation to put its weight behind those who are most seriously underprivileged and to address the root causes of the economic decline which still characterizes the situation of many countries in Africa, Asia and Latin America and is fast reaching crisis proportions in several of them. It is unacceptable that absolute poverty, hunger, disease, illiteracy and hopelessness should be the lot of one fifth of the world's population.

62.   The economic situation in Africa is of particular concern. Most Africans are poorer today than they were when their countries achieved independence in the late 1950s and 1960s. The continent as a whole accounts for 32 out of the world's 47 least developed countries. Africa is the only low-income region in the world where the number of people living in poverty is, if the current trends continue, likely to increase by the year 2000. It is also the only region of the world whose total debt equals or exceeds its economic output. The freshly

witnessed momentum for political pluralism in Africa can hardly withstand a continuing assault by desertification, famine and deprivation. Poverty is infertile soil for democracy. It breeds a search for survival that cannot be held back by national frontiers. The African countries need to become masters of their economic destiny in a more supportive global framework. In that respect, I was heartened by the fact that Member States responded positively to the call for help to combat the severe drought situation in Africa. The United Nations system must do its utmost to support the implementation of the New Agenda for the Development of Africa in the 1990s, aimed at the accelerated transformation, integration, diversification and growth of African economies through the internalization of the development process and the enhancement of self-reliance.

63.   In Eastern Europe and the former Soviet Union, the central challenge before the international community is to facilitate and assist in a smooth and peaceful management of change by countries of the region. The region needs support for the building and strengthening of democratic institutions, while meeting immediate emergency needs. Provision of humanitarian assistance with the active involvement of the United Nations system will have to be followed in the months ahead by the critical tasks of reconstructing war-torn zones and resettling displaced persons. In the longer run, the success of economic reforms in those countries will depend greatly on fiscal and monetary stability, the reshaping of industrial structures and the establishment of legal and economic institutions capable of coping with the market economy so that investment and capital formation can take place.

A.   *An integrated approach to development*

64.   Political progress and economic development are inseparable: both are equally important and must be pursued simultaneously. Political stability is needed to develop effective economic policies, but when economic conditions deteriorate too much, as events not only in developing countries but also in Eastern Europe and the Commonwealth of Independent States have shown, divisive political strife may take root.

65.   The Charter of the United Nations assigns to the Organization the major responsibility of promoting social and economic development, and the various agencies of the United Nations system do indeed make great contributions towards this end.

66.   It is essential that the United Nations continue to serve as a forum for the analysis and conceptual formulation of socio-economic problems of particular concern to the developing countries and those in transition to more open economic and

political systems. It is clear that the Organization's responsibilities and commitments in the political and security area should not be carried out at the expense of its responsibilities in the development field, and neither should be subordinated to the other. It is essential that they be pursued in an integrated, mutually supporting way.

67. There has never been a more evident need for an integrated approach to:

(a) The objectives of peace, democracy and human rights, and the requirements of development;

(b) The needs of development and the protection of the environment;

(c) The economic as well as the social dimensions of development;

(d) The interrelationships among trade, finance, investment and technology;

(e) The meeting of immediate needs for emergency and humanitarian assistance and setting the conditions for long-term development.

68. The United Nations is the only institution capable of comprehensively addressing global problems in their political, humanitarian and socio-economic dimensions. In the new climate of international relations, we must not miss the opportunity to develop the necessary international consensus and policy instruments—and also to adapt United Nations structures, and interactions within the United Nations system—to promote this integrated approach. We must have the necessary vision and political will.

69. The prospects for achieving these objectives will, of course, be brighter in a more robust global economy. In this respect, the past year has not been encouraging. The success stories in some parts of the world notwithstanding, world output as a whole declined in 1991 and there were too few signs of recovery in 1992.

70. In assisting the global economy back on the path of strong recovery, the United Nations is gradually considering a more integrated approach towards development. Conceptually, such an approach recognized linkages between the economic and social dimensions of development. Functionally, it implies mutual feedback among the trade, finance, investment and technology sectors. The aim here should be to ensure that the policy advice and the services which the Organization as a whole provides to Governments are coherent; and that target-bound results replace proliferation of activity.

71. The work of the United Nations should be rooted in sound analysis and understanding of development and global trends—relying on the fact-finding capabilities of the United Nations system. It should possess an "early warning" function, able to detect threats to security and well-being from energy crises to the burden of debt, from the risk of famine to the spread of disease.

72. Since taking office, I have participated in two major United Nations conferences in the economic and social development field: the eighth session of the United Nations Conference on Trade and Development (UNCTAD), held at Cartagena in February 1992, and the United Nations Conference on Environment and Development—the Earth Summit—held at Rio de Janeiro in June 1992. In July 1992, I addressed the high-level segment of the Economic and Social Council. These gatherings have already shown a new spirit of vitality and a readiness to break fresh ground in development cooperation.

Eighth session of the United Nations
Conference on Trade and Development

73. At the eighth session of UNCTAD, participating Governments called upon countries at all stages of development to create a new partnership for development based on the recognition of sovereign equality, mutual interest and shared responsibilities. Central to this partnership is the need for strengthened multilateral cooperation to help translate the broad commitments undertaken by countries into sustained growth in the world economy and a reactivation of development throughout the developing world. I am convinced that it is only through such a partnership that the global community can erase the scourge of poverty and deprivation, provide international support for national reform programmes, encourage efficient use of precious global resources, and address economic and social problems through coherent and mutually reinforcing policies. The eighth session of the Conference was also remarkable for the willingness shown on all sides to use the occasion of the Conference to rethink the directions of the work of the organization and to start with a fresh agenda.

74. At the global level, the interrelationships between trade and development are the central focus of the contribution of UNCTAD. In the present economic context, a greater appreciation of the linkages between trade, foreign investment, and the globalization of economic activities and corporate operations is critical. The role of the United Nations in that respect and its contribution to development and poverty alleviation will be strengthened as a result of the reoriented work programme of the Conference stemming from its eighth session.

United Nations Conference on
Environment and Development

75. The Earth Summit held at Rio de Janeiro in June marked an important milestone in awakening the world to the need for a development process that does not jeopardize future generations.

76. The Rio Conference achieved consensus in more than one area: first, it secured a set of agreements between Governments which marks a significant advance in international cooperation on development and environment issues. Second, it marshalled political commitment to these arrangements at the highest level and placed the issue of sustainable development at the heart of the international agenda. Third, it opened new paths for communication and cooperation between official and non-official organizations working towards developmental and environmental goals. Fourth, it led to an enormous increase in public awareness of the issues that were tackled in the process—an awareness that ought to facilitate the adoption of policies and the allocation of additional resources to fulfil the task.

77. A comprehensive and far-reaching programme for sustainable development is Agenda 21, which constitutes the centrepiece of international cooperation and coordination activities within the United Nations system for many years to come. Its role in galvanizing international cooperation will be crucial. Building on the spirit of Rio, the implementation of Agenda 21 must be seen as an investment in our future. I call upon the donor community to ensure a flow of new resources which will serve the common interests of the whole world.

78. The adoption of the United Nations Framework Convention on Climate Change, which launches a process of cooperation aimed at keeping greenhouse gases in the atmosphere within safe limits, was a major achievement. I urge Governments to ratify it as soon as possible.

79. The establishment of a high-level Commission on Sustainable Development in follow-up to the United Nations Conference on Environment and Development will be crucial for achieving the vital environmental and developmental goals outlined in Agenda 21.

United Nations Environment Programme

80. This year marked the culmination of a number of major efforts by the United Nations Environment Programme (UNEP): the strengthening of its Earthwatch Programme; the publication of the State of the Environment 1972-1992; the completion of a comprehensive assessment of desertification; and the entry into force of provisions strengthening the Montreal Protocol on Substances that Deplete the Ozone Layer. UNEP made important contributions to the entire preparatory process for the United Nations Conference on Environment and Development and in particular towards the negotiation of the Convention on Biological Diversity, which was adopted at Rio.

The 1992 substantive session of the Economic and Social Council

81. New approaches to the role of the United Nations system in enhancing international cooperation for development were discussed at the July meeting of the high-level segment of the Economic and Social Council. I was pleased that members of the Council viewed the objectives of securing peace, development and justice as indivisible and equally essential. They also reiterated that international development cooperation and the eradication of poverty are inextricably linked with the preservation of peace. The two must be pursued with equal vigour.

82. The Economic and Social Council has adopted significant improvements in its methods of work, including a high-level policy segment and the identification of "coordination" and "operational activities" as the main areas of concentration. I have already recommended that the Security Council invite a reinvigorated and restructured Economic and Social Council to provide reports, in accordance with Article 65 of the Charter of the United Nations, on those economic and social developments that may, unless mitigated, threaten international peace and security. I urge Governments to pursue this recommendation.

83. During the high-level segment, I also suggested that the Economic and Social Council might introduce a flexible high-level inter-sessional mechanism in order to facilitate a timely response to evolving socio-economic realities. Through such a mechanism, the Council would, in a continuing dialogue with the organizations of the system, build and expand agreement on common ends and objectives and adapt the economic and social policy agendas to changing requirements. In the framework of an integrated approach to the objectives of the United Nations, such a mechanism would enable the Council to play a central monitoring and surveillance role within the United Nations. I will urge Member States represented in the high-level inter-sessional mechanism to send experts and representatives of stature, who have access to top decision makers and can speak for their Governments on issues of global concern.

84. I fully share the emphasis placed by the Council on the need for enhanced inter-agency cooperation and, in that context, a closer and improved relationship between the United Nations and the Bretton Woods institutions. Through such a closer relationship, the United Nations would bring to bear its overall global responsibilities in the political, humanitarian and socio-economic sphere on the work and the policies of the Bretton Woods institutions. They in turn would lend their analytical and financial support to the achievement of the overall United Nations objectives.

85. The members of the Council expressed concern about levels of official development assistance. I fully share these concerns. There is also a need to take a critical look at its modalities; it is imperative that this assistance be used for fully productive purposes. In recent years, less than one tenth of official development assistance was directed to programmes in the critical human development areas, such as basic education, primary health care, supply of safe water, family planning and nutrition.

B. *Action undertaken for development*

Global economic cooperation

86. Data gathering and analysis, the review of global economic trends and policies, and the provision of analytical support to the Economic and Social Council and the General Assembly in the economic and social fields are key elements of the continuing functions of the Secretariat, as is the substantive support required by these organs and by the Secretary-General in the exercise of overview functions in relation to the work of the United Nations system as a whole. Both the research and the technical cooperation activities undertaken by the Secretariat in New York have increased over the years and have expanded to cover a growing number of areas—science and technology, natural resources, energy, the environment, the role of transnational corporations, public administration and economic management. These activities were consolidated, in the first phase of the reorganization to which I have referred in the second section of this report, in a single Department of Economic and Social Development at Headquarters.

Regional cooperation

87. The United Nations regional commissions have assumed an ever greater role in support of Member States in their respective regions over the years. In April 1992, I addressed the Economic Commission for Europe at Geneva and the Economic and Social Commission for Asia and the Pacific at Beijing. In July, I appointed a new Executive Secretary for the Economic Commission for Africa. I will chair the Executive Secretaries Meeting at Addis Ababa in December 1992, at which representatives of the regional commissions will come together. At a time when regional cooperation holds, in many different ways, the key not only to conflict resolution but also to economic and social progress, these regional entities represent more than ever an important asset for the Organization.

88. The capacity of each region to harness its collective strength with respect to trade, investment and technological opportunity will undoubtedly be increasingly essential to their development. The commissions play a major role in this process.

Making better use of their potential, for the benefit of both their respective constituencies and the Organization as a whole, will be one of my principal objectives in the forthcoming phases of the restructuring of the economic and social sectors.

Social development

89. Traditionally, United Nations social development activities have concentrated primarily on the most vulnerable groups. In the emerging trend to view the social and economic dimensions of development in a more integrated way, the Organization is also beginning to take a closer look at specific phenomena affecting social cohesion. Once again there are much larger areas of mutually shared concerns among both the developed and the developing countries than have been hitherto recognized. The degrees of social cohesion and the levels of development do not necessarily coincide.

90. The demographic trends in some developed countries indicate that, in the future, a larger number of dependent people is likely to have to be supported by a smaller workforce. Among the developing countries, the very efforts at modernization are tugging at the traditions and institutions which held the social fabric together. As societies at different levels of development cope with increasing pressures on basic social structures, like the family unit, their exposure to the media becomes an additional factor for adaptation. Issues of cultural, religious, ethnic and linguistic diversity are so closely related today to the prospects of political stability and economic advancement that the involvement of the United Nations in the area of social development is acquiring a qualitatively different nature.

91. A particular emphasis in the Organization's work over the past year has been given to promoting the full participation of women in the development process by helping devise policies that facilitate their access to the basic tools of production, credit and technology and enable them to share in the decision-making process. Efforts have been made to address the problems of discrimination and poverty affecting both rural and urban women, and to bridge the gap between equality *de jure* and de facto by increasing the awareness of women's legal rights. Considerable progress has been registered in developing a draft declaration on the issue of violence against women. Preparations are already under way for the Fourth World Conference on Women to be held at Beijing in 1995 to review progress made in the implementation of the Nairobi Forward-looking Strategies for the Advancement of Women.

92. The integration of vulnerable groups into the mainstream of development efforts is a valid goal in itself, but it also serves as a guarantee of social peace and political stability. The promotion

of respect for minority rights and the designation of 1993 as the International Year of the World's Indigenous People will create the necessary impetus to address their concerns. In addition, the United Nations is fostering awareness in developed and developing countries of the need to integrate the elderly and persons with disabilities into a productive social life.

93. One major development in the last year has been the world-wide mobilization of support for the implementation of the commitments adopted by the World Summit for Children. The Declaration endorsed by the Summit, which has now been signed by some 140 heads of State or Government, sets goals, through which we can save the lives of some 50 million children by the decade's end and improve the lives of millions more. Over 130 countries have prepared or are in the process of developing national programmes of action detailing their strategies to achieve these goals. The United Nations Children's Fund (UNICEF) is mobilizing analytical and operational capacity from a wide range of United Nations organizations in support of these efforts, which are focused on a broad range of issues, including health, basic education, nutrition, water and sanitation, and the rights of women and children. Non-governmental organizations and the private sector have also been actively involved.

Operational activities

94. Operational activities constitute the practical means by which the mandates of the United Nations in the economic and social fields are put into action. I am committed to using the operational capabilities of the Organization to the fullest to transform into reality our vision of equitable and sustainable development.

95. The basic strengths of the United Nations in the economic and social field lie in its neutrality, impartiality and cultural sensitivity. The focus of development assistance must be continuously adjusted to changes in the world in which it operates. The extensive field network of the United Nations, with offices in the majority of developing countries, should enable the Organization to respond flexibly and rapidly to changing national priorities. The United Nations Development Programme (UNDP) is working across all sectors to assist developing countries in strengthening national capacities for managing all phases of the development process from formulation, design and planning of policies and programming to execution and implementation.

96. The United Nations is increasingly involved in helping to continue the process of democratization and providing technical assistance for the electoral process in a number of countries. I am particularly pleased to respond to the requests for support in this process that I am receiving from Governments. In 1992, the United Nations has provided technical assistance for elections in Albania, the Congo, El Salvador, Ethiopia, Guinea, Guyana, Liberia, Madagascar, Mali, Rwanda and Togo, and most notably in Angola. The United Nations is assisting as well in preparations for referendums planned for Eritrea and Western Sahara.

97. Population growth in developing countries is a source of deep and justified concern. Numerous United Nations agencies under the aegis of the United Nations Population Fund (UNFPA) are engaged in the promotion of family planning and other population policies. The collaborative work of UNDP, UNICEF, the World Health Organization and UNFPA in maternal and child health care and family planning in support of national population frameworks is promising. The International Conference on Population and Development to be held in 1994 will be an important occasion to review progress made in this critical area.

98. The symbiosis between drugs and many social and political ills is evident. In addition, the ploughing back of vast proceeds from illicit drug trafficking into international money markets is having increasingly destabilizing consequences for national economies. The question of drug control requires coordinated international effort and, indeed, international legislation. The United Nations International Drug Control Programme encourages Governments to consider drug problems in their totality and also in relation to other social, economic and developmental issues. It provides Governments with guidance and technical cooperation regarding all aspects of drug control, income substitution, law enforcement, treatment and rehabilitation, legislative and institutional reform at the national, subregional and regional levels. The connection between drug trafficking and crime and approaches to crime prevention and criminal justice are reflected in a strengthened United Nations crime programme.

99. The recent increase in emergencies has served to highlight the important contribution of the World Food Programme in providing assistance to affected populations. Over the last two years, the Programme has increased its resources by 50 per cent and is moving increasingly towards integrating food aid with national development strategies. In addition to the provision of food, its logistical support has become an indispensable part of the international response to large-scale relief operations. It is coordinating, within the United Nations system, the transport and logistic efforts for the drought emergency in southern Africa.

Human rights and development

100. The protection of vulnerable groups is only one aspect of the commitment of the United Nations to human rights in general. Human rights are an essential component of sustainable development. Sustainable development is not possible without

respect for human rights. Human rights are meaningless in an environment of poverty and deprivation. The Charter of the United Nations places the promotion of human rights as one of our priority objectives, along with promoting development and preserving international peace and security. Achievements to date include the development of a significant body of international standards of universal applicability based on the Universal Declaration of Human Rights and the two International Human Rights Covenants, as well as a wide-ranging system supervising the compliance by States with their international human rights obligations. Particularly significant has been the work of the Centre for Human Rights at Geneva.

101.   However, if standards and procedures exist for normal situations, the United Nations has not been able to act effectively to bring to an end massive human rights violations. Faced with the barbaric conduct which fills the news media today, the United Nations cannot stand idle or indifferent. The long-term credibility of our Organization as a whole will depend upon the success of our response to this challenge. I suggest that we explore ways of empowering the Secretary-General and expert human rights bodies to bring massive violations of human rights to the attention of the Security Council, together with recommendations for action.

102.   Preventing violations before they occur is also of primary importance. The United Nations must be able to identify situations which could degenerate into violations and to take preventive measures. For example, we are studying those elements which have in the past helped to overcome situations of tension related to minorities. Our impartial intervention based on widely accepted standards could dissipate misunderstandings and help build a framework for living together. An impressive quantity of information on human rights is already available within the United Nations system submitted by Governments, non-governmental organizations and individuals to committees, commissions, the Secretary-General or various other bodies. The challenge is now to bring this information together in a focused way so as to understand complex situations better and thus be in a position to suggest appropriate action. The World Conference on Human Rights to be held at Vienna in 1993 will be important in this regard.

103.   Our long-term objective must be to achieve respect for human rights in every country. Building human rights institutions and promoting the human rights culture necessary for the functioning of such institutions is crucial here in connection with the transition of many countries to democracy. In the recent past, we have learned of the importance of strengthening respect for the rule of law and human rights in general through training, education, information and furnishing of expert advice. Many aspects of country programmes in this area could be carried out within the broader development programmes of United Nations agencies or bilateral donors. At the same time, the manifestations of concern for human rights and democracy must go hand in hand with action on such issues as debt, terms of trade and access to development assistance.

104.   In our efforts to build a culture of human rights, we must not forget the importance of human rights workers and non-governmental organizations, nor the courage shown by many who risk their lives and security for the rights of others. Those who work in the field understand that development provides the foundation for human rights advances, and that, equally, human rights are the key which unlocks the creative energies of people so central to economic progress.

C. *An agenda for development*

105.   An integrated approach to this wide range of issues, in sum an agenda for development, can only be promoted through a stronger United Nations. It has to become:

(a)   An organization which views its objectives in respect of economic and social cooperation and development with the same sense of responsibility and urgency as its commitments in the political and security area;

(b)   An organization where the intergovernmental bodies promote policy coherence, and where the Economic and Social Council plays the central role envisaged for it in the Charter of the United Nations;

(c)   An organization which takes full advantage of the central coordinating capacity available to it on economic, social and humanitarian issues, and of the intersectoral capabilities at its disposal in the regional commissions and in the various United Nations programmes and organs;

(d)   An organization whose extensive operational capabilities—available through UNDP, the World Food Programme, UNICEF and UNFPA—are fully supportive of its policy objectives, and where economic and social research and policy analysis, operational activities, humanitarian assistance and the promotion of human rights support and reinforce each other.

106.   The further phases of the reorganization of United Nations Secretariat structures in the economic and social field will be geared to those objectives.

107.   At the level of the United Nations system, my goal is not only to strengthen the coordination of the contributions which the various organizations of the system are in a position to make, it

is also—and perhaps more importantly—to ensure that the overall capacities of the system for research and policy analysis, finance for development and technical assistance are mobilized in a mutually reinforcing, concerted way.

108. I warmly welcome the proposal to convene a world summit for social development in 1995, which has now been endorsed by the Economic and Social Council. Consultations on the preparatory process have already begun. I am confident that the summit would provide leadership at the highest level for a shared world-wide commitment to put people at the centre of development and international cooperation. It would also surely act as a source of inspiration for new ideas and proposals towards the development of a more comprehensive approach to actions of the United Nations system in the social sphere.

109. Respect for human rights is clearly important in order to maintain international peace and security and to achieve social and economic development. In turn, without development, long-term enjoyment of human rights and democracy will prove illusory, and war, of course, is the antithesis of both. Good governance, democracy, participation, an independent judiciary, the rule of law, and civil peace create conditions necessary to economic progress. Increasingly, each area of our Organization sees the relevance of human rights in its own objectives and programmes. The Vienna World Conference on Human Rights in 1993 will bring together world leaders at the highest level. We look to this conference to reaffirm the need for the full implementation of economic, social and cultural rights, together with civil and political rights, and to reaffirm the link between development and the enjoyment of all human rights.

IV. *Peace endeavours*

A. *An overview of United Nations activities*

110. With the collective security role of the United Nations impaired in the post–Second World War era by the deep divisions between the two major nuclear nations, the United Nations created a new procedure to advance the cause of peace. "Peace-keeping" entered the international vocabulary with a fairly specific meaning: the employment of troops under United Nations command in non-violent operations, with the consent of parties to a conflict, for the purpose of maintaining stability in numerous areas of tension around the world.

111. The cold war confronted the international community with a singular threat to security; now, a widely varying array of resentments, ambitions, rivalries and hatreds masked for decades have come to the fore to threaten international harmony and shared purpose.

112. The nature of peace-keeping operations has evolved rapidly in recent years. The established principles and practices of peace-keeping have responded flexibly to new demands. The most notable feature of change in dealing with regional conflicts is that peace-keeping is no longer solely a military function. It is now almost always the case that operations undertaken by the United Nations must include civilian police, electoral personnel, human rights experts, information specialists and a significant number of political advisory staff. In Asia, Europe, Africa and in the western hemisphere new forms of conflict require a comprehensive approach.

113. Just as today no two conflicts are the same, so the design of cooperation and the division of labour in the service of peace, stability and renewal after conflict must be approached with flexibility and creativity adapted to each particular situation. In this regard, regional arrangements and agencies have new contributions to make.

114. Chapter VIII of the Charter of the United Nation envisages a clear role for regional arrangements and agencies as part of a structure for coping with international peace and security issues. In the past, regional arrangements were created because of the absence of a universal system for collective security; thus, their activities often worked at cross-purposes with the sense of solidarity required for the effectiveness of the world Organization. The cold war crippled the proper use of Chapter VIII and indeed, in that era regional arrangements worked on occasion against resolving disputes in the manner foreseen by the Charter. But in the post–cold–war period, regional organizations can play a crucial role, if their activities are undertaken in a manner consistent with the principles of Chapter VIII.

115. This is a critical moment to advance this concept and fulfil this opportunity. In many of the instances in which the United Nations has been active during 1992, regional organizations have played a part, particularly on the peacemaking side. My aim is to see that, in any new division of labour, the United Nations retains its primacy in the maintenance of international peace and security, while its burden is lightened, and its mission reinforced and underlined by the active involvement of appropriate regional arrangements and agencies. The exact modalities of this division of labour remain to be worked out, as regional organizations, no less than the United Nations itself, redefine their missions in the post–cold–war period.

116. The range of conflict we see today is immense. To provide a sense of this, the following review, based on events as of the end of August, surveys most, but not all, peace operations under way at present as represented on the map (see fig-

ure 6). The United Nations attaches equal importance to all these conflicts; when it comes to death and misery, no one situation takes priority over another.

Cyprus

117. The intensive efforts over the past year to reach agreement on the set of ideas on an overall framework agreement on Cyprus culminated in five weeks of meetings under my auspices with the leaders of the two communities. While these talks did not achieve the goal that one could have expected, a set of ideas has now been sufficiently developed to enable the two sides to reach an overall agreement. I share the Security Council's expectation, reflected in its resolution 774(1992), that when the talks resume on 26 October 1992, the two leaders will pursue direct and uninterrupted negotiations to reach an agreement.

Ethiopia and Eritrea

118. In order to promote democracy, I have been actively engaged in efforts to provide the Government of Ethiopia with assistance in the organization of regional elections. In the same vein, and as part of transitional assistance, I have been actively engaged in consultations aiming at the provision of United Nations assistance for the conduct of the planned referendum in Eritrea. A technical team visited Eritrea in August to collect information required for the involvement of the United Nations in the referendum process. Shortly, I shall assign two officers to Asmara to assist in the initial preparations and I shall report to the General Assembly in order to obtain a mandate for further action.

Haiti

119. Following the overthrow of President Aristide in September 1991, the Organization of American States (OAS) has taken the lead in restoring democracy in Haiti. The United Nations has supported OAS in that regard, and my mandate, by General Assembly resolution 46/7 of 11 October 1991, has been to provide the Secretary-General of that Organization with the support he might seek. I accepted his proposal to include a representative of the Secretary-General in a high-level mission of OAS to Haiti, which took place from 18 to 21 August. Nothing that the mission heard in Haiti during its visit indicates that the parties are closer to agreement than before. The Secretary-General of OAS has proposed to deploy to Haiti a first group of observers. In my view, the deployment of a mission, adequately staffed, with a well-defined mandate and the ability to visit the entire country, could play a useful role. I intend to continue to cooperate with OAS and to stand ready to help in any other way to solve the Haitian crisis.

Liberia

120. My representatives and I have been in regular contact with the leadership of the Economic Community of West African States (ECOWAS) and with other leaders in the region. In this connection, I support the efforts of ECOWAS towards a peaceful settlement of the Liberian situation. At its fifteenth session, held at Dakar from 27 to 29 July 1992, the heads of State and Government of ECOWAS invited the United Nations to facilitate the verification and monitoring of the electoral process. Between May and July 1992, I sent two consultants to Liberia to evaluate the availability of population data and the situation of constituency maps and to provide support to the Electoral Commission of Liberia. I am continuing with my endeavours to assist in the organization and conduct of the planned election.

Libyan Arab Jamahiriya

121. At the request of the Security Council, I have been endeavouring to persuade the Government of the Libyan Arab Jamahiriya to comply with resolutions for the purpose of establishing responsibility for the terrorist acts against Pan American flight 103 and Union de transports aériens flight 772, and contributing to the elimination of international terrorism. In the context of Security Council resolution 731(1992), I have dispatched six United Nations missions to the Libyan Arab Jamahiriya: on 26 January, 24 February, 27 February, 7 April, 11 May and 20 August. On each occasion, my envoy carried a letter from me to Colonel Muammar Qaddafi. These missions so far have not produced a full and effective response to the Council requests. This effort to achieve compliance with the resolutions of the Council will continue.

The Middle East

122. Developments of the past year have had stark consequences for the Palestinian people, including the 2.6 million refugees served by the United Nations Relief and Works Agency for Palestine Refugees in the Near East (UNRWA). The aftermath of the Gulf crisis has continued to cause hardship for tens of thousands of Palestinians who lost jobs and employment opportunities in Kuwait and other Arab Gulf States. Their influx into camps and towns in Jordan, the Syrian Arab Republic, Lebanon and the occupied territories has further tightened the already overstretched financial resources of UNRWA.

123. New challenges are arising from the more positive developments of the past year in the Middle East, namely, the start of substantive discussions between Israel, its Arab neighbours and the Palestinians over the framework of a peace settlement. The situation calls for a spirit of compromise and a mutual building of confidence.

Republic of Moldova

124. The conflict which erupted between the Dniester region's separatists and the Government has been at the centre of the peaceful settlement efforts of the Republic of Moldova, Romania, the Russian Federation and Ukraine. Concerned about the escalation of violence, I sent a fact-finding mission to the area at the end of June. On 21 July, an agreement was signed by the Moldovan and Russian presidents, resulting in the consolidation of a cease-fire monitored by a trilateral peace-keeping force. Following the Republic of Moldova's request for a United Nations observer mission, I sent the fact-finding mission back to the Republic of Moldova from 25 to 29 August. The mission noted that the situation in the Republic of Moldova had greatly improved; the escalation of violence has been reversed; and the parties to the conflict have been cooperating in the implementation of most of the provisions of the 21 July Agreement, including mechanisms such as the trilateral peace-keeping force. However, the prevailing conditions remain fragile and could rapidly deteriorate if negotiations towards an overall settlement do not progress more quickly.

Mozambique

125. At the invitation of the Government of Mozambique, issued in June, the United Nations is participating as an observer in the Italian-mediated talks between the Government and the Resistência Nacional Moçambicana, joining France, Portugal, the United Kingdom of Great Britain and Northern Ireland and the United States of America. The talks have been going on in Rome since 1990, and the recent declaration by the two parties establishing an October deadline for the cease-fire augurs well for the peace process. I have made it clear that the United Nations stands ready to support the envisaged electoral process as necessary, including the provision of electoral specialists and other relevant assistance. An electoral mission left for Mozambique on 4 September; it was followed by a technical team on 6 September. The Organization's efforts with Mozambique will be important in the region as a whole and the measures required must be approached as a comprehensive package.

Nagorno-Karabakh

126. The four-and-a-half-year-long conflict in and around Nagorno-Karabakh has left some 3,000 dead and over half a million refugees and displaced persons. Concern over the deteriorating situation and the threat to regional peace and security led to two United Nations fact-finding missions being sent to the area, from 16 to 21 March and from 21 to 28 May, in support of the efforts of the Conference on Security and Cooperation in Europe (CSCE) to achieve a peaceful settlement. A third mission was dispatched from 4 to 10 July to investigate Azerbaijani claims that Armenia had used chemical weapons, but found no evidence to that effect. Preliminary peace talks in Rome, sponsored by CSCE, were attended by a United Nations observer to look at arrangements for a cease-fire.

South Africa

127. Following the Boipatong massacre in June, I discussed the situation in South Africa with the Minister for Foreign Affairs, R. F. Botha, Chief Mangosuthu Buthelezi and Mr. Nelson Mandela, respectively. During the course of my official visit at the end of June to Abuja (Nigeria) and my attendance at the summit meeting of the Organization of African Unity held at Dakar (Senegal), I continued talks with these leaders and, in addition, with the representative of the Pan Africanist Congress of Azania, Mr. Clarence Makwetu. I urged them to resume negotiations and reported on my discussions to the Security Council.

128. On 16 July 1992, after hearing statements by the principal representatives of the above-mentioned parties, all of whom were in attendance, the Security Council unanimously adopted resolution 765(1992), which invited the Secretary-General to appoint a special representative. I named Mr. Cyrus R. Vance, who visited South Africa immediately after the adoption of the resolution. Also, at the request of the parties, 10 United Nations observers witnessed mass action during the week commencing 3 August 1992. The United Nations observers worked in close cooperation with the National Peace Secretariat during that week to observe mass mobilization, demonstrations and political rallies.

129. Following the adoption of Security Council resolution 772(1992) on 17 August 1992, 50 United Nations observers have been deployed in order to address effectively the areas of concern noted in my report of 7 August 1992, in coordination with the structures set up by the National Peace Accord. The international community must continue to assist the people of South Africa as a whole in their effort to bring an effective end to the violence and create conditions for negotiations leading towards a peaceful transition to a democratic, non-racial and united South Africa.

Western Sahara

130. In my efforts to reactivate the implementation of the settlement plan, I have tried to overcome the obstacles to the holding of a referendum. The differences over the criteria for eligibility to vote persist. My special representative has continued efforts to break the deadlock in which the settlement plan has found itself since the beginning

of this year. Since my report on the subject of 20 August 1992, my special representative has started negotiations with the two parties concerned in order to reach an agreement on the interpretation of the criteria relating to voter eligibility. The outcome of these negotiations will be reported to the Security Council.

B. *An analysis of five conflicts*

131. As the preceding list indicates, involvement by the United Nations has taken many forms, depending both on the nature of the situation itself and on the role which the United Nations has been called upon to perform. We have dispatched fact-finding missions and special representatives; observer teams have been deployed under United Nations auspices; there have been peace-keeping operations involving substantial numbers of United Nations troops and police; major humanitarian operations, sometimes involving millions of refugees and displaced persons, have been organized; and an active role in peace-building has brought involvement by the United Nations in the establishment of electoral machinery and participatory processes and even, in some cases, in providing advice and assistance on the writing of constitutions. The response has involved many agencies and has been multidisciplinary. The multiplicity of responses by the United Nations has therefore been as remarkable as the number and complexity of the situations with which we have been asked to deal.

132. To illustrate more fully the current range of challenges to United Nations peace operations, five conflicts warrant analysis: Cambodia, Yugoslavia, Somalia, Angola and El Salvador. These undertakings were all initiated, or have witnessed major developments, since I took office. All involve non-State parties whose cooperation is crucial for success. Each has a special character, yet all, in one way or another, require a comprehensive approach to peace-keeping or peace-building. The integrated approach described in section III of the present report applies not only to structural and developmental matters but to peace and security issues as well. In Asia, in Europe, in Africa and in the western hemisphere, new forms of conflict are giving rise to new forms of peace operations. The operations in Cambodia, Angola, Somalia, El Salvador and the former Yugoslavia, which I wish to highlight in this section, epitomize, in my view, the Organization's role in peace-keeping in the broader sense in which it now is coming to be understood.

133. Increasingly, United Nations peace-keeping forces are being established in situations where the success of the operation depends on the cooperation of non-governmental entities or irregular groups. This presents the Organization with a whole new set of problems, such as the lack of a unified or single chain of command, and difficulty in identifying the real source of authority and in establishing direct dialogue with the real as opposed to the formal leadership of these movements, factors which in turn may result in agreements not being honoured at lower levels. Frequently, these entities or groups, lacking international recognition, encounter obstacles in obtaining participation in peace conferences or intergovernmental consultations and have thus not always been parties to the political agreements underpinning the establishment of a peace-keeping force. It is also not uncommon for the leadership of these groups to be located in geographically remote areas lacking an established liaison with the United Nations Force Commander. Their very nature may lead them in turn to a generally mistrustful view of the outside world and of the intergovernmental community in particular, and to their being less susceptible to outside influence, while their often clandestine status sometimes makes it all the more difficult to obtain, where the need arises, reliable information about the locations, number of combatants or inventories of weapons.

Cambodia

134. As a result of the Agreements on a Comprehensive Political Settlement, concluded at the Paris Conference of October 1991, the United Nations has undertaken in Cambodia one of the most ambitious and complex peace-keeping operations of its history. The mandate entrusted to the United Nations Transitional Authority in Cambodia (UNTAC) and its estimated cost, if not its size, are indeed unprecedented. On the military side, the operation involves performing the difficult tasks of supervision, monitoring and verification of the cease-fire, the withdrawal of foreign troops, and the regrouping, cantonment, disarming and subsequent demobilization of the armed forces of the four Cambodian factions. On the civilian side, it includes innovative responsibilities, such as the control and supervision of the activities of the existing administrative structures and police forces, as well as measures to promote respect for human rights and fundamental freedoms, including the investigation and redress of human rights violations.

135. The United Nations has also been given, for the first time, the responsibility of organizing and conducting free and fair elections, which are scheduled to take place in late April or early May 1993. The repatriation of some 360,000 refugees and displaced persons is a critical element of the overall settlement and is being carried out as an integral part of the operation, with the Office of the United Nations High Commissioner for Refu-

gees acting as the lead agency. In addition, UNTAC is responsible for the coordination of a major programme of rehabilitation assistance launched during my visit to Phnom Penh last April. In other words, the United Nations is faced with the daunting task of nurturing national reconciliation, fostering the democratic process and building peace and stability in a country ravaged by two decades of war.

136. Since the establishment of the operation by the Security Council on 28 February 1992, over 18,000 United Nations military and civilian personnel have been deployed in the country. The presence of the United Nations is now felt in all the provinces and UNTAC has begun to carry out the various aspects of its wide-ranging mandate. In that connection, it is worth noting that, as of the end of August, more than 100,000 refugees and displaced persons had been successfully repatriated.

137. The progress of the operation has, however, been hampered by the refusal of one of the Cambodian parties to implement the second phase of the cease-fire, under which the armed forces of all the factions must be regrouped, cantoned and disarmed. After a careful consideration of the situation, I instructed my special representative to initiate Phase II on schedule on 13 June, so as to maintain the momentum of the operation. I took this decision with the conviction that the international community cannot allow the impressive diplomatic efforts, and the vast human and material resources it has devoted to the pursuit of peace and reconstruction in Cambodia to be negated by the unwillingness of one party to honour its obligations. At the end of July, the Security Council took a clear position on the matter and reiterated the firm commitment of the international community to the full implementation of the Paris Agreements.

138. Some 50,000 troops belonging to three of the Cambodian factions have now been regrouped and cantoned under the supervision of UNTAC. Various initiatives have been taken by my special representative and member countries of the Paris Conference, with a view to convincing the fourth Cambodian party to join the second phase of the cease-fire and extend the necessary cooperation to UNTAC.

139. It is my earnest hope that these efforts will soon reach fruition, for time is now of the essence. We are indeed reaching the stage where any further delay in the implementation of the second phase of the cease-fire would seriously impair the ability of UNTAC to carry out its mandate in accordance with the timetable set by the Security Council and would jeopardize the whole peace process. UNTAC will continue to work closely with the parties and the Supreme National Council of Cambodia to prevent such a predicament. The Cambodian people have endured enough suffering. They must be given the opportunity to determine freely their own political destiny and to enjoy the peace, stability and well-being to which they have aspired for so long.

The former Yugoslavia

140. The upheaval in the former Yugoslavia illustrates how the closing of the cold war opened a Pandora's box of causes and conflicts that had been kept down by the ideological struggle of that era. Old disputes, ambitions and hatreds have burst forth. In the years just past, such activities would have been regarded as points of loss or gain in the calculations of the bipolar Powers. Without the cold war structure to deal with them, it is left to us to provide the approaches and ultimately the answers. Territories of the former Yugoslavia, now the theatre of military operations, have recently been recognized by the international community and have taken their place in the General Assembly of the United Nations as Member States.

141. This is, then, a conflict with an international dimension. The future shape and security of one or more Member States—indeed their very existence—has come under threat. The unfolding of the crisis in the former Yugoslavia is also being watched closely by others who, in similar conditions of instability and new confrontations, could resort to war and destruction rather than choose the road of negotiation and dialogue. They must be led to understand and accept that the only route for change is one that is legal, peaceful, and contributes to a structure of international peace and security.

142. In response to this crisis, the United Nations has undertaken an intensive and extensive array of actions. The Security Council has expressed itself through a series of resolutions. My personal envoy, Mr. Cyrus R. Vance, has undertaken missions on behalf of the international community's effort to stop the fighting and find a peaceful solution. The United Nations Protection Force (UNPROFOR) has been established and steps have been taken to aid refugees, deliver relief supplies to people afflicted by the fighting and to provide help for the huge number of persons displaced by this conflict.

143. It must be realized that the expectations of the international community—which has been shocked by the horror of the conflict in Bosnia and Herzegovina—continue to exceed the resources and capacity of UNPROFOR. Under these circumstances, a wider international effort in support of the requirements of the Charter of the United Nations is warranted.

144. A Conference on the former Yugoslavia was held on 26 and 27 August in London under

the co-chairmanship of Prime Minister John Major, in his capacity as President of the Council of Ministers of the European Community, and myself. The purpose of the Conference is to broaden and intensify the search for a solution to the crisis in the former Yugoslavia in all its aspects. The decisions taken at the London Conference have embodied a framework within which a comprehensive settlement may be achieved through continuous and uninterrupted effort. The Conference established a Steering Committee, and appointed as co-chairmen Mr. Cyrus Vance and Lord Owen; they will direct the six working groups and prepare the basis for a general settlement. An effective mechanism has thus been provided for dealing with the problem in all its aspects. It is my earnest hope that the political will evident at London translates itself in the future into tangible actions.

Somalia

145. Somalia poses a particularly difficult challenge to the United Nations. A means must be found of responding to the urgent and overwhelming needs of a population increasingly desperate in the face of widespread hunger, the absence of national administration, almost complete destruction of basic infrastructure and acute insecurity.

146. As in the former Yugoslavia, United Nations personnel in Somalia face the problem of having to deal with irregular forces and nongovernmental groups. The breakdown of central authority has brought virtually the entire population of Somalia, some 6 million people, into the conflict in one way or another. A vicious circle of insecurity and hunger is at work in Somalia. Lack of security prevents the delivery of food, while food shortages contribute significantly to the level of violence and insecurity. Meanwhile, refugees from the senseless killing and famine have exported the problem to neighbouring States. There again, our humanitarian action is necessary to save lives and preserve the resources of Somalia's neighbours.

147. The effort to break this circle brings together a comprehensive programme of action covering humanitarian relief, the consolidation of cease-fires, the reduction of organized and unorganized violence and national reconciliation. Thus, action must be comprehensive and multifaceted. There will need to be measures to demobilize regular and irregular forces and to establish law and order, initially on a local basis. And equal consideration must be given to reintegrating the militia forces into civil society. A wide range of supporting intervention will be required to help re-establish local police forces: training, uniforms, communications and other equipment as well as advisory services. The programme of action will also have to include educational and vocational training programmes to provide people eventually with alternatives to armed action for their survival.

148. In short, the task involves nothing less than the reconstruction of an entire society and nation. For this task, it is necessary to broaden the scope of United Nations military involvement beyond the limited deployment, restricted to Mogadishu, which was previously considered sufficient. For the same purpose, the United Nations is working with the Organization of African Unity, the League of Arab States and the Organization of the Islamic Conference on arrangements for convening a conference on national reconciliation and unity in Somalia.

Angola

149. The peace process in Angola remains one of the most remarkable and challenging developments in Africa. For three decades, the United Nations has been deeply committed to the quest for peace and to social development in Angola and the process has now entered its most critical phase. It has been over a year since the end of the war and multiparty elections are scheduled to take place at the end of September. We have been providing the services of the United Nations peacekeeping forces and in 1992 have also begun to assist in the electoral process in an endeavour to help bring about a permanent solution. The registration of eligible voters, despite the logistical difficulties, was a remarkable achievement.

150. I appointed a special representative in February 1992 and, with the recent expansion by the Security Council of the United Nations Angola Verification Mission II, more than 500 United Nations observers—electoral, police and military—are assisting in the transition. A large technical assistance project related to the electoral process, involving cost-sharing arrangements with several countries, was prepared between November 1991 and March 1992. The project began in March 1992, followed more recently by the electoral component of the United Nations Angola Verification Mission II. Both are now completely operational.

151. A sizeable effort is being made to feed the tens of thousands of demobilizing troops and to provide for their vocational training, as well as to help the returning refugees. Further, the Special Relief Programme for Angola continues and bilateral assistance has been mobilized with the help of the United Nations. On the military side, the cease-fire has been maintained, although there has recently been an increase in violent incidents throughout the country. Nevertheless, with the help of the Verification Mission, the joint monitoring machinery has so far managed to keep these under control. Notwithstanding all difficulties,

both sides are to be congratulated on the progress they have achieved in implementing the Peace Accords. It is important now that they cooperate more closely with each other and with the United Nations, in order to establish a climate of confidence and ensure the success of elections.

El Salvador

152. Negotiations under the aegis of the United Nations culminated successfully at the beginning of the year and I had the pleasure of participating in the signature of the final peace agreement between the Government of El Salvador and the Frente Farabundo Martí para la Liberación Nacional as one of my first missions away from Headquarters. The Mexico agreement and others previously signed during the two-year negotiating process constitute a blueprint for the comprehensive, positive transformation of Salvadoran society, which was required to bring about national reconciliation. A new nation equipped with reformed institutions is to emerge after a period of transition, which is likely to last through the general elections in early 1994.

153. The Organization is playing a major and unprecedented role in this transition, in verifying the implementation of all agreements, including the nationwide monitoring of respect for human rights, which had begun last year. New verification mandates relate to the separation of forces and the cease-fire, the concentration of combatants, and the reintegration of the members of the Frente Farabundo Martí para la Liberación Nacional into society, as well as those relating to the reduction and reform of the armed forces and the reform of the judiciary and the electoral system. A new civilian police is being created, as a substitution for previous security bodies controlled by the armed forces. The United Nations is playing a central role in coordinating international assistance in this project. The United Nations is also overseeing action in regard to land and other economic and social issues. An ad hoc commission composed of distinguished Salvadorans appointed by my predecessor is reviewing the entire officer corps of the armed forces to make binding recommendations regarding their future on the basis of their respect for human rights, professional competence and aptitude for service under the new, peacetime criteria for the functioning of that institution. The Commission on the Truth, composed of three eminent non-Salvadorans, also designated by my predecessor, is investigating serious acts of violence that have occurred since 1980 and "whose impact on society urgently demands that the public should know the truth".

154. The implementation of this complex series of agreements was to have been carried out in accordance with an intricate calendar painstak-ingly negotiated by the parties. While the cease-fire is being respected, considerable problems have arisen in respect of the implementation of other agreements, to the point where adherence to the calendar, already twice revised, may be in question. The United Nations Observer Mission in El Salvador is working closely with the parties to make certain that, through continued dialogue, differences can be smoothly resolved.

155. These five conflicts reveal the paradox of present-day conflict: each is unique, requiring a specific response, yet all require a comprehensive approach that takes into account the wide range of substantive issues and calls for a coordinated and multidimensional international effort.

C. *Conflicts and humanitarian assistance*

156. Natural disasters continue to cause massive destruction and suffering, requiring relief aid. Increasingly, however, there is a need to assist people suffering from man-made devastation and warfare. The international community has thus been called upon to respond to massive new demands involving the provision of urgent humanitarian assistance in conditions of violent civil conflict. The magnitude and complexities of the crises make these efforts especially difficult. To the extent possible, humanitarian action is being integrated with efforts to resolve the underlying causes of the crisis.

157. The difficulty of providing humanitarian assistance to the needy has nowhere been more painfully exhibited than in Somalia and the former Yugoslavia. At the onset of the crisis, my predecessor designated the Office of the United Nations High Commissioner for Refugees as the lead agency for providing assistance to the refugees and displaced persons in the former Yugoslavia. The role of that organization has since vastly expanded. Even after repeated attempts by the international community, assured mechanisms for providing assistance to the needy are still not available. In Somalia, where the entire social infrastructure has collapsed, relief personnel from the United Nations and other organizations, the International Committee of the Red Cross and non-governmental organizations have been repeatedly subject to assault. The World Food Programme has carried the principal responsibility, with its logistical support, of providing food aid and helping transport non-food aid items along with UNICEF under these difficult circumstances. Both in the case of Somalia and in the former Yugoslavia there have been instances where the provision of relief assistance was deliberately prevented, thus perpetuating the misery of innocent victims held in ransom by the parties to the conflict.

158. Humanitarian assistance must be provided regardless of whether or not there is an immediate political solution. However, the secu-

rity and protection of staff and the safe and effective delivery of relief materials are major concerns with regard to humanitarian efforts in conflict situations. Indeed, the situations in Somalia and the former Yugoslavia have demonstrated that it may not be a question of the capacity to deliver, but rather the security conditions pertaining to distribution of relief supplies, which determines whether humanitarian assistance can be provided. Volatile security situations have in several cases led to the suspension of operations. In other cases, relief operations have continued, but at considerable hazard for those involved. United Nations and other humanitarian relief workers are often exposed to great dangers and many are risking their lives on a daily basis. I greatly admire the courage and humanitarian commitment of these dedicated colleagues. I am, however, very conscious of the heavy responsibility I bear in exposing them to fatal danger. Each situation is unique, requiring caution, as well as imagination and flexibility of approach. In finding viable solutions, I shall need the full cooperation of all parties concerned.

159. In cases of man-made emergencies, essential humanitarian assistance must be accompanied by measures to address the root causes through peacemaking and peace-building efforts. Providing succour to the victims of conflict through effective relief programmes can positively assist peacemaking efforts. Corridors of peace and zones of tranquillity for relief delivery can reinforce peacemaking processes. By expanding or broadening such concepts—with the consent of the parties—momentum can be generated for political dialogue and peace efforts. In insisting on close cooperation, I see a dynamic link between peacemaking, peacekeeping and humanitarian assistance, constituting the essence of humanitarian diplomacy.

160. The mechanisms for refugee assistance that emerged in the light of experience in the postwar period have served us well. But with ever-increasing numbers of internally displaced persons—in fact exceeding the number of refugees—there is a need to bring clarity to institutional mandates. This problem has been addressed on an ad hoc basis, but it is now timely to devise a clear United Nations system-wide approach to it.

161. A well-coordinated and coherent United Nations system response to emergencies requires close cooperation among the key operational organizations, the International Committee of the Red Cross, the regional and subregional organizations, and the non-governmental organizations, working together as a team dedicated to the achievement of a shared objective. I am making every effort to ensure that this cooperation and collaboration is achieved, both at the policy level and in the field. This requires changes in attitude, and a broad global rather than institutional approach

to addressing problems of coordination. I am pleased to say that, even in this short time, considerable progress has been achieved. This is reflected in the newly established inter-agency process for carrying out needs assessment, the preparation of consolidated appeals, the mobilization of resources and follow-up.

162. In accordance with General Assembly resolution 46/182, the Central Emergency Revolving Fund has been established for use in "start-up" emergency operations. Its ultimate success will depend on the cooperation of the operational organizations and the international community. The former must ensure that funds advanced are replenished promptly in accordance with the established guidelines, while the response of the latter to consolidated appeals for emergency assistance will be of critical importance.

163. Disaster preparedness and mitigation constitute major objectives for the United Nations. These are also the focus of the International Decade for Natural Disaster Reduction. The cooperation and involvement of development organizations will be vital to the realization of these objectives. Indeed, enhancement of the preparedness capacity of developing countries is perhaps one of the most important elements of humanitarian response to major natural disasters.

164. The capacity of the system to provide effective and timely assistance is largely dependent upon the resources available to it. I was pleased to see that the international community responded positively to the $854 million appeal for assistance to the drought-stricken countries of southern Africa when it pledged almost $600 million at the Pledging Conference in June. In contrast, however, most operational organizations continue to face serious financial difficulties, in view of less generous responses to appeals for assistance. My appeal for emergency humanitarian assistance for Afghanistan is a case in point, where less than one third of the $180 million sought has so far been pledged. I call upon the international community to look once again with solidarity upon those less fortunate and to redouble its financial commitments for the benefit of humanitarian programmes in all parts of the world.

V. *Conclusion: Democratization and development*

165. The challenge to the United Nations is comprehensive: to become at last an effective collective instrument of global peace and security, to foster responsible relations within the community of States, to ensure the respect of the rights of all peoples for self-determination, to achieve international cooperation in the solution of economic, social, intellectual, ecological and humanitarian problems.

166. The old international order has been swept away by a tidal wave of democratization. Thirst for

democracy has been a major cause of change, and it will continue to be a force for the construction of a better world. The United Nations must foster, through its peace-building measures, the process of democratization in situations characterized by long-standing conflicts, both within and among nations.

167. I am committed, as Secretary-General, to reform the Organization to ensure that each of its organs employs its fullest capabilities in the balanced and harmonious fashion envisioned by the Charter of the United Nations. The pace of reform must be increased if the United Nations is to keep ahead of the acceleration of history that characterizes this age. All organs of the United Nations must be accorded and play their full and proper role so that the trust of all nations and peoples will be retained and deserved.

168. In that regard, the United Nations is of particular significance to the developing countries. It is not only a forum where their voices can be heard; it also provides a means of consensus-building aimed at securing the socio-economic underpinnings of political freedom. The United Nations has a crucial responsibility to monitor economic and social trends that may become sources of political tensions, violence and repression. Stark poverty, economic deprivation, political denial, and social alienation provide little nourishment for the growth of democracy. The United Nations must push for a global partnership to promote the integration of the developing countries, and those in transition, into the world economy. International financial and developmental agencies are a powerful instrument for realizing a people-centred vision of development that goes beyond the statistics of economic performance among the industrialized and the developing countries. The promotion of universal political participation and world-wide economic recovery are not distant goals; they are the foundations of a healthy and effective movement for democracy.

169. Democracy within the family of nations means the application of its principles within the world Organization itself. I am committed to a broad dialogue between the Member States and the Secretary-General. Preserving the moral authority of the United Nations requires the fullest consultation, participation and engagement of all States, large and small, in the work of the United Nations. That in turn requires the empowerment of people in civil society, providing help where it is needed by supporting indigenous communities, non-governmental organizations, citizens' groups and the private sector.

170. Here then, in 1992, a better world is within our reach. It is the time to move forward deliberately and conscientiously towards the realization of the vast potential of this unique Organization and to bring new life to the world of the Charter.

Boutros BOUTROS-GHALI
Secretary-General

Figure 1

Security Council: number of official meetings,* resolutions
and Presidential statements, 1987-1992

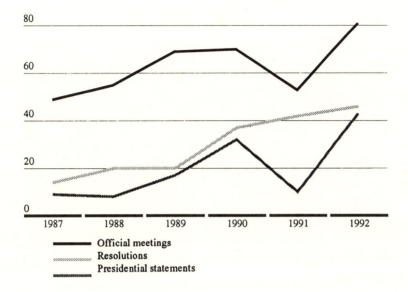

* 1990 includes one resumed meeting.
  1991 includes six closed sessions of the same meeting
  in addition to an open session of the meeting.
  1992 includes one resumed meeting.

Figure 2

Security Council: number of consultations of the whole and
bilateral consultations,* 1987–1992

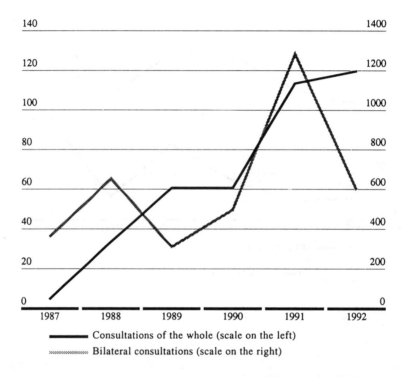

——— Consultations of the whole (scale on the left)
∞∞∞∞∞∞ Bilateral consultations (scale on the right)

* 1990 includes one resumed meeting.

Figure 3

Annual assessments and paid contributions:
regular budget and peace-keeping combined, 1987–1991

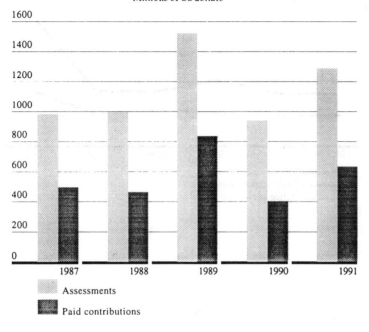

Millions of US dollars

Figure 4

Peace-keeping activities: number of personnel deployed,
1987–1992

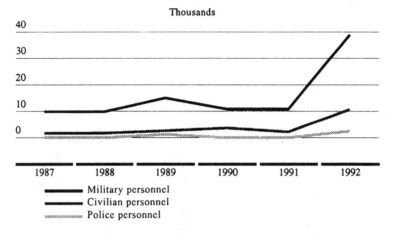

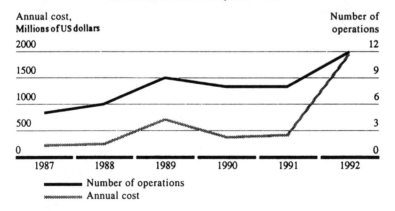

Figure 5

Peace-keeping activities: number of operations deployed
and their annual cost, 1987–1992

Figure 6

Peace-keeping forces and observer missions, 1948–1992

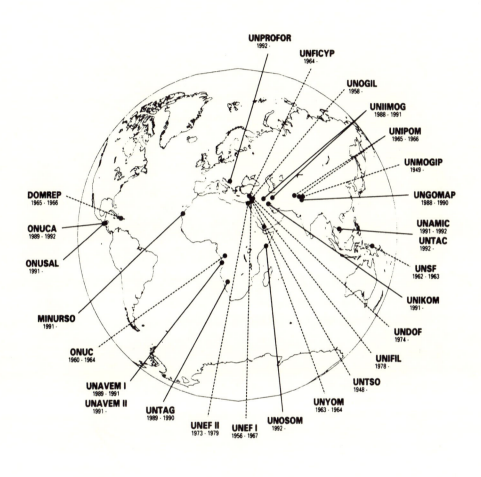

BEFORE 1988   SINCE 1988

MAP NO. 3687.1 Rev. 1   UNITED NATIONS
OCTOBER 1992

PART ONE

Political and security questions

Chapter I

International peace and security

The United Nations continued in 1992 to safeguard international peace and security. During the year, a record number of 12 peace-keeping operations were deployed in various regions of the world, with nearly 40,000 authorized military personnel serving under United Nations command.

For the first time ever, the Security Council held a summit at the level of heads of State and Government to consider its responsibility in the maintenance of international peace and security. It adopted conclusions concerning the commitment to collective security, peacemaking and peace-keeping, and disarmament, arms control and weapons of mass destruction. The Secretary-General responded to the summit with "An Agenda for Peace", outlining concepts and measures of preventive diplomacy, peacemaking and peace-keeping, to which he added the concept of post-conflict peace-building. The Council examined "An Agenda for Peace" in detail throughout the year, as did the General Assembly at its 1992 regular session.

The Assembly's consideration of that item resulted in the adoption of resolution 47/120, which dealt with the peaceful settlement of disputes, preventive diplomacy and confidence-building measures, including fact-finding, an early-warning mechanism and humanitarian assistance.

On the basis of the report of the Special Committee on Peace-keeping Operations, the Assembly, by resolution 47/71, adopted a series of recommendations and conclusions on peace-keeping matters, such as personnel, material and technical resources and financing.

Both the Council and the Assembly condemned the rising number of attacks against United Nations staff serving in various peace-keeping operations. The Assembly put forward a number of recommendations to help protect peace-keeping personnel better.

The Security Council, in January, urged the Libyan Arab Jamahiriya to respond to requests in connection with two aerial incidents—the bombing in December 1988 of Pan Am flight 103 over Lockerbie in southern Scotland and the crash in September 1989 of Union de transports aériens flight 772 over the Ténéré desert in the Niger—in which Libyan nationals were alleged to have been involved. In March 1992, the Council imposed an air and arms embargo against the Jamahiriya.

Maintenance of international security and strengthening of the international security system

Heads of State and Government Security Council summit

For the first time in its history, the Security Council on 31 January met at the level of heads of State and Government. The meeting, convened at the initiative of the United Kingdom in its capacity as Council President for January, was attended by 13 heads of State or Government (Austria, Belgium, Cape Verde, China, Ecuador, France, India, Japan, Morocco, Russian Federation, United Kingdom, United States, Venezuela) and 2 Foreign Ministers (Hungary and Zimbabwe) of the Council's 15 members. In a statement by the President at the conclusion of the day-long meeting, the Council asked the Secretary-General to recommend ways to strengthen and make more efficient the United Nations capacity for preventive diplomacy, peacemaking and peace-keeping, within the framework and provisions of the United Nations Charter. The Council also reaffirmed its commitment to the Charter's collective security system to deal with threats to peace and reverse acts of aggression.

SECURITY COUNCIL ACTION

Following statements by the Secretary-General and all the Council members, the Council's action came in the form of a statement by the Council President on behalf of the members:[1]

Meeting number. SC 3046.

"The Security Council met at the Headquarters of the United Nations in New York on 31 January 1992, for the first time at the level of heads of State and Government. The members of the Council considered, within the framework of their commitment to the United Nations Charter, 'The responsibility of the Security Council in the maintenance of international peace and security'.

"The members of the Security Council consider that their meeting is a timely recognition of the fact that there are new favourable international circumstances under which the Security Council has begun to fulfil more effectively its primary responsibility for the maintenance of international peace and security.

''*A time of change*

''This meeting takes place at a time of momentous change. The ending of the cold war has raised hopes for a safer, more equitable and more humane world. Rapid progress has been made, in many regions of the world, towards democracy and responsive forms of government, as well as towards achieving the purposes set out in the Charter. The completion of the dismantling of apartheid in South Africa would constitute a major contribution to these purposes and positive trends, including to the encouragement of respect for human rights and fundamental freedoms.

''Last year, under the authority of the United Nations, the international community succeeded in enabling Kuwait to regain its sovereignty and territorial integrity, which it had lost as a result of Iraqi aggression. The resolutions adopted by the Security Council remain essential to the restoration of peace and stability in the region and must be fully implemented. At the same time the members of the Council are concerned by the humanitarian situation of the innocent civilian population of Iraq.

''The members of the Council support the Middle East peace process, facilitated by the Russian Federation and the United States, and hope that it will be brought to a successful conclusion on the basis of Council resolutions 242(1967) and 338(1973).

''They welcome the role the United Nations has been able to play under the Charter in progress towards settling long-standing regional disputes, and will work for further progress towards their resolution. They applaud the valuable contribution being made by United Nations peace-keeping forces now operating in Asia, Africa, Latin America and Europe.

''The members of the Council note that United Nations peace-keeping tasks have increased and broadened considerably in recent years. Election monitoring, human rights verification and the repatriation of refugees have, in the settlement of some regional conflicts, at the request or with the agreement of the parties concerned, been integral parts of the Security Council's effort to maintain international peace and security. They welcome these developments.

''The members of the Council also recognize that change, however welcome, has brought new risks for stability and security. Some of the most acute problems result from changes to State structures. The members of the Council will encourage all efforts to help achieve peace, stability and cooperation during these changes.

''The international community therefore faces new challenges in the search for peace. All Member States expect the United Nations to play a central role at this crucial stage. The members of the Council stress the importance of strengthening and improving the United Nations to increase its effectiveness. They are determined to assume fully their responsibilities within the United Nations Organization in the framework of the Charter.

''The absence of war and military conflicts amongst States does not in itself ensure international peace and security. The non-military sources of instability in the economic, social, humanitarian and ecological fields have become threats to peace and security. The United Nations membership as a whole, working through the appropriate bodies, needs to give the highest priority to the solution of these matters.

''*Commitment to collective security*

''The members of the Council pledge their commitment to international law and to the United Nations Charter. All disputes between States should be peacefully resolved in accordance with the provisions of the Charter.

''The members of the Council reaffirm their commitment to the collective security system of the Charter to deal with threats to peace and to reverse acts of aggression.

''The members of the Council express their deep concern over acts of international terrorism and emphasize the need for the international community to deal effectively with all such acts.

''*Peacemaking and peace-keeping*

''To strengthen the effectiveness of these commitments, and in order that the Security Council should have the means to discharge its primary responsibility under the Charter for the maintenance of international peace and security, the members of the Council have decided on the following approach.

''They invite the Secretary-General to prepare, for circulation to the Members of the United Nations by 1 July 1992, his analysis and recommendations on ways of strengthening and making more efficient within the framework and provisions of the Charter the capacity of the United Nations for preventive diplomacy, for peacemaking and for peace-keeping.

''The Secretary-General's analysis and recommendations could cover the role of the United Nations in identifying potential crises and areas of instability as well as the contribution to be made by regional organizations in accordance with Chapter VIII of the United Nations Charter in helping the work of the Council. They could also cover the need for adequate resources, both material and financial. The Secretary-General might draw on lessons learned in recent United Nations peace-keeping missions to recommend ways of making more effective Secretariat planning and operations. He could also consider how greater use might be made of his good offices, and of his other functions under the United Nations Charter.

''*Disarmament, arms control and weapons of mass destruction*

''The members of the Council, while fully conscious of the responsibilities of other organs of the United Nations in the fields of disarmament, arms control and non-proliferation, reaffirm the crucial contribution which progress in these areas can make to the maintenance of international peace and security. They express their commitment to take concrete steps to enhance the effectiveness of the United Nations in these areas.

''The members of the Council underline the need for all Member States to fulfil their obligations in relation to arms control and disarmament; to prevent the proliferation in all its aspects of all weapons of mass destruction; to avoid excessive and destabilizing accumulations and transfers of arms; and to resolve peacefully in accordance with the Charter any problems concerning these matters threatening or disrupting the maintenance of regional and global stability. They emphasize the importance of the early ratification and implementation by the States concerned of all international and regional arms control arrangements, especially the START and CFE Treaties.

"The proliferation of all weapons of mass destruction constitutes a threat to international peace and security. The members of the Council commit themselves to working to prevent the spread of technology related to the research for or production of such weapons and to take appropriate action to that end.

"On nuclear proliferation, they note the importance of the decision of many countries to adhere to the Non-Proliferation Treaty and emphasize the integral role in the implementation of that Treaty of fully effective IAEA safeguards, as well as the importance of effective export controls. The members of the Council will take appropriate measures in the case of any violations notified to them by IAEA.

"On chemical weapons, they support the efforts of the Geneva Conference with a view to reaching agreement on the conclusion, by the end of 1992, of a universal convention, including a verification regime, to prohibit chemical weapons.

"On conventional armaments, they note the General Assembly's vote in favour of a United Nations register of arms transfers as a first step, and in this connection recognize the importance of all States providing all the information called for in the General Assembly's resolution.

"In conclusion, the members of the Security Council affirm their determination to build on the initiative of their meeting in order to secure positive advances in promoting international peace and security. They agree that the United Nations Secretary-General has a crucial role to play. The members of the Council express their deep appreciation to the outgoing Secretary-General, His Excellency Mr. Javier Pérez de Cuéllar, for his outstanding contribution to the work of the United Nations, culminating in the signature of the El Salvador peace agreement. They welcome the new Secretary-General, His Excellency Dr. Boutros Boutros-Ghali, and note with satisfaction his intention to strengthen and improve the functioning of the United Nations. They pledge their full support to him, and undertake to work closely with him and his staff in fulfilment of their shared objectives, including a more efficient and effective United Nations system.

"The members of the Council agree that the world now has the best chance of achieving international peace and security since the foundation of the United Nations. They undertake to work in close cooperation with other United Nations Member States in their own efforts to achieve this, as well as to address urgently all the other problems, in particular those of economic and social development, requiring the collective response of the international community. They recognize that peace and prosperity are indivisible and that lasting peace and stability require effective international cooperation for the eradication of poverty and the promotion of a better life for all in larger freedom.''

"An Agenda for Peace": preventive diplomacy, peacemaking and peace-keeping

Report of the Secretary-General. In June 1992,[2] the Secretary-General responded to the request of the Security Council summit in January, outlining an agenda for peace: preventive diplomacy, peacemaking and peace-keeping, to which he added the concept of post-conflict peace-building.

In the previous few years, the Secretary-General said, the immense ideological barrier that for decades had given rise to distrust and hostility collapsed. Even as issues between States north and south grew more acute, the improvement between States east and west afforded new possibilities to meet successfully threats to common security.

The global transition was marked by uniquely contradictory trends. Regional and continental associations of States were evolving ways to deepen cooperation and ease some of the contentious characteristics of sovereign and nationalistic rivalries. At the same time, new assertions of nationalism and sovereignty sprang up, and the cohesion of States was threatened by ethnic, religious, social, cultural or linguistic strife.

While the concept of peace was easy to grasp, that of international security was more complex, with a pattern of contradictions that had arisen. As major nuclear Powers had begun to negotiate arms reductions agreements, the proliferation of weapons of mass destruction threatened to increase and conventional arms continued to be amassed in many parts of the world.

The Secretary-General emphasized that since 31 May 1990, and with the end of the cold war, there had been no vetoes in the Security Council and demands on the United Nations had surged. Its security arm had emerged as a central instrument for the prevention and resolution of conflicts and for the preservation of peace. The aims of the United Nations must be to identify at the earliest possible stage situations that could produce conflict, and to try through diplomacy to remove the sources of danger before violence resulted. Where conflict erupted, the United Nations should engage in peacemaking aimed at resolving the issues that had led to conflict, and preserve peace through peace-keeping. The Organization must stand ready to assist in peace-building in its differing contexts and, in the largest sense, to address the deepest causes of conflict: economic despair, social injustice and political oppression.

The Secretary-General defined preventive diplomacy as action to prevent disputes from arising between parties, to prevent existing disputes from escalating into conflicts, and to limit the spread of the latter when they occurred. Peacemaking was action to bring hostile parties to agreement, essentially through such peaceful means as those foreseen in Chapter VI of the Charter. Peacekeeping was the deployment of a United Nations presence in the field, with the consent of the parties concerned, normally involving United Nations military and/or police personnel and frequently civilians as well. Post-conflict peace-building was defined as action to identify and support structures which strengthened and solidified peace to avoid a relapse into conflict. Preventive diplomacy sought to resolve disputes before violence broke out; peacemaking and peace-keeping were required to halt conflicts and preserve peace once it was attained. If successful, they strengthened the opportunity for post-conflict peace-building, which could prevent the recurrence of violence among nations and peoples.

Preventive diplomacy. Preventive diplomacy could be performed by the Secretary-General personally or through senior staff or specialized agencies and programmes, by the Security Council or the General Assembly, and by regional organizations in cooperation with the United Nations. It required measures to create confidence; it needed early warning based on information gathering and fact-finding; it might also involve preventive deployment and, in some situations, demilitarized zones.

Peacemaking. Under peacemaking, the report discussed greater reliance on the International Court of Justice; amelioration through assistance; sanctions and special economic problems; use of military force; and the utilization of peace-enforcement units.

When peacemaking required the imposition of sanctions under Article 41 of the Charter, it was important that States confronted with special economic problems not only had the right to consult the Security Council under Article 50, but also had the realistic possibility of having their difficulties addressed. The Secretary-General recommended that the Council devise a set of measures involving financial institutions and other components of the United Nations system that could be put in place to insulate States from such difficulties, as a matter of equity and a means of encouraging States to cooperate with Council decisions.

Peace-keeping. Peace-keeping could rightly be called the invention of the United Nations, having brought stability to numerous areas of conflict around the world. In view of the volume and unpredictability of peace-keeping contributions, the Secretary-General strongly supported proposals in some States that their peace-keeping contributions be financed from defence, rather than foreign affairs, budgets. He recommended such action to others and urged the General Assembly to encourage that approach. He again requested all States to indicate what military personnel they were in principle prepared to make available. He recommended that arrangements be reviewed and improved for training civilian, police or military peace-keeping personnel and that the strength and capability of military staff serving in the Secretariat be augmented to meet new and heavier requirements.

Post-conflict peace-building. In the aftermath of international war, post-conflict peace-building might take the form of concrete cooperative projects linking two or more countries in a mutually beneficial undertaking. That could not only contribute to economic and social development but also enhance the confidence fundamental to peace. The concept of peace-building as the construction of a new environment should be viewed as the counterpart of preventive diplomacy, which sought to avoid the breakdown of peaceful conditions. Preventive diplomacy was to avoid a crisis; post-conflict peace-building was to prevent a recurrence.

Cooperation with regional arrangements and organizations. Regional arrangements or organizations in many cases possessed a potential that should be utilized in preventive diplomacy, peace-keeping, peacemaking and post-conflict confidence-building. Under the Charter, the Security Council had and would continue to have primary responsibility for maintaining international security, but regional action as a matter of decentralization, delegation and cooperation with United Nations efforts could contribute to a deeper sense of participation, consensus and democratization in international affairs.

Agenda for peace. Concluding with "An Agenda for Peace", the Secretary-General stressed that the Security Council must never again lose the collegiality that was essential to its proper functioning. A genuine sense of consensus deriving from shared interests must govern its work, not the threat of the veto or the power of any group of nations. The Secretary-General recommended that the heads of State and Government of members of the Council meet in alternate years, just before the start of the general debate in the General Assembly, and that the Council meet at the Foreign Minister level whenever the situation warranted such meetings.

The Secretary-General cautioned against unilateralism and isolationism and stressed that democracy required respect for human rights and fundamental freedoms as set forth in the Charter. He stated that democracy within the family of nations required fullest consultation, participation and engagement of all States in the work of the Organization and that the principles of the Charter must be applied consistently, not selectively. Swift and impartial reaction of the Organization presupposed an efficient and independent international civil service and an assured financial basis.

In addition, involvement of non-governmental organizations, academic institutions, parliamentarians, business and professional communities, the media and the public at large would help strengthen the Organization's ability to reflect the concerns of its widest constituency.

The Security Council took note of the Secretary-General's agenda for peace on 30 June. Following consultations, the President made a statement on behalf of the Council members:[3]

Meeting number. SC 3089.

"The Security Council has noted with interest and appreciation the report of the Secretary-General on ways of strengthening and making more efficient within the framework and provisions of the Charter of the United Nations the capacity of the United Nations for preventive diplomacy, for peacemaking and for peace-keeping, prepared pursuant to the statement adopted on 31 January 1992 at the conclusion of the meeting held for the first time by the Security Council at the level of heads of State and Government. It is grateful to the Secretary-General for his report, which is a comprehensive reflection on the ongoing process of strengthening the Organization. In this connection, the Council welcomes the efforts made by the Secretary-General.

"In reading the report, the Security Council has noted a set of interesting proposals addressed to the various organs of the United Nations and to Member States and regional organizations. The Council therefore trusts that all organs and entities, in particular the General Assembly, will devote particular attention to the report and will study and evaluate the elements of the report that concern them.

"Within the scope of its competence, the Security Council will, for its part, examine in depth and with due priority the recommendations of the Secretary-General.

"The Security Council also takes this opportunity to reiterate its readiness to cooperate fully with the Secretary-General in the strengthening of the Organization in accordance with the provisions of the Charter."

In a statement issued on 25 September following a meeting with the Secretary-General,[4] the five permanent members of the Council addressed a number of regional conflicts and noted with appreciation the Secretary-General's agenda for peace.

The Council began its in-depth examination of "An Agenda for Peace" on 29 October. Following consultations, the President made a statement on behalf of the Council members:[5]

Meeting number. SC 3128.

"Pursuant to the President's statement of 30 June 1992, the Security Council has begun to examine the Secretary-General's report entitled 'An Agenda for Peace'.

"This examination of 'An Agenda for Peace' by the Security Council will be coordinated with the discussions carried out in the General Assembly. The Council welcomes in this regard the contact already established between the Presidents of the two organs and invites its President to continue and intensify such contacts.

"The Security Council intends to examine the proposals of the Secretary-General which concern it or are addressed to it. For this purpose, the members of the Council have decided to hold a meeting at least once a month on the report, such meetings being prepared for, as necessary, by a working group.

"One objective of this examination is to arrive at conclusions which would be considered during a special meeting of the Security Council. The Council will determine the date of this meeting, bearing in mind the progress of the work at the present session of the General Assembly, but it hopes to hold the meeting by next spring at the latest.

"The Security Council has followed with close interest the views expressed by Member States in the General Assembly during the general debate as well as during the discussion on item 10 of the agenda of the General Assembly. It has also noted the report of the special session of the Special Committee on Peace-keeping Operations. It has now identified the Secretary-General's proposals which concern it or are addressed to it.

"Without prejudice to the further examination of other proposals of the Secretary-General, and taking into account the greatly increased number and complexity of peace-keeping operations authorized by the Council during recent months, the Council believes that two suggestions contained in 'An Agenda for Peace' should be considered at this moment:

"The Security Council, in accordance with the recommendations contained in paragraph 51 of the Secretary-General's report, encourages Member States to inform the Secretary-General of their willingness to provide forces or capabilities to the United Nations for peace-keeping operations and the type of units or capabilities that might be available at short notice, subject to overriding national defence requirements and the approval of the Governments providing them. It further encourages the Secretariat and those Member States which have indicated such willingness to enter into direct dialogue so as to enable the Secretary-General to know with greater precision what forces or capabilities might be made available to the United Nations for particular peace-keeping operations, and on what time-scale;

"The Security Council shares the view of the Secretary-General in paragraph 52 of his report concerning the need for an augmentation of the strength and capability of military staff serving in the Secretariat and of civilian staff dealing more generally with peace-keeping matters in the Secretariat. The Council suggests to the Secretary-General that he report to it, as well as to the General Assembly, on this subject as soon as possible. The Secretary-General might consider in his report the establishment in the Secretariat of an enhanced peace-keeping planning staff and an operations centre in order to deal with the growing complexity of initial planning and control of peace-keeping operations in the field. The Council further suggests to Member States that they consider making available to the Secretariat appropriately experienced military or civilian staff, for a fixed period of time, to help with work on peace-keeping operations.

"Moreover, the Security Council intends to study those paragraphs which are addressed to it, including paragraph 41 concerning the special economic problems which may concern other States when sanctions are imposed on a State, paragraphs 64 and 65 concerning the role of regional organizations, and paragraph 25 concerning resort by the United Nations to fact-finding.''

Following consultations, the President made a statement on 30 November on behalf of the Council members:[6]

"The members of the Security Council had continued the examination of the Secretary-General's report entitled 'An Agenda for Peace'.

"The members of the Security Council welcome and support the proposals in paragraph 25 of 'An Agenda for Peace' on fact-finding. They are of the view that an increased resort to fact-finding as a tool of preventive diplomacy, in accordance with the Charter and General Assembly Declaration on Fact-finding (resolution 46/59), particularly its guidelines, can result in the best possible understanding of the objective facts of a situation which will enable the Secretary-General to meet his responsibilities under Article 99 of the Charter and facilitate Security Council deliberations. They agree that various forms of fact-finding can be employed according to the requirements of a situation, and that a request by a State for the dispatch of a fact-finding mission to its territory should be considered without undue delay. They encourage all Member States in a position to do so to provide the Secretary-General with the detailed information needed on issues of concern, so as to facilitate effective preventive diplomacy.

"The members of the Security Council, being aware of the increased responsibilities of the United Nations in the area of preventive diplomacy, invite the Secretary-General to consider the appropriate measures necessary to strengthen the capacity of the Secretariat for information gathering and in-depth analysis. They also invite the Member States and the Secretary-General to consider the secondment of experts to help in this regard. They urge the Secretary-General to take appropriate measures to ensure the availability at short notice of eminent persons who might share, with senior officials of the Secretariat, the burden of fact-finding missions. They note the positive role of regional organizations and arrangements in fact-finding within their areas of competence and welcome its intensification and close coordination with fact-finding efforts by the United Nations.

"Bearing in mind the Declaration on Fact-finding and the Secretary-General's recommendations in 'An Agenda for Peace', the members of the Security Council for their part will facilitate and encourage every appropriate use of fact-finding missions on a case-by-case basis in accordance with the purposes and principles of the Charter of the United Nations.

"In this context, the members of the Security Council note and endorse the Secretary-General's view that in some cases a fact-finding mission can help defuse a dispute or situation, indicating to those concerned that the United Nations and in particular the Security Council is actively seized of the matter as a present or potential threat to international peace and security. Such action in the early stages of a potential dispute can be particularly effective. They welcome the Secretary-General's readiness to make full use of his powers under Article 99 of the Charter to draw the attention of the Security Council to any matter which in his opinion may threaten international peace and security. They note with satisfaction the recent greater use of fact-finding missions, as exemplified by the missions to Moldova, Nagorno-Karabakh, Georgia, Uzbekistan and Tajikistan.

"The members of the Security Council intend to continue their work on the Secretary-General's report as indicated in the President's statement of 29 October 1992.''

The Security Council again considered "An Agenda for Peace" on 30 December. Following consultations, the President made a statement on behalf of the Council members:[7]

Meeting number. SC 3154.

"In pursuance of the President's statement of 29 October 1992 in connection with the Secretary-General's report entitled 'An Agenda for Peace', according to which 'the Security Council intends to study those paragraphs which are addressed to it, including paragraph 41 concerning the special economic problems which may concern other States when sanctions are imposed on a State', the Security Council examined the question of special economic problems of States as a result of sanctions imposed under Chapter VII of the Charter.

"The Security Council shares the observation made by the Secretary-General in paragraph 41 of his report that when such sanctions are imposed under Chapter VII of the Charter, it is important that States confronted with special economic problems have the right to consult the Security Council regarding such problems, as provided in Article 50. The Council agrees that appropriate consideration should be given to their situation.

"The Security Council notes the Secretary-General's recommendation that the Council devise a set of measures, involving the financial institutions and other components of the United Nations system, that can be put in place to insulate States from such difficulties.

"The Security Council, while noting that this matter is being considered in other forums of the United Nations, expresses its determination to consider this matter further and invites the Secretary-General to consult the heads of the international financial institutions, other components of the United Nations system and Member States of the United Nations, and to report to the Security Council as early as possible.

"The Security Council intends to continue its work on the Secretary-General's report as indicated in the President's statement of 29 October 1992.''

GENERAL ASSEMBLY ACTION

The General Assembly on 18 December adopted **resolution 47/120** without vote.

An Agenda for Peace: preventive diplomacy and related matters

The General Assembly,

Recalling the statement of 31 January 1992, adopted at the conclusion of the first meeting held by the

Security Council at the level of heads of State and Government, in which the Secretary-General was invited to prepare, for circulation to the States Members of the United Nations by 1 July 1992, an ''analysis and recommendations on ways of strengthening and making more efficient within the framework and provisions of the Charter the capacity of the United Nations for preventive diplomacy, for peacemaking and for peace-keeping'',

Welcoming the timely presentation of the forward-looking report of the Secretary-General entitled ''An Agenda for Peace'', in response to the summit meeting of the Security Council, as a set of recommendations that deserve close examination by the international community,

Recognizing the need to maintain the increased interest in and momentum for revitalization of the Organization to meet the challenges of the new phase of international relations in order to fulfil the purposes and principles of the Charter of the United Nations,

Stressing that the implementation of the concepts and proposals contained in ''An Agenda for Peace'' should be in strict conformity with the provisions of the Charter, in particular its purposes and principles,

Recalling also its resolution 2625(XXV) of 24 October 1970, the annex to which contains the Declaration on Principles of International Law concerning Friendly Relations and Cooperation among States in accordance with the Charter of the United Nations, and its resolution 43/51 of 5 December 1988, the annex to which contains the Declaration on the Prevention and Removal of Disputes and Situations Which May Threaten International Peace and Security and on the Role of the United Nations in this Field,

Emphasizing that international peace and security must be seen in an integrated manner and that the efforts of the Organization to build peace, justice, stability and security must encompass not only military matters, but also, through its various organs within their respective areas of competence, relevant political, economic, social, humanitarian, environmental and developmental aspects,

Stressing the need for international action to strengthen the socio-economic development of Member States as one of the means of enhancing international peace and security and, in this regard, recognizing the need to complement ''An Agenda for Peace'' with ''An Agenda for Development'',

Acknowledging that timely application of preventive diplomacy is the most desirable and efficient means of easing tensions before they result in conflict,

Recognizing that preventive diplomacy may require such measures as confidence-building, early-warning, fact-finding and other measures in which consultations with Member States, discretion, confidentiality, objectivity and transparency should be combined as appropriate,

Emphasizing the need to strengthen the capacity of the United Nations in the field of preventive diplomacy, through, *inter alia*, allocating appropriate staff resources and financial resources for preventive diplomacy, in order to assist Member States to resolve their differences in a peaceful manner,

Reaffirming the fundamental importance of a sound and secure financial basis for the United Nations in order, *inter alia*, to enable the Organization to play an effective role in preventive diplomacy,

Emphasizing the importance of cooperation between the United Nations and regional arrangements and organizations for preventive diplomacy within their respective areas of competence,

Emphasizing also that respect for the principles of sovereignty, territorial integrity and political independence of States is crucial to any common endeavour to promote international peace and security,

Recalling further other resolutions adopted by the Assembly during its forty-seventh session concerning various aspects of ''An Agenda for Peace'',

Emphasizing the need for all organs and bodies of the United Nations, as appropriate, to intensify their efforts to strengthen the role of the Organization in preventive diplomacy, peacemaking, peace-keeping and peace-building and to continue the discussion of the report of the Secretary-General with a view to adequate action being taken,

Stressing the need for adequate protection of personnel involved in preventive diplomacy, peacemaking, peace-keeping and humanitarian operations, in accordance with relevant norms and principles of international law,

Noting the definition of preventive diplomacy provided by the Secretary-General in his report entitled ''An Agenda for Peace'',

I

Peaceful settlement of disputes

Emphasizing the need to promote the peaceful settlement of disputes,

1. *Invites* Member States to seek solutions to their disputes at an early stage through such peaceful means as provided for in the Charter of the United Nations;

2. *Decides* to explore ways and means for a full utilization of the provisions of the Charter whereby the General Assembly may recommend measures for the peaceful adjustment of any situation, regardless of origin, which is deemed likely to impair the general welfare or friendly relations among nations;

3. *Encourages* the Security Council to utilize fully the provisions of Chapter VI of the Charter on procedures and methods for peaceful settlement of disputes and to call upon the parties concerned to settle their disputes peacefully;

4. *Encourages* the Secretary-General and the Security Council to engage at an early stage in close and continuous consultation in order to develop, on a case-by-case basis, an appropriate strategy for the peaceful settlement of specific disputes, including the participation of other organs, organizations and agencies of the United Nations system, as well as regional arrangements and organizations as appropriate, and invites the Secretary-General to report to the General Assembly on such consultations;

II

Early-warning, collection of information
and analysis

Recognizing the need to strengthen the capacity of the United Nations for early-warning, collection of information and analysis,

1. *Encourages* the Secretary-General to set up an adequate early-warning mechanism for situations which are likely to endanger the maintenance of international peace and security, in close cooperation with Member States and United Nations agencies, as well as regional arrangements and organizations, as appropriate, making use of the information available to

these organizations and/or received from Member States, and to keep Member States informed of the mechanism established;

2. *Invites* the Secretary-General to strengthen the capacity of the Secretariat for the collection of information and analysis to serve better the early-warning needs of the Organization and, to that end, encourages the Secretary-General to ensure that staff members receive proper training in all aspects of preventive diplomacy, including the collection and analysis of information;

3. *Invites* Member States and regional arrangements and organizations to provide timely early-warning information, on a confidential basis when appropriate, to the Secretary-General;

4. *Encourages* the Secretary-General to continue, in accordance with Article 99 of the Charter of the United Nations, to bring to the attention of the Security Council, at his discretion, any matter which in his opinion may threaten the maintenance of international peace and security, together with his recommendations thereon;

5. *Invites* Member States to support the efforts of the Secretary-General in preventive diplomacy, including by providing assistance he may require;

6. *Encourages* the Secretary-General, in accordance with the relevant provisions of the Charter, to notify the General Assembly, as appropriate, of any situation which is potentially dangerous or might lead to international friction or dispute;

7. *Invites* the Secretary-General to bring to the attention of Member States concerned, at an early stage, any matter which in his opinion may adversely affect relations between States;

III
Fact-finding

Recalling the statements made by the President of the Security Council, on behalf of the Council, on 29 October and 30 November 1992, and its own resolutions 1967(XVIII) of 16 December 1963, 2104(XX) of 20 December 1965, 2182(XXI) of 12 December 1966 and 2329(XXII) of 18 December 1967 on the question of methods of fact-finding,

1. *Reaffirms* its resolution 46/59 of 9 December 1991, the annex to which contains the Declaration on Fact-finding by the United Nations in the Field of the Maintenance of International Peace and Security, particularly its guidelines;

2. *Recommends* to the Secretary-General that he should continue to utilize the services of eminent and qualified experts in fact-finding and other missions, selected on as wide a geographical basis as possible, taking into account candidates with the highest standards of efficiency, competence and integrity;

3. *Invites* Member States to submit names of suitable individuals whom the Secretary-General might wish to use at his discretion in fact-finding and other missions;

4. *Recommends* that a request by a Member State for the dispatch of a fact-finding mission to its territory should be considered expeditiously;

5. *Invites* the Secretary-General to continue to dispatch fact-finding and other missions in a timely manner in order to assist him in the proper discharge of his functions under the Charter of the United Nations;

IV
Confidence-building measures

Recognizing that the application of appropriate confidence-building measures, consistent with national security needs, would promote mutual confidence and good faith, which are essential to reducing the likelihood of conflicts between States and enhancing prospects for the peaceful settlement of disputes,

Recalling its resolutions 43/78 H of 7 December 1988 and 45/62 F of 4 December 1990, as well as its resolution 47/54 D of 9 December 1992 on the implementation of the guidelines for appropriate types of confidence-building measures,

Recognizing that confidence-building measures may encompass both military and non-military matters, including political, economic and social matters,

Stressing the need to encourage Member States, and regional arrangements and organizations where relevant and in a manner consistent with their mandates, to play a leading role in developing confidence-building measures appropriate to the region concerned and to coordinate their efforts in this regard with the United Nations in accordance with Chapter VIII of the Charter of the United Nations,

1. *Invites* Member States and regional arrangements and organizations to inform the Secretary-General through appropriate channels about their experiences in confidence-building measures in their respective regions;

2. *Supports* the intention of the Secretary-General to consult on a regular basis with Member States and regional arrangements and organizations on further confidence-building measures;

3. *Encourages* the Secretary-General to consult with parties to existing or potential disputes, the continuance of which is likely to endanger the maintenance of international peace and security, and with other interested Member States and regional arrangements and organizations, as appropriate, on the possibility of initiating confidence-building measures in their respective regions and to keep Member States informed thereon in consultation with the parties concerned;

4. *Commends* such confidence-building measures as the promotion of openness and restraint in the production, procurement and deployment of armaments, the systematic exchange of military missions, the possible formation of regional risk reduction centres, arrangements for the free flow of information and the monitoring of regional arms control and disarmament agreements;

V
Humanitarian assistance

Recalling its resolution 45/100 of 14 December 1990 on humanitarian assistance to victims of natural disasters and similar emergency situations and its resolution 46/182 of 19 December 1991 on the strengthening of the coordination of emergency humanitarian assistance of the United Nations,

Welcoming the increasing role of the United Nations system in providing humanitarian assistance,

Noting that, in certain circumstances, programmes of impartially-provided humanitarian assistance and peace-keeping operations can be mutually supportive,

1. *Encourages* the Secretary-General to continue to strengthen the capacity of the Organization in order to

ensure coordinated planning and execution of humanitarian assistance programmes, drawing upon the specialized skills and resources of all parts of the United Nations system, as well as those of non-governmental organizations, as appropriate;

2. *Also encourages* the Secretary-General to continue to address the question of coordination, when necessary, between humanitarian assistance programmes and peace-keeping or related operations, preserving the non-political, neutral and impartial character of humanitarian action;

3. *Invites* the Secretary-General to bring to the attention of appropriate organs of the United Nations any situation requiring urgent humanitarian assistance in order to prevent its deterioration, which might lead to international friction or dispute;

VI
Resources and logistical aspects of preventive diplomacy

Recognizing the need for adequate resources in support of the United Nations efforts in preventive diplomacy,

1. *Invites* Member States to provide political and practical support to the Secretary-General in his efforts for the peaceful settlement of disputes, including early-warning, fact-finding, good offices and mediation;

2. *Also invites* Member States, on a voluntary basis, to provide the Secretary-General with any necessary additional expertise and logistical resources that he might require for the successful execution of these functions of increasing importance;

VII
The role of the General Assembly in preventive diplomacy

Emphasizing that, together with the Security Council and the Secretary-General, it has an important role in preventive diplomacy,

Recognizing that, having an important role in preventive diplomacy, it has to work in close cooperation and coordination with the Security Council and the Secretary-General in accordance with the Charter of the United Nations and consistent with their respective mandates and responsibilities,

Decides to explore ways and means to support the recommendations of the Secretary-General in his report entitled "An Agenda for Peace" to promote the utilization of the General Assembly, in accordance with the relevant provisions of the Charter of the United Nations, by Member States so as to bring greater influence to bear in pre-empting or containing any situation which is potentially dangerous or might lead to international friction or dispute;

VIII
Future work

Bearing in mind that owing to time constraints it could not examine all the proposals contained in the report of the Secretary-General entitled "An Agenda for Peace",

1. *Decides* to continue early in 1993 its examination of other recommendations on preventive diplomacy and related matters contained in the report of the Secretary-General entitled "An Agenda for Peace", including preventive deployment, demilitarized zones and the International Court of Justice, as well as implementation of the provisions of Article 50 of the Charter of the United Nations, in conformity with the Charter and taking into account the relevant developments and practices in the competent organs of the United Nations;

2. *Also decides* to discuss and consider other proposals contained in "An Agenda for Peace".

General Assembly resolution 47/120
18 December 1992   Meeting 91   Adopted without vote

Draft by President (A/47/L.50); agenda item 10.

Maintenance of international security

On 9 December, following the recommendation of the First Committee, the General Assembly adopted **resolution 47/60 B** by recorded vote.

Maintenance of international security

The General Assembly,

Noting that, with the end of the era of the cold war and of bipolar confrontation, the United Nations faces new tasks in the areas of maintaining international peace and security and achieving social progress and better standards of life in larger freedom,

Aspiring to promote a greater convergence of views among Member States as to the priorities of the United Nations in shaping a more stable international order,

Noting with appreciation that the Secretary-General submitted ideas and proposals in his report entitled "An Agenda for Peace", in particular dealing with the strengthening and enhancement of the effectiveness, within the framework and in accordance with the provisions of the Charter of the United Nations, of the United Nations potential in the area of preventive diplomacy, peacemaking, peace-keeping and post-conflict peace-building,

Noting also the ideas and proposals of the Secretary-General contained in his report entitled "New dimensions of arms regulation and disarmament in the post-cold war era",

1. *Decides* to continue consideration of the question of maintenance of international security, taking into account new international realities and new tasks before the United Nations in the area of strengthening collective efforts to maintain international peace and security;

2. *Invites* all Member States to provide their views on further consideration of the question of maintenance of international security, taking into account, *inter alia*, appropriate provisions of the reports of the Secretary-General entitled "An Agenda for Peace" and "New dimensions of arms regulation and disarmament in the post-cold war era", and requests the Secretary-General to submit a relevant report to the General Assembly at its forty-eighth session;

3. *Decides* to include in the provisional agenda of its forty-eighth session an item entitled "Maintenance of international security".

General Assembly resolution 47/60 B
9 December 1992   Meeting 81   79-0-84 (recorded vote)

Approved by First Committee (A/47/699) by recorded vote (56-0-67), 20 November (meeting 37); 31-nation draft (A/C.1/47/L.47/Rev.1); agenda item 69.
Sponsors: Albania, Australia, Austria, Belgium, Bulgaria, Canada, Croatia, Czechoslovakia, Denmark, Finland, France, Germany, Greece, Hungary, Italy, Japan, Kazakhstan, Luxembourg, Malta, Netherlands, New Zealand, Norway, Poland, Portugal, Romania, Russian Federation, Slovenia, Spain, Turkey, United Kingdom, United States.
Meeting numbers. GA 47th session: 1st Committee 3-30, 37; plenary 81.

Recorded vote in Assembly as follows:

In favour: Angola, Argentina, Armenia, Australia, Austria, Azerbaijan, Bahrain, Belarus, Belgium, Bhutan, Bolivia, Bulgaria, Burkina Faso, Canada, Costa Rica, Czechoslovakia, Denmark, Dominica, El Salvador, Fiji, Finland, France, Gambia, Germany, Greece, Hungary, Iceland, Ireland, Israel, Italy, Japan, Jordan, Kazakhstan, Kuwait, Kyrgyzstan, Latvia, Liechtenstein, Lithuania, Luxembourg, Malawi, Maldives, Mali, Malta, Marshall Islands, Mauritius, Micronesia, Mozambique, Netherlands, New Zealand, Norway, Oman, Panama, Papua New Guinea, Poland, Portugal, Qatar, Republic of Korea, Republic of Moldova, Romania, Russian Federation, Saint Kitts and Nevis, Saint Lucia, Samoa, San Marino, Saudi Arabia, Seychelles, Slovenia, Spain, Swaziland, Sweden, Turkey, Turkmenistan, Ukraine, United Arab Emirates, United Kingdom, United States, Uruguay, Vanuatu, Zaire.

Against: None.

Abstaining: Afghanistan, Algeria, Antigua and Barbuda, Bahamas, Bangladesh, Barbados, Belize, Benin, Botswana, Brazil, Brunei Darussalam, Burundi, Cameroon, Cape Verde, Central African Republic, Chad, Chile, Colombia, Comoros, Congo, Côte d'Ivoire, Cuba, Cyprus, Democratic People's Republic of Korea, Dominican Republic, Ecuador, Egypt, Estonia, Ethiopia, Gabon, Ghana, Grenada, Guatemala, Guinea, Guinea-Bissau, Guyana, Haiti, Honduras, India, Indonesia, Iran, Iraq, Jamaica, Kenya, Lao People's Democratic Republic, Lebanon, Lesotho, Liberia, Libyan Arab Jamahiriya, Madagascar, Malaysia, Mauritania, Mexico, Mongolia, Morocco, Myanmar, Namibia, Nicaragua, Niger, Nigeria, Pakistan, Paraguay, Peru, Philippines, Rwanda, Saint Vincent and the Grenadines, Sao Tome and Principe, Senegal, Singapore, Sri Lanka, Sudan, Suriname, Syrian Arab Republic, Thailand, Togo, Trinidad and Tobago, Tunisia, Uganda, United Republic of Tanzania, Venezuela, Viet Nam, Yemen, Zambia, Zimbabwe.

Introducing the text, the Russian Federation said its main thrust was to give impetus to the First Committee's consideration of the item relating to security in the light of the new tasks facing the United Nations in an era when cold war and bipolar confrontation had ended. Another reason for its importance was the decision to merge consideration in the First Committee of the items on disarmament and international security.

Implementation of the 1970 Declaration

In December 1992, the General Assembly reaffirmed the validity of its 1970 Declaration on the Strengthening of International Security[8] and urged States to take further immediate steps to promote and use the system of collective security as envisaged in the Charter.

The Secretary-General, in October 1992,[9] transmitted replies from two Member States to a 1991 Assembly invitation[10] to submit their views on the implementation of the Declaration.

GENERAL ASSEMBLY ACTION

On 9 December, in accordance with the recommendation of the First Committee, the General Assembly adopted **resolution 47/60 A** by recorded vote.

Review of the implementation of the Declaration on the Strengthening of International Security

The General Assembly,

Recalling its resolution 2734(XXV) of 16 December 1970 on the Declaration on the Strengthening of International Security, as well as all its resolutions on the review of the implementation of the Declaration,

Bearing in mind the final documents of the Tenth Conference of Heads of State or Government of Non-Aligned Countries, held at Jakarta from 1 to 6 September 1992,

Expressing its firm belief that disarmament, the relaxation of international tension, respect for international law and for the purposes and principles of the Charter of the United Nations, especially the principles of the sovereign equality of States and the peaceful settlement of disputes and the injunction to refrain from the use or threat of use of force in international relations, respect for the right to self-determination and national independence, economic and social development, the eradication of all forms of domination and respect for basic human rights and fundamental freedoms, as well as the need for preserving the environment, are closely related and provide the basis for an enduring and stable universal peace and security,

Welcoming the recent positive changes in the international landscape, characterized by the end of the cold war, the relaxation of tensions on the global level and the emergence of a new spirit governing relations among nations,

Welcoming also the wide-ranging dialogue between the Russian Federation and the United States of America, with its positive effects on world developments, and expressing its hope that these developments will lead to the renunciation of strategic doctrines based on the use of nuclear weapons and to the elimination of weapons of mass destruction, thereby making a real contribution to global security,

Expressing the hope that the positive trends that started in Europe, where a new system of security and cooperation is being built through the process of the Conference on Security and Cooperation in Europe, will continue and will encourage similar trends in other parts of the world,

Expressing at the same time its serious concern over the persistence of tensions and conflicts and the emergence of new threats to international peace and security and its support for all efforts towards a peaceful and just resolution of hotbeds of crisis in the world, including further military disengagement,

Stressing the need for the strengthening of international security through disarmament, particularly nuclear disarmament leading to the elimination of all nuclear weapons, and restraints on the qualitative and quantitative escalation of the arms race,

Stressing also the growing importance of the relationship between disarmament and development in current international relations,

Recognizing that peace and security are dependent on socio-economic factors as well as on political and military elements,

Also recognizing that the right and responsibility for making the world safe for all should be shared by all,

Stressing further that the United Nations is the fundamental instrument for regulating international relations and resolving global problems for the maintenance and effective promotion of peace and security, disarmament and social and economic development,

1. *Reaffirms* the continuing validity of the Declaration on the Strengthening of International Security, and calls upon all States to contribute effectively to its implementation;

2. *Reaffirms also* that all States must respect, in their international relations, the principles enshrined in the Charter of the United Nations;

3. *Emphasizes* that, until an enduring and stable universal peace based on a comprehensive, viable and

readily implementable structure of international security is established, peace, the achievement of disarmament and the settlement of disputes by peaceful means continue to be the first and foremost task of the international community;

4. *Calls upon* all States to refrain from the use or threat of use of force, aggression, intervention, interference, all forms of terrorism, suppression, foreign occupation or measures of political and economic coercion that violate the sovereignty, territorial integrity, independence and security of other States, as well as the permanent sovereignty of peoples over their natural resources;

5. *Recognizes*, among other things, the validity of the concepts of confidence-building measures, particularly in regions of high tension, balanced security at lower levels of armaments and armed forces, as well as the elimination of destabilizing military capabilities and imbalances;

6. *Calls* for regional dialogues, where appropriate, to promote security and economic, environmental, social and cultural cooperation, taking into account the particular characteristics of each region;

7. *Stresses* the importance of global and regional approaches to disarmament, which should be pursued simultaneously to promote regional and international peace and security;

8. *Reaffirms* the fundamental role of the United Nations in the maintenance of international peace and security, and expresses the hope that it will continue to address all threats to international peace and security in accordance with the Charter;

9. *Urges* all States to take further immediate steps aimed at promoting and using effectively the system of collective security as envisaged in the Charter, as well as halting effectively the arms race with the aim of achieving general and complete disarmament under effective international control;

10. *Stresses also* the urgent need for more balanced development of the world economy and for redressing the current asymmetry and inequality in economic and technological development between the developed and developing countries, which are basic prerequisites for the strengthening of international peace and security;

11. *Considers* that respect for and promotion of basic human rights and fundamental freedoms, as well as the recognition of the inalienable right of peoples to self-determination and independence, will strengthen international peace and security, and reaffirms the legitimacy of the struggle of peoples under foreign occupation and their inalienable right to self-determination and independence;

12. *Reaffirms* that the democratization of international relations is an imperative necessity, and stresses its belief that the United Nations offers the best framework for the promotion of this goal;

13. *Invites* Member States to submit their views on the question of the implementation of the Declaration on the Strengthening of International Security, particularly in the light of recent positive developments in the global political and security climate, and requests the Secretary-General to submit a report to the General Assembly at its forty-eighth session on the basis of the replies received;

14. *Decides* to include in the provisional agenda of its forty-eighth session the item entitled "Review of the implementation of the Declaration on the Strengthening of International Security".

General Assembly resolution 47/60 A

9 December 1992   Meeting 81   122-1-43 (recorded vote)

Approved by First Committee (A/47/699) by recorded vote (88-1-40), 20 November (meeting 37); draft by Indonesia for Non-Aligned Movement (A/C.1/47/L.45/Rev.1), orally revised; agenda item 69.

Meeting numbers. GA 47th session: 1st Committee 3-30, 37; plenary 81.

Recorded vote in Assembly as follows:

In favour: Algeria, Angola, Antigua and Barbuda, Azerbaijan, Bahamas, Bahrain, Bangladesh, Barbados, Belarus, Belize, Benin, Bhutan, Bolivia, Botswana, Brazil, Brunei Darussalam, Burkina Faso, Cameroon, Cape Verde, Central African Republic, Chad, Chile, China, Colombia, Comoros, Congo, Costa Rica, Côte d'Ivoire, Cuba, Democratic People's Republic of Korea, Djibouti, Dominica, Dominican Republic, Ecuador, Egypt, El Salvador, Ethiopia, Fiji, Gabon, Gambia, Ghana, Grenada, Guatemala, Guinea, Guinea-Bissau, Guyana, Haiti, Honduras, India, Indonesia, Iran, Iraq, Jamaica, Jordan, Kenya, Kuwait, Lao People's Democratic Republic, Lebanon, Lesotho, Liberia, Libyan Arab Jamahiriya, Madagascar, Malawi, Malaysia, Maldives, Mali, Marshall Islands, Mauritania, Mauritius, Mexico, Micronesia, Mongolia, Morocco, Mozambique, Myanmar, Namibia, Nepal, Nicaragua, Niger, Nigeria, Oman, Pakistan, Panama, Papua New Guinea, Paraguay, Peru, Philippines, Qatar, Rwanda, Saint Kitts and Nevis, Saint Lucia, Saint Vincent and the Grenadines, Samoa, Sao Tome and Principe, Saudi Arabia, Senegal, Seychelles, Sierra Leone, Singapore, Sri Lanka, Sudan, Suriname, Swaziland, Syrian Arab Republic, Thailand, Togo, Trinidad and Tobago, Tunisia, Turkmenistan, Uganda, Ukraine, United Arab Emirates, United Republic of Tanzania, Uruguay, Vanuatu, Venezuela, Viet Nam, Yemen, Zaire, Zambia, Zimbabwe.

Against: United States.

Abstaining: Afghanistan,* Argentina, Armenia, Australia, Austria, Belgium, Bulgaria, Burundi, Canada, Czechoslovakia, Denmark, Estonia, Finland, France, Germany, Greece, Hungary, Iceland, Ireland, Israel, Italy, Japan, Kazakhstan, Kyrgyzstan, Latvia, Liechtenstein, Lithuania, Luxembourg, Netherlands, New Zealand, Norway, Poland, Portugal, Republic of Korea, Republic of Moldova, Romania, Russian Federation, San Marino, Slovenia, Spain, Sweden, Turkey, United Kingdom.

*Later advised the Secretariat it had intended to vote in favour.

Science and peace

The General Assembly's Special Political Committee considered the question of science and peace on 20 October 1992,[11] in accordance with a 1990 Assembly resolution.[12] Acting on the Committee's recommendation, the Assembly, by **decision 47/423** of 14 December 1992, deferred consideration of the item until its 1993 session.

Introducing the draft decision in Committee, Costa Rica, on behalf of the sponsors, said it would prefer that consideration of the item be postponed to comply with the Secretary-General's guidelines on rationalization of work, since the item could be combined with that on education and information for disarmament which was to be considered anew in 1993. In addition, a greater number of pertinent reports would be available following the June 1992 United Nations Conference on Environment and Development and subsequent adoption of Agenda 21 (see PART THREE, Chapter VIII).

Previously, the Assembly had adopted a resolution on the topic in 1988,[13] in the framework of follow-up activities to the 1986 International Year of Peace.[14]

REFERENCES

(1)S/23500. (2)A/47/277-S/24111. (3)S/24210. (4)S/24587. (5)S/24728. (6)S/24872. (7)S/25036. (8)YUN 1970, p. 105, GA res. 2734(XXV), 16 Dec. 1970. (9)A/47/505 & Add.1. (10)YUN 1991, p. 17, GA dec. 46/414, 6 Dec. 1991. (11)A/47/608. (12)GA res. 45/70, 11 Dec. 1990. (13)YUN 1988, p. 32, GA res. 43/61, 6 Dec. 1988. (14)YUN 1986, p. 115.

Review of peace-keeping operations

In 1992, a record number of 12 United Nations peace-keeping operations were under way. In addition to a significant increase in the number of such operations, the scope of the Organization's peace-keeping responsibilities expanded from monitoring cease-fires and supervising elections to providing humanitarian relief and assistance.

In mid-1992, nearly 40,000 military personnel were serving under United Nations command, as were 9,461 international and local civilian personnel. Peace-keeping operations approved were estimated to cost in excess of $2.5 billion in 1992.

Peace-keeping forces continued in 1992 to operate in Cyprus, Lebanon and the Golan Heights between Israel and the Syrian Arab Republic, as did two long-standing military observer missions, the United Nations Truce Supervision Organization in the Middle East (see PART TWO, Chapter V) and the United Nations Military Observer Group in India and Pakistan. In addition, the United Nations Angola Verification Mission (UNAVEM II), expanded in 1991, was active to verify the peace accords between the Angolan Government and the guerrilla forces in the country (see PART TWO, Chapter I), and the United Nations Mission for the Referendum in Western Sahara, established in 1991, continued to verify the cease-fire and cessation of hostilities there (see PART FOUR, Chapter I). Also established in 1991 and active in 1992 were the United Nations Iraq-Kuwait Observation Mission (see PART TWO, Chapter III) and the United Nations Observer Mission in El Salvador (see PART TWO, Chapter II).

In February 1992, the Security Council created the United Nations Protection Force (UNPROFOR), which was deployed in March on the territory of the former Yugoslavia (see PART TWO, Chapter IV). Peace-keeping forces started operating in March under the mandate of the United Nations Transitional Authority in Cambodia (UNTAC) (see PART TWO, Chapter III), preceded by the United Nations Advance Mission in Cambodia, and in April with the United Nations Operation in Somalia (see PART TWO, Chapter I).

In 1992, the Special Committee on Peace-keeping Operations held six meetings in New York between 24 April and 1 June.[1] To examine the substance of its mandate, it established an open-ended working group, which submitted conclusions and recommendations for the Committee's approval and transmittal to the General Assembly. The recommendations concerned ways to improve the organization and effectiveness of peace-keeping operations, including transferring certain functions of the Secretariat's Field Operations Di-

vision to the Department of Peace-keeping Operations, strengthening the Military Adviser's Office and designating a central body for liaison with Member States. A number of suggestions were also made regarding standardization of operating procedures and unit types and delegating administrative authority to force commanders and special representatives.

As the basis for its discussions, the Committee had before it a report of the Secretary-General[2] containing further observations and suggestions on peace-keeping, as requested by the Assembly in 1991.[3] As at 24 April 1992, replies were received from seven Governments, one responding on behalf of the European Community and another, the Nordic countries. Also before the Committee was a draft working document prepared by its Bureau, based on submissions of States to the Secretary-General and containing a list of specific items and elements for possible consideration by the Committee.

In addition to its annual session, the Special Committee and its open-ended working group met between 17 and 25 August to discuss the Secretary-General's agenda for peace[4] (see above) and to prepare a special report[5] on the topic. Delegations were unanimous in welcoming and appreciating "An Agenda for Peace", which they deemed a valuable and timely contribution aimed at strengthening the role of the United Nations in the maintenance of international peace and security.

The Secretary-General, in response to a 1991 Assembly resolution,[3] submitted in October 1992 a report[6] containing information from 21 States concerning peace-keeping training and similar activities, and another report on the feasibility, including costs, of establishing an annual peace-keeping fellowship programme for national peace-keeping trainers, to be administered by the Secretariat.[7]

The information received showed that peace-keeping training took place generally in the context of participation in a particular peace-keeping operation. Four Nordic countries (Denmark, Finland, Norway, Sweden) were an exception to that, with their joint training programmes. Several countries had specialized courses for different categories of personnel, notably military observers. With the duration of training from a few days to two months, the content varied accordingly. A number of programmes included refresher training of basic military skills, and some courses covered the full range of subjects listed in the training guidelines issued by the United Nations Secretariat in 1991.

GENERAL ASSEMBLY ACTION

On 14 December, following the recommendation of the Special Political Committee, the

General Assembly adopted **resolution 47/71** without vote.

Comprehensive review of the whole question of peace-keeping operations in all their aspects

The General Assembly,

Recalling its resolution 2006(XIX) of 18 February 1965 and all other relevant resolutions,

Recalling, in particular, its resolution 46/48 of 9 December 1991,

Welcoming the progress made by the Special Committee on Peace-keeping Operations during its recent sessions,

Convinced that peace-keeping operations are enhancing the effectiveness of the United Nations in the maintenance of international peace and security,

Recognizing that the peacemaking activities of the Secretary-General and of organs of the United Nations, which are actions to bring hostile parties to agreement, essentially through such peaceful means as those foreseen in Chapter VI of the Charter of the United Nations, constitute an essential function of the United Nations and are among the important means for the prevention, containment and resolution of disputes and for maintaining international peace and security,

Taking into account that increasing activities in the field of United Nations peace-keeping require both increasing and better managed human, financial and material resources for the Organization,

Aware of the extremely difficult financial situation of the United Nations and its peace-keeping operations and of the heavy burden on the troop contributors, especially those from developing countries,

Taking note of the report of the Secretary-General on the work of the Organization and, in particular, his report entitled ''An Agenda for Peace'',

Taking note also of the useful exchange of views on ''An Agenda for Peace'' during the inter-sessional meetings of the Special Committee devoted to that report and of the role of the Special Committee in carrying out further analysis and consideration, in particular as regards peace-keeping operations,

Recalling its debate on agenda item 10 during the forty-seventh session, and in particular the views expressed by Member States on ''An Agenda for Peace'',

Recalling also that in the statement by the President of the Security Council of 29 October 1992, on the report of the Secretary-General entitled ''An Agenda for Peace'', the Council expressed support for, *inter alia,* the suggestions contained in paragraphs 51 and 52 of the report,

Having examined the reports of the Special Committee,

1. *Takes note* of the reports of the Special Committee on Peace-keeping Operations;

Resources

2. *Notes* that only a small number of Member States have to date responded to the questionnaire issued by the Secretary-General on 21 May 1990 pursuant to General Assembly resolution 44/49 of 8 December 1989 to identify those personnel, material and technical resources and services which Member States would be ready, in principle, to contribute to United Nations peace-keeping operations, and urges Member States that have not yet replied to do so;

3. *Requests* the Secretary-General to explore the possibility of improving the formulation of his questionnaire of 21 May 1990 and to recirculate the questionnaire on a regular basis;

4. *Encourages* the Secretary-General to consider circulating a separate questionnaire on civil police and civilian experts whom Member States would be ready to contribute to United Nations peace-keeping operations;

5. *Urges* Member States to transmit promptly to the Secretary-General their replies to those questionnaires;

6. *Recommends* that the guidelines in the current questionnaire be developed and used subsequently in the ''Notes for Guidance'' in order to achieve a standard organization for type units;

7. *Calls upon* the Secretariat to consult with and assist Member States in completing the questionnaires, with a view to ensuring commonality of approach and understanding;

8. *Requests* the Secretary-General to promote, based on the questionnaires, the establishment on a voluntary basis among Member States of a pool of resources, including military units, military observers, civil police, key staff personnel and humanitarian *matériel,* that might be made readily available to United Nations peace-keeping operations, subject to national approval;

9. *Encourages* Member States to inform the Secretary-General of their willingness to provide forces or capabilities to the United Nations for peace-keeping operations and the type of units or capabilities that might be available at short notice, subject to overriding national defence requirements and the approval of the Governments providing them;

10. *Encourages* the Secretariat and those Member States which have indicated such willingness to enter into direct dialogue so as to enable the Secretary-General to know with greater precision what forces or capabilities might be made available to the United Nations for particular peace-keeping operations and on what time-scale;

11. *Stresses* the need for the United Nations to be given resources commensurate with its growing responsibilities in the area of peace-keeping, particularly with reference to the resources needed for the start-up phases of such operations;

Finances

12. *Recalls* that the financing of peace-keeping operations is the collective responsibility of all Member States in accordance with Article 17, paragraph 2, of the Charter of the United Nations, and reiterates its call upon all Member States to pay their assessed contributions in full and on time and encourages those States which can do so to make voluntary contributions that are acceptable to the Secretary-General;

13. *Reiterates* the need to maintain the accepted principles and guidelines on the financing of all United Nations peace-keeping operations;

14. *Stresses* the need to delegate increased financial and administrative authority to Force Commanders, or Special Representatives for multi-component missions, in order to increase the missions' capacity to adjust to new situations and specific requirements;

15. *Encourages* consideration in the appropriate forums of the establishment of a reserve fund or other appropriate

arrangement to improve the start-up financing of peace-keeping operations;

16. *Also stresses* the importance of the need to reimburse the outstanding dues of troop-contributing States;

17. *Considers it important* that, in establishing future peace-keeping operations, financial questions should continue to be studied seriously, particularly at the planning stage, in order to ensure the most cost-effective and efficient conduct of such operations and strict control of their expenditures;

18. *Also considers it important* to contain financial expenditures of peace-keeping operations by determining, during initial planning, the levels of personnel, materials and technical equipment required, by early definition of the sequence of each operation, and by improved estimating, during the planning stage, of operational costs;

19. *Acknowledges* the competence of the General Assembly for the appropriation and apportionment of the costs of United Nations peace-keeping operations, and also acknowledges the importance of the Security Council members being informed of the cost implications of such operations;

20. *Emphasizes* the importance of making, from the standpoint of sources of financing, a clear distinction between peace-keeping operations themselves, and the provision to States and parties to a conflict, at their request, of other assistance from the specialized agencies and departments of the United Nations not an integral part of the operation;

21. *Considers* that in view of the critical financial situation of the United Nations, as described in the report of the Secretary-General, the issue of supplementing diversified financial resources, on terms acceptable to the Secretary-General, to the assessed contributions should be further studied in all the appropriate forums;

22. *Recognizes* the need for an augmentation of the strength and capability of military staff serving in the Secretariat and of civilian staff dealing more generally with peace-keeping matters in the Secretariat;

23. *Requests* the Secretary-General to report to the General Assembly on this subject as soon as possible; in that report he might consider the establishment in the Secretariat of an enhanced peace-keeping planning staff and an operations centre in order to deal with the growing complexity of initial planning and control of peace-keeping operations in the field;

24. *Urges* Governments of host countries to take all necessary measures to create conditions that will permit United Nations forces to be kept to a minimum, and equally urges them to provide, in accordance with their capacity, the greatest possible logistic and material support for these operations;

Organization and effectiveness

25. *Invites* the Secretary-General, as Chief Administrative Officer, to consider the necessary strengthening and reform of the Secretariat units dealing with peace-keeping operations, so that they can deal effectively and efficiently with the planning, launching, ongoing management and termination of peace-keeping operations;

26. *Welcomes* the creation of the Department of Peace-keeping Operations and invites the Secretary-General to consider the creation of a unified, integrated structure within the Department to establish clear lines of responsibility and accountability, which are essential for the effective and efficient management of peace-keeping operations; in that regard, it requests the Secretary-General to consider whether relevant parts of the Field Operations Division should be transferred to that Department;

27. *Also welcomes*, in the light of the increasing use of civilian police in peace-keeping operations, the decision of the Secretary-General to appoint a Senior Police Adviser;

28. *Requests* the Secretariat to consider, in due course, the utility of training guidelines for civilian specialized units, including civilian police;

29. *Encourages* all Member States to organize national or regional training programmes, to include cross-cultural education and relevant international humanitarian law in such programmes and to promote cooperation with other national and regional peace-keeping training programmes;

30. *Takes note with appreciation* of the report of the Secretary-General on the feasibility, including costs, of establishing an annual peace-keeping fellowship programme for national peace-keeping trainers to be administered by the Secretariat, and the information he has gathered on national peace-keeping training and similar activities, and requests him to issue a regularly updated list based upon national submissions;

31. *Invites* the Secretary-General to institute proper arrangements and procedures for providing additional personnel on a short-term basis in order to ensure that the Secretariat can respond effectively and efficiently to fluctuations in its workload, particularly when new operations are planned and launched;

32. *Reiterates* its invitation to the Secretary-General to consider identifying a focal point for contacts by Member States seeking information on all facets, including operational and administrative matters, of ongoing and planned peace-keeping operations;

33. *Also invites* the Secretary-General to review, with a view to streamlining procedures and enhancing effectiveness, the applicable United Nations financial and administrative regulations concerning peace-keeping operations;

34. *Further invites* the Secretary-General to consider means whereby Special Representatives/Force Commanders and other key personnel are identified at the earliest possible time;

35. *Recommends* that the Secretary-General conduct a study on how to prevent duplication of responsibilities of civilian and military staff personnel in the field, especially in the areas of supply, communication and transportation, and how to improve their interaction and cooperation in fulfilling the tasks assigned to them;

36. *Invites* the Secretary-General immediately to envisage the adoption of all necessary arrangements to define logistics doctrine and standard operational procedures combining civilian and military aspects in order to achieve the greatest possible efficiency and cost-effectiveness, and urges Member States to cooperate with the Secretary-General in this exercise;

37. *Encourages* the Secretary-General to invite Member States to provide qualified military and civilian personnel to assist the Secretariat in the planning and management of peace-keeping operations;

38. *Expresses its appreciation* to the Secretary-General for reporting on peace-keeping operations and requests

him to report periodically on the performance of all peace-keeping operations;

39. *Requests* the Secretary-General to consider establishing a training programme for key staff personnel of peace-keeping operations with a view to creating a pool of trained personnel with knowledge of the United Nations system and its working procedures;

40. *Requests* the Secretariat immediately to make all necessary arrangements for the reissue of *The Blue Helmets* in 1995;

41. *Recommends* that the Secretariat continue the existing practice of informal consultations with contributing States more directly interested, as appropriate, and that, especially for particularly large or complex operations, these informal consultations be held on a more frequent and regular basis, with a view to providing effective follow-up and support to the operation from its initial stage to its termination;

Development of peace-keeping

42. *Welcomes* the report of the Secretary-General on ways of strengthening the capacity of the United Nations for preventive diplomacy, peacemaking and peacekeeping within the framework and provisions of the Charter, as requested by the Security Council at its meeting held at the level of heads of State and Government on 31 January 1992;

43. *Considers* that the concept of preventive peacekeeping, that is, the deployment of peace-keeping operations as a deterrent to a possible aggressor, requires development and clarification as a helpful tool for the United Nations in its pursuit of preventive diplomacy;

44. *Believes* that the Secretary-General should have the means to dispatch his own missions, with the consent of the parties concerned, where necessary in cooperation with regional organizations, and to evaluate the situation and develop his peacemaking activities as appropriate;

45. *Also believes* that the Declaration on Fact-finding by the United Nations in the Field of the Maintenance of International Peace and Security, approved by the General Assembly in its resolution 46/59 of 9 December 1991, is a valuable contribution to the Organization's preventive functions;

46. *Encourages* Member States to provide the Secretary-General with full and up-to-date information concerning tensions that could escalate into an international conflict;

47. *Believes*, in this connection, that the closest attention needs to be paid to the issue of applying the preventive potential of the United Nations more broadly and considers that the responsibilities of the Security Council, the General Assembly and the Secretary-General in this regard should be strengthened in accordance with the framework and provisions of the Charter;

48. *Recognizes* the importance of according special consideration to mechanisms and means of deterring a potential aggressor and procedures for a prompt and effective response to acts of aggression and threats to international peace and security, in accordance with the provisions of the Charter;

49. *Stresses* that the parties to a conflict have an obligation to respect the international status of United Nations operations and to refrain from encouraging or taking actions capable of disrupting or impeding United Nations personnel in the performance of their peace-keeping, peacemaking or humanitarian functions, in accordance with the Convention on the Privileges and Immunities of the United Nations and status-of-forces agreements;

50. *Urges* all Governments of host countries and parties to a conflict to take all necessary measures to ensure the safety and security of United Nations personnel and to prevent any attempts on the life and health of those personnel;

51. *Considers* that, in the light of the ever-expanding role of peace-keeping operations, it is important that the United Nations, from planning through implementation of each operation, and on an ongoing basis, assess the risks to the safety and security of its units and personnel and take all necessary measures, including the elaboration of appropriate guidelines and procedures, to ensure the highest possible levels of that safety and security;

52. *Encourages* all regional and subregional organizations to promote the maintenance of peace, security and stability in their respective regions and, where applicable, work in cooperation with the United Nations, in accordance with Chapter VIII of the Charter, contributing to peace-keeping operations there;

53. *Emphasizes* that any deployment of peace-keeping operations should be accompanied, as appropriate, by an intensification of coordinated political efforts by the States concerned, by regional organizations and by the United Nations itself as part of the political process for a peaceful settlement of the crisis situation or conflict in accordance with Chapters VI and VIII of the Charter;

54. *Believes* that consideration might be given over the next few years to the elaboration of a universally acceptable text for a declaration on United Nations peacekeeping operations, which would include the main organizational and practical aspects involved and would contain recommendations on ways of enhancing the effectiveness of such operations;

55. *Takes note* of the establishment of an informal working group, open to all Member States, on "An Agenda for Peace";

* * *

56. *Recommends* that, should any of the proposals contained in the present resolution result in budgetary implications for the biennium 1992-1993, such additional costs should be accommodated within the appropriation level approved by the General Assembly in its resolution 46/186 A of 20 December 1991;

57. *Decides* that the Special Committee, in accordance with its mandate, should continue its efforts for a comprehensive review of the whole question of peacekeeping operations in all their aspects;

58. *Encourages* the Special Committee to consider holding an inter-sessional meeting to consider at the earliest opportunity the recommendations relating to peace-keeping contained in "An Agenda for Peace";

59. *Requests* the Special Committee to submit a report on its work to the General Assembly at its forty-eighth session;

60. *Invites* Member States to submit any further observations and suggestions on peace-keeping operations to the Secretary-General by 1 March 1993, outlining proposals on specific items in order to allow for more detailed consideration by the Special Committee, with particular emphasis on practical proposals to make these operations more effective;

61. *Requests* the Secretary-General to prepare, within existing resources, a compilation of the above-mentioned observations and suggestions and to submit it to the Special Committee by 30 March 1993;

62. *Decides* to include in the provisional agenda of its forty-eighth session the item entitled "Comprehensive review of the whole question of peace-keeping operations in all their aspects".

General Assembly resolution 47/71

14 December 1992   Meeting 85   Adopted without vote

Approved by Special Political Committee (A/47/613) without vote, 20 November (meeting 22); 6-nation draft (A/SPC/47/L.7); agenda item 75.
Sponsors: Argentina, Canada, Egypt, Japan, Nigeria, Poland.
Financial implications. 5th Committee, A/47/770; S-G, A/SPC/47/L.11, A/C.5/47/60.
Meeting numbers. GA 47th session: 5th Committee 40; SPC 14-18, 22; plenary 85.

Administrative and budgetary aspects of the financing of United Nations peace-keeping operations were dealt with in **resolution 47/218.** By **resolution 47/217,** the Assembly decided to establish a peace-keeping reserve fund.

Protection of peace-keeping personnel

In "An Agenda for Peace"[4] (see above), the Secretary-General noted an unconscionable increase in fatalities among United Nations peace-keeping personnel. In view of the pressing need for adequate protection to those engaged in life-endangering circumstances, he recommended that the Security Council, unless it elected immediately to withdraw the United Nations presence to preserve the credibility of the Organization, consider what action should be taken towards those who put United Nations personnel in danger. Before deployment took place, the Council should keep open the option of considering in advance collective measures, possibly including those under Chapter VII of the Charter when a threat to international peace and security was also involved, to come into effect should the purpose of the United Nations operation systematically be frustrated and hostilities occur.

SECURITY COUNCIL ACTION

After consultations held on 2 December, the President of the Security Council made the following statement on behalf of the Council members:[8]

"The members of the Security Council wish to express their deep concern and outrage about the increasing number of attacks against United Nations personnel serving in various peace-keeping operations.

"A number of serious incidents affecting military and civilian personnel serving with UNAVEM II, UNTAC and UNPROFOR have occurred during the last few days.

"On 29 November in Uige, northern Angola, a Brazilian police observer with UNAVEM II was killed as a result of an outbreak of hostilities between UNITA and government forces, during which the UNAVEM camp was caught in the cross-fire. The members of the Council convey their deep sympathy and condolences to the Government of Brazil and to the bereaved family.

"The situation in UNPROFOR, which has already suffered over 300 casualties, 20 of them fatal, remains deeply troubling. On 30 November, two Spanish UNPROFOR soldiers in Bosnia and Herzegovina were seriously injured in a mine attack and a Danish UNPROFOR soldier was abducted by armed men today.

"On 1 December, two British UNTAC military observers and four naval observers, two from the Philippines, one from New Zealand and one from the United Kingdom, on patrol in Kompong Thom province were illegally detained by forces belonging to the National Army of Democratic Kampuchea (NADK). An UNTAC helicopter, sent to assist in the discussions for their release, was fired upon, and a French military observer on board was injured. Moreover, today, six UNTAC civilian police monitors, three Indonesians, two Tunisians and one Nepalese, were injured in two land-mine incidents in Siem Reap province.

"The members of the Council condemn these attacks on the safety and security of United Nations personnel and demand that all parties concerned take all necessary measures to prevent their recurrence. The members of the Council consider the abduction and detention of United Nations peace-keeping personnel as totally unacceptable and demand the immediate and unconditional release of the UNTAC and UNPROFOR personnel concerned."

GENERAL ASSEMBLY ACTION

On 14 December, in accordance with the recommendation of the Special Political Committee, the General Assembly adopted **resolution 47/72** without vote.

Protection of peace-keeping personnel

The General Assembly,

Acknowledging the vital importance of the involvement of United Nations personnel in preventive diplomacy, peacemaking, peace-keeping, peace-building and humanitarian operations,

Noting with grave concern the growing number of fatalities and injuries among United Nations peace-keeping and other personnel resulting from deliberate hostile actions in areas of deployment,

Bearing in mind the concern of the Secretary-General over the safety of peace-keeping personnel expressed in his report entitled "An Agenda for Peace",

Recalling its resolution 46/48 of 9 December 1991 and other relevant resolutions, as well as the recommendations contained in the report of the Special Committee on Peace-keeping Operations,

Having examined the special report of the Special Committee on Peace-keeping Operations,

Noting relevant resolutions of the Security Council,

1. *Pays tribute* to the courage, commitment and idealism of peace-keeping and other United Nations personnel in the field, who often work in difficult and dangerous circumstances;

2. *Resolutely condemns* any hostile actions against United Nations personnel, including deliberate attacks against United Nations peace-keeping operations, which have resulted in a disturbing number of casualties;

3. *Strongly demands* that host countries and all parties to a conflict take all measures possible to ensure the safety of peace-keeping and other United Nations personnel;

4. *Reminds* Governments of host countries of their responsibility for the safety of peace-keeping and other United Nations personnel on their territory;

5. *Urges* the Secretary-General to conclude, if possible at the earliest stage of a peace-keeping operation, a status-of-forces agreement with the parties concerned, emphasizing their obligations to respect the international status of United Nations operations in accordance with the Convention on the Privileges and Immunities of the United Nations;

6. *Requests* the Secretary-General, in planning future peace-keeping operations and in making recommendations for their deployment, to give particular attention to adequate protection for peace-keeping and other United Nations personnel;

7. *Recommends* that, in appropriate cases, the Security Council might make it clear to the parties when authorizing a new peace-keeping operation that it is prepared to take further steps in accordance with the Charter of the United Nations should the purpose of the operation systematically be frustrated by provocative attacks against United Nations personnel;

8. *Also recommends* that the Security Council continue, in collaboration with the Secretary-General, to collect and, where appropriate, to disseminate reliable information about attacks on the safety of peace-keeping and other United Nations personnel;

9. *Requests* the Special Committee on Peace-keeping Operations to study other measures to ensure the safety of peace-keeping and other United Nations personnel and to report thereon to the General Assembly;

10. *Requests* the Secretary-General to address the question of the safety of United Nations personnel in his periodic reports on ongoing peace-keeping operations.

General Assembly resolution 47/72

14 December 1992   Meeting 85   Adopted without vote

Approved by Special Political Committee (A/47/613) without vote, 20 November (meeting 22); 57-nation draft (A/SPC/47/L.8), orally revised; agenda item 75.
Sponsors: Algeria, Argentina, Australia, Austria, Belarus, Belgium, Bolivia, Brazil, Canada, Colombia, Costa Rica, Croatia, Czechoslovakia, Denmark, Egypt, El Salvador, Fiji, Finland, France, Germany, Greece, India, Ireland, Italy, Japan, Jordan, Kenya, Lesotho, Luxembourg, Malaysia, Mauritania, Mexico, Nepal, Netherlands, New Zealand, Niger, Nigeria, Norway, Pakistan, Peru, Philippines, Poland, Portugal, Republic of Korea, Romania, Russian Federation, Samoa, Senegal, Singapore, Spain, Sweden, Tunisia, Ukraine, United Kingdom, United States, Uruguay, Venezuela.
Meeting numbers. GA 47th session: SPC 14-18, 22; plenary 85.

REFERENCES
[1]A/47/253. [2]A/AC.121/39/Rev.1 & Add.1,2. [3]YUN 1991, p. 20, GA res. 46/48, 9 Dec. 1991. [4]A/47/277-S/24111. [5]A/47/386. [6]A/47/597. [7]A/47/604. [8]S/24884.

Regional aspects of international peace and security

Strengthening of security in the Mediterranean region

Pursuant to a General Assembly resolution of 1991,[1] the Secretary-General submitted in October 1992 a report[2] on the strengthening of security and cooperation in the Mediterranean region, containing a summary of the debate on the question during the 1991 Assembly session. Also included were replies from five Governments submitted in response to his request for their views.

The Inter-Parliamentary Conference on Security and Cooperation in the Mediterranean (Malaga, Spain, 15-20 June), in its final document,[3] recommended, among other things, that Governments concerned convene as soon as possible an intergovernmental conference on security and cooperation in the Mediterranean, which would draw on the procedures and general experience of the Conference on Security and Cooperation in Europe.

The European Council of Ministers of the European Economic Community, in a declaration on the relations between Europe and the Maghreb (Lisbon, Portugal, 25 June),[4] reaffirmed its solidarity with the Maghreb countries and its firm determination to continue contributing to the stability and prosperity of the Mediterranean region on the basis of an approach favouring partnership. It considered that its relations and those of its member States with the Maghreb countries must be founded on a common commitment to respect for international law and human rights, the establishment of democratic institutional systems, and tolerance and coexistence between cultures and religions.

The final document of the Tenth Conference of Heads of State or Government of Non-Aligned Countries (Jakarta, Indonesia, 1-6 September)[5] reaffirmed the non-aligned countries' support for the efforts to transform the Mediterranean area into a region of peace, security and cooperation and, in that context, welcomed the 1989 Treaty between Algeria, the Libyan Arab Jamahiriya, Mauritania, Morocco and Tunisia instituting the Arab Maghreb Union.

GENERAL ASSEMBLY ACTION

On 9 December, the General Assembly, on the recommendation of the First Committee, adopted **resolution 47/58** without vote.

Strengthening of security and cooperation in the Mediterranean region

The General Assembly,

Recalling its relevant resolutions, including its resolution 46/42 of 6 December 1991,

Reaffirming the primary role of the Mediterranean countries in strengthening and promoting peace, security and cooperation in the Mediterranean region,

Recognizing the efforts realized so far and the determination of the Mediterranean countries to intensify the process of dialogue and consultations with a view to resolving the problems existing in the Mediterranean region and eliminating the causes of tension and the consequent threat to peace and security,

Recognizing also the indivisible character of security in the Mediterranean and that the enhancement of cooperation among Mediterranean countries with a view to promoting the economic and social development of all peoples of the region will contribute significantly to stability, peace and security in the region,

Recognizing further that prospects for closer Euro-Mediterranean cooperation in all spheres can be enhanced by positive developments worldwide, particularly in Europe,

Expressing satisfaction at the growing awareness of the need for joint efforts by all Mediterranean countries so as to strengthen economic, social, cultural and environmental cooperation in the Mediterranean region,

Reaffirming the responsibility of all States to contribute to the stability and prosperity of the Mediterranean region and their commitment to respect the purposes and principles of the Charter of the United Nations, as well as the provisions of the Declaration on Principles of International Law concerning Friendly Relations and Cooperation among States in accordance with the Charter of the United Nations,

Expressing its concern at the persistent tension and continuing military activities in parts of the Mediterranean that hinder efforts to strengthen security and cooperation in the region,

Taking note of the report of the Secretary-General on this item,

1. *Reaffirms* that security in the Mediterranean is closely linked to European security as well as to international peace and security;

2. *Expresses satisfaction* at the continuing efforts by Mediterranean countries to contribute actively to the elimination of all causes of tension in the region and to the promotion of just and lasting solutions to the persistent problems of the region through peaceful means, thus ensuring the withdrawal of foreign forces of occupation and respecting the sovereignty, independence and territorial integrity of all countries of the Mediterranean and the right of peoples to self-determination, and therefore calls for full adherence to the principles of non-interference, non-intervention, non-use of force or threat of use of force and the inadmissibility of the acquisition of territory by force, in accordance with the Charter and the relevant resolutions of the United Nations;

3. *Welcomes* the efforts by the Mediterranean countries in the continuation of initiatives and negotiations as well as the adoption of measures that will promote confidence- and security-building as well as disarmament in the Mediterranean region, and encourages them to pursue these efforts further;

4. *Recognizes* that the elimination of the economic and social disparities in levels of development as well as other obstacles in the Mediterranean area will contribute to enhancing peace, security and cooperation among Mediterranean countries;

5. *Takes note* of the conclusions of the Tenth Conference of Heads of State or Government of Non-Aligned Countries, held at Jakarta from 1 to 6 September 1992, specifically paragraphs 36 to 39, Chapter III, of the Final Document on political issues concerning the Mediterranean;

6. *Recalls* the decisions taken by the Second Ministerial Meeting of the Western Mediterranean Countries, held at Algiers in October 1991, and the decision concerning the forthcoming summit meeting of the Western Mediterranean countries to be held at Tunis;

7. *Takes note* of the "Helsinki Document 1992—The Challenges of Change", adopted in July 1992, whereby the heads of State or Government of the States participating in the Conference on Security and Cooperation in Europe agreed, *inter alia*, to widen their cooperation and enlarge their dialogue with the non-participating Mediterranean States as a means to promote social and economic development, thereby enhancing stability in the region, in order to narrow the prosperity gap between Europe and its Mediterranean neighbours and protect the Mediterranean ecosystems;

8. *Takes note also* of the Declaration of the European Council of Ministers of the European Economic Community on relations between Europe and the Maghreb, issued at Lisbon on 25 June 1992;

9. *Welcomes* in this context the decision to convene a Mediterranean seminar of the Conference on Security and Cooperation in Europe under the auspices of the Committee of Senior Officials to consider various topics, including the environment, demographic trends or economic development and other areas of bilateral and multilateral cooperation between States participating in the Conference and non-participating Mediterranean States, reflecting the general framework of principles of cooperation in the Mediterranean region as provided for in the Final Act and other documents of the Conference;

10. *Takes note further* of the conclusions and recommendations of the first Inter-Parliamentary Conference on Security and Cooperation in the Mediterranean, held at Malaga, Spain, from 15 to 20 June 1992, which, *inter alia*, launched a pragmatic process of cooperation that would gradually gain in strength and coverage, generate a positive and irreversible momentum and facilitate the settlement of disputes;

11. *Encourages* the continued widespread support among Mediterranean countries for the convening of a conference on security and cooperation in the Mediterranean, as well as the ongoing regional consultations to create the appropriate conditions for its convening;

12. *Notes* the adoption by the Economic Commission for Europe of its decision G(47), entitled "Economic cooperation in the Mediterranean in the light of the Final Act of the Conference on Security and Cooperation in Europe", and, in this context, calls upon the Executive Secretaries of the relevant United Nations regional commissions as well as other United Nations bodies concerned to strengthen their cooperation on matters that are of common interest to the Mediterranean countries and that will have a positive impact on

the region as a whole, in particular in the economic, social, humanitarian and environmental spheres;

13. *Requests* the Secretary-General to submit a report on means to strengthen security and cooperation in the Mediterranean region;

14. *Decides* to include in the provisional agenda of its forty-eighth session the item entitled "Strengthening of security and cooperation in the Mediterranean region".

General Assembly resolution 47/58

9 December 1992   Meeting 81   Adopted without vote

Approved by First Committee (A/47/697) without vote, 20 November (meeting 37); 8-nation draft (A/C.1/47/L.46/Rev.1); agenda item 67.
Sponsors: Albania, Algeria, Cyprus, Egypt, Libyan Arab Jamahiriya, Malta, Morocco, Tunisia.
Meeting numbers. GA 47th session: 1st Committee 3-30, 37; plenary 81.

South Atlantic zone of peace

The General Assembly in 1986[6] had declared the South Atlantic a zone of peace and cooperation. In subsequent resolutions, the Assembly reaffirmed the determination of the States of the zone to enhance and accelerate their cooperation in political, economic, scientific, technical, cultural and other spheres.

In response to the latest such resolution, adopted in 1991,[7] the Secretary-General submitted in September 1992 a report, with later addenda,[8] containing replies from five Governments and the United Nations Development Programme expressing their views on the implementation of the 1986 declaration.

GENERAL ASSEMBLY ACTION

On 14 December, the General Assembly adopted **resolution 47/74** by recorded vote.

Zone of peace and cooperation of the South Atlantic

The General Assembly,

Recalling its resolution 41/11 of 27 October 1986, in which it solemnly declared the Atlantic Ocean, in the region situated between Africa and South America, the "Zone of peace and cooperation of the South Atlantic",

Recalling also its subsequent resolutions on the matter, including resolutions 45/36 of 27 November 1990 and 46/19 of 25 November 1991, in which it reaffirmed the determination of the States of the zone to enhance and accelerate their cooperation in the political, economic, scientific, technical, cultural and other spheres,

Reaffirming that the questions of peace and security and those of development are interrelated and inseparable, and considering that cooperation among all States, in particular those of the region, for peace and development is essential to promote the objectives of the zone of peace and cooperation of the South Atlantic,

Aware of the importance that the States of the zone attach to the preservation of the region's environment and recognizing the threat that pollution from any source poses to the marine and coastal environment, its ecological balance and its resources,

Noting the concern expressed on the use of fishing methods and practices that cause the over-exploitation of living marine resources, especially of highly migra-

tory and straddling fish stocks, and that it has an adverse impact on the conservation and management of living resources of the marine environment, both within and beyond the exclusive economic zones,

1. *Reaffirms* the purpose and objective of the zone of peace and cooperation of the South Atlantic;

2. *Takes note* of the report submitted by the Secretary-General, in accordance with its resolution 46/19;

3. *Welcomes* the recent initiatives aimed at the full entry into force of the Treaty for the Prohibition of Nuclear Weapons in Latin America and the Caribbean (Treaty of Tlatelolco) and stresses the relevance of such initiatives for the advancement of the objectives and principles of the zone of peace and cooperation of the South Atlantic;

4. *Affirms* the importance of the South Atlantic to global maritime and commercial transactions and its determination to preserve the region for all activities protected by relevant international law, including the freedom of navigation in the high seas;

5. *Stresses* the importance for the zone of peace and cooperation of the South Atlantic of the results of the United Nations Conference on Environment and Development, particularly the principles of the Rio Declaration on Environment and Development and the programmes set forth in Agenda 21, as well as the United Nations Framework Convention on Climate Change and the Convention on Biological Diversity, in the conviction that their implementation will strengthen the basis for cooperation within the zone and for the benefit of the international community as a whole;

6. *Notes with interest* the hope expressed by the countries of the zone to welcome in the near future a non-racial democratic South Africa into the community of South Atlantic States and, in that connection, urges all parties concerned in South Africa to cooperate with a view to ending the continuing violence and thereby create an atmosphere conducive to negotiations leading to the establishment of a non-racial democratic and united South Africa;

7. *Expresses its appreciation* to the international community for its support of the Peace Plan for Liberia of the Economic Community of West African States, most recently through the adoption of Security Council resolution 788(1992) of 19 November 1992, and hopes that the continuing efforts made at the subregional and international levels aimed at a peaceful resolution of the Liberian conflict will, within the shortest possible time, lead to national reconciliation, reconstruction and development;

8. *Calls upon* the parties to the Peace Accords for Angola to respect all the commitments undertaken in accordance with these accords, in particular with regard to the confinement of their troops and weapons, demobilization and the formation of the unified national armed force, and to refrain from any act that might heighten tension, impair the conduct of the electoral process and threaten the territorial integrity of the country;

9. *Also calls upon* the international community to increase humanitarian assistance to both Angola and Liberia;

10. *Takes note with satisfaction* of the initiative of the Government of Namibia to host a meeting of the Ministers of Trade and Industry of the countries of the zone at Windhoek in the first half of 1993;

11. *Requests* the relevant organizations, organs and bodies of the United Nations system to render all ap-

propriate assistance which States of the zone may seek in their joint efforts to implement the declaration of the zone of peace and cooperation of the South Atlantic;

12. *Requests* the Secretary-General to keep the implementation of resolution 41/11 and other subsequent resolutions on the matter under review and to submit a report to the General Assembly at its forty-eighth session, taking into account, *inter alia*, the views expressed by Member States;

13. *Decides* to include in the provisional agenda of its forty-eighth session the item entitled "Zone of peace and cooperation of the South Atlantic".

General Assembly resolution 47/74

14 December 1992   Meeting 85   144-1 (recorded vote)

23-nation draft (A/47/L.24/Rev.1 & Add.1); agenda item 26.

Sponsors: Angola, Argentina, Benin, Brazil, Cameroon, Cape Verde, Congo, Côte d'Ivoire, Gabon, Gambia, Ghana, Guinea, Guinea-Bissau, Liberia, Mauritania, Morocco, Namibia, Nigeria, Sao Tome and Principe, Senegal, Sierra Leone, Togo, Uruguay.

Meeting numbers. GA 47th session: plenary 73, 85.

Recorded vote in Assembly as follows:

In favour: Afghanistan, Albania, Algeria, Angola, Antigua and Barbuda, Argentina, Australia, Austria, Bahrain, Bangladesh, Barbados, Belarus, Belgium, Belize, Benin, Bhutan, Bolivia, Botswana, Brazil, Brunei Darussalam, Bulgaria, Burkina Faso, Cameroon, Canada, Central African Republic, Chad, China, Colombia, Comoros, Costa Rica, Côte d'Ivoire, Cuba, Cyprus, Czechoslovakia, Democratic People's Republic of Korea, Denmark, Djibouti, Dominica, Ecuador, Egypt, El Salvador, Estonia, Ethiopia, Finland, France, Gabon, Gambia, Germany, Ghana, Greece, Guatemala, Guinea-Bissau, Guyana, Haiti, Honduras, Iceland, India, Indonesia, Iran, Iraq, Ireland, Israel, Italy, Jamaica, Japan, Jordan, Kazakhstan, Kuwait, Lao People's Democratic Republic, Latvia, Lebanon, Liberia, Libyan Arab Jamahiriya, Liechtenstein, Lithuania, Luxembourg, Madagascar, Malawi, Malaysia, Maldives, Mali, Malta, Marshall Islands, Mauritania, Mauritius, Mexico, Micronesia, Mongolia, Morocco, Myanmar, Namibia, Nepal, Netherlands, New Zealand, Nicaragua, Niger, Nigeria, Norway, Oman, Pakistan, Panama, Paraguay, Peru, Philippines, Poland, Portugal, Qatar, Republic of Korea, Republic of Moldova, Romania, Russian Federation, Rwanda, Saint Kitts and Nevis, Saint Vincent and the Grenadines, Samoa, Sao Tome and Principe, Saudi Arabia, Senegal, Sierra Leone, Singapore, Slovenia, Spain, Sri Lanka, Sudan, Suriname, Swaziland, Sweden, Syrian Arab Republic, Thailand, Togo, Trinidad and Tobago, Tunisia, Turkey, Ukraine, United Arab Emirates, United Kingdom, United Republic of Tanzania, Uruguay, Vanuatu, Venezuela, Viet Nam, Yemen, Zambia, Zimbabwe.

Against: United States.

REFERENCES

[1]YUN 1991, p. 23, GA res. 46/42, 6 Dec. 1991. [2]A/47/524. [3]A/C.1/47/8. [4]A/47/310. [5]A/47/675-S/24816. [6]YUN 1986, p. 369, GA res. 41/11, 27 Oct. 1986. [7]YUN 1991, p. 24, GA res. 46/19, 25 Nov. 1991. [8]A/47/424 & Add.1-3.

Aerial incidents and the Libyan Arab Jamahiriya

Charges of air terrorism

The Security Council met on 21 January 1992 to consider December 1991 charges[1] by France, the United Kingdom and the United States that nationals and possibly officials of the Libyan Arab Jamahiriya were involved in two aerial incidents: the bombing on 21 December 1988 of Pan Am flight 103 over Lockerbie in southern Scotland and the crash on 19 September 1989 of Union de transports aériens (UTA) flight 772 over the Ténéré desert in the Niger.

In a joint declaration of November 1991,[2] the United Kingdom and the United States had demanded that the Libyan Arab Jamahiriya surrender for trial those nationals charged with bombing Pan Am flight 103, disclose all it knew of the crime, allow full access to witnesses and evidence, and pay appropriate compensation. France, placing presumptions of guilt for the attack on UTA flight 772 on several Libyan nationals, called on the Libyan Arab Jamahiriya to produce all the material evidence in its possession, facilitate contacts and meetings for the assembly of witnesses, and authorize Libyan officials to respond to requests made by the examining magistrate.[3]

Also in November 1991, the Libyan Arab Jamahiriya challenged the United States and the United Kingdom to produce convincing material and tangible evidence for their accusations, declared its readiness to cooperate fully with any impartial international judicial authority, and reserved its right to defend itself in accordance with Article 51 of the United Nations Charter.[4] It affirmed that its policy was incompatible with all forms of terrorism, declared that it would not permit the use of its territory or citizens for terrorist operations, and declared that all applications by France, the United Kingdom and the United States would receive every attention, inasmuch as the competent Libyan authorities would investigate them.[5]

By a letter of 8 January,[6] the Libyan Arab Jamahiriya affirmed that submission of the matter to the Security Council had no basis either in the Charter or in international law, which did not stipulate that the Council had the power to consider judicial cases involving individuals. It offered to enter into dialogue with the three countries, urged them to provide Libyan judges investigating the incidents with the records of the investigation, and invited the parties to reach agreement through international judicial authorities, including the International Court of Justice (ICJ).

Also before the Council were two January communications from the Jamahiriya, one transmitting a letter addressed to the United Kingdom and the United States and the other a resolution adopted by the Council of the League of Arab States (LAS) on 16 January. By the first,[7] the Jamahiriya called for implementation of article 14 of the 1971 Montreal Convention for the Suppression of Unlawful Acts against the Safety of Civilian Aviation,[8] to which all three States were parties. Under article 14, paragraph 1, any dispute between two or more contracting States that could not be settled through negotiation should be submitted to arbitration. The LAS Council again called for the establishment of a United Nations–LAS joint commission and urged the Security Council to resolve the conflict by negotiation, mediation and judicial settlement in accordance with Article 33 of the Charter.[9]

At their request, Canada, the Congo, Iran, Iraq, Italy, the Libyan Arab Jamahiriya, Mauritania, the Sudan and Yemen were invited to participate in the discussion without the right to vote, in accordance with rule 37[a] of the Council's provisional rules of procedure. At Morocco's request,[(10)] the Council extended an invitation to the League of Arab States, under rule 39.[b]

Following statements, the Council unanimously adopted **resolution 731(1992)**.

The Security Council,

Deeply disturbed by the world-wide persistence of acts of international terrorism in all its forms, including those in which States are directly or indirectly involved, which endanger or take innocent lives, have a deleterious effect on international relations and jeopardize the security of States,

Deeply concerned by all illegal activities directed against international civil aviation, and affirming the right of all States, in accordance with the Charter of the United Nations and relevant principles of international law, to protect their nationals from acts of international terrorism that constitute threats to international peace and security,

Reaffirming its resolution 286(1970) of 9 September 1970, in which it called on States to take all possible legal steps to prevent any interference with international civil air travel,

Reaffirming also its resolution 635(1989) of 14 June 1989, in which it condemned all acts of unlawful interference against the security of civil aviation and called upon all States to cooperate in devising and implementing measures to prevent all acts of terrorism, including those involving explosives,

Recalling the statement made on 30 December 1988 by the President of the Security Council on behalf of the members of the Council strongly condemning the destruction of Pan American flight 103 and calling on all States to assist in the apprehension and prosecution of those responsible for this criminal act,

Deeply concerned over the results of investigations, which implicate officials of the Libyan Government and which are contained in Security Council documents that include the requests addressed to the Libyan authorities by France, the United Kingdom of Great Britain and Northern Ireland, and the United States of America, in connection with the legal procedures related to the attacks carried out against Pan American flight 103 and Union de transports aériens flight 772,

Determined to eliminate international terrorism,

1. *Condemns* the destruction of Pan American flight 103 and Union de transports aériens flight 772 and the resultant loss of hundreds of lives;

2. *Strongly deplores* the fact that the Libyan Government has not yet responded effectively to the above requests to cooperate fully in establishing responsibility for the terrorist acts referred to above against Pan American flight 103 and Union de transports aériens flight 772;

3. *Urges* the Libyan Government immediately to provide a full and effective response to those requests so as to contribute to the elimination of international terrorism;

4. *Requests* the Secretary-General to seek the cooperation of the Libyan Government to provide a full and effective response to those requests;

5. *Urges* all States individually and collectively to encourage the Libyan Government to respond fully and effectively to those requests;

6. *Decides* to remain seized of the matter.

Security Council resolution 731(1992)
21 January 1992   Meeting 3033   Adopted unanimously

3-nation draft (S/23422).
Sponsors: France, United Kingdom, United States.

In a statement before the Council, the Libyan Arab Jamahiriya said that an ostensibly arduous four-year investigation by the United Kingdom and the United States into the Lockerbie incident had found no supporting evidence, and no proof had been made available as to the alleged responsibility of Libyan nationals. Its own judicial authorities had appointed two magistrates who initiated an investigation; they contacted investigating authorities in Scotland, the United States and France, but had been unable to make any significant progress owing to the authorities' refusal to hand over the files or submit evidence in their possession. The Libyan authorities had expressed readiness to receive investigators to participate in the investigation.

Asserting that the problem involved Libyan nationals but had nothing to do with the State, the Jamahiriya said the matter was a legal issue and the Council was not the competent forum to consider the question, as under Article 36 of the Charter legal disputes should be referred to ICJ. To treat the dispute as a political rather than a legal matter would constitute a flagrant violation of Article 27 of the Charter.

Summing up its position, the Jamahiriya stated that it condemned terrorism in all its forms, including State-sponsored terrorism, and reconfirmed its determination to put an end to that dangerous phenomenon. It strongly condemned the destruction of the two airliners and expressed willingness to cooperate with the judicial authorities in the countries concerned. It requested that the United Kingdom and the United States be invited to enter promptly into negotiations with it on proceedings leading to arbitration; if no agreement was reached in arbitration, the matter would be brought before ICJ.

In the view of the United States, the Libyan Arab Jamahiriya had sought to evade its respon-

[a]Rule 37 of the Council's provisional rules of procedure states: "Any Member of the United Nations which is not a member of the Security Council may be invited, as the result of a decision of the Security Council, to participate, without vote, in the discussion of any question brought before the Security Council when the Security Council considers that the interests of that Member are specially affected, or when a Member brings a matter to the attention of the Council in accordance with Article 35(1) of the Charter."

[b]Rule 39 of the Council's provisional rules of procedure states: "The Security Council may invite members of the Secretariat or other persons, whom it considers competent for the purpose, to supply it with information or to give other assistance in examining matters within its competence."

sibilities and to procrastinate. Resolution 731(1992) provided for the accused to be turned over to the judicial authorities of the Governments that were competent under international law to try them— requests the Jamahiriya had refused to respond to. No State could seek to hide support for international terrorism behind traditional principles of international law and State practice. France hoped that the unanimous reaction of the international community, as expressed in the resolution, would induce the Libyan authorities to respond quickly to the requests of the judicial authorities conducting the investigation into both attacks, which had claimed 441 victims.

Reports of the Secretary-General. Pursuant to Security Council resolution 731(1992), the Secretary-General submitted two reports, on 11 February[11] and on 3 March.[12]

He had sent Under-Secretary-General Vasiliy Safronchuk as his Special Envoy to the Libyan Arab Jamahiriya on 25 January to deliver to the Libyan leader, Colonel Muammar Qaddafi, a personal message, together with the text of the Council resolution and related records.

During the meeting with the Special Envoy, Colonel Qaddafi reiterated his readiness to cooperate with the Secretary-General. He explained that following receipt of the charges against two Libyan nationals said to be involved in the downing of Pan Am flight 103, Libyan authorities had immediately started legal proceedings against them. The Libyan judges would require further information from the United Kingdom and the United States. He stressed that no action could be taken that contravened the Libyan legal system and suggested that the Secretary-General invite to the Jamahiriya judges from the three countries concerned, as well as representatives of the LAS, the Organization of African Unity (OAU) and the Organization of the Islamic Conference (OIC), to observe a possible trial.

The Permanent Representative of the Libyan Arab Jamahiriya to the United Nations met with the Secretary-General on 11 February; his Government was ready to cooperate fully with the Security Council and the Secretary-General and proposed that a mechanism be created for implementing resolution 731(1992).

The Secretary-General's March report dealt mainly with suggestions by France, the United Kingdom and the United States and a response from the Libyan Arab Jamahiriya concerning a possible handing over of the two suspects and subsequent judicial procedures. During two further meetings with the Special Envoy, the Libyan leader pointed out that constitutional obstacles prevented the handing over of the suspects for trial in a foreign country, a point that was reiterated in a 2 March letter from the Secretary of the People's

Committee for Foreign Liaison and International Cooperation of the Libyan Arab Jamahiriya to the Secretary-General. That letter and another of 27 February were annexed to the report. In the 27 February letter, the Secretary proposed a mechanism for implementing resolution 731(1992): he agreed to the requests of France that a magistrate go to the Jamahiriya to investigate the case in a manner he deemed fit and that he be provided with a copy of the minutes of the investigation carried out by the Libyan judge and condemned terrorism in all its forms. He also discussed the question of compensation.

Air and arms embargo

SECURITY COUNCIL ACTION (March)

The Security Council, on 31 March, again considered the charges by France, the United Kingdom and the United States against the Libyan Arab Jamahiriya in connection with the bombing of Pan Am flight 103 and UTA flight 772, together with the February[11] and March[12] reports of the Secretary-General on the implementation of Council resolution 731(1992) (see above).

The Council President drew attention to four letters addressed to him or the Secretary-General. By the first,[13] the Libyan Arab Jamahiriya transmitted a 6 February memorandum by the International Progress Organization, stating that resolution 731(1992) was not in conformity with Article 33 of the Charter regarding the peaceful settlement of disputes, which required that parties first seek a solution by negotiation, enquiry, mediation, conciliation, arbitration or judicial settlement. The memorandum suggested applying the procedures of the 1971 Montreal Convention.[8] Portugal transmitted a 17 February statement[14] by the European Community welcoming the unanimous adoption of resolution 731(1992) and underlining the great importance of Libyan compliance with it.

By a letter of 18 March,[15] the Jamahiriya asserted that it had actively and positively cooperated with regard to that resolution. It asked the Council to urge France, the United Kingdom and the United States to hand over their dossiers so that the Libyan judges could complete their investigation. It maintained that the issue was a legal one and should thus be left to ICJ. Jordan transmitted a 22 March resolution by the LAS Council,[16] by which the League renewed its call to the Council to resolve the conflict in accordance with Article 33 of the Charter, and urged the Council to avoid the adoption of economic, military or diplomatic measures that might increase the complications and have an adverse effect on the region, and to await a decision by ICJ.

At their request, Iraq, Jordan, the Libyan Arab Jamahiriya, Mauritania and Uganda were invited to participate in the discussion without a right to vote, in accordance with rule 37ᵃ of the Council's provisional rules of procedure. At Morocco's request,[17] an invitation to OIC was extended under rule 39.ᵇ

Following statements, the Council adopted **resolution 748(1992)**.

The Security Council,

Reaffirming its resolution 731(1992) of 21 January 1992,

Noting the reports of the Secretary-General,

Deeply concerned that the Libyan Government has still not provided a full and effective response to the requests in its resolution 731(1992) of 21 January 1992,

Convinced that the suppression of acts of international terrorism, including those in which States are directly or indirectly involved, is essential for the maintenance of international peace and security,

Recalling that, in the statement issued on 31 January 1992 on the occasion of the meeting of the Security Council at the level of heads of State and Government, the members of the Council expressed their deep concern over acts of international terrorism, and emphasized the need for the international community to deal effectively with all such acts,

Reaffirming that, in accordance with the principle in Article 2, paragraph 4, of the Charter of the United Nations, every State has the duty to refrain from organizing, instigating, assisting or participating in terrorist acts in another State or acquiescing in organized activities within its territory directed towards the commission of such acts, when such acts involve a threat or use of force,

Determining, in this context, that the failure by the Libyan Government to demonstrate by concrete actions its renunciation of terrorism and in particular its continued failure to respond fully and effectively to the requests in resolution 731(1992) constitute a threat to international peace and security,

Determined to eliminate international terrorism,

Recalling the right of States, under Article 50 of the Charter, to consult the Security Council where they find themselves confronted with special economic problems arising from the carrying out of preventive or enforcement measures,

Acting under Chapter VII of the Charter,

1. *Decides* that the Libyan Government must now comply without any further delay with paragraph 3 of resolution 731(1992) regarding the requests contained in documents S/23306, S/23308 and S/23309;

2. *Decides also* that the Libyan Government must commit itself definitively to cease all forms of terrorist action and all assistance to terrorist groups and that it must promptly, by concrete actions, demonstrate its renunciation of terrorism;

3. *Decides* that on 15 April 1992 all States shall adopt the measures set out below, which shall apply until the Security Council decides that the Libyan Government has complied with paragraphs 1 and 2 above;

4. *Decides also* that all States shall:

(*a*) Deny permission to any aircraft to take off from, land in or overfly their territory if it is destined to land in or has taken off from the territory of Libya, unless the particular flight has been approved on grounds of significant humanitarian need by the Committee established by paragraph 9 below;

(*b*) Prohibit, by their nationals or from their territory, the supply of any aircraft or aircraft components to Libya, the provision of engineering and maintenance servicing of Libyan aircraft or aircraft components, the certification of airworthiness for Libyan aircraft, the payment of new claims against existing insurance contracts and the provision of new direct insurance for Libyan aircraft;

5. *Decides further* that all States shall:

(*a*) Prohibit any provision to Libya by their nationals or from their territory of arms and related material of all types, including the sale or transfer of weapons and ammunition, military vehicles and equipment, paramilitary police equipment and spare parts for the aforementioned, as well as the provision of any types of equipment, supplies and grants of licensing arrangements, for the manufacture or maintenance of the aforementioned;

(*b*) Prohibit any provision to Libya by their nationals or from their territory of technical advice, assistance or training related to the provision, manufacture, maintenance, or use of the items in (*a*) above;

(*c*) Withdraw any of their officials or agents present in Libya to advise the Libyan authorities on military matters;

6. *Decides* that all States shall:

(*a*) Significantly reduce the number and the level of the staff at Libyan diplomatic missions and consular posts and restrict or control the movement within their territory of all such staff who remain; in the case of Libyan missions to international organizations, the host State may, as it deems necessary, consult the organization concerned on the measures required to implement this subparagraph;

(*b*) Prevent the operation of all Libyan Arab Airlines offices;

(*c*) Take all appropriate steps to deny entry to or expel Libyan nationals who have been denied entry to or expelled from other States because of their involvement in terrorist activities;

7. *Calls upon* all States, including States not members of the United Nations, and all international organizations, to act strictly in accordance with the provisions of the present resolution, notwithstanding the existence of any rights or obligations conferred or imposed by any international agreement or any contract entered into or any licence or permit granted prior to 15 April 1992;

8. *Requests* all States to report to the Secretary-General by 15 May 1992 on the measures they have instituted for meeting the obligations set out in paragraphs 3 to 7 above;

9. *Decides* to establish, in accordance with rule 28 of its provisional rules of procedure, a Committee of the Security Council consisting of all the members of the Council, to undertake the following tasks and to report on its work to the Council with its observations and recommendations:

(*a*) To examine the reports submitted pursuant to paragraph 8 above;

(*b*) To seek from all States further information regarding the action taken by them concerning the effective implementation of the measures imposed by paragraphs 3 to 7 above;

(*c*) To consider any information brought to its attention by States concerning violations of the measures imposed by paragraphs 3 to 7 above and, in that context, to make recommendations to the Council on ways to increase their effectiveness;

(d) To recommend appropriate measures in response to violations of the measures imposed by paragraphs 3 to 7 above and provide information on a regular basis to the Secretary-General for general distribution to Member States;

(e) To consider and to decide upon expeditiously any application by States for the approval of flights on grounds of significant humanitarian need in accordance with paragraph 4 above;

(f) To give special attention to any communications in accordance with Article 50 of the Charter from any neighbouring or other State with special economic problems that might arise from the carrying out of the measures imposed by paragraphs 3 to 7 above;

10. *Calls upon* all States to cooperate fully with the Committee in the fulfilment of its task, including supplying such information as may be sought by the Committee in pursuance of the present resolution;

11. *Requests* the Secretary-General to provide all necessary assistance to the Committee and to make the necessary arrangements in the Secretariat for this purpose;

12. *Invites* the Secretary-General to continue his role as set out in paragraph 4 of resolution 731(1992);

13. *Decides* that the Security Council shall, every 120 days or sooner should the situation so require, review the measures imposed by paragraphs 3 to 7 above in the light of the compliance by the Libyan Government with paragraphs 1 and 2 above taking into account, as appropriate, any reports provided by the Secretary-General on his role as set out in paragraph 4 of resolution 731(1992);

14. *Decides* to remain seized of the matter.

Security Council resolution 748(1992)

31 March 1992   Meeting 3063   10-0-5

3-nation draft (S/23762).
Sponsors: France, United Kingdom, United States.
Vote in Council as follows:
    In favour: Austria, Belgium, Ecuador, France, Hungary, Japan, Russian Federation, United Kingdom, United States, Venezuela.
    Against: None.
    Abstaining: Cape Verde, China, India, Morocco, Zimbabwe.

Speaking before the Council, the Libyan Arab Jamahiriya said the dispute was of a purely legal nature and should be solved by legal means. On the basis of the 1971 Montreal Convention,[8] it had taken concrete measures and had requested arbitration. The other parties had not cooperated with Libyan judicial authorities, refusing to turn over their files on the case and the evidence in their possession.

With regard to resolution 731(1992) adopted in January, the Jamahiriya said not only was it based on incomplete investigations, but there was no justification for it, since it made no mention of the Libyan point of view and ignored Article 33 of the Charter. In addition, the procedure followed by the Council in adopting that resolution did not take into account Article 27 of the Charter, which stipulated that when decisions were adopted under Chapter VI, a party to a dispute should abstain

from voting; that was applicable to France, the United Kingdom and the United States.

The Libyan Arab Jamahiriya stated that it had no objection to surrendering the two suspects to the United Nations in Tripoli in order to facilitate investigations, or to the Secretary-General's undertaking to set up a legal committee to carry out a comprehensive investigation. If the Secretary-General were then to confirm the seriousness of the accusations, it would not object to surrendering the two suspects under his personal supervision to a third party. It further agreed with France's proposal to send a judge to the Jamahiriya to investigate and expressed readiness to have the Secretary-General or his deputy engage in fact-finding on its territory in order to disprove or confirm allegations of its purported implication in terrorist acts.

In the view of the United States, the evidence revealing Libyan involvement in the terrorist acts against the two airliners indicated a serious breach of international peace and security and fully justified measures pursuant to Chapter VII of the Charter. The means chosen were appropriate and the sanctions measured, precise and limited—a multilateral, non-violent and peaceful response to violent and brutal acts.

Given the nature of Libyan involvement with terrorism and the means it had employed, the United Kingdom considered entirely appropriate the arms ban and action against Libyan overseas missions and Libyan Arab Airlines offices. The sanctions would not be brought into force until 15 April, which would allow time for the Libyan Arab Jamahiriya to take steps in order to avoid their imposition completely. For France, the sanctions were balanced and appropriate, as the three areas they applied to— arms, aviation, and diplomatic and consular personnel—could be used to support international terrorism.

Report and communications. The Secretary-General submitted a report on 22 May with later addenda,[18] on the implementation of resolution 748(1992). As at 13 August, 82 States reported on the measures they had instituted to comply with the resolution. Later in the year, another five reported on their compliance.[19]

During the year, the Libyan Arab Jamahiriya informed the President of the Security Council or the Secretary-General on many occasions[20] of the negative effects resulting from the aerial embargo imposed in resolution 748(1992). It also renounced terrorism on several occasions and affirmed its acceptance of as well as its readiness to cooperate in implementing Security Council resolution 731(1992).

France transmitted a 16 April letter[21] from the judge in charge of investigating the bombing of UTA flight 772, stating that the Libyan documents on the enquiry into the air attack submitted to him were inconsistent and some of them even showed anomalies; therefore, they had no probative value.

Responding on 26 April,[22] the Counsellor and Investigating Judge of the Libyan Arab Jamahiriya stated that the Libyan authorities had instituted an enquiry after establishing the three subjects' identities and informing them of the charges brought against them. They had also discussed with them in detail the indictment brought by the French examining magistrate and the suspicions against them. With regard to the fourth suspect, they presented evidence, by means of official documents, to establish his true name and that he had died more than a year earlier. The Counsellor declared that the Libyan authorities were prepared to cooperate fully with the French magistrate in order to bring the truth to light.

France, the United Kingdom and the United States, in a 27 November declaration,[23] condemned the Jamahiriya's failure to comply with the Security Council's requirements; demanded prompt, complete and unequivocal compliance; expressed determination to intensify their efforts to make the Council sanctions more effective; and called on the Libyan Arab Jamahiriya to end its defiance of the international community.

The Libyan Arab Jamahiriya, on 8 December,[24] appealed to the Secretary-General to use his best endeavours to have resolution 748(1992) rescinded, in view of the steps it had taken to implement resolution 731(1992) and the proposals it had put foward regarding the legal prosecution of the two Libyan nationals suspected of being connected with the downing of Pan Am flight 103.

Following adoption of a resolution by the Basic People's Congresses (the Libyan legislative authority) to the effect that they did not object to the two suspects being brought before a just and fair tribunal, the Jamahiriya declared that it had no objection to them appearing of their own accord before United States or British courts and that it was prepared to enter into negotiations, under the Secretary-General's auspices, regarding a trial held in a neutral country.

With regard to UTA flight 772, the Jamahiriya stated that the French and Libyan investigating magistrates had met on a number of occasions, and the French magistrate had examined the records of the Libyan investigation. It was agreed that he should go to the Jamahiriya to complete his investigations, and contacts continued to renew arrangements for such a visit. The Jamahiriya said it had also cooperated with France in respect of its other requests as set forth in December 1991,[3] namely, that the Jamahiriya produce all the material evidence in its possession and facilitate access to all documents that might be useful in establishing the truth; facilitate the necessary contacts for the assembly of witnesses; and author-

ize the Libyan officials to respond to any request by the examining magistrate for judicial information.

The Jamahiriya also summed up its action taken against terrorism, namely: it had severed relations with all groups and organizations suspected of involvement in terrorist acts; it did not permit its territory, nationals or institutions to be used for such acts and was prepared to impose severe penalties on those proved to have been involved; it had cooperated with the United Kingdom to help trace those elements and organizations accused by the latter of being involved in terrorist acts; and it had facilitated talks between French and Libyan judicial authorities to determine responsibility in the case of the bombing of UTA flight 772.

SECURITY COUNCIL ACTION (August and December)

Following consultations held on 12 August and 9 December, the President made identical statements on behalf of the Council members:[25]

"The members of the Security Council held informal consultations on 12 August 1992 [9 December 1992] pursuant to paragraph 13 of resolution 748(1992), by which the Council decided to review every 120 days or sooner, should the situation so require, the measures imposed by paragraphs 3 to 7 against the Libyan Arab Jamahiriya.

"After hearing all the opinions expressed in the course of the consultations, the President of the Council concluded that there was no agreement that the necessary conditions existed for modification of the measures of sanctions established in paragraphs 3 to 7 of resolution 748(1992)."

Incident at Venezuela's Embassy in Tripoli

At the request of Venezuela,[26] the Security Council considered on 2 April 1992 the destruction of Venezuela's Embassy in Tripoli. Venezuela reported to the President of the Council[27] that that day a mob of students and people from the street broke into the Embassy shouting slogans against Venezuela because of its vote in the Council in favour of resolution 748(1992) and then ransacked and destroyed the premises. Neither the four Libyan guards assigned to protect the Embassy nor the police of Tripoli intervened to stop the looting and arson.

Following consultations, the President made a statement on behalf of members of the Council.[28]

Meeting number. SC 3064.

"The Security Council strongly condemns the violent attacks on and destruction of the premises of the Embassy of Venezuela in Tripoli that took place today. The fact that these intolerable and extremely grave events have been directed not only against the Government of Venezuela but also against and in reaction to Security Council resolution 748(1992) underlines the seriousness of the situation.

"The Council demands that the Government of the Libyan Arab Jamahiriya take all necessary measures to honour its international legal obligations to ensure the security of the personnel and to protect the property of the Embassy of Venezuela and of all other diplomatic and consular premises or personnel present in the Libyan Arab Jamahiriya, including those of the United Nations and related organizations, from acts of violence and terrorism.

"The Council further demands that the Libyan Arab Jamahiriya pay to the Government of Venezuela immediate and full compensation for the damage caused.

"Any suggestion that those acts of violence were not directed against the Government of Venezuela but against and in reaction to resolution 748(1992) is extremely serious and totally unacceptable."

On 5 April,[29] Venezuela informed the Council that, on that day, the Libyan Arab Jamahiriya had apologized for the damage to the Embassy, condemned the act and indicated that it would provide compensation.

REFERENCES

[1]A/46/825-S/23306, A/46/826-S/23307, A/46/827-S/23308, A/46/828-S/23309, A/46/831-S/23317. [2]A/46/827-S/23308. [3]A/46/825-S/23306. [4]A/46/844-S/23416. [5]A/46/845-S/23417. [6]A/46/841-S/23396. [7]S/23441. [8]YUN 1971, p. 739. [9]S/23436. [10]S/23442. [11]S/23574. [12]S/23672. [13]A/46/886-S/23641. [14]A/46/888-S/23656. [15]A/46/895-S/23731. [16]S/23745. [17]S/23764. [18]S/23992 & Add.1,2. [19]S/24374, S/24465, S/24485, S/24676, S/24972. [20]S/23855, S/23915, S/23954, S/24004, S/24072, S/24186, S/24334, S/24381, S/24427, S/24428, S/24463, S/24530, S/24629, S/24773, S/24961/Add.1. [21]S/23828. [22]S/23891. [23]A/47/758-S/24913. [24]S/24961. [25]S/24424, S/24925. [26]S/23771. [27]S/23776. [28]S/23772. [29]S/23796.

Chapter II

Disarmament

Throughout 1992, the world moved further away from the environment of the cold war. The change in the international climate and agreements on major arms reductions by the former Soviet Union and the United States had placed disarmament in a significantly different perspective. Rather than being directed at achieving a balance of power between two military alliances, arms control and disarmament were seen more in the broader context of international peace and security. Moreover, arms limitation and disarmament efforts were being woven into the larger fabric of preventive diplomacy, conflict management and peace-building. In that context, the United Nations assumed a new role in international security, arms control and disarmament.

Nuclear disarmament negotiations between the Russian Federation and the United States gained new momentum in 1992. On 1 October, the United States Senate consented to ratification of the 1991 Treaty on the Reduction and Limitation of Strategic Offensive Arms (START). The Russian Parliament, on 4 November, also approved the Treaty, with the proviso that ratification would not be completed until Belarus, Kazakhstan and Ukraine had joined the 1968 Treaty on the Non-Proliferation of Nuclear Weapons and the Russian Federation had reached accords with them on all aspects of their nuclear forces. A protocol to the START Treaty was signed at Lisbon on 23 May by Belarus, Kazakhstan, the Russian Federation, Ukraine and the United States, under which the four States of the former USSR agreed that, as successor States, they would assume the obligations of the former USSR under START.

On 17 June, at a Washington, D.C., summit meeting, President George Bush of the United States and President Boris Yeltsin of the Russian Federation agreed in principle to further far-reaching reductions in their strategic arms. By the end of 1992, a draft treaty—to be known as START II—was ready for signature by the two parties. Another significant development affecting nuclear disarmament took place on 24 September, when the United States Congress for the first time imposed limitations on nuclear testing and called for the negotiation of a multilateral comprehensive nuclear-test ban by the United States, to be concluded on or before 30 September 1996.

The Conference on Disarmament, a 39-nation multilateral negotiating body, completed, after more than a decade of negotiations, the text of the draft Convention on the Prohibition of the Development, Production, Stockpiling and Use of Chemical Weapons and on Their Destruction. The landmark agreement would ban chemical weapons and ensure the destruction of declared stocks under a comprehensive verification regime allowing for on-site inspections, by a new international organization, of any facility suspected of non-compliance. It was the first disarmament agreement negotiated within a multilateral framework that provided for eliminating an entire category of weapons of mass destruction. The General Assembly requested the Secretary-General, as depositary of the Convention, to open it for signature in Paris on 13 January 1993 and called on all States to become parties to it at the earliest possible date (resolution 47/39).

The Disarmament Commission, a deliberative body composed of all United Nations Member States, dealt with objective information on military matters; nuclear disarmament in the framework of international peace and security, with the objective of eliminating nuclear weapons; a regional approach to disarmament within the context of global security; and the role of science and technology in the context of international security, disarmament and other related fields. In 1992, the Commission successfully concluded the agenda item on objective information on military matters by adopting a set of guidelines and recommendations on the subject, which were subsequently endorsed by the Assembly (resolution 47/54 B).

UN role in disarmament

United Nations machinery

In 1992, the United Nations continued its disarmament efforts mainly through the General Assembly and its First Committee, the Disarmament Commission (a subsidiary organ of the Assembly) and the Conference on Disarmament (a multilateral negotiating forum at Geneva).

The existing disarmament machinery, which was agreed on at the Assembly's tenth special session in 1978, its first special session devoted to disarmament, remained essentially the same.[1] In an October report, *New Dimensions of Arms Regulation and Disarmament in the Post–Cold War Era*,[2] the Secretary-General, referring to the disarmament machinery, stated that the United Nations framework in which disarmament had been pursued was created during the cold war. He recommended reassessing the machinery to meet the new realities and priorities and stressed the need for a coordinated system which would allow the international community to address major disarmament problems promptly, flexibly and efficiently. In addition, the Secretary-General supported a greater role and involvement of the Security Council in disarmament matters.

As a result of widespread interest in examining the existing disarmament machinery, the Assembly, by **decision 47/422**, decided to reconvene the First Committee in March 1993.

GENERAL ASSEMBLY ACTION

On 9 December 1992, on the recommendation of the First Committee, the General Assembly adopted **decision 47/422** without vote.

Review of the implementation of the recommendations and decisions adopted by the General Assembly at its tenth special session

At its 81st plenary meeting, on 9 December 1992, the General Assembly, on the recommendation of the First Committee, decided:

(a) To reconvene meetings of the First Committee for five working days, from 8 to 12 March 1993 in New York, with the purpose of reassessing the multilateral arms control and disarmament machinery, in particular the respective roles of the First Committee, the Disarmament Commission and the Conference on Disarmament and their interrelationship, as well as the role of the Office for Disarmament Affairs of the Secretariat, including ways and means to enhance the functioning and efficiency of the said machinery, bearing in mind the competence of the Security Council in those matters. The aim of the meetings is to conduct the aforementioned reassessment with a view to reaching concrete, agreed recommendations for appropriate action. With respect to the Conference on Disarmament, it is understood that the primary responsibility for making recommendations on its future rests with that body;

(b) To invite Member States to provide their views on the report of the Secretary-General entitled "New dimensions of arms regulation and disarmament in the post–cold war era" no later than 31 January 1993, and to request the Secretary-General to submit a compilation of those views to the General Assembly for consideration at the reconvened meetings of the First Committee;

(c) To request the Secretary-General to transmit his report entitled "New dimensions of arms regulation and disarmament in the post–cold war era" to the Conference on Disarmament; and the Conference on Disarmament to transmit to the Chairman of the First Committee the results of its consideration of that report by 15 February 1993, as well as a report on the status of its ongoing review of its agenda, composition and methods of work by 20 February 1993;

(d) To request the Chairman of the First Committee, with the assistance of the other officers of the Committee, and the Secretariat, to coordinate the above actions.

General Assembly decision 47/422

9 December 1992   Meeting 81   Adopted without vote

Approved by First Committee (A/47/693) without vote, 25 November (meeting 40); draft by Chairman (A/C.1/47/L.53), orally revised; agenda item 63.
Financial implications. ACABQ, A/47/7/Add.11; 5th Committee, A/47/761; S-G, A/C.1/47/L.55, A/C.5/47/63.
Meeting numbers. GA 47th session: 1st Committee 3-21, 37, 40; 5th Committee 38; plenary 81.

Disarmament Commission

The Disarmament Commission, composed of all United Nations Member States, at its 1992 session (New York, 20 April–11 May) held eight plenary meetings under the chairmanship of André Erdös (Hungary).[3] It also held an organizational session on 8 December to elect its officers and consider the provisional agenda for its 1993 session.

The Commission's agenda included items on objective information on military matters; nuclear disarmament in the framework of international peace and security, with the objective of eliminating nuclear weapons; regional disarmament within the context of global security; and the role of science and technology in international security, disarmament and related fields. All of those items were carried over from the Commission's 1991 session.[4]

The Commission had established a Committee of the Whole and four working groups to deal with its agenda items. Working Group I dealt with objective information on military matters and adopted guidelines and recommendations on the subject which were annexed to the Commission's report to the General Assembly (see **resolution 47/54 B**). In Working Group II, discussions continued on nuclear disarmament in the framework of international peace and security, with the objective of eliminating nuclear weapons on the basis of four subjects presented by the Chairman of the Group in 1991.[5] Working Group III continued consideration of a regional approach to disarmament within the context of global security based on its Chairman's paper presented in 1991.[6] Discussion focused on the first two of the five topics in the paper: the relationship between regional disarmament and global security and arms limitation and disarmament; and principles and guidelines. Two papers presented by the Chairman were annexed to the Commission's report. Working Group IV continued to debate the role of science and technology in the context of international security, disarmament and other related fields, focusing on four aspects of the item identified in 1991.[7]

Sweden proposed the inclusion of a new item in the agenda of the 1993 session entitled "General guidelines for non-proliferation, with special emphasis on weapons of mass destruction".

GENERAL ASSEMBLY ACTION

On 9 December 1992, on the recommendation of the First Committee, the General Assembly adopted **resolution 47/54 A** without vote.

Report of the Disarmament Commission

The General Assembly,

Having considered the annual report of the Disarmament Commission,

Considering the role that the Disarmament Commission has been called upon to play and the contribution that it should make in examining and submitting recommendations on various problems in the field of disarmament and in the promotion of the implementation of the relevant decisions of the tenth special session,

Noting the support for the proposal to include a new item in the agenda of the 1993 substantive session of the Disarmament Commission, entitled "General guidelines for non-proliferation, with special emphasis on weapons of mass destruction",

Also noting the support for consideration of the inclusion of a new item in the agenda of the 1994 substantive session of the Disarmament Commission, entitled "International arms transfer, with particular reference to resolution 46/36 H of 6 December 1991",

Recognizing the need to improve further the effective functioning of the Disarmament Commission, and bearing in mind the experience of the 1992 substantive session, when the agenda item on objective information on military matters was successfully concluded,

Recalling its resolution 46/38 A of 6 December 1991,

1. *Takes note* of the annual report of the Disarmament Commission;

2. *Commends* the Disarmament Commission for its adoption by consensus of a set of guidelines and recommendations for objective information on military matters, which were recommended to the General Assembly for consideration, pursuant to the adopted "Ways and means to enhance the functioning of the Disarmament Commission";[a]

3. *Notes with satisfaction* that the Disarmament Commission has successfully implemented its reform programme and has made considerable progress on other substantive items on its agenda;

4. *Recalls* the role of the Disarmament Commission as the specialized, deliberative body within the United Nations multilateral disarmament machinery that allows for in-depth deliberations on specific disarmament issues, leading to the submission of concrete recommendations on those issues;

5. *Requests* the Disarmament Commission to continue its work in accordance with its mandate, as set forth in paragraph 118 of the Final Document of the Tenth Special Session of the General Assembly, and with paragraph 3 of resolution 37/78 H of 9 December 1982, and to that end to make every effort to achieve specific recommendations on the items on its agenda, taking into account the adopted "Ways and means to enhance the functioning of the Disarmament Commission";

6. *Stresses* the importance for the Disarmament Commission to work on the basis of a relevant agenda of disarmament topics, thereby enabling the Commission to concentrate its efforts and thus optimize its progress on specific subjects in accordance with resolution 37/78 H;

7. *Recommends* that the Disarmament Commission, at its 1992 organizational session, adopt the following items for consideration at its 1993 substantive session:

   (1) Process of nuclear disarmament in the framework of international peace and security, with the objective of the elimination of nuclear weapons;

   (2) Regional approach to disarmament within the context of global security;

   (3) The role of science and technology in the context of international security, disarmament and other related fields;

8. *Also requests* that the Disarmament Commission, at the aforementioned organizational meeting, consider the following matters:

   (a) The objective of moving the agenda of the Disarmament Commission to a three-item phased approach with one item in the first year of consideration, one item in its middle year and one item in its concluding year, with the result that, in principle, one item is added and one item is concluded, respectively, at each substantive session;

   (b) That, in furtherance of the foregoing, the 1993 substantive session should be considered as a transitional year and therefore should consider whether:

   (i) Two items on the current agenda, namely, those items referred to in paragraph 7 (2) and (3) above, respectively, should be concluded;

   (ii) One item, namely, that referred to in paragraph 7(1) above, should be held over for conclusion at the next substantive session in 1994;

   (iii) One new item should be included in the substantive agenda;

9. *Further requests* the Disarmament Commission to meet for a period not exceeding four weeks during 1993 and to submit a substantive report to the General Assembly at its forty-eighth session;

10. *Requests* the Secretary-General to transmit to the Disarmament Commission the annual report of the Conference on Disarmament, together with all the official records of the forty-seventh session of the General Assembly relating to disarmament matters, and to render all assistance that the Commission may require for implementing the present resolution;

11. *Also requests* the Secretary-General to ensure full provision to the Commission and its subsidiary bodies of interpretation and translation facilities in the official languages and to assign, as a matter of priority, all the necessary resources and services to that end;

12. *Decides* to include in the provisional agenda of its forty-eighth session the item entitled "Report of the Disarmament Commission".

---

[a]A/CN.10/137.

General Assembly resolution 47/54 A

9 December 1992   Meeting 81   Adopted without vote

Approved by First Committee (A/47/693) without vote, 20 November (meeting 37); 14-nation draft (A/C.1/47/L.4), amended by 23 nations (A/C.1/47/L.48), orally revised; agenda item 63 *(a)*.

Sponsors of draft: Armenia, Brazil, Cameroon, Egypt, Finland, Hungary, Malaysia, Nepal, Netherlands, Nigeria, Peru, Romania, Sweden, Uruguay.

Sponsors of amendments: Australia, Austria, Bolivia, Bulgaria, Canada, Colombia, Costa Rica, Denmark, Ecuador, France, Guatemala, Indonesia, Ireland, Italy, Mauritius, Mongolia, New Zealand, Nicaragua, Norway, Panama, Philippines, Portugal, Spain.

Meeting numbers. GA 47th session: 1st Committee 3-21, 37; plenary 81.

Conference on Disarmament

The Conference on Disarmament, a 39-member multilateral negotiating body, met three times in 1992 at Geneva (21 January–27 March, 11 May–26 June, 20 July–3 September).[8] It held 30 formal plenary meetings and 16 informal meetings during which it considered: a nuclear-test ban; cessation of the nuclear-arms race and nuclear disarmament; prevention of nuclear war; chemical weapons; prevention of an arms race in outer space; security assurances to non-nuclear-weapon States; radiological weapons; a comprehensive programme of disarmament; and transparency in armaments.

In 1992, intensive efforts were made to conclude, as a priority task, the draft Convention on the Prohibition of the Development, Production, Stockpiling and Use of Chemical Weapons and on their Destruction (see below under ''Major trends and developments''). Accordingly, Conference negotiations concentrated on the activities of the Ad Hoc Committee on Chemical Weapons. The Committee completed the negotiations and transmitted the draft text of the Convention to the Conference for its consideration.[9]

As far as the other items were concerned, no significant substantive progress was made. The Conference re-established ad hoc committees on security assurances to non-nuclear weapon States, radiological weapons, chemical weapons and the prevention of an arms race in outer space. (Details of those questions are discussed elsewhere in this chapter.)

At its plenary meetings, the Conference continued to consider the comprehensive programme of disarmament. Informal consultations were held, but as there had been no significant changes in the positions of delegations, they were inconclusive. It was agreed that the organizational framework for dealing with the item would be considered in 1993.

The Conference also held four informal open-ended consultations on its improved and effective functioning under the chairmanship of Ahmad Kamal (Pakistan). General agreement emerged on ways to improve its function in the areas of report writing, reduction of plenary meetings, organization of work of ad hoc committees, tenure of presidency, avoidance of duplication in documentation, and agenda and membership. As to the latter issue, the President of the Conference conducted open-ended consultations on 8 December[10] during which he noted a trend in favour of expanding the Conference by some 20 members. However, differing views were held concerning the criteria for selecting candidates. A wide majority of delegations supported or were prepared to support changes in the agenda. The President was to report to the Conference in 1993.

GENERAL ASSEMBLY ACTION

On 9 December 1992, on the recommendation of the First Committee, the General Assembly adopted **resolution 47/54 E** without vote.

Report of the Conference on Disarmament

The General Assembly,

Having considered the report of the Conference on Disarmament,

Convinced that the Conference on Disarmament, as the single multilateral disarmament negotiating forum of the international community, has the primary role in substantive negotiations on priority questions of disarmament,

Considering, in this respect, that the present international climate should give additional impetus to multilateral negotiations with the aim of reaching concrete agreements,

Welcoming the conclusion of negotiations in the Conference on Disarmament on the draft Convention on the Prohibition of the Development, Production, Stockpiling and Use of Chemical Weapons and on Their Destruction, which has reaffirmed the need for and the importance of the Conference as the single multilateral disarmament negotiating forum of the international community,

Noting with satisfaction the results achieved so far on the subject of the improved and effective functioning of the Conference on Disarmament, including the decision to carry out consultations on the issues of the membership and agenda of the Conference, and the decision of the Conference to continue the process at its 1993 session,

1. *Reaffirms* the role of the Conference on Disarmament as the single multilateral disarmament negotiating forum of the international community;

2. *Welcomes* the determination of the Conference on Disarmament to fulfil that role in the light of the evolving international situation with a view to making early substantive progress on priority items of its agenda;

3. *Encourages* the ongoing review of the agenda, membership and methods of work of the Conference on Disarmament;

4. *Requests* the Conference on Disarmament to submit a report on its work to the General Assembly at its forty-eighth session;

5. *Decides* to include in the provisional agenda of its forty-eighth session the item entitled ''Report of the Conference on Disarmament''.

General Assembly resolution 47/54 E

9 December 1992   Meeting 81   Adopted without vote

Approved by First Committee (A/47/693) without vote, 12 November (meeting 31); draft by Belgium, as President of Conference on Disarmament (A/C.1/47/L.28/Rev.1); agenda item 63 (b).

Meeting numbers. GA 47th session: 1st Committee 3-21, 28, 31; plenary 81.

The Security Council and disarmament

On 31 January 1992, the Security Council met for the first time ever at the level of heads of State and Government (see Chapter I of this section). In a statement made on behalf of all Council members,[11] the Council's President stated that the proliferation of all weapons of mass destruction constituted a threat to international peace and security. Specific concerns were expressed regarding the danger of further proliferation of nuclear and chemical weapons, as well as of conventional weapons, and the danger of the spread of military technology.

At the conclusion of a meeting held in Washington, D.C., on 28 and 29 May, the five permanent members of the Security Council adopted interim guidelines related to weapons of mass destruction,[12] by which they undertook not to assist any non-nuclear-weapon State in developing or acquiring nuclear weapons; to notify the International Atomic Energy Agency (IAEA) of the export to a non-nuclear-weapon State of any nuclear materials and to place them under IAEA safeguards; to exercise restraint in the transfer of sensitive nuclear facilities, technology and weapons-usable materials, equipment or facilities; not to assist any recipient whatsoever in developing or acquiring chemical weapons, or to export material or technology that could be used for manufacturing chemical weapons; and to observe similar restrictions concerning biological weapons. In addition, they agreed on other restrictions regarding the export of items that might be used in manufacturing weapons of mass destruction.

In his October report, *New Dimensions of Arms Regulation and Disarmament in the Post–Cold War Era*,[2] the Secretary-General stated that he supported greater Security Council involvement in disarmament matters, in particular the enforcement of non-proliferation. He recalled that under the Charter (see APPENDIX II), the Military Staff Committee was to provide assistance to the Council on all questions relating, *inter alia*, to the regulation of armaments and possible disarmament.

Disarmament agreements

Parties and signatories

In October 1992, the Secretary-General submitted to the General Assembly his annual report on the status of multilateral disarmament agreements,[13] based on information received from the depositaries of those instruments. It listed the parties to and signatories of those agreements as at 31 July 1992.

As at 31 December 1992, the following numbers of States had become parties to the multilateral agreements covered in the Secretary-General's report (listed in chronological order, with the years in which they were initially signed or opened for signature).[14]

(Geneva) Protocol for the Prohibition of the Use in War of Asphyxiating, Poisonous or Other Gases, and of Bacteriological Methods of Warfare (1925): 131 parties
The Antarctic Treaty (1959): 41 parties
Treaty Banning Nuclear Weapon Tests in the Atmosphere, in Outer Space and under Water (1963): 119 parties

Treaty on Principles Governing the Activities of States in the Exploration and Use of Outer Space, including the Moon and Other Celestial Bodies (1967):[15] 91 parties
Treaty for the Prohibition of Nuclear Weapons in Latin America and the Caribbean (Treaty of Tlatelolco) (1967): 33 parties
Treaty on the Non-Proliferation of Nuclear Weapons (1968):[16] 156 parties
Treaty on the Prohibition of the Emplacement of Nuclear Weapons and Other Weapons of Mass Destruction on the Seabed and the Ocean Floor and in the Subsoil Thereof (1971):[17] 87 parties
Convention on the Prohibition of the Development, Production and Stockpiling of Bacteriological (Biological) and Toxin Weapons and on Their Destruction (1972):[18] 124 parties
Convention on the Prohibition of Military or Any Other Hostile Use of Environmental Modification Techniques (1977):[19] 57 parties
Agreement Governing the Activities of States on the Moon and Other Celestial Bodies (1979):[20] 8 parties
Convention on Prohibitions or Restrictions on the Use of Certain Conventional Weapons Which May Be Deemed to Be Excessively Injurious or to Have Indiscriminate Effects (1981): 35 parties
South Pacific Nuclear Free Zone Treaty (Treaty of Rarotonga) (1985): 13 parties
Treaty on Conventional Armed Forces in Europe (1990): 29 parties
Treaty on Open Skies (1992): 2 parties

REFERENCES

[1]YUN 1978, p. 17. [2]*New Dimensions of Arms Regulation and Disarmament in the Post–Cold War Era*, Sales No. E.93.IX.8. [3]A/47/42. [4]YUN 1991, p. 27. [5]Ibid., p. 34. [6]Ibid., p. 60. [7]Ibid., p. 59. [8]A/47/27. [9]CD/1170. [10]A/C.1/47/14. [11]S/23500. [12]*Disarmament: A periodic review by the United Nations*, vol. XV, No. 4. [13]A/47/470 & Corr.1. [14]*The United Nations Disarmament Yearbook*, vol. 17, *1992*, Sales No. E.93.IX.1. [15]YUN 1966, p. 41, GA res. 2222(XXI), annex, 19 Dec. 1966. [16]YUN 1968, p. 17, GA res. 2373(XXII), annex, 12 June 1968. [17]YUN 1970, p. 18, GA res. 2660(XXV), annex, 7 Dec. 1970. [18]YUN 1971, p. 19, GA res. 2826(XXVI), annex, 16 Dec. 1971. [19]YUN 1976, p. 45, GA res. 31/72, annex, 10 Dec. 1976. [20]YUN 1979, p. 111, GA res. 34/68, annex, 5 Dec. 1979.

Major trends and developments

The year 1992 was marked by unprecedented achievements in arms limitation and disarmament, reflecting the broad trends of international politics at a time of global transition towards new solutions to security problems. The adversarial relationship between East and West was a thing of the past. In Europe, determined efforts were made to strengthen institutions for cooperation and peace so as to give new impetus to the realization of a community of free and democratic States. Events in other parts of the world showed that, in spite of widespread turmoil and civil strife, the main trend was towards political and economic liberalization and new approaches to peace and security.

Those broad trends were reflected and analysed in three basic post–cold war documents of 1992 dealing with matters of international security and disarmament: a statement adopted by the Security Council at its Summit Meeting on 31 January (see Chapter I of this section);[1] a report of the Secretary-General to the Security Council on preventive diplomacy, peacemaking and peace-keeping, known as *An Agenda for Peace* (see Chapter I of this section);[2] and a subsequent report of the Secretary-General, *New Dimensions of Arms Regulation and Disarmament in the Post–Cold War Era*.[3] The three documents together provided, for the first time since 1978, when the General Assembly adopted the Final Document of the first special session on disarmament,[4] a comprehensive statement on strengthening international peace and security and on the contribution that arms limitation and disarmament could make to achieve that goal.

In his October report, *New Dimensions of Arms Regulation and Disarmament in the Post–Cold War Era*,[3] the Secretary-General discussed three concepts as the foundation of an enhanced international effort in disarmament and arms regulation: integration (disarmament in the new international environment), globalization (enhancing the multilateral approach), and revitalization (building on past achievements). The Secretary-General concluded that, with the development of the disarmament process, an entirely new set of problems—post-disarmament issues—were being encountered, namely the conversion of military capacities to peaceful uses, the safe destruction of weapons and technical and financial facilities to make the transition in a balanced manner.

Chemical weapons

After more than a decade of negotiations, the Conference on Disarmament adopted the Convention on the Prohibition of the Development, Production, Stockpiling and Use of Chemical Weapons and on Their Destruction in 1992. It was the first disarmament agreement negotiated within a multilateral framework that provided for eliminating an entire category of weapons of mass destruction.

Conference on Disarmament consideration. The Ad Hoc Committee on Chemical Weapons, re-established by the Conference on Disarmament on 21 January, held 32 meetings between 24 January and 26 August under its mandate to continue negotiations on a multilateral convention on the complete and effective prohibition of the development, production, stockpiling and use of chemical weapons and on their destruction, with a view to achieving final agreement during 1992.[5] Representatives of 45 States not members of the

Conference participated in the work of the Ad Hoc Committee.

The negotiating framework established by the Committee was designed to concentrate on the main outstanding issues. It set up a working group on verification in the chemical industry, and friends of the Chair conducted consultations on legal and organizational issues; economic and technological development; technical issues; old and abandoned chemical weapons; the seat of the Organization for the Prohibition of Chemical Weapons (see below, under "Convention on chemical weapons"); the composition and decision-making process of the Executive Council of the organization; and the destruction of chemical weapons and chemical weapons production facilities. The Chairman of the Committee conducted negotiations on challenge inspection procedures, and an editing and drafting group was established.

On 3 September,[6] the Conference on Disarmament adopted the report of the Ad Hoc Committee[7] and its appendix containing the draft convention and a text on establishing a preparatory commission for the Organization for the Prohibition of Chemical Weapons (see below, under "Convention on chemical weapons"). The report also incorporated statements of members on their positions regarding the Convention as a whole and on specific provisions. The Conference agreed by consensus to transmit the draft Convention to the General Assembly.

The issue of export controls for chemical substances and equipment with a potential for use as chemical weapons constituted a difficult problem in the negotiations on the Convention. Developing States in particular had requested that all control mechanisms, which in their view were discriminatory, be abolished for States parties to the Convention, specifically an export control regime established by the Australia Group (Australia, Austria, Belgium, Canada, Denmark, Finland, France, Germany, Greece, Ireland, Italy, Japan, Luxembourg, Netherlands, New Zealand, Norway, Portugal, Spain, Sweden, Switzerland, United Kingdom, United States). In an attempt to help address those concerns, members of the Australia Group underlined, in an August statement,[8] their readiness to review, in the light of the implementation of the Convention, measures taken by them to prevent the spread of chemical substances and equipment for purposes contrary to the objectives of the Convention, with the aim of removing such measures for the benefit of States parties to the Convention acting in full compliance with their obligations under it.

Other action. Progress was registered in bilateral consultations (Washington, D.C., 17 June 1992) between Presidents George Bush of the United States and Boris Yeltsin of the Russian Federation regarding chemical weapons. In their joint statement of 17 June,[9] they stressed their continuing commitment to the global elimination of chemical weapons. The two parties underscored their support for a joint memorandum signed in Wyoming (United States) in 1989[10] on phased confidence-building measures in the area of chemical weapons destruction, and agreed to implement the new cooperative provisions for detailed data exchange and inspections included in it. They also agreed to update the bilateral chemical weapons destruction Agreement of 1990[11] and to bring it into force promptly. In addition, both States entered into the Agreement concerning the Safe and Secure Transportation, Storage and Destruction of Weapons and the Prevention of Weapons Proliferation, which, among other things, provided for assistance to the Russian Federation in destroying nuclear, chemical and other weapons; transporting and storing such weapons safely and securely in connection with their destruction; and establishing additional verification measures against the proliferation of such weapons that posed a risk of proliferation.[9] To accomplish the objectives regarding chemical weapons, both States signed the Agreement concerning the Safe, Secure and Ecologically Sound Destruction of Chemical Weapons, in Washington, D.C., on 30 July 1992.[12] Its main objective was to assist the Russian Federation to destroy chemical weapons in accordance with existing or future agreements between the two States.

On 29 May 1992, the five permanent members of the Security Council adopted, in Washington, D.C., interim guidelines related to weapons of mass destruction.[13] As to chemical weapons, they declared that they would observe and consult on the following guidelines: to not assist, directly or indirectly, in the development, acquisition, manufacture, testing, stockpiling or deployment of chemical weapons by any recipient whatsoever; and to not export equipment, materials, services or technology which could be used in the manufacture of chemical weapons except when satisfied, for example, by recipient country guarantees or confirmation by the recipient, that such exports would not contribute to the development or acquisition of chemical weapons.

A chemical weapons regional seminar (Sydney, Australia, 21-23 June), sponsored by Australia and attended by countries of South-East Asia and the South Pacific, considered progress towards eliminating chemical weapons and preventing their development.[14]

Notes by the Secretary-General. Allegations of the use of chemical weapons were reported in January by Mozambique[15] and in June by Azerbaijan.[16] The Secretary-General nominated experts to conduct missions to both countries to investigate the allegations. By notes of 12 June[17] and 24 July,[18] the Secretary-General transmitted to the Security Council the reports of the experts on the investigations in Mozambique and Azerbaijan, respectively. (For details of the reports on Mozambique and Azerbaijan, see PART TWO, Chapters I and III, respectively.)

Convention on chemical weapons

The Convention on the Prohibition of the Development, Production, Stockpiling and Use of Chemical Weapons and on Their Destruction[7] consisted of a preamble, 24 articles and three annexes. The Convention was to enter into force 180 days after the date of the deposit of the sixty-fifth instrument of ratification, but in no case earlier than two years after its opening for signature in January 1993.

The Convention established the Organization for the Prohibition of Chemical Weapons, with its headquarters at The Hague (Netherlands), to ensure the implementation of the Convention's provisions, including those for international verification of compliance with it, and to provide a forum for consultation and cooperation among States parties. The Organization comprised a Conference of the States Parties, the principal decision-making body; a 41-member Executive Council comprising representatives of five regional groups, to act as the executive organ of the Organization and to supervise its activities; and a Technical Secretariat, headed by a Director-General, to conduct the organization's practical work. The principal component of the Secretariat was its inspectorate, responsible for carrying out the Convention's verification provisions. A Preparatory Commission for the Organization was established to prepare for the implementation of the Convention and the first session of the Conference of the States Parties.

The Convention's articles dealt with the general obligations of States parties; definitions and criteria; declarations; chemical weapons; chemical weapons production facilities; activities not prohibited under the Convention; national implementation measures; the Organization for the Prohibition of Chemical Weapons; consultations, cooperation and fact-finding; assistance and protection against chemical weapons; economic and technological development; measures to redress a situation and to ensure compliance, including sanctions; the Convention's relation to other international agreements; settlement of disputes; amendments; duration and withdrawal; status of the annexes (see below); signature; ratification; accession; entry into force; reservations; depositary; and authentic texts.

Three annexes—Annex on chemicals, Annex on Implementation and Verification and Annex on the Protection of Confidential Information—formed an integral part of the Convention.

GENERAL ASSEMBLY ACTION

On 30 November 1992, the General Assembly, on the recommendation of the First Committee, adopted **resolution 47/39** without vote.

Convention on the Prohibition of the Development, Production, Stockpiling and Use of Chemical Weapons and on Their Destruction

The General Assembly,

Recalling the long-standing determination of the international community to achieve the effective prohibition of the development, production, stockpiling and use of chemical weapons, and their destruction, as well as the continuing support for measures to uphold the authority of the Protocol for the Prohibition of the Use in War of Asphyxiating, Poisonous or Other Gases, and of Bacteriological Methods of Warfare, signed at Geneva on 17 June 1925, as expressed by consensus in many previous resolutions,

Recalling in particular its resolution 46/35 C of 6 December 1991, in which the Assembly strongly urged the Conference on Disarmament, as a matter of the highest priority, to resolve outstanding issues so as to achieve a final agreement on a convention on the prohibition of the development, production, stockpiling and use of chemical weapons and on their destruction during its 1992 session,

Bearing in mind the Final Declaration of the Conference of States Parties to the 1925 Geneva Protocol and Other Interested States,[a] held in Paris from 7 to 11 January 1989, in which participating States stressed their determination to prevent any recourse to chemical weapons by completely eliminating them,

Determined to make progress towards general and complete disarmament under strict and effective international control, including the prohibition and elimination of all types of weapons of mass destruction,

Convinced, therefore, of the urgent necessity of a total ban on chemical weapons, so as to abolish an entire category of weapons of mass destruction, and thus to eliminate the risk to mankind of renewed use of these inhumane weapons,

Welcoming the draft Convention on the Prohibition of the Development, Production, Stockpiling and Use of Chemical Weapons and on Their Destruction, adopted by the Conference on Disarmament and contained in its report, the result of many years of intensive negotiations, which constitutes an historic achievement in the field of arms control and disarmament,

Also convinced that the Convention, particularly as adherence to it approaches universality, will contribute to the maintenance of international peace and improve the security of all States and that it therefore merits the strong support of the entire international community,

Further convinced that the implementation of the Convention should promote expanded international trade, technological development and economic cooperation in the chemical sector, in order to enhance the economic and technological development of all States parties,

Determined to ensure the efficient and cost-effective implementation of the Convention,

Recalling the support for the prohibition of chemical weapons expressed in the declaration by representatives of the world's chemical industry at the Government-Industry Conference against Chemical Weapons, held at Canberra from 18 to 22 September 1989,[b]

Bearing in mind the relevant references to the Convention in the final documents of the Tenth Conference of Heads of State or Government of Non-Aligned Countries, held at Jakarta from 1 to 6 September 1992,[c]

Welcoming the invitation of the President of the French Republic to participate in a ceremony to sign the Convention in Paris on 13 January 1993,

1. *Commends* the Convention on the Prohibition of the Development, Production, Stockpiling and Use of Chemical Weapons and on Their Destruction, as contained in the report of the Conference on Disarmament;

2. *Requests* the Secretary-General, as depositary of the Convention, to open it for signature in Paris on 13 January 1993;

3. *Calls upon* all States to sign and, thereafter, according to their respective constitutional processes, to become parties to the Convention at the earliest possible date, thus contributing to its rapid entry into force and to the early achievement of universal adherence;

4. *Also calls upon* all States to ensure the effective implementation of this unprecedented, global, comprehensive and verifiable multilateral disarmament agreement, thereby enhancing cooperative multilateralism as a basis for international peace and security;

5. *Also requests* the Secretary-General to provide such services as may be requested by the signatory States to initiate the work of the Preparatory Commission for the Organization on the Prohibition of Chemical Weapons;

6. *Further requests* the Secretary-General, as depositary of the Convention, to report to the General Assembly at its forty-eighth session on the status of signatures and ratifications of the Convention.

---

[a]A/44/88.
[b]A/C.1/44/4.
[c]A/47/675-S/24816.

General Assembly resolution 47/39

30 November 1992   Meeting 74   Adopted without vote

Approved by First Committee (A/47/690) without vote, 12 November (meeting 31); 145-nation draft (A/C.1/47/L.1/Rev.2); agenda item 60.
Sponsors: Afghanistan, Albania, Antigua and Barbuda, Argentina, Armenia, Australia, Austria, Azerbaijan, Bahamas, Bangladesh, Barbados, Belarus, Belgium, Belize, Benin, Bolivia, Bosnia and Herzegovina, Botswana, Brazil, Brunei Darussalam, Bulgaria, Burkina Faso, Burundi, Cameroon, Canada, Cape Verde, Central African Republic, Chad, Chile, Colombia, Comoros, Congo, Costa Rica, Côte d'Ivoire, Croatia, Cuba, Cyprus, Czechoslovakia, Denmark, Dominica, Dominican Republic, Ecuador, El Salvador, Estonia, Ethiopia, Fiji, Finland, France, Gabon, Gambia, Georgia, Germany, Ghana, Greece, Grenada, Guatemala, Guinea, Guinea-Bissau, Guyana, Haiti, Honduras, Hungary, Iceland, India, Indonesia, Iran, Ireland, Israel, Italy, Jamaica, Japan, Kazakhstan, Kenya, Kyrgyzstan, Latvia, Lesotho, Liberia, Liechtenstein, Lithuania, Luxembourg, Madagascar, Malawi, Malaysia, Maldives, Mali, Malta, Marshall Islands, Mauritius, Mexico, Micronesia, Mongolia, Mozambique, Myanmar, Namibia, Nepal, Netherlands, New Zealand, Nicaragua, Niger, Nigeria, Norway, Panama, Papua New Guinea, Paraguay, Peru, Philippines, Poland, Portugal, Republic of Korea, Republic of Moldova, Romania, Russian Federation, Rwanda, Saint Kitts and Nevis, Saint Lucia, Saint Vincent and the Grenadines, Samoa, San Marino, Sao Tome and Principe, Senegal, Sierra Leone, Singapore, Slovenia, Solomon Islands, Spain, Sri Lanka, Suriname, Swaziland, Sweden, Tajikistan, Thailand, Togo, Trinidad and Tobago, Turkey, Turkmenistan, Ukraine, United Kingdom, United States, Uruguay, Uzbekistan, Vanuatu, Viet Nam, Venezuela, Zaire, Zambia.

Financial implications. 5th Committee, A/47/704; S-G, A/C.1/47/L.43, A/C.5/47/49.
Meeting numbers. GA 47th session: 1st Committee 3-21, 28, 31; 5th Committee 29; plenary 72.

Non-proliferation

In 1992, there were some positive developments concerning nuclear non-proliferation, such as the accession of the remaining two nuclear-weapon States, China and France, to the 1968 Treaty on the Non-Proliferation of Nuclear Weapons (NPT),[19] which had entered into force on 5 March 1970, and the preparations for a conference, to be held in 1995, to review the Treaty's operation and decide on its extension. However, there were still States with significant nuclear programmes that were not parties to NPT, some of which were alleged to have nuclear weapons, and some parties to the Treaty had programmes that were not under IAEA safeguards. In addition, there were differences of view among nuclear-weapon and non-nuclear-weapon States regarding the Treaty's future.

The United Nations continued to investigate incidents of the proliferation of weapons which were prohibited under international law in general or on the basis of treaty obligations. Thus, the United Nations Special Commission and IAEA inspectors carried out inspections in Iraq on the basis of a 1991 Security Council resolution regarding nuclear, chemical and biological weapons and missiles.[20] (See PART TWO, Chapter III.)

Although no specific item concerning non-proliferation in all its aspects appeared on the agendas of either the Disarmament Commission or the Conference on Disarmament, the issue was discussed in both bodies in the context of a number of agenda items.

Communications. A number of bilateral and unilateral declarations were transmitted to the Secretary-General in 1992 by States on their policies regarding the proliferation of nuclear and other weapons of mass destruction, conventional weapons, and science and technology with military applications: by Argentina on 28 April,[21] Argentina and Brazil on 18 February,[22] the Russian Federation on 28 and 29 January,[23] and Sweden on 27 April.[24]

The Second Meeting of the Council of Ministers for Foreign Affairs of the Conference on Security and Cooperation in Europe (CSCE) (Prague, Czechoslovakia, 30 and 31 January),[25] in its Declaration on Non-Proliferation and Arms Transfers, stressed the Ministers' readiness to support international cooperation to prevent the proliferation of weapons of mass destruction and the control of missile technology. It also stated that build-ups of conventional weapons beyond defence needs posed a threat to international peace and security.

On 20 July,[26] the United States transmitted to the Conference on Disarmament a statement of 13 July by the United States President on a non-proliferation initiative. The initiative included a decision not to produce plutonium and highly enriched uranium for nuclear explosive purposes and a number of proposals to strengthen international actions against those contributing to the spread of weapons of mass destruction and the missiles that deliver them.

Non-Proliferation Treaty

Accessions

In 1992, the remaining two nuclear-weapon-States, China and France, acceded to NPT, as did Azerbaijan, Estonia, Latvia, Myanmar, Namibia, Niger, Slovenia and Uzbekistan, bringing the total number of States parties to 156 at year's end.[27]

Preparations for the 1995 Review Conference on NPT

Following the entry into force on 5 March 1970 of NPT,[19] quinquennial review conferences were held in 1975,[28] 1980,[29] 1985[30] and 1990,[31] as called for under article VIII, paragraph 3, of the Treaty.

On 22 October, the States parties to NPT formed a preparatory committee for a conference, to be held in 1995, to review the operation of the Treaty and decide on its extension. The Treaty called for holding a conference 25 years after its entry into force to decide whether it should continue in force indefinitely or be extended for an additional fixed period or periods. The preparatory committee was scheduled to hold its first meeting in May 1993.

GENERAL ASSEMBLY ACTION

On 9 December 1992, the General Assembly, on the recommendation of the First Committee, adopted **resolution 47/52 A** by recorded vote.

Preparatory Committee for the 1995 Conference of the States Parties to the Treaty on the Non-Proliferation of Nuclear Weapons

The General Assembly,

Recalling its resolution 2373(XXII) of 12 June 1968, the annex to which contains the Treaty on the Non-Proliferation of Nuclear Weapons,

Noting the provisions of article X, paragraph 2, of that Treaty, requiring the holding of a conference twenty-five years after the entry into force of the Treaty, to decide whether the Treaty shall continue in force indefinitely or shall be extended for an additional fixed period or periods,

Noting also the provisions of article VIII, paragraph 3, concerning the convening of review conferences, which provides for quinquennial review conferences,

Noting further that the last review conference took place in 1990,

Recalling that the Treaty entered into force on 5 March 1970,

Recalling also its decision 46/413 of 6 December 1991, by which it took note of the intent of the parties to form a preparatory committee in 1993 for the conference called for in article X, paragraph 2, of the Treaty,

1. *Takes note* of the decision of the parties to the Treaty on the Non-Proliferation of Nuclear Weapons, following appropriate consultations, to form a preparatory committee for a conference to review the operation of the Treaty and to decide on its extension, as called for in article X, paragraph 2, and also as provided for in article VIII, paragraph 3, of the Treaty;

2. *Notes* that the Preparatory Committee will be open to all the parties to the Treaty and, if the Preparatory Committee so decides at the outset of its first session, to States not parties, as observers, and will hold its first meeting in New York from 10 to 14 May 1993;

3. *Requests* the Secretary-General to render the necessary assistance and to provide such services, including summary records, as may be required for the 1995 Conference and its Preparatory Committee.

General Assembly resolution 47/52 A

9 December 1992   Meeting 81   168-0 (recorded vote)

Approved by First Committee (A/47/691) by recorded vote (133-0-2), 12 November (meeting 31); draft by Peru, for States parties to NPT (A/C.1/47/L.6); agenda item 61 (n).

Meeting numbers. GA 47th session: 1st Committee 3-21, 24, 31; plenary 81.

Recorded vote in Assembly as follows:

In favour: Afghanistan, Algeria, Angola, Antigua and Barbuda, Argentina, Armenia, Australia, Austria, Azerbaijan, Bahamas, Bahrain, Bangladesh, Barbados, Belarus, Belgium, Belize, Benin, Bhutan, Bolivia, Botswana, Brazil, Brunei Darussalam, Bulgaria, Burkina Faso, Burundi, Cameroon, Canada, Cape Verde, Central African Republic, Chad, Chile, China, Colombia, Comoros, Congo, Costa Rica, Côte d'Ivoire, Cuba, Cyprus, Czechoslovakia, Democratic People's Republic of Korea, Denmark, Djibouti, Dominica, Dominican Republic, Ecuador, Egypt, El Salvador, Estonia, Ethiopia, Fiji, Finland, France, Gabon, Gambia, Germany, Ghana, Greece, Grenada, Guatemala, Guinea, Guinea-Bissau, Guyana, Haiti, Honduras, Hungary, Iceland, India,* Indonesia, Iran, Iraq, Ireland, Israel, Italy, Jamaica, Japan, Jordan, Kazakhstan, Kenya, Kuwait, Lao People's Democratic Republic, Latvia, Lebanon, Lesotho, Liberia, Libyan Arab Jamahiriya, Liechtenstein, Lithuania, Luxembourg, Madagascar, Malawi, Malaysia, Maldives, Mali, Malta, Marshall Islands, Mauritania, Mauritius, Mexico, Micronesia, Mongolia, Morocco, Mozambique, Myanmar, Namibia, Nepal, Netherlands, New Zealand, Nicaragua, Niger, Nigeria, Norway, Oman, Pakistan, Panama, Papua New Guinea, Paraguay, Peru, Philippines, Poland, Portugal, Qatar, Republic of Korea, Republic of Moldova, Romania, Russian Federation, Rwanda, Saint Kitts and Nevis, Saint Lucia, Saint Vincent and the Grenadines, Samoa, San Marino, Sao Tome and Principe, Saudi Arabia, Senegal, Seychelles, Sierra Leone, Singapore, Slovenia, Solomon Islands, Spain, Sri Lanka, Sudan, Suriname, Swaziland, Sweden, Syrian Arab Republic, Tajikistan, Thailand, Togo, Trinidad and Tobago, Tunisia, Turkey, Turkmenistan, Uganda, Ukraine, United Arab Emirates, United Kingdom, United Republic of Tanzania, United States, Uruguay, Vanuatu, Venezuela, Viet Nam, Yemen, Zaire, Zambia, Zimbabwe.

Against: None.

*Later advised the Secretariat that it had intended to abstain.

Regional non-proliferation accords

Two regional nuclear non-proliferation treaties were in existence in 1992: the 1967 Treaty for the Prohibition of Nuclear Weapons in Latin America and the Caribbean (Treaty of Tlatelolco) and the 1985 South Pacific Nuclear Free Zone Treaty (Treaty of Rarotonga).

During the year, Saint Vincent and the Grenadines became party to the Treaty of Tlatelolco, bringing the total number of parties to 33 at year's end. On 24 August 1992, France ratified Additional Protocol I of the Treaty concerning the Treaty's application to territories in the region for which outside States had *de jure* or *de facto* responsibility. France had been the only one of four States to which the Protocol was open that had not ratified it prior to 1992. (Other States having ratified the Protocol were the Netherlands, the United Kingdom and the United States.) The General Assembly, by **resolution 47/61**, welcomed France's ratification of the Protocol. (For details on amendments to the Treaty adopted in 1992, see below under "Nuclear arms limitation and disarmament".)

There were no new parties to the Treaty of Rarotonga in 1992; the number of parties remained at 13.

Strengthening the security of non-nuclear-weapon States

Consideration by the Conference on Disarmament. In 1992, the Conference on Disarmament[6] considered effective international arrangements to assure non-nuclear-weapon States against the use or threat of use of nuclear weapons—also known as negative security assurances. On 21 January,[32] it re-established an ad hoc committee on the subject, which held three formal meetings between 22 June and 3 August.

In its conclusions and recommendations,[33] the Ad Hoc Committee noted that difficulties relating to differing perceptions of security interests of nuclear-weapon and non-nuclear-weapon States persisted and that the complex nature of the issues involved continued to prevent agreement on a common formula. Recognizing the importance of the question and the need to take a fresh look at it to enable the Committee to fulfil its mandate as soon as possible, it was agreed that the Ad Hoc Committee should be re-established at the beginning of the 1993 session of the Conference.

GENERAL ASSEMBLY ACTION

On 9 December 1992, the General Assembly, on the recommendation of the First Committee, adopted **resolution 47/50** by recorded vote.

Conclusion of effective international arrangements to assure non-nuclear-weapon States against the use or threat of use of nuclear weapons

The General Assembly,

Bearing in mind the need to allay the legitimate concern of the States of the world with regard to ensuring lasting security for their peoples,

Convinced that nuclear weapons pose the greatest threat to mankind and to the survival of civilization,

Welcoming the progress achieved in recent years in both nuclear and conventional disarmament,

Noting that, despite recent progress in the field of nuclear disarmament, further efforts are necessary towards the achievement of the goal of general and complete disarmament under effective international control,

Also convinced that nuclear disarmament and the complete elimination of nuclear weapons are essential to remove the danger of nuclear war,

Determined strictly to abide by the relevant provisions of the Charter of the United Nations on the non-use of force or threat of force,

Recognizing that the independence, territorial integrity and sovereignty of non-nuclear-weapon States need to be safeguarded against the use or threat of use of force, including the use or threat of use of nuclear weapons,

Considering that, until nuclear disarmament is achieved on a universal basis, it is imperative for the international community to develop effective measures and arrangements to ensure the security of non-nuclear-weapon States against the use or threat of use of nuclear weapons from any quarter,

Recognizing also that effective measures and arrangements to assure the non-nuclear-weapon States against the use or threat of use of nuclear weapons can contribute positively to the prevention of the spread of nuclear weapons,

Bearing in mind paragraph 59 of the Final Document of the Tenth Special Session of the General Assembly, the first special session devoted to disarmament, in which it urged the nuclear-weapon States to pursue efforts to conclude, as appropriate, effective arrangements to assure non-nuclear-weapon States against the use or threat of use of nuclear weapons, and desirous of promoting the implementation of the relevant provisions of the Final Document,

Recalling the relevant parts of the special report of the Committee on Disarmament,[a] submitted to the General Assembly at its twelfth special session, the second special session devoted to disarmament, and of the special report of the Conference on Disarmament submitted to the Assembly at its fifteenth special session,[b] the third special session devoted to disarmament, as well as of the report of the Conference on its 1992 session,

Recalling also paragraph 12 of the Declaration of the 1980s as the Second Disarmament Decade, contained in the annex to its resolution 35/46 of 3 December 1980, which states, *inter alia*, that all efforts should be exerted by the Committee on Disarmament urgently to negotiate with a view to reaching agreement on effective international arrangements to assure non-nuclear-weapon States against the use or threat of use of nuclear weapons,

Noting the in-depth negotiations undertaken in the Conference on Disarmament and its Ad Hoc Committee on Effective International Arrangements to Assure Non-Nuclear-Weapon States against the Use or Threat of Use of Nuclear Weapons, with a view to reaching agreement on this item,

Taking note of the proposals submitted under that item in the Conference on Disarmament, including the drafts of an international convention,

Taking note also of the decision contained in paragraph 47, chapter II, of the Final Document adopted by the Tenth Conference of Heads of State or Government of Non-Aligned Countries, held at Jakarta from 1 to 6 September 1992,[c] as well as the relevant recommendations of the Organization of the Islamic Conference reiterated in the Final Communiqué of the Twentieth Islamic Conference of Foreign Ministers, held at Istanbul from 4 to 8 August 1991,[d] calling upon the Conference on Disarmament to reach an urgent agreement on an international

convention to assure non-nuclear-weapon States against the use or threat of use of nuclear weapons,

Taking note further of the unilateral declarations made by all nuclear-weapon States on their policies of non-use or non-threat of use of nuclear weapons against non-nuclear-weapon States,

Noting the support expressed in the Conference on Disarmament and in the General Assembly for the elaboration of an international convention to assure non-nuclear-weapon States against the use or threat of use of nuclear weapons, as well as the difficulties pointed out in evolving a common approach acceptable to all,

Noting also the greater willingness to overcome the difficulties encountered in previous years,

Recalling its relevant resolutions adopted in previous years, in particular resolutions 45/54 of 4 December 1990 and 46/32 of 6 December 1991,

1.   *Reaffirms* the urgent need to reach an early agreement on effective international arrangements to assure non-nuclear-weapon States against the use or threat of use of nuclear weapons;

2.   *Notes with satisfaction* that in the Conference on Disarmament there is no objection, in principle, to the idea of an international convention to assure non-nuclear-weapon States against the use or threat of use of nuclear weapons, although the difficulties as regards evolving a common approach acceptable to all have also been pointed out;

3.   *Appeals* to all States, especially the nuclear-weapon States, to work actively towards an early agreement on a common approach and, in particular, on a common formula that could be included in an international instrument of a legally binding character;

4.   *Recommends* that further intensive efforts should be devoted to the search for such a common approach or common formula and that the various alternative approaches, including, in particular, those considered in the Conference on Disarmament, should be further explored in order to overcome the difficulties;

5.   *Recommends also* that the Conference on Disarmament should actively continue intensive negotiations with a view to reaching early agreement and concluding effective international arrangements to assure non-nuclear-weapon States against the use or threat of use of nuclear weapons, taking into account the widespread support for the conclusion of an international convention and giving consideration to any other proposals designed to secure the same objective;

6.   *Decides* to include in the provisional agenda of its forty-eighth session the item entitled ''Conclusion of effective international arrangements to assure non-nuclear-weapon States against the use or threat of use of nuclear weapons''.

---

[a]The Committee on Disarmament was redesignated the Conference on Disarmament as from 7 February 1984.
[b]A/S-15/2.
[c]A/47/675-S/24816.
[d]A/46/486-S/23055.

General Assembly resolution 47/50

9 December 1992   Meeting 81   162-0-2 (recorded vote)

Approved by First Committee (A/47/687) by recorded vote (139-0-2), 13 November (meeting 33); 8-nation draft (A/C.1/47/L.17); agenda item 57.
Sponsors: Bangladesh, Colombia, Iran, Madagascar, Nepal, Pakistan, Sri Lanka, Viet Nam.
Meeting numbers. GA 47th session: 1st Committee 3-21, 33; plenary 81.

Recorded vote in Assembly as follows:

In favour: Afghanistan, Algeria, Angola, Argentina, Armenia, Australia, Austria, Azerbaijan, Bahamas, Bahrain, Bangladesh, Barbados, Belarus, Belgium, Belize, Benin, Bhutan, Bolivia, Botswana, Brazil, Brunei Darussalam, Bulgaria, Burkina Faso, Burundi, Cameroon, Canada, Cape Verde, Central African Republic, Chad, Chile, China, Colombia, Comoros, Congo, Costa Rica, Côte d'Ivoire, Cuba, Cyprus, Czechoslovakia, Democratic People's Republic of Korea, Denmark, Djibouti, Dominica, Dominican Republic, Ecuador, Egypt, El Salvador, Estonia, Ethiopia, Fiji, Finland, France, Gabon, Gambia, Germany, Ghana, Greece, Grenada, Guatemala, Guinea, Guinea-Bissau, Guyana, Haiti, Honduras, Hungary, Iceland, India, Indonesia, Iran, Iraq, Ireland, Israel, Italy, Jamaica, Japan, Jordan, Kazakhstan, Kenya, Kuwait, Lao People's Democratic Republic, Latvia, Lebanon, Lesotho, Liberia, Libyan Arab Jamahiriya, Liechtenstein, Lithuania, Luxembourg, Madagascar, Malaysia, Maldives, Mali, Malta, Marshall Islands, Mauritania, Mauritius, Mexico, Micronesia, Mongolia, Morocco, Mozambique, Myanmar, Namibia, Nepal, Netherlands, New Zealand, Nicaragua, Niger, Nigeria, Norway, Oman, Pakistan, Panama, Papua New Guinea, Paraguay, Peru, Philippines, Poland, Portugal, Qatar, Republic of Korea, Republic of Moldova, Romania, Russian Federation, Rwanda, Saint Kitts and Nevis, Saint Lucia, Saint Vincent and the Grenadines, Samoa, San Marino, Sao Tome and Principe, Saudi Arabia, Senegal, Seychelles, Sierra Leone, Singapore, Slovenia, Spain, Sri Lanka, Sudan, Suriname, Swaziland, Sweden, Syrian Arab Republic, Tajikistan, Thailand, Togo, Trinidad and Tobago, Tunisia, Turkey, Uganda, Ukraine, United Arab Emirates, United Republic of Tanzania, Uruguay, Vanuatu, Venezuela, Viet Nam, Yemen, Zaire, Zambia, Zimbabwe.

Against: None.

Abstaining: United Kingdom, United States.

Regional disarmament

In 1992, a number of developments took place at the regional level, confirming once again that the regional approach to disarmament was a key element in the achievement of international peace and security. (For further information on regional developments in the nuclear field, see below under "Nuclear disarmament".)

Reports of the Secretary-General. In his June 1992 report on preventive diplomacy, peacemaking and peace-keeping, known as *An Agenda for Peace*,[2] the Secretary-General, in discussing essential measures for reducing the likelihood of conflict between States, asked all regional organizations to consider further confidence-building measures which might be applied in their areas. In that connection, he indicated that he would undertake periodic consultations on confidence-building measures with parties to potential, current or past disputes and with regional organizations, offering such advisory assistance as the Secretariat could provide. He emphasized that regional arrangements and organizations had an important role in early warning and invited regional organizations that had not yet sought United Nations observer status to do so and to be linked with the Organization's security mechanisms.

Subsequently, in his October report, *New Dimensions of Arms Regulation and Disarmament in the Post–Cold War Era*,[3] the Secretary-General addressed the subject of regional disarmament in the new international environment, stressing that arms limitation could have a significant role in peacekeeping and peace-building operations.

Disarmament Commission consideration. In 1992, the Disarmament Commission[34] considered the item entitled "regional approach to disarmament

within the context of global security", which was discussed by a working group of the Commission from 22 April to 8 May and in a number of informal consultations. In addition to the papers of the 1991 session,[35] the Group had before it new documents submitted by Cuba[36] and South Africa.[37] The group based its deliberations on a paper presented by its Chairman to the Commission's 1991 session,[35] while also taking new proposals into consideration. Discussions focused on two of the five topics in the Chairman's 1991 paper: the relationship between regional disarmament and global security and arms limitation and disarmament; and principles and guidelines. Following extensive consideration of the topics, the Chairman presented two papers for consideration by the Group, which were annexed to the Commission's report. Further consideration of the item was scheduled for the Commission's 1993 session.

GENERAL ASSEMBLY ACTION

On 9 December 1992, the General Assembly, on the recommendation of the First Committee, adopted **resolution 47/52 G** without vote.

Regional disarmament
The General Assembly,

Recalling its resolutions 44/116 U and 44/117 B of 15 December 1989, 45/58 M of 4 December 1990 and 46/36 F of 6 December 1991,

Considering that the regional approach to disarmament is one of the most important means by which States can contribute to the strengthening of international security, arms limitation and disarmament,

Recognizing that the regional and global approaches complement each other and can be pursued simultaneously in the promotion of regional and international peace and security,

Convinced that disarmament can be carried out only in a climate of confidence based on mutual respect and aimed at ensuring better relations founded on justice, solidarity and cooperation,

Noting that the consumption of resources for potentially destructive purposes is in stark contrast to the need for social and economic development and that reduction in military expenditure following, *inter alia*, the conclusion of regional disarmament agreements could entail benefits in both the social and economic fields,

Considering that regional disarmament measures should be aimed at establishing a military balance at the lowest level while not diminishing the security of each State and at eliminating as a matter of priority the capability for large-scale offensive action and surprise attacks,

Noting also that disarmament measures in one region should not lead to increased arms transfers to other regions or extend the military imbalances and/or tensions from one area to other areas,

Considering also that confidence-building and transparency measures are essential elements in the implementation of regional disarmament,

Persuaded that verification measures are important to ensure compliance with regional agreements on arms control and disarmament,

1. *Reaffirms* that the regional approach to disarmament is one of the essential elements in the global efforts to strengthen international peace and security, arms limitation and disarmament;

2. *Is convinced* of the importance and effectiveness of regional disarmament measures taken at the initiative of States of the region and with the participation of all States concerned and taking into account the specific characteristics of each region, in that they can contribute to the security and stability of all States, in accordance with the principles of the Charter of the United Nations and in compliance with international law and existing treaties;

3. *Affirms* that comprehensive political and peaceful settlement of regional conflicts and disputes can contribute to the reduction of tension and the promotion of regional peace, security and stability as well as of arms limitation and disarmament;

4. *Stresses* the importance of confidence-building measures, including objective information on military matters, in ensuring the success of this process;

5. *Affirms also* that multifaceted cooperation among States in the region, especially encompassing political, economic, social and cultural fields, can be conducive to the strengthening of regional security and stability;

6. *Notes with satisfaction* the important progress made in various regions of the world through the adoption of arms limitation, peace, security and cooperation agreements, including those related to the prohibition of weapons of mass destruction, and encourages States in the regions concerned to continue implementing these agreements;

7. *Recognizes* the useful role played by the regional centres of the United Nations;

8. *Encourages* States of the same region to examine the possibility of creating, on their own initiative, regional mechanisms and/or institutions for the establishment of measures in the framework of an effort of regional disarmament or for the prevention and the peaceful settlement of disputes and conflicts with the assistance, if requested, of the United Nations;

9. *Believes* that regional initiatives should enjoy the support of all States of the region concerned and the respect of those outside that region;

10. *Invites and encourages* all States to conclude, whenever possible, agreements on arms limitation and confidence-building measures at the regional level, including those conducive to avoiding the proliferation of weapons of mass destruction.

General Assembly resolution 47/52 G

9 December 1992   Meeting 81   Adopted without vote

Approved by First Committee (A/47/691) without vote, 12 November (meeting 32); 46-nation draft (A/C.1/47/L.25); agenda item 61 *(j)*.

Sponsors: Albania, Armenia, Australia, Austria, Belgium, Bolivia, Bulgaria, Burundi, Canada, Chile, Colombia, Costa Rica, Czechoslovakia, Denmark, Ecuador, France, Germany, Greece, Guatemala, Guinea, Haiti, Honduras, Hungary, Ireland, Italy, Luxembourg, Netherlands, New Zealand, Nicaragua, Norway, Paraguay, Peru, Philippines, Poland, Portugal, Republic of Korea, Romania, Senegal, Spain, Sweden, Thailand, Togo, Ukraine, United Kingdom, United States, Uruguay.

Meeting numbers. GA 47th session: 1st Committee 3-21, 23, 32; plenary 81.

Also on 9 December, the General Assembly adopted **resolution 47/52 J** by recorded vote.

Regional disarmament

The General Assembly,

Recalling its resolutions 45/58 P of 4 December 1990 and 46/36 I of 6 December 1991 on regional disarmament,

Believing that the efforts of the international community to move towards the ideal of general and complete disarmament are guided by the inherent human desire for genuine peace and security, the elimination of the danger of war and the release of economic, intellectual and other resources for peaceful pursuits,

Affirming the abiding commitment of all States to the purposes and principles enshrined in the Charter of the United Nations in the conduct of their international relations,

Noting that essential guidelines for progress towards general and complete disarmament were adopted at the tenth special session of the General Assembly,

Welcoming the prospects of genuine progress in the field of disarmament engendered in recent years as a result of negotiations between the two super-Powers,

Taking note of the recent proposals for disarmament and nuclear non-proliferation at regional and subregional levels,

Recognizing the importance of confidence-building measures for regional and international peace and security,

Convinced that endeavours by countries to promote regional disarmament, taking into account the specific characteristics of each region and in accordance with the principle of undiminished security at the lowest level of armaments, would enhance the security of smaller States and would thus contribute to international peace and security by reducing the risk of regional conflicts,

1. *Stresses* that sustained efforts are needed, within the framework of the Conference on Disarmament and under the umbrella of the United Nations, to make progress on the entire range of disarmament issues;

2. *Affirms* that global and regional approaches to disarmament complement each other and should therefore be pursued simultaneously to promote regional and international peace and security;

3. *Calls upon* States to conclude agreements, wherever possible, for nuclear non-proliferation, disarmament and confidence-building measures at regional and subregional levels;

4. *Welcomes* the initiatives towards disarmament, nuclear non-proliferation and security undertaken by some countries at regional and subregional levels;

5. *Supports and encourages* efforts aimed at promoting confidence-building measures at regional and subregional levels in order to ease regional tensions and to further disarmament and nuclear non-proliferation measures at regional and subregional levels;

6. *Decides* to include in the provisional agenda of its forty-eighth session the item entitled ''Regional disarmament''.

General Assembly resolution 47/52 J

9 December 1992   Meeting 81   168-0-1 (recorded vote)

Approved by First Committee (A/47/691) by recorded vote (130-0-4), 12 November (meeting 32); 81-nation draft (A/C.1/47/L.35); agenda item 61 *(j)*.

Sponsors: Albania, Antigua and Barbuda, Armenia, Austria, Belgium, Benin, Bolivia, Bosnia and Herzegovina, Burundi, Cameroon, Canada, Cape Verde, Central African Republic, Chile, Colombia, Comoros, Costa Rica, Côte d'Ivoire, Czechoslovakia, Ecuador, Egypt, Estonia, Gabon, Germany,

Ghana, Grenada, Guatemala, Guinea, Haiti, Hungary, Italy, Kuwait, Kyrgyzstan, Latvia, Lesotho, Liberia, Lithuania, Luxembourg, Madagascar, Mali, Marshall Islands, Mauritania, Micronesia, Nepal, Netherlands, New Zealand, Niger, Norway, Pakistan, Panama, Papua New Guinea, Paraguay, Peru, Poland, Republic of Moldova, Romania, Rwanda, Saint Kitts and Nevis, Saint Lucia, Saint Vincent and the Grenadines, Samoa, Saudi Arabia, Senegal, Slovenia, Solomon Islands, Spain, Sudan, Suriname, Swaziland, Togo, Tunisia, Turkey, Turkmenistan, Ukraine, United Kingdom, United States, Uruguay, Vanuatu, Venezuela, Zambia, Zimbabwe.

Meeting numbers. GA 47th session: 1st Committee 3-21, 32; plenary 81.

Recorded vote in Assembly as follows:

In favour: Afghanistan, Algeria, Angola, Antigua and Barbuda, Argentina, Armenia, Australia, Austria, Azerbaijan, Bahamas, Bahrain, Bangladesh, Barbados, Belarus, Belgium, Belize, Benin, Bhutan, Bolivia, Botswana, Brazil, Brunei Darussalam, Bulgaria, Burkina Faso, Burundi, Cameroon, Canada, Cape Verde, Central African Republic, Chad, Chile, China, Colombia, Comoros, Congo, Costa Rica, Côte d'Ivoire, Cuba, Cyprus, Czechoslovakia, Democratic People's Republic of Korea, Denmark, Djibouti, Dominica, Dominican Republic, Ecuador, Egypt, El Salvador, Estonia, Ethiopia, Fiji, France, Gabon, Gambia, Germany, Ghana, Greece, Grenada, Guatemala, Guinea, Guinea-Bissau, Guyana, Haiti, Honduras, Hungary, Iceland, Indonesia, Iran, Iraq, Ireland, Israel, Italy, Jamaica, Japan, Jordan, Kazakhstan, Kenya, Kuwait, Kyrgyzstan, Lao People's Democratic Republic, Latvia, Lebanon, Lesotho, Liberia, Libyan Arab Jamahiriya, Liechtenstein, Lithuania, Luxembourg, Madagascar, Malawi, Malaysia, Maldives, Mali, Malta, Marshall Islands, Mauritania, Mauritius, Mexico, Micronesia, Mongolia, Morocco, Mozambique, Myanmar, Namibia, Nepal, Netherlands, New Zealand, Nicaragua, Niger, Nigeria, Norway, Oman, Pakistan, Panama, Papua New Guinea, Paraguay, Peru, Philippines, Poland, Portugal, Qatar, Republic of Korea, Republic of Moldova, Romania, Russian Federation, Rwanda, Saint Kitts and Nevis, Saint Lucia, Saint Vincent and the Grenadines, Samoa, San Marino, Sao Tome and Principe, Saudi Arabia, Senegal, Seychelles, Sierra Leone, Singapore, Slovenia, Solomon Islands, Spain, Sri Lanka, Sudan, Suriname, Swaziland, Sweden, Syrian Arab Republic, Tajikistan, Thailand, Togo, Trinidad and Tobago, Tunisia, Turkey, Turkmenistan, Uganda, Ukraine, United Arab Emirates, United Kingdom, United Republic of Tanzania, United States, Uruguay, Vanuatu, Venezuela, Viet Nam, Yemen, Zaire, Zambia, Zimbabwe.

Against: None.

Abstaining: India.

Africa

Report of the Secretary-General. In accordance with a 1991 General Assembly request,[38] the Secretary-General in October submitted a report on regional confidence-building measures,[39] in which he stated that, on 28 May, he had established the Standing Advisory Committee on Security Questions in Central Africa under United Nations auspices to develop confidence-building measures and encourage arms limitation and development in Central Africa. He had also appointed a permanent Secretary of the Committee, which held a ministerial-level meeting (Yaoundé, Cameroon, 27-31 July) to elect its officers and adopt its rules of procedure and programme of work. The programme of work comprised the classification of confidence-building and security measures according to priority in such areas as preventive diplomacy, peace-building, peacemaking and peace-keeping, training of peace-keeping personnel and compliance and verification. The Secretary-General noted that discussions held during the Committee's meeting and its programme of work had paved the way for effective collaboration between the United Nations and the member States of the Economic Community of Central African States to promote and consolidate peace in the subregion.

On 15 December 1992, the General Assembly, on the recommendation of the First Committee, adopted **resolution 47/53 F** by recorded vote.

Regional confidence-building measures

The General Assembly,

Recalling the purposes and principles of the United Nations and its primary responsibility for the maintenance of international peace and security in accordance with its Charter,

Bearing in mind the guidelines for general and complete disarmament adopted at its tenth special session, the first special session devoted to disarmament,

Recalling also its resolutions 43/78 H and 43/85 of 7 December 1988, 44/21 of 15 November 1989, 45/58 M of 4 December 1990 and 46/37 B of 6 December 1991,

Considering the importance and effectiveness of confidence-building measures taken at the initiative and with the participation of all States concerned and taking into account the specific characteristics of each region, in that they can contribute to regional disarmament and to international security, in accordance with the principles of the Charter of the United Nations,

Convinced that the resources released by disarmament, including regional disarmament, can be devoted to economic and social development and to the protection of the environment for the benefit of all peoples, in particular those of the developing countries,

Bearing in mind the establishment by the Secretary-General on 28 May 1992 of the Standing Advisory Committee on Security Questions in Central Africa, the purpose of which is to encourage arms limitation, disarmament, non-proliferation and development in the subregion,

Bearing in mind also the appointment by the Secretary-General of a permanent Secretary of the Standing Advisory Committee on Security Questions in Central Africa,

1. *Takes note* of the report of the Secretary-General on regional confidence-building measures, which deals chiefly with the organizational meeting of the Standing Advisory Committee on Security Questions in Central Africa, held at Yaoundé from 27 to 31 July 1992 under the auspices of the United Nations;

2. *Supports and encourages* efforts aimed at promoting confidence-building measures at regional and subregional levels in order to ease regional tensions and to further disarmament and non-proliferation measures at regional and subregional levels in Central Africa;

3. *Welcomes* the programme of work including confidence-building measures adopted by the States members of the Economic Community of Central African States at the organizational meeting of the Standing Advisory Committee;

4. *Requests* the Secretary-General to continue to provide assistance to the Central African States in implementing the programme of work of the Standing Advisory Committee;

5. *Also requests* the Secretary-General to submit to the General Assembly at its forty-eighth session a report on the implementation of the present resolution;

6. *Decides* to include in the provisional agenda of its forty-eighth session the item entitled "Regional confidence-building measures".

General Assembly resolution 47/53 F

15 December 1992   Meeting 88   159-1-1 (recorded vote)

Approved by First Committee (A/47/692) by recorded vote (132-1-2), 18 November (meeting 36); 12-nation draft (A/C.1/47/L.2), orally revised; agenda item 62 *(b)*.

Sponsors: Angola, Burundi, Cameroon, Central African Republic, Chad, Congo, Equatorial Guinea, France, Gabon, Rwanda, Sao Tome and Principe, Zaire.

Financial implications. ACABQ, A/47/7/Add.11; 5th Committee, A/47/784; S-G, A/C.1/47/L.50, A/C.5/47/64.

Meeting numbers. GA 47th session: 1st Committee 3-21, 23, 36; 5th Committee 44; plenary 88.

Recorded vote in Assembly as follows:

In favour: Afghanistan, Albania, Algeria, Angola, Argentina, Australia, Austria, Azerbaijan, Bahamas, Bahrain, Bangladesh, Barbados, Belarus, Belgium, Belize, Benin, Bhutan, Bolivia, Bosnia and Herzegovina, Botswana, Brazil, Brunei Darussalam, Bulgaria, Burkina Faso, Burundi, Cameroon, Canada, Cape Verde, Central African Republic, Chad, Chile, China, Colombia, Congo, Costa Rica, Côte d'Ivoire, Croatia, Cuba, Cyprus, Czechoslovakia, Democratic People's Republic of Korea, Denmark, Djibouti, Dominica, Ecuador, Egypt, El Salvador, Estonia, Ethiopia, Fiji, Finland, France, Gabon, Gambia, Germany, Ghana, Greece, Grenada, Guatemala, Guinea, Guinea-Bissau, Guyana, Haiti, Honduras, Hungary, Iceland, India, Indonesia, Iran, Iraq, Ireland, Israel, Italy, Jamaica, Japan, Jordan, Kazakhstan, Kenya, Kuwait, Lao People's Democratic Republic, Latvia, Lebanon, Lesotho, Liberia, Libyan Arab Jamahiriya, Liechtenstein, Lithuania, Luxembourg, Madagascar, Malawi, Malaysia, Maldives, Mali, Malta, Marshall Islands, Mauritania, Mauritius, Mexico, Micronesia, Mongolia, Morocco, Mozambique, Myanmar, Namibia, Nepal, Netherlands, New Zealand, Nicaragua, Niger, Nigeria, Norway, Oman, Pakistan, Panama, Paraguay, Peru, Philippines, Poland, Portugal, Qatar, Republic of Korea, Republic of Moldova, Romania, Russian Federation, Rwanda, Saint Kitts and Nevis, Saint Lucia, Saint Vincent and the Grenadines, Samoa, San Marino, Sao Tome and Principe, Saudi Arabia, Senegal, Sierra Leone, Singapore, Slovenia, Spain, Sri Lanka, Sudan, Suriname, Swaziland, Sweden, Syrian Arab Republic, Tajikistan, Thailand, Togo, Trinidad and Tobago, Tunisia, Turkey, Uganda, Ukraine, United Arab Emirates, United Republic of Tanzania, Uruguay, Venezuela, Viet Nam, Yemen, Zambia, Zimbabwe.

Against: United States.

Abstaining: United Kingdom.

Asia

North-East Asia

In North-East Asia, the safeguards agreement between IAEA and the Democratic People's Republic of Korea entered into force on 10 April 1992. During the year, the Democratic People's Republic of Korea and the Republic of Korea, which were parties to NPT and had also signed the basic IAEA safeguards agreement, were engaged in the process of implementing two bilateral accords: the Agreement on Reconciliation, Non-aggression and Exchanges and Cooperation between the South and the North; and the Joint Declaration of the Denuclearization of the Korean Peninsula,[40] both of which entered into force in February 1992. The Agreement established a South-North Joint Military Commission with a mandate to negotiate confidence-building measures and, ultimately, a reduction in armaments. The Joint Declaration banned nuclear weapons from the peninsula as well as nuclear reprocessing and uranium enrichment facilities. As part of the Agreement, the two parties were negotiating, through a Joint Nuclear Control Commission, a bilateral inspection regime to complement IAEA inspections.

As a result of inspection activities conducted under the IAEA safeguards agreement, inconsistencies between the information provided by the Democratic People's Republic of Korea and IAEA findings began to emerge in July 1992.[41] In a meeting at Vienna (30 November and 1 December), IAEA officials advised the Minister of Atomic Energy of the Democratic People's Republic of Korea of the Agency's concerns. Subsequently, the Democratic People's Republic of Korea objected to an IAEA request to revisit a site, emphasizing that the location was on a military site not relevant to the country's nuclear activities. The IAEA Director-General stated that the Agency had no interest in military, non-nuclear aspects of any site to be visited, but that a site could not be exempted from visits or inspections on the basis of its military character if, as was the case in the Democratic People's Republic of Korea, the Agency had reason to believe such access to be relevant to the implementation of the safeguards agreement.

South-East Asia

GENERAL ASSEMBLY ACTION

On 9 December 1992, the General Assembly, on the recommendation of the First Committee, adopted **resolution 47/53 B** without vote.

Treaty of Amity and Cooperation in South-East Asia

The General Assembly,

Recalling the purposes and principles of the United Nations and its primary responsibility for the maintenance of international peace and security in accordance with its Charter,

Recalling also the Ten Principles adopted by the Asian-African Conference, held at Bandung on 25 April 1955, the Declaration of the Association of South-East Asian Nations, signed at Bangkok in August 1967, and the Singapore Declaration of 1992 adopted by the Association of South-East Asian Nations at its fourth summit meeting, held at Singapore on 27 and 28 January 1992,[a]

Noting that the Treaty of Amity and Cooperation in South-East Asia, signed at Bali on 24 February 1976, which came into force on 15 July 1976 in respect of the Republic of Indonesia, Malaysia, the Republic of the Philippines, the Republic of Singapore and the Kingdom of Thailand, and on 7 January 1984 in respect of Brunei Darussalam, was registered with the United Nations on 20 October 1976,

Noting also that Papua New Guinea acceded to the Treaty on 5 July 1989 and that the Socialist Republic of Viet Nam and the Lao People's Democratic Republic acceded to the Treaty on 22 July 1992,

Noting further that the purpose of the Treaty is to promote perpetual peace, everlasting amity and cooperation among the peoples of South-East Asia, in accordance with the principles of the Charter of the United Nations, including, *inter alia*, mutual respect for the independence, sovereignty and territorial integrity of all nations, non-interference in the internal affairs of all na-

---

[a] A/47/80-S/23502.

tions, peaceful settlement of differences and disputes and renunciation of the threat or use of force,

Aware that the Treaty includes provisions for the pacific settlement of disputes which are in accordance with the Charter of the United Nations,

Recognizing that the Treaty provides a strong foundation for regional confidence-building and for regional cooperation and that it is consistent with the call by the Secretary-General of the United Nations, in his report entitled "An Agenda for Peace", for a closer relationship between the United Nations and regional associations,

Endorses the purposes and principles of the Treaty of Amity and Cooperation in South-East Asia and its provisions for the pacific settlement of regional disputes and for regional cooperation in order to achieve peace, amity and friendship among the peoples of South-East Asia, in accordance with the Charter of the United Nations, which are consistent with the current climate of enhancing regional and international cooperation.

General Assembly resolution 47/53 B

9 December 1992   Meeting 81   Adopted without vote

Approved by First Committee (A/47/692) without vote, 12 November (meeting 31); 137-nation draft (A/C.1/47/L.24); agenda item 62 *(b)*.

Sponsors: Afghanistan, Albania, Antigua and Barbuda, Armenia, Australia, Austria, Bahamas, Bangladesh, Barbados, Belize, Benin, Bhutan, Bolivia, Bosnia and Herzegovina, Botswana, Brunei Darussalam, Bulgaria, Burkina Faso, Cambodia, Cameroon, Canada, Chile, China, Colombia, Comoros, Congo, Costa Rica, Côte d'Ivoire, Croatia, Cuba, Cyprus, Czechoslovakia, Democratic People's Republic of Korea, Djibouti, Dominica, Ecuador, Egypt, El Salvador, Equatorial Guinea, Estonia, Ethiopia, Fiji, France, Gabon, Germany, Ghana, Grenada, Guatemala, Guinea, Guinea-Bissau, Guyana, Haiti, Honduras, Hungary, India, Indonesia, Iran, Italy, Jamaica, Japan, Kazakhstan, Kenya, Kuwait, Lao People's Democratic Republic, Lesotho, Liberia, Libyan Arab Jamahiriya, Madagascar, Malawi, Malaysia, Maldives, Mali, Malta, Marshall Islands, Mauritania, Mauritius, Mexico, Micronesia, Mongolia, Morocco, Mozambique, Myanmar, Namibia, Nepal, Netherlands, New Zealand, Nicaragua, Niger, Nigeria, Norway, Oman, Pakistan, Panama, Papua New Guinea, Paraguay, Peru, Philippines, Poland, Qatar, Republic of Korea, Republic of Moldova, Romania, Russian Federation, Rwanda, Saint Kitts and Nevis, Saint Lucia, Saint Vincent and the Grenadines, Samoa, Senegal, Seychelles, Sierra Leone, Singapore, Slovenia, Solomon Islands, Sri Lanka, Sudan, Suriname, Swaziland, Sweden, Thailand, Togo, Trinidad and Tobago, Turkey, Uganda, Ukraine, United Arab Emirates, United Kingdom, United Republic of Tanzania, United States, Uruguay, Vanuatu, Venezuela, Viet Nam, Yemen, Zaire, Zambia, Zimbabwe.

Meeting numbers. GA 47th session: 1st Committee 3-21, 28, 31; plenary 81.

Europe

The 29 parties to the 1990 Treaty on Conventional Armed Forces in Europe (CFE)[42] met in 1992 and signed the Final Document of the Extraordinary Conference of the States Parties to the CFE Treaty (Oslo, Norway, 5 June).[27] The document stated in part that the understandings, notifications, confirmations and commitments contained or referred to in the Final Document and its Annexes A and B, together with the deposit of instruments of verification by all the States parties, were deemed as fulfilling the requirements for the Treaty's entry into force. Annex A contained understandings and changes to Treaty wording made necessary by the dissolution of the USSR. Annex B contained notifications, confirmations and commitments and made some further necessary adjustments.

On 10 July, at the CSCE summit (Helsinki, Finland, 9 and 10 July), the States parties to the Treaty decided to put the Treaty provisionally into force as from 17 July to allow more time for ratification by a number of States. It entered into force formally on 9 November, after all 29 States had ratified it. Shortly after its entry into force, the process of inspecting each party's baseline data began. The Concluding Act of the Negotiation on Personnel Strength of CFE, a politically binding agreement setting out limits on personnel levels decided on by each party and providing for exchanges of information on such forces, was signed on 10 July to be implemented concurrently with the application of the CFE Treaty.

Also at the CSCE meeting at Helsinki, the Heads of State or Government of the 52 participating States adopted the Helsinki Document 1992— The Challenges of Change,[43] reflecting their decision to establish a new CSCE Forum for Security Cooperation at Vienna, with a strengthened conflict-prevention centre, as an integral part of CSCE. (For further details on the CSCE Forum, see below under "Transparency, confidence-building and the Arms Register".)

GENERAL ASSEMBLY ACTION

On 9 December 1992, the General Assembly, on the recommendation of the First Committee, adopted **resolution 47/52 I** without vote.

Confidence- and security-building measures and conventional disarmament in Europe

The General Assembly,

Determined to achieve progress in disarmament,

Stressing that confidence-building and disarmament measures have a positive impact on international security,

Noting the work accomplished in 1992 by the Disarmament Commission on its agenda items entitled "Objective information on military matters" and "Regional approach to disarmament within the context of global security",

Recalling its resolutions 43/75 P of 7 December 1988, 44/116 I of 15 December 1989, 45/58 I of 4 December 1990 and 46/36 G of 6 December 1991,

Reaffirming the great importance of increasing security and stability in Europe through the establishment of a stable, secure and verifiable balance of conventional armed forces at lower levels, as well as through increased openness and predictability of military activities,

Considering that, along with the new political situation in Europe, the positive results of the negotiations on confidence- and security-building measures, as well as those on conventional armaments and forces, both within the framework of the Conference on Security and Cooperation in Europe, have considerably increased confidence and security in Europe, thereby contributing to international peace and security,

Welcoming the new measures agreed upon in these fields among the States signatories of the Treaty on Conventional Armed Forces in Europe and among the States participating in the Conference on Security and Cooperation in Europe,

Expressing the hope that the implementation of these decisions will contribute to the prevention or settlement of crises in Europe, including those due to acts of aggression or the use of military force in some parts of the continent,

1. *Notes with satisfaction* the progress achieved so far in the process of disarmament and the strengthening of confidence and security in Europe;

2. *Welcomes* in particular:

(a) The decision of the States signatories of the Treaty on Conventional Armed Forces in Europe to implement this Treaty, as well as the recent Concluding Act of the Negotiations on Personnel Strength of Conventional Armed Forces in Europe;

(b) The signature of the Treaty on Open Skies with the adoption of the Declaration on the Treaty on Open Skies;

(c) The adoption, by the States participating in the Conference on Security and Cooperation in Europe, of a new significant set of confidence- and security-building measures;

(d) The decision of the States participating in the Conference on Security and Cooperation in Europe, at the Helsinki summit meeting in July 1992, to establish a CSCE Forum for Security Cooperation with a mandate to start new negotiations on arms control, disarmament, and confidence- and security-building; to enhance regular consultation and to intensify cooperation among them on matters related to security, and to further the process of reducing the risk of conflict;

3. *Invites* all States to consider the possibility of taking appropriate measures with a view to reducing the risk of confrontation and strengthening security, taking due account of their specific regional conditions.

General Assembly resolution 47/52 I

9 December 1992   Meeting 81   Adopted without vote

Approved by First Committee (A/47/691) without vote, 12 November (meeting 32); 35-nation draft (A/C.1/47/L.29); agenda item 61 *(m)*.
Sponsors: Albania, Armenia, Austria, Belarus, Belgium, Bulgaria, Canada, Costa Rica, Czechoslovakia, Denmark, Estonia, Finland, France, Germany, Greece, Hungary, Iceland, Ireland, Italy, Lithuania, Luxembourg, Malta, Netherlands, Norway, Poland, Portugal, Republic of Moldova, Romania, Russian Federation, Spain, Sweden, Turkey, Ukraine, United Kingdom, United States.
Meeting numbers. GA 47th session: 1st Committee 3-21, 27, 32; plenary 81.

Transparency, confidence-building and the arms register

In 1992, transparency—the systematic provision of information under formal or informal international arrangements—was for the first time on the disarmament agendas of the General Assembly and the Conference on Disarmament. The sharing of information about military matters sought to enhance confidence, predictability, restraint and, as a result, stability.

Transparency

Consideration by the Conference on Disarmament. In response to 1991 General Assembly requests concerning transparency in armaments,[44] the Conference on Disarmament,[6] at the start of its 1992 session, discussed appropriate organizational arrangements to meet those requests. On 26 May, the Conference decided to add to its 1992 agenda an item entitled "transparency in arma-

ments".[45] It held five meetings between 9 and 26 June to address interrelated aspects of the excessive and destabilizing accumulation of arms, including military holdings and procurement through national production; the elaboration of non-discriminatory practical means to increase openness and transparency in the field; and the problems and the elaboration of practical means to increase openness and transparency related to transfer of high technology with military applications and weapons of mass destruction.

Report of the Secretary-General. In an August report with later addenda,[46] the Secretary-General presented information provided by 23 Member States concerning the implementation of a 1991 General Assembly resolution on transparency in armaments.[44]

Register of Conventional Arms

Report of the Secretary-General. As requested by the General Assembly in a 1991 resolution,[44] by which it established the Register of Conventional Arms, the Secretary-General in August submitted a report,[47] which dealt with expanding the Register's scope by adding further categories of equipment and including data on military holdings and procurement through national production. The report elaborated the technical procedures for standardized reporting of data on international transfers of seven categories of conventional arms identified in the Register, namely, battle tanks, armoured combat vehicles, large-calibre artillery systems, combat aircraft, attack helicopters, warships and missiles and missile launchers. In addition, the report described the manner in which Member States might communicate to the United Nations background information regarding their military holdings, procurement through national production and relevant policies. It also dealt with the resource implications of developing, upgrading and maintaining the Register and the resource requirements for the initial operation and storage of the Register's data, as well as its subsequent operation. It discussed the needs of the computerized database of the Office for Disarmament Affairs which would be used to process information submitted by Governments for inclusion in the Register.

GENERAL ASSEMBLY ACTION

On 15 December 1992, the General Assembly, on the recommendation of the First Committee, adopted **resolution 47/52 L** without vote.

Transparency in armaments

The General Assembly,

Recalling its resolution 46/36 L of 9 December 1991 entitled "Transparency in armaments",

Continuing to take the view that an enhanced level of transparency in armaments contributes greatly to confidence-building and security among States and that the establishment of the Register of Conventional Arms, contained in the annex to resolution 46/36 L, constitutes an important step forward in the promotion of transparency in military matters,

Welcoming the Secretary-General's report on the technical procedures and adjustments to the annex to resolution 46/36 L necessary for the effective operation of the Register and on the modalities for its early expansion,

Welcoming also the guidelines and recommendations for objective information on military matters as adopted by consensus in the Disarmament Commission,

Welcoming further the report of the Conference on Disarmament on its agenda item entitled "Transparency in armaments",

1. *Declares* its determination to ensure the effective operation of the Register of Conventional Arms as provided for in paragraphs 7, 9 and 10 of its resolution 46/36 L;

2. *Endorses* the recommendations contained in the Secretary-General's report on the technical procedures and adjustments to the annex to the above-mentioned resolution necessary for the effective operation of the Register;

3. *Notes* the suggestions offered in the report as a first step in the consideration of modalities for early expansion of the Register;

4. *Calls upon* all Member States to provide the requested data and information to the Secretary-General by 30 April annually, beginning in 1993;

5. *Encourages* Member States to inform the Secretary-General of their national arms import and export policies, legislation and administrative procedures, both as regards authorization of arms transfers and prevention of illicit transfers, in conformity with paragraph 18 of its resolution 46/36 L;

6. *Reaffirms* its request to the Secretary-General to prepare a report on the continuing operation of the Register and its further development with the assistance of a group of governmental experts convened in 1994 on the basis of equitable geographical representation;

7. *Requests* the Secretary-General to ensure that sufficient resources are made available for the United Nations Secretariat to operate and maintain the Register;

8. *Encourages* the Conference on Disarmament to continue its work undertaken in response to the requests contained in paragraphs 12 to 15 of resolution 46/36 L;

9. *Also requests* the Secretary-General to report on progress made in implementing the present resolution to the General Assembly at its forty-eighth session;

10. *Decides* to include in the provisional agenda of its forty-eighth session the item entitled "Transparency in armaments".

General Assembly resolution 47/52 L

15 December 1992   Meeting 88   Adopted without vote

Approved by First Committee (A/47/691) without vote, 12 November (meeting 31); 53-nation draft (A/C.1/47/L.18); agenda item 61 *(l)*.

Sponsors: Albania, Argentina, Armenia, Australia, Austria, Belgium, Bolivia, Brazil, Bulgaria, Canada, Central African Republic, Costa Rica, Czechoslovakia, Denmark, Finland, France, Germany, Greece, Guinea, Haiti, Hungary, Iceland, Ireland, Italy, Japan, Lesotho, Liechtenstein, Luxembourg, Malaysia, Mali, Malta, Nepal, Netherlands, New Zealand, Norway, Peru, Poland, Portugal, Republic of Korea, Republic of Moldova, Romania, Russian Federation, Samoa, Senegal, Singapore, Slovenia, Spain, Suriname, Sweden, Turkey, United Kingdom, United States, Venezuela.

Financial implications. ACABQ, A/47/7/Add.11; 5th Committee, A/47/784; S-G, A/C.1/47/L.44, A/C.5/47/50.

Meeting numbers. GA 47th session: 1st Committee 3-21, 25, 31; 5th Committee, 44; plenary 88.

Information on military matters

Disarmament Commission consideration. In 1992, the Disarmament Commission[(34)] completed its work on objective information on military matters, which had been on its agenda since 1990.[(48)] The subject was pursued in a working group, which, on 8 May, adopted by consensus guidelines and recommendations on the subject consisting of objectives, principles, scope, mechanisms and recommendations, which were subsequently considered by the Commission itself and submitted to the General Assembly.

GENERAL ASSEMBLY ACTION

On 9 December 1992, on the recommendation of the First Committee, the General Assembly adopted **resolution 47/54 B** without vote.

Guidelines and recommendations for objective information on military matters

The General Assembly,

Recalling its resolutions 43/75 G of 7 December 1988 and 44/116 E of 15 December 1989,

Taking note of the report of the Disarmament Commission, containing the text, adopted by the Commission at its 1992 session, of the guidelines and recommendations for objective information on military matters,

Expressing its appreciation for the work accomplished by the Disarmament Commission in finalizing the text of the guidelines and recommendations,

Reaffirming its firm conviction that a better flow of objective information on military matters can help to relieve international tension and contribute to the building of confidence among States on a global, regional or subregional level and to the conclusion of concrete disarmament agreements,

Appealing to all States to consider the widest possible use of objective information on military matters,

Noting with satisfaction the encouraging results of specific measures agreed upon and implemented in certain regions,

1. *Endorses* the guidelines and recommendations for objective information on military matters as adopted by the Disarmament Commission at its 1992 substantive session;

2. *Recommends* the guidelines and recommendations to all States for implementation, fully taking into account specific political, military and other conditions prevailing in a region, on the basis of initiatives and with the agreement of the States of the region concerned;

3. *Invites* all States to provide relevant information to the Secretary-General regarding their implementation of the guidelines and recommendations not later than 31 May 1994;

4. *Requests* the Secretary-General to submit a report on the implementation of the guidelines and recommendations, on the basis of national reports on accumulated relevant experience, to the General Assembly at its forty-ninth session;

5. *Decides* to include in the provisional agenda of its forty-ninth session an item entitled "Implementation of the guidelines and recommendations for objective information on military matters".

General Assembly resolution 47/54 B

9 December 1992   Meeting 81   Adopted without vote

Approved by First Committee (A/47/693) without vote, 12 November (meeting 31); 21-nation draft (A/C.1/47/L.8); agenda item 63 *(a)*.

Sponsors: Austria, Brazil, Cameroon, Costa Rica, Czechoslovakia, Finland, France, Germany, Greece, Hungary, Ireland, Japan, Malaysia, Nepal, Netherlands, Nigeria, Peru, Romania, Sweden, United Kingdom, Uruguay.

Meeting numbers. GA 47th session: 1st Committee 3-21, 30, 31; plenary 81.

Confidence-building measures

Report of the Secretary-General. Pursuant to a 1990 request of the General Assembly,[49] the Secretary-General presented in September[50] information received from four Governments on implementation of the guidelines for confidence-building measures adopted by the Disarmament Commission in May 1988[51] and endorsed later that year by the Assembly.[52]

GENERAL ASSEMBLY ACTION

On 9 December 1992, the General Assembly, on the recommendation of the First Committee, adopted **resolution 47/54 D** without vote.

Implementation of the guidelines for appropriate types of confidence-building measures

The General Assembly,

Recalling its resolution 45/62 F, adopted without a vote on 4 December 1990,

Reconfirming its support for the guidelines for appropriate types of confidence-building measures and for the implementation of such measures on a global or regional level as endorsed in resolution 43/78 H, adopted without a vote on 7 December 1988,

Welcoming the report of the Secretary-General on experience reported by Member States with the implementation of confidence-building measures,

Noting with satisfaction the encouraging results of specific confidence-building measures agreed upon and implemented in some regions and, in particular, of measures creating confidence by contributing to disarmament and arms control and by promoting constraint in the military field,

Realizing with deep concern that at the same time tensions in other regions rise and that in some places violent armed conflicts have erupted,

Considering that confidence-building measures, especially when applied in a comprehensive manner, can be conducive to achieving structures of security based on cooperation and openness and thus contribute to the wider objective of the renunciation of the threat or use of force,

Welcoming recent progress in the promotion of transparency in the military field as a cornerstone for confidence-building through the finalization in the Disarmament Commission at its 1992 session of its work on the agenda item entitled "Objective information on military matters" and through the inclusion of the item entitled "Transparency in armaments" in the agenda of the Conference on Disarmament,

Bearing in mind that confidence-building measures pursued at the regional level can contribute to the development of global security,

Pointing to the ongoing elaboration and implementation of confidence- and security-building measures within the framework of the Conference on Security and Cooperation in Europe with a view to building on the foundations already laid for cooperative security in Europe,

Aware that there are situations peculiar to specific regions that have a bearing on the nature of the confidence-building measures feasible in those regions,

1. *Stresses* the need for the development of confidence-building measures as a concrete and continuous process to help to prevent the use of armed force as a means of resolving political conflicts;

2. *Recommends* the guidelines for appropriate types of confidence-building measures to all States for implementation, taking fully into account the specific political, military and other conditions prevailing in a region, on the basis of initiatives and with the agreement and cooperation of the States of the region concerned;

3. *Also recommends* to all States and regions that have started to implement confidence-building measures to pursue further and strengthen this process;

4. *Appeals* to all States to consider the widest possible use of confidence-building measures in their international relations, including bilateral, regional and global negotiations, as an important step towards prevention of conflict and, in times of political tension and crisis, as an instrument for peaceful settlement of conflicts;

5. *Requests* the Conference on Disarmament to pursue actively its work on the agenda item entitled "Transparency in armaments", which includes consideration and elaboration of universal and non-discriminatory practical means to increase openness and transparency in military matters;

6. *Invites* the Secretary-General to continue to collect relevant information from all Member States;

7. *Appeals* to all Member States that have not yet done so to make their contribution to the report of the Secretary-General;

8. *Decides* to include in the provisional agenda for its forty-ninth session the item entitled "Implementation of the guidelines for appropriate types of confidence-building measures".

General Assembly resolution 47/54 D

9 December 1992   Meeting 81   Adopted without vote

Approved by First Committee (A/47/693) without vote, 12 November (meeting 32); 47-nation draft (A/C.1/47/L.22); agenda item 63 *(g)*.

Sponsors: Argentina, Australia, Austria, Bahamas, Belarus, Belgium, Bolivia, Bulgaria, Burundi, Cameroon, Canada, Colombia, Costa Rica, Czechoslovakia, Denmark, Ethiopia, Finland, France, Germany, Honduras, Hungary, Iceland, India, Ireland, Italy, Luxembourg, Malaysia, Nepal, Netherlands, New Zealand, Norway, Peru, Poland, Portugal, Republic of Korea, Republic of Moldova, Romania, Russian Federation, Samoa, Senegal, Spain, Sweden, Togo, Turkey, United Kingdom, United States.

Meeting numbers. GA 47th session: 1st Committee 3-21, 27, 32; plenary 81.

Security and cooperation in Europe

The representatives of the 52 participating States of CSCE, meeting at Helsinki, unanimously adopted, on 10 July, the Helsinki Document 1992—The Challenges of Change.[43] The Helsinki Document comprised the Helsinki Summit

Declaration and various decisions, including one on strengthening CSCE institutions and structures and one on establishing a CSCE Forum for Security Cooperation.

The CSCE members decided at the summit meeting to start a new negotiation on arms control, disarmament and confidence- and security-building, enhance regular consultation and intensify cooperation among themselves on matters related to security and further the process of reducing the risk of conflict. To carry out those tasks, they decided to establish a CSCE Forum for Security Cooperation, with a strengthened Conflict Prevention Centre, which opened at Vienna on 22 September.

In 1992, CSCE members also adopted a specific document on confidence- and security-building, known as the Vienna Document 1992, which integrated new measures on the subject with those adopted previously.

Treaty on Open Skies

The Treaty on Open Skies was completed early in 1992 and signed at Helsinki on 24 March.[53] The Treaty established a regime for conducting observation flights by States parties over the territories of other States parties, and set forth their rights and obligations in relation to such flights. The Treaty was open to Armenia, Azerbaijan, Belarus, Bulgaria, Czechoslovakia, Georgia, Hungary, Kazakhstan, Kyrgyzstan, Poland, Republic of Moldova, Romania, Russian Federation, Tajikistan, Turkmenistan, Ukraine, Uzbekistan and all members of the North Atlantic Treaty Organization (NATO) (Belgium, Canada, Denmark, France, Germany, Greece, Iceland, Italy, Luxembourg, Netherlands, Norway, Portugal, Spain, Turkey, United Kingdom, United States). By 31 December, the Treaty had been signed by Belarus, Bulgaria, Czechoslovakia, Georgia, Hungary, Kyrgyzstan, Poland, Romania, Russian Federation, Ukraine and the 16 NATO members, bringing to 26 the number of signatory States. Under article XVII of the Treaty, for six months after the Treaty's entry into force, any other State participating in CSCE could apply for accession. Six months after the Treaty's entry into force, the Open Skies Consultative Commission could consider the accession of any State which, in the judgement of the Commission, was able and willing to contribute to the objectives of the Treaty.

Verification

Report of the Secretary-General. As requested by the General Assembly in 1990,[54] the Secretary-General, in September 1992,[55] submitted a report on verification in which he described action taken by the United Nations Secretariat in implementing recommendations made in 1990 by a group of governmental experts.[56] Among the group's recommendations was the development of a United Nations data bank of published materials and data provided on a voluntary basis by Member States on all aspects of verification and compliance. The Secretary-General stated that the United Nations Office for Disarmament Affairs had established a modest data collection including chapters on the history of negotiations and treaty compliance, information on various procedures for verification and monitoring, data on techniques and instrumentation for verification and monitoring and bibliographic information and data. In addition, he noted that there were plans to compile lists of experts on verification and addresses of institutions, organizations, companies and individuals that could provide expertise, technologies and advice on aspects of verification. Such lists would be stored in a computerized database in the Office for Disarmament Affairs. The report also contained replies from six Governments on action taken to implement the group's recommendations.

Developments also took place in 1992 in the area of biological weapon verification. Following the Third (1991) Review Conference of the Parties to the Convention on the Prohibition of the Development, Production and Stockpiling of Bacteriological (Biological) and Toxin Weapons and on Their Destruction,[57] an Ad Hoc Group of Governmental Experts, open to all States parties to the Convention, met at Geneva from 30 March to 10 April and from 23 November to 4 December to identify and examine potential verification measures from a scientific and technical standpoint, with a view to strengthening the Convention. The Group's two sessions, which were attended by representatives of some 50 States parties, were devoted to examining the ability to differentiate between prohibited and permitted activities, the ability of the potential verification measures to resolve ambiguities about compliance, and the technologies of verification measures and their material, manpower and equipment requirements.

In the Final Document of the Third Review Conference, additional measures to strengthen the Convention's authority and enhance confidence in the implementation of its provisions had been endorsed. The States parties were then invited to make available information on their activities relevant to the Convention's provisions on the basis of the annex to the Final Document on confidence-building measures. Of 125 States parties (as of 31 July 1992), 36 provided information on the question in 1992.

GENERAL ASSEMBLY ACTION

On 9 December 1992, the General Assembly, on the recommendation of the First Committee, adopted **resolution 47/45** without vote.

Verification in all its aspects, including the role of the United Nations in the field of verification

The General Assembly,

Recalling its resolutions 40/152 O of 16 December 1985, 41/86 Q of 4 December 1986, 42/42 F of 30 November 1987, 43/81 B of 7 December 1988 and 45/65 of 4 December 1990,

Noting that the critical importance of verification of and compliance with arms limitation and disarmament agreements is universally recognized,

Stressing that the issue of verification of and compliance with arms limitation and disarmament agreements is a matter of concern to all nations,

Recognizing that the United Nations, in accordance with its role and responsibilities established under the Charter, can make a significant contribution in the field of verification, in particular of multilateral agreements,

Affirming its continued support for the sixteen principles of verification drawn up by the Disarmament Commission,[a]

Noting that recent developments in international relations have underscored the continuing importance of effective verification of existing and future arms limitation and disarmament agreements, and that some of these developments have significant effects on the role of the United Nations in the field of verification, which require careful and ongoing examination,

Taking note of the report of the Secretary-General pursuant to the statement of 31 January 1992 adopted at the conclusion of the first meeting held by the Security Council at the level of Heads of State and Government, containing his analysis and recommendations on ways of strengthening and making more efficient, within the framework and provisions of the Charter, the capacity of the United Nations for preventive diplomacy, peacemaking, peace-keeping and post-conflict peace-building,

Taking note also of the Final Declaration of the Third Review Conference of the Parties to the Convention on the Prohibition of the Development, Production and Stockpiling of Bacteriological (Biological) and Toxin Weapons and on Their Destruction, adopted on 27 September 1991, and the activities of the Ad Hoc Group of Governmental Experts on verification,

Welcoming the conclusion of the Convention on the Prohibition of the Development, Production, Stockpiling and Use of Chemical Weapons and on Their Destruction, which contains an unprecedented regime of verification,

Recalling that in resolution 45/65 it requested the Secretary-General to report to the General Assembly at its forty-seventh session on actions taken by Member States and by the United Nations Secretariat to implement the recommendations contained in the concluding chapter of the report of the Group of Qualified Governmental Experts to Undertake a Study on the Role of the United Nations in the Field of Verification,[b]

1. *Takes note* of the report of the Secretary-General on actions to implement the recommendations in the in-depth study on the role of the United Nations in the field of verification;

2. *Encourages* Member States to continue to give active consideration to the recommendations contained in the concluding chapter of the study and to assist the Secretary-General in their implementation where appropriate;

3. *Requests* the Secretary-General, as a follow-up to the study on the role of the United Nations in the field of verification and in view of significant developments in international relations since that study, to seek the views of Member States on:

(*a*) Additional actions that might be taken to implement the recommendations contained in the study;

(*b*) How the verification of arms limitation and disarmament agreements can facilitate United Nations activities with respect to preventive diplomacy, peacemaking, peace-keeping and post-conflict peace-building;

(*c*) Additional actions with respect to the role of the United Nations in the field of verification, including further studies by the United Nations on this subject;

4. *Also requests* the Secretary-General to submit a report on the subject to the General Assembly at its forty-eighth session;

5. *Decides* to include in the provisional agenda of its forty-eighth session the item entitled "Verification in all its aspects, including the role of the United Nations in the field of verification".

---

[a]A/S-15/3.
[b]A/45/372 & Corr.1.

General Assembly resolution 47/45

9 December 1992   Meeting 81   Adopted without vote

Approved by First Committee (A/47/682) without vote, 12 November (meeting 31); 34-nation draft (A/C.1/47/L.42/Rev.1); agenda item 52.
Sponsors: Armenia, Australia, Austria, Belgium, Bolivia, Brazil, Bulgaria, Cameroon, Canada, Costa Rica, Czechoslovakia, Denmark, Ethiopia, Finland, Greece, Hungary, Iceland, India, Italy, Japan, Kenya, Mexico, Netherlands, New Zealand, Norway, Portugal, Romania, Russian Federation, Samoa, Singapore, Slovenia, Spain, Sweden, Thailand.
Meeting numbers. GA 47th session: 1st Committee 3-21, 26, 31; plenary 81.

Nuclear arms limitation and disarmament

Unilateral and bilateral action

In 1992, international attention continued to focus on nuclear-arms limitation, nuclear disarmament and prevention of nuclear war. Positive developments in the nuclear field and especially the radical reductions of the nuclear arsenals of the two major nuclear Powers enabled the General Assembly to adopt in 1992, for the first time, a consensus resolution on bilateral nuclear-arms negotiations (resolution 47/52 K).

Reductions and limitations of the nuclear arsenals of the former USSR and the United States took place under the 1991 Treaty on the Reduction and Limitation of Strategic Offensive Arms (START), signed by the Presidents of those countries.[58] In late 1991, the nuclear arsenal of the former USSR passed into the jurisdiction of four newly formed States—Belarus, Kazakhstan, Russian Federation and Ukraine. To address the questions raised by the new situation, those States and the United States signed a Protocol to the 1991 START Treaty on 23 May at Lisbon, Portugal,[27] under which Belarus, Kazakhstan, the Russian Federation and Ukraine were to assume the obligations of the former USSR under the Treaty. As at 31 December, the START Treaty and the Lisbon Protocol had been ratified by Kazakhstan (2 July). On 1 October, the United States Senate consented to ratification and on 4 November, the Russian Federation approved the Treaty. Both States attached a number of conditions, among them the completion of implementation arrangements among the four former Soviet republics and adherence to NPT by Belarus, Kazakhstan and Ukraine. The Treaty was to enter into force upon the exchange of instruments of ratification by all five parties.

In 1992, President George Bush of the United States and President Boris Yeltsin of the Russian Federation signed, on 17 June in Washington, D.C., a Joint Understanding[(9)] by which they agreed to substantial further reductions in strategic offensive arms and to convert the provisions of the Joint Understanding into a formal treaty, to be known as START II. According to the Joint Understanding, the reductions would be implemented in two phases, the first of which would be completed within seven years of the entry into force of the START Treaty and the second by 2003, or by 2000 if the United States could contribute to financing the elimination of the Russian Federation's strategic offensive arms. The first phase included the provision that each side would reduce and limit its strategic forces to an aggregate number of warheads between 3,800 and 4,250. Under the second phase, the sides would reduce their overall totals to 3,000 to 3,500 warheads. START II was to enter into force upon the exchange of instruments of ratification, but not prior to the entry into force of START I.

Also in 1992, unilateral moratoriums on nuclear weapons testing were declared or extended by three States. On 8 April, France decided to suspend its testing of nuclear weapons until the end of 1992. On 24 September, the United States Congress decided that no underground test of nuclear weapons might be conducted after 30 September 1992 and before 1 July 1993; the legislation placed limits on the number of tests to be permitted annually after 1 July 1993 and prohibited testing after 30 September 1996 unless a foreign State conducted a nuclear test after that date. In addition, the Russian Federation decided to extend its one-year unilateral moratorium, which had been declared in October 1991,[(59)] to 1 July 1993.

GENERAL ASSEMBLY ACTION

On 9 December 1992, the General Assembly, on the recommendation of the First Committee, adopted **resolution 47/52 K** without vote.

Bilateral nuclear-arms negotiations and nuclear disarmament

The General Assembly,

Recalling its previous resolutions,

Recognizing the fundamental changes that have taken place with respect to international security, which have permitted agreements on deep reductions in the nuclear armaments of the States possessing the largest inventories of such weapons,

Mindful that it is the responsibility and obligation of all States to contribute to the process of the relaxation of international tension and to the strengthening of international peace and security,

Stressing the importance of strengthening international peace and security through disarmament,

Emphasizing that nuclear disarmament remains one of the principal tasks of our times,

Stressing also that it is the responsibility of all States to adopt and implement measures towards the attainment of general and complete disarmament under effective international control,

Appreciating a number of positive developments in the field of nuclear disarmament, in particular the intermediate-range nuclear forces agreement and the Treaty on the Reduction and Limitation of Strategic Offensive Arms,

Noting that there are still significant nuclear arsenals and that the primary responsibility for nuclear disarmament, with the objective of the elimination of nuclear weapons, rests with the nuclear-weapon States, in particular those which possess the largest nuclear arsenals,

Welcoming the steps that have already been taken by those States to begin the process of reducing the number of nuclear weapons and removing such weapons from a deployed status,

Noting also the new climate of relations between the United States of America and States of the former Soviet Union, which permits them to intensify their cooperative efforts to ensure the safety, security and environmentally sound destruction of nuclear weapons,

Urging that further cooperation be undertaken to accelerate the implementation of agreements and unilateral decisions relating to nuclear disarmament and nuclear-arms reductions,

Welcoming also the reductions made by other nuclear-weapon States in some of their nuclear-weapon programmes, and encouraging all nuclear-weapon States to consider appropriate measures relating to nuclear disarmament,

Affirming that bilateral and multilateral negotiations on disarmament should facilitate and complement each other,

1.   *Expresses its satisfaction* at the continued implementation of the treaty that was concluded between the former Union of Soviet Socialist Republics and the United States of America on the elimination of their intermediate-range and shorter-range missiles, in particular at the completion by the parties of the destruction of all their declared missiles subject to elimination under the treaty;

2.   *Welcomes* the signing of the Treaty on the Reduction and Limitation of Strategic Offensive Arms in Moscow on 31 July 1991, and the accompanying protocol that was signed in Lisbon on 23 May 1992, and urges the parties to take the steps necessary to bring this Treaty and the accompanying protocol into force at the earliest possible date;

3.   *Also welcomes* the unilateral decisions announced by the President of the United States of America and similar unilateral steps announced by the former Union

of Soviet Socialist Republics and subsequently by the President of the Russian Federation to reduce significantly the size and nature of nuclear deployments worldwide, to eliminate certain nuclear weapons and to enhance stability;

4. *Further welcomes* the Joint Understanding on Further Reductions in Strategic Offensive Arms between the United States of America and the Russian Federation that was announced in Washington on 17 June 1992, and urges that the early conversion of this Joint Understanding into a formal treaty be completed;

5. *Encourages* the United States of America, the Russian Federation, Belarus, Kazakhstan and Ukraine to continue their cooperative efforts aimed at eliminating nuclear weapons and strategic offensive arms on the basis of existing agreements, and welcomes the contributions that other States are making to such cooperation as well;

6. *Further encourages and supports* the Russian Federation and the United States of America in their efforts to reduce their nuclear armaments and to continue to give these efforts the highest priority in order to contribute to the objective of the elimination of nuclear weapons;

7. *Invites* the Russian Federation and the United States of America to keep other States Members of the United Nations duly informed of progress in their discussions and in the implementation of their strategic offensive arms agreements and unilateral decisions.

General Assembly resolution 47/52 K

| 9 December 1992 | Meeting 81 | Adopted without vote |

Approved by First Committee (A/47/691) without vote, 13 November (meeting 33); draft by Argentina, Armenia, Australia, Austria, Belarus, Belgium, Bulgaria, Canada, Costa Rica, Czechoslovakia, Denmark, Finland, France, Germany, Greece, Hungary, Iceland, Indonesia (for Non-Aligned Movement), Ireland, Italy, Japan, Kazakhstan, Luxembourg, Netherlands, New Zealand, Norway, Poland, Portugal, Republic of Korea, Romania, Russian Federation, Samoa, Spain, Sweden, Turkey, United Kingdom, United States (A/C.1/47/L.36); agenda item 61*(d)*.

Meeting numbers. GA 47th session: 1st Committee 3-21, 27, 33; plenary 81.

Also on 9 December, the General Assembly adopted **resolution 47/53 E** by recorded vote.

Nuclear-arms freeze

The General Assembly,

Recalling that, in the Final Document of the Tenth Special Session of the General Assembly, the first special session devoted to disarmament, adopted in 1978 and unanimously and categorically reaffirmed in 1982 during the twelfth special session of the General Assembly, the second special session devoted to disarmament, the Assembly expressed deep concern over the threat to the very survival of mankind posed by the existence of nuclear weapons,

Reaffirming the goal of general and complete disarmament under effective international control,

Welcoming the new trends that have led to an improvement in the international security environment,

Welcoming also the announcements of the significant measures, including unilateral steps, taken by the Russian Federation and the United States of America, which could signal the cessation and reversal of the nuclear-arms race,

Welcoming further the Treaty between the United States of America and the Union of Soviet Socialist Republics on the Reduction and Limitation of Strategic Offensive Arms, signed on 31 July 1991, and the signing of a protocol to this Treaty in which Belarus, Kazakhstan, the Russian Federation, Ukraine and the United States of America have undertaken to give effect to the Treaty,

Welcoming the Joint Understanding of 17 June 1992 between the Russian Federation and the United States of America on further reductions in their strategic offensive arms, and expressing the hope that it will be followed by an agreement at an early date in this regard,

Welcoming in addition the moratoria on nuclear-weapon tests currently observed by France, the Russian Federation and the United States of America,

Convinced of the urgency of further negotiations for the substantial reduction and qualitative limitation of existing nuclear arms,

Considering that a nuclear-arms freeze, while not an end in itself, would constitute an effective step to prevent the qualitative improvement of existing nuclear weaponry during the period when the negotiations take place, and that it would at the same time reinforce the favourable environment for the conduct of negotiations to reduce and eventually eliminate nuclear weapons,

Convinced also that the undertakings derived from the freeze can be effectively verified,

Welcoming the unilateral steps taken by the nuclear-weapon States for the cessation of the production of highly enriched uranium for nuclear weapons and for the shutting down of reactors producing weapons-grade plutonium,

Noting with concern that all nuclear-weapon States have not so far taken any collective action in response to the call made in the relevant resolutions on the question of a nuclear-arms freeze,

Convinced further that the current international situation is most conducive to nuclear disarmament,

1. *Urges* the Russian Federation and the United States of America, as the two major nuclear-weapon States, to reach agreement on an immediate nuclear-arms freeze, which would, *inter alia*, provide for a simultaneous total stoppage of any production of nuclear weapons and a complete cut-off in the production of fissionable material for weapons purposes;

2. *Calls upon* all nuclear-weapon States to agree, through a joint declaration, to a comprehensive nuclear-arms freeze, whose structure and scope would be the following:

   (*a*) It would embrace:

   (i) A comprehensive test ban on nuclear weapons and on their delivery vehicles;

   (ii) The complete cessation of the manufacture of nuclear weapons and of their delivery vehicles;

   (iii) A ban on all further deployment of nuclear weapons and of their delivery vehicles;

   (iv) The complete cessation of the production of fissionable material for weapons purposes;

   (*b*) It would be subject to appropriate and effective measures and procedures of verification;

3. *Requests once again* the nuclear-weapon States to submit a joint report, or separate reports, to the General Assembly, prior to the opening of its forty-eighth session, on the implementation of the present resolution;

4. *Decides* to include in the provisional agenda of its forty-eighth session the item entitled "Nuclear-arms freeze".

General Assembly resolution 47/53 E
9 December 1992   Meeting 81   121-19-27 (recorded vote)

Approved by First Committee (A/47/692) by recorded vote (92-18-28), 13
November (meeting 33); 6-nation draft (A/C.1/47/L.41); agenda item 62 *(c)*.
Sponsors: Bolivia, Democratic People's Republic of Korea, India, Indonesia,
Mexico, Myanmar.
Meeting numbers. GA 47th session: 1st Committee 3-21, 28, 33; plenary 81.

Recorded vote in Assembly as follows:

In favour: Afghanistan, Algeria, Angola, Antigua and Barbuda, Argen-
tina, Azerbaijan, Bahamas, Bahrain, Bangladesh, Barbados, Belarus, Be-
lize, Benin, Bhutan, Bolivia, Botswana, Brazil, Brunei Darussalam, Burkina
Faso, Burundi, Cameroon, Cape Verde, Central African Republic, Chad,
Chile, Colombia, Comoros, Congo, Costa Rica, Côte d'Ivoire, Cuba, Cyprus,
Democratic People's Republic of Korea, Djibouti, Dominica, Dominican
Republic, Ecuador, Egypt, El Salvador, Ethiopia, Fiji, Gabon, Gambia,
Ghana, Grenada, Guatemala, Guinea, Guinea-Bissau, Guyana, Haiti, Hon-
duras, India, Indonesia, Iran, Iraq, Jamaica, Jordan, Kazakhstan, Kenya,
Kuwait, Lao People's Democratic Republic, Lebanon, Lesotho, Liberia, Lib-
yan Arab Jamahiriya, Madagascar, Malawi, Malaysia, Maldives, Mali,
Mauritania, Mauritius, Mexico, Mongolia, Morocco, Mozambique, Myan-
mar, Namibia, Nepal, Nicaragua, Niger, Nigeria, Oman, Pakistan, Panama,
Papua New Guinea, Paraguay, Peru, Philippines, Qatar, Rwanda, Saint Kitts
and Nevis, Saint Lucia, Saint Vincent and the Grenadines, Sao Tome and
Principe, Saudi Arabia, Senegal, Seychelles, Sierra Leone, Singapore, Sri
Lanka, Sudan, Suriname, Swaziland, Syrian Arab Republic, Tajikistan, Thai-
land, Togo, Trinidad and Tobago, Tunisia, Turkmenistan, Uganda, Ukraine,
United Arab Emirates, United Republic of Tanzania, Uruguay, Vanuatu, Viet
Nam, Yemen, Zambia, Zimbabwe.

Against: Belgium, Bulgaria, Canada, Czechoslovakia, France, Germany,
Hungary, Israel, Italy, Luxembourg, Netherlands, Poland, Republic of Moldova, Romania, San Marino, Spain, Turkey, United Kingdom, United States.

Abstaining: Armenia, Australia, Austria, China, Denmark, Estonia, Fin-
land, Greece, Iceland, Ireland, Japan, Latvia, Liechtenstein, Lithuania,
Malta, Marshall Islands, Micronesia, New Zealand, Norway, Portugal,
Republic of Korea, Russian Federation, Samoa, Slovenia, Solomon Islands,
Sweden, Zaire.

Multilateral action

Disarmament Commission consideration. In
1992, the Disarmament Commission[34] re-
established its Working Group II to continue consideration of the item entitled "Process of nuclear
disarmament in the framework of international
peace and security, with the objective of the elimination of nuclear weapons", which it began to consider in 1991.[58] The Group held nine meetings
between 22 April and 7 May, and decided to base
its work on the following topics: the relationship
between the process of nuclear disarmament and
international peace and security; review of the
steps taken in the process of nuclear disarmament;
strengthening the process of nuclear disarmament,
necessary conditions and mechanisms required for
it; and the role of the United Nations system. New
papers on the item were submitted to the Commission by China,[60] Portugal on behalf of the
member States of the European Community
(EC)[61] and Ireland.[62] A number of other working papers were submitted to the Working Group.
The Working Group annexed to its report a list
of elements identified and elaborated under the
four subjects discussed.

**Consideration by the Conference on Disar-
mament.** The Conference on Disarmament[6]
considered the topic of nuclear-war prevention
during three informal meetings between 21 May
and 25 June. As in previous years, no consensus
was reached on a mandate proposed by the Group
of 21 neutral and non-aligned States (Algeria, Ar-

gentina, Brazil, Cuba, Egypt, Ethiopia, India, Indonesia, Iran, Kenya, Mexico, Morocco, Myanmar, Nigeria, Pakistan, Peru, Sri Lanka, Sweden,
Venezuela, Yugoslavia, Zaire) for an ad hoc committee that would consider all relevant proposals,
including appropriate and practical measures for
preventing nuclear war.

The Conference considered the item entitled
"Cessation of the nuclear-arms race and nuclear
disarmament" in four informal meetings held between 12 March and 23 July. The President of the
Conference prepared a list of topics to facilitate
a structured and orderly discussion. The Conference was again unable to agree on the establishment of an ad hoc committee under the item.

Report of the Secretary-General. In accordance with a General Assembly resolution of
1989,[63] the Secretary-General in September submitted a report containing information received
from three Member States[64] on technological
developments relating to the Treaty on the Prohibition of the Emplacement of Nuclear and Other
Weapons of Mass Destruction on the Seabed and
the Ocean Floor and in the Subsoil Thereof,[65]
and verification and compliance with the Treaty.

GENERAL ASSEMBLY ACTION

On 9 December 1992, the General Assembly,
on the recommendation of the First Committee,
adopted **resolution 47/52 C** by recorded vote.

Prohibition of the production of fissionable
material for weapons purposes

The General Assembly,

Recalling its resolution 46/36 D of 6 December 1991
and previous resolutions, in which it requested the Conference on Disarmament, at an appropriate stage of the
implementation of the Programme of Action set forth
in section III of the Final Document of the Tenth Special Session of the General Assembly and of its work
on the item entitled "Nuclear weapons in all aspects",
to consider urgently the question of adequately verified
cessation and prohibition of the production of fissionable material for nuclear weapons and other nuclear explosive devices and to keep the Assembly informed of
the progress of that consideration,

Noting that the agenda of the Conference on Disarmament for 1992 included the item entitled "Nuclear
weapons in all aspects" and that the programme of work
of the Conference for all three parts of its 1992 session
contained the item entitled "Cessation of the nuclear-
arms race and nuclear disarmament",

Recalling also the proposals and statements made in the
Conference on Disarmament on those items,

Welcoming the significant progress in reducing nuclear-
weapon arsenals as evidenced by substantive bilateral
agreements between the Russian Federation and the
United States of America and unilateral undertakings
by France, the Russian Federation, the United Kingdom of Great Britain and Northern Ireland and the
United States of America towards the reduction in some
of their nuclear-weapons programmes or of the num-

bers of nuclear weapons and their delivery systems as well as regarding the disposition of fissile material,

Welcoming also the recent decision by the United States of America not to produce plutonium or highly enriched uranium for nuclear explosive purposes,

Considering that the cessation of production of fissionable material for weapons purposes and the progressive conversion and transfer of stocks to peaceful uses would also be a significant step towards halting and reversing the nuclear-arms race,

Considering also that the prohibition of the production of fissionable material for nuclear weapons and other explosive devices would be an important measure in facilitating the prevention of the proliferation of nuclear weapons and explosive devices,

1. *Requests* the Conference on Disarmament to pursue its consideration of the question of adequately verified cessation and prohibition of the production of fissionable material for nuclear weapons and other nuclear explosive devices and to keep the General Assembly informed of the progress of that consideration;

2. *Decides* to include in the provisional agenda of its forty-eighth session the item entitled "Prohibition of the production of fissionable material for weapons purposes".

General Assembly resolution 47/52 C

9 December 1992   Meeting 81   164-0-3 (recorded vote)

Approved by First Committee (A/47/691) by recorded vote (133-0-4), 13 November (meeting 33); 22-nation draft (A/C.1/47/L.12); agenda item 61 *(g)*.

Sponsors: Australia, Austria, Bahamas, Bangladesh, Belarus, Cameroon, Canada, Denmark, Finland, Indonesia, Ireland, Japan, Netherlands, New Zealand, Norway, Philippines, Poland, Romania, Russian Federation, Samoa, Sweden, Uruguay.

Meeting numbers. GA 47th session: 1st Committee 3-21, 24, 33; plenary 81.

Recorded vote in Assembly as follows:

In favour: Afghanistan, Algeria, Angola, Antigua and Barbuda, Argentina, Australia, Austria, Azerbaijan, Bahamas, Bahrain, Bangladesh, Barbados, Belarus, Belgium, Belize, Benin, Bhutan, Bolivia, Botswana, Brazil, Brunei Darussalam, Bulgaria, Burkina Faso, Burundi, Cameroon, Canada, Cape Verde, Central African Republic, Chad, Chile, Colombia, Comoros, Congo, Costa Rica, Cote d'Ivoire, Cuba, Cyprus, Czechoslovakia, Democratic People's Republic of Korea, Denmark, Djibouti, Dominica, Dominican Republic, Ecuador, Egypt, El Salvador, Estonia, Ethiopia, Fiji, Finland, France,* Gabon, Gambia, Germany, Ghana, Greece, Grenada, Guatemala, Guinea, Guinea-Bissau, Guyana, Haiti, Honduras, Hungary, Iceland, Indonesia, Iran, Iraq, Ireland, Israel, Italy, Jamaica, Japan, Jordan, Kazakhstan, Kenya, Kuwait, Kyrgyzstan, Lao People's Democratic Republic, Latvia, Lebanon, Lesotho, Liberia, Libyan Arab Jamahiriya, Liechtenstein, Lithuania, Luxembourg, Madagascar, Malawi, Malaysia, Maldives, Mali, Malta, Marshall Islands, Mauritania, Mauritius, Mexico, Micronesia, Mongolia, Morocco, Mozambique, Myanmar, Namibia, Nepal, Netherlands, New Zealand, Nicaragua, Niger, Nigeria, Norway, Oman, Pakistan, Panama, Papua New Guinea, Paraguay, Peru, Philippines, Poland, Portugal, Qatar, Republic of Korea, Republic of Moldova, Romania, Russian Federation, Rwanda, Saint Kitts and Nevis, Saint Lucia, Saint Vincent and the Grenadines, Samoa, San Marino, Sao Tome and Principe, Saudi Arabia, Senegal, Seychelles, Sierra Leone, Singapore, Slovenia, Solomon Islands, Spain, Sri Lanka, Sudan, Suriname, Swaziland, Sweden, Syrian Arab Republic, Tajikistan, Thailand, Togo, Trinidad and Tobago, Tunisia, Turkey, Turkmenistan, Uganda, Ukraine, United Arab Emirates, United Republic of Tanzania, Uruguay, Vanuatu, Venezuela, Viet Nam, Yemen, Zaire, Zambia, Zimbabwe.

Against: None.

Abstaining: India, United Kingdom, United States.

*Later informed the Secretariat that it had intended to abstain.

Also on 9 December, the General Assembly, on the recommendation of the First Committee, adopted **resolution 47/53 C** by recorded vote.

Convention on the Prohibition of the Use of Nuclear Weapons

The General Assembly,

Convinced that the existence and use of nuclear weapons pose the greatest threat to the survival of mankind,

Convinced also that nuclear disarmament is the only ultimate guarantee against the use of nuclear weapons,

Convinced further that a multilateral agreement prohibiting the use or threat of use of nuclear weapons should strengthen international security and contribute to the climate for negotiations leading to the ultimate elimination of nuclear weapons,

Welcoming the agreement reached between the Russian Federation and the United States of America in June 1992 to reduce their warhead stockpiles to a maximum of 3,000 for the Russian Federation and 3,500 for the United States of America by the year 2003,

Conscious that the recent steps taken by the Russian Federation and the United States of America towards a reduction of their nuclear weapons and the improvement in the international climate can contribute towards the goal of complete elimination of nuclear weapons,

Recalling that in paragraph 58 of the Final Document of the Tenth Special Session of the General Assembly, it is stated that all States should actively participate in efforts to bring about conditions in international relations among States in which a code of peaceful conduct of nations in international affairs could be agreed upon and that would preclude the use or threat of use of nuclear weapons,

Reaffirming that the use of nuclear weapons would be a violation of the Charter of the United Nations and a crime against humanity, as declared in its resolutions 1653(XVI) of 24 November 1961, 33/71 B of 14 December 1978, 34/83 G of 11 December 1979, 35/152 D of 12 December 1980 and 36/92 I of 9 December 1981,

Noting with regret that the Conference on Disarmament, during its 1992 session, was not able to undertake negotiations with a view to achieving agreement on an international convention prohibiting the use or threat of use of nuclear weapons under any circumstances, taking as a basis the text annexed to General Assembly resolution 46/37 D of 6 December 1991,

1. *Reiterates its request* to the Conference on Disarmament to commence negotiations, as a matter of priority, in order to reach agreement on an international convention prohibiting the use or threat of use of nuclear weapons under any circumstances, taking as a basis the draft Convention on the Prohibition of the Use of Nuclear Weapons annexed to the present resolution;

2. *Also requests* the Conference on Disarmament to report to the General Assembly on the results of those negotiations.

ANNEX
Draft Convention on the Prohibition of the Use of Nuclear Weapons

The States Parties to this Convention,

Alarmed by the threat to the very survival of mankind posed by the existence of nuclear weapons,

Convinced that any use of nuclear weapons constitutes a violation of the Charter of the United Nations and a crime against humanity,

Convinced that this Convention would be a step towards the complete elimination of nuclear weapons leading to general and complete disarmament under strict and effective international control,

Determined to continue negotiations for the achievement of this goal,

Have agreed as follows:

Article 1

The States Parties to this Convention solemnly undertake not to use or threaten to use nuclear weapons under any circumstances.

Article 2

This Convention shall be of unlimited duration.

Article 3

1. This Convention shall be open to all States for signature. Any State that does not sign the Convention before its entry into force in accordance with paragraph 3 of this article may accede to it at any time.

2. This Convention shall be subject to ratification by signatory States. Instruments of ratification or accession shall be deposited with the Secretary-General of the United Nations.

3. This Convention shall enter into force on the deposit of instruments of ratification by twenty-five Governments, including the Governments of the five nuclear-weapon States, in accordance with paragraph 2 of this article.

4. For States whose instruments of ratification or accession are deposited after the entry into force of the Convention, it shall enter into force on the date of the deposit of their instruments of ratification or accession.

5. The depositary shall promptly inform all signatory and acceding States of the date of each signature, the date of deposit of each instrument of ratification or accession and the date of the entry into force of this Convention, as well as of the receipt of other notices.

6. This Convention shall be registered by the depositary in accordance with Article 102 of the Charter of the United Nations.

Article 4

This Convention, of which the Arabic, Chinese, English, French, Russian and Spanish texts are equally authentic, shall be deposited with the Secretary-General of the United Nations, who shall send duly certified copies thereof to the Government of the signatory and acceding States.

IN WITNESS WHEREOF, the undersigned, being duly authorized thereto by their respective Governments, have signed this Convention, opened for signature at _____ on the _____ day of _____ one thousand nine hundred and _____.

General Assembly resolution 47/53 C

9 December 1992   Meeting 81   126-21-21 (recorded vote)

Approved by First Committee (A/47/692) by recorded vote (97-21-19), 13 November (meeting 33); 15-nation draft (A/C.1/47/L.33); agenda item 62 *(d)*.

Sponsors: Algeria, Bangladesh, Bhutan, Bolivia, Costa Rica, Democratic People's Republic of Korea, Ecuador, Egypt, Ethiopia, India, Indonesia, Lao People's Democratic Republic, Malaysia, Viet Nam.

Meeting numbers. GA 47th session: 1st Committee 3-21, 28, 33; plenary 81.

Recorded vote in Assembly as follows:

In favour: Afghanistan, Algeria, Angola, Antigua and Barbuda, Argentina,* Azerbaijan, Bahamas, Bahrain, Bangladesh, Barbados, Belarus, Belize, Benin, Bhutan, Bolivia, Botswana, Brazil, Brunei Darussalam, Burkina Faso, Burundi, Cameroon, Cape Verde, Central African Republic, Chad, Chile, China, Colombia, Comoros, Congo, Costa Rica, Côte d'Ivoire, Cuba, Cyprus, Democratic People's Republic of Korea, Djibouti, Dominica, Dominican Republic, Ecuador, Egypt, El Salvador, Ethiopia, Fiji, Gabon, Gambia, Ghana, Grenada, Guatemala, Guinea, Guinea-Bissau, Guyana, Haiti, Honduras, India, Indonesia, Iran, Iraq, Jamaica, Jordan, Kazakhstan, Kenya, Kuwait, Lao People's Democratic Republic, Lebanon, Lesotho, Liberia, Libyan Arab Jamahiriya, Madagascar, Malawi, Malaysia, Maldives, Mali, Mauritania, Mauritius, Mexico, Micronesia, Mongolia, Morocco, Mozambique, Myanmar, Namibia, Nepal, Nicaragua, Niger, Nigeria, Oman, Pakistan, Panama, Papua New Guinea, Paraguay, Peru, Philippines, Qatar,

Russian Federation, Rwanda, Saint Kitts and Nevis, Saint Lucia, Saint Vincent and the Grenadines, Sao Tome and Principe, Saudi Arabia, Senegal, Seychelles, Sierra Leone, Singapore, Sri Lanka, Sudan, Suriname, Swaziland, Syrian Arab Republic, Tajikistan, Thailand, Togo, Trinidad and Tobago, Tunisia, Turkmenistan, Uganda, Ukraine, United Arab Emirates, United Republic of Tanzania, Uruguay, Vanuatu, Venezuela, Viet Nam, Yemen, Zaire, Zambia, Zimbabwe.

Against: Australia, Belgium, Bulgaria, Canada, Czechoslovakia, Denmark, France, Germany, Hungary, Iceland, Italy, Luxembourg, Netherlands, New Zealand, Norway, Poland, Portugal, Spain, Turkey, United Kingdom, United States.

Abstaining: Armenia, Austria, Estonia, Finland, Greece, Ireland, Israel, Japan, Latvia, Liechtenstein, Lithuania, Malta, Marshall Islands, Republic of Korea, Republic of Moldova, Romania, Samoa, San Marino, Slovenia, Solomon Islands, Sweden.

*Later advised the Secretariat it had intended to abstain.

Nuclear-test ban and other nuclear questions

Consideration by the Conference on Disarmament. At its 1992 session, the Conference on Disarmament[6] was unable to re-establish the Ad Hoc Committee on a Nuclear Test Ban because of continued differences among member States concerning the Committee's mandate. None the less, the Conference agreed to intensify consultations with a view to re-establishing the Committee at the beginning of its 1993 session.

On 26 May, France, the only nuclear-weapon State that had not thus far participated in the work of the Ad Hoc Committee on a Nuclear Test Ban, announced its decision to join the Ad Hoc Committee when it was re-established.

Under the item, Norway presented to the Conference the full report of an expert study on questions related to a comprehensive test-ban treaty[66] and a summary of the study,[67] which was commissioned and published by the Ministry of Foreign Affairs of Norway.

The Ad Hoc Group of Scientific Experts to Consider International Cooperative Measures to Detect and Identify Seismic Events held two sessions at Geneva in 1992 (thirty-third session, 2-13 March;[68] and thirty-fourth session, 27 July–7 August[69]). It had conducted, as agreed in 1987,[70] the main phase of its second major technical test, a large-scale international experiment on the exchange and analysis of seismic data (GSETT-2). In a report to the Conference,[71] the Group noted GSETT-2 had demonstrated that communication means and associated protocols were available which permitted extensive data exchange within a global seismic monitoring system.

On 18 August, the Conference adopted the dates of the Group's next session (15-26 February 1993) and, as suggested by the Group, the President, with the agreement of the Conference, extended an invitation to IAEA to participate in the session.

Notes by the Secretary-General. By a July note,[72] prepared in response to a 1987 General Assembly request,[73] the Secretary-General transmitted a quarterly report (January–March 1992) by Australia on presumed underground nuclear explosions, which referred to a nuclear explosion in Nevada (United States) on 26 March with an estimated yield of 40 to 150 kilotonnes. In an October note,[74] the Secretary-General presented the annual register of information provided on nuclear explosions, covering the period 15 September 1991–14 September 1992 and reporting the same explosion. No other nuclear explosive testing during the period was reported to the Secretary-General for consolidation in the register.

GENERAL ASSEMBLY ACTION

On 9 December, the General Assembly, on the recommendation of the First Committee, adopted **resolution 47/47** by recorded vote.

Comprehensive nuclear-test-ban treaty

The General Assembly,

Recalling previous resolutions that identify the complete cessation of nuclear-weapon tests and a comprehensive test ban as one of the priority objectives in the field of disarmament,

Convinced that a nuclear war cannot be won and must never be fought,

Welcoming the improved relationship between the Russian Federation and the United States of America and their consequent announcements of significant measures, including unilateral steps, which could signal the reversal of the nuclear-arms race,

Welcoming also the Treaty between the United States of America and the Union of Soviet Socialist Republics on the Reduction and Limitation of Strategic Offensive Arms, signed on 31 July 1991, and the signing of a protocol to this Treaty in which Belarus, Kazakhstan, the Russian Federation, Ukraine and the United States of America undertake to give effect to the Treaty,

Welcoming further the Joint Understanding of 17 June 1992 between the Russian Federation and the United States of America on further reductions in their strategic offensive arms,

Welcoming the decision taken by France to suspend its testing of nuclear weapons for 1992,

Endorsing the call made by France and by the Russian Federation on the other nuclear Powers to suspend their nuclear tests,

Welcoming also in addition the recent decision of the United States of America to implement a testing moratorium accompanied by a plan for achieving a multilateral, comprehensive ban on the testing of nuclear weapons,

Welcoming further the decision of the Russian Federation to extend its earlier-announced nuclear-testing moratorium,

Convinced that an end to nuclear testing by all States in all environments for all time is an essential step in order to prevent the qualitative improvement and development of nuclear weapons and their further proliferation and to contribute, along with other concurrent efforts to reduce nuclear arms, to the eventual elimination of nuclear weapons,

Noting the concerns expressed about the environmental and health risks associated with underground nuclear testing, as brought out in the Expert Study on Questions Related to a Comprehensive Test Ban Treaty in CD/1167 of 14 August 1992, which noted, *inter alia*, the environmental benefits and economic savings to be derived from a complete ban on nuclear testing,

Convinced also that the most effective way to achieve an end to nuclear testing is through the conclusion, at an early date, of a verifiable, comprehensive nuclear-test-ban treaty that will attract the adherence of all States,

Taking into account the undertakings by the original parties to the 1963 Treaty Banning Nuclear Weapon Tests in the Atmosphere, in Outer Space and under Water to seek to achieve the early discontinuance of all test explosions of nuclear weapons for all time, and also noting the reiteration of this commitment in the 1968 Treaty on the Non-Proliferation of Nuclear Weapons,

Noting with satisfaction the work being undertaken within the Conference on Disarmament by the Ad Hoc Group of Scientific Experts to Consider International Cooperative Measures to Detect and Identify Seismic Events, and in this context welcoming the results of the second technical test concerning the global exchange and analysis of seismic data, which will permit the system to be redesigned in the light of this experience,

Recalling that the Amendment Conference of States Parties to the Treaty Banning Nuclear Weapon Tests in the Atmosphere, in Outer Space and under Water was held in New York from 7 to 18 January 1991,

Expressing its disappointment that the Conference on Disarmament was unable to re-establish the Ad Hoc Committee on item 1 of its agenda, entitled "Nuclear test ban", despite the improved political climate,

1. *Reaffirms its conviction* that a treaty to achieve the prohibition of all nuclear-test explosions by all States in all environments for all time is a matter of priority which would constitute an essential step in order to prevent the qualitative improvement and development of nuclear weapons and their further proliferation, and which would contribute to the process of nuclear disarmament;

2. *Urges*, therefore, all States to seek to achieve the early discontinuance of all nuclear-test explosions for all time;

3. *Urges*:

(a) The nuclear-weapon States to agree promptly to appropriate verifiable and militarily significant interim measures, with a view to concluding a comprehensive nuclear-test-ban treaty;

(b) Those nuclear-weapon States which have not yet done so to adhere to the Treaty Banning Nuclear Weapon Tests in the Atmosphere, in Outer Space and under Water;

4. *Reaffirms* the particular responsibilities of the Conference on Disarmament in the negotiation of a comprehensive nuclear-test-ban treaty, and in this context urges the re-establishment of the Ad Hoc Committee on a Nuclear Test Ban in 1993;

5. *Requests* the Conference on Disarmament, in this context, to intensify its substantive work begun in 1990 on specific and interrelated test-ban issues, including structure and scope and verification and compliance, taking also into account all relevant proposals and future initiatives;

6. *Urges* the Conference on Disarmament:

(a) To take into account the progress achieved by the Ad Hoc Group of Scientific Experts to Consider International Cooperative Measures to Detect and Identify Seismic Events, including the experience gained from the technical test concerning the global exchange and analysis of seismic data, and other relevant initiatives;

(b) To continue efforts to establish, with the widest possible participation, an international seismic monitoring network with a view to developing further a system for the effective monitoring and verification of compliance with a comprehensive nuclear-test-ban treaty;

(c) To investigate other measures to monitor and verify compliance with such a treaty, including on-site inspections, satellite monitoring and an international network to monitor atmospheric radioactivity;

7. *Calls upon* the Conference on Disarmament to report to the General Assembly at its forty-eighth session on progress made, including its recommendations on how the objectives of the Ad Hoc Committee on item 1 of its agenda, entitled "Nuclear test ban", should be carried forward most effectively towards achieving a comprehensive test-ban treaty;

8. *Decides* to include in the provisional agenda of its forty-eighth session the item entitled "Comprehensive nuclear-test-ban treaty".

General Assembly resolution 47/47

9 December 1992   Meeting 81   159-1-4 (recorded vote)

Approved by First Committee (A/47/684) by recorded vote (136-1-4), 13 November (meeting 33); 99-nation draft (A/C.1/47/L.37), orally revised; agenda item 54.

Sponsors: Afghanistan, Albania, Antigua and Barbuda, Australia, Austria, Azerbaijan, Bahamas, Bangladesh, Barbados, Belarus, Belgium, Bolivia, Botswana, Brazil, Brunei Darussalam, Bulgaria, Cameroon, Canada, Cape Verde, Chile, Colombia, Costa Rica, Croatia, Cuba, Cyprus, Czechoslovakia, Denmark, Dominican Republic, Ecuador, Egypt, Fiji, Finland, Germany, Greece, Guatemala, Guinea, Guyana, Haiti, Honduras, Hungary, Iceland, Indonesia, Iran, Ireland, Italy, Jamaica, Japan, Kazakhstan, Latvia, Lesotho, Liberia, Liechtenstein, Lithuania, Luxembourg, Madagascar, Malaysia, Malta, Marshall Islands, Mauritius, Mexico, Mongolia, Myanmar, Nepal, Netherlands, New Zealand, Nicaragua, Nigeria, Norway, Panama, Papua New Guinea, Paraguay, Peru, Philippines, Poland, Portugal, Republic of Korea, Russian Federation, Saint Vincent and the Grenadines, Samoa, Singapore, Slovenia, Solomon Islands, Spain, Sri Lanka, Suriname, Sweden, Thailand, Togo, Turkey, Uganda, Ukraine, United Republic of Tanzania, Uruguay, Vanuatu, Venezuela, Viet Nam, Zaire, Zambia, Zimbabwe.

Meeting numbers. GA 47th session: 1st Committee 3-21, 24, 33; plenary 81.

Recorded vote in Assembly as follows:

In favour: Afghanistan, Algeria, Angola, Argentina, Armenia, Australia, Austria, Azerbaijan, Bahamas, Bahrain, Bangladesh, Barbados, Belarus, Belgium, Belize, Benin, Bhutan, Bolivia, Botswana, Brazil, Brunei Darussalam, Bulgaria, Burkina Faso, Burundi, Cameroon, Canada, Cape Verde, Central African Republic, Chad, Chile, Colombia, Comoros, Congo, Costa Rica, Côte d'Ivoire, Cuba, Cyprus, Czechoslovakia, Democratic People's Republic of Korea, Denmark, Djibouti, Dominica, Dominican Republic, Ecuador, Egypt, El Salvador, Estonia, Ethiopia, Fiji, Finland, Gabon, Gambia, Germany, Ghana, Greece, Grenada, Guatemala, Guinea, Guinea-Bissau, Guyana, Haiti, Honduras, Hungary, Iceland, India, Indonesia, Iran, Iraq, Ireland, Italy, Jamaica, Japan, Jordan, Kazakhstan, Kenya, Kuwait, Lao People's Democratic Republic, Latvia, Lebanon, Lesotho, Liberia, Libyan Arab Jamahiriya, Liechtenstein, Lithuania, Luxembourg, Madagascar, Malaysia, Maldives, Mali, Malta, Marshall Islands, Mauritania, Mauritius, Mexico, Micronesia, Mongolia, Morocco, Mozambique, Myanmar, Namibia, Nepal, Netherlands, New Zealand, Nicaragua, Niger, Nigeria, Norway, Oman, Pakistan, Panama, Papua New Guinea, Paraguay, Peru, Philippines, Poland, Portugal, Qatar, Republic of Korea, Republic of Moldova, Romania, Russian Federation, Rwanda, Saint Kitts and Nevis, Saint Lucia, Saint Vincent and the Grenadines, Samoa, San Marino, Saudi Arabia, Senegal, Seychelles, Sierra Leone, Singapore, Slovenia, Solomon Islands, Spain, Sri Lanka, Sudan, Suriname, Swaziland, Sweden, Syrian Arab Republic, Tajikistan, Thailand, Togo, Trinidad and Tobago, Tunisia, Turkey, Uganda, Ukraine, United Arab Emirates, United Republic of Tanzania, Uruguay, Vanuatu, Venezuela, Viet Nam, Yemen, Zaire, Zambia, Zimbabwe.

Against: United States.

Abstaining: China, France, Israel, United Kingdom.

Follow-up to Amendment Conference of States parties to the partial test-ban Treaty

Following the 1991 Amendment Conference[75] of the States parties to the Treaty Banning Nuclear Weapon Tests in the Atmosphere, in Outer Space and under Water (1963) (also known as the partial test-ban Treaty),[76] the President of that Conference conducted consultations. In October 1992, an understanding was reached by a majority of the parties that a special meeting of States parties would be held in the second quarter of 1993 to review the developments on the issue of nuclear testing, with a view to examining the feasibility of resuming the work of the Amendment Conference later that year, but no consensus was reached on that point. The United States and the United Kingdom continued to oppose plans to reconvene the Conference, as they had done at the Conference itself.

GENERAL ASSEMBLY ACTION

On 9 December 1992, the General Assembly, on the recommendation of the First Committee, adopted **resolution 47/46** by recorded vote.

Amendment of the Treaty Banning Nuclear Weapon Tests in the Atmosphere, in Outer Space and under Water

The General Assembly,

Recalling its resolutions 44/106 of 15 December 1989, 45/50 of 4 December 1990 and 46/28 of 6 December 1991,

Reiterating its conviction that a comprehensive nuclear-test-ban treaty is the highest-priority measure for the cessation of the nuclear-arms race and for the achievement of the objective of nuclear disarmament,

Recalling the central role of the United Nations in the field of nuclear disarmament and in particular in the cessation of all nuclear-test explosions, as well as the persistent efforts of non-governmental organizations in the achievement of a comprehensive nuclear-test-ban treaty,

Conscious of the growing environmental concerns throughout the world and of the past and potential negative effects of nuclear testing on the environment,

Recalling its resolution 1910(XVIII) of 27 November 1963, in which it noted with approval the Treaty Banning Nuclear Weapon Tests in the Atmosphere, in Outer Space and under Water, signed on 5 August 1963, and requested the Conference of the Eighteen-Nation Committee on Disarmament[a] to continue with a sense of urgency its negotiations to achieve the objectives set forth in the preamble to the Treaty,

Recalling also that more than one third of the parties to the Treaty requested the Depositary Governments to convene a conference to consider an amendment that would convert the Treaty into a comprehensive test-ban treaty,

Recalling further that a substantive session of the Amendment Conference of the States Parties to the Treaty Banning Nuclear Weapon Tests in the Atmosphere, in Outer Space and under Water was held in New York from 7 to 18 January 1991,

Reiterating its conviction that the Amendment Conference will facilitate the attainment of the objectives set forth in the Treaty and thus serve to strengthen it,

---

[a]The Committee on Disarmament was redesignated the Conference on Disarmament as from 7 February 1984.

Noting with satisfaction the unilateral nuclear-test moratoria announced by several nuclear-weapon States,

Recalling its recommendation that arrangements be made to ensure that intensive efforts continue, under the auspices of the Amendment Conference, until a comprehensive nuclear-test-ban treaty is achieved,

Recalling also the decision adopted by the Amendment Conference to the effect that, since further work needed to be undertaken on certain aspects of a comprehensive test-ban treaty, especially those with regard to verification of compliance and possible sanctions against non-compliance, the President of the Conference should conduct consultations with a view to achieving progress on those issues and to resuming the work of the Conference at an appropriate time,

Welcoming the ongoing consultations being conducted by the President of the Amendment Conference,

1. *Notes* the ongoing consultations being conducted by the President of the Amendment Conference of the States Parties to the Treaty Banning Nuclear Weapon Tests in the Atmosphere, in Outer Space and under Water and the special meeting of States parties of a brief duration to be held in New York in the second quarter of 1993 to review the developments on the issue of nuclear testing, with a view to examining the feasibility of resuming the work of the Amendment Conference later that year;

2. *Calls upon* all parties to the Treaty Banning Nuclear Weapon Tests in the Atmosphere, in Outer Space and under Water to participate in, and to contribute to the success of, the Amendment Conference for the achievement of a comprehensive nuclear-test ban at an early date, as an indispensable measure towards implementation of their undertakings in the preamble to the Treaty;

3. *Urges* all States, especially those nuclear-weapon States which have not yet done so, to adhere to the Treaty;

4. *Recommends* that arrangements should be made to ensure the fullest possible participation of non-governmental organizations in the Amendment Conference;

5. *Reiterates its conviction* that, pending the conclusion of a comprehensive nuclear-test-ban treaty, the nuclear-weapon States should suspend all nuclear-test explosions through an agreed moratorium or unilateral moratoria;

6. *Stresses once again* the importance of ensuring adequate coordination among the various negotiating forums dealing with a comprehensive nuclear-test-ban treaty;

7. *Decides* to include in the provisional agenda of its forty-eighth session the item entitled "Amendment of the Treaty Banning Nuclear Weapon Tests in the Atmosphere, in Outer Space and under Water".

General Assembly resolution 47/46

9 December 1992   Meeting 81   118-2-41 (recorded vote)

Approved by First Committee (A/47/683) by recorded vote (93-2-40), 16 November (meeting 34); 23-nation draft (A/C.1/47/L.38); agenda item 53.
Sponsors: Bahamas, Bolivia, Brunei Darussalam, Chile, Colombia, Costa Rica, Democratic People's Republic of Korea, India, Indonesia, Iran, Malaysia, Mexico, Mongolia, Nepal, Nigeria, Peru, Philippines, Senegal, Singapore, Sri Lanka, Thailand, United Republic of Tanzania, Venezuela.
Meeting numbers. GA 47th session: 1st Committee 3-21, 30, 34; plenary 81.

Recorded vote in Assembly as follows:

In favour: Afghanistan, Algeria, Angola, Azerbaijan, Bahamas, Bahrain, Bangladesh, Barbados, Belarus, Belize, Benin, Bhutan, Bolivia, Botswana, Brazil, Brunei Darussalam, Burkina Faso, Burundi, Cameroon, Cape Verde, Central African Republic, Chad, Chile, Colombia, Comoros, Congo, Costa Rica, Côte d'Ivoire, Cuba, Cyprus, Democratic People's Republic of Korea, Djibouti, Dominica, Dominican Republic, Ecuador, Egypt, El Salvador, Ethiopia, Fiji, Gabon, Gambia, Ghana, Grenada, Guatemala, Guinea, Guinea-Bissau, Guyana, Haiti, Honduras, India, Indonesia, Iran, Iraq, Jamaica, Jordan, Kazakhstan, Kenya, Kuwait, Lao People's Democratic Republic, Lebanon, Lesotho, Liberia, Libyan Arab Jamahiriya, Madagascar, Malaysia, Maldives, Mali, Mauritania, Mauritius, Mexico, Mongolia, Morocco, Mozambique, Myanmar, Namibia, Nepal, Nicaragua, Niger, Nigeria, Oman, Pakistan, Panama, Paraguay, Peru, Philippines, Qatar, Russian Federation, Rwanda, Saint Kitts and Nevis, Saint Lucia, Saint Vincent and the Grenadines, Saudi Arabia, Senegal, Seychelles, Sierra Leone, Singapore, Sri Lanka, Sudan, Suriname, Swaziland, Syrian Arab Republic, Tajikistan, Thailand, Togo, Trinidad and Tobago, Tunisia, Uganda, Ukraine, United Arab Emirates, United Republic of Tanzania, Uruguay, Vanuatu, Venezuela, Viet Nam, Yemen, Zaire, Zambia, Zimbabwe.
Against: United Kingdom, United States.
Abstaining: Argentina, Armenia, Australia, Austria, Belgium, Bulgaria, Canada, Czechoslovakia, Denmark, Estonia, Finland, Germany, Greece, Hungary, Iceland, Ireland, Israel, Italy, Japan, Latvia, Liechtenstein, Lithuania, Luxembourg, Malta, Marshall Islands, Micronesia, Netherlands, New Zealand, Norway, Papua New Guinea, Poland, Portugal, Republic of Korea, Republic of Moldova, Romania, Samoa, San Marino, Slovenia, Spain, Sweden, Turkey.

Before adopting the draft text as a whole in the Committee, paragraph 1 was adopted by a recorded vote of 86 to 2, with 43 abstentions, and paragraph 2, by a recorded vote of 89 to 2, with 41 abstentions. Separate recorded votes on those paragraphs were also requested in the Assembly where paragraph 1 was adopted by 113 to 2, with 43 abstentions, and paragraph 2, by 112 to 2, with 43 abstentions.

New types of weapons of mass destruction, including radiological weapons

Consideration by the Conference on Disarmament. The Conference on Disarmament[6] considered the item "New types of weapons of mass destruction and new systems of such weapons: radiological weapons", re-establishing the Ad Hoc Committee on Radiological Weapons[77] with a view to reaching agreement on a convention prohibiting the development, production, stockpiling and use of radiological weapons. The Ad Hoc Committee held four meetings between 17 March and 27 July and a number of informal consultations.

The Ad Hoc Committee re-established contact group A to continue to consider the prohibition of radiological weapons in the "traditional" sense and contact group B on the prohibition of attacks against nuclear facilities. The reports of the two groups were annexed to the Committee's report.[78] The Ad Hoc Committee concluded that its work had contributed further to clarifying the different approaches to the two subjects under consideration. It recommended that the Conference re-establish the Ad Hoc Committee in 1993 and give it guidance on reviewing the organization of its work with the aim of fulfilling its mandate.

GENERAL ASSEMBLY ACTION

On 9 December 1992, the General Assembly, on the recommendation of the First Committee, adopted **resolution 47/52 B** without vote.

Prohibition of the development, production, stockpiling and use of radiological weapons

The General Assembly,

Recalling its resolution 46/36 E of 6 December 1991,

1. *Takes note* of the part of the report of the Conference on Disarmament on its 1992 session that deals with the question of radiological weapons, in particular the report of the Ad Hoc Committee on Radiological Weapons;

2. *Recognizes* that in 1992 the Ad Hoc Committee made a further contribution to the clarification of different approaches that continue to exist with regard to both of the important subjects under consideration;

3. *Takes note also* of the recommendation of the Conference on Disarmament that the Ad Hoc Committee on Radiological Weapons should be re-established at the beginning of its 1993 session and that it should be given guidance on reviewing the organization of its work with the aim of fulfilling its mandate;

4. *Requests* the Conference on Disarmament to continue its substantive negotiation on the subject with a view to the prompt conclusion of its work, taking into account all proposals presented to the Conference to this end and drawing upon the annexes to the report of the Ad Hoc Committee, the result of which should be submitted to the General Assembly at its forty-eighth session;

5. *Requests* the Secretary-General to transmit to the Conference on Disarmament all relevant documents relating to the discussion of all aspects of the issue by the General Assembly at its forty-seventh session;

6. *Decides* to include in the provisional agenda of its forty-eighth session the item entitled "Prohibition of the development, production, stockpiling and use of radiological weapons".

General Assembly resolution 47/52 B

9 December 1992   Meeting 81   Adopted without vote

Approved by First Committee (A/47/691) without vote, 12 November (meeting 31); 4-nation draft (A/C.1/47/L.10); agenda item 61 *(h)*.

Sponsors: Belgium, Canada, Russian Federation, Sweden.

Meeting numbers. GA 47th session: 1st Committee 3-21, 26, 31; plenary 81.

Nuclear-weapon-free zones and zones of peace

Africa

Since 1964, when the Declaration on the Denuclearization of Africa was adopted by the Organization of African Unity (OAU),[79] the General Assembly had annually called for its implementation.

Report of the Secretary-General. In response to a General Assembly request of 1991,[80] the Secretary-General submitted in October 1992 a report on the nuclear capabilities of South Africa[81] containing the text of a resolution on the subject adopted on 25 September by the IAEA General Conference. It also contained a report by the IAEA Director General to the General Conference on the completeness of the inventory of South Africa's nuclear installations and material.

Expert group meeting. In accordance with an Assembly resolution of 1991,[82] the Secretary-General, by an October note,[83] submitted the report of the second meeting of the Group of Experts to Examine the Modalities and Elements for the Preparation and Implementation of a Convention or Treaty on the Denuclearization of Africa (Lomé, Togo, 28-30 April). The Group of Experts considered the relationship of such a convention with other international agreements and similar zones and various clauses of the future instrument. They agreed to recommend to the OAU Council of Ministers that formulation of a convention or treaty on the denuclearization of Africa begin and that it request the Assembly to consider providing assistance to OAU to enable it to conclude that task. The experts had held their first meeting in 1991.[84]

GENERAL ASSEMBLY ACTION

On 15 December 1992, the General Assembly, on the recommendation of the First Committee, adopted **resolution 47/76** without vote.

Implementation of the Declaration on the Denuclearization of Africa

The General Assembly,

Bearing in mind the Declaration on the Denuclearization of Africa adopted by the Assembly of Heads of State and Government of the Organization of African Unity at its first ordinary session, held at Cairo from 17 to 21 July 1964, in which they solemnly declare their readiness to undertake, through an international agreement to be concluded under United Nations auspices, not to manufacture or acquire control of atomic weapons,

Recalling its resolution 1652(XVI) of 24 November 1961, its earliest on the subject, as well as all its previous resolutions on the implementation of the Declaration on the Denuclearization of Africa,

Calling upon all States to consider and respect the continent of Africa and its surrounding areas as a nuclear-weapon-free zone,

Bearing in mind also the provisions of resolutions CM/Res.1342(LIV) and CM/Res.1395(LVI)/Rev.1 on the implementation of the Declaration on the Denuclearization of Africa adopted by the Council of Ministers of the Organization of African Unity at its fifty-fourth and fifty-sixth ordinary sessions, held at Abuja from 27 May to 1 June 1991 and at Dakar from 22 to 28 June 1992,[a] respectively,

Noting the accession by South Africa to the Treaty on the Non-Proliferation of Nuclear Weapons on 10 July 1991,

Noting also that the Government of South Africa has concluded a safeguards agreement with the International Atomic Energy Agency and committed itself to early and full implementation of the agreement,

Recalling resolution GC(XXXVI)/RES/577 on South Africa's nuclear capabilities, adopted on 25 September 1992 by the General Conference of the International Atomic Energy Agency,

Stressing that the full disclosure of South Africa's nuclear installations and materials is essential to the peace

---

[a]A/47/558.

and security of the region and to the success of efforts exerted towards the establishment of a nuclear-weapon-free zone for Africa,

Having considered the report of the Second Meeting of the Group of Experts to Examine the Modalities and Elements for the Preparation and Implementation of a Convention or Treaty on the Denuclearization of Africa, set up jointly by the Organization of African Unity and the United Nations, held at Lomé from 28 to 30 April 1992,

Convinced that the evolution of the international situation is conducive to the implementation of the Declaration on the Denuclearization of Africa of 1964, as well as the relevant provisions of the Declaration on Security, Disarmament and Development of 1968 of the Organization of African Unity,

1. *Reaffirms* that the implementation of the Declaration on the Denuclearization of Africa adopted by the Assembly of Heads of State and Government of the Organization of African Unity would be an important measure to prevent the proliferation of nuclear weapons and to promote international peace and security;

2. *Strongly renews its call* upon all States to consider and respect the continent of Africa and its surrounding areas as a nuclear-weapon-free zone;

3. *Takes note* of the report of the Director General of the International Atomic Energy Agency on the implementation of the safeguards agreement between the Government of South Africa and the Agency, including the verification of the completeness of the inventory of South Africa's nuclear installations and material;

4. *Calls upon* South Africa to continue to comply fully with the implementation of its safeguards agreement with the International Atomic Energy Agency;

5. *Commends* the Secretary-General for the diligence with which he has rendered effective assistance to the Organization of African Unity in organizing the meetings of the above-mentioned Group of Experts;

6. *Requests* the Secretary-General, in consultation with the Organization of African Unity, to take appropriate action to enable the Group of Experts designated by the United Nations in cooperation with the Organization of African Unity to meet during 1993 at Harare, in order to draw up a draft treaty or convention on the denuclearization of Africa, and to submit the report of the Group of Experts to the General Assembly at its forty-eighth session;

7. *Also requests* the Secretary-General to report to the General Assembly at its forty-eighth session on the progress made by the Director General of the International Atomic Energy Agency in ensuring the full implementation of the safeguards agreement with South Africa;

8. *Urges* all Member States to assist and cooperate with the Secretary-General and the Director General to this end.

General Assembly resolution 47/76

15 December 1992   Meeting 88   Adopted without vote

Approved by First Committee (A/47/689) without vote, 18 November (meeting 36); draft by Mauritania, for African Group (A/C.1/47/L.14), orally revised; agenda item 59.
Financial implications. 5th Committee, A/47/784; S-G, A/C.1/47/L.51, A/C.5/47/65.
Meeting numbers. GA 47th session: 1st Committee 3-36; 5th Committee 44; plenary 88.

Latin America

On 22 September,[85] Mexico, the depositary State of the Treaty of Tlatelolco, transmitted to the Secretary-General amendments to the Treaty adopted by the General Conference of the Agency for the Prohibition of Nuclear Weapons in Latin America and the Caribbean (Mexico City, 26 August), as proposed by Argentina, Brazil, Chile and Mexico. The amendments were intended to enhance the implementation of a number of articles relating to verification and to enable the full entry into force of the Treaty. A commentary on the amendments was submitted to the Conference on Disarmament by Argentina, Brazil and Chile.[86] Following the adoption of the amendments, Brazil made a declaration,[87] also on behalf of Argentina and Chile, indicating that, as soon as the three countries had completed the procedures for ratifying the text of the Treaty as amended, they would waive all the requirements set forth in paragraph 1 of article 28 of the Treaty that still remained to be met. (According to paragraph 2 of article 28 of the Treaty, all signatory States had the right to waive, wholly or in part, the requirements laid down in paragraph 1 of that article.)

The item on the signature and ratification of Additional Protocol I of the Treaty of Tlatelolco had been on the General Assembly's agenda since 1979. Because France had deposited its instrument of ratification of Additional Protocol I on 24 August 1992 (see under "Non-proliferation"), thus giving full force to the Protocol, and because of the adoption of the amendments to the Treaty, a new item was included on the Assembly's agenda at the request of Mexico,[88] entitled "Consolidation of the regime established by the Treaty for the Prohibition of Nuclear Weapons in Latin America and the Caribbean".

GENERAL ASSEMBLY ACTION

On 9 December 1992, the General Assembly, on the recommendation of the First Committee, adopted **resolution 47/61** without vote.

Consolidation of the regime established by the Treaty for the Prohibition of Nuclear Weapons in Latin America and the Caribbean (Treaty of Tlatelolco)

The General Assembly,

Recalling that in its resolution 1911(XVIII) of 27 November 1963 it expressed the hope that the States of Latin America would take appropriate measures to conclude a treaty that would prohibit nuclear weapons in Latin America,

Recalling also that in the same resolution it voiced its confidence that, once such a treaty was concluded, all States, and particularly the nuclear-weapon States, would lend it their full cooperation for the effective realization of its peaceful aims,

Considering that in its resolution 2028(XX) of 19 November 1965 it established the principle of an acceptable balance of mutual responsibilities and obligations between nuclear-weapon States and those which do not possess such weapons,

Recalling that the Treaty for the Prohibition of Nuclear Weapons in Latin America and the Caribbean (Treaty of Tlatelolco) was opened for signature at Mexico City on 14 February 1967,

Recalling also that in its preamble the Treaty of Tlatelolco states that military denuclearized zones are not an end in themselves but rather a means for achieving general and complete disarmament at a later stage,

Recalling further that in its resolution 2286(XXII) of 5 December 1967 it welcomed with special satisfaction the Treaty of Tlatelolco as an event of historic significance in the efforts to prevent the proliferation of nuclear weapons and to promote international peace and security,

Bearing in mind that the Treaty of Tlatelolco is open for signature to all the sovereign States of Latin America and the Caribbean and that it contains two additional protocols that are open for signature, respectively, to the States that *de jure* or de facto are internationally responsible for territories located within the zone of application of the Treaty and to the nuclear-weapon States,

Bearing in mind also that, with the adherence in 1992 of Saint Vincent and the Grenadines, the Treaty of Tlatelolco is in force for twenty-four sovereign States of the region,

Noting with satisfaction that the Government of France deposited its instrument of ratification of Additional Protocol I on 24 August 1992, thus giving full force to that Protocol,

Recalling that since 1974 Additional Protocol II has been in force for the five nuclear-weapon States,

Mindful that international conditions are more propitious for the consolidation of the regime established by the Treaty of Tlatelolco,

Also noting with satisfaction the holding of the fourth meeting of the signatories of the Treaty of Tlatelolco and the seventh special session of the General Conference of the Agency for the Prohibition of Nuclear Weapons in Latin America and the Caribbean, at Mexico City on 26 August 1992,

Welcoming the adoption on that occasion of resolution 290(VII), in which the General Conference approved and opened for signature a set of amendments to the Treaty of Tlatelolco with the aim of enabling the full entry into force of that instrument,

Noting that the Government of Cuba has declared that, in pursuit of regional unity, it would be ready to sign the Treaty of Tlatelolco once all the States of the region have assumed the undertakings of that Treaty,

1. *Welcomes* the concrete steps taken by several countries this year, the twenty-fifth anniversary of the Treaty for the Prohibition of Nuclear Weapons in Latin America and the Caribbean (Treaty of Tlatelolco), for the consolidation of the regime of military denuclearization established by that Treaty, including the adoption by acclamation on 26 August 1992 of the amendments to it;

2. *Welcomes in particular* the ratification of Additional Protocol I of the Treaty of Tlatelolco by France, thus giving full force to the additional protocols of that Treaty;

3. *Notes with satisfaction* the declaration of the Governments of Argentina, Brazil and Chile to the effect that as soon as the three countries have completed the proce-

dures for ratifying the text of the Treaty of Tlatelolco, as amended, they will waive all the requirements set forth in paragraph 1 of article 28 of the Treaty that still remain to be met;

4. *Urges* all Latin American and Caribbean States to take speedily the necessary measures to attain the full entry into force of the Treaty of Tlatelolco and, in particular, the States in respect of which the Treaty is open for signature and ratification immediately to carry out the corresponding formalities so that they may become parties to that international instrument, thus contributing to the consolidation of the regime established by that Treaty;

5. *Decides* to include in the provisional agenda of its forty-eighth session an item entitled "Consolidation of the regime established by the Treaty for the Prohibition of Nuclear Weapons in Latin America and the Caribbean (Treaty of Tlatelolco)".

General Assembly resolution 47/61

9 December 1992   Meeting 81   Adopted without vote

Approved by First Committee (A/47/700) without vote, 12 November (meeting 32); 25-nation draft (A/C.1/47/L.40); agenda item 142.

Sponsors: Antigua and Barbuda, Bahamas, Barbados, Belize, Bolivia, Colombia, Costa Rica, Dominican Republic, Ecuador, El Salvador, Guatemala, Haiti, Honduras, Jamaica, Mexico, Nicaragua, Panama, Paraguay, Peru, Saint Lucia, Suriname, Trinidad and Tobago, United States, Uruguay, Venezuela.

Meeting numbers. GA 47th session: 1st Committee 3-21, 27, 32; plenary 81.

Middle East

As requested by the General Assembly in 1991,[89] the Secretary-General reported in September[90] that he had held consultations with concerned parties to explore further the establishment of a nuclear-weapon-free zone in the Middle East. In the light of the ongoing peace initiative on the Middle East, launched at Madrid (Spain) in October 1991,[91] the Secretary-General stated that it would be premature for him to take any further action relating to the question at present.

GENERAL ASSEMBLY ACTION

On 9 December 1992, the General Assembly, on the recommendation of the First Committee, adopted **resolution 47/48** without vote.

Establishment of a nuclear-weapon-free zone in the region of the Middle East

The General Assembly,

Recalling its resolutions 3263(XXIX) of 9 December 1974, 3474(XXX) of 11 December 1975, 31/71 of 10 December 1976, 32/82 of 12 December 1977, 33/64 of 14 December 1978, 34/77 of 11 December 1979, 35/147 of 12 December 1980, 36/87 of 9 December 1981, 37/75 of 9 December 1982, 38/64 of 15 December 1983, 39/54 of 12 December 1984, 40/82 of 12 December 1985, 41/48 of 3 December 1986, 42/28 of 30 November 1987, 43/65 of 7 December 1988, 44/108 of 15 December 1989, 45/52 of 4 December 1990 and 46/30 of 6 December 1991 on the establishment of a nuclear-weapon-free zone in the region of the Middle East,

Recalling also the recommendations for the establishment of such a zone in the Middle East consistent with paragraphs 60 to 63, and in particular paragraph 63 *(d)*, of the Final Document of the Tenth Special Session of the General Assembly,

Emphasizing the basic provisions of the above-mentioned resolutions, which call upon all parties directly concerned to consider taking the practical and urgent steps required for the implementation of the proposal to establish a nuclear-weapon-free zone in the region of the Middle East and, pending and during the establishment of such a zone, to declare solemnly that they will refrain, on a reciprocal basis, from producing, acquiring or in any other way possessing nuclear weapons and nuclear explosive devices and from permitting the stationing of nuclear weapons on their territory by any third party, to agree to place all their nuclear facilities under International Atomic Energy Agency safeguards and to declare their support for the establishment of the zone and to deposit such declarations with the Security Council for consideration, as appropriate,

Reaffirming the inalienable right of all States to acquire and develop nuclear energy for peaceful purposes,

Emphasizing also the need for appropriate measures on the question of the prohibition of military attacks on nuclear facilities,

Bearing in mind the consensus reached by the General Assembly at its thirty-fifth session that the establishment of a nuclear-weapon-free zone in the region of the Middle East would greatly enhance international peace and security,

Desirous of building on that consensus so that substantial progress can be made towards establishing a nuclear-weapon-free zone in the region of the Middle East,

Welcoming all initiatives leading to general and complete disarmament, including in the region of the Middle East, and in particular on the establishment therein of a zone free of weapons of mass destruction, including nuclear weapons,

Emphasizing the essential role of the United Nations in the establishment of a nuclear-weapon-free zone in the region of the Middle East,

Having examined the report of the Secretary-General on the implementation of resolution 46/30,

1. *Urges* all parties directly concerned to consider seriously taking the practical and urgent steps required for the implementation of the proposal to establish a nuclear-weapon-free zone in the region of the Middle East in accordance with the relevant resolutions of the General Assembly, and, as a means of promoting this objective, invites the countries concerned to adhere to the Treaty on the Non-Proliferation of Nuclear Weapons;

2. *Calls upon* all countries of the region that have not done so, pending the establishment of the zone, to agree to place all their nuclear activities under International Atomic Energy Agency safeguards;

3. *Takes note* of resolution GC(XXXVI)/RES/601 of the General Conference of the International Atomic Energy Agency concerning the application of Agency safeguards in the Middle East;

4. *Invites* all countries of the region, pending the establishment of a nuclear-weapon-free zone in the region of the Middle East, to declare their support for establishing such a zone, consistent with paragraph 63 *(d)* of the Final Document of the Tenth Special Session of the General Assembly, and to deposit those declarations with the Security Council;

5. *Also invites* those countries, pending the establishment of the zone, not to develop, produce, test or otherwise acquire nuclear weapons or permit the stationing on their territories, or territories under their control, of nuclear weapons or nuclear explosive devices;

6. *Invites* the nuclear-weapon States and all other States to render their assistance in the establishment of the zone and at the same time to refrain from any action that runs counter to both the letter and the spirit of the present resolution;

7. *Takes note* of the report of the Secretary-General;

8. *Invites* all parties to consider the appropriate means that may contribute towards the goal of general and complete disarmament and the establishment of a zone free of weapons of mass destruction in the region of the Middle East;

9. *Requests* the Secretary-General to pursue further consultations with the States of the region and other concerned States, in accordance with paragraph 7 of resolution 46/30, and taking into account the evolving situation in the region, and to seek from those States their views on the measures outlined in chapters III and IV of the study annexed to his report[a] or other relevant measures, in order to move towards the establishment of a nuclear-weapon-free zone in the region of the Middle East;

10. *Also requests* the Secretary-General to submit to the General Assembly at its forty-eighth session a report on the implementation of the present resolution;

11. *Decides* to include in the provisional agenda of its forty-eighth session the item entitled "Establishment of a nuclear-weapon-free zone in the region of the Middle East".

---

[a]A/45/435.

General Assembly resolution 47/48

9 December 1992   Meeting 81   Adopted without vote

Approved by First Committee (A/47/685) without vote, 12 November (meeting 32); 2-nation draft (A/C.1/47/L.11); agenda item 55.
Sponsors: Armenia, Egypt.
Meeting numbers. GA 47th session: 1st Committee 3-21, 28, 32; plenary 81.

Israeli nuclear armament

In response to a General Assembly resolution of 1991,[92] the Secretary-General in October submitted a report containing the text of a resolution adopted on 25 September by the IAEA General Conference on the application of IAEA safeguards in the Middle East and a report of the IAEA Director General on the same subject.[93]

GENERAL ASSEMBLY ACTION

On 9 December 1992, the General Assembly, on the recommendation of the First Committee, adopted **resolution 47/55** by recorded vote.

Israeli nuclear armament

The General Assembly,

Bearing in mind its previous resolutions on Israeli nuclear armament, the latest of which is resolution 46/39 of 6 December 1991,

Recalling its resolution 44/108 of 15 December 1989, in which, *inter alia*, it called for placing all nuclear facilities in the region under International Atomic Energy

Agency safeguards, pending the establishment of a nuclear-weapon-free zone in the Middle East,

Recalling also that the Security Council, in its resolution 487(1981), called upon Israel urgently to place all its nuclear facilities under Agency safeguards,

Taking note of relevant resolutions adopted by the General Conference of the International Atomic Energy Agency, the latest of which is resolution GC(XXXVI)/RES/601 of 25 September 1992,

Taking into consideration section D, chapter II, of the Final Document on international security and disarmament adopted by the Tenth Conference of Heads of State or Government of Non-Aligned Countries, held at Jakarta from 1 to 6 September 1992,[a] and in particular its paragraph 52, which relates to Israel's nuclear capabilities,

Deeply alarmed by the information with regard to the continuing production, development and acquisition of nuclear weapons by Israel,

Concerned at the cooperation between Israel and South Africa in the military nuclear fields,

1. *Deplores* Israel's refusal to renounce possession of nuclear weapons;

2. *Urges* Israel to accede to the Treaty on the Non-Proliferation of Nuclear Weapons;

3. *Reaffirms* that Israel should promptly apply Security Council resolution 487(1981), in which the Council, *inter alia*, requested it to place all its nuclear facilities under International Atomic Energy Agency safeguards and to refrain from attacking or threatening to attack nuclear facilities;

4. *Calls upon* all States and organizations not to cooperate with or give assistance to Israel with the aim of enhancing its nuclear-weapons capability;

5. *Requests* the International Atomic Energy Agency to inform the Secretary-General of any steps Israel may take to place its nuclear facilities under Agency safeguards;

6. *Requests* the Secretary-General to follow closely Israeli nuclear activities and to report thereon to the General Assembly at its forty-eighth session;

7. *Decides* to include in the provisional agenda of its forty-eighth session the item entitled ''Israeli nuclear armament''.

---

[a]A/47/675-S/24816.

General Assembly resolution 47/55

9 December 1992   Meeting 81   64-3-90 (recorded vote)

Approved by First Committee (A/47/694) by recorded vote (54-3-70), 16 November (meeting 34); 20-nation draft (A/C.1/47/L.9/Rev.1); agenda item 64.

Sponsors: Algeria, Bahrain, Djibouti, Egypt, Iraq, Jordan, Kuwait, Libyan Arab Jamahiriya, Lebanon, Malaysia, Mauritania, Morocco, Oman, Qatar, Saudi Arabia, Sudan, Syrian Arab Republic, Tunisia, United Arab Emirates, Yemen.

Meeting numbers. GA 47th session: 1st Committee 3-21, 26, 34; plenary 81.

Recorded vote in Assembly as follows:

In favour: Afghanistan, Algeria, Angola, Azerbaijan, Bahrain, Bangladesh, Benin, Botswana, Brunei Darussalam, Burkina Faso, Burundi, Chad, China, Comoros, Cuba, Cyprus, Democratic People's Republic of Korea, Djibouti, Egypt, Gabon, Ghana, Guinea, Indonesia, Iran, Iraq, Jordan, Kuwait, Lao People's Democratic Republic, Lebanon, Lesotho, Libyan Arab Jamahiriya, Madagascar, Malaysia, Maldives, Mali, Mauritania, Mauritius, Morocco, Namibia, Niger, Nigeria, Oman, Pakistan, Philippines, Qatar, Sao Tome and Principe, Saudi Arabia, Senegal, Sri Lanka, Sudan, Swaziland, Syrian Arab Republic, Thailand, Trinidad and Tobago, Tunisia, Turkey, Uganda, United Arab Emirates, United Republic of Tanzania, Vanuatu, Viet Nam, Yemen, Zambia, Zimbabwe.

Against: Israel, Romania, United States.

Abstaining: Antigua and Barbuda, Argentina, Australia, Austria, Bahamas, Barbados, Belarus, Belgium, Belize, Bhutan, Bolivia, Brazil, Bulgaria, Cameroon, Canada, Central African Republic, Chile, Colombia, Congo, Costa Rica, Côte d'Ivoire, Czechoslovakia, Denmark, Dominica, Dominican Republic, Ecuador, Estonia, Ethiopia, Fiji, Finland, France, Germany, Greece, Grenada, Guatemala, Guyana, Haiti, Honduras, Hungary, Iceland, India, Ireland, Italy, Jamaica, Japan, Kenya, Kyrgyzstan, Latvia, Liberia, Liechtenstein, Lithuania, Luxembourg, Malawi, Malta, Marshall Islands, Mexico, Micronesia, Mongolia, Netherlands, New Zealand, Nicaragua, Norway, Panama, Papua New Guinea, Paraguay, Peru, Poland, Portugal, Republic of Korea, Republic of Moldova, Russian Federation, Rwanda, Saint Kitts and Nevis, Saint Lucia, Saint Vincent and the Grenadines, Samoa, San Marino, Singapore, Slovenia, Solomon Islands, Spain, Suriname, Sweden, Tajikistan, Togo, Ukraine, United Kingdom, Uruguay, Venezuela, Zaire.

South Asia

In accordance with a 1991 General Assembly request,[94] the Secretary-General in July submitted a report summarizing the views of one Government (United Kingdom) on the establishment of a nuclear-weapon-free zone in South Asia.[95]

GENERAL ASSEMBLY ACTION

On 9 December 1992, the General Assembly, on the recommendation of the First Committee, adopted **resolution 47/49** by recorded vote.

Establishment of a nuclear-weapon-free zone in South Asia

The General Assembly,

Recalling its resolutions 3265 B (XXIX) of 9 December 1974, 3476 B (XXX) of 11 December 1975, 31/73 of 10 December 1976, 32/83 of 12 December 1977, 33/65 of 14 December 1978, 34/78 of 11 December 1979, 35/148 of 12 December 1980, 36/88 of 9 December 1981, 37/76 of 9 December 1982, 38/65 of 15 December 1983, 39/55 of 12 December 1984, 40/83 of 12 December 1985, 41/49 of 3 December 1986, 42/29 of 30 November 1987, 43/66 of 7 December 1988, 44/109 of 15 December 1989, 45/53 of 4 December 1990 and 46/31 of 6 December 1991 concerning the establishment of a nuclear-weapon-free zone in South Asia,

Reiterating its conviction that the establishment of nuclear-weapon-free zones in various regions of the world is one of the measures that can contribute effectively to the objectives of non-proliferation of nuclear weapons and general and complete disarmament,

Believing that the establishment of a nuclear-weapon-free zone in South Asia, as in other regions, will assist in the strengthening of the security of the States of the region against the use or threat of use of nuclear weapons,

Taking note with appreciation of the declarations issued at the highest level by Governments of South Asian States that are developing their peaceful nuclear programmes, reaffirming their undertaking not to acquire or manufacture nuclear weapons and to devote their nuclear programmes exclusively to the economic and social advancement of their peoples,

Welcoming the recent proposal for the conclusion of a bilateral or regional nuclear-test-ban agreement in South Asia,

Taking note of the proposal to convene, under the auspices of the United Nations, a conference on nuclear non-proliferation in South Asia as soon as possible, with the participation of the regional and other concerned States,

Taking note also of the proposal to hold consultations among five nations with a view to ensuring nuclear non-proliferation in the region,

Considering that the eventual participation of other States as appropriate in this process could be useful,

Bearing in mind the provisions of paragraphs 60 to 63 of the Final Document of the Tenth Special Session of the General Assembly regarding the establishment of nuclear-weapon-free zones, including in the region of South Asia,

Taking note further of the report of the Secretary-General,

1. *Reaffirms* its endorsement, in principle, of the concept of a nuclear-weapon-free zone in South Asia;

2. *Urges once again* the States of South Asia to continue to make all possible efforts to establish a nuclear-weapon-free zone in South Asia and to refrain, in the meantime, from any action contrary to that objective;

3. *Calls upon* the nuclear-weapon States that have not done so to respond positively to this proposal and to extend the necessary cooperation in the efforts to establish a nuclear-weapon-free zone in South Asia;

4. *Requests* the Secretary-General to communicate with the States of the region and other concerned States in order to ascertain their views on the issue and to promote consultations among them with a view to exploring the best possibilities of furthering the efforts for the establishment of a nuclear-weapon-free zone in South Asia;

5. *Also requests* the Secretary-General to report on the subject to the General Assembly at its forty-eighth session;

6. *Decides* to include in the provisional agenda of its forty-eighth session the item entitled "Establishment of a nuclear-weapon-free zone in South Asia".

General Assembly resolution 47/49

9 December 1992   Meeting 81   144-3-13 (recorded vote)

Approved by First Committee (A/47/686) by recorded vote (117-2-12), 12 November (meeting 32); 2-nation draft (A/C.1/47/L.19); agenda item 56.
Sponsors: Bangladesh, Pakistan.
Meeting numbers. GA 47th session: 1st Committee 3-21, 32; plenary 81.

Recorded vote in Assembly as follows:

In favour: Afghanistan, Angola, Argentina, Armenia, Australia, Austria, Azerbaijan, Bahamas, Bahrain, Bangladesh, Barbados, Belarus, Belgium, Belize, Benin, Bolivia, Botswana, Brunei Darussalam, Bulgaria, Burkina Faso, Burundi, Cameroon, Canada, Cape Verde, Central African Republic, Chad, Chile, China, Colombia, Comoros, Congo, Costa Rica, Côte d'Ivoire, Czechoslovakia, Denmark, Djibouti, Dominica, Dominican Republic, Ecuador, Egypt, El Salvador, Estonia, Fiji, Finland, France, Gabon, Gambia, Germany, Ghana, Greece, Grenada, Guatemala, Guinea, Guinea-Bissau, Guyana, Haiti, Honduras, Iceland, Iran, Iraq, Ireland, Israel, Italy, Jamaica, Japan, Jordan, Kazakhstan, Kenya, Kuwait, Latvia, Lebanon, Lesotho, Liberia, Libyan Arab Jamahiriya, Liechtenstein, Lithuania, Luxembourg, Malaysia, Maldives, Mali, Malta, Marshall Islands, Mauritania, Mexico, Micronesia, Morocco, Mozambique, Namibia, Nepal, Netherlands, New Zealand, Nicaragua, Niger, Nigeria, Norway, Oman, Pakistan, Panama, Papua New Guinea, Paraguay, Peru, Philippines, Poland, Portugal, Qatar, Republic of Moldova, Romania, Russian Federation, Rwanda, Saint Kitts and Nevis, Saint Lucia, Saint Vincent and the Grenadines, Samoa, San Marino, Sao Tome and Principe, Saudi Arabia, Senegal, Sierra Leone, Singapore, Slovenia, Spain, Sri Lanka, Sudan, Suriname, Swaziland, Sweden, Tajikistan, Thailand, Togo, Trinidad and Tobago, Tunisia, Turkey, Uganda, Ukraine, United Arab Emirates, United Kingdom, United Republic of Tanzania, United States, Uruguay, Vanuatu, Venezuela, Zaire, Zambia, Zimbabwe.

Against: Bhutan, India, Mauritius.

Abstaining: Algeria, Brazil, Cuba, Cyprus, Ethiopia, Indonesia, Lao People's Democratic Republic, Madagascar, Myanmar, Republic of Korea, Seychelles, Viet Nam, Yemen.

Declaration of the Indian Ocean as a Zone of Peace

Activities of the Committee on the Indian Ocean. At its 1992 session (New York, 18-22 May),[96] the Ad Hoc Committee on the Indian Ocean continued to consider various aspects of holding a United Nations Conference on the Indian Ocean—a necessary step for achieving the implementation of the 1971 Declaration of the Indian Ocean as a Zone of Peace.[97]

The Ad Hoc Committee, acting as the preparatory body for the Conference, mainly dealt with the implementation of a 1991 General Assembly resolution[98] by which the Assembly had decided to convene the first of three stages of the Conference in 1993, or as soon as possible, at Colombo, Sri Lanka. In addition, the Assembly had called for the participation in the Conference of the permanent members of the Security Council and the major maritime users of the Indian Ocean. Following consultations with three of the permanent members of the Security Council—France, the United Kingdom and the United States—and with some of the major maritime users of the Indian Ocean, the Chairman informed the Committee on 18 May that those States would not find it possible to participate in a conference based on the 1971 Declaration, as they believed that the Declaration had been overtaken by positive developments in international political relations. Their position was that there was no longer rivalry between the great Powers in the Indian Ocean. The Committee, therefore, felt that it might not be possible to hold the Conference. It was of the view that the Assembly might wish to consider new, alternative approaches to establishing a zone of peace in the Indian Ocean.

GENERAL ASSEMBLY ACTION

On 9 December 1992, the General Assembly, on the recommendation of the First Committee, adopted **resolution 47/59** by recorded vote.

Implementation of the Declaration of the Indian Ocean as a Zone of Peace

The General Assembly,

Recalling the Declaration of the Indian Ocean as a Zone of Peace, contained in its resolution 2832(XXVI) of 16 December 1971, and recalling also its resolution 46/49 of 9 December 1991 and other relevant resolutions,

Recalling also the report on the Meeting of the Littoral and Hinterland States of the Indian Ocean held in July 1979,

Recalling further paragraphs 15 and 16, chapter III, of the Final Document adopted by the Tenth Conference of Heads of State or Government of Non-Aligned Countries, held at Jakarta from 1 to 6 September 1992,[a]

Affirming the importance of the establishment of the Indian Ocean as a zone of peace to achieve the goals contained in the Declaration of the Indian Ocean as a Zone of Peace and as considered at the Meeting of the Littoral and Hinterland States of the Indian Ocean,

Welcoming the positive developments in international political relations, which offer opportunities for enhanc-

---

[a]A/47/675-S/24816.

ing peace, security and cooperation, and expressing the hope that the new spirit of international cooperation will be reflected in the establishment of a zone of peace in the Indian Ocean and in the work of the Ad Hoc Committee on the Indian Ocean to that end,

Having considered the report of the Ad Hoc Committee on the Indian Ocean,

Noting with appreciation the offer made by the Government of Sri Lanka to host the United Nations Conference on the Indian Ocean at Colombo,

Noting also that it may not be possible to convene the first stage of the United Nations Conference on the Indian Ocean in accordance with resolution 46/49, and urging that consideration be given to the timing of such a conference at Colombo at the appropriate time,

Desirous of continuing its efforts for the establishment of a zone of peace in the Indian Ocean,

Considering the need for new alternative approaches for the establishment of a zone of peace in the Indian Ocean,

1. *Takes note* of the report of the Ad Hoc Committee on the Indian Ocean;

2. *Requests* the Ad Hoc Committee to consider new alternative approaches leading to the achievement of the goals contained in the Declaration of the Indian Ocean as a Zone of Peace and as considered at the Meeting of the Littoral and Hinterland States of the Indian Ocean held in July 1979, taking into account the changing international situation;

3. *Also requests* the Ad Hoc Committee to address the complex ramifications of the issues involved and differing perceptions on these issues as well as the future role of the Ad Hoc Committee and to make recommendations for consideration by the General Assembly at its forty-eighth session;

4. *Decides* to convene, as early as possible thereafter, the United Nations Conference on the Indian Ocean at Colombo with the participation of the permanent members of the Security Council and the major maritime users of the Indian Ocean;

5. *Calls upon* the permanent members of the Security Council and the major maritime users of the Indian Ocean to participate in the work of the Ad Hoc Committee;

6. *Requests* the Ad Hoc Committee to hold a session during 1993 with a duration of not more than ten working days;

7. *Also requests* the Ad Hoc Committee to submit to the General Assembly at its forty-eighth session a comprehensive report on the implementation of the present resolution;

8. *Requests* the Secretary-General to continue to render all necessary assistance to the Ad Hoc Committee, including the provision of summary records;

9. *Decides* to include in the provisional agenda of its forty-eighth session the item entitled "Implementation of the Declaration of the Indian Ocean as a Zone of Peace".

General Assembly resolution 47/59

9 December 1992   Meeting 81   129-3-35 (recorded vote)

Approved by First Committee (A/47/698) by recorded vote (98-3-31), 16 November (meeting 34); draft by Indonesia, for Non-Aligned Movement (A/C.1/47/L.31/Rev.1); agenda item 68.
Financial implications. ACABQ, A/47/7/Add.11; 5th Committee, A/47/762; S-G, A/C.1/47/L.49, A/C.5/47/52.
Meeting numbers. GA 47th session: 1st Committee 3-21, 32, 34; 5th Committee 38; plenary 81.

Recorded vote in Assembly as follows:

In favour: Afghanistan, Algeria, Angola, Antigua and Barbuda, Argentina, Armenia, Azerbaijan, Bahamas, Bahrain, Bangladesh, Barbados, Belarus, Belize, Benin, Bhutan, Bolivia, Botswana, Brazil, Brunei Darussalam, Burkina Faso, Burundi, Cameroon, Cape Verde, Central African Republic, Chad, Chile, China, Colombia, Comoros, Congo, Costa Rica, Côte d'Ivoire, Cuba, Cyprus, Democratic People's Republic of Korea, Djibouti, Dominica, Dominican Republic, Ecuador, Egypt, El Salvador, Ethiopia, Gabon, Gambia, Ghana, Grenada, Guatemala, Guinea, Guinea-Bissau, Guyana, Haiti, Honduras, India, Indonesia, Iran, Iraq, Jamaica, Jordan, Kazakhstan, Kenya, Kuwait, Kyrgyzstan, Lao People's Democratic Republic, Lebanon, Lesotho, Liberia, Libyan Arab Jamahiriya, Madagascar, Malawi, Malaysia, Maldives, Mali, Malta, Marshall Islands, Mauritania, Mauritius, Mexico, Micronesia, Mongolia, Morocco, Mozambique, Myanmar, Namibia, Nepal, Nicaragua, Niger, Nigeria, Oman, Pakistan, Panama, Papua New Guinea, Paraguay, Peru, Philippines, Qatar, Russian Federation, Rwanda, Saint Kitts and Nevis, Saint Lucia, Saint Vincent and the Grenadines, Samoa, Sao Tome and Principe, Saudi Arabia, Senegal, Seychelles, Sierra Leone, Singapore, Sri Lanka, Sudan, Suriname, Swaziland, Syrian Arab Republic, Thailand, Togo, Trinidad and Tobago, Tunisia, Turkmenistan, Uganda, Ukraine, United Arab Emirates, United Republic of Tanzania, Uruguay, Vanuatu, Venezuela, Viet Nam, Yemen, Zaire, Zambia, Zimbabwe.

Against: France, United Kingdom, United States.

Abstaining: Australia, Austria, Belgium, Bulgaria, Canada, Czechoslovakia, Denmark, Estonia, Fiji, Finland, Germany, Greece, Hungary, Iceland, Ireland, Israel, Italy, Japan, Latvia, Liechtenstein, Lithuania, Luxembourg, Netherlands, New Zealand, Norway, Poland, Portugal, Republic of Korea, Republic of Moldova, Romania, San Marino, Slovenia, Spain, Sweden, Turkey.

Conventional armaments and advanced technology

Efforts to curb the conventional arms race and prevent the development of more sophisticated weapons and weapons systems continued in 1992, with attention focusing on the control of exports and imports of arms, including illicit traffic; transfers of weapons, with special emphasis on the transfer of high technology with military applications; and restriction of the use of inhumane weapons.

International arms transfers

Report of the Secretary-General. Pursuant to a 1991 General Assembly request,[99] the Secretary-General submitted information received from 14 Member States concerning their national legislation and regulations on arms exports, imports and procurement and their administrative procedures regarding the authorization of arms transfers and prevention of illicit arms trade.[100] The report also contained information on seizures of arms and military equipment destined for destabilizing activities. Information provided by one other Member State (Sweden) was provided separately.[46]

On 9 December 1992, the Assembly, by **decision 47/419,** welcomed the information provided by Member States contained in the Secretary-General's report and invited those that had not yet done so to convey to him their views on the subject. It decided to include the item "International arms transfers" on its 1993 agenda.

Science and technology

In accordance with a 1991 General Assembly request,[101] the Secretary-General provided information received from 13 Member States on the transfer of high technology with military applications.[102] One other Member State (Denmark) provided information on the subject separately.[100]

By a note of 20 October,[103] the Secretariat informed Member States that, pursuant to a 1990 General Assembly resolution,[104] which recommended that the United Nations collect and disseminate information on technological developments in the area of science and technology for disarmament, information had been received from Member States and was available in the reference library of the United Nations Office for Disarmament Affairs.

Disarmament Commission consideration. The Disarmament Commission[34] established a working group to consider the agenda item on the role of science and technology in the context of international security, disarmament and related fields. The Working Group met from 22 April to 8 May and held 10 meetings in addition to informal consultations. It continued a structured debate on four aspects of the item, including scientific and technological developments and their impact on international security; science and technology for disarmament; the role of science and technology in other related fields; and the transfer of high technology with military applications. It was suggested that it might be necessary to further focus the Group's work in order to develop concrete recommendations.

Before the Commission were working papers submitted in 1991[105] and papers submitted in 1992 by Brazil[106] on the international transfer of sensitive technologies; Canada[107] on science and technology for verification purposes; Colombia[108] on scientific and technological developments and their impact on international security and the role of science and technology in other related fields; and Portugal, on behalf of the member States of EC,[109] on the role of science and technology in the context of implementing disarmament agreements.

Report of the Secretary-General. As requested by the General Assembly in 1990,[110] the Secretary-General in August submitted a report describing activities undertaken by the Disarmament Commission and the United Nations Office for Disarmament Affairs to develop a method to assess emerging new technologies.[111] He noted that the Office for Disarmament Affairs was setting up an informal network of experts on science and technology and that the subject was under discussion in the Disarmament Commission. In the light of those activities, he considered that it would be premature for any further action to be taken to develop a framework for technological assessment.

GENERAL ASSEMBLY ACTION

On 9 December 1992, the General Assembly, on the recommendation of the First Committee, adopted **resolution 47/43** by recorded vote.

Scientific and technological developments and their impact on international security

The General Assembly,

Recalling that at its tenth special session, the first special session devoted to disarmament, it unanimously stressed the importance of both qualitative and quantitative measures in the process of disarmament,

Recognizing that scientific and technological developments can have both civilian and military applications and that progress in science and technology for civilian applications needs to be maintained and encouraged,

Noting with concern the potential in technological advances for application to military purposes, which could lead to more sophisticated weapons and new weapon systems,

Stressing the interests of the international community in the subject and the need to follow closely the scientific and technological developments that may have a negative impact on the security environment and on the process of arms limitation and disarmament and to channel scientific and technological developments for beneficial purposes,

Emphasizing that the proposal contained in its resolution 43/77 A of 7 December 1988 is without prejudice to research and development efforts being undertaken for peaceful purposes,

Noting the results of the United Nations conference on New Trends in Science and Technology: Implications for International Peace and Security, held at Sendai, Japan, from 16 to 19 April 1990,[a] and recognizing, in this regard, the need for the scientific and policy communities to work together in dealing with the complex implications of technological change,

1. *Takes note* of the report of the Secretary-General entitled "Scientific and technological developments and their impact on international security";[a]

2. *Takes note also* of the interim report of the Secretary-General submitted in pursuance of resolution 45/60 of 4 December 1990;

3. *Fully agrees* that:

(a) The international community needs to position itself better to follow the nature and direction of technological change;

(b) The United Nations can serve as a catalyst and a clearing-house for ideas to this purpose;

4. *Requests* the Secretary-General to continue to follow scientific and technological developments in order to make an assessment of emerging "new technologies" and to submit to the General Assembly at its forty-eighth session a framework for technology assessment guided, *inter alia*, by the criteria suggested in his report;

5. *Decides* to include in the provisional agenda of its forty-eighth session the item entitled "Scientific and technological developments and their impact on international security".

---

[a]A/45/568.

General Assembly resolution 47/43

9 December 1992   Meeting 81   128-3-30 (recorded vote)

Approved by First Committee (A/47/680) by recorded vote (104-3-28), 16 November (meeting 34); 10-nation draft (A/C.1/47/L.32); agenda item 50.

Sponsors: Afghanistan, Belarus, Bhutan, Bolivia, Costa Rica, Hungary, India, Indonesia, Sri Lanka, Venezuela.

Meeting numbers. GA 47th session: 1st Committee, 3-21, 28, 34; plenary 81.

Recorded vote in Assembly as follows:

In favour: Afghanistan, Algeria, Angola, Argentina, Armenia, Australia, Azerbaijan, Bahamas, Bahrain, Bangladesh, Barbados, Belarus, Belize, Benin, Bhutan, Bolivia, Botswana, Brazil, Brunei Darussalam, Burkina Faso, Burundi, Cameroon, Cape Verde, Central African Republic, Chad, Chile, China, Colombia, Comoros, Congo, Costa Rica, Côte d'Ivoire, Cuba, Cyprus, Democratic People's Republic of Korea, Djibouti, Dominican Republic, Ecuador, Egypt, El Salvador, Ethiopia, Fiji, Gabon, Gambia, Grenada, Guatemala, Guinea, Guinea-Bissau, Guyana, Haiti, Honduras, Hungary, India, Indonesia, Iran, Iraq, Ireland, Jamaica, Jordan, Kazakhstan, Kenya, Kuwait, Lao People's Democratic Republic, Lebanon, Lesotho, Liberia, Libyan Arab Jamahiriya, Madagascar, Malaysia, Maldives, Mali, Marshall Islands, Mauritania, Mauritius, Mexico, Micronesia, Mongolia, Morocco, Mozambique, Myanmar, Namibia, Nepal, New Zealand, Nicaragua, Niger, Nigeria, Oman, Pakistan, Panama, Papua New Guinea, Paraguay, Peru, Philippines, Qatar, Republic of Korea, Russian Federation, Rwanda, Saint Kitts and Nevis, Saint Lucia, Saint Vincent and the Grenadines, Samoa, Saudi Arabia, Senegal, Seychelles, Sierra Leone, Singapore, Sri Lanka, Sudan, Suriname, Swaziland, Syrian Arab Republic, Tajikistan, Thailand, Togo, Trinidad and Tobago, Tunisia, Uganda, Ukraine, United Arab Emirates, United Republic of Tanzania, Uruguay, Vanuatu, Venezuela, Viet Nam, Yemen, Zaire, Zambia, Zimbabwe.

Against: France, United Kingdom, United States.

Abstaining: Austria, Belgium, Bulgaria, Canada, Czechoslovakia, Denmark, Estonia, Finland, Germany, Greece, Iceland, Israel, Italy, Japan, Latvia, Liechtenstein, Lithuania, Luxembourg, Malta, Netherlands, Norway, Poland, Portugal, Republic of Moldova, Romania, San Marino, Slovenia, Spain, Sweden, Turkey.

Also on 9 December, the General Assembly, on the recommendation of the First Committee, adopted **resolution 47/44** without vote.

The role of science and technology in the context of international security, disarmament and other related fields

The General Assembly,

Recalling its resolutions 45/61 of 4 December 1990 and 46/38 D of 6 December 1991,

Taking note of the report of the Disarmament Commission on its 1992 substantive session, in particular on the work of Working Group IV on agenda item 7, entitled "The role of science and technology in the context of international security, disarmament and other related fields",

Taking note also of the report of the Conference on Disarmament on its 1992 substantive session, in particular on the work on the agenda item entitled "Transparency in armaments", which includes, in response to resolution 46/36 L of 9 December 1991, *inter alia*, the subject of the elaboration of practical means to increase openness and transparency related to the transfer of high technology with military applications,

Recognizing that progress in the application of science and technology contributes substantially to the implementation of arms control and disarmament agreements, *inter alia*, in the fields of weapons disposal, military conversion and verification,

Recognizing also that norms or guidelines for the transfer of high technology with military applications should take into account legitimate requirements for the maintenance of international peace and security, while ensuring that they do not deny access to high-technology products, services and know-how for peaceful purposes,

Noting the interest of the international community in cooperation in the fields of disarmament-related science and technology and the transfer of high technology with military applications,

1. *Calls upon* the Disarmament Commission to intensify its work on agenda item 7 and to submit as soon as possible specific recommendations on this matter to the General Assembly;

2. *Requests* the Conference on Disarmament to pursue constructively in response to resolution 46/36 L its work on the agenda item entitled "Transparency in armaments", which includes consideration of the elaboration of practical means to increase openness and transparency related to the transfer of high technology with military applications;

3. *Invites* Member States to undertake additional efforts to apply science and technology for disarmament-related purposes and to make disarmament-related technologies available to interested States;

4. *Also invites* Member States to widen multilateral dialogue, bearing in mind the proposal for seeking universally acceptable international norms or guidelines that would regulate international transfers of high technology with military applications;

5. *Decides* to include in the provisional agenda of its forty-eighth session an item entitled "The role of science and technology in the context of international security, disarmament and other related fields".

General Assembly resolution 47/44

9 December 1992   Meeting 81   Adopted without vote

Approved by First Committee (A/47/681) without vote, 16 November (meeting 34); 36-nation draft (A/C.1/47/L.15/Rev.1); agenda items 51 & 63 (i).

Sponsors: Argentina, Australia, Austria, Belgium, Bolivia, Brazil, Bulgaria, Canada, Chile, Colombia, Costa Rica, Czechoslovakia, Denmark, Ecuador, Finland, France, Germany, Greece, Hungary, Ireland, Italy, Luxembourg, Nepal, Netherlands, New Zealand, Nigeria, Norway, Peru, Poland, Portugal, Romania, Russian Federation, Samoa, Spain, Uruguay, Venezuela.

Meeting numbers. GA 47th session: 1st Committee 3-21, 28, 34; plenary 81.

Conventional disarmament on a regional scale

In response to a 1991 General Assembly decision,[112] the Secretary-General submitted a report with later addenda presenting the views of four Member States and the United Kingdom on behalf of the member States of EC on conventional disarmament on a regional scale.[113]

On 9 December, the Assembly adopted **decision 47/420**, by which it welcomed the Secretary-General's report and invited Member States which had not done so to convey their views on the matter to him and decided to include the item in its 1993 agenda.

Convention on excessively injurious conventional weapons and its Protocol

The number of States parties stood at 35, as at 31 December,[114] to the 1980 Convention on Prohibitions or Restrictions on the Use of Certain Conventional Weapons Which May Be Deemed to Be Excessively Injurious or to Have Indiscriminate Effects and its three Protocols (dealing with non-detectable fragments; mines, booby traps and other devices; and incendiary weapons).[115] In 1992, Germany and Greece ratified the Convention and Niger acceded to it. Slovenia became a successor State to the Convention. The Convention and Protocols entered into force in 1983.[116]

In the First Committee, a representative of the International Committee of the Red Cross (ICRC) stressed the urgent need to encourage universal ratification of the Convention and to give serious thought to its applicability to non-international armed conflicts, since the majority of ongoing conflicts involved both internal and international elements. ICRC was studying the problems of the potential use of blinding laser weapons and would publish, in 1993, reports of meetings of experts on the subject. It suggested that measures to strengthen the Convention and the eventual adoption of new protocols could be undertaken at a review conference, as provided for in the Convention. Ireland, the Netherlands and Sweden expressed support for that position and suggested that consultations should be carried out with a view to convening a review conference, as 1993 would mark the tenth anniversary of the Convention's entry into force.

GENERAL ASSEMBLY ACTION

On 9 December 1992, the General Assembly, on the recommendation of the First Committee, adopted **resolution 47/56** without vote.

Convention on Prohibitions or Restrictions on the Use of Certain Conventional Weapons Which May Be Deemed to Be Excessively Injurious or to Have Indiscriminate Effects

The General Assembly,

Recalling its resolutions 32/152 of 19 December 1977, 35/153 of 12 December 1980, 36/93 of 9 December 1981, 37/79 of 9 December 1982, 38/66 of 15 December 1983, 39/56 of 12 December 1984, 40/84 of 12 December 1985, 41/50 of 3 December 1986, 42/30 of 30 November 1987, 43/67 of 7 December 1988, 45/64 of 4 December 1990 and 46/40 of 6 December 1991,

Recalling with satisfaction the adoption, on 10 October 1980, of the Convention on Prohibitions or Restrictions on the Use of Certain Conventional Weapons Which May Be Deemed to Be Excessively Injurious or to Have Indiscriminate Effects, together with the Protocol on Non-Detectable Fragments (Protocol I), the Protocol on Prohibitions or Restrictions on the Use of Mines, Booby Traps and Other Devices (Protocol II) and the Protocol on Prohibitions or Restrictions on the Use of Incendiary Weapons (Protocol III),

Reaffirming its conviction that general agreement on the prohibition or restriction of use of specific conventional weapons would significantly reduce the suffering of civilian populations and of combatants,

Taking note with satisfaction of the report of the Secretary-General,[a]

1. *Notes with satisfaction* that an increasing number of States have either signed, ratified, accepted or acceded to the Convention on Prohibitions or Restrictions on the Use of Certain Conventional Weapons Which May Be Deemed to Be Excessively Injurious or to Have Indiscriminate Effects, which was opened for signature in New York on 10 April 1981;

2. *Also notes with satisfaction* that, consequent upon the fulfilment of the conditions set out in article 5 of the Convention, the Convention and the three Protocols annexed thereto entered into force on 2 December 1983;

3. *Urges* all States that have not yet done so to exert their best endeavours to become parties to the Convention and the Protocols annexed thereto as early as possible, as well as successor States to take appropriate action so as ultimately to obtain universality of adherence;

4. *Stresses* that, under article 8 of the Convention, conferences may be convened to consider amendments to the Convention or any of the annexed Protocols, to consider additional protocols relating to other categories of conventional weapons not covered by the existing annexed Protocols, or to review the scope and operation of the Convention and the Protocols annexed thereto and to consider any proposal for amendments to the Convention or to the existing Protocols and any proposals for additional protocols relating to other categories of conventional weapons not covered by the existing Protocols;

5. *Notes,* taking into account the nature of the Convention, the potential of the International Committee of the Red Cross to consider questions pursuant to the Convention;

6. *Requests* the Secretary-General as depositary of the Convention and its three annexed Protocols to inform the General Assembly from time to time of the state of adherence to the Convention and its Protocols;

7. *Decides* to include in the provisional agenda of its forty-eighth session the item entitled "Convention on Prohibitions or Restrictions on the Use of Certain Conventional Weapons Which May Be Deemed to Be Excessively Injurious or to Have Indiscriminate Effects".

---

[a]A/44/569.

General Assembly resolution 47/56

9 December 1992   Meeting 81   Adopted without vote

Approved by First Committee (A/47/695) without vote, 12 November (meeting 31); 19-nation draft (A/C.1/47/L.21); agenda item 65.

Sponsors: Australia, Austria, Belarus, Belgium, Costa Rica, Cuba, Denmark, Finland, France, Greece, Iceland, India, Ireland, Netherlands, New Zealand, Norway, Russian Federation, Sweden, Viet Nam.

Meeting numbers. GA 47th session: 1st Committee 3-21, 26, 31; plenary 81.

Prevention of an arms race in outer space

The question of preventing an arms race in outer space continued to be considered within and outside the United Nations.

Consideration by the Conference on Disarmament. In 1992, the Conference on Disarmament[6] considered the item in the Ad Hoc Committee on outer space,[117] which held 13 meetings between 10 March and 11 August. The Committee functioned under the same non-negotiating mandate as it had done in 1991.

The Committee adopted the same programme of work as in 1991, which included examining and identifying issues relevant to the prevention of an arms race in outer space, existing agreements and proposals and future initiatives.

Many delegations expressed their regret that the Committee's mandate remained the same, and that no substantive changes had been made in the programme of work. The Group of 21 would have preferred the Committee to work under a negotiating mandate, because it believed such a mandate would help to concentrate efforts on concrete proposals.

Although a large number of members— principally non-aligned—thought it would be desirable to undertake negotiations immediately, the United States remained opposed to such a move.

Open-ended consultations conducted by the Friends of the Chair, focusing on terminological issues, verification of anti-satellites and confidence-building measures in space activities, were inconclusive.

In its report to the Conference,[118] the Committee noted that there had been continued general recognition of the importance and urgency of preventing an arms race in outer space, as well as of the significant role that the legal regime applicable to outer space was playing and the need to consolidate and reinforce it and enhance its effectiveness. The importance of strict compliance with existing agreements, both bilateral and multilateral, and of the presentations in the Committee relating to confidence-building measures and to greater transparency and openness were also recognized. It recommended that in 1993 the Conference re-establish the Committee with an adequate mandate and that the work done by the Friends of the Chair be continued.

In addition to the documents of previous sessions, the Conference had before it compendiums of plenary statements and working papers on outer space from the 1991 session of the Conference, submitted by Canada,[119] and several working papers.

Bilateral negotiations

In parallel with multilateral efforts, the Russian Federation and the United States held bilateral negotiations on ballistic missile defence. In a joint statement issued by Presidents Yeltsin and Bush on 17 June in Washington, D.C.,[9] they noted that they were continuing their discussion of the potential benefits of a global protection system against ballistic missiles. They agreed that they should work together with allies and other interested States in developing a concept for such a system as part of an overall strategy with regard to the proliferation of ballistic missiles and weapons of mass destruction. In addition, the United States and the Russian Federation signed the Agreement on Cooperation in Outer Space, which provided a broad framework for cooperation related to space activities.

GENERAL ASSEMBLY ACTION

On 9 December 1992, the General Assembly, on the recommendation of the First Committee, adopted **resolution 47/51** by recorded vote.

Prevention of an arms race in outer space
The General Assembly,

Recognizing the common interest of all mankind in the exploration and use of outer space for peaceful purposes,

Reaffirming the will of all States that the exploration and use of outer space, including the Moon and other celestial bodies, shall be for peaceful purposes, shall be carried out for the benefit and in the interest of all countries, irrespective of their degree of economic or scientific development, and shall be the province of all mankind,

Reaffirming also provisions of articles III and IV of the Treaty on Principles Governing the Activities of States in the Exploration and Use of Outer Space, including the Moon and Other Celestial Bodies,

Recalling the obligation of all States to observe the provisions of the Charter of the United Nations regarding the use or threat of use of force in their international relations, including in their space activities,

Reaffirming further paragraph 80 of the Final Document of the Tenth Special Session of the General Assembly, in which it is stated that in order to prevent an arms race in outer space further measures should be taken and appropriate international negotiations held in accordance with the spirit of the Treaty,

Recalling also its resolutions on this issue and paragraph 45, section D, chapter II, of the Final Document adopted by the Tenth Conference of Heads of State or Government of Non-Aligned Countries, held at Jakarta from 1 to 6 September 1992,[a] and taking note of the proposals submitted to the General Assembly at its tenth special session and at its regular sessions, and of the recommendations made to the competent organs of the United Nations and to the Conference on Disarmament,

Recognizing the grave danger for international peace and security of an arms race in outer space and of developments contributing to it,

Emphasizing the paramount importance of strict compliance with existing arms limitation and disarmament agreements relevant to outer space, including bilateral agreements, and with the existing legal regime concerning the use of outer space,

Considering that wide participation in the legal regime applicable to outer space could contribute to enhancing its effectiveness,

Noting that bilateral negotiations, begun in 1985 between the Union of Soviet Socialist Republics and the United States of America, have continued with the declared objective of working out effective agreements aimed, *inter alia*, at preventing an arms race in outer space,

---

[a]A/47/675-S/24816.

Welcoming the re-establishment of the Ad Hoc Committee on the Prevention of an Arms Race in Outer Space at the 1992 session of the Conference on Disarmament, in the exercise of the negotiating responsibilities of this sole multilateral body on disarmament, to continue to examine and identify, through substantive and general consideration, issues relevant to the prevention of an arms race in outer space,

Noting also that the Ad Hoc Committee on the Prevention of an Arms Race in Outer Space, taking into account its previous efforts since its establishment in 1985 and seeking to enhance its functioning in qualitative terms, continued the examination and identification of various issues, existing agreements and existing proposals, as well as future initiatives relevant to the prevention of an arms race in outer space, and that this contributed to a better understanding of a number of problems and to a clearer perception of the various positions,

Emphasizing the mutually complementary nature of bilateral and multilateral efforts in the field of preventing an arms race in outer space, and hoping that concrete results will emerge from these efforts as soon as possible,

Convinced that further measures should be examined in the search for effective and verifiable bilateral and multilateral agreements in order to prevent an arms race in outer space,

Stressing that the growing use of outer space increases the need for greater transparency and better information on the part of the international community,

Recalling in this context its resolution 45/55 B of 4 December 1990 which, *inter alia*, reaffirmed the importance of confidence-building measures as means conducive to ensuring the attainment of the objective of the prevention of an arms race in outer space,

Conscious of the benefits of confidence- and security-building measures in the military field,

1. *Reaffirms* the importance and urgency of preventing an arms race in outer space and the readiness of all States to contribute to that common objective, in conformity with the provisions of the Treaty on Principles Governing the Activities of States in the Exploration and Use of Outer Space, including the Moon and Other Celestial Bodies;

2. *Reaffirms its recognition*, as stated in the report of the Ad Hoc Committee on the Prevention of an Arms Race in Outer Space, that the legal regime applicable to outer space by itself does not guarantee the prevention of an arms race in outer space, that this legal regime plays a significant role in the prevention of an arms race in that environment, that there is a need to consolidate and reinforce that regime and enhance its effectiveness, and that it is important strictly to comply with existing agreements, both bilateral and multilateral;

3. *Emphasizes* the necessity of further measures with appropriate and effective provisions for verification to prevent an arms race in outer space;

4. *Calls upon* all States, in particular those with major space capabilities, to contribute actively to the objective of the peaceful use of outer space and of the prevention of an arms race in outer space and to refrain from actions contrary to that objective and to the relevant existing treaties in the interest of maintaining international peace and security and promoting international cooperation;

5. *Reiterates* that the Conference on Disarmament, as the single multilateral disarmament negotiating forum, has the primary role in the negotiation of a multilateral agreement or agreements, as appropriate, on the prevention of an arms race in outer space in all its aspects;

6. *Requests* the Conference on Disarmament to consider as a matter of priority the question of preventing an arms race in outer space;

7. *Also requests* the Conference on Disarmament to intensify its consideration of the question of the prevention of an arms race in outer space in all its aspects, building upon areas of convergence and taking into account relevant proposals and initiatives, including those presented in the Ad Hoc Committee at the 1992 session of the Conference and at the forty-seventh session of the General Assembly;

8. *Further requests* the Conference on Disarmament to re-establish an ad hoc committee with an adequate mandate at the beginning of its 1993 session and to continue building upon areas of convergence with a view to undertaking negotiations for the conclusion of an agreement or agreements, as appropriate, to prevent an arms race in outer space in all its aspects;

9. *Recognizes*, in this respect, the growing convergence of views on the elaboration of measures designed to strengthen transparency, confidence and security in the uses of outer space;

10. *Urges* the Russian Federation and the United States of America to pursue intensively their bilateral negotiations in a constructive spirit with a view to reaching early agreement for preventing an arms race in outer space, and to advise the Conference on Disarmament periodically of the progress of their bilateral sessions so as to facilitate its work;

11. *Decides* to include in the provisional agenda of its forty-eighth session the item entitled "Prevention of an arms race in outer space".

General Assembly resolution 47/51

9 December 1992   Meeting 81   164-0-2 (recorded vote)

Approved by First Committee (A/47/688) by recorded vote (133-0-2), 17 November (meeting 35); 31-nation draft (A/C.1/47/L.34); agenda item 58.

Sponsors: Algeria, Argentina, Australia, Bolivia, Brazil, Bulgaria, Canada, China, Colombia, Costa Rica, Democratic People's Republic of Korea, Denmark, Egypt, Ethiopia, France, India, Indonesia, Iran, Ireland, Lao People's Democratic Republic, Mexico, Myanmar, Netherlands, Nigeria, Romania, Sri Lanka, Sweden, Turkey, Ukraine, Venezuela, Viet Nam.

Meeting numbers. GA 47th session: 1st Committee 3-21, 24, 35; plenary 81.

Recorded vote in Assembly as follows:

In favour: Afghanistan, Algeria, Angola, Argentina, Armenia, Australia, Austria, Azerbaijan, Bahamas, Bahrain, Bangladesh, Barbados, Belarus, Belgium, Belize, Benin, Bhutan, Bolivia, Botswana, Brazil, Brunei Darussalam, Bulgaria, Burkina Faso, Burundi, Cameroon, Canada, Cape Verde, Central African Republic, Chad, Chile, China, Colombia, Comoros, Congo, Costa Rica, Côte d'Ivoire, Cuba, Cyprus, Czechoslovakia, Democratic People's Republic of Korea, Denmark, Djibouti, Dominica, Dominican Republic, Ecuador, Egypt, El Salvador, Estonia, Ethiopia, Fiji, Finland, France, Gabon, Gambia, Germany, Ghana, Greece, Grenada, Guatemala, Guinea, Guinea-Bissau, Guyana, Haiti, Honduras, Hungary, Iceland, India, Indonesia, Iran, Iraq, Ireland, Israel, Italy, Jamaica, Japan, Jordan, Kazakhstan, Kenya, Kuwait, Lao People's Democratic Republic, Latvia, Lebanon, Lesotho, Liberia, Libyan Arab Jamahiriya, Liechtenstein, Lithuania, Luxembourg, Madagascar, Malawi, Malaysia, Maldives, Mali, Malta, Marshall Islands, Mauritania, Mauritius, Mexico, Mongolia, Morocco, Mozambique, Myanmar, Namibia, Nepal, Netherlands, New Zealand, Nicaragua, Niger, Nigeria, Norway, Oman, Pakistan, Panama, Papua New Guinea, Paraguay, Peru, Philippines, Poland, Portugal, Qatar, Republic of Korea, Republic of Moldova, Romania, Russian Federation, Rwanda, Saint Kitts and Nevis, Saint Lucia, Saint Vincent and the Grenadines, Samoa, San Marino, Sao Tome and Principe, Saudi Arabia, Senegal, Seychelles, Sierra Leone, Singapore, Slovenia, Spain, Sri Lanka, Sudan, Suriname, Swaziland, Sweden, Syrian

Arab Republic, Tajikistan, Thailand, Togo, Trinidad and Tobago, Tunisia, Turkey, Turkmenistan, Uganda, Ukraine, United Arab Emirates, United Kingdom, United Republic of Tanzania, Uruguay, Vanuatu, Venezuela, Viet Nam, Yemen, Zaire, Zambia, Zimbabwe.
Against: None.
Abstaining: Micronesia, United States.

Before adopting the draft text as a whole, the First Committee voted separately to retain paragraph 8 by a recorded vote of 130 to 1, with 4 abstentions. The same paragraph was adopted by the Assembly by 159 to 1, with 4 abstentions.

Economic aspects of disarmament

Disarmament and development

In accordance with a 1991 General Assembly request,[120] the Secretary-General in September[121] reported on United Nations activities concerning the relationship between disarmament and development, particularly with regard to the implementation of priorities for the period 1990-1993, as determined by a high-level intra-Secretariat task force in 1990.[122] The task force had been established pursuant to the Final Document adopted at the 1987 International Conference on the Relationship between Disarmament and Development.[123] The Secretary-General described international meetings in which the United Nations Office for Disarmament Affairs had participated, namely, the Conference on International Cooperation in Peaceful Use of Military Industrial Technology (Beijing, China, 22-26 October 1991); a one-day workshop on linking financial flows to military expenditures (Washington, D.C., 28 January 1992); the International Conference on Conversion: Opportunities for Development and Environment (Dortmund, Germany, 24-27 February); and the International Conference on Aerospace Complex Conversion (Moscow, 12-16 October).

GENERAL ASSEMBLY ACTION

On 9 December 1992, the General Assembly, on the recommendation of the First Committee, adopted **resolution 47/52 F** without vote.

Relationship between disarmament and development
The General Assembly,
Recalling the provisions of the Final Document of the Tenth Special Session of the General Assembly concerning the relationship between disarmament and development,
Recalling also the adoption on 11 September 1987 of the Final Document of the International Conference on the Relationship between Disarmament and Development,
Bearing in mind the final documents of the Tenth Conference of Heads of State or Government of Non-Aligned Countries, held at Jakarta from 1 to 6 September 1992,[a]
Stressing the growing importance of the symbiotic relationship between disarmament and development in current international relations,

1. *Welcomes* the report of the Secretary-General and actions undertaken in accordance with the Final Document of the International Conference on the Relationship between Disarmament and Development;
2. *Requests* the Secretary-General to continue to take action, through appropriate organs and within available resources, for the implementation of the action programme adopted at the International Conference;
3. *Also requests* the Secretary-General to submit a report to the General Assembly at its forty-eighth session;
4. *Decides* to include in the provisional agenda of its forty-eighth session the item entitled "Relationship between disarmament and development".

---

aA/47/675-S/24816.

General Assembly resolution 47/52 F
9 December 1992   Meeting 81   Adopted without vote

Approved by First Committee (A/47/691) without vote, 12 November (meeting 31); draft by Armenia, and Indonesia for Non-Aligned Movement (A/C.1/47/L.23); agenda item 61 *(f)*.
Meeting numbers. GA 47th session: 1st Committee 3-21, 28, 31; plenary 81.

Disarmament as an investment process

By an August 1992 note,[124] the Secretary-General transmitted, as requested by the General Assembly in 1990,[125] a research report on the economic aspects of disarmament, particularly disarmament as an investment process, prepared by the United Nations Institute for Disarmament Research (UNIDIR). The report contained an executive summary setting forth 12 economic principles for disarmament which summed up the main conclusions of the research. It presented an overview of the problem, considering, in particular, defence spending and disarmament, and also dealt with key issues such as basic data, an economic approach to defence spending, military research and development, arms exports, arms limitation, development and economic adjustment and problems of conversion. The study's conclusions addressed the issue of the "peace dividend"—an investment process in which current costs were incurred in the expectation of future benefits—and the role of public policies designed to optimize it. They also examined different methods for analysing and forecasting the economic effects of disarmament and for evaluating public policies which might accompany conversion and transition processes.

The report concluded that disarmament had major economic consequences involving costs as well as benefits. On the cost side, it required a fundamental reallocation of resources from military to civilian production that was likely to result in major potential problems of unemployment or underemployment of labour, capital and other resources. As a result, the economic dividends of disarmament were likely to be small in the short term. In the long term, however, disarmament led to significant and worthwhile benefits through the production of civil goods and services as resources were reallocated to the civilian sector. Thus, in its economic aspects, disarmament was like an investment process involving short-run costs and long-run benefits.

An appendix to the report noted that the subject of defence economics, which involved the application of economic principles to defence, disarmament and peace, was a relatively new specialized field within economics. It provided a number of examples of items that could be included in a research agenda on the economic aspects of disarmament.

By **resolution 47/54 F**, the Assembly welcomed the UNIDIR report (see below).

Reduction of military budgets

In a July report with later addenda,[126] the Secretary-General presented information received from 32 Member States on their military expenditures, as requested by the General Assembly in 1985.[127] Annexed to the report was an instrument for standardized international reporting of military expenditures and general guidelines for its use.

By **decision 47/418** of 9 December, the General Assembly took note of the Secretary-General's report.

Disarmament and the environment

Convention to prohibit the hostile use of environmental modification techniques

As at 31 December,[114] there were 57 States parties to the Convention on the Prohibition of Military or Any Other Hostile Use of Environmental Modification Techniques, referred to as the ENMOD Convention, adopted by the General Assembly in 1976[128] and in force since 1978.[129] In 1992, Dominica became a successor State and Mauritius acceded to the Convention.

Second Review Conference

In its Final Declaration, the First Review Conference of the ENMOD Convention (Geneva, 1984)[130] requested the Secretary-General to solicit the views of States parties concerning a second review conference if none was held before 1994. In 1991,[131] the General Assembly noted that a majority of States parties to the Convention had expressed their wish to convene the Second Review Conference in September 1992.

The Preparatory Committee for the Review Conference, with 35 States parties participating, met at Geneva from 6 to 8 April. It set the Conference's date and venue and recommended draft rules of procedure and a provisional agenda.[132]

The Second Review Conference (Geneva, 14-18 September 1992) was attended by 40 of the 55 States parties at that time, four signatories, six observer States and two non-governmental organizations (NGOs), as well as representatives of ICRC, the League of Arab States, the Regional Organization for the Protection of the Marine Environment, the World Meteorological Organization and the United Nations Conference on Environment and Development (UNCED). (For further details on UNCED, see PART THREE, Chapter VIII.)

The general debate, during which 26 States parties explained their positions, revealed the persistence of differences concerning the scope of the Convention.

On 18 September, the Conference adopted by consensus its Final Document,[133] which contained a Final Declaration. A number of proposals that were submitted but did not receive general acceptance were annexed to the Final Document.

On 9 December 1992, the General Assembly, on the recommendation of the First Committee, adopted **resolution 47/52 E** without vote.

Second Review Conference of the Parties to the Convention on the Prohibition of Military or Any Other Hostile Use of Environmental Modification Techniques

The General Assembly,

Recalling its resolution 31/72 of 10 December 1976, in which it referred the Convention on the Prohibition of Military or Any Other Hostile Use of Environmental Modification Techniques to all States for their consideration, signature and ratification and expressed the hope for the widest possible adherence to the Convention,

Recalling also its resolution 46/36 A of 6 December 1991, in which it noted that a majority of States parties to the Convention had expressed their wish to convene the Second Review Conference of the Parties to the Convention in September 1992,

Welcoming the fact that States parties to the Convention met at Geneva from 14 to 18 September 1992 to review the operation of the Convention, with a view to ensuring that its purposes and provisions were being realized,

Having considered the Final Document of the Second Review Conference,

Noting with satisfaction that the Review Conference confirmed that the obligations assumed under article I of the Convention had been faithfully observed by the States parties,

Noting also that the Review Conference recognized the continuing importance of the Convention and its objectives and the common interest of mankind in maintaining its effectiveness in prohibiting the use of environmental modification techniques as a means of war,

Emphasizing that in its Final Declaration the Second Review Conference reaffirmed its belief that universal adherence to the Convention would enhance international peace and security,

Bearing in mind that the States parties to the Convention reaffirmed their strong common interest in preventing the use of environmental modification techniques for military or any other hostile purposes, their strong support for the Convention, their continued dedication to its principles and objectives and their commitment to implement effectively its provisions,

1. *Notes* the assessment by the Second Review Conference of the Parties to the Convention on the Prohibition of Military or Any Other Hostile Use of Environmental Modification Techniques that the Convention has been effective in preventing military or any other hostile use of any environmental modification techniques between States parties and that its provisions need to be kept under continuing review and examination in order to ensure their global effectiveness;

2. *Welcomes* the reaffirmation by the Review Conference of support for article II of the Convention and for the definition therein of the term "environmental modification techniques", which States parties to the Convention agree that, taken together with the Understandings relating to articles I and II, covers military or any other hostile use of any environmental modification techniques having widespread, long-lasting or severe effects as the means of destruction, damage or injury to any State party by another State party;

3. *Notes with satisfaction* the confirmation by the Review Conference that the military or any other hostile use of herbicides as an environmental modification technique in the meaning of article II is a method of warfare prohibited by article I if such use of herbicides upsets the ecological balance of a region, thus causing widespread, long-lasting or severe effects as the means of destruction, damage or injury to any other State party;

4. *Calls upon* all States to refrain from military or any other hostile use of any environmental modification techniques;

5. *Urges* all States that have not already done so to exert their best endeavours to become parties to the Convention as early as possible, and urges successor States to take appropriate action, so as ultimately to obtain universality of adherence;

6. *Welcomes* the reaffirmation of the undertaking, under article V, of all States parties to consult one another and to cooperate in solving any problems which may arise in relation to the objectives of, or in the application of the provisions of, the Convention;

7. *Requests* the Secretary-General to intensify efforts to assist States parties in promoting the universality of the Convention, including through the provision of appropriate advice on procedures.

General Assembly resolution 47/52 E

9 December 1992　　　　Meeting 81　　　　Adopted without vote

Approved by First Committee (A/47/691) without vote, 12 November (meeting 31); 36-nation draft (A/C.1/47/L.20/Rev.1); agenda item 61.
Sponsors: Albania, Algeria, Argentina, Australia, Bolivia, Brazil, Bulgaria, Canada, Costa Rica, Cuba, Cyprus, Czechoslovakia, Democratic People's Republic of Korea, Egypt, Finland, Germany, Greece, Haiti, Honduras, Hungary, India, Ireland, Italy, Japan, Kuwait, Netherlands, New Zealand, Norway, Pakistan, Poland, Republic of Korea, Romania, Russian Federation, Sweden, United Kingdom, United States.
Meeting numbers. GA 47th session: 1st Committee 3-21, 23, 31; plenary 81.

Protection of the environment in times of armed conflict

On 25 November, on the recommendation of the Sixth (Legal) Committee, the General Assembly adopted **resolution 47/37**, by which it urged States to ensure compliance with international law

applicable to the protection of the environment in times of armed conflict and to incorporate the provisions of such law into their military manuals and ensure their effective dissemination. (For further details on military conflicts and the environment, see PART FIVE, Chapter II.)

Radioactive wastes

In 1992, the Conference on Disarmament re-established the Ad Hoc Committee on Radiological Weapons,[77] with a view to reaching agreement on a convention prohibiting the development, production, stockpiling and use of radiological weapons, the draft articles of which dealt with the dumping of radioactive waste. (For further details, see under "Nuclear arms limitation and disarmament".)

GENERAL ASSEMBLY ACTION

On 9 December, the General Assembly, on the recommendation of the First Committee, adopted **resolution 47/52 D** without vote.

Prohibition of the dumping of radioactive wastes
The General Assembly,

Bearing in mind resolutions CM/Res.1153(XLVIII) of 1988[a] and CM/Res.1225(L) of 1989,[b] adopted by the Council of Ministers of the Organization of African Unity, concerning the dumping of nuclear and industrial wastes in Africa,

Welcoming resolution GC(XXXIII)/RES/509 on the dumping of nuclear wastes, adopted on 29 September 1989 by the General Conference of the International Atomic Energy Agency at its thirty-third regular session,

Welcoming also resolution GC(XXXIV)/RES/530 establishing a Code of Practice on the International Transboundary Movement of Radioactive Waste, adopted on 21 September 1990 by the General Conference of the International Atomic Energy Agency at its thirty-fourth regular session,

Considering its resolution 2602 C (XXIV) of 16 December 1969, in which it requested the Conference of the Committee on Disarmament,[c] *inter alia*, to consider effective methods of control against the use of radiological methods of warfare,

Recalling resolution CM/Res.1356(LIV) of 1991,[d] adopted by the Council of Ministers of the Organization of African Unity, on the Bamako Convention on the Ban on the Import of Hazardous Wastes into Africa and on the Control of Their Transboundary Movements within Africa,

Aware of the potential hazards underlying any use of radioactive wastes that would constitute radiological warfare and its implications for regional and international security, and in particular for the security of developing countries,

---

[a]A/43/398.
[b]A/44/603.
[c]The Committee on Disarmament was redesignated the Conference on Disarmament as from 7 February 1984.
[d]A/46/390.

Desirous of promoting the implementation of paragraph 76 of the Final Document of the Tenth Special Session of the General Assembly,

Aware also of the consideration in the Conference on Disarmament during its 1992 session of the question of dumping of radioactive wastes,

Gravely concerned at the recently reported efforts to dump harmful wastes in Somalia,

Recalling its resolution 46/36 K of 6 December 1991, in which it requested the Conference on Disarmament to include in its report to the General Assembly at its forty-seventh session the progress recorded in the ongoing negotiations on this subject,

1. *Takes note* of the part of the report of the Conference on Disarmament relating to a future convention on the prohibition of radiological weapons;

2. *Expresses grave concern* regarding any use of nuclear wastes that would constitute radiological warfare and have grave implications for the national security of all States;

3. *Calls upon* all States to take appropriate measures with a view to preventing any dumping of nuclear or radioactive wastes that would infringe upon the sovereignty of States;

4. *Requests* the Conference on Disarmament to take into account, in the ongoing negotiations for a convention on the prohibition of radiological weapons, radioactive wastes as part of the scope of such a convention;

5. *Also requests* the Conference on Disarmament to intensify efforts towards an early conclusion of such a convention and to include in its report to the General Assembly at its forty-eighth session the progress recorded in the ongoing negotiations on this subject;

6. *Takes note* of resolution CM/Res.1356(LIV) of 1991, adopted by the Council of Ministers of the Organization of African Unity, on the Bamako Convention on the Ban on the Import of Hazardous Wastes into Africa and on the Control of Their Transboundary Movements within Africa;

7. *Expresses the hope* that the effective implementation of the International Atomic Energy Agency Code of Practice on the International Transboundary Movement of Radioactive Waste will enhance the protection of all States from the dumping of radioactive wastes on their territories;

8. *Requests* the International Atomic Energy Agency to continue keeping the subject under active review, including the desirability of concluding a legally binding instrument in this field;

9. *Decides* to include in the provisional agenda of its forty-eighth session the item entitled ''Prohibition of the dumping of radioactive wastes''.

General Assembly resolution 47/52 D

9 December 1992   Meeting 81   Adopted without vote

Approved by First Committee (A/47/691) without vote, 18 November (meeting 36); draft by Mauritania for African Group (A/C.1/47/L.13/Rev.2); agenda item 61 *(k)*.

Meeting numbers. GA 47th session: 1st Committee 3-21, 30, 36; plenary 81.

REFERENCES

[1]S/23500. [2]A/47/277-S/24111. [3]*New Dimensions of Arms Regulation and Disarmament in the Post–Cold War Era*, Sales No. E.93.IX.8. [4]YUN 1978, p. 39, GA res, S-10/2, 30 June 1978. [5]CD/1120. [6]A/47/27. [7]CD/1170. [8]CD/1164. [9]CD/1162, CD/1166. [10]CD/973, CD/974. [11]CD/1000, CD/1001. [12]CD/1161. [13]*Disarmament: A Periodic Review by the United Nations*, vol. XV,

No. 4. [14]CD/1157. [15]A/47/78-S/23490. [16]S/24053. [17]S/24065. [18]S/24344. [19]YUN 1968, p. 17, GA res. 2373(XXII), annex, 12 June 1968. [20]YUN 1991, p. 172, SC res. 687(1991), 3 Apr. 1991. [21]A/47/181. [22]A/47/92. [23]A/47/77-S/23486 & Corr.1, A/47/79-S/23494. [24]A/47/183. [25]A/47/89-S/23576. [26]CD/1158. [27]*The United Nations Disarmament Yearbook*, vol. 17, *1992*, Sales No. E.93.IX.1. [28]YUN 1975, p. 27. [29]YUN 1980, p. 51. [30]YUN 1985, p. 56. [31]NPT CONF.IV/45/I. [32]CD/1121. [33]CD/1160. [34]A/47/42. [35]YUN 1991, p. 60. [36]A/CN.10/168. [37]A/CN.10/167. [38]YUN 1991, p. 63, GA res. 46/37 B, 6 Dec. 1991. [39]A/47/511. [40]CD/1147. [41]A/48/133-S/25556. [42]CD/1064. [43]A/47/361-S/24370. [44]YUN 1991, p. 57, GA res. 46/36 L, 9 Dec. 1991. [45]CD/1119/Add.1. [46]A/47/370 & Add.1-3. [47]A/47/342 & Corr.1,3. [48]A/45/42. [49]GA res. 45/62 F, 4 Dec. 1990. [50]A/47/417. [51]A/S-15/3. [52]GA res. 43/78 H, 7 Dec. 1988. [53]*Status of Multilateral Arms Regulation and Disarmament Agreements*, 4th edition: 1993, Sales No. E.93.IX.11. [54]GA res. 45/65, 4 Dec. 1990. [55]A/47/405 & Add.1. [56]A/45/372 & Corr.1. [57]YUN 1991, p. 52. [58]Ibid., p. 34. [59]A/46/592-S/23161. [60]A/CN.10/166. [61]A/CN.10/172. [62]A/CN.10/173. [63]GA res. 44/116 O, 15 Dec. 1989. [64]A/47/362. [65]YUN 1970, p. 18, GA res. 2660(XXV), annex, 7 Dec. 1970. [66]CD/1167. [67]CD/1151. [68]CD/1145. [69]CD/1163 & Corr.1. [70]YUN 1987, p. 50. [71]CD/1144. [72]A/47/313. [73]YUN 1987, p. 54, GA res. 42/38 C, 30 Nov. 1987. [74]A/47/482. [75]YUN 1991, p. 38. [76]YUN 1963, p. 137. [77]CD/1122. [78]CD/1159. [79]YUN 1964, p. 69. [80]YUN 1991, p. 44, GA res. 46/34 A, 6 Dec. 1991. [81]A/47/533. [82]YUN 1991, p. 44, GA res. 46/34 B, 9 Dec. 1991. [83]A/47/468. [84]YUN 1991, p. 43. [85]A/47/467. [86]CD/1172. [87]A/47/461. [88]A/47/241. [89]YUN 1991, p. 46, GA res. 46/30, 6 Dec. 1991. [90]A/47/387. [91]YUN 1991, p. 221. [92]Ibid., p. 47, GA res. 46/39, 6 Dec. 1991. [93]A/47/538. [94]YUN 1991, p. 48, GA res. 46/31, 6 Dec. 1991. [95]A/47/304. [96]A/47/29. [97]YUN 1971, p. 34, GA res. 2832(XXVI), 16 Dec. 1971. [98]YUN 1991, p. 49, GA res. 46/49, 9 Dec. 1991. [99]Ibid., p. 56, GA res. 46/36 H, 6 Dec. 1991. [100]A/47/314 & Add.1. [101]YUN 1991, p. 60, GA res. 46/38 D, 6 Dec. 1991. [102]A/47/371 & Add.1,2. [103]A/C.1/47/INF/2. [104]GA res. 45/61, 4 Dec. 1990. [105]YUN 1991, p. 60. [106]A/CN.10/171. [107]A/CN.10/170. [108]A/CN.10/169. [109]A/CN.10/165. [110]GA res. 45/60, 4 Dec. 1990. [111]A/47/355. [112]YUN 1991, p. 64, GA dec. 46/42, 6 Dec. 1991. [113]A/47/316 & Add.1,2. [114]*Multilateral Treaties Deposited with the Secretary-General as at 31 December 1992* (ST/LEG/SER.E/11), Sales No. E.93.V.11. [115]YUN 1980, p. 76. [116]YUN 1983, p. 66. [117]CD/1125. [118]CD/1165. [119]CD/1142. [120]YUN 1991, p. 32, GA res. 46/36 C, 6 Dec. 1991. [121]A/47/452. [122]A/45/592. [123]YUN 1987, p. 82. [124]A/47/346. [125]GA res. 45/62 G, 4 Dec. 1990. [126]A/47/303 & Add.1,2. [127]YUN 1985, p. 84, GA res. 40/91 B, 12 Dec. 1985. [128]YUN 1976, p. 45, GA res. 31/72, annex, 10 Dec. 1976. [129]YUN 1978, p. 964. [130]YUN 1984, p. 73. [131]YUN 1991, p. 33, GA res. 46/36 A, 6 Dec. 1991. [132]ENMOD/CONF.II/1. [133]ENMOD/CONF.II/12.

Information and studies

World Disarmament Campaign

In 1992, the General Assembly decided that the World Disarmament Campaign—launched by the General Assembly in 1982[1] to sensitize public opinion to the dangers of the arms race—and its Voluntary Trust Fund would be known in future as the United Nations Disarmament Information

Programme and the Voluntary Trust Fund for the United Nations Disarmament Information Programme, respectively. Delegations felt the change would lay the basis for broader support and would more accurately reflect the work being done.

Reports of the Secretary-General. In October,[2] the Secretary-General, in his annual report on implementing the Campaign's objectives, informed the Assembly of activities carried out by the United Nations system in the areas of training (see below), special events and publicity. The Office for Disarmament Affairs organized two regional meetings for Asia and the Pacific: a conference on disarmament issues (Hiroshima, Japan, 15-18 June), which focused on non-proliferation and confidence-building measures, and a conference on disarmament and security issues (Shanghai, China, 17-19 August). The Department of Public Information continued to inform the public of United Nations activities in the disarmament area by providing radio and television coverage, answering public inquiries, arranging briefings for NGOs and organizing events at Headquarters and at information centres around the world.

In July, the Secretary-General, reporting on the annual meeting of the Advisory Board on Disarmament Matters (twenty-third session, New York, 22-26 June),[3] noted that a new approach had been taken in implementing the Campaign's programme of activities consisting of an information programme that promoted the role of arms control and disarmament in preventive diplomacy. Some members of the Board felt that the name "World Disarmament Campaign" no longer reflected the realities of the present.

Financing

The tenth United Nations Pledging Conference for the World Disarmament Campaign was convened in New York on 30 October 1992, with 72 delegations participating.[4]

Either during the Conference or at other times during the year, the following pledges were announced for the Campaign: Australia ($A 30,000), Austria ($10,000), Chile ($1,000), Cyprus ($1,000), Greece ($5,000), Indonesia ($5,000), Italy (20,000,000 lire), Mexico ($2,500), New Zealand ($NZ 6,000), Norway ($2,500), Pakistan (125,000 rupees), Republic of Korea ($5,000), Sri Lanka ($3,000), Sweden (200,000 kronor); for UNIDIR: Australia ($A 20,000), China ($10,000), Finland (65,000 markkaa), France (1,515,800 francs), Norway ($100,000), Republic of Korea ($11,000), Spain (2,000,000 pesetas, earmarked for 1994), Switzerland (100,000 francs); for a 1992 seminar on arms proliferation and confidence- and security-building measures in Latin America: Canada ($Can 90,000); for the Latin American and Caribbean regional centre: Colombia ($1,000), Italy

(20,000,000 lire), Mexico ($2,500), Norway ($10,000), Spain (600,000 pesetas); for a 1992 seminar on confidence- and security-building measures in southern Africa, Windhoek, Namibia: Finland ($20,000), Norway ($25,000), Sweden (185,000 kronor); for a seminar on security implications of refugee flows from the Horn of Africa, Nairobi, Kenya: Finland (65,000 markkaa); for the African regional centre: France (50,000 francs), Italy (20,000,000 lire), Norway ($10,000); for authors' fees in the framework of UNIDIR's research project entitled "European Security in the 1990s": Germany ($10,000); for the Asian and Pacific regional centre: Italy (20,000,000 lire), Nepal ($7,000), New Zealand ($NZ 10,000), Norway ($10,000), Pakistan (125,000 rupees), Republic of Korea ($4,000), Thailand ($1,000); and for activities related to the Register of Conventional Arms: Italy (50,000,000 lire).

GENERAL ASSEMBLY ACTION

On 9 December 1992, the General Assembly, on the recommendation of the First Committee, adopted **resolution 47/53 D** without vote.

World Disarmament Campaign
The General Assembly,

Recalling its decision taken in 1982 at its twelfth special session, the second special session devoted to disarmament, by which the World Disarmament Campaign was launched,

Recalling also its various resolutions on the subject, including resolution 46/37 A of 6 December 1991,

Having examined the reports of the Secretary-General of 8 October 1992 on the implementation of the World Disarmament Campaign, and of 31 July 1992 on the Advisory Board on Disarmament Matters relating to the implementation of the World Disarmament Campaign, as well as the Final Act of the Tenth United Nations Pledging Conference for the Campaign, held on 30 October 1992,

Noting with appreciation the contributions that Member States have already made to the Campaign,

1. *Welcomes* the report of the Secretary-General of 8 October 1992 on the World Disarmament Campaign;

2. *Commends* the Secretary-General for his efforts to make effective use of the resources available to him in disseminating as widely as possible information on arms limitation and disarmament to elected officials, the media, non-governmental organizations, educational communities and research institutes, and in carrying out an active seminar and conference programme;

3. *Notes with appreciation* the contributions to the efforts of the Campaign by the United Nations information centres and the regional centres for disarmament;

4. *Decides* that the World Disarmament Campaign shall be known hereafter as the "United Nations Disarmament Information Programme" and the World Disarmament Campaign Voluntary Trust Fund as the "Voluntary Trust Fund for the United Nations Disarmament Information Programme";

5. *Recommends* that the Programme should further focus its efforts:

(a) To inform, to educate and to generate public understanding of the importance of and support for multilateral action, including action by the United Nations and the Conference on Disarmament, in the field of arms limitation and disarmament, in a factual, balanced and objective manner;

(b) To facilitate unimpeded access to and an exchange of information on ideas between the public sector and public interest groups and organizations, and to provide an independent source of balanced and factual information that takes into account a range of views to help further an informed debate on arms limitation, disarmament and security;

(c) To organize meetings to facilitate exchanges of views and information between governmental and non-governmental sectors and between governmental and other experts in order to facilitate the search for common ground;

6. *Invites* all Member States to contribute to the Voluntary Trust Fund for the United Nations Disarmament Information Programme;

7. *Commends* the Secretary-General for supporting the efforts of universities, other academic institutions and non-governmental organizations active in the educational field in widening the world-wide availability of disarmament education, and invites him to continue to support and cooperate with, without cost to the regular budget of the United Nations, educational institutions and non-governmental organizations engaged in such efforts;

8. *Decides* that at its forty-eighth session there should be an eleventh United Nations Pledging Conference for the United Nations Disarmament Information Programme, and expresses the hope that on that occasion all those Member States that have not yet announced any voluntary contributions will do so, bearing in mind the objectives of the Third Disarmament Decade and the need to ensure its success;

9. *Requests* the Secretary-General to submit to the General Assembly at its forty-eighth session a report covering both the implementation of the activities of the Programme by the United Nations system during 1993 and the activities of the Programme contemplated by the system for 1994;

10. *Also decides* to include in the provisional agenda of its forty-eighth session an item entitled ''United Nations Disarmament Information Programme''.

General Assembly resolution 47/53 D

9 December 1992   Meeting 81   Adopted without vote

Approved by First Committee (A/47/692) without vote, 12 November (meeting 31); 14-nation draft (A/C.1/47/L.39); agenda item 62 *(a)*.
Sponsors: Afghanistan, Bangladesh, Belarus, Bolivia, Costa Rica, Indonesia, Iran, Mexico, Myanmar, Philippines, Sri Lanka, Sweden, Ukraine, Venezuela.
Meeting numbers. GA 47th session: 1st Committee 3-21, 28, 31; plenary 81.

Regional centres for peace and disarmament

In September,[5] the Secretary-General reported to the General Assembly on the activities of the three regional centres for peace and disarmament covering Africa, Asia and the Pacific and Latin America and the Caribbean for the period August 1991 to July 1992.

The United Nations Regional Centre for Peace and Disarmament in Africa, as agreed by the Assembly in 1985,[6] was established in 1986 at Lomé, Togo.[7] The Centre focused on disseminating information on disarmament and peace and security, organizing seminars and conferences and undertaking studies. It held an international conference on the role of the media in the peaceful resolution of conflicts in Africa at Lomé from 25 to 27 May. The Centre continued to publish its quarterly newsletter, *African Peace Bulletin*.

As decided by the Assembly in 1986,[8] the United Nations Regional Centre for Peace, Disarmament and Development in Latin America and the Caribbean was established on 1 January 1987 and inaugurated at Lima, Peru, on 9 October of that year.[9] The Secretary-General noted that the Centre had widened and strengthened its contacts and cooperation with governmental and non-governmental organizations, academic and other institutions and other United Nations bodies. It continued to serve as a resource centre for students and researchers, in addition to distributing United Nations publications and making videos and films on disarmament available to universities, schools and institutions. In February, the Centre published a book, *Peace and Security in Latin America and the Caribbean in the Nineties*.

The United Nations Regional Centre for Peace and Disarmament in Asia and the Pacific, established in 1987[10] and inaugurated on 30 January 1989 at Kathmandu, Nepal, focused on disseminating information on United Nations activities concerning arms limitation and disarmament, answering public inquiries and organizing a yearly meeting. In 1992, the Centre organized a major regional meeting, for the third consecutive year, on non-proliferation and other disarmament issues in the region (Kathmandu, 27-29 January).

GENERAL ASSEMBLY ACTION

On 9 December, the General Assembly, on the recommendation of the First Committee, adopted **decision 47/421**, by which it requested the Secretary-General to report in 1993 on the activities of the regional centres. It also decided to include in the provisional agenda for its 1993 session the item entitled ''Review and implementation of the Concluding Document of the Twelfth Special Session of the General Assembly:[11] United Nations Regional Centre for Peace and Disarmament in Africa, United Nations Regional Centre for Peace and Disarmament in Asia and the Pacific and United Nations Regional Centre for Peace, Disarmament and Development in Latin America and the Caribbean''.

In the Committee, on 13 November, Bangladesh, Bolivia, China, Costa Rica, Democratic People's Republic of Korea, France, Indonesia, Iran, Mauritania (on behalf of the Group of African States), Mongolia, Myanmar, Nepal, Pakistan,

Philippines, Singapore, Sri Lanka, Thailand, Togo, Uruguay (on behalf of the Group of Latin American and Caribbean States) and Viet Nam submitted a draft on the United Nations Regional Centre for Peace and Disarmament in Africa, United Nations Regional Centre for Peace and Disarmament in Asia and the Pacific and United Nations Regional Centre for Peace, Disarmament and Development in Latin America and the Caribbean[12] by which, among other things, the Assembly would have decided that the administrative costs of the regional centres should be financed from within the existing resources of the regular budget. On the same date, the sponsors requested that no action be taken on the draft.

Disarmament Week

Disarmament Week, an annual event commencing on United Nations Day, 24 October, to foster the objectives of disarmament, was marked on 27 October at United Nations Headquarters by a special meeting of the General Assembly's First Committee. Statements were made by the Assembly President, the Chairman of the First Committee and the Secretary-General.

In a July report on the Week,[13] the Secretary-General submitted replies received from four Member States, as well as from the United Nations system and NGOs, on activities undertaken by them to promote the Week's objectives.

GENERAL ASSEMBLY ACTION

On 9 December 1992, the General Assembly, on the recommendation of the First Committee, adopted **resolution 47/54 C** without vote.

Disarmament Week

The General Assembly,

Noting the momentous developments of unprecedented magnitude that have taken place in international relations recently, and welcoming the important achievements of late in the areas of arms limitation and disarmament,

Noting with satisfaction the increasing role and prestige of the United Nations as a focal point for coordinating and harmonizing the efforts of States,

Emphasizing anew the need for and the importance of world public opinion in support of disarmament efforts in all their aspects,

Also noting with satisfaction the broad and active support by Governments and international and national organizations of the decision taken by the General Assembly at its tenth special session, the first special session devoted to disarmament, regarding the proclamation of the week starting 24 October, the day of the founding of the United Nations, as a week devoted to fostering the objectives of disarmament,

Recalling the recommendations concerning the World Disarmament Campaign contained in annex V to the Concluding Document of the Twelfth Special Session of the General Assembly, the second special session

devoted to disarmament, in particular the recommendation that Disarmament Week should continue to be widely observed,

Noting the support for the further observance of Disarmament Week expressed by Member States at the fifteenth special session of the General Assembly, the third special session devoted to disarmament,[a]

Recognizing the significance of the annual observance of Disarmament Week, including by the United Nations,

1. *Takes note with appreciation* of the report of the Secretary-General on the follow-up measures undertaken by Governments and non-governmental organizations in holding Disarmament Week;

2. *Commends* all States and international and national governmental and non-governmental organizations for their active support for and participation in Disarmament Week;

3. *Invites* all States that so desire, in carrying out appropriate measures at the local level on the occasion of Disarmament Week, to take into account the elements of the model programme for Disarmament Week prepared by the Secretary-General;

4. *Invites* Governments and international and national non-governmental organizations to continue to take an active part in Disarmament Week and to inform the Secretary-General of the activities undertaken;

5. *Invites* the Secretary-General to continue to use the United Nations information organs as widely as possible to promote better understanding among the world public of disarmament problems and the objectives of Disarmament Week;

6. *Decides* to include in the provisional agenda of its fiftieth session, the year of the fiftieth anniversary of the United Nations, the item entitled "Disarmament Week".

---

[a]A/S-15/2.

General Assembly resolution 47/54 C

9 December 1992   Meeting 81   Adopted without vote

Approved by First Committee (A/47/693) without vote, 12 November (meeting 31); 25-nation draft (A/C.1/47/L.16); agenda item 63 *(f)*.

Sponsors: Afghanistan, Belarus, Canada, China, Costa Rica, Democratic People's Republic of Korea, Indonesia, Japan, Kazakhstan, Kyrgyzstan, Malaysia, Micronesia, Mongolia, Myanmar, Nepal, New Zealand, Pakistan, Philippines, Samoa, Singapore, Tajikistan, Thailand, Turkmenistan, Ukraine, Viet Nam.

Meeting numbers. GA 47th session: 1st Committee 3-21, 23, 31; plenary 81.

Disarmament studies and research

Advisory Board on Disarmament Matters

The Advisory Board on Disarmament Matters, which met in New York from 22 to 26 June,[3] discussed current developments and trends in international affairs and their bearing on the role of the United Nations in international security and disarmament. It identified issues it believed required prompt attention, including non-proliferation, nuclear disarmament, conventional disarmament, safe disposal of weapons, transparency, verification and conversion. The Board recommended preventing the disarmament debate from becoming a North-South issue; curbing the proliferation of weapons of mass destruction and their delivery systems while not impeding the transfer of technology for peaceful purposes; moving from the limited nature of existing technology regimes to a more universal approach, with the United Nations providing the appropriate forum for such discussions; and reassessing the relevance and effectiveness of the multilateral disarmament machinery, in particular reviewing the agendas and membership/formats of the Conference on Disarmament, the First Committee and the Disarmament Commission in the light of new developments in international security.

During the year, the Advisory Board continued to act as the Board of Trustees of UNIDIR. In that capacity, it considered and approved the report of the UNIDIR Director on the Institute's activities for 1991-1992 (see below) and the research programme and proposed annual budget for 1993. The UNIDIR Director apprised the Board of UNIDIR's programme for 1994. The Board recommended a subvention from the regular United Nations budget of $220,000 for 1993 to assure the independence of the Institute. In October,[14] the Secretary-General reported to the General Assembly's Fifth (Administrative and Budgetary) Committee, noting that in 1991 the Assembly had approved a subvention of $440,000 for the 1992-1993 biennium.[15]

UN Institute for Disarmament Research

In August, the Secretary-General transmitted to the General Assembly the UNIDIR Director's report, covering the period from July 1991 to June 1992,[16] describing UNIDIR's completed and ongoing research projects. Publication of the UNIDIR *Newsletter* continued, as did its fellowship programme enabling scholars from developing countries to undertake research on disarmament. UNIDIR also continued to publish studies on national concepts of security of individual States and update its computerized information and documentation database service. Among the Institute's research projects were disarmament problems related to outer space; non-military aspects of security; verification; international law, disarmament and security issues; regional approaches to disarmament, security and stability; and nuclear disarmament. During the year, UNIDIR, in cooperation with the Ministry of Foreign Affairs of China and the Chinese People's Association for Peace and Disarmament, held a Conference of Asian and Pacific Institutes (Beijing, 23-25 March).

GENERAL ASSEMBLY ACTION

On 9 December 1992, the General Assembly, on the recommendation of the First Committee, adopted **resolution 47/54 F** by recorded vote.

United Nations Institute for Disarmament Research

The General Assembly,

Recalling its resolution 34/83 M of 11 December 1979, in which it requested the Secretary-General to establish the United Nations Institute for Disarmament Research on the basis of the recommendations contained in the report of the Secretary-General,

Reaffirming its resolution 39/148 H of 17 December 1984, in which it approved the Statute of the United Nations Institute for Disarmament Research, renewed the invitations to Governments to consider making voluntary contributions to the Institute and requested the Secretary-General to continue to give the Institute administrative and other support,

Recalling also its resolution 42/42 J of 30 November 1987, in which it took note with appreciation of the report of the Advisory Board on Disarmament Studies and noted that the establishment of the Institute offered new opportunities regarding research in the field of disarmament,

Recalling further its resolution 45/62 G of 4 December 1990, in which it requested the Institute to prepare, with the assistance of independent experts, a research report on the economic aspects of disarmament and to report to the General Assembly, through the Secretary-General, at its forty-seventh session,

Reaffirming the need for the international community to have access to independent and in-depth research on disarmament, in particular on emerging problems and the foreseeable consequences of disarmament,

Noting in this regard the importance of research on the economic aspects of disarmament,

Having considered the annual report of the Director of the Institute and the report of the Advisory Board on Disarmament Matters acting in its capacity as Board of Trustees of the Institute,

1. *Welcomes* the research report of the United Nations Institute for Disarmament Research entitled "Economic aspects of disarmament: disarmament as an investment process", as transmitted by the Secretary-General to the General Assembly;

2. *Commends* the report to the attention of Member States and encourages them to give active consideration, in particular, to the economic principles for disarmament contained in the executive summary of the report;

3. *Requests* the Secretary-General to give the report the widest possible circulation.

General Assembly resolution 47/54 F

9 December 1992   Meeting 81   166-0-2 (recorded vote)

Approved by First Committee (A/47/693) by recorded vote (132-0-3), 12 November (meeting 31); 31-nation draft (A/C.1/47/L.30); agenda item 63 *(e)*.

Sponsors: Albania, Algeria, Armenia, Austria, Cameroon, Canada, Costa Rica, Egypt, France, Germany, Greece, Hungary, India, Indonesia, Iran, Italy, Libyan Arab Jamahiriya, Nepal, Netherlands, Nigeria, Norway, Panama, Philippines, Poland, Portugal, Romania, Russian Federation, Senegal, Singapore, Spain, Sri Lanka.

Meeting numbers. GA 47th session: 1st Committee 3-21, 26, 31; plenary 81.

Recorded vote in Assembly as follows:

In favour: Afghanistan, Algeria, Angola, Antigua and Barbuda, Argentina, Armenia, Australia, Austria, Azerbaijan, Bahamas, Bahrain, Bangladesh, Barbados, Belarus, Belgium, Belize, Benin, Bhutan, Bolivia, Botswana, Brazil, Brunei Darussalam, Bulgaria, Burkina Faso, Burundi, Cameroon, Canada, Cape Verde, Central African Republic, Chad, Chile, China, Colombia, Comoros, Congo, Costa Rica, Côte d'Ivoire, Cuba, Cyprus, Czechoslovakia, Democratic People's Republic of Korea, Denmark, Djibouti, Dominica, Dominican Republic, Ecuador, Egypt, El Salvador, Estonia, Ethiopia, Fiji, Finland, France, Gabon, Gambia, Germany, Ghana, Greece, Grenada, Guatemala, Guinea, Guinea-Bissau, Guyana, Haiti, Honduras, Hungary, Iceland, India, Indonesia, Iran, Iraq, Ireland, Israel, Italy, Jamaica, Japan, Jordan, Kazakhstan, Kenya, Kuwait, Lao People's Democratic Republic, Latvia, Lebanon, Lesotho, Liberia, Libyan Arab Jamahiriya, Liechtenstein, Lithuania, Luxembourg, Madagascar, Malawi, Malaysia, Maldives, Mali, Malta, Marshall Islands, Mauritania, Mauritius, Mexico, Micronesia, Mongolia, Morocco, Mozambique, Myanmar, Namibia, Nepal, Netherlands, New Zealand, Nicaragua, Niger, Nigeria, Norway, Oman, Pakistan, Panama, Papua New Guinea, Paraguay, Peru, Philippines, Poland, Portugal, Qatar, Republic of Korea, Republic of Moldova, Romania, Russian Federation, Rwanda, Saint Kitts and Nevis, Saint Lucia, Saint Vincent and the Grenadines, Samoa, San Marino, Sao Tome and Principe, Saudi Arabia, Senegal, Seychelles, Sierra Leone, Singapore, Slovenia, Solomon Islands, Spain, Sri Lanka, Sudan, Suriname, Swaziland, Sweden, Syrian Arab Republic, Tajikistan, Thailand, Togo, Trinidad and Tobago, Tunisia, Turkey, Turkmenistan, Uganda, Ukraine, United Arab Emirates, United Republic of Tanzania, Uruguay, Vanuatu, Venezuela, Viet Nam, Yemen, Zaire, Zambia, Zimbabwe.

Against: None.

Abstaining: United Kingdom, United States.

UN disarmament studies programme

In 1992, a study on defensive security concepts was completed, and another, on confidence-building measures in outer space, was in progress.

In response to a General Assembly request of December 1990,[17] the Secretary-General appointed a group of 11 experts to assist him in carrying out a study on defensive security concepts and policies. In September, the Secretary-General transmitted to the Assembly the report of the Group of Experts,[18] which held its first session in 1991[19] and its second and third in 1992 (New York, 13-24 January; 6-17 July). The study attempted to determine the general elements in defensive security concepts and policies that could contribute to strengthening international peace and security. The study noted that defensive security was defined as a condition of peace and security attained step by step and sustained through effective and concrete measures in the political and military fields under which friendly relations among States were established and maintained; disputes were settled in a peaceful and equitable manner and the resort to force was consequently excluded; and the capacity for launching a surprise attack and initiating large-scale offensive action was eliminated through verifiable arms control and disarmament, confidence- and security-building measures and restructuring armed forces towards a defensive orientation. The study recommended, for consideration by Member States, measures that might help to create a condition in which defensive security prevailed. Those measures were outlined in an Assembly resolution.

GENERAL ASSEMBLY ACTION

On 9 December 1992, the General Assembly, on the recommendation of the First Committee, adopted **resolution 47/52 H** without vote.

Study on defensive security concepts and policies

The General Assembly,

Recalling its resolution 45/58 O of 4 December 1990, in which it requested the Secretary-General, with the assistance of qualified governmental experts, to undertake a study on defensive security concepts and policies,

Noting with satisfaction positive developments in the world, reflecting a trend towards reducing the significance of military power in ensuring national policy aims,

Realizing that threats to international peace and security caused by recurring acts of aggression underline the need for intensified efforts towards elaborating a broad range of peaceful means for the prevention of conflicts, including confidence-building measures,

Noting that defensive security concepts as well as initiatives on preventive diplomacy contribute to the strengthening of international peace and security,

Considering the importance of the development of an international dialogue on defensive security policies for the promotion of security and stability in the world,

Having examined the report of the Secretary-General containing the study on defensive security concepts and policies,

1. *Takes note* of the study on defensive security concepts and policies;

2. *Expresses its appreciation* to the Secretary-General and to the group of experts who assisted in the preparation of the study;

3. *Calls upon* all Member States to familiarize themselves with the study and its conclusions and recommendations;

4. *Recalls* that, in its resolution 45/58 O, it invited Member States to initiate or intensify the dialogue on defensive security concepts and policies at the bilateral level, particularly at the regional level and, where appropriate, at the multilateral level, and notes that the study concluded that:

"To this end, Member States could:

"*(a)* Express their views on the concept and objective of 'defensive security', as defined in the present study;

"*(b)* Examine their current situation with respect to the political and military aspects of 'defensive security';

"*(c)* Determine to what extent their international relations, their security commitments and their regional situation might enable them to consider taking measures, on the basis of reciprocity, to achieve a situation of 'defensive security' at the bilateral, regional or multilateral level. The States that share common security interests at a regional or other level might consider undertaking consultations among themselves;

"*(d)* Consider, individually or jointly, problems relating to the resources needed to fulfil collective security commitments consistent with the Charter of the United Nations;

"*(e)* Keep the Secretary-General informed of progress or initiatives in the field of 'defensive security' ";

5. *Requests* the Secretary-General to arrange for the reproduction of the study as a United Nations publication and to give it the widest possible distribution.

General Assembly resolution 47/52 H

9 December 1992   Meeting 81   Adopted without vote

Approved by First Committee (A/47/691) without vote, 12 November (meeting 31); 15-nation draft (A/C.1/47/L.27); agenda item 61 *(e)*.

Sponsors: Armenia, Argentina, Austria, Belgium, Egypt, France, Germany, Greece, Indonesia, Iran, Netherlands, Nigeria, Poland, Russian Federation, Ukraine.

Meeting numbers. GA 47th session: 1st Committee 3-21, 31; plenary 81.

Fellowship, training and advisory services programme

In October,[20] the Secretary-General submitted his annual report on the United Nations disarmament fellowship, training and advisory services programme, stating that, because of the recent expansion in the membership of the United Nations, the number of fellowships to be awarded yearly had been increased from 25 to 30. The increase was effected within existing resources, primarily by reducing the duration of the programme from 18 to 12 weeks. Twenty-nine participants took part in the programme, which started on 10 August at Geneva and concluded on 28 October in New York. The programme included lectures; speaking, drafting and simulation exercises; preparation of individual research papers; attending the Conference on Disarmament and the General Assembly; study visits to IAEA headquarters at Vienna; and, at the invitation of the States concerned, visits to offices and institutions in Czechoslovakia, Finland, Germany, Japan and Sweden.

The training and advisory services programme was established in 1985[21] with a view to making such services available regionally. However, in 1992, no regional workshops were held.

GENERAL ASSEMBLY ACTION

On 9 December 1992, the General Assembly, on the recommendation of the First Committee, adopted **resolution 47/53 A** without vote.

United Nations disarmament fellowship, training and advisory services programme

The General Assembly,

Having considered the report of the Secretary-General on the United Nations disarmament fellowship, training and advisory services programme,

Recalling its decision, contained in paragraph 108 of the Final Document of the Tenth Special Session of the General Assembly, the first special session devoted to disarmament, to establish a programme of fellowships on disarmament, as well as its decisions contained in annex IV to the Concluding Document of the Twelfth Special Session of the General Assembly, the second special session devoted to disarmament, in which it decided, *inter alia*, to continue the programme,

Noting with satisfaction that the programme has already trained an appreciable number of public officials selected from geographical regions represented in the United Nations system, most of whom are now in positions of responsibility in the field of disarmament affairs in their respective countries or Governments,

Recalling also its resolutions 37/100 G of 13 December 1982, 38/73 C of 15 December 1983, 39/63 B of 12 December 1984, 40/151 H of 16 December 1985, 41/60 H of 3 December 1986, 42/39 I of 30 November 1987, 43/76 F of 7 December 1988, 44/117 E of 15 December

1989, 45/59 A of 4 December 1990 and 46/37 E of 6 December 1991,

Noting also with satisfaction that the programme, as designed, has enabled an increased number of public officials, particularly from the developing countries, to acquire more expertise in the sphere of disarmament,

Believing that the forms of assistance available to Member States, particularly to developing countries, under the programme will enhance the capabilities of their officials to follow ongoing deliberations and negotiations on disarmament, both bilateral and multilateral,

1. *Reaffirms* its decisions contained in annex IV to the Concluding Document of the Twelfth Special Session of the General Assembly and the report of the Secretary-General approved by resolution 33/71 E of 14 December 1978;

2. *Expresses its appreciation* to the Governments of Czechoslovakia, Finland, Germany, Japan and Sweden for inviting the 1992 fellows to study selected activities in the field of disarmament, thereby contributing to the fulfilment of the overall objectives of the programme;

3. *Notes with satisfaction* that, within the framework of the programme, the Office for Disarmament Affairs of the Secretariat organized regional disarmament workshops for Africa, Asia and the Pacific, and Latin America and the Caribbean;

4. *Expresses its appreciation* to the Governments of Indonesia, Mexico and Nigeria for their support of the regional disarmament workshops, and to the Governments of New Zealand and Norway for making financial contributions;

5. *Commends* the Secretary-General for the diligence with which the programme has continued to be carried out;

6. *Requests* the Secretary-General to continue the implementation of the Geneva-based programme within existing resources and to report to the General Assembly at its forty-eighth session.

General Assembly resolution 47/53 A

9 December 1992   Meeting 81   Adopted without vote

Approved by First Committee (A/47/692) without vote, 12 November (meeting 31); 44-nation draft (A/C.1/47/L.5); agenda item 62 (e).

Sponsors: Algeria, Argentina, Australia, Benin, Bolivia, Bulgaria, Cameroon, Canada, China, Costa Rica, Cuba, Czechoslovakia, Democratic People's Republic of Korea, Finland, France, Germany, Greece, Hungary, Indonesia, Iran, Japan, Kenya, Lesotho, Liberia, Mali, Mongolia, Myanmar, Namibia, New Zealand, Nicaragua, Nigeria, Pakistan, Philippines, Republic of Korea, Russian Federation, Senegal, Sweden, Togo, Uganda, United Republic of Tanzania, United States, Venezuela, Viet Nam, Zimbabwe.

Meeting numbers. GA 47th session: 1st Committee 3-21, 24, 31; plenary 81.

REFERENCES
[1]YUN 1982, p. 31. [2]A/47/469. [3]A/47/354. [4]A/CONF.161/1. [5]A/47/359. [6]YUN 1985, p. 95, GA res. 40/151 G, 16 Dec. 1985. [7]YUN 1986, p. 85. [8]Ibid., p. 86, GA res. 41/60 J, 3 Dec. 1986. [9]YUN 1987, p. 88. [10]Ibid., p. 89, GA res. 42/39 D, 30 Nov. 1987. [11]YUN 1982, p. 18, GA dec. S-12/24, 10 July 1982. [12]A/C.1/47/L.26/Rev.2. [13]A/47/321. [14]A/C.5/47/19. [15]YUN 1991, p. 870, GA res. 46/185 C, 20 Dec. 1991. [16]A/47/345. [17]GA res. 45/58 O, 4 Dec. 1990. [18]A/47/394. [19]YUN 1991, p. 70. [20]A/47/568. [21]YUN 1985, p. 97, GA res. 40/151 H, 16 Dec. 1985.

Chapter III

Peaceful uses of outer space

International Space Year, designed to promote international cooperation in space, was commemorated in 1992 through a programme of activities carried out by the United Nations and international organizations focusing on space technology and the environment.

During the year, the Committee on the Peaceful Uses of Outer Space (Committee on outer space) and its Scientific and Technical and Legal Subcommittees continued their consideration of matters of international cooperation in the peaceful uses of outer space. The Committee held its thirty-fifth session (New York, 15-26 June). The General Assembly, in December, endorsed the Committee's recommendations and the United Nations Programme on Space Applications for 1993 (resolution 47/67). Principles Relevant to the Use of Nuclear Power Sources in Outer Space, on which the Committee reached consensus in 1992, were adopted by the Assembly in resolution 47/68.

The prevention of an arms race in outer space was considered by an ad hoc committee of the Conference on Disarmament (see PART ONE, Chapter II).

Science, technology and law

Space science and technology

The Scientific and Technical Subcommittee of the Committee on outer space held its twenty-ninth session in 1992 (New York, 25 February–5 March).[1] It continued to discuss the United Nations Programme on Space Applications, the coordination of space activities within the United Nations system and follow-up to the Second (1982) United Nations Conference on the Exploration and Peaceful Uses of Outer Space (UNISPACE-82).[2] The Subcommittee also considered matters relating to remote sensing of the Earth by satellites; the use of nuclear power sources in outer space; questions relating to space transportation; the physical nature and technical attributes of the geostationary orbit; matters relating to life sciences, including space medicine; space activities related to the Earth environment; planetary exploration; and astronomy.

In accordance with a 1991 General Assembly resolution,[3] the Subcommittee re-established the Working Group of the Whole to evaluate implementation of the recommendations of UNISPACE-82 (see below).

A special session of the Subcommittee, sponsored by the Committee on Space Research (COSPAR) of the International Council of Scientific Unions and the International Astronautical Federation (IAF), was held on 24 February 1992 to celebrate International Space Year (see below). The theme selected for special attention at the Subcommittee's 1992 session was space technology and protection of the Earth's environment.

The Subcommittee's recommendations were acted on by the Committee on outer space in June.[4]

International Space Year

The General Assembly, in 1989,[5] had endorsed the initiative of international scientific organizations and bodies to designate 1992 as International Space Year (ISY). It had also endorsed the recommendation of the Committee on outer space that international cooperation be promoted through the Year for the benefit and in the interests of all States and that the training and education capabilities of the United Nations Programme on Space Applications be utilized to bring about a meaningful role for the United Nations.

The focus of international ISY activities[6] was the use of space technology for studying and monitoring the environment, specifically the management of the resources of the Earth and its environment, long-term education programmes and public education. A number of conferences, seminars and workshops were held in support of ISY. The United Nations programme was to be complementary to the activities of international organizations such as COSPAR, IAF, the International Society for Photogrammetry and Remote Sensing and the Space Agency Forum for International Space Year.

In accordance with a 1991 Assembly resolution,[3] the Committee on outer space held a special commemorative meeting on 15 June 1992, which included a panel discussion on new approaches to international cooperation in space in a changing world. The Scientific and Technical Subcommittee's special session on 24 February, open to all Member States, included a panel discussion on space flight and global unification and a symposium on space technology and the Earth's environment, organized by COSPAR and IAF.

Among other activities organized by the United Nations were an essay competition and the issuance of a commemorative stamp.

In December,[7] the Secretariat presented a final report on United Nations ISY activities. The report stated that those activities had encouraged all countries, particularly developing ones, to participate in the applications of space technology and to undertake programmes contributing to the understanding, management and safeguarding of the environment.

The Committee on outer space noted the wide variety of national and international activities for ISY. It expressed appreciation to Austria, China, Greece, Japan, Sweden and the United States, as well as to the European Space Agency (ESA), for their voluntary contributions to ISY and urged others to support further scientific and technical activities in cooperation with the United Nations. It also recommended that the United Nations encourage the continuation of activities initiated for ISY and the involvement of more nations.

The Committee recommended that at its 1993 session Member States discuss the proposal that a third UNISPACE conference be organized in 1995, preferably in a developing country, in order to consolidate the momentum of ISY and to evolve follow-up actions and mechanisms for broadening the scope of international cooperation and increasing the participation of all developing countries in space activities.

Implementation of the recommendations of the 1982 Conference on outer space

In 1992, the Scientific and Technical Subcommittee, noting that the General Assembly in 1991[3] had again emphasized the urgency and importance of implementing fully the recommendations of UNISPACE-82, endorsed by the Assembly in 1982,[8] reconvened the Working Group of the Whole to Evaluate the Implementation of the Recommendations of UNISPACE-82, which held a series of meetings between 27 February and 4 March 1992.

In the report on its sixth session, annexed to the Subcommittee's report,[1] the Working Group put forward several recommendations, which were subsequently endorsed by the Committee and by the Assembly in **resolution 47/67**. Among its proposals were that: the organization of seminars and workshops on advanced applications of space science and technology and on new systems development should continue, taking the recent evolution of related technologies, applications and developmental priorities into account for the benefit of planners, administrators and users in developing countries; the emphasis of the United Nations Programme on Space Applications should remain on long-term, project-oriented on-the-job training in space technology and specific applications areas and, in order

to facilitate the indigenous research-and-development capabilities of developing countries, there should be a sufficient number of trainees to create national core groups of experts; the United Nations should continue making efforts to arrange funding and other support for creating regional centres for space science and technology education, and should endeavour to encourage regional cooperation and strengthen its cooperation with governmental and non-governmental organizations; countries with relevant capabilities should be encouraged to provide developing countries with financial and technical assistance for developing low-cost community receivers and power sources for communication satellites.

Other recommendations included: specific studies, including those in the areas of communications, broadcasting and forest and ocean resources management and development, should be carried out to demonstrate the potentials of space technology; the United Nations should promote better access to and experience in space-related subjects by arranging for experts to prepare an integrated national plan of action for an appropriate space applications programme; efforts were to be intensified to stimulate the growth of indigenous nuclei and an autonomous technological base in space technology in developing countries and to promote greater exchange of actual experiences with space applications.

In an August 1992 report,[9] the Secretary-General provided information on progress made in implementing the recommendations of UNISPACE-82. He noted that, as requested by the Assembly in 1991,[3] United Nations bodies and specialized agencies, particularly the United Nations Environment Programme, the Food and Agriculture Organization of the United Nations (FAO), the United Nations Educational, Scientific and Cultural Organization (UNESCO), the International Telecommunication Union (ITU), the World Meteorological Organization, the International Maritime Organization and the United Nations Industrial Development Organization, had extensive space-related programmes. Details of those programmes were covered in the Secretary-General's annual report on coordination of outer space activities in the United Nations system (see below).

In response to 1991 requests of the Working Group of the Whole, the Secretariat prepared and submitted in 1992 to the Scientific and Technical Subcommittee reports and studies on: applications of space technology for integrated land and water resources management for rural development;[10] applications of space technology to the study of desertification in developing countries;[11] activities of Member States in the context of international cooperation in the peaceful uses of outer space;[12] and an analytical review of international activities, in particular those of the United Nations, undertaken to implement UNISPACE-82 recommendations.[13]

The Committee on outer space, in endorsing the recommendations of the Working Group, noted that they called for preparation of further studies and reports of relevance to the UNISPACE-82 recommendations. In support of those recommendations, the United Nations Programme on Space Applications (see below) conducted training courses, seminars and workshops and provided technical advisory services.

The Secretariat continued its efforts to strengthen regional mechanisms of cooperation, among other things, by conducting consultations with regional commissions and countries on the establishment of regional centres for space science and technology education. Offers to host such centres had come from 21 countries. In that context, experts from Canada and Spain as well as from the United Nations undertook in May 1992 an evaluation mission to Latin America. Such missions to other regions were to be carried out as soon as funding sources were identified.

Budget allocations for
implementing UNISPACE-82 recommendations

The Committee on outer space, noting the Subcommittee's view that the respective budgetary allocations had been meagre in past years and remained the same for the current year, requested the General Assembly to make an adequate allocation to the Programme on Space Applications for full implementation of the recommendations of UNISPACE-82.

Following a request by Austria on behalf of the Working Group on International Cooperation in the Peaceful Uses of Outer Space of the Assembly's Special Political Committee, the Committee Chairman, by a letter of 30 October,[14] drew the attention of the Chairman of the Fifth (Administrative and Budgetary) Committee to the relevant paragraph in the report of the Committee on outer space.

The Working Group of the Whole of the Subcommittee also recommended that, in formulating cooperative programmes and projects, intensive participation of international and regional financial institutions be encouraged and that, in that connection, the Secretariat continue to report annually on arrangements within the United Nations system and with regional and international organizations for full utilization of available resources and for securing additional financial support from other sources.

The General Assembly, on 23 December 1992, by **resolution 47/219, section XXIII**, took note of the letter from the Chairman of the Special Political Committee regarding a budgetary allocation for the Programme on Space Applications.

UN Programme on Space Applications

In 1992, the United Nations Programme on Space Applications, under its mandate given by the General Assembly in 1982,[8] focused on developing indigenous capability in space science and technology, providing fellowships for in-depth training and technical advisory services to Member States; organizing regional and international training courses, conferences and meetings; assisting in the development of information systems; and promoting greater cooperation in space science and technology.

In a December 1992 report to the Scientific and Technical Subcommittee, the United Nations Expert on Space Applications[15] indicated that the Programme helped develop indigenous capability through the establishment and operation of centres for space science and technology education at the regional level,[16] providing in-depth education, research and applications programmes in satellite meteorology and remote sensing for environmental monitoring and natural resources management. The centres were to contribute to sustainable development of natural resources and provide a supplementary input for biodiversity conservation and other related environmental programmes.

The Programme received 19 long-term fellowship offers for 1992/93: 2 from Austria in microwave technology; 10 from Brazil in remote sensing; 2 from China in geodesy, photogrammetry and remote sensing; and 5 from ESA in satellite meteorology, space antennas, remote-sensing information and instrumentation, and communications systems.

The Programme, in collaboration with ESA, completed a survey on the remote-sensing data needs of those African countries covered by ESA's two ground-based receiving stations (Maspalomas, Canary Islands, Spain; Fucino, Italy) and selected a number of projects that could benefit from the data available in ESA's archives or being acquired by the two receiving stations. ESA provided data acquired by satellites to Guinea, Morocco, Nigeria and Tunisia in support of development programmes in irrigation, roads, water resources, land use, forestry and agriculture.

The United Nations was working with all parties associated with the Cotopaxi ground station in Ecuador to determine if the station was beneficial to the region; to analyse the cooperation and support that countries concerned could offer; and to define the technical and economic assistance that could be provided from the United Nations and other sources.

In 1992, the Programme conducted three training courses, four workshops and an international conference. In cooperation with Ecuador and Japan, it organized a workshop on space technology for resource development and environmental management for participants from the Economic Commission for Latin America and the Caribbean region, hosted by the Centro de Levantamientos Integrados de Recursos Naturales por Sensores Remotos (CLIRSEN) (Quito, 9-13 March).[17] The workshop exposed managers and planners to the possibilities of using data from current and future Earth observation systems in their decision-making, familiarized them with the functions of the CLIRSEN-Cotopaxi satellite station and discussed possible regional cooperation programmes for the 22 countries within the coverage of the station.

The second United Nations training course on remote-sensing education for educators (Stockholm and Kiruna, 11 May–12 June), organized in cooperation with Sweden and hosted by Stockholm University and the Swedish Space Corporation, was attended by 27 educators from 23 developing countries in Africa, South-East Asia and Latin America.[18]

A United Nations/United States international conference (Boulder, Colorado, 17-20 August)[19] examined issues facing developing countries in their efforts to contribute to the development and utilization of remote-sensing technology and that technology's role in resource management, environmental assessment and global-change studies. The conference, with 155 participants, also discussed the accessibility and availability of data sources and the role of remote sensing in meeting the needs of developing countries.

Participants from developing and Eastern European countries received education and practical training at the fourth United Nations training course on remote-sensing applications to geological sciences, organized jointly with Germany (Potsdam and Berlin, 28 September–16 October).[20] Participants from Africa and the Middle East were given education and practical training at a United Nations/ESA course on the use of remote-sensing systems in hydrological and agrometeorological applications (Nairobi, Kenya, 12-30 October).[21]

The second United Nations/ESA/The Planetary Society workshop on basic space science, organized with Costa Rica and Colombia and hosted by the University of the Costa Rica, the International Centre for Physics and the University of the Andes, was held at San José (2-7 November) and Santa Fé de Bogotá (9-13 November).[22] A United Nations workshop on space communications for development, organized in cooperation with and hosted by the Republic of Korea (Seoul, 24-28 November),[23] provided participants with information on the current state and future trends of satellite communication technology and its contribution to economic and social development in the Economic and Social Commission for Asia and the Pacific region.

The Programme also promoted greater cooperation in space science and technology by organizing, with the International Society for Photogrammetry and Remote Sensing, a workshop on remote-sensing data analysis methods and applications (Washington, D.C., 6 and 7 August) and, with IAF, COSPAR and the American Institute of Aeronautics and Astronautics, a symposium on space technology in developing countries (Washington, D.C., 28-30 August).

The Programme designed a number of activities to mark United Nations participation in ISY and provided technical advisory services in support of Chile's plans to host in 1993 the Second Space Conference of the Americas.

The General Assembly in 1991 had approved appropriations of $345,900 under the regular United Nations budget for implementation of Programme activities during 1992-1993. In addition, the Programme received voluntary contributions in cash and kind from Member States and their institutions, as well as from regional and international governmental and non-governmental organizations.

Both the Scientific and Technical Subcommittee and the Committee on outer space expressed concern over the limited financial resources available for the Programme and appealed for further voluntary contributions.

The Assembly, in **resolution 47/67**, endorsed the Programme for 1993, as proposed by the Expert on Space Applications,[24] and urged all States to make voluntary contributions to enhance the Programme's effectiveness.

Remote sensing of the Earth by satellites

The Scientific and Technical Subcommittee, in accordance with a 1991 General Assembly resolution,[3] continued consideration of matters relating to remote sensing of the Earth by satellites.[1] It reviewed national and cooperative programmes in remote sensing and received information on programmes in developed and developing countries based on bilateral, regional and international cooperation, including technical assistance.

The Subcommittee noted the continuing programmes for remote-sensing satellites of China, France, India, Japan, the Russian Federation, the United States and ESA and the planned systems of Brazil and Canada. It also noted the activities of FAO for mapping, assessment and management of renewable natural resources for the benefit of developing countries and those of UNESCO in the area of education and training, particularly for oceanography.

The Subcommittee reiterated that remote-sensing activities should take into account the need to provide appropriate and non-discriminatory assistance to developing countries. It emphasized the importance of making remote-sensing data and analysed information openly available, affordable and timely and recognized the continuing need for free access to data from meteorological satellites.

The Subcommittee suggested that international cooperation be encouraged through coordination of the operations of ground stations and regular meetings between satellite operators and users. It also noted the importance of compatibility and complementarity of existing and future remote-sensing systems, of sharing experiences and technologies, of cooperation through international and regional remote-sensing centres and of joint work on collaborative projects.

The Committee on outer space recognized the importance of those international efforts and encouraged all countries and agencies to continue the free distribution of meteorological information.

Nuclear power sources in outer space

In accordance with a 1991 General Assembly resolution,[3] the Scientific and Technical Subcommittee in 1992 reconvened its Working Group on the Use of Nuclear Power Sources in Outer Space. The Group met from 26 February to 5 March. Its report was annexed to the Subcommittee's report.[1]

Among other matters, the Working Group discussed revised draft principles relevant to the use of nuclear power sources in outer space, consideration of which took place in the Legal Subcommittee (see below). Revised working papers reflected discussions on the subject in the Scientific and Technical Subcommittee and its Working Group.

The Subcommittee agreed that Member States should be invited to report to the Secretary-General on national and international research concerning the safety of nuclear-powered satellites, that the problem of collision of nuclear power sources with space debris be studied further and that it be informed of the results. In that regard, the Subcommittee noted a paper submitted by the Russian Federation containing preliminary results of studies on the question.

The Committee on outer space endorsed the Subcommittee's recommendations.

Space transportation

The Scientific and Technical Subcommittee reviewed national and international cooperative programmes in space transportation systems, including expendable launchers, reusable space shuttles, space stations and research on aerospace planes, and their implications for future activities in space. In particular, it noted the progress in the various programmes in operation or planned by China, India, Japan, the Russian Federation, the United Kingdom, the United States and ESA. The Sub-

committee stressed the importance of international cooperation in space transportation to provide all countries with access to the benefits of space science and technology.

The Committee on outer space endorsed the Subcommittee's recommendation that it continue consideration of the item at its next session.

Technical aspects of the geostationary orbit

In considering the question of the utilization of the geostationary orbit—in which communications and other satellites are positioned some 36,000 kilometres above the equator—the Scientific and Technical Subcommittee reviewed national and international cooperative programmes in satellite communications, including progress in making satellite communications more accessible and affordable and increasing the communications capacity of the geostationary orbit and the electromagnetic spectrum.

In elaborating their views on the question of equitable access to the geostationary orbit, some delegations considered that its saturation should be avoided, that a special regime was required to ensure equitable access and that account should be taken in particular of the characteristics of the equatorial countries. Others considered that use of the orbit was affected by space debris, which should be minimized, and that satellites should be moved before the end of their useful lives into disposal orbits beyond the geostationary belt of orbit.

The Subcommittee took note of studies and research on the use of multiple, low-orbiting satellites for low-cost satellite communications.

The Committee on outer space expressed its appreciation to the ITU for its thirty-first annual progress report on telecommunication and the peaceful uses of outer space.[25] Some delegations stressed the important technical scope of ITU's work, while drawing attention to the Committee's competence in preparing policy decisions referring to the geostationary orbit.

Legal aspects of the geostationary orbit were considered by the Legal Subcommittee (see below).

Space and Earth environment

In 1991,[3] the General Assembly had recommended that more attention be paid to all aspects related to the protection and preservation of the outer space environment, especially those potentially affecting the Earth's environment, as well as to the problem of collisions with space debris and other aspects of space debris. In response to the Assembly's request, 17 Member States provided information to the Scientific and Technical Subcommittee on their research on space debris.[26]

The Subcommittee agreed that information on national research on space debris should continue to be provided to it, and that there was a need for further research and for the compilation and dissemination of data on space debris as well as for the development of improved monitoring technology. It also noted the importance of international cooperation in addressing those issues.

The Committee on outer space noted the importance of satellite remote sensing for monitoring the Earth's environment and, in particular, for studying and monitoring global change. It agreed that the Secretariat should prepare, for its 1993 session, an analytical report on the role the Committee could play in view of the decisions and recommendations of the United Nations Conference on Environment and Development (UNCED) (see PART THREE, Chapter VIII).

Spin-off benefits of space technology

In accordance with a 1991 General Assembly request,[3] the Committee on outer space reviewed the status of spin-off benefits of space technology and noted working papers submitted by China and the Russian Federation on their achievements in that area.

The Committee agreed that spin-offs of space technology were yielding substantial benefits, which provided new techniques for industrial measurement and control, image and data processing, non-destructive testing, temperature control and vacuum systems, computer systems, special materials and chemicals, food safety, water treatment and refrigeration.

The Committee agreed on the need to strengthen and enhance international cooperation in spin-off benefits through providing greater access, with particular attention to those benefits which addressed the needs of developing countries. It recommended that the United Nations Programme on Space Applications consider including the subject each year in its training courses, seminars or expert meetings, and reiterated its recommendation that space agencies consider making budgetary allocations to promote spin-off benefits in various countries.

Coordination in the UN system

The fourteenth Ad Hoc Inter-Agency Meeting on Outer Space Activities, convened by the Administrative Committee on Coordination (Paris, 5-7 October 1992),[27] reviewed activities requiring coordination and discussed matters of mutual interest relating to programming of activities, including those in connection with the implementation of UNISPACE-82 recommendations, follow-up to ISY and UNCED, and remote sensing.

The Committee on outer space and its Scientific and Technical Subcommittee noted that the General Assembly, in 1991,[3] had reaffirmed that all United Nations organs and organizations and other intergovernmental bodies working in the field of outer space or on space-related matters should cooperate in implementing the recommendations of UNISPACE-82.

Following consideration of the report of the 1991 Inter-Agency Meeting,[28] the Subcommittee noted the information on progress achieved in coordinating United Nations space activities. It also expressed appreciation for the Secretary-General's October 1991 report on coordination of outer space activities in the United Nations system,[29] which summarized the major activities and programmes planned by individual organizations for 1992 and 1993 in an integrated form in the areas of remote sensing, communications, meteorology and hydrology, space science, use of space technology for maritime communications and air navigation, ISY, and other activities in space science and technology and its applications.

In December 1992,[30] the Secretary-General submitted a report outlining major United Nations system activities and programmes planned for 1993, 1994 and future years.

The Committee on outer space noted that the Scientific and Technical Subcommittee had stressed the necessity of ensuring continuous and effective consultations and coordination in outer space activities. It found the reports submitted by the specialized agencies and other international organizations helpful in enabling it and its subsidiary bodies to fulfil their roles as focal point for international cooperation, especially with respect to the practical applications of space science and technology in developing countries.

Other questions

The Committee on outer space and its Scientific and Technical Subcommittee considered various other space-related questions, such as life sciences, including space medicine; progress in national and international space activities related to the Earth environment, in particular progress in the geosphere-biosphere (global change) programme; and matters relating to planetary exploration and to astronomy. The Committee noted that a number of special presentations on those items had been made to the Subcommittee by specialists from various countries.

In the area of life sciences, the Subcommittee took note of a working paper by the Russian Federation on space biology and medicine and a Secretariat study on applications of biomedical technology.[31] The Subcommittee noted the research programmes in Canada, Germany, the Russian Federation and the United States, the important advances in medical knowledge resulting from studies of human physiology under the microgravity conditions of space flight and the growing promise of space technologies in public health.

In relation to the Earth environment, the Subcommittee noted the progress made in the international geosphere-biosphere programme and the important contributions of satellite remote sensing for monitoring, preventing and reversing land degradation, and of meteorological and atmospheric research satellites for studying global climate change, including the greenhouse effect and ozone layer degradation. It noted the need for further research of environmental phenomena.

The Subcommittee welcomed the annual reports of various organizations in and outside the United Nations system[32] and the preliminary version of the thirty-first report of ITU on telecommunication and the peaceful uses of outer space.[25] It expressed appreciation to COSPAR for its report on the progress of space research in 1990-1991[33] and to IAF for its report on highlights in space technology and applications during 1991.[34]

The Committee on outer space expressed appreciation to those organizations that had submitted reports and requested that it continue to be kept informed. It also noted the participation in its work and that of its Subcommittees of various organizations.

The Committee recommended that the Secretariat invite Member States to submit annual reports on their space activities, including information on space programmes and spin-off benefits of space activities. Pursuant to that recommendation, the Secretariat in December submitted such information from 14 Member States.[35]

Space law

The Legal Subcommittee of the Committee on outer space, at its thirty-first session (New York, 23 March–10 April),[36] continued to consider draft principles relevant to the use of nuclear power sources in outer space; matters relating to the definition and delimitation of outer space and to the character and utilization of the geostationary orbit; and legal aspects related to the application of the principle that the exploration and utilization of outer space should be carried out for the benefit and in the interest of all States.

The Committee on outer space took note with appreciation of the Subcommittee's report on the work of its 1992 session.[4]

Legal aspects of nuclear power sources in spacecraft

The Legal Subcommittee continued in 1992, through its Working Group on the Use of Nuclear Power Sources in Outer Space, to elaborate draft principles relevant to the use of such power sources. In addition to working papers presented previously, the Subcommittee had before it the eleventh revision of the draft principles submitted by Canada and Germany, reflecting the discussions in the Scientific and Technical Subcommittee.

Following informal consultations, the Committee on outer space reached consensus, on the basis of a text by the Chairman, on the draft set of principles and recommended that it be adopted by the General Assembly. It further recommended that the Legal Subcommittee consider the question of the early review and possible revision of the principles.

On 14 December, the General Assembly, on the recommendation of the Special Political Committee, adopted **resolution 47/68** without vote.

Principles Relevant to the Use of Nuclear Power Sources in Outer Space

The General Assembly,

Having considered the report of the Committee on the Peaceful Uses of Outer Space on the work of its thirty-fifth session and the text of the Principles Relevant to the Use of Nuclear Power Sources in Outer Space as approved by the Committee and annexed to its report,

Recognizing that for some missions in outer space nuclear power sources are particularly suited or even essential owing to their compactness, long life and other attributes,

Recognizing also that the use of nuclear power sources in outer space should focus on those applications which take advantage of the particular properties of nuclear power sources,

Recognizing further that the use of nuclear power sources in outer space should be based on a thorough safety assessment, including probabilistic risk analysis, with particular emphasis on reducing the risk of accidental exposure of the public to harmful radiation or radioactive material,

Recognizing the need, in this respect, for a set of principles containing goals and guidelines to ensure the safe use of nuclear power sources in outer space,

Affirming that this set of Principles applies to nuclear power sources in outer space devoted to the generation of electric power on board space objects for non-propulsive purposes, which have characteristics generally comparable to those of systems used and missions performed at the time of the adoption of the Principles,

Recognizing that this set of Principles will require future revision in view of emerging nuclear power applications and of evolving international recommendations on radiological protection,

Adopts the Principles Relevant to the Use of Nuclear Power Sources in Outer Space as set forth below.

Principle 1
Applicability of international law

Activities involving the use of nuclear power sources in outer space shall be carried out in accordance with international law, including in particular the Charter of the United Nations and the Treaty on Principles Governing the Activities of States in the Exploration and Use of Outer Space, including the Moon and Other Celestial Bodies.

Principle 2
Use of terms

1. For the purpose of these Principles, the terms "launching State" and "State launching" mean the State which exercises jurisdiction and control over a space object with nuclear power sources on board at a given point in time relevant to the principle concerned.

2. For the purpose of principle 9, the definition of the term "launching State" as contained in that principle is applicable.

3. For the purposes of principle 3, the terms "foreseeable" and "all possible" describe a class of events or circumstances whose overall probability of occurrence is such that it is considered to encompass only credible possibilities for purposes of safety analysis. The term "general concept of defence-in-depth" when applied to nuclear power sources in outer space refers to the use of design features and mission operations in place of or in addition to active systems, to prevent or mitigate the consequences of system malfunctions. Redundant safety systems are not necessarily required for each individual component to achieve this purpose. Given the special requirements of space use and of varied missions, no particular set of systems or features can be specified as essential to achieve this objective. For the purposes of paragraph 2 (*d*) of principle 3, the term "made critical" does not include actions such as zero-power testing which are fundamental to ensuring system safety.

Principle 3
Guidelines and criteria for safe use

In order to minimize the quantity of radioactive material in space and the risks involved, the use of nuclear power sources in outer space shall be restricted to those space missions which cannot be operated by non-nuclear energy sources in a reasonable way.

1. *General goals for radiation protection and nuclear safety*

(*a*) States launching space objects with nuclear power sources on board shall endeavour to protect individuals, populations and the biosphere against radiological hazards. The design and use of space objects with nuclear power sources on board shall ensure, with a high degree of confidence, that the hazards, in foreseeable operational or accidental circumstances, are kept below acceptable levels as defined in paragraphs 1 (*b*) and (*c*).

Such design and use shall also ensure with high reliability that radioactive material does not cause a significant contamination of outer space.

(*b*) During the normal operation of space objects with nuclear power sources on board, including re-entry from the sufficiently high orbit as defined in paragraph 2 (*b*), the appropriate radiation protection objective for the public recommended by the International Commission on Radiological Protection shall be observed. During such normal operation there shall be no significant radiation exposure.

(*c*) To limit exposure in accidents, the design and construction of the nuclear power source systems shall take into account relevant and generally accepted international radiological protection guidelines.

Except in cases of low-probability accidents with potentially serious radiological consequences, the design for the nuclear power source systems shall, with a high degree of confidence, restrict radiation exposure to a limited geographical region and to individuals to the principal limit of 1 mSv in a year. It is permissible to use a subsidiary dose limit of 5 mSv in a year for some years, provided that the average annual effective dose equivalent over a lifetime does not exceed the principal limit of 1 mSv in a year.

The probability of accidents with potentially serious radiological consequences referred to above shall be kept extremely small by virtue of the design of the system.

Future modifications of the guidelines referred to in this paragraph shall be applied as soon as practicable.

(*d*) Systems important for safety shall be designed, constructed and operated in accordance with the general concept of defence-in-depth. Pursuant to this concept, foreseeable safety-related failures or malfunctions must be capable of being corrected or counteracted by an action or a procedure, possibly automatic.

The reliability of systems important for safety shall be ensured, *inter alia*, by redundancy, physical separation, functional isolation and adequate independence of their components.

Other measures shall also be taken to raise the level of safety.

2. *Nuclear reactors*

(*a*) Nuclear reactors may be operated:

(i) On interplanetary missions;

(ii) In sufficiently high orbits as defined in paragraph 2 (*b*);

(iii) In low-Earth orbits if they are stored in sufficiently high orbits after the operational part of their mission.

(*b*) The sufficiently high orbit is one in which the orbital lifetime is long enough to allow for a sufficient decay of the fission products to approximately the activity of the actinides. The sufficiently high orbit must be such that the risks to existing and future outer space missions and of collision with other space objects are kept to a minimum. The necessity for the parts of a destroyed reactor also to attain the required decay time before re-entering the Earth's atmosphere shall be considered in determining the sufficiently high orbit altitude.

(*c*) Nuclear reactors shall use only highly enriched uranium 235 as fuel. The design shall take into account the radioactive decay of the fission and activation products.

(*d*) Nuclear reactors shall not be made critical before they have reached their operating orbit or interplanetary trajectory.

(*e*) The design and construction of the nuclear reactor shall ensure that it can not become critical before reaching the operating orbit during all possible events, including rocket explosion, re-entry, impact on ground or water, submersion in water or water intruding into the core.

(*f*) In order to reduce significantly the possibility of failures in satellites with nuclear reactors on board during operations in an orbit with a lifetime less than in the sufficiently high orbit (including operations for transfer into the sufficiently high orbit), there shall be a highly reliable operational system to ensure an effective and controlled disposal of the reactor.

3. *Radioisotope generators*

(*a*) Radioisotope generators may be used for interplanetary missions and other missions leaving the gravity field of the Earth. They may also be used in Earth orbit if, after conclusion of the operational part of their mission, they are stored in a high orbit. In any case ultimate disposal is necessary.

(b) Radioisotope generators shall be protected by a containment system that is designed and constructed to withstand the heat and aerodynamic forces of re-entry in the upper atmosphere under foreseeable orbital conditions, including highly elliptical or hyperbolic orbits where relevant. Upon impact, the containment system and the physical form of the isotope shall ensure that no radioactive material is scattered into the environment so that the impact area can be completely cleared of radioactivity by a recovery operation.

Principle 4
Safety assessment

1. A launching State as defined in principle 2, paragraph 1, at the time of launch shall, prior to the launch, through cooperative arrangements, where relevant, with those which have designed, constructed or manufactured the nuclear power source, or will operate the space object, or from whose territory or facility such an object will be launched, ensure that a thorough and comprehensive safety assessment is conducted. This assessment shall cover as well all relevant phases of the mission and shall deal with all systems involved, including the means of launching, the space platform, the nuclear power source and its equipment and the means of control and communication between ground and space.

2. This assessment shall respect the guidelines and criteria for safe use contained in principle 3.

3. Pursuant to article XI of the Treaty on Principles Governing the Activities of States in the Exploration and Use of Outer Space, including the Moon and Other Celestial Bodies, the results of this safety assessment, together with, to the extent feasible, an indication of the approximate intended time-frame of the launch, shall be made publicly available prior to each launch, and the Secretary-General of the United Nations shall be informed on how States may obtain such results of the safety assessment as soon as possible prior to each launch.

Principle 5
Notification of re-entry

1. Any State launching a space object with nuclear power sources on board shall in a timely fashion inform States concerned in the event this space object is malfunctioning with a risk of re-entry of radioactive materials to the Earth. The information shall be in accordance with the following format:

(a) *System parameters:*
(i)   Name of launching State or States, including the address of the authority which may be contacted for additional information or assistance in case of accident;
(ii) International designation;
(iii) Date and territory or location of launch;
(iv) Information required for best prediction of orbit lifetime, trajectory and impact region;
(v)   General function of spacecraft;

(b) *Information on the radiological risk of nuclear power source(s):*
(i)   Type of nuclear power source: radioisotopic/reactor;
(ii) The probable physical form, amount and general radiological characteristics of the fuel and contaminated and/or activated components likely to

reach the ground. The term "fuel" refers to the nuclear material used as the source of heat or power.

This information shall also be transmitted to the Secretary-General of the United Nations.

2. The information, in accordance with the format above, shall be provided by the launching State as soon as the malfunction has become known. It shall be updated as frequently as practicable and the frequency of dissemination of the updated information shall increase as the anticipated time of re-entry into the dense layers of the Earth's atmosphere approaches so that the international community will be informed of the situation and will have sufficient time to plan for any national response activities deemed necessary.

3. The updated information shall also be transmitted to the Secretary-General of the United Nations with the same frequency.

Principle 6
Consultations

States providing information in accordance with principle 5 shall, as far as reasonably practicable, respond promptly to requests for further information or consultations sought by other States.

Principle 7
Assistance to States

1. Upon the notification of an expected re-entry into the Earth's atmosphere of a space object containing a nuclear power source on board and its components, all States possessing space monitoring and tracking facilities, in the spirit of international cooperation, shall communicate the relevant information that they may have available on the malfunctioning space object with a nuclear power source on board to the Secretary-General of the United Nations and the State concerned as promptly as possible to allow States that might be affected to assess the situation and take any precautionary measures deemed necessary.

2. After re-entry into the Earth's atmosphere of a space object containing a nuclear power source on board and its components:

(a) The launching State shall promptly offer and, if requested by the affected State, provide promptly the necessary assistance to eliminate actual and possible harmful effects, including assistance to identify the location of the area of impact of the nuclear power source on the Earth's surface, to detect the re-entered material and to carry out retrieval or clean-up operations;

(b) All States, other than the launching State, with relevant technical capabilities and international organizations with such technical capabilities shall, to the extent possible, provide necessary assistance upon request by an affected State.

In providing the assistance in accordance with subparagraphs *(a)* and *(b)* above, the special needs of developing countries shall be taken into account.

Principle 8
Responsibility

In accordance with article VI of the Treaty on Principles Governing the Activities of States in the Exploration and Use of Outer Space, including the Moon and Other Celestial Bodies, States shall bear international responsibility for national activities involving the use of nuclear power sources in outer space, whether such activities are carried on by governmental agencies or by non-governmental entities, and for assuring that such national activities are carried out in conformity with that Treaty and the recommendations contained in these Principles. When activities in outer space involving the use of nuclear power sources are carried on by an international organization, responsibility for compliance with the aforesaid Treaty and the recommendations contained in these Principles shall be borne both by the international organization and by the States participating in it.

Principle 9
Liability and compensation

1. In accordance with article VII of the Treaty on Principles Governing the Activities of States in the Exploration and Use of Outer Space, including the Moon and Other Celestial Bodies, and the provisions of the Convention on International Liability for Damage Caused by Space Objects, each State which launches or procures the launching of a space object and each State from whose territory or facility a space object is launched shall be internationally liable for damage caused by such space objects or their component parts. This fully applies to the case of such a space object carrying a nuclear power source on board. Whenever two or more States jointly launch such a space object, they shall be jointly and severally liable for any damage caused, in accordance with article V of the above-mentioned Convention.

2. The compensation that such States shall be liable to pay under the aforesaid Convention for damage shall be determined in accordance with international law and the principles of justice and equity, in order to provide such reparation in respect of the damage as will restore the person, natural or juridical, State or international organization on whose behalf a claim is presented to the condition which would have existed if the damage had not occurred.

3. For the purposes of this principle, compensation shall include reimbursement of the duly substantiated expenses for search, recovery and clean-up operations, including expenses for assistance received from third parties.

Principle 10
Settlement of disputes

Any dispute resulting from the application of these Principles shall be resolved through negotiations or other established procedures for the peaceful settlement of disputes, in accordance with the Charter of the United Nations.

Principle 11
Review and revision

These Principles shall be reopened for revision by the Committee on the Peaceful Uses of Outer Space no later than two years after their adoption.

General Assembly resolution 47/68

14 December 1992   Meeting 85   Adopted without vote

Approved by Special Political Committee (A/47/610) without vote, 30 October (meeting 8); draft by Austria, for Working Group (A/SPC/47/L.6); agenda item 72.

Meeting numbers. GA 47th session: SPC 5-8; plenary 85.

Legal aspects of the geostationary orbit and definition of outer space

The Legal Subcommittee, through its working group, continued consideration of matters relating to the definition and delimitation of outer space and to the character and utilization of the geostationary orbit, including ways to ensure its rational and equitable use without prejudice to the role of ITU. In addition to working papers submitted at previous sessions, the Subcommittee also had before it a working paper presented by the Russian Federation, which the Committee on outer space agreed could be a suitable basis, among others, for future discussion.

The Committee also noted the deliberations of the Legal Subcommittee and the exchange of views that had taken place on the basis of a "working nonpaper" introduced by members of the Group of 77,[37] a revised version of which was to be submitted to the Subcommittee in 1993.

Exploration of outer space

The Legal Subcommittee re-established its working group to continue consideration of the legal aspects related to the application of the principle that the exploration and utilization of outer space should be carried out for the benefit of all States, taking into particular account the needs of developing countries. In accordance with a 1991 request,[37] the Chairman of the working group submitted a background paper summarizing in an analytical manner views and information contained in replies of Member States to requests from the Secretary-General in 1988 and 1989, respectively, on priority subjects under the item and on international agreements they had entered into relevant to the principle.

In addition, the group had before it a 1991 working paper and a new working paper by Nigeria. The group's discussion of the provisions of the 1991 paper, on principles regarding international cooperation in the exploration and utilization of outer space for peaceful purposes, was set out in the report of the Chairman of the group, annexed to the Subcommittee's report.[36]

The Committee on outer space noted the constructive work carried out by the Subcommittee and the working group, the discussion based on the 1991 working paper, and the positive reaction of the co-sponsors (Argentina, Brazil, Chile, Mexico, Nigeria, Pakistan, Philippines, Uruguay, Venezuela) to comments made by other delegations, which would be taken into account in future discussions.

GENERAL ASSEMBLY ACTION

On 14 December, the General Assembly, following the recommendation of the Special Political Committee, adopted **resolution 47/67** without vote.

International cooperation in the peaceful uses of outer space

The General Assembly,

Recalling its resolution 46/45 of 9 December 1991,

Deeply convinced of the common interest of mankind in promoting the exploration and use of outer space for peaceful purposes and in continuing efforts to extend to all States the benefits derived therefrom, and of the importance of international cooperation in this field, for which the United Nations should continue to provide a focal point,

Reaffirming the importance of international cooperation in developing the rule of law, including the relevant norms of space law and their important role in international cooperation for the exploration and use of outer space for peaceful purposes,

Gravely concerned about the extension of an arms race into outer space,

Recognizing that all States, in particular those with major space capabilities, should contribute actively to the goal of preventing an arms race in outer space as an essential condition for the promotion of international cooperation in the exploration and use of outer space for peaceful purposes,

Aware of the need to increase the benefits of space technology and its applications and to contribute to an orderly growth of space activities favourable to the socio-economic advancement of mankind, in particular that of the people of developing countries,

Noting with satisfaction that the Committee on the Peaceful Uses of Outer Space, on the basis of the deliberations of its two subcommittees, had endorsed the text of the draft principles relevant to the use of nuclear power sources in outer space,

Considering that space debris is an issue of concern to all nations,

Noting the progress achieved in the further development of peaceful space exploration and application as well as in various national and cooperative space projects, which contribute to international cooperation in this field,

Taking note of the report of the Secretary-General on the implementation of the recommendations of the Second United Nations Conference on the Exploration and Peaceful Uses of Outer Space,

Having considered the report of the Committee on the Peaceful Uses of Outer Space on the work of its thirty-fifth session,

1. *Endorses* the report of the Committee on the Peaceful Uses of Outer Space;

2. *Invites* States that have not yet become parties to the international treaties governing the uses of outer space to give consideration to ratifying or acceding to those treaties;

3. *Notes* that, at its thirty-first session, the Legal Subcommittee of the Committee on the Peaceful Uses of Outer Space, in its working groups, continued its work as mandated by the General Assembly in resolution 46/45;

4. *Endorses* the recommendations of the Committee that the Legal Subcommittee, at its thirty-second session, taking into account the concerns of all countries, particularly those of developing countries, should:

(*a*) Consider, through its working group, the question of early review and possible revision of the Principles Relevant to the Use of Nuclear Power Sources in Outer Space;

(*b*) Continue, through its working group, its consideration of matters relating to the definition and delimitation of outer space and to the character and utilization of the geostationary orbit, including consideration of ways and means to ensure the rational and equitable use of the geostationary orbit without prejudice to the role of the International Telecommunication Union;

(*c*) Continue, through its working group, its consideration of the legal aspects related to the application of the principle that the exploration and utilization of outer space should be carried out for the benefit and in the interests of all States, taking into particular account the needs of developing countries;

5. *Notes* that deliberations on the question of the geostationary orbit were undertaken by the Legal Subcommittee, as reflected in its report, on the basis of recent proposals which might provide a new and enhanced basis for future work;

6. *Endorses* the recommendations of the Committee concerning the organization of work in the Legal Subcommittee;

7. *Notes* that the Scientific and Technical Subcommittee of the Committee on the Peaceful Uses of Outer Space, at its twenty-ninth session, continued its work as mandated by the General Assembly in its resolution 46/45;

8. *Endorses* the recommendations of the Committee that the Scientific and Technical Subcommittee, at its thirtieth session, taking into account the concerns of all countries, particularly those of developing countries, should:

(*a*) Consider the following items on a priority basis:

(i) United Nations Programme on Space Applications and the coordination of space activities within the United Nations system;

(ii) Implementation of the recommendations of the Second United Nations Conference on the Exploration and Peaceful Uses of Outer Space;

(iii) Matters relating to remote sensing of the Earth by satellites including, *inter alia*, applications for developing countries;

(iv) Use of nuclear power sources in outer space;

(*b*) Consider the following items:

(i) Questions relating to space transportation systems and their implications for future activities in space;

(ii) Examination of the physical nature and technical attributes of the geostationary orbit; examination of its utilization and applications, including, *inter alia*, in the field of space communications, as well as other questions relating to space communications developments, taking particular account of the needs and interests of developing countries;

(iii) Matters relating to life sciences, including space medicine;

(iv) Progress in national and international space activities related to the Earth's environment, in particular progress in the geosphere-biosphere (global change) programme;

(v) Matters relating to planetary exploration;

(vi) Matters relating to astronomy;

(vii) The theme fixed for special attention at the 1993 session of the Scientific and Technical Subcommittee: "Space-based communication: the expansion of current services and increased understanding of new systems and the services they will make possible"; the Committee on Space Research and the International Astronautical Federation, in liaison with Member States, should be invited to arrange a symposium, with as wide a participation as possible, to be held during the first week of the Subcommittee's session, to complement discussions within the Subcommittee on the special theme;

9. *Considers*, in the context of paragraph 8 *(a)* (ii) above, that it is particularly urgent to implement the following recommendations:

(a) All countries should have the opportunity to use the techniques resulting from medical studies in space;

(b) Data banks at the national and regional levels should be strengthened and expanded and an international space information service should be established to function as a centre of coordination;

(c) The United Nations should support the creation of adequate training centres at the regional level, linked, whenever possible, to institutions implementing space programmes; necessary funding for the development of such centres should be made available through financial institutions;

(d) The United Nations should organize a fellowship programme through which selected graduates or postgraduates from developing countries should get in-depth, long-term exposure to space technology or applications; it is also desirable to encourage the availability of opportunities for such exposure on other bilateral and multilateral bases outside the United Nations system;

10. *Endorses* the recommendation of the Committee that the Scientific and Technical Subcommittee should reconvene, at its thirtieth session, the Working Group of the Whole to Evaluate the Implementation of the Recommendations of the Second United Nations Conference on the Exploration and Peaceful Uses of Outer Space, to continue its work;

11. *Also endorses* the recommendations of the Working Group of the Whole of the Scientific and Technical Subcommittee, as endorsed by the Committee and as contained in the report of the Working Group of the Whole;

12. *Decides* that, during the thirtieth session of the Scientific and Technical Subcommittee, the Working Group on the Use of Nuclear Power Sources in Outer Space should be reconvened, and invites Member States to report to the Secretary-General on a regular basis with regard to national and international research concerning the safety of nuclear-powered satellites;

13. *Endorses* the United Nations Programme on Space Applications for 1993, as proposed to the Committee by the Expert on Space Applications, and urges all States to make voluntary contributions to this Programme in order to enhance its effectiveness;

14. *Emphasizes* the urgency and importance of implementing fully the recommendations of the Second United Nations Conference on the Exploration and Peaceful Uses of Outer Space as early as possible;

15. *Reaffirms* its approval of the recommendation of the Conference regarding the establishment and strengthening of regional mechanisms of cooperation and their promotion and creation through the United Nations system;

16. *Expresses its appreciation* to all Governments that have made or expressed their intention to make contributions towards carrying out the recommendations of the Conference;

17. *Invites* all Governments to take effective action for the implementation of the recommendations of the Conference;

18. *Requests* all organs, organizations and bodies of the United Nations system and other intergovernmental organizations working in the field of outer space or on space-related matters to cooperate in the implementation of the recommendations of the Conference;

19. *Requests* the Secretary-General to report to the General Assembly at its forty-eighth session on the implementation of the recommendations of the Conference;

20. *Recommends* that Member States might discuss, during the next sessions of the Committee under its agenda item "Other matters", the possibility of holding a third United Nations Conference on the Exploration and Peaceful Uses of Outer Space in the future;

21. *Also recommends* that the United Nations should actively encourage the continuation of activities initiated for International Space Year 1992 and promote broader involvement in those activities by more nations;

22. *Notes with interest* the plans of the Government of Chile to host the second Space Conference of the Americas, at Santiago, in 1993;

23. *Recommends* that more attention be paid to all aspects related to the protection and the preservation of the outer space environment, especially those potentially affecting the Earth's environment;

24. *Considers* that it is essential that Member States pay more attention to the problem of collisions of space objects, including nuclear power sources, with space debris, and other aspects of space debris, and calls for the continuation of national research on this question, for the development of improved technology for the monitoring of space debris and for the compilation and dissemination of data on space debris, and that, to the extent possible, information thereon should be provided to the Scientific and Technical Subcommittee in order to allow it to follow this area more closely;

25. *Requests* the Secretary-General to invite Member States to provide information on national research on space debris to the Scientific and Technical Subcommittee;

26. *Also considers* that space debris could be an appropriate subject for in-depth discussion by the Committee in the future;

27. *Requests* the Secretary-General to prepare, for the next session of the Committee, an analytical report on the role that the Committee could play in view of the decisions and recommendations of the United Nations Conference on Environment and Development and invites Member States to submit their views in time for inclusion in that report;

28. *Urges* all States, in particular those with major space capabilities, to contribute actively to the goal of preventing an arms race in outer space as an essential condition for the promotion of international cooperation in the exploration and uses of outer space for peaceful purposes;

29. *Takes note* of the views expressed during the thirty-fifth session of the Committee and during the forty-seventh session of the General Assembly concerning ways and means of maintaining outer space for peaceful purposes;

30. *Requests* the Committee to continue to consider, as a matter of priority, ways and means of maintaining outer space for peaceful purposes and to report thereon to the General Assembly at its forty-eighth session;

31.   *Also requests* the Committee to continue to consider, at its thirty-sixth session, its agenda item entitled "Spin-off benefits of space technology: review of current status";

32.   *Requests* the specialized agencies and other international organizations to continue and, where appropriate, enhance their cooperation with the Committee and to provide it with progress reports on their work relating to the peaceful uses of outer space;

33.   *Further requests* the Committee to continue its work, in accordance with the present resolution, to consider, as appropriate, new projects in outer space activities and to submit a report to the General Assembly at its forty-eighth session, including its views on which subjects should be studied in the future.

General Assembly resolution 47/67

14 December 1992   Meeting 85   Adopted without vote

Approved by Special Political Committee (A/47/610) without vote, 30 October (meeting 8); draft by Austria, for Working Group (A/SPC/47/L.5), orally corrected; agenda item 72.
Meeting numbers. GA 47th session: SPC 5-8; plenary 85.

REFERENCES

[1]A/AC.105/513. [2]YUN 1982, p. 162. [3]YUN 1991, p. 77, GA res. 46/45, 9 Dec. 1991. [4]A/47/20. [5]GA res. 44/46, 8 Dec. 1989. [6]A/AC.105/445 & Add.1-8. [7]A/AC.105/445/Add.9. [8]YUN 1982, p. 163, GA res. 37/90, 10 Dec. 1982. [9]A/47/383. [10]A/AC.105/490. [11]A/AC.105/501. [12]A/AC.105/505 & Add.1-3. [13]A/AC.105/504. [14]A/C.5/47/51. [15]A/AC.105/533. [16]A/AC.105/498 & A/AC.105/534. [17]A/AC.105/525. [18]A/AC.105/526. [19]A/AC.105/527. [20]A/AC.105/528. [21]A/AC.105/529. [22]A/AC.105/530. [23]A/AC.105/531. [24]A/AC.105/497. [25]A/AC.105/518. [26]A/AC.105/510 & Add.1-3. [27]ACC/1992/28. [28]ACC/1991/PG/12. [29]A/AC.105/491. [30]A/AC.105/524. [31]A/AC.105/500. [32]A/AC.105/506-509, 511&512. [33]A/AC.105/502. [34]A/AC.105/503. [35]A/AC.105/523. [36]A/AC.105/514. [37]YUN 1991, p. 76.

Spacecraft launchings

During 1992, eight countries (Czechoslovakia, France, India, Japan, Russian Federation, Sweden, United Kingdom, United States)[1] provided information to the United Nations on the launchings of objects into orbit or beyond, in accordance with a 1961 General Assembly resolution[2] and article IV of the Convention on Registration of Objects Launched into Outer Space,[3] which had entered into force in 1976.

Convention on registration of launchings

As at 31 December 1992, there were 36 States parties to the Convention on registration. In 1979, ESA had declared its acceptance of the rights and obligations of the Convention. No new accessions took place during 1992.

REFERENCES

[1]ST/SG/SER.E/248-253, 255-257. [2]YUN 1961, p. 35, GA res. 1721 B(XVI), 20 Dec. 1961. [3]YUN 1974, p. 63, GA res. 3235(XXIX), annex, 12 Nov. 1974.

Chapter IV

Other political questions

In 1992, questions relating to information, the effects of atomic radiation and Antarctica were again on the General Assembly's agenda. Promotion of communication and the free flow of information, and United Nations public information policies and activities were the subjects of two Assembly resolutions. The Assembly requested the United Nations Scientific Committee on the Effects of Atomic Radiation to continue its work on the levels, effects and risks of ionizing radiation from all sources and noted with satisfaction the Committee's increasing cooperation with the United Nations Environment Programme. The Assembly also underlined the significance of Antarctica for international peace and security, environment, global climate conditions, economy and scientific research, reiterated its concern over Antarctic environmental degradation, and appealed again for the exclusion of South Africa from the meetings of the Antarctic Treaty Consultative Parties pending the attainment of a non-racial democratic government in that country.

Thirteen new States were admitted to United Nations membership, bringing the number of Members to 179. Yugoslavia (Serbia and Montenegro) was barred from participating in the work of the Assembly until its admission to the United Nations as a new State. Boutros Boutros-Ghali of Egypt entered into a five-year term of office as Secretary-General of the United Nations on 1 January 1992.

Information

The public information activities of the United Nations continued to focus on publicizing the Organization's work and goals and enhancing the information and communication capabilities of developing countries. Those activities were carried out by the Department of Public Information (DPI) of the Secretariat, the United Nations Educational, Scientific and Cultural Organization (UNESCO) and the Joint United Nations Information Committee (JUNIC).

Information policies and activities were reviewed at the fourteenth session of the General Assembly's Committee on Information (New York, 30 March–16 April 1992).[1] Its recommendations were considered by the Special Political Committee in November and acted on by the General Assembly in December. On 14 December, the Assembly also decided to increase the membership of the Committee on Information from 79 to 81 and appointed the Republic of Korea and Senegal as members (**decision 47/424**).

Mass communication

At its 1992 session, the Committee on Information elaborated on the establishment of a new, more just and more effective world information and communication order, examined United Nations public information policies and activities in the light of the evolution of international relations, and evaluated the efforts made and progress achieved by the United Nations system in the field of information and communication.

The Committee had before it three reports of the Secretary-General, submitted in response to a 1991 General Assembly resolution.[2] The Secretary-General outlined JUNIC activities,[3] reviewed implementation of a system-wide information programme for the United Nations Conference on Environment and Development (UNCED)[4] (see PART THREE, Chapter VIII) and described the allocation of resources and host government assistance to United Nations information centres (UNICs).[5]

The Committee decided that preparation of a report on ways and means to further the development of communication infrastructures in developing countries, also requested by the Assembly in 1991,[2] should be deferred until after 1 January 1993, following submission of additional observations and suggestions by Member States.

UNESCO activities. UNESCO again pursued in 1992 its strategy for the development of communication and the free flow of information, agreed on at its General Conference in 1989. As part of a continuing effort to support freedom of the press, called for in a 1991 Conference resolution,[6] UNESCO extended its cooperation to the Convention for a Democratic South Africa and organized a round table on the independent and pluralistic media for a democratic post-apartheid South Africa (Windhoek, Namibia, 14-17 August 1992). This meeting, whose participants came from Angola, Namibia, South Africa, Zambia and Zimbabwe, was the first major follow-up to the

May 1991 Declaration of Windhoek.[7] It made a number of proposals aimed at creating an environment conducive to promoting media independence and pluralism in southern Africa.

UNESCO was continuing to provide assistance to the Pan African News Agency for its restructuring as a commercial enterprise with mixed government and private-sector shares, maintaining an independent editorial stance.

In conjunction with DPI, UNESCO organized a seminar on promoting independent and pluralistic Asian media (Alma Ata, Kazakhstan, 5-9 October 1992). The seminar adopted a Declaration,[8] which incorporated specific project proposals regarding media legislation and training programmes, as well as measures to ensure the free flow of information and safety of journalists and to encourage the development of public service broadcasting and independent professional associations. The Declaration maintained that those projects, while identified as relating to the specific needs of Central Asian media, had region-wide applications.

UNESCO was ensuring follow-up to its seminars mainly through its International Programme for the Development of Communication (IPDC), which continued to support projects aimed at meeting the needs of developing countries in the fields of communication, information and mass media infrastructures. Thirteen new IPDC projects were launched in 1992.

At its thirteenth session (Paris, 17-24 February),[9] the IPDC Intergovernmental Council paid particular attention to follow-up to the Declaration of Windhoek[7] on promoting an independent and pluralistic African press. It reviewed the activities of the Intergovernmental Council on Communication and Information in Africa, established at IPDC's initiative, and noted that UNESCO had submitted to the United Nations Development Programme (UNDP) a regional project of $1,750,000 on the development of the independent press in Africa. In response to the Declaration's request for IPDC's detailed research into a variety of press-related topics, the Council recommended that the UNESCO Director-General report in 1993 on the possibility of allotting part of the IPDC Special Account to initial studies and evaluation.

The Council approved 34 projects totalling $2,534,000 for financing under the IPDC Special Account and two projects amounting to $505,000 to be financed under funds-in-trust arrangements. It also decided to seek special funding for the development of the independent press in Africa, estimated at $5,898,000, and additional funding for the establishment and operation of a State Information Service data bank in Egypt.

Among projects approved for Africa were the creation of an African regional film and television institute (phase II) and a radio and television training institute for the Portuguese-speaking countries, the organization of a television programme festival/contest, a broadcasting training programme in Namibia and the development of national media services in Guinea-Bissau and the Niger. Asia and the Pacific received allocations for developing training capabilities of its broadcasting organizations, a Pacific press development project, a workshop on media education in South Asia (phase II), the computerization of the "ASIAVISION News Exchange", the upgrading of a farmers' newspaper in China, the training of mass-communication field investigators in India, the development of provincial radio services in the Lao People's Democratic Republic, staff development in educational mass-media production in Malaysia, video-production development in Tonga and renovation of the printing industry in Mongolia.

Projects in Latin America and the Caribbean included assistance to the Ibero-American and Caribbean television network, training programmes in Chile and the Dominican Republic, technical equipment for the FIDES news agency in Bolivia, a radio production centre for the Colombian coast and the development of communication policies and strategies for the improvement of basic education in Ecuador.

In Europe, a funds-in-trust allocation was made for the computerization of a press editorial department in Romania.

GENERAL ASSEMBLY ACTION

On 14 December 1992, the General Assembly, on the recommendation of the Special Political Committee, adopted without vote **resolution 47/73 A.**

Information in service of humanity

The General Assembly,

Taking note of the comprehensive and important report of the Committee on Information,

Also taking note of the report of the Secretary-General on questions relating to information,

Urges that all countries, organizations of the United Nations system as a whole and all others concerned, reaffirming their commitment to the principles of the Charter of the United Nations and to the principles of freedom of the press and freedom of information, as well as to those of the independence, pluralism and diversity of the media, deeply concerned by the disparities existing between developed and developing countries and the consequences of every kind arising from those disparities that affect the capability of the public, private or other media and individuals in developing countries to disseminate information and communicate their views and their cultural and ethnical values through endogenous cultural production, as well as to ensure the diversity of sources of and their free access to information, recognizing the call in this context for what in the United Nations and at various international forums has been termed "a new world information and communication order, seen as an evolving and continuous process", should:

(a) Cooperate and interact with a view to reducing existing disparities in information flows at all levels by increasing assistance for the development of communication infrastructures and capabilities in developing countries, with due regard for their needs and the priorities attached to such areas by those countries, and in order to enable them and the public, private or other media in developing countries to develop their own information and communication policies freely and independently and increase the participation of media and individuals in the communication process, and to ensure a free flow of information at all levels;

(b) Ensure for journalists the free and effective performance of their professional tasks and condemn resolutely all attacks against them;

(c) Provide support for the continuation and strengthening of practical training programmes for broadcasters and journalists from public, private and other media in developing countries;

(d) Enhance regional efforts and cooperation among developing countries, as well as cooperation between developed and developing countries, to strengthen communication capacities and to improve the media infrastructure and communication technology in the developing countries, especially in the areas of training and dissemination of information;

(e) Aim, in addition to bilateral cooperation, at providing all possible support and assistance to the developing countries and their media, public, private or other, with due regard to their interests and needs in the field of information and to action already adopted within the United Nations system, including:

(i) The development of the human and technical resources that are indispensable for the improvement of information and communication systems in developing countries and support for the continuation and strengthening of practical training programmes, such as those already operating under both public and private auspices throughout the developing world;

(ii) The creation of conditions that will enable developing countries and their media, public, private or other, to have, by using their national and regional resources, the communication technology suited to their national needs, as well as the necessary programme material, especially for radio and television broadcasting;

(iii) Assistance in establishing and promoting telecommunication links at the subregional, regional and interregional levels, especially among developing countries;

(iv) The facilitation, as appropriate, of access by the developing countries to advanced communication technology available on the open market;

(f) Provide full support for the International Programme for the Development of Communication of the United Nations Educational, Scientific and Cultural Or-

ganization, which should support both public and private media.

General Assembly resolution 47/73 A

14 December 1992   Meeting 85   Adopted without vote

Approved by Special Political Committee (A/47/614) without vote, 20 November (meeting 23); draft by Acting Chairman of Committee on Information on behalf of its Bureau (A/SPC/47/L.9); agenda item 76.
Meeting numbers. GA 47th session: SPC 18-23; plenary 85.

UN public information

DPI activities

In response to a 1991 General Assembly resolution,[2] the Secretary-General submitted in September 1992[10] a report on questions relating to information, which focused on special activities and products of DPI.

The report stated that, in accordance with the 1991 resolution, DPI continued in 1992 its cooperation with the News Agencies Pool of Non-Aligned Countries and other news agencies of and in developing countries by providing them with daily news items on a variety of issues. It disseminated information about United Nations activities pertaining to international peace and security, particularly the Secretary-General's June 1992 report on an agenda for peace (see PART ONE, Chapter I) and the 1991 Declaration on Fact-finding by the United Nations in the Field of the Maintenance of International Peace and Security.[11] It also sponsored the 1992 annual non-governmental organizations (NGOs) conference, on regional conflicts (New York, 9-11 September), and provided radio coverage of the International Conference on Yugoslavia (London, 26-28 August) (see PART TWO, Chapter IV).

During the year, DPI issued a number of booklets and press kits, periodically updated its *Information Notes* on ongoing peace-keeping missions and introduced a new radio segment entitled "The Blue Helmets" into its weekly news programmes. It pursued its programme of activities within the framework of the International Decade for the Eradication of Colonialism (1990-2000) (see PART FOUR, Chapter I) and continued its collaboration with the Division for the Advancement of Women. As part of a world-wide educational campaign to increase awareness of women's role in society, it produced an illustrated book, *Women: Challenges to the Year 2000*, in English, French and Spanish.

DPI prepared a programme to promote the 1993 World Conference on Human Rights and developed a special promotional campaign for the International Year for the World's Indigenous People (1993). As to activities on economic and social development, DPI organized the press launch in 1992 of the *World Economic Survey* and the *World Investment Report* and coordinated the production of an exhibit and provided press release coverage of the International Congress and Exhibition on Disability and a related United Nations expert meeting (Vancouver, Canada, 25-29 April). A multimedia information programme of DPI on environment and development was aimed in 1992 at preparing and servicing UNCED.

DPI pursued its activities pertaining to African economic recovery and development, based on the United Nations New Agenda for the Development of Africa in the 1990s, adopted in 1991,[12] through continuing publication of its quarterly periodical *Africa Recovery* and by producing a special media package on the Africa crisis. It also produced a number of briefing papers and pamphlets on environment and development, the economic repercussions of a free South Africa, southern Africa and the issue of African debt relief.

As part of its programme on the question of Palestine, mandated by the Assembly in 1991,[13] DPI sponsored encounters for Irish journalists (Dublin, Ireland, 5 May 1992) and European journalists (Lisbon, Portugal, 16 and 17 September). The programme included a variety of other projects, such as fact-finding missions for journalists to the Middle East and publication of special materials.

In 1992, DPI began using a totally computerized telecommunications system that connected it with nearly 150 official addresses throughout the world, including UNICs and other United Nations field offices. As at September 1992, 54 UNICs had been computerized and the number of those having access to electronic mail had increased to 29.

DPI's annual training programme for broadcasters and journalists from developing countries was held in New York (8 September–16 October). Since 1981, 209 participants from more than 115 countries had been trained under the programme.

In April 1992, DPI conducted a comprehensive survey of UNIC activities, focused on enhancing public awareness of United Nations priority themes, cooperation with other field offices and providing services to local media and NGOs. Efforts were under way to develop a data bank of activities of UNICs. DPI was actively integrating certain UNICs with UNDP field offices, in an effort to present a unified image of the United Nations.

The report also described DPI activities in connection with the World Disarmament Campaign (see PART ONE, Chapter II), the international campaign against drug abuse and illicit trafficking in narcotics (see PART THREE, Chapter XVI) and against apartheid, as well as United Nations publications during 1992, including the *UN Chronicle*, the *Yearbook of the United Nations* and *Development Forum*.

UN interim offices in new Member States

In conformity with Economic and Social Council **resolution 1992/40** of 30 July 1992, which em-

phasized the importance of a unified United Nations presence in the Commonwealth of Independent States in order to ensure practical and effective dialogue between the Organization and its new Member States, the Secretary-General notified the General Assembly[14] of his March 1992 decision to set up integrated United Nations/UNDP interim offices in Armenia, Azerbaijan, Belarus, Kazakhstan, Ukraine and Uzbekistan. Following joint missions to assess requirements for such offices, host country agreements were signed with all six countries. Subsequently, he decided to initiate action for the creation of an interim office in Georgia.

In May,[15] the Governing Council of UNDP agreed to finance its share of the cost of establishing those offices during 1992-1993. In December,[16] the Secretary-General reported to the Assembly's Fifth (Administrative and Budgetary) Committee on the financial requirements for the seven interim offices, estimated at $934,600 for the share of the United Nations during the biennium.

GENERAL ASSEMBLY ACTION

On 23 December, acting on the recommendation of the Fifth Committee, the General Assembly adopted without vote **resolution 47/219, section XVIII**.

Revised estimates under section 31 (Public Information): establishment of seven United Nations interim offices

[*The General Assembly . . .*]

1. *Takes note* of the revised estimates submitted by the Secretary-General;

2. *Requests* the Secretary-General to re-submit a complete report on the establishment and operation of the seven United Nations interim offices, including staffing, project implementation and an integrated budget with full sources of financing, at its resumed forty-seventh session, in accordance with the relevant resolutions and decisions of the competent United Nations bodies regarding operational activities and public information activities and taking into account the views expressed by the Member States in the Fifth Committee on this issue during the forty-seventh session;

. . .

General Assembly resolution 47/219, section XVIII

23 December 1992   Meeting 94   Adopted without vote

Approved by Fifth Committee (A/47/835) without vote, 17 December (meeting 47); oral proposal by Chairman; agenda item 104.

Meeting numbers. GA 47th session: 5th Committee 45, 47, plenary 94.

Coordination in the UN system

The inter-agency Joint United Nations Information Committee, which coordinated information activities in the United Nations system, held its eighteenth session in 1992 (Rome, Italy, 7-9 July).[17] Its discussions focused on the work programme and funding of the United Nations Non-

Governmental Liaison Service, issues related to *Development Forum*, and project proposals for inter-agency information programmes on upcoming events, such as the 1993 World Conference on Human Rights, the 1994 International Conference on Population and Development, the 1995 Fourth World Conference on Women and the observance of the United Nations fiftieth anniversary, also in 1995.

The Committee also reviewed its participation in UNCED, considered the arrangements to complete the *Agenda for a Small Planet IV* series of television documentaries produced by participants from both developed and developing countries, and agreed to co-sponsor another series (*Agenda V*), to be produced by 1995 and focusing on issues relating to women and development.

GENERAL ASSEMBLY ACTION

Pursuant to the recommendation of the Special Political Committee, the General Assembly on 14 December adopted without vote **resolution 47/73 B.**

United Nations public information policies and activities

The General Assembly,

Taking note of the comprehensive and important report of the Committee on Information,

Also taking note of the report of the Secretary-General on questions relating to information,

Reaffirming the primary role of the General Assembly in elaborating, coordinating and harmonizing United Nations policies and activities in the field of information,

Also reaffirming that the Secretary-General should ensure that the activities of the Department of Public Information of the Secretariat, as the focal point of the public information tasks of the United Nations, are strengthened and improved, keeping in view the purposes and principles of the Charter of the United Nations, the priority areas defined by the General Assembly and the recommendations of the Committee on Information,

1. *Decides* to consolidate the role of the Committee on Information as its main subsidiary body mandated to make recommendations relating to the work of the Department of Public Information of the Secretariat;

2. *Calls upon* the Secretary-General, in respect of United Nations public information policies and activities, to implement the following recommendations in accordance with relevant United Nations resolutions, and in this regard to ensure that the Department of Public Information:

(*a*) Continues to disseminate information about the activities of the United Nations in coordination with the information services of other relevant agencies in accordance with the United Nations medium-term plan, the programme budget and their relevant revisions, pertaining, *inter alia*, to:

(i) International peace and security;
(ii) Disarmament;
(iii) Peace-keeping operations and peacemaking;

(iv) Decolonization and the situation in the Non-Self-Governing Territories in the light of the International Decade for the Eradication of Colonialism;

(v) The promotion and protection of human rights and in that context the World Conference on Human Rights, to be held in 1993;

(vi) The elimination of all forms of racial discrimination;

(vii) The advancement of the status of women and their role in society;

(viii) The promotion of the Convention on the Rights of the Child;

(ix) Problems of economic and social development, as well as international economic cooperation aimed at resolving external debt problems;

(x) The least developed countries;

(xi) The environment and development;

(xii) The elimination of foreign occupation;

(xiii) The campaign against terrorism in all its forms in line with General Assembly resolution 40/61 of 9 December 1985;

(xiv) International efforts against drug abuse and illicit drug trafficking;

(xv) Crime prevention and criminal justice;

(xvi) Support for the United Nations New Agenda for the Development of Africa in the 1990s and for the tremendous efforts of the African countries aimed at recovery and development, as well as the positive response by the international community to alleviate the serious economic situation prevailing in Africa;

(xvii) International efforts towards the total eradication of apartheid and support for the establishment of a united, non-racial and democratic South Africa and, where necessary, the role of the United Nations in this context;

(xviii) United Nations activities pertaining to the situation in the Middle East and the question of Palestine in particular, also including current developments in that region and the ongoing peace process;

(*b*) Provides the necessary level of information support for the activities of the United Nations in situations requiring immediate and special response;

(*c*) Continues its efforts at promoting an informed understanding of the work and purposes of the United Nations system among the peoples of the world and at strengthening the positive image of the system as a whole;

(*d*) Continues its efforts to ensure timely production and dissemination of its mandated publications, in particular the *UN Chronicle*, the *Yearbook of the United Nations*, *Development Forum* and *Africa Recovery*, and continues to maintain consistent editorial independence and accuracy in reporting all the material that it produces, taking necessary measures to ensure that its output contains adequate, objective and equitable information about issues before the Organization, reflecting divergent opinions where they occur;

(*e*) Submits a report on continuous and major publications to the Committee on Information at its fifteenth session, providing the following details:

(i) The list of publications and their circulation figures;

(ii) Their cost;

(iii) The original language versions and the languages into which the publications were translated;

(iv) Target audiences, including, where possible, the intended end-use of the specific products;

(f) Continues its briefings, assistance and orientation programmes for broadcasters and journalists from developing countries focused on United Nations–related issues;

(g) Provides, on the basis of its activities, information to the United Nations Educational, Scientific and Cultural Organization about new forms of cooperation, at the regional and subregional levels, for the training of media professionals and for the improvement of the information and communication infrastructures of developing countries;

(h) Continues its policies of cooperation with all agencies of the United Nations system, in particular with the United Nations Educational, Scientific and Cultural Organization;

(i) Continues its policies of cooperation with news agencies in and of the developing countries, in particular the News Agencies Pool of Non-Aligned Countries;

3. *Requests* the Secretary-General, in the light of the increasing demands now placed on the Department of Public Information in relation to media coverage of United Nations activities, to provide at the fifteenth session of the Committee on Information an assessment regarding:

(a) Any measures considered appropriate to ensure that the working facilities provided for the media are fully adequate to meet present and future needs and, in this context, to consult with the Bureau of the Committee, spokespersons of the regional groups, the Group of Seventy-seven and China, in relation to the implementation of any significant measures in this regard;

(b) The consideration of a greater framework of coordination within the Department of Public Information in relation to the provision of facilities and services for the media, such as the work of the Executive Media Service and the provision of accreditation services;

4. *Requests*, in this context, the Secretary-General to direct the Publications Board to develop criteria and review all publications and proposals for publications to ensure, *inter alia*, that each publication fulfils an identifiable mandate and need, is timely, does not duplicate other publications inside or outside the United Nations system, and is cost-effective, and that before the publication is printed, it satisfies the criteria on the basis of which it was authorized, and to report thereon to the Committee on Information;

5. *Reaffirms* the importance attached by Member States to the role of United Nations information centres in effectively and comprehensively disseminating information about United Nations activities and the optimization of the resources allocated to the Department of Public Information;

6. *Calls upon* the Secretary-General to submit a detailed and comprehensive report on his plan of integrating United Nations information centres with other United Nations offices, while maintaining the functional autonomy of the United Nations information centres and emphasizing that they should be fully operational, as provided for in relevant resolutions, to the Committee on Information at its fifteenth session for its consideration of the different options available in this regard; in this context, consultations should take place on this matter through the informal mechanism composed of the Bureau of the Committee on Information and the spokespersons of regional groups, the Group of Seventy-seven and China, as was established in paragraph 1 *(s)* of General Assembly resolution 46/73 B of 11 December 1991;

7. *Reaffirms* the role of the General Assembly in relation to the opening of new United Nations information centres and invites the Secretary-General, as well, to make such recommendations as he may judge necessary regarding the establishment and location of new United Nations information centres;

8. *Calls upon* the Secretary-General to study ways and means of redressing differences in the allocation of resources, in particular the differences of support, in relation to the financing of United Nations information centres in various countries and to report thereon to the Committee on Information at its fifteenth session;

9. *Notes* the substantial contribution by the Government of Poland and requests the Secretary-General to finalize, in consultation with the Polish authorities, arrangements for a United Nations information component in Warsaw;

10. *Calls upon* the Secretary-General to implement fully its recommendations contained in resolution 46/73 B, including paragraphs 1 *(l)* and *(m)*, regarding the establishment of a United Nations information centre in Sana'a, as well as the reactivation of the United Nations information centre in Tehran and the enhancing of the information centres in Dar es Salaam, Dhaka and Bujumbura;

11. *Encourages* enhanced cooperation between the Department of Public Information and the University for Peace in Costa Rica as a focal point of promoting United Nations activities and disseminating United Nations information materials;

12. *Takes note* of the requests by Bulgaria, Gabon and Haiti for information components;

13. *Calls upon* the Secretary-General to enhance the efficiency of and ensure full programme delivery of all segments currently produced by all regional radio units in the Department of Public Information;

14. *Encourages* the Department of Public Information to take into account, especially in the area of electronic media production, the various standards and systems used around the world, bearing in mind the need for harmonization and efficiency;

15. *Calls upon* the Secretary-General, as of the forty-seventh session of the General Assembly, to make every effort as a matter of particular urgency to create conditions and to make them more conducive to achieving parity by appropriate utilization of existing equipment in the press coverage of meetings in English and French;

16. *Decides*, as of the forty-seventh session of the General Assembly, on the publication in the Arabic and Spanish languages, after each annual session of the General Assembly, of the press release containing the resolutions and decisions adopted by the General Assembly and the results of the voting, through reallocation of resources from the budget of the Department of Public Information;

17. *Invites* Member States to submit to the Secretary-General, by 1 January 1993, observations and suggestions on ways and means of furthering the development

of communications infrastructures and capabilities in developing countries, with a view to consolidating recent experience in the field of international cooperation aimed at enabling them to develop their own information and communication capacities, freely and independently, and requests the Secretary-General to report thereon to the Committee on Information at its fifteenth session;

18. *Decides* on procedural grounds to refer to the Economic and Social Council, for its consideration, resolution 4.3 adopted on 6 November 1991 by the General Conference of the United Nations Educational, Scientific and Cultural Organization at its twenty-sixth session and contained in the relevant note by the Secretary-General;

19. *Requests* the Secretary-General to report to the Committee on Information at its fifteenth session in 1993 on the results of the implementation of a system-wide information programme for the United Nations Conference on Environment and Development;

20. *Also requests* the Secretary-General to report to the Committee on Information at its fifteenth session in 1993 and to the General Assembly at its forty-eighth session in 1993 on the activities of the Department of Public Information and on the implementation of the recommendations contained in the present resolution as well as in resolution 46/73 B;

21. *Requests* the Committee on Information to report to the General Assembly at its forty-eighth session;

22. *Decides* to include in the provisional agenda of its forty-eighth session the item entitled "Questions relating to information".

General Assembly resolution 47/73 B

14 December 1992   Meeting 85   Adopted without vote

Approved by Special Political Committee (A/47/614) without vote, 20 November (meeting 23); draft by Acting Chairman of Committee on Information on behalf of its Bureau (A/SPC/47/L.10); agenda item 76.
Financial implications. 5th Committee, A/47/771; S-G, A/C.5/47/57, A/SPC/47/L.13.
Meeting numbers. GA 47th session: 5th Committee 40; SPC 18-23; plenary 85.

REFERENCES
[1]A/47/21. [2]YUN 1991, p. 84, GA res. 46/73 B, 11 Dec. 1991. [3]A/AC.198/1992/2. [4]A/AC.198/1992/3. [5]A/AC.198/1992/4. [6]YUN 1991, p. 82. [7]A/SPC/47/4. [8]A/SPC/47/3. [9]CII/MD/2. [10]A/47/462 & Corr.1. [11]YUN 1991, p. 843, GA res. 46/59, annex, 9 Dec. 1991. [12]Ibid., p. 402, GA res. 46/151, annex, sect. II, 18 Dec. 1991. [13]Ibid., p. 229, GA res. 46/74 C, 11 Dec. 1991. [14]A/47/419/Add.3. [15]E/1992/28 (dec. 92/29 & 92/43). [16]A/C.5/47/58. [17]ACC/1992/24.

Radiation effects

The United Nations Scientific Committee on the Effects of Atomic Radiation held its forty-first session at Vienna (15-19 June 1992).[1] It took note of a 1991 General Assembly request[2] that it continue its review of problems arising from radiation doses and effects, and welcomed the Assembly's reference to its scientific authority and independence of judgement.

The Committee examined documents prepared by the secretariat on subjects selected for further study and focused its technical discussions on natural, medical, occupational and man-made environmental radiation exposures; radiation effects on the environment and on the developing human brain; epidemiological study of radiation carcinogenesis; late deterministic effects of radiation in children; mechanisms of radiation oncogenesis; dose and dose-rate influence on stochastic radiation effects; hereditary effects of radiation; stimulatory and adaptive response to radiation in cells and organisms; and perception of radiation risks. The Committee made suggestions for the further development of those topics, in particular pointing out additional information to be considered.

In an effort to collect data on radiation exposures in countries worldwide for a more thorough analysis of the issue, the Committee invited States to respond to the secretariat's questionnaires and expressed the hope that Member States as well as the specialized agencies and the International Atomic Energy Agency would continue to assist by providing relevant information on the subjects of interest for future studies. The Committee stated its intention to conclude the evaluations of sources, effects and risks of ionizing radiation and radiation exposures, along with its reviews of biological subjects, in 1993 and to submit a comprehensive report to the General Assembly.

GENERAL ASSEMBLY ACTION

On 14 December 1992, the General Assembly, in accordance with the recommendation of the Special Political Committee, adopted without vote **resolution 47/66.**

Effects of atomic radiation
The General Assembly,

Recalling its resolution 913(X) of 3 December 1955, by which it established the United Nations Scientific Committee on the Effects of Atomic Radiation, and its subsequent resolutions on the subject, including resolution 46/44 of 9 December 1991, in which, *inter alia*, it requested the Scientific Committee to continue its work,

Taking note with appreciation of the report of the United Nations Scientific Committee on the Effects of Atomic Radiation,

Reaffirming the desirability of the Scientific Committee continuing its work,

Concerned about the potentially harmful effects on present and future generations resulting from the levels of radiation to which man is exposed,

Conscious of the continued need to examine and compile information about atomic and ionizing radiation and to analyse its effects on man and his environment,

Bearing in mind the decision of the Scientific Committee to submit, as soon as the relevant studies are completed, shorter reports with supporting scientific documents on the specialized topics mentioned by the Committee,

1. *Commends* the United Nations Scientific Committee on the Effects of Atomic Radiation for the valuable contribution it has been making in the course of the past thirty-seven years, since its inception, to wider knowledge and understanding of the levels, effects and risks of atomic radiation and for fulfilling its original mandate with scientific authority and independence of judgement;

2. *Notes with satisfaction* the continued and growing scientific cooperation between the Scientific Committee and the United Nations Environment Programme;

3. *Requests* the Scientific Committee to continue its work, including its important coordinating activities, to increase knowledge of the levels, effects and risks of ionizing radiation from all sources;

4. *Endorses* the intentions and plans of the Scientific Committee for its future activities of scientific review and assessment on behalf of the General Assembly;

5. *Also requests* the Scientific Committee to continue at its next session the review of the important problems in the field of radiation and to report thereon to the General Assembly at its forty-eighth session;

6. *Requests* the United Nations Environment Programme to continue providing support for the effective conduct of the work of the Scientific Committee and for the dissemination of its findings to the General Assembly, the scientific community and the public;

7. *Expresses its appreciation* for the assistance rendered to the Scientific Committee by Member States, the specialized agencies, the International Atomic Energy Agency and non-governmental organizations, and invites them to increase their cooperation in this field;

8. *Invites* Member States, the organizations of the United Nations system and non-governmental organizations concerned to provide further relevant data about doses, effects and risks from various sources of radiation, which would greatly help in the preparation of future reports of the Scientific Committee to the General Assembly.

General Assembly resolution 47/66

14 December 1992   Meeting 85   Adopted without vote

Approved by Special Political Committee (A/47/609) without vote, 21 October (meeting 4); 36-nation draft (A/SPC/47/L.3); agenda item 71.
Sponsors: Argentina, Australia, Austria, Azerbaijan, Belarus, Belgium, Bolivia, Canada, China, Costa Rica, Czechoslovakia, Denmark, Egypt, France, Germany, Greece, India, Indonesia, Ireland, Italy, Japan, Jordan, Luxembourg, Mongolia, Netherlands, New Zealand, Poland, Portugal, Russian Federation, Samoa, Spain, Sweden, Ukraine, United Kingdom, United States, Uruguay.
Meeting numbers. GA 47th session: SPC 3, 4; plenary 85.

REFERENCES

(1)A/47/293. (2)YUN 1991, p. 88, GA res. 46/44, 9 Dec. 1991.

Antarctica

Pursuant to a 1991 General Assembly request,[1] the Secretary-General submitted in October 1992 a report[2] evaluating the response to the Assembly's call on the 1959 Antarctic Treaty Consultative Parties to deposit with him information covering all aspects of Antarctica.

On 12 May 1992, Germany on behalf of the States parties to the Treaty (*Argentina, Australia,* Austria, *Belgium, Brazil,* Bulgaria, Canada, *Chile, China,* Colombia, Cuba, Czechoslovakia, Democratic People's Republic of Korea, Denmark, *Ecuador, Finland, France, Germany,* Greece, Hungary, *India, Italy, Japan, Netherlands, New Zealand, Norway,* Papua New Guinea, *Peru, Poland, Republic of Korea,* Romania, *Russian Federation, South Africa, Spain, Sweden,* Switzerland, *United Kingdom, United States, Uruguay* (italic indicates consultative status)) transmitted to the Secretary-General the final report of the Sixteenth Antarctic Treaty Consultative Meeting (Bonn, 7-18 October 1991), containing comprehensive information about different aspects of Antarctica. Matters discussed by the Meeting included inspections and environmental monitoring under the Antarctic Treaty; the impact of waste disposal and marine pollution on the Antarctic environment; issues related to Antarctica's specially protected areas, including new land and marine sites of special scientific interest; and promotion of international scientific and logistic cooperation in Antarctica.

The Meeting reviewed reports from a number of international bodies and conventions—such as the Commission for the Conservation of Antarctic Marine Living Resources, the Convention for the Conservation of Antarctic Seals, the Scientific Committee on Antarctic Research (SCAR), the Convention on the Regulation of Antarctic Mineral Resource Activities, the World Meteorological Organization, the International Maritime Organization and the International Hydrographic Organization—and stressed the absolute priority of the earliest possible ratification and entry into force of the Protocol on Environmental Protection to the Antarctic Treaty.

In a declaration on the thirtieth anniversary of the entry into force of the Treaty, the Contracting Parties reaffirmed that the Treaty's objective was to ensure, in the interest of all mankind, that Antarctica continued to be used exclusively for peaceful purposes and should not become the scene or object of international discord.

In addition, the Meeting adopted a series of recommendations concerning the establishment of new sites of special scientific interest, specially protected areas, areas protection and management. The Meeting recommended that an informal meeting of the Consultative Parties be convened with a view to making proposals to the Seventeenth Consultative Meeting regarding a comprehensive regulation of tourist and non-governmental activities in Antarctica.

The Meeting also discussed a proposal to establish an Antarctic Treaty secretariat; as no consensus was reached, the question was to be considered further at the next Consultative Meeting.

Concluding his report, the Secretary-General remarked that international cooperation on Antarctica had been achieved at the level of Governments, some United Nations agencies and programmes, and relevant international and non-governmental organizations. The documents submitted appeared to reflect that the existing Antarctic Treaty system continued to foster international cooperation, to adapt to changing environmental priorities and to elaborate new mechanisms in line with innovative scientific research; they also indicated interest in renewed global efforts in line with increased public awareness, particularly with regard to Antarctic ecosystems and growing worldwide environmental concerns.

GENERAL ASSEMBLY ACTION

On 9 December, the General Assembly, pursuant to the recommendation of the First Committee, adopted **resolution 47/57** by roll-call vote.

Question of Antarctica

The General Assembly,

Having considered the item entitled "Question of Antarctica",

Recalling its resolutions 38/77 of 15 December 1983, 39/152 of 17 December 1984, 40/156 A and B of 16 December 1985, 41/88 A and B of 4 December 1986, 42/46 A and B of 30 November 1987, 43/83 A and B of 7 December 1988, 44/124 A and B of 15 December 1989, 45/78 A and B of 12 December 1990 and 46/41 A and B of 6 December 1991,

Recalling also the relevant paragraphs of the final documents adopted by the second meeting of States of the Zone of Peace and Cooperation of the South Atlantic, held at Abuja from 25 to 29 June 1990, the Twentieth Islamic Conference of Foreign Ministers, held at Istanbul from 4 to 8 August 1991, the meeting of the Commonwealth Heads of Government, held at Harare from 16 to 22 October 1991 and the Tenth Conference of Heads of State or Government of Non-Aligned Countries, held at Jakarta from 1 to 6 September 1992,

Recalling further the Declaration on South Africa adopted by the Assembly of Heads of State and Government of the Organization of African Unity at its twenty-eighth ordinary session, held at Dakar from 29 June to 1 July 1992,

Taking into account the debates on this item held since its thirty-eighth session,

Reaffirming the principle that the international community is entitled to information covering all aspects of Antarctica and that the United Nations should be made the repository for all such information in accordance with General Assembly resolutions 41/88 A, 42/46 B, 43/83 A, 44/124 B, 45/78 A and 46/41 A,

Welcoming the decision of the Antarctic Treaty Consultative Parties to submit to the Secretary-General the final report of the Sixteenth Antarctic Treaty Consultative Meeting, which took place at Bonn from 7 to 18 October 1991,

Conscious of the particular significance of Antarctica to the international community in terms, *inter alia*, of international peace and security, environment, its effects on global climate conditions, economy and scientific research,

Conscious also of the interrelationship between Antarctica and the physical, chemical and biological processes that regulate the total Earth system,

Welcoming also the increasing recognition of the significant impact that Antarctica exerts on the global environment and ecosystems and of the need for a comprehensive agreement to be negotiated by the international community on the protection and conservation of the Antarctic environment and its dependent and associated ecosystems,

Reiterating the concern over the environmental degradation of Antarctica and its impact on the global environment,

Welcoming further the recognition by the United Nations Conference on Environment and Development, held at Rio de Janeiro from 3 to 14 June 1992, of the value of Antarctica as an area for the conduct of scientific research, in particular research essential to understanding the global environment,

Welcoming the increasing support, including by some Antarctic Treaty Consultative Parties, for the establishment of Antarctica as a nature reserve or world park to ensure the protection and conservation of its environment and its dependent and associated ecosystems for the benefit of all mankind,

Welcoming also the ongoing trend in acknowledging the need for internationally coordinated scientific research stations in Antarctica in order to minimize unnecessary duplication and logistical support facilities,

Welcoming further the increasing awareness of an interest in Antarctica shown by the international community, and convinced of the advantages to the whole of mankind of a better knowledge of Antarctica,

Affirming its conviction that, in the interest of all mankind, Antarctica should continue for ever to be used exclusively for peaceful purposes and that it should not become the scene or object of international discord,

Reaffirming that the management and use of Antarctica should be conducted in accordance with the purposes and principles of the Charter of the United Nations and in the interest of maintaining international peace and security and of promoting international cooperation for the benefit of mankind as a whole,

Convinced of the need for concerted international cooperation in order to protect and safeguard Antarctica and its dependent ecosystems from external environmental disturbances for future generations,

1. *Takes note* of the reports of the Secretary-General on the report of the Sixteenth Antarctic Treaty Consultative Meeting and on the participation of the apartheid minority regime of South Africa in meetings of the Antarctic Treaty Consultative Parties;

2. *Welcomes* the report of the Secretary-General on the state of the environment in Antarctica, and requests the Secretary-General to explore the possibilities of publishing, as official documents of the United Nations, extracts of data received from the various organizations in the preparation of future annual reports, within existing resources;

3. While noting the cooperation of some United Nations specialized agencies and programmes at the Sixteenth Antarctic Treaty Consultative Meeting, *expresses its regret* that, despite the numerous resolutions adopted by the General Assembly, the Secretary-General or his

representative has not been invited to the meetings of the Antarctic Treaty Consultative Parties, and urges once again the Consultative Parties to invite the Secretary-General or his representative to their future meetings;

4.   Bearing in mind that the Antarctic Treaty is, by its terms, intended to further the purposes and principles embodied in the Charter of the United Nations, with which South Africa has yet to comply fully, *calls upon* the Antarctic Treaty Consultative Parties to prevent South Africa from participating fully in their meetings pending the attainment of a non-racial democratic government in that country;

5.   While welcoming the decision of the Antarctic Treaty Consultative Parties to provide information regarding the Sixteenth Antarctic Treaty Consultative Meeting, *encourages* the Parties to provide to the Secretary-General, on a continuing basis, more information and documents covering all aspects of Antarctica, and requests the Secretary-General to submit a report on his evaluations thereof to the General Assembly at its forty-eighth session;

6.   *Welcomes* the commitment made by the Antarctic Treaty Consultative Parties under chapter 17 of Agenda 21, adopted by the United Nations Conference on Environment and Development, as provided for in article III of the Antarctic Treaty, to continue:

(a)   To ensure that data and information resulting from scientific research activities conducted in Antarctica are freely available to the international community;

(b)   To enhance access of the international scientific community and specialized agencies of the United Nations to such data and information, including the encouragement of periodic seminars and symposia;

7.   *Urges* the Antarctic Treaty Consultative Parties to build on the agreements achieved at the United Nations Conference on Environment and Development, particularly as noted in paragraph 6 of the present resolution, and, in this connection, actively to explore the possibility of organizing an annual seminar/symposium covering issues relating to the environment, commencing in 1993, with international participation as wide as possible, including that of international organizations such as the United Nations;

8.   *Also urges* the Antarctic Treaty Consultative Parties to establish monitoring and implementation mechanisms to ensure compliance with the provisions of the 1991 Madrid Protocol, on Environmental Protection;

9.   Welcoming the ban on prospecting and mining in and around Antarctica for the next fifty years by Antarctic Treaty Consultative Parties in accordance with the Madrid Protocol, *reiterates its call* for the ban to be made permanent;

10.   *Also reiterates its call* that any move at drawing up an international convention to establish a nature reserve or world park in Antarctica and its dependent and associated ecosystems must be negotiated with the full participation of the international community;

11.   While welcoming the concrete steps taken by the Secretariat through the publication on Antarctica by the Department of Public Information, *reaffirms* the need to promote further public awareness of the importance of Antarctica to the ecosystem, and in this regard requests the Secretary-General to continue to provide relevant materials on Antarctica through the Department of Public Information within existing resources;

12.   *Encourages* the Antarctic Treaty Consultative Parties to increase the level of cooperation and collaboration with a view to reducing the number of scientific stations in Antarctica;

13.   *Urges* the international community to ensure that all activities in Antarctica are carried out exclusively for the purpose of peaceful scientific investigation and that all such activities will ensure the maintenance of international peace and security and the protection of the Antarctic environment and are for the benefit of all mankind;

14.   *Urges* all States Members of the United Nations to cooperate with the Secretary-General on matters pertaining to Antarctica and to continue consultations on all aspects relating to the continent;

15.   *Decides* to include in the provisional agenda of its forty-eighth session the item entitled "Question of Antarctica".

General Assembly resolution 47/57

9 December 1992   Meeting 81   96-1-9 (roll-call vote)

Approved by First Committee (A/47/696) by roll-call vote (71-0-6), 25 November (meeting 40); draft by Antigua and Barbuda, Bangladesh, Brunei Darussalam, Guinea, Indonesia, Kenya, Lesotho, Malaysia, Mauritius for African Group, Nepal, Nigeria, Oman, Philippines, Sierra Leone, Sri Lanka, Uganda, United Republic of Tanzania, Yemen (A/C.1/47/L.54); agenda item 66.

Meeting numbers. GA 47th session: 1st Committee 38-40; plenary 81.

Roll-call vote in Assembly as follows:

In favour: Afghanistan, Algeria, Angola, Antigua and Barbuda, Bahamas, Bahrain, Bangladesh, Barbados, Belize, Benin, Bhutan, Botswana, Brunei Darussalam, Burkina Faso, Burundi, Cameroon, Cape Verde, Central African Republic, Chad, Comoros, Congo, Costa Rica, Cyprus, Djibouti, Dominica, Egypt, El Salvador, Ethiopia, Gabon, Gambia, Ghana, Grenada, Guinea, Guinea-Bissau, Guyana, Haiti, Indonesia, Iran, Iraq, Jamaica, Jordan, Kenya, Kuwait, Lebanon, Lesotho, Liberia, Libyan Arab Jamahiriya, Malawi, Malaysia, Maldives, Mali, Mauritania, Mauritius, Mexico, Mongolia, Morocco, Mozambique, Myanmar, Namibia, Nepal, Nicaragua, Niger, Nigeria, Oman, Pakistan, Panama, Philippines, Qatar, Rwanda, Saint Kitts and Nevis, Saint Lucia, Saint Vincent and the Grenadines, Sao Tome and Principe, Saudi Arabia, Senegal, Seychelles, Sierra Leone, Singapore, Sri Lanka, Sudan, Suriname, Swaziland, Syrian Arab Republic, Thailand, Togo, Trinidad and Tobago, Tunisia, Uganda, United Arab Emirates, United Republic of Tanzania, Vanuatu, Viet Nam, Yemen, Zaire, Zambia, Zimbabwe.

Against: Argentina.*

Abstaining: Azerbaijan, Bosnia and Herzegovina, Ireland, Liechtenstein, Malta, Portugal, San Marino, Turkey, Venezuela.

*Later advised the Secretariat it had intended not to participate.

During the vote in the Assembly, the following States announced that they were not participating: Armenia, Australia, Austria, Belarus, Belgium, Bolivia, Brazil, Bulgaria, Canada, Chile, China, Colombia, Côte d'Ivoire, Croatia, Cuba, Czechoslovakia, Democratic People's Republic of Korea, Denmark, Dominican Republic, Ecuador, Estonia, Finland, France, Germany, Greece, Guatemala, Honduras, Hungary, Iceland, India, Israel, Italy, Japan, Kazakhstan, Kyrgyzstan, Lao People's Democratic Republic, Latvia, Lithuania, Luxembourg, Madagascar, Marshall Islands, Micronesia, Netherlands, New Zealand, Norway, Papua New Guinea, Paraguay, Peru, Poland, Republic of Korea, Republic of Moldova, Romania, Russian Federation, Samoa, Slovenia, Solomon Islands, Spain, Sweden, Ukraine, United Kingdom, United States, Uruguay.

In the Committee, 45 States made a similar announcement.

Antarctica and the environment

In November 1992,[3] in response to a 1991 General Assembly resolution,[1] the Secretary-General reported on the state of the environment in Antarctica. The report, which took into account information from Member States and intergovernmental and non-governmental organizations, considered Antarctica's role in the global environmental system and questions relating to protection of the Antarctic environment; it emphasized that human activities had already had a major effect on the balance of the Antarctic marine ecosystem and that commercial exploitation of the continent's mineral resources might lead to irreversible damage.

According to June 1992 reports from the United Nations Environment Programme, increased levels of ultraviolet radiation resulting from ozone depletion had been shown to have a detrimental impact on the productivity of flora and fauna in Antarctica. Studies of the Antarctic ecosystems revealed a growing need for comprehensive environmental monitoring and international cooperation concerning waste disposal, contamination by oil and other toxic substances, construction and operation of facilities, science programmes, recreational activities and those affecting designated protected areas, as recommended by the Sixteenth Antarctic Treaty Consultative Meeting (see above) and by SCAR. The report also outlined SCAR's proposals on collection, storage and dissemination of environmental data.

Recognizing the significance of Antarctica in a global context, the United Nations Conference on Environment and Development (see PART THREE, Chapter VIII) called on States conducting scientific research in Antarctica to make the results available to the international community and to enhance the community's access to such information.

Participation of South Africa

In a report of October 1992,[4] the Secretary-General responded to a 1991 resolution[5] in which the General Assembly noted with regret the continuing participation of the apartheid regime of South Africa in meetings of the Antarctic Treaty Consultative Parties and appealed again to those Parties to exclude South Africa from their meetings. On 28 May 1992, the Secretary-General received a note from Germany, on behalf of the parties to the Treaty, declaring that a 1987 note from Australia[6] continued to reflect their position.

REFERENCES
[1]YUN 1991, p. 89, GA res. 46/41 A, 6 Dec. 1991. [2]A/47/541. [3]A/47/624. [4]A/47/542. [5]YUN 1991, p. 91, GA res. 46/41 B, 6 Dec. 1991. [6]YUN 1987, p. 357.

Institutional questions

Admission to UN membership

During 1992, 13 States were admitted to the United Nations, including nine republics of the former USSR, three former republics of Yugoslavia, and San Marino, bringing the total membership of the Organization to 179.

The Security Council recommended Kazakhstan for membership on 23 January,[1] and Armenia,[2] Kyrgyzstan,[3] Tajikistan[4] and Uzbekistan[5] on 29 January. The Republic of Moldova,[6] Turkmenistan[7] and Azerbaijan[8] were recommended on 5, 7 and 14 February, respectively, and San Marino on 25 February.[9] On 2 March 1992, at its resumed forty-sixth session, the General Assembly admitted these nine States to the United Nations.

Acting on Kazakhstan's application,[10] the Council adopted **resolution 732(1992)** without vote.

The Security Council,

Having examined the application of the Republic of Kazakhstan for admission to the United Nations,

Recommends to the General Assembly that the Republic of Kazakhstan be admitted to membership in the United Nations.

Security Council resolution 732(1992)

23 January 1992   Meeting 3034   Adopted without vote

Draft by Committee on Admission of New Members (S/23456).

The Assembly adopted **resolution 46/224** without vote.

Admission of the Republic of Kazakhstan to membership in the United Nations

The General Assembly,

Having received the recommendation of the Security Council of 23 January 1992 that the Republic of Kazakhstan should be admitted to membership in the United Nations,

Having considered the application for membership of the Republic of Kazakhstan,

Decides to admit the Republic of Kazakhstan to membership in the United Nations.

General Assembly resolution 46/224

2 March 1992   Meeting 82   Adopted without vote

119-nation draft (A/46/L.59 & Add.1); agenda item 20.

Sponsors: Afghanistan, Albania, Algeria, Antigua and Barbuda, Argentina, Australia, Austria, Bahrain, Bangladesh, Barbados, Belarus, Belgium, Belize, Brazil, Brunei Darussalam, Bulgaria, Burundi, Cambodia, Canada, Cape Verde, Chad, Chile, China, Colombia, Comoros, Congo, Costa Rica, Cyprus, Czechoslovakia, Democratic People's Republic of Korea, Denmark, Djibouti, Ecuador, El Salvador, Estonia, Fiji, Finland, France, Gabon, Germany, Greece, Guatemala, Guinea, Guinea-Bissau, Guyana, Honduras, Hungary, Iceland, India, Indonesia, Iran, Ireland, Israel, Italy, Jamaica, Japan, Jordan, Kenya, Kuwait, Lao People's Democratic Republic, Latvia, Lebanon, Liechtenstein, Lithuania, Luxembourg, Madagascar, Malaysia, Maldives, Mali, Malta, Marshall Islands, Mauritania, Mauritius, Mexico, Micronesia, Mongolia, Morocco, Nepal, Netherlands, New Zealand, Nicaragua, Norway, Oman, Pakistan, Panama, Philippines, Poland, Portugal, Qatar, Republic of Korea, Romania, Russian Federation, Saint Kitts and Nevis, Saint

Vincent and the Grenadines, Samoa, Sao Tome and Principe, Saudi Arabia, Senegal, Sierra Leone, Singapore, Spain, Sri Lanka, Sudan, Suriname, Sweden, Thailand, Trinidad and Tobago, Tunisia, Turkey, Uganda, Ukraine, United Kingdom, United Republic of Tanzania, United States, Uruguay, Vanuatu, Venezuela, Viet Nam, Yugoslavia.

Following consideration of Armenia's application,[11] the Council adopted **resolution 735(1992)** without vote.

The Security Council,

Having examined the application of the Republic of Armenia for admission to the United Nations,

Recommends to the General Assembly that the Republic of Armenia be admitted to membership in the United Nations.

Security Council resolution 735(1992)

29 January 1992   Meeting 3041   Adopted without vote

Draft by Committee on Admission of New Members (S/23475).

The Assembly adopted **resolution 46/227** without vote.

Admission of the Republic of Armenia to membership in the United Nations

The General Assembly,

Having received the recommendation of the Security Council of 29 January 1992 that the Republic of Armenia should be admitted to membership in the United Nations,

Having considered the application for membership of the Republic of Armenia,

Decides to admit the Republic of Armenia to membership in the United Nations.

General Assembly resolution 46/227

2 March 1992   Meeting 82   Adopted without vote

119-nation draft (A/46/L.62 & Add.1); agenda item 20.

Sponsors: Afghanistan, Albania, Algeria, Antigua and Barbuda, Argentina, Australia, Austria, Bahrain, Bangladesh, Barbados, Belarus, Belgium, Belize, Brazil, Brunei Darussalam, Bulgaria, Burundi, Cambodia, Canada, Cape Verde, Chad, Chile, China, Colombia, Comoros, Congo, Costa Rica, Cyprus, Czechoslovakia, Democratic People's Republic of Korea, Denmark, Djibouti, Ecuador, El Salvador, Estonia, Fiji, Finland, France, Gabon, Germany, Greece, Guatemala, Guinea, Guinea-Bissau, Guyana, Honduras, Hungary, Iceland, India, Indonesia, Iran, Ireland, Israel, Italy, Jamaica, Japan, Jordan, Kenya, Kuwait, Lao People's Democratic Republic, Latvia, Lebanon, Liechtenstein, Lithuania, Luxembourg, Madagascar, Malaysia, Maldives, Mali, Malta, Marshall Islands, Mauritania, Mauritius, Mexico, Micronesia, Mongolia, Morocco, Nepal, Netherlands, New Zealand, Nicaragua, Norway, Oman, Pakistan, Panama, Philippines, Poland, Portugal, Qatar, Republic of Korea, Romania, Russian Federation, Saint Kitts and Nevis, Saint Vincent and the Grenadines, Samoa, Sao Tome and Principe, Saudi Arabia, Senegal, Sierra Leone, Singapore, Spain, Sri Lanka, Sudan, Suriname, Sweden, Thailand, Trinidad and Tobago, Tunisia, Turkey, Uganda, Ukraine, United Kingdom, United Republic of Tanzania, United States, Uruguay, Vanuatu, Venezuela, Viet Nam, Yugoslavia.

The Council acted on Kyrgyzstan's application[12] by adopting **resolution 736(1992)** without vote.

The Security Council,

Having examined the application of the Republic of Kyrgyzstan for admission to the United Nations,

Recommends to the General Assembly that the Republic of Kyrgyzstan be admitted to membership in the United Nations.

Security Council resolution 736(1992)

29 January 1992   Meeting 3042   Adopted without vote

Draft by Committee on Admission of New Members (S/23476).

The Assembly adopted **resolution 46/225** without vote.

Admission of the Republic of Kyrgyzstan to membership in the United Nations

The General Assembly,

Having received the recommendation of the Security Council of 29 January 1992 that the Republic of Kyrgyzstan should be admitted to membership in the United Nations,

Having considered the application for membership of the Republic of Kyrgyzstan,

Decides to admit the Republic of Kyrgyzstan to membership in the United Nations.

General Assembly resolution 46/225

2 March 1992   Meeting 82   Adopted without vote

119-nation draft (A/46/L.60 & Add.1); agenda item 20.

Sponsors: Afghanistan, Albania, Algeria, Antigua and Barbuda, Argentina, Australia, Austria, Bahrain, Bangladesh, Barbados, Belarus, Belgium, Belize, Brazil, Brunei Darussalam, Bulgaria, Cambodia, Canada, Cape Verde, Chad, Chile, China, Colombia, Comoros, Congo, Costa Rica, Cyprus, Czechoslovakia, Democratic People's Republic of Korea, Denmark, Djibouti, Ecuador, El Salvador, Estonia, Fiji, Finland, France, Gabon, Germany, Greece, Guatemala, Guinea, Guinea-Bissau, Guyana, Honduras, Hungary, Iceland, India, Indonesia, Iran, Ireland, Israel, Italy, Jamaica, Japan, Jordan, Kenya, Kuwait, Lao People's Democratic Republic, Latvia, Lebanon, Liechtenstein, Lithuania, Luxembourg, Madagascar, Malaysia, Maldives, Mali, Malta, Marshall Islands, Mauritania, Mauritius, Mexico, Micronesia, Mongolia, Morocco, Nepal, Netherlands, New Zealand, Nicaragua, Norway, Oman, Pakistan, Panama, Philippines, Poland, Portugal, Qatar, Republic of Korea, Romania, Russian Federation, Saint Kitts and Nevis, Saint Vincent and the Grenadines, Samoa, Sao Tome and Principe, Saudi Arabia, Senegal, Sierra Leone, Singapore, Spain, Sri Lanka, Sudan, Suriname, Sweden, Thailand, Trinidad and Tobago, Tunisia, Turkey, Uganda, Ukraine, United Kingdom, United Republic of Tanzania, United States, Uruguay, Vanuatu, Venezuela, Viet Nam, Yugoslavia.

The Council considered Tajikistan's application[13] and adopted **resolution 738(1992)** without vote.

The Security Council,

Having examined the application of the Republic of Tajikistan for admission to the United Nations,

Recommends to the General Assembly that the Republic of Tajikistan be admitted to membership in the United Nations.

Security Council resolution 738(1992)

29 January 1992   Meeting 3044   Adopted without vote

Draft by Committee on Admission of New Members (S/23478).

The Assembly adopted **resolution 46/228** without vote.

Admission of the Republic of Tajikistan to membership in the United Nations

The General Assembly,

Having received the recommendation of the Security Council of 29 January 1992 that the Republic of Tajikistan should be admitted to membership in the United Nations,

Having considered the application for membership of the Republic of Tajikistan,

Decides to admit the Republic of Tajikistan to membership in the United Nations.

General Assembly resolution 46/228

2 March 1992   Meeting 82   Adopted without vote

119-nation draft (A/46/L.63 & Add.1); agenda item 20.

Sponsors: Afghanistan, Albania, Algeria, Antigua and Barbuda, Argentina, Australia, Austria, Bahrain, Bangladesh, Barbados, Belarus, Belgium, Belize, Brazil, Brunei Darussalam, Bulgaria, Burundi, Cambodia, Canada, Cape

Verde, Chad, Chile, China, Colombia, Comoros, Congo, Costa Rica, Cyprus, Czechoslovakia, Democratic People's Republic of Korea, Denmark, Djibouti, Ecuador, El Salvador, Estonia, Fiji, Finland, France, Gabon, Germany, Greece, Guatemala, Guinea, Guinea-Bissau, Guyana, Honduras, Hungary, Iceland, India, Indonesia, Iran, Ireland, Israel, Italy, Jamaica, Japan, Jordan, Kenya, Kuwait, Lao People's Democratic Republic, Latvia, Lebanon, Liechtenstein, Lithuania, Luxembourg, Madagascar, Malaysia, Maldives, Mali, Malta, Marshall Islands, Mauritania, Mauritius, Mexico, Micronesia, Mongolia, Morocco, Nepal, Netherlands, New Zealand, Nicaragua, Norway, Oman, Pakistan, Panama, Philippines, Poland, Portugal, Qatar, Republic of Korea, Romania, Russian Federation, Saint Kitts and Nevis, Saint Vincent and the Grenadines, Samoa, Sao Tome and Principe, Saudi Arabia, Senegal, Sierra Leone, Singapore, Spain, Sri Lanka, Sudan, Suriname, Sweden, Thailand, Trinidad and Tobago, Tunisia, Turkey, Uganda, Ukraine, United Kingdom, United Republic of Tanzania, United States, Uruguay, Vanuatu, Venezuela, Viet Nam, Yugoslavia.

Acting on Uzbekistan's application,[14] the Council adopted **resolution 737(1992)** without vote.

The Security Council,
Having examined the application of the Republic of Uzbekistan for admission to the United Nations,
Recommends to the General Assembly that the Republic of Uzbekistan be admitted to membership in the United Nations.

Security Council resolution 737(1992)
29 January 1992   Meeting 3043   Adopted without vote
Draft by Committee on Admission of New Members (S/23477).

The Assembly adopted **resolution 46/226** without vote.

Admission of the Republic of Uzbekistan to membership in the United Nations
The General Assembly,
Having received the recommendation of the Security Council of 29 January 1992 that the Republic of Uzbekistan should be admitted to membership in the United Nations,
Having considered the application for membership of the Republic of Uzbekistan,
Decides to admit the Republic of Uzbekistan to membership in the United Nations.

General Assembly resolution 46/226
2 March 1992   Meeting 82   Adopted without vote
119-nation draft (A/46/L.61 & Add.1); agenda item 20.
Sponsors: Afghanistan, Albania, Algeria, Antigua and Barbuda, Argentina, Australia, Austria, Bahrain, Bangladesh, Barbados, Belarus, Belgium, Belize, Brazil, Brunei Darussalam, Bulgaria, Burundi, Cambodia, Canada, Cape Verde, Chad, Chile, China, Colombia, Comoros, Congo, Costa Rica, Cyprus, Czechoslovakia, Democratic People's Republic of Korea, Denmark, Djibouti, Ecuador, El Salvador, Estonia, Fiji, Finland, France, Gabon, Germany, Greece, Guatemala, Guinea, Guinea-Bissau, Guyana, Honduras, Hungary, Iceland, India, Indonesia, Iran, Ireland, Israel, Italy, Jamaica, Japan, Jordan, Kenya, Kuwait, Lao People's Democratic Republic, Latvia, Lebanon, Liechtenstein, Lithuania, Luxembourg, Madagascar, Malaysia, Maldives, Mali, Malta, Marshall Islands, Mauritania, Mauritius, Mexico, Micronesia, Mongolia, Morocco, Nepal, Netherlands, New Zealand, Nicaragua, Norway, Oman, Pakistan, Panama, Philippines, Poland, Portugal, Qatar, Republic of Korea, Romania, Russian Federation, Saint Kitts and Nevis, Saint Vincent and the Grenadines, Samoa, Sao Tome and Principe, Saudi Arabia, Senegal, Sierra Leone, Singapore, Spain, Sri Lanka, Sudan, Suriname, Sweden, Thailand, Trinidad and Tobago, Tunisia, Turkey, Uganda, Ukraine, United Kingdom, United Republic of Tanzania, United States, Uruguay, Vanuatu, Venezuela, Viet Nam, Yugoslavia.

Following consideration of the Republic of Moldova's application,[15] the Council adopted **resolution 739(1992)** without vote.

The Security Council,
Having examined the application of the Republic of Moldova for admission to the United Nations,

Recommends to the General Assembly that the Republic of Moldova be admitted to membership in the United Nations.

Security Council resolution 739(1992)
5 February 1992   Meeting 3047   Adopted without vote
Draft by Committee on Admission of New Members (S/23511).

The Assembly adopted **resolution 46/223** without vote.

Admission of the Republic of Moldova to membership in the United Nations
The General Assembly,
Having received the recommendation of the Security Council of 5 February 1992 that the Republic of Moldova should be admitted to membership in the United Nations,
Having considered the application for membership of the Republic of Moldova,
Decides to admit the Republic of Moldova to membership in the United Nations.

General Assembly resolution 46/223
2 March 1992   Meeting 82   Adopted without vote
113-nation draft (A/46/L.58 & Add.1); agenda item 20.
Sponsors: Afghanistan, Albania, Algeria, Antigua and Barbuda, Argentina, Australia, Austria, Bahamas, Bahrain, Bangladesh, Barbados, Belarus, Belgium, Belize, Brazil, Brunei Darussalam, Bulgaria, Burundi, Cambodia, Canada, Cape Verde, Chile, China, Colombia, Comoros, Congo, Costa Rica, Cyprus, Czechoslovakia, Democratic People's Republic of Korea, Denmark, Djibouti, Ecuador, El Salvador, Estonia, Fiji, Finland, France, Gabon, Germany, Greece, Guatemala, Guinea, Guinea-Bissau, Honduras, Hungary, Iceland, India, Indonesia, Ireland, Israel, Italy, Jamaica, Japan, Jordan, Kenya, Kuwait, Lao People's Democratic Republic, Latvia, Lebanon, Liechtenstein, Lithuania, Luxembourg, Madagascar, Malaysia, Maldives, Mali, Malta, Marshall Islands, Mauritius, Mexico, Micronesia, Mongolia, Morocco, Nepal, Netherlands, New Zealand, Nicaragua, Norway, Oman, Pakistan, Panama, Philippines, Poland, Portugal, Republic of Korea, Romania, Russian Federation, Saint Kitts and Nevis, Saint Vincent and the Grenadines, Samoa, Sao Tome and Principe, Saudi Arabia, Senegal, Sierra Leone, Singapore, Spain, Sudan, Suriname, Sweden, Thailand, Trinidad and Tobago, Tunisia, Turkey, Uganda, Ukraine, United Kingdom, United Republic of Tanzania, United States, Uruguay, Vanuatu, Venezuela, Viet Nam.

The Council acted on Turkmenistan's application[16] by adopting **resolution 741(1992)** without vote.

The Security Council,
Having examined the application of Turkmenistan for admission to the United Nations,
Recommends to the General Assembly that Turkmenistan be admitted to membership in the United Nations.

Security Council resolution 741(1992)
7 February 1992   Meeting 3050   Adopted without vote
Draft by Committee on Admission of New Members (S/23523).

The Assembly adopted **resolution 46/229** without vote.

Admission of Turkmenistan to membership in the United Nations
The General Assembly,
Having received the recommendation of the Security Council of 7 February 1992 that Turkmenistan should be admitted to membership in the United Nations,
Having considered the application for membership of Turkmenistan,
Decides to admit Turkmenistan to membership in the United Nations.

General Assembly resolution 46/229

2 March 1992   Meeting 82   Adopted without vote

119-nation draft (A/46/L.64 & Add.1); agenda item 20.

Sponsors: Afghanistan, Albania, Algeria, Antigua and Barbuda, Argentina, Australia, Austria, Bahrain, Bangladesh, Barbados, Belarus, Belgium, Belize, Brazil, Brunei Darussalam, Bulgaria, Burundi, Cambodia, Canada, Cape Verde, Chad, Chile, China, Colombia, Comoros, Congo, Costa Rica, Cyprus, Czechoslovakia, Democratic People's Republic of Korea, Denmark, Djibouti, Ecuador, El Salvador, Estonia, Fiji, Finland, France, Gabon, Germany, Greece, Guatemala, Guinea, Guinea-Bissau, Guyana, Honduras, Hungary, Iceland, India, Indonesia, Iran, Ireland, Israel, Italy, Jamaica, Japan, Jordan, Kenya, Kuwait, Lao People's Democratic Republic, Latvia, Lebanon, Liechtenstein, Lithuania, Luxembourg, Madagascar, Malaysia, Maldives, Mali, Malta, Marshall Islands, Mauritania, Mauritius, Mexico, Micronesia, Mongolia, Morocco, Nepal, Netherlands, New Zealand, Nicaragua, Norway, Oman, Pakistan, Panama, Philippines, Poland, Portugal, Qatar, Republic of Korea, Romania, Russian Federation, Saint Kitts and Nevis, Saint Vincent and the Grenadines, Samoa, Sao Tome and Principe, Saudi Arabia, Senegal, Sierra Leone, Singapore, Spain, Sri Lanka, Sudan, Suriname, Sweden, Thailand, Trinidad and Tobago, Tunisia, Turkey, Uganda, Ukraine, United Kingdom, United Republic of Tanzania, United States, Uruguay, Vanuatu, Venezuela, Viet Nam, Yugoslavia.

The Council considered Azerbaijan's application[17] and adopted **resolution 742(1992)** without vote.

The Security Council,

Having examined the application of the Republic of Azerbaijan for admission to the United Nations,

Recommends to the General Assembly that the Republic of Azerbaijan be admitted to membership in the United Nations.

Security Council resolution 742(1992)

14 February 1992   Meeting 3052   Adopted without vote

Draft by Committee on Admission of New Members (S/23569).

The Assembly adopted **resolution 46/230** without vote.

Admission of the Azerbaijani Republic to membership in the United Nations

The General Assembly,

Having received the recommendation of the Security Council of 14 February 1992 that the Azerbaijani Republic should be admitted to membership in the United Nations,

Having considered the application for membership of the Azerbaijani Republic,

Decides to admit the Azerbaijani Republic to membership in the United Nations.

General Assembly resolution 46/230

2 March 1992   Meeting 82   Adopted without vote

111-nation draft (A/46/L.65 & Add.1); agenda item 20.

Sponsors: Afghanistan, Albania, Algeria, Antigua and Barbuda, Argentina, Australia, Austria, Bahrain, Bangladesh, Barbados, Belarus, Belgium, Belize, Brazil, Brunei Darussalam, Burundi, Cambodia, Canada, Cape Verde, Chile, China, Colombia, Comoros, Congo, Costa Rica, Cyprus, Czechoslovakia, Democratic People's Republic of Korea, Denmark, Djibouti, Ecuador, El Salvador, Estonia, Fiji, Finland, France, Gabon, Germany, Greece, Guatemala, Guinea-Bissau, Guyana, Honduras, Hungary, Iceland, India, Indonesia, Iran, Ireland, Israel, Italy, Jamaica, Japan, Kenya, Kuwait, Lao People's Democratic Republic, Latvia, Lebanon, Liechtenstein, Luxembourg, Madagascar, Malaysia, Maldives, Mali, Malta, Marshall Islands, Mauritania, Mauritius, Mexico, Micronesia, Mongolia, Morocco, Nepal, Netherlands, New Zealand, Nicaragua, Norway, Oman, Pakistan, Panama, Philippines, Poland, Portugal, Republic of Korea, Romania, Russian Federation, Saint Kitts and Nevis, Saint Vincent and the Grenadines, Samoa, Sao Tome and Principe, Saudi Arabia, Senegal, Singapore, Spain, Sudan, Suriname, Sweden, Thailand, Trinidad and Tobago, Tunisia, Turkey, Uganda, Ukraine, United Kingdom, United Republic of Tanzania, United States, Uruguay, Vanuatu, Venezuela, Viet Nam, Yugoslavia.

Acting on San Marino's application,[18] the Council adopted **resolution 744(1992)** without vote.

The Security Council,

Having examined the application of the Republic of San Marino for admission to the United Nations,

Recommends to the General Assembly that the Republic of San Marino be admitted to membership in the United Nations.

Security Council resolution 744(1992)

25 February 1992   Meeting 3056   Adopted without vote

Draft by Committee on Admission of New Members (S/23634).

The Assembly adopted **resolution 46/231** without vote.

Admission of the Republic of San Marino to membership in the United Nations

The General Assembly,

Having received the recommendation of the Security Council of 25 February 1992 that the Republic of San Marino should be admitted to membership in the United Nations,

Having considered the application for membership of the Republic of San Marino,

Decides to admit the Republic of San Marino to membership in the United Nations.

General Assembly resolution 46/231

2 March 1992   Meeting 82   Adopted without vote

104-nation draft (A/46/L.66 & Add.1); agenda item 20.

Sponsors: Afghanistan, Albania, Algeria, Australia, Austria, Bahamas, Bahrain, Bangladesh, Barbados, Belarus, Belgium, Belize, Brazil, Burundi, Canada, Cape Verde, Chile, China, Colombia, Comoros, Congo, Costa Rica, Cyprus, Czechoslovakia, Democratic People's Republic of Korea, Denmark, Djibouti, Ecuador, El Salvador, Fiji, Finland, France, Gabon, Germany, Greece, Guatemala, Guinea-Bissau, Honduras, Hungary, Iceland, India, Indonesia, Ireland, Israel, Italy, Jamaica, Japan, Jordan, Kenya, Kuwait, Lao People's Democratic Republic, Latvia, Lebanon, Liechtenstein, Lithuania, Luxembourg, Madagascar, Maldives, Malta, Marshall Islands, Mauritania, Mexico, Micronesia, Mongolia, Morocco, Nepal, Netherlands, New Zealand, Nicaragua, Norway, Oman, Pakistan, Panama, Paraguay, Philippines, Poland, Portugal, Republic of Korea, Romania, Russian Federation, Saint Kitts and Nevis, Saint Vincent and the Grenadines, Samoa, Sao Tome and Principe, Saudi Arabia, Senegal, Sierra Leone, Somalia, Spain, Sudan, Suriname, Sweden, Thailand, Tunisia, Turkey, Ukraine, United Kingdom, United States, Uruguay, Vanuatu, Venezuela, Yemen, Yugoslavia.

On 18 May, the Security Council recommended Croatia[19] and Slovenia,[20] former republics of Yugoslavia. Bosnia and Herzegovina, another former Yugoslav republic, was recommended on 20 May.[21] Their membership was granted by the Assembly on 22 May.

Upon consideration of Croatia's application,[22] the Council adopted **resolution 753(1992)** without vote.

The Security Council,

Having examined the application of the Republic of Croatia for admission to the United Nations,

Recommends to the General Assembly that the Republic of Croatia be admitted to membership in the United Nations.

Security Council resolution 753(1992)

18 May 1992   Meeting 3076   Adopted without vote

Draft by Committee on Admission of New Members (S/23935).

The Assembly adopted **resolution 46/238** without vote.

Admission of the Republic of Croatia to membership in the United Nations

The General Assembly,

Having received the recommendation of the Security Council of 18 May 1992 that the Republic of Croatia should be admitted to membership in the United Nations,

Having considered the application for membership of the Republic of Croatia,

Decides to admit the Republic of Croatia to membership in the United Nations.

General Assembly resolution 46/238

22 May 1992   Meeting 86   Adopted without vote

76-nation draft (A/46/L.74 & Add.1); agenda item 20.

Sponsors: Albania, Algeria, Australia, Austria, Bahamas, Bangladesh, Belarus, Belgium, Brazil, Bulgaria, Canada, Cape Verde, Chile, China, Costa Rica, Czechoslovakia, Democratic People's Republic of Korea, Denmark, Djibouti, Dominican Republic, Estonia, Fiji, Finland, France, Germany, Greece, Guatemala, Guinea, Honduras, Hungary, India, Indonesia, Ireland, Israel, Italy, Japan, Jordan, Latvia, Lebanon, Liechtenstein, Lithuania, Luxembourg, Malaysia, Maldives, Malta, Mongolia, Morocco, Nepal, Netherlands, New Zealand, Nicaragua, Norway, Oman, Pakistan, Philippines, Poland, Portugal, Romania, Russian Federation, Samoa, Saudi Arabia, Senegal, Somalia, Spain, Sudan, Suriname, Sweden, Tunisia, Turkey, Ukraine, United Arab Emirates, United Kingdom, United States, Uruguay, Yemen.

The Council acted on Slovenia's application[23] by adopting **resolution 754(1992)** without vote.

The Security Council,

Having examined the application of the Republic of Slovenia for admission to the United Nations,

Recommends to the General Assembly that the Republic of Slovenia be admitted to membership in the United Nations.

Security Council resolution 754(1992)

18 May 1992   Meeting 3077   Adopted without vote

Draft by Committee on Admission of New Members (S/23936).

The Assembly adopted **resolution 46/236** without vote.

Admission of the Republic of Slovenia to membership in the United Nations

The General Assembly,

Having received the recommendation of the Security Council of 18 May 1992 that the Republic of Slovenia should be admitted to membership in the United Nations,

Having considered the application for membership of the Republic of Slovenia,

Decides to admit the Republic of Slovenia to membership in the United Nations.

General Assembly resolution 46/236

22 May 1992   Meeting 86   Adopted without vote

79-nation draft (A/46/L.71 & Add.1); agenda item 20.

Sponsors: Albania, Algeria, Australia, Austria, Bahamas, Bahrain, Bangladesh, Belarus, Belgium, Brazil, Bulgaria, Canada, Cape Verde, Chile, China, Costa Rica, Czechoslovakia, Democratic People's Republic of Korea, Denmark, Djibouti, Dominican Republic, Ecuador, Egypt, Estonia, Fiji, Finland, France, Germany, Greece, Guatemala, Guinea, Honduras, Hungary, Iceland, India, Indonesia, Ireland, Israel, Italy, Japan, Jordan, Latvia, Lebanon, Liechtenstein, Lithuania, Luxembourg, Malaysia, Maldives, Malta, Mongolia, Morocco, Nepal, Netherlands, New Zealand, Nicaragua, Norway, Oman, Pakistan, Philippines, Poland, Portugal, Romania, Russian Federation,

Samoa, Saudi Arabia, Senegal, Somalia, Spain, Sudan, Suriname, Sweden, Tunisia, Turkey, Ukraine, United Arab Emirates, United Kingdom, United States, Uruguay, Yemen.

The Council considered the application of Bosnia and Herzegovina[24] and adopted **resolution 755(1992)** without vote.

The Security Council,

Having examined the application of the Republic of Bosnia and Herzegovina for admission to the United Nations,

Recommends to the General Assembly that the Republic of Bosnia and Herzegovina be admitted to membership in the United Nations.

Security Council resolution 755(1992)

20 May 1992   Meeting 3079   Adopted without vote

Draft by Committee on Admission of New Members (S/23974).

The Assembly adopted **resolution 46/237** without vote.

Admission of the Republic of Bosnia and Herzegovina to membership in the United Nations

The General Assembly,

Having received the recommendation of the Security Council of 20 May 1992 that the Republic of Bosnia and Herzegovina should be admitted to membership in the United Nations,

Having considered the application for membership of the Republic of Bosnia and Herzegovina,

Decides to admit the Republic of Bosnia and Herzegovina to membership in the United Nations.

General Assembly resolution 46/237

22 May 1992   Meeting 86   Adopted without vote

77-nation draft (A/46/L.73 & Add.1); agenda item 20.

Sponsors: Albania, Algeria, Australia, Austria, Bahrain, Bangladesh, Belarus, Belgium, Bulgaria, Canada, Cape Verde, Chad, Comoros, Costa Rica, Czechoslovakia, Democratic People's Republic of Korea, Denmark, Djibouti, Dominican Republic, Egypt, Estonia, Fiji, Finland, France, Germany, Greece, Guatemala, Guinea, Honduras, Hungary, Iceland, India, Indonesia, Iran, Ireland, Israel, Italy, Jordan, Kuwait, Latvia, Lebanon, Liechtenstein, Lithuania, Luxembourg, Malaysia, Maldives, Malta, Mongolia, Morocco, Nepal, Netherlands, New Zealand, Nicaragua, Norway, Oman, Pakistan, Philippines, Poland, Portugal, Qatar, Romania, Russian Federation, Samoa, Saudi Arabia, Senegal, Somalia, Spain, Sudan, Suriname, Tunisia, Turkey, Ukraine, United Arab Emirates, United Kingdom, United States, Uruguay, Yemen.

In a statement on the occasion of the admission of Slovenia, Croatia, and Bosnia and Herzegovina,[25] the Federal Republic of Yugoslavia said the fact that they had become Members in no way challenged the international legal personality and continuity of membership of the Federal Republic of Yugoslavia in the United Nations and its specialized agencies.

On 6 July, the Security Council recommended the granting of United Nations membership to Georgia, a republic of the former USSR.[26] The Assembly endorsed the recommendation on 31 July.

Acting on Georgia's application,[27] the Council adopted **resolution 763(1992)** without vote.

The Security Council,

Having examined the application of the Republic of Georgia for admission to the United Nations,

Recommends to the General Assembly that the Republic of Georgia be admitted to membership in the United Nations.

Security Council resolution 763(1992)

6 July 1992   Meeting 3091   Adopted without vote

Draft by Committee on Admission of New Members (S/24231).

The Assembly adopted **resolution 46/241** without vote.

Admission of the Republic of Georgia to membership in the United Nations

The General Assembly,

Having received the recommendation of the Security Council of 6 July 1992 that the Republic of Georgia should be admitted to membership in the United Nations,

Having considered the application for membership of the Republic of Georgia,

Decides to admit the Republic of Georgia to membership in the United Nations.

General Assembly resolution 46/241

31 July 1992   Meeting 88   Adopted without vote

76-nation draft (A/46/L.75 & Add.1); agenda item 20.

Sponsors: Afghanistan, Albania, Angola, Argentina, Armenia, Australia, Austria, Azerbaijan, Bahamas, Bangladesh, Barbados, Belarus, Belgium, Brazil, Bulgaria, Canada, Cape Verde, Chile, China, Colombia, Congo, Costa Rica, Croatia, Cyprus, Czechoslovakia, Denmark, Djibouti, Dominican Republic, Ecuador, El Salvador, Estonia, Finland, France, Gabon, Germany, Greece, Guatemala, Guinea, Honduras, Hungary, India, Ireland, Israel, Italy, Jamaica, Japan, Jordan, Kuwait, Kyrgyzstan, Lao People's Democratic Republic, Latvia, Lebanon, Lesotho, Liechtenstein, Luxembourg, Madagascar, Malaysia, Maldives, Mali, Malta, Marshall Islands, Mauritius, Mexico, Mongolia, Morocco, Nepal, Netherlands, New Zealand, Nicaragua, Nigeria, Norway, Oman, Pakistan, Panama, Paraguay, Philippines, Poland, Portugal, Republic of Korea, Republic of Moldova, Romania, Russian Federation, Saint Vincent and the Grenadines, San Marino, Sao Tome and Principe, Saudi Arabia, Slovenia, Spain, Sri Lanka, Suriname, Sweden, Thailand, Trinidad and Tobago, Turkey, Ukraine, United Kingdom, United States, Uruguay, Venezuela, Viet Nam, Yemen, Yugoslavia, Zimbabwe.

On 10 December,[28] Czechoslovakia communicated to the Secretary-General the intention of the Czech Republic and the Slovak Republic to apply for United Nations membership, following the dissolution of the Czech and Slovak Federal Republic on 31 December 1992.

Yugoslavia and UN membership

In September, the General Assembly, on the recommendation of the Security Council, ruled that the Federal Republic of Yugoslavia (Serbia and Montenegro) could not continue automatically the membership of the former Socialist Federal Republic of Yugoslavia in the United Nations and, therefore, should not participate in the work of the Assembly and should apply for membership.

In response to the creation of the Federal Republic of Yugoslavia, announced on 27 April 1992 by Serbia and Montenegro, Austria communicated on 5 May its view that there was no legal basis for the Federal Republic to continue automatically the existence of the former Socialist Federal Republic of Yugoslavia and, therefore, the Yugoslav membership in the United Nations.[29]

Also in May, Canada[30] and the United States[31] stated that Yugoslavia's participation in the activities of United Nations bodies was without prejudice to the eventual determination of the Republic's status.

Replying on 5 June to a letter of 27 May by Slovenia,[32] which demanded prompt termination of the Yugoslav membership in international organizations, Yugoslavia pointed out that Serbia and Montenegro had not seceded from the former Socialist Federal Republic, thus continuing its legal personality as members of the new State.[33]

On 29 June,[34] Belgium, France and the United Kingdom communicated to the Security Council a declaration by the European Community on the former Yugoslavia, stating, *inter alia*, that the Community did not recognize the new entity comprising Serbia and Montenegro as the successor State of the former Yugoslavia.

(For details of the Yugoslavia question, see PART TWO, Chapter IV.)

SECURITY COUNCIL ACTION

On 19 September 1992, the Security Council adopted **resolution 777(1992)**.

The Security Council,

Reaffirming its resolution 713(1991) of 25 September 1991 and all subsequent relevant resolutions,

Considering that the State formerly known as the Socialist Federal Republic of Yugoslavia has ceased to exist,

Recalling in particular resolution 757(1992) which notes that "the claim by the Federal Republic of Yugoslavia (Serbia and Montenegro) to continue automatically the membership of the former Socialist Federal Republic of Yugoslavia in the United Nations has not been generally accepted",

1. *Considers* that the Federal Republic of Yugoslavia (Serbia and Montenegro) cannot continue automatically the membership of the former Socialist Federal Republic of Yugoslavia in the United Nations; and therefore *recommends* to the General Assembly that it decide that the Federal Republic of Yugoslavia (Serbia and Montenegro) should apply for membership in the United Nations and that it shall not participate in the work of the General Assembly;

2. *Decides* to consider the matter again before the end of the main part of the forty-seventh session of the General Assembly.

Security Council resolution 777(1992)

19 September 1992   Meeting 3116   12-0-3

5-nation draft (S/24570).

Sponsors: Belgium, France, Morocco, United Kingdom, United States.

Vote in Council as follows:

In favour: Austria, Belgium, Cape Verde, Ecuador, France, Hungary, Japan, Morocco, Russian Federation, United Kingdom, United States, Venezuela.

Against: None.

Abstaining: China, India, Zimbabwe.

In a statement prior to the vote, the Russian Federation emphasized that the resolution in no way affected Yugoslavia's participation in the work of United Nations bodies other than the General

Assembly, particularly the Security Council, nor the functioning of its Permanent Mission, the issuance of documents or the keeping of the nameplate with the name Yugoslavia in the Assembly Hall and the rooms in which the Assembly's organs met. After the vote, China made a statement to the same effect, adding that the Council's decision was only a transitional arrangement.

On 9 December,[35] the Council President informed the President of the Assembly that the Council members agreed to keep the subject-matter of the 19 September resolution under continuous review and to consider it again at a later date.

GENERAL ASSEMBLY ACTION

On 22 September, the General Assembly adopted **resolution 47/1** by recorded vote.

Recommendation of the Security Council of 19 September 1992

The General Assembly,

Having received the recommendation of the Security Council of 19 September 1992 that the Federal Republic of Yugoslavia (Serbia and Montenegro) should apply for membership in the United Nations and that it shall not participate in the work of the General Assembly,

1. *Considers* that the Federal Republic of Yugoslavia (Serbia and Montenegro) cannot continue automatically the membership of the former Socialist Federal Republic of Yugoslavia in the United Nations; and therefore decides that the Federal Republic of Yugoslavia (Serbia and Montenegro) should apply for membership in the United Nations and that it shall not participate in the work of the General Assembly;

2. *Takes note* of the intention of the Security Council to consider the matter again before the end of the main part of the forty-seventh session of the General Assembly.

General Assembly resolution 47/1

22 September 1992   Meeting 7   127-6-26 (recorded vote)

45-nation draft (A/47/L.1 & Add.1); agenda item 8.

Sponsors: Afghanistan, Albania, Australia, Austria, Bahrain, Bangladesh, Belgium, Bosnia and Herzegovina, Canada, Comoros, Croatia, Denmark, Egypt, Finland, France, Germany, Greece, Iceland, Iran, Ireland, Italy, Jordan, Liechtenstein, Luxembourg, Malaysia, Malta, Mauritania, Morocco, Netherlands, New Zealand, Norway, Oman, Pakistan, Portugal, Qatar, Saudi Arabia, Senegal, Slovenia, Spain, Sweden, Tunisia, Turkey, United Arab Emirates, United Kingdom, United States.

Recorded vote in Assembly as follows:

In favour: Afghanistan, Albania, Algeria, Antigua and Barbuda, Argentina, Armenia, Australia, Austria, Azerbaijan, Bahrain, Bangladesh, Barbados, Belarus, Belgium, Belize, Benin, Bhutan, Bolivia, Bosnia and Herzegovina, Brunei Darussalam, Bulgaria, Burkina Faso, Canada, Cape Verde, Chile, Colombia, Comoros, Congo, Costa Rica, Croatia, Cyprus, Czechoslovakia, Denmark, Djibouti, Ecuador, Egypt, El Salvador, Estonia, Fiji, Finland, France, Gabon, Gambia, Germany, Greece, Grenada, Guatemala, Guinea, Guinea-Bissau, Haiti, Honduras, Hungary, Iceland, Indonesia, Iran, Ireland, Israel, Italy, Japan, Jordan, Kazakhstan, Kuwait, Kyrgyzstan, Lao People's Democratic Republic, Latvia, Liberia, Libyan Arab Jamahiriya, Liechtenstein, Lithuania, Luxembourg, Madagascar, Malawi, Malaysia, Maldives, Mali, Malta, Marshall Islands, Mauritania, Mauritius, Micronesia, Mongolia, Morocco, Nepal, Netherlands, New Zealand, Nicaragua, Niger, Nigeria, Norway, Oman, Pakistan, Panama, Paraguay, Peru, Philippines, Poland, Portugal, Qatar, Republic of Korea, Republic of Moldova, Romania, Russian Federation, Rwanda, Saint Kitts and Nevis, Saint Vincent and the Grenadines, Samoa, San Marino, Saudi Arabia, Senegal, Singapore, Slovenia, Spain, Sudan, Suriname, Sweden, Thailand, Trinidad and Tobago, Tunisia, Turkey, Turkmenistan, Ukraine, United Arab Emirates, United Kingdom, United States, Uruguay, Vanuatu, Yemen.

Against: Kenya, Swaziland, United Republic of Tanzania, Yugoslavia, Zambia, Zimbabwe.

Abstaining: Angola, Bahamas, Botswana, Brazil, Burundi, Cameroon, China, Côte d'Ivoire, Cuba, Ghana, Guyana, India, Iraq, Jamaica, Lebanon,* Lesotho, Mexico, Mozambique, Myanmar, Namibia, Papua New Guinea, Sri Lanka, Togo, Uganda, Viet Nam, Zaire.

*Later advised the Secretariat it had intended to vote in favour.

Introducing the draft on behalf of the sponsors, the United Kingdom said it was neither punitive nor designed to undermine the peace process, but a measure that had to be taken in view of the unjustified claim by the Federal Republic of Yugoslavia (Serbia and Montenegro) to represent the continuity of the Socialist Federal Republic of Yugoslavia. The situation was without precedent and had clearly not been foreseen by the authors of the Charter. That the Council had decided to consider the matter again before the end of the year should be a helpful incentive to all the parties and an effective means to support the Co-Chairmen of the International Conference on the Former Yugoslavia in their task.

Yugoslavia voiced certainty that it satisfied the conditions for membership; it had been a founding member of the Organization and had always lived up to its principles. It stressed that in a resolution adopted on the same date as the Assembly resolution, the Yugoslav Federal Assembly had expressed grave concern regarding Yugoslavia's membership.

On 25 September,[36] Bosnia and Herzegovina and Croatia, referring to the General Assembly resolution, argued that the Federal Republic of Yugoslavia was not a Member of the United Nations and that the flag and the name-plaque of the Socialist Federal Republic of Yugoslavia did not represent the new State; they requested a legal explanatory statement concerning those questions. Responding on 28 September,[37] Yugoslavia stated that there were no legal grounds for requests to remove the name-plate and flag. The Security Council's recommendation and the Assembly's decision as well as the ensuing debates dealt exclusively with Yugoslavia's non-participation in the work of the Assembly.

In his reply of 29 September to Bosnia and Herzegovina and Croatia,[38] the United Nations Legal Counsel explained that, while it was clear that representatives of the Federal Republic of Yugoslavia (Serbia and Montenegro) could no longer participate in the work of the Assembly, its subsidiary organs, or conferences and meetings convened by it, the Assembly resolution neither terminated nor suspended Yugoslavia's membership in the Organization. Consequently, the seat and name-plate remained as before, but in Assembly bodies representatives of the Federal Republic of Yugoslavia could not sit behind the sign "Yugoslavia". The Counsel also stated that the Secretariat would continue to fly the flag of the old Yugoslavia as the last flag of Yugoslavia used at the United Nations. The admission of a new Yugoslavia under Article 4 of the Charter would terminate the situation created by the Assembly resolution.

Institutional machinery

Security Council

In 1992, the Security Council held 129 meetings and adopted 74 resolutions.

Agenda

The Security Council considered 26 topics under 52 agenda items during 1992. It continued the practice of adopting at each meeting the agenda for that meeting. (For list of agenda items, see APPENDIX IV.)

On 15 September,[39] the Secretary-General notified the General Assembly, in accordance with Article 12, paragraph 2, of the Charter, of 44 matters relative to the maintenance of international peace and security that the Council had discussed since his previous annual notification.[40] He listed 142 other matters not discussed during the period but of which the Council remained seized.

By **decision 47/404** of 21 October, the Assembly took note of those matters.

Membership

In December 1992, the General Assembly acted on the question of equitable representation on and increase in the membership of the Security Council.

The item was first considered by the Assembly in 1979,[41] when it was introduced on the grounds that United Nations membership had grown to 152, compared to 113 in 1963, when the Council membership was increased from 11 to 15.[42]

In September 1992, the Tenth Conference of Heads of State or Government of Non-Aligned Countries (Jakarta, Indonesia), in its Jakarta Message,[43] called for a review of the membership of the Council, aimed at reflecting the increased membership of the United Nations and promoting a more equitable and balanced representation of its Members.

GENERAL ASSEMBLY ACTION

On 11 December, the General Assembly adopted **resolution 47/62** without vote.

Question of equitable representation on and increase in the membership of the Security Council

The General Assembly,

Recognizing the increasingly crucial role of the Security Council in maintaining international peace and security,

Recognizing also the changed international situation and the substantial increase in the membership of the United Nations, the total membership having reached one hundred and seventy-nine,

Acting in accordance with the principles and objectives of the Charter of the United Nations,

Reaffirming the principle of sovereign equality of all Members of the United Nations,

Mindful of Article 23 of the Charter of the United Nations,

Realizing the need to continue the process of revitalization and restructuring of certain organs of the United Nations,

Recalling the statements made on the subject at the forty-seventh session, as well as the statement on the same subject contained in the final documents of the Tenth Conference of Heads of State or Government of Non-Aligned Countries, held at Jakarta from 1 to 6 September 1992,

1. *Requests* the Secretary-General to invite Member States to submit, not later than 30 June 1993, written comments on a possible review of the membership of the Security Council;

2. *Requests* the Secretary-General to submit to the General Assembly at its forty-eighth session, for its consideration, a report containing comments made by Member States on the subject;

3. *Decides* to include in the provisional agenda of its forty-eighth session the item entitled "Question of equitable representation on and increase in the membership of the Security Council".

General Assembly resolution 47/62

11 December 1992   Meeting 84   Adopted without vote

37-nation draft (A/47/L.26/Rev.1 & Add.1); agenda item 40.
Sponsors: Algeria, Barbados, Bhutan, Brazil, Chile, Colombia, Cuba, Egypt, Gabon, Guyana, Honduras, India, Indonesia, Jamaica, Japan, Jordan, Lebanon, Liberia, Libyan Arab Jamahiriya, Lithuania, Malaysia, Mali, Mauritius, Mexico, Nepal, Nicaragua, Nigeria, Pakistan, Paraguay, Peru, Senegal, Togo, Tunisia, Uganda, Venezuela, Viet Nam, Zimbabwe.
Meeting numbers. GA 47th session: plenary 69, 84.

General Assembly

The General Assembly met in two sessions during 1992, to resume and conclude its forty-sixth (1991) regular session and to hold the major part of its forty-seventh session. The forty-sixth session resumed on 4 and 14 February, 2 and 19 March, 13 April, 6 and 22 May, 29 and 31 July, 24 and 25 August and 14 September 1992.

The forty-seventh session opened on 15 September and continued until its suspension on 23 December.

Representatives' credentials

At its first meeting on 8 October 1992, the Credentials Committee examined a memorandum of the previous day from the Secretary-General indicating that credentials of representatives to the General Assembly's forty-seventh session had been submitted by 131 Member States. The Legal Counsel explained that the memorandum related solely to Member States that had submitted formal credentials. The Counsel further informed that, subsequent to the memorandum, additional credentials in due form had been received in respect of the representatives of Latvia.

On 9 December, at its second meeting, the Committee examined a further memorandum from the Secretary-General, reporting that, since the first meeting, formal credentials had been received from 29 other Member States. In addition, information concerning the appointment of their representatives to the forty-seventh session had been communicated to the Secretary-General by 15 Member States, by means of a facsimile communication, letter or note verbale. The Committee Chairman proposed that the Committee accept the credentials of all those Member States, including those that had communicated by facsimile, letter or note verbale, on the understanding that the latter would submit formal credentials as soon as possible.

At each meeting, the Committee, acting without vote on an oral proposal by its Chairman, adopted a resolution by which it accepted the credentials received. The Committee also recommended to the Assembly two draft resolutions approving its first[44] and second[45] reports. The Assembly took no action on either report.

(For details on the status of the credentials of Haiti, see PART TWO, Chapter II.)

Organization of the 1992 session

On 18 September 1992, by **decision 47/401**, the General Assembly, on the recommendation of the General Committee as set forth in its first report,[46] adopted a number of provisions concerning the organization of the 1992 session.

The Committee's recommendations concerned rationalization of the Assembly's work; the closing date of the session; the schedule of meetings; the general debate; explanations of vote, right of reply, points of order and length of statements; meeting records; concluding statements; resolutions; questions related to the programme budget; documentation; observances and commemorative meetings; special conferences; and meetings of subsidiary organs.

Subsidiary organs

By **decisions 47/403 A, B and C**, adopted on 15, 18 and 30 September, respectively, on the recommendations of the Committee on Conferences[47] and the General Committee,[46] the General Assembly authorized the following subsidiary organs to hold meetings during its 1992 session: Committee for Programme and Coordination; Committee on Relations with the Host Country; Committee on the Exercise of the Inalienable Rights of the Palestinian People; Special Committee against Apartheid; Working Group on the Financing of the United Nations Relief and Works Agency for Palestine Refugees in the Near East; Committee of Trustees of the United Nations Trust Fund for South Africa; Advisory Committee on the United Nations Educational and Training Programme for Southern Africa; Executive Board of the United Nations Children's Fund; Intergovernmental Group to Monitor the Supply and Shipping of Oil and Petroleum Products to South Africa; and Board of Trustees of the United Nations Institute for Training and Research. The Assembly, acting on an oral proposal of its President, also authorized meetings of the Preparatory Committee for the Fiftieth Anniversary of the United Nations.

Agenda

At its resumed forty-sixth session, on 4 February 1992, the General Assembly included in the agenda a sub-item on the appointment of members of the International Civil Service Commission and an additional item on financing of the United Nations Transitional Authority in Cambodia; it also reopened consideration of the item on special economic and disaster relief assistance, at the request of Samoa[48] (**decision 46/402 B**). By the same decision, on 2 March, the Assembly included in the agenda an item on financing of the United Nations Protection Force. On 13 April and 6 May, respectively, the Assembly reopened consideration of the item on the United Nations Conference on Environment and Development and of the sub-item on human rights questions, including alternative approaches for improving the effective enjoyment of human rights and fundamental freedoms (**decision 46/402 C**).

The Assembly took further action on the agenda of its resumed session by **decision 46/402 D**. On 29 July, it reopened consideration of the items on financing of the United Nations Angola Verification Mission and on the United Nations common system, the latter at the request of the United States.[49] An item on the situation in Bosnia and Herzegovina was included on 24 August, on the recommendation of the General Committee.[50] On 14 September, the Assembly, on a proposal of the Chairman of the Committee on colonial countries, revised the wording of agenda item 100 of the provisional agenda of the forty-seventh session to read ''Activities of those foreign economic and other interests which impede the implementation of the Declaration on the Granting of Independence to Colonial Countries and Peoples in Territories under colonial domination and efforts to eliminate colonialism, apartheid and racial discrimination in southern Africa''.

Also on 14 September, the Assembly included in the draft agenda of its forty-seventh session items on the question of Cyprus (**decision 46/474**), the consequences of the Iraqi occupation of and aggression against Kuwait (**decision 46/475**) and the current financial crisis of the United Nations (**decision 46/476**).

By **decision 47/402**, acting on the recommendations of the General Committee,[51] the Assembly, on 18 and 25 September, 6 and 15 October, 20 and 23 November and 17 December, adopted the agenda of its forty-seventh session, which initially had 144 items, and allocated them to the appropriate Main Committee. At the Secretary-General's request,[52] the Assembly included in the agenda an item on financing of the United Nations Operation in Somalia. On the recommendations of the General Committee,[51] it further included items on: emergency assistance to Pakistan; programme budget for the biennium 1990-1991; emergency assistance to the Philippines; the situation of human rights in Estonia and Latvia; international assistance for the rehabilitation and reconstruction of Nicaragua; request for an advisory opinion from the International Court of Justice; and convening of an international conference on Somalia.

On 23 December, by **decision 47/467**, the Assembly retained 41 items or sub-items on the agenda of its forty-seventh session.

1993 agenda

By **decision 47/402**, the Assembly, on 18 September, on the General Committee's recommendation,[46] included in the provisional agenda of its forty-eighth (1993) session the questions of the Malagasy islands of Glorieuses, Juan de Nova, Europa and Bassas da India and of East Timor. On 14 December, by **decision 47/425**, it included an item on the composition of the relevant organs of the United Nations.

Deferring consideration of the item on implementation of the resolutions of the United Nations, the Assembly, by **decision 47/466** of 23 December, included it in the provisional agenda of its 1993 session. Also to be included was the question of the Falkland Islands (Malvinas), consideration of which was deferred by **decision 47/408** of 10 November. The item on science and peace was also deferred until the 1993 session (**decision 47/423** of 14 December), as was the item on the Declaration of the Assembly of Heads of State and Government of the Organization of African Unity on the aerial and naval military attack against the Libyan Arab Jamahiriya by the United States Administration in April 1986 (**decision 47/463** of 23 December).

Commemoration of the fiftieth anniversary of the United Nations in 1995

On 13 April 1992, the General Assembly decided to establish a Preparatory Committee for the Fiftieth Anniversary of the United Nations and to entrust it with considering and recommending to the Assembly at its 1992 session proposals for suitable activities in connection with the observance of the anniversary (**decision 46/472**).

The Committee held two meetings, on 22 October and 30 November 1992, to consider various programmes and activities related to the commemoration of the anniversary.[53] By **decision 47/417** of 8 December, the Assembly took note of the Committee's activities and decided that it should continue its work.

REFERENCES

[1]A/46/853. [2]A/46/859. [3]A/46/860. [4]A/46/862. [5]A/46/861. [6]A/46/870. [7]A/46/871. [8]A/46/880. [9]A/46/885. [10]A/46/834-S/23353. [11]A/46/847-S/23405. [12]A/46/842-S/23450. [13]A/46/850-S/23455. [14]A/46/843-S/23451. [15]A/46/852-S/23468. [16]A/46/856-S/23489 & Corr.1. [17]A/46/872-S/23558. [18]A/46/881-S/23619. [19]A/46/919. [20]A/46/920. [21]A/46/922. [22]A/46/912-S/23884. [23]A/46/913-S/23885. [24]A/46/291-S/23971. [25]A/46/927. [26]A/46/942. [27]A/46/938-S/24116. [28]A/47/774. [29]A/47/201-S/23876. [30]A/46/909-S/23883. [31]A/46/906 (S/23879). [32]A/47/234-S/24028. [33]A/47/258-S/24073. [34]S/24200. [35]S/24924. [36]A/47/474. [37]A/47/478-S/24599. [38]A/47/485. [39]A/47/436 & Corr.1. [40]YUN 1991, p. 98. [41]YUN 1979, p. 435. [42]YUN 1963, p. 87, GA res. 1991 A (XVIII), 17 Dec. 1963. [43]A/47/675-S/24816. [44]A/47/517. [45]A/47/517/Add.1. [46]A/47/250. [47]A/47/409 & Add.1,2. [48]A/46/865. [49]A/46/952. [50]A/46/250/Add.4. [51]A/47/250 & Add.1-5. [52]A/47/243. [53]A/47/48.

Cooperation with other organizations

League of Arab States

In response to a 1991 General Assembly resolution,[1] the Secretary-General submitted in September 1992 a report[2] on cooperation between the United Nations and the League of Arab States.

According to the report, the secretariats of both organizations continued to maintain close contact on matters of mutual concern. The report reviewed follow-up action on proposals agreed to at previous meetings and summarized the activities of 23 United Nations bodies and organizations which cooperated with the League in six sectoral areas—international peace and security; food and agriculture; labour, trade, industry and environment; social affairs; education, science, culture and information; and communications—in accordance with a decision taken at a joint meeting at Geneva in July 1990.

GENERAL ASSEMBLY ACTION

On 29 October 1992, the General Assembly adopted **resolution 47/12** by recorded vote.

Cooperation between the United Nations and the League of Arab States

The General Assembly,

Recalling its previous resolutions on the promotion of cooperation between the United Nations and the League of Arab States,

Having considered the report of the Secretary-General on cooperation between the United Nations and the League of Arab States,

Recalling the decision of the Council of the League of Arab States that it considers the League as a regional organization within the meaning of Chapter VIII of the Charter of the United Nations,

Noting with appreciation the desire of the League of Arab States to consolidate and develop the existing ties with the United Nations in all areas relating to the maintenance of international peace and security, and to cooperate in every possible way with the United Nations in the implementation of United Nations resolutions relating to Lebanon and to the question of Palestine and the situation in the Middle East,

Aware of the vital importance for the countries members of the League of Arab States of achieving a just, comprehensive and durable solution to the Middle East conflict and the question of Palestine, the core of the conflict,

Welcoming the peace process concerning the Middle East, which commenced in the convening of the conference at Madrid in 1991, with a view to achieving a comprehensive and just settlement of the Middle East conflict, the core of which is the question of Palestine,

Realizing that the strengthening of international peace and security is directly related, *inter alia*, to economic development, disarmament, decolonization, self-determination and the eradication of all forms of racism and racial discrimination,

Convinced that the maintenance and further strengthening of cooperation between the United Nations system and the League of Arab States contribute to the promotion of the purposes and principles of the United Nations,

Also convinced of the need for more efficient and coordinated utilization of available economic and financial resources to promote common objectives of the two organizations,

Recognizing the need for closer cooperation between the United Nations system and the League of Arab States and its specialized organizations in realizing the goals and objectives set forth in the Strategy for Joint Arab Economic Development adopted by the Eleventh Arab Summit Conference, held at Amman in November 1980,

Having heard the statement by the Permanent Observer for the League of Arab States to the United Nations on 29 October 1992 concerning cooperation between the United Nations and the League of Arab States, and having noted the emphasis placed therein on follow-up actions and procedures on the recommendations in the political, social, cultural and administrative fields adopted at the meetings between the representatives of the General Secretariat of the League of Arab States and its specialized organizations and the secretariats of the United Nations and other organizations of the United Nations system, as well as on the recommendations relating to political matters contained in the relevant resolutions of the General Assembly,

1. *Takes note with satisfaction* of the report of the Secretary-General;

2. *Commends* the continued efforts of the League of Arab States to promote multilateral cooperation among Arab States and requests the United Nations system to continue to lend its support;

3. *Expresses its appreciation* to the Secretary-General for the follow-up action taken by him to implement the proposals adopted at the meetings between the representatives of the secretariats of the United Nations and other organizations of the United Nations system and the General Secretariat of the League of Arab States and its specialized organizations, held at Tunis in 1983, at Amman in 1985 and at Geneva in 1988;

4. *Expresses its appreciation also* to the Secretary-General for his efforts to implement Security Council resolution 425(1978) of 19 March 1978 and commends the League of Arab States and its Tripartite High Committee for their endeavours to promote the peace process and reconstruction efforts in Lebanon;

5. *Requests* the Secretary-General to continue to strengthen cooperation with the General Secretariat of the League of Arab States for the purpose of implementing United Nations resolutions relating to the question of Palestine and the situation in the Middle East in order to achieve a just, comprehensive and durable solution to the Middle East conflict and the question of Palestine, the core of the conflict;

6. *Requests* the Secretariat of the United Nations and the General Secretariat of the League of Arab States, within their respective fields of competence, to intensify further their cooperation towards the realization of the purposes and principles of the Charter of the United Nations, the strengthening of international peace and security, economic development, disarmament, decolonization, self-determination and the eradication of all forms of racism and racial discrimination;

7. *Also requests* the Secretary-General to continue his efforts to strengthen cooperation and coordination between the United Nations and other organizations and agencies of the United Nations system and the League of Arab States and its specialized organizations in order to enhance their capacity to serve the mutual interests of the two organizations in the political, economic, social, humanitarian, cultural and administrative fields;

8. *Further requests* the Secretary-General to continue to coordinate the follow-up action to facilitate the implementation of the proposals of a multilateral nature adopted at the Tunis meeting in 1983, and to take appropriate action regarding the proposals adopted at previous meetings, including the following:

(a) Promotion of contacts and consultations between the counterpart programmes of the United Nations system;

(b) Setting up joint sectoral inter-agency working groups;

9. *Calls upon* the specialized agencies and other organizations and programmes of the United Nations system:

(a) To continue to cooperate with the Secretary-General and among themselves, as well as with the League of Arab States and its specialized organizations, in the follow-up of multilateral proposals aimed at strengthening and expanding cooperation in all fields between the United Nations system and the League of Arab States and its specialized organizations;

(b) To maintain and increase contacts and improve the mechanism of consultation with the counterpart programmes, organizations and agencies concerned regarding projects and programmes, in order to facilitate their implementation;

(c) To associate whenever possible with organizations and institutions of the League of Arab States in the execution and implementation of development projects in the Arab region;

(d) To inform the Secretary-General, not later than 15 May 1993, of the progress of their cooperation with the League of Arab States and its specialized organizations, in particular the follow-up action taken on the multilateral and bilateral proposals adopted at the previous meetings between the two organizations;

10. *Decides* that, in order to intensify cooperation and for the purpose of review and appraisal of progress as well as to prepare comprehensive periodic reports, a general meeting between the United Nations system and the League of Arab States should take place once every two years, and inter-agency sectoral meetings should be organized annually on areas of priority and wide importance in the development of the Arab States;

11. *Recommends* that the next general meeting on cooperation between the representatives of the secretariats of the United Nations system and the General Secretariat of the League of Arab States and its specialized organizations should be held during 1993, in commemoration of the tenth anniversary of the first general meeting of cooperation between the two organizations, and also requests the Secretary-General of the United Nations and the executive heads of the agencies and organizations of the United Nations system to cooperate with the Secretary-General of the League of Arab States for the success of the meeting and the realization of its objectives;

12. *Also recommends* that the United Nations and the other organizations of the United Nations system should utilize Arab expertise to the extent possible in projects undertaken in the Arab region;

13. *Requests* the Secretary-General of the United Nations, in cooperation with the Secretary-General of the League of Arab States, to encourage periodic consultation between representatives of the Secretariat of the United Nations and the General Secretariat of the League of Arab States to review and strengthen coordination mechanisms with a view to accelerating implementation and follow-up action of multilateral projects, proposals and recommendations adopted by the meetings between the two organizations;

14. *Also requests* the Secretary-General to submit to the General Assembly at its forty-eighth session a progress report on the implementation of the present resolution;

15. *Decides* to include in the provisional agenda of its forty-eighth session the item entitled "Cooperation between the United Nations and the League of Arab States".

General Assembly resolution 47/12

29 October 1992   Meeting 51   119-2-1 (recorded vote)

17-nation draft (A/47/L.12); agenda item 29.
Sponsors: Algeria, Bahrain, Djibouti, Egypt, Jordan, Kuwait, Lebanon, Libyan Araba Jamahiriya, Mauritania, Morocco, Oman, Qatar, Saudi Arabia, Syrian Arab Republic, Tunisia, United Arab Emirates, Yemen.

Recorded vote in Assembly as follows:

In favour: Afghanistan, Albania, Algeria, Antigua and Barbuda, Argentina, Australia, Austria, Bahamas, Bahrain, Bangladesh, Barbados, Belgium, Belize, Benin, Bosnia and Herzegovina, Botswana, Brazil, Brunei Darussalam, Bulgaria, Burkina Faso, Canada, Cape Verde, Chile, China, Colombia, Costa Rica, Cuba, Cyprus, Czechoslovakia, Denmark, Djibouti, Ecuador, Egypt, Equatorial Guinea, Estonia, Ethiopia, Finland, France, Gabon, Germany, Ghana, Greece, Guatemala, Guinea, Guinea-Bissau, Guyana, Haiti, Honduras, Hungary, Iceland, India, Indonesia, Iran, Iraq, Ireland, Italy, Jamaica, Japan, Jordan, Kenya, Kuwait, Lao People's Democratic Republic, Latvia, Lebanon, Libyan Arab Jamahiriya, Liechtenstein, Lithuania, Lux-

embourg, Madagascar, Malaysia, Maldives, Mali, Malta, Mexico, Micronesia, Morocco, Myanmar, Nepal, Netherlands, New Zealand, Nicaragua, Norway, Oman, Pakistan, Panama, Paraguay, Peru, Philippines, Poland, Portugal, Qatar, Republic of Korea, Romania, Russian Federation, Sao Tome and Principe, Saudi Arabia, Senegal, Sierra Leone, Singapore, Spain, Sri Lanka, Sudan, Suriname, Swaziland, Sweden, Syrian Arab Republic, Thailand, Togo, Trinidad and Tobago, Tunisia, Turkey, Ukraine, United Arab Emirates, United Kingdom, United Republic of Tanzania, Uruguay, Venezuela, Viet Nam, Yemen.
Against: Israel, United States.
Abstaining: San Marino.

Organization of the Islamic Conference

Pursuant to a 1991 General Assembly resolution,[3] the Secretary-General submitted in September 1992 a report[4] on cooperation between the United Nations and the Organization of the Islamic Conference (OIC). He reported that, during the year, the United Nations Department of Political Affairs had held regular consultations with the General Secretariat of OIC and the Office of the Permanent Observer for OIC to the United Nations, and that representatives of OIC had participated in meetings of the Security Council and the Assembly.

The report further described follow-up action in seven priority areas of cooperation: development of science and technology; development of trade; technical cooperation among Islamic countries; assistance to refugees; food security and agriculture; education and eradication of illiteracy; and investment mechanisms and joint ventures. The Secretary-General also summarized the activities of 16 United Nations bodies and organizations which cooperated with OIC in the field of economic, social and cultural development.

In response to the 1991 Assembly resolution,[3] a United Nations/OIC technical working group held a meeting on basic education and training for human resources development (Jeddah, Saudia Arabia, 17 and 18 May 1992). The group agreed on the need for continued cooperation between the two organizations in that area and noted that the situation regarding human resources development in Islamic countries remained a matter of grave concern. It concluded that, to meet the challenges of the future, Islamic countries should expand access to all sectors of education, improve and diversify its quality and meet the learning needs of all citizens. The group further set out subject areas for future action—including girls' and women's education with particular emphasis on literacy and skill-training programmes, introduction of science and technology in primary education, and literacy and skill-training for adults in non-formal education—and decided to prepare terms of reference for eventual pilot projects in those areas in OIC member States, to be considered at its 1993 meeting in Paris.

In an addendum to the report,[5] the Secretary-General described the November 1991 general meeting between the secretariats of both organizations, which had reviewed the progress achieved in implementing a two-year plan of action in the seven priority areas of cooperation and considered the report of an April 1991 sectoral meeting on basic education and training for human resources development.[6]

GENERAL ASSEMBLY ACTION

On 23 November 1992, the General Assembly adopted without vote **resolution 47/18**.

Cooperation between the United Nations and the Organization of the Islamic Conference

The General Assembly,

Having considered the report of the Secretary-General on cooperation between the United Nations and the Organization of the Islamic Conference,

Taking into account the desire of both organizations to cooperate more closely in their common search for solutions to global problems, such as questions relating to international peace and security, disarmament, self-determination, decolonization, fundamental human rights and economic and technical development,

Recalling the Articles of the Charter of the United Nations that encourage activities through regional cooperation for the promotion of the purposes and principles of the United Nations,

Noting the strengthening of cooperation between the specialized agencies and other organizations of the United Nations system and the Organization of the Islamic Conference and its specialized institutions,

Noting with satisfaction the meeting of the working group on Human Resources Development: Basic Education and Training, held at Jeddah, Saudi Arabia, on 17 and 18 May 1992,

Noting also the encouraging progress made in the seven priority areas of cooperation as well as in the identification of other areas of cooperation,

Convinced that the strengthening of cooperation between the United Nations and other organizations of the United Nations system and the Organization of the Islamic Conference contributes to the promotion of the purposes and principles of the United Nations,

Noting with appreciation the determination of both organizations to strengthen further the existing cooperation by developing specific proposals in the designated priority areas of cooperation,

Recognizing the ongoing need for closer cooperation between the specialized agencies and other organizations of the United Nations system and the Organization of the Islamic Conference and its specialized institutions in the implementation of the proposals adopted at the coordination meeting of the focal points of the lead agencies of the two organizations,

Taking into account the meeting of the focal points of the lead agencies of the United Nations system and the Organization of the Islamic Conference and its specialized institutions, held at Geneva from 27 to 29 October 1992,

Recalling its resolutions 37/4 of 22 October 1982, 38/4 of 28 October 1983, 39/7 of 8 November 1984, 40/4 of 25 October 1985, 41/3 of 16 October 1986, 42/4 of 15 October 1987, 43/2 of 17 October 1988, 44/8 of 18 October 1989, 45/9 of 25 October 1990 and 46/13 of 28 October 1991,

1. *Takes note with satisfaction* of the report of the Secretary-General;

2. *Recalls* the conclusions and recommendations of the sectoral meeting on Human Resources Development: Basic Education and Training, held at Rabat in April 1991;

3. *Notes with satisfaction* the active participation of the Organization of the Islamic Conference in the work of the United Nations towards the realization of the purposes and principles of the Charter of the United Nations;

4. *Requests* the United Nations and the Organization of the Islamic Conference to continue cooperation in their common search for solutions to global problems, such as questions relating to international peace and security, disarmament, self-determination, decolonization, fundamental human rights and economic and technical development;

5. *Encourages* the specialized agencies and other organizations of the United Nations system to continue to expand their cooperation with the Organization of the Islamic Conference, particularly by negotiating cooperation agreements, and invites them to multiply the contacts and meetings of the focal points for cooperation in priority areas of interest to the United Nations and the Organization of the Islamic Conference;

6. *Welcomes* the follow-up action of the sectoral meeting on Human Resources Development: Basic Education and Training by the United Nations system and the Organization of the Islamic Conference and its specialized institutions;

7. *Recommends* that a general meeting between representatives of the secretariats of the United Nations system and the Organization of the Islamic Conference and its specialized institutions be organized in 1993 at a date and place to be determined through consultations with the concerned organizations;

8. *Urges* the organizations of the United Nations system, especially the lead agencies, to provide increased technical and other forms of assistance to the Organization of the Islamic Conference and its specialized institutions in order to enhance cooperation;

9. *Expresses its appreciation* to the Secretary-General for his continued efforts to strengthen cooperation and coordination between the United Nations and other organizations of the United Nations system and the Organization of the Islamic Conference to serve the mutual interests of the two organizations in the political, economic, social and cultural fields;

10. *Requests* the United Nations and the Organization of the Islamic Conference to hold consultations on a regular basis between representatives of the Secretariat of the United Nations and the General Secretariat of the Organization of the Islamic Conference focusing on the implementation of programmes, projects and follow-up action;

11. *Requests* the Secretary-General of the United Nations, in cooperation with the Secretary-General of the Organization of the Islamic Conference, to continue encouraging the convening of sectoral meetings in the priority areas of cooperation, namely areas of environment, disaster relief and science and technology, as recommended by the 1989 and 1990 meetings of the focal points of the two organizations, including follow-up to the sectoral meetings;

12. *Expresses its appreciation* for the efforts of the Secretary-General in the promotion of cooperation between the United Nations and the Organization of the Islamic Conference, and expresses the hope that he will continue to strengthen the mechanisms of coordination between the two organizations;

13. *Requests* the Secretary-General to report to the General Assembly at its forty-eighth session on the state of cooperation between the United Nations and the Organization of the Islamic Conference;

14. *Decides* to include in the provisional agenda of its forty-eighth session the item entitled "Cooperation between the United Nations and the Organization of the Islamic Conference".

General Assembly resolution 47/18

23 November 1992   Meeting 69   Adopted without vote

Draft by Turkey (A/47/L.21); agenda item 25.

Conference on Security and Cooperation in Europe

Inclusion of an item on coordination of the activities of the United Nations and the Conference on Security and Cooperation in Europe (CSCE) in the General Assembly's agenda was requested by Czechoslovakia in August 1992.[7] In the accompanying explanatory memorandum, Czechoslovakia, the Chairman-in-Office of the Council of CSCE, stated that interaction between the United Nations and CSCE had acquired a new dimension after the CSCE summit (Helsinki, Finland, 9 and 10 July). At the summit, the heads of State or Government of CSCE had declared their understanding of the Conference as a regional arrangement in the sense of Chapter VIII of the United Nations Charter.

The declaration adopted at the summit contained a number of decisions on various aspects of cooperation, including strengthening of institutions and structures; the establishment of a high commissioner on national minorities; early warning, conflict prevention and crisis management; relations with international organizations and with non-participating States; the creation of a CSCE forum for security cooperation; regional and transfrontier cooperation; environmental cooperation; support for recently admitted participating States; and security and cooperation in the Mediterranean.[8]

GENERAL ASSEMBLY ACTION

On 28 October 1992, the General Assembly adopted without vote **resolution 47/10**.

Cooperation between the United Nations and the Conference on Security and Cooperation in Europe

The General Assembly,

Welcoming the declaration by the heads of State or Government of the States participating in the Conference on Security and Cooperation in Europe of their understanding that the Conference is a regional arrangement in the sense of Chapter VIII of the Charter of the United Nations, and as such provides an important link between European and global security,

Recalling the documents of the Conference, in particular the Final Act, signed at Helsinki on 1 August 1975, the Charter of Paris for a New Europe, the Prague Document on Further Development of the Institutions and Structures of the Conference on Security and Cooperation in Europe, the Vienna Document 1992 on Confidence- and Security-Building Measures and the Helsinki Document 1992,

Noting the role that the Conference plays in promoting democratic values and institutions and human rights, the development of the capabilities of the Conference in early warning, conflict prevention, conflict management and security cooperation, including peace-keeping and initiatives in the Conference for further enhancing mechanisms for the peaceful settlement of disputes, and other developments in the Conference process,

Noting also that the new tasks before the Conference require enhanced coordination and cooperation with international organizations, in particular the United Nations,

1. *Stresses the need* for enhanced cooperation and coordination between the Conference on Security and Cooperation in Europe and the United Nations;

2. *Requests* the Secretary-General to submit to the General Assembly at its forty-eighth session a report on cooperation and coordination between the United Nations and the Conference;

3. *Decides* to include in the provisional agenda of its forty-eighth session an item entitled "Cooperation between the United Nations and the Conference on Security and Cooperation in Europe".

General Assembly resolution 47/10

28 October 1992   Meeting 50   Adopted without vote

45-nation draft (A/47/L.11 & Add.1); agenda item 140.

Sponsors: Albania, Armenia, Austria, Azerbaijan, Belarus, Belgium, Bosnia and Herzegovina, Bulgaria, Canada, Croatia, Cyprus, Czechoslovakia, Denmark, Estonia, Finland, France, Germany, Greece, Hungary, Iceland, Ireland, Italy, Japan, Kazakhstan, Latvia, Liechtenstein, Lithuania, Luxembourg, Malta, Netherlands, Norway, Poland, Portugal, Republic of Moldova, Romania, Russian Federation, Slovenia, Spain, Sweden, Tajikistan, Turkey, Turkmenistan, Ukraine, United Kingdom, United States.

Observer status for the International Organization for Migration

The Geneva-based International Organization for Migration (IOM), created in 1951 as the Intergovernmental Committee for European Migration, promotes technical cooperation and serves as a mechanism for coordination and discussion of migration-related issues and activities for the benefit of Governments, intergovernmental and non-governmental organizations. In 1991, the General Assembly had issued a standing invitation to the organization to attend the coordination meetings convened by the United Nations Department of Humanitarian Affairs.[9]

In view of the fact that IOM was already cooperating with many parts of the United Nations system, including the Office of the United Nations High Commissioner for Refugees and the Commission on Human Rights, its Governing Council requested the IOM Chairman to undertake consultations with the goal of obtaining observer status for the organization in the deliberations of the General Assembly.

GENERAL ASSEMBLY ACTION

On 16 October 1992, the General Assembly adopted without vote **resolution 47/4**.

Observer status for the International Organization for Migration in the General Assembly

The General Assembly,

Noting the desire of the International Organization for Migration to intensify its cooperation with the United Nations,

1. *Decides* to invite the International Organization for Migration to participate in the sessions and the work of the General Assembly in the capacity of observer;

2. *Requests* the Secretary-General to take the necessary action to implement the present resolution.

General Assembly resolution 47/4

16 October 1992   Meeting 41   Adopted without vote

67-nation draft (A/47/L.6 & Add.1); agenda item 138.

Sponsors: Afghanistan, Albania, Angola, Argentina, Australia, Austria, Azerbaijan, Bangladesh, Belgium, Bolivia, Bulgaria, Canada, Cape Verde, Chile, Colombia, Costa Rica, Cyprus, Czechoslovakia, Denmark, Dominican Republic, Ecuador, Egypt, El Salvador, Finland, France, Germany, Greece, Guatemala, Guinea-Bissau, Honduras, Hungary, India, Israel, Italy, Japan, Jordan, Kenya, Latvia, Lithuania, Luxembourg, Mali, Morocco, Netherlands, New Zealand, Nicaragua, Norway, Pakistan, Paraguay, Peru, Philippines, Poland, Portugal, Republic of Korea, Romania, Russian Federation, San Marino, Sao Tome and Principe, Spain, Sri Lanka, Suriname, Sweden, Thailand, Turkey, United States, Uruguay, Venezuela, Viet Nam.

Other organizations

At the request of the host Governments of several intergovernmental conferences in 1992, the main documents of those meetings were transmitted to the Secretary-General for circulation as documents of the General Assembly, the Security Council or both, as follows:

—summit meeting of the member States of the Association of South-East Asian Nations (ASEAN) (Singapore, 27 and 28 January)[10] and Twenty-fifth ASEAN Ministerial Meeting (Manila, Philippines, 21 and 22 July);[11]

—Eighty-seventh Inter-Parliamentary Conference (Yaoundé, Cameroon, 3-11 April);[12]

—Ministerial Meeting of the Coordinating Bureau of the Movement of Non-Aligned Countries (Bali, Indonesia, 14-16 May)[13] and Tenth Conference of Heads of State or Government of Non-Aligned Countries (Jakarta, Indonesia, 1-6 September);[14]

—fifty-sixth session of the Council of Ministers of the Organization of African Unity (Dakar, Senegal, 22-28 June) and the twenty-eighth session of its Assembly of Heads of State and Government (Dakar, 29 June-1 July);[15]

—Thirteenth Meeting of the Conference of Heads of Government of the Caribbean Community (Port-of-Spain, Trinidad, 29 June-2 July);[16]

—sixth extraordinary session of the Islamic Conference of Foreign Ministers (Jeddah, Saudi Arabia, 1 and 2 December);[17]

—thirteenth session of the Supreme Council of the Gulf Cooperation Council (Abu Dhabi, United Arab Emirates, 21-23 December).[18]

REFERENCES

[1]YUN 1991, p. 101, GA res. 46/24, 5 Dec. 1991. [2]A/47/451. [3]YUN 1991, p. 103, GA res. 46/13, 28 Oct. 1991. [4]A/47/450. [5]A/47/450/Add.1. [6]YUN 1991, p. 102. [7]A/47/192. [8]A/47/361-S/24370. [9]YUN 1991, p. 421, GA res. 46/182, 19 Dec. 1991. [10]A/47/80-S/23502. [11]A/47/351-S/24357. [12]A/47/706. [13]A/47/225-S/23998. [14]A/47/675-S/24816. [15]A/47/558. [16]A/47/344. [17]A/47/765-S/24930. [18]A/47/845-S/25020.

PART TWO

Regional questions

Chapter I

Africa

The United Nations continued its efforts in 1992 to build a non-racial, democratic society in South Africa. The peace process was hampered, however, by delays in negotiations and the escalation of political violence. To enhance the peace process, the Security Council authorized the deployment of United Nations observers who, by the end of October, were present in all regions of the country.

The United Nations also faced severe challenges in Angola, Liberia, Mozambique and Somalia. The Security Council expanded the mandate of the second United Nations Angola Verification Mission to include observation of the first-ever multiparty elections held in September, within the framework of implementation of the Peace Accords (''Acordos de Paz para Angola''). Civil war continued to rage in Liberia, in spite of the efforts of the Economic Community of West African States to enforce a cease-fire. In order to help establish peace and stability in that country, the Council in November imposed a complete arms embargo against all parties to the conflict. After extended negotiations, the Government of Mozambique and its main rival, the Resistência Nacional Mozambicana, signed a General Peace Agreement in October. The Council in December authorized the establishment of a United Nations Operation in Mozambique for the purpose of implementing the Agreement. In Somalia, United Nations observers and security personnel were deployed to break the cycle of violence and food insecurity, which threatened the lives of a large part of the population. In view of the deteriorating situation, the Council in December decided to endorse action under Chapter VII of the Charter of the United Nations in order to establish a secure environment for relief operations. In response to that decision, the President of the United States directed the execution of Operation Restore Hope on 4 December, with the first elements of the Unified Task Force arriving at Mogadishu on 9 December.

United Nations involvement was requested to verify a referendum by which the people of Eritrea in 1993 would determine their political future. The General Assembly, in December 1992, authorized the establishment of a United Nations Observer Mission for that purpose.

The Secretary-General continued to exercise his good offices towards finding a solution to the question of the island of Mayotte. The Assembly reaffirmed the sovereignty of the Comoros over the island and urged France to accelerate negotiations with a view to ensuring the return of the island to the Comoros.

At a meeting in April, organizations of the United Nations system and the Organization of African Unity (OAU) adopted recommendations for a new joint action programme. The Assembly requested the United Nations to continue supporting OAU in its efforts to promote a peaceful settlement of disputes and conflicts and to collaborate with it in implementing the United Nations New Agenda for the Development of Africa in the 1990s.

South Africa and apartheid

Important developments continued to occur in South Africa as the country moved towards a more democratic and non-racial society. With the creation of a negotiating framework in December 1991, the political process reached a new stage.

In February 1992, following a victory by the Conservative Party in a parliamentary by-election, President F. W. de Klerk called on the white electorate to vote through a referendum on the constitutional reforms introduced over the previous two years. On 17 March, 68.7 per cent of the more than 2.8 million white voters voted ''yes'' in response to the question as to whether they supported the continuation of the reform process aimed at a new constitution through negotiations.

However, negotiations were hampered by repeated set-backs and delays, due in part to the persistent political violence, which reached new heights in June with the massacre of 40 people, including women and children, in Boipatong township near Johannesburg. In August, 348 persons died in political violence, bringing the total of victims killed since the signing of the National Peace Accord in September 1991 to more than 3,400. Twenty-eight persons were killed and nearly 200 wounded when, on 7 September, Ciskei forces opened fire on demonstrators marching on Bisho, capital of the homeland.

Following adoption by the Security Council of resolution 765(1992) in July, the Secretary-General appointed Cyrus R. Vance (United States) as his Special Representative for South Africa, who arrived in South Africa on 21 July for a 10-day mission.

At the request of the parties, 10 United Nations observers witnessed mass action during the week commencing 3 August. An additional 40 observers were deployed in accordance with Council resolution 772(1992), adopted in August.

Activities of the Special Committee against Apartheid. In its annual report covering the period September 1991 to September 1992,[1] the Special Committee against Apartheid reviewed, as in previous years, political, economic, military and other developments relating to the process towards peaceful elimination of apartheid and the establishment of a non-racial, democratic society in South Africa, based on a new constitution, negotiated and agreed on within a broad-based and democratically representative forum. It continued to monitor and analyse the response of the international community to those developments, in accordance with its mandate and the guidelines set by the 1989 Declaration on Apartheid and its Destructive Consequences in Southern Africa.[2] In that context, it continued to monitor all factors threatening to derail the negotiating process and issued early warnings when warranted.

During the period under review, the Special Committee focused its attention on the persisting political violence in the country and the grave socio-economic inequalities. It welcomed the commitment of the international community to encourage a transition to a democratic non-racial South Africa, but cautioned against removing restrictions which would undermine political leverage on the regime. It advocated a phased application of pressure against South Africa in line with positive developments there and underlined the need for increased assistance for the disadvantaged sector of the South African population. At the same time, it welcomed all positive measures taken by the South African authorities towards the creation of an appropriate climate for negotiations.

The Committee responded to developments by issuing statements and organizing encounters with the media, as well as meetings or briefings with Governments and South Africans representing different segments of society. On various occasions, the Committee Chairman met with the leaders of the national liberation movements to discuss developments and promotion of the peace process.

The Committee, together with the United Nations Centre against Apartheid, organized a seminar on South Africa's socio-economic problems and the future role of the United Nations system in helping to address them (Windhoek, Namibia, 22-24 May), which discussed measures for economic growth; the redistribution of opportunity, input, income and services; human resources development needs; and resource needs for the socio-economic restructuring of a new South Africa.

On 29 and 30 June, the Committee held consultations in New York with United States and Canadian anti-apartheid movements and other concerned non-governmental organizations (NGOs), in order to give them an opportunity to develop a new approach to their work in South Africa during the period of transition and beyond, and to help identify relevant issues and programmes of action.

On 14 and 15 July, the British Anti-Apartheid Movement, in conjunction with the Committee, organized an international hearing on political violence in South Africa and the implementation of the September 1991 National Peace Accord. The concluding statement of the hearing called for an international intervention in South Africa through the establishment of appropriate mechanisms, to ensure not only effective monitoring but also the means to end the violence.

The Committee financed a conference on educational assistance to disadvantaged South Africans, organized by the Centre Against Apartheid under the auspices of the United Nations Educational and Training Programme for Southern Africa (New York, 8 and 9 September).

As in previous years, it observed the International Day for the Elimination of Racial Discrimination (21 March), the International Day of Solidarity with the Struggling People of South Africa (16 June), the International Day of Solidarity with the Struggle of Women in South Africa (9 August) and the Day of Solidarity with South African Political Prisoners (11 October).

In its conclusions, the Committee said that any delay in bringing about a political settlement could be disastrous and the economic price of such a delay was also growing rapidly. South Africa urgently needed an interim government of national unity to prepare elections for a constitution-making body and to administer the country until a new government was elected on the basis of an agreed democratic and non-racial constitution.

Apartheid would be eradicated only with the adoption of a new constitution and the installation of a new government resulting from a free and fair election. The Committee said it could therefore not support the view that apartheid was a closed page in the history of South Africa. Old legislative and executive structures were in place and the majority of the population had not been able to exercise the right to vote. While many apartheid laws had been dismantled, the legacy of apartheid, with its glaring socio-economic disparities, continued to threaten the process of democratization and would take long years to overcome.

The Committee recommended that the Assembly reaffirm its determination to support the South African people in their legitimate struggle for the total elimination of apartheid through peaceful means and in their efforts to build a non-racial and democratic society; reaffirm the principles and goals envisaged in the 1989 consensus Declaration on Apartheid; reiterate its conviction that broad-based negotiations resulting in a new non-racial and democratic constitution would lead to the total elimination of apartheid; reiterate its strong support for the negotiation process; and note that while positive measures had been taken towards creating a better climate for negotiations, including the repeal of key apartheid laws, the revision of major security legislation and the release of remaining political prisoners, serious obstacles remained to achieving a climate conducive to free political activity.

The Committee further recommended that the Assembly welcome Security Council resolutions 765(1992) and 772(1992), its 10 September statement on the spiralling cycle of violence, the Secretary-General's report on the mission to South Africa of his Special Representative, the recommendations in his 7 August report, and the measures taken by the Secretary-General to assist the process in South Africa in strengthening the structures set up under the National Peace Accord, including the deployment of United Nations observers.

Among other recommendations were that the Assembly: urge the South African authorities to exercise fully and impartially their primary responsibility to end the violence, protect lives, security and property of all South Africans, and bring to justice those responsible for acts of violence; urge them to respect and protect the right of South Africans to demonstrate peacefully; call on the signatories to the National Peace Accord to recommit themselves to the process of peaceful change; note with satisfaction the release of prisoners held for their political beliefs or activities, and the agreements reflected in the record of understanding issued on 26 September; urge the resumption of broad-based negotiations on transitional arrangements and basic principles for reaching agreement on a new constitution and for its speedy entering into force; call on the international community to support the process in South Africa through a phased application of appropriate measures; urge the international community to respect the measures imposed by the Security Council for the purpose of bringing an early end to apartheid; appeal for an increase in humanitarian and legal assistance to apartheid victims; appeal to the international community to help create stable conditions for a rapid and peaceful attainment of a new South Africa based on a negotiated, democratic and non-racial constitution by providing material, financial and other assistance; request the Secretary-General to continue ensuring the coordination of United Nations ac-

tivities; authorize the Special Committee, in accordance with its mandate, to mobilize international support for eliminating apartheid; and appeal to Governments, intergovernmental and non-governmental organizations to continue cooperating with the Committee.

GENERAL ASSEMBLY ACTION

On 18 December, the General Assembly adopted **resolution 47/116 B** without vote.

Programme of work of the Special Committee against Apartheid

The General Assembly,

Having considered the report of the Special Committee against Apartheid,

Recognizing the important role that the Special Committee has had in mobilizing international support for the elimination of apartheid and in the adoption by consensus, on 14 December 1989, of the Declaration on Apartheid and its Destructive Consequences in Southern Africa,

1. *Takes note with appreciation* of the report of the Special Committee against Apartheid on its work, under its mandate, in support of the peaceful eradication of apartheid and of the process of a negotiated transition of South Africa to a democratic non-racial society;

2. *Commends* the Special Committee for the holding in Windhoek, from 22 to 24 May 1992, of the Seminar on South Africa's Socio-Economic Problems: Future Role of the United Nations System in Helping to Address Them, and for its full support of the holding of the Follow-up Conference on International Educational Assistance to Disadvantaged South Africans, held in New York on 8 and 9 September 1992, under the auspices of the United Nations Educational and Training Programme for Southern Africa and its Advisory Committee;

3. *Authorizes* the Special Committee, in accordance with its mandate, to mobilize international support for the elimination of apartheid through the early establishment in South Africa of a society based on an agreed democratic and non-racial constitution as envisaged in the Declaration on Apartheid and its Destructive Consequences in Southern Africa, and to this end:

(a) To continue to monitor the complex developments in South Africa, and to collect, analyse and disseminate factual information in this regard;

(b) To facilitate a peaceful and stable transition in South Africa by promoting international assistance to help South Africans overcome the negative social and economic consequences of the policies of apartheid by, *inter alia*, following up on the Windhoek Seminar through sectoral seminars on well-defined and specific topics with the participation of experts in the relevant fields and in cooperation with relevant bodies and agencies of the United Nations system, institutions and non-governmental organizations;

(c) To undertake liaison and consultations with Governments, intergovernmental and non-governmental organizations, foundations and institutions, as well as other relevant groups, both inside and outside South Africa;

4. *Appeals* to Governments and intergovernmental and non-governmental organizations to continue their

cooperation with the Special Committee, and requests all relevant components of the United Nations system to continue to cooperate with the Special Committee and the Centre against Apartheid in their activities in support of the ongoing process of the peaceful elimination of apartheid in South Africa;

5. *Decides* that the special allocation of 450,000 United States dollars to the Special Committee for 1993 from the regular budget of the United Nations should be used towards the cost of special projects aimed at promoting the process towards the elimination of apartheid through the establishment of a new society in South Africa based on a democratic and non-racial constitution, with particular emphasis on issues of human rights and constitution-building, human resources development, institutional capacity-building, health, housing and other socio-economic priority areas;

6. *Also decides* to continue to authorize adequate financial provision in the regular budget of the United Nations to enable the African National Congress of South Africa and the Pan Africanist Congress of Azania to maintain offices in New York so that they may participate effectively in the deliberations of the Special Committee and in deliberations relating to the situation in South Africa in other relevant United Nations bodies.

General Assembly resolution 47/116 B

18 December 1992   Meeting 91   Adopted without vote

Draft by Nigeria (A/47/L.29); agenda item 33.
Financial implications. 5th Committee, A/47/798; S-G, A/C.5/47/74.
Meeting numbers. GA 47th session: 5th Committee 47; plenary 62-66, 88, 91.

Report of the Secretary-General. In November 1992, in response to a 1991 General Assembly resolution,[3] the Secretary-General presented a third progress report[4] on implementation of the 1989 Declaration on Apartheid and its Destructive Consequences in Southern Africa.[2]

The report, which analysed the progress since September 1991 towards dismantling apartheid, was based on written submissions by the Government, political parties and movements and other organizations, supplemented by official statements and press releases. It dealt specifically with the release of all political prisoners and detainees, as called for by the Declaration; the removal of all troops from the townships; the repeal of legislation designed to circumscribe political activity; and the cessation of all political trials and executions. It considered other elements conducive to free political discussion and to the negotiation process, such as the creation of an atmosphere free of violence, and freedom of assembly and of the press. It dealt with matters that enhanced or obstructed the process of ending apartheid, and with the application of the guidelines for the negotiation process, as set out in the Declaration. Finally, it reviewed implementation by the international community of the programme of action put forward in the Declaration.

On a number of occasions during the year, the Secretary-General discussed with South Africa's Minister for Foreign Affairs and its Permanent Representative to the United Nations developments relating to the situation in the country, in particular the negotiation process under way. He also met with Nelson Mandela, President of the African National Congress of South Africa (ANC), Clarence Makwetu, President of the Pan Africanist Congress of Azania (PAC), and Chief Mangosuthu Buthelezi, President of the Inkatha Freedom Party (IFP). In addition, he was represented in an observer capacity at the two sessions of the Convention for a Democratic South Africa (CODESA I and II). His Special Representative, Cyrus R. Vance, visited the country in July and Virendra Dayal, Special Envoy of the Secretary-General, visited it in September to hold follow-up discussions with the relevant parties in connection with the implementation of Council resolution 772(1992) (see below).

The Secretary-General observed that the Boipatong massacre, the tragedy at Bisho and other incidents of violence (see below) called attention to the imperative need to put an end to the violence and facilitate a peaceful transition to a democratic, non-racial and united South Africa. The role of the international community in establishing such a country could be complementary only to that of the various political groups in South Africa, whose participation, good will and political courage were essential. Responsibility for achieving a just and long-lasting agreement through negotiation must rest with the South Africans themselves.

The United Nations, for its part, would continue to seek creative ways to assist the people of South Africa as a whole in attaining the goals they had set for themselves and to which the Assembly had committed itself in its 1989 Declaration. The Organization stood ready to provide a concerted system-wide response to address the economic and social disparities resulting from institutionalized racism. It was active, through the United Nations High Commissioner for Refugees (UNHCR), its trust funds for southern Africa and the specialized agencies, in facilitating the return of South African exiles and the reintegration of former political prisoners, and in providing educational and training assistance to disadvantaged South Africans.

Annexed to the report were the declaration of intent adopted by the participants at CODESA I (see below) and the joint statement and record of understanding agreed on by President de Klerk and the ANC President following a September 1992 meeting (see below).

Negotiation process

The second plenary session of the Convention for a Democratic South Africa (CODESA II) took place on 15 and 16 May 1992, with the participation of the Government of South Africa, ANC, IFP, the Governments of the so-called "independent homelands" and a number of political parties, such as the Democratic Party and the Solidarity Party. The same 19 participants had attended the first plenary session (CODESA I) in December 1991, at which they had adopted a declaration of intent committing themselves to bring about an undivided South Africa free from apartheid and to some fundamental constitutional principles. The Conservative Party, the Azanian People's Organization and PAC did not take part in the talks; PAC described the forum as undemocratic.

Five working groups established by CODESA I submitted their reports to CODESA II. They indicated that consensus had been reached on the following issues: the transition to democracy would involve two preliminary phases, with a multiparty Transitional Executive Council preparing the country for elections and an assembly elected by proportional representation and universal suffrage elaborating and adopting a new constitution; all parties agreed "in principle" to the reincorporation of "independent homelands" and the restoration of South African citizenship to their residents; all security forces should be placed under the control of the transitional governmental structures and held accountable to the public; all parties needed to recommit themselves to the letter and spirit of the National Peace Accord;[5] and the international community should be called upon for assistance to facilitate implementation of the Accord.

CODESA II, however, was unable to reach agreement on a number of issues related to the constitution-making process. This deadlock prevented consideration of the reports of the other working groups, since ANC would not accept a partial agreement. As the differences could not be resolved, CODESA II reached an impasse.

Following the collapse of the talks, ANC, together with its political allies—the Congress of South African Trade Unions and the South African Communist Party—announced a four-phase mass action plan embodying demands for an interim government and an elected constituent assembly. The first phase of the mass action began on 16 June and continued until the end of the month, the first deadline set by ANC for a break in the deadlock at CODESA and the creation of an interim government. Following the failure to do so, the second phase was set in motion on 1 July. During the month, mass action remained mostly regional, but simultaneous national actions, such as marches and sit-ins, targeted specific government institutions.

The third phase of the mass action plan started with a general strike on 3 and 4 August, when millions of South Africans stayed away from work, followed on 5 August by demonstrations and marches. The fourth phase began after the general strike; its aim was for the Government to relinquish power or at least accept demands for a representative constituent assembly and introduce legislation for the establishment of a transitional executive authority to oversee elections.

Although formal constitutional negotiations were suspended, contacts between ANC and the Government resumed at the end of July, with talks focusing on the issues of political prisoners. The deadlock, however, could not be broken, as ANC considered that the Government had not answered satisfactorily the 14 demands it had set in June 1992 as preconditions to negotiations. Those demands focused on creating an elected constitutional assembly, setting up an interim government, ending all covert operations, disbanding all special forces and detachments made up of foreign nationals, suspending and prosecuting all members of the security forces involved in the violence, ending repression in the homelands, phasing out hostels, installing fences around hostels and guarding and searching them permanently, banning all dangerous weapons, setting up an international commission of inquiry into the Boipatong massacre (see below) and other acts of violence, repealing all repressive legislation and releasing all political prisoners.

The ANC National Executive Committee, meeting on 3 September, reiterated its decision not to resume negotiations until its demands were met, underlining in particular the need to deal with the violence and to release political prisoners. It acknowledged, however, that some progress had been achieved during the informal talks, noting that the Government had indicated its support for adequate deadlock-breaking mechanisms and precise time-frames.

At the beginning of September, the Government convened a multiparty conference, to which it invited all political parties and organizations and government institutions interested in the concept of regional government in a new order. ANC declined to attend.

A meeting between Mr. Mandela and President de Klerk on 26 September resulted in a record of understanding[6] on such issues as the release of remaining political prisoners, the constitution-making process, the carrying and display of dangerous weapons at public occasions, and the fencing and policing of a number of hostels. Agreement was also reached on the need for a democratic constituent assembly/constitution-making body and constitutional continuity during the transitional period.

On 30 September, ANC announced that its National Executive Committee had decided to return to negotiations. IFP leader Mangosuthu Buthelezi, however, stated that his party was not willing to resume negotiations on the basis of the agreements reached between ANC and the Government, a position in which he was joined by the leaders of Bophuthatswana and Ciskei.

Exploratory talks resumed in August between the Government and PAC. The latter announced that substantive issues such as violence, election of a constituent assembly, the role of the international community, the transitional authority and voter registration would be discussed in October in a neighbouring country presided over by a neutral chairman. PAC reiterated that it was not opposed to negotiations, but wanted them to be conducted within a democratic forum which should write a new constitution. The convening of a constituent assembly and an alternative forum for negotiations would be a major issue on the agenda. The South African Minister of Constitutional Affairs confirmed that talks would include demands for a sovereign constitutional assembly.

PAC informed the Government that it would not join an "interim government" which in its view co-opted the liberation movements and was based on the principle of full political responsibility without full political power. It supported a transitional authority which impacted directly on the transition to a new order. Some of its duties would be to supervise elections and control the electronic media and security forces.

Meanwhile, President de Klerk outlined draft legislation that he was to table at the resumed session of Parliament in October. That legislation would enable him to appoint blacks to his Cabinet and suspend all Parliamentary by-elections, as well as transfer the functions of "own affairs" departments to general affairs and rearrange the functions of self-governing states.

The Government and PAC held bilateral discussions in Gaborone, Botswana, in early November and agreed to meet again in South Africa on 9 December to discuss the convening of a multiparty forum. Arrangements for further meetings, however, were cancelled in reaction to the position taken by the PAC political leadership with regard to reports that its armed wing, the Azanian People's Liberation Army (APLA), claimed responsibility for recent armed attacks at King William's Town and Queens Town and that APLA planned a campaign of attacks on "soft targets".

Further political developments included the emergence in October of a loose coalition of the Conservative Party and other groups on the right, and the leaders of Bophuthatswana, Ciskei and KwaZulu, under the name of Concerned South Africans Group, which was aimed at galvanizing opposition to what its members perceived as an alliance between ANC and the Government. Other

organizations and entities across the entire political spectrum were also pursuing contacts with one another.

Bilateral talks between the parties focused on the regional structure of a new South Africa, the devolution of powers and power-sharing, and the corresponding constitutional provisions.

At CODESA II, there was wide agreement in principle on the reincorporation of the homelands into South Africa, their participation in transitional arrangements, provisions for testing the will of their people regarding their reincorporation, and the "restoration" of South African citizenship to those who chose reincorporation.

The leader of Ciskei subsequently indicated his outright opposition to reincorporation, which was also rejected by Bophuthatswana. On 1 December, Chief Buthelezi presented a new draft constitution for a "federal state of Natal/KwaZulu", which was ratified the same day by the KwaZulu Legislative Assembly.

During bilateral talks in the first week of December, the Government and ANC appeared to make considerable progress in narrowing differences. The talks took place against the background of the Government's proposed timetable for the transition, which envisaged that a fully representative government of national unity was to be in place no later than the first half of 1994, and the November 1992 meeting of the ANC National Executive Committee which considered the establishment of interim governmental structures. Continuation of those talks was expected shortly and both parties emphasized that their positions were to be considered as proposals and that they were determined not to exclude other parties from the process.

At a meeting on 10 December, President de Klerk, Chief Buthelezi and the leaders of Bophuthatswana and Ciskei discussed the resumption of multiparty talks. Following an agreement reached between ANC and IFP at the 24 November meeting of the National Peace Committee, preparations started for a meeting between Chief Buthelezi and Mr. Mandela.

Violence

In spite of the National Peace Accord signed in September 1991 between 23 parties, including the South African Government, ANC and IFP, political violence continued to wreak havoc in black townships, with some 300 persons dying each month, according to the non-governmental South African Human Rights Commission. The violence reached unprecedented and dramatic levels during the period covered by the annual report of the Special Committee against Apartheid.[f] Whereas the majority of those killed seemed to have been ordinary residents of black townships, a degree of political affiliation could be identified for up to half of the fatal victims; of those, about 84 per cent appeared to be linked to ANC, while some 16 per cent were assumed to be affiliated with IFP.

On the night of 17 June 1992, armed men attacked residents in the township of Boipatong, near Johannesburg, killing at least 40 men, women and children. Numerous witnesses alleged that the attackers, who apparently came from a nearby hostel, were supporters of IFP and were assisted by members of the police. The Government and the police immediately denied being implicated in the incident. Relations between the Government and ANC were further strained after a visit to Boipatong by President de Klerk on 20 June, when angry demonstrators forced the President to leave the area. Following his departure, unprovoked firing was reported to have led to several casualties, including three members of PAC.

On 23 June, the ANC National Executive Committee held an emergency meeting, at the end of which it decided to suspend talks with the Government, as well as its participation in CODESA negotiations, while reaffirming its commitment to a negotiated resolution of the conflict. Accusing the Government of fomenting violence, ANC put forward 14 demands as preconditions for negotiations (see above). Responding on 2 July, President de Klerk denied allegations that the Government was sponsoring the violence and reiterated the warning that mass mobilization would inevitably lead to further violence.

At the end of June, Justice Richard Goldstone, Chairman of the Commission of Inquiry regarding the Prevention of Public Violence and Intimidation (Goldstone Commission), established under the terms of the National Peace Accord, had three British experts evaluate the investigation by the South African police into the Boipatong massacre. The experts found no evidence of police collusion, but described the police as suffering from serious organizational problems; according to their report, inadequate command and control in particular had allowed the massacre to be perpetrated unhindered, and it appeared that the police lacked effective intelligence and contingency planning. The investigation had been conducted in an unstructured and inadequate manner, which undermined evidence-gathering. Hostility and non-cooperation from the township residents, which had also impeded the investigation, could partly be attributed to insufficient awareness by the police of working on community relations and to their perceived bias in favour of hostel-dwellers. According to the Special Committee against Apartheid, these severe conclusions by foreign experts brought to South Africa with the authorities' approval had significant political impact.

In addition, disclosures by a prominent South African pathologist, Dr. Jonathan Gluckman, increased pressure on the authorities to investigate police actions further. In a report published by the South African press in July, Dr. Gluckman expressed his conviction that in 90 per cent of the 200 cases of deaths in police custody for which he had performed post-mortems, the prisoners had been killed by the police. He also stated that he had discussed the deaths with high-ranking officials, but no action had been taken. Reacting to his report, the Minister of Law and Order announced that he had ordered a full investigation into all deaths which had occurred in detention over the past two years. Twelve deaths in custody, however, were reported again during August, bringing the total of such deaths for 1992 to 86.

The Security Council convened on 15 and 16 July to consider the question of South Africa, in particular the escalating violence and the breakdown of negotiations (see below). The Council, by resolution 765(1992), condemned the violence, urged the South African authorities to take immediate measures to end it and called on all the parties to cooperate to that end. It also authorized the Secretary-General to dispatch urgently a Special Representative to hold discussions with the parties in South Africa, in order to recommend measures for ending the violence and creating conditions for negotiations.

Based on the findings of Cyrus Vance, his Special Representative for South Africa, the Secretary-General on 7 August issued a report to the Council. Among the recommendations in the report was that the Goldstone Commission should undertake a series of investigations into the functioning and operations of the South African army and police, the Umkhonto we Sizwe, APLA, the KwaZulu police and various independent security firms. It was also recommended that the United Nations make available observers.

Responding to increased pressure on the Government to investigate police actions and reform the police force radically, the Minister of Law and Order announced on 27 August initiatives, such as the setting up of a body to investigate crimes allegedly committed by police, the resignation or early retirement of 18 of the 55 South African police generals and the rectification of the discriminatory practices which had previously prevented black police from being promoted. ANC described the measures as a face-lift, not a substantial change, pointing out that many of the police generals suspected of wrongdoing were not included in the list of those to resign or retire. PAC, on 28 August, said the purging of 13 generals would not cleanse a morally corrupt police force; a genuine new credible police could be brought about only by a democratic majority government.

On 1 October, the International Committee of the Red Cross (ICRC) announced that the Government had agreed to allow ICRC representatives access to South African police stations.

On 7 September, Ciskei forces opened fire on ANC demonstrators marching on Bisho, capital of the homeland, leading to the killing of at least 28 participants. ANC strongly condemned what it described as unprovoked killing of unarmed demonstrators and put responsibility for the massacre on Brigadier Oupa Gqozo and the South African authorities. Mr. Mandela called for Gqozo's resignation and for an independent inquiry into the shooting. Church leaders, for their part, urged Brigadier Gqozo to submit himself to a referendum.

The shooting dampened hopes for negotiations further. President de Klerk condemned both the Ciskei authorities for breaches of the National Peace Accord and ANC for having stepped up its mass action campaign. At the same time, he acknowledged that it was not possible to negotiate constitutional issues before the question of violence had been dealt with satisfactorily and proposed that a high-level meeting be held between the Government and ANC to discuss the issue. He also announced his intention to invite all homeland leaders to an urgent discussion on the control of their security forces.

A high-level meeting between Mr. Mandela and President de Klerk on 26 September resulted in a record of understanding on certain outstanding issues and, on 30 September, ANC announced its decision to return to negotiations (see above).

The Goldstone Commission, in its second interim report issued in April 1992, stated that it had not received evidence of a third force orchestrating violence and that both ANC and IFP were guilty of many incidents that had resulted in the deaths of and injuries to large numbers of people. However, it critized the Government's failure to take sufficiently firm steps to prevent criminal conduct by members of the security forces and to punish the perpetrators.

In a September report,[7] the Special Rapporteur of the Commission on Human Rights on the question of the use of mercenaries as a means of violating human rights and impeding the exercise of the right of peoples to self-determination charged that mercenary groups had been responsible for acts of repression against liberation movement leaders and for massacres carried out in suburbs inhabited by the Black majority. Investigating commissions had established that mercenaries participated in implementing apartheid policies and were entrusted with the most violent actions.

In the view of PAC, the major source of violence in the country was the regime, and violence would continue until all mercenaries, such as the Buffalo Battalion and the Koevoet, were expelled from the country under international supervision and all death

squads were disbanded. While some anti-apartheid organizations welcomed President de Klerk's announcement on 14 July that the particularly discredited Battalions 31 and 32 and the Koevoet unit of the security forces would be disbanded, they called for wider measures, in particular for prompt implementation of the recommendations of Justice Goldstone, such as a total ban on the carrying of dangerous weapons.

SECURITY COUNCIL ACTION (July)

On 15 and 16 July, the Security Council, at the request of Madagascar for the Group of African States,[8] convened to consider the question of South Africa, in particular the escalating violence.

The Council invited Algeria, Angola, Antigua and Barbuda, Australia, Barbados, Botswana, Brazil, Canada, the Congo, Cuba, Egypt, Germany, Indonesia, Iran, Italy, Lesotho, Malaysia, Namibia, Nepal, the Netherlands, New Zealand, Nigeria, Norway, Peru, the Philippines, Portugal, Senegal, South Africa, Spain, Suriname, Sweden, Uganda, Ukraine, the United Republic of Tanzania, Zaire and Zambia, at their request, to participate in the discussion without the right to vote, under rule 37 of the Council's provisional rules of procedure.[a] An invitation under rule 39[b] was extended to the Chairman of the Special Committee against Apartheid, at his request, and, at the request of Zimbabwe, to the Secretary-General of the Organization of African Unity (OAU)[9] and the Presidents of PAC[10] and ANC.[11]

At South Africa's request,[12] the Council invited seven participants in CODESA (Mangosuthu Buthelezi, Lucas M. Mangope, Brigadier Oupa Gqozo, Dr. J. N. Reddy, E. Joosab, Kenneth M. Andrew, E. E. Ngobeni) under rule 39. At India's request,[13] it invited Bantu Holomisa, Essop Pahad, Philip Mahlangu and Manguezi Zitha, also under rule 39.

On 16 July, the Council adopted **resolution 765(1992)** unanimously.

The Security Council,

Recalling its resolutions 392(1976), 473(1980), 554(1984) and 556(1984),

Gravely concerned by the escalating violence in South Africa, which is causing a heavy loss of human life, and by its consequences for the peaceful negotiations aimed at creating a democratic, non-racial and united South Africa,

---

[a]Rule 37 of the Council's provisional rules of procedure states: "Any Member of the United Nations which is not a member of the Security Council may be invited, as the result of a decision of the Security Council, to participate, without vote, in the discussion of any question brought before the Security Council when the Security Council considers that the interests of that Member are specially affected, or when a Member brings a matter to the attention of the Council in accordance with Article 35(1) of the Charter."

[b]Rule 39 of the Council's provisional rules of procedure states: "The Security Council may invite members of the Secretariat or other persons, whom it considers competent for the purpose, to supply it with information or to give other assistance in examining matters within its competence."

Concerned that the continuation of this situation would seriously jeopardize peace and security in the region,

Recalling the consensus Declaration on Apartheid and its Destructive Consequences in Southern Africa adopted by the General Assembly at its sixteenth special session on 14 December 1989 which called for negotiations in South Africa to take place in a climate free of violence,

Emphasizing the responsibility of the South African authorities to take all necessary measures to stop immediately the violence and protect the life and property of all South Africans,

Emphasizing also the need for all parties to cooperate in combating violence and to exercise restraint,

Concerned at the break in the negotiating process and determined to help the people of South Africa in their legitimate struggle for a non-racial, democratic society,

1. *Condemns* the escalating violence in South Africa and in particular the massacre at Boipatong township on 17 June 1992, as well as subsequent incidents of violence including the shooting of unarmed protesters;

2. *Strongly urges* the South African authorities to take immediate measures to bring an effective end to the ongoing violence and to bring those responsible to justice;

3. *Calls upon* all the parties to cooperate in combating violence and to ensure the effective implementation of the National Peace Accord;

4. *Invites* the Secretary-General to appoint, as a matter of urgency, a Special Representative in order to recommend, after, *inter alia*, discussion with the parties, measures which would assist in bringing an effective end to the violence and in creating conditions for negotiations leading towards a peaceful transition to a democratic, non-racial and united South Africa, and to submit a report to the Security Council as early as possible;

5. *Urges* all parties to cooperate with the Special Representative of the Secretary-General in carrying out his mandate and to remove the obstacles to the resumption of negotiations;

6. *Underlines*, in this regard, the importance of all parties cooperating in the resumption of the negotiating process as speedily as possible;

7. *Urges* the international community to maintain the existing measures imposed by the Security Council for the purpose of bringing an early end to apartheid in South Africa;

8. *Decides* to remain seized of the matter until a democratic, non-racial and united South Africa is established.

Security Council resolution 765(1992)

16 July 1992   Meeting 3096   Adopted unanimously

Draft prepared in consultations among Council members (S/24288).
Meeting numbers. SC 3095, 3096.

Addressing the Council, the ANC President, Nelson Mandela, urged the appointment of a United Nations Special Representative on South Africa to investigate the situation there and help the Council decide on measures to end the violence, which, he said, was organized and directed against the democratic movement. Like the system of apartheid itself, the violence was a direct challenge to the authority of the Council.

The PAC President, Clarence Makwetu, invited the United Nations to send a commission to South Africa to help identify solutions for ending the violence. He called on the Council to empower the Secretary-General to identify a neutral venue for and supervise discussions on democratic elections to a constituent assembly which would then draw up a new constitution.

IFP leader Buthelezi refuted allegations that the Government and his party were responsible for the violence at Boipatong, saying that IFP members were among the victims.

South Africa's Foreign Minister said the Government accepted responsibility for maintaining order but the other parties to the National Peace Accord were not absolved from their commitments. Negotiation was the only alternative to the violence, the causes of which were complex and multidimensional.

The Chairman of the Special Committee against Apartheid emphasized that the continuing violence put in jeopardy the peaceful negotiation process and transition to a non-racial democracy. The violence and the deadlock in the political negotiations were the two critical questions the Council had to address. The blame for the violence rested primarily with the Government, which had failed in its moral responsibility for its citizens and the State. The Government had to bear full responsibility for the conduct of its agencies, which invariably resulted in inadequate police investigations, sham trials and unwarranted acquittals of perpetrators of violence, ineffective jail sentences and bails and police cover-ups. The regime had created an impediment to the negotiations which raised questions as to its sincerity and long-term commitment to a non-racial democracy in the country.

Report of the Secretary-General (August). In response to the 16 July Council resolution, the Secretary-General appointed former United States Secretary of State Cyrus R. Vance as his Special Representative for South Africa. A report on his mission, together with the Secretary-General's observations, was submitted to the Council on 7 August.[14]

Accompanied by Virendra Dayal, former Chef de Cabinet, the Special Representative visited South Africa from 21 to 31 July. The delegation met with President de Klerk and members of his Cabinet, as well as with the major political parties and participants in CODESA. It also held discussions with delegations from Bophuthatswana, Ciskei, Transkei and Venda, and with members of Parliament, prominent individuals, among them Justice Goldstone, scholars, lawyers, trade unionists, leaders of the business community, and representatives of the media, churches, civic groups and NGOs.

In his concluding observations, the Secretary-General said he was impressed by the open and responsive manner in which the United Nations had been received by all sectors of society; he viewed it as further evidence of a transformation towards a democratic, non-racial and united South Africa.

However, the violence must be brought under control and conditions established to ensure the success of the negotiating process. The unanimous adoption of Security Council resolution 765(1992) had heightened expectations that the continuous involvement of the Council in the new phase of South Africa's evolution would be marked by understanding and a readiness to contribute constructively to the process of peaceful change.

On the basis of these observations, the Secretary-General recommended that the international community support the efforts of the Goldstone Commission, whose recommendations should be fully and speedily implemented. Among them were those relating to a total ban on the public display of dangerous weapons and the security of hostels, which needed to be acted on with utmost urgency. Also, the Commission's code of conduct for mass demonstrations could do much to control violence, and the leaders of the major political parties should take firm steps to stop their supporters from participating in acts of violence.

In order to remedy the lack of political trust, the Secretary-General recommended that the Goldstone Commission investigate the functioning and operations of certain agencies, among them the army and police, the Umkontho we Sizwe, APLA, the KwaZulu police and certain private "security firms". Any further investigations and prosecutions required pursuant to the Commission's reports should be undertaken promptly by the competent government departments, and the Commission's reports should be made available to all signatories of the National Peace Accord within 24 hours of submission to the State President.

The mechanisms foreseen under the Accord needed to be greatly strengthened, and both the National Peace Committee and the National Peace Secretariat needed to be more substantially and consistently supported by the highest political levels. The Secretary-General therefore recommended that the United Nations make available some 30 observers to serve in close association with the National Peace Secretariat, in order to further the purposes of the Accord. The experience gained by the dispatch of 10 United Nations observers to cover the current mass demonstrations could help define their tasks and methods of functioning and, as necessary, their number could be supplemented by other international organizations, such as the Commonwealth, the European Community (EC)

and OAU. In addition, there was a need for the establishment of operations centres at the major "flashpoints" to defuse incipient problems; those offices or centres, staffed on a 24-hour basis, should have direct access to law enforcement agencies and should have a standing group composed of representatives of the Government, ANC, IFP and other concerned parties.

The Secretary-General urged the Government to ensure the early appointment of the Justices of Peace and the establishment of special criminal courts envisaged in the National Peace Accord. The effects of apartheid could be remedied only by rapid progress towards the creation of a democratic, non-racial and united South Africa that was the goal of the negotiations and the objective not only of CODESA but of the international community as a whole.

The conducting of the negotiations was uniquely the responsibility of the South Africans themselves; the Secretary-General was heartened by statements that the major parties were determined to return to the negotiating table as early as possible. Actions such as the immediate release of all remaining political prisoners could contribute greatly to improving the political climate and creating trust.

For all its shortcomings, the CODESA process must be pursued and improved. Those who had not joined in that process needed to be encouraged to do so. CODESA proceedings needed to be better coordinated and made more transparent. A highest-level machinery needed to be established to help resolve deadlocks, and the appointment of an eminent and impartial person to provide cohesion might be considered.

SECURITY COUNCIL ACTION (August/September)

The Security Council met on 17 August in accordance with the understanding reached at prior consultations. The Council adopted **resolution 772(1992)** unanimously.

The Security Council,

Reaffirming its resolution 765(1992) of 16 July 1992,

Having considered the report of the Secretary-General on the question of South Africa,

Determined to help the people of South Africa in their legitimate struggle for a non-racial, democratic society,

Cognizant of the expectations of the people of South Africa that the United Nations will assist with regard to the removal of all obstacles to the resumption of the process of negotiations,

Bearing in mind the areas of concern relevant to the question of violence in South Africa, including the issues of the hostels, dangerous weapons, the role of the security forces and other armed formations, the investigation and prosecution of criminal conduct, mass demonstrations and the conduct of political parties,

Further bearing in mind the need to strengthen and reinforce the indigenous mechanisms set up under the National Peace Accord, so as to enhance their capacity in the building of peace, both in the present and in the future,

Determined to assist the people of South Africa to end violence, the continuation of which would seriously jeopardize peace and security in the region,

Underlining, in this regard, the importance of all parties cooperating in the resumption of the negotiating process as speedily as possible,

1. *Welcomes* with appreciation the report of the Secretary-General of 7 August 1992;

2. *Expresses* its appreciation to all relevant parties in South Africa for the cooperation they extended to the Special Representative of the Secretary-General;

3. *Calls upon* the South African Government and all parties in South Africa to implement urgently the relevant recommendations of the Secretary-General contained in his report;

4. *Authorizes* the Secretary-General to deploy, as a matter of urgency, United Nations observers in South Africa, in such a manner and in such numbers as he determines necessary to address effectively the areas of concern noted in his report, in coordination with the structures set up under the National Peace Accord;

5. *Invites* the Secretary-General to assist in the strengthening of the structures set up under the National Peace Accord in consultation with the relevant parties;

6. *Requests* the Secretary-General to report to the Security Council quarterly, or more frequently if necessary, on the implementation of the present resolution;

7. *Calls* on the Government of South Africa, parties and organizations, and the structures set up under the National Peace Accord, to extend their full cooperation to the United Nations observers to enable them to carry out their tasks effectively;

8. *Invites* international organizations such as the Organization of African Unity, the Commonwealth and the European Community to consider deploying their own observers in South Africa in coordination with the United Nations and the structures set up under the National Peace Accord;

9. *Decides* to remain seized of the matter until a democratic, non-racial and united South Africa is established.

Security Council resolution 772(1992)

17 August 1992   Meeting 3107   Adopted unanimously

Draft prepared in consultations among Council members (S/24444).

After consultations held on 10 September, the President of the Security Council made the following statement to the media on behalf of the Council:[15]

"The members of the Security Council deplore the killing of 28 demonstrators and the wounding of nearly 200 others by security elements in South Africa on 7 September 1992. They reiterate their grave concern at the continued escalation of the violence in South Africa. They emphasize once again the responsibility of the South African authorities for the maintenance of law and order and call on them to take all measures to end the violence and to protect the right of all South Africans to engage in peaceful political activity without fear of intimidation or violence. They urge all parties in South Africa to cooperate in com-

bating violence and to exercise maximum restraint in order to help break the spiralling cycle of violence.

"The members of the Security Council emphasize the need to put an end to the violence and create conditions for negotiations leading to the establishment of a democratic, non-racial and united South Africa. They note in this regard that the Security Council, in its resolution 772(1992) of 17 August 1992, authorized the Secretary-General to deploy United Nations observers in South Africa, in coordination with the structures set up under the National Peace Accord, to provide a framework and basis for putting an end to violence in the country. They welcome the Secretary-General's decision to deploy an advance party of 13 United Nations observers in South Africa on 11 September 1992 as part of the complement of 50 observers to be deployed within one month.

"The members of the Council call upon the Government of South Africa, parties and organizations, and the structures set up under the National Peace Accord, to extend their full cooperation to the United Nations observers to enable them to carry out their tasks effectively. They reiterate their call to other relevant regional and intergovernmental organizations to consider deploying their own observers in South Africa in coordination with the United Nations and the structures set up under the National Peace Accord in order to facilitate the peace process."

Report of the Secretary-General (December). In December,[16] the Secretary-General reported to the Council on the findings of his Special Envoys, designated following consultations with the Government of South Africa and the parties after adoption of resolution 772(1992). Virendra Dayal, former United Nations Under-Secretary-General, visited South Africa from 16 to 27 September, and Tom Vraalsen, Assistant Secretary-General of the Ministry of Foreign Affairs of Norway and former Permanent Representative of Norway to the United Nations, was there from 22 November to 9 December. Their findings covered the status of negotiations and implementation of the National Peace Accord; the return of refugees; political violence and measures to reduce it; investigations into the security forces and other armed formations; the status of Battalions 31, 32 and Koevoet; prosecutions of criminal activity and efforts at police reform; the question of hostels; and the carrying and display of dangerous weapons. The Secretary-General also supplied information about the activities of the United Nations Observer Mission in South Africa (see below), as well as his own contacts and consultations.

On the basis of those consultations and the reports of his Special Envoys, the Secretary-General noted that there had been distinct progress since his 7 August report. Recent developments gave cause for guarded optimism about the prospect for progress towards a negotiated settlement; there was substantial agreement to expedite arrangements for multiparty negotiations. Those trends should be encouraged by the international community and it was essential that the Council stay actively seized of the situation, as the goal of a democratic, non-racial and united South Africa must remain a priority of the Organization.

With respect to the CODESA process, the Secretary-General said the principle of inclusiveness must be recognized as essential for a transition to democratic rule through free elections and new constitutional arrangements. It was imperative that all parties refrain from unilateral actions or public statements that rendered the process more difficult. All parties must recognize that continued uncertainty over the country's future could only lead to further violence, instability and economic decline.

While the Government had primary responsibility for maintaining law and order, all political leaders must take immediate action to curb the violence. In that context, the Secretary-General urged all parties to attend the planned meeting of signatories to the National Peace Accord in order to examine ways of putting an end to violence. Those in a position to influence the authorities of the homelands should strongly urge the repeal of repressive legislation and restraint of their security forces.

Following the 26 September meeting between President de Klerk and Mr. Mandela, a government-ANC joint committee made considerable progress regarding political prisoners and, by 15 November, the agreed date for their release, 536 cases had been disposed of by the committee. Some cases submitted by ANC had yet to be resolved, however. The Government stated that it would issue a proclamation to prohibit, country-wide, the carrying and display of dangerous weapons at all public occasions, subject to exemptions based on guidelines being prepared by the Goldstone Commission. The Secretary-General urged the Government to take steps to expedite the full implementation of the agreements on those issues and said that further consideration might be given to ways of cutting off illegal weapons supplies, over which all parties had expressed deep concern.

The Secretary-General expressed his intention to continue supporting the work of the Goldstone Commission and welcomed the Government's and ANC's assurance of cooperation with it. He urged all parties to cooperate with the Commission's forthcoming investigation into the security forces and other armed formations. He also urged expansion of the programmes for exchange of information and expertise between South Africa and other countries to help build community confidence in and develop the human resources of the South African police; police officers from various countries should be invited to advise South African police on the conduct of investigations.

GENERAL ASSEMBLY ACTION

The General Assembly on 18 September decided that the item on the policies of apartheid of the Government of South Africa would be considered directly in plenary meeting, on the understanding that representatives of OAU and of national liberation movements recognized by it would be permitted to participate in the plenary discussions and that organizations and individuals with special interest in the item would be heard by the Special Political Committee.

In accordance with that decision, the Special Political Committee on 6 November heard seven persons representing the following organizations:[17] PAC, the Lutheran Office for World Community, the Interfaith Center on Corporate Responsibility, the Sub-Committee on Southern Africa of the Non-Governmental Organizations Committee on Human Rights, the International Confederation of Free Trade Unions, the South African Non-Racial Olympic Committee and ANC. By **decision 47/410** of 17 November, the Assembly took note of the Committee's report.

Following discussion of the agenda item, the Assembly on 18 December adopted **resolution 47/116 A** without vote.

International efforts towards the total eradication of apartheid and support for the establishment of a united, non-racial and democratic South Africa

The General Assembly,

Recalling the Declaration on Apartheid and its Destructive Consequences in Southern Africa, adopted by consensus on 14 December 1989, which, *inter alia*, called for negotiations in a climate free of violence,

Reaffirming the Declaration and the need for the full implementation of its provisions,

Also recalling its decision 45/457 B of 13 September 1991 and its resolution 46/79 A of 13 December 1991,

Welcoming the initiative of the Organization of African Unity to place before the Security Council the question of violence in South Africa and welcoming Security Council resolutions 765(1992) of 16 July 1992 and 772(1992) of 17 August 1992 and especially the decision to deploy United Nations observers to further the purposes of the National Peace Accord signed on 14 September 1991,

Welcoming also the deployment of observers from the Organization of African Unity, the Commonwealth and the European Community in South Africa in response to Security Council resolution 772(1992),

Taking note of the report of the Secretary-General of 7 August 1992 on the mission of his Special Representative to South Africa,

Also taking note of the report of the Special Committee against Apartheid, and the third progress report of the Secretary-General on the implementation of the Declaration, as well as the report of the Secretary-General on the coordinated approach by the United Nations system on questions relating to South Africa,

Welcoming the safeguards agreement of 16 September 1991 between the International Atomic Energy Agency and the Government of South Africa and the report of the Director General of the International Atomic Energy Agency of 4 September 1992 on the completeness of the inventory of South Africa's nuclear installations and material, under the terms of the safeguards agreement,

Reiterating its conviction that broad-based negotiations, initially undertaken by the Convention for a Democratic South Africa, resulting in a new non-racial and democratic constitution and its early entry into force will lead to the total elimination of apartheid through peaceful means,

Noting that while positive measures have been undertaken by the South African authorities, including the repeal of key apartheid laws and the revision of major security legislation, important obstacles to achieving a climate conducive to free political activity remain,

Recognizing the responsibility of the United Nations and the international community, as envisaged in the Declaration, to help the South African people in their legitimate struggle for the total elimination of apartheid through peaceful means,

Gravely concerned that continued and escalating violence threatens to undermine the process of peaceful change, through negotiations, to a united, non-racial and democratic South Africa,

Deeply concerned at revelations of illegal covert activities carried out by military intelligence with a view to undermining a major party to the political process of peaceful change in South Africa,

Noting with concern that, despite the signing of the National Peace Accord, the tragic bloodshed in South Africa has not ended,

Bearing in mind the need to strengthen and reinforce the mechanisms set up in South Africa under the National Peace Accord and emphasizing the need for all parties to cooperate in combating violence and to exercise restraint,

Encouraging the efforts of all parties, including ongoing talks among them, aimed at facilitating the resumption of substantive broad-based negotiations towards a new constitution and arrangements on the transition to a democratic order,

Taking note with satisfaction of recent agreements between parties aimed at removing many obstacles to resuming broad-based negotiations and also noting with satisfaction the release of prisoners held for their political beliefs or activities,

Noting with concern the remaining effects of the acts of destabilization that were committed by South Africa against the neighbouring African States,

1. *Strongly urges* the South African authorities to exercise fully and impartially the primary responsibility of government to bring to an end the ongoing violence, to protect the lives, security and property of all South Africans in all of South Africa, and to bring to justice those responsible for acts of violence;

2. *Calls upon* all parties to refrain from acts of violence and to cooperate in combating violence;

3. *Strongly urges* the South African authorities to assume the full responsibility to respect and protect the right of South Africans to demonstrate peacefully in public in order to convey their views effectively;

4. *Urgently calls upon* all signatories to the National Peace Accord to recommit themselves to the process of peaceful change by fully and effectively implementing its provisions and by cooperating with each other to that end;

5. *Calls upon* all other parties to contribute to the achievement of the aims of the National Peace Accord;

6. *Takes note with approval* of the recommendations contained in the report of the Secretary-General and calls upon the Government of South Africa and all parties in South Africa to implement urgently those recommendations;

7. *Commends* the Secretary-General for those measures taken to address areas of concern noted in his report and particularly to assist in strengthening the structures set up under the National Peace Accord, including the deployment of United Nations observers in South Africa, and urges the Secretary-General to continue to address all the areas of concern noted in his report which fall within the purview of the United Nations;

8. *Welcomes* the deployment in South Africa of the observers of the Organization of African Unity, the Commonwealth and the European Community;

9. *Strongly urges* the Government of South Africa, as well as the other parties and movements, to lend their full cooperation to the Commission of Inquiry regarding the Prevention of Public Violence and Intimidation (Goldstone Commission) and to permit the Commission urgently and fully to carry out investigations into the functioning and operations of security forces and armed formations, as recommended by the Secretary-General in his report;

10. *Requests* the Secretary-General to respond positively and appropriately, as envisaged in his report, to requests for assistance from the Goldstone Commission in the context of the National Peace Accord;

11. *Urges* the representatives of the people of South Africa to resume, without further delay, broad-based negotiations on transitional arrangements and basic principles for a process of reaching agreement on a new democratic and non-racial constitution and for its speedy entry into force;

12. *Calls upon* the international community to support the vulnerable and critical process still under way in South Africa through a phased application of appropriate measures with regard to the South African authorities, as warranted by ongoing developments, and, within the context of the need to respond appropriately to them, to review existing restrictive measures as warranted by positive developments, such as agreement by the parties on transitional arrangements and agreement on a new, non-racial and democratic constitution;

13. *Calls upon* all Governments to observe fully the mandatory arms embargo, requests the Security Council to continue to monitor effectively its strict implementation and urges States to adhere to the provisions of other Council resolutions on the import of arms from South Africa and the export of equipment and technology destined for military or police purposes in that country;

14. *Appeals* to the international community to increase humanitarian and legal assistance to the victims of apartheid, returning refugees and exiles and released political prisoners;

15. *Calls upon* the international community to assist disadvantaged South African democratic anti-apartheid organizations and individuals in the academic, scientific and cultural fields;

16. *Also calls upon* the international community to assist the non-racial sports bodies, which have been endorsed by representative anti-apartheid sports organi-

zations in South Africa, in redressing the continuing structural inequalities in sports;

17. *Appeals* to the international community to help create stable conditions for the rapid and peaceful attainment of a new South Africa, based on an agreed, democratic and non-racial constitution, by providing and increasing its material, financial and other assistance to South Africans in their efforts to address the serious socio-economic problems of the disadvantaged people of South Africa, particularly in the areas of education, employment, health and housing;

18. *Also appeals* to the international community to render all possible assistance to States neighbouring South Africa to enable them to recover from the effects of destabilization and thereby to contribute to the stability and prosperity of the subregion;

19. *Requests* the Secretary-General, in consultation with the parties concerned, to undertake preliminary examination of the assistance that the United Nations might provide in the electoral process leading to a united, non-racial and democratic South Africa;

20. *Also requests* the Secretary-General to continue to ensure the coordination of activities of the United Nations and its agencies with regard to South Africa, and, as appropriate, inside that country, and to report to the General Assembly at its forty-eighth session on measures taken to facilitate the peaceful elimination of apartheid and the transition of South Africa to a non-racial and democratic society as envisaged in the Declaration on Apartheid and its Destructive Consequences in Southern Africa.

General Assembly resolution 47/116 A

18 December 1992   Meeting 91   Adopted without vote

Draft by Nigeria (A/47/L.32); agenda item 33.
Financial implications. 5th Committee, A/47/798; S-G, A/C.5/47/74.
Meeting numbers. GA 47th session: 5th Committee 47; plenary 62-66, 88, 91.

UN Observer Mission in South Africa

The terms of reference of the United Nations Observer Mission in South Africa (UNOMSA) were set out in Security Council resolution 772(1992) of 17 August, as well as in a report of the Secretary-General dated 7 August[14] (see above). Following consultations, the Secretary-General announced on 9 September his decision to deploy a mission of up to 50 United Nations observers in South Africa in implementation of the Council resolution.

Angela King, Director, Staff Administration and Training Division, Office of Human Resources Management, was appointed Chief of UNOMSA and took up her post on 23 September. The headquarters of UNOMSA was at Johannesburg, with a regional office at Durban. By the end of October, UNOMSA observers were deployed in all 11 regions of South Africa, and by the end of November, all 50 observers were deployed. UNOMSA observers were joined by observers from the Commonwealth, EC and OAU. As at 22 December, they numbered 17, 14 and 11, respectively. UNOMSA's deployment was weighted towards the Witwatersrand/Vaal and Natal/KwaZulu regions, where 70 per cent of the political violence occurred.

UNOMSA personnel observed demonstrations, marches and other forms of mass action, noting the conduct of all parties, and endeavoured to obtain information indicating the degree to which the parties' actions were consistent with the principles of the National Peace Accord and the Goldstone Commission guidelines for marches and political gatherings. Observers supplemented their field observations by establishing and maintaining informal contacts at all levels with established government structures, political parties and organizations, as well as community-based "alternative structures" such as civic associations and other groups.

The functions of the structures established under the National Peace Accord, with which UNOMSA was requested to cooperate, were varied but interrelated. The National Peace Committee was charged with the resolution of disputes concerning interpretation and alleged transgression of the code of conduct for political parties and organizations and with the promotion of social and economic reconstruction and development. The National Peace Secretariat had the responsibility to establish and coordinate the work of regional and local dispute resolution committees.

In its role of strengthening peace structures, UNOMSA initiated through the National Peace Secretariat courtesy calls and visits to homelands other than Bophuthatswana, Ciskei and KwaZulu, which were visited separately. Fact-finding trips were made to QwaQwa, Lebowa and KaNgwane. The UNOMSA observer team based at Pretoria (Northern Transvaal) made frequent visits to KwaNdebele.

In a December report,[18] the Secretary-General estimated net requirements of UNOMSA for the period from mid-September 1992 to 31 December 1993 at $13,121,300. The Advisory Committee on Administrative and Budgetary Questions, in an oral report before the General Assembly's Fifth (Administrative and Budgetary) Committee, recommended approval of the Secretary-General's estimates. It trusted that the staffing of UNOMSA would be kept under constant review and that the Secretary-General would pursue his efforts with the host Government to obtain premises at no cost.

GENERAL ASSEMBLY ACTION

On 23 December, on the recommendation of the Fifth Committee, the General Assembly adopted **resolution 47/219, section XIX**, without vote.

United Nations Observer Mission in South Africa
[*The General Assembly . . .*]

1. *Takes note* of the report of the Secretary-General and the recommendations of the Advisory Committee on Administrative and Budgetary Questions;

2. *Approves* an appropriation of 13,121,300 dollars required under section 2 (Peace-keeping operations and

special missions) of the programme budget for the biennium 1992-1993 for the United Nations Observer Mission in South Africa, from mid-September 1992 to 31 December 1993, on the understanding that these requirements would be treated outside the procedures related to the contingency fund and without prejudice to the future mode of financing;

3. *Also approves* an appropriation of 1,673,200 dollars under section 36 (Staff assessment) of the programme budget for the biennium 1992-1993, offset by the same amount under income section 1 (Income from staff assessment);

4. *Requests* the Secretary-General to submit to the Advisory Committee, at its spring session of 1993, a performance report on the Mission, including actual expenditures from its inception and revised requirements for 1993, taking into account the developments in the region;

. . .

General Assembly resolution 47/219, section XIX

23 December 1992   Meeting 94   Adopted without vote

Approved by Fifth Committee (A/47/835) without vote, 19 December (meeting 50); oral proposal by Chairman; agenda item 104.

Other aspects

Political prisoners and exiles

Among factors hindering the establishment of a climate of free political activity was the issue of political prisoners and the return of exiles. While some 1,000 political prisoners were released in 1991, such action virtually ceased at the beginning of 1992. In September 1992, the Human Rights Commission listed 395 political prisoners. More than a year after the deadline agreed in the Pretoria Minute for the release of all political prisoners, therefore, the issue had not been entirely resolved.

In his 7 August 1992 report to the Security Council,[14] the Secretary-General recommended the immediate release of all remaining political prisoners. The South African Government, reacting to the recommendation and in preparation for a meeting on 26 September between the State President and Mr. Mandela, proposed a blanket amnesty for all crimes committed by both the security forces and anti-apartheid guerrillas before October 1990, a proposal which included the release of over 400 remaining political prisoners. ANC rejected the proposal on the grounds that it equated acts of apartheid opponents with those carried out to maintain the system and that amnesty could only be put in place after investigation of State-committed atrocities by a non-racial, democratically elected government.

PAC, on 28 September, said it would not recognize legislation by which the Government would indemnify its own crimes.

Substantial progress was made with regard to the return of political exiles. By the end of August 1992, more than 5,200 exiles had returned to South Africa under the auspices of the programme by UNHCR, and the National Coordinating Committee for the Repatriation of Exiles, for its part, had brought back an additional 7,000.

Another 5,000 refugees had applied to return. UNHCR's mandate in the country was extended for another year in order to address problems of reintegration and facilitate the return of exiles. UNHCR reached agreement with the Government on the involvement of the United Nations Children's Fund in reintegration, focusing on the needs of women and children. A mission of the United Nations Development Programme (UNDP) recommended that consideration be given to establishing a modest UNDP presence in the country, within UNHCR, to assist with the rehabilitation aspects of resettling returnees.

Women and children under apartheid

On 30 July, on the recommendation of its Social Committee, the Economic and Social Council adopted **resolution 1992/15** by recorded vote.

Women and children under apartheid

The Economic and Social Council,

Recalling its resolution 1991/20 of 30 May 1991,

Reaffirming the provisions of the Declaration on Apartheid and its Destructive Consequences in Southern Africa, contained in the annex to General Assembly resolution S-16/1 of 14 December 1989,

Recalling General Assembly resolution 46/79 of 13 December 1991,

Alarmed by the grave socio-economic deprivation to which the majority of the people, especially the women and children, are subjected as a direct consequence of apartheid,

Deeply concerned about the alleged State complicity in politically motivated violence that has to date claimed thousands of lives and has left hundreds of thousands homeless, the majority of whom are women and children,

Noting the positive changes initiated by the South African authorities aimed at dismantling apartheid, which were the result of the relentless struggle waged by the people of South Africa as well as the pressure exerted by the international community,

Noting with satisfaction the signing of the National Peace Accord in September 1991 and the convening of the Convention for a Democratic South Africa in December 1991, and expressing the hope that this will constitute a major contribution towards the final ending of violence in South Africa,

Welcoming the holding of the Convention for a Democratic South Africa as an attempt to resolve the problems of South Africa by peaceful means as envisaged in the Declaration on Apartheid,

Recognizing that the equality of women and men cannot be achieved without the success of the struggle towards a united, non-racist, non-sexist and democratic South Africa,

Aware of the attention given by the United Nations, and, in particular, the Centre against Apartheid and the Division for the Advancement of Women, to the issue of assisting South African women to participate fully in the process of establishing a non-racist democracy in their country,

1. *Commends* those women both inside and outside South Africa who have resisted oppression and who have remained steadfast in their opposition to apartheid;

2. *Demands* the immediate unconditional release of all political prisoners and detainees, among whom are women and children, in accordance with the undertaking of the South African authorities;

3. *Urges* those involved in the Convention for a Democratic South Africa to place high on their agenda issues concerning women such as freedom, justice and equality, development and the environment;

4. *Also urges* the South African authorities to ratify the Convention on the Elimination of All Forms of Discrimination against Women, at the earliest possible opportunity;

5. *Appeals* to all countries and United Nations bodies, in conformity with General Assembly resolution 46/79 and in consultation with liberation movements, to increase their support for educational, health, vocational training and employment opportunities for women and children living under apartheid;

6. *Requests* the Centre against Apartheid to widen and strengthen its cooperation with the Division for the Advancement of Women, with a view to creating specific programmes of assistance to South African women to enable them to participate fully in the process of transition of their country towards a non-racist democracy;

7. *Appeals* to the international community to give its full and concerted support to the vulnerable and critical process now under way in South Africa through a phased application of appropriate pressures on the South African authorities as warranted by developments, and to provide assistance to the opponents of apartheid and the disadvantaged sectors of society in order to ensure the rapid and peaceful attainment of the objectives of the Declaration on Apartheid and its Destructive Consequences in Southern Africa;

8. *Decides* to remain seized of the issue of women and children living under apartheid;

9. *Requests* the Secretary-General to submit a report on the implementation of the present resolution to the Commission on the Status of Women at its thirty-seventh session.

Economic and Social Council resolution 1992/15

30 July 1992   Meeting 40   33-1-18 (recorded vote)

Approved by Social Committee (E/1992/105) by recorded vote (33-1-17), 21 July (meeting 14); draft by Commission on women (E/1992/24); agenda item 18.

Recorded vote in Council as follows:

In favour: Algeria, Angola, Australia, Bahrain, Bangladesh, Benin, Botswana, Brazil, Burkina Faso, Chile, China, Colombia, Ecuador, Ethiopia, Guinea, India, Jamaica, Kuwait, Madagascar, Malaysia, Mexico, Morocco, Pakistan, Peru, Philippines, Rwanda, Somalia, Syrian Arab Republic, Togo, Trinidad and Tobago, Yugoslavia, Zaire.

Against: United States.

Abstaining: Argentina, Austria, Belarus, Belgium, Bulgaria, Canada, Finland, France, Germany, Italy, Poland, Romania, Russian Federation, Spain, Sweden, Turkey, United Kingdom.

Economic and social conditions

A year after the repeal of the major apartheid laws, the impact of political changes had yet to be felt by the majority of South Africans, whose living conditions were deteriorating rapidly. Politi-

cal uncertainty and violence were contributing factors. Recession, described as the worst since 1945, accentuated the structural incapacity of the country's economy to generate employment. The number of unemployed was estimated to range from 1.9 million to 5.4 million. Forecasts of a 2 per cent growth rate in 1992 had to be revised following a negative growth rate of 0.5 per cent in 1991, and it was envisaged that South Africa's economy could register a contraction of 1 per cent in 1992.

Business confidence remained low, reflecting the unfavourable investment climate. Real gross domestic fixed investment, which declined by 8.5 per cent in 1991, was expected to fall by a further 6 per cent during 1992. Consumer spending also remained under pressure.

Hopes of a major export-led recovery in South Africa were dampened by the slower than expected recovery in world markets and the poor performance of commodity prices, especially for gold, platinum and ferroalloys. Little progress was achieved in countering the high rate of inflation, estimated at 14 per cent, compared to 15.3 per cent in 1991. Food prices increased by 28.8 per cent during the year ending March 1992, and a growing number of South Africans—estimated at 2.5 million—could not afford to pay for their basic nutritional needs. Government relief programmes were not sufficient to check the spread of poverty.

In spite of increased allocations to social, health and educational services for blacks, important disparities remained, as black education continued to be affected by a severe shortage of basic materials and qualified teachers and most medical facilities were still de facto segregated. Little progress was also achieved in addressing the redistribution of land.

Many organizations and parties joined the call for a unitary, non-racial education system. In February, the Government announced further reforms, whereby most white schools would opt for a new, semi-private status. The trend towards privatization was denounced as a new attempt to keep black children out of white schools. ANC called for a moratorium on any restructuring of the health sector until a forum with all the key players was established to develop a new health policy.

The issue of housing was the focus of intense debates, and although the Government devoted more funds to reducing the housing backlog, they were not expected to be sufficient to cover housing needs. A May report of the South African Housing Advisory Board called for a complete overhaul and rationalization of existing subsidy schemes and the merging of white and black local authorities.

There was a growing awareness among the major political parties that no political compromise would be viable without simultaneous agreement on the course to be followed to generate new growth while addressing the most urgent socio-economic needs of the majority of the population. At its first policy conference (Johannesburg, May 1992), ANC adopted a comprehensive set of guidelines on economic policy which, according to the Special Committee against Apartheid, reflected a more pragmatic approach and indicated a general shift regarding the question of public ownership and nationalization. While generally welcomed by the business sector, the guidelines drew some criticism for the proposed principle of "national treatment" to be applied to foreign investors who could be blocked from investing in certain strategic areas and would have limits placed on their local borrowing facilities.

On 31 March, the largest labour federations, including the Congress of South African Trade Unions and the National Council of Trade Unions, and key business representatives reached agreement on the setting up of a national economic forum where various economic policy options could be debated. The new Finance Minister expressed support for the initiative. However, failure to adopt in July a joint charter for peace, democracy and economic reconstruction, to help prevent further industrial unrest, soured relations between business and labour.

The Special Committee expressed full support for a negotiating forum which would seek an accord between government, business and labour and help reset economic priorities and correct socio-economic imbalances engendered by decades of apartheid. Those inequalities continued to plague the majority of the South African population.

Apartheid in sports

South Africa's participation in the Olympic Games at Barcelona, Spain, in September 1992 signalled the end of its isolation in sports. Consequently, its sports and cultural links with the rest of the world increased significantly.

In a November report to the General Assembly,[19] the Commission against Apartheid in Sports, established under the International Convention against Apartheid in Sports,[20] acknowledged that there was a strong movement towards the integration of sports in South Africa. However, it noted that blacks and other disadvantaged groups were not fully integrated in sports in general and that there were sports in which they did not participate due to remaining patterns of apartheid. The Commission urged the international community to provide assistance to the disadvantaged sectors of the South African population to help them overcome the legacy of apartheid.

As of the time of the Commission's report, there were 28 States signatories and 55 States parties to the Convention, which was adopted by the Assembly in 1985[20] and entered into force in 1988.

The Commission, which monitored implementation of the Convention by States parties, recommended that the Assembly urge them to observe all the Convention's provisions until apartheid was abolished, that it call on States, organizations and individuals to provide moral and material support to non-racial sports organizations in South Africa, and that it invite the Special Committee against Apartheid to consider using its good offices to promote fund-raising for the purpose of supporting racial integration of sports in the country.

GENERAL ASSEMBLY ACTION

On 18 December, the General Assembly adopted **resolution 47/116 G** by recorded vote.

Support for the work of the Commission against Apartheid in Sports

The General Assembly,

Recalling its resolutions on the boycott of apartheid in sports and, in particular, 32/105 M of 14 December 1977, by which it adopted the International Declaration against Apartheid in Sports, 40/64 G of 10 December 1985, the annex to which contains the International Convention against Apartheid in Sports, and 45/176 G of 19 December 1990,

Having considered the report of the Commission against Apartheid in Sports and the relevant sections of the report of the Special Committee against Apartheid,

1. *Takes note* of the report of the Commission against Apartheid in Sports and endorses its recommendations;

2. *Urges* Governments and the international sporting community to assist the non-racial sports movement in South Africa to redress the structural inequalities in sports that are among the legacies of apartheid.

General Assembly resolution 47/116 G

18 December 1992   Meeting 91   121-0-39 (recorded vote)

19-nation draft (A/47/L.46 & Add.1); agenda item 33.

Sponsors: Algeria, Angola, Barbados, Chile, Cuba, Gambia, Ghana, Guyana, Haiti, Libyan Arab Jamahiriya, Malaysia, Mozambique, Namibia, Nigeria, Syrian Arab Republic, United Republic of Tanzania, Vanuatu, Zambia, Zimbabwe.

Meeting numbers. GA 47th session: plenary 62-66, 88, 91.

Recorded vote in Assembly as follows:

In favour: Afghanistan, Algeria, Angola, Antigua and Barbuda, Armenia, Azerbaijan, Bahamas, Bahrain, Bangladesh, Barbados, Belize, Benin, Bhutan, Bosnia and Herzegovina, Botswana, Brazil, Brunei Darussalam, Burkina Faso, Burundi, Cameroon, Cape Verde, Central African Republic, Chad, Chile, China, Colombia, Comoros, Costa Rica, Côte d'Ivoire, Croatia, Cuba, Cyprus, Democratic People's Republic of Korea, Djibouti, Dominica, Ecuador, Egypt, El Salvador, Estonia, Ethiopia, Fiji, Gabon, Gambia, Ghana, Grenada, Guatemala, Guinea, Guinea-Bissau, Guyana, Honduras, India, Indonesia, Iran, Iraq, Jamaica, Jordan, Kenya, Kuwait, Lao People's Democratic Republic, Latvia, Lebanon, Lesotho, Libyan Arab Jamahiriya, Lithuania, Madagascar, Malawi, Malaysia, Maldives, Mali, Marshall Islands, Mauritania, Mauritius, Mexico, Micronesia, Mongolia, Morocco, Mozambique, Myanmar, Namibia, Nepal, Nicaragua, Niger, Nigeria, Oman, Pakistan, Panama, Papua New Guinea, Paraguay, Peru, Philippines, Qatar, Republic of Korea, Republic of Moldova, Rwanda, Saint Kitts and Nevis, Saint Lucia, Saint Vincent and the Grenadines, Sao Tome and Principe, Saudi Arabia, Sierra Leone, Singapore, Sri Lanka, Sudan, Suriname, Swaziland, Syrian Arab Republic, Thailand, Togo, Trinidad and Tobago, Tunisia, Uganda, United Arab Emirates, United Republic of Tanzania, Uruguay, Vanuatu, Venezuela, Viet Nam, Yemen, Zaire, Zambia, Zimbabwe.

Against: None.

Abstaining: Albania, Argentina, Australia, Austria, Belarus, Belgium, Bulgaria, Canada, Czechoslovakia, Denmark, Finland, France, Germany,

Greece, Hungary, Iceland, Ireland, Israel, Italy, Japan, Kazakhstan, Liechtenstein, Luxembourg, Malta, Netherlands, New Zealand, Norway, Poland, Portugal, Romania, Russian Federation, Samoa, Slovenia, Spain, Sweden, Turkey, Ukraine, United Kingdom, United States.

In **resolution 47/116 A**, the Assembly called on the international community to assist the non-racial sports bodies in redressing the continuing structural inequalities in sports.

Relations with South Africa

South Africa's isolation continued to lessen as more States decided to establish diplomatic ties with Pretoria and a number of countries lifted restrictive measures. However, following the deadlock at CODESA II in May 1992 and the massacre at Boipatong in June, a number of States and cities which had been preparing to lift their sanctions put such plans on hold.

In accordance with a decision by the Commonwealth heads of Government in October 1991[21] to lift sanctions in phases, following progress made towards negotiations on a new constitution, some Commonwealth countries lifted all people-to-people sanctions, including consular and visa restrictions, cultural, scientific and sports boycotts, bans on airlinks and restrictions on tourism promotion.

The State Department of the United States issued a statement allowing the use of United States export-import facilities in trade with South Africa. Before the stalemate at CODESA II, the Mayor of New York announced that sanctions imposed by the city in 1985 would be lifted in phases following the establishment of an interim government in South Africa. While the ANC President agreed with that course of action, PAC informed the Mayor that such a decision would harm the victims of apartheid as the regime had reneged on a number of issues and therefore could not be trusted. PAC emphasized that sanctions could be lifted only after adoption of a new constitution by a democratically elected constituent assembly.

An important aspect of South Africa's increased diplomatic activity was the extensive travelling of the State President in 1992. Politically, the most significant trip was his visit to Abuja, Nigeria, in April. The President of Kenya, Daniel arap Moi, became in June the first African head of State to visit South Africa in 21 years, and the decision of Côte d'Ivoire to open an embassy at Pretoria made Abidjan the first African capital to exchange ambassadors with Pretoria since Malawi did so more than 25 years before. Lesotho followed by establishing ties at the ambassadorial level. South Africa had consular offices/trade missions or representative offices in some 20 other African States.

Most Western countries had maintained diplomatic relations with South Africa even during the years of isolation. In Eastern Europe, diplomatic relations existed with Bulgaria, Czechoslovakia, Hungary, Poland, Romania, the Russian Federation and Ukraine. Diplomatic ties were also opened with Japan, Singapore, Taiwan and Thailand. In the Middle East, where Israel remained South Africa's long-standing ally, contacts were established with Bahrain, Dubai (the United Arab Emirates), Iran and Lebanon. Moreover, a large number of countries established interest sections in other embassies at Pretoria.

Non-governmental and other organizations, on the other hand, continued to call for application of pressure on South Africa, while pursuing their efforts to provide support to the anti-apartheid opposition and monitor the political situation in the country. When EC decided to lift the oil embargo in April, the EC Anti-Apartheid Movement strongly protested the decision.

Economic relations

Trade and finance

The years 1991 and 1992 saw a rapid reintegration of South Africa into the mainstream of world trade, the Special Committee against Apartheid noted in its annual report.[1] Especially in the early months of 1992, before the breakdown in political negotiations, potential local and foreign investors showed interest in the South African economy.

With a number of countries relaxing restrictive measures on trade as well as exploring the possibilities of establishing business operations in South Africa and the region as a whole, a significant list of trade missions held talks with the South African Government and business officials. A trade agreement was signed with Italy on economic and industrial cooperation, the first such agreement with a major European Power. As France lifted coal sanctions, major collaboration agreements with French companies were reportedly negotiated, including deals in the hotel and transport field. South Africa offered the Russian Federation a 140 million rand (R) revolving credit link to facilitate expanding trade between the two countries. The Barlows Equipment Co. of South Africa was contracted to supply mining equipment for a diamond venture in Angola, the biggest trade deal between the two countries.

Trade between South Africa and the rest of Africa grew significantly during the period under review. The reform process in South Africa prompted the formation of the Southern Africa Development Community (SADC), to replace the Southern African Development Coordination Conference, set up in 1980 to reduce dependence on South Africa. The new SADC was set to expand its role, which included a tighter unity in economic policies, regional security, foreign affairs and security issues. Meanwhile, South Africa's main trading partners remained Germany, Italy, Japan, the United Kingdom and the United States; while trade with Africa was estimated at R 10 billion in 1991, South Africa's total visible trade was R 114 billion.

Despite depressed base and precious metals prices, South Africa's major export commodities, South African exports performed well during the first quarter of 1992, with a gain of 7 per cent in January and February. The biggest contributors to that growth were jewellery and precious stones (mainly diamonds), which rose by 79 per cent during the first quarter. Exports of manufactured products also increased. Total exports of goods and services exceeded total imports, resulting in sustained favourable performance of the current account of the balance of payments. The account surplus, which reached R 7.4 billion, or 2.5 per cent of gross domestic product, in 1991, declined, however, to an annualized R 4.5 billion in the first quarter of 1992 and R 6 billion in the second.

As economic sanctions were lifted, international banks and investors re-established business relations with South Africa, improving significantly the capital account of the balance of payments. In the first quarter of 1992, the total net outflow of capital declined to R 21 million, but increased in the second quarter to R 1.9 billion, in reaction to adverse political developments.

Following South Africa's re-entry into world capital markets in September 1991, it raised several bond issues with European banks. The return of South African borrowers to international financial markets generated a great deal of controversy, and ANC appealed to major financial institutions in Europe and the Far East to keep financial sanctions in place.

While traders clearly manifested their interest in South Africa, the hope for significant foreign investment remained unfulfilled. In a move to encourage such investments, the Minister of Finance announced in June 1992 that foreign companies and individuals would no longer pay tax on interest accrued on their investment in South Africa. ANC, meanwhile, maintained that the most important way to promote foreign investment remained the establishment of a climate of political stability, economic growth and transparent and consistent economic policies.

To stimulate tourism and trade links further, South Africa announced a liberalization of its international aviation policy, including a possible relaxation of tariff control measures.

While Japan had announced during the latter part of 1991 that it was lifting its economic, financial and trade sanctions, several countries followed suit in 1992. In January, EC members lifted their last economic sanctions against South Africa—on imports of gold coins and iron and steel products—and, on 6 April, EC announced its decision to lift the oil embargo, in effect since 1985, and declared that restrictive measures in the cultural, scientific and sporting fields were formally lifted. However, the embargo on imports and exports of arms and sensitive goods for the armed forces, along with measures affecting military and nuclear cooperation, remained in effect.

The Republic of Korea lifted economic sanctions imposed since 1978, opening the way for investment by Korean companies and increased trade between the two countries. However, the ban on sales of arms and petroleum remained in place. Mexico decided to lift its trade sanctions and move towards establishing diplomatic relations with South Africa.

Singapore announced in March 1992 the lifting of its trade and investment sanctions, but decided to maintain the ban on arms sales and loans to the South African authorities and public enterprises.

Oil embargo

The Intergovernmental Group to Monitor the Supply and Shipping of Oil and Petroleum Products to South Africa, established by the General Assembly in 1986,[22] continued in 1992 collecting data and considering information on alleged violations and port calls in South Africa of ships with the capability of carrying oil and petroleum products. In pursuance of its mandate, the Group maintained contact with Governments, intergovernmental and non-governmental organizations and the shipping industry, following up cases of alleged violations.

During 1992, the Group queried 78 cases of alleged violations that occurred mainly during the 12 months since its previous report of October 1991.[21] There were 71 cases involving tankers with a total dead-weight capacity of over 16.8 million tons, with an additional seven cases involving combination carriers with a total dead-weight capacity of over 700,000 tons. Most of the cases involved oil-producing States.

Since 1987, the Group had removed a number cases of alleged violations from further consideration on the basis of one or more of the following criteria: when the certificate of discharge confirmed the delivery of oil to ports other than those in South Africa; when there was no oil-loading facility in the port concerned; and when it was certified that the ship in question was not capable of transporting oil or petroleum products.

In the conclusions to its annual report to the Assembly issued in November,[23] the Group considered it essential that oil-exporting States maintained their policies and regulations banning the export of oil and petroleum products to South

Africa, particularly the restrictions on the final destination of those products. A premature lifting of the oil embargo would be counter-productive and harmful to the negotiating process.

The Group recommended that the Assembly call on States to maintain and enforce existing measures prohibiting the supply and shipping of oil and petroleum products to South Africa, to apply strictly the oil embargo or comparable policies, and to discourage ships capable of carrying oil or petroleum products in their national registries or owned/managed by companies or individuals under their jurisdiction from engaging in activities that violated the embargo; and request States to cooperate fully with the Group, particularly in its investigation into the circumstances of alleged violations of the embargo or of port calls of ships capable of carrying oil and petroleum products, including the removal of legal impediments to such cooperation.

In April, the Chairman of the Group issued a statement expressing regret about the 6 April decision of EC to lift the ban on the export of oil to South Africa, since an agreement on transitional arrangements or on a new non-racial democratic constitution had not been achieved. The strategy of pressure and encouragement, which the Group had consistently supported, should be maintained and lifted only when the conditions set forth in the 1989 Declaration on Apartheid and its Destructive Consequences in Southern Africa[2] were met.

An addendum to the Group's report contained a list of ships and companies reported to have been involved in supplying oil to South Africa between 1987 and 1991; a summary of communications between Governments and the Group concerning alleged violations reported between 1987 and 1991; a summary of cases of alleged violations reported in 1992; and surveys of unclarified tanker calls at South African ports reported in 1991 and 1992.

GENERAL ASSEMBLY ACTION

On 18 December, the General Assembly adopted **resolution 47/116 D** by recorded vote.

Oil embargo against South Africa

The General Assembly,

Having considered the report of the Intergovernmental Group to Monitor the Supply and Shipping of Oil and Petroleum Products to South Africa,

Recalling its resolutions on the oil embargo against South Africa, in particular resolution 46/79 E of 13 December 1991,

Recognizing the importance of the oil embargo as a major contribution to the pressure exerted on South Africa towards the eradication of apartheid through negotiations, as well as the importance of maintaining pressure until there is clear evidence of profound and irreversible changes, bearing in mind the objectives of the Declaration on Apartheid and its Destructive Consequences in Southern Africa, such as the adoption of a non-racial and democratic constitution for a free South Africa,

Noting that the most effective way to enforce the oil embargo against South Africa remains the adoption by the Security Council of a mandatory embargo,

Taking note with appreciation of the draft model law for the effective enforcement of the oil embargo against South Africa, contained in the report of the Intergovernmental Group to the General Assembly at its forty-fifth session, and welcoming its consideration by Member States,

Concerned that the oil embargo against South Africa is still being violated and that South Africa, because of loopholes in the embargo such as lack of effective legislation, has been able to acquire oil and petroleum products,

Convinced that an effective oil embargo against South Africa would contribute to the efforts of the international community to bring about a negotiated settlement and the establishment of a united, non-racial and democratic South Africa,

1. *Takes note* of the report of the Intergovernmental Group to Monitor the Supply and Shipping of Oil and Petroleum Products to South Africa and endorses its recommendations;

2. *Requests* all States to adopt, if they have not already done so, and otherwise to maintain and enforce effective measures prohibiting the supply and shipping of oil and petroleum products to South Africa, whether directly or indirectly, and in particular:

(a) To apply strictly the "end users" clause and other conditions concerning restriction on destination to ensure compliance with the embargo;

(b) To compel the companies originally selling or purchasing oil or petroleum products, as appropriate to each country, to desist from selling, reselling or otherwise transferring oil and petroleum products to South Africa, whether directly or indirectly;

(c) To establish strict control over the supply of oil and petroleum products to South Africa by intermediaries, oil companies and traders by placing responsibilities for the fulfilment of the contract on the first buyer or seller of oil and petroleum products who would, therefore, be liable for the actions of these parties;

(d) To prevent South African companies from acquiring holdings in oil companies outside South Africa;

(e) To prohibit all assistance to South Africa in the oil sector, including finance, technology, equipment or personnel;

(f) To prohibit the transport of oil and petroleum products to South Africa by ships flying their flags, or by ships that are ultimately owned, managed or chartered by their nationals or by companies within their jurisdiction;

(g) To develop a system for registration of ships, registered in their territory or owned by their nationals, that have violated the oil embargo, and to discourage such ships from calling at South African ports;

(h) To impose penal action against companies and individuals that have been involved in violating the oil embargo, and to publicize cases of successful prosecutions in conformity with their national laws;

(i) To gather, exchange and disseminate information regarding violations of the oil embargo, including ways and means to prevent such violations, and to take concerted measures against violators;

(j) To discourage ships within their jurisdiction from engaging in activities that give rise to violation of the oil embargo against South Africa, taking into account legislative and other measures already adopted;

3. *Authorizes* the Intergovernmental Group to take action to promote public awareness of the oil embargo against South Africa, including, when necessary, sending missions and participating in relevant conferences and meetings;

4. *Requests* the Intergovernmental Group to submit to the General Assembly at its forty-eighth session a report on the implementation of the present resolution;

5. *Requests* all States to extend their cooperation to the Intergovernmental Group with all necessary assistance for the implementation of the present resolution.

General Assembly resolution 47/116 D

18 December 1992   Meeting 91   111-1-44 (recorded vote)

11-nation draft (A/47/L.31 & Add.1); agenda item 33.

Sponsors: Algeria, Cuba, Indonesia, Kuwait, Libyan Arab Jamahiriya, New Zealand, Nicaragua, Nigeria, Norway, Ukraine, United Republic of Tanzania.

Financial implications. 5th Committee, A/47/798; S-G, A/C.5/47/74.

Meeting numbers. GA 47th session: 5th Committee 47; plenary 62-66, 88, 91.

Recorded vote in Assembly as follows:

In favour: Afghanistan, Algeria, Angola, Antigua and Barbuda, Argentina, Armenia, Azerbaijan, Bahamas, Bahrain, Bangladesh, Barbados, Belarus, Belize, Benin, Bhutan, Bosnia and Herzegovina, Brazil, Brunei Darussalam, Burkina Faso, Burundi, Cameroon, Cape Verde, Central African Republic, Chad, Chile, China, Colombia, Comoros, Costa Rica, Côte d'Ivoire, Cuba, Cyprus, Democratic People's Republic of Korea, Djibouti, Dominica, Ecuador, El Salvador, Fiji, Gabon, Gambia, Ghana, Guatemala, Guinea, Guinea-Bissau, Guyana, Honduras, India, Indonesia, Iran, Iraq, Jamaica, Jordan, Kenya, Kuwait, Lao People's Democratic Republic, Lebanon, Libyan Arab Jamahiriya, Malaysia, Maldives, Mali, Mauritania, Mauritius, Mexico, Mongolia, Morocco, Mozambique, Myanmar, Namibia, Nepal, New Zealand, Nicaragua, Niger, Nigeria, Norway, Oman, Pakistan, Panama, Papua New Guinea, Paraguay, Peru, Philippines, Qatar, Republic of Korea, Rwanda, Saint Kitts and Nevis, Saint Lucia, Saint Vincent and the Grenadines, Sao Tome and Principe, Saudi Arabia, Sierra Leone, Sri Lanka, Sudan, Suriname, Sweden, Syrian Arab Republic, Thailand, Togo, Trinidad and Tobago, Tunisia, Uganda, Ukraine, United Arab Emirates, United Republic of Tanzania, Uruguay, Vanuatu, Venezuela, Viet Nam, Yemen, Zaire, Zambia, Zimbabwe.

Against: United States.

Abstaining: Albania, Australia, Austria, Belgium, Botswana, Bulgaria, Canada, Croatia, Czechoslovakia, Denmark, Estonia, Finland, France, Germany, Greece, Hungary, Iceland, Ireland, Israel, Italy, Japan, Kazakhstan, Latvia, Lesotho, Liechtenstein, Lithuania, Luxembourg, Malawi, Malta, Marshall Islands, Micronesia, Netherlands, Poland, Portugal, Republic of Moldova, Romania, Russian Federation, Samoa, Singapore, Slovenia, Spain, Swaziland, Turkey, United Kingdom.

Transnational corporations

In a March 1992 report to the Commission on Transnational Corporations (TNCs),[24] the Secretary-General examined the role of TNCs in the South African economy in the 1990s, the role of sanctions and the reaction of the international community to the repeal of key apartheid legislation. In another March report,[25] the Secretary-General updated the lists of TNCs with equity interests in South Africa and those which had disinvested. (For details, see PART THREE, Chapter V.)

By **resolution 1992/34**, the Economic and Social Council invited TNCs, among others, to give their full support to the demise of the apartheid system. The Council requested the Secretary-General to continue examining possible contributions of TNCs to the construction of a united and non-racial South Africa.

Military and nuclear collaboration

South Africa's defence budget for 1992-1993 was estimated at R 9.7 billion, representing less than 10 per cent of total government spending. Although declining, at 4.3 per cent of gross national product (GNP), military expenditure was still above the targeted 3.6 per cent of GNP.

As part of the ongoing restructuring and privatization of the South African arms industry, the South African Arms Corporation reorganized its manufacturing subsidiaries into the Denel Group, whose management indicated that the aim was conversion from predominatly military production (85 per cent) to the manufacture for mainly civilian markets, an endeavour to which the United States had reportedly offered its assistance. The Atlas Aircraft Corporation, now under the name SIMERA, was reorganized in a similar manner.

The United States Administration was reported to have opposed South Africa's efforts to build and launch space satellites. Houwteq, a Denel subsidiary, was said to be developing a satellite and launching capability that could be ready within five years. Some evidence also suggested that South Africa had already developed various components for satellites.

In its report, the Special Committee against Apartheid supplied information about reported imports and exports of arms and equipment to and from South Africa. Among the Committee's actions in that regard was a letter of 1 April to Chile from the Acting Chairman, expressing concern at South Africa's participation in the FIDAE '92 air exhibition at Chilean Los Cerrillos Air Force base near Santiago. On 6 April, the Acting Chairman addressed letters to Czechoslovakia, Poland and the Russian Federation concerning the participation of companies in their respective countries with the South African companies Atlas and Kentron in promoting jet fighters and related technology at the Aviation Africa '92 Aerospace Trade Fair at Johannesburg. The Russian Federation, by a 24 April letter, stated that neither fighter aircraft nor any other military technology connected with such aircraft was exhibited at the show. Czechoslovakia, by a letter of 30 April, said it complied and would continue to do so with the 1991 General Assembly resolution on military collaboration with South Africa,[26] as well as with the obligatory military embargo imposed by the Security Council in 1977.[27] Even though informal contacts might happen, no licences for arms or military technology exports to South Africa were given by the Council of State Defence.

By a letter of 9 September, the Acting Chairman expressed concern about reports that the South African Air Force had decided to purchase approximately 40 Brazilian EMB 312 aircraft. On 16 October, Brazil responded that the Brazilian firm EMBRAER had considered the possibility of selling Tucano aircraft to South Africa, but that such transaction was only to be carried out on condition that the aircraft could be used for exclusive use as pilot trainers and without any possibility of conversion for military use; however, in international bidding, the contract for the supply of trainer aircraft was not awarded to EMBRAER. Brazil carefully monitored EMBRAER's efforts at the South African market and there was no question of circumventing the mandatory sanctions imposed by the Security Council.

Following its accession to the 1968 Treaty on the Non-Proliferation of Nuclear Weapons[28] and the safeguards agreement signed in September 1991 with the International Atomic Energy Agency (IAEA),[29] South Africa resumed its participation in the proceedings of the policy-making organs of IAEA. By a resolution on South Africa's nuclear capability, adopted on 25 September 1992, the General Conference of IAEA requested South Africa to continue to cooperate with IAEA in implementing the safeguards agreement. The Conference also requested the IAEA Director General to assist African States in their efforts towards the establishment of a nuclear-weapon-free zone in Africa.

The Director General, in a September 1992 report to the General Conference, stated that no evidence had been found that the list of nuclear facilities and locations provided by South Africa under the safeguards agreement was incomplete, and IAEA was not in possession of any other information suggesting the existence of any undeclared facilities or nuclear material. The General Conference resolution and the Director General's report were annexed to the Secretary-General's October 1992 report[30] on South Africa's nuclear capability (see PART ONE, Chapter II).

GENERAL ASSEMBLY ACTION

On 18 December, the General Assembly adopted **resolution 47/116 E** by recorded vote.

Military and other collaboration with South Africa
The General Assembly,

Recalling the Declaration on Apartheid and its Destructive Consequences in Southern Africa, its resolutions 45/176 B and C of 19 December 1990 and 46/79 B and C of 13 December 1991, as well as the resolutions of the Security Council on the arms embargo and military collaboration with South Africa,

Taking note of the report of the Special Committee against Apartheid and the report of the Security Council Committee established by Council resolution 421(1977) of 9 December 1977 concerning the question of South Africa on its activities during the period 1980-1989,

Noting with appreciation the resolve and effectiveness of the Security Council in its handling of questions relating to the preservation of international peace and security,

Noting that the monitoring and enforcement mechanism of the mandatory sanctions imposed by the Security Council on South Africa in its resolution 418(1977) of 4 November 1977 would benefit from further strengthening,

Reiterating that the full implementation of the mandatory arms embargo against South Africa is an essential element of international action towards the eradication of apartheid,

Convinced that sanctions and other restrictive measures have had a significant impact on recent developments in South Africa and that the phased application of appropriate pressure remains an effective and necessary instrument in the process towards the peaceful end to apartheid,

Taking note of the report of the Director General of the International Atomic Energy Agency of 4 September 1992 on the completeness of the inventory of South Africa's nuclear installations and material, under the terms of the safeguards agreement,

Expressing serious concern about the continued violations of the mandatory arms embargo, particularly by those countries which surreptitiously trade in arms with South Africa,

Expressing concern that South Africa's external military relations, especially in the area of military technology and, in particular, in the production and testing of missiles, continue unabated, as mentioned in the report of the Special Committee against Apartheid,

Gravely concerned about the practice carried out by certain oil-producing States whereby oil is exchanged for South African arms,

1. _Deplores_ the actions of those States which, directly or indirectly, continue to violate the mandatory arms embargo and collaborate with South Africa in the military, nuclear, intelligence and technology fields, and calls upon those States to terminate forthwith any illegal acts and honour their obligations under Security Council resolution 418(1977);

2. _Urges_ all States to adopt strict legislation relating to the implementation of the arms embargo and to prohibit the supply to South Africa of nuclear and military products, as well as computer and communications equipment, technological skills and services, including military intelligence, destined for use by the military, police and security agencies of that country, until free and fair elections have been held and a democratic government has been established;

3. _Urges_ the Security Council to consider immediate steps to ensure the full implementation and the effective monitoring of the arms embargo imposed by the Council in its resolutions 418(1977) and 558(1984) of 13 December 1984, to implement the recommendations of the Committee established under Council resolution 421(1977) concerning appropriate measures in response to violations of the mandatory arms embargo and to provide information on a regular basis to the Secretary-General for general distribution to Member States;

4. _Calls upon_ all States to maintain existing financial measures and, in particular, urges Governments and private financial institutions, as well as the International Monetary Fund and the World Bank, not to extend new loans and credits to South Africa, whether to the public or private sector, until agreement has been reached on a non-racial democratic constitution or until specific recommendations are made on this matter by the tran-

sitional authorities to be established by the Convention for a Democratic South Africa;

5. *Requests* the Special Committe against Apartheid to keep the issue of military and nuclear collaboration with South Africa under constant review and to report thereon to the General Assembly and the Security Council as appropriate.

General Assembly resolution 47/116 E

18 December 1992   Meeting 91   106-2-47 (recorded vote)

22-nation draft (A/47/L.44 & Corr.1 & Add.1); agenda item 33.

Sponsors: Algeria, Angola, Chile, Cuba, Gambia, Ghana, Guatemala, Guyana, Haiti, Iran, Malaysia, Mauritania, Mozambique, Myanmar, Namibia, Nigeria, Sierra Leone, Syrian Arab Republic, United Republic of Tanzania, Vanuatu, Zambia, Zimbabwe.

Financial implications. 5th Committee, A/47/798; S-G, A/C.5/47/74.

Meeting numbers. GA 47th session: 5th Committee 47; plenary 62-66, 88, 91.

Recorded vote in Assembly as follows:

In favour: Afghanistan, Algeria, Angola, Antigua and Barbuda, Armenia, Azerbaijan, Bahamas, Bahrain, Bangladesh, Barbados, Belize, Benin, Bhutan, Bosnia and Herzegovina, Botswana, Brazil, Brunei Darussalam, Burkina Faso, Burundi, Cameroon, Cape Verde, Central African Republic, Chad, Chile, China, Colombia, Comoros, Costa Rica, Côte d'Ivoire, Cuba, Cyprus, Democratic People's Republic of Korea, Djibouti, Dominica, Ecuador, Egypt, El Salvador, Fiji, Gabon, Gambia, Ghana, Grenada, Guatemala, Guinea, Guinea-Bissau, Guyana, Honduras, India, Indonesia, Iran, Iraq, Jamaica, Jordan, Kenya, Kuwait, Lao People's Democratic Republic, Lebanon, Libyan Arab Jamahiriya, Malaysia, Maldives, Mali, Mauritania, Mexico, Mongolia, Morocco, Mozambique, Myanmar, Namibia, Nepal, Nicaragua, Niger, Nigeria, Oman, Pakistan, Panama, Papua New Guinea, Paraguay, Peru, Philippines, Qatar, Rwanda, Saint Kitts and Nevis, Saint Lucia, Saint Vincent and the Grenadines, Sao Tome and Principe, Saudi Arabia, Sierra Leone, Singapore, Sri Lanka, Suriname, Swaziland, Syrian Arab Republic, Thailand, Togo, Trinidad and Tobago, Tunisia, Uganda, United Arab Emirates, United Republic of Tanzania, Vanuatu, Venezuela, Viet Nam, Yemen, Zaire, Zambia, Zimbabwe.

Against: United Kingdom, United States.

Abstaining: Albania, Argentina, Australia, Austria, Belarus, Belgium, Bulgaria, Canada, Croatia, Czechoslovakia, Denmark, Estonia, Finland, France, Germany, Greece, Hungary, Iceland, Ireland, Israel, Italy, Japan, Kazakhstan, Latvia, Liechtenstein, Lithuania, Luxembourg, Malawi, Malta, Marshall Islands, Micronesia, Netherlands, New Zealand, Norway, Poland, Portugal, Republic of Korea, Republic of Moldova, Romania, Russian Federation, Samoa, Slovenia, Spain, Sweden, Turkey, Ukraine, Uruguay.

Israel–South Africa relations

The Special Committee, in the second part of its report, prepared in response to a 1991 General Assembly resolution,[31] dealt exclusively with relations between South Africa and Israel, especially in the military and nuclear fields. The Committee viewed the ongoing collaboration from the standpoint of its effect on concerted international efforts aimed at total eradication of apartheid and support for the establishment of a united, non-racial and democratic South Africa.

The Committee drew attention to various reports in newspapers and publications in Israel, the United Kingdom and the United States that military and nuclear cooperation was continuing. According to the Committee, South Africa was one of Israel's major arms customers. The ongoing cooperation, which violated the mandatory arms embargo imposed by the Security Council in 1977,[32] was a matter of great concern to the international community, the Committee said.

The Committee called for effective action, particularly by the Security Council, to end that violation. It recommended that the Assembly call on

Israel to cease its collaboration with South Africa, particularly in the military and nuclear fields, and that it authorize the Committee to continue monitoring relations between the two countries.

With respect to other aspects of the collaboration between them, the Special Committee noted that a November 1991 visit to Israel by President de Klerk had resulted in a February 1992 tour to South Africa by an Israeli delegation, which included representatives of the Ministries of Finance, Industry and Commerce, Agriculture and Tourism. The Committee quoted the magazine *Israeli Foreign Affairs*, which reported on 20 February that Israel had trained most of IFP's intelligence operatives, including an assistant to the party leader.

According to statistics available, Israeli exports to South Africa amounted to $98 million in 1991, with imports to Israel from there estimated at $235 million.

GENERAL ASSEMBLY ACTION

On 18 December, the General Assembly adopted **resolution 47/116 F** by recorded vote.

Relations between South Africa and Israel

The General Assembly,

Recalling its resolutions concerning the relations between South Africa and Israel and, in particular, its resolution 46/79 D of 13 December 1991,

Having considered the report of the Special Committee against Apartheid on recent developments concerning relations between South Africa and Israel, and the report of the Secretary-General on South Africa's nuclear-tipped ballistic missile capability,[a]

Noting with concern that the military relations between South Africa and Israel, especially in the area of military technology and in particular the collaboration in the production and testing of nuclear missiles, continue unabated,

1. *Strongly deplores* the collaboration of Israel with the South African regime in the military and nuclear fields;

2. *Reiterates its demand* that Israel desist from and terminate forthwith all forms of collaboration with South Africa, particularly in the military and nuclear fields;

3. *Urges* the Security Council to consider taking appropriate measures against Israel for its violation of the mandatory arms embargo against South Africa;

4. *Requests* the Special Committee against Apartheid to continue to monitor the relations between South Africa and Israel and keep them under constant review and report to the General Assembly and the Security Council as appropriate.

---

[a]A/46/357 & Add.1.

General Assembly resolution 47/116 F

18 December 1992   Meeting 91   93-39-23 (recorded vote)

19-nation draft (A/47/L.45 & Corr.3 & Add.1); agenda item 33.

Sponsors: Algeria, Angola, Cuba, Gambia, Ghana, Haiti, Iran, Libyan Arab Jamahiriya, Malaysia, Mauritania, Mozambique, Namibia, Nigeria, Sudan, Syrian Arab Republic, United Republic of Tanzania, Vanuatu, Zambia, Zimbabwe.

Financial implications. 5th Committee, A/47/798; S-G, A/C.5/47/74.

Meeting numbers. GA 47th session: 5th Committee 47; plenary 62-66, 88, 91.

Recorded vote in Assembly as follows:

In favour: Afghanistan, Algeria, Angola, Antigua and Barbuda, Bahamas, Bahrain, Bangladesh, Barbados, Belize, Bhutan, Bosnia and Herzegovina, Botswana, Brazil, Brunei Darussalam, Burkina Faso, Cape Verde, Chad, Chile, China, Colombia, Comoros, Costa Rica, Cuba, Cyprus, Democratic People's Republic of Korea, Djibouti, Ecuador, Egypt, El Salvador, Gabon, Gambia, Ghana, Grenada, Guatemala, Guinea, Guinea-Bissau, Guyana, Honduras, India, Indonesia, Iran, Iraq, Jamaica, Jordan, Kenya, Kuwait, Lao People's Democratic Republic, Lebanon, Lesotho, Libyan Arab Jamahiriya, Madagascar, Malawi, Malaysia, Maldives, Mali, Mauritania, Mexico, Morocco, Mozambique, Namibia, Nepal, Nicaragua, Niger, Nigeria, Oman, Pakistan, Paraguay, Philippines, Qatar, Rwanda, Sao Tome and Principe, Saudi Arabia, Sierra Leone, Singapore, Sri Lanka, Sudan, Suriname, Swaziland, Syrian Arab Republic, Thailand, Togo, Trinidad and Tobago, Tunisia, Uganda, United Arab Emirates, United Republic of Tanzania, Vanuatu, Venezuela, Viet Nam, Yemen, Zaire, Zambia, Zimbabwe.

Against: Australia, Austria, Belgium, Bulgaria, Canada, Croatia, Czechoslovakia, Denmark, Estonia, Finland, France, Germany, Greece, Hungary, Iceland, Ireland, Israel, Italy, Latvia, Liechtenstein, Lithuania, Luxembourg, Malta, Marshall Islands, Micronesia, Netherlands, New Zealand, Norway, Poland, Portugal, Republic of Moldova, Romania, Russian Federation, Slovenia, Spain, Sweden, United Kingdom, United States, Uruguay.

Abstaining: Albania, Argentina, Belarus, Benin, Burundi, Cameroon, Central African Republic, Côte d'Ivoire, Dominica, Fiji, Japan, Kazakhstan, Myanmar, Panama, Papua New Guinea, Peru, Republic of Korea, Saint Kitts and Nevis, Saint Lucia, Saint Vincent and the Grenadines, Samoa, Turkey, Ukraine.

Aid programmes and inter-agency cooperation

In a November 1992 report,[33] submitted in accordance with a 1991 General Assembly request,[3] the Secretary-General described current or planned activities of the United Nations system for the successful repatriation of South African refugees and exiles, the reintegration of political exiles and released political prisoners, and assistance to the disadvantaged sectors of South African society. Guidelines for a coordinated United Nations approach to questions relating to South Africa had been adopted by the Administrative Committee on Coordination in 1991.[34] To facilitate future coordination of United Nations efforts, a seminar was held on South Africa's socio-economic problems and the role of the United Nations system in helping to address them (Windhoek, 22-24 May 1992), at which 20 United Nations offices and organizations or agencies were represented. The seminar discussed the identification of priority needs, assessment of United Nations assistance in response to the needs of South Africans in the context of a new national economic development policy, an institutional framework for the delivery of assistance and the mobilization of financial resources for such assistance.

At the conclusion of the seminar, the participants approved the following observations made by the Chairman of the Special Committee: the socio-economic needs of the disadvantaged population should urgently be addressed, with resources commensurate to the seriousness of the situation; education, health, housing and job creation— areas in which the impact of apartheid was particularly devastating—were among the top priorities; South Africa's economic and social sectors required a profound restructuring if genuine development was to benefit the whole population; grass-roots organizations needed to be consulted with regard to technical cooperation in general and activities geared to the disadvantaged communities in particular; there was a need for a comprehensive national programme of redress, with strong elements of affirmative action, to tackle glaring socio-economic imbalances; there was a need for a new integrated development strategy which would promote growth and redistribution simultaneously; need for assistance had been expressed in the form of technical advice, human resources development, institutional capacity-building, relief operations, programmes and projects affecting structures, and policy formulation in areas such as industrial development, technological innovation, investment codes and subregional economic cooperation and integration; and domestic resources would have to be mobilized as a first step, but significant external financing would be required in meeting the priority needs of the population. Seminar participants were of the view that the dialogue should continue in a follow-up meeting on specific issues arising out of the seminar's discussions. It was agreed that a follow-up meeting would require concerted preparations also in South Africa.

Among other activities were a round table on independent and pluralistic media in South Africa (Windhoek, 14-17 August) under the auspices of the United Nations Educational, Scientific and Cultural Organization, and a new two-year programme by the World Bank's Economic Development Institute for training South Africans in the management of urban development projects and in the fundamentals of economic policy.

Taking note of the report, the Assembly, in **resolution 47/116 A**, called on the international community to assist disadvantaged South African democratic anti-apartheid organizations and individuals in the academic, scientific and cultural fields.

UN Trust Fund for South Africa

Five grants totalling $1,550,000 were made in 1992 from the United Nations Trust Fund for South Africa, established in 1965[35] to provide assistance to persons persecuted under the country's repressive and discriminatory legislation and relief to South African refugees. In addition, the Fund's Committee of Trustees extended three grants totalling $900,000.

According to an October 1992 report of the Secretary-General,[36] the Fund had received, since his report of October 1991,[37] $4,594,938 in voluntary contributions from 29 Member States. Total income of the Fund since its inception was $47,987,616 and the total amount of grants was

$45,970,974, including those approved in 1992. The report said pledges from 15 Governments, totalling $87,091, were outstanding as at 30 September 1992.

In accordance with a 1991 General Assembly resolution,[38] the Fund's Committee of Trustees provided assistance for the reintegration of former political prisoners and newly released prisoners into South African society, as well as assistance to voluntary agencies, mostly inside South Africa, that rendered humanitarian and legal assistance to victims of apartheid. The Committee also supported work in the legal field aimed at ensuring effective implementation of legislation, repealing major apartheid laws, redressing continuing adverse effects of those laws and encouraging increased public confidence in the rule of law. Due to the changing circumstances in the country, the Committee decided to channel its assistance henceforth exclusively through appropriate NGOs inside South Africa. The Committee's report was annexed to that of the Secretary-General.

GENERAL ASSEMBLY ACTION

On 18 December, the General Assembly adopted **resolution 47/116 C** without vote.

United Nations Trust Fund for South Africa
The General Assembly,
Recalling its resolutions on the United Nations Trust Fund for South Africa, in particular resolution 46/79 F, adopted without a vote on 13 December 1991,
Having considered the report of the Secretary-General on the United Nations Trust Fund for South Africa, to which is annexed the report of the Committee of Trustees of the Trust Fund,
Recalling, in particular, paragraph 2 of its resolution 46/79 F, relating to the reintegration of released political prisoners into South African society,
Welcoming the announcement on 26 September 1992 of the Record of Understanding reached between the African National Congress of South Africa and the Government of South Africa, which contained agreement on the release of remaining political prisoners, and the voluntary repatriation of political exiles and refugees as a result of the agreement reached between the South African authorities and the United Nations High Commissioner for Refugees,
Noting with concern that continuing political violence and other developments in South Africa are having an adverse impact on the negotiating process and on the functioning of the framework provided by the National Peace Accord signed on 14 September 1991,
Recognizing the work being carried out by broad-based, impartial voluntary organizations inside South Africa in providing legal and humanitarian assistance to the victims of apartheid and racial discrimination and noting with satisfaction the working relationship that the Trust Fund has established with those South African organizations,
Strongly convinced that continued, direct and substantial contributions to the Trust Fund and to the voluntary agencies concerned are necessary to enable them to meet the extensive needs for humanitarian, legal and relief assistance during the critical transition to a non-racial and democratic South Africa,

1. *Endorses* the report of the Secretary-General on the United Nations Trust Fund for South Africa;
2. *Supports* continued and substantial humanitarian, legal and educational assistance by the international community in order to alleviate the plight of those persecuted under discriminatory legislation in South Africa, and to facilitate the reintegration of released political prisoners and returning exiles into South African society;
3. *Supports* assistance by the Trust Fund for work in the legal field aimed at ensuring effective implementation of legislation repealing major apartheid laws, redressing the continuing adverse effects of those laws and encouraging increased public confidence in the rule of law;
4. *Endorses* the decision of the Trust Fund to channel its assistance through appropriate non-governmental organizations inside South Africa;
5. *Expresses its appreciation* to the Governments, organizations and individuals that have contributed to the Trust Fund and to the voluntary agencies engaged in rendering humanitarian and legal assistance to the victims of apartheid in South Africa;
6. *Appeals* for generous contributions to the Trust Fund;
7. *Also appeals* for direct contributions to the voluntary agencies engaged in rendering assistance to the victims of apartheid and racial discrimination in South Africa;
8. *Commends* the Secretary-General and the Committee of Trustees of the Trust Fund for their persistent efforts to promote humanitarian and legal assistance to the victims of apartheid and racial discrimination.

General Assembly resolution 47/116 C

18 December 1992   Meeting 91   Adopted without vote

37-nation draft (A/47/L.27 & Add.1); agenda item 33.
Sponsors: Angola, Argentina, Australia, Austria, Brazil, Canada, Chile, China, Costa Rica, Denmark, Egypt, Finland, France, Germany, Greece, Iceland, India, Indonesia, Iran, Ireland, Japan, Malaysia, Morocco, Mozambique, Namibia, Nepal, New Zealand, Nigeria, Norway, Pakistan, Spain, Sweden, Turkey, United Republic of Tanzania, Venezuela, Zambia, Zimbabwe.
Meeting numbers. GA 47th session: plenary 62-66, 88, 91.

In **resolution 47/116 A**, the Assembly appealed to the international community to increase humanitarian and legal assistance to the victims of apartheid, returning refugees and exiles and released political prisoners.

UN Educational and Training Programme for Southern Africa

Scholarship awards under the United Nations Educational and Training Programme for Southern Africa reached 2,108 in 1991/92, compared to 1,278 in 1990/91, according to an October 1992 report of the Secretary-General.[39] The Programme was administered by the Secretary-General in consultation with an Advisory Committee and financed from a Trust Fund made up of voluntary contributions from States, organizations and individuals. Under the 1992 Programme, scholarship assistance was granted to 1,787 students from

South Africa and, for a transitional period ending 31 December 1992, to 321 students from Namibia. New awards were granted only to students from South Africa. Originally, the Programme was established by integrating earlier special programmes to assist persons from Namibia, South Africa, Southern Rhodesia and Territories under Portuguese administration in Africa.[40]

For the period from 1 September 1991 to 31 August 1992, a total of $5,289,542 in contributions was received from 27 countries. In addition, pledges for 1992 amounted to $133,743. The 1992 contributions and pledges, totalling $5,423,285, represented a decrease of $485,535 compared to the previous year.

During the period under review, the Programme initiated a number of new projects in cooperation with scholarship agencies, educational institutions, foundations, and governmental and intergovernmental agencies. Those new projects resulted in the involvement of the Programme in more forms of training than it could have arranged on its own, and at a lower cost per award, especially in North America and Europe. At the same time, the Programme was able to grant awards to an increasing number of students from inside South Africa. Overall, those co-sponsorship arrangements proved to be beneficial to all involved—the students, the Programme and the cooperating agencies.

In accordance with recommendations of a 1989 evaluation report, the Programme continued to secure a larger intake of students from South Africa and to show greater concern for the returnability and employability of graduates, which were considered essential criteria of selection for awards. In order to help match graduates with jobs and employers, contacts were established with South African–based NGOs. Efforts were made to help strengthen black and other universities through exchange programmes for black graduates and junior faculty.

The Advisory Committee on the Programme held two meetings during the period under review, at which it considered several aspects relating to the Programme's development. In accordance with a 1991 Assembly resolution,[41] it organized jointly with the Programme a Follow-up Conference on International Educational Assistance to Disadvantaged South Africans (New York, 8 and 9 September), which was serviced by the Centre against Apartheid. The Conference, which was attended by 133 experts, representatives of major bilateral and multilateral donors, relevant intergovernmental and non-governmental organizations and observers, focused attention on the requirements for effective international educational assistance to disadvantaged South Africans during the transition to a post-apartheid society.

In four workshops at the Conference, the following points emerged that were of direct interest to the Programme: the establishment of linkages between training institutions and industry in South Africa would ensure that the institutions produced the skills necessary to meet the demands of the South African economy; there should be a linkage between scholarship awards and job opportunities; there was a need to strengthen historically disadvantaged institutions and develop their research and analytical capacities; international support could be helpful in research and networking among South African NGOs involved in providing and channelling educational assistance; the United Nations could serve as an information focal point and as catalyst for cooperation in education, particularly by improving coordination between donors and recipients, and could facilitate communication between South African institutions, aid agencies and the international community. Areas of priority for United Nations technical assistance were generally defined as capacity-building of black universities and the NGO sector, tertiary student financial assistance and basic adult education.

In the conclusions to his report, the Secretary-General stated that it was increasingly recognized that a large trained cadre of black South Africans, especially at the high and mid-management level in priority areas, would play a critical role in facilitating a transition to a non-racial and democratic South Africa. In view of the urgent need to contribute effectively to human resources development, the Secretary-General appealed for generous financial and other support to the Programme.

GENERAL ASSEMBLY ACTION

On 18 December, the General Assembly adopted **resolution 47/117** without vote.

United Nations Educational and Training Programme for Southern Africa

The General Assembly,

Recalling its resolutions on the United Nations Educational and Training Programme for Southern Africa, in particular resolution 46/80 of 13 December 1991,

Having considered the report of the Secretary-General containing an account of the work of the Advisory Committee on the United Nations Educational and Training Programme for Southern Africa and the administration of the Programme for the period from 1 September 1991 to 31 August 1992,

Noting with satisfaction that the recommendations of the evaluation of the Programme undertaken in 1989 as endorsed by the Advisory Committee continue to be implemented,

Recognizing the valuable assistance rendered by the Programme to the peoples of South Africa and Namibia,

Also noting with satisfaction that educational and technical assistance for southern Africa has become a growing concern of the international community,

Fully recognizing the need to provide continuing educational opportunities and counselling to students from South Africa in a wide variety of professional, cultural and linguistic disciplines, as well as opportunities for vocational and technical training and for advanced studies at graduate and postgraduate levels in priority fields of study, as often as possible at educational and training institutions within South Africa,

Strongly convinced that the development of the Programme is essential in order to meet the increasing demand for educational and training assistance to disadvantaged students from South Africa,

Noting that, in order to address the priority needs of disadvantaged South Africans, the Programme is continuing to allocate greater resources for the purpose of institution-building in South Africa, in particular by strengthening the historically black and other institutions of higher learning, especially through a graduate student and junior faculty enhancement programme abroad in the field of educational management and other short-term specialized training courses with built-in returnability and employability of participants,

1. *Endorses* the report of the Secretary-General on the United Nations Educational and Training Programme for Southern Africa;

2. *Commends* the Secretary-General and the Advisory Committee on the United Nations Educational and Training Programme for Southern Africa for their continued efforts to develop the Programme so that it can best meet the needs evolving from changing circumstances in South Africa, to promote generous contributions to the Programme and to enhance cooperation with governmental, intergovernmental and non-governmental agencies involved in educational and technical assistance to South Africa;

3. *Welcomes* the main thrust of the proceedings of the Follow-up Conference on International Educational Assistance to Disadvantaged South Africans, held in New York on 8 and 9 September 1992, organized by the United Nations Educational and Training Programme for Southern Africa and its Advisory Committee, with special regard to the need for:

   (a) Establishing linkages between training and educational activities and industry in South Africa;

   (b) Supporting and strengthening the historically black and other universities through exchange programmes for graduates and junior faculty;

   (c) Continuing to provide educational assistance at the tertiary level in South Africa and to strengthen the institutional technical and financial capacity as well as the decision-making of non-governmental organizations, community-based organizations and educational institutions that serve the needs and interests of disadvantaged South Africans;

4. *Notes with satisfaction* the training activities of the Programme designed to address priority needs in the areas of education and training assistance to disadvantaged South Africans;

5. *Welcomes* the expanding educational and training activities of the Programme inside South Africa and its close cooperation with South African non-governmental organizations and educational institutions;

6. *Emphasizes* that the international community has an important role in assisting the people of South Africa in bridging the economic and social disparities in South Africa during the transitional period, particularly in the field of education;

7. *Calls upon* non-governmental educational institutions, private organizations and individuals concerned to assist the Programme in facilitating the returnability and job placement of its graduates;

8. *Appeals* to Governments, intergovernmental and non-governmental organizations, international professional associations and individuals to use their influence and leverage inside South Africa to assist graduates of the Programme in obtaining access to job opportunities so that they can effectively contribute their professional competence and expertise towards the political, economic and social development of South Africa during the period of transition and beyond;

9. *Considers* that, under the changing circumstances in South Africa, the Programme should continue to have, in addition to its educational and training programmes abroad, the necessary flexibility and means to expand, in an appropriate manner, educational and training assistance to disadvantaged South Africans within the country itself;

10. *Expresses its appreciation* to all those who have supported the Programme by providing contributions, scholarships or places in their educational institutions;

11. *Appeals* to all States, institutions, organizations and individuals to offer greater financial and other assistance to the Programme to enable it to carry out its programme of activities.

General Assembly resolution 47/117

18 December 1992   Meeting 91   Adopted without vote

50-nation draft (A/47/L.15 & Add.1); agenda item 34.
Sponsors: Angola, Argentina, Australia, Austria, Bangladesh, Belarus, Belgium, Brazil, Burundi, Canada, Chile, Congo, Costa Rica, Denmark, Djibouti, Finland, France, Germany, Greece, Guyana, Iceland, India, Indonesia, Ireland, Japan, Madagascar, Malaysia, Mali, Mexico, Morocco, Mozambique, Myanmar, Netherlands, New Zealand, Nigeria, Norway, Papua New Guinea, Portugal, Romania, Spain, Sweden, Thailand, Tunisia, Turkey, Ukraine, United Republic of Tanzania, United States, Venezuela, Zambia, Zaire.

REFERENCES
[1]A/47/22. [2]GA res. S-16/1, annex, 14 Dec. 1989. [3]YUN 1991, p. 111, GA res. 46/79 A, 13 Dec. 1991. [4]A/47/574. [5]YUN 1991, p. 108. [6]A/47/494-S/24606. [7]A/47/412. [8]S/24232. [9]S/24283. [10]S/24284. [11]S/24285. [12]S/24287. [13]S/24298. [14]S/24389. [15]S/24541. [16]S/25004. [17]A/47/616. [18]A/C.5/47/79. [19]A/47/45. [20]YUN 1985, p. 166, GA res. 40/64 G, annex, 10 Dec. 1985. [21]YUN 1991, p. 114. [22]YUN 1986, p. 137, GA res. 41/35 F, 10 Nov. 1986. [23]A/47/43-S/24775 & Add.1. [24]E/C.10/1992/6. [25]E/C.10/1992/7. [26]YUN 1991, p. 118, GA res. 46/79 C, 13 Dec. 1991. [27]YUN 1977, p. 161, SC res. 418(1977), 4 Nov. 1977. [28]YUN 1968, p. 17, GA res. 2373(XXII), annex, 12 June 1968. [29]YUN 1991, p. 119. [30]A/47/533. [31]YUN 1991, p. 120, GA res. 46/79 D, 13 Dec. 1991. [32]YUN 1977, pp. 161 & 162, SC res. 418(1977) & 421(1977), 4 Nov. & 9 Dec. 1977. [33]A/47/559. [34]YUN 1991, p. 109. [35]YUN 1965, p. 115, GA res. 2054 B (XX), 15 Dec. 1965. [36]A/47/525. [37]YUN 1991, p. 124. [38]Ibid., p. 125, GA res. 46/79 F, 13 Dec. 1991. [39]A/47/513. [40]YUN 1967, p. 649, GA res. 2349(XXII), 19 Dec. 1967. [41]YUN 1991, p. 137, GA res. 46/80, 13 Dec. 1991.

Other States

forces and restoration of a central administration throughout the country.

Angola

After 16 years of civil war, both parties to the conflict in Angola—the Government and the National Union for the Total Independence of Angola (UNITA)—showed willingness to continue the peace process begun in May 1991 with the signing of the Peace Accords.[1] The first-ever multiparty elections in the country were held on 29 and 30 September 1992. The four-month electoral process, organized and directed by the National Electoral Council, was observed by the United Nations Angola Verification Mission (UNAVEM II) and supported by technical assistance from UNDP.

On 17 October, the Secretary-General's Special Representative for Angola certified the elections as generally free and fair. Results of the elections gave 49.57 per cent of the vote to Angolan President José Eduardo dos Santos, head of the Popular Movement for the Liberation of Angola (MPLA), and 40.07 per cent to Jonas Malheiro Savimbi, President of UNITA. The remainder of the vote was divided among nine other candidates. Under Angolan electoral rules, a candidate would be declared the winner with more than 50 per cent of the vote; if no candidate obtained a majority, the two top contenders would compete in a run-off.

In the parliamentary elections, the governing MPLA party received 53.74 per cent, while UNITA got 34.1 per cent.

An ad hoc Commission of the Security Council was sent to Angola from 11 to 14 October to support implementation of the Peace Accords, after reports reached the Council that one of the parties to the Accords was contesting the validity of the elections. During its meetings with, among others, the Angolan and UNITA Presidents, South Africa's Foreign Minister, the Special Representative and officials of the National Electoral Council, the Commission underscored the importance of full implementation of the Accords, including upholding the integrity of the electoral process. It noted with grave concern the increasing violence and level of tension, and appealed to the people of Angola and all parties to safeguard the peace they had achieved after years of devastating war.

On 31 October, heavy fighting broke out in many parts of the country between government and UNITA forces. A cease-fire was achieved on 2 November, but sporadic fighting continued. The Security Council, on 22 December, urged both parties to resume the direct talks begun in the southern Angolan town of Namibe on 26 November and to demonstrate their commitment with regard to confinement of troops, collection of weapons, demobilization, formation of the national armed

UNAVEM II

Communication and report of the Secretary-General (February/March). By a 6 February 1992 letter to the President of the Security Council,[2] the Secretary-General indicated that plans were being drawn up, in response to a request from the Government of Angola, for United Nations technical assistance to help prepare for and conduct presidential and legislative elections scheduled for September 1992, and for United Nations observers to follow the electoral procedure until its completion. An agreement on technical assistance had been signed with the Government and, with regard to observation of the elections, the Secretary-General announced that he would soon present to the Council the necessary operational plan and recommend that the Council authorize the addition of that function to the mandate already entrusted to him in connection with implementation of the Peace Accords.

The Secretary-General announced his intention to appoint Margaret Joan Anstee, Director-General of the United Nations Office at Vienna, as his Special Representative for Angola and Chief of UNAVEM II, established in May 1991.[3] As stated in a 7 February 1992 letter of the President,[4] the Security Council members welcomed Ms. Anstee's appointment.

In a March report,[5] the Secretary-General outlined the terms of reference and an operational plan for UNAVEM II, whose mandate was to verify the impartiality of the Angolan electoral authorities in all aspects and stages of the electoral process; the complete freedom of organization, movement, assembly and expression for all political parties and forces, as well as individuals and groups, without hindrance or intimidation; that all political parties and forces had access to State radio and television; that the electoral rolls were properly drawn; and that qualified voters were not denied registration and the right to vote. Other activities to be monitored included registration of voters, the organization of the poll, the electoral campaign, the poll itself and the counting, computing and announcement of the results.

Much had been achieved in implementing the peace process, the Secretary-General said, but the timetable for putting the Accords into effect could not be delayed further. All the parties and forces had to join in making renewed commitments until the goal of free and fair elections in September 1992 was achieved.

To ensure the success of the electoral process, the Secretary-General called for the establishment of a unified civilian police force, as well as the formation of joint military police units within the new national army, an extension of the Government's administration and restoration of security throughout the country. An early national consensus on the essential elements for organizing the elections was necessary, such as agreement on the polling date, establishment of a workable national electoral council, minimum voting age and a comprehensive budget allocated by the Government.

The Secretary-General recommended an enlargement of UNAVEM's mandate, strength and composition; the efforts to be undertaken, above all by the Angolan people themselves, in organizing their first free and fair elections—an essential precondition for peace and political stability—deserved the support not only of the United Nations, but of all those concerned with the future of Angola.

Details of the staffing requirements, as well as cost estimates for the expansion of UNAVEM II from 15 March to 31 October 1992, were provided in an addendum to the report.

SECURITY COUNCIL ACTION (March)

The Security Council met on 24 March to consider the Secretary-General's report. Angola and Portugal were invited to participate in the discussion in accordance with the Charter and rule 37 of the Council's provisional rules of procedure.[a]

On the same date, the Council adopted **resolution 747(1992)** unanimously.

The Security Council,

Recalling its resolution 696(1991) of 30 May 1991 which decided to entrust a new mandate to the United Nations Angola Verification Mission (UNAVEM II) as proposed by the Secretary-General in line with the "Acordos de Paz para Angola",

Welcoming the continuing efforts of the Secretary-General to implement fully the mandate entrusted to UNAVEM II,

Noting with satisfaction the efforts made so far by the Government of the People's Republic of Angola and the National Union for the Total Independence of Angola to maintain the cease-fire and *expressing concern* over the delays and gaps in the completion of some major tasks arising from the "Acordos de Paz",

Stressing again the importance it attaches to the fulfilment by the parties in good faith of all obligations contained in the "Acordos de Paz",

Welcoming the appointment by the Secretary-General of a Special Representative for Angola who will be in charge of all current and projected activities of the United Nations in connection with the "Acordos de Paz" and will also be the Chief of UNAVEM II,

Taking into account the further report of the Secretary-General dated 31 October 1991,

Having considered the report of the Secretary-General dated 3 March 1992 and the addendum dated 20 March 1992,

1. *Approves* the report of the Secretary-General dated 3 March 1992 and the recommendations contained therein concerning the operational plan for United Nations observation of the elections and the enlargement of UNAVEM II;

2. *Calls upon* the Angolan parties to cooperate fully with the Special Representative of the Secretary-General and with UNAVEM II, including in the discharge of its expanded mandate;

3. *Underlines* the necessity recalled in paragraph 18 of the report of the Secretary-General that the United Nations electoral mission will have the explicit agreement of the two parties to the "Acordos de Paz";

4. *Decides* to enlarge the mandate of UNAVEM II to include the mission provided for in paragraph 22 of the report of the Secretary-General for the remainder of its existing mandate period;

5. *Urges* the Angolan parties to comply scrupulously with the provisions of the "Acordos de Paz" and with the agreed deadlines; and to this end, to proceed without delay with the demobilization of their troops, formation of a unified national armed force, effective operation of joint police monitoring units, extension of the central administration and other major tasks;

6. *Calls upon* the Angolan authorities and parties to finalize political, legal, organizational and budgetary preparations for free and fair multi-party elections to be held in September 1992 and to make available as soon as possible all available resources for the electoral process;

7. *Encourages* all States to contribute voluntarily and requests the United Nations programmes and specialized agencies to provide the assistance and support necessary to prepare for free and fair multi-party elections in Angola;

8. *Urges* the parties to establish as soon as possible a precise timetable for the electoral process in Angola so that elections can take place at the date fixed and requests the Secretary-General to extend his cooperation to this end;

9. *Requests* the Secretary-General to keep the Security Council informed of developments and to submit a further report to the Council within three months of the adoption of this resolution.

Security Council resolution 747(1992)
24 March 1992   Meeting 3062   Adopted unanimously

Draft prepared in consultations among Council members (S/23743), orally revised.

Communication and report of the Secretary-General (May and June). By a 14 May letter to the Security Council President,[6] the Secretary-General reported that his Special Representative had informed him that noticeable progress had been made with regard to police monitoring, as foreseen in the Peace Accords. Three joint (government and UNITA) police monitoring groups had been established in each of 18 Angolan provinces.

[a]Rule 37 of the Council's provisional rules of procedure states: "Any Member of the United Nations which is not a member of the Security Council may be invited, as the result of a decision of the Security Council, to participate, without vote, in the discussion of any question brought before the Security Council when the Security Council considers that the interests of that Member are specially affected, or when a Member brings a matter to the attention of the Security Council in accordance with Article 35(1) of the Charter."

The Special Representative held it necessary to expand UNAVEM II's police strength in each province from four police officers to six; she also believed it to be important to expand the tasks assigned to the UNAVEM II police contingent and to include in the Mission's electoral tasks the monitoring of rallies during the political campaign and observation of the registration process and polling stations at the time of the elections. Accordingly, the Secretary-General recommended an increase in the police strength of UNAVEM II from 90 to 126 officers, at a cost of $1.175 million. The Council members expressed agreement with the recommendation, as stated in a 20 May letter of the President.[7]

In accordance with the 24 March Council resolution, the Secretary-General submitted in June a further report on UNAVEM II.[8] He observed that a great deal had been achieved in implementing the peace process, but much needed to be done, mainly by the Government and UNITA, if the goal of free and fair multiparty elections was to be achieved by the end of September. The Secretary-General remarked that the parties were being actively assisted by the three observers— Portugal, the Russian Federation and the United States—as well as by the international community and UNAVEM II.

In recent weeks, the attention of the Angolan people and their leaders had increasingly turned towards the election process and away from the major unfinished tasks of the Peace Accords, namely, the confinement of troops and weapons, demobilization, and the formation of new armed forces and police. The Secretary-General stressed that the Government and UNITA must make progress on those vital tasks if the peace process was to succeed and endure; they must work together to reduce and bring under control the current brinkmanship, since the political and security atmosphere throughout the country remained tense and could derail the peace process if not contained. It was the Angolan parties' responsibility to organize and supervise the Accords, while the United Nations was only to observe and verify the peace process and the elections.

SECURITY COUNCIL ACTION (July)

In connection with the Council's consideration of the Secretary-General's report and following consultations with its members, the President, on behalf of the Council, made the following statement on 7 July:[9]

Meeting number. SC 3092.

"The Security Council has considered carefully the report of the Secretary-General on the United Nations Angola Verification Mission (UNAVEM II), and notes the efforts of the Angolan parties to implement commitments agreed to in the "Acordos de Paz para Angola". It commends the efforts of the Angolans to move their country towards free and fair multi-party elections on 29 and 30 September 1992 in accordance with the established timetable. There is no viable alternative to this. The Security Council calls on all interested parties to cooperate fully with the electoral process to ensure that elections are free and fair.

"The Council re-emphasizes the observation of the Secretary-General in his report that Angola being a sovereign and independent country, the organization and supervision of all tasks under the Peace Accords is the responsibility of the Angolan parties themselves. Nevertheless, the Council, which has mandated United Nations observation and verification of the peace process, at the request of the Angolan parties, remains seriously concerned at some constraints holding back the process at the moment.

"The maintenance of peace since May 1991, and the commitment by all parties to the electoral process, are encouraging. Nevertheless, the Council reaffirms the importance it attaches to the fulfilment by the parties in good faith of all obligations contained in the "Acordos de Paz para Angola". In this connection, it strongly appeals to the Government and UNITA to overcome rapidly the delays and inadequacies described in the report, and increase the momentum of progress on the issues of confinement of troops and weapons, demobilization and the formation of the new armed forces and police.

"The Council also expresses its concern at the political and security situation in Angola, which requires the greatest restraint. Violent incidents, mutual accusations and hostile propaganda should be terminated and give way to tolerance, cooperation and reconciliation. It is imperative to agree, without delay, on a brief and clear Code of Electoral Conduct and to ensure that everybody is allowed freedom of movement and speech and the ability to register to vote without fear in all areas of the country. The Council calls on the Government and all parties to work closely with the Special Representative and all United Nations specialized agencies engaged in the electoral process to ensure that voter registration is conducted in accordance with established procedures and completed in a timely manner.

"The Security Council calls on both parties to devote all available resources to preparations for the elections in order that their commitment to elections on 29 and 30 September 1992 may be met and welcomes with appreciation commitments by donor countries to provide all support for all vital tasks relating to the final three months of the peace process. Since the logistical difficulties are major constraints on the process, the Council strongly appeals to the Member States concerned to provide the promised assistance expeditiously and urges Member States as well as the United Nations agencies to display flexibility and pragmatism in this cooperation to ensure that a successful conclusion of the Angolan operation leads to stability and prosperity in Angola.

"The Security Council calls on all parties to take all necessary measures to ensure the security and safety of UNAVEM staff and property.

"The Security Council will continue to keep the situation in Angola under close review and looks forward to a further report by the Secretary-General at the beginning of the electoral campaign."

Report of the Secretary-General (September).
In a September report,[10] the Secretary-General said the Angolan people must protect their achievements, such as maintaining the cease-fire and registering the majority of the adult population for the elections, by making determined efforts to demobilize the remaining government and UNITA troops, collect and centralize storage of weapons, form the new Angolan armed forces, disband the armies belonging to the parties before the voting and ensure correct operation of the police. If government and UNITA leaders maintained without reservation their determination to make the peace process succeed and prevent their country from returning to violence, anarchy and poverty, they could lay the groundwork for a prosperous democratic future.

The Secretary-General considered it essential that all political parties pledge to respect the results of the elections. He appealed to the Government and UNITA to ensure that their representatives and the media under their control did not present inaccurate, distorted or inflammatory reports during the upcoming weeks, and appealed to the Angolan and UNITA Presidents to continue honouring their commitments under the Peace Accords.

SECURITY COUNCIL ACTION (September)

On 18 September, following consultations on the Secretary-General's report, the President of the Security Council made the following statement on behalf of the Council members:[11]

Meeting number. SC 3115.

"The Security Council has noted with appreciation the further report of the Secretary-General on the United Nations Angola Verification Mission (UNAVEM II), which it has studied carefully.

"It reaffirms the importance it attaches to the full implementation of the 'Acordos de Paz para Angola', culminating in free and fair multiparty elections on 29 and 30 September 1992. It congratulates the Angolans on their success in maintaining the cease-fire and in registering the great majority of the population to vote in the elections. It is convinced of the irreversibility of this process.

"At the same time, the Council calls on the Angolan parties to take urgent and determined steps to complete certain essential measures. These include the demobilization of the remaining government and UNITA troops, the collection and centralized storage of weapons, and the rapid completion of the formation of the new National Angolan Armed Forces. It is also essential that the police should operate as a neutral, national force.

"The Council is also concerned at the recent deterioration of the political and security situation in Angola. It endorses the Secretary-General's appeal to President dos Santos and Dr. Savimbi to exercise leadership at this critical juncture and to ensure that their followers act with restraint and tolerance. The Council is encouraged by the reports of positive decisions reached by the two leaders at their meeting on 7 September 1992 and urges them to implement these without delay. Of particular importance is their reported agreement in principle to the formation of a government of national reconciliation after the elections.

"The Council calls upon the Angolan electoral authorities to ensure that all registered persons are given the opportunity to exercise their vote and to extend polling hours on the second day, if this should prove necessary. The Council also underlines the importance of adequate logistical planning and support and urges the donor community to move speedily to provide the remaining requirements identified in the Secretary-General's report.

"The Council is concerned that doubts have recently been expressed in Angola about UNAVEM's effectiveness and impartiality and welcomes the decision of the Secretary-General as expressed in paragraph 9 of his report to investigate thoroughly all matters raised in this regard. It expresses strong support for the Secretary-General and his Special Representative and commends UNAVEM II personnel who are tackling their challenging tasks with courage, impartiality and dedication. It urges the Angolan parties to continue to cooperate closely with the United Nations and to take all necessary steps to ensure the security of United Nations personnel and property.

"The Council takes note of a reported agreement between the Government and UNITA that the United Nations should be asked to extend UNAVEM's presence in Angola during the period of transition after the elections. It will be prepared to consider such a request if it is based on wide support in Angola and if it proposes for UNAVEM a mandate which is clearly defined in scope and time.

"The Security Council will continue to keep the situation in Angola under close review and looks forward to a further report by the Secretary-General after the elections."

Further developments (September/October).
By a 22 September letter to the Secretary-General,[12] Angola's Minister of External Relations requested an extension of UNAVEM II presence until 31 December 1992, in view of the possibility of a second round of voting in the presidential elections due to the large number of candidates.

The Secretary-General, on 29 October,[13] recommended extension of UNAVEM II for an interim period until 30 November. He restated that difficulties had arisen since the September elections, including the lack of agreement between the two parties to the Peace Accords on arrangements for the holding of a second round of the presidential elections. Both parties, however, had declared their wish that UNAVEM II play a role in organizing and verifying that round.

SECURITY COUNCIL ACTION (October)

On 6 October, following an oral report by the Secretary-General on UNAVEM II and after consultations with the Security Council members, the President, on behalf of the Council, made the following statement:[14]

Meeting number. SC 3120.

"The Security Council has followed closely the electoral process which took place in Angola on 29 and 30 September 1992 in accordance with resolution 696(1991), which it adopted on 30 May 1991 following the peace agreements. The Council is gratified that the presidential and parliamentary elections were held throughout the country in a calm atmosphere and with the participation of a large number of voters. It also wishes to express once again its full support for the Special Representative of the Secretary-General and its gratitude for the outstanding efforts that she has made, together with all the personnel of the United Nations Angola Verification Mission (UNAVEM II), to ensure the implementation of that resolution and in particular the smooth conduct of the electoral process.

"The Council expresses its concern at the reports it has received, according to which one of the parties to the peace agreements is contesting the validity of the elections. It is also concerned that certain Generals belonging to the same party have announced their intention of withdrawing from the new Angolan Armed Forces.

"The Council calls upon all the parties to respect the obligations they have assumed within the framework of the peace agreements, and in particular the obligation to respect the final election results. Any challenge must be settled through the mechanisms established for that purpose.

"The Security Council has decided to send to Angola as quickly as possible an ad hoc commission, composed of members of the Council, to support the implementation of the peace agreements, in close cooperation with the Special Representative of the Secretary-General. The membership of this Commission will be established in the near future following consultations among the members of the Council."

On 8 October,[15] the President announced that during consultations the Council members had agreed that the ad hoc Commission should comprise Cape Verde, Morocco, the Russian Federation and the United States.

On 19 October, the President, on behalf of the Council members, issued a statement to the media:[16]

"The members of the Security Council heard on 19 October an oral report of the members of the ad hoc Commission of the Council which was dispatched to Angola from 11 to 14 October 1992.

"They expressed gratitude to the members of this Commission and welcomed its contribution to reducing the tension in Angola and to finding a solution to the difficulties that arose after the elections of 29 and 30 September 1992.

"The members of the Security Council once again called upon the parties to abide scrupulously by all the commitments entered into within the framework of the peace agreements, in particular with regard to the demobilization of their troops and formation of the United Armed Forces, and to refrain from any action that could increase the tension.

"The members of the Security Council noted with satisfaction that in her public announcement of 17 October 1992 the Special Representative of the Secretary-General for Angola certified that, with all deficiencies taken into account, the elections held on 29 and 30 September 1992 can be considered to have been generally free and fair.

"They also noted with satisfaction that the leaders of the two parties to the peace agreements agreed to start a dialogue with a view to the completion of the presidential elections.

"The members of the Security Council look forward to the recommendations of the Secretary-General on the contribution of the United Nations to ensuring the completion of the presidential elections. They are ready to act without delay on the basis of these recommendations.

On 27 October, the President, on behalf of the Council, made the following statement:[17]

Meeting number. SC 3126.

"The Security Council has taken note of the letter dated 27 October 1992 from the Secretary-General addressed to the President of the Council concerning the situation in Angola. It expresses its serious concern at the deterioration of the political situation and the rising tension in that country.

"It once again calls on the parties to the Peace Accords to respect all the commitments undertaken in accordance with these accords, in particular with regard to the confinement of their troops and weapons, demobilization and the formation of the unified national Armed Force. It also calls on the parties to refrain from any act that might heighten tension, impair the conduct of the electoral process and threaten the territorial integrity of Angola.

"The Security Council calls on UNITA and the other parties in the electoral process in Angola to respect the results of the elections held on 29 and 30 September 1992, which the Special Representative of the Secretary-General certified as generally free and fair. It urges the leaders of two parties to the Peace Accords to engage in a dialogue without delay so as to enable the second round of the presidential elections to be held. The Security Council will hold responsible any party which refuses to take part in such a dialogue, thereby jeopardizing the entire process.

"The Security Council strongly condemns the attacks and baseless accusations made by Vorgan radio of UNITA against the Special Representative of the Secretary-General and the United Nations Angola Verification Mission (UNAVEM II). It calls for the immediate cessation of these attacks and accusations, and reiterates its full support for the Special Representative and for UNAVEM II.

"The Security Council reiterates its readiness to act without delay on the basis of recommendations that the Secretary-General might make concerning the contribution of the United Nations to the completion of the electoral process."

On 30 October, the Council met to consider the Secretary-General's 29 October letter requesting extension of UNAVEM II until 30 November.[13] With the consent of the Council, the President invited Angola, Brazil, Portugal and South Africa to participate in the discussion without the right to vote, in accordance with rule 37 of the Council's provisional rules of procedure.[a]

On the same date, the Council adopted **resolution 785(1992)** unanimously.

The Security Council,

Recalling its resolutions 696(1991) of 30 May 1991 and 747(1992) of 24 March 1992,

Recalling also the statement made on its behalf by the President of the Security Council on 27 October 1992,

Taking note of the letter of the Secretary-General dated 29 October 1992, in which he recommends an extension of the existing mandate of the United Nations Angola Verification Mission (UNAVEM II) for an interim period,

Deeply concerned at the deterioration of the political situation and the rising tension in Angola,

Deeply concerned also at the reports of the recent resumption of hostilities by UNITA in Luanda and Huambo,

Affirming that any party which fails to abide by all the commitments entered into under the ''Acordos de Paz para Angola'' will be rejected by the international community, and that the results of use of force will not be accepted,

1. *Approves* the recommendation of the Secretary-General to extend the existing mandate of UNAVEM II for an interim period, until 30 November 1992;

2. *Requests* the Secretary-General to submit to it by that date a detailed report on the situation in Angola together with long-term recommendations, accompanied by the financial implications thereof, on the mandate and strength of UNAVEM II;

3. *Strongly condemns* any such resumption of hostilities and *urgently demands* that such acts cease forthwith;

4. *Calls on* all States to refrain from any action which directly or indirectly could jeopardize the implementation of the ''Acordos de Paz'' and increase the tension in the country;

5. *Reiterates* its full support for the Special Representative of the Secretary-General and UNAVEM II, and its strong condemnation of the attacks and baseless accusations made by UNITA's radio station, Vorgan, against the Special Representative of the Secretary-General and UNAVEM II;

6. *Supports* the statement by the Special Representative of the Secretary-General certifying that the elections held on 29 and 30 September 1992 were generally free and fair and *calls upon* UNITA and the other parties to the electoral process in Angola to respect the results of the elections;

7. *Calls upon* the parties to the ''Acordos de Paz'' to abide by all the commitments entered into under the Accords, in particular with regard to the confinement of their troops and collection of their weapons, demobilization and the formation of the unified national armed force, and to refrain from any act that might heighten tension, jeopardize the continued conduct of the electoral process and threaten the territorial integrity of Angola;

8. *Urges* the leaders of the two parties to engage in a dialogue without delay so as to enable the second round of the presidential elections to be held promptly;

9. *Reaffirms* that it will hold responsible any party which refuses to take part in such a dialogue, thereby jeopardizing the entire process, and *reiterates* its readiness to consider all appropriate measures under the Charter of the United Nations to secure implementation of the ''Acordos de Paz'';

10. *Decides* to remain seized of the question.

Security Council resolution 785(1992)

30 October 1992   Meeting 3130   Adopted unanimously

Draft prepared in consultations among Council members (S/24738), orally revised.

Speaking before the Council, Angola expressed concern for the irresponsible attitude of UNITA in refusing to accept the results of the elections, an attitude that clearly violated the Peace Accords, demonstrated a lack of respect for the principles of democracy and perpetuated the suffering of the Angolan people. Strong measures were needed to force UNITA to accept the results and implement the Accords. Angola also expressed concern about information that South African forces were fighting alongside UNITA; if proved as a fact, that would have dangerous implications for the entire region.

South Africa categorically refuted the allegations and stated that it would not support any party that opted for a violent solution or perpetrated aggression in Angola. Military action there was not an option, and it had done its best to bring that home to the Angolan leaders; a democratic process was absolutely essential to solve the problems in Angola.

Report of the Secretary-General (November). In November,[18] the Secretary-General reported that the situation in Angola had deteriorated and a successful completion of the peace process and the establishment of multiparty democracy seemed farther off than at any time since the signing of the Peace Accords in May 1991. The cease-fire of 2 November 1992 was barely holding and both sides had undertaken preparations for renewed war. The situation was a cruel set-back for the Angolan people and a major disappointment for the international community. One of the root causes was the incomplete fulfilment of key provisions of the Accords, foremost among them the less than effective demobilization and storage of weapons, the delay in creating unified armed forces, the failure to re-establish effective central administration in many parts of the country and the dilatoriness in setting up a neutral police force.

Both sides, however, had also reiterated their commitment to peace and dialogue and had expressed the wish for assistance from the international community in that regard. Both had agreed on the need for an enlarged UNAVEM presence in order to create conditions in which a second round of presidential elections could take place and the peace process could be successfully concluded.

The Secretary-General stated that unless both sides could convince him of their genuine adherence to and fulfilment of the Peace Accords, he would not be prepared to recommend an enlargement of UNAVEM's mandate and strength. It would be necessary for the parties to agree on a clear timetable and on formal evaluation at regular intervals of the fulfilment of their commitments, and there had to be evidence of a genuine commitment to national reconciliation, which could not be achieved without the full participation of UNITA, whose legitimate concerns had to be addressed.

In view of the fact that it was not possible to assess at the time whether his own efforts and those of Member States would succeed in persuading the Government and UNITA to reactivate the peace process, the Secretary-General said he was not in a position to make long-term recommendations on the mandate and strength of UNAVEM II, as the Council had requested in its October resolution. He recommended another extension within the existing mandate, until 31 January 1993, by which time he would submit a further report with recommendations on the future United Nations involvement in the Angolan peace process. The cost of the two-month extension was estimated at some $12.4 million, to be borne by Member States.

Meanwhile, the Secretary-General proposed urgent steps to restore the strength of UNAVEM II to its authorized levels in order to demonstrate the international community's continuing commitment to the peace process and to improve the security of UNAVEM's personnel in the field, as well as to strengthen their ability to consolidate the cease-fire.

SECURITY COUNCIL ACTION (November)

On 30 November, the Security Council adopted **resolution 793(1992)** unanimously.

The Security Council,

Recalling its resolutions 696(1991) of 30 May 1991, 747(1992) of 24 March 1992 and 785(1992) of 30 October 1992,

Taking note of the further report of the Secretary-General of 25 November 1992,

Deeply concerned by deterioration in the political and military situation in Angola and especially by the troop movements which have taken place and by the hostilities which occurred on 31 October and 1 November 1992,

Welcoming and supporting the efforts of the Secretary-General and his Special Representative aimed at resolving the present crisis,

Disturbed by the continuing non-implementation of major aspects of the "Acordos de Paz para Angola",

Reiterating its support for the statement by the Special Representative of the Secretary-General that the elections held on 29 and 30 September 1992 were generally free and fair and *taking note* of the acceptance by UNITA of the results of the elections,

Noting the intention of the Secretary-General to continue, in this as in other peace-keeping operations, to monitor expenditures carefully during this period of increasing demands on peace-keeping resources,

1. *Approves* the recommendation of the Secretary-General to extend the existing mandate of UNAVEM II for a further period of two months until 31 January 1993;

2. *Appeals* to the troop- and police-contributing States to lend cooperation to UNAVEM II in order to restore as soon as possible its mandated strength;

3. *Welcomes* the joint declaration of the Government of Angola and UNITA made in Namibe on 26 November 1992 and *urges* them to take immediate and effective actions in accordance with the declaration;

4. *Demands* that the two parties scrupulously observe the cease-fire, immediately stop all military confrontations, and in particular offensive troop movements, and create all the conditions necessary for the completion of the peace process;

5. *Urges* the two parties to demonstrate their adherence to, and fulfilment without exception of, the "Acordos de Paz" in particular with regard to the confinement of their troops and collection of their weapons, demobilization and the formation of the unified national armed force and to refrain from any action which might heighten tension or jeopardize the return to normalcy;

6. *Strongly appeals* to the two parties to engage in a continuous and meaningful dialogue aimed at national reconciliation and at the participation of all parties in the democratic process and to agree on a clear timetable for the fulfilment of their commitments in accordance with the "Acordos de Paz";

7. *Reaffirms* that it will hold responsible any party which refuses to take part in such a dialogue, thereby jeopardizing the entire process, and *reiterates* its readiness to consider all appropriate measures under the Charter of the United Nations to secure implementation of the "Acordos de Paz";

8. *Calls on* all States to refrain from any action which directly or indirectly could jeopardize the implementation of the "Acordos de Paz" and increase the tension in the country;

9. *Requests* the Secretary-General to submit to it by 31 January 1993 a further report on the situation in Angola together with his longer-term recommendations for the further role of the United Nations in the peace process, which should be clearly defined in scope and time and based on a wide degree of support in Angola;

10. *Decides* to remain seized of the question.

Security Council resolution 793(1992)

30 November 1992   Meeting 3144   Adopted unanimously

Draft prepared in consultations among Council members (S/24863), orally revised.

Communication of the Secretary-General (December). By a letter of 18 December,[19] the Secretary-General informed the Council about the situation in Angola following adoption of the 30 November resolution. Since then, he reported, there had been little or no progress in putting the peace process back on track and, unless there was rapid improvement, it was difficult to believe that by the end of January 1993 conditions would exist for recommending an enlarged United Nations presence, which both sides to the conflict requested.

The progress begun on 26 November—when senior representatives of both sides met under UNAVEM auspices at Namibe, southern Angola—received an almost immediate set-back when, on 29 November, UNITA forces took the northern cities of Uige and Negage, the latter being the site of an important airbase. A United Nations police observer died in the crossfire. Since then, all attempts to restore a dialogue had failed. UNITA forces were largely, but not entirely, withdrawn from Uige and Negage on 4 December, after strenuous efforts by UNAVEM II. However, they continued to occupy up to two thirds of the municipalities in Angola, which the government administration had had to leave or from which it had been expelled. There was disturbing evidence that both sides were continuing preparations for a resumption of war on a large scale, a possibility of which the Government's public statements spoke openly.

On the political front, the formation of a Government of National Unity, headed by Marcolino Moco, formerly Secretary-General of the governing party, was announced on 2 December. Of the 27 posts of ministers and state secretaries which made up the new Government, the post of Minister of Cultural Affairs was offered to UNITA, together with four vice-ministerial posts in defence, agriculture, public works and social assistance. One ministerial post and six lesser positions were offered to other parties which had won seats in the new Assembly.

At a meeting of the Permanent Committee of its Political Commission (8 and 9 December), UNITA decided to take up its seats in the Assembly and nominate persons to the posts offered by the Government. It also decided to return its Generals to the structures of the new Angolan Armed Forces, from which they had withdrawn shortly after the September elections.

The hopes that a political dialogue could be resumed and agreement reached on a programme of action to complete implementation of the Peace Accords were not fulfilled, however. Recriminations continued between the two sides on a variety of issues: the situation at Uige and Negage; UNITA's refusal to withdraw its troops and its resistance to restoring government administration in municipalities which it had seized since the elections; the release of persons held by each side, in particular UNITA personalities living "under government protection" at Luanda; the exchange of bodies of those killed in recent fighting; and mutual accusations of preparations for war.

A further obstacle to progress was UNITA's legitimate concern about the security of its members at Luanda and other government-controlled parts of the country; that was a matter for which both sides would like the United Nations to assume responsibility. While it would be difficult for the United Nations to do so directly, a number of ideas were offered to both sides and, if certain conditions were fulfilled, the Secretary-General would be ready to seek the Council's authority to make some United Nations military personnel available, on a temporary basis, to facilitate the return to Luanda of Dr. Savimbi and the UNITA members of the new Government and of the elected Assembly. His Special Representative had been instructed to try to engage the two sides in discussions of practical arrangements acceptable to both.

Both sides had recently conveyed to the Special Representative their ideas about the role they would like the United Nations to play in the future. Both agreed in principle on the need to enlarge UNAVEM II's mandate and increase its strength on the ground, including the provision of armed troops. However, there were differences on the extent to which UNAVEM II should exercise good offices or mediatory function and to which it should be involved in the organization and conduct of the second round of presidential elections.

The Secretary-General said he was ready to recommend a larger mandate and strength for UNAVEM II; however, he could do that only if both sides demonstrated their continuing commitment to the Peace Accords by agreeing on a realistic plan of action to get the implementation process back on track.

In order to make a determined effort to move forward, the Secretary-General suggested to President dos Santos and Dr. Savimbi a meeting under his auspices at Geneva during the last week of December. While President dos Santos stated his willingness to meet Dr. Savimbi at Luanda, the latter expressed readiness to attend a meeting at Geneva as proposed. The Secretary-General urged President dos Santos to take into account the critical situation in the country and the danger that, unless both sides showed willingness and ability to work together, the international community would no longer feel justified in committing scarce resources to a continuation of the United Nations operation in Angola on its current scale.

In bringing the situation to the Council's attention, the Secretary-General said he would value its support, perhaps in the form of an appeal to both leaders to accept the invitation to a joint meeting at Geneva or another United Nations location, such as Addis Ababa, Ethiopia.

SECURITY COUNCIL ACTION (December)

The Security Council met on 22 December to consider the Secretary-General's letter and in accordance with the understanding reached in prior consultations. The President invited Angola to participate in the discussion without the right to vote, under rule 37 of the Council's provisional rules of procedure.[a]

Following consultations among Council members, the President made a statement on behalf of the Council:[20]

Meeting number. SC 3152.

"The Security Council has taken note of the letter dated 18 December 1992 from the Secretary-General addressed to the President of the Council concerning the situation in Angola. It expresses serious concern at the lack of progress in implementing the 'Acordos de Paz para Angola' and at the continuation of the dangerous political and security situation in the country.

"The Security Council reiterates its strong appeal to the two parties to engage in a continuous and meaningful dialogue aimed at national reconciliation and at the participation of all parties in the democratic process, and to agree on a clear timetable and programme of action to complete the implementation of the 'Acordos de Paz'. The Security Council urges that the military forces of the União Nacional para a Independência Total de Angola (UNITA) be immediately withdrawn from Uige and Negage and that the government administration be fully restored there and that the two parties resume the direct talks started in Namibe on 26 November 1992. It again urges both parties to demonstrate their commitment to the 'Acordos de Paz', in particular with regard to confinement of their troops and collection of their weapons, demobilization, formation of the national armed forces and restoration of the central administration throughout the country.

"The Security Council also considers it essential that both parties agree without delay on security and other arrangements which would allow all ministers and other high-ranking officials to occupy the posts which have been offered by the Government and for all deputies to assume their functions in the National Assembly.

"The Security Council also considers it imperative that both parties agree on a realistic plan of action for full implementation of the 'Acordos de Paz', and to facilitate a continuing United Nations presence in Angola. It underlines the need for the two sides to produce early evidence of their willingness and ability to work together to implement the 'Acordos de Paz', so that the international community would feel encouraged to continue to commit its scarce resources to the continuation of the United Nations operation in Angola on its present scale.

"The Security Council fully supports the action of the Secretary-General aimed at resolving the present crisis and appeals to President dos Santos and Dr. Savimbi to accept the Secretary-General's invitation to attend, under his auspices, a joint meeting at an agreed location, to confirm that real progress has been made in the reactivation of the Bicesse Accords with a view to their full implementation and that agreement has been reached on a continuing United Nations presence in Angola."

Financing of UNAVEM II

Report of the Secretary-General (June). In June 1992,[21] the Secretary-General submitted a report on the financing of UNAVEM II, which included the operational plan for United Nations observations of the elections and the enlargement of UNAVEM II; the status of assessed and voluntary contributions; and revised cost estimates resulting from the enlarged mandate.

The Secretary-General recommended additional appropriations of $19,428,680 gross ($18,351,500 net) for the operation of UNAVEM II from 1 January to 31 October 1992, bringing the total appropriation for the period to $62,305,400 gross ($60,413,500 net). Assessed contributions due from Member States as at 31 May 1992 amounted to $18,236,300, of which $741,700 was for UNAVEM and $17,494,600 for UNAVEM II.

ACABQ recommendations. In a July 1992 report,[22] the Advisory Committee on Administrative and Budgetary Questions (ACABQ) said it had carefully examined the cost estimates of UNAVEM II and supplementary information provided to it. The Secretary-General's report was difficult to analyse as it did not contain up-to-date information on budget performance, which would have been useful in determining future requirements. ACABQ believed that initial appropriations for the period 1 January to 31 October 1992 should have been compared with the requirements of the original mandate on the basis of actual expenditure, substantiating projected savings or additional requirements and justifying any change with supplementary information. It put forward a number of recommendations for economies to be made and finally recommended that the General Assembly appropriate, over the initial appropriation of $42.9 million gross ($42 million net), an additional $15 million gross ($14 million net) for the period 1 January to 31 October 1992, including $2.9 million authorized under a 1991 Assembly resolution on unforeseen and extraordinary expenses.[23] On that basis, total resources for UNAVEM II for the period ending 31 October 1992 would be $57.9 million gross ($56 million net). Additional requirements could be reported to the Assembly at its 1992 regular session or, if necessary, the Secretary-General could avail himself of the commitment authority (with the prior concurrence of ACABQ) granted under a 1991 Assembly resolution on financing UNAVEM II.[24]

GENERAL ASSEMBLY ACTION (July)

On 31 July 1992, on the recommendation of the Fifth Committee, the General Assembly adopted **resolution 46/195 B** without vote.

Financing of the United Nations Angola Verification Mission II

The General Assembly,

Having considered the note by the Secretary-General on the financing of the United Nations Angola Verification Mission and the related report of the Advisory Committee on Administrative and Budgetary Questions,

Bearing in mind Security Council resolution 626(1988) of 20 December 1988, by which the Council established the United Nations Angola Verification Mission, Council resolution 696(1991) of 30 May 1991, by which the Council decided to entrust a new mandate to the United Nations Angola Verification Mission (thenceforth called the United Nations Angola Verification Mission II) and Council resolution 747(1992) of 24 March 1992, by which the Council decided to enlarge the mandate to include an Electoral Division for the purpose of observing and verifying the Angolan electoral process for the remainder of the existing mandate period, that is, until 31 October 1992,

Reaffirming that the costs of the Verification Mission are expenses of the Organization to be borne by Member States in accordance with Article 17, paragraph 2, of the Charter of the United Nations,

Recalling its previous decisions regarding the fact that, in order to meet the expenditures caused by the Verification Mission, a different procedure is required from the one applied to meet expenditures of the regular budget of the United Nations,

Taking into account the fact that the economically more developed countries are in a position to make relatively larger contributions and that the economically less developed countries have a relatively limited capacity to contribute towards such an operation,

Bearing in mind the special responsibilities of the States permanent members of the Security Council, as indicated in General Assembly resolution 1874(S-IV) of 27 June 1963, in the financing of such operations,

Mindful of the fact that it is essential to provide the Verification Mission with the necessary financial resources to enable it to fulfil its responsibilities under the relevant resolutions of the Security Council,

1. *Endorses* the observations and recommendations contained in the report of the Advisory Committee on Administrative and Budgetary Questions;

2. *Urges* all Member States to make every possible effort to ensure payment of their assessed contributions to the United Nations Angola Verification Mission II in full and on time;

3. *Decides* to appropriate to the Special Account for the Verification Mission an additional amount of 15 million United States dollars gross (14 million dollars net), inclusive of the amount of 2.9 million dollars authorized with the concurrence of the Advisory Committee, under the terms of General Assembly resolution 46/187 of 20 December 1991, for the operation of the Verification Mission for the period from 1 January to 31 October 1992;

4. *Decides also*, as an ad hoc arrangement, to apportion the amounts indicated in paragraph 3 above among Member States in accordance with the composition of the groups set out in paragraphs 3 and 4 of General Assembly resolution 43/232 of 1 March 1989, as adjusted by the Assembly in its resolutions 44/192 B of 21 December 1989, 45/269 of 27 August 1991 and 46/195 A of 20 December 1991, and taking into account the scale of assessments for the years 1992, 1993 and 1994;

5. *Decides further* that, in accordance with the provisions of its resolution 973(X) of 15 December 1955, there shall be set off against the apportionment among Member States, as provided for in paragraph 4 above, their respective share in the Tax Equalization Fund of the estimated staff assessment income of one million dollars approved for the Verification Mission;

6. *Decides* to consider the contributions of Armenia, Azerbaijan, Bosnia and Herzegovina, Croatia, Georgia, Kazakhstan, Kyrgyzstan, the Republic of Moldova, San Marino, Slovenia, Tajikistan, Turkmenistan and Uzbekistan to the Verification Mission in accordance with the rates of assessment to be adopted by the General Assembly for these Member States at its forty-seventh session;

7. *Decides also* that the vehicles transferred to the Verification Mission from the United Nations Mission for the Referendum in Western Sahara should be of no cost to the Verification Mission;

8. *Decides further* that, should additional requirements arise, the Secretary-General could continue to avail himself, with the prior concurrence of the Advisory Committee, of the commitment authority granted under General Assembly resolution 46/195 A;

9. *Invites* the new Member States listed in paragraph 6 above to make advance payments against their assessed contributions to be determined;

10. *Invites* voluntary contributions to the Verification Mission in cash and in the form of services and supplies acceptable to the Secretary-General, to be administered, as appropriate, in accordance with the procedure established by the General Assembly in its resolutions 43/230 of 21 December 1988, 44/192 A of 21 December 1989 and 45/258 of 3 May 1991;

11. *Requests* the Secretary-General to take all necessary action to ensure that all United Nations activities related to the Angolan peace process, including the elections, are administered in a coordinated fashion with a maximum of efficiency and economy and in accordance with the relevant mandates.

General Assembly resolution 46/195 B

31 July 1992   Meeting 88   Adopted without vote

Approved by Fifth Committee (A/46/820/Add.1) without vote, 30 July (meeting 67); draft by Chairman (A/C.5/46/L.26); agenda item 120.
Meeting numbers. GA 46th session: 5th Committee 66, 67; plenary 88.

Report of the Secretary-General (December). In December,[25] the Secretary-General requested the Assembly to provide for the maintenance of UNAVEM II for the period beyond 30 November 1992 at a rate not exceeding $5,999,625 gross ($5,739,350 net) per month, with the prior concurrence of ACABQ, pending a decision of the Security Council to extend the Mission's mandate and a further report of the Secretary-General on the future involvement of the United Nations in the Angolan peace process.

As at 31 October, outstanding assessments of $23,432,000 were due from Member States for UNAVEM ($699,400) and UNAVEM II ($22,732,600). Expenditures for the period from 1 January to 31 October totalled $59,137,100 gross ($57,322,400 net). Recorded expenditures for the period from 3 January 1989 to 31 May 1991 showed a revised unencumbered balance of $2,492,300 gross ($2,397,900 net), consisting of $931,000 gross ($896,300 net) for the mandate period from 3

January 1989 to 2 August 1991 (UNAVEM) and $6,900 gross ($2,000 net) for the mandate period from 1 June to 31 December 1991 (UNAVEM II).

In order to meet the operating cash requirements of UNAVEM II, loans amounting to $9.7 million had been made to the Special Account for UNAVEM from the Special Account for the United Nations Transition Assistance Group in Namibia (see PART SIX, Chapter I).

Cost estimates for UNAVEM II operations from 1 November 1992 to 31 October 1993 amounted to $71,995,500 gross ($68,872,200 net).

GENERAL ASSEMBLY ACTION (December)

On 18 September, the General Assembly, on the recommendation of the General Committee, decided to include in the agenda of its forty-seventh (1992) session an item on the financing of UNAVEM II.

On 16 December, the Fifth Committee, on a proposal of its Chairman, decided, owing to a lack of time to consider the Secretary-General's December report, to recommend to the Assembly that it authorize the Secretary-General to enter into commitments up to the amount of $25,258,800 gross ($24,218,000 net) for the maintenance of UNAVEM II until 28 February 1993. That amount was to be apportioned among Member States in accordance with the scheme set out in **resolution 47/41** on the financing of the United Nations Operation in Somalia. That commitment authorization would be considered as part of the appropriation to be decided on at the resumed forty-seventh session.

The Assembly acted on the Committee's recommendations on 22 December by adopting **decision 47/450 A**.

Comorian island of Mayotte

The question of Mayotte—one of a group of four islands in the Indian Ocean Comoro Archipelago—remained on the General Assembly's agenda in 1992. The Islamic Federal Republic of the Comoros acceded to independence on 6 July 1975, following a referendum in 1974. France, the former colonial Power, had since continued to administer the island of Mayotte.

Report of the Secretary-General. In a September 1992 report,[26] the Secretary-General said he had addressed letters to the Comoros and France, drawing their attention to a 1991 General Assembly resolution on the question of Mayotte[27] and inviting them to provide him with any pertinent information. A similar communication was sent to the Secretary-General of OAU. Under the 1991 resolution, the Assembly had requested the United Nations Secretary-General to make available his good offices in the search for a negotiated solution to the problem.

France, in its response, pointed out that Mayotte's special status acquired under the December 1976 law proclaiming Mayotte a territorial collectivity of the French Republic did not close the door to any future development. France was willing to seek conditions for a solution to the problem, subject to the requirements of its own national law and those of international law. It remained prepared to contribute to a just and lasting solution consonant with its Constitution and the wishes of the people concerned. Accordingly, a continuing and constructive dialogue was being maintained at the highest level with the Comoros, as evidenced by the visit to France of the Comorian President in February 1992.

The Comoros said the United Nations recognized the independence of the Comorian State—comprising the four islands of Grande-Comore, Anjouan, Mohéli and Mayotte—and considered it as a single entity. Notwithstanding resolutions to that effect by the United Nations and other organizations, including OAU and the Organization of the Islamic Conference, France continued to maintain its presence and its administration on Mayotte, on the grounds that the population of Mayotte had voted by a two-thirds majority against independence. Under agreements reached between the two parties, France had undertaken to respect the Comoros' unity and territorial integrity.

In 1989, all the country's political factions had reaffirmed unanimously that Mayotte belonged to the Islamic Federal Republic of the Comoros and demanded that it be reincorporated into that nation. The political will demonstrated by both the French and the Comorian Governments must be supported by the international community so that a dialogue could begin quickly towards a just and lasting solution to the Comorian claim.

The OAU Secretary-General again quoted a resolution adopted by the Assembly of Heads of State and Government of OAU in June 1991, reaffirming the sovereignty of the Comoros over the island of Mayotte and appealing to the French Government to meet the legitimate demands of the Government of the Comoros. The resolution also appealed to all OAU member States and the international community to condemn any initiative by France to make the Comorian island of Mayotte participate in events as a separate entity.

GENERAL ASSEMBLY ACTION

On 27 October 1992, the General Assembly adopted **resolution 47/9** by recorded vote.

Question of the Comorian island of Mayotte
The General Assembly,

Recalling its resolutions 1514(XV) of 14 December 1960, containing the Declaration on the Granting of Independence to Colonial Countries and Peoples, and

2621(XXV) of 12 October 1970, containing the programme of action for the full implementation of the Declaration,

Recalling also its previous resolutions, in particular resolutions 3161(XXVIII) of 14 December 1973, 3291(XXIX) of 13 December 1974, 31/4 of 21 October 1976, 32/7 of 1 November 1977, 34/69 of 6 December 1979, 35/43 of 28 November 1980, 36/105 of 10 December 1981, 37/65 of 3 December 1982, 38/13 of 21 November 1983, 39/48 of 11 December 1984, 40/62 of 9 December 1985, 41/30 of 3 November 1986, 42/17 of 11 November 1987, 43/14 of 26 October 1988, 44/9 of 18 October 1989, 45/11 of 1 November 1990 and 46/9 of 16 October 1991, in which, *inter alia*, it affirmed the unity and territorial integrity of the Comoros,

Recalling, in particular, its resolution 3385(XXX) of 12 November 1975 on the admission of the Comoros to membership in the United Nations, in which it reaffirmed the necessity of respecting the unity and territorial integrity of the Comoro Archipelago, composed of the islands of Anjouan, Grande-Comore, Mayotte and Mohéli,

Recalling further that, in accordance with the agreements between the Comoros and France, signed on 15 June 1973, concerning the accession of the Comoros to independence, the results of the referendum of 22 December 1974 were to be considered on a global basis and not island by island,

Convinced that a just and lasting solution to the question of Mayotte is to be found in respect for the sovereignty, unity and territorial integrity of the Comoro Archipelago,

Convinced also that a speedy solution of the problem is essential for the preservation of the peace and security which prevail in the region,

Bearing in mind the wish expressed by the President of the French Republic to seek actively a just solution to that problem,

Taking note of the repeated wish of the Government of the Comoros to initiate as soon as possible a frank and serious dialogue with the French Government with a view to accelerating the return of the Comorian island of Mayotte to the Islamic Federal Republic of the Comoros,

Taking note of the report of the Secretary-General,

Bearing in mind also the decisions of the Organization of African Unity, the Movement of Non-Aligned Countries and the Organization of the Islamic Conference on this question,

1. *Reaffirms* the sovereignty of the Islamic Federal Republic of the Comoros over the island of Mayotte;

2. *Invites* the Government of France to honour the commitments entered into prior to the referendum on the self-determination of the Comoro Archipelago of 22 December 1974 concerning respect for the unity and territorial integrity of the Comoros;

3. *Calls for* the translation into practice of the wish expressed by the President of the French Republic to seek actively a just solution to the question of Mayotte;

4. *Urges* the Government of France to accelerate the process of negotiations with the Government of the Comoros with a view to ensuring the effective and prompt return of the island of Mayotte to the Comoros;

5. *Requests* the Secretary-General of the United Nations to maintain continuous contact with the Secretary-General of the Organization of African Unity with regard to this problem and to make available his good offices in the search for a peaceful negotiated solution to the problem;

6. *Also requests* the Secretary-General to report on this matter to the General Assembly at its forty-eighth session;

7. *Decides* to include in the provisional agenda of its forty-eighth session the item entitled ''Question of the Comorian island of Mayotte''.

General Assembly resolution 47/9

27 October 1992   Meeting 48   126-1-40 (recorded vote)

25-nation draft (A/47/L.10 & Add.1); agenda item 23.

Sponsors: Algeria, Bahrain, Benin, Burkina Faso, Comoros, Cuba, Equatorial Guinea, Gabon, Gambia, Guinea, Guinea-Bissau, Kenya, Lesotho, Libyan Arab Jamahiriya, Madagascar, Mauritius, Morocco, Oman, Sao Tome and Principe, Senegal, Uganda, United Arab Emirates, United Republic of Tanzania, Yemen, Zambia.

Recorded vote in Assembly as follows:

In favour: Afghanistan, Algeria, Angola, Antigua and Barbuda, Argentina, Armenia, Australia, Azerbaijan, Bahamas, Bahrain, Bangladesh, Barbados, Belarus, Belize, Benin, Bhutan, Bolivia, Bosnia and Herzegovina, Botswana, Brazil, Brunei Darussalam, Burkina Faso, Burundi, Cameroon, Cape Verde, Chad, Chile, China, Colombia, Comoros, Congo, Costa Rica, Côte d'Ivoire, Cuba, Democratic People's Republic of Korea, Djibouti, Ecuador, Egypt, El Salvador, Equatorial Guinea, Ethiopia, Fiji, Finland, Gabon, Gambia, Ghana, Grenada, Guatemala, Guinea, Guinea-Bissau, Guyana, Haiti, Honduras, India, Indonesia, Iran, Iraq, Jamaica, Jordan, Kazakhstan, Kenya, Kuwait, Kyrgyzstan, Lesotho, Liberia, Libyan Arab Jamahiriya, Madagascar, Malawi, Malaysia, Maldives, Mali, Marshall Islands, Mauritania, Mauritius, Mexico, Mongolia, Morocco, Mozambique, Myanmar, Namibia, Nepal, New Zealand, Nicaragua, Niger, Nigeria, Oman, Pakistan, Panama, Papua New Guinea, Paraguay, Peru, Philippines, Qatar, Russian Federation, Rwanda, Saint Kitts and Nevis, Sao Tome and Principe, Saudi Arabia, Senegal, Sierra Leone, Singapore, Sri Lanka, Sudan, Suriname, Swaziland, Sweden, Syrian Arab Republic, Tajikistan, Thailand, Togo, Trinidad and Tobago, Tunisia, Turkey, Turkmenistan, Uganda, Ukraine, United Arab Emirates, United Republic of Tanzania, Uruguay, Vanuatu, Venezuela, Viet Nam, Yemen, Zaire, Zambia, Zimbabwe.

Against: France.

Abstaining: Albania, Austria, Belgium, Bulgaria, Canada, Croatia, Cyprus, Czechoslovakia, Denmark, Dominica, Estonia, Germany, Greece, Hungary, Iceland, Ireland, Israel, Italy, Japan, Lao People's Democratic Republic, Latvia, Liechtenstein, Lithuania, Luxembourg, Malta, Micronesia, Netherlands, Norway, Poland, Portugal, Republic of Korea, Republic of Moldova, Romania, Saint Lucia, Saint Vincent and the Grenadines, San Marino, Slovenia, Spain, United Kingdom, United States.

Eritrea

The right of the Eritrean people to determine their political future by an internationally supervised referendum was formally recognized in July 1991 by the Conference on Peace and Democracy (Addis Ababa), which assembled all the political parties and relevant social actors in Ethiopia.

By a letter of 19 May 1992, the Referendum Commissioner of Eritrea invited the Secretary-General to send a United Nations delegation to observe and verify the freeness, fairness and impartiality of the referendum, from its beginning in July 1992 to its completion in April 1993. The Secretary-General, by a letter of 11 June 1992, informed the President of the General Assembly that in view of the need for further information and the limited time remaining before the start of the referendum process in July, he was dispatching a technical team to gather information for the preparation of a report on the details of a potential United Nations involvement in the Eritrean referendum. Both communications, as well as a December 1991 letter from the President of the

Transitional Government of Ethiopia expressing support for the referendum, were transmitted to the Assembly President on 29 October 1992[(28)] by the Chairman of the Third (Social, Humanitarian and Cultural) Committee.

A technical team, led by the Director of the Electoral Assistance Unit of the Department of Political Affairs of the United Nations, visited Eritrea in June for talks with the Referendum Commission, members of the provisional Government and representatives of political, social and religious organizations. During those meetings, the team detected uniform and strong support for the presence of an observation mission and a desire to have a free and fair referendum process.

On the basis of experience gained in other electoral exercises and comments received from the United Nations Centre for Human Rights, the team made a number of technical suggestions aimed at improving some operational and legal aspects of the organization of the referendum. It provided the Referendum Commission with detailed information on the characteristics and procedures of a United Nations observation mission, including standard agreements related to the mission's status and terms of reference; complete agreement was reached on those points.

Based on the fact that the referendum and the notion of its international supervision were supported by the agreements reached in July 1991 at Addis Ababa and that there had been a historical involvement of the United Nations with Eritrea, the Secretary-General, in an October 1992 report,[(29)] recommended the establishment of a United Nations Observer Mission to Verify the Referendum in Eritrea (UNOVER), with the terms of reference to verify: the impartiality of the referendum authorities and organs, including the Referendum Commission, in all aspects and stages of the referendum process; that there existed complete freedom of organization, movement, assembly and expression without hindrance and intimidation; that there was equal access to media facilities and fairness in allocation of both timing and length of broadcasts; and that the referendum rolls were properly drawn up and qualified voters were not denied identification and registration cards or the right to vote. UNOVER was further to report to the referendum authorities on complaints, irregularities and interferences, requesting them to take action if necessary, and to observe all activities related to registration of voters, organization of the poll, the referendum campaign, the poll itself, and the counting, computation and announcement of the results.

In carrying out its mandate, UNOVER was expected to gather factual information about the conduct of the referendum and, in particular, the decision of the electorate; to recognize that the ultimate judgement about the referendum process would be made by the electorate themselves and that its role was to take note of their decision; to recognize the independent character of the Referendum Commission and establish a relationship with it on that basis; and, in its observer capacity, to make constructive contributions to ensure the referendum's success at every stage of the process.

Concerning the structure of UNOVER, the Secretary-General suggested an Office of the Chief of the Mission at Asmara, to provide overall political direction, maintain contact with the provisional Government and the Referendum Commission, and deal with political and electoral matters; regional offices at Asmara, Keren and Mendefera; and mobile teams at Asmara and Keren. Given the peaceful situation in Eritrea and the lack of evidence of political tensions or conflictual positions in relation to the referendum, as well as the organization of the referendum effort already carried out by the Commission, the Secretary-General deemed a total of 21 international staff, supported by local personnel, sufficient to fulfil the verification functions. During the polling itself, 60 observation teams of two persons each would be fielded, with additional observers drawn from UNDP and other United Nations agency personnel at Asmara and in neighbouring countries, as well as from Member States and NGOs.

Three main phases of the referendum process were foreseen: the registration of voters, the referendum campaign, and the poll itself, scheduled for April 1993.

In putting forward his recommendations, the Secretary-General said he conceived of the referendum as not only an important step towards establishing democracy but also an integral part of consolidating peace in the country and contributing to the stability of the region.

In an annex to the report, the Secretary-General provided detailed cost estimates for UNOVER. In a November report to the Third Committee,[(30)] he estimated requirements for UNOVER at $2,807,000, or $181,000 less than his original estimates. In a later report,[(31)] estimated requirements were again revised downward to $2,577,000, due to the delay in the estimated start of the mission from mid-November to mid-December 1992.

GENERAL ASSEMBLY ACTION

On 16 December, on the recommendation of the Third Committee, the General Assembly adopted **resolution 47/114** without vote.

Report of the Secretary-General concerning a request to the United Nations to observe the referendum process in Eritrea

The General Assembly,

Having considered the report of the Secretary-General concerning a request to the United Nations to observe the referendum process in Eritrea,

Recalling that the authorities directly concerned have registered their commitment to respect the results of the referendum in Eritrea,

Taking into account that the authorities directly concerned have requested the involvement of the United Nations to verify the referendum in Eritrea,

1. *Takes note* of the report of the Secretary-General and of the recommendations contained therein for the establishment of a United Nations observer mission to verify the referendum scheduled to take place in Eritrea in April 1993;

2. *Decides* to authorize the Secretary-General to establish the United Nations Observer Mission to Verify the Referendum in Eritrea, which will have terms of reference as provided for in paragraph 7 of the report of the Secretary-General, and to appoint, as a matter of urgency, a Special Representative for the referendum, who will head the Observer Mission;

3. *Requests* the Secretary-General to arrange, as soon as possible, for the deployment of the Observer Mission so that it may commence its verification functions;

4. *Calls upon* the authorities directly concerned to extend their fullest cooperation to the Observer Mission in order to facilitate the accomplishment of its task, as requested by the United Nations;

5. *Requests* the Secretary-General to report to the General Assembly at its forty-eighth session on the implementation of the present resolution.

General Assembly resolution 47/114

16 December 1992   Meeting 89   Adopted without vote

Approved by Third Committee (A/47/678 & Corr.1) without vote, 16 November (meeting 41); draft by Chairman (A/C.3/47/L.20/Rev.1); agenda item 97 (b).

Financial implications. 5th Committee, A/47/786; S-G, A/C.3/47/L.25, A/C.5/47/55.

Meeting numbers. GA 47th session: 3rd Committee 35, 41; 5th Committee 44; plenary 89.

Liberia

The civil war in Liberia—an armed struggle for political power whose main protagonists were the National Patriotic Front of Liberia (NPFL) of Charles Taylor and the United Liberation Movement of Liberia (ULIMO), inspired by the memory of the former President of Liberia who was killed in that war—continued to rage in 1992. The immediate origins of the three-year war could be traced to the complete breakdown of law and order and civil authority that accompanied the overthrow in 1990 of the regime headed by President Samuel Doe. The war caused severe casualties and major displacement of the population, both internally and in terms of refugees in countries bordering Liberia. The rupture of the system of civil administration, the cessation of most forms of social services and the disruption of economic activities resulted in considerable dependence on humanitarian assistance from the United Nations and NGOs.

Since the outbreak of hostilities, the members of the Economic Community of West African States (ECOWAS), both individually and within the framework of the Community, had taken many initiatives aimed at a peaceful settlement of the conflict. Among them, the fourth Yamoussoukro (Côte d'Ivoire) meeting in October 1991 and a meeting at Geneva in April 1992 marked a significant evolution in ECOWAS efforts to establish peace. All the warring factions in Liberia accepted the proposed modalities for a peace plan, including the encampment and disarmament of all their armed troops by 14 January 1992 under the supervision of the Economic Community Monitoring Group (ECOMOG) and the organization of free, democratic elections under the supervision of foreign observers. A request for United Nations assistance in the preparation and conduct of the elections, in accordance with a 1991 General Assembly resolution,[32] was made by the Minister for Foreign Affairs of the Interim Government of National Unity of the Republic of Liberia in a letter of 11 February 1992.[33]

The peace plan, however, was blocked by many obstacles owing to numerous violations by NPFL and, despite many appeals for a cease-fire, the fighting continued, especially with the appearance of ULIMO.

At their fifteenth summit meeting (Dakar, Senegal, 27-29 July), the heads of State or Government of ECOWAS reaffirmed their commitment to work for compliance with the final communiqué of 30 October 1991 (known as the Yamoussoukro IV Accord or Yamoussoukro IV Agreement), adopted by the ECOWAS Committee of Five. A one-month deadline was set for the encampment and disarmament operations; should those measures not be implemented in that time, new ones would be devised to make the factions comply.

Following the summit, Benin, succeeding Senegal as Chairman of ECOWAS, took a series of actions officially to inform the protagonists, including NPFL and ULIMO, of the decisions taken and to make them understand the need to accept and scrupulously observe the peace plan and the Yamassoukro IV Agreement. The Chairman also approached the Secretary-General for support by the international community and the Security Council with respect to any measures ECOWAS might adopt to restore peace.

In conformity with the Dakar decisions, the first joint summit of the Standing Mediation Committee and the Committee of Five, which had been established to resolve the Liberian conflict, was held (Cotonou, Benin, 20 October 1992). Following the meeting, a new appeal was issued to the warring parties to observe a cease-fire as of midnight on 21 October. ECOMOG was made responsible for supervising compliance with the cease-fire and a 15-day deadline was established for complete implementation of the Yamoussoukro IV Agreement. A follow-up committee (Committee of Nine) was established, composed of Benin, Burkina Faso, Côte d'Ivoire, the Gambia, Ghana, Guinea, Nigeria, Senegal and Togo. It was mandated to evaluate, five days before expiration of the 15-day deadline, the extent to which the parties had implemented the Cotonou decisions; if the situation was unchanged, the Committee was mandated to implement fully the decision with respect to sanctions against the warring factions that had not complied with the Agreement. The sanctions were intended to blockade all land, sea and air points of entry into Liberia in order to prevent the delivery of war _matériel_ to those parties and the export of products from the zones they controlled.

Despite the measures adopted at Cotonou, ECO-MOG, the intervention force of ECOWAS, was the target of armed attacks by NPFL that claimed many victims in its ranks. Under those circumstances, a meeting of heads of State or Government of the Committee of Nine was held (Abuja, Nigeria, 7 November), at which a fresh appeal for an immediate cease-fire as of midnight on 10 November was issued. The meeting invited the Secretary-General to name a special representative to work with ECOWAS to implement the peace plan.

As the deadline set for implementation of the Yamoussoukro IV Agreement had expired, the heads of State or Government considered that their decision on sanctions had entered into force against all the warring factions as of 5 November.

The final communiqués of the 7 April[34] and 21 June[35] meetings of the ECOWAS Committee of Five were transmitted to the Secretary-General by Senegal, then Chairman of ECOWAS. Benin transmitted to the Security Council the ECOWAS final communiqué and decisions of 20 October,[36] the final communiqué of the 7 November summit of the Committee of Nine[37] and the Yamoussoukro IV Agreement.[38]

By a letter of 28 October,[39] Benin informed the Council of the decision taken on 20 October at Cotonou to send a ministerial mission of ECOWAS to the Council to report on the latest developments in the crisis in Liberia, to request United Nations assistance in connection with the application of sanctions and to request the presence of observers to facilitate the verification and monitoring of the electoral process. Benin also asked for an emergency meeting of the Council on 4 November, when the ministerial mission was expected to be in New York.

On 19 November, the Security Council imposed a complete embargo on the delivery of weapons and military equipment to Liberia, and, on 20 November, Trevor Gordon-Somers (Jamaica) was named Special Representative of the Secretary-General for Liberia.

The Assembly, in **resolution 47/154**, called for international aid to help resettle Liberian refugees.

SECURITY COUNCIL ACTION

On 7 May, following consultations, the President, on behalf of the Security Council, made the following statement:[40]

Meeting number. SC 3071.

"The members of the Security Council recalled the statement made by the President of the Council on behalf of the Council on 22 January 1991 concerning the situation in Liberia.

"The members of the Security Council noted with appreciation the final communiqué of the Informal Consultative Group Meeting of the Economic Community of West African States (ECOWAS) Committee of Five on Liberia issued at Geneva on 7 April 1992.

"The members of the Security Council commend ECOWAS and its various organs, in particular the Committee of Five, for their untiring efforts to bring the Liberian conflict to a speedy conclusion.

"In this connection the members of the Security Council believe that the Yamoussoukro Accord of 30 October 1991 offers the best possible framework for a peaceful resolution of the Liberian conflict by creating the necessary conditions for free and fair elections in Liberia.

"The members of the Security Council renew their call to all parties to the conflict in Liberia to respect and implement the various accords of the peace process in the framework of the ECOWAS Committee of Five, including refraining from actions which endanger the security of the neighbouring States.

"The members of the Security Council commend the efforts of the Member States, the Secretary-General and humanitarian organizations in providing humanitarian assistance to the victims of the civil war in Liberia and in this regard reaffirm their support for increased assistance."

At the request of Liberia,[41] the Council met again on 19 November to consider the situation in Liberia. Benin, Burkina Faso, Côte d'Ivoire, Egypt, the Gambia, Ghana, Guinea, Liberia, Mauritius, Nigeria, Senegal, Sierra Leone and Togo were invited to participate without the right to vote in accordance with rule 37 of the Council's provisional rules of procedure.[a]

On that date, the Council adopted **resolution 788(1992)** unanimously.

The Security Council,

Recalling the statements by the President of the Council on its behalf on 22 January 1991 and 7 May 1992 on the situation in Liberia,

Reaffirming its belief that the Yamoussoukro IV Accord of 30 October 1991 offers the best possible framework for a peaceful resolution of the Liberian conflict by creating the necessary conditions for free and fair elections in Liberia,

Taking into account the decision of the joint meeting of the Standing Mediation Committee and the Committee of Five of 20 October 1992 held at Cotonou, Benin, and the final communiqué of the first meeting of the Monitoring Committee of Nine on the Liberian conflict issued at Abuja, Nigeria, on 7 November 1992,

Regretting that parties to the conflict in Liberia have not respected or implemented the various accords to date, especially the Yamoussoukro IV Accord,

Determining that the deterioration of the situation in Liberia constitutes a threat to international peace and security, particularly in West Africa as a whole,

Recalling the provisions of Chapter VIII of the Charter of the United Nations,

Noting that the deterioration of the situation hinders the creation of conditions conducive to the holding of free and fair elections in accordance with the Yamoussoukro IV Accord,

Welcoming the continued commitment of the Economic Community of West African States (ECOWAS) to and the efforts towards a peaceful resolution of the Liberian conflict,

Further welcoming the endorsement and support by the Organization of African Unity of these efforts,

Noting the request of 29 July 1992 from ECOWAS for the United Nations to dispatch an observer group to Liberia to verify and monitor the electoral process,

Taking note of the invitation of ECOWAS of 20 October 1992, in Cotonou, Benin, for the Secretary-General to consider, if necessary, the dispatch of a group to observe the encampment and disarmament of the warring parties,

Recognizing the need for increased humanitarian assistance,

Taking into account the request made by the Permanent Representative of Benin on behalf of ECOWAS,

Taking also into account the letter of the Foreign Minister of Liberia endorsing the request made by the Permanent Representative of Benin on behalf of ECOWAS,

Convinced that it is vital to find a peaceful, just and lasting solution to the conflict in Liberia,

1. *Commends* ECOWAS for its efforts to restore peace, security and stability in Liberia;

2. *Reaffirms* its belief that the Yamoussoukro IV Accord offers the best possible framework for a peaceful resolution of the Liberian conflict by creating the necessary conditions for free and fair elections in Liberia, and *calls upon* ECOWAS to continue its efforts to assist in the peaceful implementation of this Accord;

3. *Condemns* the violation of the cease-fire of 28 November 1990 by any party to the conflict;

4. *Condemns* the continuing armed attacks against the peace-keeping forces of ECOWAS in Liberia by one of the parties to the conflict;

5. *Calls upon* all parties to the conflict and all others concerned to respect strictly the provisions of international humanitarian law;

6. *Calls upon* all parties to the conflict to respect and implement the cease-fire and the various accords of the peace process, including the Yamoussoukro IV Accord of 30 October 1991, and the final communiqué of the Informal Consultative Group Meeting of ECOWAS Committee of Five on Liberia, issued at Geneva on 7 April 1992, to which they themselves have agreed;

7. *Requests* the Secretary-General to dispatch urgently a Special Representative to Liberia to evaluate the situation, and to report to the Security Council as soon as possible with any recommendations he may wish to make;

8. *Decides*, under Chapter VII of the Charter of the United Nations, that all States shall, for the purposes of establishing peace and stability in Liberia, immedi-ately implement a general and complete embargo on all deliveries of weapons and military equipment to Liberia until the Security Council decides otherwise;

9. *Decides* within the same framework that the embargo imposed by paragraph 8 shall not apply to weapons and military equipment destined for the sole use of the peace-keeping forces of ECOWAS in Liberia, subject to any review that may be required in conformity with the report of the Secretary-General;

10. *Requests* all States to respect the measures established by ECOWAS to bring about a peaceful solution to the conflict in Liberia;

11. *Calls on* Member States to exercise self-restraint in their relations with all parties to the Liberian conflict and to refrain from taking any action that would be inimical to the peace process;

12. *Commends* the efforts of Member States, the United Nations system and humanitarian organizations in providing humanitarian assistance to the victims of the conflict in Liberia, and in this regard *reaffirms* its support for increased humanitarian assistance;

13. *Requests* the Secretary-General to submit a report on the implementation of this resolution as soon as possible;

14. *Decides* to remain seized of the matter.

Security Council resolution 788(1992)
19 November 1992   Meeting 3138   Adopted unanimously

Draft prepared in consultations among Council members (S/24827).

By a letter of 20 November,[42] the Secretary-General informed the Council of his decision to appoint Trevor Gordon-Somers as Special Representative for Liberia. The Council welcomed the Secretary-General's decision on 23 November.[43]

Mozambique

After ongoing negotiations since the signing of a partial cease-fire agreement on 1 December 1990, the Government of Mozambique and the Resistência Nacional Moçambicana (RENAMO) signed on 4 October 1992 in Rome a General Peace Agreement, which consisted of the Agreement itself and seven protocols: I (basic principles); II (criteria and arrangements for the formation and recognition of political parties); III (principles of the Electoral Act); IV (military questions); V (guarantees); VI (cease-fire); and VII (donors' conference).

The Agreement, which came into force on 15 October, further specified that four other documents formed integral parts of it, namely: a joint communiqué of 10 July 1990 by which both parties affirmed their readiness to dedicate themselves fully to the search for a working basis from which to end the war and create conditions for a lasting peace and for normalizing the life of all Mozambican citizens; an agreement of 1 December 1990 on a partial cease-fire; a declaration of 16 July 1992 by the Government and RENAMO on guiding principles for humanitarian assistance; and a joint declaration signed on 7 August by which both sides committed themselves to guarantee conditions permitting complete political freedom, in accordance with internationally recognized principles of democracy; to guarantee the personal safety of all Mozambican citizens and all members of political parties; to accept the role of the international community, particularly the United Nations, in monitoring and guaranteeing implementation of the General Peace Agreement, particularly the cease-fire and the electoral process; and fully to respect the principles of protocol I, under which the Government was to refrain from any action contrary to the provisions of the protocols or from adopting and applying laws inconsistent with them, while RENAMO was to refrain from armed combat and was instead to conduct its political struggle in conformity with the laws in force, within the framework of existing State institutions and in accordance with the conditions and guarantees established in the General Peace Agreement. The parties were further committed to safeguard political rights, establish constitutional guarantees and incorporate the protocols and guarantees, as well as the Agreement, in Mozambican law.

The General Peace Agreement was annexed to a letter of 4 October from the President of Mozambique to the Secretary-General,[44] requesting the United Nations to chair the following commissions: the Supervision and Control Commission of the implementation of the Agreement, as provided for in protocol I; the Cease-fire Commission provided for in protocol VI; and the Reintegration Commission, provided for in protocol IV. At the same time, he requested that the Security Council be informed of the need to send a United Nations team to Mozambique to monitor the Agreement until the holding of general elections which, in principle, were to take place one year after the signing of the Agreement. According to protocol IV, the United Nations was expected to start its functions of verifying and monitoring the cease-fire upon entry into force of the Agreement. The 7 August joint declaration was transmitted by Mozambique on 10 August.[45]

After the Security Council on 13 October welcomed the signing of the General Peace Agreement, the Secretary-General appointed Aldo Ajello (Italy) as interim Special Representative to assist the parties in setting up the joint machinery required for the military and other arrangements to be taken under the Agreement. The Special Representative and the head of the United Nations military observer team arrived in Maputo on 14 October, along with the first observers. On 4 November, the Special Representative appointed a Supervisory and Monitoring Commission, which on the same date appointed its three main subsidiary commissions: the Cease-fire Commission, the Reintegration Commission and the Joint Commission for the Formation of the Mozambican Defence Forces.

The Supervisory and Monitoring Commission was to guarantee implementation of the General Peace Agreement, assume responsibility for authentic interpretation of it and settle any disputes that might arise between the parties. The other commissions were responsible for supervising the cease-fire and demobilization; economic and social reintegration of demobilized military personnel; and the formation of new unified armed forces.

All four commissions were composed of government and RENAMO delegates. In addition, they included representatives of: France, Italy, Portugal, the United Kingdom, the United States and OAU (Supervisory and Monitoring Commission); Botswana, Egypt, France, Italy, Nigeria, Portugal, the United Kingdom and the United States (Cease-fire Commission); Denmark, France, Germany, Italy, the Netherlands, Norway, Portugal, South Africa, Spain, Sweden, Switzerland, the United Kingdom, the United States and the European Community (EC) (Reintegration Commission); and France, Portugal and United Kingdom (Joint Commission for the Formation of the Mozambican Defence Forces, the only Commission not chaired by the United Nations).

Immediately after the signing of the Agreement, the Secretary-General dispatched a humanitarian assistance mission to Mozambique to assess existing United Nations operations and devise a more effective response to the intended expansion of humanitarian activities. As a result of the war and continuing drought, the internally displaced population in Mozambique totalled some 3 to 4 million. About 3 million Mozambicans living in accessible areas were receiving humanitarian assistance. The signing of the Agreement created access to additional affected areas, many of which were controlled by RENAMO. As a consequence, nearly 270,000 additional beneficiaries were being provided with humanitarian assistance by the United Nations and ICRC, under the terms of a 15 July declaration on the principles of humanitarian assistance. Indications were that the number of additional beneficiaries might reach 500,000.

While 1.4 million of the estimated 1.8 million Mozambican refugees living in neighbouring countries were receiving assistance, drought was reported to have caused many other Mozambicans to seek refuge there. The expected returnee population could thus be estimated at no less than 1.8 million.

On 16 December 1992, the Security Council authorized a United Nations Operation in Mozambique until 31 October 1993. Its estimated 8,000 military and civilian personnel were to monitor withdrawal of foreign forces and help administer the electoral process and humanitarian assistance.

As agreed in protocol VII, a conference of donor countries and organizations to finance the electoral process, emergency programmes and programmes for the reintegration of displaced persons, refugees and demobilized soldiers was convened by Italy (Rome, 15 and 16 December). An appropriate share of the funds provided was to be placed at the disposal of political parties for the financing of their activities. An announcement of the conference and its conclusions were submitted by Italy, by letters of 12 November[46] and 30 December,[47] respectively.

Report of the Secretary-General (October). In October,[48] the Secretary-General reported on the status of the peace process, summarized the principal features of the General Peace Agreement, including the role proposed for the United Nations in monitoring it, and outlined an immediate plan of action. In essence, the Organization was asked to undertake certain specific functions in relation to the cease-fire, the elections and humanitarian assistance.

With regard to the cease-fire, the United Nations was asked to provide chairmen for the Cease-fire Commission and the Reintegration Commission; the former was also to verify the existence of other armed groups, including irregulars, and to authorize security arrangements for vital public and private infrastructures.

It would not be possible for the United Nations to establish more than a token presence in Mozambique by 15 October, the Secretary-General said. The viability of the cease-fire in its early stages would therefore depend on the political will and strict compliance by the two parties with the agreed modalities. In that context, he noted that the parties had not yet reached agreement on locations for the assembly areas for the separation and concentration of forces.

The Secretary-General stated his intention, subject to the approval of the Security Council, to appoint immediately an interim Special Representative in overall charge of United Nations activities in support of the Agreement, including monitoring its implementation and the specific tasks related to the military arrangements and the elections. As soon as appointed, the Special Representative was to assist the parties in setting up the joint machinery to be chaired by the United Nations and in finalizing modalities and conditions for the military arrangements. He was also to coordinate humanitarian and other related United Nations efforts, taking steps, as a priority matter, to ensure access for relief workers to all those in need of humanitarian assistance. In those initial tasks, he was to be supported by a team of up to 25 mili-

tary observers and administrative support staff. The military personnel, drawn from existing peace-keeping missions, were to establish a presence at Maputo, Beira and Nampula to carry out limited verification of the cease-fire arrangements; establish liaison with both parties in those regions and provide them with technical advice on the modalities for implementing the Agreement; facilitate the build-up of the mission; and carry out reconnaissance and other required activities.

SECURITY COUNCIL ACTION (October)

On 13 October, the Security Council met to consider the Secretary-General's report. The Council invited Mozambique to participate in the discussion without the right to vote, in accordance with rule 37 of its provisional rules of procedure.[a]

Following a statement by Mozambique, the Council unanimously adopted **resolution 782(1992)**.

The Security Council,

Welcoming the signature, on 4 October 1992 in Rome, of a General Peace Agreement between the Government of Mozambique and the Resistência Nacional Moçambicana (RENAMO),

Considering that the signature of the Agreement constitutes an important contribution to the restoration of peace and security in the region,

Taking note of the Joint Declaration dated 7 August 1992 of the President of the Republic of Mozambique and the President of RENAMO, in which the parties accept the role of the United Nations in monitoring and guaranteeing the implementation of the General Peace Agreement,

Also taking note of the report of the Secretary-General dated 9 October 1992 and of the request of the President of Mozambique,

1. *Approves* the appointment by the Secretary-General of an interim Special Representative, and the dispatch to Mozambique of a team of up to 25 military observers as recommended in paragraph 16 of the above-mentioned report;

2. *Looks forward* to the report of the Secretary-General on the establishment of a United Nations Operation in Mozambique, including in particular a detailed estimate of the cost of this operation;

3. *Decides* to remain actively seized of the matter.

Security Council resolution 782(1992)

13 October 1992   Meeting 3123   Adopted unanimously

Draft prepared in consultations among Council members (S/24650), orally revised.

On 27 October, the President made the following statement on behalf of the Council:[49]

Meeting number. SC 3125

''The Security Council has taken note of the letter dated 23 October 1992 from the Secretary-General addressed to the President of the Security Council concerning the situation in Mozambique. It expresses its gratitude to the Secretary-General and to his interim Special Representative for their efforts to ensure that the United Nations contributes to the implementation of the General Peace Agreement in accordance with the provisions of this Agreement.

"The Council remains deeply concerned by the reports of major violations of the cease-fire in several regions of Mozambique. It calls upon the parties to halt such violations immediately and scrupulously to respect the cease-fire and all the commitments entered into under the General Peace Agreement. It also urges the parties to cooperate fully with the interim Special Representative, and in particular to take all necessary measures to ensure the safety of United Nations staff in Mozambique.

"The Council wishes to reiterate its firm commitment to work towards a lasting peace in Mozambique. In this regard, it urges the parties to respect fully the cease-fire, which is a necessary condition for the speedy establishment and successful deployment of the United Nations Operation in Mozambique."

Report of the Secretary-General (December). In December,[50] the Secretary-General recommended the deployment of a United Nations Operation in Mozambique (ONUMOZ) to provide an impartial and supportive structure to help both parties break the cycle of violence and to assist in the rebuilding and development of a peaceful society.

In accordance with the General Peace Agreement, the mandate of ONUMOZ would be to facilitate impartially implementation of the Agreement, in particular by chairing the Supervisory and Monitoring Commission and its subordinate commissions; to monitor and verify the cease-fire, the separation and concentration of forces, their demobilization and the collection, storage and destruction of weapons; to monitor and verify the complete withdrawal of foreign forces as well as the disbanding of private and irregular armed groups; to authorize security arrangements for vital infrastructures; and to provide security for United Nations and other international activities in support of the peace process. ONUMOZ would also provide technical assistance for and monitor the entire electoral process, coordinate humanitarian assistance operations, in particular those relating to refugees, internally displaced persons, demobilized military personnel and the affected local population, and chair the Humanitarian Assistance Committee.

ONUMOZ's verification function was to be carried out mainly by military observer teams at the 49 assembly areas in three military regions and elsewhere in the field. They would work with, but would remain separate from, the monitoring groups composed of representatives of the two parties at each location. They would observe the manner in which those groups were carrying out their functions in order to verify that the joint monitoring machinery was working effectively. They would respond to requests for assistance and would use their good offices to resolve any problems that might arise within the monitoring groups, con-

ducting their own investigations and patrolling the assembly areas. Teams would also be deployed at airports, ports and other critical areas, including RENAMO headquarters.

The military aspects of the United Nations operation would be inescapably linked with the humanitarian efforts. Approximately 110,000 soldiers were to be disarmed, demobilized and reintegrated into civil society; they would need food and other support and the relief programmes for the assembled soldiers and civilian populations would need to be closely coordinated.

With the withdrawal of foreign troops having started after the Agreement's entry into force and in view of roaming groups of heavily armed irregulars, the Secretary-General saw an imperative need to continue ensuring the security of the transport corridors and other key routes and to protect humanitarian convoys using them; there seemed to be no alternative but for ONUMOZ to assume that responsibility and deploy five logistically self-sufficient infantry battalions for that purpose. In addition, three engineer companies were needed to assist in demining and road repair.

While the Agreement did not provide for a specific role for United Nations civilian police, the Secretary-General considered its presence desirable in order to inspire confidence that violation of civil liberties, human rights and political freedom would be avoided. A police component of up to 128 police officers could be deployed in the regions and provincial capitals; it could work in close cooperation with and provide technical advice to the National Police Affairs Commission.

With regard to elections as foreseen in the Agreement, the Secretary-General felt it was important that they should not take place until the military aspects of the Agreement were fully implemented. However, the peace process should not be drawn out indefinitely and the highest priority was to be given to timely implementation of the cease-fire, the assembly, disarmament and demobilization of troops and the formation of new armed forces.

ONUMOZ's electoral component was to verify the impartiality of the National Elections Commission and its organs; that political parties and alliances enjoyed complete freedom of organization, movement, assembly and expression and that they had fair access to State mass media; and that the electoral rolls were properly drawn up and that qualified voters were not denied identification and registration cards or the right to vote. In addition, ONUMOZ was to report to the electoral authorities on complaints, irregularities and interferences reported or observed, and, if necessary, to request action to resolve and rectify them, as well as to conduct its own investigation; to observe all activities related to voter registration, the electoral campaign, the organization of the poll and the poll itself, as well as the counting, computation and announcement of the results; to participate in the electoral education campaign; and to report periodically to the Secretary-General on the electoral process.

With regard to coordination of the humanitarian aspects of the Agreement, the Secretary-General recommended that a United Nations Office for the Coordination of Humanitarian Assistance be established as an integral part of ONUMOZ, with regional and provincial suboffices, replacing the current office of the United Nations Special Coordinator for Emergency Relief Operations.

Summing up his observations, the Secretary-General said the difficulties for ONUMOZ derived from the size of the country, its devastated infrastructure, the disruption of its economy by war and drought, and the limited capacity of the Government to cope with the new tasks arising from the General Peace Agreement and the complexity of the processes enshrined in it. An additional dimension was the critical importance of the Mozambican corridors for much of southern Africa. To achieve within one year the assembly, disarmament and demobilization of the two sides' troops, the formation of new armed forces, the resettlement of 5 to 6 million refugees and displaced persons, the provision of humanitarian relief to all parts of the country, and the organization and conduct of elections would require a huge and cooperative effort by the Government, RENAMO and the international community, with the United Nations in the lead. Very substantial resources were needed for that purpose. However, United Nations efforts could only support those of the parties. Also, it would not be possible to create the conditions for a successful election unless the military situation had been brought fully under control.

The Secretary-General recommended the deployment of: a military component, including 354 military observers and 5 infantry battalions composed of up to 850 personnel each; a civilian technical unit to support the logistic tasks relating to the demobilization programme in the assembly areas; 128 police officers to monitor civil liberties and provide technical advice to the National Police Affairs Commission, subject to the parties' concurrence; an Electoral Division consisting of up to 148 international electoral officers and support staff, followed by up to 1,200 international observers for the elections themselves; and 16 international Professional staff for the coordination and monitoring of humanitarian assistance.

In an addendum to the report, the Secretary-General estimated that $331.8 million would be required for ONUMOZ from its inception to 31 October 1993, the cost to be borne by Member States.

SECURITY COUNCIL ACTION (December)

The Security Council considered the Secretary-General's report on 16 December. In accordance with rule 37 of the Council's provisional rules of procedure,[a] Mozambique was invited to participate without the right to vote.

On the same date, the Council adopted **resolution 797(1992)** unanimously.

The Security Council,

Recalling its resolution 782(1992) of 13 October 1992,

Recalling also the statement of the President of the Security Council of 27 October 1992,

Having considered the report of the Secretary-General dated 3 December 1992,

Stressing the importance it attaches to the General Peace Agreement for Mozambique and to the fulfilment by the parties in good faith of the obligations contained therein,

Noting the efforts made so far by the Government of Mozambique and the Resistência Nacional Moçambicana to maintain the cease-fire, and expressing concern over the delays in initiating some of the major tasks arising from the General Peace Agreement,

Welcoming the appointment by the Secretary-General of an interim Special Representative for Mozambique who will be in overall charge of United Nations activities in support of the General Peace Agreement for Mozambique as well as the dispatch to Mozambique of a team of twenty-five military observers, as approved by resolution 782(1992) of 13 October 1992,

Noting the intention of the Secretary-General, in this as in other peace-keeping operations, to monitor expenditures carefully during this period of increasing demands on peace-keeping resources,

1. *Approves* the report of the Secretary-General dated 3 December 1992 and the recommendations contained therein;

2. *Decides* to establish a United Nations Operation in Mozambique as proposed by the Secretary-General and in line with the General Peace Agreement for Mozambique, and requests the Secretary-General in planning and executing the deployment of the Operation to seek economies through, *inter alia*, phased deployment and to report regularly on what is achieved in this regard;

3. *Further decides* that the United Nations Operation in Mozambique is established for a period until 31 October 1993 in order to accomplish the objectives described in the report of the Secretary-General;

4. *Calls upon* the Government of Mozambique and the Resistência Nacional Moçambicana to cooperate fully with the interim Special Representative of the Secretary-General and with the United Nations Operation in Mozambique and to respect scrupulously the cease-fire and all the commitments entered into under the Agreement, and stresses that the full respect of these commitments constitutes a necessary condition for the fulfilment by the United Nations Operation in Mozambique of its mandate;

5. *Demands* that all parties and others concerned in Mozambique take all measures necessary to ensure the safety of United Nations and all other personnel deployed pursuant to this and prior resolutions;

6. *Endorses* the approach in paragraphs 30 and 51 of the Secretary-General's report as regards the timetable

for the electoral process, and invites the Secretary-General to consult closely with all the parties on the precise timing of and preparations for the presidential and legislative elections as well as on a precise timetable for the implementation of the other major aspects of the Agreement and to report back to the Council on this as soon as possible, and in any event not later than 31 March 1993;

7. *Calls upon* the Government of Mozambique and the Resistência Nacional Moçambicana to finalize, in close coordination with the interim Special Representative, as soon as possible organizational and logistical preparations for the demobilization process;

8. *Encourages* Member States to respond positively to requests made to them by the Secretary-General to contribute personnel and equipment to the United Nations Operation in Mozambique;

9. *Further encourages* Member States to contribute voluntarily to United Nations activities in support of the General Peace Agreement for Mozambique, and requests United Nations programmes and specialized agencies to provide appropriate assistance and support for the implementation of the major tasks arising from the Agreement;

10. *Requests* the Secretary-General to keep the Security Council informed of developments and to submit a further report to the Council by 31 March 1993;

11. *Decides* to remain actively seized of the matter.

Security Council resolution 797(1992)

16 December 1992   Meeting 3149   Adopted unanimously

Draft prepared in consultations among Council members (S/24941).

Alleged use of chemical weapons

By a communiqué of 23 January 1992,[51] the Government of Mozambique charged that following a military operation on 16 January against a RENAMO stronghold in the region of Ngungue, Estompene, 5 kilometres from the border with South Africa, its forces were subjected to an attack with a chemical weapon. As a result, some soldiers died, while others were rendered paralysed, were mentally affected, or lost sight and hearing abilities. In submitting its charges, the Government urgently appealed to the international community for assistance in its efforts to determine the nature of the weapon involved, as well as the treatment of the injured persons.

After requesting further information and clarifications from the Government and having been informed of the preliminary results of an investigation carried out at the Government's request by experts from the National Defence Research Establishment of Sweden from 5 to 11 February, the Secretary-General reached the conclusion that an investigation was warranted, although the passage of a considerable amount of time since the incident was feared to have substantially diminished the possibility of determining which chemical agents, if any, might have been involved. The Government of Mozambique, on 13 March, reiterated its strong wish to have a United Nations investigation team in Maputo at the Secretary-General's earliest convenience.

Accordingly, the Secretary-General, under his own authority, appointed in March a mission of three qualified experts, from Sweden, Switzerland and the United Kingdom, to carry out an investigation. The President of the Security Council was informed of the decision in a letter of 26 March. The mission was coordinated by the Director, Office for Disarmament Affairs of the Department for Political Affairs.

The mission arrived at Maputo on 23 March. In the course of their investigation, the experts were able to go to the location identified by the authorities of Mozambique as the site of the incident, where they collected various types of samples which were later analysed independently at laboratories in Sweden, Switzerland and the United Kingdom. After concluding their investigation on 27 March, the experts submitted a joint report to the Secretary-General. They said the effect of the attack on the troops was consistent with the use of an atropine-like chemical warfare agent and also with severe heat stress. In the absence of analytical data, it could not be concluded that a chemical warfare agent had been used and, due to the considerable delay between the attack and the investigation, it might not be possible to detect traces of the agent if a chemical warfare agent had been used.

In transmitting the experts' report to the Security Council,[52] the Secretary-General noted that they determined that the government forces had sustained casualties not entirely explicable by the kind of weapons so far in use in the conflict in Mozambique. From the material available, it was not possible to determine whether or not a chemical weapon had been used. However, the mere possibility that such weapons might be used in the continuing armed conflict pointed to the urgency of finding a peaceful settlement.

Somalia

Since the ousting of President Mohammed Siad Barre—Somalia's leader for 21 years—in January 1991, the country had been embroiled in a clan-based civil war. Since November 1991, heavy fighting had persisted in Mogadishu (Mogadiscio), the capital, between the factions of Ali Mahdi Mohamed, appointed Interim President on the basis of the 1991 Djibouti Accords, and General Mohamed Farah Aidid. The Djibouti Accords were the result of two conferences on Somali national reconciliation, held in June and July 1991 in response to an appeal by the President of Djibouti. The conferences brought together all the major political factions in Somalia, with the exception of the Somali National Movement.

The conflict in Mogadishu arose mainly because General Aidid, rejecting the Accords, did not recognize Mr. Mohamed as Interim President.

During the fighting, areas inhabited by civilians were subjected to persistent direct fire, including from artillery and mortar units. At the same time, independent military operations by some of the heavily armed elements which controlled parts of the city, including the seaport and airport, increased. While some of those elements declared alliance with one or the other of the two protagonists in Mogadishu, others were not controlled by either of them.

The fighting resulted in widespread death and destruction, forced hundreds of thousands of civilians to flee the city, caused dire need of emergency humanitarian assistance and brought about a grave threat of widespread famine. It seriously impeded United Nations efforts to deliver humanitarian assistance to the affected population in and around Mogadishu, and threatened stability in the Horn of Africa. Throughout the country, almost 4.5 million of the 6 million Somalis were estimated to be threatened by severe malnutrition and related disease, with at least 1.5 million immediately at risk and 300,000 estimated to have died since November 1991 (for details, see PART THREE, Chapter III). Some 700,000 Somalis had sought refuge in neighbouring countries and another 300,000 were exiled elsewhere (for details, see PART THREE, Chapter XV).

On 23 January, the Security Council urged all parties to the conflict to cease hostilities and decided that all States should immediately implement a complete embargo on deliveries of weapons and military equipment to Somalia. A cease-fire agreed to by the two factions in Mogadishu came into effect on 3 March. After about a month of relative calm, fighting resumed between some units belonging to the two factions. The leaders of both factions moved quickly to stop the fighting and re-establish the cease-fire. However, some sporadic shooting and incidents of apparent banditry by armed elements not under the control of either faction were reported.

On 17 March, the Council supported the Secretary-General's decision to dispatch a United Nations technical team to Somalia to prepare a plan for a cease-fire monitoring mechanism. The Council also requested the team to develop a high-priority plan for the delivery of humanitarian assistance.

On 12 April, representatives of the two factions met face to face for the first time at United Nations offices at Mogadishu to discuss the formation of a joint committee for relief assistance, under the chairmanship of the Coordinator for Humanitarian Assistance. Similarly, the chiefs of staff of both factions met in connection with the monitoring of the cease-fire and the agreements reached on ensuring unimpeded delivery of humanitarian assistance.

On 24 April, the Council established a United Nations Operation in Somalia (UNOSOM) and requested the immediate deployment of 50 United Nations observers to monitor the cease-fire in Mogadishu. The Secretary-General on 28 April appointed Ambassador Mohamed Sahnoun (Algeria) as his Special Representative for Somalia. On 4 May, Mr. Sahnoun took up residence in Mogadishu, where he established the headquarters of UNOSOM. Following Mr. Sahnoun's resignation at the end of October, the Secretary-General appointed Ambassador Ismat Kittani (Iraq) as his new Special Representative.

On 27 July, the Council approved an enlargement of UNOSOM and urged all parties, movements and factions to facilitate United Nations efforts to provide urgent humanitarian assistance. On 28 August, the Council authorized an increase in UNOSOM's strength and, on 3 December, it authorized the use of all necessary means to establish as soon as possible a secure environment for humanitarian relief operations in Somalia.

SECURITY COUNCIL ACTION (January)

On 11 January 1992, Omer Arteh Qhalib, appointed interim Prime Minister for Somalia in the context of arrangements agreed on by all the Somali political parties that had participated in the Somali national reconciliation conference held at Djibouti in July 1991, requested the Chargé d'affaires a.i. of the Permanent Mission of Somalia to the United Nations to present the deteriorating situation in the country to the Security Council. By a letter of 20 January,[53] the Chargé d'affaires, noting that the civil war situation in Somalia was worsening by the day, expressed support of Mr. Arteh's appeal to the Council to convene immediately to consider the resulting human dilemma.

The Council met on 23 January. Somalia was invited to participate in the discussion without the right to vote, under rule 37 of the Council's provisional rules of procedure.[a]

On the same date, the Council unanimously adopted **resolution 733(1992)**.

The Security Council,

Considering the request by Somalia for the Security Council to consider the situation in Somalia,

Having heard the report of the Secretary-General on the situation in Somalia and commending the initiative taken by him in the humanitarian field,

Gravely alarmed at the rapid deterioration of the situation in Somalia and the heavy loss of human life and widespread material damage resulting from the conflict in the country and aware of its consequences on the stability and peace in the region,

Concerned that the continuation of this situation constitutes, as stated in the report of the Secretary-General, a threat to international peace and security,

Recalling its primary responsibility under the Charter of the United Nations for the maintenance of international peace and security,

Recalling also the provisions of Chapter VIII of the Charter of the United Nations,

Expressing its appreciation to the international and regional organizations that have provided assistance to the populations affected by the conflict and deploring that personnel of these organizations have lost their lives in the exercise of their humanitarian tasks,

Taking note of the appeals addressed to the parties by the Chairman of the Organization of the Islamic Conference on 16 December 1991, the Secretary-General of the Organization of African Unity on 18 December 1991 and the League of Arab States on 5 January 1992,

1. *Takes note* of the report of the Secretary-General on the situation in Somalia and expresses its concern with the situation prevailing in that country;

2. *Requests* the Secretary-General immediately to undertake the necessary actions to increase humanitarian assistance of the United Nations and its specialized agencies to the affected population in all parts of Somalia in liaison with the other international humanitarian organizations and to this end to appoint a coordinator to oversee the effective delivery of this assistance;

3. *Requests* the Secretary-General of the United Nations, in cooperation with the Secretary-General of the Organization of African Unity and the Secretary-General of the League of Arab States, immediately to contact all parties involved in the conflict, to seek their commitment to the cessation of hostilities to permit the humanitarian assistance to be distributed, to promote a cease-fire and compliance therewith, and to assist in the process of a political settlement of the conflict in Somalia;

4. *Strongly urges* all parties to the conflict immediately to cease hostilities and agree to a cease-fire and to promote the process of reconciliation and of political settlement in Somalia;

5. *Decides*, under Chapter VII of the Charter of the United Nations, that all States shall, for the purposes of establishing peace and stability in Somalia, immediately implement a general and complete embargo on all deliveries of weapons and military equipment to Somalia until the Security Council decides otherwise;

6. *Calls on* all States to refrain from any action which might contribute to increasing tension and to impeding or delaying a peaceful and negotiated outcome to the conflict in Somalia, which would permit all Somalis to decide upon and to construct their future in peace;

7. *Calls upon* all parties to cooperate with the Secretary-General to this end and to facilitate the delivery by the United Nations, its specialized agencies and other humanitarian organizations of humanitarian assistance to all those in need of it, under the supervision of the coordinator;

8. *Urges* all parties to take all the necessary measures to ensure the safety of personnel sent to provide humanitarian assistance, to assist them in their tasks and to ensure full respect for the rules and principles of international law regarding the protection of civilian populations;

9. *Calls upon* all States and international organizations to contribute to the efforts of humanitarian assistance to the population in Somalia;

10. *Requests* the Secretary-General to report to the Security Council as soon as possible on this matter;

11. *Decides* to remain seized of the matter until a peaceful solution is achieved.

Security Council resolution 733(1992)

23 January 1992   Meeting 3039   Adopted unanimously

Draft prepared in consultations among Council members (S/23461).

By a letter of 30 January,[54] Somalia expressed gratification at the unanimous adoption of resolution 733(1992), which it hoped would diminish human suffering and bring about a holding cease-fire, national reconciliation and lasting peace. In an annex to the letter, Somalia highlighted the political situation in the country.

Report of the Secretary-General (March). In March,[55] the Secretary-General described his efforts, in cooperation with the Secretaries-General of OAU and the League of Arab States (LAS), to secure the commitment of all parties involved in the conflict in Somalia to a cessation of hostilities in order to permit distribution of humanitarian assistance, promotion of a cease-fire, compliance with it and promotion of a political settlement.

On 31 January, the Secretary-General invited LAS, OAU, the Organization of the Islamic Conference (OIC), Interim President Mohamed and General Aidid, then Chairman of the United Somali Congress, to send representatives to New York for consultations. The talks, held from 12 to 14 February, succeeded in the two Somali factions committing themselves to an immediate cessation of hostilities and maintenance of a cease-fire in Mogadishu. They signed pledges to that effect in the presence of representatives of the United Nations, LAS, OAU and OIC. They also agreed to a visit to Mogadishu, before the end of February, of a high-level delegation from those organizations to arrange a cease-fire agreement.

The joint delegation, led by Under-Secretary-General James O. C. Jonah, arrived at Mogadishu on 29 February. It held separate talks with Interim President Mohamed and General Aidid. On 3 March, after four days of intensive negotiations, both signed an agreement on the implementation of a cease-fire.

The signing of the agreement, the text of which was annexed to the Secretary-General's report, opened the way for the dispatch of a United Nations technical team to Mogadishu to work out with military officials of the two main factions a possible monitoring mechanism aimed at stabilizing the cease-fire and to look into possible mechanisms to ensure unimpeded delivery of humanitarian assistance.

In the light of the immediate threat posed by severe food shortages to large portions of the country's population, the Secretary-General said, the relief programme should not necessarily depend on implementation of a cease-fire, and the consequences of obstructing the work of international monitors or of any United Nations observer mission should be made unmistakably clear to the leaders of the two factions.

SECURITY COUNCIL ACTION (March)

The Security Council convened on 17 March to consider the Secretary-General's report on the situation in Somalia. Italy, Kenya, Nigeria and Somalia, at their request, were invited to participate in the discussion without the right to vote, in accordance with rule 37 of the Council's provisional rules of procedure.[a] At Morocco's request, an invitation was also extended to the Permanent Observers of LAS[56] and OIC,[57] under rule 39 of the Council's provisional rules of procedure.[b]

Following statements, the Council unanimously adopted **resolution 746(1992)**.

The Security Council,

Considering the request by Somalia for the Security Council to consider the situation in Somalia,

Reaffirming its resolution 733(1992) of 23 January 1992,

Having considered the report of the Secretary-General on the situation in Somalia,

Taking note of the signing of the cease-fire agreements in Mogadiscio on 3 March 1992, including agreements for the implementation of measures aimed at stabilizing the cease-fire through a United Nations monitoring mission,

Deeply regretting that the factions have not yet abided by their commitment to implement the cease-fire and thus have still not permitted the unimpeded provision and distribution of humanitarian assistance to the people in need in Somalia,

Deeply disturbed by the magnitude of the human suffering caused by the conflict and concerned that the continuation of the situation in Somalia constitutes a threat to international peace and security,

Bearing in mind that the factors described in paragraph 76 of the Secretary-General's report must be taken into account,

Cognizant of the importance of cooperation between the United Nations and regional organizations in the context of Chapter VIII of the Charter of the United Nations,

Underlining the importance which it attaches to the international, regional and non-governmental organizations, including the International Committee of the Red Cross, continuing to provide humanitarian and other relief assistance to the people of Somalia under difficult circumstances,

Expressing its appreciation to the regional organizations, including the Organization of African Unity, the League of Arab States and the Organization of the Islamic Conference, for their cooperation with the United Nations in the effort to resolve the Somali problem,

1. _Takes note with appreciation_ of the report of the Secretary-General;

2. _Urges_ the Somali factions to honour their commitment under the cease-fire agreements of 3 March 1992;

3. _Urges_ all the Somali factions to cooperate with the Secretary-General and to facilitate the delivery by the United Nations, its specialized agencies and other hu-

manitarian organizations of humanitarian assistance to all those in need of it, under the supervision of the coordinator mentioned in resolution 733(1992);

4. _Requests_ the Secretary-General to pursue his humanitarian efforts in Somalia and to use all the resources at his disposal, including those of the relevant United Nations agencies, to address urgently the critical needs of the affected population in Somalia;

5. _Appeals_ to all Member States and to all humanitarian organizations to contribute to and to cooperate with these humanitarian relief efforts;

6. _Strongly supports_ the Secretary-General's decision urgently to dispatch a technical team to Somalia, accompanied by the coordinator, in order to work within the framework and objectives outlined in paragraphs 73 and 74 of his report and to submit expeditiously a report to the Security Council on this matter;

7. _Requests_ that the technical team also develop a high priority plan to establish mechanisms to ensure the unimpeded delivery of humanitarian assistance;

8. _Calls on_ all parties, movements and factions in Mogadiscio in particular, and in Somalia in general, to respect fully the security and safety of the technical team and the personnel of the humanitarian organizations and to guarantee their complete freedom of movement in and around Mogadiscio and other parts of Somalia;

9. _Calls upon_ the Secretary-General of the United Nations to continue, in close cooperation with the Organization of African Unity, the League of Arab States and the Organization of the Islamic Conference, his consultations with all Somali parties, movements and factions towards the convening of a conference for national reconciliation and unity in Somalia;

10. _Calls upon_ all Somali parties, movements and factions to cooperate fully with the Secretary-General in the implementation of this resolution;

11. _Decides_ to remain seized of the matter until a peaceful solution is achieved.

Security Council resolution 746(1992)

17 March 1992   Meeting 3060   Adopted unanimously

Draft prepared in consultations among Council members (S/23722), orally revised.

In Somalia's view, expressed in a letter of 26 March,[58] the resolution carried all the necessary elements for resolving the country's problem. Annexed to the letter were suggestions by Somalia for action within the resolution's context.

Report of the Secretary-General (April). In April,[59] the Secretary-General informed the Council that on 20 March he appointed David Bassiouni as Coordinator to oversee the delivery of United Nations humanitarian assistance to the affected population in all parts of Somalia, in liaison with other international humanitarian organizations. On the same date, he appointed a 15-member technical team led by Robert Gallagher

[b]Rule 39 of the Council's provisional rules of procedure states: "The Security Council may invite members of the Secretariat or other persons, whom it considers competent for the purpose, to supply it with information or to give other assistance in examining matters within its competence."

and including representatives of LAS, OAU and OIC. The team was in Somalia from 23 March to 1 April. It visited Mogadishu, Kismayo and Hargeisa and met with the authorities and clan leaders from the north-east as well as the south-west of the country. The team obtained the signatures of Interim President Mohamed and General Aidid to agreements on mechanisms for monitoring the cease-fire and on arrangements for equitable and effective distribution of humanitarian assistance. Under those agreements, the United Nations would deploy observers to monitor the cease-fire and deploy security personnel to protect its staff and safeguard its humanitarian and relief activities, providing security for equipment and escorting deliveries of supplies. The team also reached agreements with the various authorities and clan leaders for the delivery of humanitarian assistance through the collaborative efforts of the United Nations, ICRC and NGOs.

The Secretary-General observed that the crisis in the country had regional consequences, as evidenced by the flow of Somali refugees to neighbouring countries, and there were grave concerns about the destabilizing effects it could have on the Horn of Africa. In the country, there was hardly any governmental infrastructure that could be relied on. Banditry was widespread and there was wide proliferation of weapons. The port and international airport of Mogadishu were in the control of groups not under the command of either major faction.

The tragic situation with its extraordinary complexities so far had eluded conventional solutions. The threat of dramatic food shortages among particularly vulnerable groups was becoming increasingly acute. The lack of clean water and primary health care services and control of communicable diseases was exacerbating the crisis. Owing to the efforts of NGOs, supported in part by United Nations agencies, some basic health, water and disease-control services were provided, but those efforts needed to be intensified. Access to the main ports and acceptance of the principle of "corridors" and "zones of peace" would enable the provision of more assistance.

The prevailing crisis posed a paradox which must be addressed: without security, relief assistance programmes would continue to be severely constrained; yet without such programmes, prospects for security were at best precarious. Therefore, the Secretary-General emphasized the necessity for the provision of humanitarian assistance even before the full complement of United Nations security personnel and cease-fire modalities were in place.

To monitor the cease-fire and the delivery of humanitarian assistance, the Secretary-General recommended the establishment of UNOSOM.

Command of UNOSOM in the field would be entrusted to a Commanding Officer with the rank of Brigadier-General, to be appointed by the Secretary-General after consultation with the two parties and with the consent of the Security Council. The military personnel would be contributed by Member States at the Secretary-General's request, after consultation with the parties and with the Council's approval.

As an addendum to his report, the Secretary-General submitted a consolidated inter-agency 90-day plan of action for emergency humanitarian assistance to Somalia. The plan was to form the basis for immediate action to deliver food and non-food relief assistance to an estimated 1.5 million people most immediately at risk. In addition, it targeted assistance for a further 3.5 million who were in need of food, seeds, and basic health and water services. The latter group included many thousands of soldiers and other armed groups who were to be reintegrated into civilian life through disarmament and demobilization programmes.

Implementation of the plan, as well as the continuity of expanded humanitarian relief and recovery efforts, required that United Nations agencies expanded their presence throughout the country, under the United Nations Coordinator for Humanitarian Assistance in Somalia, based at Mogadishu.

In another addendum, the Secretary-General provided preliminary cost estimates for UNOSOM—consisting of 550 military and security personnel and 79 civilians—in the amount $23.1 million for an initial six-month period.

SECURITY COUNCIL ACTION (April)

On 24 April, the Security Council reconvened to consider the situation in Somalia. The President, with the consent of the Council, invited Somalia, at its request, to participate in the discussion without the right to vote.

The Council unanimously adopted **resolution 751(1992)**.

The Security Council,

Considering the request by Somalia for the Security Council to consider the situation in Somalia,

Reaffirming its resolutions 733(1992) of 23 January 1992 and 746(1992) of 17 March 1992,

Having considered the report of the Secretary-General on the situation in Somalia,

Taking note of the signing of the cease-fire agreements in Mogadishu on 3 March 1992, including agreements for the implementation of measures aimed at stabilizing the cease-fire through a United Nations monitoring mission,

Taking note also of the signing of letters of agreement in Mogadishu, Hargeisa and Kismayo on the mechanism for monitoring the cease-fire and arrangements for the equitable and effective distribution of humanitarian assistance in and around Mogadishu,

Deeply disturbed by the magnitude of the human suffering caused by the conflict and concerned that the continuation of the situation in Somalia constitutes a threat to international peace and security,

Cognizant of the importance of cooperation between the United Nations and regional organizations in the context of Chapter VIII of the Charter of the United Nations,

Underlining the importance which it attaches to the international, regional and non-governmental organizations, including the International Committee of the Red Cross, continuing to provide humanitarian and other relief assistance to the people of Somalia under difficult circumstances,

Expressing its appreciation to the regional organizations, including the Organization of African Unity, the League of Arab States and the Organization of the Islamic Conference, for their cooperation with the United Nations in the effort to resolve the Somali problem,

1. *Takes note with appreciation* of the report of the Secretary-General of 21 April 1992;

2. *Decides* to establish under its authority, and in support of the Secretary-General in accordance with paragraph 7 below, a United Nations Operation in Somalia (UNOSOM);

3. *Requests* the Secretary-General immediately to deploy a unit of 50 United Nations Observers to monitor the cease-fire in Mogadishu in accordance with paragraphs 24 to 26 of the Secretary-General's report;

4. *Agrees*, in principle, also to establish under the overall direction of the Secretary-General's Special Representative a United Nations security force to be deployed as soon as possible to perform the functions described in paragraphs 27-29 of the Secretary-General's report;

5. *Further requests* the Secretary-General to continue his consultations with the parties in Mogadishu regarding the proposed United Nations security force and, in light of those consultations, to submit his further recommendations to the Security Council for its decision as soon as possible;

6. *Welcomes* the intention expressed by the Secretary-General in paragraph 64 of his report to appoint a Special Representative for Somalia to provide overall direction of United Nations activities in Somalia and to assist him in his endeavours to reach a peaceful resolution of the conflict in Somalia;

7. *Requests* the Secretary-General as part of his continuing mission in Somalia to facilitate an immediate and effective cessation of hostilities and the maintenance of a cease-fire throughout the country in order to promote the process of reconciliation and political settlement in Somalia and to provide urgent humanitarian assistance;

8. *Welcomes* the cooperation between the United Nations and the League of Arab States, the Organization of African Unity and the Organization of the Islamic Conference in resolving the problem in Somalia;

9. *Calls upon* all parties, movements and factions in Somalia immediately to cease hostilities and to maintain a cease-fire throughout the country in order to promote the process of reconciliation and political settlement in Somalia;

10. *Requests* the Secretary-General to continue as a matter of priority his consultations with all Somali parties, movements and factions towards the convening of a conference on national reconciliation and unity in Somalia in close cooperation with the League of Arab States, the Organization of African Unity and the Organization of the Islamic Conference;

11. *Decides* to establish, in accordance with rule 28 of the provisional rules of procedure of the Security Council, a Committee of the Security Council consisting of all the members of the Council, to undertake the following tasks and to report on its work to the Council with its observations and recommendations:

(a) to seek from all States information regarding the action taken by them concerning the effective implementation of the embargo imposed by paragraph 5 of resolution 733(1992);

(b) to consider any information brought to its attention by States concerning violations of the embargo, and in that context to make recommendations to the Council on ways of increasing the effectiveness of the embargo;

(c) to recommend appropriate measures in response to violations of the general and complete embargo on all deliveries of weapons and military equipment to Somalia and provide information on a regular basis to the Secretary-General for general distribution to Member States;

12. *Notes with appreciation* the ongoing efforts of the United Nations, its specialized agencies and humanitarian organizations to ensure delivery of humanitarian assistance to Somalia, particularly to Mogadishu;

13. *Calls upon* the international community to support, with financial and other resources, the implementation of the 90-day Plan of Action for Emergency Humanitarian Assistance to Somalia;

14. *Urges* all parties concerned in Somalia to facilitate the efforts of the United Nations, its specialized agencies and humanitarian organizations to provide urgent humanitarian assistance to the affected population in Somalia and reiterates its call for the full respect of the security and safety of the personnel of the humanitarian organizations and the guarantee of their complete freedom of movement in and around Mogadishu and other parts of Somalia;

15. *Calls upon* all Somali parties, movements and factions to cooperate fully with the Secretary-General in the implementation of this resolution;

16. *Decides* to remain seized of the matter until a peaceful solution is achieved.

Security Council resolution 751(1992)

24 April 1992   Meeting 3069   Adopted unanimously

Draft prepared in consultations among Council members (S/23834), orally revised.

By a letter of 24 April,[60] the Secretary-General informed the Council of his intention to appoint Mohammed Sahnoun (Algeria) as his Special Representative for Somalia. On 28 April,[61] the Council President informed the Secretary-General that the Council members welcomed his decision.

By a letter of 15 May,[62] Somalia said it was particularly grateful that a Special Representative had been appointed in accordance with the Council's resolution. In an annex, Somalia again put forward suggestions for solving the crisis.

Communication and report of the Secretary-General (June/July). By a letter of 23 June,[63] the Secretary-General informed the Security Council that both principal factions in Mogadishu had agreed to the immediate deployment of 50 uniformed and unarmed United Nations observers, which the Council had requested in its 24 April resolution. It was anticipated, the Secretary-General said, that an advance party under the command of the Chief Military Observer would arrive in Mogadishu on 5 July, with the other observers due to arrive by 10 July.

On 22 July,[(64)] the Secretary-General reported to the Council on the activities of his Special Representative, the monitoring of the cease-fire, humanitarian assistance and rehabilitation, national reconciliation efforts and regional activities supporting them, as well as the status of the arms embargo.

In his concluding observations, he noted that Somalia was fragmented along clan and family lines, without any recognized channels for political action. The activities of independent armed groups, factions and individuals, which possessed an enormous quantity of arms, were possibly the biggest and most serious threat to both the Somalis and the expatriates working for United Nations agencies and NGOs.

The complexity of the situation and its inherent dangers, combined with the almost total absence of central, regional or local government, posed enormous operational difficulties for establishing a large-scale and effective United Nations presence. However, the threat of mass starvation and potential renewal of hostilities required an immediate and comprehensive response. United Nations efforts needed to be enlarged to help bring about an effective cease-fire throughout the country, while at the same time promoting national reconciliation. That would require the establishment of a United Nations presence in all regions, as well as the adoption of an innovative and comprehensive approach dealing with all aspects of the situation—humanitarian relief and recovery, cessation of hostilities and security, the peace process and national reconcilation—in a consolidated framework. To that effect, the Secretary-General proposed the establishment of four operational zones: the north-west (Berbera), the north-east (Bossasso), the central rangelands and Mogadishu, and the south (Kismayo).

As the security situation in Mogadishu continued to be precarious, with widespread looting and banditry and increased attacks on United Nations and NGO personnel, the Secretary-General said he had requested his Special Representative to pursue his consultations for the deployment of a security force there.

Conditions in most of the other regions of Somalia also called for immediate action; therefore, the Secretary-General intended to dispatch a technical team to Somalia to examine the possible monitoring of cease-fire arrangements in parts of the country other than Mogadishu; the possible deployment of military observers in the south-west region on Somalia's border with Kenya; the feasibility of an arms-for-food exchange programme; the need for security forces to escort and protect humanitarian aid activities and personnel in other parts of the country; and a possible role for the United Nations in helping re-establish local police forces.

All political leaders and elders in Somalia requested United Nations assistance in disarming the population and demobilizing the irregular forces. Such a programme had begun in some areas, such as Mogadishu-north and parts of the north-west and the north-east, on the initiative of the local leaders themselves. Some leaders preferred the arms to be destroyed, while others suggested that they be retained for the new regular forces. The Special Representative, with the help of the technical team, was to develop a plan in that regard for application in all four zones. The Secretary-General also considered it important that the international community continue to enforce the arms embargo as provided for in the Council's January resolution.

The conflict in Somalia could be resolved only by the people of Somalia themselves in a process of national reconciliation, the Secretary-General stated. The convening of a conference towards that end called for sustained efforts and demanded patience and understanding of the regional environment. Important progress on that matter had been made during the Special Representative's consultations with Somali leaders and elders, during which alternative venues were discussed.

The Special Representative had already shown that his personal intervention could help defuse potential local crises. Qualified UNOSOM personnel would accordingly be located in each of the zones to assist in mediation and conciliation and in arranging for consultative conferences as needed. In the two months since the establishment of UNOSOM, significant developments had taken place which must be consolidated and built upon, as there was the risk of a renewal of hostilities. The desperate and complex situation in the country required energetic and sustained efforts on the part of the international community to break the cycle of violence and hunger. The new, comprehensive approach described was intended as a catalyst for achieving the vital objective of national reconciliation and the construction of a peaceful, stable and democratic Somalia.

SECURITY COUNCIL ACTION (July)

On 27 July, the Security Council met again to consider the situation in Somalia. The President, with the Council's consent, invited Somalia to participate in the discussion without the right to vote.

On the same date, the Council adopted **resolution 767(1992)** unanimously.

The Security Council,

Considering the request by Somalia for the Security Council to consider the situation in Somalia,

Reaffirming its resolutions 733(1992) of 23 January 1992, 746(1992) of 17 March 1992 and 751(1992) of 24 April 1992,

Having considered the report of the Secretary-General on the situation in Somalia,

Considering the letter of the Secretary-General to the President of the Security Council informing him that all the parties in Mogadishu have agreed to the deployment of the fifty military observers, and that the advance party of the observers arrived in Mogadishu on 5 July 1992 and that the rest of the observers arrived in the mission area on 23 July 1992,

Deeply concerned about the availability of arms and ammunition in the hands of civilians and the proliferation of armed banditry throughout Somalia,

Alarmed by the sporadic outbreak of hostilities in several parts of Somalia leading to continued loss of life and destruction of property, and putting at risk the personnel of the United Nations, non-governmental organizations and other international humanitarian organizations, as well as disrupting their operations,

Deeply disturbed by the magnitude of the human suffering caused by the conflict and concerned that the situation in Somalia constitutes a threat to international peace and security,

Gravely alarmed by the deterioration of the humanitarian situation in Somalia and underlining the urgent need for quick delivery of humanitarian assistance in the whole country,

Recognizing that the provision of humanitarian assistance in Somalia is an important element in the effort of the Council to restore international peace and security in the area,

Responding to the urgent calls by the parties in Somalia for the international community to take measures in Somalia to ensure the delivery of humanitarian assistance in Somalia,

Noting the Secretary-General's proposals for a comprehensive decentralized zonal approach in the United Nations involvement in Somalia,

Cognizant that the success of such an approach requires the cooperation of all parties, movements and factions in Somalia,

1.   *Takes note with appreciation* of the report of the Secretary-General of 22 July 1992;

2.   *Requests* the Secretary-General to make full use of all available means and arrangements, including the mounting of an urgent airlift operation, with a view to facilitating the efforts of the United Nations, its specialized agencies and humanitarian organizations in accelerating the provision of humanitarian assistance to the affected population in Somalia, threatened by mass starvation;

3.   *Urges* all parties, movements and factions in Somalia to facilitate the efforts of the United Nations, its specialized agencies and humanitarian organizations to provide urgent humanitarian assistance to the affected

population in Somalia and reiterates its call for the full respect of the security and safety of the personnel of the humanitarian organizations and the guarantee of their complete freedom of movement in and around Mogadishu and other parts of Somalia;

4.   *Calls upon* all parties, movements and factions in Somalia to cooperate with the United Nations with a view to the urgent deployment of the United Nations security personnel called for in paragraphs 4 and 5 of its resolution 751(1992), and otherwise assist in the general stabilization of the situation in Somalia. In the absence of such cooperation, the Security Council does not exclude other measures to deliver humanitarian assistance to Somalia;

5.   *Reiterates its appeal* to the international community to provide adequate financial and other resources for humanitarian efforts in Somalia;

6.   *Encourages* the ongoing efforts of the United Nations, its specialized agencies and humanitarian organizations, including the International Committee of the Red Cross, to ensure delivery of humanitarian assistance to all regions of Somalia;

7.   *Appeals* to all parties, movements and factions in Somalia to extend full cooperation to the military observers and to take measures to ensure their security;

8.   *Requests* the Secretary-General, as part of his continuing efforts in Somalia, to promote an immediate and effective cessation of hostilities and the maintenance of a cease-fire throughout the country in order to facilitate the urgent delivery of humanitarian assistance and the process of reconciliation and political settlement in Somalia;

9.   *Calls upon* all parties, movements and factions in Somalia immediately to cease hostilities and to maintain a cease-fire throughout the country;

10. *Stresses* the need for the observance and strict monitoring of the general and complete embargo of all deliveries of weapons and military equipment to Somalia, as decided in paragraph 5 of its resolution 733(1992);

11. *Welcomes* the cooperation between the United Nations, the Organization of African Unity, the League of Arab States and the Organization of the Islamic Conference in resolving the situation in Somalia;

12. *Approves* the Secretary-General's proposal to establish four operational zones in Somalia as part of the consolidated United Nations Operation in Somalia;

13. *Requests* the Secretary-General to ensure that his Special Representative for Somalia is provided with all the necessary support services to enable him to effectively carry out his mandate;

14. *Strongly supports* the Secretary-General's decision urgently to dispatch a technical team to Somalia, under the overall direction of the Special Representative, in order to work within the framework and objectives outlined in paragraph 64 of his report and to submit expeditiously a report to the Security Council on this matter;

15. *Affirms* that all officials of the United Nations and all experts on mission for the United Nations in Somalia enjoy the privileges and immunities provided for in the Convention on the Privileges and Immunities of the United Nations of 1946 and in any other relevant instruments and that all parties, movements and factions in Somalia are required to allow them full freedom of movement and all necessary facilities;

16. *Requests* the Secretary-General to continue urgently his consultations with all parties, movements and

factions in Somalia towards the convening of a conference on national reconciliation and unity in Somalia in close cooperation with the Organization of African Unity, the League of Arab States and the Organization of the Islamic Conference;

17. *Calls upon* all parties, movements and factions in Somalia to cooperate fully with the Secretary-General in the implementation of this resolution;

18. *Decides* to remain seized of the matter until a peaceful solution is achieved.

Security Council resolution 767(1992)

27 July 1992   Meeting 3101   Adopted unanimously

Draft prepared in consultations among Council members (S/24347), orally revised.

On 12 August,[65] the Secretary-General reported to the Council that the two principal factions in Mogadishu had agreed to the deployment of a 500-strong United Nations security force in the Somali capital as part of UNOSOM; he intended to deploy the force as soon as possible. By a letter of 14 August,[66] the Council President informed the Secretary-General of the Council's agreement to the deployment.

Report of the Secretary-General (August). In an August report,[67] the Secretary-General described the steps planned or taken to mitigate the widespread starvation in the areas of Somalia most seriously affected by internal strife and drought. The report was based on the findings of a technical team led by Peter Hansen, former Assistant Secretary-General of the United Nations, which had visited various places in Somalia from 6 to 15 August, meeting with leaders and representatives of various factions and movements, as well as with elders. The team leader also held consultations with Kenyan authorities on issues of particular concern to them.

According to the report, United Nations agencies and ICRC, as well as NGOs, continued implementing the 90-day plan submitted in April (see above) and to extend their humanitarian activities. Since March, a joint World Food Programme (WFP)/United Nations Children's Fund airlift had transported over 1,300 metric tons of supplementary foods and medical supplies from Nairobi to Mogadishu, Kismayo, Boroma and Baidoa. Since the beginning of the year, WFP had delivered 36,500 metric tons of food, mainly to Mogadishu, while ICRC had delivered 83,000 metric tons to various parts of the country. Bilateral donors, such as France and Saudi Arabia, also shipped food and other assistance.

The delivery of humanitarian assistance, however, was fraught with difficulties because of the vicious cycle of insecurity and hunger. Lack of security prevented the delivery of food, while food shortages contributed significantly to violence and insecurity. The crisis was further compounded by

drought in the south and the devastation of agriculture, livestock and fisheries by the civil war.

To break the cycle of violence and food insecurity, the Secretary-General proposed a comprehensive programme of action covering humanitarian relief, cessation of hostilities, reduction of violence and national reconciliation. He reiterated the belief that "food for arms" could be an important component of efforts to improve security conditions through a disarmament and demobilization programme. The programme of action would have to include educational and vocational training and its basic thrust must be to provide alternatives for survival other than possession of arms. Equal consideration must be given to the reintegration of militia forces into society.

A stronger United Nations role in securing access, transport and distribution of relief supplies must be paralleled by an effort to involve Somali entities fully in all aspects of the process, the Secretary-General stressed. He suggested that airlift operations be substantially expanded and primarily directed to central and southern Somalia. He further proposed an emergency relief programme to halt massive displacements and refugee flows caused by the civil war and starvation. A particularly serious situation existed along the Kenyan border, where some 280,000 Somali refugees were located, with 2,000 more arriving daily. The "preventive zone" concept reflected in an updated consolidated inter-agency appeal of 15 July needed to be put into effect immediately and UNHCR was ready to take the lead in that matter. The first phase of the programme would be the establishment of an operation to deliver food and seeds from Kenya to a preventive zone on the Somali side of the border. The programme was intended to reduce significantly cross-border movements of people in search of food and to contribute to a decrease in friction that was growing in the border area.

The Secretary-General noted that the main problem was not the delivery of humanitarian relief supplies to Somali ports and airports but the protection of the transport convoys. The technical team confirmed the Secretary-General's earlier recommendation that such protection should be provided by United Nations security personnel. An agreement for the earliest possible deployment in Mogadishu of a 500-strong security force had been reached on 12 August, and a similar agreement was obtained for the deployment of security units in two other parts of the country.

The technical team also evaluated the possible extension of UNOSOM's cease-fire activities at Mogadishu to other parts of Somalia. The Secretary-General reported that the 50 military observers who completed their deployment in Mogadishu on 23 July were able to play a valuable role in helping both sides there maintain the cease-fire. On 2 August, UNOSOM was able to arrange the first meeting of a joint cease-fire monitoring committee, chaired by the Chief Military Observer.

The Secretary-General recommended the deployment of four additional United Nations security units, each with a strength of up to 750, for the protection of the humanitarian convoys and distribution centres throughout Somalia. He reiterated an earlier proposal that UNOSOM establish four operational zones to cover all parts of the country.

SECURITY COUNCIL ACTION (August and October)

On 28 August, the Security Council met to consider the Secretary-General's report. Somalia was invited to participate without the right to vote. The Council unanimously adopted **resolution 775(1992)**.

The Security Council,

Considering the request by Somalia for the Security Council to consider the situation in Somalia,

Reaffirming its resolutions 733(1992) of 23 January 1992, 746(1992) of 17 March 1992, 751(1992) of 24 April 1992 and 767(1992) of 27 July 1992,

Having considered the report of the Secretary-General on the situation in Somalia,

Deeply concerned about the availability of arms and ammunition and the proliferation of armed banditry throughout Somalia,

Alarmed by the continued sporadic outbreak of hostilities in several parts of Somalia leading to continued loss of life and destruction of property, and putting at risk the personnel of the United Nations, non-governmental organizations and other international humanitarian organizations, as well as disrupting their operations,

Deeply disturbed by the magnitude of the human suffering caused by the conflict and concerned that the situation in Somalia constitutes a threat to international peace and security,

Gravely alarmed by the deterioration of the humanitarian situation in Somalia and underlining the urgent need for quick delivery of humanitarian assistance in the whole country,

Reaffirming that the provision of humanitarian assistance in Somalia is an important element in the effort of the Council to restore international peace and security in the area,

Welcoming the ongoing efforts by the United Nations organizations as well as the International Committee of the Red Cross, non-governmental organizations and States to provide humanitarian assistance to the affected population in Somalia,

Welcoming in particular the initiatives to provide relief through airlift operations,

Convinced that no durable progress will be achieved in the absence of an overall political solution in Somalia,

Taking note in particular of paragraph 24 of the report of the Secretary-General,

1. *Takes note with appreciation* of the report of the Secretary-General of 24 August 1992 on the findings of the technical team and the recommendations of the Secretary-General contained therein;

2. *Invites* the Secretary-General to establish four zone headquarters as proposed in paragraph 31 of the Secretary-General's report;

3. *Authorizes* the increase in strength of the United Nations Operation in Somalia and the subsequent deployment as recommended in paragraph 37 of the Secretary-General's report;

4. *Welcomes* the decision of the Secretary-General to increase substantially the airlift operation to areas of priority attention;

5. *Calls upon* all parties, movements and factions in Somalia to cooperate with the United Nations with a view to the urgent deployment of the United Nations security personnel called for in paragraphs 4 and 5 of its resolution 751(1992) and as recommended in paragraph 37 of the Secretary-General's report;

6. ·*Welcomes* also the material and logistical support from a number of States and *urges* that the airlift operation be effectively coordinated by the United Nations as described in paragraphs 17 to 21 of the report of the Secretary-General;

7. *Urges* all parties, movements and factions in Somalia to facilitate the efforts of the United Nations, its specialized agencies and humanitarian organizations to provide urgent humanitarian assistance to the affected population in Somalia and reiterates its call for the full respect of the security and safety of the personnel of these organizations and the guarantee of their complete freedom of movement in and around Mogadishu and other parts of Somalia;

8. *Reiterates its appeal* to the international community to provide adequate financial and other resources for humanitarian efforts in Somalia;

9. *Encourages* ongoing efforts of the United Nations, its specialized agencies and humanitarian organizations including the International Committee of the Red Cross and non-governmental organizations to ensure delivery of humanitarian assistance to all regions of Somalia and *underlines* the importance of coordination between these efforts;

10. *Requests* also the Secretary-General to continue, in close cooperation with the Organization of African Unity, the League of Arab States and the Organization of the Islamic Conference, his efforts to seek a comprehensive political solution to the crisis in Somalia;

11. *Calls upon* all parties, movements and factions in Somalia immediately to cease hostilities and to maintain a cease-fire throughout the country;

12. *Stresses* the need for the observance and strict monitoring of the general and complete embargo on all deliveries of weapons and military equipment to Somalia, as decided in paragraph 5 of its resolution 733(1992);

13. *Calls upon* all parties, movements and factions in Somalia to cooperate fully with the Secretary-General in the implementation of this resolution;

14. *Decides* to remain seized of the matter until a peaceful solution is achieved.

Security Council resolution 775(1992)

28 August 1992   Meeting 3110   Adopted unanimously

Draft prepared in consultations among Council members (S/24497), orally corrected.

Following consultations on 16 October, the President, on behalf of the Council members, made a statement to the media:[68]

"The Security Council heard today a communication from Mr. Sahnoun, the Special Representative of the Secretary-General in Somalia. On this occasion, the members of the Security Council reiterated their full support for the action of the Secretary-General and his Special Representative. They also expressed the wish that the appeal recently made in Geneva for an increase in the humanitarian assistance to Somalia should be heeded.

"The members of the Council expressed their deep concern over the information communicated to them by Mr. Sahnoun, particularly regarding the difficulties he is encountering in the delivery of humanitarian assistance. In this regard, the rapid deployment of UNOSOM personnel is essential. The members of the Council consider that persons hampering the deployment of UNOSOM would be responsible for aggravating an already unprecedented humanitarian disaster."

Communications (November). With the situation in Somalia deteriorating by the day, the Secretary-General outlined in a 24 November letter to the Council[69] the difficulties UNOSOM faced in implementing its mandate, such as the absence of a government or governing authority capable of maintaining law and order; the failure of the various factions to cooperate with UNOSOM; the extortion of large sums of cash from donor agencies and organizations to allow them to operate; the hijacking of vehicles, looting of relief convoys and warehouses; and the detention of expatriate personnel.

Unless problems relating to security and protection of relief supplies were effectively addressed, United Nations agencies and NGOs would not be able to provide the relief assistance urgently needed. The Secretary-General stated that he was giving urgent consideration to that state of affairs and did not exclude the possibility that it might become necessary to review the basic premises and principles of the United Nations effort in Somalia.

The Security Council members discussed the letter during informal consultations on 25 November. They expressed the view that the situation was intolerable and voiced doubts as to whether the methods employed by the United Nations would be capable of bringing the situation under control. Strong support was expressed for the Secretary-General's view that the time had come to move into Chapter VII of the Charter. The Council members therefore welcomed the Secretary-General's reference to a re-examination of basic premises and principles and asked him to come forward with specific recommendations on how the United Nations could remedy the situation.

On 29 November,[70] the Secretary-General outlined five options for creating the conditions for uninterrupted delivery of supplies. The first was to continue and intensify efforts to deploy UNOSOM in accordance with its existing mandate, under which force was to be used only in self-defence. Without any central authority with which UNOSOM could effectively negotiate, however, continuation of the current course would be an inadequate response. Under the second option, the use of international military personnel would be abandoned and humanitarian agencies would negotiate arrangements with the various factions and clan leaders for distribution of relief assistance; the experience of recent months, when agencies without military protection had felt obliged to pay protection money to the various factions and clans, showed that this could lead to less and less aid reaching vulnerable groups and lawless trading in aid could become the foundation of Somalia's economy.

The third option would be for UNOSOM to mount a show of force to discourage attacks on relief efforts, which would be a major military undertaking and give rise to difficult questions with regard to organization, command and control. The fourth option was a country-wide enforcement operation by a group of Member States under the authority of the Security Council. In that context, the Secretary-General noted an offer by the United States to organize and lead such an operation. The fifth option was country-wide enforcement action under United Nations command and control, along the lines of peace-keeping operations, or some other arrangement on which the Council might decide.

In view of the prevailing situation, the Secretary-General recommended that the Council take a very early decision to adjust its approach to the crisis; the Council's focus should be on creating conditions in which relief supplies could be delivered to those in need. Experience showed that that could not be achieved by a United Nations operation based on the accepted principles of peace-keeping.

The Secretary-General concluded that there was no alternative but to resort to the enforcement provisions under Chapter VII of the Charter, with parallel action to promote national reconciliation in order to remove the main factors that created the human emergency. Such forceful action should preferably be under United Nations command and control; if that was not feasible, an alternative would be an operation undertaken by Member States with Security Council authorization. In either case, the objectives of the operation must be precisely defined and limited in time, in order to prepare the way for a return to peace-keeping and post-conflict peace-building.

Canada and Pakistan, by letters of 27 November[71] and 3 December,[72] respectively, voiced their expectation that as troop contributors they would be consulted by the Council and the Secretariat on any measures that might affect UNOSOM's mandate.

SECURITY COUNCIL ACTION (December)

On 3 December, the Security Council met to consider the deteriorating situation in Somalia. As at previous meetings, the President invited Somalia to participate without the right to vote.

The Council adopted **resolution 794(1992)** unanimously.

The Security Council,

Reaffirming its resolutions 733(1992) of 23 January 1992, 746(1992) of 17 March 1992, 751(1992) of 24 April 1992, 767(1992) of 27 July 1992 and 775(1992) of 28 August 1992,

Recognizing the unique character of the present situation in Somalia and *mindful* of its deteriorating, complex and extraordinary nature, requiring an immediate and exceptional response,

Determining that the magnitude of the human tragedy caused by the conflict in Somalia, further exacerbated by the obstacles being created to the distribution of humanitarian assistance, constitutes a threat to international peace and security,

Gravely alarmed by the deterioration of the humanitarian situation in Somalia and *underlining* the urgent need for the quick delivery of humanitarian assistance in the whole country,

Noting the efforts of the League of Arab States, the Organization of African Unity, and in particular the proposal made by its Chairman at the forty-seventh regular session of the General Assembly for the organization of an international conference on Somalia, and the Organization of the Islamic Conference and other regional agencies and arrangements to promote reconciliation and political settlement in Somalia and to address the humanitarian needs of the people of that country,

Commending the ongoing efforts of the United Nations, its specialized agencies and humanitarian organizations and of non-governmental organizations and of States to ensure delivery of humanitarian assistance in Somalia,

Responding to the urgent calls from Somalia for the international community to take measures to ensure the delivery of humanitarian assistance in Somalia,

Expressing grave alarm at continuing reports of widespread violations of international humanitarian law occurring in Somalia, including reports of violence and threats of violence against personnel participating lawfully in impartial humanitarian relief activities; deliberate attacks on non-combatants, relief consignments and vehicles, and medical and relief facilities; and impeding the delivery of food and medical supplies essential for the survival of the civilian population,

Dismayed by the continuation of conditions that impede the delivery of humanitarian supplies to destinations within Somalia, and in particular reports of looting of relief supplies destined for starving people, attacks on aircraft and ships bringing in humanitarian relief supplies, and attacks on the Pakistani UNOSOM contingent in Mogadishu,

Taking note with appreciation of the letters of the Secretary-General of 24 November 1992 and of 29 November 1992,

Sharing the Secretary-General's assessment that the situation in Somalia is intolerable and that it has become necessary to review the basic premises and principles of the United Nations effort in Somalia, and that UNOSOM's existing course would not in present circumstances be an adequate response to the tragedy in Somalia,

Determined to establish as soon as possible the necessary conditions for the delivery of humanitarian assistance wherever needed in Somalia, in conformity with resolutions 751(1992) and 767(1992),

Noting the offer by Member States aimed at establishing a secure environment for humanitarian relief operations in Somalia as soon as possible,

Determined further to restore peace, stability and law and order with a view to facilitating the process of a political settlement under the auspices of the United Nations, aimed at national reconciliation in Somalia, and *encouraging* the Secretary-General and his Special Representative to continue and intensify their work at the national and regional levels to promote these objectives,

Recognizing that the people of Somalia bear ultimate responsibility for national reconciliation and the reconstruction of their own country,

1. *Reaffirms* its demand that all parties, movements and factions in Somalia immediately cease hostilities, maintain a cease-fire throughout the country, and cooperate with the Special Representative of the Secretary-General as well as with the military forces to be established pursuant to the authorization given in paragraph 10 below in order to promote the process of relief distribution, reconciliation and political settlement in Somalia;

2. *Demands* that all parties, movements and factions in Somalia take all measures necessary to facilitate the efforts of the United Nations, its specialized agencies and humanitarian organizations to provide urgent humanitarian assistance to the affected population in Somalia;

3. *Also demands* that all parties, movements and factions in Somalia take all measures necessary to ensure the safety of United Nations and all other personnel engaged in the delivery of humanitarian assistance, including the military forces to be established pursuant to the authorization given in paragraph 10 below;

4. *Further demands* that all parties, movements and factions in Somalia immediately cease and desist from all breaches of international humanitarian law including from actions such as those described above;

5. *Strongly condemns* all violations of international humanitarian law occurring in Somalia, including in particular the deliberate impeding of the delivery of food and medical supplies essential for the survival of the civilian population, and *affirms* that those who commit or order the commission of such acts will be held individually responsible in respect of such acts;

6. *Decides* that the operations and the further deployment of the 3,500 personnel of the United Nations Operation in Somalia (UNOSOM) authorized by paragraph 3 of resolution 775(1992) should proceed at the discretion of the Secretary-General in the light of his assessment of conditions on the ground; and *requests* him to keep the Council informed and to make such recommendations as may be appropriate for the fulfilment of its mandate where conditions permit;

7. *Endorses* the recommendation by the Secretary-General in his letter of 29 November 1992 that action under Chapter VII of the Charter of the United Nations should be taken in order to establish a secure en-

vironment for humanitarian relief operations in Somalia as soon as possible;

8. *Welcomes* the offer by a Member State described in the Secretary-General's letter to the Council of 29 November 1992 concerning the establishment of an operation to create such a secure environment;

9. *Welcomes also* offers by other Member States to participate in that operation;

10. *Acting* under Chapter VII of the Charter of the United Nations, *authorizes* the Secretary-General and Member States cooperating to implement the offer referred to in paragraph 8 above to use all necessary means to establish as soon as possible a secure environment for humanitarian relief operations in Somalia;

11. *Calls* on all Member States which are in a position to do so to provide military forces and to make additional contributions, in cash or in kind, in accordance with paragraph 10 above and *requests* the Secretary-General to establish a fund through which the contributions, where appropriate, could be channelled to the States or operations concerned;

12. *Authorizes* the Secretary-General and the Member States concerned to make the necessary arrangements for the unified command and control of the forces involved, which will reflect the offer referred to in paragraph 8 above;

13. *Requests* the Secretary-General and the Member States acting under paragraph 10 above to establish appropriate mechanisms for coordination between the United Nations and their military forces;

14. *Decides* to appoint an ad hoc commission composed of members of the Security Council to report to the Council on the implementation of this resolution;

15. *Invites* the Secretary-General to attach a small UNOSOM liaison staff to the Field Headquarters of the unified command;

16. Acting under Chapters VII and VIII of the Charter, *calls upon* States, nationally or through regional agencies or arrangements, to use such measures as may be necessary to ensure strict implementation of paragraph 5 of resolution 733(1992);

17. *Requests* all States, in particular those in the region, to provide appropriate support for the actions undertaken by States, nationally or through regional agencies or arrangements, pursuant to this and other relevant resolutions;

18. *Requests* the Secretary-General and, as appropriate, the States concerned to report to the Council on a regular basis, the first such report to be made no later than fifteen days after the adoption of this resolution, on the implementation of this resolution and the attainment of the objective of establishing a secure environment so as to enable the Council to make the necessary decision for a prompt transition to continued peace-keeping operations;

19. *Requests* the Secretary-General to submit a plan to the Council initially within fifteen days after the adoption of this resolution to ensure that UNOSOM will be able to fulfil its mandate upon the withdrawal of the unified command;

20. *Invites* the Secretary-General and his Special Representative to continue their efforts to achieve a political settlement in Somalia;

21. *Decides* to remain actively seized of the matter.

Security Council resolution 794(1992)
3 December 1992   Meeting 3145   Adopted unanimously
Draft prepared in consultations among Council members (S/24880).

Further developments. In response to the Council resolution of 3 December, the President of the United States directed the execution of Operation Restore Hope on 4 December. The United States central command was given the mission of conducting joint and combined military operations in Somalia, under United Nations auspices, to secure major airports and seaports, key installations and food distribution points, to provide open passage of relief supplies and security for convoys, and to assist the United Nations and NGOs in providing humanitarian relief.

The first elements of the Unified Task Force (UNITAF), led by United States marines, arrived at Mogadishu on 9 December. United States forces were to number eventually 28,000, augmented by over 17,000 troops from 20 other countries. A report on Operation Restore Hope was annexed to a 17 December letter from the United States to the Security Council President.[73]

Phase I of Operation Restore Hope was completed on 16 December, with the airfield and port facilities at Mogadishu and the airfields at Baidoa and Bale Dogle secured. Phase II was completed on 28 December with the securing of all eight major relief centres, including Bardera, Belet Weyne, Gialalassi, Kismayo and Oddur. On 31 December, United States and Italian forces secured the coastal city of Marka. Coalition forces continued to expand security operations in Mogadishu and the other major relief centres.[74]

Parallel with the establishment of a secure environment, efforts to achieve a political settlement continued, the Secretary-General reported on 19 December to the Security Council.[75] Accordingly, he invited 12 political Somali movements to participate in an informal preparatory meeting for a conference on national reconciliation, to be held at Addis Ababa in January 1993. In order to create conditions for the process of national reconciliation, the Secretary-General considered it necessary to establish or consolidate agreements with the leaders of all the organized factions for effective cease-fires; those agreements were to include provisions for the concentration of all the heavy weapons at designated locations, where they could be brought under international control, exercised initially by UNITAF and thereafter by UNOSOM. In that context, he noted that the leaders of the two principal factions in Mogadishu had recently agreed to a new cease-fire and to the concentration of their weapons. In addition, the Secretary-General felt it was necessary to disarm the lawless gangs that had been the principal threat to humanitarian operations.

During discussions with United States authorities, it was suggested that the mandate of UNOSOM be enlarged in conceptual and other terms, once UNOSOM took over from UNITAF, and that it cover the whole territory of Somalia. The United States envisaged that the mandate, concept of operations, level of armament and rules of engagement of the new UNOSOM would be little different from those of UNITAF; that approach of a peace-enforcement operation, the first such operation under United Nations command, would require, in the Secretary-General's view, a further decision by the Security Council under Chapter VII of the Charter and would be analogous to the fifth option for which he had expressed preference in his 29 November letter (see above).

The question that would have to be addressed was whether such an operation would be feasible and how many Member States would be ready to participate in it. Progress in the peace process had to be taken into account in deciding how and when UNITAF should be replaced by a new UNOSOM. Another consideration was the fact that the international community faced a long haul in helping the Somali people to put their country on its feet again. To that effect, an integrated approach containing all the elements of post-conflict peace-building was needed, such as restoration of security, political reconciliation, re-creation of institutions, return of refugees, rehabilitation and reconstruction.

For all those reasons, the Secretary-General recommended that the Council defer a decision until the situation on the ground became clearer.

On 23 December,[76] Somalia expressed support for the Secretary-General's request to the Council to defer any new decisions until he had obtained the views of all factions. It encouraged his efforts to continue translating his conceptual framework into concrete plans for presentation to the Somali factions in the near future, perhaps during the informal meeting scheduled for January 1993. Among other measures, it suggested that the Council mandate the Secretary-General to put together an international peace-keeping force, under United Nations command, with the capacity to enforce peace, and that the United States ensure that the United Nations eventually took over responsibility from the Unified Military Command. It further appealed to Member States to provide resources for a successful transition and national reconcilation process.

Somalia stressed that international presence and assistance should be available to all parts of Somalia. Speedy implementation of programmes to rehabilitate basic social and economic services and basic infrastructure, restore local civil administration, resettle displaced persons and repatriate refugees could be a catalyst for peace and stability that would minimize the need for forceful measures.

Composition of UNOSOM

By a letter of 22 June,[77] the Secretary-General proposed that the military elements of UNOSOM be composed of contingents from Austria, Bangladesh, Czechoslovakia, Egypt, Fiji, Finland, Indonesia, Jordan, Morocco and Zimbabwe. On 25 June,[78] the President of the Security Council reported that Council members agreed with the proposal.

On 23 June,[79] the Secretary-General proposed that Brigadier-General Imtíaz Shaheen (Pakistan) be appointed as Chief Military Observer of UNOSOM.

In pursuance of resolution 775(1992) of 28 August, by which the Security Council authorized an increase in the strength of UNOSOM, the Secretary-General undertook consultations with Australia, Austria, Belgium, Canada, Denmark, Egypt, Germany, Nigeria, Sweden and Switzerland. By a letter of 1 September,[80] he sought the Council's approval of the list of prospective troop contributors. The Council gave its approval on 8 September.[81]

Also on 1 September,[82] the Secretary-General requested the Council to authorize an increase in UNOSOM strength to cover the logistic support units; consequently, the total strength of UNOSOM should be 4,219 all ranks (3,500 security personnel, including the unit of 500 already authorized for Mogadishu, and 719 for the logistic units). The Council members expressed their agreement in a letter of 8 September.[83]

On 21 October,[84] the Secretary-General informed the Council that, of the countries listed in his 1 September letter, Belgium, Canada and Egypt each pledged to provide one battalion to UNOSOM and Australia agreed to provide personnel for the logistical unit. As Norway and New Zealand had also offered logistic personnel, the Secretary-General sought the Council's agreement that they be added to the list of troop contributors. On 26 October,[85] the Council President conveyed to the Secretary-General the Council members' agreement.

On 19 November,[86] the Secretary-General requested the addition of Ireland to the list of troop-contributing countries. The Council gave its consent on 24 November.[87]

On 1 December,[88] Egypt stated its agreement to participate in UNOSOM.

Financing of UNOSOM

Initial commitments

In order to provide for the immediate requirements for the deployment of 50 United Nations observers, requested by Security Council resolution 751(1992) of 24 April, the Chairman of ACABQ informed the Secretary-General, by a letter of 20 May, that ACABQ concurred with his proposal to enter into commitments for UNOSOM of up to $7,410,000 under the terms of a 1991 General Assembly resolution on unforeseen and extraordinary expenses for 1992-1993,[23] until an appropriation for UNOSOM was made available by the Assembly. That amount included the cost of the March 1992 technical survey mission. Resources from the Trust Fund in Support of United Nations Peacemaking and Peace-keeping Activities were utilized, to the extent possible, to meet UNOSOM's cash flow requirements.

By a letter of 14 September, ACABQ further concurred with the Secretary-General's proposal to enter into additional commitments of $10 million under the terms of the 1991 Assembly resolution, in order to provide for the most urgent requirements of UNOSOM, following the Security Council's authorization of an increase in troop strength to 4,219, all ranks. As a result, $17,410,000 was thus authorized.

Cost estimates of UNOSOM

In a November report,[89] the Secretary-General estimated the total cost of UNOSOM for the period 1 May 1992 to 31 October 1993, including the pre-implementation phase, at $208,122,700 gross ($204,585,700 net). Details of expenditure were contained in annexes to the report. The Secretary-General also outlined the operational plan for UNOSOM. He appealed to Member States to make advances, on a voluntary basis, to meet the initial expenses of UNOSOM, pending formal action by the General Assembly. He noted that the Government of the United States had offered to airlift military personnel, as a voluntary contribution-in-kind.

ACABQ, also in November,[90] recommended appropriation of $6,953,100 gross ($6,741,600 net) for the six months from 1 May to 31 October 1992 and $102,698,900 gross ($101,171,200 net) for the period from 1 November 1992 to 30 April 1993, adding that commitment authorization and appropriation for the period after 30 April 1993 should be subject to action by the Security Council concerning a continuation of UNOSOM's mandate.

GENERAL ASSEMBLY ACTION

On 18 September,[91] the Secretary-General requested inclusion in the agenda of the 1992 regular session of the General Assembly an additional item on the financing of UNOSOM.

On 1 December, on the recommendation of the Fifth Committee, the Assembly adopted **resolution 47/41 A** without vote.

Financing of the United Nations Operation in Somalia

The General Assembly,

Having considered the report of the Secretary-General on the financing of the United Nations Operation in Somalia and the related report of the Advisory Committee on Administrative and Budgetary Questions,

Bearing in mind Security Council resolution 751(1992) of 24 April 1992, by which the Council, *inter alia*, decided to establish under its authority a United Nations Operation in Somalia, requested the Secretary-General to deploy military observers to monitor the cease-fire in Mogadishu and agreed, in principle, to the deployment of a United Nations security force under the overall direction of the Special Representative of the Secretary-General to provide security and to escort deliveries of humanitarian supplies,

Bearing in mind also Security Council resolution 767(1992) of 27 July 1992, by which the Council, *inter alia*, approved the establishment of four operational zones in Somalia as part of the consolidated Operation in Somalia and Council resolution 775(1992) of 28 August 1992, by which the Council, *inter alia*, authorized the increase in the strength of the Operation in Somalia,

Recognizing that the costs of the Operation in Somalia are expenses of the Organization to be borne by Member States in accordance with Article 17, paragraph 2, of the Charter of the United Nations,

Recognizing also that, in order to meet the expenditures caused by the Operation in Somalia, a different procedure is required from the one applied to meet expenditures of the regular budget of the United Nations,

Taking into account the fact that the economically more developed countries are in a position to make relatively larger contributions and that the economically less developed countries have a relatively limited capacity to contribute towards such an operation,

Bearing in mind the special responsibilities of the States permanent members of the Security Council, as indicated in General Assembly resolution 1874(S-IV) of 27 June 1963, in the financing of such operations,

Mindful of the fact that it is essential to provide the Operation in Somalia with the necessary financial resources to enable it to fulfil its responsibilities under the relevant resolutions of the Security Council,

1. *Endorses* the observations and recommendations contained in the report of the Advisory Committee on Administrative and Budgetary Questions;

2. *Requests* the Secretary-General to establish firm internal control on all financial transactions, including detailed and up-to-date recording and close monitoring by certifying officers and supervisory staff in accordance with the recommendation contained in paragraph 38 of the report of the Advisory Committee;

3. *Urges* all Member States to make every possible effort to ensure payment of their assessed contributions to the United Nations Operation in Somalia in full and on time;

4. *Affirms* that it is important that the question of the duration of the mandate of the Operation in Somalia should be resolved as soon as possible;

5. *Notes*, in this context, the intention of the Secretary-General to submit a report to the Security Council on the situation in Somalia within the next six months;

6. *Decides*, at this stage, to appropriate, in accordance with the recommendation contained in paragraph 42 of the report of the Advisory Committee, a total amount of 109,652,000 United States dollars gross (107,912,800 dollars net), inclusive of the amount of 17,410,000 dollars authorized with the prior concurrence of the Advisory Committee, for the period from 1 May 1992 to 30 April 1993, and requests the Secretary-

General to establish a Special Account for the United Nations Operation in Somalia in accordance with paragraph 23 of his report;

7. *Decides also*, as an ad hoc arrangement, to apportion the amount of 6,953,100 dollars gross (6,741,600 dollars net) for the period from 1 May to 31 October 1992 and the amount of 102,698,900 dollars gross (101,171,200 dollars net) for the period from 1 November 1992 to 30 April 1993 among Member States in accordance with the composition of groups set out in paragraphs 3 and 4 of General Assembly resolution 43/232 of 1 March 1989, as adjusted by the Assembly in its resolutions 44/192 B of 21 December 1989, 45/269 of 27 August 1991 and 46/198 A of 20 December 1991, and taking into account the scale of assessments for the years 1992, 1993 and 1994;

8. *Decides further* that, in accordance with the provisions of its resolution 973(X) of 15 December 1955, there shall be set off against the apportionment among Member States, as provided for in paragraph 7 above, their respective share in the Tax Equalization Fund of the estimated staff assessment income of 211,500 dollars for the period from 1 May to 31 October 1992 and 1,527,700 dollars for the period from 1 November 1992 to 30 April 1993 approved for the Operation in Somalia;

9. *Authorizes* the Secretary-General to enter into commitments for the operation of the Operation in Somalia, if necessary and pending the appropriation by the General Assembly, at a rate not to exceed 14 million dollars gross (13.7 million dollars net) per month for the initial months beginning 1 May 1993, should the Security Council decide to continue the operation beyond 30 April 1993, subject to obtaining the prior concurrence of the Advisory Committee for the actual level of commitments to be entered into for the period beyond 30 April 1993, the said amount to be apportioned among Member States in accordance with the scheme set out in the present resolution;

10. *Decides* to consider the contributions of Armenia, Azerbaijan, Bosnia and Herzegovina, Croatia, Georgia, Kazakhstan, Kyrgyzstan, the Republic of Moldova, San Marino, Slovenia, Tajikistan, Turkmenistan and Uzbekistan to the Operation in Somalia in accordance with the rates of assessment to be adopted by the General Assembly for these Member States at its forty-seventh session;

11. *Invites* the new Member States listed in paragraph 10 above to make advance payments against their assessed contributions, to be determined;

12. *Invites* voluntary contributions to the Operation in Somalia in cash and in the form of services and supplies acceptable to the Secretary-General, to be administered, as appropriate, in accordance with the procedure established by the General Assembly in its resolutions 43/230 of 21 December 1988, 44/192 A of 21 December 1989 and 45/258 of 3 May 1991;

13. *Requests* the Secretary-General to take all necessary action to ensure that all United Nations activities related to the Operation in Somalia are administered under the authority of his Special Representative in a coordinated fashion with a maximum of efficiency and economy and in accordance with the relevant mandates, and to include in his report on the financial performance of the Operation in Somalia information on the arrangement made in this regard;

14. *Decides* to include in the provisional agenda of its forty-eighth session the item entitled "Financing of the United Nations Operation in Somalia".

General Assembly resolution 47/41

1 December 1992   Meeting 76   Adopted without vote

Approved by Fifth Committee (A/47/734) without vote, 27 November (meeting 33); draft by Netherlands (A/C.5/47/L.3); agenda item 145.
Meeting numbers. GA 47th session: 5th Committee 31, 33; plenary 76.

Humanitarian assistance

In order to accelerate relief efforts and pave the way for eventual recovery of the Somali society, the Under-Secretary-General for Humanitarian Affairs in September led a high-level inter-agency mission to the country. A major outcome of the mission was the drafting of a 100-day Action Programme for Accelerated Humanitarian Assistance for the period ending December 1992. Its eight components included massive infusion of food aid (some 50,000 tons per month), provision of basic health services, clean water, sanitation and shelter materials, prevention of further refugee flows and civil society rehabilitation. Funding requirements were estimated at $82.7 million.

The Programme was reviewed twice, at the first (Geneva, 12 and 13 October) and second (Addis Ababa, 3-5 December) United Nations coordination meetings on humanitarian assistance to Somalia. The latter, in its final conclusions, noted that the Programme had failed to generate sufficient resources. It proposed that food be monetarized to stimulate the economy and encourage local production. Emphasis was laid on resettling displaced farmer families and on a massive rehabilitation programme, including accelerated mine clearing. One of the conclusions of the meeting was that the 100-day Programme should be followed by a new plan for 1993, and a third meeting was planned for early that year.

(For details of humanitarian and emergency assistance to Somalia, see PART THREE, Chapter III.)

Proposed international conference on Somalia

By a letter of 10 December 1992,[92] Senegal requested inclusion in the General Assembly's agenda of an additional item on the convening of an international conference on Somalia. An *aide-mémoire* annexed to the letter stated that the proposal for such a conference had been made on 30 September by the Senegalese President, as Chairman of OAU, during the general debate of the Assembly. The proposal had been welcomed by the Ministers for Foreign Affairs of OIC during their special session (Jeddah, Saudi Arabia, 1 and 2 December), as well as by most regional groups and by the Movement of Non-Aligned Countries' working group on Somalia. The conference should fall within the framework of the action currently being undertaken by the Security Council, the Secretary-General and humanitarian organizations; it could provide, subsequent to the initial stages defined by the Council and the Secretary-

General, an appropriate framework for a comprehensive political settlement of the Somali crisis.

Supporting Senegal's request, Morocco transmitted on 14 December[93] a draft resolution adopted by the Group of African States on the convening of a conference.

GENERAL ASSEMBLY ACTION

On 18 December, the General Assembly adopted **resolution 47/167** without vote.

Convening of an international conference on Somalia

The General Assembly,

Deeply concerned about the tragic situation in Somalia,

Taking into account the statement made in the General Assembly by the current Chairman of the Assembly of Heads of State and Government of the Organization of African Unity on 30 September 1992 and especially his proposal to convene an international conference on Somalia,

Taking note of relevant Security Council resolutions, in particular resolution 794(1992) of 3 December 1992,

Taking note also of the outcome of the Second Coordination Meeting on Somalia, held at Addis Ababa from 3 to 5 December 1992,

Realizing that lasting peace, stability and unity in the country can be achieved through a process of national reconciliation culminating in a final, comprehensive, politically negotiated settlement among all the political entities and segments of the Somali people,

Deeply convinced that a final negotiated settlement of the Somali conflict is an ultimate responsibility of the Somalis themselves,

Recognizing that the idea of convening an international conference on Somalia has gained widespread acceptance and is viewed as part of the important initiatives currently being undertaken by the Secretary-General, the Security Council and the international community to contribute to creating the conditions necessary for national reconciliation, peace and stability and for reconstruction of the national economy of Somalia,

Welcoming in this regard the efforts being exerted by the Security Council, the Secretary-General and the international community,

Welcoming also the efforts of the Organization of African Unity, the Organization of the Islamic Conference, the League of Arab States, the Movement of Non-Aligned Countries and the Standing Committee of the States of the Horn of Africa on Somalia,

Stressing the need to coordinate the efforts being made by the international community towards the restoration of national unity and peace and the reconstruction of the national economy of Somalia,

1. *Affirms* the need for a comprehensive and lasting solution to the Somali crisis;

2. *Welcomes* the idea of convening an international peace conference on Somalia under the auspices of the United Nations and in cooperation with the Organization of African Unity, the Organization of the Islamic Conference, the League of Arab States, the Standing Committee of the States of the Horn of Africa on Somalia and governmental and non-governmental organizations, which would contribute to the establishment of peace and security in the subregion;

3. *Recognizes* that the restoration of much-needed peace and stability in Somalia must be governed, *inter alia,* by the following considerations: strict observance of a cease-fire, full cooperation with United Nations peace-keeping forces, national reconciliation, assistance for refugees, displaced persons and returnees, a constitution that guarantees democracy, freedom and justice, and free and fair elections;

4. *Welcomes* the efforts of the Secretary-General, in close cooperation with the Organization of African Unity, the Organization of the Islamic Conference, the League of Arab States, the Standing Committee of the States of the Horn of Africa on Somalia and with the support of other governmental and non-governmental organizations, aimed at national reconciliation in Somalia, and emphasizes the need to consider the practical modalities for convening an international conference on Somalia as soon as possible;

5. *Requests* the Secretary-General to report to the General Assembly during its current session on this matter.

General Assembly resolution 47/167

18 December 1992   Meeting 92   Adopted without vote

38-nation draft (A/47/L.48 & Add.1); agenda item 152.

Sponsors: Algeria, Angola, Bangladesh, Benin, Bosnia and Herzegovina, Burkina Faso, Burundi, Cape Verde, Comoros, Congo, Côte d'Ivoire, Djibouti, Egypt, Ethiopia, Gabon, Gambia, Guinea, Guinea-Bissau, Indonesia, Kuwait, Madagascar, Mali, Mauritania, Mauritius, Mongolia, Morocco, Namibia, Niger, Pakistan, Rwanda, Senegal, Sierra Leone, Togo, Tunisia, Turkey, Ukraine, United Arab Emirates, Yemen.

REFERENCES

[1]YUN 1991, p. 127. [2]S/23556. [3]YUN 1991, p. 127, SC res. 696(1991), 30 May 1991. [4]S/23557. [5]S/23671 & Add.1. [6]S/23985. [7]S/23986. [8]S/24145 & Corr.1. [9]S/24249. [10]S/24556. [11]S/24573. [12]S/24585. [13]S/24736. [14]S/24623. [15]S/24639. [16]S/24683. [17]S/24720. [18]S/24858 & Add.1. [19]S/24996. [20]S/25002. [21]A/46/934 & Add.1. [22]A/46/945. [23]YUN 1991, p. 869, GA res. 46/187, 20 Dec. 1991. [24]Ibid., p. 129, GA res. 46/195 A, 20 Dec. 1991. [25]A/47/744. [26]A/47/459. [27]YUN 1991, p. 131, GA res. 46/9, 16 Oct. 1991. [28]A/C.3/47/5. [29]A/47/544. [30]A/C.3/47/L.25. [31]A/C.5/47/55. [32]YUN 1991, p. 426, GA res. 46/147, 17 Dec. 1991. [33]A/47/91-S/23585. [34]S/23863. [35]S/24218. [36]S/24811. [37]S/24812. [38]S/24815. [39]S/24735. [40]S/23886. [41]S/24825. [42]S/24834. [43]S/24835. [44]S/24635. [45]S/24406. [46]S/24813. [47]S/25044. [48]S/24642. [49]S/24719. [50]S/24892 & Corr.1. & Add.1. [51]A/47/78-S/23490. [52]S/24065. [53]S/23445. [54]S/23507 & Corr.1. [55]S/23693 & Corr.1. [56]S/23724. [57]S/23723. [58]S/23763. [59]S/23829 & Add.1,2. [60]S/23851. [61]S/23852. [62]S/23957. [63]S/24179. [64]S/24343. [65]S/24451. [66]S/24452. [67]S/24480 & Add.1. [68]S/24674. [69]S/24859. [70]S/24868. [71]S/24867. [72]S/24893. [73]S/24976. [74]S/25126. [75]S/24992. [76]S/25014. [77]S/24177. [78]S/24178. [79]S/24180. [80]S/24533. [81]S/24534. [82]S/24531. [83]S/24532. [84]S/24714. [85]S/24715. [86]S/24849. [87]S/24850. [88]S/24878. [89]A/47/607. [90]A/47/674. [91]A/47/243. [92]A/47/780. [93]A/47/780/Add.1.

Cooperation between OAU and the UN system

Cooperation between the United Nations and the Organization of African Unity was described by the Secretary-General, pursuant to a 1991 General Assembly resolution,[1] in a September

1992 report.[2] In 1991, the Assembly had called on the Secretaries-General of both organizations to work in close cooperation, in particular regarding the follow-up to and review of implementation of the United Nations New Agenda for the Development of Africa in the 1990s.[3]

The report gave an overview of consultations and exchange of information between the two organizations and of cooperation in the field of economic and social development as well as in other areas.

In order to evaluate progress achieved in implementing the proposals and recommendations for cooperation agreed on in 1990 and 1991, and to adopt new joint action, a meeting was held between organizations and agencies of the United Nations system and OAU (Addis Ababa, Ethiopia, 2-4 April 1992).

The meeting called for cooperation in popularizing the Treaty establishing the African Economic Community, signed in 1991, by, among other measures, establishing national committees for that purpose, organizing meetings and disseminating the Treaty in African languages with the help of specialized agencies. The meeting also called on the agencies to continue to assist OAU in preparing the protocols of the Economic Community.

With regard to refugees, returnees and displaced persons, the meeting focused on a number of priority issues, including root causes, durable solutions, emergency preparedness and response, collaborative, integrated and coordinated approaches to humanitarian assistance, the humanitarian dimension of the New Agenda and follow-up to the 1988 International Conference on Refugees, Returnees and Displaced Persons in Southern Africa.

The meeting identified human rights abuses, conflicts and adverse socio-economic conditions as the main root causes of the problems of refugees and internally displaced persons in Africa. Special mention was made of Rwanda and Somalia where OAU and the United Nations system had worked closely. The meeting appealed to the United Nations system to provide increased resources to African countries to enable them to cope more effectively with those problems. It urged OAU members to ratify the African Charter on Human and Peoples' Rights, adopted in 1981, as well as the 1969 OAU Convention on Refugees; appealed to those members concerned to adopt legal measures to enable the smooth and safe reintegration of refugees; called for integration of returnee programmes into national development plans; called on OAU and UNHCR to organize seminars to educate the public on the root causes of asylum-seeking on the continent; and urged OAU, UNHCR and others to finalize as soon as possible the plan of action for Rwandese refugees.

The meeting also discussed follow-up and monitoring of implementation of the New Agenda, at the national and international levels. It suggested that OAU participate fully in all meetings of the proposed United Nations inter-agency task force to monitor implementation of a system-wide plan of action for African economic recovery and development and that it be invited to address high-level inter-agency machinery.

The meeting agreed that OAU should continue contacts with various United Nations agencies with a view to reviewing specific sectoral activities and that sectoral meetings should be organized as and when required. It also recommended that the OAU specialized agencies be invited to participate in implementation of New Agenda-related activities.

The meeting noted that OAU could provide political support to United Nations efforts in getting additional resources to be used in activities aimed at African economic recovery and development. It requested OAU to ensure that the New Agenda was placed on the agenda of subsequent meetings between OAU and the United Nations.

GENERAL ASSEMBLY ACTION

On 18 December, the General Assembly adopted **resolution 47/148** without vote.

Cooperation between the United Nations and the Organization of African Unity

The General Assembly,

Having considered the report of the Secretary-General on cooperation between the United Nations and the Organization of African Unity,

Recalling its resolutions on the enhancement of cooperation between the United Nations and the Organization of African Unity, in particular resolutions 43/12 of 25 October 1988, 43/27 of 18 November 1988, 44/17 of 1 November 1989, 45/13 of 7 November 1990 and 46/20 of 26 November 1991,

Recalling also the agreement of 15 November 1965 on cooperation between the United Nations and the Organization of African Unity as updated and signed on 9 October 1990 by the Secretaries-General of the two organizations,

Taking note of the resolutions, decisions and declarations adopted by the Council of Ministers of the Organization of African Unity at its fifty-sixth ordinary session, held at Dakar from 22 to 28 June 1992, and by the Assembly of Heads of State and Government of that organization at its twenty-eighth ordinary session, held at Dakar from 29 June to 1 July 1992,

Considering the important statement made by the current Chairman of the Assembly of Heads of State and Government of the Organization of African Unity before the General Assembly on 30 September 1992,

Noting in particular the efforts of the Organization of African Unity to promote the peaceful settlement of disputes and conflicts in Africa and the harmonious continuation of the democratization process,

Noting with satisfaction the support and assistance of the United Nations for the democratization process in Africa,

Also noting the efforts of the United Nations to contribute to resolving conflicts in Africa,

Further noting with satisfaction decision AHG/Dec.1 (XXVIII) adopted by the Assembly of Heads of State and Government of the Organization of African Unity, with a view to setting up machinery for the prevention, settlement and management of conflicts in Africa,

Mindful of the need for continued and closer cooperation between the United Nations and the specialized agencies and the Organization of African Unity, in particular in the political, economic, social, technical, cultural and administrative fields,

Also mindful of political developments in South Africa and conscious of the need to provide increased assistance to the people of South Africa and to their national liberation movements in their legitimate struggle to eradicate apartheid, and to the independent States of southern Africa that are victims of the system of apartheid,

Deeply concerned that, despite the policies of reform being implemented by African countries, their economic situation remains critical and African recovery and development continue to be severely hindered by the collapse of commodity prices, the heavy debt burden and the paucity of funding possibilities, as well as by the devastating drought affecting certain regions of the continent,

Considering that the implementation of the United Nations Programme of Action for African Economic Recovery and Development 1986-1990 did not live up to expectations,

Welcoming the adoption in 1991 of the United Nations New Agenda for the Development of Africa in the 1990s, while regretting that the machinery for its implementation has not yet begun operating,

Aware of the efforts under way by the Organization of African Unity and its member States in the area of economic integration and, in particular, the adoption by the Assembly of Heads of State and Government of the Organization of African Unity on 3 June 1991 at Abuja of the Treaty establishing the African Economic Community,

Recalling further that in its resolution 46/20 it, *inter alia*, urged the Secretary-General of the United Nations and the relevant agencies of the United Nations system to extend their support for the establishment of an African economic community,

Deeply concerned about the gravity of the situation of refugees and displaced persons in Africa and the urgent need for increased international assistance to help refugees and, subsequently, African countries of asylum,

1. *Takes note* of the report of the Secretary-General on cooperation between the United Nations and the Organization of African Unity and of his efforts to strengthen that cooperation and to implement the relevant resolutions;

2. *Notes with appreciation* the increasing and continued participation of the Organization of African Unity in the work of the United Nations and the specialized agencies and its constructive contribution to that work;

3. *Commends* the continued efforts of the Organization of African Unity to promote multilateral cooperation and economic integration among African States and requests United Nations organizations to continue to support those efforts;

4. *Requests* the United Nations to continue to support the Organization of African Unity in its efforts to promote the peaceful settlement of disputes and conflicts and peacefully to manage change in Africa;

5. *Urges* the United Nations to provide cooperation and assistance, as appropriate, to the Organization of African Unity should the latter decide to launch a peace-keeping operation;

6. *Calls upon* the Secretary-General of the United Nations to continue to cooperate closely with the Secretary-General of the Organization of African Unity on the question of decolonization;

7. *Reiterates* the determination of the United Nations, in cooperation with the Organization of African Unity, to continue its efforts for the early eradication of racial discrimination and apartheid, taking into consideration the democratic process emerging in South Africa, and to provide the appropriate assistance to that end;

8. *Calls upon* the United Nations organs—in particular the Security Council, the Economic and Social Council, the Special Committee on the Situation with regard to the Implementation of the Declaration on the Granting of Independence to Colonial Countries and Peoples and the Special Committee against Apartheid— to continue to involve the Organization of African Unity closely in all their activities concerning Africa;

9. *Urges* all Member States and regional and international organizations, in particular those of the United Nations system, as well as non-governmental organizations, to provide the necessary and appropriate economic, financial and technical assistance to refugees, as well as to African countries of asylum;

10. *Notes* that the economic, technical and development assistance provided to Africa by the organizations of the United Nations system must continue, and emphasizes the current need for those organizations to accord priority to Africa in this field;

11. *Reaffirms* that the implementation of the United Nations New Agenda for the Development of Africa in the 1990s will necessitate the full participation of the international community, in particular of the Governments, organizations and programmes of the United Nations system, as well as intergovernmental and non-governmental organizations, and emphasizes the urgency of the need to adopt appropriate measures to ensure its implementation in accordance with General Assembly decisions;

12. *Calls upon* the Secretary-General of the United Nations to work in close coordination and cooperation with the Secretary-General of the Organization of African Unity, in particular on follow-up to and review and evaluation of the implementation of the New Agenda;

13. *Requests* the Secretary-General of the United Nations to invite the representative of the Secretary-General of the Organization of African Unity to participate in the meetings of all United Nations organizations, commissions, committees and working groups on follow-up to and monitoring and assessment of the New Agenda;

14. *Calls upon* the Secretary-General to adopt appropriate measures, in consultation with the international organizations and financial institutions concerned, as well as with donor countries, to assist in the mobilization of the resources needed to support the efforts of the African States to implement, at the national and regional levels, Agenda 21 and other relevant decisions adopted by the United Nations Conference on Environment and Development;

15. *Urges* the Secretary-General of the United Nations and the relevant organizations of the United Nations system to extend their support and cooperation to the member States and the Secretary-General of the Organization of African Unity for the effective organizational arrangement and smooth functioning of the African Economic Community;

16. *Also urges* all Member States and regional and international organizations, as well as non-governmental organizations, to provide support as appropriate to the establishment of the African Economic Community, and to assist in economic integration and cooperation in Africa, in particular by providing financial and technical assistance to African regional and subregional organizations, as well as to African organizations for drought and desertification control;

17. *Notes with appreciation* the assistance provided by the United Nations and its organizations to the African countries in the context of the democratization process, as well as in organizing and holding pluralistic, free and fair elections, and encourages the provision, in the future, of such assistance to countries that request it;

18. *Reiterates its appreciation* to the Secretary-General for his continued efforts to mobilize international support for special programmes of economic assistance to African States facing grave economic difficulties or victims of the policies of apartheid, and requests him to continue to keep the Organization of African Unity informed periodically of measures taken by the United Nations agencies and by the international community to help implement these programmes;

19. *Endorses* the agreement reached between the organizations of the United Nations system and the Organization of African Unity on the convening of a meeting between the secretariats of those organizations, to be held in 1993, to review and evaluate the progress made in implementing the proposals and recommendations agreed upon in April 1991 and 1992 on cooperation between them in 1992-1993 and to adopt new and effective joint action;

20. *Requests* the Secretary-General of the United Nations to support the efforts of the Secretary-General of the Organization of African Unity with a view to holding sectoral meetings in the priority areas of cooperation, particularly the establishment of the African Economic Community and the strengthening of the African regional and subregional organizations;

21. *Requests* the United Nations and the Organization of African Unity to ensure that the representatives of their secretariats continue to hold regular close consultations, particularly on the follow-up to the present resolution;

22. *Calls upon* the relevant organs of the United Nations to ensure the effective, fair and equitable representation of Africa at senior and policy levels at their respective headquarters and in their regional field operations;

23. *Also requests* the Secretary-General to ensure that the United Nations information network continues to disseminate information so as to increase public awareness of the situation prevailing in southern Africa, as well as of the social and economic problems and needs of African States and of their regional and subregional institutions;

24. *Further requests* the Secretary-General to report to the General Assembly at its forty-eighth session on the implementation of the present resolution and on the development of cooperation between the Organization of African Unity and organizations of the United Nations system.

General Assembly resolution 47/148

18 December 1992   Meeting 92   Adopted without vote

Draft by Mauritius (A/47/L.14/Rev.1); agenda item 27.
Meeting numbers. GA 47th session: plenary 60, 92.

REFERENCES

(1)YUN 1991, p. 138, GA res. 46/20, 26 Nov. 1991. (2)A/47/453 & Add.1. (3)YUN 1991, p. 402, GA res. 46/151, annex, sect. II, 18 Dec. 1991.

Chapter II

Americas

United Nations efforts to help resolve the remaining protracted conflicts in Central America bore fruit in 1992 with respect to El Salvador. A final peace agreement was concluded in January between the Government and the Frente Farabundo Martí para la Liberación Nacional, the opposition movement in the country, formally bringing the 12-year armed conflict between them to an end in December.

In the light of this development and given the undergirding joint course of action adopted by the Central American States in the Managua Agenda for the progressive transformation of the subregion into one of peace, democracy and development, the Security Council terminated the United Nations Observer Group in Central America. The Council enlarged and extended the mandate of the United Nations Observer Mission in El Salvador, however, to enable it to verify compliance with all of the agreements concluded between the parties during their negotiations for a comprehensive settlement of their conflict. It subsequently extended the Mission's mandate a second time, to 31 May 1993.

During the year, the General Assembly adopted several resolutions relating to the Americas. It urged the Governments of Central America to continue their efforts to consolidate a firm and lasting peace in the subregion and reiterated the importance of stepping up the negotiating process between the Government of Guatemala and the Unidad Revolucionaria Nacional Guatemalteca, the opposition movement, on the basis of the Mexico City and Querétaro Agreements of 1991. In a resolution concerning the need to end the economic embargo imposed by the United States against Cuba, the Assembly called for the repeal of laws whose extraterritorial effects affected States' sovereignty and freedom of trade and navigation. It condemned anew the attempted illegal replacement of the constitutional President of Haiti. It requested continued consultations between the United Nations and the Organization of American States with a view to signing a cooperation agreement in 1993.

In a related action, the Assembly sought continued international support for Nicaragua to overcome the aftermath of war and of recent natural disasters in the country, as well as to stimulate reconstruction and development.

Central America situation

The Central American States of Costa Rica, El Salvador, Guatemala, Honduras, Nicaragua and Panama pressed forward in 1992 with their programme for the consolidation of peace in Central America and for the economic integration and development of the subregion. They held a summit at Managua, Nicaragua, on 4 and 5 June 1992,[1] the twelfth since they first gathered at Esquipulas, Guatemala, in 1986,[2] in search of a peaceful resolution of their differences.

The six countries adopted a detailed agenda, referred to as the Managua Agenda, covering a wide range of issues in the political, social and economic domains. A number of them related to the establishment of the Preparatory Commission for the implementation of the Tegucigalpa Protocol, so as to bring into operation the Central American Integration System;[3] the renewal of the mandate of the Security Commission, established by the 1990 Security Commission Agreement,[4] to include a deeper scrutiny into the questions of arms trafficking and confidence-building; the continuance of policies to advance national reconciliation, with emphasis on the role of the national commissions set up for the purpose; and improvement of the democratic institutions and mechanisms for guaranteeing human rights. Also on the Agenda were appeals to the international community in general for increased support for democracy and peace in Central America, and to the European Economic Community in particular for specific assistance in the trade, energy and finance sectors.

(For the question of the Central American refugees and displaced persons, see PART THREE, Chapter XV.)

GENERAL ASSEMBLY ACTION

On 18 December 1992, the General Assembly adopted without vote **resolution 47/118.**

The situation in Central America: procedures for the establishment of a firm and lasting peace and progress in fashioning a region of peace, freedom, democracy and development

The General Assembly,

Recalling Security Council resolutions 530(1983) of 19 May 1983, 562(1985) of 10 May 1985, 637(1989) of 27 July 1989, 644(1989) of 7 November 1989, 650(1990) of

27 March 1990, 653(1990) of 20 April 1990, 654(1990) of 4 May 1990, 656(1990) of 8 June 1990, 714(1991) of 30 September 1991, 719(1991) of 6 November 1991, 729(1992) of 14 January 1992, 784(1992) of 30 October 1992 and 791(1992) of 30 November 1992, and its resolutions 38/10 of 11 November 1983, 39/4 of 26 October 1984, 41/37 of 18 November 1986, 42/1 of 7 October 1987, 43/24 of 15 November 1988, 44/10 of 23 October 1989, 44/44 of 7 December 1989, 45/15 of 20 November 1990 and 46/109 of 17 December 1991,

Bearing in mind the importance of the commitments assumed by the Central American Presidents under the agreement signed at Guatemala City on 7 August 1987 at the Esquipulas II summit meeting; the declarations adopted at Alajuela, Costa Rica, on 16 January 1988 and at Costa del Sol, El Salvador, on 14 February 1989; the agreements concluded at Tela, Honduras, on 7 August 1989, at San Isidro de Coronado, Costa Rica, on 12 December 1989, at Montelimar, Nicaragua, on 3 April 1990, at Antigua, Guatemala, on 17 June 1990, at Puntarenas, Costa Rica, on 17 December 1990, and at Tegucigalpa on 13 December 1991; and the Managua Agenda of 5 June 1992,

Aware that the agreement on "Procedures for the establishment of a firm and lasting peace in Central America", signed at Guatemala City on 7 August 1987 by the Presidents of the Republics of Costa Rica, El Salvador, Guatemala, Honduras and Nicaragua, at the Esquipulas II summit meeting, is the outcome of the decision by Central Americans to take up fully the historical challenge of forging a peaceful destiny for Central America,

Convinced of the political will that inspires the peoples of Central America to achieve peace, reconciliation, development and justice, as well as the commitment to settle their differences by means of dialogue, negotiation and respect for the legitimate interests of all States, in accordance with their own decision and their own historical experience and without sacrificing the principles of self-determination and non-intervention,

Recognizing the importance of all aspects of the peace-keeping operations that have been carried out in Central America, pursuant to the decisions of the Security Council and with the support of the Secretary-General, and the need to preserve and enhance the results obtained,

Reaffirming the belief that peace is one, undivided and indivisible, and thus inseparable from freedom, democracy and development, and that these goals are essential for consolidating the transformations which will guarantee sustained, participatory and equitable development in Central America, as well as the need to redefine the manner in which the Central American economies are linked to the rest of the world,

Considering that, at the Puntarenas summit meeting, the Presidents declared Central America to be a region of peace, freedom, democracy and development, and that in the Tegucigalpa Declaration they established the Central American Integration System, the fundamental objective of which is to ensure the integration of Central America and its establishment as a region of peace, freedom, democracy and development,

Also considering the importance of the decisions concerning human and social development adopted by the Central American Presidents at Tegucigalpa in December 1991, as well as the significance of the Managua Agenda, adopted by the Presidents in Nicaragua in June 1992, when they also evaluated the results of the last eleven summit meetings and adopted a joint course of action for follow-up and consolidation of the agreements concluded,

Further considering the commitments that have been entered into during the negotiations on security, verification, and control and limitation of arms and military personnel, within the Security Commission established under the agreement signed at the Esquipulas II summit meeting, for the purpose of achieving a stable and lasting peace in Central America,

Convinced that the Peace Agreement reached on 16 January 1992 at Mexico City between the Government of El Salvador and the Frente Farabundo Martí para la Liberación Nacional reflects that country's profound aspiration for peace and justice, and that scrupulous compliance therewith will not only permit an end to the armed conflict through political means but also lay the foundation for major political, legal, economic and social changes that must involve all sectors of the country in the consolidation of a democratic and cohesive society,

Noting with satisfaction that both parties have scrupulously observed the cease-fire, overcoming delays and difficulties in the process of implementing the peace agreements in El Salvador, and, through the mediation of the Secretary-General and his representatives, have adopted agreements leading to the final cessation of the armed conflict on 15 December 1992,

Taking note of the report of the Secretary-General on the United Nations Observer Mission in El Salvador of 23 November 1992,

Convinced of the importance of continued talks between the Government of Guatemala and the Unidad Revolucionaria Nacional Guatemalteca, under the auspices of the National Reconciliation Commission of Guatemala and in the presence of the Representative of the Secretary-General, in order to end the internal armed confrontation at the earliest opportunity and to bring about national reconciliation, with full respect for the human rights of all Guatemalans,

Emphasizing the importance of the end of the armed conflict in Nicaragua and the need to consolidate peace in that country, as well as the urgent need for the international community and the United Nations system to continue providing Nicaragua with the support required to promote rehabilitation and economic and social reconstruction, for the purpose of strengthening democracy and overcoming the aftermath of the war and the adverse consequences of recent natural disasters,

Recognizing the valuable and effective contribution of the United Nations and of various governmental and non-governmental mechanisms to the process of democratization, pacification and development in Central America, as well as the importance for the progressive transformation of Central America into a region of peace, freedom, democracy and development of both the political dialogue and the economic cooperation set in motion by the Ministerial Conference on Political Dialogue and Economic Cooperation between the European Community and the Central American countries and the joint initiatives of the industrialized countries (Group of Twenty-four) and the group of cooperating countries (Group of Three) in Latin America, through a partnership for democracy and development in Central America,

Bearing in mind that there remain in Central America major obstacles to the full exercise of peace, freedom, democracy and development, the final overcoming of which requires a global frame of reference that would enable the international community to focus its support on efforts towards collective affirmation and democratic progress being made by the Central American countries,

1. *Commends* the effort made by the Central American countries to achieve peace through the implementation of the agreement on "Procedures for the establishment of a firm and lasting peace in Central America", signed at Guatemala City on 7 August 1987, as well as of the agreements adopted at subsequent summit meetings;

2. *Expresses its strongest support* for these agreements and urges the Governments to continue their efforts to consolidate firm and lasting peace in Central America, and requests the Secretary-General to continue to afford the fullest possible support to the Central American Governments in their efforts to consolidate peace, democracy and development;

3. *Reaffirms* the decision of the Presidents of the Central American countries to declare Central America a region of peace, freedom, democracy and development, and encourages the initiatives of the Central American countries to consolidate Governments which base their development on democracy, peace, cooperation and strict respect for human rights;

4. *Welcomes* the agreements reached by the Security Commission of the Central American countries in the creation of a new security model based on coordination, communication and prevention, confidence-building between the States of the region, as well as the progress made on security, verification, and control and limitation of arms and military personnel;

5. *Expresses its satisfaction* at the steps taken to implement the vital Peace Agreement between the Government of El Salvador and the Frente Farabundo Martí para la Liberación Nacional, and at the flexibility shown by both parties in overcoming obstacles and differences and in maintaining the close linkage between the implementation of the various commitments assumed by them, in order to ensure the full and scrupulous implementation of all the agreements;

6. *Welcomes with particular satisfaction* the holding of the National Reconciliation Ceremony on 15 December 1992, which brought to an end definitively the armed confrontation in El Salvador, and urges all sectors of Salvadorian society to continue to act with the greatest responsibility and spirit of *détente* and national reconciliation in order to ensure implementation of the commitments still to be fulfilled, thus making it possible to complete successfully the pacification process and develop normal living conditions throughout the country, particularly in the areas most affected by the armed conflict;

7. *Expresses its appreciation* for the effective and timely mediation of the Secretary-General and his representatives and extends its support to them so that they can continue to take all necessary steps to contribute to the successful implementation of all the peace agreements in El Salvador;

8. *Also expresses its appreciation* to the Governments of Colombia, Mexico, Spain and Venezuela, which make up the Group of Friends of the Secretary-General, as well as to the Government of the United States of America, for their constant support and contribution to the efforts to reach the Peace Agreement and implement the commitments which are laid down in it, and urges them to continue to support them until the full implementation of these agreements, which reflect the will and aspirations of the Salvadorian people, is brought about;

9. *Reiterates* the importance of stepping up the negotiating process between the Government of Guatemala and the Unidad Revolucionaria Nacional Guatemalteca in order to achieve the goals laid down in the agreements signed at Mexico City on 26 April 1991 and at Querétaro, Mexico, on 25 July 1991, and urges scrupulous implementation of the agreed procedures and progress towards the adoption of commitments on all the issues set forth in the agreements signed at Mexico City, particularly the signing of the Comprehensive Agreement on Human Rights which they have been considering, in order to achieve, in the near future, national reconciliation and a firm and lasting peace with the continued support of the international community and the United Nations; expresses appreciation, likewise, to the Secretary-General and his Representative for the support that they are giving to the negotiating process and encourages them to continue to provide it;

10. *Supports* the efforts that the Government of Nicaragua is making to consolidate peace and endorses the provision concerning exceptional circumstances so that the international community and funding agencies will provide their support for rehabilitation, economic and social reconstruction and the strengthening of reconciliation and democracy in that country;

11. *Stresses* the importance that the continuity and outcome of the political dialogue and economic cooperation between the European Community and its member States, the States of Central America and Panama and the group of cooperating countries (Group of Three), as well as the initiative of the industrialized countries (Group of Twenty-four), through the Partnership for Democracy and Development in Central America, have for the efforts of the Central American countries to achieve peace and to consolidate democracy and economic development;

12. *Requests* the Secretary-General and the organizations of the United Nations system to provide, as appropriate and from within existing resources, the necessary technical and financial support to the Central American Governments, and calls upon the international community to increase its support for peace, freedom, democracy and development in Central America by providing resources for their consolidation, so that the region's material limitations do not diminish or reverse the progress made;

13. *Reiterates* the importance that the Special Plan of Economic Cooperation for Central America, which the General Assembly welcomed in its resolution 42/231 of 12 May 1988, has for the implementation of this resolution, in particular because it provides the underpinning for the implementation of the Central American Economic Plan of Action;

14. *Decides* to include in the provisional agenda of its forty-eighth session the item entitled "The situation in Central America: procedures for the establishment of a firm and lasting peace and progress in fashioning a region of peace, freedom, democracy and development";

15. *Requests* the Secretary-General to submit a report to the General Assembly at its forty-eighth session on the implementation of the present resolution.

General Assembly resolution 47/118

18 December 1992   Meeting 91   Adopted without vote

25-nation draft (A/47/L.34/Rev.1 & Rev.1/Add.1), orally revised; agenda item 36.
Sponsors: Argentina, Belgium, Brazil, Chile, Colombia, Costa Rica, Denmark, El Salvador, France, Germany, Greece, Guatemala, Honduras, Ireland, Italy, Luxembourg, Mexico, Netherlands, Nicaragua, Panama, Portugal, Spain, United Kingdom, United States, Venezuela.
Financial implications. 5th Committee, A/47/799; S-G, A/C.5/47/73.
Meeting numbers. GA 47th session: 5th Committee 47; plenary 80, 91.

UN Observer Group in Central America

Based on a recommendation by the Secretary-General, the Security Council terminated, with effect from 17 January 1992, the United Nations Observer Group in Central America (ONUCA), established in 1989[5] to verify compliance with the security undertakings agreed upon by five Central American countries in 1987.[6] Its mandate had been last extended in November 1991[7] and review of its operations since then was undertaken by the Secretary-General early in January 1992, in the light of recent positive developments in Central America and in keeping with the widely held view that a given peace-keeping operation should be set up for a specific task and period and then be disbanded.

Report of the Secretary-General. Following his review of ONUCA, the Secretary-General informed the Security Council on 14 January 1992[8] that the only notable incident in which ONUCA played a role took place on 19 December 1991. When it provided helicopter support to help recover the bodies of nine Honduran military personnel who had died when their helicopter, which had strayed into El Salvador, had been mistaken for an aircraft of that country's armed force and shot down by the Frente Farabundo Martí para la Liberación Nacional (FMLN).

More significantly, major progress had been achieved in the negotiations on a comprehensive settlement of the armed conflict in El Salvador between the Government and FMLN. The parties had concluded further agreements that, together with those concluded earlier, would put a definitive end to the conflict. Having formally recorded this fact in the New York Act of 31 December 1991, the parties were set to sign a final Peace Agreement in Mexico City on 16 January 1992.[9]

In view of these developments, the Secretary-General recommended the termination of ONUCA and proposed redeployment of some of its personnel and equipment to the United Nations Observer Mission in El Salvador (ONUSAL) by 1 February. In so doing, he paid tribute to the Chief Military Observer, Brigadier-General Víctor Suanzes Pardo (Spain), and to all other military and civilian personnel who had served with ONUCA.

SECURITY COUNCIL ACTION

On 16 January 1992, the Security Council, having considered the Secretary-General's report, unanimously adopted **resolution 730(1992)**.

The Security Council,
Recalling its resolution 719(1991) of 6 November 1991,
Recalling also its resolution 729(1992) of 14 January 1992,
1. *Approves* the report of the Secretary-General of 14 January 1992;
2. *Decides,* in accordance with the recommendation in paragraph 7 of the report, to terminate the mandate of the United Nations Observer Group in Central America with effect from 17 January 1992.

Security Council resolution 730(1992)

16 January 1992   Meeting 3031   Adopted unanimously

Draft prepared in consultations among Council members (S/23427).

Financing

In October 1992,[10] the Secretary-General provided information covering the status, as at 30 September, of contributions assessed on Member States for the financing of ONUCA from its inception on 7 November 1989 to 30 April 1992, the date to which its mandate had last been extended; the resources made available to it, the operating costs and the resultant unutilized balance in the ONUCA Special Account; and the disposition of ONUCA personnel and assets.

Of a total assessment of $94,961,864 apportioned among Member States, $82,223,800 had been received, leaving a balance due of $12,738,064.

Resources made available for the period 7 November 1989 to 30 April 1992 amounted to $115,726,900 gross ($112,817,400 net), including appropriations of $114,163,900 gross ($111,254,400 net) and voluntary contributions in kind from Germany and Venezuela valued at $1,563,000; interest and miscellaneous income totalled $4,313,685. Deducting operating costs for the same period of $89,357,172 gross ($87,139,662 net) and $17,337,700 gross ($17,106,600 net) in credits to Member States against their assessed contributions left a net unencumbered balance of $12,884,823. However, owing to the outstanding assessed contributions of $12,738,064, the ONUCA Special Account showed a net unutilized balance of $146,759.

On 24 January 1992, 131 military observers were transferred to ONUSAL. Twenty-nine (of 45) international and 53 (of 81) local staff were retained to supervise the closing of ONUCA, all of whom, except for one of the international staff, were phased out over three and a half months; 16 international staff were reassigned or returned to their parent duty stations. On 31 January, 28 local staff were terminated. The assignment of one international staff member was extended until 30 September to settle financial obligations at United Nations Headquarters. Also transferred to ONUSAL was equipment with a depreciated value of $3,561,547.

El Salvador situation

The complex negotiations that began in 1990 to end the armed conflict in El Salvador culminated in the signing of the Peace Agreement by the Government of El Salvador and FMLN in Mexico City on 16 January 1992.[9]

That event was preceded by the signing, at midnight on 31 December 1991, of the New York Act, concluded in negotiations between the parties at United Nations Headquarters through the good offices of outgoing Secretary-General Javier Pérez de Cuéllar. By the Act, the parties declared that they had reached definitive agreements which, combined with the 1990 San José Agreement on Human Rights[11] and 1991 Mexico[12] and New York[13] Agreements, completed the negotiations on all substantive items called for by the 1990 Caracas Agenda[14] and by the Compressed Negotiations that formed an integral part of the 1991 New York Agreement. The parties agreed that the process of ending the armed conflict was to begin formally on 1 February 1992 and be completed by 31 October. They further agreed to finalize, by 14 January at the latest, the timetable for implementing the agreements and the procedure for dismantling the military structure of FMLN and the reintegration of its members into El Salvador's civil, political and institutional life.

On 13 January, following an intensive final round of negotiations at Headquarters under the leadership of the Secretary-General's Personal Representative for the Central American Peace Process, Alvaro de Soto, the parties signed New York Act II, recording their agreement on all other outstanding issues.

The texts of the Acts were transmitted by El Salvador to the Secretary-General on 27 January.[15]

SECURITY COUNCIL ACTION

Following consultations of the Security Council members on 3 January 1992, the President, on behalf of the Council, made the following statement:[16]

"The members of the Security Council have noted with appreciation the briefing provided by the Secretary-General on the agreement signed late in the night of 31 December by the Government of El Salvador and the FMLN which, when implemented, will put a definite end to the Salvadorian armed conflict. The members of the Council warmly welcomed the agreement, which is of vital importance for the normalization of the situation in El Salvador and in the region as a whole. They place on record their thanks and appreciation for the enormous contribution of Señor Pérez de Cuéllar and his Personal Representative, Alvaro de Soto, their collaborators, and all the Governments, especially those of Colombia, Mexico, Spain and Venezuela, that have assisted Señor Pérez de Cuéllar in his efforts.

"The members of the Council urge the parties to show maximum flexibility in resolving the pending issues in the negotiations at United Nations Headquarters starting this weekend. They also urge the parties to exercise maximum restraint and to take no action in the coming days which would be contrary to the agreement reached in New York and to the excellent spirit in which these talks took place.

"They welcomed the Secretary-General's intention, stated today, to submit a written report and proposals early next week with a view to Council action both regarding verification of cease-fire arrangements and the monitoring of the maintenance of public order pending the establishment of the new National Civil Police. This will require the approval by the Council of new tasks for ONUSAL. The members of the Council stand ready to deal expeditiously with any recommendations that the Secretary-General may make."

Report of the Secretary-General. In a report of 30 November 1992,[17] Secretary-General Boutros Boutros-Ghali attributed the success that led to the Salvadorian Peace Agreement primarily to the determination of El Salvador's President, Alfredo F. Cristiani, and the FMLN leadership to achieve a negotiated solution to the conflict. He expressed appreciation to his predecessor, Javier Pérez de Cuéllar, who helped to ensure that success, as well as to Colombia, Mexico, Spain and Venezuela—referred to as the Group of Friends of the Secretary-General—for their support during the negotiations.

The Secretary-General described the Peace Agreement as a comprehensive package of inter-related undertakings by the parties, aimed not only at the cessation of the 12-year civil war in El Salvador, but also at tackling the root causes of the conflict by promoting democratization, respect for human rights and reconciliation among Salvadorians. Those endeavours would lay the groundwork for general elections in 1994.

The Agreement[9] provided for the reform of the armed forces of El Salvador (FAES) in terms of doctrine, structure, professional training and size; the replacement of the existing security bodies and intelligence services; the creation of a new National Civil Police under exclusive civilian control and of a new National Public Security Academy; the reform of the judicial system, including the creation of an Office of the National Counsel for the Defence of Human Rights; amendments to the Electoral Code and appointment of a Supreme Electoral Tribunal to prepare for the 1994 elections; economic and social development, the minimum commitments for which included agrarian reform, legal settlement of the land-tenure situation in the conflict zones and a national reconstruction plan; and legislative and other action to guarantee political participation by FMLN.

The Agreement further specified the interlocking steps to be carried out by the Government and FMLN for ending the armed conflict and for dismantling the FMLN structure, as well as the related verification tasks to be performed by ONUSAL. It called for United Nations verification of compliance, not only with the Peace Agreement, but also with the 1990 San José and 1991 Mexico and New York Agreements. It set forth an implementation timetable, with the stipulation that any adjustments required should be decided by ONUSAL in consultation with the parties. This was followed by a final declaration expressing the parties' firm determination to fulfil in good faith all the undertakings outlined by the Agreement and to cooperate with ONUSAL.

UN Observer Mission in El Salvador

The mandate of the United Nations Observer Mission in El Salvador, established by the Security Council in May 1991,[18] was extended thrice in 1992: on 14 January, when it was also enlarged, on 30 October and on 30 November. The extensions, for periods ending, respectively, on 31 October and 30 November 1992 and on 31 May 1993, were based on the Secretary-General's reports on all operational aspects of ONUSAL before the expiry of each mandate period.

Report of the Secretary-General (January). On 10 January 1992,[19] the Secretary-General informed the Security Council that the agreements referred to in the New York Act included two in particular that, subject to the Council's approval, would require an immediate and substantial increase in the strength of ONUSAL if it was to fulfil the verification and monitoring functions desired by the parties. One agreement related to the cessation of the armed confrontation to begin on 1 February, which envisaged that ONUSAL would verify all the aspects of the cease-fire and the separation of forces; the other, relating to the creation of a new National Civil Police, envisaged that ONUSAL would monitor the maintenance of public order until that new body was in place. Those functions, together with the time-frames involved, were described in detail.

The Secretary-General thus proposed increasing ONUSAL's strength by adding to the existing Human Rights Division two other divisions under the overall control of the Chief of Mission: a Military Division and a Police Division. The Military Division would have a core strength of 244 military observers through 31 October (when the process of ending the armed hostilities was to be completed), with another 128 to be deployed in connection with the 30-day (1 February–2 March) implementation of the separation of forces. It would be headquartered in San Salvador and would maintain four regional offices colocated with the current regional offices of the Human Rights Division.

The Police Division would require a core strength of 631 police observers until 31 December, to be deployed in all departments of El Salvador. It would likewise be headquartered in San Salvador and would have four regional offices colocated in the existing ONUSAL regional offices. It would set up sub-offices that would correspond to National Police deployment.

ONUSAL additionally required 95 civilian staff to provide administrative, transport, communication and procurement support; premises and accommodation, transport and air operations; communication and miscellaneous equipment; and supplies and services.

It was the Secretary-General's intention to meet most of these requirements by the transfer of personnel and equipment from ONUCA, whose termination was imminent (see above, under "UN Observer Group in Central America").

On 13 January,[20] the Secretary-General gave a preliminary estimate of approximately $58.9 million as the cost of ONUSAL for the 10-month period from 1 January to 31 October 1992, should the Council decide to expand the ONUSAL mandate as recommended. That amount was to be considered an expense of the Organization, to be borne by Member States in accordance with the relevant provisions of the Charter of the United Nations. The assessments to be levied on Member States were to be credited to the ONUSAL Special Account.

SECURITY COUNCIL ACTION (January)

On 14 January 1992, the Security Council, having considered the Secretary-General's report, unanimously adopted **resolution 729(1992)**.

The Security Council,
Recalling its resolution 637(1989) of 27 July 1989,
Recalling also its resolution 714(1991) of 30 September 1991, as well as the statement made by the President of the Council on behalf of the members of the Council on 3 January 1992 following the signature of the Act of New York on 31 December 1991,
Recalling further its resolution 693(1991) of 20 May 1991 by which it established the United Nations Observer Mission in El Salvador,
Welcoming the conclusion of agreements between the Government of El Salvador and the Frente Farabundo Martí para la Liberación Nacional, which are to be signed in Mexico City on 16 January 1992 and which, when implemented, will put a definitive end to the Salvadorian armed conflict, and will open the way for national reconciliation,
Calling upon both parties to continue to exercise maximum moderation and restraint and to take no action which would be contrary to or adversely affect the agreements to be signed in Mexico City,
Expressing its conviction that a peaceful settlement in El Salvador will make a decisive contribution to the Central American peace process,
Welcoming the intention of the Secretary-General to convey shortly to the Council his recommendation on the termination of the mandate of the United Nations Observer Group in Central America,

1. *Approves* the report of the Secretary-General contained in document S/23402;

2. *Decides*, on the basis of the Secretary-General's report and in accordance with the provisions of its resolution 693(1991) of 20 May 1991, to enlarge the mandate of the United Nations Observer Mission in El Salvador to include the verification and monitoring of the implementation of all the agreements once these are signed in Mexico City between the Government of El Salvador and the Frente Farabundo Martí para la Liberación Nacional, in particular the Agreement on the Cessation of the Armed Conflict and the Agreement on the Establishment of a National Civil Police;

3. *Also decides* that the mandate of the United Nations Observer Mission in El Salvador, enlarged in accordance with this resolution, will be extended to 31 October 1992 and that it will be reviewed at that time on the basis of recommendations to be presented by the Secretary-General;

4. *Requests* the Secretary-General to take the necessary measures to increase the strength of the United Nations Observer Mission in El Salvador as recommended in his report;

5. *Calls upon* both parties to respect scrupulously and to implement in good faith the commitments assumed by them under the agreements which are to be signed in Mexico City, and to cooperate fully with the United Nations Observer Mission in El Salvador in its task of verifying the implementation of these agreements;

6. *Reaffirms* its support for the Secretary-General's continuing mission of good offices with regard to the Central American peace process, and in particular for his observations in paragraphs 17, 18 and 19 of the report regarding his intention to continue, as was foreseen in the Geneva Agreement of 4 April 1990 concerning the process which is to end definitively the armed conflict, to rely on the Governments of Colombia, Mexico, Spain and Venezuela, as well as other States and groups of States, to support him in the exercise of his responsibilities;

7. *Requests* the Secretary-General to keep the Council fully informed of developments relating to the implementation of this resolution and to report on the operations of the United Nations Observer Mission in El Salvador before the expiry of the new mandate period.

Security Council resolution 729(1992)

14 January 1992   Meeting 3030   Adopted unanimously

Draft prepared in consultations among Council members (S/23411).

On 17 January,[21] the Council agreed to the Secretary-General's proposal[22] to appoint the former Chief Military Observer of ONUCA, Brigadier-General Víctor Suanzes Pardo (Spain), Chief Military Observer of ONUSAL.

Financing (January-October 1992)

On 22 April 1992,[23] the Secretary-General presented to the General Assembly a report on the total requirements of ONUSAL for the period 1 January to 31 October 1992.

He stated that, to enable him to act speedily on the Security Council decision to enlarge and extend the ONUSAL mandate pending approval of the budget for the enlarged operation, the Advisory Committee on Administrative and Budgetary Questions (ACABQ) had concurred with his proposal to enter into commitments for ONUSAL not to exceed $10 million under a 1991 Assembly resolution[24] on unforeseen and extraordinary expenses for the 1992-1993 biennium.

The total cost for the period 1 January to 31 October 1992 was estimated at $48,784,000 gross ($46,374,000 net). That amount covered requirements relating to the original mandate (to verify compliance with the 1990 San José Agreement on Human Rights[11]) and to the enlarged mandate, and included the commitment authority of up to $10 million.

As to financing from 1 July to 31 December 1991, assessments totalling $13,242,993 had been apportioned among Member States, of which $7,060,446 had been received, leaving an unpaid balance of $6,182,547 as at 31 March 1992. Initial appropriations and related expenditures for the same period resulted in an estimated unencumbered balance of $3,561,500 gross ($3,347,700 net), or about 25 per cent of the authorized appropriations. Against the contributions received was a net expenditure of $9,652,300 for the period ending 31 December 1991; this resulted in an operating deficit of $2,591,854.

In the light of the deficit and of the unpaid assessed contributions, the Secretary-General recommended that no action be taken regarding the net unencumbered balance and that it be retained in the ONUSAL Special Account.

Following a detailed examination of the cost estimates, and taking account not only of those areas where savings could be made, but also of the net unencumbered balance, ACABQ[25] recommended that, for the period from 1 January to 31 October 1992, the Assembly appropriate and assess $39 million gross ($37 million net) inclusive of the $10 million it had previously authorized.

ACABQ requested that the Secretary-General report to the Assembly on the feasibility and implications of merging the accounts of ONUCA and ONUSAL, in view of the functional relationship of the two operations and of the large number of personnel and equipment that had been transferred from ONUCA to ONUSAL.

GENERAL ASSEMBLY ACTION

Acting on the recommendation of the Fifth (Administrative and Budgetary) Committee, the General Assembly adopted **resolution 46/240** without vote on 22 May 1992.

Financing of the United Nations Observer Mission in El Salvador

The General Assembly,

Having considered the report of the Secretary-General on the financing of the United Nations Observer Mission in El Salvador and the related report of the Advisory Committee on Administrative and Budgetary Questions,

Bearing in mind Security Council resolution 693(1991) of 20 May 1991, by which the Council established the United Nations Observer Mission in El Salvador and Council resolution 729(1992) of 14 January 1992, by which the Council decided to extend the mandate of the Mission until 31 October 1992 and to enlarge it to include the verification and monitoring of the implementation of all the agreements signed at Mexico City between the Government of El Salvador and the Frente Farabundo Martí para la Liberación Nacional,

Reaffirming that the costs of the Mission are expenses of the Organization to be borne by Member States in accordance with Article 17, paragraph 2, of the Charter of the United Nations,

Recalling its previous decisions regarding the fact that, in order to meet the expenditures caused by the Mission, a different procedure is required from the one applied to meet expenditures of the regular budget of the United Nations,

Taking into account the fact that the economically more developed countries are in a position to make relatively larger contributions and that the economically less developed countries have a relatively limited capacity to contribute towards such an operation,

Bearing in mind the special responsibilities of the States permanent members of the Security Council, as indicated in General Assembly resolution 1874(S-IV) of 27 June 1963, in the financing of such operations,

Mindful of the fact that it is essential to provide the Mission with the necessary financial resources to enable it to fulfil its responsibilities under the relevant resolutions of the Security Council,

1. *Concurs* with the observations and recommendations made by the Advisory Committee on Administrative and Budgetary Questions in its report, subject to the provisions of paragraphs 2, 8 and 9 below;

2. *Notes* that the payment of assessed contributions since 31 March 1992 has reduced the outstanding assessments;

3. *Urges* all Member States to make every possible effort to ensure payment of their assessed contributions to the United Nations Observer Mission in El Salvador in full and on time;

4. *Decides* to appropriate to the Special Account for the United Nations Observer Mission in El Salvador an amount of 39 million United States dollars gross (37 million dollars net), inclusive of the amount of 10 million dollars authorized with the concurrence of the Advisory Committee, under the terms of General Assembly resolution 46/187 of 20 December 1991, for the operation of the Mission for the period from 1 January to 31 October 1992;

5. *Decides also*, as an ad hoc arrangement, to apportion the amounts referred to in paragraph 4 above among Member States in accordance with the composition of the groups set out in paragraphs 3 and 4 of General Assembly resolution 43/232 of 1 March 1989, as adjusted by the Assembly in its resolutions 44/192 B of 21 December 1989, 45/269 of 27 August 1991 and 46/198 A of 20 December 1991, and taking into account the scale of assessments for the years 1992, 1993 and 1994;

6. *Requests* the Secretary-General to report to the General Assembly at its forty-seventh session on anoma-

lies in the allocation of countries to the four groups set out in Assembly resolution 43/232, as adjusted by the Assembly in its resolutions 44/192 B, 45/269 and 46/198 A and applied as an ad hoc arrangement to the financing of the Mission, taking into account Assembly resolution 46/206 of 20 December 1991 and other relevant resolutions of the Assembly, including resolution 3101(XXVIII) of 11 December 1973;

7. *Decides* that, in accordance with the provisions of its resolution 973(X) of 15 December 1955, there shall be set off against the apportionment among Member States, as provided for in paragraph 5 above, their respective share in the Tax Equalization Fund of the estimated staff assessment income of 2 million dollars approved for the Mission;

8. *Decides also* that 2 million dollars of the unencumbered balance of appropriation shall be retained in the Special Account and that the balance of 1,347,700 dollars shall be set off against the apportionment among Member States as provided for in paragraph 5 above;

9. *Decides further*, in principle, that the special accounts for the United Nations Observer Group in Central America and the United Nations Observer Mission in El Salvador shall be merged;

10. *Decides* to consider the contributions of Armenia, Azerbaijan, Kazakhstan, Kyrgyzstan, the Republic of Moldova, San Marino, Tajikistan, Turkmenistan and Uzbekistan to the Mission in accordance with the rates of assessment to be adopted for these Member States by the General Assembly at its forty-seventh session;

11. *Invites* the new Member States listed in paragraph 10 above to make advance payments against their assessed contributions to be determined;

12. *Invites* voluntary contributions to the Mission in cash and in the form of services and supplies acceptable to the Secretary-General, to be administered, as appropriate, in accordance with the procedure established by the General Assembly in its resolutions 43/230 of 21 December 1988, 44/192 A of 21 December 1989 and 45/258 of 3 May 1991;

13. *Requests* the Secretary-General to take all necessary action to ensure that the Mission is administered with a maximum of efficiency and economy;

14. *Decides* to include in the provisional agenda of its forty-seventh session the item entitled "Financing of the United Nations Observer Mission in El Salvador".

General Assembly resolution 46/240

22 May 1992   Meeting 86   Adopted without vote

Approved by Fifth Committee (A/46/924) without vote, 21 May (meeting 65); draft by Vice-Chairman (A/C.5/46/L.24), orally revised following informal consultations; agenda item 139.
Meeting numbers. GA 46th session: 5th Committee 64, 65; plenary 86.

Composition

According to the Secretary-General's reports of 25 February[26] and 26 May 1992,[27] the Military Division of ONUSAL was set up and fully deployed by 31 January among four regional military offices and 15 verification centres. Its strength, authorized at 380 military observers, stood at 368 as at 25 February. It was reduced to 292 by 26 May from 10 countries: Brazil, Canada, Colombia, Ecuador, India, Ireland, Norway, Spain, Sweden and Venezuela. On the Secretary-General's recommendation, the Security Council agreed to maintain the Division's strength at that level until 1 September.[28] A further gradual reduction was expected during the remainder of the year.

The Police Division was constituted at the beginning of February with 147 of the 631 authorized police observers. By 26 May, its strength had been raised to 304 observers, deployed among six regional offices and four regional sub-offices.

The Human Rights Division was staffed with 51 civilian professionals and 14 police observers assigned from the Police Division.

In addition to the above, eight medical officers were provided by Argentina to assist ONUSAL.

Report of the Secretary-General (May). The Secretary-General, on 26 May 1992,[27] reported on ONUSAL operations since the cease-fire went into effect on 1 February, as well as on the status of compliance with the undertakings prescribed by the peace agreements.

As from the cease-fire date, the Military Division began to monitor the first steps to end the armed conflict, namely, the separation of FAES and FMLN troops and their peace-time concentration in designated locations. It verified troop and weapons inventories furnished by the two forces, authorized and accompanied the movements of both, and investigated complaints of violations. It conducted air and land patrols over the area under its responsibility.

The functions of the Police Division related to government compliance with the replacement of the three existing public security bodies: the National Guard and the Treasury Police, which were to be abolished and their members incorporated into the Army for inclusion in a review aimed at purifying FAES; and the National Police, which was to be progressively replaced by the new National Civil Police. Pending completion of these processes, the Division lent support to the National Police in the discharge of its duties as the sole body responsible for law and order, monitoring its activities through an average of 100 visits and patrols each day.

The Human Rights Division of ONUSAL continued to verify compliance with the 1990 San José Agreement on Human Rights.[11] (For the reports issued by the Division in 1992, see PART THREE, Chapter X.)

ONUSAL provided assistance in overcoming some of the difficulties encountered by the parties in the course of implementing the agreements. It participated in the work of the National Commission for the Consolidation of Peace (COPAZ), established by the 1991 New York Agreement[13] to draft legislative measures related to the accords and to supervise their execution. ONUSAL continued to be assisted by the Group of Friends of the Secretary-General and by other interested Governments.

The Secretary-General observed that the goal set by the agreements to end the 12-year civil conflict in El Salvador, to consolidate peace and to return to a normal political process that should lead to free and fair elections in 1994 was not easy to achieve. The agreements were complex and demanded compromise and fundamental adjustments in political and social attitudes. While commending the parties for their strict observance of the cease-fire and noting that no major incident had threatened the fragile first phase of national reconciliation, the Secretary-General pointed to serious delays in implementation, which had undermined each side's confidence in the other's good faith.

Of concern was the continuing failure of both sides to concentrate all of their forces in the designated locations, a process that was to have been completed on 2 March. Despite its timely presentation of troop and weapons inventories, FMLN had yet to present a weapons inventory that accurately reflected its true holdings, given the widespread suspicion that it retained clandestine caches of arms and ammunition. Of equal concern was the failure of the Government to set up the National Public Security Academy and to begin recruitment for the National Civil Police, of FMLN to return the first 20 per cent of its combatants to civilian life, and of the Government to initiate the legalization of FMLN as a political party—all of which should have taken place by 1 May.

Contradictory interpretations of specific provisions further impeded implementation. This was true with the land-tenure issue, which, in the absence of a precise definition of "conflict zones" in the Peace Agreement, had resulted in land seizures and dispossessions. This was also true with the restoration of public administration in those zones, where the return of certain judges and mayors met with opposition from FMLN, the community and non-governmental organizations. Based on its interpretation of the letter, the Government saw no problem with the manner in which it had abolished the Treasury Police and National Guard, or in transferring to the National Police large numbers of their members—actions that ONUSAL regarded as contrary to the spirit of the Agreement.

Because of the atmosphere of deep distrust between the parties, ONUSAL's insistence on impartiality had sometimes been perceived by one side as partiality towards the other. The Secretary-General reported in this connection that anonymous threats had recently been made against the security of ONUSAL and its personnel, of which the Salvadorian authorities had been informed. He also stated that the failure of the two sides to comply fully with the timetable had been brought to the attention of the President and the FMLN

General Command, who assured him that they would take steps to break the impasse and get the implementation process back on course.

After consultations held on 3 June, the President of the Security Council made the following statement[29] to the media on behalf of the Council members in connection with the item entitled "Central America: efforts towards peace":

> "The members of the Security Council have taken note of the report of the Secretary-General on the United Nations Observer Mission in El Salvador (ONUSAL).
>
> "They are pleased that the cease-fire is holding and there has not been a single violation since it came into force on 1 February 1992.
>
> "However, the members of the Council are deeply concerned about the many delays by both parties in implementing agreements concluded between the Government of El Salvador and the FMLN and the climate of mutual suspicion that still remains. If that situation were to continue, it would jeopardize the very foundation of the agreements.
>
> "They urge both parties to demonstrate good faith in implementing the agreements fully, to abide by the agreed time-limits, to exert every effort to bring about national reconciliation in El Salvador and to implement the process of demobilization and reform.
>
> "The members of the Council reaffirm their full support for the efforts made by the Secretary-General and his Special Representative, Mr. Iqbal Riza, with the assistance of the 'Friends of the Secretary-General' and other Governments concerned. They commend the staff of ONUSAL, who are working under very difficult conditions, and express their concern about the threats to their safety. They remind the parties of their obligation to take all necessary measures to guarantee the safety of ONUSAL and its members.
>
> "The members of the Council will continue to monitor closely developments in the implementation of the peace agreements in El Salvador."

Report of the Secretary-General (June). On 19 June,[30] the Secretary-General informed the Security Council that the issues that had delayed the implementation process had been resolved. According to arrangements finalized on 12 June, those steps that had not been complied with were to be fulfilled by dates reprogrammed as follows.

By 25 June, concentration of the two sides' forces at locations designated for them was to be completed. By 30 June: (1) reintegration of the first FMLN contingent into civilian life was to begin and be completed, as originally scheduled, by 31 October; (2) the Government was to present to the Legislative Assembly a bill for the definitive abolition of the National Guard and Treasury Police, and create a two-unit Special Brigade for Military Security, one unit for frontier protection duties and the other for military police duties (the Brigade would have no public security responsibilities in the civilian sphere, and personnel of the former two security bodies would not be eligible for recruitment into the new National Civil Police, nor could there be further transfers of such personnel to the existing National Police); (3) the Government was also to propose to the Legislative Assembly reforms to the Electoral Code to facilitate the legalization of FMLN as a political party; and (4) COPAZ was to begin verification of the FMLN land inventory, giving priority to properties subject to legal process.

By 15 July, the National Public Security Academy was to begin training recruits for the new National Civil Police, to include personnel from the existing National Police and former FMLN combatants in agreed proportions. Also by 15 July, the Government was to finalize programmes to facilitate reintegration of FMLN combatants into civilian life, providing contingency plans to benefit those who reintegrated earlier.

The Secretary-General subsequently reported[31] that, in the face of further delays, a second reprogramming was agreed upon on 19 August, following a visit to El Salvador by the Under-Secretary-General for Peace-keeping Operations. In this second reprogramming, the fulfilment by 31 October of two key government commitments had to be postponed beyond that date: the provision of agricultural land in the former zones of conflict, originally to have been completed by 31 July; and the establishment of the National Public Security Academy, which had been due on 1 May, to train recruits for the new National Civil Police for deployment no later than 28 October.

In reaction to these government delays, FMLN decided to suspend demobilization, asserting that the dismantling of its military structure, scheduled for completion by 31 October, would likewise have to be reprogrammed in order to maintain the link in the original timetable between the key undertakings of the two parties. Until then, only 40 per cent of FMLN combatants had returned to civilian life; the remaining 60 per cent, who were still armed, had been scheduled to leave their assembly sites, one third on 30 September, another third on 15 October and the final third on 31 October.

Activities of the Secretary-General. The Secretary-General informed the President of the Security Council on 19 October[32] that, as a result of the finding that the land issue was a main obstacle to the timely implementation of the second reprogramming, intense consultations were mounted inside and outside the United Nations system on the issue. He sent the Under-Secretary-General for Peace-keeping Operations to El Salvador to help the parties search for solutions. On 13 October, he presented them with a proposal deemed an equitable compromise between their positions. It set out terms and conditions for the transfer of land to former combatants of both sides and for the formalization of the land-tenure system; or, if necessary, for the relocation on new land of persons who during the hostilities had moved onto land in the conflict zones. FMLN and the Government accepted the proposal on 15 and 16 October, respectively, and confirmed their commitment to its early implementation.

As to the dismantling of FMLN's military structure, the Secretary-General felt that, due to the complications of demobilizing in 15 different locations, the process could not possibly be completed by 31 October. Thus, on 23 October, he reprogrammed for a third time the schedule for compliance, whereby the final phase of the FMLN demobilization would begin by 31 October and be completed by 15 December. FMLN accepted the proposal provided the Government also accepted it. Owing to its reservations on a number of aspects and questions as to the FMLN weapons inventory and the schedule for implementing the recommendations of the Ad Hoc Commission on the Purification of the Armed Forces, the Government decided to suspend its restructuring, reduction and demobilization of FAES. Clarification of these matters with the parties was in progress at the time of reporting.

Lacking the information required to formulate long-term recommendations on ONUSAL's mandate and strength, the Secretary-General, on 28 October,[33] recommended an extension of the current mandate for an interim period of one month, until 30 November.

SECURITY COUNCIL ACTION (October)

On 30 October 1992, the Security Council unanimously adopted **resolution 784(1992)**.

The Security Council,
Recalling its resolution 637(1989) of 27 July 1989,
Recalling also its resolutions 693(1991) of 20 May 1991, 714(1991) of 30 September 1991 and 729(1992) of 14 January 1992,
Taking note of the letter from the Secretary-General dated 19 October 1992, in which he announced a delay in the schedule laid down in resolution 729(1992),
Noting also the letter from the Secretary-General dated 28 October 1992, in which he proposed an interim extension of the current mandate of the United Nations Observer Mission in El Salvador (ONUSAL),
1. *Approves* the proposal of the Secretary-General to extend the current mandate of ONUSAL for a period ending on 30 November 1992;
2. *Requests* the Secretary-General to submit to it, between now and that date, recommendations on the period of extension of the mandate, on the mandate and strength that ONUSAL will need, taking into account progress already made, in order to verify the implementation of the final phases of the peace process in El Salvador together with their financial implications;
3. *Urges* both parties to respect scrupulously and to implement in good faith the commitments assumed by

them under the agreements signed on 16 January 1992 at Mexico City and to respond positively to the Secretary-General's latest proposals to them aimed at overcoming the current difficulties;
4. *Decides* to remain seized of the matter.

Security Council resolution 784(1992)
30 October 1992   Meeting 3129   Adopted unanimously
Draft prepared in consultations among Council members (S/24737).

Report of the Secretary-General (November). On 23 November,[31] the Secretary-General reported on the status of the implementation of the agreements and the related ONUSAL activities.

As he informed the Council President on 11 November,[34] his Personal Representative for the Central American Peace Process—who, along with the Under-Secretary-General for Peace-keeping Operations, travelled to San Salvador to consult with the parties regarding his 23 October proposal—subsequently reported that arrangements had been concluded which, if implemented, would formally bring the armed conflict to an end on 15 December. These included government implementation of the recommendations of the Ad Hoc Commission on Purification of the Armed Forces within a specified time-frame; FMLN presentation to ONUSAL, on 30 November, of its final weapons inventory; and the concentration by that date of the inventoried weapons in designated zones, for destruction beginning on 1 December. Upon confirmation of the completion of these measures, the Government would promptly resume the dissolution of its military units.

Agreement on these arrangements was recorded in letters exchanged by the Personal Representative with the President and the FMLN General Command, stipulating for the first time that compliance with certain key points in the calendar by one side was contingent upon compliance with specific undertakings by the other.

The Military Division of ONUSAL continued to ensure observance of the cease-fire and assumed further verification tasks related to the reduction of FAES. It participated in a working group on the problem of minefields and provided support to a UNICEF public-awareness campaign on the dangers they posed. It determined that the majority of demobilized personnel were released directly into civilian life and verified that personnel transfers to other military service were not in conflict with the accords. It continued to ensure the effective dissolution of the Territorial Service and followed up on regulations to implement the recently promulgated law establishing an armed forces reserve system. It verified the official disbandment of the National Intelligence Department and the creation of the new State Intelligence Agency. It had requested, but had yet to receive, a plan for the recall of military weapons in private hands.

As to public security matters, the Police Division cooperated in verifying that the dissolution of civil defence units was effective and in locating illegal arms caches. It confirmed its finding that demobilized, self-contained FAES units had been integrated into the National Police, in contravention of the spirit of the agreements. It conducted special inquiries required by the Human Rights Division and ensured that special security measures were provided for FMLN leaders. Over ONUSAL's objections, the Academic Council had accepted the applications of former Treasury Police and National Guard personnel to the National Public Security Academy, in contravention of the accords; the Council had moreover given university credit for prior training and service in the National Police. For an effective monitoring of the Academy's functioning, the Division pressed for its attendance at Academic Council meetings. It provided guidance, instruction and logistical support to the Auxiliary Transitory Police, which was deployed in 12 posts by mid-November.

Regarding the complex land-tenure issue, new occupations of lands in the former conflict zones, some by former FMLN combatants, had given rise to new tensions that, on one occasion, threatened the cease-fire but was averted through intervention by ONUSAL and the Archbishop of San Salvador. While FMLN had called a halt to such activity, reports to the contrary continued to be received and investigated by ONUSAL. It continued to press for the completion of procedures for implementing the reintegration programmes. Since the Government accorded FMLN the status of a "political party in formation" on 30 July, steps towards its full political participation had been in progress. In consultation with both sides, ONUSAL, on 16 September, finalized a programme for the restoration of public administration in the former zones of conflict and initiated contacts between mayors in exile and local organizations resisting their return.

The Secretary-General observed that, despite the problems encountered in the course of implementing the intricate agreements within a climate of distrust and polarization, implementation of the peace process had advanced steadily and many obstacles had been overcome. That observance of the cease-fire was impeccable and that FMLN was enabled to engage in political activities in advance of its full legalization as a political party were an impressive demonstration of the will of both parties to consolidate peace in their country. In those instances when the implementation process had been put at serious risk, the United Nations exerted considerable effort to steer the process back on track, with help from the Group of Friends of the Secretary-General, the United States and other interested Governments.

Pointing to certain major undertakings that were to extend into 1994, such as the reduction of FAES and the deployment of the National Civil Police, the Secretary-General said it could be anticipated that ONUSAL would complete its mission by mid-1994. In the meantime, he recommended that its mandate be extended for a further period of six months, to 31 May 1993. He indicated a preliminary cost estimate of some $20.6 million for that period,[35] which should be considered a United Nations expense to be borne by Member States.

SECURITY COUNCIL ACTION (November)

Having studied the Secretary-General's report, the Security Council unanimously adopted **resolution 791(1992)** on 30 November 1992.

The Security Council,
Recalling its resolution 637(1989) of 27 July 1989,
Recalling also its resolutions 693(1991) of 20 May 1991, 714(1991) of 30 September 1991, 729(1992) of 14 January 1992 and 784(1992) of 30 October 1992,
Having studied the report of the Secretary-General dated 23 November 1992,
Noting with appreciation the continuing efforts of the Secretary-General to support implementation of the several agreements signed between 4 April 1990 and 16 January 1992 by the Government of El Salvador and the Frente Farabundo Martí para la Liberación Nacional (FMLN) to re-establish peace and promote reconciliation in El Salvador,
Noting the intention of the Secretary-General to continue, in this as in other peace-keeping operations, to monitor expenditures carefully during this period of increasing demands on peace-keeping resources,
1. *Approves* the report of the Secretary-General;
2. *Decides* to extend the mandate of the United Nations Observer Mission in El Salvador (ONUSAL) as defined in resolutions 693(1991) and 729(1992), for a further period of six months ending on 31 May 1993;
3. *Welcomes* the intention of the Secretary-General to adapt the future activities and strength of ONUSAL, taking into account progress made in implementing the peace process;
4. *Urges* both parties to respect scrupulously and to implement in good faith the solemn commitments they have assumed under the agreements signed on 16 January 1992 at Mexico City and to exercise the utmost moderation and restraint, both at present and following the conclusion of the cease-fire phase, in order to respect the new deadlines agreed upon by them for the successful completion of the peace process and for the restoration of normal conditions, especially in the zones of former conflict;
5. *Shares*, in this context, the preoccupations expressed by the Secretary-General in paragraph 84 of his report;
6. *Reaffirms* its support for the Secretary-General's use of his good offices in the El Salvador peace process and calls upon both parties to cooperate fully with the Secretary-General's Special Representative and ONUSAL in their tasks of assisting and verifying the parties' implementation of their commitments;

7. *Requests* all States, as well as the international institutions in the fields of development and finance, to continue to support, in particular through voluntary contributions, the peace process;

8. *Requests* the Secretary-General to keep the Security Council fully informed of further developments in the El Salvador peace process and to report, as necessary, on all aspects of ONUSAL's operations, at the latest before the expiry of the new mandate period.

Security Council resolution 791(1992)

30 November 1992   Meeting 3142   Adopted unanimously

Draft prepared in consultations among Council members (S/24861).

Financing (December 1992–May 1993)

On 4 December 1992,[36] following the extension of ONUSAL's mandate for a further six-month period, from 1 December 1992 to 31 May 1993, the Secretary-General reported to the General Assembly on the requirements of ONUSAL for that period. He also summarized the budget performance of the two previous mandate periods, from 1 January to 31 October and from 1 to 30 November 1992, as well as the status of contributions for ONUSAL financing as at 30 November.

In his summary of the appropriations provided for the 10-month period from 1 January to 31 October 1992 and the related expenditures during the 11-month period from 1 January to 31 October and from 1 to 30 November 1992, the Secretary-General indicated an unencumbered balance of $1,624,200 gross ($1,484,700 net).

He estimated the cost for the period 1 December 1992 to 31 May 1993 at $19,339,500 gross ($17,999,700 net). Based on that level of expenditure, he further estimated that continued maintenance of ONUSAL beyond 31 May 1993 would cost an average monthly rate not to exceed $3,223,250 gross ($2,999,950 net).

Of the assessments totalling $49,503,028 that had been apportioned among Member States for the period 1 July 1991 to 31 October 1992, $37,894,597 had been received and $3,296,972 had been credited to Member States, leaving an unpaid balance of $11,608,431. As a result of merging the Special Account of ONUCA, which had a net unutilized balance of $146,759, with that of ONUSAL, which had a net deficit of $7,953,242, the combined ONUCA/ONUSAL Special Account resulted in a net operating deficit of $7,806,483. To meet operating cash requirements, loans amounting to $5 million had been made available to ONUSAL from the United Nations Iran-Iraq Military Observer Group Special Account.

In view of that loan and pending receipt of the outstanding assessed contributions for both ONUCA and ONUSAL, the Secretary-General recommended that no action be taken as to the income of $4,484,174 ($1,990,206 in interest and $2,493,968 in miscellaneous income combined) and that it be retained in the ONUSAL/ONUCA Special Account.

Owing to lack of time, the Fifth Committee could not consider the Secretary-General's report, which was before it on 16 December 1992. It therefore recommended measures for the continued maintenance of ONUSAL until 28 February 1993. These were embodied in **decision 47/452**, adopted by the General Assembly without vote on 22 December.

Financing of the United Nations Observer Mission in El Salvador

At its 93rd plenary meeting, on 22 December 1992, the General Assembly, on the recommendation of the Fifth Committee:

(*a*) Authorized the Secretary-General to enter into commitments up to the amount of 8,045,600 United States dollars gross (7,514,200 dollars net) for the maintenance of the United Nations Observer Mission in El Salvador for the period ending 28 February 1993;

(*b*) Apportioned, as an ad hoc arrangement, the amount indicated in subparagraph (*a*) above among Member States, in accordance with the scheme set out in its resolution 47/41 of 1 December 1992;

(*c*) Deferred to its resumed forty-seventh session the consideration of the item entitled "Financing of the United Nations Observer Mission in El Salvador".

General Assembly decision 47/452

Adopted without vote

Approved by Fifth Committee (A/47/797) without vote, 16 December (meeting 46); oral proposal by Chairman; agenda item 122.

Report of the Secretary-General (December). In a report of 23 December 1992,[37] the Secretary-General informed the Security Council that the armed conflict between the Government of El Salvador and FMLN was formally brought to an end on 15 December, the date fixed by the latest adjusted timetable. The event, preceded the previous day by the legalization of FMLN as a political party, was marked by a ceremony attended by the President of El Salvador, who presided over it, FMLN, the Secretary-General, and representatives of Spain, on behalf of the Group of Friends of the Secretary-General, of Guatemala, on behalf of the Central American States, and of the United States. The Secretary-General's statement at the ceremony was annexed to his report.

The Secretary-General noted that the parties had generally complied with their commitments according to the adjusted timetable, and that COPAZ and the Legislative Assembly had made a determined effort to complete the related legislation. He made special mention of the timely demobilization of the fifth and final FMLN contingent, which brought the total number of demobilized combatants to 8,876 as at 17 December, and of handicapped and injured combatants to 3,486, also demobilized; of the destruction of 50 per cent of the total FMLN arms inventory, with the remainder to be destroyed by year's end and those located outside El Salvador by early January 1993; of the punctual presentation of the administrative decisions for implementing the recommendations of the Ad Hoc Commission on the Purification of the Armed Forces; and of the completion of the investigations by the Commission on Truth. (Mandated by the 1991 Mexico Agreements[12] to investigate serious acts of violence committed since the outbreak of armed confrontation in 1980 and whose impact on society demanded that the public know the truth, the Commission on Truth was formally constituted in New York on 13 July. It was composed of three eminent persons: Belisario Betancur (Colombia), former President; Reinaldo Figueredo (Venezuela), former Minister for Foreign Affairs; and Thomas Buergenthal (United States), former President of the Inter-American Court for Human Rights and Honorary President of the Inter-American Institute for Human Rights. The Commission's secretariat was set up in San Salvador.)

The Secretary-General also noted, however, the Government's failure to ensure the recovery of weapons in private hands, which was to have been accomplished by 8 December, adding that less than 100 of an estimated several thousand weapons had been recovered by that date. The Government had assured ONUSAL that it would intensify efforts in that regard.

Noting that a number of provisions remained to be implemented, the Secretary-General pointed to six that merited emphasis: the land-transfer programme, including guarantees for the non-eviction of current landholders pending a legal solution; the programmes for the reintegration into civilian life of ex-combatants of both sides, including the war-disabled; the international supervision of the National Public Security Academy and its establishment in permanent premises; the establishment of the National Civilian Police and its progressive deployment in lock step with the phasing out of the existing National Police; the planned reduction of FAES; and the coordination of long-term plans for the economic and social development of El Salvador.

Aid programmes

The United Nations Development Programme (UNDP) played a principal role in providing technical assistance and mobilizing financial resources to make possible the implementation of some of the major provisions of the Peace Agreement. Notably, it coordinated an inter-agency mission for the formulation of a National Reconstruction Plan. It provided technical support for the formation and strengthening of democratic institutions, including the National Public Security Academy,

the National Ombudsman for the Protection of Human Rights, the National Commission for the Consolidation of Peace and the new Supreme Electoral Council. It also provided technical and financial support for the reintegration programmes for demobilized FMLN ex-combatants in the areas of emergency assistance at relocation points, agricultural training, education and health.

Assistance from the international community was being sought to enable the Salvadorian Government to implement the National Reconstruction Plan.

(For additional information on the foregoing, see PART THREE, Chapter III.)

El Salvador–Honduras

On 11 September 1992, the International Court of Justice delivered its Judgment in the case concerning the ''Land, Island and Maritime Frontier Dispute (El Salvador/Honduras; Nicaragua intervening)''. The case was submitted to the Court in 1986[38] by a special agreement between El Salvador and Honduras which defined the questions for decision. In dispute were certain sections of land along the border between the two countries, the islands of the Gulf of Fonseca and the maritime spaces within and outside the closing line of that Gulf, which touched the coastline of El Salvador, Honduras and Nicaragua on the Pacific.

(For details of the Judgment, see PART FIVE, Chapter I.)

Guatemala situation

In his November 1992 report on the situation in Central America,[17] the Secretary-General described the status of the peace process in Guatemala, initiated in 1990 by the Government and the Unidad Revolucionaria Nacional Guatemalteca (URNG), the opposition movement, when they concluded the Basic Agreement for the Search for Peace by Political Means.[39]

The Secretary-General stated that, in January 1992, the parties reached agreement on several provisions for inclusion in a future agreement on human rights, including the principle of international verification by the United Nations. Serious differences emerged, however, regarding human rights issues as they related to the protection of the civilian population and wounded and captured combatants, to the proposed voluntary civil defence committees on freedom of association and movement, and to the proposed commission to inquire into human rights violations since the conflict began. A proposal to resolve those differences was presented to the parties in May by the Conciliator (Chairman of the National Reconciliation Commission), which the Government accepted.

Also in May, URNG put forward a comprehensive set of proposals relating to a number of items on the agenda agreed upon in 1991.[40] In an equally comprehensive response of 30 June,[41] the Government, in addition to outlining the status of the peace negotiations, clarified its position with respect to civilian authority and the army's role in a democratic society like Guatemala, the rights of the indigenous population, constitutional amendments and the electoral system, and social and economic problems in such areas as education, land entitlement and redistribution, and resettlement of population groups displaced by the armed conflict. The Government noted that the proposals advanced by URNG failed to state its position on such fundamental issues as a definitive cease-fire, a timetable for implementing agreements, arrangements for verification of implementation, and demobilization.

To give greater impetus to the negotiations based on their proposals, the Government suggested that the Conciliator, the Observer (Personal Representative of the Secretary-General) and the parties consider themselves in permanent session as from the second fortnight of July, meeting during alternate weeks until the agenda had been exhausted and a final peace agreement had been signed.

In August, progress was achieved on the issue of voluntary civil defence committees, with the parties deciding to make public the text of the relative provision agreed upon. Noting that there had been little progress since, the Secretary-General urged the parties to reinvigorate the process and redouble their efforts towards the goal of a firm and lasting peace.

GENERAL ASSEMBLY ACTION

In **resolution 47/118**, the General Assembly reiterated the importance of stepping up the negotiating process between the Government of Guatemala and URNG in order to achieve the goals laid down in the 1991 Mexico City and Querétaro Agreements.[40] It urged scrupulous implementation of the agreed procedures and progress towards the adoption of commitments on all the issues set forth in the Mexico City Agreement, particularly the signing of the Comprehensive Agreement on Human Rights which they had been considering.

Nicaragua

In 1992, assistance continued to be sought for the rehabilitation and reconstruction of Nicaragua, which were necessary for overcoming the aftermath of war and for the consolidation of peace and democracy already achieved in the country. The appeal for such assistance, from the international community and from international funding agencies, had its origins in the National Conciliation Agreement on Economic and Social Matters concluded in Nicaragua in 1990[42] (phase I) and 1991 (phase II), which the General Assembly welcomed, supporting in particular the agreements regarding property rights and privatization in phase II of the Agreement.

In **resolution 47/118**, the Assembly supported efforts by Nicaragua to consolidate peace. In **resolution 47/169**, it asked for continued support to that country to enable it to overcome the aftermath not only of war but also of recent natural disasters (see PART THREE, Chapter III), and to stimulate the process of reconstruction and development. It requested the Secretary-General to provide Nicaragua with all possible assistance to support the consolidation of peace in such areas as the settlement of displaced and demobilized persons and refugees, rural land ownership and land tenure, direct care for war victims, mine clearance and the restoration of the country's productive areas.

Nicaragua-Honduras

As a result of an out-of-court agreement between Nicaragua and Honduras aimed at enhancing their good-neighbourly relations, the case pending before the International Court of Justice concerning "Border and Transborder Armed Actions (Nicaragua v. Honduras)" was brought to an end during 1992 on the initiative of Nicaragua. It had filed the Application instituting proceedings against Honduras in 1986.[43] (For details on the discontinuance of the case, see PART FIVE, Chapter I.)

REFERENCES

[1]A/46/954-S/24354. [2]YUN 1986, p. 177. [3]YUN 1991, p. 141. [4]A/44/970-S/21504. [5]SC res. 644(1989), 7 Nov. 1989. [6]YUN 1987, p. 188. [7]YUN 1991, p. 145, SC res. 719(1991), 6 Nov. 1991. [8]S/23421. [9]A/46/864-S/23501. [10]A/47/556. [11]A/44/971-S/21541. [12]YUN 1991, p. 147. [13]Ibid., p. 148. [14]A/46/552-S/23129. [15]A/46/863-S/23504. [16]S/23360. [17]A/47/739-S/24871. [18]YUN 1991, p. 149, SC res. 693(1991), 20 May 1991. [19]S/23402. [20]S/23402/Add.1. [21]S/23434. [22]S/23433. [23]A/46/900. [24]YUN 1991, p. 869, GA res. 46/187, 20 Dec. 1991. [25]A/46/904. [26]S/23642. [27]S/23999. [28]S/23988. [29]S/24058. [30]S/23999/Add.1. [31]S/24833. [32]S/24688. [33]S/24731. [34]S/24805. [35]S/24833/Add.1. [36]A/47/751. [37]S/25006. [38]YUN 1986, p. 984. [39]A/45/706-S/21931. [40]YUN 1991, p. 151. [41]A/47/334. [42]A/45/818. [43]YUN 1986, pp. 181 & 983.

The Caribbean

Cuba–United States

Cuba, on 27 April 1992,[1] requested the Security Council to convene as soon as possible in order to consider the terrorist activities being promoted, encouraged or tolerated by the United States against Cuba. In this context, Cuba referred to terrorists within the United States who were openly organizing and training military groups for the purpose of invading Cuba, and recalled the 1976 explosion of a Cuban civil aircraft, from a bomb planted in it, shortly after take-off from Barbados that killed the 73 persons on board. According to Cuba, the criminal proceedings instituted by Venezuela in 1976 against the four men implicated in the crime ended in 1987, 11 years later. The two Venezuelan nationals accused of planting the bomb were sentenced to 20 years in prison. One of the two Cuban nationals accused of masterminding the crime, Orlando Bosch, was "acquitted". No verdict was rendered in the case of the other Cuban, Luis Posada Carriles, who reportedly left his place of detention under peculiar circumstances. Cuba alleged that the United States had withheld information from Venezuela that would have convicted Orlando Bosch and that the two Cubans were currently in the United States enjoying that country's protection.

Underscoring the Council's statement of 31 January 1992 on the need for the international community to deal effectively with acts of international terrorism, such as the attacks on Pan Am flight 103 in 1988 and on UTA (Union de transports aériens) flight 772 in 1989 (see PART ONE, Chapter I), Cuba demanded that the Council condemn the destruction of the Cuban airliner and that it ask the United States to deliver the two Cuban nationals to Cuba and take immediate steps to eliminate all terrorist activities carried out against Cuba from the United States.

On 8 May,[2] Cuba reiterated its request for a meeting, providing further information as to why the Council was duty-bound to examine its allegations. On 13 May,[3] Cuba disputed a statement reportedly made by the Secretary-General's spokesman that the Council had discussed its request and would continue consultations on the issue, and that Cuba had been so informed. Asserting that such discussion could not have transpired, Cuba reiterated that the Council should convene without further delay.

The United States, on 21 May,[4] replied that the opposite of Cuba's allegations against it was true. It traced the legal actions taken by the United States against Orlando Bosch, beginning with his 1968 trial and conviction for involvement with terrorist activities, which resulted in his sentencing to 10 years in prison; his parole in 1972; his incarceration in 1988 for violating that parole and the consequent recommendation for his exclusion from the United States (he fled the country in 1974 while on parole and illegally re-entered in 1988). The United States asserted that it had no record

of having received a request from Venezuela for evidence or testimony in connection with its criminal proceedings against the two Cubans. Although found excludable from the United States, Orlando Bosch had remained in its custody, at his residence in Miami, Florida, with restrictions on his movements and activities. He had not been deported to Cuba, where, the United States said, he faced certain execution, having been tried *in absentia* and sentenced to death.

SECURITY COUNCIL CONSIDERATION

The Security Council convened on 21 May 1992 to consider the matter brought before it by Cuba, which was invited, at its request, to participate without the right to vote under rule 37[a] of the Council's provisional rules of procedure.

Meeting number. SC 3080.

In essence, Cuba's statement before the Council was that the United States had covered up for Orlando Bosch by withholding information from Venezuela that would have led to his conviction for the 1976 bombing of the Cuban airliner, and that it continued to withhold information on his other terrorist activities for which he should be brought to justice. Cuba alleged that, notwithstanding the Justice Department's determination that Orlando Bosch should be deported, he was allowed to remain in the United States by a higher authority, that is, by the President of the United States.

Cuba provided information on the whereabouts of Luis Posada Carriles and on his activities in the service of the United States Department of State and Central Intelligence Agency, after leaving his place of detention in Venezuela. In addition, it provided radio and press accounts, dated as recently as April 1992, of terrorist activities against Cuba launched from the United States.

Responding, the United States emphasized that it was not insensitive to the sorrow of those whose relatives or friends had died in the 1976 airline bombing. It labelled as absurd Cuba's attempt to portray the United States as a supporter of international terrorism and harbourer of terrorists, and regretted Cuba's misuse of the Council to make such baseless allegations. To the best of its knowledge, Luis Posada was not in the United States but believed to be somewhere in Latin America. The facts relating to Orlando Bosch, as it had communicated in detail to the Council, belied the canard that the United States had supported his illegal activities.

[a]Rule 37 of the Council's provisional rules of procedure states: "Any Member of the United Nations which is not a member of the Security Council may be invited, as the result of a decision of the Security Council, to participate, without vote, in the discussion of any question brought before the Security Council when the Security Council considers that the interests of that Member are specially affected, or when a Member brings a matter to the attention of the Security Council in accordance with Article 35(1) of the Charter."

The United States restated its position in respect of Cuba: it supported peaceful democratic change in that country and had no aggressive intentions towards it. The United States neither supported nor condoned preparations or efforts within its territory for the violent overthrow of Cuba's Government or for fomenting violence in Cuba; suggestions to the contrary were untruthful and unacceptable. The United States categorically rejected any assertion that its economic policy measures towards Cuba were inconsistent with international law, stressing that every Government had the right to choose with whom it wished to maintain relations. The United States had chosen to have neither full diplomatic nor commercial relations with Cuba because of the lack of democracy there and of the Government's flagrant abuse of human rights.

The Council concluded its meeting without taking action on a draft resolution proposed but not pressed to the vote by Cuba.[5] The draft would have had the Council condemn the 1976 sabotage of the Cuban airliner, declare that all States in a position to do so had an obligation to contribute to a full investigation of the incident, request the Secretary-General to seek United States cooperation in providing information to facilitate such an investigation and punishment of the guilty parties, urge the United States to release information on the activities of Luis Posada since leaving detention and on his current whereabouts, and further urge it to prevent the use of its territory for terrorist acts against Cuba.

United States embargo against Cuba

In accordance with its 1991 decision,[6] the General Assembly included in its 1992 agenda an item on the necessity of ending the economic, commercial and financial embargo imposed by the United States against Cuba.

The embargo was the subject of several communications from Cuba to the Secretary-General during the year. Of note was the transmittal on 11 June[7] of a letter to the Congress of the United States, a *démarche* to the Department of State and a letter to a United States senator, all from the Delegation of the Commission of the European Communities. These expressed the objections of the European Community (EC) to four pieces of legislation pending before the United States Congress that would have the effect of prohibiting United States–owned subsidiary companies incorporated and domiciled outside the United States from trading with Cuba. The Delegation set out in detail the elements which EC regarded as having no basis in international law.

Also of note was a 6 November letter from Cuba[8] drawing attention to the Cuban Democracy Act of 1992, signed into law on 23 Oc-

tober by the President of the United States. Among the Act's provisions, Cuba cited the categorical prohibition of third-country companies owned or controlled by United States nationals from engaging in any transactions with Cuba. It prohibited third-country vessels from loading or unloading goods at United States ports for 180 days after they had entered Cuban ports for trade in goods or services. It made clear to other countries that, in determining its relations with them, the United States would take into account their willingness to cooperate with its sanctions programme against Cuba.

The Delegation of the Commission of the European Communities had likewise expressed EC objections to the Act when it was pending before Congress.[9] It cited the unacceptability of, among the Act's other provisions, the extraterritorial extension of United States jurisdiction as a matter of law and policy; and of the discriminatory tax penalties against United States companies with overseas subsidiaries which traded with Cuba, thereby providing a Draconian economic disincentive against transactions that would be permitted in other jurisdictions.

GENERAL ASSEMBLY ACTION

On 24 November 1992, the General Assembly adopted **resolution 47/19** by recorded vote.

**Necessity of ending the economic, commercial
and financial embargo imposed
by the United States of America against Cuba**

The General Assembly,

Determined to encourage strict compliance with the purposes and principles enshrined in the Charter of the United Nations,

Reaffirming, among other principles, the sovereign equality of States, non-intervention and non-interference in their internal affairs and freedom of trade and international navigation, which are also enshrined in many international legal instruments,

Concerned about the promulgation and application by Member States of laws and regulations whose extraterritorial effects affect the sovereignty of other States and the legitimate interests of entities or persons under their jurisdiction, as well as the freedom of trade and navigation,

Having learned of the recent promulgation of measures of that nature aimed at strengthening and extending the economic, commercial and financial embargo against Cuba,

1. *Calls upon* all States to refrain from promulgating and applying laws and measures of the kind referred to in the preamble to the present resolution in conformity with their obligations under the Charter of the United Nations and international law and with the commitments that they have freely entered into in acceding to international legal instruments that, *inter alia,* reaffirm the freedom of trade and navigation;

2. *Urges* States that have such laws or measures to take the necessary steps to repeal or invalidate them as soon as possible in accordance with their legal regime;

3. *Requests* the Secretary-General to submit to the General Assembly at its forty-eighth session a report on the implementation of the present resolution;

4. *Decides* to include the item in the provisional agenda of its forty-eighth session.

General Assembly resolution 47/19

24 November 1992   Meeting 70   59-3-71 (recorded vote)

Draft by Cuba (A/47/L.20/Rev.1); agenda item 39.

Recorded vote in Assembly as follows:

In favour: Algeria, Angola, Barbados, Benin, Brazil, Burkina Faso, Burundi, Canada, Central African Republic, Chile, China, Colombia, Comoros, Congo, Cuba, Democratic People's Republic of Korea, Ecuador, Equatorial Guinea, France, Ghana, Guinea, Guinea-Bissau, Haiti, India, Indonesia, Iran, Iraq, Jamaica, Kenya, Lao People's Democratic Republic, Lebanon,* Lesotho, Libyan Arab Jamahiriya, Madagascar, Malaysia, Mali, Malta, Mexico, Myanmar, Namibia, New Zealand, Niger, Nigeria, Pakistan, Papua New Guinea, Spain, Sudan, Swaziland, Syrian Arab Republic, Uganda, Ukraine, United Republic of Tanzania, Uruguay, Vanuatu, Venezuela, Viet Nam, Yemen, Zambia, Zimbabwe.

Against: Israel, Romania, United States.

Abstaining: Albania, Antigua and Barbuda, Argentina, Armenia, Australia, Austria, Azerbaijan, Bahamas, Bangladesh, Belarus, Belgium, Belize, Bolivia, Brunei Darussalam, Bulgaria, Cameroon, Chad, Costa Rica, Côte d'Ivoire, Czechoslovakia, Denmark, El Salvador, Ethiopia, Fiji, Finland, Gabon, Germany, Greece, Guatemala, Guyana, Honduras, Hungary, Iceland, Ireland, Italy, Japan, Jordan, Kuwait, Liechtenstein, Luxembourg, Maldives, Marshall Islands, Micronesia, Nepal, Netherlands, Nicaragua, Norway, Panama, Paraguay, Peru, Philippines, Poland, Portugal, Republic of Korea, Republic of Moldova, Russian Federation, Rwanda, Saint Lucia, Saint Vincent and the Grenadines, Samoa, San Marino, Singapore, Slovenia, Sri Lanka, Suriname, Sweden, Thailand, Trinidad and Tobago, Turkey, United Kingdom, Zaire.

*Later advised the Secretariat it had intended to abstain.

Haiti

Efforts continued in 1992 to restore the legitimate Government of President Jean-Bertrand Aristide of Haiti, overthrown by a military coup in 1991[10] and currently in exile in the United States. Despite the measures taken by the Organization of American States (OAS), which had assumed the leading role in those efforts, that objective had not been realized.

President Aristide thus wrote to the Secretary-General on 3 June 1992, expressing hope that the United Nations would assist OAS in achieving effective implementation of its resolutions to compel restoration of the legitimate Government, particularly compliance with the embargo imposed against Haiti and the dispatch to it of a multidimensional mission. He asked that a personal representative of the Secretary-General be sent to inquire into human rights violations in Haiti and determine its humanitarian needs. It was imperative, he stressed, that the Office of the United Nations High Commissioner for Refugees (UNHCR) ensure full compliance with article 33 of the 1951 Convention relating to the Status of Refugees, prohibiting expulsion or forceable return to the frontiers of territories where the refugee's life or freedom would be threatened.[11]

The Secretary-General stated on 18 June that he would seek the opinion of OAS on those requests, as his mandate was limited to supporting OAS action. Meanwhile, he gave assurances that

UNHCR was taking steps to alleviate the plight of the Haitian refugees.

The OAS Secretary-General replied on 10 July that the crisis in Haiti—an internal problem of a country in the American hemisphere caused by a disruption of its democratic process—called for joint action in accordance with the commitments by which OAS members were bound and in keeping with the tradition and legal foundations of the regional system of the Americas. The intense effort that OAS accordingly mounted included several initiatives: suspending economic, financial and trade ties with Haiti; endeavouring to protect human rights; cooperating with UNHCR to tackle the Haitian refugee problem; coordinating its efforts with those of the United Nations, including those of UNDP; and, through missions to Haiti, making contact with all sectors of Haitian society. OAS hoped that support from the United Nations membership would be forthcoming, in accordance with a 1991 General Assembly request.[12]

This exchange of communications, transmitted to the Security Council on 15 July,[13] was taken note of by the Council at informal consultations held on 20 July.[14]

(For information on special emergency assistance to Haiti, human rights violations there and the Haitian refugees, see PART THREE, Chapters III, X and XV, respectively.)

Report of the Secretary-General. As requested by the General Assembly in 1991,[12] the Secretary-General, on 3 November 1992,[15] presented a comprehensive report on the situation in Haiti since the 1991 coup.[10] The report gave a chronological account of the international community's efforts to resolve the Haitian crisis and summarized the communications between the Secretary-General, President Aristide and OAS (see above). It also covered the situation relating to humanitarian assistance, human rights and the Haitian refugees, and restated the Assembly's position on Haiti's credentials (see below).

In addition to action taken by the Security Council and the General Assembly in 1991, the Haitian Parliament, under pressure from the military, named an ''Acting President'' to organize new elections and appointed a ''Prime Minister'', while the Haitian Army reiterated that the return of President Aristide was not negotiable. OAS adopted two resolutions: one demanded the immediate reinstatement of President Aristide and recommended diplomatic, economic and financial isolation of the de facto authorities and suspension of any aid except for humanitarian purposes; the other condemned the illegal replacement of President Aristide, declared unacceptable any government resulting from that situation, urged OAS members to freeze the financial assets of the Haitian State and to impose a trade embargo except for humanitarian aid, and constituted a civilian mission to re-establish constitutional democracy in Haiti. The mission visited Haiti in August and September 1992, and held a meeting in Washington, D.C., in between.

Meanwhile, Colombia's Minister for Foreign Affairs, acting on behalf of OAS, succeeded in arranging several meetings, between November 1991 and February 1992, between President Aristide and the Presidents of the two chambers of the Haitian Parliament. The meetings resulted in the signing of two protocols of agreement at Washington, D.C., on 23 and 25 February. The first protocol provided for President Aristide's reinstatement and for the proclamation of a general amnesty, but not applicable to common criminals; the second called for the confirmation of the Prime Minister-designate, René Théodore, who thereafter would create the conditions for President Aristide's return.

Neither protocol was ratified by the Haitian National Assembly. Instead, a tripartite agreement was concluded on 8 May on the formation of a Government of consensus and public redemption for the consolidation of democracy, which mentioned neither President Aristide nor the protocols of agreement, but left the office of President unfilled until a definitive solution to the crisis was found. Under a revised tripartite agreement, a new ''Government'' was formed; the ''Acting President'' resigned and Marc Bazin, previously chosen ''Prime Minister'' by consensus, was sworn in.

On 17 May, OAS adopted another resolution (MRE/RES.3/92) reinforcing the embargo and recommending that its members deny port access to ships that had engaged in trade with Haiti, prevent violations of the embargo by air and punish the perpetrators and supporters of the coup by denying them visas and freezing their financial assets.

A June meeting between President Aristide and the Haitian community in Miami adopted the Florida Declaration, by which they denounced the tripartite agreement and the pressure brought to bear on Parliament, and called for a dialogue among Haitians aimed at forming a Government of unity and allowing the return to Haiti of the constitutional President. On the basis of the Declaration, a 10-member Presidential Commission was established in Haiti on 6 July, which issued a set of proposals, presented as a codification of the Washington protocols as updated in the Florida Declaration.

On 10 September, the Secretary-General informed the Security Council at informal consultations that his representative had taken part in the OAS mission, that the parties did not seem to have come closer together, that OAS was planning to deploy a first group of observers in Haiti and

that it had decided to maintain the embargo. The Secretary-General stated his intention to cooperate with OAS and readiness to lend any other assistance that might lead to a solution of the crisis.

The Secretary-General noted that Haiti's economy was in a state of free fall. The normally high unemployment rate had risen even higher. Many small farmers had used up their seed reserves and sold their animals and tools, or even their land. Consumer prices had risen. Shrinking food and fertilizer imports, and the scarcity of fuel to transport goods to consumers, had caused the food situation to deteriorate further. This was exacerbated by the threat of famine in the north-west region due to two years of drought. The lack of safe drinking-water and medicines, as well as the serious disruption of immunization programmes, had put public health at risk. The financial difficulties under which the educational system operated had led to school closures, teacher resignations and a decline in pupil attendance. An estimated 135,000 children had left school as a result of the crisis. An inter-agency committee, set up by eight United Nations agencies maintaining a presence in Haiti, had drawn up a draft integrated plan of humanitarian assistance under the direction of the Secretariat's Department of Humanitarian Affairs. OAS had also set up a coordinating committee for humanitarian assistance to Haiti.

In an addendum of 4 November to his report,[16] the Secretary-General transmitted the replies from nine Member States to his request for information on measures they had taken in support of the 1991 OAS resolutions described above.

GENERAL ASSEMBLY ACTION

When the General Assembly considered the Secretary-General's report, it also took account of an additional resolution adopted by the OAS Permanent Council on 10 November (CP/RES.594 (923/92). The resolution urged United Nations Members to adopt the measures specified in the previous three OAS resolutions and to increase their humanitarian assistance to the Haitian people. It also requested United Nations participation in the OAS civilian mission to Haiti.

On 24 November, the General Assembly adopted without vote **resolution 47/20 A**.

The situation of democracy and human rights in Haiti

The General Assembly,

Having considered the item entitled ''The situation of democracy and human rights in Haiti'',

Recalling its resolutions 46/7 of 11 October 1991 and 46/138 of 17 December 1991, as well as the relevant resolutions and decisions adopted by the Economic and Social Council, the Commission on Human Rights and by other international forums,

Welcoming resolutions MRE/RES.1/91, MRE/RES.2/91 and MRE/RES.3/92 adopted on 3 and 8 October 1991 and 17 May 1992, respectively, by the Ministers for Foreign Affairs of the member countries of the Organization of American States,

Also welcoming resolution CP/RES.594(923/92) on the re-establishment of democracy in Haiti, adopted by the Permanent Council of the Organization of American States on 10 November 1992,

Considering that, despite the efforts of the international community, the legitimate Government of President Jean-Bertrand Aristide has not yet been re-established and that civil and political liberties continue to be trampled upon in Haiti,

Greatly alarmed at the persistence and worsening of gross violations of human rights, in particular summary and arbitrary executions, involuntary disappearance, reports of torture and rape, arbitrary arrests and detentions, as well as the denial of freedom of expression, of assembly and of association,

Concerned that the persistence of this situation contributes to a climate of fear of persecution and economic dislocation which could increase the number of Haitians seeking refuge in neighbouring Member States and convinced that a reversal of this situation is needed to prevent its negative repercussions on the region,

Welcoming the measures taken by the Secretary-General of the United Nations to lend his support to the Organization of American States, in particular the participation of his personal representative in the mission of the Secretary-General of the Organization of American States to Haiti, from 19 to 21 August 1992,

Taking into account its resolution 47/11 of 29 October 1992 on cooperation between the United Nations and the Organization of American States,

Taking note of the report of the Secretary-General on the situation of democracy and human rights in Haiti,

Taking note also of the statement by the Secretary-General in his report on the work of the Organization, in which he declares that he stands "ready to help in any other way to resolve the Haitian crisis",

Aware that, in accordance with the Charter of the United Nations, the Organization promotes and encourages respect for human rights and fundamental freedoms for all, and that the Universal Declaration of Human Rights states that "the will of the people shall be the basis of the authority of government",

Recognizing the urgent need for an early, comprehensive and peaceful settlement of the situation in Haiti in accordance with the Charter of the United Nations and international law,

1. *Strongly condemns again* the attempted illegal replacement of the constitutional President of Haiti, the use of violence and military coercion and the violation of human rights in that country;

2. *Reaffirms* as unacceptable any entity resulting from that illegal situation and demands the restoration of the legitimate Government of President Jean-Bertrand Aristide, together with the full application of the National Constitution and hence the full observance of human rights in Haiti;

3. *Takes note* of the efforts by the Secretary-General of the Organization of American States to seek the implementation of the resolutions adopted by that organization;

4. *Affirms* that the solution of the Haitian crisis should take into account resolutions MRE/RES.1/91, MRE/RES.2/91, MRE/RES.3/92 and CP/RES.594 (923/92) of the Organization of American States;

5. *Requests* the Secretary-General of the United Nations to take the necessary measures in order to assist, in cooperation with the Organization of American States, in the solution of the Haitian crisis;

6. *Urges* the States Members of the United Nations to renew their support, within the framework of the Charter of the United Nations and international law, by adopting measures in accordance with resolutions MRE/RES.1/91, MRE/RES.2/91, MRE/RES.3/92 and CP/RES.594(923/92) adopted by the Organization of American States, especially as they relate to the strengthening of representative democracy, the constitutional order and to the embargo on trade with Haiti;

7. *Also urges* the States Members of the United Nations and other international organizations to increase their humanitarian assistance to the Haitian people and to support all efforts to resolve the problems associated with displaced persons, and encourages, in this context, the strengthening of the institutional coordination established among United Nations agencies, as well as between the United Nations and the Organization of American States;

8. *Calls upon* the international community to refrain from supplying materials for the use of military forces or police in Haiti, including arms, ammunition and petroleum, until the present crisis has been resolved;

9. *Emphasizes* that an increase in technical, economic and financial cooperation, when constitutional order is restored in Haiti, will be necessary to support its economic and social development efforts in order to strengthen its democratic institutions;

10. *Requests* the Secretary-General to submit to the General Assembly by mid-February, at a resumed session, a report on the implementation of the present resolution;

11. *Decides* to keep open the consideration of this item until a solution to the situation is found.

General Assembly resolution 47/20 A

24 November 1992   Meeting 71   Adopted without vote

14-nation draft (A/47/L.23 & Add.1), orally revised; agenda item 22.
Sponsors: Belgium, Canada, Denmark, France, Germany, Greece, Ireland, Italy, Luxembourg, Netherlands, Portugal, Spain, United Kingdom, Venezuela.

Report of the Secretary-General. In keeping with the Assembly's request, the Secretary-General, on 11 December 1992, appointed Dante Caputo (Argentina) as his Special Envoy for Haiti,[17] to assist, in cooperation with the OAS Secretary-General, in the solution of the Haitian crisis.

Between 17 and 22 December, the Special Envoy held a series of preliminary consultations in Washington, D.C., with President Aristide, and at Port-au-Prince with the following: the Coordinator and members of the Presidential Commission, the Commander-in-Chief of the Haitian Armed Forces and other members of the Army High Command, the Prime Minister of the de facto Government, and the Presidents of the two chambers of the National Assembly of Haiti. The Special Envoy also met in New York with representatives of Canada, France, the United States and Venezuela, whom the Secretary-General had requested to assist him in his endeavours; and in Washington, D.C., with the OAS Secretary-General.

Credentials

The Secretary-General's report of 3 November 1992[15] provided information on the matter of Haiti's credentials. As reported by his spokesman, communications received from the "Government of Haiti" included one on the credentials of its delegation to the forty-seventh session of the General Assembly. Since in 1991[12] the Assembly had affirmed as unacceptable any entity resulting from the attempted illegal replacement of the constitutional President of Haiti and had demanded the immediate restoration of the legitimate Government of President Aristide, the purported credentials from the so-called Government of Haiti in Port-au-Prince were not receivable from the legal point of view and were of no legal consequence to the United Nations.

REFERENCES
[1]S/23850. [2]S/23890. [3]S/23913. [4]S/23989. [5]S/23990. [6]YUN 1991, p. 151, GA dec. 46/407, 13 Nov. 1991. [7]A/47/272. [8]A/47/654. [9]A/47/273. [10]YUN 1991, p. 151. [11]YUN 1951, p. 522. [12]YUN 1991, p. 152, GA res. 46/7, 11 Oct. 1991. [13]S/24340. [14]S/24361. [15]A/47/599 & Corr.1. [16]A/47/599/Add.1. [17]A/47/908.

Other questions relating to the Americas

Cooperation with OAS

In an October 1992 report,[1] the Secretary-General described measures taken to further cooperation between the United Nations and the Organization of American States, in accordance with a 1990 General Assembly resolution.[2]

The report outlined the consultations and information exchanges undertaken between the two organizations from 1991. At a general meeting that year (New York, 15-17 May),[3] specific recommendations were made under eight areas identified for cooperation: environment, drug abuse control, women and development, disaster prevention, children and development, rural development and agriculture, Indian people and development, and strengthening cooperation between the two systems at the national level. Also identified were the lead agencies for each area.

Consultations continued in 1992 and representatives of the secretariats of both organizations and the associated institutions attended each other's meetings and cooperated on matters of mutual interest, including the situation in Central America and the crisis in Haiti. In addition, OAS continued its representation on the Support Committee, on the Policies and Project Committee and in sectoral meetings of the Special Plan of Economic Cooperation for Central America.[4]

The report provided updated information on the collaborative activities and projects undertaken with OAS by six United Nations bodies and programmes—INSTRAW, UNDP, UNEP, UNHCR, WFC and WFP; by a regional commission—ECLAC; and by nine specialized agencies—FAO, UNESCO, WHO, IMF, ICAO, ITU, IMO, IFAD and GATT.

GENERAL ASSEMBLY ACTION

The General Assembly adopted without vote **resolution 47/11** on 29 October 1992.

Cooperation between the United Nations and the Organization of American States
The General Assembly,

Recalling its resolution 45/10 of 25 October 1990 relating to the promotion of cooperation between the United Nations and the Organization of American States,

Having examined the report of the Secretary-General on cooperation between the United Nations and the Organization of American States,

Taking into account the report of the Secretary-General entitled "An Agenda for Peace" and the related consultations within the United Nations and with regional organizations on this subject,

Recalling that the purposes of the United Nations are, *inter alia*, to achieve international cooperation in solving international problems of an economic, social, cultural or humanitarian character and in promoting and encouraging respect for human rights and fundamental freedoms, and to be a centre for harmonizing the actions of nations in the attainment of these common ends,

Bearing in mind that the Charter of the United Nations provides for the existence of regional arrangements and agencies for dealing with such matters relating to the maintenance of international peace and security as are appropriate for regional action, and whose activities are consistent with the purposes and principles of the United Nations,

Recalling also that the Charter of the Organization of American States reaffirms these purposes and principles, and provides that that organization is a regional agency under the terms of the Charter of the United Nations,

Noting with satisfaction that the first general meeting held between the representatives of the United Nations system and of the Organization of American States was held at United Nations Headquarters from 15 to 17 May 1991, and was inaugurated by the Secretaries-General of the two organizations,

Welcoming the meeting of the two Secretaries-General during the United Nations Conference on Environment and Development, held in Rio de Janeiro in June 1992,

Bearing in mind the adoption by the General Assembly of the Organization of American States on 23 May 1992 of resolution AG/RES.1199(XXII-O/92), also on cooperation between the Organization of American States and the United Nations,

Recalling its resolution 46/7 of 11 October 1991 on the situation of democracy and human rights in Haiti and taking into account the letter dated 15 July 1992 in which the Secretary-General informed the President of the Security Council of an exchange of correspondence with the President of Haiti and the Secretary-General of the Organization of American States, and of his decision to accept the offer for the participation of United Nations officials in the mission of the Secretary-General of the Organization of American States to Haiti,

Aware that the effective consolidation of a new international order requires regional action in harmony with that of the United Nations,

1. *Takes note with satisfaction* of the report of the Secretary-General on cooperation between the United Nations and the Organization of American States, as well as his efforts to strengthen that cooperation;

2. *Welcomes* the offer of the Chairman of the Permanent Council of the Organization of American States to the President of the Security Council concerning the readiness of the Organization of American States to cooperate with the United Nations in its efforts to improve collective measures for the prevention and solution of international conflicts;

3. *Expresses its satisfaction* at the close cooperation between the two organizations in the verification of the electoral process in Nicaragua from August 1989 to February 1990 and recognizes the effectiveness of that cooperation;

4. *Recognizes* the importance of the participation of the International Support and Verification Commission in the demobilization of the irregular forces of the Nicaraguan resistance and takes note with satisfaction of the fundamental role of the United Nations Observer Group in Central America in the military aspects of the process and of the activities of the United Nations High Commissioner for Refugees in the operational area;

5. *Welcomes* the continued participation of the Organization of American States in the Support Committee and the Policies and Projects Committee of the Special Plan of Economic Cooperation for Central America, established by General Assembly resolution 42/231 of 12 May 1988 and extended by General Assembly resolution 45/231 of 21 December 1990;

6. *Requests* both Secretaries-General, or their representatives, to continue their consultations with a view to signing in 1993 an agreement for cooperation between the United Nations and the Organization of American States;

7. *Approves* the conclusions and recommendations of the first general meeting between the representatives of the two organizations held in May 1991 and urges the relevant authorities of both organizations to take the necessary steps to implement those recommendations and promote further cooperation;

8. *Recommends* that a second general meeting between representatives of the United Nations system and of the Organization of American States be held in 1993 to review and appraise progress, and that inter-agency sectoral and focal point meetings be held on areas of priority or mutually agreed issues;

9. *Takes note* of the participation of senior officials of the United Nations in the mission of the Secretary-General of the Organization of American States to Haiti in August 1992;

10. *Expresses its appreciation* for the efforts of the Secretary-General in the promotion of cooperation between the United Nations and the Organization of American States and expresses the hope that he will continue to strengthen the mechanisms for cooperation between the two organizations;

11. *Requests* the Secretary-General to submit to the General Assembly at its forty-ninth session a report on the implementation of the present resolution;

12. *Decides* to include in the provisional agenda of its forty-ninth session the item entitled "Cooperation between the United Nations and the Organization of American States".

General Assembly resolution 47/11

29 October 1992   Meeting 51   Adopted without vote

26-nation draft (A/47/L.13 & Add.1); agenda item 21.

Sponsors: Argentina, Barbados, Belize, Bolivia, Brazil, Canada, Colombia, Costa Rica, Chile, Dominican Republic, Ecuador, El Salvador, Guatemala, Guyana, Haiti, Honduras, Jamaica, Mexico, Nicaragua, Panama, Paraguay, Peru, Suriname, Trinidad and Tobago, Uruguay, Venezuela.

REFERENCES

[1]A/47/498. [2]GA res. 45/10, 25 Oct. 1990. [3]A/47/498/Add.1. [4]GA res. 42/231, 12 May 1988, & 45/231, 21 Dec. 1990.

Chapter III

Asia and the Pacific

The United Nations in 1992 steadfastly maintained the momentum of its peace-keeping and peace-building activities in Asia.

In Korea, the implementation of the 1953 Armistice Agreement continued and the United Nations Command submitted its annual report to the Security Council.

In accordance with the 1991 settlement agreements (Paris agreements) that brought about an official cease-fire in Cambodia and called for their implementation under United Nations auspices, the Security Council early in the year established and deployed the United Nations Transitional Authority in Cambodia, one of the Organization's most ambitious and complex peace-keeping operations. Despite the refusal of one of the four signatories to the Paris agreements to implement the second phase of the cease-fire, the Transitional Authority, which became operational in March, forged steadily ahead in discharging its mandate with the ultimate goal of preparing the country for free and fair elections towards the middle of 1993.

United Nations efforts to promote peace among the conflicting factions in Afghanistan were outpaced by political and military events in the country. Although forced to withdraw its personnel from Kabul due to the wide-scale fighting that erupted there in July and August, the United Nations maintained its presence in other parts of the country.

The Secretary-General continued his mission of good offices in Cyprus with the goal of achieving overall agreement between the Greek Cypriot and Turkish Cypriot communities.

In March and November, the Security Council conducted a comprehensive review of Iraq's compliance with the series of related Council resolutions, beginning with resolution 687(1991), which embodied the terms of the cease-fire that formally ended the 1991 military action to compel Iraq's withdrawal from Kuwait. The key reporting bodies for the reviews were the Special Commission created by the cease-fire resolution and the International Atomic Energy Agency. Both remained resolute, in the face of alternating Iraqi cooperation and resistance, in carrying out their task of uncovering and eliminating Iraq's capability to manufacture or use nuclear and other weapons of mass destruction. The Council reviews concluded that Iraq still was not in full and unconditional compliance with its obligations. Insisting that it had complied with its substantive obligations under the cease-fire resolution, Iraq requested the Council to lift the sanctions imposed on it since 1990.

East Asia

Korean question

The United States, on behalf of the Unified Command, submitted the annual report of the United Nations Command (UNC) concerning the maintenance in 1991 of the 1953 Armistice Agreement[1] to the Security Council on 15 June 1992.[2]

According to the report, the Military Armistice Commission (MAC), set up to supervise the implementation of the Agreement and to settle any violations of it through negotiations with the Korean People's Army (KPA) and the Chinese People's Volunteers (CPV), held one meeting during 1991, at which KPA demanded, as it had in previous years, that UNC cease its annual joint training exercise "Team Spirit" with the Republic of Korea, despite UNC's reiteration that the Agreement did not address military training exercises. Since the appointment in March[3] of Major-General Hwang Won-Tak of the Republic of Korea as the senior member representing UNC, no formal plenary meeting had been held for the remainder of the year. However, the UNC and KPA/CPV commanders maintained communication through the Joint Duty Office "hot line" and through meetings of the MAC Secretaries.

In June, the Democratic People's Republic of Korea returned 11 sets of what it said were "United States war remains" to a United States congressional delegation at the Joint Security Area (Panmunjom), in disregard of the provision of an Understanding stipulating that delivery and reception of such remains should be arranged through MAC. In December, KPA informally advised that another 30 UNC war remains recently discovered would be returned in the near future.

Regarding the accord on reconciliation, non-aggression and denuclearization of the Korean peninsula signed by the two Koreas in December

1991,[3] the report noted that UNC, while not directly involved, provided administrative and security assistance to the related negotiations held between the two sides at the Joint Security Area. In this connection, UNC stated that the Democratic People's Republic should abandon its nuclear-weapons programme and accept full-scope nuclear safeguards under the International Atomic Energy Agency. As a confidence-building measure, it should move its armed forces and advanced weapons from their offensive posture.

On 15 June 1992,[4] the United States, on behalf of UNC, drew to the Council's attention a serious Armistice violation that occurred on 21 and 22 May. A group of heavily armed men from a KPA guard post crossed the military demarcation line into the south side. Upon their encounter with a UNC security police patrol, an exchange of fire ensued in which two of the infiltrators were killed and a UNC policeman was wounded. Later, a third infiltrator died in a similar encounter and exchange of fire, in which another UNC policeman was wounded. UNC called a meeting of MAC on 29 May for a joint investigation of the incident, which KPA/CPV boycotted.

The Democratic People's Republic, on 28 September,[5] characterized the two reports as extremely distorted and attributed the paralysis of the supervisory mechanism of MAC to the appointment of Major-General Hwang Won-Tak and to UNC's refusal to hold negotiations on its challenge that a legal institutional mechanism should replace the UNC senior member of MAC. As to the reported infiltration incident, the Democratic People's Republic argued that the incident had nothing to do with it, but was a drama concocted by the Republic of Korea designed to stop the developing dialogue between them.

REFERENCES

[1]YUN 1953, p. 136, GA res. 725(VIII), annex, 7 Dec. 1953. [2]S/24466. [3]YUN 1991, p. 154. [4]S/24467. [5]S/24598.

South-East Asia

Within the context of the call by the Secretary-General in his "An Agenda for Peace" for a closer relationship between the United Nations and regional associations, the General Assembly, by **resolution 47/53 B** of 9 December 1992, endorsed the purposes and principles of the 1976 Treaty of Amity and Cooperation in South-East Asia for the peaceful settlement of regional disputes and regional cooperation towards peace, amity and friendship among the peoples of South-East Asia.

Cambodia situation

Pursuant to the 1991 settlement agreements (Paris agreements)[1] that brought about the official cease-fire in Cambodia and called for their implementation under United Nations auspices, the Security Council early in 1992 established and deployed the United Nations Transitional Authority in Cambodia (UNTAC). In carrying out its mandate, UNTAC coordinated its activities with the Supreme National Council (SNC), on which were represented the four parties to the Cambodian conflict and signatories to the agreements: (1) the People's Revolutionary Party of Kampuchea, renamed the Cambodian People's Party (CPP) and later also referred to as the party of the State of Cambodia (SOC); (2) the National United Front for an Independent, Neutral, Peaceful and Cooperative Cambodia (FUNCINPEC, from its French title, Front Uni National pour un Cambodge Indépendent, Neutre, Pacifique et Coopératif); (3) the Khmer People's National Liberation Front (KPNLF), renamed on 22 May as the Buddhist Liberal Democratic Party (BLDP); and (4) the Party of Democratic Kampuchea (PDK).

The armed forces of the four parties were, respectively, the Cambodian People's Armed Forces (CPAF), the National Army of Independent Kampuchea (ANKI), the Khmer People's National Liberation Armed Forces (KPNLAF) and the National Army of Democratic Kampuchea (NADK).

UN Advance Mission in Cambodia

At its second meeting of 8 January, the Security Council had before it a report of the Secretary-General of 1991[2] proposing, pending the establishment of UNTAC, the expansion of the mandate of the United Nations Advance Mission in Cambodia (UNAMIC) to include, in addition to the existing mine-awareness programme, the training of Cambodians in mine clearance and the initiation of a mine-clearance programme. Following consideration of the report, the Council unanimously adopted **resolution 728(1992)**.

The Security Council,

Recalling its resolutions 668(1990) of 20 September 1990, 717(1991) of 16 October 1991 and 718(1991) of 31 October 1991,

Welcoming the fact that the United Nations Advance Mission in Cambodia (UNAMIC) has become operational as reported by the Secretary-General in his report of 14 November 1991,

Welcoming also the progress that has been made in implementing the provisions of the Agreements on a Comprehensive Political Settlement of the Cambodia Conflict relating to the functioning of the Supreme National Council of Cambodia under the chairmanship of His Royal Highness Samdech Norodom Sihanouk and the maintenance of the cease-fire,

Concerned that the existence of mines and minefields in Cambodia poses a serious hazard to the safety of people in Cambodia, as well as an obstacle to the smooth and timely implementation of the Agreements on the Comprehensive Political Settlement, including the early return of Cambodian refugees and displaced persons,

Noting that UNAMIC's mandate as approved by the Security Council in its resolution 717(1991) provides, *inter alia*, for the establishment of a mine awareness programme, and that the Agreements provide for the United Nations Transitional Authority in Cambodia (UNTAC) to undertake, *inter alia*, a programme of assisting with clearing mines and undertaking training programmes in mine clearance and a mine awareness programme among the Cambodian people,

Considering that the establishment of training programmes in mine clearance, in addition to the existing mine awareness programme undertaken by UNAMIC, and the early initiation of mine clearance are required for the effective implementation of the Agreements on the Comprehensive Settlement,

Having considered the report of the Secretary-General proposing that the mandate of UNAMIC be expanded to include training in mine clearance and the initiation of a mine clearance programme,

1. *Approves* the report of the Secretary-General, especially the provision of assistance in mine clearing by Cambodians;

2. *Calls upon* the Supreme National Council of Cambodia, and all the Cambodian parties, to continue to cooperate fully with the United Nations Advance Mission in Cambodia, including in the discharge of its expanded mandate;

3. *Reiterates* its call to all the Cambodian parties to comply scrupulously with the cease-fire and to lend all necessary assistance to UNAMIC;

4. *Requests* the Secretary-General to keep the Security Council informed of further developments.

Security Council resolution 728(1992)

8 January 1992   Meeting 3029   Adopted unanimously

Draft prepared in consultations among Council members (S/23383).

The Secretary-General subsequently obtained Council agreement[3] to his proposal[4] that Bangladesh, the Netherlands and Thailand be added to the States contributing troops to UNAMIC, to meet the increase in troop strength required by the expanded mandate. He thereafter confirmed the appointment of Under-Secretary-General Yasushi Akashi as Special Representative for Cambodia,[5] an action the Council welcomed.[6]

Financing

At the request of the Secretary-General,[7] the agenda item of the General Assembly's forty-sixth (1991) session on the financing of UNAMIC was reopened by the Assembly on 4 February 1992 to enable consideration of the additional requirements entailed by UNAMIC's expanded responsibilities.

In his report of 31 January 1992[8] relating to those requirements, the Secretary-General estimated a total cost of $22,893,000 gross ($22,813,000 net)

for the period from 15 January to 30 April 1992. That included the initial commitment authority of up to $10 million for the immediate emplacement of additional UNAMIC personnel and equipment, as concurred with by the Advisory Committee on Administrative and Budgetary Questions (ACABQ) under the provisions of a 1991 Assembly resolution.[9] The cost of maintaining UNAMIC for six months beyond 30 April 1992 would amount to $38,874,000 gross ($38,139,000 net), or $6,479,000 gross ($6,356,500 net) a month.

Military personnel required for the mine training and de-mining tasks included a planning and liaison unit of 40 officers at Phnom Penh headquarters, a field engineer battalion of 750 all ranks, a mine-clearing team of 200 expert trainers and a 150-man logistical support unit. Thirty-four civilian (24 international and 10 local) staff were needed to provide additional administrative, transport, communication, procurement, security and interpretation support to UNAMIC. Premises and accommodations, transport, air support, communication, and miscellaneous equipment, supplies and services were also required.

Contributions in kind were provided by Thailand (two fork-lift trucks) and France (a fixed-wing aircraft, two utility helicopters and 41 crew and maintenance personnel).

In view of the additional voluntary contributions ($2,029,000) and savings resulting from delays in staff deployment ($1,607,000), ACABQ[10] recommended to the General Assembly the appropriation and assessment of an additional amount of $19,257,000 gross ($19,204,000 net) for the expanded UNAMIC operations from 15 January to 30 April 1992. As to the estimates for operations beyond 30 April, ACABQ regarded them as indicative and pointed to the likelihood of UNAMIC's merger with UNTAC before then.

GENERAL ASSEMBLY ACTION

Acting without vote on the recommendation of the Fifth (Administrative and Budgetary) Committee, the General Assembly adopted **resolution 46/198 B** on 14 February 1992.

Financing of the United Nations Advance Mission in Cambodia

The General Assembly,

Having considered the report of the Secretary-General on the financing of the United Nations Advance Mission in Cambodia and the related report of the Advisory Committee on Administrative and Budgetary Questions,

Bearing in mind Security Council resolution 717(1991) of 16 October 1991, by which the Council established the United Nations Advance Mission in Cambodia,

Recalling its resolution 46/198 A of 20 December 1991 on the financing of the Advance Mission,

Bearing in mind also Security Council resolution 728(1992) of 8 January 1992, by which the Council approved the proposal of the Secretary-General to expand the mandate of the Advance Mission,

Recognizing that the costs of the Advance Mission are expenses of the Organization to be borne by Member States in accordance with Article 17, paragraph 2, of the Charter of the United Nations,

Recognizing also that, in order to meet the expenditures caused by the Advance Mission, a different procedure is required from the one applied to meet expenditures of the regular budget of the United Nations,

Taking into account the fact that the economically more developed countries are in a position to make relatively larger contributions and that the economically less developed countries have a relatively limited capacity to contribute towards such an operation,

Bearing in mind the special responsibilities of the States permanent members of the Security Council, as indicated in General Assembly resolution 1874(S-IV) of 27 June 1963, in the financing of such operations,

Noting with appreciation that voluntary contributions have been made to the Advance Mission by certain Member States,

Mindful of the fact that it is essential to provide the Advance Mission with the necessary financial resources to enable it to fulfil its responsibilities under the relevant resolutions of the Security Council,

1. *Concurs* with the observations and recommendations contained in the report of the Advisory Committee on Administrative and Budgetary Questions;

2. *Urges* all Member States to make every possible effort to ensure payment of their assessed contributions to the United Nations Advance Mission in Cambodia in full and on time;

3. *Decides* to appropriate an amount of 19,257,000 United States dollars gross (19,204,000 dollars net), inclusive of the amount of 10 million dollars authorized by the Advisory Committee under the terms of General Assembly resolution 46/187 of 20 December 1991 for the expansion of the Advance Mission for the period from 15 January to 30 April 1992;

4. *Decides also*, as an ad hoc arrangement, to apportion the amount of 19,257,000 dollars gross (19,204,000 dollars net) among Member States in accordance with the composition of groups set out in paragraphs 3 and 4 of General Assembly resolution 43/232 of 1 March 1989, as adjusted by the Assembly in its resolutions 44/192 B of 21 December 1989, 45/269 of 27 August 1991 and 46/198 A, and taking into account the scale of assessments for the years 1992, 1993 and 1994;

5. *Decides further* that, in accordance with the provisions of its resolution 973(X) of 15 December 1955, there shall be set off against the apportionment among Member States, as provided for in paragraph 4 above, their respective share in the Tax Equalization Fund of the estimated staff assessment income of 53,000 dollars approved for the period from 15 January to 30 April 1992, inclusive;

6. *Authorizes* the Secretary-General to enter into commitments for the Advance Mission at a rate not to exceed 6,176,900 dollars gross (6,054,000 dollars net) per month for the period beyond 30 April 1992, subject to the concurrence of the Advisory Committee, should the Security Council decide to continue the Advance Mission beyond that date, the said amount to be apportioned among Member States in accordance with the scheme set out in the present resolution;

7. *Invites* voluntary contributions to the Advance Mission in cash and in the form of services and supplies acceptable to the Secretary-General, to be administered, as appropriate, in accordance with the procedure established by the General Assembly in its resolution 44/192 A of 21 December 1989;

8. *Requests* the Secretary-General to take all necessary action to ensure that the Advance Mission is administered with a maximum of efficiency and economy.

General Assembly resolution 46/198 B

14 February 1992   Meeting 81   Adopted without vote

Approved by Fifth Committee (A/46/823/Add.1) without vote, 13 February (meeting 59); draft by Chairman (A/C.5/46/L.21), orally amended by Japan; agenda item 146.

Meeting numbers. GA 46th session: 5th Committee 58, 59; plenary 81.

UN Transitional Authority in Cambodia

Under the terms of the Agreement on a Comprehensive Political Settlement of the Cambodia Conflict, one of the four instruments of the Paris agreements of 1991,[1] the mandate foreseen for UNTAC during the transitional period in Cambodia included the promotion and protection of human rights, the organization and conduct of free and fair general elections, the establishment of military arrangements to stabilize security and build confidence among the four Cambodian parties to the conflict, the setting up of a civil administration to ensure a neutral political environment conducive to free and fair elections, the maintenance of law and order, the repatriation and resettlement of the Cambodian refugees and displaced persons, and the rehabilitation of essential Cambodian infrastructure (food security, health, housing, training, education, transport network, public utilities).

The transitional period was defined as the period commencing with the entry into force of the Agreement and terminating when the constituent assembly, elected in conformity with the Agreement, had approved the new Cambodian constitution and transformed itself into a legislative assembly, and when a new Cambodian Government had been elected. The Agreement entered into force upon signature by the parties concerned, on 23 October 1991.

The focal point of the United Nations relationship in Cambodia was SNC—under the Agreement, the unique legitimate body and source of authority in which, throughout the transitional period, the sovereignty, independence and unity of Cambodia were enshrined. By the Agreement, SNC had delegated to the United Nations all powers necessary to ensure implementation of the Agreement. The head of UNTAC, the Special Representative of the Secretary-General, would maintain dialogue with SNC regarding UNTAC activities.

Report of the Secretary-General. Pursuant to a 1991 Security Council request,[11] the Secretary-General, on 19 February 1992,[12] submitted an implementation plan to serve as the basis for the establishment of UNTAC.

Under the plan, UNTAC would consist of seven distinct components: the human rights, electoral, military, civil administration, police, repatriation and rehabilitation components, each with appropriate functions and structure.

The human rights component would discharge UNTAC's responsibility for fostering an environment conducive to respect for human rights. This included the development of a human rights education programme to promote understanding of and respect for human rights; overseeing the exercise of general human rights in all of the existing administrative structures in Cambodia, particularly in those areas exercising law-enforcement and judicial functions; and providing a mechanism for investigating alleged human rights violations and for effective redress, especially redress of violations relating to participation in the electoral process. A human rights office set up at headquarters at Phnom Penh would be the central policy-making and coordinating body with staff specialists in human rights advocacy, civic education and investigation, and liaison.

The task of organizing and conducting free and fair general elections would be the responsibility of the electoral component. It would design a system for every phase of the election of 120 members to the constituent assembly; establish, in consultation with SNC, a legal framework consisting of an electoral law and regulations to govern the electoral process and an electoral code of conduct to ensure freedom of speech, assembly and movement; mount a civic education programme, as well as an orientation and training programme for staff and political party agents; and design a system of voter registration and procedures for political party registration and for balloting and polling.

Voter registration would take place over three months at fixed, temporary or mobile registration stations and, for military personnel, at cantonments. Polling stations would be in the same location as registration stations. About 200 international staff in two-member teams would be required to supervise an estimated 800 local registration personnel working in five-member teams and to canvass all districts in Cambodia.

The Special Representative of the Secretary-General, who would have the task of organizing and conducting the elections, would be assisted by a chief electoral officer and a three-member electoral advisory committee, headquartered at Phnom Penh. Deployment of the international electoral staff would take place in March and April. A proposed election calendar recommended that voter registration begin in October 1992 and that elections extend from late April to early May 1993.

Military arrangements, to be discharged by the military component, were aimed at stabilizing the security situation and building confidence among the parties to the conflict. They were grouped into four categories: verification of the withdrawal and non-return of all categories of foreign forces and their arms and equipment, to be accomplished by posting military observers at 24 fixed ingress/egress points and deployment of mobile monitoring teams to investigate allegations of the presence of foreign forces; supervision of the cease-fire and related measures, including regroupment, cantonment, disarming and demobilization; weapons control, including monitoring the cessation of outside military assistance, locating and confiscating caches of weapons and military supplies throughout Cambodia, and storing of the arms and equipment of the cantoned and demobilized military forces; and management of training programmes in mine-awareness, mine-clearance and related activities.

The military component would need to canton about 200,000 soldiers, disarm about 450,000 soldiers and militia, secure more than 300,000 weapons and monitor the security of Cambodia's borders and territorial waters. To perform those tasks, the component would require the full cooperation of the Cambodian parties and the scrupulous fulfilment of their commitments under the Paris agreements, as well as freedom of movement and communication and other rights and facilities. It would be provided with enough personnel and resources to enable it to establish an effective and credible presence.

A proposed calendar recommended that full deployment of the military component of about 15,900 troops of all ranks be completed by the end of May, and that the regroupment and cantonment processes, as well as demobilization of at least 70 per cent of the cantoned forces, be completed by 30 September.

The responsibility for ensuring a neutral political environment conducive to free and fair general elections rested with the civil administration component, whose functions would include: identification of agencies, bodies and offices of existing administrative structures in five areas to be placed under its direct control—foreign affairs, national defence, finance, public security and information; identification of administrative structures—education, public health, transport and communications—that could influence the outcome of the elections and over which a lesser degree of scrutiny could be exercised; training of Cambodian administrative personnel in connection with codes of conduct and management guidelines to ensure observance of those instruments; and setting up complaints mechanisms and investigation procedures concerning actions by administrative structures that were inconsistent with or militated against the objectives of the comprehensive political settlement.

Offices would be set up to deal with each of the five areas identified for direct control. Twenty-one provincial offices would be established at provincial and municipal centres, paralleling the existing structures in the country, to each of which five to seven international staff would be assigned. About 200 subprovincial offices, mostly at the district level, were foreseen.

Law enforcement would be the responsibility of the police component, which would exercise supervision over the civil police in order to ensure law and order and protect human rights. Some 50,000 Cambodian civil police were expected to be supervised by the UNTAC police monitors. The structure of the UNTAC civilian police component would include a policy and management unit at headquarters, 21 units at the provincial level and 200 at the district level. The latter would operate as mobile teams. A total of about 3,600 UNTAC civilian police monitors would be required.

Under the terms of the Agreement, the Office of the United Nations High Commissioner for Refugees (UNHCR) would be the lead agency for the repatriation and resettlement of Cambodians. It was stipulated in this connection that Cambodians must return voluntarily to Cambodia to destinations of their choice, with their human rights and fundamental freedoms fully respected. Appropriate border crossing points and routes would be designated and cleared of mines and other hazards. A memorandum of understanding signed between UNHCR and the Government of Thailand defined modalities of cooperation on all aspects of the repatriation operation.

The objectives set for the repatriation of more than 360,000 potential returnees included: organized repatriation within a nine-month period; identification and provision of agricultural and settlement land, and installation assistance and food for up to 360,000 returnees for up to 18 months and for up to 30,000 "spontaneous" returnees for up to one year; and limited reintegration assistance for up to 360,000 returnees and upgrading of services in returnee-concentrated areas through quick-impact projects.

Repatriation would be in three stages: the movement of returnees from border camps to the final destinations of their choice in Cambodia; the provision of immediate assistance (shelter, materials, household kits) and food for an average of 12 months; and a reintegration programme.

Under the Declaration on the Rehabilitation and Reconstruction of Cambodia, one of the four instruments comprising the 1991 Paris agreements,[1] particular attention was to be given to food security, health, housing, training, education,

the transport network and the restoration of existing infrastructure and public utilities. The rehabilitation effort would be headed by a Coordinator for Rehabilitation in Cambodia, appointed by the Secretary-General and reporting to the Special Representative. The Coordinator would be responsible for assessing needs and for ensuring that these were met without duplication and with efficiency.

The implementation plan underscored four essential conditions for the effective and impartial discharge of UNTAC's responsibilities: full Security Council support, full cooperation of the Cambodian parties at all times, full freedom of movement and communications, and adequate and timely financial resources.

In an addendum to his report, dated 26 February,[13] the Secretary-General stated that the preliminary indicative costs of UNTAC, inclusive of the initial appropriation of $200 million, were estimated at approximately $1,900 million gross ($1,876 million net). That did not include the repatriation-programme costs. A breakdown of the major objects of expenditure was annexed to the report. The estimates covered a period of approximately 15 months, assuming a new Cambodian Government would be created within three months of the elections as foreseen by the Agreement, or by 31 July 1993.

Based on the implementation plan and the reports of several survey missions, UNTAC structure and personnel requirements were as follows.

UNTAC would be headed by the Special Representative of the Secretary-General, assisted by a deputy, an executive management, coordination and liaison team, human rights, political, legal and economic advisers and an information service. The number of international personnel required was estimated at 76, including support staff. In addition, UNTAC would have an administrative support division of some 450 international staff.

The human rights and civil administration components, consisting of some 224 specialists, assisted by 84 international support staff, would operate at the central levels, from offices to be established at the 21 provincial and municipal centres and, particularly as regards dissemination of information and civic education, from offices at all of the estimated 200 districts in Cambodia.

The military component, headed by a Force Commander, would have a strength of about 15,900 all ranks, consisting of: force headquarters and sector headquarters staff of 204, a military observer group of 485, 12 infantry battalions of 10,200 all ranks, a naval element of 376 and logistics and specialized support elements of about 4,500. The infantry element and the observer group would be reduced from 10,200 and 485 to 5,100 and 300, respectively, by 30 September 1992.

The police component would consist of some 3,600 civilian police monitors operating throughout the territory from offices to be established in 21 provincial and municipal centres and in some 200 district offices.

The electoral component would consist of 72 international personnel operating from headquarters and 126 personnel at 21 provincial and municipal centres. Under the supervision of headquarters and provincial electoral personnel, 400 United Nations Volunteers would operate from each of the 200 districts. Electoral personnel would be supplemented by 800 Cambodian teams (4,000 personnel) during the three- to four-month period of voter registration, and, for the polling process, by 1,000 international supervisors and 8,000 Cambodian polling teams (56,000 personnel). The electoral component would be phased out shortly after certification of the results of the election.

All UNTAC components would be assisted by an estimated 7,000 locally recruited support personnel, including some 2,500 interpreters, and by additional temporary staff as may be required for the conduct of the electoral process and other tasks.

SECURITY COUNCIL ACTION

On 28 February, the Security Council, having examined the Secretary-General's report, unanimously adopted **resolution 745(1992)**.

The Security Council,

Reaffirming its resolutions 668(1990) of 20 September 1990, 717(1991) of 16 October 1991, 718(1991) of 31 October 1991 and 728(1992) of 8 January 1992,

Reaffirming also its full support for the Agreements signed in Paris on 23 October 1991,

Noting the report of the Secretary-General of 19 February 1992 submitted pursuant to resolution 718(1991),

Desiring to contribute to the restoration and maintenance of peace in Cambodia, to the promotion of national reconciliation, to the protection of human rights, and to the assurance of the right to self-determination of the Cambodian people through free and fair elections,

Convinced that free and fair elections are essential to produce a just and durable settlement to the Cambodia conflict, thereby contributing to regional and international peace and security,

Mindful of Cambodia's recent tragic history and determined that the policies and practices of the past will not be repeated,

Expressing appreciation for the work of the United Nations Advance Mission in Cambodia (UNAMIC) in the maintenance of the cease-fire, in mine awareness and mine clearance, and in preparation for the deployment of a United Nations Transitional Authority in Cambodia (UNTAC),

Noting with appreciation the efforts of His Royal Highness Samdech Norodom Sihanouk and the Supreme National Council under his chairmanship in regard to the implementation of the provisions of the Agreements,

Welcoming the appointment by the Secretary-General of a Special Representative for Cambodia to act on his behalf,

1. *Approves* the report of the Secretary-General of 19 February 1992 containing his plan, which is subject to re-examination in the light of experience, for implementing the mandate envisaged in the Agreements;

2. *Decides* that UNTAC shall be established under its authority in accordance with the above-mentioned report for a period not to exceed eighteen months;

3. *Decides* that it is vital that elections be held in Cambodia by May 1993 at the latest as recommended by the Secretary-General in paragraph 38 of his report;

4. *Requests* the Secretary-General to deploy UNTAC as rapidly as possible to implement the above decision, urges that both the deployment and the further implementation of his plan be done in the most efficient and cost-effective way possible, and invites him to that end to keep the operation under continuous review, bearing in mind the fundamental objectives of the Agreements;

5. *Calls upon* the Supreme National Council of Cambodia to fulfil its special responsibilities set out in the Agreements;

6. *Calls further upon* all parties concerned to comply scrupulously with the terms of the Agreements, to cooperate fully with UNTAC in the implementation of its mandate, and to take all necessary measures to ensure the safety and security of all United Nations personnel;

7. *Calls further upon* the Supreme National Council and all Cambodians on behalf of the host country to provide all necessary assistance and facilities to UNTAC;

8. *Strongly urges* the Cambodian parties to agree to the complete demobilization of their military forces prior to the end of the process of registration for the elections as well as to the destruction of the weapons and ammunition deposited into UNTAC custody in excess of those, if any, which may be deemed necessary by UNTAC for the maintenance of civil order and national defence, or which may be required by the new Cambodian Government;

9. *Appeals* to all States to provide all voluntary assistance and support necessary to the United Nations and its programmes and specialized agencies for the preparations and operations to implement the Agreements, including for rehabilitation and for the repatriation of refugees and displaced persons;

10. *Requests* the Secretary-General to report to the Security Council by 1 June 1992 and subsequently to report to the Council in September 1992, January 1993 and April 1993 on progress to date in the implementation of the present resolution and on tasks still to be performed in the operation, with particular regard to the most effective and efficient use of resources;

11. *Decides* to remain seized of the matter.

Security Council resolution 745(1992)

28 February 1992   Meeting 3057   Adopted unanimously

Draft prepared in consultations among Council members (S/23651).

On 11 March, the Secretary-General obtained Security Council agreement[14] to his proposed appointment of Lieutenant-General John M. Sanderson (Australia) as Force Commander of the UNTAC military component and of Brigadier-

General Michel Loridon (France) as Deputy Force Commander.[15] He thereafter obtained Council agreement[16] to his proposals[17] that the military elements would be composed of contingents from Algeria, Argentina, Australia, Austria, Bangladesh, Bulgaria, Cameroon, Canada, Chile, China, France, Ghana, India, Indonesia, Ireland, Italy, Malaysia, the Netherlands, New Zealand, Pakistan, the Philippines, Poland, the Russian Federation, Senegal, Thailand, Tunisia, the United Kingdom and Uruguay. The addition of Japan and Brunei Darussalam to these troop-contributing countries, as he later proposed,[18] was also agreed to by the Council.[19]

Financing

As he informed the Security Council President on 18 January 1992,[20] the Secretary-General intended to propose that the General Assembly should provide an initial appropriation of $200 million, to be made available immediately upon Council approval of the implementation plan for the establishment of UNTAC. That decision, duly noted by the Council President,[21] was taken in the context of the need, repeatedly stressed by the Cambodian parties and the international community, for the urgent emplacement of UNTAC in order to prevent any erosion of the peace process.

On 31 January, the Secretary-General submitted his proposal[22] for the appropriation and apportionment of the $200 million, giving a general breakdown by object of expenditure for the priority items of accommodation, vehicles, water transport, communications and miscellaneous items. He described the tasks of UNTAC as distributed among some of its components in order to provide an idea of its likely magnitude and cost. The request for such a substantial appropriation in advance of the General Assembly's review and approval of detailed cost estimates was prompted by the magnitude of the tasks to be performed by UNTAC and the consequent need to obtain in a timely manner the large quantities of equipment and services it required, the near absence in Cambodia of a support infrastructure and the inadequacy of the current financial commitment authority available to the Secretary-General to provide for the anticipated pre-implementation goods and services.

Aware of the exigencies of the situation, ACABQ[23] acknowledged that there was sufficient justification for seeking such a substantial appropriation in advance of Security Council adoption of the plan of implementation for UNTAC and of the General Assembly's review and approval of a detailed cost estimate. It therefore had no objection to approval of the request and noted the Secretary-General's intention to set up a special account for UNTAC. It requested him to ensure that commitments were entered into only in respect of those requirements that were absolutely essential and in line with actual requirements as they emerged.

GENERAL ASSEMBLY ACTION (February)

In response to the Secretary-General's request,[24] the General Assembly, on the recommendation of the General Committee, decided on 4 February to include in the agenda of its resumed forty-sixth (1991) session an item on the financing of UNTAC and to allocate it to the Fifth Committee.

On 14 February, the Assembly, acting on the recommendation of the Fifth Committee, adopted **resolution 46/222 A** without vote.

Financing of the United Nations Transitional Authority in Cambodia

The General Assembly,

Recalling its resolutions 46/18 of 20 November 1991 and 46/198 A of 20 December 1991,

Having considered the report of the Secretary-General on the financing of the initial phase of the implementation plan of the United Nations Transitional Authority in Cambodia and the related report of the Advisory Committee on Administrative and Budgetary Questions,

Bearing in mind Security Council resolution 717(1991) of 16 October 1991, by which the Council established the United Nations Advance Mission in Cambodia to be emplaced immediately after the signing of the agreements on a comprehensive political settlement of the Cambodia conflict,

Bearing in mind also Security Council resolution 718(1991) of 31 October 1991, by which the Council expressed its full support for the agreements on a comprehensive political settlement of the Cambodia conflict (Paris agreements), signed in Paris on 23 October 1991, which, *inter alia*, call for the establishment of a United Nations Transitional Authority in Cambodia,

Noting that the unusual approach of seeking a substantial appropriation in advance of the review and approval by the General Assembly of the detailed cost estimate of the Transitional Authority is prompted by the extraordinary circumstances of the tasks to be performed by the Transitional Authority and the consequent need to obtain in a timely manner the large quantities of equipment and services it will require, as reflected in the statement of the Secretary-General in his report and the exchange of letters between the Secretary-General and the President of the Security Council reproduced therein, and in the statement by the representative of the Secretary-General to the Fifth Committee at its 58th meeting,

Noting also that the plan for implementing the mandate envisaged in the Paris agreements is under preparation and is to be submitted to the Security Council at the earliest possible date,

Recognizing that the costs to prepare for the deployment of the Transitional Authority are part of the total expenses of the operation and as such are expenses of the Organization to be borne by Member States in accordance with Article 17, paragraph 2, of the Charter of the United Nations,

Recognizing also that, in order to meet the expenditures for the deployment of the Transitional Authority, a different procedure is required from the one applied to meet expenditures of the regular budget of the United Nations,

Taking into account the fact that the economically more developed countries are in a position to make relatively larger contributions and that the economically less developed countries have a relatively limited capacity to contribute towards such an operation,

Bearing in mind the special responsibilities of the States permanent members of the Security Council, as indicated in General Assembly resolution 1874(S-IV) of 27 June 1963, in the financing of such operations,

Mindful of the fact that it is essential to provide the necessary financial resources to enable the Secretary-General to fulfil the tasks envisaged in the Paris agreements as supported by the Security Council and the General Assembly in their respective resolutions and to prepare for the deployment of the Transitional Authority,

1. *Endorses* the observations and recommendations contained in the report of the Advisory Committee on Administrative and Budgetary Questions;

2. *Urges* all Member States to ensure payment of their assessed contributions in full and on time;

3. *Decides* to appropriate an amount of 200 million United States dollars to meet the initial, unavoidable requirements, as indicated in the reports of the Secretary-General and of the Advisory Committee, to enable the Secretary-General to initiate the action necessary for a timely deployment of the United Nations Transitional Authority in Cambodia consistent with the eventual plan of implementation, and requests the Secretary-General to establish a special account for the Transitional Authority;

4. *Decides also* to take into account the amount of 200 million dollars appropriated above against the full assessments to be levied on Member States upon the approval of the total cost estimates of the Transitional Authority;

5. *Decides further,* as an ad hoc arrangement, to apportion the amount of 200 million dollars among Member States in accordance with the composition of groups set out in paragraphs 3 and 4 of General Assembly resolution 43/232 of 1 March 1989, as adjusted by the Assembly in its resolutions 44/192 B of 21 December 1989, 45/269 of 27 August 1991 and 46/198 A, and taking into account the scale of assessments set out in Assembly resolution 46/221 A of 20 December 1991;

6. *Invites* voluntary contributions to the Transitional Authority in cash and in the form of services and supplies acceptable to the Secretary-General, to be administered, as appropriate, in accordance with the procedure established by the General Assembly in its resolution 44/192 A of 21 December 1989;

7. *Requests* the Secretary-General to take all necessary action to ensure that resources to prepare for the deployment of the Transitional Authority are administered with a maximum of efficiency and economy, and bearing in mind paragraph 11 of the report of the Advisory Committee and the status of the Security Council actions on the Transitional Authority;

8. *Also requests* the Secretary-General to submit to the General Assembly during its forty-sixth session, through the Advisory Committee, the full and detailed budget of the Transitional Authority.

General Assembly resolution 46/222 A

14 February 1992   Meeting 81   Adopted without vote

Approved by Fifth Committee (A/46/879) without vote, 13 February (meeting 59); draft by Chairman (A/C.5/46/L.22), orally revised; agenda item 148.

Meeting numbers. GA 46th session: 5th Committee 58, 59; plenary 80, 81.

Report of the Secretary-General. Based on his implementation plan for UNTAC, the Secretary-General, on 7 May 1992,[25] submitted a report to the General Assembly on the financing of UNAMIC and UNTAC. He proposed that, since UNAMIC was absorbed by UNTAC as of 15 March, the individual accounts of the two operations should be consolidated into the UNTAC Special Account and that the expenditures relating to both be combined. The financial accounts would be kept for the period from the inception of UNAMIC on 1 November 1991 to the end of the current UNTAC mandate on 31 July 1993.

The total cost of the two operations was currently estimated at $1,721,596,700 gross ($1,699,512,600 net). That amount comprised UNAMIC expenditures from 1 November 1991 to 14 March 1992, estimated at $20,023,200 gross ($19,777,200 net), and the full cost of UNTAC for the period 15 March 1992 to 31 July 1993, estimated at $1,701,573,500 gross ($1,679,735,400 net), inclusive of the $200 million already appropriated by the Assembly. A breakdown by object of expenditure was annexed to the report. The UNTAC estimated costs included $14 million for rehabilitation/reintegration assistance to the demobilized military forces of the Cambodian parties.

As to repatriation costs, which were not provided for, it was the Secretary-General's intention to launch a separate appeal for the further financing of this component of the operation, but he would recommend alternative arrangements should a shortfall in funding occur.

Appropriations for both missions had so far amounted to $233,576,200 gross, while assessments of $233,294,400 had been apportioned among Member States. As ACABQ was later informed,[26] payments received for both missions as at 6 May reduced the unpaid balance for UNAMIC to $8.9 million and for UNTAC to $57.6 million, or to a combined unpaid balance of $66.5 million.

Given the above figures, the Secretary-General recommended that $764,058,800 gross ($757,117,700 net) should be appropriated and apportioned for UNTAC operations through 31 October 1992. Adding the amounts already appropriated for UNAMIC and UNTAC totalling $233,576,200 gross ($233,171,300 net), the total appropriations for the combined operations of UNAMIC and UNTAC through 31 October 1992 would amount to $997,635,000 gross ($990,289,000 net).

ACABQ noted that it would have been helpful if the requirements for UNTAC for the period 15

March to 31 October 1992 had been separately indicated rather than incorporated in the estimates for 15 March 1992 to 31 July 1993, since this would have clarified the basis for the requested appropriation. Having identified a large number of areas where savings could be made, ACABQ believed that an additional appropriation and assessment of $606 million gross ($600 million net) for UNTAC through 31 October 1992 should be adequate. That figure, plus the $233.6 million gross ($233.2 million net) already appropriated would make available a total of $839.6 million gross ($833.2 million net) for UNTAC operation for the period indicated.

GENERAL ASSEMBLY ACTION (May)

Acting on the recommendation of the Fifth Committee, the General Assembly adopted **resolution 46/222 B** on 22 May 1992 without vote.

Financing of the United Nations Advance Mission in Cambodia and the United Nations Transitional Authority in Cambodia

The General Assembly,

Recalling its resolutions 46/18 of 20 November 1991, 46/198 A of 20 December 1991 and 46/198 B and 46/222 A of 14 February 1992,

Bearing in mind Security Council resolution 717(1991) of 16 October 1991, by which the Council established the United Nations Advance Mission in Cambodia, and Council resolution 728(1992) of 8 January 1992, by which the Council approved the proposal of the Secretary-General to expand the mandate of the Advance Mission, especially with regard to the provision of assistance in mine clearing by Cambodians,

Bearing in mind also Security Council resolution 718(1991) of 31 October 1991, by which the Council expressed its full support for the agreements on a comprehensive political settlement of the Cambodia conflict (Paris agreements), signed in Paris on 23 October 1991, and Council resolution 745(1992) of 28 February 1992, by which the Council established the United Nations Transitional Authority in Cambodia in accordance with the report of the Secretary-General of 19 February 1992 for a period not to exceed eighteen months,

Having considered the report of the Secretary-General on the financing of the Advance Mission and the Transitional Authority and the related report of the Advisory Committee on Administrative and Budgetary Questions,

Noting that the budgetary estimates for the Advance Mission and the Transitional Authority as contained in the report of the Secretary-General amount to 1,721,596,700 United States dollars gross (1,699,512,600 dollars net) for the period from 1 November 1991 to 31 July 1993,

Noting also that the duration of the mandate of the Advance Mission extended from the signature of the Paris agreements until the establishment of the Transitional Authority by the Security Council, at which time the Advance Mission was absorbed into the Transitional Authority,

Recognizing that the costs of the Advance Mission and the Transitional Authority, as indicated in paragraph 7 of the report of the Secretary-General, are expenses of the Organization to be borne by Member States in accordance with Article 17, paragraph 2, of the Charter of the United Nations,

Recognizing also that, in order to meet the expenditures caused by the Advance Mission and the Transitional Authority, a different procedure is required from the one applied to meet expenditures of the regular budget of the United Nations,

Taking into account the fact that the economically more developed countries are in a position to make relatively larger contributions and that the economically less developed countries have a relatively limited capacity to contribute towards such an operation,

Bearing in mind the special responsibilities of the States permanent members of the Security Council, as indicated in General Assembly resolution 1874(S-IV) of 27 June 1963, in the financing of such operations,

Mindful of the fact that it is essential to provide the Advance Mission and the Transitional Authority with the necessary financial resources to enable them to fulfil their responsibilities under the relevant resolutions of the Security Council,

1. *Endorses* the observations and recommendations made by the Advisory Committee on Administrative and Budgetary Questions in its report;

2. *Urges* all Member States to make every possible effort to ensure payment of their assessed contributions to the United Nations Advance Mission in Cambodia and the United Nations Transitional Authority in Cambodia in full and on time;

3. *Requests* the Secretary-General to consolidate the special account for the Advance Mission into the special account for the Transitional Authority;

4. *Decides*, at this stage, to appropriate, in accordance with the recommendation contained in paragraph 78 of the report of the Advisory Committee, an amount of 606 million United States dollars gross (600 million dollars net) for the operation of the Transitional Authority through 31 October 1992, in addition to the total amount of 233,576,200 dollars gross (233,171,300 dollars net) already appropriated for the Advance Mission and the Transitional Authority by the General Assembly in its resolutions 46/198 A and B and 46/222 A;

5. *Decides also*, as an ad hoc arrangement, to apportion the amount of 606 million dollars gross (600 million dollars net) among Member States in accordance with the composition of groups set out in paragraphs 3 and 4 of General Assembly resolution 43/232 of 1 March 1989, as adjusted by the Assembly in its resolutions 44/192 B of 21 December 1989, 45/269 of 27 August 1991 and 46/198 A of 20 December 1991, and taking into account the scale of assessments for the years 1992, 1993 and 1994;

6. *Requests* the Secretary-General to report to the General Assembly at its forty-seventh session on anomalies in the allocation of countries to the four groups set out in General Assembly resolution 43/232, as adjusted by the Assembly in its resolutions 44/192 B, 45/269 and 46/198 A and applied as an ad hoc arrangement to the financing of the Transitional Authority, taking into account Assembly resolution 46/206 of 20 December 1991 and other relevant resolutions of the Assembly, including resolution 3101(XXVIII) of 11 December 1973;

7. *Decides* that, in accordance with the provisions of its resolution 973(X) of 15 December 1955, there shall

be set off against the apportionment among Member States, as provided for in paragraph 5 above, their respective share in the Tax Equalization Fund of the estimated staff assessment income of 6 million dollars approved for the Advance Mission and the Transitional Authority;

8. *Decides also* to consider the contributions of Armenia, Azerbaijan, Kazakhstan, Kyrgyzstan, the Republic of Moldova, San Marino, Tajikistan, Turkmenistan and Uzbekistan to the Advance Mission and the Transitional Authority in accordance with the rates of assessment to be adopted for these Member States by the General Assembly at its forty-seventh session;

9. *Invites* the new Member States listed in paragraph 8 above to make advance payments against their assessed contributions to be determined;

10. *Reiterates* the need for increased use of civilian personnel provided by Governments in relevant sectors of peace-keeping operations, as called for in General Assembly resolutions 44/192 A of 21 December 1989 and 45/258 of 3 May 1991, and requests the Secretary-General to encourage the participation of such personnel in the civilian components of the Transitional Authority in accordance with the recommendations contained in paragraphs 24 and 25 of the report of the Advisory Committee;

11. *Takes note* of the views expressed by the Secretary-General in paragraph 46 of his report with respect to the repatriation programme to be undertaken by the Office of the United Nations High Commissioner for Refugees, and, since the implementation and integrity of the electoral process is dependent upon the prior repatriation of Cambodian refugees, calls upon Member States and others to make voluntary contributions in support of the repatriation programme;

12. *Calls upon* Member States and others to make voluntary contributions to the rehabilitation programme referred to in paragraph 47 of the report of the Secretary-General;

13. *Invites* voluntary contributions to the Transitional Authority in cash and in the form of services and supplies acceptable to the Secretary-General, to be administered, as appropriate, in accordance with the procedure established by the General Assembly in its resolutions 43/230 of 21 December 1988, 44/192 A and 45/258;

14. *Requests* the Secretary-General to take all necessary action to ensure that the Transitional Authority is administered with a maximum of efficiency and economy;

15. *Also requests* the Secretary-General to submit to the General Assembly, no later than at its forty-seventh session, a report on such additional requirements as may be necessary and to include in the report detailed and up-to-date information on the performance of the Transitional Authority;

16. *Decides* to include in the provisional agenda of its forty-seventh session the item entitled "Financing of the United Nations Transitional Authority in Cambodia".

General Assembly resolution 46/222 B

22 May 1992   Meeting 86   Adopted without vote

Approved by Fifth Committee (A/46/879/Add.1) without vote, 21 May (meeting 65); draft by Vice-Chairman (A/C.5/46/L.25), orally revised; agenda items 146 & 148.

Meeting numbers. GA 46th session: 5th Committee 64, 65; plenary 86.

Activities

Reports of the Secretary-General (May and June). As requested by the Security Council when it established UNTAC, the Secretary-General, on 1 May 1992,[27] issued the first in a series of progress reports on UNTAC operations. It was based on his visit to Cambodia from 18 to 20 April.

According to the report, the arrival in Phnom Penh on 15 March of the Special Representative of the Secretary-General for Cambodia marked the initial deployment of UNTAC and UNAMIC's absorption into it. All senior officials of UNTAC had assumed their duties and its various components had begun discharging their responsibilities.

Lines of communication between UNTAC and SNC were being set up. Both agreed that a technical advisory committee, chaired by a senior UNTAC official, would be set up in some areas under UNTAC responsibility to function as an SNC subsidiary. A "hot line" service was installed on 1 April linking the Special Representative and the Force Commander with each of the four Cambodian parties.

The human rights component began its first training programmes for UNTAC police monitors in April. A quick-response mechanism, composed of members of the human rights, civil administration and police components, had been established to investigate alleged human rights violations. At its 20 April meeting, SNC acceded to the International Covenant on Civil and Political Rights and the International Covenant on Economic, Social and Cultural Rights.[28] That was the first in a series of measures designed to create a free and neutral political environment within Cambodia. (For the reports of the human rights component, see PART THREE, Chapter X.)

A draft electoral law presented by UNTAC was discussed by SNC at three meetings. The Advance Election Planning Unit had completed initial visits to 19 of 21 provinces for the purpose of compiling socio-demographic and cartographic data. Preparation for voter registration and polling was proceeding, but equipment procurement was being hampered by procedural requirements.

Deployment of the military component proceeded at a slower rate than expected, with 3,694 troops deployed by the end of April. Considerable difficulty was experienced in emplacing and securing necessary equipment. Of the 24 checkpoints planned (along the borders with Thailand (7), with Viet Nam (9), with the Lao People's Democratic Republic (2), at the Kompong Som and Phnom Penh ports (1 each), at the airports in Phnom Penh, Battambang, Siem Reap and Stung Treng (1 each)), 3 had been set up along the border with Viet Nam.

The cease-fire had generally been maintained, except at Kompong Thom, where the forces of all four Cambodian parties were present and where a number of armed clashes had occurred since mid-January. On 26 February, an UNTAC helicopter on reconnaissance in the area came under fire and an officer of the Australian contingent was wounded. Following an investigation, the cease-fire was restored. Up to 244 United Nations troops were later stationed at Kompong Thom. As to implementation of cease-fire measures, it was agreed to set up 55 cantonment areas: 33 for CPAF, 14 for NADK, 5 for KPNLAF and 3 for ANKI.

SNC agreed to the creation of a Cambodian Mine Action Centre to be managed by a Governing Council of five Cambodian and five UNTAC members. Six mine-clearing training teams had been deployed in north-western Cambodia. The military component had provided convoy escorts for the repatriation of refugees from camps on the Thai border and set up a security presence at each of the refugee reception centres.

The civil administration component had initiated contacts with the existing administrative structure and had drawn up operating procedures for the exercise of the right of assembly and association, which SNC approved.

At the end of April, 193 civilian police monitors had been deployed, giving priority to deployment at Sisophon and Battambang, where refugee resettlement was in progress.

The repatriation component began its activities on 30 March with the return to Cambodia of 526 refugees. As at the end of April, 5,763 persons had been repatriated. Owing to the difficulty of finding suitable land for returnee resettlement, a geographical widening of land settlement options and non-agricultural solutions for returnees were being actively pursued. (For supplementary information on the activities of UNHCR relating to the repatriation of Cambodian refugees, see PART THREE, Chapter XV.)

The Secretary-General, on 20 April, formally launched an appeal to the international community for $593 million for rehabilitation assistance in the areas of food, health services, shelter, education, training and restoration of basic infrastructure, public utilities and support institutions.

In a special report of 12 June,[29] the Secretary-General drew the Council's attention to the fact that implementation of the 1991 Paris agreements had reached a critical stage. The ability of UNTAC to adhere to the implementation of phase II of the cease-fire, scheduled to begin on 13 June, was being seriously compromised by lack of cooperation from PDK.

In preparation for phase II, the Commander of the UNTAC military component, on 9 May, obtained assurances from each of the four Cambodian parties that it would (a) grant freedom of movement to UNTAC personnel, vehicles and aircraft; (b) mark minefields in the areas it controlled; (c) provide information by 20 May on its troops, arms, ammunition and equipment; and (d) adhere to the Paris agreements, in particular not interfere with troops moving to regroupment and cantonment areas and inform its troops of the regroupment and cantonment plan.

Two parties promptly provided the information requested and a third made a bona fide effort to comply substantially. The fourth party, PDK, continued to deny full access and freedom of movement to UNTAC, preventing it from conducting reconnaissance of 6 of the 16 cantonment sites envisaged for NADK, the PDK army. It failed to provide the information requested, and also failed to mark minefields in areas under its control; it had also re-mined other areas. The PDK army was believed to have been responsible for many of the cease-fire violations that continued to occur in Kompong Thom, Kompong Cham and elsewhere.

PDK explained that, because foreign military personnel remained present in Cambodia and until their withdrawal and non-return had been verified by UNTAC, its own security required that fulfilment of its obligations had to be deferred. While firmly rejecting that view, UNTAC undertook to allay any legitimate concerns by installing 10 border checkpoints on the Cambodia–Viet Nam border, inviting the four parties to participate in manning them and launching mobile military teams to investigate any alleged presence of foreign forces. In reply to a list of such allegations submitted by PDK, UNTAC asked PDK to join it in investigating those allegations; PDK had yet to comply with that request.

Despite the unsatisfactory outcome of the SNC meetings and of his personal appeal to the PDK President on the question, the Secretary-General concluded that phase II of the cease-fire must proceed as scheduled on 13 June. Accordingly, the Special Representative was consulting the three parties which had expressed readiness to begin regroupment and cantonment of their forces, so as to ensure that the conduct of that process would minimize any military disadvantage they would suffer vis-à-vis PDK.

The Secretary-General urged every effort to persuade PDK to join the other parties in good faith in implementing the Paris agreements. He suggested that the Security Council might wish to consider what action it could take to achieve that objective.

SECURITY COUNCIL ACTION (May and June)

The Security Council, on 14 May 1992,[30] took note of the Secretary-General's first progress report on UNTAC[27] and welcomed the announcement that phase II of the cease-fire arrangements would begin on 13 June.

On 12 June, the Council met to consider the Secretary-General's special report of the same date.[29] Following consultations among its members, the President made the following statement,[31] on behalf of the Council:

Meeting number. SC 3085.

"Having read the report of the Secretary-General, the Security Council is deeply concerned by the difficulties that the United Nations Transitional Authority in Cambodia (UNTAC) is encountering in the implementation of the Paris agreements, on the eve of moving to the second phase of the cease-fire. In particular, the Council notes that, during the meeting of the Supreme National Council on 10 June 1992, one party was not able to allow the necessary deployment of UNTAC in areas under its control. The Council believes that any delay could jeopardize the whole peace process to which all Cambodian parties have agreed under the auspices of the United Nations and the Paris Conference.

"The Council reaffirms the importance of the full and timely implementation of the Paris agreements. The Council commends the efforts of the Secretary-General's Special Representative and UNTAC in this regard. It reaffirms that the Supreme National Council, under the chairmanship of HRH Prince Norodom Sihanouk, is the unique legitimate body and source of authority in which, throughout the transitional period, the sovereignty, independence and unity of Cambodia are enshrined. In this regard, section III of part I of the Paris agreements should be implemented as soon as possible.

"The Council stresses the need that the second phase of the military arrangements should begin on 13 June 1992, as determined in accordance with the agreements. In this connection, the Council urges the Secretary-General to accelerate the deployment of the full UNTAC peace-keeping force to Cambodia and within the country.

"The Council calls upon all parties to comply strictly with the commitments they have accepted, including cooperation with UNTAC. It specifically calls upon all parties to respond affirmatively to the latest demands for cooperation in implementation of the agreements put to them by UNTAC."

Report of the Secretary-General (July). In a second special report, of 14 July 1992,[32] the Secretary-General stated that, as at 10 July, the armies of the four Cambodian parties had cantoned 13,512 of their troops, as follows: CPAF, 9,003; ANKI, 3,187; KPNLAF, 1,322; NADK, 0. As the data showed, PDK had so far failed to canton any of its troops. It had moreover failed to grant UNTAC free and unrestricted access to the zones it controlled, to mark the minefields there and to stop cease-fire violations. It insisted on making its compliance with those obligations conditional upon verification of the withdrawal from and non-return to Cambodia of foreign forces and strengthening the role and powers of SNC according to its interpretations of those provisions.

An 11-point informal proposal for discussion to meet some of PDK's concerns was accordingly put forward at a Ministerial Conference on the Rehabilitation and Reconstruction of Cambodia (Tokyo, 20 and 22 June). The proposal was drawn up by the five permanent Security Council members, the Co-Chairmen of the Paris Conference on Cambodia[1] and other Conference participants, including the Special Representative. Following its discussion by all four parties at SNC meetings (22 June, 8 July) and a working session (2 July), the proposal was accepted by all but PDK, which countered with its own proposal regarding SNC's powers and role and the administrative structures in the CPP-controlled zone. Meanwhile, UNTAC strengthened its border checkpoints and mobile military investigation teams to follow up on any reports of the presence of foreign forces or evidence of outside military assistance.

Besides giving priority to the recruitment and deployment of its civil administration staff, UNTAC actively sought PDK agreement on the establishment of a mechanism for keeping the four Cambodian parties informed of and involved with its exercise of direct control over the existing key administrative structures of foreign affairs, national defence, finance, public security and information. In this regard, PDK, through its President, Khieu Samphan, elaborated its position on the relationship between SNC and UNTAC and on UNTAC's exercise of authority in Cambodia, and called for the dissolution of the administrative structures in the CPP zone. The Special Representative explained that the Paris agreements provided that UNTAC control be exercised through the "existing administrative structures" of each of the four Cambodian parties; the Phnom Penh authorities formed part of those structures, which could not be abolished or dismantled.

The UNTAC military deployment was almost complete, with some 14,300 troops already in the country; UNTAC civilian police monitors currently numbered 1,780. A total of 50,000 refugees and displaced persons had been repatriated. Over 100 cases of human rights investigations had been successfully carried out in the CPP zone, with investigations soon to begin in the FUNCINPEC and KPNLF (BLDP) zones. The draft electoral law submitted by UNTAC to SNC in April was under extensive discussion. Pledges of $880 million had resulted from the Tokyo Ministerial Conference—substantially in excess of the $593 million appealed for.

Despite lack of cooperation from PDK, phase II of the cease-fire began on 13 June. While the regroupment and cantonment process should have been completed on 11 July, barely 5 per cent of the estimated 200,000 Cambodian troops had been cantoned by that date. In his instructions to press forward with the process wherever possible, the Special Representative was asked to ensure that the cooperating parties suffered no military disadvantage. Implementation would thus be pursued in areas posing no military confrontation; and some cantoned troops might be permitted to retain their weapons until the situation was clarified. The Secretary-General warned, however, that the process could not go on indefinitely with the cooperation of only three of the parties. He said three points needed to be considered: steps to persuade PDK to comply with its obligations under the Paris agreements; action to underscore the international community's determination to implement the agreements according to the timetable set by the Secretary-General's implementation plan; and ways to obtain the full and active support of the signatories of the agreements.

SECURITY COUNCIL ACTION (July)

At its meeting on 21 July 1992, the Security Council had before it, in addition to the Secretary-General's report, the texts of the Tokyo Declaration on the Cambodia Peace Process and the Tokyo Declaration on the Rehabilitation and Reconstruction of Cambodia, issued at the conclusion of the Ministerial Conference on the Rehabilitation and Reconstruction of Cambodia on 22 June.[33]

By the first Declaration, the Conference stressed the importance of full and timely implementation of the Paris agreements and the need for all the signatories to comply with their provisions so as to allow UNTAC to exercise, in consultation with SNC, all powers with which it was mandated by the agreements in accordance with the mechanisms and time schedule specified; and it gave a clear signal that there was full international support for the peace process and reaffirmed the importance it attached to its effective and expeditious implementation. By the second Declaration, the Conference set the guidelines for assistance in Cambodia.

Following consideration of the Secretary-General's report and the foregoing texts, the Council unanimously adopted **resolution 766(1992)**.

The Security Council,

Reaffirming its resolutions 668(1990) of 20 September 1990, 717(1991) of 16 October 1991, 718(1991) of 31 October 1991, 728(1992) of 8 January 1992 and 745(1992) of 28 February 1992,

Recalling the statement made by the President of the Security Council on 12 June 1992,

Recalling also that any difficulty arising in the implementation of the Paris Agreements should be settled through close consultation between the SNC and UNTAC and must not be allowed to undermine the principles of these Agreements, or to delay the timetable for their implementation,

Taking note of the report of the Secretary-General dated 14 July 1992, and in particular of the fact that CPP, FUNCINPEC and KPNLF have agreed to proceed with phase II of the cease-fire as laid down in annex 2 of the first Paris Agreement and that the Party of Democratic Kampuchea has so far refused to do so,

Taking note also of the declaration on the Cambodia Peace Process adopted in Tokyo on 22 June 1992, and the other efforts made there by the countries and parties concerned for the implementation of the Paris Agreements,

1. *Expresses* its deep concern at the difficulties met by UNTAC in the implementation of the Paris Agreements;

2. *Underlines* that all signatories of the Agreements are bound by all their obligations thereunder;

3. *Deplores* the continuing violations of the cease-fire and *urges* all parties to cease all hostilities forthwith, to cooperate fully with UNTAC in the marking of all minefields and to refrain from any deployment, movement or other action intended to extend the territory they control or which might lead to renewed fighting;

4. *Reaffirms* the international community's firm commitment to a process under which UNTAC, operating freely throughout all of Cambodia as authorized by the Paris Agreements, can verify the departure of all foreign forces and ensure full implementation of the Agreements;

5. *Demands* that all parties respect the peaceful nature of UNTAC's mission and take all necessary measures to ensure the safety and security of all United Nations personnel;

6. *Urges* all parties to cooperate with UNTAC in broadcasting information helpful to implementation of the Paris Agreements;

7. *Strongly deplores* the continuing refusal by one of the parties to permit the necessary deployment of all components of UNTAC to the areas under its control to enable UNTAC to carry out its full functions in the implementation of the Paris Agreements;

8. *Urges* all States, in particular neighbouring countries, to provide assistance to UNTAC to ensure the effective implementation of the Paris Agreements;

9. *Approves* the efforts of the Secretary-General and his Special Representative to continue to implement the Agreements despite the difficulties;

10. *Invites* in particular the Secretary-General and his Special Representative to accelerate the deployment of UNTAC's civilian components, especially the component mandated to supervise or control the existing administrative structures;

11. *Demands* that the Party that has failed so far to do so permit without delay the deployment of UNTAC in the areas under its control, and implement fully phase II of the plan as well as the other aspects of the Paris Agreements;

12. *Requests* the Secretary-General and his Special Representative to ensure that international assistance to the rehabilitation and reconstruction of Cambodia from now on only benefits the parties which are fulfilling their obligations under the Paris Agreements and cooperating fully with UNTAC;

13. *Decides* to remain actively seized of the matter.

Security Council resolution 766(1992)

21 July 1992   Meeting 3099   Adopted unanimously

Draft prepared in consultations among Council members (S/24320).

Report of the Secretary-General (September). According to the Secretary-General's second progress report, of 21 September 1992,[34] UNTAC continued to enjoy the full cooperation of the SNC President. Its relations with SNC had generally been harmonious and productive despite constraints from the failure of PDK to participate fully in the peace process.

The human rights component remained active in three broad areas: encouraging SNC to adhere to international human rights instruments and reviewing existing judicial and penal systems in the light of those instruments; mounting an extensive human rights information and education campaign; and investigating complaints related to human rights, taking corrective measures where applicable. Of the 250 complaints it had examined of harassment and intimidation, arbitrary arrest, wrongful injury or death and destruction of property, it referred 130 to other UNTAC components and found 13 unsubstantiated. It began work on prison reform; since the creation of a Prisons Control Commission, 258 detainees had been released by August.

The electoral component had deployed some 150 international staff at UNTAC headquarters and in the provinces, and 400 United Nations Volunteers at the district level. It was in the process of deploying some 1,000 locally recruited staff. The draft electoral law, having been amended, was finally adopted and promulgated by SNC on 12 August. The amendments related to the definition of "Cambodian persons" entitled to register and to overseas voting by Cambodians. Provisional registration of political parties began on 15 August. Voter registration was scheduled to begin in October. According to latest estimates, the voting population was about 5 million—larger than the previously estimated 4.3 million.

The electoral component was currently examining a proposal to hold a presidential election simultaneously with the election for a constituent assembly. Since such an election was not provided for in the Paris agreements, it would require Security Council authorization and additional resources.

The almost fully deployed military component had a strength of about 15,100 all ranks, with 12 infantry battalions, military observers, engineers, signals, naval, air and other elements. It completed setting up nine checkpoints on Cambodia's border with Viet Nam, two on the border with the Lao People's Democratic Republic and seven on the border with Thailand. It also installed checkpoints at airports and at the port of Sihanoukville, as well as on all major routes. It reported several incidents of firings at UNTAC helicopters, believed to have come from areas under PDK control, which remained inaccessible to UNTAC. On 17 September, NADK, after an absence of three months, rejoined the Mixed Military Working Group, the mechanism to resolve cease-fire issues.

As at 10 September, 52,292 Cambodian troops had been cantoned, as follows: CPAF, 42,368; ANKI, 3,445; KPNLAF, 6,479; NADK, 0. Approximately 50,000 weapons had been taken into custody. Eleven mine-clearance training centres had been established and had fully trained some 850 soldiers. About 350 were currently employed by UNTAC in mine-clearance activities.

The civil administration component had completed deployment of some 200 international and 600 locally recruited staff. With the exception of PDK, each party had submitted a list of its current laws for UNTAC review. At UNTAC's initiative, SNC adopted laws enshrining the rights of freedom of association and assembly. It also approved a set of principles relating to the legal system, penal law and penal procedure, setting minimum standards applicable throughout Cambodia. On 1 July, the component, whose personnel were deployed in Phnom Penh's ministries of foreign affairs, national defence, public security, finance and information, began to exercise full control over those key administrative areas. By 15 July, UNTAC civil administration offices were in operation in all 21 provinces.

Activities in foreign affairs related to issuance of entry visas to Cambodia, passport and identity card validation, and control over foreign aid. Investigations in national defence revealed a high level of SOC (formerly CPP) political activity within the armed forces, which had to be curtailed. In public security, the Public Security Service, in addition to compiling existing laws and modifying those found to be incompatible with the Paris agreements, had drafted codes of conduct. Direct control over finance had been fully established by early September, which extended to individual expenditures and to main sources of revenue, such as customs duties. Financial controls were also being exercised in the FUNCINPEC and KPNLF (BLDP) zones. In information, the component drafted a media charter governing freedom of the press and media rights and obligations for consideration by a media working group composed of the Cambodian parties. The Inquiries and Complaints Service, working with the civilian police, electoral and human rights components, had processed some 50 information-related complaints.

The civilian police component, comprising 2,500 police officers (out of a projected strength of 3,600), had extended its activities to all provinces. It had established a highly visible presence in Phnom Penh and at the provincial level, and was setting up police stations in the districts and conducting regular patrols in the villages. It also maintained a permanent presence in the FUNCINPEC and KPNLF (BLDP) zones. PDK had begun cooperating with the UNTAC police in seven Cambodian provinces under its control.

Since 30 March, more than 115,000 refugees and displaced Cambodians had been repatriated under the auspices of UNHCR, the lead agency of the repatriation component. With repatriations expected to rise from 30,000 to 40,000 monthly during the coming dry season, the remaining 250,000 refugees would very likely be repatriated in time to take part in the elections. PDK had neither obstructed nor interfered with the 35,000 or so persons who returned to Cambodia from camps under its control; in fact, it had cooperated in certain respects with the repatriation process.

While PDK had initially refused to cooperate with the SNC Technical Advisory Committee set up to facilitate approval of rehabilitation projects by consensus, it had adopted a more positive attitude following the Tokyo Ministerial Conference. Ten programmes of more than $187 million presented by UNTAC in July were approved by the SNC President. The largest of these was a three-year programme of cooperation ($89 million), to be funded and executed by the United Nations Children's Fund, aimed at improving drinking-water supply and sanitation, schools, health services and food security. The second largest was an *aide-mémoire* for an Asian Development Bank loan ($74.4 million), covering projects in transport, power, agriculture and education. By September, SNC had approved 13 other programmes totalling over $42 million. A recommendation for a country-wide moratorium on the export of logs from Cambodia was under consideration.

Through UNTAC's information campaign, its activities were becoming increasingly familiar to Cambodians throughout the country. In the six months since its inception and despite constraints imposed by PDK's refusal to participate fully in the peace process, UNTAC had made substantial strides towards its goals. As a result, the Secretary-General remained determined that the electoral process should be carried out as scheduled. As to PDK's failure to meet its obligations under the Paris agreements, he made known his intention, subject to Security Council approval, to request the Co-Chairmen of the Paris Conference on Cambodia to undertake, within a definite time-frame, consultations with the aim of breaking the current impasse, or, failing that, exploring steps to ensure the realization of the agreements' fundamental objectives.

SECURITY COUNCIL ACTION (October)

On 29 September 1992,[35] the President of the Security Council notified the Secretary-General that a number of Council members required some time to study his report to determine what action was required.

The Council met on 13 October, when it unanimously adopted **resolution 783(1992)**.

The Security Council,

Reaffirming its resolutions 668(1990) of 20 September 1990, 717(1991) of 16 October 1991, 718(1991) of 31 Oc-

tober 1991, 728(1992) of 8 January 1992, 745(1992) of 28 February 1992 and 766(1992) of 21 July 1992,

Recalling the statement made by the President of the Security Council on 12 June 1992,

Recalling also the declaration on the Cambodia peace process adopted in Tokyo on 22 June 1992,

Paying tribute to His Royal Highness Prince Norodom Sihanouk, President of the Supreme National Council, for his efforts to restore peace and national unity in Cambodia,

Taking note of the cooperation extended to UNTAC, by the parties of SOC, FUNCINPEC and KPNLF, and of the fact that the PDK still fails to meet obligations it assumed when it signed the Paris Agreements, as reflected in the report of the Secretary-General dated 21 September 1992,

Reaffirming that UNTAC must have full and unrestricted access to the areas controlled by each of the parties,

Welcoming the achievements of UNTAC in the implementation of the Paris Agreements, concerning, *inter alia*, military deployment almost throughout the whole country, the promulgation of the electoral law, the provisional registration of political parties, the beginning of voter registration, safe repatriation of over 150,000 refugees, progress in rehabilitation programmes and projects and the campaign in favour of respect for human rights,

Welcoming the accession of the SNC to a number of international human rights conventions,

Welcoming also the progress made by UNTAC in strengthening supervision and control over administrative structures as set out in the Paris Agreements, and recognizing the importance of this part of UNTAC's mandate,

Welcoming further the fact that the SNC functions in accordance with the Paris Agreements,

Expressing appreciation to the States and international financial institutions which announced, during the Tokyo Conference on 22 June 1992, financial contributions to Cambodia's reconstruction and rehabilitation,

Expressing its gratitude to the Governments of Thailand and Japan for their efforts to find solutions to the current problems relating to the implementation of the Paris Agreements,

Deeply concerned by difficulties faced by UNTAC caused in particular by security and economic conditions in Cambodia,

1. *Approves* the report of the Secretary-General;

2. *Confirms* that, in conformity with paragraph 66 of the report, the electoral process shall be carried out in accordance with the timetable laid down in the implementation plan and thus that the election for a constituent assembly will be held no later than May 1993;

3. *Supports* the intention of the Secretary-General, expressed in paragraph 67 of his report, concerning checkpoints in the country and along its borders with neighbouring countries;

4. *Expresses its gratitude* to the Secretary-General and his Special Representative for their efforts as well as to Member States which have cooperated with UNTAC in order to solve the difficulties it has met and urges all States, in particular neighbouring countries, to provide assistance to UNTAC to ensure the effective implementation of the Paris Agreements;

5. *Deplores* the fact that the PDK, ignoring the requests and demands contained in its resolution 766(1992), has not yet complied with its obligations;

6. *Demands* that the party mentioned in paragraph 5 fulfil immediately its obligations under the Paris Agreements; that it facilitate without delay full deployment of UNTAC in the areas under its control; and that it implement fully phase II of the plan, particularly cantonment and demobilization, as well as all other aspects of the Paris Agreements, taking into account that all parties in Cambodia have the same obligations to implement the Paris Agreements;

7. *Demands* full respect for the cease-fire, calls upon all parties in Cambodia to cooperate fully with UNTAC to identify minefields and to refrain from any activity aimed at enlarging the territory under their control, and further demands that these parties facilitate UNTAC investigations of reports of foreign forces, foreign assistance and cease-fire violations within the territory under their control;

8. *Reiterates* its demands that all parties take all necessary measures to ensure the safety and security of all United Nations personnel and refrain from any threat or violent act against them;

9. *Emphasizes*, in accordance with article 12 of the Paris Agreements, the importance of the elections being held in a neutral political environment, encourages the Secretary-General and his Special Representative to continue their efforts to create such an environment, and in that context requests, in particular, that the UNTAC radio broadcast facility be established without delay and with access to the whole territory of Cambodia;

10. *Encourages* the Secretary-General and his Special Representative to make use fully of all possibilities offered by UNTAC's mandate, including annex 1, section B, paragraph 5 (*b*), of the Paris Agreements to enhance the effectiveness of existing civil police in resolving the growing problems relating to the maintenance of law and order in Cambodia;

11. *Invites* States and international financial institutions to make available as soon as possible the contributions they had already announced during the Tokyo Conference on 22 June 1992, giving priority to those which produce quick impact;

12. *Invites* the Governments of Thailand and Japan, in cooperation with the Co-Chairmen and in consultation with any other Government as appropriate, to continue their efforts to find solutions to the current problems relating to the implementation of the Paris Agreements and to report to the Secretary-General and the Co-Chairmen of the Paris Conference by 31 October 1992 on the outcome of their efforts;

13. *Invites* the Secretary-General, in accordance with the intention expressed in paragraph 70 of his report, to ask the Co-Chairmen of the Paris Conference immediately on receipt of the report referred to in paragraph 12 of this resolution to undertake appropriate consultations with a view to implementing fully the peace process;

14. *Requests* the Secretary-General to report to the Security Council as soon as possible, and no later than 15 November 1992, on the implementation of this resolution and, if the present difficulties have not been overcome, undertakes to consider what further steps are necessary and appropriate to ensure the realization of the fundamental objectives of the Paris Agreements;

15. *Decides* to remain actively seized of the matter.

Security Council resolution 783(1992)

13 October 1992   Meeting 3124   Adopted unanimously

Draft prepared in consultations among Council members (S/24652).

Report of the Secretary-General (November). On 15 November,[36] the Secretary-General reported on the outcome of efforts to find solutions to the full implementation of the Paris agreements. Japan and Thailand, responding to the Security Council's invitation of 13 October to continue such efforts, held further tripartite consultations with PDK so as to meet the central concerns it had repeatedly raised regarding (1) verification of foreign troop withdrawal and non-return; and (2) strengthening the role of SNC and the effective supervision and control of existing administrative structures.

At the first such consultation (Bangkok, 17 July), PDK noted that UNTAC had made considerable progress in meeting the first point but that measures taken to address the second were unsatisfactory. Based on an assessment of PDK's contention regarding the second point, Japan and Thailand, at a second consultation (Bangkok, 22 August), suggested that an Administrative Consultative Body be set up under UNTAC auspices to deliberate on any requests, suggestions and possible complaints regarding all administrative matters related to UNTAC control of existing administrative structures stipulated in the Paris agreements. The new body would be set up when all the Cambodia parties entered into phase II of the cease-fire. At a third consultation (Bangkok, 27 August), PDK merged that suggestion with its own proposal for the creation of consultative committees within the existing administrative structures and the police forces of all the Cambodia parties. Viewing the conditions under which those committees were to be created as going beyond the framework of the Paris agreements, Japan and Thailand suggested that they be set up instead as subsidiaries of the proposed Administrative Consultative Body.

In a revised suggestion designed to ensure the neutrality of administrative actions, Japan and Thailand proposed that, in addition to the system of bodies made up of the Administrative Consultative Body and Consultative Committees as regional subsidiaries, UNTAC would keep SNC meticulously informed every month of its activities in supervising and controlling existing administrative structures. The revised suggestion was handed to PDK (Phnom Penh, 22 October) for discussion at a fourth consultation (Phnom Penh, 29 October), to which representatives of the Co-Chairmen of the Paris Conference on Cambodia and UNTAC were invited as observers. Rather than address the contents of the revised suggestion at that consultation, PDK once again reverted to talking about the broader context of implementation of the Paris agreements as an integral whole as the fundamental issue to be addressed, making it difficult, if not impossible, to pinpoint specific remedial measures. In the circumstances, Japan and Thailand concluded that the tripartite consultations were no longer the appropriate means to address the impasse in the peace process.

The Co-Chairmen of the Paris Conference, responding also to the Council's request that they undertake appropriate consultations, did so (Beijing, China, 7 and 8 November) with the SNC President, the Special Representative and heads of the four Cambodian parties, together with the permanent members of the Security Council, Australia, Germany, Japan and Thailand. It became clear from the consultations that three parties—FUNCINPEC, KPNLF (BLDP) and SOC (CPP)—remained fully committed to implementing the peace process. PDK, on the other hand, confirmed that it was still not prepared to cooperate so long as what it claimed to be improper implementation of certain aspects of the agreements was not resolved, specifically as to the verification of foreign (Vietnamese) troop withdrawal and their non-return and the status and functioning of SNC. It would not take part in the electoral process and in subsequent elections so long as a neutral political condition as provided for in the Paris agreements was not ensured.

The Co-Chairmen thus offered several courses of action for consideration by the Council: to reaffirm that the peace process must continue to be implemented and that the timetable leading to elections in April/May 1993 must be maintained; to call on PDK to comply with its obligations; to leave the door open to that party to rejoin the process; to adjust the implementation plan so as to ensure realization of the fundamental objectives of the Paris agreements; to ask the Secretary-General to take steps to complete the establishment of checkpoints; to appeal to the general public and to all the parties to ensure the safety and security of all United Nations personnel; and to define measures to be taken against PDK should it hamper the continuation of the peace plan.

The Co-Chairmen also drew attention to the strong interest expressed by FUNCINPEC, KPNLF and SOC in an election by universal suffrage of a Cambodian head of State, in addition to the general elections for a constituent assembly. A presidential election would contribute to the process of national reconciliation and provide an anchor of stability in the interim period after the general elections and before a new Government of Cambodia could emerge.

Having weighed the practical consequences of the alternatives—putting the process on hold until PDK cooperation was obtained, or withdrawing UNTAC in the conclusion that it was impossible to pursue the process—the Secretary-General concurred with the Co-Chairmen that implementation of the peace process must continue and that the timetable leading to free and fair elections no

later than May 1993 must be maintained. This meant that the required demobilization by election time of at least 70 per cent of all Cambodian troops would not be met and that the population in the PDK-controlled areas would be deprived of the opportunity to vote. It also meant that the projected reduction of the UNTAC military component would no longer be feasible. Accordingly, he proposed that the component's present level of deployment be maintained until the elections, so as to foster a general sense of security and enhance the component's ability to protect the electoral process. He would report shortly on the financial implications of that adjustment.

In the meantime, UNTAC would continue to maintain active dialogue with PDK with a view to persuading it to comply with its obligations under the Paris agreements. It would remain prepared to accommodate PDK's entry into the process as long as that was feasible.

As to UNTAC operations, about a million Cambodians had been registered since voter registration began on 5 October. Information to encourage the broadest participation in the elections was being disseminated by radio. The civilian police component had reached a strength of 3,400 police personnel, of which up to 65 per cent were engaged full time in voter registration. The component was also engaged in training local police in basic police methods, including traffic control and implementation of the new penal code, and in cooperating with the human rights and civil administration components on public security issues.

Scattered cease-fire and human rights violations continued to be reported. The recent past had seen a disturbing number of what appeared to be politically motivated acts of harassment, intimidation and violence and an increase in banditry and crime. After a period of relative quiet during the rainy season, tension increased in the central and northern parts of Cambodia following a series of artillery exchanges. Attacks on UNTAC personnel had also increased, such as firings on its helicopters and an attack on 7 November on the village of Choan Khsan, Preah Vihear province, forcing UNTAC to evacuate an electoral team and 11 civilian police monitors. Some 55,000 Cambodian troops had entered canton sites and handed over their weapons. While PDK had ordered its troops not to canton, some 200 of its army had spontaneously presented themselves to UNTAC.

UNTAC continued to devote serious attention to the question of foreign forces, although it had found no evidence of the presence of any formed units of such forces in areas to which it had access. None the less, it was drawing up plans to strengthen border controls. In the light of recent killings of Vietnamese-speaking villagers and fishermen in Tuk Meas village and in Koh Kong province, the issue of foreign residents and immigrants had become a matter of deep concern to many Cambodians. Investigations indicated that NADK was responsible for the killings. UNTAC was therefore considering setting up a technical advisory committee to gather factual information for discussion at SNC.

SECURITY COUNCIL ACTION (November)

Following its consideration of the Secretary-General's report, the Security Council, on 30 November, adopted **resolution 792(1992)**.

The Security Council,

Reaffirming its resolutions 668(1990) of 20 September 1990, 717(1991) of 16 October 1991, 718(1991) of 31 October 1991, 728(1992) of 8 January 1992, 745(1992) of 28 February 1992, 766(1992) of 21 July 1992 and 783(1992) of 13 October 1992,

Taking note of the report of the Secretary-General dated 15 November 1992 in response to its resolution 783(1992),

Paying tribute to His Royal Highness Prince Norodom Sihanouk, President of the Supreme National Council, for his continuing efforts to restore peace and national unity in Cambodia,

Reaffirming its commitment to implement the Paris Agreements and its determination to maintain the implementation timetable of the peace process, leading to elections for a constituent assembly in April/May 1993, the adoption of a constitution and the formation of a new Cambodian Government thereafter,

Recognizing the need for all Cambodian parties, the States concerned and the Secretary-General to maintain close dialogue in order to implement the peace process effectively,

Recalling that all Cambodians have, in accordance with article 12 of the Agreement on a Comprehensive Political Settlement of the Cambodia Conflict, the right to determine their own political future through the free and fair election of a constituent assembly and that political parties wishing to participate in the election can be formed in accordance with paragraph 5 of annex 3 to the Agreement,

Noting the discussion during the consultations held in Peking on 7 and 8 November 1992 by the Co-Chairmen of the Paris Conference regarding a presidential election, and the views of the Co-Chairmen shared by the Secretary-General that such an election could contribute to the process of national reconciliation and help to reinforce the climate of stability in Cambodia,

Welcoming the achievements of the Special Representative of the Secretary-General and UNTAC in the implementation of the Paris Agreements,

Welcoming in particular the good progress made in voter registration,

Welcoming also the efforts of UNTAC to strengthen its relationship with the Supreme National Council (SNC) and its supervision and control over the existing administrative structures, *inter alia*, to ensure the widest possible agreement on essential regulations for elections, natural resources, rehabilitation, national heritage and human rights, on relations with the international financial institutions, and on the question of foreign residents and immigrants,

Noting also the efforts of UNTAC to address the concerns raised by the PDK, including steps to verify the withdrawal of all foreign forces, advisers and military personnel from Cambodia, close cooperation between UNTAC and the SNC as the embodiment of Cambodian sovereignty, the creation of Technical Advisory Committees to advise the SNC and UNTAC, the extension of UNTAC supervision and control over the five key administrative areas mandated in the Paris Agreements in the areas to which UNTAC has access, and the creation of Working Groups in these areas to enable the parties to be involved in and informed about UNTAC's activities in these five key areas,

Expressing its appreciation for the efforts of Japan and Thailand to find solutions to current problems relating to the implementation of the Paris Agreements,

Expressing also its appreciation for the efforts of the Co-Chairmen of the Paris Conference, in consultations with all parties pursuant to resolution 783(1992) to find a way to implement fully the Paris Agreements,

Deploring the failure of the PDK to meet its obligations under the Paris Agreements, notably as regards unrestricted access by UNTAC to the areas under PDK control for voter registration and other purposes of the Agreements and as regards the application of phase II of the cease-fire concerning cantonment and demobilization of its forces,

Deploring recent violations of the cease-fire and their implications for the security situation in Cambodia, emphasizing the importance of maintaining the cease-fire and calling on all parties to comply with their obligations in this regard,

Condemning attacks against UNTAC, in particular the recent firings upon UNTAC helicopters and on electoral registration personnel,

Concerned by the economic situation in Cambodia and its impact on the implementation of the Paris Agreements,

1. *Endorses* the report of the Secretary-General dated 15 November 1992;

2. *Confirms* that the election for a constituent assembly in Cambodia will be held not later than May 1993;

3. *Notes* the decision of the Secretary-General to instruct his Special Representative to make contingency plans for the organization and conduct by UNTAC of a presidential election, and moreover, noting that such an election must be held in conjunction with the planned election for a constituent assembly, requests the Secretary-General to submit any recommendations for the holding of such an election to the Council for decision;

4. *Calls upon* all Cambodian parties to cooperate fully with UNTAC to create a neutral political environment for the conduct of free and fair elections and prevent acts of harassment, intimidation and political violence;

5. *Determines* that UNTAC shall proceed with preparations for free and fair elections to be held in April/May 1993 in all areas of Cambodia to which UNTAC has full and free access as at 31 January 1993;

6. *Calls on* the Supreme National Council to continue to meet regularly under the chairmanship of His Royal Highness Prince Norodom Sihanouk;

7. *Condemns* the failure by the PDK to comply with its obligations;

8. *Demands* that the PDK fulfil immediately its obligations under the Paris Agreements; that it facilitate

without delay full deployment of UNTAC in the areas under its control; that it not impede voter registration in those areas; that it not impede the activities of other political parties in those areas; and that it implement fully phase II of the cease-fire, particularly cantonment and demobilization, as well as all other aspects of the Paris Agreements, taking into account that all parties in Cambodia have the same obligations to implement the Paris Agreements;

9. *Urges* the PDK to join fully in the implementation of the Paris Agreements, including the electoral provisions, and requests the Secretary-General and States concerned to remain ready to continue dialogue with the PDK for this purpose;

10. *Calls on* those concerned to ensure that measures are taken, consistent with the provisions of article VII of annex 2 to the Paris Agreements, to prevent the supply of petroleum products to the areas occupied by any Cambodian party not complying with the military provisions of those Agreements and requests the Secretary-General to examine the modalities of such measures;

11. *Undertakes* to consider appropriate measures to be implemented should the PDK obstruct the implementation of the peace plan, such as the freezing of the assets held by the PDK outside Cambodia;

12. *Invites* UNTAC to establish all necessary border checkpoints, requests neighbouring States to cooperate fully in the establishment and maintenance of those checkpoints and requests the Secretary-General to undertake immediate consultations with States concerned regarding their establishment and operation;

13. *Supports* the decision of the Supreme National Council dated 22 September 1992 to set a moratorium on the export of logs from Cambodia in order to protect Cambodia's natural resources; requests States, especially neighbouring States, to respect this moratorium by not importing such logs; and requests UNTAC to take appropriate measures to secure the implementation of such moratorium;

14. *Requests* the Supreme National Council to consider the adoption of a similar moratorium on the export of minerals and gems in order to protect Cambodia's natural resources;

15. *Demands* that all parties comply with their obligations to observe the cease-fire and calls upon them to exercise restraint;

16. *Requests* UNTAC to continue to monitor the cease-fire and to take effective measures to prevent the recurrence or escalation of fighting in Cambodia, as well as incidents of banditry and arms smuggling;

17. *Demands also* that all parties take all action necessary to safeguard the lives and the security of UNTAC personnel throughout Cambodia including by issuing immediate instructions to this effect to their commanders forthwith and reporting their action to the Special Representative;

18. *Requests* the Secretary-General to consider the implications for the electoral process of the failure by the PDK to canton and demobilize its forces and, in response to this situation, to take all appropriate steps to ensure the successful implementation of the electoral process;

19. *Requests* the Secretary-General to investigate and report upon the implications for security in post-election Cambodia of the possible incomplete implementation

of the disarmament and demobilization provisions of the Paris Agreements;

20. *Invites* the States and international organizations providing economic assistance to Cambodia to convene a meeting to review the current state of economic assistance to Cambodia in the wake of the Conference on Reconstruction and Rehabilitation of Cambodia held in Tokyo in June 1992;

21. *Requests* the Secretary-General to report to the Council as soon as possible and no later than 15 February 1993 on the implementation of this resolution, and on any further measures that may be necessary and appropriate to ensure the realization of the fundamental objectives of the Paris Agreements;

22. *Decides* to remain actively seized of the matter.

Security Council resolution 792(1992)

30 November 1992   Meeting 3143   14-0-1

6-nation draft (S/24865).

Sponsors: Belgium, France, Japan, Russian Federation, United Kingdom, United States.

Vote in Council as follows:

In favour: Austria, Belgium, Cape Verde, Ecuador, France, Hungary, India, Japan, Morocco, Russian Federation, United Kingdom, United States, Venezuela, Zimbabwe.

Against: None.

Abstaining: China.

Explaining its abstention, China said it agreed with some of the elements of the draft resolution, such as the call on the parties to fulfil their commitments to the cease-fire and to exercise restraint. It also contained elements, however, that China felt were at variance with the Paris agreements: sanctions and a three-party election. The first would further increase differences and sharpen contradictions, and thus could lead to new, complicated problems. The second could have possible adverse consequences, regarding which China was deeply anxious. It added that sanctions could affect neighbouring States, in which case their sovereignty should be respected and their opinions on the matter fully heeded.

Financing (December)

In December 1992,[37] the Secretary-General submitted a report to the General Assembly containing details of additional resource requirements for UNTAC, including updated information on its financial performance.

The report indicated outstanding assessments, as at 31 October, of $4,935,000 for UNAMIC and $210,928,300 for UNTAC, or a combined total of $215,863,300. As ACABQ was later informed during its review of the report, that total had been reduced to $215,211,000 as at 30 November.

Voluntary contributions in kind were received as follows: three medium transport aircraft and six utility helicopters with an estimated value of $29.9 million, which had been budgeted for; 1.5 million meals with an estimated value of $570,000, not budgeted for; and air ambulance service, not utilized during the period under review. Other contributions (television sets, videotape recorders, portable generators plus spare parts, emergency health kits) were currently of undetermined value.

The financial performance of UNTAC for the period 1 November 1991 to 31 October 1992 showed a revised apportionment for the combined UNAMIC and UNTAC operations of $677,215,400 gross ($672,215,300 net) compared to the initial apportionment of $839,561,200 gross ($833,156,300 net), resulting in an unencumbered balance of $162,345,800 gross ($160,941,000 net) for the period. That balance was accounted for in large part by substantial savings under premises and accommodation ($81.3 million), late deployment of military contingents ($23.8 million) and of international and local staff ($10.6 million), and savings in air and surface freight ($26.7 million).

The Secretary-General estimated the requirements for the nine-month period from 1 November 1992 to 31 July 1993 at $925,802,500 gross ($906,632,100 net). The requirements were indicated separately for the six-month period from 1 November 1992 to 30 April 1993 in the amount of $633,961,200 gross ($620,808,500 net) and the subsequent three-month period from 1 May to 31 July 1993 in the amount of $291,841,300 gross ($285,823,600 net).

The revised cost estimates for the period from 1 November 1991 to 31 July 1993 amounted to $1,603,018,000 gross ($1,578,847,500 net), representing a reduction of $118,578,700 gross ($120,665,100 net) from the initial cost estimates submitted in May.[25]

In addition, the Secretary-General noted that contingency plans were being drawn up for the organization and conduct by UNTAC of an election for a head of State of Cambodia, to be held in conjunction with the planned election for a constituent assembly. That would require, in due course, Security Council authorization and additional resources.

In summary, the Secretary-General recommended: an appropriation, and apportionment, of $633,961,200 gross ($620,808,500 net) for the continued operation of UNTAC from 1 November 1992 to 30 April 1993; a decision to credit to Member States the unencumbered balance of $162,345,800 gross ($160,941,000 net) in respect of the period 1 November 1991 to 31 October 1992 against their assessments for the period beginning on 1 November 1992; and commitment authorization in the amount of $291,841,300 gross ($285,823,600 net) for UNTAC's continued operation from 1 May to 31 July 1993 and for the apportionment thereof.

In its review of the Secretary-General's report and the additional information provided by his representatives, ACABQ[38] took account of the unencumbered balance from the initial period and identified a number of budget items where savings could be achieved. It thus reduced the cost

estimates by $200 million, recommending that the Assembly appropriate and assess an additional amount of $483,961,200 gross ($470,808,500 net) for the continued operation of UNTAC from 1 November 1992 to 30 April 1993; and provide commitment authorization not to exceed $241,841,300 gross ($235,823,600 net) for 1 May to 31 July 1993, with prior ACABQ concurrence.

ACABQ further recommended that the Secretary-General be permitted the usual flexibility to transfer credits between items of expenditure as necessary, adding that, should he experience difficulties with the reduced level of resources, he might submit additional requirements to address any eventual shortfall. ·ACABQ also concurred with the Secretary-General's proposal for the disposition of the unencumbered balance.

GENERAL ASSEMBLY ACTION

Acting on the recommendation of the Fifth Committee, the General Assembly, on 22 December 1992, adopted **resolution 47/209** without vote.

Financing of the United Nations Transitional Authority in Cambodia

The General Assembly,

Recalling its resolutions 46/18 of 20 November 1991, 46/198 A of 20 December 1991, 46/198 B and 46/222 A of 14 February 1992 and 46/222 B of 22 May 1992,

Bearing in mind Security Council resolution 717(1991) of 16 October 1991, by which the Council established the United Nations Advance Mission in Cambodia, and Council resolution 728(1992) of 8 January 1992, by which the Council approved the proposal of the Secretary-General to expand the mandate of the Advance Mission, especially with regard to the provision of assistance in mine clearing by Cambodians,

Bearing in mind also Security Council resolution 718(1991) of 31 October 1991, by which the Council expressed its full support for the agreements on a comprehensive political settlement of the Cambodia conflict (Paris agreements), signed in Paris on 23 October 1991, and Council resolution 745(1992) of 28 February 1992, by which the Council established the United Nations Transitional Authority in Cambodia, in accordance with the report of the Secretary-General of 19 February 1992, for a period not to exceed eighteen months,

Taking note of Security Council resolution 766(1992) of 21 July 1992, by which the Council approved the efforts of the Secretary-General and his Special Representative to continue to implement the Paris agreements despite the difficulties,

Taking note also of Security Council resolutions 783(1992) of 13 October 1992 and 792(1992) of 30 November 1992, by which the Council confirmed that the electoral process should be carried out in accordance with the timetable laid down in the implementation plan and thus that the election for a constituent assembly would be held no later than May 1993,

Taking further note of Security Council resolution 792(1992), by which the Council requested the Secretary-General to submit any recommendations for the holding of a presidential election to the Council for decision,

Having considered the report of the Secretary-General on the financing of the United Nations Transitional Authority in Cambodia and the related report of the Advisory Committee on Administrative and Budgetary Questions,

Noting that the revised budgetary estimates for the Advance Mission and for the Transitional Authority as contained in the report of the Secretary-General amount to 1,603,018,000 United States dollars gross (1,578,847,500 dollars net) for the period from 1 November 1991 to 31 July 1993, a reduction of 118,578,700 dollars gross (120,665,100 dollars net) from the initial cost estimates contained in the previous report of the Secretary-General,

Noting also that the duration of the mandate of the Advance Mission extended from the signature of the Paris agreements until the establishment of the Transitional Authority by the Security Council, at which time the Advance Mission was absorbed into the Transitional Authority,

Recognizing that the costs of the Advance Mission and of the Transitional Authority are expenses of the Organization to be borne by Member States in accordance with Article 17, paragraph 2, of the Charter of the United Nations,

Recognizing also that, in order to meet the expenditures caused by the Advance Mission and the Transitional Authority, a different procedure is required from the one applied to meet expenditures of the regular budget of the United Nations,

Taking into account the fact that the economically more developed countries are in a position to make relatively larger contributions and that the economically less developed countries have a relatively limited capacity to contribute towards such operations,

Bearing in mind the special responsibilities of the States permanent members of the Security Council, as indicated in General Assembly resolution 1874(S-IV) of 27 June 1963, in the financing of such operations,

Mindful of the fact that it is essential to provide the Transitional Authority with the necessary financial resources to enable it to fulfil its responsibilities under the relevant resolutions of the Security Council,

Noting with appreciation that voluntary contributions have been made to the Advance Mission and the Transitional Authority by certain Governments,

1. *Endorses* the observations and recommendations made by the Advisory Committee on Administrative and Budgetary Questions in its report;

2. *Urges* all Member States to make every possible effort to ensure payment of their assessed contributions to the United Nations Advance Mission in Cambodia and the United Nations Transitional Authority in Cambodia in full and on time;

3. *Decides*, at this stage, to appropriate, in accordance with the recommendation contained in paragraph 62 of the report of the Advisory Committee, an amount of 483,961,200 dollars gross (470,808,500 dollars net) for the continued operation of the Transitional Authority for the period from 1 November 1992 to 30 April 1993, in addition to the amount of 839,576,200 dollars gross (833,171,300 dollars net) already appropriated for the Advance Mission and the Transitional Authority;

4. *Decides also*, as an ad hoc arrangement, to apportion the amount of 483,961,200 dollars gross (470,808,500 dollars net) among Member States in accordance with the composition of groups set out in paragraphs 3 and 4 of General Assembly resolution 43/232 of 1 March 1989, as adjusted by the Assembly in its resolutions 44/192 B of 21 December 1989, 45/269 of 27 August 1991 and 46/198 A, and taking into account the scale of assessments for the years 1992, 1993 and 1994;

5. *Decides further* that, in accordance with the provisions of its resolution 973(X) of 15 December 1955, there shall be set off against the apportionment among Member States, as provided for in paragraph 4 above, their respective share in the Tax Equalization Fund of the estimated staff assessment income of 13,152,700 dollars approved for the Transitional Authority;

6. *Decides* that the unencumbered balance of 162,345,800 dollars gross (160,941,000 dollars net) in respect of the period from 1 November 1991 to 31 October 1992 shall be set off against the apportionment among Member States as provided for in paragraph 4 above;

7. *Authorizes* the Secretary-General to enter into commitments for the operation of the Transitional Authority at a rate not to exceed 241,841,300 dollars gross (235,823,600 dollars net) for the period from 1 May to 31 July 1993, subject to obtaining the prior concurrence of the Advisory Committee, the said amount to be apportioned among Member States in accordance with the scheme set out in the present resolution;

8. *Decides* to consider the contributions of Armenia, Azerbaijan, Bosnia and Herzegovina, Croatia, Georgia, Kazakhstan, Kyrgyzstan, the Republic of Moldova, San Marino, Slovenia, Tajikistan, Turkmenistan and Uzbekistan to the Transitional Authority in accordance with the rates of assessment to be adopted by the General Assembly for these Member States at its forty-seventh session;

9. *Invites* the new Member States listed in paragraph 8 above to make advance payments against their assessed contributions, to be determined;

10. *Invites* voluntary contributions to the Transitional Authority in cash and in the form of services and supplies acceptable to the Secretary-General, to be administered, as appropriate, in accordance with the procedure established by the General Assembly in its resolutions 43/230 of 21 December 1988, 44/192 A of 21 December 1989 and 45/258 of 3 May 1991;

11. *Requests* the Secretary-General to take all necessary action to ensure that the Transitional Authority is administered with a maximum of efficiency and economy;

12. *Also requests* the Secretary-General to submit to the General Assembly at its forty-eighth session a detailed performance report on the budget of the Transitional Authority, including the planned disposal of the assets of the operation;

13. *Decides* to include in the provisional agenda of its forty-eighth session the item entitled "Financing of the United Nations Transitional Authority in Cambodia".

General Assembly resolution 47/209

22 December 1992   Meeting 93   Adopted without vote

Approved by Fifth Committee (A/47/824) without vote, 19 December (meeting 50); draft by Chairman (A/C.5/46/L.15); agenda item 123.
Meeting numbers. GA 47th session: 5th Committee 46, 50; plenary 93.

Personnel safety

After consultations among the members of the Security Council, its President, in a statement to the press on 2 December 1992, expressed the Council's deep concern and outrage over the increasing number of attacks against United Nations personnel serving in various peace-keeping operations. Among these were two military and four naval observers serving with UNTAC, who were illegally detained by NADK in Kompong Thom province on 1 December. An UNTAC helicopter, sent to assist in their release, was fired upon, injuring a military observer on board. Also, on 2 December, six UNTAC civilian police monitors were injured in two land-mine incidents in Siem Reap province. Another instance of illegal detention occurred on 20 December, followed by release the next day.

SECURITY COUNCIL ACTION

The Council met on 22 December and, following consultations among its members, the President was authorized to make the following statement[39] on behalf of the Council:

Meeting number. SC 3153.

"The Security Council strongly condemns the illegal detention of UNTAC personnel by elements of the Party of Democratic Kampuchea and acts of threat and intimidation against these personnel. It demands that such actions and any other hostile acts against UNTAC cease immediately, and that all parties take all action necessary to safeguard the lives and the security of UNTAC personnel throughout Cambodia.

"The Council urges all the parties to abide scrupulously by their obligations under the Paris Agreement to cooperate fully with UNTAC and to respect all the relevant resolutions of the Security Council."

REFERENCES

[1]YUN 1991, p. 155. [2]Ibid., p. 158. [3]S/23415. [4]S/23414. [5]S/23428. [6]S/23429. [7]A/46/867. [8]A/46/855. [9]YUN 1991, p. 869, GA res. 46/187, 20 Dec. 1991. [10]A/46/873. [11]YUN 1991, p. 155, SC res. 718(1991), 31 Oct. 1991. [12]S/23613. [13]S/23613/Add.1. [14]S/23696. [15]S/23695. [16]S/23775. [17]S/23773 & S/23774. [18]S/24397 & S/24706. [19]S/24398 & S/24707. [20]S/23458. [21]S/23459. [22]A/46/235/Add.1. [23]A/46/874. [24]A/46/235. [25]A/46/903. [26]A/46/916. [27]S/23870 & Corr.1,2. [28]YUN 1966, pp. 423 & 419, GA res. 2200 A (XXI), annex, 16 Dec. 1966. [29]S/24090. [30]S/23928. [31]S/24091. [32]S/24286. [33]A/47/285-S/24183. [34]S/24578. [35]S/24607. [36]S/24800. [37]A/47/733. [38]A/47/763. [39]S/25003.

South Asia

Papua New Guinea–Solomon Islands

On 17 September 1992,[1] Solomon Islands drew to the attention of the President of the Security Council an act of aggression by the armed forces of neighbouring Papua New Guinea that violated its territorial integrity and caused the death of two of its citizens, the abduction of another and the wounding of a child. It requested the Council to take several actions, including a call on Papua New Guinea to offer a public apology, to return the abducted citizen, to pay compensation for liabilities resulting from the aggression and to seek a peaceful resolution to the crisis, as well as a request for an investigation of the incident by the good offices of the Secretary-General.

The incident, which occurred on 12 September, was a spillover from an ongoing secessionist movement on Bougainville, an island in Papua New Guinea's North Solomons province. Papua New Guinea, which withdrew from the island as a result of an uprising in 1989, imposed a strict military blockade in 1990 that resulted in continuing allegations of human rights violations (see PART THREE, Chapter X).

The Council informally considered the matter on 24 September, when the President reported that Papua New Guinea had already addressed several of the points raised by Solomon Islands and had proposed that the two Governments enter into a formal agreement governing all aspects of their relations, a fact confirmed by Papua New Guinea on 29 September.[2] The Council concurred that the matter should be resolved through bilateral talks as quickly as possible.

To encourage such a dialogue and to express United Nations concern for the security of small island States, the Secretary-General, on his own initiative, dispatched a good-will mission to Solomon Islands and neighbouring States from 2 to 15 November.

In December, Solomon Islands informed the United Nations that the two Governments were in the process of agreeing to resume their dialogue in January 1993 at several levels. The talks would be aimed at an eventual formal agreement on the maintenance of their common maritime borders.

REFERENCES

[1]S/24572. [2]S/24603.

Southern and Western Asia

Afghanistan situation

Early in 1992, the Secretary-General, through his Personal Representative in Afghanistan and Pakistan, set in motion arrangements for the convening of an Afghan gathering for the purpose of reaching agreement on a transition period and mechanism that would lead to the establishment of a broad-based Government through free and fair elections. This was in response to the 1991 General Assembly request[1] that he and his Personal Representative continue to encourage and facilitate the early realization of a comprehensive political settlement in Afghanistan in accordance with the provisions of the 1988 Agreements on the Settlement of the Situation Relating to Afghanistan.[2]

Those efforts, however, were quickly overtaken by political and military events in Afghanistan that led to the installation of a new Government in April, when the proposed Afghan gathering was to take place. The change of government led not only to massive voluntary repatriations of Afghans from Iran and Pakistan, but also to wide-scale fighting among various factions that erupted in July and August in and around Kabul, accompanied by heavy rocket attacks on the city. The repatriations increased the country's humanitarian needs. The assault on Kabul caused a large number of casualties, vast material damage and hundreds of thousands of city residents to flee their homes and become displaced.

(For information on emergency international assistance for the reconstruction of war-stricken Afghanistan and the activities of the Office for the Coordination of United Nations Economic and Humanitarian Assistance Programmes relating to Afghanistan; on human rights violations there; and on the Afghan refugee situation, see PART THREE, Chapters III, X and XV, respectively.)

Statements by the Secretary-General. In a statement delivered at Geneva on 10 April, the Secretary-General, referring to the round of consultations carried out by his Personal Representative, stated that the proposal for convening an Afghan gathering had received widespread support among the Afghans consulted, including political, religious and tribal leaders, resistance commanders and prominent Afghan personalities residing in Afghanistan, in Islamabad and Peshawar (Pakistan) and in Tehran (Iran), as well as Afghans residing outside the region. He welcomed as a major contribution to the peace process President Mohammed Najibullah's announcement on 18 March[3] of his decision not to insist on his personal participation in the proposed Afghan gathering and of his agreement that, once an understanding was reached through the United Nations process for the establishment of an interim Government in Kabul, all powers and all executive authority would be transferred to that Government as of the first day of the transition period.

An agreement in principle had accordingly been reached to establish, as soon as possible, a pre-transition council composed of impartial personalities to which all powers and all executive authority would be transferred. An Afghan gathering, combined with the one originally envisaged, would be organized to work out arrangements for the transition period and establishment of the interim Government. An understanding had also been reached that once the council assumed power in Kabul, there would be a cessation of hostilities, a declaration of general amnesty, guarantees of safety and security for all Afghans, respect for human rights, protection of property, and opening of all major routes to commercial traffic.

The Secretary-General urged appropriate international guarantees to enable the council to carry out effectively its responsibilities and that all Governments concerned recognize and support it as the legitimate authority in Afghanistan during the transition period until the interim Government was established.

The Secretary-General referred to the humanitarian response by Iran, Pakistan and the United States to his appeal of 6 April for food and funds to alleviate the suffering in Afghanistan, and urged all other Governments to respond likewise. He also urged all Afghans to set aside their differences and exercise maximum restraint in order to safeguard lives and the country's unity and territorial integrity.

In a further statement of 16 April, the Secretary-General expressed concern about events that occurred on the night of 15/16 April, including the aborted departure of President Najibullah and his taking refuge in United Nations premises in Kabul, creating a delicate situation. The Secretary-General expected that the safety of all United Nations personnel would be respected and that they would be allowed freedom of movement in and out of the country as their responsibilities required.

SECURITY COUNCIL ACTION

After consultations held on 16 April 1992, the President of the Security Council issued the following statement[4] on behalf of the Council members:

"The members of the Security Council strongly endorse the statement on the situation in Afghanistan issued by the Secretary-General on 10 April 1992 and share the Secretary-General's concern about the recent events there expressed in his statement of 16 April 1992. In this regard, it is imperative that all concerned display restraint and support the efforts of his Personal Representative towards a political solution to the Afghanistan crisis, to which there is no viable alternative. Such a solution has been proposed by the Secretary-General with the objective of bringing an end to bloodshed and violence, promoting national reconciliation, and safeguarding the unity and territorial integrity of Afghanistan. Failure to do so could only perpetuate the suffering of the Afghan people. The members of the Council urge all parties in Afghanistan to assure the safety of all, especially United Nations personnel and their complete freedom of movement and the safety of the personnel of all diplomatic missions, as well as the safe departure of those who have chosen to leave."

Communication. Afghanistan, on 17 April,[5] referring to the Security Council's statement of 16 April, acknowledged that there was no alternative to a political settlement of the country's situation. It stated its conviction that, with Mohammed Najibullah having stepped aside, the ground had been paved for the cessation of war and establishment of peace in the country. In full compliance with the international agreements and conventions on diplomatic rights and immunities, Afghanistan would spare no effort to ensure the security, safety and full freedom of movement of United Nations employees and diplomatic personnel. It would further spare no effort in cooperating towards realizing the Council's urgings and requested the cooperation of the *Jehadi* formations and local commanders in that respect.

Report of the Secretary-General. In response to a 1991 General Assembly request,[1] the Secretary-General submitted a report in November 1992[6] on the progress of his efforts and those of his Personal Representative towards a settlement of the protracted conflict in Afghanistan.

He stated that his Personal Representative, in addition to the round of bilateral consultations he had undertaken with Afghan representatives, held tripartite consultations at Tehran on 30 March with the Minister for Foreign Affairs of Iran and the Minister of State for Foreign Affairs of Pakistan. He also held regular consultations with the Special Representative of the Secretary-General of the Organization of the Islamic Conference. The object was to convene an Afghan gathering during the second half of April, at Geneva or Vienna, inviting some 150 middle-level representatives, acceptable to all sides, from all segments of Afghan society. Those efforts were outpaced, however, by accelerated political and military events in Kabul.

Following President Najibullah's resignation and refuge in United Nations premises on 16 April, the Islamic Unity Party of Afghanistan, an alliance of various Afghan resistance groups based in Tehran, including the *mujahideen*, was formed. On 24 April, most of the Afghan resistance groups concluded the Peshawar Agreement, according to which the power vested in the Government of the Republic of Afghanistan was to be transferred to the Islamic State of Afghanistan, with Sebghatullah Mojaddedi, leader of the Afghan National Liberation Front, as Acting President and Chairman of a 51-member *Jehadi* Council, for a term of two months. That transfer took place on 28 April at a ceremony in Kabul, with officials of the outgoing Government in attendance. The new leadership proclaimed the establishment of the Islamic State of Afghanistan, declared general amnesty and introduced several institutional changes.

On 28 June, Burhanuddin Rabbani, leader of the Islamic League of Afghanistan, succeeded Mojaddedi. Under the Peshawar Agreement, he was to serve concurrently as head of the Islamic Leadership Council and as head of the Islamic State of Afghanistan for four months. Thereafter, an Islamic Council would be formed, which would decide on the form of the future interim Government, with the understanding that it would hold elections within 18 months to two years.

In the meantime, the Secretary-General held discussions on the Afghanistan situation with the President and Foreign Minister of Pakistan (25 April), as well as of Iran (26 and 27 April), and with the Islamic Unity Party of Afghanistan. Apart from emphasizing the imperative of promoting national unity and safeguarding Afghanistan's territorial integrity, sovereignty and independence, the Secretary-General also emphasized the need for an immediate cease-fire, a declaration of general amnesty for all, respect for human rights and guarantees for personal safety, security and property. He further reiterated the readiness of the United Nations to assist in the country's reconstruction and rehabilitation.

Despite the establishment of the interim Council, fighting and violence escalated in and around Kabul in July and August, indicating that a national consensus had not been achieved. On 10 August, the Secretary-General appealed to the warring factions to lay down their arms and begin a dialogue forthwith, as well as to neighbouring Governments to use their influence to help end the tragedy. He asked that the safety and protection of United Nations personnel be assured if their humanitarian and other operations in Afghanistan were to continue. The Security Council repeated that appeal on 12 August (see below).

Owing to the deteriorating situation, the Secretary-General, on 22 August, instructed the remaining United Nations personnel to evacuate Kabul temporarily. In return for his assurances that he would spare no effort to mobilize international humanitarian assistance to the Afghan people, President Rabbani assured him that the Afghan Government would ensure the safety and security of all diplomatic missions and United Nations personnel, premises and property.

At the same time, the Secretary-General's Personal Representative cooperated with interested Governments in encouraging a temporary cease-fire to allow the safe evacuation of diplomatic personnel from Kabul. A cease-fire was agreed on 29 August, although scattered fighting continued in parts of the city. A peace commission was created and a neutral Afghan buffer force was deployed between warring factions. Improved security permitted several fact-finding and technical assistance missions of United Nations international staff to visit Kabul for consultations with government officials and to assist in restoring basic services.

On 31 October, the Afghan Leadership Council extended President Rabbani's term for an additional period of 45 days and decided that his main task was to organize and convene the Council of Learned People Who Can Resolve and Decide on 10 December.

The Secretary-General observed that operational constraints continued to be experienced owing to unstable security situations in the country. Although United Nations international staff in Kabul had been withdrawn, the United Nations had strengthened its presence in other provinces. He appealed for the release of prisoners of war, Afghan and non-Afghan, including former USSR servicemen, who continued to be held by various groups, stating that the International Committee of the Red Cross (ICRC) stood ready to provide assistance in that regard. In his view, the general amnesty declared in April should apply to all. International efforts should focus on the country's massive needs in the humanitarian, economic and social sectors, to enable the Afghans to consolidate peace with rehabilitation and reconstruction.

SECURITY COUNCIL ACTION

Following Security Council consultations on 12 August 1992, the Council President made the following statement[7] to the media on behalf of Council members:

"The members of the Security Council express their utmost concern over the wide-scale fighting which has broken out in Kabul and which has already resulted in heavy loss of life and property, including to foreign missions and their personnel.

"The members of the Security Council urge that the Government of Afghanistan take every measure to ensure the safety and security of all diplomatic and international missions, as well as their personnel in Kabul, and call upon all those involved in the hostilities to cease such hostilities and establish the necessary conditions for the safe evacuation of foreign personnel."

Office of the Secretary-General in Afghanistan and Pakistan

The Office of the Secretary-General in Afghanistan and Pakistan[6] continued to assist the Secretary-General in his efforts towards a comprehensive political settlement in Afghanistan. The Office was headed by the Personal Representative of the Secretary-General in Afghanistan and Pakistan, Benon V. Sevan, who, after 7 August 1992, was succeeded by Sotirios Mousouris. The Office maintained two small headquarters units, one in Kabul and the other in Islamabad. The sub-office in Peshawar was closed on 30 June.

A Military Advisory Unit, comprising 10 military advisers from Austria, Canada, Denmark, Fiji, Finland, Ghana, Ireland, Nepal, Poland and Sweden, continued to provide the Personal Representative with military advice, as required, and maintained continuous assessment of the security situation in Afghanistan. The military advisers were temporarily detached, with the concurrence of their respective Governments, from the United Nations Truce Supervision Organization, the United Nations Disengagement Observer Force and the United Nations Interim Force in Lebanon.

REFERENCES

[1]YUN 1991, p. 161, GA res. 46/23, 5 Dec. 1991. [2]S/19835. [3]A/47/128. [4]S/23818. [5]A/47/165-S/23823. [6]A/47/705-S/24831. [7]S/24425.

Cyprus question

The Secretary-General continued in 1992 his mission of good offices in Cyprus, with the objective of achieving a comprehensive settlement between the Greek and Turkish Cypriot communities. Discussions were held with the leaders of the two communities as well as with government representatives of Greece and Turkey.

The Security Council twice extended the mandate of the United Nations Peace-keeping Force in Cyprus (UNFICYP), in June and December. The troop-contributing countries began reducing their contingents in the Force due to its deepening financial crisis.

Although the question of Cyprus was included in the agenda of the forty-seventh (1992) General Assembly session (**decisions 46/474** of 14 September and **47/402** of 18 September), it was not discussed, but the Assembly retained it on its agenda (**decision 47/467** of 23 December).

Cyprus and Turkey addressed communications to the Secretary-General on various aspects of the situation throughout the year. Those from Turkey forwarded letters from the Turkish Cypriot community signed by Osman Ertug as "representative of the Turkish Republic of Northern Cyprus" and those from Cyprus referred to George Vassiliou as President of the Republic of Cyprus.

On 2 April 1992, the Committee of Ministers of the Council of Europe decided to make public a report by the European Commission of Human Rights of October 1983 regarding Application No. 8007/77, Cyprus v. Turkey. The report stated, *inter alia*, that the recognition by Turkey of the Turkish Cypriot administration in the northern part of the island as the "Turkish Federated State of Cyprus" did not affect the continuing existence of the Republic of Cyprus as a single State and that, consequently, the "Turkish Federated State of Cyprus" could not be regarded as an entity which exercised "jurisdiction" over any part of Cyprus, within the meaning of article 1 of the European Convention for the Protection of Human Rights and Fundamental Freedoms. Cyprus presented excerpts of the report in May[1] and the full report in September.[2]

Between July and November, Turkey and Cyprus transmitted a series of communications to the Secretary-General concerning the question of human rights in Cyprus,[3] and a resolution on the demographic structure of the Cypriot communities, based on the report of the Council of Europe's Committee on Migration, Refugees and Demography.[4] The resolution by the Parliamentary Assembly of the Council of Europe requested the Republic of Cyprus and the Turkish Cypriot administration to keep the arrival of aliens on the island under strict control, and appealed to the latter to reconsider its legislation on naturalization. It stated that the population in the southern part of the island had increased by 13.7 per cent since 1974, from 505,700 to 575,000 at the end of 1990; in the northern part, the population increase was 48.35 per cent, from 115,600 to 171,500.

In November, Mr. Vassiliou indicated his acceptance of the confidence-building measures proposed by the Secretary-General[5] and reiterated his willingness to proceed with the demilitarization of Cyprus.[6] If complete demilitarization was not in itself sufficient guarantee for the security of the Turkish Cypriot community, he would be ready to accept a United Nations force.

In order to put the proposal of demilitarization into a proper context, Mr. Ertug pointed out that, according to the Greek Cypriot Defence Minister, the Greek Cypriot National Guard was equipped with sophisticated weaponry and was not prepared for the static defence of Cyprus, but poised for a prompt and decisive victory in the island.[7]

Oscar Camilión continued his functions as the Secretary-General's Special Representative in Cyprus.

Secretary-General's good offices

The Secretary-General's mission of good offices in Cyprus focused on ensuring an overall framework agreement between the Greek Cypriot and Turkish Cypriot communities, based on a set of ideas that emerged from talks held in 1991.[8] Those ideas provided for the establishment of a bi-communal and bi-zonal federation represented in international relations as a single, sovereign and independent State comprising two politically equal communities; outlined the structure and functioning of its legislative, executive and judicial branches of government; elaborated on the guarantees of human rights and security of both communities; and provided for transitional arrangements to implement such an agreement.

Outstanding issues to which a solution needed to be found were territorial adjustments and displaced persons. Despite differences on those and other issues, however, the leaders of both communities expressed willingness to continue their dialogue.

Report of the Secretary-General (April). In an April 1992 report,[9] the Secretary-General recounted the efforts made during the preceding two years to prepare a set of ideas for an overall framework agreement. He summarized the ideas that had emerged from extended contact with the parties, stating that, in his opinion, they provided elements of a fair solution. He added that if similar progress could be made on the outstanding issues, in particular territorial adjustments and displaced persons, an overall solution would be within reach.

In order to review the Cyprus question, the Secretary-General met in January with the leaders of the two communities. He stressed the importance of the momentum achieved in 1991 and reiterated the need to proceed with discussions in order to complete the set of ideas for an overall framework agreement. Both Greece and Turkey had assured him of their full support.

A first round of talks in February and March, however, did not succeed in bringing matters forward; on the contrary, there was regression in some areas. In his conclusions, the Secretary-General emphasized that it was vital that the parties be willing to clarify equally all the elements of the agreement and adhere to the principles laid down by the Security Council; the current effort could not be expected to continue indefinitely if all concerned were not willing to contribute to a compromise solution. The usefulness of the parties' endorsement of Council resolutions was undermined by the interpretations they had given them; it was, however, essential that their views be in harmony with the Council's position.

The lack of progress in his mission of good offices was compounded by developments related to UNFICYP (see below), the Secretary-General added, which made it unlikely that the United Nations would be able for much longer to maintain its peace-keeping presence in Cyprus on the current scale.

SECURITY COUNCIL ACTION (April and July)

On 10 April 1992, having considered the Secretary-General's report, the Security Council adopted **resolution 750(1992)** unanimously.

The Security Council,

Having considered the report of the Secretary-General of 3 April 1992 on his mission of good offices in Cyprus,

Reaffirming its previous resolutions on Cyprus,

Noting with concern that there has been no progress in completing the set of ideas for an overall framework agreement since the Secretary-General's report of 8 October 1991 and that in some areas there has even been regression,

Welcoming the assurances given to the Secretary-General over the past two months by the leaders of the two communities and the Prime Ministers of Greece and Turkey of their desire to cooperate with him and his representatives,

1. *Commends* the Secretary-General for his efforts, and expresses its appreciation for his report;

2. *Reaffirms* the position, set out in resolutions 649(1990) of 12 March 1990 and 716(1991) of 11 October 1991, that a Cyprus settlement must be based on a State of Cyprus with a single sovereignty and international personality and a single citizenship, with its independence and territorial integrity safeguarded, and comprising two politically equal communities as defined in paragraph 11 of the Secretary-General's report in a bicommunal and bi-zonal federation, and that such a settlement must exclude union in whole or in part with any other country or any form of partition or secession;

3. *Calls again upon* the parties to adhere fully to these principles and to negotiate without introducing concepts that are at variance with them;

4. *Endorses* the set of ideas described in paragraphs 17 to 25 and 27 of the Secretary-General's report as an appropriate basis for reaching an overall framework agreement, subject to the work that needs to be done on the outstanding issues, in particular on territorial adjustments and displaced persons, being brought to a conclusion as an integrated package mutually agreed upon by both communities;

5. *Requests* all concerned to cooperate fully with the Secretary-General and his representatives in clarifying without delay these outstanding issues;

6. *Reaffirms* that the Secretary-General's mission of good offices is with the two communities, whose participation in the process is on an equal footing to assure the well-being and security of both communities;

7. *Decides* to remain seized of the Cyprus question on an ongoing and direct basis in support of the effort to complete the set of ideas referred to in paragraph 4 above and to conclude an overall framework agreement;

8. *Requests* the Secretary-General to pursue his intensive efforts to complete the set of ideas referred to in paragraph 4 above during May and June 1992, to keep the Council closely informed of his efforts and to seek the Council's direct support whenever necessary;

9. *Continues to believe* that, following the satisfactory conclusion of the Secretary-General's intensive efforts to complete the set of ideas referred to in paragraph 4 above, the convening of a high-level international meeting chaired by the Secretary-General in which the two communities and Greece and Turkey would participate represents an effective mechanism for concluding an overall framework agreement;

10. *Also requests* the Secretary-General to submit a full report to the Council on the outcome of his efforts by July 1992 at the latest and to make specific recommendations for overcoming any outstanding difficulty;

11. *Reaffirms* the important mandate entrusted to the United Nations Peace-keeping Force in Cyprus and looks forward to receiving the report on the Force that the Secretary-General proposes to submit in May 1992.

Security Council resolution 750(1992)

10 April 1992   Meeting 3067   Adopted unanimously

Draft prepared in consultations among Council members (S/23797).

Following an oral report by the Secretary-General on 24 June on his mission of good offices, the Council met on 13 July in accordance with the understanding reached in its prior consultations. The President issued the following statement on behalf of the Council members:[10]

Meeting number. SC 3094.

"The Security Council recalls the oral report presented on 24 June 1992 on the Secretary-General's mission of good offices in Cyprus. It welcomes the separate meetings which the Secretary-General had with the leaders of the two communities from 18 to 23 June. It notes with satisfaction that the discussions focused on the issues of territorial adjustments and displaced persons and that the other six issues that make up the set of ideas on an overall framework agreement were also reviewed. It is unanimous in expressing its full support of the procedure adopted by the Secretary-General for implementing resolution 750(1992).

"The Council reaffirms its endorsement of the set of ideas as an appropriate basis for reaching an overall framework agreement as mentioned in paragraph 4 of resolution 750(1992).

"The Council notes with satisfaction the acceptance by the leaders of the two communities to resume on 15 July their meetings with the Secretary-General and to remain for such reasonable duration as may be necessary to complete the work.

"The Council considers that the forthcoming meetings represent a determining phase in the Secretary-General's effort and calls on both leaders to be ready to take the necessary decisions to reach agreement on each of the issues as dealt with in the set of ideas as an integrated whole on an overall framework agreement.

"The Council endorses the Secretary-General's intention to invite the two leaders to a joint meeting as soon as the proximity talks reveal that the two sides are within agreement range on the set of ideas; and, subject to the successful completion of the work of the joint meeting, to convene an international high-level meeting to conclude the overall framework agreement.

"The Council calls upon all concerned to fulfil their responsibilities and cooperate fully with the Secretary-General to ensure the success of these meetings.

"The Council reaffirms its decision to remain seized of the Cyprus question on an ongoing and direct basis in support of the effort to complete the set of ideas and to conclude an overall framework agreement.

"The Council requests that the Secretary-General provide it with an ongoing assessment of the progress being made at the meetings beginning on 15 July so as to enable the Council to determine, as the talks unfold, how it might best lend its full and direct support.

"The Council looks forward to receiving at the conclusion of these meetings a full report from the Secretary-General as requested in operative paragraph 10 of resolution 750(1992)."

Report of the Secretary-General (August). Reporting to the Council on 21 August,[11] the Secretary-General described the proximity talks he conducted with the two leaders in New York from 18 to 23 June and from 15 July to 11 August, as well as the joint meetings under his chairmanship which began on 12 August with the purpose of negotiating an agreement on the basis of the set of ideas, including the Secretary-General's suggestions regarding territorial adjustments and displaced persons. The meetings adjourned on 14 August and were to be reconvened in October.

The Secretary-General felt that the set of ideas, which was annexed to his report, was now sufficiently developed to enable the two sides to reach an overall agreement. On territorial adjustments, substantive discussions had taken place for the first time, but the Turkish Cypriot side needed to show willingness to foresee an adjustment more or less in line with the suggestions embodied in the set of ideas.

While accepting certain principles contained in the set, the Turkish Cypriot side expressed apprehension about the impact of the suggested adjustments on its community and indicated that its position formulated in 1984 and 1986 remained unchanged. The Greek Cypriot side agreed to negotiate an agreement on the basis provided by the set, though it did not consider the suggested territorial adjustments to be equitable.

The Secretary-General said there was no question of the population living in the affected area becoming displaced or refugees, as no one would be required to move; those who wished to move to the federated State that would come under Turkish Cypriot administration would only do so when adequate housing and economic rehabilitation had been provided.

Continuation of the status quo not being a viable option, the Secretary-General concluded that, should no agreement emerge from the talks scheduled for October, it would be necessary for the Security Council seriously to consider alternative courses of action for resolving the Cyprus problem.

SECURITY COUNCIL ACTION (August)

The Security Council on 26 August unanimously adopted **resolution 774(1992)**.

The Security Council,

Having considered the report of the Secretary-General of 21 August 1992 on his mission of good offices in Cyprus,

Reaffirming all its previous resolutions on Cyprus,

Noting that some progress has been achieved, in particular the acceptance by both sides of the right of return and the right to property, and in a narrowing of the gap by both sides on territorial adjustments,

Expressing concern nevertheless that it has not yet been possible, for reasons explained in the report, to achieve the goals set out in resolution 750(1992),

1. *Endorses* the report of the Secretary-General and commends him for his efforts;

2. *Reaffirms* its position that a Cyprus settlement must be based on a State of Cyprus with a single sovereignty and international personality and a single citizenship, with its independence and territorial integrity safeguarded, and comprising two politically equal communities as defined in paragraph 11 of the Secretary-General's report of 3 April 1992 in a bi-communal and bi-zonal federation, and that such a settlement must exclude union in whole or in part with any other country or any form of partition or secession;

3. *Endorses* the set of ideas including suggested territorial adjustments reflected in the map contained in the annex to the Secretary-General's report as the basis for reaching an overall framework agreement;

4. *Agrees* with the Secretary-General that the set of ideas as an integrated whole has now been sufficiently developed to enable the two sides to reach an overall agreement;

5. *Calls on* the parties to manifest the necessary political will and to address in a positive manner the observations of the Secretary-General for resolving the issues covered in his report;

6. *Urges* the parties, when they resume their face-to-face talks with the Secretary-General on 26 October 1992, to pursue uninterrupted negotiations at United Nations Headquarters until an overall framework agreement is reached on the basis of the entire set of ideas;

7. *Reaffirms* its position that the Secretary-General convene, following the satisfactory conclusion of the face-to-face talks, a high-level international meeting chaired by him to conclude an overall framework agreement, in which the two communities and Greece and Turkey would participate;

8. *Requests* all concerned to cooperate fully with the Secretary-General and his representatives in preparing the ground prior to the resumption of the direct talks in October to facilitate the speedy completion of the work;

9. *Expresses the expectation* that an overall framework agreement will be concluded in 1992 and that 1993 will be the transitional period during which the measures set out in the annex to the set of ideas will be implemented;

10. *Reaffirms* that, in line with previous resolutions of the Security Council, the present status quo is not acceptable, and, should an agreement not emerge from the talks that will reconvene in October, calls on the Secretary-General to identify the reasons for the failure and to recommend to the Council alternative courses of action to resolve the Cyprus problem;

11. *Requests* the Secretary-General to submit, prior to the end of 1992, a full report on the talks that will resume in October.

Security Council resolution 774(1992)

26 August 1992   Meeting 3109   Adopted unanimously

Draft prepared in consultations among Council members (S/24487).

Report of the Secretary-General (November). The Secretary-General submitted a further report in November[12] on the face-to-face talks between the leaders of the two communities, which resumed in New York from 28 October to 11 November. Matters discussed included displaced persons, constitutional aspects of the federation, territorial adjustments, overall objectives of the framework agreement and guiding principles, security and guarantee of the federal republic and of the federated states, economic development and safeguards, and transitional arrangements.

The report described the parties' positions on each issue. The Greek Cypriot side accepted the set of ideas and the map setting out the territories of the federated states as a basis for an agreement. While affirming its basic acceptance of 91 out of the 100 paragraphs of the set, the Turkish Cypriot side stated a lack of agreement on seven issues incorporated in the nine remaining paragraphs, dealing with the executive branch of government and the federal council of ministers, elimination of economic disparities, the principle of "one sovereignty" and its modalities, participation of Cyprus in international organizations where Turkey and Greece were not both members, the establishment of a transitional Government and the issue of displaced persons. The Turkish Cypriot side also held to its position on territorial adjustments, refusing to accept the suggested map endorsed by the Council.

Noting that no agreement resulted from the talks, the Secretary-General formulated a number of confidence-building measures to be embraced by the parties before the scheduled resumption of negotiations in March 1993. His proposals provided for the reduction of armed forces and armaments; the unmanning of all military positions in the buffer zone; inclusion of Varosha in the United Nations–controlled area; reduced travel restrictions across the buffer zone for both Cypriots and foreign visitors; promotion of intercommunal cooperation; a Cyprus-wide census under United Nations auspices; and feasibility studies on the resettlement and rehabilitation of Turkish Cypriots affected by territorial adjustments as part of the overall agreement.

The time may have come, the Secretary-General said, to give fuller form to the decision of the Security Council, reflected in its April 1992 resolution, to be seized of the matter on an ongoing and more direct basis.

SECURITY COUNCIL ACTION (November)

On 25 November, the Security Council unanimously adopted **resolution 789(1992)**.

The Security Council,

Having considered the report of the Secretary-General of 19 November 1992 on his mission of good offices in Cyprus,

Noting with satisfaction that the two leaders discussed all the issues in the set of ideas with the result that there were areas of agreement as noted in the report,

Welcoming the agreement by the two sides to meet again with the Secretary-General in early March 1993 to complete the work on an agreed set of ideas,

1. *Reaffirms* all its previous resolutions on Cyprus, including resolutions 365(1974), 367(1975), 541(1983), 550(1984) and 774(1992);

2. *Endorses* the report of the Secretary-General and commends him for his efforts;

3. *Reaffirms also* its endorsement of the set of ideas including the territorial adjustments reflected in the map contained in the annex to the report of the Secretary-General of 21 August 1992 as the basis for reaching an overall framework agreement;

4. *Reaffirms further* its position that the present status quo is not acceptable and that an overall agreement in line with the set of ideas should be achieved without further delay;

5. *Notes* that the recent joint meetings did not achieve their intended goal, in particular because certain positions adopted by the Turkish Cypriot side were fundamentally at variance with the set of ideas;

6. *Calls upon* the Turkish Cypriot side to adopt positions that are consistent with the set of ideas on those issues identified by the Secretary-General in his report, and for all concerned to be prepared in the next round of talks to make decisions that will bring about a speedy agreement;

7. *Recognizes* that the completion of this process in March 1993 would be greatly facilitated by the implementation by each side of measures designed to promote mutual confidence;

8. *Urges* all concerned to commit themselves to the confidence-building measures set out below:

(a) That, as a first step towards the withdrawal of non-Cypriot forces envisaged in the set of ideas, the number of foreign troops in the Republic of Cyprus undergo a significant reduction and that a reduction of defence spending be effected in the Republic of Cyprus;

(b) That the military authorities on each side cooperate with the United Nations Peace-keeping Force in Cyprus in order to extend the unmanning agreement of 1989 to all areas of the United Nations–controlled buffer zone where the two sides are in close proximity to each other;

(c) That, with a view to the implementation of resolution 550(1984), the area at present under the control of the United Nations Peace-keeping Force in Cyprus be extended to include Varosha;

(d) That each side take active measures to promote people-to-people contact between the two communities by reducing restrictions to the movement of persons across the buffer zone;

(e) That restrictions imposed on foreign visitors crossing the buffer zone be reduced;

(f) That each side propose bi-communal projects, for possible financing by lending and donor Governments as well as international institutions;

(g) That both sides commit themselves to the holding of a Cyprus-wide census under the auspices of the United Nations;

(h) That both sides cooperate to enable the United Nations to undertake, in the relevant locations, feasibility studies (i) in connection with the resettlement and rehabilitation of persons who would be affected by the territorial adjustments as part of the overall agreement, and (ii) in connection with the programme of economic development that would, as part of the overall agreement, benefit those persons who would resettle in the area under Turkish Cypriot administration;

9. *Requests* the Secretary-General to follow up on the implementation of the above confidence-building measures and to keep the Security Council informed as appropriate;

10. *Also requests* the Secretary-General to maintain such preparatory contacts as he considers appropriate before the resumption of the joint meetings in March 1993, and to propose for the Security Council's consideration revisions in the negotiating format to make it more effective;

11. *Further requests* the Secretary-General, during the March 1993 joint meetings, to assess developments on a regular basis with the Council with a view to considering what further action may be needed by the Council;

12. *Requests* the Secretary-General to submit a full report after the conclusion of the joint meetings that will resume in March 1993.

Security Council resolution 789(1992)

25 November 1992   Meeting 3140   Adopted unanimously

Draft prepared in consultations among Council members (S/24841).

UNFICYP

The United Nations Peace-keeping Force in Cyprus, established by the Security Council in 1964,[13] continued throughout 1992. It supervised the cease-fire lines of the Cyprus National Guard and the Turkish and Turkish Cypriot forces, keeping the area between the lines—the buffer zone—under constant surveillance through a system of 151 observation posts, with 51 of them permanently manned as at 30 November 1992.

UNFICYP also continued to facilitate humanitarian activities on the island, provide emergency medical services and support United Nations relief operations. It delivered foodstuffs and other supplies to the 250 Maronites and the Greek Cypriots in northern Cyprus, whose number decreased from 551 to 544 during the year; visited regularly Turkish Cypriots residing in the south; and facilitated five voluntary transfers and 899 visits of Greek Cypriots to the south. The Force also remained seized of the situation in the mixed village of Pyla, located in the buffer zone. In an effort to reduce demands on its declining manpower, UNFICYP recommended that Red Cross representatives of both parties resume their original responsibilities for the delivery of mail, medical supplies and Red Cross messages across cease-fire lines.

The number of cease-fire violations increased slightly in the second half of the year. UNFICYP reported 210 overflights of the zone by civilian, military and police aircraft, including 17 by aircraft of other countries, and continuing crossings of the maritime security line by Greek Cypriot tourist and fishing boats, which on one occasion led to warning shots. Despite protests by the Turkish Cypriot side and reservations expressed by the Force, the Cyprus National Guard intensified construction work on its defensive positions along the cease-fire lines and often refused to cooperate in UNFICYP's investigations and inspection of its positions.

Safety and security in the buffer zone were also threatened as a result of hunting by Greek Cypriots in certain areas and by mines that had not been removed despite representations by UNFICYP and the Government's commitment to do so. The 1989 agreement concerning the unmanning of certain positions in Nicosia continued to hold, with only a few violations. As part of the confidence-building measures recommended in a November report on his good offices mission (see above), the Secretary-General requested the UNFICYP Commander to initiate discussions on a possible extension of the agreement to all areas of the zone where the troops of both sides remained in close proximity to each other. The Security Council, in its 25 November resolution, urged both sides to commit themselves to these measures.

UNFICYP's military personnel were reduced during 1992 from 2,103 in May to 2,040 in November, with the strength of civilian police remaining 38. The Force's size was further reduced significantly in December, which necessitated a major restructuring and reorganization, including a decrease in the number of permanently manned observation posts.

In March,[14] the Security Council agreed to the change in the UNFICYP command proposed by the Secretary-General;[15] on 8 April, Major-General Clive Milner of Canada handed over command of the Force to Major-General Michael F. Minehane of Ireland.

Report of the Secretary-General (May). In response to a 1991 Security Council resolution,[16] the Secretary-General submitted a report[17] on the United Nations operation in Cyprus, covering the period from 1 December 1991 to 31 May 1992. The report brought up to date the activities of UNFICYP and the Secretary-General's mission of good offices. It showed that UNFICYP had continued to perform its functions, often under difficult circumstances.

The Secretary-General recommended an extension of the UNFICYP mandate for a further period of six months, subject to possible changes in its size and mandate, on which he was holding consultations with the troop contributors. Those discussions had been made necessary in view of UNFICYP's deepening financial crisis, which imposed an unfair burden on the troop-contributing countries (Austria, Canada, Denmark, Finland, Ireland, Sweden, United Kingdom). Discussing the future of UNFICYP in view of an impending reduction of its contingents, he noted that that would deny it the troops necessary for execution of the existing mandate.

SECURITY COUNCIL ACTION (June)

On 12 June, the Security Council unanimously adopted **resolution 759(1992)**.

The Security Council,

Noting the report of the Secretary-General on the United Nations operation in Cyprus of 31 May 1992,

Noting also the recommendation by the Secretary-General that the Security Council extend the stationing of the United Nations Peace-keeping Force in Cyprus for a further period of six months,

Noting further that the Government of Cyprus has agreed that in view of the prevailing conditions in the island, it is necessary to keep the Force in Cyprus beyond 15 June 1992,

Reaffirming the provisions of resolution 186(1964) of 4 March 1964 and other relevant resolutions,

1. *Extends once more* the stationing in Cyprus of the United Nations Peace-keeping Force established under resolution 186(1964) for a further period ending on 15 December 1992;

2. *Requests* the Secretary-General, after consulting the troop-contributing Governments as envisaged in paragraph 56 of the report, to submit specific proposals to the Security Council no later than 1 September 1992 on the restructuring of the Force, such proposals to be based on the realistic options available in current circumstances;

3. *Requests* the Secretary-General to continue his mission of good offices, to keep the Security Council informed of the progress made and to submit a report on the implementation of the present resolution by 30 November 1992;

4. *Calls upon* all the parties concerned to continue to cooperate with the Force on the basis of the present mandate.

Security Council resolution 759(1992)

12 June 1992   Meeting 3084   Adopted unanimously

Draft prepared in consultations among Council members (S/24084).

Reports of the Secretary-General (September and December). Reporting to the Council in September,[18] the Secretary-General reviewed his consultations of 9 and 10 September with representatives of the troop-contributing countries. While acknowledging that a critical moment had been reached in the efforts to achieve a settlement in Cyprus, the majority of the contributors believed that UNFICYP could maintain its mandate with fewer resources, relying on the use of military observers instead of infantry units. Five contributing Governments—Austria, Canada, Denmark, Finland and the United Kingdom—had already indicated that they would be reducing their contingents. The Secretariat argued that the Force's mandate implied not only observation but also rapid intervention in peace-threatening incidents, and that its tasks might become more extensive and require its current strength for a fixed transitional period, should the parties conclude an agreement in 1993.

The Secretary-General noted that the Force Commander had been instructed to absorb as much as possible the effects of the forthcoming reductions, but pointed out that UNFICYP in its current form would shortly become unviable unless the Council changed the basis of its financing.

By a letter of 28 September,[19] the Security Council President stated that the Council members had taken note of the report. They looked forward to the holding of further consultations with the troop-contributing States and to the Secretary-General's report containing specific proposals on the restructuring of the Force. They recalled that in December 1991 they had agreed to keep the question of UNFICYP financing under review as a matter of urgency. (For details on UNFICYP financing, see below.)

The Secretary-General submitted a report in December covering the United Nations operation in Cyprus from 1 June to 30 November 1992.[20] He stated that in the face of a forthcoming troop reduction by 28 per cent, UNFICYP was undergoing restructuring, commencing on 16 November with the withdrawal of 63 Austrian personnel and to be completed by 15 December. Following the restructuring, the territory under UNFICYP's control would be divided into three sectors instead of four and the number of permanently manned observation posts would be reduced from 51 to 39. Further reductions in the contingents were planned during 1993.

The Secretary-General, however, expressed the belief that UNFICYP's continued presence on the island remained indispensable to achieve the objectives set by the Security Council, and recommended an extension of its mandate for another six months. He noted that the contributing Governments had been asked to maintain the current strength of their contingents throughout the new mandate period.

SECURITY COUNCIL ACTION

On 14 December, the Security Council adopted **resolution 796(1992)** unanimously.

The Security Council,

Noting the report of the Secretary-General on the United Nations operation in Cyprus of 1 December 1992,

Noting also the recommendation by the Secretary-General that the Security Council extend the stationing of the United Nations Peace-keeping Force in Cyprus for a further period of six months,

Noting further that the Government of Cyprus has agreed that, in view of the prevailing conditions in the island, it is necessary to keep the Force in Cyprus beyond 15 December 1992,

Reaffirming the provisions of resolution 186(1964) of 4 March 1964 and other relevant resolutions,

1. *Extends once more* the stationing in Cyprus of the United Nations Peace-keeping Force established under resolution 186(1964) for a further period ending on 15 June 1993;

2. *Requests* the Secretary-General to continue his mission of good offices, to keep the Security Council informed of the progress made and to submit a report on the implementation of the present resolution by 31 May 1993;

3. *Welcomes* the intention of the Secretary-General expressed in paragraph 46 of his report to pursue his con-

sultations with the troop-contributing Governments about a restructuring of the Force and to report on this to the Council as soon as possible;

4. *Calls upon* all the parties concerned to continue to cooperate with the Force on the basis of the present mandate.

Security Council resolution 796(1992)

14 December 1992   Meeting 3148   Adopted unanimously

Draft prepared in consultations among Council members (S/24949).

Financing of UNFICYP

For the two mandate periods of UNFICYP ending in 1992, voluntary contributions from Governments to the part of the Force's financing borne by the United Nations amounted to only $7.8 million, against anticipated expenditures of some $30.8 million. As a result of chronic shortfalls, the reimbursement claims from the troop-contributing countries had been met only up to December 1981, and the accumulated deficit in the UNFICYP Special Account was expected to reach approximately $197.1 million for the periods since the inception of the Force.

Based on the revised strength and responsibilities of the Force due to contingent reductions, UNFICYP expenditures for the six-month period ending on 15 June 1993 was estimated at $9.5 million. On 10 March[21] and 24 November 1992,[22] the Secretary-General appealed to all Member States and members of the specialized agencies for voluntary contributions, stressing UNFICYP's vital peace-keeping role and its critical financial situation.

In his December report[20] on the United Nations operation in Cyprus (see above), the Secretary-General said it had been predicted for several years that unless the financing of UNFICYP was assured by assessed contributions, it would prove impossible to maintain the Force. Following a review of UNFICYP's financial crisis and adoption of a Security Council resolution in December 1990,[23] the Secretariat had cooperated actively with the Council in its deliberations on the issue and identified a new method of defining and rationalizing those costs incurred by the troop contributors for which the United Nations would be responsible. Unfortunately, the necessary agreement did not exist in the Council for a decision on a change in UNFICYP financing, with the consequences now evident.

As a result, the Secretary-General was pursuing consultations with the troop-contributing Governments about a restructuring of the Force and was also exploring the possibility of additional countries which could agree to contribute troops to replace those being withdrawn. Currently, however, his impression was that even if UNFICYP was radically restructured, it was likely that a viable arrangement could be made only on the basis of financing by assessed contributions.

GENERAL ASSEMBLY ACTION

By **resolution 47/218**, section IV, of 23 December 1992, on administrative and budgetary aspects of the financing of United Nations peace-keeping operations, the General Assembly, having noted the Secretary-General's report of December on UNFICYP financing and its appeal for voluntary contributions, invited all Member States to respond positively.

REFERENCES

[1]A/47/204-S/23887 & Corr.1. [2]A/47/527-S/24660. [3]A/47/329-S/24289. [4]A/47/536-S/24667. [5]A/47/736-S/24862. [6]A/47/759-S/24914. [7]A/47/618-S/24747. [8]YUN 1991, p. 92. [9]S/23780. [10]S/24271. [11]S/24472. [12]S/24830. [13]YUN 1964, p. 165, SC res. 186(1964), 4 Mar. 1964. [14]S/23753. [15]S/23752. [16]YUN 1991, p. 94, SC res. 723(1991), 12 Dec. 1991. [17]S/24050 & Add.1. [18]S/24581. [19]S/24594. [20]S/24917 & Add.1. [21]S/23735. [22]S/24938. [23]SC res. 682(1990), 21 Dec. 1990.

Iran

Iran-Iraq

Throughout 1992, Iran and Iraq transmitted to the Secretary-General numerous communications containing allegations of violations of the terms of the cease-fire between them.

Iran reported several instances of Iraqi border encroachments and infiltrations; airspace violations; firing of light weapons, including at facilities in Khorramshahr, once; and, along and inside the area of separation between the two countries, frequent traffic of Iraqi military vehicles and armed soldiers patrolling, monitoring, moving ammunition boxes, digging trenches and canals, constructing bunkers and restoring others, deploying automatic machine-gun positions, laying mines and installing the Iraqi flag. Iran also reported the kidnapping of four Iranian soldiers from their sentry posts.[1]

Iraq made particularly numerous allegations of Iranian violations, including airspace violations, mostly by helicopters and at times by fighter planes; border incursions, including abduction of a farmer, as well as of 12 Iraqi fishermen fishing in Iraqi territorial waters; frequent random rifle firings, some shelling and machine-gun firings across the border into Iraqi territory; and various Iranian activities along and inside the area of separation, mainly building guard posts or fortifying them with barbed wire and sandbags, digging slit trenches, constructing defensive positions with high sandbag embankments, and setting up monitoring posts and machine-gun emplacements.

The most significant of Iraq's allegations was communicated to the President of the Security

Council on 5 April,[2] to the effect that, on that day, Iran's Air Force carried out four air raids inside Iraq near Al-Khalis, a town 90 kilometres from the border and 70 kilometres north-east of Baghdad. One of the eight bombers was shot down and its two-man crew taken prisoner. Iran, also on 5 April,[3] claimed that the raids were in self-defence, responding to the armed attacks launched from Iraq earlier that day on the Iranian villages of Beshkan and Bayani that killed four civilians and wounded seven others, as well as to the simultaneous attacks on several Iranian diplomatic missions abroad, violating premises, injuring officials, taking hostages and damaging property. Those attacks, Iran alleged, were organized and coordinated by terrorist mercenaries operating in Iraq, whose headquarters was the target of the Iranian raids.

Iraq reported on 20 April[4] that, according to the two captured Iranian pilots, preparations for the raids took place a month before they were carried out, thus invalidating Iran's claim of action taken in self-defence. On 27 April,[5] Iraq stated that the three military observers from the United Nations Office of the Secretary-General in Iraq (UNOSGI), based at Baghdad, who inspected the bombed supply depots at Al Azim on 14 April verified that 500-pound rockets and cluster bombs were among the projectiles used. On 12 September,[6] Iraq also alleged that a number of captured Iraqi military deserters confessed to having been enlisted by Iran to carry out acts of sabotage within Iraq. It later substantiated its allegation with what it claimed were videotapes of those confessions.[7]

Prisoners of war

In identical letters of 12 May 1992[8] to the Secretary-General and the President of the Security Council, Iraq drew attention to what it called Iran's persistent refusal to release all Iraqi prisoners of war (POWs) in accordance with the 1949 Geneva Convention relative to the Treatment of Prisoners of War (third Geneva Convention). Whereas no Iranian POW remained in Iraq other than those who had refused repatriation and whose refusal had been notified to ICRC, Iran released Iraqi POWs on a one-for-one basis—an action neither legitimate nor realistic, since the number of Iraqi prisoners in Iran far exceeded that of Iranian prisoners in Iraq. As a result, thousands of Iraqi POWs remained in Iran despite the almost four years since the conclusion of the 1988 ceasefire between the two countries.

According to Iraq's record of Iraqi POWs held by Iran, 41,655 had been repatriated. Of those remaining in Iran, 10,225 were registered with ICRC and bore ICRC numbers; a further 9,558 were registered with ICRC through correspondence; and 66,161 were missing in action.

As a result of a joint technical committee meeting held at the invitation of ICRC (Geneva, 12-14 February), Iran and Iraq agreed upon and signed an action plan outlining the steps for their resumption of the repatriation process and verification of the fate of all missing persons. Because of Iran's failure to comply with the plan and its termination of ICRC activities in Iran on 26 March, another joint technical committee meeting was held (Geneva, 15 and 16 April), at which both parties agreed to resume repatriation by 1 May. Iran subsequently postponed the repatriation process without setting another date for its resumption.

UN Iran-Iraq Military Observer Group

By **decision 46/478** of 14 September 1992, the General Assembly included in the draft agenda of its forty-seventh session the item entitled "Financing of the United Nations Iran-Iraq Military Observer Group" (UNIIMOG).

In October, the Secretary-General submitted a report to the Assembly[9] on the status of the liquidation costs and disposition of assets of UNIIMOG, which was terminated in 1991.[10] The report updated information on the status of unpaid assessed contributions, total expenditures for the duration of the operation and the unencumbered balance and miscellaneous income. Among the annexes to the report was a description and valuation of additional property transferred to existing United Nations peace-keeping and other operations, including UNOSGI in Iran and Iraq.

As at 30 September 1992, unpaid assessed contributions to UNIIMOG totalled $1,060,886. Resources made available since its inception on 9 August 1988 until its termination on 28 February 1991 totalled $213,827,900 gross ($210,509,900 net), while operating costs amounted to $171,387,911 gross ($167,286,511 net), leaving a balance of $42,439,989 gross ($43,223,389 net—a figure higher than the gross because expenditures for staff assessment exceeded the amount budgeted). The sum of $24,481,000 gross ($23,627,000 net) from that balance was credited to Member States against their assessed contributions for the last four mandate periods (between 1 April 1990 and 28 February 1991) in accordance with a 1990 Assembly decision,[11] thus adjusting the unutilized appropriations to $19,596,389.

Interest income amounted to $9,999,427 and miscellaneous income to $8,272,872 (including an amount of $6,364,150 from the sale of equipment), making a total of $18,272,299. This amount plus the unutilized appropriations, minus the unpaid assessed contributions, left a total unencumbered balance of $36,807,802 in the UNIIMOG Special Account.

In view of the foregoing, the Secretary-General proposed the following: that an appropriation of

$2,384,000 gross ($2,178,000 net) be authorized and apportioned in respect of the period 1 to 28 February 1991 and that the same amount from the unencumbered balance be credited to Member States against their assessments; that the unutilized appropriations balance be credited to Member States; and, in view of the outstanding assessed contributions, that $17,211,413 of the total interest and miscellaneous income be retained in the Special Account pending an Assembly decision on the proposed Peace-keeping Reserve Fund (see PART SIX, Chapter I).

ACABQ[12] did not object to those proposals. It noted, however, that the unutilized appropriations balance of $19,596,389 was subject to further adjustment upon liquidation of the $3,003,407 in obligations indicated by the Secretary-General as outstanding as at 30 September 1992. In addition, cash resources backing those obligations continued to accrue interest, as did the $17,211,413 proposed to be retained in the Special Account. Consequently, future credits to Member States and other adjustments might be necessary.

GENERAL ASSEMBLY ACTION

Acting on the recommendation of the Fifth Committee, the General Assembly, on 22 December 1992, adopted **resolution 47/206** without vote.

Financing of the United Nations Iran-Iraq Military Observer Group

The General Assembly,

Having considered the report of the Secretary-General on the financing of the United Nations Iran-Iraq Military Observer Group and the related report of the Advisory Committee on Administrative and Budgetary Questions,

Bearing in mind Security Council resolution 619(1988) of 9 August 1988, by which the Council established the United Nations Iran-Iraq Military Observer Group, and the subsequent resolutions by which the Council extended the mandate of the Military Observer Group, the latest of which was resolution 685(1991) of 31 January 1991,

Recalling its resolution 42/233 of 17 August 1988 on the financing of the Military Observer Group and its subsequent resolutions thereon, the latest of which was resolution 45/245 of 21 December 1990,

Reaffirming that the costs of the Military Observer Group are expenses of the Organization to be borne by Member States in accordance with Article 17, paragraph 2, of the Charter of the United Nations,

Recalling its previous decisions regarding the fact that, in order to meet the expenditures caused by the Military Observer Group, a different procedure is required from the one applied to meet expenditures of the regular budget of the United Nations,

Taking into account the fact that the economically more developed countries are in a position to make relatively larger contributions and that the economically less developed countries have a relatively limited capacity to contribute towards such an operation,

Bearing in mind the special responsibilities of the States permanent members of the Security Council, as indicated in General Assembly resolution 1874(S-IV) of 27 June 1963, in the financing of such operations,

Noting with appreciation that voluntary contributions have been made to the Military Observer Group by certain Governments,

1. _Endorses_ the observations and recommendations contained in the report of the Advisory Committee on Administrative and Budgetary Questions;

2. _Urges_ all Member States to make every possible effort to ensure payment in full of their assessed contributions to the United Nations Iran-Iraq Military Observer Group;

3. _Decides_ to appropriate to the Special Account referred to in General Assembly resolution 42/233 the amount of 2,384,000 United States dollars gross (2,178,000 dollars net) authorized by the Assembly in its resolution 45/245 and apportioned in accordance with paragraphs 11 to 13 thereof for the operation of the Military Observer Group for the period from 1 to 28 February 1991;

4. _Decides also_ that there shall be set off against the apportionment among Member States, as provided for in paragraph 3 above, their respective share in the unencumbered balance of 2,384,000 dollars gross (2,178,000 dollars net) in respect of the period from 1 to 28 February 1991;

5. _Decides further_ that 19,596,389 dollars of the unutilized balance in the Special Account for the United Nations Iran-Iraq Military Observer Group shall be credited to Member States;

6. _Decides_ to transfer the balance remaining in the Special Account for the United Nations Iran-Iraq Military Observer Group to the Peace-keeping Reserve Fund.

General Assembly resolution 47/206

22 December 1992   Meeting 93   Adopted without vote

Approved by Fifth Committee (A/47/821) without vote, 19 December (meeting 50); draft by Chairman (A/C.5/47/L.4); agenda item 116.
Meeting numbers. GA 47th session: 5th Committee 36, 50; plenary 93.

Iran-Israel

On 1 July 1992,[13] Iran drew the Secretary-General's attention to a 15 June statement by the Chief of Israel's Air Force which, it said, contained unfounded allegations, as well as threats of armed aggression against Iran and other countries. (The subject of the statement appeared to be Iran's nuclear energy programme.)

Iran stated that it was a party to the 1968 Treaty on the Non-Proliferation of Nuclear Weapons[14] and as such had concluded a safeguards agreement with the International Atomic Energy Agency (IAEA). It referred to a February 1992 IAEA inspection whose findings corroborated the fact that Iran was in full compliance with its international obligations in respect of its nuclear programme. It further recalled its long-standing advocacy of a Middle East free from nuclear and other weapons of mass destruction, adding that, as common knowledge had it, that was not the case with Israel, whose nuclear-weapons programme flew in the face of all international instruments.

Through the Secretary-General, IAEA, on 10 July,[15] provided the Security Council with a copy of its 14 February press release officially setting out the nature and results of the visit of a four-member IAEA team to Iran from 7 to 12 February, undertaken at that country's request. The team familiarized itself with the current status of the Iranian Nuclear Research and Development Programme and visited the Bushehr Nuclear Power Project, the Esfahan Nuclear Technology Centre, the Tehran Nuclear Research Centre and the Karaj Agricultural and Medical Research Centre. It also visited the site of a uranium exploration project at Saghand in Yazd province and a facility under construction in the mountains north of Tehran near Mo'allem Kalayeh.

The press release stated that the activities reviewed at those facilities and sites were found to be consistent with the peaceful application of nuclear energy and ionizing radiation, and that the team's conclusions were limited to those facilities and sites and of relevance only to the time of the visit.

Iran–United Arab Emirates

The question of sovereignty over the three islands of Abu Musa, Greater Tunb and Lesser Tunb in the Gulf was brought anew to the attention of the Security Council and the General Assembly in 1992. The claimants to the islands were Iran and the United Arab Emirates. Iran militarily occupied the islands towards the end of 1971,[16] when the United Kingdom terminated its treaties with Bahrain, Qatar and the seven Trucial States (Abu Dhabi, Aijman, Dubai, Fujairah, Ras al Khaimah, Sharjah, Umm al Qaiwain), which since became known as the United Arab Emirates. Iran claimed its action to be a re-establishment of its rightful authority over the islands after a long interruption of colonial domination of the Persian Gulf. The United Arab Emirates asserted sovereignty over the islands as integral parts of its federation and was backed by other Arab States which affirmed the islands to be Arab. The question was again brought before the United Nations in 1972[17] and 1980.[18]

By a resolution adopted on 13 September 1992, the Council of Ministers for Foreign Affairs of the League of Arab States decided: to stand by the United Arab Emirates in its claim to full sovereignty over the three islands and to denounce their illegal occupation by Iran; to state the Council's unqualified support for all measures taken by the United Arab Emirates to assert its sovereignty over the islands and to place the issue of Iranian violations, which endangered the region's security and stability, before the United Nations; and to call on Iran to respect the pacts and covenants it had concluded with the United Arab Emirates and the

latter's sovereignty over the three islands. The resolution was transmitted to the Security Council on 2 October[19] and the Assembly on 6 October.[20]

REFERENCES

[1]S/24696. [2]S/23785. [3]S/23786. [4]S/23827. [5]S/23856. [6]S/24562. [7]S/24591 & S/24853. [8]S/23909. [9]A/47/560. [10]YUN 1991, p. 164. [11]GA res. 45/245, 21 Dec. 1990. [12]A/47/606. [13]S/24239. [14]YUN 1968, p. 17, GA res. 2373(XXII), annex, 12 June 1968. [15]S/24301. [16]YUN 1971, p. 209. [17]YUN 1972, p. 208. [18]YUN 1980, p. 319. [19]S/24609. [20]A/47/516.

Iraq-Kuwait situation

During 1992, the Security Council twice conducted a comprehensive review of the status of compliance by Iraq with resolution 687(1991),[1] setting forth the terms of the cease-fire that formally brought to an end the 1991 military action taken against Iraq to compel it to withdraw from Kuwait and providing for other conditions essential to the restoration of peace and security in the Gulf region. Compliance with subsequent related resolutions was also reviewed, chief among which were resolutions 707(1991)[2] and 715(1991)[3] directly linked with and elaborating upon certain provisions of the cease-fire resolution.

For the purpose of the reviews, several entities were called upon to present their assessments, key among which were the Special Commission established under the cease-fire resolution and IAEA, both mandated to ensure Iraq's compliance with its weapons-related obligations. At the request of Iraq, it was represented at the two reviews by a high-level official delegation headed by the Deputy Prime Minister of Iraq.

Cease-fire compliance

Report of the Secretary-General (January). In accordance with a December 1991 statement by the President of the Security Council,[4] the Secretary-General submitted on 25 January 1992[5] a factual report on Iraq's compliance with all the obligations placed upon it by Council resolution 687(1991) and subsequent relevant resolutions. The information was updated by a further report submitted in March (see below). The reports focused only on those provisions in the resolutions that placed mandatory obligations on Iraq, grouped into three categories: general, specific and other obligations.

The general obligations required Iraq's acceptance of the provisions of the entire resolution 687(1991) (para. 33) and compliance with all its international obligations (resolution 707(1991), para. 5). The report noted that Iraq complied with the first in 1991[6] and that it was not specifically required to confirm compliance with the second.

There were nine specific obligations, which included respect for the inviolability of the international border and allocation of islands between Iraq and Kuwait (resolution 687(1991), para. 2); obligations relating to conventional, biological or chemical weapons and such materials for warfare (resolution 687(1991), paras. 8, 9 *(a)* and 10; resolution 707(1991), para. 3; resolution 715(1991), para. 5), to nuclear capability development programmes (resolution 687(1991), paras. 10 and 12; resolution 707(1991), para. 3; resolution 715(1991), para. 5), and to repatriation of and access to all Kuwaiti and third-country nationals in Iraq (resolution 687(1991), para. 30); liability under international law for loss or damage resulting from Iraq's unlawful invasion and occupation of Kuwait (resolution 687(1991), para. 16); adherence to all obligations concerning servicing and repayment of Iraq's foreign debt (resolution 687(1991), para. 17); non-entitlement to claims deriving from the effects of the measures taken by the Council in resolution 661(1990)[7] and related resolutions (resolution 687(1991), para. 29); liability for the full cost of the tasks authorized under section C of resolution 687(1991) (resolution 699(1991),[8] para. 4); and provision of monthly statements of gold and foreign currency reserves (resolution 706(1991),[9] para. 7).

Two other items concerned the undertaking not to commit or support any international terrorist act (resolution 687(1991), para. 32) and obligations under the 1968 Treaty on the Non-Proliferation of Nuclear Weapons[10] (NPT) (resolution 707(1991), para. 5). The Secretary-General was unable to offer any guiding information to the Council as to the first item, but referred to Iraq's 1991 communication affirming that it had never pursued a policy favourable to international terrorism.[11] As to the second item, Iraq's 1991 letter accepting resolution 687(1991) also stated that it was a party to NPT and referred to IAEA reports confirming that it was in observance of all NPT provisions.

The January report, besides stating that Iraq had respected the demilitarized zone (DMZ), annexed detailed assessments of compliance with the specific obligations cited.

The Special Commission covered compliance with respect to the elimination of capabilities in regard to chemical and biological weapons, ballistic missiles and long-range guns; ongoing monitoring and verification to ensure that acquisition and development of such weapons were not resumed; the related reporting obligations; and obligations in connection with the facilities, privileges and immunities of the Commission and IAEA.

The Special Commission stated in summary that significant progress had been made in implementing section C of resolution 687(1991) but that much remained to be done. It had not been able to complete the first phase of its work—inspection and survey—as Iraq had not met its reporting obligations comprehensively. Furthermore, it had no confidence that the full, final and complete disclosure called for by resolution 707(1991) would be forthcoming in the immediate future, given Iraq's recent indication that it would respond only to specific items of evidence of undisclosed weapons, facilities and materials. The second phase—disposal of weapons of mass destruction and the facilities for their production—was being carried out with significant progress in the area of ballistic missiles, with Iraq having destroyed its declared missiles and launchers under Commission supervision. Planning for the destruction of chemical weapons was in an advanced stage with active Iraqi cooperation. As to the third phase—ongoing monitoring and verification—Iraq had not made a clear acknowledgement of the plans for that phase. Instead, it arrogated to itself the determination of what it considered to be required of it. (For measures undertaken by the Commission and the Security Council on the subject, see below, under "Special Commission activities".)

The IAEA assessment covered Iraq's compliance with respect to the disclosure of its activities in nuclear-weapons development, its holdings of nuclear-weapons-usable material and its nuclear facilities and equipment; granting IAEA access and inspection rights; and the removal and rendering harmless of all items related to clandestine nuclear programmes. IAEA stated that Iraq's response to the IAEA inspections had been marked by a pattern of denial of clandestine activities until forced into acknowledgement when presented with overwhelming evidence, followed by cooperation until the next case of concealment was revealed. Consequently, it was not possible to be confident that the full extent of prohibited nuclear activities in Iraq had been disclosed. IAEA thus deemed it necessary to continue the inspections in parallel with the monitoring programme. (See also below, under "IAEA inspections".)

ICRC had helped in the return of 6,909 prisoners of war and civilians from Iraq to their home countries since March 1991. It had registered about 3,700 persons currently in Iraq whose nationality could not be established with certainty but who claimed residence in Kuwait and wished to return. Their personal data had been transmitted to Kuwait for determination of repatriation eligibility. Kuwait on 12 October 1991 had submitted a list of 2,101 missing persons, and had repeatedly stressed that those names were not identical with the 3,700 persons mentioned above.

Through ICRC, Saudi Arabia had sent Iraq detailed testimonies by former Saudi prisoners to the effect that some of the 17 Saudi nationals reported missing in Iraq had been seen in Iraqi captivity. ICRC had not yet received information from Iraq on the whereabouts of persons reported missing in Iraq, the outcome of the search by Iraq for those persons and identification of persons who had died while in custody. (See also below, under "Repatriation of Kuwaitis and third-country nationals".)

The Governing Council of the United Nations Compensation Commission stated that Iraq's compliance with its liability under international law for loss or damage resulting from its unlawful invasion and occupation of Kuwait, which was dependent on the resumption of its exports of petroleum and petroleum products, had not taken place because the 1990 economic sanctions imposed upon it remained in force. The sales regime established by resolutions 706(1991) and 712(1991)[12] to meet the humanitarian requirements of the Iraqi civilian population while the sanctions were in place, as well as the costs of various United Nations activities undertaken in implementation of resolution 687(1991), was objected to by Iraq, which stated that, since it had satisfied all conditions specified in paragraph 22 of the latter resolution, the sanctions should be lifted. (See also below, under "UN Compensation Commission and Compensation Fund".)

The International Monetary Fund (IMF) noted that Iraq was in arrears in the sum of SDR (special drawing rights) 7.3 million as at 31 December 1991 and had yet to submit any report on its gold and foreign currency reserves. It had been advised that Iraq's attempts to meet its obligations had failed due to the sanctions. Iraq's debt with certain members of the Paris Club of creditor countries totalled $13,420 million as at 1 April 1991.

No information was provided by the Security Council Committee established by resolution 661(1990) (Committee on sanctions) with respect to paragraphs 10 and 12 of resolution 687(1991). With respect to paragraph 29 of the same resolution, however, information received from Denmark indicated that Iraq had attempted to make a claim in connection with a contract affected by the coming into effect of the 1990 economic sanctions.

Appended to the report was a summary of Iraq's financial obligations in respect of the operations involved in implementing resolution 687(1991), including appropriate payment to the United Nations Compensation Fund, the full costs of destroying Iraq's weapons of mass destruction, the full costs incurred by the United Nations in facilitating the return of all Kuwaiti properties, and half the costs of the Iran-Iraq Boundary Demarcation Commission. Iraq, which had yet to signify its willingness to comply with the provisions of resolutions 706(1991) and 712(1991), indicated that

it was not prepared to resume the production and export of petroleum and petroleum products on the basis of the procedures outlined in those resolutions.

As at 31 December 1991, financial commitments to meet the costs mentioned above amounted to $17.2 million. That amount was provided through a commitment authority of $10 million granted by ACABQ under a 1989 General Assembly resolution on unforeseen and extraordinary expenses[13] and contributions of $7.2 million by Member States. Iraqi reimbursement of these amounts was the subject of two rounds of discussions held with Iraq (Baghdad, 22 and 23 November 1991; Vienna, 8-10 January 1992), which were inconclusive.

SECURITY COUNCIL ACTION (5 February)

On 5 February 1992, the President of the Security Council issued the following statement[14] to the media on behalf of the Council members in connection with the item entitled "The situation between Iraq and Kuwait":

"The members of the Security Council held informal consultations on 28 January and 5 February 1992 pursuant to paragraph 21 of resolution 687(1991). The members of the Council express their thanks to the Secretary-General for his factual report on Iraq's compliance with all the obligations placed upon it by resolution 687(1991) and subsequent relevant resolutions (S/23514).

"After taking note of the Secretary-General's report and hearing all the opinions expressed in the course of the consultations, the President of the Council concluded that there was no agreement that the necessary conditions existed for a modification of the regime established in paragraph 20 of resolution 687(1991), as referred to in paragraph 21 of that resolution.

"In the context of compliance, the Council members note with concern the recent incident at Baghdad, which demonstrates a lack of Iraqi cooperation in complying with the resolutions of the Council.

"In connection with the Secretary-General's factual report on Iraq's compliance with all the obligations placed upon it by resolution 687(1991) and subsequent relevant resolutions, the members of the Security Council note that while much progress has been made, much remains to be done. There is serious evidence of Iraqi non-compliance over its programmes for weapons of mass destruction and the repatriation of Kuwaitis and other third-country nationals detained in Iraq. There is still much Kuwaiti property to be returned. The members of the Council are disturbed by the lack of Iraqi cooperation. Iraq must implement fully resolution 687(1991) and subsequent relevant resolutions, as was stated in the statement read out by the President of the Council on behalf of its members in the meeting held on 31 January 1992 with the participation of the heads of State and Government (S/23500).

"The members of the Security Council note that with a view to alleviating the humanitarian conditions of the civilian population of Iraq and facilitating the utilization of paragraph 20 of resolution 687(1991), the Security Council Committee established by resolution 661(1990) had been requested to prepare a study of those materials and supplies for essential civilian and humanitarian needs, other than medicines which have not been subject to sanctions and food shipments which have been permitted to move freely, that might be transferred from the 'no objection' procedure to a simple notification procedure. The members of the Council also note the report of the Chairman of the Committee in this regard. They express their appreciation for the efforts the Chairman has made to reach a conclusion and encourage him to continue his consultations with the members of the Committee on the study and to report to the Council at an early date.

"The members of the Council strongly deplore that the Iraqi authorities have decided and communicated that decision to the Secretariat to discontinue contacts with the Secretariat regarding implementation of resolutions 706(1991) and 712(1991), which give to Iraq the possibility for oil sales to finance the purchase of foodstuffs, medicines and materials and supplies for essential civilian needs for the purpose of providing humanitarian relief. They underscore that the Government of Iraq, by acting in this way, is forgoing the possibility of meeting the essential needs of its civilian population and therefore bears the full responsibility for their humanitarian problems. They hope that a resumption of these contacts may lead to the early implementation of the scheme set out in those resolutions to enable humanitarian supplies to reach the Iraqi people."

Communications. Iraq, on 23 January 1992,[15] transmitted a comprehensive and detailed report on the measures it had implemented pursuant to resolution 687(1991). Its obligations were in five main areas: demarcation of boundaries between Iraq and Kuwait, including cooperation with the United Nations Iraq-Kuwait Observation Mission (UNIKOM); nuclear weapons; weapons of mass destruction, including chemical and biological weapons and ballistic missiles; return of Kuwaiti property; and repatriation of Kuwaiti and third-country nationals. Iraq restated its position on the question of the Iraq-Kuwait boundary made known in 1991,[16] adding that it had participated in all four meetings of the Iraq-Kuwait Boundary Demarcation Commission. It had further fully cooperated with UNIKOM to ensure the success of its task to monitor the DMZ and deter violations or potentially hostile action from either side.

On its NPT and nuclear-weapons-related obligations, Iraq emphasized that it had never sought to acquire or develop nuclear weapons. It cited six letters to IAEA containing declarations, with tables and annexes, of amounts and types of nuclear material and nuclear-related items and their locations. It further cited an additional 26 letters containing answers to questions raised by the IAEA inspection teams regarding its nuclear programme, which, it stressed, was devoted to peace-

ful purposes. In April 1991, it agreed to place all of its nuclear-weapons-usable materials under IAEA control and itemized those disposed of by the inspectors. It enumerated the services extended to them by their Iraqi counterparts in facilitating the destruction, rendering harmless, or removal of nuclear materials and related equipment. It named the more than 50 sites inspected by the first to eighth (1991) IAEA inspections and confirmed that it had halted all nuclear-related activities, including the transfer and unilateral destruction of nuclear-related materials and equipment.

Iraq maintained that it had declared, within the prescribed period, all information regarding its chemical weapons and related production sites, laboratories and stocks of chemical agents, as well as non-filled ammunition. It mentioned all the sites visited by the six chemical weapons inspections conducted in 1991 by the Special Commission. It also stated that it had declared its research programme in biological weapons to be for defensive purposes and that Al-Salman, the programme site, and other associated facilities had been inspected; that it had likewise declared information on its Scud missiles, together with their conventional and chemical warheads, accessories, support systems and launchers; and that it had made additional declarations of mobile launchers, missile storage areas, production, testing and modification sites, and missile research and development programme (Fahad 300, Fahad 500, Al-Hijara, Condor, Al-Abbas, Tamuz and the long-range gun). Under Special Commission instruction and supervision, it had destroyed missiles and related equipment. Its obligation to abandon any activity related to ballistic missiles had been practically verified by the seven 1991 ballistic missile inspection teams.

In addition to Kuwaiti property returned during 1991,[17] Iraq was in the process of arranging for delivery to Kuwait of Hawk missiles and related equipment, along with other military hardware. Delivery delays were due, Iraq stressed, not to its reluctance, but to United Nations procedures and staff shortage.

Iraq indicated that it had carefully and earnestly facilitated the repatriation of all Kuwaiti and third-country nationals. It provided updated information on the subject in February, including the number of those repatriated through ICRC, the measures it had taken and those it had intended to take to expedite the search for persons still missing, as communicated to ICRC on 20 February and on the basis of which it stated that it had met its obligations under paragraphs 30 and 31 of resolution 687(1991). (See also below, under "Repatriation of Kuwaitis and third-country nationals".)

Finally, Iraq reiterated its 1991 statement that it had registered its firm rejection of international terrorism.[11]

Report of the Secretary-General (March). In a further report of 7 March 1992,[18] the Secretary-General updated information on the status of Iraq's compliance with obligations as outlined in his January report[15] and incorporated information contained in Iraq's letter of 23 January.

Under the first of the two obligations of a general nature, the Secretary-General referred to Iraq's statement that, as of 31 December 1991, it had met a very large part of the conditions, restrictions and measures imposed on it by Security Council resolution 687(1991).

New information was presented under the group of specific obligations, as follows. Regarding respect for the inviolability of the international border and allocation of islands between Iraq and Kuwait, reference was made to the measures that Iraq said it had taken in its dealings with UNIKOM; its statement regarding its cooperation with the Mission was quoted. According to the Iraq-Kuwait Boundary Demarcation Commission, Iraq had fully participated in the Demarcation Commission's work: it attended all meetings, took part in voting procedures and in drafting the report, and in no way hindered the preliminary field work of surveying and mapping, concluded in November 1991.

As to obligations relating to conventional, biological or chemical weapons, the Special Commission listed the following as outstanding from Iraq: acknowledgement of its obligations under resolutions 707(1991) and 715(1991) and under the plans, approved by the latter, for ongoing monitoring and verification; the declarations required under those plans; agreement to implement unconditionally all its obligations under section C of resolution 687(1991) and resolutions 707(1991) and 715(1991); information required under resolutions 687(1991) and 707(1991) in order for the Commission and IAEA to have the full, final and complete picture of all aspects of Iraq's programmes for weapons of mass destruction and ballistic missiles with a range greater than 150 kilometres; arrangements necessary for the implementation of certain of the facilities, privileges and immunities of the Commission, such as airport landing rights; and compliance with Commission instructions to destroy items and facilities used in proscribed ballistic missile programmes.

With respect to obligations relating to nuclear capability development programmes, IAEA stated that, whereas the initial information required of Iraq should cover the period from 1 January 1989, the information received reflected the situation as of the date of reporting, namely, November 1991, after the military operations in the Gulf, during which certain facilities and equipment had been damaged, and subsequent to Iraq's unilateral de-struction of items. Moreover, the list of items reported was limited to those in the possession of the Iraqi Atomic Energy Commission (IAEC), whereas it should have included all items of the kind in question existing in Iraq. The Iraqi technical team advised IAEA that, while modifications of the initial information could be made in order to reflect the situation as of 1 January 1989, it could not comply with the second requirement, deeming it practically impossible to extend the list to cover all the items in question.

On obligations relating to repatriation of and access to all Kuwaiti and third-country nationals, the Secretary-General restated the information provided by Iraq in January and February 1992 as to the series of measures it had taken and intended to take. Attention was drawn to a March letter from France, Kuwait, Saudi Arabia, the United Kingdom and the United States, describing Iraq's February letter as no more than a belated and restrictive declaration of intent.

As to Iraq's liability under international law for loss or damage resulting from its unlawful invasion and occupation of Kuwait, the United Nations Compensation Commission reported that, at the fourth (20-24 January) session of its Governing Council, Iraq had requested a five-year grace period for its contribution to the Compensation Fund in view of its financial obligations and urgent food and medicine requirements. The Governing Council decided that the request be addressed to the Security Council, the competent authority on the matter.

IMF indicated that, as at 29 February, Iraq's arrears to IMF had increased to SDR 8.6 million.

Information from the United Nations Coordinator for the return of Kuwaiti property was that, to date, properties of Kuwait's Central Bank, Central Library, National Museum, News Agency, Airways Corporation and Air Force had been returned. A number of additional items were ready to be returned. Lists of properties from other Kuwaiti ministries, corporations and individuals had been submitted and were being pursued. The Iraqi and Kuwaiti officials involved in the return process had extended maximum cooperation to the United Nations.

In addition, annexed to the report were comments by the Office of the Executive Delegate of the Secretary-General relating to the Security Council's demand that Iraq end the repression of the Iraqi civilian population, including in Kurdish-populated areas. Reference was made to restrictions on essential commodities, particularly food and fuel, imposed by the Government since October 1991 on the three northern governorates of Dohuk, Erbil and Suleimaniya, to the non-payment of civil servants' salaries in those governorates since November, and to distribution of less than half of the regular food rations since December.

The Executive Delegate and the executive heads of UNHCR, UNICEF, the World Food Programme (WFP) and the World Health Organization (WHO) informed the Government in December of their inability to replace essential services and provide the goods denied to the Kurdish population at large. The Government's position was that the restrictions were due to the inability of the Kurdish leadership to maintain security and protect government personnel and resources. Discussions between the Government and the Kurdish leadership had so far not succeeded in ending the restrictions. (See also below, under "Kurds and other minority populations".)

The 1991 Memorandum of Understanding (see below, under "Inter-agency humanitarian programme"), which expired on 31 December 1991, was extended to the end of June 1992. Under the extended Memorandum, the Government committed itself to facilitating access where necessary in most parts of Iraq by United Nations and other relief agencies. However, the Government had refused to approve the establishment of humanitarian centres at Kirkuk in the north and Nasariya and Hammar in the south. The Government's position in this respect was that, according to the Memorandum, establishment of such centres and determination of humanitarian needs were to be undertaken in agreement and cooperation with the Government and with due respect for Iraq's independence, sovereignty and territorial integrity. Given the need for agreement, the Government's refusal was not to be construed as a unilateral act.

Under the original Memorandum, Iraq contributed 1.5 million Iraqi dinar (ID) to cover the inter-agency programme's in-country operational costs. The ID 1 million it undertook to make available under the extended Memorandum had not been received as at 17 January 1992.

SECURITY COUNCIL ACTION (11 and 12 March)

As agreed in prior consultations, the Security Council convened on 11 March 1992 and invited Iraq and Kuwait to participate, in accordance with Article 31 of the Charter of the United Nations and rule 37[a] of the Council's provisional rules of procedure. It also invited, under rule 39,[b] the Director General of IAEA, Hans Blix, and the Executive Chairman of the Special Commission, Rolf Ekéus. A high-level Iraqi technical team and the Deputy Prime Minister of Iraq, Tariq Aziz, appeared before the Council to respond to questions on all aspects of Iraq's compliance with resolution 687(1991) and other relevant resolutions.

After consultations among Council members, the President was authorized to make the following introductory statement[(19)] on behalf of the Council:

Meeting number. SC 3059 (with resumptions 1 and 2).

"I.   General obligation

"1.   The resolutions concerning the situation between Iraq and Kuwait impose a number of general and specific obligations upon Iraq.

"2.   As regards the general obligation, Iraq is required, under paragraph 33 of Security Council resolution 687(1991), to give official notification to the Secretary-General and to the Security Council of its acceptance of the provisions of that entire resolution.

"3.   Iraq signified its unconditional acceptance in letters dated 6 and 10 April 1991 (S/22456 and S/22480, respectively) and 23 January 1992 (S/23472).

"4.   When the Security Council met at the level of heads of State and Government on 31 January 1992, the concluding statement made by the President of the Council, on behalf of its members (S/23500), contained the following passage:

" 'Last year, under the authority of the United Nations, the international community succeeded in enabling Kuwait to regain its sovereignty and territorial integrity, which it had lost as a result of Iraqi aggression. The resolutions adopted by the Security Council remain essential to the restoration of peace and stability in the region and must be fully implemented. At the same time the members of the Council are concerned by the humanitarian situation of the innocent civilian population of Iraq.'

"5.   On 5 February 1992, the President of the Security Council issued a statement on behalf of its members (S/23517) in which he stated, among other things:

" 'In connection with the Secretary-General's factual report (S/23514) on Iraq's compliance with all the obligations placed upon it by resolution 687(1991) and subsequent relevant resolutions, the members of the Security Council note that while much progress has been made, much remains to be done. . . . The members of the Council are disturbed by the lack of Iraqi cooperation. Iraq must implement fully resolution 687(1991) and subsequent relevant resolutions, as was stated in the statement read out by the President of the Council on behalf of its members in the meeting held on 31 January 1992 with the participation of the heads of State and Government (S/23500).'

"6.   In a statement made on behalf of the Council on 28 February 1992 (S/23663), the President said:

[a]Rule 37 of the Council's provisional rules of procedure states: "Any Member of the United Nations which is not a member of the Security Council may be invited, as the result of a decision of the Security Council, to participate, without vote, in the discussion of any question brought before the Security Council when the Security Council considers that the interests of that Member are specially affected, or when a Member brings a matter to the attention of the Security Council in accordance with Article 35(1) of the Charter."

[b]Rule 39 of the Council's provisional rules of procedure states: "The Security Council may invite members of the Secretariat or other persons, whom it considers competent for the purpose, to supply it with information or to give other assistance in examining matters within its competence."

" 'The members of the Council demand that Iraq immediately implement all its obligations under Council resolution 687(1991) and subsequent resolutions on Iraq. The members of the Council require the Government of Iraq to communicate directly to the Council without further delay an authoritative and unconditional acknowledgement of its agreement to accept and implement the above noted obligations, including specifically to comply with the determination of the Special Commission requiring the destruction of ballistic missile-related equipment. The members of the Council emphasize that Iraq must be aware of the serious consequences of continued material breaches of resolution 687(1991).'

"7.   I must also draw attention to the further report of the Secretary-General on the status of compliance by Iraq with the obligations placed upon it (S/23687).

"8.   From the aforementioned statements by the President and in view of the reports of the Secretary-General, it will be seen that, despite Iraq's statements of unconditional acceptance of Security Council resolution 687(1991), the Security Council has determined that Iraq is not in full compliance with all of its obligations.

"II.   Specific obligations

"9.   In addition to the general obligation to accept the provisions of resolution 687(1991) in their entirety, several Security Council resolutions impose specific obligations upon Iraq.

"(a)   Respect for the inviolability of the international boundary

"10.   By paragraph 2 of resolution 687(1991) the Security Council demands that Iraq respect the inviolability of the international boundary and the allocation of islands previously agreed upon between Iraq and Kuwait. Pursuant to paragraph 3 of that resolution, the Secretary-General established a Boundary Demarcation Commission to demarcate the boundary between Iraq and Kuwait. Paragraph 5 of the same resolution requires Iraq and Kuwait to respect a demilitarized zone (DMZ) established by the Security Council. The Council has been informed that Iraq has respected the DMZ and that it has fully participated in the work of the Boundary Demarcation Commission. It has also been informed that Iraq refuses to withdraw a number of police posts that are not in line with UNIKOM's principle that both sides should stay 1,000 metres from the boundary line shown on UNIKOM's map.

"(b)   Weapons-related obligations

"11.   Section C of resolution 687(1991) imposes certain specific obligations upon Iraq with respect to its chemical and biological weapons programmes, its ballistic missile programmes with a range greater than 150 kilometres and its nuclear programmes. These obligations are elaborated upon in resolutions 707(1991) and 715(1991). The obligations are defined in paragraphs 8, 9, 10, 11, 12 and 13 of resolution 687(1991) and they are elaborated upon in paragraphs 3 and 5 of resolution 707(1991) and paragraph 5 of resolution 715(1991).

"12.   The information relevant to Iraq's compliance with the obligations laid down in the paragraphs of the Security Council resolutions to which I have just referred is reproduced in annex I to the Secretary-General's report (S/23687).

"13.   By resolution 699(1991), the Security Council decided that the Government of Iraq shall be liable for the full costs of carrying out the tasks authorized by section C of resolution 687(1991). No funds have so far been received from Iraq to meet this liability.

"14.   The Council has noted that since the adoption of resolution 687(1991) progress has been made in the implementation of section C of that resolution but that much remains to be done. There is serious non-compliance with the obligations concerning the programmes for weapons of mass destruction and ballistic missiles and the members of the Council have found this to be a continuing material breach of resolution 687(1991).

"15.   The Special Commission has informed the Council about the outstanding matters that would at the present time appear to be the most important. The Council's attention is invited again to annex I of the Secretary-General's report, S/23687, of 7 March 1992.

"16.   The Council has also noted the statement by the International Atomic Energy Agency (IAEA) contained in the Secretary-General's report of 25 January 1992 (S/23514, section C of the annex). The attention of the Council is drawn to information annexed to the further report of the Secretary-General, S/23687 (annex II), of 7 March 1992, relative to the two last inspections by the IAEA, on Iraq's compliance with its obligations under United Nations Security Council resolutions as they relate to nuclear activities.

"17.   In a statement issued on behalf of the members of the Council (S/23609), the President stated on 19 February 1992 that:

" 'Iraq's failure to acknowledge its obligations under resolutions 707(1991) and 715(1991), its rejection up until now of the two plans for ongoing monitoring and verification and its failure to provide the full, final and complete disclosure of its weapons capabilities constitute a continuing material breach of the relevant provisions of resolution 687(1991).'

"18.   In a further statement made on 28 February 1992 on behalf of the Council (S/23663), the President said:

" 'The members of the Council deplore and condemn the failure of the Government of Iraq to provide the Special Commission with full, final and complete disclosure, as required by resolution 707(1991), of all aspects of its programmes to develop weapons of mass destruction and ballistic missiles with a range greater than 150 kilometres, including launchers, and of all holdings of such weapons, their components and production facilities and locations, as well as all other nuclear programmes; and the failure of Iraq to comply with the plans for ongoing monitoring and verification approved by resolution 715(1991). . . . Furthermore, the members of the Council equally deplore and condemn Iraq's failure, within the time prescribed by the Special Commission at the request of Iraq, to commence destruction of ballistic missile-related equipment designated for destruction by the Special Commission. The members of the Council reaffirm that it is for the Special Commission alone to determine which items must be destroyed under paragraph 9 of resolution 687(1991).'

"*(c)* Repatriation of and access to Kuwaiti and third-country nationals in Iraq

"19. As regards Kuwaiti and third-country nationals in Iraq, Security Council resolutions 664 (1990), 666(1990), 667(1990), 674(1990), 686(1991) and 687(1991) impose an obligation on Iraq to release, facilitate repatriation of, and arrange for immediate access to them, as well as the return of the remains of any deceased personnel of the forces of Kuwait and of the Member States cooperating with Kuwait pursuant to resolution 678(1990). Furthermore, paragraph 30 of resolution 687(1991) requires Iraq to extend all necessary cooperation to the International Committee of the Red Cross (ICRC) in facilitating the search for Kuwaiti and third-country nationals still unaccounted for.

"20. The Security Council was informed by the ICRC in January 1992 that almost 7,000 persons have returned from Iraq to their countries since the beginning of March 1991. The ICRC also stated that despite all its efforts, there are still thousands of persons reported missing by the parties to the conflict.

"21. A special commission composed of the representatives of France, Iraq, Kuwait, Saudi Arabia, the United Kingdom and the United States has met under the auspices of the ICRC to try to reach an agreement on, among other things, the implementation of paragraph 30 of resolution 687(1991). However, the ICRC has informed the Council that it has not yet received any information as to the whereabouts of the persons reported missing in Iraq. Nor has it received detailed and documented information on the search conducted by the Iraqi authorities. Finally, it is also still awaiting information on persons who have died while in custody.

"22. The attention of the Council is drawn to section 4, paragraphs 12 to 14, of the Secretary-General's report contained in document S/23687 of 7 March 1992.

"*(d)* Iraq's liability under international law

"23. Another obligation concerns Iraq's liability under international law. In resolution 674(1990), the Security Council reminds Iraq 'that under international law it is liable for any loss, damage or injury arising in regard to Kuwait and third States and their nationals and corporations, as a result of the invasion and illegal occupation of Kuwait by Iraq'. Its liability under international law is reaffirmed in paragraph 2 *(b)* of resolution 686(1991) and paragraph 16 of resolution 687(1991). Resolution 687(1991) further specifies that it 'is liable under international law for any direct loss, damage, including environmental damage and the depletion of natural resources, or injury to foreign Governments, nationals and corporations, as a result of Iraq's unlawful invasion and occupation of Kuwait'.

"24. By paragraph 18 of the same resolution, the Security Council created a Fund to pay compensation for claims that fall within paragraph 16, to be financed by a percentage of the value of the exports of petroleum and petroleum products from Iraq. In view of the existing economic sanctions against Iraq under resolution 661(1990), Iraq was permitted by the Security Council under resolutions 706(1991) and 712(1991) to sell a limited quantity of oil, as an exception, a portion of the proceeds from which would be used to provide financial resources for the Fund. To date, it has not availed itself of this possibility. The Council notes that this authorization is due to lapse on 18 March 1992. The members of the Council are aware of a request by Iraq for a five-year moratorium on meeting its financial obligations, including payments into the Compensation Fund.

"*(e)* Repayment and servicing of Iraq's foreign debt

"25. With regard to another obligation, the Security Council, in paragraph 17 of resolution 687(1991), demands that Iraq scrupulously adhere to all of its obligations concerning servicing and repayment of its foreign debt.

"26. The attention of the Council is drawn to paragraphs 17 and 18 of the Secretary-General's report (S/23687) of 7 March 1992.

"*(f)* Return of property

"27. I now turn to the question of return of property. The Security Council, in paragraph 2 *(d)* of resolution 686(1991), demands that Iraq immediately begin to return all Kuwaiti property seized by it, to be completed in the shortest possible period. The members of the Council have noted with satisfaction that, as stated in the further report of the Secretary-General, Iraqi officials involved with the return of property have extended maximum cooperation to the United Nations to facilitate the return.

"*(g)* Monthly statements of gold and foreign currency reserves

"28. Another obligation is set out by paragraph 7 of resolution 706(1991), under which the Government of Iraq is required to provide to the Secretary-General and appropriate international organizations monthly statements of its gold and foreign currency reserves. To date, no such statements have been provided to the Secretary-General or to the IMF.

"*(h)* Undertaking not to commit or support acts of international terrorism

"29. By paragraph 32 of resolution 687(1991), Iraq is required not to commit or support acts of international terrorism or allow any organization directed towards commission of such acts to operate within its territory and to condemn unequivocally and renounce all acts, methods, and practices of terrorism.

"30. The Council notes Iraq's statements contained in letters dated 11 June 1991 (S/22687 and S/22689) and 23 January 1992 (S/23472) that it is a party to international conventions against terrorism and that it has never pursued a policy favourable to international terrorism as defined by international law.

"*(i)* Security Council action with respect to the Iraqi civilian population

"31. Resolutions 706(1991) and 712(1991) provide a means for Iraq to meet its obligations to supply its civilian population with needed humanitarian assistance, particularly food and medicine. To date, Iraq has refused to implement these resolutions. In fact, after initiating discussions with Secretariat representatives on implementation, Iraq abruptly terminated the discussions.

"III. Security Council resolution 688(1991)

"32. I should now like to refer to the demands by the Security Council with respect to the Iraqi civilian population. In paragraph 2 of resolution 688(1991), the Security Council demands that Iraq, as a contribution to removing the threat to international peace and security in the region, end the repression of its civilian population. In paragraphs 3 and 7, the Security Council insists that it allow immediate access by international humanitarian organizations to all those in need of assistance in all parts of Iraq, and demands its cooperation with the Secretary-General to these ends.

"33. The Security Council remains deeply concerned at the grave human rights abuses that, despite the provisions of resolution 688(1991), the Government of Iraq continues to perpetrate against its population, in particular in the northern region of Iraq, in southern Shi'a centres and in the southern marshes (Commission on Human Rights resolution 1992/71 of 5 March 1992). The Security Council notes that this situation is confirmed by the report of the Special Rapporteur of the Commission on Human Rights (E/CN.4/1992/31, also to be circulated in document S/23685) and by the comments of the Office of the Executive Delegate of the Secretary-General contained in the further report of the Secretary-General.

"34. The members of the Council are particularly concerned at the reported restrictions on the supplies of essential commodities, in particular food and fuel, which have been imposed by the Government of Iraq on the three northern governorates of Dohuk, Erbil and Suleimaniya. In this regard, as the Special Rapporteur has noted in his report, inasmuch as the repression of the population continues, the threat to international peace and security in the region mentioned in resolution 688(1991) remains.

"IV. Concluding observation

"35. In view of the observations on the record of Iraq's performance, the Security Council has considered itself justified in concluding that Iraq has not fully complied with the obligations placed upon it by the Council. It is the Council's hope and expectation that this meeting will prove an invaluable opportunity to advance in the consideration of this issue as required in the interest of world peace and security, as well as that of the Iraqi people."

Iraq, in the person of its Deputy Prime Minister, Tariq Aziz, referred to resolution 687(1991) as laying down measures and conditions without precedent in United Nations history, for they transcended by a large degree the initial limits and declared objectives of Council resolutions 660(1990)[20] and 686(1991).[21] It recalled that, as an independent sovereign State, Iraq made known its views on resolution 687(1991), based on the Charter, international law and principles of fairness and justice, but accepted the resolution to ward off the dangers that were threatening the Iraqi people. As demonstrated by its comprehensive letter of 23 January,[15] Iraq had since implemented to a large extent the fundamental provisions of that resolution.

Focusing on aspects that had been the source of problems, Iraq stated that the prohibited weapons had been totally destroyed; whatever remained was scheduled for destruction according to a plan about which Iraq and the United Nations inspection teams had no argument. Equipment used or allegedly used

to produce such weapons had been identified, examined and placed under seal to ensure its non-use. From April 1991 to February 1992, 29 inspection teams of about 400 inspectors conducted 415 inspections in Iraq, including 127 surprise ones, for a total of 240 days. The teams used the most advanced and sophisticated means of detection, communication, reconnaissance and transport, including extensive helicopter aerial surveys—about 45 of them, plus another 120 flights, each of between four and eight hours' duration. United States U-2 planes flew 32 reconnaissance missions, averaging three to four hours each.

The inspection teams supervised 40 operations of destruction of missile systems, chemical weapons, equipment and their accessories, totalling around 14,000 items, ranging from half-manufactured parts to missiles and rocket launchers, from machines and equipment to empty chemical-munition shells. Iraq itself had destroyed more than 270,000 items of equipment and machine parts. More than 1,500 tonnes of raw materials had also been destroyed. Machines and equipment placed under seal numbered nearly 1,000, not to mention those destroyed during the 1991 military operations. The conclusion to be drawn was that Iraq was no longer in possession of any weapons, munitions, or major or minor systems prohibited by resolution 687(1991).

Iraq repeated the information it communicated to the Council President in February regarding the repatriation of Kuwaiti and third-country nationals and to the Secretary-General on 28 January regarding the return of Kuwaiti properties.

Iraq restated that it had fulfilled the most fundamental provisions of sections A, B, D and H of resolution 687(1991). Those provisions that required some time to implement fully were being implemented with Iraq's serious and professional cooperation. Iraq noted that, after each compliance review since June 1991, the Council had declared that it was not yet in full compliance; the embargo thus remained in force and the suffering of 18 million Iraqis continued unmitigated. It asserted that the extent of its compliance, repeatedly notified to the Council, had been ignored under pressure from a small but influential and perhaps even tyrannical number of Council members, which had exploited resolution 687(1991) for political ends.

As to the Council President's statement of 28 February (see below, under "Special Commission activities"), Iraq declared its readiness to take several steps—all in relation to resolution 687(1991)—based on respect for its sovereignty and dignity and non-infringement of its national security. It would continue to cooperate with the Special Commission and IAEA in accomplishing the tasks specified and in providing information to complete the picture of its prohibited programmes; it was ready to reach a practical solution to the question of verifying Iraq's capabilities to produce prohibited weapons, as well as a practical mechanism to render harmless the equipment specified in paragraph 8 of the resolution.

With regard to completing information and data, Iraq proposed a technical meeting between itself, the Special Commission and the Security Council, at which the Commission's demands and questions relating to resolution 687(1991) would be submitted; the information and documentation to be presented by Iraq would be reviewed; and a comprehensive report would be submitted to the Council within a fixed period. By this means the Council's demand for a full, complete and final declaration would be met scientifically, objectively and reliably.

In order to resolve the issue of ongoing monitoring and verification, Iraq proposed that the related plans be discussed—a proposal for which the inspection teams evinced an understanding. As to equipment capable of dual use, Iraq felt it possible to arrive at a reasonable formula for verifying that such equipment was not used to produce prohibited weapons while at the same time preserving Iraq's legitimate rights, its sovereignty and security, rather than resorting to the extremist approach calling only for destruction. To that end Iraq proposed that the Commission submit to the Council a complete and final list of all the machines and equipment to be destroyed or rendered harmless. Iraq would determine whether or not, in its view, the equipment could be used for prohibited purposes. Alternatively, every Member State could be represented by experts capable of verifying the information and views of both sides.

Finally, Iraq sought clarification from the Council as to its position on the subject of the economic embargo imposed on Iraq, saying that despite the extent to which it had implemented resolution 687 (1991), the Council had not budged an inch. Therefore, Iraqis remained deprived of their right to a normal life and had to import all their humanitarian needs. It called on the Council to abandon that position in favour of an objective and fair one.

IAEA, in the person of its Director General, stated its mandate under the series of Council resolutions beginning with resolution 687(1991): to map nuclear programmes and facilities in Iraq intended, or susceptible to being used, to produce nuclear weapons or weapons-usable material; to remove, destroy or render harmless proscribed items; and to plan and perform future ongoing monitoring and verification of Iraq's compliance with all Council resolutions in the nuclear sphere.

IAEA stated that considerable work had been accomplished, which would not have been possible without Iraq's cooperation; however, the results would have come sooner and with much less pain had Iraq fully and spontaneously complied with its obligations under the resolutions. It noted in this connection that Iraq's behaviour had often been marked by denial of clandestine activities until the evidence was overwhelming, followed by cooperation until the next case of concealment was revealed. He recalled serious incidents of confrontation when IAEA inspection teams were denied unrestricted access to sites or when pertinent documents were removed from them. In the face of these attitudes, IAEA could not have carried out the mapping of Iraq's nuclear programme but for the firm and consistent support of the Council.

After 10 months of work, including 10 inspections, after many sessions of intense questioning of Iraqi technical teams, after the screening of masses of documents and assessment of the analytical investigations of many hundreds of samples taken in Iraq, a fairly consistent and coherent picture was emerging of the Iraqi nuclear programme. That picture was by no means a simple reflection of the information supplied by Iraq; it was based on direct observation and inspection of nuclear facilities, equipment and material, on authentic documents and proven information from other countries and on the IAEA experts' considerable experience of nuclear programmes. Some gaps or grey areas remained, however. In view of these and Iraq's track record of non-revelation, inspections needed to continue even as future ongoing monitoring and verification was under way.

A general shortcoming in Iraq's attitude had been the lack of full and explicit acceptance of resolutions 707(1991) and 715(1991)—an expression not only of reluctance but also of resistance that was incompatible with the binding nature of those resolutions. The Council's insistence on the matter was important, not only as a question of its authority but as a matter underlying the many specific points of non-compliance that had been noted. Lack of cooperation and non-compliance still persisted in respect of information on procurement sources of critical material and equipment. Further, the initial information needed to establish the future ongoing plan for monitoring and verification, required to be supplied by Iraq under resolution 715(1991), had been provided only partially. A statement by Iraq of readiness to provide procurement information and to complete the information required under resolution 705(1991) would eliminate serious hurdles.

As to the removal, destruction or rendering harmless of proscribed nuclear items, a large part of Iraq's nuclear facilities, including most of those known to have been used in the nuclear-weapons development programme, was either fully destroyed or heavily damaged in the course of the 1991 military operations in the Gulf. This was true of Al-Tuwaitha, the main research and development centre of the Iraqi nuclear programme; of Tarmiya, the industrial complex for electromagnetic isotope separation (EMIS) enriched uranium production; of Ash Sharqat, the intended second site for EMIS industrial-scale activities; of Al-Jesirah, the large chemical complex, where the natural uranium feed material for enrichment activities was produced; and of Al-Qaim, where uranium concentrates from indigenous uranium-bearing phosphate ores were produced.

In addition, by admission of the Iraqi authorities, a number of items, such as components and equipment, were subsequently damaged or destroyed by the Iraqi military in an attempt to remove evidence of the clandestine nuclear programme. In spite of this extensive destruction, there were still sites, facilities, equipment and material that suffered little or no damage and therefore fell into the category of items requiring destruction, removal or rendering harmless under resolution 687(1991). A case in point was the Al-Atheer site, specifically designed for weaponization activities, and of some buildings at Tarmiya and Ash Sharqat.

IAEA summarized progress as follows. Material in the form of fresh and irradiated fuel elements for the Iraqi research reactors was removed from Iraq in November 1991; negotiations were under way to remove the remaining irradiated fuel. A large number of components of calutrons and ultracentrifuges relevant to producing enriched uranium had been destroyed under IAEA supervision. Hot cells, glove boxes, remote-handling manipulators and other equipment used in research activities for laboratory-scale separation of plutonium from irradiated fuel had been destroyed or rendered harmless. Dedicated equipment and machine tools for the manufacture of those components had also been destroyed. Dual-use items were being inventoried and placed under IAEA seal. Buildings, such as laboratories, plants and other facilities where research and development, production or testing directly relevant to activities prohibited under resolution 687(1991) were conducted, were being assessed for destruction.

IAEA noted that large facilities and amounts of equipment for the production of nuclear weapons and nuclear-weapons-usable material had been destroyed, removed or rendered harmless. New facilities could not be built easily without detection, and the import or production of new relevant equipment would meet great obstacles. What certainly remained in Iraq, however, was a large cadre of highly trained scientists and engineers who had been engaged in its nuclear programme. It was important, the Director General said, that that cadre, reported to be currently engaged in the civilian reconstruction of Iraq, remain engaged in nonproscribed activities.

The Special Commission, in the person of the Executive Chairman, emphasized that the Commission had one fundamental aim: to be able to report to the Council as soon as possible that Iraq had fully met all its obligations under section C of resolution 687(1991) as elaborated upon in resolutions 707(1991) and 715(1991). The speed with which the Commission could report the successful execution of its task was largely determined by the degree of Iraq's cooperation, openness and transparency, which fell short of what was required. All the necessary information that Iraq claimed to have provided was neither complete nor systematized, for the Commission had evidence of the continued existence and concealment of undeclared weapons and means of their delivery. The very fact that Iraq had not acknowledged resolution 707(1991), which called for full, final and complete disclosure of its prohibited programmes in all their aspects, undermined the credibility of the information it had provided.

Instead of providing the disclosure called for, Iraq had proposed a dialogue whereby the Commission would elicit information through an inquisitorial approach and thus shift the onus placed on Iraq to present the information it possessed onto the Commission to seek and compile that information. The Commission stressed that Iraq must provide: all information on the evolution of the programmes and the links among all the elements in each; all information on procurement to support the programmes, including a detailed year-by-year breakdown of production and imports plus sources; full records of the use of all relevant weapons and their components; credible, detailed information on items unilaterally destroyed by Iraq; and sufficient, credible supporting documentation and physical evidence for all declarations made to date. Since resolution 687(1991) provided for the disposal of prohibited items only under international supervision, the Commission had requested, but had yet to receive, a list fully accounting for the 270,000 items declared as having been unilaterally destroyed.

Regarding the Commission's responsibility to destroy, remove or render harmless Iraq's weapons and capabilities in the proscribed areas, the destruction of weapons already declared was under way with Iraqi cooperation, duly noted as having been good. Regarding disposal of production capabilities, however, in particular certain missile-producing ones identified for destruction after a long process of exchanges with Iraq on a case-by-case basis, a ballistic missile inspection team charged with overseeing the destruction had to be withdrawn due to Iraq's refusal to proceed. As the Council statement of 28 February clearly reaffirmed, it was for the Commission alone to determine what items must be destroyed under paragraph 9 of resolution 687(1991).

To Iraq's argument that, rather than destroy the facilities specifically designed to produce weapons of mass destruction, they should be converted to civilian use so as not to deprive the country of its civilian industrial base, the Executive Chairman replied that the Commission would be failing in its responsibility to the Council if it did not ensure that such facilities were either destroyed, removed or rendered harmless. The latter would involve modification to render the facilities incapable of being reconverted for prohibited activities.

The Commission drew attention to the existing impasse with respect to the third stage of its responsibility: ongoing monitoring and verification of Iraq's compliance with its obligations under section C of resolution 687(1991). In January 1992, Iraq confirmed its position to the Commission that the objectives of the monitoring and verification plans were incompatible with the letter and spirit of the United Nations Charter, the norms of international law, and international and humanitarian pacts and covenants. While Iraq claimed that that statement did not amount to a rejection, the Commission could not but understand it as such in the light of its language. Further confirming that rejection was Iraq's failure so far to submit two declarations required under the Commission's plans for ongoing monitoring and verification, without which a satisfactory monitoring regime could not be set up and monitoring could not be instituted.

The Commission explained that the intrusive elements in the general provisions of the plans were approved by the Council against a background of Iraqi concealment, movement of proscribed items and violation of the privileges and immunities of inspection teams. Those elements would not be invoked provided Iraq cooperated. In any event, the Commission and IAEA had no need to justify plans unanimously endorsed by the Council in resolution 715(1991), adopted under Chapter VII of the Charter.

The successful implementation of the work of the Commission and of IAEA required that their facilities, privileges and immunities be respected, flowing as they did from Council resolutions, from relevant international conventions to which Iraq was party, and from the express provisions of the status agreement between the United Nations and Iraq, which entered into force on 14 May 1991.[22] If Iraq had a real interest in the full cooperation necessary to expedite implementation of section C of resolution 687(1991), it should stop meeting with silence the Commission's approaches to resolve the difficulties interposed in regard to its operations and aircraft landing rights. Aerial surveillance flights were undertaken with full Commission control and command. It was correct that a large number of them had taken place over Baghdad for the simple reason that a number of facili-

ties to which resolution 687(1991) related were in its vicinity. The Commission had to act in accordance with Council resolutions, the provisions of which it could not negotiate away.

In the absence of the undertaking by Iraq to comply fully with the Council's decisions, and until practical experience was gained to confirm that such an undertaking was being honoured, the Special Commission would be seriously hindered in those phases of its operations concerning identification and destruction of proscribed items and would be precluded from instituting the ongoing monitoring and verification phase. In such a situation, the possibility of the Special Commission's certifying Iraq's compliance with its obligations under section C of resolution 687(1991) could not even arise.

At a resumed meeting on 12 March, Iraq responded to the questions and concerns put forward.

Addressing the matter of respect for the international boundary between Iraq and Kuwait, Iraq said there was not a fundamental problem but rather a minor one concerning five police posts set up by Iraq on Kuwait's side of the boundary. He said Iraq had asked that their withdrawal be deferred until the demarcation had been completed.

On the weapons-related obligations, Iraq asserted that all weapons prohibited under resolution 687(1991) and their subsystems had been destroyed. Iraq was ready to make full, comprehensive and final declarations of all of its weapons programmes specified in that resolution, and, for that purpose, suggested that technical meetings be held with the Special Commission and IAEA. As to the "destruction or rendering harmless" of specified items and facilities, Iraq said it was committed to the provisions of resolution 687(1991) as they stood, but reiterated its observation that the current interpretation of that phrase was not in line with the text of the resolution. It asserted that destruction must be limited to equipment that could be used only to produce prohibited weapons and called on the Council to meet Iraq's legitimate request that other equipment that could be converted for non-prohibited purposes be simply rendered harmless. Verification of such use could be provided for.

Through its acceptance of resolution 687(1991), Iraq had accepted the principle of future verification of compliance, but reaffirmed in this connection that the requirements of its national sovereignty and territorial integrity be respected.

Iraq restated the measures it had taken and was taking to arrange visits to prisons and detention camps and to obtain information on missing Kuwaitis and third-country nationals. It had accepted the resolutions on the question of its liability under international law. Iraq emphasized that, as the party directly concerned in the claims for losses and damage being filed against it, it should be represented in the machinery dealing with those claims. Under the law, a relationship between fault and damage should be established and justice demanded proof of fault for liability. As to its obligation to pay its debts and interest, Iraq could not do so under the all-out embargo against it.

As to suspicions that if Iraq were allowed to export oil to finance its humanitarian needs it might use the proceeds for other purposes, a practical way to dispel those suspicions was to sell oil to Council members which had been purchasers of Iraqi oil and Iraq could confine its purchases to the permanent Council members so that they could keep track of the transactions. For Iraq, the sales regime laid out in resolution 706(1991) had political implications that, wittingly or not, would lead to interference in Iraq's internal affairs. Therefore, it was ready to enter into serious talks to find an acceptable alternative solution. It was ready to pursue the contacts begun at Vienna in February, but without preconditions, so as to reach agreement on practical arrangements for the export of an appropriate amount of Iraqi oil and to secure transparency on future imports and exports. Iraq hoped that such arrangements would not be embodied in a resolution.

Regarding the Kurds in the north and the Shiites in the south, as well as the alleged blockade against the three governorates and international relief efforts, Iraq's position on resolution 688(1991)[23] on the matter was that it constituted blatant interference in Iraq's internal affairs. Dialogue with the Kurdistan Front, while resulting in a new formula for autonomy for the Iraqi Kurds, was not signed by the Front. Subsequent acts of destruction and sabotage against Government authorities in the governorates made it imperative for the Government to withdraw the administrative apparatus from the area. Thus Erbil was bereft of a mechanism whereby to pay the salaries of civil employees, although salaries could be collected at Mosul or Kirkuk. The governorates were likewise bereft of the apparatus to distribute supply rations so that distribution was being made to Kurdish-controlled caterers. The question of proper distribution thus fell outside the central Government's responsibility. There was no blockade of the governorates, Iraq asserted, only precautionary measures in the form of checkpoints to prevent smuggling into bordering countries.

Iraq had reaffirmed its commitment against terrorism, and there was not a shred of evidence that it had taken part in terrorist operations.

Finally, Iraq requested that it be allowed to appear before the Council at every review of its compliance in order to have the opportunity to explain its position on matters raised.

After consultations among the Council members during a brief suspension of the meeting, the President was authorized to make the following statement[24] on the Council's behalf:

"In concluding the present stage of the consideration of the item on the agenda, I have been authorized, following consultations among members of the Security Council, to make the following statement on behalf of the Council:

" 'The views of the Security Council having been expressed through its President and by the statements of its members on the extent of compliance by the Government of Iraq with its obligations under the relevant Security Council resolutions, the Security Council has listened with close attention to the statement by the Deputy Prime Minister of Iraq and his responses to the questions posed by Council members.

" 'The members of the Security Council wish to reiterate their full support for the statement made by the President of the Council on their behalf at the opening of the 3059th meeting (S/23699).

" 'In the view of the Security Council, the Government of Iraq has not yet complied fully and unconditionally with those obligations, must do so and must immediately take the appropriate actions in this regard. It hopes that the goodwill expressed by the Deputy Prime Minister of Iraq will be matched by deeds.' "

Report of the Special Commission. On 22 May 1992,[25] the Secretary-General transmitted to the Security Council a report by the Executive Chairman of the Special Commission on the status of Iraq's compliance with its obligations under section C of resolution 687(1991) and resolutions 707(1991) and 715(1991), prepared for the Council's 60-day review of the sanctions imposed on Iraq.

The report stated that the Office of the Executive Chairman explained in detail to Iraq's high-level delegation to the Council in March the format and modalities required by the plan for ongoing monitoring and verification under its different sections and annexes, and emphasized that the plan required full information. The Iraqi team promised to provide the information by early April—although not information on the sources of imported items and the operational deployment or disposition of relevant weapons—as well as the full, final and complete disclosure of all aspects of Iraq's proscribed weapons programmes as required under resolution 707(1991). To an invitation to visit Baghdad to review both sets of draft declarations, the Commission indicated acceptance provided it received beforehand the draft texts and Iraq's clear acknowledgement of its obligations arising from resolutions 707(1991) and 715(1991). Neither that formal acknowledgement nor the draft declarations had been received.

The Executive Chairman summarized the Commission's inspection activities with respect to Iraq's chemical and biological weapons and ballistic missiles. He again drew attention to the Commission's unsuccessful efforts to obtain landing rights at Rasheed airport, to Iraq's continuing protests against the use of the U-2 high-altitude surveillance aircraft, and to the fact that not all the documents forcibly removed from a nuclear inspection team in 1991 had yet been returned.

On 26 May 1992,[26] Iraq transmitted a letter of the same date from the Minister for Foreign Affairs of Iraq in response to a 21 May letter from the Executive Chairman of the Special Commission.

As to the required full, final and complete disclosure, the Minister said such disclosure in the nuclear field was submitted directly to the IAEA Director General on 12 March. At the time it was agreed that it would be seen as a draft for discussion and revision in the light of IAEA comments. The draft was subsequently revised after discussions with the inspectors of the eleventh (April) nuclear inspection. The Minister recalled that the Commission had been advised in March that the draft of the full, final and complete disclosure relating to chemical and biological weapons and ballistic missiles was ready for submission in Arabic, and that the English version would be submitted to a Commission delegation that was to have visited Baghdad in April but never did. The report was ready and Iraq awaited the Executive Chairman's views as to whether it should be transmitted by mail or through Commission representatives.

With regard to Iraq's acknowledgement of its obligations under resolution 707(1991) and 715(1991) approving the plans for ongoing monitoring and verification, the Minister recalled the Deputy Prime Minister's statement before the Council emphasizing Iraq's readiness to reach a practical solution regarding the verification specified and the possibility of identifying a reasonable formula that would achieve the plans' objectives while preserving Iraq's legitimate rights, sovereignty and security.

As to providing the declarations called for under the plans, he explained that those in the nuclear field were made in November 1991, as later updated. Declarations on chemical, biological and ballistic activities were to be discussed with a Commission technical team that was never sent to Baghdad. What remained to be met of the Commission's demands were the names of suppliers of materials related to those activities, which Iraq had declined to divulge on the grounds of trading ethics. On the question of ongoing monitoring to ensure that prohibited (ballistic, chemical and nuclear) weapons were not produced in the future, it was Iraq's demand that agreement be reached between it, the Commission and IAEA, under Security Council auspices, on practical guarantees

to ensure that the methods employed would not infringe upon Iraq's sovereignty, threaten its internal security, lead to interference in its internal affairs or deny it the prospects for scientific, technological and industrial progress in both the civilian and military spheres not prohibited under resolution 687(1991).

In the light of Iraq's responses, the Secretary-General, on 3 June,[27] circulated to the Security Council the Executive Chairman's letters of 1 and 2 April to the Vice-Chairman of the Military Industrial Corporation of Iraq and of 21 May to the Minister of State for Foreign Affairs of Iraq. The 1 April letter contained the Executive Chairman's conditions for accepting Iraq's invitation to review the draft declarations in Baghdad. The 2 April letter reviewed the preliminary draft declarations made available to the Commission on an unofficial basis by the Iraqi technical team in March and explained the concept behind the plan for ongoing monitoring and verification in relation to the revisions necessary to make the declarations conform with the parameters established by the provisions of the plans. The 21 May letter set out the three items that remained to be provided by Iraq, stressing that if not received, the Commission would have no alternative but to conclude that no progress had been made in obtaining them from Iraq.

IAEA report. IAEA, on 26 May 1992,[28] submitted a report on the status of Iraq's compliance with its obligations under section C of resolution 687(1991) and resolutions 707(1991) and 715(1991), likewise prepared for the 60-day review by the Security Council of the sanctions imposed on Iraq.

IAEA stated that, on 12 and 13 March, it discussed outstanding issues with a team headed by the IAEC Chairman and drawn from Iraq's high-level delegation to the Council. Further meetings were held (Vienna, Austria, 20-24 March) at the request of Iraq for the purpose of clarifying the role and functions of the Al-Atheer Centre in an effort to spare it from destruction. Convinced, however, that the technical core of the Al-Atheer–Al-Hatteen facility had been designed to accommodate nuclear-weapons development, IAEA informed Iraq on 25 March that the destruction of the facility had to proceed in conjunction with the eleventh (April) nuclear inspection (see below, under "IAEA inspections").

IAEA concluded that, before it could report to the Council that Iraq was in substantial compliance with its obligations, it had to fulfil the following: accept its obligations under resolutions 707(1991) and 715(1991); make a full, final and complete disclosure of all aspects of its nuclear programme, including procurement details, as called for by resolution 707(1991); and provide, under the IAEA plan adopted through resolution 715(1991), a complete list of equipment and materials used for prohibited purposes and of equipment and materials having dual-use capability. The removal, destruction and rendering harmless called for by resolution 687(1991) had to be completed to the full satisfaction of IAEA, and monitoring and verification to ensure that Iraq did not reacquire capabilities prohibited under resolution 687(1991) must be initiated and must proceed smoothly.

SECURITY COUNCIL ACTION (May and September)

After consultations held on 27 May 1992, the President of the Security Council issued the following statement[29] on behalf of the Council members in connection with the item entitled "The situation between Iraq and Kuwait":

"The members of the Security Council held informal consultations on 27 May 1992 pursuant to paragraph 21 of resolution 687(1991).

"After hearing all the opinions expressed in the course of the consultations, the President of the Council concluded that there still was no agreement that the necessary conditions existed for a modification of the regime established in paragraph 20 of resolution 687(1991), as referred to in paragraph 21 of that resolution."

Likewise, after consultations on 24 September, the President issued a similar statement[30] on behalf of the Council members in connection with the same item.

Communications from Iraq. On 28 October 1992,[31] Iraq called on the Security Council in the strongest terms to revise its position and attitude towards Iraq. It accused the Council, the Special Commission and IAEA of waging a ferocious and unparalleled campaign to exact from Iraq compliance with obligations imposed on it under resolution 687(1991). For the sake of truth and the historical record, it was obliged to state that most of the inspection teams that visited Iraq were hostile. They engaged in effrontery and provocation and had no regard for the sovereignty, dignity and security of Iraq. They contrived problems and their inspection plans were based, not on scientific, technical and logical considerations, but on tendentious reports aimed at furthering the well-known political designs of certain States against Iraq. The teams behaved more like medieval inquisitors than technical inspectors carrying out the well-defined objectives of resolution 687(1991).

Iraq asserted that the United Nations was applying a shameful double standard. In its pursuit of the enforcement of provisions that punished and restricted Iraq well beyond the wording of the resolution, the provision calling for the establishment of a Middle East zone free of weapons of mass destruction and all missiles for their delivery was being ignored. Israel and Iran were engaged in building their arsenals of mass destruction, resulting in the emergence of a dangerous disequilibrium of forces in the region that threatened its security and stability. The Council, whose resolution 687(1991) allegedly was the result of the Iraq-Kuwait issue, had further chosen to ignore Iran's military occupation of the Gulf islands belonging to the United Arab Emirates (see above, under "Iran–United Arab Emirates").

In the interest of justice and fairness, Iraq deemed it essential for the Council to conduct a radical review of the provisions of resolutions 707(1991) and 715(1991), saying they were intrusive and constituted a violation of its sovereignty. At issue were the Commission's aerial surveillance by helicopter and U-2 aircraft, which Iraq claimed were intelligence-gathering missions on behalf of certain Governments endeavouring to undermine the country's internal situation and eliminate its national leadership. In addition, Iraq registered its vigorous protest against the gratuitous imposition of no-fly zones north of the 36th parallel and south of the 32nd—by France, the United Kingdom and the United States. Iraq called for the condemnation of such autocratic action, which undermined the legitimacy of the Council resolutions so long as the Council failed to address this issue.

Finally, Iraq recalled its requests for the lifting of the economic embargo imposed against it under resolution 661(1990),[7] stating that, whereas its lifting was originally linked to compliance with resolution 660(1990)[20] demanding Iraq's withdrawal from Kuwait, it became linked to new conditions incorporated in resolution 687(1991). Iraq referred to its statement before the Council in March that the high proportion of obligations it had fulfilled warranted a full or partial lifting of the sanctions, regardless of any difference of opinion as to the extent to which those obligations had been fulfilled. Citing deprivations suffered by the Iraqis and death rates of children in various age groups, Iraq asserted that continuance of the sanctions was tantamount to genocide against its people and called for an end to such a squalid operation.

Iraq, on 10 November,[32] reiterated that it was incumbent on the Council to begin lifting the embargo and all the exceptional measures imposed on Iraq. It stated its wish to send a high-level delegation to New York on the occasion of the Council's November review of the status of its compliance with its obligations. On 19 November,[33] Iraq submitted a factual report on further measures it had taken to implement section C of resolution 687(1991), covering the period between January and November 1992. The report gave a detailed account of activities in conjunction with the 1992 IAEA and Special Commission inspections.

The Security Council met on 23 November 1992 for its second review of the status of Iraq's compliance with resolution 687(1991) and other related resolutions. As agreed in earlier consultations, it invited Iraq and Kuwait to participate in the debate in accordance with Article 31 of the United Nations Charter and rule 37[a] of the Council's provisional rules of procedure. It also invited, under rule 39,[b] the IAEA Director General, Hans Blix, the Special Commission Executive Chairman, Rolf Ekéus, the Under-Secretary-General for Humanitarian Affairs and the Emergency Relief Coordinator, Jan Eliasson, and the Special Rapporteur on human rights, Max van der Stoel.

China and Zimbabwe registered their view that it was inappropriate for the Council to invite the Special Rapporteur to its deliberations on the grounds that the human rights question fell within the purview of the Commission on Human Rights and the General Assembly. China further entered its reservations on the references to the interim report of the Special Rapporteur contained in the statement below.

Following consultations among the Council members, the President was authorized to make the following introductory statement[(34)] on behalf of the Council:

Meeting number. SC 3139 (with resumptions 1 and 2).

"I. General obligation

"1. The resolutions concerning the situation between Iraq and Kuwait impose a number of general and specific obligations upon Iraq.

"2. As regards the general obligations, Iraq is required, under paragraph 33 of Security Council resolution 687(1991), to give official notification to the Secretary-General and to the Security Council of its acceptance of the provisions of that entire resolution.

"3. Iraq signified its unconditional acceptance in letters dated 6 and 10 April 1991 (S/22456 and S/22480, respectively) and 23 January 1992 (S/23472).

"II. Specific obligations

"4. In addition to the general obligation to accept the provisions of resolution 687(1991) in their entirety, several Security Council resolutions impose specific obligations upon Iraq.

"(a) Respect for the inviolability of the international boundary

"5. By paragraph 2 of resolution 687(1991) the Security Council demands that Iraq respect the inviolability of the international boundary and the allocations of islands previously agreed upon between Iraq and Kuwait. Pursuant to paragraph 3 of that resolution, the Secretary-General established a Boundary Demarcation Commission to demarcate the boundary between Iraq and Kuwait. Paragraph 5 of the same resolution requires Iraq and Kuwait to respect a demilitarized zone (DMZ) established by the Security Council.

"6. Iraq did not participate in the work of the Boundary Demarcation Commission at its July 1992 and October 1992 sessions. Iraq has refused up to now to withdraw a number of police posts that are not in line with UNIKOM's principle that both sides should stay 1,000 metres from the boundary line shown on UNIKOM's map. The Council in paragraph 2 of resolution 773(1992) welcomed the Commission's land demarcation decisions and, by paragraph 5, the intention of the Secretary-General to carry out at the earliest practicable time the realignment of the DMZ to correspond to the international boundary demarcated, by the Commission, with the consequent removal of the Iraqi police posts.

"7. In response to the Iraqi Foreign Minister's 21 May 1992 letter to the Secretary-General (S/24044), the Security Council in a 17 June 1992 statement (S/24113) stressed to Iraq the inviolability of the international boundary between Iraq and Kuwait being demarcated by the Commission and guaranteed by the Council pursuant to resolution 687(1991). The Presidential statement also noted with dismay that the Iraqi Foreign Minister's letter recalled past Iraqi claims to Kuwait without also recalling Iraq's subsequent repudiation of these claims. The members of the Council firmly rejected any suggestion that tended to dispute the existence of Kuwait. Resolution 773(1992) underlined the Council's guarantee of the above-mentioned international boundary and its decision to take as appropriate all necessary measures to that end in accordance with the Charter, as provided for in paragraph 4 of resolution 687(1991).

"(b) Weapons-related obligations

"8. Section C of resolution 687(1991) imposes certain specific obligations upon Iraq with respect to its chemical and biological weapons programmes, its ballistic missile programmes with a range greater than 150 kilometres and its nuclear programmes. These obligations are elaborated upon in resolutions 707(1991) and 715(1991). The obligations are defined in paragraphs 8, 9, 10, 11, 12 and 13 of resolution 687(1991) and they are elaborated upon in paragraphs 3 and 5 of resolution 707(1991) and paragraph 5 of resolution 715(1991).

"9. By resolution 699(1991), the Security Council decided that the Government of Iraq shall be liable for the full costs of carrying out the tasks authorized by section C of resolution 687(1991). No funds have so far been received from Iraq to meet this liability.

"10. The Council has noted that since the adoption of resolution 687(1991) progress has been made in the implementation of section C of that resolution but that much remains to be done. In particular, Iraq needs to provide the full, final and complete disclosure of all aspects of its programmes for weapons of mass destruction and ballistic missiles with a range greater than 150 kilometres. There is a particular and vital requirement for complete information, including credible documentary evidence on Iraq's past production, suppliers and consumption of all prohibited items, and its past capacity to produce such items.

"11. Iraq must also acknowledge clearly its obligations under Security Council resolution 715(1991) and the two plans for ongoing monitoring and verification approved thereunder. It must agree to implement these obligations unconditionally. In this connection the Council notes the letter of 28 October 1992 from Iraq's Minister for Foreign Affairs to the Secretary-General seeking a review of the terms and provisions not only of resolution 715(1991) but also Security Council resolution 707(1991). It is accordingly clear that Iraq seems unprepared to comply with the obligations already prescribed.

"12. The Special Commission has informed the Council about the outstanding matters that would at the present time appear to be the most important. The Council has noted document S/24661 of 19 October 1992 entitled 'The status of the implementation of the plan for the ongoing monitoring and verification of Iraq's compliance with relevant parts of section C of Security Council resolution 687(1991)'.

"13. The Council has also noted document S/24722 of 28 October 1992 containing the second report of the Director General of the International Atomic Energy Agency (IAEA) on the implementation of the Agency's plan for the future ongoing monitoring and verification of Iraq's compliance with paragraph 12 of resolution 687(1991).

"14. In a statement issued on behalf of the members of the Council (S/23803) on the Special Commission's right to conduct aerial surveillance flights in Iraq, the President stated on 10 April 1992 that:

" 'The members of the Council wish to point out that the surveillance flights are carried out under the authority of Security Council resolutions 687(1991), 707(1991) and 715(1991). Reaffirming the right of the Special Commission to conduct such aerial surveillance flights, the members of the Council call upon the Government of Iraq to take all the necessary steps to ensure that the Iraqi military forces will not interfere with or threaten the security of the flights concerned and to comply with its responsibilities to secure the safety of the Special Commission's aircraft and personnel flying over Iraq.'

"The President also said that:

" 'The members of the Council warn the Government of Iraq of the serious consequences which would ensue from any failure to comply with these obligations.'

"15. The Special Commission, on 15 October 1992, informed the Council of actions endangering the safety and security of the Commission's inspection teams in Iraq, including a systematic campaign of harassment, acts of violence, vandalism to property and verbal denunciations and threats at all levels. The President of the Council issued on the same day a statement to the press stressing the Council's particular concern for the safety of the Commission's inspectors.

"16. In a further statement made on 6 July 1992 on behalf of the Council (S/24240) concerning the Government of Iraq's refusal to permit access to certain premises by a team of inspectors, the President said:

" 'Iraq's present refusal to permit access to the Inspection Team currently in Iraq to the premises designated by the Special Commission constitutes a material and unacceptable breach by Iraq of a provision of resolution 687(1991) which established

the cease-fire and provided the conditions essential to the restoration of peace and security in the region. The members of the Council demand that the Government of Iraq immediately agree to the admission to the premises concerned of the inspectors of the Special Commission as required by the Chairman of the Special Commission, so that the Special Commission may establish whether or not any documents, records, materials, or equipment relevant to the responsibilities of the Commission are located therein.'

"Security Council resolution 707(1991) demands that Iraq allow the Special Commission, the IAEA and their inspection teams immediate, unconditional and unrestricted access to any and all areas, facilities, equipment, records and means of transportation which they wish to inspect. Therefore, the Council cannot accept Iraq's insistence that there must be a limit on access by the inspection teams.

"(c)   Repatriation of and access to Kuwaiti and third-country nationals in Iraq

"17. As regards Kuwaiti and third-country nationals in Iraq, Security Council resolutions 664(1990), 666(1990), 667(1990), 674(1990), 686(1991) and 687(1991) impose an obligation on Iraq to release, facilitate repatriation of, and arrange for immediate access to them, as well as the return of the remains of any deceased personnel of the forces of Kuwait and of the member States cooperating with Kuwait pursuant to resolution 678(1990). Furthermore, paragraph 30 of resolution 687(1991) requires Iraq to extend all necessary cooperation to the International Committee of the Red Cross (ICRC) in facilitating the search for Kuwaiti and third-country nationals still unaccounted for.

"18. In spite of ICRC's best ongoing efforts, ICRC has not received information as to the whereabouts of the persons reported missing in Iraq. Nor has it received detailed and documented information on the search conducted by the Iraqi authorities. Following the 11-12 March 1992 Council meeting with the Iraqi Deputy Prime Minister, Iraq published in its press lists of those believed missing/detained inside Iraq. ICRC has still not received permission to visit Iraqi prisons and detention centres in accordance with standard ICRC criteria. Very few missing persons/detainees have been released since March 1992, while hundreds are believed still to be inside Iraq.

"(d)   Iraq's liability under international law

"19. Another obligation concerns Iraq's liability under international law. In resolution 674(1990), the Security Council reminds Iraq that under international law it is liable for any loss, damage or injury arising in regard to Kuwait and third States and their nationals and corporations, as a result of the invasion and illegal occupation of Kuwait by Iraq. Its liability under international law is reaffirmed in paragraph 2 (b) of resolution 686(1991) and paragraph 16 of resolution 687(1991). Resolution 687(1991) further specifies that it 'is liable under international law for any direct loss, damage, including environmental damage and the depletion of natural resources, or injury to foreign governments, nationals and corporations, as a result of Iraq's unlawful invasion and occupation of Kuwait'.

"20. By paragraph 18 of the same resolution, the Security Council created a fund to pay compensation for claims that fall within paragraph 16, to be financed by a percentage of the value of the exports of petroleum and petroleum products from Iraq. In view of the existing economic sanctions against Iraq under resolution 661(1991), Iraq was permitted by the Security Council under resolutions 706(1991) and 712(1991) to sell a limited quantity of oil, as an exception, a portion of the proceeds from which would be used to provide financial resources for the fund. To date, it has not availed itself of this possibility. The Council noted that this authorization lapsed on 18 March 1992 but indicated its readiness to authorize the regime for the sale of Iraqi petroleum and petroleum products for a like period of time as that specified in the resolutions and also its readiness to consider possible further extensions (S/23732, 19 March 1992). Since then Iraq has not shown any willingness to resume discussions about implementing these resolutions. The members of the Council are aware of a previous request by Iraq for a five-year moratorium on meeting its financial obligations, including payments into the Compensation Fund.

"21. In view of Iraq's refusal to cooperate in the implementation of resolutions 706(1991) and 712(1991) after several rounds of technical discussions with the Secretariat, the Security Council adopted resolution 778(1992) which mandates that certain frozen Iraqi assets be transferred to a United Nations escrow account. A portion of these funds will be transferred to the Compensation Fund.

"*(e)* Repayment and servicing of Iraq's foreign debt

"22. With regard to another obligation, the Security Council, in paragraph 17 of resolution 687(1991), demands that Iraq scrupulously adhere to all of its obligations concerning servicing and repayment of its foreign debt.

"*(f)* Non-entitlement to claims deriving from the effects of the measures taken by the Security Council in resolution 661(1990) and related resolutions (para. 29 of resolution 687(1991)) of the Security Council

"23. According to information received with regard to this item, Iraq has attempted to enforce some claims under which it would have benefited from a contract frustrated by the coming into effect of the terms of resolution 661(1990), in particular, through the confiscation of the property of foreign companies and organizations left in Iraq.

"*(g)* Return of property

"24. I now turn to the question of return of property. The Security Council, in paragraph 2 *(d)* of resolution 686(1991), demands that Iraq immediately begin to return all Kuwaiti property seized by it, to be completed in the shortest possible period. The members of the Council have previously noted with satisfaction that Iraqi officials involved with the return of property have extended cooperation to the United Nations to facilitate the return. However, much property, including military equipment and private property, remains to be returned.

"*(h)* Monthly statements of gold and foreign currency reserves

"25. Another obligation is set out by paragraph 7 of resolution 706(1991), under which the Government of Iraq is required to provide to the Secretary-General and appropriate international organizations monthly statements of its gold and foreign currency reserves. To date, no such statements have been provided to the Secretary-General or to the IMF.

"*(i)* Undertaking not to commit or support acts of international terrorism

"26. By paragraph 32 of resolution 687(1991), Iraq is required not to commit or support acts of international terrorism or allow any organization directed towards commission of such acts to operate within its territory and to condemn unequivocally and renounce all acts, methods and practices of terrorism.

"27. The Council notes Iraq's statements contained in letters dated 11 June 1991 (S/22687 and S/22689) and 23 January 1992 (S/23472) that it is a party to international conventions against terrorism and that it has never pursued a policy favourable to international terrorism as defined by international law.

"*(j)* Security Council action with respect to the Iraqi civilian population

"28. Resolutions 706(1991) and 712(1991) provide a means for Iraq to meet its obligations to supply its civilian population with needed humanitarian assistance, particularly food and medicine. Resolution 778(1992) mandates that certain frozen Iraqi assets be transferred to a United Nations escrow account and urges States to contribute funds from other sources to the escrow account. A portion of these funds will be used for humanitarian assistance.

"III.   Security Council resolution 688(1991)

"29. I should now like to refer to the demands by the Security Council with respect to the Iraqi civilian population. In paragraph 2 of resolution 688(1991), the Security Council demands that Iraq, as a contribution to removing the threat to international peace and security in the region, end the repression of its civilian population. In paragraphs 3 and 7, the Security Council insists that it allow immediate access by international humanitarian organizations to all those in need of assistance in all parts of Iraq, and demands its cooperation with the Secretary-General to these ends.

"30. The Security Council remains deeply concerned at the grave human rights abuses that, despite the provisions of resolution 688(1991), the Government of Iraq continues to perpetrate against its population, in particular in the northern region of Iraq, in southern Shi'a Centres and in the southern marshes (Commission on Human Rights resolution 1992/71 of 5 March 1992). The Security Council notes that this situation is confirmed by the reports of the Special Rapporteur of the Commission on Human Rights (E/CN.4/1992/31, also circulated as document S/23685 and Add.1, and part I of the interim report circulated as document S/24386). The members of the Council recall their public meeting with Mr. Max van der Stoel on 11 August 1992.

"31. The members of the Security Council take note of the renewal on 22 October 1992 of the Memorandum of Understanding providing the framework for urgent humanitarian assistance throughout the country between the United Nations and the Government of Iraq.

"IV. Concluding observation

"32. In view of the observations on the record of Iraq's performance, and without prejudice to further action by the Security Council on the question of the implementation of its relevant resolutions by Iraq, the Security Council has considered itself justified in concluding that Iraq has up to now only selectively and then partially complied with the obligations placed upon it by the Council. It is the Council's hope that this meeting will prove a valuable opportunity to impress once again upon Iraq the imperative need for full compliance and to obtain from Iraq undertakings which would constitute an advance in the consideration of this issue as required in the interest of world peace and security, as well as that of the Iraqi people."

In its address to the Council on 23 November, Iraq, in the person of its Deputy Prime Minister, Tariq Aziz, stated that, in the past eight months, 16 additional inspections were carried out by the Special Commission and IAEA, during which 9,983 pieces of weaponry (shells, bombs, warheads, propellant charges), as well as many installations and equipment that could have been converted for civilian industrial purposes, were destroyed. Iraq referred to its factual report of 19 November giving details of what had been accomplished during the preceding eight-month period in further fulfilment of its obligations under section C of resolution 687(1991). Recapitulating the figures since that resolution was adopted, Iraq said that, in all, it had received 46 inspection teams comprising 1,056 inspectors who had spent a total of 11,816 inspection days in Iraq. They conducted 884 inspection operations including 237 surprise visits. They also conducted no less than 64 aerial survey missions involving 371 helicopter flights of four to eight hours duration and 97 U-2 surveillance flights, averaging three to four hours each.

The inspection teams supervised 44 destruction operations during which the number of items destroyed reached 26,865, including semi-manufactured items, missiles and launchers, as well as equipment, devices and empty chemical-munition shells. Also destroyed were quantities of raw materials weighing in excess of 1,500 tonnes. In addition to huge quantities of documentation that were either presented or seized before Iraq submitted its complete and comprehensive report, hundreds of hours of dialogue had been held with the inspectors, during which Iraq answered innumerable questions and proved false the vicious allegations that it was hiding missiles and had an underground reactor. In this connection, it quoted part of its 28 October letter[31] comparing the inspectors to medieval inquisitors and accusing the Council of applying double standards and overlooking the larger goal of security and stability in the Gulf area and in the Middle East.

Despite all this, the iniquitous embargo imposed on Iraq remained in force, denying the Iraqi people the essentials of human existence. Moreover, the Council in recent months had placed obstacles to Iraq's use of its assets abroad, which Council members continued to keep frozen even as the Committee on sanctions had allowed them to free those assets. The United States had also imposed on the Council adoption of resolution 778(1992)—another in the series of unjust Council resolutions—which allowed the arbitrary use of parts of those assets. While the Council placed heavy emphasis on the alleged loss of property of claimants who had not substantiated or sufficiently documented their claims, it deliberately squandered assets that were clearly Iraq's.

Iraq asserted that keeping the embargo in place amounted to the perpetration of the crime of genocide. For example, the embargo had caused the death of thousands of Iraqi children, deprived students of their education needs, led to the deterioration of the environment, and prevented Iraqis, including the sick, from travelling by fixed-wing aircraft.

Iraq reiterated its call for a halt to the Commission's use of the U-2 aircraft—referring to it as a United States spy plane—and its proposal that aircraft from a neutral State or Iraqi aircraft currently lying idle be used instead. Iraq would never tolerate any act intended to encroach on its sovereignty and trample its dignity. Stressing the importance of security and stability in the Gulf area and the need to deal in a balanced manner with all of the countries in the region, it demanded that the measures provided for in resolution 687(1991) be applied equally to all of them, not to Iraq alone. Iraq was ready for constructive and responsible cooperation towards that end.

IAEA, in the person of its Director General, stated that, since March, IAEA had made five more inspections and carried out considerable further investigative and other work. As a result, IAEA had fulfilled important parts of its first two tasks and had begun implementing elements of the third.

As to the first task—the complete mapping of Iraq's nuclear capabilities—while the picture of the nuclear programme that had emerged was comprehensive and detailed, IAEA could not be certain that it was complete. Due to Iraq's unwillingness to reveal foreign sources of equipment, material and technology, it was difficult to ascertain whether all nuclear-related imported equipment and material had been identified. Also, new information could point to sites requiring inspection. Therefore, IAEA saw a need for continued on-site inspection.

Since March, much work had been devoted to the second task, that of ensuring the destruction, removal or rendering harmless, as appropriate, of facilities and equipment related to the clandestine nuclear programme. With the active cooperation of the Iraqi authorities, key buildings, equipment and material at Al-Atheer, Tarmiya and Ash Sharqat had been destroyed or rendered harmless. The only nuclear-weapons-usable material known to remain in Iraq was the highly enriched uranium in irradiated reactor fuel assemblies, arrangements for the removal of which were under way.

The third task—long-term monitoring and verification of Iraq's compliance with the requirement not to reacquire or develop a nuclear-weapons capability—had met with some cooperation and some resistance. Iraq continued to challenge the legitimacy of the plans approved under resolution 715(1991). Of particular concern was Iraq's letter of 28 October[31] restating in strong terms its non-acceptance of resolutions 707(1991) and 715(1991). IAEA reiterated that the lack of acceptance of those resolutions ignored their binding nature and appeared also to ignore Iraq's own explicit acceptance of resolution 687(1991), paragraph 12 of which laid on Iraq the obligation to accept the plan for monitoring and verification.

Iraq continued to delay compliance with repeated requests for clear and complete information on items to be reported to IAEA under the plan. Only recently did it indicate its readiness to submit before the end of the year information on all nuclear-related items existing in Iraq as of 1 January 1989.

In the circumstances, IAEA was unable to report to the Council that Iraq had fully complied with its obligations under the relevant resolutions.

The Special Commission, in the person of its Executive Chairman, referred to the two biannual reports on the Commission's activities in the discharge of its threefold responsibilities. The first stage—identification of Iraq's weapons of mass destruction in the chemical, biological and ballistic missile areas—remained incomplete. The information that according to Iraq constituted the full, final and comprehensive report of all aspects of its programmes to develop weapons of mass destruction was unanimously found by the Commission, at its fourth plenary (October) session, to be flawed and incomplete. Almost the entire documentation needed to substantiate Iraq's account of its chemical, biological and bacteriological programmes had been denied to the Commission. The same was true in the missile field.

However, some progress had been made in compiling more information on Iraq's programmes for weapons of mass destruction as they existed at the outbreak of the military operations in the Gulf. Once again, this was largely due to further pains-taking inspection in conjunction with lengthy seminar-type meetings with senior Iraqi officials.

On the disposal of the capabilities for the production of weapons of mass destruction, the impediments to destruction of certain missile-producing capabilities reported in March had been overcome. This second stage of the Commission's activities remained incomplete, however, pending final decision on the disposal of many items and facilities that were currently under seal.

As to the third stage—ongoing monitoring and verification—the impasse reported in March had yet again been confirmed and even more forcefully. Iraq had consistently refused to acknowledge the existence of its obligations under resolutions 707(1991) and 715(1991) and under the plans approved by the latter. From the outset, Iraq had indicated willingness only to accept ongoing monitoring and verification in principle and on its own terms. Those terms appeared to be Iraq's exclusive understanding of paragraphs 10 and 12 of resolution 687(1991), which placed the most severe limitations—expressed as considerations of sovereignty, national security, dignity and non-interference in Iraq's internal affairs and industrial development—on any form of monitoring. This position could not be more clearly enunciated than by Iraq's letter of 28 October, which called on the Council to conduct a radical review, based on justice and fairness, of the terms and provisions of those two resolutions.

That letter further objected to the essential aspects of the Commission's operations in Iraq, in particular its air transportation, helicopter and high-altitude surveillance activities—all clearly authorized by Council resolutions adopted under Chapter VII of the Charter. Thus, if sanctions and the oil embargo were to end without Iraq's unconditional acceptance of its obligations under the two resolutions, the Commission's air transportation and aerial surveillance would be halted by withdrawal of Iraq's de facto acquiescence, and monitoring and verification would be reduced purely to visits to such installations as Iraq selected and at such times as it permitted.

Since March, the Commission had to defend vigorously the privileges and immunities of its staff and inspectors in Iraq, in particular their safety and security (see below, under "Special Commission activities"). Currently, however, there were fewer incidents of individual harassment.

Responding to the remarks regarding the conduct of its inspectors and staff, the Commission said they deserved tribute for their competence, dedication and courage. In seeking to identify and map out Iraq's weapons programmes, they had acted in the most professional manner, often under difficult and trying circumstances. The apparent intrusiveness of their activities on occasion was brought about by lack of Iraqi cooperation and by their desire to ensure that the Council's mandates were carried out.

If Iraq pursued its current course of action, particularly where resolutions 707(1991) and 715(1991) were concerned, the Special Commission would be constrained to repeat its March assessment, namely, that the possibility of the Commission's certifying Iraq's compliance with its obligations under section C of resolution 687(1991) did not even arise.

The Under-Secretary-General for Humanitarian Affairs and the Emergency Relief Coordinator referred to the Memorandum of Understanding between the United Nations and the Government of Iraq, which he had signed on behalf of the Secretary-General on 22 October, covering a six-month period ending 31 March 1993. The plan of action included components corresponding to more than $250 million and covered all regions of Iraq with emphasis on assistance delivery to the northern governorates due to the supply restrictions imposed on them and the impending harsh winter.

The Under-Secretary-General reported that, between July and the signing of the new Memorandum in October, United Nations personnel in the north experienced security problems and harassment. Their visas were not extended and travel permits were not granted. By September, they numbered less than 200. There was no United Nations presence in the south. Programme implementation under the new Memorandum was a struggle for time. Visas had been extended for the duration of the action plan, to be reviewed at the beginning of 1993. A total of 195 United Nations guards were currently deployed; another 105 were expected by December, the majority to be posted in the northern provinces.

Ten million litres of kerosene valued at $2.9 million were in the process of being delivered to Erbil and Suleimaniya. In cooperation with CARE, a non-governmental organization (NGO), UNICEF would shortly purchase another 20 million litres. In addition, it had just launched a nationwide vaccination campaign. WHO planned to distribute some $2 million worth of medicines to various areas. WFP had stocked 5,200 tonnes of food in the country, of which 2,000 tonnes were in the north; an additional 20,000 tonnes were in the process of being shipped to Iraq through Turkey. The WFP plan was to supply 27,000 tonnes of wheat flour to the north and 16,200 tonnes to the rest of the country.

For the success of the programme, it was essential to have the full cooperation of the Iraqi Government and the financial support of Member States. If the United Nations was to deliver humanitarian aid on an urgent basis, it was important that substantial contributions be made in the very near future. (See also below, under "Interagency humanitarian programme".)

The Special Rapporteur of the Commission on Human Rights stated that, based on evidence (statements of witnesses, documents, audio and video cassettes) he had to conclude that Iraq continued to refuse compliance with resolution 688(1991),[23] which demanded that Iraq immediately end the repression of the Iraqi civilian population. Iraq had repeatedly labelled that conclusion a subjective and biased one, although it was arrived at by using the yardsticks of the international human rights instruments to which Iraq had acceded: the 1966 International Covenant on Civil and Political Rights and Optional Protocol,[35] the 1966 International Covenant on Economic, Social and Cultural Rights,[36] and the 1948 Convention on the Prevention and Punishment of the Crime of Genocide.[37]

The Special Rapporteur said that even in the special circumstances invoked by Iraq (the Iran-Iraq armed conflict, the 1991 military operations in the Gulf and Iraqi uprisings, the economic embargo), the norms of applicable international law did not allow summary or arbitrary executions and forced disappearances or torture—all of which had happened in Iraq, not incidentally, but on a massive scale. The Special Rapporteur recalled that United Nations personnel participating in the inter-agency, humanitarian programme had repeatedly been subjected to harassment, vandalism and violence. Those incidents had occurred mostly in government-controlled areas, several at government checkpoints and others in the presence of local police or government security personnel who had failed to intervene.

Notwithstanding Iraq's explicit assurances to the contrary, discrimination existed with respect to access to food and health care. The population in the marshlands to the south were subjected to a complete blockade. The supply of food and fuel in the three Kurdish governorates in the north had steadily diminished, especially in Erbil and Suleimaniya. In the course of the year, a virtually complete embargo had been applied on fuel supplies to those governorates. Contrary to the Government's promise to facilitate the safe and rapid passage of humanitarian assistance throughout the country, it took nearly a month before 12 lorries carrying 400,000 litres of heating and cooking oil arrived in the north, where the fuel requirements for the 3 million Kurds during the four winter months had been estimated at 47 million litres of kerosene.

The Special Rapporteur concluded that when a Government tried to deny the right to life to a specific community within the State, the question inevitably arose as to whether it was engaging in genocidal practices as defined in the 1948 Convention on the Prevention and Punishment of the Crime of Genocide. (See also below, under ''Kurds and other minority populations''.)

On 24 November, Iraq vigorously insisted that, despite the unjust and arbitrary nature of resolution 687(1991) and other related resolutions, it had met the obligations they had imposed, particularly the substantive ones relating to the economic embargo. On the question of the Iraq-Kuwait boundary, Iraq decided not to participate in the activities of the Boundary Demarcation Commission since Iraq's view, as substantiated by historical evidence and realities, was not listened to. None the less, Iraq had not hindered the Demarcation Commission's activities. (See also below, under ''Iraq-Kuwait boundary''.)

On the question of missing persons, Iraq reaffirmed that it had cooperated sincerely and objectively with ICRC and that it detained no one, Kuwaiti or otherwise. The responsibility for those missing, it said, belonged to those who waged the war called Desert Storm.

With regard to its liability under international law, Iraq was emphatic that there be no vengeance claims or claims trumped up for material gain. That Iraq was not represented in the machinery dealing with such claims was incompatible with international law or with precedents in this area. Due process of law demanded a clear-cut link between fault and damage and stressed that compensation should be the direct result of that liability. Justice demanded proof and the party concerned should be represented directly. As to its foreign debt, Iraq repeated that it could neither repay debt nor service interest because of the economic embargo.

Concerning claims of government expropriation of the property of other countries and companies, Iraq informed those concerned that certain equipment would be used in agricultural and service projects in order to mitigate the suffering of the Iraqis caused by the embargo and that all rights accruing to them from such use would be fully respected, in accordance with their contracts with Iraq.

Regarding the return of Kuwaiti property, Iraq stated that from March through 25 October 1992, it had returned the following: four Skyhawk aircraft and one dual-use aircraft, type 383; Kuwaiti Airlines reserve equipment, 68 marine units; property belonging to Kuwait's Ministries of Health, of Social Affairs, and of Housing, its Institute of Planning and Air Force. Arrangements were under way for the return of remaining weapons and military equipment. Iraq stated that it had not received any demands whatsoever regarding private property.

Iraq repeated that at no time did it engage in acts of terrorism. It asserted that resolutions 706(1991) and 712(1991) were adopted with the aim of interfering in its internal affairs, and that in the three rounds of negotiations with the United Nations, Iraq failed to reach agreement on a reasonable arrangement that would meet the urgent humanitarian needs of its people. Talk of those two resolutions after Iraq had met so many of its obligations relating to economic embargo was but an attempt to divert attention from the essential issue of lifting the economic embargo in keeping with paragraph 22 of resolution 687(1991). Iraq further repeated that resolution 688(1991) was also a blatant interference in its internal affairs.

Commenting on other issues brought out during the debate, Iraq said that the Iraqi population's attitude towards the inspection teams reflected their bitterness over the continued sanctions, which the Iraqi officials could not control.

On the issue of the alleged repression of the Kurds and Shiites, Iraq asserted that it was the only country where recognition of the Kurds' national and cultural rights was enshrined in the constitution and in law and where the Kurds shared power. In a country where Arabs, Christians, Kurds, Muslims and Shiites lived together, the Shiites had never been the object of sectarian persecution. Concerning the Special Rapporteur's allegations about the situation in the southern marshes, Iraq asked why the Council had not sent a mission of eminent persons to verify the situation, as Iraq had suggested. The no-fly zone imposed by the United States was never meant to protect the Shiites or the marsh-dwellers of southern Iraq but to create a military crisis with Iraq during the United States presidential elections.

Finally, Iraq argued that the assertion that it was feeding its army but not its people was absurd, for the Iraqi army could not possibly be consuming the millions of tonnes of food cited by the United States as having entered Iraq. That could be true only if the 18 million Iraqis constituted the Iraqi army.

After consultations among Council members during a suspension of the meeting, the President was authorized to make the following statement[38] on behalf of the Council:

''The views of the Security Council having been expressed through its President and by the statements of its members on the extent of compliance by the Government of Iraq with its obligations under the relevant Security Council resolutions, the Council has listened with close attention to the statements by the Deputy Prime Minister of Iraq. The Council regrets the lack of any indication in the statements by the Deputy Prime Minister of Iraq of how the Government of Iraq intends to comply with the resolutions of the Council. It also regrets the baseless threats, allegations and attacks launched by the Deputy Prime Minister of Iraq against the Council, the Special Commission, the International Atomic Energy Agency

(IAEA), the Iraq-Kuwait Boundary Demarcation Commission and the Committee established by resolution 661(1990). The Council rejects *in toto* these threats, allegations and attacks.

"Having heard all the interventions in the debate, the Council reiterates its full support for the statement made by the President of the Council on its behalf at the opening of the 3139th meeting (S/24836).

"In the view of the Security Council, while there have been some positive steps, the Government of Iraq has not yet complied fully and unconditionally with its obligations, must do so and must immediately take the appropriate actions in this regard."

Iraq-Kuwait boundary

Communications. On 15 May 1992,[39] Kuwait drew the Secretary-General's attention to recent statements by Iraq's Deputy Prime Minister in a Jordanian newspaper and by the Speaker of the National Assembly in a British newspaper in Baghdad to the effect that a decision adopted by the Iraq-Kuwait Boundary Demarcation Commission in April was not based on legally valid documentation. Therefore, Iraq would not accept the new border, which gave some of its territory to Kuwait. Iraq needed direct talks with Kuwait, and if a third party was to be involved, it should be the League of Arab States.

Iraq, on 21 May,[40] referred to its position on the international boundary, as communicated to the Secretary-General in 1991,[41] and set forth in detail its views on the decisions adopted by the Demarcation Commission on 14 April, at its fifth session. It asserted that the Commission, having based its work on United Kingdom sources and interpretations (Security Council document S/22412 specified in resolution 687(1991)), had come out with a boundary line that was worse for Iraq than that drawn by the United Kingdom using the same sources. The coordinates arrived at contradicted geographical as well as historical facts. Iraq maintained that, throughout the nineteenth century and until the First World War, the small village settled some two centuries ago on the banks of the Arabian Gulf under the name of "Kuwait", an Iraqi term for "a small settlement of people", was an Iraqi Qadhaa' (district) belonging to the province of Basrah. Under Ottoman administrative law, Kuwait was an integral part of Iraq, subject to that province. By the 1916 Sykes-Picot Agreement, the United Kingdom had drawn artificial boundaries severing a part (Kuwait) of Iraq and its natural access to the Arabian Gulf.

SECURITY COUNCIL ACTION

Following consultations held by the Security Council on 17 June 1992, its President issued the following statement[42] on behalf of the Council members:

"The members of the Security Council have noted the letter of 17 April 1992 from the Chairman of the Iraq-Kuwait Boundary Demarcation Commission to the Secretary-General and express their complete support for the work of the Secretary-General and the Boundary Demarcation Commission in implementing paragraph 3 of resolution 687(1991). They recall in this connection that through the demarcation process the Boundary Demarcation Commission is not reallocating territory between Kuwait and Iraq, but is simply carrying out the technical task necessary to demarcate the precise coordinates of the boundary between Kuwait and Iraq for the first time. This task is being carried out in the special circumstances following Iraq's invasion of Kuwait and pursuant to resolution 687(1991) and the Secretary-General's report (S/22558) for implementing paragraph 3 of that resolution. They look forward to the completion of the work of the Commission.

"The members of the Council have noted with particular concern the letter of 21 May 1992 from the Minister of Foreign Affairs of the Republic of Iraq to the Secretary-General (S/24044) concerning the work of the Boundary Demarcation Commission, which appears to call into question Iraq's adherence to Security Council resolution 687(1991). The members of the Council are concerned in particular that the letter from Iraq of 21 May 1992 may be interpreted as rejecting the finality of the Boundary Demarcation Commission's decisions notwithstanding the terms of resolution 687(1991) and the Secretary-General's report for implementing paragraph 3 of that resolution, both of which were formally accepted by Iraq.

"They note with dismay that the letter recalls past Iraqi claims to Kuwait without also recalling Iraq's subsequent repudiations of these claims, *inter alia* through its acceptance of resolution 687(1991). The members of the Council firmly reject any suggestion that tends to dispute the very existence of Kuwait, a member State of the United Nations.

"The members of the Council remind Iraq of its obligations under resolution 687(1991), and in particular paragraph 2 thereof, and under other relevant resolutions of the Council.

"The members of the Council also remind Iraq of its acceptance of the resolutions of the Council adopted pursuant to Chapter VII of the United Nations Charter, which forms the basis for the cease-fire. The members of the Council wish to stress to Iraq the inviolability of the international boundary between Iraq and Kuwait being demarcated by the Commission and guaranteed by the Council pursuant to resolution 687(1991), and the grave consequences that would ensue from any breach thereof."

Upon issuance of that statement, Ecuador[43] quoted the views it had expressed to explain its abstention on resolution 687(1991), stating that Article 36 of the Charter did not give the Council authority under Chapter VII to pronounce on the territorial limits between Iraq and Kuwait or to stipulate arrangements demarcating the boundary in question; that the Council could not be given powers greater than those laid down in the Charter and the means of implementing the Council resolutions must be in full conformity with the norms of international law; and that, as many Council members had expressed, the relevant paragraphs of resolution 687(1991) did not constitute a precedent that could be invoked subsequently. However, Ecuador did not wish to obstruct actions agreed upon by the Council in implementation of that resolution.

Communications. On 12 July 1992,[44] Iraq, referring to a notification of the forthcoming sixth session (New York, 15-24 July) of the Boundary Demarcation Commission, restated that the outcome of the Commission's work was a predetermined one imposed by Powers that controlled the Security Council and the United Nations, in particular the United Kingdom and the United States. Iraq was convinced that its views would not be heard in the Commission, as confirmed by the fact that the Council, instead of giving Iraq's 21 May letter careful consideration, was induced to adopt a statement by its President containing interpretations lacking in objectivity and threats. For these reasons, Iraq concluded that its participation in the Commission's work would be to no avail.

Kuwait, on 5 August,[45] drew to the attention of the Council President the escalation of Iraqi propaganda against the sovereignty and territorial integrity of Kuwait. It stated that Iraqi official pronouncements and media—newspapers, radio, television, magazines and even a university publication said to contain historical evidence—were making increasing references to Kuwait as being an integral part of Iraq and an Iraqi governorate, to Kuwait's restoration to its mother country, Iraq, and to its union with Iraq. It said that the Council's responsibility to ensure international security and stability required this grave matter to be taken up and adequately addressed.

SECURITY COUNCIL ACTION

The Security Council met on 26 August 1992 in connection with a recent report of the Iraq-Kuwait Boundary Demarcation Commission and adopted **resolution 773(1992)**.

The Security Council,

Reaffirming its resolution 687(1991) of 3 April 1991, and in particular paragraphs 2, 3 and 4 thereof, and its resolution 689(1991) of 9 April 1991,

Recalling the report of the Secretary-General dated 2 May 1991 concerning the establishment of the United Nations Iraq-Kuwait Boundary Demarcation Commission (the Commission) and the subsequent exchange of letters of 6 and 13 May 1991,

Having considered the Secretary-General's letter of 12 August 1992 to the President of the Security Council transmitting the further report of the Commission,

Recalling in this connection that through the demarcation process the Commission is not reallocating territory between Kuwait and Iraq, but it is simply carry-

ing out the technical task necessary to demarcate for the first time the precise coordinates of the boundary set out in the Agreed Minutes between the State of Kuwait and the Republic of Iraq regarding the restoration of Friendly Relations, Recognition and Related Matters signed by them on 4 October 1963, and that this task is being carried out in the special circumstances following Iraq's invasion of Kuwait and pursuant to resolution 687(1991) and the Secretary-General's report for implementing paragraph 3 of that resolution,

1. *Welcomes* the Secretary-General's letter of 12 August to the President of the Council and the further report of the Commission enclosed therewith;

2. *Expresses its appreciation* to the Commission for its work on the demarcation of the land boundary, and welcomes its demarcation decisions;

3. *Welcomes* also the decision of the Commission to consider the Eastern section of the boundary, which includes the offshore boundary, at its next session and urges the Commission to demarcate this part of the boundary as soon as possible and thus complete its work;

4. *Underlines* its guarantee of the inviolability of the above-mentioned international boundary and its decision to take as appropriate all necessary measures to that end in accordance with the Charter, as provided for in paragraph 4 of resolution 687(1991);

5. *Welcomes further* the Secretary-General's intention to carry out at the earliest practicable time the realignment of the demilitarized zone referred to in paragraph 5 of resolution 687(1991) to correspond to the international boundary demarcated by the Commission, with the consequent removal of the Iraqi police posts;

6. *Urges* the two States concerned to cooperate fully with the work of the Commission;

7. *Decides* to remain seized of the matter.

Security Council resolution 773(1992)

26 August 1992   Meeting 3108   14-0-1

4-nation draft (S/24488), orally revised.
Sponsors: France, Russian Federation, United Kingdom, United States.
Vote in Council as follows:
     In favour: Austria, Belgium, Cape Verde, China, France, Hungary, India, Japan, Morocco, Russian Federation, United Kingdom, United States, Venezuela, Zimbabwe.
     Against: None.
     Abstaining: Ecuador.

In explanation of its abstention, Ecuador referred to its views[43] quoted in connection with the Council President's statement of 17 June[42] (see above) as being applicable also with respect to the resolution just adopted.

UN Iraq-Kuwait Observation Mission

The United Nations Iraq-Kuwait Observation Mission (UNIKOM), established by the Security Council in 1991,[46] was mandated to monitor the Khawr Abd Allah waterway and the DMZ established by the Council along the boundary between Iraq and Kuwait, to deter DMZ violations through surveillance, and to observe any hostile or potentially hostile action mounted from the territory of one State into the other.

For operational purposes, UNIKOM divided the DMZ into three sectors—north, centre and south—each with a headquarters and six patrol/observation bases. Operations were conducted through those bases, observation points, vehicular and aerial patrols, investigation teams and liaison with Iraqi and Kuwaiti authorities at all levels. The Governments of both parties extended the cooperation necessary for UNIKOM to carry out its mandate.

On the Secretary-General's recommendation, the Council extended the UNIKOM mandate twice in 1992, each for a six-month period: from 9 April until 8 October 1992 and from 9 October 1992 until 8 April 1993.

Reports of the Secretary-General (March and October). In 1992, the Secretary-General provided the Security Council with two reports on the activities of UNIKOM in connection with the six-month review of its mandate in March and October. The first report covered the period 3 October 1991 to 31 March 1992;[47] the second, 1 April to 30 September.[48]

During those two periods, the engineering unit cleared and marked 250 kilometres of patrol tracks, disposed of 6,050 pieces of unexploded ordnance and reconfirmed the safety of previously cleared routes. It continued to improve security and working conditions at the northern (Umm Qasr) headquarters and its extension, Camp Khor, and built seven landing strips and 16 concrete helicopter landing pads, as well as observation towers, in the DMZ. The logistics unit continued to provide transport, distribute logistic supplies, and maintain heavy-duty vehicles. The medical unit operated a sick-bay facility at Umm Qasr and first-aid posts at the other two sectors. Mine-clearance, contracted for by Kuwait, was under way on its side of the DMZ, which was particularly badly littered with unexploded ordnance.

UNIKOM maintained contact with and provided support to other United Nations missions working in Iraq and Kuwait, in particular the United Nations Boundary Demarcation Commission and the United Nations Return of Property from Iraq to Kuwait.

UNIKOM observed three types of violations: minor incursions on the ground by small groups of soldiers, often just one or two; overflights by military aircraft of the type used by Kuwait and by forces of Member States cooperating with Kuwait; and policemen carrying weapons other than the prescribed sidearms. Tabulated summaries of these violations indicated a total of 9 by Iraq, 39 by Kuwait, 11 by Member States cooperating with Kuwait and 20 by unidentified parties. As of 31 March, 100 violations were ascribed to Kuwait and Member States cooperating with it. Since the declaration of the ''no-fly zone'' in southern Iraq, a number of overflights had been too high to identify. The Governments concerned

with that zone were asked to avoid actions that might compromise the demilitarized status of the DMZ and adversely affect the work of UNIKOM.

UNIKOM received and investigated 61 written complaints from Iraq and 35 from Kuwait. Efforts had been unsuccessful to persuade Iraq to pull back either its five police posts on the Kuwaiti side of the boundary line or the two on its side that were closer than 1,000 metres to the line. Iraq was firm in its position that those posts remain in place until the border had been demarcated.

Four incidents gave cause for concern. On 10 October 1991, Kuwait detained 55 Iraqi fishermen north-east of Failaka Island, claiming they were inside Kuwaiti territorial waters; they were returned to Iraq eventually through ICRC. Eight days later, Iraq alleged that a Kuwaiti patrol entered Iraq near Safwan, fired on an Iraqi police post there, wounded a local farmer with rifle fire and detained two others. While it could not verify the attack on the post, UNIKOM determined that the incident took place on the Kuwaiti side of the DMZ in an area close to the boundary where Iraqis used to farm prior to the 1990 Iraqi occupation of Kuwait. On 2 November, armed Kuwaitis intercepted 12 Iraqi policemen *en route* towards Talha on a road criss-crossing the boundary, detained them and confiscated their vehicle, arms and money; they were returned to Iraq on 7 December through ICRC. On 7 January 1992, two Kuwaiti policemen were apprehended at one of the five Iraqi police posts on the Kuwaiti side of the boundary line. UNIKOM determined that they had lost their way and approached the post by mistake; they were returned to Kuwait by ICRC on 25 January.

The latter part of the second period was marked by a gradual heightening of tension in the DMZ. The work of the Boundary Demarcation Commission drew attention to the fact that some of the areas farmed by Iraqis in the northern sector were actually on Kuwaiti territory. Suspicions that the farmers were Iraqi military or security personnel resulted in a number of firing incidents between them and the Kuwaitis, during one of which (30 August) a UNIKOM military observer was injured while trying to restore calm. To enable it to monitor the situation, UNIKOM asked Iraq for a register of its farmers in the area. Increased Iraqi fishing in the Khawr Abd Allah also resulted in complaints by Kuwait of violations of its territorial waters and by Iraq of detention of its nationals.

Since July, the safety of United Nations staff in Iraq, including UNIKOM, had been put at risk by Iraqi demonstrations, threatening telephone calls, and vandalizing of their cars.

The Secretary-General was of the view that UNIKOM's high level of vigilance was essential for ensuring respect for the DMZ and maintaining calm in the area. He therefore recommended that UNIKOM be extended for a further six months from 9 April to 8 October 1992 in the first instance, with which the Council concurred;[49] and from 9 October 1992 to 8 April 1993 in the second, with which the Council also concurred.[50]

Composition

As of September 1992, UNIKOM had a strength of 413.[48] Of these, 254 were military observers from 33 Member States and 159 were personnel comprising four administrative and logistics units provided by Canada, Chile, Denmark and Norway. Of the 300 military observers authorized, 46 were on stand-by in their countries. The total strength of the four units had been reduced by 41 since April.[47]

The civilian staff numbered 186—90 international and 96 local recruits—representing a reduction of 10 since April. For personnel and equipment transport between Baghdad and Kuwait, UNIKOM had the use of two small fixed-wing civilian aircraft and a military helicopter unit.

Financing

In a report of November 1992 on the financing of UNIKOM,[51] the Secretary-General stated that assessments totalling $121,166,424 had been apportioned among Member States for UNIKOM from its inception on 9 April 1991 to 8 October 1992. Contributions received for the same period amounted to $95,784,205, leaving a shortfall of $25,382,219. Voluntary contributions in kind were received from Switzerland in the form of two fixed-wing aircraft with crew, valued at about $1,587,300, and from Sweden in the form of airlift of military personnel at the beginning of UNIKOM operations, later valued at $250,000.

In the interest of administrative efficiency, the Secretary-General proposed that the special financial period of UNIKOM be for a period of 12 calendar months, from 1 November of one year to 31 October of the next, with effect from 1 November 1992. He further proposed that the third financial period be extended by 23 days up to and including 31 October 1992, making that period 9 April to 31 October 1992.

Resources made available from 9 April 1991 to 31 October 1992 totalled $123,077,000 gross ($120,347,200 net), comprising appropriations of $94,577,000 gross ($92,649,000 net) and commitment authorization of $28,500,000 gross ($27,698,200 net). Estimated expenditures for the same period amounted to $112,828,735 gross ($119,838,324 net), resulting in an unencumbered balance of $10,248,265 gross ($9,508,876 net). Interest income totalled $675,259 and miscellaneous income, $61,359.

The cost of UNIKOM from 1 November 1992 to 31 October 1993 was estimated at $4,141,100 gross

($4,006,500 net) a month. On that basis, the Secretary-General requested that the General Assembly provide appropriations for the six months from 1 November 1992 to 30 April 1993—amounting to $24,846,600 gross ($24,039,000 net)—and for a further six months, from 1 May to 31 October 1993, should the Security Council decide to continue UNIKOM.

In view of the outstanding contributions, the Secretary-General proposed that no action should be taken with respect to the unencumbered balance. He also proposed that the special arrangements approved for UNIIMOG should be applied to UNIKOM, whereby appropriations required in respect of obligations owed to troop-contributing States be retained beyond the period stipulated under the relevant regulations of the Financial Regulations of the United Nations.

ACABQ[52] recommended deferment of the latter proposal without prejudice to existing arrangements and concurred with the retention of the unencumbered balance in the UNIKOM Special Account. In the light of that and of savings that might be realized in line with experience gained during the previous mandate, ACABQ recommended that appropriations for 1 November 1992 to 30 April 1993 should not exceed $20,000,000 gross ($19,192,400 net). For the period beyond 30 April 1993, it recommended that the Secretary-General be authorized to enter into commitments not to exceed $3.3 million gross ($3.1 million net) a month, subject to its prior concurrence.

GENERAL ASSEMBLY ACTION

On 22 December 1992, the General Assembly, on the recommendation of the Fifth Committee, adopted **resolution 47/208** without vote.

Financing of the United Nations Iraq-Kuwait Observation Mission

The General Assembly,

Having considered the report of the Secretary-General on the financing of the United Nations Iraq-Kuwait Observation Mission and the related report of the Advisory Committee on Administrative and Budgetary Questions,

Bearing in mind Security Council resolutions 687(1991) of 3 April 1991 and 689(1991) of 9 April 1991, by which the Council decided to set up the United Nations Iraq-Kuwait Observation Mission and to review the question of its termination or continuation every six months,

Recalling its resolutions 45/260 of 3 May 1991 and 46/197 of 20 December 1991 on the financing of the Observation Mission,

Reaffirming that the costs of the Observation Mission are expenses of the Organization to be borne by Member States in accordance with Article 17, paragraph 2, of the Charter of the United Nations,

Recalling its previous decision regarding the fact that, in order to meet the expenditures caused by the Observation Mission, a different procedure is required from the one applied to meet expenditures of the regular budget of the United Nations,

Taking into account the fact that the economically more developed countries are in a position to make relatively larger contributions and that the economically less developed countries have a relatively limited capacity to contribute towards such an operation,

Bearing in mind the special responsibilities of the States permanent members of the Security Council, as indicated in General Assembly resolution 1874(S-IV) of 27 June 1963, in the financing of such operations,

Noting with appreciation that voluntary contributions have been made to the Observation Mission by certain Governments,

Mindful of the fact that it is essential to provide the Observation Mission with the necessary financial resources to enable it to fulfil its responsibilities under the relevant resolutions of the Security Council,

1. *Endorses* the observations and recommendations contained in the report of the Advisory Committee on Administrative and Budgetary Questions;

2. *Urges* all Member States to make every possible effort to ensure payment of their assessed contributions to the United Nations Iraq-Kuwait Observation Mission in full and on time;

3. *Decides* that the authorization provided by its resolution 46/197 for the period from 9 April to 8 October 1992, inclusive, shall be extended to include the period up to and including 31 October 1992;

4. *Decides also* to appropriate to the Special Account referred to in General Assembly resolution 45/260 an amount of 28.5 million United States dollars gross (27,698,200 dollars net) authorized and apportioned by the Assembly in paragraph 14 of its resolution 46/197 for the operation of the Observation Mission from 9 April to 31 October 1992;

5. *Decides further* to appropriate to the Special Account the amount of 20 million dollars gross (19,192,400 dollars net) for the operation of the Observation Mission from 1 November 1992 to 30 April 1993, inclusive, subject to the review by the Security Council of the mandate of the Mission in respect of the period beyond 8 April 1993;

6. *Decides*, as an ad hoc arrangement, to apportion the amount of 20 million dollars gross (19,192,400 dollars net) for the above-mentioned period among Member States in accordance with the composition of groups set out in paragraphs 3 and 4 of General Assembly resolution 43/232 of 1 March 1989, as adjusted by the Assembly in its resolutions 44/192 B of 21 December 1989, 45/260 and 46/197, and taking into account the scale of assessments for the years 1992, 1993 and 1994;

7. *Decides also* that, in accordance with the provisions of its resolution 973(X) of 15 December 1955, there shall be set off against the apportionment among Member States, as provided for in paragraph 6 above, their respective share in the Tax Equalization Fund of the estimated staff assessment income of 807,600 dollars for the period from 1 November 1992 to 30 April 1993, inclusive, approved for the Observation Mission;

8. *Authorizes* the Secretary-General to enter into commitments for the operation of the Observation Mission at a rate not to exceed 3.3 million dollars gross (3.1 million dollars net) per month for the period from 1 May to 31 October 1993, inclusive, subject to the review by the Security Council of the mandate of the Mission in respect of the period beyond 8 April 1993, and subject to obtaining the prior concurrence of the Advisory Committee for the actual level of commitments to be entered into for the period beyond 30 April 1993, the said amounts to be apportioned among Member States in accordance with the scheme set out in the present resolution;

9. *Decides* to consider the contributions of Armenia, Azerbaijan, Bosnia and Herzegovina, Croatia, Georgia, Kazakhstan, Kyrgyzstan, the Republic of Moldova, San Marino, Slovenia, Tajikistan, Turkmenistan and Uzbekistan to the Observation Mission in accordance with the rates of assessment to be adopted by the General Assembly for these Member States at its forty-seventh session;

10. *Invites* the new Member States listed in paragraph 9 above to make advance payments against their assessed contributions, to be determined;

11. *Decides* to retain the unencumbered balance in the Special Account for the United Nations Iraq-Kuwait Observation Mission;

12. *Decides also* that the special financial period of the Observation Mission shall be for twelve months, beginning 1 November of one year and ending on 31 October of the next, effective as from 1 November 1992, subject to the continuation of the Mission by the Security Council;

13. *Invites* voluntary contributions to the Observation Mission in cash and in the form of services and supplies acceptable to the Secretary-General, to be administered, as appropriate, in accordance with the procedure established by the General Assembly in its resolutions 43/230 of 21 December 1988, 44/192 A of 21 December 1989 and 45/258 of 3 May 1991;

14. *Requests* the Secretary-General to take all necessary action to ensure that the Observation Mission is administered with a maximum of efficiency and economy;

15. *Decides* to include in the provisional agenda of its forty-eighth session the item entitled ''Financing of the activities arising from Security Council resolution 687(1991): United Nations Iraq-Kuwait Observation Mission''.

General Assembly resolution 47/208

22 December 1992   Meeting 93   Adopted without vote

Approved by Fifth Committee (A/47/823) without vote, 19 December (meeting 50); draft by Chairman (A/C.5/47/L.5), orally revised by United Kingdom; agenda item 120 *(a)*.

Meeting numbers. GA 47th session: 5th Committee 38, 50; plenary 93.

On-site inspections

IAEA inspections

During 1992, IAEA, with the assistance and cooperation of the Special Commission of the United Nations, conducted eight on-site nuclear inspections in Iraq—the ninth to sixteenth since it began such inspections in accordance with the relevant provisions of Security Council resolution 687(1991) of April 1991. The sites inspected were designated by the Special Commission and the inspection findings were summarized in reports transmitted to the Council by the Secretary-General.

The ninth inspection (11-14 January)[53] confirmed data obtained from Germany that, between

January and May 1990, it had delivered large quantities of stock material intended for Iraq's centrifuge manufacturing programme. In addition, Iraq declared the procurement of 100 tonnes of 350-grade maraging steel and aluminium forgings sufficient for the manufacture of several thousand top and bottom flanges for centrifuge vacuum housings. It made no previous declaration of these materials and components since it had unilaterally destroyed or rendered them harmless by melting and crushing just before the IAEA inspections began. The team's rough, on-site estimate of the quantities of melted steel pieces and powder from the crushed ferrite magnets appeared consistent with the quantities procured.

The team thoroughly re-inspected the Rashdiya complex, located near the Baghdad North Bridge, to verify the existence of some machine tools that might have been associated with the centrifuge enrichment programme. Part of the complex had been modified into an Engineering Design Centre, staffed by 250 technical and administrative personnel, whose work was described as water treatment and quality management, but marked by a complete absence of paper records. Ten per cent of the southern part of the complex was used to store fertilizers, pesticides and seeds, from which samples were taken; the rest of the area was empty. No physical evidence suggested that the facility served a purpose other than that declared.

The tenth inspection (5-13 February)[54] focused on 10 sites: the Salah-al-Din General Establishment (SAAD-13); the Tuwaitha Transportation Centre and the Engineering Services Centre; the "Future Design Centre"; the Latifiya Agricultural Farm; and six sites near Mosul indicated to IAEA as potential locations for heavy water production facilities. The first two sites had been inspected previously.

The team obtained a detailed description of the development and purpose of SAAD-13. It thoroughly inspected all the buildings, the open ground between the plant site and the river, the water intake, and the treatment and discharge facilities for both the plant and the village, the underground shelters and a heating/cooling facility. It conducted a helicopter survey of the site with video and still camera. A team of divers collected water samples above and below the discharge canal and sediment samples from points along the bottom of the river. Pending analysis of those samples, it appeared unlikely that an undergound reactor had been constructed there. The six sites near Mosul yielded no evidence of nuclear-related activity. Inspection of the "ingots" of melted maraging steel and ferrite powder stored at the Iskandariya State Enterprise for Mechanical Industries, as well as of the aluminium stock materials declared as having been melted at the

Ur Establishment (the only aluminium smelter in Iraq), yielded data in reasonable agreement with Iraqi declarations.

The team continued work on reconciling inconsistencies between IAEA findings and Iraqi declarations of nuclear material. It sought clarification of Iraq's position as to its obligation to provide information as required under resolution 715(1991), with which it had yet to comply. It made plans for the transfer of irradiated fuel from the Tamuz 2 and IRT-5000 reactors stored in a farm north of Tuwaitha into new tanks due to an increasing risk of a radiological incident (the fuel cladding was corroding from seepage of salt-containing groundwater into the tanks), as well as for the transfer of uranium wastes being held in an oil storage tank at the Al-Jezira UO 2 plant pending recovery and analysis of the uranium content.

In addition, the team provided technical support to a Special Commission inspection of the central computer facility at the Ministry of Industry and Minerals in central Baghdad.

An important objective of the eleventh inspection (7-15 April)[55] was the destruction of key technical installations at the Al-Atheer–Al-Hatteen complex southwest of Baghdad, identified by IAEA as the main research centre where Iraq intended to pursue development of nuclear weapons. Eight buildings covering a surface of approximately 35,000 square metres and 26 major equipment items, some consisting of several components, were marked for destruction. Owing to the extensive preparatory work required for the demolition, only about 24,000 square metres of buildings were demolished, but most of the equipment was destroyed. Iraq provided all the manpower, equipment and materials that efficiently accomplished the task under the inspectors' supervision. The remaining buildings and equipment were being prepared for destruction during the next inspection.

The inspection team supervised the transfer of the irradiated fuel from the farm near Tuwaitha to new concrete containers above ground—an operation that took Iraqi technicians four days to execute. The team's attempts to resolve a variety of inconsistencies in Iraq's declarations relating to nuclear materials resulted in a new declaration of sources and quantities, subsequent processing and end-use for related work carried out at Al-Tuwaitha. This substantially changed IAEA's assessment of the flow and associated production (type and location) of nuclear materials in Iraq.

Replies to the team's repeated questioning about inconsistencies in declarations regarding Iraq's uranium enrichment programme indicated that the political decision to open this file to the inspectors had yet to be taken. Sources of carbon fibre rotors and maraging steel and of centrifuge technology advice, as well as information on the scope of the Iraqi chemical enrichment work, remained to be identified.

In further efforts to determine the extent of Iraqi experiments and studies in weapons development, the team focused on the production of plane-wave explosive lenses and on testing facilities for high explosives, and removed from Iraq the pressing die declared to have been used for lens production. It revisited 12 sites previously inspected, to complete the inventory and manufacturer identification of key equipment and machine tools used or capable of use in Iraq's nuclear programme. It held discussions on a draft text of the "full, final and complete report" submitted by Iraq in March on its nuclear programme and on the implementation of the plan for future ongoing monitoring and verification. Iraq proposed another meeting before finalizing that report and requested IAEA clarification of a number of items identified in an annex to the long-term plan.

The twelfth inspection (26 May–4 June)[56] supervised the completion of the destruction by Iraqi technicians of the remaining buildings (approximately 11,000 square metres in surface area) and equipment at the Al-Atheer–Al-Hatteen complex and removal of the protective berm around Building 33 firing site. It set in motion preparations for the destruction of selected buildings at the two EMIS sites at Tarmiya and Ash Sharqat and for other associated activities. The inspection team completed work to identify the machine tools and to better understand the overall capabilities of facilities declared to have been involved in the IAEC programme. The information was intended to help establish the basis for the long-term monitoring programme.

The amount of undeclared nuclear material processed in a safeguarded fuel fabrication facility, in violation of the safeguards agreement between Iraq and IAEA, was revised upwards by Iraq from 19 kilograms to 60 kilograms of natural uranium dioxide. The team removed the remaining quantity of fresh highly enriched uranium fuel (473 grams of U-235) from Iraq. Through written questions, meetings and interviews, it obtained some clarification of issues related to Iraq's weaponization and uranium enrichment programmes and nuclear material declarations. Certain questions on Iraq's centrifuge enrichment programme and the extent of chemical enrichment work remained open.

The final version of Iraq's "full, final and complete" report, dated May 1992, regarding all activities relating to weapons of mass destruction was handed to the team on 4 June for transmission to the Special Commission. The covering letter requested that, because of its nature, the report should be treated as confidential. The nuclear portion of the report was being translated.

The team noted that Iraq's cooperation in carrying out the destruction operations mentioned above could not be faulted. A definite stiffening in Iraqi attitude had become evident, however, as exemplified by numerous attempts to prohibit or limit photograph-taking and placing of seals, and by a slow-down in arrangements for meetings, transportation and other activities. The reason, Iraq explained, was that their active cooperation during previous inspections had not resulted in an improvement in the sanctions situation.

The thirteenth inspection (14-21 July)[57] supervised the destruction of key installations at the two EMIS sites, including eight buildings (four at each site). As in similar operations in the past, Iraq supplied the necessary manpower, equipment and materials required to execute the task. With the completion before the end of August of a few remaining activities at the sites, all known technical facilities and equipment for research and production of enriched uranium using EMIS technology would have been destroyed or rendered harmless. The sites would continue to be inspected, however, under the long-term monitoring plan.

The 95 irregular chunks of melted maraging steel in open-air storage at the Iskandariya State Enterprise for Mechanical Industries were individually identified and photographed preparatory to their transfer to a foundry for remelting and dilution with equal amounts of high carbon steel during a future mission in order to render the material harmless.

The inspection team twice revisited the State Enterprise for Heavy Engineering Equipment at Daura to collect additional technical data and contract numbers needed to identify or confirm the identities of manufacturers or procurement routes for the furnaces and the electron beam welder intended for use in Iraq's centrifuge manufacture programme.

The fourteenth inspection (31 August–7 September)[58] verified completion of the destruction of the eight buildings at the EMIS sites. In the context of the long-term monitoring plan, the team began a project aimed at the periodic control of radionuclides and other selected, stable nuclides of the main bodies of water in Iraq. A number of sites had been identified where water and sediment samples would be periodically collected. Highly sensitive analytical techniques applied to the samples would yield information on any sizeable nuclear activity. The first sampling, begun by the inspection team and to be completed during the next inspection, would provide the baseline against which future sampling results would be compared. Samples were taken from 15 sites.

The identification and tagging of a number of high-temperature laboratory furnaces and other non-released equipment stored at the Ash Shaykilii warehouse was completed. These had been removed from Tuwaitha prior to the inspections authorized under resolution 687(1991) and, at IAEA request, were collected for storage. Previously inspected sites were revisited for monitoring purposes. The maraging steel pieces were transferred to a Basrah foundry. The uranium-containing wastes at Al-Jezira and the water level in the spent-fuel storage tanks near Tuwaitha were monitored.

The inspection team held several meetings with Iraqi authorities on the radiometric hydrologic survey as a component of the long-term monitoring plan, on the completeness of the "full, final and complete" Iraqi report and on annex 3 of the long-term monitoring plan.

The fifteenth inspection (8-18 November)[59] concluded the sampling of the waterways of Iraq, begun during the previous inspection. The 37 sites visited brought to 52 the total number of sites sampled along the full length of the Tigris-Euphrates watershed. A detailed assessment was made of the conditions for the removal of the irradiated fuel stored near Tuwaitha. It included an evaluation of fuel design, exposure history and current storage conditions. Removal of the fuel was estimated to take from four to six months. Under the observation of the inspectors, the 100 tonnes of maraging steel at Basrah was destroyed by remelting and diluting it with equal amounts of high carbon steel. The R24 experimental EMIS magnet system was destroyed with cutting torches. The system included nine double-pole magnets, a coil-winding machine and transport rails.

Iraq acknowledged to the inspectors that the Engineering Design Centre at Rashdiya played a role in the design of the centrifuge enrichment programme. It also identified the role of certain key technical staff, interviews with whom resulted in a more credible picture of Iraq's centrifuge programme. The importance of procurement data for the establishment of a basis for the long-term monitoring programme was again emphasized to no avail. The current process of obtaining that information through Member States continued to produce results, but that process was inherently slow.

Work to identify and catalogue key machine tools in various Iraqi State engineering establishments continued. Under resolution 715(1991), Iraq was to update every six months a declaration regarding facilities, materials and equipment starting from the situation as it existed on 1 January 1989. Its reporting obligation covered all sites in Iraq, not just those belonging to IAEC. Iraq advised that it would officially submit a declaration covering IAEC facilities as soon as possible after the end of the inspection. A draft was provided to the inspection team and a commitment was made to amend the declaration to cover the country as a whole by year's end.

The uranium waste material recovered at Al-Jezira and removed to Al-Tuwaitha was weighed, sampled for verification and removed for storage under IAEA seal. Re-verification of irradiated fuel at the IRT-5000 reactor and remedial actions to improve storage conditions for the irradiated fuel near Tuwaitha were completed. A number of additional nuclear material samples were taken from previously verified material to evaluate further Iraqi declarations regarding the processing of nuclear materials at Al-Tuwaitha.

The inspection team visited 30 other locations throughout Iraq, including known nuclear facilities, State industrial establishments, support or storage facilities and other sites not previously inspected. Some were visited on short notice, with prior notifications of between five minutes and two hours.

The inspection report noted that the team was not harassed at any of the sites inspected, nor did tight security interfere with inspection work. Arrangements to accommodate the inspection activities were made efficiently throughout the inspection period.

The inspectors of the sixteenth inspection (5-8 December),[60] with support from a chemical-biological weapons team from the Special Commission, inspected a complex of buildings used by the Military Industrial Committee as an Engineering Design Centre to rebuild Iraqi industry. The complex included the former headquarters of "Petrochemical Three", the code name for Iraq's project for developing an implosion-type nuclear weapon.[61] The inspectors were in search of documents pertaining to that project and to Iraq's programme for developing chemical and biological weapons of mass destruction. While the inspection team found neither activity nor documents relevant to resolution 687(1991), it observed the removal of documents from the site on its arrival. Confronted with videotape footage of the situation, the chief Iraqi counterpart promised an immediate investigation of the incident, which he ascribed to the personal initiative of panic-stricken individuals.

Short-notice inspections were also made of an IAEC guest house in the Tuwaitha area and of a warehouse at Al-Atheer. On 7 December, the IAEA Chief Inspector met with the IAEC Chairman, who read a written statement on the question of the procurement sources for Iraq's centrifuge enrichment programme. The statement first reiterated Iraq's position regarding the "grey areas", expressed to the Security Council on 23 November, and then noted that Iraq had so far named a total of 80 companies (35 in the "full, final and complete" report, 30 in inspection reports and 15 named as a result of the survey of machines, equipment and other items in IAEC workplaces and support facilities), representing 90 per cent of Iraq's sources. Questions on the remaining 10 per cent could be submitted to Iraq in writing, which would be dealt with positively. Accordingly, IAEA on 18 December submitted a request for the names of the manufacturers and suppliers of the maraging steel; Iraq's reply of 22 December failed to provide the requested information.

IAEA reports. During 1992, IAEA issued the second and third semi-annual reports on its implementation of the plan for the destruction, removal or rendering harmless of items listed in paragraph 12 of Security Council resolution 687(1991). The second report covered the period 17 December 1991 to 17 June 1992, and the third, the period 17 June to 17 December. They were transmitted to the Council in June[62] and December[63] respectively.

According to the reports, the 12.24 kilograms of U-235 contained in the fresh fuel for the IRT-5000 research reactor, removed from Iraq in November 1991,[64] was transferred to the Russian Federation, where it was transformed, through isotopic dilution, into approximately 61 kilograms of uranium, enriched to slightly less than 20 per cent in U-235. It was then transferred to a storage facility, where it will remain under IAEA safeguards pending its resale. French-origin MTR type plates and Russian-origin pins containing, respectively, 372 grams and 116.1 grams of U-235 were removed from Iraq in June 1992 and were in storage at the IAEA laboratory in Seibersdorf, Austria.

Other irradiated enriched research reactor fuel containing a total of 35.58 kilograms of U-235 was held in storage in the Russian reactor building at Al-Tuwaitha and a location nearby. Negotiations with a consortium of commercial companies from France and the United Kingdom for the removal and reprocessing of this fuel had met with legal, technical and financial difficulties. Consequently, IAEA, on 27 November, called for new proposals for the removal, transportation and disposal of the material. The removal, to take place during the first half of 1993, could be accomplished without major difficulties, but required the substantial involvement of Iraqi personnel.

IAEA continued to pursue its inquiry into the Iraqi nuclear material flow declarations, in particular with regard to activities declared to have taken place at Al-Tuwaitha. Additional samples were taken of the filters, declared feed and waste materials.

As to installations, equipment and other materials relevant to enriched uranium production, materials procured from Germany and new Iraqi declarations of other stocks of materials procured were described in detail by the ninth (January) IAEA inspection.[53] The destruction of EMIS

uranium enrichment production capabilities at the Tarmiya and Ash Sharqat sites, including the associated electrical power distribution capability, had been verified as complete. EMIS components, consistent with Iraqi declarations and independently acquired procurement data, had been verified as destroyed; 51 return irons of 30 tonnes each were removed from Tarmiya to a nearby storage area. Electrical power to the site was reduced by a factor of three.

With respect to Iraq's weaponization activities, the Al-Atheer–Al-Hatteen sites had been re-inspected since completion of the destruction of the weaponization-related facilities and equipment there. At Iraq's invitation, cameras and associated accessories declared in 1991 were inventoried and were being evaluated as to their utility for high explosives testing. Approximately 250 tonnes of HMX, a high-melting-point explosive, was in storage under IAEA seal at Al-Qa'qa' pending a determination of its disposition.

Future activities included: arrangements for the removal from Iraq of 35 kilograms of U-235 contained in the irradiated fuel elements of the Tamuz 2 and IRT-5000 research reactors; and determination of the disposition of the approximately 700 machine tools inventoried by IAEA, some of which met the specifications for annex 3 of the IAEA plan for ongoing monitoring of Iraq's compliance with relevant Council resolutions.

In all, IAEA had carried out, with Special Commission assistance and cooperation, 16 inspections in Iraq of more than 70 sites that resulted in the gradual disclosure of a broad-based nuclear programme aimed at the production of enriched uranium and development of nuclear-weapon capabilities. In the course of the inspections, IAEA interviewed numerous Iraqi authorities and secured thousands of pages of documents from which it had been able to draw a reasonably coherent and consistent picture of Iraq's nuclear programme. Doubts remained, however, as to whether that picture was complete.

Special Commission activities

The Special Commission established under resolution 687(1991)[1] continued to maintain three offices: the Office of the Executive Chairman in New York, a field office at Manama, Bahrain, and another at Baghdad. Agreements concluded by the United Nations with Bahrain and Iraq governing the status, privileges and immunities of the Commission[22] remained in force. According to the two 1992 reports on the Commission's activities (see below), issued by the Executive Chairman, Rolf Ekéus, the agreement with Bahrain was extended twice during the year, each for a six-month period, to 29 September 1992 and thereafter to 31 March 1993.

The question of the Commission's financing, currently met by contributions in cash and in kind (personnel, services, equipment) from a number of Member States, required attention in the absence of an Iraqi agreement to sell oil under the terms of resolution 706(1991).[9] The first contribution to the escrow account established by that resolution was received on 10 December from Saudi Arabia in the amount of $30 million specifically earmarked for the Commission.

Special mission (January)

As reported by the Secretary-General on 25 January 1992,[5] the Special Commission dispatched a special mission to Iraq from 27 to 29 January. Led by two Commission members, the mission was to emphasize to Iraq the most serious concern at its failure to provide information required under resolution 715(1992)[3] and to urge it, in accordance with resolution 707(1991),[2] to disclose, fully and completely, information on its programmes related to chemical and biological weapons and ballistic missiles with a range greater than 150 kilometres.

The Commission's Executive Chairman, in a special report transmitted to the Security Council on 18 February,[65] stated that, while the mission obtained some of the information that Iraq should have supplied on its own initiative as part of its compliance with resolution 707(1991), it had to do so by an interrogative procedure whereby specific questions were addressed to Iraq to which it replied. The mission had no success as to the requirement that Iraq unconditionally comply with its obligations under the two plans for ongoing monitoring and verification approved by resolution 715(1991). The Commission thus concluded that Iraq had no intention of meeting those obligations and that it recognized only its own understanding of its obligations under paragraphs 10 and 12 of resolution 687(1991), which fell far short of what was called for by resolution 715(1991).

The Executive Chairman drew attention to additional matters of serious concern that illustrated Iraq's refusal to acknowledge its obligations under resolution 707(1991) and impinged on the privileges and immunities of the Commission. One was Iraq's insistence that incoming and outgoing inspection flights to and from Bahrain or Kuwait use Habbaniyah airfield, coupled with the imposition of increasingly onerous conditions that not only had considerably delayed loading and offloading but had also come close to harassment. Given those difficulties and the 100-kilometre distance of Habbaniyah from the Commission's centre of operations in Baghdad, the Commission on 23 January officially proposed using Muthanna or Rasheed airfields, which were operational and within city limits. Of further concern were Iraq's constant objection to the aerial surveillance flights by the Commission and Iraq's continuing failure to deliver to IAEA the documents forcibly removed from the sixth nuclear inspection team in September 1991.[61]

The Executive Chairman stated that, were the Commission to initiate the ongoing monitoring and verification phase of its mandate under these circumstances, it would be sending a message that, in fact if not in law, it was prepared to conduct this phase of its responsibilities under Iraq's conditions, not the Council's. The Commission was neither legally able nor prepared to adopt such an approach, which experience had demonstrated was fraught with serious inadequacies. It was therefore seeking instructions from the Council, adding that the longer firm action was delayed, the more intransigent Iraq's position was likely to become.

SECURITY COUNCIL ACTION (19 February)

After consultations held on 19 February 1992, the President of the Security Council issued the following statement[66] on behalf of Council members in connection with the item entitled "The situation between Iraq and Kuwait":

"The members of the Security Council express their gratitude to the Secretary-General for the report submitted to the Security Council on 18 February 1992 (S/23606).

"The members of the Security Council note that while progress has been made, much still remains to be done to implement the relevant resolutions of the Council. The members of the Council are gravely concerned by Iraq's continued failure to acknowledge all its obligations under Council resolutions 707(1991) and 715(1991), and its continued rejection of the plans of the Secretary-General and of the Director General of the International Atomic Energy Agency (S/22871/Rev.1 and S/22872/Rev.1 and Corr.1) as approved by resolution 715(1991) for ongoing monitoring and verification of Iraq's compliance with its obligations under paragraphs 10, 12 and 13 of resolution 687(1991).

"Ongoing monitoring and verification of Iraq's obligations is an integral part of Security Council resolution 687(1991), which established a cease-fire and provided the conditions essential to the restoration of peace and security in the region. Such ongoing monitoring and verification is a step of the utmost importance towards the goal set out in paragraph 14 of that resolution.

"Iraq's failure to acknowledge its obligations under resolutions 707(1991) and 715(1991), its rejection up until now of the two plans for ongoing monitoring and verification and its failure to provide the full, final and complete disclosure of its weapons capabilities constitute a continuing material breach of the relevant provisions of resolution 687(1991). Unconditional agreement by Iraq to implement these obligations is one of the essential preconditions to any reconsideration by the Council under paragraphs 21 and 22 of resolution 687(1991) of the prohibitions referred to in those paragraphs.

"The members of the Council support the decision of the Secretary-General to dispatch a special mission headed by the Executive Chairman of the Special Commission to visit Iraq immediately to meet and discuss with the highest levels of the Iraqi Government for the purpose of securing the unconditional agreement by Iraq to implement all its relevant obligations under resolutions 687(1991), 707(1991) and 715(1991). The mission should stress the serious consequences if such agreement to implement is not forthcoming. The Secretary-General is requested to report on the results of the special mission to the Security Council upon its return."

Special mission (February)

Following the statement by the President of the Security Council, a five-member special mission[67] headed by the Executive Chairman of the Special Commission visited Baghdad from 21 to 24 February 1992. The mission held four meetings with officials of the Government of Iraq at the highest levels, including the Deputy Prime Minister; the Minister for Foreign Affairs; the Minister of State for Foreign Affairs; and the Adviser to the Minister, as well as the Foreign Ministry's Director of Disarmament Section, Head of Research Department, and Chief of Department of International Organizations; the Vice-Chairman of the Military Industrial Corporation; and the IAEC Chairman. As agreed at the second meeting on 22 February, both sides clarified their respective positions through an exchange of written statements.

In the mission's statement, the Executive Chairman noted that progress had been made but much remained to be done to implement the Council's resolutions. The Council was gravely concerned at Iraq's continued failure to acknowledge its obligations under resolutions 707(1991) and 715(1991) and viewed its rejection of the ongoing monitoring and verification plans as a continuing material breach of the relevant provisions of resolution 687(1991). Full disclosure of Iraq's weapons programmes, with supporting documentary and physical evidence, was required under resolution 707(1991) to advance implementation of resolution 715(1991). Monitoring and verification of Iraq's obligations were integral to resolution 687(1991) and of the utmost importance in achieving in the Middle East a zone free from weapons of mass destruction and all missiles for their delivery. Unconditional agreement by Iraq to implement its obligations under all relevant Council resolutions was one of the essential preconditions for any Council reconsideration of the sanctions. The special mission's purpose was to obtain Iraq's unconditional agreement to implement all its obligations under resolutions 687(1991), 707(1991) and 715(1991) and to stress the serious consequences

if such agreement was not forthcoming, including a delay in the lifting of sanctions and destruction of more of Iraq's dual-capable production facilities than would otherwise be required.

The Executive Chairman stressed that dialogue on Iraq's compliance would be meaningful only on the basis of a full, final and complete disclosure of its weapons programmes. He drew attention to the Special Commission's rights to operate its own aircraft and use airfields of its choice, as elaborated upon in resolution 707(1991) and in the plans for ongoing monitoring and verification, offering to explore practical arrangements to accommodate Iraq's legitimate concerns in this regard. He further drew attention to a request by a chemical-weapons destruction team then in Iraq to land a fixed-wing aircraft at Al-Tallil airfield at Nasiriyah, for medical evacuation in case of an emergency during the destruction of a large number of chemically-armed rockets at Khamisiyah. Having explained in depth the background of the ongoing monitoring and verification plans, the Executive Chairman stressed that their implementation could be relatively easy with complete declarations and full cooperation.

The Iraqi statement asserted that Iraq had provided all the necessary information required of it under resolution 687(1991) but suggested presenting it again in a consolidated format to give a better overall picture. If that information still proved unsatisfactory, Iraq proposed that the Special Commission and IAEA should then address specific questions to Iraqi experts at a seminar that should deal once and for all with the overall picture of Iraq's weapons programmes. The seminar would take place within a fixed timetable and should result in a jointly signed statement, to which a definitive list of outstanding issues could be appended, and in a report to the Council that Iraq was in compliance with its obligations under stage 1 of the Special Commission's work. To facilitate completion of that stage, the Commission should draw up a final list of the precise equipment that needed to be destroyed.

Iraq did not respond to the Commission's point about operating its own aircraft and using airfields of its choice. In the discussions, however, Iraqi concerns in this regard appeared to be linked to the question of sovereignty, territorial integrity and national security. The mission learned on leaving Baghdad that Iraq had agreed to the request for emergency landings at the Al-Tallil airfield.

While it had earlier expressed objections to resolution 687(1991), Iraq nevertheless admitted its obligations to permit ongoing monitoring of its obligations not to reacquire the weapons systems destroyed under section C of that resolution. It did not reject the two plans for ongoing monitoring and verification approved under resolution

715(1991); it merely expressed its position on that resolution. From its standpoint, the main problem with the plans lay in the general provisions, which continued into the indefinite future the privileges, immunities and facilities for the Special Commission and IAEA, agreed as part of the cease-fire arrangements, and as such infringed Iraq's sovereignty, territorial integrity, national security and industrial capabilities.

Iraq proposed that the Commission provide a detailed description of how the ongoing monitoring and verification plans would be implemented, the better to identify a mode of implementation acceptable to both sides. It insisted on a linkage between its cooperation with the Special Commission and the easing or lifting of sanctions. It asked that a clear distinction be made between stage 1 of the Commission's work—the identification and destruction of weapons systems specified in resolution 687(1991) and identification of the related production equipment for future monitoring—and stage 2—the long-term monitoring plans under resolution 715(1991). Sanctions should be progressively eased as implementation of stage 1 progressed. Stage 2 should not be used as a mandate in perpetuity by Council members empowered with a veto.

After a careful review of the Iraqi statement and taking account of the discussions held, the Executive Chairman regretfully concluded that, at that stage, he was not able to report to the Council that he had secured unconditional agreement by Iraq to implement all its obligations under resolutions 687(1991), 707(1991) and 715(1991). He was of the view that Iraq's offer to consolidate what it called "all the necessary information" it had already provided would not constitute the full, final and complete disclosure called for by resolution 707(1991), which would give a complete picture and understanding of all of Iraq's prohibited weapons programmes.

The Executive Chairman would continue to press for landing rights at Rasheed airport so that the Commission's fixed-wing and helicopter operations might be consolidated at one place not far from its field office at Baghdad. Iraq accepted only the "principle" of ongoing monitoring and verification under resolution 715(1991), subject to considerations of sovereignty, territorial integrity, national security and non-infringement of its industrial capabilities—a statement the Executive Chairman could not interpret as constituting unconditional agreement by Iraq to implement its obligations under those plans. Short of such agreement, the practical implementation of resolution 715(1991) and the plans it approved could not be undertaken in a credible manner.

The Iraqi statement indicated that a delegation to be dispatched to talk to the Council in March would convey Iraq's position on resolutions 707(1991) and 715(1991). The Executive Chairman concluded that only through successful implementation in the field, based on adequate declarations and periodic reporting by Iraq, could those resolutions be carried out to the point where the Special Commission and IAEA would be in a position to report to the Council that Iraq was in substantial compliance with its obligations under section C of resolution 687(1991).

In a 24 January letter to the Secretary-General,[68] Iraq recapitulated the points it had made to the special mission and reiterated its proposal for an expert-level dialogue for the following purposes: to present to the Special Commission information required from Iraq in consolidated form and to respond to any questions relating to it; to enable adequate material balances to be established for all weapons and their components; to provide credible detailed information on items destroyed unilaterally by Iraq; to respond to specific requests for available evidence relating to Iraqi declarations; and to discuss the scope of destruction proposed by the Special Commission, so as to ensure irreversibly the non-prohibited use of facilities, equipment, materials and components.

Iraq confirmed that it did not reject the plans for ongoing monitoring and verification. It reaffirmed that, by recognizing resolution 687(1991), it had accepted the principle that the Security Council should ascertain and verify that Iraqi industry was in no way directed towards the production of prohibited weapons. In this regard, Iraq could deal with the Council and the Special Commission on the basis of respect for its sovereignty and national security requirements, and of non-infringement of its industrial capabilities devoted to purposes not prohibited by resolution 687(1991).

SECURITY COUNCIL ACTION (28 February)

Following consultations among Security Council members, the President made the following statement[69] on behalf of the Council, at its meeting on 28 February 1992, in connection with its consideration of the item entitled "The situation between Iraq and Kuwait":

"The members of the Security Council express their gratitude to the Secretary-General for the report submitted to the Council on 27 February 1992 (S/23643), transmitting the results of the special mission dispatched to Iraq by the Secretary-General pursuant to the statement of the President of the Council of 19 February 1992 (S/23609). The members of the Council approve in full the conclusions of the special mission as contained in the report and in particular its finding that Iraq is not prepared to give its unconditional agreement to implement all of its obligations under resolutions 687(1992), 707(1991) and 715(1991).

"The members of the Council deplore and condemn the failure of the Government of Iraq to provide the special mission with full, final and complete disclosure, as required by resolution 707(1991), of all aspects of its programmes to develop weapons of mass destruction and ballistic missiles with a range greater than 150 kilometres, including launchers, and of all holdings of such weapons, their components and production facilities and locations, as well as all other nuclear programmes; and the failure of Iraq to comply with the plans for ongoing monitoring and verification (S/22871/Rev.1 and S/22872/Rev.1 and Corr.1) approved by resolution 715(1991). In the statement made on 19 February 1992 (S/23609) prior to the dispatch of the special mission to Iraq, the Council noted that Iraq's behaviour constituted a material breach of resolution 687(1991). Regrettably, this continues to be the case.

"Furthermore, the members of the Council equally deplore and condemn Iraq's failure, within the time prescribed by the Special Commission at the request of Iraq, to commence destruction of ballistic missile-related equipment designated for destruction by the Special Commission. The members of the Council reaffirm that it is for the Special Commission alone to determine which items must be destroyed under paragraph 9 of resolution 687(1991). Therefore, the Government of Iraq's letter of 28 February 1992 to the Executive Chairman of the Special Commission is unacceptable. Iraq's refusal to implement the determinations of the Special Commission constitutes a further material breach of the relevant provisions of resolution 687(1991).

"The members of the Council demand that Iraq immediately implement all its obligations under Council resolution 687(1991) and subsequent resolutions on Iraq. The members of the Council require the Government of Iraq to communicate directly to the Council without further delay an authoritative and unconditional acknowledgement of its agreement to accept and implement the above noted obligations, including specifically to comply with the determination of the Special Commission requiring the destruction of ballistic missile-related equipment. The members of the Council emphasize that Iraq must be aware of the serious consequences of continued material breaches of resolution 687(1991).

"The members of the Council note that an Iraqi delegation is prepared to come to New York as soon as it is invited to do so. The members of the Council have asked its President to extend such an invitation to the delegation to come to New York without further delay. The members of the Council intend in any event to continue their consideration of this question no later than the week beginning 9 March 1992."

Meeting number. SC 3058.

Report of the Special Commission (June).

The Executive Chairman of the Special Commission submitted two reports—its third and fourth—in 1992, which the Secretary-General transmitted to the Security Council. The third report, issued in June and covering the period 4 December 1991 to 10 June 1992,[70] summarized the principal developments and activities since the Commission's report of December 1991.[71] It restated the negative outcome of the special mission to Iraq in February and its implications for the implementation of resolution 715(1991).

The Special Commission and IAEA continued to conduct vigorous inspections of sites declared by Iraq or designated by the Commission. The inspections were the main source for compiling a picture of Iraq's weapons of mass destruction and capabilities for producing them. Although Iraq had in most instances extended cooperation to inspectors in the field, it had not been uniformly forthcoming with information on its weapons programmes as a whole. Three problems that emerged in the first five months of Commission operations had crystallized, shifting the emphasis of the Commission's work from conducting inspections to seeking compliance with Council resolutions, and thus delaying the fulfilment of its mandate.

First, an obstruction to the Commission's progressive discharge of its work as envisioned—from inspection and survey to destruction, and thence to long-term ongoing monitoring and verification to ensure that Iraq did not reacquire proscribed weapons—emerged in November 1991 with Iraq's written confirmation of its position that the plans for future ongoing monitoring and verification were illegal, as it had stated before the Council resolution 715(1991) approving those plans was adopted.[17] Second, Iraq had failed to provide the initial declarations required under the plans, which were important for identifying which facilities, materials and activities needed to be monitored. In June, however, it submitted to the twelfth (May/June) IAEA inspection team documents containing what it characterized as a comprehensive and complete version of its nuclear, chemical, biological and ballistic-missile activities. Those documents, currently being assessed, should correspond to the full, final and complete disclosures required under resolution 707(1991). Third, Iraq had continued putting obstructions in the way of the Commission's landing rights for fixed-wing aircraft and stepping up criticisms and protests against its high-altitude surveillance flights.

The protests, reported to the Security Council on a number of occasions, escalated to a point where, by a letter of 9 April, Iraq referred to a recent incursion into Iraqi airspace by Iranian aircraft and called a halt to all Commission aerial surveillance flights "in order to avoid any unfortunate incidents"; it further referred to the possibility that the flights might "now endanger the aircraft itself and its pilot". In his response of 10 April, the Executive Chairman expressed the gravest concern that those remarks appeared to constitute a threat to the security of the Commission's surveillance flights, which derived from resolution 687(1991) and was expressly authorized under resolutions 707(1991) and 715(1991) and in the 1991 status agreement between the United Nations and Iraq.[22] Unless the Commission received immediate assurances from Iraq that its military forces would not interfere with or threaten the security of the flights, the modalities for those unescorted flights would have to be reviewed. The exchange of correspondence was transmitted to the Council for consideration (see below).

During the period under review, the Special Commission conducted two chemical-weapons inspections: the seventh and eighth. The 10 sites inspected during the seventh inspection (27 January–5 February) revealed no evidence of activities or items relevant to resolution 687(1991). At Al-Muthanna, where the central chemical weapon destruction facility was under construction, the team verified the return to the facility of chemical-bomb-making equipment from a sugar factory at Mosul. After observing an experimental test run of a procedure for the controlled destruction of nerve agents by caustic hydrolysis, the team concluded that further test runs were necessary.

The eighth inspection (15-29 April) covered 14 sites to verify declarations submitted on 28 March relating to chemical weapon items that Iraq claimed to have unilaterally destroyed in July 1991. It also inspected without prior notice a suspected documentation centre and visited the former headquarters of the Centre for Technical Research. It found no activity of relevance to resolution 687(1991) at either site.

Meanwhile, a team directed and controlled the destruction at Khamisiyah (21 February–24 March) of 425 chemically filled and 38 unfilled rockets. Another team monitored preparations for the destruction facility at Al-Muthanna (5-13 April), providing technical guidance for the construction of a mustard-agent incinerator, which was 70 per cent complete, and a large-scale nerve-agent hydrolysis plant, which needed further modification. By a decision of the Commission, all ballistic-missile-related chemicals used in the production of solid rocket propellant were to be transferred from their current locations to Al-Muthanna for destruction.

Between December 1991 and June 1992, the Special Commission conducted six ballistic-missile inspections. The first inspection (1-9 December 1991) was to verify destruction of fixed launch sites, mainly in the western zone, and of "supergun" components. The team inspected 17 missile sites, of which seven were undeclared. Equipment assessed to have been primarily intended for ballistic-missile production and testing was found at two of the undeclared sites. Iraq agreed to destroy four

Scud-missile transporters that were re-inspected and to blow up four similar ones remaining at Al-Taji.

The second inspection (9-17 December 1991) visited 14 suspected missile concealment sites— one in Baghdad and the rest in the western zone— in search of documentary evidence relating to missiles and associated equipment.

The main task of the third inspection (21-28 February 1992) was to supervise destruction by Iraq of ballistic-missile production and repair facilities, together with related equipment, identified by the Executive Chairman in a 14 February letter to Iraq's Minister of State for Foreign Affairs. The team inspected a total of seven sites and found the facilities for the missile-solid-propellant project to have been extensively rebuilt. It also found and catalogued prohibited items in a number of areas that had been inaccessible to previous inspection teams due to war damage. Owing to Iraq's refusal to execute destruction as specified in the letter, the Executive Chairman ordered the team to withdraw from Iraq. As a result of the Council's consideration of the matter in formal session on 11 and 12 March (see under "Ceasefire compliance"), Iraq on 19 March declared additional numbers of ballistic missiles, chemical weapons and associated items and stated its readiness to go along with the required destruction.

In addition to initiating the destruction concerned, the fourth inspection (21-30 March) was charged with verifying Iraq's claim to having unilaterally destroyed 89 ballistic missiles and certain associated equipment in the summer of 1991, and with conducting a number of undeclared inspections. The team was handed a revised accounting of the number of missiles Iraq had received from the former USSR and a downward revision of the number of missiles Iraq fired at Iran during their 1980-1988 armed conflict. The fifth inspection (13-21 April) continued supervising destruction of ballistic-missile production equipment. Forty-five items and 10 buildings were destroyed, representing the majority of the items listed in the Executive Chairman's letter of 14 February, as extended by his letter of 4 April.

The sixth inspection (14-22 May) continued with the verification, begun by the previous inspection, of Iraq's declaration of 19 March. It inventoried equipment designed for the production of nozzles for the BADR-2000 ballistic missile, miscellaneous components, and missile transport dollies. It verified destruction of six items of various types of test vehicles as well as a maintenance vehicle, the erector arm of a training launcher, nine oxidizer and four propellant vehicles, a spot welder and a rolling machine. It identified five sets of Iraqi manufactured missile guidance components, which were to be removed from Iraq for technical analysis. The remains of guidance components unilaterally destroyed by Iraq were found scattered in and around a canal 10 kilometres long. The team found a number of documents relating to the construction of facilities probably associated with missile systems. It removed for analysis copies of 33 pages of documents concerning construction at SAAD-16.

SECURITY COUNCIL ACTION (10 April)

The exchange of correspondence between Iraq and the Special Commission regarding the latter's aerial surveillance flights was the subject of Security Council consultations held on 10 April 1992.

After those consultations, the Council President issued the following statement[74] on behalf of the Council members in connection with the item entitled "The situation between Iraq and Kuwait":

"The members of the Security Council have learned with grave concern from the Executive Chairman of the Special Commission of recent developments which appear to call for a halt in and consitute a threat to the safety and security of the Special Commission's aerial surveillance flights over Iraq. The members of the Council wish to point out that the surveillance flights are carried out under the authority of Security Council resolutions 687(1991), 707(1991) and 715(1991). Reaffirming the right of the Special Commission to conduct such aerial surveillance flights, the members of the Council call upon the Government of Iraq to take all the necessary steps to ensure that the Iraqi military forces will not interfere with or threaten the security of the flights concerned and to comply with its responsibilities to secure the safety of the Special Commission's aircraft and personnel while flying over Iraq. The members of the Council warn the Government of Iraq of the serious consequences which would ensue from any failure to comply with these obligations."

Report of the Special Commission (December). The fourth report of the Special Commission covered its activities during the period 10 June to 14 December 1992.[73] Five appendices contained descriptions of: organizational and administrative issues; security issues; further inspections of Iraq's proscribed weapons activities in the areas of chemical and biological weapons and ballistic missiles; aerial surveillance by high-altitude aircraft and helicopter; and activities relating to the destruction of Iraq's chemical agents and munitions. A sixth appendix listed all inspections and special missions undertaken by the Commission since its inception.

The report provided a detailed account of the main problems that had impeded the Commission's operations and thus the fulfilment of its mandate. They included: Iraq's position that the plans for ongoing monitoring and verification were unlawful and that a solution to address their substance in a manner acceptable to Iraq should be negotiated between Iraq, the Security Council, the Special Commission and IAEA; Iraq's "full, final and complete" disclosures due under resolution 707(1991) and its initial declarations, due under the plans for ongoing monitoring and verification, found to contain major shortcomings, needed to be rectified if they were to form the basis for a definite material balance of Iraq's past programmes of weapons of mass destruction and for effective monitoring and verification of compliance; and Iraq's failure to substantiate information it had provided on its prohibited programmes. The Commission had accepted the declarations made by Iraq on these issues as a basis for dialogue with its authorities in the hope of eventually obtaining complete disclosures.

As to observance of the Commission's status, privileges and immunities, the problems related to its right to operate aircraft anywhere within Iraq continued. A most serious instance was the Iraqi authorities' refusal to accept that an appropriately notified aerial surveillance flight should take place. A formal complaint was lodged with Iraq's Foreign Ministry and the incident was brought to the Security Council's attention on 10 December (see below). A disturbing new development was the sharp deterioration of the security of Commission personnel and property in Iraq. An appendix to the report summarized the types of security-related incidents, including hostile demonstrations, harassment, telephone threats, verbal abuse and physical attacks on Commission inspectors and property. The report stated that, while some incidents might have been spontaneous, it was difficult not to believe that the decrease in security was the result of a centrally coordinated government campaign to intimidate and humiliate Commission staff.

Three chemical weapons inspections—the ninth to the eleventh—were conducted during the period under review. The ninth inspection (26 June–10 July) was essentially in search of documentation on proscribed weapons activities at declared and undeclared sites, some of which were possibly concerned with biological weapons and ballistic missiles. The team also surveyed and recorded reconstruction activity at the Fallujah sites, where chemical weapon precursors were formerly produced. In addition, it supervised the destruction of a majority of the chemical bomb-making equipment identified to date. The inspection ended with a stand-off at the Ministry of Agriculture and Irrigation, where the Iraqi authorities refused access to the building. The team, which had been monitoring the building's exits to ensure that evidence was not removed, had to be withdrawn eventually.

The tenth inspection (21-29 September) verified that, with the exception of mortar rounds at Fallujah and whatever might remain in the damaged and unsafe bunkers at Muhammadiyat, Iraq had fully carried out Commission instructions to move all identified chemical munitions and agents to the destruction facility at Al-Muthanna. A comprehensive inventory of the items, currently under way, would form the baseline for destruction operations.

The eleventh inspection (6-14 December) comprised two sub-teams which undertook inspections relating to chemical and bacteriological weapons. A report on that inspection remained to be submitted.

In the area of ballistic missiles, the Commission conducted three inspections. The team of the first inspection (11-29 July) replaced that of the ninth chemical weapons inspection. Its task was to keep watch outside the Ministry of Agriculture and Irrigation until such time as access was allowed. The team was forced to withdraw from the vicinity of the building on 22 July after an attack on one of the inspectors, which Iraqi security officials did nothing to prevent. Following discussions on modalities in New York between the Executive Chairman and the Permanent Representative of Iraq to the United Nations, access to the Ministry was granted and a full inspection was conducted. No proscribed items were found, although indications were that such items might have been removed.

The findings of the second inspection (7-18 August), which investigated Iraq's ability to acquire or produce indigenously proscribed ballistic missiles, especially missile guidance and control systems, including gyroscopes, were negative. The team obtained further information, however, on the scope and extent of Iraq's programmes to acquire or produce prohibited ballistic missiles and components, the interrelationship between the various projects and organizations in the ballistic missile programme, and foreign involvement in certain of the programme's aspects.

The third inspection (16-30 October) had a two-fold objective: to determine whether Iraq retained an inventory of or the capability to produce fuels for ballistic missiles and to obtain information on the operational use of those missiles. Iraq adopted a more open approach to providing data on the operational use of its ballistic missiles since 1980. The team obtained information on Iraq's past plans to acquire fuel and oxidizer for prohibited missiles but found no evidence of the capability to produce such fuels indigenously.

SECURITY COUNCIL ACTION (6 July)

After Security Council consultations held on 6 July 1992, the President issued the following statement[74] on behalf of the Council members in connection with the item entitled "The situation between Iraq and Kuwait":

"The members of the Security Council have learned with concern of the refusal of the Government of Iraq to permit a team of inspectors sent to Iraq by the Special Commission to enter certain premises designated by the Special Commission for inspection.

"The members of the Council recall that, under paragraph 9 (b) (i) of section C of Security Council resolution 687(1991), Iraq is required to permit the Special Commission to undertake immediate on-site inspection of any locations designated by the Commission. This obligation is imposed as a result of a decision of the Council, taken under Chapter VII of the Charter. Furthermore, Iraq has agreed to such inspections as a condition precedent to the establishment of a formal cease-fire between Iraq and Kuwait and the Member States cooperating with Kuwait in accordance with Security Council resolution 678(1990). The members of the Council further recall that by paragraph 2 (ii) of resolution 707(1991) the Council has reaffirmed the relevant provision of resolution 687(1991) and expressly demanded that Iraq 'allow the Special Commission . . . and their Inspection Teams immediate, unconditional, and unrestricted access to any and all areas, facilities, equipment, records, and means of transportation which they wish to inspect.'

"Iraq's present refusal to permit access to the Inspection Team currently in Iraq to the premises designated by the Special Commission constitutes a material and unacceptable breach by Iraq of a provision of resolution 687(1991), which established the cease-fire and provided the conditions essential to the restoration of peace and security in the region. The members of the Council demand that the Government of Iraq immediately agree to the admission to the premises concerned of the inspectors of the Special Commission as required by the Chairman of the Special Commission, so that the Special Commission may establish whether or not any documents, records, materials, or equipment relevant to the responsibilities of the Commission are located therein."

Mission (July)

The Special Commission undertook a third mission to Iraq, from 17 to 19 July 1992, in order to secure from the Iraqi Government immediate and full access to the premises of the Ministry of Agriculture and Irrigation and to obtain Iraq's undertaking to implement its obligations under all relevant Security Council resolutions. Access to the Ministry had been denied to the ninth chemical weapons inspection team on 5 July.

The four-member mission, headed by the Executive Chairman, held four meetings, on 18 and 19 July: with the Minister of State for Foreign Affairs, along with the IAEC Chairman, the Director of the Military Industrial Corporation, and the Permanent Representative designate of Iraq to the United Nations, on the first day; and with the Foreign Minister and the Deputy Prime Minister, along with the Permanent Representative designate, on the next.

The Executive Chairman explained that the Ministry had been designated for inspection because of a well-founded concern that the facility contained material of relevance to section C of resolution 687(1991). He reiterated the Council demand that Iraq immediately agree to admit the Commission inspectors to the premises, warning that if the situation was not rectified, a new legal situation regarding the cease-fire arrangement might be created. The obstruction by Iraq amounted to a challenge to the Council's authority.

Iraq's legal argument was that Council decisions taken under Chapter VII of the Charter of the United Nations could not be invoked to impose on a Member State conditions that infringed on its national sovereignty. Thus, Iraq did not accept that resolutions 687(1991) and 707(1991) placed an obligation on it to give the Commission unimpeded access to any place in Iraq. The building in question was a ministerial building symbolizing Iraq's sovereignty. To permit its inspection would create a precedent for access to other ministry buildings and politically sensitive sites, which was an unacceptable infringement of Iraq's sovereignty.

In an effort to find what he called an honourable solution to the impasse, the Deputy Prime Minister proposed that a team of weapons experts from neutral and non-aligned countries within the Security Council should be allowed to conduct, independently of the Commission and not under the terms of the Council resolutions, a full inspection of the premises and report to the Council. The Executive Chairman, recalling that such a proposal had been firmly rejected by the Council in March, stated that the idea could be considered provided that the inspection took place under the auspices of the relevant Council resolutions and that the experts were approved as competent and thoroughly trained and briefed by the Commission. He then outlined other procedures for determining whether the facility contained anything related to resolution 687(1991), Iraqi reaction to which was inconclusive.

The Executive Chairman's report on the mission,[75] which concluded that it had failed to obtain its objectives, was transmitted to the Council President by the Secretary-General.

Iraq, on 19 July,[76] conveyed to the Council President its proposal to invite a group of experts from members of the Movement of Non-Aligned Countries and possibly from Austria, China and Sweden, to conduct the inspection, outside the Special Commission's mandate, to ascertain that no materials relevant to resolution 687(1991) were in the premises. On 22 July, when the inspection team was withdrawn from its watch of the Ministry of Agriculture and Irrigation because of attempted physical violence on an inspector, which Iraq failed to prevent, Iraq transmitted to the Secretary-General a statement by a Foreign Ministry spokesman[77] contending that the decision to withdraw stemmed rather from the dilemma in which the Commission found itself after Iraq had expressed readiness to accept inspection by a neutral team to prove the falsity of the alleged presence of prohibited materials in the building.

Communications. On 17 December,[78] the Security Council President circulated to Council members a letter of 10 December from the Deputy Executive Chairman of the Special Commission, Pierce S. Corden, providing details of adverse developments that affected the ability of the Special Commission and IAEA to carry out their mandates.

One development concerned Iraq's refusal of an aerial surveillance mission of which the appropriate Iraqi authorities were notified on 2 December. The reason given for the refusal was that part of the designated flight area fell within Baghdad city limits. To the Commission's request for a reconsideration of that position, Iraq on 9 December confirmed the negative decision, stating moreover that such flights would not be permitted "one metre inside Baghdad".

On 6 December, during the sixteenth IAEA inspection, conducted jointly with the Special Commission,[59] the joint inspection team, while seeking admission to a designated site, observed a number of individuals hurriedly leaving the site with documents. In response to protests by the Chief Inspector, Johan Stantesson (Sweden), the Iraqi authorities claimed that those individuals had acted on their own initiative. Certain documents, purportedly those removed, were subsequently produced for the inspectors. Further, the inspectors were denied permission to remove or copy blueprints of pharmaceutical plants found at the site, with the Iraqi authorities demanding that the inspectors first prove the documents' direct relevance to resolution 687(1991). To resolve the conflict, the Chief Inspector inventoried and tagged the blueprints for examination by a Commission expert due to arrive in the course of the inspection.

The Special Commission and IAEA were lodging protests with Iraq's Foreign Ministry regarding deprivation of their rights to aerial surveillance, to secure and review documents without interference and alone to determine the relevance of documentary evidence to their mandate and when to remove or copy documents.

Also circulated was an account of an 8 December meeting between the Chief Inspector and General Amer Muhammad Rashid, Director of the Military Industrial Corporation, which reflected a serious deterioration in Iraq's willingness to fulfil its obligations. The General strongly criticized the Special Commission, in particular its November report to the Council. He stated that regardless of what Iraq provided, the Commission demanded more. Whereas the report of the October ballistic missile inspection[73] expressed complete satisfaction that Iraq's ballistic missile programme was totally finished, the Executive Chairman's speech before the Council made no mention of it. The purpose of the Commission's helicopter surveillance, the General asserted, was to gather intelligence information and humiliate the Iraqi people; consequently, he would never allow the helicopter one metre inside Baghdad. Iraq had trusted the Commission but had been deceived; therefore, the game was over. Iraq would provide nothing more and would punish any of its people who provided information to the Commission.

In 14 December,[79] Iraq wrote to set the record straight by apprising the Council of the true facts of the meeting between the Chief Inspector and General Amer Muhammad Rashid. The letter stated that the General affirmed Iraq's candour and frankness in its dealings with the Commission regarding implementation of resolution 687(1991), despite the malevolent game in progress, behind which were certain influential Council members bent on prolonging the inspections in order to maintain the embargo against Iraq. It was evident, he said, that the inspection teams were reiterating requests for information already provided, as if the inspections had begun again from zero. The General asked why the Executive Chairman's statement before the Council in November made no reference to the positive results of the October inspection that had closed the file on Iraq's ballistic missile programme. When the General indicated that he would punish any Iraqi who undertook to provide the inspection teams with information bearing no relation to resolution 687(1991), his intention was clear: to stop the teams from harassing their Iraqi counterparts with questions and inquiries that bore no relation to that resolution.

The General stressed that he was conveying to the Chief Inspector the Iraqi people's anger and deep distress towards the inspection teams so that the Commission might understand their feelings regarding the embargo. Despite detailed and complete information provided by Iraq, the Commission had persisted in presenting new requests under suspicions raised by parties hostile to Iraq. This had engendered the prevailing belief that the inspection teams served political and intelligence-related goals that had nothing to do with Council resolutions.

In view of Iraq's request for adherence to the agreement reached with the aerial inspection team regarding the boundaries of the City of Baghdad and his feeling that the aerial inspections were intelligence-gathering missions, the General regarded the flight requests unwarranted and provocative and said the sites could be investigated by ground-based inspection teams.

It saddened the General that the reports of his meeting with the Chief Inspector ignored his affirmations of Iraq's desire to cooperate with the Commission, leading to the perception that the aim of those reports was to distort the position of Iraq and do it a disservice. He pointed out that the inspection teams had seen and verified everything relating to resolution 687(1991) and that all weapons and equipment proscribed by that resolution had been destroyed. That could not have been done without Iraq's full assistance and cooperation. As a result, Iraq had expected the Commission to fulfil its own obligations under the resolution by recommending that the economic embargo against Iraq be lifted. Regrettably, nothing of the kind had happened.

Monitoring and verification

The long-term monitoring and verification of Iraq's compliance with relevant parts of Security Council resolution 687(1991), as set forth in the Special Commission and IAEA plans[80] approved by resolution 715(1991), continued to be challenged by Iraq in 1992. As a follow-up to the objection it raised before the Council when the plans were approved,[81] Iraq formally restated its position in a letter of 19 November 1991 to the Council President, namely, that it did not recognize any obligations under resolution 715(1991) and attacked the plans, describing them as unlawful and aimed at objectives incompatible with the letter and spirit of the United Nations Charter, the norms of international law and international and humanitarian pacts and covenants.

The Special Commission's plan covered long-term monitoring and verification of Iraq's compliance with its unconditional obligations not to use, retain, possess, develop, construct or otherwise acquire any weapons or related facilities and items prohibited by the Council under resolution 687(1991), relating to proscribed ballistic missiles, chemical and biological weapons and facilities. The plan provided for inspections in Iraq of both military and civilian sites, facilities, material and other items or activities that could be used in contravention of those obligations, as well as for aerial overflights and submission by Iraq of information to enable the Commission to discharge its mandate.

Under the IAEA plan, Iraq was obliged to provide the Agency with inventories of: all nuclear material in Iraq; all facilities, installations and sites where nuclear activities of any kind, including but not limited to research facilities, laboratory-scale installations and pilot plants suitable for carrying out such activities; all material, equipment and items in Iraq identified in annex 3 of the plan; all isotopes in Iraq used for medical, agricultural or industrial applications; and all facilities, installations and sites provided with any means of supply of electricity exceeding 10 MW (megawatts). Iraq was also to provide information on existing and proposed programmes of nuclear activities for the next five years. Annex 2 of the plan set forth the information requirements of these inventories, including the requirement that the initial information be provided in English within 30 days of the plan's adoption and should cover the period from 1 January 1989, with subsequent complete information to be provided each 15 January and 15 July. Annex 3 contained the list of items to be reported to IAEA.

On 14 July 1992, IAEA informed the Council, through the Secretary-General, that annex 3 to its plan was being revised and that it would so inform Iraq. Its revision was warranted in the light of experience gained in the implementation of resolutions 687(1991) and 707(1991), and of an agreement by a group of 27 nuclear-supplier countries that export controls should be applied to a list of nuclear-related dual-use equipment, materials and associated technology. The revised annex, together with an appendix of detailed specifications for machine tools, was transmitted to the Council on 16 July.[82]

During the year, the Secretary-General, on behalf of the Special Commission, submitted two reports to the Council, as did the IAEA Director General, prepared pursuant to a provision of resolution 715(1991) that both submit reports at least every six months on the implementation of the plans.

Reports of the Secretary-General (April and October). On 10 April 1992,[83] the Secretary-General submitted his first report on the implementation of the Special Commission's plan during the period 11 October 1991 to 8 April 1992.

He recalled that under the plan, Iraq was to submit, by 10 November 1991, *(a)* initial information on the specific dual-purpose activities, facilities and items outlined in the plan and its annexes; and *(b)* a report on the legislative and administrative measures taken to implement resolutions 687(1991), 707(1991), other relevant Council resolutions and the plan. Iraq was further obliged to update the information in *(a)* each 15 January and 15 July and to report further on *(b)* when requested by the Special Commission. Remaining firm in its position and arrogating to itself the right to decide what information to provide the Commission, Iraq in late November 1991 submitted what it described as the information required under resolution 687(1991) that fell under the Commission's

mandate. The information did little more than repeat what had already been supplied, and no information was given on any legislative and administrative measures taken by Iraq.

Iraq failed to respond to the Commission's request that it provide not only the specified initial information but also the first semi-annual declaration under the plan due on 15 January 1992. The Secretary-General outlined the steps that the Commission took to obtain Iraq's compliance, including its missions to Iraq in January and February, the corresponding Council statement after being apprised of the results of each mission, as well as Iraq's reiteration of its position and alternative proposals (see above, under "Special Commission activities"). He restated what the Commission regarded as the most important outstanding matters, and recounted the Commission's statement to the Council in March,[18] as well as the meeting immediately thereafter between the Iraqi technical team and the Commission and its outcome (see above, under "Cease-fire compliance").

The Commission communicated to Iraq on 20 December 1991 that it could not decide upon Iraq's requests for the reuse of certain dual-purpose items until it received all information and data under the plan for ongoing monitoring and verification and obtained clear and unequivocal acceptance by Iraq of resolution 715(1991) and the plan. Any such items that might be released by the Commission for reuse, after being rendered harmless, needed to be covered by appropriate monitoring and verification procedures envisaged in the plan.

Thus, as of the reporting date, the Secretary-General concluded that, during the period covered, Iraq was not in compliance with resolution 715(1991) and that, without clear acknowledgement of its obligations under that resolution and the plans it approved, as well as its agreement to implement unconditionally those obligations, the Commission would neither legally nor practically be able to initiate and operate its monitoring and verification plan.

A second report, transmitted on 19 October,[84] provided information on developments between 10 April and 10 October 1992. It recapitulated the Council decisions adopted in the light of Iraq's non-compliance, which further served to define the Council's position in respect of the ongoing monitoring and verification and to provide guidance to the Commission in seeking to carry out its mandate. Those decisions, embodied in statements issued by the Council President on behalf its members, included the findings that: full implementation of the Council's resolutions on the situation between Iraq and Kuwait was essential to the restoration of peace and security in the region (statement of the heads of State and Government at the Security Council summit on 31 January—see PART ONE, Chapter I); Iraq's failure to acknowledge its obligations under resolutions 707(1991) and 715(1991) and to provide the necessary declarations constituted a continuing material breach of resolution 687(1991) (19 February);[66] that Iraq's unconditional agreement to implement its obligations under those two resolutions was an essential precondition to any reconsideration of the lifting of sanctions under paragraphs 21 and 22 of resolution 687(1991) (19 February)[66] and was necessary for the initiation and credible practical implementation of ongoing monitoring and verification (28 February);[69] and Iraq had not complied fully and unconditionally with all its obligations, must do so and immediately take appropriate actions.[24]

The Secretary-General described, among other developments, Iraq's demand made before the Council on 11 March that agreement should be reached between it, the Special Commission and IAEA, under Council auspices, to ensure that the measures and methods of ongoing monitoring would not infringe on Iraq's sovereignty, threaten its internal security, lead to interference in its internal affairs or deny it the prospects of scientific, technological and industrial progress in the civilian and military fields. The report noted that Iraq missed the first two reporting requirements; however, on 27 June, it formally submitted what it termed its "report on future compliance verification", assessed by a group of international experts as inadequate for the purpose of commencing ongoing monitoring and verification activities.

The report concluded that the conditions for the initiation in full of the Commission's plan for ongoing monitoring and verification had still not been met. There had been no movement in Iraq's underlying position on the plan and resolution 715(1991) to suggest a change in the Commission's assessment that Iraq was seeking to ensure that implementation of the plan proceeded on the basis of its interpretation of its obligations rather than on the Council's resolutions. Thus, while the Commission had already been performing some essentially monitoring functions, for the time being it remained constrained from going beyond preparatory work into full-scale monitoring and verification until it was clear that Iraq would comply with such monitoring on the Council's terms. The Council directives on this point were unequivocal and must be complied with by both the Commission and Iraq.

IAEA reports (April and October). The first IAEA report, submitted on 11 April 1992,[85] stated that approximately 190 pages of Arabic text including five tables and one appendix relating to Iraq's nuclear capabilities were delivered to the Special Commission in Baghdad on 20 Novem-

ber 1991. Following a meeting with the Iraqi Resident Representative to IAEA (Vienna, 3 December 1991), an additional 52 pages, also in Arabic, were transmitted to IAEA on 11 December "in compliance with Security Council resolution 715(1991)"—the only occasion on which Iraq referred to submitting information under that particular resolution. The texts were described as: table 1—Iraq's obligations and action taken; table 2—Inventory of nuclear material in Iraq, with a notation that uniform tables were being prepared for all information contained in declarations mentioned; table 3—Information on nuclear sites, facilities and installations; table 4—Inventory of radioactive sources of IAEC; table 5—Inventory of radioactive sources in Iraqi installations and establishments other than IAEC; and table 6—actually an appendix to table 3.

Although the information submitted was declared to be that required by the plan, its scope did not conform with the information requirements set forth in annex 2 of the plan in so far as it included only items belonging to IAEC, rather than all relevant items located in Iraq. Nor did the information reflect the situation as of 1 January 1989—a requirement that Iraq later said would be practically impossible to meet. It also refused to identify facilities, installations and sites provided with an electricity supply exceeding 10 MW, except for two IAEC facilities.

In January 1992, another table, also in Arabic and listing "equipment and devices related to the Iraqi nuclear programme in accordance with resolution 687(1991)", was submitted with a letter referring to a number of items whose required inclusion Iraq considered as exceeding its obligations under that resolution.

The report noted that it had been made clear to Iraq that IAEA would not negotiate modifications to the terms of the plans approved by resolution 715(1991); and that, until Iraq provided full and complete details of its nuclear programme, IAEA would be unable to establish a firm basis for effectively carrying out monitoring and verification of the scope and nature approved by the Council.

The second IAEA report, submitted on 30 September,[86] stated that, during the twelfth (May-June) IAEA inspection, Iraq provided a revised declaration of its nuclear programme, referred to as the "full, final and complete report" required by resolution 707(1991), but refused to provide information on the suppliers of its enrichment equipment and technology. Following additional clarifications of the revisions to annex 3 of the plan, IAEA expected Iraq to submit updated inventories.

Two Iraqi requests were received for the import of specified radioisotopes for use in nuclear medicine applications (11 December 1991) and in 44 research projects (26 March 1992). Following receipt of additional information from Iraq, IAEA, with prior clearance from the Committee on sanctions, gave its technical approval to the first request and to 42 of the projects listed in the second. IAEA was of the opinion that the remaining two projects could be linked to proscribed research and development activities.

There were indications that information was being compiled in full compliance with the plan's requirements. In the meantime, IAEA had begun to implement those components of the plan that were not dependent on the availability of additional information, including: periodic checks of IAEA seals applied to nuclear and other materials, equipment and machine tools; visits to sites previously identified as related to Iraq's nuclear weapons programme to verify that no nuclear activity was resumed; analysis of high- and low-altitude imagery of known nuclear sites to identify the purpose of new buildings or to detect activities that might require further on-site inspection; and periodic radiometric surveys of the main water bodies in Iraq for the detection of the presence or resurgence of major nuclear activities.

Kuwaiti property

The Secretary-General, in his report of March 1992[18] updating information on the status of Iraq's compliance with its obligations under the series of Security Council resolutions beginning with resolution 687(1991), stated that properties belonging to a number of Kuwaiti Government and public institutions had been returned and that the return of additional Kuwaiti property was continuing. Iraq's January report[15] on its compliance activities listed the items it had returned between May and December 1991[17] to the same Kuwaiti entities cited by the Secretary-General.

Kuwait, on 6 November 1992,[87] transmitted to the Secretary-General a document signed by officials of Iraq and Kuwait, including a representative of each country's Ministry of Health, and by a United Nations representative, attesting to Iraq's return of Kuwaiti property listed in annex A, with the condition of each item described in annex B, on 26 August at Ar'ar, Saudi Arabia. The parties acknowledged that inspection of the returned property was not feasible and that Kuwait reserved the right to submit to the United Nations any observations pertaining to alleged loss, damage or alteration in respect of the items listed.

UN Compensation Commission and Compensation Fund

The United Nations Compensation Commission, established by the Security Council in 1991[88] for the resolution and payment of claims against Iraq for losses and damage resulting from its invasion and occupation of Kuwait, submitted its first annual report to the Council on 21 September 1992.[89]

The report summarized the activities of the Commission and of the Governing Council, its policy-making organ, during the period July 1991 to June 1992. It listed the six sessions held by the Governing Council and annexed a list of the decisions (1 to 11) it adopted, with decisions 3 to 9 reproduced. The report also described the status of the Commission's financing.

The Commission maintained its headquarters at Geneva. Under the direction of the Executive Secretary, its secretariat organized the Governing Council sessions and prepared the relevant documentation. It advised Governments and international organizations on questions related to the preparation and submission of claims.

Activities of the Governing Council. The Governing Council held five sessions in 1992, all at Geneva: the fourth (20-24 January) and resumed fourth (6 March),[90] fifth (16-20 March),[91] sixth (22-26 June),[92] seventh (21-24 September)[93] and eighth (14-18 December)[94] sessions.

As a result of its work during those sessions, the Governing Council adopted a number of decisions on topics as follows: on 24 January and 6 March —determination of ceilings for compensation for mental pain and anguish (decision 8) and propositions and conclusions on compensation for business losses: types of damages and their valuation (decision 9); on 26 June—provisional rules for claims procedure (decision 10) and eligibility for compensation of members of the Allied Coalition Armed Forces (decision 11); on 24 September— claims for which established filing deadlines were extended (decision 12) and further measures to avoid multiple recovery of compensation by claimants (decision 13); on 18 November— establishment of the United Nations Compensation Commission Committee on Administrative Matters (decision 14), compensation for business losses resulting from Iraq's unlawful invasion and occupation of Kuwait where the trade embargo and related measures were also a cause (decision 15) and awards of interest (decision 16).

As listed in the Commission report, the decisions adopted by the Governing Council in 1991 included: guidelines for the conduct of its work; criteria for expedited processing of urgent claims (decision 1), arrangements for ensuring payment to the Compensation Fund (decisions 2 and 6), personal injury and mental pain and anguish (decision 3), business losses of individuals eligible for consideration under the expedited procedures (decision 4), guidelines relating to paragraph 19 of the criteria for expedited processing of urgent claims (decision 5) and criteria for additional categories of claims (decision 7).

Iraq, on 17 December 1992,[95] stated that the Governing Council, in adopting decision 10, failed to follow the Secretary-General's 1991 recommendations[17] stressing that Iraq be informed of all claims and be given the right to present its views to the panels of commissioners within time-limits fixed by the Governing Council—recommendations which the Security Council directed it to take into account.[88] The Executive Secretary's report of 30 October 1992, although circulated to Iraq, did not provide the necessary details on which to base its views: it contained numbers without details or explanation, or even the claimants' names and nationalities. Decision 10 thus denied Iraq of its legal and logical right, despite the fact that Iraq was the only party of crucial importance in the matter of compensation payment.

Iraq called on the Security Council to correct the situation and ensure compliance with its relevant instructions.

Arms and related sanctions

Reports of the Committee on sanctions. The Committee established by Security Council resolution 661(1990)[7] (Committee on sanctions) issued four reports—one every 90 days—during 1992, pursuant to the responsibilities entrusted to it under the guidelines approved by the Council[96] for monitoring the prohibitions against the sale or supply of arms to Iraq and related sanctions. They were transmitted to the Council President on 12 March,[97] 10 June,[98] 8 September[99] and 4 December.[100]

Each report stated that, during the period under review, the Committee had received no information relating to possible violations of the arms and related sanctions against Iraq committed by other States or foreign nationals. It had not been consulted by States or international organizations on either the sale or supply of items to Iraq that might fall within the categories of proscribed items or of dual- or multiple-use items, nor had any allegations of violations in this regard been reported to it. No international organization had reported any relevant information that might have come to its attention.

SECURITY COUNCIL ACTION

Following each consultation held by the Security Council on 27 March,[101] 27 July[102] and 24 November[103] 1992, on the March, June and September reports of the Committee on sanctions, respectively, the Council President issued a statement to the effect that informal consultations were held pursuant to paragraphs 21 and 28 of resolution 687(1991) and paragraph 6 of resolution 700(1991);[96] that, after hearing all the opinions expressed in the course of the consultations, the President concluded that there still was no agreement that the necessary conditions existed for a modification of the regimes established in paragraph 20 of resolution 687(1991), as referred to in paragraph 21 of that resolution; in paragraphs 22, 23, 24 and 25 of resolution 687(1991), as referred to in paragraph 28 of that resolution; and in paragraph 6 of resolution 700(1991).

The March report of the Committee on sanctions indicated that the same statement was issued following the Council's consideration of the December 1991 report.[104]

Repatriation of Kuwaitis and third-country nationals

Further to the information provided by Iraq to the Security Council on 23 January 1992[15] on the repatriation of Kuwaitis and third-country nationals who had remained unaccounted for in Iraq since the 1991 military operations in the Gulf, Iraq, on 28 February,[105] submitted updated information according to which it had repatriated, in cooperation with ICRC, 6,520 Kuwaiti and other nationals since 4 March 1991. Some 3,594 Kuwaitis currently living free in Iraq were awaiting Kuwait's agreement to their repatriation. So far, Kuwait had agreed to repatriate only 460 of them. Thus, despite Iraq's cooperation, Kuwait had refused to receive its nationals. An examination of the Kuwaiti list of 2,242 persons believed to be in Iraq revealed that 233 had already been repatriated under ICRC supervision and 59 were among those awaiting repatriation approval from Kuwait. To make the international community aware of the developments in the matter and at the request of Iraq, the League of Arab States sent a team to Iraq to conduct on-site investigations to ascertain the situation of Kuwaitis in Iraq.

As a result of a 1991 meeting between Iraq and the coalition States held under ICRC auspices (Geneva, 16 and 17 October), the participants signed a protocol by which Iraq was to publish the names of the missing in the Iraqi media, with a request that any information on those persons be conveyed to ICRC, and to repeat publication as necessary. Accordingly, Iraq informed ICRC of its agreement to: disseminate in one Iraqi newspaper the names of missing Kuwaitis and Saudis and seek information on their fate; provide ICRC with lists of detention sites and prisons so that it could visit each of them once; and have the visits coordinated with the competent Iraqi agencies and Foreign Ministry. Based on the principle of reciprocity, Iraq asked that the same procedures be instituted by Kuwait and Saudi Arabia in the search for missing Iraqis. Iraq said that, in view of the negative reply from the coalition States, it alternatively proposed that ICRC draw up a plan to be agreed upon between it and the coalition States concerning methods and procedures for tracing Iraqi, Kuwaiti, Saudi and other nationals on the basis of the provisions of the 1949 Geneva Conventions.

To dispel the widespread belief engendered by a media campaign that Iraq continued to hold large numbers of Kuwaitis in detention, Iraq communicated its position to ICRC thus: its competent authorities were prepared to publish the names of missing Kuwaitis, Saudis and others in Iraqi newspapers; to arrange visits by ICRC to detention sites and prisons; and to reach agreement with the ICRC head at Baghdad regarding these measures. Having done so, Iraq stated that it had met its obligations as stipulated in paragraphs 30 and 31 of resolution 687(1991).

On 6 March,[106] the third countries concerned—France, Kuwait, Saudi Arabia, the United Kingdom and the United States—stated that Iraq's letter of 28 February was yet another attempt to delay fulfilling its commitments under the Geneva Conventions and the relevant Council resolutions. It had neither published any names in any of its media nor lived up to its commitment made at Riyadh, Saudi Arabia, on 7 March 1991 to grant ICRC the facilities necessary to enable it to gather information to establish the whereabouts of missing persons. It had not effectively responded to individual inquiry files submitted by Kuwait and Saudi Arabia in October 1991, having merely returned them on 18 February 1992 without information as to specific measures taken to trace the cases. Nor had it responded to ICRC inquiries outlined in the Secretary-General's 25 January report.[5] Its unilateral assumption that it had met its obligations by submitting a letter of intent only underlined Iraq's disdain towards this humanitarian issue.

Regarding that assumption, Iraq, on 19 March,[107] explained that it meant that it had given effect to the practical measures required by paragraphs 30 and 31 of resolution 687(1991) and that that was to be considered an achieved stage in its efforts to close the file on the matter, in cooperation with the United Nations, ICRC and the other parties concerned. Iraq stated that: on 10 and 17 March, it published the names of missing Kuwaitis in *Al-Thawrah*, *Al-Jumhuriyah* and *Al-Iraq* and would repeat their publication; on 12 March, it notified ICRC that it would be allowed to conduct open and unrestricted visits to all detention places; it returned the 13 inquiry files to ICRC with an official reply to every question entered; and, except for one case of death of a Kuwaiti in detention, of which ICRC had been informed, no other cases of death had been reported by the competent Iraqi authorities.

Humanitarian assistance

Iraq

SECURITY COUNCIL ACTION (March)

The Security Council met on 19 March 1992 in connection with its resolutions 706(1991)[9] and 712(1991),[12] setting up a scheme and appropriate machinery whereby Iraq was authorized to sell petroleum and petroleum products, to finance, *inter alia*, the purchase of foodstuffs, medicines and materials and supplies to meet Iraq's urgent humanitarian needs.

Following consultations among Council members, the President was authorized to make the following statement,[108] on behalf of the Council:

"The Security Council welcomes the announcement of the Iraqi authorities that they will resume discussions with the United Nations Secretariat concerning implementation of the scheme of sales of Iraqi petroleum and petroleum products, as provided for in Security Council resolutions 706(1991) and 712(1991), and for the use of the proceeds of such sales in accordance with the Secretary-General's report of 4 September 1991 (S/23006) and the above-mentioned resolutions.

"The Council also welcomes the Secretary-General's intention that these discussions be organized without delay.

"The Council is prepared to authorize the regime for the sale of Iraqi petroleum and petroleum products on the above basis for a like period of time as that specified in these resolutions as soon as the Secretary-General indicates that the Iraqi authorities are prepared to proceed on a date certain with the export of petroleum and petroleum products in accordance with the scheme.

"The members of the Council are prepared at an appropriate time to consider possible further extensions of time based upon Iraq's cooperation with the above and the Council's ongoing assessment of the needs and requirements in accordance with paragraph 1 *(d)* of Security Council resolution 706(1991)."

Communication. On 13 July 1992,[109] Iraq stated that the idea of meeting Iraq's humanitarian needs, already on scale so modest as to fall short of what was required to ensure a minimum of humanity to its people, evolved into two resolutions—706(1991) and 712(1991)—containing many political conditions and restrictions that sought to strip Iraq of its sovereignty. The issue had developed into controversy with the result that, in mid-1992, the essential needs of the Iraqi people for the second half of the previous year had yet to be met. Negotiations with the United Nations Secretariat between January and June had led Iraq to conclude that the purpose of the formula for meeting those needs was to impair Iraq's independence and interfere in its internal affairs.

The most recent formula resulting from three rounds of negotiations contained numerous restrictions and complexities exposing the purchase, shipment and distribution of food and medicine to possible hindrances and stoppage, to say nothing of the consequent high prices that would reduce the purchasing power of the already paltry sum that would be made available to Iraq through such outlandish procedure.

Iraq asserted that the sound and workable course was for the Security Council to allow Iraq to export its petroleum in the regular manner that it had done before the events of August 1990 so that its people might have their humanitarian due.

SECURITY COUNCIL ACTION (October)

The Security Council convened on 2 October 1992 in accordance with an understanding reached in prior consultations and adopted **resolution 778(1992)**.

The Security Council,

Recalling its previous relevant resolutions and in particular resolutions 706(1991) and 712(1991),

Taking note of the letter of 15 July 1992 from the Secretary-General to the President of the Security Council on Iraq's compliance with the obligations placed on it by resolution 687(1991) and subsequent resolutions,

Condemning Iraq's continued failure to comply with its obligations under relevant resolutions,

Reaffirming its concern about the nutritional and health situation of the Iraqi civilian population, and the risk of a further deterioration of this situation, and recalling in this regard its resolutions 706(1991) and 712(1991), which provide a mechanism for providing humanitarian relief to the Iraqi population, and resolution 688(1991), which provides a basis for humanitarian relief efforts in Iraq,

Having regard to the fact that the period of six months referred to in resolutions 706(1991) and 712(1991) expired on 18 March 1992,

Deploring Iraq's refusal to cooperate in the implementation of resolutions 706(1991) and 712(1991), which puts its civilian population at risk, and which results in the failure by Iraq to meet its obligations under relevant Security Council resolutions,

Recalling that the escrow account provided for in resolutions 706(1991) and 712(1991) will consist of Iraqi funds administered by the Secretary-General which will be used to pay contributions to the Compensation Fund, the full costs of carrying out the tasks authorized by section C of resolution 687(1991), the full costs incurred by the United Nations in facilitating the return of all Kuwaiti property seized by Iraq, half the costs of the Boundary Commission, and the cost to the United Nations of implementing resolution 706(1991) and of other necessary humanitarian activities in Iraq,

Recalling that Iraq, as stated in paragraph 16 of resolution 687(1991), is liable for all direct damages resulting from its invasion and occupation of Kuwait, without prejudice to its debts and obligations arising prior to 2 August 1990, which will be addressed through the normal mechanisms,

Recalling its decision in resolution 692(1991) that the requirement for Iraqi contributions to the Compensation Fund applies to certain Iraqi petroleum and petroleum products exported from Iraq before 2 April 1991, as well as to all Iraqi petroleum and petroleum products exported from Iraq after 2 April 1991,

Acting under Chapter VII of the Charter of the United Nations,

1. *Decides* that all States in which there are funds of the Government of Iraq, or its State bodies, corporations, or agencies, that represent the proceeds of sale of Iraqi petroleum or petroleum products, paid for by or on behalf of the purchaser on or after 6 August 1990, shall cause the transfer of those funds (or equivalent amounts) as soon as possible to the escrow account provided for in resolutions 706(1991) and 712(1991); provided that this paragraph shall not require any State to cause the transfer of such funds in excess of 200 million dollars or to cause the transfer of more than fifty per cent of the total funds transferred or contributed pursuant to paragraphs 1, 2 and 3 of this resolution; and further provided that States may exclude from the operation of this paragraph any funds which have already been released to a claimant or supplier prior to the adoption of this resolution, or any other funds subject to or required to satisfy the rights of third parties, at the time of the adoption of this resolution;

2. *Decides* that all States in which there are petroleum or petroleum products owned by the Government of Iraq, or its State bodies, corporations, or agencies, shall take all feasible steps to purchase or arrange for the sale of such petroleum or petroleum products at fair market value, and thereupon to transfer the proceeds as soon as possible to the escrow account provided for in resolutions 706(1991) and 712(1991);

3. *Urges* all States to contribute funds from other sources to the escrow account as soon as possible;

4. *Decides* that all States shall provide the Secretary-General with any information needed for the effective implementation of this resolution and that they shall take the necessary measures to ensure that banks and other bodies and persons provide all relevant information necessary to identify the funds referred to in paragraphs 1 and 2 above and details of any transactions relating thereto, or the said petroleum or petroleum products, with a view to such information being utilized by all States and by the Secretary-General in the effective implementation of this resolution;

5. *Requests* the Secretary-General:

(*a*) To ascertain the whereabouts and amounts of the said petroleum and petroleum products and the proceeds of sale referred to in paragraphs 1 and 2 of this resolution, drawing on the work already done under the auspices of the Compensation Commission, and report the results to the Security Council as soon as possible;

(*b*) To ascertain the costs of United Nations activities concerning the elimination of weapons of mass destruction, the provision of humanitarian relief in Iraq, and the other United Nations operations specified in paragraphs 2 and 3 of resolution 706(1991); and

(*c*) To take the following actions:

(i) Transfer to the Compensation Fund, from the funds referred to in paragraphs 1 and 2 of this resolution, the percentage referred to in paragraph 10 of this resolution; and

(ii) Use of the remainder of funds referred to in paragraphs 1, 2 and 3 of this resolution for the costs of United Nations activities concerning the elimination of weapons of mass destruction, the provision of humanitarian relief in Iraq, and the other United Nations operations specified in paragraphs 2 and 3 of resolution 706(1991), taking into account any preference expressed by States transferring or contributing funds as to the allocation of such funds among these purposes;

6. *Decides* that for so long as oil exports take place pursuant to the system provided in resolutions 706(1991) and 712(1991) or to the eventual lifting of sanctions pursuant to paragraph 22 of resolution 687(1991), implementation of paragraphs 1 to 5 of this resolution shall be suspended and all proceeds of those oil exports shall immediately be transferred by the Secretary-General in the currency in which the transfer to the escrow account had been made, to the accounts or States from which funds had been provided under paragraphs 1, 2 and 3 of this resolution, to the extent required to replace in full the amounts so provided (together with applicable interest); and that, if necessary for this purpose, any other funds remaining in the escrow account shall similarly be transferred to those accounts or States; provided, however, that the Secretary-General may retain and use any funds urgently needed for the purposes specified in paragraph 5 *(c)* (ii) of this resolution;

7. *Decides* that the operation of this resolution shall have no effect on rights, debts and claims existing with respect to funds prior to their transfer to the escrow account; and that the accounts from which such funds were transferred shall be kept open for retransfer of the funds in question;

8. *Reaffirms* that the escrow account referred to in this resolution, like the Compensation Fund, enjoys the privileges and immunities of the United Nations, including immunity from legal proceedings, or any forms of attachment, garnishment or execution; and that no claim shall lie at the instance of any person or body in connection with any action taken in compliance with or implementation of this resolution;

9. *Requests* the Secretary-General to repay, from any available funds in the escrow account, any sum transferred under this resolution to the account or State from which it was transferred, if the transfer is found at any time by him not to have been of funds subject to this resolution; a request for such a finding could be made by the State from which the funds were transferred;

10. *Confirms* that the percentage of the value of exports of petroleum and petroleum products from Iraq for payment to the Compensation Fund shall, for the purpose of this resolution and exports of petroleum or petroleum products subject to paragraph 6 of resolution 692(1991), be the same as the percentage decided by the Security Council in paragraph 2 of resolution 705(1991), until such time as the Governing Council of the Compensation Fund may decide otherwise;

11. *Decides* that no further Iraqi assets shall be released for purposes set forth in paragraph 20 of resolution 687(1991) except to the sub-account of the escrow account, established pursuant to paragraph 3 of resolution 712(1991), or directly to the United Nations for humanitarian activities in Iraq;

12. *Decides* that, for the purposes of this resolution and other relevant resolutions, the term "petroleum products" does not include petrochemical derivatives;

13. *Calls upon* all States to cooperate fully in the implementation of this resolution;

14. *Decides* to remain seized of this matter.

Security Council resolution 778(1992)

| 2 October 1992 | Meeting 3117 | 14-0-1 |

7-nation draft (S/24605).

Sponsors: Belgium, France, Hungary, Japan, Russian Federation, United Kingdom, United States.

Vote in Council as follows:

In favour: Austria, Belgium, Cape Verde, Ecuador, France, Hungary, India, Japan, Morocco, Russian Federation, United Kingdom, United States, Venezuela, Zimbabwe.

Against: None.

Abstaining: China.

Explaining its abstention, China stated that the issue of payments to the United Nations Compensation Fund, the costs of carrying out the tasks authorized by section C of resolution 687(1991), the costs incurred in the return of all Kuwaiti property seized by Iraq, half the costs of the Iraq-Kuwait Boundary Demarcation Commission and the financing of the humanitarian needs of the Iraqi people should be resolved by making full use of the machinery established by resolutions 706(1991) and 712(1991). China thus believed it unnecessary to resort to so extraordinary a measure as the seizure of Iraq's frozen assets overseas.

During the remainder of the year, some 40 States wrote to the Secretary-General in connection with paragraphs 1 and 2 of the resolution. Of these, 34 stated that, under their jurisdiction, there were no petroleum or petroleum products or funds of the Government of Iraq, or of its State bodies, corporations, or agencies that represented the proceeds of sale of Iraqi petroleum or petroleum products subject to the provisions of the resolution.

Inter-agency humanitarian programme

In view of the expiry at the end of 1991 of the Memorandum of Understanding that provided the basic framework for the United Nations humanitarian presence and action in Iraq,[110] the Executive Delegate for the United Nations Inter-Agency Humanitarian Programme for Iraq, Kuwait and the Iraq/Turkey and Iraq/Iran border areas, Sadruddin Aga Khan, reached agreement with Iraq's Foreign Minister, on 24 November 1991,[18] to extend the Memorandum for a further six-month period up to the end of June 1992, including the continued deployment in Iraq of the United Nations Guards Contingent for the same period.

As he informed the Security Council in November (see above, under "Cease-fire compliance"), the Under-Secretary-General for Humanitarian Affairs, acting on behalf of the Secretary-General, signed in New York on 22 October a new Memorandum of Understanding between the United Nations and Iraq, covering a six-month period ending 31 March 1993. Based on that Memorandum, a plan of action was finalized covering all regions of the country, with emphasis on assistance to the northern provinces.

In the period between the end of the extended Memorandum and the signing of the new 1992 Memorandum, assistance delivery to the northern governorates (Dohuk, Erbil and Suleimaniyah) ground to a halt due to lack of fuel, travel and visa restrictions, security problems, and an unacceptable wave of harassment of United Nations personnel.

SECURITY COUNCIL ACTION

Following consultations held with members of the Security Council on 17 July 1992, the President made the following statement[111] on behalf of the Council, in connection with its consideration of the item entitled "The situation between Iraq and Kuwait":

"The Security Council deeply deplores the murder of a member of the United Nations Guards Contingent in Iraq on 16 July 1992 in the Governorate of Dohuk. It supports the Secretary-General's decision to order an immediate and thorough investigation of this appalling crime. Members of the Council wish to express their sincere condolences to the family of the victim, Mr. Ravuama Dakia, and to the Government of Fiji.

"The Security Council wishes to register its profound concern at the deteriorating security conditions affecting the safety and well-being of United Nations personnel in Iraq. The Council demands that attacks perpetrated against the United Nations Guards Contingent and other humanitarian personnel deployed in Iraq cease immediately and that maximum cooperation be extended by the authorities in the investigation of this crime, as well as in the protection of United Nations personnel."

Iraq, in a letter to the Secretary-General of 17 July 1992,[112] stated that the regrettable incident of 16 July occurred where there was no Government presence. The Governorate of Dohuk was controlled by Kurdish irregulars supported by the United States and its allies. The heinous incident, for which the Government of Iraq bore no responsibility, was a consequence of interference by the United States and its allies in Iraq's internal affairs.

Commenting on a statement by the Spokesman for the Secretary-General issued on 9 July concerning the series of incidents affecting the safety of personnel assigned to the United Nations Humanitarian Programme, Iraq, on the same date,[113] observed that the statement avoided identifying the locations of the incidents because they were occurring in the northern governorates, where Government administration had been withdrawn and were thus wide open to brigands, thieves and irresponsible elements supported and encouraged by the United States and its allies.

Communication from the Secretary-General. On 24 August 1992,[114] the Secretary-General informed the Security Council President of the progress of United Nations efforts to obtain from Iraq an extension or renewal of the Memorandum of Understanding governing the Inter-Agency Humanitarian Programme in Iraq. The Under-Secretary-General for Humanitarian Affairs, assisted by the Coordinator and senior officials from United Nations entities and agencies participating in the Programme—UNHCR, UNICEF, WFP and WHO—held five rounds of talks with Iraq's Foreign Minister and other officials (Baghdad, 17-21 August), including a meeting with the Deputy Prime Minister. Further meetings were held at the technical level.

Iraq took the position that circumstances had changed since the first Memorandum so that the Programme should be based on transitional arrangements leading from an emergency operation to regular cooperation with United Nations agencies. Therefore, the exceptional measures previously provided for would no longer apply. United Nations sub-offices would no longer be permitted, although access on a functional basis would be granted for project implementation; NGO participation would only be allowed under a separate agreement between each NGO and the Government of Iraq; the Guards Contingent would be limited to a maximum strength of 150, to be deployed only in the three northern Governorates, with the Contingent Chief and four or five assistants to be located in Baghdad; a separate radio communications system for the Programme would no longer be permitted; and the new Memorandum would no longer provide for a local-currency contribution by the Government. The period covered could not go beyond 31 December 1992. Iraq also urged that every effort be made to exempt humanitarian requirements from the ongoing sanctions in view of the suffering they inflicted on the civilian population.

The United Nations maintained that sub-offices or field stations were essential for effective implementation of the Programme throughout Iraq; NGO participation was an important operational requirement, but separate individual agreements could be considered subject to the successful adoption of a Memorandum; a ceiling of 500 Guards was necessary to ensure the protection of Programme personnel; a radio communications system was an essential component of all United Nations emergency humanitarian operations; and, in the absence of a special currency exchange rate for humanitarian operations, a Government contribution in local currency was necessary. In view of the time lost since the expiration of the extended Memorandum and the importance of assistance during the winter months, the duration of the new Memorandum should extend to 31 March 1993.

The United Nations agreed to take into consideration and reflect in an eventual Memorandum Iraq's request for joint preparation of the action plan and for its implementation under a Coordination Committee consisting of Programme and Iraqi Government representatives, as well as of Iraq's requirement for separate agreements with NGOs. Iraq, however, was not prepared to modify its position on the question of sub-offices and on the deployment of Guards.

Iraq's Deputy Prime Minister, expressing concern at the impending imposition of an exclusion zone for Iraqi aircraft below the 32nd parallel (see below), explicitly linked that eventuality to the continued presence of the Inter-Agency Humanitarian Programme in the south of the country and of the maintenance of sub-offices under a renewed agreement. Because of possible demonstrations in the Basrah area if the no-fly zone was put into effect, the remaining humanitarian personnel in the south—eight Guards and a UNICEF staff member—were recalled to Baghdad at the Deputy Prime Minister's behest.

As a result of representations by the Under-Secretary-General for Humanitarian Affairs regarding the unacceptable wave of harassment of United Nations staff based in Baghdad, the Foreign Minister gave his assurance that every effort would be made to prevent further harassment.

While no agreement was reached, the Foreign Minister stated that there would shortly be another opportunity to agree on a formula for a new Memorandum. In the meantime, he gave his Government's assurance that a de facto Memorandum existed, that visas and travel permits would be renewed for staff currently assigned to Iraq, although none would be granted for additional staff, and that the 120 Guards could remain, but no replacements or additional deployment would be permitted. Offices outside Baghdad and the northern Governorates should be closed forthwith and NGO presence terminated for the time being.

The Secretary-General stated that, in the absence of a United Nations presence in the south, a reliable assessment of conditions prevailing in that region would not be possible. Since the Programme's implementation had been brought to a halt in the northern governorates owing to lack of fuel supply, the population there would be placed at serious risk unless adequate food and fuel were prepositioned by November.

SECURITY COUNCIL ACTION

The Security Council met on 2 September 1992 to consider the Secretary-General's communication. After consultations among Council members, the President was authorized to make the following statement[115] on behalf of the Council:

"The Security Council is deeply concerned at the current situation of the Inter-Agency Humanitarian Programme in Iraq, as outlined in the Secretary-General's letter of 24 August 1992 to the President of the Council (S/24509), including its reference to Iraq's failure to renew its Memorandum of Understanding with the United Nations.

"The Security Council recalls the statement of 17 July 1992 (S/24309), in which the Council expressed its profound concern at the deteriorating conditions affecting the safety and well-being of United Nations personnel in Iraq. The Council is particularly disturbed by Iraq's continuing failure to ensure the safety of United Nations personnel and the personnel of non-governmental organizations (NGOs).

"The Security Council expresses its concern regarding the conduct and statements of Iraq on the Inter-Agency Humanitarian Programme which are inconsistent with the previous Security Council resolutions that demand that Iraq cooperate with the international humanitarian organizations.

"The Security Council affirms that the critical humanitarian needs of vulnerable groups in Iraq require the speedy conclusion of arrangements that would ensure the continuation of the Inter-Agency Humanitarian Programme. In this respect, the Council considers unrestricted access throughout the country and the assurance of adequate security measures as essential prerequisites for the effective implementation of the Programme. To this end, the Council fully endorses the Secretary-General's insistence upon appropriate field offices for participating United Nations agencies and programmes and the continuing deployment of the United Nations Guards. The Council strongly supports the Secretary-General's continuing efforts to sustain a United Nations and NGO humanitarian presence throughout Iraq, and urges him to continue to use all resources at his disposal to help all those in need in Iraq. The Council urges Iraq in the strongest possible terms to cooperate with the United Nations."

Meeting number. SC 3112.

Iraq, on 3 November,[116] drew attention to what it described as a serious development in connection with the use of the humanitarian assistance programme as a pretext to interfere in Iraq's internal affairs and undermine its security and stability. As reported by the Turkish press, a shipment of military *matériel* was discovered on board a French C-160 aircraft refueling at Diyarbakir military airfield. The report was corroborated by a spokesman of the Ministry of Foreign Affairs of Turkey who said that a United Kingdom–based NGO licensed by the European Council and cleared by the Committee on sanctions was behind the affair. Iraq called the incident a violation of its sovereignty and territorial integrity and of the rules governing the Committee's work.

Kurds and other minority populations

Report of the Special Rapporteur. In the context of Security Council resolution 688(1991),[23] part I of an interim report on human rights violations in Iraq was transmitted to the Council on

3 August 1992.[117] The preliminary text of the interim report had been transmitted earlier, on 5 March.[118] Prepared by Max van der Stoel (Netherlands), the Special Rapporteur of the Commission on Human Rights on the situation of human rights in Iraq, part I of the report was exclusively concerned with the situation in the southern marshes and elaborated on a previously recommended system of human rights monitoring in Iraq as part of an exceptional response to an exceptional situation.

The Special Rapporteur drew attention to reliable and disconcerting information that, beginning in July, the Iraqi military had launched a series of attacks against the civilian population in the southern marshes bordering Iran, which appeared to demonstrate a preconceived policy. These included indiscriminate bombardments of civilian settlements, disappearances, forced relocation of the Marsh Arabs who were also Shi'a muslims, and a de facto internal economic blockade. Perhaps the enormous water diversion programme known as the Third River Project posed the greatest threat to the inhabitants. The creation of another central waterway in the region, ostensibly to irrigate salted flats, would result in the draining of the marsh area. This would threaten the immediate livelihood of its inhabitants, which was fishing, and the survival of their ancient culture.

In the Special Rapporteur's opinion, regardless of Iraq's reply to his appeal of 29 July that it cease all activities that might constitute violations of its obligations under international law, the water diversion project ought to be stopped and there was an urgent need to send a team of human rights monitors to the area to serve as an independent source of reliable information. He described the recommended system of human rights monitoring, including the composition of the teams, their duties and mode of operation, organizational setup, logistical and financial requirements and the role of the Government of Iraq.

Iraq wrote on 6 August[119] to express surprise at the Special Rapporteur's transmittal of his interim report and letter to the Security Council President, rather than to the General Assembly, in line with established procedure, as well as at the transmittal even of the preliminary text. Iraq called into question the impartiality and objectivity of the Rapporteur and accused him of participating in the propaganda campaign against Iraq by leaking the report to the press and holding seminars and television and newspaper interviews directed against the country with which he was supposed to be cooperating.

Stating that the report was full of allegations and fallacies, Iraq explained in detail the purpose of the Third River project on which the Rapporteur's report focused. It traced the origins of the project

to 1952 as part of a major programme to divert high-salinity drainage water from agricultural enterprises in central and southern Iraq into one main drain and channel it into the Arabian Gulf without intermixture with any of the country's rivers. Its aim was to transform land rendered unfit for cultivation by salt accumulation, particularly in the southern areas, into agriculturally productive land. The project, which had gone through many phases, was resumed after the 1991 military operations in the Persian Gulf.

The paucity of water in the marshlands was caused by the reduction of water in the Euphrates from the Kayban and Karakaya dams in Turkey and the Tabqah dam in the Syrian Arab Republic, and by a project, begun in 1990, to fill the reservoir of Turkey's Ataturk dam.

Iraq peremptorily rejected the recommended system of human rights monitoring as interference in its internal affairs.

In addition, Iraq, on 28 August,[120] drew attention to what it called a dangerous decision by France, the United Kingdom and the United States to prevent Iraqi aircraft from flying in southern Iraq below the 32nd parallel. It said that the true objective of that decision, taken under the pretext of protecting the Shiite population of the marshlands, was to divide the country on an ethnic and confessional basis in order to control it, plunder its wealth and enslave its people. Iraq called on the Secretary-General to assume his responsibilities and prevent this new act of aggression against Iraq.

SECURITY COUNCIL ACTION

At the urgent request of Belgium,[121] France,[122] the United Kingdom,[123] and the United States,[124] the Security Council met on 11 August to consider the continuing repression of the civilian population in several parts of Iraq. Those States recalled that, by resolution 688(1991), the Council decided to remain seized of the matter.

Iraq, at its request, was invited to participate in the discussion without the right to vote, in accordance with the relevant provisions of the Charter and with rule 37[a] of the Council's provisional rules of procedure. At the request of the same States that asked for the meeting, the Council invited Max van der Stoel, the Special Rapporteur on the human rights situation in Iraq, to participate in his personal capacity under rule 39.[b] China, India and Zimbabwe entered reservations about his invitation on the grounds that human rights matters should be more appropriately discussed by the Commission on Human Rights, the Economic and Social Council or the General Assembly.

In addition, the Council had before it a 10 August letter[125] from Iran stating that the campaign of total annihilation of large segments of the Iraqi population—in the recent past mostly against the Shiite inhabitants of the southern marshlands—could lead to conditions threatening regional and international peace and security.

Max van der Stoel stated that information from Iraq's Ministry of Health suggested that the health of the Iraqi population was rapidly deteriorating. The incidence of respiratory diseases was seven to eight times higher than in the past and deaths from dysentery five to six times higher. Infant mortality had risen sharply. Some 1,270 cholera cases required treatment and dozens had died. The Government food-rationing programme provided only 1,400 calories per person daily and food prices in the open market were too high for most of the population. The situation underlined the need for a quick breakthrough in the negotiations for a "food-for-oil" formula based on resolutions 706(1991) and 712(1991).

Against that background, Max van der Stoel expressed alarm that the humanitarian programme in Iraq was inexorably grinding to a halt due to the Government's refusal to issue visas to incoming staff or renew visas of those remaining, who were moreover subjected to harassment. Travel and fuel supply restrictions made delivery of aid difficult. He cited the Government's economic blockade of the Kurds in the northern governorates and of the Shiites in the southern marshes, the military attacks on both the north and the south, the forced relocation of the marsh inhabitants, and the threat to their fishing areas and to the survival of their ancient culture by the causeways that were under construction. He concluded that the Government was in the process of undertaking a major operation to subdue the indigenous population of the marshes, recalling in this connection the "Anfal operations" in the north against the Kurds in the 1980s to underscore how ruthless such an operation could be.

Given the gravity of those allegations, Iraq asked why the Special Rapporteur did not verify his information by a country survey or with the Government, to satisfy himself and convince others of his objectivity, seriousness and independence. Iraq repeated the contents of its 6 August letter on the Rapporteur's report[119] and hoped for a correction of its data, including that on the Third River Project. It clarified that Government forces occasionally raided the marshes, not for the reasons alleged but to ferret out deserters, murderers, smugglers and infiltrators hiding within the safety of the tall reeds. Iraq's appearance before the Council, however, was to state that the report,

regardless of its merits or demerits, was an illegal attempt to help accomplish an illegal aim: to dismember Iraq by calling for permanent human rights observers and eventually to establish another so-called safe haven in the south.

Meeting number. SC 3105.

Other assistance

Emergency relief was provided under the auspices of the United Nations Development Programme for the group of countries affected by the Iraq-Kuwait situation, and international cooperation attempted to mitigate the environmental consequences on Kuwait and other neighbouring countries resulting from the hostilities in the Persian Gulf (see PART THREE, Chapters III and VIII).

REFERENCES

[1]YUN 1991, p. 172, SC res. 687(1991), 3 Apr. 1991. [2]Ibid., p. 188, SC res. 707(1991), 15 Aug. 1991. [3]Ibid., p. 194, SC res. 715(1991), 11 Oct. 1991. [4]Ibid., p. 199. [5]S/23514. [6]YUN 1991, p. 176. [7]SC res. 661(1990), 6 Aug. 1990. [8]YUN 1991, p. 184, SC res. 699(1991), 17 June 1991. [9]Ibid., p. 207, SC res. 706(1991), 15 Aug. 1991. [10]YUN 1968, p. 17, GA res. 2373(XXII), annex, 12 June 1968. [11]YUN 1991, p. 200. [12]YUN 1991, p. 209, SC res. 712(1991), 19 Sep. 1991. [13]GA res. 44/203, 2 Dec. 1989. [14]S/23517. [15]S/23472. [16]YUN 1991, p. 177. [17]Ibid., p. 195. [18]S/23687. [19]S/23699. [20]SC res. 660(1990), 2 Aug. 1990. [21]YUN 1991, p. 171, SC res. 686(1991), 2 Mar. 1991. [22]Ibid., pp. 183 & 191. [23]Ibid., p. 204, SC res. 688(1991), 5 Apr. 1991. [24]S/23709. [25]S/23993. [26]S/24002. [27]S/24056. [28]S/24036. [29]S/24010. [30]S/24584. [31]S/24726. [32]S/24822. [33]S/24829. [34]S/24836. [35]YUN 1966, p. 423, GA res. 2200 A (XXI), annex, 16 Dec. 1966. [36]Ibid., p. 419, GA res. 2200 A (XXI), annex, 16 Dec. 1966. [37]YUN 1948-49, p. 959, GA res. 260 A (III), annex, 9 Dec. 1948. [38]S/24839. [39]S/23970. [40]S/24044. [41]YUN 1991, p. 176 & 177. [42]S/24113. [43]S/24117. [44]S/24275. [45]S/24387. [46]YUN 1991, p. 178, SC res. 689(1991), 9 Apr. 1991. [47]S/23766. [48]S/24615. [49]S/23789. [50]S/24649. [51]A/47/637. [52]A/47/735. [53]S/23505. [54]S/23644. [55]S/23947. [56]S/24223. [57]S/24450. [58]S/24593. [59]S/24981. [60]S/25013. [61]YUN 1991, p. 190. [62]S/24110. [63]S/24988. [64]YUN 1991, p. 191. [65]S/23606. [66]S/23609. [67]S/23643. [68]S/23636. [69]S/23663. [70]S/24108 & Corr.1. [71]YUN 1991, p. 192. [72]S/23803. [73]S/24984. [74]S/24240. [75]S/24443. [76]S/24321. [77]S/24336. [78]S/24985. [79]S/24964. [80]YUN 1991, p. 193. [81]Ibid., p. 194. [82]S/24300. [83]S/23801. [84]S/24661. [85]S/23813. [86]S/24722. [87]S/24806. [88]YUN 1991, p. 196, SC res. 692(1991), 20 May 1991. [89]S/24589. [90]S/23734. [91]S/23765. [92]S/24363. [93]S/24611. [94]S/25135. [95]S/24989. [96]YUN 1991, p. 198, SC res. 700(1991), 17 June 1991. [97]S/23708. [98]S/24083. [99]S/24545. [100]S/24912. [101]S/23761. [102]S/24352. [103]S/24843. [104]YUN 1991, p. 199. [105]S/23661. [106]S/23686. [107]S/23738. [108]S/23732. [109]S/24276. [110]YUN 1991, p. 206. [111]S/24309. [112]S/24311. [113]S/24335. [114]S/24509. [115]S/24511. [116]S/24757. [117]S/24386. [118]S/23685 & Add.1. [119]S/24388. [120]S/24475. [121]S/24393. [122]S/24394. [123]S/24395. [124]S/24396. [125]S/24414.

Chapter IV

Europe

The United Nations intensified its efforts in 1992 to resolve the armed conflict in the former Yugoslavia. The situation—triggered in 1991 by the breakaway of four of the six republics that constituted Yugoslavia—grew progressively complex and more violent during the year.

At the beginning of 1992, the United Nations became actively involved in the crisis between Croatia and the truncated Yugoslavia (comprising the republics of Serbia and Montenegro) by deploying a peace-keeping mission to Croatia. By April, the ethnic conflicts between Bosnian Serbs, Muslims and Croats grew increasingly violent, causing massive civilian deaths and dislocations.

United Nations efforts to contain the crisis and alleviate the suffering included the military protection of humanitarian convoys, as well as the control and supervision of Sarajevo's airport to allow for the airlift of humanitarian assistance. These activities were carried out in close cooperation with the Office of the United Nations High Commissioner for Refugees, which supervised the relief assistance.

Throughout the year, the Secretary-General and his Personal Envoy, Cyrus R. Vance, worked in close coordination with the European Community to co-sponsor a settlement plan for the crisis in Bosnia and Herzegovina. In the face of the escalating violence, the Security Council adopted 22 resolutions directly related to the conflicts in the former Yugoslavia, while the General Assembly adopted four resolutions on the matter. The Council in December authorized the establishment of a small presence of the United Nations Protection Force in the former Yugoslav Republic of Macedonia to monitor developments in the border areas, which could undermine confidence and stability in Macedonia and threaten its territory.

With regard to the events in the former USSR, the General Assembly called for withdrawal of all foreign military forces from the Baltic States of Estonia, Latvia and Lithuania. The Secretary-General sent United Nations good-offices and other missions to the Commonwealth of Independent States and other States of the former USSR experiencing internal strife and conflict. He also dispatched a fact-finding mission to help reach a peaceful settlement to the deteriorating situation in and around Nagorno-Karabakh, an enclave in Azerbaijan marked by over four years of fighting between its Armenian and Azerbaijani inhabitants.

Yugoslavia situation

By January 1992, the United Nations had taken several actions in its efforts to settle the conflict in the former Yugoslavia, resulting from the unilateral declarations of independence in 1991 of four—Bosnia and Herzegovina, Croatia, Macedonia and Slovenia—of six of its constituent republics.

Violence erupted over the issues of border delineations between Bosnia and Herzegovina and Croatia, on the one side, and Serbia, on the other. Large portions of the Yugoslav People's Army (JNA), under the command of the truncated Yugoslavia (Serbia and Montenegro), supported the Serb factions in the two former republics.

By resolution 743(1992) of 21 February, the Security Council established, under its authority and for an initial period of 12 months, a United Nations Protection Force (UNPROFOR), in accordance with a 15 February report of the Secretary-General and a December 1991 United Nations peace-keeping plan. In successive resolutions, the Council added to the responsibilities of UNPROFOR; as a result, UNPROFOR grew considerably throughout the year, in numbers and in the range and variety of its tasks.

Bosnia and Herzegovina, Croatia and Slovenia were admitted to United Nations membership in May 1992 (see PART ONE, Chapter IV). Based on a recommendation of the Security Council, the General Assembly ruled that Yugoslavia (Serbia and Montenegro) could not continue automatically the membership of the former Socialist Federal Republic of Yugoslavia, that it should apply for membership and should not participate in the Assembly's work.

The United Nations and the European Community (EC), through their appointed envoys, continued mediation efforts to bring about dialogue and resolution of the conflict in Bosnia and Herzegovina. The EC-sponsored talks for future constitutional arrangements in Bosnia and Herzegovina were suspended on 27 May 1992, when representatives of the Muslim SDA Party withdrew in protest against the continuing shelling of Sarajevo by Bosnian Serb forces. In subsequent statements, President Izetbegovic and members of the presidency of Bosnia and Herzegovina expressed inability to undertake further negotiations with representatives of the Serbian SDS Party led by Radovan Karadzic and reaffirmed that they could resume participation in the talks only if the basis for discussions was changed.

International Conference on Yugoslavia. The International Conference on the Former Yugoslavia combined the efforts of the United Nations and EC, as well as other international organizations such as the Conference on Security and Cooperation in Europe (CSCE) and the Organization of the Islamic Conference (OIC). Building on the work already done by the EC Conference on Yugoslavia, it was organized to remain in existence until a final settlement of the problems of the former Yugoslavia was reached. Its permanent Co-Chairmen were the head of State or Government of the presidency of EC and the United Nations Secretary-General.

Meeting in London from 26 to 28 August, the Conference adopted a statement of principles for a negotiated settlement. Parties to the conflict represented at the London Conference were Bosnia and Herzegovina, Croatia, Macedonia, Slovenia and Yugoslavia (Serbia and Montenegro). Other countries present included Albania, Austria, Belgium, Bulgaria, Canada, China, Denmark, France, Germany, Greece, Hungary, Ireland, Italy, Japan, Luxembourg, the Netherlands, Portugal, Romania, the Russian Federation, Saudi Arabia, Spain, Turkey and the United States. Also represented were CSCE, OIC and the International Committee of the Red Cross (ICRC).

The Conference established a Steering Committee to manage its operational work. It was cochaired by a representative of the Secretary-General, Cyrus R. Vance (United States), and of the presidency of EC, Lord Owen (United Kingdom). The Committee's membership included representatives of a troika of EC, a troika of CSCE, the five permanent members of the Security Council, an OIC representative, two representatives from neighbouring States, and Lord Carrington (United Kingdom), Chairman of the EC Conference on Yugoslavia.

Mr. Vance and Lord Owen were assisted by the Chairmen of the Conference's six working groups: on Bosnia and Herzegovina; on humanitarian issues; on ethnic and national communities and minorities; on succession issues; on economic issues; and on confidence and security-building and verification measures. The groups met in continuous session at the United Nations Office at Geneva. In addition to their own activities, the Co-Chairmen directed the working groups and prepared the basis for a general settlement and associated measures. The Conference also had an Arbitration Commission and a small secretariat.

In 1992, the Steering Committee held three meetings, all at Geneva: on 3 September, 27 October and 16 December. The Secretary-General reported to the Security Council on the activities of the Conference on 11 November[1] and 24 December.[2]

The Co-Chairmen closely monitored the humanitarian situation in the former Yugoslavia and issued several appeals for protection of and assistance to the victims of the conflict, particularly in Bosnia and Herzegovina. As a result of their efforts, humanitarian flights to Sarajevo, which were suspended following the shooting down of an Italian aircraft on 3 September, were resumed on 3 October.

The Co-Chairmen engaged in extensive diplomatic activities, keeping steady contact with the principal leaders in the former Yugoslavia, as well as leaders of the neighbouring countries, in order to promote peace and a resolution of humanitarian problems, priority being the conflict in Bosnia and Herzegovina. They contacted Governments in a position to assist the peace process and brought together at Geneva Presidents Cosic (Federal Republic of Yugoslavia) and Tudjman (Croatia) on the one hand, and Presidents Cosic and Izetbegovic (Bosnia and Herzegovina) on the other. In the light of the 1991 conflict between Croats and Serbs, they also sought to deal with the central relationship between Croatia and the Federal Republic of Yugoslavia. Close attention was further given to the potentially explosive situations in the Serbian province of Kosovo and in Macedonia.

With regard to the conflict in Bosnia and Herzegovina, the efforts of the Co-Chairmen were directed simultaneously at two basic objectives: a cessation of hostilities and the preparation of options for the republic's constitutional future. In order to help improve relations between the Federal Republic of Yugoslavia and Croatia, the Co-Chairmen organized two sets of meetings at Geneva between Presidents Cosic and Tudjman on 30 September and 20 October. Following each meeting, the two Presidents signed joint declarations containing statements of principle and arrangements for practical cooperation. Results of that process included the demilitarization of the Prevlaka peninsula and the establishment of liaison offices at Belgrade and Zagreb.

Croatia

Under the terms of the original United Nations peace-keeping plan, UNPROFOR was intended to be an interim arrangement to create conditions of peace and security required for the negotiation of an overall settlement of the crisis in the former Yugoslavia. To that end, it was deployed in three United Nations protected areas (UNPAs) in Croatia—Eastern Slavonia, Western Slavonia and Krajina—which corresponded largely to areas where intercommunal tensions had led to armed conflict. The plan accepted by the parties to the conflict rested on two central elements: on the one hand, withdrawal of JNA from all of Croatia and the demilitarization of the UNPAs; on the other, the continued functioning, on an interim basis, of the existing local authorities and police, under United Nations supervision, pending the achievement of an overall political solution to the Yugoslav crisis under the auspices of the EC Conference on Yugoslavia. UNPROFOR was required to ensure that the UNPAs remained demilitarized and that all persons residing in them were protected from armed attack. In addition to military personnel, United Nations civilian police (UNCIVPOL) monitors were to ensure that the local police carried out their duties without discrimination against any nationality and with full respect for the human rights of all UNPA residents. The Force was also to provide support to facilitate the return to their homes of all persons displaced by the hostilities who wished to return.

By resolution 762(1992) of 30 June, the Council additionally authorized UNPROFOR to undertake monitoring functions in the so-called "pink zones" of Croatia, which were Serb-controlled areas lying outside the UNPAs where hostilities continued. It also recommended establishment of a Joint Commission chaired by UNPROFOR and consisting of representatives of the Government of Croatia and of the local authorities of the region, with the participation of the European Community Monitoring Mission (ECMM), to oversee and monitor the process of the restoration of the Croatian Government's authority in the "pink zones". The tasks assigned to UNPROFOR included verifying immediate withdrawal of the Croatian Army, territorial defence forces (TDFs) and any irregular units from the "pink zones", particularly the Miljevici plateau; supervising the restoration of authority by the Croatian police and the reestablishment of the local police in proportion to the demographic structure of the areas prior to the conflict; and monitoring the maintenance of law and order by the existing police forces, particularly with regard to minorities.

By resolution 769(1992) of 7 August, the Council authorized UNPROFOR to carry out immigration and customs functions at the international borders of certain areas in Croatia where the boundaries of UNPAs coincided with international frontiers. Finally, by resolution 779(1992) of 6 October, the Council authorized UNPROFOR to assume responsibility for monitoring the withdrawal of JNA from Croatia and the demilitarization of the Prevlaka peninsula near Dubrovnik.

UNPROFOR's principal success in Croatia was ensuring the complete withdrawal of JNA from the territory of that republic, including the Prevlaka peninsula. Its presence also helped prevent a recurrence of hostilities in the UNPAs and "pink zones". However, non-cooperation by the local Serb authorities prevented it from achieving the demilitarization of the UNPAs and the disarming of Serb TDFs and irregular forces. The Serb local authorities took the position that official and public threats by Croatian authorities to resort to force, as well as frequent cease-fire violations and repeated armed incursions, made it impossible for them to implement full demilitarization.

In consequence, UNPROFOR was not able to establish conditions of peace and security that would have permitted the voluntary return of refugees and displaced persons. Nor was it able to establish the border controls called for by resolution 769(1992). The civilian aspect of UNPROFOR's activities, notably the efforts of UNCIVPOL to prevent discrimination and abuse of human rights, did not prove fully successful. During the year, the Secretary-General informed the Council on a number of occasions of an atmosphere of terror and intimidation existing in many parts of the four UNPROFOR sectors. However, from November onwards, the situation improved in all but a few areas. The maintenance of law and order was gradually enhanced through the reorganization and redeployment of the local police. The carrying of "long arms", in breach of the agreed plan, greatly diminished.

By a letter of 9 December,[3] the Croatian President expressed regret that the joint efforts of the United Nations and EC had not produced the anticipated results; on the contrary, after initial positive steps, subsequent progress and the peace plan were frustrated by extreme Serbian elements in the UNPAs which had been encouraged and politically and materially supported by the authorities in Belgrade. Aggression against Croatia continued in spite of the engagement of UNPROFOR, and brutal terrorism still reigned in Sectors East, North and South. Even in Sector West there had been recent attempts to offset the modest results achieved, as Serbian extremists from Knin as well as from Bosnia and Herzegovina visited the area in question and publicly stated that they would establish the rule of anarchy equal to that in other UNPA sectors.

Report of the Secretary-General (5 January). On 5 January 1992,[4] the Secretary-General submitted a report pursuant to a November 1991 Security Council resolution,[5] giving an overview of the activities of his Personal Envoy, who conducted his fifth mission to the former Yugoslavia from 28 December 1991 to 4 January 1992. On his way, he conferred at Lisbon with Joao de Deus

Pinheiro, the Foreign Minister of Portugal and incoming President of the EC Council of Ministers, and Lord Carrington.

In Belgrade, the Personal Envoy met with President Slobodan Milosevic of the Republic of Serbia; General Veljko Kadijevic, Federal Secretary for National Defence of Yugoslavia (Serbia and Montenegro); and Branko Jovic, Chairman of the Yugoslav (Serbia and Montenegro) State Committee for Cooperation with the United Nations on Peace-keeping Matters. All confirmed their acceptance of the concept of a peace-keeping operation as outlined in the plan annexed to a December 1991 report of the Secretary-General.[6]

Croatian President Franjo Tudjman stated to the Personal Envoy his Government's full acceptance of the plan and its commitment to an absolute cease-fire. Mr. Jovic expressed the Federal Presidency's desire for an immediate cease-fire and said the Presidency would order all JNA and territorial units not to return fire, even in the event of attack.

Under the chairmanship of the Personal Envoy, military representatives of Croatia and JNA signed at Sarajevo on 2 January an implementing accord for an unconditional cease-fire as agreed on 23 November 1991, to become effective at 1800 hours on 3 January 1992. While in Sarajevo, Mr. Vance also met with President Alija Izetbegovic of Bosnia and Herzegovina, who reiterated his support for the outlined peace-keeping operation and requested once more that 2,000 to 3,000 United Nations peace-keepers be sent to his country to help prevent further hostilities.

As a follow-up to the Personal Envoy's mission, the Secretary-General stated his intention to send immediately to the former Yugoslavia a group of up to 50 military liaison officers, initially drawn from existing peace-keeping operations, to help maintain the cease-fire by facilitating communication between the two sides, resolving difficulties that might arise and determining measures to avoid cease-fire violations or restoring the status quo after such violations. The officers would be attached to the general headquarters of JNA and the Croatian People's Guard and their respective field headquarters. Their mission would take place on the assumption that the cease-fire would quickly establish itself, that the other necessary conditions for deploying a peace-keeping force would be met and that the military liaison group would thus be superseded by a larger operation.

However, a United Nations peace-keeping force could not be established without sustained evidence of the willingness and ability of both sides to ensure respect of the cease-fire; also, the concept for a peace-keeping operation as described in the December 1991 report had to be accepted by all those on whose cooperation the implementation of a peace-keeping mandate depended. With regard to the request of the President of Bosnia and Herzegovina that a substantial United Nations peace-keeping presence be immediately deployed in the republic, the December 1991 concept envisaged United Nations military observers there, the Secretary-General pointed out; for the time being, the question should be approached within the concept of an overall peace-keeping operation.

In an addendum to his report, the Secretary-General estimated the cost for emplacement and maintenance of the military liaison officers' group, including civilian support staff, at some $2 million for the first month and approximately $0.7 million monthly thereafter.

SECURITY COUNCIL ACTION (7 and 8 January)

Following the shooting down on 7 January of an ECMM helicopter over the former Yugoslavia, killing five people, the Security Council convened on the same day. The Council invited Yugoslavia (Serbia and Montenegro), at its request, to participate without vote under rule 37[a] of the Council's provisional rules of procedure.

After consultations, the Council authorized its President to make the following statement:[7]

Meeting number. SC 3027.

"The members of the Security Council discussed on 7 January the tragic incident that occurred in Yugoslavia earlier in the day, in which helicopters of the European Community Monitoring Mission in Yugoslavia were shot down by a Yugoslav aircraft, killing four Italian members and one French member of the Monitoring Mission.

"The members of the Council condemned this callous attack on unarmed civilian personnel. They extended their most sincere condolences to the families of those who had lost their lives. They noted that the Yugoslav authorities had accepted responsibility for this flagrant breach of the cease-fire, had said that they would take the necessary disciplinary action against those responsible, and had reiterated their commitment to observe the cease-fire fully. The members of the Council called on the Yugoslav authorities to take all steps necessary to ensure that this act does not go unpunished and that such incidents do not occur again.

[a]Rule 37 of the Council's provisional rules of procedure states: "Any Member of the United Nations which is not a member of the Security Council may be invited, as the result of a decision of the Security Council, to participate, without vote, in the discussion of any question brought before the Security Council when the Security Council considers that the interests of that Member are specially affected, or when a Member brings a matter to the attention of the Security Council in accordance with Article 35(1) of the Charter."

"The members of the Council reiterated their urgent call on all parties to the conflict in Yugoslavia to respect their cease-fire commitments. They underlined the continuing importance of the role played by the EC Monitoring Mission, as emphasized in the Secretary-General's report of 5 January. They expressed their deep appreciation for the work done by members of the Mission and they called on the Yugoslav parties to ensure that members of the Mission and United Nations personnel be allowed to fulfil their role with the full cooperation of all sides.''

The Council again convened on 8 January to consider the Secretary-General's 5 January report. It invited Yugoslavia (Serbia and Montenegro), at its request, to participate without the right to vote. On the same date, the Council unanimously adopted **resolution 727(1992)**.

The Security Council,

Reaffirming its resolutions 713(1991) of 25 September 1991, 721(1991) of 27 November 1991 and 724(1991) of 15 December 1991,

Noting the report of the Secretary-General of 5 January 1992 submitted pursuant to resolution 721(1991),

Recalling its primary responsibility under the Charter of the United Nations for the maintenance of international peace and security,

Recalling also the provisions of Chapter VIII of the Charter of the United Nations, and *noting* the continuing role that the European Community will play in achieving a peaceful solution in Yugoslavia,

Deploring the tragic incident on 7 January 1992 which caused the death of five members of the European Community Monitoring Mission,

1. *Approves* the report of the Secretary-General of 5 January 1992 and expresses its appreciation to the Secretary-General for it;

2. *Welcomes* the signing, under the auspices of the Secretary-General's Personal Envoy, of an Implementing Accord at Sarajevo on 2 January 1992 concerning modalities for implementing the unconditional cease-fire agreed to by the parties at Geneva on 23 November 1991;

3. *Endorses* the Secretary-General's intention as a follow-up to his Personal Envoy's latest mission to send immediately to Yugoslavia a group of up to 50 military liaison officers to promote maintenance of the cease-fire; in this connection, takes note in particular of the views expressed in paragraphs 24, 25, 28, 29 and 30 of the Secretary-General's report and the criteria reflected in paragraphs 3 and 4 of resolution 724(1991);

4. *Urges* all parties to honour the commitments made at Geneva and Sarajevo with a view to effecting a complete cessation of hostilities;

5. *Requests* all the parties to take all the necessary measures to ensure the safety of the personnel sent by the United Nations and of the members of the European Community Monitoring Mission;

6. *Reaffirms* the embargo applied in paragraph 6 of resolution 713(1991) and in paragraph 5 of resolution 724(1991), and decides that the embargo applies in accordance with paragraph 33 of the Secretary-General's report;

7. *Encourages* the Secretary-General to pursue his humanitarian efforts in Yugoslavia;

8. *Decides* to remain actively seized of the matter until a peaceful solution is achieved.

Security Council resolution 727(1992)

8 January 1992   Meeting 3028   Adopted unanimously

Draft prepared in consultations among Council members (S/23382), orally revised.

Report of the Secretary-General (4 February). Following the adoption of Council resolution 727(1992), a United Nations military liaison mission headed by Colonel John Wilson (Australia) and consisting of unarmed officers arrived in the former Yugoslavia on 14 January, the Secretary-General reported on 4 February.[8]

In New York, the Secretary-General met on 23 January with Mr. Jovic and the Prime Minister of Croatia; both reiterated the commitment of their respective authorities to the cease-fire and requested the earliest possible deployment of a peace-keeping operation. The Secretary-General responded that there remained a number of obstacles in the way of such a deployment but that he had asked the Under-Secretary-General for Special Political Affairs, Marrack Goulding, to make an on-site assessment of the cease-fire and to examine how those obstacles could be removed.

During his mission to the former Yugoslavia from 26 to 30 January, Mr. Goulding held discussions to that end with political and military leaders. He pointed out to the parties that before a peace-keeping operation could be deployed, it would be necessary for them to observe an unconditional and effective cease-fire; to accept fully the December 1991 plan; and to make an unconditional commitment to cooperate fully with such a force.

The military liaison officers, during their two weeks on the ground, received daily allegations of sporadic cease-fire violations. None the less, since the Sarajevo accord went into effect on 3 January, the cease-fire had been generally observed. There were almost no complaints of movements of formations of platoon size or larger and commanders on both sides showed evidence of a readiness to respect the cease-fire. Unfortunately, the military forces on both sides included irregular armed elements who were not fully under the control of the established commands and who were responsible for a substantial portion of the alleged cease-fire violations. However, both parties assured Mr. Goulding that they would strengthen measures to bring those elements under their control.

At a meeting in Zagreb on 28 January, the Croatian President said the operation must provide for immediate restoration of the full authority of his Government in the UNPAs, thus retracting his full acceptance of the United Nations plan given to the Special Envoy in December 1991.

Those positions, as well as allegations that the arms embargo imposed by the Security Council in September 1991[9] was not being observed, led to the Secretary-General's conclusion that deployment of a peace-keeping operation was not recommendable for the time being. However, he felt that the military liaison group, which had contributed significantly to maintaining the cease-fire, should be kept and enlarged to 75 officers.

By a letter of 3 February 1992, annexed to the Secretary-General's report, the Vice-President of the Federal Republic of Yugoslavia (Serbia and Montenegro) stated that the competent bodies of his Government guaranteed the unhindered reception of United Nations forces, irrespective of the proposals made by representatives of the Serbian population during their talks with Mr. Goulding.

SECURITY COUNCIL ACTION (7 February)

The Security Council, at a meeting on 7 February, to which it invited Yugoslavia (Serbia and Montenegro) to participate without the right to vote under rule 37[a] of its provisional rules of procedure, considered the report of the Secretary-General and unanimously adopted **resolution 740(1992)**.

The Security Council,

Reaffirming its resolutions 713(1991) of 25 September 1991, 721(1991) of 27 November 1991, 724(1991) of 15 December 1991 and 727(1992) of 8 January 1992,

Noting the further report of the Secretary-General of 5 February 1992 submitted pursuant to resolution 721(1991) and welcoming his report that the cease-fire has been generally observed thus removing one of the obstacles to the deployment of a peace-keeping operation,

Taking note that the letter of President Franjo Tudjman of 6 February 1992, in which he accepts fully and unconditionally the Secretary-General's concept and plan which defines the conditions and areas where the United Nations force would be deployed, removes a further obstacle in that respect,

Further noting that the implementation of the United Nations peace-keeping plan will facilitate the task of the Conference on Yugoslavia in reaching a political settlement,

Recalling its primary responsibility under the Charter of the United Nations for the maintenance of international peace and security,

Recalling also the provisions of Chapter VIII of the Charter of the United Nations,

Expressing concern at the indications that the arms embargo established by the Security Council in resolution 713(1991) is not being fully observed, as noted in paragraph 21 of the report of the Secretary-General,

1. *Reaffirms* its approval set out in resolution 724(1991) of the United Nations peace-keeping plan contained in the report of the Secretary-General of 11 December 1991;

2. *Welcomes* the continuing efforts of the Secretary-General and his Personal Envoy to remove the remaining obstacle in the way of the deployment of a peace-keeping operation;

3. *Approves* the Secretary-General's proposal to increase the authorized strength of the military liaison mission to a total of 75 officers;

4. *Requests* the Secretary-General to expedite his preparations for a United Nations peace-keeping operation so as to be prepared to deploy immediately after the Security Council decides to do so;

5. *Expresses its concern* that the United Nations peace-keeping plan contained in the report of the Secretary-General of 11 December 1991 has not yet been fully and unconditionally accepted by all in Yugoslavia on whose cooperation its success depends;

6. *Calls upon* all States to continue to take all appropriate steps to ensure that the Yugoslav parties implement their unqualified acceptance of the United Nations peace-keeping plan, fulfil their commitments in good faith and cooperate fully with the Secretary-General;

7. *Calls upon* the Yugoslav parties to cooperate fully with the Conference on Yugoslavia in its aim of reaching a political settlement consistent with the principles of the Conference on Security and Cooperation in Europe and reaffirms that the United Nations peace-keeping plan and its implementation is in no way intended to prejudge the terms of a political settlement;

8. *Calls upon* all States to cooperate fully with the Committee established by resolution 724(1991), including reporting any information brought to their attention concerning violations of the embargo;

9. *Decides* to remain actively seized of the matter until a peaceful solution is achieved.

Security Council resolution 740(1992)

7 February 1992   Meeting 3049   Adopted unanimously

Draft prepared in consultations among Council members (S/23534), orally revised.

Report of the Secretary-General (15 February). In a report of 15 February,[10] the Secretary-General described recent developments regarding the positions of Croatia and of the local leaders in the province of Krajina, which he had identified in his 4 February report and which constituted the major obstacles to the deployment of a United Nations peace-keeping force. He also dealt with certain aspects of the concept and plan for such a force, put forward in December 1991, and described the structures and resources required for implementing that plan.

The President of Croatia, having been requested by the Personal Envoy to reconfirm full acceptance of the plan, did so in a letter of 11 February 1992. Nevertheless, several technical questions in the status-of-forces agreement needed to be resolved, including substantive issues relating to the extension of the authority of the Croatian Government over the UNPAs in areas such as traffic, trade, banking and currency, maintenance of law and order and the return of refugees. The Secretary-General decided to accept the President's initial assurances and to leave those technical questions to be resolved within the letter and spirit of the plan; if they were not, however, the plan's implementation would be endangered.

The Assembly of the Serbian Krajina Republic, the highest organ of authority in that area, had voted to endorse the plan unconditionally. A rival assembly in Krajina, headed by Milan Babic, decided to hold a referendum on the subject on 22 and 23 February, which, in the Secretary-General's view, was a potential danger to the plan; therefore, it was all the more important that the concerns of the Serbian community in Krajina be considered at the EC Conference on Yugoslavia.

As almost all political groups in Yugoslavia expressed support for a United Nations peace-keeping operation, the Secretary-General recommended the establishment of UNPROFOR, headquartered at Sarajevo, with sub-offices at Belgrade and Zagreb and a logistics base at Banja Luka, Bosnia and Herzegovina.

It would be deployed in the three UNPAs, which, for United Nations purposes, would be divided into four sectors: Sector East (Eastern Slavonia including Baranja and Western Srem), Sector North (northern Krajina), Sector South (southern Krajina) and Sector West (Western Slavonia). In addition, military observers would be deployed in certain parts of Bosnia and Herzegovina adjacent to Croatia.

UNPROFOR would include military, police and civilian components. The military component would consist of 12 enlarged infantry battalions (10,400 all ranks); headquarters, logistics and other support elements totalling about 2,840 all ranks; and 100 military observers. The police component (UNCIVPOL) would number about 530 personnel commanded by a Police Commissioner, who would be appointed by the Secretary-General and would report to the Force Commander. The civilian component, headed by the Director of Civil Affairs, would consist largely of United Nations staff performing a wide range of political, legal, information and administrative functions.

The role of UNPROFOR with regard to local administration and maintenance of public order would be: to identify the existing arrangements in the UNPAs, together with any existing regional structures; to use its good offices to ensure that any changes to the status quo with regard to administration were consistent with the spirit of the December 1991 plan and posed no threat to public order; to monitor the work of the local police; and to confirm that the composition of the existing police forces reflected the national composition of the population that lived in the area concerned before the recent hostilities and to arrange changes as might be necessary.

Those arrangements, the Secretary-General emphasized, would be of an interim nature, pending an overall settlement. The success of the operation would depend on the readiness of all concerned to exercise restraint and refrain from actions that could disturb public order in the UNPAs.

UNPROFOR would remain in the former Yugoslavia until a negotiated settlement was achieved. However, it was recommended to establish the Force for a period of 12 months, with a provision for its mandate to be renewed if necessary.

Underlining that the December 1991 plan continued to provide a solid basis for the Force, the Secretary-General discussed certain aspects related to its implementation, such as the drawing of the exact boundaries of the UNPAs, to be decided by an advance party of the Force; the possibility of weapons being handed over to the United Nations for safe custody; the overall command of the operation by the Force Commander instead of a civilian chief of mission as originally proposed; the establishment of a mixed military working group consisting of senior representatives of JNA and the Croatian Army, under the chairmanship of the Force Commander; and the implications of the deployment of the Force for the mandate of ECMM.

The two central elements of the plan—the continued functioning of existing local authorities and police under United Nations supervision, pending an overall political solution to the Yugoslav crisis, and the demilitarization of the UNPAs—must be strictly respected, the Secretary-General stressed; otherwise, the plan would be undermined and there would be a grave risk of resumed fighting. The Security Council and all the Yugoslav parties concerned should be alerted to that danger from the outset.

Another major undertaking which required the full cooperation of all the parties was the return of displaced persons; the Secretary-General had requested the United Nations High Commissioner for Refugees (UNHCR) to assume responsibility for designing and implementing a scheme to permit those who wished to do so to return to their homes as soon as possible after the deployment of UNPROFOR.

Concluding, the Secretary-General stressed that a working cease-fire and unconditional acceptance of the plan by all concerned, with clear assurances of their readiness to cooperate in its implementation, were required if UNPROFOR was to succeed in consolidating the cease-fire and thus facilitate the negotiation of an overall political settlement. There remained a number of unanswered questions about the extent to which UNPROFOR would in practice receive the necessary cooperation; however, the danger of failure of a peace-keeping operation due to lack of cooperation was less grievous than the danger that a delay in its dispatch would lead to a breakdown of the cease-fire and a new conflagration.

SECURITY COUNCIL ACTION (21 February)

The Security Council convened on 21 February to consider the Secretary-General's report. The Council invited Yugoslavia (Serbia and Montenegro), at its request, to participate in the discussion without the right to vote under rule 37ᵃ of the Council's provisional rules of procedure. On the same date, the Council unanimously adopted **resolution 743(1992)**.

The Security Council,
Reaffirming its resolutions 713(1991) of 25 September 1991, 721(1991) of 27 November 1991, 724(1991) of 15 December 1991, 727(1992) of 8 January 1992 and 740(1992) of 7 February 1992,
Noting the report of the Secretary-General of 15 February 1992 submitted pursuant to resolution 721(1991) and the request of the Government of Yugoslavia of 26 November 1991 for a peace-keeping operation referred to in that resolution,
Noting in particular that the Secretary-General considers that the conditions permitting the early deployment of a United Nations Protection Force (UNPROFOR) are met and welcoming his recommendation that this Force should be established with immediate effect,
Expressing its gratitude to the Secretary-General and his Personal Envoy for their contribution to the achievement of conditions facilitating the deployment of a United Nations Protection Force and their continuing commitment to this effort,
Concerned that the situation in Yugoslavia continues to constitute a threat to international peace and security as determined in resolution 713(1991),
Recalling its primary responsibility under the Charter of the United Nations for the maintenance of international peace and security,
Recalling also the provisions of Article 25 and Chapter VIII of the Charter of the United Nations,
Commending again the efforts undertaken by the European Community and its member States, with the support of the States participating in the Conference on Security and Cooperation in Europe, through the convening of a Conference on Yugoslavia, including the mechanisms set forth within it, to ensure a peaceful political settlement,
Convinced that the implementation of the United Nations peace-keeping plan will assist the Conference on Yugoslavia in reaching a peaceful political settlement,

1. *Approves* the report of the Secretary-General of 15 February 1992;

2. *Decides* to establish, under its authority, a United Nations Protection Force (UNPROFOR) in accordance with the above-mentioned report and the United Nations peace-keeping plan and requests the Secretary-General to take the measures necessary to ensure its earliest possible deployment;

3. *Decides* that, in order to implement the recommendations in paragraph 30 of the report of the Secretary-General, the Force is established in accordance with paragraph 4 below, for an initial period of 12 months unless the Council subsequently decides otherwise;

4. *Requests* the Secretary-General immediately to deploy those elements of the Force which can assist in developing an implementation plan for the earliest possible full deployment of the Force for approval by the Council and a budget which together will maximize the contribution of the Yugoslav parties to offsetting its costs and in all other ways secure the most efficient and cost-effective operation possible;

5. *Recalls* that, in accordance with paragraph 1 of the United Nations peace-keeping plan, the Force should be an interim arrangement to create the conditions of peace and security required for the negotiation of an overall settlement of the Yugoslav crisis;

6. *Invites* accordingly the Secretary-General to report as appropriate and not less than every six months on progress towards a peaceful political settlement and the situation on the ground, and to submit a first report on the establishment of the Force within two months of the adoption of this resolution;

7. *Undertakes*, in this connection, to examine without delay any recommendations that the Secretary-General may make in his reports concerning the Force, including the duration of its mission, and to adopt appropriate decisions;

8. *Urges* all parties and others concerned to comply strictly with the cease-fire arrangements signed at Geneva on 23 November 1991 and at Sarajevo on 2 January 1992, and to cooperate fully and unconditionally in the implementation of the peace-keeping plan;

9. *Demands* that all parties and others concerned take all the necessary measures to ensure the safety of the personnel sent by the United Nations and of the members of the European Community Monitoring Mission;

10. *Calls again upon* the Yugoslav parties to cooperate fully with the Conference on Yugoslavia in its aim of reaching a political settlement consistent with the principles of the Conference on Security and Cooperation in Europe and reaffirms that the United Nations peace-keeping plan and its implementation is in no way intended to prejudge the terms of a political settlement;

11. *Decides* within the same framework that the embargo imposed by paragraph 6 of Security Council resolution 713(1991) shall not apply to weapons and military equipment destined for the sole use of UNPROFOR;

12. *Requests* all States to provide appropriate support to UNPROFOR, in particular to permit and facilitate the transit of its personnel and equipment;

13. *Decides* to remain actively seized of the matter until a peaceful solution is achieved.

Security Council resolution 743(1992)

21 February 1992   Meeting 3055   Adopted unanimously

Draft prepared in consultations among Council members (S/23620), orally revised.

Report of the Secretary-General (2 April). On 2 April,[11] the Secretary-General reported to the Council on the deployment of UNPROFOR.

Force Commander Lieutenant-General Satish Nambiar arrived in Belgrade on 8 March, as did

Deputy Force Commander Major-General Philippe Morillon, the Director of Civil Affairs, Cedric Thornberry, Chief of Staff Brigadier-General Lewis MacKenzie, Chief Administrative Officer Keith Walton and other senior members of UNPROFOR. The Force established its headquarters at Sarajevo on 13 March and reconnaissance teams were sent to the four UNPA sectors.

During discussions with the Force Commander, each of the authorities at Belgrade, Zagreb and Sarajevo emphasized the need to stabilize a very delicate situation. Breaches of the cease-fire and continuing tension had been reported on a daily basis in a number of areas, even after the arrival of UNPROFOR's advance elements, and conditions remained far from stable. The Force Commander's finding confirmed the original operational concept for UNPROFOR; however, certain variations in deployment could be made without seriously prejudicing the implementation of the mandate.

As to the military component of the operation, the 12 battalions would be assigned as originally planned: two in Sector East, four in Sector West and three each in Sectors North and South. Logistic bases would be located at Banja Luka, Belgrade and Zagreb. Combat engineers would be based initially in Sector West, concurrently addressing the serious mine-clearing tasks in Sectors West and East. After two months, that unit would shift to Sectors North and South. The construction engineer battalion would be based at Banja Luka, to support all four sectors.

Police headquarters and three sector headquarters were established as at 30 March with 100 police deployed, although with limited logistical support. The Secretary-General recommended that the original provision for 530 police be maintained, but that in order to reduce costs only 320 be deployed at the initial stage, in some 31 locations. Regarding the police tasks in the UNPAs as well as those of the civil affairs element and humanitarian agencies, the Secretary-General expressed deep concern at the continuing reports of mass expulsions and other forms of coercion against certain communities on both sides of the conflict. Strong representations were made on that issue to the respective authorities by both the Secretary-General and UNHCR.

The Secretary-General concluded by sharing the sense of urgency in deploying UNPROFOR, as expressed by all the authorities who had had dialogue with the Force Commander. The cease-fire remained fragile, with alleged violations averaging about 100 per day and occasionally exceeding 200. Tensions were aggravated by reports, not all of them substantiated, that persons of various nationalities were expelled from their homes.

An implementation plan for full deployment of UNPROFOR was annexed to the report. The plan reflected the difficulties that had arisen, largely for budgetary reasons, in making arrangements for transporting some of the more distant battalions and their equipment to the former Yugoslavia. As a result, UNPROFOR would not be fully deployed until mid-May 1992, assuming that the Security Council took a very early decision to authorize full deployment.

SECURITY COUNCIL ACTION (7 April)

The Security Council convened on 7 April to consider the Secretary-General's report. The Council invited Yugoslavia (Serbia and Montenegro), at its request, to participate in the discussion without the right to vote under rule 37[a] of its provisional rules of procedure. On that same date, the Council adopted **resolution 749(1992)** unanimously.

The Security Council,

Reaffirming its resolutions 713(1991) of 25 September 1991, 721(1991) of 27 November 1991, 724(1991) of 15 December 1991, 727(1992) of 8 January 1992, 740(1992) of 7 February 1992 and 743(1992) of 21 February 1992,

Noting the report of the Secretary-General of 2 April 1992 submitted pursuant to resolution 743(1992),

Recalling its primary responsibility under the Charter of the United Nations for the maintenance of international peace and security,

Welcoming the progress made towards the establishment of the United Nations Protection Force (UNPROFOR) and the continuing contacts by the Secretary-General with all parties and others concerned to stabilize the cease-fire,

Expressing its concern about reports on the daily violations of the cease-fire and the continuing tension in a number of regions even after the arrival of UNPROFOR's advance elements,

1. *Approves* the report of the Secretary-General of 2 April 1992;

2. *Decides* to authorize the earliest possible full deployment of UNPROFOR;

3. *Urges* all parties and others concerned to make further efforts to maximize their contributions towards offsetting the costs of UNPROFOR, in order to help secure the most efficient and cost-effective operation possible;

4. *Further urges* all parties and others concerned to take all action necessary to ensure complete freedom of aerial movement for UNPROFOR;

5. *Calls upon* all parties and others concerned not to resort to violence, particularly in any area where UNPROFOR is to be based or deployed;

6. *Appeals* to all parties and others concerned in Bosnia and Herzegovina to cooperate with the efforts of the European Community to bring about a cease-fire and a negotiated political solution.

Security Council resolution 749(1992)

7 April 1992   Meeting 3066   Adopted unanimously

Draft prepared in consultations among Council members (S/23788), orally revised.

Reports of the Secretary-General (24 April and 12 May). On 24 April,[12] the Secretary-General reported to the Council on progress made towards full deployment of UNPROFOR. At that time, the Force had a strength of 8,332, including 7,975 military personnel. The majority—i.e., some 350—of the headquarters military personnel was already located at Sarajevo.

In Sector East, the UNPROFOR military component of 1,293 personnel consisting of battalions from Belgium and the Russian Federation was at full strength on the ground as at 18 April. In Sector West, the Canadian infantry battalion was fully deployed. For budgetary reasons, deployment of three other battalions from Argentina, Jordan and Nepal would be carried out primarily by surface means; those battalions would not arrive until mid-May, leaving the current military strength in Sector West at 1,373.

A total of 2,046 military personnel—from Denmark and Poland—were deployed in Sector North, with the arrival of the third battalion from Nigeria expected by the end of May. In Sector South, a total of 1,505 personnel consisting of battalions from Czechoslovakia and France were fully deployed, with a third battalion from Kenya expected in mid-May. The full complement of 102 United Nations military observers was present in the area of operations; 40 of them were to be sent to the Mostar area in Bosnia and Herzegovina on 30 April.

A total of 290 UNCIVPOL officers were in the mission area, with the remaining 230 expected to arrive in the second half of May.

The infantry battalions were already engaged in active patrols throughout the sectors, maintaining a United Nations presence even in areas not yet permanently manned. Battalions already assigned to their areas were establishing liaisons with both sides at various levels, arranging crossing points, preparing positions, patrolling and siting checkpoints and observation posts. On the recommendation of the Force Commander, no logistic base was established at Banja Luka; the elements to be placed there were to be deployed at the two other logistics bases at Belgrade and Zagreb. The other deployment plans proposed in December 1991 and elaborated in two later reports, of 15 February[10] and 2 April 1992,[11] remained substantially in force.

A final text for a status-of-forces arrangement with the parties to the conflict was agreed to by the authorities of Bosnia and Herzegovina, and a tentative agreement was reached with the Croatian authorities. However, protracted negotiations continued with Yugoslavia (Serbia and Montenegro), with key differences relating to the provision of goods and services to UNPROFOR by the parties to the conflict.

Disturbing cases were reported in both the UNPAs and in Bosnia and Herzegovina, with combatants on both sides of the conflict using United Nations insignia on their vehicles and uniforms. If such abuse persisted, the Secretary-General warned, the parties' genuineness to cooperate with UNPROFOR would be called into question. Also reported were incidents of small-arms fire directed at Force personnel in the UNPAs, with some perpetrated allegedly by drunken Croatian and JNA soldiers. Firings close to Force personnel had reached unacceptable levels, and UNPROFOR's freedom of movement both by land and air was restricted on several occasions. All such incidents were protested to the authorities concerned.

Discussions were held with both sides on the establishment of an "air corridor" that would permit UNPROFOR flights to and from Belgrade, Sarajevo and Zagreb, as well as over the UNPAs. On 22 April, a technical agreement was concluded with the cooperation of the International Civil Aviation Organization, confirming the following three provisions: freedom to fly in the Sarajevo-Belgrade-Zagreb triangle; freedom for medical evacuation and aircraft-maintenance movement from the UNPAs to their various destinations; and freedom to fly into Zagreb for logistical purposes. Agreement on freedom to fly above the UNPAs had been reached in principle, but further discussions were required on certain aspects of an overall regime for the "UN Special Use Airspace".

The Secretary-General indicated that UNPROFOR would not be in a position to assume its full responsibilities in all the UNPAs for another two to three weeks. During that time, it was crucial that the parties conformed to the letter and spirit of the approved concept, a principle that had not been universally observed.

JNA had started to withdraw from some locations in the UNPAs; while doing so, it had been observed transferring arms to the local TDFs, which were due to be demobilized as soon as UNPROFOR was fully deployed. It was also seen transferring vehicles and personnel to the local police; although Belgrade authorities explained that those were police personnel who had been temporarily attached to JNA and were now being returned to their normal posts, such action was a cause for concern.

UNPROFOR also confirmed reports of forcible evacuation of minority populations from their homes, especially in Eastern Slavonia. Advance warning of such activity enabled the Force to prevent some incidents. Citing specific cases involving over 200 expulsions, the Secretary-General said a pattern of systematic harassment of minority populations seemed to be emerging. All reported incidents were vigorously protested and the Belgrade authorities were requested to investigate. UNPROFOR also stepped up patrols in Sector East.

As Bosnia and Herzegovina slid into anarchy (see below), the situation in Sarajevo continued to deteriorate, making operations more and more difficult. Movement in and out of the city was extremely difficult and within the city became increasingly dangerous. UNPROFOR was using its limited resources at headquarters to provide humanitarian support to the needy citizens affected by the fighting. On a number of occasions, it helped evacuate wounded civilians. However, it lacked adequate resources to carry out all humanitarian operations in Bosnia and Herzegovina, the Secretary-General noted.

He observed that some of the difficulties encountered by UNPROFOR were endemic to most new peace-keeping operations. Others raised concern about the commitment of the parties to the basic principles of the UNPROFOR concept, namely the demilitarization of the UNPAs, maintenance of the existing arrangements for local administration and public order, and voluntary return of displaced persons to their homes.

In discussions with UNPROFOR, both sides raised issues beyond the provisions of the peace-keeping plan. Authorities in Belgrade and Zagreb pointed to the problem of certain areas in Croatia which were currently controlled by JNA but which were outside the agreed boundaries of the UNPAs. The federal authorities proposed that those areas, inhabited primarily by Serbs and later to be known as ''pink zones'', be included within the UNPAs, while the Croatian side sought UNPROFOR's help with regard to the presence of Serb irregular forces in those areas.

The Secretary-General submitted on 12 May[13] a report on the mission by Under-Secretary-General Marrack Goulding to the former Yugoslavia from 4 to 10 May, of which he had informed the Council in advance by a letter of 29 April[14] and received Council approval the following day.[15]

At Lisbon, Mr. Goulding met with Lord Carrington and his Plenipotentiary for Bosnia and Herzegovina, José Cutileiro of Portugal. In the former Yugoslavia, he met with political and military leaders of Bosnia and Herzegovina and Croatia, as well as with Colm Doyle, representing Lord Carrington, and the head of ECMM. He was briefed by representatives of UNHCR and ICRC, visited UNPROFOR in Sector East and met with local civic, military and militia leaders on both sides.

The full deployment of UNPROFOR was one week behind its original schedule, as a result of the conditions in Sarajevo, the complexities of transporting infantry battalions and equipment from distant countries, and the difficulties in assigning civilian staff and procuring the necessary equipment. However, the Force Commander had informed the two sides that he would assume his full responsibilities in Sector East at 0800 hours on 15 May. Thus, the nightly cease-fire violations

there would end, particularly in Osijek, which was suffering serious casualties at the hands of JNA. Also, expulsions of non-Serbs from the JNA-controlled areas of Eastern Slavonia would be stopped. UNPROFOR had obtained evidence that JNA and the local police were acting in complicity in those expulsions, although such involvement was denied by both Belgrade and the local authorities.

The two parties had conflicting positions with regard to areas in Croatia outside the UNPAs, controlled by JNA and largely populated by Serbs. Belgrade authorities strongly pressed for those areas to be included in the UNPAs; otherwise, they argued, the Serb residents of those areas would resist the restoration of Croatian authority after the withdrawal of JNA and fighting would resume, with the defence units in neighbouring UNPAs coming to the aid of their fellow Serbs. Croatian authorities, however, were completely opposed to changes in the UNPA boundaries.

As a result, the Force Commander reported, the Sector Commanders, especially in Sectors North and South, were encountering serious difficulties, which threatened the viability of UNPROFOR's mandate. In those areas, Serb territorial defence units were preventing UNPROFOR from setting up checkpoints and observation posts and refused to demobilize unless the additional areas concerned were brought into the UNPAs. Mr. Goulding's attempts to persuade the Belgrade authorities to convince the Serb populations in the areas outside the UNPAs of their safety once Croatian authority was restored and to persuade the Croatian authorities to accept some modifications of the UNPA boundaries were unsuccessful. However, the Croatian President agreed to the deployment of United Nations military observers and police monitors in the areas in question.

Mr. Goulding was informed by JNA leaders that, following the declaration on 27 April of the new Federal Republic of Yugoslavia (Serbia and Montenegro), all JNA personnel who were citizens of that Republic were to be withdrawn from all other republics of the former Yugoslavia, leaving behind the others to be demobilized or join the armed forces of the new republics. That policy was already applied in Bosnia and Herzegovina, where about 80 per cent of JNA troops were citizens of that republic. It would similarly be employed in Sectors North and South, which would greatly enlarge the number of troops to be demobilized. UNPROFOR would continue to plan for that difficult task on the basis of full support by JNA, as had been negotiated. If those enlarged local forces refused to demobilize, the very basis of the peace-keeping plan would be undermined.

The Secretary-General saw no alternative but to instruct the Force Commander to assume his responsibilities in accordance with the United Nations plan, while continuing to appeal to JNA and Serbian authorities to calm the fears of the Serb communities outside the UNPAs and ensure a successful demilitarization of the UNPAs.

With respect to humanitarian programmes in the entire former Yugoslavia, the Secretary-General said that, in the absence of agreements between the parties, armed escorts were necessary and would be permitted to open fire if a convoy of relief supplies were attacked. A protection operation similar to the one proposed for Mogadishu, Somalia, on 21 April (see PART TWO, Chapter I) would be needed, which would require armed troops in addition to UNPROFOR's existing strength. However, such an operation could risk involving the Force in hostile encounters with those on whose cooperation it depended in order to fulfil its mandate; he did not recommend that the Security Council currently pursue that option.

Other aspects covered by the Secretary-General's report were the situation in Bosnia and Herzegovina and the feasibility of a United Nations peace-keeping operation there (see below).

SECURITY COUNCIL ACTION (15 May)

By **resolution 752(1992)** of 15 May, the Security Council noted the progress made in the deployment of UNPROFOR. It welcomed the fact that the Force had assumed its full responsibility in Eastern Slavonia and requested the Secretary-General to ensure that it would do so similarly in all UNPAs as soon as possible. The Council urged all parties and others concerned to cooperate in every way with UNPROFOR in accordance with the United Nations plan and to comply strictly with the plan in all its aspects, in particular the disarming of all irregular forces, whatever their origin, in the UNPAs.

Report of the Secretary-General (26 June). Tensions were rising in the so called "pink zones", most acutely in those adjacent to Sectors North and South, the Secretary-General reported on 26 June.[16]

UNPROFOR assumed its full responsibilities in Sector East on 15 May and in Sector West on 20 June. At the same time, the Force Commander continued to search for a solution to the problem of the "pink zones", holding discussions with the parties. JNA finally withdrew most of its forces from the areas in question, while leaving equipment and many members who were placed under the command of the local defence forces. Until a solution was found to the "pink zones", the Force Commander noted, it would prove extremely difficult for UNPROFOR to assume its full responsibilities in Sectors North and South.

On 1 June, with the consent of both parties, the Force Commander directed UNPROFOR military and police teams to begin moving into the "pink zones" in order to commence preliminary reconnaissance and patrol activities, pending a final agreement. Although that move helped lower the tension, developments in the region as a whole, including certain statements by national leaders, exacerbated the situation and the parties again adopted intransigent positions. None the less, the Force Commander announced that UNPROFOR would assume responsibility in Sectors North and South on 25 June.

On 21 June, the Croatian Army attacked positions of the Serb TDFs near Drnis in the "pink zone" south of Sector South, moving forward several kilometres. Serb forces retaliated by bombarding the town of Sibenik and, on 22 June, the Croatian Army bombarded Knin in Sector South. The advance of the Croatian Army, apparently conducted by two brigades in a well-planned manner, was the second in the area in a month. Both were in breach of the 2 January Sarajevo accord governing modalities of the implementation of the cease-fire. They were protested by UNPROFOR and ECMM, each of which called for the withdrawal of the Croatian Army to the former line of confrontation.

During discussions with the Force Commander on 23 June, the Vice-Premier of Croatia and the Croatian Chief of Defence Staff said the 21 June action had occurred unplanned, in reaction to mounting Serb provocations; none the less, the Croatian Army would not accede to the request to withdraw to its previous positions.

That offensive seriously set back implementation of the United Nations plan, stated the Force Commander, and confidence building among the parties would have to start afresh. Although the Croatian Government did not accept his suggestion of a conference on the issue of the "pink zones", to include Croatian authorities, representatives of Serb inhabitants of area and members of ECMM, it accepted the idea of a presence of UNPROFOR and ECMM monitors in the "pink zones" after the Government had reassumed authority there, in order to reassure the Serb population.

Also on 23 June, the Commander of UNPROFOR in Sector South reported growing tension, with general mobilization on the Serb side, and increasing intensity of shelling by both parties. Substantial casualties had been incurred and it was reported that a Serb TDF counter-attack had taken place. The Sector Commander warned of the risk of the conflict spilling over into the whole of the "pink zones".

In a meeting with the Force Commander on 24 June, the Chairman of the Yugoslav (Serbia and Montenegro) State Committee for Cooperation with the United Nations on Peace-keeping Matters warned that the conflict would escalate if the United Nations plan could not be implemented. His Government remained open to solutions which, however, had to be accepted by the local inhabitants of the "pink zones" who greatly feared Croatian rule.

A representative of the local authorities at Knin also called on UNPROFOR to assume authority in the area as a whole, including the UNPAs and "pink zones", as soon as possible. He claimed that Croatia intended to launch further offensives in the near future. Under the circumstances, his side could not be expected to disarm and withdraw. His authorities were open to any UNPROFOR proposal for a solution, but wanted the issue of the restoration of the Croatian government authority in the "pink zones" to be left open.

The Secretary-General drew three conclusions: the restoration of Croatian authority in the "pink zones" without effective preparation and re-establishment of confidence among its inhabitants did not appear achievable without the serious danger of a resumption of armed conflict; the instability caused in Sectors North and South by the "pink zone" situation had been increased by the conflict in adjacent areas of Bosnia and Herzegovina; and UNPROFOR's assumption of responsibility in the Sectors and the implementation of the December 1991 plan had little likelihood of success if the question of the "pink zones" remained unresolved.

Based on a recommendation of the Force Commander, the Secretary-General proposed several courses of action, including the establishment of a Joint Commission under the chairmanship of UNPROFOR and consisting of representatives of the Government of Croatia and the local authorities in the region, with the participation of ECMM, to oversee and monitor the restoration of Croatian government authority in the "pink zones".

He proposed further that UNPROFOR assume its full responsibilities in Sectors North and South as soon as feasible and, simultaneously, undertake monitoring functions in the "pink zones". There would be an immediate withdrawal of the Croatian Army, TDFs and any irregular units from the "pink zones", including the area of the 21 June incursion. No such elements would re-enter the "pink zones" (with the exception of those disbanded and demobilized in those areas), their withdrawal being verified by United Nations military observers. Any remaining JNA elements would be withdrawn to Yugoslavia (Serbia and Montenegro).

Under those circumstances, the Croatian Army would disengage from the line of confrontation in a manner and to a distance established by the Joint Commission. An appropriate number of United Nations military observers would be deployed along the line of confrontation and within the "pink zones", and mobile patrols would be conducted from Sectors North and South.

UNCIVPOL would be deployed throughout the "pink zones" to monitor the maintenance of law and order by the existing police forces, with particular regard to the well-being of minority groups. At a time deemed appropriate but as soon as possible, UNCIVPOL would supervise the restoration of authority by the Croatian police and the re-establishment of the local police in proportion to the demographic structure of the areas prior to the conflict.

ECMM personnel would be deployed on both sides of the line of confrontation but outside the UNPAs, on the basis of a division of labour with UNPROFOR to be agreed within the Joint Commission.

Finally, prior to the reinstatement of Croatian authority in the "pink zones", a general amnesty in regard to events associated with the conflict would be declared by the Government of Croatia, thus helping to create a climate of security in which displaced persons could return to their homes.

Those measures were to be applied under UNPROFOR's authority and supervision, for the purpose of ensuring an internationally monitored, step-by-step reintroduction of the Croatian Government's authority to an area currently controlled by Serb forces and with a substantial Serb population, in such a manner as to minimize the danger of further hostilities and destabilization of the adjoining region. An addition to UNPROFOR of some 60 military observers and 120 UNCIVPOL monitors would be needed to implement those measures.

Each party to the conflict had, at some time, expressed acceptance of some of the elements outlined by the Secretary-General, who was aware that certain aspects would not appeal to one or the other side. In particular, Croatia strongly held that restoration of its authority in the "pink zones" related to its own sovereign territory and was not a matter for negotiation. None the less, the Secretary-General pointed out that unilateral Croatian action as had occurred around 21 June was likely to have a severely destabilizing effect on the UNPAs and jeopardize the viability of UNPROFOR. The collapse of the United Nations plan in Sectors North and South would have grave consequences not only in the other UNPAs but throughout the region.

In a reply of 30 June[17] to the Secretary-General's report, Croatia said the reference to the "pink zones" as areas populated largely by Serbs was not correct, as illustrated by demographic data. It was ready to discuss the Secretary-General's proposals but objected to an imposition of any of the proposed measures through the Security Council, which would mean a formal modification of the peace plan and was therefore legally unacceptable.

SECURITY COUNCIL ACTION (30 June)

The Security Council, convening on 30 June to consider the Secretary-General's report, unanimously adopted **resolution 762(1992)**.

The Security Council,

Reaffirming its resolutions 713(1991) of 25 September 1991, 721(1991) of 27 November 1991, 724(1991) of 15 December 1991, 727(1992) of 8 January 1992, 740(1992) of 7 February 1992, 743(1992) of 21 February 1992, 749(1992) of 7 April 1992, 752(1992) of 15 May 1992, 757(1992) of 30 May 1992, 758(1992) of 8 June 1992, 760(1992) of 18 June 1992 and 761(1992) of 29 June 1992,

Noting the report of the Secretary-General of 26 June 1992 submitted pursuant to resolution 752(1992),

Recalling its primary responsibility under the Charter of the United Nations for the maintenance of international peace and security,

Welcoming the progress made as a result of the assumption of responsibilities by the United Nations Protection Force in Sectors East and West, and concerned about the difficulties encountered by the Force in Sectors North and South,

Commending again the efforts undertaken by the European Community and its member States, with the support of the States participating in the Conference on Security and Cooperation in Europe, through the convening of a Conference on Yugoslavia, including the mechanisms set forth within it, to ensure a peaceful political settlement,

1. *Approves* the report of the Secretary-General of 26 June 1992;

2. *Urges* all parties and others concerned to honour their commitments to effect a complete cessation of hostilities and to implement the United Nations peace-keeping plan;

3. *Also urges*, in accordance with paragraph 4 of resolution 727(1992), the Government of Croatia to withdraw its army to the positions held before the offensive of 21 June 1992 and to cease hostile military activities within or adjacent to the United Nations Protected Areas;

4. *Urges* the remaining units of the Yugoslav People's Army, the Serb territorial defence forces in Croatia and others concerned to comply strictly with their obligations under the United Nations peace-keeping plan, in particular with regard to the withdrawal and the disarming of all forces in accordance with the plan;

5. *Urges* the Government of Croatia and others concerned to follow the course of action outlined in paragraph 16 of the Secretary-General's report and appeals to all parties to assist the United Nations Protection Force in its implementation;

6. *Recommends* the establishment of the Joint Commission described in paragraph 16 of the Secretary-General's report, which should consult, as may be necessary or appropriate, with the Belgrade authorities in performing its functions;

7. *Authorizes* the strengthening of the United Nations Protection Force by the addition of up to sixty military observers and one hundred and twenty civilian police to perform the functions envisaged in paragraph 16 of the Secretary-General's report, with the agreement of the Government of Croatia and others concerned;

8. *Reaffirms* the embargo applied in paragraph 6 of resolution 713(1991), paragraph 5 of resolution 724(1991) and paragraph 6 of resolution 727(1992);

9. *Supports* the views expressed in paragraph 18 of the Secretary-General's report about the grave consequences which the collapse of the United Nations peace-keeping plan would have throughout the region;

10. *Encourages* the Secretary-General to pursue his efforts to fulfil as soon as possible the terms of paragraph 12 of resolution 752(1992);

11. *Calls again upon* all parties concerned to cooperate fully with the Conference on Yugoslavia and its aim of reaching a political settlement consistent with the principles of the Conference on Security and Cooperation in Europe and reaffirms that the United Nations peace-keeping plan and its implementation is in no way intended to prejudge the terms of a political settlement;

12. *Decides* to remain actively seized of the matter until a peaceful solution is achieved.

Security Council resolution 762(1992)
30 June 1992   Meeting 3088   Adopted unanimously
Draft prepared in consultations among Council members (S/24207).

Report of the Secretary-General (27 July). The Secretary-General, in a report of 27 July,[18] discussed progress made by UNPROFOR in Croatia, as well as several major problems confronting it.

A major achievement was the elimination of cease-fire violations involving the use of heavy weapons, facilitated through simultaneous withdrawal by both sides of such weapons to a distance of 30 kilometres from the line of confrontation. Tension in all three UNPAs had also lessened, though occasional cease-fire violations continued. Another major achievement was seen in the withdrawal of JNA from all sectors, except for one infantry battalion in Sector East, which was set to leave within a few days. Simultaneously, a number of Croatian Army units had been withdrawn from the front line.

All TDF units in Sectors East and West, which had received many of JNA's heavy weapons, had handed them over for storage in a number of locations under the control of UNPROFOR. Similar action was in progress in Sectors North and South, including the "pink zones", to be completed within a few days. The next step in the demilitarization process—the withdrawal of the infantry, who were now armed only with light weapons, to be followed by the lifting of mines by unarmed parties of the Croatian Army and JNA under UNPROFOR protection—was already under way in Sector West and would be undertaken in other sectors shortly.

The demobilization of the TDF units had been complicated by the parallel emergence of strengthened police and militia organizations, designated as "special police", "border police", etc., which possessed automatic rifles and sometimes machine-guns, in violation of the United Nations peace plan. In many cases, those groups had taken over from JNA or Serb TDFs on the front lines, and needed to be withdrawn and disbanded. The matter had been repeatedly taken up with the local authorities, but as yet with no satisfactory results.

In the "pink zones", the withdrawal of heavy weapons by both sides had begun, as called for in resolution 762(1992). However, delays continued to occur in some areas, with each side insisting on the prior withdrawal of the other. Moreover, Croatian authorities had replaced their military in certain areas with Croatian police, which they refused to withdraw. The increased strength and armament of police and militia on the Serb side also remained a matter of concern.

JNA forces remained in the Dubrovnik area, despite repeated efforts by UNPROFOR to secure their withdrawal. In meetings with Belgrade authorities, the Force Commander was informed that in view of the strategic importance of the Prevlaka peninsula east of Dubrovnik, which controlled the entrance to the Gulf of Kotor, JNA withdrawal would be contingent on a demilitarization of the peninsula and on the guarantee that Croatian heavy weapons would not be located in its proximity. The Belgrade authorities requested UNPROFOR presence in the area to ensure its demilitarization until the case they had submitted to the EC Conference on Yugoslavia on the delineation of State borders was resolved as part of an overall settlement, or until a decision was taken on the matter by the International Court of Justice. UNPROFOR conveyed the views of the Belgrade authorities to those in Zagreb on 14 July. The Croatian Government indicated its willingness to consider the non-emplacement of heavy arms in the area, on condition of reciprocal abstention by Serbia and Montenegro, with the situation being monitored by UNPROFOR military observers. Discussions on the matter were being conducted by UNPROFOR as a matter of urgency.

On the positive side, the Croatian Government and the Serb authorities accepted the establishment of a Joint Commission to oversee and monitor restoration of the Croatian Government's authority in the "pink zones". Its composition was announced on 17 July, following consultation with both sides and ECMM. Its first meeting was expected to take place within a week, although its location was not yet agreed on and one of the parties declined to participate until Croatia withdrew all its personnel from the Drnis area.

The Secretary-General also reported on developments of concern during recent months which, he said, had radically altered many of the premises on which the United Nations peace-keeping plan was based and which, if they were to be addressed effectively, would require further modifications to UNPROFOR's mandate. Among those developments were expulsions, coercion and intimidation, the control of international borders and the humanitarian situation in the UNPAs. In the Force Commander's judgement, UNPROFOR's mandate needed to be further enlarged if it was to succeed in establishing peaceful, just and stable conditions in the UNPAs, pending an overall political settlement. Specifically, he recommended that UNPROFOR be given authority to control the entry of civilians into the UNPAs and to perform immigration and customs functions at the UNPA borders where they coincided with international frontiers. He also recommended an increase in the strength of UNPROFOR's civil affairs component. If approved by the Council, those enlargements of the Force's mandate and strength would come on top of two previous enlargements in connection with Sarajevo airport and the "pink zones", by resolutions 758(1992) and 762(1992), respectively. In addition, the Secretary-General said, there was the possibility that UNPROFOR would be asked to establish a military presence on the Prevlaka peninsula to ensure that it remained demilitarized.

UNPROFOR continued to take part in the rescue and care of refugees from the fighting in Bosnia and Herzegovina, although that task was technically outside its mandate. Serbs within the UNPAs were increasingly involved in the conflict in Bosnia and Herzegovina, making it more difficult for the Force to demilitarize those areas. The conflict in Bosnia and Herzegovina (see below) had largely interrupted the economic links between the UNPAs and other former Yugoslav republics; as a result, the Secretary-General received requests for humanitarian aid to the UNPA populations. Those requests were coordinated by the United Nations Department of Humanitarian Affairs, while requests to send aid from Belgrade were referred to the Sanctions Committee of the Security Council, which granted approval on the understanding that the shipments would be inspected by UNHCR, UNPROFOR and ICRC.

Summing up his observations, the Secretary-General expressed gratitude to Croatia for its flexibility in responding to the Force Commander's efforts to find a solution to the question of the "pink zones". Problems nevertheless remained, especially with regard to the excessive armament of the local police in the UNPAs, the continuing persecution of non-Serbs in some areas and the destruction of Serb property in others. It was too early to report, the Secretary-General said, that UNPROFOR had succeeded in demilitarizing the UNPAs and establishing its full authority there or that conditions existed for the voluntary return of displaced persons to their homes.

The Force Commander's latest recommendations relating to the UNPAs illustrated the extent to which UNPROFOR was being drawn into quasi-governmental functions which went beyond normal peace-keeping practice. They had major resource implications and might stimulate demands for still deeper United Nations involvement. The Secretary-General viewed that trend with some misgiving, in the light of the many other demands on the Organization's attention and resources. However, he believed that, on balance, the Force Commander's recommendations had to be accepted if the effort already invested in Croatia was not to be undermined as a result of UNPROFOR's mandate being limited to control of military movements only.

The Secretary-General estimated the cost associated with enlarging UNPROFOR's mandate to include the additional responsibilities of controlling the entry of civilians into the UNPAs and performing immigration and customs functions at the UNPA borders, together with an increase in the strength of UNPROFOR's civil affairs component, at some $30.9 million for the two months from mid-August to mid-October; thereafter, the monthly cost relating to those activities would be approximately $5.9 million.

SECURITY COUNCIL ACTION (7 August)

On 7 August, the Security Council convened to consider the Secretary-General's report. The Council invited Croatia, at its request, to participate without the right to vote under rule 37[a] of the Council's provisional rules of procedure. On the same day, the Council unanimously adopted **resolution 769(1992)**.

The Security Council,

Reaffirming its resolution 743(1992) and all subsequent resolutions relating to the United Nations Protection Force (UNPROFOR),

Having examined the report of the Secretary-General of 27 July 1992 in which the Secretary-General recommended certain enlargements in the mandate and strength of UNPROFOR,

Taking note of the letter dated 7 August 1992 from the Deputy Prime Minister of the Republic of Croatia to the President of the Security Council,

1. *Approves* the Secretary-General's report;

2. *Authorizes* the enlargements of UNPROFOR's mandate and strength recommended by the Secretary-General in that report;

3. *Reiterates* its demand that all parties and others concerned cooperate with UNPROFOR in implementing the mandate entrusted to it by the Security Council;

4. *Condemns resolutely* the abuses committed against the civilian population, particularly on ethnic grounds, as referred to in paragraphs 14-16 of the above-mentioned report of the Secretary-General.

Security Council resolution 769(1992)

7 August 1992   Meeting 3104   Adopted unanimously

Draft prepared in consultations among Council members (S/23482).

Report of the Secretary-General (28 September). In a report of 28 September,[19] the Secretary-General provided an update on UNPROFOR's progress in Croatia, as well as on the establishment of a Joint Commission to oversee the return of Croatian authority to the "pink zones". He outlined a number of major difficulties encountered by the Force since his report of 27 July, including violations of the cease-fire; problems in the UNPAs with demilitarization, terrorist acts, refugees and displaced persons; the situation at Dubrovnik; and difficulties caused by inaccurate and inflammatory information.

He noted that UNPROFOR had not fully implemented the United Nations plan in three of the UNPAs, nor had it been able to restore a degree of inter-ethnic tolerance, due to the fact that the conflicting parties had not fully cooperated. The situation had to be corrected as soon as possible, otherwise there would be a real danger of renewed widespread conflict.

The situation along the confrontation line was generally stable, with some incidents occurring and occasional small-arms fire. Tension was high in Sector South, particularly in the areas of the Peruca dam, Miljevci plateau and Zemunik airport, where heavy machine-guns and light mortars had sometimes been used.

Four major incidents had occurred in the UNPAs since the end of July. On 7 August, fighting erupted in the south-east end of Sector West when armed elements from the Croatian side apparently attempted to cross the Sava River to attack armed Bosnian Serbs. United Nations forces sustained no casualties, but were caught in an exchange of fire which included the use of tanks, artillery and mortars. Nine bodies in a variety of uniforms found on the southern side of the river were not claimed by either side, giving rise to the suspicion of the use of mercenaries. On 13 August, a group of Serbs from the village of Markusica in Sector East were attacked by the Croatian Army as they harvested maize in an area just across the confrontation line. Four people were killed and 19 taken prisoner. UNPROFOR quickly defused the situation and secured the release of the 19 individuals. On 21 August, three Serb so-called "border militia" personnel were shot dead in the vicinity of the confrontation line of Sector East.

In the last week of August, a large group of armed personnel attempting to infiltrate through Sector North into Bosnia and Herzegovina were encountered by local Serb militia, who killed or captured several of them. Prisoners interviewed by UNPROFOR said they had been mobilized and trained by the Croatian Army and were being infiltrated in small groups into Bosnia and Herzegovina. When the matter was raised with the Croatian President by Under-Secretary-General

Goulding on 31 August, the President stated that such practices would no longer be permitted. However, tension in the area remained high.

In the UNPAs, the demilitarization process had been delayed by the creation of new Serb militia forces, made up of former JNA members, TDFs and irregular elements. Those militia, under the names of "special police", "border police" or "multi-purpose police brigades", comprised up to 16,000 armed men equipped with personnel carriers, mortars and machine-guns. The Force Commander considered that their level of armament and almost total ignorance of police work demonstrated that, in reality, they were paramilitary forces. Efforts by UNPROFOR to demobilize the newly created units had largely succeeded in Sector West, but not in the other sectors. Such paramilitary units were engaged in acts of terrorism against minorities, especially in Sector East and to a lesser extent in Sector South, and appeared to enjoy complete impunity.

Deteriorating conditions in Sector East had led to a general breakdown in law and order, with no functioning court system. Harassment, intimidation and aggression against the non-Serb population continued and even increased in the Baranja area. While terrorism was mostly directed against non-Serbs, on 29 August four Serb militiamen were killed by other Serbs and three villagers were wounded. Crime was also rising in the Sector, often with elderly people as the victims. A number of brutal murders had occurred, frequently at the hands or with the collusion of the "special police". Unemployment was up as well, with non-Serbs often being the first to lose jobs, either for true economic reasons or so that their jobs could be taken by newly arrived Serb refugees. There was a similar situation in Sector South, with an increase of incidents against the non-Serb population, such as the destruction of houses and churches, looting, intimidation and even murder. Such events were often matched by actions against Serbs across the confrontation line.

A slight improvement was seen in the Croatian-controlled part of Sector West, with fewer burnings of Serb houses. However, numerous cases of intimidation and arrest of Serb residents by the Croatian authorities were documented. Some Serbs had been removed from UNPROFOR protection to a military prison at Bjelovar, outside the Sector, before being indirectly expelled through an involuntary "prisoner-of-war" exchange. Photographic and medical evidence of serious beatings of several Serbs while in custody was presented to the Croatian authorities, who said they had turned it over to the Public Attorney's Office for proceedings. Few, if any, of those acts in the four sectors had led to prosecution and punishment of the offenders.

The regular civil police in the UNPAs, though often well-trained and professional, were inactive and seemed more or less impotent in the face of the "special police". Under those conditions, UNCIVPOL's role had become even more important. Increasingly, the local population was turning to UNCIVPOL for assistance—as crime victims, for security, or for humanitarian help.

The Joint Commission established by resolution 762(1992) to oversee the restoration of the Croatian Government's authority in the "pink zones" had held five meetings since its inception. Comprised of representatives of UNPROFOR, ECMM, the Croatian Government and the local Serb authorities at Knin, it had, after a slow start, begun to make progress. In the second week of September, subcommissions began meeting on cease-fire and security, and on humanitarian and economic issues. "Hot lines" were established between the parties regarding security issues, and experts on both sides had drawn up agreed plans for the repair of utilities and other economic installations in the "pink zones".

After Serb authorities at Knin agreed to withdraw their "special police" forces from the Peruca dam, UNPROFOR brought in international consultants to inspect the installation. Their disturbing report led to the decision, following talks at Belgrade conducted by Personal Envoy Vance on 12 September, to have UNPROFOR take over full control of the dam, effective as of 14 September. Upon assumption of that authority, UNPROFOR took emergency measures to lower the water level and reduce the pressure, allowing briefly for an adequate flow of water to power stations downstream to generate power for much of the adjoining region. However, Serb forces had apparently laid explosives around the dam prior to their withdrawal, and cooperation of the authorities in Belgrade and Knin had been sought to deal with that danger.

The Secretary-General directed UNPROFOR to remain in charge of the dam until it was fully safeguarded and could be handed over to the appropriate authorities. Despite previous assurances, it was unclear whether the Serb authorities in Knin would respect that arrangement. Senior members had told UNPROFOR that they would insist on restoring their "authority" over the dam. Currently, UNPROFOR troops from two contingents were in control of the dam and its immediate vicinity; several hundred Serb "special militia" were also deployed around it.

The tragedies in the region were often inspired and exacerbated by propaganda, rumour and disinformation, which were employed by some of the national leaders. Distorted and inflammatory accounts of the conflict, and of gross human rights violations, were presented daily in the media. UNPROFOR had sought, within its limited means, to explain its mission through print, radio and television. However, its mandate remained widely misunderstood, and authorities in the former Yugoslavia provided inconsistent support for such communication. In particular, Croatian authorities had banned several UNPROFOR radio broadcasts and prevented the Force from televising a programme explaining its mandate. In response, the Force had developed a plan for providing timely and objective information, countering misinformation and explaining its functions and tasks.

Concluding, the Secretary-General observed that there were positive elements, notably the agreement on the Prevlaka peninsula. UNPROFOR's proposal for the withdrawal of JNA forces from there was accepted on 12 September by the Prime Minister of Yugoslavia (Serbia and Montenegro) and the JNA Chief of Staff, and on 15 September by the Croatian President. The agreement called for complete withdrawal of JNA from Croatia, the demilitarization of the Prevlaka peninsula, and the removal of heavy weapons from neighbouring areas of Croatia and Montenegro.

On the other hand, it had not been possible for UNPROFOR, despite strenuous efforts, to achieve full implementation of the United Nations plan in the three UNPAs or to restore a degree of normalcy and interethnic tolerance. The situation had to be corrected urgently, otherwise there was a real danger of renewed widespread conflict.

The Secretary-General regarded it as particularly distressing that the deteriorating security situation had made it impossible for UNPROFOR and UNHCR to start major programmes for the return of refugees and displaced persons. The Security Council might wish to consider action in response to the many cases in which persons had been coerced into signing away their property and rights of residence, declaring such acts, taken under duress, to be null and void.

The situation in the "pink zones" was also a cause of considerable concern. The Secretary-General noted the readiness of both sides, especially the Serbian one, to cut power and water supplies as a means of putting pressure on their opponents. In his view, completion of the restoration of the Croatian Government's authority in the zones would remove the causes of many of the cease-fire violations, permit many displaced persons to return and help rebuild confidence between the parties.

SECURITY COUNCIL ACTION (6 October)

The Security Council convened on 6 October to consider the Secretary-General's report. Croatia, at its request, was invited to participate in the Council discussion without vote, under rule 37[a] of the Council's provisional rules of procedure.

The Council unanimously adopted **resolution 779(1992)**.

The Security Council,

Reaffirming its resolution 743(1992) of 21 February 1992 and all subsequent resolutions relating to the activities of the United Nations Protection Force in Croatia,

Having examined the report of the Secretary-General of 28 September 1992 submitted pursuant to resolution 743(1992) and 762(1992),

Concerned about the difficulties encountered by the United Nations Protection Force in the implementation of resolution 762(1992) due to cease-fire violations and in particular to the creation of paramilitary forces in the United Nations protected areas in violation of the United Nations peace-keeping plan,

Expressing grave alarm at continuing reports of "ethnic cleansing" in the UNPAs and of forcible expulsion of civilians and deprivation of their rights of residence and property,

Welcoming the Joint Declaration signed in Geneva on 30 September 1992 by the Presidents of the Republic of Croatia and the Federal Republic of Yugoslavia (Serbia and Montenegro),

Welcoming in particular the agreement, reaffirmed in the Joint Declaration, concerning the demilitarization of the Prevlaka peninsula,

Recalling the provisions of Chapter VIII of the Charter of the United Nations,

1. *Approves* the report of the Secretary-General including the steps taken to ensure the control of the Peruca dam by the United Nations Protection Force;

2. *Authorizes* the United Nations Protection Force to assume responsibility for monitoring the arrangements agreed for the complete withdrawal of the Yugoslav Army from Croatia, the demilitarization of the Prevlaka peninsula and the removal of heavy weapons from neighbouring areas of Croatia and Montenegro, in cooperation, as appropriate, with the European Community Monitoring Mission, looks forward to the report of the Secretary-General on how this is implemented, and calls on all parties and others concerned to cooperate fully with UNPROFOR in its performance of this new task;

3. *Calls on* all parties and others concerned to improve their cooperation with the United Nations Protection Force in the performance of the tasks it is already undertaking in the UNPAs and in the areas adjacent to the United Nations protected areas;

4. *Urges* all parties and others concerned in Croatia to comply with their obligations under the United Nations peace-keeping plan, especially with regard to the withdrawal and the disarming of all forces, including paramilitary forces;

5. *Endorses* the principles agreed by the Presidents of the Republic of Croatia and the Federal Republic of Yugoslavia (Serbia and Montenegro) on 30 September 1992 that all statements or commitments made under duress, particularly those relating to land and property, are wholly null and void and that all displaced persons have the right to return in peace to their former homes;

6. *Strongly supports* the current efforts of the co-chairmen of the International Conference on Former Yugoslavia to ensure the restoration of power and water supplies before the coming winter, as mentioned in paragraph 38 of the report of the Secretary-General, and calls on all the parties and others concerned to cooperate in this regard;

7. *Decides* to remain actively seized of the matter until a peaceful solution is achieved.

Security Council resolution 779(1992)

6 October 1992   Meeting 3118   Adopted unanimously

Draft prepared in consultations among Council members (S/24617), orally revised.

Report of the Secretary-General (24 November). In a report of 24 November,[20] the Secretary-General updated information on progress made by UNPROFOR in implementation of its mandate, mainly in Croatia. In particular, he dealt with violations of the cease-fire, demilitarization of the UNPAs, terrorism, the return of refugees and displaced persons, border control, the situation at the Peruca dam, the withdrawal of JNA from the Prevlaka peninsula and the Joint Commission.

Summing up his observations, the Secretary-General stated that the situation in the UNPAs and "pink zones" had not improved since his report of 28 September. Although neither side had fully implemented its undertakings under the United Nations plan and each was guilty of irresponsible and provocative conduct, the root cause of UNPROFOR's inability to make further progress had been the Knin authorities' growing and increasingly outspoken defiance of the Security Council and UNPROFOR. The Knin authorities' refusal to accept the demilitarization of the UNPAs and the return of refugees and displaced persons undermined two of the fundamental principles of the peace-keeping plan. Particularly distressing was their apparent intention to establish in Sector West, where UNPROFOR had been making some progress, the conditions of brutal lawlessness which, despite all UNPROFOR efforts, existed in Sectors East, North and South. Although the Croatian authorities from time to time had raised tension in the UNPAs and the "pink zones" by injudicious public statements and provocative military moves, responsibility for non-implementation of the peace-keeping plan rested squarely with the Knin authorities. They had abused the law and order powers entrusted to the local authorities by the plan and instead had created or perpetuated conditions of lawlessness and disorder. They had exploited UNPROFOR's presence and the resulting cessation of hostilities in order to assert their pretensions of sovereignty and statehood, instead of cooperating to create conditions in which a negotiated accommodation of their legitimate concerns could be achieved. They had refused to withdraw their forces from the "pink zones" and had blocked full implementation of resolution 762(1992) by pursuing the aim of consolidating the status quo in those areas rather than facilitating the orderly restoration of Croatian authority there.

The question thus arose as to what further action could be taken to persuade the Knin authorities to honour the commitments arising from their previously declared acceptance of the peace-keeping plan (though some of their more recent statements called the plan itself into question). It had appeared for a brief time that the improving climate of relations between Belgrade and Zagreb might make it possible to overcome the various obstacles in the way of effective implementation of the plan, but that hope was not fulfilled. Unless a way could quickly be found to obtain the cooperation of the Knin authorities, UNPROFOR in Croatia would confront the Security Council with the same dilemma as had other operations, notably the one in southern Lebanon, which had been prevented by the non-cooperation of one or more of the parties from fulfilling their original short-term mandate but nevertheless succeeded in controlling the suffering of the civilian population. In such situations, the Council had to make the difficult choice between withdrawing the operation, in the knowledge that doing so would be likely to lead to a resumption of fighting, or keeping it in place, which might involve the Council in a large and expensive commitment for an indefinite period of time, without any certainty that the mandate of the operation would be fulfilled.

(For details of the Secretary-General's report on the activities of UNPROFOR in Bosnia and Herzegovina, see below.)

Bosnia and Herzegovina

The situation in Bosnia and Herzegovina worsened markedly during the year. The European Community, which recognized Bosnia and Herzegovina as an independent and sovereign State as of 7 April,[21] supported efforts to bring about a peaceful solution through negotiations on future constitutional arrangements. From 26 to 28 August, the International Conference on the Former Yugoslavia, successor to the EC Conference on the Former Yugoslavia, convened in London under the co-chairmanship of the Secretary-General of the United Nations and the Prime Minister of the United Kingdom, in his capacity as President of the Council of Ministers of EC. The Conference adopted a statement of principles for a negotiated settlement of the conflict and reached a number of agreements among the parties. At the London session, the parties agreed to a ban on all military flights over Bosnia and Herzegovina. The ban was broken on numerous occasions, with population centres in the republic sometimes being heavily bombarded, as charged by Bosnia and Herzegovina in several communications.[22]

The Conference's working group on Bosnia and Herzegovina took up its tasks to promote a cessation of hostilities and a constitutional settlement in the republic on 18 September 1992. The discussions led to an agreement, announced on 30

September, that military commanders and local authorities of the three sides would meet under the auspices of UNPROFOR and the International Conference to work towards a demilitarization of Sarajevo and a cessation of hostilities in the city. The Mixed Military Working Group met for the first time on 23 October at Sarajevo airport. The three sides, meeting in the Group, signed on 10 November a cease-fire for all of Bosnia and Herzegovina effective at midnight on 11 November. By resolution 787(1992) of 16 November, the Security Council called on all parties to fulfil their commitments to put into effect an immediate cessation of hostilities and to negotiate in the Mixed Military Working Group, continuously and in uninterrupted session, in order to end the blockades of Sarajevo and other towns and to demilitarize them, with heavy weapons to be placed under international supervision.

Consultations were conducted separately with the parties on a possible constitutional structure for Bosnia and Herzegovina. The Co-Chairmen, in proposals presented to the parties, foresaw that the republic would be a decentralized State, with 7 to 10 autonomous provinces whose boundaries would take into account ethnic and other considerations. The parties in turn were requested to provide, in the form of maps if possible, their conceptions as to those boundaries. By resolution 787(1992), the Security Council called on the parties to continue negotiations, in uninterrupted session, for constitutional arrangements on the basis of the Co-Chairmen's draft outline constitution. In preparation for peace talks scheduled for January 1993, the Co-Chairmen held, on 27 and 28 December 1992, consultations with the parties, which concentrated on the provincial structure in Bosnia and Herzegovina.

The peace-keeping plan approved by the Council in resolution 743(1992) of 12 February envisaged that the headquarters of UNPROFOR would be located in Bosnia and Herzegovina and that UNPROFOR military observers would patrol certain limited areas of the republic following the demilitarization of the UNPAs in Croatia. Accordingly, in March, UNPROFOR established its headquarters at Sarajevo, which was chosen as a neutral location unaffected by the conflict in Croatia. It was also hoped that its presence might serve as a stabilizing factor amidst increasing tension, a hope that was rapidly belied by the outbreak of fighting in Bosnia and Herzegovina, which severely handicapped UNPROFOR's senior command in executing its primary mandate relating to the UNPAs. The bulk of UNPROFOR's headquarters staff was therefore relocated temporarily to Belgrade on 16 and 17 May. UNPROFOR subsequently established its headquarters at Zagreb.

Despite the relocation of its headquarters, the Force left behind some 120 persons at Sarajevo under the command of the Chief Military Observer. That UNPROFOR group became the only international presence in Bosnia and Herzegovina when ECMM and ICRC withdrew their personnel after violence was directed against them, causing one fatality each. As a result, UNPROFOR found itself not only facilitating, but also leading, negotiations between the parties, both on specific ad hoc problems and on arrangements for an overall cease-fire, as well as lending its good offices to promote humanitarian actions for which it did not, strictly speaking, have a mandate from the Security Council. Once UNPROFOR had concluded an agreement on 5 June permitting the reopening of Sarajevo airport under its auspices, its formal mandate in Bosnia and Herzegovina followed, and was defined by, that agreement.

By resolution 761(1992) of 29 June, the Council authorized UNPROFOR to take over full operational responsibility for the functioning and security of Sarajevo airport. That responsibility included ensuring the immediate security of the airport and its installations, supervising its operations, controlling its facilities and organization, facilitating the unloading of humanitarian cargo and ensuring the safe movement of humanitarian aid and related personnel. In addition, UNPROFOR was to verify the withdrawal of anti-aircraft weapons systems from within range of the airport and its approaches and to monitor the concentration of artillery, mortar and ground-to-ground missile systems in specified areas. That task was performed initially by one large, and subsequently three smaller, infantry battalions, together with necessary support elements, including military observers and civilian police.

Following widespread reports of attacks on civilians, human rights abuses and shortages of food and medicine throughout the republic, the Council, on 13 August, by resolution 770(1992), acting under Chapter VII of the Charter of the United Nations, called on States to take all measures necessary to facilitate the delivery of humanitarian assistance in Bosnia and Herzegovina. In further discussions, however, it was decided that that task should be entrusted to UNPROFOR. By resolution 776(1992) of 14 September, which made no reference to Chapter VII, the Council authorized UNPROFOR to support UNHCR efforts to deliver humanitarian relief throughout the republic, and in particular to provide protection where and when UNHCR considered it necessary. The Council noted with appreciation the offers of a number of Member States to make available military personnel for that purpose without cost to the Organization. It also authorized UNPROFOR to protect convoys of released detainees if requested to do so by ICRC. A separate Bosnia and Herzegovina Command was established within UNPROFOR to implement resolution 776(1992), with a total of some 7,800 of all ranks in addition to Sector Sarajevo.

By resolution 781(1992) of 9 October, the Council established a ban on military flights in the airspace of Bosnia and Herzegovina and requested UNPROFOR to monitor compliance with it, including by placing observers where necessary at airfields in the territory of the former Yugoslavia. It also instructed UNPROFOR to ensure, through an appropriate approval and inspection mechanism, that the purpose of flights to and from Bosnia and Herzegovina, other than those banned, was consistent with its resolutions. The ban and the above arrangements were reaffirmed in resolution 786(1992) of 10 November. An additional 75 United Nations military observers were authorized for the task.

Despite interruptions as a result of hostile military action against humanitarian aircraft, UNPROFOR succeeded in keeping Sarajevo airport open during the year to allow the delivery of much-needed relief supplies. The operation under resolution 776(1992) to protect humanitarian convoys throughout the republic was persistently thwarted by obstruction, mines, hostile fire and the refusal of the parties on the ground, particularly—but not exclusively—the Bosnian Serb party, to cooperate with UNPROFOR. None the less, from the deployment of additional UNPROFOR battalions for that purpose in November 1992 until January 1993, a total of some 34,600 tons of relief supplies were delivered to an estimated 800,000 beneficiaries in 110 locations throughout Bosnia and Herzegovina.

However, UNPROFOR's efforts in the republic were characterized by a tendency on the part of the host Government to blame it for a variety of shortcomings, whether real or imagined. Criticism of UNPROFOR's performance in the republic was largely directed at its failure to fulfil tasks it was not mandated, authorized, equipped or staffed for. There were a number of attacks on UNPROFOR by the Government and by elements answerable to it, both in public statements and, more seriously, through violence. Deliberate attacks on UNPROFOR personnel led to the deaths of six soldiers and injuries to over 100 more in the performance of their duties in the republic. Despite formal protests by UNPROFOR, no action was taken by the Government to identify and punish those responsible.

The interdiction of military flights in the airspace of Bosnia and Herzegovina was violated, apparently by all three parties, on many occasions since its imposition. However, the ban achieved its principal purpose of preventing the use of air power in military combat in the republic. UNPROFOR observers on the ground and monitors using AWACS information made available by the North Atlantic Treaty Organization (NATO) found no evidence to suggest that any party flew combat air missions, or conducted hostilities from the air, since the interdiction regime was established by the Council.

SECURITY COUNCIL ACTION (7 and 10 April)

In **resolution 749(1992)** of 7 April, the Security Council appealed to all parties and others concerned in Bosnia and Herzegovina to cooperate with the EC's efforts to bring about a cease-fire and a negotiated political solution.

The Council convened on 10 April to consider the situation in the republic. After consultations, the President of the Council made the following statement:[23]

Meeting number. SC 3068.

"The Security Council, alarmed by reports on rapid deterioration of the situation in Bosnia and Herzegovina, reiterates the appeal in Security Council resolution 749(1992) to all parties and others concerned in Bosnia and Herzegovina to stop the fighting immediately. It invites the Secretary-General to dispatch urgently to the area his Personal Envoy to act in close cooperation with representatives of the European Community whose current efforts are aimed at stopping the fighting and at bringing about a peaceful solution to the crisis, and to report to the Council."

Report of the Secretary-General (24 April). In response to the Security Council's appeal in resolution 749(1992), the Secretary-General, in a report of 24 April,[24] discussed the possibility of deploying a peace-keeping force in Bosnia and Herzegovina.

He had met at Geneva on 10 April with the Foreign Minister of the republic, who requested that such a force be sent to his country. The Secretary-General suggested that it might be more appropriate for EC to expand its presence and activities there, since it occupied the role of peacemaker for the former Yugoslavia, with the United Nations mandate being limited to Croatia.

The Secretary-General's Personal Envoy undertook his seventh mission to the region from 14 to 18 April. At Belgrade, he was briefed by the Commander of UNPROFOR. He also met with, among others, Colonel-General Blagoje Adzic, the Acting Defence Minister and JNA Chief of Staff, and President Milosevic of Serbia. At Sarajevo, he met with President Izetbegovic of Bosnia and Herzegovina, as well as with leaders of the other communities in the republic and with the regional JNA commander. At Zagreb, he conferred with President Franjo Tudjman and other senior Croatian officials. In Slovenia, he met with President Milan Kucan.

On his return to New York, the Personal Envoy met at Lisbon with the President of the Council of Ministers of EC and the Plenipotentiary for Bosnia and Herzegovina of the Chairman of the Conference on Yugoslavia to discuss the political, military and humanitarian aspects of the situation in Bosnia and Herzegovina.

All parties believed that a civil war there would be a great tragedy that could yield no victor and all agreed that no alternative existed to the tripartite talks taking place under EC auspices. All specifically supported the cease-fire agreement reached at Sarajevo on 12 April by the three main parties. The text of the agreement was annexed to the Secretary-General's report.

There was no consensus on the origins of or responsibility for the fighting, and no agreement concerning the situation on the ground. According to the President of Serbia, the principal responsibility for the fighting lay with the President of Bosnia and Herzegovina and hostilities had been initiated by units from Croatia. The best solution to the problem, in his view, would be the cantonization of Bosnia and Herzegovina within its existing borders along ethnic lines.

The firm position of the Croatian President was that regular Croatian Army troops were not engaged in the fighting in the republic. However, he acknowledged that Croat irregulars were involved, particularly in the Croat-majority region of western Herzegovina. The President of Serbia acknowledged the presence of Serb irregulars, particularly along the west bank of the Drina River.

According to JNA leadership, all three communities in Bosnia and Herzegovina had some type of paramilitary forces and contained extremist elements which were difficult to control. JNA warned, however, that its troops would react with force if its garrisons and other installations were attacked, as they had been in Croatia.

The President of Bosnia and Herzegovina reiterated the request for immediate deployment of a United Nations peace-keeping force. In his opinion, the Serbian leadership in his country had sought forcibly to alter the republic's demographic composition, with the support of JNA elements, in order to prejudge the outcome of a future division along ethnic lines. He stated that JNA sided with the Serb territorials under the control of the Serb community leader, Radovan Karadzic. He suggested that JNA leadership be restructured in Bosnia and Herzegovina to include Muslims and Croats in the army's higher command structure. The only way to reach a final settlement would be to have outside experts draw a map cantonizing the country, together with the internal communities, the President said. At the same time, he pointed to excessive territorial claims of the Serbs as the source of the conflict.

According to Croatian Democratic Community (HDZ) leaders at Sarajevo, their community in Bosnia and Herzegovina wished the republic, which was their homeland, to be independent. Croatia had recognized Bosnia and Herzegovina's independence and the Republic of Serbia should do the same. While accusing JNA of siding with Serb territorials, they stressed that JNA was the crucial element in a peaceful solution.

Serb community leaders denied responsibility for the violence at Sarajevo and in other parts of Bosnia and Herzegovina, and disclaimed control of the territorials operating in the hills surrounding the city. They charged that the President of Bosnia and Herzegovina wanted to create a fundamentalist Islamic State, and that he resisted the establishment of geographically defined ethnic communities which, in their opinion, was the most urgent issue.

Massive mistrust was underlying the entire conflict in Bosnia and Herzegovina, the Secretary-General concluded; all sides tended to blame the others and the cycle of violence was escalating. It was essential that a cease-fire be effected immediately, based on the 12 April agreement, and there was no alternative to concluding and implementing the constitutional arrangements being developed at the tripartite talks under EC auspices. It was also essential that work at the Conference on Yugoslavia continue to be pressed forward, together with EC endeavours to bring about a peaceful settlement.

The Secretary-General also expressed concern about the deteriorating humanitarian situation in Bosnia and Herzegovina, where the fighting made it increasingly difficult, if not impossible, to provide for the most basic needs of the victims of the conflict.

Although concurring with his Personal Envoy that the deployment of a peace-keeping force in Bosnia and Herzegovina was not feasible under circumstances making it impossible to define a workable concept for such an operation, the Secretary-General announced that he would advance the dispatch of 41 unarmed military observers to the municipalities of Capljina, Mostar, Stolac and Trebinje.

SECURITY COUNCIL ACTION (24 April)

At the urgent requests of Austria[25] and France,[26] the Security Council convened on 24 April to consider the deteriorating situation in Bosnia and Herzegovina. Following consultations, the Council authorized its President to make a statement:[27]

Meeting number. SC 3070.

"In advance of its consideration of the report of the Secretary-General pursuant to Security Council resolution 749(1992), the Security Council has had an exchange of views in the course of which various proposals were made with regard to the situation in Bosnia-Hercegovina.

"The Security Council notes with deep concern the rapid and violent deterioration of the situation in Bosnia-Hercegovina, which in addition to causing an increasing number of deaths of many innocent victims further risks compromising peace and security in the region.

"It welcomes the recent efforts of the European Community and the Secretary-General aimed at prevailing upon the parties to respect fully the cease-fire signed on 12 April 1992 under the auspices of the European Community. It notes with satisfaction the decision of the Secretary-General to accelerate the deployment in Bosnia-Hercegovina of the 100 military observers from UNPROFOR, 41 to be deployed in the Mostar region immediately. The presence of these military observers, like that of the monitors of the European Community, should help the parties to implement their commitment, undertaken on 23 April 1992, to respect the cease-fire. The Council welcomes the support given by the CSCE to the efforts of the European Community and the United Nations.

"The Council demands that all forms of interference from outside Bosnia-Hercegovina cease immediately. In this respect, it specifically calls upon Bosnia-Hercegovina's neighbours to exercise all their influence to end such interference. The Council condemns publicly and unreservedly the use of force, and calls upon all regular or irregular military forces to act in accordance with these principles. It emphasizes the value of close and continuous coordination between the Secretary-General and the European Community in order to obtain the necessary commitments from all parties and others concerned.

"The Council urges all the parties to respect immediately and fully the cease-fire, and condemns all breaches of the cease-fire from whatever quarter.

"The Council supports the efforts undertaken by the European Community in the framework of discussions on constitutional arrangements for Bosnia-Hercegovina under the auspices of the Conference on Yugoslavia. It urges the three communities in Bosnia-Hercegovina to participate actively and constructively in these talks and to conclude and implement the constitutional arrangements being developed at the tripartite talks.

"The Council calls upon all parties and others concerned to facilitate humanitarian assistance and cooperate so that deliveries of humanitarian assistance reach their destination.

"The Council has decided to remain actively seized of the matter, and to continue its consideration of the further contribution that the Security Council can make to the restoration of peace and security in Bosnia-Hercegovina."

Report of the Secretary-General (12 May). In a report of 12 May,[28] the Secretary-General further reviewed the situation in Bosnia and Herzegovina, covering the findings of Under-Secretary-General Goulding during his mission to the former Yugoslavia from 4 to 10 May. At Sarajevo, Mr. Goulding met with the President of Bosnia and Herzegovina, leaders of the HDZ party and the Muslim Party of Democratic Action (SDA), the commander of JNA at Sarajevo and the Commander of UNPROFOR. At Belgrade, he held consultations with Radovan Karadzic, leader of the Serbian Democratic Party (SDS) of Bosnia and Herzegovina.

Throughout the republic, the state of affairs was grim, Mr. Goulding reported, and conditions in Sarajevo continued to disintegrate. The city suffered heavy shelling and sniper fire each night from Serb irregulars in the surrounding hills; they used mortars and light artillery allegedly made available to them by JNA. Muslim forces had blockaded JNA locations in the city and regularly attacked a Serb stronghold in the suburb of Ilidza. There was no public transportation and streets were virtually deserted. Food and other essential supplies were growing short as a result of the blockade of the city by Serb forces. Many lives had been lost and property destroyed. Intense hostilities were also taking place elsewhere in the republic.

The general consensus among international observers was that a concerted effort was made by the Serbs to create "ethnically pure" areas within the EC-proposed cantons throughout Bosnia and Herzegovina. Territory was seized by military force and the non-Serb population was then intimidated. A partial cease-fire signed between Croat and Serb leaders on 6 May revived suspicions that the two parties would attempt to carve up the republic, leaving minimal territory for Muslims, who comprised 44 per cent of the population. Further concern was caused by the decision of the Belgrade authorities to withdraw from Bosnia and Herzegovina by 18 May all JNA personnel who were not citizens of that republic; that would leave behind about 50,000 mostly Serb troops and their weapons with no effective political control.

Fighting and intimidation led to massive displacement of civilians, with the number of displaced persons reaching an estimated 520,000 (over 12 per cent of the republic's population) at 8 May, 360,000 of whom had taken refuge in neighbouring republics. The international community's efforts to aid the displaced were strongly obstructed by the fighting, with relief supplies being stolen, vehicles hijacked and international aid workers threatened and abused.

Under the circumstances, it had not been possible to implement the cease-fire agreement of 12 April, which had been reaffirmed on 23 April during a visit to Sarajevo of Lord Carrington and his Plenipotentiary for Bosnia and Herzegovina, Ambassador Cutileiro. Following the killing of one of its members near Mostar on 1 May, ECMM withdrew completely from the republic. EC protested to the authorities in Belgrade the action which it believed had been carried out by JNA and called for an investigation.[29]

Meanwhile, Ambassador Cutileiro continued his efforts to induce the leaders of the Croat, Muslim and Serb communities to agree on constitutional arrangements for the republic, in particular to the drafting of maps for the cantonal boundaries. However, because of the deteriorating security situation in Sarajevo, he postponed the reconvening of a conference on the matter.

Operations of UNPROFOR military observers, who had been conducting patrols in Bosnia and Herzegovina since 1 May, were suspended after one observer was wounded at Mostar on 6 May and an observer vehicle was struck by a rocket on 12 May, with the occupants escaping unharmed.

Although it was outside its mandate, UNPROFOR responded positively to requests for help to control the conflict and mitigate its worst consequences. Reacting to humanitarian emergencies arising from the shelling of Sarajevo, it provided some support to international humanitarian agencies and made its good offices available, with the EC representatives, in crisis situations, including those directly arising from military conflict between two of the parties. UNPROFOR headquarters had become the only meeting place accepted by all the parties in the EC-led efforts to implement the cease-fire.

Mr. Goulding's discussions on the feasibility of a United Nations peace-keeping operation in Bosnia and Herzegovina focused on two possible timeframes: an immediate operation to help end the fighting, and an operation to help implement possible constitutional agreements. While President Izetbegovic, HDZ and SDA advocated immediate United Nations intervention, Mr. Goulding's interlocutors at Belgrade, including the leader of SDS, saw no role for a United Nations peacekeeping force under the circumstances and considered the current deployment of UNPROFOR military observers in the Mostar area to be of limited utility. They were doubtful about prospects for negotiating any interim agreements that could form an acceptable basis for a United Nations operation, in advance of an agreement on new constitutional arrangements. The Commander of the JNA Sarajevo corps and Ambassador Joao Salgueiro, head of ECMM, expressed similar views.

A possible United Nations role in resolving specific problems, such as those relating to the closure of Sarajevo airport, on the basis of local or ad hoc agreements among the warring parties, was found acceptable only by President Izetbegovic. Colm Doyle, Lord Carrington's representative, stated that, should he succeed in obtaining adherence to the cease-fire agreed on 12 April, the ceasefire would continue to be monitored by EC, within its existing mandate and using ECMM.

With regard to United Nations peace-keepers supporting international humanitarian activities, the Force Commander and Mr. Goulding noted that no agreements had been negotiated for unhindered distribution of humanitarian aid. In those circumstances, and given the parties' uncooperative attitude to the movement of relief convoys, they judged that armed troops would be required to implement such a mandate.

Some degree of consensus, however, emerged on a possible role for United Nations peace-keepers in helping to implement a constitutional agreement. The President of Bosnia and Herzegovina said he reluctantly accepted the cantonization principle as preferable to war and would welcome a peace-keeping force to separate the warring factions, monitor the future internal borders and verify that no military personnel or equipment crossed those borders. The Belgrade authorities and JNA leadership in both Belgrade and Sarajevo agreed to that concept. In the opinion of the leader of SDS, UNPROFOR military observers could conceivably perform those functions. The President of Croatia expressed similar views.

Following Mr. Goulding's visit, President Izetbegovic, in a letter of 8 May to the Secretary-General, requested the deployment of a United Nations peace-keeping force with specific goals and a limited workable mandate to control Sarajevo airport, protect humanitarian aid deliveries and keep open roads, bridges and border crossings. Commenting on that request, the Secretary-General stated that if it proved possible, contrary to the general expectation, to obtain the other parties' agreement to such interim arrangements, there might be a role for UNPROFOR military observers in monitoring their implementation. However, the chaotic military situation and apparent inability of the protagonists to get their forces to respect the cease-fire agreements would probably make it necessary to deploy armed troops; the protective force might also find that it had to take control of extensive territory.

United Nations military observers could also monitor implementation of agreements, binding on all the armed parties, to allow the unhindered delivery of humanitarian supplies. In the absence of such agreements, however, it would be necessary to provide convoys with armed escorts whose rules of engagement would permit them to open fire in case of an attack, along the lines of the protection operation proposed for Mogadishu, Somalia (see PART TWO, Chapter I).

Based on Mr. Goulding's findings that the situation in Bosnia and Herzegovina was dangerous, violent and confused, the Secretary-General did not believe that the conflict in the republic was, in its current phase, susceptible to United Nations peace-keeping, as any such operation had to be based on some agreement between the hostile parties. Without such an agreement—which could range from a simple cease-fire to a comprehensive settlement—a workable mandate for a peacekeeping operation was impossible. If EC's efforts to reach agreements succeeded, opportunities for United Nations peacemaking might emerge, although it might be more appropriate for EC rather than the United Nations to undertake the peacekeeping as well as the peacemaking.

Successful peace-keeping required the parties to respect the United Nations, its personnel and its mandate; none of the parties in Bosnia and Herzegovina satisfied that condition. The establishment of UNPROFOR's headquarters at Sarajevo had not prevented the outbreak of a savage conflict there and the Force Commander's repeated appeals for restraint had been ignored. United Nations personnel were routinely harassed, the Organization's property stolen and its emblems and uniforms misappropriated.

Despite those conditions, the Secretary-General did not believe that an enforcement action, as had been requested by President Izetbegovic, to end the fighting was a practicable proposition.

Drawing the conclusion that it was currently not feasible to undertake peace-keeping activities beyond UNPROFOR's limited involvement in Sarajevo and the Mostar area, where the security of United Nations personnel was already precarious, the Secretary-General suggested that the Council continue to support the peacemaking activities of EC. The possibilities for an effective United Nations role would depend on the success of the EC negotiators.

Due to the problems encountered on a daily basis by UNPROFOR at Sarajevo, the Force Commander had moved most of the civilian administrative staff to Belgrade and Zagreb. In addition, he proposed temporary relocation of significant elements of headquarters staff pending the restoration of calm in the city, a proposal with which the Secretary-General agreed.

SECURITY COUNCIL ACTION (15 May)

The Security Council met on 15 May to consider the Secretary-General's report. By a unanimous vote, it adopted **resolution 752(1992)**.

The Security Council,

Reaffirming its resolutions 713(1991) of 25 September 1991, 721(1991) of 27 November 1991, 724(1991) of 15 December 1991, 727(1992) of 8 January 1992, 740(1992) of 7 February 1992, 743(1992) of 21 February 1992 and 749(1992) of 7 April 1992,

Expressing its appreciation for the reports of the Secretary-General of 24 April 1992 and 12 May 1992 pursuant to resolution 749(1992),

Deeply concerned about the serious situation in certain parts of the former Socialist Federal Republic of Yugoslavia, and in particular about the rapid and violent deterioration of the situation in Bosnia-Hercegovina,

Recalling its primary responsibility under the Charter of the United Nations for the maintenance of international peace and security,

Recalling also the provisions of Chapter VIII of the Charter of the United Nations, and the continuing role that the European Community is playing in achieving a peaceful solution in Bosnia-Hercegovina, as well as in other republics of the former Socialist Federal Republic of Yugoslavia,

Having considered the announcement in Belgrade on 4 May 1992 described in paragraph 24 of the report of the Secretary-General of 12 May 1992 concerning the withdrawal of Yugoslav People's Army (JNA) personnel from republics other than Serbia and Montenegro and the renunciation of authority over those who remain,

Noting the urgent need for humanitarian assistance and the various appeals made in this connection, in particular by the President of Bosnia-Hercegovina,

Deploring the tragic incident on 4 May 1992 which caused the death of a member of the European Community Monitor Mission,

Deeply concerned about the safety of United Nations personnel in Bosnia-Hercegovina,

1. *Demands* that all parties and others concerned in Bosnia-Hercegovina stop the fighting immediately, respect immediately and fully the cease-fire signed on 12 April 1992, and cooperate with the efforts of the European Community to bring about urgently a negotiated political solution respecting the principle that any change of borders by force is not acceptable;

2. *Welcomes* the efforts undertaken by the European Community in the framework of the discussions on constitutional arrangements for Bosnia-Hercegovina under the auspices of the Conference on Yugoslavia, urges that the discussions be resumed without delay, and urges the three communities in Bosnia-Hercegovina to participate actively and constructively in these discussions on a continuous basis as recommended by the Secretary-General and to conclude and implement the constitutional arrangements being developed at the tripartite talks;

3. *Demands* that all forms of interference from outside Bosnia-Hercegovina, including by units of the Yugoslav People's Army (JNA) as well as elements of the Croatian Army, cease immediately, and that Bosnia-Hercegovina's neighbours take swift action to end such interference and respect the territorial integrity of Bosnia-Hercegovina;

4. *Demands* that those units of the Yugoslav People's Army (JNA) and elements of the Croatian Army now in Bosnia-Hercegovina must either be withdrawn, or be subject to the authority of the Government of Bosnia-Hercegovina, or be disbanded and disarmed with their weapons placed under effective international monitoring, and requests the Secretary-General to consider without delay what international assistance could be provided in this connection;

5. *Demands also* that all irregular forces in Bosnia-Hercegovina be disbanded and disarmed;

6. *Calls upon* all parties and others concerned to ensure that forcible expulsions of persons from the areas where they live and any attempts to change the ethnic composition of the population, anywhere in the former Socialist Federal Republic of Yugoslavia, cease immediately;

7. *Emphasizes* the urgent need for humanitarian assistance, material and financial, taking into account the

large number of refugees and displaced persons and fully supports the current efforts to deliver humanitarian aid to all the victims of the conflict and to assist in the voluntary return of displaced persons to their homes;

8. *Calls* on all parties and others concerned to ensure that conditions are established for the effective and unhindered delivery of humanitarian assistance, including safe and secure access to airports in Bosnia-Hercegovina;

9. *Requests* the Secretary-General to keep under active review the feasibility of protecting international humanitarian relief programmes, including the option mentioned in paragraph 29 of his report of 12 May 1992, and of ensuring safe and secure access to Sarajevo airport, and to report to the Security Council by 26 May 1992;

10. *Further requests* the Secretary-General, having regard to the evolution of the situation and to the results of the efforts undertaken by the European Community, to continue to keep under review the possibility of deploying a peace-keeping mission in Bosnia-Hercegovina under the auspices of the United Nations;

11. *Demands* that all parties and others concerned cooperate fully with UNPROFOR and the European Community Monitoring Mission, and respect fully their freedom of movement and the safety of their personnel;

12. *Notes* the progress made thus far in the deployment of UNPROFOR, welcomes the fact that UNPROFOR has assumed the full responsibility called for by its mandate in Eastern Slavonia, and requests the Secretary-General to ensure that UNPROFOR will assume its full responsibilities in all the United Nations Protected Areas (UNPAs) as soon as possible and to encourage all parties and others concerned to resolve any problems remaining in this connection;

13. *Urges* all parties and others concerned to cooperate in every way with UNPROFOR in accordance with the United Nations Plan and to comply strictly with the Plan in all its aspects, in particular the disarming of all irregular forces, whatever their origin, in the UNPAs;

14. *Decides* to remain actively seized of the matter and to consider further steps to achieve a peaceful solution in conformity with relevant resolutions of the Council.

Security Council resolution 752(1992)
15 May 1992   Meeting 3075   Adopted unanimously
Draft prepared in consultations among Council members (S/23927), orally revised.

Report of the Secretary-General (26 May). In a report of 26 May,[30] the Secretary-General addressed the feasibility of having the United Nations protect international humanitarian relief programmes in Bosnia and Herzegovina where devastation was continuing, with displacement of civilians occurring on levels not seen since the Second World War. The plight of those trapped in cities besieged by irregular forces—and in some cases by JNA—was deteriorating. In Sarajevo alone, from 300,000 to 400,000 people were estimated to be in need of emergency relief. The situation was further complicated by repeated failure to implement agreements for the withdrawal of JNA troops surrounding Bosnian territorial forces in Sarajevo.

UNHCR had, until recently, been successful in organizing humanitarian relief convoys to various cities, including Sarajevo. The deteriorating security situation, however, had lately prevented UNHCR from continuing its aid to the city. Relief to other areas in Bosnia, organized out of Belgrade and Zagreb, was made only after protracted negotiations for safe passage with all regular and irregular forces and other parties concerned. Nevertheless, the convoys were stopped at roadblocks and allowed to continue only after further negotiations. On 22 May, UNHCR had 12 of its trucks commandeered by local armed elements, to be returned only after arduous negotiations with Serbian authorities in Pale, Belgrade and Banja Luka.

Following the death on 18 May of one of its delegates, resulting from an attack on one of its convoys at Sarajevo, ICRC was reassessing its plan of action in Bosnia and Herzegovina. Representatives of all parties to the conflict met at Geneva from 21 to 23 May under ICRC auspices and signed an agreement on the application of the basic principles of humanitarian law in the conflict.

Approximately 90 UNPROFOR personnel remained at Sarajevo, while about two thirds were temporarily relocated. Those remaining continued to perform such tasks as arranging, hosting and sometimes chairing meetings between the hostile parties on cease-fires; accompanying delegations to such meetings; arranging exchanges of prisoners of war, wounded and war dead; and such other humanitarian tasks as the Chief Military Observer judged feasible. The staff's well-being was increasingly at risk; on several occasions, they had been the deliberate target of mortar and small-arms fire from various sides.

Analysing the options available for protecting humanitarian relief efforts, the Secretary-General cited respect for agreements, binding on all the armed parties, as the best protection. Their implementation could be monitored by United Nations military observers. However, the feasibility of that approach depended on agreements being negotiated and honoured; the hostile parties, while having concluded a number of agreements, had poor records when it came to honouring them. The presence of international observers did not appear to curb their behaviour.

Air delivery of relief supplies would demand an agreement from all parties for the opening of the necessary airports. In that connection, the President of Bosnia and Herzegovina had informed the Secretary-General on 19 May that civilian and military airports were being destroyed by JNA. UNPROFOR had raised with JNA and the Serb side the possibility of opening Sarajevo airport for humanitarian deliveries, with the latter two agreeing to consider that option provided all shipments were checked to ensure that no weapons were included. The Commander of Serbian forces in Sarajevo confirmed on 26 May that he was ready to participate in immediate negotiations on the subject; that was being followed up by UNPROFOR. A further possible way of delivering supplies would be by airdrops from helicopters, which would require negotiated agreements to ensure their safety.

Armed protection was the second option discussed by the Secretary-General to ensure the delivery of humanitarian relief. It would require the deployment of troops to clear the route in advance and protect each convoy's passage. As inflicting hardship on civilians was a strategy of war for some of the parties, the use of force by those troops to fulfil their task would very likely be predisposed. In order to guarantee the security of Sarajevo airport, a considerable body of United Nations troops and armaments would be needed to secure the surrounding hills, from which the airport could be easily shelled; that too would be a potential combat operation.

Providing armed protection for convoys of humanitarian supplies *en route* from Sarajevo airport to the distribution centres within the city was a less ambitious option, which would require an agreement that no party would fire at the airport or its approaches while such supplies were arriving. That option would necessitate an addition to UNPROFOR's mandate, as well as extra troops and consultations with troop-contributing Governments if existing UNPROFOR personnel were proposed for that purpose. However, any mandate requiring United Nations troops to take coercive action in Bosnia and Herzegovina could make it more difficult to secure the cooperation which UNPROFOR needed in the UNPAs in Croatia, the Secretary-General pointed out.

A more promising course would be to persuade the warring parties to conclude and honour agreements permitting unimpeded delivery of relief supplies. Recent developments, including a more receptive attitude by the Serb military leader in Sarajevo and the willingness of the authorities in Belgrade, expressed in a 26 May letter,[31] to use their influence to help unhindered engagement of the United Nations and international humanitarian organizations in Bosnia and Herzegovina, suggested that conditions might be more propitious for such agreements than in previous weeks. The Chief Military Observer of UNPROFOR, who led the sole remaining international presence at Sarajevo, would continue to do all he could to arrange negotiations to that effect. The Secretary-General had also requested the United Nations Emergency Relief Coordinator to take any steps necessary to facilitate the early negotiation of agreements that would allow unimpeded delivery of humanitarian supplies, in close consultation with UNHCR, ICRC and other agencies involved.

SECURITY COUNCIL ACTION (30 May)

On 30 May, following an urgent request from Canada,[32] the Security Council convened to consider the situation in Bosnia and Herzegovina and adopted **resolution 757(1992)**.

The Security Council,

Reaffirming its resolutions 713(1991) of 25 September 1991, 721(1991) of 27 November 1991, 724(1991) of 15 December 1991, 727(1992) of 8 January 1992, 740(1992) of 7 February 1992, 743(1992) of 21 February 1992, 749(1992) of 7 April 1992 and 752(1992) of 15 May 1992,

Noting that in the very complex context of events in the former Socialist Federal Republic of Yugoslavia all parties bear some responsibility for the situation,

Reaffirming its support for the Conference on Yugoslavia, including the efforts undertaken by the European Community in the framework of the discussions on constitutional arrangements for Bosnia and Herzegovina, and recalling that no territorial gains or changes brought about by violence are acceptable and that the borders of Bosnia and Herzegovina are inviolable,

Deploring the fact that the demands in resolution 752(1992) have not been complied with, including its demands:

—That all parties and others concerned in Bosnia and Herzegovina stop the fighting immediately,

—That all forms of interference from outside Bosnia and Herzegovina cease immediately,

—That Bosnia and Herzegovina's neighbours take swift action to end all interference and respect the territorial integrity of Bosnia and Herzegovina,

—That action be taken as regards units of the Yugoslav People's Army (JNA) in Bosnia and Herzegovina, including the disbanding and disarming with weapons placed under effective international monitoring of any units that are neither withdrawn nor placed under the authority of the Government of Bosnia and Herzegovina,

—That all irregular forces in Bosnia and Herzegovina be disbanded and disarmed,

Deploring further that its call for the immediate cessation of forcible expulsions and attempts to change the ethnic composition of the population has not been heeded, and reaffirming in this context the need for the effective protection of human rights and fundamental freedoms, including those of ethnic minorities,

Dismayed that conditions have not yet been established for the effective and unhindered delivery of humanitarian assistance, including safe and secure access to and from Sarajevo and other airports in Bosnia and Herzegovina,

Deeply concerned that those United Nations Protection Force (UNPROFOR) personnel remaining in Sarajevo have been subjected to deliberate mortar and small-arms fire, and that the United Nations Military Observers deployed in the Mostar region have had to be withdrawn,

Deeply concerned also at developments in Croatia, including persistent cease-fire violations and the continued expulsion of non-Serb civilians, and at the obstruction of and lack of cooperation with UNPROFOR in other parts of Croatia,

Deploring the tragic incident on 18 May 1992 which caused the death of a member of the ICRC team in Bosnia and Herzegovina,

Noting that the claim by the Federal Republic of Yugoslavia (Serbia and Montenegro) to continue automatically the membership of the former Socialist Federal Republic of Yugoslavia in the United Nations has not been generally accepted,

Expressing its appreciation for the report of the Secretary-General of 26 May 1992 pursuant to resolution 752(1992),

Recalling its primary responsibility under the Charter of the United Nations for the maintenance of international peace and security,

Recalling also the provisions of Chapter VIII of the Charter of the United Nations, and the continuing role that the European Community is playing in working for a peaceful solution in Bosnia and Herzegovina, as well as in other republics of the former Socialist Federal Republic of Yugoslavia,

Recalling its decision in resolution 752(1992) to consider further steps to achieve a peaceful solution in conformity with relevant resolutions of the Council, and affirming its determination to take measures against any party or parties which fail to fulfil the requirements of resolution 752(1992) and its other relevant resolutions,

Determined in this context to adopt certain measures with the sole objective of achieving a peaceful solution and encouraging the efforts undertaken by the European Community and its member States,

Recalling the right of States, under Article 50 of the Charter, to consult the Security Council where they find themselves confronted with special economic problems arising from the carrying out of preventive or enforcement measures,

Determining that the situation in Bosnia and Herzegovina and in other parts of the former Socialist Federal Republic of Yugoslavia constitutes a threat to international peace and security,

Acting under Chapter VII of the Charter of the United Nations,

1. *Condemns* the failure of the authorities in the Federal Republic of Yugoslavia (Serbia and Montenegro), including the Yugoslav People's Army (JNA), to take effective measures to fulfil the requirements of resolution 752(1992);

2. *Demands* that any elements of the Croatian Army still present in Bosnia and Herzegovina act in accordance with paragraph 4 of resolution 752(1992) without further delay;

3. *Decides* that all States shall adopt the measures set out below, which shall apply until the Security Council decides that the authorities in the Federal Republic of Yugoslavia (Serbia and Montenegro), including the Yugoslav People's Army (JNA), have taken effective measures to fulfil the requirements of resolution 752(1992);

4. *Decides* that all States shall prevent:

(a) The import into their territories of all commodities and products originating in the Federal Republic of Yugoslavia (Serbia and Montenegro) exported therefrom after the date of the present resolution;

(b) Any activities by their nationals or in their territories which would promote or are calculated to promote the export or transshipment of any commodities or products originating in the Federal Republic of Yu-goslavia (Serbia and Montenegro); and any dealings by their nationals or their flag vessels or aircraft or in their territories in any commodities or products originating in the Federal Republic of Yugoslavia (Serbia and Montenegro) and exported therefrom after the date of the present resolution, including in particular any transfer of funds to the Federal Republic of Yugoslavia (Serbia and Montenegro) for the purposes of such activities or dealings;

(c) The sale or supply by their nationals or from their territories or using their flag vessels or aircraft of any commodities or products, whether or not originating in their territories, but not including supplies intended strictly for medical purposes and foodstuffs notified to the Committee established pursuant to resolution 724(1991), to any person or body in the Federal Republic of Yugoslavia (Serbia and Montenegro) or to any person or body for the purposes of any business carried on in or operated from the Federal Republic of Yugoslavia (Serbia and Montenegro), and any activities by their nationals or in their territories which promote or are calculated to promote such sale or supply of such commodities or products;

5. *Decides* that all States shall not make available to the authorities in the Federal Republic of Yugoslavia (Serbia and Montenegro) or to any commercial, industrial or public utility undertaking in the Federal Republic of Yugoslavia (Serbia and Montenegro) any funds or any other financial or economic resources, and shall prevent their nationals and any persons within their territories from removing from their territories or otherwise making available to those authorities or to any such undertaking any such funds or resources and from remitting any other funds to persons or bodies within the Federal Republic of Yugoslavia (Serbia and Montenegro), except payments exclusively for strictly medical or humanitarian purposes and foodstuffs;

6. *Decides* that the prohibitions in paragraphs 4 and 5 above shall not apply to the transshipment through the Federal Republic of Yugoslavia (Serbia and Montenegro) of commodities and products originating outside the Federal Republic of Yugoslavia (Serbia and Montenegro) and temporarily present in the territory of the Federal Republic of Yugoslavia (Serbia and Montenegro) only for the purpose of such transsshipment, in accordance with guidelines approved by the Committee established by resolution 724(1991);

7. *Decides* that all States shall:

(a) Deny permission to any aircraft to take off from, land in or overfly their territory if it is destined to land in or has taken off from the territory of the Federal Republic of Yugoslavia (Serbia and Montenegro), unless the particular flight has been approved, for humanitarian or other purposes consistent with the relevant resolutions of the Council, by the Committee established by resolution 724(1991);

(b) Prohibit, by their nationals or from their territory, the provision of engineering and maintenance servicing of aircraft registered in the Federal Republic of Yugoslavia (Serbia and Montenegro) or operated by or on behalf of entities in the Federal Republic of Yugoslavia (Serbia and Montenegro) or components for such aircraft, the certification of airworthiness for such aircraft, and the payment of new claims against existing insurance contracts and the provision of new direct insurance for such aircraft;

8. *Decides* that all States shall:

(a) Reduce the level of the staff at diplomatic missions and consular posts of the Federal Republic of Yugoslavia (Serbia and Montenegro);

(b) Take the necessary steps to prevent the participation in sporting events on their territory of persons or groups representing the Federal Republic of Yugoslavia (Serbia and Montenegro);

(c) Suspend scientific and technical cooperation and cultural exchanges and visits involving persons or groups officially sponsored by or representing the Federal Republic of Yugoslavia (Serbia and Montenegro);

9. *Decides* that all States, and the authorities in the Federal Republic of Yugoslavia (Serbia and Montenegro), shall take the necessary measures to ensure that no claim shall lie at the instance of the authorities in the Federal Republic of Yugoslavia (Serbia and Montenegro), or of any person or body in the Federal Republic of Yugoslavia (Serbia and Montenegro), or of any person claiming through or for the benefit of any such person or body, in connection with any contract or other transaction where its performance was affected by reason of the measures imposed by this resolution and related resolutions;

10. *Decides* that the measures imposed by this resolution shall not apply to activities related to UNPROFOR, to the Conference on Yugoslavia or to the European Community Monitoring Mission, and that States, parties and others concerned shall cooperate fully with UNPROFOR, the Conference on Yugoslavia and the European Community Monitoring Mission and respect fully their freedom of movement and the safety of their personnel;

11. *Calls upon* all States, including States not Members of the United Nations, and all international organizations, to act strictly in accordance with the provisions of the present resolution, notwithstanding the existence of any rights or obligations conferred or imposed by any international agreement or any contract entered into or any licence or permit granted prior to the date of the present resolution;

12. *Requests* all States to report to the Secretary-General by 22 June 1992 on the measures they have instituted for meeting the obligations set out in paragraphs 4 to 9 above;

13. *Decides* that the Committee established by resolution 724(1991) shall undertake the following tasks additional to those in respect of the arms embargo established by resolutions 713(1991) and 727(1992):

(a) To examine the reports submitted pursuant to paragraph 12 above;

(b) To seek from all States further information regarding the action taken by them concerning the effective implementation of the measures imposed by paragraphs 4 to 9 above;

(c) To consider any information brought to its attention by States concerning violations of the measures imposed by paragraphs 4 to 9 above and, in that context, to make recommendations to the Council on ways to increase their effectiveness;

(d) To recommend appropriate measures in response to violations of the measures imposed by paragraphs 4 to 9 above and provide information on a regular basis to the Secretary-General for general distribution to Member States;

(e) To consider and approve the guidelines referred to in paragraph 6 above;

(f) To consider and decide upon expeditiously any applications for the approval of flights for humanitarian or other purposes consistent with the relevant resolutions of the Council in accordance with paragraph 7 above;

14. *Calls upon* all States to cooperate fully with the Committee in the fulfilment of its tasks, including supplying such information as may be sought by the Committee in pursuance of the present resolution;

15. *Requests* the Secretary-General to report to the Security Council, not later than 15 June 1992 and earlier if he considers it appropriate, on the implementation of resolution 752(1992) by all parties and others concerned;

16. *Decides* to keep under continuous review the measures imposed by paragraphs 4 to 9 above with a view to considering whether such measures might be suspended or terminated following compliance with the requirements of resolution 752(1992);

17. *Demands* that all parties and others concerned create immediately the necessary conditions for unimpeded delivery of humanitarian supplies to Sarajevo and other destinations in Bosnia and Herzegovina, including the establishment of a security zone encompassing Sarajevo and its airport and respecting the agreements signed in Geneva on 22 May 1992;

18. *Requests* the Secretary-General to continue to use his good offices in order to achieve the objectives contained in paragraph 17 above, and invites him to keep under continuous review any further measures that may become necessary to ensure unimpeded delivery of humanitarian supplies;

19. *Urges* all States to respond to the Revised Joint Appeal for humanitarian assistance of early May 1992 issued by the United Nations High Commissioner for Refugees, the United Nations Children's Fund and the World Health Organization;

20. *Reiterates* the call in paragraph 2 of resolution 752(1992) that all parties continue their efforts in the framework of the Conference on Yugoslavia and that the three communities in Bosnia and Herzegovina resume their discussions on constitutional arrangements for Bosnia and Herzegovina;

21. *Decides* to remain actively seized of the matter and to consider immediately, whenever necessary, further steps to achieve a peaceful solution in conformity with relevant resolutions of the Council.

Security Council resolution 757(1992)

30 May 1992   Meeting 3082   13-0-2

6-nation draft (S/24037).

Sponsors: Belgium, France, Hungary, Morocco, United Kingdom, United States.

Vote in Council as follows:

In favour: Austria, Belgium, Cape Verde, Ecuador, France, Hungary, India, Japan, Morocco, Russian Federation, United Kingdom, United States.
Against: None.
Abstaining: China, Zimbabwe.

Reports of the Secretary-General (30 May and 6 June). Pursuant to Council resolution 752(1992), the Secretary-General submitted on 30 May a report[33] on the status of the withdrawal of JNA and Croatian Army forces from Bosnia and Herzegovina.

On 4 May, Belgrade authorities had announced their decision to withdraw by 18 May all JNA personnel who were not citizens of Bosnia and Herzegovina. On 13 May, the Vice-President of Yugoslavia (Serbia and Montenegro) proposed to the President of Bosnia and Herzegovina that talks be resumed with the participation of representatives of the Bosnian Serb and Croat communities. That same day, authorities of the so-called "Serbian Republic of Bosnia and Herzegovina" announced the formation of their own army, composed of former JNA units and under the command of General Ratko Mladic (formerly of JNA).

On 17 May, the JNA Chief of General Staff requested assistance from the Secretary-General in withdrawing JNA troops from Bosnia and Herzegovina, referring to a 10 May agreement signed on UNPROFOR premises at Sarajevo by Bosnia and Herzegovina, JNA, ECMM and the representative of the Chairman of the Conference on Yugoslavia. On 21 May, the Vice-President of Yugoslavia (Serbia and Montenegro) again wrote to the Secretary-General, asking that he request Bosnia and Herzegovina to unblock the JNA garrisons at Sarajevo. By a letter of 25 May, the President of Bosnia and Herzegovina requested that UNPROFOR supervise the withdrawal of part of the JNA personnel and weapons, in accordance with the 10 May agreement.

However, the majority of JNA personnel deployed in Bosnia and Herzegovina were actually citizens of that republic and therefore not covered by Belgrade's decision to withdraw JNA. Apparently, most joined the army of the "Serbian Republic of Bosnia and Herzegovina", while others became members of the Territorial Defence of Bosnia and Herzegovina, which was under the political control of the presidency of that republic. Still others might have joined various irregular forces. The barely 20 per cent of JNA forces who were not citizens were mostly believed to have already withdrawn into Serbia or Montenegro. Others, however, remained at various garrisons in Bosnia and Herzegovina, especially in Serb-controlled areas, including two installations on the outskirts of Sarajevo; a further category consisted of personnel blockaded in their barracks by the Territorial Defence or hostile irregular forces, mostly in the Sarajevo area.

Clearly, the Secretary-General said, the withdrawal of remaining JNA troops from their barracks had become tied to other problems in the conflict; in particular, it was complicated by problems relating to the withdrawal of heavy weapons. While JNA leadership in Belgrade had indicated its willingness to leave the bulk of those weapons behind, the leaders of the army of the "Serbian Republic of Bosnia and Herzegovina" would not. Uncertainty about who exercised political control

over the Serb forces in Bosnia and Herzegovina further complicated the situation. Initially, the President of Bosnia and Herzegovina had been reluctant to engage in talks on those and other issues with the leadership of the "Serbian Republic of Bosnia and Herzegovina" and insisted on direct talks with the Belgrade authorities, but it became clear that the word of the latter was not binding on the army of General Mladic; for example, it appeared that the heavy shelling of Sarajevo on the night of 28/29 May was ordered by the latter, in direct contravention of the instructions issued by General Nedeljko Boskovic and JNA leadership in Belgrade.

Given the doubts about the ability of the Belgrade authorities to influence General Mladic, efforts were made by UNPROFOR to appeal to him directly, as well as through the political leadership of the "Serbian Republic of Bosnia and Herzegovina". As a result, he agreed on 30 May to stop the bombardment of Sarajevo. President Izetbegovic had since agreed to deal with General Mladic, but not with the political leadership of the "Serbian Republic of Bosnia and Herzegovina."

No withdrawal of the Croatian Army from Bosnia and Herzegovina had taken place. The Croatian authorities consistently took the position that the soldiers involved there had left the Croatian Army and were not subject to its authority. International observers believed, however, that portions of Bosnia and Herzegovina were under the control of Croatian military units, whether belonging to the local Territorial Defence, to paramilitary groups or to the Croatian Army. It was unclear under the circumstances how their withdrawal or disbandment, as required by the Council, could be achieved, the Secretary-General said.

Resolution 752(1992) outlined three possible alternatives for units of JNA and Croatian Army elements in Bosnia and Herzegovina: they could be withdrawn; be subject to the authority of the Government of the republic; or be disbanded and disarmed, with their weapons placed under international monitoring. International assistance could play a role in implementing each of those alternatives; however, it was contingent on agreements being respected by all parties, especially by the commanders of the units and elements concerned. Such agreements would need to specify clearly which military personnel were deemed "units of JNA" or "elements of the Croatian Army"—a difficult task given the positions of the Croatian and Belgrade authorities and of the other parties involved. Those providing international assistance would also need to be given details, accepted by the principal parties, of the numbers, locations and armament of all troops to which the agreements applied.

International assistance could take various forms, such as monitoring and verifying implementation of agreements. International military personnel could be deployed to help build confidence as troops were assembled and moved out of the republic or to locations where they would pass under the Government's authority, or be disarmed and disbanded. All those forms, however, assumed voluntary agreements by those in political and operational control of the troops concerned, with the latter carrying out the orders they received.

The Council's decision in resolution 757(1992) to impose sanctions on Yugoslavia (Serbia and Montenegro) created a new situation. It was not yet clear what implications the decision would have, but it was to be hoped that it would make it easier to negotiate the necessary agreements.

On 6 June,[34] the Secretary-General reported to the Security Council on progress made in creating conditions for unimpeded delivery of humanitarian aid to Bosnia and Herzegovina, including the establishment of a security zone encompassing Sarajevo and its airport, as had been demanded by the Council in resolution 757(1992).

In keeping with the Council's request in that resolution that the Secretary-General continue using his good offices to achieve those objectives, the Commander of UNPROFOR sent Cedric Thornberry, UNPROFOR Director of Civil Affairs, on 2 June, to negotiate with the parties to the conflict. Mr. Thornberry, assisted by Colonel John Wilson, the Chief Military Observer at UNPROFOR headquarters in Sarajevo, engaged in intensive discussions over a three-day period with representatives of the presidency of that republic, leaders of the Croatian Democratic Party, Radovan Karadzic and other leaders of the self-proclaimed "Serbian Republic of Bosnia and Herzegovina", as well as General Mladic.

The discussions centred on reopening Sarajevo airport for humanitarian purposes, under exclusive United Nations authority. On 5 June, an agreement to that effect was signed by all members of the presidency of Bosnia and Herzegovina, and separately by Mr. Karadzic for the Bosnian Serb side.

The agreement, the text of which was annexed to the Secretary-General's report, called for UNPROFOR to take over full operational responsibility for the airport, supervising operations, controlling its facilities and organization, facilitating the unloading of humanitarian cargo and ensuring the safe movement of cargo and related personnel. UNPROFOR would also verify the withdrawal of anti-aircraft weapons systems from within range of the airport and its approaches and monitor the concentration of artillery, mortar and ground-to-ground missile systems in specified

areas. Such an additional mandate would require the consent of the Council, which would have to approve a corresponding increase in UNPROFOR's strength.

A four-phase plan was envisaged by the Force Commander to implement the agreement. In phase 1, United Nations military observers would be deployed to Sarajevo to supervise the withdrawal of anti-aircraft weapons and the concentration of heavy weapons at agreed locations. Simultaneously, technical personnel would evaluate the airport's serviceability, the condition of its equipment and measures required to control and receive aircraft, unload stores and control the flow of humanitarian aid. In phase 2, an infantry battalion would be deployed to ensure the airport's security. During phase 3, civilian personnel required to operate the airport, as well as representatives of humanitarian agencies, would be deployed there. In phase 4, the airport would be opened for humanitarian and official flights. The four phases were expected to take 10 days to implement, following a decision of the Council. The special regime would be maintained until normal conditions were restored to Sarajevo.

In order to undertake those tasks, the Force Commander proposed to establish a fifth UNPROFOR sector headquarters at Sarajevo, without prejudice to the re-establishment of UNPROFOR headquarters there as soon as security conditions permitted. The additional strength needed would require a reinforced infantry battalion of 1,000 persons; 60 military observers; additional military and civilian staff for Sarajevo Sector headquarters; 40 civilian police to supervise the functioning of the airport; and possibly some technical personnel, engineers and airport staff. Armoured personnel carriers and other vehicles, as well as communications equipment and defence stores, would also be needed.

Although only a first step towards fulfilment of the requirements of resolution 757(1992), the agreement represented a significant breakthrough in the conflict in Bosnia and Herzegovina, the Secretary-General believed. In keeping with that resolution, he had requested the Force Commander to pursue negotiation of a broader security zone encompassing the city of Sarajevo as a whole.

The opportunity afforded by the willingness of the parties to agree to the reopening of Sarajevo airport should be seized, the Secretary-General said. Given that heavy weapons would remain in the hills overlooking Sarajevo and its airport, albeit supervised by UNPROFOR, the viability of the agreement depended on the parties, especially the Bosnian Serb party, scrupulously honouring their commitments. It would also be necessary to elaborate further the question of security corridors, initially between the airport and city and in due course beyond, in order to permit the distribution of the humanitarian supplies flown in.

The proposed operation involved significant risks, as many past agreements had been broken. However, the humanitarian emergency grew more severe by the day, creating an ever-increasing need to bring the fighting under control. Successful implementation of the 5 June agreement, which also reaffirmed the existing cease-fire agreement, would serve both humanitarian and political objectives.

The Secretary-General estimated that enlarging the mandate of UNPROFOR as recommended would cost an additional $20.1 million for the first four months until mid-October, and approximately $3 million for each month thereafter.

SECURITY COUNCIL ACTION (8 June)

On 8 June, the Security Council convened to consider the Secretary-General's 6 June report and unanimously adopted **resolution 758(1992).**

The Security Council,

Reaffirming its resolutions 713(1991) of 25 September 1991, 721(1991) of 27 November 1991, 724(1991) of 15 December 1991, 727(1992) of 8 January 1992, 740(1992) of 7 February 1992, 743(1992) of 21 February 1992, 749(1992) of 7 April 1992, 752(1992) of 15 May 1992 and 757(1992) of 30 May 1992,

Noting that the Secretary-General has secured the evacuation of the Marshal Tito barracks in Sarajevo,

Noting also the agreement of all the parties in Bosnia and Herzegovina to the reopening of Sarajevo airport for humanitarian purposes, under the exclusive authority of the United Nations, and with the assistance of the United Nations Protection Force (UNPROFOR),

Noting further that the reopening of Sarajevo airport for humanitarian purposes would constitute a first step in establishing a security zone encompassing Sarajevo and its airport,

Deploring the continuation of the fighting in Bosnia and Herzegovina which is rendering impossible the distribution of humanitarian assistance in Sarajevo and its environs,

Stressing the imperative need to find an urgent negotiated political solution for the situation in Bosnia and Herzegovina,

1. *Approves* the report of the Secretary-General of 6 June 1992 submitted in accordance with paragraphs 17 and 18 of resolution 757(1992);

2. *Decides* to enlarge the mandate and strength of UNPROFOR, established under resolution 743(1992), in accordance with the Secretary-General's report;

3. *Authorizes* the Secretary-General to deploy, when he judges it appropriate, the military observers and related personnel and equipment required for the activities referred to in paragraph 5 of his report;

4. *Requests* the Secretary-General to seek Security Council authorization for the deployment of the additional elements of UNPROFOR, after he has reported to the Council that all the conditions necessary for them to carry out the mandate approved by the Security Council, including an effective and durable cease-fire, have been fulfilled;

5. *Strongly condemns* all those parties and others concerned that are responsible for violations of the cease-fire reaffirmed in paragraph 1 of the agreement of 5 June 1992 annexed to the Secretary-General's report;

6. *Calls upon* all parties and others concerned to comply fully with the above-mentioned agreement and in particular to respect strictly the cease-fire reaffirmed in paragraph 1 thereof;

7. *Demands* that all parties and others concerned cooperate fully with UNPROFOR and international humanitarian agencies and take all necessary steps to ensure the safety of their personnel;

8. *Demands* that all parties and others concerned create immediately the necessary conditions for unimpeded delivery of humanitarian supplies to Sarajevo and other destinations in Bosnia and Herzegovina, including the establishment of a security zone encompassing Sarajevo and its airport and respecting the agreements signed in Geneva on 22 May 1992;

9. *Requests* the Secretary-General to continue to use his good offices in order to achieve the objectives contained in paragraph 8 above, and invites him to keep under continuous review any further measures that may become necessary to ensure unimpeded delivery of humanitarian supplies;

10. *Requests* the Secretary-General to report to the Security Council on his efforts no later than seven days after the adoption of this resolution;

11. *Decides* to remain actively seized of the matter.

Security Council resolution 758(1992)
8 June 1992   Meeting 3083   Adopted unanimously
Draft prepared in consultations among Council members (S/24078).

Report of the Secretary-General (15 June). On 15 June,[35] the Secretary-General reported to the Council on implementation of the cease-fire of 12 April and other aspects of resolution 752(1992), as well as on the efforts to reopen Sarajevo airport, as requested by resolution 758(1992).

Following repeated cease-fire violations, a new cease-fire was negotiated by UNPROFOR on 1 June, which again was broken within hours of its signing. It was subsequently reaffirmed in the 5 June agreement on the reopening of Sarajevo airport, which too was not respected for several days.

As a result of the evacuation of JNA from the previously blockaded Marshal Tito barracks at Sarajevo, the Territorial Defence force of Bosnia and Herzegovina was reported to have acquired artillery, which it used to try to extend the territory under its control. Bosnian Serb forces continued to use their own artillery to bombard Sarajevo, causing further severe damage. On 11 June, Mr. Karadzic, one of the signatories to the airport agreement, announced a further "unilateral cease-fire" effective 15 June, which President Izetbegovic denounced in a 13 June letter to the Secretary-General as an attempt to deceive the United Nations and world opinion. None the less, on 14 June both sides reaffirmed a new cease-fire as of 0600 hours on 15 June, which appeared to be generally holding.

With regard to cooperation with the EC efforts to bring about a negotiated political solution, the Secretary-General reported that the EC-sponsored talks on future constitutional arrangements in Bosnia and Herzegovina were suspended on 27 May, when the Muslim SDA Party withdrew in protest against the continued shelling of Sarajevo by Bosnian Serb forces. Subsequently, the leaders of SDA reiterated their unwillingness to return to the negotiating table and, by a letter of 8 June to Lord Carrington, President Izetbegovic expressed his inability to negotiate further with the Serbian SDS Party. In reply, Lord Carrington urged him to participate fully and expressed the hope that the President would attend the next round of discussions to be convened in the near future. Members of the presidency of Bosnia and Herzegovina reaffirmed that they could resume participation in the talks only if the basis for discussion were changed. Mr. Karadzic, leader of the Serbian SDS Party, confirmed his willingness to participate in the talks and urged that they be reconvened immediately.

Throughout that process, the Secretary-General assured Lord Carrington of continued support for his efforts towards an overall political settlement and of his conviction that the strengthening of the political process was a *sine qua non* for finding a solution to the tragic impasse and for arresting further bloodshed and destruction. On 12 June, Lord Carrington reiterated his intention to resume the talks and announced that he and Ambassador Cutileiro would go to Sarajevo as soon as the airport was reopened.

Interference from forces outside Bosnia and Herzegovina had continued over the preceding two weeks, despite the Council's demand in resolution 752(1992) that such activities stop. Authorities in Belgrade and Zagreb insisted that they were not interfering militarily in the republic and that the armed Serbs and Croats there were citizens of Bosnia and Herzegovina and not under their authority. A matter of great concern remained that both sides had been permitted to retain control over their tanks, armoured personnel carriers, artillery, personal weapons and uniforms, and there was reason to believe that both Serb and Croat combatants continued to receive at least part of their financial and logistic support from outside.

Delivery of humanitarian assistance to an increasingly deprived population was gravely complicated by persistent fighting. On 24 May, UNHCR suspended deliveries of humanitarian relief supplies within the republic when it became clear that the security guarantees negotiated with political and military leaders were not respected by local gunmen manning a profusion of roadblocks. ICRC, having stopped its relief operations since the killing of one of its delegates on 18 May, negotiated a new security agreement with the parties to the conflict on 6 June at Geneva. Both organizations intended to resume operations in Bosnia and Herzegovina shortly.

Following the adoption of resolution 758(1992) regarding reopening of Sarajevo airport, the Force Commander on 10 June dispatched his Chief of Staff, Brigadier-General Lewis MacKenzie, to Sarajevo as Commander-designate of UNPROFOR's new Sarajevo Sector. General MacKenzie was accompanied by some United Nations military observers and Canadian reconnaissance elements. On 12 June, he was joined by a 50-person airport security team provided by France. A further 60 military observers, drawn from two existing peace-keeping operations, were to arrive at Sarajevo on 16 June. The task of General MacKenzie's advance party was to establish the cease-fire, start evaluating conditions at the airport and verify the withdrawal of anti-aircraft and heavy weaponry as provided for in the 5 June agreement.

For the first three days, it proved impossible for General MacKenzie's advance mission to reach the airport, partly due to widespread fighting in areas they had to cross *en route*, but also because they came under fire from Bosnian Serb elements who appeared not to accept the 5 June agreement and were seemingly not prepared to allow the airport to be placed under United Nations control.

On 14 June, however, General MacKenzie was able to achieve three of his immediate objectives: he obtained separate reaffirmations of the cease-fire from the presidency of Bosnia and Herzegovina as well as from the Bosnian Serb side; the resulting cease-fire came into effect at 0600 hours on 15 June and, at least initially, appeared to be holding. With the cooperation of the Bosnian Serb side and under its escort, he was able to dispatch a 30-man reconnaissance team to the airport. Lastly, he made significant progress in discussing the withdrawal of heavy weapons from within airport range; a definitive agreement on that question was expected to be signed shortly.

In spite of the limited progress made in controlling and resolving the conflict in Bosnia and Herzegovina, the Secretary-General believed that the international community should remain firm in its determination to put into effect the mechanisms it had established to end the fighting, relieve human suffering and broker a just and lasting political settlement. For the time being, the opposing parties displayed no willingness to honour the agreements they had signed or to utilize the problem-solving mechanisms provided by the international community.

Political negotiation offered the only real hope of restoring peace, the Secretary-General said. He therefore joined Lord Carrington in appealing to all concerned to return to the negotiating table.

Following consideration of the Secretary-General's report, the Security Council, on 18 June, unanimously adopted **resolution 760(1992)**.

The Security Council,

Recalling its resolutions 752(1992) of 15 May 1992, 757(1992) of 30 May 1992 and 758(1992) of 8 June 1992, and in particular paragraph 7 of resolution 752(1992), in which it emphasized the urgent need for humanitarian assistance and fully supported the current efforts to deliver humanitarian aid to all the victims of the conflict,

Acting under Chapter VII of the Charter of the United Nations,

Decides that the prohibitions in paragraph 4 *(c)* of resolution 757(1992) concerning the sale or supply to the Federal Republic of Yugoslavia (Serbia and Montenegro) of commodities or products, other than medical supplies and foodstuffs, and the prohibitions against financial transactions related thereto, contained in resolution 757(1992), shall not apply, with the approval of the Committee established by resolution 724(1991) under the simplified and accelerated "no objection" procedure, to commodities and products for essential humanitarian need.

Security Council resolution 760(1992)

18 June 1992   Meeting 3086   Adopted unanimously

Draft prepared in consultations among Council members (S/24114).

Oral reports of the Secretary-General (26 and 29 June). Pursuant to resolution 758(1992), the Secretary-General made statements to the Security Council on 26 and 29 June[36] on the situation in Sarajevo and the most recent developments surrounding its airport.

The situation in the city had deteriorated considerably on 26 June, he said. Bosnian Serb forces had increased their bombardment of the area of Dobrinja, clearly attempting to capture that suburb of Sarajevo close to the airport. Tank and infantry attacks were carried out and heavy artillery was used against civilians, despite a public agreement of the previous day to stop shelling civilian areas. The forces of the Government of Bosnia and Herzegovina retaliated, but UNPROFOR had no doubt that primary responsibility for the current bloodshed lay with the Serb forces.

The Secretary-General condemned the attacks and called for an end to them. A further military advance into Dobrinja was incompatible with the 5 June agreement, the basis for UNPROFOR's endeavour to open Sarajevo airport. Unless the current military offensive ended and there was evidence over the next 48 hours of actual relocation of heavy weaponry to areas of concentration supervised by UNPROFOR, the Secretary-General said he would have to reassess the feasibility of the Force's implementing the 5 June agreement; it would then be up to the Council to determine what other means would be required to bring relief to the suffering people of Sarajevo.

By 29 June, considerable progress towards UNPROFOR's assuming responsibility for the airport was reported by the Force Commander. Serb forces had been withdrawing from the airport and both sides had begun to concentrate their heavy weapons in locations to be supervised by UNPROFOR. An absolute cease-fire had yet to be achieved, but the Force Commander recommended that UNPROFOR seize the opportunity afforded by those developments. Accordingly, the Secretary-General requested the Council to grant him the authorization foreseen in resolution 758(1992) to deploy the additional UNPROFOR elements needed to secure the airport and make it operational.

If the Council agreed, the Secretary-General would instruct the Force Commander to redeploy to Sarajevo airport on an interim basis the Canadian battalion currently in Sector West of Croatia; request France to make available immediately the air-traffic and airlift control elements it had offered; and request the countries concerned to deploy three smaller battalions to Sarajevo. Those battalions would replace the Canadian battalion, which would return to its duties in Croatia.

In view of the pattern of recent fighting, the Secretary-General requested that the Council join him in appealing to the Government of Bosnia and Herzegovina to exercise utmost restraint, in particular not to seek any military advantage from the Serb withdrawal; the humanitarian objectives of UNPROFOR's action must be kept firmly in mind by all parties. In that connection, President Mitterrand of France had informed the Secretary-General in advance of his visit to Sarajevo on 28 June and later briefed him on the results, stressing that his objectives coincided with those of the United Nations.

As requested by the Force Commander, the Secretary-General urged Member States to delay humanitarian flights to Sarajevo until the airport was fully under UNPROFOR control and all heavy weapons were concentrated at UNPROFOR-supervised locations. Arrangements for operation of the airport and for the reception and distribution of humanitarian supplies were not yet complete; he would report on 1 July on progress achieved in that regard.

The Security Council met on 29 June to consider the Secretary-General's oral reports in accordance with an understanding reached in prior consultations. The Council unanimously adopted **resolution 761(1992)**.

The Security Council,

Reaffirming its resolutions 713(1991) of 25 September 1991, 721(1991) of 27 November 1991, 724(1991) of 15 December 1991, 727(1992) of 8 January 1992, 740(1992) of 7 February 1992, 743(1992) of 21 February 1992, 749(1992) of 7 April 1992, 752(1992) of 15 May 1992, 757(1992) of 30 May 1992, 758(1992) of 8 June 1992 and 760(1992) of 18 June 1992,

Noting the considerable progress reported by the Secretary-General towards securing the evacuation of Sarajevo airport and its reopening by UNPROFOR and feeling the need to maintain this favourable momentum,

Underlining the urgency of a quick delivery of humanitarian assistance to Sarajevo and its environs,

1. *Authorizes* the Secretary-General to deploy immediately additional elements of the United Nations Protection Force (UNPROFOR) to ensure the security and functioning of Sarajevo airport and the delivery of humanitarian assistance in accordance with his report dated 6 June 1992;

2. *Calls upon* all parties and others concerned to comply fully with the agreement of 5 June 1992 and in particular to maintain an absolute and unconditional cease-fire;

3. *Appeals* to all sides to cooperate fully with UNPROFOR in the reopening of the airport, to exercise the utmost restraint and not to seek any military advantage in this situation;

4. *Demands* that all parties and others concerned cooperate fully with UNPROFOR and international humanitarian agencies and organizations and take all necessary steps to ensure the safety of their personnel; in the absence of such cooperation, the Security Council does not exclude other measures to deliver humanitarian assistance to Sarajevo and its environs;

5. *Calls upon* all States to contribute to the international humanitarian efforts in Sarajevo and its environs;

6. *Decides* to remain actively seized of the matter.

Security Council resolution 761(1992)

29 June 1992   Meeting 3087   Adopted unanimously

Draft prepared in consultations among Council members (S/24199).

Communication and report of the Secretary-General (1 and 10 July). As indicated in his statement of 29 June, the Secretary-General reported to the Security Council in a letter of 1 July[37] on developments with regard to the reopening of Sarajevo airport. Fighting continued in the area around the airport and in the nearby suburb of Dobrinja, endangering the safety of both personnel and aircraft. The process of heavy-weapons concentration to locations supervised by United Nations military observers was not complete. There was debris on the runway, and mines remaining in several parts of the airport were susceptible to accidental detonation.

The Canadian battalion travelling from UNPROFOR Sector West in Croatia to take up security functions at the airport had encountered unexpected difficulties and was expected to arrive on 2 July. Air-traffic and airlift control elements offered by France had arrived, as had an infantry company from France. An UNPROFOR convoy arriving from Belgrade had brought in movement-control and technical personnel as well as a detachment of marines who were being deployed at the airport. Rudimentary air-traffic control functions were being performed by a skeleton staff and manual discharging of cargo was taking place, while UNHCR was endeavouring to make the necessary arrangements for onward distribution of supplies that might be landed at the airport.

In order to avoid any slackening of the momentum generated by the withdrawal of Serb forces from the airport, UNPROFOR operated the airport within those constraints. Several French aircraft had been able to fly in under visual flight rules, bringing military personnel as well as some humanitarian aid, which was distributed under the auspices of UNHCR. Efforts continued to improve security, establish more complete air-traffic control and improve arrangements for the unloading and distribution of relief items.

On 10 July,[38] the Secretary-General reported that despite the endeavours of UNPROFOR's Sector Commander, General MacKenzie, the cease-fire agreed to on 1 June and reaffirmed on 5 June had not been fully established. Artillery, mortar, tank and small-arms exchanges had taken place each day since the United Nations flag was raised on 29 June and the airport was opened by the first flight carrying humanitarian aid. Nor had the concentration of weaponry under UNPROFOR observation been completed. While humanitarian aid had been moved into the city by convoys of UNPROFOR and UNHCR, secure corridors had not been established.

On a number of occasions since 29 June, fighting had come very close to the airport, although installations, aircraft and airport personnel themselves had not the less been intense at times and sniper fire had been directed at UNPROFOR vehicles, although UNHCR aid vehicles were not attacked.

By 9 July at 2200 hours, more than 100 planes from 15 countries carrying over 1,000 metric tons of food and humanitarian aid had arrived at the airport. On some days, as many as 17 had landed; on 5 July, 300 tons of aid were brought in and unloaded, and, despite manual ground-handling only, 240 tons were moved that day to distribution points in the city, and many aircraft were able to depart within an hour of arrival. Such high standards had been maintained in spite of considerable constraints, as mentioned in the Secretary-General's 1 July letter.

There had been a gradual buildup of UNPROFOR personnel in the Sector. The first group of 30 was deployed to the airport on 28 June. French troops began to arrive on 1 July and the Canadian battalion—which was to be replaced upon the arrival of battalions from Egypt, France and Ukraine around 20 to 25 July—arrived on 2 July. By 3 July, all available United Nations military observers and troops were deployed at the airport, with the two sides, and at other locations in Sarajevo. Current UNPROFOR personnel in the Sector, including military, UNCIVPOL and civilians, numbered 1,104.

UNHCR staff at the airport were working with UNPROFOR in the control of relief flights, having been granted by Governments the full facilitation of this coordinating role, as requested by the Secretary-General. UNHCR then ensured the expeditious dispatch of relief items to Sarajevo and its environs. Sadako Ogata, the United Nations High Commissioner for Refugees, visited Sarajevo on 8 July to review the relief operations.

On 5 July, the Force Commander inspected the UNPROFOR operation in the Sarajevo Sector. He noted that despite highly difficult circumstances, General MacKenzie and the elements under his leadership were doing a magnificent job. As the operation was taking shape, however, it was apparent that the initial personnel estimates for an UNPROFOR take-over of the airport, as put forward in the Secretary-General's 6 June report[34] and approved by the Council in resolution 758(1992), would not be enough. The updated estimate was 1,600 additional personnel— as opposed to the original 1,000—in order to provide for three small battalions rather than one reinforced battalion, as well as for air-traffic control and handling elements, an artillery-locating radar platoon, a helicopter unit, and a signals and a medical platoon. The revised staff costs would amount to $22.7 million instead of $20.1 million from mid-July to mid-October; thereafter the monthly cost would be approximately $3.8 million.

Despite an encouraging start of the operation, the Secretary-General warned that the surrounding circumstances remained worrisome. Three of the basic conditions of the 5 June agreement— cease-fire, complete concentration of heavy weaponry under UNPROFOR monitoring and establishment of security corridors—had not been complied with by either side. Several UNPROFOR military staff members had been slightly wounded by gunfire and one soldier lost part of his leg in a mine explosion on 9 July. Fighting continued, with only temporary lulls in Sarajevo and all around the airport itself. Forces opposed to those of the Serbian SDS Party appeared to be seeking to leverage the advantage resulting from the transfer of the airport to UNPROFOR. SDS forces in turn continued to respond with heavy weapons into populated areas. A military advance by Croatian forces towards Sarajevo was reported by several sources, but could not be independently verified by UNPROFOR.

Due to limited resources and security, UNPROFOR was unable to respond to the many requests it had received for humanitarian evacuation. The situation at the airport, on the outskirts and in the city, coupled with operational considerations, made it impossible to consider initiatives for the evacuation by air of cases of special humanitarian concern. Nevertheless, options for the evacuation of critical medical cases were being reviewed; if feasible, they would take place in close coordination between UNPROFOR and UNHCR, in cooperation with ICRC.

At a meeting with the Force Commander, the UNPROFOR Director of Civil Affairs and the Sarajevo Sector Commander on 5 July, the President of Bosnia and Herzegovina continued to call for the establishment of a security zone around Sarajevo, but agreed that the basic conditions for implementing even the more limited airport agreement had not been fully satisfied. While he favoured demilitarizing the contested area of Dobrinja adjacent to the airport, he felt that other SDS-held neighbourhoods should be similarly demilitarized and placed under UNPROFOR control.

Serb forces were attempting to maintain a unilateral cease-fire, but were compelled to respond to the worst provocations of the opposing side, leaders of SDS and the Army Commander of the "Serbian Republic of Bosnia and Herzegovina" told the Force Commander on 5 July. Allegations were made of a large Croatian military intervention. The SDS leaders said that their handing over of the airport to UNPROFOR had not led to peace; they were willing to negotiate directly with the President of Bosnia and Herzegovina but had been refused. The Force Commander noted those statements, but stressed that such issues lay outside UNPROFOR's mandate.

The situation in Sarajevo and the many reports on deteriorating conditions throughout Bosnia and Herzegovina were greatly perturbing, the Force Commander said. The current success of the airport operation was an outstanding tribute to all those participating in it; however, their endeavours had not stimulated a corresponding initiative from the conflicting parties to seek a political settlement.

The Secretary-General concluded that the Sarajevo airport operation was based on foundations of utmost fragility, as the continuing military conflict in the area could at any moment encroach on the airport and disrupt the arrival and distribution of relief goods. Meanwhile, the provision of humanitarian aid to the rest of the country was sparse, intermittent and hazardous. While efforts by humanitarian agencies to open up routes to other parts of Bosnia and Herzegovina continued, vast areas of the republic remained in desperate need of assistance. Only urgent efforts of the international community to address the basic causes of the conflict, including negotiations with all the parties involved, could resolve what had emerged as one of the worst humanitarian emergencies.

SECURITY COUNCIL ACTION (13 and 17 July)

The Security Council, meeting on 13 July, invited Bosnia and Herzegovina, at its request, to participate without the right to vote under rule 37ᵃ of the Council's provisional rules of procedure. The Council considered the Secretary-General's report and unanimously adopted **resolution 764(1992)**.

The Security Council,

Reaffirming its resolutions 713(1991) of 25 September 1991, 721(1991) of 27 November 1991, 724(1991) of 15 December 1991, 727(1992) of 8 January 1992, 740(1992) of 7 February 1992, 743(1992) of 21 February 1992, 749(1992) of 7 April 1992, 752(1992) of 15 May 1992, 757(1992) of 30 May 1992, 758(1992) of 8 June 1992, 760(1992) of 18 June 1992, 761(1992) of 29 June 1992 and 762(1992) of 30 June 1992,

Noting with appreciation the further report of the Secretary-General,

Disturbed by the continuing violation of the Sarajevo airport agreement of 5 June 1992, in which the parties agreed, *inter alia:*

—That all anti-aircraft weapon systems would be withdrawn from positions from which they could engage the airport and its air approaches;

—That all artillery, mortar, ground-to-ground missile systems and tanks within the range of the airport would be concentrated in areas agreed by the United Nations Protection Force (UNPROFOR) and subject to UNPROFOR observation at the firing line;

—To establish security corridors between the airport and the city, under UNPROFOR's control, to ensure the safe movement of humanitarian aid and related personnel;

Deeply concerned about the safety of UNPROFOR personnel,

Cognizant of the magnificent work being done in Sarajevo by UNPROFOR and its leadership, despite the conditions of great difficulty and danger,

Aware of the enormous difficulties in the evacuation by air of cases of special humanitarian concern,

Deeply disturbed by the situation which now prevails in Sarajevo and by many reports and indications of deteriorating conditions throughout Bosnia and Herzegovina,

Commending the determination and courage of all those who are participating in the humanitarian effort,

Deploring the continuation of the fighting in Bosnia and Herzegovina which is rendering difficult the provision of humanitarian assistance in Sarajevo and its environs, as well as in other areas of the Republic,

Noting that the reopening of Sarajevo airport for humanitarian purposes constitutes a first step in establishing a security zone encompassing Sarajevo and its airport,

Recalling the obligations under international humanitarian law, in particular the Geneva Conventions of 12 August 1949,

Stressing once again the imperative need to find an urgent negotiated political solution for the situation in Bosnia and Herzegovina,

1. *Approves* the report of the Secretary-General of 10 July 1992;

2. *Authorizes* the Secretary-General to deploy immediately additional elements of the United Nations Protec-

tion Force (UNPROFOR) to ensure the security and functioning of Sarajevo airport and the delivery of humanitarian assistance, in accordance with paragraph 12 of his report dated 10 July 1992;

3. *Reiterates its call* on all parties and others concerned to comply fully with the agreement of 5 June 1992, and to cease immediately any hostile military activity in Bosnia and Herzegovina;

4. *Commends* the untiring efforts and the bravery of UNPROFOR for its role in securing humanitarian relief in Sarajevo and its environs;

5. *Demands* that all parties and others concerned cooperate fully with UNPROFOR and international humanitarian agencies to facilitate the evacuation by air of cases of special humanitarian concern;

6. *Calls on* all parties and others concerned to cooperate with UNPROFOR and international humanitarian agencies to facilitate the provision of humanitarian aid to other areas of Bosnia and Herzegovina which remain in desperate need of assistance;

7. *Reiterates* its demand that all parties and others concerned take the necessary measures to secure the safety of UNPROFOR personnel;

8. *Calls again on* all parties concerned to resolve their differences through a negotiated political solution to the problems in the region and to that end to cooperate with the renewed efforts of the European Community and its member States, with the support of the States participating in the Conference on Security and Cooperation in Europe, within the framework of the Conference on Yugoslavia, and in particular to respond positively to the invitation of the Chairman of the Conference to talks on 15 July 1992;

9. *Requests* the Secretary-General to keep close contact with the developments within the framework of the Conference on Yugoslavia and to assist in finding a negotiated political solution for the conflict in Bosnia and Herzegovina;

10. *Reaffirms* that all parties are bound to comply with the obligations under international humanitarian law and in particular the Geneva Conventions of 12 August 1949, and that persons who commit or order the commission of grave breaches of the Conventions are individually responsible in respect of such breaches;

11. *Requests* the Secretary-General to keep under continuous review any further measure that may be required to ensure unimpeded delivery of humanitarian assistance;

12. *Decides* to remain actively seized of the matter.

Security Council resolution 764(1992)

13 July 1992   Meeting 3093   Adopted unanimously

Draft prepared in consultations among Council members (S/24267), orally corrected.

Following the signing of a cease-fire agreement on 17 July[39] by representatives of the three opposing parties, at a meeting held in London within the framework of the Conference on Yugoslavia, the Security Council convened on the same date. The agreement was to be effective as of 19 July for a period of 14 days, during which time all parties would explore measures for strengthening the cease-fire in the longer term. They also agreed to place all heavy weapons under international supervision, under arrangements to be made by the

Council. In addition, all refugees would be permitted to return to the places from which they had been expelled and civilians caught in military situations would be given freedom of movement.

The Council invited Bosnia and Herzegovina, at its request, to participate in the discussion without the right to vote, under rule 37[a] of the Council's provisional rules of procedure. Following consultations, the President of the Council made a statement:[(40)]

Meeting number. SC 3097.

"The Security Council welcomes the agreement between the parties in Bosnia and Herzegovina, signed at London on 17 July 1992 within the framework of the Conference on Yugoslavia.

"The Council calls on the parties to comply fully with the agreement in all its aspects. In particular, it calls on all parties and others concerned to observe scrupulously the cease-fire throughout the entire territory of Bosnia and Herzegovina.

"The Council has decided in principle to respond positively to the request for the United Nations to make arrangements for the supervision by the United Nations Protection Force (UNPROFOR) of all heavy weapons (combat aircraft, armour, artillery, mortars, rocket-launchers, etc.) in accordance with the agreement of 17 July 1992. It calls on the parties to declare immediately to the Force Commander of UNPROFOR the locations and quantities of the heavy weapons to be placed under supervision. It requests the Secretary-General to report by 20 July on the implementation and resource implications of this decision.

"The Council welcomes the provisions in the agreement concerning the return of all refugees and freedom of movement for civilians caught up in or trapped by the military situation. It also welcomes the efforts being made to mobilize international assistance in handling the refugee problem under the aegis of UNHCR. It invites the Secretary-General and the United Nations humanitarian agencies concerned to make the maximum use of the cease-fire now proclaimed to bring humanitarian relief and supplies to all parts of Bosnia and Herzegovina.

"The Council expresses its satisfaction that the talks on future constitutional arrangements for Bosnia and Herzegovina are to resume in London on 27 July 1992, and urges all the parties to contribute actively and positively to these talks so that a peaceful solution is achieved as soon as possible.

"The Council stresses the need for full compliance with all the requirements of the relevant resolutions of the Council towards which the agreement reached in London on 17 July 1992 is an important step. It reaffirms its decision to remain actively seized of the matter and to consider immediately, whenever necessary, further steps to achieve a peaceful solution in conformity with those resolutions."

Report of the Secretary-General (21 July). In accordance with the Council's decision in principle to respond positively to the parties' request for international supervision of all their heavy weapons, the Force Commander immediately instructed his Sector Commander at Sarajevo to contact the parties with a view to identifying the locations and quantities of heavy weapons to be supervised, the Secretary-General reported on 21 July.[(41)] However, no relevant information was made available by any of the parties, two of which had not responded at all. In those circumstances, the Force Commander submitted on 19 July a proposed concept of operations for UNPROFOR to supervise the parties' heavy weapons, on the basis of information available to him from public sources.

The concept, as outlined in an annex to the Secretary-General's report, envisaged the deployment of United Nations military observers throughout the territory of Bosnia and Herzegovina, other than Sarajevo where separate arrangements were in effect. The observers would supervise the heavy weapons of all parties to the conflict. Some 1,100 of them would be required; they would be based in 62 equipment-collection points, grouped into seven patrol areas. Teams of six observers at each collection point would conduct patrols on a 24-hour basis. The observers would need vehicles, communications equipment, office equipment and working space, as well as technical and administrative support.

Based on the assumption that implementation of the 17 July agreement would open up access to many areas where there were pressing humanitarian needs and that UNPROFOR would be expected to help the agencies respond to those needs, the concept envisaged that the observers would have an important role in helping UNHCR and other humanitarian agencies identify requirements for humanitarian relief.

The success of such an operation depended on the cooperation of the parties, who would be required to declare all the heavy weapons in their possession and to cooperate with UNPROFOR in concentrating them at locations where they could be monitored. It would also be necessary for the parties to demonstrate a genuine commitment to a sustained cease-fire.

The Secretary-General felt that conditions did not exist for him to recommend that the Security Council accept the request to supervise the heavy weapons to be declared by the parties. The request called into question the relationship of the United Nations to regional organizations, which was set up in the Charter to allow for the Council to utilize such organizations, with no provision for the reverse. Also, the United Nations had not participated in the agreement and the respective roles of the United Nations and EC in its implementation were unclear. In addition, the 19 July cease-fire had not come into effect in Sarajevo, nor apparently anywhere else in Bosnia and Herzegovina.

UNPROFOR was already stretched to the breaking-point and could not assume functions beyond its current capability. The United Nations was already massively engaged in the former Yugoslavia, and continued extensive concentration on that problem might be at the expense of the Organization's ability to help resolve equally dangerous conflicts elsewhere.

SECURITY COUNCIL ACTION (24 July and 4 August)

The Security Council met on 24 July to consider the Secretary-General's report. The Council invited Bosnia and Herzegovina, at its request, to participate in the discussion without the right to vote.

Following consultations, the President made a statement on behalf of the Council:[42]

Meeting number. SC 3100.

"The Security Council recalls the statement of its President of 17 July 1992 concerning the Agreement signed in London on 17 July by the parties in Bosnia and Herzegovina.

"The Security Council takes note with appreciation of the Secretary-General's report submitted to it, in response to its request of 17 July 1992, together with a Concept of Operations.

"The Council invites the Secretary-General to contact all Member States, particularly the Member States of the relevant regional organizations in Europe, to ask them to make urgently available to the Secretary-General information about the personnel, equipment and logistic support which they would be prepared to contribute, individually or collectively, to the supervision of heavy weapons in Bosnia and Herzegovina as described in the Secretary-General's report.

"In the light of the outcome of these contacts, the Secretary-General will undertake the further preparatory work needed on the supervision of the heavy weapons in Bosnia and Herzegovina.

"Recalling the provisions of Chapter VIII of the United Nations Charter, the Council invites the European regional arrangements and agencies concerned, particularly the European Community, to enhance their cooperation with the Secretary-General in their efforts to help to resolve the conflicts that continue to rage in the former Yugoslavia. In particular, it would welcome the participation of the Secretary-General in any negotiations under European Community auspices.

"The Council further invites the European Community in cooperation with the Secretary-General of the United Nations to examine the possibility of broadening and intensifying the present Conference with a view to providing a new momentum in the search for negotiated settlements of the various conflicts and disputes in the former Yugoslavia.

"The Council underlines the importance of the parties to the Agreement signed at London on 17 July 1992 honouring fully the terms of that Agreement and calls on others concerned also to respect the Agreement. It emphasizes in particular the need for the parties to respect and maintain a cease-fire throughout the entire territory of Bosnia and Herzegovina, and for them to declare immediately to the Force Commander of UNPROFOR the locations and quantities of the heavy weapons to be placed under supervision. It further demands that the parties and others concerned cooperate fully with UNPROFOR and the humanitarian agencies and take all necessary steps to ensure the safety of their personnel.

"The Council stresses the need for full compliance with all the requirements of its relevant resolutions and stands ready to consider immediately, whenever necessary, further steps to achieve a peaceful solution in conformity with its relevant resolutions.

"The Council requests the Secretary-General to report back to it on the further work being undertaken and remains actively seized of the matter."

On 4 August, the Council met at the urgent requests of the United States[43] and Venezuela[44] over reports in the media on concentration camps and the torture of citizens in Bosnia and Herzegovina. That republic, at its request, participated in the meeting without vote under rule 37[a] of the Council's provisional rules of procedure.

Following consultations, the President made a statement on behalf of the Council:[45]

Meeting number. SC 3103.

"The Security Council is deeply concerned at the continuing reports of widespread violations of international humanitarian law and in particular reports of the imprisonment and abuse of civilians in camps, prisons and detention centres within the territory of the former Yugoslavia and especially in Bosnia and Herzegovina. The Council condemns any such violations and abuses and demands that relevant international organizations, and in particular the International Committee of the Red Cross, be granted immediate, unimpeded and continued access to all such places and calls upon all parties to do all in their power to facilitate such access. The Council further calls upon all parties, States, international organizations and non-governmental organizations to make immediately available to the Council any further information they might possess regarding these camps and access to them.

"The Council reaffirms that all parties are bound to comply with the obligations under international humanitarian law and in particular the Geneva Conventions of 12 August 1949, and that persons who commit or order the commission of grave breaches of the Conventions are individually responsible in respect of such breaches.

"The Council will remain actively seized of this issue."

On the same date, the Council President made a statement to the press:[46]

"The members of the Security Council condemn the recent cowardly attack on UNPROFOR positions in Sarajevo resulting in loss of life and injuries among the Ukrainian servicemen. The members of the Council note that UNPROFOR has already commenced investigation of this incident.

"The members of the Council express their condolences to the family of the officer killed and to the Government of Ukraine.

"The members of the Council also express their condolences to the families of the two French officers of UNPROFOR killed in Croatia and to the Government of France.

"The members of the Council call upon all parties to ensure that those responsible for these intolerable acts are quickly called to account.

"The members of the Council reiterate their demand that all parties and others concerned take the necessary measures to secure the safety of UNPROFOR personnel."

Information contained in two UNPROFOR memoranda, on the evident existence of concentration camps, "ethnic cleansing" and other violations of international humanitarian law in Bosnia and Herzegovina, was transmitted by that republic's Government to the President of the Security Council on 5[47] and 7 August,[48] pursuant to the request made by the President in his 4 August statement. Five concentration camps holding Muslims and Croatians in the republic were identified. The treatment of Muslims and other minorities in the camps was reported to be atrocious, with regular beatings, deprivation of food and water and poor shelter, among other things. The situation was deteriorating and even spilling over to the UNPAs. In an announcement published by the News Agency of Bosnia and Herzegovina on 1 August, annexed to the letter of 5 August, it was charged that, according to reliable information, similar detention camps existed in Serbia and Montenegro. Some 130,000 citizens of Bosnia and Herzegovina were estimated to be in 96 camps there.

SECURITY COUNCIL ACTION (13 August)

On 13 August, the Security Council met at the urgent request of Bosnia and Herzegovina,[49] as well as of Bahrain,[50] the Comoros,[51] Egypt,[52] Iran,[53] Kuwait,[54] Malaysia,[55] Pakistan,[56] Qatar,[57] Saudi Arabia,[58] Senegal,[59] Turkey[60] and the United Arab Emirates.[61] In forwarding its request, Bosnia and Herzegovina cited serious violations of human rights and international law. It requested that the Council consider taking measures provided for in Chapter VII of the United Nations Charter to restore peace and security in the region.

The Council invited Bosnia and Herzegovina, at its request, to participate without vote under rule 37[a] of the Council's provisional rules of procedure.

The Council adopted **resolution 770(1992)**.

The Security Council,

Reaffirming its resolutions 713(1991) of 25 September 1991, 721(1991) of 27 November 1991, 724(1991) of 15 December 1991, 727(1992) of 8 January 1992, 740(1992) of 7 February 1992, 743(1992) of 21 February 1992, 749(1992) of 7 April 1992, 752(1992) of 15 May 1992, 757(1992) of 30 May 1992, 758(1992) of 8 June 1992, 760(1992) of 18 June 1992, 761(1992) of 29 June 1992, 762(1992) of 30 June 1992, 764(1992) of 13 July 1992 and 769(1992) of 7 August 1992,

Noting the letter dated 10 August 1992 from the Permanent Representative of the Republic of Bosnia and Herzegovina to the United Nations,

Underlining once again the imperative need for an urgent negotiated political solution to the situation in the Republic of Bosnia and Herzegovina to enable that country to live in peace and security within its borders,

Reaffirming the need to respect the sovereignty, territorial integrity and political independence of the Republic of Bosnia and Herzegovina,

Recognizing that the situation in Bosnia and Herzegovina constitutes a threat to international peace and security and that the provision of humanitarian assistance in Bosnia and Herzegovina is an important element in the Council's effort to restore international peace and security in the area,

Commending the United Nations Protection Force (UNPROFOR) for its continuing action in support of the relief operation in Sarajevo and other parts of Bosnia and Herzegovina,

Deeply disturbed by the situation that now prevails in Sarajevo, which has severely complicated UNPROFOR's efforts to fulfil its mandate to ensure the security and functioning of Sarajevo airport and the delivery of humanitarian assistance in Sarajevo and other parts of Bosnia and Herzegovina pursuant to resolutions 743(1992), 749(1992), 761(1992) and 764(1992) and the reports of the Secretary-General cited therein,

Dismayed by the continuation of conditions that impede the delivery of humanitarian supplies to destinations within Bosnia and Herzegovina and the consequent suffering of the people of that country,

Deeply concerned by reports of abuses against civilians imprisoned in camps, prisons and detention centres,

Determined to establish as soon as possible the necessary conditions for the delivery of humanitarian assistance wherever needed in Bosnia and Herzegovina, in conformity with resolution 764(1992),

Acting under Chapter VII of the Charter of the United Nations,

1. *Reaffirms* its demand that all parties and others concerned in Bosnia and Herzegovina stop the fighting immediately;

2. *Calls upon* States to take nationally or through regional agencies or arrangements all measures necessary to facilitate in coordination with the United Nations the delivery by relevant United Nations humanitarian organizations and others of humanitarian assistance to Sarajevo and wherever needed in other parts of Bosnia and Herzegovina;

3. *Demands* that unimpeded and continuous access to all camps, prisons and detention centres be granted immediately to the International Committee of the Red Cross and other relevant humanitarian organizations and that all detainees therein receive humane treatment, including adequate food, shelter and medical care;

4. *Calls upon* States to report to the Secretary-General on measures they are taking in coordination with the United Nations to carry out this resolution, and *invites* the Secretary-General to keep under continuous review any further measures that may be necessary to ensure unimpeded delivery of humanitarian supplies;

5. *Requests* all States to provide appropriate support for the actions undertaken in pursuance of this resolution;

6. *Demands* that all parties and others concerned take the necessary measures to ensure the safety of United Nations and other personnel engaged in the delivery of humanitarian assistance;

7. *Requests* the Secretary-General to report to the Council on a periodic basis on the implementation of this resolution;

8. *Decides* to remain actively seized of the matter.

Security Council resolution 770(1992)

13 August 1992   Meeting 3106   12-0-3

5-nation draft (S/24421).
Sponsors: Belgium, France, Russian Federation, United Kingdom, United States.
Vote in Council as follows:

In favour: Austria, Belgium, Cape Verde, Ecuador, France, Hungary, Japan, Morocco, Russian Federation, United Kingdom, United States, Venezuela.
Against: None.
Abstaining: China, India, Zimbabwe.

The Council unanimously adopted **resolution 771(1992)**.

The Security Council,

Reaffirming its resolutions 713(1991) of 25 September 1991, 721(1991) of 27 November 1991, 724(1991) of 15 December 1991, 727(1992) of 8 January 1992, 740(1992) of 7 February 1992, 743(1992) of 21 February 1992, 749(1992) of 7 April 1992, 752(1992) of 15 May 1992, 757(1992) of 30 May 1992, 758(1992) of 8 June 1992, 760(1992) of 18 June 1992, 761(1992) of 29 June 1992, 762(1992) of 30 June 1992, 764(1992) of 13 July 1992, 769(1992) of 7 August 1992 and 770(1992) of 13 August 1992,

Noting the letter dated 10 August 1992 from the Permanent Representative of the Republic of Bosnia and Herzegovina to the United Nations,

Expressing grave alarm at continuing reports of widespread violations of international humanitarian law occurring within the territory of the former Yugoslavia and especially in Bosnia and Herzegovina including reports of mass forcible expulsion and deportation of civilians, imprisonment and abuse of civilians in detention centres, deliberate attacks on non-combatants, hospitals and ambulances, impeding the delivery of food and medical supplies to the civilian population, and wanton devastation and destruction of property,

Recalling the statement of the President of the Council of 4 August 1992,

1. *Reaffirms* that all parties to the conflict are bound to comply with their obligations under international humanitarian law and in particular the Geneva Conventions of 12 August 1949, and that persons who commit or order the commission of grave breaches of the Conventions are individually responsible in respect of such breaches;

2. *Strongly condemns* any violations of international humanitarian law, including those involved in the practice of "ethnic cleansing";

3. *Demands* that all parties and others concerned in the former Yugoslavia, and all military forces in Bosnia and Herzegovina, immediately cease and desist from all breaches of international humanitarian law including from actions such as those described above;

4. *Further demands* that relevant international humanitarian organizations, and in particular the International Committee of the Red Cross, be granted immediate, unimpeded and continued access to camps, prisons and detention centres within the territory of the former Yugoslavia and *calls upon* all parties to do all in their power to facilitate such access;

5. *Calls upon* States and, as appropriate, international humanitarian organizations to collate substantiated information in their possession or submitted to them relating to the violations of humanitarian law, including grave breaches of the Geneva Conventions, being committed in the territory of the former Yugoslavia and to make this information available to the Council;

6. *Requests* the Secretary-General to collate the information submitted to the Council under paragraph 5 and to submit a report to the Council summarizing the information and recommending additional measures that might be appropriate in response to the information;

7. *Decides,* acting under Chapter VII of the Charter of the United Nations, that all parties and others concerned in the former Yugoslavia, and all military forces in Bosnia and Herzegovina, shall comply with the provisions of the present resolution, failing which the Council will need to take further measures under the Charter;

8. *Decides* to remain actively seized of the matter.

Security Council resolution 771(1992)

13 August 1992   Meeting 3106   Adopted unanimously

5-nation draft (S/24422).
Sponsors: Belgium, France, Russian Federation, United Kingdom, United States.

Human Rights Commission action (13 and 14 August). By a letter of 5 August, the United States requested the convening of the Commission on Human Rights to discuss the dangerous situation in the former Yugoslavia. The majority of the Commission's members being in agreement, the Commission held its first special session on 13 and 14 August (see PART THREE, Chapter X), at which it adopted a resolution on the human rights situation in the former Yugoslavia, which was endorsed by the Economic and Social Council in **decision 1992/305.** The Sub-Commission on Prevention of Discrimination and Protection of Minorities dealt with human rights violations, including "ethnic cleansing", in a decision of 13 August. In accordance with the Commission resolution, a Special Rapporteur was appointed to investigate first-hand the human rights situation in the former Yugoslavia.

GENERAL ASSEMBLY ACTION (25 August)

On 25 August, at its resumed forty-sixth session, the General Assembly adopted **resolution 46/242** by recorded vote.

The situation in Bosnia and Herzegovina

The General Assembly,

Having considered the item entitled "The situation in Bosnia and Herzegovina",

Reaffirming the purposes and principles of the Charter of the United Nations and guided by the need to implement them,

Aware of its responsibility to promote and encourage respect for international legitimacy,

Considering that the United Nations, pursuant to the provisions of its Charter, has a major role to play in, and responsibility for, the maintenance of international peace and security,

Recalling the relevant resolutions of the Security Council, the United Nations Educational, Scientific and Cultural Organization and the Commission on Human Rights, as well as Economic and Social Council decision 1992/305 of 18 August 1992,

Noting that a large number of States have reserved their position regarding the succession of the Socialist Federal Republic of Yugoslavia by the Federal Republic of Yugoslavia (Serbia and Montenegro),

Deploring the grave situation in Bosnia and Herzegovina and the serious deterioration of the living conditions of the people there, especially the Muslim and Croat populations, arising from the aggression against the territory of the Republic of Bosnia and Herzegovina, which constitutes a threat to international peace and security,

Alarmed by the prospect of further escalation of the fighting in the region,

Expressing grave alarm at continuing reports of widespread violations of international humanitarian law occurring within the territory of the former Yugoslavia and especially in Bosnia and Herzegovina, including reports of mass forcible expulsion and deportation of civilians, imprisonment and abuse of civilians in detention centres and deliberate attacks on non-combatants, hospitals and ambulances, impeding the delivery of food and medical supplies to the civilian population, as well as wanton devastation and destruction of property,

Strongly condemning the abhorrent practice of "ethnic cleansing", which constitutes a grave and serious violation of international humanitarian law,

Recalling the report of the Secretary-General of 12 May 1992, in which he states that "all international observers agree that what is happening is a concerted effort by the Serbs of Bosnia and Herzegovina, with the acquiescence of, and at least some support from, the Yugoslav People's Army, to create 'ethnically pure' regions in the context of negotiations on the 'cantonization' of the Republic in the Conference of the European Community on Bosnia and Herzegovina'',

Expressing grave concern that, despite the relevant resolutions of the Security Council, no effective measure has been implemented to stop the abhorrent practice of "ethnic cleansing", or to reverse and discourage the policies and proposals that might encourage it,

Appalled by the continuing reports of widespread, massive and grave violations of human rights perpetrated within the territory of the former Yugoslavia and especially in Bosnia and Herzegovina, including reports of summary and arbitrary executions, forced disappearances, torture, rape and other cruel, inhuman or degrading treatment, as well as arbitrary arrest and detention,

Expressing grave concern that, despite repeated demands by the Security Council, the cease-fire agreed upon by all parties has not been respected,

Concerned that other demands made by the Security Council in its relevant resolutions, especially resolutions 752(1992) of 15 May 1992, 757(1992) of 30 May 1992, 764(1992) of 13 July 1992 and 770(1992) and 771(1992) of 13 August 1992, have not been complied with,

Reaffirming the necessity of respecting the sovereignty, territorial integrity, political independence and national unity of the Republic of Bosnia and Herzegovina, and rejecting any attempt to change the boundaries of that Republic,

Reaffirming also the inherent right of the Republic of Bosnia and Herzegovina to individual or collective self-defence in accordance with Article 51 of the Charter,

Underlining the imperative need for an urgent peaceful solution to the situation in Bosnia and Herzegovina, in conformity with the Charter and the principles of international law, in particular the principles of respect for sovereignty and territorial integrity of States, non-recognition of the fruits of aggression and non-recognition

of the acquisition of territory by force, and welcoming in this context the International Conference on the Former Yugoslavia, scheduled to be convened in London on 26 August 1992,

Commending the efforts of the Secretary-General, the Security Council, United Nations agencies, including the Office of the United Nations High Commissioner for Refugees, and other international and relief organizations, including the Organization of the Islamic Conference, the European Community, the Conference on Security and Cooperation in Europe and the International Committee of the Red Cross,

Commending also the United Nations Protection Force for its continuing action in support of the relief operation in Sarajevo and other parts of Bosnia and Herzegovina,

Deeply concerned about the safety of the personnel of the United Nations Protection Force and expressing sympathy for the losses suffered by them,

1. *Demands* that all parties to the conflict immediately stop fighting and find a peaceful solution in line with the Charter of the United Nations and the principles of international law, in particular the principles of respect for sovereignty and territorial integrity of States, non-recognition of the fruits of aggression and non-recognition of the acquisition of territory by force;

2. *Demands also* that all forms of interference from outside the Republic of Bosnia and Herzegovina cease immediately;

3. *Demands further* that those units of the Yugoslav People's Army and elements of the Croatian Army now in Bosnia and Herzegovina must either be withdrawn, or be subject to the authority of the Government of Bosnia and Herzegovina, or be disbanded and disarmed with their weapons placed under effective international monitoring, and requests the Secretary-General to consider without delay what kind of international assistance could be provided in this connection;

4. *Reaffirms* its support for the Government and people of the Republic of Bosnia and Herzegovina in their just struggle to safeguard their sovereignty, political independence, territorial integrity and unity;

5. *Urges* the Security Council to consider, on an urgent basis, taking further appropriate measures, as provided in Chapter VII of the Charter, to put an end to the fighting and to restore the unity and the territorial integrity of the Republic of Bosnia and Herzegovina;

6. *Condemns* the violation of the sovereignty, territorial integrity and political independence of the Republic of Bosnia and Herzegovina as well as the massive violations of human rights and international humanitarian law, in particular the abhorrent practice of "ethnic cleansing", and demands that this practice be brought to an end immediately and that further steps be taken, on an urgent basis, to stop the massive and forcible displacement of population from and within the Republic of Bosnia and Herzegovina, as well as all other forms of violation of human rights in the former Yugoslavia;

7. *Affirms* that States are to be held accountable for violations of human rights which their agents commit upon the territory of another State;

8. *Calls upon* all States and international organizations not to recognize the consequences of the acquisition of territory by force and of the abhorrent practice of "ethnic cleansing";

9. *Demands* that the International Committee of the Red Cross be granted immediate, unimpeded and continued access to all camps, prisons and other places of detention within the territory of the former Yugoslavia and that all parties ensure complete safety and freedom of movement for the International Committee and otherwise facilitate such access;

10. *Demands also* the safe, unconditional and honourable repatriation of the refugees and deportees to their homes in Bosnia and Herzegovina and recognizes their right to receive reparation for their losses;

11. *Calls upon* organs of the United Nations and all international relief agencies to facilitate the return of the displaced people to their homes in the Republic of Bosnia and Herzegovina, as well as their rehabilitation;

12. *Commends* the untiring efforts and the bravery of the United Nations Protection Force in securing the relief operation in the Republic of Bosnia and Herzegovina, as well as the efforts of the Office of the United Nations High Commissioner for Refugees and other relief agencies;

13. *Urges* all parties and others concerned to take the necessary measures to secure the safety of the United Nations Protection Force and all other United Nations personnel;

14. *Urges* all States to support the ongoing efforts to be taken in accordance with the relevant Security Council resolutions to facilitate the delivery of humanitarian assistance to all parts of the Republic of Bosnia and Herzegovina;

15. *Requests* the Secretary-General to report to the General Assembly at its forty-seventh session on the implementation of the present resolution;

16. *Decides* to remain seized of the matter and to continue its consideration of this item at its forty-seventh session.

General Assembly resolution 46/242

25 August 1992   Meeting 91   136-1-5 (recorded vote)

44-nation draft (A/46/L.76 & Add.1); agenda item 150.

Sponsors: Afghanistan, Albania, Algeria, Austria, Azerbaijan, Bangladesh, Bosnia and Herzegovina, Colombia, Comoros, Costa Rica, Croatia, Djibouti, Egypt, El Salvador, Estonia, Germany, Guinea, Guinea-Bissau, Indonesia, Iran, Italy, Jordan, Kuwait, Latvia, Lithuania, Malaysia, Malta, Marshall Islands, Mauritania, Micronesia, Morocco, Netherlands, Niger, Oman, Pakistan, Peru, Qatar, Saudi Arabia, Senegal, Slovenia, Sudan, Tunisia, Turkey, United Arab Emirates.
Meeting numbers. GA 46th session: plenary 89-91.

Recorded vote in Assembly as follows:

In favour: Afghanistan, Albania, Algeria, Angola, Argentina, Armenia, Australia, Austria, Azerbaijan, Bahamas, Bahrain, Bangladesh, Barbados, Belarus, Belgium, Belize, Bolivia, Bosnia and Herzegovina, Botswana, Brazil, Brunei Darussalam, Bulgaria, Burkina Faso, Cameroon, Canada, Cape Verde, Chile, China, Colombia, Comoros, Congo, Costa Rica, Côte d'Ivoire, Croatia, Cuba, Cyprus, Czechoslovakia, Denmark, Djibouti, Ecuador, Egypt, El Salvador, Estonia, Fiji, Finland, France, Gabon, Germany, Greece, Grenada, Guatemala, Guinea, Guinea-Bissau, Guyana, Honduras, Hungary, Iceland, India, Indonesia, Iran, Iraq, Ireland, Israel, Italy, Jamaica, Japan, Jordan, Kuwait, Kyrgyzstan, Latvia, Lebanon, Libyan Arab Jamahiriya, Liechtenstein, Lithuania, Luxembourg, Madagascar, Malaysia, Maldives, Malta, Marshall Islands, Mauritania, Mexico, Micronesia, Mongolia, Morocco, Mozambique, Myanmar, Nepal, Netherlands, New Zealand, Nicaragua, Nigeria, Norway, Oman, Pakistan, Panama, Paraguay, Peru, Philippines, Poland, Portugal, Qatar, Republic of Korea, Republic of Moldova, Romania, Rwanda, Saint Kitts and Nevis, Saint Vincent and the Grenadines, San Marino, Saudi Arabia, Senegal, Singapore, Slovenia, Spain, Sri Lanka, Sudan, Suriname, Sweden, Syrian Arab Republic, Thailand, Togo, Trinidad and Tobago, Tunisia, Turkey, Uganda, Ukraine, United Arab Emirates, United Kingdom, United Republic of Tanzania, United States, Uruguay, Venezuela, Viet Nam, Yemen, Zambia, Zimbabwe.

Against: Yugoslavia.

Abstaining: Ghana, Lesotho, Malawi, Namibia, Russian Federation.

An amendment by the Russian Federation,[62] which would have included in the eleventh preambular paragraph reference to a statement in the Secretary-General's report of 30 May[33] that international observers did not, however, doubt that portions of Bosnia and Herzegovina were under the control of Croatian military or paramilitary units, was rejected by 69 votes to 9, with 50 abstentions, following a motion by Turkey.

Yugoslavia (Serbia and Montenegro) said it supported the resolution's call for an immediate and effective cease-fire, as well as the condemnation of human rights violations and "ethnic cleansing". Regrettably, the resolution contained some statements which distorted facts and some of its portions were not consonant with the real wish to restore peace. The sixth preambular paragraph contained a statement that had no connection to the item under discussion. The seventh preambular paragraph was discriminatory, emphasizing the serious deterioration of living conditions of Muslims and Croats, but excluding the Serbs, who constituted one third of Bosnia and Herzegovina's population. The fact that neither side in the civil war was blameless with regard to human rights violations and "ethnic cleansing" should have been clearly reflected in the eleventh preambular paragraph. With regard to paragraph 3, JNA had ceased to exist and not a single soldier of the Federal Republic of Yugoslavia remained on the territory of Bosnia and Herzegovina. The dangerous request for military intervention would result in more bloodshed and destruction. In addition, the resolution failed to support strong negotiations and a peaceful settlement between the three constituent nations living in Bosnia and Herzegovina.

In a letter of 2 September to the Security Council,[63] the President of the General Assembly summarized the views prevailing in the Assembly during its debate on the situation in Bosnia and Herzegovina. While commending the role being played by the Secretary-General, the Council, UNPROFOR and United Nations agencies, it was felt that the United Nations as a whole could do much more to find an urgent solution, to safeguard the republic's sovereignty, territorial integrity, political independence and national unity, and to put an end to the fighting and the grave violations of international humanitarian law. A great number of Member States also felt that the arms embargo precluded Bosnia and Herzegovina's inherent right to self-defence and that action should be taken to rectify that. Further, it was stressed that the time factor was vital, as it was working against the victims and to the advantage of the Bosnian Serbs. Those views were reflected in several provisions of the Assembly resolution.

The Assembly President expressed the hope that the Council would take urgent action on the resolution, which represented the collective will of an overwhelming majority of the United Nations membership.

Replying on 14 September,[64] the Council President said the Council had dealt with the problems in former Yugoslavia virtually on a continuous basis over the past 12 months and would do its utmost to bring about an end to them.

SECURITY COUNCIL ACTION (9 September)

Following an incident on 3 September that cost the lives of four Italian airmen delivering humanitarian aid to Sarajevo and an attack on a humanitarian aid convoy on 8 September, during which two French soldiers were killed and five others wounded, the Security Council President, after consultations on 9 September, made the following statement on behalf of the Council:[65]

Meeting number. SC 3113.

''The Security Council has noted with deep concern the attack which cost the lives of two French soldiers of UNPROFOR near Sarajevo, during which five other soldiers were wounded. It conveys its deep-felt sympathy and condolences to the Government of France and to the bereaved families. It strongly condemns this deliberate attack against UNPROFOR personnel.

''The Council invites the Secretary-General to inform it as soon as possible on the findings of the inquiry into the circumstances of this attack as well as other similar incidents involving the United Nations activities in Bosnia and Herzegovina, in particular the incident which cost the lives of four Italian airmen in charge of the transportation of humanitarian relief to Sarajevo airport. It invites him also to pass on to it any information which he could gather on the responsibility for these incidents.

''The serious incidents underline the urgent need for reinforcing the security and protection of UNPROFOR personnel as well as of all personnel involved in the United Nations activities in Bosnia and Herzegovina. The Security Council expresses its readiness to adopt without delay measures to this end.''

In a statement of 10 September,[66] Yugoslavia (Serbia and Montenegro) strongly condemned the attack on the French soldiers, saying that it endangered the ongoing peace process. It pointed out that it had fulfilled its obligations and secured free and safe passage of the convoy on the road from Belgrade to Sarajevo.

Report and communication of the Secretary-General (10 September). Proposals for the delivery of humanitarian assistance under the protection of UNPROFOR to Sarajevo and other parts of Bosnia and Herzegovina were outlined by the Secretary-General in a report of 10 September.[67] Following adoption of resolution 770(1992) on 13 August, the Secretary-General explained, a number of its co-sponsors had communicated to him their views on how the delivery of such assistance could be facilitated through protective support by

UNPROFOR, a function that could be added to UNPROFOR's mandate and carried out by military personnel, under the UNPROFOR Commander. Some of the Member States concerned indicated their readiness to provide the necessary military personnel, equipment and logistic support at no cost to the United Nations. The Secretary-General welcomed that approach, especially with regard to its financial aspects.

The proposals recognized UNHCR as lead agency for humanitarian activities in the former Yugoslavia. UNPROFOR's task, under its enlarged mandate, would be to support and protect the efforts of UNHCR, which would determine priorities and schedules for the delivery of relief, organize the convoys, negotiate safe passage along intended routes (with UNPROFOR assistance as required), and coordinate requests from non-governmental organizations (NGOs) and other agencies wishing to join its convoys. UNHCR would establish regional storage and distribution centres at 11 locations in Bosnia and Herzegovina, including Sarajevo, which would be accessible from Croatia and/or Serbia and Montenegro. UNPROFOR would protect convoys moving to the regional centres and to local distribution points; it would also protect United Nations facilities, including UNHCR storage centres. Additional military elements would include a transport battalion to be used when UNHCR determined specific routes to be particularly difficult; in other cases, UNHCR trucks would be escorted by UNPROFOR military vehicles and personnel.

Operational decisions relating to a protected convoy, including action to be taken in the event of obstacles to delivery, would be made by the UNPROFOR escort commander, in consultation with the senior UNHCR representative. In providing protection, UNPROFOR troops would follow normal peace-keeping rules of engagement and would thus be authorized to use force in self-defence, including in situations where attempts were made by armed persons to prevent its troops from fulfilling their mandate.

Overall command and control of the operation would be exercised by the Force Commander. A new Bosnia and Herzegovina Command, based at Sarajevo, would assume responsibility for all peace-keeping operations in the republic. The Command would consist of Sector Sarajevo, which would continue to carry out the tasks outlined in Council resolutions 758(1992) and 761(1992), and four or five new zones to be defined after further consultation with UNHCR. Each zone would be assigned an infantry battalion group and civilian staff to undertake political, information and liaison functions.

If approved by the Security Council, the proposals would require a fourfold or fivefold increase in the number of troops and other UNPROFOR personnel currently in the republic. Upon Council approval, the Secretary-General would ask the Member States contributing additional elements to UNPROFOR to form a joint planning team and then finalize implementation arrangements together with the Force Commander and UNHCR.

The outlined concept seemed to provide the best possibility for ensuring increased deliveries of humanitarian relief to the suffering population of Bosnia and Herzegovina, the Secretary-General said. It would assure the Council's control of the operation, while avoiding additional financial burdens on the Organization.

By a letter of 10 September,[68] the Secretary-General informed the Council that he had been requested by Mr. Vance to seek Council authorization to use existing UNPROFOR resources to protect some 4,000 or more Muslim and Croat detainees who were expected to be released shortly from Serb detention camps at Manjaca and Trnopolje in the northern part of Bosnia and Herzegovina and to be taken to transit facilities in Croatia. Such assistance, the Secretary-General noted, would have to await the deployment of additional units he had recommended in his report.

The Council President, on 12 September,[69] conveyed the Council's agreement to the proposal.

SECURITY COUNCIL ACTION (14 September and 6 October)

On 14 September, the Security Council convened to consider the Secretary-General's report. The Council invited Bosnia and Herzegovina, at its request, to participate in the discussion without vote under rule 37[a] of the Council's provisional rules of procedure.

The Council adopted **resolution 776(1992)**.

The Security Council,

Reaffirming its resolution 743(1992) of 21 February 1992 and all subsequent resolutions relating to the United Nations Protection Force (UNPROFOR),

Expressing its full support for the Statement of Principles adopted and other agreements reached at the London Conference, including the agreement of the parties to the conflict to collaborate fully in the delivery of humanitarian relief by road throughout Bosnia and Herzegovina,

Having examined the report of the Secretary-General of 10 September 1992,

Noting with appreciation the offers made by a number of States, following the adoption of its resolution 770(1992) of 13 August 1992, to make available military personnel to facilitate the delivery by relevant United Nations humanitarian organizations and others of humanitarian assistance to Sarajevo and wherever needed in other parts of Bosnia and Herzegovina, such personnel to be made available to the United Nations without cost to the Organization,

Reaffirming its determination to ensure the protection and security of UNPROFOR and United Nations personnel,

Stressing in this context the importance of air measures, such as the ban on military flights to which all parties to the London Conference committed themselves, whose

rapid implementation could, *inter alia*, reinforce the security of humanitarian activities in Bosnia and Herzegovina,

1. *Approves* the report of the Secretary-General;

2. *Authorizes*, in implementation of paragraph 2 of resolution 770(1992), the enlargements of UNPROFOR's mandate and strength in Bosnia and Herzegovina recommended by the Secretary-General in that report to perform the functions outlined in the report, including the protection of convoys of released detainees if requested by the International Committee of the Red Cross;

3. *Further urges* Member States, nationally or through regional agencies or arrangements, to provide the Secretary-General with such financial or other assistance as he deems appropriate to assist in the performance of the functions outlined in his report;

4. *Decides* to remain actively seized of the matter in particular with a view to considering, as required, what further steps might be necessary to ensure UNPROFOR's security and to enable it to fulfil its mandate.

Security Council resolution 776(1992)

14 September 1992   Meeting 3114   12-0-3

5-nation draft (S/24554).

Sponsors: Belgium, France, Russian Federation, United Kingdom, United States.

Vote in Council as follows:

In favour: Austria, Belgium, Cape Verde, Ecuador, France, Hungary, Japan, Morocco, Russian Federation, United Kingdom, United States, Venezuela.

Against: None.

Abstaining: China, India, Zimbabwe.

On 6 October, the Council, in accordance with the understanding reached in prior consultations, met again to consider the issue of human rights violations in Bosnia and Herzegovina. An urgent meeting had been requested on 5 October by the Contact Group of OIC,[70] representing 47 States members and mandated by the Islamic Conference of Foreign Ministers to follow up the situation in Bosnia and Herzegovina and to keep developments in the former Yugoslavia under review.

The Council invited Bosnia and Herzegovina as well as Croatia, at their request, to participate without vote under rule 37[a] of the provisional rules of procedure.

The Council had before it, among other documents, a report on the situation of human rights in the former Yugoslavia by the Special Rapporteur of the Commission on Human Rights (see PART THREE, Chapter X), transmitted by the Secretary-General on 3 September.[71]

The Council adopted **resolution 780(1992)** unanimously.

The Security Council,

Reaffirming its resolution 713(1991) of 25 September 1991 and all subsequent relevant resolutions,

Recalling paragraph 10 of its resolution 764(1992) of 13 July 1992, in which it reaffirmed that all parties are bound to comply with the obligations under international humanitarian law and in particular the Geneva Conventions of 12 August 1949, and that persons who commit or order the commission of grave breaches of the Conventions are individually responsible in respect of such breaches,

Recalling also its resolution 771(1992) of 13 August 1992, in which, *inter alia*, it demanded that all parties and others concerned in the former Yugoslavia, and all military forces in Bosnia and Herzegovina, immediately cease and desist from all breaches of international humanitarian law,

Expressing once again its grave alarm at continuing reports of widespread violations of international humanitarian law occurring within the territory of the former Yugoslavia and especially in Bosnia and Herzegovina, including reports of mass killings and the continuance of the practice of ''ethnic cleansing'',

1. *Reaffirms* its call, in paragraph 5 of resolution 771(1992), upon States and, as appropriate, international humanitarian organizations to collate substantiated information in their possession or submitted to them relating to the violations of humanitarian law, including grave breaches of the Geneva Conventions being committed in the territory of the former Yugoslavia, and requests States, relevant United Nations bodies, and relevant organizations to make this information available within thirty days of the adoption of the present resolution and as appropriate thereafter, and to provide other appropriate assistance to the Commission of Experts referred to in paragraph 2 below;

2. *Requests* the Secretary-General to establish, as a matter of urgency, an impartial Commission of Experts to examine and analyse the information submitted pursuant to resolution 771(1992) and the present resolution, together with such further information as the Commission of Experts may obtain through its own investigations or efforts, of other persons or bodies pursuant to resolution 771(1992), with a view to providing the Secretary-General with its conclusions on the evidence of grave breaches of the Geneva Conventions and other violations of international humanitarian law committed in the territory of the former Yugoslavia;

3. *Also requests* the Secretary-General to report to the Council on the establishment of the Commission of Experts;

4. *Further requests* the Secretary-General to report to the Council on the conclusions of the Commission of Experts and to take account of these conclusions in any recommendations for further appropriate steps called for by resolution 771(1992);

5. *Decides* to remain actively seized of the matter.

Security Council resolution 780(1992)

6 October 1992   Meeting 3119   Adopted unanimously

7-nation draft (S/24618).

Sponsors: Belgium, France, Hungary, Morocco, United Kingdom, United States, Venezuela.

Commission of Experts. Pursuant to the Security Council's request in resolution 780(1992), the Secretary-General established a Commission of Experts to examine information containing evidence of grave breaches of the 1949 Geneva Conventions and other violations of international law committed in the former Yugoslavia, particularly in Bosnia and Herzegovina. In establishing the Commission, the Secretary-General said in a report of 14 October,[72] he had taken into account the mandate and work of the Special Rapporteur of the Commission on Human Rights, in order to minimize a duplication of efforts, maximize the efficient use of resources and reduce costs.

The Commission was to be located at Geneva. It was composed, in the first instance, of five members serving in their personal capacity. On 23 October, the Secretary-General informed the Council that he had appointed Professor Fritz Kalshoven (Netherlands) as President of the Commission, and Professor Cherif Bassiouni (Egypt), William Fenrick (Canada), Judge Kéba Mbaye (Senegal) and Professor Torkel Opsahl (Norway) as members.

The Commission held its first meeting on 4 and 5 November. It met with the Secretary-General, as well as with Hans Corell of Sweden, a member of the CSCE Mission under the Moscow Human Dimension Mechanism, whose report and recommendations it reviewed. It decided to analyse existing reports as well as examine applicable law, and was identifying practical problems inherent in investigating alleged incidents. It had before it information on alleged violations from Governments and United Nations sources, as well as from the International Conference on the Former Yugoslavia, CSCE and NGOs, including Helsinki Watch and Amnesty International.

SECURITY COUNCIL ACTION (9 and 30 October)

At a meeting on 9 October, the Security Council invited Bosnia and Herzegovina, at its request, to participate without vote under rule 37[a] of the Council's provisional rules of procedure, and adopted **resolution 781(1992)**.

The Security Council,

Reaffirming its resolution 713(1991) of 25 September 1991 and all subsequent relevant resolutions,

Determined to ensure the safety of humanitarian flights to Bosnia and Herzegovina,

Noting the readiness of the parties, expressed in the framework of the London Conference, to take appropriate steps in order to ensure the safety of humanitarian flights and their commitment at that Conference to a ban on military flights,

Recalling in this context the Joint Declaration signed at Geneva on 30 September 1992 by the Presidents of the Republic of Croatia and the Federal Republic of Yugoslavia (Serbia and Montenegro), and in particular paragraph 7 thereof,

Recalling also the agreement reached on air issues at Geneva on 15 September 1992 among all the parties concerned in the framework of the Working Group on Confidence and Security-building and Verification Measures of the London Conference,

Alarmed at reports that military flights over the territory of Bosnia and Herzegovina are none the less continuing,

Noting the letter of 4 October 1992 from the President of the Republic of Bosnia and Herzegovina addressed to the President of the Security Council,

Considering that the establishment of a ban on military flights in the airspace of Bosnia and Herzegovina constitutes an essential element for the safety of the delivery of humanitarian assistance and a decisive step for the cessation of hostilities in Bosnia and Herzegovina,

Acting pursuant to the provisions of resolution 770(1992) aimed at ensuring the safety of the delivery of humanitarian assistance in Bosnia and Herzegovina,

1. *Decides* to establish a ban on military flights in the airspace of Bosnia and Herzegovina, this ban not to apply to United Nations Protection Force flights or to other flights in support of United Nations operations, including humanitarian assistance;

2. *Requests* the United Nations Protection Force to monitor compliance with the ban on military flights, including the placement of observers where necessary at airfields in the territory of the former Yugoslavia;

3. *Also requests* the United Nations Protection Force to ensure, through an appropriate mechanism for approval and inspection, that the purpose of flights to and from Bosnia and Herzegovina other than those banned by paragraph 1 above is consistent with Security Council resolutions;

4. *Requests* the Secretary-General to report to the Council on a periodic basis on the implementation of the present resolution and to report immediately any evidence of violations;

5. *Calls upon* States to take nationally or through regional agencies or arrangements all measures necessary to provide assistance to the United Nations Protection Force, based on technical monitoring and other capabilities, for the purposes of paragraph 2 above;

6. *Undertakes* to examine without delay all the information brought to its attention concerning the implementation of the ban on military flights in Bosnia and Herzegovina and, in the case of violations, to consider urgently the further measures necessary to enforce this ban;

7. *Decides* to remain actively seized of the matter.

Security Council resolution 781(1992)

9 October 1992   Meeting 3122   14-0-1

7-nation draft (S/24636).

Sponsors: Austria, Belgium, France, Morocco, Russian Federation, United Kingdom, United States.

Vote in Council as follows:

In favour: Austria, Belgium, Cape Verde, Ecuador, France, Hungary, India, Japan, Morocco, Russian Federation, United Kingdom, United States, Venezuela, Zimbabwe.

Against: None.

Abstaining: China.

The agreement of 15 September on implementation of aerial confidence measures, including the ban on military use of aircraft, together with the report of the Chairman of the Working Group on Confidence and Security-building and Verification Measures, was transmitted to the Council by the United Kingdom.[73]

Presenting allegations on several occasions that the flight ban had been violated,[74] Bosnia and Herzegovina requested the Council to examine without delay all information brought to its attention concerning implementation of the ban and to consider urgently further measures necessary to enforce that ban.

On 30 October, the Council met again to consider the situation in Bosnia and Herzegovina and invited that country, at its request, to participate without vote under rule 37a of the Council's provisional rules of procedure.

Before the Council was a letter of 29 October from Bosnia and Herzegovina stating that the besieged city of Jajce had fallen to the aggressor and requesting UNPROFOR protection for fleeing civilians.[75]

Following consultations, the President made a statement authorized by the Council:[76]

"The Security Council remains concerned by the continuing conflict in the Republic of Bosnia and Herzegovina with its resultant loss of life and material damage, which threaten international peace and security, and by reports of egregious violations of international humanitarian law by whomsoever committed.

"The Security Council is appalled by the most recent reports that Serb militia in the Republic of Bosnia and Herzegovina are attacking civilians fleeing from the city of Jajce.

"The Council strongly condemns any such attacks which constitute grave violations of international humanitarian law, including the Geneva Conventions, and reaffirms that persons who commit or order the commission of grave breaches of these Conventions are individually responsible for such breaches. The Council wishes that such violations be brought to the attention of the Commission of Experts mentioned in resolution 780(1992).

"The Council demands that all such attacks cease immediately."

By a letter of 30 October,[77] President Izetbegovic reported continuing attacks on Jajce; over 20,000 women, children and elderly were fleeing the city.

Report of the Secretary-General (5 November). A plan for further deployment of UNPROFOR to monitor compliance with the ban on military flights over Bosnia and Herzegovina was set out in a 5 November report of the Secretary-General.[78] In order to monitor compliance and approve and inspect non-military flights to and from the republic, UNPROFOR developed a concept combining the deployment of military observers at selected airfields with information obtained from technical sources.

A Monitoring Coordination and Control Centre (MCCC), set up at UNPROFOR headquarters at Zagreb, would oversee all UNPROFOR activities arising from the new mandate set out in Council resolution 781(1992). All flights using the airspace of Bosnia and Herzegovina would be required to obtain prior approval from MCCC, with UNHCR liaison personnel clearing humanitarian assistance flights. All flights to Bosnia and Herzegovina would be required to depart from Belgrade, Zagreb or Split, Croatia, where they would be inspected. Inspections in Belgrade would be undertaken by UNPROFOR civilian police, while in Zagreb, they would be the responsibility of ECMM. The airfield at Split would be reserved for humanitarian assistance flights to be inspected by UNHCR.

Teams of up to five observers each would be deployed at 13 airfields in Bosnia and Herzegovina, Croatia and Yugoslavia (Serbia and Montenegro) to monitor all flight movements and inspect on arrival and departure aircraft whose flights into or out of Bosnia and Herzegovina had been approved by UNPROFOR. They would also have a mobile component available to travel to other airfields if so needed. MCCC would be notified of all flights detected over the republic, and then verify that they were UNPROFOR-approved. Any non-approved flights would be reported to the Security Council.

At the time of the report, UNPROFOR was in the process of establishing guidelines as to which categories of non-military flights, apart from humanitarian assistance, would be permitted.

To meet the immediate requirements arising from the new mandate, currently, 30 military observers from four existing peace-keeping operations were temporarily redeployed, and the measures described for monitoring compliance with the flight ban became operational to a limited extent as of 31 October.

The Force Commander estimated that 75 additional military observers with air-force experience, including 25 specialists with pilot and/or air-traffic controller qualifications, would be required, and three or four officers for MCCC.

The Presidents of Croatia and Yugoslavia (Serbia and Montenegro) welcomed the early stationing of international observers on airfields in their respective countries as a confidence-building measure. On 10 October, at the Working Group on Confidence and Security-building and Verification Measures of the International Conference on the Former Yugoslavia, both Governments agreed on certain practical aspects of the deployment of ECMM and UNPROFOR military observers.

On 31 October and 1 November, respectively, UNPROFOR concluded agreements with Yugoslavia (Serbia and Montenegro) and Croatia, regarding arrangements for the deployment of military observers on their respective airfields. The agreements provided for: access to the airfield flight-control system; observation of preparations for and performance of the flying missions of aircraft at the requested airfields; and inspection of all aircraft whose flights had been authorized by UNPROFOR. Similar agreements were signed with Bosnia and Herzegovina on 3 November, granting UNPROFOR unrestricted access to airfields in the republic, and separately with Radovan Karadzic regarding two airfields in the Banja Luka area.

Additional costs to cover the proposed enlargement of the Force's mandate were estimated at $4,485,000 for the six-month period from 1 November 1992 to 30 April 1993. The monthly cost thereafter would be approximately $520,000.

Information on possible violations of the ban on military flights over Bosnia and Herzegovina was presented to the President of the Security Council by the Secretary-General in a letter of 6 November,[79] pursuant to resolution 781(1992). According to reports from UNPROFOR, some 24 flights of fixed- or rotary-wing aircraft had taken place in the restricted airspace since 22 October. It had not been possible to determine from which airports the aircraft concerned were operating nor if those flights were military in nature and, therefore, fell under the ban. However, the specific allegations of an air attack on two villages on 31 October, made by Bosnia and Herzegovina on 2 November,[80] could not be confirmed. A log of the detected flights was annexed to the Secretary-General's report.

SECURITY COUNCIL ACTION (10 November)

On 10 November, the Security Council met to consider the Secretary-General's report. It invited Bosnia and Herzegovina, at its request, to participate without vote under rule 37[a] of the Council's provisional rules of procedure.

The Council unanimously adopted **resolution 786(1992)**.

The Security Council,

Reaffirming its resolution 781(1992) of 9 October 1992,

Taking note of the report of the Secretary-General of 5 November 1992 and his subsequent letter of 6 November 1992 submitted pursuant to resolution 781(1992),

Considering that the establishment of a ban on military flights in the airspace of Bosnia and Herzegovina constitutes an essential element for the safety of the delivery of humanitarian assistance and a decisive step for the cessation of hostilities in Bosnia and Herzegovina,

Taking into account the need for a speedy deployment of monitors on the ground for observation and verification purposes,

Gravely concerned at the indication in the Secretary-General's letter of 6 November 1992 of possible violations of its resolution 781(1992) and of the impossibility of corroborating the information on such violations by technical means presently available to the United Nations Protection Force,

Determined to ensure the safety of humanitarian flights to Bosnia and Herzegovina,

1. *Welcomes* the current advance deployment of military observers of the United Nations Protection Force and the European Community Monitoring Mission at airfields in Bosnia and Herzegovina, Croatia and the Federal Republic of Yugoslavia (Serbia and Montenegro);

2. *Reaffirms* its ban on military flights in the airspace of Bosnia and Herzegovina, which applies to all flights, whether of fixed-wing or rotary-wing aircraft, subject to the exceptions contained in paragraph 1 of its resolution 781(1992), and reiterates that all parties and others concerned must comply with this ban;

3. *Endorses* the general concept of operations described in the Secretary-General's report and calls on all parties and others concerned, including all Governments operating aircraft in the area, to cooperate fully with the United Nations Protection Force in its implementation;

4. *Calls upon* all parties and others concerned henceforth to direct all requests for authorizations of flights

pursuant to paragraph 3 of its resolution 781(1992) to the United Nations Protection Force, with special provisions being made for flights of the Protection Force, and all other flights in support of United Nations operations, including humanitarian assistance;

5. *Approves* the recommendation in paragraph 10 of the Secretary-General's report that the strength of the United Nations Protection Force be increased, as proposed in paragraph 5 of the report, in order to permit it to implement the concept of operations;

6. *Reiterates its determination* to consider urgently, in the case of violations when further reported to it in accordance with its resolution 781(1992), the further measures necessary to enforce the ban on military flights in the airspace of Bosnia and Herzegovina;

7. *Decides* to remain actively seized of the matter.

Security Council resolution 786(1992)

10 November 1992   Meeting 3133   Adopted unanimously

Draft prepared in consultations among Council members (S/24784), orally revised.

Eleven more reports of unauthorized flights over the "no flight zone" were issued by the Secretary-General in 1992. From 5 to 12 November, 34 flights were detected.[81] At that point, monitors of UNPROFOR or ECMM were deployed in the majority of their assigned areas. Further reported were: 73 flights from 13 to 19 November;[82] 55 from 20 to 26 November;[83] and 132 from 27 November to 28 December.[84]

Report of the Secretary-General (11 November). The Secretary-General on 11 November reported to the Security Council on the International Conference on the Former Yugoslavia,[1] including the activities of the Steering Committee and its Co-Chairmen and the six working groups. In particular, he provided information on the efforts being pursued within the Conference to promote a peaceful solution to the conflict in Bosnia and Herzegovina. A draft outline constitution, recently submitted to the parties by the Co-Chairmen of the Steering Committee, was annexed to the report.

The Secretary-General called for full cooperation of all the parties involved as well as the support of the international community for the work being pursued by the Co-Chairmen and the working groups. (For details on the work of the Conference, see above.)

SECURITY COUNCIL ACTION (13 and 16 November)

The Security Council convened four meetings on 13 and 16 November to consider the situation in Bosnia and Herzegovina, at its request,[85] as well as at the requests of Belgium,[86] France[87] and Egypt, Iran, Pakistan, Saudi Arabia, Senegal and Turkey, as members of the Contact Group of OIC.[88]

The President invited Afghanistan, Albania, Algeria, Azerbaijan, Bangladesh, Bosnia and Herzegovina, Canada, the Comoros, Croatia, Egypt, Germany, Greece, Indonesia, Iran, Italy, Jordan,

Kuwait, Lithuania, Malaysia, Malta, Norway, Pakistan, Qatar, Romania, Senegal, Slovenia, Tunisia, Turkey, Ukraine and the United Arab Emirates, at their request, to participate in the discussion without the right to vote under rule 37[a] of the Council's provisional rules of procedure. Also granted was a request of Foreign Minister Ilija Djukic, who identified himself as the Foreign Minister of the Federal Republic of Yugoslavia, to address the Council in the course of the discussion.

The President informed the Council of a letter[89] from the Permanent Observer of Palestine to the United Nations, requesting that, in accordance with the Council's previous practice, an invitation be extended to him to participate in the discussion without the right to vote. He would be speaking in his capacity as Chairman of the Arab Group for the month of November. The President added that the request was not made pursuant to rule 37[a] or rule 39[b] of the Council's provisional rules of procedure but that, if approved, the Council would invite the Permanent Observer to participate, not under rule 37 or 39, but with the same rights of participation of rule 37.

The request was approved by 10 votes in favour to 1 against (United States), with 4 abstentions (Belgium, France, Hungary, United Kingdom).

Prior to the vote, the United States, which had requested it, stated its opposition, saying the Council did not have before it a valid request and the Palestine Liberation Organization should be granted permission to speak only if the request complied with rule 39. The United States was opposed to special, ad hoc departures from orderly procedures and did not agree with recent practice, which appeared selectively to try to enhance, through a departure from the rules of procedure, the prestige of those wishing to speak in the Council.

Invitations to participate under rule 39 were extended to both Co-Chairmen of the Steering Committee of the International Conference on the Former Yugoslavia, the United Nations High Commissioner for Refugees and the Special Rapporteur of the Commission on Human Rights. The reports of the Special Rapporteur on his first and second missions to the territory of the former Yugoslavia were transmitted to the Council by the Secretary-General on 3 September and 6 November;[90] a report on the human rights situation in the former Yugoslavia was transmitted on 17 November[91] (for details, see PART THREE, Chapter X).

Both China and Zimbabwe expressed reservations about inviting the Special Rapporteur. Human rights fell under the purview of the Com-

[b]Rule 39 of the Council's provisional rules of procedure states: "The Security Council may invite members of the Secretariat or other persons, whom it considers competent for the purpose, to supply it with information or to give other assistance in examining matters within its competence."

mission and the General Assembly rather than of the Council, and the invitation was therefore not appropriate, China felt. The growing tendency of the Council to interfere' with the work of other United Nations organs was a cause of great concern to Zimbabwe, at a time when efforts were being made to streamline the work of the Organization and improve the functional capacity of its constitutional parts.

On 16 November, the Council adopted **resolution 787(1992)**.

The Security Council,

Reaffirming its resolution 713(1991) of 25 September 1991 and all subsequent relevant resolutions,

Reaffirming its determination that the situation in the Republic of Bosnia and Herzegovina constitutes a threat to the peace, and reaffirming that the provision of humanitarian assistance in the Republic of Bosnia and Herzegovina is an important element in the Security Council's effort to restore peace and security in the region,

Deeply concerned at the threats to the territorial integrity of the Republic of Bosnia and Herzegovina, which, as a State Member of the United Nations, enjoys the rights provided for in the Charter of the United Nations,

Reaffirming also its full support for the International Conference on the Former Yugoslavia as the framework within which an overall political settlement of the crisis in the former Yugoslavia may be achieved, and for the work of the Co-Chairmen of the Steering Committee of the Conference,

Recalling the decision by the International Conference on the Former Yugoslavia to examine the possibility of promoting safe areas for humanitarian purposes,

Recalling the commitments entered into by the parties and others concerned within the framework of the International Conference on the Former Yugoslavia,

Reiterating its call on all parties and others concerned to cooperate fully with the Co-Chairmen of the Steering Committee,

Noting the progress made so far within the framework of the International Conference, including the Joint Declarations signed at Geneva on 30 September 1992 and 20 October 1992 by the Presidents of the Republic of Croatia and the Federal Republic of Yugoslavia (Serbia and Montenegro); the Joint Statement made at Geneva on 19 October 1992 by the Presidents of the Republic of Bosnia and Herzegovina and the Federal Republic of Yugoslavia (Serbia and Montenegro); the Joint Communiqué issued on 1 November 1992 at Zagreb by the Presidents of the Republic of Croatia and the Republic of Bosnia and Herzegovina; the establishment of the Mixed Military Working Group in the Republic of Bosnia and Herzegovina; and the production of a draft outline constitution for the Republic of Bosnia and Herzegovina,

Noting with grave concern the report of the Special Rapporteur appointed following a special session of the Commission on Human Rights to investigate the human rights situation in the former Yugoslavia, which makes clear that massive and systematic violations of human rights and grave violations of international humanitarian law continue in the Republic of Bosnia and Herzegovina,

Welcoming the deployment of additional elements of the United Nations Protection Force for the protection of humanitarian activities in the Republic of Bosnia and Herzegovina, in accordance with its resolution 776(1992) of 14 September 1992,

Deeply concerned about reports of continuing violations of the embargo imposed by its resolutions 713(1991) and 724(1991) of 15 December 1991,

Deeply concerned also about reports of violations of the measures imposed by its resolution 757(1992) of 30 May 1992,

1. *Calls upon* the parties in the Republic of Bosnia and Herzegovina to consider the draft outline constitution as a basis for negotiating a political settlement of the conflict in that country and to continue negotiations for constitutional arrangements on the basis of the draft outline, under the auspices of the Co-Chairmen of the Steering Committee, these negotiations to be held in continuous and uninterrupted session;

2. *Reaffirms* that any taking of territory by force or any practice of "ethnic cleansing" is unlawful and unacceptable, and will not be permitted to affect the outcome of the negotiations on constitutional arrangements for the Republic of Bosnia and Herzegovina, and insists that all displaced persons be enabled to return in peace to their former homes;

3. *Strongly reaffirms* its call on all parties and others concerned to respect strictly the territorial integrity of the Republic of Bosnia and Herzegovina, and affirms that any entities unilaterally declared or arrangements imposed in contravention thereof will not be accepted;

4. *Condemns* the refusal of all parties in the Republic of Bosnia and Herzegovina, in particular the Bosnian Serb paramilitary forces, to comply with its previous resolutions, and demands that they and all other concerned parties in the former Yugoslavia fulfil immediately their obligations under those resolutions;

5. *Demands* that all forms of interference from outside the Republic of Bosnia and Herzegovina, including infiltration into the country of irregular units and personnel, cease immediately, and reaffirms its determination to take measures against all parties and others concerned which fail to fulfil the requirements of resolution 752(1992) and its other relevant resolutions, including the requirement that all forces, in particular elements of the Croatian army, be withdrawn, or be subject to the authority of the Government of the Republic of Bosnia and Herzegovina, or be disbanded or disarmed;

6. *Calls upon* all parties in the Republic of Bosnia and Herzegovina to fulfil their commitments to put into effect an immediate cessation of hostilities and to negotiate in the Mixed Military Working Group, continuously and in uninterrupted session, to end the blockades of Sarajevo and other towns and to demilitarize them, with heavy weapons under international supervision;

7. *Condemns* all violations of international humanitarian law, including in particular the practice of "ethnic cleansing" and the deliberate impeding of the delivery of food and medical supplies to the civilian population of the Republic of Bosnia and Herzegovina, and reaffirms that those that commit or order the commission of such acts will be held individually responsible in respect of such acts;

8. *Welcomes* the establishment of the Commission of Experts provided for in paragraph 2 of its resolution 780(1992) of 6 October 1992, and requests the Commis-

sion to pursue actively its investigations with regard to grave breaches of the Geneva Conventions and other violations of international humanitarian law committed in the territory of the former Yugoslavia, in particular the practice of "ethnic cleansing";

9. *Decides*, acting under Chapter VII of the Charter of the United Nations, in order to ensure that commodities and products transshipped through the Federal Republic of Yugoslavia (Serbia and Montenegro) are not diverted in violation of resolution 757(1992), to prohibit the transshipment of crude oil, petroleum products, coal, energy-related equipment, iron, steel, other metals, chemicals, rubber, tyres, vehicles, aircraft and motors of all types unless such transshipment is specifically authorized on a case-by-case basis by the Committee established by resolution 724(1991) under its no-objection procedure;

10. *Further decides*, acting under Chapter VII of the Charter of the United Nations, that any vessel in which a majority or controlling interest is held by a person or undertaking in or operating from the Federal Republic of Yugoslavia (Serbia and Montenegro) shall be considered, for the purpose of implementation of the relevant resolutions of the Security Council, a vessel of the Federal Republic of Yugoslavia (Serbia and Montenegro) regardless of the flag under which the vessel sails;

11. *Calls upon* all States to take all necessary steps to ensure that none of their exports are diverted to the Federal Republic of Yugoslavia (Serbia and Montenegro) in violation of resolution 757(1992);

12. Acting under Chapters VII and VIII of the Charter of the United Nations, *calls upon* States, acting nationally or through regional agencies or arrangements, to use such measures commensurate with the specific circumstances as may be necessary under the authority of the Security Council to halt all inward and outward maritime shipping in order to inspect and verify their cargoes and destinations and to ensure strict implementation of the provisions of resolutions 713(1991) and 757(1992);

13. *Commends* the efforts of those riparian States which are acting to ensure compliance with resolutions 713(1991) and 757(1992) with respect to shipments on the Danube, and reaffirms the responsibility of riparian States to take necessary measures to ensure that shipping on the Danube is in accordance with resolutions 713(1991) and 757(1992), including such measures commensurate with the specific circumstances as may be necessary to halt such shipping in order to inspect and verify their cargoes and destinations and to ensure strict implementation of the provisions of resolutions 713(1991) and 757(1992);

14. *Requests* the States concerned, nationally or through regional agencies or arrangements, to coordinate with the Secretary-General, *inter alia*, on the submission of reports to the Security Council regarding actions taken in pursuance of paragraphs 12 and 13 of the present resolution to facilitate the monitoring of the implementation of the present resolution;

15. *Requests* all States to provide in accordance with the Charter of the United Nations such assistance as may be required by those States acting nationally or through regional agencies and arrangements in pursuance of paragraphs 12 and 13 of the present resolution;

16. *Considers* that, in order to facilitate the implementation of the relevant Security Council resolutions, ob-

servers should be deployed on the borders of the Republic of Bosnia and Herzegovina, and requests the Secretary-General to present to the Council as soon as possible his recommendations on this matter;

17. *Calls upon* all international donors to contribute to the humanitarian relief efforts in the former Yugoslavia, to support the United Nations Consolidated Inter-Agency Programme of Action and Appeal for the former Yugoslavia and to speed up the delivery of assistance under existing pledges;

18. *Calls upon* all parties and others concerned to cooperate fully with the humanitarian agencies and with the United Nations Protection Force to ensure the safe delivery of humanitarian assistance to those in need of it, and reiterates its demand that all parties and others concerned take the necessary measures to ensure the safety of United Nations and other personnel engaged in the delivery of humanitarian assistance;

19. *Invites* the Secretary-General, in consultation with the United Nations High Commissioner for Refugees and other relevant international humanitarian agencies, to study the possibility of and the requirements for the promotion of safe areas for humanitarian purposes;

20. *Expresses its appreciation* for the report presented to the Council by the Co-Chairmen of the Steering Committee of the International Conference on the Former Yugoslavia, and requests the Secretary-General to continue to keep the Council regularly informed of developments and of the work of the Conference;

21. *Decides* to remain actively seized of the matter until a peaceful solution is achieved.

Security Council resolution 787(1992)

16 November 1992   Meeting 3137   13-0-2

5-nation draft (S/24808/Rev.1), orally revised.
Sponsors: Belgium, France, Russian Federation, United Kingdom, United States.
Meeting numbers. SC 3134-3137.

Vote in Council as follows:

In favour: Austria, Belgium, Cape Verde, Ecuador, France, Hungary, India, Japan, Morocco, Russian Federation, United Kingdom, United States, Venezuela.
Against: None.
Abstaining: China, Zimbabwe.

Report of the Secretary-General (24 November). In a report of 24 November,[20] the Secretary-General provided updated information on UNPROFOR activities in Bosnia and Herzegovina. Progress had been made in deploying the newly established Bosnia and Herzegovina Command and the units under its control, but the deployment of military observers and civil affairs personnel was delayed due to budgetary problems.

Throughout the reporting period, Sector Sarajevo contrived to carry out its mandate of keeping open and operating Sarajevo airport and escorting convoys of relief supplies from the airport to the city. A total of 1,619 humanitarian flights, carrying 19,660 metric tons of aid, had been flown into the airport. The Sector also coordinated efforts to restore electricity, gas and water supplies in the city, with UNPROFOR personnel protecting civilian workers and completing many of the repairs themselves. UNPROFOR military observers continued to monitor the heavy-weapons positions of the parties in the hills around Sarajevo. In addition, the Sector had to devote much effort to providing support to high-ranking delegations who had requested armed and armoured escort during visits to the city.

The establishment of the Mixed Military Working Group, which had held six meetings since 23 October, was a step forward, although negotiations had been slow and arduous. The three parties— the presidency of Bosnia and Herzegovina, Bosnian Croats and Bosnian Serbs—had declared their resolve to achieve results which could lead to a cessation of hostilities and facilitate the provision of humanitarian aid throughout the conflict area, but that resolve had not been translated into concrete agreements. So far, the three sides had mostly used the Working Group to state their points of view on various issues or to lay down conditions that were unacceptable to the others. The cease-fire agreement of 10 November was a positive development, but had already been violated by all sides on a large number of occasions, and it remained to be seen whether the parties were really willing and able to implement such an agreement on the ground.

The challenge facing UNPROFOR in Bosnia and Herzegovina should not be underestimated, the Secretary-General warned. The frequent autumn rains, which had led to flooding and mobility problems, were being followed by periods of falling temperatures and snowfalls on Sarajevo and many mountain areas. Roads, bridges and railways had been without normal maintenance for nearly a year; many had suffered major damage from the fighting, making road surfaces unsafe. The implications for humanitarian operations were severe.

Overall, the Secretary-General observed, the situation in Bosnia and Herzegovina was disquieting, with a complicated and savage conflict raging and a large number of people remaining vulnerable to starvation and displacement during an arduous winter whose rigours had only just begun. Security Council resolutions calling for the withdrawal of foreign forces remained largely unimplemented. The Croatian Army was reliably reported to be engaged extensively in the republic, particularly in Herzegovina and in the Orasje area. Serb forces in Bosnia and Herzegovina continued to rely on logistical support from Yugoslavia (Serbia and Montenegro).

The Secretary-General noted, however, that UNPROFOR's mandate in Bosnia and Herzegovina was more practicable than in Croatia. The first four weeks of the ban on military flights had produced no confirmed evidence of combat activity, though they had shown that many flights of military aircraft, mostly helicopters, were taking place from Serb-controlled airfields and that unapproved flights occurred regularly, mostly at night, from Croatia into government-controlled areas of Bosnia and Herzegovina.

The bulk of UNPROFOR's activity in Bosnia and Herzegovina, however, was in support of efforts to relieve the suffering of the civilian population. United Nations troops were pioneering a new dimension of United Nations peace-keeping as they took on the task of protecting the delivery of humanitarian supplies. That task did not in the Secretary-General's view require a revision of peace-keeping rules of engagement, which already entitled United Nations troops to use force if prevented by armed persons from carrying out their mandate. However, in convoy protection duties, United Nations troops might have to move beyond their usual impartiality, an aspect the Secretary-General was watching carefully.

Turning to the arrangements agreed on for the expansion of UNPROFOR under resolution 776(1992), the Secretary-General said they were quite innovative; the addition to UNPROFOR of contingents financed and supported entirely by their national Governments had given rise to some teething troubles, especially with regard to command and control. He had had to seek the help of contributing Governments in ensuring that all concerned recognized that the new units were an integral part of UNPROFOR, under the overall command of the Force Commander, and that newly arrived troops wearing United Nations insignia passed under United Nations command as soon as they reached the mission area. Their subsequent activities had to comply with UNPROFOR policy, as laid down by the Force Commander, in all operational, legal, information and administrative matters. The lack of budgetary provision for United Nations civilian personnel, including administrators and military observers, had deprived the Bosnia and Herzegovina Command of experienced United Nations personnel; for that reason, the Secretary-General had decided to recommend to the General Assembly that the Command's requirements for civilian staff and related support be provided through assessed contributions levied on all Member States.

SECURITY COUNCIL ACTION (9 and 18 December)

On 9 December, the Security Council met at the request of Bosnia and Herzegovina,[92] which the Council invited, at its request, to participate without the right to vote under rule 37ᵃ of the Council's provisional rules of procedure.

In presenting its request, Bosnia and Herzegovina cited a dramatic increase in aggression against Sarajevo, Bihac and other cities in the central area and the northern corridor of the republic.

Following consultations, the President of the Council made a statement:[93]

Meeting number. SC 3146.

"The Security Council is alarmed by the most recent reports that Serb militia in the Republic of Bosnia and Herzegovina have renewed their offensive in Bosnia and Herzegovina, and in particular against the city of Sarajevo, resulting in further loss of life and material damage as well as in endangering the security of UNPROFOR and international relief workers, thus threatening international peace and security.

"The Security Council is particularly alarmed by reports that the Serb militia in the Republic of Bosnia and Herzegovina are forcing the inhabitants of Sarajevo to evacuate the city. The Council warns that actions aimed at impeding the distribution of humanitarian assistance and at forcing the inhabitants of Sarajevo to leave the city, including the possibility of ethnic cleansing, would have grave consequences for the overall situation in that country.

"The Security Council strongly condemns these attacks as violations of its relevant resolutions and of previous commitments, in particular with regard to the cessation of hostilities, the ban on military flights in the airspace of the Republic of Bosnia and Herzegovina, the safety of humanitarian assistance to the civilian population and the restoration of power and water supplies.

"The Security Council demands the immediate cessation of these attacks and of all actions aimed at impeding the distribution of humanitarian assistance and at forcing the inhabitants of Sarajevo to leave the city.

"If such attacks and actions continue, the Security Council will consider, as soon as possible, further measures against those who commit or support them to ensure the security of UNPROFOR and of international relief workers, the ability of UNPROFOR to fulfil its mandate and compliance with the Council's relevant resolutions.

"The Security Council will remain actively seized of the matter."

The Council again met on 18 December and by unanimous vote adopted **resolution 798(1992)**.

The Security Council,

Recalling its resolutions 770(1992) and 771(1992) of 13 August 1992 as well as other relevant resolutions of the Security Council,

Appalled by reports of the massive, organized and systematic detention and rape of women, in particular Muslim women, in Bosnia and Herzegovina,

Demanding that all the detention camps and, in particular, camps for women should be immediately closed,

Taking note of the initiative taken by the European Council on the rapid dispatch of a delegation to investigate the facts received until now,

1.   *Expresses its support* for the above-mentioned initiative of the European Council;

2.   *Strongly condemns* these acts of unspeakable brutality;

3.   *Requests* the Secretary-General to provide such necessary means of support as are available to him in the area to enable the European Community delegation to have free and secure access to the places of detention;

4.   *Requests* the member States of the European Community to inform the Secretary-General of the work of the delegation;

5.   *Invites* the Secretary-General to report to it within fifteen days of the adoption of the present resolution on measures taken to support the delegation;

6.   *Decides* to remain actively seized of the matter.

Security Council resolution 798(1992)
18 December 1992   Meeting 3150   Adopted unanimously
4-nation draft (S/24977).
Sponsors: Belgium, France, Morocco, United Kingdom.

The EC delegation, which the Secretary-General was requested by the Council to support, was headed by Dame Anne Warburton and included Simone Veil and a number of experts in forensic psychiatry, clinical psychology, law, social development and social anthropology. It visited Geneva and Zagreb between 18 and 24 December and had extensive discussions with representatives of UNHCR, the United Nations Centre for Human Rights and the Commission of Experts on War Crimes in the Former Yugoslavia.[94]

Reports of the Secretary-General (December). Pursuant to resolution 787(1992), the Secretary-General in a report of 21 December[95] presented three alternative concepts for deploying observers on the borders of Bosnia and Herzegovina in order to facilitate implementation of relevant Council resolutions. Bosnia and Herzegovina itself had repeatedly expressed itself in favour of effective monitoring of its borders, and Croatia and Yugoslavia (Serbia and Montenegro) had agreed to it in principle during and since the London stage of the International Conference on the Former Yugoslavia.

The relevant resolutions were: 713(1991) of 25 September 1991, which established a general and complete embargo on all deliveries of weapons and military equipment to Yugoslavia; 752(1992) of 5 May 1992, which demanded that all forms of interference from outside Bosnia and Herzegovina, including units of JNA as well as elements of the Croatian Army, cease immediately, and that Bosnia and Herzegovina's neighbours take swift action to end such interference and respect the republic's territorial integrity; 757(1992) of 30 May, which imposed comprehensive mandatory economic sanctions against Yugoslavia (Serbia and Montenegro); and 787(1992) of 16 November, which again demanded that all forms of interference from outside Bosnia and Herzegovina, including infiltration into the country of irregular units and personnel, cease immediately.

The three operational concepts outlined by UNPROFOR were: observing and reporting of traffic; observing and searching of vehicles and persons crossing the border in either direction, and reporting; and observing, searching, denying passage or confiscating weapons or sanctioned goods, and reporting. All three, but especially the last option, which the Force Commander favoured, would require considerable additional material and human resources, the Secretary-General said.

An additional command, communication and logistics structure would be required to control and supply border personnel, who would be deployed at the 123 widely dispersed crossing points along borders which extended nearly 1,100 kilometres through predominantly difficult terrain. Two or more sub-headquarters in Croatia and Yugoslavia (Serbia and Montenegro) would be needed to report through cells in Belgrade and Zagreb to UNPROFOR headquarters. For a variety of political and practical reasons, the Force Commander believed that it would be best for the United Nations observers to carry out their functions on the Croatia or Serbia/Montenegro side of the border; the full cooperation of those States' authorities would be required, especially when non-authorized vehicles or persons were turned back by the observers.

The option preferred by the Force Commander and the Secretary-General would require approximately 10,000 troops, including the necessary logistic, medical and engineering support. In addition, there could also be a need for United Nations civilian police and customs officers. UNPROFOR's logistic infrastructure would have to be extensively upgraded and enlarged.

The Secretary-General estimated the costs associated with the additional responsibilities at $694,125,000 for an initial six-month period, and the monthly costs thereafter at approximately $69,155,000. He recommended that the additional costs be borne by Member States and that the assessments to be levied on them be credited to the UNPROFOR Special Account.

In a report of 24 December,[2] the Secretary-General provided information on the activities of the International Conference on the Former Yugoslavia since his previous report of 11 November. (For details on the Conference, see above.)

He reported on the situation in Bosnia and Herzegovina to the General Assembly on 3 December,[96] pursuant to its August request. In submitting the report, he stated it was complemented by his reports to the Security Council and the reports of the Special Rapporteur to the Commission on Human Rights (see PART THREE, Chapter X). The Secretary-General's report dealt with efforts to end hostilities and achieve a peaceful solution to the conflict, as well as the withdrawal of foreign forces; action taken by the Security Council during the year; violations of human rights and humanitarian law; the release of prisoners and detainees; and humanitarian assistance.

GENERAL ASSEMBLY ACTION

On 18 December, the General Assembly adopted **resolution 47/121** by recorded vote.

The situation in Bosnia and Herzegovina

The General Assembly,

Having considered the item entitled "The situation in Bosnia and Herzegovina",

Taking note of the report of the Secretary-General,

Reaffirming its resolution 46/242 of 25 August 1992,

Recalling all the resolutions adopted by the Security Council regarding the Republic of Bosnia and Herzegovina, and other parts of the former Yugoslavia,

Appreciating all the ongoing international efforts to restore peace in the Republic of Bosnia and Herzegovina, particularly those efforts being pursued by the United Nations, the European Community, the International Conference on the Former Yugoslavia, the Conference on Security and Cooperation in Europe and the Organization of the Islamic Conference,

Commending the untiring efforts and bravery of the United Nations Protection Force in securing relief operations in the Republic of Bosnia and Herzegovina, as well as the efforts of the Office of the United Nations High Commissioner for Refugees and other relief and humanitarian agencies, and expressing its condemnation of the recent attacks on the United Nations Protection Force in Sarajevo by Serbian forces resulting in loss of life and injuries to some of its personnel,

Taking note of the report of the Special Rapporteur of the Commission on Human Rights on the situation of human rights in the territory of the former Yugoslavia dated 6 November 1992, in which he stated, *inter alia,* that "ethnic cleansing" did not appear to be the consequence of the war, but rather its goal,

Taking note also of the report of the Special Rapporteur dated 17 November 1992, in which he stated, *inter alia,* that another factor which had contributed to the intensity of "ethnic cleansing" in areas under Serbian control was the marked imbalance between the weaponry in the hands of the Serbian and the Muslim population of Bosnia and Herzegovina,

Gravely concerned about the deterioration of the situation in the Republic of Bosnia and Herzegovina owing to intensified aggressive acts by the Serbian and Montenegrin forces to acquire more territories by force, characterized by a consistent pattern of gross and systematic violations of human rights, a burgeoning refugee population resulting from mass expulsions of defenceless civilians from their homes and the existence in Serbian and Montenegrin controlled areas of concentration camps and detention centres, in pursuit of the abhorrent policy of "ethnic cleansing", which is a form of genocide,

Strongly condemning Serbia and Montenegro and their surrogates in the Republic of Bosnia and Herzegovina for their continued non-compliance with all relevant United Nations resolutions,

Deeply regretting that the sanctions imposed by the Security Council have not had the desired effect of halting the aggressive acts by Serbian and Montenegrin irregular forces and the direct and indirect support of the Yugoslav People's Army for the aggressive acts in the Republic of Bosnia and Herzegovina,

Recalling that the Government of the Republic of Bosnia and Herzegovina has accepted the constitutional principles proposed by the Co-Chairmen of the International Conference on the Former Yugoslavia,

Convinced that the situation in the Republic of Bosnia and Herzegovina warrants the implementation of decisive actions under Chapter VII of the Charter of the United

Nations to oblige Serbia and Montenegro and their surrogates in the Republic of Bosnia and Herzegovina to comply with the relevant Security Council resolutions,

Reaffirming the principle of the inadmissibility of the acquisition of territory by force and the right of all Bosnian refugees to return to their homes in conditions of safety and honour,

Reaffirming also that the Republic of Bosnia and Herzegovina has the inherent right to individual or collective self-defence in accordance with Chapter VII, Article 51, of the Charter, until the Security Council has taken the measures necessary to maintain international peace and security,

Determined to restore peace in the Republic of Bosnia and Herzegovina as well as to preserve its unity, sovereignty, political independence and territorial integrity,

1. *Reaffirms* its support for the Government and people of the Republic of Bosnia and Herzegovina in their just struggle to safeguard their sovereignty, political independence, territorial integrity and unity;

2. *Strongly condemns* Serbia, Montenegro and Serbian forces in the Republic of Bosnia and Herzegovina for violation of the sovereignty, territorial integrity and political independence of the Republic of Bosnia and Herzegovina, and their non-compliance with existing resolutions of the Security Council and the General Assembly, as well as the London Peace Accords of August 1992;

3. *Demands* that Serbia and Montenegro and Serbian forces in the Republic of Bosnia and Herzegovina immediately cease their aggressive acts and hostility and comply fully and unconditionally with the relevant resolutions of the Security Council, in particular resolutions 752(1992) of 15 May 1992, 757(1992) of 30 May 1992, 770(1992) and 771(1992) of 13 August 1992, 781(1992) of 9 October 1992 and 787(1992) of 16 November 1992, General Assembly resolution 46/242 and the London Peace Accords of August 1992;

4. *Demands* that, in accordance with Security Council resolution 752(1992), all elements of the Yugoslav People's Army still in the territory of the Republic of Bosnia and Herzegovina must be withdrawn immediately, or be subject to the authority of the Government of the Republic of Bosnia and Herzegovina, or be disbanded and disarmed with their weapons placed under effective United Nations control;

5. *Demands also* that, in accordance with Security Council resolution 752(1992), all elements of the Croatian Army that may be in the Republic of Bosnia and Herzegovina and that are already not operating in accord with the authority of the Government of the Republic of Bosnia and Herzegovina must be withdrawn immediately, or be subject to the authority of that Government, or be disbanded and disarmed with their weapons placed under effective United Nations control;

6. *Supports* the consideration by the Security Council of the immediate enforcement of Council resolution 781(1992) banning all military flights over the Republic of Bosnia and Herzegovina;

7. *Urges* the Security Council, within its responsibility to maintain international peace and security, to again call upon the Serbian and Montenegrin forces to comply with all relevant resolutions and to bring to an end the aggressive acts against the Republic of Bosnia and Herzegovina, to implement and enforce all existing resolutions with respect to the Republic of Bosnia and Herzegovina and the former Yugoslavia and, specifically, fur-

ther to consider measures, including the following, on an urgent basis, but no later than 15 January 1993:

(a) In the event that Serbian and Montenegrin forces fail to comply fully with all relevant resolutions of the Security Council, under the provisions of Chapter VII of the Charter of the United Nations, to authorize Member States, in cooperation with the Government of the Republic of Bosnia and Herzegovina, to use all necessary means to uphold and restore the sovereignty, political independence, territorial integrity and unity of the Republic of Bosnia and Herzegovina;

(b) To exempt the Republic of Bosnia and Herzegovina from the arms embargo as imposed on the former Yugoslavia under Security Council resolution 713(1991) of 25 September 1991;

8. *Also urges* the Security Council to consider taking measures to open more airports/airfields for international humanitarian relief flights, to pursue emergency airdrops as a stop-gap measure and to study the possibility of and the requirements for the promotion of safe areas for humanitarian purposes;

9. *Further urges* the Security Council to consider what resources may be required to improve the implementation of all relevant resolutions, and calls upon Member States to notify the Secretary-General regarding the availability of personnel and *matériel* to assist and facilitate in this effort;

10. *Urges* the Security Council to consider recommending the establishment of an ad hoc international war crimes tribunal to try and punish those who have committed war crimes in the Republic of Bosnia and Herzegovina when sufficient information has been provided by the Commission of Experts established by Council resolution 780(1992) of 6 October 1992;

11. *Requests* the Co-Chairmen of the International Conference on the Former Yugoslavia to conclude expeditiously the work of the Working Group on the Republic of Bosnia and Herzegovina, to report on the reasons for the lack of progress and to submit proposals to overcome obstacles in the fulfilment of their mandate by 18 January 1993;

12. *Requests* the Secretary-General to report to the General Assembly by 18 January 1993 on the implementation of the present resolution;

13. *Decides* to remain seized of the matter and to continue the consideration of this item.

General Assembly resolution 47/121

18 December 1992   Meeting 91   102-0-57 (recorded vote)

44-nation draft (A/47/L.47/Rev.1); agenda item 143.

Sponsors: Afghanistan, Albania, Algeria, Antigua and Barbuda, Azerbaijan, Bahrain, Bangladesh, Bolivia, Bosnia and Herzegovina, Brunei Darussalam, Colombia, Comoros, Costa Rica, Croatia, Djibouti, Egypt, Estonia, Gambia, Guinea, Honduras, Indonesia, Iran, Jordan, Kuwait, Latvia, Lebanon, Lithuania, Malaysia, Mali, Mauritania, Morocco, Niger, Oman, Pakistan, Qatar, Saudi Arabia, Senegal, Sudan, Tajikistan, Tunisia, Turkey, United Arab Emirates, Venezuela, Yemen.

Meeting numbers. GA 47th session: plenary 86-88, 91.

Recorded vote in Assembly as follows:

In favour: Afghanistan, Albania, Algeria, Antigua and Barbuda, Australia, Austria, Azerbaijan, Bahamas, Bahrain, Bangladesh, Barbados, Belize, Bhutan, Bolivia, Bosnia and Herzegovina, Botswana, Brunei Darussalam, Burkina Faso, Cape Verde, Chad, Chile, Colombia, Comoros, Costa Rica, Croatia, Cyprus, Djibouti, Dominica, Ecuador, Egypt, El Salvador, Estonia, Fiji, Gabon, Gambia, Grenada, Guatemala, Guinea, Guinea-Bissau, Guyana, Honduras, Hungary, Indonesia, Iran, Jamaica, Jordan, Kuwait, Latvia, Lebanon, Liberia, Libyan Arab Jamahiriya, Lithuania, Madagascar, Malaysia, Maldives, Mali, Malta, Marshall Islands, Mauritania, Mauritius, Micronesia, Mongolia, Morocco, Mozambique, Nepal, Nicaragua, Niger, Nigeria, Oman, Pakistan, Panama, Paraguay, Peru, Philippines, Qatar, Republic of

Moldova, Rwanda, Saint Kitts and Nevis, Saint Lucia, Saint Vincent and
the Grenadines, Samoa, Sao Tome and Principe, Saudi Arabia, Senegal,
Sierra Leone, Singapore, Slovenia, Solomon Islands, Sri Lanka, Sudan, Suriname, Syrian Arab Republic, Thailand, Trinidad and Tobago, Tunisia, Turkey, United Arab Emirates, United Republic of Tanzania, United States, Vanuatu, Venezuela, Yemen.

Against: None.

Abstaining: Angola, Argentina, Belarus, Belgium, Benin, Brazil, Bulgaria,
Burundi, Cameroon, Canada, Central African Republic, China, Côte d'Ivoire,
Cuba, Czechoslovakia, Denmark, Dominican Republic, Finland, France, Ger-
many, Ghana, Greece, Iceland, India, Ireland, Israel, Italy, Japan, Kazakh-
stan, Kenya, Lesotho, Liechtenstein, Luxembourg, Malawi, Mexico, Namibia,
Netherlands, New Zealand, Norway, Papua New Guinea, Poland, Portugal,
Republic of Korea, Romania, Russian Federation, Spain, Swaziland, Sweden,
Togo, Uganda, Ukraine, United Kingdom, Uruguay, Viet Nam, Zaire, Zam-
bia, Zimbabwe.

Further developments. In view of the heightened international concern over the situation in Bosnia and Herzegovina, the Co-Chairmen of the Steering Committee invited the three parties to Geneva
to discuss from 2 January 1993 onwards a sustainable
cessation of hostilities; the demilitarization of
Sarajevo; an agreement on a pull-back from the military front line in a way that would reinforce an overall
political settlement; ensuring free access of all citizens
in and out of besieged cities and towns; and free
movement of humanitarian aid. Croatia and Yugoslavia (Serbia and Montenegro) were also invited.

In preparation for those discussions, the Co-
Chairmen invited the Presidents of Croatia and Bosnia and Herzegovina to Geneva on 27 and 28 December 1992 for consultations, concentrating on
the provincial structure of Bosnia and Herzegovina
as an intrinsic part of future constitutional arrangements. Consultations also took place on 28 December
between the Presidents of Croatia and Yugoslavia
(Serbia and Montenegro).

During individual talks with the three Presidents,
the Secretary-General expressed his grave concern
over the developments in the republic and the risks
of escalation and expansion of the conflict, and appealed to each of them to help the Co-Chairmen
in their search for peaceful solutions.

Those discussions led the Secretary-General to
the conclusion that the designation of Sarajevo as
a demilitarized open city could be advantageous
to the peace process. On 30 December, he wrote
to the Security Council President describing his impression that there were subtle signs of progress and
stating his conviction that the growing momentum
for stronger military measures by the international
community in Bosnia and Herzegovina should be
slowed in order to allow the still fragile peace process an opportunity to take root.

Implementation of the weapons
embargo and sanctions

A mandatory weapons embargo with respect to
all the constituent republics of the former Socialist
Federal Republic of Yugoslavia was established by
the Security Council in September 1991.[9] In 1992,
the Council significantly expanded the scope of its
mandatory sanctions relative to the Federal Republic

of Yugoslavia (Serbia and Montenegro): by resolution 757(1992), of 30 May, the Council, acting
under Chapter VII of the Charter, imposed a wide
range of sanctions; by resolution 760(1992) of 18
June, it expanded the exceptions to the prohibitions
in resolution 757(1992) relating to the sale or supply of any commodities or products, conditioned
on the Sanction Committee's approval on a case-
by-case basis; and by resolution 787(1992) of 16
November, the Council, again acting under Chapter
VII, tightened procedures for implementing the
mandatory sanctions.

As reported by the Secretary-General,[97] a total
of 111 replies from 107 States was received as at 29
May 1992 on measures they had initiated to implement a general and complete embargo on all deliveries of weapons to Yugoslavia. In December
1991,[98] the Council had requested reports from
States on such measures and had established a reporting machinery.

In another report,[99] the Secretary-General
stated that, as at 9 October 1992, 97 States had submitted information pertaining to the implementation
of expanded sanctions under resolution 757(1992).

Security Council
Committee on the former Yugoslavia

The Security Council Committee, established pursuant to resolution 724(1991) of 15 December
1991,[98] which consisted of all Council members,
outlined its activities in two reports to the Council, of 13 April[100] and 30 December 1992.[101]

The Committee's original mandate was to monitor
the implementation by States of the mandatory arms
embargo against the former Yugoslavia. In accordance with its approved guidelines, the Committee,
in an initial appeal of 7 February, requested all States
to provide information relating to any violation or
alleged violation of the arms embargo. A similar
appeal was addressed to individuals and governmental and non-governmental organizations, both
national and international, by means of a press release of 24 February.

Expanding the scope of mandatory sanctions by
resolutions 757(1992), 760(1992) and 787(1992), the
Council expanded the Committee's mandate accordingly. In June, the Committee adopted a new
set of guidelines for its work, which were subsequently
amended and transmitted to all States and international organizations. Following adoption of resolution 787(1992), it formulated additional guidelines incorporating further amendments.

The Committee held 47 meetings in 1992, following its first meeting on 20 December 1991. Three
meetings were held on an emergency basis (to consider requests for approval of imminent flights from,
or back to, Yugoslavia). The Committee devoted
most of its time to consideration of matters arising from more than 2,000 communications submitted

to it by States, international organizations and, in 16 instances, by NGOs and individuals. The communications consisted for the most part of notifications of the import of foodstuffs and medical supplies to Yugoslavia; requests for approval for supply to that country of commodities and products for essential humanitarian needs; applications for exemptions from the sanctions, where permitted by the Council; requests for approval of transshipments of certain commodities and products through Yugoslavia; reports of sanctions violations or suspected violations; and general questions with regard to implementation of the sanctions regime. In addition, the Committee studied material from published sources, on the basis of which it decided on three occasions to address letters to States requesting that investigations be undertaken into the suspect activities reported.

The Committee adopted a general principle that, in considering requests from States or international organizations under the various sanctions and embargo resolutions, it would not grant generic or standing but case-by-case approval. In a number of instances, it granted general approval, provided advance notification was given, with respect to the following: payment of foreign pension benefits to persons in Yugoslavia; fees and dues collectible by embassies and consulates of Yugoslavia; goods and mail going to Yugoslavia for the use of diplomatic and consular missions there; fees or customs dues for commercial traffic in transit through Yugoslavia; certain requests by international humanitarian organizations, with respect to which the Committee agreed that several shipments of aid materials might be effected to Yugoslavia within a given time (alternatively, specific amounts of such materials might be approved for shipment on any number of trips); and flights by UNPROFOR, as well as by the Secretary-General's Special Representative and the Co-Chairmen of the International Conference on the Former Yugoslavia, as authorized under resolution 757(1992).

The Committee also formulated general principles regarding the repatriation of goods from Yugoslavia and the transfer of personal belongings to and from that country.

In the course of its deliberations, it reached a number of decisions relating to the implementation of sanctions, among them the prohibition of commercial activities of vessels owned by interests in Yugoslavia, regardless of which flag they sailed under; also prohibited were related payments and port services. That matter was settled by the Security Council in resolution 787(1992). By the same resolution, the Council enforced the Committee's position that riparian States of the Danube had the authority and obligation to enforce the sanctions on the Danube.

At several meetings, the Committee considered a number of communications from Yugoslavia requesting authorization for the import of a certain amount of oil derivatives and natural gas exclusively for the operation of humanitarian institutions and services. The Committee suggested that Yugoslavia contact the relevant United Nations humanitarian organizations in order to prepare a plan that would verify and meet the humanitarian needs described and would provide measures to ensure that any permitted products were to be distributed and consumed only to satisfy those needs.

The Committee responded positively to a request by Montenegro for authorization of the import of certain items and machinery in the aftermath of flash floods following heavy rains in October; the Committee's decision was predicated on the agreement by the United Nations Department of Humanitarian Affairs to coordinate the supervision of the import, delivery and proper use. The Committee declined, however, a request of Yugoslavia to repatriate certain works of art following their exhibition in France, having received information that there was a dispute as to the ownership of some of the items among various republics of the former Socialist Federal Republic of Yugoslavia. The Committee considered that it was not in a position to determine ownership, nor was it able to authorize shipment to Yugoslavia (Serbia and Montenegro) of items in dispute.

Faced with several requests concerning participation by athletes from Yugoslavia in international sports events, including the 1992 Olympic Games at Barcelona, Spain, the Committee established a series of conditions for such participation: the athletes were not to appear together or participate as part of a team, nor should they appear in uniform, under any banner or flag, or have any anthem dedicated to them; the international organizations hosting the sports events must assume responsibility for the selection of participating athletes, who might be accompanied by coaches, technical assistants or trainers, but not by any other personnel or officials; and the athletes must not make any political statements or gestures.

In its April report, the Committee dealt with only one specific case of reported sanctions violations, which was brought to its attention by Yugoslavia; since then, the Committee opened 45 new cases, on the basis of information from Yugoslavia and Romania, as well as on the basis of periodic reports submitted by the NATO/Western European Union (WEU) monitoring teams in the Adriatic Sea, from press reports and other sources. In response to the information presented by Yugoslavia, the Committee requested 31 States to undertake investigations, 19 of which had replied as at 29 December. The information supplied by Romania resulted in five States being requested to undertake investigations; based on NATO/WEU reports, such requests were sent to 21 States, of which 11 replied.

In two specific cases still under consideration by the Committee, it was established that sanctions violations did occur. One concerned the delivery of weapons and military equipment by an Iranian transport aircraft at Zagreb on 4 September. The Committee decided that the weapons and equipment seized should be destroyed; their destruction by Croatian authorities was witnessed and confirmed by UNPROFOR. The matter was drawn to the attention of the Security Council, while the Committee was still awaiting an explanation from Iran.

The second case involved illegal trade in pharmaceuticals between Slovenia and Yugoslavia. The Committee put on hold further exports of medical precursors to the companies involved in Yugoslavia until full explanations were submitted by the two Governments.

The Committee also pursued inquiries into the activities of three oil tankers (of Greek, Maltese and Panamanian registry), which were reported by the NATO/WEU monitoring teams to have delivered large quantities of oil and gasoline to Yugoslavia. Inquiries into the remaining specific cases were ongoing; however, in its December report, the Committee stated that as long as replies from the States concerned had not been received, it was not possible to determine whether, or to what extent, sanctions violations had occurred.

In its final observations in December, the Committee noted that the monitoring of sanctions had not been easy and that the effective implementation of sanctions had had an adverse impact on economies, particularly of those neighbouring the territory of the former Yugoslavia. The Committee expressed concern that a number of States had not responded to requests regarding measures they were expected to institute for meeting the obligations set out in the relevant sanction resolutions. It expressed disappointment at the lack of information on sanctions violations, especially from those States that were well placed to have access to such information, and emphasized that the success of the sanctions programme as a measure for settling international disputes peacefully depended on the active cooperation of all States.

While the Committee's role was to offer all possible assistance to States in undertaking their responsibility with regard to sanctions, the absence of an independent monitoring mechanism inhibited its ability to obtain original information and follow up on the investigations requested from States. The Committee considered that resolution 787(1992) had gone a long way in redressing that gap by authorizing States, acting nationally or through regional agencies or arrangements, to stop and search maritime vessels or vessels on the Danube in order to establish the bona fides of the cargoes on board. The Committee expressed gratitude to the NATO/WEU monitoring teams in the Adriatic for

their cooperation and said it would seek the assistance of the sanctions assistance missions operating in certain countries of the region, to verify the bona fides of commodities and products going to and from regions of the former Yugoslavia.

UNPROFOR financing

The General Assembly, by **resolution 46/233** of 19 March 1992, appropriated $251.5 million gross ($250 million net) for the operation of UNPROFOR until October 1992. With the Security Council enlarging the mandate of the Force by seven separate decisions, additional appropriations were needed. In respect of the estimated $30.9 million cost associated with the enlargement of UNPROFOR for border control, the Secretary-General sought and received the concurrence of the Advisory Committee on Administrative and Budgetary Questions (ACABQ) to enter into commitments of $10 million in order to meet the most urgent requirements of that enlargement. No additional appropriation was sought for the costs (estimated at some $27.1 million gross) associated with the reopening of Sarajevo airport and the monitoring of the so-called ''pink zones''.

By **resolution 47/210** of 22 December, the Assembly appropriated $290,049,500 gross ($288,313,900 net), inclusive of the $10 million authorized with the prior concurrence of ACABQ, for the operation of UNPROFOR for the period from 15 October 1992 to 20 February 1993.

Report of the Secretary-General (March). On 27 February,[102] the Secretary-General requested inclusion of the item on the financing of UNPROFOR in the agenda of the resumed forty-sixth session of the General Assembly, for allocation to the Fifth (Administrative and Budgetary) Committee. The financial requirements of the Force were outlined in a report of 6 March.[103]

In order to act immediately on the Security Council's agreement in resolution 727(1992) to send 50 military liaison officers to promote maintenance of the cease-fire in the former Yugoslavia, the Secretary-General had authorized budgetary commitments of up to $1 million, under the authority of a 1991 Assembly resolution on unforeseen and extraordinary expenses of the Organization.[104] He subsequently sought the concurrence of ACABQ to enter into commitments not to exceed $10 million, including the $1 million already authorized, to meet expenses of the military liaison mission starting on 12 January.

The total cost of UNPROFOR was estimated at $620,676,000 gross ($616,280,000 net) for the period from 12 January 1992 to 14 April 1993.

The Secretary-General also outlined the operational plan for UNPROFOR throughout the UNPAs. He also appealed to Member States to make advances to meet the initial expenses of UNPROFOR, and to make voluntary contributions in support of the emplacement and continuing operation of the Force. He recommended the establishment of a special account for UNPROFOR under the authority of financial regulation 6.6 for the purpose of accounting for income received and expenditures made.

Evaluating the Secretary-General's estimates, ACABQ, in a report of 13 March,[105] cited a number of areas in which it believed savings could be achieved, including mission subsistence allowance, travel and transportation, redistribution and reduction of civilian staff, rental and maintenance of premises, air operations, communications and equipment, and supplies and services. It recommended that the Assembly appropriate $250 million net, including the $10 million already authorized, which it considered adequate pending the Secretary-General's submission for additional requirements beyond October 1992.

GENERAL ASSEMBLY ACTION (March)

On 19 March, on the recommendation of the Fifth Committee, the General Assembly adopted **resolution 46/233** without vote.

Financing of the United Nations Protection Force

The General Assembly,

Having considered the report of the Secretary-General on the financing of the United Nations Protection Force and the related report of the Advisory Committee on Administrative and Budgetary Questions,

Bearing in mind Security Council resolutions 727(1992) of 8 January 1992 and 740(1992) of 7 February 1992, which endorsed the sending of a group of military liaison officers to Yugoslavia to promote maintenance of the cease-fire,

Bearing in mind also Security Council resolution 743(1992) of 21 February 1992, by which the Council established the United Nations Protection Force for an initial period of twelve months,

Recognizing that the costs of the Force are expenses of the Organization to be borne by Member States in accordance with Article 17, paragraph 2, of the Charter of the United Nations,

Recognizing also that, in order to meet the expenditures caused by the Force, a different procedure is required from the one applied to meet expenditures of the regular budget of the United Nations,

Taking into account the fact that the economically more developed countries are in a position to make relatively larger contributions and that the economically less developed countries have a relatively limited capacity to contribute towards such an operation,

Bearing in mind the special responsibilities of the States permanent members of the Security Council, as indicated in General Assembly resolution 1874(S-IV) of 27 June 1963, in the financing of such operations,

Mindful of the fact that it is essential to provide the Force with the necessary financial resources to enable it to fulfil its responsibilities under the relevant resolutions of the Security Council,

1. *Concurs* with the observations and recommendations contained in the report of the Advisory Committee on Administrative and Budgetary Questions;

2. *Urges* all Member States to make every possible effort to ensure payment of their assessed contributions to the United Nations Protection Force in full and on time;

3. *Decides* at this stage to appropriate, in accordance with the recommendation contained in paragraph 30 of the report of the Advisory Committee an amount of 251.5 million United States dollars gross (250 million dollars net), inclusive of the amount of 10 million dollars authorized with the concurrence of the Advisory Committee under the terms of General Assembly resolution 46/187 of 20 December 1991 for the expenses of the Force, and requests the Secretary-General to establish a special account for the Force in accordance with paragraph 15 of his report;

4. *Decides also*, as an ad hoc arrangement, to apportion the amounts referred to in paragraph 3 above among Member States in accordance with the composition of groups set out in paragraphs 3 and 4 of General Assembly resolution 43/232 of 1 March 1989, as adjusted by the Assembly in its resolutions 44/192 B of 21 December 1989, 45/269 of 27 August 1991 and 46/198 A of 20 December 1991, and taking into account the scale of assessments for the years 1992, 1993 and 1994;

5. *Decides further* that, in accordance with the provisions of its resolution 973(X) of 15 December 1955, there shall be set off against the apportionment among Member States, as provided for in paragraph 4 above, their respective share in the Tax Equalization Fund of the estimated staff assessment income of 1.5 million dollars approved for the Force;

6. *Decides* to consider the contributions of Armenia, Azerbaijan, Kazakhstan, Kyrgyzstan, the Republic of Moldova, San Marino, Tajikistan, Turkmenistan and Uzbekistan to the Force in accordance with the rates of assessment to be adopted for these Member States by the General Assembly at its forty-seventh session;

7. *Invites* the new Member States listed in paragraph 6 above to make advance payments against their assessed contributions to be determined;

8. *Invites* voluntary contributions to the Force in cash and in the form of services and supplies acceptable to the Secretary-General, to be administered, as appropriate, in accordance with the procedure established by the General Assembly in its resolution 44/192 A of 21 December 1989;

9. *Requests* the Secretary-General to take all necessary action to ensure that the Force is administered with a maximum of efficiency and economy;

10. *Decides* to include in the provisional agenda of its forty-seventh session the item entitled ''Financing of the United Nations Protection Force'';

11. *Requests* the Secretary-General to submit to the General Assembly by the start of its forty-seventh session a report on such additional requirements as may be necessary and to include in the report detailed and up-to-date information on the performance of the Force.

General Assembly resolution 46/233

19 March 1992   Meeting 83   Adopted without vote

Approved by Fifth Committee (A/46/894) without vote, 18 March (meeting 62); draft by Netherlands (A/C.5/46/L.23); agenda item 149.
Meeting numbers. GA 46th session: 5th Committee 61, 62; plenary 83.

Report of the Secretary-General (December).
In a 2 December report,[106] the Secretary-General estimated the cost of UNPROFOR at $292,811,400 gross ($290,924,100 net) for the period from 15 October 1992 to 20 February 1993, including $10 million in commitment authorization granted by ACABQ for the maintenance of UNPROFOR during the period beyond 14 October 1992. For the year from 21 February 1993 to 20 February 1994, he projected monthly costs of $48,112,350 gross ($47,462,350 net).

As at 31 October 1992, assessments totalling $250,455,801 had been apportioned among Member States for the operation of UNPROFOR from 12 January to 14 October. Contributions received totalled $186,975,292, leaving a shortfall of $63,480,509 in unpaid assessments. Full reimbursement to troop-contributing States for the initial six months of UNPROFOR had been delayed; only $19.3 million had been reimbursed and, as at 14 October, a balance of $64.7 million remained to be paid.

ACABQ, in a report of 11 December,[107] recommended savings through the use of available resources, carrying out UNPROFOR's various mandates in an integrated manner. It therefore recommended that the Assembly appropriate $290,049,500 gross ($288,313,900 net) for the period from 15 October 1992 to 20 February 1993 and, after that, the Secretary-General be given commitment authorization for seven months, i.e., until 20 September 1993, in the amount of $47,064,525 gross ($46,492,334 net) per month.

GENERAL ASSEMBLY ACTION (December)

On 22 December 1992, on the recommendation of the Fifth Committee, the General Assembly adopted **resolution 47/210** without vote.

Financing of the United Nations Protection Force

The General Assembly,

Having considered the report of the Secretary-General on the financing of the United Nations Protection Force and the related report of the Advisory Committee on Administrative and Budgetary Questions,

Bearing in mind Security Council resolutions 727(1992) of 8 January 1992 and 740(1992) of 7 February 1992, in which the Council endorsed the sending of a group of military liaison officers to Yugoslavia to promote maintenance of the cease-fire,

Bearing in mind also Security Council resolution 743(1992) of 21 February 1992, by which the Council established the United Nations Protection Force for an initial period of twelve months, and Council resolutions 758(1992) of 8 June 1992, 761(1992) of 29 June 1992, 762(1992) of 30 June 1992, 764(1992) of 13 July 1992, 769(1992) of 7 August 1992, 776(1992) of 14 September 1992, 779(1992) of 6 October 1992, 781(1992) of 9 October 1992, 786(1992) of 10 November 1992, 787(1992) of 16 November 1992 and 795(1992) of 11 December 1992, by which the Council enlarged the mandate of the Force,

Recalling its resolution 46/233 of 19 March 1992 on the financing of the Force,

Reaffirming that the costs of the Force are expenses of the Organization to be borne by Member States in accordance with Article 17, paragraph 2, of the Charter of the United Nations,

Recalling its previous decision regarding the fact that, in order to meet the expenditures caused by the Force, a different procedure is required from the one applied to meet expenditures of the regular budget of the United Nations,

Taking into account the fact that the economically more developed countries are in a position to make relatively larger contributions and that the economically less developed countries have a relatively limited capacity to contribute towards such an operation,

Bearing in mind the special responsibilities of the States permanent members of the Security Council, as indicated in General Assembly resolution 1874(S-IV) of 27 June 1963, in the financing of such operations,

Noting with appreciation that voluntary contributions have been made to the Force by certain Governments,

Mindful of the fact that it is essential to provide the Force with the necessary financial resources to enable it to fulfil its responsibilities under the relevant resolutions of the Security Council,

1. *Endorses* the observations and recommendations contained in the report of the Advisory Committee on Administrative and Budgetary Questions;

2. *Urges* all Member States to make every possible effort to ensure payment of their assessed contributions to the United Nations Protection Force in full and on time;

3. *Decides* to appropriate to the Special Account referred to in General Assembly resolution 46/233 an amount of 10 million United States dollars authorized with the concurrence of the Advisory Committee under the terms of General Assembly resolution 46/187 of 20 December 1991, for the period from 12 January to 14 October 1992;

4. *Decides also* to appropriate to the Special Account an amount of 290,049,500 dollars gross (288,313,900 dollars net), inclusive of the amount of 10 million dollars authorized with the prior concurrence of the Advisory Committee, for the operation of the Force for the period from 15 October 1992 to 20 February 1993, inclusive;

5. *Decides further*, as an ad hoc arrangement, to apportion the amount of 10 million dollars for the period from 12 January to 14 October 1992 and the amount of 290,049,500 dollars gross (288,313,900 dollars net) for the period from 15 October 1992 to 20 February 1993 among Member States in accordance with the composition of groups set out in paragraphs 3 and 4 of General Assembly resolution 43/232 of 1 March 1989, as adjusted by the Assembly in its resolutions 44/192 B of 21 December 1989, 45/269 of 27 August 1991 and 46/198 A of 20 December 1991, and taking into account the scale of assessments for the years 1992, 1993 and 1994;

6. *Decides* that, in accordance with the provisions of its resolution 973(X) of 15 December 1955, there shall be set off against the apportionment among Member States, as provided for in paragraph 5 above, their respective share in the Tax Equalization Fund of the estimated staff assessment income of 1,735,600 dollars for the period from 15 October 1992 to 20 February 1993 approved for the Force;

7. *Authorizes* the Secretary-General to enter into commitments for the operation of the Force at a rate not to exceed 47,064,525 dollars gross (46,492,334 dollars net) per month for the period from 21 February to 20 September 1993, should the Security Council decide to continue the Force beyond 20 February 1993, subject to obtaining the prior concurrence of the Advisory Committee for the actual level of commitments to be entered into for the period beyond 20 February 1993, the said amounts to be apportioned among Member States in accordance with the scheme set out in the present resolution;

8. *Decides* to consider the contributions of Armenia, Azerbaijan, Bosnia and Herzegovina, Croatia, Georgia, Kazakhstan, Kyrgyzstan, the Republic of Moldova, San Marino, Slovenia, Tajikistan, Turkmenistan and Uzbekistan to the Force in accordance with the rates of assessment to be adopted by the General Assembly for these Member States at its forty-seventh session;

9. *Invites* the new Member States listed in paragraph 8 above to make advance payments against their assessed contributions, to be determined;

10. *Invites* voluntary contributions to the Force in cash and in the form of services and supplies acceptable to the Secretary-General, to be administered, as appropriate, in accordance with the procedure established by the General Assembly in its resolutions 43/230 of 21 December 1988, 44/192 A of 21 December 1989 and 45/258 of 3 May 1991;

11. *Requests* the Secretary-General to take all necessary action to ensure that the Force is administered with a maximum of efficiency and economy;

12. *Decides* to include in the provisional agenda of its forty-eighth session the item entitled "Financing of the United Nations Protection Force".

General Assembly resolution 47/210

22 December 1992   Meeting 93   Adopted without vote

Approved by Fifth Committee (A/47/825) without vote, 19 December (meeting 50); draft by Kenya (A/C.5/47/L.16); agenda item 137.
Meeting numbers. GA 47th session: 5th Committee 46, 50; plenary 93.

Former Yugoslav Republic of Macedonia

By a letter of 23 November 1992 to the Security Council President,[108] the Secretary-General proposed that the Commander of UNPROFOR dispatch a dozen military, police and civilian personnel on an exploratory mission to the former Yugoslav Republic of Macedonia, in order to assess the need for possible UNPROFOR deployment there. A request for such deployment had been presented to the Secretary-General by Kiro Gligorov, President of Macedonia, on 11 November. The Co-Chairmen of the Steering Committee of the International Conference on the Former Yugoslavia, on 19 November, had recommended deployment to the capital, Skopje, of a small group of UNPROFOR military and police observers, with supporting political staff. Their immediate mandate would be to visit Macedonia's border areas with Albania and Serbia and to prepare a report on how a larger deployment of United Nations military and police personnel might help strengthen security and confidence there.

The Security Council's agreement with the proposal was conveyed to the Secretary-General on 25 November.[109]

Concern about the situation in the former Yugoslav Republic of Macedonia, particularly of the Albanians, who made up 40 per cent of the entire population there, was expressed by Albania in a letter of 14 November.[110] Recent violent clashes had left 4 persons dead, 30 wounded and more than 80 arrested. Albania recognized Macedonia's territorial integrity, but insisted that the legitimate rights of the Albanians living there be exercised. Albania requested that the region be put under international observation to avoid more bloodshed.

Report of the Secretary-General. An exploratory mission visited the former Yugoslav Republic of Macedonia from 28 November to 3 December 1992, the Secretary-General stated in a 9 December report.[111] The mission recommended that a small UNPROFOR presence be established on the inside of the Republic's borders with Albania and Yugoslavia (Serbia and Montenegro), with an essentially preventive mandate of monitoring any developments which could undermine stability. That task could be performed by an infantry battalion and 35 United Nations military observers.

The mission also recommended that a small group of United Nations civilian police be deployed in the border areas to monitor the Macedonian border police, as incidents arising from illegal attempts to cross the border had recently led to increased tension. However, unlike the military deployment, that proposal had not yet been accepted by the authorities of the former Republic.

The Commander of UNPROFOR endorsed the mission's proposals, and the Secretary-General accordingly recommended that the Security Council authorize a further enlargement of UNPROFOR's mandate and strength. The mission's report and recommendations were annexed to the Secretary-General's report.

The start-up costs for the deployment in the former Republic of Macedonia would initially be met from the resources made available for UNPROFOR by the General Assembly at its 1992 regular session.

SECURITY COUNCIL ACTION

On 11 December, the Security Council met to consider the Secretary-General's report. By unanimous vote, the Council adopted **resolution 795(1992)**.

The Security Council,

Recalling its resolution 743(1992) of 21 February 1992,

Recalling the letter of the President of the Security Council dated 25 November 1992 conveying its agreement to the

Secretary-General's proposal to send an exploratory mission to the former Yugoslav Republic of Macedonia,

Noting the report of the Secretary-General dated 9 December 1992,

Concerned about possible developments which could undermine confidence and stability in the former Yugoslav Republic of Macedonia or threaten its territory,

Welcoming the presence of a mission of the Conference on Security and Cooperation in Europe (CSCE) in the former Yugoslav Republic of Macedonia,

Considering the request by the Government in the former Yugoslav Republic of Macedonia for a United Nations presence in the former Yugoslav Republic of Macedonia,

Recalling Chapter VIII of the Charter of the United Nations,

1. *Approves* the report of the Secretary-General;

2. *Authorizes* the Secretary-General to establish a presence of the United Nations Protection Force (UNPRO-FOR) in the former Yugoslav Republic of Macedonia, as recommended by him in his report, and so to inform the authorities of Albania and those of the Federal Republic of Yugoslavia (Serbia and Montenegro);

3. *Requests* the Secretary-General to deploy immediately the military, civil affairs and administrative personnel recommended in his report, and that he deploy the police monitors immediately upon receiving the consent of the Government in the former Yugoslav Republic of Macedonia to do so;

4. *Urges* the UNPROFOR presence in the former Yugoslav Republic of Macedonia to coordinate closely with the CSCE mission there;

5. *Requests* the Secretary-General to keep the Council regularly informed of the implementation of this resolution;

6. *Decides* to remain seized of the matter.

Security Council resolution 795(1992)

11 December 1992   Meeting 3147   Adopted unanimously

Draft prepared in consultations among Council members (S/24940).

REFERENCES

[1]S/24795. [2]S/25015. [3]S/24934. [4]S/23363 & Add.1. [5]YUN 1991, p. 217, SC res. 721(1991), 27 Nov. 1991. [6]Ibid., p. 218. [7]S/23389. [8]S/23513. [9]YUN 1991, p. 215, SC res. 713(1991), 25 Sep. 1991. [10]S/23592 & Add.1. [11]S/23777. [12]S/23844. [13]S/23900. [14]S/23860. [15]S/23861. [16]S/24188 & Add.1. [17]S/24212. [18]S/24353 & Add.1. [19]S/24600. [20]S/24848. [21]A/47/158-S/23793. [22]S/24616, S/24640, S/24651, S/24675, S/24703, S/24709, S/24717, S/24734, S/24750. [23]S/23802. [24]S/23836. [25]S/23833. [26]S/23838. [27]S/23842. [28]S/23900. [29]S/23872. [30]S/24000. [31]S/24007. [32]S/23997. [33]S/24049. [34]S/24075 & Add.1. [35]S/24100 & Corr.1. [36]S/24201. [37]S/24222. [38]S/24263 & Add.1. [39]S/24305. [40]S/24307. [41]S/24333. [42]S/24346. [43]S/24376. [44]S/24377. [45]S/24378. [46]S/24379. [47]S/24404. [48]S/24405. [49]S/24401. [50]S/24439. [51]S/24439. [52]S/24423. [53]S/24410. [54]S/24416. [55]S/24412. [56]S/24419. [57]S/24440. [58]S/24415. [59]S/24413. [60]S/24409. [61]S/24431. [62]A/46/L.77. [63]A/46/967-S/24517. [64]A/46/972-S/24555. [65]S/24539. [66]A/46/968-S/24547. [67]S/24540. [68]S/24549. [69]S/24550. [70]S/24620. [71]S/24516. [72]S/24657. [73]S/24634. [74]S/24709, S/24717, S/24734, S/24750. [75]S/24740. [76]S/24744. [77]A/47/619-S/24749. [78]S/24767 & Add.1. [79]S/24783. [80]S/24750. [81]S/24810. [82]S/24840. [83]S/24870. [84]S/24900 & Add.1-7. [85]S/24761. [86]S/24785. [87]S/24786. [88]S/24620. [89]S/24804. [90]A/47/418-S/24516, A/47/635-S/24766. [91]A/47/666-S/24809. [92]S/24916.

[93]S/24932. [94]S/25052. [95]S/25000 & Add.1. [96]A/47/747. [97]S/23358 & Add.1-4. [98]YUN 1991, p. 219, SC res. 724(1991), 15 Dec. 1991. [99]S/24221 & Add.1,2. [100]S/23800. [101]S/25027. [102]A/46/236. [103]A/46/236/Add.1. [104]YUN 1991, p. 869, GA res. 46/187, 20 Dec. 1991. [105]A/46/893. [106]A/47/741. [107]A/47/778. [108]S/24851. [109]S/24852. [110]A/47/671-S/24814. [111]S/24923.

Baltic States

The Conference on Security and Cooperation in Europe, in its Helsinki summit Declaration of 10 July 1992,[1] expressed support for the efforts of participating States to remove peacefully problems that remained from the past, such as the stationing of foreign armed forces in the Baltic States—Estonia, Latvia and Lithuania—without the required consent of those countries. CSCE called on the participating States to conclude without delay bilateral agreements, including timetables, for the early, orderly and complete withdrawal of such foreign troops.

The Baltic States, collectively and individually, sent several communications to the Secretary-General regarding the unauthorized presence of Russian Federation forces in their territory. In August,[2] they requested that the issue be included on the agenda of the 1992 session of the General Assembly, bilateral negotiations on the subject having been largely unsuccessful.

GENERAL ASSEMBLY ACTION

On 25 November, the General Assembly adopted without vote **resolution 47/21**.

Complete withdrawal of foreign military forces from the territories of the Baltic States

The General Assembly,

Having considered the item entitled "Complete withdrawal of foreign military forces from the territories of the Baltic States",

Considering that the United Nations, pursuant to the provisions of its Charter, has a major role to play in, and responsibility for, the maintenance of international peace and security,

Recalling with particular satisfaction that independence was restored in Estonia, Latvia and Lithuania through peaceful and democratic means,

Recognizing that the stationing of foreign military forces on the territories of Estonia, Latvia and Lithuania without the required consent of those countries is a problem remaining from the past that must be resolved in a peaceful manner,

Welcoming recent agreements on the complete withdrawal of foreign military forces from the territory of Lithuania,

Welcoming also the bilateral talks on the complete withdrawal of foreign military forces from the territories of Estonia and Latvia,

Concerned about the continuing absence of any agreements for the complete withdrawal of foreign military forces from the territories of Estonia and Latvia,

Taking note of the report of the Secretary-General entitled "An Agenda for Peace", pursuant to the statement of 31 January 1992 adopted at the conclusion of the meeting held by the Security Council at the level of heads of State and Government,

Mindful that the timely application of preventive diplomacy is the most desirable and efficient means to ease tensions before they result in conflict,

Welcoming the "Helsinki Document 1992—The Challenges of Change", in particular paragraph 15, agreed upon at the Conference on Security and Cooperation in Europe, held at Helsinki on 9 and 10 July 1992,

Recognizing that the Conference on Security and Cooperation in Europe is a regional arrangement in the sense of Chapter VIII of the Charter of the United Nations, and as such provides an important link between European and global security,

Recognizing also that regional organizations participating in complementary efforts with the United Nations may encourage States outside the region to act supportively,

1. *Expresses support* for the efforts made by the States participating in the Conference on Security and Cooperation in Europe to remove the foreign military forces stationed on the territories of Estonia, Latvia and Lithuania without the required consent of those countries, in a peaceful manner and through negotiations;

2. *Calls upon* the States concerned, in line with the basic principles of international law and in order to prevent any possible conflict, to conclude without delay appropriate agreements, including timetables, for the early, orderly and complete withdrawal of foreign military forces from the territories of Estonia and Latvia;

3. *Urges* the Secretary-General to use his good offices to facilitate the complete withdrawal of foreign military forces from the territories of Estonia, Latvia and Lithuania;

4. *Requests* the Secretary-General to keep Member States informed of progress towards the implementation of the present resolution and to report thereon to the General Assembly at its forty-eighth session;

5. *Decides* to include in the provisional agenda of its forty-eighth session the item entitled "Complete withdrawal of foreign military forces from the territories of the Baltic States".

General Assembly resolution 47/21

25 November 1992   Meeting 72   Adopted without vote

3-nation draft (A/47/L.19); agenda item 139.
Sponsors: Estonia, Latvia, Lithuania.

Introducing the draft on behalf of the Baltic States, Latvia said that stationed in their territories were approximately 100,000 former Soviet military forces. Contrary to earlier agreements, new recruits had been rotated in order to replace departing troops. Military aircraft conducted unauthorized sorties in Baltic skies, endangering civil aviation, and continued to carry out bombing exercises with live ordnance. Cargo aircraft entered and departed Baltic territory without the knowledge and permission of the respective Government. Ports were used by foreign military naval forces, and vessels that operated from those bases were outside the control of local government and had on occasion been transferred to third countries. Nuclear reactors, controlled by

the foreign military forces in Estonia, were accessible neither to the Estonian Government nor to international inspectors.

Following the July 1992 Helsinki summit, agreements signed between Lithuania and the Russian Federation provided that the former Soviet military forces stationed in Lithuania would be completely withdrawn by 31 August 1993. However, those agreements were called into question when the President of the Russian Federation, by decree, suspended the withdrawal of military forces from the Baltic States and made the implementation of economic agreements between the Russian Federation and those States conditional on the granting of social guarantees to the foreign military forces. Equally disturbing were provisions of the decree that appeared to link the Russian Federation's commitment to withdraw its forces completely with the resolution of other issues.

The Russian Federation stated that it was attempting to complete the withdrawal as quickly as was feasible in the light of the need for simultaneous troop withdrawal from other foreign States. Having already agreed on a timetable for complete withdrawal from Lithuania by 31 August 1993, the Russian Federation proposed an accelerated withdrawal from Estonia and Latvia before the end of 1994, with the understanding that agreements would be reached on issues to ensure an orderly withdrawal and normal function of the troops during withdrawal. The temporary suspension of such withdrawal should not be seen as a political decision but as a measure for creating social protection for the military personnel involved. The Russian Federation was determined to settle all the problems between itself and the Baltic States in a responsible and constructive manner and in a spirit of cooperation and good-neighbourliness.

REFERENCES
[1]A/47/361. [2]A/47/191.

Other States

Armenia-Azerbaijan

Armenia and Azerbaijan, two newly independent States recently admitted to membership of the United Nations, had become involved in the situation in and around Nagorno-Karabakh, an enclave in Azerbaijan marked by over four years of fighting between its Armenian and Azerbaijani inhabitants.[1]

The situation was brought to the attention of the Secretary-General on 13 March 1992[2] by Ukraine, which described it as having reached a critical point, causing untold suffering among the population and dangerously destabilizing the situation in the region. Ukraine declared its support for the peace efforts of CSCE and the recommendations of its Committee of Senior Officials, and called for the withdrawal from the region of all armed formations, including the armed forces of the Commonwealth of Independent States. Escalation of the fighting was confirmed by Azerbaijan on 9 May,[3] when it reported that Armenian forces had occupied and destroyed Nagorno-Karabakh's city of Shusha, cutting off the only road linking that city with the rest of Azerbaijan; it made reference to a separatist movement instigated by ardent nationalists from Khankendi and their protectors, including Armenia, which were fuelling hatred and war. Earlier, on 27 March,[4] Iran reported on its efforts, at a tripartite meeting with Armenia and Azerbaijan at Tehran, to mediate an extension of a cease-fire in Nagorno-Karabakh.

SECURITY COUNCIL ACTION (May)

On 11 May,[5] Armenia requested an emergency meeting of the Security Council to consider the escalating conflict. Accordingly, the Council met on 12 May. Following consultations among Council members, the President made a statement[6] on behalf of the Council:

Meeting number. SC 3072.

"The members of the Security Council are deeply concerned by recent reports on the deterioration of the situation relating to Nagorno-Karabakh and by violations of cease-fire agreements which have caused losses of human life and widespread material damage, and by their consequences for the countries of the region.

"The members of the Security Council commend and support the efforts undertaken within the framework of the Conference on Security and Cooperation in Europe (CSCE), as well as other efforts aimed at assisting the parties in arriving at a peaceful settlement and at providing humanitarian assistance.

"They welcome the urgent dispatch by the Secretary-General of a mission to the region for fact-finding and to study ways and means to speedily assist the efforts undertaken within the framework of the CSCE to help the parties to reach a peaceful settlement. This mission will also include a technical element to look into ways the international community could provide prompt humanitarian assistance.

"The members of the Security Council call upon all concerned to take all steps necessary to bring the violence to an end, to facilitate the work of the Secretary-General's mission and to ensure the safety of its personnel. They recall the statements made on their behalf by the President of the Council on 29 January and 14 February 1992 on the admission respectively of Armenia and Azerbaijan to the United Nations, in particular the reference to the Charter principles relating to the peaceful settlement of disputes and the non-use of force."

Communications (May-August). Between May and August, Azerbaijan alleged continuing Armenian aggression, with Armenian military forces at-

tacking the town of Lachin, not within Nagorno-Karabakh,[7] and other Azerbaijani areas along the Armenia-Azerbaijan border in order to create a perimeter of "scorched territory" uninhabited by Azerbaijanis.[8] It subsequently reported that Armenia had carried out military operations along the entire length of the Armenia-Azerbaijan frontier, seizing Lachin, Shusha, Yukharyt-Askipara, Barkhudarly and Kiarka—to which Azerbaijan had been compelled to respond by exercising its right of self-defence to preserve its sovereignty and territorial integrity—and that CSCE had put forward proposals for a 60-day cease-fire.[9]

Armenia, referring to the alleged attacks and territorial seizures, contended that self-defence units from Nagorno-Karabakh were simply securing a road extending from Nagorno-Karabakh to Armenia to make it a safe corridor for the transport of humanitarian aid to Armenians in Nagorno-Karabakh.[10] On 20 August,[11] Armenia informed the Security Council President that, despite the fact-finding mission dispatched by the United Nations to the region in May to study ways of assisting CSCE negotiations towards resolving the conflict, the situation in Nagorno-Karabakh had rapidly deteriorated; it was therefore requesting an urgent meeting of the Council to consider ways to stabilize the situation.

SECURITY COUNCIL ACTION (26 August)

Following consultations among the members of the Security Council on 26 August, the President made a statement[12] on behalf of the Council, in connection with the item entitled "The situation relating to Nagorno-Karabakh":

"The members of the Security Council are deeply concerned by recent reports on the deterioration of the situation relating to Nagorno-Karabakh with heavy losses of human life and widespread material damage.

"The members of the Council strongly appeal to all parties and others concerned for an immediate cease-fire and support the efforts of the Minsk Conference on the question of Nagorno-Karabakh within the framework of the CSCE, as well as the preparatory negotiations held in Rome. They urge all parties and others concerned to cooperate closely with the CSCE and to participate positively in the negotiations with a view to reaching a peaceful settlement of their disputes as early as possible. They have noted that the Secretary-General dispatched fact-finding missions to the region and was ready to send observers to the above CSCE negotiations. The members of the Council will consider further the role of the United Nations in Nagorno-Karabakh at an appropriate time in the light of the development of the situation in the area."

Communications (October). Armenia on 12 October[13] stated that a cease-fire agreement as proposed by CSCE was unfortunately not concluded. However, a recent meeting with the Russian Federation, Kazakhstan, Armenia and Azerbaijan

(Sochi, Russian Federation, 21 September) resulted in a cease-fire agreement, with effect from 26 September, but that had been seriously violated. With Azerbaijan's explicit expression of willingness to enter into a cease-fire agreement and of consent to the deployment of observers in the region, Armenia requested the United Nations to send observers to assist both parties to implement a cease-fire. Certain that the appropriate time for such involvement was immediate, Armenia requested an urgent meeting of the Security Council to consider its request.

Azerbaijan, on 15 October,[14] advised that two cease-fire agreements had been signed: at Alma Ata, Kazakhstan, on 27 August; and at Sochi, on 21 September. A protocol covering the cease-fire arrangements and deployment of observers had also been signed in Moscow on 25 September. The first group of observers were deployed in the conflict zone and began operations on 28 September, and CSCE was continuing to strengthen the negotiating process between the parties.

SECURITY COUNCIL ACTION (October)

Responding to Armenia's request, the Security Council met on 27 October. Before it was a statement from Azerbaijan,[15] expressing grounds for optimism with regard to accelerating the settlement process within the CSCE framework.

Following consultations among Council members, the President was authorized to make a statement[16] on behalf of the Council:

Meeting number. SC 3127.

"The Security Council is deeply concerned by the grave situation which continues to prevail in Nagorno-Karabakh and surrounding districts, and also by the resulting loss of human life and destruction of property, despite the cease-fire agreement concluded at Sochi on 21 September 1992.

"The Security Council reaffirms the terms of its statement of 26 August 1992 on the situation concerning Nagorno-Karabakh, and in particular its support for the efforts of the Minsk Conference on the Nagorno-Karabakh question within the framework of the Conference on Security and Cooperation in Europe (CSCE). It strongly urges all the parties and others concerned to implement the cease-fire forthwith and to lift all blockades. It requests that the Minsk Conference be convened immediately and that political negotiations be undertaken in accordance with the President's rules of procedure. It urges all the parties and others concerned to cooperate closely with the CSCE and to participate positively in the Conference in order to reach an overall settlement of their disputes as soon as possible.

"The Security Council welcomes the intention of the Secretary-General to send a representative to the region to evaluate the contribution which the United Nations might make in supporting the efforts of the CSCE and in providing humanitarian assistance."

Welcoming the Council statement, Armenia said on 29 October[17] it accepted fully and unconditionally the Council's renewed call for an immediate cessation of hostilities and was ready to cooperate with the United Nations and CSCE in that regard. Subsequently, Armenia,[18] referring to a de facto economic blockade by Azerbaijan, appealed for humanitarian assistance, while Azerbaijan[19] reported new aggressions by Armenia in areas along their common border. Moreover, Azerbaijan[20] registered its vigorous objection with the Security Council President to the use of "Nagorno-Karabakh Republic" in a 31 October letter circulated as a Council document at Armenia's request,[21] and categorically rejected any attempt to introduce into United Nations usage, even in veiled form, the concept of an administrative-territorial entity which did not exist in Azerbaijan.

Alleged chemical-weapons use

Report of an investigative mission. By a note of 24 July,[22] the Secretary-General transmitted the report of a mission he had appointed, of three experts assisted by two Secretariat members, to investigate reports of chemical-weapons use in Azerbaijan. The mission was dispatched in response to two communications from Azerbaijan in June:[23] one alleged chemical attacks by Armenia on Nakhichevan, an Azerbaijani enclave in Armenia; the other transmitted, among other documents, the results of laboratory analyses of blood and other samples relating to the attacks. The mission's report described the methodology used, the on-site inspections where chemically armed artillery bombardments were alleged to have taken place, and chemical analyses of the samples taken.

The report observed that the initial information of chemical-weapons use was ambiguous at best; the finding of cyanide ion in chemical analyses could have a number of natural explanations; the events described as suggestive of such use were in no way typical of chemical attacks; the cases examined were instances of chemical injuries combined with those from conventional weapons, which were small in number and randomly dispersed over zones of conflict; and it was unlikely that chemical warfare agents would be used in such a way that no clusters of contaminated persons without conventional injury would have occurred. Furthermore, neither the histories told nor the signs and symptoms observed pointed to any of the recognized chemical warfare agents.

The report concluded that the events described could also be readily explained by causes other than chemical weapons; none agreed with any pattern that would be expected from a chemical attack. In sum, no evidence of chemical-weapons use was presented to the team.

Georgia

During 1992, the United Nations was apprised of an armed conflict that had broken out in Abkhazia, in the north-western part of Georgia, another newly independent State recently admitted to the United Nations.

SECURITY COUNCIL ACTION (September)

After consultations held by the Security Council on 10 September, its President made the following statement[24] to the media on behalf of the Council:

"The members of the Security Council, having heard the information provided by the Secretary-General and having considered the final document of the Moscow meeting between the President of the Russian Federation and the Chairman of the State Council of the Republic of Georgia on 3 September 1992, express their satisfaction with the efforts of the participants of the meeting aimed at achieving an immediate cease-fire, overcoming the crisis situation and creating conditions for a comprehensive political settlement in Abkhazia, which had become an area of armed conflict.

"The members of the Council, stressing the urgent necessity for a political settlement of the conflict by peaceful means, through negotiations, reaffirm the inadmissibility of any encroachment upon the principle of territorial integrity and upon Georgia's internationally recognized borders, and the necessity of respecting the rights of all people of all ethnic groups in the region. They welcome the resumption of the normal functioning of the legitimate authorities in Abkhazia.

"In this connection the members of the Council welcome the principles of the settlement contained in the above-mentioned final document and commend concrete measures aimed at the settlement in Abkhazia envisaged in it. They call upon all the parties in the conflict and all others concerned to observe strictly the agreements achieved in Moscow.

"The members of the Council take note of the intention of the Secretary-General to send a goodwill mission and request him to inform the Council periodically of the developments in Abkhazia."

Mission of good offices (September)

The Secretary-General, on 7 October,[25] transmitted to the President of the Security Council the report of the mission of good offices to Georgia. Led by the Director of the Europe Division, Department of Political Affairs, the mission extended from 12 to 20 September. At Tbilisi, it met with Eduard Shevardnadze, Chairman of the State Council, the Minister for Foreign Affairs, the Deputy Prime Minister and representatives of the State Council and several political parties. Thereafter, it met with members of the Supreme Council of Abkhazia, including its first Deputy President, at the Abkhazian capital of Sukhumi, and its President, at

Gudauta, with whom lengthy discussions were held. The mission also met with ICRC representatives. On its return to Tbilisi, it again met with Mr. Shevardnadze and held talks with the diplomatic community.

The report stated that the immediate crisis in Abkhazia could be attributed to two developments early in the year: widespread sabotage and looting that resulted in some 11 billion roubles in lost goods and in the virtual severance of Georgia's links with the Russian Federation, its main trading partner; and to actions by the ethnic Abkhaz leadership issuing from its 1990 declaration of the former Abkhaz Autonomous Soviet Socialist Republic as an independent republic.

The report described Abkhazia's 540,000 population as 47 per cent Georgian, 18 per cent Abkhaz (ethnically related to the north Caucasian mountain tribes and mostly Islamic), 18 per cent Armenian and 13 per cent Russian. The decades-long on-and-off tense relations between Georgians and Abkhaz resurfaced in 1978 when the Abkhaz launched a campaign to separate the Autonomous Republic of Abkhazia from the Georgian Soviet Socialist Republic and to incorporate it in the Russian Federative Socialist Republic. Although rejected by the latter and Georgia, the event resulted in significant concessions to the Abkhaz, including a disproportionate representation in the Supreme Soviet of Abkhazia, a preferential treatment perceived by Georgians as unfair to them.

Georgian opposition to new demands in 1989 that Abkhazia be separated from Georgia and granted the status of full Union Republic, which it had enjoyed from 1921 to 1930, led to the first of a series of violent incidents causing a significant number of deaths. In August 1990, the Abkhaz Supreme Soviet declared Abkhazia a sovereign republic of the Soviet Union independent of Georgia, an action immediately annulled by the Georgian Supreme Soviet.

In December 1991, a new Supreme Council of Abkhazia, elected under an electoral law agreed on by the Abkhaz leadership and the Georgian Government during Zviad Gamsakhurdia's presidency, allocated the seats on that Council as follows: 28 to Abkhazians, 26 to Georgians and 11 to the remaining Armenians and Russians. Instead of easing political tensions, this split the Council into two opposing factions so that it ceased to function as a whole.

In mid-1992, in the face of sabotage and looting too widespread for the police to control, Georgia sent 2,000 troops into Abkhazia to protect the railway and communication links. Fierce fighting broke out. Some 200 persons died, hundreds were wounded and up to 40,000 persons became refugees or displaced. While acknowledging that the Abkhaz had legitimate grievances, Georgia stressed that the attack against its troops was unprovoked and planned in advance. The Abkhaz leadership, which relocated to Gudauta, contended that the true purpose of the troops was to oppress the Abkhazians.

On 3 September, an agreement was signed in Moscow by the President of the Russian Federation, Boris Yeltsin, and Chairman Shevardnadze, and agreed to by the Abkhazian leadership. The agreement, the text of which was submitted to the Security Council on 8 September,[26] provided, *inter alia*, for: the territorial integrity of Georgia, a cease-fire effective 5 September, a Monitoring and Inspection Commission composed of representatives of Georgia, Abkhazia and the Russian Federation to ensure compliance with the agreement, the disarming and withdrawal of all outside illegal armed formations, the reduction of Georgia's armed forces in Abkhazia, the exchange of detainees, prisoners and hostages by 10 September, the removal of all impediments to the free movement of goods and persons, the return of refugees and the search for missing persons, and the resumption of the normal functions of the legitimate authorities of Abkhazia by 15 September. The agreement also appealed for United Nations and CSCE support for the principles it embodied.

Georgia agreed to the need to preserve Abkhazia's autonomy and its self-government status, but stressed that a solution had to preserve Georgia's territorial integrity and be acceptable to both Abkhaz and Georgians. The Abkhaz leadership, which alleged having been forced to sign the 3 September agreement, insisted that Abkhazia was not part of Georgia; thus, references to Georgia's territorial integrity did not affect Abkhazia. It conditioned implementation of the agreement—including withdrawal of the north Caucasian elements and resumption of the Abkhazian authorities' functions—on the withdrawal of all Georgian troops from Abkhazia. It called for direct negotiations with Georgia in order to establish some kind of confederation or federation.

The report observed that the situation in Abkhazia remained tense and explosive and could easily transcend Georgia's borders. The 3 September agreement remained largely unimplemented and law and order had broken down to a serious degree. The agreement should remain the foundation for a peaceful settlement. The international community could help to encourage both sides to abide by the agreement and negotiate a political settlement.

Communications. On 6 October,[27] the First Deputy Minister for Foreign Affairs of Georgia requested an urgent meeting of the Security Council to consider the grave and deteriorating situation in the country as a result of armed conflict unleashed in Abkhazia, threatening regional and international peace and security.

That request had been made four days earlier[28] by the Vice-Chairman of the State Council of Georgia, who informed the Secretary-General that, on 1 October, Abkhaz separatists, in conjunction with mercenary terrorists from the north Caucasian regions of the Russian Federation, mounted a large-scale offensive against the town of Gagra and advanced towards the Georgian-Russian Federation border, cutting off the northern part of Abkhazia from the rest of Georgia. The attackers were armed with state-of-the-art tanks and other weaponry of the kind with which the Russian army was equipped. The Vice-Chairman underscored the apparent conspiracy of the Abkhaz separatists with reactionary forces in Russia. An accompanying appeal for help to CSCE added that the aggression against Georgia climaxed on 3 October when an attempt was made on the life of the State Council Chairman.

In a statement of 7 October,[29] Georgia's First Deputy Foreign Minister recounted the events occurring in Abkhazia and its implications for Georgia's sovereignty and territorial integrity. He spoke of the Russian military's collaboration with separatists and direct aggression against Georgia, which the Government of the Russian Federation was unable to curb. He requested that a small United Nations peace-keeping force, or 10 to 15 military observers, be sent to the region.

On 8 October,[30] the Chairman of the State Council reported that, according to reliable sources from Abkhazia, mass executions of the Georgian civilian population, widespread torture, rape and other atrocities were being committed. He appealed to the Security Council to consider setting up a war crimes commission, with which Georgia was ready to cooperate in furnishing material evidence that might be deemed appropriate.

SECURITY COUNCIL ACTION (October)

In response to Georgia's request, the Security Council convened on 8 October. At its request, Georgia was invited to participate under rule 37a of the Council's provisional rules of procedure.

Following consultations among Council members, the President made a statement[31] on behalf of the Council:

Meeting number. SC 3121.

"The Security Council has noted with concern the report of the Secretary-General regarding the situation in Georgia dated 7 October 1992. It thanks the

Secretary-General for the useful information contained in that document. It expresses its grave preoccupation regarding the recent deterioration of the situation in Georgia. It calls on all the parties to cease the fighting forthwith and to observe the terms of the agreement concluded on 3 September 1992 in Moscow which affirms that the territorial integrity of Georgia shall be ensured, which provides for the establishment of a cease-fire, the commitment by the parties not to resort to the use of force, and which constitutes the basis for an overall political solution.

"The Council supports the decision of the Secretary-General to send, in response to the request of the Government of Georgia, another mission to Georgia, headed by an Under-Secretary-General, which will be accompanied by members of the Secretariat, some of whom will remain on the spot. It endorses the mandate proposed by the Secretary-General in his letter of 7 October. It looks forward to the report to be submitted by the Secretary-General upon the return of his mission from Georgia and is prepared to consider the recommendations which the Secretary-General plans to submit to it concerning the contribution which the United Nations could make to the implementation of the agreement of 3 September.

"The Council notes that the current Chairman of the CSCE intends to dispatch a mission to Georgia in the near future and underlines the need to ensure coordination between the efforts of the United Nations and those of the CSCE aimed at restoring peace."

Mission of good offices (October)

On 10 November,[32] the Secretary-General informed the Security Council President that he had sent a second mission to Georgia, from 13 to 16 October, headed by the Director-General of the United Nations Office at Geneva and including the Director of the Europe Division of the Department of Political Affairs.

A summary of the mission's report stated that the situation in Abkhazia had seriously deteriorated since the first mission. Severe fighting had broken out, the military build-up had intensified, Georgians and Abkhazians were accusing each other of the most serious human rights violations and a war mentality seemed to be taking hold. Relations had deteriorated between Georgia and the Russian Federation, mediator of the 3 September agreement, thus handicapping the peace process. Besides capturing the town of Gagra on 1 October and gaining control of the area from the northern cease-fire line along the Bzib River to the Russian Federation border to the north and west, the Abkhaz forces, supported by northern Caucasian fighters, had attacked Ochamchira, 55 kilometres south-east of Sukhumi. Ochamchira's capture could lead to the fall of Sukhumi and bring almost 80 per cent of Abkhazia under Abkhaz control. That could trigger a major military action in the area that could involve neighbouring countries.

The 3 September agreement appeared to have completely broken down and attempts during the first half of October to put it back on track proved unsuccessful. Georgia continued to support full implementation of the agreement, but called for restoration of the status quo prior to 1 October, when the Abkhaz resumed the fighting. It underlined that a crucial question was whether the international community accepted Georgia's territorial integrity and therefore recognized its right to deploy troops within its own borders. It expressed deep concern about the hostile intentions of the illegal "Confederation of Mountain Peoples of the Caucasus" established in the north Caucasus region of the Russian Federation, including its intention to make Sukhumi its capital. It stated that no action had been taken to ensure the withdrawal of the illegal north Caucasian elements from Abkhazia and that their numbers had increased to about 3,000.

The Abkhaz leadership agreed to the implementation of the 3 September agreement but insisted that, according to its interpretation, all Georgian troops were to be withdrawn from Abkhazia, which turned out not to be the case. Therefore, it preferred to conclude a new agreement explicitly stipulating such withdrawal. It recognized the principle of territorial integrity but insisted that the principle of self-determination also had to be respected. Above all, Abkhazia had declared its own "sovereignty" prior to Georgia's admission to the United Nations, of which the Organization had taken no notice. The United Nations, it stated, could play a very important role in Abkhazia, provided it fairly addressed the issues of concern to the Abkhaz.

The mission observed that the potentially explosive situation described by the first mission had clearly worsened. If not reversed and if confidence in the peace process of the 3 September agreement was not rebuilt, large-scale fighting appeared inevitable.

Communications. By a letter transmitted on 11 November,[33] Georgia said the fact-finding mission was an important step towards a peaceful settlement. However, confrontation was intensifying and the number of casualties increased daily, as the Abkhaz separatists, along with mercenaries from other countries, continued to carry out military operations. The rest of Georgia was engulfed by a surge of refugees originating in Abkhazia. Georgia still invested its greatest hopes in international organizations, first and foremost in a prompt and effective response by the Security Council.

On 25 December,[34] Georgia informed the Secretary-General that the military-political situation in the country had somewhat changed. It called for inclusion of the issue on the 1993 agenda of the Security Council and suggested that it be the subject of a formal Council debate. Any Council resolution adopted on it should provide for a United Nations peace-keeping force in the Abkhazian region, as well as for an appeal to neighbouring States to support the efforts for a peaceful settlement of the Abkhaz problem, to refrain from actions that might cause a further escalation of the confrontation and not to allow any encroachment on Georgia's territorial integrity. Georgia also suggested that coordination of Council efforts with those of various regional and subregional international organizations could be highly effective.

Tajikistan

The Secretary-General, on 29 October 1992,[35] informed the President of the Security Council of his decision to send a United Nations good-offices mission to Tajikistan and other countries in Central Asia. That decision was in response to two communications, of 29 September and 15 October, from Tajikistan and in the context of a report of a United Nations fact-finding mission to Uzbekistan and Tajikistan from 13 to 23 September.

The mission, to be led by a Director in the Secretariat's Department of Political Affairs, was scheduled to leave New York on 1 November for Moscow and thence to Tajikistan, Uzbekistan, Kyrgyzstan and Kazakhstan. The actual visit to Tajikistan and neighbouring countries took place from 4 to 13 November, with a stopover for consultations in Moscow on 3 and 14 November.

Tajikistan informed the Council President earlier, on 21 October,[36] of the armed confrontations among various factions in the country and consequent death and destruction, and urgently requested that a mission be dispatched to help settle the conflicts and provide emergency humanitarian aid. Kyrgyzstan[37] and the Russian Federation[38] also drew attention to the civil strife and to the threat of its further escalation and expansion, with catastrophic consequences for Tajikistan's territorial integrity and the security of the whole Central Asian region. On 29 October,[39] Tajikistan informed the Secretary-General that several officers of the Russian Federation's military command in the country had been won over by one of the local factions and that armoured vehicles and tanks stolen from the Russian command were being used in the fighting.

SECURITY COUNCIL ACTION

On 30 October, the Security Council met to discuss the Tajikistan situation. After consultations among Council members, the President was authorized to make the following statement[40] on behalf of the Council:

Meeting number: SC 3131.

"The Security Council has considered the communications received from the Government of Tajikistan.

"The Security Council expresses its very grave concern about the continuing deterioration in the situation in Tajikistan, which is causing considerable loss of human life and serious material damage. It notes with concern the consequences for peace and security in the region that this crisis might entail.

"The Security Council calls on all parties to the conflict to end the fighting. It urges the Government of Tajikistan, local authorities, party leaders and other groups concerned to enter into a political dialogue with a view to reaching an overall settlement of the conflict by peaceful means. It calls on parties in neighbouring countries to refrain from any action which might contribute to increasing tension and to impeding a settlement.

"The Security Council welcomes the efforts made by the member countries of the Commonwealth of Independent States, on the initiative of the Republic of Kyrgyzstan, and those undertaken by other States to help Tajikistan to resolve the crisis. It invites the Government of Tajikistan and all other parties to the conflict to cooperate actively with all these efforts.

"The Security Council welcomes the Secretary-General's decision to send a goodwill mission, including a humanitarian assistance mission, to Tajikistan and Central Asia, in response to the requests of the Governments of the region, within the next few days as a contribution by the United Nations to resolving the conflict.

"The Security Council calls on all parties to the conflict and the neighbouring countries to facilitate the work of the Secretary-General's mission and to ensure the safety of its personnel."

Subsequently, in December, Kazakhstan[41] informed the Council President of a further dangerous development, namely, that one of the warring factions had occupied a number of government buildings and announced a change of power in Tajikistan; and Tajikistan[42] advised the Secretary-General of repeated violations of its borders by Afghanistan.

REFERENCES

[1]A/47/1. [2]A/47/122-S/23716. [3]S/23894. [4]S/23760. [5]S/23896. [6]S/23904. [7]S/23926. [8]S/24112. [9]S/24486. [10]S/24029. [11]S/24470. [12]S/24493. [13]S/24656. [14]S/24671. [15]S/24713. [16]S/24721. [17]S/24730. [18]S/24915. [19]S/24952. [20]S/24771. [21]S/24751. [22]S/24344. [23]S/24053, S/24103. [24]S/24542. [25]S/24633. [26]S/24523. [27]S/24619. [28]S/24626. [29]S/24632. [30]S/24641. [31]S/24637. [32]S/24794. [33]A/47/664-S/24802. [34]S/25026. [35]S/24739. [36]S/24699. [37]S/24692. [38]S/24725. [39]S/24741. [40]S/24742. [41]S/24881. [42]S/25025.

Chapter V

Middle East

United Nations efforts to bring about a comprehensive settlement of the complex Middle East conflict remained unswerving throughout 1992. The parties to the conflict were themselves engaged in an ongoing peace process sponsored by the Russian Federation and the United States, to the multilateral negotiations of which the United Nations had been invited as a full participant. Several Member States welcomed as a positive contribution to that process the fact that the General Assembly, deviating from past practice, did not adopt a general resolution on the Middle East during the year. The Assembly expressed the need, however, for the United Nations to play an expanded role in that process.

Concerted action by various United Nations bodies focused on the question of Palestine; on the policies and practices of Israel in the Palestine territory, including Jerusalem, and other Arab territories it had occupied since 1967; and on assistance to the Palestine refugees. To help keep the region's volatility in check, the Security Council extended the mandate of the United Nations Interim Force in Lebanon, as well as that of the United Nations Disengagement Observer Force in the Golan Heights, so that both peace-keeping operations remained in place throughout the year.

The Committee on the Exercise of the Inalienable Rights of the Palestinian People (Committee on Palestinian rights) continued to press for the implementation of its original (1976) recommendations—on the rights of the Palestinians to return to their homes and property and to achieve self-determination, national independence and sovereignty in Palestine—and for the convening of an international peace conference under United Nations auspices. The Assembly considered that such a conference should take place, at a certain stage, in the light of the Secretary-General's assessment that sufficient agreement did not exist to permit its imminent convening.

The Special Committee to Investigate Israeli Practices Affecting the Human Rights of the Palestinian People and Other Arabs of the Occupied Territories (Committee on Israeli practices) drew to the Assembly's attention the worsening situation in the occupied territories owing to Israeli policies and practices there and to the occupation itself. The Commission on Human Rights reiterated the Palestinians' right to self-determination and called on Israel to desist from human rights violations in the territories.

The United Nations Relief and Works Agency for Palestine Refugees in the Near East continued to provide a wide-ranging programme of education, health, relief and social services for the Palestine refugees. It appealed for more funds from the donor community to enable it to expand its services to meet rising demands from a refugee population that had swelled to an estimated 2.73 million by the end of the year.

By a series of resolutions, the Assembly addressed specific aspects of the refugee problem and of the situation in the occupied territories. By mid-1992, those territories had been under Israeli occupation for a quarter of a century. Throughout that time, the territories' Palestinian and other Arab inhabitants had refused to accept the occupation as a permanent fact. The persistent uprising, born of that refusal, and its suppression by Israeli military force and collective punishment led the Assembly once more to request the Security Council urgently to consider measures to provide international protection to the Palestinian civilians in those territories. The Security Council condemned the renewed cycle of violence between March and April. It convened in January to consider Israel's resumption of deportations, on that occasion of 12 Palestinians accused of inciting terrorism. It met again in December strongly to condemn Israel's deportation of hundreds of Palestinians into Lebanon, to demand their safe and immediate return to the territories, and to ask the Secretary-General to consider dispatching a representative to discuss the matter with the Government of Israel. Of the 418 Palestinians under deportation orders, 383 were deported into southern Lebanon despite that country's unwillingness to receive them.

The Economic and Social Council, as well as the Assembly, deplored Israel's confiscation of land, its appropriation of water resources and depletion of other economic resources. A number of other United Nations organs and specialized agencies maintained their programmes of economic and social assistance for the Palestinians during the year.

Middle East situation

The General Assembly, deviating from past practice, in 1992 did not adopt a resolution on the general situation in the Middle East—a gesture welcomed by several Member States as a positive contribution to the ongoing peace process launched at Madrid, Spain, in 1991.[1] While welcoming that process, the Assembly reaffirmed the urgency of achieving a comprehensive settlement of the Arab-Israeli conflict—the core of which was the question of Palestine—and considered that the convening, at a certain stage, of an International Peace Conference on the Middle East under United Nations auspices would contribute to the promotion of peace in the region (resolution 47/64 D).

It was the Secretary-General's assessment, however, that sufficient agreement did not exist to permit convening such a conference in the foreseeable future. In the meantime, the United Nations had become a full participant in the multilateral negotiations on regional matters of the ongoing peace process.

Reports of the Secretary-General. In response to a General Assembly request of 1991,[2] the Secretary-General reported to the Assembly and the Security Council on developments in the Middle East situation during the period 16 November 1991 to 20 November 1992.[3] He gave an overview of all aspects of the situation, including the various peace-keeping operations in the region, the situation in the occupied territories, the Palestine question and the Palestine refugees.

The Secretary-General stated that he had followed closely the Peace Conference on the Middle East in progress in Washington, D.C., had maintained contact with its co-sponsors (the United States and the Russian Federation) and the parties concerned (Israel, Lebanon, the Syrian Arab Republic and a joint Jordanian-Palestinian delegation), and had underlined United Nations readiness to assist in any way useful. He believed that the United Nations, with its wide experience in peace-keeping, humanitarian relief and technical assistance, was in a position to play a more substantive and integrated role in the Middle East. He recalled that United Nations peace-keeping had its origins in the region, where for decades it had contributed to peace and stability, and where, in the economic and social domains, United Nations agencies and programmes had a solid record of assistance. He noted that Security Council resolutions 242(1967)[4] and 338(1973),[5] long recognized as the cornerstone of a comprehensive settlement of the Arab-Israeli conflict, were the basis of the current negotiating process.

The Secretary-General also stated that, on 20 November 1992, following the invitation extended to the United Nations as a full participant in the multilateral negotiations of the Peace Conference, he had appointed Chinmaya Rajaninath Gharekhan (India), with effect from January 1993, as his Special Representative to coordinate the role of the United Nations in the working groups on arms control and regional security, economic and regional development, environment, refugees and water.

The Secretary-General submitted a second report[6] reproducing replies, received as of 16 November from four States, to his request for information regarding implementation of the Assembly's 1991 call on all States not to provide Israel with any assistance to be used specifically in connection with settlements in the occupied Palestinian territory and other occupied Arab territories.[2]

GENERAL ASSEMBLY CONSIDERATION

During the General Assembly's consideration of the agenda item on the Middle East situation on 11 December 1992, Indonesia, on behalf also of Afghanistan, Cuba, Malaysia, Mauritania, Morocco, Oman, Pakistan, the Sudan, the Syrian Arab Republic, Viet Nam and Yemen, introduced a draft resolution[7] embodying the text of the resolution traditionally adopted on the item. As in the past, its provisions included a reaffirmation of the Assembly's conviction that the question of Palestine was the core of the conflict in the Middle East and that no comprehensive, just and lasting peace in the region would be achieved without the full exercise by the Palestinian people of its inalienable national rights and the immediate withdrawal of Israel from the Palestinian territory occupied since 1967, including Jerusalem, and other occupied Arab territories.

The sponsors recommended, however, that the Assembly not take action on the draft, although they reserved the right to request action on it later in the current session. Canada, Japan and the United Kingdom welcomed that recommendation as a positive contribution towards the ongoing Middle East peace process. Because the text was repetitive of the previous year's resolution on the subject,[2] the Russian Federation joined in welcoming the sponsors' decision.

Proposed peace conference under UN auspices

As requested by General Assembly resolution 46/75 of 1991, calling for an international peace conference on the Middle East,[8] the Secretary-General submitted a progress report on 27 November 1992[9] on developments concerning the prospects for such a conference, first endorsed by the Assembly in 1983.[10] The report stated that the Security Council had yet to reply to the Secretary-General's request for its views on the matter. However, Israel, Lebanon, the Syrian Arab Republic and the Palestine Liberation Organization (PLO) had communicated their positions, in response to a similar request made of them and of Egypt and Jordan as participants in such a conference.

In its note of 9 November, Israel pointed out that it had consistently voted against Assembly resolutions calling for an international peace conference, having long advocated direct negotiations as the only framework to advance peace in the Middle East. It was currently engaged in direct, face-to-face negotiations with its neighbours in bilateral and multilateral frameworks, in the multilateral negotiations of which the United Nations had become a participant. Israel described resolution 46/75 as detached from reality and anachronistic, and found unacceptable its inclusion of PLO as a conference participant, for it was a terrorist organization and as such could not be considered a partner in peace negotiations. Resolution 46/75, by reaffirming a series of principles that prejudged the very principles contained in Council resolutions 242(1967) and 338(1973), stood in opposition to any genuine notion of peace, thus contradicting itself.

Lebanon's note of 16 November stressed the following points: it supported the convening of an international conference and agreed in principle to attend, although its primary interest lay in the liberation of all of its territory; its attendance should in no way imply a link between the resolution of its problem and that of the Middle East as a whole; it rejected any attempt to settle Palestinians in Lebanese territory; it insisted that the problem of Israel's occupation of Lebanese territory must be solved by implementing Council resolution 425(1978)[11] calling for the immediate cessation of Israel's military action against Lebanon's territorial integrity and withdrawal of Israel's forces from all Lebanese territory; and it insisted on adherence to all provisions of the 1949 General Armistice Agreement.[12] Lebanon noted that its participation in the current Peace Conference was in response to a United States invitation stating the need for implementing resolution 425(1978).

The Syrian Arab Republic advised on 19 November that, in continuance of its efforts to help establish a comprehensive peace based on Council resolutions 242(1967) and 338(1973), it agreed to participate in the current Peace Conference. It stressed that a failure of that Conference to arrive at an agreement would not affect its commitment to Assembly resolution 46/75 or to other United Nations resolutions on the Arab-Israeli conflict and on the Palestine question. It stated its belief that the Assembly should reaffirm the need for continued international efforts to achieve a comprehensive peace that secured Israel's full withdrawal from all occupied Arab territories and guaranteed the national rights of the Palestinian people.

PLO, in its note of 3 November, expressed support for the peace process currently under way and

had authorized Palestinian participation in it. Unfortunately, a year had passed and the negotiations had not achieved any tangible results—because, as the chairman of the observer delegation of Palestine noted in his statement on 30 November before the Assembly, of Israel's intransigent posture. Consequently, PLO believed that an international peace conference represented the most effective means of achieving peace in the Middle East. In view of the complexity of the issues relating to the Palestine question and the Middle East situation, PLO deemed it imperative that such a conference must be convened at a certain stage.

From the foregoing communications, the Secretary-General concluded that sufficient agreement did not exist to permit the convening of an international peace conference as outlined in resolution 46/75. It was important to note, he added, that the negotiations begun at Madrid had continued throughout the year and had been widened to include full United Nations participation in the multilateral working groups on regional issues.

On the other hand, the Committee on Palestinian rights,[13] in adopting its work programme, continued to give utmost priority to the convening of an international peace conference under United Nations auspices.

GENERAL ASSEMBLY ACTION

The General Assembly, on 11 December 1992, adopted **resolution 47/64 D** by recorded vote.

The General Assembly,

Recalling its resolutions 43/176 of 15 December 1988, 44/42 of 6 December 1989, 45/68 of 6 December 1990 and 46/75 of 11 December 1991,

Having considered the report of the Secretary-General of 27 November 1992,

Having heard the statement made on 30 November 1992 by the chairman of the observer delegation of Palestine,

Stressing that achieving a comprehensive settlement of the Middle East conflict, the core of which is the question of Palestine, will constitute a significant contribution to international peace and security,

Noting the convening at Madrid, on 30 October 1991, of the Peace Conference on the Middle East and the subsequent bilateral negotiations, as well as meetings of the multilateral working groups,

Noting also that the United Nations has participated as a full, extraregional participant in the work of the multilateral working groups,

Preoccupied by the increasingly serious situation in the occupied Palestinian territory, including Jerusalem, as a result of persistent policies and practices of Israel, the occupying Power,

1. *Reaffirms* the urgent need to achieve a just and comprehensive settlement of the Arab-Israeli conflict, the core of which is the question of Palestine;

2. *Welcomes* the ongoing peace process, which started at Madrid, and expresses the hope that it will lead to the establishment of a comprehensive, just and lasting peace in the region;

3.   *Expresses* the need for the United Nations to play a more active and expanded role in the current peace process;

4.   *Considers* that the convening, at a certain stage, of an International Peace Conference on the Middle East, under the auspices of the United Nations, with the participation of all parties to the conflict, including the Palestine Liberation Organization, on an equal footing, and the five permanent members of the Security Council, based on Council resolutions 242(1967) of 22 November 1967 and 338(1973) of 22 October 1973 and the legitimate national rights of the Palestine people, primarily the right to self-determination, would contribute to the promotion of peace in the region;

5.   *Reaffirms* the following principles for the achievement of comprehensive peace:

(*a*)   The withdrawal of Israel from the Palestinian territory occupied since 1967, including Jerusalem, and from the other occupied Arab territories;

(*b*)   Guaranteeing arrangements for peace and security of all States in the region, including those named in resolution 181(II) of 29 November 1947, within secure and internationally recognized boundaries;

(*c*)   Resolving the problem of the Palestine refugees in conformity with General Assembly resolution 194(III) of 11 December 1948, and subsequent relevant resolutions;

(*d*)   Dismantling the Israeli settlements in the territories occupied since 1967;

(*e*)   Guaranteeing freedom of access to Holy Places, religious buildings and sites;

6.   *Notes* the expressed desire and endeavours to place the Palestinian territory occupied since 1967, including Jerusalem, under the supervision of the United Nations for a transitional period or, alternatively, to provide international protection for the Palestinian people there, as part of the peace process;

7.   *Requests* the Secretary-General to continue his efforts with the parties concerned, and in consultation with the Security Council, for the promotion of peace in the region, and to submit progress reports on developments in this matter.

General Assembly resolution 47/64 D

11 December 1992   Meeting 84   93-4-60 (recorded vote)

26-nation draft (A/47/L.38 & Add.1); agenda item 30.
Sponsors: Afghanistan, Algeria, Bangladesh, Comoros, Cuba, Guinea, India, Indonesia, Jordan, Lao People's Democratic Republic, Lebanon, Madagascar, Malaysia, Mali, Malta, Mauritania, Morocco, Pakistan, Qatar, Saudi Arabia, Senegal, Sudan, Tunisia, Vanuatu, Viet Nam, Yemen.
Meeting numbers. GA 47th session: plenary 74-77, 84.

Recorded vote in Assembly as follows:

In favour: Afghanistan, Algeria, Angola, Azerbaijan, Bahrain, Bangladesh, Barbados, Bhutan, Botswana, Brazil, Brunei Darussalam, Burkina Faso, Burundi, Cameroon, Central African Republic, Chad, Chile, China, Colombia, Comoros, Côte d'Ivoire, Cuba, Cyprus, Democratic People's Republic of Korea, Djibouti, Ecuador, Egypt, El Salvador, Ethiopia, Fiji, Gabon, Gambia, Ghana, Guinea, Guyana, Haiti, Honduras, India, Indonesia, Iran, Iraq, Jamaica, Jordan, Kenya, Kuwait, Lao People's Democratic Republic, Lebanon, Lesotho, Libyan Arab Jamahiriya, Madagascar, Malaysia, Maldives, Mali, Malta, Mauritania, Mauritius, Mexico, Mongolia, Morocco, Myanmar, Namibia, Nepal, Nicaragua, Niger, Nigeria, Oman, Pakistan, Paraguay, Peru, Philippines, Qatar, Rwanda, Saudi Arabia, Senegal, Sierra Leone, Singapore, Sri Lanka, Sudan, Suriname, Syrian Arab Republic, Thailand, Togo, Tunisia, Turkey, Uganda, United Arab Emirates, United Republic of Tanzania, Vanuatu, Venezuela, Viet Nam, Yemen, Zambia, Zimbabwe.
Against: Israel, Marshall Islands, Micronesia, United States.
Abstaining: Albania, Antigua and Barbuda, Argentina, Australia, Austria, Bahamas, Belarus, Belgium, Belize, Benin, Bolivia, Bosnia and Herzegovina, Bulgaria, Canada, Costa Rica, Croatia, Czechoslovakia, Denmark, Dominica, Dominican Republic, Estonia, Finland, France, Germany, Greece, Guatemala, Hungary, Iceland, Ireland, Italy, Japan, Kazakhstan, Latvia, Liechtenstein, Lithuania, Luxembourg, Malawi, Netherlands, New Zealand, Norway, Panama, Poland, Portugal, Republic of Korea, Republic of Moldova, Romania, Russian Federation, Saint Kitts and Nevis, Saint Lucia, Saint Vincent and the Grenadines, Samoa, San Marino, Slovenia, Solomon Islands, Spain, Swaziland, Sweden, Ukraine, United Kingdom, Uruguay.

Before adopting the text as a whole, the Assembly adopted operative paragraphs 4, 5 and 6 by recorded votes of, respectively: 87 to 5, with 58 abstentions; 87 to 6, with 59 abstentions; and 90 to 5, with 57 abstentions.

The Russian Federation, a co-sponsor of the current peace talks, suggested earlier that, instead of presenting the traditional and outdated draft resolution on the convening of an international peace conference, the Assembly should adopt a brief resolution aimed at promoting the Arab-Israeli negotiations currently under way without touching on the substance of questions discussed. Such a resolution might reaffirm the urgent need for the achievement of a comprehensive, just and lasting settlement of the Arab-Israeli conflict, welcome the negotiation process within the framework of the Peace Conference taking place at a bilateral level and also in multilateral working groups, call on all parties to those negotiations to demonstrate a constructive and responsible approach and on all other parties concerned to endeavour to ensure a favourable atmosphere to promote the successful conclusion of the ongoing negotiations.

Israel felt that, in the view of the current peace talks and the Secretary-General's assessment that sufficient agreement did not exist to permit the convening of an international peace conference, there was no reason for the resolution just adopted. The text was changed to call for the convening of such a conference "at a certain stage" to create the impression that the resolution and the current peace process were somehow compatible, which they were not. The resolution laid down five principles for the achievement of peace that predetermined the outcome of the proposed international conference, in contradiction of any fair notion of peace. On the other hand, the peace process begun at Madrid and continuing at Washington, D.C., was based on the principle of direct negotiations without preconditions between Israel and its Arab neighbours.

After the vote, a representative of the Permanent Observer Mission of Palestine to the United Nations underscored the importance of three principles: permanent United Nations responsibility in relation to the question of Palestine until the question was resolved in all its aspects; the effective implementation of United Nations resolutions, particularly those of the Security Council, that were binding regardless of developments in the current, or in any other, peace process; and any positive change in the international community's stance towards Israel should be meticulously concurrent with and equal to genuine progress in the peace process and in the actual situation in the occupied territories.

United Nations Truce Supervision Organization

As described by the Secretary-General in his November report on the situation in the Middle East,[3] three peace-keeping operations remained in place in the region: two peace-keeping forces—the United Nations Disengagement Observer Force (UNDOF) (see below, under "Israel and the Syrian Arab Republic") and the United Nations Interim Force in Lebanon (UNIFIL) (see below, under "Lebanon")—and an observer mission, the United Nations Truce Supervision Organization (UNTSO). Headquartered in Jerusalem, with liaison offices in Amman, Jordan, and Beirut, Lebanon, UNTSO continued to assist UNDOF and UNIFIL in the performance of their tasks.

UNTSO was in the process of gradually reducing its strength, from 298 to some 220 military observers. The observers were from the following countries: Argentina, Australia, Austria, Belgium, Canada, Chile, China, Denmark, Finland, France, Ireland, Italy, Netherlands, New Zealand, Norway, Russian Federation, Sweden, Switzerland, United States.

REFERENCES
[1]YUN 1991, p. 221. [2]Ibid., p. 222, GA res. 46/82 A, 16 Dec. 1991. [3]A/47/672-S/24819. [4]YUN 1967, p. 257, SC res. 242(1967), 22 Nov. 1967. [5]YUN 1973, p. 213, SC res. 338(1973), 22 Oct. 1973. [6]A/47/673. [7]A/47/L.41 & Add.1. [8]YUN 1991, p. 224, GA res. 46/75, 11 Dec. 1991. [9]A/47/716-S/24845. [10]YUN 1983, p. 278, GA res. 38/58 C, 13 Dec. 1983. [11]YUN 1978, p. 312, SC res. 425(1978), 19 Mar. 1978. [12]YUN 1948-49, p. 185. [13]A/47/35.

Palestine question

The question of Palestine remained a subject of debate and of several resolutions by the General Assembly in 1992.

Besides reaffirming the question to be the core of the Middle East conflict (resolution 47/64 D), the Assembly, following its consideration of the annual report of the Committee on Palestinian rights, endorsed the Committee's recommendations and drew the attention of the Security Council to the fact that action on them was still awaited (47/64 A); requested resources for the Division for Palestinian Rights, as well as continued cooperation with it (47/64 B); and further requested the Department of Public Information (DPI) to continue its special information programme on the question during the 1992-1993 biennium (47/64 C). It again determined that Israel's 1980

decision[1] to impose its laws, jurisdiction and administration on Jerusalem was illegal and therefore null and void (47/63 B).

Having reviewed the assistance provided by the United Nations system to Palestinians throughout the year, the Assembly, on the recommendation of the Economic and Social Council (1992/58), asked for sustained and increased international assistance to the Palestinian people, in cooperation with PLO (47/170). It requested the United Nations Conference on Trade and Development (UNCTAD) to maintain its programme of assistance in its current form, also in cooperation with PLO (decision 47/445).

In related actions, the Assembly demanded that Israel acknowledge the *de jure* applicability of the 1949 Geneva Convention relative to the Protection of Civilian Persons in Time of War (fourth Geneva Convention) to the occupied Palestinian territory and other Arab territories, that it desist from changing their legal status, geographical nature or demographic composition, and that it allow the Committee on Israeli practices access to them (see below, under "Territories occupied by Israel"); the Assembly also proposed the establishment of a university for Palestine refugees (see also below, under "Palestine refugees").

Communications. The Permanent Observer of Palestine, on 4 March 1992,[2] transmitted to the Secretary-General a document presented by the Palestinian delegation (the Palestinian side of the joint Palestinian-Jordanian delegation) to Israel on 3 March during the round of negotiations in progress in Washington, D.C. The document outlined the model for a Palestinian Interim Self-Governing Authority (PISGA) as part of interim arrangements for self-government, based on free elections under international supervision and entailing the orderly transfer to PISGA of the powers and responsibilities currently exercised by Israel in the occupied Palestinian territory, including Jerusalem. PISGA would provide a framework in which Palestinians, in the occupied territory or in exile, would be able to participate, on an equal footing, in all negotiations leading to the permanent resolution of the Palestinian question in all its aspects.

The document emphasized that acceptance of the proposed interim arrangements by the Palestinians would in no way prejudice the exercise of their legitimate right to self-determination, as embodied in the Charter of the United Nations and relevant United Nations resolutions, and as stipulated by the Assembly in 1947.[3] It further emphasized the Palestinian resolve to establish an independent State of Palestine, alongside the State of Israel, and that, once established, it would opt for a confederal relationship with Jordan. The document defined the powers and responsibilities to be vested in PISGA and outlined the modalities for electing a legislative assembly, together with specific measures to be undertaken by Israel in advance of the elections.

Israel, in its statement before the Special Political Committee on 24 November, referred to its offer of interim arrangements for Palestinian self-government within a relatively short period, having put forward a series of proposals that would enable the Palestinians to conduct their own affairs under an administrative-executive council, which could be chosen by elections. Negotiations on a permanent settlement, based on Council resolutions 242(1967)[4] and 338(1973),[5] would begin in the third year of such arrangements. The proposed autonomy, being less than independence, was acknowledged earlier as imperfect by Israel's Minister for Foreign Affairs, but was clearly a way out of the existing impasse.

In December, during the debate on the question of Palestine, Israel expanded on its concept of the elected Palestinian council. Its broad powers and responsibilities would include administration of 15 spheres of operation: justice; personnel matters; agriculture; ecology; education and culture; finance, budget and taxation; health; industry and commerce; labour; local police; local transportation and communications; municipal affairs; religious affairs; social welfare; and tourism.

Activities of the Committee on Palestinian rights. The Committee on Palestinian rights, established in 1975,[6] continued in 1992 to follow developments in the Israeli-occupied territory and actions by Israel which the Committee regarded as violations of international law or of United Nations resolutions. It brought such actions— including Israeli settlements, Israeli exploitation of Arab-owned land, human rights violations and other matters affecting Palestinian rights—to the attention of the General Assembly and the Security Council.[7] It submitted a report on its activities to the Assembly in November.[8]

The Committee and, under its guidance, the Division for Palestinian Rights, continued to expand cooperation with non-governmental organizations (NGOs) in order to promote awareness of the Palestine question and create conditions favourable for the implementation of its recommendations. To that end, the Committee carried out its approved programme of regional NGO symposia and seminars for 1992.

The Asian symposium (Nicosia, Cyprus, 20-24 January) was on the theme of developing solidarity activities by Israeli and other organizations with Palestinian women, physicians, health workers and students; the event was combined with an Asian regional seminar on the topics of a just settlement of the Palestine question, protection of the Palestinian people in occupied Palestinian territory, and international and regional is-

sues. The North American symposium (New York, 24-26 June) centred on the themes of overcoming the obstacles of 25 years of Israeli occupation and of preparing the way for Palestine; it was preceded by a North American regional seminar (New York, 22 and 23 June) that focused on enforcing the 1949 fourth Geneva Convention. The European symposium (Geneva, 24 and 25 August) had as its theme "Working for peace: European coordination"; it was followed by an international NGO meeting (Geneva, 26-28 August) on the subject of protection and statehood and by a European regional seminar (Qawra, Malta, 27-29 July) that explored international action to ensure the safety and protection of Palestinians in the occupied Palestinian territory and efforts to promote implementation of United Nations resolutions on Palestine and the Middle East.

The Committee reiterated its conviction that Security Council action on its recommendations, first made in 1976,[9] would contribute to promoting a peaceful settlement of the Palestine question, the core of the Arab-Israeli conflict in the Middle East. While welcoming the Peace Conference on the Middle East begun at Madrid in 1991 and the subsequent 1992 bilateral and multilateral talks, the Committee continued to promote the convening of an international peace conference under United Nations auspices. It called on Israel to respond positively to the Palestinian peace initiative put forward by the PLO Chairman before the Assembly in 1988 and subsequent proposals, and to recognize the inalienable national rights of the Palestinian people, particularly self-determination.

The Committee expressed concern at the continuing deterioration of the situation in the occupied Palestinian territory and repressive measures imposed by Israel in violation of the fourth Geneva Convention. It deplored Israel's reliance on military force to suppress the Palestinian uprising, the *intifadah*, already in its fifth year, and condemned Israel's intensified pursuit of its policy of land confiscation and settlement in the occupied territories, including Jerusalem, and its imposition of curfews and collective punishment and restrictions on Palestinians' freedom of movement and economic activities.

The Committee reaffirmed that Israel's continued occupation of Palestinian and other Arab territories and denial of the Palestinians' inalienable rights to self-determination, to national independence and to return to their homes and property constituted the principal obstacles to the achievement of a just peace. It restated its full support for the *intifadah* to end that occupation and to implement the 1988 proclamation of independence.[10] It reaffirmed the principles it had recommended in 1976, subsequently elaborated by the International Conference on the Question of

Palestine,[11] including Israel's withdrawal from the occupied territories, respect for the right of all States in the region to live in peace within secure and internationally recognized boundaries, and recognition of the national rights of the Palestinians.

In expressing hope for radical changes in Israeli policies under the new Government of Israel, the Committee called on it immediately to cease all land confiscation and settlement activities; release political prisoners; end deportations, administrative detention, ill-treatment and torture of prisoners and extrajudicial killings; restore freedom of movement and other civil liberties; and repeal the military orders through which it controlled every area of Palestinian daily life. Pending a political settlement, it pointed to the urgency of action to ensure that Israel, as occupying Power, abide by its obligations under the fourth Geneva Convention, as called for by the Security Council in 1990.[12]

Finally, the Committee reiterated its call on the United Nations system, Governments and intergovernmental and non-governmental organizations to increase their economic and social assistance to the Palestinians.

GENERAL ASSEMBLY ACTION

Following consideration of the report of the Committee on Palestinian rights, the General Assembly adopted four resolutions on the question of Palestine. **Resolution 47/64 A** was adopted on 11 December by recorded vote.

The General Assembly,

Recalling its resolutions 181(II) of 29 November 1947, 194(III) of 11 December 1948, 3236(XXIX) of 22 November 1974, 3375(XXX) and 3376(XXX) of 10 November 1975, 31/20 of 24 November 1976, 32/40 A of 2 December 1977, 33/28 A and B of 7 December 1978, 34/65 A of 29 November 1979 and 34/65 C of 12 December 1979, ES-7/2 of 29 July 1980, 35/169 A and C of 15 December 1980, 36/120 A and C of 10 December 1981, ES-7/4 of 28 April 1982, 37/86 A of 10 December 1982, 38/58 A of 13 December 1983, 39/49 A of 11 December 1984, 40/96 A of 12 December 1985, 41/43 A of 2 December 1986, 42/66 A of 2 December 1987, 43/175 A of 15 December 1988, 44/41 A of 6 December 1989, 45/67 A of 6 December 1990 and 46/74 A of 11 December 1991,

Having considered the report of the Committee on the Exercise of the Inalienable Rights of the Palestinian People,

Affirming that the United Nations has a permanent responsibility with respect to the question of Palestine until the question is resolved in all its aspects in a satisfactory manner in accordance with international legitimacy,

1. *Expresses its appreciation* to the Committee on the Exercise of the Inalienable Rights of the Palestinian People for its efforts in performing the tasks assigned to it by the General Assembly;

2. *Endorses* the recommendations of the Committee contained in paragraphs 85 to 94 of its report and draws the attention of the Security Council to the fact that action on the recommendations of the Committee, as repeatedly endorsed by the General Assembly at its thirty-first session and subsequently, is still awaited;

3. *Requests* the Committee to continue to keep under review the situation relating to the question of Palestine as well as the implementation of the Programme of Action for the Achievement of Palestinian Rights and to report and make suggestions to the General Assembly or the Security Council, as appropriate;

4. *Authorizes* the Committee to continue to exert all efforts to promote the implementation of its recommendations, including representation at conferences and meetings and the sending of delegations, to make such adjustments in its approved programme of work as it may consider appropriate and necessary, to give special emphasis to the need to mobilize public opinion in Europe and North America, and to report thereon to the General Assembly at its forty-eighth session and thereafter;

5. *Also requests* the Committee to continue to extend its cooperation to non-governmental organizations in their contribution towards heightening international awareness of the facts relating to the question of Palestine and creating a more favourable atmosphere for the full implementation of the recommendations of the Committee, and to take the necessary steps to expand its contacts with those organizations;

6. *Requests* the United Nations Conciliation Commission for Palestine, established under General Assembly resolution 194(III), as well as other United Nations bodies associated with the question of Palestine, to continue to cooperate fully with the Committee and to make available to it, at its request, the relevant information and documentation which they have at their disposal;

7. *Decides* to circulate the report of the Committee to all the competent bodies of the United Nations and urges them to take the necessary action, as appropriate, in accordance with the programme of implementation of the Committee;

8. *Requests* the Secretary-General to continue to provide the Committee with all the necessary facilities for the performance of its tasks.

General Assembly resolution 47/64 A

11 December 1992   Meeting 84   115-3-40 (recorded vote)

27-nation draft (A/47/L.35 & Add.1); agenda item 30.
Sponsors: Afghanistan, Algeria, Bangladesh, Comoros, Cuba, Guinea, India, Indonesia, Jordan, Lao People's Democratic Republic, Lebanon, Madagascar, Malaysia, Mali, Malta, Mauritania, Morocco, Pakistan, Qatar, Saudi Arabia, Senegal, Sudan, Tunisia, Ukraine, Vanuatu, Viet Nam, Yemen.
Meeting numbers. GA 47th session: plenary 74-77, 84.

Recorded vote in Assembly as follows:

In favour: Afghanistan, Algeria, Angola, Antigua and Barbuda, Azerbaijan, Bahamas, Bahrain, Bangladesh, Barbados, Belarus, Belize, Benin, Bhutan, Bolivia, Bosnia and Herzegovina, Botswana, Brazil, Brunei Darussalam, Burkina Faso, Burundi, Cameroon, Cape Verde, Central African Republic, Chad, Chile, China, Colombia, Comoros, Côte d'Ivoire, Cuba, Cyprus, Democratic People's Republic of Korea, Djibouti, Dominica, Ecuador, Egypt, El Salvador, Ethiopia, Fiji, Gabon, Gambia, Ghana, Greece, Guatemala, Guinea, Guyana, Haiti, India, Indonesia, Iran, Iraq, Jamaica, Jordan, Kazakhstan, Kenya, Kuwait, Lao People's Democratic Republic, Lebanon, Lesotho, Liberia, Libyan Arab Jamahiriya, Madagascar, Malaysia, Maldives, Mali, Malta, Mauritania, Mauritius, Mexico, Mongolia, Morocco, Myanmar, Namibia, Nepal, Nicaragua, Niger, Nigeria, Oman, Pakistan, Panama, Paraguay, Peru, Philippines, Qatar, Republic of Korea, Rwanda, Saint Kitts and Nevis, Saint Lucia, Saint Vincent and the Grenadines, Samoa, Saudi Arabia, Senegal, Sierra Leone, Singapore, Spain, Sri Lanka, Sudan, Suriname, Swaziland, Syrian Arab Republic, Thailand,

Togo, Tunisia, Turkey, Uganda, Ukrainian SSR, United Arab Emirates, United Republic of Tanzania, Uruguay, Vanuatu, Venezuela, Viet Nam, Yemen, Zambia, Zimbabwe.
Against: Israel, Micronesia, United States.
Abstaining: Albania, Argentina, Australia, Austria, Belgium, Bulgaria, Canada, Costa Rica, Croatia, Czechoslovakia, Denmark, Dominican Republic, Estonia, Finland, France, Germany, Honduras, Hungary, Iceland, Ireland, Italy, Japan, Latvia, Liechtenstein, Lithuania, Luxembourg, Marshall Islands, Netherlands, New Zealand, Norway, Poland, Portugal, Republic of Moldova, Romania, Russian Federation, San Marino, Slovenia, Solomon Islands, Sweden, United Kingdom.

Also on 11 December, the Assembly adopted **resolution 47/64 B** by recorded vote.

The General Assembly,

Having considered the report of the Committee on the Exercise of the Inalienable Rights of the Palestinian People,

Taking note, in particular, of the relevant information contained in paragraphs 41 to 65 of that report,

Recalling its resolutions 32/40 B of 2 December 1977, 33/28 C of 7 December 1978, 34/65 D of 12 December 1979, 35/169 D of 15 December 1980, 36/120 B of 10 December 1981, 37/86 B of 10 December 1982, 38/58 B of 13 December 1983, 39/49 B of 11 December 1984, 40/96 B of 12 December 1985, 41/43 B of 2 December 1986, 42/66 B of 2 December 1987, 43/175 B of 15 December 1988, 44/41 B of 6 December 1989, 45/67 B of 6 December 1990 and 46/74 B of 11 December 1991,

1. *Takes note with appreciation* of the action taken by the Secretary-General in compliance with its resolution 46/74 B;

2. *Requests* the Secretary-General to provide the Division for Palestinian Rights of the Secretariat with the necessary resources to strengthen its programme of research, studies and publications, through the establishment of an adequately staffed and equipped computer-based information system on the question of Palestine, and to ensure that it continues to discharge the tasks detailed in paragraph 1 of resolution 32/40 B, paragraph 2 *(b)* of resolution 34/65 D, paragraph 3 of resolution 36/120 B, paragraph 3 of resolution 38/58 B, paragraph 3 of resolution 40/96 B, paragraph 2 of resolution 42/66 B, paragraph 2 of resolution 44/41 B and paragraph 2 of resolution 46/74 B, in consultation with the Committee· on the Exercise of the Inalienable Rights of the Palestinian People and under its guidance;

3. *Also requests* the Secretary-General to ensure the continued cooperation of the Department of Public Information and other units of the Secretariat in enabling the Division for Palestinian Rights to perform its tasks and in covering adequately the various aspects of the question of Palestine;

4. *Invites* all Governments and organizations to lend their cooperation to the Committee on the Exercise of the Inalienable Rights of the Palestinian People and the Division for Palestinian Rights in the performance of their tasks;

5. *Takes note with appreciation* of the action taken by Member States to observe annually on 29 November the International Day of Solidarity with the Palestinian People and requests them to continue to give the widest possible publicity to the observance.

General Assembly resolution 47/64 B

11 December 1992   Meeting 84   119-2-37 (recorded vote)

27-nation draft (A/47/L.36 & Add.1); agenda item 30.
Sponsors: Afghanistan, Algeria, Bangladesh, Comoros, Cuba, Guinea, India, Indonesia, Jordan, Lao People's Democratic Republic, Lebanon, Madagas-

car, Malaysia, Mali, Malta, Mauritania, Morocco, Pakistan, Qatar, Saudi Arabia, Senegal, Sudan, Tunisia, Ukraine, Vanuatu, Viet Nam, Yemen.
Meeting numbers. GA 47th session: plenary 74-77, 84.

Recorded vote in Assembly as follows:

In favour: Afghanistan, Algeria, Angola, Antigua and Barbuda, Azerbaijan, Bahamas, Bahrain, Bangladesh, Barbados, Belarus, Belize, Benin, Bhutan, Bolivia, Bosnia and Herzegovina, Botswana, Brazil, Brunei Darussalam, Burkina Faso, Burundi, Cameroon, Cape Verde, Central African Republic, Chad, Chile, China, Colombia, Comoros, Costa Rica, Côte d'Ivoire, Cuba, Cyprus, Democratic People's Republic of Korea, Djibouti, Dominica, Ecuador, Egypt, El Salvador, Ethiopia, Fiji, Gabon, Gambia, Ghana, Greece, Guatemala, Guinea, Guyana, Haiti, Honduras, India, Indonesia, Iran, Iraq, Jamaica, Jordan, Kazakhstan, Kenya, Kuwait, Lao People's Democratic Republic, Lebanon, Lesotho, Liberia, Libyan Arab Jamahiriya, Madagascar, Malaysia, Maldives, Mali, Malta, Mauritania, Mauritius, Mexico, Mongolia, Morocco, Myanmar, Namibia, Nepal, Nicaragua, Niger, Nigeria, Oman, Pakistan, Panama, Paraguay, Peru, Philippines, Qatar, Republic of Korea, Russian Federation, Rwanda, Saint Kitts and Nevis, Saint Lucia, Saint Vincent and the Grenadines, Samoa, Saudi Arabia, Senegal, Sierra Leone, Singapore, Solomon Islands, Spain, Sri Lanka, Sudan, Suriname, Swaziland, Syrian Arab Republic, Thailand, Togo, Tunisia, Turkey, Uganda, Ukraine, United Arab Emirates, United Republic of Tanzania, Uruguay, Vanuatu, Venezuela, Viet Nam, Yemen, Zambia, Zimbabwe.
Against: Israel, United States.
Abstaining: Albania, Argentina, Australia, Austria, Belgium, Bulgaria, Canada, Croatia, Czechoslovakia, Denmark, Dominican Republic, Estonia, Finland, France, Germany, Hungary, Iceland, Ireland, Italy, Japan, Latvia, Liechtenstein, Lithuania, Luxembourg, Marshall Islands, Micronesia, Netherlands, New Zealand, Norway, Poland, Portugal, Republic of Moldova, Romania, San Marino, Slovenia, Sweden, United Kingdom.

The third resolution (47/64 C) concerned United Nations information activities on the question of Palestine (see below); the fourth (47/64 D) was on the convening of an international peace conference on the Middle East (see above, under "Proposed peace conference under UN auspices").

Public information activities

The Committee on Palestinian rights[8] followed up on the implementation of a 1991 General Assembly request[13] that DPI continue in 1992-1993 its special information programme on the Palestine question, with emphasis on public opinion in Europe and North America.

DPI in 1992 accordingly continued to provide press coverage of all United Nations meetings relevant to the question of Palestine, including those of the Security Council and the Committee, and issued press releases on the symposia and seminars organized by the Committee (see above). It provided feature coverage of various aspects of the question in news bulletins, radio programmes and *World Chronicle,* a 30-minute panel discussion video programme. DPI sponsored an international encounter for European journalists (Lisbon, Portugal, 16 and 17 September) that reviewed the ongoing peace process and explored, from a European perspective, ways and means to build peace in the Middle East. It also prepared for a news mission to that region, scheduled for December.

DPI distributed a total of 14,639 copies, in Arabic, English, French, German and Spanish, of three booklets: *Human Rights for Palestinians: The Work of the Special Committee to Investigate Israeli Practices Af-*

fecting the Human Rights of the Population of the Occupied Territories;[14] *The United Nations and the Question of Palestine;*[15] and a revised version of *For the Rights of Palestinians: Work of the Committee on the Exercise of the Inalienable Rights of the Palestinian People.*[16] In addition, it issued two new publications, in English and French, titled *Prospects for Peace in the Middle East: An Israeli-Palestinian Dialogue*[17] and *Life of the Palestinians under Israeli Occupation.*[18]

Following up also on a 1991 Assembly request that the Division for Palestinian Rights be provided with a computer-based information system,[19] the Committee noted that a feasibility study of the proposed system had been prepared, initial hardware components had been acquired and development of the system was proceeding.

GENERAL ASSEMBLY ACTION

On 11 December 1992, the General Assembly adopted **resolution 47/64 C** by recorded vote.

The General Assembly,

Having considered the report of the Committee on the Exercise of the Inalienable Rights of the Palestinian People,

Taking note, in particular, of the information contained in paragraphs 66 to 84 of that report,

Recalling its resolutions 46/74 C and 46/75 of 11 December 1991,

Convinced that the world-wide dissemination of accurate and comprehensive information and the role of non-governmental organizations and institutions remain of vital importance in heightening awareness of and support for the inalienable rights of the Palestinian people,

1. *Takes note with appreciation* of the action taken by the Department of Public Information of the Secretariat in compliance with General Assembly resolution 46/74 C;

2. *Requests* the Department of Public Information, in full cooperation and coordination with the Committee on the Exercise of the Inalienable Rights of the Palestinian People, to continue, with the necessary flexibility as may be required by developments affecting the question of Palestine, its special information programme on the question of Palestine for the biennium 1992-1993, with particular emphasis on public opinion in Europe and North America and, in particular:

(a) To disseminate information on all the activities of the United Nations system relating to the question of Palestine, including reports of the work carried out by the relevant United Nations organs;

(b) To continue to issue and update publications on the various aspects of the question of Palestine, including Israeli violations of the human rights of the Palestinian people and other Arab inhabitants of the occupied territories as reported by the relevant United Nations organs;

(c) To expand its audiovisual material on the question of Palestine, including the production of such material;

(d) To organize and promote fact-finding news missions for journalists to the area, including the occupied territories;

(e) To organize international, regional and national encounters for journalists.

General Assembly resolution 47/64 C

11 December 1992   Meeting 84   152-2-3 (recorded vote)

26-nation draft (A/47/L.37/Rev.1 & Rev.1/Add.1); agenda item 30.
Sponsors: Afghanistan, Algeria, Bangladesh, Comoros, Cuba, Guinea, India, Indonesia, Jordan, Lao People's Democratic Republic, Lebanon, Madagascar, Malaysia, Mali, Malta, Mauritania, Morocco, Pakistan, Qatar, Saudi Arabia, Senegal, Sudan, Tunisia, Vanuatu, Viet Nam, Yemen.
Meeting numbers. GA 47th session: plenary 74-77, 84.

Recorded vote in Assembly as follows:

In favour: Afghanistan, Albania, Algeria, Angola, Antigua and Barbuda, Argentina, Australia, Austria, Azerbaijan, Bahamas, Bahrain, Bangladesh, Barbados, Belarus, Belgium, Belize, Benin, Bhutan, Bolivia, Bosnia and Herzegovina, Botswana, Brazil, Brunei Darussalam, Bulgaria, Burkina Faso, Burundi, Cameroon, Canada, Cape Verde, Central African Republic, Chad, Chile, China, Colombia, Comoros, Costa Rica, Côte d'Ivoire, Cuba, Cyprus, Czechoslovakia, Democratic People's Republic of Korea, Denmark, Djibouti, Dominica, Ecuador, Egypt, El Salvador, Estonia, Ethiopia, Fiji, Finland, France, Gabon, Gambia, Germany, Ghana, Greece, Guatemala, Guinea, Guyana, Haiti, Honduras, Hungary, Iceland, India, Indonesia, Iran, Iraq, Ireland, Italy, Jamaica, Japan, Jordan, Kazakhstan, Kenya, Kuwait, Lao People's Democratic Republic, Latvia, Lebanon, Lesotho, Liberia, Libyan Arab Jamahiriya, Liechtenstein, Lithuania, Luxembourg, Madagascar, Malaysia, Maldives, Mali, Malta, Mauritania, Mauritius, Mexico, Mongolia, Morocco, Myanmar, Namibia, Nepal, Netherlands, New Zealand, Nicaragua, Niger, Nigeria, Norway, Oman, Pakistan, Panama, Paraguay, Peru, Philippines, Poland, Portugal, Qatar, Republic of Korea, Republic of Moldova, Romania, Russian Federation, Rwanda, Saint Kitts and Nevis, Saint Lucia, Saint Vincent and the Grenadines, Samoa, San Marino, Saudi Arabia, Senegal, Sierra Leone, Singapore, Slovenia, Solomon Islands, Spain, Sri Lanka, Sudan, Suriname, Swaziland, Sweden, Syrian Arab Republic, Thailand, Togo, Tunisia, Turkey, Uganda, Ukraine, United Arab Emirates, United Kingdom, United Republic of Tanzania, Uruguay, Vanuatu, Venezuela, Viet Nam, Yemen, Zambia, Zimbabwe.
Against: Israel, United States.
Abstaining: Dominican Republic, Marshall Islands, Micronesia.

Jerusalem

In a report of November 1992,[20] the Secretary-General reproduced replies received from four Member States to his request for information on steps taken or envisaged to implement a 1991 resolution of the General Assembly deploring the transfer by some States of their diplomatic missions to Jerusalem and calling on them to abide by the relevant United Nations resolutions.[21] Of those States, Ecuador pointed out that it maintained its Embassy in Tel Aviv.

GENERAL ASSEMBLY ACTION

On 11 December 1992, the General Assembly adopted **resolution 47/63 B** by recorded vote.

The General Assembly,

Recalling its resolutions 36/120 E of 10 December 1981, 37/123 C of 16 December 1982, 38/180 C of 19 December 1983, 39/146 C of 14 December 1984, 40/168 C of 16 December 1985, 41/162 C of 4 December 1986, 42/209 D of 11 December 1987, 43/54 C of 6 December 1988, 44/40 C of 4 December 1989, 45/83 C of 13 December 1990 and 46/82 B of 16 December 1991, in which it determined that all legislative and administrative measures and actions taken by Israel, the occupying Power, which had altered or purported to alter the character and status of the Holy City of Jerusalem, in particular the so-called "Basic Law" on Jerusalem and the proclamation of Jerusalem as the capital of Israel, were null and void and must be rescinded forthwith,

Recalling Security Council resolution 478(1980) of 20 August 1980, in which the Council, *inter alia*, decided not to recognize the "Basic Law" and called upon those

States that had established diplomatic missions at Jerusalem to withdraw such missions from the Holy City,

Having considered the report of the Secretary-General of 25 November 1992,

1. *Determines* that Israel's decision to impose its laws, jurisdiction and administration on the Holy City of Jerusalem is illegal and therefore null and void and has no validity whatsoever;

2. *Deplores* the transfer by some States of their diplomatic missions to Jerusalem in violation of Security Council resolution 478(1980), and their refusal to comply with the provisions of that resolution;

3. *Calls once more upon* those States to abide by the provisions of the relevant United Nations resolutions, in conformity with the Charter of the United Nations;

4. *Requests* the Secretary-General to report to the General Assembly at its forty-eighth session on the implementation of the present resolution.

General Assembly resolution 47/63 B

11 December 1992   Meeting 84   140-1-5 (recorded vote)

16-nation draft (A/47/L.43 & Add.1); agenda item 35.
Sponsors: Afghanistan, Algeria, Cuba, Egypt, Indonesia, Jordan, Malaysia, Mauritania, Morocco, Oman, Pakistan, Sudan, Syrian Arab Republic, Tunisia, Viet Nam, Yemen.
Meeting numbers. GA 47th session: plenary 78, 79, 84.

Recorded vote in Assembly as follows:

In favour: Afghanistan, Albania, Algeria, Antigua and Barbuda, Argentina, Australia, Austria, Azerbaijan, Bahamas, Bahrain, Bangladesh, Barbados, Belarus, Belgium, Belize, Benin, Bhutan, Bolivia, Botswana, Brazil, Brunei Darussalam, Bulgaria, Burkina Faso, Burundi, Cameroon, Canada, Cape Verde, Central African Republic, Chad, Chile, China, Colombia, Comoros, Côte d'Ivoire, Cuba, Cyprus, Czechoslovakia, Democratic People's Republic of Korea, Denmark, Djibouti, Dominica, Ecuador, Egypt, Estonia, Ethiopia, Fiji, Finland, France, Gabon, Gambia, Germany, Ghana, Greece, Guatemala, Guinea, Guyana, Haiti, Honduras, Hungary, Iceland, India, Indonesia, Iran, Iraq, Ireland, Italy, Jamaica, Japan, Jordan, Kazakhstan, Kuwait, Kyrgyzstan, Lao People's Democratic Republic, Latvia, Lebanon, Lesotho, Libyan Arab Jamahiriya, Liechtenstein, Lithuania, Luxembourg, Madagascar, Malaysia, Maldives, Malta, Mauritania, Mauritius, Mexico, Mongolia, Morocco, Myanmar, Nepal, Netherlands, New Zealand, Nicaragua, Niger, Nigeria, Norway, Oman, Pakistan, Panama, Paraguay, Peru, Philippines, Poland, Portugal, Republic of Korea, Republic of Moldova, Romania, Russian Federation, Rwanda, Saint Lucia, Saint Vincent and the Grenadines, Samoa, San Marino, Saudi Arabia, Senegal, Sierra Leone, Singapore, Slovenia, Spain, Sri Lanka, Sudan, Suriname, Swaziland, Sweden, Syrian Arab Republic, Thailand, Tunisia, Turkey, Uganda, Ukraine, United Arab Emirates, United Kingdom, United Republic of Tanzania, Uruguay, Vanuatu, Venezuela, Viet Nam, Yemen, Zimbabwe.
Against: Israel.
Abstaining: Croatia,* Marshall Islands, Micronesia, Togo, United States.
*Later advised the Secretariat it had intended to vote in favour.

Assistance to Palestinians

The United Nations system continued in 1992 to provide assistance to the Palestinian people, as the General Assembly had requested in 1991.[22] Summaries of the assistance activities undertaken by 10 organs and six specialized agencies of the system were contained in a report submitted by the Secretary-General to the Assembly, through the Economic and Social Council, in June 1992,[23] as updated by the following year's report on the subject.[24]

Report of the Secretary-General. According to the Secretary-General's June report, towards the end of the year, the United Nations Centre for Human Settlements (Habitat) completed a plan for implementing a housing development strategy for the Palestinian people, for consideration by the Commission on Human Settlements in 1993. The plan gave an overview of Palestinian land and population, as well as of the housing sector, including supply and demand, surveyed future housing delivery mechanisms, proposed a Palestinian housing strategy and action plan, and suggested housing institutions and an investment plan.

The United Nations Children's Fund focused on assistance for Palestinian children and women in Jordan, Lebanon, the Syrian Arab Republic, the West Bank and the Gaza Strip. In collaboration with the United Nations Relief and Works Agency for Palestine Refugees in the Near East (UNRWA) and other United Nations organs, it supported programmes in the areas of health, pre-school and primary education, women's development, water supply and sanitation, and rehabilitation for the disabled. The objective was to reduce infant and maternal mortality and morbidity through primary health care, immunization, control of diarrhoeal diseases and respiratory infections, health education and safe child-delivery practices. A five-year (1992-1996) programme of assistance in those areas was submitted to the Executive Board in 1992 for the benefit of Palestinians in Lebanon, while a three-year (1992-1994) programme was submitted for the West Bank and the Gaza Strip.

(For assistance provided by UNCTAD, see below.)

The Programme of Assistance to the Palestinian People under the United Nations Development Programme (UNDP)[25] achieved a level of activity in 1992 unmatched in its 12-year history, with expenditures totalling $12 million. By a decision adopted in May,[26] the UNDP Governing Council called on the Administrator to continue his efforts to provide development assistance to the Palestinian people and invited Governments and other donors to expand further financial and other support for the Programme.

A number of large UNDP-financed projects were completed during the year: the extension and renovation of the Princess Alia Hospital in Hebron; the construction of a packing and grading facility for fruits and vegetables in Gaza; the installation of a honey-processing plant in Jericho; the construction of a sewage-collection network in the Balata refugee camp of Nablus; and the installation of a sewage collection, treatment and disposal system in the northern region of the Gaza Strip, to serve a population of about 120,000. Two infrastructural projects in the West Bank were also completed: water-supply schemes—improvement of wells, construction of pumping stations and reservoirs, and installation of distribution networks and house connections—in 14 villages, benefiting 80,000 villagers; and installation of electricity generators, including maintenance training, in eight villages with a population of 45,000.

Ongoing income-generating projects included: the construction of new irrigation channels in the El-Duyuk area in the West Bank, to benefit some 200 farmers, and distribution of modern irrigation equipment to 1,000 others in the Gaza Strip; the construction of a marketing centre and industrial zone in Nablus; and the manufacture of equipment for a citrus-processing plant with a 20-tonne-per-hour capacity to be installed in the Gaza Strip.

The Business Development Centre continued its training activities in management, feasibility studies and marketing, from which 13 management consultants benefited during the year. In addition, training workshops were organized at Nablus, Bethlehem and Gaza, in which 150 trade unionists took part. Other workshops offered special technical training at the community level to 80 Palestinian women, new education techniques to 15 university educators, and technical and pedagogical training to 90 vocational trainees. At Bir Zeit University at Ramallah, 20 engineers and technicians, engaged in the operation and maintenance of the Gaza Strip sewage system, underwent specialized training.

An assessment of the technical cooperation and capital assistance needs conducted in the first quarter of 1992 identified priority areas for new activities: formulation of development and environmental policies; reactivation of productive sectors, particularly agriculture and industry; and human resources development, with emphasis on women's role in the development process. As a follow-up to its earlier initiatives in information exchange among donors, UNDP issued in April the first compendium of ongoing technical assistance projects in the occupied Palestinian territories.

In the latter part of the year, the Programme underwent a broad review; the findings were being taken into account in the new programming and operational initiatives in progress under the direction of the UNDP Special Representative at Jerusalem.

The Economic and Social Commission for Western Asia (ESCWA),[24] at its sixteenth session (see PART TWO, Chapter VI), adopted two resolutions on Palestinian development. One called for support for the ESCWA secretariat's activities (including studies, conferences, seminars and workshops) giving priority to rebuilding the institutional framework for development.[27] The other, which declared the period 1994-2003 a reconstruction and rehabilitation decade for Western Asia, requested ESCWA to provide technical assistance during the decade for the implementation of projects in various countries and areas, including the occupied Palestinian territory.[28]

ESCWA began implementing those resolutions through field missions to the occupied territories, undertaken in coordination with the UNDP office at Jerusalem. One such mission, made by the ESCWA Regional Adviser on Development Issues and Policies, was aimed at analysing the current situation in the territories and proposing an integrated work programme. A joint FAO/ESCWA mission was dispatched for the purpose of preparing a report on the rehabilitation of the agricultural sector and of identifying priority projects. In addition, a training workshop on planning and appraisal of rural development projects (Jerusalem, 26 July–12 August) was organized by the joint FAO/ESCWA Division, in collaboration with UNDP/Jerusalem; it was attended by 32 trainees from the West Bank and the Gaza Strip.

The United Nations Population Fund assisted Palestinian NGOs engaged in providing expanded maternal health services in the same two areas. The objectives, to be fulfilled by 1995, were: increased coverage of prenatal and postnatal care; increased hospital delivery for high-risk women; research and baseline studies essential for evaluating and planning maternal and reproductive health care; family planning services; and dissemination of information on the need for birth spacing in relation to maternal and reproductive care.

UNRWA maintained an extensive programme of education, health and relief services and other humanitarian assistance to Palestine refugees (see below, under ''Palestine refugees'').

The project of assistance of the World Food Programme (WFP), totalling $871,900, provided food aid and cash for the purchase of local food for Palestinians in the West Bank and Gaza Strip. Begun in September 1991 and terminated by the end of March 1992, it was channelled through local institutions to hospital patients, orphanages and destitute families. As of the date of reporting, WFP had not received an official response from the Israeli civil administration authorities to its note of January 1992 notifying them of its intention to continue assistance to targeted beneficiaries.

As to assistance by specialized agencies, the technical cooperation activities of the International Labour Organisation (ILO) in the occupied territories, which began in 1980, centred on two types of projects in 1992. One was on trade union training, for which courses were given to 30 trainees at Nablus, Bethlehem and Gaza. The other was a three-year vocational training project for handicapped persons, organized jointly with UNDP and UNRWA and begun in 1991, under which three ILO consultants held specialized six-week seminars for persons engaged in the vocational training and placement of the handicapped.

In response to a request of the 1991 Conference of the Food and Agriculture Organization of the United Nations (FAO),[29] negotiations were held in 1992 regarding a joint FAO/UNDP mission to formulate an umbrella technical assistance project. Contacts were being made with potential donors, multilateral funding agencies, regional development banks and funds to identify and formulate agricultural investment projects in the occupied territories.

Following adoption of a resolution by the Fourth (1991) General Conference of the United Nations Industrial Development Organization (UNIDO), requesting increased technical assistance to the Palestinian people in close cooperation with PLO, UNIDO established a focal point to monitor developments in the Palestinian industrial sector and coordinate technical assistance activities. As a result of a mission to the West Bank and Gaza Strip that also held consultations with UNDP/Jerusalem in February 1992, UNIDO approved two projects before the end of the year: a project of technical advisory services ($49,000) under the Industrial Development Fund and a training project for small-scale industrial enterprises ($180,000) under a trust fund from Japan.

(For assistance to Palestinian women, see PART THREE, Chapter XIII.)

ECONOMIC AND SOCIAL COUNCIL ACTION

On 31 July 1992, the Economic and Social Council adopted **resolution 1992/58** by recorded vote.

Assistance to the Palestinian people

The Economic and Social Council

Recommends to the General Assembly the adoption of the following draft resolution:

[Same text as General Assembly resolution 47/170 below, except for the last preambular paragraph and paragraph 4, which were added.]

Economic and Social Council resolution 1992/58

31 July 1992   Meeting 42   52-1-1 (recorded vote)

13-nation draft (E/1992/L.35), orally revised following informal consultations; agenda item 6 *(b)*.
Sponsors: Algeria, Egypt, Iraq, Jordan, Lebanon, Libyan Arab Jamahiriya, Malaysia, Mauritania, Morocco, Suriname, Syrian Arab Republic, Tunisia, Yemen.
Meeting numbers. ESC 38, 42.

Recorded vote in Council as follows:

In favour: Algeria, Angola, Argentina, Australia, Austria, Bahrain, Bangladesh, Belarus, Belgium, Benin, Botswana, Brazil, Bulgaria, Burkina Faso, Canada, Chile, China, Colombia, Ecuador, Ethiopia, Finland, France, Germany, Guinea, India, Iran, Italy, Jamaica, Japan, Kuwait, Madagascar, Malaysia, Mexico, Morocco, Pakistan, Peru, Philippines, Poland, Romania, Rwanda, Somalia, Spain, Suriname, Swaziland, Sweden, Syrian Arab Republic, Togo, Trinidad and Tobago, Turkey, United Kingdom, Yugoslavia, Zaire.

Against: United States.
Abstaining: Russian Federation.

GENERAL ASSEMBLY ACTION

On 22 December 1992, acting on the recommendation of the Second (Economic and Financial) Committee, the General Assembly adopted **resolution 47/170** by recorded vote.

Assistance to the Palestinian people

The General Assembly,

Recalling its resolution 46/201 of 20 December 1991,

Taking into account the *intifadah* of the Palestinian people in the occupied Palestinian territory against the Israeli occupation, including Israeli economic and social policies and practices,

Rejecting Israeli restrictions on external economic and social assistance to the Palestinian people in the occupied Palestinian territory,

Concerned about the economic losses of the Palestinian people as a result of the Gulf crisis,

Aware of the increasing need to provide economic and social assistance to the Palestinian people,

Affirming that the Palestinian people cannot develop their national economy as long as the Israeli occupation persists,

Welcoming the Middle East peace process started at Madrid on 30 October 1991 and expressing the hope that, despite the difficulties, all sides will pursue this path,

1. *Takes note* of the report of the Secretary-General;

2. *Expresses its appreciation* to the States, United Nations bodies and intergovernmental and non-governmental organizations that have provided assistance to the Palestinian people;

3. *Requests* the international community, the United Nations system and intergovernmental and non-governmental organizations to sustain and increase their assistance to the Palestinian people, in close cooperation with the Palestine Liberation Organization, taking into account the economic losses of the Palestinian people as a result of the Gulf crisis;

4. *Urges* the Government of Israel to accept *de jure* applicability of the Geneva Convention relative to the Protection of Civilian Persons in Time of War, of 12 August 1949, to all territories occupied by Israel since 1967 and to abide scrupulously by the provisions of that Convention;

5. *Calls* for treatment on a transit basis of Palestinian exports and imports passing through neighbouring ports and points of exit and entry;

6. *Also calls* for the granting of trade concessions and concrete preferential measures for Palestinian exports on the basis of Palestinian certificates of origin;

7. *Further calls* for the immediate lifting of Israeli restrictions and obstacles hindering the implementation of assistance projects by the United Nations Development Programme, other United Nations bodies and others providing economic and social assistance to the Palestinian people in the occupied Palestinian territory;

8. *Reiterates its call* for the implementation of development projects in the occupied Palestinian territory, including the projects referred to in its resolution 39/223 of 18 December 1984;

9. *Calls* for facilitation of the establishment of Palestinian development banks in the occupied Palestinian territory, with a view to promoting investment, production, employment and income therein;

10. *Recognizes* the need for convening a seminar on assistance to the Palestinian people in the occupied Palestinian territory, and, in this regard, suggests to the Committee on the Exercise of the Inalienable Rights of the Palestinian People to consider, in its programme for 1992-1993, convening such a seminar, taking into account the assistance needs of the Palestinian people in the light of the developments in the region;

11. *Requests* the Secretary-General to report to the General Assembly at its forty-eighth session, through

the Economic and Social Council, on the progress made in the implementation of the present resolution.

General Assembly resolution 47/170

22 December 1992   Meeting 93   155-2-3 (recorded vote)

Approved by Second Committee (A/47/717/Add.1) by recorded vote (107-2-2), 11 December (meeting 50); draft recommended by ESC resolution 1992/58 (A/C.2/47/L.5/Rev.1), orally revised; agenda item 12.

Meeting numbers. GA 47th session: 2nd Committee 34-37, 40, 42, 43, 45, 46, 50; plenary 93.

Recorded vote in Assembly as follows:

In favour: Afghanistan, Algeria, Angola, Antigua and Barbuda, Argentina, Australia, Austria, Azerbaijan, Bahamas, Bahrain, Bangladesh, Barbados, Belarus, Belgium, Belize, Benin, Bhutan, Bolivia, Bosnia and Herzegovina, Botswana, Brazil, Brunei Darussalam, Bulgaria, Burkina Faso, Burundi, Cameroon, Canada, Cape Verde, Chad, Chile, China, Colombia, Comoros, Costa Rica, Côte d'Ivoire, Croatia, Cuba, Cyprus, Czechoslovakia, Democratic People's Republic of Korea, Denmark, Djibouti, Dominica, Ecuador, Egypt, Estonia, Ethiopia, Fiji, Finland, France, Gabon, Gambia, Germany, Ghana, Greece, Guatemala, Guinea, Guinea-Bissau, Guyana, Haiti, Honduras, Hungary, Iceland, India, Indonesia, Iran, Iraq, Ireland, Italy, Jamaica, Japan, Jordan, Kazakhstan, Kenya, Kuwait, Kyrgyzstan, Lao People's Democratic Republic, Latvia, Lebanon, Lesotho, Liberia, Libyan Arab Jamahiriya, Liechtenstein, Lithuania, Luxembourg, Madagascar, Malawi, Malaysia, Maldives, Mali, Malta, Mauritania, Mauritius, Mexico, Mongolia, Morocco, Mozambique, Myanmar, Namibia, Nepal, Netherlands, New Zealand, Nicaragua, Niger, Norway, Oman, Pakistan, Panama, Papua New Guinea, Paraguay, Peru, Philippines, Poland, Portugal, Qatar, Republic of Korea, Republic of Moldova, Romania, Russian Federation, Rwanda, Saint Lucia, Saint Vincent and the Grenadines, Sao Tome and Principe, Saudi Arabia, Senegal, Sierra Leone, Singapore, Slovenia, Spain, Sri Lanka, Sudan, Suriname, Swaziland, Sweden, Syrian Arab Republic, Tajikistan, Thailand, Togo, Trinidad and Tobago, Tunisia, Turkey, Turkmenistan, Uganda, Ukraine, United Arab Emirates, United Kingdom, United Republic of Tanzania, Uruguay, Vanuatu, Venezuela, Viet Nam, Yemen, Zaire, Zambia, Zimbabwe.

Against: Israel, United States.

Abstaining: Marshall Islands, Micronesia, Samoa.

UNCTAD activities

Beginning in March 1992, the UNCTAD secretariat intensified its assistance activities for Palestinians in four main areas: monitoring and analysis of Israeli policies and practices hampering Palestinian economic development; investigation of their impact on the main economic sectors; development of a database on the economy in the occupied territories and information dissemination; and coordination of activities with other United Nations organs responding to General Assembly resolutions on assistance to Palestinians and on economic and social conditions in the occupied Palestinian territory.

An eighth report,[30] prepared in accordance with a decision by UNCTAD VIII (see PART THREE, Chapter IV) that UNCTAD assistance to the Palestinian people would be continued in its current form, was submitted to the Trade and Development Board in September. As in previous years, part I of the report examined the overall policy environment, including Israeli, Palestinian, regional and international dimensions, that influenced the performance of the Palestinian economy, as well as main economic trends; assessed aggregate and sectoral performance; and identified measures for immediate action to promote the revival of an economy that was in serious deterioration. Part II reviewed progress of work being carried out by the Special Economic Unit (Palestinian people), in particular with respect to the intersectoral project

investigating prospects for sustained economic and social development of the Palestinian territory of the West Bank and Gaza Strip. Initiated in 1990, the project involved preparation of studies in 25 economic and social sectors, scheduled for completion during the second half of 1992.

A meeting of international and Palestinian experts (Geneva, 19-22 May), attended also by representatives of the United Nations and regional organizations, was held to discuss and adopt the findings of part one of each of the 25 studies, which made up a consolidated report on the prevailing economic and social situation in the occupied territories, with specific measures suggested for immediate action by the Israeli authorities, Palestinian inhabitants of the West Bank and Gaza, and the international community. Also considered was the quantitative framework for the preparation of parts two and three of the individual studies dealing with future prospects of the Palestinian economy.

The Unit continued development of a database on the Palestinian economy, including the compilation and computerization of statistical data—on national income, population, labour and employment, balance of payments and external trade—standardized and classified according to the specifications of the secretariat's Economic Time Series. The Unit also issued a "Select bibliography on the economy of the occupied Palestinian territory (West Bank and Gaza Strip)",[31] "Selected national accounts series of the occupied Palestinian territory (West Bank and Gaza Strip), 1968-1987"[32] and "The tourism sector and related services in the Palestinian territory under Israeli occupation".[33]

UNCTAD continued to cooperate with the UNCTAD/GATT International Trade Centre (ITC) on finalizing a project document for a proposed marketing centre for Palestinian agricultural goods. Consultations were under way with ITC, UNDP and UNIDO for fielding a mission of experts to prepare a feasibility study on a similar centre for industrial goods.

GENERAL ASSEMBLY ACTION

The Second Committee had before it a Secretariat note of 10 December 1992[34] reproducing the revised text of a draft resolution transmitted in October[35] by UNCTAD VIII for consideration by the General Assembly. The draft had been submitted to UNCTAD by Iran on behalf of the Group of 77 developing countries.

Based on the recommendation of the Second Committee, the Assembly, in December, adopted **decision 47/445** by recorded vote.

Programmes of the United Nations Conference on Trade and Development for the Palestinian people

At its 93rd plenary meeting, on 22 December 1992, the General Assembly, on the recommendation of the Second Committee, decided:

(a) To request the United Nations Conference on Trade and Development to sustain its programme for the Palestinian people in its current form in close cooperation with the Palestine Liberation Organization;

(b) To urge that Conference staff and experts be given access to the occupied Palestinian territory;

(c) To invite the Trade and Development Board to consider making appropriate reporting arrangements to enable them to be informed by the Secretary-General of the United Nations Conference on Trade and Development on the progress made in the implementation of the present decision.

General Assembly decision 47/445

159-2-2 (recorded vote)

Approved by Second Committee (A/47/718/Add.2) by recorded vote (133-2-2), 16 December (meeting 51); 15-nation draft (A/C.2/47/L.84); agenda item 78 *(a)*.

Sponsors: Afghanistan, Algeria, Djibouti, Egypt, Iraq, Jordan, Malaysia, Mauritania, Morocco, Pakistan, Qatar, Sudan, Syrian Arab Republic, Tunisia, Yemen.

Meeting numbers. GA 47th session: 2nd Committee 40, 42, 43, 48-51; plenary 93.

Recorded vote in Assembly as follows:

In favour: Afghanistan, Algeria, Angola, Antigua and Barbuda, Argentina, Australia, Austria, Azerbaijan, Bahamas, Bahrain, Bangladesh, Barbados, Belarus, Belgium, Belize, Benin, Bhutan, Bolivia, Bosnia and Herzegovina, Botswana, Brazil, Brunei Darussalam, Bulgaria, Burkina Faso, Burundi, Cameroon, Canada, Cape Verde, Chad, Chile, China, Colombia, Comoros, Congo, Costa Rica, Côte d'Ivoire, Croatia, Cuba, Cyprus, Czechoslovakia, Democratic People's Republic of Korea, Denmark, Djibouti, Dominica, Dominican Republic, Ecuador, Egypt, Estonia, Ethiopia, Fiji, Finland, France, Gabon, Gambia, Germany, Ghana, Greece, Guinea, Guinea-Bissau, Guyana, Haiti, Honduras, Hungary, Iceland, India, Indonesia, Iran, Iraq, Ireland, Italy, Jamaica, Japan, Jordan, Kazakhstan, Kenya, Kuwait, Kyrgyzstan, Lao People's Democratic Republic, Latvia, Lebanon, Lesotho, Liberia, Libyan Arab Jamahiriya, Liechtenstein, Lithuania, Luxembourg, Madagascar, Malawi, Malaysia, Maldives, Mali, Malta, Mauritania, Mauritius, Mexico, Mongolia, Morocco, Mozambique, Myanmar, Namibia, Nepal, Netherlands, New Zealand, Nicaragua, Niger, Nigeria, Norway, Oman, Pakistan, Panama, Papua New Guinea, Paraguay, Peru, Philippines, Poland, Portugal, Qatar, Republic of Korea, Republic of Moldova, Romania, Russian Federation, Rwanda, Saint Kitts and Nevis, Saint Lucia, Saint Vincent and the Grenadines, Samoa, Sao Tome and Principe, Saudi Arabia, Senegal, Sierra Leone, Singapore, Slovenia, Spain, Sri Lanka, Sudan, Suriname, Swaziland, Sweden, Syrian Arab Republic, Tajikistan, Thailand, Togo, Trinidad and Tobago, Tunisia, Turkey, Turkmenistan, Uganda, Ukraine, United Arab Emirates, United Kingdom, United Republic of Tanzania, Uruguay, Vanuatu, Venezuela, Viet Nam, Yemen, Zaire, Zambia, Zimbabwe.

Against: Israel, United States.

Abstaining: Marshall Islands, Micronesia.

REFERENCES

[1]YUN 1980, p. 399. [2]A/47/115-S/23680. [3]YUN 1947-48, p. 247, GA res. 181 A (II), 29 Nov. 1947. [4]YUN 1967, p. 257, SC res. 242(1967), 22 Nov. 1967. [5]YUN 1973, p. 213, SC res. 338(1973), 22 Oct. 1973. [6]YUN 1975, p. 248, GA res. 3376(XXX), 10 Nov. 1975. [7]A/46/837-S/23374, A/46/875-S/23570, A/46/933-S/24045, A/46/947-S/24304, A/46/896-S/23782, A/46/958-S/24436, A/47/522-S/24648, A/47/793-S/24974. [8]A/47/35. [9]YUN 1976, p. 235. [10]A/43/827-S/20278. [11]YUN 1983, p. 274. [12]SC res. 681(1990), 20 Dec. 1990. [13]YUN 1991, p. 229, GA res. 46/74 C, 11 Dec. 1991. [14]DPI/974. [15]DPI/994. [16]DPI/1304. [17]*Prospects for Peace in the Middle East: An Israeli-Palestinian Dialogue* (DPI/1230), Sales No. E.92.I.25. [18]*Life of the Palestinians under Israeli Occupation* (DPI/1192), Sales No. E.92.I.27. [19]YUN 1991, p. 228, GA res. 46/74 B, 11 Dec. 1991. [20]A/47/673. [21]YUN 1991, p. 230, GA res. 46/82 B, 16 Dec. 1991. [22]Ibid., p. 235, GA res. 46/201, 20 Dec. 1991. [23]A/47/212-E/1992/54. [24]A/48/183-E/1993/74. [25]DP/1993/19. [26]E/1992/28 (dec. 92/21). [27]E/1992/34 (res. 184(XVI)). [28]Ibid. (res. 182(XVI)). [29]YUN 1991, p. 234. [30]TD/B/39(1)/4. [31]UNCTAD/RDP/SEU/5. [32]UNCTAD/RDP/SEU/6. [33]UNCTAD/RDP/SEU/7. [34]A/C.2/47/L.84. [35]A/C.2/47/6.

Incidents and disputes involving Arab countries and Israel

Iraq and Israel

By **decision 47/464** of 23 December 1992, the General Assembly deferred consideration of the item on armed Israeli aggression against the Iraqi nuclear installations and included it in the provisional agenda of its forty-eighth (1993) session. The item had been inscribed yearly on the Assembly's agenda since 1981,[1] following the bombing by Israel of a nuclear research centre near Baghdad.

Lebanon

The situation in Lebanon was marked by continued violence throughout 1992. The southern part of the country, north of the border with Israel, and the western Bekaa were theatres for frequent armed confrontations between Israeli and South Lebanon Army troops on the one hand, and Islamic and other resistance groups on the other. However, a slow but gradual improvement in the security situation had begun to emerge.

Two German nationals, the last of 11 Westerners who had been held hostage in Lebanon, were released in Beirut on 17 June. After their release—hailed a victory by the Secretary-General for all who believed in the rights and dignity of the human person—Giandomenico Picco, the Secretary-General's special envoy who had been instrumental in obtaining the release of the first nine hostages in 1991,[2] stressed that the file on the hostage issue was not closed. He was referring to Lebanese, Iranian and Israeli nationals who continued to be held hostage, as well as to the remains of some Western hostages that had yet to be returned.

While developments on the security front offered encouragement, the national economy failed to show the level of recovery hoped for. The value of the Lebanese pound fell, and the country received little of the promised foreign aid for reconstruction and development, thus limiting the scope for investment and narrowing employment opportunities. Consequently, the number of families under the poverty line increased.

Israel and Lebanon

Lebanon continued in 1992 to press for the withdrawal of Israel from that part of southern Lebanon proclaimed a "security zone" by Israel and manned by Israel Defence Forces (IDF), with the assistance of the so-called South Lebanon Army, referred to also as the de facto forces (DFF). In justification of its refusal to withdraw, Israel maintained that its presence in the area was to prevent terrorist access to its northern borders. Israel's long-standing contention was that southern Lebanon served as a staging area for attacks on northern Israel by what it claimed were several terrorist factions, singling out the Shiite Muslim group Hezbollah, which the Government of Lebanon was either incapable of preventing or unwilling to prevent.

The boundaries of the Israeli-controlled Lebanese territory—an area along the armistice demarcation line—were determined by the forward positions of DFF and IDF. In 1992, both forces maintained 69 military positions, up from 65 in 1991.

Communications. Lebanon, on 17 January 1992,[3] requested that the mandate of the United Nations Interim Force in Lebanon, due to expire on 31 January, be extended for a further six months. In so doing, Lebanon pointed out that, as a result of its efforts to steer the country towards normal conditions, it had strengthened and restructured its army and internal security units into a more cohesive force in the south of the country adjacent to Israel's self-proclaimed security zone. The army had confiscated heavy and medium weapons and banned all forms of armed presence in the areas under its control, including in the Palestinian refugee camps, and had achieved perfect coordination with UNIFIL, with which it was in consultation to determine how best to take over from UNIFIL.

Lebanon alleged that, despite these positive developments, Israel was more than ever adamant in its refusal to withdraw from southern Lebanon. Together with its proxies, it had conducted a series of bombardments and assaults on the area's civilian population during the past year. Lebanon implored the Security Council to take new steps decisively to end the violence. On 21 January,[4] it reported continued Israeli bombings on villages in the area, forcing 80 per cent of their inhabitants to flee, and the incorporation of Rashaf into the so-called security zone. Lebanon reiterated its plea for Council action to stop the escalating attacks.

Responding on 27 January,[5] Israel pointed to the escalation of terrorist activities and resulting casualties in southern Lebanon since the deployment of the Lebanese army in the south, as well as to Lebanon's failure to mention the destabilizing role of Hezbollah, the Islamic faction largely responsible for the unstable situation in the area. The true cause of the civilian population's suffering, Israel asserted, lay in the use by Hezbollah and other terrorist organizations of civilian centres as bases of operation. By refusing to disarm those elements and by praising their acts of bloodshed, the Government of Lebanon had shown itself un-

willing to abide by its international obligation to prevent violence and terror within its territory and across Israel's northern border.

Israel was emphatic in its reiteration that it had no claims on any part of Lebanese territory but found it necessary to undertake security functions within a narrow zone of southern Lebanon owing to that country's failure to prevent the use of that part of its territory as a staging area for acts of terrorism against Israel. The appropriate forum for resolving issues between it and Lebanon lay in direct face-to-face negotiations, without preconditions, within the framework of the ongoing peace process.

Israel, on 29 May,[6] clarifying further the state of affairs prevailing in southern Lebanon, alleged that, frustrated by the continuing peace talks between Israel and its neighbours, Hezbollah and others had stepped up their campaign of terror. In view of Lebanon's unwillingness to act to prevent the continuous attacks against it, Israel had been compelled to engage in defensive operations, in exercise of its legitimate right to self-defence.

Lebanon, in two letters of 17 February,[7] requested an urgent meeting of the Security Council to consider what it said were the latest acts of aggression by Israel against the sovereignty and territorial integrity of Lebanon and Israel's continuing occupation of southern Lebanon and part of the Bekaa valley. Lebanon was referring to the previous day's air bombardment of the Palestinian refugee camps of Ein el-Hilweh near Sidon and Rashidieh near Tyre, and the fatal attack from the air on the motorcade carrying Hezbollah's Secretary-General and his family. It also referred to the continued bombardment of southern villages by artillery, tank rounds and machine-gun fire, as well as to violations of its airspace over the southern area.

SECURITY COUNCIL ACTION

Responding to Lebanon's request, the Security Council convened on 19 February 1992 to consider the situation in southern Lebanon. After consultations among Council members, the President made the following statement[8] on behalf of the Council:

Meeting number. SC 3053.

"The members of the Council are deeply concerned about the renewed and rising cycle of violence in southern Lebanon and elsewhere in the region. The Council deplores in particular the recent killings and the continued violence, which threatens to claim additional lives and to destabilize the region further.

"The members of the Council call upon all those involved to exercise maximum restraint in order to bring such violence to an end.

"They reaffirm their commitment to the full sovereignty, independence, territorial integrity and national unity of Lebanon within its internationally recognized boundaries, as set out in resolution 425(1978). In this context they assert that any State shall refrain from the threat or use of force against the territorial integrity or political independence of any State, or in any other manner inconsistent with the purposes of the United Nations.

"The members of the Council express their continued support for all efforts to bring peace to the region on the basis of resolutions 242(1967) and 338(1973). The members of the Council urge all the parties concerned to work vigorously to enhance the ongoing peace process."

UNIFIL

The mandate of UNIFIL was extended twice by the Security Council during 1992, in January and July, each time for a six-month period.

Established by the Council in 1978[9] following Israel's invasion of Lebanon in March of that year,[10] UNIFIL was entrusted with confirming the withdrawal of Israeli forces, restoring international peace and security, and assisting the Government of Lebanon in ensuring the return of its effective authority in the area. A second Israeli invasion, launched in June 1982,[11] radically altered the situation in which UNIFIL had to function. Shortly thereafter, the Council authorized the Force to carry out, in addition to its original mandate, the interim tasks of providing protection and humanitarian assistance to the local population, while maintaining its positions in its area of deployment.[12]

The Force was assisted by the Observer Group Lebanon (OGL), composed of unarmed military observers organized from UNTSO and under the operational control of the UNIFIL Commander.

Composition

As at January 1992, UNIFIL had a strength of 5,764 military personnel, provided by nine countries: Fiji, Finland, France, Ghana, Ireland, Italy, Nepal, Norway, Sweden. By July, at the beginning of the second mandate period, troop strength increased to 5,807, with Poland becoming the tenth troop-contributing country. Plans for a 10 per cent reduction in troop strength, as well as a 17 per cent reduction in the number of internationally recruited civilian staff, were to be implemented during this second period.

Under the command of Lieutenant-General Lars-Eric Wahlgren (Sweden) since 1988, UNIFIL remained deployed in southern Lebanon in six sectors: the Fijian, Finnish, Ghanaian, Irish, Nepalese and Norwegian battalion sectors. Parts of the Fijian, Nepalese, Irish and Finnish sectors and the entire Norwegian sector were within the Israeli-controlled area. The 65-member OGL manned five observations posts along the Lebanese side of the Israel-Lebanon armistice demarcation line and operated four mobile teams in the Israeli-

controlled section of the UNIFIL area of operation. Two observers were assigned to UNIFIL headquarters.

Military logistic support was provided by the Swedish logistic battalion, elements of the French composite battalion, the Norwegian maintenance company, the Ghanaian engineer company, the Italian helicopter unit and by some civilian staff, especially in communications and vehicle maintenance. Civilian support was provided by a staff of 530, of whom 165 were recruited internationally and 365 locally. By July, the numbers had changed, respectively, to 515, 142 and 373.

The Force Mobile Reserve, a composite mechanized company consisting of elements from seven contingents (Fiji, Finland, Ghana, Ireland, Nepal, Norway, Sweden), served to reinforce UNIFIL battalions when serious incidents occurred and during rotations.

The medical unit temporarily consisted of a small team for emergencies provided jointly by Norway and Sweden since October 1991. In January 1992, the Secretary-General proposed,[13] and the Security Council agreed,[14] to accept Poland's offer to provide the unit. The change-over took effect towards the end of April.

In November,[15] the Secretary-General informed the Council President that, subject to the usual consultations and to the Council's extension of UNIFIL, he intended to appoint Major-General Trond Furuhovde (Norway), with effect from 23 February 1993, to succeed the current Commander, scheduled to leave his post the day before. The Council agreed to that appointment in December 1992.[16]

The foregoing information on the UNIFIL composition and deployment was contained in the Secretary-General's reports of January and July below.

Activities

Report of the Secretary-General (January). The Secretary-General gave an account of developments in the UNIFIL area between 21 July 1991 and 21 January 1992.[17] During that period, UNIFIL casualties due to firings and explosions included 3 soldiers (Ireland, Nepal, Sweden) dead and 14 others wounded. Another soldier (Ghana) died and 3 others were injured due to traffic accidents. This brought the number of soldiers who had died since UNIFIL's inception to 184 and the wounded to 272.

In addition to providing the data on the composition and deployment of UNIFIL above, the report stated that, as a result of discussions begun in 1991 between the Lebanese military authorities and UNIFIL,[18] for the gradual transfer to the Lebanese army of responsibility for security in the UNIFIL area of deployment, arrangements were under way to hand over to the Lebanese army that part of the Ghanaian battalion sector west of Marakah, some 32 square kilometres in area and encompassing the villages of Burj Rahhal, Bidyas, Dayr Qanun an Nahr, Abbasiyah, Tura, Tayr Dibbah and Al Bazuriyah. UNIFIL troops in the area would be redeployed to the east and south where the need for their presence was greater. The Council, on 28 January,[19] welcomed that development, of which it had been notified earlier by the Secretary-General.[20]

UNIFIL continued its programme of protective works throughout its area of deployment, opposing attempts by armed elements to enter or operate within it. This led to confrontations at checkpoints and to several serious incidents, which claimed the lives of three UNIFIL soldiers and injured nine others.

While for some time IDF and DFF maintained respect for UNIFIL's injunction to refrain from engaging in military operations in the Norwegian battalion sector, which had come entirely within the Israeli-controlled area since Israel's move into Lebanon in 1982,[21] a change in Israeli policy occurred so that, during the reporting period, both forces frequently fired into or within the sector, where they had also begun to conduct patrols. At Chebaa, Kafr Hammam and Kafer Chouba, Israeli security services set up civil administrations, theretofore successfully prevented by UNIFIL.

Resistance groups opposed to the presence of IDF and DFF in Lebanon undertook 52 operations against them, using roadside bombs, rockets, rocket-propelled grenades and small firearms. Retaliation from the two forces, especially when sustaining casualties, was described as indiscriminate bombardment of nearby villages with artillery, tank and helicopter-gunship fire. Some nine villages came under such attack, claiming the lives of seven civilians and wounding 30 others. A nine-day retaliatory shelling of Brashit in August 1991 caused several thousand people to flee their homes. A bomb explosion in Rashaf in December that claimed DFF casualties resulted in travel restrictions to neighbouring villages to the north. A similar explosion in January 1992 that caused further DFF casualties incurred attacks on Yatar, Haddathah and Tibnin.

IDF/DFF firings at or close to UNIFIL positions were reported to have increased substantially, from 90 in the previous period to 263. At Tiri, in November 1991, DFF shot and killed an Irish soldier; others narrowly escaped death when two tank-rounds hit a UNIFIL position there in December. These incidents were vigorously protested to the Israeli military authorities.

UNIFIL carried out 46 controlled explosions in connection with a programme to clear its deployment area of various types of unexploded ordnance. In cooperation with the Lebanese authorities, United Nations organs and agencies operating in the country, the International Committee of the Red Cross (ICRC) and NGOs, it continued to extend humanitarian assistance in the form of food, fuel, water, electricity, clothing, medical supplies, engineering work and building repairs. From resources made available by troop-contributing countries, it provided water projects, school materials and equipment, and supplies for social services. UNIFIL medical centres, mobile teams and a dental programme rendered care to an average of 3,000 patients a month.

The Secretary-General observed that the current period had been more difficult than preceding periods for both UNIFIL and the inhabitants of southern Lebanon. Hostilities between Lebanese resistance groups and IDF/DFF had intensified, with a consequent rise in casualties. The imminent transfer of responsibility to the Lebanese army for a part of the UNIFIL deployment area was an encouraging step towards restoring the Government's authority in southern Lebanon. In view of UNIFIL's contribution to stability in such a volatile area, the Secretary-General recommended that the Council accept Lebanon's request for an extension of the UNIFIL mandate for another six months, until 31 July 1992.

SECURITY COUNCIL ACTION (January)

The Security Council met on 29 January 1992 to consider the Secretary-General's report, following which the Council unanimously adopted **resolution 734(1992)**.

The Security Council,

Recalling its resolutions 425(1978) and 426(1978) of 19 March 1978, 501(1982) of 25 February 1982, 508(1982) of 5 June 1982, 509(1982) of 6 June 1982 and 520(1982) of 17 September 1982, as well as all its resolutions on the situation in Lebanon,

Having studied the report of the Secretary-General on the United Nations Interim Force in Lebanon of 21 January 1992 and taking note of the observations expressed therein,

Recalling the addendum to the Secretary-General's report of 22 January 1991,

Taking note of the letter dated 17 January 1992 from the Permanent Representative of Lebanon to the United Nations addressed to the Secretary-General,

Responding to the request of the Government of Lebanon,

1. *Decides* to extend the present mandate of UNIFIL for a further interim period of six months, that is until 31 July 1992;

2. *Approves* the overall objective of the Secretary-General, as set out in paragraph 33 of his report, aimed at promoting the greater effectiveness of UNIFIL;

3. *Approves in particular* the recommendations summarized in subparagraphs 59 *(c)* (i) and (ii) of the report contained in the addendum to the Secretary-General's report of 22 January 1991;

4. *Invites* the Secretary-General to consider further, in consultation with the troop-contributing countries, how to achieve the overall objective referred to in paragraph 2 above, and to take action on the objectives in paragraphs 2 and 3 above;

5. *Reiterates* its strong support for the territorial integrity, sovereignty and independence of Lebanon within its internationally recognized boundaries;

6. *Re-emphasizes* the terms of reference and general guidelines of the Force as stated in the report of the Secretary-General of 19 March 1978, approved by resolution 426(1978), and calls upon all parties concerned to cooperate fully with the Force for the full implementation of its mandate;

7. *Reiterates* that the Force should fully implement its mandate as defined in resolutions 425(1978), 426(1978) and all other relevant resolutions;

8. *Requests* the Secretary-General to continue consultations with the Government of Lebanon and other parties directly concerned with the implementation of the present resolution and to report to the Security Council thereon.

Security Council resolution 734(1992)

29 January 1992   Meeting 3040   Adopted unanimously

Draft prepared in consultations among Council members (S/23483).

Upon adoption of the resolution and after consultations among Council members, the President made the following statement[22] on behalf of the Council:

"The members of the Security Council have noted with appreciation the report of the Secretary-General on the United Nations Interim Force in Lebanon (UNIFIL) submitted in conformity with resolution 701(1991).

"They reaffirm their commitment to the full sovereignty, independence, territorial integrity and national unity of Lebanon within its internationally recognized boundaries. In this context, they assert that any State shall refrain from the threat or use of force against the territorial integrity or political independence of any State, or in any other manner inconsistent with the purposes of the United Nations.

"As the Security Council extends the mandate of UNIFIL for a further interim period on the basis of resolution 425(1978), the members of the Council again stress the need for the implementation of that resolution in all its aspects. They reiterate their full support for the Taif Agreement and commend the Lebanese Government for its continuous successful efforts to deploy units of its army in the south of the country in full coordination with UNIFIL. The members of the Council urge all the parties concerned fully to support UNIFIL.

"The members of the Security Council express their concern over the continuing violence in southern Lebanon and urge all parties to exercise restraint.

"The members of the Security Council take this opportunity to express their appreciation for the continuing efforts of the Secretary-General and his staff in this regard and commend UNIFIL's troops and troop-contributing countries for their sacrifices and commitment to the cause of international peace and security under difficult circumstances."

Report of the Secretary-General (July). In his report to the Security Council on developments during the six-month period from 22 January to 21 July 1992,[23] the Secretary-General noted that one soldier (Fiji) died and eight others were injured from firings or explosions, and that another soldier (Ghana) died and seven others were injured in traffic accidents. This brought the number of UNIFIL dead to 186 and of wounded to 287.

The Secretary-General, in addition to noting changes in the composition of UNIFIL, also noted that the hand-over to the Lebanese army of the western part of UNIFIL's Ghanaian battalion sector, which involved vacating eight military positions, was completed on 9 April. The boundary of the sector was accordingly redrawn and the battalion headquarters was moved to the vicinity of Bir Sanasil.

UNIFIL recorded 28 attacks by resistance groups on IDF/DFF positions north of the Litani River and near the Akiya Bridge in the Finnish battalion sector. In retaliation, the two forces subjected seven villages to shelling. Using helicopter gunships, they also targeted individual houses in six villages, as well as the Palestinian refugee camp at Rashidieh. The resultant civilian casualties numbered seven dead and five wounded.

On 16 February, Israeli forces staged an ambush from the air north of the Litani River on a motorcade carrying the Hezbollah Secretary-General, his wife and son, killing all three. Exchanges of intense artillery and rocket fire ensued between armed Lebanese elements and Israeli forces. Caught in the crossfire were many villages in the Nepalese and Irish battalion sectors and several towns in northern Israel.

IDF/DFF firings at or close to UNIFIL positions, of which 175 were recorded for the period, continued to be a subject of UNIFIL protests to Israeli authorities. In one instance, a UNIFIL position south of Kabrikha in the Irish battalion sector sustained five tank rounds; in another, a position in nearby Tulin came under artillery fire. In February, a two-company Israeli force with tanks and armoured carriers, assisted by IDF with bulldozers, launched an incursion into Kafra in the Nepalese battalion sector. Although blocked by UNIFIL for two and a half hours, the Israeli force successfully bulldozed its way to Kafra, where armed elements engaged it. Protective cover was provided by IDF/DFF artillery and mortar fire from helicopter gunships. An exploding missile wounded five Fijian soldiers, one of whom later died. The Secretary-General strongly protested to Israel against the incursion. On his instructions, the Under-Secretary-General and Assistant Secretary-General for Peace-keeping Operations travelled to the area for discussions with Lebanese and Israeli officials, as well as with the Force Commander.

They visited Kafra to inspect the heavy damage it sustained from shelling.

UNIFIL conducted 65 controlled explosions under its mine-clearing programme. Its humanitarian assistance for the period included distribution of 117 tonnes of WFP food to 60 villages and 2,500 families. With UNDP funds, it replaced livestock and crops and repaired greenhouses, and, with $9,000 from UNIFIL personnel, it provided a bus for an orphanage in Tibnin and school books. Its medical centres, mobile teams and field dental programme continued rendering services to an average of 3,000 patients a month.

The Secretary-General observed that the incidents described underscored the continued volatility in the area. He stated that the firings directed at UNIFIL itself severely hampered the discharge of its tasks and he reiterated his appeal for respect of its international and impartial status. He reminded the Israeli authorities that IDF/DFF positions close to population centres should be withdrawn and taken over by UNIFIL. Referring to UNIFIL's contribution to stability in the area, he recommended that the Council accept Lebanon's request of 15 July[24] for an extension of the Force for a further six months.

SECURITY COUNCIL ACTION (July)

On 30 July 1992, the Security Council, having considered the Secretary-General's report, unanimously adopted **resolution 768(1992)**.

The Security Council,

Recalling its resolutions 425(1978) and 426(1978) of 19 March 1978, 501(1982) of 25 February 1982, 508(1982) of 5 June 1982, 509(1982) of 6 June 1982 and 520(1982) of 17 September 1982, as well as all its resolutions on the situation in Lebanon,

Having studied the report of the Secretary-General on the United Nations Interim Force in Lebanon of 21 July 1992 and taking note of the observations expressed therein,

Taking note of the letter dated 15 July 1992 from the Permanent Representative of Lebanon to the United Nations addressed to the Secretary-General,

Responding to the request of the Government of Lebanon,

1. *Decides* to extend the present mandate of UNIFIL for a further interim period of six months, that is until 31 January 1993;

2. *Reiterates* its strong support for the territorial integrity, sovereignty and independence of Lebanon within its internationally recognized boundaries;

3. *Re-emphasizes* the terms of reference and general guidelines of the Force as stated in the report of the Secretary-General of 19 March 1978, approved by resolution 426(1978), and calls upon all parties concerned to cooperate fully with the Force for the full implementation of its mandate;

4. *Reiterates* that the Force should fully implement its mandate as defined in resolutions 425(1978), 426(1978) and all other relevant resolutions;

5. *Requests* the Secretary-General to continue consultations with the Government of Lebanon and other parties directly concerned with the implementation of the present resolution and to report to the Security Council thereon.

Security Council resolution 768(1992)
30 July 1992   Meeting 3102   Adopted unanimously

Draft prepared in consultations among Council members (S/24360).

After the vote and consultations among Council members, the President made the following statement[25] on behalf of the Council:

"The members of the Security Council have noted with appreciation the report of the Secretary-General on the United Nations Interim Force in Lebanon (UNIFIL) submitted in conformity with resolution 734(1992).

"They reaffirm their commitment to the full sovereignty, independence, territorial integrity and national unity of Lebanon within its internationally recognized boundaries. In this context, they assert that any State shall refrain from the threat or use of force against the territorial integrity or political independence of any State, or in any other manner inconsistent with the purposes of the United Nations.

"As the Security Council extends the mandate of UNIFIL for a further interim period on the basis of resolution 425(1978), the members of the Council again stress the urgent need for the implementation of that resolution in all its aspects. They reiterate their full support for the Taif Agreement and for the continued efforts of the Lebanese Government to consolidate peace, national unity and security in the country. The members of the Council commend the Lebanese Government for its successful efforts to deploy units of its army in the south of the country in full coordination with UNIFIL.

"The members of the Security Council express their concern over the continuing violence in southern Lebanon, regret the loss of civilian life and urge all parties to exercise restraint.

"The members of the Security Council take this opportunity to express their appreciation for the continuing efforts of the Secretary-General and his staff in this regard and commend UNIFIL's troops and troop-contributing countries for their sacrifices and commitment to the cause of international peace and security under difficult circumstances."

Financing

The Secretary-General's report of November 1992 on the financing of UNIFIL[26] indicated that assessments totalling $2,003.6 million had been apportioned among Member States from UNIFIL's inception on 19 March 1978 to 31 January 1993, against which contributions of $1,846.4 million had been received. It also indicated an additional commitment authority of $147 million and applied credits of $19.9 million. The resulting outstanding balance of $284.3 million included an amount of $19.6 million due from China, transferred to a special account in accordance with a General

Assembly resolution of 1981,[27] leaving $264.7 million due as at 31 October 1992.

Voluntary contributions in services and supplies not budgeted for in the cost estimates continued to be received from Switzerland. Cash contributions to the Suspense Account created in 1979[28] amounted to $8.4 million as at 31 October 1992.

The budget performance for the period from 1 February 1992 to 31 January 1993 reflected overall commitments higher than the level concurred in by the Advisory Committee on Administrative and Budgetary Questions (ACABQ). The additional requirements amounted to $1,723,000 gross ($1,525,000 net), for which the Secretary-General was seeking supplemental commitment authorization. The revised apportionment for the same period indicated a total of $148,708,000 gross ($145,677,000 net), inclusive of the requested supplemental commitment.

Should the UNIFIL mandate be extended beyond 31 January 1993, the Secretary-General estimated operational costs for a 12-month period beginning on 1 February 1993 at $12,190,000 gross ($11,931,500 net) per month, based on an average Force strength of 5,250 troops. The estimate incorporated the full impact of the ongoing Force reductions of 10 per cent in military strength, and 17 per cent and 10 per cent in the numbers, respectively, of internationally and locally recruited staff.

The audited UNIFIL financial statement for 1 February 1990 to 31 January 1991 indicated a "surplus" balance of $6,851,976, representing excess of income over expenditure. The Secretary-General recommended that that amount, which under certain provisions of the Financial Regulations of the United Nations would have to be surrendered as credits to Member States, be entered in the Suspense Account until the $264.7 million in outstanding assessed contributions was reduced.

Owing to delays or the withholding of contributions by certain Member States, the Secretary-General said UNIFIL was unable to meet its obligations on time, particularly those due to the troop-contributing States, which had never been paid on time and in full according to established rates. The UNIFIL Suspense Account, set up to alleviate the financial burden on those States, had not achieved that purpose. As at 31 October 1992, an estimated $108.7 million was due to former and current troop-contributing States for troop costs; an estimated $10.7 million was also due to Governments for contingent-owned equipment.

ACABQ[29] concurred with the Secretary-General as to the surplus balance and, to permit its transfer to the Suspense Account, recommended that the Assembly suspend the relevant financial regulations. It also recommended approval of commitment authority in the monthly amount indicated for any mandate extension during the 12 months beginning 1 February 1993 and that the Secretary-General be allowed the usual flexibility to transfer credits between items of expenditure.

GENERAL ASSEMBLY ACTION

On 22 December 1992, acting on the recommendation of the Fifth (Administrative and Budgetary) Committee, the General Assembly adopted **resolution 47/205** without vote.

Financing of the United Nations Interim Force in Lebanon

The General Assembly,

Having considered the report of the Secretary-General on the financing of the United Nations Interim Force in Lebanon and the related report of the Advisory Committee on Administrative and Budgetary Questions,

Bearing in mind Security Council resolution 425(1978) of 19 March 1978, by which the Council established the United Nations Interim Force in Lebanon, and the subsequent resolutions by which the Council extended the mandate of the Force, the latest of which was resolution 768(1992) of 30 July 1992,

Recalling its resolution S-8/2 of 21 April 1978 on the financing of the Force and its subsequent resolutions thereon, the latest of which was resolution 46/194 of 20 December 1991,

Reaffirming its previous decisions regarding the fact that, in order to meet the expenditures caused by the Force, a different procedure is required from the one applied to meet expenditures of the regular budget of the United Nations,

Taking into account the fact that the economically more developed countries are in a position to make relatively larger contributions and that the economically less developed countries have a relatively limited capacity to contribute towards such operations involving heavy expenditures,

Bearing in mind the special responsibilities of the States permanent members of the Security Council, as indicated in General Assembly resolution 1874(S-IV) of 27 June 1963, in the financing of such operations,

Having regard to the financial position of the Special Account for the United Nations Interim Force in Lebanon, as set forth in the report of the Secretary-General, and referring to paragraph 26 of the report of the Advisory Committee,

Recalling its resolution 34/9 E of 17 December 1979 and the subsequent resolutions in which it decided that the provisions of regulations 5.2 *(b)*, 5.2 *(d)*, 4.3 and 4.4 of the Financial Regulations of the United Nations should be suspended, the latest of which was resolution 46/194,

Mindful of the fact that it is essential to provide the Force with the necessary financial resources to enable it to fulfil its responsibilities under the relevant resolutions of the Security Council,

Noting with appreciation that voluntary contributions have been made to the Force by certain Governments,

Concerned that the Secretary-General continues to face difficulties in meeting the obligations of the Force on a current basis, including reimbursement to current and former troop-contributing States, resulting from the withholding of contributions by certain Member States,

Concerned also that the surplus balances in the Special Account for the Force have, in effect, been drawn upon to the full extent to supplement the income received from contributions for meeting expenses of the Force,

Concerned further that the implementation of the provisions of regulations 5.2 *(b)*, 5.2 *(d)*, 4.3 and 4.4 of the Financial Regulations of the United Nations would aggravate the already difficult financial situation of the Force,

1. *Decides* to appropriate to the Special Account referred to in section I, paragraph 1, of General Assembly resolution S-8/2 the amount of 148,708,000 United States dollars gross (145,677,000 dollars net) authorized and apportioned by the Assembly in paragraphs 2 and 3 of its resolution 46/194 for the operation of the United Nations Interim Force in Lebanon from 1 February 1992 to 31 January 1993, inclusive;

2. *Authorizes* the Secretary-General to enter into commitments for the operation of the Force at a rate not to exceed 12,190,000 dollars gross (11,931,500 dollars net) per month for the period beginning 1 February 1993, should the Security Council decide to continue the Force beyond the period of six months authorized under its resolution 768(1992);

3. *Decides*, as an ad hoc arrangement, to apportion the amounts referred to in paragraph 2 above among Member States in accordance with the composition of groups set out in paragraphs 3 and 4 of General Assembly resolution 43/232 of 1 March 1989, as adjusted by Assembly resolutions 44/192 B of 21 December 1989, 45/244 of 21 December 1990 and 46/194, and taking into account the scale of assessments for the years 1992, 1993 and 1994;

4. *Decides also* to consider the contributions of Armenia, Azerbaijan, Bosnia and Herzegovina, Croatia, Georgia, Kazakhstan, Kyrgyzstan, the Republic of Moldova, San Marino, Slovenia, Tajikistan, Turkmenistan and Uzbekistan to the Force in accordance with the rates of assessment to be adopted by the Assembly for these Member States at its forty-seventh session;

5. *Invites* the new Member States listed in paragraph 4 above to make advance payments against their assessed contributions, to be determined;

6. *Decides* that the provisions of regulations 5.2 *(b)*, 5.2 *(d)*, 4.3 and 4.4 of the Financial Regulations of the United Nations shall be suspended in respect of the amount of 6,851,976 dollars, which otherwise would have to be surrendered pursuant to those provisions, this amount to be entered into the account referred to in the operative part of General Assembly resolution 34/9 E and held in suspense until a further decision is taken by the Assembly;

7. *Requests* the Secretary-General to take all necessary measures to ensure that the Force is administered with a maximum of efficiency and economy;

8. *Renews its invitation* to Member States and other interested parties to make voluntary contributions to the Force both in cash and in the form of services and supplies acceptable to the Secretary-General, to be administered, as appropriate, in accordance with the procedure established by the General Assembly in its resolutions 43/230 of 21 December 1988, 44/192 A of 21 December 1989 and 45/258 of 3 May 1991, and also to make voluntary contributions in cash to the Suspense Account established in accordance with Assembly resolution 34/9 D of 17 December 1979;

9. *Decides* to consider at its forty-eighth session the question of the financing of the United Nations Interim Force in Lebanon.

General Assembly resolution 47/205

22 December 1992   Meeting 93   Adopted without vote

Approved by Fifth Committee (A/47/820) without vote, 19 December (meeting 50); draft by Chairman (A/C.5/47/L.13); agenda item 115 *(b)*.
Meeting numbers. GA 47th session: 5th Committee 46, 50; plenary 93.

Israel and the Syrian Arab Republic

The General Assembly continued in 1992 to call for Israel's withdrawal from the Golan Heights, a part of the Syrian Arab Republic near its borders with Israel and Lebanon, which came under Israeli occupation in 1967. It was effectively annexed by Israel when it decided to extend its laws, jurisdiction and administration to that territory towards the end of 1981.[30] The de facto annexation of the Syrian Arab Golan was further confirmed by a decision of the Israeli Knesset on 11 November 1991.

The issue of Israeli practices affecting the human rights of the population in the Syrian Arab Golan continued to be monitored by the Committee on Israeli practices and was the subject of resolutions by the Commission on Human Rights and the General Assembly (see below, under "Territories occupied by Israel").

Report of the Committee on Israeli practices. In its report covering developments in the occupied territories between 23 August and 30 November 1991,[31] the Committee on Israeli practices, citing the *Jerusalem Post* of 12 November 1991, stated that, on the previous day, the Israeli Knesset, by a vote of 26 to 12, called for the continuation of Israeli sovereignty over the Golan Heights and the expansion of settlements there. Long-term plans for such expansion and the region's development had reportedly been submitted to the Israeli Prime Minister in October, for which he had expressed his support.

GENERAL ASSEMBLY ACTION

On 11 December, the General Assembly adopted **resolution 47/63 A** by recorded vote.

The General Assembly,

Having considered the item entitled "The situation in the Middle East",

Taking note of the report of the Secretary-General of 25 November 1992,

Recalling Security Council resolution 497(1981) of 17 December 1981,

Recalling its relevant resolutions, the last of which is 45/83 B of 13 December 1990,

Recalling also its resolution 3314(XXIX) of 14 December 1974, in the annex to which it defined an act of aggression, *inter alia*, as "the invasion or attack by the armed forces of a State of the territory of another State, or any military occupation, however temporary, resulting from such invasion or attack, or any annexation by the use of force of the territory of another State or part thereof'' and provided that ''no consideration of whatever nature, whether political, economic, military or otherwise, may serve as a justification for aggression'',

Reaffirming the fundamental principle of the inadmissibility of the acquisition of territory by force,

Reaffirming once more the applicability of the Geneva Convention relative to the Protection of Civilian Persons in Time of War, of 12 August 1949, to the occupied Syrian Golan and the Palestinian territory occupied since 1967, including Jerusalem, and the other occupied Arab territories,

Noting that Israel has refused, in violation of Article 25 of the Charter of the United Nations, to accept and carry out the numerous relevant resolutions of the Security Council, in particular resolution 497(1981),

Deeply concerned that Israel has not withdrawn from the Syrian Golan, which has been under occupation since 1967, contrary to the relevant Security Council and General Assembly resolutions,

Taking note with satisfaction of the convening at Madrid of the Peace Conference on the Middle East on the basis of Security Council resolutions 242(1967) of 22 November 1967 and 338(1973) of 22 October 1973, but regretting that the desired substantial results have not been achieved,

1. *Declares* that Israel has failed so far to comply with Security Council resolution 497(1981) and the relevant resolutions of the General Assembly;

2. *Declares once more* that Israel's decision to impose its laws, jurisdiction and administration on the occupied Syrian Golan is illegal and therefore null and void and has no validity whatsoever;

3. *Declares* that the Knesset decision of 11 November 1991 annexing the occupied Syrian Golan constitutes a grave violation of Security Council resolution 497(1981) and therefore is null and void and has no validity whatsoever;

4. *Declares* all Israeli policies and practices of, or aimed at, annexation of the occupied Arab territories and the Palestinian territories occupied since 1967, including Jerusalem, and the occupied Syrian Golan to be illegal and in violation of international law and of the relevant United Nations resolutions;

5. *Determines once more* that all actions taken by Israel to give effect to its decisions relating to the occupied Syrian Golan are illegal and invalid and shall not be recognized;

6. *Reaffirms its determination* that all relevant provisions of the Regulations annexed to the Hague Convention IV of 1907, and the Geneva Convention relative to the Protection of Civilian Persons in Time of War, of 12 August 1949, continue to apply to the Syrian territory occupied by Israel since 1967, and calls upon the parties thereto to respect and ensure respect for their obligations under these instruments in all circumstances;

7. *Determines once more* that the continued occupation of the Syrian Golan since 1967 and its de facto annexation by Israel on 14 December 1981, following Israel's decision to impose its laws, jurisdiction and administration on that territory, constitute a continuing threat to peace and security in the region;

8. *Firmly emphasizes once more* its demand that Israel, the occupying Power, rescind forthwith its illegal decision of 14 December 1981 to impose its laws, jurisdiction and administration on the Syrian Golan, and its

decision of 11 November 1991, which resulted in the effective annexation of that territory;

9. *Demands once more* that Israel withdraw from the occupied Syrian Golan in implementation of the relevant Security Council and General Assembly resolutions;

10. *Calls upon* the international community to urge Israel to withdraw from the occupied Syrian Golan and other occupied Arab territories for the establishment of a just, comprehensive and lasting peace in the region;

11. *Requests* the Secretary-General to report to the General Assembly at its forty-eighth session on the implementation of the present resolution.

General Assembly resolution 47/63 A

11 December 1992   Meeting 84   72-3-70 (recorded vote)

13-nation draft (A/47/L.42 & Add.1); agenda item 35.

Sponsors: Afghanistan, Cuba, Indonesia, Jordan, Malaysia, Mauritania, Morocco, Oman, Pakistan, Sudan, Syrian Arab Republic, Viet Nam, Yemen.

Meeting numbers. GA 47th session: plenary 78, 79, 84.

Recorded vote in Assembly as follows:

In favour: Afghanistan, Algeria, Azerbaijan, Bahrain, Bangladesh, Belize, Bhutan, Botswana, Brunei Darussalam, Burkina Faso, Burundi, Cameroon, Central African Republic, Chad, China, Comoros, Cuba, Cyprus, Democratic People's Republic of Korea, Djibouti, Egypt, Ethiopia, Gabon, Gambia, Ghana, Guatemala, Guinea, Guyana, Haiti, Honduras, India, Indonesia, Iran, Iraq, Jordan, Kuwait, Lao People's Democratic Republic, Lebanon, Libyan Arab Jamahiriya, Madagascar, Malaysia, Maldives, Mauritania, Mauritius, Mongolia, Morocco, Myanmar, Nepal, Nicaragua, Niger, Nigeria, Oman, Pakistan, Philippines, Rwanda, Saudi Arabia, Senegal, Sierra Leone, Sri Lanka, Sudan, Suriname, Syrian Arab Republic, Togo, Tunisia, Turkey, Uganda, United Arab Emirates, United Republic of Tanzania, Vanuatu, Viet Nam, Yemen, Zimbabwe.

Against: Israel, Micronesia, United States.

Abstaining: Albania, Antigua and Barbuda, Argentina, Australia, Austria, Bahamas, Barbados, Belarus, Belgium, Benin, Brazil, Bulgaria, Canada, Chile, Colombia, Côte d'Ivoire, Croatia, Czechoslovakia, Denmark, Dominica, Ecuador, Estonia, Fiji, Finland, France, Germany, Greece, Hungary, Iceland, Ireland, Italy, Jamaica, Japan, Kazakhstan, Kenya, Kyrgyzstan, Latvia, Lesotho, Liechtenstein, Lithuania, Luxembourg, Malta, Marshall Islands, Mexico, Netherlands, New Zealand, Norway, Panama, Paraguay, Peru, Poland, Portugal, Republic of Korea, Republic of Moldova, Romania, Russian Federation, Saint Lucia, Saint Vincent and the Grenadines, Samoa, San Marino, Singapore, Slovenia, Spain, Swaziland, Sweden, Thailand, Ukraine, United Kingdom, Uruguay, Venezuela.

UNDOF

The United Nations Disengagement Observer Force, established by the Security Council in 1974,[32] as called for by the Agreement on Disengagement of Forces between Israel and the Syrian Arab Republic concluded that year,[33] was charged with supervising the observance of the cease-fire between the two countries in the Golan Heights area and ensuring that there were no military forces in the area of separation between their forces. Assisting the Force as required were UNTSO observers assigned to the Israel-Syria Mixed Armistice Commission.

The UNDOF mandate was renewed twice in 1992, in May and November, each time for a six-month period.

Composition

As of November 1992, UNDOF had a strength of 1,130 military observers (reduced from 1,296 in May) from Austria, Canada, Finland and Poland. Five of them (reduced from seven in May) were on assignment from the United Nations Truce Supervision Organization.

UNDOF, under the command of Major-General Roman Misztal (Poland), remained deployed within and close to the area of separation, where it maintained 11 observation posts. Its headquarters was at Damascus. The Austrian battalion manned 19 positions (reduced from 20 in May) and 7 outposts, conducting 28 patrols daily at irregular intervals on predetermined routes in the area of separation north and inclusive of the Damascus-Quneitra road. South of that road, the Finnish battalion manned 17 positions and 7 outposts (increased from 16 and 6, respectively, in May), patrolling 26 times daily. The UNTSO observers manned 11 observation posts.

The Austrian battalion base camp was located near Wadi Faouar, 8 kilometres east of the separation area, while west of it near Ziouani was that of the Finnish battalion. The Polish and Canadian logistic units shared Camp Faouar and Camp Ziouani, respectively. The Canadian signal unit had a detachment at each camp, as well as at Damascus headquarters. The military police was under redeployment to the two camps and to Checkpoint C (formerly position 28). Most of the military component of UNDOF headquarters relocated to the two camps. The civilian administration remained at Damascus, where the Force Commander maintained an office.

The foregoing information was contained in the May and November reports of the Secretary-General below.

Activities

Reports of the Secretary-General (May and November). Before the expiration of the mandate of UNDOF on 31 May and 30 November 1992, the Secretary-General reported to the Security Council on UNDOF activities for the mandate periods from 21 November 1991 to 19 May 1992[34] and from 20 May to 19 November 1992.[35] UNDOF suffered three fatalities during the two periods: 2 from accidents and 1 from other causes. This brought the number of deaths to 31 since UNDOF's inception, 19 as a result of hostile action or accidents and 12 from other causes.

The reports noted that UNDOF had continued to perform its functions effectively with the cooperation of Israel and the Syrian Arab Republic, that the situation in the area of separation between them had remained generally quiet and that the cease-fire had been maintained without serious incidents.

UNDOF continued to supervise the area of separation from permanently manned positions and observation posts and by foot and mobile patrols operating day and night at irregular intervals on predetermined routes. Temporary outposts were set up as required and the system of patrol paths along the cease-fire lines was further expanded.

Inspection teams made fortnightly inspections of armaments and forces in the area of limitation with the assistance of liaison officers from the two parties. UNDOF pursued the lifting of restrictions on its activities and movement in certain areas that continued to be imposed by both parties.

The November report noted that the Syrian authorities continued to lay mines and replace old ones in minefields along the eastern edge of the separation area, and that, during August and September, they also made improvements to several anti-tank ditches. Repeated UNDOF representations to the Syrian authorities about these infringements had not met with a positive response. However, representations to IDF over Israeli firings at grazing livestock that endangered the lives of their Syrian shepherds brought that dangerous practice to a halt.

The mine-clearing teams of the Polish battalion cleared a total area of 110,760 square metres and destroyed a number of other unexploded ordnance. UNDOF assisted ICRC with mail delivery and safe passage of persons and personal effects across the area of separation. It also provided medical treatment to the local population within available means.

Despite the relative quiet in the Israel–Syrian Arab Republic sector, the Secretary-General cautioned that the Middle East situation as a whole remained potentially dangerous, unless and until a comprehensive Middle East settlement was reached. Stating in each report that he considered UNDOF's continued presence in the area to be essential, the Secretary-General, with the Syrian Arab Republic's assent and Israel's agreement, recommended that its mandate be extended for a further six months, until 30 November 1992 in the first instance and until 31 May 1993 in the second.

SECURITY COUNCIL ACTION (May and November)

At a meeting on 29 May 1992, the Security Council, without debate, unanimously adopted **resolution 756(1992)**.

The Security Council,

Having considered the report of the Secretary-General on the United Nations Disengagement Observer Force,

Decides:

(a) To call upon the parties concerned to implement immediately its resolution 338(1973) of 22 October 1973;

(b) To renew the mandate of the United Nations Disengagement Observer Force for another period of six months, that is, until 30 November 1992;

(c) To request the Secretary-General to submit, at the end of this period, a report on the developments in the situation and the measures taken to implement Security Council resolution 338(1973).

Security Council resolution 756(1992)
29 May 1992   Meeting 3081   Adopted unanimously
Draft prepared in consultations among Council members (S/24026).

The President stated that, in connection with the resolution just adopted, he had been authorized to make the following complementary statement[36] on behalf of the Council:

[Same text as statement following resolution 790(1992) below.]

At a meeting on 25 November, the Council, also without debate, unanimously adopted **resolution 790(1992)**.

The Security Council,

Having considered the report of the Secretary-General on the United Nations Disengagement Observer Force,

Decides:

(a)   To call upon the parties concerned to implement immediately its resolution 338(1973) of 22 October 1973;

(b)   To renew the mandate of the United Nations Disengagement Observer Force for another period of six months, that is, until 31 May 1993;

(c)   To request the Secretary-General to submit, at the end of this period, a report on the developments in the situation and the measures taken to implement Security Council resolution 338(1973).

Security Council resolution 790(1992)
25 November 1992   Meeting 3141   Adopted unanimously
Draft prepared in consultations among Council members (S/24842).

The President again stated that, in connection with the resolution just adopted, he had been authorized to make the following complementary statement[37] on behalf of the Council:

"As is known, the report of the Secretary-General on the United Nations Disengagement Observer Force states, in paragraph 20: 'Despite the present quiet in the Israel-Syria sector, the situation in the Middle East as a whole continues to be potentially dangerous and is likely to remain so, unless and until a comprehensive settlement covering all aspects of the Middle East problem can be reached.' That statement of the Secretary-General reflects the view of the Security Council."

Financing

In a November 1992 report on the financing of UNDOF,[38] the Secretary-General indicated that assessed contributions apportioned to Member States in respect of UNDOF—from inception in 1974[32] to 30 November 1992—and of the United Nations Emergency Force II (UNEF II) (from inception at the end of 1973 and liquidation in 1980)—totalled $992 million, against which $935.7 million had been received as at 30 September 1992. The resultant balance of $56.3 million included $36 million due from China, which was transferred to a special account pursuant to a General Assembly resolution of 1981,[27] leaving $20.3 million in unpaid contributions.

The audited UNDOF/UNEF II financial statement, as at 31 December 1991, covering the 12 months from 1 December 1990 to 30 November 1991, showed a "surplus" balance of $4,520,635, representing excess of income (including assessed contributions, irrespective of collectibility) over expenditure. The Secretary-General proposed that, until the level of unpaid contributions was reduced, that surplus, which otherwise would be surrendered as credits to Member States under certain provisions of the Financial Regulations, be entered into the Suspense Account set up by the Assembly in 1978.[39]

The UNDOF performance record for 1 December 1991 to 30 November 1992 showed an unencumbered balance of $911,000 gross ($841,000 net), which the Secretary-General recommended for credit to Member States against their assessments for future mandate periods.

The Secretary-General gave an estimate of $3,034,000 gross ($2,953,000 net) per month for a 12-month period beginning on 1 December 1992, in the event of an extension of the current mandate beyond its expiration on 30 November 1992. On that basis, he requested commitment authorization, as appropriate, for the maintenance of UNDOF from 1 December 1992 to 30 November 1993. He stated that the estimate reflected the full impact of the streamlining of the Force by a 15 per cent reduction in strength of each military contingent and of the internationally recruited civilian staff, with attendant savings in transport and accommodations.

The Secretary-General also stated that appropriation was required in the amount of $21,384,000 gross ($20,835,000 net) to cover commitments for 1 June to 30 November 1992, authorized by the Assembly in 1991,[40] and for apportionment among Member States.

ACABQ[29] concurred with the proposed disposition of the unencumbered balance. It noted that, UNDOF's streamlining notwithstanding, estimates of various items remained over-budgeted, singling out premises/accommodation and transport, the very items that should reflect the impact of the streamlining. Subject to its observations on the need for economy, ACABQ recommended an appropriation for UNDOF in the amount of $18,206,500 gross ($17,718,000 net) for 1 December 1992 to 31 May 1993, and, subject to a mandate renewal after 31 May, commitment authority up to the level of $3,034,000 gross ($2,953,000 net) per month for six months beginning on 1 June 1993. It further recommended suspension of the relevant financial regulations to allow the transfer of the surplus balance to the Suspense Account.

GENERAL ASSEMBLY ACTION

On 22 December 1992, acting on the recommendation of the Fifth Committee, the General Assembly adopted **resolution 47/204** without vote.

Financing of the United Nations Disengagement Observer Force

The General Assembly,

Having considered the report of the Secretary-General on the financing of the United Nations Disengagement Observer Force and the related report of the Advisory Committee on Administrative and Budgetary Questions,

Bearing in mind Security Council resolution 350(1974) of 31 May 1974, by which the Council established the United Nations Disengagement Observer Force, and the subsequent resolutions by which the Council extended the mandate of the Force, the latest of which was resolution 790(1992) of 25 November 1992,

Recalling its resolution 3211 B (XXIX) of 29 November 1974 on the financing of the United Nations Emergency Force and the United Nations Disengagement Observer Force and its subsequent resolutions thereon, the latest of which was resolution 46/193 of 20 December 1991,

Reaffirming its previous decisions regarding the fact that, in order to meet the expenditures caused by the United Nations Disengagement Observer Force, a different procedure is required from the one applied to meet expenditures of the regular budget of the United Nations,

Taking into account the fact that the economically more developed countries are in a position to make relatively larger contributions and that the economically less developed countries have a relatively limited capacity to contribute towards such operations involving heavy expenditures,

Bearing in mind the special responsibilities of the States permanent members of the Security Council, as indicated in General Assembly resolution 1874(S-IV) of 27 June 1963, in the financing of such operations,

Having regard to the financial position of the Special Account for the United Nations Emergency Force and the United Nations Disengagement Observer Force, as set forth in the report of the Secretary-General, and referring to paragraphs 24 and 26 of the report of the Advisory Committee,

Recognizing that, as a consequence of the withholding of contributions by certain Member States, the surplus balances in the Special Account for the United Nations Emergency Force and the United Nations Disengagement Observer Force have, in effect, been drawn upon to supplement the income received from contributions for meeting expenses of the Forces,

Mindful of the fact that it is essential to provide the United Nations Disengagement Observer Force with the necessary financial resources to enable it to fulfil its responsibilities under the relevant resolutions of the Security Council,

Noting with appreciation that a voluntary contribution has been made to the United Nations Disengagement Observer Force by a Government,

1. *Decides* to appropriate to the Special Account referred to in section II, paragraph 1, of General Assembly resolution 3211 B (XXIX) the amount of 21,384,000 United States dollars gross (20,835,000 dollars net) authorized and apportioned by the General Assembly in paragraph 14 of its resolution 46/193 for the operation of the United Nations Disengagement Observer Force for the period from 1 June to 30 November 1992, inclusive;

2. *Decides also* to appropriate to the Special Account an amount of 18,206,500 dollars gross (17,718,000 dollars net) for the operation of the United Nations Disengagement Observer Force for the period from 1 December 1992 to 31 May 1993, inclusive;

3. *Decides further*, as an ad hoc arrangement, to apportion the amount of 18,206,500 dollars gross (17,718,000 dollars net) for the above-mentioned period among Member States in accordance with the composition of groups set out in paragraphs 3 and 4 of General Assembly resolution 43/232 of 1 March 1989, as adjusted by Assembly resolutions 44/192 B of 21 December 1989, 45/243 of 21 December 1990 and 46/193, and taking into account the scale of assessments for the years 1992, 1993 and 1994;

4. *Decides* that there shall be set off against the apportionment among Member States, as provided for in paragraph 3 above, their respective share in the estimated income of 7,500 dollars other than staff assessment income approved for the period from 1 December 1992 to 31 May 1993, inclusive;

5. *Decides also* that, in accordance with the provisions of its resolution 973(X) of 15 December 1955, there shall be set off against the apportionment among Member States, as provided for in paragraph 3 above, their respective share in the Tax Equalization Fund of the estimated staff assessment income of 481,000 dollars approved for the period from 1 December 1992 to 31 May 1993, inclusive;

6. *Decides further* that there shall be set off against the apportionment among Member States, as provided for in paragraph 3 above, their respective share in the unencumbered balance of 911,000 dollars gross (841,000 dollars net) for the period from 1 December 1991 to 30 November 1992, inclusive;

7. *Authorizes* the Secretary-General to enter into commitments for the United Nations Disengagement Observer Force at a rate not to exceed 3,034,000 dollars gross (2,953,000 dollars net) per month for the period from 1 June to 30 November 1993, inclusive, should the Security Council decide to continue the Force beyond the period of six months authorized under its resolution 790(1992), the said amount to be apportioned among Member States in accordance with the scheme set out in the present resolution;

8. *Decides* that the provisions of regulations 5.2 *(b)*, 5.2 *(d)*, 4.3 and 4.4 of the Financial Regulations of the United Nations shall be suspended in respect of the surplus balance as at 31 December 1991 covering the period from 1 December 1990 to 30 November 1991 in the amount of 4,520,635 dollars, which otherwise would have to be surrendered pursuant to those provisions, this amount to be entered into the Suspense Account established pursuant to General Assembly resolution 33/13 E of 14 December 1978, until a further decision is taken by the Assembly;

9. *Decides also* to consider the contributions of Armenia, Azerbaijan, Bosnia and Herzegovina, Croatia, Georgia, Kazakhstan, Kyrgyzstan, the Republic of Moldova, San Marino, Slovenia, Tajikistan, Turkmenistan and Uzbekistan to the United Nations Disengagement Observer Force in accordance with the rates of assessment to be adopted by the General Assembly for these Member States at its forty-seventh session;

10. *Invites* the new Member States listed in paragraph 9 above to make advance payments against their assessed contributions, to be determined;

11. *Invites* voluntary contributions to the United Nations Disengagement Observer Force in cash and in the

form of services and supplies acceptable to the Secretary-General, to be administered, as appropriate, in accordance with the procedure established by the General Assembly in its resolutions 43/230 of 21 December 1988, 44/192 A of 21 December 1989 and 45/258 of 3 May 1991;

12. *Requests* the Secretary-General to take all necessary action to ensure that the United Nations Disengagement Observer Force is administered with a maximum of efficiency and economy;

13. *Decides* to consider at its forty-eighth session the question of the financing of the United Nations Disengagement Observer Force.

General Assembly resolution 47/204

22 December 1992   Meeting 93   Adopted without vote

Approved by Fifth Committee (A/47/819) without vote, 19 December (meeting 50); draft by Chairman (A/C.5/47/L.12); agenda item 115 *(a)*.
Meeting numbers. GA 47th session: 5th Committee 46, 50; plenary 93.

REFERENCES

[1]YUN 1981, p. 275. [2]YUN 1991, p. 236. [3]S/23435. [4]A/46/849-S/23453. [5]S/23479. [6]S/24032. [7]S/23604 & S/23618. [8]S/23610. [9]YUN 1978, p. 312, SC res. 425(1978), 19 Mar. 1978. [10]Ibid., p. 296. [11]YUN 1982, p. 428. [12]Ibid., p. 450, SC res. 511(1982), 18 June 1982. [13]S/23439. [14]S/23440. [15]S/24950. [16]S/24951. [17]S/23452. [18]YUN 1991, p. 237. [19]S/23485. [20]S/23484. [21]YUN 1982, p. 433. [22]S/23495. [23]S/24341. [24]S/24293. [25]S/24362. [26]A/47/740. [27]YUN 1981, p. 1299, GA res. 36/116 A, 10 Dec. 1981. [28]YUN 1979, p. 352, GA res. 34/9 D, 17 Dec. 1979. [29]A/47/782. [30]YUN 1981, p. 309. [31]A/47/76. [32]YUN 1974, p. 205, SC res. 350(1974), 31 May 1974. [33]Ibid., p. 198. [34]S/23955. [35]S/24821. [36]S/24030. [37]S/24846. [38]A/47/620. [39]YUN 1978, p. 323, GA res. 33/13 E, 14 Dec. 1978. [40]YUN 1991, p. 246, GA res. 46/193, 20 Dec. 1991.

Territories occupied by Israel

The Palestine territory and other Arab territories occupied by Israel as a result of previous armed conflicts in the Middle East comprised the West Bank of the Jordan River, including East Jerusalem, the Gaza Strip, and the Golan Heights in the Syrian Arab Republic. By mid-1992, those territories had been under Israeli occupation for a quarter of a century. Throughout that time, the territories' inhabitants had refused to accept the occupation as a permanent fact—a refusal expressed in sporadic waves of general unrest and violence that exploded into widespread uprising (*intifadah*) towards the end of 1987 and persisted into 1992.

Israel's policies and practices in the territories remained under constant monitoring by the Committee on Israeli practices, whose reports in 1992 reflected the extremely tense situation and high level of violence engendered by the uprising and Israel's suppression of it by military force and collective punishment, including mass deportations of Palestinians.

The Security Council, in a statement on the situation in the occupied territories, condemned all violence and urged maximum restraint. It further condemned Israel's resumption of deportations in early January (resolution 726(1992)) and demanded the immediate return of the 383 Palestinians deported to Lebanon in December (799(1992)).

The General Assembly, in a series of resolutions adopted in December, demanded that Israel, as the occupying Power, desist from those policies and practices that were in violation of the 1949 fourth Geneva Convention and called on the High Contracting Parties to ensure Israel's respect for that Convention (47/64 E). It reaffirmed that occupation itself was a grave violation of the Palestinians' human rights and condemned Israel's policies and practices affecting every aspect of Palestinian life (47/70 A), demanded that Israel accept the applicability to the occupied territories of the fourth Geneva Convention (47/70 B) and called on it to rescind its deportation orders and to facilitate the immediate return of the deportees (47/70 E). The Assembly called on Israel to release all Palestinians and other Arabs arbitrarily detained or imprisoned (47/70 D) and to rescind all measures taken against Palestinian educational institutions (47/70 G). It condemned Israel's persistence in changing the physical character, demographic composition, institutional structure and legal status of the occupied Syrian Golan (47/70 F) and demanded that Israel desist from such action in all of the occupied territories (47/70 C).

In addition, Israel's confiscation of land, its appropriation of water resources and depletion of other economic resources and displacement and deportation of the territories' population were deplored by the Economic and Social Council (resolution 1992/57) and by the Assembly (47/172).

Earlier, in February, the Commission on Human Rights adopted four resolutions by which it again called on Israel to desist from all forms of human rights violations and to withdraw from the Palestine territory and other occupied Arab territories, as well as to refrain immediately from deporting Palestinians and to return all deportees without delay. It reaffirmed that the occupation of Palestine was a gross violation of human rights and an act of aggression against the peace and security of mankind, and determined that all Israeli measures purporting to alter the character and legal status of the Syrian Golan had no legal effect and that the installation of Israeli civilians in the occupied territories was illegal and a violation of the fourth Geneva Convention.

Communications. Several communications addressed to the Secretary-General in March and early April 1992 drew attention to an escalation of Israeli acts of repression, resulting in many casualties. The communications called on the United Nations to end Israel's continued violation of the fourth Geneva Convention and to provide international protection for the Palestinians living under Israeli occupation.

On 16 March,[1] the Deputy Permanent Observer for Palestine to the United Nations reported that, on the previous day, a large Israeli contingent stormed the Askar refugee camp, in the West Bank, from several directions, killing three Palestinians and injuring a fourth. On 20 March,[2] the Observer further reported that the Israeli army killed six youths and injured many others during the previous two days. Those repressive acts culminated in Israel's announcement, also on 20 March, of its intention completely to seal off the occupied Gaza Strip, where 800,000 Palestinians lived, until further notice. It declared Jerusalem closed to West Bank residents and set up roadblocks on all roads leading to and out of the West Bank.

The Observer wrote on 1 April[3] that Israeli undercover army units and other security forces deliberately opened fire on Palestinians in the Shaborah neighbourhood of Rafah, killing at least four and injuring more than 50, many seriously— a crime that added fuel to an extremely explosive and dangerous situation in occupied Palestine. Referring to the same incident, the Chairman of the Committee on Palestinian rights, on 3 April,[4] named the Israeli border police as the perpetrators of the killing, who additionally injured about 80 persons while chasing a Palestinian car in the market of the Rafah refugee camp. The Chairman referred to a Reuters report according to which 21 other Palestinians were shot and wounded by the Israeli army on 2 April in a clash with protesters in the Gaza Strip, as well as to a British Broadcasting Corporation account of that incident, which spoke of a woman run over and killed by an army jeep, of indiscriminate firing at Palestinians and of ambulances carrying the wounded being denied passage. He cited an article in *Ha'aretz* of 17 March to the effect that the Israeli Knesset (Parliament), in the latest of a series of legislation aimed at giving wider latitude in respect of its "open-fire" policy, passed a law allowing Israeli settlers and soldiers to chase and shoot at stone-throwing Palestinians. The Chairman asked that Israel immediately cease the killing and injuring of Palestinians and accept the *de jure* applicability of the fourth Geneva Convention.

Responding on 6 April,[5] Israel explained that, since the beginning of the peace process launched at Madrid in 1991, Israel had been subjected to a wave of terrorist attacks against its citizens at home and abroad that had left 17 Israelis dead and more than 250 wounded, including Jews and Arabs, schoolchildren and diplomats serving overseas. Terrorist leaders of the *intifadah* had stepped up their calls for violence against Israelis and had urged an intensification of attacks. It was in the context of *intifadah* violence and bloodshed, Israel stressed, that the incident at Rafah in the Gaza District should be viewed.

The incident was the result of a hand-grenade thrown at an IDF lookout post in southern Rafah. A local vehicle fleeing the scene ran over at least three local residents and hurled three fire-bombs at IDF troops giving chase; two of the attackers were killed in return fire. Mass disturbances ensued in several locations in the area and local residents leapt on vehicles of the security forces, compelling them to open fire. In all, four residents were killed (two of whom had hurled fire-bombs at IDF) and 11 others were wounded; 12 more were injured in riots the following day.

SECURITY COUNCIL ACTION

The Security Council met on 4 April to consider the latest waves of violence in the Gaza Strip. Before it were the foregoing communications, as well as a request of 3 April[6] from the Permanent Observer for Palestine that he be invited to participate in the meeting. The President noted that if the request met with approval, the Observer would be invited, not under rule 37[a] or 39[b] of the Council's provisional rules of procedure, but with the same rights of participation as those conferred by rule 37. On the proposal of the United States, the request was put to a vote. It was approved by 10 votes to 1 (United States), with 4 abstentions (Belgium, France, Hungary, United Kingdom).

Speaking before the vote, the United States maintained that the Council did not have before it a valid request to speak, and that the PLO representative should be granted permission to speak only if the request complied with rule 39. It pointed to the long-established practice that an Observer had no right to speak in the Council at its own request; rather, a request must be made on its behalf by a Member State. The United States saw no justification for a departure from that practice, nor was there anything in General Assembly resolutions to warrant a change in Council practice, including the 1988 resolution[7] that purported to change the designation of the PLO Mission but did not constitute recognition of any State of Palestine. The United States insisted

---

[a]Rule 37 of the Council's provisional rules of procedure states: "Any Member of the United Nations which is not a member of the Security Council may be invited, as the result of a decision of the Security Council, to participate, without vote, in the discussion of any question brought before the Security Council when the Security Council considers that the interests of that Member are specially affected, or when a Member brings a matter to the attention of the Security Council in accordance with Article 35(1) of the Charter."

[b]Rule 39 of the Council's provisional rules of procedure states: "The Security Council may invite members of the Secretariat or other persons, whom it considers competent for the purpose, to supply it with information or to give other assistance in examining matters within its competence."

on its opposition to special and ad hoc departures from orderly procedure, whence its proposal to put the request to a vote.

After consultations among Council members, the President made the following statement[8] on behalf of the Council:

Meeting number. SC 3065.

"The members of the Security Council are gravely concerned by the continued deterioration of the situation in the Gaza Strip, especially by the current serious situation in Rafah in which several Palestinians have been killed and many more injured.

"The members of the Security Council condemn all these acts of violence at Rafah. They urge maximum restraint in order to bring violence to an end.

"The members of the Security Council urge Israel to abide at all times by its obligations under the Fourth Geneva Convention relative to the Protection of Civilian Persons in Time of War of 12 August 1949 and to respect and to act in accordance with the relevant resolutions of the Security Council. The members of the Security Council are concerned that any escalation of violence would have serious implications for the peace process, especially at a time when negotiations to achieve a comprehensive, just and lasting peace are under way.

"The members of the Security Council request the Secretary-General to use his good offices, in accordance with resolution 681(1990), regarding this situation concerning Palestinian civilians under Israeli occupation."

Recommendations of the Secretary-General. In the light of the worsening situation in the Palestinian and other Arab territories occupied by Israel since 1967, attention was once more focused on the Secretary-General's recommendations on ways to ensure the safety and protection of the Palestinian civilians under Israeli occupation, as contained in his reports of 1988,[9] 1990[10] and 1991.[11]

The 1988 report recommended that, pending a political settlement that responded both to the refusal of the Palestinian population of the territories to accept a future under Israeli occupation and to Israel's determination to ensure its security and the well-being of its people, the international community should make a concerted effort to persuade Israel to accept the *de jure* applicability of the fourth Geneva Convention to the occupied territories and to correct its practices in full compliance with that Convention. Meanwhile, temporary measures were urgently needed, including: IDF training in the rules of international humanitarian law, with orders to its personnel to permit, during disturbances, rapid evacuation of the wounded and delivery of essential foods and medical supplies to the civilian population; and an increase in the number of the international staff, within UNRWA's existing administrative structures, to improve the general assistance provided to the refugee population.

In the 1990 and 1991 reports, the Secretary-General stressed that, for any measure of protection to be ensured, the cooperation of the Israeli authorities was absolutely essential. Nevertheless, given the special responsibility of the High Contracting Parties for ensuring respect for the Convention, the Security Council might wish to call for a meeting of the Parties to discuss possible measures that might be taken under the Convention. The Palestinian appeals for an impartial presence in the territories, properly mandated by the United Nations, was a matter for the Council to decide.

GENERAL ASSEMBLY ACTION

On 11 December 1992, the General Assembly adopted **resolution 47/64 E** by recorded vote.

The General Assembly,

Aware of the uprising *(intifadah)* of the Palestinian people since 9 December 1987 against Israeli occupation, which has received significant attention and sympathy from world public opinion,

Deeply concerned about the alarming situation in the Palestinian territory occupied since 1967, as a result of the continued occupation by Israel, the occupying Power, and of its persistent policies and practices against the Palestinian people,

Reaffirming that the Geneva Convention relative to the Protection of Civilian Persons in Time of War, of 12 August 1949, is applicable to the Palestinian territory occupied by Israel since 1967, including Jerusalem, and to the other occupied Arab territories,

Expressing its profound shock at the continued measures by Israel, the occupying Power, including the killing and wounding of Palestinian civilians, and at the acts of violence committed by the Israeli security forces, which took place on 8 October 1990 at the Haram al-Sharif in Jerusalem, resulting in injuries and loss of human lives, and on 29 December 1990 at Rafah,

Stressing the need to promote international protection to the Palestinian civilians in the occupied Palestinian territory,

Recognizing the need for increased support to, and aid for and solidarity with, the Palestinian people under Israeli occupation,

Having considered the recommendations contained in the reports of the Secretary-General of 21 January 1988, 31 October 1990 and 9 April 1991,

Recalling its relevant resolutions as well as the relevant Security Council resolutions, in particular Council resolution 681(1990) of 20 December 1990, in paragraph 6 of which the Council requested "the Secretary-General, in cooperation with the International Committee of the Red Cross, to develop further the idea, expressed in his report, of convening a meeting of the High Contracting Parties to the said Convention to discuss possible measures that might be taken by them under the Convention and, for this purpose, to invite the Parties to submit their views on how the idea could contribute to the goals of the Convention, as well as on other relevant matters, and to report thereon to the Council",

1. *Condemns* those policies and practices of Israel, the occupying Power, which violate the human rights of the

Palestinian people in the occupied Palestinian territory, including Jerusalem, and, in particular, such acts as the opening of fire by the Israeli army and settlers that result in the killing and wounding of defenceless Palestinian civilians, the beating and breaking of bones, the deportation of Palestinian civilians, the imposition of restrictive economic measures, the demolition of houses, the ransacking of real or personal property belonging individually or collectively to private persons, collective punishment and detentions, and so forth;

2. *Demands* that Israel, the occupying Power, abide scrupulously by the Geneva Convention relative to the Protection of Civilian Persons in Time of War, of 12 August 1949, and desist immediately from those policies and practices which are in violation of the provisions of the Convention;

3. *Calls upon* all the High Contracting Parties to the Convention to ensure respect by Israel, the occupying Power, for the Convention in all circumstances, in conformity with their obligation under article 1 thereof;

4. *Strongly deplores* the continuing disregard by Israel, the occupying Power, of the relevant decisions of the Security Council;

5. *Reaffirms* that the occupation by Israel of the Palestinian territory since 1967, including Jerusalem, and of the other Arab territories in no way changes the legal status of those territories;

6. *Requests* the Security Council to examine with urgency the situation in the occupied Palestinian territory with a view to considering measures needed to provide international protection to the Palestinian civilians in the Palestinian territory occupied by Israel since 1967, including Jerusalem;

7. *Invites* Member States, the organizations of the United Nations system, governmental, intergovernmental and non-governmental organizations, and the mass communications media to continue and enhance their support for the Palestinian people;

8. *Requests* the Secretary-General to examine the present situation in the Palestinian territory occupied since 1967, including Jerusalem, by all means available to him and to submit periodic reports thereon, the first such report as soon as possible.

General Assembly resolution 47/64 E

11 December 1992   Meeting 84   146-3-10 (recorded vote)

24-nation draft (A/47/L.39 & Add.1); agenda item 30.
Sponsors: Afghanistan, Algeria, Bangladesh, Comoros, Cuba, Guinea, Indonesia, Jordan, Lao People's Democratic Republic, Lebanon, Madagascar, Malaysia, Malta, Mauritania, Morocco, Pakistan, Qatar, Saudi Arabia, Senegal, Sudan, Tunisia, Vanuatu, Viet Nam, Yemen.
Meeting numbers. GA 47th session: plenary 74-77, 84.

Recorded vote in Assembly as follows:

In favour: Afghanistan, Albania, Algeria, Angola, Antigua and Barbuda, Argentina, Australia, Austria, Azerbaijan, Bahamas, Bahrain, Bangladesh, Barbados, Belarus, Belgium, Belize, Benin, Bhutan, Bosnia and Herzegovina, Botswana, Brazil, Brunei Darussalam, Bulgaria, Burkina Faso, Burundi, Cameroon, Canada, Cape Verde, Central African Republic, Chad, Chile, China, Colombia, Comoros, Cuba, Cyprus, Czechoslovakia, Democratic People's Republic of Korea, Denmark, Djibouti, Dominica, Ecuador, Egypt, El Salvador, Estonia, Ethiopia, Fiji, Finland, France, Gabon, Gambia, Germany, Ghana, Greece, Guatemala, Guinea, Guyana, Haiti, Honduras, Hungary, Iceland, India, Indonesia, Iran, Iraq, Ireland, Italy, Jamaica, Japan, Jordan, Kazakhstan, Kenya, Kuwait, Lao People's Democratic Republic, Latvia, Lebanon, Lesotho, Liberia, Libyan Arab Jamahiriya, Liechtenstein, Lithuania, Luxembourg, Madagascar, Malaysia, Maldives, Mali, Malta, Mauritania, Mauritius, Mexico, Mongolia, Morocco, Myanmar, Namibia, Nepal, Netherlands, New Zealand, Nicaragua, Niger, Nigeria, Norway, Oman, Pakistan, Panama, Paraguay, Peru, Philippines, Poland, Portugal, Qatar, Republic of Korea, Republic of Moldova, Romania, Rwanda, Saint Kitts and Nevis, Saint Lucia, Saint Vincent and the Grenadines, Samoa,

San Marino, Saudi Arabia, Senegal, Sierra Leone, Singapore, Slovenia, Solomon Islands, Spain, Sri Lanka, Sudan, Suriname, Swaziland, Sweden, Syrian Arab Republic, Thailand, Tunisia, Turkey, Uganda, Ukraine, United Arab Emirates, United Kingdom, United Republic of Tanzania, Vanuatu, Venezuela, Viet Nam, Yemen, Zambia, Zimbabwe.
Against: Israel, Micronesia, United States.
Abstaining: Bolivia, Costa Rica, Côte d'Ivoire, Croatia, Dominican Republic, Malawi, Marshall Islands, Russian Federation, Togo, Uruguay.

Reports of the Committee on Israeli practices. In 1992, the Special Committee to Investigate Israeli Practices Affecting the Human Rights of the Palestinian People and Other Arabs of the Occupied Territories presented three periodic reports—in January,[12] July[13] and October[14]—covering developments in the occupied territories between 23 August 1991 and 26 August 1992. The reports incorporated excerpts or details of written information from various sources, including individuals, organizations and the local press; oral testimonies of persons with firsthand experience of the human rights situation in the territories, obtained through hearings organized by the Committee at Damascus (Syrian Arab Republic), Amman (Jordan), Cairo (Egypt) and Geneva; and official Israeli statements reflecting Israeli policies in the territories, as well as reports on measures taken to implement them.

On the basis of the information before it, the Committee concluded that the situation of basic human rights and fundamental freedoms in the occupied territories continued to be extremely serious. The ongoing peace process, begun at Madrid in 1991,[15] had had no significant effect on the overall enjoyment of those rights and freedoms. The physical and psychological stress endured by the Palestinians and other Arabs remained a threat to international peace and security.

The October report reflected the extremely tense situation that had prevailed in the occupied territories since the *intifadah* began in December 1987.[16] The repression of that struggle had maintained the dramatic level of violence reached in the territories. The occupation itself engendered a situation where human rights violations would occur. The period under review again witnessed a heavy toll of casualties among all categories of the civilian population, due to the indiscriminate and violent methods employed to suppress the popular uprising. To quell demonstrations or strikes, especially in detention centres, disproportionate and at times unnecessary force was resorted to, including beating and the use of tear-gas canisters and live ammunition, causing numerous deaths and injuries that often led to permanent incapacitation. The fear and tension prevailing in the occupied territories was exacerbated by the introduction of undercover units as death squads and the relaxation of open-fire regulations against activists involved in the uprising.

The hardships suffered by a population already living on the threshold of mere survival, brought about by a steady deterioration of the economic, social and health conditions, were compounded by such measures of collective punishment as the periodic closure of educational institutions, the demolition of houses, the deliberate policy of economic pressure and administrative obstacles. Freedom of education was further infringed upon by increasingly restrictive identity-card regulations in respect of students in the West Bank and the Gaza Strip. Curfews and restrictions on movement inside and outside the occupied territories continued to have an adverse effect on the employment of tens of thousands of Arab workers. The non-recognition of diplomas earned in off-campus teaching owing to school closures resulted in a generation of young Palestinians and other Arabs unable to obtain employment. Further aggravating the employment situation was the continual influx of Jewish immigrants who were competing for the same employment opportunities.

The climate of uncertainty and frustration increased as acts of aggression by Israeli settlers multiplied and as settlements increased under the annexationist policy pursued by Israel. The Committee thus welcomed declarations by the new Israeli Government concerning those settlements, but remained preoccupied by the overwhelming preponderance of "security" over "political" settlements, particularly in the Jordan Valley and the Syrian Arab Golan. The settlers' increased physical and psychological harassment of Palestinians and other Arabs seemed deliberately intended to make them leave their homeland.

The expulsion of Palestinians from the territories for alleged security reasons continued, in violation of the fourth Geneva Convention and despite renewed international protests, as did the expulsion of persons without valid residence permits. Drawn to the Committee's attention was a form of "disguised" deportation of certain students wanting to study abroad, by obliging them to leave for three years.

Other Israeli policies and practices described as persistent included: the increasing transfer of the administration of justice to the military, as had been the case with recent traffic offences; arbitrary administrative detention, ostensibly for preventive purposes; denial of basic legal rights, including the right to a fair trial; imposition of sentences harsher than those imposed on Israelis for the same offences; the detention of several thousand Palestinians, including minors, in prisons and detention centres characterized by overcrowding and inadequate food and medical care; detention of minors over 12 years old in the same areas with adult, often common-law, prisoners; the routine use of torture, including electric shock during interrogation, and ill-treatment of the detained and imprisoned; and severe repression of prison strikes, including hurling tear-gas canisters into closed spaces.

To prevent an exacerbation of the already dramatic situation in the occupied territories, renewed efforts by the international community were required to convince Israel to end its practices affecting human rights. In the meantime, the Committee recommended: full application by Israel of the fourth Geneva Convention, the main international instrument of humanitarian law applicable to the territories, as repeatedly reaffirmed by the Security Council and the General Assembly; full compliance with all resolutions relevant to the Palestine question adopted by the United Nations and by ILO, UNESCO and WHO; the creation of conditions conducive to promoting respect for human rights; full Israeli cooperation with ICRC in its efforts to gain access to detained persons in the occupied territories; full support by Member States of ICRC activities on behalf of the detained, as well as of UNRWA activities on behalf of the refugee population; and full respect by the Israeli authorities of the privileges and immunities of UNRWA as an international body providing humanitarian services to Palestinian refugees in the occupied territories.

Report of the Secretary-General. The Secretary-General reported to the General Assembly in October 1992[17] that Israel had not replied to his July request for information on steps taken or envisaged to implement a 1991 Assembly resolution[18] demanding that Israel desist from certain policies and practices in the occupied territories. He had also drawn the attention of States and international organizations, including the specialized agencies, to the Assembly's call not to recognize any changes carried out by Israel in the territories and to avoid actions, including those in the field of aid, that might be used by Israel in its annexation or other policies.

The Secretary-General further stated that, in response to the resolution's request that he ensure the widest circulation of the reports of the Committee on Israeli practices and of information on its activities and findings, DPI had published a booklet on the life of Palestinians under Israeli occupation, in Arabic, English, French, German, Russian and Spanish, drawing extensively from the Committee's reports. DPI included in its 1992-1993 work programme the updating of the 1989 edition of a booklet on human rights for Palestinians, publicizing the Committee's work. It also publicized the Committee's 1992 mission to the Middle East. (For details of the publications mentioned, see above, under "Public information activities".)

GENERAL ASSEMBLY ACTION

On 14 December 1992, acting on the recommendation of the Special Political Committee, the General Assembly adopted **resolution 47/70 A** by recorded vote.

The General Assembly,

Guided by the purposes and principles of the Charter of the United Nations and by the principles and provisions of the Universal Declaration of Human Rights,

Aware of the uprising *(intifadah)* of the Palestinian people since 9 December 1987 against Israeli occupation, which has received significant attention and sympathy from world public opinion,

Deeply concerned about the alarming situation in the Palestinian territory occupied since 1967, including Jerusalem, as well as in the other occupied Arab territories, as a result of their continued occupation by Israel, the occupying Power, and of its persistent policies against the Palestinian people,

Bearing in mind the provisions of the Geneva Convention relative to the Protection of Civilian Persons in Time of War, of 12 August 1949, as well as of other relevant conventions and regulations,

Taking into account the need to consider measures for the impartial protection of the Palestinian people under Israeli occupation,

Recalling the relevant resolutions of the Security Council,

Recalling specifically Security Council resolution 681(1990) of 20 December 1990, in paragraph 6 of which the Council requested "the Secretary-General, in cooperation with the International Committee of the Red Cross, to develop further the idea, expressed in his report, of convening a meeting of the High Contracting Parties to the said Convention to discuss possible measures that might be taken by them under the Convention and, for this purpose, to invite the Parties to submit their views on how the idea could contribute to the goals of the Convention, as well as on other relevant matters, and to report thereon to the Council",

Recalling also all its resolutions on the subject, the most recent of which was resolution 46/47 A of 9 December 1991,

Recalling further the relevant resolutions adopted by the Commission on Human Rights, including its resolutions 1992/1, 1992/2 A and B, 1992/3 and 1992/4 of 14 February 1992 and 1992/70 of 4 March 1992,

Having considered the reports of the Special Committee to Investigate Israeli Practices Affecting the Human Rights of the Palestinian People and Other Arabs of the Occupied Territories, which contain, *inter alia*, self-incriminating public statements made by officials of Israel, the occupying Power,

Having also considered the reports of the Secretary-General of 21 January 1988, 31 October 1990, 9 April 1991 and 23 October 1992,

1. *Commends* the Special Committee to Investigate Israeli Practices Affecting the Human Rights of the Palestinian People and Other Arabs of the Occupied Territories for its efforts in performing the tasks assigned to it by the General Assembly and for its impartiality;

2. *Deplores* the continued refusal by Israel to allow the Special Committee access to the occupied Palestinian territory, including Jerusalem, and other Arab territories occupied by Israel since 1967, and demands that Israel allow the Special Committee access to those territories;

3. *Reaffirms* the fact that occupation itself constitutes a grave violation of the human rights of the Palestinian people in the occupied Palestinian territory, including Jerusalem, and other Arab territories occupied by Israel since 1967;

4. *Condemns* the continued and persistent violation by Israel of the Geneva Convention relative to the Protection of Civilian Persons in Time of War, of 12 August 1949, and other applicable international instruments, and condemns in particular those violations which the Convention designates as "grave breaches" thereof;

5. *Reaffirms*, in accordance with the Convention, that the Israeli military occupation of the Palestinian territory, including Jerusalem, and other Arab territories is of a temporary nature, thus giving no right whatsoever to the occupying Power over the territorial integrity of the occupied territories;

6. *Condemns*, in particular, the Israeli policies and practices of collective punishment, destruction and demolition of houses, use of undercover units as death squads and ill-treatment and torture of prisoners;

7. *Strongly condemns* the imposition of Israeli laws, jurisdiction and administration on the occupied Syrian Golan, which has resulted in the effective annexation of that territory;

8. *Condemns* the Israeli repression against and closing of the educational institutions in the occupied Syrian Golan, particularly prohibiting Syrian textbooks and the Syrian educational system, preventing Syrian students from pursuing their higher education in Syrian universities, denying the right of return to Syrian students receiving their higher education in the Syrian Arab Republic, forcing Hebrew on Syrian students, imposing courses that promote hatred, prejudice and religious intolerance and dismissing teachers, all in clear violation of the Convention;

9. *Strongly condemns* the arming of Israeli settlers in the occupied territories to perpetrate and commit acts of violence against Palestinians and other Arabs, causing deaths and injuries;

10. *Urges* the Security Council to consider the current situation in the Palestinian territory occupied by Israel since 1967, taking into account the recommendations contained in the reports of the Secretary-General, with a view to securing international protection for the defenceless Palestinian people until the withdrawal of Israel, the occupying Power, from the occupied Palestinian territory;

11. *Reaffirms* that Israel's policy of settling parts of its population and new immigrants in the occupied territories constitutes a flagrant violation of the Convention and of the relevant resolutions of the United Nations;

12. *Calls upon* Israel, the occupying Power, to allow the reopening of the Roman Catholic Medical Facility Hospice at Jerusalem in order to continue to provide needed health and medical services to the Palestinians in the city;

13. *Also calls upon* Israel, the occupying Power, to take immediate steps for the return of all displaced Arab and Palestinian inhabitants to their homes or former places of residence in the territories occupied by Israel since 1967, in implementation of Security Council resolution 237(1967) of 14 June 1967;

14. *Urges* international organizations, including the specialized agencies, in particular the International Labour Organisation, the United Nations Educational, Scientific and Cultural Organization and the World

Health Organization, to continue to examine the educational and health conditions in the occupied Palestinian territory, including Jerusalem, and other Arab territories occupied by Israel since 1967;

15. *Reiterates its call* upon all States, in particular those States parties to the Convention, in accordance with article 1 thereof, and upon international organizations, including the specialized agencies, not to recognize any changes carried out by Israel, the occupying Power, in the occupied territories and to avoid actions, including those in the field of aid, that might be used by Israel in its pursuit of the policies of annexation and colonization or any of the other policies and practices referred to in the present resolution;

16. *Requests* the Special Committee, pending early termination of the Israeli occupation, to continue to investigate Israeli policies and practices in the occupied Palestinian territory, including Jerusalem, and other Arab territories occupied by Israel since 1967, to consult, as appropriate, with the International Committee of the Red Cross according to its regulations in order to ensure that the welfare and human rights of the peoples of the occupied territories are safeguarded and to report to the Secretary-General as soon as possible and whenever the need arises thereafter;

17. *Also requests* the Special Committee to submit regularly to the Secretary-General periodic reports on the present situation in the occupied Palestinian territory;

18. *Further requests* the Special Committee to continue to investigate the treatment of prisoners in the occupied Palestinian territory, including Jerusalem, and other Arab territories occupied by Israel since 1967;

19. *Condemns* Israel's refusal to permit persons from the occupied Palestinian territory to appear as witnesses before the Special Committee and to participate in conferences and meetings held outside the occupied Palestinian territory;

20. *Demands* that Israel, the occupying Power, return immediately all documents and papers that were taken away from the Sharia Islamic Court in occupied Jerusalem, to the officials of the said Court;

21. *Requests* the Secretary-General:

(a) To provide all necessary facilities to the Special Committee, including those required for its visits to the occupied territories, so that it may investigate the Israeli policies and practices referred to in the present resolution;

(b) To continue to make available such additional staff as may be necessary to assist the Special Committee in the performance of its tasks;

(c) To circulate regularly and periodically the reports mentioned in paragraph 17 above to Member States;

(d) To ensure the widest circulation of the reports of the Special Committee and of information regarding its activities and findings, by all means available, through the Department of Public Information of the Secretariat and, where necessary, to reprint those reports of the Special Committee that are no longer available;

(e) To report to the General Assembly at its forty-eighth session on the tasks entrusted to him in the present resolution;

22. *Decides* to include in the provisional agenda of its forty-eighth session the item entitled "Report of the Special Committee to Investigate Israeli Practices Affecting the Human Rights of the Palestinian People and Other Arabs of the Occupied Territories".

General Assembly resolution 47/70 A

14 December 1992   Meeting 85   83-5-55 (recorded vote)

Approved by Special Political Committee (A/47/612) by recorded vote (74-6-43), 25 November (meeting 27); 10-nation draft (A/SPC/47/L.25); agenda item 74.
Sponsors: Afghanistan, Bangladesh, Brunei Darussalam, Comoros, Cuba, Indonesia, Madagascar, Malaysia, Pakistan, Zambia.
Meeting numbers. GA 47th session: SPC 24-27; plenary 85.

Recorded vote in Assembly as follows:

In favour: Afghanistan, Algeria, Angola, Azerbaijan, Bahrain, Bangladesh, Bhutan, Bosnia and Herzegovina, Botswana, Brazil, Brunei Darussalam, Burkina Faso, Chad, Chile, China, Colombia, Comoros, Cuba, Cyprus, Democratic People's Republic of Korea, Djibouti, Ecuador, Egypt, El Salvador, Ethiopia, Gabon, Gambia, Guatemala, Guinea-Bissau, Guyana, Haiti, Honduras, India, Indonesia, Iran, Jordan, Kuwait, Lao People's Democratic Republic, Lebanon, Libyan Arab Jamahiriya, Madagascar, Malaysia, Maldives, Mali, Mauritania, Mauritius, Mexico, Morocco, Mozambique, Myanmar, Namibia, Nepal, Niger, Nigeria, Oman, Pakistan, Peru, Philippines, Qatar, Republic of Korea, Rwanda, Sao Tome and Principe, Saudi Arabia, Senegal, Sierra Leone, Singapore, Sri Lanka, Sudan, Swaziland, Syrian Arab Republic, Thailand, Togo, Trinidad and Tobago, Tunisia, Turkey, Ukraine, United Arab Emirates, Vanuatu, Venezuela, Viet Nam, Yemen, Zambia, Zimbabwe.
Against: Israel, Marshall Islands, Romania, United States, Uruguay.
Abstaining: Albania, Antigua and Barbuda, Argentina, Australia, Austria, Barbados, Belarus, Belgium, Belize, Benin, Bolivia, Bulgaria, Cameroon, Canada, Costa Rica, Cote d'Ivoire, Czechoslovakia, Denmark, Dominica, Estonia, Finland, France, Germany, Greece, Hungary, Iceland, Ireland, Italy, Jamaica, Japan, Kazakhstan, Latvia, Liberia, Liechtenstein, Lithuania, Luxembourg, Malta, Micronesia, Mongolia, Netherlands, New Zealand, Norway, Panama, Paraguay, Poland, Portugal, Republic of Moldova, Russian Federation, Saint Lucia, Saint Vincent and the Grenadines, Samoa, Spain, Suriname, Sweden, United Kingdom.

Human Rights Commission action. The Commission on Human Rights, on 14 February 1992, adopted two resolutions on the question of the violation of human rights in the occupied Arab territories, including Palestine.[19] It again called on Israel to desist from its policies and practices that violated the human rights of the Palestinians, to withdraw from the occupied territories, and to refrain forthwith from deporting Palestinians and to allow all deportees to return to their homes without delay. (See also PART THREE, Chapter X.)

Fourth Geneva Convention

Report of the Committee on Israeli practices. In its October 1992 report,[14] the Committee on Israeli practices stressed that the overall hardships confronting the population of the occupied territories derived from the fact that occupation itself constituted a violation of human rights. Israel continued to impose its laws, jurisdiction and administration on the occupied territories, in violation of its obligations as a State party to the fourth Geneva Convention, which stipulated that military occupation was to be considered a temporary, de facto situation giving no right whatsoever to the occupying Power over the territorial integrity of the territories it occupied.

Israel had consistently held, however, that it did not recognize the Convention's *de jure* applicability to the territories but asserted that it was acting in de facto accordance with the humanitarian provisions of that Convention. It continued to claim that certain of the territories it had occupied since 1967 constituted a part of Israel—a claim unanimously refuted by the international community.

Report of the Secretary-General. In October 1992,[20] the Secretary-General informed the Assembly that Israel had not replied to his July request for information on steps taken or envisaged to implement a 1991 Assembly resolution[21] demanding that Israel accept the *de jure* applicability of the Convention and comply with its provisions in the occupied Palestinian territory, including Jerusalem, and other Arab territories it had occupied since 1967.

GENERAL ASSEMBLY ACTION

On 14 December 1992, on the recommendation of the Special Political Committee, the General Assembly adopted **resolution 47/70 B** by recorded vote.

The General Assembly,

Recalling Security Council resolution 465(1980) of 1 March 1980, in which, *inter alia*, the Council affirmed that the Geneva Convention relative to the Protection of Civilian Persons in Time of War, of 12 August 1949, is applicable to the Arab territories occupied by Israel since 1967, including Jerusalem,

Recalling also Security Council resolutions 672(1990) of 12 October 1990, 673(1990) of 24 October 1990 and 681(1990) of 20 December 1990,

Recalling further its resolutions 3092 A (XXVIII) of 7 December 1973, 3240 B (XXIX) of 29 November 1974, 3525 B (XXX) of 15 December 1975, 31/106 B of 16 December 1976, 32/91 A of 13 December 1977, 33/113 A of 18 December 1978, 34/90 B of 12 December 1979, 35/122 A of 11 December 1980, 36/147 A of 16 December 1981, 37/88 A of 10 December 1982, 38/79 B of 15 December 1983, 39/95 B of 14 December 1984, 40/161 B of 16 December 1985, 41/63 B of 3 December 1986, 42/160 B of 8 December 1987, 43/58 B of 6 December 1988, 44/48 B of 8 December 1989, 45/74 B of 11 December 1990 and 46/47 B of 9 December 1991,

Recalling the reports of the Secretary-General of 21 January 1988, 31 October 1990 and 9 April 1991, and taking note of the report of the Secretary-General of 23 October 1992,

Considering that the promotion of respect for the obligations arising from the Charter of the United Nations and other instruments and rules of international law is among the basic purposes and principles of the United Nations,

Bearing in mind the provisions of the Convention,

Noting that Israel and the concerned Arab States whose territories have been occupied by Israel since June 1967 are parties to that Convention,

Taking into account that States parties to the Convention undertake, in accordance with article 1 thereof, not only to respect but also to ensure respect for the Convention in all circumstances,

1. *Reaffirms* that the Geneva Convention relative to the Protection of Civilian Persons in Time of War, of 12 August 1949, is applicable to the occupied Palestinian territory, including Jerusalem, and other Arab territories occupied by Israel since 1967;

2. *Condemns once again* the failure of Israel, the occupying Power, to acknowledge the applicability of the Convention to the territories it has occupied since 1967, including Jerusalem;

3. *Strongly demands* that Israel accept the *de jure* applicability of the Convention and comply with its provisions in the occupied Palestinian territory, including Jerusalem, and other Arab territories occupied by Israel since 1967;

4. *Urgently calls upon* all States parties to the Convention to exert all efforts in order to ensure respect for and compliance with its provisions in the occupied Palestinian territory, including Jerusalem, and other Arab territories occupied by Israel since 1967;

5. *Requests* the Secretary-General to report to the General Assembly at its forty-eighth session on the implementation of the present resolution.

General Assembly resolution 47/70 B

14 December 1992   Meeting 85   141-1-4 (recorded vote)

Approved by Special Political Committee (A/47/612) by recorded vote (118-1-5), 25 November (meeting 27); 10-nation draft (A/SPC/47/L.26); agenda item 74.

Sponsors: Afghanistan, Bangladesh, Brunei Darussalam, Comoros, Cuba, Indonesia, Madagascar, Malaysia, Pakistan, Zambia.

Meeting numbers. GA 47th session: SPC 24-27; plenary 85.

Recorded vote in Assembly as follows:

In favour: Afghanistan, Albania, Algeria, Angola, Antigua and Barbuda, Argentina, Australia, Austria, Azerbaijan, Bahrain, Bangladesh, Barbados, Belarus, Belgium, Belize, Benin, Bhutan, Bolivia, Bosnia and Herzegovina, Botswana, Brazil, Brunei Darussalam, Bulgaria, Burkina Faso, Cameroon, Canada, Central African Republic, Chad, Chile, China, Colombia, Comoros, Costa Rica, Cuba, Cyprus, Czechoslovakia, Democratic People's Republic of Korea, Denmark, Djibouti, Dominica, Ecuador, Egypt, El Salvador, Estonia, Ethiopia, Finland, France, Gabon, Gambia, Germany, Greece, Guatemala, Guinea-Bissau, Guyana, Haiti, Honduras, Hungary, Iceland, India, Indonesia, Iran, Ireland, Italy, Jamaica, Japan, Jordan, Kazakhstan, Kuwait, Lao People's Democratic Republic, Latvia, Lebanon, Liberia, Libyan Arab Jamahiriya, Liechtenstein, Lithuania, Luxembourg, Madagascar, Malawi, Malaysia, Maldives, Mali, Malta, Marshall Islands, Mauritania, Mauritius, Mexico, Mongolia, Morocco, Mozambique, Myanmar, Namibia, Nepal, Netherlands, New Zealand, Niger, Nigeria, Norway, Oman, Pakistan, Panama, Paraguay, Peru, Philippines, Poland, Portugal, Qatar, Republic of Korea, Republic of Moldova, Romania, Rwanda, Saint Lucia, Saint Vincent and the Grenadines, Samoa, Sao Tome and Principe, Saudi Arabia, Senegal, Sierra Leone, Singapore, Spain, Sri Lanka, Sudan, Suriname, Swaziland, Sweden, Syrian Arab Republic, Thailand, Togo, Trinidad and Tobago, Tunisia, Turkey, Ukraine, United Arab Emirates, United Kingdom, United Republic of Tanzania, Uruguay, Vanuatu, Venezuela, Viet Nam, Yemen, Zambia, Zimbabwe.

Against: Israel.

Abstaining: Côte d'Ivoire, Micronesia, Russian Federation, United States.

Before voting on the text as a whole, the Assembly and the Committee retained paragraph 1 by recorded votes of 143 to 1, with 1 abstention, and 123 to 1, respectively.

Expulsion and deportation of Palestinians

Report of the Committee on Israeli practices. In its report of October 1992,[14] the Committee on Israeli practices noted the continued issuance of deportation orders for alleged security reasons against inhabitants of the occupied territories, in violation of the fourth Geneva Convention. Despite repeated international protests, the case involving 11 persons under deportation orders since the beginning of 1992 remained pending before the High Court of Justice of Israel. Also continuing was the recently introduced "conditional

banishment'' of alleged leading activists of the uprising, as in the expulsion to Jordan of six Palestinian students on 17 July, following a five-day siege
of Al-Najah National University at Nablus in the
West Bank, as well as expulsions for lack of a valid
''staying visa'', often of non-resident wives and
children.

SECURITY COUNCIL ACTION (January)

The Security Council convened on 6 January 1992
in the wake of the most recent mass deportation
of Palestinians from the occupied territories. At their
request, Egypt, Israel and the Syrian Arab Republic
were invited to participate in the discussion without the right to vote, in accordance with rule 37[a]
of the Council's provisional rules of procedure.

The President drew attention to a letter from
the Permanent Observer for Palestine[22] requesting that, in accordance with the Council's previous practice, he be invited to participate in the discussion. The President noted that the request was
not made pursuant to rule 37 or rule 39,[b] but
that, if approved, the Observer would have the
same rights of participation as those conferred by
rule 37. The request was approved by 10 votes to
1 (United States), with 4 abstentions (Belgium,
France, Hungary, United Kingdom).

The United States, which requested the vote,
stated its opposition, as it normally had regarding similar requests in the past, to granting PLO
the same rights to participate in Council proceedings as if it represented a Member State of the
United Nations. It underscored its generous interpretation of rule 39 over four decades and would
not have raised any objection had the request been
appropriately made under that rule.

Before the Council were two letters, from the
Observer[23] and from the Acting Chairman of
the Committee on Palestinian rights,[24] dated 3
and 6 January, respectively, drawing attention to
and condemning the expulsion of 12 Palestinian
civilians suspected of directing and taking part in
violent acts against Israel. They were identified as
Marwan Afaneh, Iyhab al-Ashkar, Ahmed Nimr
Hamdan, Ghassan Jarrar, Iyad Abed al-Raouf
Judeh, Khader Atieh Khader, Ali Faris al-Khatib,
Ra'afet al-Najar, Omar Assaf Safi, Ahmad Abu
Sa'if, Sami Abu Samhadaneh and Hassan Abed
Alla Shaban. The Acting Chairman cited *The New
York Times* of 3 January as reporting that, since the
intifadah began, Israel had deported at least 66
Palestinians, excluding the 12 mentioned above.

Following statements by five speakers, including the Observer for Palestine, the Council unanimously adopted **resolution 726(1992)**.

The Security Council,

Recalling the obligations of Member States under the
United Nations Charter,

Recalling its resolutions 607(1988), 608(1988),
636(1989), 641(1989) and 694(1991),

Having been apprised of the decision of Israel, the occupying Power, to deport twelve Palestinian civilians
from the occupied Palestinian territories,

1. *Strongly condemns* the decision of Israel, the occupying Power, to resume deportations of Palestinian
civilians;

2. *Reaffirms* the applicability of the Fourth Geneva
Convention of 12 August 1949 to all the Palestinian ter-
ritories occupied by Israel since 1967, including
Jerusalem;

3. *Requests* Israel, the occupying Power, to refrain
from deporting any Palestinian civilian from the occupied territories;

4. *Also requests* Israel, the occupying Power, to ensure
the safe and immediate return to the occupied territories of all those deported;

5. *Decides* to keep the matter under review.

Security Council resolution 726(1992)

6 January 1992   Meeting 3026   Adopted unanimously

Draft prepared in consultations among Council members (S/23372).

The Observer for Palestine asserted that the
policy of deportation had its roots in the ideological position that rejected not only the Palestinian
national identity, but the very existence of Palestine. That position insisted on regarding the existence of Palestinians in their own country as a transient situation that must be changed and on the
need to depopulate the territory of its Palestinian
inhabitants through a policy of transfer, in order
to annex the territory while keeping the pure Jewish nature of the State.

Israel asserted that the decision to expel the 12
Palestinians who were heavily implicated in organizing terror was not hastily taken. The 12 were
active members of three terrorist groups: the Popular Front, which had taken responsibility for
several serious attacks involving firearms; the
Hamas group, which had admitted to 67 attacks;
and the PLO Fatah group, which had committed
approximately 320 terrorist acts—all in the past
year. Israel pointed out that the expulsion orders
were not immediate, each of the 12 having been
given the opportunity to submit an appeal, first
to an advisory committee attached to the Regional
Commander, and then to the Israeli Supreme
Court sitting as the High Court of Justice. Israel
said expulsion orders were a rarely used but highly
effective deterrent, the last ones having been issued against four Gaza District residents in May
1991.[25] The expulsion of extremists actively engaged in wrecking the ongoing peace process
would help create the security and calm so essential for serious peace talks.

Israel went on to say that its expulsion orders
were in accord with the legal framework in force
in Judaea, Samaria and the Gaza District. Pending a political solution to the problem as a whole,
Israel was responsible, according to international

law, for the administration of the territories and as such obliged to determine the manner of restoring and maintaining order. Most of the security measures adopted by the Military Government in the administered areas were based on local Jordanian or Egyptian legislation, of which the Defence (Emergency) Regulations 1945 formed part. Those regulations were enacted by the British Government in 1945 and applied to the whole area under the Mandate, including the administered areas. Regulation 112, under which expulsion orders were issued, had been held valid in the administered areas by the Israeli Supreme Court. It had been argued that expulsion was prohibited by the fourth Geneva Convention; however, the Convention was not applicable to Judaea, Samaria and the Gaza District since they were not taken, as formulated in the Convention, from any legal sovereign. Nevertheless, Israel voluntarily applied the Convention's humanitarian provisions, which, as interpreted by the Israeli Supreme Court, did not include any prohibition of the expulsion of individuals involved in terrorist activities.

The United States believed that deportation of individuals from the occupied territories was a violation of the fourth Geneva Convention as it pertained to the treatment of inhabitants of those territories. Any person charged with wrongdoing should be brought before a court of law and given a fair trial affording full judicial process. The United States said it had repeatedly urged Israel to cease deportations immediately and permanently and to comply fully with the Convention in all of the territories it had occupied since 1967.

Communications. The Chairman of the Committee on Palestinian rights, on 17 December 1992,[26] drew the Secretary-General's attention to a Reuters dispatch, as well as to press releases issued by the Gaza Centre for Rights and Law and the Palestine Human Rights Information Centre (PHRIC), to the effect that, on the previous day, Israel had ordered the summary deportation of 418 Palestinians from the occupied territories for two years, apparently in punishment for the recent killing of a kidnapped Israeli soldier. Alleged to be activists with Islamic groups, they had not been formally charged with any offence but had been taken to Israel's northern border in anticipation of their deportation into southern Lebanon. They were reportedly waiting on buses, blindfolded and handcuffed, pending a court ruling from Jerusalem.

The move came in the wake of mass arrests of some 2,000 Palestinians during the preceding three days, of a round-the-clock curfew imposed on the Gaza Strip and of the sealing of the Gaza Strip and West Bank as closed military zones. The Chairman conveyed the Committee's renewed call for international protection for Palestinians living under Israeli occupation and for intensified efforts towards the achievement of a just and lasting settlement.

The Observer for Palestine, on 18 December,[27] reported that 383 of those slated for deportation had effectively been deported, in complete disregard of world-wide appeals and in violation of the fourth Geneva Convention. He asked for immediate action to guarantee their safe return and the return of all other Palestinian deportees.

Lebanon, also on 18 December,[28] requested an urgent meeting of the Security Council to discuss the grave situation resulting from the mass deportation into Lebanese territory, urging the Council to compel Israel to reverse its action.

SECURITY COUNCIL ACTION (December)

The Council convened on 18 December 1992 in response to Lebanon's request.[28] Egypt, Israel, Jordan, Lebanon and the Syrian Arab Republic were invited, at their request, to participate in the deliberations without the right to vote, in accordance with rule 37[a] of the Council's provisional rules of procedure.

Regarding a request from the Permanent Observer for Palestine[29] to participate in accordance with the Council's previous practice, the President again noted that it had not been made pursuant to rule 37 or rule 39,[b] and that, if approved, the Observer would be invited to participate with the same rights of participation as those conferred by rule 37. The request was approved by 10 votes in favour to 1 against (United States), with 4 abstentions (Belgium, France, Hungary, United Kingdom). The United States, which had requested the vote, reiterated its objection to the participation of PLO for the same reasons it had cited at the Council's January meeting (see above).

The Council unanimously adopted **resolution 799(1992)**.

The Security Council,

Recalling the obligations of Member States under the United Nations Charter,

Reaffirming its resolutions 607(1988), 608(1988), 636(1989), 641(1989), 681(1990), 694(1991) and 726(1992),

Having learned with deep concern that Israel, the occupying Power, in contravention of its obligations under the Fourth Geneva Convention of 1949, deported to Lebanon on 17 December 1992 hundreds of Palestinian civilians from the territories occupied by Israel since 1967, including Jerusalem,

1. *Strongly condemns* the action taken by Israel, the occupying Power, to deport hundreds of Palestinian civilians, and *expresses* its firm opposition to any such deportation by Israel;

2. *Reaffirms* the applicability of the Fourth Geneva Convention of 12 August 1949 to all the Palestinian territories occupied by Israel since 1967, including Jerusa-

lem, and *affirms* that deportation of civilians constitutes a contravention of its obligations under the Convention;

3. *Reaffirms also* the independence, sovereignty and territorial integrity of Lebanon;

4. *Demands* that Israel, the occupying Power, ensure the safe and immediate return to the occupied territories of all those deported;

5. *Requests* the Secretary-General to consider dispatching a representative to the area to follow up with the Israeli Government with regard to this serious situation and to report to the Security Council;

6. *Decides* to keep the matter actively under review.

Security Council resolution 799(1992)

18 December 1992   Meeting 3151   Adopted unanimously

Draft prepared in consultations among Council members (S/24987).

The Observer for Palestine remarked that perhaps one of the most serious political consequences of Israel's action was its potential for sabotaging or even completely destroying the ongoing peace process. The Palestinian delegation to the talks had been compelled to boycott the previous day's meeting, the last in the eighth round of talks, pending a final decision by the PLO leadership on whether to continue with its participation in the process, for it could not agree to participate in peace talks while Israel pursued its illegal and repressive policies against Palestinians, especially its deportation policy.

Calling Israel's action an act of defiance of the United Nations, a challenge to the Council and a serious breach of the sovereignty and rights of States, Lebanon noted that the Palestinian deportees were left stranded in the open on Lebanese soil under harsh weather conditions, despite its announcement that it would not receive them on its territory.

In defence of the deportations, Israel stated that since March the Islamic fundamentalist group Hamas had carried out 30 terrorist attacks against Israelis that had left 11 dead and 9 wounded. It went on to describe the circumstances and dates of death by stabbing of 3 Israelis (22 February and 24 and 27 May); of 3 soldiers killed by Hamas terrorists, who later paraded through Gaza City proclaiming responsibility for the attack (7 December); of the death of a driver and the wounding of 2 soldiers when Hamas opened fire on their moving vehicle (12 December); and of the kidnapping of an Israeli soldier, later strangled and stabbed to death and whose body was dumped on the Jerusalem-Jericho highway (15 December).

Hamas and Islamic Jihad, Israel claimed, had engaged in gunfire attacks on Israeli civilians and soldiers, in the murder of suspected Palestinian collaborators, in kidnappings and hostage-taking, and in shrill anti-Semitic rhetoric. Moreover, in a leaflet issued in 1991, Hamas declared its unyielding opposition to the very notion of a Middle East peace conference and called for "a serious and effective move at all levels to foil the capitulation conference". Despite these, some Council members were condemning Israel for protecting its citizens and taking measures in self-defence. In view of these terrorist activities, Israel decided to issue temporary removal orders, for a period not to extend beyond two years, against hundreds of members of the terrorist Hamas and Islamic Jihad organizations, including their political and military leaders, whose actions endangered, or incited others to endanger, human lives. The Supreme Court of Israel allowed the temporary-removal measures to proceed, following a careful 14-hour examination of the legal issues involved.

To sum up its position, Israel quoted its Prime Minister, who stated at a special Knesset session on 15 December: "We have only one course, and it is a dual one: a search for peace and an uncompromising war on terrorism. Despite the pain, we continue to cling to the pursuit of peace."

Explaining its affirmative vote, the United States expressed regret that Israel had gone ahead with the deportations, for, by so doing, it played into the hands of those whose goal was to scuttle the peace process. It also imposed an unfair burden on Lebanon. The United States, however, could not ignore, and equally and strongly condemned, the brutal murder of Israelis by Hamas that preceded the deportations and were part of a deliberate strategy to undermine the peace process.

Subsequent communications. On 21 December,[30] the Observer for Palestine drew attention to the extremely harsh conditions of the area in which the deportees were located, making necessary an even more rapid implementation of the resolution just adopted.

Israel, on 23 December,[31] expressed its regret over the Council resolution, which not only failed to recognize Israel's compelling need to defend and protect its citizens against a brutal wave of terrorist activity but also in no way condemned the acts of terror by Hamas and Islamic Jihad elements against Arab and Jew alike. Nevertheless, Israel agreed to the Secretary-General's suggestion to send his representative to Israel on a goodwill mission in the very near future.

Israel restated that it took the exceptional step of temporarily excluding the operatives of the two organizations so as to curtail their network to a degree that would enable the peace talks to proceed in the desired direction. It pointed out that the Supreme Court of Israel sitting as the High Court of Justice had twice considered the petitions for the return of those subjected to the exclusion orders, who had been allowed recourse to individual appeals within 60 days of their removal.

Report of the Secretary-General. The Secretary-General informed the General Assembly in October 1992[32] that no reply had been received from Israel to his July request for information on steps it had taken or envisaged to implement the 1991 Assembly demand[33] that Israel rescind the illegal measure of deporting Palestinians and facilitate their immediate return.

GENERAL ASSEMBLY ACTION

On 14 December 1992, the General Assembly, on the recommendation of the Special Political Committee, adopted **resolution 47/70 E** by recorded vote.

The General Assembly,

Recalling Security Council resolutions 605(1987) of 22 December 1987, 607(1988) of 5 January 1988, 608(1988) of 14 January 1988, 636(1989) of 6 July 1989, 641(1989) of 30 August 1989, 672(1990) of 12 October 1990, 673(1990) of 24 October 1990, 681(1990) of 20 December 1990, 694(1991) of 24 May 1991 and 726(1992) of 6 January 1992,

Recalling also the reports of the Secretary-General of 21 January 1988, 31 October 1990 and 9 April 1991, and taking note of the report of the Secretary-General of 23 October 1992,

Recalling further the Geneva Convention relative to the Protection of Civilian Persons in Time of War, of 12 August 1949, in particular article 1 and the first paragraph of article 49, which read as follows:

"Article 1

"The High Contracting Parties undertake to respect and to ensure respect for the present Convention in all circumstances."

"Article 49

"Individual or mass forcible transfers, as well as deportations of protected persons from occupied territory to the territory of the occupying Power or to that of any other country, occupied or not, are prohibited, regardless of their motive . . .",

Reaffirming the applicability of the Convention to the occupied Palestinian territory, including Jerusalem, and other Arab territories occupied by Israel since 1967,

1.   *Strongly deplores* the continuing disregard by Israel, the occupying Power, of the relevant resolutions and decisions of the Security Council and resolutions of the General Assembly;

2.   *Demands* that the Government of Israel, the occupying Power, rescind the illegal measures taken by its authorities in deporting Palestinians and that it facilitate their immediate return;

3.   *Calls upon* Israel, the occupying Power, to cease forthwith the deportation of Palestinians and to abide scrupulously by the provisions of the Geneva Convention relative to the Protection of Civilian Persons in Time of War, of 12 August 1949;

4.   *Requests* the Secretary-General to report to the General Assembly as soon as possible, but not later than the beginning of its forty-eighth session, on the implementation of the present resolution.

General Assembly resolution 47/70 E

14 December 1992   Meeting 85   143-1-3 (recorded vote)

Approved by Special Political Committee (A/47/612) by recorded vote (118-1-4), 25 November (meeting 27); 11-nation draft (A/SPC/47/L.29); agenda item 74.

Sponsors: Afghanistan, Bangladesh, Brunei Darussalam, Comoros, Cuba, India, Indonesia, Madagascar, Malaysia, Pakistan, Zambia.
Meeting numbers. GA 47th session: SPC 24-27; plenary 85.

Recorded vote in Assembly as follows:

In favour: Afghanistan, Albania, Algeria, Angola, Antigua and Barbuda, Argentina, Australia, Austria, Azerbaijan, Bahrain, Bangladesh, Barbados, Belarus, Belgium, Belize, Benin, Bhutan, Bolivia, Bosnia and Herzegovina, Botswana, Brazil, Brunei Darussalam, Bulgaria, Burkina Faso, Cameroon, Canada, Central African Republic, Chad, Chile, China, Colombia, Comoros, Costa Rica, Côte d'Ivoire, Cuba, Cyprus, Czechoslovakia, Democratic People's Republic of Korea, Denmark, Djibouti, Dominica, Ecuador, Egypt, El Salvador, Estonia, Ethiopia, Finland, France, Gabon, Gambia, Germany, Greece, Guatemala, Guinea-Bissau, Guyana, Haiti, Honduras, Hungary, Iceland, India, Indonesia, Iran, Ireland, Italy, Jamaica, Japan, Jordan, Kazakhstan, Kuwait, Lao People's Democratic Republic, Latvia, Lebanon, Liberia, Libyan Arab Jamahiriya, Liechtenstein, Lithuania, Luxembourg, Madagascar, Malawi, Malaysia, Maldives, Mali, Malta, Marshall Islands, Mauritania, Mauritius, Mexico, Mongolia, Morocco, Mozambique, Myanmar, Namibia, Nepal, Netherlands, New Zealand, Niger, Nigeria, Norway, Oman, Pakistan, Panama, Paraguay, Peru, Philippines, Poland, Portugal, Qatar, Republic of Korea, Republic of Moldova, Romania, Rwanda, Saint Lucia, Saint Vincent and the Grenadines, Samoa, Sao Tome and Principe, Saudi Arabia, Senegal, Sierra Leone, Singapore, Slovenia, Spain, Sri Lanka, Sudan, Suriname, Swaziland, Sweden, Syrian Arab Republic, Thailand, Togo, Trinidad and Tobago, Tunisia, Turkey, Ukraine, United Arab Emirates, United Kingdom, United Republic of Tanzania, Uruguay, Vanuatu, Venezuela, Viet Nam, Yemen, Zambia, Zimbabwe.
Against: Israel.
Abstaining: Micronesia, Russian Federation, United States.

Palestinian detainees

Report of the Committee on Israeli practices. The Committee on Israeli practices[14] noted serious shortcomings in the administration of justice, increasingly exercised by military courts, even in traffic offences. The number of Arab civilians in detention, administrative or otherwise, remained very high due to the policy of "quick justice". As Amnesty International reported in September 1991, more than 14,000 Palestinians had spent some time in administrative detention since the *intifadah* began.

Court proceedings were described as summary and arbitrary, denying basic legal safeguards, such as the right to a fair trial. Extracting confessions under duress was common practice. Family members of detainees were also arbitrarily detained so as to exert psychological pressure on them. Contact with legal counsel was not permitted during interrogation periods, which could last several months. Lawyers complained of difficulties in gaining access to their clients' files and of procedural obstacles during trial. In addition, relatives of arrested persons were systematically subjected to economic and psychological pressures, such as the denial or cancellation of work and travel permits. Lawyers and families were often not notified of the place of incarceration or of the transfer of prisoners from one detention centre to another.

The Committee was concerned by the severity of sentences imposed on the Arab population, often disproportionate to the offence, in marked contrast with the leniency from which Israeli citizens benefited, even when charged with the killing or ill-treatment of Arab civilians, in flagrant violation of the fundamental right of equality before courts and tribunals. An additional grave deficiency was the practice of imposing dual punishment on Palestinians, who not only received harsh sentences but also had their houses demolished. Such measures of collective punishment, prohibited by the fourth Geneva Convention, also affected innocent family members or relatives.

The Committee noted a further deterioration in the treatment of prisoners, characterized by systematic torture and ill-treatment, both physical and psychological, such as food and sleep deprivation, being tied up in painful positions and confined to extremely reduced spaces. Such practices often resulted in severe injuries, permanent incapacitation or even death, as in the case of Mustapha al-Akawi, aged 35, who died on 4 February while under interrogation at Hebron Prison in the West Bank. Detained on 22 January, he was brought before the military court at Hebron at the request of the Israeli secret service, Shin Bet. Mr. al-Akawi complained of having been beaten during interrogation, showing the judge deep bruises on his arms and shoulders. Israeli authorities admitted subjecting him to standard treatment—beatings, sleep deprivation, forced postures, confinement to a tiny cell and exposure to extreme cold. A lawyer was not permitted to speak with him during his detention and court appearances. On 4 February, his father was summoned to the Jerusalem police station, where the lawyer telephoned Hebron Prison and learned of Mr. al-Akawi's death. No information on the cause of death was given.

A particularly disquieting development was the alleged use of electric shock during interrogation. The newspaper *Hadashot* (February 1991) quoted police sources as confirming the allegation to be substantially correct and that electric shock was in use at several prisons to extract information from stone-throwers. An ICRC press release of 21 May 1992 called for an immediate halt to the ill-treatment of detainees during interrogations, stressing that confessions obtained under duress precluded a fair trial.

Contrary to the fourth Geneva Convention, detainees continued to be held in prisons and detention centres inside Israel itself, such as Ketziot, in the Negev, in southern Israel, where conditions were said to be harsh throughout the year and where facilities, food, clothing and medical services were inadequate. Owing to insufficient food intake—only 1,400 calories daily—prisoners fell easy prey to disease. Many were reported to have died of deliberate medical negligence. Although Israel had ratified the 1984 Convention against Torture and Other Cruel, Inhuman or Degrading Treatment or Punishment,[34] it had a record of detaining and torturing minors. Evidence indicated that even children aged 12 were arrested, beaten and tortured for several days on end.

Communications. In October, the Chairman of the Committee on Palestinian rights[35] and the Permanent Observer for Palestine[36] drew attention to press reports that, since 27 September, at least 3,000 Palestinian prisoners in the Israeli prisons at Jneid, Nablus, Ashkelon, Bir Saba' and Nafha had been on a hunger strike in protest against ill-treatment and deteriorating conditions of detention. The prisoners were demanding an end to long periods of solitary confinement and other arbitrary individual and collective punishments; the closure of special punishment dungeons; a reinstatement of adequate food rations; a halt to overcrowding; access to proper medical treatment; and an end to beatings and tear-gassing in the cells and to demeaning strip searches.

The Committee deplored that the Israeli authorities had so far refused to address these legitimate grievances, treating them as a security problem rather than as a human rights issue, and that support demonstrations had been suppressed with live ammunition and rubber bullets, resulting in at least 90 Palestinians shot and injured in the Gaza Strip. The Committee further stated that a PHRIC press release estimated the number of Palestinians currently detained or imprisoned at 12,500. Up to 1,000 more might be under short detention orders, although not registered with detention centres or police lock-ups.

The Observer reported[37] that, on 6 October, Israeli forces indiscriminately fired on Palestinian civilians in the Gaza Strip and West Bank and raided the ICRC office at Rafah, where a number of Palestinians had previously assembled in solidarity with the ongoing hunger strike. They also attacked other solidarity gatherings at Rafah with gunfire, gas bombs and other means, resulting in 108 casualties.

Report of the Secretary-General. The Secretary-General informed the General Assembly in October 1992[38] that Israel had not replied to his July request for information on steps taken or envisaged to implement an Assembly resolution of 1991[39] calling on Israel to release all Palestinians and other Arabs arbitrarily detained or imprisoned.

GENERAL ASSEMBLY ACTION

The General Assembly, acting on the recommendation of the Special Political Committee, adopted **resolution 47/70 D** by recorded vote on 14 December.

The General Assembly,

Recalling Security Council resolution 605(1987) of 22 December 1987,

Recalling also its resolutions 38/79 A of 15 December 1983, 39/95 A of 14 December 1984, 40/161 A of 16 December 1985, 41/63 A of 3 December 1986, 42/160 A of 8 December 1987, 43/21 of 3 November 1988, 43/58 D of 6 December 1988, 44/2 of 6 October 1989, 44/48 D of 8 December 1989, 45/74 D of 11 December 1990 and 46/47 D of 9 December 1991,

Taking note of the reports of the Special Committee to Investigate Israeli Practices Affecting the Human Rights of the Palestinian People and Other Arabs of the Occupied Territories,

Recalling the reports of the Secretary-General of 21 January 1988 and 31 October 1990, and taking note of the report of the Secretary-General of 23 October 1992,

1. *Deplores* the arbitrary detention or imprisonment by Israel of thousands of Palestinians as a result of their resistance to occupation in order to attain self-determination;

2. *Calls upon* Israel, the occupying Power, to release all Palestinians and other Arabs arbitrarily detained or imprisoned;

3. *Requests* the Secretary-General to report to the General Assembly as soon as possible, but not later than the beginning of its forty-eighth session, on the implementation of the present resolution.

General Assembly resolution 47/70 D

14 December 1992   Meeting 85   142-2-2 (recorded vote)

Approved by Special Political Committee (A/47/612) by recorded vote (118-2-3), 25 November (meeting 27); 11-nation draft (A/SPC/47/L.28); agenda item 74.
Sponsors: Afghanistan, Bangladesh, Brunei Darussalam, Comoros, Cuba, India, Indonesia, Madagascar, Malaysia, Pakistan, Zambia.
Meeting numbers. GA 47th session: SPC 24-27; plenary 85.

Recorded vote in Assembly as follows:

In favour: Afghanistan, Albania, Algeria, Angola, Antigua and Barbuda, Argentina, Australia, Austria, Azerbaijan, Bahrain, Bangladesh, Barbados, Belarus, Belgium, Belize, Benin, Bhutan, Bolivia, Bosnia and Herzegovina, Botswana, Brazil, Brunei Darussalam, Bulgaria, Burkina Faso, Cameroon, Canada, Central African Republic, Chad, Chile, China, Colombia, Comoros, Costa Rica, Côte d'Ivoire, Cuba, Cyprus, Czechoslovakia, Democratic People's Republic of Korea, Denmark, Djibouti, Dominica, Ecuador, Egypt, El Salvador, Estonia, Ethiopia, Finland, France, Gabon, Gambia, Germany, Greece, Guatemala, Guinea-Bissau, Guyana, Haiti, Honduras, Hungary, Iceland, India, Indonesia, Iran, Ireland, Italy, Jamaica, Japan, Jordan, Kazakhstan, Kuwait, Lao People's Democratic Republic, Latvia, Lebanon, Liberia, Libyan Arab Jamahiriya, Liechtenstein, Lithuania, Luxembourg, Madagascar, Malawi, Malaysia, Maldives, Mali, Malta, Marshall Islands, Mauritania, Mauritius, Mexico, Mongolia, Morocco, Mozambique, Myanmar, Namibia, Nepal, Netherlands, New Zealand, Niger, Nigeria, Norway, Oman, Pakistan, Panama, Paraguay, Peru, Philippines, Poland, Portugal, Qatar, Republic of Korea, Republic of Moldova, Romania, Rwanda, Saint Lucia, Saint Vincent and the Grenadines, Samoa, Sao Tome and Principe, Saudi Arabia, Senegal, Sierra Leone, Singapore, Slovenia, Spain, Sri Lanka, Sudan, Suriname, Swaziland, Sweden, Syrian Arab Republic, Thailand, Togo, Trinidad and Tobago, Tunisia, Turkey, Ukraine, United Arab Emirates, United Kingdom, United Republic of Tanzania, Vanuatu, Venezuela, Viet Nam, Yemen, Zambia, Zimbabwe.
Against: Israel, United States.
Abstaining: Micronesia, Russian Federation.

Israeli measures against educational institutions

Report of the Committee on Israeli practices. The Committee on Israeli practices noted in its October 1992 report[14] that freedom of education continued to be restricted by the frequent closure of academic institutions, some of which had remained closed since the beginning of the popular uprising. Those allowed to reopen were subjected to periodic closures. A case in point was Al-Najah University at Nablus, sealed off by the army on 14 July on suspicion that armed fugitives were on

the premises. As a result, approximately 2,000 students, professors, employees and several children found themselves confined to the campus for days. A curfew imposed on the town at the same time affected its almost 150,000 inhabitants. The long-term effects of closures and curfews had led to a dramatic decline in the once high academic standards and educational level of the Palestinians. Restrictions on movement curtailed one's choice of schools, as in the case of students from Gaza who wanted to study in the West Bank but needed permission to do so from its military governor.

The Committee was informed of severe shortages of classrooms and teaching materials and of restrictions on the importation of books, even of books in use at Israeli university libraries. An additional difficulty that Palestinian students faced was that diplomas awarded by universities subjected to official closures, based on academic requirements fulfilled outside their premises, were not recognized by Israeli authorities; consequently, students holding such diplomas were unable to find employment. Although regarded illegal by the Israeli military authorities, almost all universities had begun off-campus teaching to maintain a connection between students and teachers and some semblance of a university.

Report of the Secretary-General. The Secretary-General informed the General Assembly in October 1992[40] that no reply had been received from Israel to his July request for information on steps it had taken or envisaged to implement the 1991 Assembly demand[41] that it rescind all actions and measures against educational institutions, ensure their freedom and refrain from hindering their effective operation.

GENERAL ASSEMBLY ACTION

On 14 December 1992, on the recommendation of the Special Political Committee, the General Assembly adopted **resolution 47/70 G** by recorded vote.

The General Assembly,

Bearing in mind the Geneva Convention relative to the Protection of Civilian Persons in Time of War, of 12 August 1949,

Deeply concerned about the continued and intensified harassment by Israel, the occupying Power, directed against educational institutions in the occupied Palestinian territory,

Recalling Security Council resolutions 605(1987) of 22 December 1987, 672(1990) of 12 October 1990, 673(1990) of 24 October 1990 and 681(1990) of 20 December 1990,

Recalling also its resolutions 38/79 G of 15 December 1983, 39/95 G of 14 December 1984, 40/161 G of 16 December 1985, 41/63 G of 3 December 1986, 42/160 G of 8 December 1987, 43/21 of 3 November 1988, 43/58 G of 6 December 1988, 44/2 of 6 October 1989, 44/48 G of 8 December 1989, 45/74 G of 11 December 1990 and 46/47 G of 9 December 1991,

Recalling further the reports of the Secretary-General of 21 January 1988, 31 October 1990 and 9 April 1991, and taking note of the report of the Secretary-General of 23 October 1992,

Taking note of the relevant decisions adopted by the Executive Board of the United Nations Educational, Scientific and Cultural Organization concerning the educational and cultural situation in the occupied Palestinian territory,

1. *Reaffirms* the applicability of the Geneva Convention relative to the Protection of Civilian Persons in Time of War, of 12 August 1949, to the occupied Palestinian territory, including Jerusalem, and other Arab territories occupied by Israel since 1967;

2. *Condemns* Israeli policies and practices against Palestinian students and faculty members in schools, universities and other educational institutions in the occupied Palestinian territory, especially the opening of fire on defenceless students, causing many casualties;

3. *Also condemns* the systematic Israeli campaign of repression against and closing of universities, schools and other educational and vocational institutions in the occupied Palestinian territory, in large numbers and for prolonged periods, restricting and impeding the academic activities of Palestinian universities by subjecting the selection of courses, textbooks and educational programmes, the admission of students and the appointment of faculty members to the control and supervision of the military occupation authorities, in flagrant contravention of the Convention;

4. *Demands* that Israel, the occupying Power, comply with the provisions of that Convention, rescind all actions and measures taken against all educational institutions, ensure the freedom of those institutions and refrain forthwith from hindering the effective operation of the universities, schools and other educational institutions;

5. *Requests* the Secretary-General to report to the General Assembly as soon as possible, but not later than the beginning of its forty-eighth session, on the implementation of the present resolution.

General Assembly resolution 47/70 G

14 December 1992   Meeting 85   143-2-4 (recorded vote)

Approved by Special Political Committee (A/47/612) by recorded vote (116-2-5), 25 November (meeting 27); 10-nation draft (A/SPC/47/L.31); agenda item 74.
Sponsors: Afghanistan, Bangladesh, Brunei Darussalam, Comoros, Cuba, Indonesia, Madagascar, Malaysia, Pakistan, Zambia.
Meeting numbers. GA 47th session: SPC 24-27; plenary 85.

Recorded vote in Assembly as follows:

In favour: Afghanistan, Albania, Algeria, Angola, Antigua and Barbuda, Argentina, Australia, Austria, Azerbaijan, Bahrain, Bangladesh, Barbados, Belarus, Belgium, Belize, Benin, Bhutan, Bolivia, Bosnia and Herzegovina, Botswana, Brazil, Brunei Darussalam, Bulgaria, Burkina Faso, Cameroon, Central African Republic, Chad, Chile, China, Colombia, Comoros, Costa Rica, Cuba, Cyprus, Czechoslovakia, Democratic People's Republic of Korea, Denmark, Djibouti, Dominica, Ecuador, Egypt, El Salvador, Estonia, Ethiopia, Finland, France, Gabon, Gambia, Germany, Greece, Guatemala, Guinea-Bissau, Guyana, Haiti, Honduras, Hungary, Iceland, India, Indonesia, Iran, Iraq, Ireland, Italy, Jamaica, Japan, Jordan, Kazakhstan, Kuwait, Lao People's Democratic Republic, Latvia, Lebanon, Liberia, Libyan Arab Jamahiriya, Liechtenstein, Lithuania, Luxembourg, Madagascar, Malawi, Malaysia, Maldives, Mali, Malta, Marshall Islands, Mauritania, Mauritius, Mexico, Mongolia, Morocco, Mozambique, Myanmar, Namibia, Nepal, Netherlands, New Zealand, Niger, Nigeria, Norway, Oman, Pakistan, Panama, Paraguay, Peru, Philippines, Poland, Portugal, Qatar, Republic of Korea, Republic of Moldova, Romania, Rwanda, Saint Kitts and Nevis, Saint Lucia, Saint Vincent and the Grenadines, Samoa, Sao Tome and Principe, Saudi Arabia, Senegal, Sierra Leone, Singapore, Slovenia, Spain, Sri Lanka, Sudan, Suriname, Swaziland, Sweden, Syrian

Arab Republic, Thailand, Togo, Trinidad and Tobago, Tunisia, Turkey, Ukraine, United Arab Emirates, United Kingdom, United Republic of Tanzania, Uruguay, Vanuatu, Venezuela, Viet Nam, Yemen, Zambia, Zimbabwe.
Against: Israel, United States.
Abstaining: Canada, Côte d'Ivoire, Micronesia, Russian Federation.

Golan Heights

Report of the Committee on Israeli practices. The October 1992 report of the Committee on Israeli practices[14] included information on the policies and practices pursued by Israel in the occupied Syrian Golan, as provided by the Syrian Arab Republic. The report cited the *Jerusalem Post* of 15 July, which carried an item on "security" settlements to be established in the Golan Heights and the Jordan Valley, contrary to changes in the settlements policy announced by the newly elected Israeli Government. Land in the region of Buq'ata village was reported to have recently been confiscated, on which military outposts were set up, thus excluding it from grazing. Land was further expropriated from the remaining Syrian Arab villages of Al-Fajr, Ayn Qunyah, Majdal Shams and Mas'adah.

Other practices mentioned included: the continual reduction of irrigation water for Golan Arabs owing to its diversion to farmlands in Jewish settlements; restrictions on digging new wells; the uprooting of fruit trees and saplings of landowners who had not obtained permits from the so-called Israel Land Administration; setting fire to Arab orchards and wooded areas surrounding Arab villages; burning grazing areas and planting mines around them; levying high property and income taxes; replacing Syrian Arab educational curricula with one hostile to the population's national and spiritual heritage; restrictions on travel out of the Golan for medical treatment; and the use of force to quell demonstrations and resistance to Israeli occupation.

Report of the Secretary-General. In October 1992,[42] the Secretary-General informed the General Assembly that no reply had been received from Israel to his July request for information on steps it had taken or envisaged to implement the 1991 Assembly call[43] on Israel to desist from repressive measures against the Golan population.

GENERAL ASSEMBLY ACTION

On 14 December, the General Assembly, on the Special Political Committee's recommendation, adopted **resolution 47/70 F** by recorded vote.

The General Assembly,

Deeply concerned that the Arab territories occupied since 1967 have been under continued Israeli military occupation,

Recalling Security Council resolution 497(1981) of 17 December 1981,

Recalling also its resolutions 36/226 B of 17 December 1981, ES-9/1 of 5 February 1982, 37/88 E of 10 December 1982, 38/79 F of 15 December 1983, 39/95 F of 14 December 1984, 40/161 F of 16 December 1985, 41/63 F of 3 December 1986, 42/160 F of 8 December 1987, 43/21 of 3 November 1988, 43/58 F of 6 December 1988, 44/2 of 6 October 1989, 44/48 F of 8 December 1989, 45/74 F of 11 December 1990 and 46/47 F of 9 December 1991,

Having considered the report of the Secretary-General of 23 October 1992,

Recalling its previous resolutions, in particular resolutions 3414(XXX) of 5 December 1975, 31/61 of 9 December 1976, 32/20 of 25 November 1977, 33/28 and 33/29 of 7 December 1978, 34/70 of 6 December 1979 and 35/122 E of 11 December 1980, in which, *inter alia,* it called upon Israel to put an end to its occupation of the Arab territories and to withdraw from all those territories,

Reaffirming once more the illegality of Israel's decision of 14 December 1981 to impose its laws, jurisdiction and administration on the occupied Syrian Golan, which has resulted in the effective annexation of that territory,

Reaffirming that the acquisition of territory by force is inadmissible under the Charter of the United Nations and that all territories thus occupied by Israel must be returned,

Recalling the Geneva Convention relative to the Protection of Civilian Persons in Time of War, of 12 August 1949,

Reaffirming the applicability of that Convention to the occupied Syrian Golan,

Bearing in mind Security Council resolution 237(1967) of 14 June 1967,

1. *Strongly condemns* Israel, the occupying Power, for its refusal to comply with the relevant resolutions of the General Assembly and the Security Council, particularly Council resolution 497(1981), in which the Council, *inter alia,* decided that the Israeli decision to impose its laws, jurisdiction and administration on the occupied Syrian Arab Golan was null and void and without international legal effect and demanded that Israel, the occupying Power, should rescind forthwith its decisions;

2. *Condemns* the persistence of Israel in changing the physical character, demographic composition, institutional structure and legal status of the occupied Syrian Golan;

3. *Determines* that all legislative and administrative measures and actions taken or to be taken by Israel, the occupying Power, that purport to alter the character and legal status of the occupied Syrian Golan are null and void, constitute a flagrant violation of international law and of the Geneva Convention relative to the Protection of Civilian Persons in Time of War, of 12 August 1949, and have no legal effect;

4. *Strongly condemns* Israel for its attempts forcibly to impose Israeli citizenship and Israeli identity cards on the Syrian citizens in the occupied Syrian Golan, and calls upon it to desist from its repressive measures against the population of the occupied Syrian Golan;

5. *Deplores* the violations by Israel of the Convention;

6. *Calls once again upon* Member States not to recognize any of the legislative or administrative measures and actions referred to above;

7. *Requests* the Secretary-General to report to the General Assembly at its forty-eighth session on the implementation of the present resolution.

General Assembly resolution 47/70 F

14 December 1992   Meeting 85   142-1-4 (recorded vote)

Approved by Special Political Committee (A/47/612) by recorded vote (116-1-5), 25 November (meeting 27); 9-nation draft (A/SPC/47/L.30); agenda item 74.

Sponsors: Afghanistan, Bangladesh, Brunei Darussalam, Comoros, Cuba, Indonesia, Madagascar, Malaysia, Pakistan.

Meeting numbers. GA 47th session: SPC 24-27; plenary 85.

Recorded vote in Assembly as follows:

In favour: Afghanistan, Albania, Algeria, Angola, Antigua and Barbuda, Argentina, Australia, Austria, Azerbaijan, Bahrain, Bangladesh, Barbados, Belarus, Belgium, Belize, Benin, Bhutan, Bolivia, Bosnia and Herzegovina, Botswana, Brazil, Brunei Darussalam, Bulgaria, Burkina Faso, Cameroon, Canada, Central African Republic, Chad, Chile, China, Colombia, Comoros, Costa Rica, Cuba, Cyprus, Czechoslovakia, Democratic People's Republic of Korea, Denmark, Djibouti, Dominica, Ecuador, Egypt, El Salvador, Estonia, Ethiopia, Finland, France, Gabon, Gambia, Germany, Greece, Guatemala, Guinea-Bissau, Guyana, Haiti, Honduras, Hungary, Iceland, India, Indonesia, Iran, Ireland, Italy, Jamaica, Japan, Jordan, Kazakhstan, Kuwait, Lao People's Democratic Republic, Latvia, Lebanon, Liberia, Libyan Arab Jamahiriya, Liechtenstein, Lithuania, Luxembourg, Madagascar, Malaysia, Maldives, Mali, Malta, Marshall Islands, Mauritania, Mauritius, Mexico, Mongolia, Morocco, Mozambique, Myanmar, Namibia, Nepal, Netherlands, New Zealand, Niger, Nigeria, Norway, Oman, Pakistan, Panama, Paraguay, Peru, Philippines, Poland, Portugal, Qatar, Republic of Korea, Republic of Moldova, Romania, Rwanda, Saint Kitts and Nevis, Saint Lucia, Saint Vincent and the Grenadines, Samoa, Sao Tome and Principe, Saudi Arabia, Senegal, Sierra Leone, Singapore, Slovenia, Spain, Sri Lanka, Sudan, Suriname, Swaziland, Sweden, Syrian Arab Republic, Thailand, Togo, Trinidad and Tobago, Tunisia, Turkey, Ukraine, United Arab Emirates, United Kingdom, United Republic of Tanzania, Uruguay, Vanuatu, Venezuela, Viet Nam, Yemen, Zambia, Zimbabwe.

Against: Israel.

Abstaining: Côte d'Ivoire, Micronesia, Russian Federation, United States.

Human Rights Commission action. The Commission on Human Rights, on 14 February, adopted a resolution by which it determined that all legislative and administrative measures and actions taken or to be taken by Israel, purporting to alter the character and legal status of the Syrian Golan, were null and void, constituted a flagrant violation of international law and the fourth Geneva Convention, and had no legal effect.[44] (See also PART THREE, Chapter X.)

Israeli settlements

Report of the Committee on Israeli practices. In its October 1992 report,[14] the Committee on Israeli practices observed that, from the information before it, Israeli settlement activities had intensified through land expropriation and the transfer of Israeli citizens to the occupied territories, particularly of recent Jewish immigrants from Eastern Europe and the former USSR. These and related practices to induce Palestinian and other Arab population to leave their homeland (diversion of water resources, destruction of fields, uprooting of fruit trees, expropriation of grazing land and closing other land areas as military zones, and excessive use of environmentally harmful pesticides and other chemicals) indicated a clear intent to modify the territories' demographic composition. Settlements were often built between Arab villages, cutting off contact among them. Newly built roads and highways linked the settlements but bypassed Palestinian towns and villages.

The Committee cited press reports to show the direction of Israel's settlements policy. Two reports noted the quadrupling in 1991 of building starts in the territories (*Ha'aretz* and *Jerusalem Post*, 6 April), and the transfer of some $10.5 million earmarked for roads under the Ministry of Housing's regular budget to a parallel budget for road construction specifically for security reasons (*Ha'aretz*, 6 May). Announcements were made of the imminent launching of a major campaign to attract more settlers to the Golan Heights, following declarations by the outgoing Prime Minister and the incoming one that Israel would keep the Golan for its strategic importance (*Jerusalem Post*, 18 June); and of the possible establishment of new "security" settlements in the Golan Heights and the Jordan Valley, defined as border settlements directly connected with warding off attacks and whose residents were organized to defend the sector (*Jerusalem Post*, 15 July).

On the other hand, Prime Minister Yitzhak Rabin was reported as having proposed a shift away from budget allocations for settlements, but ruled out a complete freeze, and as making a clear distinction between "political" and "security" settlements (*Jerusalem Post*, 25 June). The Government was reported to have imposed a de facto freeze on all new public housing construction and on all unsigned building contracts throughout the country, including the West Bank and the Gaza Strip (*Ha'aretz*, 16 July; *Jerusalem Post*, 17 July). The new cabinet, at its first session in July, voted to carry out previously approved settlement projects only upon their re-approval by the new Government (*Jerusalem Post*, 20 July; *Ha'aretz*, 21 July). The Ministers of Finance and Housing ordered the cancellation of construction work on nearly 7,000 new housing units in the territories and on a dozen highways (*Ha'aretz*, *Jerusalem Post*, 24 July); and the Prime Minister gave final approval to a plan calling a halt to the construction of 5,364 houses in the territories and of 6,617 units planned to be built inside the Green Line (*Jerusalem Post*, 28 July).

Meanwhile, numerous cases of harassment and violence involving Israeli settlers continued to be reported. On several occasions, settlers raided villages and refugee camps, attacking the inhabitants, destroying their property and uprooting trees, with the Israeli armed forces often unable to control such outbursts of aggression.

Report of the Secretary-General. The Secretary-General informed the General Assembly in October 1992[45] that no reply had been received from Israel to his July request for information on steps it had taken or envisaged to implement the 1991 Assembly demand[46] that it desist from taking any action that would result in changing the legal status, geographical nature or demographic composition of the territories.

On 14 December 1992, the General Assembly, on the basis of the Special Political Committee's recommendation, adopted **resolution 47/70 C** by recorded vote.

The General Assembly,

Recalling Security Council resolutions 465(1980) of 1 March 1980, 605(1987) of 22 December 1987, 672(1990) of 12 October 1990, 673(1990) of 24 October 1990, 681(1990) of 20 December 1990 and 726(1992) of 6 January 1992,

Recalling also its resolutions 32/5 of 28 October 1977, 33/113 B of 18 December 1978, 34/90 C of 12 December 1979, 35/122 B of 11 December 1980, 36/147 B of 16 December 1981, 37/88 B of 10 December 1982, 38/79 C of 15 December 1983, 39/95 C of 14 December 1984, 40/161 C of 16 December 1985, 41/63 C of 3 December 1986, 42/160 C of 8 December 1987, 43/58 C of 6 December 1988, 44/48 C of 8 December 1989, 45/74 C of 11 December 1990 and 46/47 C of 9 December 1991,

Expressing grave anxiety and concern about the serious situation prevailing in the occupied Palestinian territory, including Jerusalem, and other Arab territories occupied by Israel since 1967, as a result of the continued Israeli occupation and the measures and actions taken by Israel, the occupying Power, designed to change the legal status, geographical nature and demographic composition of those territories,

Recalling the reports of the Secretary-General of 21 January 1988, 31 October 1990 and 9 April 1991, and taking note of the report of the Secretary-General of 23 October 1992,

Confirming that the Geneva Convention relative to the Protection of Civilian Persons in Time of War, of 12 August 1949, is applicable to all occupied Palestinian territory, including Jerusalem, and other Arab territories occupied by Israel since 1967,

1. *Determines* that all such measures and actions taken by Israel in the occupied Palestinian territory, including Jerusalem, and other Arab territories occupied by Israel since 1967 are in violation of the relevant provisions of the Geneva Convention relative to the Protection of Civilian Persons in Time of War, of 12 August 1949, constitute a serious obstacle to the efforts to achieve a comprehensive, just and lasting peace in the Middle East and therefore have no legal validity;

2. *Strongly deplores* the persistence of Israel in carrying out such measures, in particular the establishment of settlements in the occupied Palestinian territory, including Jerusalem, and other Arab territories occupied by Israel since 1967;

3. *Demands* that Israel comply strictly with its international obligations in accordance with the principles of international law and the provisions of the said Convention;

4. *Demands once more* that Israel, the occupying Power, desist forthwith from taking any action that would result in changing the legal status, geographical nature or demographic composition of the occupied Palestinian territory, including Jerusalem, and other Arab territories occupied by Israel since 1967;

5. *Urgently calls upon* all States parties to the Convention to respect and to exert all efforts in order to ensure

respect for and compliance with its provisions in all occupied Palestinian territory, including Jerusalem, and other Arab territories occupied by Israel since 1967;

6. *Requests* the Secretary-General to report to the General Assembly at its forty-eighth session on the implementation of the present resolution.

General Assembly resolution 47/70 C

14 December 1992   Meeting 85   143-1-3 (recorded vote)

Approved by Special Political Committee (A/47/612) by recorded vote (119-1-3), 25 November (meeting 27); 11-nation draft (A/SPC/47/L.27); agenda item 74.
Sponsors: Afghanistan, Bangladesh, Brunei Darussalam, Comoros, Cuba, India, Indonesia, Madagascar, Malaysia, Pakistan, Zambia.
Meeting numbers. GA 47th session: SPC 24-27; plenary 85.

Recorded vote in Assembly as follows:

In favour: Afghanistan, Albania, Algeria, Angola, Antigua and Barbuda, Argentina, Australia, Austria, Azerbaijan, Bahrain, Bangladesh, Barbados, Belarus, Belgium, Belize, Benin, Bhutan, Bolivia, Bosnia and Herzegovina, Botswana, Brazil, Brunei Darussalam, Bulgaria, Burkina Faso, Cameroon, Canada, Central African Republic, Chad, Chile, China, Colombia, Comoros, Costa Rica, Côte d'Ivoire, Cuba, Cyprus, Czechoslovakia, Democratic People's Republic of Korea, Denmark, Djibouti, Dominica, Ecuador, Egypt, El Salvador, Estonia, Ethiopia, Finland, France, Gabon, Gambia, Germany, Greece, Guatemala, Guinea-Bissau, Guyana, Haiti, Honduras, Hungary, Iceland, India, Indonesia, Iran, Ireland, Italy, Jamaica, Japan, Jordan, Kazakhstan, Kuwait, Lao People's Democratic Republic, Latvia, Lebanon, Liberia, Libyan Arab Jamahiriya, Liechtenstein, Lithuania, Luxembourg, Madagascar, Malawi, Malaysia, Maldives, Mali, Malta, Marshall Islands, Mauritania, Mauritius, Mexico, Mongolia, Morocco, Mozambique, Myanmar, Namibia, Nepal, Netherlands, New Zealand, Niger, Nigeria, Norway, Oman, Pakistan, Panama, Paraguay, Peru, Philippines, Poland, Portugal, Qatar, Republic of Korea, Republic of Moldova, Romania, Rwanda, Saint Lucia, Saint Vincent and the Grenadines, Samoa, Sao Tome and Principe, Saudi Arabia, Senegal, Sierra Leone, Singapore, Slovenia, Spain, Sri Lanka, Sudan, Suriname, Swaziland, Sweden, Syrian Arab Republic, Thailand, Togo, Trinidad and Tobago, Tunisia, Turkey, Ukraine, United Arab Emirates, United Kingdom, United Republic of Tanzania, Uruguay, Vanuatu, Venezuela, Viet Nam, Yemen, Zambia, Zimbabwe.
Against: Israel.
Abstaining: Micronesia, Russian Federation, United States.

Human Rights Commission action. The Commission on Human Rights, on 14 February,[47] reaffirmed that the installation of Israeli civilians in the occupied territories was illegal and constituted a violation of the fourth Geneva Convention; it urged Israel to abstain from installing settlers, including immigrants, in the occupied territories. (See also PART THREE, Chapter X.)

Economic and social repercussions of Israeli settlements

In a report of July 1992,[48] the Secretary-General summarized the economic and social consequences of the establishment of settlements by Israel in the Palestinian territory, including Jerusalem, and the Syrian Golan. Prepared in response to a General Assembly request of 1991,[49] it was submitted to the Assembly through the Economic and Social Council.

According to the report, the establishment of settlements had accelerated since the beginning of 1991. Massive Jewish immigration to Israel from the Commonwealth of Independent States, Eastern Europe and Ethiopia (about 200,000 in 1990 and another 200,000 in 1991) led to unprecedented housing construction in the West Bank, including East Jerusalem, the Gaza Strip and the Syrian

Golan. In 1991, 5,565 mobile and prefabricated homes were installed. Under a long-term plan, a ring of new housing was to be built in the Jerusalem, Jericho and Nablus areas in the West Bank, and at Tulkarim in the Gaza Strip. By September 1991, there were about 19,000 units at various stages of construction.

Rising prices and a tight housing market in Israel on the one hand, and government financial and tax incentives, concessionary loans and free infrastructure on the other, led many Israelis to move to settlements in the occupied territories. The Council of Jewish Communities launched a major campaign in April 1992 to encourage tens of thousands of Jews to move to houses currently under construction in the territories, with the aim of settling 70,000 persons within a year.

The indigenous Arab community in the occupied territories—governed by a civil administration under the authority of the Israeli Ministry of Defence and subject to specific legislation—developed separately from the newly established Jewish Israeli community. This dual legal and administrative system applicable to the two peoples was highlighted in a 1990 report on human rights practices by the United States Department of State. It emphasized that Palestinians—both Muslim and Christian—were treated less favourably than Israeli settlers on a broad range of issues, including equality before the law, right to residence, freedom of movement, sale of crops and goods, land and water use, and access to health and social services.

The Palestinian human rights organization Al-Haq pointed out that the benefits and subsidies granted to settlers were components of a situation in which 65 per cent of the Arab lands in the West Bank were illegally confiscated by the authorities, and where Palestinian towns and villages were encircled and isolated by settlement developments. There were no urban or rural development projects for the improvement or expansion of Palestinian agglomerations.

Apart from being subject to continued expropriation, Arab land was also subject to restrictions under a specific military order, applicable where the land surrounded settlements, camps, military installations or access routes to settlements. In some areas, fertile Palestinian land had been sacrificed to secure access routes, as in the case of many vineyards between Bethlehem and Hebron. Land confiscated between June 1967 and the end of 1990 through the application of Israeli laws and regulations totalled as follows: 2,895,642 dunums (52.6 per cent) in the occupied West Bank, 153,475 dunums (42.3 per cent) in the Gaza Strip, and 69.4 per cent of the land area of the Syrian Golan. In January 1992, Israel's Ministry of Finance put the number of Jewish settlers at 130,000 in the West Bank, at 120,000 in East Jerusalem, at between 4,000 and 5,000 in the Gaza Strip and at more than 13,000 in the Syrian Golan, making a total of some 268,000 settlers in the occupied territories. The number of settlements was estimated at 194—136 in the West Bank, 33 in the Syrian Golan, 17 in the Gaza Strip and 8 in East Jerusalem.

The report noted that the development of Jewish settlements had worsened the socio-economic conditions of the Palestinians and was a source of tension. Clashes between the two communities occurred with increasing frequency, the Israeli settlers having organized themselves into an armed militia. It cited an UNCTAD study[50] indicating that Israeli policy and practices in the West Bank and the Gaza Strip had brought about radical changes in the structure of the economy that adversely affected economic growth and development and reduced Palestinian contribution to the gross domestic product. The study found that the total cultivated area decreased in the West Bank from 36 per cent in 1966 to 27 per cent in 1984, and, in the Gaza Strip, from 55 per cent in 1966 to 28 per cent in 1985.

Land confiscation in both territories meant an inevitable decline in agricultural production, and hence a decline in agricultural income: in the West Bank, from $237 million in 1981 to $204 million in 1985, and, in the Gaza Strip, from $66 million to $61 million in the same period, the increased use of modern agricultural technologies notwithstanding. Agricultural employment likewise fell in both territories, from 38.7 per cent of the total workforce in 1970 to 24.4 per cent in 1985.

Also cited was a 1990 ILO report, according to which endogenous development efforts were frequently frustrated or undone for administrative or security reasons. Thousands of workers had left because they or their employers had lost their land or could not expand for lack of water; or because they could not compete in the home market with subsidized imports from Israel; or because they encountered barriers to buying farm inputs or to selling their products abroad. Land confiscation and restrictions on water resources meant that a large proportion of the population normally earning a living by traditional agriculture gradually began seeking employment in Israel as unskilled workers because of a lack of alternative jobs in the territories. That appeared to be partially responsible for the territories' economic dependence on Israel, particularly for agricultural produce.

As to water resources, Israel had issued a series of orders to guarantee its complete monopoly and control over those resources, with respect to water transfer, extraction, consumption, sales and distribution, use, water sharing and rationing, well drilling and construction of water installations. Arab inhabitants of the Syrian Golan were forced to demolish some of their own reservoirs; the Is-raeli army had dynamited a number of others. Only three or four reservoirs, out of some 400 in existence in the Golan, were currently authorized for use. Restrictions on water use were such that the permits granted were for drilling wells not exceeding 60 metres and for domestic purposes only, while Israeli settlers were allowed to drill to depths of up to 500 metres. Several hundred Arab-owned water pumps in the Jordan Valley were destroyed for security reasons, as were irrigation canals supplying water to Arab farms in the Al-Jiftlik area. Ram Lake, the largest body of water in the Syrian Golan, was seized by Israeli authorities and its water diverted to serve agricultural and industrial projects in Israeli settlements; consequently, Golan villages suffered a critical shortfall in drinking and irrigation water.

The report described the consequences of Israeli water policies and practices thus: a state of conflict and competition over land and water resources prevailed—such as that between Israeli settlements in the Jordan Valley and the Arab villages of the West Bank—with adverse impact on the living conditions of Palestinians. Of estimated usable groundwater reserves of 600 million cubic metres per year in the West Bank, approximately 500 million cubic metres were being pumped by the Israeli occupation authorities, leaving only 100 million cubic metres, or 16.6 per cent of the total water available, for West Bank use. The deep wells drilled by Israeli authorities reduced the water level in Arab wells, in turn reducing productive capacity and gradually drying up those wells and agricultural lands dependent on them for irrigation. Over-exploitation of groundwater in the Gaza Strip and the dramatic increase in water consumption by Israeli settlers had increased salinity through sea-water intrusion so that about 50 per cent of the Gaza wells had become unfit for human use and most of them unfit for irrigation. As in the West Bank and Gaza Strip, Israel's arbitrary practices in land confiscation and control of water resources in the Syrian Golan had reduced the area under cultivation, curtailed local development and lowered income from agriculture.

ECONOMIC AND SOCIAL COUNCIL ACTION

On 31 July 1992, the Economic and Social Council, on the recommendation of its Economic Committee, adopted **resolution 1992/57** by recorded vote.

Economic and social repercussions of the Israeli settlements on the Palestinian people in the Palestinian territory, including Jerusalem, occupied since 1967, and on the Arab population of the Syrian Golan

The Economic and Social Council,

Recalling General Assembly resolution 46/199 of 20 December 1991,

Guided by the principles of the Charter of the United Nations, and affirming the inadmissibility of the acquisition of territory by force and Security Council resolutions 242(1967) of 22 November 1967 and 497(1981) of 17 December 1981,

Recalling also Security Council resolution 465(1980) of 1 March 1980 and other resolutions affirming the applicability of the Geneva Convention relative to the Protection of Civilian Persons in Time of War, of 12 August 1949, to the occupied Palestinian territory, including Jerusalem, and other Arab territories occupied by Israel since 1967,

Expressing its concern at the establishment by Israel, the occupying Power, of settlements in the occupied Palestinian territory and other Arab territories occupied since 1967, including the settlements of new immigrants therein,

1. *Takes note* of the report of the Secretary-General;

2. *Deplores* the establishment of settlements by Israel in the Palestinian territory, including Jerusalem, and the other Arab territories occupied since 1967, and regards the settlements as unlawful and without any legal effect;

3. *Recognizes* the economic and social repercussions of the Israeli settlements on the Palestinian people in the Palestinian territory, including Jerusalem, occupied by Israel since 1967, and on the Arab population of the Syrian Golan;

4. *Strongly deplores* Israel's practices in the occupied Palestinian territory and other Arab territories occupied since 1967, in particular its confiscation of land, its appropriation of water resources, its depletion of other economic resources and its displacement and deportation of the population of those territories;

5. *Reaffirms* the inalienable right of the Palestinian people and the population of the Syrian Golan to their natural and all other economic resources, and regards any infringement thereof as being without any legal validity;

6. *Requests* the Secretary-General to submit to the General Assembly at its forty-eighth session, through the Economic and Social Council, a report on the progress made in the implementation of the present resolution.

Economic and Social Council resolution 1992/57

31 July 1992   Meeting 42   47-2-2 (recorded vote)

Approved by Economic Committee (E/1992/110) by recorded vote (47-2-3), 28 July (meeting 16); 12-nation draft (E/1992/C.1/L.9), orally amended by Vice-Chairman; agenda item 13.

Sponsors: Algeria, Bahrain, Egypt, Iraq, Jordan, Lebanon, Libyan Arab Jamahiriya, Mauritania, Morocco, Syrian Arab Republic, Tunisia, Yemen.

Recorded vote in Council as follows:

In favour: Algeria, Angola, Argentina, Australia, Austria, Bahrain, Bangladesh, Belarus, Belgium, Benin, Botswana, Brazil, Bulgaria, Burkina Faso, Chile, China, Colombia, Ecuador, Ethiopia, Finland, France, Germany, Guinea, India, Iran, Italy, Jamaica, Kuwait, Madagascar, Malaysia, Mexico, Morocco, Pakistan, Peru, Philippines, Poland, Romania, Rwanda, Somalia, Spain, Suriname, Sweden, Togo, Trinidad and Tobago, Turkey, United Kingdom, Yugoslavia.

Against: Russian Federation, United States.

Abstaining: Canada, Japan.

GENERAL ASSEMBLY ACTION

On 22 December 1992, the General Assembly, acting on the recommendation of the Second Committee, adopted **resolution 47/172** by recorded vote.

Economic and social repercussions of the Israeli settlements on the Palestinian people in the Palestinian territory, including Jerusalem, occupied since 1967, and on the Arab population of the Syrian Golan

The General Assembly,

Taking note of Economic and Social Council resolution 1992/57 of 31 July 1992,

Recalling its resolution 46/199 of 20 December 1991,

Guided by the principles of the Charter of the United Nations, affirming the inadmissibility of the acquisition of territory by force and recalling Security Council resolutions 242(1967) of 22 November 1967 and 497(1981) of 17 December 1981,

Recalling also Security Council resolution 465(1980) of 1 March 1980 and other resolutions affirming the applicability of the Geneva Convention relative to the Protection of Civilian Persons in Time of War, of 12 August 1949, to the occupied Palestinian territory, including Jerusalem, and other Arab territories occupied by Israel since 1967,

Expressing its concern at the establishment by Israel, the occupying Power, of settlements in the occupied Palestinian territory and other Arab territories occupied since 1967, including the settlements of new immigrants therein,

Welcoming the Middle East peace process started at Madrid on 30 October 1991 and recognizing that a complete freeze of settlement activity would significantly enhance the prospects for progress in this process,

1. *Takes note* of the report of the Secretary-General;

2. *Deplores* the establishment of settlements by Israel in the Palestinian territory, including Jerusalem, and other Arab territories occupied since 1967, and regards the settlements as illegal and an obstacle to peace;

3. *Recognizes* the economic and social repercussions of the Israeli settlements on the Palestinian people in the Palestinian territory, including Jerusalem, occupied by Israel since 1967, and on the Arab population of the Syrian Golan;

4. *Strongly deplores* Israel's practices in the occupied Palestinian territory and other Arab territories occupied since 1967, in particular its confiscation of land, its appropriation of water resources, its depletion of other economic resources and its displacement and deportation of the population of those territories;

5. *Reaffirms* the inalienable right of the Palestinian people and the population of the Syrian Golan to their natural and all other economic resources, and regards any infringement thereof as being without any legal validity;

6. *Requests* the Secretary-General to submit to the General Assembly at its forty-eighth session, through the Economic and Social Council, a report on the progress made in the implementation of the present resolution.

General Assembly resolution 47/172

22 December 1992   Meeting 93   150-3-5 (recorded vote)

Approved by Second Committee (A/47/717/Add.1) by recorded vote (101-3-5), 11 December (meeting 50); 20-nation draft (A/C.2/47/L.29/Rev.1); agenda item 12.

Sponsors: Afghanistan, Algeria, Cuba, Djibouti, Egypt, Indonesia, Iraq, Jordan, Kuwait, Lebanon, Libyan Arab Jamahiriya, Malaysia, Mauritania, Morocco, Pakistan, Saudi Arabia, Syrian Arab Republic, Tunisia, United Arab Emirates, Yemen.

Meeting numbers. GA 47th session: 2nd Committee 34-37, 40, 42, 43, 50; plenary 93.

Recorded vote in Assembly as follows:

In favour: Afghanistan, Algeria, Angola, Antigua and Barbuda, Australia, Austria, Azerbaijan, Bahamas, Bahrain, Bangladesh, Barbados, Belarus, Belgium, Belize, Benin, Bhutan, Bolivia, Bosnia and Herzegovina, Botswana, Brazil, Brunei Darussalam, Bulgaria, Burkina Faso, Burundi, Cameroon, Canada, Cape Verde, Chad, Chile, China, Colombia, Comoros, Costa Rica, Cuba, Cyprus, Czechoslovakia, Democratic People's Republic of Korea, Denmark, Djibouti, Dominica, Ecuador, Egypt, Estonia, Ethiopia, Fiji, Finland, France, Gabon, Gambia, Germany, Ghana, Greece, Guatemala, Guinea, Guinea-Bissau, Guyana, Haiti, Honduras, Hungary, Iceland, India, Indonesia, Iran, Iraq, Ireland, Italy, Jamaica, Japan, Jordan, Kazakhstan, Kenya, Kuwait, Kyrgyzstan, Lao People's Democratic Republic, Latvia, Lebanon, Lesotho, Liberia, Libyan Arab Jamahiriya, Liechtenstein, Lithuania, Luxembourg, Madagascar, Malawi, Malaysia, Maldives, Mali, Malta, Mauritania, Mauritius, Mexico, Mongolia, Morocco, Mozambique, Myanmar, Namibia, Nepal, Netherlands, New Zealand, Nicaragua, Niger, Norway, Oman, Pakistan, Panama, Papua New Guinea, Paraguay, Peru, Philippines, Poland, Portugal, Qatar, Republic of Korea, Republic of Moldova, Romania, Rwanda, Saint Lucia, Saint Vincent and the Grenadines, Sao Tome and Principe, Saudi Arabia, Senegal, Sierra Leone, Singapore, Slovenia, Spain, Sri Lanka, Sudan, Suriname, Swaziland, Sweden, Syrian Arab Republic, Tajikistan, Thailand, Togo, Trinidad and Tobago, Tunisia, Turkey, Turkmenistan, Uganda, Ukraine, United Arab Emirates, United Kingdom, United Republic of Tanzania, Vanuatu, Venezuela, Viet Nam, Yemen, Zaire, Zambia, Zimbabwe.

Against: Israel, Micronesia, United States.

Abstaining: Croatia, Marshall Islands, Russian Federation, Samoa, Uruguay.

REFERENCES

[1]A/47/123-S/23721. [2]A/47/129-S/23740. [3]A/47/139-S/23770. [4]A/46/896-S/23782. [5]S/23790. [6]S/23781. [7]GA res. 43/177, 15 Dec. 1988. [8]S/23783. [9]S/19443. [10]S/21919 & Corr.1. [11]YUN 1991, p. 251. [12]A/47/76. [13]A/47/262. [14]A/47/509. [15]YUN 1991, p. 221. [16]YUN 1987, pp. 253 & 306. [17]A/47/545. [18]YUN 1991, p. 252, GA res. 46/47 A, 9 Dec. 1991. [19]E/1992/22 (res. 1992/2 A & B). [20]A/47/546. [21]YUN 1991, p. 257, GA res. 46/47 B, 9 Dec. 1991. [22]S/23373. [23]A/46/836-S/23369. [24]A/46/837-S/23374. [25]YUN 1991, p. 259. [26]A/47/793-S/24974. [27]A/47/805-S/24983. [28]S/24980. [29]S/24979. [30]A/47/829-S/24997. [31]A/47/844-S/25017. [32]A/47/549. [33]YUN 1991, p. 260, GA res. 46/47 E, 9 Dec. 1991. [34]YUN 1984, p. 813, GA res. 39/46, annex, 10 Dec. 1984. [35]A/47/522-S/24648. [36]A/47/526-S/24659. [37]A/47/507-S/24630. [38]A/47/548. [39]YUN 1991, p. 259, GA res. 46/47 D, 9 Dec. 1991. [40]A/47/551. [41]YUN 1991, p. 261, GA res. 46/47 G, 9 Dec. 1991. [42]A/47/550. [43]YUN 1991, p. 262, GA res. 46/47 F, 9 Dec. 1991. [44]E/1992/22 (res. 1992/1). [45]A/47/547. [46]YUN 1991, p. 264, GA res. 46/47 C, 9 Dec. 1991. [47]E/1992/22 (res. 1992/3). [48]A/47/294-E/1992/84. [49]YUN 1991, p. 267, GA res. 46/199, 20 Dec. 1991. [50]TD/B/1142.

Palestine refugees

The number of Palestine refugees registered with the United Nations Relief and Works Agency for Palestine Refugees in the Near East, as at 30 June 1992, was 2,648,707.[1] They lived in and outside camps in the Israeli-occupied West Bank (459,147) and Gaza Strip (560,207), Jordan (1,010,719), Lebanon (319,427) and the Syrian Arab Republic (299,207). UNRWA noted, however, that the refugees present in those five areas almost certainly numbered less than the population recorded. By the end of 1992, UNRWA put the total number of refugees at 2.73 million.

The various aspects of the Palestine refugee problem, as well as the activities of UNRWA, were addressed by the General Assembly through 11 resolutions adopted in December on: assistance to Palestine refugees (47/69 A) and to displaced persons (47/69 C); the Working Group on the Financing of UNRWA (47/69 B); scholarships for higher education and vocational training (47/69 D); refugees in Israeli-occupied territory (47/69 E); resumption of the ration distribution to Palestine refugees (47/69 F); return of displaced population and refugees (47/69 G); revenues from refugees' properties (47/69 H); refugee protection (47/69 I); proposed University of Jerusalem "Al-Quds" for Palestine refugees (47/69 J); and protection of Palestinian students and educational institutions and safeguarding of UNRWA facilities (47/69 K).

UN Agency for Palestine refugees

In 1992, UNRWA continued to provide a wide-ranging programme of education, health, relief and social services for the Palestine refugees in the five areas of UNRWA operation. In addition, it undertook extraordinary measures of assistance for Lebanon and the occupied territories. Details of this assistance were contained in the Commissioner-General's report covering the period 1 July 1991 to 30 June 1992.[1]

The education programme, UNRWA's largest activity, served a total of 374,406 elementary and preparatory pupils during the reporting period, 8,800 more than in the previous year. Vocational training, encompassing two-year post-preparatory trade courses and post-secondary technical and teacher-training courses, increased to 5,202 training places, from 5,146 in the preceding period, as did university scholarships, to 661 from 641. The programme followed the host Governments' curricula, in close cooperation with UNESCO, which seconded 14 of its senior staff to UNRWA. Some 9,750 Palestine refugee pupils who returned in 1991 from Kuwait and other Gulf States were absorbed by UNRWA schools, mostly in Jordan (6,200) and Gaza (1,300). The schools in Gaza absorbed another 2,000 pupils originally expected to attend government schools.

As a result of school closures in the occupied territories, due to military orders, curfews and general strikes, the Agency's 98 schools in the West Bank lost 17 per cent of school days, while its 153 schools in the Gaza Strip lost 12 per cent. Its four training centres lost 20 per cent of training days. To compensate for lost days, UNRWA developed self-learning and audiovisual materials for distance education.

The 197 UNRWA schools in Jordan, serving 140,000 pupils, as well as the two training centres, operated normally. The 77 schools in Lebanon, attended by a total of 34,400 pupils, lost less than 6 per cent of school days. Several school construction projects were completed: the renovation of all school premises at Nahr el-Bared camp and of Mansoura school, the reconstruction of Mount Tabor school and the establishment of two learning resource centres in central Lebanon. The 111 schools in the Syrian Arab Republic, serving a student population of 58,800, and the Damascus Training Centre, which provided 776 training places, operated without interruption.

A significant academic development was the Agency's participation in standardized, internationally recognized mathematics and science tests held in Jordan and the West Bank in April and May. Consistent with the findings of an external evaluation made of its vocational and technical education programme, and in view of the region's depressed labour market, UNRWA introduced short-term vocational training. It decided to phase out its two-year pre-service teacher-training programme by 1994, owing to the inability of large numbers of the programme's graduates to find posts and to the imminent requirement of a four-year university degree by Jordan, Gaza and the West Bank.

The Agency health programme provided primary health care, health protection and promotion services; environmental health services in camps; and nutrition and supplementary feeding to vulnerable population groups. Overcrowding at clinics was met by introducing patient-flow analysis and appointment systems, as well as by constructing additional health centres, renovating those that had deteriorated and increasing the number of laboratories, dental and special-care clinics and diagnostic equipment. Medical service was extended to localities not previously covered, especially in the West Bank and Lebanon. A second afternoon shift rendering a full range of preventive and curative services was introduced in five out of eight refugee camps in Gaza. UNRWA emergency operations provided primary and hospital care to *intifadah*-related casualties. The joint UNRWA/UNICEF physiotherapy programme continued in UNRWA health centres in the West Bank and Gaza. Greater attention was given to planning for the care of the mentally and psychologically disturbed segment of the refugee population. Besides taking over a joint UNRWA/WHO mental health programme begun in 1991, UNRWA jointly arranged with WHO a 12-month training course in community mental health, beginning in October in the United Kingdom.

Under the UNRWA/WHO short-term action plan for HIV/AIDS prevention and control, two interfield training workshops were conducted in July 1991 and January 1992 in blood transfusion for Agency senior staff and technologists in the West Bank and Gaza, and on epidemiological surveillance for senior staff from all five areas of Agency operation. Meanwhile, WHO provided HIV examination kits for non-governmental hospitals in the West Bank and for the Central Blood Bank Society in Gaza. The expanded UNRWA programme of immunization was strengthened by a supply of measles, mumps, rubella and hepatitis-B vaccines from the Public Health Department of the West Bank.

Demand for social and relief services increased significantly, with the number of refugees qualifying for special hardship assistance rising to 178,000 from 162,000. The increase was largest in Gaza, where economic and social dislocation was especially severe. Of the families receiving such assistance, 42 per cent were headed by women. Development programmes expanded for those with special needs, particularly women and the disabled.

Women's programme centres functioned as multi-purpose focal points. Women and girls from special hardship families received priority for informal training in skills, literacy and numeracy, health education, child development, household maintenance, technical skills to generate or conserve income, basic business skills and legal literacy. With the opening of eight new centres, the number of women's centres rose to 65 and women participants to 9,100, from 4,700. While UNRWA staff were attached to each centre to facilitate the programme, women's committees raised funds to supplement the core budget provided by the Agency. A special contribution enabled the Agency to launch a Palestinian Women's Initiative Fund, under which technical support, grants and loans were made available to productive enterprises and support services, including a women's community bank, a pilot marketing and distribution centre for items produced by women, and training in operating specialized machinery.

A similar community-based, participatory approach was employed in the rehabilitation of the disabled. In the five areas of operation, 14 community rehabilitation centres each offered basic rehabilitation services to an average of 34 children, supported their families and involved disabled persons in community life.

In Jordan, where the number of refugees increased from 960,000 to nearly 1,011,000 due to the return of Palestinians from Kuwait and other Gulf States, 141 families took part in self-support projects, 97 of which achieved sufficient success and were thus removed from the ration rolls. A social service office was set up at Aqaba, together with a women's programme centre offering training in marketable skills. In Lebanon, grants and technical support were given for 154 small income-generating enterprises; of the participating families, 98 became independent of the ration rolls. In the Syrian Arab Republic, recipients of direct relief had increased by 28 per cent over the previous year, necessitating a substantial increase in the allocation of food rations. Assistance for the rehabilitation of dilapidated housing was increased and 176 shelters were repaired or rebuilt. Two new women's centres and several day-care facilities were opened, as was the first community rehabilitation centre at Nairab camp.

In addition to its regular activities, UNRWA, for the fifth successive year, ran a programme of extraordinary measures to alleviate the difficulties experienced by the refugee population in the context of the *intifadah* and the Israeli response. These included the refugee affairs officer programme, a legal assistance scheme, emergency food distribution, cash grants to families in distress and a variety of emergency health services, including increased hospitalization subsidies.

The situation of the estimated 25,000 to 30,000 Palestinians in Kuwait continued to require UNRWA's attention, particularly of those Palestinians from Gaza who had only Egyptian travel documents and who could have nowhere to go were they to be required to leave Kuwait for lack of employment. UNRWA remained in contact with Kuwait and other concerned Governments on this issue.

UNRWA continued efforts to obtain some liberalization of employment restrictions imposed on Palestinians in Lebanon as a result of economic set-backs in that country. The Government, however, suspended the Lebanese-Palestinian dialogue on Palestinian civil and social rights in Lebanon, pending the outcome of the ongoing peace talks. In the circumstances, UNRWA carried out three emergency food distributions to some 220,000 refugees throughout the country, and a fourth distribution to some 60,000 refugees in Bekaa and Tyre. Other emergency operations in Lebanon were especially directed towards alleviating the suffering of the 7,000 Palestinian families displaced by various rounds of fighting, of which 4,000 remained in makeshift accommodations.

For 1992, UNRWA budgeted over $1 million for the West Bank and Gaza for temporary assistance to families suffering uprising-related death, injury or detention, or whose shelters had been demolished or sealed. An additional $100,000 was provided for Gaza families whose houses had been demolished or sealed in the early days of the uprising but had yet to find suitable accommodations. Another $100,000 worth of roofing sheets and cement was provided for repairs to shelter damage caused by the winter of 1991/92. The Agency continued to operate emergency clinics in the West Bank and Gaza, in spite of the reductions in staff. Subsidies for additional beds or patient expenses in those two areas were budgeted at $300,000, with another $300,000 earmarked for medical supplies for emergency cases. The Agency provided skimmed milk and baby cereals or dry

rations to 34,500 additional nutritionally-at-risk infants, school-age children and pregnant or nursing women. UNRWA earmarked $100,000 for education in the West Bank and Gaza, with an additional $100,000 reserved for the production of self-learning materials for elementary and preparatory school students.

Under the expanded programme of assistance (EPA), set up in 1988 with a target of $65 million, some $45 million had been received or pledged by mid-1992. An additional $6.4 million had been received in response to two fund-raising appeals launched to expand the programme further, to cope with rising demands for Agency services by the thousands of jobless migrant workers and their families returning to the UNRWA areas of operation. The funds were to cover construction projects, equipment and medical supplies, and small-scale income-generating projects.

The Agency employed approximately 18,500 staff, the majority of whom were themselves Palestine refugees, and was thus one of the largest employers in the Middle East. The events in the region considerably affected the Agency's work during the reporting period.

GENERAL ASSEMBLY ACTION

On 14 December 1992, on the recommendation of the Special Political Committee, the General Assembly adopted **resolution 47/69 A** by recorded vote.

Assistance to Palestine refugees

The General Assembly,

Recalling its resolution 46/46 A of 9 December 1991 and all its previous resolutions on the question, including resolution 194(III) of 11 December 1948,

Taking note of the report of the Commissioner-General of the United Nations Relief and Works Agency for Palestine Refugees in the Near East, covering the period from 1 July 1991 to 30 June 1992,

1. *Notes with deep regret* that repatriation or compensation of the refugees as provided for in paragraph 11 of General Assembly resolution 194(III) has not been effected, that no substantial progress has been made in the programme endorsed by the Assembly in paragraph 2 of its resolution 513(VI) of 26 January 1952 for the reintegration of refugees either by repatriation or resettlement and that, therefore, the situation of the refugees continues to be a matter of serious concern;

2. *Expresses its thanks* to the Commissioner-General and to all the staff of the United Nations Relief and Works Agency for Palestine Refugees in the Near East, recognizing that the Agency is doing all it can within the limits of available resources, and also expresses its thanks to the specialized agencies and to private organizations for their valuable work in assisting the refugees;

3. *Reiterates its request* that the headquarters of the Agency should be relocated to its former site within its area of operations as soon as practicable;

4. *Notes with regret* that the United Nations Conciliation Commission for Palestine has been unable to find a means of achieving progress in the implementation of paragraph 11 of General Assembly resolution 194(III), and requests the Commission to exert continued efforts towards the implementation of that paragraph and to report to the Assembly as appropriate, but no later than 1 September 1993;

5. *Directs attention* to the continuing seriousness of the financial position of the Agency, as outlined in the report of the Commissioner-General;

6. *Notes with profound concern* that, despite the commendable and successful efforts of the Commissioner-General to collect additional contributions, this increased level of income to the Agency is still insufficient to cover essential budget requirements in the present year and that, at currently foreseen levels of giving, deficits will recur each year;

7. *Calls upon* all Governments, as a matter of urgency, to make the most generous efforts possible to meet the anticipated needs of the Agency, particularly in the light of the budgetary deficit projected in the report of the Commissioner-General, and therefore urges non-contributing Governments to contribute regularly and contributing Governments to consider increasing their regular contributions;

8. *Decides* to extend the mandate of the Agency until 30 June 1996, without prejudice to the provisions of paragraph 11 of General Assembly resolution 194(III).

General Assembly resolution 47/69 A

14 December 1992   Meeting 85   136-0-2 (recorded vote)

Approved by Special Political Committee (A/47/611) by recorded vote (122-0-1), 25 November (meeting 27); draft by United States (A/SPC/47/L.14); agenda item 73.
Meeting numbers. GA 47th session: SPC 9-12, 27; plenary 85.

Recorded vote in Assembly as follows:

In favour: Afghanistan, Algeria, Angola, Antigua and Barbuda, Argentina, Australia, Austria, Azerbaijan, Bahrain, Bangladesh, Barbados, Belarus, Belgium, Benin, Bhutan, Bolivia, Bosnia and Herzegovina, Botswana, Brazil, Brunei Darussalam, Bulgaria, Burkina Faso, Cameroon, Canada, Chad, Chile, China, Colombia, Costa Rica, Côte d'Ivoire, Cuba, Cyprus, Czechoslovakia, Democratic People's Republic of Korea, Denmark, Djibouti, Ecuador, Egypt, El Salvador, Estonia, Ethiopia, Finland, France, Gabon, Gambia, Germany, Greece, Guatemala, Guinea-Bissau, Guyana, Haiti, Honduras, Hungary, Iceland, India, Indonesia, Iran, Ireland, Italy, Jamaica, Japan, Jordan, Kazakhstan, Kuwait, Lao People's Democratic Republic, Latvia, Lebanon, Liberia, Libyan Arab Jamahiriya, Liechtenstein, Lithuania, Luxembourg, Madagascar, Malawi, Malaysia, Maldives, Mali, Malta, Marshall Islands, Mauritania, Mauritius, Mexico, Mongolia, Morocco, Mozambique, Myanmar, Namibia, Nepal, Netherlands, New Zealand, Niger, Nigeria, Norway, Pakistan, Panama, Paraguay, Peru, Philippines, Poland, Portugal, Qatar, Republic of Korea, Republic of Moldova, Romania, Russian Federation, Rwanda, Saint Lucia, Saint Vincent and the Grenadines, Samoa, Sao Tome and Principe, Saudi Arabia, Senegal, Singapore, Spain, Sri Lanka, Sudan, Suriname, Swaziland, Sweden, Syrian Arab Republic, Thailand, Togo, Trinidad and Tobago, Tunisia, Turkey, Ukraine, United Arab Emirates, United Kingdom, United States, Uruguay, Vanuatu, Venezuela, Viet Nam, Yemen, Zambia, Zimbabwe.
Against: None.
Abstaining: Dominica,* Israel.
*Later advised the Secretariat it had intended to vote in favour.

UNRWA financing

The UNRWA Commissioner-General, in his report to the General Assembly,[1] stated that, beginning with the 1992-1993 biennium, the Agency had shifted from an annual to a biennial budgetary cycle, bringing it in line with the majority of United Nations organizations. In another change, ACABQ became involved for the first time in the

budgetary process. Both changes were reflected in amendments to its financial regulations. A four-year forward planning process was also introduced, the first period to be covered being 1994-1997.

The Agency's relatively healthy financial condition in 1991 began to deteriorate in 1992, with the year ending with a deficit of about $10 million. The gradual emergence of a budget problem was ascribed to increasing claims on limited donor funds from a growing number of global crises and to a downturn in the economies of many of the Agency's major donors.

The General Fund budget approved for the 1992-1993 biennium amounted to $572 million; with the additional sums earmarked for extraordinary measures for Lebanon and the occupied territory (EMLOT), EPA and the Gaza Hospital project, the grand total for the biennium amounted to $644.7 million.

In 1992, a total of $254,068,726 was received under the UNRWA General Fund ($221,917,276 in cash and $32,151,450 in kind). In addition, $13,246,059 was received for ongoing activities ($9,634,204 in cash and $3,611,855 in kind). Expenditures for the year totalled $256,679,308 under the General Fund, and $11,015,293 for ongoing activities—compared to expenditures of $308.1 million in 1991. For the 1994-1995 biennium, expenditures under the General Fund were estimated at $623 million (including $70 million in food donations), representing an increase of $51 million, or 8.9 per cent, over the approved General Fund budget for 1992-1993.

The regular budget was not completely funded for 1992 and substantial amounts were still required for EMLOT, EPA and the Gaza Hospital project. Only limited success was achieved in broadening the Agency's donor base. None the less, donor and host government support remained strong. Agency services alone would not be sufficient to maintain even basic life-sustaining needs were they not complemented by millions of dollars worth of host government assistance for the refugees.

Working Group on UNRWA financing

In a report covering its meetings of 2 September and 22 October 1992,[2] the Working Group on the Financing of UNRWA noted that UNRWA received sufficient funds in 1991 to implement its regular programme in accordance with established plans. For the 1992 regular programme, however, income already received and expected to be received during the remainder of the year indicated that it would be under-funded, in the order of $3 million to $4 million, which would have to be covered by the working capital reserve (which stood at $33.7 million at the end of 1991).

The EMLOT fund showed an unencumbered balance of $5.5 million at the end of 1991; an additional $2.9 million was received or pledged for 1992. Programme expenditures for 1992 were expected to amount to $13 million, which meant an anticipated shortfall of between $4 million and $5 million. The EMLOT fund financed additional medical and relief services, as well as other forms of general assistance in Lebanon, the West Bank and Gaza.

Regarding a $35-million project for the construction of a 232-bed general hospital in the Gaza Strip, to include equipment, furnishings and operating costs for three years, the Agency in 1992 obtained a pledge of some $18 million from the European Community for the financing of the construction phase. With another $1.8 million already received, the project was able to enter the pre-tendering phase. This left an unfunded balance of $15.2 million to cover the other phases of the project.

Funding continued to be solicited for EPA, under which some 200 projects were currently under implementation with a total budget of some $32 million.

Of the biennial budget of $572 million for core activities, the 1992 share of financial requirements was budgeted at $274.8 million. This included some $14.4 million for capital and special projects, for which only $9 million had been received; thus, a number of construction projects might have to be deferred to 1993 or later. Of the 1992 requirements, some $28.3 million was expected in the form of contributions in kind.

Sharing the Commissioner-General's concern about the funding prospects for 1993, the Working Group strongly urged Governments to continue making generous contributions and to consider making additional contributions in support of emergency-related programmes and special projects.

GENERAL ASSEMBLY ACTION

On 14 December 1992, on the recommendation of the Special Political Committee, the General Assembly adopted **resolution 47/69 B** without vote.

Working Group on the Financing of the United Nations Relief and Works Agency for Palestine Refugees in the Near East

The General Assembly,

Recalling its resolutions 2656(XXV) of 7 December 1970, 2728(XXV) of 15 December 1970, 2791(XXVI) of 6 December 1971, 46/46 B of 9 December 1991 and the previous resolutions on this question,

Recalling also its decision 36/462 of 16 March 1982, whereby it took note of the special report of the Working Group on the Financing of the United Nations Relief and Works Agency for Palestine Refugees in the Near East, and adopted the recommendations contained therein,

Having considered the report of the Working Group,

Taking into account the report of the Commissioner-General of the United Nations Relief and Works Agency for Palestine Refugees in the Near East, covering the period from 1 July 1991 to 30 June 1992,

Deeply concerned about the critical financial situation of the Agency, which has affected and affects the continuation of the provision of the necessary Agency services to the Palestine refugees, including the emergency-related programmes,

Emphasizing the continuing need for extraordinary efforts in order to maintain, at least at the present minimum level, the activities of the Agency, as well as to enable the Agency to carry out essential construction,

1. *Commends* the Working Group on the Financing of the United Nations Relief and Works Agency for Palestine Refugees in the Near East for its efforts to assist in ensuring the financial security of the Agency;

2. *Takes note with approval* of the report of the Working Group;

3. *Requests* the Working Group to continue its efforts, in cooperation with the Secretary-General and the Commissioner-General, for the financing of the Agency for a further period of one year;

4. *Requests* the Secretary-General to provide the necessary services and assistance to the Working Group for the conduct of its work.

General Assembly resolution 47/69 B

14 December 1992   Meeting 85   Adopted without vote

Approved by Special Political Committee (A/47/611) without vote, 25 November (meeting 27); 23-nation draft (A/SPC/47/L.15); agenda item 73.
Sponsors: Australia, Austria, Bangladesh, Belgium, Canada, Denmark, France, Germany, Greece, Indonesia, Ireland, Italy, Luxembourg, Malaysia, Netherlands, New Zealand, Pakistan, Philippines, Portugal, Spain, Sweden, Turkey, United Kingdom.
Meeting numbers. GA 47th session: SPC 9-12, 27; plenary 85.

Accounts for 1991

The Board of Auditors, following its audit of the UNRWA financial statements for the year ended 31 December 1991, made several observations,[3] summarized also by the Secretary-General in an August 1992 note.[4] These related to the liability for losses and damages to UNRWA equipment in all of its field offices, the employment of internal auditors in line functions and cash management, regarding which ACABQ commented in October.[5]

The General Assembly, by **resolution 47/211**, accepted the financial report and audited financial statements of UNRWA and the Board's audit opinions and report on them, and requested that the Commissioner-General report in 1993 on steps taken to implement the Board's recommendations.

Legal matters

UNRWA staff

The Commissioner-General reported that, for the period 1 July 1991 to 30 June 1992,[1] the number of UNRWA staff members arrested or detained without trial declined in the occupied territories, as well as in Lebanon and the Syrian Arab Republic, but increased in Jordan. Of the 61 staff members detained during the period, 51 were arrested and released without trial and 10 remained in detention. One staff member in the Gaza Strip remained under deportation order as at 30 June. Of the 418 Palestinians who received deportation orders into southern Lebanon in December, 16 were reported to be UNRWA staff members. Two local staff members in the Gaza Strip were killed for allegedly collaborating with the Israeli authorities.

The Agency remained unable to obtain adequate and timely information on the reasons for the arrest and detention of its staff members. It could thus not ascertain whether the staff members' official functions were involved. However, it had access to 18 staff members from Gaza and six from the West Bank who were in prisons and detention centres in the occupied territories and in Israel. It was unable to visit staff in detention in Jordan, Lebanon and the Syrian Arab Republic, despite its representations to the Governments of those countries.

Of continuing concern was the mistreatment of staff in detention, of which 58 cases were recorded in Gaza and 70 in the West Bank. Mistreatment in the performance of their duties took the form of beatings, threats, insults, intimidation and temporary detention.

UNRWA continued to encounter difficulties with respect to staff movement in and out of the West Bank and the Gaza Strip. These included substantial delays in the clearance of staff travelling on official duty and, in some cases, refusal of clearance. Staff movement within the occupied territory remained seriously curtailed by frequent curfews and the designation of areas as closed military zones, with Israel insisting that local staff could operate only if in possession of curfew permits from the civil administration, as well as by periodic restrictions on access to Israel and East Jerusalem imposed on staff residing in the West Bank and Gaza. UNRWA experienced particular difficulty in obtaining for its local drivers entry to Israel's Ben Gurion International Airport, despite assurances from the authorities that their entry would be facilitated.

UNRWA services and premises

The Commissioner-General reported[1] that between 1 July 1991 and 30 June 1992 Israeli security forces made 117 incursions into UNRWA installations in the West Bank and 210 in the Gaza Strip, at times resulting in injury to staff and damage to property. There were 94 recorded intrusions into health clinic premises. Israeli security forces on occasion also used Agency premises during military operations. The Agency continued to protest against such incursions as constituting abuse of its privileges and immunities.

Of particular concern were incidents in which Agency medical and ambulance services were interfered with or prevented. There were 31 such incidents in the Gaza Strip alone, during which ambulances were stopped, searched or shot at, with the drivers beaten up and their identity documents confiscated. Israeli authorities continued to object to the Agency's reconstruction of demolished camp shelters, despite assurances by Israel's Ministry of Foreign Affairs that there would be no objection to it. Construction projects were also subjected to detailed and time-consuming procedures. Restrictions were imposed on the quantity of items imported for the Agency's essential operations and incoming goods were often subjected to delays at the port of entry.

As at 30 June 1992, the Government of Israel owed the Agency $7.7 million in arrears for the payment of clearance, warehousing and transport charges for which Israel was responsible in respect of Agency supplies under the terms of the 1967 Comay-Michelmore agreement. Payment of those charges, suspended by Israel from 1988 to 1991, were advanced by the Agency.

In **resolution 47/69 K**, the General Assembly condemned the repeated Israeli raids on UNRWA premises and installations and called on Israel to refrain from such acts.

Compensation claims

In 1992, UNRWA reported[1] that no progress had been made with regard to its claims against the Governments of: Israel (for loss and damage to UNRWA property during the 1967 Middle East hostilities, Israel's invasion of Lebanon in 1982 and its military action before then); Jordan (arising from the 1967 hostilities and the disturbances of 1970 and 1971); and the Syrian Arab Republic (relating mainly to the levy of certain taxes from which UNRWA believed it was exempt under existing agreements). Those claims had been reported in 1986.[6] The Secretary-General, in October 1992,[7] also stated that there had been no progress with regard to UNRWA claims against Israel resulting from its 1982 invasion of Lebanon.

In **resolution 47/69 I**, the General Assembly called anew on Israel to compensate UNRWA for damages to its property and facilities resulting from its invasion of Lebanon, without prejudice to Israel's responsibility for all damages resulting from that invasion.

Other aspects

Displaced persons

Approximately 12,000 displaced registered refugees were known by UNRWA to have returned to the occupied territories since June 1967.[1] A particularly acute problem were marriages entered into by West Bank residents with women, mainly from Jordan, who had applied for West Bank residence but had obtained only short-term, renewable visitor permits. Deportations carried out by Israeli military authorities of women and children deemed ineligible for resident status created considerable uncertainty for newlyweds and prospective couples, who remained subject to military administrative decisions, with little scope for legal recourse.

Humanitarian assistance

In 1992, in addition to providing relief in the form of basic food commodities, blankets, clothing, shelter repair and cash grants, UNRWA continued to provide a small measure of humanitarian assistance to persons who had been displaced as a result of the June 1967 war and subsequent hostilities in the Middle East but who were not registered with UNRWA as refugees.

GENERAL ASSEMBLY ACTION

On 14 December 1992, the General Assembly, on the recommendation of the Special Political Committee, adopted **resolution 47/69 C** without vote.

Assistance to persons displaced as a result of the June 1967 and subsequent hostilities
The General Assembly,

Recalling its resolution 46/46 C of 9 December 1991 and all its previous resolutions on the question,

Taking note of the report of the Commissioner-General of the United Nations Relief and Works Agency for Palestine Refugees in the Near East, covering the period from 1 July 1991 to 30 June 1992,

Concerned about the continued human suffering resulting from the hostilities in the Middle East,

1. *Reaffirms* its resolution 46/46 C and all its previous resolutions on the question;

2. *Endorses,* bearing in mind the objectives of those resolutions, the efforts of the Commissioner-General of the United Nations Relief and Works Agency for Palestine Refugees in the Near East to continue to provide humanitarian assistance as far as practicable, on an emergency basis and as a temporary measure, to other persons in the area who are at present displaced and in serious need of continued assistance as a result of the June 1967 and subsequent hostilities;

3. *Strongly appeals* to all Governments and to organizations and individuals to contribute generously for the above purposes to the United Nations Relief and Works Agency for Palestine Refugees in the Near East and to the other intergovernmental and non-governmental organizations concerned.

General Assembly resolution 47/69 C

14 December 1992   Meeting 85   Adopted without vote

Approved by Special Political Committee (A/47/611) without vote, 25 November (meeting 27); 22-nation draft (A/SPC/47/L.16); agenda item 73.
Sponsors: Austria, Bangladesh, Belgium, Canada, Cyprus, Denmark, Finland, Germany, Greece, India, Indonesia, Ireland, Italy, Japan, Malaysia, Mali, Netherlands, Norway, Pakistan, Philippines, Sri Lanka, Sweden.
Meeting numbers. GA 47th session: SPC 9-12, 27; plenary 85.

Repatriation of refugees

The Secretary-General reported in October 1992[8] regarding compliance with the General Assembly's 1991 call on Israel to take immediate steps for the return of all displaced inhabitants and to desist from measures obstructing their return.[9] By a note of 30 June, Israel stated that its position on the matter had been set out fully in successive annual replies, the latest of which was the subject of a 1991 report by the Secretary-General;[10] because of its continued effort to review individual cases of resettlement based on the merits of each case, approximately 79,368 persons had already returned to the administered territories.

The Secretary-General also included information from UNRWA on the return of refugees registered with it. Since UNRWA was not involved in arrangements for either refugees or displaced persons not registered as refugees, its information was based on requests by returning registered refugees for the transfer of their service entitlements to their areas of return; UNRWA was not necessarily aware of the return of registered refugees who had not made such requests. Its records indicated that, between 1 July 1991 and 30 June 1992, 310 registered refugees had returned to the West Bank and 83 to the Gaza Strip. Some of them might not have been displaced in 1967 but might be family members of a displaced registered refugee whom they had accompanied on return or later joined. Displaced refugees known by UNRWA to have returned to the occupied territories since June 1967 numbered about 12,400. UNRWA was unable to estimate the total number of displaced inhabitants who had returned, as it kept records only of registered refugees, and even those records, particularly with respect to location of registered refugees, might be incomplete.

GENERAL ASSEMBLY ACTION

On 14 December 1992, on the recommendation of the Special Political Committee, the General Assembly adopted **resolution 47/69 G** by recorded vote.

Return of population and refugees displaced since 1967
The General Assembly,

Recalling Security Council resolution 237(1967) of 14 June 1967,

Recalling also its resolutions 2252(ES-V) of 4 July 1967, 2452 A (XXIII) of 19 December 1968, 2535 B (XXIV) of 10 December 1969, 2672 D (XXV) of 8 December 1970, 2792 E (XXVI) of 6 December 1971, 2963 C and D (XXVII) of 13 December 1972, 3089 C (XXVIII) of 7 December 1973, 3331 D (XXIX) of 17 December 1974, 3419 C (XXX) of 8 December 1975, 31/15 D of 23 November 1976, 32/90 E of 13 December 1977, 33/112 F of 18 December 1978, 34/52 E of 23 November 1979, ES-7/2 of 29 July 1980, 35/13 E of 3 November 1980, 36/146 B of 16 December 1981, 37/120 G of 16 December 1982, 38/83 G of 15 December 1983, 39/99 G of 14 December 1984, 40/165 G of 16 December 1985, 41/69 G of 3 December 1986, 42/69 G of 2 December 1987, 43/57 G of 6 December 1988, 44/47 G of 8 December 1989, 45/73 G of 11 December 1990 and 46/46 G of 9 December 1991,

Having considered the report of the Secretary-General,

Having also considered the report of the Commissioner-General of the United Nations Relief and Works Agency for Palestine Refugees in the Near East, covering the period from 1 July 1991 to 30 June 1992,

1. *Reaffirms* the inalienable right of all displaced inhabitants to return to their homes or former places of residence in the territories occupied by Israel since 1967, and declares once more that any attempt to restrict, or to attach conditions to, the free exercise of the right to return by any displaced person is inconsistent with that inalienable right and is inadmissible;

2. *Considers* any and all agreements embodying any restriction on, or condition for, the return of the displaced inhabitants as null and void;

3. *Strongly deplores* the continued refusal of the Israeli authorities to take steps for the return of the displaced inhabitants;

4. *Calls once more upon* Israel:

   (*a*) To take immediate steps for the return of all displaced inhabitants;

   (*b*) To desist from all measures that obstruct the return of the displaced inhabitants, including measures affecting the physical and demographic structure of the occupied territories;

5. *Requests* the Secretary-General, after consulting with the Commissioner-General of the United Nations Relief and Works Agency for Palestine Refugees in the Near East, to report to the General Assembly, before the opening of its forty-eighth session, on the compliance of Israel with paragraph 4 above.

General Assembly resolution 47/69 G

14 December 1992   Meeting 85   103-2-37 (recorded vote)

Approved by Special Political Committee (A/47/611) by recorded vote (87-2-32), 25 November (meeting 27); 12-nation draft (A/SPC/47/L.20); agenda item 73.

Sponsors: Afghanistan, Bangladesh, Brunei Darussalam, Comoros, Cuba, India, Indonesia, Madagascar, Malaysia, Mali, Pakistan, Zambia.

Meeting numbers. GA 47th session: SPC 9-12, 27; plenary 85.

Recorded vote in Assembly as follows:

In favour: Afghanistan, Algeria, Angola, Antigua and Barbuda, Azerbaijan, Bahrain, Bangladesh, Barbados, Belarus, Belize, Benin, Bhutan, Bosnia and Herzegovina, Botswana, Brazil, Brunei Darussalam, Burkina Faso, Cameroon, Chad, Chile, China, Colombia, Comoros, Costa Rica, Côte d'Ivoire, Cuba, Cyprus, Democratic People's Republic of Korea, Djibouti, Ecuador, Egypt, El Salvador, Ethiopia, Gabon, Gambia, Greece, Grenada, Guatemala, Guinea-Bissau, Guyana, Haiti, Honduras, India, Indonesia, Iran, Jamaica, Japan, Jordan, Kazakhstan, Kuwait, Lao People's Democratic Republic, Lebanon, Liberia, Libyan Arab Jamahiriya, Madagascar, Malawi, Malaysia, Maldives, Mali, Malta, Mauritania, Mauritius, Mexico, Mongolia, Morocco, Mozambique, Myanmar, Namibia, Nepal, Niger, Nigeria, Pakistan, Panama, Paraguay, Peru, Philippines, Qatar, Republic of Korea, Rwanda, Sao Tome and Principe, Saudi Arabia, Senegal, Singapore, Spain, Sri Lanka, Sudan, Suriname, Swaziland, Syrian Arab Republic, Thailand, Togo, Trinidad and Tobago, Tunisia, Turkey, Ukraine, United Arab Emirates, Uruguay, Vanuatu, Venezuela, Viet Nam, Yemen, Zambia, Zimbabwe.

Against: Israel, United States.

Abstaining: Albania, Argentina, Australia, Austria, Belgium, Bolivia, Bulgaria, Canada, Czechoslovakia, Denmark, Dominica, Estonia, Finland, France, Germany, Hungary, Iceland, Ireland, Italy, Latvia, Liechtenstein, Lithuania, Luxembourg, Marshall Islands, Netherlands, New Zealand, Norway, Poland, Portugal, Republic of Moldova, Romania, Russian Federation, Saint Lucia, Saint Vincent and the Grenadines, Samoa, Sweden, United Kingdom.

Food aid

The Secretary-General reported in October 1992[11] that UNRWA continued to provide food assistance to the neediest of the refugee population, known as special hardship cases, who numbered 167,602 persons in December 1991. It also continued emergency distributions of basic commodities, such as flour, rice, sugar, animal protein and skimmed milk to the needy, including non-registered Palestinians, in the occupied territory and Lebanon. In 1991, 25,896 tonnes of those commodities were distributed in the Gaza Strip, 25,527 tonnes in the West Bank and 3,307 tonnes in Lebanon. Given the lack of additional resources, it had not been possible for the Commissioner-General to consider resuming the interrupted general distribution of basic food rations to all refugees, as requested by the Assembly in several resolutions, most recently in 1991.[12]

GENERAL ASSEMBLY ACTION

On 14 December, on the recommendation of the Special Political Committee, the General Assembly adopted **resolution 47/69 F** by recorded vote.

Resumption of the ration distribution to Palestine refugees

The General Assembly,

Recalling its resolutions 36/146 F of 16 December 1981, 37/120 F of 16 December 1982, 38/83 F of 15 December 1983, 39/99 F of 14 December 1984, 40/165 F of 16 December 1985, 41/69 F of 3 December 1986, 42/69 F of 2 December 1987, 43/57 F of 6 December 1988, 44/47 F of 8 December 1989, 45/73 F of 11 December 1990, 46/46 F of 9 December 1991 and all its previous resolutions on the question, including resolution 302(IV) of 8 December 1949,

Having considered the report of the Secretary-General,

Having also considered the report of the Commissioner-General of the United Nations Relief and Works Agency for Palestine Refugees in the Near East, covering the period from 1 July 1991 to 30 June 1992,

Deeply concerned about the interruption by the Agency, owing to financial difficulties, of the general ration distribution to Palestine refugees in all fields,

1. *Regrets* that its resolutions 37/120 F, 38/83 F, 39/99 F, 40/165 F, 41/69 F, 42/69 F, 43/57 F, 44/47 F, 45/73 F and 46/46 F have not been implemented;

2. *Calls once again upon* all Governments, as a matter of urgency, to make the most generous efforts possible and to offer the necessary resources to meet the needs of the United Nations Relief and Works Agency for Palestine Refugees in the Near East, particularly in the light of the interruption by the Agency of the general ration distribution to Palestine refugees in all fields, and therefore urges non-contributing Governments to contribute regularly and contributing Governments to consider increasing their regular contributions;

3. *Requests* the Commissioner-General of the United Nations Relief and Works Agency for Palestine Refugees in the Near East to resume on a continuing basis the interrupted general ration distribution to Palestine refugees in all fields;

4. *Requests* the Secretary-General, in consultation with the Commissioner-General, to report to the General Assembly at its forty-eighth session on the implementation of the present resolution.

General Assembly resolution 47/69 F

14 December 1992   Meeting 85   103-24-14 (recorded vote)

Approved by Special Political Committee (A/47/611) by recorded vote (86-22-14), 25 November (meeting 27); 12-nation draft (A/SPC/47/L.19); agenda item 73.

Sponsors: Afghanistan, Bangladesh, Brunei Darussalam, Comoros, Cuba, India, Indonesia, Madagascar, Malaysia, Mali, Pakistan, Zambia.

Meeting numbers. GA 47th session: SPC 9-12, 27; plenary 85.

Recorded vote in Assembly as follows:

In favour: Afghanistan, Algeria, Angola, Antigua and Barbuda, Azerbaijan, Bahrain, Bangladesh, Barbados, Belarus, Belize, Benin, Bhutan, Bolivia, Bosnia and Herzegovina, Botswana, Brazil, Brunei Darussalam, Burkina Faso, Cameroon, Chad, Chile, China, Colombia, Comoros, Costa Rica, Côte d'Ivoire, Cuba, Cyprus, Democratic People's Republic of Korea, Djibouti, Ecuador, Egypt, El Salvador, Ethiopia, Gabon, Gambia, Grenada, Guatemala, Guinea-Bissau, Guyana, Haiti, Honduras, India, Indonesia, Iran, Jamaica, Jordan, Kazakhstan, Kuwait, Lao People's Democratic Republic, Lebanon, Liberia, Libyan Arab Jamahiriya, Madagascar, Malawi, Malaysia, Maldives, Mali, Malta, Mauritania, Mauritius, Mexico, Mongolia, Morocco, Mozambique, Myanmar, Namibia, Nepal, Niger, Nigeria, Pakistan, Panama, Paraguay, Peru, Philippines, Qatar, Republic of Korea, Russian Federation, Rwanda, Saint Lucia, Sao Tome and Principe, Saudi Arabia, Senegal, Singapore, Sri Lanka, Sudan, Suriname, Swaziland, Syrian Arab Republic, Thailand, Togo, Trinidad and Tobago, Tunisia, Turkey, Ukraine, United Arab Emirates, Uruguay, Vanuatu, Venezuela, Viet Nam, Yemen, Zambia, Zimbabwe.

Against: Australia, Belgium, Canada, Denmark, Estonia, Finland, France, Germany, Hungary, Iceland, Ireland, Israel, Italy, Japan, Latvia, Lithuania, Luxembourg, Netherlands, New Zealand, Norway, Portugal, Sweden, United Kingdom, United States.

Abstaining: Albania, Argentina, Austria, Bulgaria, Czechoslovakia, Greece, Liechtenstein, Marshall Islands, Poland, Republic of Moldova, Romania, Saint Vincent and the Grenadines, Samoa, Spain.

Education and training services

Protection of Palestinian students and educational institutions

In October 1992,[13] the Secretary-General reproduced Israel's reply of 30 June to a 1991 General Assembly resolution[14] calling on Israel to open immediately all closed educational and vocational institutions, a large number of which were operated by UNRWA, and to refrain from closing them thereafter.

Describing the resolution as unbalanced, Israel said it distorted the Government's role and policy, which had always been to encourage development of the educational system in Judaea, Samaria and the Gaza District. During its administration, the level of education and literacy in those territories had markedly improved and many new institutions of learning had been established. Since December 1987, however, the schools had frequently been exploited as centres for organizing and launching violent activities. Measures taken by the authorities were in reaction to activities having nothing to do with education. Those measures had enabled Israel to permit the reopening of all educational institutions, including all seven institutions of higher education, as recently recognized by UNESCO.

The Secretary-General also cited the UNRWA Commissioner-General's report[1] stating that, of the 117 cases of unauthorized entry into UNRWA premises in the West Bank during the period 1 July 1991 to 30 June 1992, 62 related to schools; of the 210 such cases in the Gaza Strip, 118 related to schools.

During the same period, one death and 138 cases of injury among students and trainees occurred at UNRWA educational institutions in the West Bank, and five deaths and 637 injuries at institutions in the Gaza Strip—all attributable to beatings, tear-gas inhalation, rubber bullets and live ammunition. In addition, 259 students and trainees in the West Bank and 43 in Gaza were detained, of whom 144 and 37, respectively, were released by 30 June 1992.

During the 1991/92 academic year, an average of 21 per cent of training time was lost at the Kalandia and Ramallah men's and women's training centres in the West Bank due to general strikes, curfews and severe weather conditions. In March 1992, West Bank trainees interrupted instruction in solidarity with Gaza trainees whom Israeli authorities prevented from attending the West Bank centres for lack of permits to stay in the West Bank. The permits, which were a new requirement, were subsequently obtained by UNRWA; none were granted, however, for 17 of the trainees. The Gaza training centre lost 18 per cent of training days to strikes, 1 per cent to curfews, 1 per cent to military closure orders and 4 per cent to closure by UNRWA for security reasons.

Between September 1991 and June 1992, 17.2 per cent of school days were lost in the West Bank and 12.4 per cent in the Gaza Strip owing primarily to military closures, general strikes and curfews. On 27 May, following the stabbing of an Israeli from the Kfar Darom settlement in Gaza, settlers attacked the UNRWA school at Deir el-Balah, where more than 200 children were taking final examinations. In another attack, the settlers bulldozed the school fence to the ground. Military authorities eventually restored calm and UNRWA evacuated the children.

GENERAL ASSEMBLY ACTION

On 14 December, on the recommendation of the Special Political Committee, the General Assembly adopted **resolution 47/69 K** by recorded vote.

Protection of Palestinian students and educational institutions and safeguarding of the security of the facilities of the United Nations Relief and Works Agency for Palestine Refugees in the Near East in the occupied Palestinian territories

The General Assembly,

Recalling Security Council resolution 605(1987) of 22 December 1987,

Recalling also its resolutions 43/21 of 3 November 1988, 43/57 I of 6 December 1988, 44/2 of 6 October 1989, 44/47 K of 8 December 1989, 45/73 K of 11 December 1990 and 46/46 K of 9 December 1991,

Taking note of the report of the Secretary-General dated 21 January 1988, submitted in accordance with Security Council resolution 605(1987), the report dated 31 October 1990, submitted in accordance with Council resolution 672(1990), and the report dated 9 April 1991, submitted in accordance with Council resolution 681(1990),

Having considered the report of the Secretary-General,

Having also considered the report of the Commissioner-General of the United Nations Relief and Works Agency for Palestine Refugees in the Near East, covering the period from 1 July 1991 to 30 June 1992,

Taking note, in particular, of paragraph 111 of that report, in which it is stated that during the reporting period "there were 117 incursions into Agency installations by members of the Israeli security forces in the West Bank and 210 such incursions in the Gaza Strip" and that "the Agency recorded 94 incidents in which the Agency's clinic and hospital premises were entered" and that "on 26 November 1991, border police personnel fired tear gas into the [Agency's] girls' school in Shu'fat camp in the West Bank, necessitating medical treatment for affected students and teachers, including two pregnant teachers who required hospital treatment",

Gravely concerned and alarmed by the deteriorating situation in the Palestinian territory occupied by Israel since 1967, including Jerusalem,

1. *Condemns* the repeated Israeli raids on the premises and installations of the United Nations Relief and Works Agency for Palestine Refugees in the Near East, and calls upon Israel, the occupying Power, to refrain from such raids;

2. *Deplores* the policy and practices of Israel, the occupying Power, which have led to the prolonged closure of educational and vocational institutions, a large number of which are operated by the Agency, and the repeated disruption of medical services;

3. *Calls upon* Israel, the occupying Power, to open immediately all closed educational and vocational institutions and to refrain from closing them thereafter;

4. *Requests* the Secretary-General to report to the General Assembly at its forty-eighth session on the implementation of the present resolution.

General Assembly resolution 47/69 K

14 December 1992   Meeting 85   141-2 (recorded vote)

Approved by Special Political Committee (A/47/611) by recorded vote (119-2), 25 November (meeting 27); 11-nation draft (A/SPC/47/L.24); agenda item 73.

Sponsors: Afghanistan, Bangladesh, Brunei Darussalam, Comoros, Cuba, Indonesia, Madagascar, Malaysia, Mali, Pakistan, Zambia.

Meeting numbers. GA 47th session: SPC 9-12, 27; plenary 85.

Recorded vote in Assembly as follows:

In favour: Afghanistan, Albania, Algeria, Angola, Antigua and Barbuda, Argentina, Australia, Austria, Azerbaijan, Bahrain, Bangladesh, Barbados, Belarus, Belgium, Belize, Benin, Bhutan, Bolivia, Bosnia and Herzegovina, Botswana, Brazil, Brunei Darussalam, Bulgaria, Burkina Faso, Cameroon, Canada, Chad, Chile, China, Colombia, Comoros, Costa Rica, Côte d'Ivoire, Cuba, Cyprus, Czechoslovakia, Democratic People's Republic of Korea, Denmark, Djibouti, Dominica, Ecuador, Egypt, El Salvador, Estonia, Ethiopia, Finland, France, Gabon, Gambia, Germany, Greece, Grenada, Guatemala, Guinea-Bissau, Guyana, Haiti, Honduras, Hungary, Iceland, India, Indonesia, Iran, Ireland, Italy, Jamaica, Japan, Jordan, Kazakhstan, Kuwait, Lao People's Democratic Republic, Latvia, Lebanon, Liberia, Libyan Arab Jamahiriya, Liechtenstein, Lithuania, Luxembourg, Madagascar, Malawi, Malaysia, Maldives, Mali, Malta, Marshall Islands, Mauritania, Mauritius, Mexico, Mongolia, Morocco, Mozambique, Myanmar, Namibia, Nepal, Netherlands, New Zealand, Niger, Nigeria, Norway, Pakistan, Panama, Paraguay, Peru, Philippines, Poland, Portugal, Qatar, Republic of Korea, Republic of Moldova, Romania, Russian Federation, Rwanda, Saint Lucia, Saint Vincent and the Grenadines, Samoa, Sao Tome and Principe, Saudi Arabia, Senegal, Sierra Leone, Singapore, Spain, Sri Lanka, Sudan, Suriname, Swaziland, Sweden, Syrian

Arab Republic, Thailand, Togo, Trinidad and Tobago, Tunisia, Turkey, Ukraine, United Arab Emirates, United Kingdom, Uruguay, Vanuatu, Venezuela, Viet Nam, Yemen, Zambia, Zimbabwe.

Against: Israel, United States.

Proposed University of Jerusalem "Al Quds"

In keeping with a General Assembly request of 1991,[15] the Secretary-General reported in October 1992[16] on the establishment of a university for Palestine refugees at Jerusalem. The proposed university, first considered by the Assembly in 1980,[17] had since been the subject of annual reports by the Secretary-General with regard to measures taken towards its establishment, including a functional feasibility study.

To assist in the preparation of the study and at the Secretary-General's request, the United Nations University made available the services of an expert who would visit the area and meet with Israeli officials. By a note verbale of 15 September 1992, the Secretary-General requested Israel to facilitate the expert's visit at a mutually convenient time. Recalling the position of Israel on the proposed university and the questions it had raised, as well as the clarifications already given by the Secretariat, the Secretary-General expressed the opinion that those questions could best be discussed during the proposed visit.

Israel replied on 23 October that its position remained unchanged, and recalled its note of 30 June underscoring its consistent vote against the Assembly resolutions calling for the establishment of the proposed university, whose sponsors sought to exploit higher education in order to politicize issues totally extraneous to genuine academic pursuits. In the opinion of Israel, a visit by the expert would serve no useful purpose.

The Secretary-General thus concluded that the feasibility study could not be completed as planned.

GENERAL ASSEMBLY ACTION

On 14 December 1992, on the basis of the Special Political Committee's recommendation, the General Assembly adopted **resolution 47/69 J** by recorded vote.

University of Jerusalem "Al-Quds" for Palestine refugees

The General Assembly,

Recalling its resolutions 36/146 G of 16 December 1981, 37/120 C of 16 December 1982, 38/83 K of 15 December 1983, 39/99 K of 14 December 1984, 40/165 D and K of 16 December 1985, 41/69 K of 3 December 1986, 42/69 K of 2 December 1987, 43/57 J of 6 December 1988, 44/47 J of 8 December 1989, 45/73 J of 11 December 1990 and 46/46 J of 9 December 1991,

Having considered the report of the Secretary-General,

Having also considered the report of the Commissioner-General of the United Nations Relief and Works Agency for Palestine Refugees in the Near East, covering the period from 1 July 1991 to 30 June 1992,

1. *Emphasizes* the need for strengthening the educational system in the Palestinian territory occupied by Israel since 5 June 1967, including Jerusalem, and specifically the need for the establishment of the proposed university;

2. *Requests* the Secretary-General to continue to take all necessary measures for establishing the University of Jerusalem "Al-Quds", in accordance with Assembly resolution 35/13 B of 3 November 1980, giving due consideration to the recommendations consistent with the provisions of that resolution;

3. *Calls once more upon* Israel, the occupying Power, to cooperate in the implementation of the present resolution and to remove the hindrances that it has put in the way of establishing the University of Jerusalem "Al-Quds";

4. *Also requests* the Secretary-General to report to the General Assembly at its forty-eighth session on the progress made in the implementation of the present resolution.

General Assembly resolution 47/69 J

14 December 1992   Meeting 85   139-2-1 (recorded vote)

Approved by Special Political Committee (A/47/611) by recorded vote (119-2-1), 25 November (meeting 27); 13-nation draft (A/SPC/47/L.23); agenda item 73.

Sponsors: Afghanistan, Bangladesh, Brunei Darussalam, Comoros, Cuba, India, Indonesia, Jordan, Madagascar, Malaysia, Mali, Pakistan, Zambia.

Meeting numbers. GA 47th session: SPC 9-12, 27; plenary 85.

Recorded vote in Assembly as follows:

In favour: Afghanistan, Albania, Algeria, Angola, Antigua and Barbuda, Argentina, Australia, Austria, Azerbaijan, Bahrain, Bangladesh, Barbados, Belarus, Belgium, Belize, Benin, Bhutan, Bolivia, Bosnia and Herzegovina, Botswana, Brazil, Brunei Darussalam, Bulgaria, Burkina Faso, Cameroon, Canada, Chad, Chile, China, Colombia, Comoros, Costa Rica, Côte d'Ivoire, Cuba, Cyprus, Czechoslovakia, Democratic People's Republic of Korea, Denmark, Djibouti, Dominica, Ecuador, Egypt, El Salvador, Estonia, Ethiopia, Finland, France, Gabon, Gambia, Germany, Greece, Guatemala, Guinea-Bissau, Guyana, Haiti, Honduras, Hungary, Iceland, India, Indonesia, Iran, Ireland, Italy, Jamaica, Japan, Jordan, Kazakhstan, Kuwait, Lao People's Democratic Republic, Latvia, Lebanon, Liberia, Libyan Arab Jamahiriya, Liechtenstein, Lithuania, Luxembourg, Madagascar, Malawi, Malaysia, Maldives, Mali, Malta, Marshall Islands, Mauritania, Mauritius, Mexico, Mongolia, Morocco, Mozambique, Myanmar, Namibia, Nepal, Netherlands, New Zealand, Niger, Nigeria, Norway, Pakistan, Panama, Paraguay, Peru, Philippines, Poland, Portugal, Qatar, Republic of Korea, Republic of Moldova, Romania, Rwanda, Saint Lucia, Saint Vincent and the Grenadines, Samoa, Sao Tome and Principe, Saudi Arabia, Senegal, Sierra Leone, Singapore, Spain, Sri Lanka, Sudan, Suriname, Swaziland, Sweden, Syrian Arab Republic, Thailand, Togo, Trinidad and Tobago, Tunisia, Turkey, Ukraine, United Arab Emirates, United Kingdom, Uruguay, Vanuatu, Venezuela, Viet Nam, Yemen, Zambia, Zimbabwe.

Against: Israel, United States.

Abstaining: Russian Federation.

Scholarships

The Secretary-General reported in October 1992[18] on responses to the General Assembly's appeal of 1991[19] to augment special allocations for scholarships and grants to Palestine refugees, for which UNRWA acted as recipient and trustee.

In the academic year 1991/92, Japan offered, through UNRWA, 16 vocational fellowships in Japan for Palestine refugees in UNRWA's employ. Under the UNRWA university scholarship programme for secondary school graduates, 140 Palestine refugee students were recipients of scholarship awards made possible by Japan's contribution of $1 million in 1989, to be spread over five years. Another 136 Palestinians were awarded scholarships under the same programme, made possible

by Switzerland's contributions to the programme of $180,000 in 1989, $213,000 in 1990 and $197,300 in 1991. Those awards, while not specifically in response to Assembly resolutions, were in keeping with their spirit.

In 1991, seven Palestinians were awarded international fellowships under the WHO postgraduate fellowship programme aimed at developing technical and managerial skills of UNRWA's Department of Health staff and at meeting future replacement needs under various health disciplines. Three other Palestinians were granted fellowships to study in Belgium in 1990-1991: one for a full scholastic year in paediatric cardiology, and two for a four-month study in oncology. The World Intellectual Property Organization followed up its award of 15 fellowships in the period 1980-1990, with the offer of a further award in 1992.

GENERAL ASSEMBLY ACTION

On 14 December, on the recommendation of the Special Political Committee, the General Assembly adopted **resolution 47/69 D** by recorded vote.

Offers by Member States of grants and scholarships for higher education, including vocational training, for Palestine refugees

The General Assembly,

Recalling its resolution 212(III) of 19 November 1948 on assistance to Palestine refugees,

Recalling also its resolutions 35/13 B of 3 November 1980, 36/146 H of 16 December 1981, 37/120 D of 16 December 1982, 38/83 D of 15 December 1983, 39/99 D of 14 December 1984, 40/165 D of 16 December 1985, 41/69 D of 3 December 1986, 42/69 D of 2 December 1987, 43/57 D of 6 December 1988, 44/47 D of 8 December 1989, 45/73 D of 11 December 1990 and 46/46 D of 9 December 1991,

Cognizant of the fact that the Palestine refugees have, for the last four decades, lost their homes, lands and means of livelihood,

Having considered the report of the Secretary-General,

Having also considered the report of the Commissioner-General of the United Nations Relief and Works Agency for Palestine Refugees in the Near East, covering the period from 1 July 1991 to 30 June 1992,

1. *Urges* all States to respond to the appeal contained in its resolution 32/90 F of 13 December 1977 and reiterated in subsequent relevant resolutions in a manner commensurate with the needs of Palestine refugees for higher education, including vocational training;

2. *Strongly appeals* to all States, specialized agencies and non-governmental organizations to augment the special allocations for grants and scholarships to Palestine refugees, in addition to their contributions to the regular budget of the United Nations Relief and Works Agency for Palestine Refugees in the Near East;

3. *Expresses its appreciation* to all Governments, specialized agencies and non-governmental organizations that responded favourably to its resolutions 41/69 D, 42/69 D, 43/57 D, 44/47 D, 45/73 D and 46/46 D;

4. *Invites* the relevant specialized agencies and other organizations of the United Nations system to continue,

within their respective spheres of competence, to extend assistance for higher education to Palestine refugee students;

5. *Appeals* to all States, specialized agencies and the United Nations University to contribute generously to the Palestinian universities in the Palestinian territory occupied by Israel since 1967, including, in due course, the proposed University of Jerusalem "Al-Quds" for Palestine refugees;

6. *Also appeals* to all States, specialized agencies and other international bodies to contribute towards the establishment of vocational training centres for Palestine refugees;

7. *Requests* the Agency to act as the recipient and trustee for the special allocations for grants and scholarships and to award them to qualified Palestine refugee candidates;

8. *Requests* the Secretary-General to report to the General Assembly at its forty-eighth session on the implementation of the present resolution.

General Assembly resolution 47/69 D

14 December 1992   Meeting 85   139-0-1 (recorded vote)

Approved by Special Political Committee (A/47/611) by recorded vote (122-0-1), 25 November (meeting 27); 13-nation draft (A/SPC/47/L.17); agenda item 73.
Sponsors: Afghanistan, Bangladesh, Brunei Darussalam, Comoros, Cuba, India, Indonesia, Jordan, Madagascar, Malaysia, Mali, Pakistan, Zambia.
Meeting numbers. GA 47th session: SPC 9-12, 27; plenary 85.

Recorded vote in Assembly as follows:

In favour: Afghanistan, Algeria, Angola, Antigua and Barbuda, Argentina, Australia, Austria, Azerbaijan, Bahrain, Bangladesh, Barbados, Belarus, Belgium, Benin, Bhutan, Bolivia, Bosnia and Herzegovina, Botswana, Brazil, Brunei Darussalam, Bulgaria, Burkina Faso, Cameroon, Canada, Chad, Chile, China, Colombia, Comoros, Costa Rica, Côte d'Ivoire, Cuba, Cyprus, Czechoslovakia, Democratic People's Republic of Korea, Denmark, Djibouti, Dominica, Ecuador, Egypt, El Salvador, Estonia, Ethiopia, Finland, France, Gabon, Gambia, Germany, Greece, Grenada, Guatemala, Guinea-Bissau, Guyana, Haiti, Honduras, Hungary, Iceland, India, Indonesia, Iran, Ireland, Italy, Jamaica, Japan, Jordan, Kazakhstan, Kuwait, Lao People's Democratic Republic, Latvia, Lebanon, Liberia, Libyan Arab Jamahiriya, Liechtenstein, Lithuania, Luxembourg, Madagascar, Malawi, Malaysia, Maldives, Mali, Malta, Marshall Islands, Mauritania, Mauritius, Mexico, Mongolia, Morocco, Mozambique, Myanmar, Namibia, Nepal, Netherlands, New Zealand, Niger, Nigeria, Norway, Pakistan, Panama, Paraguay, Peru, Philippines, Poland, Portugal, Qatar, Republic of Korea, Republic of Moldova, Romania, Russian Federation, Rwanda, Saint Lucia, Saint Vincent and the Grenadines, Samoa, Sao Tome and Principe, Saudi Arabia, Senegal, Singapore, Spain, Sri Lanka, Sudan, Suriname, Swaziland, Sweden, Syrian Arab Republic, Thailand, Togo, Trinidad and Tobago, Tunisia, Turkey, Ukraine, United Arab Emirates, United Kingdom, United States, Uruguay, Vanuatu, Venezuela, Viet Nam, Yemen, Zambia, Zimbabwe.
Against: None.
Abstaining: Israel.

Property rights

Report of the Secretary-General. In response to a General Assembly resolution of 1991,[20] the Secretary-General, in September 1992,[21] submitted a report on the status of steps taken for the protection and administration of Arab property, assets and property rights in Israel and for the setting up of a fund for the receipt of income derived therefrom, on behalf of the rightful owners. The Secretary-General indicated that he had transmitted the resolution to Israel and to all other Member States for their comments, as well as to the Chairman of the United Nations Conciliation Commission for Palestine.

According to Israel's reply of 1 July, reproduced in the report, the 1991 resolution demonstrated its sponsors' misuse of the Assembly for the goals of an ongoing propaganda campaign against Israel. Its position had been set out in statements to the Special Political Committee on three occasions and in a 1991 report of the Secretary-General.[22] Israel again asserted that there was no legal basis for taking the steps proposed, as property rights within the borders of a sovereign State were subject exclusively to that State's domestic laws; the right of States to regulate and dispose of property within their territory (and income derived from that property) was a generally accepted principle. Significantly, the resolution's sponsors had not proposed that similar steps be taken regarding the confiscated Jewish property in Arab countries—suggesting that Israel's sovereignty was limited or restricted by some provision that did not apply to other Members of the United Nations. The property left behind by approximately 800,000 Jewish refugees who resettled in Israel as a result of the 1948 war, estimated to be in the billions of dollars, was expropriated by the Arab countries in which they had lived. Israel stressed that there could be no difference in law, justice or equity between the claims of Arab and Jewish property owners.

The Secretary-General added that no reply had been received from any other Member State regarding implementation of the resolution.

Report of the Conciliation Commission. The United Nations Conciliation Commission for Palestine, in its report covering the period from 1 September 1991 to 31 August 1992,[23] stated that the circumstances that unfortunately had limited its possibilities of action regarding compensation for Palestine refugee properties remained unchanged. The events that had occurred in the area since the preceding reporting period had further complicated an already very complex situation. The Commission continued to hope, nevertheless, that the situation and related circumstances in the region would improve towards a comprehensive, just and lasting Middle East peace, thus enabling it to carry forward its work in accordance with the 1948 Assembly resolution defining its mandate.[24]

Referring to prospects for implementing paragraph 11 of that resolution, by which the Assembly resolved that the refugees wishing to return to their homes should be permitted to do so at the earliest practicable date, and that compensation should be paid for the property of those choosing not to return and for loss or damage to property, the Commission noted that the examination of various ways in which it might be possible to intensify its efforts towards that end had compelled the conclusion that all the ways envisaged presupposed substantial changes in the situation.

GENERAL ASSEMBLY ACTION

On 14 December, on the recommendation of the Special Political Committee, the General Assembly adopted **resolution 47/69 H** by recorded vote.

Revenues derived from Palestine refugees' properties

The General Assembly,

Recalling its resolutions 35/13 A to F of 3 November 1980, 36/146 C of 16 December 1981, 37/120 H of 16 December 1982, 38/83 H of 15 December 1983, 39/99 H of 14 December 1984, 40/165 H of 16 December 1985, 41/69 H of 3 December 1986, 42/69 H of 2 December 1987, 43/57 H of 6 December 1988, 44/47 H of 8 December 1989, 45/73 H of 11 December 1990, 46/46 H of 9 December 1991 and all its previous resolutions on the question, including resolution 194(III) of 11 December 1948,

Taking note of the report of the Secretary-General,

Taking note also of the report of the United Nations Conciliation Commission for Palestine, covering the period from 1 September 1991 to 31 August 1992,

Recalling that the Universal Declaration of Human Rights and the principles of international law uphold the principle that no one shall be arbitrarily deprived of his or her private property,

Considering that the Palestine Arab refugees are entitled to their property and to the income derived therefrom, in conformity with the principles of justice and equity,

Recalling in particular its resolution 394(V) of 14 December 1950, in which it directed the United Nations Conciliation Commission for Palestine, in consultation with the parties concerned, to prescribe measures for the protection of the rights, property and interests of the Palestine Arab refugees,

Taking note of the completion of the programme of identification and evaluation of Arab property, as announced by the United Nations Conciliation Commission for Palestine in its twenty-second progress report, and of the fact that the Land Office had a schedule of Arab owners and file of documents defining the location, area and other particulars of Arab property,

1. *Requests* the Secretary-General to take all appropriate steps, in consultation with the United Nations Conciliation Commission for Palestine, for the protection and administration of Arab property, assets and property rights in Israel and to establish a fund for the receipt of income derived therefrom, on behalf of the rightful owners;

2. *Calls once more upon* Israel to render all facilities and assistance to the Secretary-General in the implementation of the present resolution;

3. *Calls upon* the Governments of all the other Member States concerned to provide the Secretary-General with any pertinent information in their possession concerning Arab property, assets and property rights in Israel, which would assist the Secretary-General in the implementation of the present resolution;

4. *Deplores* the refusal of Israel to cooperate with the Secretary-General in the implementation of the resolutions on the question;

5. *Requests* the Secretary-General to report to the General Assembly at its forty-eighth session on the implementation of the present resolution.

General Assembly resolution 47/69 H

14 December 1992   Meeting 85   100-2-39 (recorded vote)

Approved by Special Political Committee (A/47/611) by recorded vote (85-2-34), 25 November (meeting 27); 11-nation draft (A/SPC/47/L.21); agenda item 73.

Sponsors: Afghanistan, Bangladesh, Brunei Darussalam, Comoros, Cuba, Indonesia, Madagascar, Malaysia, Mali, Pakistan, Zambia.

Meeting numbers. GA 47th session: SPC 9-12, 27; plenary 85.

Recorded vote in Assembly as follows:

In favour: Afghanistan, Algeria, Angola, Antigua and Barbuda, Azerbaijan, Bahrain, Bangladesh, Barbados, Belarus, Belize, Benin, Bhutan, Bosnia and Herzegovina, Botswana, Brazil, Brunei Darussalam, Burkina Faso, Cameroon, Chad, Chile, China, Colombia, Comoros, Costa Rica, Côte d'Ivoire, Cuba, Cyprus, Democratic People's Republic of Korea, Djibouti, Ecuador, Egypt, El Salvador, Ethiopia, Gabon, Gambia, Greece, Guatemala, Guinea-Bissau, Guyana, Haiti, Honduras, India, Indonesia, Iran, Jamaica, Jordan, Kazakhstan, Kuwait, Lao People's Democratic Republic, Lebanon, Liberia, Libyan Arab Jamahiriya, Madagascar, Malawi, Malaysia, Maldives, Mali, Malta, Mauritania, Mauritius, Mexico, Mongolia, Morocco, Mozambique, Myanmar, Namibia, Nepal, Niger, Nigeria, Pakistan, Panama, Paraguay, Peru, Philippines, Qatar, Republic of Korea, Rwanda, Sao Tome and Principe, Saudi Arabia, Senegal, Singapore, Spain, Sri Lanka, Sudan, Suriname, Swaziland, Syrian Arab Republic, Thailand, Trinidad and Tobago, Tunisia, Turkey, Ukraine, United Arab Emirates, Uruguay, Vanuatu, Venezuela, Viet Nam, Yemen, Zambia, Zimbabwe.

Against: Israel, United States.

Abstaining: Albania, Argentina, Australia, Austria, Belgium, Bolivia, Bulgaria, Canada, Czechoslovakia, Denmark, Dominica, Estonia, Finland, France, Germany, Hungary, Iceland, Ireland, Italy, Japan, Latvia, Liechtenstein, Lithuania, Luxembourg, Marshall Islands, Netherlands, New Zealand, Norway, Poland, Portugal, Republic of Moldova, Romania, Russian Federation, Saint Lucia, Saint Vincent and the Grenadines, Samoa, Sweden, Togo, United Kingdom.

Refugee protection

The Secretary-General reported in October 1992[7] on implementation of a General Assembly resolution of 1991[25] holding Israel responsible for the security of the Palestine refugees in the occupied territory and calling on it to compensate UNRWA for the damage to its property and facilities resulting from Israel's 1982 invasion of Lebanon.

The report reproduced Israel's reply of 30 June 1992 to the Secretary-General's request for information on steps taken or envisaged to comply with the resolution. Israel said that it had fully set forth its position on the subject in statements to the Special Political Committee and in a 1991 report of the Secretary-General.[26] The adoption of the resolution was hypocritical, anachronistic and out of place. Despite its withdrawal from Lebanon in 1985, Israel was still being blamed for the "suffering" of Palestinians there and, not surprisingly, for Arab persecution of Palestinian refugees. In recent years, thousands of Palestinians had been killed and wounded in Lebanese refugee camps in vicious fighting totally unconnected with Israel; likewise, Palestinian refugee camps in Jordan and the Syrian Arab Republic were the scenes of considerable human misery. The selective and distorted presentation of the Palestinian refugees' situation in Arab countries clearly illustrated the resolution's double standards and its blatant disregard for the refugees' general welfare. Israel emphasized that, in keeping with international law, it alone was competent to ensure full protection to all inhabitants of Judaea, Samaria and the Gaza District.

The Secretary-General cited the UNRWA Commissioner-General's report for the period 1 July 1991 to 30 June 1992,[1] to the effect that the Commissioner-General had continued his efforts in support of the Palestine refugees' safety and legal and human rights. UNRWA international staff, in particular the Refugee Affairs Officers, continued to help reduce tension and prevent maltreatment of refugees, especially vulnerable groups such as women and children. The Commissioner-General also protested to Israel against the excessive use of force and collective punishments, such as the demolition and sealing of shelters, as a failure on Israel's part to uphold standards required under international humanitarian law. As part of the Commissioner-General's efforts in that regard, legal advice and financial assistance were provided for refugees seeking to assert their legal rights.

GENERAL ASSEMBLY ACTION

On 14 December, on the recommendation of the Special Political Committee, the General Assembly adopted **resolution 47/69 I** by recorded vote.

Protection of Palestine refugees

The General Assembly,

Recalling in particular recent Security Council resolutions 605(1987) of 22 December 1987, 607(1988) of 5 January 1988, 608(1988) of 14 January 1988, 636(1989) of 6 July 1989, 641(1989) of 30 August 1989, 672(1990) of 12 October 1990, 673(1990) of 24 October 1990, 681(1990) of 20 December 1990, 694(1991) of 24 May 1991 and 726(1992) of 6 January 1992,

Also recalling its resolutions ES-7/5 of 26 June 1982, ES-7/6 and ES-7/8 of 19 August 1982, ES-7/9 of 24 September 1982, 37/120 J of 16 December 1982, 38/83 I of 15 December 1983, 39/99 I of 14 December 1984, 40/165 I of 16 December 1985, 41/69 I of 3 December 1986, 42/69 I of 2 December 1987, 43/21 of 3 November 1988, 43/57 I of 6 December 1988, 44/47 I of 8 December 1989, 45/73 I of 11 December 1990 and 46/46 I of 9 December 1991,

Taking note of the report of the Secretary-General dated 21 January 1988, submitted in accordance with Security Council resolution 605(1987), the report dated 31 October 1990, submitted in accordance with Council resolution 672(1990), and the report dated 9 April 1991, submitted in accordance with Council resolution 681(1990),

Having considered the report of the Secretary-General,

Having also considered the report of the Commissioner-General of the United Nations Relief and Works Agency for Palestine Refugees in the Near East, covering the period from 1 July 1991 to 30 June 1992,

Gravely concerned and alarmed by the deteriorating situation in the Palestinian territory occupied by Israel since 1967, including Jerusalem,

Taking into account the need to consider measures for the impartial protection of the Palestinian civilian population under Israeli occupation,

Referring to the humanitarian principles of the Geneva Convention relative to the Protection of Civilian Persons in Time of War, of 12 August 1949, and to the obligations arising from the regulations annexed to the Hague Convention IV of 1907,

Deeply distressed that, notwithstanding the improved security situation owing to the deployment of the Lebanese army, the Palestinian and Lebanese population are still suffering from continuing Israeli acts of aggression against Lebanon and from other hostile acts,

1. *Holds* Israel responsible for the security of the Palestine refugees in the occupied Palestinian territory, including Jerusalem, and other Arab territories occupied by Israel since 1967, and calls upon it to fulfil its obligations as the occupying Power in this regard, in accordance with the pertinent provisions of the Geneva Convention relative to the Protection of Civilian Persons in Time of War, of 12 August 1949;

2. *Calls upon* all the High Contracting Parties to the Convention to take appropriate measures to ensure respect by Israel, the occupying Power, for the Convention in all circumstances, in conformity with their obligation under article 1 thereof;

3. *Strongly urges* the Security Council to consider the current situation in the occupied Palestinian territory, taking into account the recommendations contained in the reports of the Secretary-General dated 21 January 1988, 31 October 1990 and 9 April 1991;

4. *Urges* the Secretary-General and the Commissioner-General of the United Nations Relief and Works Agency for Palestine Refugees in the Near East to continue their efforts in support of the upholding of the safety and security and the legal and human rights of the Palestine refugees in all the territories under Israeli occupation since 1967;

5. *Calls once again upon* Israel to desist forthwith from acts of aggression against the Lebanese and Palestinian population in Lebanon, in violation of the Charter of the United Nations and the norms of international law;

6. *Demands* that Israel, the occupying Power, release forthwith all arbitrarily detained Palestine refugees, including the employees of the United Nations Relief and Works Agency for Palestine Refugees in the Near East;

7. *Calls once again upon* Israel to compensate the Agency for damages to its property and facilities resulting from the invasion of Lebanon by Israel in 1982, without prejudice to the responsibility of the latter for all damages resulting from that invasion, as well as for other damages resulting from the policies and practices of Israel, the occupying Power, in the occupied Palestinian territory;

8. *Requests* the Secretary-General, in consultation with the Commissioner-General, to report to the General Assembly, before the opening of its forty-eighth session, on the implementation of the present resolution.

General Assembly resolution 47/69 I

14 December 1992   Meeting 85   138-2-1 (recorded vote)

Approved by Special Political Committee (A/47/611) by recorded vote (119-2-1), 25 November (meeting 27); 12-nation draft (A/SPC/47/L.22); agenda item 73.

Sponsors: Afghanistan, Bangladesh, Brunei Darussalam, Comoros, Cuba, Indonesia, Madagascar, Malaysia, Mali, Pakistan, Sudan, Zambia.

Meeting numbers. GA 47th session: SPC 9-12, 27; plenary 85.

Recorded vote in Assembly as follows:

In favour: Afghanistan, Albania, Algeria, Angola, Antigua and Barbuda, Argentina, Australia, Austria, Azerbaijan, Bahrain, Bangladesh, Barbados, Belarus, Belgium, Belize, Benin, Bhutan, Bolivia, Bosnia and Herzegovina, Botswana, Brazil, Brunei Darussalam, Bulgaria, Burkina Faso, Cameroon, Canada, Chad, Chile, China, Colombia, Comoros, Costa Rica, Côte d'Ivoire,

Cuba, Cyprus, Czechoslovakia, Democratic People's Republic of Korea, Denmark, Djibouti, Dominica, Ecuador, Egypt, El Salvador, Estonia, Ethiopia, Finland, France, Gabon, Gambia, Germany, Greece, Guatemala, Guinea-Bissau, Guyana, Haiti, Honduras, Hungary, Iceland, India, Indonesia, Iran, Ireland, Italy, Jamaica, Japan, Jordan, Kazakhstan, Kuwait, Lao People's Democratic Republic, Latvia, Lebanon, Liberia, Libyan Arab Jamahiriya, Liechtenstein, Lithuania, Luxembourg, Madagascar, Malawi, Malaysia, Maldives, Mali, Malta, Marshall Islands, Mauritania, Mauritius, Mexico, Mongolia, Morocco, Mozambique, Myanmar, Namibia, Nepal, Netherlands, New Zealand, Niger, Nigeria, Norway, Pakistan, Panama, Paraguay, Peru, Philippines, Poland, Portugal, Qatar, Republic of Korea, Republic of Moldova, Romania, Rwanda, Saint Lucia, Saint Vincent and the Grenadines, Samoa, Sao Tome and Principe, Saudi Arabia, Senegal, Singapore, Spain, Sri Lanka, Sudan, Suriname, Swaziland, Sweden, Syrian Arab Republic, Thailand, Togo, Trinidad and Tobago, Tunisia, Turkey, Ukraine, United Arab Emirates, United Kingdom, Uruguay, Vanuatu, Venezuela, Viet Nam, Yemen, Zambia, Zimbabwe.

Against: Israel, United States.

Abstaining: Russian Federation.

Removal and resettlement of refugees

In a report of October 1992,[27] the Secretary-General reproduced Israel's reply of 30 June to a 1991 General Assembly resolution[28] demanding that Israel desist from removing and resettling Palestine refugees in the Palestinian territory occupied by it since 1967 and from destroying their shelters. The reply stated that Israel's position had been made known in successive annual replies to the Secretary-General in recent years, the latest of which was contained in his 1991 report on the subject.[29]

Israel considered the resolution unbalanced and distorted in that it intentionally ignored the improved living conditions in Gaza since 1967. Nothing could be more indicative of that approach than the resolution's condemnation of refugee rehabilitation projects. Since 1967, Israel had initiated community development projects in Gaza, enabling some 20,000 families (approximately 150,000 persons), to leave the refugee camps on a voluntary basis and relocate to nearby residential areas. Israel's vital role in planning and implementing those housing projects had been recognized in 1985 by the Secretary-General[30] and the UNRWA Commissioner-General. The resolution's request that the Secretary-General resume issuing identity cards irrespective of the refugees' need for them was yet another indication of its patent political bias. Notwithstanding subversive efforts to the contrary, Israel was determined to pursue the task of improving the refugees' living conditions through projects such as the refugee housing programmes, and would welcome all assistance from the international community in that regard.

The Secretary-General stated that, according to information from UNRWA,[1] the Israeli authorities continued their practice of inflicting collective punishment by demolishing and sealing refugee shelters in the West Bank and Gaza. As at 30 June 1992, of the refugee families affected by the 1971 demolitions,[31] 12 continued to live in conditions of hardship and 19 remained in unsatisfactory housing. UNRWA's representations with Israeli authorities for the rehousing of those 31 families had not met with success.

The situation of the families living on the northern perimeter of Jabalia camp[32] who had been told to remove some of their shelter extensions remained the same: no demolitions had taken place, but the shelters remained isolated by a sand-hill bulldozed around them. Of the 35 families whose shelters on the perimeter of Beach camp were demolished in 1983,[33] 18 families had been allocated plots of land at Sheikh Radwan and Beit Lahiya housing projects; one was housed in a vacant shelter at Beach camp; and the other 16 families remained in the same situation as previously reported—in temporary shelters near the camp site.

Of the 13 families at Rafah camp who had agreed to relocate to the Israeli-sponsored Tel-es-Sultan housing project but remained waiting at the camp,[34] one finally moved to Tel-es-Sultan. Nine families (91 persons) from Canada camp in Egypt returned to Gaza to accommodations at the same housing project.

Statistics on Israeli resettlement of refugees were as reported in 1991.[35]

As to the Assembly's request that the Commissioner-General address the acute situation of the Palestine refugees, he advised that UNRWA, in addition to extending to them its regular services plus emergency food, medical and other assistance, also pursued its long-term programme to upgrade infrastructure, especially in the camps, and, in general, to improve the economic and social welfare of the refugees.

The Secretary-General regretted his inability to comply with the Assembly's request that he resume issuing identification cards to all Palestine refugees and their descendants in the occupied territory, whether or not they were recipients of UNRWA rations and services. Under an arrangement in effect in the last 40 years, all refugee families registered with UNRWA were in possession of Agency-issued registration cards. While indicating the number of family members and their eligibility for services, those cards were not identification cards and had a more limited purpose: to reflect data about the refugee family concerned, which was entered on the registration roll at the time of registration. While appreciating the need for documentation, the Commissioner-General did not have the means to issue identity cards. However, he would keep the matter under review to see whether appropriate documentation regarding the registration status of individual members of refugee families could be issued.

GENERAL ASSEMBLY ACTION

On 14 December 1992, on the recommendation of the Special Political Committee, the General

Assembly adopted **resolution 47/69 E** by recorded vote.

Palestine refugees in the Palestinian territory occupied by Israel since 1967

The General Assembly,

Recalling Security Council resolution 237(1967) of 14 June 1967,

Recalling also its resolutions 2792 C (XXVI) of 6 December 1971, 2963 C (XXVII) of 13 December 1972, 3089 C (XXVIII) of 7 December 1973, 3331 D (XXIX) of 17 December 1974, 3419 C (XXX) of 8 December 1975, 31/15 E of 23 November 1976, 32/90 C of 13 December 1977, 33/112 E of 18 December 1978, 34/52 F of 23 November 1979, 35/13 F of 3 November 1980, 36/146 A of 16 December 1981, 37/120 E and I of 16 December 1982, 38/83 E and J of 15 December 1983, 39/99 E and J of 14 December 1984, 40/165 E and J of 16 December 1985, 41/69 E and J of 3 December 1986, 42/69 E and J of 2 December 1987, 43/57 E of 6 December 1988, 44/47 E of 8 December 1989, 45/73 E of 11 December 1990 and 46/46 E of 9 December 1991,

Having considered the report of the Secretary-General,

Having also considered the report of the Commissioner-General of the United Nations Relief and Works Agency for Palestine Refugees in the Near East, covering the period from 1 July 1991 to 30 June 1992,

Recalling the provisions of paragraph 11 of its resolution 194(III) of 11 December 1948, and considering that measures to resettle Palestine refugees in the Palestinian territory occupied by Israel since 1967 away from their homes and property from which they were displaced constitute a violation of their inalienable right of return,

Alarmed by the reports received from the Commissioner-General that the Israeli occupying authorities, in contravention of the obligation of Israel under international law, persist in their policy of demolishing shelters occupied by refugee families,

1. *Strongly reiterates its demand* that Israel desist from the removal and resettlement of Palestine refugees in the Palestinian territory occupied by Israel since 1967 and from the destruction of their shelters;

2. *Requests* the Commissioner-General of the United Nations Relief and Works Agency for Palestine Refugees in the Near East to address the acute situation of the Palestine refugees in the Palestinian territory occupied by Israel since 1967 and accordingly to extend all the services of the Agency to those refugees;

3. *Requests* the Secretary-General, in cooperation with the Commissioner-General, to resume issuing identification cards to all Palestine refugees and their descendants in the occupied Palestinian territory, irrespective of whether or not they are recipients of rations and services of the Agency;

4. *Also requests* the Secretary-General, after consulting with the Commissioner-General, to report to the General Assembly, before the opening of its forty-eighth session, on the implementation of the present resolution and, in particular, on the compliance of Israel with paragraph 1 above.

General Assembly resolution 47/69 E

14 December 1992   Meeting 85   138-2 (recorded vote)

Approved by Special Political Committee (A/47/611) by recorded vote (119-2), 25 November (meeting 27); 11-nation draft (A/SPC/47/L.18); agenda item 73.

Sponsors: Afghanistan, Bangladesh, Brunei Darussalam, Comoros, Cuba, Indonesia, Madagascar, Malaysia, Mali, Pakistan, Zambia.

Meeting numbers. GA 47th session: SPC 9-12, 27; plenary 85.

Recorded vote in Assembly as follows:

In favour: Afghanistan, Algeria, Angola, Antigua and Barbuda, Argentina, Australia, Austria, Azerbaijan, Bahrain, Bangladesh, Barbados, Belarus, Belgium, Belize, Benin, Bhutan, Bolivia, Bosnia and Herzegovina, Botswana, Brazil, Brunei Darussalam, Bulgaria, Burkina Faso, Cameroon, Canada, Chad, Chile, China, Colombia, Comoros, Costa Rica, Côte d'Ivoire, Cuba, Cyprus, Czechoslovakia, Democratic People's Republic of Korea, Denmark, Djibouti, Dominica, Ecuador, Egypt, El Salvador, Estonia, Ethiopia, Finland, France, Gabon, Gambia, Germany, Greece, Grenada, Guatemala, Guinea-Bissau, Guyana, Haiti, Honduras, Hungary, Iceland, India, Indonesia, Iran, Ireland, Italy, Jamaica, Japan, Jordan, Kazakhstan, Kuwait, Lao People's Democratic Republic, Latvia, Lebanon, Liberia, Libyan Arab Jamahiriya, Liechtenstein, Lithuania, Luxembourg, Madagascar, Malawi, Malaysia, Maldives, Mali, Malta, Marshall Islands, Mauritania, Mauritius, Mexico, Mongolia, Morocco, Mozambique, Myanmar, Namibia, Nepal, Netherlands, New Zealand, Niger, Nigeria, Norway, Pakistan, Panama, Paraguay, Peru, Philippines, Poland, Portugal, Qatar, Republic of Korea, Republic of Moldova, Romania, Russian Federation, Rwanda, Saint Lucia, Saint Vincent and the Grenadines, Samoa, Sao Tome and Principe, Saudi Arabia, Senegal, Singapore, Spain, Sri Lanka, Sudan, Suriname, Swaziland, Sweden, Syrian Arab Republic, Thailand, Togo, Trinidad and Tobago, Tunisia, Turkey, Ukraine, United Arab Emirates, United Kingdom, Vanuatu, Venezuela, Viet Nam, Yemen, Zambia, Zimbabwe.

Against: Israel, United States.

In the Special Political Committee, Israel said that, by its negative vote, it expressed its consistent opposition to paragraph 11 of Assembly resolution 194(III)[24] and paragraph 2 of Assembly resolution 513(VI).[36] The multilateral working group on refugee issues of the ongoing peace process had recently held a session in Ottawa, Canada, with the participation of some 40 countries and the United Nations. It was through the bilateral and multilateral talks, rather than the one-sided United Nations resolutions, that the question of Arab and Jewish refugees would be discussed and hopefully resolved. Israel would continue to cooperate with UNRWA to enable it to fulfil its important humanitarian task.

REFERENCES

[1]A/47/13. [2]A/47/576. [3]A/47/5/Add.3. [4]A/47/315. [5]A/47/500. [6]YUN 1986, p. 342. [7]A/47/492. [8]A/47/491. [9]YUN 1991, p. 276, GA res. 46/46 G, 9 Dec. 1991. [10]Ibid., p. 276. [11]A/47/490. [12]YUN 1991, p. 277, GA res. 46/46 F, 9 Dec. 1991. [13]A/47/493. [14]YUN 1991, p. 278, GA res. 46/46 K, 9 Dec. 1991. [15]Ibid., p. 279, GA res. 46/46 J, 9 Dec. 1991. [16]A/47/601. [17]YUN 1980, p. 443, GA res. 35/13 B, 3 Nov. 1980. [18]A/47/488. [19]YUN 1991, p. 280, GA res. 46/46 D, 9 Dec. 1991. [20]Ibid., p. 281, GA res. 46/46 H, 9 Dec. 1991. [21]A/47/438. [22]YUN 1991, p. 281. [23]A/47/413. [24]YUN 1948-49, p. 174, GA res. 194(III), 11 Dec. 1948. [25]YUN 1991, p. 282, GA res. 46/46 I, 9 Dec. 1991. [26]Ibid., p. 282. [27]A/47/489. [28]YUN 1991, p. 285, GA res. 46/46 E, 9 Dec. 1991. [29]Ibid., p. 283. [30]YUN 1985, p. 367. [31]YUN 1971, p. 198. [32]YUN 1985, p. 366. [33]YUN 1983, p. 358. [34]YUN 1986, p. 351. [35]YUN 1991, p. 284. [36]YUN 1951, p. 315, GA res. 513(VI), 26 Jan. 1952.

Chapter VI

Regional economic and social activities

The five United Nations regional commissions held their regular sessions during 1992, in continuing efforts to promote economic and social development in their respective regions.

The Economic Commission for Africa (ECA) held its twenty-seventh session/eighteenth meeting of the Conference of Ministers at Addis Ababa, Ethiopia, from 20 to 23 April and the thirteenth meeting of the Technical Preparatory Committee of the Whole from 13 to 18 April; the Economic and Social Commission for Asia and the Pacific (ESCAP) held its forty-eighth session at Beijing, China, from 14 to 23 April; the Economic Commission for Europe held its forty-seventh session at Geneva from 7 to 15 April; the Economic Commission for Latin America and the Caribbean held its twenty-fourth session at Santiago, Chile, from 8 to 15 April; and the Economic and Social Commission for Western Asia held its sixteenth session at Amman, Jordan, from 30 August to 3 September.

In July, the Economic and Social Council admitted as members of ESCAP Kazakhstan and Uzbekistan (resolution 1992/46), the Democratic People's Republic of Korea (1992/47), the Federated States of Micronesia and the Marshall Islands (1992/48), and Azerbaijan, Kyrgyzstan, Tajikistan and Turkmenistan (1992/50). French Polynesia and New Caledonia were admitted as associate members of ESCAP (1992/49).

The Council endorsed the programme for the Second Industrial Development Decade for Africa, 1991-2000 (1992/44), which was subsequently adopted by the General Assembly at its forty-seventh (1992) session and adjusted to cover the years 1993-2002 (resolution 47/177). United Nations activities in Africa were also addressed by the Council in its resolutions on strengthening ECA to face Africa's development challenges in the 1990s (1992/51); strengthening the role and functions of ECA in the context of the restructuring and revitalization of the United Nations in the economic and social fields (1992/52); and cooperation in fisheries in Africa (1992/54).

The Council also adopted resolutions on activities of the United Nations system in the Baltic States and the Commonwealth of Independent States (1992/40); strengthening the role of the regional commissions (1992/43); and the Europe-Africa permanent link through the Strait of Gibraltar (1992/45).

In October, the General Assembly urged United Nations agencies and organizations to continue and intensify their support for and cooperation with the activities of the Latin American Economic System (47/13).

Regional cooperation

Strengthening the role of the regional commissions

On 7 February 1992, the Economic and Social Council decided to consider at its 1992 substantive session, under the item on regional cooperation, the question of strengthening the role of the regional commissions to promote subregional, regional and interregional cooperation (**decision 1992/206**).

GENERAL ASSEMBLY ACTION

On 13 April 1992, at its resumed forty-sixth (1991) session, the General Assembly adopted measures for the restructuring and revitalization of the United Nations system in the economic, social and related fields (**resolution 46/235**). The Assembly considered, *inter alia*, that the effectiveness of the regional commissions should be strengthened and that the regional commissions, particularly those located in developing countries, should also be strengthened in terms of their activities and participation in operational activities of the United Nations system. The commissions were requested to provide recommendations for consideration by the Assembly at its forty-seventh (1992) session.

In a statement to the Assembly of 2 November, the Secretary-General stressed the importance of decentralizing United Nations activities at both national and regional levels and delegating greater authority to the regional commissions while enhancing their accountability. He indicated his intention to strengthen the role and contribution of the commissions, emphasizing at the same time the need for them to operate within a coherent organizational strategy.

Regional commissions action. During 1992, four of the five regional commissions responded to the General Assembly's request. By a 15 April resolution,[1] the Economic Commission for Latin America and the Caribbean (ECLAC) recommended increased decentralization in the execution of United Nations activities; improved coordination between the regional commissions and other United Nations organizations and agencies through intensified joint activities and joint programming exercises and meetings; a clear division of responsibilities regarding regional technical cooperation activities between the commissions and the United Nations funding agencies; and improved effectiveness of those activities in the region by decentralizing more of the budget resources allotted to ECLAC and by strengthening its capacity as an executing agency at the regional level.

By a resolution of 23 April,[2] the Economic and Social Commission for Asia and the Pacific (ESCAP) directed its Advisory Committee of Permanent Representatives and Other Representatives Designated by Members of the Commission to respond to the Assembly request on behalf of the Commission. At its August/September session, the Economic and Social Commission for Western Asia (ESCWA) recommended[3] that its potential for coordinating, initiating and carrying out development activities be strengthened through decentralization of those activities that could be more effectively undertaken by the regional commissions and through improved coordination inside and outside the United Nations system. The Commission also recommended the promotion of joint programming of United Nations activities involving the regional commissions and the commissions' active participation in the programming and budgeting process, as well as strengthening their role as executing agencies for regional and subregional technical cooperation projects. The Economic Commission for Africa (ECA), recalling its 1991 resolution on the revitalization of its mandate and operational framework[4] and a 1991 Economic and Social Council decision[5] on that resolution, in April 1992 adopted a resolution[6] which formed the basis of Council **resolution 1992/52** (see below).

Report of the Secretary-General. In a June report to the Economic and Social Council on regional cooperation,[7] the Secretary-General outlined the work of the five regional commissions, including matters and decisions requiring action by the Council or brought to the Council's attention, and elaborated on the question of strengthening the role of the commissions. That issue, he said, must be viewed in the broader context of the restructuring of the economic and social sectors of the United Nations system as a whole; the Organization's success at the regional level depended heavily on concerted and coordinated action throughout the system, within the framework of

an integrated multidisciplinary and regional approach to development. As most issues on the new development agenda were of a cross-sectoral nature, that approach had become increasingly important both in terms of dealing with differentiated social and economic problems and as a basis for promoting concerted action among Member States. In that context, greater regionalization and subregionalization of the United Nations system could be expected to occur, and the regional commissions would be called on to play an increasingly active role in promoting regional and subregional cooperation.

As for the relationship between the regional commissions and United Nations agencies, the commissions believed that, based on the experience so far, closer coordination could be maintained and strengthened through greater use of such established mechanisms as joint units, meetings, programming exercises and regular exchanges of information, the Secretary-General reported. He noted that the regional commissions, in their role as team leader under a 1977 General Assembly resolution,[8] developed a variety of arrangements for inter-agency coordination, including inter-agency committees and task forces on various multisectoral subjects, which were beneficial in avoiding duplication of work and in enhancing complementarity in joint planning of activities. However, greater coordination between the regional commissions and the United Nations funding agencies appeared necessary, especially in cases where the traditional role and mandate of the commissions were surpassed by the efforts of global bodies to extend their regional presence. The Secretary-General stated that the tendency on the part of funding agencies to organize substantive regional meetings further reinforced the need for the Assembly and the Economic and Social Council to redefine the relationship and respective mandates of the two sets of organizations.

As the activities and role of the regional commissions expanded to assist countries in transition to a market economy and countries undertaking economic restructuring or recovering from regional conflicts, closer cooperation and coordination between the commissions and non–United Nations organizations active in their respective regions became of paramount importance, to ensure their full integration in development assistance programmes in the economic and social fields. The Secretary-General recommended that various programming, administrative and management practices of the United Nations system be adjusted to enhance the ability of the commissions to respond to the needs of their members. He noted that neither the Council nor the Assembly had considered how resources would be mobilized for carrying out the new tasks assigned to the regional commissions, nor had they made provision for the allocation of additional resources for that purpose.

UNCTAD action. The United Nations Conference on Trade and Development, at its eighth session (UNCTAD VIII) (Cartagena de Indias, Colombia, 8-25 February) (see PART THREE, Chapter IV), adopted the Cartagena Commitment,[9] which provided a framework for economic cooperation among developing countries. The Commitment underscored the importance of regional integration for such cooperation and called on United Nations agencies and organizations to support interregional, regional and subregional integration programmes and infrastructural projects. It stated that structural adjustment programmes financed from bilateral and multilateral sources should take into account their impact on regional cooperation and integration, and that the allocation of aid resources should support regional trade liberalization among developing countries.

ECONOMIC AND SOCIAL COUNCIL ACTION

On 31 July, the Economic and Social Council, acting on the recommendation of its Economic Committee, adopted **resolution 1992/43** without vote.

Strengthening the role of the regional commissions

The Economic and Social Council,

Recalling General Assembly resolutions 45/264 of 13 May 1991 and 46/235 of 13 April 1992 on the restructuring and revitalization of the United Nations in the economic, social and related fields, 46/145 of 17 December 1991 on regional economic integration among developing countries, and other relevant Assembly resolutions,

Taking note of the report of the Secretary-General on regional cooperation, including his views on the role of the regional commissions within the framework of an integrated approach to enhancing the effectiveness of the United Nations system,

Bearing in mind that regional economic integration is important in expanding trade and investment, particularly in developing countries, and that regional economic integration has the potential to strengthen global economic and social development,

1. *Urges* the regional commissions to take steps to enable them fully to play their role in assisting their member States, in particular the developing countries, to promote accelerated and sustainable development through an integrated approach;

2. *Recommends* that, when preparing regional technical cooperation programmes, all relevant bodies of the United Nations system dealing with development coordinate their work with the regional commissions with a view to achieving a better and more focused use of available resources, greater coherence of action and, therefore, greater and more concentrated impact;

3. *Also recommends* that the regional commissions participate fully in the programme budget process at United Nations Headquarters;

4. *Urges* that priority setting for programming by the regional commissions should take fully into account the views of member States;

5. *Urges* the regional commissions, at the request of their member States, together with the United Nations Conference on Trade and Development, and in accordance with the Cartagena Commitment, to contribute to the identification, preparation and implementation of specific projects to facilitate economic integration and to submit them to bilateral donors, regional economic integration organizations, regional development banks and financial institutions for their consideration;

6. *Requests* each regional commission to study the possibility of assisting its member States, as appropriate, to participate fully and effectively at its sessions;

7. *Stresses* the role and important contribution of the regional commissions, within their mandates, in the follow-up and implementation of the decisions adopted by the United Nations Conference on Environment and Development, in particular those contained in Agenda 21;

8. *Stresses also* the importance of the regional commissions being part of the continued reform process in the economic and social fields, bearing in mind General Assembly resolutions 45/264 and 46/235;

9. *Requests* the Secretary-General to submit a report to the Economic and Social Council at its substantive session of 1993 on the progress made in the implementation of the present resolution.

Economic and Social Council resolution 1992/43

31 July 1992   Meeting 42   Adopted without vote

Approved by Economic Committee (E/1992/108) without vote, 28 July (meeting 16); draft by Vice-Chairman (E/1992/C.1/L.20), based on informal consultations on draft by Pakistan for Group of 77 (E/1992/C.1/L.2); agenda item 11.

On the same date the Council, on the recommendation of its Economic Committee, adopted **resolution 1992/52** without vote.

Restructuring and revitalization of the United Nations in the economic and social fields: strengthening the role and functions of the Economic Commission for Africa

The Economic and Social Council,

Recalling the terms of reference of the Economic Commission for Africa, as adopted by the Economic and Social Council in its resolution 671(XXV) of 29 April 1958 and amended by resolutions 974 D (XXXVI), section I, of 5 July 1963, 1343(XLV) of 18 July 1968 and 1978/68 of 4 August 1978,

Recalling also its decision 1991/302 of 26 July 1991, in which it endorsed resolution 718(XXVI) of 12 May 1991 of the Conference of Ministers of the Economic Commission for Africa on the revitalization of the mandate and operational framework of the regional commission for Africa,

Bearing in mind General Assembly resolutions 45/177 of 19 December 1990, 45/264 of 13 May 1991 and 46/235 of 13 April 1992 on the restructuring and revitalization of the United Nations in the economic, social and related fields, in which it was stated that the regional commissions should be enabled fully to play their role under the authority of the General Assembly and the Economic and Social Council, and that those regional commissions located in developing countries should be strengthened in the context of the overall objectives of the ongoing restructuring and revitalization process,

Convinced that the Economic Commission for Africa plays a vital catalytic role in the coordination and execution of intercountry programmes and projects aimed at strengthening regional cooperation and integration, especially by fostering the goals of the African Economic Community,

1. *Reaffirms* the continuing validity of the role of the regional commissions as important organs of the United Nations for promoting the socio-economic development of their respective regions;

2. *Appeals* to the Secretary-General to ensure that, in the context of the ongoing restructuring and revitalization of the United Nations in the economic and social fields, due recognition is accorded to the vital role of the regional commissions.

Economic and Social Council resolution 1992/52

31 July 1992   Meeting 42   Adopted without vote

Approved by Economic Committee (E/1992/108) without vote, 28 July (meeting 16); draft by Conference of Ministers of ECA (E/1992/65), orally amended; agenda item 11.

Also on 31 July, the Council, by **decision 1992/295**, took note of a number of documents pertaining to regional cooperation, including a note by the Secretary-General on the Second Industrial Development Decade for Africa;[10] the second report of the Joint Inspection Unit on the cost-benefit of office accommodation at ECLAC, Port of Spain (Trinidad and Tobago), and the Secretary-General's comments thereon;[11] the Secretary-General's report on the Transport and Communications Decade for Asia and the Pacific, 1985-1994;[12] and a letter of 2 July 1992 from the Chairman of the Economic Commission for Europe (ECE) to the President of the Economic and Social Council[13] on the situation within ECE caused by the lack of human resources and its effect on the efficiency of the Commission's activities.

Regional activities in environment and sustainable development

In an April report[14] to the General Assembly and the Economic and Social Council, submitted in response to a 1989 Assembly request,[15] the Secretary-General summarized further substantive follow-up by Governments and United Nations bodies to two 1987 Assembly resolutions[16] pertaining to the question of the environment and sustainable development. The report noted that United Nations activities in sustainable development focused on preparations for and contribution to the 1992 United Nations Conference on Environment and Development (UNCED), and outlined, among other things, activities of the regional commissions (see PART THREE, Chapter VIII).

ECA gave priority to achieving food self-sufficiency and security; reversing deforestation and conserving wildlife; preventing and reversing desertification and mitigating the impact of drought; ensuring effective management and use of water resources; managing coastal and marine resources; securing greater energy self-sufficiency; and managing demographic change, population pressure and human settlements.

ESCAP concentrated on environmental awareness-building; the greening of the development process; management of terrestrial ecosystems; and protection of the marine environment. Activities of ECE covered promotion of environmental impact assessment; economic instruments; linkages between environmental and trade policies; the Energy Efficiency 2000 programme; environmentally sound technologies; energy-labelling systems; and environmental improvement of transportation. ECLAC's activities included preparations of environmental management plans for sustainable agriculture in mountain ecosystems and for solid and toxic waste management in urban development; provision of guidelines and training in environmental impact assessment and environmental accounting; valuation of environmental management of marine resources; and technical cooperation to strengthen member countries' capability to implement environmentally sound and sustainable development.

By **decision 47/444** of 22 December, the General Assembly took note of the Secretary-General's report.

REFERENCES

[1]E/1992/35 (res. 520(XXIV)). [2]E/1992/31 (res. 48/12). [3]E/1992/34 (res. 191(XVI)). [4]YUN 1991, p. 288. [5]Ibid., ESC dec. 1991/302, 26 July 1991. [6]E/1992/33 (res. 728(XXVII)). [7]E/1992/65 & Add.1. [8]YUN 1977, p. 438, GA res. 32/197, 20 Dec. 1977. [9]TD/364. [10]E/1992/14 & Add.1 (Parts I & II). [11]E/1992/21 & Add.1. [12]E/1992/61 & Add.1. [13]E/1992/101 & Corr.1. [14]A/47/121-E/1992/15. [15]GA res. 44/227, 22 Dec. 1989. [16]YUN 1987, p. 661, GA res. 42/186, 11 Dec. 1987; p. 679, GA res. 42/187, 11 Dec. 1987.

Africa

In accordance with Economic and Social Council **decision 1992/213** of 7 February, ECA held its twenty-seventh session/eighteenth meeting of the Conference of Ministers at Addis Ababa, Ethiopia, from 20 to 23 April,[1] to focus on new directions in the 1990s. The Ministers undertook a preliminary review of the continent's economic and social performance in 1991 and prospects for 1992, including its transformation, recovery and adjustment, and considered the Commission's on-

going and planned activities and work programmes as reflected in reports of its subsidiary
bodies.

In his message to the Conference of Ministers,
the Secretary-General stated that African economies had, in the past decade, suffered dramatic
deterioration characterized by disproportionate
population growth, serious declines in standards
of living, worsening terms of trade and debt-
servicing burdens. The revitalization and strengthening of African economies was part of the global
perspective for international economic development, which included as a priority narrowing the
gap between the rich North and poor South
through solutions to the debt problem and strategies for development within a sustainable environment. In that regard, the New Agenda for the Development of Africa in the 1990s (UNNADAF),
adopted by the General Assembly in 1991[2] as a
successor arrangement to the United Nations Programme of Action for African Economic Recovery and Development 1986-1990 (UNPAAERD),[3]
could be used to build on past initiatives, serving
as instruments for the economic transformation
of the continent. Although some countries were
still plagued with civil strife, border disputes, environmental degradation, famine and refugee
problems, the Secretary-General was confident
that Africa would succeed in moving ahead with
its recovery and in improving the socio-economic
conditions of its people.

The Acting Executive Secretary of ECA observed in his statement that there was increasing
recognition of the need to step up intra-African
cooperation in order to accelerate economic integration, but cautioned that promoting the continent's economic and social transformation in the
1990s would become difficult as the attention of
Africa's major development partners shifted towards other regions, particularly Eastern Europe.
He noted that the Commission would devote the
forthcoming decade to the practical pursuit of priorities, focusing on specific problems of member
countries within the context of the various
subregional economic groupings.

The Conference of Ministers was preceded by
the thirteenth meeting of the Technical Preparatory Committee of the Whole (Addis Ababa, 13-
18 April), which adopted ECA's policy and
management framework for facing Africa's development challenges in the 1990s.[4] The framework
provided adjustments in the Commission's policy
orientation, programmes and management capacity, and identified the following areas of focus for
ECA's programme delivery: strengthening its advisory role on socio-economic questions; promoting regional cooperation and integration; enhancing the efficiency of the public sector; promoting
private initiatives and entrepreneurship; develop-

ing, disseminating and utilizing science and technology; ensuring a desirable balance between food
supply, population, human settlements and environment; fostering human-centred development;
achieving structural transformation and diversification of African economies; and promoting
women in development.

The Committee recommended the streamlining and rationalization of the Commission's structure and activities, and the revitalization of its
Multinational Programming and Operational
Centres (MULPOCs) to improve their service to the
subregional economic groupings. It endorsed the
first revision[5] of the Commission's medium-term
plan for 1992-1997[6] (see below) and updated the
1992-1993 programme of work. Noting the alarming decline in the level of extrabudgetary resources
for ECA's operational activities, the Committee requested the secretariat to alleviate the financial crisis through the promotion of income-generating
actions, use of restrictive budgetary measures and
resource mobilization targeted at multilateral and
bilateral donors. It further noted the establishment
of the Multidisciplinary Regional Advisory Group
as part of the new orientation of ECA advisory
services during the 1990s and endorsed its 1992
work programme.

The Committee reviewed the continent's socio-
economic development in 1991 and considered a
progress report on the implementation of regional
development strategies,[7] including the Lagos
Plan of Action,[8] the African Alternative Framework to Structural Adjustment Programmes for
Socio-economic Recovery and Transformation
(AAF-SAP)[9] and the African Charter for Popular
Participation in Development and Transformation,
adopted in 1990.[10]

The Conference of Ministers amended and endorsed the Committee's report,[11] including its
resolutions and decisions. The Ministers also took
note of the report and resolutions of the eleventh
meeting of the Conference of Ministers of the African Least Developed Countries (LDCs) (Addis
Ababa, 17-19 April),[12] and endorsed the African
Common Position on the African Programme for
Environment and Development as a regional input
to UNCED.

In its resolutions on strengthening the follow-
up mechanism of the Lagos Plan of Action in the
1990s[13] and on implementation of the Treaty establishing the African Economic Community,[14]
signed at Abuja, Nigeria, in June 1991,[15] the
Conference called on ECA, the Organization of
African Unity (OAU) and the African Development Bank (AfDB) to monitor and assist in the implementation of those initiatives through their joint
secretariat. The Ministers also adopted resolutions
concerning the restructuring and revitalization of
the United Nations in the economic and social

fields[16] and the strengthening of ECA to face Africa's development challenges in the 1990s,[17] and submitted them to the Economic and Social Council for action. By other resolutions and decisions, the Conference approved the 1992-1994 budget of the African Centre of Meteorological Applications for Development,[18] approved appointments to the Governing Council of the Institute for Economic Development and Planning[19] and endorsed amendments to the Statutes of the United Nations African Institute for the Prevention of Crime and the Treatment of Offenders concerning the composition of its Governing Board and financial resources.[20]

The conclusions of the twenty-seventh session of ECA/eighteenth meeting of the Conference of Ministers were summarized in their Final Declaration, which was communicated to the Secretary-General in June.[21]

ECONOMIC AND SOCIAL COUNCIL ACTION

On 31 July, on the recommendation of its Economic Committee, the Economic and Social Council adopted **resolution 1992/51** without vote.

Strengthening the Economic Commission for Africa to face Africa's development challenges in the 1990s

The Economic and Social Council,

Recalling the terms of reference of the Economic Commission for Africa, as adopted by the Economic and Social Council in its resolution 671(XXV) of 29 April 1958 and amended by resolutions 974 D (XXXVI), section I, of 5 July 1963, 1343(XLV) of 18 July 1968 and 1978/68 of 4 August 1978,

Recalling also the various resolutions that have implications on the mandate and operations of the Commission, including, in particular, General Assembly resolution 32/197 of 20 December 1977 on the restructuring of the economic and social sectors of the United Nations system, and Assembly resolutions 33/202 of 29 January 1979 and 44/211 of 21 December 1989,

Recalling further its endorsement in its decision 1991/302 of 26 July 1991 of resolution 718(XXVI) of 12 May 1991 of the Conference of Ministers of the Economic Commission for Africa on the revitalization of the mandate and operational framework of the regional commission for Africa,

Bearing in mind General Assembly resolutions 45/177 of 19 December 1990, 45/264 of 13 May 1991 and 46/235 of 13 April 1992 on the restructuring and revitalization of the United Nations in the economic, social and related fields, in which it was stated that the regional commissions should be enabled fully to play their role under the authority of the General Assembly and the Economic and Social Council, and that those regional commissions located in developing countries should be strengthened in the context of the overall objectives of the ongoing restructuring and revitalization process,

Reiterating the validity of the general orientation of the programme of work of the Commission, as outlined in the medium-term plan for the period 1992-1997, including the identified individual subprogrammes,

Convinced that the many and important changes that are taking place in the member States of the Commission, in the international environment and in the United Nations system as a whole will necessitate new approaches by the Commission in carrying out its mandate and new relationships with its constituency and partners, with a view to increasing its impact,

Having examined the in-depth analysis made by the Acting Executive Secretary of the Commission as contained in the document entitled "The Economic Commission for Africa in the 1990s: a policy and management framework for facing Africa's development challenges",

1. *Congratulates* the Acting Executive Secretary of the Economic Commission for Africa for taking the initiative to establish a task force to review and appraise the policy orientation, programmes and management capacity of the Commission and for his excellent analysis of the pertinent issues and the useful and innovative proposals he has made;

2. *Requests* the Executive Secretary of the Commission to ensure that there is a clear and concrete balance between the research and operational activities of the secretariat of the Commission and to focus all such activities on the specific realities and characteristics of the African region and on individual subregions;

3. *Also requests* the Executive Secretary of the Commission to ensure that its activities are fully grounded in sound data and information systems, through the strengthening of the Pan-African Documentation and Information System and providing it with adequate financial resources;

4. *Further requests* the Executive Secretary to ascertain that the implementation of all subprogrammes contained in the programme of work of the Commission is solidly based on the full attainment of the identified basic indicators of achievement of the objectives of the Commission, namely, strengthening the advisory role of the Commission on socio-economic questions; promoting regional cooperation and integration; enhancing the efficiency of the public sector; promoting private initiatives and entrepreneurship; development, dissemination and utilization of science and technology; ensuring a desirable balance between food supply, population, human settlements and environment; fostering human-centred development; achieving structural transformation and diversification of African economies; and promotion of women in development;

5. *Welcomes* the process of frequent and close consultations by the secretariat with member States and donors, including with their representatives at Addis Ababa, through regular briefing sessions;

6. *Recommends* the establishment, within existing resources, of a consultative mechanism that would advise the Executive Secretary on the grouping of conferences along specific themes, including the scheduling and preparation of conferences, meetings, seminars and workshops, taking into account the need to harmonize them with those of the Organization of African Unity and the African Development Bank to avoid duplication and achieve greater efficiency;

7. *Urges* the Executive Secretary to explore all possibilities for establishing or strengthening the relationships of the Commission with African intergovernmental organizations, the specialized agencies of the United Nations system, bilateral and multilateral development cooperation agencies and non-governmental organi-

zations, including, in particular, the possibility of establishing joint units or special programmes with the specialized agencies and the creation of a special unit within the secretariat of the Commission to coordinate the increased joint activities of the Commission with non-governmental organizations;

8. *Expresses appreciation* to the General Assembly for providing additional resources to the Multinational Programming and Operational Centres, and consequently recommends that, in conformity with resolution 702(XXV) of 19 May 1990 of the Conference of Ministers of the Economic Commission for Africa on transforming and strengthening the Multinational Programming and Operational Centres of the Commission, the Centres should be further strengthened through the redeployment of resources, should be given specific assignments with respect to technical assistance and advisory services for the execution of joint projects of member States within the framework of the intergovernmental organizations in their respective subregions, and should be enabled to act as the major subregional focal points for collecting and disseminating information on all aspects of economic cooperation and integration;

9. *Expresses its gratitude* to the General Assembly for providing the African Institute for Economic Development and Planning with four additional posts for the biennium 1992-1993, thus enabling the Institute to contribute to the process of strengthening the operational capacity of the Commission in meeting the challenges facing Africa in the 1990s, and requests the redeployment of resources which would enable the Institute to assume additional responsibility;

10. *Requests* the Executive Secretary, in close cooperation with the Secretary-General of the Organization of African Unity, to undertake a thorough examination of the problems and constraints facing the institutions sponsored by the Commission and subsequently to make concrete proposals aimed at alleviating the different problems and to consider alternative solutions such as merging some of the institutions;

11. *Appeals* to bilateral and multilateral donors to increase their financial and other forms of assistance to the Economic Commission for Africa to enable it to shoulder its responsibilities to member States in the form of extrabudgetary operational activities;

12. *Also requests* the Executive Secretary to undertake, as necessary, reforms in the structure of the secretariat so as to achieve full consistency with the new orientations recommended in the present resolution and attain greater efficiency and increased capacity for the secretariat to serve as an effective organ for the economic and social development of Africa;

13. *Further requests* the Executive Secretary to report on the implementation of the present resolution to the Conference of Ministers of the Economic Commission for Africa at its nineteenth meeting.

Economic and Social Council resolution 1992/51

31 July 1992   Meeting 42   Adopted without vote

Approved by Economic Committee (E/1992/108) without vote, 28 July (meeting 16); draft by Conference of Ministers of ECA (E/1992/65); agenda item 11.

Economic and social trends

Economic trends

Africa's overall economic performance, measured in terms of trends in total output, payments position, fiscal situation, external debt and price trends, was generally weak, according to a summary of the survey of economic and social conditions in Africa.[22] In 1992, the regional real output grew by only 1.5 per cent, down from an already discouraging gross domestic product (GDP) rate of 2.3 per cent in 1991. The combined output of the continent's 42 non–oil-exporting countries declined by 1.1 per cent, but that was partially compensated by a 3 per cent growth rate in the oil-exporting countries. Economic performance in a number of countries, notably Algeria, Liberia, Mozambique, Somalia, Togo and Zaire, was seriously affected by the unsettled political situation. Adverse international factors also continued to play a decisive role, mainly recessionary conditions in the countries members of the Organisation for Economic Cooperation and Development (OECD), Africa's major trading partners.

Despite considerable policy adjustments, the manufacturing sector grew by only 2 per cent in 1992, after a 0.3 per cent decline the previous year. Capacity utilization remained at a low 30 to 50 per cent level in most African countries, which continued to face a high degree of import dependence and constraining factors associated with structural adjustment programmes. The sector was adversely affected by poor agricultural performance, constrained foreign exchange situation and low foreign direct investment inflow, coupled with drastically reduced public investment in many countries. Structural limitations contributed to an overall decline of 0.8 per cent in the mining sector, while the production of oil increased by less than 1 per cent against 1991, totalling 338 million tonnes. The production level stagnated in the States members of the Organization of Petroleum Exporting Countries (OPEC), but rose by 3.4 per cent among the non-OPEC economies (Angola, Congo and Egypt), with Angola producing 27.4 million tonnes—a 10 per cent increase over 1991. The year saw intensified oil- and gas-exploration activities and efforts to improve the investment climate for foreign oil companies. In the non-fuel mining sector, however, prices fell due to the weakening of the base metal market, and the volume of zinc, gold and silver output grew only by 2.2, 2 and 0.4 per cent, respectively.

Annual inflation rates reached 63 per cent in 1992, compared with 36.3 per cent in 1991, excluding the economies of the franc zone (Benin, Cameroon, Central African Republic, Chad, Comoros, Congo, Côte d'Ivoire, Equatorial Guinea, Gabon, Mali, Niger, Senegal, Togo), which averaged 3.6

per cent inflation. The increase was greatest in Central Africa, due to hyper-inflation in Zaire, and in West Africa. In eastern and southern Africa, drought led to an average inflation rate of 60.5 per cent.

Macroeconomic policy in 1992 emphasized the liberalization and stabilization of economic systems, with particular focus on financial and fiscal sectors, factor markets, the price system and the role of the public and private sectors. Reform measures focused on fiscal discipline and resource rationalization, improvement of the expenditure/revenue ratio and ways to increase revenues, and tax reform. Some countries undertook measures to rationalize expenditure through containing growth in wages and, partly, reducing civil strife. Reform of the financial system concentrated on improving monetary control and coordination, enhancing the mobilization and allocation of domestic savings, and removing the rigidities of the banking system in general. There was also increased recourse to financial instruments, with a number of countries revising their interest and exchange-rate policies. During the year, currencies were devalued in Ethiopia, Malawi, Mauritania, Nigeria, the Sudan and Zambia, while exchange control was liberalized in Botswana, Mauritius, Nigeria and Uganda. The policy of State disengagement from the public sector continued as loss-making public enterprises were being sold in Chad, Morocco, Mozambique, Nigeria, the Sudan and Uganda. Privatization, however, was constrained by the indebtedness of those enterprises and the narrow capital base of the domestic private sector.

Prospects for 1993 depended critically on the removal of current external resource constraints through increased export earnings and investment flows, improved commodity prices and debt reduction. There were encouraging signs of a possible recovery in agriculture, with a considerable rebound forecast for southern Africa after the 1992 drought. Yet prospects were tainted by the existing uncertainty concerning peace and security in the region and by the stagnation in external trade.

External debt

By the end of 1992, the outstanding external debt of developing Africa was $281.8 billion, only $0.8 billion higher than in 1991, and accounted for 92.6 per cent of regional GDP, down from 94 per cent the previous year. Debt servicing represented 23.7 per cent of goods and services exports and continued to constrain import capacity and growth. Accumulations of arrears remained unabated, preventing African countries from creating an environment to attract foreign investment, particularly from private sources.

In addition to Egypt's measures to write off and reschedule a part of its debt, which generally levelled out the continent's external debt obligations, part of the long-term public debt was cancelled in the amount of $1 billion for Zambia and $200 million for Ethiopia. Similarly, Nigeria secured a review of terms for paying back $7 billion, while Algeria concluded a refinancing agreement for $2 billion. The net long-term financial flows to sub-Saharan Africa, estimated at $17.8 billion by the World Bank, contracted by $100 million against 1991, and budgetary problems in donor countries were increasingly affecting aid programmes and external development finance for Africa, even though UNNADAF estimated that beginning from 1992, a minimum of $30 billion would have to be mobilized for Africa every year, growing in real terms at a 4 per cent annual rate.

In April, the ECA Conference of Ministers welcomed the decision of the Secretary-General to make alleviation of the debt burden of the world's poorest countries a major priority for the United Nations, and called on members of the Commission to devote greater effort to debt management at the national level.[23]

Agriculture

In developing Africa, agricultural production declined by 1.5 per cent in 1992, compared to a 3.8 per cent increase in 1991, owing largely to the catastrophic drought in eastern and southern Africa, where output fell by 7.7 per cent. Dry conditions also prevailed in North Africa, mainly in Algeria and Morocco, causing a decline in production in those countries as well. Central and western Africa, however, registered growth of 2.3 and 4.2 per cent, respectively. Food was the sector most seriously affected by the poor agricultural performance. Aggregate cereal output in developing Africa dropped by 14.1 per cent to 75 million tonnes—falling an estimated 65 per cent in Morocco and 42.5 per cent in southern Africa. As a result, 40 million people faced food shortages in sub-Saharan Africa, and food import requirements for the region in 1992 amounted to 6 million tonnes, compared to 2 million in a normal year. For developing Africa as a whole, those requirements were estimated at 20.2 million tonnes, and the food aid needed was set at 5.5 million tonnes.

Except for tobacco, a negative growth rate was recorded for all other major industrial crops, including cocoa (-5.3 per cent), coffee (-6.1 per cent), tea (-10.3 per cent), cotton (-7.1 per cent) and sugar (-3.7 per cent), while prices either fell or remained depressed. Agricultural policy continued to focus on transformation through sound investment and liberalization measures; increased attention was also given to drought relief and rehabilitation, and environmental protection was emphasized in the agricultural policies of some countries.

Trade

The volume of exports for the region, totalling $70.8 billion, fell in 1992 by 6 per cent, and their value declined by 6.1 per cent. The purchasing power of exports registered a 9 per cent decline, compared with 3.4 per cent in 1991. As a result, developing Africa's share in world trade remained minimal and showed a decrease in export values of 2 per cent. Oil-exporting countries accounted for 70.5 per cent of the region's exports in 1992, but their earnings declined by 1.5 per cent because of a drop in oil prices and in export volumes. At the same time, import values rose by 9.3 per cent to reach $81 billion, with prices increasing by 3.2 per cent and volume by 3.6 per cent. The increase in import prices was essentially due to a 4.6 per cent rise in the prices of manufactured goods. Although the price of wheat increased by 17.7 per cent, food import prices increased only 1.6 per cent. As the value of exports dropped and imports expanded, the region's trade deficit swelled to $10.2 billion in 1992, up from $1.7 billion the previous year. Yet the services deficit improved from $19.7 billion to $18.7 billion, and unrequited transfers contracted by nearly $3 billion, as a result of reduced level of private transfers.

Commodity prices overall decreased by 1.3 per cent, up from a 14.3 per cent drop in 1991. Excluding oil prices, the decline was 7.3 per cent, against 4.7 per cent the previous year. Prices of beverages fell by 12.3 per cent, although tea prices recovered in 1992. Agricultural raw material prices improved by an average of 2.5 per cent, but cotton recorded a 24.1 per cent decline because of a large supply/demand imbalance on the world market. Metals and minerals prices dropped 2.6 per cent, with copper losing 2.3 per cent on average; nickel, 14 per cent; and iron ore, 4.9 per cent.

Subregional economic performance

Among the continent's subregions, the best results in 1992 were achieved in West Africa, where output grew by 3.3 per cent, although slightly lower than the 3.5 per cent recorded in 1991. Several countries, such as Ghana and Nigeria, showed a satisfactory performance, while others performed poorly and some experienced negative growth, notably Côte d'Ivoire and the Niger. Economic activity increased at a 5.8 per cent rate in the Sahelian subgroup, with the Sudan recording an exceptional GDP growth of some 11 per cent. The growth rates averaged 1.4 per cent in sub-Saharan Africa and 2.1 per cent in North Africa, where only Egypt and Tunisia recorded significant growth rates. In Central Africa, output fell by 1.2

per cent, largely due to the crisis in Zaire and the slow-down in Cameroon and Gabon. The decline in East Africa (2.2 per cent) and southern Africa (3.1 per cent) was largely due to civil strife in Angola, Mozambique and Somalia and the disastrous drought in most countries of the area.

In the least developed countries (LDCs) of Africa, real GDP growth decreased by 0.9 per cent after a drop of 0.4 per cent in 1991. Drought and political instability in Ethiopia, Zaire and Zambia and civil strife in Liberia, Rwanda, Somalia and southern Sudan were among the factors contributing to the poor performance. Agricultural output rose by only 0.8 per cent in 1992, down from 2.7 per cent in 1991, with as many as 14 African LDCs facing the threat of large-scale famine, according to the Food and Agriculture Organization of the United Nations (FAO). The financial distress in many LDCs was aggravated by a further drop in an already low rate of domestic savings, averaging some 7 per cent in 1991-1992.

Social trends

According to an ECA report on the African social situation,[24] the severe economic crisis that had engulfed Africa's social sector in the 1980s had not abated. Regional per capita incomes and real wages continued to decline, resulting in widespread malnutrition and starvation and leaving a large segment of the population to face primary poverty. Urban unemployment, which was 14 million in 1991, continued to rise and was projected to reach 44 million by the year 2000. The education, health, and food and nutrition sectors, among others, were characterized by social retrogression, compounded by unprecedented population growth rates and negative effects of inadequate structural adjustment programmes.

Severe budgetary pressures resulted in the reduction of real expenditure on education and health, leading to increasing school closures, declining school enrolment and attendance ratios, mounting repetition of classes, falling educational standards and shortages of teaching materials and teachers. The health situation was aggravated by the resurgence of previously controlled diseases, a rise in meningitis and malaria, lack of universal immunization, and depressed consumer imports of medicines and medical equipment. Mortality rates increased among all age groups, and the prevalence of the human immunodeficiency virus/acquired immunodeficiency syndrome (HIV/AIDS) had grown into a public health crisis; at current rates, it was estimated that close to 20 million Africans could be infected with the disease by 2000. In addition, the droughts affecting much of the continent caused mass displacements of people and posed a threat of hunger and starvation for millions in more than 11 countries.

Political instability, civil strife and military conflicts, coupled with domestic policy failures, contributed significantly to the continued crisis in the African social situation. The persisting problem of refugees exerted additional pressure on the continent's social sector: it was estimated that Africa was hosting close to 50 per cent of the total world refugee population in 1992. Another adverse factor was the fall in the region's commodity prices and the decline in terms of trade, the burden of external debt and inadequate resource flows, which necessitated a severe and prolonged compression of consumer imports.

On the positive side, increased recognition of Africa's problems and rising democratic activity in the region, although accompanied in some cases by unrest, were believed to be contributing to a gradual restoration of stability in African society.

Activities in 1992

Development policy and regional economic cooperation activities

The 1992 development policy and regional economic cooperation activities were geared towards implementation of the 1991 Abuja Treaty establishing the African Economic Community,[15] according to ECA's annual report covering 24 April 1992 through 6 May 1993.[25] The ECA secretariat and its MULPOCs provided assistance to African intergovernmental organizations and their member countries to promote the continent's economic integration. Advisory services dealt with the formulation and programming of integration projects under the United Nations Development Programme (UNDP) fifth (1992-1996) programming cycle, trade and maritime coastal links in Central Africa, the Rusumo hydroelectric centre and human resources capacity and capability development in eastern and southern Africa. A seminar on the production and marketing of embroidery products in the Economic Community of the Great Lakes Countries was organized for Central African countries, while workshops and field projects in eastern and southern Africa focused on human resources development, local production of school and university textbooks and the operationalization of the Eastern and Southern African Development and Information System. In West Africa, a number of seminars were held on issues related to integration through production.

The ECA Regional Multidisciplinary Advisory Group provided technical support to 12 training workshops and seminars on policy and development in such sectors as agriculture, energy, science and technology, human resources, and public administration. The Group also undertook 18 country missions and 20 advisory missions to intergovernmental organizations, including an exploratory mission to South Africa to create a framework for reintegrating that country into the rest of Africa. In response to requests from Governments and organizations, the Group carried out a variety of activities related to subregional economic community schemes, policy and development issues, development projects, training programmes, a multidisciplinary approach to the establishment of public administration and management institutions, application of national accounts to development and strategies for combating desertification and integrating environmental dimensions into economic planning.

In the field of socio-economic research and planning, the secretariat prepared biennial surveys of the economic and social conditions and social trends in Africa as a whole and in the African LDCs, and an annual economic report on the region. Other publications dealt with the mobilization and use of household savings in the African least developed, island and land-locked countries as well as with their food and agricultural policies, and with social security schemes and national development in Africa. The secretariat also provided advice on the modalities of the proposed African Foundation for Research and Development and the Research and Development Forum for Science-Led Development in Africa, whose trust became operational in October.

Statistical development

In its annual report covering 14 May 1991 through 23 April 1992,[1] ECA noted that the level and quality of African statistics had deteriorated during the past two decades due to economic crises that led to public spending cuts; weak interest in quantitative information for economic planning; competition between external and internal demands for statistical data; inadequate infrastructure for data collection, analysis and dissemination; and poor management of statistical services.

Issues related to statistical development and economic planning and forecasting were examined by the Joint Conference of African Planners, Statisticians and Demographers at its seventh session (Addis Ababa, 2-7 March), which considered the Strategy for the Implementation of the Addis Ababa Plan of Action for Statistical Development in Africa in the 1990s.[26] In April,[27] the ECA Conference of Ministers adopted the Strategy and urged its members to set up needs assessment/programme review and strategy development teams to identify needs and priorities and to formulate draft five- to ten-year national statistical development plans. Also in April,[28] the Ministers requested the secretariat to continue strengthening and expanding its work on short-term economic forecasting in Africa and called on bilateral and multi-lateral donors to support the establishment of forecasting systems in African countries.

Activities in 1992 were centred on building national statistical capability and self-reliance. The secretariat undertook technical advisory missions in the areas of training and household surveys, and provided technical support in census project development/census organization, census cartography, sampling, data processing and civil registration/vital statistics. It prepared publications on vertical and horizontal collaboration in data processing within national statistical offices and on alternatives to population censuses in small area statistics, and continued to issue the *Statistical Training Programme for Africa (STPA) News* and the *Foreign Trade Statistics for Africa* series. Among other publications were African socio-economic indicators for 1989 and for 1990-1991; the African compendium of environment statistics for 1991; a directory of African statisticians for 1992; and the *African Statistical Yearbook, 1988-1989, Part 4 — East and Southern Africa*.

The Coordinating Committee on African Statistical Development held its second annual meeting in Kenya in November.

Information for development

The Technical Preparatory Committee of the Whole, noting that data and information were central to socio-economic development planning, observed that the information infrastructure in Africa was largely unprepared to meet information needs in the 1990s, owing to inadequate organization of existing data and information, insufficient use of facilities and resources, insensitivity of information structures to the needs of development planners, and lack of attention given to the role of information by decision-makers in many countries. While information technology, particularly computers, was well-disseminated, its impact on the quality of socio-economic information in the region had been negligible. In that regard, the Committee noted with satisfaction the work of the Pan-African Development Information System (PADIS) in sensitizing African countries to the use of information technology for development, as well as the creation of a Working Group on ECA's Information Systems to help the secretariat integrate its activities in this area.

In April,[29] the ECA Conference of Ministers set out measures for its members to adopt in order to ensure the delivery of technical assistance by PADIS, called on them to adopt policies related to the acquisition and use of appropriate information technology and requested PADIS to continue coordinating development information to respond to the continent's pressing problems. The secretariat was requested to collaborate with OAU and AfDB in harmonizing and standardizing information sources and systems to facilitate regional economic cooperation.

During 1992, PADIS continued to provide technical assistance (advisory services and training) to member States. Training courses were offered at Addis Ababa in reprography techniques (10 October–13 November), selected aspects of information technology (19-20 November) and database development (November/December). Workshops on digital communications and on science and technology networking were held (Nairobi, Kenya, August) to discuss the use of digital radio and packet satellite technology in development communications and electronic networks in Africa, including training in project development. Preparations were initiated for a joint project of PADIS and the International Development Research Centre (Canada) (Ottawa, October), and an African pilot project for an economic and commercial information network, established by the Chambers of Commerce and Industry of Developing Countries members of the Group of 77, was launched in Cameroon in December. The Development Information Day was celebrated on 18 November at ECA headquarters. A subregional workshop on processing, analysis and dissemination of household survey data was organized for English-speaking African countries in cooperation with the International Labour Organisation (ILO).

Other activities included a meeting on information processing using Arabic letters (Tunis, Tunisia, 29 June–12 July); a review of the database and information system development project for the Kagera Basin Organization (Kigali, Rwanda, May); and training courses on PADIS methodologies and the use of computer software, and on electronic mail and computer-mediated communications. The secretariat maintained databases on socio-economic, scientific and technical aspects of Africa's development and on African experts in those fields, and provided technical assistance to UNDP in establishing a database of Nigerian experts. It also published its quarterly *Newsletter* and four issues of the *Divindex-Africa*, and updated the *Directory of African Experts*, the *Directory of ECA-sponsored Institutions*, and the *Directory of Development Institutions*.

The System's role and functioning was reviewed by the Regional Technical Committee for PADIS and the Standing Committee on the Harmonization and Standardization of Documentation and Information Systems, which met from 18 to 20 November.

Public administration and finance

ECA provided assistance to its members in improving and strengthening their public administration, management and fiscal systems, institutions and processes as well as the performance of public enterprises, public financial management and the promotion of entrepreneurship. The secretariat completed technical publications on measures to stimulate, develop, and promote indigenous entrepreneurial capability in Africa, as well as measures to improve management capacity, motivation and productivity in African public enterprises, and on current trends in Africa's public expenditure programming. Other publications dealt with public administration and management innovations to enhance popular participation in the design and implementation of national development programmes; current trends in the restructuring of taxation systems for adequate mobilization of domestic resources; and the impact of automation and modern technology on financial management in public enterprises.

Regional training workshops were held on strengthening the managerial and administrative capacity of public enterprises and various approaches to privatization in Africa (Khartoum, the Sudan, September), and on improvement in tax administration (Yaoundé, Cameroon, June). Two senior policy workshops and a regional conference were organized under the Special Action Programme for Administration and Management in Africa, funded by UNDP. National training workshops in 1992 focused on reforming taxation systems, policies and tax administration (Lusaka, Zambia, September/October) and on senior financial management in the public sector (Lusaka, March).

International trade and development finance

ECA's activities in trade and development finance focused on mobilizing financial resources for development through indigenous banking and financial institutions and improving the region's position in world trade and at international multilateral trade negotiations.

The Technical Preparatory Committee of the Whole, considering issues related to UNCTAD VIII (see above), noted that Africa's interests were not reflected in the common position of the Group of 77 at the session due to the continent's poor participation. The Committee further observed that negotiation frameworks offered by UNCTAD and the General Agreement on Tariffs and Trade (GATT) were important for the region, and that it should strive to improve its negotiating position.

The ECA Conference of Ministers noted with concern that most African financial institutions had been ineffective in mobilizing resources to finance the development process, and that imbalances between the volume of savings and investment requirements remained large and perpetuated the continent's overdependence on external development financing. The Ministers

called upon African countries to implement financial reform programmes and pursue policies aimed at raising real incomes and savings, especially in rural areas, and requested the secretariat to undertake case studies on obstacles to the mobilization of financial resources.[30] By another resolution,[31] ECA, OAU, AfDB and the African Centre for Monetary Studies were requested to assist member States in monitoring the evolution of international monetary systems, particularly the European Monetary System, and in evaluating their possible impact on the monetary and financial arrangements in African countries. In an effort to give impetus to Africa's monetary integration, the Conference called on its members to accelerate the ratification of the Treaty establishing the African Economic Community.

In 1992, the secretariat prepared a number of studies on the continent's external debt situation and the impact of initiatives for alleviating the debt burden, as well as on the creation of an ECA database on Africa's debt profile and on the impact of recent international developments on net resource transfers to African countries. It also continued to issue information on trade opportunities for African businessmen and the *African Trade Bulletin*, and published a study on the role of financial institutions in facilitating and promoting intra-African trade.

Workshops were organized in southern and eastern Africa on facilitation of trade and investment flows and payments in the subregion (Mauritius, June); savings and development of small-scale enterprises (Gaborone, Botswana, June); and facilitation of intra-regional economic activity (Harare, Zimbabwe, 30 November–2 December). A meeting of the Working Party of the African Governors of the World Bank and the International Monetary Fund (Arusha, United Republic of Tanzania, August) discussed issues related to monetary and financial policies. AfDB and the subregional committees of the Association of African Central Banks for West Africa and eastern and southern Africa also held their meetings in 1992.

Other activities included a fourth Trade Fair of the Preferential Trade Area of Eastern and Southern African States (Dar-es-Salaam, United Republic of Tanzania, July); a ninth East African Central Banks course (Nairobi, 6 July–14 August); an international conference on promoting capital markets in Africa (Abuja, November); and a sixth all-Africa Trade Fair (Bulawayo, Zimbabwe, 2-10 September), organized by OAU.

Industrial development

The secretariat pursued activities aimed at revitalizing and restructuring the industrial sector through supporting national and multinational resource-based and core industries. In the context of the second Industrial Development Decade for Africa, emphasis was placed on strengthening the technological and entrepreneurial capabilities of African countries. The secretariat prepared a review of African industry, a directory of project profiles on small-scale industries and a manual for entrepreneurship-development trainers in those industries, and issued publications on national and subregional industrial priorities, the structure of industrial enterprises in the informal sector, sustainable financing of selected industrial projects, the role of industrial free zones in African industrialization, guidelines for the manufacture of agricultural tools and other equipment by small-scale engineering industries and possibilities and perspectives for the production of basic chemicals from natural gas. Seminars on comparative advantage for industrial development and on policies for the promotion of small-scale industries were held in West Africa.

Second Industrial Development Decade for Africa

In April,[32] the ECA Conference of Ministers endorsed the resolution adopted by the Conference of African Ministers of Industry at its tenth meeting, held in July 1991,[33] adopting the draft programme for the second Industrial Development Decade for Africa (IDDA II), 1991-2000. In a separate resolution,[34] the Conference of Ministers adopted the programme and requested ECA to submit it through the Economic and Social Council for adoption by the General Assembly at its 1992 session. It also decided to establish a ten-member working group to monitor implementation of the programme, and appealed to the Assembly and United Nations funding agencies to provide adequate financial support to programme-related activities. The General Conference of the United Nations Industrial Development Organization (UNIDO) had also endorsed the programme in November 1991 and recommended it for adoption by the Assembly in 1992.

In May, the Secretary-General submitted the programme to the Economic and Social Council.[35]

The programme of IDDA II incorporated strategic approaches and an action-oriented programme for self-sustained development through industrialization, focusing on the industrial expansion of major sectors, promotion of small- and medium-scale industries and entrepreneurship development, development of physical and institutional infrastructure and human resources and consolidation programmes aimed at rehabilitating and regenerating existing industries, improving the performance of public enterprises and enhancing complementarity between the public and private sector. It also included programmes for the

industrialization of Africa's LDCs, proposed ways of financing the Decade, set out possible mechanisms for coordinating and monitoring the implementation of IDDA II and provided breakdowns by subregion.

ECONOMIC AND SOCIAL COUNCIL ACTION

On 31 July 1992, by **decisions 1992/293** and **1992/295**, respectively, the Economic and Social Council took note of the decision of the ECA Conference of Ministers on industrial development in Africa[32] and the Secretary-General's note.[35]

On the same date, the Council, on the recommendation of its Economic Committee, adopted **resolution 1992/44** without vote.

Second Industrial Development Decade for Africa (1991-2000)

The Economic and Social Council,

Recalling General Assembly resolution 44/237 of 22 December 1989, in which the Assembly proclaimed the period 1991-2000 the Second Industrial Development Decade for Africa, and Assembly decision 46/458 of 20 December 1991 on the programme for the Second Decade,

Recalling also General Assembly resolution 46/151 of 18 December 1991, in which the Assembly adopted the United Nations New Agenda for the Development of Africa in the 1990s, which identifies the Second Decade as a major programme for African regional economic integration,

Recalling further its resolution 1991/81 of 26 July 1991 on the Second Decade,

Stressing the need to integrate the programme for the Second Decade into the overall framework of the United Nations New Agenda for the Development of Africa in the 1990s, in particular the commitment of African countries and the international community to promote domestic and foreign direct investment in Africa, as reflected in the relevant paragraphs of the New Agenda,

Recalling the relevant provisions of Agenda 21, adopted by the United Nations Conference on Environment and Development, held at Rio de Janeiro from 3 to 14 June 1992,

Considering resolution GC.4/Res.8 of 22 November 1991 of the Fourth General Conference of the United Nations Industrial Development Organization, in which the General Conference adopted the programme for the Second Decade as one of the top priority programmes of that organization and recommended its adoption by the General Assembly at its forty-seventh session, through the Economic and Social Council at its substantive session of 1992,

Considering also resolution 739(XXVII) of 22 April 1992 of the Conference of Ministers of the Economic Commission for Africa, in which the Conference of Ministers adopted the programme for the Second Decade, and decision 1(XXVII) of 22 April 1992, in which the Conference of Ministers recommended the adoption of the programme by the General Assembly at its forty-seventh session, through the Economic and Social Council at its substantive session of 1992, and the provision to the Economic Commission for Africa of adequate resources to enable it to support the African countries and subregional organizations in the implementation of their programmes for the Second Decade,

Cognizant of the appeal made by the Council of Ministers of the Organization of African Unity, in resolution CM/Res.1399(LVI) of 28 June 1992, to the General Assembly to adopt, at its forty-seventh session, the programme for the Second Decade, and of the endorsement of the programme by the Assembly of Heads of State and Government of the Organization of African Unity in its decision AHG/Dec.2 (XXVIII) of 1 July 1992,

1. *Endorses* the programme for the Second Industrial Development Decade for Africa, including the national, subregional and regional components;

2. *Recommends* that the General Assembly, at its forty-seventh session, adopt the programme for the Second Decade;

3. *Recommends* that the General Assembly adjust the period for the programme for the Second Decade, established in its resolution 44/237, to cover the years 1993-2002;

4. *Notes* the efforts already undertaken in Africa to establish an environment to attract domestic and foreign investment, calls for further efforts in this regard, and urges the international community to take the necessary steps to encourage direct foreign investment and support the policy changes undertaken in African countries;

5. *Recommends also* that the General Assembly urge the African countries, financial institutions and the specialized agencies of the United Nations system to adopt an integrated approach to the implementation of the programme for the Second Decade, taking full account of the United Nations New Agenda for the Development of Africa in the 1990s;

6. *Recommends further* that the General Assembly urge the Director-General of the United Nations Industrial Development Organization, the Executive Secretary of the Economic Commission for Africa, the institutions and agencies of the United Nations system, the African States and subregional and regional organizations to integrate the relevant provisions of Agenda 21, adopted by the United Nations Conference on Environment and Development, in the implementation of the Second Decade;

7. *Appeals* to the international community, particularly bilateral and multilateral funding institutions, to increase significantly their contributions to the industrial sector in African countries so as to ensure the successful and sustained implementation of the programme for the Second Decade;

8. *Urges* international financial institutions, in particular the World Bank, the International Monetary Fund and the African Development Bank, to ensure full support for the programme for the Second Decade and the effective implementation of that programme at the national and subregional levels;

9. *Reiterates its recommendation* that the General Assembly provide the Economic Commission for Africa with adequate resources to enable it to assist African countries and organizations effectively in the implementation of the programme for the Second Industrial Development Decade for Africa.

Economic and Social Council resolution 1992/44

31 July 1992   Meeting 42   Adopted without vote

Approved by Economic Committee (E/1992/108) without vote, 28 July (meeting 16); draft by Vice-Chairman (E/1992/C.1/L.17), based on informal consultations on draft by Pakistan for Group of 77 (E/1992/C.1/L.3); agenda item 11.

GENERAL ASSEMBLY ACTION

On 22 December 1992, on the recommendation of the Second (Economic and Financial) Committee, the General Assembly adopted **resolution 47/177** without vote.

Second Industrial Development Decade for Africa (1991-2000)

The General Assembly,

Recalling its resolution 44/237 of 22 December 1989, by which it proclaimed the period 1991-2000 the Second Industrial Development Decade for Africa, and its decision 46/458 of 20 December 1991 on the programme for the Second Decade,

Recalling also its resolution 46/151 of 18 December 1991, by which it adopted the United Nations New Agenda for the Development of Africa in the 1990s, which identifies the Second Decade as a major programme for African regional economic integration,

Recalling further Economic and Social Council resolution 1991/81 of 26 July 1991 on the Second Decade,

Stressing the need to integrate the programme for the Second Decade into the overall framework of the United Nations New Agenda for the Development of Africa in the 1990s, in particular the commitment of African countries and the international community to promote domestic and foreign direct investment in Africa, as reflected in the relevant paragraphs of the New Agenda,

Recalling the relevant provisions of Agenda 21, adopted by the United Nations Conference on Environment and Development,

Considering resolution GC.4/Res.8 of 22 November 1991 of the fourth General Conference of the United Nations Industrial Development Organization, in which the General Conference adopted the programme for the Second Decade as one of the top priority programmes of that organization and recommended its adoption by the General Assembly at its forty-seventh session, through the Economic and Social Council at its substantive session of 1992,

Considering also resolution 739(XXVII) of 22 April 1992 of the Conference of Ministers of the Economic Commission for Africa, in which the Conference of Ministers adopted the programme for the Second Decade, and decision 1(XXVII) of 22 April 1992, in which the Conference of Ministers recommended the adoption of the programme by the General Assembly at its forty-seventh session, through the Economic and Social Council at its substantive session of 1992, and the provision to the Economic Commission for Africa of adequate resources to enable it to support the African countries and subregional organizations in the implementation of their programmes for the Second Decade,

Taking into account the industrial development aspects of the Special Programme for Africa of the World Bank,

Cognizant of the appeal made to the General Assembly by the Council of Ministers of the Organization of African Unity in its resolution CM/Res. 1399(LVI) of 28 June 1992 to adopt, at its forty-seventh session, the programme for the Second Decade, and of the endorsement of the programme by the Assembly of Heads of State and Government of the Organization of African Unity in its decision AHG/Dec. 2(XXVIII) of 1 July 1992,

Considering Economic and Social Council resolution 1992/44 of 31 July 1992, in which the Council endorsed the programme and recommended, *inter alia*, that the General Assembly, at its forty-seventh session, adopt the programme,

1. *Adopts* the programme for the Second Industrial Development Decade for Africa, including the national, subregional and regional components contained therein;

2. *Decides* to adjust the period for the programme for the Second Decade, established in its resolution 44/237, to cover the years 1993-2002;

3. *Takes note* of the efforts already undertaken in Africa to establish an environment to attract domestic and foreign investment, calls for further efforts in this regard and urges the international community to take the necessary steps to encourage direct foreign investment and support the policy changes undertaken in African countries;

4. *Urges* the African countries, financial institutions and specialized agencies of the United Nations system to adopt an integrated approach to the implementation of the programme for the Second Decade, taking full account of the United Nations New Agenda for the Development of Africa in the 1990s;

5. *Urges* the Director-General of the United Nations Industrial Development Organization, the Executive Secretary of the Economic Commission for Africa, the institutions and agencies of the United Nations system and the African States and subregional and regional organizations to integrate the relevant provisions of Agenda 21, adopted by the United Nations Conference on Environment and Development, in the implementation of the Second Decade;

6. *Appeals* to the international community, particularly bilateral and multilateral funding institutions, to increase significantly their contributions to the industrial sector in African countries so as to ensure the successful and sustained implementation of the programme for the Second Decade;

7. *Urges* international financial institutions, in particular the World Bank, the International Monetary Fund and the African Development Bank, to ensure full support for the programme for the Second Decade and the effective implementation of the programme at the national and subregional levels;

8. *Requests* the Secretary-General to provide the Economic Commission for Africa with adequate resources to enable it to assist African countries and organizations effectively in the implementation of the current programme for the Second Decade;

9. *Also requests* the Secretary-General, in cooperation with the Director-General of the United Nations Industrial Development Organization, the relevant institutions and agencies of the United Nations system and the African States and subregional and regional organizations to undertake a mid-term evaluation of the implementation of the programme for the Second Decade, in 1998, and to submit a report thereon to the General Assembly at its fifty-fourth session, and also to submit to the Assembly biennial progress reports on the implementation of the present resolution.

General Assembly resolution 47/177

22 December 1992   Meeting 93   Adopted without vote

Approved by Second Committee (A/47/717/Add.1) without vote, 11 December (meeting 50); draft by Vice-Chairman (A/C.2/47/L.79), based on informal consultations on draft by Mauritius for African States (A/C.2/47/L.50); agenda item 12.

Meeting numbers. GA 47th session: 2nd Committee 3-9, 34-37, 40, 42, 43, 45, 46, 48-50; plenary 93.

Transport and communications

Activities in the transport and communications sector included a seminar on the establishment of a multinational company for transport operations on Lakes Kivu and Tanganyika, a technical consultative meeting on transit traffic, a second special meeting of the Conference of African Ministers responsible for Telecommunications (Abidjan, Côte d'Ivoire, May), a meeting of the African information and telecommunication study group (Nairobi, July) and the African regional telecommunications conference (Gaborone). Intergovernmental meetings of experts were held on the development of cooperation among African ports, trans-African highways and gas transportation. A regional seminar on railway restructuring was organized by the World Bank. An ad hoc expert group meeting reviewed proposals and guidelines for the development of subregional and regional cooperation in shipping, prepared by ECA. The Ministerial Conference of West and Central African States on Maritime Transport, the Port Management Association for West and Central Africa and the General Assembly and Symposium of the Union of African Railways also met during the year.

The secretariat issued guidelines on the establishment of inland container depots along the main transport corridors in Africa, and for the improvement of clearing and forwarding operations to facilitate seaborne trade. It also prepared a study on African gas pipelines and draft statutes for the Trans-African Highways Bureau. Other publications focused on port dues and charges for cargo handling and their impact on port efficiency, development of standardized maintenance management systems, rehabilitation and modernization programmes for railway services, and improvement of maintenance and repair workshops for rolling stock in African railways networks.

Transport and Communications Decade

In April, the Technical Preparatory Committee of the Whole[11] considered a progress report[36] on the implementation of the second United Nations Transport and Communications Decade in Africa (UNTACDA II),[37] which was adopted by the Economic and Social Council in July 1991[38] and endorsed by the General Assembly later that year.[39]

The Committee recommended that the programme be implemented in a way that ensured proper linkages with other economic sectors. Calling for more coordination between UNTACDA II and IDDA II, it urged ECA to prepare a plan of action for harmonizing the activities of the two Decades. The Committee also requested finalization of a review of guidelines for project identification, especially those related to railway projects, and recommended that more emphasis be placed on research in transport equipment maintenance, transport modes and applied research for alleviating the burden on women transporting goods from rural to urban areas. It particularly welcomed the memorandum signed between the World Bank and ECA inviting donor participants in sub-Saharan Africa's Special Transport Programme to launch activities compatible with the UNTACDA II programme.

The ECA Conference of Ministers, having taken note of the Committee's deliberations related to the implementation of the Decade, urged its members to establish national coordination committees and to revitalize the operation of the existing ones, and requested the General Assembly to provide the Commission, as the Decade's lead agency, with the necessary regular budgetary resources.[40] By **decision 1992/294** of 31 July, the Economic and Social Council endorsed the decision of the Conference.

Initial activities of the Decade included the first meeting of the UNTACDA II working group on strategies for development of transport and communications equipment, organized by ECA and attended by OAU, UNDP and UNIDO, as well as a training workshop on the design and management of road safety programmes.

Europe-Africa permanent link through the Strait of Gibraltar

A 1989 cooperation agreement between Morocco and Spain included a study of institutional schemes for implementing the project of linking Europe and Africa through the Strait of Gibraltar, as well as measures for its promotion at the international level. The Economic and Social Council, in 1991, had requested the Executive Secretaries of ECA and ECE to prepare an evaluation report for submission to the Council in 1993.[41]

ECONOMIC AND SOCIAL COUNCIL ACTION

On 31 July 1992, the Economic and Social Council, acting on the recommendation of its Economic Committee, adopted **resolution 1992/45** without vote.

Europe-Africa permanent link through the Strait of Gibraltar

The Economic and Social Council,

Recalling its resolution 1991/74 of 26 July 1991 and other relevant resolutions concerning the Europe-Africa permanent link through the Strait of Gibraltar, and the ac-

tivities that the Executive Secretaries of the Economic Commission for Africa and the Economic Commission for Europe were requested to carry out regarding the preparation of an evaluation report on the studies relating to the project in the period 1982-1993 for submission to the Economic and Social Council at its substantive session of 1993,

Conscious of the contribution of the project to the development of transport and to physical integration at the regional and interregional levels,

Noting that its resolution 1991/74 does not impose any financial burden on the budgets of the two Commissions concerned, since the Governments of Morocco and Spain are making available most of the financial resources needed to perform the activities mandated in that resolution,

Bearing in mind the necessary involvement of experts from the Economic Commission for Africa and the Economic Commission for Europe in coordinating the evaluation process requested in Council resolution 1991/74,

Recalling that in that resolution it called upon the Secretary-General to allocate as far as possible sufficient resources to the two Commissions, within existing priorities, for the preparation of the above-mentioned evaluation report,

Noting that the Secretary-General has not been able to allocate the necessary resources from within existing appropriations,

Requests the Secretary-General, taking account of relevant priorities, to provide the Economic Commission for Africa and the Economic Commission for Europe, within existing resources for the relevant sections of the programme budget for the biennium 1992-1993, with the necessary budgetary resources to enable them to prepare effectively and efficiently the evaluation report requested by the Economic and Social Council in its resolution 1991/74.

Economic and Social Council resolution 1992/45

31 July 1992   Meeting 42   Adopted without vote

Approved by Economic Committee (E/1992/108) without vote, 28 July (meeting 16); draft by Vice-Chairman (E/1992/C.1/L.16), based on informal consultations on draft sponsored by France, Greece, Italy, Morocco, Spain (E/1992/C.1/L.6); agenda item 11.

Science and technology

Acting on the conclusions of the Intergovernmental Committee of Experts for Science and Technology Development at its seventh meeting, held at Addis Ababa in November 1991, the ECA Conference of Ministers requested the Executive Secretary to prepare a report on the possibilities of establishing a Conference of Ministers of Science and Technology for Development.[42] In a separate resolution,[43] the Conference urged members of ECA to take explicit individual and collective measures to build up their endogenous capabilities in science and technology.

During 1992, activities focused on strengthening policies and institutional infrastructure for science and technology in African countries and promoting regional and interregional cooperation in that area. A high-level expert meeting on science and technology (Bujumbura, Burundi, May) discussed the role of technology in industrialization and regional economic integration. An ad hoc expert group meeting (Addis Ababa, October) considered various applications of nuclear science and technology for agricultural production and food preservation. A technical publication on guidelines and methodologies for the planning and management of science and technology policies for development was issued by the secretariat.

Marine affairs

In the field of marine affairs, the secretariat prepared a technical study on current status, policies, strategies and legal framework for developing marine resources in selected African countries, and provided advisory services and technical assistance to several States regarding development of institutions, human resources and science and technology in the marine sector.

Natural resources

Activities in the field of mineral resources were geared towards improving institutional capacity for mineral resources development, policy formulation in small-scale mining strategies and dissemination of information for the mining sector. Advisory services were provided on the development of gold deposits in the Liptako-Gourma region; restructuring of the national mining survey and improvement of the small-scale gold-mining sector in Equatorial Guinea; feasibility of establishing a mineral processing plant in Burkina Faso; and negotiations with donors regarding environmental aspects of developing the Mount Nimba iron deposit in Guinea. Technical assistance was extended to the Undugu Group (an intergovernmental economic group of Sahelian countries) in drafting a framework for cooperation, to the Central African Mineral Resources Development Centre in defining strategies to revitalize the institution and to the Eastern and Southern African Mineral Resources Development Centre to prepare project documents for submission to potential donors. The secretariat participated in an international seminar on the role of the mineral sector in Africa's economic development, organized by UNCTAD (Ouarzazate, Morocco, 27-30 April), and prepared technical publications on the establishment of African mineral associations of mining and related industrial operators; the status of small-scale mining in Africa and strategies for its development; and the environment and mineral resources development and use.

Under the water resources subprogramme, the secretariat assisted member States in coordinating and harmonizing their activities in the development of natural resources within the transboundary river/lake basin areas. It published an information bulletin on water activities in the region and a directory of African water specialists, and offered advisory services to Cameroon to re-

view the creation of water points in the Menchoum region.

ECA's efforts in cartography and remote sensing focused on the development of technological, institutional and human resources capabilities in data acquisition, analysis and use for natural resources and environmental management, as well as on policies and strategies in surveying, mapping and remote sensing in Africa. The *Cartography and Remote Sensing Bulletin for Africa* was issued in 1992. Technical assistance was provided to the African Organization for Cartography and Remote Sensing, the Regional Centre for Training in Aerospace Surveys and the Regional Centre for Services in Surveying, Mapping and Remote Sensing.

Energy

ECA continued to assist its members in energy planning and management. The secretariat issued guidelines on petroleum legislation in African countries and a compendium of rules and regulations in the continent's oil-producing States, and provided technical advice to the African Regional Centre for Solar Energy in Burundi in coping with its managerial and financial difficulties. It also cooperated with the World Bank in formulating and monitoring a project on rationalization of petroleum supply in sub-Saharan Africa, including a meeting of governmental experts from eastern African countries on the subject (Nairobi, 20-21 January), and in organizing a seminar on energy policy and the environment (Addis Ababa, 9-11 November), which focused on strengthening energy policy research and management in Africa. ECA held discussions with other regional commissions on interregional project development within the framework of the Global Energy Efficiency 21/Energy Efficiency 2000 project (Geneva, October), following an ad hoc meeting on the subject (Geneva, 3-5 March).

Food and agriculture

Activities in the area of food and agriculture included seminars on training needs in agricultural development planning and programming, four meetings for Central and West African countries on critical food security issues and workshops and field projects in eastern and southern Africa on food self-sufficiency and food processing and storage. Advisory services were provided to improve control of the tsetse fly under the Kagera basin project and to test livestock models in Central and West Africa, with the aim of expanding the region's livestock resources.

In 1992, the secretariat distributed to member States a progress report on the application of AAF-SAP in the agricultural sector, published two issues of the *Rural Progress* newsletter and a manual on measures for expanding food availability through the exploitation of non-conventional food resources, and issued a comparative analysis of the structural advantages of African and South-East Asian agricultural export products as well as guidelines for loss reduction in the cattle subsector with emphasis on reproductive wastage.

Other technical publications dealt with the impact of the 1992 European economic integration measures on African agriculture, assessment of inland and marine aquaculture development programmes, the impact of biotechnology on agricultural development, measures to coordinate maize research networks in eastern and southern Africa, the impact of structural adjustment programmes on the food situation in West Africa, measures to develop institutional aspects of rural transformation in selected African countries, the impact of food aid on the continent's food security and self-sufficiency and the role of agricultural marketing in economic development.

Fisheries

In response to a 1990 request of the General Assembly,[44] the Secretary-General in June submitted a report on cooperation in fisheries in Africa,[45] prepared in close consultation with FAO. The report provided an overview of African fishery development and reviewed the status and prospects for cooperation, including short- and medium-term cooperation needs in resource management; development planning and programming; training; technology transfers and support to private entrepreneurs; and coordination of regional and subregional fishery programmes.

According to the report, the total potential of African waters, both marine and inland, was estimated at some 9 million tonnes per year. Of that amount, marine fisheries accounted for 6.8 million tonnes, with West Africa (from Morocco to Namibia) accounting for nearly 74 per cent. As the continent's fishery exports had increased threefold over the past decade, the fishery sector had become a vital source of foreign exchange, job creation and investment potential as well as protein supply. It was generating considerable social and economic benefits, and could be considered one of the healthiest sectors in Africa, with its economic indicators showing positive trends.

At the same time, marine and inland fishery resources were under severe pressure almost everywhere in Africa. Given fiercer competition and increasingly demanding health and ecological standards on world markets, the continent also needed urgent action to sustain and improve its trade position and to speed up technological advances in its fishery sector. As most African countries had no high-sea fishing fleets and shared stocks among several exclusive economic zones, cooperation was

essential at the international, regional and subregional levels to negotiate fishing agreements, to evaluate and monitor stocks, to develop regulations for and carry out joint administration and control of fisheries and to meet training needs. The report stated that national and regional development-planning and resource-management efforts had to be urgently reinforced in order to meet those challenges without further endangering the resource base, as well as to solve the complex problems related to the environment and to the unbalanced distribution of expertise, experience and technical and financial resources.

The Secretary-General noted that the framework for sustained international and regional collaboration in fishery management had been laid by the 1982 United Nations Convention on the Law of the Sea[46] and developed through the Strategy for Fisheries Management and Development, adopted by the World Conference on Fisheries Management and Development in 1984,[47] and the Regional Convention on Fisheries Cooperation and the Programme of Action, adopted by the Ministerial Conference on Cooperation in Fisheries among the African States Bordering the Atlantic Ocean in 1991.[48] He underscored the importance of complementarity between such organizations as ECA and FAO for developing effective cooperation in Africa, and pointed to various existing and emerging regional bodies and economic groupings concerned with marine fisheries, which demonstrated the resolve of African countries to strengthen their capabilities for cooperation in this field.

In conclusion, the Secretary-General recommended that African Governments adopt fishery planning and management standards, with greater reliance on subregional approaches, and that regional and subregional coordination mechanisms be reinforced, particularly among groupings and bodies with overlapping fishery management areas. He also recommended that a greater portion of fish export earnings be used for importing the fishing inputs necessary to increase the productivity of small-scale fishermen, and called for the exchange of African expertise as well as more effective use of regional training centres. Other recommendations provided for enhancing and harmonizing relevant statistical and information bases and devising options and strategies for generating maximum social and economic benefits from the various African fishery subsectors.

By **decision 47/444** of 22 December, the General Assembly took note of the Secretary-General's report.

A number of regional projects continued to be implemented during the year in several African subregions. A programme on aquaculture for local community development; research projects on applied hydrobiology and on management of the Lake Tanganyika fisheries; and a project for inland fisheries planning, development and management in eastern, central and southern Africa contributed to the development of the Rift Valley fisheries. The development of small-scale fisheries in West Africa was boosted through a project on the integrated development of artisanal fisheries, the reduction of post-harvest losses and the regional fish trade information and cooperation services.

The ECA secretariat held a seminar for North African countries on improved capacity for fishery planning and management, and issued technical publications on ameliorating fishery policies and management, enhancing fishery institutional capacities, and strengthening cooperation for the exploitation and management of shared inland fishery resources. Activities planned as a follow-up to the 1991 Ministerial Conference[48] included workshops on: the maritime data bank; monitoring, control and surveillance; and institutional options for the establishment of a permanent secretariat for the Conference.

ECONOMIC AND SOCIAL COUNCIL ACTION

On 31 July 1992, on the recommendation of its Economic Committee, the Economic and Social Council adopted **resolution 1992/54** without vote.

Cooperation in fisheries in Africa

The Economic and Social Council,

Recalling General Assembly resolution 45/184 of 21 December 1990,

Recalling also its resolutions 1990/77 of 27 July 1990 and 1991/73 of 26 July 1991,

Aware of the importance of regional and subregional agreements for the development of fishery resources,

Considering the need to encourage these initiatives, which are directed towards attaining food self-sufficiency, improving nutrition, diversifying exports, promoting employment and ensuring the sustainable development of fishery resources,

Welcoming the convening, at Rabat in 1989 and at Dakar in 1991, of the first and second sessions of the Ministerial Conference on Cooperation in Fisheries among the African States Bordering the Atlantic Ocean,

1. *Takes note with satisfaction* of the report of the Secretary-General on cooperation in fisheries in Africa and the oral report by the Director-General of the Food and Agriculture Organization of the United Nations;

2. *Welcomes* the progress achieved in implementing the cooperation programmes of the Ministerial Conference on Cooperation in Fisheries among the African States Bordering the Atlantic Ocean;

3. *Invites* the Conference to intensify its activities with a view to ensuring the sustainable development of fishery resources, in particular through the adoption of effective norms in the area of fisheries planning and management, further encouragement for the compilation and dissemination of fishery statistics as well as marine scientific research and for the protection and continued monitoring of the marine resources of the region;

4. *Welcomes* the support shown by the organizations of the United Nations system and by donor countries for the achievement of Conference objectives;

5. *Reiterates its appeal* to the international community, organizations of the United Nations system, donor countries and international and regional financial institutions to contribute generously to the implementation of Conference programmes and projects;

6. *Requests* the Secretary-General to submit to the Economic and Social Council, at its substantive session of 1994, a report by the Director-General of the Food and Agriculture Organization of the United Nations, working in cooperation with the other relevant organizations and in close consultation with the Acting Chairman of the Conference, on the progress achieved in the implementation of the present resolution and on the outcome of the third session of the Ministerial Conference on Cooperation in Fisheries among the African States Bordering the Atlantic Ocean, to be held in Cape Verde in 1993;

7. *Decides* to include in the agenda of its substantive session of 1994 an item entitled "Cooperation in fisheries in Africa".

Economic and Social Council resolution 1992/54

31 July 1992   Meeting 42   Adopted without vote

Approved by Economic Committee (E/1992/109) without vote, 28 July (meeting 16). Draft by Angola, Benin, Cameroon, Cape Verde, Congo, Côte d'Ivoire, Guinea, Guinea-Bissau, Mauritania, Morocco, Nigeria, Senegal, Sierra-Leone, Suriname, Togo, Zaire (E/1992/C.1/L.8), orally amended; agenda item 12.

Environment

In April, the ECA Conference of Ministers endorsed the African Common Position on the African Programme on Environment and Development as a regional input to UNCED. The areas covered in the Programme included food self-sufficiency and security; efficient and equitable use of water resources; management of marine and coastal resources; energy self-sufficiency; control of demographic changes and pressure; development of human settlement planning and management; optimization of industrial production and pollution control; management of biological and bio-technological diversity; mitigation of global warming and climatic change; protection and regeneration of the tropical forest; reversal of desertification; human resources development; popular participation; development of environmental legislation; enhancement of environmental awareness; management of solid and toxic wastes; environmental revival; elimination of poverty; drought monitoring; development of science and technology; health; mitigation of the effects of natural disasters; environmental measures in land-locked countries; and minimization of the effects of refugees on environment and development.

During 1992, the secretariat continued to publish its quarterly *Environment Newsletter*, and focused on the follow-up of UNCED within the framework of the Conference's main document, Agenda

21.[49] Its coordination activities were directed towards the ECA-sponsored African Centre of Meteorological Applications for Development in Niamey (Niger). ECA also collaborated with OAU to develop an African approach to negotiations for an international convention on desertification, and maintained contact with non-governmental organizations on matters relating to preparations for UNCED and its follow-up. Advisory services were provided to the Permanent Inter-State Committee on Drought Control in the Sahel and the Intergovernmental Authority on Drought and Development.

Social development and humanitarian affairs

In April, the ECA Conference of Ministers urged its members to give priority to the human dimension and to the implementation of an integrated approach to human resources planning and development within the Regional Framework for Human Resources Development and Utilization in Africa, prepared by a United Nations Inter-Agency Task Force on the subject.[50] The Ministers also urged UNDP to implement its pilot programme on integrated human resources development, requested the Executive Secretary to carry out the regional pilot programme for the exchange of African experts and called on the Intergovernmental Committee for Migration to increase its support to the ECA's Return of Skills Programme for Africa.

In 1992, the secretariat undertook a number of activities aimed at promoting the development of human resources. It produced technical publications on: trends and issues in African education, focusing on constraints and challenges of education development over the past three decades and Africa's response to them; strategies for increasing the effectiveness of human resources in priority sectors for socio-economic development; and resource mobilization and utilization in higher education institutions. Member States and other interested parties were informed of job vacancies in the region for qualified and trained personnel available for recruitment under the Return of Skills Programme for Africa. The secretariat also issued the *Training Information Notice*, providing information on ECA training programmes, and prepared publications on non-formal education in Africa and on measures for solving the problem of unemployment among the educated. A national seminar in Nigeria (15-19 June) considered an integrated long-term manpower and employment policy in that country. National training workshops were held on curriculum development and evaluation in Swaziland (18-29 May) and on employment planning and productivity enhancement in Ethiopia (6-10 July). The Ministerial Follow-up Committee of Ten of the Conference of Ministers Respon-

sible for Human Resources Planning, Development and Utilization held its seventh meeting at Addis Ababa (18 and 19 April).

Activities in the field of social programmes and services focused on issues concerning youth, the family and disabled persons. In response to ECA's request, the secretariat undertook a feasibility study on the establishment of an African fund for youth.[51] It issued innovative strategies for dealing with youth unemployment in the region, a directory of youth organizations in Africa and a publication on the interrelationship between youth, health and the continent's development and transformation. As part of its efforts to promote the United Nations Decade of Disabled Persons (1983-1992) (see PART THREE, Chapter XI), the secretariat continued to publish the *Equal Time* newsletter, highlighting activities for and by disabled persons. It prepared a study on the impact of economic and social changes on the African family, and continued to provide technical and substantive support to the United Nations African Institute for the Prevention of Crime and the Treatment of Offenders, in Kampala, Uganda.

Among the international and regional meetings convened by other United Nations bodies in 1992 were a regional meeting on human rights (Tunisia, November), the third biennial meeting of Africa Employment Planners (Arusha, November/December) and an International Conference on African Children (Dakar, Senegal, December). ECA also collaborated with the United Nations system in organizing a meeting on the ramifications of the HIV/AIDS pandemic on the long-term socio-economic development of the region.

Population

The Technical Preparatory Committee of the Whole, noting the deteriorating living conditions and physical environment in Africa aggravated by rapid population growth, insufficient and inequitably distributed goods and services, the AIDS pandemic and mass displacement of people as a result of man-made and natural calamities, encouraged African countries to formulate population and development policies aimed at balancing their economic and population growth rates and to integrate them in their development plans. In addition, the Committee urged ECA members to intensify population education programmes from the primary level to the post-formal education stages and to involve both men and women in family-planning programmes and policies.

During the year, the secretariat provided advisory and backstopping services to member States and ECA-sponsored institutions in the field of population, and produced the *Demographic Handbook for Africa, 1992,* as well as technical publications on strategies for improving contraceptive use to influence demographic trends in African countries; assessment of mortality levels, trends and differentials in selected countries in relation to the goal of health for all by the year 2000; and assessment of the methodology and data from the world fertility and demographic surveys. It held a training workshop on methodologies and uses of subnational and sectoral population projections (Ghana, November/December), and provided advisory services in evaluation analysis and dissemination of data from population censuses, survey and vital registration systems, as well as in formulation execution, assessment of population-related projects and programmes and integration of population factors into development planning and policy formulation.

In preparing for the International Conference on Population and Development, to be held at Cairo, Egypt, in 1994, the secretariat presented a document on major population and environment problems in Africa to an expert group meeting on population, environment and development (New York, 20-24 January), and organized the third African Population Conference (Dakar, 7-12 December). The Conference reviewed implementation of the 1984 Kilimanjaro Programme of Action for African Population and Self-Reliant Development[52] and adopted the Dakar/Ngor Declaration on Population, Family and Sustainable Development.[53]

The Declaration provided a set of 36 recommendations for African Governments pertaining to population, socio-economic growth and sustainable development; family; fertility and family planning; mortality, morbidity and AIDS; urbanization, migration and physical planning; refugees and displaced persons; women in development; children; youth; data collection and analysis, information dissemination, training and research; information, education and communication; and private and non-governmental organizations. Other recommendations were addressed to subregional and regional groupings, ECA, United Nations Fund for Population Activities (UNFPA) and the international community. The Declaration called on African Governments to integrate population policies and programmes in their development strategies and to strengthen the social sectors, giving special attention to environmental issues and food security.

Among the targets set in the Declaration were reducing the annual population growth rate from the prevailing 3 to 2.5 per cent by the year 2000 and to 2 per cent by 2010; increasing average life expectancy at birth for the region to at least 55 years by 2000; decreasing infant mortality to less than 50 per 1,000 and maternal mortality by 50 per cent; and increasing contraceptive prevalence to 20 per cent by 2000 and 40 per cent by 2010.

Human settlements

Activities in the area of human settlements focused on redressing the rural/urban imbalance in the region. In that regard, ECA developed and promoted guidelines for the formulation and implementation of national policies on settlements aimed at balanced spatial distribution of population and economic activities in the context of a sound environment, land reforms, promotion of rural townships and strengthening of the indigenous construction sector. The secretariat organized an ad hoc expert group meeting on the protection of the natural and man-made environment by regulating human settlement development, issued a publication on strengthening the development of intermediate towns and establishing growth poles in African countries, and launched a UNDP-funded field project on the commercial manufacture and use of soil-stabilized blocks in Senegal, fibre concrete roofing tiles in Cameroon and Guinea, and lime in Uganda.

Integration of women in development

In April, the ECA Conference of Ministers endorsed a 1991 proposal to establish a federation of African women entrepreneurs,[54] and recommended that ECA, along with OAU and AfDB, study the possibility of creating an African Bank for Women. The Ministers appealed to United Nations funding agencies to provide financial, material and technical support for those initiatives.[55] The Ministers urged member States to revise their legal texts by drafting family codes, strengthening the schooling of young girls, eliminating illiteracy among women, establishing a data bank for women, promoting trade in products produced by women and creating the necessary policy environment for the operation of small and medium-sized enterprises initiated by women. In addition, the Ministers called on States which had not implemented the Abuja Declaration on Participatory Development: The Role of Women in the 1990s, adopted by the 1989 Conference on the Integration of Women in Development and endorsed by the Conference of Ministers in 1990,[56] to consider taking the necessary steps to do so. By another resolution,[57] the Ministers urged Governments to ensure the participation of women in all peace initiatives and negotiations at all levels, and supported Uganda's proposal to hold a regional Conference on Women for Peace. By a separate decision,[58] the Conference of Ministers requested the Secretary-General to appoint an African woman as Secretary-General for the fourth World Conference on Women, to be held in Beijing, China, in September 1995.

The Africa Regional Coordinating Committee for the Integration of Women in Development held its thirteenth meeting (Addis Ababa, 9 and 10 April), and a Franco-African Conference on Women in Development was held in Paris in November. A round table for women in business in eastern and southern Africa (Lusaka, July) recommended strengthening the existing associations of business women in the Preferential Trade Area subregion and establishing a revolving loan fund for that purpose.

The African Training and Research Centre for Women (ATRCW) published guidelines for improving the role of women in production and management in the informal sector and an annotated bibliography on African women in development, as well as two issues of the *ATRCW Update* newsletter. Other activities included a joint ECA/AfDB/FAO international consultation on increasing rural women's access to credit, and seminars on policies for the promotion of women in development in West Africa and on the elaboration of a rural national plan of action for women in the Niger.

Programme, administrative and organizational questions

Medium-term plan for 1992-1997

In April, the ECA Technical Preparatory Committee of the Whole endorsed proposed revisions[5] to the medium-term plan for 1992-1997,[6] covering follow-up to UNPAAERD and issues arising from the adoption of UNNADAF; a follow-up to UNCED and UNCTAD VIII; update of the industrial development subprogramme with regard to IDDA II and adjustments to the transport and communications subprogramme to include UNTACDA II; and updating of legislative authorities arising from the Programme of Action for LDCs in the 1990s, endorsed by the General Assembly in 1990.[59] The revised plan included new subprogrammes on development issues and policies; trade, regional economic cooperation and integration; poverty alleviation through sustainable development; development administration and management; human resources development and social transformation; statistical and information systems development; natural resources and energy development; infrastructural and structural transformation; and women in development.

In October, the Committee for Programme and Coordination (CPC)[60] further revised the medium-term plan, which the General Assembly adopted by **resolution 47/214**.

Venue of 1993 session

At its 1992 session, the ECA Conference of Ministers approved Zambia's offer to host the 1993 session of the Conference. On 31 July, by **decision 1992/292**, the Economic and Social Council decided that the twenty-eighth session of the Commission/nineteenth meeting of the Conference of Ministers should be held at Lusaka in April 1993.

REFERENCES

[1]E/1992/33. [2]YUN 1991, p. 402, GA res. 46/151, annex, sect. II, 18 Dec. 1991. [3]YUN 1986, p. 446, GA res. S-13/2, annex, 1 June 1986. [4]E/ECA/CM.18/4. [5]E/ECA/CM.18/20. [6]A/45/6 (Prog. 45). [7]E/ECA/CM.18/5. [8]YUN 1980, p. 548. [9]GA res. 44/24, 17 Nov. 1989. [10]A/45/427. [11]E/ECA/CM.18/22. [12]E/ECA/CM.18/23. [13]E/1992/33 (res. 733(XXVII)). [14]Ibid. (res. 727(XXVII)). [15]A/46/390, annex II. [16]Ibid. (res. 728(XXVII)). [17]Ibid. (res. 726(XXVII)). [18]Ibid. (res. 741(XXVII)). [19]Ibid. (dec. 5(XXVII)). [20]Ibid. (dec. 3(XXVII)). [21]E/1992/93. [22]E/1993/53. [23]E/1992/33 (res. 729(XXVII)). [24]E/ECA/CM.19/CRP.1. [25]E/1993/38. [26]YUN 1991, p. 304. [27]E/1992/33 (res. 734(XXVII)). [28]Ibid. (res. 735(XXVII)). [29]Ibid. (res. 732(XXVII)). [30]Ibid. (res. 730(XXVII)). [31]Ibid. (res. 731(XXVII)). [32]Ibid. (dec. 1(XXVII)). [33]YUN 1991, p. 296. [34]E/1992/33 (res. 739(XXVII)). [35]E/1992/14 & Add.1 (Parts I and II). [36]E/ECA/CM.18/11. [37]YUN 1991, p. 301. [38]Ibid., ESC res. 1991/83, 26 July 1991. [39]YUN 1991, p. 302, GA dec. 46/456, 20 Dec. 1991. [40]E/1992/33 (dec. 2(XXVII)). [41]YUN 1991, p. 303, ESC res. 1991/74, 26 July 1991. [42]E/1992/33 (dec. 4(XXVII)). [43]Ibid. (res. 738(XXVII)). [44]GA res. 45/184, 21 Dec. 1990. [45]A/47/279-E/1992/79 & Corr.1. [46]YUN 1982, p. 178. [47]YUN 1984, p. 672. [48]YUN 1991, p. 298. [49]*Report of the United Nations Conference on Environment and Development, Rio de Janeiro, 3-14 June 1992*, vol. I, Sales No. E.93.I.8. [50]E/1992/33 (res. 740(XXVII)). [51]E/ECA/CM.19/10. [52]YUN 1984, p. 616. [53]E/ECA/CM.19/12. [54]YUN 1991, p. 300. [55]E/1992/33 (res. 736(XXVII)). [56]E/1990/42 (res.686(XV)). [57]E/1992/33 (res. 737(XXVII)). [58]Ibid. (dec. 6(XXVII)). [59]GA res. 45/206, 21 Dec. 1990. [60]A/47/16.

Asia and the Pacific

ESCAP, at its forty-eighth session (Beijing, 14-23 April),[1] had as its theme topic "Regional economic cooperation in the ESCAP region: prospects, priorities and policy options". On 23 April,[2] the Commission adopted the Beijing Declaration on Regional Economic Cooperation, in which it set out the following guiding principles to impart new impetus to economic cooperation in the region: to ensure the region's sustained growth and development for the good of its people; to promote economic cooperation on the basis of equality and mutual benefit; to reaffirm ESCAP members' commitment to an open world trading system; to take into account the diversity of the region; and to follow the principles of equality and consensus-building in consultations and dialogue.

The Commission urged that high priority be accorded to promoting intraregional trade and investment, to greater cooperation in science and technology and to the development of infrastructure. In the context of revising its intergovernmental subsidiary structure, the Commission welcomed the establishment of the Committee for

Regional Economic Cooperation and directed it to examine trends and developments in the region and develop measures for enhancing regional cooperation.

The Commission adopted a resolution revising its conference structure and frequency of meetings in order to enhance its effectiveness in responding to increasingly complex development problems.[3] It also adopted a framework for its own programming and established a subsidiary structure comprising three thematic committees (on regional economic cooperation, on environment and sustainable development and on poverty alleviation through economic growth and social development), two other committees (on statistics and on transport and communications) and two special bodies (on least developed and land-locked developing countries and on Pacific island developing countries). It also set up a high-level steering group for the Committee for Regional Economic Cooperation, abolished the Special Body on Land-locked Countries and amended provisions for convening ad hoc conferences and intergovernmental meetings. The terms of reference of the thematic and other committees and special bodies were annexed to the Commission's resolution.

The Commission invited the ESCAP Executive Secretary, under the direction of the Secretary-General, to reorganize the ESCAP secretariat to enhance the servicing of the Commission's subsidiary structure and to forward to ESCAP members his assessment of the organizational, staffing and financial implications of the revised intergovernmental structure. The Executive Secretary was asked to report to the Commission in 1994 on the implementation of its resolution.

By a resolution on the role and functions of ESCAP in the context of restructuring the economic and social fields of the United Nations,[4] the Commission, taking note of General Assembly **resolution 46/235**, which stated that the regional commissions should be strengthened (see PART THREE, Chapter XVIII), directed the Advisory Committee of Permanent Representatives and Other Representatives Designated by Members of the Commission to seek the views of members and associate members on the Assembly resolution, draft a response and submit it for consideration by members and associate members, convey the response to the Assembly through the ESCAP Executive Secretary and report to the Commission in 1993 on the implementation of its resolution.

In other action, the Commission adopted resolutions on the Asian and Pacific Decade of Disabled Persons, 1993-2002; the Fourth Asian and Pacific Population Conference, 1992; the Social Development Strategy for the ESCAP Region Towards the Year 2000 and Beyond; regional cooperation in the implementation of the Jakarta Plan of Action on Human Resources Development in the ESCAP Region; guidelines for consumer protection; problems faced by the transitional disadvantaged economies in the ESCAP region; strengthening ESCAP assistance to the Pacific island countries; the Asia-Pacific International Trade Fair (1994); and road and rail transport modes in relation to facilitation measures. (For further information on those resolutions, see below under subject headings.)

In a message to the session, the Secretary-General said that the end of the cold war provided the international community with an opportunity to lay a basis for balanced and sustained development in all regions of the world. The vigorous economic performance of some Asian and Pacific countries, their remarkable resilience and economic dynamism in the face of serious external and domestic difficulties were an encouraging indication that developing countries could achieve rapid progress. However, a number of economies in the region, particularly the least developed and Pacific island countries, had been unable to achieve significant growth and still needed special support and assistance. A major challenge facing the region in the 1990s was breaking the cycle of stagnation and poverty and ensuring access to opportunities for all, thus reducing the differences within and between countries. The Secretary-General called on the Asian and Pacific nations to make a collective effort to eradicate poverty and illiteracy and to improve social conditions in the region as a prerequisite for sustained economic development.

The ESCAP Executive Secretary noted with satisfaction that, despite the lack of an immediate recovery in the world economy, the region's economic growth rate remained high, although there were considerable variations among countries. Strong growth in intraregional trade and domestic demand played an increasingly important role in overall economic development; however, the resultant growth in imports caused deterioration in the external trade and balance-of-payments situation, and necessitated a quick revival of export demand. As the average per capita income in Asia and the Pacific remained low, the reputed dynamism and prosperity in the region was limited to a small, though expanding, group of countries, while the least developed and Pacific island economies continued to be generally weak.

He noted that poverty remained the region's main challenge, with absolute poverty existing in most developing countries of Asia and the Pacific. Many of them continued to be burdened with high rates of population growth and unbalanced demographic distribution, and their development was seriously hindered by inadequate physical and social infrastructure. In addition, uncontrolled exploitation of natural resources and environmental degradation had become increasingly serious problems. The Executive Secretary urged ESCAP members to formulate appropriate regional strategies in those and other areas.

Pointing to the emergence of regional cooperation arrangements in many parts of the world, he said that enhanced regional cooperation could stimulate accelerated development in an open multilateral trading system, supported by the ESCAP region, and that the Commission could make a strong plea for a speedy and successful conclusion of the Uruguay Round of multilateral trade negotiations.

ECONOMIC AND SOCIAL COUNCIL ACTION

On 31 July 1992, the Economic and Social Council, by **decision 1992/290**, approved ESCAP's resolution on restructuring its conference structure.

Economic and social trends

Economic trends

The *Economic and Social Survey of Asia and the Pacific, 1992*[5] comprised two volumes: recent economic and social developments in the region, and expansion of investment and intraregional trade as a vehicle for enhancing regional economic cooperation and development.

According to a summary of the survey,[6] the region sustained high growth performance in 1992, despite an overall sluggishness of the world economy. The average rate of growth for its developing economies was estimated at 6.9 per cent, against 6.1 per cent in 1991. China's growth rate reached 12 per cent, compared with 7.7 per cent in 1991, while India's economy was expected to pick up to slightly above 4 per cent, after a dip to 2.5 per cent in 1991. However, a large number of economies in the region remained weak and fragile after decades of development effort, in a perpetual state of low performance caused by a complex of both long- and short-term factors. With the exception of China, rates of economic growth in East and South-East Asia varied between 5 and 8 per cent, and decreased in some countries. In South Asia, Iran's GDP growth rate was expected to decline to 8 per cent in 1992 from 9.9 per cent in 1991, while Pakistan's increased to 6.4 per cent from 5.6 per cent in 1991. The small island economies of the Pacific were experiencing tightening rather than easing of the usual constraints on their growth and development, and the performance of the region's LDCs, with the exception of Maldives, remained lacklustre in most cases.

In 1992, the three developed economies of the region were at different stages of recession. Australia, whose economy went into full recession in 1991 and experienced negative growth (−1.9 per cent), was undergoing a slow recovery, with the 1992 growth rate estimated at 2.6 per cent. Japan's rate of economic growth (4.5 per cent in 1991) fell to an estimated 1.8 per cent in 1992, the lowest since 1980. Although the easing of monetary policy and fiscal conditions as well as low inflation and expanding export markets had been expected to bring growth back to 2.5 per cent by the end of the year, low personal consumption and corporate investment rates had an adverse impact on the pace of recovery. In New Zealand, GDP fell by 2.1 per cent in 1991. Declining domestic demand caused imports to fall by 6 per cent in 1991, but projections for 1992 showed a modest increase of between 2.5 and 3 per cent. Inflation was projected to decline to around 2 per cent. However, fiscal consolidation suffered a set-back as the recession caused a decrease in tax revenues.

With the exception of the Democratic People's Republic of Korea and Mongolia, the economies of East Asia remained geared to a high performance in 1992. Hong Kong's economic growth accelerated from 4.2 per cent in 1991 to an estimated 6 per cent in 1992, and its economy became increasingly linked with that of China. The Republic of Korea, whose GDP grew by 8.4 per cent in 1991, achieved a growth rate of 7.3 per cent in 1992. A reduced growth target had been set by the Government as part of its stabilization policies to reduce inflation and balance-of-payments deficits. Taiwan's growth rate reached 7.3 per cent in 1991 and was projected at 7 per cent for 1992.

The economy of the Democratic People's Republic of Korea grew at an estimated annual rate of 2 to 3 per cent during the first three years of its 1987-1993 plan and contracted in 1990-1991. In Mongolia, which was undergoing a transition from a centrally planned to a market system, GDP continued to fall, declining by 9.2 per cent in 1991 and an estimated 5 per cent in 1992.

The six Central Asian republics of the former USSR, which became members of ESCAP in 1992 (see below), were also experiencing serious problems of transition to a market economy, with losses of output, excessive inflation and rising unemployment, resulting from a breakdown of the centrally planned system, the collapse of trade with the former members of the Council for Mutual Economic Assistance, the dissolution of the USSR and price liberalization measures by the Russian Federation. The net material product (NMP), which declined in 1991 by 9.6 per cent in Kazakhstan, 8.7 per cent in Tajikistan, and between 0.6 and 2 per cent in Azerbaijan, Kyrgyzstan, Turkmenistan and Uzbekistan, was expected to fall more steeply in 1992.

In South-East Asia, only Singapore experienced a substantial deceleration in its growth rate, from 6.7 per cent in 1991 to 4.7 per cent in 1992, while Viet Nam's GDP was expected to rise from 4 per cent in 1991 to some 7 per cent in 1992. The Philippines succeeded in reversing the 1991 contraction of its economy; however, its growth rate remained at less than 2 per cent in 1992, leading to a further decline in average per capita income. Indonesia's rate of GDP growth slowed to 6.6 per cent in 1991 from 7.1 per cent in 1990, and a further deceleration to 5.9 per cent was projected for 1992. Malaysia's economic growth in 1992 was estimated at 8.5 per cent, compared with 8.6 per cent in 1991. Thailand's economy sustained an overall growth rate of 7.5 per cent in 1992, despite a period of political uncertainty from February 1991 until the general election in September 1992, policy changes such as the introduction of the value-added tax on 1 January 1992, and supply-side constraints emerging from the previous years of rapid growth, which adversely affected consumption and investment activities.

Of the subregion's LDCs, the Lao People's Democratic Republic's GDP growth rate slowed from 6.6 per cent in 1990 to 4 per cent in 1991, largely due to a drought affecting agricultural production. The rate rose to 6 per cent in 1992, as the industrial sector continued to grow rapidly, spurred by liberal reforms in investment, trade and prices. Myanmar's GDP, which achieved a 3.7 per cent growth rate in 1990, decreased its growth to 2.7 per cent in 1991 and to 1.3 per cent in 1992, the result of a decline in agricultural output.

With regard to the five LDCs of South Asia, Afghanistan's economy showed no apparent improvement after the GDP decrease in 1987-1989; its agricultural production index registered a further decline of 6 per cent in 1991. Although GDP in Bangladesh grew at the rate of 4 per cent in 1992 against 3.6 per cent in 1991, agricultural and industrial growth rates were marginally lower than in the previous year. Bhutan's rate of growth was estimated at 4 per cent in 1992, up from just over 3 per cent in 1990 and 1991. The economy of Maldives, which performed exceptionally well during the 1980s, showed an estimated growth rate of 15.1 per cent in 1990 and 8 per cent in 1991, with manufacturing output increasing by 40 per cent between 1987 and 1990. Nepal's GDP increased by only 3.1 per cent in 1992, down from 5.5 per cent for 1991; the non-agricultural sector, however, was expected to grow at the rate of 7 per cent, compared with 5.7 per cent in 1991.

The economies of the Pacific island countries came under severe pressure from recessionary conditions prevailing in the industrialized nations in 1991-1992, especially in Australia and New Zealand. The situation was further compounded by extensive cyclone damage to some of them; however, many of those countries maintained positive rates of growth, although reduced in some cases. Papua New Guinea, with a 9.5 per cent growth in 1991, sharply reversed a cumulative contraction of its economy by more than 4 per cent during the previous two years; for 1992, the rate was estimated at over 5 per cent. Tonga recorded a 3.9 per cent GDP growth in 1991, and its economy was projected to grow by more than 4 per cent in 1992. GDP growth in the Solomon Islands also increased to 3.9 per cent in 1991, but was expected to slow to 3.6 per cent in 1992. Vanuatu registered a growth rate of over 4 per cent in 1991, and the 1992 projections for the industry and service sectors showed a further increase, although the agricultural sector, expected to contract by 11 per cent, was slowing overall economic growth to 2.9 per cent. After its 1991 contraction, the economy of Fiji was expected to rebound in 1992 with a 4.2 per cent growth rate. That of Samoa, however, continued to decline for the third consecutive year, owing to the damage from two highly destructive cyclones in 1990 and 1991.

The nature of the problems faced by the disadvantaged economies of the region varied in both kind and intensity. Of the 13 LDCs, four countries (Afghanistan, Bhutan, Lao People's Democratic Republic and Nepal) suffered the additional disadvantage of being land-locked, while Afghanistan, Cambodia and the Lao People's Democratic Republic also had to cope with difficulties related to their transition to a market system, with the former two remaining the most distressed economically and politically. The six Asian republics of the former USSR had similar problems adjusting to a market system, as their traditional international links had been severed and needed recasting. Six LDCs, including Maldives, were island economies suffering from their smallness, remoteness and openness to international market influences.

Despite the global recession, the international trade of the region's developing countries was buoyant in 1991-1992 as a result of improved production efficiency, low rates of domestic inflation and wage increases, diversification of markets, and consolidated and expanded policy reforms involving trade and investment regimes.

Exports from the region as a whole in 1991 totalled $872.3 billion, representing 25.3 per cent of world exports, compared with $715.4 billion, or 21.1 per cent, in the previous year. The developing economies' share in the regional total was 58 per cent, while their share in world trade reached 15.5 per cent. At the same time, intraregional exports in 1991 rose to $395.1 billion, accounting for 45.3 per cent of the regional total.

Over the period 1975-1991, exports from the ESCAP region grew at 12.1 per cent annually, against the world rate of 8.7 per cent, so that the region had become its own dynamic market. Although the performance of different groups of economies and individual countries varied greatly, the overall situation in intraregional trade was characterized by a decline in the dominant role of the developed countries of the region and an improvement in the position of the newly industrializing economies (NIEs) (Hong Kong, Republic of Korea, Singapore and Taiwan), the four larger countries of the Association of South-East Asian Nations (ASEAN-4) (Indonesia, Malaysia, the Philippines and Thailand) and China. In 1991, the NIEs' share in the region's exports to world markets rose to 35 per cent and that of China to 8 per cent, while ASEAN-4 accounted for 11.5 per cent and South Asia for about 3.5 per cent of the regional total. At the same time, exports to regional markets from Australia, New Zealand and Japan represented 63.5, 52.6 and 35.5 per cent, respectively, of their global exports.

Regional trade links were also strengthened by investment flows. After 1986, the ESCAP region became the largest recipient of foreign direct investment (FDI) in the developing world, of which more than 90 per cent went to NIEs, ASEAN-4 and China. Although Japan was the most important source of FDI in the region, the United States and the European Community (EC) had a more visible presence in some developing economies, and the investment flow from NIEs to the region also increased significantly, notably to China.

However, intraregional trade and investment expansion encountered a number of constraints. Endogenous obstacles stemmed from three main sources—the macroeconomic environment, regulations of foreign investment and inadequate infrastructural support—which were within the purview of domestic policy. Non-tariff barriers and product standardization requirements imposed by importing countries represented the main exogenous obstructions.

Enhancing regional economic cooperation was an option for stimulating the growth process across the region, as coordinated regional strategies based on export-led growth would encourage more efficient use of capital and capital flows within the region, and expand both intraregional and interregional markets. It was essential to direct policy efforts towards removing or easing constraints to the free flow of goods, services and investment; providing decision makers and the business community with information about markets, technologies and investment opportunities; encouraging foreign investment in regional and world, rather than domestic, markets to ensure positive balance-of-payments effects; enhancing, through trade and

investment, export capacities in the domestic private sectors of host countries; devising such mechanisms as payment arrangements and capital flows; and according due attention to the problems of the Pacific island countries, LDCs and the economies in transition.

Increasing intraregional linkages in trade and investment also underlined the need for greater macroeconomic consultation, cooperation and synchronization, especially on monetary, fiscal and external commercial issues, as well as a cooperative action to lower trade barriers in the region. The move towards trade liberalization, in its turn, required strengthening the regional transportation and communications infrastructure and removing hindrances in the movement of goods and people. In order to strengthen the operation of the trade-investment nexus in the region and ensure the spread of its beneficial impact to the less dynamic developing economies, the *Survey* suggested a number of initiatives dealing with increased regional trade information dissemination; establishment of a regional trade-related network of research institutions and a regional investment information and promotion service; regional cooperation in trade in services; human resources development; harmonization of customs procedures; and regional programmes on quality assurance, development of small- and medium-scale enterprises, and special assistance to the economies in transition and to LDCs.

Social trends

The summary of the economic and social survey[6] noted that the health of the region's 3.1 billion people was one of the most significant issues in social development. Although many more people were enjoying higher living standards, better education and improved social services, poverty and malnutrition still predominated in many parts of Asia and the Pacific, with an estimated 800 million people living below the poverty line in 1990. Infectious and communicable diseases, many associated with substandard living conditions, continued to undermine productivity, while social and economic inequities fueled the vicious circle leading from poverty to malnutrition and disease to loss of employment and productivity, thereby perpetuating poverty. In more developed areas, non-communicable diseases linked to stress and environmental factors became major public health problems. Drug addiction, which earlier existed in a limited form, was threatening to acquire menacing new dimensions, and AIDS was emerging as perhaps the foremost health challenge in the region.

Those problems notwithstanding, life expectancy increased significantly in most developing nations of Asia and the Pacific and, in some countries, almost reached the developed country levels, while infant mortality rates, although still relatively high, declined in all countries. The highest under-five mortality rates of 292 and 193 deaths per 1,000 live births were recorded in 1990 in war-torn Afghanistan and Cambodia; in the same year, Hong Kong and Singapore registered the lowest rates in the region, of 7 and 9, respectively. Maternal mortality rates had also declined, to 50 deaths per 100,000 live births in Sri Lanka and 60 in Thailand by 1988, but remained as high as 1,310 per annum in Bhutan for the period 1980-1990. In the Asian republics of the former USSR, where family-planning services were virtually non-existent and the frequency of abortions in many communities equalled or exceeded the rate of live births, maternal mortality rates ranged between 40 and 120 per 100,000.

As primary health care was widely recognized as the key to achieving health for all by the year 2000, most countries of the region incorporated health policies in their national development strategies and made concerted efforts to reorient their health systems. The primary-health-care approach sought to meet the needs of all population groups through integrated programmes, multisectoral collaboration and maximum community and individual participation. Most national health-care systems in the region included extended hospital emergency medical care and general public-health services supplemented by a private health sector and a network of health centres with limited ambulatory and home visiting services supported by referral institutions. Steps were also taken to shift emphasis from the curative to the preventive aspects of health care, decentralize services and focus on reaching underserved and vulnerable populations, particularly in rural areas and urban slums.

The percentage of total government expenditure devoted to health services indicated their relative priority over other sectors. As a proportion of gross national product (GNP), however, it was very low for many of the region's developing economies, ranging in 1990 from 0.2 per cent in Pakistan to 2.7 per cent in Papua New Guinea and 2.8 per cent in Vanuatu. The exception was Maldives, which allocated 9.8 per cent of its GNP to the health sector. Yet, regardless of trends in national economic growth and the share of national income allocated to health, the combined effects of inflation and population growth often resulted in declining real public spending for health per capita, and vast amounts of additional resources were required to ensure improvements in the health status and well-being of the region's population.

In addition to resource allocation considerations, the critical role of population growth for attaining the goals of economic development and health for all demanded greater attention. The average annual population growth rate in the region was 1.7 per cent, which translated to an additional 53 million people each year. Most countries were taking steps to control their population growth through the promotion of integrated family-planning and health programmes, but integration efforts often left much to be desired. In the absence of an adequately integrated approach, family-planning programmes could divert resources from other sectors having a bearing on fertility determinants and ultimately on health and population growth.

Activities in 1992

Development policy and regional economic cooperation

During 1992, ESCAP prepared a theme study on prospects, priorities and policy options for regional cooperation.[7] The report, which examined policy options for strengthening regional cooperation in the areas of investment and development finance, complementarities and intraregional trade, science and technology, and infrastructure development, was discussed at ESCAP's 1992 session[1] in the debate leading up to the adoption of the Beijing Declaration (see above). The Commission also devoted attention to activities in support of the developing Asian and Pacific nations, as well as to policy reforms and economic restructuring efforts under way in many countries of the region, including social consequences of those measures and the problems of economies in transition to a market system.

The newly established Committee for Regional Economic Cooperation held its first session at Bangkok, Thailand, on 19 October and from 22 October to 2 November 1992[8] to discuss modalities for implementing its mandate. The Committee's Steering Group, at its first meeting (New Delhi, India, 24-27 November),[9] adopted an action programme for regional economic cooperation in trade and investment, giving high priority to a macro study on intraregional trade patterns and a study on sectoral inflows of FDI. The programme also provided for a number of subsidiary studies addressing particular issues of regional concern, such as the outcome of the Uruguay Round of multilateral trade negotiations, trade regimes in manufactures and non-tariff barriers. It incorporated recommendations for strengthening the regional trade expansion infrastructure, including ESCAP's Regional Trade Information Network and a network of trade-related research institutions, and for promoting standardization and quality control in the manufacturing process. The action programme further called for the establishment of a regional investment information and promotion service, and focused on the development of small and medium-sized enterprises and cooperation among them; trade, investment and environmental issues; regional cooperation in assisting the economies in transition to overcome macroeconomic problems and requirements for their integration into the region; and inter-subregional cooperation. The action programme would be given final consideration by the Committee for Regional Economic Cooperation in 1993.

Implementation of the Programme of Action for LDCs

In contrast to the overall dynamism of the ESCAP region, the socio-economic conditions of LDCs continued to deteriorate, mainly due to their chronic structural weakness and fragile economic base. The uncertain global economic environment, mounting obstacles faced by exports from LDCs, a heavy debt burden and other external shocks and natural disasters added to their difficulties. Several countries also faced major dislocations stemming from wars, civil unrest and ethnic strife, and had to cope with serious economic, social and humanitarian problems created by large masses of refugees and displaced persons.[10] As a consequence, the GDP growth rate of the least developed and land-locked developing countries of Asia and the Pacific as a group fell below 1 per cent in 1991, impeding progress in implementing the Programme of Action for LDCs for the 1990s, adopted in 1990 by a United Nations conference (known as the Paris Conference)[11] and endorsed by the General Assembly later that year.[12]

However, there were substantial differences in individual country performance, from Afghanistan, which was plagued by a series of calamities, to countries like Bhutan and Maldives, which registered significant economic gains in recent years. Generally, low growth characterized the economies of Bangladesh, the Lao People's Democratic Republic, Myanmar and Nepal, and growth was marginal or slowing down in the Pacific island LDCs, except for Kiribati. In an effort to reactivate their development process, the least developed and land-locked developing countries of the region launched far-reaching reform programmes, ranging from improved policies for development and modernization of the economic base to mobilization and effective use of domestic resources. Measures were taken to enhance the efficiency of the private sector, strengthen human and institutional capabilities, promote private initiative for development, foster motivation and participation of the population and link poverty alleviation to environmental concerns. Bangladesh, the Lao People's Democratic Republic and Nepal also adopted structural adjustment policies to

strengthen their competiveness and raise their actual and potential growth rates. Many LDCs undertook unilateral trade liberalization measures; however, they needed to be matched by supportive action of their trading partners.

Efforts by LDCs needed to be complemented by external support measures, particularly official development assistance (ODA), as envisaged in the Programme of Action for the 1990s. While ODA resources played a vital role in building social and physical infrastructure in those countries, stagnation and decline in ODA flows in the early 1990s remained a matter of considerable concern and fueled the need for donor nations to increase substantially their assistance. There was also a need for strengthened international efforts to alleviate the debt burden of LDCs, as well as for expanded activities enabling those countries to exploit fully the special treatment offered to them under the generalized system of preferences (GSP) schemes (see PART THREE, Chapter IV). The special problems of LDCs were also considered by other United Nations bodies (see PART THREE, Chapter I).

Special problems of Pacific island countries

A note by the ESCAP secretariat to the Commission[13] described the special barriers to development unique to Pacific island countries, such as smallness of land area, geographical fragmentation and isolation, great vulnerability to natural disasters and lack of human and natural resources

The Commission, noting those constraints, endorsed the need for technology-intelligence services and training, emphasizing an intercountry approach to supplement national arrangements and to take advantage of economies of scale and economic diversity. It expressed concern at the decline in technical assistance activities for those countries and urged the secretariat to reverse that trend. The Commission also noted with gratification financial assistance and expert services provided by Australia, France, Japan and New Zealand to the ESCAP Pacific Operations Centre, and welcomed announcements by France of its provision of a replacement expert and by Australia of possible funding of the post of statistical adviser.

The ESCAP Pacific Operations Centre continued to discharge its technical assistance activities in the Pacific. During the year, Australia, France and the Republic of Korea provided personnel to the Centre in the areas of statistics, macroeconomics and planning, and trade promotion, respectively. A number of countries, namely Australia, China, France, Indonesia, Japan, Kiribati, Micronesia, Papua New Guinea, the Philippines and the Republic of Korea, pledged financial support for the Pacific Trust Fund, which was established to ensure the participation of Pacific island countries in ESCAP's annual sessions. The Commission appealed to ESCAP members for financial assistance to the Fund to transform it into a self-supporting endowment body.

On 23 April,[14] the Commission asked the ESCAP Executive Secretary to redeploy three Professional staff members from ESCAP headquarters to the Pacific Operations Centre in Vanuatu for three years commencing in 1993. Those staff members would complement the available expertise at the Centre and provide assistance in economic and financial management, structural adjustment and economic reform; social development problems stemming from economic adjustment and reform programmes; and market development and trade promotion.

Other United Nations bodies also considered the problems of island developing countries (see PART THREE, Chapter I).

By **resolution 47/186**, the General Assembly appealed to the international community to assist island developing countries and, by **resolution 47/189**, decided to convene, in 1994, a global conference on the sustainable development of small island developing States.

ESCAP transition economies

On 23 April,[15] the Commission welcomed several Asian Republics of the Commonwealth of Independent States (Azerbaijan, Kyrgyzstan, Tajikistan and Turkmenistan) as new members (see below). Kazakhstan and Uzbekistan also joined ESCAP in 1992. Taking into account that the early stabilization of the social and economic situation in those countries, which were facing problems of transition from centrally planned to market economies, coincided with the interests of ESCAP members, the Commission recommended that activities relating to countries with transitional disadvantaged economies should be included in ESCAP's programme of work as soon as possible and that the medium-term plan for 1992-1997 should be revised to take their needs into account. The secretariat was asked to provide consultancy and technical assistance in economic reform, structural adjustment and the social development problems that accompanied economic reform. The Commission recommended that the Executive Secretary ask for voluntary contributions to enable the full participation of the transitional economies in ESCAP meetings and invited ESCAP members to contribute generously and promptly.

Economic and technical cooperation

During 1992, ESCAP received $19.5 million in contributions to implement its technical cooperation activities, 23 per cent less than in 1991.[16] The decrease was mainly due to reduced funding by UNDP. Also in 1992, donor States and developing member countries provided 300.25 workmonths of expert services, compared with 388 in 1991. The Project Review Committee considered 135 new project proposals for bilateral funding in 1993 (compared with 111 in 1991), and recommended 94 of them, totalling $10 million, for approval and submission to potential donors. A corps of 10 regional advisers undertook 37 missions to 26 developing countries of the region.

The Commission urged its secretariat to exert further efforts to promote ECDC/TCDC (economic and technical cooperation among developing countries), particularly to enhance the availability of information on TCDC potential and opportunities for the benefit of the least developed, landlocked and island developing countries, and endorsed a proposal to conduct a TCDC survey on the needs of those countries. It urged members of ESCAP and other donors to contribute to the ESCAP TCDC supplementary fund in order to expand operational TCDC activities in the region. In total, the secretariat implemented more than 80 ECDC/TCDC activities, comprising 12 study tours in specific areas of interest to ESCAP members, 18 workshops and seminars and 3 demonstration projects to promote further cooperation. With the support of China, the Netherlands, Norway and the Republic of Korea to the ESCAP TCDC supplementary fund, the secretariat supported 33 operational TCDC activities, 10 of which were for the benefit of the least developed, land-locked and island developing countries. Fields of interest included agriculture, natural resources development, industry and human settlements, the environment, population, social development and science and technology.

International trade and finance

In 1992, although there was an emerging global consensus on liberalization of international trade and investment regimes, trade barriers persisted and non-tariff barriers proliferated in areas that were comparatively advantageous to developing countries.

In November,[9] the Steering Group of the Committee for Regional Economic Cooperation adopted an action programme for regional economic cooperation in trade and investment (see above, under "Development policy and regional economic cooperation"). Other major activities in 1992 included the Intergovernmental Meeting on Policy Issues and Measures Arising from the Effects of Graduation under GSP (Bangkok, 28-30 January), the ESCAP/UNCTAD/UNDP Expert Group Meeting on a Regional Investment Information and Promotion Service for Asia and the Pacific (Seoul, Republic of Korea, 23-25 June) and the Intercountry Consultation on

Trade in the Asia-Pacific Region (New Delhi, 11 and 12 August). The secretariat fielded a joint ESCAP/Asian Development Bank advisory mission to newly independent Asian republics of the former USSR, and provided technical assistance in such areas as commodities, intraregional trade and investment, including in the mineral sector; market and product diversification; trade facilitation; trade expansion in manufactures; and promotion of exports, including the Asian International Silk Fair '92 (Dusseldorf, Germany, 6-9 September).

On 23 April,[17] the Commission decided that the fifth Asia-Pacific International Trade Fair would be held in Beijing in 1994. It asked the ESCAP Executive Secretary to assist the Fair and to approach the UNDP Administrator and bilateral donors for financial support for it. The Commission called on Governments of ESCAP members and associate members to support the Fair and to encourage their industrial and commercial organizations to participate in it.

Consumer protection

On 23 April,[18] the Commission commended the Executive Secretary on ESCAP's efforts to promote the implementation of the guidelines for consumer protection adopted by the General Assembly in 1985.[19] The Executive Secretary was asked, in cooperation with non-governmental organizations (NGOs) and relevant parts of the United Nations system, to promote implementation of the guidelines, initiate activities to follow up on the recommendations of a 1990 regional seminar on consumer protection for Asia and the Pacific and to seek extrabudgetary contributions for that purpose.

Transnational corporations

The potential contribution of transnational corporations (TNCs) to the socio-economic development of many developing countries in the region was recognized by the Commission, which, at its April session, stressed the need for greater regional cooperation to attract foreign investment in Asia and the Pacific. However, ESCAP expressed concern at the environmental impact of TNC activities in host countries, and noted that joint action was needed to solve those problems.

During the year, the ESCAP/TCMD (United Nations Transnational Corporations and Management Division) Joint Unit on Transnational Corporations continued efforts to facilitate mutually beneficial linkages through a better understanding of TNCs and their impact on host countries in Asia and the Pacific, and to provide policy recommendations and assist the region's developing countries in attracting foreign investment. The Joint Unit continued to prepare policy recommendations for publication and distribution among members of ESCAP, and to collect data on FDI in the region for a *World Investment Directory* to be published by the Division (see also PART THREE, Chapter V).

Transport and communications

ESCAP's major achievement in the transport and communications area in 1992 was the formulation of the regional action programme for phase II (1992-1996) of the Transport and Communications Decade for Asia and the Pacific (see below). The secretariat continued to develop computer models and manuals for strengthening national capabilities in transport research and planning, focusing particularly on shipping and ports. It also intensified efforts to implement the integrated project on Asian land transport infrastructure development, comprising the Asian Highway, the Trans-Asian Railway and the facilitation of land transport projects.

In addition, the secretariat fielded a number of route survey missions to selected countries in the region and fact-finding missions to the newly independent Asian republics, and provided advisory services on transit transport facilitation to several land-locked countries. It continued assistance in national capacity-building for multimodal transport by providing training for national trainers and in developing and improving information and statistical systems on inland water transport and upgrading dredging capabilities. In support of environmental development, the secretariat issued two publications relating to the environmental impact of dredging and port development and successfully completed a five-year demonstration project in Karachi, Pakistan, on the use of compressed natural gas in urban transport.

Other activities included a subregional seminar on performance improvement of inter-island shipping (Suva, Fiji, 12-15 May) a seminar-cum-study tour on commercial aspects of railway modernization (Tokyo, Sendai and Hokodate, Japan, 20-27 October) and a regional expert group meeting on utilization of compressed natural gas in urban transport (Karachi, 30 and 31 December). ESCAP also organized a number of country-level workshops on various aspects of transport and communications.

On 23 April,[20] the Commission adopted a resolution on road and rail transport modes in relation to facilitation measures, in which it recommended that countries of the region that had not yet done so consider acceding to a number of transport-related international conventions. It also recommended that the ESCAP secretariat examine the needs of countries or groups of countries in relation to the adoption of facilitation measures in road and rail transport, provide advisory services and convene expert group meetings to consider problems, bottlenecks and facilitation measures in that area.

Transport and Communications
Decade for Asia and the Pacific

The second session of the Meeting of Ministers Responsible for Transport and Communications (Bangkok, 3-5 June)[21] considered a regional action programme for phase II (1992-1996) of the Transport and Communications Decade for Asia and the Pacific, 1985-1994.[22] In preparation for the meeting, a meeting of senior government officials was held on 1 and 2 June. The Decade covered the area of two regional commissions, ESCAP and ESCWA. In 1991,[23] the Assembly changed the period of the Decade's second quinquennium to 1992-1996 to coincide with the period of the medium-term plan (1992-1997).

The Ministers emphasized the importance of strengthening the transport network of the region and the elimination of missing links and non-physical barriers, as well as the promotion of greater private-sector participation in transport and communications infrastructure development and services. They endorsed the following issues for the action programme: institutional development; transport and communications operations; human resources development; multimodal transport and logistics; commercialization of transport and communications operations; environment, health and safety in transport; and urban transport.

On 5 June, the Ministers adopted a declaration and officially launched phase II of the Decade. The report of its meeting was submitted to the Economic and Social Council.[24]

During 1992, the ESCAP secretariat carried out two missions to Amman, Jordan, for consultations with the ESCWA secretariat on developing inter-regional projects within the framework of the Decade. The secretariat also began implementing some regional action programme activities. The first meeting of the Inter-agency Steering Committee on Phase II of the Decade was held at Geneva from 2 to 4 December.

In response to a 1984 request of the Economic and Social Council,[25] the Secretary-General in June submitted to the Council a biennial report on implementation of the Decade.[26] The report described activities undertaken by ESCAP and the conclusions of the 1991 mid-term review of the Decade,[27] as well as preparations for Phase II. The report went on to describe activities undertaken by the ESCWA secretariat, as the Western Asia region was also covered by the Decade.

By **decision 1992/295** of 31 July, the Council took note of the Secretary-General's report and of the report of the Meeting of Ministers.

Tourism

International tourism in Asia and the Pacific grew at rates higher than in other regions of the world. It became a principal source of foreign exchange for a number of countries and played a significant role in generating employment opportunities. In 1992, the Commission suggested that the secretariat expand its assistance to tourism projects at the country level and continue to assist members and associate members in collecting data on the impact of tourism on economic development. The secretariat's work programme emphasized research on the economic, socio-cultural and environmental impact of tourism, as well as human resources development, tourism marketing, promotion of tourism investment and regional and subregional cooperation in tourism development.

During the year, the secretariat continued to assist developing countries of the region in deriving greater socio-economic benefit from the planned and systematic development of tourism. Research studies were prepared on the impact of tourism on the national economy and the environment in Bangladesh, Pakistan, the Republic of Korea and Sri Lanka. Other activities included advisory services on tourism promotion and the dissemination of technical information and data on tourism development through the *ESCAP Tourism Review* and the *ESCAP Tourism Newsletter.*

Industrial and technological development

At its 1992 session, the Commission adopted the Seoul Plan of Action for Promoting Industrial Restructuring in Asia and the Pacific, which it had welcomed at its 1991 session.[28]

The Seoul Plan of Action (1992-2001) served as a basis for the Regional Strategy and Action Plan for Industrial and Technological Development, adopted by the Meeting of Ministers of Industry and Technology (Tehran, Iran, 28 and 29 June).[29] The meeting, which was preceded by a preparatory meeting of senior officals (Tehran, 23-25 June), was held in conjunction with the Industrial and Technological Exhibition (23-29 June). A private-sector symposium was held on 26 June. The Meeting also adopted the Tehran Declaration on Strengthening Regional Cooperation for Technology-led Industrialization in Asia and the Pacific.

The main objective of the regional strategy was to enhance the quality and pace of national industrial and technological developments and, through its multiplier effects on other sectors, stimulate the growth and expansion of trade, transport and communications, services, human resources development and agriculture. Its key elements included national and regional facilities, trade and investment, science and technology, problems and issues of disadvantaged economies, development of small and medium-scale industries and improvement of the public sector, the environment, women in industry and technological development, human resources development, and cooperation with the United Nations and other international organizations.

The Tehran Declaration called for further strengthening of regional cooperation to accelerate industrialization in Asia and the Pacific, urged members of ESCAP to take the action necessary for this purpose, and identified areas for such action.

During the year, the secretariat provided assistance to LDCs and the newly independent Asian republics in strengthening national capacity for industrial and technological development, and organized training workshops on industrial project preparations and management. Major activities included a training workshop on industrial projects preparation and management for LDCs and island developing countries of the region (Bangkok, 14-26 September) and a training workshop on industrial project preparation and management for private-sector representatives from selected LDCs, island developing countries and transitional disadvantaged economies of the region (Bangkok, 8-15 December).

Asian and Pacific Development Centre

The Asian and Pacific Development Centre (APDC), in implementing its fifth phase work programme (1991-1994), carried out 16 projects during 1992 in its seven programme areas: energy planning, industrial development, information technology, poverty alleviation, public management, regional cooperation, and women in development. Six projects were funded by UNDP and 10 by other countries and agencies, including such major bilateral donors as Australia, Canada, the Netherlands and Sweden. Total funds available to APDC for 1992 amounted to $3 million, an increase of 22.2 per cent over 1991. The increase was mainly due to an increase in Malaysia's contribution. Malaysia, the host Government, had also provided additional grants for upgrading the Centre's facilities. By the end of the year, 188 institutions from 33 countries, including 10 from outside the region, were associated with APDC networks.

Natural resources and marine affairs

Mineral resources

During 1992, many developing countries in the ESCAP region initiated nationwide resource assessment programmes for the discovery and development of their mineral endowments. The ESCAP secretariat assisted members in attracting foreign investment in the mining industry.

Regional mineral assessment programmes were continued in 1992 on important mineral commodities such as epithermal gold mineralization, nonmetallic and fertilizer minerals and construction materials. The secretariat focused its activities on geological resource assessment in selected countries of the region, and provided assistance in formulating national mineral development strategies, integrating geoscientific knowledge in land-use planning and applying environmental geology to sustainable development in urban centres and in the Asian and Pacific new economic zones. Other activities during the year included a seminar on future directions in mineral resources development in LDCs (Bangkok, 29 June-1 July), a workshop on a mineral information database system for the ESCAP region and installation of four country databases (Colombo, Sri Lanka, 20-25 July) and a workshop-cum-study tour on industrial minerals development (Nagoya, Japan, 27 August-2 September).

The 1992 activities of the Committee for Coordination of Joint Prospecting for Mineral Resources in Asian Offshore Areas (CCOP) in the areas of energy and minerals included work on oil and gas management, application of computer technology to map compilation, and interpretation of geological and geophysical data.

Water resources

ESCAP activities in 1992 in the area of water resources included the continued TCDC programme and a study on the assessment of water resources and water demand by user sectors in Thailand. The Interagency Task Force on Water for Asia and the Pacific met at Bangkok (15 May and 19 November), as did a workshop on testing the training modules on women, water supply and sanitation (21-25 September).

Marine affairs

In the marine affairs area, attention was directed to the problems of managing and developing coastal zones. The ESCAP secretariat continued to promote the establishment of a new ocean regime within the framework of the 1982 United Nations Convention on the Law of the Sea[30] (see PART FIVE, Chapter III) by assisting member countries to develop an integrated and multisectoral marine policy with special emphasis on the protection of the marine environment to achieve sustainable development. A number of training courses, workshops and advisory missions related to applied geosciences and coastal zone management were organized by CCOP, including a seminar on the removal and disposal of obsolete offshore installations and structures in the exclusive economic zone and the continental shelf (Jakarta, Indonesia, 25-28 May).

Mekong River basin development

The Committee for Coordination of Investigations of the Lower Mekong Basin[31] had, since 1978, functioned with interim status without the participation of Cambodia. Cambodia rejoined the Committee in November 1991, allowing full operations in that country to be resumed. In 1992, the Committee initiated consultations among the four riparian States (Cambodia, the Lao People's Democratic Republic, Thailand and Viet Nam) on its future role, mandate, structure and operations. Substantial progress was made at the Committee's meeting in October (Hong Kong). At a December meeting (Kuala Lumpur, Malaysia), the four countries approved the Committee's 1993 work programme and agreed on basic principles for future cooperation and on the modality for elaborating a new cooperative framework.

New donor commitments for the Committee totalled more than $17 million in 1992, compared with an average of $8 to $12 million during the previous decade. During 1991 and 1992, Austria, Canada and Denmark joined or rejoined the Committee's donor community.

Energy

In 1992, activities under the UNDP-funded Regional Energy Development Programme included a regional workshop on sectoral energy demand studies and energy scenarios, a workshop on co-generation and advisory missions to Cambodia on training for power sector rehabilitation and to Viet Nam on the use of computers in power system management. However, operational activities were greatly curtailed compared with the previous biennium, as UNDP had temporarily suspended support.

TCDC activities were conducted between China and Sri Lanka and Viet Nam in wind energy technology, and between Thailand and China, India, the Republic of Korea and Viet Nam in acid rain and emissions, while Australia funded a project on environmentally sound coal utilization. In October, missions were fielded to China, India and Japan to collect information and hold discussions on clean coal technology. In a concerted effort to promote the enhancement of energy efficiency, ESCAP, together with the other regional commissions, initiated the Global Energy Efficiency 21 project, as follow-up to the 1992 United Nations Conference on Environment and Development (see PART THREE, Chapter VIII.).

A workshop on the legal framework for co-generation of electricity and process heat (Bangkok, 30 June–2 July) was organized jointly by ESCAP and the German Agency for Technical Cooperation.

Agricultural and rural development

During 1992, ESCAP activities in agriculture and rural development continued to focus on the alleviation of rural poverty, integrated rural development and interdivisional, inter-agency and multisectoral activities. The ESCAP/FAO/UNIDO Fertilizer Advisory, Development and Information Network for Asia and the Pacific carried out national and regional training programmes in India, Indonesia, the Lao People's Democratic Republic, Nepal, Thailand and Viet Nam under the regional fertilizer distribution and marketing assistance programme and the project on environmentally friendly fertilizer use. The agricultural requisites scheme for Asia and the Pacific continued to collect pesticide index information and launched, in April, a project to create a database on pesticides and the environment, funded by ECE. Field work on employment strategies to involve the rural poor in income-generating activities was continued in Bangladesh, Nepal and Viet Nam as part of an inter-agency programme within the framework of the Inter-agency Coordinated Plan of Action for Integrated Rural Development in the ESCAP Region.

Other activities included an expert group meeting on a centre on rival enterprises (Beijing, 13-15 May) and a meeting of the Inter-agency Task Force on Integrated Rural Development for Asia and the Pacific (Bangkok, 26 August).

Science and technology

ESCAP continued its activities aimed at strengthening technological capabilities and institutional infrastructure for science and technology in its member States. It accorded high priority to the transfer and diffusion of technology, especially with regard to energy conservation and renewable sources of energy, as well as to biotechnology and information technology. It provided advisory services to the region's LDCs to improve their capability to import technology. In the field of biotechnology, special importance was placed on greater regional cooperation, women's involvement in development, the transfer and adaptation of technology and the extension of biotechnology to small-scale farmers.

The Governing Board of the Asian and Pacific Centre for Transfer of Technology held its seventh session at New Delhi on 27 and 28 November.[32] The Centre's main activity continued to be a UNDP-supported project on technology transfer and management with particular relevance to clean technologies. Workshops included one on the identification and formulation of intercountry projects in the field of biotechnology (Taejon, Republic of Korea, 14-18 September) and a regional training workshop on the application and extension of the technology atlas (Bangkok, 14-18 December).

Remote sensing

The second phase of the UNDP-funded ESCAP Regional Remote Sensing Programme was completed on 30 June 1992. It began to function as a regular budget programme activity within

ESCAP and included seminars, short- and long-term training activities and information exchange. The Programme maintained a national focal points network covering 30 member countries, a regional information service network in 17 countries and an education and training network in 17 countries of the region. Technical advisory assistance was strengthened with the appointment of a regional adviser on remote sensing and geographic information systems. The Programme's activities helped update and maintain a higher standard in the application of space remote sensing and geographic information systems for the sustainable development of environmental resources in Asia and the Pacific.

Social development

Activities in the area of social development focused on implementing the Social Development Strategy for the ESCAP Region towards the Year 2000 and Beyond. On 23 April,[33] the Commission welcomed the Strategy's adoption in 1991[34] by the Fourth Ministerial Conference on Social Welfare and Social Development and urged all members and associate members to take early action to implement it. It called on donor countries and funding agencies, United Nations bodies and specialized agencies and intergovernmental and non-governmental organizations to provide substantive and financial support. The Commission requested the Executive Secretary to examine modalities for implementing the Strategy, convene a meeting of experts to obtain advice on the matter and establish an inter-agency task force to promote intersectoral participation and ensure effective coordination of the United Nations system in implementing the Strategy; establish a forum of concerned NGOs to promote their participation; convene in 1994 a regional conference of senior government officials, United Nations bodies and agencies and other organizations to review progress achieved towards attaining the Strategy's aims and objectives; and prepare a progress report for submission to the Fifth Asian and Pacific Ministerial Conference on Social Welfare and Social Development to be held in 1996.

As requested by the Commission, an expert group meeting on implementation of the Social Development Strategy was held at Bangkok from 8 to 11 December, and the Inter-agency Task Force meeting on the Strategy's implementation was held, also at Bangkok, on 14 December. An expert group meeting on a survey of the quality of life in the ESCAP region met twice in 1992 (Seoul, 11-15 August; Bangkok, 26-30 October).

In the social development field, in addition to activities in the areas of human resources development, assistance to disabled persons, population, human settlements and women (see below),

ESCAP organized a number of meetings on drug abuse control and the special problems of youth and the elderly. They included a Pacific subregional workshop on the training of trainers in rural and urban youth work (Honiara, Solomon Islands, 5-19 July), a community-level training course on the development of integrated community-based approaches to drug abuse demand reduction (Manila, 2-6 September; Kandhala, India, 18-24 September; Bangkok, 26-30 October; Manila, 4-8 November), a meeting to design country studies on policies and programmes concerning the integration of elderly persons in development (Bangkok, 29 September–2 October) and a seminar on the effects of new technologies on the working life of young people (Zhuhai, China, 20-24 October).

The ESCAP secretariat held an expert group meeting to examine and advise on the modalities for implementing the regional strategy on social development and established an inter-agency task force on its implementation. Advisory services were provided to assist Governments and NGOs in planning and delivering social services, in strengthening demand-reduction activities to fight drug abuse and in crime prevention and criminal justice. The secretariat also contributed to strengthening a regional network of national focal points on drug abuse demand reduction, extending community-based action on drug abuse to the border area of two countries in the region and developing integrated community-based approaches to tackle the problem through information collection and pilot planning and training workshops.

Human resources development

On 23 April,[35] the Commission called on all its members and associate members to intensify their efforts to promote human resources development by implementing the 1988 Jakarta Plan of Action on Human Resources Development in the ESCAP Region.[36] All bilateral and multilateral development partners were invited to support and participate in the regional initiative, and UNDP was urged to provide adequate funding. The Commission requested the Executive Secretary to continue to provide support to the activities of the ESCAP Network of National Focal Points for Human Resources Development, particularly in strengthening linkages among government agencies and between them and NGOs and the private sector; adopting an integrated approach to human resources development; building a human resources development information base; promoting the training of public sector and NGO personnel in human resources development–related skills; enhancing public awareness of human resources development as elaborated in the Jakarta Plan of Action; establishing, in each country and area, a national advisory mechanism to provide conceptual guidance to human resources development initiatives at the national level; and monitoring and evaluating the Jakarta Plan of Action's implementation. He was also asked to prepare standardized procedures for use by Governments in monitoring and evaluating the implementation of the Plan of Action, review the status of its implementation, convene an expert group meeting to re-examine the Plan of Action with a view to refining it to ensure its continued relevance, and refine it in conformity with the findings of that expert group for submission to the Commission in 1994.

As requested, the ESCAP secretariat developed guidelines to assist in the systematic monitoring and evaluation of the Jakarta Plan of Action and initiated a project to involve the business sector in skills-training programmes to enhance the productivity of the rural poor.

Disabled persons

On 23 April,[37] the Commission proclaimed the Asian and Pacific Decade of Disabled Persons, 1993-2002, with a view to giving fresh impetus to implementing the 1982 World Programme of Action concerning Disabled Persons[38] (see also PART THREE, Chapter XI) in the ESCAP region beyond 1992 and strengthening regional cooperation to resolve issues affecting the achievement of the World Programme of Action's goals, especially those concerning the full participation and equality of persons with disabilities. The Economic and Social Council and General Assembly were asked to endorse the Commission's resolution and to encourage support for its implementation. The Commission urged all members and associate members to review the situation of disabled persons in their countries and areas, with a view to developing measures to enhance their equality and full participation, including: formulating and implementing national policies and programmes to promote the participation of disabled persons in economic and social development; establishing and strengthening national coordinating committees on disability matters; assisting in enhancing community-based support services for disabled persons and their families; and promoting special efforts to foster positive attitudes towards children and adults with disabilities, and undertaking measures to improve their access to rehabilitation, education, employment, cultural and sports activities and the physical environment. The Commission urged members of the United Nations system to examine their ongoing programmes and projects in the region with a view to integrating disability concerns into their work programmes. It called on NGOs to utilize their experience and expertise to strengthen the capabilities and activities of organizations of disabled persons, and urged the latter organizations to cooperate with government agencies in helping disabled citizens to realize their full potential and in strengthening linkages among disabled persons in developed and developing countries to enhance their self-help capacity. The Executive Secretary was asked to assist members and associate members to develop and pursue national programmes of action during the Decade and to formulate and implement technical guidelines and legislation to promote access by disabled persons to buildings, public facilities, transport and communications systems, information, education and training, and technical aids. He was also asked to report to the Commission biennially until the Decade's end on progress made in implementing the resolution.

During 1992, the ESCAP secretariat fostered regional support for implementing the resolution by preparing case-studies and technical guidelines on promoting non-handicapping environments for disabled and elderly persons. It also published a directory of self-help organizations of disabled persons and reports on a series of national training workshops. A meeting to launch the Asian and Pacific Decade of Disabled Persons, 1993-2002, was held at Beijing from 1 to 5 December, and the Sixth Meeting of the Asia-Pacific Inter-organizational Task Force on Disability-related Concerns was held at Bangkok on 1 September.

By **decision 1992/289** of 31 July, the Economic and Social Council endorsed the Commission's resolution proclaiming the Decade. By **resolution 47/88** of 16 December, the General Assembly welcomed the Commission's proclamation.

Population

On 23 April,[39] the Commission called on member and associate member Governments to review and appraise population trends and policies in their countries and areas in order to report to the Fourth Asian and Pacific Population Conference to be held later in the year. It urged them to participate, at the ministerial level, in its deliberations, which were aimed at determining goals, strategies and directions for the achievement of sustainable development in the twenty-first century. The Executive Secretary was asked to undertake follow-up activities based on the Conference's recommendations and provide assistance to members in implementing those recommendations. He was also asked to present the Conference's findings to the International Conference on Population and Development to be held in 1994.

The Fourth Asian and Pacific Population Conference was held in two parts at Bali, Indonesia: a meeting of senior officials (19-24 August) followed by a ministerial meeting (26 and

27 August).[40] The Preparatory Committee for the Conference held its third session, also at Bali, from 16 to 18 August.

The Conference reviewed the population situation in the region and adopted the Bali Declaration on Population and Sustainable Development,[41] which included a set of 67 recommendations on policy and programme development, population data and policy research, information and population awareness and human resources development in population. It also formulated proposals on follow-up strategies for consideration by the Commission in 1993, which included activities to improve the awareness and understanding of population and sustainable development issues among planners, policy makers and programme managers; the data, information and knowledge base relating to population, use of resources, the environment, development and their interrelationships; the policies, plans and programmes reflective of those linkages; the implementation, monitoring and evaluation of those programmes; and the national skills to respond effectively to the emerging challenges.

Other ESCAP activities in the area of population in 1992 included training on mangement, analysis and synthesis of population data and information (Bangkok, 4-15 May), an expert group meeting on population change, women's role and status, and development (Bangkok, 12-15 May), a study programme on technology and management of population data processing services (Hong Kong, 15 June-3 July) and an expert group meeting on trends, patterns and implications of rural-urban migration (Bangkok, 3-6 November).

Human settlements

ESCAP activities during 1992 in the human settlements area included missions to Ho Chi Minh City (Viet Nam) and Ahmedabad (India) to discuss the modalities and applied methodological approach to regional planning, an advisory services mission on housing finance and credit systems to Vientiane (Lao People's Democratic Republic), a regional training course on applicable construction technology and material (Chengdu, China) in April and a regional seminar-cum-study visit on solid waste management (Bandung, Indonesia) which addressed solid waste collection, treatment and disposal; privatization; and innovative approaches to solid waste management. The Regional Network of Local Authorities for the Management of Human Settlements (CITYNET), established by ESCAP with UNDP support, became independent and continued to promote cooperation and exchange of know-how in areas of urban management.

In preparation for the Ministerial Conference on Urbanization, to be held in 1993, ESCAP convened a Consultative Meeting on Establishing an Inter-organizational Task Force on Urbanization for Asia and the Pacific (Bangkok, 9 September).[42] A report on the state of urbanization in the region to be submitted to the Conference was under preparation.

Other activities included a policy-level seminar on subnational area planning through action-oriented research (Bangkok, 15-18 June), workshops, in Chiang Mai, Thailand, on urban economy and productivity (6 and 7 July) and on urban poverty (10 and 11 July) and an intergovernmental expert group meeting on urbanization (Colombo, 30 March-1 April).

Women in development

In preparation for the Second Asian and Pacific Ministerial Conference on Women and Development, to be held in 1994, ESCAP convened an interdivisional meeting on 8 September and an inter-agency meeting on 10 September, both at Bangkok.[43] In addition, a seminar on the participation of women in politics as an aspect of human resources development in the ESCAP region, funded by the Republic of Korea, took place at Seoul from 18 to 20 November. The seminar adopted the Seoul Statement on Empowering Women in Politics.[44]

Activities undertaken by ESCAP to promote and strengthen national capabilities for the integration of women's concerns into development planning included advisory services to Governments and NGOs; background studies on women's concerns; and policy recommendations relating to household operations, the market system and the government sector. In an effort to promote awareness of the need for equal rights legislation and its implementation, it organized a series of national workshops on legal literacy, followed by campaigns to improve the legal status of women. Meetings included a Pacific subregional workshop on the technical processing of information concerning women in development (Suva, Fiji, 4-15 May) and a national legal literacy workshop (Kuala Lumpur, 5 and 6 September).

Environment

The focus of ESCAP's environmental activities in 1992 was on the achievement of environmentally sound and sustainable development in the region. In an effort to integrate the objectives and recommendations of the 1992 United Nations Conference on Environment and Development (see PART THREE, Chapter VIII) into its work, the secretariat concentrated on implementing the Regional Strategy on Environmentally Sound and Sustainable Development, endorsed by the Commission in 1991,[45] as well as the recommendations of the 1990 Ministerial-level Conference on Environment and Development in Asia and the Pacific.

A project on desertification control gave priority to national capacity-building and the elaboration of desertification assessment and mapping methodology in the region. A regional working group on the marine environment and oceanographic studies was set up, and studies were undertaken to develop guidelines for environmentally sound coastal tourism development. Other activities included an ESCAP/UNDP consultative policy meeting on the regional network of environment and economic policy research institutions on environmentally sound and sustainable development (Bangkok, 13-16 July), a meeting of the Interagency Committee on Environment and Development in Asia and the Pacific (Bangkok, 8 September), a meeting on the regional working group on marine environment and oceanographic studies (Guangzhou, China, 28 September-3 October), a workshop to consider models for sustainable development and application of environmental development principles (Bangkok, 25-27 November), an expert group meeting on appropriate methodologies for hazardous waste management in Asia and the Pacific (Bangkok, 1-4 December), and an ESCAP/UNDP consultative meeting on models for environmentally sound and sustainable development (Bangkok, 8-10 December).

Natural disaster reduction

The Typhoon Committee, at its twenty-fifth session (Zhuhai, China, 8-14 December),[46] restated the importance of telecommunications in its activities and the need for a consolidated telecommunications system that would standardize and integrate some of its operational activities. The Committee appealed to ESCAP to consider allocating manpower and other resources to implement natural disaster reduction activities.

Statistics

The Committee on Statistics, at its eighth session (Bangkok, 16-20 November),[47] reviewed statistical and governmental computerization activities in the region and focused on issues relating to the development of national statistical capabilities; the promotion of computerization in the public sector; and the development of economic statistics, statistics in support of regional economic cooperation, social and demographic statistics, including those in support of poverty alleviation, and environmental and energy statistics. The Committee endorsed its programmes of work for 1992-1993 and 1994-1995 as well as the revised medium-term plan for 1992-1997. It identified important areas of its work in government computerization, including the promotion of standards and coding systems for integration of government information systems and the establishment of national policies and strategies for the development of government computerization. It also decided to hold an expert group meeting to review computerization development in the public sector.

Other meetings on statistics in 1992 included a workshop on the development and improvement of environment statistics (Kathmandu, Nepal, 31 May-4 June), a workshop on ESCAP regional specifications for phase VI of the International Comparison Programme (Beijing, 21-25 September) and a seminar on the development of statistical estimating procedures and techniques as a means of improving the timeliness of data (Bangkok, 26-30 October).

Statistical Institute for Asia and the Pacific

The Statistical Institute for Asia and the Pacific[48] (Tokyo) continued to train statisticians in government services. During the year, 166 people participated in its training courses on practical statistics, automatic data processing and analysis and interpretation of statistics, and in its five in-country courses. The Institute completed the fifth phase of its work in March and agreed on the framework of the sixth phase.

Organizational questions

Membership

In a June note,[49] the Secretary-General informed the Economic and Social Council that Kazakhstan and Uzbekistan had applied for full membership in ESCAP.

ECONOMIC AND SOCIAL COUNCIL ACTION

By **resolution 1992/46** of 31 July, the Council recommended that Kazakhstan and Uzbekistan be included in the geographical scope of the Commission and be admitted as members, and decided to amend the Commission's terms of reference accordingly.

By two other resolutions of 31 July, the Council, noting that the Democratic People's Republic of Korea (**resolution 1992/47**) and the Federated States of Micronesia and the Marshall Islands (**resolution 1992/48**) had become members of ESCAP, decided to amend the Commission's terms of reference accordingly. By **resolution 1992/49**, also of 31 July, the Council, noting that French Polynesia and New Caledonia had become associate members of ESCAP, decided to amend the Commission's terms of reference accordingly. By **resolution 1992/50** of the same date, the Council, noting that ESCAP had recommended the inclusion of Azerbaijan, Kyrgyzstan, Tajikistan and Turkmenistan in its geographical scope and their admission as members of the Commission, approved that recommendation and decided to amend the Commission's terms of reference accordingly.

Forty-ninth ESCAP session

At its forty-eighth session, the Commission decided to hold its forty-ninth session at Bangkok in March or April 1993, and chose "expansion of investment and intraregional trade as a vehicle for enhancing regional economic cooperation and development" as its theme topic for that session.

REFERENCES

[1]E/1992/31. [2]Ibid. (res. 48/1). [3]Ibid. (res. 48/2). [4]Ibid. (res. 48/12). [5]*Economic and Social Survey of Asia and the Pacific, 1992* (ST/ESCAP/1243, Parts I & II), Sales No. E.93.II.F.6. [6]E/1993/52. [7]E/ESCAP/826. [8]E/ESCAP/897. [9]E/ESCAP/898. [10]E/ESCAP/899. [11]A/CONF.147/18. [12]GA res. 45/206, 21 Dec. 1990. [13]E/ESCAP/873 & Corr.1. [14]E/1992/31 (res. 48/9). [15]Ibid. (res. 48/8). [16]E/ESCAP/920. [17]E/1992/31 (res. 48/10). [18]Ibid. (res. 48/7). [19]YUN 1985, p. 571, GA res. 39/248, annex, 9 Apr. 1985. [20]E/1992/31 (res. 48/11). [21]E/ESCAP/892. [22]YUN 1984, p. 624, GA res. 39/227, 18 Dec. 1984. [23]YUN 1991, p. 313, GA dec. 46/453, 20 Dec. 1991. [24]E/1992/61/Add.1. [25]YUN 1984, p. 623, ESC res. 1984/78, 27 July 1984. [26]E/1992/61. [27]YUN 1991, p. 312. [28]YUN 1991, p. 313. [29]E/ESCAP/893. [30]YUN 1982, p. 181. [31]E/ESCAP/911. [32]E/ESCAP/906. [33]E/1992/31 (res. 48/5). [34]YUN 1991, p. 316. [35]E/1992/31 (res. 48/6). [36]E/1988/35 (res. 274 (XLIV)). [37]E/1992/31 (res. 48/3). [38]YUN 1982, p. 980. [39]E/1992/31 (res. 48/4). [40]ST/ESCAP/1198. [41]ST/ESCAP/1195. [42]E/ESCAP/905. [43]E/ESCAP/907. [44]E/ESCAP/926. [45]YUN 1991, p. 318. [46]E/ESCAP/912. [47]E/ESCAP/896. [48]E/ESCAP/909. [49]E/1992/88.

Europe

The forty-seventh session of the Economic Commission for Europe took place at Geneva from 7 to 15 April 1992, at a time when the ECE region had to face new challenges calling for cooperative solutions. Following the disintegration of the former USSR and Yugoslavia and the consequent creation of newly independent States, the old East-West partition of Europe was replaced by new structures for cooperation and economic links, as countries in Central and Eastern Europe continued on the road towards parliamentary democracy and a market economy. Equally significant were the integration processes in Western Europe, highlighted by the signing of the Maastricht Treaty in February, which set guidelines for political, monetary and economic union, and the establishment of economic cooperation and free-trade agreements between countries from all parts of the region. However, the euphoria of 1989 gave way to a growing realization that the economic and political transformation of the region would be a long and arduous task.

During the year since the 1991 session, there was a general weakening of output growth in Europe, with several countries remaining in or moving into recession. The overall slow-down resulted in rising unemployment and increasing inflationary pressures. Changes in the economic system, introduction of stabilization measures and the collapse of trade among countries belonging to the former CMEA contributed significantly to the recession in Eastern Europe, causing an accelerating fall in output and a rise in unemployment. As the transition to a market economy proved more painful and complex than originally expected, bilateral and multilateral initiatives were needed to secure the success of reforms and mitigate the hardships experienced by the countries in transition, as well as to promote their integration into the European and global economy.

The Helsinki Declaration, adopted at the summit of the Conference on Security and Cooperation in Europe (CSCE) in July 1992, recognized the Commission's key role in the construction of a new Europe. As an agency for the multilateral implementation of the relevant provisions of CSCE, including its Final Act, the Charter of Paris for a New Europe, adopted at the 1990 CSCE summit, and the final document of the 1990 Bonn Conference on Economic Cooperation in Europe, ECE continued to make substantive contributions to the CSCE process. In 1992, particular attention was given to cooperation with Mediterranean countries not members of ECE, with a view to developing projects of common interest promoting economic and social development and enhancing stability in the region.

At its April session,[1] the Commission reviewed the implementation of its 1990 decisions on restructuring within ECE and considered its activities and future work in the five priority areas, namely, environment, transport, statistics, trade facilitation and economic analysis, as well as activities designed to assist countries in transition to a market economy and issues relating to sustainable development. Noting that its membership had increased from 34 to 40 countries between April 1991 and April 1992, ECE welcomed Estonia, Israel, Latvia, Lithuania, the Republic of Moldova and San Marino as its new members.

It adopted seven decisions, six of which pertained to the provision of adequate resources for the servicing of ECE's priority sectors;[2] fundamental principles of official statistics in the region;[3] its work concerning economies in transition in Central and Eastern Europe;[4] cooperation in the field of environment and sustainable development;[5] cooperation in the field of transport;[6] and economic cooperation in the Mediterranean in the light of the Final Act of CSCE.[7] By the seventh decision, the Commission approved its programme of work for 1992-1993 and endorsed in principle, subject to review at its forty-eighth (1993) session, its programme of work for 1992-1996.[8]

In response to a 1991 Commission request,[9] its Chairman continued to convene ad hoc informal meetings of ECE to consult on policy matters, assist in preparations for the annual sessions, monitor progress in the work programmes and offer guidance to the Executive Secretary.

As agreed at an ad hoc informal meeting on 25 June, the Commission, at a special session on 5 October,[10] considered the question of strengthening its role and functions and adopted pertinent recommendations.[11] Noting the applications of Armenia, Azerbaijan, Kyrgyzstan, Turkmenistan and Uzbekistan for admission to full membership, ECE stated that it would welcome those newly independent republics of the former USSR as its members, and welcomed their immediate participation in its activities, pending approval by the Economic and Social Council of any necessary amendments to ECE's terms of reference.

During the year under review, the Commission continued to provide a bridge between the United Nations and other economic institutions active in the region, such as EC, OECD, the Council of Europe and the European Bank for Reconstruction and Development. During 1992, five countries (Bosnia and Herzegovina, Croatia, the Republic of Moldova, San Marino and Slovenia) became members of ECE by virtue of their admission to the United Nations, bringing the Commission's membership to 43 by year's end.

By a letter of 2 July,[12] the ECE Chairman communicated to the Economic and Social Council an appeal of the ECE members to maintain budgetary resources allotted to ECE and to find a rapid solution to the situation created by the lack of personnel in its secretariat, in the light of unprecedented and increasing needs for cooperation and assistance in the region. Annexed to the letter was a resolution adopted by the Conference of European Statisticians in June (see below), calling for priority filling of vacancies in ECE's Statistical Division.

By **decision 1992/295** of 31 July, the Council took note of the letter.

Economic trends

Economic developments in Europe were disappointing in 1992, as economic conditions in Western Europe deteriorated significantly, with high and rising unemployment and a financial crisis in the public sector. According to the summary of the economic survey of Europe in 1992-1993,[13] average output growth stagnated at a rate of 1 per cent, coupled with a sharp weakening of economic activity in the second half of the year, while unemployment rose to just under 10 per cent from 8.9 per cent in 1991. The 1993 projections for the four major economies in Western Europe showed that real GDP was likely to fall in France, Germany and Italy, and was expected to grow, albeit slowly, only in the United Kingdom. Major factors behind that economic downturn were high interest rates, resulting from a tightening of monetary policy in Germany, and the commitment to fixed exchange rates under the EC Exchange Rates Mechanism. The situation in the smaller countries was characterized by a pervasive slow-down in economic growth, with a number of economies close to stagnation or even an absolute fall in total output. Against a background of turbulent foreign-exchange markets, and with the German economy moving into recession, consumer and business confidence were at very low levels. In an effort to enhance the scope for output and employment growth through a coordinated macroeconomic policy, the EC summit at Edinburgh, United Kingdom, in December adopted a package of measures to stimulate investment demand; however, the overall impact was expected to be rather modest.

Economic performance in Central and Eastern Europe was characterized by increasing diversity among the countries in transition, although the overall economic crisis deepened further during the year. GDP/net material product fell on average by some 10 per cent, bringing the aggregate decline since 1989 to more than 30 per cent, with the 1992 estimated falls ranging from 27 per cent in the Federal Republic of Yugoslavia (Serbia and Montenegro) to 4-6 per cent in Hungary, whereas in Czechoslovakia the decline appeared to have come to an end. A slow recovery was also indicated in Poland. In the former USSR/Commonwealth of Independent States (CIS), the falls in output ranged from 11 per cent in Belarus and 19 per cent in the Russian Federation to 28 per cent in Estonia, 35 per cent in Lithuania, over 40 per cent in Armenia and 44 per cent in Latvia. Agricultural output also declined, by 9-13 per cent in Eastern Europe and 10 per cent in CIS.

Nearly 6.5 million people in Eastern Europe were unemployed in December 1992, up from 5 million in 1991, with rates varying from 5 per cent in Czechoslovakia to 14 per cent in Poland and nearly 25 per cent in the Federal Repubic of Yugoslavia. In CIS and the Baltic States, where unemployment was less than 1 per cent, except in Armenia, Estonia and Latvia (2 to 3.5 per cent), there was a significant increase in the number of people officially classified as living in poverty, which in Russia more than doubled towards the end of 1992 from 12 to 29 per cent of the population. Annual inflation rates fell to 80 per cent in Bulgaria, 43 per cent in Poland, 23 per cent in Hungary and 11 to 10 per cent in Czechoslovakia, but accelerated to over 200 per cent in Albania, Romania and Slovenia. Hyperinflation was registered in the Federal Republic of Yugoslavia, with a rising annual rate of more than 9,000 per cent. In Russia and most of CIS, prices were rising at some 25 per cent a month, while the Baltic States reduced their monthly inflation to some 3 to 5 per cent by the end of the year.

At the same time, the private sector in the economies in transition grew rapidly, particularly in agriculture, construction, trade and other services. Its share in domestic output increased from 9 per cent in 1991 to 20 per cent in 1992 in Czechoslovakia and from 5 to 10 per cent in Bulgaria, and reached some 25-35 per cent of GDP in Hungary, 26 per cent in Romania and 45-50 per cent in Poland. Eastern Europe also sustained a significant growth of exports to Western markets, while trade between those markets and CIS, as well as intra-Eastern trade, continued to fall.

Ethnic strife in some parts of the region, which followed the breakup of the USSR and Yugoslavia, provided economic and social problems on a different scale, as more than 200,000 people were killed, some 85 per cent of whom were in Yugoslavia, and nearly 3 million were displaced.

Western economic assistance to Eastern Europe

Economic assistance to the region's 17 countries in transition to a market economy focused on technical aid to help create appropriate institutional structures and train people to operate them effectively, backed up by improved access for Eastern exports to Western markets and by short-run financing for private investment to take over the task of economic restructuring. According to the summary of the economic survey,[13] some $40 billion of financing was made available to those countries in 1992; however, only a small portion of it was grant aid or concessional finance, while special financing (debt write-offs, rescheduling, deferrals and arrears) accounted for about one half of the amount, totalling $5 billion in Eastern Europe and $14 billion in CIS and the Baltic States. A further $1 billion was provided by the International Monetary Fund (IMF) to Russia. A large portion of financing came in bilateral credits, which were debt-creating and carried market interest rates. The total flow of those resources was estimated at $12 billion for Russia in 1992 and $20 billion for Eastern Europe in 1991. At the same time, multilateral financing in that subregion fell from $8.5 billion in 1991 to less than $5 billion in 1992.

Political uncertainties, incomplete market infrastructures and delays in resolving basic problems such as property rights in the economies in tran-sition, as well as much delayed recovery of activity there and a deepening recession in Western Europe, led Western companies to reassess their investments in the East and postpone new investments. Those problems notwithstanding, foreign direct investment (FDI) to those countries rose from $0.6 billion in 1990 to some $3 billion in 1992, although the bulk of it (some 90 per cent) was concentrated in Czechoslovakia and Hungary. FDI also increased in 1992 in Poland and Slovenia, but the amounts remained relatively small.

In April, the seven major industrial nations announced a $24 billion aid package to Russia; according to IMF, that obligation was essentially met during the year. Yet the delivery of financial aid as well as rapidly expanding technical assistance activities revealed an urgent need for improved monitoring and coordination and for broader national transition frameworks, to match assistance with the specific economic needs of each country. Among other problems facing both the countries in transition and Western economies were debt servicing, the uneven distribution of financial assistance, further liberalization of trade, effects of United Nations sanctions on trade with the Federal Republic of Yugoslavia and increasing emigration to Western Europe.

Despite those difficulties, there was room for optimism as the reforms were starting to bear fruit and economic indicators were improving. During the year, association agreements designed to reduce trade barriers and improve market access were signed between EC and Bulgaria, Czechoslovakia, Hungary, Poland and Romania. EC also signed trade and economic cooperation agreements with Albania, the Baltic States and Slovenia, and opened negotiations on partnership and cooperation agreements with CIS countries on a broad range of political, economic and commercial relations. An early and successful conclusion of the Uruguay Round of multilateral trade negotiations could also provide important benefits to the countries of Central and Eastern Europe.

In February, the UNDP Governing Council approved the allocation of indicative planning figures under the fifth programming cycle (1992-1996) for Belarus, Estonia, Latvia, Lithuania and Ukraine, and authorized the Administrator to proceed with programme development in those five countries.[14] A similar action was taken in May for Armenia, Azerbaijan, Kazakhstan, Kyrgyzstan, the Republic of Moldova, the Russian Federation, Turkmenistan and Uzbekistan.[15] Also in May, the Governing Council, having considered ways of establishing a United Nations presence in the Baltic States and CIS, requested the Administrator, in collaboration with United Nations bodies, to elaborate an integrated United Nation system approach to and presence in the countries concerned and provide them with operational support during 1992-1993, and approved, on an exceptional basis, the use of up to $3 million during that period to open a limited number of UNDP offices in those regions.[16]

The Executive Board of the United Nations Children's Fund (UNICEF), at its 1992 regular session, recognized the need to enhance the role of UNICEF in Central and Eastern Europe, the Baltic States and CIS and approved recommendations of its Executive Director to that effect (for details, see PART THREE, Chapter XIV).

ECONOMIC AND SOCIAL COUNCIL ACTION

On 30 July, the Economic and Social Council adopted **resolution 1992/40** without vote.

Activities of the United Nations system in the Baltic States and the Commonwealth of Independent States

The Economic and Social Council,

Recalling decision 92/43, adopted on 26 May 1992 by the Governing Council of the United Nations Development Programme at its thirty-ninth session, and decision 1992/19, adopted by the Executive Board of the United Nations Children's Fund at its regular session of 1992, concerning the activities of the United Nations system in the Baltic States and the Commonwealth of Independent States,

Reaffirming the importance it attaches to an integrated United Nations system approach to, and presence in, the region,

1. *Requests* the various bodies of the United Nations system, in order to ensure an integrated United Nations system approach to, and presence in, the Baltic States and the Commonwealth of Independent States:

(a) In consultation with the Administrative Committee on Coordination and the Joint Consultative Group on Policy, to reach an early agreement that will ensure such an integrated approach and presence in the countries concerned, including common administrative support arrangements;

(b) In providing assistance to the countries concerned, to take account of the national priorities of those countries and of the comparative advantages of each of the bodies of the United Nations system;

2. *Invites* the Secretary-General to prepare a report on ways of ensuring such an integrated approach and presence in the countries concerned and the steps already taken to do so, which would be annexed to the report for the triennial comprehensive policy review of operational activities of the United Nations system at the forty-seventh session of the General Assembly.

Economic and Social Council resolution 1992/40

30 July 1992   Meeting 41   Adopted without vote

Draft by Austria, Belarus, Canada, Estonia, Finland, Japan, Latvia, Lithuania, New Zealand, Norway, Russian Federation, Sweden, Switzerland, Turkey, United Kingdom (for EEC), United States (E/1992/L.34); agenda item 4.
Meeting numbers. ESC 38, 41.

Activities in 1992

Assistance to the Central and Eastern European economies continued to be at the core of ECE activities in 1992,[17] which was reflected in the establishment of a United Nations/ECE Trust Fund for Assistance to Countries in Transition. ECE organized 34 workshops in those countries on issues relating to energy, transport, statistics, human settlements, industrial development, agriculture and timber, and, to a lesser extent, trade, environment and economic analysis. Its subsidiary bodies established special assistance programmes in their respective areas. Efforts were made to ensure close cooperation with other international organizations and their participation in the assistance programme.

Another area of activities was the ECE's continuing assistance to developing countries of other regions and its contribution to United Nations global programmes,[18] as well as its active participation in and contribution to the CSCE process.[19]

International trade

The ECE Committee on the Development of Trade (forty-first session, Geneva, 8-10 December 1992)[20] reviewed the economic and trading situation in the region, with an emphasis on trade facilitation and promotion of trade with the transition economies. It welcomed the secretariat proposal for an assistance programme in trade facilitation as well as its decision to establish an inter-secretariat task force between ECE, UNCTAD and the International Trade Centre to ensure greater cooperation and coordination of related work. It decided to hold three workshops in Eastern Europe in 1993 on promotion of FDI; progress in foreign trade and payments reform; and implication of privatization, including the role of small and medium-sized enterprises, for international trade and investment. The secretariat was requested to prepare studies on successful measures and negative experiences of the Eastern economies in the field of privatization, and on the establishment of conditions conducive to expanding trade among those countries. The Committee decided to continue its work in the field of trade in services and on information sources relevant to trade and investment activities in Central and Eastern Europe and needed by business operators.

The Committee adopted a revised programme of work for 1992-1995, reformulating it under three main headings: trade facilitation, trade promotion and trade analysis. It examined the report of a workshop on the management of East-West joint ventures (Rome, Italy, June 1992) and a *Guide on Management Requirements and Training for East-West Joint Ventures,* and noted that the secretariat's quarterly newsletter, *East-West Joint Ventures News,* continued to be published under the title *East-West Investment News*. It decided to select a discussion theme for each session, and chose the impact of trade facilitation on trade in the ECE region as the theme for its 1993 session.

The Committee reviewed the work carried out by the Working Party on International Contract Practices in Industry, which included the publication of a *Guide on Legal Aspects of Privatization in Industry* and the preparation of a new guide on financing East-West trade and privatization in Central and Eastern Europe. It also assessed the rapid progress achieved by the Working Party on Facilitation of International Trade Procedures, which approved a number of new messages to be submitted to trial and testing to increase the practical application of the United Nations Electronic Data Interchange for Administration, Commerce and Transport (UN/EDIFACT) as a standard for world trade. In total, there were 124 messages at various stages of development by the Working Party. A steering group was set up to streamline EDIFACT procedures so as to enhance the production of messages, and the team of regional rapporteurs, constituting regional EDIFACT boards, was being expanded with an agreed establishment of an African Board. During 1992, Brazil became a full member and Chile and Colombia associate members of the North American EDIFACT Board, which changed its name to Pan American EDIFACT Board, while Estonia, Latvia, Lithuania and the Russian Federation joined the Eastern European Board. The Western European Board was expanded to include Luxembourg as a member and Malta as an observer.

The Working Party also analysed international trade transactions to give countries in transition a tool for developing efficient trade procedures in order to be more competitive in Western markets, and continued implementing its comprehensive work programme in the legal field.

Industry

The Working Party on the Chemical Industry held its second session at Geneva from 7 to 9 October 1992.[21] It endorsed the reports of the meeting of experts on the periodic survey of the chemical industry and of the annual meeting of rapporteurs on aromatic hydrocarbons and olefins, and took note of the progress made in preparing a study on management of plastic wastes in the region and the *ECE Directory of Chemical Producers and Products*. The Working Party adopted its programme of work for 1993-1997, including the priority ranking of programme elements, and agreed to include in the programme a study on trends in structural and ownership changes in the chemical industries of the economies in transition.

It also considered the report of a high-level meeting on cooperation and sustainable development in the chemical industry (Warsaw, Poland, 10-12 March 1992), which reviewed development strategies for the chemical industry in the 1990s in the areas of environment, health and safety; availability and efficient use of raw materials and energy; investment and industrial cooperation; and follow-up activities in the countries in transition. ECE decided to present the conclusions of the meeting to UNCED.

The Working Party welcomed the conclusions of the meeting as guidelines for its future work and discussed possible follow-up action geared towards sustainable economic and ecological development of the chemical industry. Acting on a proposal by Poland to establish a regional environmental management centre for the chemical industry, it decided to convene a meeting of experts at Warsaw in April 1993 to examine the modalities of that project. The Working Party also recognized the need for a pilot project demonstrating the environmental clean-up of selected chemical production sites, and agreed to undertake two comparative studies, one on chemical legislation in ECE member countries and the other on the complex utilization of raw materials using advanced low- and non-waste process technologies.

A study on substitutes for tripolyphosphate in detergents was completed for sale in 1992, while the publication of the annual review of the chemical industry (1991) and the annual bulletin of trade in chemical products was delayed due to insufficient secretariat resources. The Working Party urged the secretariat to finalize and publish the review in early 1993. Preparations were made for workshops on waste treatment in industrial parks and on the rational use of raw materials and energy in the chemical industry.

In April, ECE reviewed activities of the Working Party on Engineering Industries and Automation and welcomed the preparations for seminars on environment-related topics in the countries in transition, as well as the results of workshops on rehabilitation engineering. Support was expressed for the development of internationally comparable engineering statistics and for the annual review and a study on the medium- and long-term trends and prospects in engineering industries and automation.

A workshop on strategies in privatization and management in engineering industries in Belarus was held (Minsk, 10-14 February). The third in a series of workshops on rehabilitation engineering (Trebon Spa, Czechoslovakia, 24-27 May) stressed the importance of education, information and international cooperation in the development of rehabilitation infrastructures in Central and Eastern Europe. A seminar on new materials and their application in engineering industries (Kiev, Ukraine, 13-16 October) agreed on the potential of such materials to contribute to sustainable industrial development and protection of the environment.

The Working Party on Steel, at its second session (Geneva, 21-23 October), focused on the management of the evolution of the steel industry, questions of interest to countries in transition and protection of the environment. It reviewed short- and medium-term trends in the steel market and endorsed the report of a June meeting of experts on the subject, noting a general decline in market activity, export difficulties and falling prices for most iron and steel products. The resultant decrease in industrial steel production in the most affected economies in transition was estimated at 20 per cent in Czechoslovakia, 15 per cent in Romania and Russia, and 9 per cent in Hungary.

With regard to steel statistics, the Working Party endorsed the report of a meeting of experts on the subject and asked the secretariat to rationalize and streamline further the United Nations/ECE Steel Statistical System. It noted the preparation of a study on problems arising from the use of iron and steel scrap and the completion of a study on steel product quality and maximum utilization of scrap. In 1992, the secretariat published the *Annual Bulletin of Steel Statistics for 1990* and *The Steel Market in 1991*.

The Working Party endorsed the reports of a seminar on restructuring and management techniques in steel industries in countries in transition (Szczyrk, Poland, 18-22 May) and of the first preparatory meeting on 17 June for a seminar on metallurgy and ecology, scheduled for 1993. It was informed of a workshop on the restructuring of the Romanian steel industry (Tirgoviste, 16-20 February) and the International Symposium on Steel Scrap (Algiers, Algeria, 26-30 April). It adopted its programme of work for 1992-1996.

In April, ECE endorsed the 1992-1996 programmes of work and the revised terms of reference of the Working Party on Steel and the Working Party on the Chemical Industry.

Transport

The Inland Transport Committee (fifty-fourth session, Geneva, 3-7 February 1992) analysed the transport situation in member countries and emerging development trends, considered activities regarding assistance to economies in transition, and discussed specific issues related to road, rail and inland water transport. The Committee, having examined the secretariat's proposals on follow-up action to the Pan-European Transport Conference (Prague, Czechoslovakia, 29-31 October 1991) and amendments thereto by an informal group of high-level experts, modified its programme of work for 1992-1996 and its structure

accordingly. It was informed of a series of workshops on combined transport issues, held in 1991 in some Eastern European countries, as well as a workshop on multimodal transport (Volos, Greece, November 1991) aimed at providing technical assistance to the economies in transition. It reviewed activities of its subsidiary bodies related to transport infrastructure, safety and facilitation, harmonization of transport requirements, vehicle construction, transport policy and economics, customs questions, and issues concerning the transportation of people and merchandise, including dangerous goods and perishable foodstuffs.

In April, ECE stressed the importance of international cooperation and coordination in the field of transport in the region, and felt that the Committee should contribute actively to the development of an integrated all-European transport concept. It endorsed the Committee's revised programme of work and welcomed the initiatives to translate the provisions of the Prague Declaration, adopted at the Pan-European Transport Conference, into concrete action within the framework of that programme.

During the year, the ECE secretariat continued to promote international agreements, conventions and resolutions to achieve a coherent, efficient and well-balanced all-European transport system. It participated in the elaboration of a European Transport Charter, finalized the draft of a convention on customs treatment of pool containers used in international transport, and updated regulations and provisions for combined transport on inland waterways and the transport of dangerous goods. Progress was made on the Trans-European North-South Motorway network and the Trans-European Railways project, which were revised to include east-west connections. A number of workshops were held on transition issues in the field of inland transport: on responsibilities of the State and the railways in a market economy (Rouen, France, 30 June–2 July); on road transport safety (Benesov, Czechoslovakia, 6-9 October); and two on combined transport (Bonn, Germany, 6-9 October; Moscow, 21 and 22 October).

Rail transport issues were addressed by an ad hoc meeting on the facilitation of border crossing in international rail transport (Geneva, 2-4 September) and a newly established ad hoc intersecretariat group, which analysed the factors causing delays in international rail traffic. A seminar on road safety (Geneva, 23 and 24 March) assessed positively the results of the first Road Safety Week in the region (October 1990) and submitted its conclusions to the Inland Transport Committee. A global seminar on the impact of increasing dimensions of loading units on combined transport (Geneva, 1-4 September 1992) considered issues related to the introduction of larger containers and adopted recommendations on their maximum size. The Working Party on Combined Transport, at its seventeenth session (7 and 8 September), provided clarifications and comments on the seminar's recommendations.

Energy

At its second session (Geneva, 10-12 November 1992), the Committee on Energy considered the energy situation and prospects in the region, with particular focus on assistance to the economies in transition, and adopted its draft programme of work for 1992-1996 in the areas of energy reforms in Central and Eastern Europe; rational use of energy, efficiency and conservation; interface between energy and the environment; energy policies and prospects; energy demand and supply issues for sustainable development; and energy trade, trade facilitation and infrastructure. The Committee reviewed energy conservation policies and prospects in the region and evaluated the impact of multilateral intergovernmental assistance to the countries of Central and Eastern Europe. It was informed of the status of negotiations to implement the European Energy Charter, providing for cooperation in the fields of energy economy and efficiency; interconnection and extension of gas and electric power systems, respectively; and technologies for the clean combustion of low-calorie-value solid fuels. The Committee noted the progress achieved in cooperation with the other regional commissions in preparing the project entitled "Global Energy Efficiency 21: An Interregional Approach" and the conclusions of an ad hoc meeting on the project (19 and 20 October).

In 1992, the Working Parties on Coal, Gas and Electric Power held their second sessions. The Working Party on Coal (2-4 November) focused on the transition of the coal industry in Central and Eastern Europe from central planning to a market economy and reviewed the coal situation in the region, including environmental concerns, international cooperation and safety in mines.

The Working Party on Gas (20-22 January) concentrated on the transition of the gas industry in Central and Eastern Europe to market economy. A study on the interconnection of gas networks in Europe was completed in 1992. Workshops were held on coal-bed methane exploration, extraction and use (Katowice, Poland, March), gas tariff-making in Italy (Turin, May) and integration of the liquefied petroleum gas industry in the energy markets of economies in transition (Prague, November).

The Working Party on Electric Power (10-12 February) initiated a joint study with the Working Party on Gas on demand for gas for electric power generation, and was preparing workshops on achievement and future development of cogeneration and district heating; possibilities of refurbishing fossil-fired power stations; and one entitled "Power to Communicate".

The Steering Committee of the "Energy Efficiency 2000" project, aimed at reducing the gap between the energy-intensive industries in Eastern Europe and the energy-saving technologies of the West, held its second session (3-5 March). Activities since the commencement of the project in June 1991[22] included a symposium on energy efficiency measures in industry (Bled, Slovenia, September/October 1991), two ad hoc meetings on energy efficiency demonstration zones (Moscow, May 1992; Rome, October 1992), a meeting on electricity and energy efficiency technology and demand management (Oslo, Norway, June), and a book on East-West energy efficiency, published in September. In November, the Committee on Energy invited its members to complete or pledge their contributions to the project trust fund, and endorsed the initiative of Central, East and South European members to work more extensively on energy efficiency demonstration zones.

Science and technology

The Senior Advisers to ECE Governments on Science and Technology (twentieth session, Geneva, 23-25 September 1992) discussed managerial aspects and the relationship between national and regional bodies in promoting innovation and reviewed changes in national science and technology policies, priorities and institutions, including those relating to international cooperation. They also considered the report of a workshop on State policy on science and technology in economies in transition aimed at promoting innovations in industry (Warsaw, 22 and 23 June), and discussed the possibility of convening a follow-up seminar aimed at encouraging research, development and innovation in industry and enterprises. The Senior Advisers reviewed progress in the establishment of an inventory of safety guidelines in biotechnology. They considered a proposal for a compendium of laws, principal legal instruments and mechanisms regulating national and international research and development activities of ECE members under market-economy conditions. They agreed to encourage one of the economies in transition to hold a workshop on commercialization of research and development and to discuss specific legislative aspects related to science and technology at a future session. The secretariat was requested to elaborate science and technology indicators for the countries in transition and prepare a study on the investment goods trade in 1985-1993, concentrating on imports into Central and Eastern Europe. The Senior Advisers adopted their programme of work for 1993-1997, including the priority ranking of programme elements.

Agriculture

The Committee on Agriculture (forty-third session, Geneva, 9-12 March 1992) reviewed recent developments and prospects for agriculture in the region and consequences of its future activities, with emphasis on the economies in transition. It adopted its programme of work for 1992-1996, focusing on economic analysis of the agri-food sector, agriculture and the environment, standardization of perishable produce and quality developments, and food and agricultural statistics. The Committee also reviewed European trade in agricultural products and the market situation of selected commodities, including grains, livestock and meat, and milk and dairy products. It was informed of the preparations for a symposium on quality of products in the agri-food sector (Murcia, Spain, 5-9 October) and for a workshop on specific problems of the transformation of collective farms into viable market-oriented units (Gödöllö, Hungary, 22-26 June). Hungary was also preparing to hold a preparatory workshop in September on the establishment of a European liaison centre for the harmonization of soil-monitoring systems.

The Committee approved the terms of reference and programmes of work of the new Working Party on Economics of the Agri-Food Sector and Farm Management and Working Party on Relations between Agriculture and the Environment, adopted at their first (constituent) sessions in October and September 1991, respectively. Acting on a recommendation of the Working Party on Standardization of Perishable Produce and Quality Developments at its forty-seventh session (October/November 1991), the Committee adopted a resolution on the role of international harmonized commercial standards. The Study Group on Food and Agricultural Statistics in Europe concentrated its activities on priority needs of the countries in transition and organization of a workshop on the preparation of agricultural censuses in those countries (Bulgaria, May 1992); creation of an intersecretariat working group for the harmonization of the international collection of agricultural statistics; and elaboration of a conceptual framework for statistics on relations between agriculture and the environment.

In April, ECE endorsed the Committee's programme of work and accepted the terms of reference of its two new Working Parties. During the year, the Committee continued its cooperative activities with FAO, which were discussed at an informal meeting of representatives of the two bodies (Rome, November). A workshop on agro-technical methods to improve soils contaminated by radionuclides was held in Minsk in September.

The Timber Committee held two sessions during 1992. At its forty-ninth session (Geneva, 27-30 January), it discussed the consequences of increased waste-paper recycling for the forest and forest products sector as its special topic, revised its terms of reference and approved its programme of work for 1992-1996 in six priority areas: analysis of developments for forestry and forest products; collection, dissemination and improvement of forest and forest products statistics; forest technology, management and training; issues related to a sound and sustainable development of the forest and forest products sector; assistance to the economies in transition; and a special priority issue of radiation contamination problems in the forestry and forest industry sector, particularly from the Chernobyl disaster.

In April, ECE endorsed the Committee's programme of work and terms of reference.

At its fiftieth session (Geneva, 20-23 October), the Committee considered market developments in 1992 and prospects for 1993, discussed as its special topic the implication of selected environmental and ecological developments on the forest and forest products sector in the region, reviewed its programme of assistance to the economies in transition and approved its revised programme of work for 1993-1997. The Committee was informed of the main findings of a 1990 FAO/ECE forest resource assessment (temperate zones) and resultant publications, and endorsed the proposal of the Joint FAO/ECE Working Party on Forest Economies and Statistics for a pilot study on long-term changes in temperate-zone forest resources. It assessed progress on the European timber trends and prospects study, endorsed the proposals of an informal meeting of experts on the outlook for economies in transition in the study, and added Estonia, Latvia and Lithuania to its scope.

The Joint FAO/ECE/ILO Committee on Forest Technology, Management and Training, at its nineteenth session (Croce di Magara, Italy, 29 September–2 October 1992), agreed to set up a team of specialists to act on the recommendations of the first meeting of experts on forestry and forest industry problems arising from radiation contamination (Gomel, Belarus, March) and a meeting of experts on the impact of the Chernobyl accident (Minsk, July). In May, a study tour and a workshop on forest regeneration in areas exposed to air pollution was carried out in Czechoslovakia. An informal FAO/ECE meeting on public relations in the forestry and forest industry sector (United Kingdom, June 1992) adopted recommendations for further activities. Assistance to the countries in transition included workshops on privatization in forestry and forest industries (Germany, June) and on problems of those countries (Russia, September), and an informal FAO/ECE meeting on strategies for and coordination of such assistance (Ossiach, Austria, 5-8 October).

Economic analysis

The Senior Economic Advisers to ECE Governments (twenty-eighth session, Geneva, 1-5 June 1992) held a round table on the conditions for economic recovery in Central and Eastern Europe, considered issues related to the prospects of economic growth and sustainable development in the region, and adopted its programme of work for 1992-1996, including a priority ranking of programme elements. Among the matters discussed were the impact of the economic slow-down in Western Europe on transition economies and related stabilization measures; restructuring of public enterprises and privatization; structural changes in employment, labour productivity and working patterns and their impact on economic growth; and growth conditions for 1991-1995 and their long-term implications, including the results of workshops on foreign trade and payment reforms in the economies in transition (Snagov, Romania, 16-19 September 1991) and on restructuring State-owned enterprises in economies in transition and main policy issues (Baden, Austria, 9-11 March 1992).

The Senior Advisers were informed of progress made in the development of a specialized macro-economic database and implementation of the telecommunication network between the secretariat, ECE members and other international organizations. The second ad hoc meeting on international trade and structural changes (Geneva, 1-3 April) agreed to focus its future work on macroeconomic development scenarios for the global and ECE economies and their implication for the transition countries, the relation between industrial restructuring and international trade, and financial implications of transition policies.

Environment

The Senior Advisers to ECE Governments on Environmental and Water Problems (fifth session, Geneva, 3-6 March 1992) assessed progress made in cooperation in water management, air pollution, environmental technology and waste management, bilateral and multilateral financial cooperation, and systems for obtaining and exchanging reliable environmental information. They adopted a Code of Practice for the Conservation of Threatened Animals and Plants and Other Species of International Significance, and took note of the Indicative Lists of Birds and Mammals of International Significance, to be attached to the Code. The Senior Advisers were informed of the preparations for the April 1993 Conference "Environment for Europe" and a May 1993 seminar on low-waste technology and environmentally sound products; and, in the area of management of hazardous chemicals, a workshop on the OECD principles of good laboratory practice (GLP) and compliance (Hungary, October 1992) and a third OECD workshop on the application of GLP (Switzerland, October). They decided to set up a task force on environmental rights and obligations and to discontinue the activities of the Working Party on Air Pollution Problems, discussed a proposal to develop a strategic planning and management framework, and adopted their programme of work, including a priority ranking of programme elements.

The Senior Advisers' recommendations to ECE members pertained to ecosystems-based water management and the protection of inland waters against eutrophication, the five R policies (reduction, replacement, recovery, recycling and reutilization of industrial waste), and the use and application of the OECD guidelines for testing of chemicals and the OECD principles of GLP.

At their resumed fifth session (Helsinki, Finland, 17 and 18 March), the Senior Advisers adopted the Convention on the Protection and Use of Transboundary Watercourses and International Lakes and the Convention on the Transboundary Effects of Industrial Accidents. During the year, the Conventions were signed by 25 and 26 Governments and EC, respectively. The Meeting of Signatories to the latter Convention (May) and the Working Party on Water Problems at its sixth session (November) considered measures for implementing the Conventions and elaborated relevant work plans. The number of signatories to the Convention on Environmental Impact Assessment in a Transboundary Context rose to 28 plus EC in 1992, with three ratifications, while the protocol on volatile organic compounds had been signed by 22 Governments and EC and ratified by one country, as at the end of 1992.

In April, ECE endorsed the Senior Advisers' programme of work, welcomed the adoption of the Conventions, and stressed the need for more support to the economies in transition to implement ECE environmental conventions and integrate environmental concerns in the process of economic reform. The Commission requested its Executive Secretary to pursue his efforts in facilitating consultations on the Mediterranean Technical Assistance Programme and the Mediterranean Special Programme of Action to strengthen environmental management and development in the region, and suggested defining elements of sustainable development there.

At its tenth session (Geneva, 17-19 November), the Executive Body for the Convention on Long-range Transboundary Air Pollution amended the mandate of the Working Group on Strategies to include provisions for proposals on financial burden-sharing, and requested it to report to the Conference "Environment for Europe" (see above) on progress in negotiating a second protocol on the reduction of sulphur emissions. The Executive Body requested the Working Group to review technical annexes to the protocol on control of nitrogen oxide emissions and future protocols, approved the revised scale of contributions to the cooperative programme for monitoring and evaluation of the long-range transmission of air pollutants in Europe, and considered effects of major air pollutants on human health and the environment and related international cooperative programmes. It also reviewed activities of the Working Group on Technology (first session) in preparing a draft technical annex to a second sulphur protocol, progress reports of the Task Forces on Persistent Organic Pollutants and on Emissions of Heavy Metals, and the results of the first workshop on facilitation of exchange of technology for the purpose of second generation protocols on emission reductions (Budapest, September). The problem of pollution was also dealt with at a workshop on integrated pollution prevention and control (Geneva, 18-20 November).

Human settlements

The Committee on Human Settlements (fifty-third session, Lisbon, Portugal, 15-17 September) discussed the human settlements situation in the region and related current trends and policies, and reviewed the work accomplished or in progress on assistance to the countries in transition, sustainable development of human settlements in the region, housing policies and building, urban and regional planning and research, human settlements policies in southern Europe and human settlements statistics. Following informal consultations with the heads of delegations at Geneva (February) and Lisbon (September), the Committee agreed that its work should focus on promoting sustainable development of human settlements and assisting the transition process in Central and Eastern Europe. It decided to discontinue the three former Working Parties and to set up two new Working Parties, on Housing Modernization and Management and on Sustainable Human Settlements Planning, and agreed on its own draft terms of reference.

During the period from September 1991 to December 1992, 14 seminars/workshops were organized on various issues related to human settlements, including a workshop on human settlements and sustainable development (Örebro, Sweden, May 1992) and the seventh Conference on Urban and Regional Research on the ecological challenge in urban planning (Ankara, Turkey, 29 June–3 July).

Standardization

The Working Party on Standardization Policies (second session, Geneva, 12-14 May) reviewed developments in the field of standardization, including coordination, harmonization, conformity assessment and metrology in testing. It adopted its revised terms of reference, an explanatory note on its role as an international standards-related forum with governmental representation with the objective of reducing non-tariff standards-related trade barriers, and its programme of work for 1992-1996.

The Working Party adopted the third revision of the ECE Standardization List, endorsed the sixth edition of the guide on standardization terms and definitions of the International Organization for Standardization and the International Electrotechnical Commission, and considered a draft recommendation on metrological assurance of testing and the proposal of an ad hoc meeting on energy efficiency standards (January 1992) for holding in May 1993 a seminar on energy efficiency standards and labelling systems. It was informed that a meeting of rapporteurs and coordinators would be held at Prague on 14 and 15 September 1992.

During 1992, the Working Party conducted five workshops—one in Bulgaria and four in Czechoslovakia—dealing with technical barriers to trade and conformity assessment, and initiated preparations for 1993 workshops on transition issues in Croatia, Cyprus and Israel.

Statistics

The Conference of European Statisticians (fortieth session, Geneva, 15-19 June) expressed satisfaction with the approval by ECE of fundamental principles of official statistics in the region[3] and reviewed activities in its programme areas, with a focus on new statistical systems emerging in the countries in transition. The Conference noted that the so-called "Steering Document" was designed to enable ECE countries to keep abreast of directions taken by statistical systems in transition economies and underlined the importance of monitoring and evaluating those systems. A workshop on the evaluation of transition processes in statistical offices was held (Bucharest, Romania, 2-5 November). The Conference was informed of the status of a project on applied statistical computing, designed to assist transition countries in adapting statistical computing techniques to the standards of market economies.

The Conference expressed support for the development of electronic data interchange for statistical use, stressed the importance of continuing work on the European Comparison Programme (a comparative analysis of national accounts), confirmed the direction of its work programme in social and demographic statistics, took note of the results achieved in natural resource and environment statistics, discussed experiences from the 1990 round of population censuses and reviewed ECE statistical publications. Noting with concern the discrepancy between the increasing amount of work and available staff, the Conference adopted a resolution on secretariat resources, requesting that United Nations Headquarters give highest priority to resolving the staffing problems of ECE's Statistical Division.

The Bureau of the Conference, at a meeting with the participation of the Statistical Office of EC (Eurostat) and OECD (Geneva, 26 and 27 October), reviewed cooperation and coordination between ECE, Eurostat and OECD and world-level organizations carried out through intersecretariat working groups in selected fields of statistics and joint programme review meetings.

REFERENCES

[1]E/1992/32. [2]Ibid. (dec. B(47)). [3]Ibid. (dec. C(47)). [4]Ibid. (dec. D(47)). [5]Ibid. (dec. E(47)). [6]Ibid. (dec. F(47)). [7]Ibid. (dec. G(47)). [8]Ibid. (dec. A(47)). [9]YUN 1991, p. 320. [10]E/1992/117. [11]Ibid. (res. 1(1992-S)). [12]E/1992/101 & Corr.1. [13]E/1993/54. [14]E/1992/28 (dec. 92/8). [15]Ibid. (dec. 92/29). [16]Ibid. (dec. 92/43). [17]E/ECE/1272. [18]E/ECE/1280. [19]E/ECE/1273. [20]ECE/TRADE/184. [21]ECE/CHEM/86. [22]YUN 1991, p. 323.

Latin America and the Caribbean

ECLAC held its twenty-fourth session at Santiago, Chile, from 8 to 15 April.[1] The Commission focused its deliberations on general economic conditions in the region and strategic approaches to achieve economic growth coupled with social equity, and considered two basic documents, entitled *Social Equity and Changing Production Patterns: An Integrated Approach* and *Education and Knowledge: Basic Pillars of Changing Production Patterns with Social Equity*, the latter prepared in cooperation with the United Nations Educational, Scientific and Cultural Organization (UNESCO).

By a resolution on bases for changing production patterns with social equity in Latin America and the Caribbean,[2] the Commission emphasized the possibility and necessity of achieving socially equitable, environmentally sustainable growth within a democratic framework, and requested its secretariat, in its efforts to take an integrated approach to economic and social matters, to give priority to regional cooperation and modalities of integration; demographic issues, especially those relating to migration, population growth, family planning, urbanization and public services; international economic trends, particularly in trade and exports; domestic and external development finance; and modernization of the public sector and the role of the State in changing production patterns with social equity on a demographic and sustainable basis.

By another resolution, dealing with human resources, changing production patterns and social equity,[3] ECLAC welcomed the document on the subject and instructed the Executive Secretary to continue working with the UNESCO Regional Office for Education to make further progress in studying, adapting and implementing the proposals contained in it and to ensure its extensive dissemination. The Commission adopted a resolution[4] on UNCED[5] (see PART THREE, Chapter VIII) recommending that its members promote the incorporation of the environmental dimension into the work of regional and subregional organizations and into regional and subregional agreements. It further urged[6] the Latin American and Caribbean countries to implement viable programmes for cooperation between the two subregions and requested the Executive Secretary to formulate a structured cooperation programme focusing on trade and issues concerning the attraction of foreign investment to the Caribbean.

Other resolutions of ECLAC pertained to support for the reorientation of the Latin American and Caribbean Institute for Economic and Social Planning (ILPES);[7] the Commission's programme of work for 1994-1995[8] and the calendar of conferences for 1992-1994;[9] and recommendations on the role and functions of ECLAC in the light of restructuring and revitalization of the United Nations in the economic and social fields.[10] The Commission also adopted resolutions on strengthening intraregional cooperation;[11] the Latin American Demographic Centre (CELADE);[12] preparatory activities for the 1994 International Conference on Population and Development[13] and regional preparations for the 1995 World Conference on Women;[14] cooperation among developing countries and regions;[15] and the damage caused by the eruption of the Cerro Negro volcano in Nicaragua.[16]

In his closing statement, the Executive Secretary said that by recognizing the linkage between economic growth, social equity, environmental sustainability and democracy, the Commission sent an encouraging message about the possibility of making simultaneous progress towards those four objectives and the practical ways of applying public policies to attain them. Progress had also been made in formulating guidelines for the work of ECLAC and the United Nations, especially with regard to strengthening the relationship between democracy and development. He pointed out the need to disseminate the Commission's proposals and initiate a discussion of development at all levels of the societies of the region, particularly relating to education and knowledge, and drew attention to the richness and diversity of the existing situations in Latin America and the Caribbean, saying that they were a great asset to the region in terms of knowledge and creativity.

ECLAC continued close cooperation with other United Nations bodies and specialized agencies, and established joint programmes and units with some of them. It also maintained coordination with academic and other institutions and with subregional and regional organizations active in fields related to the Commission's programme of work.

Economic trends

In 1992, economic activity in Latin America and the Caribbean as a whole grew by 2.4 per cent, according to a summary of the 1992 economic survey of Latin America and the Caribbean.[17] Excluding Brazil, the output of the region's economies increased by 4.3 per cent, while regional per capita GDP rose by nearly 2.3 per cent. The average annual inflation rate, excluding Brazil, declined to 22 per cent, less than half the 1991 level. Inflation rates in the region varied from Brazil's high of 1,130 per cent to about 60 per cent in Ecuador, Peru and Uruguay, almost 30 per cent in Colombia and Venezuela and below 20 per cent in the rest of the region.

In view of widespread global recession, such growth was a considerable achievement; however, there was a divergence in the performance of various economies. In Chile, GDP increased by 9.5 per cent, continuing its steady expansion for the ninth consecutive year. Economic activity in Argentina, the Dominican Republic, Panama, Uruguay and Venezuela grew by 6 to 8 per cent, while in Costa Rica, El Salvador, Guatemala and Honduras, output rose by 4 to 5 per cent. The growth rate was some 3 per cent in Bolivia, Colombia, Ecuador, Guyana and Mexico, and 1 to 2 per cent in the Bahamas, Jamaica and Paraguay. It remained unchanged in Nicaragua, Suriname and Trinidad and Tobago, and fell by an estimated 1.5 per cent in Brazil, 2.5 per cent in Barbados and Peru, and 5 per cent in Haiti. The smaller countries of the Organization of Eastern Caribbean States (OECS) (Antigua and Barbuda, Dominica, Grenada, Saint Kitts and Nevis, Saint Lucia, and Saint Vincent and the Grenadines) maintained their growth rate of previous years, registering an average increase of some 4 per cent.

Economic expansion generally exceeded population growth, with increases in per capita output of 1 to 3 per cent in eight countries and over 4 per cent in six. In 11 States, that indicator increased just marginally or fell. The unemployment rate remained largely unchanged and declined significantly only in Chile, Panama and Venezuela, while Argentina, Brazil, Colombia and Uruguay registered higher unemployment.

The sluggishness of world trade in 1992 was reflected in a further decline of the terms of trade in goods to more than 3 per cent in almost all the countries of the region, with Argentina being the sole exception. The Central American economies were particularly hard hit by that deterioration; however, a considerable number of States, notably Brazil, Chile, Costa Rica and Honduras, expanded the volume of their exports. Total exports from the region grew by 6 per cent in volume and 4 per cent in value, reaching $126 billion. The value of exports from the oil-producing countries contracted slightly but was partially offset by increasing volumes, while the non–oil-exporting economies saw an increase in the value of their exports, which was 12 per cent in Brazil and Chile. At the same time, the vigorous expansion of imports continued and even accelerated in some cases, stimulated by tariff liberalization and the appreciation of local currencies, which, in turn, induced a negative merchandise trade balance of nearly $6 billion for the first time in many years. The value of merchandise imports in Latin America and the Caribbean rose to $132 billion, representing an increase of 18 per cent.

The negative effects of deterioration in the terms of trade were offset by considerable capital inflows for the second year in a row, amounting to more than $57 billion in 1992, which represented the most prominent feature of the regional economic picture. The bulk of capital entering the region consisted of various types of investments from private non-banking sources, including financial placements, short-term credits and acquisition of stocks. FDI increased significantly in Mexico, followed by Argentina, Brazil, Chile and Venezuela.

The net inflow of capital contributed to domestic stabilization measures, as it was used to close fiscal gaps through the acquisition of government bonds and privatized public enterprises, to spur a non-inflationary expansion of credit to the private sector for both investment and consumption and to shore up the region's international reserves. Most countries also sustained or tightened the drastic fiscal adjustments of the previous three years and stabilized the interest burden on fiscal budgets, which varied from 1 to 4 per cent of GDP. The adjustment processes were backed by negotiations to regularize external debt servicing, the decline in international interest rates and institutional reforms aimed at reinforcing export-oriented growth and trade liberalization, deregulation of the price system, consolidation of fiscal equilibria and more prudent management of monetary policy.

Domestic price stabilization efforts continued to be the focal point of macroeconomic policy, with only Brazil standing in sharp contrast to the rest of the region. Those efforts were particularly successful in Argentina and Nicaragua, which reduced the rate of consumer price increases to an annual 18 per cent and 2 per cent, respectively, although the adjustment, stabilization and restructuring programme in Nicaragua kept its economy in recession. The economies undergoing structural adjustment, such as Bolivia, Chile and Mexico, made further progress towards stabilization within a framework of sustained growth. Stabilization processes were also consolidated in Central America and the Caribbean, where annual inflation fell below 10 per cent except in Costa Rica, El Salvador and Haiti.

External debt

After stagnating in 1991, the region's external debt rose by 2 per cent in 1992, reaching $451 billion. Among various factors leading to that expansion were new bond placements abroad for the amount of $10 billion, official credits, a proliferation of short-term credit operations and accumulated arrears in interest payments. At the same time, the rising dollar exchange rate in international markets reduced the dollar value of debt denominated in other currencies, and various debt-reduction schemes were implemented in many Latin American and Caribbean countries. Debt growth was also restrained by the dynamism of non–debt-related capital movements, especially foreign direct and indirect (equity capital) investment, as well as the flow of resources to short-term deposits in the region's banking systems, reflecting in part a repatriation of capital.

Indicators of the region's external debt burden continued to fall during 1992, prolonging the trend towards improvement observed in recent years. The share of debt interest in total exports from Latin America and the Caribbean fell to 20 per cent, the lowest since 1980, although interest payments still absorbed an excessive portion of the region's export earnings. The total debt/export ratio, a more structural indicator of the debt burden, decreased to 282 per cent from 290 per cent in 1991. The structure of debt payments was also improved by extending payback periods under various official restructuring exercises.

The average price of the region's bank debt on the secondary market rose from 45 cents in December 1991 to 46 cents in November 1992, which basically reflected a perception in the market that the authorities of some countries in arrears were in a better position to renegotiate their debt with creditor banks. None the less, only five countries in 1992 had a debt/exports coefficient lower than the critical threshold of 200 per cent.

Activities in 1992

Development policy and regional economic cooperation

The ECLAC secretariat's work in economic development covered both the analysis of activities undertaken by the Economic Development Division and those related to information and documentation for economic and social development carried out by the Latin American Centre for Economic and Social Documentation (CLADES). The Economic Development Division monitored the economic performance of ECLAC members and examined their development policies and strategies likely to harmonize macroeconomic stability with social equity and structural change.

As part of its ongoing activities, ECLAC published the annual *Economic Panorama of Latin America*, *Preliminary Overview of the Latin American Economy*, and *Economic Survey of Latin America and the Caribbean*, which presented, respectively, a timely overview of the economic trends in the nine major economies of the region for the first half of the year and projections for the remaining months, the performance of the entire region during 1992 and complete and comparable breakdowns on the region's economic trends. ECLAC also analysed economic policies aimed at securing an expansionary adjustment and lowering inflation without inducing recession, with particular attention to the strategies adopted by some countries to reduce the external debt.

CLADES provided technical assistance to member countries and institutions connected with information and documentation, and initiated preparations for a training course on information management under the new network of Latin American information networks project. It continued to issue periodically the *Informativo IN-FOPLAN* and the *Informativo Terminológico*. In March, as a contribution to UNCED, CLADES published the review *Reseñas de Documentos sobre Desarrollo Ambientalmente Sustentable*, which listed documents on environmentally sustainable development in Latin America issued by international and regional agencies.

In 1992, consultations were initiated on the terms of collaboration between the Centre's regional programme designed to strengthen cooperation among National Information Networks and Systems for Development in Latin America and the Caribbean (INFOLAC), the project on the status of regional cooperation and the Simón Bolívar programme on Latin American technological innovation. Other activities included a meeting on "social intelligence" (Havana, Cuba, 1 and 2 June) and a regional meeting of experts on macrothesaurus and information management (Santiago, 18-20 November).

The Committee of High-level Government Experts (CEGAN), at its eighteenth session (San José, Costa Rica, 3-6 March), continued to discuss guidelines for the development of the Latin American and Caribbean countries during the 1990s, focusing on the two basic documents prepared by ECLAC's secretariat for the twenty-fourth session of the Commission (see above). It was agreed that, although adjustment and stabilization efforts of the previous decade were beginning to yield results, they were not founded on an adequate basis of sustained increases in productivity and were often offset by an irreversible deterioration of natural resources. The Committee therefore recognized the need for economic and social policy to concentrate on resolving short-term problems and made no medium-term projections. It further endorsed additional guidelines for future studies, identifying their priority topics as population and development, modernization of the state apparatus, regional cooperation and integration, the immediate international situation, technology and productivity, environmental sustainability, investment, and development financing.

At its eighth session, the Conference of Ministers and Heads of Planning of Latin America and the Caribbean (Madrid, Spain, 22-26 March) examined the link between Ibero-America and EC with regard to development plans, policies and strategies. The Regional Council for Planning, which met for its ninth session (Madrid, 24 March) within the framework of the Conference, recommended that the work programme of ILPES focus on priority issues taken up by Governments, specializing in strategic State management, and proposed that ILPES introduce changes in its training, technical cooperation and research components. In April, ECLAC endorsed the Council's recommendations.[7]

During the year, ILPES revised its training strategy to introduce a flexible, modular system of medium-length courses on specific topics in response to government requirements. Under the new system, the Institute organized a course on formulation and appraisal of social policies and projects (Santiago, 21 September–23 October) and a high-level regional development training programme and Integrated Laboratory on the Design of Regional Strategies (Santiago, 26 October–27 November). ILPES also held a seminar on models and instruments for evaluating budgetary policies (Buenos Aires, Argentina, 23-26 June) and prepared a number of studies on the subject, and provided advisory services to national planning bodies in organizing seminars and courses on project appraisal, in preparing technical documents and methodology manuals and in systems operation. The Institute maintained close cooperation with the Latin American Economic System (SELA) in the area of forward planning.

Among the numerous training activities in 1992 were 4 courses on decentralization, land-use management and siting of investments; 4 courses on project preparation and appraisal; 19 courses on decentralized municipal administration; and a seminar on national regional development funds. A fourth regional seminar on fiscal policy, stabilization and adjustment (Santiago, 27-30 January) evaluated tax reforms and programmes for restricting public expenditure. A workshop on planning activities (Santiago, 6-8 July) established analytical methods and determined the final programme of work for the regional project on fiscal decentralization. A regional seminar on public policy reform (Santiago, 3-5 August) discussed relationships among the fiscal, strategic, instrumental and political, and institutional aspects of reforms and their interaction in State restructuring processes. Technical national seminars on fiscal policy were held in Uruguay (Montevideo, 21 July) and Costa Rica (San José, 11 August).

Other activities in economic and social planning included courses and classes on social project formulation and appraisal (Temuco, Chile, 13-25 January; Caracas, Venezuela, 10-21 August; Buenos Aires, 16-20 November); a course-workshop on economics and health (Santiago, 4-9 May); an international course on Ibero-America, today and tomorrow (Canary Islands, Spain, 18-26 July); a course on poverty reduction (La Serena, Chile, 19 and 20 October); and classes on regional development (Neuquén, Argentina, 20-25 September). ECLAC and ILPES also promoted regional cooperation in investment programming and project banks and in the search for alternative development scenarios in the fishing industry. Under the joint ECLAC/International Centre for Living Aquatic Resources Management project, a technical meeting was organized (Santiago, 22-24 September) on the bio-economic valuation of development scenarios for pelagic fisheries in northern Chile and southern Peru.

Industrial, scientific and technological development

The Joint ECLAC/UNIDO Industry and Technology Division was responsible for activities in the industrial, scientific and technological fields. The Division placed special emphasis on industrial restructuring to build competitiveness, channelling its efforts through the ECLAC/UNDP project on designing policies to strengthen the capacity for technological innovation and enhance the international competitiveness of the Latin American entrepreneurial environment. Joint activities with the Latin American Association of Capital Goods Industries under a project to promote that industry focused on consolidating focal points for demand and promoting the technical and productive capacity of the regional capital goods sector. Technical advisory services were provided to Brazil, Chile, the Dominican Republic and Peru on non-conventional financial instruments to support small and medium-scale industry, and a study was conducted on paper recycling in the region.

The Division's publications in 1992 included a document on trends in quality and productivity for the 1990s, a regional directory of manufacturers of machinery and equipment covering 436 corporations in 11 countries, and two issues (Nos. 12 and 13) of the journal *Industrialización y Desarrollo Tecnológico*.

The Latin American Commission on Science and Technology (COLCYT) continued cooperating with SELA in technological forecasting under a regional research and training programme and initiated preparations for their joint participation in a United Nations seminar on technology monitoring, assessment and forecasting, scheduled for Paris in January 1993. SELA's activities in industrial and technological policy and integration focused on implementing the Regional Plan of Action on Industrialization, adopted at the 1991 Regional Conference on Industrialization, through the Permanent Regional Forum on Industrial and Technological Policy and Integration established on the recommendation of the Conference. The United Nations University (UNU) Institute for New Technologies launched a study on the role of political factors in technological policies in the region, and was commissioning a number of Latin American country studies.

International trade and development finance

The ECLAC International Trade and Development Division centred its work on four major subject areas: international economic relations; interregional economic relations; economic integration and regional cooperation; and development finance. Activities concentrated on formulating policies and defining mechanisms to continue expanding and improving the region's trade position in the world economy and included the preparation of 12 documents on various aspects of trade and regional economic integration, which examined prevailing trade policies in both developed and developing countries, analysed Latin American economic relations and integration processes and offered guidelines for promoting the region's exports and integration.

Jointly with UNCTAD and SELA, ECLAC began preparing a UNDP-funded programme of technical cooperation on international trade and trade relations for Latin America and the Caribbean.

In cooperation with the Inter-American Development Bank (IDB), ECLAC sponsored a second colloquium on global questions related to hemispheric trade liberalization (Washington, D.C., 30 April and 1 May). A third colloquium on the subject was held at Toronto, Canada, from 31 May to 2 June. The ECLAC secretariat also participated in a meeting of agencies and experts on Latin American and Caribbean integration and cooperation, hosted by SELA on 25 and 26 June. An informal inter-agency meeting on trade-related activities, held on 9 September in conjunction with the eighteenth meeting of the Latin American Council of SELA (Caracas, 7-11 September), reviewed the activities of various agencies and identified priorities of inter-institutional cooperation in international trade, regional integration, support mechanisms for Governments and other actors in the region, trade relations with the United States and regional relations with Europe and Asia.

In 1992, SELA and other regional organizations held consultations with UNCTAD to determine the best way of adapting payment and clearing arrangements without distorting normal flows of trade, investment and technology. Training programmes and advisory services were elaborated with the participation of SELA member States to encourage the involvement of regional enterprises in environmentally sound trade and development activities. A seminar on GATT was held in Ecuador in February, and officials from SELA member States participated in a trade policy course in Spanish, organized by GATT, during the first half of the year.

Foreign trade officials of member countries of the Latin American Integration Association, at their fifth meeting (Santiago, 23 and 24 November), considered issues related to Latin American integration, negotiations and international economic relations, and relations with developed economies.

Activities in development finance included studies on bank regulation and supervision (Brazil, El Salvador, Honduras, Trinidad and Tobago) and on pension reform systems (Argentina, El Salvador, Honduras, Jamaica, Paraguay, Trinidad and Tobago), as well as seminars on those subjects (Santo Domingo, Dominican Republic, 23 November; Santiago, 3 and 4 December) and on indexing financial funds in Latin America (Santiago, 3 and 4 August). ECLAC, UNU, the World Institute for Development Economics Research and UNCTAD jointly organized an international seminar on savings and financial policy issues in African, Asian, and Latin American and Caribbean countries (Santiago, 5 and 6 October). Among 1992 publications were project documents on reducing inflation rates in the region and on financing exports, a review of regional experiences in bank regulation and supervision and five issues of the *Financiamiento del Desarrollo* series on development finance.

Natural resources and energy

ECLAC's activities in support of natural resource and energy management concentrated on four subject areas: mineral resources, water resources, marine resources and energy. The secretariat continued its support to the Latin American Mining Organization in implementing the second phase of the Latin American Regional Mining Information and Documentation System and assessed the mining situation in several countries. Assistance was provided in calculating the economic value of natural resources and assessing their use in the region, preparing legal and institutional analyses of natural resource management and maintaining a statistical database on international trade, prices, output and reserves of mining resources.

The secretariat analysed recommendations of UNCED pertaining to marine resources, with a view to assisting countries in formulating appropriate marine policies, and offered a course-workshop on development management of basins and micro-regions in Latin America (Santa Fe de Bogotá, Colombia, 19-22 May). Advisory services were delivered to a number of countries to help establish a cooperation network on integrated water resource management, and a postgraduate course on the subject was offered (Mendoza, Argentina, 28 September–23 October).

Transport

A regional technical cooperation project on transport, distribution, commercialization and competitiveness of exports concluded in 1992 with the publication of a document summarizing the findings of project studies and proposing a methodology for an overall analysis of a corridor for world trade. The work completed under another project, on control and organization of urban public transport systems in Latin America, was reviewed in a document on the impact of subsidies, regulation and different forms of ownership on the quality of service and operational efficiency of urban bus systems. A publication on restructuring public-sector enterprises in the case of the region's ports inspired studies on rationalizing port activities in 14 countries.

A regional technical cooperation project on road maintenance resulted in a book providing a new approach to road network management and conservation, which was widely distributed in Latin America and followed by national seminars on the subject in seven countries. Regional seminars on the same topic were held in Chile (Santiago, 27 and 28 April) and Mexico (Mexico City, 18 and 19 May). A seminar on institutional aspects of mass urban transport (Lima, Peru, 19-22 May) addressed issues related to transport deregulation.

The Commission provided support to Argentina, Bolivia, Brazil, Colombia, Chile, Ecuador, Paraguay, Peru, Uruguay and Venezuela in establishing and institutionalizing the Conference of Ministers of Transport, Communications and Public Works of South America (Santiago, 27-29 May) as a permanent regional forum. Transport-related issues were also considered at a meeting of Ministers of Transport, Communications and Public Works of the Andean Group (Caracas, 22-24 October) and at a meeting of Ministers of Public Works and Transport of the Southern Cone Countries (Punta del Este, Uruguay, 9-14 November).

Within the framework of the General Assembly of the Latin American Railways Association at its eighteenth session, a symposium was held on the restructuring and privatization of Latin America's railways (Santiago, 17-19 November).

Social development

In the early 1990s, nearly 200 million Latin Americans were unable to meet their basic needs and poverty continued to increase. As the Governments of the region were attaching growing importance to the study of the nature and evolution of poverty and policies to combat it, the ECLAC Social Development Division concentrated on preparations for the Third Regional Conference on Poverty in Latin America and the Caribbean (Santiago, 23-25 November).[18]

The Conference, in which 25 ECLAC member States and several United Nations bodies and agencies participated, assessed the levels and characteristics of poverty and poverty-reduction efforts in Latin America and the Caribbean, considered policies to promote higher productivity among the rural and urban poor, and discussed targeting of social policies to reduce poverty in the region. Noting the need for various institutions, policies and programmes to fight poverty from different angles and the need to coordinate action at regional and international levels, the Conference proposed the establishment of an intergovernmental information network on anti-poverty social policies and the creation of an advisory system within its framework. It also pointed out the need to maintain the continuity of regional cooperation, avoid duplication of efforts and take full advantage of available resources in the framework of national anti-poverty strategies.

The third informal inter-agency meeting on integrated social policies and economic adjustment

(Caracas, 7 and 8 May), convened by SELA, resulted in important agreements on joint activities, including the final revision of the meeting's basic document, on the social dimensions of changing production patterns with social equity, prepared by ECLAC; establishment of a social project bank and an information and communications network; inter-agency missions and projects on social policy; and organization of a regional meeting to prepare for a world summit for social development.

ECLAC contributed to the Latin American and Caribbean regional meeting in preparation for the International Year of the Family (1994) (Cartagena de Indias, 10-13 August) and prepared a number of studies on family issues. It also offered a workshop on methodologies for analysing the situation of the family in Latin America (Mexico City, 27-30 October). Cooperation activities in the field of youth were reviewed at the fourth informal inter-agency meeting on youth in Latin America and the Caribbean (Seville, Spain, 14 September), while another meeting discussed the methodology of a project on popular participation and community organization, organized jointly with three universities in Spain (Santiago, 9 June). Various courses on social development and a lecture on adjustment, restructuring and social security in the region were also offered in 1992.

Integration of women

The Commission attached great importance to activities related to the integration of women into development, including the elaboration of a new regional programme of action for women in Latin America and the Caribbean, 1995-2001, and preparing an assessment of the status of women. In April, ECLAC urged the Economic and Social Council and the General Assembly to allocate the resources needed for regional activities in preparing for the 1995 World Conference on Women.[14] Those activities, as well as measures and mechanisms for their coordination, were evaluated at a meeting of specialized agencies and other bodies of the United Nations system (Santiago, 3 and 4 September),[19] which identified priority issues for future action to promote the integration of women into Latin American and Caribbean development. The meeting agreed that the integration of gender analysis into policy formulation should be promoted as a guiding principle, that future activities should be defined by the integration of women into global processes and that women's participation must be ensured at all levels of decision-making. It was also agreed that the United Nations should give priority to in-house gender training, that there was a need to analyse the family from the perspective of women and that men and boys as well as girls and young women

must be mobilized and sensitized if effective changes were to be made through education.

The Presiding Officers of the Regional Conference on the Integration of Women into the Economic and Social Development of Latin America and the Caribbean met twice during 1992. At their fourteenth meeting (Curaçao, Netherlands Antilles, 18 and 19 June)[20] they reviewed national and regional activities undertaken since 1 June 1991; considered actions taken to implement the resolutions of the Conference at its fifth session held in September 1991,[21] and set up a group of experts to prepare a new regional programme of action on the integration of women into economic and social development. That group (Mexico City, 26-28 October)[22] discussed the objective and structure of the regional programme of action and identified its priority areas, including the relationship between women and power and issues related to power-sharing and social equity. It was decided that the programme should cover the period 1995-2001 and focus on changing current society as a prerequisite for achieving social equity.

The Presiding Officers, at their fifteenth meeting (Mexico City, 29 and 30 October),[23] reviewed the new regional programme of action, evaluated their work for 1991-1992 and considered future activities in preparation for the sixth session of the Regional Conference.

The improvement of the legal and institutional framework for incorporating women into development was the subject of a technical meeting (Tegucigalpa, Honduras, 13 and 14 February) and national and regional workshops (Asunción, Paraguay, 1 and 2 August; Santiago, 14-16 October). The legal status of women was also discussed at a national seminar in Ecuador (Quito, 4 and 5 May). Among other 1992 activities were a working meeting on women and violence (Santiago, 29 April) and a seminar on gender and identity (Santiago, 18 and 19 August).

Environment

The ECLAC Environment and Human Settlements Division centred its efforts on finding alternative instruments for the promotion of sustainable economic growth through policies designed to enhance the quality of life in the region's human settlements. It initiated activities to improve information and statistics on the urban environment, and provided assistance under a project on technical cooperation for environmental planning and management in Latin America and the Caribbean, financed by the United Nations Environment Programme (UNEP). The Division also provided technical assistance through the execution of projects related to guidelines and advisory services on controlled environmentally sound waste management and on urban management in selected middle-sized Latin American cities.

The management of hazardous wastes in the context of environmentally sustainable development was the subject of a national seminar in Argentina (Buenos Aires, 21 and 22 April) and an international course in Chile (Santiago, 30 June–10 July). Another national seminar (Santiago, 22-24 June) examined management of sustainable agricultural development in marginal areas of Chile. A seminar/workshop on environmentally sound waste management for sustainable development (Cartagena de Indias, 3 and 4 September) was followed by a national seminar on 7 and 8 September, which considered a case-study on the subject. Another seminar in Chile (Santiago, 16-20 March) formulated an action plan for environmental education in that country.

Human settlements

A Regional Meeting of Ministers and High-level Authorities of the Housing and Urban Development Sector in Latin America and the Caribbean (Santiago, 16-20 March)[24] reviewed the regional situation in that sector; considered international financing for housing, concentration of resources on low-cost housing and cost-recovering capacity, restoration and repopulation of deteriorated city centres and modalities for a permanent regional experience-sharing mechanism; and adopted the Santiago Declaration. The Declaration provided for the establishment of an advisory and coordinating body among the participants of the meeting and requested the ECLAC secretariat to strengthen its role in coordinating United Nations activities in the area of housing and human settlements. The participants agreed to hold regular biennial meetings to analyse the main trends in housing development, share experience and know-how and define cooperation objectives.

Other activities included a regional meeting on selected middle-sized Latin American cities (Santiago, 11-15 May); a course on State, region and municipality (Santiago, April-June); an international course on Government and municipal administration (Rio de Janeiro, Brazil, 22-29 November); and a training course for municipal officials under the municipal management and training support programme (Talca, Chile, 26 November–3 December).

Population

During 1992, CELADE, the institution within ECLAC responsible for the regional population programme, fielded 41 missions to 16 countries and provided technical assistance in the areas of the elderly population; census processing; demographic analysis; maternal and child mortality; applications of the "previous child" computer pro-

gramme, developed by the Centre to help hospitals establish a database on health conditions of previous children of women in maternity wards; population and environment; population projections; spatial distribution; demographic dynamics of poverty; population policies; computerized documentation on population and bibliographic searches; and the use of a computerized data retrieval system interfacing with geographical and demographic information systems.

The Centre's training and teaching activities included a second course on population and development under the UNFPA Global Plan of Training in Population and Development (Santiago, 3 March–3 December), evaluated at the Scientific Advisory Committee meeting (Santiago, 20 and 21 October); the fifteenth intensive regional course on demographic analysis for development (San José, 3 August–4 December); a workshop on policies for the care of the elderly (Santiago, 2-6 November); a regional workshop on in-depth analysis of the results of a demographic and health survey (Santiago, 27 February–27 March); and courses on the population dimension in development strategies (Santiago, 22 June–6 July) and on spatial planning (Santiago, July-August). Training courses were organized in specific fields, including a course-workshop on socio-demographic analysis of census data (Bolivia, 30 November–11 December), a one-week workshop on subnational population projections (Valdivia, Chile, January) and a seminar-workshop on the use of demographic-economic models in policy formulation.

A Meeting of Government Experts on Population and Development in Latin America and the Caribbean (Saint Lucia, 6-9 October),[25] held in preparation for the 1994 International Conference on Population and Development, examined socio-economic trends and implications of population growth, structure and distribution in the region, and formulated recommendations on a wide variety of population issues, such as population dynamics, development and equity, fertility and mortality, and spatial distribution and migrations; population policies and programmes; population growth and distribution in relation to development and the environment; women and population dynamics; and family planning, health and family well-being.

Food and agriculture

A number of documents published by ECLAC in 1992 gave an overview of agriculture and forestry development in the region. Several missions were conducted in Chile to obtain information for a case study on agro-industrial changes and relations, using a methodology to be applied in similar studies in the Dominican Republic, El Salvador, Nicaragua and Paraguay. Projects on the modernizing impact of agro-industry in Paraguay and on the use of forestry resources within the concept of sustainable development, both financed from extrabudgetary resources, were prepared during the year.

FAO provided assistance to Central American countries to strengthen their food control programmes as a means of contributing to the region's economic development and integration and reducing non-tariff barriers. Similar projects were being implemented in Peru and other Latin American and Caribbean countries. Another project was being prepared to strengthen food standardization and import/export control in the Southern Cone Common Market. Within the framework of a joint FAO/UNEP/World Health Organization food contamination and assessment programme, two subregional networks were developed for the monitoring of food contaminants, especially pesticide residues, in Central and South America.

Statistics and economic projections

The ECLAC Statistics and Projections Division concentrated its work on enlarging the regional network of statistical information; statistical development and quantitative analysis; regional cooperation, dissemination and transfer of new computer technologies to the countries; prospective medium- and long-term studies on Latin American and Caribbean development; and analysis of the region's position in world production and trade. The Division launched the first stage of a database of short-term indicators, incorporated new international statistical classifications into the regional data bank on external trade and created a database on external debt, covering the period 1970-1980. It also added new survey results to the household survey data bank, refined and augmented the database on social statistics and started replacing the 1980 base year used in national accounts with a more recent year in preparation for adopting a new system of national accounts.

Special importance was attached to refining the methods of updating sampling frames and sample designs; the development of household survey databases to facilitate the application of more advanced methods of measuring poverty; a study of computerized systems to be used in the region; and the analysis and definition of social indicators included each year in the *Panorama Social de América Latina*. The Division collaborated with Governments and other United Nations bodies in organizing seminars and indicator databases and assisted in the data compilation and computer processing of statistical information. Two seminars were held on the renovation of sampling frames and sample

designs (Caracas, 22-24 September; Port of Spain, Trinidad and Tobago, 29 September–1 October), and one on Central American foreign trade statistics (Guatemala City, 7-11 September).

Work in the field of economic projections focused on analysing the external economic factors influencing the region and on updating medium- and long-term prospects for Latin American and Caribbean countries. As for the region's global integration, emphasis was placed on studying the situation and the evolution of the world economy and its possible impact on regional development.

Activities in the area of statistics were reviewed at a meeting of Directors of Statistics of the Americas (Madrid, 11-13 November),[26] which discussed national experiences in conducting the 1990s round of censuses and examined the latest revision of the national accounts system. It considered the current status and future outlook of administrative records and the architecture of regional statistical data banks and geographical information systems as its special topics, and evaluated activities currently pursued in various statistical areas, including the informal sector, social and poverty indicators, short-term indicators and statistics, foreign trade statistics and the environment.

Transnational corporations

The joint unit of ECLAC and the United Nations Centre on Transnational Corporations continued to carry out research, information and technical cooperation activities to identify contributions (and the repercussions thereof) by TNCs to the development of the Latin American and Caribbean countries, and elaborating case-studies on specific countries and sectors, focusing on the interests and concerns of the Governments and economic agents of ECLAC members. A number of working papers were completed under a project on the role of foreign capital in the process of industrial restructuring in the region, and questionnaires were administered to the major foreign-owned manufacturing companies of Brazil, Chile and Colombia. The joint unit initiated three special studies involving the collection, processing and analysis of background information on the role of foreign direct investment by TNCs in industrial restructuring in Argentina, Mexico and Peru.

The contribution of TNCs to growth and development in the region was the central theme of a high-level symposium (Santiago, 19 and 20 October).

Technical cooperation and assistance

During 1992, the ECLAC Programme Planning and Operations Division completed five regional, three subregional and seven country projects and launched 20 new projects for a total amount of some $4.8 million. Technical assistance was provided to Chile, Colombia and the Dominican Republic in the area of food and agriculture, and similar assistance was extended to Argentina, Brazil, Chile, Colombia, Ecuador, El Salvador, Jamaica, Mexico, Nicaragua, the Dominican Republic, Uruguay and Venezuela on economic development and economic and social planning.

ECLAC collaborated with the Latin American Integration Association in designing a project to establish an integrated system of information and support for the region's foreign trade, and offered assistance to member countries in other programme areas, including industrial, scientific and technological development; international trade and development finance; natural resources and energy; environment and human settlements; population; social development and the integration of women into the socio-economic development of the region; transport; and statistics and economic projections.

Technical assistance in promoting linkages between regional economies and foreign markets was also provided by the Department of Economic and Social Development (DESD) of the United Nations Secretariat, and included the formulation and implementation of policies and laws in foreign investment, foreign trade and technology transfer, and the establishment of linkages between specific companies in the region and TNCs in natural resources, agriculture, manufacturing and services.

Technical cooperation among developing countries

The Division continued to carry out various activities within the framework of the 1978 Buenos Aires Plan of Action for Promoting and Implementing Technical Cooperation among Developing Countries.[27] Those activities were coordinated through a regional mechanism, set up for that purpose by ECLAC and SELA with UNDP support, and reviewed at a regional meeting of national directors for international technical cooperation (Caracas, 7-9 September) and by a seasonal committee on TCDC, which discussed the main guidelines of work in this field for the following biennium.

ECLAC continued to promote TCDC initiatives related to technical cooperation projects in specific sectors and prepared a document on the guidelines and regional strategies for TCDC in the 1990s. In July, the Commission hosted a regional meeting on TCDC in health technologies, within the framework of the "project convergence" exercise, intended to stimulate the development of health technology in the region. The meeting was preceded by subregional meetings on the subject

in Central America (Antigua, Guatemala, 9-12 March) and in the Caribbean (Bridgetown, Barbados, 27-30 April).

ECLAC also collaborated with the Administrative Committee for the Coordination of Information Systems in preparing the United Nations Register of Development Projects for 1991 and in publishing the quarterly bulletin *Cooperation and Development* (Nos. 37-39), which described technical cooperation initiatives carried out by the Commission.

Subregional activities

Caribbean

The ECLAC subregional headquarters for the Caribbean, at Port of Spain, Trinidad and Tobago, analysed issues relevant to the promotion of socio-economic development in the Caribbean Development and Cooperation (CDCC) countries and focused on the initiation and implementation of projects pertinent to them. It continued to prepare economic analyses of Caribbean countries, including overviews of their economic activity for 1990 and 1991; develop and maintain electronic databases on information collection and dissemination and amplify the coverage of its database in terms of countries and subject matter; issue a quarterly bulletin on trade and related activities; and support the activities of the Caribbean Council for Science and Technology, which held its eleventh session in 1992 (Saint Lucia, 12-14 September). The CDCC secretariat also developed population units and contributed to population policy formulation in various Caribbean countries, concluded a project on training policies to identify problems of public-sector services, prepared a document on implications of the proposed North American Free Trade Agreement from the Caribbean perspective, and provided assistance in organizing a Subregional Conference on Poverty in the Caribbean (Dominican Republic, 30 September–2 October).

A project on socio-cultural and environmental management issues in Caribbean tourism, completed in 1992, included one regional and two national workshops in Trinidad and Tobago (13 and 14 February), Barbados (12 and 13 March) and Saint Lucia (18 and 19 March), respectively, to develop a plan of action on tourism in the subregion and forecasting models on tourist arrivals for 26 Caribbean countries.

CDCC held consultations on national science and technology activities in Saint Lucia (21-24 April) and Belize (27 April–1 May), followed by a regional seminar/workshop to develop a plan of action for science and technology (Saint Lucia, 8-11 September). It also organized a workshop for its national focal points (Port of Spain, 15 and 16 July) and provided training on the UNEP/ECLAC Electronic Environment Information System (Port of Spain, 30 November–2 December). A number of other training workshops dealt with the application of computer programs and with the analysis of census data using such programs. A working group on Non-Independent Caribbean Countries held its first meeting in conjunction with a meeting on inter-organizational collaboration (Grenada, 7 December).

Mexico and Central America

The ECLAC subregional headquarters for Mexico and Central America, at Mexico City, carried out activities in Central America, Cuba, the Dominican Republic, Haiti and Mexico, with the aim of reviving and transforming the subregion's economies and consolidating Central American integration. A significant share of the work was devoted to analysing economic developments in 1991.

As a contribution to the modernization of the manufacturing sector, project profiles and studies were elaborated on capital formation in some countries, and research was initiated on the feasibility of producing agricultural raw materials for the pharmaceutical industry. In the field of energy, ECLAC continued its research on the supply of oil for electricity generation and its activities in support of Central American electrical integration. Documents were prepared on the energy crisis, methods of saving energy and electrical interconnection, and simulation models to optimize petroleum supply to Central America were considered at a seminar/workshop in Nicaragua (Managua, 6-11 June) under a technical cooperation project for enhancing the petroleum subsector. At the request of Nicaragua, the Commission collaborated with UNDP in evaluating the damage caused by the eruption of the Cerro Negro volcano and the subsequent tsunami that struck the country. In the area of social development, research was begun on savings and financing mechanisms for low-income groups.

Food and agricultural activities in 1992 were closely connected to issues related to international and intraregional trade in agricultural commodities and trade liberalization. Advisory services on the subject were provided to the Central American countries in the Uruguay Round, and a study was conducted on recent trends in the trade of some Central American products and their consequences for the subregion, coupled with a seminar on production of traditional agricultural exports (Mexico City, 10 and 11 December). Economic relations between Mexico and Central America were reviewed at a meeting of Central American Vice-Ministers of Economic Affairs (Mexico City, 30 March), which evaluated the progress achieved in implementing the trade liberalization programme with Mexico and its prospects. The impact of trade liberalization on Mexican agriculture was analysed under a technical cooperation project, which also provided alternative scenarios for the organization of production and the application of differentiated public policies.

Other activities during the year included a seminar on small- and medium-scale industry (San José, 19 October), followed by the first Central American Congress on Micro-, Small- and Medium-scale Industry (San Pedro Sula, Honduras, 23 and 24 October), a seminar/workshop on liberalization of the petroleum trade in Central America (Tegucigalpa, 26-28 August) and the fourth meeting on the petroleum supply in the subregion (Panama, 12 and 13 November). Training was provided on rural modernization in Mexico and on new Mexican agrarian policies.

Cooperation between the United Nations and the Latin American Economic System

In response to a 1991 General Assembly resolution,[28] the Secretary-General submitted, in October 1992, a report[29] on cooperation between the United Nations and the Latin American Economic System. Collaboration between the two entities, which had been growing stronger and broader in scope since the establishment of SELA in 1975, was further strengthened through a cooperation agreement signed in September 1991, which spurred new activities with a wider range of United Nations bodies.

An essential part of those activities continued to be carried out through ECLAC, which provided support to various SELA projects and participated in SELA meetings. ECLAC and SELA maintained ongoing consultations in the fields of social policies and economic planning, information, trade development and other areas of economic cooperation; on the promotion of a convergence among various Latin American economic integration modalities; on environment and development; and on the execution of a special cooperation programme on external trade.

Cooperation between SELA and UNDP concentrated on activities related to international trade negotiations, industrialization, integration, external debt, and regional cooperation and convergence. Further activities in those and other fields, such as external economic relations, foreign trade and financing, innovation, and competitiveness and social equity were incorporated in a new UNDP/SELA project for an amount of $550,000, to be included in the UNDP fifth programming cycle (1992-1996) for an initial period of two years (1993-

1994). Jointly with UNDP, SELA co-sponsored and hosted a regional workshop on the application of the Montreal Protocol on Substances that Deplete the Ozone Layer[30] (12-15 May). UNDP also assisted SELA in defining a working strategy to strengthen national focal points for technical cooperation and in identifying related priority areas, which facilitated the promotion of programming exercises and TCDC negotiations in specific fields.

The SELA/UNESCO/IDB regional Simón Bolívar Programme, aimed at achieving technological development, innovation and industrial competitiveness through new linkages among the scientific, academic, business and public sectors in Latin America and the Caribbean, was launched on 31 March. Another project, analysing the status of the Uruguay Round of multilateral trade negotiations in terms of the interests of the countries in the region, was being carried out by SELA in collaboration with UNCTAD. DESD implemented a substantial technical cooperation programme in developing countries that were SELA members and continued to work closely with SELA in the research and analysis of development issues of global and regional concern.

SELA hosted the third meeting of the Latin American and Caribbean Forum on Intellectual Property Policies (20 and 21 July), which considered the general situation and international trends in intellectual property protection; the Uruguay Round and trade-related aspects of intellectual property rights; the 1970 Patent Cooperation Treaty; the possibilities of advancing towards a Latin American patent system; and elements of a possible SELA/TCDC programme on industrial property. The SELA/UNIDO programme of cooperation, agreed on in 1989, accorded priority to industrial and technological development activities in the region.

The SELA Action Committee for the Economic and Social Development of Central America (CADESCA) received assistance from FAO in calculating production costs and producer subsidy equivalents for maize, sorghum, rice and beans and in organizing workshops on the calculation of such equivalents for basic grains and standardization of the calculation methodology. Another area of cooperation between CADESCA and FAO was the preparation of national studies on producer subsidy equivalents and on marketing foodstuffs in rural areas of Central America and Panama, as well as workshops on management and analysis of data on food consumption for food and nutrition surveillance. SELA and FAO also planned to cooperate in establishing a fertilizer information network for Latin America and the Caribbean.

In conclusion, the report stressed that cooperation between SELA and the United Nations system became increasingly diversified during the year and helped to optimize existing resources for the benefit of the countries in the region.

GENERAL ASSEMBLY ACTION

On 29 October, the General Assembly, having considered the Secretary-General's report, adopted **resolution 47/13** without vote.

Cooperation between the United Nations and the Latin American Economic System

The General Assembly,

Recalling its resolution 46/12 of 28 October 1991 on cooperation between the United Nations and the Latin American Economic System,

Having considered the report of the Secretary-General on cooperation between the United Nations and the Latin American Economic System,

Bearing in mind the Agreement between the United Nations and the Latin American Economic System, in which they agree to strengthen and expand their cooperation in matters which are of common concern in the field of their respective competence pursuant to their constitutional instruments,

Considering that the Economic Commission for Latin America and the Caribbean has developed ties of cooperation with the Latin American Economic System which have grown stronger in recent years,

Bearing in mind that the Permanent Secretariat of the Latin American Economic System has carried out several programmes with the support of the United Nations Development Programme in areas that are considered of priority for the economic development of the region,

Considering also that the Latin American Economic System is developing joint activities with the specialized agencies and other organizations and programmes of the United Nations system, such as the United Nations Conference on Trade and Development, the United Nations Educational, Scientific and Cultural Organization, the United Nations Industrial Development Organization, the World Meteorological Organization, the World Health Organization, the World Intellectual Property Organization, the United Nations Environment Programme, the Department of Economic and Social Development, the Office of the United Nations Disaster Relief Coordinator, the United Nations Institute for Training and Research and the International Telecommunication Union,

1. *Takes note with satisfaction* of the report of the Secretary-General;

2. *Urges* the Economic Commission for Latin America and the Caribbean to continue broadening and deepening its coordination and mutual support activities with the Latin American Economic System;

3. *Urges* the United Nations Development Programme to strengthen and broaden its support to the programmes that the Permanent Secretariat of the Latin American Economic System is carrying out, aimed at complementing the technical assistance activities conducted by the Latin American Economic System;

4. *Urges* the specialized agencies and other organizations and programmes of the United Nations system to continue and intensify their support for and cooperation with the activities of the Latin American Economic System;

5. *Requests* both the Secretary-General of the United Nations and the Permanent Secretary of the Latin American Economic System to assess, at the appropriate time, the implementation of the Agreement between the United Nations and the Latin American Economic System, and to report to the General Assembly thereon at its forty-eighth session;

6. *Requests* the Secretary-General to submit to the General Assembly at its forty-eighth session a report on the implementation of the present resolution.

General Assembly resolution 47/13

29 October 1992   Meeting 51   Adopted without vote

27-nation draft (A/47/L.7); agenda item 24.

Sponsors: Argentina, Barbados, Belize, Bolivia, Brazil, Chile, Colombia, Costa Rica, Cuba, Dominican Republic, Ecuador, El Salvador, Grenada, Guatemala, Guyana, Haiti, Honduras, Jamaica, Mexico, Nicaragua, Panama, Paraguay, Peru, Suriname, Trinidad and Tobago, Uruguay, Venezuela.

Organizational questions

JIU report

By an April note,[31] the Secretary-General transmitted to the Economic and Social Council a second report of the Joint Inspection Unit (JIU) on the cost-benefit of the Commission's office accommodation at Port of Spain, prepared as a follow-up to a 1987 JIU report on the rational use of space and location of offices at the Commission's headquarters at Santiago. JIU noted that the subregional office at Port of Spain was limited in its capacity for expansion, efficiency and effectiveness due to the size and location of the premises. In the light of the offer of Trinidad and Tobago to make a piece of land available for the use of interested international organizations at no cost, JIU recommended that ECLAC begin negotiations leading to the donation of the land, followed by in-situ arrangements for the construction of offices. It also recommended that all agencies paying rent to third parties alert their organizations to the savings and benefits to be realized from locating all the agencies in the same place.

The Secretary-General, in a July addendum to the report, notified the Council that ECLAC would begin consultations on the subject and examine the construction costs and viability of the project as soon as a firm commitment was obtained from Trinidad and Tobago to donate the property to the United Nations. By **decision 1992/295** of 31 July, the Council took note of the JIU report and the Secretary-General's comments thereon.

Venue of the twenty-fifth session of ECLAC

On 31 July, the Economic and Social Council, acting on a recommendation of ECLAC,[32] decided that the Commission's twenty-fifth session should be held at Cartagena de Indias in 1994 (**decision 1992/291**).

REFERENCES

[1]E/1992/35. [2]Ibid. (res. 519(XXIV)). [3]Ibid. (res. 521(XXIV)). [4]Ibid. (res. 528(XXIV)). [5]*Report of the United Nations Conference on Environment and Development, Rio de Janeiro, 3-14 June 1992*, vols.I-III, Sales No. E.93.I.8. [6]E/1992/35 (res. 518(XXIV)). [7]Ibid. (res. 529(XXIV)). [8]Ibid. (res. 524(XXIV)). [9]Ibid. (res. 525(XXIV)). [10]Ibid. (res. 520(XXIV)). [11]Ibid. (res. 522(XXIV)). [12]Ibid. (res. 526(XXIV)). [13]Ibid. (res. 527(XXIV)). [14]Ibid. (res. 523(XXIV)). [15]Ibid. (res. 530(XXIV)). [16]Ibid. (res. 531(XXIV)). [17]E/1993/46. [18]LC/G.1766(CONF.82/8). [19]LC/L.712. [20]LC/L.699(MDM.14/4). [21]YUN 1991, p. 329. [22]LC/L.736. [23]LC/L.735(MDM.15/2). [24]LC/G.1726(Sem.66/3). [25]LC/G.1756(CONF.81/3). [26]LC/G.1753. [27]YUN 1978, p. 467. [28]YUN 1991, p. 333, GA res. 46/12, 28 Oct. 1991. [29]A/47/463. [30]YUN 1987, p. 700. [31]E/1992/21 & Add.1. [32]E/1992/35 (res. 532(XXIV)).

Western Asia

In a January 1992 letter to the Secretary-General,[1] Bahrain confirmed its offer to host in April the sixteenth session of the Economic and Social Commission for Western Asia, which had been postponed for one year by a 1991 decision of the Economic and Social Council,[2] owing to the interruption of work by the Persian Gulf hostilities and the subsequent temporary repatriation of staff. Activities of the Commission had been officially resumed in August 1991.[3] On 7 February 1992, the Council decided that the session would be held in Bahrain from 27 to 30 April 1992 (**decision 1992/212**).

The Secretariat was subsequently informed of the withdrawal of Bahrain's invitation. By a June note,[4] the Secretary-General notified the Council accordingly and proposed a new date and venue for the session. By **decision 1992/224** of 29 June, the Council endorsed the Secretary-General's proposal.

In accordance with the Council's decision, the Commission held its sixteenth session at Amman, Jordan, from 30 August to 3 September 1992.[5] The Commission assessed progress in implementing its programme of work for 1990-1991 and reviewed follow-up action on its resolutions adopted at the fifteenth (1989) session.[6] It also examined regional follow-up to United Nations world conferences and ESCWA regional meetings, and issues related to cooperation among developing countries and regional organizations. The Commission commended the secretariat's efforts to continue its work during the Persian Gulf hostilities.[7]

Noting with deep concern the devastating effects of man-made destruction and natural disasters on economic and social conditions in ESCWA countries, the Commission declared[8] 1994-2003 a

Reconstruction and Rehabilitation Decade for Western Asia, and requested its secretariat, in close coordination with concerned regional and international organizations, to intensify efforts to promote regional cooperation in the areas of reconstruction, rehabilitation and manpower, and to organize a meeting to assess the progress made and formulate appropriate policies. It also adopted resolutions on: the reconstruction of Lebanon;[9] the economic and social condition of Palestinian Arabs in the occupied Palestinian territories[10] and the Syrian people in the occupied Syrian Golan;[11] preparations for the International Year of the Family, 1994;[12] support for the Regional Household Survey Project;[13] the impact of a single European market on Western Asia;[14] and the restructuring and revitalization of the United Nations in the economic, social and related fields.[15] (For other resolutions on specific issues, see below.)

In an October addendum to his report on regional cooperation,[16] the Secretary-General communicated to the Economic and Social Council the Commission's resolutions that required action by the Council or were brought to its attention.

Economic trends

The overall economic performance and outlook of the region improved considerably in 1992, according to a summary of the survey of economic and social developments in the ESCWA region, 1992.[17] Among the contributing factors were: the progress in implementing economic reform programmes in Egypt and Jordan; the spread of privatization and policies of "opening up" to the Syrian Arab Republic, Yemen and other countries; the resiliency of Jordan and other economies in coping with the aftermath of the Persian Gulf hostilities; progress in the reconstruction of Kuwait; and a continuing commitment to the Middle East peace negotiations. With the exception of Iraq, which continued to be adversely affected by United Nations sanctions, the region showed higher aggregate output and per capita income levels, a marked improvement in the internal and external balance situation, and reduced inflationary pressures.

After declining in 1990-1991, regional GDP was estimated to have grown by 4.5 per cent in 1992, with all ESCWA members, except Iraq and Yemen, achieving positive growth rates. Economic activity in the Gulf Cooperation Council (GCC) group of countries grew by 5.2 per cent, compared with a 0.8 per cent decline in the previous year. The fastest growth, 30 per cent, was recorded by Kuwait, which had a 40 per cent fall in output in 1991. Kuwait's rebound was largely due to a sharp increase in oil production and a boom in construc-

tion activity to rebuild the country's infrastructure and basic services. Oman's GDP growth rate was estimated at 9 per cent, against 7.5 per cent in the previous year. Growth in the non-oil sector was the major contributing factor to Oman's performance. Saudi Arabia's economy was expected to grow by 4 per cent, down from 6 per cent in 1991.

With one of the region's more diversified economies, Jordan achieved the highest growth, 8 per cent, after a marginal 1.1 per cent in 1991. Jordan also reduced inflation from 8.2 to about 4 per cent. The central contributing factors were a boom in the construction sector, boosted by sharp rises in demand and investment, financed mainly through the repatriated savings of returnees, increased investment in the manufacturing sector and a favourable agricultural season. The GDP growth rate in the Syrian Arab Republic was estimated at 5 per cent. Egypt's economy grew by 3.5 per cent, driven by higher oil revenues, record earnings from tourism and Suez Canal dues, an improved balance of payments, and increased private sector investment.

Privatization gained further momentum in 1992 as the Syrian Arab Republic and Yemen adopted investment promotion laws, and Egypt and Jordan pursued privatization under structural adjustment programmes. A recovery in non-oil sector activities in the Persian Gulf, the return of capital that was repatriated during the crisis, as well as good agricultural harvests in some countries gave an added boost to the region's development.

Many serious obstacles to development persisted, however. The Persian Gulf hostilities had adverse effects on regional trade and aid and labour flows, and it strained relations even among countries with traditionally close economic and cultural ties. The crisis also accentuated the priority attached to security and defence, helping to widen budget deficits, increase external debt, and hinder the consolidation of institutions and policies needed to implement Yemen's unification agreement of May 1990. Income disparities within and between Western Asian economies remained a problem, together with inflation and unemployment, the latter running at double-digit rates in Egypt, Jordan and Yemen.

Sharply reduced remittances and aid flows, lower oil revenues and a series of strikes by civil-servants and trade unions, coupled with a massive influx of refugees and returnees from the Gulf crisis, contributed to depressed economic activity in Yemen. GDP in Yemen declined for the third year, although at a lower rate, 2 per cent, while inflation was estimated to have risen from 40 per cent in 1991 to 50 per cent. Iraq's economy also continued to suffer from high inflation, fuelled by severe supply constraints and excessive money supply. Inflation averaged 120 per cent in Lebanon, ranging as high as 200 per cent in the first 6 months of the year, but subsided in some other countries, notably Egypt and Jordan.

Government budgeting and financial planning in Western Asia continued to suffer the impact of the hostilities in the Persian Gulf, though to a lesser degree than in 1990-1991.

The budgets of most ESCWA countries in 1992 were aimed at restoring financial order and economic balance. Budget deficits were largely contained by increases in oil revenues and the trimming of expenditures associated with the crisis. The total debt of the GCC countries was estimated at about $90 billion at the end of 1992, of which $65 billion was domestic.

The total external debt of the ESCWA region was estimated at more than $180 billion at the end of 1992, with Egypt, Iraq, Kuwait and Saudi Arabia accounting for a significant portion. While the debt of GCC member countries could be serviced from their substantial foreign financial resources, indebtedness remained a heavy burden on other Western Asian countries. A number of these, however, were able to reschedule significant portions of their debt, and in Jordan the ratio of external debt to gross national product fell from 220 per cent in 1991 to 150 per cent in 1992.

Sectoral developments

Oil and natural gas

Oil markets in 1992 remained calm compared with 1990 and the first half of 1991. Average oil prices were virtually unchanged at $18.50 per barrel. There was a gradual return of Kuwait's oil production to almost equal its pre-Gulf crisis level, and production by members of the Organization of Petroleum Exporting Countries (OPEC) reached 24.4 million barrels a day, the highest level since 1980. Demand, however, grew by less than 1 per cent, reflecting the overall sluggishness of the global economy.

Total crude oil production in the ESCWA region, after declining by 4.2 per cent in 1991, rose by 8.2 per cent in 1992, bringing oil revenues for the year to $77.5 billion, 13.8 per cent higher than in 1991 ($68 billion) but still 5.2 per cent below the 1990 level of $81.7 billion. The largest increase was recorded in Kuwait, where oil revenues reached $4.1 billion compared with $500 million in 1991. Saudi Arabia followed with 3 per cent growth in production and a 10.7 per cent gain in revenues. The Syrian Arab Republic had increases of 7.7 and 3.8 per cent in output and revenues, respectively, while the United Arab Emirates registered 2.9 and 2.4 per cent declines, respectively. Yemen's output and revenues fell by 10.2 and 16.3 per cent, respectively. Oil production rose by 2.4 per cent

in Bahrain. Iraq's output grew by 53.9 per cent, but the volume was still only about one seventh that of its pre-Gulf crisis level, and oil exports were blocked by United Nations sanctions, except for 50,000 barrels a day that were exported to Jordan in repayment of debt.

The region's share of total OPEC production increased from 56.3 per cent in 1991 to 61.3 per cent in 1992 but remained 1.2 per cent below its 1990 level. The share of ESCWA countries in total OPEC revenues grew from 52.7 per cent in 1991 to 56.7 per cent in 1992.

Proven oil reserves in the region remained virtually unchanged at 574.8 billion barrels, accounting for 57.7 per cent of the world total and 77.4 per cent of the OPEC total. Saudi Arabia accounted for 45.3 per cent of the regional total and 26.1 per cent of global oil reserves, followed by Iraq with 17.4 per cent of the regional total and 10 per cent of the world total. Iraq, Kuwait, Saudi Arabia and the United Arab Emirates combined accounted for 55.5 per cent of the world's proven oil reserves.

Proven gas reserves in the ESCWA region grew by 14 per cent in 1992 to be slightly more than 17 per cent of the world total. This was mainly due to discoveries in Egypt, Oman, Qatar and Yemen. Although most of this production was intended for local consumption, Western Asian countries with large gas reserves were looking for export markets in Europe and Asia. A number of gas purchase agreements were concluded with European and Asian countries in 1992.

Agriculture

Growth in the agricultural production index ranged from 1.7 per cent in Egypt to 48 per cent in Jordan. Despite a 5.2 per cent increase in the area under cultivation, the region's cereal production fell by 3.5 per cent against the 1991 harvest. However, the production of fruits grew by 1.8 per cent, the output of vegetables was up 3.8 per cent due to the expanded use of greenhouses in most ESCWA countries, and there was some increase in the production of red meat and poultry, eggs and dairy products, as well as in the production of pulse crops, potatoes and sugar beets. A decline was recorded in the output of oil crops.

Agricultural commodities accounted for some 17.1 per cent of total regional imports in 1991 and a mere 2.6 per cent of exports. The deficit in agricultural trade, however, decreased from $12.5 billion in 1990 to some $11 billion in 1991, due mainly to the Persian Gulf hostilities.

Industrial development

With the exception of Kuwait and Iraq, where manufacturing activities focused mainly on reconstruction and restoration, the region's industrial performance remained strong, registering a growth rate of 8.8 per cent, led by the food, beverage, clothing and construction industries.

The transportation sector also performed strongly in 1992, with most countries giving transportation projects a high priority. Efforts were being made to reduce nations' dependence on foreign resources for project implementation, extend transportation networks and optimize services, giving consideration to conditions for competition or complementarity between various transport modes. Maritime transport, however, continued to suffer the effects of the Persian Gulf conflict as reflected in the reduced deadweight tonnage of the region's merchant fleet.

Trade

The trade performance of Western Asia was adversely affected during the year by the decline of oil prices to pre-Gulf crisis levels, the disruptive impact of sanctions against Iraq, the global recession, and deepening financial difficulties in the former USSR and countries of Eastern Europe. The total value of exports from the region, excluding Iraq and Kuwait, declined by 12.9 per cent in 1991 to $89.3 billion, with the sharpest falls registered in Yemen (28.8 per cent) and the Syrian Arab Republic (22.6 per cent). Decreases in exports from the GCC countries ranged from 9.4 per cent in Bahrain to 6.5 per cent in Oman. Saudi Arabia and Qatar, however, recorded increases of 10 and 6.4 per cent, respectively. Egypt reported 41 per cent growth following a 50 per cent increase in its oil exports and Jordan's export total grew by 6.5 per cent despite the economic isolation of Iraq, its largest market.

Exports from Western Asia remained heavily weighted in favour of the developed market economies, although their total share fell from 54 per cent in 1991 to 51.7 per cent in 1992. Intraregional exports rose from 9 per cent in 1990 to 9.5 per cent, while exports to developing countries grew from 23 to 24 per cent of the total.

Imports to the region, excluding Iraq, totalled more than $72 billion in 1991, a 2.9 per cent improvement over 1990. With the exception of Egypt and Jordan, where imports fell by 15.7 and 3.5 per cent, respectively, imports increased in all ESCWA countries at rates ranging from 9.4 per cent in Bahrain to 45.4 per cent in Lebanon. The developed countries increased their share of the regional total from 60.7 per cent in 1991 to 61.7 per cent in 1992, with the United States accounting for 17.6 per cent of that amount. While the share of EC declined, it remained the region's leading supplier. The largest reduction was in intraregional imports, from 7.7 to 4.7 per cent.

The combined current account balance of the region, excluding Iraq, Kuwait and Lebanon, regressed into a $21.8 billion deficit in 1991, after surpluses of $3.9 billion in 1989 and $4.3 billion in 1990. The deficit reflected a decline in the trade surplus from $29.6 billion to $26.9 billion, accompanied by an expansion of the services deficit from $15.8 billion to $30.8 billion and the unrequited transfers deficit from $9.5 billion to about $18 billion. The surplus fell by more than 50 per cent in the Syrian Arab Republic, but grew in the non-oil economies from $1.9 billion in 1990 to $3.1 billion in 1991. Egypt led the improvement with a surplus rising from $0.2 billion to $1.9 billion, followed by Jordan, which succeeded in transforming a $0.1 billion deficit in 1990 into a $0.4 billion surplus in 1991. At the same time, the aggregate international reserves of Western Asia, excluding Iraq, the Syrian Arab Republic and Yemen, reached $36.4 billion in 1991, compared with $31.4 billion in 1990. Of this amount, $24.9 billion belonged to GCC countries and $11.4 billion to Egypt. The reserve/import ratio for the region as a whole grew from 5.3 months in 1990 to 6.6 months in 1991.

Social trends

The Western Asian countries in 1992 were adjusting to significant social changes in the wake of the Persian Gulf hostilities, which aggravated unemployment, disparities in living standards, poverty, drug abuse, disability and the flow of refugees and returnees. High population growth rates, a massive influx of returnees, and reduced aid flows in a number of countries had an adverse effect on employment opportunities, savings generation and the delivery of health, education and other social services, particularly in rural areas.

Deteriorating rural conditions continued to encourage the massive displacement of people and worsen urban poverty. In Iraq, poverty increased dramatically as a result of the Persian Gulf hostilities and economic sanctions, and in Jordan, where almost 30 per cent of the population was already considered to be living below the poverty line, the Gulf crisis added further strain. Indications from Yemen were that increasing poverty had been precipitated by the return of more than 850,000 people from the Gulf region, and 40,000-60,000 refugees from Somalia and other parts of Eastern Africa. Another expanding problem in the ESCWA region was the large caseload of human disability, as a result of armed conflicts such as the Persian Gulf hostilities and the suppression of the *intifadah* in the Israeli-occupied territories. (see PART TWO, Chapter V). Diseases leading to impairments were also on the increase, due to a lack of vaccines and poor sanitary conditions.

Despite these problems, education and health conditions overall in Western Asia continued to improve. Health plans and programmes were being implemented by almost every country and expanding education opportunities were reflected in higher adult literacy rates and gross enrolment ratios in primary education, as well as in the establishment of new and specialized higher education institutions, with the participation of the private sector. In most ESCWA countries, better health care was prolonging life expectancy, reducing infant mortality and improving labour productivity. In Iraq, however, the health situation deteriorated due to inadequate medical supplies and services. The infant mortality rate quadrupled and cholera and typhoid returned.

Rapid urbanization, industrialization, migration, armed conflicts and political disturbances continued to undermine family structures and traditional values in the region, although the family was still considered the primary source of cohesion and support for its individual members. The typical family was still dominated by children and youth—more than 61.7 per cent—with very high economic dependency ratios.

Activities in 1992

The Persian Gulf hostilities cost ESCWA a full year of work and led to the postponement of some 25 per cent of its activities under the 1990-1991 plan until the 1992-1993 biennium. However, despite the disruption and difficult working conditions, 36 per cent of total outputs were completed as planned, and an additional 8 per cent were concluded after being reformulated.

The Commission's medium-term plan for 1992-1997 was reviewed by an intergovernmental meeting convened for that purpose (Cairo, Egypt, 8 and 9 February 1992), and subsequently amended by the ESCWA Technical Committee at its seventh session (Amman, 30 August–3 September). Among the key issues and problems addressed under the plan were: rehabilitation and reconstruction of war-affected areas; economic restructuring; transfer of technology; employment; urbanization; population dynamics; rural poverty; housing, especially low-cost housing; social welfare, particularly with regard to the handicapped; the changing role of the family; women in society; and the new social structure. Programme areas covered in the plan included: food and agriculture; development issues and policies; environment; human settlements; industrial development; international trade and development finance; natural resources; energy issues; population; public administration and finance; science and technology; social development and welfare; women and development; statistics; and transport and communications.

In September, the Commission approved its revised medium-term plan for 1992-1997[18] and the programme budget for 1992-1993,[19] as amended on the recommendation of its Technical Committee.

The secretariat continued to strengthen its relations with the specialized agencies and other United Nations organizations, while cooperating closely with various regional and interregional institutions. The Commission cooperated with the Organization of the Islamic Conference in priority areas such as food security and agriculture, science and technology, and trade and investment mechanisms among Islamic countries. In February 1992, the ESCWA Executive Secretary and the Deputy Secretaries-General of the economic, social, political and Palestinian affairs offices of the League of Arab States (LAS) held discussions on strengthening joint activities and cooperation between the two bodies.

During the period under review, from mid-1989 to mid-1992, ESCWA signed a number of agreements and exchanged memoranda of understanding with various regional and interregional bodies, including the Arab Cooperation Council, the International Council for Building Research Studies and Documentation, the General Federation of Arab Chambers of Commerce, Agriculture and Industry in the Arab countries, and the Arab Atomic Energy Organization.

Development planning, development finance and international trade

Several studies and reports were undertaken under the development planning subprogramme, with emphasis on the state of the regional economy in the aftermath of the Persian Gulf hostilities. They included the annual survey of economic and social developments in the ESCWA region and technical publications dealing with the hostilities' impact on Western Asian economies, with breakdowns by country and sector.

In the area of international trade and development finance, the secretariat issued a review of developments and trends in the monetary and financial sectors in the region for 1991 and completed a regional study on financial resources availability and management. It also prepared the sixth issue of the *External Trade Bulletin of the ESCWA Region* and a review of developments in the external sector of Western Asia, dealing with the performance of new export products in the 1980s, and carried out studies on export finance and the implications of the Uruguay Round on the region's economies.

Food and agriculture

ESCWA continued to issue its annual publication *Agriculture and Development in Western Asia* and completed two country studies and a regional study in preparation for an ad hoc expert group meeting on rural development at the regional level, scheduled for Amman in October 1993. The secretariat assisted in formulating national plans of action to combat desertification in Bahrain and in Yemen, and initiated activities to prepare a similar plan for the United Arab Emirates. A socio-economic survey of the Baalbeck-Hirmil region, published in 1992, dealt with the eradication of illicit crops and rehabilitation of Lebanon's agricultural sector. Work was completed on projects addressing issues related to rural credit institutions and extension, and education for agriculture and rural development. In cooperation with FAO, several training workshops and seminars were held on the use of computers in agricultural policy analysis, farm management surveys, data processing and project planning, and agricultural marketing at the regional and international levels. Also jointly with FAO, the Commission undertook studies on agricultural marketing in Iraq, Jordan and the Syrian Arab Republic, and extension institutions in Jordan.

Industrial development

The joint ESCWA/UNIDO Industry and Technology Division continued to promote industrial development in the Arab countries. Activities in 1992 included an expert group meeting on interconnection technologies for the Western Asian electronics industries (Damascus, Syrian Arab Republic, 4 and 5 July); a review of recent developments in the region's manufacturing sector; studies on promoting entrepreneurship in small-scale industrial enterprises and the strengthening of industrial training institutions in the region; and a regional seminar on motivation, orientation and training techniques for enhancing industrial entrepreneurship in Western Asia. Several projects were also initiated by UNDP to develop engineering infrastructure and strengthen national capabilities to organize industrial projects for the use of natural gas.

Natural resources and energy

The secretariat's activities under this subprogramme focused on implementation of renewable energy projects and the expansion of the regional information network on new and renewable energy sources. During the year, the secretariat issued a bulletin on energy data for the ESCWA region for 1991, a directory of new and renewable energy resources, and a survey and assessment of energy-related activities for 1990-1991. It continued to cooperate with UNEP in carrying out a project on the assessment of water resources using remote-sensing techniques, and completed a study on water-loss prevention measures in West-

ern Asian irrigation schemes. A regional water resources database and a study on issues of rural energy were also published in 1992, and a preliminary document was prepared on the impact of the ongoing Arab-Israeli peace negotiations on the region's water sector. Country studies on energy demand in the household sector were prepared for Egypt, Jordan and the Syrian Arab Republic.

An interregional symposium on gas development and market prospects by the year 2000 and beyond (Damascus, 20-26 June 1992) adopted a set of recommendations for the development of natural gas projects and an expansion of natural gas usage and trade. A UNDP-sponsored seminar on domestic energy policies and management in the Arab countries, in October 1992, focused on improving the efficiency of energy use, promoting the development of conventional and renewable energy resources, and strengthening regional cooperation.

Science and technology

The Commission's science and technology subprogramme was responding to the enhanced interest of ESCWA members in scientific and technological activities aimed at protecting the environment and developing environmentally sound technologies. A number of activities were undertaken in the areas of ozone-depleting substances and the use of space technology for monitoring desert environments. A high-level workshop on the implications of new advanced materials technologies for Western Asian economies (Damascus, 21-24 September) was organized jointly with UNIDO's new technology and Arab region programme. The secretariat also had before it a proposal to establish a regional centre for space science and technology education.

Transport and communications

Activities in Western Asia within the framework of the Transport and Communications Decade for Asia and the Pacific (1985-1994), proclaimed by the General Assembly in 1984,[20] focused in 1992 on: the impact of privatization, deregulation and subsidy policies in the transport sector; manpower policies and training for transport operations; and maritime transport problems. In addition to the annual *ESCWA Transport Bulletin*, four documents on transport development were published in 1992, addressing the privatization and deregulation of selected transport modes, the training needs of transport authorities in Western Asia, subsidy issues, and the pricing policies of port services. A study on road maintenance issues and problems in the ESCWA countries was also issued. Other activities included a seminar on modern pricing policies for the region's ports and an expert group meeting on training requirements in the transport sector.

Environment

During 1992, ESCWA continued to promote the integration of environmental aspects into the development policies of its members and to implement related capacity-building programmes, including a UNEP-funded project to strengthen environmental management and planning capabilities in Jordan. Work also started on a preliminary assessment of environment and development conditions and trends in selected ESCWA countries.

In September, the Commission endorsed[21] the Arab Declaration on Environment and Development and Future Prospects, adopted by the 1991 Arab Ministerial Conference on Environment and Development.[22] The Declaration incorporated the Arab perspective on, and programme of action for, environmentally sound and sustainable development in the Arab countries and served as a regional input to UNCED. The Commission also called for the establishment of an Arab and international inter-agency committee to coordinate promotional activities for environmentally sound and sustainable development in the region. Two preparatory meetings on the terms of reference, functions and mandate of a joint committee on environment and development in the Arab region were held in 1992 in cooperation with LAS. In December, the secretariat issued a review of reports on the environment and sustainable development submitted by selected countries to UNCED.

Social development and the role of women

At its 1992 session, the Commission, noting the deteriorating social situation in the region, with particular regard to poverty, unemployment, disability, crime and drug abuse, shelter and health care costs, and access to basic education, adopted a resolution on the forthcoming world summit for social development,[23] endorsing Economic and Social Council **resolution 1992/27** and requesting ESCWA's active involvement in the summit and its preparations. In another resolution,[24] the Commission stressed the need to strengthen national and regional institutional mechanisms for the advancement of women. It appealed to its members and to regional and international donors to support a 1994 regional preparatory meeting for the Fourth World Conference on Women, to be convened in 1995.

As a follow-up to the 1989 Conference on the Capabilities and Needs of Disabled Persons in the ESCWA region, a Cultural Event of Disabled Persons was organized in Amman in October 1992 to promote public awareness of the capabilities of disabled persons.

Technical studies on the introduction, adaptation and transfer of appropriate technologies for disabled persons in the region and on the second-round monitoring of the implementation of the 1982 World Programme of Action concerning Disabled Persons[25] were included in the Commission's 1992-1993 programme of work.

Among other activities related to social development and the integration of women were a review of social security systems in Western Asia, an assessment of the impact of socio-economic changes on the Arab family, and a document on working women in the ESCWA region. Five case-studies were completed on the participation of women in the food and textile industries of five Western Asian countries, and executive summaries of nine other studies on the participation of women in development were issued for the benefit of other United Nations bodies and funding organizations.

Population and human settlements

In preparing for the 1994 International Conference on Population and Development, the ESCWA and LAS secretariats and UNFPA agreed in 1992 to convene a joint Arab Population Conference at Amman in April 1993, including a three-day intergovernmental expert group meeting followed by a two-day ministerial meeting. In September 1992, the Commission endorsed the agreement and requested its members to take an active part in the Conference.[26]

During the year, the secretariat carried out research on returnees from Kuwait and other Persian Gulf countries, and started preparing for expert group meetings on unemployment in the Arab world and on human development. Technical publications were issued on national policies for crime prevention and drug abuse control, and on the situation of marginalized youth groups in the region. Work continued on a review and appraisal of national policies and measures related to population distribution in selected Western Asian countries and on a bibliography of population literature in the Arab world. Case-studies on manpower planning in the industry sector were completed for Saudi Arabia and the Syrian Arab Republic. A symposium on low-cost housing in the Arab region (Sanaa, Yemen, 24-28 October) called for an intensified exchange of information and experiences and the coordination of policies and programmes to alleviate housing problems. The secretariat also published a study on the role of geographic information systems in planning appropriate human settlements in Western Asia.

Statistics

Following the 1989 session of the Commission, the secretariat participated in a number of technical and policy-oriented meetings on statistics, including a regional seminar for senior statisticians on household surveys (Cairo, Egypt, 14-21 December 1992) and meetings of the LAS Statistical

Committee and the Board of Directors of the Arab Institute for Training and Research in Statistics. The third edition of the *Unified Arab Statistical Abstract* was published under the agreement on cooperation in statistics between ESCWA and LAS. Other publications included the *Statistical Abstract of the ESCWA Region* and the *Bulletin of National Accounts*.

In September, the Commission established a committee of heads of the ESCWA members' central statistical organizations to coordinate statistical activities and the exchange of related data, and to standardize national statistics and provide advice to member States on training requirements. It was decided that the Statistical Committee would meet biennially.[27]

Technical cooperation

ESCWA continued technical cooperation activities in the region through short-term regional advisory services and the monitoring and substantive support of technical assistance projects. During 1992, the secretariat issued a review and analysis of progress made by Yemen in carrying out the 1990 Programme of Action for the Least Developed Countries for the 1990s, and provided advice on data processing, energy, environment, human resource development, industrial development, national accounts and economic statis-tics, development planning, science and technology, transport and communications, and water resources development.

Organizational questions

In September, ESCWA decided that sessions of its Technical Committee would be convened in the years when no Commission session was held, starting with a three-day meeting in 1993.[28] The Commission requested its Executive Secretary to study offers from Jordan and Lebanon to host ESCWA's permanent headquarters, and decided to discuss the question at a special session in Beirut, Lebanon, to be held within one year.[29] It thanked Iraq for the facilities it had provided to the Commission and Jordan for hosting the Commission on a temporary basis since August 1991.

REFERENCES

[1]E/1992/7. [2]YUN 1991, p. 339, ESC dec. 1991/207, 7 Feb. 1991. [3]Ibid., p. 334. [4]E/1992/87. [5]E/1992/34. [6]E/1989/36 (res. 165-177(XV)). [7]E/1992/34 (res. 193(XVI)). [8]Ibid. (res. 182(XVI)). [9]Ibid. (res. 183(XVI)). [10]Ibid. (res. 184(XVI)). [11]Ibid. (res. 185(XVI)). [12]Ibid. (res. 186(XVI)). [13]Ibid. (res. 181(XVI)). [14]Ibid. (res. 190(XVI)). [15]Ibid. (res. 191(XVI)). [16]E/1992/65/Add.1. [17]E/1993/48. [18]E/1992/34 (res. 194(XVI)). [19]Ibid. (res. 195(XVI)). [20]YUN 1984, p. 624, GA res. 39/227, 18 Dec. 1984. [21]E/1992/34 (res. 180(XVI)). [22]YUN 1991, p. 338. [23]E/1992/34 (res. 187(XVI)). [24]Ibid. (res. 188(XVI)). [25]YUN 1982, p. 980. [26]E/1992/34 (res. 189(XVI)). [27]Ibid. (res. 179(XVI)). [28]Ibid. (res. 178(XVI)). [29]Ibid. (res. 192(XVI)).

PART THREE

Economic and social questions

Chapter I

Development policy and international economic cooperation

World economic growth continued to be slow in 1992, after having contracted in 1991—the first such contraction in the post-war era. The sluggishness of world output was largely a reflection of the slow-down in some large developed market economies and the sharp decline in the transition economies of Eastern Europe and the former USSR. Although the developing countries as a whole were experiencing an acceleration in growth, not all were sharing in it; strong growth rates were almost entirely concentrated in Asia.

In July, at the high-level segment of its substantive session, the Economic and Social Council discussed the role of the United Nations system in enhancing international cooperation for development. The General Assembly, in December, reaffirmed the unique position of the United Nations as a forum for promoting such cooperation and requested the Secretary-General to make recommendations on ways to enhance that role (resolution 47/181). During its coordination segment, the Council considered the policies and activities of the specialized agencies and other bodies of the system as they related to assistance in eradicating poverty and supporting vulnerable groups. The Assembly, in December, declared that 17 October would be observed as International Day for the Eradication of Poverty beginning in 1993 (resolution 47/196).

Concerning least developed countries (LDCs), the Assembly discussed the application of new criteria for identifying those countries in the implementation of the Programme of Action for the Least Developed Countries for the 1990s. It noted donors' determination to implement their commitments with regard to official development assistance to the 47 countries included in the list of LDCs and the intention of the Trade and Development Board of the United Nations Conference on Trade and Development (UNCTAD) to examine the effects of the newly added countries on the additional resource requirements of the group as a whole (resolution 47/173). In February, the eighth session of UNCTAD discussed a wide range of international economic issues, including the special problems of LDCs.

With regard to small island developing countries, the Assembly decided to convene, in April 1994, the first global conference on their sustainable development (resolution 47/189).

International economic relations

Development and international economic cooperation

The General Assembly, the Economic and Social Council and other United Nations bodies in 1992 discussed many issues related to development and international economic cooperation.

CDP activities. At its April 1992 session,[1] the Committee for Development Planning (CDP) noted that the expectation of an early recovery from the recession in the industrial market economies had not materialized and, although relatively unaffected by the Iraq-Kuwait situation, their performance was sluggish. Demand in Canada and the United States did not recover as expected, restructuring in the eastern part of Germany placed a considerable burden on the economy of that country and Japan had not overcome the set-backs created by financial market shocks. Recovery was expected to be slower than in earlier recessions, which was unhelpful for the developing countries and those in Eastern Europe. In the latter, output contracted and unemployment rose. However, in Czechoslovakia, Hungary and Poland where structural changes were taking place, inflation was being brought under control and balance-of-payments indicators were modestly sturdy. In the other countries of Central and Eastern Europe, economic problems were much larger and major domestic policy initiatives and considerable international support would be required for them to overcome the problems of transition.

Developing countries continued to experience widely divergent patterns of growth and some showed a rise in performance well above that of the industrial market economies. China showed considerable success in its stabilization policies and India initiated a comprehensive liberalization programme. A number of other developing countries in all regions were overcoming some major macro- and micro-economic difficulties, becoming more stable and internationally competitive. In Latin America, more countries experienced increases in their gross domestic product (GDP) growth rates in 1991 and an increasing number of them were succeeding in their domestic stabilization efforts. Growth was stronger in Argentina, Chile, Mexico and Venezuela. In Africa, somewhat higher growth rates were achieved by countries participating in the World Bank's Special Programme of Assistance for debt-distressed and low-income countries in sub-Saharan Africa. However, the economic problems of the poorest and least developed countries continued and were exacerbated by high population growth rates.

With regard to the role of the United Nations in the framework of international economic cooperation, CDP stated that political events and the cumulative effect of economic and technological processes had reshaped the world economy, added new issues to the international agenda and enhanced the role of the United Nations in the economic, social and political arenas. To meet that challenge, the United Nations system was in need of reform. Its specialized agencies were to a great extent self-contained and, in spite of their sectoral mandates, their activities frequently overlapped, often resulting in spontaneous cooperation but sometimes in conflict. The United Nations itself, which revolved around the General Assembly, the Security Council and the Economic and Social Council, was complicated in structure and lacked transparency.

CDP recommended that coordination of the activities of the specialized agencies be improved by: flexible cooperation among agencies with interrelated spheres of interest; more consistent positions by member States in the various governing bodies of which they were members; and the revitalization of the Economic and Social Council to enhance its overview function. The complicated structure of the United Nations needed to be streamlined and made more transparent and more coordination was needed between the Economic and Social Council and the Assembly to streamline their agendas and make them more relevant. CDP also recommended strengthening the research functions of the Secretariat in the economic and social fields.

Economic Committee consideration. The Economic Committee of the Economic and Social Council considered the question of development and international economic cooperation in June/July 1992.[2]

The Committee had before it the *World Economic Survey 1992*,[3] prepared by the United Nations Department of Economic and Social Development. The *Survey* examined the state of the world economy and trends in global output and policies. It also discussed international trade, saving, investment and the international transfer of resources, developments and emerging trends in energy, conversion and the peace dividend, and entrepreneurship and the development challenges of the 1990s.

Also before the Committee was the Secretary-General's report on the main research findings of the system in major global economic and social trends, policies and emerging issues.[4] In accord-

ance with a 1986 resolution,[5] by which the Council had requested that the report be submitted on a biennial basis, it was prepared on the basis of information received from concerned bodies of the United Nations system, together with a review of their major publications. It highlighted findings published in the preceding few years, including some issues and projections of future conditions for the 1990s, and identified areas warranting further analysis. The report considered in particular global output and policies; debt adjustment, growth and human resource protection and development; population and human settlements; science and technology; and environment and development.

The report concluded that research carried out in the system over the preceding two years had focused on such questions as the nature, parameters and policy implications of changing concepts of growth and development, the reversal of environmental degradation in a developmental context and the improvement of the quality of life.

Subjects that seemed to warrant further investigation included: the need for more reliable data on Eastern European economies in order to monitor their transitional process and define policies to support transition; grass-roots participation as an element of the development process; and the use of human resources for capacity-building, self-reliance and sustainability. Although major strides had been made in factoring environmental concerns into the development process, the secretariat of the 1992 United Nations Conference on Environment and Development (UNCED) (see PART THREE, Chapter VIII) had suggested further intersectoral research in a number of areas.

The report noted that the objectivity and impartiality of research work carried out by entities such as the World Institute for Development Economics Research of the United Nations University and the United Nations Research Institute for Social Development generated new insights and information into major policy issues. Their contributions could be further promoted through enhanced collaboration both between them and with research-oriented units within the system.

On the basis of the recommendations of the Committee, the Economic and Social Council, by **decision 1992/296** of 31 July 1992, took note of the Secretary-General's report,[4] the *World Economic Survey 1992*[3] and the CDP report.[1]

High-level segment of the Economic and Social Council. In accordance with a 1991 General Assembly resolution[6] on the restructuring and revitalization of the United Nations in the economic, social and related fields, the Economic and Social Council held a high-level segment of its substantive session from 6 to 9 July 1992. On 7 February (**decision 1992/203**), the Council decided that the high-level segment would consider the theme "Enhancing international cooperation for development: the role of the United Nations system".

The segment, which was attended by Ministers and high-level representatives, had before it CDP's report on its 1992 session[1] (see above), the *World Economic Survey 1992*[3] and a note by the Secretary-General on strengthening the operational activities of the United Nations system, including the governance and financing thereof[7] (see PART THREE, Chapter II).

It also had before it a report of the Secretary-General on the role of the United Nations in enhancing international cooperation for development.[8] The report reviewed the dramatic changes in the international environment that had set the new context for development cooperation, and attempted to identify key development objectives for the 1990s, such as revitalizing growth and development; the reform of national policies and the establishment of stable rules for market access and an enhanced mechanism for the settlement of trade disputes; and the interrelated aims of human development, eradication of poverty, diffusion of technology and protection of the environment.

The report's principal focus was on the role of the United Nations system in facilitating the attainment of those objectives, including what action the international community could take, through the system, to advance international cooperation and ways to improve the system to serve as an effective instrument to that end. It stated that the development dialogue in the United Nations forums in the key areas of trade, finance, technology and sustainable development needed to be strengthened. The General Assembly's political role in the development dialogue and the Council's overview functions had to be made more effective, and there was a need for more fruitful cooperation among the various bodies of the system. The system had to continue to provide multilateral assistance to support economic reforms and structural adjustment programmes, as well as long-term development objectives of developing countries, but that assistance had to be refocused on the basis of more clearly defined goals and priorities. Greater impact could be achieved if funding institutions, specialized agencies and Governments worked together to help developing countries to formulate and implement common development strategies. Arrangements for governance needed to be examined to ensure a strong intergovernmental capacity to set clear directions and policy guidance. Financing of operational activities needed to be placed on a more adequate, assured and stable basis and field level coordination needed to be improved.

Summarizing the proceedings of the high-level segment, the President of the Council noted that a broad convergence of views on several key aspects of the theme had emerged. International development cooperation and the eradication of poverty were inextricably linked with the preservation of peace and security and needed to be pursued with equal vigour. Member States had expressed concern over the stalled world economy, stressing that persistent problems of limited access to markets and technology, excessive debt burdens, inadequate official development assistance (ODA) and an unfavourable international economic environment continued to hamper development. The first priority was a concerted global effort to reinvigorate growth and development.

The successful transition and restoration of growth in Eastern Europe and newly independent States, seen by participants in the high-level segment as beneficial for growth and development in the world economy, and the urgency of international support for the accompanying political and economic reforms were highlighted. Assurances were given that resources for development assistance would not be diverted to support the transition economies.

With the concept of development emerging as human-centred, equitable and socially and environmentally sustainable, the high-level segment pointed to the eradication of poverty as a priority objective and stressed the need to integrate social goals into structural adjustment programmes and development strategies. Reference was also made to adjustment programmes and economic reform policies, including more open and liberalized trade policies, being pursued by developing countries, and international support for their success was called for.

With regard to the restructuring and reform of the United Nations system, caution was expressed against redefining the development priorities of developing countries or limiting the scope of technical cooperation carried out through the system. The importance of better coordination of United Nations activities in the economic, social and related fields was stressed, including the enhancement of the roles of resident coordinators and of the regional commissions. The high-level segment also noted the need for a closer and improved relationship between the United Nations and its agencies and the Bretton Woods institutions (the International Monetary Fund (IMF) and the World Bank). The role of the Administrative Committee on Coordination (ACC) was seen as central in improving coordination in the system.

At the end of the high-level segment, the President of the Council established an ad hoc open-ended working group to hold consultations, prior to the opening of the General Assembly's 1992 session, on the role of the United Nations system in enhancing international economic cooperation with a view to making recommendations to the Assembly for its consideration and action. Since the working group did not complete its work in time for it to report to the Assembly, it continued its consultations under the Assembly's auspices.

GENERAL ASSEMBLY ACTION

In his annual report on the work of the Organization (see p. 3), the Secretary-General discussed the wide range of development issues before the international community and outlined a possible approach to those issues—an agenda for development.

On 22 December 1992, on the recommendation of the Second (Economic and Financial) Committee, the General Assembly adopted **resolution 47/181** without vote.

An agenda for development

The General Assembly,

Recalling the Charter of the United Nations, in particular the commitment to employ international machinery for the promotion of the economic and social advancement of all peoples,

Taking note of the report of the Secretary-General on the work of the Organization, in particular the reference to an agenda for development,

Reaffirming the unique position of the United Nations as a forum for the promotion of international cooperation for development,

Emphasizing the need to give due consideration to the broad scope of themes related to international cooperation and international economic relations in order to address effectively the issue of development, particularly of developing countries,

Stressing the importance of continuing to strengthen the capacity of the United Nations to foster international cooperation in order to address fully the wide range of issues pertaining to development, particularly that of developing countries,

Stressing also that the objectives and commitments with regard to development adopted by the General Assembly, especially the Declaration on International Economic Cooperation, in particular the Revitalization of Economic Growth and Development of the Developing Countries, the International Development Strategy for the Fourth United Nations Development Decade, the Cartagena Commitment, the United Nations New Agenda for the Development of Africa in the 1990s, the Programme of Action for the Least Developed Countries for the 1990s, and the various consensus agreements and conventions, especially Agenda 21, adopted by the United Nations Conference on Environment and Development at the level of heads of State or Government, which mark the beginning of a new global partnership for sustainable development, all together provide the overall framework of international cooperation for development,

Recalling the restructuring and revitalization process initiated by its resolution 45/264 of 13 May 1991, in particular its commitment to promote the achievement of the objectives and priorities of the United Nations in the economic, social and related fields, as set forth in other relevant resolutions,

Requests the Secretary-General to submit to the General Assembly at its forty-eighth session, in consultation with Member States, a report on an agenda for development, taking fully into consideration the objectives and agreements on development adopted by the Assembly, containing an analysis of and recommendations on ways to enhance the role of the United Nations and the relationship between the United Nations and the Bretton Woods institutions in the promotion of international cooperation for development, within the framework and provisions of the Charter of the United Nations and the articles of agreement of the Bretton Woods institutions, and to include therein, *inter alia*, a comprehensive annotated list of substantive themes and areas to be addressed by the United Nations in the agenda, as well as his views on priorities among them, for the consideration of Member States.

General Assembly resolution 47/181

22 December 1992   Meeting 93   Adopted without vote

Approved by Second Committee (A/47/718/Add.1) without vote, 9 December (meeting 49); draft by Vice-Chairman (A/C.2/47/L.71), based on informal consultations on draft by Pakistan for Group of 77 (A/C.2/47/L.44); agenda item 78.

Meeting numbers. GA 47th session: 2nd Committee 25, 30, 45, 46, 49; plenary 93.

The Second Committee considered the issues of development and international economic cooperation during the Assembly's 1992 regular session and made recommendations on a number of topics (see APPENDIX IV, agenda item 78). The Assembly took note of part I of the Committee's report on the item[9] by **decision 47/441** of 22 December.

In other action, by **decision 47/465** of 23 December, the Assembly deferred consideration of the launching of global negotiations on international economic cooperation for development and decided to include it in the provisional agenda of its forty-eighth (1993) session.

Integration of economies in transition into the world economy

The *World Economic Survey 1992* examined the transition process of the centrally planned economies of Eastern Europe and the former USSR to market economies. Although the old order had broken up as of early 1992, the new system had not crystallized. Severe economic disruption was taking place, with output dropping by 16 per cent in 1991 and investment falling to the levels of the mid-1970s. The *Survey* noted that the excitement in 1989 over the political opening for the full economic transformation of the centrally planned economies of Europe had been tempered by the realization of the arduous nature of the transformation. The breakup of the USSR into 15 independent States intensified the disruption of economic activity, with no new mechanisms to replace the traditional ones for economic exchange and distribution. Those successor States had only just started their economic transformation, but neither the path of the transition nor the character of the mix of State and private activity towards which they were aiming was clear. The other Eastern European countries had already started the transition to market economies and the stabilization-cum-liberalization policies implemented had started to bear fruit in those countries that began the process first. The *Survey* analysed the situation in the countries of the former USSR and the prospects and challenges for them.

Report of the Secretary-General. In response to a 1991 request of the General Assembly,[10] the Secretary-General submitted a report on the impact of the evolution of East-West relations on global growth and development.[11] It described the state of economic transformation and recent developments in East-West economic relations and discussed the implications of Eastern Europe's transition to market orientation for the developing countries.

The report concluded that efforts to introduce far-reaching structural changes in the Eastern European economies deserved international assistance. However, that assistance had to be managed in such a way as to produce positive effects on the transition, while containing negative repercussions for other countries, including developing ones.

From country to country, the transitions had exhibited major differences in scope, depth and range, but it was widely recognized that the timetable stretched far into the future. It was likely to be much longer for most of the successor Soviet republics, where transition policies remained a subject of socio-political debate, than for the Central European countries where steps towards macroeconomic stabilization, institution-building and structural change had already been taken.

For the transition economies to reach the stage where they could play a constructive role in coordinating global affairs in the interest of all parts of the world economy, the international community would need to provide temporary technical and financial assistance to deflect the most negative aspects of transformation policies for their populations. In addition, since a successful transition hinged on the ability of the Eastern European countries to penetrate world markets competitively, it was necessary to restore and reinforce basic elements of a multilateral trading world with minimal non-tariff inhibitions.

Although both national Governments and multilateral financial organizations had generally adhered to their commitments to assist the transitional economies, it seemed likely that the Eastern European countries would need assistance over a longer period and on a larger scale than originally envisaged. Over the medium term, major donor countries might find it necessary to merge

assistance budgets. The report stated that that should be avoided, as assisting the Eastern European countries was a different proposition from assisting the development process of the less advantaged countries. It noted that more open, liberal trade policies would be of immense significance to most of the transition economies and, in the long term, considerably boost trade with developing countries.

GENERAL ASSEMBLY ACTION

On 22 December, on the recommendation of the Second Committee, the General Assembly adopted **resolution 47/187** without vote.

Integration of the economies in transition into the world economy

The General Assembly,

Reaffirming its resolutions S-18/3 of 1 May 1990, the annex to which contains the Declaration on International Economic Cooperation, in particular the Revitalization of Economic Growth and Development of the Developing Countries, and 45/199 of 21 December 1990, the annex to which contains the International Development Strategy for the Fourth United Nations Development Decade, and recalling the Cartagena Commitment, adopted by the United Nations Conference on Trade and Development at its eighth session,[a] and Agenda 21, adopted by the United Nations Conference on Environment and Development,[b]

Aware of the fundamental changes taking place in the countries that are transforming their economies from centrally planned to market-oriented ones, and of the problems they are facing in this regard,

Taking note of the *World Economic Survey 1992,*

1. *Recognizes* that the full integration of the economies in transition into the world economy should have a positive impact on world trade, economic growth and development, including that of the developing countries;

2. *Also recognizes* the need for the international community to support the successful process of bringing about economic reforms and restructuring in the economies in transition, with due regard to the developing countries among them, without adversely affecting development assistance to other developing countries;

3. *Requests* the Secretary-General to coordinate and strengthen the ability of the United Nations system to conduct analytical and policy advice activities regarding changes that take place in the economies in transition as they integrate into the world economy;

4. *Requests* the Secretary-General therefore to prepare, within existing resources, with the full cooperation of the relevant organizations and bodies of the United Nations system, including the World Bank and the International Monetary Fund, a report on the role of the United Nations system in addressing problems facing the economies in transition, including the difficulties that the economies in transition are encountering in their integration into the world economy, and to submit the report to the General Assembly at its forty-eighth session;

---

[a]TD/364.
[b]A/CONF.151/26.

5. *Decides* to include in the agenda of its forty-eighth session a sub-item entitled "Integration of the economies in transition into the world economy" under the item entitled "Development and international economic cooperation".

General Assembly resolution 47/187

22 December 1992   Meeting 93   Adopted without vote

Approved by Second Committee (A/47/718/Add.2) without vote, 11 December (meeting 50); 23-nation draft (A/C.2/47/L.35/Rev.1); agenda item 78 (a).

Sponsors: Afghanistan, Albania, Armenia, Azerbaijan, Belarus, Bosnia and Herzegovina, Bulgaria, Croatia, Czechoslovakia, Estonia, Finland, Iceland, Kazakhstan, Latvia, Lithuania, Poland, Republic of Moldova, Romania, Russian Federation, Tajikistan, Turkey, Turkmenistan, Ukraine.

Meeting numbers. GA 47th session: 2nd Committee 40, 42, 43, 48-50; plenary 93.

On the same date, also on the recommendation of the Second Committee, the Assembly adopted **resolution 47/175** without vote.

Impact of the recent evolution of the economies in transition on the growth of the world economy, in particular on the economic growth and development of the developing countries, as well as on international economic cooperation

The General Assembly,

Reaffirming its resolutions S-18/3 of 1 May 1990, the annex to which contains the Declaration on International Economic Cooperation, in particular the Revitalization of Economic Growth and Development of the Developing Countries, and 45/199 of 21 December 1990, the annex to which contains the International Development Strategy for the Fourth United Nations Development Decade, and taking note of the Cartagena Commitment, adopted by the United Nations Conference on Trade and Development at its eighth session,

Recalling its resolutions 45/182 of 21 December 1990 and 46/202 of 20 December 1991,

Taking note of the report of the Secretary-General on the impact of the evolution of East-West relations on global growth and development,

Taking note also of the Declaration of the Ministers for Foreign Affairs of the States members of the Group of Seventy-seven adopted on the occasion of their sixteenth annual meeting, held in New York on 1 October 1992,[a] in which the Ministers recalled the conclusions of the Special High-level Meeting of the Economic and Social Council held at Geneva on 4 and 5 July 1991,

1. *Takes note* of the report of the Secretary-General on the impact of the evolution of East-West relations on global growth and development;

2. *Urges* the developed countries and multilateral financial institutions to continue to ensure that the resources allocated to the economies in transition do not reduce or divert official development assistance allocated to the developing countries;

3. *Calls upon* the international community to consider assisting the developing countries whose economies have been most affected by the changes in their economic relations with the economies in transition to adapt to those changes;

4. *Requests* the Secretary-General to continue to review and analyse, in close consultation and coordination with the United Nations Conference on Trade and Development, the impact of the evolution of the economies in transition on the growth of the world economy, in particular on the economic growth and development of the developing countries, as well as on international economic cooperation, and to submit to the General Assembly at its forty-eighth session a report containing, *inter alia*, an assessment of the progress made in the implementation of the present resolution.

————
[a]A/47/499.

General Assembly resolution 47/175

22 December 1992   Meeting 93   Adopted without vote

Approved by Second Committee (A/47/717/Add.1) without vote, 11 December (meeting 50); draft by China, Japan, Pakistan for Group of 77 (A/C.2/47/L.40/Rev.1); agenda item 12.

Meeting numbers. GA 47th session: 2nd Committee 3-9, 34-37, 40, 42, 43, 45, 46, 48-50; plenary 93.

International cooperation for economic growth and development

In response to a 1991 request,[12] the Secretary-General submitted to the General Assembly the report of the President of the Economic and Social Council[13] on the outcome of an informal exchange of views on the 1991 report of the Commonwealth Group of Experts on the Impact of Global Economic and Political Change on the Development Process.[14] The informal exchange of views took place on 22 July 1992. By **decision 47/444** of 22 December, the Assembly took note of the Council President's report.

Implementation of the 1990 Declaration on International Economic Cooperation

In response to a 1991 request of the General Assembly,[15] the Secretary-General submitted an analytical report on the implementation of the commitments and policies agreed upon in the Declaration on International Economic Cooperation, in particular the Revitalization of the Economic Growth and Development of the Developing Countries.[16] The report examined national and international action that had implications for the implementation of the Declaration, adopted by the Assembly in 1990,[17] and concluded that so far results of the implementation had been mixed.

Economic growth and policies in industrialized countries, developing countries and countries with economies in transition were discussed. The report also addressed the issues of betterment of the human condition, the debt problem of the developing countries, external resources for development, regional integration among developing countries, international trade, the environment, science and technology, integrating the transition economies into the global economy, reduction of military expenditure and the role of the United Nations system.

In a series of conclusions, the report stated that, although many developing countries had instituted or continued major economic reforms, there was a widening perception of old and new problems, such as poverty eradication and environmental protection, and the gap between international commitment and action remained large. Initiatives taken included some progress towards solving the debt problem of the developing countries; countries with economies in transition continued efforts to integrate themselves into the world economy; and world military expenditure declined, creating the potential for economic and social development. However, there had not been a commensurate international initiative to create a supportive economic environment; international economic cooperation to revitalize growth in developing countries lacked the momentum envisaged in the Declaration; the revival of the transition economies was more difficult than envisaged; and the stalemate in the Uruguay Round of multilateral trade negotiations cast doubts on the future of the multilateral trading system and inhibited trade-related investment.

International Development Strategy for the Fourth UN Development Decade

The International Development Strategy for the Fourth United Nations Development Decade (the 1990s), adopted by the General Assembly in 1990,[18] provided for a process of review and appraisal. Accordingly, the Secretary-General submitted to the Economic and Social Council and the Assembly in June 1992 the first biennial review of the Strategy's implementation.[19]

Since its launching, some of the Strategy's basic premises had been threatened by the situation in the Persian Gulf, recession in the developed market economies and the dissolution of the USSR. Although the Persian Gulf situation had left little impact at the global level, the recession in the developed market economies had been deeper and more persistent than predicted and the recovery was weak. The resumption of growth in the industrialized economies, a major premise on which the Strategy had based its objective of accelerated development in developing countries, had not materialized and the international economic environment was not conducive to growth and development in other respects.

The Strategy had seen reform and restructuring in Eastern Europe as a potential new source of growth and development for developing countries, largely through expanded trade, but that seemed unlikely to happen in the first half of the decade. The pattern of growth in the developing countries remained essentially unchanged in 1991.

Despite the Strategy's emphasis on the need for additional financial resources, development finance remained scarce. Since some major donors were burdened with large fiscal deficits and deteriorating social and economic conditions, their ability and willingness to provide and increase resources were constrained.

The Strategy had stressed the need for domestic economic reform, and many developing countries had undertaken major policy reforms aiming at greater reliance on market forces and the private sector, stabilization and monetary and fiscal discipline, more realistic exchange rates and trade liberalization.

It was too early to discern major changes in the Strategy's priority areas of poverty and hunger eradication, human resources development, slowing population growth and environmentally sound and sustainable development. However, despite developments in the early 1990s, the goals and objectives of the Strategy remained valid since the Strategy had set broad goals in critical areas and recognized that many of its objectives could be realized only in the medium and long term. The review identified a number of concerns which had become more prominent than at the time of the Strategy's adoption. They included the repercussions for international economic relations of the disintegration of the USSR, the integration of Eastern European countries into the world economy, the environment and international migration. The review noted that a reversal of trends in the first 18 months of the decade would require decisive efforts in virtually all countries. Developing countries should continue their economic reform process and developed countries should restore the primacy of economic growth.

The Economic and Social Council took note of the Secretary-General's report by **decision 1992/297** of 31 July.

GENERAL ASSEMBLY ACTION

On 18 December, on the recommendation of the Second Committee, the General Assembly adopted **resolution 47/152** without vote.

International cooperation for economic growth and development

The General Assembly,

Reaffirming the Declaration on International Economic Cooperation, in particular the Revitalization of Economic Growth and Development of the Developing Countries, contained in the annex to its resolution S-18/3 of 1 May 1990, and the International Development Strategy for the Fourth United Nations Development Decade, contained in the annex to its resolution 45/199 of 21 December 1990, which provide the overall framework for economic growth and development,

Recalling its resolution 46/144 of 17 December 1991 on the implementation of the commitments and policies agreed upon in the Declaration,

Taking into account the Cartagena Commitment, the United Nations New Agenda for the Development of Africa in the 1990s, the Programme of Action for the Least Developed Countries for the 1990s, and Agenda

21, and all the relevant decisions of the United Nations Conference on Environment and Development,

1. *Takes note with interest* of the reports submitted by the Secretary-General on the subject;

2. *Encourages* Member States to submit their reports on the implementation of the commitments and policies agreed upon in the Declaration on International Economic Cooperation, in particular the Revitalization of Economic Growth and Development of the Developing Countries;

3. *Requests* the Secretary-General to provide, at its forty-ninth session, an analytical and comprehensive report on the implementation of the commitments and policies agreed upon in the Declaration and on the implementation of the International Development Strategy for the Fourth United Nations Development Decade, including his assessment of the steps taken by Governments of developed and developing countries, individually and collectively, and by organs, organizations and bodies of the United Nations system, including the regional commissions;

4. *Decides*, in order to keep the implementation of the Declaration and the International Development Strategy under review, to include in the provisional agenda of its forty-eighth session the item entitled "International cooperation for economic growth and development: (*a*) Implementation of the commitments and policies agreed upon in the Declaration on International Economic Cooperation, in particular the Revitalization of Economic Growth and Development of the Developing Countries; (*b*) Implementation of the International Development Strategy for the Fourth United Nations Development Decade".

General Assembly resolution 47/152

18 December 1992   Meeting 92   Adopted without vote

Approved by Second Committee (A/47/724) without vote, 24 November (meeting 45); draft by Pakistan for Group of 77 (A/C.2/47/L.9); agenda item 84.
Meeting numbers. GA 47th session: 2nd Committee 3-9, 12, 13, 22, 45; plenary 92.

The private sector in development

Entrepreneurship and private-sector development

The *World Economic Survey 1992*,[3] in a section on entrepreneurship and the development challenges of the 1990s, stated that there was a growing consensus that interaction between government activities and market forces provided the most conducive environment for tackling the complex problems of sustained economic development and the alleviation of global poverty. A long-term vision of change in which entrepreneurship had a key role could open new perspectives on the challenge of development. The *Survey* examined the key features of entrepreneurship and its role in bolstering productive potential and promoting rapid restructuring. It reassessed the concept of entrepreneurship, outlined the nature of an enabling environment for private enterprise and suggested specific institutional requirements and policy measures in support of productive entrepreneurship. Experiences with entrepreneurship in Africa, Asia and Latin America, as well as the transition economies in Eastern Europe, were presented.

UNDP action. In response to a 1991 request,[20] the Administrator of the United Nations Development Programme (UNDP) reported to the UNDP Governing Council on UNDP's role in private-sector development.[21] The report indicated that the private sector had come to play a central role in nations' development strategies, which included mobilizing entrepreneurs to achieve self-sustaining growth in national development efforts. That trend was reflected in many national development plans reviewed by UNDP field offices. UNDP, in cooperation with other United Nations agencies, had assisted a variety of private sector–related activities in response to requests from Governments arising from major changes in their development strategies. The report suggested that communication with and coordination of United Nations system activities would be strengthened by UNDP involvement at the country level through the resident representatives and resident coordinators with support from UNDP's Division for the Private Sector in Development. The allocation of $4 million in Special Programme Resources would support private-sector initiatives of a catalytic nature during UNDP's fifth programming cycle (1992-1996).

The report discussed UNDP's comparative advantage in providing assistance in private-sector development and outlined UNDP's strategy for the private sector in development. The strategy included seeking to create a favourable environment for private investment and business, and supporting the development of the intellectual infrastructure, institutions and skills needed to expand and improve efficiency. The report also addressed the need to strengthen coordination among United Nations bodies and other organizations involved in matters relating to the private sector.

On 26 May,[22] the Governing Council endorsed UNDP's role and strategy in assisting Governments to promote the role of the private sector in their development efforts and requested UNDP to focus its activities on national capacity-building and policy formulation. It asked the Administrator to define further UNDP's role in promoting assistance in private-sector development in order to clarify its comparative advantage, to strengthen communication and cooperation within the United Nations system and to harmonize UNDP activities with other multilateral organizations and bilateral donors when promoting entrepreneurship and private-sector development.

Privatization

Private-sector development had become a central concern for many developing countries and economies in transition. During 1992,[23] the Transnational Corporations and Management Division of the Department of Economic and Social

Development (formerly the Centre on Transnational Corporations) assisted Governments in developing a network of institutions, agencies and mechanisms to support the functioning of markets and encourage entrepreneurial activities.

UNCTAD action. The eighth session of the United Nations Conference on Trade and Development (UNCTAD VIII) (see PART THREE, Chapter IV), in its final document (the Cartagena Commitment),[24] noted the growing recognition that reform of State economic enterprises would contribute to an increase in savings and investment in developing countries. Privatization, accompanied by an effective regulatory framework to foster competition and efficiency and prevent the emergence of private· monopolies, could play an important role. The Conference encouraged officials responsible for the privatization programmes adopted by many countries to share their experience and expertise. It recommended that developing countries should further improve their policy and regulatory environment so as to attract foreign direct investment, the return of flight capital and other non-debt-creating financial flows. Policies were also required to sustain economic development and expand internal market opportunities and export activities.

On 7 May,[25] the UNCTAD Trade and Development Board established the Ad Hoc Working Group on Comparative Experiences with Privatization. The Group's terms of reference were: to review countries' experience with privatization; to consider medium- and long-term objectives of privatization processes; to consider factors pertinent to the design and implementation of privatization programmes; to elaborate possible guidelines for formulating privatization programmes and plans; and to serve as a forum for the presentation of national privatization programmes and plans and for the exchange and dissemination of information and national experiences. It would also identify areas in which technical cooperation could be strengthened.

ECONOMIC AND SOCIAL COUNCIL ACTION

On 30 July, on the recommendation of its Economic Committee, the Economic and Social Council adopted **resolution 1992/36** without vote.

Privatization and foreign investment in the context of economic restructuring

The Economic and Social Council,

Recognizing the fact that numerous countries attach growing importance to privatization of enterprises, administrative deregulation, increased competition, open markets and demonopolization of their economic activities as a means to increase economic efficiency, growth and development, in the context of their economic restructuring policies,

Stressing the important role that foreign direct investment can play in the process of privatization in those countries,

Noting the difficulties those countries encounter in the process of privatization, administrative deregulation and demonopolization of their economic activities,

Noting also the work the former United Nations Centre on Transnational Corporations has performed so far in analysing new approaches to the process of privatization, administrative deregulation and demonopolization of economic activities,

1. *Requests* the Secretary-General, in coordination with other relevant international organizations, to enhance technical cooperation activities in order to assist all interested countries in attracting foreign investment and transnational corporations so as to contribute to the implementation of privatization programmes, in the context of their economic reforms;

2. *Invites* the Secretary-General to explore further, through case-by-case studies of foreign investment, new approaches to the process of privatization, administrative deregulation and demonopolization of economic activities;

3. *Recognizes* the need to diversify sources of funding for research and technical cooperation activities, and, to that end, invites voluntary contributions to the Trust Fund for the Technical Cooperation Programme of the former United Nations Centre on Transnational Corporations, and requests the Secretary-General to seek to mobilize resources from various sources, including non-governmental organizations, and to report to the Commission on Transnational Corporations at its twentieth session.

Economic and Social Council resolution 1992/36

30 July 1992   Meeting 41   Adopted without vote

Approved by Economic Committee (E/1992/109/Add.3) without vote, 28 July (meeting 16); draft by Commission on TNCs (E/1992/26); agenda item 12 *(e)*.

GENERAL ASSEMBLY ACTION

On 22 December, on the recommendation of the Second Committee, the General Assembly adopted **resolution 47/171** without vote.

Privatization in the context of economic restructuring, economic growth and sustainable development

The General Assembly,

Reaffirming its resolution S-18/3 of 1 May 1990, the annex to which contains the Declaration on International Economic Cooperation, in particular the Revitalization of Economic Growth and Development of the Developing Countries, and its resolution 45/199 of 21 December 1990, the annex to which contains the International Development Strategy for the Fourth United Nations Development Decade, as well as other relevant United Nations resolutions,

Taking note of the Cartagena Commitment, adopted by the United Nations Conference on Trade and Development at its eighth session, and Trade and Development Board decision 398(XXXVIII) of 7 May 1992, by which, *inter alia,* the Ad Hoc Working Group on Comparative Experiences with Privatization was established, and looking forward to the contribution of the Ad Hoc Working Group,

Taking note also of Economic and Social Council resolution 1992/36 of 30 July 1992 on privatization and foreign investment in the context of economic restructuring,

Recognizing the sovereign right of each State to decide on the development of its private and public sectors, taking into account the comparative advantages of each sector,

Noting that the private sector plays a positive role in mobilizing resources and promoting economic growth and sustainable development,

Noting also that many countries are attaching growing importance, in the context of their economic restructuring policies, to the privatization of enterprises and the demonopolization and administrative deregulation of economic activities, as well as market-oriented reforms, increased competition, the elimination of price-distorting mechanisms, and open markets, all as a means to increase economic efficiency, growth and sustainable development,

Noting further the difficulties these countries encounter in those policies and that various practical modalities and approaches towards privatization can be considered by them,

1. *Welcomes* the activities being undertaken by relevant organs, organizations and bodies of the United Nations system in supporting national efforts aimed at increasing economic efficiency, growth and sustainable development through privatization, demonopolization, administrative deregulation of economic activities and other relevant policies, and urges them:

   (a) To support, when requested, the national efforts of countries in implementing privatization, demonopolization, administrative deregulation and other relevant policies in the context of their economic reforms and the opening of their economies;

   (b) To strengthen their communication and cooperation in supporting the national efforts of countries in privatizing enterprises, demonopolizing and deregulating their economic activities and implementing other relevant policies, and invites the Secretary-General to give due attention to coordination of the United Nations system in this field, through, *inter alia*, the Economic and Social Council and other relevant United Nations bodies;

   (c) To take into account, in implementing their respective mandates, the work already undertaken by the organs, organizations and bodies of the United Nations system in order to maximize the efficiency of the system, mindful of the ongoing process of restructuring the system;

2. *Calls upon* interested Member States to enhance the exchange of information among themselves and all relevant organs, organizations and bodies of the United Nations system on their activities, programmes and experiences concerning privatization, demonopolization, administrative deregulation and other relevant policies in order to increase the efficiency and coordination of technical cooperation in this field;

3. *Requests* the Secretary-General to improve, within existing resources, research activities on all areas of privatization, demonopolization, administrative deregulation and other relevant policies, to enhance cooperation with national and international research institutions and to include all pertinent findings in relevant United Nations publications, including the *World Economic Survey;*

4. *Also requests* the Secretary-General to include in his report to the General Assembly at its forty-eighth session, to be submitted pursuant to its resolution 46/166 of 19 December 1991 on entrepreneurship, recommendations for action by the United Nations system in support of the present resolution.

General Assembly resolution 47/171

22 December 1992   Meeting 93   Adopted without vote

Approved by Second Committee (A/47/717/Add.1) without vote, 11 December (meeting 50); draft by Vice-Chairman (A/C.2/47/L.78), based on informal consultations on 48-nation draft (A/C.2/47/L.23); agenda item 12.
Meeting numbers. GA 47th session: 2nd Committee 3-9, 34-37, 40, 42, 43, 45, 46, 48-50; plenary 93.

Industrial development cooperation

In response to General Assembly requests of 1990[26] and 1991,[27] the Secretary-General submitted a report on measures taken by the United Nations Industrial Development Organization (UNIDO) to enhance industrial development cooperation and the diversification and modernization of productive activities in developing countries.[28] As requested by the Assembly in 1990,[26] a study was planned by UNIDO, to be undertaken jointly with the United Nations Secretariat, on scientists, engineers and entrepreneurs, which was expected to culminate in an action plan on ways to promote the enhancement of United Nations training activities. However, the study's preparation was postponed due to financial constraints and it was proposed that it be submitted to the Assembly in 1994.

The Secretary-General reported that UNIDO's industrial cooperation activities were being strengthened within an integrated framework comprising the human factor; modernization: the challenge of technology; and diversification: industrial recovery. UNIDO's human resources development objective was to build up in developing countries coherent and sustainable systems for upgrading local technological, managerial and entrepreneurial capabilities for industrial development. Programmes had given priority to the transfer of new and high technologies, the enhancement of economic and technical cooperation among developing countries, the integration of women in human resource development activities and managerial training. The primary objectives of the UNIDO development and transfer of technology programme were to: increase developing countries' awareness of the implications of emerging technological changes; facilitate their access to technology sources; assist them in strengthening their domestic technological capabilities; promote broader participation by them in international technological development; and improve regional cooperation. With regard to revitalizing industry in developing countries, UNIDO aimed to find new ways to increase the international flow of finance to productive industrial investment by supporting investment policy formulation, including investment codes attractive to foreign capital. It also aimed to work closely with financial institutions in developing countries, identify, appraise and promote industrial investment opportunities and promote enterprise-to-enterprise cooperation through direct foreign investment and technical cooperation agreements.

GENERAL ASSEMBLY ACTION

On 18 December, the Assembly, on the recommendation of the Second Committee, adopted **resolution 47/153** without vote.

Industrial development cooperation

The General Assembly,

Reaffirming its resolutions S-18/3 of 1 May 1990, the annex to which contains the Declaration on International Economic Cooperation, in particular the Revitalization of Economic Growth and Development of the Developing Countries, 45/199 of 21 December 1990, the annex to which contains the International Development Strategy for the Fourth United Nations Development Decade, and 46/151 of 18 December 1991, the annex to which contains the United Nations New Agenda for the Development of Africa in the 1990s,

Reaffirming also its resolutions 45/196 of 21 December 1990 and 46/146 of 17 December 1991, taking note of Economic and Social Council resolution 1992/44 of 31 July 1992, and reaffirming other relevant resolutions in the field of industrial development cooperation,

Noting with satisfaction the outcome of the United Nations Conference on Environment and Development,

Recognizing that the creation of a supportive international economic environment, through, *inter alia*, effective relief measures to address external debt problems and an open and non-restrictive world trading system, is essential to promoting the industrialization efforts of developing countries,

Convinced that, in order to promote the industrial development of developing countries, their indigenous capabilities in such areas as entrepreneurship, management, technology, financing and marketing need to be built up or strengthened, and that technical and financial assistance in support of the national efforts of developing countries would need to be extended for this purpose,

Taking note of the note by the Secretary-General on industrial development cooperation and the diversification and modernization of productive activities in developing countries,

1. *Stresses* the importance of international cooperation in supporting efforts at the regional, subregional and national levels in industrial development, in particular in the fields of human resources development, investment and export promotion, technology transfer, industrial conversion and development of national capacities, in order to diversify and modernize productive activities in developing countries;

2. *Calls upon* organizations of the United Nations system, in particular the United Nations Industrial Development Organization, to take due account in their programmes, projects and activities, in the context of industrial development cooperation, of the commitments to further sustainable development agreed upon in the United Nations Conference on Environment and Development process, especially by ensuring provision of the means of implementation, as set forth in section IV of Agenda 21, stressing in particular the importance of financial resources and mechanisms, the transfer of environmentally sound technology, cooperation and capacity-building and international institutional arrangements, in order to achieve sustainable development in all countries;

3. *Recommends* that the United Nations Industrial Development Organization, in the context of its medium-term plan and the decision taken by the Industrial Development Board, on 6 November 1992, on relative priorities among the activities included within that plan, bearing in mind the Organization's financial and technical capacity and with due regard to national priorities, strengthen its cooperation with organizations in the public and private sectors, especially in developing countries, in particular with those organizations working in human resource development, investment and export promotion and technological capacity-building;

4. *Urges* the international community, including the United Nations system and the regional commissions, and, in particular, multilateral financial institutions and regional banks, to support industrial development programmes and projects, especially in developing countries;

5. *Notes with concern* that the study of long-term world industrial structure could not be carried out;

6. *Reiterates its call* to the United Nations Industrial Development Organization and other relevant United Nations organizations to encourage and support technical cooperation among developing countries in the field of industrialization;

7. *Requests* the Secretary-General to invite the Director-General of the United Nations Industrial Development Organization to report, through the Secretary-General, to the General Assembly at its forty-ninth session on the implementation of the present resolution;

8. *Decides* to include in the provisional agenda of its forty-ninth session an item entitled "Industrial development cooperation".

General Assembly resolution 47/153

18 December 1992   Meeting 92   Adopted without vote

Approved by Second Committee (A/47/725) without vote, 11 December (meeting 50); draft by Vice-Chairman (A.C.2/47/L.74), based on informal consultations on draft by Pakistan for Group of 77 (A/C.2/47/L.14); agenda item 85.
Meeting numbers. GA 47th session: 2nd Committee 3-9, 18, 28, 50; plenary 92.

Eradication of poverty

By **decision 1992/204** of 7 February 1992, the Economic and Social Council decided that part of its 1992 segment on coordination should be devoted to the coordination of the policies and activities of the specialized agencies and other bodies of the United Nations system related to assistance in the eradication of poverty and support to vulnerable groups, including assistance during the implementation of structural adjustment programmes.

In a May report,[29] the Secretary-General provided the Council with a brief review of recent developments in the area of poverty relevant to coordination issues, paying particular attention to the impact of structural adjustment programmes on poverty. Based on information from various parts of the United Nations system, it outlined the strategies, priorities, policy orientations and programmatic activities of the system in poverty eradication, including promotion of growth with poverty alleviation, support to vulnerable groups and amelioration of negative impacts of structural adjustment programmes. The report also drew on the discussions and conclusions on the subject of the ACC Task Force on Long-term Development Objectives (Geneva, 3-6 March).[30]

The report also presented some broad themes related to the nature and scope of coordination in the United Nations system in poverty alleviation and eradication, and formulated specific suggestions to improve and strengthen coordination processes and structures. It identified the need to develop a coherent system-wide framework for action and strengthen the existing mechanisms for inter-agency coordination and cooperation and their mandates to ensure coverage of the whole range of issues related to poverty. In recognition of the importance of accurate and up-to-date data and the development of poverty indicators, it was also suggested that an inter-agency meeting be organized to devise common understandings and approaches towards a set of social indicators that could be used for data collection by the system. At the country level, it was suggested that the role of the resident coordinator be strengthened and that programmes and projects of the United Nations system be better harmonized with those of recipient Governments to enhance the efficiency of delivery.

Summarizing the results of the Council's coordination segment,[2] the President stated that a number of recommendations had emerged. At the global level, ACC should develop a common system-wide approach to policies and activities for poverty eradication and review existing arrangements for system-wide coordination in the area of poverty, modifying them to encompass poverty issues more comprehensively. At the country level, the system should assist developing countries to enhance their institutional capacity for policy formulation and coordination of the implementation of programmes to eradicate poverty. In all countries, a common strategy, prepared under the leadership of the resident coordinator, should be developed on ways in which the organizations of the system could work together to help alleviate poverty. Coordinated approaches should be devised for data collection and the development of social indicators to facilitate shared analysis and assessment of country situations. The organizations of the system, including the World Bank and

IMF, should collaborate closely to ensure that poverty alleviation and human development goals were incorporated into their programmes and into structural adjustment programmes. It was recommended that the Secretary-General should report in 1993 on progress made in implementing the Council's recommendations.

On 31 July, the Council, by **decision 1992/300**, took note of the Secretary-General's report.

In response to a 1991 request,[31] the Secretary-General, in October 1992,[32] reported to the General Assembly, informing it of the Council's consideration of the matter. He submitted to it for consideration his report on progress made in coordinating policies and activities for the eradication of poverty in developing countries[29] and drew attention to the Council President's summary of recommendations for action by the United Nations system on poverty eradication.[2]

UNCTAD action. The Cartagena Commitment, adopted by UNCTAD VIII in February[24] (see PART THREE, Chapter IV), stated that a consensus had developed on a number of priority aspects of development, including the eradication of poverty and hunger. It was agreed that major efforts by all countries were necessary to evolve approaches to growth that would substantially alleviate poverty and promote ecologically sound and sustainable development. In the context of the need for institutional adaptation by UNCTAD in order for it to address new developments in international economic cooperation, UNCTAD VIII agreed that a number of new committees of the Trade and Development Board should be established, including a standing committee on poverty alleviation.

On 7 May,[25] the Board adopted the terms of reference of the Standing Committee on Poverty Alleviation, which would contribute to national and international efforts to prevent, alleviate and reduce poverty and to the formulation of national and international policies, bearing in mind the diversity of country situations including the particular problems of LDCs and the most vulnerable population groups. To that end, the Committee, among other things, would: review existing information and analyses on the characteristics, causes, location, dimensions and dynamics of poverty; exchange and review national experiences in dealing with poverty and identify impediments to poverty alleviation and policy options for the prevention and alleviation of poverty; exchange views on the impact of development assistance and cooperation programmes on the alleviation and reduction of poverty and develop approaches to promote effective programmes; consider questions related to the financing and organization of social development programmes in developing countries, particularly in the areas of health, education, housing and sanitation; examine the impact of trade expansion on poverty alleviation; identify linkages between poverty alleviation and the achievement of sustainable development; and examine the relationship between migration and other demographic factors and poverty alleviation. The Committee would also identify areas where technical cooperation should be strengthened.

On 22 December, on the recommendation of the Second Committee, the General Assembly adopted **resolution 47/197** without vote.

International cooperation for the eradication of poverty in developing countries

The General Assembly,

Reaffirming the Declaration on International Economic Cooperation, in particular the Revitalization of Economic Growth and Development of the Developing Countries, contained in the annex to its resolution S-18/3 of 1 May 1990, the International Development Strategy for the Fourth United Nations Development Decade, contained in the annex to its resolution 45/199 of 21 December 1990, the Paris Declaration and Programme of Action for the Least Developed Countries for the 1990s, adopted by the Second United Nations Conference on the Least Developed Countries, the United Nations New Agenda for the Development of Africa in the 1990s and the Cartagena Commitment, adopted by the United Nations Conference on Trade and Development at its eighth session, in February 1992,

Reaffirming also principle 5 of the Rio Declaration on Environment and Development, chapter 3 of Agenda 21, principle 7 *(a)* of the Non-legally Binding Authoritative Statement of Principles for a Global Consensus on the Management, Conservation and Sustainable Development of All Types of Forests, and all other decisions and recommendations adopted by the United Nations Conference on Environment and Development relating to the eradication of poverty,

Reaffirming further its resolutions 43/195 of 20 December 1988, 44/212 of 22 December 1989, 45/213 of 21 December 1990 and 46/141 of 17 December 1991,

Noting that the eradication of poverty in all countries, in particular in developing countries, has become one of the priority development objectives for the 1990s,

Stressing that effective national policies supported by a favourable international economic environment can promote sustained and sustainable development in all countries, in particular in developing countries, thus increasing their capacity to undertake social and economic programmes to eradicate poverty,

Noting with concern the negative effects of large debt burdens and their impact on poorer sections of society in many developing countries,

Recognizing that poverty is a complex and multidimensional problem with origins in both the national and international domains, and that its eradication constitutes an important factor to ensure sustainable development,

Noting that the efforts made at the national and international levels need to be enhanced to ensure the eradication of poverty,

1. *Takes note* of the note by the Secretary-General on the subject;

2. *Stresses* the importance of domestic policies, including effective budgetary policies, to mobilize and allocate domestic resources for the eradication of poverty through, *inter alia*, the creation of employment and income-generating programmes, with particular reference to households headed by women, the implementation of food security, health, education, housing and population programmes and the strengthening of national capacity-building execution programmes;

3. *Encourages* all countries to undertake national strategies and programmes for the eradication of poverty, in particular devoted to the poorest strata of society, and involving a more active participation of the targeted communities in the initiative for and implementation, follow-up and evaluation of specific projects;

4. *Reaffirms* that a supportive international economic environment which takes into account the review of resource flows and structural adjustment programmes, integrating social and environmental dimensions, is crucial to the success of efforts of developing countries to deal with the eradication of poverty;

5. *Reiterates its request* to the international community to adopt specific, effective measures designed to increase financial flows to developing countries, and urges the developed countries, which have reaffirmed their commitment to reach the accepted United Nations target of 0.7 per cent of gross national product for official development assistance, to the extent that they have not yet achieved that target, to agree to augment their aid programmes in order to reach that target as soon as possible, some developed countries having agreed to reach the target by the year 2000; other developed countries, in line with their support for reform efforts in developing countries, agree to make their best efforts to increase their level of official development assistance;

6. *Urges* all donors to contribute generously to the tenth replenishment of the International Development Association, to the fourth replenishment of the International Fund for Agricultural Development and to other international financial institutions, with a view to ensuring that those institutions continue in their fight against poverty, especially in rural areas;

7. *Urges* the international community to continue to undertake technical cooperation programmes with a view to strengthening income and job creation capacities, improving food security, health, education and housing, and meeting other basic needs of the populations of developing countries, in particular the poorest groups among them, and, in that context, reaffirms that, with respect to the transfer of technology on favourable terms, including concessional and preferential terms, as mutually agreed, taking into account the need to protect intellectual property rights as well as the special needs of developing countries for the implementation of Agenda 21, effective modalities should be examined with a view to implementing and enhancing that transfer as soon as possible;

8. *Encourages* the international community, including the organs, organizations and bodies of the United Nations system, to continue to support development programmes in all countries, in particular developing countries, including human resources development programmes, in order to strengthen endogenous technical

capacity and generate opportunities for production and employment;

9. *Welcomes* the decision of the United Nations Conference on Trade and Development at its eighth session to set up a Standing Committee on Poverty Alleviation and to request the Trade and Development Board to attach high priority to its work in the framework of its agreed terms of reference;

10. *Requests* the Secretary-General to report to the General Assembly at its forty-eighth session on the progress made in coordinating action, in cooperation with governmental and non-governmental organizations and other multilateral bodies, to formulate improved and enhanced action-oriented technical cooperation programmes for the eradication of poverty in all countries, particularly in developing countries, within the framework of the United Nations system, in accordance with the policies, priorities and strategies of those countries;

11. *Decides* to include in the provisional agenda of its forty-eighth session the item entitled "International cooperation for the eradication of poverty in developing countries".

General Assembly resolution 47/197

22 December 1992   Meeting 93   Adopted without vote

Approved by Second Committee (A/47/721) without vote, 16 December (meeting 51); draft by Vice-Chairman (A/C.2/47/L.88), based on informal consultations on draft by Pakistan for Group of 77 (A/C.2/47/L.53) and orally revised; agenda item 81.
Meeting numbers. GA 47th session: 2nd Committee 3-9, 38, 39, 46, 51; plenary 93.

International day for the eradication of poverty

On 22 December 1992, on the recommendation of the Second Committee, the General Assembly adopted **resolution 47/196** without vote.

Observance of an international day for the eradication of poverty

The General Assembly,

Noting that the eradication of poverty and destitution in all countries, in particular in developing countries, has become one of the priorities of development for the 1990s, and considering that the promotion of the eradication of poverty and destitution requires public awareness,

Welcoming the fact that certain non-governmental organizations, on the initiative of one non-governmental organization, have in recent years in many States observed 17 October as World Day for Overcoming Extreme Poverty,

1. *Decides* to declare 17 October International Day for the Eradication of Poverty, to be observed beginning in 1993;

2. *Notes* that activities undertaken with respect to the Day will take into account those undertaken each 17 October by certain non-governmental organizations;

3. *Invites* all States to devote the Day to presenting and promoting, as appropriate in the national context, concrete activities with regard to the eradication of poverty and destitution;

4. *Invites* the Secretary-General to make recommendations on ways and means by which the Secretariat could, within existing resources and without prejudice to ongoing activities, assist States in organizing their national activities for the observance of International Day for the Eradication of Poverty;

5. *Invites* intergovernmental and non-governmental organizations to assist States, at their request, in organizing national activities for the observance of International Day for the Eradication of Poverty, paying due attention to the specific problems of the destitute;

6. *Requests* the Secretary-General to take, within existing resources, the measures necessary to ensure the success of the observance by the United Nations of International Day for the Eradication of Poverty;

7. *Also requests* the Secretary-General to report to the General Assembly at its fiftieth session on the implementation of the present resolution.

General Assembly resolution 47/196

22 December 1992   Meeting 93   Adopted without vote

Approved by Second Committee (A/47/721) without vote, 16 December (meeting 51); draft by Vice-Chairman (A/C.2/47/L.87), based on informal consultations on draft by Pakistan for Group of 77 (A/C.2/47/L.52); agenda item 81.
Meeting numbers. GA 47th session: 2nd Committee 3-9, 38, 39, 46, 51; plenary 93.

Agrarian reform and rural development

ACC action. The ACC Task Force on Rural Development (New York, 22-24 April)[33] considered the work accomplished by various agencies and bodies of the United Nations system during 1991 in rural development and related areas. The issues discussed were monitoring and evaluation of rural development, people's participation, industrial contribution to rural development, coordination and collaboration on rural development and agrarian reform, impact of national macroeconomic policies on the rural poor, implementation of the 1985 Nairobi Forward-looking Strategies for the Advancement of Women[34] as they related to rural women, and an enabling approach to shelter improvement in rural areas as a contribution to sustainable rural development and poverty alleviation.

The Task Force agreed that agencies should provide information on the impact of their rural development efforts and, in their next reports, place their rural development activities in perspective and review progress, shortcomings and obstacles. It reviewed agency reports on their planned activities for 1992-1993, noting that people's participation, environmental sustainability, food security and nutrition, the private sector, employment, integration of women in development and rural poverty alleviation had received high priority in most agencies. The Task Force agreed that in future reports attention should also be paid to rural-urban linkages. It noted the activities of UNDP in the Niger and the United Republic of Tanzania on the impact of national macroeconomic policies on the rural poor and, in particular, on the implications of the UNDP/World Bank Social Dimensions of Adjustment programme for rural women, and suggested closer cooperation on issues relating to women in development. Having considered the suggestion of the ACC Task Force on Long-term Development Objectives[30] that the mandate of the Task Force on Rural Development be extended to cover all issues related to poverty, the Task Force concluded that, although its mandate should remain firmly anchored in rural development, it could be enlarged to review linkages between rural and urban poverty.

UNCTAD and other action. In February,[24] UNCTAD VIII expressed support for and solidarity with the Summit on the Economic Advancement of Rural Women, to be held later that month, and underlined the importance of strengthening the productive role of rural women to promote food security, alleviate poverty and accelerate development.

On 30 June,[35] Belgium transmitted to the Secretary-General the Geneva Declaration for Rural Women, adopted at that Summit (Geneva, 25 and 26 February) (see PART THREE, Chapter XIII).

In **resolution 1992/53** of 31 July, the Economic and Social Council urged States to work to achieve the Geneva Declaration's goals. It urged the United Nations system to take those goals into account in carrying out programmes and invited governing bodies to consider measures to address the special needs of rural women.

FAO report. In response to a 1981 request,[36] the Secretary-General submitted to the Economic and Social Council in April 1992 the third review and analysis of agrarian reform and rural development.[37] The report, prepared by the Food and Agriculture Organization of the United Nations (FAO) in collaboration with other concerned organizations and bodies of the United Nations system, was the third in the series, the first having been submitted in 1984[38] and the second in 1988.[39] The report discussed the major dimensions and trends of rural poverty alleviation; reviewed progress in agrarian reforms and their impact on rural poverty; considered patterns and trends in rural employment and the implications of agricultural policy reforms for market prices and access to inputs; analysed the impact of human resource development on poverty and rural development; and discussed the relationship between environment, public policy and poverty. It also drew together the main lessons from the experience of developing countries in their efforts to implement poverty alleviation strategies in the light of the Programme of Action adopted by the 1979 World Conference on Agrarian Reform and Rural Development.[40]

The report found that the negative effects of structural adjustment programmes on the rural poor could be effectively minimized through appropriate government policies. Improvements in social indicators and a decline in the proportion of the poor in the total rural population could also be achieved through increased social services expenditure and improved targeting to the poor.

Considerable disparities persisted between rural and urban areas and between males and females, particularly with respect to school enrolment and literacy rates. Thus, greater effort was required in many countries to remove the bias against rural areas and women. There was strong justification for agrarian reforms based on equity, but effective implementation of redistributive land reforms was contingent on political will and the introduction of complementary policies and measures to provide beneficiaries with improved technologies and supporting services. Greater attention was needed to remove barriers to effective implementation of labour legislation and more innovative and concerted efforts were needed to reach rural youth and women in skill-formation training programmes. Special measures were also needed to promote technology adoption by small farmers and for research and development of appropriate farming systems and technologies for resource-poor, environmentally degraded agro-ecological areas. People's participation was vital to successful environmental conservation or rehabilitation.

By **decision 1992/280** of 30 July, the Economic and Social Council took note of the FAO report.

REFERENCES

[1]E/1992/27. [2]A/47/3/Rev.1. [3]*World Economic Survey 1992: Current Trends and Policies in the World Economy* (E/1992/40), Sales No. E.92.II.C.1. [4]E/1992/46. [5]YUN 1986, p. 884, ESC res. 1986/51, 22 July 1986. [6]YUN 1991, p. 749, GA res. 45/264, 13 May 1991. [7]E/1992/64. [8]E/1992/82 & Add.1. [9]A/47/718. [10]YUN 1991, p. 345, GA res. 46/202, 20 Dec. 1991. [11]A/47/403. [12]YUN 1991, p. 344, GA dec. 46/461, 20 Dec. 1991. [13]A/47/477. [14]A/C.2/46/12 & Add.1. [15]YUN 1991, p. 346, GA res. 46/144, 17 Dec. 1991. [16]A/47/397. [17]GA res. S-18/3, annex, 1 May 1990. [18]GA res. 45/199, annex, 21 Dec. 1990. [19]A/47/270-E/1992/74. [20]YUN 1991, p. 349. [21]DP/1992/15. [22]E/1992/28 (dec. 92/17). [23]E/C.10/1993/9. [24]TD/364. [25]A/47/15, vol. I (dec. 398(XXXVIII)). [26]GA res. 45/196, 21 Dec. 1990. [27]YUN 1991, p. 351, GA res. 46/146, 17 Dec. 1991. [28]A/47/535. [29]E/1992/47. [30]ACC/1992/7. [31]YUN 1991, p. 350, GA res. 46/141, 17 Dec. 1991. [32]A/47/530. [33]ACC/1992/18. [34]YUN 1985, p. 937. [35]A/47/308-E/1992/97. [36]YUN 1981, p. 400, ESC dec. 1981/185, 23 July 1981. [37]E/1992/38. [38]YUN 1984, p. 411. [39]E/1988/56. [40]YUN 1979, p. 501.

Economic and social trends and policy

Economic surveys and trends

The *World Economic Survey 1992*[1] stated that the gross global product—the total world output of goods and services—dipped by 0.5 per cent in 1991, a rare occurrence. The dip was mainly due to the fact that the economies of Eastern Europe and the former USSR plunged even deeper into disruption than in 1990. However, growth also slowed in the large industrial economies and several of them were in recession. African economies, on average, barely kept up with population growth. On the other hand, Latin American economies seemed to revive from a decade of stagnation, and growth in Asia remained widespread and fast, despite the slow-down in world trade.

Although in late 1991 many indicators suggested that recovery was finally under way in the United States and a number of other countries, economic activity began weakening in Germany and Japan. Political instability in several parts of the world and the difficulties encountered in the transition in Eastern Europe and the former USSR obscured the economic prospects in those regions. Uncertainties also prevailed in world markets, notably with regard to interest rates. The large investment requirements of the European transition economies and the needs of the Gulf States were leading to an increased world demand for credit, over and above the current-account deficits of the United States. Also, in some major developed market economies, commercial banks, shaken by falling equity prices and large bankruptcies among borrowers, were reluctant to lend even to credit-worthy traditional customers. Thus, interest rates could remain high and credit scarce.

In a note giving an update of the world economy at the end of 1992,[2] the Secretary-General stated that it grew only 0.4 per cent in 1992, resulting from a 1.5 per cent increase in industrial countries, a 4.5 per cent increase in developing countries and a decline of 18.4 per cent in the transition economies of Eastern Europe and the former USSR. An improvement was forecast for 1993, mainly due to projected better conditions in transition economies, high growth rates for developing countries and slow but improving growth in industrial countries.

World trade grew 4.5 per cent in 1992, a strong result given slow output growth; imports surged in the developing countries of Asia and Latin America. Japan's net transfer of financial resources to other countries jumped by 55 per cent to some $90 billion in 1992, while the United States absorbed $39 billion from the rest of the world for a second year of smaller inflows. Developing countries absorbed $25 billion in net financial transfers for a second year of big inflows after almost a decade of outflows.

In its review of the situation and prospects for the world economy, the *Trade and Development Report, 1992*[3] noted that the world economy was in a period of uncoordinated, disparate and overall weak growth, with little prospect of vigorous recovery in the near future, continuing a trend that had become evident in 1989 and 1990. Some of the key problems facing the world economy were structural in nature and specific to particular country groups or regions. The clearest example was that of Central and Eastern Europe, where new political, economic and social institutions had to be built. Institution-building would also be important to the economic future of the European Economic Community, and the United Kingdom and the United States also faced major tasks of rebuilding deteriorated infrastructures. In Asia, growth in many of the newly industrialized economies would be increasingly constrained by environmental deterioration and too little investment in infrastructure. In contrast, the development process had scarcely been launched in Africa.

In all regions, problems stemming from demographic changes and pressures required urgent attention. Measures to put the world economy on a balanced and sustainable path of development required not only macroeconomic policy coordination, but also approaches that were carefully tailored to the specific need of individual countries and regions while being mutually supportive and taking account of global interdependence.

REFERENCES

[1] *World Economic Survey 1992: Current Trends and Policies in the World Economy* (E/1992/40), Sales No. E.92.II.C.1. [2] E/1993/INF/1. [3] *Trade and Development Report, 1992* (UNCTAD/TDR/12), Sales No. E.92.II.D.7.

Development planning and public administration

Development planning

The Committee for Development Planning held its twenty-eighth session in Kuwait (18-22 April 1992).[1] It stated that while the short-term outlook for the world economy remained fragile, the medium-term outlook inspired cautious optimism. In the industrial countries, the major factors underlying that assessment were the policy reforms introduced in the 1980s, completion of the European Community single-market programme and the creation of the European Economic Area, establishment of a North American free trade area and continuing rapid technical progress, making for rising economies of scale, greater competitiveness and increasing productivity. For other countries to benefit, however, it was important that neither a "fortress Europe" nor a "fortress America" emerged.

In the developing countries, acceleration of growth would depend on the industrial countries and their own continuing domestic policy reforms aimed at macroeconomic stability and outward-oriented trade regimes. There was a danger that privileged access of the Central and Eastern European countries to the markets of Western Europe could harm the trade prospects of developing countries and that those countries could also "crowd out" some groups of countries in international capital markets. CDP observed that, since the rising pressure on global savings would raise interest rates and the cost of capital, a medium-term policy objective of developed market economies should be to raise national savings rates, by reducing fiscal deficits and easing the stance of monetary policy. For developing countries, dependent on ODA for the bulk of their development financing, the prospects for growth in ODA were poor, particularly in view of the likelihood of a diversion of existing ODA levels to the countries with economies in transition.

Addressing the question of economic reforms being implemented in developing countries, CDP concluded that for structural adjustment packages to be sustainable and conducive to longer-term growth, they must include measures to cope with transitory social costs and ensure satisfactory levels of investment in physical infrastructure and human resource development. Experience also indicated that in many developing countries a variety of fundamental structural and institutional changes were needed to ensure growth. Furthermore, structural adjustment programmes that did not explicitly incorporate measures addressing long-term development goals, such as the alleviation of poverty, improvement in the distribution of income, and the socio-economic attainments of women, were likely to fail since a broad-based consensus in support of reform was unlikely to become firmly established. Equally, a comprehensive reform programme that did not address issues of short-term stabilization and medium-term growth-oriented structural reform was likely to result in failure and premature abandonment of the programme. Within a framework of macroeconomic stability, most decision-making in economic matters should be decentralized, consistent with the country's basic socio-economic objectives, requiring measures in a range of policy areas, including fiscal, trade, exchange rates, industrial, labour, social and others.

With regard to fiscal policies, public-sector investment and social spending needed to be rationalized to sustain adequate levels of investment in infrastructure, agriculture and energy and to increase access of the poor to health, education and adequate nutrition. Besides overhauling fiscal systems, States could contribute more effectively to economic development by modifying their approach to development, from one involving heavy governmental intervention and regulation to a more indicative approach.

Industrial and labour policies also needed to be reviewed and reformed, with adequate employment termination benefits and job retraining programmes replacing efforts to preserve employment by keeping loss-making enterprises afloat through public subsidies.

Since growth and welfare benefits of comprehensive reform programmes were realized only after a considerable period of time, many countries needed to pursue political reforms to foster a sense of participation in decision-making at the grass-roots level. Improvements were also needed in the basic elements of governance—adherence to the rule of law, transparency in the use of public funds, and accountability to the governed—so that States could become effective agents of development.

CDP concluded that, although the implementation of developing countries' reform programmes would depend on their own efforts, a favourable external environment would enhance their chance of success. Donor countries could also assist reform efforts by encouraging developing countries to programme measures and establish performance targets over a long-term horizon, supporting such programmes with a multi-year financial commitment.

By **decision 1992/296** of 31 July, the Economic and Social Council took note of CDP's report.[1]

Public administration

The Secretary-General, in April 1992, presented to the Economic and Social Council the report of the Tenth Meeting of Experts on the United Nations Programme in Public Administration and Finance (New York, 4-11 September 1991).[2] The Meeting reviewed current issues in public administration and finance in developing countries, the United Nations work programme in public administration and finance and medium-term plan for 1992-1997, and technical cooperation activities of the United Nations in public administration and finance and prospects for technical cooperation among developing countries. It made recommendations for action at the national and international levels.

In their review of current issues, the Experts noted that the 1990s would present extraordinary challenges to public administration and finance systems throughout the world where national Governments were faced with a complex environment for decision-making. They reviewed those challenges and emphasized that public management would continue to play a vital role in national development. They recommended a number of policy and programme actions to strengthen management approaches, techniques and skills in the areas of administrative reform; human resource management; resource mobilization and expenditure control; financial management; public enterprises; environmental management; information technologies in public management; and commitment and transparency in public management. They also reviewed the constraints facing public administration and finance systems in making them relevant and effective in the 1990s and beyond.

Commenting on the Experts' recommendations, the Secretary-General agreed that there was a need for closer collaboration between the United Nations central programme and new programmes in public management initiated by other United Nations agencies. He stated that the Experts' recommendations were sound and reflected the priority interests and pressing needs of developing countries; their implementation would help to increase the efficiency and effectiveness of public administration and finance measures in developing countries. Actions at the international level would be implemented within current available resources and every attempt would be made to incorporate the recommendations within the framework of the United Nations medium-term plan for 1992-1997. The Secretary-General suggested that future Meetings of Experts should focus mainly on prevailing public management issues, especially in the context of global concerns such as governance, transformation, responsiveness and resource management, with a view to providing timely policy and technical guidance to developing countries.

By **decision 1992/287** of 30 July, the Economic and Social Council took note of the Secretary-General's report and requested him to convene the Eleventh Meeting of Experts in 1993.

REFERENCES

[1]E/1992/27. [2]E/1992/13.

Developing countries

Least developed countries

The special problems of the officially designated least developed countries were considered in several United Nations forums during 1992, including UNCTAD VIII, the UNCTAD Trade and Development Board, CDP and ACC.

The number of countries on the United Nations list of LDCs remained at 47: Afghanistan, Bangladesh, Benin, Bhutan, Botswana, Burkina Faso, Burundi, Cambodia, Cape Verde, Central African Republic, Chad, Comoros, Djibouti, Equatorial Guinea, Ethiopia, Gambia, Guinea, Guinea-Bissau, Haiti, Kiribati, Lao People's Democratic Republic, Lesotho, Liberia, Madagascar, Malawi, Maldives, Mali, Mauritania, Mo-

zambique, Myanmar, Nepal, Niger, Rwanda, Samoa, Sao Tome and Principe, Sierra Leone, Solomon Islands, Somalia, Sudan, Togo, Tuvalu, Uganda, United Republic of Tanzania, Vanuatu, Yemen, Zaire, Zambia.

Application of the criteria for identification of LDCs

In April,[1] in accordance with the criteria recommended by it in 1991 for the identification of LDCs and noted by the General Assembly later that year,[2] CDP considered the requests of the Republic of the Marshall Islands and the Federated States of Micronesia for inclusion in the list of LDCs. CDP examined the economic and social situation of both countries, paying particular attention to the extremely high level of aid dependency. However, in both cases, according to the data provided, per capita income exceeded the income threshold (per capita GDP of $600 or less) and the value of the augmented physical quality of life index exceeded the cut-off point (a value of 47 or less) for that indicator. Accordingly, the Committee did not recommend the two countries for inclusion in the list.

CDP agreed on the need to consider further possible improvements in the criteria for identifying LDCs and their application and requested the Secretariat to prepare a note on the subject for consideration at its 1994 session.

Programme of Action for the 1990s

During 1992, several United Nations bodies reviewed progress in implementing the Programme of Action for the Least Developed Countries for the 1990s, adopted by the Second (1990) United Nations Conference on the Least Developed Countries (Paris Conference)[3] and endorsed by the General Assembly the same year.[4]

In response to a 1991 request of the General Assembly,[2] the Secretary-General in June 1992[5] submitted, through the Economic and Social Council, a note by the UNCTAD Secretary-General on the resource and other implications of the application of the new criteria for identifying LDCs on the implementation of the Programme of Action. The UNCTAD Secretary-General noted that, as a result of the addition in 1990 of Liberia[6] and of five new LDCs in 1991,[2] the increase in external capital requirements of LDCs as a group was in the order of 20 per cent.

In a report on the subject[7] to UNCTAD VIII (see PART THREE, Chapter IV), which the UNCTAD Secretary-General attached to his note, it was stated that a steady improvement in living standards could be seen in 11 LDCs (with 58 million population) and that an additional six countries (with 124 million population) had realized modest per capita GDP gains. However, those relatively high growth rates were in stark comparison with the group average. Their performance was due in part to strong gains in the purchasing power of their exports and the ability to expand the volume of imports and maintain high domestic investment, high levels and effective use of concessional assistance, expansion of agricultural production and efficient management of external debt. Other factors included large emigrant remittances, strong tourism earnings and, for the six Asian LDCs, the spillover effects of sharply accelerated growth in neighbouring countries.

At the other extreme were the countries with rapid declines in growth and in various human development indicators; they suffered from varying combinations of war, turmoil and unrest, exacerbated in many cases by a heavy inflow of refugees, severely declining export earnings, onerous debt, high inflation and accompanying devaluations, severe declines in investment and sharp falls in import value. Comparing the two extremes, the report noted that countries that were included in the list of LDCs from the beginning (1971)[8] had generally performed better during the 1980s than those included more recently. That analysis supported the declaration made by participants in the Paris Conference that deterioriation in the situation of LDCs could be reversed if the Programme of Action was expeditously and fully implemented by all concerned.

With regard to the implications of the new criteria on the implementation of the Programme of Action, the report stated that, with the addition of five countries in 1991,[2] the population of the LDC group had increased by 15 per cent, rising from 445 million to over 500 million. Since the 1990 Programme of Action was designed for the 41 LDCs on the list at that time, the subsequent increase called for a corresponding revision of the volume of external support and scope of international action on their behalf. Also, the added countries would be expected to fulfil the commitments undertaken at the Conference by other LDCs. Examining the implications, the report focused on international action with respect to resources, debt and trade. The Secretary-General's note described the response of UNCTAD VIII to the situation and action by the Trade and Development Board and the UNDP Governing Council (see below).

UNCTAD action. On 11 February,[9] UNCTAD VIII held a special meeting on LDCs to review progress in implementing the Programme of Action and the implications for the Programme of additions to the list of LDCs. Two proposals emerged from the meeting: that studies be initiated within UNCTAD on the possible repercussions of new developments in LDCs (increase in number and political and economic changes in the international environment); and that the concerns expressed at the special meeting be taken into account and included in the final act of UNCTAD VIII (the Cartagena Declaration).

The Declaration reaffirmed the need to give priority to the problems facing LDCs due to the fragility of their economies and their particular vulnerability to external shocks and natural calamities. In a section of the Cartagena Commitment dealing with the follow-up of the Programme of Action, UNCTAD VIII stated that LDCs should continue to enhance the implementation of national policies and measures in line with the Programme of Action. Their development partners should effectively and expeditiously implement commitments undertaken or measures proposed in the Programme in all areas of international support.

UNCTAD reiterated that external financial support to complement domestic efforts and appropriate policies should be sufficient in volume and quality, and reaffirmed that a significant and substantial increase in the aggregate level of external support should be made available to LDCs, taking into account those countries recently added to the list. In that regard, donor countries reaffirmed their determination to implement the commitments undertaken in the Programme of Action with regard to ODA to the 41 LDCs on the list at the time of the Paris Conference. As to the consequences of the inclusion of the six additional countries, UNCTAD recommended that the Trade and Development Board, at its spring 1992 session, consider the implications of appropriate adjustments to the commitments contained in the Programme in respect of targets and levels of ODA. The UNDP Governing Council was invited to consider adjusting the total allocation of indicative planning figures (IPFs) to LDCs in the light of the additions to the list. It was noted that the call in the Programme of Action for increasing the resources of the United Nations Capital Development Fund by 20 per cent a year should be adjusted.

UNCTAD identified a number of areas for priority action: external debt problems; mobilization of resources for development; attention to the problems of LDCs in the Uruguay Round of multilateral trade negotiations (see PART SEVEN, Chapter XVIII); implementation by preference-giving countries of the Programme of Action's provisions in respect of measures under the generalized system of preferences in favour of LDCs; support by the international community for LDCs' efforts towards diversification; and the introduction of further compensatory-financing mechanisms to assist LDCs affected by commodity-related shortfalls in export earnings.

The Conference stressed the importance of the monitoring, follow-up and review process envisaged in the Programme and called on Governments, UNCTAD and other members of the United Nations system to make early preparations for a mid-term review of the Programme in 1995.

The Conference stated that the problems of LDCs should remain a priority topic in all relevant international forums. It invited UNCED to give special attention to their problems of poverty and environmental degradation.

During the September/October session of the Trade and Development Board,[10] a special sessional committee conducted the second annual review of progress in implementing the Programme of Action for LDCs. It decided that the special issues of domestic and external resource mobilization, including debt situation and management, and improving trading opportunities would be reviewed at the Board's spring session in 1993, when the question of the effects that the countries newly added to the list of LDCs would have on additional resource requirements would also be considered. The Committee urged donors to consider providing extrabudgetary resources to facilitate participation of LDC delegations in future reviews of the Programme of Action by the Board.

UNDP action. In an April report to the Governing Council,[11] the UNDP Administrator indicated that IPFs for the five countries obtaining LDC status in 1991—Cambodia, Madagascar, Solomon Islands, Zaire, Zambia—had been recalculated to take account of additional supplementary points awarded to LDCs.

UNCED action. Agenda 21, adopted by UNCED in June[12] (see PART THREE, Chapter VIII), stated that particular efforts in implementing recommendations in four programme areas—promoting sustainable development through trade, making trade and environment mutually supportive, providing adequate financial resources to developing countries and encouraging economic policies conducive to sustainable development—were warranted in view of the especially acute environmental and developmental problems of LDCs.

Inter-agency consultation. The second inter-agency consultation on the follow-up to the Programme of Action for LDCs (Geneva, 25 and 26 June 1992)[13] discussed the implications of recent developments in the world economy and of the enlarged list of LDCs for the implementation of the Programme of Action, action by individual organizations in implementing the Programme within their fields of competence, follow-up arrangements at the regional and national levels, including the outcome of country review meetings, and action at the global level for review and monitoring of progress in implementing the Programme. The consultation made recommendations to ACC through its Organizational Committee on the resource situation of LDCs, access to resources under

UNDP intercountry programmes, and acquired immunodeficiency syndrome and LDC development in the 1990s.

GENERAL ASSEMBLY ACTION

On 22 December, on the recommendation of the Second Committee, the General Assembly adopted **resolution 47/173 without vote.**

Implications of the application of the new criteria for identifying the least developed countries in the implementation of the Programme of Action for the Least Developed Countries for the 1990s

The General Assembly,

Recalling its resolution 45/206 of 21 December 1990, in which it endorsed the Paris Declaration and the Programme of Action for the Least Developed Countries for the 1990s, adopted by the Second United Nations Conference on the Least Developed Countries, resolution 46/156 of 19 December 1991 on the implementation of the Programme of Action and resolution 46/206 of 20 December 1991 on the report of the Committee for Development Planning: criteria for identifying the least developed countries,

Taking note of the document entitled "A New Partnership for Development: The Cartagena Commitment", adopted by the United Nations Conference on Trade and Development at its eighth session,

Reaffirming that the least developed countries have the primary responsibility for the formulation and effective implementation of national policies and priorities for their growth and development, and should continue to implement the commitments they undertook at the Paris Conference, and that the international community, in particular the donor countries, should implement fully and expeditiously their commitments in all areas, as set out in the Programme of Action,

Reiterating the need to strengthen international cooperation for sustainable development in order to support and complement the efforts of the least developed countries,

Noting the donors' determination, reflected in the Cartagena Commitment, to implement the commitments that they undertook in the Programme of Action with regard to official development assistance to the forty-one countries which were included in the list of the least developed countries at the time of the Second United Nations Conference on the Least Developed Countries,

Noting also that the Trade and Development Board, at the first part of its thirty-ninth session, conducted the second annual review of progress in the implementation of the Programme of Action and also reviewed the question of appropriate adjustment of commitments in respect of targets and levels of official development assistance to the least developed countries in the light of the addition of six countries to the list of those countries after the Second United Nations Conference on the Least Developed Countries,

Noting further that, at the same session of the Trade and Development Board, donors expressed their intention to examine the effects that the countries newly added to the list of the least developed countries were having on the additional resource requirements of the least developed country group as a whole,

1. *Reaffirms* that the Programme of Action for the Least Developed Countries for the 1990s should be implemented fully, effectively and on a timely basis by all parties;

2. *Also reaffirms* that all least developed countries should continue to enhance the implementation of national policies and measures in line with the Programme of Action, including through macroeconomic policies conducive to long-term, sustained growth and sustainable development, the promotion of individual initiative and broad-based popular participation in the development process, the enhancement of human and institutional capacities and the expansion and modernization of the economic base, and that their development partners should effectively and expeditiously implement the commitments undertaken or the measures proposed in the Programme of Action in all areas of international support, including official development assistance, debt relief and external trade;

3. *Further reaffirms* that a significant and substantial increase in the aggregate level of external support should be made available to the least developed countries, taking into account those countries recently added to the list of the least developed countries;

4. *Takes note* of decision 92/30 of 26 May 1992 of the Governing Council of the United Nations Development Programme concerning adjustment of the allocation of indicative planning figures to the least developed countries in the light of the additions to the list of the least developed countries;

5. *Welcomes* the outcome of the second annual review of progress in the implementation of the Programme of Action undertaken by the Trade and Development Board at the first part of its thirty-ninth session, and notes the decision, *inter alia*, that the Board, at the second part of its thirty-ninth session, should:

(a) Review in depth two special issues, namely, domestic and external resource mobilization, including debt situation and management, and improvement of trading opportunities;

(b) Consider the question of appropriate adjustment of the commitments, as requested by the United Nations Conference on Trade and Development at its eighth session, taking into account the views expressed and the decisions made at the first part of the thirty-ninth session of the Trade and Development Board;

6. *Invites* the least developed countries and their development partners, including international organizations and financial institutions, to participate adequately and effectively in the second part of the thirty-ninth session of the Trade and Development Board, to be held at Geneva from 15 to 26 March 1993;

7. *Urges* donors to consider providing, pursuant to its resolution 46/156, extrabudgetary resources to facilitate the participation of representatives of the least developed countries at future reviews of the Programme of Action by the Trade and Development Board;

8. *Requests* the Secretary-General to submit to the General Assembly at its forty-eighth session a report on the implementation of the present resolution, including an assessment of the outcome of the third annual review of the Programme of Action by the Trade and Development Board.

General Assembly resolution 47/173

22 December 1992   Meeting 93   Adopted without vote

Approved by Second Committee (A/47/717/Add.1) without vote, 7 December (meeting 48); draft by Vice-Chairman (A/C.2/47/L.66), based on informal consultations on draft by Pakistan for Group of 77 (A/C.2/47/L.34) and orally revised; agenda item 12.

Meeting numbers. GA 47th session: 2nd Committee 3-9, 34-37, 40, 42, 43, 45, 46, 48; plenary 93.

Island developing countries

In response to a 1990 General Assembly request,[14] the Secretary-General submitted in September 1992 a report[15] on the specific problems and needs of island developing countries. The report drew on the observations of a meeting of a group of experts (Geneva, 15 and 16 July) appointed by the UNCTAD Secretary-General to review recent trends in the socio-economic performance of island developing countries and prospects for their growth and development; to assess the nature and magnitude of island-specific vulnerabilities; to identify areas of development potential and comparative advantage of island developing countries; and to make policy recommendations for national, regional and international action.

The report examined recent economic performance of island developing countries and their specific vulnerabilities, transport problems, the challenges for the 1990s, and areas of development potential, including service exports, flexible specialization as an approach to organizing production and marine resources of exclusive economic zones.

In a series of policy recommendations for national, regional and international action, the report noted that the key to reducing the vulnerability of island developing countries and to achieving sustainable development was in developing the capacity to respond to shocks and changes in the external environment. National development policy should therefore be outward-oriented and encourage flexibility. Island developing countries should seek to increase their international competitiveness and, in that regard, Governments should provide a broad focus for the economy and establish an enabling environment to encourage and support entrepreneurial activity. They should explore the concept of flexible specialization as the basis for a development strategy linked to world trade and capable of responding to new consumer-driven demand. Countries should actively explore service export strategies, especially in the tourism sector, where linkages within the domestic economy to agriculture, marine resource development, local manufacturing, construction, transport and other service sectors should be encouraged. In achieving the strategic objectives of island developing countries, the importance of human resource development and infrastructural investment should be emphasized, as well as the importance of environmental management. There was also scope for increased regional cooperation measures, particularly among those countries in close geographical proximity, which would help to address the problem of being high-cost economies by developing common services.

With regard to international action, the report recommended removing protectionist measures in developed countries, making available financial resources at concessional rates to complement trade preferences, providing international assistance to mitigate the consequences of global warming and sealevel rise and establishing a family of statistical indicators to reflect adequately the special vulnerabilities of island developing countries.

The expert group suggested a number of areas for specific studies and identified UNCTAD as the appropriate forum to carry them out.

An addendum to the Secretary-General's report[16] provided information from 7 countries, 18 United Nations bodies and specialized agencies and 5 intergovernmental organizations on action taken in response to General Assembly requests in respect of island developing countries.

The sustainable development of small islands was considered by UNCED in June,[12] identifying it as one of the programme areas in the chapter of Agenda 21 dealing with the protection of the oceans. Small island developing States and islands supporting small communities were considered a special case for both environment and development because of their small size, limited resources, geographic dispersion and isolation. The ocean and coastal environment was of strategic importance for them and constituted a valuable development resource. Because their development options were limited, there were special challenges to planning for and implementing sustainable development.

States committed themselves to addressing the problems of sustainable development of small island developing States and identified a number of management-related activities. At the level of international and regional cooperation and coordination, UNCED recommended that, with the support of international organizations, small island developing States should develop and strengthen inter-island, regional and interregional cooperation and information exchange, including periodic regional and global meetings on sustainable development of small island developing States. International organizations should recognize their special development requirements and give adequate priority in providing assistance, particularly with regard to developing and implementing sustainable development plans.

GENERAL ASSEMBLY ACTION

On 22 December, on the recommendation of the Second Committee, the General Assembly adopted **resolution 47/186** without vote.

Specific measures in favour of island developing countries

The General Assembly,

Recognizing that, in addition to the general problems facing developing countries, many island developing countries experience handicaps arising from the interplay of such factors as their smallness, remoteness, geographical dispersion, vulnerability to natural disasters, the fragility of their ecosystems, constraints on transport and communications, great distances from market centres, a highly limited internal market, lack of natural resources, weak indigenous technological capacity, the acute problem of obtaining fresh water supplies, heavy dependence on imports and a small number of commodities, depletion of non-renewable resources, migration, particularly of personnel with high-level skills, shortages of administrative personnel and heavy financial burdens,

Recognizing also that many of these factors occur concurrently in island developing countries, resulting in economic and social vulnerability and dependence, particularly in those countries which are small and/or geographically dispersed,

Noting that many island developing countries are least developed countries,

Mindful of the fact that island developing countries are facing in the 1990s an international economic environment which may strongly affect their ability to achieve sustainable development, particularly in small island developing countries which have extremely open and volatile economies,

Concerned about the adverse effects on island developing countries of sealevel rise resulting from climate change,

Taking note of Agenda 21, which was adopted by the United Nations Conference on Environment and Development, in particular chapter 17, section G thereof, relating to the sustainable development of small island developing States,

Welcoming the decision to convene in 1994 a global conference on the sustainable development of small island developing States,

1. *Reaffirms* its resolution 45/202 of 21 December 1990 and other relevant resolutions of the General Assembly and of the United Nations Conference on Trade and Development, and calls for their immediate and effective implementation;

2. *Expresses its appreciation* to States and to organizations and bodies, within and outside the United Nations system, that have responded to the special needs of island developing countries;

3. *Welcomes* the initiative of the Secretary-General of the United Nations Conference on Trade and Development in having convened a meeting of the Group of Experts on Island Developing Countries at Geneva on 14 and 15 July 1992;

4. *Takes note* of the report of the Secretary-General on the specific problems and needs of island developing countries;

5. *Welcomes* the efforts made by island developing countries to adopt policies that address their specific problems, including efforts at regional cooperation and integration, and calls upon those countries to continue to pursue, in accordance with their national objectives, policies and priorities, further measures to increase their

international competitiveness, render their economies less vulnerable by developing the capacity to respond to shocks due to natural disasters and external economic changes, and promote sustainable development;

6. *Appeals* to the international community:

(a) To maintain and, if possible, increase the level of concessional financial and technical assistance provided to island developing countries;

(b) To optimize access of island developing countries to concessional financial and technical assistance by taking into account, *inter alia*, the specific development needs and problems facing those countries;

(c) To consider reviewing the mechanisms of existing procedures used in providing concessional resources to island developing countries, taking into account their situation and development potential;

(d) To ensure that assistance conforms to the national and, as appropriate, regional priorities of island developing countries;

(e) To provide support to island developing countries over a mutually agreed and, where appropriate, longer time-frame to enable them to achieve economic growth and development;

(f) To consider improving trade and/or other existing arrangements for assisting island developing countries in redressing adverse effects on their export earnings and to consider wider adoption of such arrangements;

(g) To continue to ensure that a concerted effort is made to assist island developing countries, at their request, in improving their institutional and administrative capacities and in satisfying their overall needs with regard to the development of human resources;

(h) To provide assistance, where appropriate, to island developing countries to mitigate the consequences of climate change and sealevel rise;

7. *Invites* island developing countries to intensify further their regional and subregional cooperative arrangements, particularly to address the problem of high-cost economies, by developing, where appropriate, common services to reduce the high per capita costs of infrastructure and public services and by developing regional transport and communications systems;

8. *Urges once again* relevant organizations of the United Nations system to take adequate measures to respond positively to the particular needs of island developing countries and continue to report on such measures through the United Nations Conference on Trade and Development, as appropriate;

9. *Urges* the United Nations Conference on Trade and Development to strengthen its role, within its mandate, as the focal point for specific action at the global level in favour of island developing countries and to act as a catalyst in this regard, *inter alia*, by organizing and facilitating the cross-regional interchange of information and experience, in full cooperation with regional and subregional organizations, both within and outside the United Nations system, as appropriate;

10. *Requests* the Secretary-General, taking into account work already done on this issue, as well as that provided for in the context of the preparation for and follow-up to the global conference on the sustainable development of small island developing States, to continue to monitor and review in a coordinated manner, *inter alia*, within the Inter-Agency Committee on Sustainable Development and the secretariats of the Commis-

sion on Sustainable Development and the United Nations Conference on Trade and Development, the problems of island developing countries, in particular those of small island developing countries;

11. *Also requests* the Secretary-General to report to the General Assembly at its forty-ninth session on the implementation of the present resolution.

General Assembly resolution 47/186

22 December 1992   Meeting 93   Adopted without vote

Approved by Second Committee (A/47/718/Add.2) without vote, 7 December (meeting 48); draft by Vice-Chairman (A/C.2/47/L.68), based on informal consultations on draft by Pakistan for Group of 77 (A/C.2/47/L.33); agenda item 78 *(a)*.

Meeting numbers. GA 47th session: 2nd Committee 40, 42, 43, 48; plenary 93.

On the same date, the Assembly adopted, on the recommendation of the Second Committee, **resolution 47/189** without vote.

Convening of a global conference on the sustainable development of small island developing States

The General Assembly,

Recalling its resolution 44/228 of 22 December 1989, in which it decided to convene the United Nations Conference on Environment and Development to, *inter alia*, elaborate strategies and measures aimed at promoting sustainable and environmentally sound development in all countries,

Recalling also its resolution 45/202 of 21 December 1990, in which it called upon island developing countries to continue to adopt suitable development policies designed to overcome their specific vulnerabilities and to adopt measures aimed at protecting and rehabilitating their fragile ecosystems, and at the same time appealed to the international community to extend cooperation in this regard,

Taking note of Agenda 21, adopted by the United Nations Conference on Environment and Development, in particular chapter 17, section G thereof, on the sustainable development of small island developing States,

Taking into account relevant work in this area carried out by other organs, programmes and organizations of the United Nations system,

Recognizing that small island developing States and islands supporting small communities are a special case with regard to both environment and development, that they are ecologically fragile and vulnerable, that their small size, limited resources, geographic dispersion and isolation from markets place them at a disadvantage economically and limit economies of scale, and that for small island developing States the ocean and coastal environment is of strategic importance and constitutes a valuable development resource,

Also recognizing that the geographic isolation of small island developing States has resulted in their habitation by comparatively large numbers of unique species of flora and fauna, giving them a very large share of global biodiversity,

Aware that small island developing States have rich and diverse cultures with special adaptations to island environments and knowledge of sound management of island resources,

Aware also that small island developing States have all the environmental problems and challenges of the coastal zone concentrated in a limited land area,

Noting that small island developing States are considered extremely vulnerable to the impact of potential climate change and sealevel rise, with certain small low-lying island developing States facing the increasing threat of the loss of their entire national territories,

Gravely concerned that most tropical islands are currently experiencing the more immediate impacts of an increasing frequency of cyclones, storms and hurricanes associated with climate change, which are causing major set-backs to their socio-economic development,

Stressing that, because the development options of small island developing States are limited, there are special challenges to planning for and implementing sustainable development, and that small island developing States will be constrained in meeting those challenges without the cooperation and assistance of the international community,

Affirming the relevance of the environmental issues identified in paragraph 12, section I, of its resolution 44/228 to the sustainable development of small island developing States,

Reaffirming the recommendation in Agenda 21 that small island developing States, with the support, as appropriate, of international organizations, whether subregional, regional or global, should develop and strengthen inter-island, regional and interregional cooperation and information exchange, including periodic regional and global meetings on the sustainable development of such States,

1. *Decides* to convene in April 1994 the first Global Conference on the Sustainable Development of Small Island Developing States, which shall be of two weeks' duration and shall have the highest possible level of participation;

2. *Accepts with deep appreciation* the generous offer of the Government of Barbados to host the Conference;

3. *Affirms* that the Conference should elaborate strategies and measures to enhance the sustainable development of small island developing States in the context of increased national and international efforts to promote sustainable and environmentally sound development worldwide;

4. *Decides* that the Conference shall have the following objectives:

   (*a*) To adopt plans and programmes to support the sustainable development of small island developing States and the utilization of their marine and coastal resources, which includes meeting essential human needs, maintaining biodiversity and improving the quality of life for island people;

   (*b*) To adopt measures that will enable small island developing States to cope effectively and creatively and in a sustainable manner with environmental changes and to mitigate the impacts on and reduce the threats posed to marine and coastal resources;

5. *Also decides* that the Conference, in pursuit of those objectives, shall examine strategies for national and international action with a view to arriving at specific agreements and commitments by Governments and by intergovernmental organizations for defined activities to promote sustained and environmentally sound development of small island developing States; the Conference shall, *inter alia:*

   (*a*) Review current trends in the socio-economic development of small island developing States and the prospects, constraints and further options for their sustainable development, taking into consideration the relevant programmes and recommendations in chapter 17, section G, of Agenda 21;

   (*b*) Examine the nature and magnitude of the specific vulnerabilities of small island developing States with a view to defining and/or formulating specific indicators of vulnerability in a way that has operational applicability;

   (*c*) Define a number of specific actions and policies relating to environmental and development planning to be undertaken by small island developing States, with the assistance of the international community, to facilitate the sustainable development of such States;

   (*d*) Identify the elements that small island developing States need to include in their medium- and long-term sustainable development plans, including their response strategies, taking into account the importance of integrating environmental, social and economic factors in the maintenance of cultural and biological diversity and the conservation of endangered species and critical habitats on both land and sea;

   (*e*) Recommend measures for enhancing the endogenous capacity of small island developing States, in particular the development of human resources and the promotion of access to environmentally sound technology for sustainable development within such States;

   (*f*) Review whether institutional arrangements at the international level enable small island developing States to give effect to the relevant provisions of Agenda 21, and make recommendations as needed in this regard;

6. *Requests* the Secretary-General to prepare a report for the substantive session of the Preparatory Committee established in paragraph 8 below, containing a review of existing global and regional programmes of action with regard to their applicability to and their combined effect on the sustainable development of small island developing States, with specific recommendations on any changes to those programmes of action which may be needed to establish greater consistency with the principles of Agenda 21 with respect to the sustainable development of small island developing States;

7. *Also requests* the Secretary-General to invite to the Conference those listed in paragraph 9 of General Assembly resolution 46/168 of 19 December 1991, as well as representatives of relevant regional and subregional organizations;

8. *Decides* to establish the Preparatory Committee for the Global Conference on the Sustainable Development of Small Island Developing States, which shall be open to all the participants referred to in paragraph 7 above, in accordance with the established practice of the Assembly;

9. *Welcomes* the candidature of Ambassador Penny Wensley (Australia) for the chairmanship of the Preparatory Committee;

10. *Decides* that the Preparatory Committee shall hold a two-day organizational session at United Nations Headquarters, not later than April 1993, for the following purposes:

    (*a*) The election of its chairman and the other officers, namely, four vice-chairmen, including a rapporteur, giving due regard to equitable geographical representation;

    (*b*) The organization of its work;

11. *Also decides* that the Preparatory Committee shall hold a substantive session of two weeks' duration in Au-

gust 1993 at United Nations Headquarters, at which time it shall:

(a) Draft the provisional agenda for the Conference, in accordance with the provisions of the present resolution, on the basis of recommendations to be submitted by the Secretary-General;

(b) Receive and consider the substantive contributions referred to in paragraphs 6, 16 and 17 of the present resolution;

(c) Prepare draft decisions to be submitted to the Conference for consideration and adoption;

12. *Further decides* that the host country of the Conference shall be ex officio an officer of the Preparatory Committee;

13. *Requests* the Secretary-General, within the context of the administrative arrangements to be put in place to coordinate the implementation of Agenda 21 and the servicing of the Commission on Sustainable Development, and in close cooperation with the United Nations Environment Programme, the United Nations Development Programme, the United Nations Conference on Trade and Development, the United Nations Educational, Scientific and Cultural Organization, the Food and Agriculture Organization of the United Nations and other relevant organizations and programmes of the United Nations system, to establish a focal point with a senior official, at an appropriate level and with the necessary specialized expertise, to service fully the preparations for and holding of the Conference and to ensure such follow-up action as may result therefrom;

14. *Also requests* the Secretary-General to prepare a report, to be submitted to the Preparatory Committee at its organizational session, containing recommendations on an adequate preparatory process, taking into account the provisions of the present resolution and the views expressed by Governments during the United Nations Conference on Environment and Development;

15. *Further requests* the Secretary-General to prepare draft rules of procedure for the consideration of the Preparatory Committee at its organizational session, and, in this context, to include proposals for the participation of representatives of associate members of the regional commissions, outside the negotiating process, and, in accordance with the rules of procedure of the General Assembly, to allow them to contribute to the Conference and its preparatory process;

16. *Stresses* the importance of holding regional technical meetings on the sustainable development of small island developing States as a means of preparing substantive contributions to the Conference, and invites relevant regional and subregional bodies, in close cooperation with the United Nations Environment Programme, the United Nations Development Programme, the United Nations Conference on Trade and Development, the Food and Agriculture Organization of the United Nations, the United Nations Educational, Scientific and Cultural Organization and other agencies, organs, organizations and programmes of the United Nations system, to organize such meetings as soon as practicable, preferably in the first half of 1993;

17. *Requests* the Secretary-General to ensure the coordination of contributions from the United Nations system through the Administrative Committee on Coordination;

18. *Invites* relevant non-governmental organizations from developed and developing countries, in particular those from small island developing States, including those related to major groups, to contribute to the Conference, within the areas of their competence and expertise, on the basis of the procedures for their accreditation followed for the United Nations Conference on Environment and Development, as recommended in paragraph 38.44 of Agenda 21;

19. *Decides* that, subject to the relevant provisions of General Assembly resolutions 40/243 of 18 December 1985, 41/213 of 19 December 1986 and 42/211 of 21 December 1987, the funds necessary for the preparatory process and the Conference itself should be made available within the programme budget without adversely affecting other ongoing activities and without prejudice to the provision of extrabudgetary resources;

20. *Also decides* to establish a voluntary fund for the purpose of assisting small island developing States and the least developed countries to participate fully and effectively in the Conference and its preparatory process, and invites Governments to contribute to the fund;

21. *Requests* the Secretary-General to bring the present resolution to the attention of the relevant specialized agencies and other relevant organs, organizations and programmes of the United Nations system;

22. *Decides* to include in the provisional agenda of its forty-eighth session a sub-item entitled "Global Conference on the Sustainable Development of Small Island Developing States" under an item entitled "Implementation of decisions and recommendations of the United Nations Conference on Environment and Development".

General Assembly resolution 47/189

22 December 1992	Meeting 93	Adopted without vote

Approved by Second Committee (A/47/719) without vote, 16 December (meeting 51); draft by Malaysia (A/C.2/47/L.47), orally revised; agenda item 79.

Financial implications. 5th Committee, A/47/814; S-G, A/C.2/47/L.90, A/C.5/47/81.

Meeting numbers. GA 47th session: 2nd Committee 51; 5th Committee 49; plenary 93.

REFERENCES

[1]E/1992/27. [2]YUN 1991, p. 356, GA res. 46/206, 20 Dec. 1991. [3]A/CONF.147/18. [4]GA res. 45/206, 21 Dec. 1990. [5]A/47/278-E/1992/77. [6]GA dec. 45/437, 21 Dec. 1990. [7]TD/359. [8]YUN 1971, p. 232. [9]TD/364. [10]A/47/15, vol. II. [11]DP/1992/22. [12]*Report of the United Nations Conference on Environment and Development, Rio de Janeiro, 3-14 June 1992*, vol. I (A/CONF.151/26/Rev.1 (vol. I)), Sales No. E.93.I.8. [13]ACC/1992/21. [14]GA res. 45/202, 21 Dec. 1990. [15]A/47/414. [16]A/47/414/Add.1.

PUBLICATION

The Least Developed Countries—1992 Report (TD/B/392/10), Sales No. E.93.II.3.

Chapter II

Operational activities for development

A comprehensive policy review of United Nations operational activities for development took place in 1992 at a critical juncture for developing countries and international development cooperation. The operational activities of the United Nations system were undergoing important changes to adapt to the circumstances of the 1990s. The question of strengthening the operational activities of the United Nations system was discussed by the Economic and Social Council in July, while the triennial policy review of operational activities was carried out by the General Assembly later in the year. In December (resolution 47/199), the Assembly stressed the need for a substantial increase in resources for operational activities for development and made a number of recommendations for improvements in the system, including the strengthening of the resident coordinator function. As part of his efforts to restructure the Secretariat, the Secretary-General established the Department of Economic and Social Development (DESD), incorporating the former Department of Technical Cooperation for Development.

During 1991, the most recent year for which figures were available, expenditures by the United Nations system on operational activities for development totalled $8.4 billion. Of that amount, $4.3 billion was in the form of development grants and $4.1 billion in concessional loans.

The United Nations Development Programme (UNDP)—the central funding body for providing technical assistance to developing countries—spent $1 billion on programme activities in 1992, a decline from $1.1 billion in 1991. The organizational entities of the United Nations—mainly through DESD—delivered a technical cooperation programme of $243 million in 1992, compared with $285 million in 1991.

Expenditures in 1992 by the United Nations Capital Development Fund, a multilateral agency providing small-scale capital assistance to the least developed countries, amounted to some $57.5 million.

With regard to technical cooperation among developing countries, the Economic and Social Council, in July, called for increased use by developed countries of consultants from developing countries to improve the cost-effectiveness of technical cooperation projects, and urged UNDP to intensify efforts to build national capacity for human resources development in developing countries (resolution 1992/41).

General aspects

Strengthening operational activities. In accordance with a 1991 General Assembly decision,[1] the Secretary-General, by a June note,[2] submitted to the Economic and Social Council a report on strengthening the operational activities of the United Nations system, including the governance and financing aspects thereof, prepared by two consultants. The Council considered the report and others during its high-level segment (6-9 July), devoted to the theme "enhancing international cooperation for development: the role of the United Nations system" (see PART THREE, Chapter I), and during its operational activities segment.

The report discussed the need to reform the United Nations system as well as those reform and restructuring efforts that had already taken place. It also considered issues in governance and finance and other issues in strengthening operational activities. To assist the Council in its review of the subject of governance, the report presented four models representing four different governance structures, including the current situation, ranging from a highly centralized, unified structure to a highly decentralized one. In an appendix, the report discussed two reform initiatives and proposals—the Nordic United Nations project and a research programme of the United Nations Association of the United States, *A Successor Vision: The United Nations of Tomorrow.*

By **decision 1992/301** of 31 July, the Council took note of the Secretary-General's note transmitting the consultants' report.

Triennial policy review. In September/ October, the Secretary-General submitted to the General Assembly a report on the triennial comprehensive policy review of the operational activities of the United Nations system.[3] The report discussed changes in United Nations operational activities, resources for development, human development, programming, the resident coordinator system and country representation, national execution, and coordinated training strategies and national capacity. Addenda surveyed the contribution of operational activities to the enhancement of science and technology in developing countries (see PART III, Chapter VII), provided statistical data for 1991, and described the activities of the United Nations system in the Baltic States and the Commonwealth of Independent States.

Among the changes taking place in the United Nations development system were the reforms initiated by a General Assembly resolution of 1989,[4] which recognized that the 1990s required greater coherence of action and new approaches to programming operational activities, with greater emphasis on integrated and multidisciplinary support and advice.

Guiding the reforms was the resolution's call for more coordinated programming of United Nations system cooperation; harmonization of programming processes at country levels; a shift away from small projects to more concentrated and integrated programmes; the strengthening of the resident coordinator system; more decentralized capacity of the United Nations at the country level, including maximum use of national capacities; and measures to enable Governments to assume the execution of programmes funded by the United Nations. The system had taken action to comply with the resolution on many fronts.

In 1992, the Secretary-General initiated the first phase of the restructuring of the economic and social sectors of the United Nations and was in the process of consulting with a panel of high-level advisers on the future course of United Nations development activities.

The report's analysis of the country-level performance of the system's operational activities was based on the findings of four expert missions to 12 developing countries between 8 February and 11 March; 101 responses to questionnaires sent to United Nations resident coordinators; responses to a questionnaire sent to United Nations organizations and as a result of direct consultations within the Consultative Committee on Substantive Questions (Operational Activities) of the Administrative Committee on Coordination (ACC); and 71 responses to questions sent to Governments of both developing and developed countries.

The principal findings were as follows: the provisions of the 1989 Assembly resolution on operational activities[4] remained valid, although the United Nations system had taken numerous steps to implement the resolution at the intergovernmental level; differences remained in understanding and applying operational concepts; and the remaining task was to implement more fully the central ideas of the resolution and to take further steps to respond to developing countries' requirements through support from the best sources both within and outside the system.

The report reviewed the historical and international economic factors that had an impact on the availability of resources for development, noting that the International Development Strategy for the Second United Nations Development Decade, adopted by the Assembly in 1970,[5] had set a target for each developed country of 0.7 per cent of its gross national product (GNP) to be provided as official development assistance. Several smaller developed countries had met or surpassed the target, but overall the flow of assistance had remained at half the target level.

Debate on the magnitude of resources for development had gone well beyond discussion of the desirable level of assistance and was currently addressing the following major issues: international debt; trade; environment; population; development assistance and basic needs; investment flows; and institutional framework.

With regard to the role of operational activities in human development, the policy review stated that all development effort, whether national, bilateral or multilateral, had been traditionally justified on the grounds that it would improve the lives of people. However, at national and international levels, the focus on human development remained inadequate. Developing countries had not been able to make their needs felt as an imperative in shaping global economic priorities nor had the poorer sections of the population been able to do so at the national level.

The new focus on human development in the United Nations was directed at providing the poor with the means to improve their condition. That meant improving their access to food, water, housing, health services and education. It also meant empowering them to improve their technical skills, conserve their environment, enlarge their intellectual world and protect their human rights.

Cross-sectoral dimensions had been added to the concept of human development. For example, UNDP and the United Nations Children's Fund (UNICEF), in collaboration with the United Nations Educational, Scientific and Cultural Organization (UNESCO), the International Labour Organisation (ILO) and the United Nations Population Fund (UNFPA) were assisting Governments to prepare country strategies for human development that placed social concerns on an equal basis with economic growth.

As to programming of operational activities, the shift from a project to a programme approach was considered in the policy review. It was noted that the 1990s demanded greater inter-agency cooperation and integration of United Nations programmes with national strategies. The programme approach was an integral part of the national effort, and the national organization managing the programme needed to have the capacity to implement cross-sectoral programmes.

Some progress had been achieved in synchronizing all programming cycles of United Nations funds and programmes and adapting them to national requirements. Further progress should be achieved, particularly on the basis of work being done by the Joint Consultative Group on Policy (UNDP, UNFPA, UNICEF and the World Food Programme (WFP)), by establishing an agreed plan and by stressing substantive, thematic collaboration. Further steps should be taken to improve the assessment of impact, sustainability and self-reliance in evaluating programme and project performance.

The policy review also discussed the responsibility of the United Nations resident coordinator to provide leadership in integrating and coordinating the system's response to developing countries' needs.

Resident coordinators worked in differing environments, providing development services, technical advice, humanitarian assistance and information. The resident coordinator system had been strengthened during the past three years, but further progress was needed. Several elements were essential for its improved functioning: a process to communicate United Nations goals and strategies at the country level; clearer guidelines for the functioning of the resident coordinator system; technical capacity to provide high-quality and timely support to the Government; better access to data required for country programmes; and further decentralization to the field level, delegation of authority and flexibility.

Many achievements of the resident coordinator system had relied too much on ad hoc initiatives and not enough on a systematic approach. More coherent guidance from the headquarters of various United Nations organizations was required on major policy questions, and support should come in a coordinated manner and on the basis of processes agreed upon by ACC and other co-ordinating entities, such as the Joint Consultative Group on Policy.

To respond more effectively to requirements for multidisciplinary advice, there was a need to give the resident coordinator the authority to constitute multidisciplinary teams and to reinforce collaborative cross-sectoral programmes through co-ordination and harmonization of the policies of United Nations organizations.

Wider application of the national execution modality was occurring in various countries, the policy review stated. In UNICEF, the International Fund for Agricultural Development (IFAD) and WFP, national execution was the norm. That also largely applied to the World Health Organization (WHO). For UNFPA, the proportion varied, but was much higher than for UNDP.

Current rules and procedures relating to administration and programme and project identification, formulation, appraisal, monitoring and evaluation required by the United Nations system inhibited greater national participation. Greater harmonization and simplification of United Nations rules and procedures would facilitate national participation, enhance efficiency and make better use of scarce resources.

Addressing the issue of training strategies and national capacity, the policy review observed that the impact and the success or failure of operational activities was related to the Government's ability to provide human and financial resources. Deficiencies took various forms, among which the following were particularly relevant: shortages of qualified human resources in the public sector; lack of legal, accounting, audit and financial management personnel; lack of funding; lack of training resources; and delays in decision-making, cumbersome national bureaucracies and lack of delegation of authority.

A training strategy in operational activities could involve training for enhanced national development management within the framework of national execution and national capacity-building and workshops on the management of field coordination for senior United Nations representatives.

A scheme for the training of trainers was needed. While project-by-project funded training schemes should continue, there was a need to mobilize a separate fund to underwrite the start-up cost and the continuing organizing expenses of a global multi-agency trainers' programme.

GENERAL ASSEMBLY ACTION

On 22 December 1992, the General Assembly, on the recommendation of the Second (Economic and Financial) Committee, adopted **resolution 47/199** without vote.

Triennial policy review of operational activities for development within the United Nations system
The General Assembly,

Recalling its resolutions 44/211 of 22 December 1989 and 46/219 of 20 December 1991, and other relevant resolutions,

Concerned that the full and coordinated implementation of resolution 44/211 has not been achieved by the United Nations system,

Noting with concern that, while some progress has been made in implementing parts of its resolution 44/211, both by individual organs, organizations and bodies of the United Nations system and by coordination mechanisms of the system, many of the provisions of that resolution have still to be implemented,

Urging developed countries, in particular those countries whose overall performance is not commensurate with their capacity, taking into account established official development assistance targets, including targets established at the Second United Nations Conference on the Least Developed Countries, and current levels of contribution, to increase their official development assistance substantially, including contributions to the operational activities of the United Nations system,

Stressing that national plans and priorities constitute the only viable frame of reference for the national programming of operational activities for development within the United Nations system,

Stressing also that the fundamental characteristics of the operational activities of the United Nations system should be, *inter alia*, their universal, voluntary and grant nature, neutrality and multilateralism, and the ability to respond to the needs of the developing countries in a flexible manner, and that the operational activities of the United Nations system are carried out for the benefit of the developing countries, at the request of those countries and in accordance with their own policies and priorities for development,

Reaffirming that the operational activities for development within th e nited Nations system have a critical and unique role to play in enabling developing countries to take a lead role in the management of their own development process,

Stressing further that, in order to achieve the objective set out above, processes and procedures of the United Nations system should be streamlined and rationalized, especially in the interrelated areas of programming, execution, decentralization, monitoring and evaluation, thus making the United Nations system more relevant and responsive to the national plans, priorities and objectives of developing countries and more efficient in its delivery systems,

Emphasizing the importance it attaches to a more effective and coherent coordinated approach by the United Nations system to the needs of recipient countries, particularly at the field level,

1. *Takes note* of the report of the Secretary-General on the triennial comprehensive policy review of operational activities of the United Nations system;

2. *Reaffirms* its resolution 44/211 and stresses the need to implement all the elements of that resolution in a coherent manner, keeping in mind their interlinkages;

3. *Stresses* the need for a substantial increase in resources for operational activities for development on a predictable, continuous and assured basis, commensurate with the increasing needs of developing countries;

4. *Reaffirms* the need for priority allocation of scarce grant resources to programmes and projects in low-income countries, particularly the least developed countries;

5. *Stresses* the need for an overall improvement of the effectiveness and efficiency of the United Nations system in delivering its development assistance;

6. *Also stresses* that, in the context of the administrative reform of the Secretariat and the restructuring and revitalization of the intergovernmental process, the mandates of the separate sectoral and specialized entities, funds, programmes and specialized agencies should be respected and enhanced, taking into account their complementarities;

7. *Emphasizes* that the recipient Government has the primary responsibility for coordinating, on the basis of national strategies and priorities, all types of external assistance, including that provided by multilateral organizations, in order effectively to integrate the assistance into its development process;

8. *Reaffirms* that the multisectoral, sectoral and/or subsectoral strategies prepared by the recipient countries, on the basis of priorities identified by them, should provide a coherent and coordinated programme framework for all external assistance;

9. *Stresses* that, on the basis of the priorities and plans of recipient countries, and in order to ensure the effective integration of assistance provided by the United Nations system into the development process of countries, with enhanced accountability, and to facilitate the assessment and evaluation of the impact and sustainability of that assistance, a country strategy note should be formulated by interested recipient Governments, with the assistance of and in cooperation with the United Nations system, under the leadership of the resident coordinator, in all recipient countries where the Government so chooses, taking into account the following:

(a) The country strategy note should outline the contribution the operational activities for development within the United Nations system could make to respond to the requirements identified by recipient countries in their plans, strategies and priorities;

(b) The contribution of the United Nations system to the country strategy note should be formulated under the leadership of the resident coordinator, in order to promote greater coordination and cooperation at the field level;

(c) The country strategy note should be transmitted to the governing body of each funding organization as a reference for the consideration of its specific country programme;

(d) The specific activities of each funding organization of the United Nations system, within the broad framework of the country strategy note, should be outlined in a specific country programme prepared by the recipient Government with the assistance of the funding organizations;

10. *Reaffirms* that, within the context of the Joint Consultative Group on Policies, the funding organizations of the United Nations system, the United Nations Development Programme, the United Nations Children's Fund, the United Nations Population Fund, the World Food Programme and the International Fund for Agricultural Development and the funds administered by the United Nations Development Programme should harmonize their cycles and, where appropriate, adapt them to national budget cycles, plans and strategies;

11. *Decides* that assistance should be based on an agreed division of responsibility among the funding organizations, under the coordination of the Government, in order to integrate their response into the development needs of recipient countries;

12. *Takes note* of decision 92/23 of 26 May 1992 and of all other relevant decisions of the Governing Council of the United Nations Development Programme regarding the programme approach;

13. *Requests* the Secretary-General to promote an early agreement on a common interpretation of the programme approach, including an effective methodology for evaluation, to be applied by the United Nations system, with due regard to country-specific circumstances, and to report thereon to the Economic and Social Council at its substantive session of 1993;

14. *Requests* the Economic and Social Council to examine the report mentioned above at its substantive session of 1993 and to determine whether effective and coordinated actions are being taken on the matter by the United Nations system dealing with development;

15. *Reiterates* that national execution should be the norm for programmes and projects supported by the

United Nations system, taking into account the needs and capacities of recipient countries;

16. *Also reiterates* that it is the principal responsibility of recipient countries to determine their capacity to execute programmes and projects supported by the United Nations system;

17. *Stresses* the need for the United Nations system to strengthen its capacity to provide policy and technical support and advice at the request of recipient countries;

18. *Also stresses* the urgent need for the United Nations system to give increased priority to assisting recipient countries in building and/or enhancing the capacity necessary to undertake national execution, including the provision of support services, as required, at the field level;

19. *Recognizes* the important role of the specialized agencies of the United Nations system within their specific areas of competence and the need for a clear division of labour in facilitating and providing the necessary technical and substantive expertise for programmes and projects supported by the United Nations system;

20. *Requests* the Economic and Social Council, through the Commission on Science and Technology for Development at its session in 1993, to consider the report of the Secretary-General on the comprehensive policy review of operational activities of the United Nations system as a means to examine the contribution of the operational activities of the United Nations system to the enhancement of the national capacities of developing countries in the field of science and technology, and to make appropriate recommendations thereon;

21. *Takes note* of decision 92/22 of 26 May 1992 and of all other relevant decisions of the Governing Council of the United Nations Development Programme regarding the definition of programme/project execution and implementation concepts;

22. *Requests* the Secretary-General to promote an early agreement on a common interpretation of national execution to be applied by the United Nations system and to report thereon to the Economic and Social Council at its substantive session of 1993;

23. *Requests* the Economic and Social Council to examine the report mentioned above at its substantive session of 1993 and to determine whether effective and co-ordinated actions are being taken on the matter by the United Nations system dealing with development;

24. *Decides* that, in order to enhance coherence in programming and resource utilization, programme development and component approval, capacity and authority should be further decentralized to the field offices, which should be provided with the necessary technical and substantive expertise;

25. *Strongly urges*, in this context, that governing bodies of all funds, programmes and specialized agencies should ensure that the prescribed limits on field-level authority for cancelling, modifying and adding activities within approved programmes and for shifting resources within approved budget lines of individual components of a programme and among components of a programme, with the approval of national authorities, should be expanded to become equal and uniform, to the maximum extent possible, in the context of enhanced accountability;

26. *Stresses* that the United Nations system should use, to the fullest extent possible, available national expertise and indigenous technologies;

27. *Also stresses* that the procurement of expertise and equipment and the placing of fellowships should be decentralized to the country level to the maximum extent possible to avoid delays, reflect national needs and ensure cost-effectiveness, and stresses further that, in this context, the procurement of expertise and equipment should be decentralized, with due regard to the principles of international competitive bidding, while acknowledging the commitment to increase substantially procurement from developing countries and the need for effective accountability mechanisms;

28. *Acknowledges* the commitment to procurement from underutilized major donor countries, in accordance with the principles of international competitive bidding;

29. *Stresses* that common formats, rules and procedures are critical to meet the requirements of the shift to a programme approach, and that all formats, rules and procedures and periodicity of reports should be simplified and harmonized to promote national capacity-building, so as to assist the Government to integrate external assistance from different sources into its development process;

30. *Decides* that the financial and programme auditing capacity and accounting systems of recipient Governments should be strengthened, with assistance from the United Nations system, as requested by Governments;

31. *Also decides* that, within the context of the programme approach, formats designed for programme, programme component and project development, monitoring and evaluation should take into account interrelated and cross-sectoral linkages between individual strategies of recipient countries and between the individual components of a strategy;

32. *Further decides* that budgeting and related rules, procedures, processes and formats should be redefined to become, within the context of the sustainability of programmes supported by the United Nations system and their components and projects, oriented towards output, impact or performance rather than towards input or supply, and that, accordingly, evaluation and monitoring systems should be reoriented, while the use of evaluation and monitoring findings should be strengthened, thereby creating a feedback system;

33. *Requests* inter-agency coordination mechanisms, in particular the Joint Consultative Group on Policies, to give priority to simplifying, harmonizing and increasing the transparency of their procedures relating to programme component and project formulation, appraisal, implementation, monitoring and evaluation, taking into account the need to focus on the impact and sustainability of projects and programmes, and to reach agreement on a common United Nations system-wide manual for such procedures by 1 July 1994;

34. *Also requests* the members of inter-agency coordination mechanisms, in particular the Joint Consultative Group on Policies, to put in place as soon as possible, and no later than 1 January 1995, measures to enhance accountability at the field level, including effective harmonized programme monitoring, evaluation and management audit systems;

35. *Stresses* the need for funds and programmes to take into account the decisions of the General Assembly on auditing standards;

36. *Also stresses* that the strengthened resident co-ordinator function is necessary to assist the Government

in mobilizing technical expertise from both inside and outside the United Nations system and ensuring co-ordination at the country level through, *inter alia*, the country strategy note, in order to respond to national needs and priorities in the most cost-effective and effi-cient manner and to maximize the impact of the United Nations system on the development process;

37. *Further stresses* that, in order to achieve the ob-jective set out above, particular attention should be paid in the selection of the resident coordinators to quality, relevant broad development experience, managerial and team-building skills, and the capacity to integrate in-dividual components and strategies into the overall de-velopment process of the country, as well as to develop effective and coherent coordination by the United Na-tions system as a whole;

38. *Emphasizes* that an effectively functioning resident coordinator system will be dependent on a number of factors, including the following:

(a) The separate funds, programmes and special-ized agencies must make a commitment to work together to integrate assistance provided by the United Nations system into the development process of the recipient countries in a fully coordinated manner;

(b) The United Nations system at the country level should be tailored, taking into account the views of the recipient Government, to the specific developmental needs of the country in such a way that they correspond to ongoing and projected cooperation programmes rather than to the institutional structure of the United Nations;

(c) The separate identities and, where appropriate, representation of funds and programmes at the coun-try level should be ensured in the framework of a clear and improved division of labour, in accordance with their mandates;

(d) The resident coordinator should, if required, es-tablish close cooperation with the funds, programmes and specialized agencies at the regional and subregional levels, in order to respond to specific requests by recip-ient Governments;

(e) In strengthening the resident coordinator system, the creation of an additional bureaucratic layer should be avoided;

39. *Requests* the Secretary-General, with due regard to General Assembly resolutions 34/213 of 19 Decem-ber 1979 and 46/182 of 19 December 1991 and paragraph 38 above, to strengthen the resident coordinator system with the aim of:

(a) Improving the efficiency and effectiveness of the United Nations system at the field level, through a fully coordinated multidisciplinary approach to the needs of recipient countries under the leadership of the resident coordinator, bearing in mind the complementarity of the system and the need for a division of labour within the respective spheres of competence of individual spe-cialized agencies, programmes and funds;

(b) Establishing, in consultation with recipient Governments, a clearer division of responsibilities for the resident coordinator and individual funds, pro-grammes and specialized agencies;

(c) Ensuring that, in the context of the country strategy note, where in place, representatives of the members of the Joint Consultative Group on Policies at the field level and, in due course, of all funds, pro-grammes and specialized agencies with field operations

inform, consult with and take account of any views of the resident coordinator in the context of major pro-gramming exercises before reporting to their headquar-ters on major programming and policy issues;

(d) Widening the pool of qualified development professionals eligible for appointment as United Nations Development Programme resident representatives/resi-dent coordinators to include the members of the Joint Consultative Group on Policies, together with increased transparency in the selection process;

(e) Encouraging individual specialized agencies at the field level to participate fully in all aspects of the resident coordinator system;

(f) Defining the responsibility of the relevant inter-agency coordination mechanisms, in particular the Joint Consultative Group on Policies, in close consultation with the funds, programmes and specialized agencies of the United Nations system, for providing clear guid-ance to resident coordinators and for ensuring that they are provided with the necessary support both at the headquarters level and in the field;

(g) Enhancing the responsibility and authority of the resident coordinator for the planning and coordination of programmes as well as allowing him or her to pro-pose, in full consultation with the Government, to the heads of the funds, programmes and specialized agen-cies, the amendment of country programmes and major projects and programmes, where required, to bring them into line with the country strategy note;

40. *Calls upon* resident coordinators to take the neces-sary steps, in those countries where the scale of the ac-tivities of the United Nations and the number of funds, programmes and specialized agencies so justify, to es-tablish, in consultation with host Governments, an ap-propriate field-level committee, which will normally comprise all resident United Nations system represen-tatives and which, under the leadership of the resident coordinator, will serve as a United Nations coordinating mechanism in the countries concerned;

41. *Calls upon* the coordinating mechanism men-tioned above, in consultation with the host Government, to undertake advisory functions including, *inter alia*, the provision of guidance and advice on proposed pro-grammes of funding organizations, the review of agency sector strategies and evaluations and the investigation of specific problems and issues requiring a coordinated response;

42. *Welcomes* the decision of the Joint Consultative Group on Policies to set a target for increasing the number of common premises, while emphasizing that this should be achieved in cooperation with host Governments in a way that increases efficiency through, *inter alia*, consoli-dation of administrative infrastructures of organizations concerned, without increasing the costs for the United Nations system or for developing countries;

43. *Emphasizes* the necessity of continuing to develop common innovative and integrated system-wide train-ing programmes, at Headquarters and, especially, at the field level, while taking into account the use of regional cooperation arrangements, for government officials and other nationals, as well as for the staff of the United Na-tions system field offices, to facilitate the shift from the project to the programme approach and to promote ef-fective and innovative execution modalities;

44. *Also emphasizes* that those training programmes should be joint and common, include on-the-job train-

ing, involve the establishment of a training capacity internal to each country, including a scheme for the training of national trainers, and be provided on a continuous basis as an integral function of the United Nations system field office structure;

45. *Stresses* that those training programmes should aim to develop capacities, especially in the areas of the programme approach, national execution, programme accountability and financial audit, support costs and evaluation and monitoring;

46. *Urges* the United Nations system to give appropriate attention to establishing and maintaining national institutional expertise, particularly in the areas mentioned in paragraph 45 above, through, *inter alia*, the increased participation in training programmes of national staff and members of relevant national institutions;

47. *Reaffirms* the importance of human development, including human resources development, and requests the United Nations system to strengthen the support given by its operational activities for development, at the request of recipient countries, to sectors vital to human development;

48. *Recognizes* that the United Nations system has a role to play in assisting countries that are undergoing deep economic and social reforms;

49. *Requests* the Secretary-General to ensure that the operational activities for development within the United Nations system carried out in new recipient countries are undertaken, from the outset, on the basis of an integrated, unified, cost-effective and innovative approach to development cooperation and presence in the countries concerned and to ensure effective support to them, while ensuring that such support is not to the detriment of existing programmes for developing countries;

50. *Stresses* the need for the Economic and Social Council to examine the operational activities of the United Nations system with a view to ensuring implementation of the present resolution and making recommendations thereon;

51. *Calls upon* the governing bodies of the funds, programmes and specialized agencies of the United Nations system to take appropriate action for the full implementation of the present resolution, and requests the executive heads of those funds, programmes and specialized agencies to submit a yearly progress report to their governing bodies on measures taken and to be taken for its implementation;

52. *Requests* the Secretary-General to ensure that the provisions of the present resolution are fully implemented by all the organs, organizations and bodies of the United Nations system;

53. *Also requests* the Secretary-General, after consultations with the funds, programmes and specialized agencies of the United Nations system, to present to the Economic and Social Council at its substantive session of 1993 an appropriate management process containing clear guidelines, targets, benchmarks and timeframes for the full implementation of the present resolution;

54. *Further requests* the Secretary-General to submit to the Economic and Social Council at its substantive sessions of 1993 and 1994 a progress report on the implementation of the present resolution, incorporating, *inter alia*, the reports mentioned in paragraph 51 above

to be prepared by the funds, programmes and specialized agencies of the United Nations system;

55. *Requests* the Secretary-General to submit to the General Assembly at its fiftieth session, through the Economic and Social Council, in the context of the triennial policy review, a comprehensive analysis of the implementation of the present resolution and to make appropriate recommendations.

General Assembly resolution 47/199

22 December 1992   Meeting: 93   Adopted without vote

Approved by Second Committee (A/47/723) without vote, 16 December (meeting 51); draft by Vice-Chairman (A/C.2/47/L.92), based on informal consultations on drafts (A/C.2/47/L.21 & L.22), as orally corrected and revised; agenda item 83.
Meeting numbers: GA 47th session: 2nd Committee 21-24, 36, 38, 48, 51; plenary 93.

Financing of operational activities

Expenditures

In an addendum to his report on the triennial comprehensive policy review of operational activities,[6] the Secretary-General provided detailed statistical data for 1991 on resources channelled through United Nations organizations. During 1991, expenditures by the United Nations system on operational activities totalled $8.4 billion. Of that amount, $4.3 billion was distributed in grants and $4.1 billion was disbursed in concessional loans by the International Development Association (IDA) ($4 billion) and IFAD ($115 million). Non-concessional loans, disbursed through the World Bank and the International Finance Corporation (IFC), had a negative balance of $4 billion in 1991. Grants to finance refugee, humanitarian, special economic and disaster relief activities amounted to $1.4 billion.

Of the total expenditures on grant-financed development activities, WFP accounted for approximately 31.2 per cent in 1991; UNDP and UNDP-administered funds, 28.9 per cent; specialized agencies, 15.5 per cent; UNICEF, 13.8 per cent; regular budgets, 6.7 per cent; and UNFPA, 4 per cent.

Regionally, approximately 47.6 per cent of the expenditures went to Africa; 39.4 per cent to Asia and the Pacific; 8.2 per cent to the Americas; 4 per cent to Western Asia; and 0.7 per cent to Europe.

Expenditures by sector were as follows: health, 24 per cent; humanitarian aid and relief, 23 per cent; agriculture, forestry and fisheries, 16 per cent; general development issues, policy and planning, 8 per cent; industry, 5 per cent; natural resources, population, and transport and communications, 4 per cent each; education, 3 per cent; employment, international trade and development finance, science and technology, and social conditions and equity, 2 per cent each; and culture and human settlements, 1 per cent each.

Contributions

Contributions from Governments and other sources for operational activities of the United Nations system, including IFAD and the World Bank group (World Bank, IDA and IFC), totalled $10 billion in 1991.[6]

In addition, contributions for refugees, humanitarian, special economic and disaster relief activities totalled $1.9 billion and for the Environment Fund of the United Nations Environment Programme (UNEP), $61 million.

UN Pledging Conference for Development Activities

The 1992 United Nations Pledging Conference for Development Activities was held in New York on 3 and 4 November to receive government pledges for 1993 to United Nations funds and programmes concerned with development and related assistance.

In a September note[7] to the General Assembly, the Secretary-General listed contributions pledged or paid as at 30 June 1992 to 22 United Nations funds and programmes at the 1991 pledging conference, totalling approximately $1,557 million, with $832 million designated for UNDP.

REFERENCES

[1]YUN 1991, p. 366, GA dec. 46/465, 20 Dec. 1991. [2]E/1992/64. [3]A/47/419 & Add.1-3. [4]GA res. 44/211, 22 Dec. 1989. [5]YUN 1970, p. 319, GA res. 2626(XXV), 24 Oct. 1970. [6]A/47/419/Add.2. [7]A/CONF.158/2.

Technical cooperation through UNDP

In his annual report for 1992,[1] the UNDP Administrator noted that there was an emerging international consensus that development was aimed at improving the human condition rather than achieving growth *per se*, and that while economic growth was a necessary condition of human development, it could not take place at the cost of future generations.

Shifts in the development paradigm made for complex relationships between development and humanitarian assistance and for considerable institutional uncertainty, the Administrator said. UNDP was re-examining its mandate, focus, tools and modalities and was collaborating with its partners in the United Nations system in an attempt to make the system more effective. The mandate and functions of UNDP seemed certain to remain valid as a need would remain for a multisectoral, country-based organization supporting national, regional and global efforts for sustainable development with sufficient funding resources to ensure its coordination role as well as its credibility with recipient countries.

In 1992, estimated UNDP income was some $1,620 million, an increase from $1,222 million in 1991. Of the 1992 total, $1,178 million came from voluntary pledges, compared to $949 million in 1991. Other major sources included cost-sharing contributions by recipient Governments ($294 million), trust funds established by the Administrator, excluding the Global Environment Facility (GEF) ($51 million), GEF trust fund ($64 million), contributions to local office costs ($17 million) and government cash counterpart contributions ($11 million).

UNDP also administered eight funds which provided an additional $76.4 million during 1992, bringing total income to $1,696 million. The funds were the United Nations Capital Development Fund (UNCDF), the United Nations Revolving Fund for Natural Resources Exploration (UNRFNRE), the United Nations Sudano-Sahelian Office (UNSO), the United Nations Volunteers (UNV), the United Nations Fund for Science and Technology for Development (UNFSTD), the United Nations Development Fund for Women (UNIFEM), the UNDP Energy Account and the UNDP Study Programme.

At the November 1992 Pledging Conference, Austria and the United States announced increases in their contributions of 10 per cent and 16 per cent, respectively, surpassing the UNDP Governing Council target of 8 per cent per annum. Luxembourg increased its contribution by 25 per cent. Other major donors that made pledges were Belgium, Canada, Denmark, Finland, France, Germany, the Netherlands, Norway, Spain, Sweden and the United Kingdom. Denmark and the Netherlands pledged contributions at levels higher than their 1992 contributions.

Of the recipient countries that made pledges, Benin, Bhutan, Botswana, Djibouti, Fiji, Guinea, India, Kenya, Lesotho, the Maldives, Mauritius, Mongolia, Nigeria, Panama, Romania, Thailand, the United Republic of Tanzania and Viet Nam surpassed the Council's growth target. Nine recipient countries pledged $1 million or more each: China, Cuba, India, Indonesia, Mexico, the Republic of Korea, Saudi Arabia, Sri Lanka and Thailand.

Field programme expenditures, including indicative planning figures (IPFs), Special Programme Resources (SPR), the Special Measures Fund for the Least Developed Countries, cost-sharing and government cash counterpart contributions were reported at $1,027 million in 1992. Of total field programme expenditures, 52 per cent went for project personnel, which included internationally and nationally recruited personnel and UNV specialists, 18 per cent for subcontracts, 15 per cent for project equipment, 11 per cent for training and 4 per cent for miscellaneous expenses such as maintenance and operational costs.

Regionally, Africa absorbed 33.4 per cent of field programme expenditures in 1992; Asia and the Pacific, 28.5 per cent; Latin America and the Caribbean, 22.9 per cent; the Arab States, 7.6 per cent; Europe and the Commonwealth of Independent States, 1 per cent; and global and interregional projects, 6.6 per cent.

Project approvals during 1992 totalled 972, a decline from 1,129 the previous year. The value of new project approvals was about $642 million, compared to $690 million in 1991.

UNDP Governing Council

In 1992, the UNDP Governing Council held both its organizational meeting and a special session to discuss pending issues from 10 to 14 February 1992 in New York; it held its thirty-ninth session from 4 to 26 May at Geneva.[2]

At the organizational meeting, the Council adopted decisions on its schedule of meetings in 1992 and other organizational matters,[3] rationalization of its work[4] and its venue.[5] At the special session, it adopted eight decisions. Those not dealt with in this chapter were on assistance to Djibouti, Ethiopia, Kenya, Somalia, the Sudan and Yemen; the UNDP Gulf Task Force; and special assistance to Samoa (see next chapter).

During its thirty-ninth session, the Council adopted 36 decisions. Those not dealt with in this chapter were on the human immunodeficiency virus/acquired immunodeficiency syndrome (HIV/AIDS), environment and development, the private sector in development, the International Year for the World's Indigenous People, a New Agenda for the Development of Africa in the 1990s, humanitarian programmes, assistance to the Palestinian people; UNFPA, and UNFPA financial, budgetary and administrative matters.

On 4 May,[6] the Council approved the agenda and organization of work for its thirty-ninth session. On 26 May,[7] it decided to review the venue of its sessions at its fortieth (1993) session and asked the UNDP Administrator to provide further information on attendance and the cost of holding sessions for both Geneva and New York. The Advisory Committee on Administrative and Budgetary Questions (ACABQ) was asked to report to the Council on the matter in 1993. Also on 26 May, the Council took note of a number of reports and documents;[8] adopted a provisional agenda for its fortieth session;[9] and agreed to the schedule of its future sessions and those of its subsidiary bodies.[10]

By **decision 1992/301** of 31 July, the Economic and Social Council took note of an extract from the Governing Council's report on its 1992 meetings.[11]

Standing Committee for Programme Matters. The Standing Committee for Programme Matters held an in-sessional meeting during the special session of the Governing Council (10-14 February).[12] The Committee recommended that the Council adopt draft decisions on SPR and on country, intercountry and global programmes.

On 26 May,[8] the Council took note of the report of the Standing Committee on its 1992 in-session meeting.

The Standing Committee also held an in-sessional meeting during the thirty-ninth session of the Council (4-26 May),[13] covering field visits, the social dimensions of adjustment, country and intercountry programmes and projects, UNFPA, evaluation and its future programme of work. The Committee recommended that the Council adopt draft decisions on country, intercountry and global programmes, country programming and mid-term reviews, programme approach, evaluation, assistance to Myanmar and the UNDP programme in the former Yugoslavia.

UNDP operational activities

Country and intercountry programmes

On 14 February,[14] the UNDP Governing Council approved country programmes for nine countries: Chad, Colombia, Democratic People's Republic of Korea, Ecuador, Maldives, Peru, Senegal, Sri Lanka and Viet Nam. It also approved the country programme for Zambia on condition that an advance mid-term review would be held in 1993. It took note of the extension by one year of country programmes for Anguilla, Burundi, the Congo, Ghana, Pakistan and Rwanda.

On 26 May,[15] the Council approved country programmes for 57 countries: 13 in Africa, 6 in Arab States, 3 in Europe, 12 in Asia and the Pacific and 23 in Latin America and the Caribbean. It also approved a five-year programme for Malawi, subject to a policy review after one year of the social and political environment. It took note of the extensions of 44 country programmes: 16 for Africa, 3 for Asia and the Pacific, 8 for the Arab States, 4 for Europe and 13 for Latin America and the Caribbean, and approved the extensions of the country programmes for Gabon, Iran and Turkey for a period of two years. It also took note of intercountry programmes in Africa, Asia and the Pacific, Europe, and Latin American and the Caribbean, and of the extension of the regional programme for Arab States. It authorized the UNDP Administrator to approve projects on a project-by-project basis for Afghanistan, Cambodia, Haiti, Kuwait, Lebanon, Liberia, Myanmar and the former Yugoslavia, as he had requested.

The Council further approved the global and interregional programmes for the fifth programming cycle (1992-1996). The global programmes included health and food research, food and natural resources research and health research. The interregional programmes covered social development and poverty alleviation, environment and natural resources and public-sector management. The Council approved eight global projects in health and environmentally sustainable food production totalling $62.7 million.

With regard to the country programme for Myanmar, the Administrator, in an April note,[16] sought the Council's authorization to approve assistance on a project-by-project basis (see above). On 26 May,[17] the Council asked the Administrator to review with Myanmar reallocations of fourth programming cycle (1987-1991) IPF resources and to approve personally higher priority projects likely to have greater impact at the grass-roots level. He was also asked to conduct a review of the fifth country programme for Myanmar, including an evaluation of the impact of all projects implemented under it, and to present a report to the Council in 1993 together with recommendations on programming for Myanmar under the fifth programming cycle. The Council deferred further action on Myanmar's sixth country programme until it had considered and accepted the review and recommendations requested.

As to the former Yugoslavia, the Council, also on 26 May,[18] noted the Administrator's proposal to draw on the small balance of fourth-cycle programme resources carried forward solely for the preparation of urgent humanitarian projects on a case-by-case basis and authorized him to proceed.

Mid-term reviews. On 26 May,[19] the Governing Council, reaffirming the need for the Administrator to carry out mid-term reviews of all country, regional, interregional and global programmes, welcomed the new format of country programme documents presented for its consideration. It asked the Administrator to include in mid-term review documents an analysis of levels of national execution; UNDP assistance in national capacity-building at the policy and programme formulation, management and evaluation levels; experience with the new support costs arrangements; and experience with the programme approach, including the use of alternative programme support mechanisms. He was asked to include in future country programme documents more consistent information on lessons learned from previous programming cycles and mid-term reviews and more comprehensive performance indicators. He was also asked to continue to increase the focus of country programmes on a smaller number of concentration areas according to recipient country needs.

The Administrator was invited to submit to the Council's 1993 special session a tentative timetable for mid-term reviews to be carried out in 1993-

1995, together with proposals on how he would report the outcomes of those reviews. He was asked to report to the Council's regular 1993 session on progress achieved in harmonizing programme cycles and programming procedures among members of the Joint Consultative Group on Policy (JCGP) and to increase his efforts to stagger the scheduling of country programmes throughout the programming cycle.

Country programmes by region

Africa

The management plan of the UNDP Regional Bureau for Africa for 1992 was aligned with the major objectives of the United Nations New Agenda for the Development of Africa in the 1990s (see next chapter), adopted by the General Assembly in 1991.[20] Under the National Long-Term Perspective Studies Programme, which aimed to create a national process for establishing long-term development strategies and priorities, plans were launched in 9 countries and a further 20 countries submitted requests for studies. The African Capacity-Building Foundation, a joint initiative of UNDP, the World Bank and the African Development Bank, sought to strengthen regional and national capacities to formulate and manage national economic policies and programmes and to support the internalization of long-term development planning.

During the year UNDP supported democratization and electoral processes in 22 African countries with advisory services, resource mobilization, logistical support and follow-up (observers), and development of social funds or social safety nets. Electoral support in Ethiopia, Mali and Namibia was successful, while in Angola, where UNDP coordinated some $5 million in cost-sharing support for the election, the results were not accepted by all parties and fighting resumed. In Ethiopia, UNDP assisted in demobilizing troops and reintegrating them into the private sector; an estimated 350,000 ex-servicemen benefited from donor contributions, including $7.87 million from UNDP.

UNDP provided emergency assistance to drought-affected countries in southern Africa and to 40,000 persons who were displaced by the political upheaval and resumed fighting in Liberia. In Mozambique, technical support was provided to national and provincial emergency commissions, and a large multi-donor programme to reintegrate displaced persons and returning refugees was supported.

Under GEF, seven UNDP-sponsored projects, amounting to $18 million, were approved. A range of innovative projects were being implemented, including a project in Mauritania to establish infrastructure to deliver wind-based rural electric power. In a semi-arid zone of Burkina Faso, a pilot project to demonstrate how biodiversity could be conserved within wildlife ranching systems was designed in collaboration with village associations and local and international non-governmental organizations (NGOs).

UNDP assisted Governments to formulate economic management and capacity-building programmes, four of which were inaugurated, in Burkina Faso, Côte d'Ivoire, the Gambia and Zambia. Furthest advanced was the programme to develop national economic management capacity in the Gambia.

With respect to HIV/AIDS, UNDP played an advocacy role through the country programmes, including the sensitization of African policy makers and community organizations to the implications—human, social and developmental—of the pandemic. Some 30 projects, ranging from support for multisectoral national programmes to survivor assistance, were developed.

Asia and the Pacific

Use of the programme approach gained momentum in Asia and the Pacific. UNDP assisted national authorities to develop national programme frameworks, a prelude to programme formulation. In China, eight programmes in agriculture, forestry, industry and natural resources development were approved. In India, jute and leather programmes became operational. In Thailand, a subprogramme on human resources development focused on increasing the relevance of and access to education.

UNDP assistance was increasingly sought to translate the principles of human development into national development strategies. For example, following a one-year UNDP-assisted study, Bangladesh published a human development report and undertook to integrate its concerns into a five-year plan. In Pakistan, a human development initiative led to a report that was distributed to government officials, the private sector, NGOs and foreign missions and influenced a $700,000 human development project. In the Philippines, UNDP helped to organize a network of human development advocates among academicians, practitioners and professionals in both the public and private sectors to promote the concept and prepare a national human development report.

In the area of aid coordination, round-table meetings were organized for Bhutan and the Lao People's Democratic Republic. The shortfall in resources for Bhutan's sixth five-year plan was estimated at $370 million, and donors expressed willingness to support that country's development schemes. Priority projects in the Lao People's Democratic Republic were estimated to cost $745

million, against which donors pledged some $600 million in concessional loans and grants.

In north-eastern Asia, the Tumen River Area Development Programme was a comprehensive approach by China, the Democratic People's Republic of Korea, Mongolia, the Republic of Korea and the Russian Federation to develop resources in their border areas. UNDP provided assistance not only in articulating common interests and objectives, but in facilitating contacts with and coordinating the inputs of donors and investors.

UNDP co-chaired a Ministerial Conference on the Rehabilitation and Reconstruction of Cambodia (Tokyo, June), which resulted in donor pledges of $880 million and which constituted the International Committee on Reconstruction of Cambodia, with UNDP as its secretariat.

In Afghanistan, UNDP initiated a rehabilitation strategy exercise to identify immediate and medium-term needs and draw up a rehabilitation and reconstruction programme.

JCGP introduced coordination mechanisms and undertook joint actions in many countries of the region. In China, UNDP organized a United Nations Inter-Agency Working Group on Poverty Issues with 11 agencies participating. In the Democratic People's Republic of Korea, a rural health plan was formulated by JCGP and WHO. In Indonesia, United Nations specialized agencies formed an Inter-Agency Coordination Committee.

Through a regional project, 14 country-level and a number of intercountry workshops and seminars were initiated on HIV/AIDS. The regional project also co-sponsored the Second International Congress on AIDS in Asia and the Pacific (New Delhi, India, November).

IPF resources for the fifth cycle for the region (1992-1996) amounted to $1.5 billion; cost-sharing contributions by recipient countries and third parties were expected to provide another $200 million. Some 200 new projects and programmes were approved, with the total IPF and cost-sharing funds committed amounting to about $140 million. Total programme expenditure for the region in 1992 was estimated at $260 million.

More than 105 nationally executed projects valued at $84 million were approved. China and India were the leading countries in national execution: in China, 52 per cent of the projects approved were nationally executed; in India, 33 per cent. Training of government staff in the operational and financial management of projects continued.

UNDP emphasized sustainable development and environmental issues in its country and intercountry programmes. A regional sustainable development project was initiated with an IPF commitment of $837,000. Work also commenced on nine national and two subregional Sustainable Development Networks (SDNs) to facilitate information exchange in support of environmentally sound national development activities. SDNs became operational in Pakistan, the Philippines and the South Pacific. The regional GEF portfolio, managed by UNDP, helped to meet obligations under the conventions on climate change and biodiversity (see PART THREE, Chapter VIII), and included a large-scale ($9.5 million) project on developing a least-cost greenhouse gas emission plan in Asia. Projects on ozone-layer depletion worth $2.9 million were programmed and implemented in five countries.

Arab States

In 1992, many Arab countries moved to rehabilitate their economies after the Gulf war of 1991, to accelerate a trend towards civil reform and more open market economies, and to introduce greater pluralism in their societies.

In Egypt and Lebanon, UNDP coordinated with the Governments and the World Bank to assess technical cooperation requirements. In Algeria, UNDP assisted the Government to review its investment policy and identify areas where legal restrictions could be reduced. In Tunisia, UNDP helped to design an anti-poverty strategy for about 100,000 families, and, with the World Bank, assisted the Government to restructure the industrial sector for privatization. UNDP assistance in Egypt focused on building its capacity for national economic reform and structural adjustment, and in Jordan was aimed at development planning and data and policy analysis.

Emergency assistance was provided to Somalia and the Sudan. In Somalia, which faced a combination of collapse of civil society, political and military disorder and extreme famine, UNDP established itself at Mogadishu and Hargeisa and provided staffing and logistical support to the Special Representative of the Secretary-General. Other UNDP activities included managing and providing air transport for the United Nations and NGOs; rehabilitating the water-supply system in Mogadishu; financing missions to identify the needs of the displaced in the agricultural sector; and participating in civil aviation and de-mining projects.

In the Sudan, the Resident Representative served as Special Representative of the Secretary-General for relief operations. He was supported by an emergency coordination unit funded and managed by UNDP.

While development programmes remained suspended in Iraq, a number of activities were approved and implemented with the concurrence of the Security Council's Sanctions Committee (see PART TWO, Chapter III). Under a regional project for the eradication of rinderpest, $400,000 was allocated for vaccination campaigns in the northern part of the country; assistance was provided to a rehabilitation project for the handicapped; and logistical and administrative support was given to United Nations humanitarian activities.

In Kuwait, UNDP assisted in planning and civil service reform, with emphasis on greater use of Kuwaiti indigenous skills and the private sector. In Saudi Arabia, UNDP helped to train 2,700 Saudis in the civil aviation sector and assisted in establishing two telecommunications institutes. In Qatar, UNDP assisted in a study of how to replenish the aquifer. In the United Arab Emirates, it helped to establish a Central Forecasting Office for Meteorological Services.

Resident representatives in the region agreed to decentralize programme activities and to strengthen field offices; to draw up subregional strategies for clusters of countries; to emphasize resource mobilization and coordination efforts; and to increase the promotion of networking and regional linkages.

Europe and the Commonwealth of Independent States

Six field offices were in operation in Europe and the Russian Federation by the end of 1992. Four were headed by a United Nations Representative, who was also the UNDP Resident Representative, and the other two by field staff from a United Nations Information Centre, supported by a Deputy United Nations Representative, who was also the UNDP Resident Representative.

Institutions implementing national privatization strategies benefited from expert advice provided through a UNDP regional privatization network. In Romania, UNDP assisted the Government to build up the capacity for privatization through a UNDP-funded centre to counsel small-scale entrepreneurs during the start-up phase of their businesses.

A regional programme based on providing turnaround teams of corporate leaders from countries outside the region was prepared. The teams would be on call for visits over a two-year period to resolve senior management problems.

Albania requested a UNDP team to assist with electoral procedures and to organize the participation of other international organizations and international observers. UNDP cooperated with the European Community (EC) in preparing studies for a meeting between EC and Albania to determine support for restructuring the Albanian economy. EC channelled $1 million in humanitarian assistance to Albania through UNDP.

There was also close cooperation with EC on the environment, particularly with regard to activities in the Danube River basin and the Black Sea area. Two projects funded by GEF were developed by

UNDP: environmental management of the Danube basin to enhance institutional capabilities in riparian countries of the Danube, and environmental protection of the Black Sea to enable riparian countries of the Black Sea and the Sea of Azov to develop a comprehensive management strategy.

Latin America and the Caribbean

In Latin America and the Caribbean, UNDP began to participate with other institutions such as the Inter-American Development Bank (IDB) in promoting democracy. The advancement of governance was being achieved through public-sector reform and decentralization efforts as well as by fostering private-sector support of human development. Efforts to reduce poverty were basic to governance and social peace, and numerous programmes were addressed to the plight of the poor. Social emergency funds in Bolivia and Central America, established under agreements with the World Bank and IDB, continued to operate. Chile put in place a UNDP-supported development facility in each of its 12 regions, which had an important poverty-alleviation component. A UNDP initiative in Peru helped to establish a fund to provide financial support to communities for employment generation and basic infrastructure.

The importance of external resource flows was increasingly recognized and a new slant was given to the national technical cooperation assessment and programmes (NATCAPs) exercise when Guatemala decided to use UNDP aid coordination to promote a national peace plan. UNDP cooperation was sought by several countries to improve their competitiveness in international markets. Brazil implemented a $28 million cost-shared project for the coordination of research and the promotion of informatics exports. Chile implemented a cost-shared project to integrate the research capacity in Government, the private sector and universities.

In the environmental sector, two new GEF projects were approved and a third IPF project for Brazil was revised, producing additional IPF and cost-sharing funds for strengthening the capacity of Governments for environmental management. One GEF project supported the Peruvian Centre for Energy Conservation, and the other would demonstrate the commercial feasibility of using biomass as a feedstock for power generation in Brazil through applying biomass-integrated gasification/gas-turbine technology.

Global and interregional programmes

The UNDP global programme supported high-level research on food production and health, and the interregional programme promoted sharing of knowledge on such questions as management, debt, trade, energy, water and sanitation, HIV and development, and electoral administration.

The United Nations received 31 requests for electoral assistance, two thirds of which were for first-time elections in Africa, between October 1991 and September 1992. UNDP prepared the publication *Guidelines on Special Arrangements for Electoral Assistance.* In addition, it established an electoral assistance trust fund, advanced the funding for seven urgent needs-assessment missions, co-funded the first conference on the coordination of international assistance in the electoral field and funded a training course for United Nations officials.

UNDP and the International Monetary Fund Institute initiated a programme to train middle-level managers in the basic skills to deal with the transition from centrally planned to market economies. The programme attracted support from Japan, Portugal and EC. The Division for Global and Interregional Programmes was instrumental in launching a new programme to strengthen the capacity of developing countries to manage their external assets and liabilities. The programme had a number of innovative features, including the fact that for the first time two major providers of technical cooperation—the United Nations Conference on Trade and Development (UNCTAD) and the World Bank—agreed to pool their assistance. In addition, the programme nurtured initiatives at the subregional level, including an effort by anglophone countries of East and southern Africa to create their own pool of advisory services which would be attached to the Reserve Bank of Zimbabwe. Other subregional initiatives were being formulated for Central America, Eastern Europe and the Commonwealth of Independent States.

At the beginning of 1992, UNDP established an HIV and Development Programme to increase global awareness of the threat that the pandemic posed to development. The programme involved communities, academic institutions, NGOs, Governments and the United Nations system. In cooperation with the library of Columbia University School of Public Health (New York), the programme initiated the HIVDEV database. A memorandum of understanding for implementing the WHO/UNDP Alliance to Combat AIDS was agreed upon, with a pledge to develop multisectoral approaches.

A UNDP/World Bank programme established a new strategy with regard to water and sanitation to build support for sustainable investments and disseminate lessons learned. For example, in Kumasi, Ghana's second-largest city, people were asked how much, if anything, they would pay for sanitation facilities. A new sanitation plan, based on demand-driven, privately provided services, was developed. The approach was to be tested in other countries of the developing world.

Other areas addressed in the UNDP global and interregional programmes included the environment, privatization, urban management, education and assistance to the Palestinian people.

Programme planning and management

Since the General Assembly adopted a resolution in 1989 on operational activities,[21] there had been considerable discussion of the terms "programme approach" and "programme-oriented mechanism". However, no clear definitions of those terms were available. UNDP had attempted to arrive at an understanding of them, and in March 1992,[22] the UNDP Administrator submitted a report to the Governing Council stressing that the programme referred to was a national programme, not a UNDP programme or that of any other outside partner. The approach was the way in which national authorities attempted to achieve a national objective, not through discrete or ad hoc projects, but through a carefully thought-out, articulated programme. The programme contained all the elements needed to reach and sustain the national objective. External cooperation supported national programmes. Within the programme approach, the advantages of UNDP, stemming from the political and sectoral neutrality and universality of its mandate, appeared to lie in areas such as policy and programme formulation and management.

The programme support mechanism in principle ensured that externally provided resources were available where they were most needed, rather than being confined to a particular component of a programme.

Guidelines would be issued in due course for cooperation in formulating and managing national programmes; for the programme support mechanism; for a revised project document format; and for revised monitoring and evaluation procedures. The Administrator suggested a number of ways in which a country could start to follow the programme approach in the areas of identifying national objectives, formulating a national programme and implementing and managing it.

On 26 May,[23] the Governing Council stressed that the programme approach should be applied on a country-specific basis and that UNDP should ensure the smooth implementation of country programmes. It encouraged UNDP to continue formulating principles for the programme approach. It further stressed the need to develop baseline data and success indicators for monitoring and evaluating UNDP-assisted projects/programmes and the need to involve United Nations specialized agencies at the early stages of the design of programme assistance. The Administrator was asked to hold consultations on the draft guiding principles and to submit a progress report in 1993.

National execution

The Administrator, in response to a 1991 request of the Governing Council,[24] in April 1922 submitted a report on national execution[25] containing guidelines on assisting Governments to formulate and implement national capacity-building strategies, on the respective roles of UNDP, agencies and Governments in national execution and implementation and on use for national execution of the technical support resources agreed upon by the Council in 1991.[26]

The overall UNDP strategy for capacity-building would provide a unifying framework for UNDP mechanisms such as the round-table process, the Management Development Programme (MDP) and NATCAPs. UNDP recognized the need for developing countries to develop their own long-term perspectives. In addition, it recognized a distinction between institution-building and capacity-building. Capacity-building need not be confined to one institution but may refer to the strengthening of national capacities across sectors such as policy formulation, scientific research, information technology and financial management.

The strategic entry points at which UNDP would interface with national systems would increasingly be the following: dialogue on overall goals and policies, sectoral strategies and programmes; assistance to Governments to strengthen their ability to define and prepare national programmes; and integration of global priorities and initiatives. The role and responsibilities of Government, United Nations specialized agencies, UNDP, UNDP field offices and the Office for Project Services (OPS) in the capacity-building process were also discussed. Guidelines specifying the roles of the various partners in the national execution process would be updated after a period of testing in the field and then incorporated into the UNDP Programmes and Projects Manual.

On 26 May,[27] the Governing Council noted the definitions in the Administrator's report and clarified the following: execution was defined as the overall management, by national government authorities or by a United Nations agency, of the programme/project, along with responsibility for outputs, achievement of objectives and use of resources; implementation was defined as the procurement and delivery of programme/project inputs and their conversion into outputs; administrative and operational support services were defined as the procurement and delivery of UNDP-financed programme/project inputs and thus constituted only an aspect of implementation.

With regard to execution and implementation, the Council agreed that national government authorities responsible for programme/project execution needed to have the necessary national management staff, and that the cost of managing nationally executed programmes/projects should be borne by the Government; UNDP assistance in the building of sustainable capacity for national execution could be financed from country IPF resources or SPR; UNDP field office staff might provide administrative assistance to executing agents as long as that did not interfere with their primary tasks; and the involvement of OPS in national execution should be limited to providing non-technical implementation services and to building up national managerial and administrative capacities.

The Council endorsed the Administrator's approval to delegate to resident representatives the authority for approving national execution and urged the Administrator to improve the financial accounting, reporting and auditing of nationally executed projects.

Programme evaluation

In March 1992,[28] the Administrator submitted to the Governing Council the ninth annual report on programme evaluation. The report covered the principal evaluation issues that had emerged during 1991 and reviewed the work of the Central Evaluation Office over the fourth programming cycle (1987-1991). The report also considered the evolving role of evaluation in UNDP during the last five years; discussed the feedback of evaluation results into UNDP's work; recorded what had been done to promote national monitoring and evaluation systems; gave an account of other evaluation work; and discussed collaboration with other institutions. It also presented a work plan for evaluation activities for 1992-1993.

On 26 May,[29] the Council welcomed the change in approach in evaluation activities towards more impact- and result-oriented assessments as well as towards increased strategy- and policy-oriented evaluation of UNDP activities during the fifth programming cycle (1992-1996). It urged the Administrator to strengthen the capacity of the Central Evaluation Office to undertake policy, strategy and programme evaluations in line with the findings and recommendations of a planning exercise and workload study and to backstop the evaluation capacity of the Regional Bureaux, keeping in mind the necessity to involve the recipient Governments in evaluation activities. It requested the Administrator to expand measures to ensure genuine feedback and use of results attained through evaluations and assessments to the programming activities of UNDP and the Governments concerned.

Field visits

The Governing Council, in 1991, had provided for up to four field visits per year by members of its Standing Committee for Programme Matters.

Each mission was to cover not more than two countries; costs would be shared by UNDP (80 per cent) and UNFPA (20 per cent).

At its February in-sessional meeting,[12] the Standing Committee, on the basis of experience gained through the first three visits (January 1992) to a total of six countries (Botswana/United Republic of Tanzania, Indonesia/Sri Lanka and Egypt/Morocco), prepared standard terms of reference to facilitate future visits. The terms were used in preparing forthcoming field visits. The report on the visit to Bhutan/India (March) was considered at the Standing Committee's May in-sessional meeting.[13] Further visits to the Syrian Arab Republic/Yemen and Bolivia/Paraguay took place in August/September 1992.[30]

Fourth and fifth programming cycles

On 14 February,[31] the Governing Council took note of an oral presentation by the Administrator on the resource outlook for the fifth programming cycle (1992-1996). It requested him to prepare a detailed analysis of the resource outlook and its impact on IPFs, and decided to consider those questions at its thirty-ninth (1992) session.

In response to that request, the Administrator in April submitted a report on matters relating to the fourth (1987-1991) and fifth programming cycles.[32] The report examined the resource outlook for the fifth cycle and discussed new and revised IPFs for it. The Administrator noted that the fifth cycle unallocated account of $100 million could not accommodate all the estimated additional requirements of $117.5 million. The addition by the General Assembly in 1991[33] of five countries to the list of least developed countries (LDCs) and the emergence of new republics from the former USSR that would probably request recipient status was likely to have an impact on fifth cycle resources. However, since the additional resources needed over and above the $100 million were likely to be small, the Administrator proposed postponing any adjustments to IPFs and SPR until the mid-term (1994) review had been carried out.

The report also provided information on the status of fourth cycle net contributor obligations.

On 26 May,[34] the Council decided that IPFs for future programming cycles should be established as of the first day of each cycle. It further decided that country IPF revisions and IPFs for new recipients should be allocated in proportion to the number of years remaining in each cycle. The Council authorized the Administrator to continue to issue allocations for the fifth cycle within the overall planning framework established by the Council in 1990,[35] and urged Governments to increase their contributions to UNDP in line with the planning assumptions contained in that framework. The Administrator was asked to inform the Council in 1993 of the complete list of IPFs for the fifth cycle.

Also on 26 May,[36] the Council requested the Administrator, in the context of a 1991 Council decision,[37] on an exceptional one-time basis and where he decided it was warranted, to extend until 31 December 1992 the period for finalizing accounts for fourth cycle obligations and payments for the purpose of calculating fifth cycle entitlements.

New recipient countries

On 14 February,[38] the Governing Council welcomed the Republics of Belarus, Estonia, Latvia, Lithuania and Ukraine as recipient countries in UNDP. It approved the allocation of IPFs and asked the Administrator to inform it in 1993 of any revised basic data and its effect on the computation of IPFs. He was also authorized to proceed with programme development in the five countries, taking into account the need for impact sustainability, effective use of resources and other development activities being undertaken there. The Council requested the Administrator to submit a report to its 1993 regular session with proposals on ways to establish a United Nations presence in those countries, with particular regard to cost-effectiveness. In preparing the report, he was asked to consult with members of ACC and JCGP.

In response to that request, the Administrator in April submitted a report[39] in which he noted that, in addition to the five countries for which the Council had established IPFs in February, requests for recipient status had been received from a further seven countries of the former USSR. He had therefore broadened the parameters within which he was responding to the Council's February decision.

The Administrator recommended that the basic UNDP structure in the region should consist of one international senior staff member per country, with the minimum office logistical support required and access to a wide-area communications network. UNDP's role dictated a set-up that would meet the following characteristics: the host country would share in the cost of nationally recruited professionals in support of the international senior officer, with possible support from other sources; and, while heads of offices would primarily serve their country of accreditation, they might also advise other offices in the region in such areas as electoral processes, social and economic dimensions of transition, information management, support to entrepreneurship, aid flow management and the role of local government.

The Administrator gave a breakdown of estimated start-up and recurrent costs to UNDP

through December 1993 per country and, applying those costs to the five countries given recipient status in February, noted that the total cost over 18 months would be $2.75 million. Assuming that the 10 remaining countries would acquire recipient status, the total net cost through 1993 for all 15 countries would be $8.25 million. He therefore recommended that that amount be provided from the UNDP administrative budget and proposed to offset a large part of it with any income received through special contributions.

On 26 May,[40] the Council, welcoming Armenia, Azerbaijan, Kazakhstan, Kyrgyzstan, the Republic of Moldova, the Russian Federation, Turkmenistan and Uzbekistan as recipient countries in UNDP, approved the allocation of IPFs and asked the Administrator to inform it in 1993 of any revised basic data and its effect on the computation of IPFs. It authorized the Administrator to proceed with programme development in the eight countries, taking into account other development activities being undertaken there.

Also on 26 May, [41] the Council noted the Administrator's intention to submit country programmes for the 13 new recipient countries in 1993. It asked him to work with those countries, other interested Governments and relevant bodies to ensure that UNDP's work in the region was focused on areas where it had a comparative advantage and to continue efforts to clarify the country-specific role and comparative advantages of UNSO in the countries concerned. He was also asked to work with the United Nations Secretariat and other United Nations bodies, particularly ACC and JCGP, to ensure an integrated United Nations system presence in those countries.

The Administrator was further asked to provide those countries with operational support during 1992-1993 and was authorized to open temporary and/or regional UNDP offices. In that regard, he was asked to give priority to countries with the lowest relative levels of per capita GNP and the highest levels of IPF and aggregate programme resources, and to follow an innovative and cost-effective approach when opening offices and/or providing operational support.

The Council approved, on an exceptional basis, the use during 1992-1993 of up to $3 million from savings in the original appropriation for the 1992-1993 core budget to enable the Administrator to open the temporary offices, and urged him to negotiate cost-sharing arrangements with host countries with the aim of covering expenses incurred in local currency. The Administrator was encouraged to seek to complement the country IPFs through other programmable resources. The Council decided to review action taken by the Administrator at its 1993 special session.

Financing

In his annual review of the financial situation,[42] the Administrator reported that total income in 1992 was $1.5 billion, while expenditures totalled $1.4 billion, with a resulting surplus of $100 million. As a result of the surplus, the balance of UNDP general resources increased from $152.9 million at 31 December 1991 to $220.6 million at 31 December 1992. Income from voluntary contributions totalled $1.2 billion. Miscellaneous income, mainly composed of income from UNDP placements of funds in short-term financial instruments and adjustments resulting from exchange rate changes, decreased from $13.1 million in 1991 to $0.5 million in 1992, reflecting lower interest rates on investments and substantial foreign exchange losses at a time of high foreign exchange rate volatility and the significant devaluation of a number of currencies of donor countries.

Cost-sharing contributions grew from $218.8 million to almost $300 million, and were expected to continue to increase. While that source of funding enabled a larger total programme expenditure in selected countries, it did not make up for shortfalls in voluntary contributions necessary for financing IPFs.

IPF expenditures declined from $867 million in 1991 to $727 million in 1992. Expenditures under the Special Measures Fund for LDCs decreased from $13 million in 1991 to $6.5 million in 1992. Expenditures under cost-sharing contributions increased from $195.9 million in 1991 to $225.2 million in 1992 and under SPR from $43 million in 1991 to $50.6 million in 1992.

The Administrator reiterated that it had become evident that the target for annual increases in contributions of 8 per cent was unlikely to be achieved. He had been obliged to assume an annual rate of growth in resources of 4 per cent; to instruct UNDP field offices to provide for a programme reserve of 10 per cent of IPFs in the country programmes; and to establish annual expenditure targets for 1992 and 1993 of $780 million and $760 million, respectively. There were also indications that contributions for 1993 would amount to only $930 million, a reduction of 13.5 per cent from 1992.

On 26 May,[43] the Governing Council took note of the Administrator's annual review of the financial situation for 1991[44] and of the Council's decision[36] on the fourth and fifth programming cycles (see above). It noted with concern the impact of exchange rate fluctuations on the dollar value of contributions in 1991 and on the level of resources anticipated by the Administrator in 1992 and 1993 and that real growth in contributions had not reached the level projected by the Council in 1990.[35] It further noted the reduction in the Administrator's expenditure forecasts resulting from the level of anticipated resources.

The Council approved the format of the *ex post facto* report on support costs contained in the Administrator's 1991 review of the financial situation and asked him to submit such a report on a biennial basis, starting in 1994. It also approved changes to the financial regulations proposed in the same document and annexed them to its decision. It deferred consideration of a request for additional support cost reimbursement from the World Meteorological Organization, and urged member organizations of JCGP to pursue the possibility of using common premises.

Budgets

Revised 1992-1993 budget

In March,[45] the Administrator submitted to the Governing Council revised budget estimates for 1992-1993. The revised estimates for UNDP core activities amounted to $478 million gross and $446 million net. In net terms, that represented a decrease of $4 million (0.9 per cent) in relation to the original appropriation approved in 1991.[46] The revised estimates for UNDP core and non-core activities as a whole amounted to $607 million gross and $575 million net. With regard specifically to non-core activities, that represented in gross terms a reduction of $0.4 million.

Cost adjustments relating to the core budget amounted to a total reduction of $4.7 million. A currency release of $6.3 million and a downward inflation adjustment of $1.5 million were partially offset by cost adjustments amounting to $3 million. The currency release related to the impact of the difference in exchange rates between February 1991, when the original 1992-1993 estimates were formulated, and February 1992, the basis for the revised estimates.

The downward adjustment in inflation rates reflected adjustments in United Nations projections for both Headquarters and the field. Cost adjustments related to the following staff cost categories: home leave ($0.6 million); security ($0.8 million); pension contributions ($1.4 million); and medical insurance ($0.7 million). That was partially offset by a reduction in the education grant of $0.5 million.

ACABQ presented its observations on the revised budget estimates for 1992-1993 to the Council in an April report.[47]

On 26 May,[48] the Council approved the cost adjustments reflected in the revised 1992-1993 biennial budget estimates. It also approved the continuation of one core post (at the P-5 level) for the Humanitarian Programme until the end of the 1992-1993 biennium and decided to apply the same procedure to an existing D-2 post in that Programme. It decided, in that context, to review the staffing level of the Programme, stressing the need for a clear division of responsibility between the United Nations Department for Humanitarian Affairs and the UNDP Humanitarian Programme.

1994-1995 budget

In his March report on revised budget estimates for the 1992-1993 biennium,[45] the Administrator also presented his budget strategy for 1994-1995. His strategy was based on two goals: further administrative cost reduction and increased transparency regarding the nature of services rendered by UNDP field offices to non-UNDP-financed programmes and their costs.

On 26 May,[48] the Council welcomed the Administrator's 1994-1995 budget strategy, including a proposed volume reduction of $30 million to $40 million and, in order to give priority to the allocation of resources for programming and to protect fully the integrity of UNDP, urged the Administrator to achieve the maximum possible savings. In that regard, the Council requested the Administrator to take into account the need to ensure that regional service centres did not introduce a new bureaucratic layer or duplicate headquarters functions and the need to reduce significantly the ratio of General Service to Professional staff.

The Council requested the Administrator, in the context of the 1994-1995 budget strategy, to report to it in 1993. The report should include an analysis of the UNDP field structure, taking the following elements into consideration: the levels of IPFs and extrabudgetary resources, the impact of the composition of resources on the field structure and the impact of different options for decentralization of OPS. It requested the Administrator to make recommendations regarding the possibility of a more flexible and cost-effective approach to the UNDP field presence, including the option of closing field offices and making use of regional offices.

Further, the Council stressed the importance of common system-wide approaches on personnel entitlement issues and on job-classification issues and decided that proposals by the Administrator on reclassification should have no adverse financial implications and should not lead to grade creep. It approved his proposals on a pilot basis for one year, and decided to review the arrangement in 1993. It also endorsed the Administrator's proposals relating to increased transparency of the nature of the services rendered by UNDP field offices to non-UNDP-financed programmes and the associated costs, approved in principle his proposals relating to OPS and requested him to review the question of savings through mergers of the administrative and other functions of the trust funds. The Administrator was asked to report on those matters in 1993, taking into account also the

review of the senior management structure to be submitted in 1993 (see below).

Audit reports

The Governing Council considered the interim audit report of the Board of Auditors on UNDP for the first year of the biennium 1990-1991[49] as well as the comments of ACABQ thereon.[50] It also reviewed the audited financial statements of the executing agencies for the year ended 31 December 1990, the reports of the external auditors and comments of the Administrator on the audit reports of the executing agencies,[51] and the report of the Administrator on the interim report of UNDP itself.[52]

On 26 May,[53] the Council noted that the Administrator had taken and was taking action to correct the situations identified by the auditors, and urged him to conclude all standard basic executing agency agreements by 31 December 1992. The Council also noted the comments of ACC regarding the views of the Board of Auditors on agency accountability, and requested the Board to pursue the issue of submission of complete audit information to the Board by the external auditors of the agencies. It requested the Administrator to intensify efforts to achieve full implementation of the recommendations of the Board of Auditors on OPS and to report to the Council thereon in 1993. He was urged to work with other United Nations organizations and specialized agencies to achieve common accounting principles and standards.

Status of management services

In March,[54] the Administrator submitted to the Governing Council his biennial report, covering 1990 and 1991, on the status of management services provided to Governments by UNDP. He noted that the use of management services continued to grow, though at a slower pace, with no significant new trends emerging since his 1990 report.[55] Development bank borrowers and bilateral aid recipients engaged UNDP in 59 new agreements during the period, bringing the total value of active management services projects at OPS to $305 million by the end of 1991. The Administrator stated that, by providing management services, UNDP assisted Governments in utilizing development funds and in mobilizing greater resources; such services also strengthened UNDP's role in coordinating aid at the country level.

On 26 May,[56] the Council concluded that the principles and guidelines in regard to management services enumerated in a 1983 Council decision[57] remained valid; that management services constituted a flexible mechanism for increasing the capacity of recipient countries to absorb external assistance; and that the use of management services enhanced the aid coordination role of UNDP at the field level.

The Council requested the Administrator to continue to observe the 1983 principles and guidelines; to bear in mind that management services should be viewed as assistance to developing countries in response to their specific needs; to ensure, with respect to bilaterally funded Management Service Agreements, fuller use of rules for international competitive bidding; and to ensure that the appropriate UNDP contract review process was followed, including the so-called double check mechanism. It authorized the Administrator in the coming years to respond to requests for management services in relation to programmes funded by sources other than UNDP. The Council recommended that in the future information on the status of management services be submitted as part of the annual financial report and as part of the OPS annual report, to be reviewed triennially by the Council.

Financial regulations

In January,[58] the Administrator submitted a report on proposed financial regulation 4.6, which defined the term "readily usable" with regard to the currency of voluntary contributions, and other matters on which consensus had not been reached. The report provided the Governing Council with the texts of those items for its consideration.

On 26 May,[59] the Governing Council took note of the report of the Administrator and decided that its Budgetary and Finance Committee would consider, at the Council's 1993 regular session, the proposed financial regulation and the other matters on which consensus had not been reached.

UNDP-administered funds

During 1992, 11 new trust funds were established by the Administrator on behalf of UNDP.[60] They were the Family Health International Trust Fund, Rehabilitation Assistance to Anhui Province (China) following Flood Disaster, Trust Fund for the Frente Farabundo Martí para la Liberación Nacional Relocation Points in El Salvador, UNDP Trust Fund for Humanitarian and Rehabilitation Assistance for Cambodia, International Development Research Centre Trust Fund for Information Management Training Series, UNDP Trust Fund for Technical Assistance to Electoral Processes, Trust Fund to Mainstream Human Development into Operational Activities, UNDP Trust Fund for the Baltic Republics, Trust Fund for the Inter-Parliamentary Union, UNDP Trust Fund for the Mozambique Demobilization Programme and the Capacity 21 Trust Fund. Contributions received for those funds during the year totalled $30.6 million. Three sub-trust funds were established under the Trust Fund for Humanita-

rian and Rehabilitation Assistance for Cambodia. They were the UNDP/Sweden Trust Fund for the Rehabilitation of Infrastructure in Cambodia, the UNDP/United States Trust Fund for Cambodia and the UNDP/Netherlands Trust Fund for Cambodia. Contributions to those funds during 1992 totalled $7.1 million.

Sixteen sub-trust fund arrangements were established on behalf of UNCDF (2) and UNV (14). The value of those arrangements was approximately $15.5 million.

During 1992, contributions to the 75 trust funds and sub-trust funds in operation totalled $118.3 million, while expenditures amounted to $42.7 million.[61]

Special Programme Resources

SPR represented resources set aside by the Governing Council to finance specified types of programme activities during each programming cycle. In 1991,[62] the Council increased the SPR allocation from $189.5 million in the fourth cycle to $313 million in the fifth.

Total SPR expenditures during 1992[42] amounted to $83.2 million, of which $32.6 million was charged against cost-sharing contributions, resulting in a net expenditure of $50.6 million.

In accordance with a 1991 Council decision,[63] the UNDP Administrator submitted a report to the Council's special session[64] containing the programming documents for the 26 subcategories of SPR, which were grouped under six major clusters: disaster mitigation; thematic activities; other special and/or new activities; aid coordination; programme development; and assistance to the Palestinian people.

On 14 February,[65] the Council approved the programming documents for allocating SPR on the understanding that comments by delegations would be taken into consideration for action during programme design and that the subcategory on social dimensions of adjustment would be redesigned and resubmitted to the Council.

Support cost successor arrangements

In response to a 1991 Governing Council decision,[26] by which it established a new system of reimbursing specialized agencies for support services provided to UNDP-financed programmes and projects, the Administrator in April 1992 submitted his first annual progress report on the new support cost successor arrangements system.[66] He stated that, since the new arrangements had gone into effect only as of 1 January 1992, his report covered preparatory actions taken since June 1991 to implement the system and other issues on which the Council's guidance was requested. He noted that UNDP, in consultation with specialized agencies, had developed a set of operational guidelines for implementation of the new system. Those guidelines were issued in January and had gone into effect. They would be field-tested for one year and would then be updated and amended as necessary. The report also discussed the policy framework for execution and implementation; status of financial provisions; the results of a 1991 cost study;[62] technical support services at the programme level (TSS-1); issues relating to agencies not subject to the new regime; application to trust funds and other funds under the Administrator; currency fluctuations; flexibility arrangements; and monitoring and evaluation. An addendum to the report listed TSS-1 for 1992-1993.

On 26 May,[27] the Council requested the Administrator, while implementing successor arrangements, to take into account differences among recipient countries with respect to the size of IPFs and the administrative capacity of the field office.

The Council approved the TSS-1 work plan for 1992-1993; authorized the Administrator to make such changes as were necessary to the work plan during its implementation; requested that a TSS-1 work plan for 1994-1995 be submitted to the Council in 1993; encouraged, through the catalytic use of TSS-1, more effective use of the agencies' analytical capacities in support of Governments at the policy and programme levels; and requested the Administrator to provide an update of the cost study, taking into account the cost of technical services provided specifically under TSS-1.

With regard to administrative and operational support services, the Council decided that if non-United Nations agents were designated as providers of support services, they would be reimbursed from the IPF sub-line at rates not to exceed those established for the United Nations agencies subject to the new regime as well as for OPS. National NGOs responsible for programme/project implementation should h ve the necessary management staff and might be reimbursed for their services from project budgets.

The Council approved a proposal made by the Administrator to provide the five agencies subject to the new regime (Food and Agriculture Organization of the United Nations, ILO, UNESCO, United Nations Industrial Development Organization and the former Department of Technical Cooperation for Development (DTCD)) with a reasonable degree of protection from exchange rate movements, taking into account the principle of symmetry in compensatory payments between UNDP and the agencies. The Administrator was asked to include in his annual review of the financial situation information on actual payments made or recoveries achieved in connection with the scheme.

Net contributor status

In response to a 1991 Governing Council decision on preparations for the fifth programming cycle,[37] the Administrator submitted a report[67] on consultations with countries having a per capita GNP of above $3,000 (except for small island developing countries) regarding their being asked to contribute to the costs of field offices located there. By an addendum to his report, the Administrator transmitted a communication from Bahrain indicating that it would bear the costs of the UNDP office there and pay 60 per cent of the principal of arrears.

On 14 February,[68] the Council noted Bahrain's proposed settlement of outstanding field cost obligations. It approved the proposed method for distributing local office costs between countries covered by a field office with regional responsibilities and the host country, namely that field office costs attributable to countries other than the host would be covered by the country concerned. The Administrator was asked to inform the Council of the manner in which countries had met their fourth cycle (1987-1991) net contributor obligations, the final IPFs for the countries concerned and the projected implications of the implementation of the 1991 decision[37] on the maintenance of field offices in those countries and on the 1994-1995 budget.

Organizational issues

Staff-related matters

In response to a 1991 Governing Council decision,[63] the Administrator in March 1992 submitted a report[69] on the senior management structure of UNDP. The report outlined the legislative background, as well as the context in which efforts to improve effectiveness and efficiency within UNDP had been undertaken. It described modalities aimed at strengthening UNDP's policy and strategy formulation capacity and dealt with issues relating to improved programme quality and accountability. The report also described a pilot exercise in enhanced divisional management and outlined the structure and functions of the new Bureau of External Relations, which included the Governing Council secretariat, the legal status of which was defined. Issues concerning OPS were also discused.

The Administrator concluded that a restructured UNDP, with a clearly defined mission, focused strategic approach and strengthened management capacity, was in a strong position to respond to the increasing development challenges facing the international community. He intended to keep UNDP's functioning under review.

On 26 May,[70] the Council asked the Administrator to continue to review the senior management structure and to report to it in 1993. It reaffirmed the need to strengthen UNDP's capacity for institutional strategic planning and the need to take full advantage of management decentralization. It invited the Administrator to designate an existing UNDP unit to have overall responsibility for institutional strategic planning and urged him to continue to improve the managerial qualities and capacities of his staff. Recognizing the steps taken to launch a new Division Chief concept, the Council encouraged the Administrator to continue to develop the concept, and in formulating proposals to increase decentralization of authority to the field, to ensure adequate monitoring, accounting, auditing, backstopping and personnel appraisal, and clear lines of responsibility. The Administrator was asked to invite the Board of External Auditors to UNDP to examine the accountability arrangements for and the effectiveness of the new Division Chief concept and to report to the Council in 1993 on the implementation of the decision.

Proposal on the location of UNDP

On 26 May,[71] the Governing Council noted with appreciation the proposal by Germany to host the headquarters of UNDP, of its affiliated funds and of UNFPA in Bonn from 1996 onwards. The Council requested the Administrator to: examine in consultation with UNDP members the potential impact of such relocation on the objective of reforming the United Nations system of operational activities for development; to consult with UNDP members on the full range of logistical and related financial, administrative and representational implications of such a relocation; and to provide to the Council, not later than February 1993, a report on the results of the implementation of the decision.

Coordination with other organizations

On 26 May,[72] the Governing Council encouraged the Administrator to strengthen UNDP's interaction with other development institutions, including international and regional finance institutions, to establish the greatest possible coordination, avoid duplication and achieve the best use of comparative advantage in technical cooperation, within the context of the national development priorities of recipient countries. It asked the Administrator to report to the Council on the issue in 1993.

REFERENCES

[1]DP/1993/10 & Add.1-5. [2]E/1992/28. [3]Ibid. (dec. 92/1). [4]Ibid. (dec. 92/2). [5]Ibid. (dec. 92/3). [6]Ibid. (dec. 92/12). [7]Ibid. (dec. 92/41). [8]Ibid. (dec. 92/45). [9]Ibid. (dec. 92/46). [10]Ibid. (dec. 92/47). [11]E/1992/L.23. [12]DP/1992/47. [13]DP/1992/70. [14]E/1992/28 (dec. 92/10). [15]Ibid. (dec. 92/25). [16]DP/1992/63. [17]E/1992/28 (dec. 92/26). [18]Ibid. (dec. 92/27). [19]Ibid. (dec. 92/28). [20]YUN 1991, p. 397, GA res. 46/151, annex, 18 Dec. 1991.
[21]GA res. 44/211, 22 Dec. 1989. [22]DP/1992/46. [23]E/1992/28 (dec. 92/23). [24]YUN 1991, p. 375. [25]DP/1992/21. [26]YUN 1991, p. 382. [27]E/1992/28 (dec. 92/22). [28]DP/1992/20. [29]E/1992/28 (dec. 92/24). [30]DP/1993/66. [31]E/1992/28 (dec. 92/9). [32]DP/1992/22. [33]YUN 1991, p. 356, GA res. 40/206, 20 Dec. 1991. [34]E/1992/28 (dec. 92/30). [35]E/1990/29 (dec. 90/34). [36]E/1992/28 (dec. 92/31). [37]YUN 1991, p. 377. [38]E/1992/28 (dec. 92/8). [39]DP/1992/51. [40]E/1992/28 (dec. 92/29). [41]Ibid. (dec. 92/43). [42]DP/1993/44 & Add.1-3 & Corr.1. [43]E/1992/28 (dec. 92/36). [44]YUN 1991, p. 378. [45]DP/1992/40. [46]YUN 1991, p. 380. [47]DP/1992/39. [48]E/1992/28 (dec. 92/37). [49]A/46/5/Add.1. [50]A/46/510. [51]DP/1992/42 & Add.1. [52]DP/1992/41. [53]E/1992/28 (dec. 92/38). [54]DP/1992/43. [55]DP/1990/67. [56]E/1992/28 (dec. 92/39). [57]YUN 1983, p. 462. [58]DP/1992/44. [59]E/1992/28 (dec. 92/40). [60]DP/1993/44/Add.3. [61]DP/1993/44/Add.2. [62]YUN 1991, p. 383. [63]Ibid., p. 384. [64]DP/1992/7. [65]E/1992/28 (dec. 92/7). [66]DP/1992/23 & Add.1. [67]DP/1992/6 & Add.1. [68]E/1992/28 (dec. 92/6). [69]DP/1992/45. [70]E/1992/28 (dec. 92/42). [71]Ibid. (dec. 92/44). [72]Ibid. (dec. 92/15).

Other technical cooperation

UN programmes

On 1 March, the Department of Economic and Social Development (DESD) was established as part of the restructuring of the United Nations Secretariat by the Secretary-General. The new Department's responsibilities included those of the former Department of Technical Cooperation for Development (DTCD). In addition to DESD, organizations engaged in providing technical cooperation assistance for economic and social development during 1992 included the regional commissions, the Centre for Human Rights, the United Nations Office at Vienna, the United Nations International Drug Control Programme, the Office of Legal Affairs, the United Nations Centre for Human Settlements, UNCTAD and UNEP.

In 1992, the organizational entities of the United Nations delivered a technical cooperation programme of $243 million, compared with $285 million in 1991, representing a 15 per cent decrease in project expenditures.

DESD activities

In his annual report to the UNDP Governing Council on technical cooperation activities,[1] the Secretary-General stated that, in 1992, DESD had 918 technical cooperation projects under execution, with a total delivery of some $140.7 million against budgets of $185 million.

Projects financed by UNDP represented $87.2 million; those by trust funds, $28.7 million; those by UNFPA, $14.1 million; and by the United Nations regular programme of technical cooperation, $10.7 million.

On a geographical basis, the DESD-executed programme included expenditures of $61.9 million in Africa; $37.6 million in the Middle East, Mediterranean, Europe and for interregional programmes; $34.6 million in Asia and the Pacific; and $6.6 million in the Americas. Project delivery in Africa remained the largest, with a 39 per cent share of the total sum.

Distribution of expenditures by substantive sectors was as follows: natural resources and energy, $47.3 million; development policy, $28.7 million; public administration and finance, $25.3 million; statistics, $16.7 million; population, $7.6 million; the United Nations Educational and Training Programme for Southern Africa (UNETPSA), $5.8 million; social development, $4.5 million; and others, $4.8 million. Natural resources and energy, which included work in minerals, energy, water and infrastructure, comprised 34 per cent of the total $140.7 million.

By component, DESD delivery included $83.9 million for project personnel; $21.2 million for training; $19.8 million for equipment; $8.8 million for subcontracted services; and $7 million for miscellaneous expenses.

In addition to a number of new initiatives, such as peace-building, improvement of governance, electoral administration, privatization, investing in Central American development and assistance to economies in transition and to newly independent States, DESD continued its efforts in relation to Africa and LDCs, environment, evaluation, women in development and technical cooperation among developing countries (TCDC).

In-depth evaluations were undertaken in respect of 29 projects during 1992. Problems identified in the evaluations included shortcomings in project selection and design; scarcity and too-rapid turnover of national staff; and lack of detail and analysis in the area of human resources development.

Expenditures for fellowships and training amounted to $21.2 million in 1992. Africa had the largest share, 54 per cent, or $11.4 million; Asia and the Pacific, 27 per cent, or $5.8 million; the Mediterranean, Middle East and interregional programmes, 18 per cent, or $3.7 million; and the Americas, 0.1 per cent, or $0.3 million.

DESD implemented a total of 3,438 training awards, including fellowships, study tours, seminars and workshops. Most placements were in the United States, followed by South Africa, the United Kingdom and Australia.

The tenth meeting of Senior Fellowship Officers, held under DESD auspices at the ILO International Training Centre (Turin, Italy, 24-26 March), reconfirmed the role of the DESD office in Geneva as the focal point for the United Nations system inter-agency fellowships.

DESD continued to cooperate with the United Nations Department of Political Affairs on UNETPSA. In 1992, contributions and pledges amounted to over $5.3 million, a decrease from the previous year's $5.9 million. Policy directives for funding in South Africa and abroad emphasized building the institutional capacity of NGOs to provide black leadership skills training to facilitate the transition to a non-racial, democratic system and training black lawyers and judges for the administration of justice in post-apartheid South Africa.

In response to a 1991 Governing Council request,[2] the Administrator in April submitted a report[3] on options for closer cooperation between the former DTCD and UNDP. He stated that its conclusions had been overtaken by the restructuring within the United Nations. Consequently, he proposed that the Council's consideration of the issue should be postponed until DESD was fully established.

On 26 May,[4] the Council took note of the Secretary-General's report on the 1991 technical cooperation activities of the United Nations[5] and of the report of the Administrator on cooperation between the former DTCD and UNDP. It noted the Administrator's view that the issue of in-depth consideration of closer cooperation between the new DESD and UNDP should be taken up again after the Department was fully established. It requested the Administrator to provide information on options of cooperation between DESD and UNDP, if possible for the Council's 1993 session.

The Council stressed the importance of collaboration between DESD and UNDP in those areas where the Department had already developed the necessary technical expertise, capacity and experience. It welcomed DESD's efforts to help increase national capacities for programme management and project execution, and invited it to continue its activities relating to LDCs, environment, TCDC, women in development, economies in transition and other initiatives.

United Nations Volunteers

On 26 May,[6] the Governing Council, having considered the Administrator's report on UNV for 1990-1991,[2] requested him to continue to strengthen the universal character of recruitment for the UNV programme, including increasing the participation of volunteers from underrepresented countries, of women and of older persons; to make full use of more detailed post and job descriptions for better matching of skills with assignments; to expand training and briefing for volunteers; and to help to formulate programmes in which UNV specialists and Domestic Development Services field workers contributed to development activities, with special emphasis on responding to ideas from local, low-income communities to build up their capacity to deal with their development needs.

The Council encouraged UNV to seek a more clearly defined role for volunteers in development cooperation and to develop its current and future strategy regarding the focus of work. It reiterated its request to the Administrator to find means to support Domestic Development Services activities and their regional networks, and encouraged him to apply funding where appropriate from SPR.

It urged the Administrator to work with Governments and the United Nations system in raising awareness of the potential contribution that volunteers could make to development, and to promote greater mobilization of human resources in developing countries through, among other things, support to local NGOs and community-based organizations and mixed teams of international and national volunteers in UNV activities. The Council welcomed UNV's involvement in the humanitarian relief area and related fields, ranging from capacity-building in disaster prevention, preparedness and mitigation to rehabilitation and reconstruction activities.

The Administrator was requested to ensure that UNV activities would be consistent with the coordination to be exercised by the United Nations Department of Humanitarian Affairs (DHA); to consider ways of securing start-up funding for the early fielding of volunteers in time of emergencies, particularly through access to DHA's central emergency revolving fund; and to ensure funding for middle- and long-term UNV involvement through access to SPR and to trust funds. The Council decided that, except in situations where special financing was available for volunteers, the external costs of UNV specialists should be charged to project budgets on the basis of a pro forma cost, starting with new contracts as at 1 July 1992. It also decided that the income accruing annually to the Special Voluntary Fund as of 1 January 1992 from voluntary general contributions and interest income be utilized to support such activities as pilot and experimental projects; the briefing of UNV specialists and training of Domestic Development Services country specialists and field workers, government officials and NGO representatives; and special recruitment campaigns. The Council invited all UNDP members to increase contributions to the Special Voluntary Fund and asked the Administrator to report to it in 1994 on the implementation of the decision.

Technical cooperation among developing countries

In his annual report for 1992,[7] the UNDP Administrator stated that solid progress had been made in the promotion of TCDC. Information activities on TCDC were intensified, targeting Governments, the United Nations development system, intergovernmental organizations, NGOs and other key actors in the development process using a training-of-trainers scheme. A comprehensive trainers' guide was prepared and distributed to field offices and Governments, and information kits on TCDC were provided. Four issues of the *Cooperation South* magazine were published, and a newsletter was produced on a regular basis.

A number of intercountry workshops took place covering, for example, air transport (Ethiopia); networking among grass-roots women's organizations (Ghana); TCDC aid coordination and resource mobilization (Seychelles); meat-preservation technologies (Senegal); macroeconomic planning for island countries (Fiji); spare parts reconditioning (Cuba); technical cooperation for transition (Commonwealth of Independent States, the Baltic States and Poland); urban management (Malaysia), and intellectual property and trade (Philippines).

Two regional workshops (Latin America and the Arab region) were held to strengthen the role of TCDC national focal points in promoting and advising on the application of TCDC. The fifth TCDC Focal Point Meeting of United Nations organizations (New York, 15 and 16 July) worked on draft guidelines for the review of policies and procedures in the United Nations development system concerning TCDC.

DESD worked with the UNDP Special Unit for TCDC in providing support to Ecuador and 21 other countries for an exercise, held at Quito, to identify possible TCDC arrangements in connection with mining and its environmental impact. In preparation for the exercise, missions were conducted to several countries in Latin America and the Caribbean and in Asia. The exercise resulted in 177 project agreements.

Secretary-General's report. In response to **decision 1992/205** of 7 February, by which the Economic and Social Council placed an item on TCDC on the agenda of its 1992 substantive session, the Secretary-General in June submitted to the Council a report[8] on TCDC as a modality in formulating, preparing, executing and evaluating projects implemented by the United Nations system in the economic, social and related fields. The report noted that the relevance of TCDC as a modality in strengthening national capabilities and building collective self-reliance had been given special impetus with the 1978 adoption of the Buenos Aires Plan of Action for Promoting and Implementing

TCDC.[9] The continuing validity of the Plan of Action had been repeatedly reaffirmed by various United Nations bodies.

The report discussed application of the modality, noting that it had not been fully put to use. TCDC needed to be seen as a key to the whole development effort, not as an alternative, but as a complement to the more conventional forms of development assistance.

The report recommended that all parties should inspire a change in attitude whereby TCDC would become appreciated and applied as an effective, less costly and relevant modality of cooperation. They should simplify the gathering and accessing of data on capacity availability in developing countries, use demonstration and pilot projects to test new approaches and refine initiatives, and strengthen the national TCDC focal points. It recommended that Governments encourage and facilitate the use of TCDC for programme and project implementation, adopt national policies favourable to its use in national development plans, strengthen or establish national focal points for TCDC, identify and facilitate sectors where TCDC could be more widely applied, sensitize officials in governmental institutions, the private sector and NGOs on the comparative advantages of TCDC for the exchange of technology, expertise and experience, and strengthen and streamline the matching of technical cooperation needs and capacities.

As to the United Nations development system, it should use TCDC in implementing programmes and projects by ensuring that it was given first consideration, both during the formulation and implementation process and through the involvement of field offices during project identification; ensure more focused efforts in using the capacities of developing countries; enhance the role of agencies in assisting Governments to identify needs and capacities for cooperation among developing countries; improve and expand the TCDC Information Referral System; encourage Governments, public and private institutions and NGOs to consider using TCDC in projects and to adopt policies favourable to its wider use; and assist Governments to apply the TCDC modality in preparing projects and programmes for cooperation regardless of the source of funds.

ECONOMIC AND SOCIAL COUNCIL ACTION

On 30 July 1992, the Economic and Social Council adopted **resolution 1992/41** without vote.

Technical cooperation among developing countries
The Economic and Social Council,

Reaffirming the continued validity and importance of all the recommendations of the Buenos Aires Plan of Action for Promoting and Implementing Technical Cooperation among Developing Countries in promoting technical cooperation among developing countries,

Reaffirming also the recommendation that the entire United Nations system dealing with development must be permeated by the spirit of technical cooperation among developing countries and that all relevant organizations of the United Nations system should play a prominent role as promoters and catalysts of technical cooperation among developing countries,

Recalling General Assembly resolutions 45/191 of 21 December 1990 and 46/143 of 17 December 1991 on developing human resources for development,

Recognizing that increased cooperation is taking place among developing countries and their institutions through the sharing of expertise, experience and facilities,

Recognizing also that technical cooperation among developing countries is an effective tool for implementing development programmes and projects through the use of relevant experience and expertise and could also facilitate trade among developing countries,

Reiterating that developing countries have a primary responsibility for promoting technical cooperation among themselves, and that developed countries and the United Nations system should assist and support such activities and should play a prominent role as promoters and catalysts of technical cooperation among developing countries, in accordance with the Buenos Aires Plan of Action,

Noting with appreciation the recent measures taken by organizations of the United Nations system to identify technical cooperation among developing countries as a priority theme, to provide increased support to promotional activities and to arrange for monitoring technical cooperation among developing countries through the mechanisms established for project appraisal and approval,

Concerned, however, that technical cooperation among developing countries since the adoption of the Buenos Aires Plan of Action has not been widespread and is still marginally applied in the implementation of programmes and projects,

1. *Calls upon* all parties in the development effort to make concerted, planned and vigorous endeavours to benefit from utilization of the capacities of developing countries by giving their full support and first consideration to the use of the modality of technical cooperation among developing countries;

2. *Urges* all parties to enhance the scope and application of the modality in work carried out at all stages of the project cycle;

3. *Requests* all parties to increase support activities aimed at enhancing awareness in government institutions, the private sector and non-governmental organizations of the modality of technical cooperation among developing countries;

4. *Calls for* increased use, where appropriate, by developed country partners of consultants from developing countries so as, *inter alia*, to improve the cost-effectiveness of projects and programmes;

5. *Urges* the United Nations Development Programme and other organizations of the United Nations system dealing with development to consider improvements to the working and scope of the Information Referral System, to improve and expand data and information on existing technical capabilities in developing countries through that System and to enhance access to such information;

6. *Also urges* the United Nations Development Programme and other organizations of the United Nations system dealing with development to intensify, within existing resources, their efforts to build national capacity for human resources development in developing countries;

7. *Invites* all countries and organizations of the United Nations system dealing with development to review further their policies and practices to facilitate the use of technical cooperation among developing countries in the design, formulation, implementation and evaluation of programmes and projects supported by them;

8. *Urges* developing countries to encourage greater use of technical cooperation among developing countries in the implementation of national development activities and projects, including procurement practices;

9. *Invites* developing countries to strengthen their national focal points for technical cooperation among developing countries to enable them to promote more effectively and monitor progress in such cooperation;

10. *Requests* the Secretary-General to report to the Economic and Social Council at its substantive session of 1994 on his assessment of the implementation of the present resolution.

Economic and Social Council resolution 1992/41

30 July 1992   Meeting 41   Adopted without vote

Draft by Vice-President (E/1992/L.39), based on informal consultations on draft by Pakistan for Group of 77 and China (E/1992/L.29); agenda item 5.
Meeting numbers. ESC 36, 41.

REFERENCES

[1]DP/1993/39 & Add.1-3. [2]YUN 1991, p. 387. [3]DP/1992/36. [4]E/1992/28 (dec. 92/34). [5]YUN 1991, p. 385. [6]E/1992/28 (dec. 92/35). [7]DP/1993/10/Add.1. [8]E/1992/75. [9]YUN 1978, p. 467.

UN Capital Development Fund

During 1992,[1] an estimated $48.7 million in resources was made available to UNCDF, a multilateral agency providing small-scale assistance to officially designated LDCs and other countries regarded as LDCs. The total comprised $39.6 million in voluntary contributions, $8 million in other income, $700,000 in loan repayments, and a $400,000 reduction in operational reserve. A further $101.2 million was available from previous years.

Resources used during the year totalled $57.5 million, including $48 million in project expenditures, $4.5 million in administrative expenditures and $5 million in loans disbursed.

Seventeen new projects were approved by UNCDF in 1992. They included an aquaculture project in Bangladesh, support to rural self-help development activities and a water supply and sanitation project in the Central African Republic, rural water supply and sanitation projects in Equatorial Guinea and Guinea-Bissau, a fisheries rehabilitation project in Eritrea, a guarantee fund and credit line for micro-enterprises in Madagascar, a rural motorized transport project in Malawi, road rehabilitation in Mozambique, a small marketing infrastructure project in Nepal, construction of a bridge in Nicaragua, integrated rural development in the Niger and road reconstruction and rehabilitation in Sierra Leone.

In his annual report for 1992,[2] the UNDP Administrator stated that an internal management review was conducted both at headquarters and in the field to analyse UNCDF programme development and delivery. A strategy based on area development emerged, although its implementation was constrained by a lack of resources. That strategy sought to take advantage of trends towards democratization and decentralization by working with Governments, community groups and NGOs in order to intensify participatory activities at the grass-roots level. With grass-roots level poverty reduction in LDCs as its major thrust, UNCDF continued to incorporate other themes into its programming, particularly the environment and women in development.

REFERENCES
[1]DP/1993/42. [2]DP/1993/10/Add.1.

Chapter III

Special economic, humanitarian and disaster relief assistance

In 1992, in response to an escalation of natural disasters, civil strife and other emergencies, the United Nations implemented a more unified and strengthened approach to special economic, humanitarian and disaster relief assistance. The Secretary-General created a new Department of Humanitarian Affairs (DHA), absorbing the Office of the United Nations Disaster Relief Coordinator, in order to deal more comprehensively with the consequences of humanitarian emergencies which required ever-mounting humanitarian relief assistance. The General Assembly emphasized the leadership role of the Secretary-General in ensuring rapid and coordinated response of the United Nations system to these humanitarian emergencies and invited States to increase the resources of the Central Emergency Revolving Fund (resolution 47/168).

A System-Wide Plan of Action for African Economic Recovery and Development, developed to contribute to the implementation of the United Nations New Agenda for the Development of Africa in the 1990s, succeeded the United Nations Programme of Action for African Economic Recovery and Development 1986-1990. Special economic assistance was provided to Benin, the Central African Republic, Chad, Djibouti, Madagascar and the frontline States bordering South Africa, as well as to Vanuatu and Yemen. Organizations of the United Nations system, under the coordination of DHA, provided humanitarian and emergency assistance to countries of the Horn of Africa through the Special Emergency Programme for that subregion. Angola, Liberia, Mozambique, Somalia and the Sudan also received assistance.

DHA and United Nations agencies also provided assistance for the drought emergency in southern Africa, to the countries of sub-Saharan Africa and to the Sudano-Sahelian region.

Countries that received United Nations disaster relief assistance in 1992 included a number of South Pacific countries following cyclones, Nicaragua following a volcanic eruption and an earthquake, Pakistan following storms and floods and the Philippines in the light of the continued activity of the Mount Pinatubo volcano.

The Organization continued to provide rehabilitation and reconstruction assistance to Afghanistan, Lebanon and Liberia and to aid efforts to mitigate the consequences of the Chernobyl nuclear powerplant disaster.

Special economic assistance

The United Nations continued in 1992 to provide special assistance to a number of developing countries faced with particularly severe economic problems. A wide range of adverse economic conditions, often accompanied by damaging climatic events, armed conflict or civil strife, jeopardized development in those countries. Several organizations of the United Nations system participated in implementing the United Nations New Agenda for the Development of Africa in the 1990s and elaborating the System-Wide Plan of Action for African Economic Recovery and Development.

Critical situation in Africa

New agenda for African development

During 1992, several United Nations forums discussed implementation of the United Nations New Agenda for the Development of Africa in the 1990s, adopted by the General Assembly in 1991.[1] The New Agenda resulted from the 1991 final review and appraisal[2] of the United Nations Programme of Action for African Economic Recovery and Development 1986-1990, adopted by the Assembly in 1986.[3]

In an effort to advance implementation of the New Agenda, the Secretary-General established the Panel of High-Level Personalities on African Development to assist and advise him. The 12-member panel, comprising specialists on African development issues from both within and outside the United Nations, held its first meeting at Geneva on 28 December 1992.

UNCTAD action. In February,[4] the United Nations Conference on Trade and Development, at its eighth session (UNCTAD VIII) (see next chapter), adopted the Cartagena Commitment, in which it identified the New Agenda and the United Nations System-Wide Plan of Action for African Economic Recovery and Development (see below) as areas requiring intensified international cooperation for development. It requested the UNCTAD Trade and Development Board (TDB) to respond fully to requests by the General Assembly for consideration of particular issues, notably UNCTAD's contribution to the New Agenda.

In a July note,[5] the UNCTAD Secretary-General presented to TDB proposals for action to be taken as UNCTAD's contribution to the implementation of the New Agenda and the System-Wide Plan of Action. The report also examined the implications of the proposals for UNCTAD's work and gave the background to the development of the System-Wide Plan. The report identified a number of areas where UNCTAD could make a contribution to the New Agenda's implementation: achievement of sustained and sustainable growth; population, environment and development; intensification of the democratization process; the human dimension; promotion of regional cooperation and integration; South/South cooperation; agriculture, rural development and food security; trade, commodities and diversification; trade; solution of Africa's debt problem; resource flows; investment promotion; technology; the role of non-governmental organizations (NGOs); and follow-up, monitoring and implementation.

On 14 October,[6] TDB took note of the report of its Sessional Committee II on the New Agenda and endorsed its decision that the UNCTAD Secretary-General should be requested to undertake Africa-specific studies and to present progress reports on UNCTAD's contribution to the New Agenda's implementation to TDB's 1993 spring session. In addition, the UNCTAD secretariat should give priority to Africa in developing available technical cooperation resources and ensure that its technical cooperation activities, within the context of the New Agenda, responded to the needs of African countries. Extrabudgetary resources should also be sought to intensify UNCTAD's contribution to the New Agenda. The work of UNCTAD intergovernmental bodies should take the New Agenda into account and TDB should evaluate UNCTAD's contribution to its implementation every two years, taking into account the follow-up and monitoring mechanisms and timetable set up by the General Assembly.

UNDP action. In response to a 1991 decision of the United Nations Development Programme (UNDP) Governing Council,[7] the UNDP Administrator submitted in March 1992 a report[8] on UNDP's role in African economic recovery and development.

For the fifth programming cycle (1992-1996), UNDP allocated over 50 per cent of indicative planning figure (IPF) resources to Africa. It would also support the New Agenda through its country programmes, the intercountry programme for Africa and activities under Special Programme Resources (SPR). It was pursuing an integrated approach focusing on human development in country programmes and six areas listed in a 1990 Governing Council decision[9]—poverty eradication and grass-roots participation in development; environ-

mental problems and natural resource management; management development; technical cooperation among developing countries; transfer and adaptation of technology for development; and women in development. At the regional level, UNDP would assist African economic recovery through its fifth intercountry programme, which concentrated on three major areas of the New Agenda: regional cooperation and integration; long-term strategic planning; and fostering an enabling environment for human development. In addition, UNDP proposed to use part of the $10 million of SPR funds allocated for African economic recovery and development to assist African countries in drawing up national long-term perspectives to provide a framework for their development in the 1990s and beyond. SPR funding would also help to support a continental programme for African capacity-building. It would continue to promote the coordination of activities covered by the Regional Bureau for Africa.

In his annual report for 1992,[10] the Administrator noted that the entire management plan of the Regional Bureau for Africa for the year was aligned with the major objectives of the New Agenda.

On 26 May,[11] the Governing Council requested the Administrator to work in concert with the United Nations system to implement all elements of the New Agenda; to work closely with the Under-Secretary-General for Humanitarian Affairs to ensure a coordinated and effective international response to the devastating drought situation, especially in eastern and southern Africa; and to assist in mobilizing additional resources, in particular from consultative groups, round-table meetings and co-financing, for programmes in the African region during the fifth programming cycle. It also requested him to report to the Council at its 1993 session, providing an analysis of the linkages and relationships among national long-term perspective studies, the UNDP/World Bank African Capacity-Building Initiative and human development strategies, and how they related to the application of the programme approach. The Council called on African countries to pursue vigorously their responsibility and commitment under the New Agenda to achieve sustained and sustainable growth and development, to promote cooperation and regional and subregional integration, to intensify the process of democratization, to encourage investment and to integrate population issues into the development process. It called on the international community to assist African countries to achieve accelerated growth and human-centred development on a sustainable basis through finding durable solutions to the African debt crisis, providing adequate resource flows, diversification of economies, enhanced market access, and support of regional integration.

System-Wide Plan of Action

In August 1992, the Secretary-General submitted to the Committee for Programming and Coordination (CPC) a report on the System-Wide Plan of Action for African Economic Recovery and Development,[12] prepared in response to a recommendation of CPC at its 1990 session and endorsed later that year by the Economic and Social Council.[13] The Plan encompassed the financial institutions and operational funds and programmes of the United Nations system, as well as the technical cooperation activities of the specialized agencies. Its objectives were to provide a dynamic and flexible framework for concerted and coordinated action by the system to assist Africa in achieving sustained and sustainable growth and development in the 1990s and beyond; to create a more supportive international economic environment; and to assist African Governments in their efforts to transform the structure of their economies and promote economic integration, collective self-reliance, popular participation, adequate human and institutional capacities and employment creation.

The Plan's overall strategy was to maximize the system's contribution to African countries and the international community in their efforts to realize the objectives of the New Agenda for African Development.

CPC action. CPC[14] recommended that the Secretary-General launch, at the earliest possible time, the System-Wide Plan of Action and the New Agenda for the Development of Africa; that the Plan's priorities be used as guidelines for the system's activities in the area of African development; that the Plan be monitored and updated within the framework of the United Nations Inter-Agency Task Force for African Economic Recovery and Development; and that the process of updating the Plan should be carried out after each review, by the General Assembly, of the implementation of the New Agenda.

Assistance to Benin, the Central African Republic and Madagascar

In response to a 1990 General Assembly resolution,[15] the Secretary-General submitted in August 1992 a report,[16] prepared by UNDP, on special economic assistance to Benin, the Central African Republic, Madagascar and a number of other countries (see below). The report stated that, as a result of a severe financial crisis, social and economic development in Benin had suffered a severe slow-down. With UNDP assistance, Benin held a Round-Table Conference of Donors (Geneva, 2 and 3 April), at which Benin's macro-economic policies, sectoral strategies, social development strategy and programme of technical assistance were discussed. Benin reported on the positive results of the implementation of its first structural adjustment programme and indicated that the second structural adjustment programme aimed to bring its public finances closer to equilibrium, promote the banking and private sectors, continue reform in the public sector and rationalize the institutional framework. Total pledges to Benin by donors at the Round-Table Conference, at which sectoral strategies and priorities were presented, exceeded requirements for the period 1992-1994. As a follow-up to the Conference, the specific needs of each sector would be considered at sectoral consultations.

Among the leading priorities of the Central African Republic's development plan and structural adjustment programme were a sustainable increase in national output; strengthening of the public administration system; overcoming constraints to external trade and communications imposed by the land-locked situation; social and human resources development; environmental preservation; and strengthening of national planning and socio-economic management. As follow-up to a 1991 Round-Table Conference of Donors, consultations on the health sector between the Government and donors were scheduled for November, with consultations on education, training and employment planned for a later stage. Estimates of needs to be met in 1992 amounted to 59.8 billion CFA francs.

During the 1991-1992 period, Madagascar experienced both a cyclone and drought. International assistance focused first on food aid, medicines and medical supplies to meet the emergency situation. Priority for subsequent action was the rehabilitation of the Dabara canal, for which a food-for-work programme was established with assistance provided by UNDP, the World Food Programme (WFP), the French Caisse centrale de Coopération économique, Swiss Cooperation and USAID. In April 1992, an assessment mission, funded by Swiss Cooperation, evaluated the situation and drew up information to enable donors to decide on their follow-up activities. The mission's report observed good donor response and concluded that the food-for-work programme proved to be a good option. The two remaining areas of need were the total rehabilitation of the irrigation network and the establishment of a rational, well-structured system of water management. In mid-May, donor agencies and institutions entered into consultations with a view to selecting from proposals and making commitments for the continuation of work.

With regard to the drought, a joint government/multi-donor mission in May identified two priorities for action: provision of emergency food and formulation of medium- and long-term development policies for the south.

GENERAL ASSEMBLY ACTION

On 18 December 1992, the General Assembly, on the recommendation of the Second (Economic and Financial) Committee, adopted **resolution 47/159** without vote.

Assistance to Benin, the Central African Republic and Madagascar

The General Assembly,

Recalling its resolution 45/230 of 21 December 1990, on assistance to Benin, the Central African Republic, Ecuador, Madagascar and Vanuatu, and its previous resolutions on assistance to those countries,

Having considered the relevant report of the Secretary-General,

Concerned at the continuing need for assistance in those countries, particularly since they are adversely affected by natural disasters,

Noting that, despite the structural adjustment programmes carried out by those countries, on the whole their economic and financial performance for the past two years has continued to be poor, and stressing the need for vigorous support of these programmes and for action to alleviate the impact of natural disasters and of the adjustment policies being implemented, especially in the social sphere,

Noting also that the financial crisis that Benin is undergoing has led to a slowing down of its economic and social development, and that the disastrous consequences of repeated floods during the past ten years, alternating with periods of drought and pluviometric disturbances, are a major impediment to the implementation of development policies and strategies,

Noting further the grave difficulties that the Government of the Central African Republic has continued to face since 1982 in achieving the objectives of its development programme, owing to the harmful effects of the international economic situation, and recognizing the need to provide it with supplementary resources so as to enable it to achieve those objectives,

Noting the particularly difficult problems faced by island developing countries in responding to negative and special economic circumstances, referred to in the report of the Secretary-General called for in General Assembly resolution 45/202 of 21 December 1990, that the economic and social development efforts of Madagascar, an island developing country, are being thwarted by the adverse effects of the cyclones, floods and drought that afflict that country periodically and that the implementation of reconstruction and rehabilitation programmes requires the mobilization of substantial resources that are beyond the real means of the country,

Concerned at the devastating effects of natural and other disasters on the environment and their adverse effects on the economy,

Recalling its resolution 44/236 of 22 December 1989 on the International Decade for Natural Disaster Reduction,

Having heard the statements of Member States at its forty-seventh session on the situations currently prevailing in those countries,

1. *Expresses its appreciation* to the Secretary-General, Member States, the specialized agencies and other organizations of the United Nations system, and regional, interregional, intergovernmental and non-governmental organizations for the assistance they have provided or pledged to those countries;

2. *Notes* the efforts undertaken by the Governments of those countries to overcome their economic and financial difficulties and to alleviate the catastrophic effects of natural disasters;

3. *Reaffirms* that all Governments and international organizations should fulfil the commitments undertaken within the framework of the Declaration on International Economic Cooperation, in particular the Revitalization of Economic Growth and Development of the Developing Countries, contained in the annex to its resolution S-18/3 of 1 May 1990, the International Development Strategy for the Fourth United Nations Development Decade, contained in the annex to its resolution 45/199 of 21 December 1990, the Paris Declaration and the Programme of Action for the Least Developed Countries for the 1990s, the United Nations New Agenda for the Development of Africa in the 1990s, the Cartagena Commitment, the Rio Declaration on Environment and Development, and Agenda 21;

4. *Notes with concern* that the assistance made available to those countries has not always been adequate to meet their urgent requirements and that additional assistance is needed;

5. *Appeals* to States, the international financial institutions of the United Nations, humanitarian organizations and voluntary agencies to respond generously and urgently to the needs of those countries and to continue and increase their assistance in response to the reconstruction, economic recovery and development needs of those countries;

6. *Requests* the Secretary-General to continue to take the steps necessary and to mobilize the resources needed, in collaboration with the relevant organs, agencies and programmes of the United Nations system, in accordance with General Assembly resolution 45/230 on special programmes of economic assistance, to provide assistance for all disasters, natural or otherwise, striking those countries, in order to:

    (a) Meet any reconstruction needs resulting from disasters that have already occurred;

    (b) Implement preventive programmes to reduce the effects of future disasters, taking into account the International Framework of Action for the International Decade for Natural Disaster Reduction contained in the annex to General Assembly resolution 44/236;

7. *Also requests* the Secretary-General to submit to the General Assembly at its forty-ninth session a report on the implementation of the present resolution, containing:

    (a) The identification of priorities for action by the international community in those countries;

    (b) An assessment of the assistance actually received by those countries;

    (c) An assessment of needs still unmet and specific proposals for responding to them effectively.

General Assembly resolution 47/159

18 December 1992   Meeting 92   Adopted without vote

Approved by Second Committee (A/47/727/Add.1) without vote, 7 December (meeting 48); 29-nation draft (A.C.2/47/L.28/Rev.1), orally revised; agenda item 87 *(b)*.

Sponsors: Algeria, Angola, Bangladesh, Benin, Burkina Faso, Cameroon, Central African Republic, Congo, Côte d'Ivoire, Cuba, Djibouti, Ecuador, Egypt, El Salvador, Guinea-Bissau, Kuwait, Lesotho, Madagascar, Mali, Mauritania, Mozambique, Namibia, Nigeria, Senegal, Sri Lanka, Suriname, Togo, Tunisia, Yemen.
Meeting numbers. GA 47th session: 2nd Committee 25, 26, 28, 30, 34, 38, 40, 42, 45, 46, 48; plenary 92.

Chad

In response to a 1991 General Assembly resolution,[17] the Secretary-General submitted an August 1992 report,[16] prepared by UNDP, containing information on special economic assistance to Chad. The report stated that Chad's economy remained extremely fragile despite internal efforts and external assistance to redress the situation. The output of cereals continued to fall short of the subsistence needs of Chad's population, which was rapidly growing due to high fertility and the large number of returning Chadian refugees. To meet overall food needs, 106,000 tons of cereals were being sought from the international community.

Pursuant to the third (1990) Round-Table Conference of Donors to Chad, an agenda for consultations on the following sectors was drawn up for the 1992-1993 period during an in-country meeting in March 1992: health and social affairs (June 1992); promotion of the private sector (October 1992); environment and desertification (December 1992); rural development, food security and hydraulic resources (January 1993); and urban development (January 1993).

Among other assistance, the Office of the United Nations High Commissioner for Refugees (UNHCR) continued to promote voluntary repatriation and reintegration. In 1992, some 12,000 Chadians, out of a total case-load of 20,000, registered for voluntary repatriation and, by mid-May, 3,412 had been repatriated. UNHCR provided transportation to final destinations, domestic utensils, seeds and agricultural tools for repatriated Chadians. The Food and Agriculture Organization of the United Nations (FAO) covered such areas as food security, environmental conservation, combating desertification, strengthening rural institutions, development of human resources and promotion of better nutrition. With technical assistance from FAO, Chad was preparing a comprehensive food security programme. FAO was executing 19 field projects in Chad, at a total value of $28.6 million, of which eight projects valued at $1.2 million were funded through its technical cooperation programme.

WFP had three development projects under implementation in Chad in education, food for vulnerable groups and rural development, valued respectively at $23.9 million, $4.5 million and $2.4 million. The United Nations Department of Economic and Social Development was executing a total of 12 projects in Chad, valued at $3.7 million, covering social development, statistics, energy, and water and mineral resources.

GENERAL ASSEMBLY ACTION

On 18 December 1992, the General Assembly, on the recommendation of the Second Committee, adopted **resolution 47/156** without vote.

Special economic assistance to Chad

The General Assembly,

1. *Takes note* of the report of the Secretary-General;

2. *Invites* all States and competent United Nations organizations and programmes that participated actively in the conference of friends of Chad, held in Paris in 1991, to participate in the various round tables to be held at N'Djamena in 1993;

3. *Calls upon* the Secretary-General to keep the situation in Chad under review and to report thereon to the General Assembly at its forty-ninth session.

General Assembly resolution 47/156
18 December 1992   Meeting 92   Adopted without vote
Approved by Second Committee (A/47/727/Add.1) without vote, 24 November (meeting 45); 32-nation draft (A.C.2/47/L.19/Rev.1); agenda item 87*(b)*.
Sponsors: Algeria, Angola, Benin, Bosnia and Herzegovina, Burkina Faso, Cameroon, Cape Verde, Central African Republic, Chad, China, Colombia, Comoros, Congo, Costa Rica, Côte d'Ivoire, Djibouti, Egypt, Gabon, Guatemala, Guinea, Honduras, Mali, Mauritania, Morocco, Niger, Nigeria, Senegal, Singapore, Suriname, Togo, Zaire.
Meeting numbers. GA 47th session: 2nd Committee 25, 26, 28, 30, 34, 38, 40, 42, 45; plenary 92.

Djibouti

In response to a 1991 General Assembly resolution,[18] the Secretary-General submitted in August a report,[16] prepared by UNDP, containing information on special economic assistance to Djibouti. The situation in the Horn of Africa had resulted in an influx of over 100,000 refugees and displaced persons into Djibouti, swelling its population by 20 per cent and exacerbating the already serious food shortage caused by drought. Following a review of the situation in January, a consolidated inter-agency appeal for the Special Emergency Programme for the Horn of Africa (SEPHA) was launched on 1 February (see below, under "Humanitarian assistance activities") to support urgent activities to be undertaken in the region by the United Nations system and secure the resources required for their implementation in 1992. While the funding requested was substantial, the needs identified represented only a small part of the total humanitarian assistance required.

Six projects in Djibouti were proposed by the United Nations for priority funding, totalling an estimated $10.6 million: multisectoral assistance to 33,000 refugees in camps in Djibouti, strengthening camp infrastructure and providing primary education ($2.3 million); food assistance for refugees ($2.1 million); port and railroad rehabilitation ($5 million); strengthening health, nutrition, water and sanitation services ($500,000); recovery of peripheral health services ($280,000); and tuberculosis control ($306,000).

A second multi-donor development project for the reconstruction and development of Djibouti City was approved in the course of 1991-1992. Valued at $45.5 million, the project would provide the city with sanitation facilities and low-cost housing schemes. UNDP and the United Nations Capital Development Fund were financing a $4.5 million low-cost housing project to set up self-help construction schemes in the poorest areas of Djibouti City. There was also an ongoing $13.3 million sanitation and drainage project, funded by the African Development Bank, to protect urban water-supply systems from pollution.

GENERAL ASSEMBLY ACTION

On 18 December 1992, the General Assembly, on the recommendation of the Second Committee, adopted **resolution 47/157** without vote.

Assistance for the reconstruction and development of Djibouti

The General Assembly,

Recalling its resolution 46/175 of 19 December 1991 and its previous resolutions on economic assistance to Djibouti,

Recalling also the Paris Declaration and the Programme of Action for the Least Developed Countries for the 1990s, adopted by the Second United Nations Conference on the Least Developed Countries on 14 September 1990, as well as the mutual commitments undertaken on that occasion and the importance to be attached to the follow-up to that Conference,

Noting that the economic and social development efforts of Djibouti, which is included in the list of least developed countries, are constrained by the extremes of the local climate, for example, cyclical droughts and torrential rains, and floods such as those which occurred in 1989, and that the implementation of reconstruction and development programmes requires the deployment of resources that exceed the real capacities of the country,

Noting with concern that the situation in Djibouti has been adversely affected by recent events in the Horn of Africa, and noting the recent influx of over 100,000 refugees and persons displaced from their countries, which has, on the one hand, placed serious strains on the fragile economic, social and administrative infrastructure of the country and, on the other, raised serious security concerns,

Noting the extremely critical economic situation of Djibouti resulting from its geographical location and from the number of priority development projects that have been suspended in the light of the new critical international situation,

Taking note of the report of the Secretary-General,

Noting with gratitude the support provided to emergency relief operations during the floods in 1989 by various countries and intergovernmental and non-governmental organizations,

1. *Declares its solidarity* with the Government and people of Djibouti in the face of the devastating consequences of the torrential rains and floods and the new economic realities of Djibouti resulting in particular from the new critical situation in the Horn of Africa;

2. *Expresses its appreciation* to the Secretary-General for his efforts to make the international community aware of the difficulties faced by Djibouti in particular and the Horn of Africa in general;

3. *Invites* the United Nations system, in particular the United Nations Development Programme, to assist the Government of Djibouti, in the context of the scheduled round-table meeting, the Government of Djibouti in preparing an urgent programme of rehabilitation and reconstruction, as well as a sustainable and adequate long-term development programme;

4. *Calls upon* all States, all regional and interregional organizations, non-governmental organizations and other intergovernmental agencies, in particular the United Nations Development Programme, the United Nations Children's Fund, the World Food Programme, the United Nations Industrial Development Organization, the Food and Agriculture Organization of the United Nations, the International Fund for Agricultural Development and the World Bank, to provide Djibouti with substantial appropriate assistance, on both a bilateral and a multilateral basis, to enable it to cope with its special economic difficulties;

5. *Requests* the Secretary-General to continue his efforts to mobilize the resources necessary for an effective programme of financial, technical and material assistance to Djibouti;

6. *Also requests* the Secretary-General to prepare a study of the economic situation of Djibouti and of the progress made in the organization and implementation of the new special programme of economic assistance for that country, in time for the question to be considered by the General Assembly at its forty-eighth session.

General Assembly resolution 47/157

18 December 1992   Meeting 92   Adopted without vote

Approved by Second Committee (A/47/727/Add.1) without vote, 25 November (meeting 46); 32-nation draft (A/C.2/47/L.20/Rev.1), orally revised; agenda item 87 *(b)*.

Sponsors: Algeria, Bahrain, Bangladesh, Benin, Bosnia and Herzegovina, Burkina Faso, Cameroon, Chad, China, Colombia, Djibouti, Egypt, Ethiopia, Gabon, Jordan, Kuwait, Lebanon, Libyan Arab Jamahiriya, Madagascar, Mali, Mauritania, Morocco, Oman, Pakistan, Saudi Arabia, Senegal, Singapore, Sudan, Syrian Arab Republic, United Arab Emirates, United Republic of Tanzania, Yemen.

Meeting numbers. GA 47th session: 2nd Committee 25, 26, 28, 30, 34, 38, 40, 42, 45, 46; plenary 92.

Front-line States

In October, the Secretary-General submitted a report[19] on special assistance to front-line States and other States bordering on South Africa in response to a 1991 General Assembly resolution.[20] The report contained information from 10 Member States and 17 United Nations organizations describing activities undertaken by them to support the national and collective development and emergency programmes of the front-line States and neighbouring States.

Following a joint United Nations/Southern African Development Community (SADC) Consolidated Appeal, a pledging conference took place in June to address the drought emergency in southern Africa (DESA) (see below, under "Disasters").

On 18 December 1992, the General Assembly, on the recommendation of the Second Committee, adopted **resolution 47/163** without vote.

Special assistance to the front-line States

The General Assembly,

Recalling its resolution 46/172 of 19 December 1991,

Having considered the report of the Secretary-General on special assistance to front-line States and other bordering States,

Reaffirming the provisions of the Declaration on Apartheid and its Destructive Consequences in Southern Africa, contained in the annex to its resolution S-16/1 of 14 December 1989, in particular paragraph 9(e) thereof, in which the States Members of the United Nations decided to render all possible assistance to the front-line and neighbouring States to enable them to rebuild their economies, which have been adversely affected by past acts of aggression and destabilization,

Aware that the apartheid system in South Africa has aggravated economic and social problems confronting the front-line States and other neighbouring States,

Welcoming the recent positive developments in the region, including the holding of elections in Angola and the recently concluded General Peace Agreement for Mozambique, signed at Rome on 4 October 1992,

Recognizing the urgent and imperative need for all the parties in South Africa to implement fully the relevant provisions of Security Council resolutions 765(1992) of 16 July 1992 and 772(1992) of 17 August 1992,

Gravely concerned about the effects of the devastating drought that is currently ravaging the southern African region,

Welcoming with appreciation the positive response of the international community at the Pledging Conference for the Drought Emergency in Southern Africa, held at Geneva on 1 and 2 June 1992,

Conscious of the urgent need and responsibility of the international community to continue to deal with the drought situation and other problems affecting the region,

Mindful of Security Council resolutions 568(1985) of 21 June 1985, 571(1985) of 20 September 1985 and 581(1986) of 13 February 1986, in which the Council, *inter alia*, requested the international community to render assistance to the front-line States and other neighbouring States,

1. *Expresses its appreciation* to the Secretary-General for his efforts regarding assistance to the front-line States and other neighbouring States;

2. *Notes with appreciation* the assistance being rendered to the front-line States by donor countries and intergovernmental and non-governmental organizations;

3. *Expresses its appreciation* to the Secretary-General, donor countries and non-governmental organizations for the invaluable assistance they are rendering towards the alleviation of the effects of the drought in the southern African region;

4. *Expresses its deep concern* about the continuing adverse effects of past acts of aggression and destabilization in the region;

5. *Strongly urges* the international community to continue to provide, in a timely and effective manner, the financial, material and technical assistance necessary to enhance the individual and collective capacity of the front-line States and other neighbouring States to cope with those effects;

6. *Requests* the Secretary-General and organizations and bodies of the United Nations system to respond, as appropriate, to such requests for assistance as might be forthcoming from individual States or the appropriate subregional organizations, and urges all States and intergovernmental and non-governmental organizations to respond favourably to such requests;

7. *Reiterates* the urgent need for the removal of all remaining obstacles to the resumption of constitutional negotiations on a non-racial democratic South Africa;

8. *Appeals* to all States and appropriate intergovernmental and non-governmental organizations to support, in the context, *inter alia*, of the current drought situation, the national and joint emergency programmes prepared by the front-line States and other neighbouring States to overcome their critical humanitarian and emergency problems, taking into account the special circumstances of the most affected countries;

9. *Appeals* to the international community to extend appropriate assistance to the front-line States and other neighbouring States to enable them to advance the process of regional economic integration, as envisaged in the Treaty of 17 August 1992 establishing the Southern African Development Community, including the eventual participation of a non-racial democratic South Africa;

10. *Requests* the Secretary-General to report to the General Assembly at its forty-ninth session on the progress made in the implementation of the present resolution.

General Assembly resolution 47/163

18 December 1992   Meeting 92   Adopted without vote

Approved by Second Committee (A/47/727/Add.1) without vote, 7 December (meeting 48); 31-nation draft (A/C.2/47/L.49/Rev.1); agenda item 87(b).

Sponsors: Algeria, Angola, Benin, Bolivia, Botswana, Brazil, Burkina Faso, Cape Verde, China, Cuba, Finland, Ghana, Guinea-Bissau, India, Indonesia, Lesotho, Libyan Arab Jamahiriya, Malawi, Mozambique, Namibia, Nigeria, Norway, Senegal, Sudan, Swaziland, Sweden, Uganda, United Republic of Tanzania, Venezuela, Zambia, Zimbabwe.

Meeting numbers. GA 47th session: 2nd Committee 25, 26, 28, 30, 34, 38, 40, 42, 45, 46, 48; plenary 92.

Other economic assistance

Vanuatu

In response to a General Assembly resolution of 1990,[21] the Secretary-General submitted in August a report,[16] prepared by UNDP, containing information on economic assistance to Vanuatu, an island developing country. The report listed, as major constraints to the country's development, a high population growth rate; lack of skilled manpower; inadequate infrastructure; and high dependency on external aid to fund the bulk of the State capital budget. It identified as priority areas for action by the international community: national planning and policy formulation; economic and financial management, adjustment and reform; institutional strengthening of the Vanuatu Development Bank; tourism, agriculture and industry; policies to mobilize domestic savings;

building of infrastructure; health and population; professional and technical expertise; and training and the provision of scholarships. The report concluded that much remained to be done before Vanuatu became economically and institutionally self-sustaining. (See PART THREE, Chapter I, for further details on island developing countries.)

GENERAL ASSEMBLY ACTION

On 18 December 1992, the General Assembly, on the recommendation of the Second Committee, adopted **resolution 47/161** without vote.

Economic assistance to Vanuatu

The General Assembly,

Recalling its resolution 45/230 of 21 December 1990 on economic assistance to Vanuatu and other specified countries, in which it requested the Secretary-General to mobilize the resources necessary to provide assistance to Vanuatu and those other countries,

Recalling also its resolution 45/202 of 21 December 1990 on specific measures in favour of island developing countries,

Taking into account that Vanuatu, an island developing country that is also included in the list of least developed countries, continues to experience, as a consequence of periodic natural disasters, significant economic and social disadvantages of the type referred to in resolution 45/202,

Taking note of Agenda 21, adopted by the United Nations Conference on Environment and Development, in particular chapter 17, section G thereof, relating to the sustainable development of small island developing States,

1. *Calls the attention* of the international community to the report of the Secretary-General on the specific problems and needs of island developing countries, and specifically to those confronting Vanuatu;

2. *Expresses its appreciation* to the Secretary-General for the steps he has taken to mobilize assistance for Vanuatu and to those States and organizations which have provided assistance to it;

3. *Also expresses its appreciation* to the United Nations Development Programme, the specialized agencies of the United Nations and the donor community for their participation in the first round-table meeting to assist Vanuatu, and notes the proposed convening of a second such meeting in 1993;

4. *Appeals* to Member States, international financial institutions and the specialized agencies, organizations and programmes of the United Nations system to respond generously to the needs of Vanuatu, particularly in the nine priority areas identified in the report of the Secretary-General;

5. *Invites* the appropriate parts of the United Nations system, at the next meetings of their various governing bodies, to consider, as appropriate, the special needs of Vanuatu and to report the decisions of those bodies to the Secretary-General;

6. *Requests* the Secretary-General:

(a) To continue his efforts to mobilize the necessary resources for an effective programme of financial, technical and material assistance to Vanuatu;

(b) To report to the General Assembly at its forty-ninth session on the progress made in organizing international assistance for Vanuatu and on developments in the economic situation of that country.

General Assembly resolution 47/161

18 December 1992   Meeting 92   Adopted without vote

Approved by Second Committee (A/47/727/Add.1) without vote, 7 December (meeting 48); 74-nation draft (A/C.2/47/L.37/Rev.1); agenda item 87 *(b)*.

Sponsors: Angola, Antigua and Barbuda, Argentina, Australia, Bahamas, Bangladesh, Barbados, Belize, Benin, Brazil, Brunei Darussalam, Cape Verde, Chile, China, Comoros, Costa Rica, Côte d'Ivoire, Cuba, Cyprus, Djibouti, Egypt, El Salvador, Fiji, Greece, Grenada, Guinea-Bissau, Guyana, India, Indonesia, Jamaica, Kenya, Kuwait, Lesotho, Malaysia, Marshall Islands, Mauritania, Mauritius, Mexico, Micronesia, Mozambique, Namibia, New Zealand, Nigeria, Oman, Pakistan, Panama, Papua New Guinea, Philippines, Portugal, Republic of Korea, Romania, Saint Kitts and Nevis, Samoa, Sao Tome and Principe, Singapore, Sri Lanka, Solomon Islands, Spain, Suriname, Swaziland, Thailand, Togo, Trinidad and Tobago, Tunisia, Uganda, United Arab Emirates, United Kingdom, United Republic of Tanzania, Uruguay, Vanuatu, Venezuela, Yemen, Zambia, Zimbabwe.

Meeting numbers. GA 47th session: 2nd Committee 25, 26, 28, 30, 34, 38, 40, 42, 45, 46, 48; plenary 92.

Yemen

In response to a 1990 General Assembly resolution,[22] and to a 1991 Economic and Social Council resolution,[23] the Secretary-General submitted a June report[24] to the Assembly, through the Council, on assistance to Yemen. The report reviewed the post-unification situation in Yemen and the mobilization of international assistance. The Yemen Arab Republic and the People's Democratic Republic of Yemen, two least developed countries, had merged in May 1990.

It was noted that the cost of unification, the negative effects of war and upheaval in the Gulf and Horn of Africa region, drought and earthquake, the return of Yemeni expatriates, coupled with unsettled financial obligations inherited from Yemen's predecessors, far outweighed the available resources. Therefore, the need for financial, capital and technical assistance to Yemen persisted.

In an August report,[16] prepared by UNDP, containing information on economic assistance to Yemen, the Secretary-General stated that the first Round-Table Conference of Donors to Yemen, convened with the assistance of UNDP, was held at Geneva on 30 June and 1 July. Follow-up sectoral meetings would construct detailed programming frameworks for key economic and social sectors.

The report noted that approximately a million Yemeni expatriates had returned to their country as a result of the situation between Iraq and Kuwait, causing the resident population to increase suddenly by 7 per cent and imposing a severe strain on social services and infrastructure. With the assistance of UNDP and the International Development Association (IDA), Yemen had formulated an emergency recovery programme to meet the long-term needs arising from the large-scale repatriation. The programme aimed to strengthen the social infrastructure, create employment opportunities in such areas as road construction and increase food production in agriculture and fisheries. The programme's first phase, which would focus on road construction, agriculture, education and housing, was estimated to cost $60 million, $52.6 million of which would be provided by donor Governments and institutions as follows: IDA, $33 million; USAID, $15 million; Germany, $4.2 million; and UNDP, $0.4 million.

Other assistance by the United Nations system included the coordination by UNDRO of humanitarian aid from specialized international agencies for some 125,000 returnees, UNDP funding of a $400,000 project to strengthen the project management unit of the emergency recovery programme, as well as continued support from the United Nations Children's Fund (UNICEF). In May, the International Labour Organisation co-sponsored with UNDP a seminar on the capacities of Yemen and other countries in the region to manage labour migration in the wake of the Gulf crisis. During the year, UNHCR provided assistance for refugees from the Horn of Africa valued at $900,000 and was extending its camps to deal with the continuing influx. WFP provided emergency food assistance for the refugees, in addition to medicines and medical supplies, field personnel and consulting doctors. The Islamic Development Bank established a school for refugee children.

ECONOMIC AND SOCIAL COUNCIL ACTION

On 31 July 1992, the Economic and Social Council adopted **resolution 1992/61** without vote.

Assistance to Yemen

The Economic and Social Council,

Taking note of the report of the Secretary-General on assistance to Yemen,

Noting the social and economic challenges for Yemen arising from the merging of the two parts of that country, the returning Yemeni expatriates and the increasing number of refugees from Somalia,

1. *Notes with interest* the Round-table Conference for Yemen, which was held at Geneva on 30 June and 1 July 1992, the sectoral follow-up meetings and the next round-table conference, scheduled for late 1993;

2. *Calls upon* Governments and all regional and international organizations to continue their efforts to provide their special assistance to Yemen so that it may overcome the difficulties arising from the above-mentioned challenges;

3. *Requests* the Secretary-General to inform the Economic and Social Council at its substantive session of 1993 of the progress made in the implementation of the present resolution.

Economic and Social Council resolution 1992/61

31 July 1992   Meeting 42   Adopted without vote

Draft by Vice-President (E/1992/L.41), based on informal consultations held on 12-nation draft (E/1992/L.33); agenda item 9.

On 22 December 1992, the General Assembly, on the recommendation of the Second Committee, adopted **resolution 47/179** without vote.

Assistance to Yemen

The General Assembly,

Taking note of the report of the Secretary-General,

Recalling its resolutions 46/174 of 19 December 1991 and 45/193 and 45/222 of 21 December 1990, as well as Economic and Social Council resolution 1991/62 of 26 July 1991 and decisions 91/19 and 91/20 of 25 June 1991 of the Governing Council of the United Nations Development Programme,

Noting the importance of implementing all relevant General Assembly and Economic and Social Council resolutions, and relevant decisions of the Governing Council of the United Nations Development Programme,

Noting also the social and economic challenges still facing Yemen as a result of unification, the return of Yemeni expatriates, the continuous flow of thousands of refugees from the Horn of Africa, in particular from Somalia, and recent natural disasters,

1. *Calls upon* States, United Nations organizations, governmental organizations, international non-governmental organizations and financial institutions to extend, as rapidly as possible, their assistance to Yemen to enable that country to deal with these challenges;

2. *Calls upon* the Secretary-General, in cooperation with the relevant organs and organizations of the United Nations system, to provide assistance to the Government and people of Yemen in their efforts to find a solution to the serious situation created by these challenges and, especially, by the returnees and refugees;

3. *Requests* the Secretary-General to submit to the General Assembly at its forty-eighth session a comprehensive report on the implementation of the present resolution.

General Assembly resolution 47/179

22 December 1992   Meeting 93   Adopted without vote

Approved by Second Committee (A/47/718/Add.1) without vote, 24 November (meeting 45); 33-nation draft (A/C.2/47/L.11); agenda item 78.

Sponsors: Afghanistan, Algeria, China, Colombia, Costa Rica, Cuba, Djibouti, Egypt, Guyana, India, Indonesia, Iran, Iraq, Jordan, Lebanon, Libyan Arab Jamahiriya, Madagascar, Mauritania, Mexico, Morocco, Nepal, Oman, Peru, Philippines, Spain, Sri Lanka, Sudan, Suriname, Syrian Arab Republic, Tunisia, Uruguay, Viet Nam, Yemen.

Meeting numbers. GA 47th session: 2nd Committee 25, 30, 45; plenary 93.

REFERENCES

[1]YUN 1991, p. 402, GA res. 46/151, annex II, 18 Dec. 1991. [2]Ibid., p. 395. [3]YUN 1986, p. 446, GA res. S-13/2, annex, 1 June 1986. [4]TD/364. [5]TD/B/39(1)/5. [6]A/47/15 (vol. II). [7]YUN 1991, p. 396. [8]DP/1992/17. [9]E/1990/29 (dec. 90/34). [10]DP/1993/10/Add.1. [11]E/1992/28 (dec. 92/19). [12]E/AC.51/1992/5. [13]ESC res. 1990/83, 27 July 1990. [14]A/47/16. [15]GA res. 45/230, 21 Dec. 1990. [16]A/47/337. [17]YUN 1991, p. 407, GA res. 46/171, 19 Dec. 1991. [18]Ibid., p. 408, GA res. 46/175, 19 Dec. 1991. [19]A/47/573. [20]YUN 1991, p. 410, GA res. 46/172, 19 Dec. 1991. [21]GA res. 45/230, 21 Dec. 1990. [22]GA res. 45/193, 21 Dec. 1990. [23]YUN 1991, p. 435, ESC res. 1991/62, 26 July 1991. [24]A/47/283-E/1992/83.

Humanitarian assistance and disaster relief

Coordination of humanitarian assistance and disaster relief

In accordance with a 1991 General Assembly resolution on strengthening the coordination of humanitarian emergency assistance of the United Nations,[1] the Secretary-General, in March, established the Department of Humanitarian Affairs (DHA) and, in April, appointed Jan Eliasson as Under-Secretary-General for Humanitarian Affairs and Emergency Relief Coordinator. In an October report to the Assembly,[2] he stated that, as called for by the Assembly in 1991,[1] the Central Emergency Revolving Fund (CERF) and the Inter-Agency Standing Committee had also been established.

DHA, designed to strengthen a coordinated and coherent system-wide approach, was staffed through the redeployment of resources, combining the former UNDRO with other existing capacities within the United Nations. The Department was also supported by staff seconded from WFP, UNICEF, UNHCR and UNDP. DHA had offices in both New York and Geneva. The New York office concentrated on policy issues pertaining to the international community's response to emergencies, monitored developments and acted as an early warning system, while the Geneva office was responsible for all matters relating to natural disasters, including relief mobilization, coordination and disaster mitigation. The secretariat of the International Decade for Natural Disaster Reduction (IDNDR) also became an integral part of DHA.

DHA launched initiatives to improve the system's preparedness, including the establishment of a Central Register of Disaster Management Capacities, two parts of which, namely the Directory of Emergency Response Officers and the Directory of International Search and Rescue Teams, were already in existence. The Register of Stockpiles of Disaster Relief Items and the Register of Disaster Management Expertise were being prepared. The Department was also establishing a register of stand-by capacity encompassing available resources, both inside and outside the United Nations system, to be drawn upon in cases of emergency. Discussions on the use of military and civil defence assets in sudden natural disasters were initiated and measures taken to strengthen the participation of other United Nations agencies in the activities of the DHA-UNDRO warehouse in Pisa (Italy). With respect to the relief-to-development continuum, DHA took steps to bring development and related financial organizations, including the World Bank and the International Monetary Fund (IMF), into the early stages of planning of humanitarian assistance, especially in the design of relief programmes, to ensure a smooth transition from relief to rehabilitation and long-term sustainable development.

The joint DHA-UNDP Disaster Management Training Programme was expanded to over 70 disaster-prone developing countries. Five regional and 17 country workshops were held in four developing regions. The programme received special contributions from States, totalling $2.75 million.

In reviewing emergency response activities, the Secretary-General indicated that DHA began to monitor world-wide developments to provide early warning and mobilize resources for effective and timely humanitarian responses to natural and man-made emergencies. During the first months of its operation, the Department addressed emergencies in Afghanistan, along the Bangladesh/Myanmar border, in Haiti, the Horn of Africa, Iraq, Kenya, Liberia, Mozambique, Nagorno-Karabakh, Somalia, the Sudan, Tajikistan and the former Yugoslavia. Its relief coordination activities were required in several natural disasters, and a major programme was put into place for the countries affected by the drought in southern Africa.

In his concluding observations, the Secretary-General noted that since its establishment DHA had addressed and coordinated the international community's response to an increasing number of acute emergencies. However, the earmarking of contributions for specific relief activities continued to limit the possibilities of a coherent humanitarian response to complex emergencies. Additional resources were essential if DHA's work was to be successfully accomplished. A major concern was the security and protection of staff in delivering humanitarian relief materials, and he advocated that all measures be taken to ensure their security. The Secretary-General observed that a notable feature in the humanitarian activities of the United Nations was the increased involvement of the Security Council, which had accorded humanitarian assistance high priority and had developed modalities to ensure the safe and effective delivery of relief assistance.

In July,[3] the Secretary-General submitted to the General Assembly a report on UNDRO's activities in 1990-1991.[4] By **decision 47/437** of 18 December, the Assembly took note of the report.

Central Emergency Revolving Fund. CERF became operational on 22 May 1992, having reached its target of $50 million in pledges with contributions from 25 Member States. CERF's establishment had been called for by the General Assembly in 1991[1] to enable operational organizations to ensure prompt response to emergencies. By October, disbursements totalling some $11 million had been made.

Consolidated appeals. The process of consolidated appeals was employed to prepare and launch appeals describing the United Nations response to particular emergencies and identifying needed resources. Under the aegis of DHA, needs assessments were carried out and consolidated inter-agency appeals were launched in the following cases: the Consolidated United Nations/SADC Appeal for DESA; the Consolidated Appeal for Emergency Humanitarian Assistance for Afghanistan; the Special Consolidated United Nations Inter-Agency Appeal for Kenya; the Updated Consolidated Inter-Agency Appeal for SEPHA; the United Nations Consolidated Inter-Agency Programme of Action and Appeal for Former Yugoslavia; and the Inter-Agency Humanitarian Programme—Plan of Action for Iraq (1 July 1992–31 March 1993).

Inter-agency coordination. The Secretary-General stated that the Inter-Agency Standing Committee, envisaged by the Assembly in its 1991 resolution[1] as an important coordination tool, had become operational. UNHCR, UNICEF, WFP, UNDP, FAO and the World Health Organization (WHO) were participating in the Standing Committee, and the International Committee of the Red Cross (ICRC), the International Federation of Red Cross and Red Crescent Societies (IFRC) and the International Organization for Migration were associated with its work. Representatives of NGOs had been invited to participate on an ad hoc basis. An Inter-Agency Working Group had also been established for regular consultations at the middle-management level at Geneva.

The Ad Hoc Working Group on Early Warning of New Flows of Refugees and Displaced Persons of the Administrative Committee on Coordination (ACC) proposed the creation of an inter-agency consultative mechanism as a first step towards establishing an early warning system to assist the international community to deal more efficiently and effectively with situations that could result in new flows of refugees and displaced persons. The Working Group designated DHA as the focal point of the new mechanism, which was expected to begin functioning in 1993.

UNDP action. In response to a 1991 Governing Council decision,[5] the UNDP Administrator submitted a March report[6] on activities carried out under UNDP's Humanitarian Programme, established in 1991. A joint planning exercise between UNDP and UNHCR concerning returnee aid and development, with particular reference to the reintegration of returning refugees, was held in January 1992. UNDP and UNHCR signed, also in January, a Memorandum of Understanding to provide the framework for cooperation between the two organizations in repatriating and resettling displaced persons in Cambodia. The UNDP Office of Project Services developed special methods and capacity to design and execute projects for the Development Programme for Refugees, Returnees, and Displaced Persons in Central America, as well as for similar operations in Cambodia and Mozambique.

The Administrator, in his annual report for 1992,[7] stated that UNDP was attempting to bring to bear its multisectoral human development expertise to put in place rehabilitation and recovery measures. The measures were designed to give practical effect to the relief-to-development continuum, whose concept was to move as quickly as possible from emergency-phase activities through recovery and rehabilitation to resumed sustainable development. UNDP was developing procedures to allow for the rapid deployment of personnel, equipment and funds in response to emergencies while preserving accountability through a mechanism of *ex post facto* reporting.

On 26 May,[8] the Council encouraged the Administrator to work closely with DHA and the relevant United Nations relief organizations to enhance their coordinated approach to the continuum from relief to rehabilitation to reconstruction. The Council urged the Administrator to cooperate fully with the Under-Secretary-General for Humanitarian Affairs in formulating a detailed, comprehensive United Nations humanitarian assistance plan specifying the respective roles and outlining the comparative advantages of DHA, UNDP and other United Nations organs, in all aspects of humanitarian emergency-related assistance, including disaster prevention, preparedness and mitigation activities, refugee assistance and other elements within the continuum from relief to rehabilitation and development. It emphasized the need for UNDP to develop a clear strategy on linking emergency assistance and sustainable development. The Administrator was requested to develop further UNDP capacities to promote the transition from relief to development and to make rapid implementation of reintegration programmes, particularly quick impact projects, a priority objective in future humanitarian programmes. The Council approved the extension of UNDP's humanitarian programme, with approved staffing from the regular budget, to cover the balance of the 1992-1993 biennium.

GENERAL ASSEMBLY ACTION

On 22 December, the General Assembly adopted **resolution 47/168** without vote.

Strengthening of the coordination of humanitarian emergency assistance of the United Nations

The General Assembly,

Reaffirming its resolution 46/182 of 19 December 1991 and the annex thereto, in particular the section on the guiding principles, as well as those sections concerning prevention, preparedness, stand-by capacity, consolidated appeals, coordination, cooperation and leadership and continuum from relief to rehabilitation and development,

Deeply concerned about the magnitude and ruinous effects of disasters and emergency situations, which call, *inter alia*, for more international cooperation to mitigate the human suffering of their victims and to expedite the rehabilitation and reconstruction processes,

Underlining the need for an adequate, coordinated and prompt response by the international community to disasters and emergency situations,

Noting the increasing number and complexity of disasters and humanitarian emergencies,

Also underlining the need for availability of adequate financial resources to ensure a prompt response by the United Nations to humanitarian emergency situations,

Welcoming the establishment of the Department of Humanitarian Affairs and the appointment of an Under-Secretary-General for Humanitarian Affairs and Emergency Relief Coordinator, as envisaged in resolution 46/182,

Emphasizing the importance of the primary role of the Emergency Relief Coordinator, including with the support of the Inter-Agency Standing Committee, in ensuring better preparation for, as well as rapid and coherent response to, natural disasters and other emergencies, in particular emergencies involving the supply of food, medicines, shelter and health care, taking into account the need to promote, in close collaboration with concerned agencies and international financial institutions, a smooth transition from relief to rehabilitation, reconstruction and development,

Stressing the need for adequate protection of personnel involved in humanitarian operations, in accordance with relevant norms and principles of international law and within the context of General Assembly resolution 47/120 of 18 December 1992,

Encouraging the Secretary-General to continue discussions with Governments and the organizations of the United Nations system on various issues related to United Nations involvement in complex and dangerous emergencies in terms of the measures set forth in paragraph 76 of his report,

1. *Takes note* of the report of the Secretary-General;

2. *Emphasizes* the leadership role of the Secretary-General in ensuring the rapid and coordinated response of the United Nations system to humanitarian emergencies, including in mobilizing the necessary resources, and invites all concerned operational organizations and agencies to continue to extend their full support for full the implementation of General Assembly resolution 46/182;

3. *Invites* those States in a position to do so to consider increasing the resources of the Central Emergency Revolving Fund based on voluntary contributions, in order to assist further the United Nations system in its efforts to respond rapidly to humanitarian emergencies, and calls upon those that have already pledged contributions to the Fund urgently to fulfil their commitments;

4. *Calls upon* potential donors to adopt the necessary measures to increase and expedite their contributions, including setting aside, on a stand-by basis, financial and other resources that can be disbursed quickly to the United Nations system in response to the consolidated appeals of the Secretary-General;

5. *Requests* the Secretary-General to continue to examine all possible ways and means to provide adequate qualified personnel and administrative resources to the Department of Humanitarian Affairs from within existing resources of the regular budget of the United Nations and, where appropriate, through the secondment of national humanitarian disaster relief experts;

6. *Also requests* the Secretary-General, in his annual report on the coordination of humanitarian emergency assistance, to review the effectiveness and achievements of the new institutional arrangements of the United Nations humanitarian assistance system, including the arrangements for the functioning between Headquarters offices and at the field level, in accordance with General Assembly resolution 46/182, as well as the progress made in the implementation of that resolution and the present resolution and to make appropriate recommendations as to how to give full effect to the provisions of these resolutions;

7. *Further requests* the Secretary-General, after consultations with Governments and United Nations organs and specialized agencies, to report on arrangements between the United Nations and interested Governments and intergovernmental and non-governmental organizations that would enable the United Nations to have more expeditious access, when necessary, to their emergency relief capacities, including food reserves, emergency stockpiles and personnel, as well as logistical support;

8. *Requests* the Secretary-General, after consultations with Governments, to report on ways and means to improve further United Nations capability in the areas of prevention and preparedness in relation to natural disasters and other emergencies, in particular emergencies involving food, medicines, shelter and health care, as provided for in General Assembly resolution 46/182;

9. *Also requests* the Secretary-General to explore the possibilities, advantages and disadvantages of the establishment of warehouses for emergency items at the regional as well as global levels, taking into account existing facilities, and to report thereon in his next annual report;

10. *Further requests* the Secretary-General to submit his annual report on the coordination of humanitarian emergency assistance to the General Assembly at its forty-eighth session and to present an oral report to the Economic and Social Council at its substantive session of 1993.

General Assembly resolution 47/168

22 December 1992   Meeting 93   Adopted without vote

Draft by New Zealand (A/47/L.51); agenda item 37.

Another draft resolution on strengthening the coordination of humanitarian emergency assistance,[9] submitted by Pakistan, was withdrawn.

Facilitation of the delivery of humanitarian assistance

In response to a 1990 General Assembly request,[10] the Secretary-General submitted an October report on humanitarian assistance to victims of natural disasters and similar emergency situations.[11] The report, based on informal meetings and questionnaires sent to Member States, United Nations agencies and NGOs, noted that, during

discussions on improving the delivery of humanitarian assistance, the issue of access to victims
of emergencies invariably came into opposition
with the principle of sovereignty. Different viewpoints on that issue persisted among Governments and international and non-governmental
organizations.

There was, however, overall agreement about
the usefulness of relief corridors as a means to
reach people trapped by armed conflicts and civil
disturbances. Agreed upon by all parties to the
conflict, corridors had been set up and successfully used in El Salvador, Ethiopia, Somalia, the
Sudan and the former Yugoslavia.

The Secretary-General considered relief corridors an indispensable tool in the successful
delivery of humanitarian assistance to conflict
zones and recommended widening the concept
whenever possible by seeking political solutions,
including conflict-solving measures, as indicated
by the Assembly in 1990.[10] Concerning the
possible establishment of a list of persons and
bodies with expert knowledge in emergency humanitarian assistance, he suggested that the creation of a detailed list might be extremely difficult, time-consuming and costly, with possible
duplication of already existing rosters by operational agencies. However, to strengthen the capacity for immediate assessment at the onset of
an emergency, DHA was studying the possibility
of creating United Nations Disaster Assessment
and Coordination (UNDAC) Stand-by Teams.
Under the UNDAC concept, DHA-Geneva, in
cooperation with national emergency relief
services, would identify skilled and experienced
persons, together with its regular staff, for a
stand-by cadre forming a core group of UNDAC
mission leaders. DHA had taken other initiatives, particularly the compilation of a Directory
of International Search and Rescue Teams. It
was also working on a project to prepare a register of stockpiles of disaster relief items available
for international assistance.

New international humanitarian order

In response to a 1990 General Assembly resolution,[12] the Secretary-General submitted an
August report[13] containing replies to his note
verbale requesting views or information on the
promotion of a new international humanitarian
order and on the report of the Independent
Commission on International Humanitarian Issues.[14] Replies were received from the Central
African Republic, Ecuador, the Holy See, the
Niger, Panama, the United Nations Subcommission on the Prevention of Discrimination and
Protection of Minorities, UNESCO, WHO and the
United Nations Volunteers.

GENERAL ASSEMBLY ACTION

On 16 December, the General Assembly, on
the recommendation of the Third Committee,
adopted **resolution 47/106** without vote.

New international humanitarian order
The General Assembly,

Recalling its resolutions 36/136 of 14 December 1981,
37/201 of 18 December 1982, 38/125 of 16 December
1983, 40/126 of 13 December 1985, 42/120 of 7 December 1987, 43/129 of 8 December 1988 and 45/101 of 14
December 1990 relating to the promotion of a new international humanitarian order,

Recalling also its resolutions 42/121 of 7 December
1987, 43/130 of 8 December 1988 and 45/102 of 14 December 1990 relating to the promotion of international
cooperation in the humanitarian field,

Taking note of the reports of the Secretary-General
and the comments made by various Governments,
specialized agencies and non-governmental organizations,

Noting the actions being taken by the specialized
agencies and programmes of the United Nations system with regard to humanitarian issues, examined by
the Independent Commission on International Humanitarian Issues, that fall within their respective
mandates,

Convinced that solving humanitarian problems requires international cooperation and harmonization of
actions taken by Governments and intergovernmental
and non-governmental organizations as well as individuals,

Recognizing with concern the continuing need further to
strengthen international responses to growing humanitarian challenges, and to undertake creative humanitarian action at the international, regional and national levels to alleviate human suffering and to
promote durable solutions to humanitarian problems,

Recognizing further the need for active follow-up to the
recommendations and suggestions made by the Independent Commission and the role being played in
this regard by the Independent Bureau for Humanitarian Issues, set up for the purpose,

1. *Expresses its appreciation* to the Secretary-General
for his continuing active support to the efforts to promote a new international humanitarian order;

2. *Urges* Governments as well as governmental and
non-governmental organizations that have not yet
done so to provide their comments and expertise to the
Secretary-General regarding the humanitarian order
and the report of the Independent Commission on International Humanitarian Issues;

3. *Invites* Governments to make available to the
Secretary-General, on a voluntary basis, information
and expertise on humanitarian issues of concern to
them in order to identify opportunities for future
action;

4. *Calls upon* Governments, the United Nations
system and intergovernmental and non-governmental
organizations further to develop international cooperation in the humanitarian field;

5. *Reiterates* that international cooperation in the
humanitarian field will facilitate better understanding,
mutual respect, confidence and tolerance among
countries and peoples, thus contributing to a more just
and non-violent world;

6. *Invites* the Independent Bureau for Humanitarian Issues to continue and further strengthen its essential role in following up the work of the Independent Commission;

7. *Encourages* the international community to contribute substantially and regularly to the international humanitarian activities required to promote a new humanitarian order;

8. *Requests* the Secretary-General to remain in contact with Governments as well as governmental and non-governmental organizations and the Independent Bureau for Humanitarian Issues and to report on the progress made by them to the General Assembly at its forty-ninth session;

9. *Decides* to review at its forty-ninth session the question of a new international humanitarian order.

General Assembly resolution 47/106

16 December 1992   Meeting 89   Adopted without vote

Approved by Third Committee (A/47/715) without vote, 18 November (meeting 43); 29-nation draft (A/C.3/47/L.37); agenda item 96.

Sponsors: Bangladesh, Cyprus, Djibouti, Egypt, France, Gambia, Honduras, Indonesia, Italy, Jamaica, Jordan, Lebanon, Libyan Arab Jamahiriya, Mauritania, Mongolia, Morocco, Nigeria, Oman, Pakistan, Peru, Philippines, Qatar, Romania, Russian Federation, Sierra Leone, Sudan, Togo, Tunisia, Yemen.

Meeting numbers. GA 47th session: 3rd Committee 34-39, 41-43; plenary 89.

REFERENCES

[1]YUN 1991, p. 421, GA res. 46/182, annex, 19 Dec. 1991. [2]A/47/595. [3]A/47/288-E/1992/94. [4]YUN 1991, p. 413. [5]Ibid., p. 707. [6]DP/1992/19. [7]DP/1993/10. [8]E/1992/28 (dec. 92/20). [9]A/47/L.22. [10]GA res. 45/100, 14 Dec. 1990. [11]A/47/540. [12]GA res. 45/101, 14 Dec. 1990. [13]A/47/352. [14]YUN 1987, p. 792.

Humanitarian assistance activities

Africa

Special Emergency Programme for the Horn of Africa

In an overview of emergencies and natural disasters in 1992, DHA reported that, despite a marked improvement in crop production in Ethiopia, Eritrea and the Sudan, improved security in Ethiopia and peace in Eritrea after 25 years of warfare, the situation in the region was still critical due to continuing civil conflict in southern Sudan and the deteriorating situation in Somalia. The effects of the conflict in Somalia spilled across borders into the neighbouring countries of Djibouti, Ethiopia and Kenya. They included large numbers of refugees and significant security problems.

Humanitarian efforts in the Sudan focused mainly on those affected by drought and by the civil war in the south. In Ethiopia, the United Nations used a cross-mandate approach for a mixed population of refugees from Somalia and Ethiopians affected by local conflicts. Although Eritrea's 1992 harvest was the best in years, it was only sufficient to meet half the country's food needs. In Djibouti, major humanitarian assistance needs arose from the problems in Somalia and from its own internal conflicts. A major component of humanitarian assistance in Kenya was for drought relief, but the country also hosted hundreds of thousands of refugees from Somalia.

On 28 January, the Secretary-General issued a Consolidated Inter-Agency Appeal for the Horn of Africa, which received pledges of almost $576 million against identified needs of $621 million. On 11 June, Kenya requested the United Nations to bring the plight of drought-affected Kenyans and of refugees from Ethiopia, Somalia and the Sudan to the attention of the international community. In response, a Special Consolidated United Nations Inter-Agency Appeal for Kenya was launched, pending an update of the Horn of Africa appeal. A revised appeal, which subsumed the Kenya appeal, was issued on 15 July.

A November 1992 situation report by DHA on the six countries of the Horn of Africa that were included in the Special Emergency Programme for the Horn of Africa (SEPHA) appeal process—Djibouti, Ethiopia, Eritrea, Kenya, Somalia and the Sudan—stated that, against revised 1992 requirements of $1.15 billion, $788 million or almost 70 per cent had been pledged by donors during the first 10 months of the year. Among United Nations agencies, WFP received pledges covering 78 per cent of its total requests under SEPHA. UNHCR also received strong donor response, while response to other agencies and in the non-food sector was less strong.

On 27 April,[1] Ethiopia transmitted to the Secretary-General the Declaration, Framework of Cooperation and Programme of Action adopted at the summit of heads of State and Government of the countries of the Horn of Africa (Addis Ababa, 8 and 9 April), which, *inter alia*, pledged assurance of access by impartial humanitarian organizations to civilian populations, to comply fully with international humanitarian law and to cooperate with the international community in the field of humanitarian assistance.

UNDP action. In response to a 1991 Governing Council request,[2] the UNDP Administrator submitted a report on UNDP's role in assisting Djibouti, Ethiopia, Kenya, Somalia, the Sudan and Yemen.[3]

The Administrator described action by UNDP and other United Nations organizations to coordinate assistance in the region, noting that his Senior Adviser for Humanitarian Affairs was leading the SEPHA unit in the United Nations Secretariat. He also outlined the level and forms of assistance provided to the countries of the region by UNDP.

On 14 February,[4] the Council requested the Administrator to present proposals in 1993 for future funding of the new liaison office, established to provide logistical support to Djibouti, Ethiopia, Kenya, Somalia, the Sudan and Yemen.

Angola

In response to a 1991 General Assembly request,[5] the Secretary-General submitted an October report on international assistance for the economic rehabilitation of Angola.[6] The report provided information on assistance to the peace process, the Special Relief Programme for Angola (SRPA), repatriation of refugees, the regional drought emergency, plans for progress from emergency to rehabilitation and assistance by the United Nations system, Member States and other donors. The Secretary-General stated that the 1991 signing of the Peace Accord[7] by the Government of Angola and the União Nacional para la Independência Total de Angola enabled the United Nations to assist Angola in the peace process, the movement towards democracy, the expansion of emergency relief activities and planning of resettlement and rehabilitation programmes.

The mandate of the United Nations Angola Verification Mission (UNAVEM II) included the observation and verification of elections (see PART TWO, Chapter I). The Secretary-General appointed a Special Representative to head UNAVEM II, who was responsible for coordinating all United Nations operations relating to the peace process and the holding of elections in September. UNDP assisted in the electoral process through a technical team in Luanda. Further United Nations support was given through the programme of assistance to soldiers and families awaiting demobilization, for which an appeal for $27 million had been launched in October 1991. WFP responded quickly to the critical situation in the assembly areas by using emergency food resources to feed cantoned soldiers, while UNICEF supplied non-food items, such as bed sheets, tents, family kits, hoes, machetes and seeds.

SRPA's second phase (SRPA-II), launched by the Secretary-General in December 1991, emphasized long-range rehabilitation of infrastructure and basic services. Its main objectives were the reintegration of 1.4 million persons affected by the war; assistance to abandoned children and disabled persons; improvement of basic services, including water and sanitation; and the extension of immunization coverage throughout the country. Against a total appeal of $167 million, only $58 million had been pledged through mid-July.

WFP programmed 64,800 tons of food aid for internally displaced persons and Angolan returnees at a cost of $36.6 million and also supplied 21,300 tons of food to 250,000 demobilized Angolan troops and their families at a cost of $11 million.

By the end of August, some 77,500 Angolan refugees had returned. A UNHCR appeal for international assistance to carry out an organized programme of repatriation was launched in June, with the greater part of the requested $55.3 million to be spent in Angola. Transit centres with shelter and sanitation facilities were established in northern and eastern Angola. Additionally, Angola was affected in 1992 by the drought emergency in southern Africa (see below, under "Disasters"), the consolidated appeal for which collected $30 million of the $81 million sought for Angola. While that provided further evidence of the international community's support for Angola, it was clear that the most vital needs of the affected population were still not being adequately addressed.

GENERAL ASSEMBLY ACTION

On 18 December 1992, the General Assembly, on the recommendation of the Second Committee, adopted **resolution 47/164** without vote.

International assistance for the economic rehabilitation of Angola

The General Assembly,

Recalling its resolutions 46/142 of 17 December 1991, 45/233 of 21 December 1990 and 44/168 of 15 December 1989 on international assistance for the economic rehabilitation of Angola,

Recalling also Security Council resolutions 387(1976) of 31 March 1976, 475(1980) of 27 June 1980, 628(1989) of 16 January 1989 and other resolutions of the Council regarding international assistance for the economic rehabilitation of Angola, in which, *inter alia,* the international community was requested to render assistance to Angola,

Deeply concerned about the serious economic and political situation prevailing in Angola,

Concerned about the continuous drought that ravages the central and southern regions of the country and adversely affects millions of lives,

Taking into consideration the fact that the implementation of the Peace Accords for Angola would create favourable conditions for the economic and social rehabilitation of the country,

Conscious of the need for continuing effort and engagement on the part of the international community to assist Angola in rehabilitating its economy,

1. *Takes note* of the report of the Secretary-General;

2. *Calls upon* all parties to do their utmost to achieve the full and effective implementation of the Peace Accords for Angola and national reconciliation goals, thus creating conditions conducive to the economic rehabilitation of the country;

3. *Expresses its appreciation* to Member States, United Nations organizations and other donors for the emergency humanitarian assistance rendered to Angola through the Special Relief Programme for Angola, and appeals for continued and generous contributions for emergency humanitarian assistance;

4. *Reiterates its appeal* to the international community to continue to render the material, technical and finan-

cial assistance necessary for the economic rehabilitation of Angola;

5. *Requests* the Secretary-General, in cooperation with the international community, to continue to mobilize organizations and organs of the United Nations system in order to ensure an appropriate level of economic assistance for Angola;

6. *Welcomes* the decision of the Government of Angola to organize a donors' round-table conference for the rehabilitation and reconstruction of Angola in 1993, in collaboration with the United Nations Development Programme, the African Development Bank, the Government of Portugal and other interested countries;

7. *Requests* the Secretary-General to report to the General Assembly at its forty-eighth session on the implementation of the present resolution;

8. *Decides* to include in the provisional agenda of its forty-eighth session the item entitled "International assistance for the economic rehabilitation of Angola".

General Assembly resolution 47/164

18 December 1992   Meeting 92   Adopted without vote

Approved by Second Committee (A/47/728) without vote, 7 December (meeting 48); 44-nation draft (A/C.2/47/L.17/Rev.1); agenda item 88.

Sponsors: Algeria, Angola, Antigua and Barbuda, Argentina, Benin, Bosnia and Herzegovina, Brazil, Burkina Faso, Burundi, Cameroon, Cape Verde, Chad, China, Congo, Cuba, Djibouti, Egypt, El Salvador, Ethiopia, Gabon, Guatemala, Guinea, Guinea-Bissau, Honduras, Madagascar, Malawi, Mali, Mauritania, Mexico, Mozambique, Namibia, Niger, Nigeria, Portugal, Sao Tome and Principe, Senegal, Spain, Togo, Tunisia, Uganda, United Republic of Tanzania, Zaire, Zambia, Zimbabwe.

Meeting numbers. GA 47th session: 2nd Committee 25, 26, 34, 40, 48; plenary 92.

Liberia

In response to a 1991 General Assembly request,[8] the Secretary-General submitted an October report on emergency assistance for the rehabilitation and reconstruction of Liberia.[9] The report described emergency assistance activities being carried out by the United Nations system in response to Liberia's civil conflict. It also outlined efforts by seven Member States (Canada, Denmark, Germany, Japan, Norway, Saudi Arabia and Sweden) to assist Liberia.

The Office of the United Nations Special Coordinator for Emergency Relief Operations in Liberia (UNSCOL), based at Monrovia, coordinated all institutional and operational arrangements for relief programmes and other humanitarian activities. The Office included representatives of UNICEF, UNDP, WFP, UNHCR, FAO and WHO.

Four United Nations operational centres were opened in strategic rural areas to enhance the delivery capacity of the organizations concerned, and a viable country-wide emergency assistance programme was instituted. Nevertheless, security and logistical problems continued to hamper relief operations. The renewal of armed hostilities in August hindered relief work in affected areas and gave rise to new mass displacements.

Some 115,000 Sierra Leonean refugees fled to the western Liberia border counties, to which UNHCR responded with an emergency assistance programme of $2.5 million covering July to December 1992. A further 20,000 to 25,000 displaced persons arrived in Monrovia in late August, including 5,000 Sierra Leonean refugees, adding to a population of 4,000 refugees from Sierra Leone already in Monrovia.

For the period December 1990 to September 1992, UNSCOL recorded contributions totalling $102 million against appeal targets of $149.9 million. Food aid requirements identified in the appeals of the Secretary-General totalled $86.6 million, against which $64.8 million was pledged. In April, the first lot of 500 metric tons of rice was sold under an experimental pilot monetization scheme intending to wean the population from total emergency food aid dependency and help revitalize the commercial market. In May, the WFP Committee on Food Aid Policies and Programmes approved the extension of food aid deliveries under a protracted refugee operation, with a total value of $170 million, covering 1993. The Global Information and Early Warning System on Food and Agriculture continued its intensive monitoring of the food supply situation.

The health situation in Liberia remained alarming with a high incidence of disease, especially among women and children. With UNICEF and WHO as lead agencies, United Nations emergency intervention in the health and medical sector was both extensive and multifaceted, ranging from supporting vaccination campaigns and a major field hospital to providing essential drugs and medical equipment to NGO partners working the interior. WHO planned to continue its programme of data collection and prevention and treatment of communicable and non-communicable diseases, costing $200,000, plus a separate component of $300,000 to prevent the spread of the human immunodeficiency virus (HIV).

Educational efforts resulted in a gradual increase of school enrolment, reaching 70 per cent of the pre-war level in greater Monrovia and 28 per cent in the country as a whole. The Special Emergency Life Food (SELF) community structure, established in Monrovia, developed a unique housing enumeration scheme which provided the basis for general food distribution and other community-based rehabilitation programmes. SELF was also being used for health and education programmes, reception of returnees, school feeding, food-for-work and vulnerable group programmes.

In his annual report for 1992,[10] the Administrator stated that UNDP provided emergency assistance to 40,000 displaced persons in Liberia, undertook an assessment of needs to be addressed and provided logistical support to deploy relief supplies and equipment. A main concern of UNDP was to facilitate the transition from relief to rehabilitation and reconstruction, and eventually to normal development activities. Such efforts ranged from distribution of agricultural seeds and tools to promotion of local NGOs, both in an immediate relief role and in larger post-relief activities.

GENERAL ASSEMBLY ACTION

On 18 December 1992, the General Assembly, on the recommendation of the Second Committee, adopted **resolution 47/154** without vote.

Assistance for the rehabilitation and reconstruction of Liberia

The General Assembly,

Recalling its resolutions 45/232 of 21 December 1990 and 46/147 of 17 December 1991,

Recalling also the statement of the Security Council of 7 May 1992 on the situation in Liberia, in which the Council indicated, *inter alia*, indicated that the Yamoussoukro Accord of 30 October 1991 offered the best possible framework for a peaceful resolution of the Liberian conflict by creating the necessary conditions for free and fair elections in Liberia, and called on all parties to the conflict to respect and implement the various accords of the peace process, including refraining from actions that endangered the security of the neighbouring States,[a]

Having considered the report of the Secretary-General,

Noting that, even though a viable country-wide emergency assistance programme has been instituted, security and logistical problems continue to hamper relief operations and have prevented the transition from emergency relief to reconstruction and development,

Noting with deep concern the devastating effects of the protracted conflict on the socio-economic conditions in Liberia and the urgent need to rehabilitate, in an atmosphere of peace and stability, basic sectors of the country in order to restore normalcy,

Recalling the agreement reached at the fourth meeting of the Committee of Five on the Liberian crisis and other members of the Standing Mediation Committee of the Economic Community of West African States, held at Yamoussoukro on 29 and 30 October 1991, on the immediate demobilization of combatants and the holding of democratic elections,[b]

Noting the recent decision of the Authority of Heads of State and Government of the Economic Community of West African States at its fifteenth session, regarding the imposition of comprehensive sanctions against any of the parties failing to implement fully the Yamoussoukro Accord,

1. *Expresses its gratitude* to the States and intergovernmental and non-governmental organizations that have responded and continue to respond to appeals by the Government of Liberia, as well as to appeals by the Secretary-General for emergency and other assistance;

2. *Expresses its gratitude* to the Secretary-General for his efforts in mobilizing the international community, the United Nations system and other organizations to provide emergency assistance to Liberia, and urges that such assistance be continued, as necessary;

3. *Calls upon* the international community and intergovernmental and non-governmental organizations to continue to provide Liberia with technical, financial and other assistance for the repatriation and resettlement of Liberian refugees, returnees and displaced persons and for the rehabilitation of combatants, which constitute important elements for facilitating the holding of democratic elections in Liberia;

4. *Appeals* to the international community and intergovernmental and non-governmental organizations to provide adequate assistance to programmes and projects identified in the report of the Secretary-General;

5. *Requests* the Secretary-General:

(a) To continue his efforts to coordinate the work of the United Nations system and to mobilize financial, technical and other assistance for the rehabilitation and reconstruction of Liberia;

(b) To undertake, when conditions permit, in close collaboration with the authorities of Liberia, an overall assessment of needs, with the objective of holding, when appropriate, a round-table conference of donors for the rehabilitation and reconstruction of Liberia;

6. *Also requests* the Secretary-General to report to the General Assembly at its forty-eighth session on the implementation of the present resolution.

[a]S/23886.
[b]S/24815.

General Assembly resolution 47/154
18 December 1992   Meeting 92   Adopted without vote

Approved by Second Committee (A/47/727/Add.1) without vote, 24 November (meeting 45); draft by Mauritania on behalf of the African States and the United States (A/C.2/47/L.15/Rev.1); agenda item 87 *(b)*.
Meeting numbers. GA 47th session: 2nd Committee 25, 26, 28, 30, 34, 38, 40, 42, 45; plenary 92.

Mozambique

In response to a 1990 General Assembly request,[11] the Secretary-General submitted an October report,[12] prepared in consultation with the Government of Mozambique, on the implementation of the emergency and rehabilitation programmes for that country. The report documented the role of the United Nations in support of Mozambique emergency programmes; emergency requirements for 1992-1993; international support for the 1990-1991 and 1991-1992 periods; global development assistance to Mozambique; and assistance rendered by United Nations organizations and by 11 Member States.

Immediately following the October signing of the General Peace Agreement for Mozambique[13] (see PART TWO, Chapter I), a DHA mission was dispatched to establish a comprehensive mechanism to ensure a more effective response to the emergency situation in the light of new realities. The Secretary-General appointed an interim Special Representative and dispatched a team of military advisers to Mozambique. In addition to the war having stripped the country of much of its economic and social infrastructure, severely constricting the Government's already limited capacity to respond quickly and effectively to the emergency situation, Mozambique was also affected by the drought in the region (see below). Simultaneously with the joint United Nations/SADC appeal for the drought emergency in southern Africa, an appeal was launched at Maputo presenting the priority requirements for the internally displaced and the drought-affected populations.

Emergency assistance for 1992-1993 was estimated at more than $400 million. The total number of persons in need of direct support in 1992-1993 was 3.1 million. In April 1992, estimates of total food aid needs were 1.3 million tons for the 1992-1993 period. WFP assistance amounted to $57.4 million in food aid and logistics support, of which $28.2 million was used to support primary education and the forestry sector and $39.2 million for emergency feeding of displaced people. In response to the joint United Nations/SADC appeal, WFP would provide additional food aid assistance and internal transportation costs valued at $71 million for the crop year 1992/93.

Health sector requirements for 1991-1992 were valued at $6.1 million, of which $5.5 million, or 68 per cent, had been pledged. Emergency health services were integrated within the national health system and donor support was allocated through bilateral agreements and ongoing development assistance, with UNICEF and WHO being among the main channels of support.

GENERAL ASSEMBLY ACTION

On 9 December 1992, the General Assembly, on the recommendation of the Second Committee, adopted **resolution 47/42** without vote.

Assistance to Mozambique

The General Assembly,

Recalling Security Council resolution 386(1976) of 17 March 1976 and taking note of Council resolution 782(1992) of 13 October 1992,

Recalling also its relevant resolutions, in particular resolution 45/227 of 21 December 1990, in which it urged the international community to respond effectively and generously to the call for assistance to Mozambique,

Reaffirming the principles for humanitarian assistance contained in the annex to its resolution 46/182 of 19 December 1991,

Noting the signing at Rome, on 16 July 1992, of the Declaration on Guiding Principles for Humanitarian Assistance, which permits the expansion of relief programmes to cover all affected people in Mozambique, and urging all parties concerned to implement the Declaration,

Welcoming the signing at Rome, on 4 October 1992, of the General Peace Agreement for Mozambique, whose main goals are the establishment of lasting peace, the enhancement of democracy and the promotion of national reconciliation in that country,

Stressing the need for a sustained effort by the international community to respond to the increasing and urgent emergency humanitarian needs of the people of Mozambique, in the light of the current severe drought and the evolving process of repatriation of refugees and normalization of the lives of displaced persons,

Stressing also that a proper response to the current situation in Mozambique requires substantial international assistance in a comprehensive and integrated manner, linking emergency relief aid with additional rehabilitation and development assistance,

Having considered the report of the Secretary-General,

1. *Takes note* of the report of the Secretary-General;

2. *Expresses its appreciation* to the Secretary-General and the relevant organizations of the United Nations system for the measures taken to organize international assistance programmes for Mozambique;

3. *Expresses its gratitude* to all States and regional, intergovernmental and non-governmental organizations that have rendered assistance to Mozambique;

4. *Expresses its satisfaction* at the entry into force, on 15 October 1992, of the General Peace Agreement for Mozambique, in particular the cease-fire, which creates favourable conditions for the implementation of programmes of economic and social rehabilitation and the overall process of national reconstruction;

5. *Urges* the international community, in particular the United Nations system, to extend its full support and contribute to the peace-building process in Mozambique in accordance with the General Peace Agreement, providing, *inter alia*, assistance for the electoral process, emergency and rehabilitation assistance for refugees and displaced persons and support for programmes of demobilization of armed forces;

6. *Also urges* the international community, in the context of paragraph 5 above, to support and participate actively in the forthcoming conference of donor countries and organizations, to be held at Rome on 15 and 16 December 1992;

7. *Notes with appreciation* the establishment, in Mozambique, of a Committee on Humanitarian Assistance, with the participation of the United Nations, and the formulation of a unified plan for the delivery of relief assistance throughout the country;

8. *Draws the attention* of the international community to the unmet funding needs referred to in the 1992/93 Emergency Programme for Mozambique and the United Nations/Southern Africa Development Community Consolidated Appeal for the Drought Emergency in Southern Africa;

9. *Calls upon* all States, regional and interregional organizations, other intergovernmental organizations and international non-governmental organizations to intensify their development cooperation and assistance in support of the process of national reconstruction of Mozambique;

10. *Requests* the Secretary-General, in close cooperation with the Government of Mozambique:

   (a) To continue his efforts to mobilize the international assistance required by Mozambique;

   (b) To ensure the coordination of the work of the United Nations system for an adequate response to the emergency, rehabilitation and development needs of Mozambique;

   (c) To prepare a report on assistance to Mozambique for submission to the General Assembly at its forty-ninth session.

General Assembly resolution 47/42

9 December 1992   Meeting 81   Adopted without vote

Approved by Second Committee (A/47/727) without vote, 24 November (meeting 45); 47-nation draft (A/C.2/47/L.26/Rev.1); agenda item 87 *(b)*.

Sponsors: Algeria, Angola, Argentina, Bangladesh, Benin, Botswana, Brazil, Burkina Faso, Burundi, Cape Verde, China, Colombia, El Salvador, Finland, Gabon, Guatemala, Guinea-Bissau, India, Indonesia, Iran, Italy, Kenya,

Lesotho, Malawi, Mali, Mauritania, Mozambique, Namibia, Nepal, Nigeria, Norway, Poland, Portugal, Senegal, Singapore, Spain, Suriname, Sweden, Thailand, Tunisia, Uganda, United Kingdom, United Republic of Tanzania, United States, Vanuatu, Zambia, Zimbabwe.
Meeting numbers. GA 47th session: 2nd Committee 25, 26, 28, 30, 34, 38, 40, 42, 45; plenary 81.

Somalia

In accordance with a 1991 General Assembly request,[14] the Secretary-General submitted an October report on emergency assistance for humanitarian relief and the economic and social rehabilitation of Somalia.[15] The report contained information on the impact of the crisis, initiatives taken by the United Nations for emergency relief and rehabilitation, progress achieved and assistance by 12 Member States and the United Nations system.

In the 22 months since the overthrow of the Government, the situation in Somalia had continued to deteriorate. Almost 4.5 million people were threatened by severe malnutrition and related diseases. Of those, at least 1.5 million were at immediate mortal risk, with 300,000 people having already died since November 1991. No functioning government existed in most parts of the country and inter- and intra-clan violence abounded. The power struggle hampered the delivery of vitally needed humanitarian assistance and increasingly threatened relief workers.

Despite a situation which for most of the year bordered on anarchy, ICRC and a determined band of NGOs had maintained a continuous presence, principally at Mogadishu and Hargeisa. UNICEF re-established its presence in Mogadishu on 24 December 1991, while WFP re-established its operations in March 1992. Deliveries of humanitarian assistance were subject to extensive theft and looting, with relief workers labouring under extremely hazardous conditions. The breakdown in law and order had resulted in the deaths of many local and expatriate relief staff.

United Nations initiative for emergency relief and rehabilitation

In March, following a series of meetings in Mogadishu and New York, the United Nations successfully negotiated a cease-fire between the two factions contesting Mogadishu, making it possible for humanitarian assistance to reach both sides of the divided city. In May, it negotiated and established a vital route along the beach for convoys to pick up food from the port. On 18 March, the Secretary-General appointed a United Nations Coordinator for Humanitarian Assistance for Somalia. The Security Council, in April (see PART TWO, Chapter I), approved deployment of a 50-member observer force to monitor the cease-fire; agreed to the deployment of a 500-member security force to protect relief goods and personnel; and endorsed a 90-Day Plan of Action for Emergency Humanitarian Assistance to Somalia, as proposed by a technical mission that had visited the country. Those elements were brought under the aegis of the United Nations Operation in Somalia (UNOSOM), and the Secretary-General appointed a Special Representative for Somalia to provide overall direction of United Nations activities and assist in promoting peace and national reconciliation. The 50 military observers were deployed in July and August, while the 500-member security force arrived at Mogadishu in September.

A United Nations technical team visited Somalia from 6 to 15 August to examine ways to expand UNOSOM's scope and effectiveness. On the basis of the team's findings, the Secretary-General recommended to the Security Council[16] a substantial increase in airlift operations; the establishment of a preventive zone on the Kenya-Somalia border for special deliveries of food and seed to reduce famine-induced population movements; deployment of four additional security units of up to 750 persons each in different parts of the country; and the establishment of four UNOSOM zone headquarters headed by civilian officials as the operational basis for a comprehensive approach to the Somali problem. By **resolution 775(1992)** of 28 August, the Security Council endorsed those proposals and called on all parties, movements and factions to cooperate fully with the Secretary-General. Earlier, in **resolution 767(1992)** of 27 July, the Council had asserted that, in the absence of cooperation of the parties concerning deployment of United Nations security personnel, other measures to deliver humanitarian assistance to Somalia were not excluded.

100-day Action Programme for Somalia

The Under-Secretary-General for Humanitarian Affairs led a high-level inter-agency mission, including high-level officials of FAO, UNDP, UNHCR, UNICEF, WFP and WHO, to Somalia from 10 to 12 September, meeting with political leaders, clan elders, ICRC, NGOs and United Nations relief workers. A major outcome of the mission was the decision to develop the 100-day Action Programme for Accelerated Humanitarian Assistance for Somalia, covering the period until the end of 1992. The Programme was drafted and refined through a collaborative process involving United Nations agencies, NGOs and other entities and reviewed at a coordination meeting on humanitarian assistance for Somalia (Geneva, 12 and 13 October). The Programme's priority actions included: massive infusion of food aid; expansion of supplementary feeding; provision of basic health services and a mass immunization campaign; urgent provision of clean water, sanitation and hygiene and of shelter material, including blankets and clothes; simultaneous delivery of seeds, tools and animal vaccines with food rations; prevention of further refugee outflows and displacements and initiation of returnee programmes; and promotion of rebuilding of civil society and local institutions, economic and social recovery and rehabilitation.

Resources of up to $83 million were required to implement the Programme, which called for some 50,000 metric tons of food per month to be delivered and distributed in Somalia.

In a December review of the 100-day Action Programme, DHA noted that deaths from starvation had been substantially reduced in most of the worst-affected famine areas, but remained, overall, at unacceptably high levels. The response from the donor community had been prompt and generous: of the $83 million requested under the Programme, $53 million was either received or pledged by early December. While food requirements were fully resourced, in some sectors underfunding or slow honouring of pledges prevented the start of activities.

A follow-up meeting to review the 100-day Action Programme was held at Addis Ababa from 3 to 5 December. Participants discussed constraints in the Programme's implementation and how to enhance collaboration between the international community and Somali society. They accepted the importance of deploying humanitarian protection forces and recommended that the focus of the forces should be on protecting key installation gateways to Somalia, including airports and overland delivery routes, the delivery process, international and Somali aid workers and their facilities and the beneficiaries of relief assistance. They recognized that the Programme's original targets needed to be reassessed, assistance to Somalia's north needed to be stepped up and, in addition to food aid, greater efforts should be made on monetization of food to stimulate the economy and encourage local food production.

In a 29 October statement to the Second Committee,[17] the Under-Secretary-General for Humanitarian Affairs said he was convinced of the great need for urgent action in Somalia. He expressed appreciation to the World Bank for a grant of $20 million for the Somali people.

GENERAL ASSEMBLY ACTION

On 18 December 1992, the General Assembly, on the recommendation of the Second Committee, adopted **resolution 47/160** without vote.

Emergency assistance for humanitarian relief and the economic and social rehabilitation of Somalia

The General Assembly,

Recalling its resolutions 43/206 of 20 December 1988, 44/178 of 19 December 1989, 45/229 of 21 December 1990 and 46/176 of 19 December 1991 and the resolutions and decisions of the Economic and Social Council on emergency assistance to Somalia,

Taking note of Security Council resolutions 733(1992) of 23 January 1992, 746(1992) of 17 March 1992, 751(1992) of 24 April 1992, 767(1992) of 27 July 1992 and 775(1992) of 28 August 1992, in which the Council, *inter alia*, urged all parties, movements and factions in Somalia to facilitate the efforts of the United Nations, its specialized agencies and humanitarian organizations to provide urgent humanitarian assistance to the affected population in Somalia and reiterated the call for the full respect of the security and safety of the personnel of those organizations and the guarantee of their complete freedom of movement in and around Mogadishu and other parts of Somalia,

Noting with appreciation the cooperation between the United Nations, the Organization of African Unity, the League of Arab States and the Organization of the Islamic Conference in their efforts to resolve the humanitarian, security and political crisis in Somalia,

Noting the efforts of the countries of the Horn of Africa and the countries of the Non-Aligned Movement to alleviate the situation in Somalia,

Noting with appreciation the measures taken by the Secretary-General to mobilize international assistance for Somalia,

Deeply concerned at the magnitude of human suffering in Somalia, the extensive damage to and destruction of villages, towns and cities, the heavy damage inflicted by the civil conflict on the infrastructure of the country and the widespread disruption of public facilities and services,

Gravely concerned about the continually deteriorating situation in Somalia, which underlines the urgent need for the accelerated delivery of adequate humanitarian assistance to all parts of the country,

Taking note of the report of the Secretary-General on emergency assistance to Somalia and the statement made before the Second Committee of the General Assembly on 29 October 1992 by the Under-Secretary-General for Humanitarian Affairs on special economic and disaster relief assistance,

Deeply appreciative of the humanitarian assistance rendered by a number of Member States to alleviate the hardship and suffering of the affected population,

Recalling the principle enunciated in the annex to its resolution 46/182 of 19 December 1991, which states that contributions for humanitarian assistance should be provided in a way that is not to the detriment of resources made available for international cooperation for development,

Noting the importance of the four operational zones for more effective humanitarian and relief assistance under current conditions in the country,

Noting with great satisfaction the humanitarian efforts being made by the various entities of the United Nations system and by intergovernmental and non-governmental organizations,

Noting with concern the disastrous impact that the conflict is having on the educational system of the country and the total disruption of schooling for all students at the primary, secondary and university levels,

Recognizing the importance of rehabilitating the basic social and economic services at the local level in all operational zones,

Cognizant that the exodus and displacement of skilled and professional manpower is eliminating the human resources of the country, which are much needed for rehabilitation, reconstruction and development,

Welcoming the policy initiatives taken by some Member States in providing educational assistance and scholarships to eligible Somali asylum seekers,

Further recognizing that emergency assistance must be provided in ways that will be supportive of recovery and long-term development,

1. *Expresses its gratitude* to the Member States and the intergovernmental and non-governmental organizations that have responded to the appeals of the Secretary-General and others by extending emergency assistance to Somalia;

2. *Expresses its appreciation* to the Secretary-General for the measures taken to mobilize emergency assistance to the affected population in Somalia;

3. *Appeals* to all States and relevant intergovernmental and non-governmental organizations to continue to extend emergency assistance to Somalia, taking into account the report of the Secretary-General and the 100-day Action Programme for Accelerated Humanitarian Assistance endorsed at the Coordination Meeting for Humanitarian Assistance for Somalia held at Geneva on 12 and 13 October 1992;

4. *Welcomes* the ongoing efforts of the United Nations, the Organization of African Unity, the League of Arab States, the Organization of the Islamic Conference, the countries of the Horn of Africa and the countries of the Non-Aligned Movement to resolve the situation in Somalia;

5. *Urges* all States and relevant intergovernmental and non-governmental organizations to assist in embarking on the rehabilitation of basic social and economic services as well as institution-building assistance aimed at the restoration of civil administration at the local level in all those parts of Somalia where peace, security and stability prevail;

6. *Encourages* all Member States, United Nations entities and non-governmental organizations to ensure that all assistance programmes draw as much as possible on local and regional priorities and build on indigenous capacities, making maximum use of educationally qualified and skilled Somalis from within and outside the country;

7. *Appeals* to all States and relevant intergovernmental and non-governmental organizations to provide financial and material assistance for the reopening of primary and secondary schools in those areas where conditions permit;

8. *Decides* to establish, through extrabudgetary resources, a United Nations scholarship programme for Somali undergraduate university students whose studies have been disrupted by the ongoing civil strife, so as to enable them to complete their studies at higher institutes and universities abroad and thus enhance the human resource capacity of Somalia, and to review the situation when the Somali university and higher institutes re-open, and urges Member States and relevant intergovernmental and non-governmental organizations to contribute to this programme;

9. *Requests* the Secretary-General to ensure, within existing regular budgetary resources, that information about the scholarships that have been offered will be disseminated to those Somali students, within and outside Somalia, who might qualify for such scholarships;

10. *Urges* the specialized agencies and other organizations of the United Nations system concerned, in particular the United Nations Development Programme,

the Office of the United Nations High Commissioner for Refugees, the United Nations Children's Fund, the World Health Organization, the Food and Agriculture Organization of the United Nations, the World Food Programme, the United Nations Centre for Human Settlements and the United Nations Environment Programme, to continue to implement their assistance programmes in their respective fields of competence, within the framework of the United Nations Operation in Somalia, on the most urgent basis, in order to alleviate the suffering of the affected population in all parts of Somalia;

11. *Appeals* to all parties concerned to terminate hostilities and to engage in a national reconciliation process that will lead to the re-establishment of peace, order and stability and also facilitate relief and rehabilitation efforts;

12. *Calls upon* the Secretary-General to continue to mobilize international humanitarian assistance for Somalia;

13. *Calls upon* all parties, movements and factions in Somalia to respect fully the security and safety of personnel of the United Nations and its specialized agencies and of non-governmental organizations, and to guarantee their complete freedom of movement throughout Somalia;

14. *Requests* the Secretary-General, in view of the critical situation in Somalia, to take all measures necessary for the implementation of the present resolution, to apprise the Economic and Social Council at its substantive session of 1993 of the progress made and to report thereon to the General Assembly at its forty-eighth session.

General Assembly resolution 47/160

18 December 1992   Meeting 92   Adopted without vote

Approved by Second Committee (A/47/727/Add.1) without vote, 7 December (meeting 48); draft by Bangladesh, China, Egypt, India, Indonesia, Jamaica, Kuwait, Mauritius, on behalf of the African States, Myanmar, Oman, Peru, Philippines, Saudi Arabia, Singapore, Somalia, Sri Lanka, Sudan, Suriname, Thailand, Trinidad and Tobago, Turkey, United Arab Emirates, Yemen (A/C.2/47/L.36/Rev.1); agenda item 87 *(b)*.
Meeting numbers. GA 47th session: 2nd Committee 25, 26, 28, 30, 34, 38, 40, 42, 45, 46, 48; plenary 92.

By **resolution 794(1992)**, the Security Council demanded that all parties, movements and factions in Somalia take the necessary measures to facilitate efforts of the United Nations and of humanitarian organizations to provide urgent humanitarian assistance to the affected population (see PART TWO, Chapter I).

Sudan

In response to a 1991 General Assembly request,[18] the Secretary-General submitted an October report on emergency assistance to the Sudan and Operation Lifeline Sudan.[19] The report reviewed the situation in the Sudan and the implementation of emergency operations. It also described the refugee situation; relief food and non-food assistance; and action taken by eight Member States (Denmark, Germany, Indonesia, Norway, Poland, the Republic of Korea, Sweden and Turkey) and by United Nations organizations. The report stated that the plight of those affected by drought, civil conflict and displacement had worsened. The overall food supply situation remained extremely difficult and in some areas critical. FAO reported that rainfall was average to above average through most of the Sudan with prospects of a good harvest. However, ongoing conflict in southern Sudan still precluded normal agricultural activity.

The situation for the increasing numbers of newly displaced people, returnees and other war-affected people had become desperate. An FAO/WFP assessment had indicated that some 5.2 million drought-affected persons and 1.9 million displaced persons would need assistance in 1992.

Emergency requirements, including those under Operation Lifeline Sudan,[20] were reflected in the Consolidated Inter-Agency Appeals for the Horn of Africa (see above). Urgent requirements identified in those appeals totalled $281.5 million. After the arrival of 270,000 returnees to the Sobat basin and Pochalla in June, Operation Lifeline Sudan committed almost all its resources to assisting them. With significant NGO collaboration, basic services, including deliveries of WFP food supplies by airlift, were provided. The southern operations of Operation Lifeline Sudan expanded in the 12 months before January 1992. However, by mid-June, the Operation's international presence in southern areas had been reduced because of lack of security or inaccessibility. United Nations flights, which were suspended for two months because of lack of clearance by all parties concerned, resumed to certain locations in June. All relief activities in the Bor-Kongor area were suspended in September when two UNICEF staff members, an NGO worker and a journalist were killed there while on mission.

The late arrival of food donated to the 1992 relief operation constrained WFP and NGO ability to pre-position food in affected areas early in 1992. It was not until May that the first ship arrived in Port Sudan carrying 1992 food aid.

The United Nations and NGOs also provided emergency assistance to displaced persons and squatters relocated by the Government of the Sudan. A World Bank–funded Khartoum structure plan was developed, which outlined viable actions Government authorities should take regarding the displaced and squatter problem. In addition, the United Nations developed medium-term and long-term proposals, including a project to improve urban management.

The Under-Secretary-General for Humanitarian Affairs held high-level discussions with the Government of the Sudan between 13 and 16 September on means to improve the delivery of humanitarian assistance. In a joint statement of 16 September,[21] the Sudan and the United Nations reaffirmed the critical importance of access to all people in need of humanitarian assistance, respect for the neutrality of relief operations and the fundamental necessity for transparency. Agreement was also reached on the use of corridors for prompt delivery and distribution of humanitarian assistance, efforts to facilitate procedures so as to expedite the entry, travel and work of NGOs, the need to support the voluntary return of Sudanese refugees, repatriation and reuniting of unaccompanied minors with their families, mobilization of resources to support the transition to recovery, rehabilitation and development, and the appointment of a Special Emissary for follow-up with the Government of the Sudan.

GENERAL ASSEMBLY ACTION

On 18 December 1992, the General Assembly, on the recommendation of the Second Committee, adopted **resolution 47/162** without vote.

Emergency assistance to the Sudan

The General Assembly,

Recalling its resolutions 43/8 of 18 October 1988, 43/52 of 6 December 1988, 44/12 of 24 October 1989, 45/226 of 21 December 1990 and 46/178 of 19 December 1991 on assistance to the Sudan,

Taking note of the Declaration, Framework of Cooperation, and Programme of Action, adopted at the Summit of the Heads of State and Government of the countries of the Horn of Africa, held at Addis Ababa on 8 and 9 April 1992, and the principles embodied therein,

Noting with deep concern the continuing negative impact of armed conflict on the socio-economic infrastructure of the Sudan and the displacement of a large number of persons,

Noting with satisfaction the projected increase in cereal production in the Sudanese harvest for 1992/93, which should first be used to meet the needs of the people,

Recognizing, however, that there continues to be a need in the Sudan for strong and continued international solidarity and humanitarian support as a complement to its own efforts to meet its urgent needs in 1993,

Taking note of the report of the Secretary-General,

1. *Notes* the agreement between the Government of the Sudan and the United Nations, as reflected in the joint statement issued on 16 September 1992 during the visit of the Under-Secretary-General for Humanitarian Affairs to Khartoum, and calls upon all parties to adhere to this agreement;

2. *Expresses its deep gratitude and appreciation* to the States and the intergovernmental and non-governmental organizations that are providing assistance to the country in the context of the Sudan Emergency Operation and Operation Lifeline Sudan;

3. *Expresses its full appreciation* to the Secretary-General and the organizations of the United Nations system for their efforts to coordinate and mobilize resources and support for the Sudan Emergency Operation and Operation Lifeline Sudan and requests them to continue these efforts;

4. *Calls upon* the international community to continue to contribute generously to the emergency needs of the country, especially in the areas of supplementary feeding, non-food items, storage, transportation and emergency recovery;

5. *Appeals* to all parties concerned to pursue dialogue and negotiations and to terminate hostilities to allow for the re-establishment of peace, order and stability and also to facilitate relief efforts;

6. *Stresses* the importance of assuring safe access for personnel providing relief assistance to all in need;

7. *Urges* all parties involved to offer all feasible assistance, including facilitating the movement of relief supplies and personnel, to guarantee maximum success of the Sudan Emergency Operation in all parts of the country;

8. *Requests* the Secretary-General to continue to assess the emergency situation in the Sudan and to report thereon to the General Assembly at its forty-eighth session.

General Assembly resolution 47/162

18 December 1992   Meeting 92   Adopted without vote

Approved by Second Committee (A/47/727/Add.1) without vote, 7 December (meeting 48); 17-nation draft (A/C.2/47/L.48/Rev.1); agenda item 87 *(b)*.

Sponsors: Afghanistan, Benin, China, Ethiopia, Iraq, Jordan, Libyan Arab Jamahiriya, Malaysia, Mali, Mauritania, Oman, Sri Lanka, Sudan, Suriname, Syrian Arab Republic, United Republic of Tanzania, Yemen.

Meeting numbers. GA 47th session: 2nd Committee 25, 26, 28, 30, 34, 38, 40, 42, 45, 46, 48; plenary 92.

Asia

Afghanistan

In response to a 1991 General Assembly request,[22] the Secretary-General submitted a November report on the situation in Afghanistan.[23] In addition to reviewing his efforts and those of his Personal Representative in Afghanistan and Pakistan towards a comprehensive political settlement (see PART TWO, Chapter III), the report also discussed the humanitarian activities of the United Nations system, coordinated by the United Nations Office for the Coordination of Humanitarian and Economic Assistance Programmes Relating to Afghanistan (UNOCA).

The Secretary-General observed that 14 years of war had resulted in more than 1 million people dead, 2 million disabled, tens of thousands of orphans and widows, over 5 million refugees and more than 2 million internally displaced persons in a country that had been subjected to total devastation. Afghanistan, one of the least developed countries even before its destructive war, faced an emergency of immense proportions, compounded by the huge number of returning refugees.

To address the severe humanitarian situation, UNOCA had issued in November 1991 the Operation Salam Programme for 1992, with a proposed budget of $133.7 million. On 6 April 1992, in response to the deteriorating situation in Kabul, the Secretary-General appealed to the international community for 30,000 tons of emergency food assistance. Based on the report of a UNOCA-led inter-agency assessment mission, which visited Afghanistan from 11 to 15 May to identify emergency humanitarian needs, the Secretary-General

launched, on 5 June, a Consolidated Appeal for Emergency Humanitarian Assistance for Afghanistan, requesting $180 million for the period 1 June to 31 December 1992, including $76 million representing the shortfall in funding for the Operation Salam Programme, 1992. The Appeal's main sectors comprised food aid ($45.1 million); voluntary repatriation ($52.8 million); health, including water supply and sanitation ($30.6 million); and mine clearance ($15 million). As at 30 October, Governments had pledged or contributed $59.2 million towards the $180 million sought.

Continued hostilities in Kabul during July and August resulted in further large-scale destruction and death. On 25 August, the Secretary-General's Personal Representative issued a Note on Immediate Needs in Afghanistan, which requested $10 million, within the context of the 5 June Consolidated Appeal, for urgent relief necessitated by the Kabul hostilities. The Note was presented to the donor community in Geneva, Islamabad and New York.

Following discussions with the authorities during a visit to Kabul on 21 October, the Personal Representative, on 1 November, issued a Note on Emergency Winter Needs for Afghanistan, seeking a further $17.6 million for winter programmes within the context of the 5 June Appeal.

Meanwhile, the change of Government in April, accompanied by the cessation of hostilities in most areas outside Kabul, led to an enormous increase in voluntary refugee repatriations from both Iran and Pakistan. By the end of October, over 1.2 million people had benefited from a UNHCR/WFP repatriation grant programme. A UNOCA-executed mine-clearance programme provided basic mine-awareness training and actual mine clearance. The 5 June Consolidated Appeal had requested $15 million for this essential programme, against which only $5.8 million was pledged. On 2 and 3 September, floods caused by heavy rainfall in the Hindu Kush mountains inundated villages, killing many and destroying houses and agricultural land. A United Nations team immediately proceeded to the area to assess the damage and deliver emergency food and medical and shelter supplies. DHA received pledges totalling $180,000 towards the relief effort.

The Secretary-General regretted that the response to the 5 June Consolidated Appeal had been far from satisfactory, and cautioned that unless needs could be adequately and effectively addressed in the early stages, the possibilities for overcoming Afghanistan's humanitarian emergency in the foreseeable future would be limited.

GENERAL ASSEMBLY ACTION

On 18 December 1992, the General Assembly adopted **resolution 47/119** without vote.

Emergency international assistance for the reconstruction of war-stricken Afghanistan

The General Assembly,

Noting that the establishment of the Islamic State in Afghanistan provides a new opportunity for reconstruction of the country,

Wishing the people of Afghanistan peace and prosperity,

Expressing the hope that the Islamic State will continue its efforts towards further stabilization of the security situation in the country, so as to contribute to the safe delivery of international aid,

Deeply concerned about the massive destruction of properties and the serious damage to the economic and social infrastructure of Afghanistan caused by the fourteen years of war,

Underlining the importance of the rehabilitation and reconstruction of Afghanistan for the prosperity of its people, who have suffered many hardships during fourteen years of war and devastation and who have lost the chance for development throughout the conflict,

Aware that Afghanistan continues to suffer from an extremely critical economic situation as a land-locked and least developed country,

Affirming the urgent need to initiate international action to assist Afghanistan in restoring basic services and in rebuilding the country,

Noting with sympathy the urgent appeal for international humanitarian assistance made to the international community by the Government of the Islamic State of Afghanistan,

Expressing its hope that the international community will respond adequately to the Consolidated Appeal for Emergency Humanitarian Assistance for Afghanistan, launched by the Secretary-General on 5 June 1992,

Thanking all Governments that have rendered assistance to Afghan refugees, in particular the Governments of Pakistan and the Islamic Republic of Iran, and recognizing the need for international assistance for the repatriation and resettlement of refugees and internally displaced persons,

Expressing its appreciation to the States and the intergovernmental and non-governmental organizations that have responded and continue to respond to the humanitarian needs of Afghanistan and to the Secretary-General and his Personal Representative for mobilizing and coordinating the delivery of appropriate humanitarian assistance,

1. *Encourages* the efforts of the Government and people of the Islamic State of Afghanistan towards rehabilitation and reconstruction;

2. *Welcomes with appreciation* the efforts undertaken by the Secretary-General in drawing the attention of the international community to the acute problems of Afghanistan and in mobilizing assistance for rehabilitation and reconstruction of the country;

3. *Urgently appeals* to all States, organizations and programmes of the United Nations, specialized agencies, and other intergovernmental and non-governmental organizations to provide, on a priority basis, all possible financial, technical and material assistance for the repatriation and resettlement of refugees and internally displaced persons, full restoration of basic services and reconstruction of Afghanistan, having in mind the availability of the Afghanistan Emergency Trust Fund as referred to in paragraph 5 below;

4. *Requests* the Secretary-General:

(a) To ensure the continued operation and further strengthening of "humanitarian and economic assistance programmes relating to Afghanistan";

(b) To dispatch, as soon as possible, a team of experts to Afghanistan to evaluate the situation in the light of the war damage and destruction and to prepare a comprehensive report, in cooperation with the Government of Afghanistan, on requirements for the rehabilitation and reconstruction of the country;

(c) To initiate a plan for mobilizing financial, technical and material assistance, including the convening of a conference of donor States and international financial institutions;

5. *Also appeals* to all Member States, in particular donor countries, to provide emergency financial assistance to the Afghanistan Emergency Trust Fund established in August 1988 and to consolidated appeals by the Secretary-General for emergency humanitarian assistance for Afghanistan;

6. *Invites* the international financial institutions and specialized agencies, organizations and programmes of the United Nations system, where appropriate, to bring the special needs of the Islamic State of Afghanistan to the attention of their respective governing bodies for their consideration and to report on the decisions of those bodies to the Secretary-General;

7. *Invites* the Secretary-General to continue to monitor the overall situation in Afghanistan and make available his good offices as required and to report to the General Assembly at its forty-eighth session;

8. *Requests* the Secretary-General to report to the General Assembly at its forty-eighth session on the progress made in the implementation of the present resolution;

9. *Decides* to include in the provisional agenda of its forty-eighth session the item entitled "Emergency international assistance for the reconstruction of war-stricken Afghanistan".

General Assembly resolution 47/119

18 December 1992   Meeting 91   Adopted without vote

35-nation draft (A/47/L.25/Rev.1 & Add.1); agenda item 141.

Sponsors: Afghanistan, Bahrain, Bangladesh, Bosnia and Herzegovina, Brunei Darussalam, Chad, Chile, China, Costa Rica, Cyprus, El Salvador, Honduras, India, Indonesia, Iran, Jordan, Kuwait, Lebanon, Libyan Arab Jamahiriya, Malaysia, Nicaragua, Oman, Pakistan, Russian Federation, Saudi Arabia, Sri Lanka, Sudan, Suriname, Tajikistan, Thailand, Turkey, United Arab Emirates, United States, Uruguay, Yemen.

Financial implications. 5th Committee, A/47/801; S-G, A/C.5/47/72.

Meeting numbers. GA 47th session: 5th Committee 47; plenary 73, 91.

Gulf Task Force

The UNDP Administrator submitted to the Governing Council a report giving an overview of proposals for the socio-economic and environmental recovery of countries affected by the Persian Gulf crisis of 1990-1991.[24] He noted that, in 1991,[25] he had established a Gulf Task Force to assist in the move from emergency relief to development.

Regional proposals included a human development and returnee programme for the Arab region and Asia ($8 million) and a Gulf war recovery programme for women ($3 million). Country-specific and territory-specific proposals were submitted for Jordan ($4.5 billion); the occupied Palestinian territories ($86.5 million); the Syrian Arab Republic ($1.8 million); the Sudan ($7.6 million); Viet Nam ($3.9 million); and Yemen ($245 million). Other proposals covered environmental rehabilitation and management of the economic impact of the Gulf crisis.

Another report[26] proposed a funding strategy for the affected countries, which had been developed at a December 1991 meeting of the international community.[25]

On 14 February,[27] the Council endorsed the proposed funding strategy for the socio-economic and environmental recovery of countries affected by the Gulf crisis and expressed continuing concern at the impact of the crisis on the affected countries and at the lack of sufficient funds to enable recovery. It noted the importance of collective action to assist the affected countries and of collaboration between them, donor countries, the United Nations system, multilateral financial institutions and NGOs. The Council requested the Administrator to continue to assist all affected countries in formulating and pursuing proposals for recovery at the national, regional and interregional levels, through UNDP field offices, its bureaux and units and in dialogue with donors at the country level, particularly regarding the human problem of returning labour migrants and management of the economic and environmental impact of the crisis.

Iraq

In April 1992, DHA assumed responsibility for the coordination of the United Nations Inter-Agency Humanitarian Programme for Iraq, established by the Secretary-General in 1991.[28] At the invitation of Iraq, the Under-Secretary-General for Humanitarian Affairs visited Baghdad from 17 to 22 August to negotiate an extension of the Memorandum of Understanding governing the Programme, which had expired on 30 June. Since final agreement could not be reached, negotiations resumed in Baghdad from 14 to 17 October, resulting in an agreement *ad referendum* on a new Memorandum of Understanding providing a framework for a humanitarian programme until 31 March 1993. The agreement was signed in New York on 22 October. Based on the findings of an inter-agency mission in September, a Winter Plan for Northern Iraq totalling over $85.5 million was drawn up in October to meet the basic survival needs of the most vulnerable groups. A plan of action covering all of Iraq was also prepared and agreed upon with the Government. Urgent requirements covering the period up to 31 March 1993 were estimated at $217 million. The total budget of the plan was revised to $206 million, of which $166 million was mobilized and ef-

fectively delivered. Under the plan, pre-positioning of food, fuel and other basis needs, provision of road repairs, shelter materials and medical supplies, immunization programmes, water and sanitation services, supply of agricultural inputs, education, rehabilitation and psycho-social support for disabled children were proposed (see also PART TWO, Chapter III).

Lebanon

In response to requests made in 1991 by the General Assembly[29] and the Economic and Social Council,[30] the Secretary-General submitted a July report on assistance for the reconstruction and development of Lebanon.[31]

The report stated that Lebanon's encouraging economic results of 1991 were not sustainable beyond the short term in so far as its exchange rate and price stabilization policy implied a major fiscal adjustment. The injection of a large dose of liquidity, as a result of a 120 per cent salary increase in the public sector, led to a depreciation in the value of the Lebanese pound and the abandonment of the stabilization policy in February 1992. The Government subsequently announced an emergency plan to deal with the economic crisis centring on control of the fiscal deficit. Also in February, a government initiative was announced towards solving the problem of the more than 500,000 displaced persons, roughly 20 per cent of the population. Lebanon's Council for Development and Reconstruction activated and accelerated preparations to initiate reconstruction and mobilize the required resources.

United Nations economic assistance to Lebanon was managed at the central level by the Under-Secretary-General for Political Affairs. At the field level, the programme of United Nations Assistance for the Reconstruction and Development of Lebanon (UNARDOL) functioned as the United Nations coordinator's office. In accordance with a 1991 Assembly invitation,[29] the Secretary-General nominated a Resident Coordinator in Beirut. The Coordinator assumed duty in January 1992 and immediately took action to create a coherent framework for enhanced coordination and expanded activities of economic and technical assistance. In addition, UNDP reactivated its operations and appointed a Resident Representative who simultaneously functioned as UNARDOL Resident Coordinator. A new WHO representative and coordinator was also appointed. In support of its representative, UNICEF appointed a Programme Officer. The UNESCO Regional Office for Education in the Arab States reopened in Beirut in April.

UNARDOL participated in the World Bank Economic Assessment Mission to Lebanon (20 April–1 May) and maintained close contacts with the

World Bank group and IMF. An Economic and Social Commission for Western Asia (ESCWA) team visited Lebanon from 10 to 12 March and identified six target areas for assistance: survey of Lebanese expatriates; strengthening of statistics; framework of macroeconomic policies; housing problems and priority programmes; industrial survey and development of industrial estates; and rehabilitation of the agricultural sector, with emphasis on agricultural credit and replacement of undesirable crops. UNICEF finalized with the Lebanese Government a five-year programme of cooperation (1992-1996) that was submitted to its Executive Board in June for a commitment of $5 million from general resources and $20 million from external funding to be sought.

During the reporting period (1 August 1991–31 May 1992), UNDP activities concentrated on preparatory work for the third country programme for Lebanon and on management of ongoing programme activities, including identification and formulation of programmes for rehabilitation of priority sectors. Total fourth (1987-1991) and fifth (1992-1996) cycle IPF or core UNDP resources committed by May amounted to $3.8 billion, leaving $15 million uncommitted. UNDP provided $50,000 from SPR for emergency assistance for the victims of severe winter snowstorms.

ECONOMIC AND SOCIAL COUNCIL ACTION

On 30 July 1992, the Economic and Social Council adopted **resolution 1992/42** without vote.

Assistance for the reconstruction and development of Lebanon

The Economic and Social Council,

Recalling General Assembly resolution 46/173 of 19 December 1991 on assistance for the reconstruction and development of Lebanon, as well as previous resolutions adopted by the Economic and Social Council in which the specialized agencies and other organizations and bodies of the United Nations system were called upon to expand and intensify their programmes of assistance in response to the urgent needs of Lebanon,

Aware of the deteriorating economic conditions of Lebanon and the magnitude of the country's prevailing needs,

Noting with great concern the high rate of inflation in Lebanon during the past few years, the catastrophic erosion of the value of the country's currency and the severe destruction of its infrastructure,

1. *Appeals* to all Member States and all organizations of the United Nations system to intensify their efforts to mobilize all possible assistance for the Government of Lebanon in its reconstruction and development efforts, in accordance with the relevant resolutions and decisions of the General Assembly and the Economic and Social Council;

2. *Invites* the Secretary-General to inform the Economic and Social Council at its substantive session of 1993 of the progress made in the implementation of the present resolution.

Economic and Social Council resolution 1992/42

30 July 1992   Meeting 41   Adopted without vote

12-nation draft (E/1992/L.31), as orally revised; agenda item 9.
Sponsors: Algeria, Egypt, France, Italy, Jordan, Kuwait, Lebanon, Morocco, Pakistan, Spain, Suriname, Syrian Arab Republic.

GENERAL ASSEMBLY ACTION

On 18 December 1992, the General Assembly, on the recommendation of the Second Committee, adopted **resolution 47/155** without vote.

Assistance for the reconstruction and development of Lebanon

The General Assembly,

Recalling its resolution 46/173 of 19 December 1991 and its previous resolutions on assistance for the reconstruction and development of Lebanon, taking note of Economic and Social Council resolution 1992/42 of 30 July 1992 and recalling other relevant resolutions and decisions previously adopted by the Council,

Taking note of the report of the Secretary-General,

Aware of the severe destruction of the infrastructure of Lebanon, and the continuing deterioration of its economic situation and basic services and the detrimental effects of such destruction and deterioration on social conditions and on the reconstruction and rehabilitation efforts of the country,

Reaffirming the urgent need to initiate regional and international action to assist the Government of Lebanon in rebuilding the country and restoring its human and economic capacities,

1. *Expresses its appreciation* to the Secretary-General for his report and for his endeavours to mobilize assistance to Lebanon;

2. *Commends* the Under-Secretary-General for Political Affairs for his coordination of system-wide assistance to Lebanon;

3. *Calls upon* Member States and international and regional organizations to provide financial and technical assistance to Lebanon in their programmes of assistance for rehabilitation and reconstruction whenever possible;

4. *Calls upon* all organizations and programmes of the United Nations system to intensify their assistance in response to the urgent needs of Lebanon and to take the steps necessary to ensure that their offices in Beirut are adequately staffed as soon as possible;

5. *Invites* the Secretary-General to intensify his efforts to mobilize all possible assistance to Lebanon and to report to the General Assembly at its forty-eighth session on the progress made in the implementation of the present resolution.

General Assembly resolution 47/155

18 December 1992   Meeting 92   Adopted without vote

Approved by Second Committee (A/47/727/Add.1) without vote, 25 November (meeting 46); 20-nation draft (A/C.2/47/L.18/Rev.1); agenda item 87 *(b)*.
Sponsors: Algeria, Bahrain, Brazil, Chile, Cyprus, Djibouti, Egypt, El Salvador, Honduras, Jordan, Kuwait, Lebanon, Libyan Arab Jamahiriya, Mexico, Saudi Arabia, Spain, Syrian Arab Republic, Tunisia, United Arab Emirates, Yemen.
Meeting numbers. GA 47th session: 2nd Committee 25, 26, 28, 30, 34, 38, 40, 42, 45, 46; plenary 92.

Europe

Croatia

By a letter of 27 August,[32] Croatia reported that the major military operations of the war in Croatia, which had started in June 1991, halted during January 1992, when a fragile cease-fire was reached (see PART TWO, Chapter IV). However, attacks against specific cities and regions were continuing and the United Nations Protection Force (UNPROFOR), under whose mandate four areas of Croatia fell, was not capable of resolving the problems of the heavy burden of human casualties, material destruction and the tide of refugees and displaced persons. More than 4,200 people had died and more than 20,000 had been wounded as a result of military operations, with the estimate of missing persons exceeding 18,000. Several cities were heavily damaged and many villages totally destroyed. The total war damage in Croatia was estimated at around $40 billion. Croatia was providing food, medical assistance and accommodation for more than 270,000 internally displaced persons, in addition to 360,000 refugees from Bosnia and Herzegovina. Croatia deemed it essential that it be granted disaster area status and that all necessary assistance be provided by the international community as soon as possible. In a 20 October letter,[33] Croatia communicated to the Secretary-General a further assessment of the war damage.

Following the International Conference on the Former Yugoslavia (London, 26-28 August 1992) (see PART TWO, Chapter IV), a high-level meeting of the Humanitarian Issues Working Group[34] was held on 4 December. The Working Group was informed that there were some 3 million refugees, displaced persons and other victims of the conflict in the former Yugoslavia, who were in need of humanitarian assistance. A UNHCR/DHA-coordinated inter-agency mission visited the former Yugoslavia from 9 to 16 August. In the framework of the United Nations Consolidated Inter-Agency Programme of Action and Appeal for the Former Yugoslavia, which was launched by the Secretary-General on 4 September and requested $434 million for 2.7 million affected people in all areas of the former Yugoslavia, Croatia's requirements were estimated at $92.1 million.

GENERAL ASSEMBLY ACTION

On 18 December 1992, the General Assembly, on the recommendation of the Second Committee, adopted **resolution 47/166** without vote.

International cooperation and assistance to alleviate the consequences of war in Croatia and to facilitate its recovery

The General Assembly,

Recalling its resolution 46/182 of 19 December 1991 and the annex thereto,

Deeply concerned about the serious aggravation of the humanitarian situation as a direct consequence of the ongoing conflict in the former Yugoslavia,

Conscious of the extensive material destruction of major sectors of the national infrastructure, dwellings, the environment and the cultural heritage in Croatia,

Aware that, owing to the constant increase in the number of refugees in Croatia, emergency assistance and humanitarian relief should be continued and expanded,

Deeply concerned about the suffering of the victims of war and of the tides of refugees and displaced persons,

Noting the efforts of the Government of Croatia to solve the problems of the postwar reconstruction of the national infrastructure and, at the same time, to solve the problem of refugees, displaced persons and victims of war within the Republic of Croatia,

Expressing concern about the potential effects of the deepening of the crisis in the former Yugoslavia in the event that, *inter alia*, no rapid process of postwar recovery in Croatia is established,

Recognizing the importance of the interrelationship between economic recovery and peaceful inter-ethnic relations,

Recognizing that the Office of the United Nations High Commissioner for Refugees, the United Nations Children's Fund and other organizations and programmes of the United Nations system are providing emergency humanitarian relief assistance to all areas of the former Yugoslavia, including the Republic of Croatia, and that such humanitarian aid should be organized in such a way as to facilitate the recovery of Croatia,

1. *Appeals* to all States, regional organizations, intergovernmental and non-governmental organizations and other relevant bodies to provide cooperation in various forms and special and other assistance, in particular in the most severely affected areas and with a view to facilitating the return of refugees and internally displaced persons to those areas;

2. *Requests* the Secretary-General, having regard for the continuum ranging from emergency relief to the longer-term development needs of the war-torn region, to initiate, in cooperation with the Government of Croatia, an assessment of needs for the rehabilitation, reconstruction and development of Croatia, and to introduce, if appropriate, an international appeal for the funding of a programme for rehabilitation, reconstruction and development;

3. *Also requests* the Secretary-General to submit a comprehensive report to the General Assembly at its forty-eighth session on the implementation of the present resolution.

General Assembly resolution 47/166

18 December 1992   Meeting 92   Adopted without vote

Approved by Second Committee (A/47/731) without vote, 7 December (meeting 48); 21-nation draft (A/C.2/47/L.41/Rev.1); agenda item 144.

Sponsors: Albania, Argentina, Austria, Bosnia and Herzegovina, Chile, Costa Rica, Czechoslovakia, El Salvador, Guatemala, Hungary, Jordan, Latvia, Mexico, New Zealand, Pakistan, Panama, Poland, Republic of Korea, Slovenia, Ukraine, Uruguay.

Meeting numbers. GA 47th session: 2nd Committee 25, 26, 40, 44, 48; plenary 92.

Latin America and the Caribbean

El Salvador

UNDP began preparations for the post-war period in El Salvador seven months before the signing of the January 1992 Peace Accord[35] (see

PART TWO, Chapter II). Technical assistance was provided to the Government in formulating a National Reconstruction Plan (NRP) and in creating opportunities for dialogue and consensus-building to ensure the viability of its execution. Immediately after the signing of the Accord, UNDP began to assist with the emergency plan for humanitarian assistance for former Frente Farabundo Martí para la Liberación Nacional (FMLN) combatants in the process of demobilization. It also provided assistance with the initial execution of NRP, the establishment of new democratic institutions emerging from the Peace Accord, the strengthening of existing ones and management of financing those programmes. UNDP coordinated an inter-agency mission to El Salvador in February, which elaborated recommendations on technical aspects of NRP in the areas of health, nutrition and sanitation; education, culture and communications; agricultural reactivation and natural resources; social compensation, poverty and housing; and employment and micro-enterprises.

During the first meeting of the consultative group of donors for El Salvador (Washington, D.C., 23-26 March), in which the Government of El Salvador and FMLN participated, the international community pledged more than $800 million to support NRP. UNDP also launched an appeal to 15 countries for financial support of a programme of humanitarian assistance for the concentration and demobilization of FMLN. In response, Canada, Denmark, Japan, Norway, Sweden, Switzerland and the United States donated more than $3.1 million.

GENERAL ASSEMBLY ACTION

On 18 December 1992, the General Assembly, on the recommendation of the Second Committee, adopted **resolution 47/158** without vote.

Assistance for the reconstruction and development of El Salvador

The General Assembly,

Taking note of Security Council resolution 784(1992) of 30 October 1992 and recalling the previous Council resolutions on El Salvador,

Noting with satisfaction the signing, on 16 January 1992 at Mexico City, of the Chapultepec Agreement between the Government of El Salvador and the Frente Farabundo Martí para la Liberación Nacional, which put an end to the Salvadorian armed conflict within the framework of the negotiating process begun on 4 April 1990 under the auspices of the Secretary-General,

Recognizing the valuable support given to the peace process by the countries that constitute the "four friends of the Secretary-General" and by other States and groups of States concerned,

Gravely concerned at the destruction of a large part of the country's economic and social infrastructure and the deterioration of the environment caused by the military activity and by other factors relating to the armed conflict,

Taking into account the fact that the National Reconstruction Plan has as its main objectives the integrated development of zones affected by the conflict, satisfaction of the most immediate needs of the population hardest hit by the conflict and of former combatants of both parties, and the reconstruction of the economic and social infrastructure,

Aware of the need for greater involvement of the international community in the reconstruction and development of El Salvador through the granting of economic, technical and financial assistance,

Bearing in mind El Salvador's resource constraints and financial difficulties affecting the implementation of the commitments assumed under the peace agreement,

Reaffirming the urgent need for the international community to take action in support of the peace agreement at this crucial stage in its implementation,

1. _Expresses its appreciation_ to the Secretary-General and the "four friends", namely, Colombia, Mexico, Spain and Venezuela, and to other States and groups of States for their efforts in helping to bring to an end the armed conflict in El Salvador;

2. _Notes_ the preparation by the Government of El Salvador of the National Reconstruction Plan, which reflects the collective wishes of the country, having taken into account the recommendations and suggestions of various political and social forces, including the Frente Farabundo Martí para la Liberación Nacional, and which was presented at the Consultative Group meeting held at the World Bank on 23 March 1992, and the current implementation by the Government of that Plan;

3. _Notes with satisfaction_ the assistance promised to El Salvador by the international community at the Consultative Group meeting;

4. _Appeals_ to all States, the relevant organizations and agencies of the United Nations system, regional and interregional intergovernmental organizations and nongovernmental organizations to provide the requisite assistance, on the most favourable terms possible, for the reconstruction and development of El Salvador;

5. _Requests_ the Secretary-General, in close coordination with the Government of El Salvador, to make all possible efforts to encourage the international community to increase the level of economic, financial and technical assistance to El Salvador;

6. _Also requests_ the Secretary-General to submit a report to the General Assembly at its forty-eighth session on the implementation of the present resolution;

7. _Decides_ to include in the provisional agenda of its forty-eighth session an item entitled "Assistance for the reconstruction and development of El Salvador".

General Assembly resolution 47/158

18 December 1992   Meeting 92   Adopted without vote

Approved by Second Committee (A/47/727/Add.1) without vote, 9 December (meeting 49); 94-nation draft (A/C.2/47/L.25/Rev.1); agenda item 87 _(b)_.

Sponsors: Afghanistan, Algeria, Angola, Antigua and Barbuda, Argentina, Armenia, Austria, Bahamas, Bangladesh, Barbados, Belarus, Belize, Benin, Bolivia, Bosnia and Herzegovina, Brazil, Bulgaria, Canada, Cape Verde, Chile, Colombia, Costa Rica, Côte d'Ivoire, Croatia, Cuba, Cyprus, Czechoslovakia, Dominica, Dominican Republic, Ecuador, El Salvador, Equatorial Guinea, Estonia, Ethiopia, Gabon, Grenada, Guatemala, Guinea-Bissau, Guyana, Haiti, Honduras, Hungary, India, Indonesia, Jamaica, Japan, Kazakhstan, Kenya, Kuwait, Kyrgyzstan, Latvia, Lebanon, Lithuania, Madagascar, Malaysia, Mali, Mauritania, Mexico, Mongolia, Morocco, Mozambique, Nicaragua, Nigeria, Oman, Panama, Papua New Guinea,

Paraguay, Peru, Philippines, Poland, Portugal, Republic of Korea, Republic of Moldova, Russian Federation, Saint Kitts and Nevis, Saint Lucia, Saint Vincent and the Grenadines, Samoa, Senegal, Spain, Sri Lanka, Suriname, Tajikistan, Thailand, Trinidad and Tobago, Tunisia, Turkey, Ukraine, United States, Uruguay, Uzbekistan, Vanuatu, Venezuela, Zimbabwe.

Meeting numbers. GA 47th session: 2nd Committee 25, 26, 28, 30, 34, 38, 40, 42, 45, 46, 48, 49; plenary 92.

Haiti

In response to a 1991 General Assembly request,[36] the Secretary-General submitted a November report on the situation of democracy and human rights in Haiti.[37] In addition to describing major developments in Haiti since the political crisis in 1991 (see PART TWO, Chapter II), the report discussed the humanitarian situation there. The 1991 *coup d'état*[38] had resulted in the freezing of Haiti's financial assets and the imposition of a trade embargo, except for humanitarian aid. The country's economy was in a state of free fall, said the Secretary-General, and the crisis had led to the collapse of the industrial and service sectors, to an increase in the already high rates of unemployment and to the deterioration of agriculture and of the food situation generally. Together with the partial suspension of priority programmes financed through external cooperation, the health situation also worsened. In addition, the crisis caused an estimated 135,000 children to leave school and thousands of refugees to flee by boat.

Also in response to a 1991 Assembly request,[39] the eight United Nations agencies still maintaining a presence in Haiti established, under the direction of DHA, an inter-agency committee, which drew up a draft integrated plan of humanitarian action for Haiti. In addition, in July, the Organization of American States (OAS) established a coordinating committee for humanitarian assistance to Haiti.

On 24 November, in **resolution 47/20**, and on 18 December, in **resolution 47/143**, the Assembly urged Member States and international organizations to increase their humanitarian assistance to the Haitian people and to support all efforts to resolve the problems associated with displaced persons. In that context, it encouraged the strengthening of institutional coordination among United Nations specialized agencies and between the United Nations and OAS.

REFERENCES

[1]A/47/182. [2]YUN 1991, p. 707. [3]DP/1992/3. [4]E/1992/28 (dec. 92/4). [5]YUN 1991, p. 425, GA res. 46/142, 17 Dec. 1991. [6]A/47/531. [7]YUN 1991, p. 127. [8]Ibid., p. 426, GA res. 46/147, 17 Dec. 1991. [9]A/47/528. [10]DP/1993/10/Add.1. [11]GA res. 45/227, 21 Dec. 1990. [12]A/47/539. [13]S/24635. [14]YUN 1991, p. 428, GA res. 47/176, 19 Dec. 1991. [15]A/47/553. [16]S/24480 & Add.1. [17]A/C.2/47/SR.25. [18]YUN 1991, p. 430, GA res. 46/178, 19 Dec. 1991. [19]A/47/554. [20]YUN 1991, p. 429. [21]A/C.2/47/5. [22]YUN 1991, p. 161, GA res. 46/23, 5 Dec. 1991. [23]A/47/705-S/24831. [24]DP/1992/4. [25]YUN 1991, p. 433. [26]DP/1992/5. [27]E/1992/28 (dec. 92/5). [28]YUN 1991, p. 205. [29]Ibid., p. 434, GA res. 46/173, 19 Dec. 1991. [30]Ibid., ESC res. 1991/61, 26 July 1991. [31]A/47/291-E/1992/95. [32]A/47/242. [33]A/C.2/47/2. [34]S/25015. [35]A/46/864-S/23501. [36]YUN 1991, p. 152, GA res. 46/7, 11 Oct. 1991. [37]A/47/599 & Corr.1. [38]YUN 1991, p. 151. [39]Ibid., p. 433, GA res. 45/257 B, 17 May 1991.

Disasters

Disaster relief activities

Drought-stricken areas

Southern Africa

In 1992, southern Africa faced the most severe drought to affect the region in the twentieth century. The drought devastated crops, reduced already scarce water availability and placed the lives of 18 million people from the most vulnerable population groups at risk from starvation and disease. It affected 10 countries of the region (Angola, Botswana, Lesotho, Malawi, Mozambique, Namibia, Swaziland, United Republic of Tanzania, Zambia, Zimbabwe), with the hardest hit countries recording maize crop failure of 70 to 90 per cent. In addition to food losses, water shortages threatened lives, livelihoods and livestock.

DHA, in cooperation with SADC, operational agencies of the United Nations system, the World Bank group and concerned NGOs, launched an urgent joint United Nations/SADC appeal to meet the anticipated needs of the drought victims. Following the official launching of the Consolidated Appeal on 26 May by the President of Botswana, on behalf of SADC, at Gaborone, and by the Secretary-General in New York, a formal pledging conference took place (Geneva, 1 and 2 June), bringing pledges amounting to $570 million of the $854 million sought. The main components of the appeal were the provision of 1.6 million metric tons of targeted food aid, 2.5 million tons of programme food aid, and non-food aid to assure the availability of water, health care and agricultural and livestock inputs.

With the support and participation of SADC and the Organization of African Unity (OAU), the joint DHA-UNDP Disaster Management Training Programme conducted a workshop at Harare, Zimbabwe, for representatives from a number of drought-affected countries. Less than six months after the appeal was issued, 82 per cent of the emergency food needs and 78 per cent of the programme food needs of the region were met. However, additional assistance estimated at $50 million was required for water interventions, refugee populations, agriculture and livestock activities.

In his report for 1992,[1] the UNDP Administrator stated that UNDP had allocated $50,000 for each affected country for institutional support dealing with the emergency situation. The Resident Representative in Zimbabwe was designated as liaison between resident coordinators, the SADC Food Security Unit in Harare and DHA. UNDP field offices provided IPF funding for projects in Malawi estimated at $1.9 million to coordinate drought disaster preparedness and relief and to strengthen the institutional response capacity of NGOs.

Sub-Saharan Africa

The Special Programme for Sub-Saharan African Countries Affected by Drought and Desertification (SPA) of the International Fund for Agricultural Development (IFAD) was established in 1986,[2] with a funding target of $300 million for the first three years. In view of the continuing need for special support, the IFAD Governing Council had, in 1991,[3] approved the continuation of the Programme into a second and terminal phase. Under the second phase (SPA-II), initiated in 1992, three new projects in Mauritania, Sierra Leone and the Sudan were presented for approval, with nine projects under preparation for 1993. IFAD held its Sixth Session of Consultation on SPA in 1992 (Rome, 20 January). The Council of Ministers of OAU (Dakar, Senegal, 22-28 June)[4] appealed to the international donor community to contribute generously to SPA-II.

ECONOMIC AND SOCIAL COUNCIL ACTION

On 30 July 1992, the Economic and Social Council, on the recommendation of its Economic Committee, adopted **resolution 1992/31** without vote.

Second phase of the Special Programme for Sub-Saharan African Countries Affected by Drought and Desertification of the International Fund for Agricultural Development

The Economic and Social Council,

Recalling its resolution 1989/88 of 26 July 1989, in which it stressed the urgent need for substantial progress in stimulating food production in developing countries, and its resolution 1991/95 of 26 July 1991 on the second phase of the Special Programme for Sub-Saharan African Countries Affected by Drought and Desertification of the International Fund for Agricultural Development,

Recalling also General Assembly resolution 45/207 of 21 December 1990, in which the Assembly urged the international community to support the efforts of developing countries by increasing even more the flow of resources, including concessional flows for agricultural development,

Bearing in mind General Assembly resolution 46/151 of 18 December 1991, in which the Assembly adopted the United Nations New Agenda for the Development of Africa in the 1990s,

Recalling resolution CM/Res.1416(LVI) on the second phase of the Special Programme, adopted by the Council of Ministers of the Organization of African Unity at its fifty-sixth ordinary session and endorsed by the Assembly of Heads of State and Government of the Organization of African Unity at its twenty-eighth ordinary session, held at Dakar in July 1992,

Noting with satisfaction the effective implementation of the first phase of the Special Programme, including the mobilization of the target level of $300 million,

Recalling also resolution 67/XIV of the Governing Council of the International Fund for Agricultural Development on the establishment of a second phase of the Special Programme and its decision, *inter alia*, to take note of the appeal made by the African members that every effort should be made to reach a target of $300 million for the second phase of the Special Programme and to appeal to all members in a position to do so to contribute generously, on a voluntary basis, to the Special Resources for Sub-Saharan Africa for the second phase of the Special Programme of three years, bearing in mind the level of resources mobilized for the first phase and its successful implementation,

Noting the progress made on the preparatory activities for the launching of the second phase of the Special Programme, including the development of a pipeline of projects in an advanced stage of preparation,

Expressing its deep appreciation for the contributions pledged by a number of industrialized and developing Member States to the second phase of the Special Programme,

1. *Appeals* to the international community to contribute generously, on a voluntary basis, to the second phase of the Special Programme for Sub-Saharan African Countries Affected by Drought and Desertification of the International Fund for Agricultural Development;

2. *Appeals also* to those donors that have generously made firm pledges for the second phase of the Special Programme to deposit their instruments of contribution so as to permit the second phase of the Special Programme to become effective as soon as possible in 1992.

Economic and Social Council resolution 1992/31

30 July 1992   Meeting 41   Adopted without vote

Approved by Economic Committee (E/1992/109/Add.2) without vote, 28 July (meeting 16); draft by Madagascar on behalf of the African States (E/1992/C.1/L.11/Rev.1); agenda item 12 *(c)*.

By **resolution 47/188**, the Assembly decided to establish an Intergovernmental Negotiating Committee to elaborate an international convention to combat desertification in countries experiencing serious drought and/or desertification, particularly in Africa (see PART THREE, Chapter VIII).

Sudano-Sahelian region

In a report on the activities of the United Nations Sudano-Sahelian Office (UNSO) during 1991 and 1992,[5] the UNDP Administrator stated that the decisions of the 1992 United Nations Conference on Environment and Development (UNCED) (see PART THREE, Chapter VIII) resulted in a redefinition of UNSO's goals and a reorientation of major areas of its activities, emphasizing its role as a dryland activity centre serving African countries affected by drought and desertification and as UNDP's focal point on drought and desertification issues. UNSO promoted the sound management of natural resources in 22 countries of the Sudano-Sahelian region to assist Governments and communities in tackling drought and desertification, which were the major environmental issues constraining sustainable development. The programme focused on three major themes: strengthening or creation of national capacity in planning and coordination for the improved management of natural resources; operational field activities; and, pursuant to a 1989 General Assembly resolution,[6] preparations for UNCED.

In 1992, UNSO launched, in cooperation with UNDP, the World Bank and the African Development Bank (AfDB), a Joint Regional Programme Facility, based at Abidjan (Côte d'Ivoire), to strengthen national capacities to integrate the environmental dimension into all aspects of development planning. A network of African experts and institutions was to be established to foster technical cooperation among African countries. During 1991-1992, 52 new projects were approved in all Sudano-Sahelian countries, except Somalia, at a value of $22.4 million, in agro-pastoral development, land protection, desertification control, land-rehabilitation and environmental education and sensitization activities.

On 26 May,[7] the Governing Council requested the Administrator to present to it in 1993 proposals on specific ways and means to combat desertification and drought, including strengthening the coordination and effectiveness of the United Nations system to meet this objective, taking into account the role identified for UNSO by UNCED's Preparatory Committee.

In a September report to the General Assembly on combating desertification and drought,[8] the Secretary-General stated that UNSO was working closely with subregional organizations, particularly the Permanent Inter-State Committee on Drought Control in the Sahel and the Intergovernmental Authority on Drought and Development, in their programming and coordination activities, including support to the Sudano-Sahelian countries for the UNCED preparatory process. UNSO's detailed study, *Assessment of Desertification and Drought in the Sudano-Sahelian Region 1985-1991*, was issued in January. The study called for concerted action in the Sudano-Sahelian region to deal with the twin environmental problems of desertification and drought, including the promotion of alternative livelihood systems that could relieve pressure on the land and help alleviate poverty by providing alternative and supplementary sources of income.

By **decision 47/444** of 22 December, the Assembly took note of the Secretary-General's report.

Storms and floods

Cyclone-affected South Pacific countries

The 1991/92 cyclone season caused considerable damage to a number of island developing countries in the South Pacific region. Cyclone Val in December 1991 was followed by cyclones Betsy in January and Fran in March.

On 13 April, Micronesia, on behalf of the members of the South Pacific Forum, described the devastation caused by the cyclones and typhoons that were increasingly prevalent in the region.

UNDP action. On 14 February,[9] the UNDP Governing Council, noting the damage caused during the cyclone season to several island developing countries in the South Pacific, particularly the devastation caused by cyclone Val in Samoa, commended the Administrator for his prompt action in allocating funds from SPR to alleviate the immediate effects of the emergency in Samoa. It called on the Administrator to continue consultations with the Samoan Government with a view to extending further assistance for its rehabilitation and reconstruction efforts and called on States and international organizations to further support Samoa and other South Pacific countries affected.

GENERAL ASSEMBLY ACTION

On 13 April 1992, the General Assembly adopted **resolution 46/234** without vote.

Reconstruction and rehabilitation of cyclone-affected South Pacific countries

The General Assembly,

Noting with concern the damage caused by recent cyclones in several island developing countries in the South Pacific, namely the Federated States of Micronesia, the Republic of the Marshall Islands, Samoa, Solomon Islands and Vanuatu, and their severe adverse impacts on the efforts of those countries to achieve sustainable economic growth and development,

Noting, in particular, the loss of life and comprehensive material damage in Samoa,

Taking note of decision 92/11 of 14 February 1992 of the Governing Council of the United Nations Development Programme, entitled "Special assistance to Samoa",

1. *Acknowledges with appreciation* both the efforts of the Governments and people to deal with the emergencies within their limited resources and the assistance so far provided by organizations of the United Nations system, other Governments and non-governmental bodies;

2. *Urges* the continuing assistance of organizations of the United Nations system, international financial institutions and the international community in the development of disaster preparedness and mitigation programmes in the above-named affected countries, in the identification of their medium- and long-term rehabilitation and reconstruction needs and in the mobilization of resources to meet those needs.

General Assembly resolution 46/234

13 April 1992   Meeting 84   Adopted without vote

57-nation draft (A/46/L.69 & Add.1); agenda item 84.
Sponsors: Antigua and Barbuda, Australia, Bangladesh, Barbados, Belize, Bra-
zil, Brunei Darussalam, Cape Verde, Chile, China, Costa Rica, Cyprus,
Czechoslovakia, Dominica, Fiji, France, Grenada, Hungary, Iceland, India,
Indonesia, Ireland, Italy, Japan, Jordan, Lao People's Democratic Repub-
lic, Madagascar, Malaysia, Maldives, Malta, Marshall Islands, Micronesia,
Mongolia, Nepal, New Zealand, Nicaragua, Pakistan, Papua New Guinea,
Peru, Philippines, Republic of Korea, Saint Lucia, Saint Vincent and the
Grenadines, Samoa, San Marino, Seychelles, Singapore, Solomon Islands,
Sri Lanka, Suriname, Sweden, Thailand, Trinidad and Tobago, Ukraine,
United Kingdom, United States, Vanuatu.

Pakistan

By a 30 September letter,[10] Pakistan reported
to the Secretary-General that there had been unprecedented rainfall in Pakistan's northern areas
and in Azad Jammu and Kashmir during the second week of September. The intensity of the rain
was the highest ever experienced in the region,
leading to exceptionally high flows in the catch-
ment areas of rivers and resulting in extensive
floods and colossal damage. Thousands of villages
were inundated and floods and landslides swept
away bridges, roads, railway tracks and the
telecommunication network. The major highway
linking Pakistan and China was severely damaged
and closed for traffic. Preliminary estimates of
damages and losses were put at 1,022 persons dead
or missing; 6 million displaced; 176,117 houses destroyed or damaged; and 122,000 cattle and other
livestock lost. The total damage was estimated at
more than $1 billion.

GENERAL ASSEMBLY ACTION

On 7 October 1992, the General Assembly
adopted **resolution 47/2** without vote.

Emergency assistance to Pakistan

The General Assembly,

Deeply concerned about the extensive damage and
devastation in Pakistan caused by the unprecedented
floods in that country,

Noting with concern the destruction of thousands of dwellings and the damage to major sectors of the national
infrastructure,

Acknowledging the efforts of the Government of Pakistan to provide relief and emergency assistance to the
people affected by the flood,

Noting that the earnest efforts of the Government of
Pakistan to promote economic growth and development
will be hampered by this calamity,

1. *Declares its solidarity* with the Government and the
people of Pakistan in this hour of trial;

2. *Notes with appreciation* the efforts of the Government
of Pakistan to provide speedy relief to the flood victims
from national resources;

3. *Commends* the efforts of the international community to supplement the efforts of the Government of Pakistan in relief operations and emergency assistance;

4. *Calls upon* the Secretary-General, in cooperation
with the relevant organs and organizations of the United
Nations system and in close collaboration with the

Government authorities, to assist in the rehabilitation
efforts of the Government of Pakistan;

5. *Requests* all States and international organizations
and other intergovernmental agencies to extend emergency support to Pakistan to alleviate the plight of the
afflicted people of Pakistan, including their economic
and financial burden.

General Assembly resolution 47/2

7 October 1992   Meeting 28   Adopted without vote

63-nation draft (A/47/L.2 & Add.1); agenda item 146.
Sponsors: Afghanistan, Algeria, Argentina, Bahamas, Bangladesh, Benin,
Bhutan, Bolivia, Brazil, Brunei Darussalam, Cape Verde, China, Colombia,
Comoros, Costa Rica, Cyprus, Djibouti, Egypt, El Salvador, Equatorial
Guinea, Ethiopia, Gabon, Grenada, Guatemala, Guinea-Bissau, Honduras,
Indonesia, Iran, Jordan, Kuwait, Lebanon, Libyan Arab Jamahiriya,
Madagascar, Malaysia, Maldives, Mali, Marshall Islands, Morocco, Myan-
mar, Nepal, New Zealand, Oman, Pakistan, Paraguay, Peru, Philippines,
Russian Federation, Saudi Arabia, Senegal, Spain, Sri Lanka, Sudan, Su-
riname, Sweden, Togo, Trinidad and Tobago, Tunisia, Turkey, Uganda, United
Arab Emirates, United Kingdom, Uruguay, Yemen.

Other disasters

Aftermath of war and natural disasters in Nicaragua

On 13 April, Nicaragua informed the General
Assembly of the eruption of the Cerro Negro volcano, which was taking place at that time. The
eruption was affecting 150,000 people in the
Chinandega and León departments in one of the
country's main productive regions. Sand- and ash-
storms caused serious damage to 4,500 families,
totalling 20,000 victims; immediate material damage was estimated at $4 million.

GENERAL ASSEMBLY ACTION

On 22 May 1992, the General Assembly
adopted **resolution 46/239** without vote.

Emergency assistance to Nicaragua following the eruption of the Cerro Negro volcano

The General Assembly,

Recalling its resolutions 43/131 of 8 December 1988 and
45/100 of 14 December 1990 concerning humanitarian
assistance to victims of natural disasters and similar
emergency situations,

Deeply concerned about the serious consequences of the
eruption of the Cerro Negro volcano in Nicaragua,
which has given rise to an emergency situation in the
affected areas, and about the urgent need to restore normal conditions for the population,

Recognizing that the great efforts that the Government
of Nicaragua is making to promote economic and social development and the process of national reconciliation have been hampered by this natural disaster,

Considering the generous assistance that has been
provided by the United Nations system, and by some
States, to alleviate this emergency situation in Nicaragua,

1. *Requests* the Secretary-General, to the extent of his
authority, to support the rehabilitation efforts that are
being made by the Government of Nicaragua in the affected areas;

2. *Invites* Member States, international financial institutions, organizations, programmes and specialized

agencies of the United Nations system to continue to contribute and to respond generously for the duration of the emergency and of the rehabilitation process in Nicaragua.

General Assembly resolution 46/239

22 May 1992   Meeting 86   Adopted without vote

8-nation draft (A/46/L.72 & Add.1); agenda item 84.

Sponsors: Belize, Costa Rica, El Salvador, Guatemala, Honduras, Nicaragua, Panama, Samoa.

On 1 September, a powerful earthquake measuring 7.2 on the Richter scale, followed by a tidal wave (tsunami) with waves reaching 15 metres in height, struck the Pacific coast of Nicaragua.

In a 12 November letter to the Secretary-General,[11] Nicaragua stated that the tidal wave had caused damage all along its coastline, including major ports, and had affected several coastal towns with a total population of some 70,000. Approximately 150 people had been killed, 500 had disappeared and immediate material losses were valued at around $25 million. In addition, Nicaragua drew attention to the fact that it was still suffering the consequences of the armed conflicts that had taken place there before 1990 (see also PART TWO, Chapter II).

GENERAL ASSEMBLY ACTION

On 22 December, the General Assembly adopted **resolution 47/169** without vote.

International assistance for the rehabilitation and reconstruction of Nicaragua: aftermath of the war and natural disasters

The General Assembly,

Recalling its resolutions 45/15 of 20 November 1990 and 46/109 A and B of 17 December 1991 concerning the item entitled "The situation in Central America: threats to international peace and security and peace initiatives", in which it welcomed the implementation of phases I and II of the National Conciliation Agreement on Economic and Social Matters concluded in Nicaragua on 26 October 1990 and 15 August 1991, and endorsed, in particular, the provision concerning exceptional circumstances and the invitation to the international community and the international funding agencies to provide effective and efficient support for the implementation of the Agreement,

Deeply concerned at the fact that the recent natural disasters are impeding Nicaragua's efforts to overcome the consequences of the war within the framework of a democracy and in the macroeconomic conditions already achieved,

Taking into account the serious consequences of the destruction of crops and of thousands of homes and the damage caused to important sectors of the national infrastructure, as well as the growing needs of thousands of displaced persons and refugees who must be incorporated into the country's economic activities,

Recognizing the efforts of the international community and the Government of Nicaragua to provide relief and emergency assistance to persons affected by the aftermath of the war, the floods, the volcanic eruption and the recent tidal wave,

Recognizing also that the intensive efforts of the Government of Nicaragua to promote economic reactivation within the framework of a process of adjustment with economic growth and development have been hindered by the aftermath of the war and natural disasters,

1. *Commends* the efforts made by the international community, including the organs and organizations of the United Nations system, to supplement the action undertaken by the Government of Nicaragua in the task of rehabilitation and national reconstruction, as well as in providing emergency assistance;

2. *Requests* all Member States, the international funding agencies and regional, intraregional and non-governmental organizations, to continue providing support to Nicaragua at the required levels in order both to overcome the aftermath of the war and natural disasters and to stimulate the process of reconstruction and development;

3. *Requests* the Secretary-General, in cooperation with the relevant organs and organizations of the United Nations system and in close cooperation with the Nicaraguan authorities, to provide all necessary assistance to activities for the rehabilitation, reconstruction and development of that country and to continue to ensure the timely, comprehensive and effective formulation and coordination of programmes of the United Nations system in Nicaragua, given the importance of those activities for the consolidation of peace;

4. *Calls upon* the Secretary-General to provide Nicaragua, at the request of the Government of Nicaragua, with all possible assistance to support the consolidation of peace, in areas such as the settlement of displaced and demobilized persons and refugees, land ownership and land tenure in rural areas, direct care for war victims, mine clearance and the overcoming of difficulties in the restoration of the productive areas of the country, and, in general, a process of sustained recovery and development that will render the peace and democracy achieved irreversible;

5. *Requests* the Secretary-General to submit a report to the General Assembly at its forty-eighth session on the action taken to implement the present resolution;

6. *Decides* to include in the provisional agenda of its forty-eighth session the item entitled "International assistance for the rehabilitation and reconstruction of Nicaragua: aftermath of the war and natural disasters".

General Assembly resolution 47/169

22 December 1992   Meeting 93   Adopted without vote

48-nation draft (A/47/L.40/Rev.2/Add.1); agenda item 150.

Sponsors: Afghanistan, Antigua and Barbuda, Argentina, Bangladesh, Barbados, Belize, Bolivia, Brazil, Chile, Colombia, Costa Rica, Cuba, Cyprus, Djibouti, Ecuador, El Salvador, Fiji, Grenada, Guatemala, Guyana, Haiti, Honduras, Indonesia, Iran, Jamaica, Mauritius, Mexico, Nepal, Nicaragua, Norway, Pakistan, Panama, Paraguay, Peru, Philippines, Russian Federation, Saint Lucia, Samoa, Spain, Sri Lanka, Suriname, Sweden, Trinidad and Tobago, Turkey, United States, Uruguay, Venezuela, Yemen.

Aftermath of Mount Pinatubo volcanic eruption and typhoons in the Philippines

In a 7 October letter,[12] the Philippines informed the Secretary-General that the Mount Pinatubo volcano, which first erupted in June 1991,[13] continued to wreak havoc and destruction in Central Luzon. The gravest and most immediate threats to life and property, however, came from mud flows and flash flooding of heavily silted rivers, exacerbated by a spate of typhoons that struck the northern Philippines, leaving, as at 9 September, 36 persons dead, 10 injured, 15 missing and some 940,000 displaced and over 6,350 homes destroyed or damaged. Some 1,254 hectares of land planted with rice, 1,476 hectares of sugarcane and 87 hectares of vegetables were damaged and 4,851 head of livestock were lost. Damage was estimated at approximately $74.2 million.

GENERAL ASSEMBLY ACTION

On 21 October 1992, the General Assembly adopted **resolution 47/7** without vote.

Emergency assistance to the Philippines

The General Assembly,

Recalling its resolution 46/177 of 19 December 1991 on emergency assistance to the Philippines,

Deeply concerned about the extensive damage and devastation in the Philippines caused by the massive mudflows from the volcanic ash deposits of the recent eruptions of Mount Pinatubo volcano,

Noting with concern the destruction of thousands of dwellings and the damage to major sectors of the national infrastructure, as well as the mounting needs of hundreds of thousands of displaced persons,

Acknowledging the efforts of the Government of the Philippines to provide relief and emergency assistance to the people affected by the mudflows and recent volcanic eruptions,

Noting that the earnest efforts of the Government of the Philippines to promote economic growth and development will be hampered by this continuing calamity,

1. *Commends* the efforts of the international community, including the organs and organizations of the United Nations system, to supplement the efforts of the Government of the Philippines in relief operations and emergency assistance;

2. *Calls upon* the Secretary-General, in cooperation with the relevant organs and organizations of the United Nations system and in close collaboration with the Government authorities, to assist in the rehabilitation efforts of the Government of the Philippines;

3. *Requests* all States and international organizations to extend, on an urgent basis, further support to the Philippines in ways that would alleviate, for the duration of the emergency and the ensuing rehabilitation process, the economic and financial burden borne by the Philippine people.

General Assembly resolution 47/7

21 October 1992   Meeting 44   Adopted without vote

64-nation draft (A/47/L.8 & Add.1); agenda item 148.

Sponsors: Afghanistan, Algeria, Angola, Argentina, Bangladesh, Benin, Bolivia, Brazil, Brunei Darussalam, Chile, China, Costa Rica, Cuba, Cyprus, Czechoslovakia, El Salvador, Ethiopia, Gabon, Guatemala, Guinea-Bissau, Honduras, India, Indonesia, Iran, Jamaica, Japan, Jordan, Lao People's Democratic Republic, Lesotho, Libyan Arab Jamahiriya, Madagascar, Malaysia, Mali, Mauritius, Mexico, Micronesia, Mongolia, Morocco, Myanmar, Nicaragua, Nigeria, Pakistan, Papua New Guinea, New Zealand, Peru, Philippines, Republic of Korea, Sao Tome and Principe, Senegal, Singapore, Spain, Sri Lanka, Sudan, Suriname, Thailand, Togo, Trinidad and Tobago, Tunisia, Turkey, Uruguay, United States, Vanuatu, Zambia.

Screw-worm infestation

In response to a 1991 request,[14] the Secretary-General transmitted to the Economic and Social Council a June report,[15] prepared by the Director-General of FAO, in cooperation with IFAD, on the screw-worm eradication programme in North Africa. The report stated that to combat the new world screw-worm, which was first detected in the Libyan Arab Jamahiriya in 1988, sterile insect technique operations—field tested in a $2.8 million pilot programme approved by IFAD in 1989—were extended to the entire infested area in February 1991. The number of screw-worm myiasis cases dropped from over 12,000 in 1990 to 6 in 1991, the last being detected on 7 April 1991. Following six months of continued dispersal of millions of sterile flies, the operation was suspended on 15 October 1991.

The last remaining international staff of the eradication programme left the Libyan Arab Jamahiriya in June 1992. Subsequent field operations were limited to surveillance activities carried out by the Libyan authorities for a further year, with the financial closure of the programme being expected in 1993. The original estimate of international funds required to complete the programme was revised downward to a final estimate of $34 million in response to the rapid success being achieved. By June 1992, donors had contributed $32.4 million and a further $2.9 million was expected, thus assuring the required funding for the programme's completion.

The FAO Director-General termed the campaign an example of effective cooperation among a large number of partners in an emergency operation. He concluded that the successful campaign demonstrated that cooperation among technical agencies, financing institutions, bilateral agencies, NGOs and affected countries could effectively address a disaster situation, in a coordinated manner.

By **decision 1992/280** of 30 July 1992, the Economic and Social Council took note of the report of the Director-General.

Chernobyl aftermath

On 23 March,[16] the heads of State of Belarus, the Russian Federation and Ukraine transmitted an appeal (Kiev, Ukraine, 20 March) to the United Nations concerning the provision of assistance in mitigating the consequences of the Chernobyl catastrophe. The heads of State called on the international community to give renewed impetus to the international programme to minimize the consequences of the 1986 nuclear powerplant disaster.

In a response to a 1991 General Assembly request,[17] the Secretary-General submitted a July report[18] on strengthening international cooperation and coordination to study, mitigate and minimize the consequences of the Chernobyl disaster, which updated information submitted to the Assembly in October 1991.[19] The report described the accident at the nuclear powerplant, measures taken by the authorities of the former USSR and by the newly independent States to counteract the disaster, and activities of the United Nations system.

The report indicated that, consequent to the 1991 Assembly resolution on the Chernobyl disaster,[17] a small secretariat was established at the United Nations to work on negotiations with donors and recipients on projects to be implemented utilizing resources from the United Nations Chernobyl Trust Fund, pledges for which had been made at the Chernobyl Pledging Conference in 1991.[20]

In the light of the political changes in the former USSR, the implementation of the 1991 International Programme on the Health Effects of the Chernobyl Accident (IPHECA) was reviewed and an agreement was signed in April 1992 by WHO and the Ministries of Health of the affected States, under which the parties were to carry out the programme on the basis of equal involvement of the three States. International participation was encouraged and all relevant Chernobyl health-related projects were to be either incorporated into IPHECA or closely coordinated with it. Together with the Russian Federation and in association with the Chernobyl secretariat, the United Nations Educational, Scientific and Cultural Organization initiated a multifaceted project for socio-economic rehabilitation in a 300-square-kilometre zone. An international seminar on the topic was held at Wolfsburg, Germany, in June.

In November, the United Nations Deputy Coordinator for Chernobyl held meetings with authorities from Belarus, the Russian Federation and Ukraine, which culminated in the signing by the affected States of a document indicating the following priorities for assistance: creation of medical centres for examination and treatment; equipping of medical institutions in the contaminated zone; formulations of plans, definition of special economic conditions and advantages for foreign investors; creation of centres for children and teenagers for socio-psychological rehabilitation; and production of uncontaminated food products and products containing special additives.

The Inter-Agency Task Force for Chernobyl decided to take full account of these priorities and considered that the coordination and management of Chernobyl programmes and projects should increasingly become the responsibility of the three Governments.

On 30 July 1992, by **decision 1992/286**, the Economic and Social Council took note of the Secretary-General's report.

UNICEF action. At its June 1992 session,[21] the UNICEF Executive Board urged the Executive Director to continue consideration of possible technical and other special assistance to children and mothers living in the areas most affected by the Chernobyl accident, and requested him to continue to provide all appropriate support and assistance to the victims.

ECONOMIC AND SOCIAL COUNCIL ACTION

On 30 July 1992, the Economic and Social Council, on the recommendation of its Economic Committee, adopted **resolution 1992/38** without vote.

International cooperation and coordination of efforts to address and mitigate the consequences of the disaster at the Chernobyl nuclear power plant

The Economic and Social Council,

Reaffirming its resolutions 1990/50 of 13 July 1990 and 1991/51 of 26 July 1991,

Recalling General Assembly resolutions 45/190 of 21 December 1990 and 46/150 of 18 December 1991,

Taking note with appreciation of the decisions adopted by the organs, organizations and programmes of the United Nations system in the implementation of General Assembly resolutions 45/190 and 46/150,

Taking note of the relevant recommendations contained in the report of the Committee for Programme and Coordination on the first part of its thirty-second session,

Noting with appreciation the contribution made by Member States and by organizations of the United Nations system in the development of cooperation to mitigate and minimize the consequences of the Chernobyl disaster, and encouraging further contributions, including contributions to projects under the joint plan executed by the organizations of the United Nations system,

Expressing profound concern about the ongoing effects on the lives and health of people, especially children, in the affected areas of Belarus, the Russian Federation and Ukraine and also in other countries affected by the Chernobyl disaster,

Aware of the need to strengthen further the coordination of active efforts, through international and, in particular, national measures, to mitigate and minimize the radiological, health, socio-economic, psychological and environmental consequences of that disaster, as well as its possible long-term effects, including those resulting from transboundary contamination,

Stressing the importance of providing extensive information on all aspects of the Chernobyl disaster and its causes for the purpose of avoiding similar calamities in the future,

Stressing also the responsibility of each State, particularly through its safety authorities and its plant operators, for the safety of its nuclear power plants, and encouraging cooperation to this end throughout the world, in particular in Central and Eastern Europe, and emphasizing the high priority that should be given by the countries concerned to eliminating this danger through safety improvements and other appropriate measures with the support of the international community,

1. *Notes* the practical measures that have been taken by the Secretary-General to coordinate the activities of the organs, organizations and programmes of the United Nations system, as well as other measures to implement General Assembly resolutions 45/190 and 46/150;

2. *Appeals* to all Member States, intergovernmental and non-governmental organizations, charity founda-

tions, the business community, scientific bodies and individuals to make contributions and to provide all possible social, medical, food and other humanitarian assistance for the purpose of rehabilitation of the population in the affected areas of Belarus, the Russian Federation and Ukraine;

3. *Requests* the Secretary-General and the United Nations Coordinator of International Cooperation for Chernobyl to report to the General Assembly at its forty-seventh session on the implementation of resolutions 45/190 and 46/150.

Economic and Social Council resolution 1992/38

30 July 1992   Meeting 41   Adopted without vote

Approved by Economic Committee (E/1992/111) without vote, 28 July (meeting 16); 35-nation draft (E/1992/C.1/L.7); agenda item 14.

Sponsors: Algeria, Argentina, Australia, Austria, Belarus, Belgium, Brazil, Bulgaria, Canada, Czechoslovakia, Denmark, Finland, France, Germany, Greece, Hungary, Ireland, Italy, Japan, Luxembourg, Mexico, Netherlands, New Zealand, Norway, Poland, Portugal, Romania, Russian Federation, Spain, Suriname, Sweden, Turkey, Ukraine, United Kingdom, Yugoslavia.

GENERAL ASSEMBLY ACTION

On 18 December 1992, the General Assembly, on the recommendation of the Second Committee, adopted **resolution 47/165** without vote.

Strengthening of international cooperation and coordination of efforts to study, mitigate and minimize the consequences of the Chernobyl disaster

The General Assembly,

Reaffirming its resolutions 45/190 of 21 December 1990 and 46/150 of 18 December 1991,

Recalling Economic and Social Council resolutions 1990/50 of 13 July 1990 and 1991/51 of 26 July 1991, and taking note of Council resolution 1992/38 of 30 July 1992,

Taking note of the decisions adopted by the organs, organizations and programmes of the United Nations system in the implementation of resolutions 45/190 and 46/150,

Taking note with appreciation of the contribution made by Member States and by organizations of the United Nations system in the development of cooperation to mitigate and minimize the consequences of the Chernobyl disaster, and encouraging further contributions,

Bearing in mind the appeal of 20 March 1992 by the Heads of State of Belarus, the Russian Federation and Ukraine to the United Nations concerning provision of assistance in mitigating the consequences of the Chernobyl catastrophe,

Expressing profound concern about the ongoing effects on the lives and health of people, especially children, in the affected areas of Belarus, the Russian Federation and Ukraine and also in other countries affected by the Chernobyl disaster,

Taking note with concern of the recent authoritative findings of the World Health Organization relating to the health effects of the Chernobyl radioactive fallout,

Aware of the need to strengthen further the coordination of active efforts, through international and, in particular, national measures, to mitigate and minimize the radiological, health, socio-economic, psychological and environmental consequences of the Chernobyl disaster,

as well as its possible long-term effects, including those resulting from transboundary contamination,

Stressing the responsibility of each State, particularly through its safety authorities and its plant operators, for the safety of its nuclear power plants, encouraging cooperation to this end throughout the world, in particular in Central and Eastern Europe, and emphasizing the high priority that should be given by the countries concerned to eliminating these dangers through improvements in safety and other appropriate measures, with the support of the international community,

1. *Takes note* of the report of the Secretary-General on the implementation of General Assembly resolution 46/150 and the recommendations contained therein on priority areas of international cooperation in studying, mitigating and minimizing the consequences of the Chernobyl disaster;

2. *Requests* the Secretary-General to continue the activities related to the follow-up to resolutions 45/190 and 46/150, taking into consideration the subsequent social, economic and other changes that have occurred in the countries most affected by the Chernobyl disaster;

3. *Also requests* the Secretary-General, in the light of his recommendations on priority areas, to undertake an analytical review of all United Nations activities to study, mitigate and minimize the consequences of the Chernobyl disaster in those countries most affected, including related secretariat arrangements, taking full account of ongoing programmes and other relevant activities, including those of regional and other organizations, and the principle of comparative advantage;

4. *Further requests* the Secretary-General to report to the General Assembly at its forty-eighth session on the implementation of the present resolution, including the conclusions of the analytical review requested in paragraph 3 above, and to submit an oral report to the Economic and Social Council at its substantive session of 1993;

5. *Decides* to consider at its forty-eighth session the question of the biennialization of the agenda item, entitled "Strengthening of international cooperation and coordination of efforts to study, mitigate and minimize the consequences of the Chernobyl disaster".

General Assembly resolution 47/165

18 December 1992   Meeting 92   Adopted without vote

Approved by Second Committee (A/47/730) without vote, 11 December (meeting 50); draft by Vice-Chairman (A/C.2/47/L.67) based on informal consultations on draft by Belarus, Russian Federation and Ukraine (A/C.2/47/L.55); agenda item 90.

Financial implications. 5th Committee, A/47/800; S-G, A/C.2/47/L.72, A/C.5/47/75.

Meeting numbers. GA 47th session: 2nd Committee 3-9, 43, 46, 50; 5th Committee 47; plenary 92.

REFERENCES

[1]DP/1993/10/Add.1. [2]YUN 1986, p. 1195. [3]YUN 1991, p. 414. [4]A/47/558. [5]DP/1993/43. [6]GA res. 44/172, 19 Dec. 1989. [7]E/1992/28 (dec. 92/16). [8]A/47/393. [9]E/1992/28 (dec. 92/11). [10]A/47/244. [11]A/47/248. [12]A/47/246. [13]YUN 1991, p. 417. [14]Ibid., p. 418, ESC res. 1991/59, 26 July 1991. [15]E/1992/72. [16]A/47/132. [17]YUN 1991, p. 420, GA res. 46/150, 18 Dec. 1991. [18]A/47/322-E/1992/102 & Add.1,2. [19]YUN 1991, p. 418. [20]Ibid., p. 419. [21]E/1992/29 (dec. 1992/20).

Chapter IV

International trade, finance and transport

The deceleration of international trade expansion which began in 1989 continued through 1992. Among the main contributing factors were the recession in North America and the United Kingdom, weakening investment trends in Japan, economic slow-down in Western Europe and the sharp output contractions in Central and Eastern Europe and the former USSR.

The eighth session of the United Nations Conference on Trade and Development, a high-level meeting held at Cartagena de Indias, Colombia, from 8 to 25 February, included in its final document "A New Partnership for Development: The Cartagena Commitment", which stressed the importance of strengthening multilateral cooperation in order to translate the broad policy commitments undertaken by countries into sustained economic growth and development. In December, the General Assembly endorsed the outcome of the Conference and called on the international community to assist in promoting measures in pursuit of the revitalization of international trade and development, particularly in the developing countries (resolution 47/183).

The Assembly noted, with regard to the strengthening of international organizations in the area of multilateral trade, that the Uruguay Round of multilateral negotiations had not been completed and expressed the hope that it would be rapidly concluded (47/184).

The Assembly examined the various aspects of international trade, finance and development, including the importance of the commodity sector to economic growth and transformation in developing countries (47/185), the promotion of an adequate flow of resources to developing countries and the need to achieve a higher degree of stability in financial markets in order to promote an international financial system more conducive to stable economic growth (47/178). It urged creditor countries, private banks and multilateral financial institutions to consider the extension of appropriate new financial support to developing countries, in particular low-income countries that continued, at great cost, to service their debt and meet their international obligations (47/198). The Assembly also continued to explore the issue of convening an international conference on the financing of development (decision 47/436).

Eighth session of UNCTAD

International trade and development issues for world economic revitalization and growth received greater focus in 1992, by the convening, in accordance with a General Assembly resolution of 1991,[1] of a high-level eighth session of the United Nations Conference on Trade and Development (UNCTAD-VIII), at Cartagena de Indias, Colombia, from 8 to 25 February 1992.[2]

The UNCTAD Trade and Development Board (TDB), which served as a preparatory committee for UNCTAD VIII, convened the first part of its seventeenth special session in December 1991.[3] The second part of that session was held from 15 to 24 January 1992 to finalize the preparations for the Conference.[4] In addition to finalizing the organizational and procedural arrangements, the special session discussed a number of substantive issues, including the outcome of a number of informal encounters and seminars held during 1991 in preparation for UNCTAD VIII.

At the intergovernmental level, three regional ministerial meetings were held: the Latin American Group of the Group of 77 (the developing countries) (Caracas, Venezuela, 26-30 August and 4 September 1991), which adopted a declaration entitled "Latin America and the Caribbean and UNCTAD VIII"; the Seventh Ministerial Meeting of the Asian Group of the Group of 77 (Pyongyang, Democratic People's Republic of Korea, 10-12 September 1991), which adopted the "Pyongyang Final Document"; and the Seventh Ministerial Meeting of the African Group of the Group of 77 (Lusaka, Zambia, 19 and 20 September 1991), which adopted the "Lusaka Declaration". The results of those meetings were considered at the Seventh Ministerial Meeting of the Group of 77 (Tehran, Iran, 16-23 November 1991), which adopted the Tehran Final Documents[5] containing the Tehran Declaration entitled "Towards a new partnership for development", the "Substantive platform of the Group of 77 for international cooperation" and the "Statement of Ministers on economic cooperation among developing countries".

Other documents circulated in connection with the substantive work of the Conference included a text by Australia on its approach to institutional issues and the role of UNCTAD; a position paper by China[6] on basic considerations on issues on the agenda of UNCTAD VIII; a communication from Italy, on behalf of States members of Group B (developed market economies),[7] on trade, development and the new international challenges: towards a programme of action for strengthened multilateral cooperation and sustainable development; and a text from the Nordic countries (Denmark, Finland, Norway and Sweden) containing their contribution to the discussions on the revitalization of UNCTAD.

A pre-Conference meeting of senior officials was held at Cartagena de Indias on 6 and 7 February.

The Conference's main substantive agenda item was the strengthening of national and international action and multilateral cooperation for a healthy, secure and equitable world economy.

Proceedings of UNCTAD VIII

The Conference was attended by 126 member States of UNCTAD, one observer State (Kiribati), Palestine and the Pan African Congress of Azania, as well as by representatives of the United Nations Secretariat, the regional commissions and other United Nations organizations, eight specialized agencies, the General Agreement on Tariffs and Trade (GATT) and the International Trade Centre (UNCTAD/GATT). Also represented were 15 intergovernmental organizations, eight non-governmental organizations (NGOs) and the Airlines Worldwide Telecommunications and Information Service.

At its opening meeting, on 8 February, the Conference elected as its President Juan Manuel Santos, Minister of Foreign Trade of Colombia; it also elected a Rapporteur and 32 Vice-Presidents.

The Conference's inaugural ceremony was addressed by Cesar Gaviria Trujillo, President of Colombia, who welcomed delegates on behalf of his Government, and by Bernard T. G. Chidzero, Senior Minister of Finance, Economic Planning and Development of Zimbabwe and President of the Conference's seventh session (1987).[8]

The United Nations Secretary-General, in his address to the inaugural ceremony, stated that, in recent years, the burden of foreign debt had hindered development in a considerable number of developing countries. Many of the poorest countries had been obliged to transfer vast resources to the rich countries and the resulting economic crisis in the poor countries was jeopardizing their democratic institutions and threatening their national stability and political future. He noted that the causes of the threats facing the environment, and the causes of large-scale migrations and the spread of epidemics, were to be found in poverty and income disparities between peoples and nations. In the economic and social field, a global

consensus in favour of development was still in the process of elaboration. The Secretary-General concluded that if the major objective of peace through development was to be pursued, the political will of Member States needed to be strengthened. New resources were also needed, as well as a more coordinated, more integrated system between the United Nations on the one hand and the specialized agencies and NGOs on the other.

On 10 February, the Conference established a Main Committee to consider and report on matters referred to it by the plenary. The Main Committee established two Working Groups to consider parts of the basic negotiating text.

The Conference had before it a report of the UNCTAD Secretary-General entitled "Accelerating the development process: challenges for national and international policies in the 1990s",[9] the Programme of Action for the Least Developed Countries (LDCs) for the 1990s,[10] an analytical report by the UNCTAD secretariat,[11] the report of the Pre-Conference Meeting of Senior Officials[12] and a number of documents submitted by member States and groups of member States.

In accordance with a proposal of the Pre-Conference Meeting, the Conference held a special meeting on 11 February on LDCs (see PART THREE, Chapter I).

UNCTAD VIII Declaration and final document. On 25 February, the Conference adopted a Declaration entitled "The Spirit of Cartagena" and a five-part final document entitled "A New Partnership for Development: the Cartagena Commitment": Part I outlined the challenges and potentials for international trade and development in the 1990s in the context of the evolving international political and economic situation and the growing convergence on development issues and priorities and a new partnership for development; Part II dealt with the broad policy orientations on the issues of good management at the national and international levels and with sustainable development; Part III discussed the role of UNCTAD in a changing political and economic environment, focusing on a wide range of issues, including institutional adaptation, UNCTAD's functions, adapting, reorienting and consolidating its substantive work, strengthening its intergovernmental machinery and improving its methods of work; Part IV reviewed policies and measures, particularly in the areas of finance, trade, commodities, technology and services and their interlinkages; and Part V focused on economic cooperation among developing countries (ECDC), noting that such cooperation could enable developing countries to exploit more effectively the latest complementarities in their economies, promote a fuller and more effective mobilization of their resources, gain access to additional resources and knowledge, and enhance the negotiating weight necessary to advance their common interests.

Other UNCTAD VIII action. In addition to the Declaration and the final document, UNCTAD VIII, by resolution 170(VIII) of 24 February, approved the report of the Credentials Committee, accepting the credentials of the representatives to the Conference. On 25 February, it adopted resolution 171(VIII), expressing its gratitude to the Government and people of the Republic of Colombia. The Conference also adopted a text by which it invited the UNCTAD Secretary-General to hold consultations on the question of convening a world commodity conference and a message from UNCTAD VIII to the 1992 United Nations Conference on Environment and Development (UNCED) (see below). The Conference also addressed a message to the 1992 Summit for the Economic Advancement of Rural Women (see PART THREE, Chapter I) and agreed to transmit to the General Assembly a draft resolution on assistance to the Palestinian people. It further agreed that UNCTAD assistance to the Palestinian people would be continued in its current form.

UNCTAD VIII follow-up

In the Cartagena Commitment,[2] UNCTAD VIII proposed a number of institutional reforms for UNCTAD, particularly its intergovernmental machinery. It called on TDB, at its first session following the Conference, to take the necessary follow-up measures to ensure speedy implementation of the agreed institutional reforms. On 7 May,[13] TDB adopted guidelines for its executive sessions and established the terms of reference for four Standing Committees: the Standing Committee on Commodities; the Standing Committee on Poverty Alleviation; the Standing Committee on ECDC; and the Standing Committee on Developing Services Sectors: Fostering Competitive Services Sectors in Developing Countries. It also established the terms of reference for the following Ad Hoc Working Groups: the Ad Hoc Working Group on Investment and Financial Flows—non-debt-creating finance for development; new mechanism for increasing investment and financial flows; the Ad Hoc Working Group on Trade Efficiency; the Ad Hoc Working Group on Comparative Experiences with Privatization; the Ad Hoc Working Group on Expansion of Trading Opportunities for Developing Countries; and the Ad Hoc Working Group on the Interrelationship between Investment and Technology Transfer. TDB agreed that the Standing Committees and the Ad Hoc Working Groups, in their work, would take into account the results of the review and follow-up by TDB of progress in implementing the Programme of Action for LDCs for the 1990s (see PART THREE, Chapter I). TDB would also consider establishing

a working group to explore questions related to structural adjustment for the transition to disarmament and the implications for economic growth and development of reductions of military expenditures.

On 9 October,[14] TDB established an Ad Hoc Working Group to explore the issue of structural adjustment for the transition to disarmament. It requested the UNCTAD Secretary-General to prepare a report on the activities of other United Nations organizations in this area, indicate where UNCTAD could best play a role, provide an estimate of the resource implications of establishing the Working Group and prepare draft terms of reference. It would also, at its first session in 1993, establish the timetable for the Group, taking into account the timetable of existing working groups and the availability of resources.

GENERAL ASSEMBLY ACTION

On 22 December 1992, on the recommendation of the Second (Economic and Financial) Committee, the General Assembly adopted **resolution 47/183** without vote.

Eighth session of the United Nations Conference on Trade and Development

The General Assembly,

Reaffirming the importance and continued validity of the Declaration on International Economic Cooperation, in particular the Revitalization of Economic Growth and Development of the Developing Countries, the International Development Strategy for the Fourth United Nations Development Decade, the United Nations New Agenda for the Development of Africa in the 1990s, the Programme of Action for the Least Developed Countries for the 1990s, and the various agreements, especially Agenda 21, that were adopted during the process of the United Nations Conference on Environment and Development,

Recalling its resolution 1995(XIX) of 30 December 1964, as amended, on the establishment of the United Nations Conference on Trade and Development (UNCTAD) as an organ of the General Assembly, and its resolution 45/261 of 3 May 1991, in which it decided to convene the eighth session of the Conference at Cartagena de Indias, Colombia, from 8 to 25 February 1992,

Having considered the final documents adopted by the United Nations Conference on Trade and Development at its eighth session, in particular the Declaration and the document entitled "A New Partnership for Development: The Cartagena Commitment", and noting with satisfaction the highly successful outcome of the eighth session of the Conference and the spirit of genuine cooperation and solidarity—the Spirit of Cartagena—that emerged therefrom,

Expressing its deep gratitude to the Government and the people of Colombia for the hospitality extended to the participants at the eighth session of the United Nations Conference on Trade and Development and for the facilities for holding the session,

Noting the importance of follow-up and of keeping under review the implementation of the policies and measures adopted by the United Nations Conference on Trade and Development at its eighth session,

Emphasizing that the concerns of the international community about the current world economic situation, trade and development issues, and the difficulties of many countries in achieving satisfactory rates of development deserve continuing attention, in particular as far as the developing countries are concerned,

Reaffirming, in this context, the need to give priority to problems facing the least developed countries owing to the fragility of their economies and their particular vulnerability to external shocks and natural calamities,

Reiterating that the Uruguay Round of multilateral trade negotiations should result in a substantial and balanced outcome in all areas involved, and expressing concern that those negotiations have not yet been completed but hopeful that they will come to a successful conclusion rapidly, taking into account the specific interests of developing countries,

I

1.   *Endorses* the outcome of the eighth session of the United Nations Conference on Trade and Development, in particular the commitments agreed upon, and emphasizes the importance of the New Partnership for Development, initiated by the Conference at that session, where countries will join actively in cooperative work to address the development challenges of the 1990s, and expresses its political will and responsibility to implement the agreed commitments;

2.   *Welcomes* the far-reaching institutional reform measures adopted by the Conference at its eighth session regarding the functions, intergovernmental machinery, methods of work and substantive orientations of the United Nations Conference on Trade and Development (UNCTAD), and agrees that those measures are a valuable contribution to the process of restructuring the economic and social sectors of the United Nations launched by the General Assembly;

3.   *Reaffirms* the important role of UNCTAD, as a principal organ of the General Assembly in the field of trade and development and as the most appropriate focal point within the United Nations proper for the integrated treatment of development and interrelated issues in key areas, including trade, commodities, finance, investment, services and technology, in the interests of all countries, particularly those of developing countries;

4.   *Welcomes* the agreement by UNCTAD to refocus its substantive work on four areas, namely, a new partnership for development, global interdependence, paths to development and sustainable development, which should serve as orientations for developing both fresh approaches to long-standing issues and insights for pursuing relevant new lines of work, and acknowledges the efforts that have been made in this respect and encourages further efforts in this regard;

5.   *Also welcomes* the high priority given by UNCTAD to commodities, poverty alleviation, services development, economic cooperation among developing countries, investment and financial flows, privatization, trading opportunities for developing countries, investment and technology transfers, and trade efficiency;

6.   *Stresses* the important contribution that UNCTAD can make to sustainable development in the context of the implementation of Agenda 21, *inter alia*, on trade-related environmental, poverty alleviation, commodity and technology issues, and, in this context, requests UNCTAD to work closely with the Commission on Sustainable Development;

7.   *Invites* all organs, organizations and bodies of the United Nations system to respond positively to the requests addressed to them in the relevant parts of the commitments of the Conference at its eighth session;

II

8.   *Takes note* of the reports of the Trade and Development Board on the second part of its thirty-eighth session and the first part of its thirty-ninth session and calls upon all States to take appropriate action to implement the outcome of those sessions;

9.   *Expresses its satisfaction* with the action initiated by the Trade and Development Board for the implementation of the new institutional arrangements and of the substantive orientations agreed upon by UNCTAD, and welcomes Trade and Development Board decision 398(XXXVIII) of 7 May 1992 on the follow-up to the recommendations adopted by the Conference at its eighth session;

10.   *Takes note* of the agreement by the Conference at its eighth session to suspend the existing Committees of the Trade and Development Board, with the exception of the Special Committee on Preferences and the Intergovernmental Group of Experts on Restrictive Business Practices;

11.   *Endorses* the establishment and the terms of reference of the new standing committees and of the new ad hoc working groups, as contained in the annex to Trade and Development Board decision 398(XXXVIII), as well as the convening of executive sessions of the Board aimed at strengthening its policy function;

12.   *Takes note* of Trade and Development Board decision 399(XXXIX) of 9 October 1992 on the establishment of an ad hoc working group to explore the issue of structural adjustment for the transition to disarmament;

13.   *Welcomes* the streamlining and strengthening of the intergovernmental machinery of UNCTAD and the improvement of methods of work aimed at providing an enriched substantive and technical basis for the functions of UNCTAD, as agreed at the eighth session of the Conference;

14.   *Endorses* the convening in 1994, within existing resources, of a United Nations international symposium of one week's duration on trade efficiency and requests the Secretary-General of the United Nations Conference on Trade and Development to make all the necessary arrangements for that symposium, taking into account the preparatory work of the Ad Hoc Working Group on Trade Efficiency of UNCTAD;

15.   *Takes note* of the valuable contribution made by the Trade and Development Board, underpinned by the *Trade and Development Report, 1992*, to the understanding of the international implications of macroeconomic policies and issues concerning global interdependence, with particular reference to the recent evolution of development problems and prospects, and welcomes the outcome of the deliberations of the Board on this matter;

16.   *Also takes note* of the recognition on the part of the Conference at its eighth session and of the Trade and Development Board that Governments should consider,

as part of fighting protectionism and as appropriate, the establishment of transparent mechanisms at the national level;

III

17. *Calls upon* the international community to assist in promoting measures necessary for the revitalization of the development process in the developing countries, in pursuit of the objective of revitalizing international trade, sustained economic growth and development;

18. *Urges* all countries to fulfil their commitments to halt and reverse protectionism and to reach a final agreement on the remaining issues of the Uruguay Round, and reaffirms that the balanced and comprehensive conclusion of the multilateral trade negotiations is crucial and is needed in order to strengthen the rules and disciplines of the international trading system and significantly enhance the prospects for trade, economic growth and development of all countries, especially developing countries.

General Assembly resolution 47/183

22 December 1992   Meeting 93   Adopted without vote

Approved by Second Committee (A/47/718/Add.2) without vote, 11 December (meeting 50); draft by Vice-Chairman (A/C.2/47/L.82), based on informal consultations on draft by Pakistan for Group of 77 (A/C.2/47/L.30), as orally corrected; agenda item 78 (a).
Financial implications. S-G, A/C.2/47/L.45.
Meeting numbers. GA 47th session: 2nd Committee 40, 42, 43, 48, 50; plenary 93.

REFERENCES

[1]YUN 1991, p. 458, GA res. 45/261, 3 May 1991. [2]TD/364. [3]YUN 1991, p. 458. [4]TD/B/1319. [5]TD/356. [6]TD/357. [7]TD/355. [8]YUN 1987, p. 465. [9]TD/354/Rev.1. [10]TD/359. [11]TD/358. [12]TD/360. [13]A/47/15, vol. I (dec. 398 (XXXVIII)). [14]A/47/15, vol. II (dec. 399(XXXIX)).

International trade

The *Trade and Development Report, 1992*[1] stated that world trade grew by only 3 per cent in 1991, continuing the deceleration of world trade expansion that began in 1989. The recession in North America and the United Kingdom, weakening investment trends in Japan, the economic slow-down in Western Europe and the sharp output contraction in Central and Eastern Europe and the former USSR all influenced international trade negatively. However, rapid growth and buoyant domestic activity bolstered imports in East Asian countries, and strong import demand was experienced in the Persian Gulf area, on account of reconstruction in some economies. The economic recovery in Latin America boosted world demand and the unification process in Germany substantially raised import demand.

As to the world trade pattern, the volume of exports of developed market economies as a group increased by slightly more than 3 per cent in 1991, compared with over 5 per cent in 1990, while imports grew by less than 2 per cent, against over 4 per cent in 1990. Export expansion slowed in virtually all the major industrialized countries in volume terms, except for the United States where, at over 6 per cent, it was about double the world average. However, imports to the United States fell slightly, owing to depressed domestic demand. The unification of Germany led to a diversion of production to internal markets and a sharp rise in imports. Exports declined by 2 per cent in 1991, in contrast to an import volume growth of over 9 per cent. Japan, despite a sluggish domestic economy, experienced some export growth but an import growth of only 1 per cent, against over 6.5 per cent the previous year. In the developing countries, which provided the major impetus to world trade in 1991, the volume of exports and imports grew significantly, especially in the Asian region. China raised its market share and integrated into the world economy, with a rapid growth in both export and import volume, averaging around 12 per cent per year. Latin America recorded a growth of imports of over 10 per cent in 1991, while for developing countries in Africa, the sharp fall in commodity prices resulted in a fall in the volume of imports of over 5 per cent. High import levels were maintained in the Persian Gulf region, while West Asia recorded a 10 per cent decline in the value of exports and an increase of over 18 per cent in imports. The decision to transact their mutual trade in hard currency led to a virtual collapse of trade among member countries of the former Council for Mutual Economic Assistance (CMEA). This loss was partially compensated by the expansion of trade with other markets, notably Western Europe.

The *World Economic Survey 1992*[2] reported that the 3 per cent growth in the volume of world trade in 1991 was the smallest gain since 1985. It was none the less remarkable in a year when world output declined.

A revival of world trade would clearly depend on the speed of recovery of the industrial economies from the current recession, said the *Survey*. The pent-up import demand in Eastern Europe and the republics of the former USSR should lead, if properly financed, to increased imports into that area. Efforts at trade liberalization in the developing countries should also make a modest contribution to the resuscitation of world trade. However, continuing protectionist trends could dampen those possibilities.

The outcome of the Uruguay Round of trade negotiations (see PART SEVEN, Chapter XVIII) remained uncertain, with agriculture continuing to be the biggest sticking-point. While there was little abatement of protectionism among the major trading nations, a number of developing countries—especially in Latin America—were undertaking significant liberalization of their trade regimes.

Trade policy

The *Trade and Development Report, 1992*[1] noted that a large number of developing countries had liberalized their trade regimes in the late 1980s and early 1990s as part of a more comprehensive set of structural adjustment measures to accelerate economic growth in response to economic crisis and disenchantment with excessive State intervention. The result had been an increase in the number of developing countries with fairly free trade regimes. Developing countries used different strategies to build export success and were able to combine protection for the domestic market with export promotion in many different ways. However, aside from liberalization of imported inputs used by the export sectors, other forms of import liberalization had not necessarily been an ingredient of successful trade policies.

The *World Economic Survey 1992*[2] reported that 1991 saw a continuing trend towards the formation of trading blocs in the form of regional and subregional arrangements in both the developed and the developing regions of the world.

UNCTAD VIII action. In the Cartagena Commitment,[3] UNCTAD VIII stated that the international trading environment had been affected by a number of developments which created new challenges and opportunities, making multilateral cooperation of even greater importance. World exports had continued to grow faster than world output in recent years, but its expansion had been unevenly spread; only a limited number of developing countries had been capable of achieving appreciable growth in their exports. Therefore, UNCTAD VIII stressed that the objectives of the international community should be to halt and reverse protectionism in order to bring about further liberalization and expansion of world trade to the benefit of all countries, particularly the developing ones; to provide for an equitable, secure, non-discriminatory and predictable international trading system; to facilitate the integration of all countries into the world economy and the international trading system; to ensure that environment and trade policies were mutually supportive, with a view to achieving sustainable development; and to strengthen the international trading system through an early, balanced, comprehensive and successful outcome of the Uruguay Round.

It outlined the measures and action needed to fulfil these objectives and urged all countries to implement previous commitments to halt and reverse protectionism and further expand market access, particularly in areas of interest to developing countries, which would be facilitated by appropriate structural adjustment in developed countries. Developing countries should continue their trade-policy reforms and structural adjustments and should progressively reduce their import barriers,

consistent with their trade, financial and development needs. These efforts should be supported by the international community through adequate improved market access and increased flows of financial resources. UNCTAD VIII invited member countries to support the transition of countries in Central and Eastern Europe to a market economy and to liberalize their trade regimes *vis-à-vis* all of them. It stressed the need to abolish discriminatory measures aimed at those countries and to relax non-tariff measures (NTMs) on a most-favoured-nation basis.

The Conference said that the international trading system should support the observance by all countries of their international commitments on the granting of differential and more favourable treatment to developing countries and provide for their increasing integration into the system. The international community should implement measures to grant substantially improved market access for exports of LDCs and provide special trade treatment for them. The Conference also called for action with regard to protectionism and the generalized system of trade preferences (GSP) (see below).

UNCTAD VIII agreed that TDB should continue to review annually global developments in the evolution of production of and trade in manufactures, commodities and services. The review should comprise analysis of the principal elements and effects of structural adjustment and trade policies and policy options, taking into account the special interests of developing countries.

Uruguay Round

The *World Economic Survey 1992*[2] reported that the Uruguay Round—the eighth round of multilateral trade negotiations, launched in 1986[4] under the aegis of GATT (see PART SEVEN, Chapter XVIII)—which was suspended in December 1990, was restarted in early 1991. However, the outcome of the negotiations remained uncertain.

UNCTAD VIII action. In the Cartagena Commitment,[3] UNCTAD VIII urged all participants, in particular the major trading partners, to make determined efforts to arrive at an early, balanced, comprehensive and successful outcome of the Uruguay Round, taking into account the specific interests of the developing countries. It reaffirmed the commitment to an open, viable and durable multilateral trading system to bring about further liberalization and expansion of world trade to the benefit of all countries, especially the developing ones. It requested TDB to analyse and assess the outcome of the Uruguay Round, in particular in areas of interest or concern to developing countries, and its impact on the international trading system. In that context, TDB should examine, on the basis of analyses by the UNCTAD Secretary-

General, the problems and opportunities faced by the developing countries as well as the economies in transition in Central and Eastern Europe in increasing their participation in international trade in the 1990s. The Conference acknowledged the appreciation expressed by developing countries for support provided by the United Nations Development Programme (UNDP), through UNCTAD, to facilitate their effective participation in the Uruguay Round.

Strengthening institutional trade arrangements

Responding to a 1991 General Assembly request,[5] the Secretary-General submitted a progress report on strengthening international organizations in the area of multilateral trade.[6] He reported that the UNCTAD Secretary-General had received no replies from international organizations in response to his 1991 request for their views, apart from the six reported on in 1991.[7] However, the UNCTAD Secretary-General had received responses to his note from nine Governments and the Commission of the European Communities. The responses emphasized that, given the still unclear situation in the Uruguay Round of multilateral trade negotiations, the time might not be ripe to define a clear line of action or to draw correct conclusions as to the institutional needs of a global trading system. Several replies did focus on ensuring complementarity between activities of UNCTAD and GATT. In particular, the Commission of the European Communities stressed that the roles of GATT and UNCTAD were and should remain complementary and that it was essential to maintain adequate coordination between the activities of the two institutions.

The Secretary-General further reported that the draft final act embodying the results of the Uruguay Round, submitted to participants in December 1991, included a draft agreement establishing a multilateral trade organization—considered to be the most effective and pragmatic mechanism for implementing the results of the Round.

The Secretary-General concluded that it would be advisable to review the matter again at the Assembly's 1993 session on the basis of an updated report on the subject, on the assumption that the Uruguay Rould would be concluded by that time.

GENERAL ASSEMBLY ACTION

On 22 December 1992, on the recommendation of the Second Committee, the General Assembly adopted **resolution 47/184** without vote.

Strengthening international organizations in the area of multilateral trade

The General Assembly,

Reaffirming the Declaration on International Economic Cooperation, in particular the Revitalization of Economic Growth and Development of the Developing Countries, and the International Development Strategy for the Fourth United Development Decade,

Recalling its resolutions 45/201 of 21 December 1990 and 46/207 of 20 December 1991,

Welcoming the successful outcome of the eighth session of the United Nations Conference on Trade and Development, in particular the organization's institutional reform,

Taking note of the progress report by the Secretary-General concerning institutional developments related to the strengthening of international organizations in the area of multilateral trade,

Expressing concern that the current negotiations of the Uruguay Round of multilateral trade negotiations have not yet been completed, but hoping that they will rapidly reach a balanced and substantial conclusion in all areas involved,

1. *Once again urges* all Governments and the executive heads of the specialized agencies and other organizations and programmes of the United Nations system to endeavour to present their views to the Secretary-General on this matter;

2. *Requests* the Secretary-General to prepare, for submission to the General Assembly at its forty-eighth session, an updated report taking into account the positive outcome and developments of the eighth session of the United Nations Conference on Trade and Development and the developments in the Uruguay Round of multilateral trade negotiations.

General Assembly resolution 47/184

22 December 1992   Meeting 93   Adopted without vote

Approved by Second Committee (A/47/718/Add.2) without vote, 9 December (meeting 49); draft by Vice-Chairman (A/C.2/47/L.70), based on informal consultations on draft by Pakistan for Group of 77 (A/C.2/47/L.31); agenda item 78 *(a).*

Meeting numbers. GA 47th session: 2nd Committee 40, 42, 43, 48, 49; plenary 93.

Protectionism and structural adjustment

UNCTAD VIII action. In the Cartagena Commitment,[3] UNCTAD VIII agreed that UNCTAD should promote the establishment by Governments of transparent mechanisms at the national level to evaluate protectionist measures sought by firms/sectors, and the implications of such measures for the domestic economy and their effects on the export interests of developing countries. The UNCTAD secretariat should provide technical assistance to interested countries in connection with the establishment of such mechanisms. The Conference also recommended that countries give attention to increasing the transparency of their trade regimes and to replacing NTMs by tariffs where possible.

National transparency mechanisms

In July, the UNCTAD secretariat presented a report to TDB on issues relating to national transparency mechanisms in the context of the fight against protectionism.[8] The report noted that the need to establish or to enhance domestic transparency of trade-related policy-making was now widely recognized and had been supported by intensive investigation and analysis by the Organisation for Economic Cooperation and Development (OECD), GATT and UNCTAD. It described the set of issues concerning national transparency mechanisms and summarized the analytical work accomplished. It discussed the trade-policy bias towards protection and the implications of transparency mechanisms for developing countries. The report further reviewed the experiences of transparency mechanisms in Australia, Canada, New Zealand and the United States, the nature of the analytical activities of a transparency agency, the techniques used to evaluate the costs to and benefits of protection on the sectors affected as well as on the economy as a whole. It listed the basic features of an effective transparency mechanism and discussed the role of technical assistance in its establishment.

Trade preferences

Generalized system of preferences

TDB's Special Committee on Preferences held its nineteenth session at Geneva from 18 to 22 May 1992.[9] It considered the fifteenth general report[10] by the UNCTAD secretariat on the implementation of GSP schemes. The report described changes and improvements that had taken place in the various schemes since the last review and updated information on the trade effects of the system. It noted that the European Economic Community (EEC) GSP scheme for 1991, with the exception of a few technical changes and an increase in the amounts in European Currency Units (ECU) of sensitive industrial products, would be applied *mutatis mutandis* from 1 January to 31 December 1992. Yugoslavia (Serbia and Montenegro) had been excluded from the beneficiary list under the schemes of EEC and Norway. Czechoslovakia had been added to the beneficiary lists of Australia, Austria, Canada and the United States. Namibia became a beneficiary under the schemes of Australia, Austria, Canada, Finland and the United States. Finland and Switzerland added Albania to their beneficiary lists. The United States considered that the Sudan did not meet the standards of workers' rights and therefore excluded it from its scheme. Poland adjusted and modified its scheme and established a new list of beneficiary countries. Hungary revised its scheme, adding several industrial products and giving preferential duty-free treatment to tropical products already covered, or increasing the preferential tariff margins on them. It also established a new list of beneficiaries. The question arose as to the form in which the GSP scheme of the former USSR would be applied in the future.

The Special Committee also considered an UNCTAD secretariat report[11] on the incidence of NTMs on imports of GSP-covered products which updated earlier information on the subject. It indicated that over one fifth ($26 billion or 21.3 per cent) of GSP-covered products ($122 billion) of the 11 OECD schemes, in terms of 1988 trade flows, were found to be subject to NTMs. GSP-covered products faced a wide variety of NTMs in the markets of preference-giving countries and heavy reliance was placed by certain preference-giving countries on the use of "hard-core" NTMs to limit imports eligible for preferential tariff treatment, including variable levies, quotas, non-automatic licences and restrictions under the Multifibre Arrangement (MFA). Percentages of GSP-covered imports facing NTMs for each of the major beneficiaries under the various schemes were found to be extremely high in all cases. The report indicated that NTMs could be an important deterrent to imports of GSP-covered products and recommended that, as a means of improving utilization of GSP, preference-giving countries could consider exempting GSP-covered products from NTMs.

In a concluding statement attached to the Special Committee's report,[9] the Chairman said that it was felt that graduation/differentation in the treatment of beneficiary countries under GSP would be arbitrary and restrictive and that objective and rational criteria for their treatment would be the best way to avoid such unwanted and often discriminatory results. A positive effect of graduation/differentiation could be a better spread of benefits among developing countries, however, and it could open the way for increased product coverage. Country/product differentation was also considered preferable to complete country exclusion because such a macroeconomic policy decision could create problems at the microeconomic level for the graduated country. With regard to the rules of origin, it was considered that the question of harmonization should be treated as a separate issue from other possible improvements, such as simplification and liberalization. Many countries felt that extension of the use of the donor-country concept would be consistent with national and international trends towards trade liberalization. Full global cumulation was seen as having positive effects on cooperation among beneficiary countries, particularly those outside regional groupings. Technical assistance was of continuing importance for meeting the growing needs of countries, as an increasing number were in a position to use GSP. There was broad consensus that, in line with agreed policy, ways should be sought to offer special benefits to all LDCs in view of their limited industrial base and export power.

Technical cooperation

The delivery of technical cooperation for GSP and other trade laws remained high in 1992[12] as a result of increased interest in GSP shown by beneficiaries and facilitated by UNDP and trust fund contributions to the GSP programme by UNCTAD member States. Extrabudgetary funding for global GSP activities in 1992 totalled $1,141,500, of which UNDP funds accounted for approximately $538,400 or 47 per cent, with the remainder ($603,100) coming from trust fund contributions. Trust fund contributions for specific purposes amounted to $343,800, in-kind contributions to $96,000 and central trust fund contributions to $163,320, or 27 per cent of total funding. During the year, 58 activities were undertaken in all regions of the world, including 22 training seminars/workshops, 16 advisory/consultation missions and 7 field research missions aimed primarily at assisting preference-receiving countries. In all, 853 participants from 20 preference-receiving countries benefited from these training activities.

Countries in Africa and Central and Eastern Europe were showing increasing awareness and interest in GSP, leading to more requests for training. It was expected that, following the conclusion of the Uruguay Round of multilateral trade negotiations, there would be more requests, particularly from Asian and Latin American countries, for seminars and advisory missions.

UNCTAD VIII action. In the Cartagena Commitment,[3] UNCTAD VIII noted that many developing countries had benefited from GSP treatment and encouraged preference-giving countries to continue to improve and renew the schemes and extend their operation periods. It recommended that preference-giving countries should comply with the multilaterally agreed principles of GSP, consider appropriate adjustments in country coverage and, if possible, consider comprehensive product coverage. It further recommended minimizing limitations and restrictions on preferential imports, as well as withdrawals of preferential benefits. The rules of origin should be simplified and harmonized, where possible, to impart stability, transparency and greater credibility to the schemes, and to reduce their complexity. The Conference expressed concern over the incidence of NTMs on benefits deriving from GSP schemes, and urged preference-giving countries to reduce or eliminate such barriers. It also called on preference-giving countries to implement fully the provisions of the Paris Declaration, adopted by the Second (1990) United Nations Conference on LDCs,[13] in respect of GSP measures in favour of LDCs. It urged UNDP and potential donor countries to increase their contributions to the UNCTAD technical assistance programme on GSP in order to allow developing countries to benefit fully. Those preference-giving countries and their exporters which had not yet fully taken advantage of GSP should participate actively in these technical assistance activities. The Special Committee on Preferences was requested to examine the scope

and possible modalities for extending preferential treatment to developing countries with respect to goods, in accordance with the principles and objectives underlying GSP. In expectation of MFN rates being brought down pending a successful conclusion of the Uruguay Round of multilateral negotiations, preference-giving countries should consider increasing preferential margins and duty-free treatment offered under existing preferential schemes.

Rules of origin

In order to facilitate discussions and find solutions to questions relating to the rules of origin under GSP, the UNCTAD secretariat submitted a report[14] containing an examination of definitions of "substantial transformation" and implications of harmonization: possible initiatives in regard to simplification and liberalization. It examined and compared the two definitions of "substantial transformation", namely, the "process" criterion and the limitations which its applications placed upon the use of imported materials, components and parts in the manufacture of a product. In order to improve the rules of origin, the report also discussed the possibilities and implications of introducing harmonization of the current definition and other initiatives.

In August,[15] the UNCTAD secretariat submitted responses to its questionnaire on this issue received from eight preference-giving countries. The questionnaire had sought information on practical problems encountered by manufacturers in seeking to produce goods to satisfy various origin rules and comments by manufacturers and certifying authorities.

Trade promotion and facilitation

In 1992, United Nations bodies continued to assist developing countries to promote their exports and facilitate the movement of goods in international commerce, with the main originator of technical cooperation projects in that area being the International Trade Centre (ITC).

International Trade Centre

During 1992, ITC, under the joint sponsorship of UNCTAD and GATT, continued its technical cooperation activities, serving as a focal point for United Nations assistance to developing countries in formulating and implementing trade promotion programmes. In response to a 1991 recommendation of its Joint Advisory Group (JAG), ITC conducted an independent programme evaluation of its activities in commodity trade, development and promotion[16] for the purpose of assessing the relevance, effectiveness and impact of ITC's objectives and related strategy in the area of commodities, examining the factors associated with its results and formulating recommendations concerning future orientation and methodologies of its work in these areas.

The report concluded that ITC was the only organization which specialized in the marketing and distribution aspects of commodities and its exposure/effectiveness was very high; its commodity work was oriented to the specific needs of developing countries and met most of the United Nations global priorities; and it had been realistic in its project design and in getting the message across to the people doing the actual work. However, ITC was working under financial constraints as its resources never matched its technical cooperation requirements.

The evaluation recommended as a commodity strategy that the commodity-specific interregional approach should be continued and the commodity work/strategy extended to ensure follow-up on interregional work at the national level; more attention should be given to solving funding constraints by generating extra business; a strategic marketing group should be formed; the thinking of the country desk officers and the commodity group needed to be reoriented; more use should be made of dissemination seminars and workshops to demonstrate ITC capabilities; the commodity group should produce a series of commodity-specific modules; and ITC publications should be more widely distributed. In relation to commodity coverage, the evaluation recommended that minerals and metals should be assessed like other commodities; a minimum of one or two interregional projects at a time should be ensured in each commodity; market surveys in Eastern Europe should be expanded and seed money found for pilot projects, new project ideas and the investigation of other commodities. Other recommendations were made to improve ITC's project design and implementation and to address the financial implications of its strengthened mandate in commodities.

JAG action. JAG held its twenty-fifth session at Geneva on 26 and 27 November 1992.[17] It considered the report on ITC's 1991 activities[18] and underlined the key role played by ITC in assisting developing countries in their trade promotion and export development efforts. It stressed the importance of filling, as soon as possible, the ITC vacant post of Executive Director and other top management and professional vacancies to permit the organization to continue to provide steady support to developing countries' trade promotion efforts. It expressed particular concern about resource constraints that had affected the Centre's work in 1991 and exhorted the ITC trust fund donor community and UNDP to do their utmost to ensure an adequate flow of resources to ITC commensurate

with the increasing trade promotion requirements of developing countries. JAG also singled out specific areas of global concern, such as the environment, as requiring special ITC emphasis.

Global trust fund

An ITC technical meeting was held at Geneva from 27 to 29 January 1992[19] to consider proposals for setting up a global trust fund and a consultative committee. The meeting recommended that JAG should accept the proposals for establishing a global trust fund and a consultative committee and invited the donor country representatives to consult with their capitals with a view to announcing possible contributions to the global fund at JAG's twenty-fifth session.

Financial report

In accordance with a 1991 General Assembly request,[20] the Secretary-General submitted an October report on ITC's administrative system.[21] He reported that a joint review had been conducted by ITC and United Nations Secretariat officials and the resulting understanding on financial issues was communicated to the ITC Executive Director. Subsequently, a corresponding revision to the administrative instruction on the delegation of authority in financial matters was issued in February 1992 and a revised delegation of authority on matters related to personnel administration was conveyed to the Centre. Based on the clear understanding that both the Staff Regulations and Rules and the Financial Regulations and Rules of the United Nations were applicable to ITC, the Secretary-General was of the view that the review's results constituted a reasonable and viable framework for ITC's administrative system. In the financial report and audited financial statements for ITC for the biennium ended 31 December 1991,[22] the Board of Auditors indicated that the United Nations Secretariat decision did not receive the approval of ITC and GATT and, consequently, certain issues were still under discussion. However, in the opinion of the Secretary-General, the only issue to be considered in the review requested by the Assembly was the degree of authority delegated by the Secretary-General to the Centre's Executive Director.

On 23 December 1992, by **resolution 47/211**, the Assembly accepted the financial report and audited financial statements for the biennium ended 31 December 1991 and took note of the Secretary-General's report on ITC's administrative system.

Trade efficiency

UNCTAD VIII action. In the Cartagena Commitment,[3] UNCTAD VIII noted that new techniques, such as electronic data interchange (EDI) and other procedures in international trade transactions, were capable of producing substantial time and money savings. It recommended that UNCTAD programmes should give special attention to integrating less advanced countries and regions into this process to give them access to new sources of trade competitiveness. It requested the UNCTAD Secretary-General to initiate consultations with member States to establish an expert group on trade efficiency. The culmination of the expert group's work, said the Conference, should be a 1994 international symposium on trade efficiency, which should reinforce international discussion on harmonized national and regional infrastructures for trade and trade efficiency, focusing especially on the need to involve all countries in efficient trade and to promote the participation of small and medium-sized enterprises in international trade.

Transparency in trade-related information should be fostered by increasing awareness of opportunities to access publicly available market information. Efforts to establish EDI standards should be supported so that the business interests and concerns of all countries, in particular developing countries, were represented and complemented through international cooperation. UNCTAD should continue to strengthen its analytical and technical cooperation in trade efficiency, including through experiments carried out jointly with the private and public sectors of pilot countries. The Conference urged countries to increase trade efficiency through the use of information technology, especially in the areas of trade facilitation and customs automation. All countries were encouraged to adopt laws, regulations and policies to reduce barriers to trade facilitation through the use of information technology.

Ad Hoc Working Group on Trade Efficiency

On 7 May,[23] TDB established an Ad Hoc Working Group on Trade Efficiency and decided on its terms of reference. At its first meeting (Geneva, 16-20 November),[24] the Working Group adopted its programme of work, which aimed at fostering greater participation in international trade, in particular by small and medium-sized enterprises, giving special attention to countries and regions less advanced in the area of trade efficiency. The main areas of the Group's work would include information flows to build trade efficiency, facilitating trade, working towards trade efficiency, implementing a pilot "Trade Point" programme, providing technical assistance and preparing for the 1994 international symposium on trade efficiency. The UNCTAD Secretary-General was invited to assess the workload and financial implications of the programme's activities, formulate proposals, identify additional funding needs and encourage extrabudgetary contributions. He was requested to establish a core advisory group of experts.

Trade and economic cooperation among developing countries

UNCTAD VIII action. In a section of the Cartagena Commitment[3] on ECDC, UNCTAD VIII stated that, in the new context of market-oriented reforms and export-oriented growth strategies being pursued by most developing countries, ECDC should be seen as a means to secure the integration of developing countries into the world economy and to increase their capacity to produce, achieve economies of scale and become internationally competitive.

Within subregional and regional groupings, the expansion of trade depended on reducing tariffs, eliminating non-tariff barriers, introducing more transparent and simple customs procedures, macroeconomic policy coordination to ensure convergence of national price trends and exchange-rate stability, and effective clearing and payments arrangements, as well as improving physical infrastructure. The allocation of aid resources should support regional trade liberalization among developing countries, and the international community should support the efforts of regional and subregional groupings of developing countries to promote and encourage enterprise and entrepreneurship. Work on the main impediments and disincentives to the expansion of trade among developing countries should be pursued. The secretariat and intergovernmental machinery of UNCTAD should examine the benefits to be derived by developing countries from reducing trade barriers and improving cooperation among them.

In the area of monetary and financial impediments to trade, UNCTAD VIII urged the UNCTAD secretariat to assist developing countries to strengthen and develop their national finance mechanisms. All countries and relevant institutions were invited to cooperate fully with the UNCTAD Secretary-General in his consultations on the feasibility of establishing an interregional trade finance mechanism among developing countries.

Other UNCTAD action. On 7 May,[23] TDB established, in accordance with the Cartagena Commitment,[3] the Standing Committee on ECDC and adopted its terms of reference. The aims of the Committee's activities were to strengthen cooperation, enhance economic growth, increase trade liberalization and transparency, promote developing-country enterprises, facilitate the integration of developing countries into the world economy so as to reduce impediments and disincentives that adversely affected the expansion of cooperation among them, and promote policies aimed at expanding trade.

Expansion of trading opportunities

On 7 May,[23] TDB established an Ad Hoc Working Group on Expansion of Trading Opportunities for Developing Countries. At its first meeting (Geneva, 14-18 December 1992),[25] the Working Group established its programme of work, under which it intended to study global trends and issues affecting the trading opportunities of developing countries, analyse prospects for expanding trade opportunities and consider technical cooperation issues.

Restrictive business practices

The UNCTAD Intergovernmental Group of Experts on Restrictive Business Practices held its eleventh session at Geneva from 23 to 27 November 1992.[26] It had before it a note by the UNCTAD secretariat[27] containing replies from 18 States and the Commission of the European Communities on steps taken by them to meet their commitment to the Set of Multilaterally Agreed Equitable Principles and Rules for the Control of Restrictive Business Practices (known as the Set).[28] Other notes submitted by the secretariat were on studies related to the provisions of the Set and technical assistance, advisory and training programmes[29] and on information and consultations procedures on restrictive business practices;[30] proposed amendments to the revised draft of possible elements for articles of a model law or laws, and commentaries on the elements;[31] and the compilation of a handbook on restrictive business practices legislation.[32] The secretariat also submitted a revised report on the concentration of market power, through mergers, take-overs, joint ventures and other acquisitions of control, and its effects on international markets, in particular the markets of developing countries.[33] Communications were received from France[34] and OECD.[35]

On 27 November,[26] the Group of Experts adopted its conclusions, agreeing that the secretariat should finalize the study on concentration of market power and prepare a study on competition policy and economic reforms in developing and other countries; revise the check-list for requests for information and consultations; prepare and circulate an updated directory on competition authorities; improve the dissemination of information on restrictive business practices in goods and services through its annual and quarterly reports and keep other bodies of UNCTAD informed as appropriate; continue the elaboration of the model law or laws and handbook; continue to provide technical assistance, advisory and training services in the area of competition policy to developing countries and countries in transition; and undertake a review of technical cooperation activities in the field of competition policy by member States and international organizations to enable the Group of Experts at its twelfth (1993) session to evaluate ways to improve the effectiveness of UNCTAD's technical assistance.

UNCTAD VIII action. In the Cartagena Commitment,[3] UNCTAD VIII agreed that UNCTAD should pursue, through the Intergovernmental Group of Experts on Restrictive Business Practices, its work with regard to policies and rules for the control of restrictive business practices in order to encourage competition, promote the proper functioning of markets and resource allocation, and bring about further liberalization of international trade. Efforts should be made by national Governments or regional authorities to implement fully the provisions of the Set and develop cooperation between national competition authorities, including competent authorities of regional groupings. UNCTAD's work should cover goods and services and its secretariat and developed countries should provide upon request developing and other countries with technical cooperation in the area of competition policy.

Commodities

The *World Economic Survey 1992*[2] stated that the average price of non-fuel commodities, as measured by the combined index of nominal dollar prices of UNCTAD, declined by 6.3 per cent in 1991. Measured in special drawing rights (SDRs), the decline was 7.4 per cent, reflecting the slight overall depreciation of the dollar. In real terms, the decline in prices was around 6 per cent, as the prices of manufactured goods exports of industrialized countries remained practically unchanged. The continuing fall of commodity prices, which started to weaken in 1989, mainly reflected demand conditions as a consequence of the recession in developed market economies. Commodity prices were also influenced by the supply and demand shocks to several markets resulting from the breakup of the USSR and increased participation of Eastern European economies in Western commodity markets. The dismantling of the Council for Mutual Economic Assistance (CMEA) and other trading arrangements between the former USSR and several developing countries created other types of market dislocations.

Among the major commodity groups, food prices declined by 6.6 per cent. Sugar led the decline with a loss of 27 per cent of free-market prices. Wheat prices recovered but tropical beverages fell. Surpluses of coffee and cocoa took prices to their lowest levels in 16 years. The vegetable oils and oilseeds commodity group was the only one to register an increase in prices. Prices of most agricultural raw materials declined, leading to an overall decline in the UNCTAD index of those prices of 8.1 per cent. The composite index of minerals, ores and metals prices declined by 9.4 per cent, the steepest decline of all commodity groups.

Negotiations aimed at reviving stalled price-stabilization schemes produced no significant results.

The *Trade and Development Report, 1992*[1] stated that the considerable difference in the behaviour of primary commodity export prices between the developed market economies and the developing economies in 1990 and 1991, with prices in the latter having risen more in 1990 and fallen more in 1991, was primarily due to large changes in petroleum prices over those two years and the greater importance of petroleum exports for the developing world. The fall in international prices of fuels was explained largely by the behaviour of crude oil prices.

In response to a 1990 General Assembly request,[36] the UNCTAD Secretary-General submitted a September report on world commodity trends and prospects, with particular emphasis on commodity-dependent developing countries in the light of the outcome of UNCTAD VIII.[37] It summarized developments in the commodity situation and outlook since his 1990 report to the Assembly,[38] and the agreed commitments on commodities at UNCTAD VIII (see below). It discussed recent developments in the functioning and transparency of commodity markets, changes in the commodity sector, with particular relevance to commodity export dependency, and developments in market access for commodity products. It also addressed the issue of management of natural resources in the context of sustainable development.

UNCTAD VIII action. The Cartagena Commitment[3] agreed that the international community's goals should be to improve the functioning of the commodity market by reducing distortions affecting supply and demand; optimize the contribution of the commodities sector to development; achieve a gradual reduction in excessive dependence on the export of primary commodities through horizontal and vertical diversification of production and exports; improve market access for commodity products through a progressive removal of barriers to international trade and improve market transparency; and ensure proper management of natural resources to achieve sustainable development. The Conference further agreed to a number of policy measures to achieve those goals. It urged producers and consumers of individual commodities to examine ways and means to reinforce and improve their cooperation towards solving problems in the commodity area. It recommended that an optimal functioning of commodity markets should be sought through,

inter alia, improved market transparency involving exchanges of views and information on investment plans, prospects and markets for individual commodities. Substantive negotiations between producers and consumers should be pursued to achieve viable and more efficient international agreements, taking into account market trends or arrangements, and with particular attention being paid to the agreements on cocoa, coffee, sugar and tropical timber.

The Conference underlined the importance of full and active participation by consumers and producers in international commodity agreements and arrangements, taking into account occupational health and safety matters, technology transfer and services associated with production, marketing and promotion of commodities, as well as environmental considerations. Cooperation among producers and consumers should be strengthened, especially in situations of large stock overhangs.

Comprehensive commodity-sector strategies should be put in place within a macroeconomic policy framework, taking into consideration a country's economic structure, resource endowments and market opportunities. Such strategies should include the setting up of an enabling national environment to encourage the mobilization of domestic and international finance; the provision of specific incentives to encourage private enterprise and private investment; the development and maintenance of commodity-related power, transport and communications infrastructure; the provision of support services and training for human resources development; and support for commodity research arrangements. Strategies should equally encompass measures to improve the competitiveness of traditional commodity exports and programmes and action to encourage diversification, particularly in countries highly dependent on commodities for export earnings. Particular attention should also be paid to the financial and physical support structures for trading commodities, and new market possibilities should be assessed and exploited.

Concerning international support for national commodity policies, the Conference called for concerted efforts by developed countries and international organizations to support national commodity policies in developing countries and in countries undergoing transition to a market economy, including providing technical cooperation for commodity development. It was urgent to improve market access conditions, notably the progressive removal of barriers restricting imports, particularly from developing countries, of commodity products in primary and processed forms, as well as the substantial and progressive reduction of types of support that induced uncompetitive production, such as production and export subsidies. Improved market access through a successful conclusion to the Uruguay Round would contribute to a favourable international trading environment, and improved flows of technology to developing countries were important for lowering commodity production costs and encouraging economic development. The free flow of information and science to allow innovation and transfer of technology should be promoted and supported through policies to promote increased collaboration among firms in developing and developed countries.

The Conference affirmed the need for adequate official bilateral, multilateral and private resources, including private investment, to finance diversification projects and programmes, and the promotion and development of resource-based industries, including commodity-related services activities. In that regard it agreed support should be directed towards institution-building, promotion of entrepreneurship, horizontal diversification and crop substitution, and increased participation in processing, marketing and distribution, including transportation, as well as towards achieving a gradual reduction of excessive commodity dependency. It recognized that increased coordination among donor country Governments and international institutions was essential and should avoid inconsistencies in advice and potential overinvestment in particular sectors.

Welcoming compensatory mechanisms introduced by the International Monetary Fund (IMF) and the European Economic Community (EEC), UNCTAD VIII invited other countries to consider introducing such mechanisms and called on Governments and institutions to improve those already existing. It recommended the avoidance of market manipulation in determining international commodity prices.

It also recognized the importance of commodities for sustainable development and recommended the manner in which prices of natural commodities and their synthetic competitors could reflect environmental costs and resource values; the means by which the competitiveness of natural products with environmental advantages could be improved, the commodity sector developed, and environmental concerns made mutually reinforcing; and additional international financial and technical support to developing countries for the development and dissemination of technologies to cope with environment problems at were specific to commodity production and processing.

With regard to UNCTAD's role, the Conference stated that UNCTAD should remain the principal forum and continue to coordinate the activities of all the bodies involved in the commodity field, including conducting periodic and global reviews of the situation of, and prospects for, commodities so as to be able to recommend appropriate actions for consideration by Governments and institutions. In order to evolve an international commodity policy for the 1990s, the UNCTAD secretariat should undertake a thorough review of the international commodity economy and policy and define a possible course of action for submission to TDB. UNCTAD should continue to assist in diversification, processing, marketing and distribution programmes, the improvement of information flows to aid investment decisions, and technical cooperation projects and programmes, particularly for human resources development. It agreed that UNCTAD should keep under continuous review the problems of shortfalls in the commodity export earnings of developing countries arising from market fluctuations and matters relating to compensatory financing of export earnings shortfalls.

The UNCTAD secretariat should follow developments in various compensatory financing schemes and their implications for developing countries. It should explore various mechanisms, including marked-linked price-hedging mechanisms, such as commodity futures, options, swaps and bonds, and obstacles to their potential use, including sovereign risk and problems of creditworthiness. UNCTAD should also explore the modalities for overcoming those obstacles and provide information and assistance in this regard. At the level of governmental and non-governmental experts, UNCTAD should examine the technical and regulatory conditions for encouraging maximum participation in, and usage of, commodity exchanges by both buyers and sellers of commodities and proposals to address these conditions. UNCTAD should also explore the links between commodity policies, use and management of natural resources and sustainable development and provide information and technical cooperation.

UNCED action. In its recommendations for improving international cooperation in commodity trade and the diversification of the sector, UNCED[39] echoed the conclusions and recommendations of UNCTAD VIII on commodity policies for the 1990s aimed at strengthening national capabilities for the design and implementation of commodity policy, the use and management of natural resources and the gathering and utilization of information on commodity markets. (For further details on UNCED, see PART THREE, Chapter VIII.)

Standing Committee on Commodities. In accordance with the Cartagena Commitment,[3] TDB, on 7 May 1992,[23] established the Standing Committee on Commodities and decided on its terms of reference. At its first meeting (Geneva, 19-23 October),[40] the Committee adopted its work programme covering the situation and prospects for commodities, its contribution to improving the functioning of commodity markets, compensatory financing mechanisms, reducing excessive dependence on primary commodities, fostering sustainable development in the commodity field and technical cooperation. The Committee established, as its subsidiary organs, the Intergovernmental Group of Experts on Tungsten and the Intergovernmental Group of Experts on Iron Ore.

Common Fund for Commodities

The Agreement Establishing the Common Fund for Commodities, a mechanism intended to stabilize the commodities market by helping to finance buffer stocks of specific commodities as well as commodity development activities such as research and marketing, entered into force in 1989, and the Fund became operational that year. The Common Fund for Commodities informed the Secretary-General that, pursuant to article 30 of the Agreement, Australia had notified it on 15 August 1991 of its decision to withdraw from the Fund with effect from 20 August 1992.

Signatures and ratifications

As at 31 December 1992,[41] taking into account Australia's withdrawal, the 1980 Agreement Establishing the Common Fund for Commodities had been signed by 118 States and EEC and, with the accession of Thailand on 6 August 1992, 105 States and EEC had become parties to it.

UNCTAD VIII action. In the Cartagena Commitment,[3] UNCTAD VIII welcomed the coming into force of the Common Fund for Commodities and its potential contribution to support international commodity cooperation. It urged maximum participation in the Fund and stressed that its resources should be fully exploited. Arrears in the payment of subscriptions to the Fund's capital, which could be an impediment to the achievement of its objectives, should be paid up as soon as possible; resources of its Second Account should be increased, particularly through the fulfilment of pledges of voluntary contributions, as soon as possible; efforts to elaborate and consider appropriate project proposals, including those for diversification, for financing through the Second Account should be speeded up; and every effort should be made to ensure that the account became fully operational as soon as possible to benefit, in particular, LDCs and the commodities of interest to developing countries, particularly those of small producers-exporters.

Individual commodities

Agricultural commodities

Cocoa. The United Nations Cocoa Conference, 1992, held three sessions at Geneva (21 April to 1 May, 6 to 24 July and 2 to 13 November 1992) to negotiate a successor arrangement to the International Cocoa Agreement, 1986,[42] which had been extended in part for two years, effective 1 October 1990.

On 13 November,[43] the Conference affirmed the determination of producing and consuming countries to conclude the negotiation of a new international cocoa agreement at the next meeting of the Conference, scheduled for early 1993. It requested the Conference's President to maintain contacts with producing and consuming countries with a view to assisting the Conference in achieving a successful conclusion.

Olive oil. The International Agreement on Olive Oil and Table Olives, 1986, due to expire on 31 December 1992, was prolonged until 31 December 1993. The International Olive Oil Council prepared a draft protocol for extending the 1986 Agreement with amendments which would be submitted to the United Nations Conference on Olive Oil and Table Olives, 1993.

Rubber. The International Natural Rubber Agreement, 1987, which entered into force provisionally on 29 December 1988 and definitively on 3 April 1989, would expire on 28 December 1993 unless extended before then by the International Natural Rubber Council. The Council held its twenty-fifth session from 25 to 27 May 1992, at which it set up a working group to consider the renegotiation of the 1987 Agreement. On 1 December 1992, the Council decided, *inter alia*, that a decision to renegotiate the Agreement would be taken not later than 30 March 1993.

Sugar. The International Sugar Agreement, 1987, due to expire on 31 December 1992, was extended to 31 December 1993 to allow for the negotiation of a new agreement. A working group, which met on 28 February to consider the terms of a new administrative agreement, prepared a revised draft text and submitted it to the United Nations Sugar Conference, 1992, held from 16 to 20 March 1992. The Conference established the text as the International Sugar Agreement, 1992,[44] which was open for signature at United Nations Headquarters from 1 May until 31 December 1992. The new Agreement would come into force on 1 January 1993 if instruments of ratification had been deposited by Governments holding 60 per cent of the votes allocated by the Conference. The agreement could be extended beyond 31 December 1995 for successive periods, not exceeding two years on each occasion.

As at 31 December 1992,[41] the International Sugar Agreement, 1992, had been signed by 27 States, 8 States had formally ratified, accepted or approved it, and 7 States had provided notifications of provisional application.

Minerals and metals

Copper. In accordance with the terms of reference of the International Copper Study Group, a meeting was held at Geneva on 23 and 24 January 1992[45] of States and intergovernmental organizations that had already notified their provisional or definitive acceptance of the terms of reference and other States that had attended the United Nations Conference on Copper, 1988, to decide whether to put the terms of reference into force provisionally or definitively. On 23 January,[46] Belgium/Luxembourg, Chile, China, Finland, France, Germany, Greece, Italy, the Netherlands, Norway, Peru, the Philippines, Poland, Portugal, Spain, the United States and EEC decided to put the terms of reference into force definitively among themselves in whole as of that date. The meeting also decided to hold the Study Group's inaugural meeting in July 1992 and requested members to send their views on the draft rules and amendments thereto to the UNCTAD secretariat before then.

The inaugural meeting of the International Copper Study Group took place at Geneva from 22 to 26 June 1992.[47] The Group established an Industry Advisory Panel and a Standing Committee, adopted its rules of procedure and amended its terms of reference. It postponed action on the location of its headquarters and on the appointment of its Secretary-General.

Iron ore. The first session of the Intergovernmental Group of Experts on Iron Ore, established in accordance with a decision of the Standing Committee on Commodities,[40] was held at Geneva from 26 to 28 October 1992.[48] The meeting reviewed iron ore statistics, the current situation and outlook for iron ore and reviewed a bibliography of relevant studies on iron ore.

Tin. As at 31 December 1992, 12 countries and EEC, representing one third of world trade in tin, had notified their definitive or provisional acceptance of the terms of reference of the International Tin Study Group, adopted by the United Nations Tin Conference, 1988. Entry into force of the terms of reference required States accounting for 70 per cent of trade in tin to notify their acceptance.

An informal meeting of tin-producing and -consuming countries took place at Geneva on 10 December 1992. It requested the UNCTAD secretariat to continue to publish the *International Tin Statistics Quarterly Bulletin*.

Tungsten. In accordance with a 1991 decision of the Committee on Tungsten,[49] an Ad Hoc Meeting on Tungsten was held at Geneva on 2 and 3 July 1992.[50] It considered project proposals by Governments for possible financing under the Second Account of the Common Fund for Commodities. The Meeting examined a revised project by China[51] and proposals by the International Tungsten Industry Association.[52]

In accordance with the decision of the Committee on Commodities[37] to establish an Intergovernmental Group of Experts on Tungsten to succeed the former Committee on Tungsten, the Group held its first session from 7 to 11 December 1992,[53] and had before it an UNCTAD secretariat report on recent developments and the short-term outlook in the tungsten market.[54] The Group of Experts examined statistics and reviewed the current market situation of and outlook for the tungsten industry; considered industry views on particular aspects of tungsten; ways and means to improve the functioning and stability of the tungsten market through strengthened international cooperation between Governments and industries of producing and consuming countries; and considered project proposals by Governments and industry for possible financing under the Second Account of the Common Fund for Commodities.

GENERAL ASSEMBLY ACTION

On 22 December 1992, in accordance with the recommendation of the Second Committee, the General Assembly adopted **resolution 47/185** without vote.

Commodities

The General Assembly,

Recalling its resolutions 1995(XIX) of 30 December 1964, as amended, on the establishment of the United Nations Conference on Trade and Development, 41/168 of 5 December 1986, 43/27 of 18 November 1988, 44/218 of 22 December 1989 and 45/200 of 21 December 1990, as well as United Nations Conference on Trade and Development resolutions 93(IV) of 30 May 1976, on the Integrated Programme for Commodities, 124(V) of 3 June 1979, and 155(VI) and 157(VI) of 2 July 1983, the Final Act adopted by the Conference at its seventh session, held at Geneva from 9 July to 3 August 1987, and the Agreement Establishing the Common Fund for Commodities, which entered into force on 19 June 1989, and taking note of a document entitled "A New Partnership for Development: The Cartagena Commitment", adopted by the Conference at its eighth session, held at Cartagena de Indias, Colombia, from 8 to 25 February 1992,

Recalling also the Rio Declaration on Environment and Development, adopted by the United Nations Conference on Environment and Development, and welcoming the importance attached in Agenda 21 to issues related to commodities in the context of sustainable development,

Recognizing that commodity exports continue to play a key role in the economies of developing countries as a whole, as a major source of export earnings, investment and livelihood, although recognizing also that this role should decrease as diversification expands,

Concerned about the difficulties experienced by developing countries in financing and implementing diversification programmes,

Concerned also that the prevalence of declining prices for most commodities contributes to many countries' problems with export earnings,

Recalling the proposal, made by the Government of Colombia at the eighth session of the United Nations Conference on Trade and Development, to consider convening a world conference on commodities which would bring together producers, consumers, marketing enterprises and other market actors and would be organized by the United Nations Conference on Trade and Development, recognizing that such a conference could contribute to shaping a coherent international commodity strategy that would take into account the specific problems of selected commodity sectors,

Welcoming the agreed conclusions establishing the work programme of the Standing Committee on Commodities,

1. *Takes note with interest* of the report of the Secretary-General of the United Nations Conference on Trade and Development on world commodity trends and prospects, with particular emphasis on commodity-dependent developing countries in the light of the outcome of the eighth session of the United Nations Conference on Trade and Development;

2. *Emphasizes* the need for developing countries that are heavily dependent on primary commodities to continue to promote a domestic policy and an institutional environment that encourage diversification and enhance competitiveness, and stresses the need for international cooperation effectively to complement and support those national efforts and policies, *inter alia*, by way of creating a more favourable international economic and trading environment;

3. *Stresses* that the solution to commodity problems calls for sound, compatible and consistent policies at the national and international levels, bearing in mind the broad aims of the Integrated Programme for Commodities;

4. *Urges* producers and consumers of individual commodities to continue to explore ways and means of reinforcing their cooperation and to consider actively participating in international commodity agreements and arrangements that take into account market trends in order to achieve more efficient international commodity cooperation;

5. *Notes* the decision taken by the United Nations Conference on Trade and Development at its eighth session to invite the Secretary-General of the Conference to hold consultations on the question of a world conference on commodities;

6. *Expresses its conviction* that supportive international policies, such as the use of commodity exchanges and commodity price risk management instruments, more stable and predictable conditions in commodity trade, and efficient and transparent price setting, all contribute significantly to the efforts of commodity-dependent countries to revitalize their development;

7. *Emphasizes* the importance of maximizing the contribution of the commodity sector to economic growth and transformation in commodity-dependent developing countries by ensuring that development in the commodity sector contributes effectively to the generation of growth and development in other sectors of the economy, as well as to the eradication of poverty, and, in this context, also stresses the importance of the diversification efforts of commodity-exporting developing countries;

8. *Requests* the Secretary-General of the United Nations Conference on Trade and Development to iden-

tify, on the basis of relevant national experiences, potential developmental linkages between the commodity sector and other sectors of the economy, as well as appropriate actions required at the national and international levels to establish and develop such linkages in the context of an effective diversification policy, and to include them in his report to the General Assembly at its forty-ninth session;

9. *Recognizes the need* to strengthen efforts to analyse shortfalls in the commodity export earnings of developing countries with a view to addressing this problem, and takes note of the decision of the Standing Committee on Commodities that the issue of shortfalls in export earnings and compensatory financing should figure as a specific issue for consideration at its future sessions, in accordance with its terms of reference and work programme;

10. *Reiterates once again its conviction* that more stable and predictable market conditions for commodities would be conducive to the social and economic development of developing countries and could, *inter alia*, contribute to the international campaign against illicit production of, trafficking in and abuse of narcotic drugs, thus supporting the efforts undertaken by countries to combat such illicit activities;

11. *Emphasizes* that, in line with Agenda 21, sustainable development of the commodity sector may require, *inter alia*, the reflection of environmental and resource costs in prices, improvements in the market access and competitiveness of natural products from developing countries, with environmental advantages, and improvements in their access to international financial and technical support, including environmentally sound technologies to cope with environmental problems specific to commodity production and processing;

12. *Urges once again* all the parties involved, especially those developed countries that have not yet done so, to meet their agreed commitments and to work for a balanced, equitable, meaningful and satisfactory outcome to the multilateral trade negotiations within the Uruguay Round so as to ensure that the successful conclusion of the negotiations brings about further expansion and liberalization of trade in commodities, taking into account the special and differential treatment for developing countries, as well as all other principles contained in the Ministerial Declaration on the Uruguay Round;

13. *Notes with satisfaction* the establishment of the Common Fund for Commodities, urges its full exploitation and notes the hope expressed by member countries of the Fund that further voluntary contributions will be forthcoming;

14. *Notes* the desire of the members of the Common Fund that countries, particularly major exporters and consumers of commodities, that have not yet ratified the Agreement Establishing the Common Fund for Commodities should do so as soon as possible;

15. *Decides* to include the question of commodities in the agenda of its forty-ninth session.

General Assembly resolution 47/185

22 December 1992   Meeting 93   Adopted without vote

Approved by Second Committee (A/47/718/Add.2) without vote, 7 December (meeting 48); draft by Vice-Chairman (A/C.2/47/L.69), based on informal consultations on draft by Pakistan for Group of 77 (A/C.2/47/L.32), as orally amended; agenda item 78 *(a)*.

Meeting numbers. GA 47th session: 2nd Committee 40, 42, 43, 48; plenary 93.

Environment and trade

The *World Economic Survey 1992*[2] noted that issues of the environment had become increasingly important at both national and international levels in recent years and international trade had important implications for the environment. Rules governing the multilateral trading system had not ignored environmental issues. Although GATT had no specific rules for the protection of the environment, its provisions allowed exceptions to the normal rules on environmental grounds. The Agreement on Technical Barriers to Trade under the Tokyo Round of multilateral trade negotiations also allowed signatories to deviate from international regulations and standards for health, safety and environmental considerations. A number of other areas of negotiations under the ongoing Uruguay Round involved issues relating to the environment. GATT had also established groups to promote environmental awareness in the trade sector. The United Nations Environment Programme listed 152 international agreements and instruments relating to environmental matters linked indirectly to international trade. However, the *Survey* contended that the protection of the environment and promotion of trade needed a set of rules that were acceptable to all trading nations.

UNCTAD VIII action. In the Cartagena Commitment,[3] UNCTAD VIII recognized that improved market access for developing-country exports, in conjunction with sound environmental policies, would have a positive environmental impact. It stressed that environmental policies should deal with the root causes of environmental degradation, thus preventing environmental measures from resulting in unnecessary restrictions to trade. Trade policy measures for environmental purposes should not constitute a means of arbitrary or unjustifiable discrimination or a disguised restriction on international trade. Environmental measures addressing transborder or global environmental problems should, as far as possible, be based on an international consensus. The Conference also identified certain rules and principles which should apply should trade policies be required to enforce environmental policies.

The Conference recommended that UNCTAD, at both the intergovernmental and secretariat levels, should undertake in-depth work on clarifying the linkages between trade and environment and on the need for environmental protection to coexist with liberal trade policies and free market access. It should also contribute to consensus building with regard to appropriate principles and rules. The Conference also requested the UNCTAD secretariat to undertake studies, analyse policy measures and carry out technical cooperation in the area of trade and sustainable development. In particular, the secretariat should analyse the rela-

tionship between environmental policy and trade and the impact of developments in this field on developing countries, taking into account the work of GATT, OECD, UNCED and other relevant forums.

UNCTAD should continue to collect, analyse and disseminate information on environmental regulations and measures which could have an impact on trade, especially that of developing countries. It requested donor countries to continue contributing extrabudgetary resources to further strengthen UNCTAD's work on interlinkages between environment, trade and sustainable development, including the adjustment of the Trade Control Measures Information System.

The Conference, in its message to UNCED (see PART THREE, Chapter VIII), noted that UNCTAD was uniquely placed to undertake analysis and build consensus on relevant policies on the interrelated areas of trade and development and protection of the environment. It outlined action already taken by UNCTAD with respect to sustainable development, including environmental measures and trade rules, declaring that a revitalized UNCTAD could contribute to the implementation of the programmes to be adopted by UNCED.

Following UNCED in June, the UNCTAD secretariat submitted to TDB in August a report[55] on sustainable development. It discussed cross-sectoral issues and sectoral links, including commodities, industry, energy and the promotion of the transfer, adaptation and generation of environmentally sound technologies.

UNCED action. Agenda 21, adopted by UNCED,[39] dealt with the issue of international cooperation to accelerate sustainable development in developing countries and related domestic policies. It stressed that the international economy should provide a supportive international climate for achieving environment and development goals by promoting sustainable development through trade liberalization, making trade and environment mutually supportive. This would also provide adequate financial resources to developing countries to deal with international debt and encourage macroeconomic policies conducive to environment and development. In that regard, it identified two programme areas: promoting sustainable development through trade and making trade and environment mutually supportive. Governments should strive, through multilateral forums, to make international trade and environment policies mutually supportive in favour of sustainable development, clarify the role of GATT, UNCTAD and other international organizations in dealing with trade and environment-related issues, including conciliation procedures and dispute settlement, and encourage international productivity and competitiveness and a constructive role on the part of industry in dealing with environment and development issues.

UNCED recommended that Governments encourage GATT, UNCTAD and other international and regional economic institutions to examine a number of propositions and principles, namely: to elaborate adequate studies for the better understanding of the relationship between trade and environment; to promote a dialogue between trade, development and environment communities; in those cases where trade measures related to environment were used, to ensure transparency and compatibility with international obligations; to deal with the root causes of environment and development problems to avoid adopting environmental measures resulting in unjustified restrictions on trade; to avoid the use of trade restrictions or distortions as a means to offset differences in costs arising from differences in environmental standards and regulations; to ensure that environment-related regulations or standards, including those related to health and safety standards, did not constitute a means of arbitrary or unjustifiable discrimination or a disguised restriction on trade; to ensure that special factors affecting environment and trade policies in the developing countries were borne in mind in applying environmental standards and in using any trade measures, since standards valid in most advanced countries could be inappropriate and of unwarranted social cost for the developing countries; to encourage participation of developing countries in multilateral agreements through such mechanisms as special transition rules; and to avoid unilateral actions to deal with environmental challenges outside the jurisdiction of the importing country.

Environment measures addressing transborder or global environment problems should, as far as possible, be based on an environmental consensus. Should trade policy measures be found necessary to enforce environment policies, certain principles and rules should apply, including the principle of non-discrimination; development of more precision and clarification of the relationship between GATT provisions and some of the multilateral measures adopted in the environment areas; ensuring public input into the formation, negotiation and implementation of trade policies as a means of fostering increased transparency in the light of country-specific conditions; and developing environmental policies that provided the appropriate legal and institutional framework to respond to new needs for the protection of the environment, resulting from changes in production and trade specialization.

In a chapter dealing with international institutional arrangements, UNCED stated that UNCTAD should play an important role in implementing Agenda 21, taking into account the importance of the interrelationship between development, international trade and the environment, in accordance with its mandate in the area of sustainable development.

The General Assembly, on 22 December, by **resolution 47/191**, requested TDB to examine the relevant provisions of Agenda 21 at its next session and report to the Assembly in 1993 on specific plans to implement them.

Consumer protection

In accordance with a 1990 Economic and Social Council request,[56] the Secretary-General submitted a July report on consumer protection.[57] The report covered activities relating to the implementation of the guidelines for consumer protection, adopted by the General Assembly in 1985.[58] The report discussed implementation of those guidelines by Governments and regional and international cooperation in their implementation, as well as the activities of NGOs. It examined the issue of the environment, financial services and the consumer and concluded that there was growing recognition that consumer policy was essential to the effective workings of modern market economies.

Within the United Nations Secretariat, the Department of Economic and Social Development had elaborated project proposals within the scope of the programme of action through 1995. However, the demand for assistance, particularly by developing and emerging market economies, far exceeded the current capacity of the Secretariat to meet it from the regular budget. In addition, many Governments made requests for regional seminars, training and advisory services and education and information programmes based on the guidelines. There were no resources to carry out the international programme for consumer protection and the report suggested that Member States might wish to consider, on the basis of progress already achieved and the continuing need for assistance, adopting the necessary measures to provide the resources required to carry out the programme activities envisaged.

By **decision 1992/284** of 30 July 1992, the Economic and Social Council took note of the Secretary-General's report.

Services

UNCTAD VIII action. In the Cartagena Commitment,[3] UNCTAD VIII agreed that developing countries should pursue policies to develop the services sectors of their economies, particularly producer services. Policies to be adopted by developing countries could include modernization and expansion of infrastructure, particularly telecommunications and information services;

development of human resources and of knowledge-intensive services; measures to encourage investment and cross-border trade in the services sector and to make use of services from competitive domestic suppliers in developing countries; the progressive liberalization of the services sector and the formulation of strategies to improve domestic services capabilities and for internationally competitive services; enhancing cooperation at the interregional, regional and subregional levels, including mutual trade liberalization, and the improvement of skills and infrastructures to promote services exports; and improving the infrastructure to support effective participation in negotiations on services at the regional and multilateral levels.

With regard to international policies, UNCTAD VIII agreed that Governments should support progressive multilateral liberalization, under the draft General Agreement on Trade in Services, in order to promote economic growth and expand world trade in services, and to increase the participation of developing countries. The Conference endorsed the obligation that developed countries, and other national Governments, should maintain contact points, as established under the draft General Agreement on Trade in Services, to facilitate the access of developing countries' services providers to information related to their respective markets.

It further agreed that the international community should continue support for concerted policy actions, including providing financial assistance on concessional terms, promoting training and the acquisition and transfer of technology on terms and conditions agreed by the parties concerned, building up technological and human capabilities of developing countries to enhance their ability to absorb relevant technologies, and constructing and/or improving basic services infrastructures, including subregional and regional transportation, particularly in low-income countries and LDCs.

UNCTAD, in cooperation with other United Nations organizations dealing with services, should continue to promote international cooperation to help developing countries overcome their handicaps, enhance their international competitiveness in order to increase their participation in world trade in services, promote environmentally friendly services and enhance the contribution of services to their sustainable development. Attention should also be given to improving the role of services in countries undergoing transition to a market economy and increasing their trade in services.

The Conference also recognized that technology had increasingly become a determinant of the ability to participate in world trade in manufactures and services and recommended a series of measures for developing technology in developing countries (see PART THREE, Chapter VII).

Standing Committee on Developing Services Sectors. As recommended by UNCTAD VIII,[3] TDB, on 7 May,[23] established the Standing Committee on Developing Services Sectors: Fostering Competitive Services Sectors in Developing Countries, and adopted its terms of reference.

The Standing Committee held its first meeting (Geneva, 26-30 October 1992),[59] at which it established its programme of work, the elements of which were promoting transparency, fostering competitive services sectors and strengthening technical cooperation.

REFERENCES

[1]*Trade and Development Report, 1992* (UNCTAD/TDR/12), Sales No. E.92.II.D.7. [2]*World Economic Survey 1992: Current Trends and Policies in the World Economy* (E/1992/40), Sales No. E.92.II.C.1. [3]TD/364. [4]YUN 1986, p. 1210. [5]YUN 1991, p. 440, GA res. 46/207, 20 Dec. 1991. [6]A/47/410. [7]YUN 1991, p. 440. [8]TD/B/39(1)/3. [9]TD/B/39(1)/2. [10]TD/B/C.5/142. [11]TD/B/C.5/142/Suppl.1. [12]TD/B/SCP/2. [13]A/CONF.147/18. [14]TD/B/C.5/141 & Corr.1. [15]TD/B/C.5/141/Add.1. [16]ITC/AG(XXVI)/135. [17]ITC/AG(XXV)/134. [18]YUN 1991, p. 443. [19]ITC/AG(XXV)/131. [20]YUN 1991, p. 884, GA res. 46/183, 20 Dec. 1991. [21]A/47/460. [22]A/47/5, vol. II. [23]A/47/15, vol. I (dec. 398(XXXVIII)). [24]TD/B/39(2)/9. [25]TD/B/39(2)/15. [26]TD/B/39(2)/7. [27]TD/B/RBP/89 & Add.1. [28]YUN 1980, p. 626. [29]TD/B/RBP/90. [30]TD/B/RBP/78/Rev.1 & Corr.1. [31]TD/B/RBP/81/Rev.1 & Corr.1. [32]TD/B/RBP/87 & Add.1. [33]TD/B/RBP/80/Rev.1 & Corr.1. [34]TD/B/RBP/91. [35]TD/B/RBP/88. [36]GA res. 45/200, 21 Dec. 1990. [37]A/47/398 & Corr.1. [38]A/45/442. [39]*Report of the United Nations Conference on Environment and Development, Rio de Janeiro, 3-14 June 1992*, vol. I, Sales No. E.93.I.8 (vol.I). [40]TD/B/39(2)/4. [41]*Multilateral Treaties Deposited with the Secretary-General: Status as at 31 December 1992* (ST/LEG/SER.E/11), Sales No. E.93.V.11. [42]YUN 1986, p. 502. [43]TD/COCOA.8/11. [44]TD/SUGAR.12/6. [45]TD/COPPER/18. [46]TD/COPPER/17/Rev.1. [47]ICSG(I)/7. [48]TD/B/CN.1/5. [49]YUN 1991, p. 448. [50]TD/B/CN.1/TUNGSTEN/2. [51]TD/B/CN.1/TUNGSTEN/AC.2. [52]TD/B/CN.1/TUNGSTEN/AC.3. [53]TD/B/CN.1/7. [54]TD/B/CN.1/TUNGSTEN/3 and Corr.1. [55]TD/B/39(1)/7. [56]ESC res. 1990/85, 27 July 1990. [57]E/1992/48. [58]YUN 1985, p. 571, GA res. 39/248, 9 Apr. 1985. [59]TD/B/39(2)/2.

Finance

Financial policy

The Committee for Development Planning, in the report on its April 1992 session,[1] noted that, in the developed market economies, the slide to stagnation and, in some cases, recession and rising unemployment had not been followed by decisive steps on the fiscal or monetary fronts. Policy issues in the countries of Eastern Europe and the former USSR were dominated by the problems of transition from a command economy to a market economy. In developing countries, amidst a great diversity of situations ranging from prolonged stagnation or sharp decline to very high rates of growth, the focus of policy had in many cases shifted to economic liberalization.

The *World Economic Survey 1992*[2] noted that world economic growth was expected to be restrained in the medium term, not by a shortage of savings, but by an inadequate allocation of the world's resources to investment projects. Some developing countries had demonstrated the "virtuous cycles" that resulted from high investment, high growth policy in the context of relatively well-managed financial and fiscal systems. In other cases, debt overhang and fragile economic situations held back possible investment and growth levels. Among the developed market economies, government investment needed to be increased and international flows augmented to support capital formation in developing and transition economies.

UNCTAD VIII action. UNCTAD VIII[3] agreed that at the national level all countries should deploy sustained efforts to mobilize domestic savings for investment, growth and development to achieve macroeconomic stability and predictability, increased monetary control and greater financial discipline. However, monetary policy should not be overburdened, and use of a wider gamut of policy instruments was needed. Financial liberalization should be accompanied by appropriate institutional reform and by domestic supervisory and prudential arrangements required for a sound national banking system operating in a liberal and secure international financial system. It should be introduced in a context of macroeconomic stability and be compatible with the competitiveness and institutional development of capital markets. Liberalization in those circumstances could help to maximize the contribution of the financial sector to economic development.

UNCTAD VIII agreed that an economically and institutionally efficient public sector would contribute to fostering growth and development. In many countries, public sector reform was essential for improved mobilization and use of savings. Fiscal reform should be introduced, aimed at rationalizing and simplifying the taxation system, protecting government revenues from erosion by inflation and strengthening tax administration. Structural adjustment programmes and international cooperation programmes should take full account of the priorities of the development of human resources, especially with regard to women, particularly to improve the status of rural women, and the provision of basic public goods, including investment in infrastructure, and social services, such as health and education. It also recommended that the efforts of developing countries to improve their policy and regulatory environment so as to attract foreign direct investment (FDI), the return of flight capital and other non-

debt-creating financial flows should be further strengthened.

It reiterated the need for developed countries to implement necessary adjustment measures to create a more favourable international economic environment so as to stimulate economic growth in developing countries. They were also encouraged to reduce external and fiscal imbalances and adopt appropriate mixes of fiscal and monetary policies conducive to a decline in interest rates consistent with price stability and an increased stability of exchange rates. UNCTAD VIII called on all countries to consider the possibilities for reducing military expenditure and for channelling the resulting savings towards socially productive uses. It welcomed reductions under way or planned by developed countries and urged them to continue those efforts in order to accelerate the reduction of external and fiscal imbalances and increase the availability of development finance. The Conference urged developing countries to reduce military spending, recognizing the positive effects that such a reduction could have on budgetary policies to accelerate growth and development.

Net transfer of resources

A significant turn-round in the transfer of resources between developed and developing countries took place in 1991. The *World Economic Survey 1992*[2] stated that the developed market economies transferred $25 billion to the developing and transition economies, whereas the year before the advanced industralized countries had received $24 billion and a similiar transfer of $25 billion the year before that. The developing countries, on the other hand, had made transfers abroad of $24 billion to $36 billion in each of the previous four years.

The developing countries did not all share in the inflow. The "capital-surplus" exporters of oil received $19 billion, largely financed by the sale of official reserves and other assets, as well as by capital-market borrowing, mainly to finance reconstruction activities in the Persian Gulf. However, the "capital-importing" countries also shared in the inflow. That was the first positive net transfer to that group of countries since the beginning of the debt crisis in 1982. Most of the change involved a group of countries that had been making very large net resource transfers since 1983, including 15 heavily indebted countries originally associated with a debt-restructuring plan. Aside from those countries, most changes in the net transfer in 1991 were not large, except for the group of "recent surplus countries", the first generation of Asian exporters of manufactures.

In accordance with a 1990 General Assembly resolution,[4] the Secretary-General submitted in

September 1992 a report[5] on the net transfer of resources between developing and developed countries, including consideration of the issue at the United Nations. It examined the reversal in the net financial flows of developing countries, their composition, the terms of trade and their relationship to net resource availability. The report concluded that it was unclear whether the positive trend in the transfer of financial resources to the developing countries would continue. The prospects depended on the international economic environment as well as the continuing confidence in those economies which had recently been attracting the flow of financial resources. On the whole, the reversal of the outflow was a highly welcome development, but its short-term nature created problems of macroeconomic management in some countries and the positive flow of financial resources to the capital-importing developing countries appeared far less impressive when the losses resulting from terms of trade were taken into account. Therefore, an improved international environment could help smooth out financial and terms-of-trade shocks.

The seven major industrial nations, at their eighteenth annual summit (Munich, Germany, 6-8 July),[6] called for an early decision by IMF on the extension for one year of its Enhanced Structural Adjustment Facility and for the full examination of options for the subsequent period, including renewal of the Facility.

GENERAL ASSEMBLY ACTION

On 22 December, the General Assembly, on the recommendation of the Second Committee, adopted **resolution 47/178** without vote.

Net transfer of resources between developing countries and developed countries

The General Assembly,

Reaffirming its resolutions S-18/3 of 1 May 1990, the annex to which contains the Declaration on International Economic Cooperation, in particular the Revitalization of Economic Growth and Development of the Developing Countries, and 45/199 of 21 December 1990, the annex to which contains the International Development Strategy for the Fourth United Nations Development Decade,

Recalling its resolutions 44/232 of 22 December 1989, on trends in the transfer of resources to and from the developing countries and their impact on the economic growth and sustained development of those countries, and 45/192 of 21 December 1990, on the net transfer of resources between developing countries and developed countries, as well as Economic and Social Council resolutions 1989/112 of 28 July 1989 and 1990/56 of 26 July 1990,

Recalling also its resolution 43/197 of 20 December 1988 and taking note of Agenda 21, adopted by the United Nations Conference on Environment and Development, which address the question of the fulfilment of the in-

ternationally agreed commitment for official development assistance,

Taking note of the *World Economic Survey 1992*, in particular chapter IV thereof, entitled "Saving, investment and the international transfer of resources", and the report of the Secretary-General on the net transfer of resources between developing and developed countries,

Recognizing that the international community has a responsibility to give strong support to the efforts of the developing countries to solve their grave economic and social problems through the creation of a favourable international economic environment,

Noting the fact that the net transfer of resources to the developing countries has been positive for the past two years and that its future course depends on a supportive international economic environment and domestic efforts,

Concerned about the insufficiency of resources of most developing countries over the past decade, in particular their inadequacies of savings and investment, which leaves developing countries with serious shortfalls in financial resources for development,

Noting the successful outcome of the eighth session of the United Nations Conference on Trade and Development and the spirit of multilateralism that permeated the Conference, as reflected in its final document entitled "A New Partnership for Development: The Cartagena Commitment",

Bearing in mind that the major industrialized countries, which have significant weight in influencing world economic growth and the international economic environment, should continue their efforts to promote sustained growth and to narrow imbalances so as to enhance the ability of the developing countries to address and alleviate their major problems in the areas of money, finance, resource flows, trade, commodities and external indebtedness,

Noting the call by the group of seven major industrialized countries at the Munich Economic Summit, held from 6 to 8 July 1992, for a full examination of the options available for the forthcoming period of the Enhanced Structural Adjustment Facility of the International Monetary Fund, including the renewal of the Facility,

1. *Stresses* the need to enhance international efforts to ensure adequate resources for the reactivation of economic growth and sustainable development in the developing countries, taking into account the following:

   (a) The developed countries should consider increasing financial flows to assist the developing countries in their diversification and structural adjustment efforts through, *inter alia*, an expansion of multilateral credits, promoting foreign direct investment and increasing concessional and non-debt resources;

   (b) Where appropriate, national economic measures that are conducive to capital formation should be taken by the developing countries with insufficient savings and flow of external resources, including increasing domestic savings, raising investment and human resources development;

   (c) Governments of the developed countries and of other countries in a position to do so should promote an adequate flow of resources to developing countries; developed countries, which have reaffirmed their commitment to reach the accepted United Nations target of 0.7 per cent of gross national product for official development assistance, to the extent that they have not

yet achieved that target, should agree to augment their aid programmes in order to reach that target as soon as possible; some developed countries have agreed to reach the target by the year 2000; other developed countries, in line with their support for reform efforts in developing countries, should agree to make their best effort to increase their level of official development assistance;

(d) The developed countries should expedite negotiations towards the realization of the tenth replenishment of the International Development Association;

(e) Since, in a large number of developing countries, the burden of debt and debt service constitutes a major obstacle to the revitalization of growth and development, there is a need for further progress towards the solution of the external debt problems of those countries;

(f) Governments should work towards a more open, free, equitable and disciplined international trading system that improves access to all markets for the exports of the developing countries so as to ensure an increase in their export earnings; in this connection, the urgent need for a balanced and successful outcome of the Uruguay Round of multilateral trade negotiations should be stressed;

(g) Producers and consumers of individual commodities should continue to explore ways and means of reinforcing their cooperation and consider participating actively in international commodity agreements and arrangements that take into account market trends in order to achieve more efficient international commodity cooperation;

(h) All Governments, particularly those of the developed countries, should cooperate more closely to achieve a higher degree of stability in financial markets, reduce the risk of financial crisis, such as high volatility in exchange rates, and help to promote an international financial system more conducive to stable economic growth;

(i) Appropriate measures should be taken by all Governments, particularly those of the developed countries, to create an international economic environment, to stabilize and lower real interest rates and to reduce uncertainties of financial flows;

(j) All Governments, particularly those of the developed countries, should strive to enhance the effectiveness of multilateral surveillance aimed at correcting existing external and fiscal imbalances so as to expand multilateral trade and foreign investment, particularly in the developing countries;

2. *Requests* the Secretary-General to continue to monitor developments in respect of the net transfer of resources between developing and developed countries and utilize all relevant reports, such as those prepared by the World Bank, the International Monetary Fund and the regional banks, and to report thereon in the *World Economic Survey 1993*; and also requests the Secretary-General to report to the General Assembly at its forty-ninth session on the implementation of the present resolution.

General Assembly resolution 47/178

22 December 1992   Meeting 93   Adopted without vote

Approved by Second Committee (A/47/718/Add.1) without vote, 11 December (meeting 50); draft by Vice-Chairman (A/C.2/47/L.86), based on informal consultations on draft by Pakistan for Group of 77, and China (A/C.2/47/L.10) and orally revised; agenda item 78.
Meeting numbers. GA 47th session: 2nd Committee 25, 30, 45, 46, 50; plenary 93.

Development financing

The *World Economic Survey 1992*[2] stated that official development finance grew in 1990 and 1991, principally owing to the expansion of grants to countries seriously affected by the situation between Iraq and Kuwait. In 1990, grants more than doubled to $29 billion and, in 1991, they rose to $32 billion. In 1992, they were expected to begin to fall back as the international crisis ebbed, but the need for highly concessional development assistance remained, especially in countries needing to reconstruct in the aftermath of civil war and for low-income countries to undertake their proper global responsibilities in environmental protection and clean-up. There was insufficient aid being provided and the members of the Development Assistance Committee of OECD noted that, given the strong efforts towards democratization and economic policy reform throughout the developing world, substantial additional aid efforts would be required both quantitatively and qualitatively. Available evidence suggested that the real value of total official development assistance (ODA) in 1991 was the same as in 1990. However, the prospects for 1992 and years ahead were not encouraging. A major test of the prospects for ODA lay in the negotiations under way for the tenth replenishment of the International Development Association, the concessional lending facility of the World Bank, to cover the period July 1993 to June 1996.

UNCTAD VIII action. In the Cartagena Commitment,[3] UNCTAD VIII declared that the process of structural adjustment in developing countries needed to be supported and funded, and a substantial increase in the aggregate level of resources, particularly concessional resources, would provide a needed boost to that process. The related macroeconomic and structural policies should take account of the specificity of the economic needs and conditions of developing countries. The Conference underscored the substantial additional efforts required to enhance the quantity and quality of support for developing countries and the importance of official finance in its various forms. It urged the developed country donors to implement their undertakings to attain the agreed international target of devoting 0.7 per cent of gross national product to ODA. Other developed donor countries, in line with their support for reform efforts in developing countries, agreed to increase their level of ODA. In addition, other countries in a position to assist would share in the global efforts, each according to its capacity. Donors reaffirmed the commitment undertaken in the Paris Declaration, adopted by the Second (1990) United Nations Conference on LDCs,[7] to bring about a significant and substantial increase in the aggregate level of external support to those countries, taking into account that, since the Paris Conference, six States had been added to the list of LDCs.[8]

The effectiveness of aid should be strongly enhanced by both donor and recipient countries. On the recipient side, a stable policy environment would contribute to increasing the effective use of aid. On the donor side, aid effectiveness would be enhanced by improved aid coordination, by further untying of aid and by targeting aid on the genuine promotion of long-term development, in particular human resource development. Aid efforts should take into account the increasing differentiation among developing countries: while highly concessional assistance should be focused primarily on low-income countries, resources for cooperation with other developing countries in need of assistance could be of a less concessional character. Efforts to provide financial assistance to the countries of Central and Eastern Europe should not diminish the determination of the international community to give high priority to developing countries.

The resources of the World Bank's Special Programme of Assistance for debt-distressed low-income countries, and those of IMF's Structural Adjustment Facility and Enhanced Structural Adjustment Facility, should continue to play a key role in providing medium-term concessional loans to low-income countries.

The Conference recommended that industrialized and developing countries should encourage mutually beneficial flows of FDI to the developing world, including membership in, and wide utilization of, programmes under the Multilateral Investment Guarantee Agency and the International Finance Corporation, the conclusion of bilateral investment and double taxation treaties, and the provision of direct incentives. Consideration should also be given to innovative incentives and promotional measures that could be adopted by developed countries and the World Bank. The Conference recognized that the problems of the poor countries of Africa, especially the debt problem, needed special treatment, and urged the international community, particularly the donor developed countries and the multilateral financing institutions, to implement fully the measures agreed in the United Nations New Agenda for the Development of Africa in the 1990s,[9] following the final review of the United Nations Programme of Action for African Economic Recovery and Development 1986-1990,[10] as well as the United Nations System-wide Plan of Action for African Economic Recovery and Development (see PART THREE, Chapter III). The Conference urged the speedy and full consideration of the Secretary-General's proposal to convene an international conference on the financing of development (see below). It agreed that the UNCTAD secretariat

should undertake analysis and make proposals, as well as provide technical assistance to developing countries, in the above-mentioned areas. UNCTAD should be a forum to promote discussions and negotiate basic consensuses on the treatment of resources for development in the different competent organizations of the international economic system.

Environment and development finance

UNCTAD VIII action. In the Cartagena Commitment,[3] UNCTAD VIII stated that, for developing countries to achieve sustainable development and address the pressing problems of economic growth needed to combat poverty and improve environmental management domestically, they must have access to the financial resources necessary to meet those challenges. Donors pledged their continuing efforts to ensure that external resources available from both the public and private sectors and through existing bilateral and multilateral channels should be increased and used effectively and efficiently. For developing countries to play their full part in coping with global environmental problems, the Conference considered that appropriate additional financial resources should be made available to them as part of a strengthened partnership and agreed on the need for more funding to implement sustainable development policies at the national level. The Conference emphasized that government intervention for the protection of the environment and the achievement of sustainable development should pay more attention to, *inter alia*, control mechanisms that made use of market signals and generated additional financial flows. Creditor countries, multilateral financial institutions, developing countries and NGOs should cooperate in efforts to implement debt conversion schemes devised by debtor countries for the protection of the environment.

The Conference also agreed on the need to examine the terms and conditions under which developing countries could resort to economic and regulatory tools to integrate environmental costs into economic activities, without hampering their economic growth and development and jeopardizing their competitive position on international markets; as well as the need to study the implications for developing countries of principles such as the polluter-pays and user-pays principles and the use of a precautionary approach where uncertainty existed.

International conference on financing for development

In response to a 1991 General Assembly request,[11] the Secretary-General submitted a report in November 1992 on a proposal to convene an international conference on the financing of development.[12] The report gave the background to the proposal and examined development finance in relation to the current international financial situation, including the questions of ODA, net transfer of resources and private financing, treatment of the debt of debt-crisis countries, fear of crowding out development, supply of savings in developing countries and the global savings shortage. It also reviewed the conclusions and recommendations on development financing of UNCTAD VIII, UNCED and the Joint Ministerial Committee of the Board of Governors of the World Bank and IMF (Washington, D.C., 21 September). Annexed to the report were the views of the multilateral financial institutions consulted in its preparation.

In his report to the high-level segment of the Economic and Social Council, devoted to the theme of enhancing international cooperation for development,[13] the Secretary-General stressed the link between peace, security and social development.

On 18 December 1992, the General Assembly, by **decision 47/436**, decided to continue exploring the issue of the convening of an international conference on the financing of development, in close consultation and cooperation with the World Bank, IMF, the regional development banks and UNCTAD. In that regard, it requested the Secretary-General to submit in 1993 a report on the situation of the potential sources of financing for development. In related action, the Assembly, by **decision 47/442** of 22 December, deferred until its fiftieth (1995) session consideration of a draft resolution entitled "International conference on money and finance for development".[14]

Debt problems of developing countries

The *World Economic Survey 1992*[2] stated that the current international debt strategy recognized that many heavily indebted countries could not work themselves out of their "debt overhang" and that some of the debt had to be written off as uncollectible, which creditors had been willing to do when debtor countries undertook the structural changes required for adjustment. The specific techniques of debt reduction had become extremely complex and varied, primarily to accommodate banks and official lenders operating under different legal, tax and regulatory systems.

Although the application of the new strategy had not brought about a major net reduction in the debt itself, progress towards resolution of the debt problem seemed well on the way. Certain heavily indebted countries that had been closed out of the financial markets were again considered creditworthy, secondary market quotations on bank debt had risen and the return of flight capital in some countries also pointed to renewed con-

fidence in those economies. The situation in smaller economies, however, still seemed fragile and evidence that the situation had improved was still tenuous. The big improvement in the net transfer of resources of the heavily indebted countries indicated what seemed to be the principal benefit of the debt regularization process: new direct investment, the return of flight capital, foreign portfolio investment and new lending. Continuation of those flows depended on prospects for export earnings and the growth of the world economy, the unhampered access to major markets, continued progress in adjustment reforms with greater social equity, and political stability.

In accordance with a 1991 General Assembly resolution,[15] the Secretary-General submitted a report in September 1992 on recent experience under the international debt strategy.[16] The report examined the current state of indebtedness, the impact on net financial transfers, progress in adjustment of heavily indebted countries, the social dimensions of adjustment under debt, the international economic environment, and negotiations with commercial banks and official creditors.

The report concluded that, after a decade of international debt crisis, the outlook was finally improving, in particular for the middle-income countries. The net transfer of financial resources had turned positive on the strength of private flows to the largest heavily indebted countries, but remained stagnant to low-income countries. Official as well as private creditors acknowledged the existence of debt overhang requiring debt reduction in various circumstances. Domestic adjustment had also prepared the ground for more sustainable growth in many developing countries. However, there was no formal mechanism to restructure the debt owed to multilateral creditors and it was not clear if the debt and debt-service reduction agreements would end the cycles of debt negotiations for the participating countries. Those agreements had raised expectations in the financial community about the future prospects of the heavily indebted middle-income countries. A substantial part of the new capital inflows to the heavily indebted countries appeared to be highly speculative funds and there was concern that the inflow of funds had only to a limited degree found its way into higher aggregate investment in new plants and equipment and the rate of growth had remained sluggish.

The *Trade and Development Report, 1992*[17] stated that official debt reschedulings within the Paris Club, an informal group of creditors meeting at the French Treasury, slowed down in 1991. However, the reduced frequency of reschedulings did not reflect a substantial lessening of debt difficulties. In fact, for many Paris Club debtors, especially those which had repeatedly rescheduled their debt, debt-service ratios tended to increase. On the other hand, problems faced by a number of countries in obtaining new IMF arrangements had caused delays in reaching agreements with Paris Club creditors.

In December 1991, the low-income countries were granted new concessional terms (enhanced concessional treatment, by which the options of both debt reduction and interest rate reduction should result in a reduction of 50 per cent of net present value), which provided for larger debt reductions than the 1988 "Toronto terms". In terms of rescheduling practice, Paris Club creditors, in agreements with Egypt and Poland, for the first time in 20 years agreed to deal with the whole stock of eligible debt (all debt contracted before the cut-off date). In addition, the new agreements reached with low-income countries under the enhanced concessional treatment contained a provision whereby Paris Club creditor countries would consider the matter of the stock of debt three or four years after the date of the first agreement under the new terms. That could be understood as a commitment to consider a reduction of the entire stock of debt, conditional upon satisfactory performance of the debtor countries under appropriate arrangements with IMF.

The UNCTAD secretariat made a preliminary assessment of the likely impact of the enhanced concessional treatment on the projected debt-service ratio of 22 low-income debtor countries, which had so far benefited from the "Toronto terms" or were likely to benefit from enhanced concessional treatment. The assessment showed that for half of the potential beneficiaries the new terms would help to reduce considerably their debt-service ratios, to a level compatible with their capacity to pay. For the other half, however, the debt burden would still remain high, even after the full implementation of the new terms.

The seven major industrial nations, at their Munich summit[6] (see above), welcomed the enhanced debt relief extended to the poorest countries by the Paris Club. They noted that the Paris Club had conditionally agreed to consider the stock-of-debt approach for the poorest countries that were prepared to adjust, and encouraged it to recognize the special situation of some highly indebted lower-middle-income countries on a case-by-case basis.

UNCTAD VIII action. In the Cartagena Commitment,[3] UNCTAD VIII recommended that the international community continue to provide support, including, on a case-by-case basis, further debt relief for countries implementing sound economic reform programmes. With regard to external debt incurred with commercial banks, it encouraged more rapid implementation of the strengthened debt strategy, noting that some coun-

tries had already benefited from a combination of sound adjustment policies and commercial bank debt reduction or equivalent measures. It further encouraged other countries with heavy bank debts to negotiate similiar reductions with their creditors. Parties to such a negotiation should take due account of both the medium-term debt reduction and new money requirements of the debtor country; multilateral institutions actively engaged in the strengthened international debt strategy were to continue to support debt-reduction packages related to commercial bank debt with a view to ensuring that the magnitude of such financing was consonant with the evolving debt strategy. Creditor banks were urged to participate in debt and debt-service reduction, and policies were to be strengthened to attract direct investment, avoid unsustainable levels of debt and foster the return of flight capital.

With regard to debt owed to official bilateral creditors, the Conference welcomed the substantial bilateral debt reduction undertaken by some creditor countries and encouraged others in a position to do so to take similiar action. It recommended that particular attention be paid to the resource needs of low-income countries and other debt-distressed developing countries that continued to service their debt, safeguard their creditworthiness and meet their external obligations.

With regard to multilateral debt, the Conference urged that serious attention be given to continuing the work towards growth-oriented solutions to the problems of developing countries with serious debt-servicing difficulties. The use of support groups should be continued in providing resources to clear arrears of countries embarking on vigorous economic reform programmes supported by IMF and the World Bank. The international community should explore ways to improve coordination between all creditors, official and private, and donors to help meet, in an integrated manner and based on solid economic considerations, financing requirements of debtor countries in relation to their medium-term development programmes. The Conference urged continued technical cooperation among developing countries in the area of external debt, as well as UNCTAD's cooperation with developing countries in debt negotiation and in providing advice on debt issues.

UNCED action. UNCED,[18] in its consideration of international cooperation to accelerate sustainable development in developing countries and related domestic policies, also addressed the debt issue and made recommendations in line with those of UNCTAD VIII. In its proposals for financial resources and mechanisms to implement Agenda 21, UNCED recommended that all creditors in the Paris Club promptly implement the agreement of December 1991 to provide debt relief for the poorest heavily indebted countries pursuing structural adjustment; debt relief measures were to be kept under review to address their continuing difficulties.

GENERAL ASSEMBLY ACTION

On 22 December, the General Assembly, on the recommendation of the Second Committee, adopted **resolution 47/198** by recorded vote.

International debt crisis and development: enhanced international cooperation towards a durable solution to the external debt problems of developing countries

The General Assembly,

Recalling its resolutions 41/202 of 8 December 1986, 42/198 of 11 December 1987, 43/198 of 20 December 1988, 44/205 of 22 December 1989, 45/214 of 21 December 1990 and 46/148 of 18 December 1991,

Reaffirming the Declaration on International Economic Cooperation, in particular the Revitalization of Economic Growth and Development of the Developing Countries, contained in the annex to its resolution S-18/3 of 1 May 1990, the International Development Strategy for the Fourth United Nations Development Decade, contained in the annex to its resolution 45/199 of 21 December 1990, the Programme of Action for the Least Developed Countries for the 1990s, adopted by the Second United Nations Conference on the Least Developed Countries, the United Nations New Agenda for the Development of Africa in the 1990s, contained in the annex to its resolution 46/151 of 18 December 1991, the document entitled "A New Partnership for Development: The Cartagena Commitment", adopted by the United Nations Conference on Trade and Development at its eighth session, and the provisions on a durable solution to the external debt crisis, contained in the relevant chapters of Agenda 21, adopted by the United Nations Conference on Environment and Development,

Noting that, owing to uneven developments, further progress is needed towards the solution of the external debt problems of a large number of developing countries, in the context of the evolving international debt strategy,

Noting also that a few indebted developing countries have regained relative access to international financial markets under the difficulties described in the report of the Secretary-General,

Noting with concern the continuing debt and debt-service problems of lower-middle-income developing countries, which adversely affect their development efforts and economic growth, and reiterating the need to address the continuing debt problems of those countries through effective debt-relief measures, bearing in mind, in this context, the special situation of lower-middle-income and certain middle-income African countries,

Also noting with concern the continuing existence of the heavy debt and debt-service burdens of low-income countries,

Noting with appreciation the recent initiatives towards the solution of the debt problems of some developing countries, such as the adoption by the Paris Club of the "enhanced terms" and the conclusion of several agreements on commercial debt and debt-service reduction,

Noting the substantial debt relief and debt reduction in favour of two middle-income countries agreed to by the Paris Club,

Stressing the importance of alleviating the debt and debt-service burdens of low- and middle-income developing countries with public debt problems,

Stressing also, in this context, the necessity of a supportive international economic environment, including an open and transparent multilateral trading system,

Emphasizing the importance for debtor developing countries to continue to pursue and intensify their efforts in their economic reform, stabilization and structural adjustment programmes, in order to raise savings and investment, reduce inflation and improve economic efficiency, taking into account their individual characteristics and the vulnerability of the poorer strata of their populations,

Expressing its concern that, in many developing countries, the burden of debt and debt service constitutes one of the major obstacles to the revitalization of growth and development, despite the often strenuous economic reforms of those countries,

Noting that those developing countries which have continued, at great cost, to meet their international debt and debt-service obligations in a timely fashion have done so despite severe external and domestic financial constraints,

1. *Takes note* of the report of the Secretary-General concerning the external debt crisis and development;

2. *Welcomes* the conclusion of several agreements on commercial bank debt and debt-service reduction under the evolving international debt strategy and takes note of relevant declarations recognizing the debt problems of some highly indebted lower-middle-income countries, taking into account their special and specific situations;

3. *Also welcomes* the write-off by certain donors of a significant part of the bilateral official debt of the least developed countries, and urges those countries that have not done so to cancel or provide equivalent relief for the official development assistance debt of the least developed countries;

4. *Expresses its appreciation* for the initiatives taken by developed countries, including recent initiatives to address the debt problems of some middle-income African countries, encourages the implementation thereof and invites all creditor countries to consider taking relevant measures for middle-income debtor developing countries;

5. *Stresses* the need for the broadest and most expeditious implementation of the recent initiatives and the need to continue to build upon them, in order, *inter alia*, to prevent the proliferation of debt problems;

6. *Also stresses* the need for the implementation of additional debt-relief measures, including further cancellation or reduction of debt and debt service related to official debt, and for more urgent action with regard to the remaining commercial debt owed by developing countries;

7. *Recognizes* the urgent need to continue to provide a social safety net to vulnerable groups most adversely affected by the implementation of economic reform programmes in the debtor countries, in particular low-income groups, in order to ensure social and political stability;

8. *Emphasizes* the importance for developing countries to continue their efforts to promote a favourable environment for attracting foreign investment, thereby promoting economic growth and sustainable development;

9. *Recognizes* the need of debtor developing countries for a supportive international economic environment as regards, *inter alia*, terms of trade, commodity prices, improved market access and trade practices, and, in this connection, stresses the urgent need for a balanced and successful outcome of the Uruguay Round of multilateral trade negotiations, which would result in the liberalization and expansion of world trade to the benefit of all countries, in particular the developing countries;

10. *Reiterates* the need for the implementation of initiatives involving developing debtor countries, developed creditor countries, commercial banks and multilateral financial institutions, with a view to easing the debt and debt-service burdens of severely indebted developing countries, which would contribute to recovery, growth and development in developing countries;

11. *Stresses* the need, in addition to debt-relief measures that include debt and debt-service reduction, for new financial flows to debtor developing countries, and urges the creditor countries and the multilateral financial institutions to continue to extend concessional financial assistance, as appropriate, in order to support the implementation by the developing countries of their economic reform, stabilization and structural adjustment programmes so as to enable them to extricate themselves from the debt overhang and to assist them in achieving economic growth and development;

12. *Urges* the international community to consider wider application of innovative measures, such as debt-for-equity swaps, debt-for-nature swaps and debt-for-development swaps;

13. *Stresses* the need for sustained action in addressing the debt problems of low-income countries and, in this regard, calls for early, expeditious and wide implementation of the enhanced terms currently offered to low-income countries by the Paris Club, as well as, where necessary, the extension thereof;

14. *Calls upon* private creditors to renew and expand initiatives and efforts in order to tackle the commercial debt problems of low- and middle-income developing countries;

15. *Urges* creditor countries, private banks and, within their prerogatives, multilateral financial institutions to consider the extension of appropriate new financial support to developing countries, in particular the low-income countries with substantial debt burdens that continue, at great cost, to service the debt and meet their international obligations;

16. *Requests* the Secretary-General to report to the General Assembly at its forty-eighth session on the implementation of the present resolution.

General Assembly resolution 47/198

22 December 1992   Meeting 93   158-1 (recorded vote)

Approved by Second Committee (A/47/722) by recorded vote (109-1), 16 December (meeting 51); draft by Vice-Chairman (A/C.2/47/L.16/Rev.1), based on informal consultations on draft by Pakistan for Group of 77 (A/C.2/47/L.16), orally revised; agenda item 82.
Meeting numbers. GA 47th session: 2nd Committee 19, 20, 28, 51; plenary 93.

Recorded vote in Assembly as follows:

In favour: Afghanistan, Algeria, Angola, Antigua and Barbuda, Argentina, Armenia, Australia, Austria, Azerbaijan, Bahamas, Bahrain, Bangladesh, Barbados, Belarus, Belgium, Benin, Bhutan, Bolivia, Bosnia and Herzegovina, Botswana, Brazil, Brunei Darussalam, Bulgaria, Burkina Faso, Burundi, Cameroon, Canada, Cape Verde, Chad, Chile, China, Colombia, Congo, Costa Rica, Côte d'Ivoire, Croatia, Cuba, Cyprus, Democratic Peo-

ple's Republic of Korea, Denmark, Djibouti, Dominica, Ecuador, Egypt, Ethiopia, Fiji, Finland, France, Gabon, Gambia, Germany, Ghana, Greece, Grenada, Guatemala, Guinea, Guinea-Bissau, Guyana, Haiti, Honduras, Hungary, Iceland, India, Indonesia, Iran, Iraq, Ireland, Israel, Italy, Jamaica, Japan, Jordan, Kenya, Kuwait, Lao People's Democratic Republic, Latvia, Lebanon, Lesotho, Liberia, Libyan Arab Jamahiriya, Liechtenstein, Lithuania, Luxembourg, Madagascar, Malawi, Malaysia, Maldives, Mali, Malta, Marshall Islands, Mauritania, Mauritius, Mexico, Micronesia, Mongolia, Morocco, Mozambique, Myanmar, Namibia, Nepal, Netherlands, New Zealand, Nicaragua, Niger, Nigeria, Norway, Oman, Pakistan, Panama, Papua New Guinea, Paraguay, Peru, Philippines, Poland, Portugal, Qatar, Republic of Korea, Republic of Moldova, Romania, Russian Federation, Rwanda, Saint Kitts and Nevis, Saint Lucia, Saint Vincent and the Grenadines, Samoa, Sao Tome and Principe, Saudi Arabia, Senegal, Sierra Leone, Singapore, Slovenia, Spain, Sri Lanka, Sudan, Suriname, Swaziland, Sweden, Syrian Arab Republic, Tajikistan, Thailand, Togo, Trinidad and Tobago, Tunisia, Turkey, Turkmenistan, Uganda, Ukraine, United Arab Emirates, United Kingdom, United Republic of Tanzania, Uruguay, Vanuatu, Venezuela, Viet Nam, Yemen, Zaire, Zambia, Zimbabwe.

Against: United States.

Investment and financial flows

According to the *World Economic Survey 1992*,[2] the total savings in the world would not be large enough to meet global investment needs over the 1990s. There was an inadequate allocation of the world's resources to investment projects. Developing countries, particularly in Asia, had demonstrated the "virtuous cycles" that resulted from a high-investment, high-growth policy in a context of well-managed financial and fiscal systems. In other cases, debt overhang and fragile economic situations held back possible investment and growth levels. Among the formerly centrally planned economies, disruptions of the transition process were deterring investment. Among the developed market economies, government investment needed to be increased and international flows augmented to support capital formation in developing and transition economies.

In accordance with a decision of UNCTAD VIII,[3] TDB, on 7 May,[19] established an ad hoc working group on investment and financial flows, non-debt-creating finance for development, and new mechanisms for increasing investment and financial flows. The Ad Hoc Working Group held its first session at Geneva from 9 to 13 November 1992[20] and adopted its work programme in the areas of global trends and issues, policies and measures to promote FDI, portfolio equity investment and new mechanisms, and strengthening technical cooperation.

The Group agreed that it would give particular attention to the situation of LDCs and suggest ways to improve their capacity. It recommended that it hold two sessions in 1993 and a final session in 1994. The 1993 sessions would focus on foreign investors' motivations, case-studies prepared by member States, country policies, multilateral measures and portfolio investment and new mechanisms. The Group noted the concerns expressed by several developing countries about the current constraints to country studies and recommended that multilateral and bilateral donors should consider making funds available to assist those countries.

Taxation

The Secretary-General submitted a report in March 1992[21] on the work of the Ad Hoc Group of Experts on International Cooperation in Tax Matters, which had held its sixth meeting in December 1991.[22] The Group directed a set of recommendations to the tax administrations of developed and developing countries to enable them to enhance the formulation and working of double taxation conventions, maximize tax compliance, improve tax equity, minimize the cost of tax collection, decrease and/or eliminate tax evasion and avoidance and promote international cooperation in tax matters. The Group also recommended that its meeting should be held annually instead of biennially, because of the rapid rate of changes in international taxation issues, bearing on the globalization and regionalization of the world economy.

By **decision 1992/281** of 30 July, the Economic and Social Council took note of the Secretary-General's report.

REFERENCES

[1]E/1992/27. [2]*World Economic Survey 1992: Current Trends and Policies in the World Economy* (E/1992/40), Sales No. E.92.II.C.1. [3]TD/364. [4]GA res. 45/192, 21 Dec. 1990. [5]A/47/404. [6]A/47/375-S/24429. [7]A/CONF.147/18. [8]YUN 1991, p. 356. [9]Ibid., p. 402, GA res. 46/151, annex II, 18 Dec. 1991. [10]YUN 1986, p. 446, GA res. S-13/2, annex, 1 June 1986. [11]YUN 1991, p. 450, GA res. 46/205, 20 Dec. 1991. [12]A/47/575. [13]E/1992/82/Add.1. [14]A/C.2/47/L.3. [15]YUN 1991, p. 452, GA res. 46/148, 18 Dec. 1991. [16]A/47/396. [17]*Trade and Development Report, 1992* (UNCTAD/TDR/12), Sales No. E.92.II.D.7. [18]*Report of the United Nations Conference on Environment and Development, Rio de Janeiro, 3-14 June 1992*, vol. I, Sales No. E.93.I.8. [19]A/47/15, vol. I (dec. 398(XXXVIII)). [20]TD/B/39(2)/6. [21]E/1992/8. [22]YUN 1991, p. 454.

Transport

Maritime transport

Shipping

UNCTAD VIII[1] decided to suspend the existing main committees of TDB, including the Committee on Shipping, and to include its current terms of reference in those of the newly created Standing Committee on Developing Services Sectors: Fostering Competitive Services Sectors in Developing Countries. Accordingly, TDB, on 7 May,[2] established the Standing Committee and decided on its terms of reference, stating that its main task in the field of shipping, ports and multimodal transport should be, *inter alia*, the review of shipping policies so as to identify elements leading to the development of competitive shipping sectors, in order to enhance the participation of developing countries in world shipping.

The Standing Committee on Developing Services Sectors (Shipping) held its first session at Geneva from 2 to 6 November 1992.[3] It considered its draft work programme[4] and a number of reports that had been requested by the former Committee on Shipping: an UNCTAD secretariat report on industry and policy developments in world shipping and their impact on developing countries;[5] the report of an expert group on shipping policy;[6] the review of maritime transport in 1991;[7] and an UNCTAD secretariat note on a review of activities in the field of shipping, ports and multimodal transport.[8] The Standing Committee adopted its work programme and decided that the UNCTAD secretariat should provide TDB with a list of specific outputs and activities, as well as estimated dates of completion of work for each of the elements of the work programme.

Multimodal transport

The Group of Experts on Multimodal Transport met at Geneva from 9 to 13 March 1992[9] and considered developments in the field of multimodal transport, containerization and technological development, as well as a draft work programme in those areas. It decided to keep the subject of container standards as a core element in the programme and suggested that the UNCTAD secretariat continue to monitor developments in that area and liaise with the International Standards Organization so as to draw attention to the specific problems of developing countries. It noted the new UNCTAD/International Chamber of Commerce (ICC) rules for multimodal transport documents[10] and suggested that the ICC Ad Hoc Working Group on Multimodal Transport continue to promote their use. It further recommended that the UNCTAD secretariat strengthen its assistance to Governments, transport operators and traders in the improved use of existing resources, as well as focus on changes in behavioural patterns leading to a high degree of action-oriented management; continue, through its technical assistance programme, to support efforts to improve the institutional and legal environment within which multimodal transport generally existed; and continue to work closely with ICC and other commercial parties in a programme whereby traders, government officials and transport providers could recognize the potential benefits arising from the control of the transport chain. In the light of the decisions of UNCTAD VIII, the Expert Group decided to submit its draft programme of work to the Secretary-

General of UNCTAD for subsequent transmission to the Standing Committee on Developing Services Sectors.

Ports

The UNCTAD secretariat, through a programme of research, training and technical cooperation, sought to improve the performance of ports in developing countries and to raise the awareness of the benefits to be achieved by ports acting as trading centres.

As requested by the Ad Hoc Intergovernmental Group of Port Experts, the secretariat prepared a study on the management and development of human resources in ports.[11] It also completed another study on the legal and regulatory aspects of port management, presenting the essential legal principles required for the effective operation of a port.[12] Two monographs were prepared, on the planning and management of multi-purpose terminals[13] and on the use of computers to manage the container terminal.[14]

Technical assistance and training

UNCTAD's activities in technical cooperation and training in shipping, ports and multimodal transport declined from a total of 37 projects with a gross expenditure of $3.2 million in 1991 to 32 projects with a total expenditure of $2 million in 1992.

Half of those projects were under the TRAINMAR programme and were designed to help training centres in developing countries provide a wide range of maritime management training, using a methodology that established professional standards at local centres and provided mechanisms for cooperation among those centres. Two new subregional projects, one in South America and one in the Caribbean, were initiated, while eight were terminated. Implementation of the Advance Cargo Information System continued in several African countries, and work was under way in Burkina Faso, Senegal and the Sudan. Other projects initiated in 1992 included a national project to develop multimodal transport in Pakistan, a subregional project to establish TRAINMAR in southern Latin America and a project to develop and deliver a new policy seminar on the commercial role of ports.

REFERENCES

[1]TD/364. [2]A/47/15, vol. I (dec. 398(XXXVIII)). [3]TD/B/39(2)/5. [4]TD/B/CN.4/4. [5]TD/B/CN.4/5. [6]TD/B/CN.4/6. [7]TD/B/CN.4/8 & Corr.1,2. [8]UNCTAD/SHIP/643. [9]TD/B/1320. [10]TRADE/WP.4/INF.117/Corr.1. [11]UNCTAD/SHIP/644. [12]UNCTAD/SHIP/639. [13]UNCTAD/SHIP/494(9). [14]UNCTAD/SHIP/494(10).

UNCTAD structure, programme and finances

Institutional matters

In the Cartagena Commitment,[1] UNCTAD VIII stated that institutional adaptation and revitalization were urgently needed to enable UNCTAD to seize the new opportunities to foster international cooperation for development. UNCTAD should promote international consensus on principles and strategies for policy action at the national and international levels to enhance development prospects of member States, particularly those of developing countries, and provide a forum for the exchange of experiences among member States. The substantive work of UNCTAD should involve the initial identification of a relevant set of issues; the carrying out of high-quality analytical work; and the conduct of intergovernmental consultations on areas of convergence and, when appropriate, negotiations. Consensus-building was an important function of UNCTAD, flowing from the identification of issues and the analytical work carried out by the secretariat to clarify the main aspects of such issues and shared perceptions.

On issues where other institutions were vested with the necessary powers of decision-making, UNCTAD should provide constructive approaches and viewpoints, and generate political impulses on matters within its purview, for consideration by those institutions. TDB should make the necessary arrangements to ensure that the outcomes of those processes were translated into concrete action. Technical cooperation should be strengthened, expanded within the resources available and integrated into all relevant areas of UNCTAD's work, taking into account the need for effective interaction among its main functions and for effective coordination with other technical cooperation agencies of the United Nations system. UNCTAD's policy review of technical cooperation activities midway between Conferences should assess the results and, as necessary, ensure continued support of those activities. Developing countries, in the context of their national priorities, should arrange for adequate provision to be made for technical cooperation as regards trade and development in the context of UNDP country and intercountry programmes and programmes financed by bilateral and other multilateral donors. The Conference invited interested countries to make use of the services of UNCTAD and ITC in that respect. UNCTAD and ITC should continue their efforts to achieve complementarity in their technical cooperation activities and UNCTAD, in particular, in accordance with its mandate, should continue to address long-standing trade and development problems.

UNCTAD intergovernmental structure

UNCTAD VIII, in the Cartagena Commitment,[1] agreed that UNCTAD's intergovernmental structure should consist of the Trade and Development Board, standing and special committees, and ad hoc working groups. The Board would continue to address annually matters relating to the international implications of macroeconomic policies and issues concerning interdependence, using the *Trade and Development Report* as background, as well as to consider topics relating to trade policies, structural adjustment and economic reform. Additional topics focusing on other key areas, including a new international partnership for development, global interdependence, other paths to development and sustainable development, should also be addressed at each annual session. TDB should also consider UNCTAD's contribution to the United Nations New Agenda for the Development of Africa in the 1990s.[2] In addition, the Board would undertake, during the spring segment of its annual sessions, the review of the progress in the implementation of the Programme of Action for the Least Developed Countries for the 1990s,[3] using the *LDC Annual Report* as background.

To strengthen its policy function, promote greater efficiency and give impetus to ongoing work, the Board would meet in short one-day or half-day sessions at the level of permanent representatives immediately before its regular sessions and periodically in between. The Board would conduct, midway between Conferences, a review and evaluation of the work programme of the intergovernmental machinery, including its own; of technical assistance programmes; and, bearing in mind the calendar established in this regard, of the programme budget and medium-term-plan, so as to ensure full integration of all work undertaken by UNCTAD and to establish or adjust priorities for the period up to the next Conference. In order to facilitate the full participation of representatives of LDCs in consideration of the implementation of the Programme of Action for LDCs for the 1990s, the Board should establish, in advance, the specific organizational arrangements and dates for such work.

UNCTAD VIII decided that, with the exception of the Special Committee on Preferences and the Intergovernmental Group of Experts on Restrictive Business Practices, the existing committees of the Board should be suspended and standing committees should be established on commodities, poverty alleviation, economic cooperation among developing countries and developing services sectors: fostering competitive services sectors in developing countries. The standing committees should be geared to assist TDB in the effective discharge of its functions. The terms of reference of the Committee on Shipping and the Committee on Invisibles and Financing related to Trade would be included in the Standing Committee on Developing Services Sectors.

UNCTAD VIII also requested TDB, as an initial step, to establish ad hoc working groups for an initial period of two years to deal with investment and financial flows, non-debt-creating finance for development, new mechanisms for increasing investment and financial flows; trade efficiency; comparative experiences with privatization; expansion of trading opportunities for developing countries; and the interrelationship between investment and technology transfers. These groups would report directly or through the relevant committee to the Board for further action.

Methods of work

UNCTAD VIII[1] decided that, to enhance the effectiveness of the existing system of consultations with representatives of member States between sessions of the Board and to promote greater efficiency in the intergovernmental process, the informal consultative mechanism established by the Board in 1981[4] should be strengthened for the purpose of preparing and following up its work. The preparatory process for the informal consultative mechanism should take the form of exchanges of views by the UNCTAD Secretary-General with representatives of members of the TDB Bureau and should be held as often as necessary, so as to enable the Secretary-General to submit recommendations for approval by the informal consultative mechanism. At the same time, the Secretary-General should be granted a greater measure of discretion in preparing proposals on the sequencing and duration of meetings of the subsidiary bodies of the Board for the consideration of Governments, through the informal consultative mechanism. Non-governmental and other international bodies could be invited to participate in an advisory capacity at public meetings of the Board and its standing and special committees and ad hoc working groups.

The Conference invited the United Nations Secretary-General to consider granting UNCTAD greater operational flexibility in financial and administrative matters, and called on TDB to take the necessary follow-up measures to ensure the speedy implementation of the institutional reforms.

UNCTAD programme

The Trade and Development Board held three sessions in 1992: the second part of its seventeenth special session from 15 to 24 January,[5] the second part of its thirty-eighth session from 21 April to 7 May,[6] and the first part of its thirty-ninth session from 28 September to 14 October.[7] The January session was largely to discuss the preparations for UNCTAD VIII. On 7 May,[8] the Board adopted a decision establishing the standing committees and the ad hoc working groups. On 9 October, it established an ad hoc working group to explore the issue of structural adjustment for the transition to disarmament[9] and adopted an agreed conclusion on the subprogrammes to be designated high priority.[10]

In accordance with its new working methods, the Board, in September/October, considered the international implications of macroeconomic policies and issues concerning interdependence—the recent evolution of development problems and prospects; paths to development—performance, problems and reform of public enterprises; sustainable development, including UNCTAD's contribution to the implementation of UNCED's conclusions and recommendations; trade policies, structural adjustment and economic reform—issues relating to national transparent mechanisms in the context of the fight against protectionism; review of progress in the implementation of the Programme of Action for LDCs for the 1990s; UNCTAD's contribution to the implementation of the United Nations New Agenda for the Development of Africa in the 1990s; assistance to the Palestinian people in the light of the Cartagena decision; and other matters relating to trade and development.

On 7 February, the Economic and Social Council, by **decision 1992/208 A**, decided to consider at its substantive session of 1992 the report of TDB on the second part of its thirty-eighth session and to authorize the Secretary-General to transmit directly to the General Assembly the report of the Board on the first part of its thirty-ninth session.

On 31 July, by **decision 1992/298**, the Council took note of the TDB report on the second part of its thirty-eighth session.

Programme budget

At its twenty-first session (Geneva, 31 August–8 September),[11] the UNCTAD Working Party on the Medium-term Plan and the Programme Budget reviewed the proposed revisions and adopted amendments to the UNCTAD sections of the United Nations medium-term plan for 1992-1997.[12] On the question of prioritizing the subprogrammes, the Working Party agreed, in the light of the decisions taken at UNCTAD VIII on the reorientation of UNCTAD's work, that the matter of priority setting was for the whole membership of UNCTAD to determine; it proposed that the question be further addressed, after consideration

by all member States of UNCTAD, at the next session of TDB.

The Committee for Programme and Coordination (CPC), in September 1992,[13] recommended approval by the General Assembly of the revisions to the medium-term plan of sections relating to UNCTAD. The Assembly approved them on 23 December by **resolution 47/214**.

In September,[14] in response to a 1991 Assembly request,[15] the Secretary-General submitted a report on the 13 posts formerly attached to the subprogramme on trade among countries having different economic and social systems. The report noted that 12 posts were redeployed to other subprogrammes and the incumbent of the D-2 post assumed responsibility for activities under the subprogramme on cross-sectoral issues and for assistance in the overall direction and supervision of international trade programmes in general. In the light of the results of UNCTAD VIII, the Secretary-General proposed to extend the 13 posts through 1993 on a temporary basis and to make proposals concerning their future status in the context of the programme budget proposals for the biennium 1994-1995. ACABQ[16] endorsed the proposal on the understanding that the financing details would be provided in respect of the redeployment of the posts and that no additional appropriations would be required.

On 23 December, by **resolution 47/220 A**, the Assembly approved a revised appropriation of $92,514,000 for UNCTAD in the framework of the 1992-1993 budget. On the same date, by **resolution 47/219 A section XXVII**, it took note of the Secretary-General's report on the 13 posts and endorsed the recommendations of CPC and ACABQ.

Technical cooperation

In 1992, about $20 million were allocated to UNCTAD technical cooperation activities. Although UNDP remained the most important source of funds, there was increasing financial support from bilateral donors and other sources. Activities relating to trade included support to developing countries participating in the Uruguay Round of multilateral trade negotiations; development of the services sector; trade policy reform; utilization of GSP; competition policies and the control of restrictive business practices; transfer of technology; and trade between developing countries and countries with economies in transition. UNCTAD's programme for the development of human resources for trade became fully operational and the programme on helping developing countries to manage their external debt liabilities continued to expand, in cooperation with the World Bank. Further assistance was provided in the areas of insurance, selected international monetary issues, and commodity production, diversification and marketing, including better management of food grain imports. Work was undertaken on the transit problems of land-locked countries in Africa, the development of shipping services, including assistance for better management of ports, multimodal transport, and the human resource development programme for the maritime sector. UNCTAD's largest single technical cooperation programme assisted over 50 countries to improve their management of customs.

The Working Party on the Medium-term Plan and the Programme Budget conducted its biennial review of the technical cooperation programme of UNCTAD for the period 1989-1991.[11] It had before it an UNCTAD secretariat report[17] reviewing activities by programme area and examining the related issues and developments. The Working Party welcomed the increase in the level of UNCTAD's technical cooperation activities over the past few years as well as their relevance and effectiveness. It requested the secretariat to develop proposals in the areas identified in the Cartagena Commitment, bearing in mind the need to ensure balanced distribution among regions and countries, particularly LDCs, land-locked and island developing countries. It invited UNDP to continue to provide support for UNCTAD's intercountry technical cooperation and appealed to UNDP's Governing Council, in its mid-term review of the fifth programming cycle (1992-1996), to consider restoring the proportionate level of resources allocated for regional programmes. It also invited bilateral donors, multilateral agencies and all member States in a position to do so to increase the level of their budgetary contributions to UNCTAD for technical cooperation purposes.

REFERENCES

[1]TD/364. [2]YUN 1991, p. 402, GA res. 46/151, annex II, 18 Dec. 1991. [3]A/CONF.147/18. [4]YUN 1981, p. 536. [5]TD/B/1319. [6]A/47/15, vol. I. [7]A/47/15, vol. II. [8]A/47/15, vol. I (dec. 398(XXXVIII)). [9]A/47/15, vol. II (dec. 399(XXXIX)). [10]Ibid. (conclusion 400(XXXIX)). [11]TD/B/39(1)/8. [12]A/47/6. [13]A/47/16. [14]A/C.5/47/7. [15]YUN 1991, p. 871, GA res. 46/185 C, sect. IX, 20 Dec. 1991. [16]A/47/7/Add.1. [17]TD/B/WP/76 & Corr.1 & Add.1 & Add.1/Corr.1.

Chapter V

Transnational corporations

Transnational corporations (TNCs) continued to exert a major influence on the global economy in 1992. Changes in the structure of international economic relations and policies in the early 1990s created conditions that placed TNCs in a position to play a significant role in development. Private sector development had become a major concern for many developing countries and countries in transition to market economies, while foreign direct investment was increasingly important as a force for promoting and integrating international flows of capital and of trade and technology.

The Commission on TNCs met twice in 1992. In January, it discussed its contribution to the United Nations Conference on Environment and Development. In April, the Commission conducted a general discussion on TNCs in the world economy and trends in foreign direct investment in developing countries. It also considered international agreements relating to TNCs and the activities of the former United Nations Centre on TNCs. Following the restructuring of the Secretariat in 1992, the Centre was incorporated into the new Transnational Corporations and Management Division of the Department of Economic and Social Development. The Intergovernmental Working Group of Experts on International Standards of Accounting and Reporting met in March.

In July, the Economic and Social Council invited TNCs to take measures to achieve the eradication of apartheid in South Africa and requested the Secretary-General to collect information on the activities of TNCs there (resolution 1992/34). The Council called on the TNCs and Management Division to strengthen its work on cooperation related to technology transfer, and requested it to assist developing countries to create a favourable investment climate and to develop their endogenous capacity to encourage foreign investment (1992/35).

Draft code of conduct

The Commission on TNCs, in April 1992, continued to consider work related to a draft code of conduct on TNCs, first considered in 1975.[1]

In a February report to the Commission on an international framework for TNCs,[2] the Secretary-General reviewed international principles and standards that had been elaborated during the second half of the century and evaluated the extent to which those norms were still relevant in the light of recent policy changes affecting foreign direct investment. He summarized the settled issues, including observance by TNCs of local laws and their non-interference in the internal affairs of host countries; fair and equitable treatment of TNCs by host countries and minimum protection under the law, including laws governing nationalization and expropriation; and specialized standards on business and trade practices, consumer and environmental protection, working conditions and labour safety. It was noted, however, that the manner in which those principles were applied by Governments and TNCs had changed, as Governments were liberalizing restrictions on the entry of foreign investment. The report also outlined a number of issues on which consensus was still to be achieved, such as foreign investment and international law, compensation for expropriation, extraterritoriality, national treatment, reciprocity, and the right of entry and establishment as an emerging standard.

Increased emphasis was being placed on a number of issues as a result of the changed economic climate in Eastern Europe and in many developing countries. Those issues included: privatization and competition; securities, banking and insurance supervision; transfer pricing; corrupt practices in international transactions; and environment and investment.

The report concluded that a global framework for the 1990s would integrate and consolidate what had been achieved so far and address the new issues arising in the international agenda. Those issues would give new perspectives to traditional standards, while defining new ones, and would complete the overall outline of the emerging international framework for foreign direct investment in the 1990s.

By a note of September 1992,[3] the Secretary-General transmitted to the General Assembly a report by the President of the forty-sixth (1991) Assembly session on the outcome of informal consultations aimed at achieving an agreement on the draft code of conduct. He stated that he had convened a new round of consultations (New York, 21-23 July 1992) pursuant to an understanding reached in 1991.[4] It was the view of delegations that no consensus was possible on the draft code at that time. Delegations felt that a fresh approach should be examined, given the changed international economic environment. It was suggested that guidelines or any other international instrument on foreign investment should be prepared at the next (1993) session of the Commission on TNCs as part of that new approach.

In **decision 47/439** of 22 December 1992, the Assembly took note of the Secretary-General's note transmitting the report of the Assembly President.

Bilateral, regional and international arrangements

In his report on an international framework for TNCs,[2] the Secretary-General noted that regional and global movements towards economic integration greatly affected the existing and future modalities of foreign direct investment. Concepts of home and host State jurisdiction, extraterritoriality, national treatment and right of establishment would lose some significance when certain aspects of national sovereignty were surrendered to regional economic institutions. Many States had commenced or concluded regional free trade agreements or frameworks for free trade agreements, developments that would inevitably be reflected in investment policy with a number of significant potential consequences. The report discussed some of those possible consequences, including whether regional arrangements would partially disrupt the global approach to investment and trade exemplified in the Uruguay Round of trade negotiations (see PART SEVEN, Chapter XVIII), the question of comity, harmonization, export of law, and uniform law and model law.

The report noted that in all those areas, the negotiations in the Uruguay Round, as well as the stream of bilateral and regional trade agreements, played both a causal and a consequential role. Unless investment was able to proceed easily across boundaries and was assured of equitable treatment once within foreign borders, trade could not flourish. Successful conclusion of the Uruguay Round would contribute to the harmonization of national investment and trade regimes, which would facilitate a symbiotic flow of productive investment across national boundaries.

REFERENCES
[1]YUN 1975, p. 484. [2]E/C.10/1992/8. [3]A/47/446. [4]YUN 1991, p. 460.

Standards of accounting and reporting

At its tenth session (New York, 5-13 March 1992),[1] the Intergovernmental Working Group of Experts on International Standards of Accounting and Reporting had before it reports by the Secretary-General on current developments at the global[2] and national[3] levels in the field of accounting and reporting by TNCs; an international survey of environmental information disclosure by TNCs;[4] accounting problems arising during privatization;[5] and accountancy development in Francophone Africa[6] and in Central and Eastern Europe.[7]

The Group reviewed progress made in harmonizing national accounting standards and discussed efforts to reduce the options in such standards worldwide and increase their use by regulators of securities markets and international trade. The Group decided that it should analyse the adequacy of accounting and auditing standards for financial institutions at the national and international levels. It also decided to keep under review the direction of change in Central and Eastern Europe, the comparability of their new standards and further improvements that could be necessary.

According to the survey of corporate environmental reporting, 191 out of 222 TNCs studied reported at least some information on their environmental impact. The Group decided to transmit its conclusions on corporate environmental accounting and reporting to the Secretary-General of the United Nations Conference on Environment and Development (UNCED) (see below).

In addressing accounting problems during privatization, the Group took up seven country case-studies (Czechoslovakia, France, Germany, Hungary, Mexico, Poland, United Kingdom). The report on the subject[5] noted that lack of good accounting information and poor accounting practices of the past, which led to inaccurate valuations of the enterprises to be privatized, were the major causes of such problems. A distinction was made between privatization in countries with an established market infrastructure and those in transition to a market economy.

With regard to accounting training and education in Africa and in Central and Eastern Europe, the Group discussed the results of the first International Conference on Accountancy Development in Africa (Dakar, Senegal, 14-17 October 1991) and reviewed various programmes for countries in transition. It decided to devote its 1993 session to education and the strengthening of the profession.

In April,[8] the Commission on TNCs took note of the Group's report.[1]

REFERENCES
[1]E/C.10/1992/12. [2]E/C.10/AC.3/1992/2. [3]E/C.10/AC.3/1992/4. [4]E/C.10/AC.3/1992/3. [5]E/C.10/AC.3/1992/5 & Add.1-7. [6]E/C.10/AC.3/1992/6. [7]E/C.10/AC.3/1992/7. [8]E/1992/26.

Commission on TNCs

The Commission on TNCs held its eighteenth session in New York in two parts, from 23 to 25 January and from 8 to 16 April 1992.[1] The January meeting was devoted to finalizing its recommendations to the Preparatory Committee for UNCED (see below). In April, the Commission discussed TNCs in the world economy and trends in foreign direct investment in developing countries, TNCs in South Africa, international arrangements and agreements relating to TNCs, activities of the former Centre on TNCs and the question of expert advisers. It also considered the provisional agenda for its nineteenth (1993) session.

On 30 July, the Economic and Social Council took note of the Commission's report on its eighteenth session[1] (**decision 1992/283**) and approved the provisional agenda and documentation for its nineteenth session (**decision 1992/282**).

TNCs in South Africa

A March report of the Secretary-General on the role of TNCs in South Africa[2] examined the role of sanctions in the South African economy that contributed to the Government's repeal of key apartheid legislation and the reaction of the international community to the repeal in terms of measures repealed and those remaining in force. It also examined disinvestments/investments undertaken by TNCs and analysed the domestic market and external constraints on attracting investments from TNCs. In addition, the report presented an optimistic scenario for attracting TNCs in the context of the medium- to long-term prospects of the South African economy and dealt with the role of TNCs in employment and education of black South Africans.

The Secretary-General noted that the pace of disinvestment in South Africa had slowed sharply since the end of 1989, with only two companies having disinvested in 1991. In the preceding two years, much international attention had switched from the issue of direct investment to that of non-equity ties. Again, the area of non-equity links between TNCs and South African business entities showed little change. Following the repeal of certain apartheid legislation,[3] some Governments lifted their economic sanctions and increased trade with South Africa, filling the gap caused by trade sanctions.

The report emphasized that economic sanctions and restrictive measures against South Africa had been successful in exerting pressure on its economy. South Africa's heavy dependence on foreign capital markets had made financial sanctions very

effective. Coupled with the financial sanctions was the decision by many TNCs to disinvest from South Africa. Although such disinvestment had had consequences for the economy and society in South Africa, the persistence of non-equity links, such as licensing and franchise agreements, might have negated the intentions of those who supported sanctions. The withdrawal of many TNCs from South Africa might also have undermined the country's efforts on behalf of rapid economic growth in the short term.

In another March report,[4] the Secretary-General provided a list of TNCs based in 18 countries that had disposed of their equity interests in South Africa and a list of TNCs from 15 countries which had equity interests there of more than 10 per cent. The report also listed companies from five countries (France, Germany, Switzerland, United Kingdom, United States) engaged in social responsibility programmes benefiting employees and their families or benefiting the entire population or specified local communities.

In April,[1] the Commission on TNCs took note of the two reports.

ECONOMIC AND SOCIAL COUNCIL ACTION

On 30 July, the Economic and Social Council, on the recommendation of its Economic Committee, adopted **resolution 1992/34** without vote.

**Activities of transnational corporations
in South Africa**

The Economic and Social Council,

Recalling its resolution 1991/54 of 26 July 1991,

Taking note with appreciation of the report of the Secretary-General on the role of transnational corporations in South Africa,

Recalling the Declaration on Apartheid and its Destructive Consequences in Southern Africa, adopted by the General Assembly at its sixteenth special session, which contains guidelines on how to end apartheid through genuine negotiations,

Welcoming the recent developments in South Africa, including the repeal or amendment of the major apartheid laws, the formation of the Patriotic/United Front, the ongoing process of negotiations, *inter alia*, under the auspices of the Convention for a Democratic South Africa, and the outcome of the whites-only referendum of 17 March 1992,

Gravely concerned about the escalation of politically inspired violence in South Africa despite the signing of the National Peace Accord on 14 September 1991,

Reiterating the urgent need for the removal of the remaining obstacles to the creation of an atmosphere conducive to constitutional negotiations,

Mindful of its obligations towards the complete eradication of apartheid, reaffirmed in General Assembly resolutions 44/244 of 17 September 1990, 45/176 A of 19 December 1990 and 46/79 A of 13 December 1991,

1. *Welcomes* the recent positive political developments in South Africa, which enhance the possibilities for the total eradication of apartheid in South Africa;

2. *Reaffirms* that Governments, entrepreneurs and enterprises, including transnational corporations, have contributed to the demise of the apartheid system, and invites them to give their full and concerted support to this end, as well as to take appropriate measures regarding the vulnerable and critical process now under way in South Africa, with a view to achieving the total eradication of the apartheid system and the establishment of a united non-racial and democratic South Africa;

3. *Requests* the Secretary-General:

(a) In close cooperation with the relevant organs of the United Nations, to continue the work of collecting and disseminating information on the activities of transnational corporations in South Africa, including the list of transnational corporations conducting operations there;

(b) To continue preparing studies on the level, form and responsibilities of operation of transnational corporations in South Africa, including their non-equity business arrangements and their involvement in particular sectors of the South African economy;

(c) To continue examining possible contributions of transnational corporations to the construction of a united and non-racial democratic South Africa in the economic and social fields, taking into account the special need for development in the areas of human resources, particularly the training of black South African entrepreneurs, employment, housing and health;

(d) To report to the Commission on Transnational Corporations at its nineteenth session, the Economic and Social Council and the General Assembly on the implementation of the present resolution.

Economic and Social Council resolution 1992/34

30 July 1992   Meeting 41   Adopted without vote

Approved by Economic Committee (E/1992/109/Add.3) without vote, 28 July (meeting 16); draft by Commission on TNCs (E/1992/26); agenda item 12 *(e)*.

Contribution to UNCED

In response to a 1991 resolution of the Economic and Social Council,[5] the Secretary-General submitted to the January meeting of the Commission on TNCs a report on TNCs and sustainable development.[6] The report contained recommendations by the Executive Director of the former Centre on TNCs in five programme areas in which large enterprises, including TNCs, could contribute to the goals of sustainable development: global corporate environmental management; risk and hazard minimization; environmentally sounder consumption patterns; full-cost environmental accounting; and environmental conventions, standards and guidelines. The specific recommendations under each programme area, derived from the existing practices of environmentally leading businesses, also addressed Governments and international organizations, since incentives and regulatory standards could allow markets to function more effectively.

Particular recommendations included the establishment of clear corporate environmental policies, institutional structures and reporting systems for monitoring progress made towards sustainable development; minimization of hazardous processes through the assessment and anticipation of environmental risks, analysis and monitoring of environmental problems and awareness-building measures; identification of new markets, products and investments to replace environmentally degrading activities, and an increase in information flows on the environmental effects of such activities and products; incorporation of environmental costs into the production of goods and services, and creation of accounting methods to encompass sustainable development considerations; and compliance with and further development of international, regional and national environmental guidelines and instruments, as well as industry trade association standards and guidelines.

On 25 January,[7] the Commission on TNCs requested its Chairman to transmit the Secretary-General's report, the Commission's recommendations and the views expressed by member and observer States to the Preparatory Committee for UNCED (see PART THREE, Chapter VIII).

The Intergovernmental Working Group of Experts on International Standards of Accounting and Reporting[8] had before it a report of the Secretary-General[9] providing an international survey of corporate reporting practices. The survey found that TNCs demonstrated an awareness of environmental issues, even though their disclosures remained qualitative, descriptive and inconsistent across industries. The report also provided information on environmental policies and programmes of TNCs, key environmental improvements in their activities, emission levels, government legislation, legal proceedings and notes to the accounts, financial effects of environmental protection measures, and the availability of environmental information in special reports and information on environmental audits.

In its conclusions,[8] which were transmitted to the Secretary-General of UNCED, the Working Group listed a number of items that could be considered by a board of directors in its report or in management discussions: type of environmental issues pertinent to the enterprise and its industry; formal policies and programmes adopted by the enterprise with respect to environmental protection measures; improvements made in key areas since the introduction of environmental policies; environmental emission targets set by the enterprise for itself, and how the enterprise was performing relative to those targets; the extent to which environmental protection measures were undertaken due to governmental legislation and the extent to which governmental requirements were being achieved; any material proceedings under environmental law; the financial or operational effect of environmental protection measures on the capital expenditures and earnings of the enterprise; and the amount charged to operations and a description of the environmental measures to which they related, such as liquid effluent treatment, waste gas and air treatment, solid waste treatment, analysis, control and compliance, remediation and recycling. The Working Group suggested that financial statements could include the following environment-related accounting policy notes: recording liabilities and provisions; setting up catastrophe reserves; and disclosure of contingent liabilities. The following environment-related items could be included in contingent liabilities disclosures: liabilities, provisions and reserves set for the current period, and amounts accumulated to date; and contingent liabilities, with an estimate of the amount involved, unless the event was not likely to occur.

TNCs and international economic relations

In addressing questions relating to TNCs and international economic relations, the Commission on TNCs in April had before it three reports of the Secretary-General, requested by the Commission in 1991.[10]

A February report[11] surveyed global and regional trends in foreign direct investment, indicating the continued growth of world-wide flows in 1990 despite reduced economic growth in a number of large economies.

The report noted that, in 1990, world-wide foreign direct investment outflows increased by 7 per cent over 1989, reaching $225 billion, while inflows fell to $184 billion. The slow-down in the growth of outflows in 1990 was largely attributable to a slow-down in the growth of outflows from Japan, a possible plateauing of outflows from the United States and a decline in outflows from the United Kingdom. Outflows of foreign direct investment from developed countries other than those three grew by 27 per cent in 1990, a growth rate equivalent to the global average for the period 1983-1990. Outflows from developing countries declined in 1990 compared with 1989, having grown substantially in the late 1980s, driven by the growth in outflows from the Asian newly industrializing economies.

Inflows of foreign direct investment to developing countries grew by 7 per cent in 1990; they received 17 per cent of all inflows, which was equal to their share for the last half of the 1980s. Foreign direct investment to Central and Eastern Europe increased sharply, but remained at low levels.

The report stated that the continuing growth of foreign direct investment was an important element in the economies of most of the world's regions. Its relative importance could be shown in such indicators as its share in domestic capital for-

mation and the growth of foreign sales by TNCs as a means of delivering goods and services to foreign markets.

In a report on TNCs and economic growth through technology,[12] the Secretary-General noted that evidence from both developed and developing countries demonstrated that technology was a key determinant of growth. The report analysed contributions by TNCs to technological change in host nations through increased research and development expenditures, higher factor productivity and change in the composition of manufactured output and exports in favour of research-and-development intensive products.

In discussing policy implications, the report noted that research and development by TNCs in developing countries was mainly located in countries already possessing some level of technological competence and a supply of trained personnel. Policy measures to induce TNCs to undertake greater research and development in host economies should be conceived. Although foreign direct investment had made a notable contribution to technology transfer, performance variations of TNCs again appeared to be related to host economies' indigenous technological capacities.

Also, while foreign direct investment was a useful means of quickly benefiting from the results of new innovation through the transfer of production, it did not necessarily imply dissemination of technological knowledge to domestic producers, raising the question of the choice between foreign direct investment and externalized forms as mode of transfer. Where TNCs were willing to transfer technologies in externalized forms, technology purchasers should be provided with information on available alternatives, as excessive payment implied a drain on domestic resources. Highly restricted policies towards foreign direct investment could limit the scope for acquiring technology through other channels, unless the country concerned had a strong bargaining position because of its large market size or the capacity to develop technologies independent of an association with TNCs.

The report emphasized that the growth-promoting impact of technologies acquired through foreign direct investment and other forms of association with TNCs was ultimately dependent on the incentive structure faced by both foreign and domestic enterprises in acquiring, adapting, innovating upon and diffusing technologies. That structure required the formulation of public policies regarding physical infrastructure, human resources development, research and development, technology and foreign direct investment, competition, international trade, factor pricing, venture capital and subsidies. Without that kind of approach, the contribution of TNCs to growth through technology transfer would fall short of its potential.

In a report on TNCs in the new world economy,[13] the Secretary-General discussed major economic changes in the 1990s. The expanded role of the private sector, the rapid pace of new technological developments and the central role of TNCs in organizing technological activity, globalization of enterprises and regionalization of business activity around the three Triad members (the European Community, Japan and the United States) enabled TNCs as integrating agents of those activities to affect significantly the economic performance of host developing countries.

The report noted that the ongoing phase of world economic growth and integration was likely to be driven by the activities of TNCs to a greater extent than ever before, with a corresponding rise in the impact of foreign direct investment on host countries' growth and development. Despite the major role of foreign direct investment in international economic relations, there was no mechanism through which Governments could provide information to other Governments and interested parties on their foreign direct investment policies. The report outlined measures to improve transparency in that area which, if adopted, would result in the establishment and dissemination of the policy statements, laws, regulations and administrative guidelines that comprised reporting countries' foreign direct investment policy frameworks. Such a reporting system could also provide the basis for improving investment policies through policy evaluations and reviews. Such policy reviews could amplify the efforts of countries to maximize the benefits of foreign direct investment to their economies.

In April,[1] the Commission took note of the Secretary-General's reports and requested the Secretariat to continue its work on foreign direct investment and the role of TNCs in development and to report in 1993.

ECONOMIC AND SOCIAL COUNCIL ACTION

On 30 July, the Economic and Social Council adopted **resolution 1992/36** on privatization and foreign investment in the context of economic restructuring (see PART THREE, Chapter I).

REFERENCES

[1]E/1992/26. [2]E/C.10/1992/6 and Corr.1. [3]YUN 1991, p. 108. [4]E/C.10/1992/7. [5]YUN 1991, p. 463, ESC res. 1991/55, 26 July 1991. [6]E/C.10/1992/2. [7]E/1992/26 (res. 1992/1). [8]E/C.10/1992/12. [9]E/C.10/AC.3/1992/3. [10]YUN 1991, p. 466. [11]E/C.10/1992/3. [12]E/C.10/1992/4. [13]E/C.10/1992/5.

PUBLICATIONS

Foreign Direct Investment and Technology Transfer in India, Sales No. E.92.II.A.3. *Foreign Direct Investment and Industrial Restructuring in Mexico*, Sales No. E.92.II.A.9. *Transnational Banks and the External Indebtedness of Developing Countries: Impact of Regulatory Changes*, Sales No. E.92.II.A.10. *World Investment Directory 1992: vol. 1—Asia and the Pacific*, Sales No. E.92.II.A.11. *Bilateral Investment Treaties*, Sales No. E.92.II.A.16. *World Investment Report 1992: Transnational Corporations as Engines of Growth*, Sales No. E.92.II.A.19. *The East-West Business Directory 1991/1992*, Sales No. E.92.II.A.20. *Formulation and Implementation of Foreign Investment Policies: Selected Key Issues*, Sales No. E.92.II.A.21. *Environmental Accounting: Current Issues, Abstracts and Bibliography*, Sales No. E.92.II.A.23. *World Investment Report 1992: Transnational Corporations as Engines of Growth—An Executive Summary*, Sales No. E.92.II.A.24. *World Investment Directory 1992: vol. 2—Central and Eastern Europe*, Sales No. E.93.II.A.1.

Centre on TNCs

In April,[1] the Commission on TNCs considered three reports of the Secretary-General dealing with the 1991 activities of the Centre on TNCs and its joint units established with the regional commissions.

In a February report,[2] the Secretary-General described work being done by the Centre to secure an effective code of conduct and other international arrangements and agreements relating to TNCs (see above); to minimize the negative effects of TNCs and enhance their contributions to development; and to strengthen the capabilities of host developing countries to deal with matters related to TNCs. With regard to the scope of the programme during the 1990s, the Secretary-General stated that the Centre planned to implement the proposed medium-term plan for the period 1992-1997, which identified the basic scope of the United Nations programme on TNCs in foreign direct investment, trade, transition of certain countries to a market economy and technical cooperation.

In 1991, the Centre offered unpaid internships to approximately 50 students of business, economics and law from Germany, Hong Kong, India, the Netherlands, Romania, Thailand, Trinidad and Tobago, Turkey and the United States, among others. The interns were able to make a useful contribution to the Centre's work, while gaining insight into the functioning of the Organization.

Information system

The Centre continued to develop its information system covering individual TNCs, industries and sectors, laws and regulations, contracts, macroeconomic data and information sources. The system provided access to directory, financial and historical information on more than 100,000 public and private companies worldwide. In 1991, it received some 2,700 requests for information, plus approximately 2,500 short, usually verbal, queries from Governments, intergovernmental, trade union and business organizations, academic institutions, and media and public interest groups.

The Centre added to the system a database covering environmental policies of 170 TNCs and finalized a computerized analytical inventory of more than 400 non-petroleum contracts and agreements. It provided information system expertise for the development of the Investment Promotion Centre in Namibia, the Registry of Foreign Investment Agreements in Ghana, a monitoring system of foreign investment projects in Thailand and an information system on technology transfer in Nepal. The Centre also made an information technology assessment for a CD-ROM database on company information in the Democratic People's Republic of Korea, and trained a number of officials from Nepal and the former USSR in the evaluation and use of information resources.

In a February report on information requirements for assessing the performance of corporate obligations,[3] the Secretary-General examined the need for reporting systems and information exchange between Governments or local enterprises and TNCs to track company performance and to ensure compliance with local laws and accountability of transborder operations. The report noted the increasing importance of access to corporate information for evaluating the financial state of companies, monitoring their development and environmental impact, and assessing the effectiveness of their operations. It reviewed national and international mechanisms for the specification of reporting requirements and the definition of accounting standards, and discussed the sharing of information within and between countries, as well as the locus of responsibility for data collection and analysis. The report assessed performance tracking systems being developed and recommended that Governments review existing legislation and administrative practices to ensure adequacy of information obtained and to consolidate their own reporting systems, introduce standardized reporting procedures and accounting regulations, analyse the collected information and make it accessible, and promote regular information exchange with other Governments.

Joint units with the regional commissions

The joint units established by the Centre on TNCs with the five regional commissions, serving as focal points of its activities in the respective regions, continued to make contributions in the fields of research, information and liaison with Governments.[2]

The Joint Unit with the Economic Commission for Africa (ECA) focused its research on corporate operations in the region and issues related to development financing. It also studied the role of TNCs in technology transfer to the African developing countries and in agricultural export products, and collected data on foreign direct investment with a view to establishing a regional database on TNCs. It also provided technical support to ECA, particularly in the area of environment and services. Missions were undertaken to Burundi, Senegal and Zambia to review the development of information systems on TNCs and related problems, to collect data on corporate foreign investment and to assess the role of TNCs in technology transfer.

The Joint Unit with the Economic Commission for Europe focused on projects related to foreign direct investment, privatization and restructuring of State-owned enterprises in Central and Eastern Europe. An ad hoc expert group meeting on the last subject was held at Geneva in September 1991. The Unit assisted in analysing the environmental impact of TNCs and represented the Centre at international meetings and conferences held in the region. It continued to support international organizations, Governments and government agencies on matters related to TNCs.

The Joint Unit established with the Economic and Social Commission for Asia and the Pacific (ESCAP) undertook and prepared for publication the following research projects: the impact of TNCs on the international trade of primary commodities; TNCs in selected service industries of developing countries in the region; and the contribution of TNCs to technology transfer in export processing zones and science parks in developing countries of Asia and the Pacific. The Unit also completed for publication a study of transnational technology towards the year 2000 and a review of the Asia-Pacific TNCs. It organized ad hoc expert group meetings on the role of TNCs in the international trade of primary commodities (Bangkok, Thailand 25-27 November 1991) and on the activities of TNCs and selected service industries of Asian and Pacific developing countries (Bangkok, 2-4 December). The Unit continued to collect, analyse and disseminate information and data on the activities of TNCs in the region. It also provided technical and information assistance and advisory services and disseminated information to ESCAP member States and its 13 focal points in the region.

The Joint Unit with the Economic Commission for Latin America and the Caribbean (ECLAC) placed particular emphasis on examining the role of foreign investment in changing production patterns and industrial restructuring in the region. The project included country case-studies on Brazil, Chile, Colombia and Mexico. The Unit continued its research on national policy frameworks on foreign direct investment in the region and related policy changes and published a number of manuals concerning transnational banks. It also carried out a study on investment opportunities in the former USSR and prepared a manual for a pilot computer programme on domestic information systems for decision-making on foreign investment (SITOD). The Unit continued to provide technical assistance to ECLAC member States, including a SITOD pilot project in Chile, legal advisory services to Peru and Venezuela and a technical cooperation project with Peru.

In September 1991, the Joint Unit with the Economic and Social Commission for Western Asia resumed its activities, suspended in August 1990 owing to the events in the Persian Gulf. Research projects due for completion included a two-volume technical paper on Arab petrochemicals and related protectionist policies of the European Community. The Unit also contributed to the Centre's project on TNCs and industrial restructuring in developing countries.

Research

In 1991, in cooperation with the United Nations Conference on Trade and Development (UNCTAD), the Centre on TNCs launched a project on the role of TNCs in world trade and exports from developing countries and undertook a study on the role of TNCs in the promotion of manufactured exports from developing countries through joint ventures and non-equity links, as well as a subsequently published study dealing with the impact of trade-related investment measures on trade and development.[4] A project on foreign direct investment, trade and international migration was initiated jointly with UNCTAD, the International Organization for Migration and the Friedrich Ebert Foundation. Together with the World Bank, the Centre began work on the *Handbook: Issues in the Liberalization of International Transactions in Services.* It also continued research on the role of small and medium-sized TNCs in the world economy.

The Centre published or completed for publication more than 80 studies, technical papers and parliamentary documents. The *World Investment Report 1991: The Triad in Foreign Direct Investment*[5] was the first in a series of annual reports on global trends in foreign direct investment and analyses of TNC-related subjects. The first two studies were issued in a new series on environmental responsibilities of TNCs, one of which recommended disclosure legislation for developing countries to enable accident prevention and emergency response.[6] The other focused on six transnational energy-producing and energy-consuming industries, in which corporate practices had an impact on global climate change.[7] The question of human resources development was addressed in

a three-volume university curriculum on TNCs[8] that provided a basis for long-term training of government and public sector officials in economic development and international business and law. The Centre also prepared a 1991 review of international accounting and reporting issues[9] and published studies on the influence of government policies on foreign investment[10] and factors that caused TNCs to undertake investments abroad.[11]

The implications of free economic zones for foreign direct investment in Central and Eastern Europe were examined in *The Challenge of Free Economic Zones in Central and Eastern Europe: International Perspectives,*[12] issued in early 1991. As a follow-up to the study, the Centre organized a series of international workshops on free economic zones in Ukraine (13-24 May 1991) and an international conference on the subject (Saint Petersburg, Russia, 10-14 December).

The Centre complemented its reference library with a selective bibliography on TNCs for 1988-1990[13] and a manual on transnational business information.[14] It completed for publication the ninth volume of *National Legislation and Regulations relating to Transnational Corporations*[15] and initial issues of the six-volume *World Investment Directory*[16] covering Asia and the Pacific, developed countries, Latin America and the Caribbean, Africa and Western Asia, Central and Eastern Europe, and global trends of foreign investment. The Centre also finalized a *Compendium of Selected International Instruments on Foreign Investment,* reproducing about 80 multilateral and regional instruments, and began work on the *Directory of the World's Largest Service Companies—Series Two.* It continued research for the *Fifth Survey on Transnational Corporations in World Development* and on the 20 volumes of its *UNCTC Library on Transnational Corporations.*

Technical cooperation

In 1991, the Centre on TNCs continued to focus its technical assistance activities on matters relating to economic reform, human resources and private sector development, and environment and natural resources management. In addition to developing countries, countries in transition to a market economy and those that had recently liberalized their policies to attract foreign investment also received assistance. Advisory, information and training assistance was provided to Afghanistan, Albania, Angola, Bulgaria, Côte d'Ivoire, Cuba, the Democratic People's Republic of Korea, Ethiopia, Ghana, Guinea, Guyana, Mongolia, Mozambique, Myanmar, Namibia, Nicaragua, Nigeria, Romania, Seychelles and Thailand, as well as members of the Commonwealth of Independent States.

The Centre provided advisory services to the African National Congress in formulating investment policies and an investment code for a new South Africa, and assisted in harmonizing fisheries arrangements in West Africa and investment laws in the eastern Caribbean, as well as economic integration in East and southern Africa. Training workshops addressed project analysis and evaluation, biotechnology, accounting, international procurement, technology transfer, joint ventures, international banking, privatization, free economic zones and international auditing. The Centre extended its programme to promote the creation and growth of small and medium-sized enterprises using linkages with TNCs to Zimbabwe, and planned to undertake feasibility studies for Botswana, Egypt, Kenya, Malawi and Mozambique. It also provided training assistance and advisory services on financial systems, access to capital markets and privatization activities, and organized a high-level round table on fiscal and administrative strategies for petroleum exploration and development. The Centre continued to assist developing countries to implement structural adjustment programmes aimed at achieving a more efficient use of their resources.

In February 1992, the Secretary-General reported to the Commission on experience gained in technical assistance activities involving the formulation of negotiation strategies to be adopted by developing countries when negotiating with TNCs.[17] The report focused on two aspects of major concern to developing countries—the sharing of financial benefits derived from TNCs' investment projects and the relationship between TNCs' activities and national development policy goals. It also highlighted the growing importance of environmental concerns in the negotiating process and the need of developing countries for technical assistance in formulating negotiating strategies. The report concluded that developing countries still faced serious limitations in obtaining up-to-date legal, economic and financial information and having available the expertise necessary to structure an appropriate contractual framework. The importance of efforts by the international community to provide such assistance on a priority basis was emphasized.

In April 1992,[1] the Commission requested the Secretary-General to submit to it in 1993 a report on the implementation of the programme on TNCs, including the activities of the joint units established with the regional commissions.

Financing

The resources for implementing the programme on TNCs were made available from the United Nations regular budget and from extrabudgetary funds from donor States.

During 1991, seven States contributed or pledged some $1.5 million to the Trust Fund of the Centre on TNCs. Expenditures in 1991 totalled $1.5 million; the Fund's balance at year's end was $2.7 million. Projects executed by the Centre under the fourth programming cycle (1987-1991) of the United Nations Development Programme (UNDP) totalled approximately $8.9 million. In 1991, some $3.5 million of UNDP funds were expended by the Centre on its technical cooperation programme.

ECONOMIC AND SOCIAL COUNCIL ACTION

On 30 July 1992, the Economic and Social Council, on the recommendation of its Economic Committee, adopted **resolution 1992/35** without vote.

Activities of the former United Nations Centre on Transnational Corporations and of its successor, the Transnational Corporations and Management Division of the Department of Economic and Social Development

The Economic and Social Council

1. *Takes note* of the reports of the Secretary-General on the question of trends in foreign direct investment, transnational corporations and economic growth through technology, transnational corporations in the new world economy: issues and policy implications, the international framework for transnational corporations and the activities of the former United Nations Centre on Transnational Corporations and of the joint units established with the regional commissions;

2. *Reaffirms* that the Commission on Transnational Corporations and the Transnational Corporations and Management Division of the Department of Economic and Social Development of the Secretariat are focal points within the United Nations system for matters concerning foreign direct investment as it relates to transnational corporations and that the mandate of the former United Nations Centre on Transnational Corporations is fully subsumed under this Division;

3. *Emphasizes* the importance of the research, technical cooperation, advisory services, training programmes and information services provided by the former United Nations Centre on Transnational Corporations to the States Members of the United Nations, and, to this end, affirms the importance of maintaining these activities and programmes as well as improving upon them, as appropriate, under the new administrative arrangements;

4. *Notes* the need for the Commission to examine, during its nineteenth session, the activities and programme of work of the Division in the field of foreign direct investment as it relates to transnational corporations in order to ensure coordination with, and avoid duplication of, the activities of other United Nations bodies;

5. *Stresses* the importance of transparency in the area of foreign direct investment, and requests the Division to contribute towards increasing that transparency in the framework of its technical assistance and information activities;

6. *Takes note* of the report of the Intergovernmental Working Group of Experts on International Standards of Accounting and Reporting, and reaffirms the importance of its work in contributing towards greater transparency in the activities of transnational corporations;

7. *Requests* the Division to assist developing countries in the creation of a favourable investment climate and, to that end, in the development of their endogenous capacity conducive to the encouragement of foreign investment;

8. *Also requests* the Division to continue to include in its technical cooperation activities advice on the interrelationship between foreign direct investment and interregional, regional and subregional economic integration;

9. *Further requests* the Division to examine ways and means of assisting member States, in particular developing countries, in attracting foreign investment, *inter alia*, through the setting up of joint ventures and free economic zones;

10. *Calls upon* the Division to strengthen its work concerning cooperation in and related to the transfer of technology;

11. *Requests* the Division to strengthen its activities in matters relating to the role of transnational corporations in the development of small and medium-sized enterprises;

12. *Also requests* the Division to study the effects of deregulation and privatization policies in developing countries on attracting foreign direct investment flows and, in this context, to make appropriate recommendations thereon;

13. *Takes note* of the consultations being undertaken by the President of the General Assembly in accordance with Assembly resolution 45/186 of 21 December 1990 on the code of conduct on transnational corporations;

14. *Encourages* the Division to strengthen and further develop the functions of the joint units established with the regional commissions, especially by developing programmes that are adapted to the needs of the respective regions;

15. *Invites* donor countries, particularly developed countries, to provide extra financial support for research, and the advisory and information work of the Division so as to contribute further to a better understanding between transnational corporations and developing countries;

16. *Requests* the Division to pay attention in particular to developing countries, especially the least developed countries and other countries in Africa that have faced a drop in foreign direct investment inflows, and to report thereon to the Commission at its nineteenth session;

17. *Takes note* of the conclusions of the United Nations symposium on globalization and developing countries, held at The Hague on 30 March 1992, and requests the Secretary-General, in collaboration with the United Nations Conference on Trade and Development and other organizations, to develop a joint programme on the interrelationship of investment, trade, technology and development, with a view to enhancing the contribution of transnational corporations to the development of developing countries through trade and investment, for consideration by the Commission at its nineteenth session.

Economic and Social Council resolution 1992/35

30 July 1992   Meeting 41   Adopted without vote

Approved by Economic Committee (E/1992/109/Add.3) without vote, 28 July (meeting 16); draft by Commission on TNCs (E/1992/26); agenda item 12 *(e)*.

REFERENCES

[1]E/1992/26. [2]E/C.10/1992/9. [3]E/C.10/1992/11. [4]*The Impact of Trade-related Investment Measures on Trade and Development: Theory, Evidence and Policy Implications*, Sales No. E.91.II.A.19. [5]*World Investment Report 1991: The Triad in Foreign Direct Investment*, Sales No. E.91.II.A.12. [6]*Transnational Corporations and Industrial Hazards Disclosure*, Sales No. E.91.II.A.18. [7]*Climate Change and Transnational Corporations: Analysis and Trends*, Sales No. E.92.II.A.7. [8]*University Curriculum on Transnational Corporations*, Sales Nos. E.91.II.A.5, E.91.II.A.6 & E.91.II.A.7. [9]*International Accounting and Reporting Issues: 1991 Review*, Sales No. E.92.II.A.8. [10]*Government Policies and Foreign Direct Investment*, Sales No. E.91.II.A.20. [11]*The Determinants of Foreign Direct Investment: A Survey of the Evidence*, Sales No. E.92.II.A.2. [12]*The Challenge of Free Economic Zones in Central and Eastern Europe: International Perspectives*, Sales No. E.90.II.A.27. [13]*Transnational Corporations: A Selective Bibliography, 1988-1990*, Sales No. E.91.II.A.10. [14]*Transnational Business Information: A Manual of Needs and Sources*, Sales No. E.91.II.A.13. [15]ST/CTC/105. [16]ST/CTC/66. [17]E/C.10/1992/10.

Chapter VI

Natural resources, energy and cartography

Natural resources exploration and energy resources development continued to be considered by a number of United Nations bodies in 1992, with the environmental aspects of increased exploitation of such resources receiving particular attention. The Committee on New and Renewable Sources of Energy met in February and considered, among other subjects, a paper on solar energy: a strategy in support of environment and development, which was submitted to the Preparatory Committee for the United Nations Conference on Environment and Development.

In January, the International Conference on Water and the Environment, in the Dublin Statement on Water and Sustainable Development, noted that scarcity and misuse of fresh water posed a serious and growing threat to sustainable development and protection of the environment. In December, the General Assembly declared that the World Day for Water would be observed on 22 March of each year, starting in 1993 (resolution 47/193).

In his annual report to the Assembly, the Director General of the International Atomic Energy Agency (IAEA) observed that expanded use of nuclear energy was an option for increasing energy generation without significantly adding to carbon dioxide emissions. The Assembly, in October, urged States to cooperate in carrying out IAEA's work and in promoting the use of nuclear energy and the application of measures to strengthen the safety of nuclear installations and to minimize risks to life, health and the environment.

The Sixth United Nations Conference on the Standardization of Geographical Names was held in New York in August/September 1992.

Natural resources

Exploration

**UN Revolving Fund for
Natural Resources Exploration**

During 1992, the United Nations Revolving Fund for Natural Resources Exploration (UNRFNRE), established by the General Assembly in 1973,[1] continued to assist developing countries in natural resources exploration and development.

Administered by the United Nations Development Programme (UNDP), the Fund was financed from voluntary contributions and donations in cash and kind, and replenishment contributions were required to be made from successful exploration projects, based on the proceeds of production. The first such replenishment was received in 1991.[2]

In 1992, pre-investment follow-up activities for successful mineral discoveries were carried out in the Congo, Guatemala and Honduras. The Yuscaran gold-silver deposit in Honduras attracted several private investors. The Fund assisted Guatemala to prepare a call for bids to develop its El Pato gold deposit. It also initiated steps to collect a $200 million reimbursable loan to the Congo for a feasibility study of an offshore phosphorite deposit; as at the end of the year, no payment had been received.

UNRFNRE had mineral exploration projects ongoing in five countries in 1992: the final report of the exploration for gold in the Suches area of Bolivia was completed; a report on the exploration for pyrophyllite deposits was submitted to China; chromite exploration in the Philippines continued with test pitting in the Mahayahay target area and the Fund announced its readiness to explore for epithermal gold deposits in northern Surigao; and, in the United Republic of Tanzania, exploration for gold began in the Canuck and Geita areas.

The Fund received requests for assistance in mineral exploration programmes from the Democratic People's Republic of Korea, Guinea, Mongolia, Myanmar, Namibia, Sri Lanka and Viet Nam, as well as for geothermal projects in China, Costa Rica, Mexico and Nicaragua. It was hoped that funds would become available to enable UNRFNRE to support those activities.

Committee on Natural Resources

Continuing its efforts to restructure and revitalize the United Nations in the economic, social and related fields (see PART THREE, Chapter XVIII), the General Assembly, at its resumed forty-sixth session in 1992, considered the status of its subsidiary bodies and those of the Economic and Social Council in those fields.

By **resolution 46/235** of 13 April, the Assembly proposed that the Committee on Natural

Resources should comprise 24 government-nominated experts from different Member States, elected by the Council for four-year terms. The Committee would have two working groups, one on minerals and one on water resources. Its mandate with respect to energy would be assumed by the Committee on New and Renewable Sources of Energy and on Energy for Development (see below). The Committee would meet for two weeks every two years and report to the Council with policy options and recommendations.

By **decision 1992/218** of 30 April, the Council abolished its standing Committee on Natural Resources and established a new expert Committee of the same name. It requested the Secretary-General to submit recommendations for the new Committee's programme of work, and decided that it should hold its first session from 22 March to 2 April 1993.

By **resolution 1992/62** of 31 July, the Council reaffirmed the mandate of the new Committee and approved the draft provisional agenda and programme of work for its first session.

Coordination of UN activities

In response to a 1991 Economic and Social Council request,[3] the Secretary-General, in his capacity as Chairman of the Administrative Committee on Coordination (ACC), included in ACC's annual overview report[4] a section on the most effective ways of enhancing coordination in the mineral and energy sectors.

Replying to a request by the Secretary-General, ACC members provided their views on the subject. New institutions and mechanisms were suggested by some organizations, while others felt that existing arrangements were adequate.

ACC members indicated a need for close coordination and cooperation among various parts of the system. In the past, ad hoc inter-agency consultations for specific purposes had been held as the need arose, a modality that should be retained.

The question of establishing new formal coordination mechanisms in the mineral and energy sectors would be taken up following action on restructuring by the General Assembly.

Mineral resources

In 1992,[5] the United Nations Department of Economic and Social Development (DESD) carried out 79 projects, with a total delivery of $13.1 million, in 40 countries in all phases of mineral development—prospecting, geological mapping, airborne geophysical surveys, establishment of a geological computerized database using the Geographic Information System, mineral policy and investment promotion advice, mineral economic

surveys, mine design and engineering, and environment protection and management. Many projects included institutional and human resources development components. Africa received 66 per cent of assistance provided, with the needs of least developed and land-locked countries, notably in the Sahel area, being stressed.

Some 20 short-term advisory missions took place, providing assistance in such areas as mineral-sector review, impact assessment of geological, geographic and environmental factors on life and poverty, the role of geological surveys in mitigating risks, evaluation of geological hazards, strategies for mitigation of volcanic hazards, formulation of legislative regulation, diamond exploration methodology and promotion, on-site evaluation and small-scale mining.

Most projects included a mining investment promotion component, including the constitution of user-friendly computerized geo-scientific databases, and many included the provision of legal and investment promotion services. Projects were implemented in Angola, Bolivia, Burkina Faso, Chad, Gabon, Guinea-Bissau, Jamaica, Mali, Mozambique, the Niger, Pakistan, the Philippines, Togo, Uganda and Yemen. DESD organized an Interregional Seminar on Foreign Investment and Joint Ventures in the Mining Sector (Haikou, China, 7-11 December).

Small-scale mining activities gained recognition, particularly as a means of providing employment opportunities in rural areas: in Mali, river-beds were dredged for mining cooperatives; in Burkina Faso, auriferous alluvials were processed; in the Lao People's Democratic Republic, alluvial gold targets were evaluated and testing for sluice recovery of gold from the Mekong River was about to start; and in Jamaica, a mobile mining task force successfully opened seven marble quarry sites. Projects also included training components: in Ethiopia, national personnel would be trained to provide advisory services to mines and prepare models for demonstrations at selected sites; and, in Mozambique, coal degasification techniques were taught.

The protection of the environment was a major concern in formulating new projects. Environmental baseline studies were carried out as a part of feasibility studies of mineral deposits in Nepal, Pakistan and Thailand.

Water resources

During the year, DESD executed 95 projects in water resources development, with a total delivery of $15.4 million. Projects and advisory missions covered water resources planning, engineering, legislation, rural water supply (including well drilling), maintenance and community participation and computer applications to surface and groundwater development and management.

Innovative large-scale projects were developed in the Central African Republic and Guinea-Bissau, financed by the United Nations Capital Development Fund and UNDP, focusing on the socio-economic aspects of water supply and sanitation in rural areas, with special emphasis on community participation and the role of women. The goal of a project in southern Africa was the integrated and environmentally sound management of the area's water resources to allow sustainable development. Projects in China, Pakistan and the Lake Chad basin (involving Cameroon, Chad, the Niger and Nigeria) also had a strong environmental component.

Interregional workshops were organized on the role of women in environmentally sound and sustainable development (Beijing, China, 9-15 September) and on the testing of training modules on women, water supply and sanitation (Bangkok, Thailand, 21-25 September).

International Conference on Water and the Environment

The International Conference on Water and the Environment (Dublin, Ireland, 26-31 January 1992) adopted, at its closing session, the Dublin Statement on Water and Sustainable Development. In March,[6] the Conference's Secretary-General submitted the Statement and the report of the Conference to the Preparatory Committee for the United Nations Conference on Environment and Development (UNCED) (see PART THREE, Chapter VIII). The Dublin Conference, attended by 500 participants, including government-designated experts from 100 countries and representatives of 80 international, intergovernmental and non-governmental organizations, was convened by the World Meteorological Organization on behalf of the organizations of the United Nations represented in the ACC Intersecretariat Group for Water Resources.

The Dublin Statement noted that scarcity and misuse of fresh water posed a serious and growing threat to sustainable development and protection of the environment. Human health and welfare, food security, industrial development and the ecosystems on which they depended were all at risk unless water and land resources were managed more effectively. The Statement listed four guiding principles on which action recommended in the Conference report was based: fresh water was a finite and vulnerable resource, essential to sustain life, development and the environment; water development and management should be based on a participatory approach, involving users, planners and policy makers; women played a central part in providing, managing and safeguarding

water; and water had an economic value and should be recognized as an economic good.

Based on those principles, the Statement proposed an action agenda covering alleviation of poverty and disease, protection against natural disasters, water conservation and reuse, sustainable urban development, agricultural production and rural water supply, protecting aquatic ecosystems and resolving water conflicts. It also addressed the need for an enabling environment to implement the action agenda and the need for follow-up mechanisms.

The report of the Conference contained further recommendations dealing with integrated water resources development and management, water resources assessment and impacts of climate change on water resources, protection of water resources, water quality and aquatic ecosystems, water and sustainable urban development and drinking-water supply and sanitation in the urban context, water for sustainable food production and rural development and drinking-water supply and sanitation in the rural context, mechanisms for implementation and coordination at international, national and local levels, and options for follow-up.

UN Conference on Environment and Development

Agenda 21, adopted in June 1992 by UNCED,[7] contained a chapter on the protection of the quality and supply of freshwater resources: application of integrated approaches to the development, management and use of water resources.

The Conference proposed a number of programme areas: integrated water resources development and management; water resources assessment; protection of water resources, water quality and aquatic ecosystems; drinking-water supply and sanitation; water and sustainable urban development; water for sustainable food production and rural development; and impacts of climate change on water resources. For each programme area, the Conference set a number of objectives and recommended activities to achieve them.

Inter-agency coordination

The ACC Intersecretariat Group for Water Resources (New York, 7-9 October 1992)[8] discussed strengthening coordination and cooperation in the field of water resources, including follow-up action on issues stemming from the Dublin Conference and UNCED.

GENERAL ASSEMBLY ACTION

On 22 December 1992, on the recommendation of the Second (Economic and Financial) Committee, the General Assembly adopted without vote **resolution 47/193.**

Observance of World Day for Water

The General Assembly,

Recalling the relevant provisions of chapter 18 of Agenda 21, adopted by the United Nations Conference on Environment and Development,

Considering that the extent to which water resource development contributes to economic productivity and social well-being is not widely appreciated, although all social and economic activities rely heavily on the supply and quality of fresh water,

Considering also that, as populations and economic activities grow, many countries are rapidly reaching conditions of water scarcity or facing limits to economic development,

Considering further that the promotion of water conservation and sustainable management requires public awareness at local, national, regional and international levels,

1. *Decides* to declare 22 March of each year World Day for Water, to be observed starting in 1993, in conformity with the recommendations of the United Nations Conference on Environment and Development contained in chapter 18 of Agenda 21;

2. *Invites* States to devote the Day, as appropriate in the national context, to concrete activities such as the promotion of public awareness through the publication and diffusion of documentaries and the organization of conferences, round tables, seminars and expositions related to the conservation and development of water resources and the implementation of the recommendations of Agenda 21;

3. *Invites* the Secretary-General to make recommendations on ways and means by which the United Nations Secretariat could, within existing resources and without prejudice to ongoing activities, assist countries in organizing their national activities for the observance of World Day for Water;

4. *Requests* the Secretary-General to make the necessary arrangements in order to ensure the success of the observance of World Day for Water by the United Nations;

5. *Also requests* the Secretary-General to focus observance of World Day for Water by the United Nations on a particular theme relating to the conservation of water resources;

6. *Recommends* that the Commission on Sustainable Development, in the execution of its mandate, attach priority to the implementation of chapter 18 of Agenda 21.

General Assembly resolution 47/193

22 December 1992   Meeting 93   Adopted without vote

Approved by Second Committee (A/47/719) without vote, 16 December (meeting 51); draft by Malaysia (A/C.2/47/L.63), orally amended by Morocco; agenda item 79.

REFERENCES

[1]YUN 1973, p. 408, GA res. 3167(XXVIII), 17 Dec. 1973. [2]YUN 1991, p. 469. [3]Ibid., p. 472, ESC. res. 1991/90, 26 July 1991. [4]E/1992/11. [5]DP/1993/39/Add.1. [6]A/CONF.151/PC/112. [7]*Report of the United Nations Conference on Environment and Development, Rio de Janeiro, 3-14 June 1992*, vol.I (A/CONF.151/26/Rev.1, vol. I), Sales No. E.93.I.8. [8]ACC/1992/29 & Corr.1.

Energy

In June,[1] UNCED (see PART THREE, Chapter VIII) adopted Agenda 21, which contained a chapter dealing with changing consumption patterns. The Conference recommended a number of activities to encourage greater efficiency in the use of energy and resources, noting that reducing the amount of energy and materials used per unit in producing goods and services could contribute to both the alleviation of environmental stress and greater economic and industrial productivity and competitiveness. It was therefore recommended that Governments should encourage the dissemination of existing environmentally sound technologies and promote research and development in such technologies, assist developing countries to use those technologies efficiently and develop technologies suited to their own circumstances, encourage the environmentally sound use of new and renewable sources of energy, and encourage the environmentally sound and sustainable use of renewable natural resources.

Energy resources development

In response to a General Assembly resolution of 1990,[2] the Secretary-General submitted in May 1992 a report on energy exploration and development trends in developing countries.[3] The report analysed trends in energy consumption, exploration, development and production and made projections for future financial requirements and investments. Forecasts to the year 2010 indicated that energy demand in the developing countries would grow at an average annual rate of 4.4 per cent, much higher than the expected rate of 1.8 per cent in the developed market economies. Half of the increase in world energy demand would be in the developing countries. However, on a per capita basis, only marginal improvement could be expected in the current situation, where the level of energy consumption in those countries was about 10 per cent of that in the developed market economies.

Oil would continue to dominate consumption in the developing world. Coal would retain its overall position and be of great importance to a few countries, particularly China and India. Natural gas, the third most important fuel, would be more widely used, and the fast growth in electricity consumption would continue. In the absence of technological breakthroughs in new and renewable sources of energy, their contribution would remain static. Massive capital investments and the application of modern technologies would be required in the developing countries to meet domestic demand. New arrangements would be needed to promote international cooperation in the energy area of the world economy.

Technical cooperation

During 1992,[4] DESD carried out 50 missions to developing countries to provide advice on energy policy, resource evaluation and exploration, project design and feasibility studies in the areas of petroleum, coal, natural gas, electric power, energy planning and conservation, geothermal, solar, wind and multi-source renewable energy packages, information systems and microcomputer-based energy analysis. The Department executed 89 projects in the energy field with a total delivery of $10.5 million.

On the basis of a survey at sites in 41 developing countries during the 1980s, DESD in 1992 launched a programme on enhancement of small-scale hydropower resources in developing countries. The programme included environmental and socio-economic considerations. DESD continued to review and update existing studies and to select sites for further investigation.

At their request, DESD assisted the countries of Eastern Europe and the Commonwealth of Independent States to restructure energy-sector institutions, in energy/environmental impact assessment and with energy efficiency advisory services. In Viet Nam, DESD and the World Bank undertook a review of energy-sector investments and policies, covering energy/economic interactions, the feasibility of building a refinery and developments in the coal sector. It also analysed an option to interconnect the northern and southern electricity grids, and assessed the condition and investment requirements of existing hydro and thermal powerplants.

Embarking on a programme to expand and improve coal utilization, China assigned priority to implementing the following DESD-formulated programme elements: control of environmental pollution from coal combustion in four cities; transfer and development of methods to predict, mitigate and eliminate karst water inflows into coal beds under development; and access to and training in high-production mining techniques in thick coal seams through seminars, visits to productive mines and technical workshops with manufacturers of high-seam equipment.

Meetings organized by DESD included a study tour on small-scale hydropower (China, 14-27 June) and reinjection of geothermal fluids (Costa Rica, 10-12 November).

ECONOMIC AND SOCIAL COUNCIL ACTION

On 31 July 1992, on the recommendation of its Economic Committee, the Economic and Social Council adopted without vote **resolution 1992/56**.

Development of the energy resources of developing countries

The Economic and Social Council,

Reaffirming the critical importance of the development of energy resources of developing countries and the need for measures by the international community to assist and support the efforts of developing countries, in particular the energy-deficient among them, to develop their energy resources in order to meet their needs through cooperation, assistance and investment in the fields of conventional and of new and renewable sources of energy, consistent with their national policies, plans and priorities,

Reaffirming also that the developing countries have the primary responsibility for the strategies and policies for exploration and development of their energy resources,

Recognizing the importance of sustainable development,

1. *Takes note with appreciation* of the report of the Secretary-General on energy exploration and development trends in developing countries;

2. *Reaffirms* that an adequate flow of external resources in support of the national efforts of developing countries, in particular the energy-deficient among them, is needed to finance, within the legislative framework of each country, the exploration and development of their energy resources;

3. *Requests* the Secretary-General to keep the matter under constant review and to submit to the Economic and Social Council at its substantive session of 1994 a report on the efforts made in this regard;

4. *Also requests* the Secretary-General to report to the Economic and Social Council at its substantive session of 1994 on the role of the United Nations in devising ways and means of mobilizing the international community to increase efforts for comprehensive national, bilateral and multilateral measures to accelerate the exploration and development of energy resources in developing countries, with full respect for their national sovereignty;

5. *Further requests* the Secretary-General to draw this matter to the attention of the Committee on New and Renewable Sources of Energy and on Energy for Development at its first substantive session.

Economic and Social Council resolution 1992/56

31 July 1992   Meeting 42   Adopted without vote

Approved by Economic Committee (E/1992/109/Add.1) without vote, 28 July (meeting 16); draft by Vice-Chairman (E/1992/C.1/L.18), based on informal consultations on draft by Pakistan for Group of 77 (E/1992/C.1/L.1); agenda item 12 (h).

GENERAL ASSEMBLY ACTION

By **decision 47/435** of 18 December, the General Assembly took note of the Secretary-General's report on energy exploration and development trends in developing countries.

New and renewable energy resources

The Committee on the Development and Utilization of New and Renewable Sources of Energy, established by the General Assembly in 1982,[5] held its sixth session in New York from 3 to 14 February 1992.[6] The Committee discussed the implementation of the 1981 Nairobi Programme of Action for the Development and Utilization of New and Renewable Sources of Energy[7] and mobilization of financial resources for its implementation. It also considered two substantive themes: the contribution of new and renewable sources of energy to decentralized energy systems and to specific multi-purpose medium- to large-scale applications; and promotion of rapid and effective transfer of technology in new and renewable sources of energy to developing countries. The Secretary-General submitted reports on the first[8] and second[9] themes. He also submitted a report on the activities of the United Nations system regarding the two themes.[10]

Also before the Committee were reports by the Secretary-General on the following subjects: a strategy for solar energy in support of environment and development;[11] activities being carried out by the entities within the United Nations system in the field of new and renewable sources of energy;[12] mobilization of financial resources and inter-agency coordination;[13] and progress achieved in the follow-up of substantive themes selected for detailed consideration by the Committee at its 1988 and 1990 sessions.[14] The Committee also considered the report of the 1991 meeting of the Intergovernmental Group of Experts on New and Renewable Sources of Energy[15] and the report of an October 1991 symposium on hydropower, held at Oslo, Norway.[16]

On 14 February, the Committee adopted two decisions. By the first,[17] it requested the Secretary-General to transmit to the Preparatory Committee for UNCED his report on solar energy,[11] the report of the Intergovernmental Group of Experts on New and Renewable Sources of Energy,[15] the report of the symposium on hydropower[16] and a pre-feasibility survey on a proposed network of centres of excellence on new and renewable sources of energy. By the second decision,[18] the Committee approved the provisional agenda and documentation for its seventh (1994) session.

The ACC Inter-Agency Group on New and Renewable Sources of Energy (New York, 3 and 4 February)[19] also discussed the substantive themes chosen for consideration by the Committee.

On 7 February, the Economic and Social Council, by **decision 1992/207**, decided that, when considering the report of the Committee on its sixth session, it would not consider new draft proposals, except for specific recommendations that required action by the Council and proposals related to coordination aspects of the Committee's work. By **decision 1992/299** of 31 July, the Council took note of the Committee's report.

On 18 December, the General Assembly also took note of the Committee's report by **decision 47/434**.

Committee name change

As part of the process of restructuring and revitalization of the United Nations in the economic, social and related fields, the General Assembly, by **resolution 46/235** of 13 April, changed the name of the Committee on the Development and Utilization of New and Renewable Sources of Energy to the Committee on New and Renewable Sources of Energy and on Energy for Development. In addition to its current mandate, the new Committee would take over the mandate of the old Committee on Natural Resources (see above) as it pertained to energy.

By **decision 1992/218** of 30 April, the Economic and Social Council established the Committee on New and Renewable Sources of Energy and on Energy for Development. On 31 July, by **resolution 1992/62**, the Council reaffirmed the mandate of the new Committee.

Energy use and air emissions

In response to a 1988 General Assembly request,[20] the Secretary-General submitted in October 1992 a report[21] on structural change in the world economy and the implications for energy use and emissions of carbon dioxide, sulphur dioxide and nitrogen oxides. The report discussed macroeconomic trends and gave projections of production and air emissions to the year 2020 under three different scenarios for economic growth, with particular reference to the energy-intensive economic sectors. Based on the same scenarios, future structural changes in the world economy were also considered; the possible changes were determined by projected trends in the level and composition of investment, foreign trade and consumption, and by assumed interregional patterns of moderate technology diffusion. In turn, those projected trends were used to determine different rates of growth of economic activities and thus of energy and materials requirements and levels of air emissions.

The report concluded that output of energy-intensive materials such as metals, chemicals, cement, fertilizers and paper typically grew rapidly during the intermediate stage of industrialization. That pattern of structural transformation was already taking place in a number of developing countries and was expected to continue. Even with considerable increases in energy-use efficiency and reductions in air emissions per unit of gross domestic product, the world's annual consumption of fossil fuels would double by the year 2020. Emissions of carbon dioxide and nitrogen oxides would increase proportionately, while emissions of sulphur dioxide would rise by more than 40 per cent.

To reduce or at least limit the long-term growth of global emissions, especially of carbon dioxide, options considered needed to be extended beyond slowing the world's economic growth. Technologies already existed to reduce nitrogen oxides and sulphur dioxide emissions substantially at costs that would be acceptable with high economic growth. The growth of carbon dioxide emissions could be limited through higher efficiency in energy use and lower inputs of materials in various production processes, and through a better mix of carbon fuels and substitution of other, carbon-free energy sources.

Reductions of carbon dioxide emissions through fuel switching would be feasible in many regions, especially those with large natural gas reserves. A massive change-over from coal and oil to natural gas, however, would require greatly expanded exploration and production, and the collaboration of the world's major coal and oil users. High capital investment would be required to develop an integrated system for world trade in natural gas and to develop the vast hydropower potential of developing countries, which was estimated to equal half of the world's annual consumption of oil.

By **decision 47/444** of 22 December, the General Assembly took note of the Secretary-General's report.

Nuclear energy

IAEA report

In an August note,[22] the Secretary-General transmitted the 1991 report of the International Atomic Energy Agency to the General Assembly. Presenting and updating the report in the Assembly on 21 October, the IAEA Director General recalled that IAEA had been established 35 years earlier to promote the peaceful uses of the atom for development and to verify that commitments to exclusively peaceful uses were respected (see PART SEVEN, Chapter I, for further information on IAEA activities).

The Director General addressed the issue of non-proliferation of nuclear weapons (see PART ONE, Chapter II), IAEA's safeguards system, including inspections to monitor Iraq's compliance with Security Council resolutions (see PART TWO, Chapter III), peaceful applications, environmental protection and nuclear safety and public opinion.

The peaceful applications of nuclear technology were significant. For example, 17 per cent of the world's electricity came from nuclear-power reactors; every third patient in industrialized countries was being examined or treated by a nuclear-related method; and the cotton crop in Pakistan and the rice crop in Indonesia had been boosted by the use of suitable mutagens, new strains produced through mutations induced by irradiating seeds.

Nuclear techniques were also being used to monitor and protect the environment. Isotopes were a tool in the fight against groundwater and soil contamination through excessive use of fertilizers; they allowed precise measurement of the amount of fertilizer that went into the plant so that

the most appropriate fertilizer regime could be established. Similarly, nuclear techniques allowed the determination of the amount of nitrogen that different crop plants obtained from the soil, leading to better fertilizer strategies. Most controversial was the question of how helpful nuclear power could be in generating the increasing amounts of electricity which the world would need without emitting carbon dioxide into the atmosphere and thereby contributing to a possible global warming. There was a growing awareness that expanded use of nuclear energy was one of the few options for increasing energy generation without significantly adding to carbon dioxide emissions.

However, it was still true that the use of nuclear power was opposed by a sizeable segment of public opinion for fear of accidental radioactive releases or from concern about the disposal of nuclear wastes. A draft convention on nuclear safety was being negotiated within IAEA and efforts were under way to work out internationally agreed radioactive-waste safety standards.

GENERAL ASSEMBLY ACTION

On 22 October 1992, the General Assembly adopted **resolution 47/8** by recorded vote.

Report of the International Atomic Energy Agency

The General Assembly,

Having received the report of the International Atomic Energy Agency to the General Assembly for the year 1991,

Taking note of the statement of the Director General of the International Atomic Energy Agency of 21 October 1992, which provides additional information on the main developments in the activities of the Agency during 1992,

Recognizing the importance of the work of the Agency to promote further the application of atomic energy for peaceful purposes, as envisaged in its statute,

Also recognizing the special needs of the developing countries for technical assistance by the Agency in order to benefit effectively from the application of nuclear technology for peaceful purposes as well as from the contribution of nuclear energy to their economic development,

Conscious of the importance of the work of the Agency in the implementation of safeguards provisions of the Treaty on the Non-Proliferation of Nuclear Weapons and other international treaties, conventions and agreements designed to achieve similar objectives, as well as in ensuring, as far as it is able, that the assistance provided by the Agency or at its request or under its supervision or control is not used in such a way as to further any military purpose, as stated in article II of its statute,

Further recognizing the importance of the work of the Agency on nuclear power, applications of nuclear methods and techniques, nuclear safety, radiological protection and radioactive waste management, including its work directed towards assisting developing countries in planning for the introduction of nuclear power in accordance with their needs,

Again stressing the need for the highest standards of safety in the design and operation of nuclear plants so as to minimize risks to life, health and the environment,

Noting the statements and actions of the Agency concerning non-compliance by Iraq with its non-proliferation obligations,

Bearing in mind resolutions GC(XXXVI)/RES/577 on the nuclear capabilities of South Africa, GC(XXXVI)/RES/579 on non-compliance by Iraq with its safeguards obligations, GC(XXXVI)/RES/582 on measures to strengthen international cooperation in matters relating to nuclear safety and radiological protection, GC(XXXVI)/RES/583 on revision of the Basic Safety Standards for Radiation Protection, GC(XXXVI)/RES/584 on education and training in radiation protection and nuclear safety, GC(XXXVI)/RES/585 on liability for nuclear damage, GC(XXXVI)/RES/586 on strengthening the effectiveness and improving the efficiency of the safeguards system, GC(XXXVI)/RES/587 on strengthening of the main activities of the Agency, GC(XXXVI)/RES/588 on practical utilization of food irradiation in developing countries, GC(XXXVI)/RES/592 entitled "Plan for producing potable water economically", and GC(XXXVI)/RES/601 on the application of safeguards of the Agency in the Middle East, adopted on 25 September 1992 by the General Conference of the Agency at its thirty-sixth regular session,

1. *Takes note* of the report of the International Atomic Energy Agency;

2. *Affirms* its confidence in the role of the Agency in the application of nuclear energy for peaceful purposes;

3. *Urges* all States to strive for effective and harmonious international cooperation in carrying out the work of the Agency, pursuant to its statute; in promoting the use of nuclear energy and the application of the necessary measures to strengthen further the safety of nuclear installations and to minimize risks to life, health and the environment; in strengthening technical assistance and cooperation for developing countries; and in ensuring the effectiveness and efficiency of the safeguards system of the Agency;

4. *Welcomes* the decisions taken by the Agency to strengthen its safeguards system;

5. *Welcomes also* the decisions taken by the Agency to strengthen its technical assistance and cooperation activities;

6. *Commends* the Director General of the Agency and his staff for their strenuous efforts in the implementation of Security Council resolutions 687(1991) of 3 April 1991, 707(1991) of 15 August 1991 and 715(1991) of 11 October 1991, in particular the detection and destruction or otherwise rendering harmless of equipment and material which could be used for nuclear weapons;

7. *Requests* the Secretary-General to transmit to the Director General of the Agency the records of the forty-seventh session of the General Assembly relating to the activities of the Agency.

General Assembly resolution 47/8

22 October 1992   Meeting 45   146-0-5 (recorded vote)

42-nation draft (A/47/L.9/Rev.1 & Add.1); agenda item 14.

Sponsors: Albania, Argentina, Australia, Belarus, Belgium, Bolivia, Botswana, Bulgaria, Canada, Chile, Colombia, Costa Rica, Czechoslovakia, Denmark, Estonia, Finland, Germany, Greece, Hungary, Italy, Japan, Latvia, Lithuania, Luxembourg, Malawi, Malta, Netherlands, New Zealand, Norway, Poland, Portugal, Republic of Korea, Romania, Russian Federation, Samoa, Spain, Sweden, Togo, Turkey, Ukraine, United Kingdom, United States.

Meeting numbers. GA 47th session: plenary 44, 45.

Recorded vote in Assembly as follows:

In favour: Afghanistan, Albania, Algeria, Angola, Antigua and Barbuda, Argentina, Armenia, Australia, Austria, Azerbaijan, Bahrain, Bangladesh, Barbados, Belarus, Belgium, Belize, Bhutan, Bolivia, Botswana, Brazil, Brunei Darussalam, Bulgaria, Burkina Faso, Cameroon, Canada, Cape Verde, Chile, China, Colombia, Comoros, Congo, Costa Rica, Côte d'Ivoire, Croatia, Cyprus, Czechoslovakia, Democratic People's Republic of Korea, Denmark, Djibouti, Ecuador, Egypt, El Salvador, Estonia, Ethiopia, Fiji, Finland, France, Gabon, Gambia, Germany, Ghana, Greece, Grenada, Guatemala, Guinea, Guinea-Bissau, Guyana, Haiti, Honduras, Hungary, Iceland, India, Indonesia, Iran, Ireland, Israel, Italy, Jamaica, Japan, Kazakhstan, Kenya, Kuwait, Lao People's Democratic Republic, Latvia, Lebanon, Lesotho, Liberia, Libyan Arab Jamahiriya, Liechtenstein, Lithuania, Luxembourg, Malaysia, Maldives, Mali, Malta, Marshall Islands, Mauritania, Mauritius, Mexico, Micronesia, Mongolia, Morocco, Mozambique, Myanmar, Namibia, Nepal, Netherlands, New Zealand, Niger, Nigeria, Norway, Oman, Pakistan, Panama, Papua New Guinea, Peru, Philippines, Poland, Portugal, Qatar, Republic of Korea, Republic of Moldova, Romania, Russian Federation, Rwanda, Saint Lucia, Samoa, Sao Tome and Principe, Saudi Arabia, Senegal, Singapore, Slovenia, Solomon Islands, Spain, Sri Lanka, Suriname, Swaziland, Sweden, Syrian Arab Republic, Thailand, Togo, Tunisia, Turkey, Uganda, Ukraine, United Arab Emirates, United Kingdom, United Republic of Tanzania, United States, Uruguay, Vanuatu, Venezuela, Viet Nam, Zaire, Zambia, Zimbabwe.

Against: None.

Abstaining: Cuba, Iraq, Jordan, Sudan, Yemen.

Before the vote on the draft text as a whole, separate votes were registered on two paragraphs. The eighth preambular paragraph was adopted by a recorded vote of 123 to 1 (Iraq), with 10 abstentions. Operative paragraph 6 was retained by 124 votes to 1 (Iraq), with 10 abstentions.

REFERENCES

[1]*Report of the United Nations Conference on Environment and Development, Rio de Janeiro, 3-14 June 1992*, vol. I (A/CONF.151/26/Rev.1, vol.I), Sales No. E.93.I.8. [2]GA res. 45/209, 21 Dec. 1990. [3]A/47/202-E/1992/51. [4]DP/1993/39/Add.1. [5]YUN 1982, p. 896, GA res. 37/250, 21 Dec. 1982. [6]A/47/36. [7]YUN 1981, p. 689. [8]A/AC.218/1992/2. [9]A/AC.218/1992/3. [10]A/AC.218/1992/4. [11]A/AC.218/1992/5/Rev.1. [12]A/AC.218/1992/6. [13]A/AC.218/1992/7. [14]A/AC.218/1992/8. [15]YUN 1991, p. 478. [16]A/AC.218/1992/10. [17]A/47/36 (dec. 1(VI)). [18]Ibid. (dec. 2(VI)). [19]ACC/1992/4. [20]GA res. 43/194, 20 Dec. 1988. [21]A/47/388. [22]A/47/374.

Cartography

During 1992,[1] DESD assisted various developing countries in applying remote sensing techniques for mapping and map updating. In Uganda, for example, satellite imagery was taken of the entire territory of the country. Comparison of that imagery with existing 30-year-old maps facilitated the preparation of revised and updated maps. Surveys of deep-sea areas were completed in Trinidad and Tobago. The country would be able to undertake work to manage and protect its marine environment effectively, particularly with regard to offshore hazards and the definition of sea lanes to cope with the heavy traffic of crude-oil carriers in the area.

In collaboration with the Earth Observation Satellite Company (United States) and the International Society for Photogrammetry and Remote Sensing, DESD organized a seminar on photogrammetry and remote sensing (Washington, D.C., 2-14 August) to benefit developing countries.

Standardization of geographical names

The Sixth United Nations Conference on the Standardization of Geographical Names, held in New York from 25 August to 3 September 1992,[2] was attended by 154 representatives and observers from 67 countries, the Holy See, the United Nations Educational, Scientific and Cultural Organization and the Commission of the European Communities (for participating States, see APPENDIX III). The Permanent Observer Mission of Palestine to the United Nations and five international scientific organizations also took part.

The Conference considered reports of linguistic/geographical divisions and of Governments on the situations in their regions and countries and on progress made in the standardization of geographical names since the Fifth (1987) Conference.[3]

It established three committees—on national, technical, and international programmes—to consider national standardization, the creation of toponymic data files, the reduction of exonyms, terminology, the naming of features beyond a single sovereignty, romanization and conversion into non-Roman writing systems, and toponymic education and practice. The Conference also considered the economic and social benefits of national and international standardization of geographical names, measures taken and proposed to implement United Nations resolutions on the standardization of geographical names, technical assistance and international cooperation.

The Conference adopted 15 resolutions. It recommended that an Africa South Division, a Baltic Division, and an Eastern Europe, Northern and Central Asia Division of the United Nations Group of Experts on Geographical Names be established, reflecting changes in those regions. Noting that the linguistic/geographical division of Latin America was not represented at the Conference, it recommended that Brazil, El Salvador, Mexico, Portugal, Spain and Venezuela reactivate the division. It also noted the increasing number of countries having toponymic guidelines for map editors and advised the United Nations to publish them in combined volumes. Owing to political changes in certain Member States, the Conference recommended that the affected countries should provide the Expert Group with information on changes of geographical names every six months. Given the sensitivity to deliberate changing of geographical names, the Conference reaffirmed a resolution of the Third (1977) Conference,[4] which had emphasized that geographical names given and/or standardized by a body other than the nationally authorized one should not be recognized by the United Nations. To facilitate uniform terminology, the Conference recommended that the Secretariat should translate the glossary of toponymic terminology, prepared in English by the Expert Group, into the five other official languages of the Organization. It also recommended that the United Nations should provide financial assistance to developing countries to organize seminars and training courses on applied toponymy.

The Conference approved the statute of the United Nations Group of Experts on Geographical Names and recommended that the Economic and Social Council also approve it. It also recommended to the Council that the Seventh Conference be held in 1997, that it accept Iran's offer to act as host and that it request the Secretary-General to take measures to implement the Sixth Conference's recommendations.

Group of Experts. The United Nations Group of Experts on Geographical Names held its sixteenth session in New York on 24 August and 4 September 1992.[5] On 24 August, it discussed the organization of the Sixth Conference and reviewed its own statute. On 4 September, it discussed the implementation of the Conference's recommendations, the status of its various working groups and the provisional agenda of its seventeenth (1994) session.

REFERENCES

[1]DP/1993/39/Add.1. [2]E/1993/21. [3]YUN 1987, p. 575. [4]YUN 1977, p. 813. [5]GEGN/16.

Chapter VII

Science and technology

In 1992, the United Nations continued its efforts to strengthen the scientific and technological areas of development. As a result of the restructuring of the United Nations Secretariat, the activities of the Centre for Science and Technology for Development were incorporated into the new Science, Technology, Energy, Environment and Natural Resources Division of the Department of Economic and Social Development. In April, as decided by the General Assembly, the Economic and Social Council established a new Commission on Science and Technology for Development to replace the Assembly's Intergovernmental Committee on Science and Technology for Development and its subsidiary body, the Advisory Committee on Science and Technology for Development.

During the year, two major United Nations conferences—the eighth session of the United Nations Conference on Trade and Development (Cartagena de Indias, Colombia, 8-25 February) and the United Nations Conference on Environment and Development (Rio de Janeiro, Brazil, 3-14 June)—contributed significantly to the new perspectives and directions of science and technology. The Cartagena Commitment and the Rio Declaration adopted by these Conferences made recommendations for the enhancement of the role of science and technology in developing countries, particularly with regard to the transfer and development of technology and transfer of environmentally sound technology.

Science and technology for development

Implementation of the Vienna Programme of Action

General aspects

Throughout 1992, several United Nations bodies and organizations continued to implement the 1979 Vienna Programme of Action on Science and Technology for Development.[1] The Programme of Action, whose goals were reaffirmed by the General Assembly in 1989 following an end-of-decade review,[2] had as its objectives: strengthening the scientific and technological capacities of developing countries by mobilizing financial resources; upgrading institutional arrangements; improving the balance of international flows of technology; and restructuring the existing pattern of international scientific and technological relations.

In 1990,[3] the Committee for Programme and Coordination (CPC) had requested the Secretary-General to submit in 1992 a conclusive report on problems associated with the implementation of the Programme of Action. In March 1992,[4] the Secretary-General indicated that, in view of the need to take into account the decisions on the legislative organs expected to be taken by the General Assembly in April (see below), it would be untimely to prepare the requested report. The Department of Economic and Social Development (DESD) would therefore submit an oral report.

At the first part of its thirty-second session (May),[5] CPC heard DESD's oral report and expressed regret that the report it had requested had not been prepared. It decided to discuss at the resumed session the issue of science and technology for development in the context of revisions to the medium-term plan for 1992-1997 and the revised estimates of the 1992-1993 programme budget.

At the resumed session (August/September),[5] CPC recommended approval of revisions to programme 17 of the medium-term plan, dealing with science and technology for sustainable development. It also recommended that the General Assembly review the proposed revisions to the titles of the programme and its subprogramme 1 in the light of relevant mandates; pending an Assembly decision on the issue, the existing titles should remain.

Proposed global information network

In response to a 1991 Economic and Social Council request,[6] the Secretary-General submitted in June 1992 a report,[7] containing information provided by organizations and agencies of the United Nations system on their international cooperation activities in the field of informatics, and on arrangements for cooperation and coordination with other parts of the system.

The report noted that the informatics activities reported reflected the diversity of the agencies' mandates and covered a broad range of informatics' wide spectrum. They included: general research and development with potential application in developing countries, including strategies and policies for informatics; technology dissemination; and development of international databases and information systems in specific fields, such as management, technical/scientific systems, bibliographic systems, statistics, and information networking and communications.

In terms of coordination, mechanisms existed, in intergovernmental bodies and under the aegis of the Administrative Committee on Coordination (ACC), to coordinate technical cooperation in statistical data processing and informatics. Applications in developing countries were an ongoing concern of those bodies and coordination in developing countries' applications could be reinforced.

An ACC body—the Advisory Committee for the Coordination of Information Systems—provided advisory services to United Nations organizations on proposals for creating new information systems and for substantial modifications to existing ones. It also promoted the use of common standards to enhance compatibility of information systems.

Although various mechanisms existed for inter-agency coordination of work on management information systems, bibliographic and other specialized technical systems, publications and communications systems, there was no general framework for their overall coordination and consideration of applications in developing countries. It was suggested that such a framework could be considered by the DESD, which was the system's focal point for general research, policy and coordination issues affecting developing countries and whose responsibilities and programmes cut across a wide range of informatics and data-processing concerns.

Such a framework would require regular coordinating arrangements that would contribute to the effectiveness and quality of the system's activities for developing countries. The objectives of such arrangements would be: to identify problem areas in informatics suitable for tackling through inter-agency coordination for the benefit of developing countries (standardization of equipment, software, data or procedures); and to propose common informatics projects/programme activities at the national/regional level to foster the use of modern informatics technology for economic and social development.

The Secretary-General analysed the causes of the situation with respect to United Nations informatics systems in a report on harmonization and improvement of those systems for optimal utilization and accessibility by all States[8] (see PART SIX, Chapter III). On 31 July, the Economic and Social Council adopted **resolution 1992/60** on the topic.

Strengthening technological capacity in developing countries

The Cartagena Commitment, adopted by the eighth session of the United Nations Conference on Trade and Development (UNCTAD VIII) in February[9] (see PART THREE, Chapter IV), noted that technology had increasingly become a determinant of the ability of countries to participate in world trade in manufactures and services. The Conference recognized technological capability as a fundamental factor for social and economic development and recommended that emphasis be put on policies and measures to promote technological innovation in developing countries. High priority should be given to stimulating technology flows to developing countries, facilitating their access to it and enhancing their capacity to modify and adapt technology to local conditions and to generate and develop technology locally. Policies should also aim to expand and adapt educational systems, build up scientific and technological research and development capabilities, and encourage the diffusion of technology within developing countries. National technology policies should promote entrepreneurship and encourage technology transfer, including foreign direct investment, and provide incentives for investment in technology capacity-building, including research and development, innovation, adaptation and development of technologies to support national objectives and priorities.

Given the importance of technologies to the development process, developed countries should consider ways to facilitate technology cooperation with the developing world. Those countries should also encourage improved cooperation between their enterprises and scientific and technological institutions and those of developing countries. The Conference recognized the need to explore ways to provide developing countries with technical cooperation and support to enable them to undertake research and development and skill formation, including training programmes, as well as to import foreign technological inputs as a complement to local technological efforts. Multilateral and international financial institutions were encouraged to take account of the technological needs of developing countries.

High-level meeting of experts

A Meeting of High-level Experts on Science and Technology for Development was held at Bujumbura, Burundi, from 4 to 8 May 1992.[10] The substantive theme of the Meeting, which was attended by 14 high-level experts and 5 representatives from organizations and agencies of the United Nations system, was the role of science and technology in the development of the least developed countries (LDCs). The Meeting also discussed technology in industrialization, specifically privatization of publicly funded industrial research and development institutions and the role of technological cooperation in fostering regional economic integration. In addition, it reviewed the experience of the former Advisory Committee on Science and Technology for Development and expressed its views on the new Commission on Science and Technology for Development (see below).

With regard to science and technology for LDCs, the Meeting noted that the debate on the issue reflected the need for a new policy approach, in line with the changing global context and the new understanding of endogenous capacity in science and technology for development. That approach should address all aspects of science and technology policy, including those of application, development and transfer, which had previously been neglected or underemphasized.

The Meeting made a series of recommendations for action at the national and international policy levels in four areas: management of resources and building of endogenous capacities; infrastructures for and linkages of technology in science and technology policy; science and technology development and technology transfer as a response to demand; and generation of domestic demand for science and technology. As to implementation, the Meeting proposed a number of guidelines for consideration by entrepreneurs and policy makers at the political level.

Science for sustainable development

The United Nations Conference on Environment and Development (UNCED) in June[11] adopted the Rio Declaration on Environment and Development, in which it proclaimed that States should cooperate to strengthen endogenous capacity-building for sustainable development by improving scientific understanding through exchanges of scientific and technological knowledge, and by enhancing the development, adaptation, diffusion and transfer of technologies, including new and innovative technologies.

UNCED also adopted Agenda 21, a chapter of which dealt with science for sustainable development, focusing on the role and use of the sciences in support of the prudent management of the environment and development for the daily survival and future development of humanity. Noting that scientists were improving their understanding in areas such as climatic change, growth in resource consumption rates, demographic trends and environmental degradation, UNCED stated that changes in those areas needed to be taken into account in working out long-term strategies for development.

UNCED identified four programme areas—strengthening the scientific basis for sustainable management, enhancing scientific understanding, improving long-term scientific assessment, and building up scientific capacity and capability—and outlined objectives, activities and means of implementation for each.

Another chapter of Agenda 21, on the scientific and technological community, addressed the question of how to enable the scientific and technological community to make a more open and effective contribution to the decision-making processes concerning environment and development. UNCED outlined objectives, activities and means of implementation for two programme areas—improving communication and cooperation among the scientific and technological community, decision makers and the public, and promoting codes of practice and guidelines related to science and technology.

(For details of UNCED, see PART THREE, Chapter VIII.)

UN Fund for Science and Technology for Development

During 1992, the United Nations Fund for Science and Technology for Development received an estimated $1.56 million in resources from voluntary, cost-sharing and sub-trust fund contributions and from interest and other income. A total of $4.24 million was carried over from 1991. During the year, the Fund's expenditure amounted to some $2.01 million, leaving a balance of $3.79 million, less $2.42 million in unspent project allocations.

The Fund organized six policy meetings in 1992, in Cape Verde, Jamaica, Pakistan, Togo, Uganda and Viet Nam, to stimulate country-specific portfolios of science and technology activities to be supported by a combination of national, bilateral and multilateral resources. A pilot technology incubator scheme was implemented in 15 countries; it offered small businesses shared office services, marketing assistance and access to new capital. The repair and maintenance of scientific instruments programme, highly successful in southern Africa, was extended to West Africa and South Asia. A computerized referral system for journalists was launched in Asia to bring together scientists and journalists in order to improve the quality of scientific reporting in the media.

Operational activities

As requested by the General Assembly in 1991,[12] the Secretary-General submitted in September 1992 a comprehensive policy review of operational activities of the United Nations system, an addendum to which[13] comprised an assessment of and recommendations on the contribution of the system's operational activities to the enhancement of national capacities of developing countries in science and technology. The report defined the concept of science and technology capacity and the functions of the United Nations organizations in science and technology. The latter included financing (funding of projects, programmes and training); capacity-building (funding of institution-building, policy analysis, and provision of technical experts and of management, administrative or legal expertise or support); and global policy coordination (providing forums for exchange of views on policy matters and for negotiations with donors). The report also provided data on financial flows to research and development and to development, noting that the large disparities in expenditures on research and development between industrialized and developing countries underlay the basis of the accelerating gap in development dividing the two groups of countries. It also included an assessment of transfer of technology and an evaluation of capacity-building.

Operational issues identified in the report as requiring attention included the growing role of the private sector in national development, ownership rights to intellectual property developed in United Nations–financed projects, coordination within the United Nations system and information management.

REFERENCES

[1]YUN 1979, p. 636. [2]GA res. 44/14 A, 26 Oct. 1989.
[3]A/45/16. [4]E/AC.51/1992/4. [5]A/47/16. [6]YUN 1991, p. 484,
ESC res. 1991/71, 26 July 1991. [7]E/1992/55. [8]E/1992/78.
[9]TD/364. [10]E/CN.16/1993/6. [11]*Report of the United Nations
Conference on Environment and Development, Rio de Janeiro, 3-14 June
1992*, vol. I, Sales No. E.93.I.8. [12]YUN 1991, p. 364, GA
res. 46/219, 20 Dec. 1991. [13]A/47/419/Add.1.

Technology transfer

UNCTAD activities. In February,[1] UNCTAD VIII recognized that, in order to stimulate transfer of technology and the development of endogenous technological capabilities, developing countries should emphasize policies to enhance their scientific and technological capability and devote adequate resources to that end. Policies should range from expanding and adapting their educational systems to building up their scientific and technological research and development capabilities, and should include measures to encourage diffusion of technology within developing countries, especially to small and medium-sized companies. UNCTAD VIII recommended that developed countries, in their trade and technology

policies, should facilitate access of developing countries to efficient, best-practice and needed technologies. It identified public guarantee schemes to promote joint ventures, licensing agreements, and research and development collaboration agreements as means to encourage technology flows to developing countries, and considered that bilateral investment and double taxation agreements could provide a supportive framework for investment flows, inviting transfer of technology and collaborative research and development arrangements between firms of developed and developing countries. Bilateral and multilateral assistance programmes should give priority to the transfer of appropriate technology.

The Conference recognized that the establishment and implementation of internationally agreed standards of protection for intellectual property rights should facilitate international flows of technology and cooperation and create market incentives for indigenous innovation and the transfer, adaptation and diffusion of technologies. It also considered that attention needed to be given to the technological requirements of the transition economies of Central and Eastern Europe and other regions.

UNCTAD should focus its economic development and technology transfer work programme on: research and analysis of the interrelationship of technology issues with trade in goods and services, investment, finance and environment; analysis of technology transfer and the issue of transfer of environmentally sound technology to developing countries and LDCs; and technical cooperation activities in support of developing countries to enhance their technological capacities.

In a section of the Cartagena Commitment dealing with institutional matters, UNCTAD VIII decided that the work programme of the Trade and Development Board's Committee on the Transfer of Technology would be assumed by an ad hoc working group on the interrelationship between investment and technology transfer.

On 7 May,[2] the Trade and Development Board established the Ad Hoc Working Group on Interrelationship between Investment and Technology Transfer. The Group's terms of reference were: to examine the interrelationship between investment flows, particularly to developing countries, including LDCs, and the transfer, absorption and generation of technology and related policy measures; to identify factors conducive to technology transfer through foreign investment and analyse the role of intellectual property protection; to examine the role played by private firms, Governments and international organizations in the transfer of technology; to consider the impact of technological change, including new and emerging technologies; and to examine and encourage new initiatives and exchange of experiences on policies to overcome constraints and facilitate technology transfer through investment.

Transfer of environmentally sound technology

UNCTAD VIII agreed that the transfer and development of environmentally sound technologies was an essential component of a successful strategy for sustainable development, and requested that effective modalities for the creation, development, favourable access to and transfer of such technologies, particularly to developing countries, including on concessional and preferential terms, be examined.

In Agenda 21,[3] UNCED recognized that the availability of scientific and technological information and access to and transfer of environmentally sound technology were essential requirements for sustainable development. Providing adequate information on the environmental aspects of existing and state-of-the-art technologies required upgrading information on such technologies, including their environmental risks, and improving access to environmentally sound technologies.

UNCED proposed a number of objectives, including helping to ensure access, in particular of developing countries, to scientific and technological information and to promote, facilitate and finance access to and transfer of environmentally sound technologies and corresponding know-how on favourable terms. Other objectives were: facilitating the maintenance and promotion of environmentally sound indigenous technologies; supporting endogenous capacity-building, particularly in developing countries, through human resource development, strengthening institutional capacities for research and development and programme implementation, and integrated sector assessments of technology needs; and promoting long-term technological partnerships between holders of environmentally sound technologies and potential users.

Programme activities proposed by UNCED were aimed at developing international information networks to link national, subregional, regional and international systems; supporting and promoting access to transfer of technology; improving the capacity to develop and manage environmentally sound technologies; establishing a collaborative network of research centres; supporting programmes of cooperation and assistance; promoting technology assessment to support the management of environmentally sound technologies; and developing collaborative arrangements and partnerships between enterprises of developed and developing countries to develop such technologies.

Draft code of conduct

In response to a 1991 General Assembly request,[4] the UNCTAD Secretary-General, in November 1992,[5] submitted a report on consultations carried out in 1992 on an international code of conduct on the transfer of technology. The report stated that UNCTAD VIII reviewed the work carried out on a draft code and the results of consultations held in 1991.[6] It recognized that conditions did not exist to reach full agreement on outstanding issues in the draft code; should Governments indicate that there was the convergence of views necessary to agree on those issues, the Trade and Development Board should continue its work to facilitate agreement on the code.

Subsequent to the adoption of the Cartagena Commitment by UNCTAD VIII, the UNCTAD Secretary-General requested Governments to provide him with their views on the issues outstanding in the draft code, particularly on the acceptability of the exclusive application of competition law principles to the evaluation of restrictive practices, and adherence to freedom of contract and freedom of choice in respect to applicable law and forum for dispute settlement. Since only 10 Governments had replied (Canada, China, Czechoslovakia, Iraq, Netherlands, Niger, Philippines, Saint Lucia, Switzerland, United States), the Secretary-General indicated that he intended to collect a wider sample of views and to prepare a more comprehensive report to the Assembly in 1993.

GENERAL ASSEMBLY ACTION

On 22 December 1992, the General Assembly, on the recommendation of the Second (Economic and Financial) Committee, adopted **resolution 47/182** without vote.

International code of conduct on the transfer of technology

The General Assembly,

Recalling its resolution 46/214 of 20 December 1991, on an international code of conduct on the transfer of technology,

1. *Takes note* of the report of the Secretary-General of the United Nations Conference on Trade and Development on the consultations carried out in 1992 on an international code of conduct on the transfer of technology;

2. *Invites* the Secretary-General of the United Nations Conference on Trade and Development, in line with the relevant provisions of the Cartagena Commitment, adopted by the United Nations Conference on Trade and Development at its eighth session, to continue his consultations with Governments on the future course of action on an international code of conduct and to report to the General Assembly at its forty-eighth session on the outcome of those consultations.

General Assembly resolution 47/182

22 December 1992   Meeting 93   Adopted without vote

Approved by Second Committee (A/47/718/Add.2 & Corr.1) without vote, 7 December (meeting 48); draft by Chairman (A/C.2/47/L.24); agenda item 78 *(a)*.

Meeting numbers. GA 47th session: 2nd Committee 40, 42, 43, 48; plenary 93.

The Assembly also adopted **resolution 47/43** on scientific and technological developments and their impact on international security and **resolution 47/44** on the role of science and technology in the context of international security, disarmament and other related fields.

REFERENCES

[1]TD/364. [2]A/47/15, vol. I (dec. 398(XXXVIII)). [3]*Report of the United Nations Conference on Environment and Development, Rio de Janeiro, 3-14 June 1992*, vol. I, Sales No. E.93.I.8. [4]YUN 1991, p. 487, GA res. 46/214, 20 Dec. 1991. [5]A/47/636. [6]YUN 1991, p. 487.

Organizational matters

Institutional arrangements

As part of the process of restructuring and revitalizing the United Nations in the economic and social fields, the General Assembly, by **resolution 46/235** of 13 April 1992, decided to transform the Intergovernmental Committee on Science and Technology for Development and its subsidiary body, the Advisory Committee on Science and Technology for Development, into a functional commission of the Economic and Social Council.

By **decision 1992/218** of 30 April, the Council established the Commission on Science and Technology for Development and requested the Secretary-General to submit to its substantive session of 1992 a draft provisional agenda for the Commission. On 31 July, by **resolution 1992/62**, the Council reaffirmed the Commission's mandate and approved the draft provisional agenda and programme of work for its first session, to be held in 1993.

Restructuring of the UN Secretariat

On 1 March, as part of the restructuring of the United Nations Secretariat, the Centre for Science and Technology for Development became part of the Science, Technology, Energy, Environment and Natural Resources Division of DESD.

DESD activities

In a report on DESD activities in science and technology for development,[1] the Secretary-General noted that the role of science and technology in the development process had received new impetus in 1991-1992 due to changes within the United Nations system designed to revitalize activities in the economic, social and related fields and to a new role attributed by UNCED to technology cooperation between developed and developing countries.

Since the 1991 meeting of the Intergovernmental Committee on Science and Technology for Development,[2] considerable work had been undertaken in endogenous capacity-building and resource mobilization and in technology assessment. Additional projects for improving capacities in science and technology were initiated with Cape Verde, Jamaica, Pakistan, Togo, Uganda and Viet Nam, and DESD held a series of policy dialogues and specialized expert group meetings in those countries, based on their specific interests.

As the focal point for technology assessment within the United Nations system, DESD's Advanced Technology Assessment System (ATAS) carried out studies in different technological areas (biotechnology, micro-electronics, information technology, new materials, energy and environmentally sound technology, as well as technology assessment methodology) through ad hoc networks of experts on an international level. ATAS publications in 1992 included the *ATAS Bulletin* and the *ATAS News*, a regular supplement to the quarterly newsletter *Update*. In further pursuance of its technology assessment mandate, the former Centre for Science and Technology for Development, in cooperation with the United Nations Environment Programme, the French Ministry of the Environment and the United States Environmental Protection Agency, organized an expert group meeting on opportunities and risks for the environment of new technologies (Geneva, 13 and 14 January). Applications of technology assessment were also the focus of two conference series—on conversion of the military/industrial complex to peaceful uses and on clean coal technologies. In the conversion series, conferences were held on opportunities for development and environment (Dortmund, Germany, 24-27 February) and on conversion of the aerospace industry (Moscow, 12-16 October). Clean coal technology meetings were held at Madras, India, in January, and Berlin, Germany, in May. Together with the International Society for Photogrammetry and Remote Sensing, DESD cosponsored an interregional seminar on remote sensing and the transfer of technology (Washington, D.C., 2-14 August).

DESD continued to maintain a registry of national science and technology focal points identified by Member States and kept them informed about ongoing activities within the system. It studied a proposal by the United Nations University (UNU) that a United Nations register of research be established by UNU and DESD.

Coordination in the UN system

The ACC Task Force on Science and Technology for Development held its thirteenth session in 1992 (New York, 30 November–2 December).[3]

The Task Force discussed and made suggestions regarding its own functions and objectives, interaction between it and the new Commission on Science and Technology for Development, possible options for a coalition of resources for the promotion of science and technology in developing countries, capacity-building in science and technology, and new and emerging areas of science and technology for development.

REFERENCES

(1)E/CN.16/1993/5. (2)YUN 1991, p. 485. (3)ACC/1992/19.

Chapter VIII

Environment

With the global environment having grown worse than it was two decades previously, despite all efforts deployed, the United Nations Conference on Environment and Development (UNCED) in 1992 adopted the Rio Declaration on Environment and Development, seeking international agreements to protect the integrity of the global environmental and developmental systems. The Conference also adopted Agenda 21, reflecting a global consensus on development and environment cooperation, and a statement of principles on the management, conservation and sustainable development of all types of forests. Two conventions—the United Nations Framework Convention on Climate Change and the Convention on Biological Diversity—were opened for signature at the Conference.

The General Assembly adopted resolutions endorsing the results of UNCED (resolution 47/190), establishing institutional arrangements to follow it up (47/191) and inviting the United Nations Development Programme to help developing countries to improve their capacity to implement Agenda 21 (47/194). The Assembly also welcomed the adoption of the Convention on Climate Change (47/195).

The Assembly established an intergovernmental negotiating committee to elaborate by 1994 a convention to combat desertification (47/188). It decided to convene an intergovernmental conference on straddling and highly migratory fish stocks in 1993 (47/192) and a global conference on the sustainable development of small island developing States in 1994 (47/189).

The Assembly appealed for international cooperation to mitigate the environmental consequences resulting from the situation between Iraq and Kuwait (47/151).

UN Conference on Environment and Development

The United Nations Conference on Environment and Development, or "Earth Summit", took place at Rio de Janeiro, Brazil, from 3 to 14 June 1992.[1] On 14 June, it adopted the Rio Declaration on Environment and Development; Agenda 21, a comprehensive plan of action for the sustainable development of the Earth into the twenty-first century; and a statement of principles for a global consensus on the management, conservation and sustainable development of forests. The United Nations Framework Convention on Climate Change and the Convention on Biological Diversity were opened for signature at UNCED and signed by 154 States and 156 States, respectively; each Convention was also signed by one regional economic integration organization.

UNCED coincided with World Environment Day (5 June),[2] which was also the twentieth anniversary of the opening of the 1972 United Nations Conference on the Human Environment.[3]

Representatives of 176 States and Territories (see APPENDIX III), the European Economic Community (EEC), Palestine and seven associate members of the regional commissions (American Samoa, Aruba, Hong Kong, Netherlands Antilles, Niue, Puerto Rico, United States Virgin Islands) attended the Conference. Two national liberation movements—the African National Congress and the Pan Africanist Congress of Azania—were represented, along with the secretariats of four of the regional commissions, several United Nations offices, organizations and specialized agencies, 35 intergovernmental organizations and some 1,500 non-governmental organizations (NGOs).[4]

The Conference elected as its President Fernando Collor, President of Brazil. Also elected were 39 Vice-Presidents, one *ex-officio* Vice-President from the host country, a Rapporteur-General and a Main Committee Chairman.

Action taken by the Conference

Rio Declaration on Environment and Development

The Rio Declaration aimed to establish a new and equitable global partnership on environment and development through cooperation among States, key sectors of society and individuals. It was hoped that the Declaration would serve as a basis for future negotiation of an Earth Charter that could be approved on the fiftieth anniversary of the United Nations in 1995. The Declaration consisted of the following 27 principles:

1. Human beings are at the centre of concerns for sustainable development. They are entitled to a healthy and productive life in harmony with nature.
2. States have, in accordance with the Charter of the United Nations and the principles of international

law, the sovereign right to exploit their own resources pursuant to their own environmental and developmental policies, and the responsibility to ensure that activities within their jurisdiction or control do not cause damage to the environment of other States or of areas beyond the limits of national jurisdiction.

3. The right to development must be fulfilled so as to equitably meet developmental and environmental needs of present and future generations.

4. In order to achieve sustainable development, environmental protection shall constitute an integral part of the development process and cannot be considered in isolation from it.

5. All States and all people shall cooperate in the essential task of eradicating poverty as an indispensable requirement for sustainable development, in order to decrease the disparities in standards of living and better meet the needs of the majority of the people of the world.

6. The special situation and needs of developing countries, particularly the least developed and those most environmentally vulnerable, shall be given special priority. International actions in the field of environment and development should also address the interests and needs of all countries.

7. States shall cooperate in a spirit of global partnership to conserve, protect and restore the health and integrity of the Earth's ecosystem. In view of the different contributions to global environmental degradation, States have common but differentiated responsibilities. The developed countries acknowledge the responsibility that they bear in the international pursuit of sustainable development in view of the pressures their societies place on the global environment and of the technologies and financial resources they command.

8. To achieve sustainable development and a higher quality of life for all people, States should reduce and eliminate unsustainable patterns of production and consumption and promote appropriate demographic policies.

9. States should cooperate to strengthen endogenous capacity-building for sustainable development by improving scientific understanding through exchanges of scientific and technological knowledge, and by enhancing the development, adaptation, diffusion and transfer of technologies, including new and innovative technologies.

10. Environmental issues are best handled with the participation of all concerned citizens, at the relevant level. At the national level, each individual shall have appropriate access to information concerning the environment that is held by public authorities, including information on hazardous materials and activities in their communities, and the opportunity to participate in decision-making processes. States shall facilitate and encourage public awareness and participation by making information widely available. Effective access to judicial and administrative proceedings, including redress and remedy, shall be provided.

11. States shall enact effective environmental legislation. Environmental standards, management objectives and priorities should reflect the environmental and developmental context to which they apply. Standards applied by some countries may be inappropriate and of unwarranted economic and social cost to other countries, in particular developing countries.

12. States should cooperate to promote a supportive and open international economic system that would lead to economic growth and sustainable development in all countries, to better address the problems of environmental degradation. Trade policy measures for environmental purposes should not constitute a means of arbitrary or unjustifiable discrimination or a disguised restriction on international trade. Unilateral actions to deal with environmental challenges outside the jurisdiction of the importing country should be avoided. Environmental measures addressing transboundary or global environmental problems should, as far as possible, be based on an international consensus.

13. States shall develop national law regarding liability and compensation for the victims of pollution and other environmental damage. States shall also cooperate in an expeditious and more determined manner to develop further international law regarding liability and compensation for adverse effects of environmental damage caused by activities within their jurisdiction or control to areas beyond their jurisdiction.

14. States should effectively cooperate to discourage or prevent the relocation and transfer to other States of any activities and substances that cause severe environmental degradation or are found to be harmful to human health.

15. In order to protect the environment, the precautionary approach shall be widely applied by States according to their capabilities. Where there are threats of serious or irreversible damage, lack of full scientific certainty shall not be used as a reason for postponing cost-effective measures to prevent environmental degradation.

16. National authorities should endeavour to promote the internalization of environmental costs and the use of economic instruments, taking into account the approach that the polluter should, in principle, bear the cost of pollution, with due regard to the public interest and without distorting international trade and investment.

17. Environmental impact assessment, as a national instrument, shall be undertaken for proposed activities that are likely to have a significant adverse impact on the environment and are subject to a decision of a competent national authority.

18. States shall immediately notify other States of any natural disasters or other emergencies that are likely to produce sudden harmful effects on the environment of those States. Every effort shall be made by the international community to help States so afflicted.

19. States shall provide prior and timely notification and relevant information to potentially affected States on activities that may have a significant adverse transboundary environmental effect and shall consult with those States at an early stage and in good faith.

20. Women have a vital role in environmental management and development. Their full participation is therefore essential to achieve sustainable development.

21. The creativity, ideals and courage of the youth of the world should be mobilized to forge a global partnership in order to achieve sustainable development and ensure a better future for all.

22. Indigenous people and their communities and other local communities have a vital role in environmental management and development because of their knowledge and traditional practices. States should recognize and duly support their identity, culture and interests and enable their effective participation in the achievement of sustainable development.

23. The environment and natural resources of people under oppression, domination and occupation shall be protected.

24. Warfare is inherently destructive of sustainable development. States shall therefore respect international law providing protection for the environment in times of armed conflict and cooperate in its further development, as necessary.

25. Peace, development and environmental protection are interdependent and indivisible.

26. States shall resolve all their environmental disputes peacefully and by appropriate means in accordance with the Charter of the United Nations.

27. States and people shall cooperate in good faith and in a spirit of partnership in the fulfilment of the principles embodied in this Declaration and in the further development of international law in the field of sustainable development.

Agenda 21

The preamble of Agenda 21 stated that humanity was confronted with a worsening of poverty, hunger, ill-health and illiteracy and the continuing deterioration of the ecosystems. Integration of environment and development concerns would lead to the fulfilment of basic needs, improved living standards for all, better protected and managed ecosystems and a safer, more prosperous future. Agenda 21 reflected a global consensus and political commitment at the highest level on development and environment cooperation. International cooperation should support and supplement national strategies and plans. In that context, the United Nations system had a key role to play. The objectives of Agenda 21 would require a substantial flow of financial resources to developing countries. The 115 programme areas defining areas of action under Agenda 21 were described in terms of the basis for action, objectives, activities and means of implementation.

Social and economic dimensions

Section I of Agenda 21 covered its social and economic dimensions. The Conference called for an international climate that would promote sustainable development through trade liberalization, make trade and environment mutually supportive, provide adequate financial resources to developing countries and deal with international debt, and encourage macroeconomic policies conducive to environment and development. It recommended halting and reversing protectionism, improving the competitiveness of the commodity sector, and diversifying to reduce dependence on commodity exports.

The Conference declared that an environmental policy focusing on the conservation and protection of resources would have to take into account those who depended on the resources for their livelihoods. A development policy focusing on increasing the production of goods without addressing the sustainability of the resources on which production was based would run into declining productivity. The United Nations system should make poverty alleviation a major priority and assist Governments in formulating action programmes on poverty alleviation and sustainable development.

Changing consumption patterns in regard to natural resources would require a multipronged strategy focusing on demand, meeting the basic needs of the poor, and reducing wastage and the use of finite resources in the production process. Governments should assist individuals and households in making environmentally informed choices.

The Conference agreed that the growth in world population and production combined with unsustainable consumption practices was placing increasingly severe stress on the life-supporting capacities of the planet. Demographic trends should be incorporated in the global analysis of environment and development issues, with full recognition of women's rights.

The Conference said that Agenda 21 should address the primary health needs of the world's population. Countries were urged to develop priority action plans based on the cooperative efforts of various levels of government, NGOs and local communities. Programme areas relating to health dealt with meeting rural health-care needs, controlling communicable diseases, protecting vulnerable groups, meeting the urban health challenge and reducing health risks from environmental pollution and hazards.

On the subject of promoting sustainable human settlements, the Conference called for providing shelter for all, improved management of settlements, sustainable land-use planning and management, the integrated provision of environmental infrastructure (water, sanitation, drainage and solid-waste management), sustainable energy and transport systems, planning and management of settlements in disaster-prone areas, sustainable construction industry activities and human resource development and capacity-building for human settlement development.

Conservation and management of resources for development

Section II of Agenda 21 covered the conservation and management of resources for development. It included four programme areas: improving the scientific basis for decision-making; promoting sustainable development; preventing stratospheric ozone depletion; and transboundary atmospheric pollution.

The Conference called for an integrated approach to the planning and management of soils, minerals, water and biota. Noting major weaknesses in the policies, methods and mechanisms adopted to support and develop the ecological, economic, social and cultural roles of trees, forests and forest lands, it recommended the following: enhancing the protection, management and conservation of all forests, as well as the greening of degraded areas, through rehabilitation, afforestation, reforestation and other means; promoting efficient utilization and assessment to recover the full valuation of the goods and services provided by forests, forest lands and woodlands; and establishing or strengthening capacities for the planning, assessment and systematic observations of forests.

Three chapters dealt with managing fragile ecosystems: combating desertification and drought, mountain development, and sustaining small islands and coastal areas. Agenda 21 called for strengthening the desertification knowledge base, developing information and monitoring systems for regions prone to desertification and drought, combating land degradation and promoting alternative livelihood systems in areas prone to desertification. In addition, the Conference proposed integrating comprehensive anti-desertification programmes into national development and environmental plans, developing comprehensive drought preparedness and drought-relief schemes for drought-prone areas, designing programmes to cope with environmental refugees and promoting education on desertification control and management of the effects of drought. The Conference called for the General Assembly to establish an intergovernmental negotiating committee to elaborate an international convention to combat desertification in countries experiencing serious drought and/or desertification.

Mountains were susceptible to accelerated erosion, landslides and rapid loss of habitat and genetic diversity. Programme areas covered strengthening knowledge about the ecology and sustainable development of mountain ecosystems and promoting integrated watershed development and alternative livelihood opportunities.

The protection and development of the marine environment, including the oceans, seas and adjacent coastal areas, was to be carried out in accordance with the 1982 United Nations Convention on the Law of the Sea.[5] Agenda 21 called for the integrated management and sustainable development of coastal areas, including exclusive economic zones; marine environmental protection; the sustainable use and conservation of marine liv-

ing resources; addressing critical uncertainties for the management of the marine environment and climate change; strengthening international cooperation and coordination; and the sustainable development of small islands. It identified small island developing States as a special case for both environment and development, given their vulnerability to global warming and sealevel rise, as well as their degree of biodiversity. The Conference called for a global conference on the sustainable development of island States and for an intergovernmental conference on straddling and highly migratory fish stocks (see below).

To protect the quality and supply of freshwater resources, the Conference proposed the following programme areas: integrated water resources development and management; water resources assessment; protection of water resources, water quality and aquatic ecosystems; drinking-water supply and sanitation; water and sustainable urban development; water for sustainable food production and rural development; and impacts of climate change on water resources.

In relation to promoting sustainable agriculture and rural development, the Conference stated that by the year 2025, 83 per cent of the expected global population of 8.5 billion would be living in developing countries. Major adjustments were needed in agricultural, environmental and macroeconomic policy to create sustainable agriculture and rural development. Agenda 21 included the following programme areas, among others: agricultural policy review, planning and integrated programming; human resource development for sustainable agriculture; improving of farm production and farming systems through diversification of farm and non-farm employment and infrastructure development; land-resource planning information and education for agriculture; land conservation and rehabilitation; and water for food production and rural development.

Regarding the conservation of biological diversity, the Conference observed that the planet's essential goods and services depended on the variety and variability of genes, species, populations and ecosystems. In its view, the current decline in biodiversity was largely the result of human activity and represented a serious threat to human development. Agenda 21 sought to improve the conservation of biological diversity and the sustainable use of biological resources, and to support the Convention on Biological Diversity (see below).

The Conference considered the environmentally sound management of toxic chemicals. It proposed six programme areas: expanding international assessment of chemical risks; harmonization of classification and labelling of chemicals; information exchange on toxic chemicals and chemical risks;

establishment of risk-reduction programmes; strengthening of national capacities for management of chemicals; and prevention of illegal international traffic in toxic and dangerous products.

With respect to hazardous wastes, countries were urged to ratify the 1989 Basel Convention on the Control of Transboundary Movements of Hazardous Wastes and Their Disposal and the 1991 Bamako Convention on the Ban of the Import of All Forms of Hazardous Wastes into Africa and the Control of Transboundary Movements of Such Wastes Generated in Africa.

For safe and environmentally sound management of radioactive wastes, the Conference said that States, in cooperation with international organizations, should limit the generation of such wastes; support efforts within the International Atomic Energy Agency to develop radioactive-waste safety standards or guidelines and codes of practice; and promote safe storage, transportation and disposal of radioactive wastes, and proper planning of their management, including emergency procedures.

Strengthening the role of major groups

The third section of Agenda 21 dealt with strengthening the role of various groups in implementing its objectives and policies. The commitment and involvement of all social groups was seen as critical to the success of the programmes. Among the groups addressed were women, children and youth, indigenous people, NGOs, local authorities, workers and trade unions, business and industry, the scientific and technological community, and farmers.

Means of implementation

The fourth and final section of Agenda 21 discussed means of financing its programmes. The Conference secretariat estimated that the average cost of implementing Agenda 21 in developing countries between 1993 and 2000 would exceed $600 billion per year, including $125 billion on grant or concessional terms from the international community.

The Conference stated that for developing countries, official development assistance (ODA) was a main source of external funding; substantial new funding would be required. Developed countries reaffirmed their commitment to reach the target of 0.7 per cent of gross national product for ODA. All available funding sources would be used, including multilateral development banks, the Global Environment Facility (see below), specialized agencies and other United Nations bodies, multilateral institutions, bilateral assistance programmes, debt relief and private funding.

The intergovernmental follow-up to the Conference was to take place within the framework of the United Nations system, with the General Assembly being the principal policy-making and appraisal organ. The Assembly would organize a regular review of the implementation of Agenda 21, and could consider holding a special session for that purpose not later than 1997. The Economic and Social Council would oversee the system-wide coordination and integration of environmental and developmental aspects of United Nations policies and programmes. The Conference recommended the creation of a high-level Commission on Sustainable Development to ensure effective follow-up (see below). The Commission, which would report to the Council, would enhance international cooperation, examine progress in implementing Agenda 21 at the national, regional and international levels, provide for the active involvement of organs, programmes and organizations of the United Nations system, international financial institutions and other intergovernmental organizations, and encourage the participation of NGOs.

Statement of Principles on forests

The Non-legally Binding Authoritative Statement of Principles for a Global Consensus on the Management, Conservation and Sustainable Development of All Types of Forests declared that States had the sovereign right to utilize, manage and develop their forests, including the right to convert them to other uses, in accordance with their own development needs and level of socio-economic development. Governments were urged to manage their forest resources and lands so as to meet the social, economic, ecological, cultural and spiritual needs of current and future generations for wood, water, food, fodder, medicine, fuel, shelter, employment, recreation, wildlife habitats, landscape diversity, carbon reservoirs and other forest products.

The Statement called on Governments to recognize that forests played a vital role in protecting fragile ecosystems and water resources, were sources of genetic material for biotechnology products and met energy requirements. In addition, all countries, notably developed countries, were urged to take action towards reforestation, afforestation and forest conservation.

Representative or unique examples of forests that were ecologically viable should be protected, while access to biological resources, including genetic material, should be provided with due regard for the sovereign rights of the countries where the forests were located.

GENERAL ASSEMBLY ACTION

On 22 December, the General Assembly, on the recommendation of the Second (Economic and Financial) Committee, adopted **resolution 47/190** without vote.

Report of the United Nations Conference on Environment and Development

The General Assembly,

Recalling its resolutions 43/196 of 20 December 1988, 44/172 A and B of 19 December 1989, 44/228 of 22 December 1989, 45/211 of 21 December 1990 and 46/168 of 19 December 1991,

Having considered the report of the United Nations Conference on Environment and Development,

Expressing its satisfaction that the Conference and its Preparatory Committee provided for the active participation of all States Members of the United Nations and members of its specialized agencies at the highest level, of observers and various intergovernmental organizations, as well as of non-governmental organizations representing all the regions of the world,

Reaffirming the need for a balanced and integrated approach to environment and development issues,

Reaffirming also a new global partnership for sustainable development,

Expressing its profound gratitude to the Government and the people of Brazil for the hospitality extended to the participants of the Conference and for the facilities, staff and services placed at their disposal,

1. *Takes note with satisfaction* of the report of the United Nations Conference on Environment and Development;

2. *Endorses* the Rio Declaration on Environment and Development, Agenda 21 and the Non-legally Binding Authoritative Statement of Principles for a Global Consensus on the Management, Conservation and Sustainable Development of All Types of Forests, as adopted by the United Nations Conference on Environment and Development on 14 June 1992;

3. *Notes with satisfaction* that the United Nations Framework Convention on Climate Change and the Convention on Biological Diversity were opened for signature and were signed by a large number of States at the United Nations Conference on Environment and Development, and stresses the need for these Conventions to come into force as soon as possible;

4. *Urges* Governments and organs, organizations and programmes of the United Nations system, as well as other intergovernmental and non-governmental organizations, to take the necessary action to give effective follow-up to the Rio Declaration on Environment and Development, Agenda 21 and the Non-legally Binding Authoritative Statement of Principles for a Global Consensus on the Management, Conservation and Sustainable Development of All Types of Forests;

5. *Calls upon* all concerned to implement all commitments, agreements and recommendations reached at the United Nations Conference on Environment and Development, especially by ensuring provision of the means of implementation under section IV of Agenda 21, stressing in particular the importance of financial resources and mechanisms, the transfer of environmentally sound technology, cooperation and capacity-building, and international institutional arrangements, in order to achieve sustainable development in all countries;

6. *Takes note with appreciation* of the initial financial commitments made at its forty-seventh session by some developed countries and urges those countries which have not done so to announce their commitments in accordance with paragraph 33.19 of Agenda 21;

7. *Decides* to include in the provisional agenda of its forty-eighth and subsequent sessions an item entitled "Implementation of decisions and recommendations of the United Nations Conference on Environment and Development";

8. *Also decides* to convene, not later than 1997, a special session for the purpose of an overall review and appraisal of Agenda 21 and, in this context, requests the Secretary-General to submit to the General Assembly at its forty-ninth session a report containing recommendations for consideration by the Assembly on the format, scope and organizational aspects of such a special session.

General Assembly resolution 47/190

22 December 1992   Meeting 93   Adopted without vote

Approved by Second Committee (A/47/719) without vote, 16 December (meeting 51); draft by Malaysia (A/C.2/47/L.51); agenda item 79.

The Assembly, by **resolution 47/189**, decided to convene a global conference on the sustainable development of small island developing States, as called for in Agenda 21. The conference was to be held in Barbados in 1994.

Preparations for UNCED

The UNCED Preparatory Committee held its fourth session in 1992 (New York, 2 March–3 April)[6] to finalize the proposals to be submitted to UNCED. The Committee adopted decisions allowing the participation of NGOs and observers at UNCED; appealing for contributions to facilitate the participation of developing countries; and adopting draft chapters of Agenda 21, the Statement of Principles on forests and the Rio Declaration. It also made recommendations to the General Assembly regarding the dates of the Conference, observer status for associate members of regional commissions, the status of EEC at UNCED and draft provisional rules of procedure of the Conference.

On 7 April,[7] the Secretary-General transmitted the four decisions containing those recommendations to the Assembly for action.

GENERAL ASSEMBLY ACTION

On 13 April 1992, the Assembly adopted the four decisions recommended by the UNCED Preparatory Committee. Noting that the Moslem Feast of Ed-Al-Adha would start on 10 or 11 June, the Assembly, by **decision 46/468**, changed the dates of UNCED from 1 to 12 June 1992 to 3 to 14 June, with pre-session consultations to take place on 1 and 2 June. By **decision 46/469**, the Assembly requested the Secretary-General to invite associate members of regional commissions to participate in the Conference as observers and amended the draft provisional rules accordingly. By **decision 46/470**, the Assembly amended the rules to allow EEC to participate fully in the Conference and, by **decision 46/471**, revised the rule relating to the election of Conference officers.

Other action. Also in preparation for UNCED, the Department of Public Information implemented a system-wide information programme, described in a January report of the Secretary-General[8] submitted to the Committee on Information in response to a 1991 request of the Assembly.[9]

In other action, the Governing Council of the United Nations Environment Programme (UNEP) held its third special session (Nairobi, Kenya, 3-5 February)[10] to consider reports to be submitted to UNCED concerning the state of the environment,[11] desertification[12] and follow-up to previous Assembly resolutions on sustainable development.[13]

The Economic and Social Council, by **decision 1992/296** of 31 July, and the Assembly, by **decision 47/444** of 22 December, took note of the report of the Governing Council on its third special session.

The United Nations Conference on Trade and Development (UNCTAD), in the report on its eighth session (see PART THREE, Chapter IV), stressed the importance of UNCED and affirmed its readiness to participate in the follow-up process.

Follow-up to the Conference

Institutional arrangements

In October, the Secretary-General submitted a report to the General Assembly on institutional arrangements to follow up UNCED,[14] which had recommended an institutional structure aimed at ensuring the implementation of Agenda 21. The Secretary-General discussed proposals related to the organization of a high-level Commission on Sustainable Development, inter-agency coordination arrangements, the role of a high-level advisory board on sustainable development, and the secretariat support structure. In an addendum, the Administrative Committee on Coordination (ACC) offered its views on those institutional arrangements.

In December,[15] the Secretary-General announced the future establishment in New York of a Department for Policy Coordination and Sustainable Development.

GENERAL ASSEMBLY ACTION

On 22 December, on the recommendation of the Second Committee, the Assembly adopted without vote **resolution 47/191**.

Institutional arrangements to follow up the United Nations Conference on Environment and Development

The General Assembly,

Welcoming the adoption by the United Nations Conference on Environment and Development of Agenda 21, in particular chapter 38, entitled "International in-

stitutional arrangements", which contains a set of important recommendations on institutional arrangements to follow up the Conference,

Stressing the overall objective of the integration of environment and development issues at the national, subregional, regional and international levels, including the United Nations system institutional arrangements, and the specific objectives recommended by the Conference in paragraph 38.8 of Agenda 21,

Taking note of the report of the Secretary-General, prepared with the assistance of the Secretary-General of the United Nations Conference on Environment and Development, on institutional arrangements to follow up the Conference, as well as the recommendations and proposals contained therein,

1. *Endorses* the recommendations on international institutional arrangements to follow up the United Nations Conference on Environment and Development as contained in chapter 38 of Agenda 21, particularly those on the establishment of a high-level Commission on Sustainable Development;

Commission on Sustainable Development

2. *Requests* the Economic and Social Council, at its organizational session for 1993, to set up a high-level Commission on Sustainable Development as a functional commission of the Council, in accordance with Article 68 of the Charter of the United Nations, in order to ensure effective follow-up to the Conference, as well as to enhance international cooperation and rationalize the intergovernmental decision-making capacity for the integration of environment and development issues and to examine the progress of the implementation of Agenda 21 at the national, regional and international levels, fully guided by the principles of the Rio Declaration on Environment and Development and all other aspects of the Conference, in order to achieve sustainable development in all countries;

3. *Recommends* that the Commission have the following functions, as agreed in paragraphs 38.13, 33.13 and 33.21 of Agenda 21:

(a) To monitor progress in the implementation of Agenda 21 and activities related to the integration of environmental and developmental goals throughout the United Nations system through analysis and evaluation of reports from all relevant organs, organizations, programmes and institutions of the United Nations system dealing with various issues of environment and development, including those related to finance;

(b) To consider information provided by Governments, for example, in the form of periodic communications or national reports regarding the activities they undertake to implement Agenda 21, the problems they face, such as problems related to financial resources and technology transfer, and other environment and development issues they find relevant;

(c) To review the progress in the implementation of the commitments set forth in Agenda 21, including those related to the provision of financial resources and transfer of technology;

(d) To review and monitor regularly progress towards the United Nations target of 0.7 per cent of the gross national product of developed countries for official development assistance; this review process should systematically combine the monitoring of the implementation of Agenda 21 with the review of financial resources available;

(*e*) To review on a regular basis the adequacy of funding and mechanisms, including efforts to reach the objectives agreed in chapter 33 of Agenda 21, including targets where applicable;

(*f*) To receive and analyse relevant input from competent non-governmental organizations, including the scientific and the private sector, in the context of the overall implementation of Agenda 21;

(*g*) To enhance the dialogue, within the framework of the United Nations, with non-governmental organizations and the independent sector, as well as other entities outside the United Nations system;

(*h*) To consider, where appropriate, information regarding the progress made in the implementation of environmental conventions, which could be made available by the relevant conferences of parties;

(*i*) To provide appropriate recommendations to the General Assembly, through the Economic and Social Council, on the basis of an integrated consideration of the reports and issues related to the implementation of Agenda 21;

(*j*) To consider, at an appropriate time, the results of the review to be conducted expeditiously by the Secretary-General of all recommendations of the Conference for capacity-building programmes, information networks, task forces and other mechanisms to support the integration of environment and development at regional and subregional levels;

4. *Also recommends* that the Commission:

(*a*) Promote the incorporation of the principles of the Rio Declaration on Environment and Development in the implementation of Agenda 21;

(*b*) Promote the incorporation of the Non-legally Binding Authoritative Statement of Principles for a Global Consensus on the Management, Conservation and Sustainable Development of All Types of Forests in the implementation of Agenda 21, in particular in the context of the review of the implementation of chapter 11 thereof;

(*c*) Keep under review the implementation of Agenda 21, recognizing that it is a dynamic programme that could evolve over time, taking into account the agreement to review Agenda 21 in 1997, and make recommendations, as appropriate, on the need for new cooperative arrangements related to sustainable development to the Economic and Social Council and, through it, to the General Assembly;

5. *Decides* that the Commission, in the fulfilment of its functions, will also:

(*a*) Monitor progress in promoting, facilitating and financing, as appropriate, access to and transfer of environmentally sound technologies and corresponding know-how, in particular to developing countries, on favourable terms, including on concessional and preferential terms, as mutually agreed, taking into account the need to protect intellectual property rights as well as the special needs of developing countries for the implementation of Agenda 21;

(*b*) Consider issues related to the provision of financial resources from all available funding sources and mechanisms, as contained in paragraphs 33.13 to 33.16 of Agenda 21;

6. *Recommends* that the Commission consist of representatives of fifty-three States elected by the Economic and Social Council from among the Members of the United Nations and members of its specialized agencies for three-year terms, with due regard to equitable geographical distribution; the regional allocation of seats could be the same as that of the Commission on Science and Technology for Development, as decided by the Economic and Social Council in its decision 1992/222 of 29 May 1992; representation should be at a high level, including ministerial participation; other Members of the United Nations and members of its specialized agencies, as well as other observers of the United Nations, may participate in the Commission in the capacity of observer, in accordance with established practice;

7. *Also recommends* that the Commission:

(*a*) Provide for representatives of various parts of the United Nations system and other intergovernmental organizations, including international financial institutions, GATT, regional development banks, subregional financial institutions, relevant regional and subregional economic and technical cooperation organizations and regional economic integration organizations, to assist and advise the Commission in the performance of its functions, within their respective areas of expertise and mandates, and participate actively in its deliberations; and provide for the European Community, within its areas of competence, to participate fully—as will be appropriately defined in the rules of procedure applicable to the Commission—without the right to vote;

(*b*) Provide for non-governmental organizations, including those related to major groups as well as to industry and the scientific and business communities, to participate effectively in its work and contribute within their areas of competence to its deliberations;

8. *Requests* the Secretary-General, in the light of paragraph 7 above, to submit, for the consideration of the Economic and Social Council at its organizational session for 1993, his proposals on the rules of procedure applicable to the Commission, including those related to participation of relevant intergovernmental and non-governmental organizations, as recommended by the Conference, taking into account the following:

(*a*) The procedures, while ensuring the intergovernmental nature of the Commission, should allow its members to benefit from the expertise and competence of relevant intergovernmental and non-governmental organizations;

(*b*) The procedures should permit relevant intergovernmental organizations inside and outside the United Nations system, including multilateral financial institutions, to appoint special representatives to the Commission;

(*c*) The rules of procedure of the Economic and Social Council and those of its functional commissions;

(*d*) The rules of procedure of the United Nations Conference on Environment and Development;

(*e*) Decisions 1/1 and 2/1 of the Preparatory Committee for the United Nations Conference on Environment and Development;

(*f*) Paragraphs 38.11 and 38.44 of Agenda 21;

9. *Recommends* that the Commission shall meet once a year for a period of two to three weeks; the first substantive session of the Commission will be held in New York in 1993, without prejudice to the venue of future sessions at Geneva and/or in New York;

10. *Requests* the Committee on Conferences to consider the need for readjusting the calendar of meetings

in order to take account of the interrelationship between the work of the Commission and the work of other relevant United Nations intergovernmental subsidiary organs, in order to ensure timely reporting to the Economic and Social Council;

11. *Recommends* that in 1993, as a transitional measure, the Commission hold a short organizational session in New York; at that session, the Commission will elect the officers of the Commission, namely, a chairman, three vice-chairmen and a rapporteur, one from each of the regional groups, decide on the agenda of its first substantive session and consider all other organizational issues as may be necessary; the agenda of the organizational session of the Commission shall be decided on by the Economic and Social Council at its organizational session for 1993;

12. *Also recommends* that the Commission, at its first substantive session, adopt a multi-year thematic programme of its work that will provide a framework to assess progress achieved in the implementation of Agenda 21 and ensure an integrated approach to all of its environment and development components as well as linkages between sectoral and cross-sectoral issues; this programme could be of clusters that would integrate in an effective manner related sectoral and cross-sectoral components of Agenda 21 in such a way as to allow the Commission to review the progress of the implementation of the entire Agenda 21 by 1997; the programme of work could be adjusted, as the need arises, at subsequent sessions of the Commission;

13. *Requests* the Secretary-General to submit his proposals for such a programme of work during the organizational session of the Commission;

14. *Recommends* that in order to carry out its functions and implement its programme of work effectively the Commission consider organizing its work on the following lines:

(*a*) Financial resources, mechanisms, transfer of technology, capacity-building and other cross-sectoral issues;

(*b*) Review of the implementation of Agenda 21 at the international level, as well as at the regional and national levels, including the means of implementation, in accordance with paragraph 12 above and the functions of the Commission, taking into account, where appropriate, information regarding progress in the implementation of relevant environmental conventions;

(*c*) A high-level meeting, with ministerial participation, to have an integrated overview of the implementation of Agenda 21, to consider emerging policy issues and to provide necessary political impetus to the implementation of the decisions of the Conference and the commitments contained therein; Review and consideration of the implementation of Agenda 21 should be in an integrated manner;

15. *Requests* the Secretary-General to provide for each session of the Commission, in accordance with the programme of work mentioned in paragraph 12 above and with its organizational modalities, analytical reports containing information on relevant activities to implement Agenda 21, progress achieved and emerging issues to be addressed;

16. *Also requests* the Secretary-General to prepare, for the first substantive session of the Commission, reports containing information and proposals, as appropriate, on the following issues:

(*a*) Initial financial commitments, financial flows and arrangements to give effect to the decisions of the Conference from all available funding sources and mechanisms;

(*b*) Progress achieved in facilitating and promoting transfer of environmentally sound technologies, cooperation and capacity-building;

(*c*) Progress in the incorporation of recommendations of the Conference in the activities of international organizations and measures undertaken by the Administrative Committee on Coordination to ensure that sustainable development principles are incorporated into programmes and processes within the United Nations system;

(*d*) Ways in which, upon request, the United Nations system and bilateral donors are assisting countries, particularly developing countries, in the preparation of national reports and national Agenda 21 action plans;

(*e*) Urgent and major emerging issues that may be addressed in the course of the high-level meeting;

17. *Decides* that organizational modalities for the Commission should be reviewed in the context of the overall review and appraisal of Agenda 21 during the special session of the General Assembly and adjusted, as may be required, to improve its effectiveness;

Relationship with other United Nations intergovernmental bodies

18. *Recommends* that the Commission, in discharging its functions, submit its consolidated recommendations to the Economic and Social Council and, through it, to the General Assembly, to be considered by the Council and the Assembly in accordance with their respective responsibilities as defined in the Charter of the United Nations and with the relevant provisions of paragraphs 38.9 and 38.10 of Agenda 21;

19. *Also recommends* that the Commission actively interact with other intergovernmental United Nations bodies dealing with matters related to environment and development;

20. *Emphasizes* that the ongoing restructuring and revitalization of the United Nations in the economic, social and related fields should take into account the organizational modalities for the Commission, with a view to optimizing its work and the work of other intergovernmental United Nations bodies dealing with matters related to environment and development;

Coordination within the United Nations system

21. *Requests* all specialized agencies and related organizations of the United Nations system to strengthen and adjust their activities, programmes and medium-term plans, as appropriate, in line with Agenda 21, in particular regarding projects for promoting sustainable development, in accordance with paragraph 38.28 of Agenda 21, and make their reports on steps they have taken to give effect to this recommendation available to the Commission and the Economic and Social Council in 1993 or, at the latest, in 1994, in accordance with Article 64 of the Charter;

22. *Invites* all relevant governing bodies to ensure that the tasks assigned to them are carried out effectively, including the elaboration and publication on a regular basis of reports on the activities of the organs, programmes and organizations for which they are responsible, and that continuous reviews are undertaken of their policies, programmes, budgets and activities;

23. *Invites* the World Bank and other international, regional and subregional financial and development institutions, including the Global Environment Facility, to submit regularly to the Commission reports containing information on their experience, activities and plans to implement Agenda 21;

24. *Requests* the Secretary-General to submit to the Commission, at its substantive session of 1993, recommendations and proposals for improving coordination of programmes related to development data that exist within the United Nations system, taking into account the provisions of paragraph 40.13 of Agenda 21, *inter alia* regarding ''Development Watch'';

United Nations Environment Programme, United Nations Development Programme, United Nations Conference on Trade and Development and United Nations Sudano-Sahelian Office

25. *Requests* the Governing Council of the United Nations Environment Programme, the Governing Council of the United Nations Development Programme and the Trade and Development Board to examine the relevant provisions of chapter 38 of Agenda 21 at their next sessions and to submit to the General Assembly at its forty-eighth session, through the Commission and the Economic and Social Council, reports on their specific plans to implement Agenda 21;

26. *Takes note* of the work of the United Nations Centre for Urgent Environmental Assistance, established by the Governing Council of the United Nations Environment Programme on an experimental basis, and invites the Governing Council to report to the General Assembly at its forty-eighth session on the experience gained within the Centre;

Regional commissions

27. *Requests* United Nations regional commissions to examine the relevant provisions of chapter 38 of Agenda 21 at their next sessions and to submit reports on their specific plans to implement Agenda 21;

28. *Requests* the Economic and Social Council to decide on the arrangements required for the reports of regional commissions with the conclusions related to such a review to be made available to the Commission on Sustainable Development in 1993, or at the latest in 1994;

High-level Advisory Board

29. *Endorses* the view of the Secretary-General that the High-level Advisory Board should consist of eminent persons broadly representative of all regions of the world, with recognized expertise on the broad spectrum of issues to be dealt with by the Commission, drawn from relevant scientific disciplines, industry, finance and other major non-governmental constituencies, as well as various disciplines related to environment and development, and that due account should also be given to gender balance;

30. *Decides* that the main task of the Advisory Board is to give broad consideration to issues related to implementation of Agenda 21, taking into account the thematic multi-year programme of work of the Commission, and provide expert advice in that regard to the Secretary-General and, through him, to the Commission, the Economic and Social Council and the General Assembly;

31. *Takes note* of the views of the Secretary-General regarding the functions of the Advisory Board and of the Committee for Development Planning, and requests him to submit appropriate proposals to the Economic and Social Council at its organizational session for 1993, including the possibility of establishing rosters of experts;

Secretariat support arrangements

32. *Takes note* of the decision of the Secretary-General to establish a new Department for Policy Coordination and Sustainable Development, headed at the Under-Secretary-General level, and in this context calls upon the Secretary-General to establish a clearly identifiable, highly qualified and competent secretariat support structure to provide support for the Commission, the Inter-Agency Committee on Sustainable Development and the High-level Advisory Board, taking into account gender balance at all levels, the paramount importance of securing the highest standards of efficiency, competence and integrity, and the importance of recruiting staff on as wide a geographical basis as possible in accordance with Articles 8 and 101 of the Charter and the following criteria:

(*a*) It should draw on the expertise gained and the working methods and organizational structures developed during the preparatory process for the Conference;

(*b*) It should work closely with United Nations and other expert bodies in the field of sustainable development and should cooperate closely and cooperatively with the economic and social entities of the Secretariat and the secretariats of the relevant organs, organizations and bodies of the United Nations system, including the secretariats of international financial institutions, and it should provide for effective liaison with relevant non-governmental organizations, including those related to major groups, in particular non-governmental organizations from developing countries;

(*c*) The secretariat, which will be located in New York, should ensure to all countries easy access to its services and effective interaction with secretariats of other international organizations, financial institutions and relevant conventions whose secretariats have been established definitively or on an interim basis, and should have a relevant office at Geneva to establish close links with activities related to follow-up to legal instruments signed at or mandated by the Conference and to maintain liaison with agencies in the fields of environment and development; the secretariat should also have a liaison office at Nairobi, on the basis of arrangements made at the Conference;

(*d*) It should be headed by a high-level official designated by the Secretary-General to work closely and directly with him and with assured access to him, as well as with the heads of relevant organizations of the United Nations system, including the multilateral financial and trade organizations, dealing with the implementation of Agenda 21;

(*e*) It should be funded from the United Nations regular budget and depend to the maximum extent possible upon existing budgetary resources;

(*f*) It should be supplemented or reinforced, as appropriate, by secondments from other relevant bodies and agencies of the United Nations system, especially the United Nations Environment Programme, the United Nations Development Programme and the World Bank, taking into account the need to ensure that the work programmes of those organizations are not negatively affected, and from national Governments, as well as by appropriate specialists on limited-term contracts from outside the United Nations in such areas as may be required;

(g) It should take into account relevant resolutions and decisions of the General Assembly and the Economic and Social Council regarding women in the United Nations Secretariat;

(h) Sustainable development should be integrated and coordinated with other economic, social and environmental activities of the Secretariat; organizational decisions should be consistent with consensus resolutions in the context of the restructuring and revitalization of the United Nations in the economic, social and related fields;

33. *Requests* the Secretary-General to make the necessary interim secretariat arrangements to ensure adequate preparations and support for the first session of the Commission and the work of the Inter-Agency Committee;

34. *Also requests* the Secretary-General to report to the General Assembly at its forty-eighth session on the implementation of the present resolution.

General Assembly resolution 47/191

22 December 1992   Meeting 93   Adopted without vote

Approved by Second Committee (A/47/719) without vote, 16 December (meeting 51); draft by Malaysia (A/C.2/47/L.61), orally revised; agenda item 79.

Financial implications. 5th Committee, A/47/814; S-G, A/C.2/47/L.90, A/C.5/47/81.

Meeting numbers. GA 47th session: 2nd Committee 51; 5th Committee 49; plenary 93.

The Secretary-General estimated that **resolution 47/191** would entail an expenditure of $1.8 million for 1993.

Capacity-building

In an April 1992 report to the Governing Council of the United Nations Development Programme (UNDP),[16] the UNDP Administrator outlined a programme of support to developing countries as part of the planned follow-up to UNCED. UNDP, through its field offices, would organize United Nations capacity-building efforts, mobilize donor resources on behalf of Governments for capacity-building, assist countries in identifying and mobilizing domestic financial resources, raise awareness of the role of women and promote the participation of all parts of society, particularly NGOs and the private sector. UNDP support for Agenda 21 would focus on helping developing countries to prepare national sustainable development strategies and on building capacities for sustainable development.

On 26 May,[17] taking into account the report of the Joint Inspection Unit assessing the environmental focus of projects financed by UNDP and other agencies,[18] the Governing Council requested the Administrator to assist developing countries in strengthening their capacity to for-

mulate and implement policies and programmes for sustainable development.

During the year, UNDP launched an initiative known as Capacity 21, which, according to the Administrator,[19] would complement existing programmes and be used to facilitate the integration of environmental considerations in all programmes. A goal of $100 million had been set for the pilot phase of the programme.[20]

GENERAL ASSEMBLY ACTION

On 22 December, on the recommendation of the Second Committee, the Assembly adopted **resolution 47/194** without vote.

Capacity-building for Agenda 21

The General Assembly,

Welcoming the adoption by the United Nations Conference on Environment and Development of Agenda 21, in particular chapter 37 thereof, which contains a set of important recommendations on capacity-building,

Noting with interest the launching by the Administrator of the United Nations Development Programme of the "Capacity 21" initiative,

1. *Invites* the Governing Council of the United Nations Development Programme, taking into account the national policies, priorities and plans of recipient countries, to give due consideration to the adoption of concrete programmes and measures to implement Agenda 21 recommendations on capacity-building through, *inter alia*, the "Capacity 21" initiative, with a view to promoting early action in support of developing countries, in particular the least developed countries, in the area of capacity-building;

2. *Invites* all relevant United Nations agencies, within their mandates, to promote early action to implement the provisions of chapter 37 of Agenda 21;

3. *Requests* the Commission on Sustainable Development, in execution of its mandate, to give urgent consideration to the implementation of the provisions of Agenda 21 on capacity-building.

General Assembly resolution 47/194

22 December 1992   Meeting 93   Adopted without vote

Approved by Second Committee (A/47/719) without vote, 16 December (meeting 51); draft by Malaysia (A/C.2/47/64); agenda item 79.

Coordination within the UN system

In a November report to the UNEP Governing Council,[21] ACC reported that the Secretary-General had established an Inter-Agency Task Force on Environment and Development, composed of the Executive Heads of the Food and Agriculture Organization of the United Nations, the United Nations Educational, Scientific and Cultural Organization, the World Health Organization, the World Meteorological Organization (WMO), the World Bank, UNDP and UNEP, with UNCED invited to attend as an *ex-officio* member. The Task Force submitted to ACC recommendations relating to the allocation and sharing of responsibilities of the United Nations system stemming from Agenda 21.

ACC, in October, established an Inter-Agency Committee for Sustainable Development, comprising the member organizations of the Task Force and two additional organizations to be designated by the Secretary-General.

REFERENCES

[1]Report of the United Nations Conference on Environment and Development, Rio de Janeiro, 3-14 June 1992, vol. I-III, Sales No. E.93.I.8. [2]GA res. 44/228, 22 Dec. 1989. [3]YUN 1972, p. 318. [4]A/CONF.151/PC/L.28 & Add.1-14. [5]YUN 1982, p. 181. [6]A/CONF.151/PC/128. [7]A/46/897. [8]A/AC.198/1992/3. [9]YUN 1991, p. 84, GA res. 46/73 B, 11 Dec. 1991. [10]A/47/25. [11]UNEP/GCSS.III/2 & Corr.1,2 and Add.1,2. [12]UNEP/GCSS.III/3 & Corr.1/Rev.1 & Add.1. [13]UNEP/GCSS.III/4 & Corr.1 & Add.1. [14]A/47/598 & Add.1. [15]A/47/753. [16]DP/1992/14. [17]E/1992/28 (dec. 92/16). [18]A/47/457 & Add.1. [19]DP/1993/11. [20]DP/1993/10. [21]UNEP/GC.17/12.

General aspects

Sustainable development

In April,[1] the Secretary-General, in response to a 1989 General Assembly resolution,[2] submitted a report on the follow-up to two 1987 resolutions dealing with sustainable development. One of the resolutions[3] had established a framework for the achievement of environmentally sound development, and the other[4] had emphasized the need for sustainable development.

In preparing the report, the Executive Director of UNEP, on behalf of the Secretary-General, had requested information from Governments and United Nations organizations on implementation of the two resolutions. In all, 38 countries and 28 United Nations bodies replied. The report concluded that while progress had been made, it was limited and uneven in relation to what was needed, and would remain so unless the structural aspects of the state of the world's environment and development received the attention of political leaders. Necessary structural changes included adjustments in the composition and distribution of production and consumption, population control, adjustments in international economic relations, alleviation of poverty and improvement of the quality and means of governance to minimize waste and injustice and maximize the creative involvement of people.

The UNEP Governing Council, on 5 February,[5] had taken note of an earlier version of the report[6] and called on Governments to devote more attention to achieving sustainable development and to allocate the necessary resources. It requested the Executive Director to report to the Council on the implementation of the decision in 1993.

The Economic and Social Council, on 31 July, by **decision 1992/296**, and the General Assembly, on 22 December, by **decision 47/444**, took note of the Secretary-General's report.

In other action, the Council, by **decision 1992/252**, approved the preparation of a progress report on human rights and the environment by a Special Rapporteur (see PART THREE, Chapter X).

UNCTAD action. In August,[7] the UNCTAD secretariat submitted to the Trade and Development Board a report on sustainable development, including UNCTAD's contribution to the implementation of UNCED's conclusions and recommendations. The report covered cross-sectoral issues, including policy principles, tradeable permits and poverty, and sectoral links, including commodities, industry and other sectors, energy policy and tradeable emission entitlements and the promotion of environmentally sound technologies.

International conventions

Climate change convention

The United Nations Framework Convention on Climate Change[8] was opened for signature on 4 June. During the year it was signed by 158 States and EEC, and ratified by nine States.[9] The Convention was to remain open for signing in New York from 20 June 1992 to 19 June 1993. It would enter into force on the ninetieth day after the date of deposit of the fiftieth instrument of ratification, acceptance, approval or accession.

The objective of the Convention was to stabilize atmospheric concentrations of "greenhouse gases", which absorbed and re-emitted infrared radiation, at a level that would prevent dangerous anthropogenic interference with the climate system. Developed countries and countries undergoing transition to a market economy were to set a goal of limiting the emission of greenhouse gases, including carbon dioxide, to 1990 levels. The developed countries were to provide financial and technological resources to the developing countries to assist them in implementing the Convention. The Convention defined a mechanism for providing financial resources on a grant or concessional basis through the Global Environment Facility (see below).

All parties to the Convention were to report periodically on national inventories of anthropogenic emissions and to cooperate in the development of processes that controlled them.

The Convention was drafted by an Intergovernmental Negotiating Committee, which was open to all United Nations Members or members of the specialized agencies, established pursuant to a 1990 General Assembly mandate.[10] One hundred and fifty-seven countries, including 118 developing countries, participated in the negotiations.

The Committee held its fifth session in two parts (New York, 18-28 February and 30 April–9 May),[11] in accordance with a 1991 Assembly resolution,[12] to finalize the drafting of the Convention, which it adopted on 9 May.

In June, the Chairman of the Committee, pursuant to a 1990 Assembly request[10] reiterated in 1991,[12] submitted a report to UNCED on the results of the Committee's negotiations, for early entry into force of the Convention.[13]

In October, the Secretary-General, pursuant to a 1991 Assembly resolution,[12] submitted a report on implementation of the resolution and possible requirements for future work.[14] He said the Convention could be considered a first step, providing a framework for further elaboration as new scientific evidence became available.

The Committee held its sixth session at Geneva (7-10 December)[15] to prepare for the first session of the Conference of the Parties and to draw up an interim work plan.

Voluntary funds. A review[16] of the two funds established pursuant to a 1990 Assembly resolution[10]—the special voluntary fund to support the participation of developing countries and the trust fund for the negotiating process[17]—stated that, as at 18 November, contributions to assist developing countries totalled about $3 million. Contributions received or pledged towards support of the negotiating process stood at about $420,000.

GENERAL ASSEMBLY ACTION

On 22 December, the General Assembly adopted **resolution 47/195** without vote.

Protection of global climate for present and future generations of mankind

The General Assembly,

Recalling its resolutions 43/53 of 6 December 1988 and 44/207 of 22 December 1989, in which it recognized climate change as a common concern of mankind,

Recalling also its resolutions 45/212 of 21 December 1990, by which it established an Intergovernmental Negotiating Committee to prepare an effective framework convention on climate change, and any related legal instruments as might be agreed upon, for signature during the United Nations Conference on Environment and Development, and 46/169 of 19 December 1991, by which it provided for the continuation of work on climate change until the end of 1992,

Taking note with appreciation of the reports of the Intergovernmental Negotiating Committee for a Framework Convention on Climate Change on its work up to May 1992 and the report prepared on behalf of the Committee, by its Chairman, for submission to the United Nations Conference on Environment and Development,

Taking note of resolution 15(EC-XLIV), adopted by the Executive Council of the World Meteorological Organization at its forty-fourth session,

Noting that, in accordance with paragraph 4 of its resolution 46/169 and pursuant to resolution INC/1992/1 adopted by the Intergovernmental Negotiating Committee on 9 May 1992, arrangements were made for the sixth session of the Intergovernmental Negotiating Committee,

Noting also that the sixth session of the Intergovernmental Negotiating Committee was held at Geneva from 7 to 10 December 1992,

Noting further the interim arrangements contained in article 21 of the United Nations Framework Convention on Climate Change, including the provision that the secretariat established by the General Assembly in resolution 45/212 should be the interim secretariat of the Convention until the completion of the first session of the Conference of the Parties to the Convention,

Noting with appreciation the support provided for the operation of the secretariat during 1992 by the United Nations Conference on Trade and Development, the United Nations Development Programme, the United Nations Environment Programme and the World Meteorological Organization, as well as by bilateral contributors,

Having considered the report of the Secretary-General, with particular reference to the possible requirements for intergovernmental and secretariat work on the implementation of the Convention in the period up to and including the first session of the Conference of the Parties to the Convention,

1. *Welcomes* the adoption, on 9 May 1992, of the United Nations Framework Convention on Climate Change by the Intergovernmental Negotiating Committee for a Framework Convention on Climate Change and its signing by a large number of States;

2. *Considers* the Convention one of the achievements of the international community working through the United Nations and a first step in a cooperative response to the common concern for the change in the Earth's climate and its adverse effects;

3. *Calls upon* States that have not done so to sign or accede to the Convention, as appropriate, and all signatories that have not yet done so to ratify, accept or approve it, so that it may enter into force;

4. *Invites* signatories of the Convention to communicate to the head of the interim secretariat of the Convention, as soon as feasible, information regarding measures consistent with the provisions of the Convention, pending its entry into force;

5. *Urges* States to support and contribute to the activities at the national, subregional, regional and international levels related to the basic scientific and technical needs specified in the Convention, including those activities carried out under the World Climate Programme and the Global Climate Observing System;

6. *Decides* that the Intergovernmental Negotiating Committee shall continue to function in order to prepare for the first session of the Conference of the Parties, as specified in the Convention, and, in that context, to contribute to the effective operation of the interim arrangements set out in article 21 of the Convention;

7. *Invites* the Intergovernmental Negotiating Committee, in this regard, to implement expeditiously the plan of preparatory work drawn up at its sixth session, and requests the Secretary-General to make arrangements within the overall calendar of conferences for the

Committee to hold sessions, in accordance with the needs of that plan;

8. *Requests* the Intergovernmental Negotiating Committee to promote a coherent and coordinated programme of activities by competent bodies aimed at supporting the entry into force and effective implementation of the Convention, including strengthening the capacities of developing and all other countries to prepare for their participation in the Convention;

9. *Calls upon* the organs, organizations and bodies of the United Nations system involved in work relating to climate change, including the interim secretariat of the Convention, to initiate and strengthen such activities, where possible in collaboration with each other, and invites them to make information on these activities and on any coordination arrangements regularly available to the Intergovernmental Negotiating Committee, through its secretariat;

10. *Invites* the Intergovernmental Negotiating Committee to convey information on its work to the General Assembly, as well as to the Economic and Social Council and the Commission on Sustainable Development, as appropriate, in particular in the context of chapter 9 of Agenda 21;

11. *Requests* the Secretary-General to strengthen the secretariat established by the General Assembly in its resolution 45/212 so that it may function as the interim secretariat of the Convention until the completion of the first session of the Conference of the Parties to the Convention and, in that capacity, provide adequate support to the evolving work of the Intergovernmental Negotiating Committee, and also requests him to make provisions for this purpose within the current and forthcoming programme budgets;

12. *Invites* the United Nations Environment Programme, the World Meteorological Organization and other United Nations bodies with relevant expertise, to continue to cooperate closely with, and to contribute staff to assist, the head of the interim secretariat;

13. *Requests* bilateral sources to continue to assist the interim secretariat as hitherto;

14. *Requests* the head of the interim secretariat to maximize opportunities for collaborative work with other secretariat entities, including the secretariat of the Commission on Sustainable Development;

15. *Requests* the Secretary-General to maintain the special voluntary fund established under paragraph 10 of General Assembly resolution 45/212 to support the participation of developing countries, in particular the least developed among them and small island developing countries, as well as developing countries stricken by drought and desertification, in the work of the Intergovernmental Negotiating Committee and in the first session of the Conference of the Parties to the Convention, bearing in mind, *inter alia*, resolution INC/1992/1 of the Intergovernmental Negotiating Committee;

16. *Also requests* the Secretary-General to maintain the trust fund established under paragraph 20 of General Assembly resolution 45/212 to contribute to the costs of the interim secretariat of the Convention;

17. *Takes note with appreciation* of the contributions made to these extrabudgetary funds and invites further adequate and timely contributions to both funds;

18. *Decides* that, subject to the relevant provisions of General Assembly resolutions 40/243 of 18 December 1985, 41/213 of 19 December 1986 and 42/211 of 21 December 1987, the costs of the work of the Committee and the interim secretariat should be funded within the current and forthcoming programme budgets, without adversely affecting the programmed activities of the United Nations, and through voluntary contributions to the trust fund, as appropriate;

19. *Welcomes* the invitation by the Government of Germany to host the first session of the Conference of the Parties to the Convention;

20. *Invites* the Chairman of the Intergovernmental Negotiating Committee to submit a final report to the General Assembly on behalf of the Committee on the completion of the Committee's work, following the conclusion of the first session of the Conference of the Parties to the Convention;

21. *Requests* the Secretary-General to report to the General Assembly at its forty-ninth session on the implementation of the present resolution;

22. *Decides* to include in the provisional agenda of its forty-ninth session the item entitled "Protection of global climate for present and future generations of mankind".

General Assembly resolution 47/195

22 December 1992   Meeting 93   Adopted without vote

Draft by Uruguay (A/47/L.49), orally amended; agenda item 80.
Financial implications. 5th Committee, A/47/815; S-G, A/C.5/47/83.
Meeting numbers. GA 47th session: 5th Committee 49; plenary 93.

On the same date, the Assembly, by **decision 47/446**, took note of a report of the Second Committee,[18] which had considered two draft resolutions on protection of the global climate. The Committee decided to take no action on one draft,[19] but the Chairman announced that he would submit it, with amendments, directly to the Assembly in plenary meeting. The other draft text[20] was subsequently withdrawn by its sponsor.

Convention on Biological Diversity

The Convention on Biological Diversity was opened for signature at the Earth Summit on 5 June and was to remain open in New York until 4 June 1993. During the year it was signed by 160 States and EEC and ratified by six States.[9] The Convention would enter into force on the ninetieth day after the deposit of the thirtieth instrument of ratification, acceptance, approval or accession.

The Convention's objectives were the conservation of biological diversity, the sustainable use of its components and the fair and equitable sharing of the benefits arising from the use of genetic resources. Its 42 articles covered, among other things, the use of terms; jurisdictional scope; cooperation; identification and monitoring; *in-situ* and *ex-situ* conservation; sustainable use of components of biological diversity; incentive measures; research and training; public education; impact assessment and minimizing adverse impacts; access to genetic resources; access to and transfer of technology; exchange of information; technical and scientific cooperation; handling of biotechnology and distribution of its benefits; financial resources; settlement of disputes; and adoption of protocols.

The Convention was drafted by the Intergovernmental Negotiating Committee for a Convention on Biological Diversity, which held two sessions in 1992 (Nairobi, 6-15 February[21] and 11-22 May[22]). It was adopted by the Conference for the Adoption of the Agreed Text of the Convention on Biological Diversity (Nairobi, 22 May). The Conference also adopted resolutions inviting the Global Environment Facility (see below) to serve as the interim financial mechanism for the Convention, calling for international cooperation in the conservation of biological diversity, and describing the interrelationship between the Convention and the promotion of sustainable agriculture.

Montreal Protocol

The parties to the 1987 Montreal Protocol on Substances that Deplete the Ozone Layer,[23] which entered into force on 1 January 1989, held their fourth meeting from 23 to 25 November at Copenhagen, Denmark.[24] They agreed to accelerate the Protocol's schedule for phasing out several ozone-depleting substances, including chlorofluorocarbons, carbon tetrachloride, halons and methyl chloroform. They also amended the Protocol to include hydrochlorofluorocarbons, hydrobromofluorocarbons and methyl bromide among the substances to be regulated. The amendment would enter into force on 1 January 1994, provided that 20 States parties to the Protocol had approved it. In addition, a multilateral fund was created to assist developing countries in eliminating the controlled substances. At the end of the year, 97 States and EEC were parties to the Protocol.[9]

The 1990 London Amendment to the Montreal Protocol[25] entered into force on 10 August 1992 with the ratification, acceptance, approval or accession of 27 States during the year. Forty-one States and EEC had become parties to the Amendment by the end of the year.[9]

Global Environment Facility

The Global Environment Facility (GEF), a joint effort of the World Bank, UNDP and UNEP, was established in 1991[26] to help developing countries respond to environmental problems in four programme areas: climate change, ozone depletion, pollution of international waters and biodiversity. UNCED, in Agenda 21, recommended that GEF be restructured to facilitate its financing of environmental activities.

GEF participants held two meetings during the year (Washington, D.C., 29 and 30 April; Abid-

jan, Côte d'Ivoire, 3-5 December) to begin the process of evaluation and restructuring to meet those requirements.[27]

In April, participating Governments decided that land degradation issues, primarily desertification and deforestation, as they related to the four established programme areas, would be eligible for financing by GEF.[28] It was also agreed that GEF would operate as the funding mechanism for the climate change and biodiversity conventions signed at UNCED.

At the December meeting, participants reiterated the April decision, but did not reach consensus on including land degradation in GEF as a priority area.

REFERENCES
[1]A/47/121-E/1992/15. [2]GA res. 44/227, 22 Dec. 1989. [3]YUN 1987, p. 661, GA res. 42/186, 11 Dec. 1987. [4]Ibid., p. 679, GA res. 42/187, 11 Dec. 1987. [5]A/47/25 (dec. SS.III/2). [6]UNEP/GCSS.III/4 & Corr.1 & Add.1. [7]TD/B/39(1)/7. [8]A/AC.237/18(Part II)/Add.1 & Corr.1. [9]*Multilateral Treaties Deposited with the Secretary-General: Status as at 31 December 1992* (ST/LEG/SER.E/11), Sales No. E.93.V.11. [10]GA res. 45/212, 21 Dec. 1990. [11]A/AC.237/18(Parts I & II). [12]YUN 1991, p. 491, GA res. 46/169, 19 Dec. 1991. [13]A/CONF.151/8. [14]A/47/466. [15]A/AC.237/24 & Corr.1. [16]A/AC.237/20. [17]A/AC.237/23 & Corr.1 & Add.1. [18]A/47/720. [19]A/C.2/47/L.58. [20]A/C.2/47/L.38/Rev.1. [21]UNEP/Bio.Div/N6-INC.4/4. [22]UNEP/Bio.Div/N7-INC.5/4 & Corr.1. [23]YUN 1987, p. 686. [24]UNEP/OzL.Pro.4/15. [25]YUN 1991, p. 493. [26]Ibid., p. 505. [27]UNEP/GC.17/23. [28]UNEP/GC.17/14.

Environmental activities

State of the environment

A report entitled "The state of the environment (1972-1992): saving our planet—challenges and hopes"[1] was prepared for presentation to UNCED by the UNEP Executive Director, pursuant to a 1989 request of the Governing Council.[2] It comprised five parts: the state of the environment; development activities and environment; human conditions and well-being; perceptions, attitudes and responses; and challenges and priorities for action.

The report said that the most significant concerns were the lack of many of the prerequisites for informed decision-making and good environmental management, in particular: the database was still of variable quality, with a shortage of data from developing countries; despite advances in the technical ability to monitor the world environment, those advances had not been generally applied, mainly because of a lack of equipment and trained personnel in many countries; there had been no agreement on the socio-economic indicators of a healthy relationship between people and their environment or on standards for a decent environment; and comprehensive assessments of the environmental situation and of the Earth's carrying capacity were, in consequence, difficult.

In his opening statement to the UNEP Governing Council (Nairobi, 3-5 February),[3] the Executive Director said the report showed that, despite the efforts undertaken, the global environment was worse than it had been 20 years earlier. Not one major environmental issue raised at the 1972 United Nations Conference on the Human Environment[4] had been solved, while new problems of planetary dimensions had emerged. The report, he said, outlined achievable targets that could constitute an agenda for action for the next decade.

On 5 February,[5] the Council took note of the report and requested the Executive Director to bring it to the attention of UNCED.

Protection against harmful products and wastes

The Secretary-General submitted in June 1992 a report[6] on products harmful to health and the environment, containing the third triennial review of the consolidated list of products whose consumption and/or sale had been banned, withdrawn, severely restricted or not approved by Governments. The first such review was submitted in 1986.[7]

In accordance with a 1989 General Assembly resolution,[8] the report reviewed the list and discussed issues and future directions. It concluded that the list should continue to refer to all the relevant work being accomplished within the United Nations system and ensure that for each product entry reference was made to the complementary publications and international conventions. The fourth issue of the list, published at the end of 1991, covered regulatory action taken by 92 Governments on more than 600 products.

The Economic and Social Council, by **decision 1992/296** of 31 July, and the Assembly, by **decision 47/439** of 22 December, took note of the report.

The Basel Convention on the Control of Transboundary Movements of Hazardous Wastes and their Disposal, adopted in 1989, entered into force on 5 May 1992. It was ratified or acceded to by 19 States during the year.[9]

Ecosystems

Desertification and drought control

In response to a 1989 request of the General Assembly,[10] the UNEP Executive Director submitted a report[11] to UNCED on the status of desertification and implementation of the 1977 United Nations Plan of Action to Combat Desertification

(PACD).[12] The report considered the world status of desertification, PACD, policy guidelines and course of action for combating desertification, and financing. Currently, desertification affected about 3.6 billion hectares—70 per cent of the total drylands, or nearly a quarter of the total land area of the world—and affected about one sixth of the world's population.

The report presented five preventive, corrective and rehabilitation measures, as well as six supporting measures.

On 5 February,[13] the Governing Council took note of the report and endorsed the preventive and corrective activities. It recommended that Governments provide additional financial and technical assistance on the most favourable terms, in particular to the developing countries, to deal with desertification, and invited countries participating in GEF to consider financing anti-desertification programmes. The Council further recommended that Agenda 21 address desertification and the financing of programmes to combat it, and requested the Executive Director to transmit the report to the UNCED Secretary-General for consideration by the Preparatory Committee. The Council also requested the Executive Director to give emphasis to refining the assessment of the status of desertification, promoting the adoption as well as the monitoring and evaluation of the effectiveness of the report's policy guidelines and course of action and assigning benchmarks and indicators of progress. The Executive Director was to report to the Council in 1993 on implementation of the decision.

Studies by the Secretary-General. In June 1992, in response to a 1991 request of the Economic and Social Council,[14] the Secretary-General presented an interim report on combating aridity, soil erosion, salinity, waterlogging, desertification and the effects of drought in South Asia.[15] Although the Council had requested him, in collaboration with the heads of UNEP, UNDP, UNCED and other organizations, to assess the problem and its effects on the peoples of the region, it was determined that a study of such magnitude could not be completed in the timeframe specified. The report was therefore limited to informing the Council of arrangements being made for the preparation of the study, and was submitted on the understanding that the full study would be presented in 1993.

In September, in response to a 1991 General Assembly request,[16] the Secretary-General submitted a report highlighting the requirements for implementing Agenda 21 in the areas of desertification and drought.[17] The Secretary-General hoped that the international community would increase assistance to such activities, and suggested that the Assembly might consider calling for a percentage of the expected increase in ODA funds to be specifically allocated to them.

UNEP activities. In a report[18] to the UNEP Governing Council on the implementation of PACD in 1991 and 1992, the Executive Director stated that UNEP, during that period, assisted Argentina, Bahrain, Mongolia, Oman, Peru, the United Arab Emirates and Yemen in developing national plans of action to combat desertification. In addition, UNEP, through its Desertification Control Programme Activity Centre, continued to provide assistance to Mozambique and Zimbabwe for the formulation and initiation of pilot village projects. In support of the African Ministerial Conference on Environment pilot village programme, which trained African villagers and technicians in ecological farming, UNEP in October organized a training workshop at Nanjing, China, for 20 participants from 17 French-speaking African countries.

The Desertification Control Research and Training Network for Asia and the Pacific (DESCONAP) was given high priority during the period. In February, the third DESCONAP regional consultative meeting and tripartite review meeting was held in Thailand, and, in November, an expert group meeting for the Asia-Pacific and West Asia regions was held at Tehran, Iran, with the aim of developing a unified approach to desertification assessment and mapping. In addition, UNEP participated in the organization of four regional seminars and workshops on desertification control. An international symposium on soil resilience and sustainable land use (Budapest, Hungary, 28 September–2 October) was attended by 164 scientists representing 33 countries and 18 international organizations.

UNEP continued to conduct training programmes on combating desertification. In 1991-1992, 231 participants from Africa, Asia and Latin America were trained in the management of dryland natural resources, sustainable food production, monitoring and assessment of desertification, increased application of new technologies and public information. A project was initiated to accumulate data on successful desertification control projects, with a view to their replication elsewhere.

UNEP continued to disseminate information on programme results and problems related to desertification control worldwide. Issues 20 and 21 of the *Desertification Control Bulletin* were published in 1992, and the *World Atlas of Desertification*, containing maps of thematic indicators of desertification, was published and distributed to Governments at UNCED.

During the year, the Governments participating in GEF decided that desertification projects would be eligible for financing by GEF (see above).

UNDP action. On 26 May,[19] the UNDP Governing Council requested the Administrator to report in 1993 on proposals on specific ways to combat desertification and drought, including strengthening the coordinated operations of the United Nations system.

ECONOMIC AND SOCIAL COUNCIL ACTION

On 31 July, the Economic and Social Council, acting on a recommendation of its Economic Committee, adopted **resolution 1992/55** without vote.

Combating aridity, soil erosion, salinity, water-logging, desertification and the effects of drought in South Asia

The Economic and Social Council,

Recalling its resolution 1991/97 of 26 July 1991,

Taking note of the interim note by the Secretary-General on the implementation of Economic and Social Council resolution 1991/97,

Stressing that South Asia, one of the most populous regions in the world, contains significant areas subject to aridity, soil erosion, salinity, water-logging, desertification and the effects of drought, which affect the lives of millions of people and the entire environment of the region,

Stressing also the importance of the study requested in its resolution 1991/97 in the context of national and international cooperative efforts,

1. *Notes with concern* that the complete implementation of resolution 1991/97 could not be carried out and its results presented to the Council at its substantive session of 1992;

2. *Urges* the Secretary-General, in full compliance with resolution 1991/97, to submit the study to the General Assembly at its forty-seventh session.

Economic and Social Council resolution 1992/55

31 July 1992   Meeting 42   Adopted without vote

Approved by Economic Committee (E/1992/109) without vote, 28 July (meeting 16); 4-nation draft (E/1992/C.1/L.10), orally revised following informal consultations; agenda item 12.

Sponsors: Bangladesh, India, Iran, Pakistan.

The Council, by **resolution 1992/31**, appealed to the international community to contribute generously, on a voluntary basis, to the second phase of the Special Programme for Sub-Saharan African Countries Affected by Drought and Desertification of the International Fund for Agricultural Development.

GENERAL ASSEMBLY ACTION

On 22 December, the General Assembly, on the recommendation of the Second Committee, adopted without vote **resolution 47/188.**

Establishment of an intergovernmental negotiating committee for the elaboration of an international convention to combat desertification in those countries experiencing serious drought and/or desertification, particularly in Africa

The General Assembly,

Recalling its resolutions 44/172 A of 19 December 1989, 44/228 of 22 December 1989 and other relevant General

Assembly resolutions, as well as decisions adopted by the United Nations Conference on Environment and Development, in particular the recommendation by which the Conference invited the General Assembly to establish at its forty-seventh session, under its auspices, an intergovernmental negotiating committee for the elaboration of an international convention to combat desertification in those countries experiencing serious drought and/or desertification, particularly in Africa, with a view to finalizing such a convention by June 1994,

1. *Welcomes with satisfaction* the results and the recommendations of the United Nations Conference on Environment and Development, particularly chapter 12 of Agenda 21, entitled "Managing fragile ecosystems: combating desertification and drought";

2. *Decides* to establish, under its auspices, an Intergovernmental Negotiating Committee for the elaboration of an international convention to combat desertification in those countries experiencing serious drought and/or desertification, particularly in Africa, taking into account proposals that may be submitted by States participating in the negotiating process, with a view to finalizing such a convention by June 1994, and welcomes the candidature of Ambassador Bo Kjellen (Sweden) for the chairmanship of the Committee;

3. *Also decides* that the Intergovernmental Negotiating Committee shall be open to all States Members of the United Nations or members of the specialized agencies, with the participation of observers in accordance with the established practice of the General Assembly;

4. *Further decides* that the Intergovernmental Negotiating Committee shall hold, in addition to an organizational session, five substantive sessions, each lasting for two weeks, at Geneva and Nairobi, in New York and, in accordance with paragraph 5 of General Assembly resolution 40/243 of 18 December 1985, in Paris; the dates of these sessions will be determined by the Committee at its organizational session, subject to review of the timetable at the end of each negotiating session and taking into account the schedule of other related meetings;

5. *Decides* that at the first session of the Intergovernmental Negotiating Committee, to be held at Nairobi, the first week shall be devoted to the sharing of technical information and assessments, with the involvement of experts, on drought and desertification;

6. *Decides* that provision shall be made for an organizational session of up to one week's duration, to be held in New York not later than February 1993, in order to organize the work of the Intergovernmental Negotiating Committee and to elect its officers, which shall consist of a chairman, three vice-chairmen and a rapporteur, each of the five regional groups being represented by one officer;

7. *Requests* the Secretary-General to establish at Geneva as soon as possible an ad hoc secretariat of appropriate size and calibre, drawing, *inter alia*, on staff resources of the United Nations system, in order to ensure that the ad hoc secretariat embodies the requisite technical expertise to assist the Intergovernmental Negotiating Committee in the fulfilment of its mandate;

8. *Invites* the United Nations Development Programme, the United Nations Sudano-Sahelian Office, the United Nations Environment Programme, the Food and Agriculture Organization of the United Nations, the International Fund for Agricultural Development, the World Health Organization, the World Meteorological Organization, the United Nations Conference on Trade and Development, the United Nations Educational, Scientific and Cultural Organization and other relevant international organizations dealing with desertification, drought and development, to make appropriate contributions to the work of the Intergovernmental Negotiating Committee in the fulfilment of its mandate;

9. *Decides* that the Secretary-General shall appoint as head of the ad hoc secretariat a senior official at an appropriate level who shall act under the guidance of the Intergovernmental Negotiating Committee;

10. *Requests* the Secretary-General, through the head of the ad hoc secretariat, to prepare draft rules of procedure to be considered by the Intergovernmental Negotiating Committee at its organizational session;

11. *Requests* the head of the ad hoc secretariat to make available to the Intergovernmental Negotiating Committee, at the first substantive session, the most relevant and recent information available, in conformity with its mandate as stated in paragraph 2 above;

12. *Decides* to establish a multidisciplinary panel of experts to assist the ad hoc secretariat and, under its authority, to provide the necessary expertise in the scientific, technical, legal and other related fields, making full use of the resources and expertise within and available to Governments and/or organizations of the United Nations system dealing with drought and desertification;

13. *Also decides* that the negotiation process shall be funded through existing United Nations budgetary resources, without negatively affecting its programmed activities, and through voluntary contributions to a trust fund established specifically for that purpose for the duration of the negotiations and administered by the head of the ad hoc secretariat, under the authority of the Secretary-General;

14. *Urges* Governments, regional economic integration organizations and other interested organizations, including non-governmental organizations, to contribute generously to the trust fund;

15. *Decides* to establish a special voluntary fund, to be administered by the head of the ad hoc secretariat, under the authority of the Secretary-General, to assist developing countries affected by desertification and drought, in particular the least developed countries, to participate fully and effectively in the negotiation process, and invites Governments, regional economic integration organizations and other interested organizations, including non-governmental organizations, to contribute generously to the fund;

16. *Invites* relevant or interested organizations, organs, programmes and agencies of the United Nations system and intergovernmental, subregional and regional organizations to participate actively in the work of the Intergovernmental Negotiating Committee;

17. *Urges* States to organize, in close collaboration with the regional commissions and national, subregional and regional organizations, activities to support the Intergovernmental Negotiating Committee process, with the involvement of the scientific and industrial communities, trade unions, the relevant non-governmental organizations and other interested groups;

18. *Invites* the United Nations Sudano-Sahelian Office to assist the countries covered under its mandate in their preparations for and participation in the negotiating process and to mobilize resources for this purpose;

19. *Invites* all relevant non-governmental organizations and, especially, encourages non-governmental organizations from developing countries to contribute constructively to the success of the negotiating process in accordance with the rules of procedure of the Intergovernmental Negotiating Committee and taking into account procedures followed in the United Nations Conference on Environment and Development process;

20. *Requests* the Chairman of the Intergovernmental Negotiating Committee to submit progress reports to the Commission on Sustainable Development and other appropriate bodies;

21. *Requests* the Secretary-General to bring the present resolution to the attention of all Governments, intergovernmental and non-governmental organizations and relevant scientific institutions;

22. *Also requests* the Secretary-General to submit to the General Assembly at its forty-eighth session a report on the implementation of the present resolution;

23. *Decides* to include in the provisional agenda of its forty-eighth session a sub-item entitled "Elaboration of an international convention to combat desertification in those countries experiencing serious drought and/or desertification, particularly in Africa" under an item entitled "Implementation of decisions and recommendations of the United Nations Conference on Environment and Development".

General Assembly resolution 47/188

22 December 1992   Meeting 93   Adopted without vote

Approved by Second Committee (A/47/719) without vote, 16 December (meeting 51); draft by Malaysia (A/C.2/47/L.46); agenda item 79.
Financial implications. 5th Committee, A/47/814; S-G, A/C.2/47/L.90, A/C.5/47/81.
Meeting numbers. GA 47th session: 2nd Committee 51; 5th Committee 49; plenary 93.

Also on 22 December, by **decision 47/444**, the Assembly took note of the Secretary-General's report on implementing Agenda 21 in the areas of desertification and drought.[17]

Marine ecosystems

Straddling and highly migratory fish stocks

The problems relating to straddling fish stocks (those occurring within the exclusive economic zones of two or more coastal States or both within the exclusive economic zone and in an area beyond and adjacent to it) and highly migratory fish stocks were considered in 1992 by UNCED and the General Assembly.

On 21 May, Mexico transmitted to UNCED the text of the Declaration of Cancun, adopted by the International Conference on Responsible Fishing (Cancun, Mexico, 6-8 May),[20] which called on States to take steps to ensure the supply of fish products and to improve management systems and scientific knowledge.

UNCED noted in Agenda 21 that during the past decade fisheries on the high seas had expanded considerably. There were problems of unregulated fishing, excessive fleet size, the reflagging of vessels to escape controls, insufficiently selective fishing gear, unreliable databases and lack of sufficient cooperation between States. Agenda 21 said that States should convene an intergovernmental conference to promote implementation of the provisions of the 1982 United Nations Convention on the Law of the Sea[21] on straddling and highly migratory fish stocks.

GENERAL ASSEMBLY ACTION

On 22 December, the General Assembly, on the recommendation of the Second Committee, adopted without vote **resolution 47/192**.

United Nations Conference on Straddling Fish Stocks and Highly Migratory Fish Stocks

The General Assembly,

Recalling Agenda 21, adopted at the United Nations Conference on Environment and Development, in particular chapter 17, programme area C, relating to the sustainable use and conservation of marine living resources of the high seas,

Recalling also the Strategy for Fisheries Management and Development, adopted by the World Conference on Fisheries Management and Development,

Taking note of the Declaration of Cancun, adopted at the International Conference on Responsible Fishing held at Cancun, Mexico, from 6 to 8 May 1992,

Inviting all members of the international community, particularly those with fishing interests, to strengthen their cooperation in the conservation and management of living marine resources, in accordance with the provisions of the United Nations Convention on the Law of the Sea,

Taking note of relevant recent discussions on international fisheries,

1. *Decides* to convene in 1993, under United Nations auspices and in accordance with the mandate agreed upon at the United Nations Conference on Environment and Development, an intergovernmental conference on straddling fish stocks and highly migratory fish stocks, which should complete its work before the forty-ninth session of the General Assembly;

2. *Also decides* that the intergovernmental conference, in accordance with the said mandate, shall take into account relevant activities at the subregional, regional and global levels, with a view to promoting effective implementation of the provisions of the United Nations Convention on the Law of the Sea on straddling fish stocks and highly migratory fish stocks, and that, drawing, *inter alia*, on scientific and technical studies by the Food and Agriculture Organization of the United Nations, it should:

(a) Identify and assess existing problems related to the conservation and management of such fish stocks;

(b) Consider means of improving fisheries cooperation among States;

(c) Formulate appropriate recommendations;

3. *Reaffirms* that the work and results of the conference should be fully consistent with the provisions of the United Nations Convention on the Law of the Sea, in particular the rights and obligations of coastal States and States fishing on the high seas, and that States should give full effect to the high seas fisheries provisions of the Convention with regard to fisheries popu-

lations whose ranges lie both within and beyond exclusive economic zones (straddling fish stocks) and highly migratory fish stocks;

4. *Requests* the Secretary-General to invite to the conference those listed in paragraph 9 of its resolution 46/168 of 19 December 1991 and in its decisions 46/469 and 46/470 of 13 April 1992, and also to invite regional and subregional fisheries organizations to attend as observers;

5. *Decides* that in 1993 the conference shall hold an organizational session of up to five days at United Nations Headquarters for the purposes of electing a chairman and other officers, namely, three vice-chairmen and a rapporteur, giving due regard to equitable geographical representation, and of organizing its work;

6. *Requests* the Secretary-General to make appropriate secretariat arrangements;

7. *Decides* that in 1993 the conference shall hold a session of three weeks' duration in July at United Nations Headquarters to deal with substantive matters;

8. *Requests* the Secretary-General to prepare draft rules of procedure for the consideration of the conference at its organizational session;

9. *Decides* to establish a voluntary fund for the purpose of assisting developing countries, especially those most concerned by the subject-matter of the conference, in particular the least developed among them, to participate fully and effectively in the conference, and invites Governments and regional economic integration organizations to contribute to the fund;

10. *Also decides* that the funds necessary for the preparatory process and the conference itself should, subject to the relevant provisions of General Assembly resolutions 40/243 of 18 December 1985, 41/213 of 19 December 1986 and 42/211 of 21 December 1987, be made available within the programme budget without adversely affecting other ongoing activities and without prejudice to the provision of extrabudgetary resources;

11. *Invites* relevant specialized agencies, particularly the Food and Agriculture Organization of the United Nations, and other appropriate organs, organizations and programmes of the United Nations system, as well as regional and subregional fisheries organizations, to contribute relevant scientific and technical studies and reports and to organize regional and subregional technical meetings in order to contribute to the work of the conference;

12. *Invites* relevant non-governmental organizations from developed and developing countries to contribute to the conference, within the areas of their competence and expertise, on the basis of procedures for their accreditation used for the United Nations Conference on Environment and Development, as recommended in paragraph 38.44 of Agenda 21;

13. *Requests* the Secretary-General to submit to the General Assembly at its forty-eighth session a report on the work of the conference;

14. *Requests* the Secretary-General to bring the present resolution to the attention of all members of the international community, relevant intergovernmental organizations, agencies, programmes and bodies within the United Nations system, regional and subregional fisheries organizations and relevant non-governmental organizations;

15. *Decides* to include in the provisional agenda of its forty-eighth session, under an item entitled "Implemen-

tation of the decisions and recommendations of the United Nations Conference on Environment and Development", a sub-item entitled "Sustainable use and conservation of the marine living resources of the high seas: United Nations Conference on Straddling Fish Stocks and Highly Migratory Fish Stocks".

General Assembly resolution 47/192

22 December 1992   Meeting 93   Adopted without vote

Approved by Second Committee (A/47/719) without vote, 16 December (meeting 51); draft by Malaysia (A/C.2/47/L.62), orally revised; agenda item 79.

Financial implications. 5th Committee, A/47/811; S-G, A/C.2/47/L.85, A/C.5/47/78.

Meeting numbers. GA 47th session: 2nd Committee 51; 5th Committee 49; plenary 93.

Drift-net fishing

In accordance with a 1991 General Assembly resolution,[22] the Secretary-General, in October 1992,[23] submitted a report on large-scale pelagic drift-net fishing and its impact on the living marine resources of the world's oceans and seas. The report reviewed region by region the activities of intergovernmental organizations and States that had been called on to implement a global moratorium on all large-scale pelagic drift-net fishing.

The Assembly, by **decision 47/443** of 22 December, took note of the report and requested a further report in 1993.

REFERENCES

[1]UNEP/GCSS.III/2 & Corr.1,2 & Add.1,2. [2]A/44/25 (dec. 15/13 A). [3]A/47/25. [4]YUN 1972, p. 318. [5]A/47/25 (dec. SS.III/3). [6]A/47/222-E/1992/57 & Corr.1. [7]YUN 1986, p. 654. [8]GA res. 44/226, 22 Dec. 1989. [9]*Multilateral Treaties Deposited with the Secretary-General: Status as at 31 December 1992* (ST/LEG/SER.E/11), Sales No. E.93.V.11. [10]GA res. 44/172, 19 Dec. 1989. [11]UNEP/GCSS.III/3 & Corr.1/Rev.1 & Add.1. [12]YUN 1977, p. 509. [13]A/47/25 (dec. SS.III/1). [14]YUN 1991, p. 501, ESC res. 1991/97, 26 July 1991. [15]E/1992/53. [16]YUN 1991, p. 501, GA res. 46/161, 19 Dec. 1991. [17]A/47/393. [18]UNEP/GC.17/14. [19]E/1992/28 (dec. 92/16). [20]A/CONF.151/15. [21]YUN 1982, p. 181. [22]YUN 1991, p. 503, GA res. 46/215, 20 Dec. 1991. [23]A/47/487.

Programme and finances of UNEP

On 8 December, on the recommendation of the Secretary-General,[1] the General Assembly appointed Elizabeth Dowdeswell of Canada as UNEP Executive Director for a four-year term beginning on 1 January 1993.

Finances

Environment Fund

As at 31 December 1992,[2] $62.5 million had been paid to the Environment Fund by 44 countries for 1992; another 32 countries were expected to make contributions totalling $1.2 million for the year. The estimated total of $63.7 million represented an increase of 6.8 per cent over the 1991 contributions of $60 million, but was significantly short of the Governing Council's target of $100 million.

1990-1991 accounts

On 23 December, the General Assembly, by **resolution 47/211**, accepted the financial report and audited financial statements of the Environment Fund for the biennium ended 31 December 1991[3] and the audit opinions and report of the Board of Auditors regarding the Fund.

Trust funds

Forty-five general and technical cooperation trust funds,[4] administered by UNEP, spent $32.7 million during the 1990-1991 biennium.

REFERENCES

[1]A/47/752.   [2]UNEP/GC.17/16.   [3]A/47/5/Add.6.
[4]UNEP/GC.17/19.

Environmental aspects of political, economic and other issues

Pursuant to a 1991 request of the General Assembly,[1] the Secretary-General submitted in June 1992 a report[2] on international cooperation to mitigate the environmental consequences on Kuwait and other countries in the region resulting from the situation between Iraq and Kuwait. The United Nations inter-agency plan of action to respond to the environmental crisis was led by UNEP, in cooperation with the Regional Organization for the Protection of the Marine Environment (ROPME) and a number of specialized agencies.

The Secretary-General reported that as a result of the massive oil spill in the Persian Gulf, estimated at between 6 million and 8 million barrels, about 600 kilometres of coastline along the Saudi coast from Khafgi to Abu Ali Island were severely damaged. At least 30,000 marine birds died; 20 per cent of the mangroves on the eastern coast of Saudi Arabia were oiled and about 50 per cent of the coral reefs were affected. The Iranian, Iraqi and Kuwaiti coasts were affected to a lesser extent.

Oil pollution was not limited to oil spills. Fallout from burning oil formed slicks on the surface of the water, releasing polycyclic aromatic hydrocarbons and heavy metal–laden soot particles into the water column. Beaches were destroyed through the construction of defence installations. The destruction of sewage-treatment plants in Kuwait resulted in the release of more than 50,000 cubic metres per day of raw sewage into Kuwait Bay, threatening the intertidal ecosystem.

The United Nations effort to assess the state of the marine environment culminated in the launching, in late February 1992, of a 100-day cruise in the ROPME sea area by the *Mount Mitchell*, a 231-foot research vessel of the United States National Oceanic and Atmospheric Administration.

Air pollution from the burning oil wells in Kuwait represented a potential health hazard. About 6 million barrels of oil were being burnt daily from more than 600 burning wells. However, a WMO/UNEP meeting of experts (Geneva, 25-29 May) analysed the atmospheric effects of the oil fires and found that the smoke had no effect on the weather or climate outside the region.

The destruction of terrestrial ecosystems was extensive, particularly in Iraq, Kuwait and Saudi Arabia. In Kuwait, the impact on soil and vegetation was very serious owing to the formation of huge oil pools, extending over vast areas of the desert. Moreover, a layer of oil droplets and soot covered hundreds of square kilometres. In some areas, pulverization of the surface soil by off-road military vehicles had destabilized the soil, increasing its vulnerability to wind erosion. In addition, the presence of land-mines and unexploded ordnance and munitions still presented a serious hazard to human life and the environment.

In Iraq, the military activities devastated large areas of land and adversely affected the agricultural production and livestock of the country, while in Saudi Arabia, the main terrestrial impact was due to the fallout of soot, particularly south of the Saudi/Kuwaiti border.

While inter-agency activities were carried out at the technical level, further attention was given to the political and financial aspects of the environmental crisis. Following a request from Kuwait, Margaret Joan Anstee, Director-General of the United Nations Office at Vienna, was dispatched in October 1991 to Kuwait as the Personal Representative of the Secretary-General to coordinate United Nations efforts.

In March 1992, Joseph Verner Reed was named to succeed Miss Anstee, with the title of Special Representative. He visited Kuwait and other countries of the region to reassess the situation after the burning oil wells were capped. He assured the Kuwaiti Government of the continued support of the United Nations to redress the environmental damage in Kuwait and the region.

An environmental rehabilitation programme was prepared by UNEP in cooperation with ROPME. The programme included project proposals covering marine, atmospheric and terrestrial pollution, technical cooperation aspects and the needs of the countries of the region for oil clean-up, recovery and restoration.

On 30 July, the Economic and Social Council, by **decision 1992/285**, took note of the Secretary-General's report.[2]

UNEP action. On 5 February,[3] the UNEP Governing Council invited the international community, Governments and intergovernmental organizations to participate technically and financially in rehabilitation programmes aimed at mitigating the environmental deterioration of the region and in strengthening ROPME's capability to coordinate and implement those programmes.

GENERAL ASSEMBLY ACTION

On 18 December, on the recommendation of the Second Committee, the General Assembly adopted **resolution 47/151** by recorded vote.

International cooperation to mitigate the environmental consequences on Kuwait and other countries in the region resulting from the situation between Iraq and Kuwait

The General Assembly,

Aware of the disastrous situation caused in Kuwait and neighbouring areas by the torching and destruction of hundreds of its oil wells and of the other environmental consequences on the atmosphere and on land and marine life,

Bearing in mind all relevant Security Council resolutions, in particular section E of resolution 687(1991) of 3 April 1991,

Having taken note of the report submitted by the Secretary-General to the Security Council describing the nature and extent of the environmental damage suffered by Kuwait,[a]

Recalling decision 16/11 A adopted by the Governing Council of the United Nations Environment Programme on 31 May 1991,

Recalling also its resolution 46/216 of 20 December 1991,

Taking note of the report of the Secretary-General,

Profoundly concerned at the degradation of the environment as a consequence of the damage, especially the threat posed to the health and well-being of the people of Kuwait and the people of the region, and the adverse impact on the economic activities of Kuwait and other countries of the region, including the effects on livestock, agriculture and fishing, as well as on wildlife,

Welcoming the recent Mount Mitchell Research Cruise, which was organized under the sponsorship of the Intergovernmental Oceanographic Commission of the United Nations Educational, Scientific and Cultural Organization, the Regional Organization for the Protection of the Marine Environment and the United Nations Environment Programme, to make a scientific assessment of environmental conditions in the region,

Awaiting the meetings due to be held in 1993, at which the results of the Mount Mitchell Research Cruise will be discussed and evaluated,

Acknowledging the fact that dealing with this catastrophe goes beyond the capabilities of the countries of the region and, in that regard, recognizing the need for strengthened international cooperation to deal with the situation,

Noting with appreciation the appointment by the Secretary-General of an Under-Secretary-General as his Personal Representative to coordinate United Nations efforts in this field,

Also noting with appreciation the efforts already undertaken by the Member States of the region, other States, the organizations of the United Nations system and governmental and non-governmental organizations to study, mitigate and minimize the consequences of this environmental catastrophe,

Bearing in mind the effective work of the Regional Organization for the Protection of the Marine Environment and the inter-agency task force established under the leadership of the United Nations Environment Programme especially to consider the environmental situation in the region, as well as the plan of action,

Expressing its special appreciation to the Governments that have extended financial support to the two trust funds established for the purpose by the Secretary-General of the International Maritime Organization and the Executive Director of the United Nations Environment Programme, and to the Governments and organizations that supported the recent international research cruise organized under the auspices of the Intergovernmental Oceanographic Commission, the Regional Organization for the Protection of the Marine Environment and the United Nations Environment Programme,

1. *Appeals* to all States Members of the United Nations, intergovernmental and non-governmental organizations, scientific bodies and individuals to provide assistance for programmes aimed at the study and mitigation of the environmental degradation of the region and for strengthening the Regional Organization for the Protection of the Marine Environment and its role in coordinating the implementation of these programmes;

2. *Calls upon* the organizations and programmes of the United Nations system, in particular the International Maritime Organization and the United Nations Environment Programme, to pursue their efforts to assess the short-term as well as the long-term impact of the environmental degradation of the region and to consider measures that may be needed to counteract these effects;

3. *Requests* the Secretary-General, through his Personal Representative, to render assistance to the members of the Regional Organization for the Protection of the Marine Environment in the formulation and implementation of a coordinated and consolidated programme of action comprising costed project profiles, to help identify all possible resources for the programme of action and, *inter alia*, for strengthening the environmental capacities of the members of the Regional Organization for the Protection of the Marine Environment to deal with this problem, and to allocate, within existing resources, the minimum resources required to enable his Personal Representative to continue to help coordinate the activities of the United Nations system to that end;

4. *Also requests* the Secretary-General to submit to the General Assembly at its forty-ninth session, through the Economic and Social Council, a report on the implementation of the present resolution;

5. *Decides* to include in the provisional agenda of its forty-ninth session the sub-item entitled "International

---

[a]S/22535 & Corr.1,2.

cooperation to mitigate the environmental consequences on Kuwait and other countries in the region resulting from the situation between Iraq and Kuwait'' under the item entitled ''Development and international economic cooperation''.

General Assembly resolution 47/151

18 December 1992   Meeting 92   159-0-2 (recorded vote)

Approved by Second Committee (A/47/718/Add.6) by recorded vote (133-0-1), 9 December (meeting 49); 101-nation draft (A/C.2/47/L.7/Rev.1), orally amended by Vice-Chairman; agenda item 78 *(e)*.

Sponsors: Afghanistan, Algeria, Argentina, Azerbaijan, Bahamas, Bahrain, Bangladesh, Barbados, Belarus, Belize, Benin, Bhutan, Bosnia and Herzegovina, Botswana, Bulgaria, Burkina Faso, Burundi, Cameroon, Cape Verde, Chile, China, Comoros, Congo, Costa Rica, Côte d'Ivoire, Cyprus, Czechoslovakia, Democratic People's Republic of Korea, Djibouti, Dominican Republic, Ecuador, Egypt, El Salvador, Fiji, Gabon, Gambia, Ghana, Grenada, Guatemala, Guinea, Guinea-Bissau, Honduras, Hungary, India, Iran, Jamaica, Kazakhstan, Kenya, Kuwait, Latvia, Lebanon, Lesotho, Madagascar, Malaysia, Maldives, Mali, Mauritania, Mongolia, Namibia, Nepal, Nicaragua, Niger, Nigeria, Oman, Pakistan, Panama, Paraguay, Peru, Philippines, Poland, Qatar, Republic of Korea, Romania, Rwanda, Saint Kitts and Nevis, Saint Lucia, Saint Vincent and the Grenadines, Samoa, San Marino, Sao Tome and Principe, Saudi Arabia, Senegal, Sierra Leone, Singapore, Spain, Sri Lanka, Suriname, Syrian Arab Republic, Tajikistan, Thailand, Togo, Tunisia, Turkey, United Arab Emirates, United Kingdom, United Republic of Tanzania, Uruguay, Vanuatu, Venezuela, Zaire, Zimbabwe.

Meeting numbers. GA 47th session: 2nd Committee 17, 49; plenary 92.

Recorded vote in Assembly as follows:

In favour: Afghanistan, Algeria, Angola, Antigua and Barbuda, Argentina, Armenia, Australia, Austria, Azerbaijan, Bahamas, Bahrain, Bangladesh, Barbados, Belarus, Belgium, Belize, Benin, Bhutan, Bolivia, Botswana, Brazil, Brunei Darussalam, Bulgaria, Burkina Faso, Burundi, Cameroon, Canada, Cape Verde, Central African Republic, Chad, Chile, China, Colombia, Comoros, Congo, Costa Rica, Côte d'Ivoire, Croatia, Cuba, Cyprus, Czechoslovakia, Democratic People's Republic of Korea, Denmark, Djibouti, Dominica, Dominican Republic, Ecuador, Egypt, Estonia, Ethiopia, Fiji, Finland, France, Gabon, Gambia, Germany, Ghana, Greece, Grenada, Guatemala, Guinea, Guinea-Bissau, Guyana, Haiti, Honduras, Hungary, Iceland, India, Indonesia, Iran, Ireland, Israel, Italy, Jamaica, Japan, Jordan, Kazakhstan, Kenya, Kuwait, Lao People's Democratic Republic, Latvia, Lebanon, Lesotho, Liberia, Liechtenstein, Lithuania, Luxembourg, Madagascar, Malawi, Malaysia, Maldives, Mali, Malta, Marshall Islands, Mauritania, Mauritius, Mexico, Mongolia, Morocco, Mozambique, Myanmar, Namibia, Nepal, Netherlands, New Zealand, Nicaragua, Niger, Nigeria, Norway, Oman, Pakistan, Panama, Papua New Guinea, Paraguay, Peru, Philippines, Poland, Portugal, Qatar, Republic of Korea, Republic of Moldova, Romania, Russian Federation, Rwanda, Saint Kitts and Nevis, Saint Lucia, Saint Vincent and the Grenadines, Samoa, Sao Tome and Principe, Saudi Arabia, Senegal, Seychelles, Sierra Leone, Singapore, Slovenia, Solomon Islands, Spain, Sri Lanka, Suriname, Swaziland, Sweden, Syrian Arab Republic, Thailand, Togo, Trinidad and Tobago, Tunisia, Turkey, Uganda, Ukraine, United Arab Emirates, United Kingdom, United Republic of Tanzania, United States, Uruguay, Vanuatu, Venezuela, Viet Nam, Zambia, Zimbabwe.

Against: None.

Abstaining: Iraq, Sudan.

By **resolution 47/37**, the Assembly urged States to ensure compliance with the existing international law applicable to the protection of the environment in times of armed conflict.

REFERENCES

[1]YUN 1991, p. 506, GA res. 46/216, 20 Dec. 1991. [2]A/47/265-E/1992/81. [3]A/47/25 (dec. SS.III/3).

Chapter IX

Population and human settlements

The United Nations Population Fund (UNFPA) in 1992, while addressing the problems of population growth, distribution and movement, continued to support the right of women and men to family planning. Inadequate resources remained a major constraint, however, and despite significant improvements in reproductive health and increasing acceptance of family planning, the global population continued to grow at a rate of about 93 million per year.

The Economic and Social Council in 1992 decided to convene the International Conference on Population and Development from 5 to 13 September 1994 at Cairo, Egypt (decision 1992/37), and the General Assembly emphasized the need for comprehensive national population policies that were compatible with sustainable economic growth and development (resolution 47/176).

The United Nations Centre for Human Settlements, also known as Habitat, continued to assist developing countries in all aspects of human settlements activities through research and development and technical cooperation projects and information dissemination.

The General Assembly noted that the continuing deterioration of living environments in many countries was being aggravated by rapid population growth and urbanization, and decided to convene the United Nations Conference on Human Settlements (Habitat II) from 3 to 14 June 1996 to address the human settlements problems and reassess related policies and programmes (47/180). The Assembly decided that the objectives of the Conference should be to arrest or reverse the deterioration of global living environments, to adopt a general statement of principles and commitments to sustainable improvements in human habitats and to formulate a global plan of action to guide national and international efforts through the first two decades of the next century.

Population

1994 International Conference on Population and Development

Following its 1989[1] and 1991[2] resolutions to convene an international meeting on population,

the Economic and Social Council decided, in July 1992, to hold the International Conference on Population and Development, at Cairo, Egypt, from 5 to 13 September 1994; in December, the General Assembly endorsed that decision.

Preparatory activities

During 1992, preparatory activities for the 1994 International Conference on Population and Development, undertaken by UNFPA and the Population Division of the Secretariat's Department of Economic and Social Development (DESD), focused on the priority issues to be addressed, including population growth and demographic structure; population policies and programmes; population, environment and development; population distribution and migration; status of women and population; and family-planning programmes, health and family well-being. The Population Commission, acting as the Preparatory Committee for the Conference, was scheduled to hold its second session in August 1993.

In May,[3] the United Nations Development Programme (UNDP) Governing Council noted with satisfaction the overall theme and objectives of the Conference, and encouraged Governments and organizations to prepare for it. The Council requested the Economic and Social Council to facilitate the participation of developing countries in the preparatory process.

Report of the Secretary-General of the Conference. In response to a 1991 Economic and Social Council resolution,[2] the Secretary-General of the Conference, Dr. Nafis Sadik, Executive Director of UNFPA, submitted a report in June 1992[4] reviewing the status of preparations and related financial and organizational questions.

The report noted that UNFPA and DESD had launched the seventh United Nations population inquiry to compile the views and policies of Member States pertaining to population. At the end of 1992,[5] about 40 Member States had replied to the inquiry, the results of which would be made available to the Conference. To ensure universal participation, the Conference Secretary-General had requested that national committees be established in each country as focal points for preparatory activities and to prepare national reports on the population situation, policies and programmes of the country concerned. The national reports would also highlight constraints on implementing the 1974 World Population Plan of Action[6] and the recommendations adopted at the 1984 International Conference on Population.[7]

The Conference Secretary-General reported that all United Nations agencies and organizations involved in population had appointed a focal point to coordinate their participation. She also reported that the Administrative Committee on Coordination had established an ad hoc task force for the Conference in 1991 to ensure inter-agency coordination and participation by United Nations bodies in the Conference and its preparatory process. The Task Force held its first formal meeting in New York on 6 July 1992[8] to review the preparations and related activities of the specialized agencies and organizations of the United Nations system.

DESD in 1992 organized a meeting of United Nations autonomous research institutes to discuss and coordinate their contributions to the Conference (New York, 2 October). The United Nations University was to act as a focal point, bringing together and synthesizing the inputs into a collective contribution to be transmitted to the Preparatory Committee.[5]

As part of its information programme, the Conference secretariat in 1992 published four issues of *Population 94*, a newsletter covering preparations for the Conference.

Expert group meetings

In 1991,[2] the Economic and Social Council had authorized the Secretary-General of the Conference to convene six expert group meetings on population and development issues. Five of those meetings, each including 15 internationally renowned experts, were held in 1992. They were described in a progress report on Conference preparations by the Secretary-General of the Conference.[5] The expert group meeting on population, environment and development (New York, 20-24 January) adopted 18 recommendations to the Conference Preparatory Committee; the meeting on population policies and programmes (Cairo, 12-16 April) adopted 21 recommendations; the meeting on population and women (Gaborone, Botswana, 22-26 June) adopted 32 recommendations; the meeting on family planning, health and family well-being (Bangalore, India, 26-29 October) adopted 35 recommendations; and the meeting on population growth and demographic structure (Paris, 16-20 November) adopted 19 recommendations. The sixth meeting, on population distribution and migration, was to be held in Bolivia in January 1993.

Regional activities

Also in 1991[2] the Economic and Social Council had invited the regional commissions to convene conferences on the status of population policies and programmes in their regions.[5]

The first of these conferences, the Fourth Asian and Pacific Population Conference (Bali, Indonesia, 19-27 August), jointly sponsored by the Economic and Social Commission for Asia and the Pacific (ESCAP) and UNFPA, focused on the theme of population and sustainable development: goals and strategies into the twenty-first century. The Conference adopted the Bali Declaration on Population and Sustainable Development, which, according to a report of the UNFPA Executive Director,[9] called on countries in the region to make a firm political and financial commitment to incorporate population and environmental concerns fully into all national efforts towards sustainable development. It also urged countries with rapid population growth to reduce their fertility rates to 2.2 children per woman by 2010, to reduce infant mortality to 40 per 1,000 during the same period and to cut maternal mortality by at least half in those countries with high maternal death rates.

The Third African Population Conference (Dakar, Senegal, 7-12 December), was organized by the Economic Commission for Africa (ECA), the Organization of African Unity and UNFPA. The Conference adopted the Dakar Declaration on Population, Family and Sustainable Development, which called for a reduction in the rate of population growth in the region to 2.5 per cent by 2000 and 2 per cent by 2010, and an increase in the contraceptive prevalence rate to 20 per cent by 2000 and 40 per cent by 2010 for Africa as a whole. It also called for an increase in life expectancy from 45 to 55 years by 2000 and a 50 per cent decrease in maternal mortality.

The Economic Commission for Europe (ECE), the Economic Commission for Latin America and the Caribbean (ECLAC) and the Economic and Social Commission for Western Asia (ESCWA) scheduled their population conferences for 1993 (see PART TWO, Chapter VI).

Trust funds

Two trust funds were established by the United Nations Secretary-General to support the Conference.[4] The first, the Trust Fund for the 1994 International Conference on Population and Development, was to be used for Conference preparatory activities. By June 1992, approximately $1 million had been contributed to the fund, and an additional $103,834 had been pledged. The second, the Voluntary Fund for Supporting Developing Countries' Participation in the Conference had received approximately $101,585 and an additional $250,000 had been pledged. A UNFPA Trust Fund was also established to support national preparatory activities, including meetings, studies and activities to increase awareness of the Conference.

The fund had received $235,320 and another $250,000 had been pledged.

ECONOMIC AND SOCIAL COUNCIL ACTION

On 30 July, the Economic and Social Council, on the recommendation of its Economic Committee, adopted **resolution 1992/37** without vote.

International Conference on Population and Development

The Economic and Social Council,

Recalling its resolutions 1989/91 of 26 July 1989 and 1991/93 of 26 July 1991,

1. *Takes note* of the report of the Secretary-General of the International Conference on Population and Development on the status of preparatory activities for the Conference;

2. *Accepts with gratitude* the offer of the Government of Egypt to host the Conference;

3. *Decides* to convene the Conference in Cairo from 5 to 13 September 1994.

Economic and Social Council resolution 1992/37

30 July 1992   Meeting 41   Adopted without vote

Approved by Economic Committee (E/1992/109/Add.4) without vote, 28 July (meeting 16); draft by Chairman (E/1992/C.1/L.4); agenda item 12 *(f)*.

GENERAL ASSEMBLY ACTION

On 22 December 1992, the General Assembly, on the recommendation of the Second (Economic and Financial) Committee, adopted **resolution 47/176** without vote.

International Conference on Population and Development

The General Assembly,

Recalling its resolutions 3344(XXIX) of 17 December 1974 on the World Population Conference, 39/228 of 18 December 1984 on the International Conference on Population, 44/210 of 22 December 1989 on future needs in the field of population, including the development of resource requirements for international population assistance, S-18/3 of 1 May 1990, the annex to which contains the Declaration on International Economic Cooperation, in particular the Revitalization of Economic Growth and Development of the Developing Countries, 45/199 of 21 December 1990, the annex to which contains the International Development Strategy for the Fourth United Nations Development Decade, 45/206 of 21 December 1990 on the implementation of the Programme of Action for the Least Developed Countries for the 1990s, 45/216 of 21 December 1990 on population and development and 40/108 of 13 December 1985 on the implementation of the Nairobi Forward-looking Strategies for the Advancement of Women,

Recalling also Economic and Social Council resolution 1989/91 of 26 July 1989, in which the Council decided, in principle, to convene in 1994, under the auspices of the United Nations, an international meeting on population,

Recalling further Economic and Social Council resolution 1991/93 of 26 July 1991, in which the Council decided that the international meeting on population should thenceforth be called the International Conference on Population and Development,

Endorsing fully the objectives of the Conference, as decided by the Economic and Social Council in its resolution 1991/93, and its overall theme of population, sustained economic growth and sustainable development, as stated in that resolution,

Recognizing the important contribution that regional conferences will play in preparations for the Conference, particularly through evaluation and updating of regional population plans of action,

Noting with satisfaction the appointment by the Secretary-General of the United Nations of the Executive Director of the United Nations Population Fund as Secretary-General of the International Conference on Population and Development, and of the Director of the Population Division of the Department of Economic and Social Development of the Secretariat as the Deputy Secretary-General of the Conference,

Emphasizing the national sovereignty of all countries in formulating, adopting and implementing policies relating to population, mindful of their cultures, values and traditions, as well as of their social, economic and political conditions, and consistent with human rights and with the responsibilities of individuals, couples and families,

Conscious of the important contribution made by research and information dissemination institutions to a clear understanding of the interrelationship between population and development,

Recognizing the importance of the outcome of the United Nations Conference on Environment and Development, including those sections of Agenda 21 concerning population, in the preparations for the International Conference on Population and Development,

1. *Emphasizes* the need for comprehensive national population policies based on national priorities and compatible with sustained economic growth and sustainable development;

2. *Also emphasizes* the need to increase and strengthen the level of awareness of population issues in the international agenda and their treatment as an integral part of sustained economic growth and sustainable development;

3. *Endorses* Economic and Social Council resolution 1992/37 of 30 July 1992, in which the Council decided to convene the International Conference on Population and Development at Cairo from 5 to 13 September 1994;

4. *Accepts with deep appreciation* the generous offer of the Government of Egypt to act as host to the Conference;

5. *Recommends* that the Conference be convened at the ministerial level;

6. *Stresses* the importance of the active participation of Member States in the Preparatory Committee for the International Conference on Population and Development and, in this context, invites the Preparatory Committee at its second session to elect its officers with due regard to equitable geographical representation;

7. *Decides* that the host country to the Conference, Egypt, shall be ex officio an officer of the Preparatory Committee;

8. *Invites* the Economic and Social Council, at its organizational session for 1993, taking fully into consideration the views expressed during the forty-seventh session of the General Assembly, to consider the possibility of adjusting, within existing budgetary resources and without prejudice to the utilization of resources avail-

able through voluntary contributions to the trust funds, the proposed timing and duration of the second and third sessions of the Preparatory Committee, taking fully into account the need to ensure the success of the Conference in fulfilling its mandate and, for this purpose, to ensure an adequate intergovernmental preparatory process for it;

9. *Calls upon* all organs, organizations and programmes of the United Nations system, as well as other relevant intergovernmental organizations, to contribute fully to the preparations for the Conference;

10. *Welcomes* the decision of the Secretary-General of the United Nations to ensure the necessary coordination of contributions within the United Nations system through the Administrative Committee on Coordination;

11. *Invites* all States to take an active part in the preparations for the Conference and to promote broad-based national preparatory processes;

12. *Recognizes* the importance of the participation in the Conference and its preparatory process of all relevant non-governmental organizations from developed and developing countries;

13. *Requests* the Economic and Social Council, at its organizational session for 1993, to formulate and adopt modalities to ensure the participation in and contribution to the Conference and its preparatory process of relevant non-governmental organizations, in particular those from developing countries, taking into account the procedures followed in the United Nations Conference on Environment and Development process and the experience gained in this regard during previous United Nations population conferences;

14. *Stresses* the significance of the various regional perspectives that exist on issues of population and development, and welcomes in this context the convening by the regional commissions and the United Nations Population Fund of regional population conferences, whose outcome will contribute significantly to the preparations for the International Conference on Population and Development;

15. *Notes* the establishment of voluntary trust funds in support of the Conference and for the purpose of assisting developing countries, in particular the least developed among them, to participate fully and effectively in the Conference and in its preparatory process;

16. *Expresses its appreciation* to contributors to the funds, and invites Governments in a position to do so to contribute generously to those funds;

17. *Calls upon* the Secretary-General of the International Conference on Population and Development to continue to make every effort to raise extrabudgetary resources for the Conference;

18. *Requests* the Secretary-General of the Conference, in the light of the need for thorough preparation for the Conference, to ensure the timely circulation of the documentation for the regional conferences, expert meetings and the Preparatory Committee;

19. *Requests* the Secretary-General of the United Nations to take appropriate steps, as part of the preparatory process, to ensure that the Conference and the issues to be discussed at it are widely publicized;

20. *Also requests* the Secretary-General of the United Nations, in close consultation with the Secretary-General of the Conference, to submit to the General Assembly at its forty-eighth session, through the Economic and Social Council, a progress report on the implementation of the present resolution;

21. *Decides* to include in the provisional agenda of its forty-eighth session an item entitled "International Conference on Population and Development".

General Assembly resolution 47/176

22 December 1992   Meeting 93   Adopted without vote

Approved by Second Committee (A/47/717/Add.1) without vote, 9 December (meeting 49); draft by Vice-Chairman (A/C.2/47/L.73), based on informal consultations on draft by Pakistan for Group of 77, China and Japan (A/C.2/47/L.42); agenda item 12.

Meeting numbers. GA 47th session: 2nd Committee 3-9, 34-37, 40, 42, 43, 45, 46, 48, 49; plenary 93.

UN Population Fund

UNFPA activities

According to a report of the Executive Director on 1992 activities,[10] the bulk of UNFPA assistance once again went to family-planning services, followed by communication and education programmes, population policy formulation and evaluation, population dynamics, basic data collection, special programmes and multisectoral activities.

At the end of 1992, the Fund was assisting 1,499 projects—503 in Africa, 400 in Asia and the Pacific, 232 in Latin America and the Caribbean, 203 in the Arab States and Europe, and 161 interregional projects.

Assistance to family-planning programmes totalled $80.7 million, almost half of the total allocation of $163.6 million. UNFPA supported numerous activities to strengthen and expand family-planning services, especially in rural and remote areas, by integrating family planning into maternal and child health care and into reproductive health programmes. Such programmes sought, *inter alia*, to provide a wide choice of safe and effective contraceptive methods as well as information and counselling to help users select and practise contraception effectively; to make clinical and referral services available for those methods requiring them; and to train service providers in family-planning techniques and counselling and in responsible sexual behaviour and parenthood.

In 1992, the Fund revised its policy guidelines on family-planning programme support to give greater emphasis to reproductive health and the Safe Motherhood Initiative, an inter-agency effort, begun in 1987,[11] to reduce maternal deaths by at least half by 2000. UNFPA continued to support skill-developing programmes in maternal and child health care and family planning (MCH/FP) in cooperation with Laval University, the University of Montreal (Canada), the Tunis Centre of International Family Planning Training (Tunisia) and the Mauritius Institute of Health. It also collaborated with the Université Libre de Bruxelles (Belgium) to produce a family-planning training manual in French, covering clinical techniques and programme management.

One of the Fund's primary activities during the year was to help Governments procure and distribute contraceptive supplies. With financial assistance from the Swedish International Development Authority (SIDA), the Rockefeller Foundation and the World Bank, UNFPA set up a unit to oversee the implementation of its Global Initiative on Contraceptive Requirements and Logistics Management Needs in developing countries.[12] The unit organized in-depth studies in India, Nepal, Pakistan and Zimbabwe to assess logistics management systems and contraceptive requirements. The study identified an urgent need for intra-uterine devices (IUDs) in Pakistan, and UNFPA provided 650,000 units.

The Fund noted a number of significant donations during 1992. The British Overseas Development Administration provided $1.2 million for injectables and oral contraceptives in Ghana; SIDA funded the procurement of 2 million IUDs for India and procured, through UNFPA, some $1.6 million in contraceptives for Angola, Nicaragua, Sri Lanka, Uganda, Viet Nam, Zambia and Zimbabwe; Austria provided over $422,000 for injectables for Rwanda; the World Bank provided 2 million doses of injectables and 15 million cycles of oral contraceptives for Bangladesh; and the Finnish International Development Agency signed an agreement to allocate some $2.4 million over three years for supplies of NORPLANT contraceptive implants for Nepal. Germany provided some $233,000 in emergency contraceptive supplies to Kazakhstan, Kyrgyzstan, Turkmenistan and Uzbekistan. The Fund also prepared a guide for concerned government departments setting out procurement options and describing the procedures and structure needed for each of them.

During the year, the Fund supported human immunodeficiency virus/acquired immunodeficiency syndrome (HIV/AIDS) prevention activities in 70 countries, compared with 41 in 1991. Activities focused on: the inclusion of AIDS-related components in population, family life and family-planning education and communication programmes; information and counselling on AIDS prevention and the distribution of condoms; the inclusion of AIDS education and information components in training programmes; and the conduct of socio-demographic, operational and biomedical research. (See also PART THREE, Chapter XI.)

UNFPA assistance for information, education and communication (IEC) activities amounted to $27.2 million, or 16.6 per cent of all programme allocations. Activities were aimed at helping countries develop comprehensive national IEC strategies; sensitizing decision makers and religious and community leaders about family planning as both a basic human right and a health measure; integrating information and education components into MCH/FP and reproductive health programmes; incorporating population and family-life education into school curricula and out-of-school programmes; and research to help in the design of messages to reach target groups. Peer education and youth-to-youth counselling on adolescent reproductive health proved to be particularly successful in a number of countries.

In a programme advisory note on youth, UNFPA recommended that more attention be paid to meeting young people's reproductive health needs and services and to facilitating their participation in population and development programmes. The note also stressed the importance of developing comprehensive national strategies on youth, population and development, combining IEC activities with reproductive health and family-planning services for youth. Such strategies should seek to involve young men in family planning and responsible parenthood, as well as to improve the health, welfare and status of young women.

The Fund provided support to the Mexican Family-Planning Federation to further develop and refine a sex education course and expanded its assistance to include some 60 formal population education activities worldwide. The content of population education also continued to expand, as most developing countries widened the scope to include such topics as responsible sexual behaviour; the role and status of women in society and development; and the interrelationship between population, the environment and resources. UNFPA collaborated with Egypt, Nigeria and Pakistan in formulating and implementing population education programmes aimed at workers and trade union leaders. In several countries, it supported projects to improve communication between parents and their children on such issues as human sexuality, family planning and contraception.

The Fund allocated some $14.7 million, or 9 per cent of its assistance, to population dynamics programmes, and some $14.8 million for the formulation, evaluation and implementation of population policies and programmes. High-quality technical assistance, provided by country support teams, was essential to the success of national execution and decentralization. In 1992, six such teams became operational—two in Africa, two in Asia, one in the Arab States and one in Latin America and the Caribbean. They conducted technical backstopping missions to 23 countries.

Basic data collection received some $9.9 million in assistance, or 6 per cent of the total allocation. The Fund continued to help developing countries generate population data and improve their capacity to collect, analyse and disseminate information on a timely basis. It kept abreast of new technologies and emerging issues in census design and helped to develop computer software packages to support population activities. UNFPA provided specialized training to some 75 professionals from 48 developing countries through the Global Programme of Training in Population and Development, and supported four multi-year studies on migration. To gain a better understanding of the population factor in economic development, UNFPA organized a consultative meeting of economists in September. The Fund also participated in a series of international meetings on ageing, two of which provided inputs for the 1994 International Conference on Population and Development. A 400-page study on changing population age structures, 1990-2015, in Europe, was jointly published by UNFPA and ECE. Other allocations included some $8.5 million, or 5.2 per cent of total assistance, for special programmes and $7.8 million, or 4.8 per cent, for multisectoral activities.

UNFPA continued to support improvements in the role and status of women in society and in development. As part of its efforts to improve the role and status of African women, the Fund supported some 40 projects addressing their reproductive and productive needs in 28 countries. In cooperation with the Arab Gulf Programme for United Nations Development Organizations, UNDP and the International Planned Parenthood Federation, it worked on establishing the Arab Women's Centre for Training and Research in Tunis to train Arab women in population-related activities. The Fund also helped several countries to establish income-generating activities for women and to provide training in micro-enterprise management and family welfare.

In line with its strategy to strengthen the Fund's capacity to deal with issues concerning women, population and development, UNFPA updated its sectoral policy guidelines as well as its guidelines for project formulation and appraisal to make them more gender-sensitive. Two training workshops on women, population and development helped UNFPA staff to incorporate gender into each of the Fund's programme areas. A status report on the strategy[13] was included in the Executive Director's 1992 annual report. To improve the technical aspect of women, population and development activities, UNFPA issued publications on women and micro-enterprise development; women, population and the environment; together with a training guide on incorporating women's issues into population and development programmes.

UNFPA continued to enhance its coordination with agencies and organizations within and outside the United Nations system. It actively participated in the work of several coordination committees and groups and entered into a number of new cooperative agreements to improve collaboration on population programme activities and help to ensure a regular exchange of information. The Fund also contributed to preparations for several international conferences, most notably the 1992 United Nations Conference on Environment and Development (UNCED) (see PART THREE, Chapter VIII) and the 1994 International Conference on Population and Development (see above). As a follow-up to UNCED, it identified chapters and programme areas of Agenda 21[14] that had programmatic, institutional and financial implications for UNFPA, and began to develop guidelines on integrating environmental goals and considerations into national population policies and programmes.

In February,[15] the Executive Directors of UNFPA and the United Nations Children's Fund (UNICEF) summarized their collaborative programming activities. The report examined the need and rationale for close collaboration between the two organizations and analysed their field- and headquarters-level collaboration.

On 26 May,[3] the Governing Council took note of the report and urged UNFPA and UNICEF to expand and strengthen their collaborative activities. It requested the two organizations to include a status report on those activities in the Executive Director's annual report to the Council.

In June, UNFPA launched a new monthly magazine, *POPULI*, in English, French and Spanish, which combined its quarterly journal with the same title with its monthly newsletter *Population*. UNFPA's 1992 *State of World Population* report, entitled "A World in Balance", called for immediate and determined action to balance population, consumption and development patterns as a prerequisite to ending absolute poverty.

UNDP Governing Council action. On 26 May 1992,[3] the UNDP Governing Council took note of the UNFPA Executive Director's report on the 1991 activities of the Fund[16] and requested her to take appropriate steps to increase voluntary contributions to UNFPA. The Council commended the progress made on the Fund's Global Initiative on Contraceptive Requirements and Logisitics Management Needs, and requested that it submit a report on the subject at its forty-first (1994) session. On the same date,[17] the Council took note of a proposal by Germany to host the headquarters of UNFPA, along with UNDP and its affiliated funds, at Bonn from 1996 onwards, and requested the Administrator to hold consultations on the issue and report to the Council at its fortieth (1993) session.

In February, by **decision 1992/208 C**, the Economic and Social Council decided not to consider the part of the UNDP Governing Council's report dealing with UNFPA, except for recommendations that required action by the Council.

Country and intercountry programmes

In a March report,[18] the Executive Director provided the status of financial implementation of UNDP Governing Council–approved UNFPA country programmes and projects for the period 1986-1991, plus estimates for 31 new programmes to be submitted to the Council in 1992. The total amount estimated for the new submissions was $318.6 million, including $224.1 million from regular funds. The balance of UNFPA commitments for ongoing and new programmes amounted to $549.8 million.

The Governing Council, on 26 May,[19] approved the 31 multi-year assistance programmes—16 in sub-Saharan Africa, 8 in Asia and the Pacific, 4 in the Arab States and 3 in Latin America.

UNFPA concentrated on programmes in 58 priority countries (32 in Africa, 17 in Asia and the Pacific, 5 in Latin America and the Caribbean and 4 in the Arab States), which received $96.7 million, or 74.2 per cent, of the $130.3 million allocated to country programmes overall.[10] Allocations for intercountry activities (regional and interregional) totalled $33.2 million, or 20.3 per cent of the total, in 1992. The resources allocated to priority country programmes increased by 1.1 per cent over 1991, but the combined amount allocated to country and intercountry programmes dropped sharply, from $172 million in 1991 to $163.6 million in 1992.

Programmes for sub-Saharan Africa received $48.6 million in 1992, a decline from $55.1 million in 1991. The decline in support made it necessary for UNFPA to scale down plans to expand activities and to seek resources from other donors to cover projects that had already been developed. Most resources for the region (58.2 per cent) were allocated to family-planning and communication and education programmes.

A status report[13] on the implementation of the strategy for UNFPA assistance to sub-Saharan Africa[20] provided an overview of UNFPA expenditures for activities in the region between 1986 and 1992 and the progress made and constraints encountered in the main areas of the programme during 1990-1992. The report concluded that of the 41 countries covered by UNFPA for which fertility information was available, 11 had seen a decline in the total fertility rate; 6 showed an increase and 24 remained more or less unchanged. Evidence suggested however that the investment in population programmes had set the stage for declining fertility and population growth, reflected in part by an upswing in contraceptive use in most countries of the region.

The Arab States and Europe received $16.1 million in 1992, compared with $14.9 million in 1991. Improved access to family-planning services, particularly in rural areas, was a primary objective of programmes in most Arab States. In 1992, family-planning programmes accounted for 45.7 per cent of the total allocation for the Arab States and Europe.

In Europe, UNFPA assistance continued to focus on efforts to reduce the high incidence of abortion and relatively high rates of infant and maternal mortality. About one quarter of the $4 million allocated to Europe was earmarked for activities in Albania. UNFPA activities were suspended in the former Yugoslavia, and the UNFPA representative there was temporarily relocated to Vienna.

Asia and the Pacific received $60.7 million in 1992, compared with $57 million in 1991. Family-planning programmes accounted for 67 per cent of UNFPA resources allocated to the region. Ageing and AIDS prevention received special emphasis.

UNFPA resources allocated to Latin America and the Caribbean increased slightly in 1992—to $18 million from $17.3 million in 1991. Of that, 43.9 per cent was allocated to family-planning programmes. Illegal abortion and adolescent pregnancy were among the region's most pressing population problems. The Fund devised a strategy that concentrated on improving women's reproductive health, to address those issues.

Allocations for interregional and global programmes in 1992 totalled some $20.1 million, of which $7.8 million, or 38.9 per cent, went to family-planning programmes, focusing on contraceptive research.

Work programmes

In a February report on the Fund's work plan for 1993-1996 and request for programme expenditure authority,[21] the Executive Director provided information on UNFPA's current and projected resources, overall resource utilization and the distribution of programmable resources for 1993-1996 among country and intercountry activities.

On 26 May,[22] the Council approved the work plan for 1993-1996 and the request for new programme expenditure authority of $188.1 million for 1993. It endorsed the following estimates for new programmable resources for 1994-1996, subject to actual contributions: $207.4 million for 1994, $225 million for 1995 and $244.4 million for 1996.

Programme planning and evaluation

Reporting on the UNFPA medium-term operational strategy,[23] the Executive Director provided background information on the Fund's growth from its beginning in 1969 through 1991; its current organizational adaptations and staffing requirements; its goals, mandate and objectives; its actions at the policy and programme level, and the resources needed to meet ongoing and emerging needs in the 1990s. The report outlined areas requiring the increased attention of the Fund, namely maternal and child health and family planning; support for women, population and development activities; training in population issues; AIDS prevention; integration of population-related issues into the substantive programmes of other United Nations organizations; and collection and analysis of programme data. It was estimated that by the year 2000, $9 billion would be required to fund population activities in developing countries, of which $4 billion was to come from the international community, including $1 billion to be channelled through UNFPA.

On 26 May 1992,[3] the UNDP Governing Council took note of the UNFPA medium-term operational strategy.

During the year, UNFPA further strengthened and refined its programme implementation, focusing on strategic programming and its requisite technical assistance, national execution, decentralization, evaluation, coordination and procurement. The Programme Review and Strategy Development (PRSD) exercise was key to the success of strategic programming.[10]

The exercises, which normally lasted for two years and culminated in a four- to six-week PRSD mission to the country, analysed the country's population status and needs, assessed past population activities and recommended action in terms of an overall national strategy.

In 1992, the Fund organized 12 PRSD missions— 9 in sub-Saharan Africa and 3 in Latin America and the Caribbean—published 13 PRSD reports, bringing their total number to 25, and finalized the PRSD guidelines.

Evaluation remained a regular and integral part of UNFPA's programming process. The Fund undertook two major thematic evaluations during the year. The first examined efforts to implement IEC strategies in support of family-planning service delivery, and the second focused on UNFPA-supported income-generating activities for women.

In a February report,[24] the Executive Director reviewed the Fund's evaluation activities in 1990-1991, including project evaluations, independent, in-depth evaluations, programme review and strategy development, and feedback and use of evaluation results. The report noted that in the period under review, UNFPA had undertaken 47 PRSD exercises, expanding their use to help countries develop coherent frameworks for national population programmes.

On 26 May,[3] the UNDP Governing Council took note of the report and requested the Executive Director to increase the number of independent evaluations. The Council also called for a re-

view of the PRSD exercise and requested that the Executive Director include the findings in a report to the Council at its forty-first (1994) session.

The Executive Director in March submitted a report[25] on national execution guidelines, which analysed UNFPA's experience with national execution, describing the lessons learned and steps taken and proposing policy and operational guidelines.

On 26 May,[3] the Governing Council endorsed the proposed national execution policy guidelines, and requested the Population Fund to continue to provide financial support for personnel training, national institutional capacity-building and necessary equipment.

Financial and administrative questions

According to the annual financial review of the Population Fund,[26] its total income in 1992 amounted to $238.2 million. Expenditures totalled $193.6 million, resulting in an excess of income over expenditure of $44.6 million. During the year, 105 Governments contributed $233.8 million, an increase of $13.1 million (5.9 per cent) over the amount pledged in 1991. Interest on income amounted to $3.1 million. Other miscellaneous income and adjustments totalled $1.3 million. The 6.3 per cent overall increase in income, however, was largely due to favourable exchange rates.

As at 1 January 1992, the unexpended balance of the 26 trust funds managed by UNFPA was $7.6 million, which, when added to the total income of $43.1 million received under the funds-in-trust agreements, resulted in $50.7 million available for programming. Total expenditures in 1992 were $39.8 million. Transfers back to donor Governments in respect of completed projects totalled $0.1 million, leaving an unexpended balance as at 31 December of $11 million, which was available to finance trust fund activities in 1993.

In May,[27] the UNDP Governing Council took note of the annual review of the activities financed by UNFPA in 1991,[28] the audit reports for the year ended 31 December 1990[29] and the interim report of the Board of Auditors for the first year of the biennium 1990-1991.[30] The Council noted that the Fund's 1991 expenditure had exceeded its income, which, along with the income projected for 1992, fell considerably short of the original estimates. It urged UNFPA to ensure that future estimates of income reflected actual trends and that future expenditure plans accorded with those estimates. It also noted with concern the continued increase in the proportion of the Fund's administrative expenditures in relation to programme expenditures, and requested the Executive Director to propose steps to reduce that proportion, to strengthen internal financial management and control and to report to the Governing Council on those activities in 1993.

Also before the Council was a progress report[31] on UNFPA successor support cost arrangements.[32] Acting on the report, the Governing Council urged the Executive Director to ensure that technical support services teams be established with clear lines of accountability, management structures, reporting and working relationships, and requested UNFPA to provide it with a progress report in 1993.

The Council also confirmed its 1991 decision[32] to keep the annual level of the Fund's operational reserve at 20 per cent.[27] It further approved a new financial regulation and requested the Executive Director to submit in 1993 proposed amendments to those regulations permitting her to enter into cost-sharing arrangements with recipient Governments and external donors.

In its financial report and audited financial statements on UNFPA for the biennium ended 31 December 1991,[33] the Board of Auditors expressed concern over the increase in the ratio of operational costs to programme expenditure from 28.8 per cent in 1988 to 33.4 per cent in 1991. It also indicated that in two trust funds, project expenditure had exceeded the funds available, contrary to UNFPA financial regulations. The Advisory Committee on Administrative and Budgetary Questions (ACABQ), in an October report on the Board's report,[34] recommended that UNFPA should programme and commit funds only up to the level of pledges received, and endorsed the Board's view that it had to reduce, suspend or terminate project activity if no funds were received from the respective donor. The Board's report also identified major weaknesses with regard to property control at the field-office level, which it said management was addressing in its new policies and procedures manual. ACABQ noted the Board's view that audit coverage of headquarters activities was particularly inadequate in view of the considerable expansion of operations, and recommended that steps be taken immediately to establish and enhance the capability of internal audit in UNFPA.

Other population activities

Technical cooperation

In a report to the UNDP Governing Council on the 1992 technical cooperation programme of DESD,[35] the Secretary-General said the Department had executed 112 population projects in 67 developing countries, with a total delivery of $7.6 million. It had also undertaken 48 project-related or direct technical advisory missions to 34 countries. Some 43 projects were in population training and research, and 34 in population

dynamics, with a major emphasis on the evaluation and analysis of data from the 1990 round of population censuses and demographic surveys. DESD, in cooperation with other international bodies, organized for African demographers and planners a four-month training programme in demographic data analysis, dissemination and utilization, and two workshops on the use of microcomputers and software for analysis of census data. Managerial and substantive backstopping was provided in 30 countries in the fields of population policy and population and development. Project activities included the strengthening of institutional arrangements, demographic research and studies, population policy formulation, the integration of population variables in development planning, and the training of national staff in the use of demo-economic models and related software for development planning.

UN Population Award

In September, the Secretary-General presented the 1992 United Nations Population Award to J. R. D. Tata (India), an industrialist and a pioneer in India's population movement, and to the Population Council, a United States-based international research NGO renowned for providing technical assistance in national population programmes and for its work in developing new contraceptives. Each received a diploma, a gold medal and a monetary prize. The award, established by the General Assembly in 1981,[36] is presented annually to individuals or institutions that have made outstanding contributions towards increasing awareness of population problems and to their solutions. The award's trust fund totalled $608,480 as at 31 December 1991.

By a note of 23 July,[37] the Secretary-General transmitted to the General Assembly the UNFPA Executive Director's report on the status of the Award. The Assembly, by **decision 47/439**, took note of the Secretary-General's note.

REFERENCES

[1]ESC res. 1989/91, 26 July 1989. [2]YUN 1991, p. 510, ESC res. 1991/93, 26 July 1991. [3]E/1992/28 (dec. 92/32 A). [4]E/1992/60. [5]E/1993/49. [6]YUN 1974, p. 552. [7]YUN 1984, p. 714. [8]ACC/1992/22. [9]DP/1993/29, Part II. [10]Ibid., Part I. [11]YUN 1987, p. 1222. [12]DP/1993/29, Part I. [13]DP/1993/29, Part III. [14]*Report of the United Nations Conference on Environment and Development, Rio de Janeiro, 3-14 June 1992*, vol. I, Sales No. E.93.I.8. [15]DP/1992/28. [16]YUN 1991, p. 511. [17]E/1992/28 (dec. 92/44). [18]DP/1992/27. [19]E/1992/28 (dec. 92/32 C). [20]YUN 1987, p. 634. [21]DP/1992/26. [22]E/1992/28 (dec 92/32 B). [23]DP/1992/31. [24]DP/1992/25. [25]DP/1992/29. [26]DP/1993/36. [27]E/1992/28 (dec 92/33). [28]DP/1992/32. [29]DP/1992/33. [30]A/46/5/Add.7. [31]DP/1992/30. [32]YUN 1991, p. 515. [33]A/47/5/Add.7. [34]A/47/500. [35]DP/1993/39/Add.1. [36]YUN 1981, p. 792. [37]A/47/338.

Human settlements

Conference on human settlements

In September 1992, in response to a General Assembly request,[1] the Secretary-General submitted a report[2] on a proposed United Nations conference on human settlements (Habitat II). The report evaluated the state of human settlements around the world and progress since the 1976 human settlements conference (Vancouver, Canada).[3] It reviewed the objectives, scope and content of the proposed Habitat II and discussed its preparation and financial requirements.

By way of background to the call for Habitat II, the Secretary-General noted that the enormous strides made since 1976 towards solving the shelter problem had not been enough to arrest the deterioration of living conditions in many countries, where rapid urbanization, increasing landlessness and declining income yields from agriculture had led to increasing poverty in both urban and rural areas. The world's population was expanding by about one billion people per decade, with 94.1 per cent of this growth in the current decade in developing countries. Cities in the developing world were expected to absorb some 90 per cent of that population growth but already faced enormous backlogs in the availability of housing, infrastructure and services, and were confronted with overcrowded transportation systems, insufficient water supply, deteriorating sanitation and environmental pollution. One third of the urban population in those countries were living in slums or squatter settlements. The lack of access to modern amenities, the growing scarcity of affordable building materials, and the inadequacy of domestic energy sources were creating equally dramatic conditions for the rural poor. The Secretary-General said the health consequences of the situation were both tragic and appalling, with some 2.5 billion people suffering from ailments related to contaminated water and the lack of sanitation. He further noted that the external debt of developing countries and structural adjustment programmes aimed at strengthening their economies had in fact undermined prospects for improved living conditions in many countries. He also noted that conventional econometric models had failed to measure correctly the economic returns on investments in human settlements which had been given low priority in the mistaken belief that they were ''social welfare''.

Since Habitat I, Governments had made substantial advances in improving living conditions, and within the United Nations, the human settlements programme had shown considerable gains, he said. Such progress was accompanied by an evolution in thinking with respect to the problems of human settlements development and their solutions. He noted that the 1992 United Nations Conference on Environment and Development (UNCED)[4] had decided to address human settlements as a substantive framework for sustainable development and that programme areas, such as atmosphere, land, coastal areas, freshwater and waste management should include the human settlements dimension (see PART THREE, Chapter VIII).

Referring to the objectives of Habitat II, the Secretary-General recommended that the conference formulate a global plan of action to arrest the deterioration of living conditions and facilitate their improvement, recognizing that the emphasis in solutions to the shelter problem had shifted in the past two decades from direct governmental involvement to government support for private-sector initiatives and the participation of communities and NGOs. He made recommendations on a variety of issues, including the role of Government and NGOs; the mobilization of financial resources; capacity-building and human resources development; sustainable development; new technologies; communications; transportation; water resources; waste management; energy; and information.

GENERAL ASSEMBLY ACTION

On 22 December 1992, the Assembly, on the recommendation of the Second Committee, adopted without vote **resolution 47/180**.

United Nations Conference on Human Settlements (Habitat II)

The General Assembly,

Recalling the recommendations adopted by Habitat: United Nations Conference on Human Settlements, and its resolution 43/181 of 20 December 1988 on the Global Strategy for Shelter to the Year 2000, as well as its resolution 46/164 of 19 December 1991, in which it expressed its conviction that a world-wide conference with broad, multidisciplinary and high-level participation could provide a suitable forum for considering the current situation in the planning, development and management of human settlements, and decided to consider at its forty-seventh session the question of convening, possibly in 1997, a United Nations conference on human settlements (Habitat II), with a view to taking a decision on the objectives, content, scope and timing of such a conference and the modalities and financial implications of holding it,

Noting the outcome of the United Nations Conference on Environment and Development, which recognized the proper management of human settlements as a prerequisite to the attainment of the overall goals for sustainable development, the centre-piece of which must be the human being,

Convinced of the need to reassess and systematically review the multifaceted aspects of human settlement policies and programmes in the light of important changes in the perception of human settlements problems and the solutions thereto since Habitat: United Nations Conference on Human Settlements, particularly the introduction of the concept of enabling strategies, and in the light of new developments and trends in international economic relations and population and migration patterns, as well as the recurrence of natural disasters,

Noting with concern that in many countries, especially many developing ones, the achievements in terms of policies, programmes and projects at the national level in the field of human settlements have not been sufficient to arrest or reverse the deterioration in the living environment of the people because, *inter alia*, of the pressure of population growth and urbanization and because the resource requirements for human settlement programmes far exceed the availability of resources in developing countries,

Cognizant of the fact that the continuing rapid rate of urbanization and population increase in the developing countries is contributing to the emergence and spread of large urban agglomerations, with adverse implications for the supply of adequate shelter, environmental infrastructure and services for the people, as well as for their employment prospects,

Recognizing the importance of giving due consideration to country-specific characteristics, such as the natural environment, the economic structure, the endogenous material base and culture, in the development and application of technology, planning and management in the area of human settlements,

Fully aware of the need for adequate resources to address the problems of human settlements and for more effective policies, programmes and projects, including public/private partnerships, as appropriate, to address those problems, and of the importance of improved management at the national and local levels,

Noting that the provision of external financial resources needed to implement the programmes set forth in chapter 7 of Agenda 21 would facilitate the mobilization of resources locally,

Stressing the need, for the implementation of Agenda 21, to promote, facilitate and finance, as appropriate, access to and transfer of environmentally sound technologies and corresponding know-how, in particular to developing countries on favourable terms, including concessional and preferential terms, as mutually agreed, taking into account the need to protect intellectual property rights as well as the special needs of developing countries,

Bearing in mind the need to take into consideration the work of other recent and planned United Nations conferences on related subjects,

Having considered the report of the Secretary-General on a United Nations conference on human settlements (Habitat II),

1. *Decides* to convene the United Nations Conference on Human Settlements (Habitat II) from 3 to 14 June 1996, at the highest possible level of participation;

2. *Also decides* that the Conference, in addressing human settlements issues in the context of sustainable development, shall have the following objectives:

(*a*) In the long term, to arrest the deterioration of global human settlements conditions and ultimately create conditions for achieving improvements in the living environment of all people on a sustainable basis, with special attention to the needs and contributions of women and vulnerable social groups whose quality of life and participation in development have been hampered by exclusion and inequality, which affect the poor in general;

(*b*) To adopt a general statement of principles and commitments and formulate a related global plan of action suitable for guiding national and international efforts through the first two decades of the next century; such a plan of action should include:

(i) A comprehensive set of programmes and subprogrammes, with realistic targets and timetables and provision for monitoring and evaluation of performance;

(ii) Guidelines for national settlement policies and strategies that can effectively contribute to the alleviation of urban and rural poverty and the promotion of a sustainable economic development process, with due consideration given to the growth and distribution of population, urban transition, natural disasters, the availability of land and other resources and the interests of women and major groups;

(iii) Programmes and subprogrammes relating to new and emerging issues in the field of technology, including the impact of the current communication and informatics revolution, energy, transportation and environmental infrastructure, that is, water-supply, sanitation and waste management;

(iv) Programmes and subprogrammes that would carry forward relevant elements of Agenda 21 to promote the development of environmentally sustainable human settlements in the future;

(v) Proposals for mobilizing, nationally and internationally, the necessary human, financial and technical resources, taking into account the enabling concept and the commitment of new and additional resources, as well as funding from countries' own public and private sectors, for the implementation of Agenda 21 programmes;

(vi) Measures for the reorganization and strengthening of national, metropolitan and municipal institutions and machinery to enhance the development of human settlements and operational capabilities;

(vii) Recommendations on ways in which the role of the United Nations and existing institutional arrangements for international cooperation and coordination in human settlements can be strengthened;

3. *Affirms* that the Conference shall, *inter alia*:

(*a*) Review trends in policies and programmes undertaken by countries and international organizations to implement the recommendations adopted by Habitat: United Nations Conference on Human Settlements;

(*b*) Conduct a mid-term review of the implementation of the Global Strategy for Shelter to the Year 2000 and make recommendations for the attainment of its objectives by the target date;

(*c*) Review the contribution to the implementation of Agenda 21 of national and international action in the area of human settlements;

(*d*) Review current global trends in economic and social development as they affect the planning, development and management of human settlements, and make recommendations for future action at the national and international levels;

4. *Decides* to establish a preparatory committee of the General Assembly for the second United Nations Conference on Human Settlements (Habitat II); the Preparatory Committee will be open to all States Members of the United Nations and members of the specialized agencies, with the participation of observers in accordance with the established practice of the General Assembly;

5. *Invites* relevant or interested organizations, organs, programmes and agencies of the United Nations system and intergovernmental, subregional and regional organizations to participate actively in the preparatory process;

6. *Invites* non-governmental organizations, particularly those from developing countries and including those related to major groups, to participate in and contribute to the Conference and its preparatory process, and, to this end, decides that the Preparatory Committee shall formulate and adopt modalities for the accreditation and participation of those organizations, taking into account the procedures followed at the United Nations Conference on Environment and Development;

7. *Decides* that an organizational session of the Preparatory Committee of three days' duration shall be held at United Nations Headquarters in March 1993 and that two preparatory sessions should be held, the first early in 1994 at Geneva or in New York, and the second in conjunction with the 1995 session of the Commission on Human Settlements, with the detailed arrangements for the preparatory discussions to be determined at the organizational session;

8. *Also decides* that, in the event of there being a clear need for further preparatory discussions, an appropriate request might be made by the Preparatory Committee to the General Assembly;

9. *Further decides* that the Preparatory Committee, at its organizational session, shall elect, with due regard to equitable geographical representation, a chairman, three vice-chairmen and a rapporteur;

10. *Notes with appreciation* the generous offer made by the Government of Turkey to act as host to the Conference, and decides that the Conference will be held in Turkey in 1996;

11. *Decides* that the host country shall be ex officio an officer of the Preparatory Committee;

12. *Requests* the Secretary-General, following the organizational session of the Preparatory Committee, in accordance with resolutions 41/213 of 19 December 1986 and 42/211 of 21 December 1987, to establish, through redeployment to the maximum extent possible and within existing resources, an ad hoc secretariat for the Conference, which shall be organizationally part of the United Nations Centre for Human Settlements (Habitat);

13. *Decides* that the ad hoc secretariat will be headed by the Secretary-General of the Conference, who will be appointed by the Secretary-General of the United Nations;

14. *Requests* the Secretary-General of the United Nations to prepare a report for the organizational session of the Preparatory Committee containing recommendations on an adequate preparatory process, taking into account the provisions of the present resolution and the views expressed by Governments in the discussion of this matter at the forty-seventh session of the General Assembly;

15. *Decides* that the Preparatory Committee shall:

(a) Draft the provisional agenda of the Conference, in accordance with the provisions of the present resolution;

(b) Adopt guidelines to enable States to take a harmonized approach in their preparations and reporting;

(c) Prepare draft decisions, including the plan of action, for the Conference and submit them to the Conference for consideration and adoption;

16. *Requests* all organs, organizations and programmes of the United Nations system, as well as other relevant intergovernmental organizations, to cooperate with the secretariat of the Conference and contribute fully to the preparations for the Conference on the basis of guidelines and requirements to be established by the Preparatory Committee;

17. *Requests* the Secretary-General of the United Nations to ensure the coordination of contributions from the United Nations system, through the Administrative Committee on Coordination;

18. *Invites* all States to take an active part in the preparations for the Conference, to prepare national reports, as appropriate, to be submitted to the Preparatory Committee in a timely manner and to promote international cooperation and broad-based national preparatory processes involving the scientific community, industry, trade unions and non-governmental organizations concerned;

19. *Recommends* that regional and subregional preparatory meetings should be held in conjunction with meetings of subregional and regional intergovernmental bodies, wherever possible;

20. *Decides* that the preparatory process and the Conference itself shall be funded through existing United Nations budgetary resources, without negatively affecting its programmed activities, and through voluntary contributions to a trust fund established specifically for that purpose;

21. *Also decides* to establish a separate voluntary fund for the purpose of supporting developing countries, in particular the least developed among them, in participating fully and effectively in the Conference and in its preparatory process, and invites Governments to contribute to the fund;

22. *Requests* the Secretary-General to report to the General Assembly at its forty-ninth and fiftieth sessions on the progress of work of the Preparatory Committee;

23. *Decides* to include in the provisional agenda of its forty-ninth and fiftieth sessions an item entitled "United Nations Conference on Human Settlements (Habitat II)".

General Assembly resolution 47/180

22 December 1992   Meeting 93   Adopted without vote

Approved by Second Committee (A/47/718/Add.1) without vote, 16 December (meeting 51); draft by Vice-Chairman (A/C.2/47/L.75), based on informal consultations on draft by Pakistan for Group of 77 (A/C.2/47/L.12); agenda item 78.

Financial implications. 5th Committee, A/47/810; S-G, A/C.2/47/L.89, A/C.5/47/80.

Meeting numbers. GA 47th session: 2nd Committee 25, 30, 45, 46, 49-51; plenary 93.

UN Centre for Human Settlements (Habitat)

Activities

In 1992, UNCHS supported 262 technical cooperation projects and programmes in 96 countries, with an overall budget in excess of $43 million. An additional 85 projects in 44 countries were awaiting funding. Sectoral support missions were sent to Angola, Cambodia, Ecuador, Fiji, the Gambia, Guatemala, Panama, Papua New Guinea, the United Republic of Tanzania and the Caribbean subregion, and the Centre supported human settlements sector analysis and needs assessment missions to Albania, Bangladesh, Cambodia, the Central African Republic, Ecuador, Fiji, the Gambia, Ghana, Indonesia, Nepal, Nigeria, Panama, Rwanda, the United Republic of Tanzania, Zambia and the Caribbean subregion.

The 1992-1993 UNCHS work programme once again had eight subprogrammes: global issues and strategies; national policies and instruments; integrated settlements management; financial resources; land management; infrastructure development and operation; housing production; and the construction sector. Those activities were described in a report of the Executive Director to the Commission on Human Settlements.[5]

Under the first subprogramme, the Centre assisted developing countries in formulating and implementing national shelter strategies in accordance with the Global Strategy for Shelter to the Year 2000, adopted by the General Assembly in 1988.[6] As part of its series of subregional seminars, UNCHS sponsored the Arab States Regional Conference on National Shelter Strategies (Cairo, Egypt, December). A pilot project was being carried out in Kenya under the City Data Programme to test a preliminary urban data framework and to train municipalities in the collection and computerized storage of key urban data. A workshop for mayors and town clerks of the pilot study cities was held in June.

Under the second subprogramme, emphasis was given to the analysis of national human settlements policies and instruments; the preparation of options and guidelines for sustainable human settlements policies and programmes; assistance with methods and instruments for investment planning; and translation of the global strategy at the national level. Within the framework of the UNCHS/World Bank Housing Indicators Programme, the Centre hosted an international seminar (Nairobi, 27-30 January) which reviewed data and information from a number of countries in Africa, Europe and North America. A concise list of global indicators was prepared for consideration by the Commission on Human Settlements at its fourteenth (1993) session. In 1992, UNCHS carried out 82 ongoing projects and programmes in 47 countries, with a budget of over $10.7 million. Many of these programmes focused on the strengthening of human settlements management in the national development planning process.

The third subprogramme was the Centre's largest in terms of financial resources, with over $12.5 million budgeted for 1992 within its integrated settlements management projects and programmes. During the year, UNHCS collaborated with 36 developing countries on 66 settlements management projects and programmes. Activities focused on metropolitan, secondary-centre and subnational-systems management, as well as human resource development. In cooperation with the League of Arab States, the Centre held a training of trainers workshop in urban finance and management for Arab States from the Mashrig subregion (Cairo, April). A senior-level seminar on national policies for local government training in South Asia was held at Colombo, Sri Lanka, in November.

Under the financial resources subprogramme, a housing in development workshop was held (Bandung, Indonesia, May) for officials and practitioners from Asian countries, with a follow-up course for the same target group (Leuven, Belgium, October). The Centre supported eight technical cooperation projects and programmes on the mobilization of financial resources for human settlements development, and provided advisory services to Indonesia, Nepal, Pakistan, Papua New Guinea, the Philippines, Sri Lanka, Uganda, the United Arab Emirates and Yemen. Activities included the training of trainers workshops in municipal economic development (Costa Rica, February), in local government management for Central and Eastern Europe (Hungary, April/May), in local government institutional development (Peru, June), in local government training methods and techniques (Ecuador, August), and in needs assessment and the use of training materials (Morocco, December). In addition, a pilot training course was held for local government-elected officials (Uganda, October/November) to train mayors and councillors in the skills required for improved management of cities.

Activities under the land-management subprogramme in 1992 focused on developing mechanisms and instruments to address land-management problems and to ensure the availability of a steady, adequate and affordable supply of land to meet all settlement needs. Work continued on reviewing and updating technical and administrative requirements for improving the operation of land-registration systems as a prerequisite for effective land policies, including land title-registration. The Centre supported eight technical cooperation projects and programmes in eight countries.

UNCHS emphasized management and financing issues relevant to improved infrastructural services. The Centre's activities under this subprogramme expanded considerably in 1992, with the development of an integrated approach to the provision, development and maintenance of environmental infrastructure. This resulted in the consolidation of existing and new UNCHS initiatives and activities under the umbrella of the Centre's Settlement Infrastructure and Environment Programme, to meet the infrastructure needs of the urban and rural poor in a sustainable way. As part of its contribution to Agenda 21,[4] UNCHS conducted a research project on strategies for solid waste recycling and reuse in developing countries and organized, in August and September, workshops in five cities (Kanpur, India; Karachi, Pakistan; Bangkok, Thailand; Manila, Philippines; Jakarta, Indonesia). The Centre undertook missions to Ghana, Guinea-Bissau and Indonesia to formulate a research project on the relationship between crowding and health in low-income settlements. Developing policies and practices to facilitate the delivery of infrastructure services was the focus of 38 technical cooperation projects and programmes in 22 countries.

The work programme for housing production paid special attention to the needs and potentials of the poorest groups. In collaboration with the World Bank and the Institute for Housing and Development Studies, UNCHS arranged an expert group meeting (Rotterdam, Netherlands, 12-15 February) to discuss the development and implementation of policies to guide the relocation process. The Centre had 30 ongoing technical cooperation projects and programmes in 18 countries, which focused on support for both the informal and formal private sector in housing development.

In the construction sector, work concentrated on the transfer of small-scale technologies to local building-materials industries as well as on skills development and upgrading. The Centre convened an expert group meeting on appropriate, intermediate, cost-effective building materials, technologies and transfer mechanisms for housing delivery (Madras, India, February). The Centre's 23 projects in 13 countries helped to develop standards, technologies and regulatory frameworks to encourage the use and production of durable local building materials.

The Centre's information activities included the production of technical publications, audiovisual aids, press releases and information kits, as well as several periodicals and newsletters.

The 1992 Habitat Scroll of Honour Awards to recognize outstanding contributions by individuals, organizations and projects to the advancement of the shelter delivery process, were presented to Laurie Baker, Yona Friedman, Evgueni Rozanov, John F. C. Turner and Mayor Jaime Lerner of Curitiba (Brazil), as well as to the Shenzhen Housing Bureau of China, the Habitat International Coalition and the Intermediate Technology Development Group of the United Kingdom. Awards were also presented to seven projects: the East Wahdat Upgrading Project in Jordan, the Earthquake Emergency Reconstruction and Rehabilitation Programme in Nepal, the Rural Housing Reconstruction with Appropriate Technologies in Ecuador, the Namuwongo Upgrading and Low-cost Housing Project in Uganda, the New Communities Programme in Egypt, the World Relief El Salvador Housing Reconstruction Project, and the Woodless Construction Project in the Niger.

Coordination

Coordination and cooperation activities within the United Nations system[7] and with intergovernmental and non-governmental organizations[8] were described by the Executive Director in separate reports to the Commission on Human Settlements.

During the year, the Centre continued to work with other organizations on urban and rural development projects, including the Urban Management Programme and the Sustainable Cities Programme. UNCHS participated in the Seventh Conference on Urban and Regional Research (Ankara, Turkey, July), the twentieth meeting of the Administrative Committee on Coordination (ACC) Task Force on Rural Development (New York, April), an international seminar on local and regional development options for the next decade focusing on eastern and southern Africa (Nairobi, September), and co-sponsored an international seminar on rural centre and settlements planning with the Economic and Social Commission for Asia and the Pacific (Tehran, Iran, July). The Centre continued its collaboration with the World Food Programme in projects related to human settlements development that required food-assisted activities. In February, the Centre participated in the eleventh session of the Inter-agency Group on New and Renewable Sources of Energy and the sixth session of the Committee on the Development and Utilization of New and Renewable Sources of Energy. In the area of science and technology, UNCHS participated in the thirteenth session of the ACC Task Force on Science and Technology (New York, November), which discussed the organization of resources for the promotion of science and technology in developing countries, the review of endogenous capacity-building projects and the contribution of biotechnology to sustainable development. The Centre also participated in the International Symposium on Transfer of Environmentally Sound Technology (Osaka and Otsu, Japan, October), which considered the promotion of the transfer of environmentally sound technologies and the establishment of global networks.

UNCHS actively participated in the preparatory process of the Earth Summit and in the formulation of several of the action programmes of Agenda 21[4] (see PART THREE, Chapter VIII). In the areas of water and sanitation, UNCHS served as a member of the Steering Committee for the International Conference on Water and Environment (Dublin, Ireland, January), which provided the major input on freshwater problems to UNCED, and assisted in the preparation of the chapter of Agenda 21 dealing with solid wastes. It also provided input to Agenda 21 in the area of transport, especially in the context of air pollution, through its participation in the International Seminar on Sustainable Transportation (Rio de Janeiro, Brazil, June).

In 1992, UNCHS launched the Settlement Infrastructure and Environment Programme (SIEP) to help Governments, the private sector and communities in planning, providing, maintaining and managing environmental infrastructure, and in August, UNCHS and the United Nations Environment Programme approved a framework for cooperation in the integrated planning and management of coastal areas.

The Centre and the Caribbean Community (CARICOM) co-sponsored a subregional meeting (Georgetown, Guyana, October) to analyse countries' priorities in the human settlements field as a basis for project formulation.

The Meeting on Governmental–Non-Governmental Cooperation in the Field of Human Settlements (The Hague, Netherlands, 2-6 November) identified the following priorities for action: defining the roles and responsibilities of the different actors in human settlements; providing sustainable support at the community level; providing access to land and finance for low-income groups; alleviation of poverty; supporting the role of women in human settlements development; and decentralization of powers, responsibilities and resources from central to local levels.

Global Parliamentarians on Habitat

The Conference of Global Parliamentarians on Human Settlements and Development (Vancouver, Canada, 15-20 March)[9] adopted the Vancouver 1992 Declaration of Global Parliamentarians on Habitat (Human Settlements and Sustainable Development). The Declaration recommended action in such areas as human settlements management, effective land-resource management, adequate shelter for all, integrated provision of environmental infrastructure, sustainable transport and energy systems, human resources development and capacity-building, promoting human settlements planning and management in disaster-prone areas and promoting sustainable construction industry activities. It

also made recommendations in such areas as management of the atmosphere, coastal area conservation, deforestation, biodiversity preservation, public health, protection of the water supply and waste management, and called for the implementation of a Global Human Settlements Strategy.

Women and human settlements

In response to a request of the Commission on Human Settlements, the Executive Director in December submitted a report[10] on women's participation in the Global Strategy for Shelter to the Year 2000.[6]

The Women in Human Settlements Development Programme, launched by UNCHS in 1990, was directed at: involving women in the formulation and implementation of human settlements policies and programmes; opening up employment opportunities for women in the human settlements sector; improving women's access to credit for both property ownership and business development; protecting and improving women's shelter and land tenure; and improving the living and working environment of women, especially low-income women, their families and their communities. The Centre emphasized training in gender awareness; capacity-building for women already involved in the settlements sector; hands-on training in construction skills; improved access to land by changing laws related to land tenure and housing finance; training for women as educators on the subjects of environmental protection and natural resources management; improving women's access to the mass media; support for women's exchange networks; and the development of training materials to foster a clearer gender perspective in human settlements and enable women's active involvement.

Three workshops were held on gender-aware approaches to human settlements development (United Republic of Tanzania and Bolivia, February, and Colombia, March), and two workshops addressed issues related to women and sustainable development in Latin America (Bolivia, February; Colombia, March). A gender-specific component was incorporated into a workshop on training local government elected officials (Kampala, Uganda, October/November), and a workshop on gender-aware approaches to human settlements development was held (Dar-es-Salaam, United Republic of Tanzania, February). In addition, the Centre held an ad hoc expert group meeting on the Global Strategy for Shelter to the Year 2000 in Action: Enhancing the Role of Women in Community Development (Nairobi, 7-9 December).

Financing

During 1992, the Centre's work programme was financed from the United Nations regular budget and from extrabudgetary resources. Programme support income from projects financed by UNDP and trust funds amounted to $3.6 million, while income for the United Nations Habitat and Human Settlements Foundation was $11.3 million.

UNCHS project delivery amounted to $41.2 million, including projects financed by UNDP ($31.8 million), the Foundation ($4.8 million) and other sources ($4.6 million). In 1992, the Foundation received contributions totalling $8 million from 40 countries.

UN Habitat and Human Settlements Foundation

Income for the Foundation for the biennium ended 31 December 1991[11] amounted to $15,889,460, while expenditures totalled $17,187,260, resulting in a deficit of $1,297,800. The Board of Auditors noted overspending of allotments issued for contractual services, the untimely review of unliquidated obligations, restrictive procurement practices in the award of publications contracts to local printers, lack of prompt updating of project records, delays in the closing of operationally completed projects, the lack of a centralized roster of consultants, the lack

of effective procedures for recording and monitoring non-expendable property, and long delays in the liquidation of travel advances. The Board recommended that: expenditures on contractual services should be kept within appropriations through effective monitoring; stringent procedures should be introduced to ensure adequate control of non-expendable property; competition for publications contracts should be encouraged among the identified local printers; the systematic use of a centralized roster of consultants by all units should be enforced; project implementation should be further improved through adequate record-keeping and the timely closure of completed projects; and regular reviews of unliquidated obligations should be conducted.

In an October report,[12] ACABQ considered the Board of Auditors' report and reviewed the Administration's responses to its recommendations.

REFERENCES

[1]YUN 1991, p. 521, GA res. 46/164, 19 Dec. 1991. [2]A/47/360. [3]YUN 1976, p. 441. [4]*Report of the United Nations Conference on Environment and Development, Rio de Janeiro, 3-14 June 1992*, vol. I, Sales No. E.93.I.8. [5]HS/C/14/2. [6]GA res. 43/181, 20 Dec. 1988. [7]HS/C/14/12. [8]HS/C/14/13. [9]HS/C/14/INF.4. [10]HS/C/14/2/Add.3. [11]A/47/5/Add.8 & Corr.1. [12]A/47/500.

Chapter X

Human rights

In 1992, the United Nations continued its efforts to promote and protect universally recognized human rights and fundamental freedoms.

The General Assembly, in December, proclaimed the Declaration on the Protection of All Persons from Enforced Disappearance as a set of principles for all States (resolution 47/133) and adopted the Declaration on the Rights of Persons Belonging to National or Ethnic, Religious and Linguistic Minorities (47/135).

On 10 December 1992 (Human Rights Day), the International Year of the World's Indigenous People (1993) was launched under the theme "Indigenous people—a new partnership". The Working Group on Indigenous Populations continued work on the draft declaration on the rights of indigenous peoples. Elaboration of the declaration on the right and responsibility of individuals, groups and organs of society to promote and protect universally recognized human rights and fundamental freedoms moved forward. In March, the Commission on Human Rights established a working group to elaborate a draft optional protocol to the Convention against Torture and Other Cruel, Inhuman or Degrading Treatment or Punishment, which would establish a system of visits to places of detention.

Alleged violations of human rights on a large scale in several countries were again examined. During 1992, the Commission held two special sessions (13 and 14 August 1992, 30 November and 1 December) to consider the situation of human rights in the former Yugoslavia, as well as its forty-eighth session (27 January–6 March). Its Subcommission on Prevention of Discrimination and Protection of Minorities held its forty-fourth session (3-28 August).

Discrimination

Racial discrimination

Second Decade to Combat Racism and Racial Discrimination (1983-1993)

Implementation of the Programme for the Decade

In 1992, United Nations efforts to implement the Programme of Action for the Second Decade to Combat Racism and Racial Discrimination continued to be carried out in accordance with the plan of activities for 1985-1989 put forward in 1984[1] and the plan approved by the General Assembly in 1987,[2] covering the remainder of the Decade, 1990-1993.

Reports of the Secretary-General. In response to a 1991 request of the Commission on Human Rights,[3] the Secretary-General, in January 1992,[4] reported on progress made in carrying out the plan of activities. He described action taken by United Nations bodies, coordination of United Nations activities under the Decade, seminars, training courses and workshops, the status of the Trust Fund for the Programme for the Decade and the implementation of activities for the Decade, including seminars, publications, studies and future activities.

In accordance with Economic and Social Council requests of 1985[5] and 1991,[6] the Secretary-General submitted in June 1992,[7] his annual report summarizing activities carried out or planned by Governments, United Nations bodies, specialized agencies, and regional, intergovernmental and non-governmental organizations (NGOs) to achieve the Decade's objectives.

As requested by the Council in **resolution 1992/13** of 20 July (see below), the Secretary-General submitted to the General Assembly in September a report on the implementation of the Programme of Action for the Second Decade and a draft programme of action for a third decade (1993-2003).[8] He stated that the activities that were not completed for the second half of the Second Decade owing to a lack of resources could be integrated into the proposed programme for a third decade. It was suggested that the goals and objectives of the third decade be those adopted by the Assembly in 1973 for the first Decade.[9] The elements for the programme of action for the third decade were: action to combat apartheid; action to combat racism and racial discrimination at the international, national and regional levels; basic research and studies on racism and racial discrimination; coordination of and reporting on the implementation of the programme and evaluation of its activities; and annual consultations between the United Nations, specialized agencies and NGOs to review and plan decade-related activities. Annexed to the Secretary-General's report was a table showing the status of government contributions to the Trust Fund for the Programme for the Second Decade as at 7 August 1991.

Human Rights Commission action. On 21 February 1992,[10] the Commission commended all States that had ratified or acceded to the international instruments relevant to the Decade and appealed to others to do the same. It asked Governments, international organizations and NGOs to increase and intensify their activities to combat racism, racial discrimination and apartheid and appealed for generous contributions to the Trust Fund. Within the 1990-1993 plan of activities, the Commission recalled having selected as its topic for 1992 the treatment of political prisoners and detainees in South Africa, particularly women and children; it decided that a global study on the extent of dissemination of the 1965 International Convention on the Elimination of All Forms of Racial Discrimination[11] would be its topic for 1993.

The Commission recommended that the General Assembly take steps to launch a third decade, to begin in 1993, and asked the Secretary-General to finalize the text of the model legislation to guide Governments in enacting further legislation against racial discrimination and the handbook of recourse procedures for victims of racial discrimination and to publish and distribute those texts. It welcomed the publication of the global compilation of national legislation against racism and racial discrimination[12] and asked the Secretary-General to transmit it to Governments as soon as possible. The Commission also asked him to continue to keep it informed of measures taken to ensure that resources for implementing the Second Decade's activities were included in the proposed 1992-1993 budget and to inform it in 1993 of progress made in carrying out the 1992-1993 plan of activities. It took note of the report of a 1991 meeting of experts to review the experience of countries in the operation of schemes of internal self-government for indigenous peoples,[13] and asked the Secretary-General to continue to study the effects of racial discrimination on children of minorities, particularly migrant workers, in the areas of education, training and employment, and to submit recommendations on measures to combat those effects.

Subcommission action. On 21 August 1992,[14] the Subcommission on Prevention of Discrimination and Protection of Minorities took note of a July report by the Secretary-General[15] describing current trends in racism, racial discrimination, intolerance and xenophobia and decided to submit it to the Commission in 1993. It recommended that the General Assembly take steps to launch a third decade to combat racism and racial discrimination, beginning in 1993, and that the Commission appoint a special rapporteur to address contemporary forms of racism, racial discrimination and xenophobia.

Other action. In August,[16] the Committee on the Elimination of Racial Discrimination requested the Centre for Human Rights to revise the 1991 draft model legislation to guide Governments in enacting legislation against racial discrimination in view of comments made by its members, and to present the revised draft in 1993. The Committee appointed a working group to consider measures to ensure that legal remedies were effective in reducing discrimination and exchanged views on a possible third decade to combat racism and racial discrimination.

ECONOMIC AND SOCIAL COUNCIL ACTION

On 30 July 1992, the Economic and Social Council, on the recommendation of its Social Committee, adopted **resolution 1992/13** without vote.

Implementation of the Programme of Action for the Second Decade to Combat Racism and Racial Discrimination

The Economic and Social Council,

Recalling its resolution 1991/2 of 29 May 1991,

Reaffirming the purpose set forth in the Charter of the United Nations of achieving international cooperation in solving international problems of an economic, social, cultural or humanitarian character and in promoting and encouraging respect for human rights and fundamental freedoms for all, without distinction as to race, sex, language or religion,

Recalling the proclamation by the General Assembly, in its resolution 38/14 of 22 November 1983, of the Second Decade to Combat Racism and Racial Discrimination,

Recalling also the Programme of Action for the Second Decade to Combat Racism and Racial Discrimination, approved by the General Assembly in its resolution 38/14 and contained in the annex thereto, to achieve the objectives of the Second Decade,

Reaffirming the plan of activities for the period 1990-1993, to be implemented by the Secretary-General in accordance with General Assembly resolution 42/47 of 30 November 1987, to which it is annexed, and recalling the activities that were proposed for the period 1985-1989,

Conscious of the responsibility conferred upon it by the General Assembly for coordinating and, in particular, evaluating the activities undertaken in the implementation of the Programme of Action for the Second Decade,

Bearing in mind, in particular, its mandate under General Assembly resolution 41/94 of 4 December 1986 to submit to the Assembly, during the period of the Second Decade, annual reports on the activities undertaken or contemplated to achieve the objectives of the Second Decade,

Having examined the report of the Secretary-General,

Noting that despite the efforts of the international community, the principal objectives of the first Decade for Action to Combat Racism and Racial Discrimination and the first years of the Second Decade have not been attained, and that millions of human beings continue to be victims of varied forms of racism, racial discrimination and apartheid,

Emphasizing that it continues to be the responsibility of the Government of South Africa to take all necessary measures to stop immediately the violence in that country and protect the life and property of all South Africans,

Emphasizing also the need for all parties to cooperate in combating violence and to exercise restraint,

Bearing in mind the Declaration on Apartheid and its Destructive Consequences in Southern Africa, adopted by the General Assembly in its resolution S-16/1 of 14 December 1989 and contained in the annex thereto,

Convinced that international pressure exerted by the United Nations, Governments, individual citizens and organizations has had and continues to have a significant impact on developments in South Africa,

Deeply concerned about the prevalence of racism and racial tensions as well as the rising tide of xenophobia,

Stressing the need to continue the coordination of activities undertaken by various United Nations bodies and specialized agencies for the purpose of implementing the Programme of Action for the Second Decade,

1. *Reaffirms* the importance of achieving the objectives of the Second Decade to Combat Racism and Racial Discrimination;

2. *Takes note with appreciation* of the report of the Secretary-General, in particular the recommendations contained therein;

3. *Urges* the Government of South Africa to exercise its responsibility to end the violence in that country and thus sustain the emerging political climate, which is conducive to the abolition of the system of apartheid;

4. *Calls upon* all the parties in South Africa to cooperate to ensure the effective implementation of the National Peace Accord in order to end the violence in that country;

5. *Appeals* to the international community to give its full and concerted support to the vulnerable and critical process now under way in South Africa through a phased application of appropriate pressure on the South African authorities, as warranted by developments;

6. *Requests* the Secretary-General to continue with the implementation of the activities for the period 1990-1993, and further requests him to continue to accord the highest priority to measures to combat apartheid;

7. *Invites* all Governments to take or continue to take all necessary measures to combat all forms of racism and racial discrimination and to support the work of the Second Decade by making contributions to the Trust Fund for the Programme for the Decade for Action to Combat Racism and Racial Discrimination, in order to ensure further implementation of the activities for the Second Decade;

8. *Calls upon* all Member States to consider signing and ratifying or acceding to the International Convention on the Protection of the Rights of All Migrant Workers and Members of Their Families[a] as a matter of priority, and expresses the hope that it will enter into force at an early date;

9. *Welcomes once again* the proclamation of the International Year for the World's Indigenous People by the General Assembly in its resolution 45/164 of 18 December 1990;

10. *Reaffirms* the need to continue giving particular attention to the specific activities of the Programme of Action for the Second Decade that are directed towards the elimination of apartheid, which is the most destructive and vicious form of institutionalized racism;

11. *Also reaffirms* the importance of public information activities in combating racism and racial discrimination and in mobilizing public support for the objectives of the Second Decade, and commends the efforts of the Coordinator for the Second Decade to Combat Racism and Racial Discrimination;

12. *Requests* the Secretary-General to ensure the effective and immediate implementation of the activities proposed for the first half of the Second Decade that have not yet been undertaken;

13. *Also requests* the Secretary-General, in his reports, to continue to pay special attention to the situation of migrant workers and members of their families;

14. *Reaffirms* the need for continued coordination of the full range of programmes being implemented by the United Nations system as they relate to the objectives of the Second Decade;

15. *Recommends* that, in 1993, the General Assembly proclaim a third decade to combat racism and racial discrimination;

16. *Requests* the Secretary-General to prepare a draft programme of action for the third decade and to submit it to the General Assembly at its forty-seventh session, taking into account, *inter alia*, the elements of the Programme of Action for the Second Decade that have not yet been completed;

17. *Decides* to continue to accord the highest priority to the item entitled "Implementation of the Programme of Action for the Second Decade to Combat Racism and Racial Discrimination".

---

[a]GA res. 45/158, annex, 18 Dec. 1990.

Economic and Social Council resolution 1992/13

30 July 1992   Meeting 40   Adopted without vote

Approved by Social Committee (E/1992/104) without vote, 22 July (meeting 16); draft by Madagascar for African States (E/1992/C.2/L.5/Rev.1); agenda item 16.

GENERAL ASSEMBLY ACTION

On 16 December, the General Assembly, on the recommendation of the Third (Social, Humanitarian and Cultural) Committee, adopted **resolution 47/77** without vote.

Second Decade to Combat Racism and Racial Discrimination

The General Assembly,

Reaffirming its objective set forth in the Charter of the United Nations to achieve international cooperation in solving international problems of an economic, social, cultural or humanitarian character and in promoting and encouraging respect for human rights and fundamental freedoms for all without distinction as to race, sex, language or religion,

Reaffirming also its firm determination and its commitment to eradicate totally and unconditionally racism in all its forms, racial discrimination and apartheid,

Recalling the Universal Declaration of Human Rights, the International Convention on the Elimination of All Forms of Racial Discrimination, the International Convention on the Suppression and Punishment of the Crime of Apartheid, and the Convention against Discrimination in Education adopted by the United Nations Educational, Scientific and Cultural Organization on 14 December 1960,

Recalling also its resolution 3057(XXVIII) of 2 November 1973, on the first Decade for Action to Combat Racism and Racial Discrimination, and its resolution 38/14 of 22 November 1983, on the Second Decade to Combat Racism and Racial Discrimination,

Recalling further the two World Conferences to Combat Racism and Racial Discrimination, held at Geneva in 1978 and 1983,

Bearing in mind the *Report of the Second World Conference to Combat Racism and Racial Discrimination,*

Convinced that the Second World Conference represented a positive contribution by the international community towards attaining the objectives of the Decade, through its adoption of a Declaration and an operational Programme of Action for the Second Decade to Combat Racism and Racial Discrimination,

Noting with grave concern that despite the efforts of the international community, the principal objectives of the two Decades for Action to Combat Racism and Racial Discrimination have not been attained and that millions of human beings continue to this day to be the victims of varied forms of racism, racial discrimination and apartheid,

Deeply concerned about the current trend of the evolution of racism into discriminatory practices based on culture, nationality, religion or language,

Recalling, in particular, its resolution 46/85 of 16 December 1991,

Emphasizing once again the necessity of attaining all the objectives of the Second Decade,

Having considered the report submitted by the Secretary-General within the framework of the implementation of the Programme of Action for the Second Decade,

Firmly convinced of the need to take more effective and sustained international measures for the elimination of all forms of racism and racial discrimination and the total eradication of apartheid in South Africa,

Recognizing the importance of strengthening, where necessary, national legislation and institutions for the promotion of racial harmony,

Aware of the importance and the magnitude of the phenomenon of migrant workers, as well as the efforts undertaken by the international community to improve the protection of the human rights of migrant workers and members of their families,

Recalling the adoption at its forty-fifth session of the International Convention on the Protection of the Rights of All Migrant Workers and Members of Their Families,

Reaffirming the Declaration on Apartheid and its Destructive Consequences in Southern Africa, unanimously adopted by the General Assembly at its sixteenth special session, on 14 December 1989, which offers guidelines on how to end apartheid,

1. *Declares once again* that all forms of racism and racial discrimination, particularly in their institutionalized form, such as apartheid, or resulting from official doctrines of racial superiority or exclusivity, are among the most serious violations of human rights in the contemporary world and must be combated by all available means;

2. *Urges* all Governments to take all necessary measures to combat new forms of racism, in particular by ongoing adjustment of the methods used to combat them;

3. *Decides* that the international community, in general, and the United Nations, in particular, should continue to give the highest priority to programmes for combat-

ing racism, racial discrimination and apartheid and intensify their efforts, during the latter part of the Second Decade to Combat Racism and Racial Discrimination, to provide assistance and relief to the victims of racism and all forms of racial discrimination and apartheid;

4. *Appeals* to all Governments and to international and non-governmental organizations to increase and intensify their activities to combat racism, racial discrimination and apartheid and to provide relief and assistance to the victims of these evils;

5. *Notes and commends* the efforts made to coordinate all the programmes currently under implementation by the United Nations system that relate to the objectives of the Second Decade, and encourages the Coordinator for the Second Decade to Combat Racism and Racial Discrimination to continue his efforts;

6. *Requests* the Secretary-General to continue to accord special attention to the situation of migrant workers and members of their families and to include regularly in his reports all information on such workers;

7. *Calls upon* all Member States to consider signing and ratifying or acceding to the International Convention on the Protection of the Rights of All Migrant Workers and Members of Their Families as a matter of priority, to enable its early entry into force;

8. *Requests* the Secretary-General to continue the study on the effects of racial discrimination on the children of minorities, in particular those of migrant workers, in the field of education, training and employment, and to submit, *inter alia,* specific recommendations for the implementation of measures to combat the effects of that discrimination;

9. *Also requests* the Secretary-General to revise and finalize the draft model legislation for the guidance of Governments in the enactment of further legislation against racial discrimination, in the light of comments made by members of the Committee on the Elimination of Racial Discrimination at its fortieth and forty-first sessions and to publish and distribute the text as soon as possible;

10. *Renews its invitation* to the United Nations Educational, Scientific and Cultural Organization to expedite the preparation of teaching materials and teaching aids to promote teaching, training and education activities on human rights and against racism and racial discrimination, with particular emphasis on activities at the primary and secondary levels of education;

11. *Considers once again* that all the parts of the Programme of Action for the Second Decade to Combat Racism and Racial Discrimination should be given equal attention in order to attain the objectives of the Second Decade;

12. *Regrets* that most of the activities scheduled for the period 1992-1993 have not been implemented because of lack of adequate resources;

13. *Calls upon* the international community to provide the Secretary-General with appropriate financial resources for efficient action against racism and racial discrimination;

14. *Requests* the Secretary-General to accord the highest priority to activities of a programme of action for a third decade to combat racism and racial discrimination, aiming at monitoring the transition from apartheid to a non-racist society in South Africa;

15. *Also requests* the Secretary-General, pursuant to General Assembly resolutions 42/47 of 30 November

1987, 44/52 of 8 December 1989 and 45/105 of 14 December 1990, to ensure that the necessary and additional resources are included in the programme budget for the biennium 1992-1993 to provide for the implementation of the activities of the Second Decade;

16. *Further requests* the Secretary-General to continue to accord the highest priority, in executing the plan of activities, to measures for combating apartheid;

17. *Calls upon* Governments to encourage further positive change in South Africa based on the guidelines set out in the Declaration on Apartheid and its Destructive Consequences in Southern Africa, in particular by maintaining effective and sustained international pressure against South Africa;

18. *Invites* all Governments, United Nations bodies, the specialized agencies and other intergovernmental organizations, as well as interested non-governmental organizations in consultative status with the Economic and Social Council, to participate fully in the activities scheduled for the period 1990-1993 which have not yet been carried out;

19. *Considers* that voluntary contributions to the Trust Fund for the Programme for the Decade for Action to Combat Racism and Racial Discrimination are indispensable for the implementation of the above-mentioned programmes;

20. *Notes with regret* that, since its establishment, contributions to the Fund have been scarce despite repeated appeals by the Secretary-General;

21. *Strongly appeals*, therefore, to all Governments, organizations and individuals in a position to do so to contribute generously to the Fund, and to this end requests the Secretary-General to continue to undertake appropriate contacts and initiatives to encourage contributions;

22. *Takes note* of the report of the Secretary-General on the implementation of the Programme of Action for the Second Decade and the launching of a third decade to combat racism and racial discrimination, and requests him to prepare a draft programme of action for the third decade and to submit it to the General Assembly at its forty-eighth session, taking into account, *inter alia*, the elements of the Programme of Action for the Second Decade that have not yet been implemented;

23. *Invites* the Commission on Human Rights at its forty-ninth session to recommend activities to be undertaken during the third decade to combat racism and racial discrimination;

24. *Decides* to keep the item entitled "Elimination of racism and racial discrimination" on its agenda and to consider it as a matter of highest priority at its forty-eighth session.

General Assembly resolution 47/77

16 December 1992   Meeting 89   Adopted without vote

Approved by Third Committee (A/47/658) without vote, 5 November (meeting 30); draft by Mauritius for African Group (A/C.3/47/L.3/Rev.1), orally revised; agenda item 91.
Meeting numbers. GA 47th session: 3rd Committee 3-10, 13, 16, 20, 25, 30; plenary 89.

Convention on the Elimination of All Forms of Racial Discrimination

Accessions and ratifications

As at 31 December 1992,[17] there were 133 parties to the International Convention on the Elimination of All Forms of Racial Discrimination, adopted by the General Assembly in 1965[11] and in force since 1969.[18] Croatia, Latvia and Slovenia became parties during 1992.

The Commission on Human Rights, in February,[10] appealed to those States that had not done so to ratify, accede to and implement the Convention, among other international instruments to combat racism.

In September,[19] the Secretary-General reported to the Assembly on the status of the Convention as at 14 August 1992.

GENERAL ASSEMBLY ACTION

On 16 December, the General Assembly, on the recommendation of the Third Committee, adopted **resolution 47/78** without vote.

Status of the International Convention on the Elimination of All Forms of Racial Discrimination
The General Assembly,

Recalling its relevant resolutions adopted since 1973, the most recent of which is resolution 45/89 of 14 December 1990,

Expressing its satisfaction once again at the entry into force, on 3 December 1982, of the competence of the Committee on the Elimination of Racial Discrimination to receive and consider communications from individuals or groups of individuals under article 14 of the International Convention on the Elimination of All Forms of Racial Discrimination,

Bearing in mind the decision taken at the Fourteenth Meeting of States Parties to the Convention on 15 January 1992 to amend paragraph 6 of article 8 of the Convention and to add a new paragraph as paragraph 7 of article 8, by which the members of the Committee established under the Convention would henceforth receive emoluments from United Nations resources on such terms and conditions as may be decided by the General Assembly,

1. *Takes note* of the report of the Secretary-General on the status of the International Convention on the Elimination of All Forms of Racial Discrimination;

2. *Expresses its satisfaction* at the number of States that have ratified the Convention or acceded thereto;

3. *Reaffirms once again its conviction* that ratification of or accession to the Convention on a universal basis and implementation of its provisions are necessary for the realization of the objectives of the Second Decade to Combat Racism and Racial Discrimination and for action beyond the Decade;

4. *Requests* those States which have not yet become parties to the Convention to ratify it or accede thereto;

5. *Requests* the States parties to the Convention to consider the possibility of making the declaration provided for in article 14 of the Convention;

6. *Requests* the Secretary-General to submit to the General Assembly at its forty-ninth session a report concerning the status of the Convention, in accordance with Assembly resolution 2106 A (XX) of 21 December 1965.

General Assembly resolution 47/78

16 December 1992   Meeting 89   Adopted without vote

Approved by Third Committee (A/47/658) without vote, 28 October (meeting 20); 38-nation draft (A/C.3/47/L.6); agenda item 91.

Sponsors: Algeria, Argentina, Australia, Bahamas, Belgium, Botswana, Brazil, Bulgaria, Canada, Cuba, Cyprus, Czechoslovakia, Denmark, Ecuador, Egypt, Ethiopia, France, Germany, Greece, Hungary, India, Italy, Luxembourg, Morocco, Netherlands, New Zealand, Norway, Poland, Portugal, Romania, Russian Federation, Rwanda, Senegal, Spain, Sweden, Togo, United Kingdom, Uruguay.
Meeting numbers. GA 47th session: 3rd Committee 3-10, 13, 16, 20; plenary 89.

Implementation of the Convention

The Committee on the Elimination of Racial Discrimination (CERD), set up under article 8 of the Convention, held its forty-first session at Geneva from 3 to 14 August 1992.[16] The Committee, which normally held two three-week sessions annually, cancelled its session scheduled for March 1992 and curtailed its August session to two weeks owing to the critical financial situation arising from the non-payment of assessed contributions by a number of States parties.

Most of CERD's work was devoted to examining reports submitted by States parties on measures taken to implement the Convention's provisions. Under article 9 of the Convention, it considered the updated reports of Austria, Bangladesh, Belgium, Chile, Colombia, Costa Rica, Ghana, Greece, Maldives and Yemen. The review of the implementation of the Convention by Botswana, Cape Verde, Lesotho, Papua New Guinea, Saint Vincent and the Grenadines, Solomon Islands and Viet Nam, whose last reports had been submitted in 1983, was based on their previous reports. The same applied to Burkina Faso and the Lao People's Democratic Republic, from which no reports had been received since 1984. At the request of Somalia, the Committee decided to defer consideration of the Convention's implementation there for one year. Consideration of the eleventh and twelfth periodic reports of Ecuador and the seventh periodic report of the Republic of Korea was postponed until 1993 at their request. States parties were urged to fulfil their reporting obligations as soon as possible and reminded that they could request technical assistance from the United Nations Centre for Human Rights in preparing their reports.

In its report,[16] CERD provided a summary of its members' views on each country report and of statements made by the States parties concerned. Regarding reporting obligations under article 9, the Committee requested the Secretary-General to continue sending reminders to States parties from which two or more reports were due but had not been received before 14 August—the closing date of its session—asking them to submit their reports by 31 December 1992. Also in accordance with article 9, the Committee, on 12 August, requested further information by 1 March 1993 from Burundi[20] and Rwanda,[21] where continuing ethnic conflict was cause for concern. It also requested further information from Papua New Guinea on the situation in Bougainville (for de-

tails on the situation in Bougainville, see below, under "Human rights violations").

The Committee also considered, in conformity with article 14, communications from individuals or groups of individuals claiming violation of their rights under the Convention by a State party recognizing CERD competence to receive and consider such communications. Sixteen States parties—Algeria, Costa Rica, Denmark, Ecuador, France, Hungary, Iceland, Italy, the Netherlands, Norway, Peru, the Russian Federation, Senegal, Sweden, Ukraine and Uruguay—had declared such recognition. In 1992, the Committee decided to send two communications before it to the States parties concerned for information and observations.

CERD also considered activities to implement the Programme of Action for the Second Decade to Combat Racism and Racial Discrimination (see above).

Owing to a lack of time, the Committee did not consider petitions and other information relating to Trust and Non-Self-Governing Territories (see PART FOUR, Chapter I) in accordance with article 15 of the Convention.

Concerning a special session of the Commission on Human Rights, being convened to consider developments in the former Yugoslavia (see below, under "Human rights violations"), the Committee approved a letter to the Commission's Chairman, stating its readiness to cooperate in ending human rights violations and human suffering and providing protection for civilians within the mandate entrusted to it by the Convention.

The fourteenth meeting of the States parties was held on 15 January 1992 in New York and, as requested by the General Assembly in 1991,[22] considered an amendment proposed by Australia in respect of article 8, paragraph 6, of the Convention, by which States parties were responsible for the expenses of CERD members while they were performing CERD duties. The States parties adopted the proposed amendment,[23] replacing paragraph 6 with a paragraph stating that the Secretary-General would provide the necessary staff and facilities for the effective performance of the functions of the Committee under the Convention, and adding a new paragraph, stating that CERD members would, with the approval of the General Assembly, receive emoluments from United Nations resources on the terms and conditions decided by the Assembly. In addition, the States parties recommended that the Assembly approve the amendment in 1992 and decided that it would enter into force when approved by the Assembly and accepted by a two-thirds majority of States parties.

In a January note to the meeting of the States parties,[24] the Secretary-General stated that the delayed payment or non-payment of financial assessments by a significant number of States parties had seriously impeded the functioning of CERD for several years and had given rise to concern about the Committee's ability to carry out its responsibilities efficiently. In October,[25] he informed the Assembly that, as at 31 August 1992, outstanding assessments and arrears totalled $195,288 from 76 States. Annexed to the report was a list of States parties and assessments outstanding as at 31 August and the text of the decision adopted by the States parties on amending article 8.

On 21 February,[26] the Commission on Human Rights asked meetings of States parties to consider ways to strengthen the collection of contributions and to make procedures more effective, and, if necessary, to reconsider the position of States parties that were substantially in default on their assessed contributions.

GENERAL ASSEMBLY ACTION

On 16 December 1992, the General Assembly, on the recommendation of the Third Committee, adopted **resolution 47/79** without vote.

Report of the Committee on the Elimination of Racial Discrimination

The General Assembly,

Recalling its previous resolutions concerning the reports of the Committee on the Elimination of Racial Discrimination and its resolutions on the status of the International Convention on the Elimination of All Forms of Racial Discrimination,

Reiterating the importance of the International Convention on the Elimination of All Forms of Racial Discrimination, which is one of the most widely accepted human rights instruments adopted under the auspices of the United Nations,

Aware of the importance of the contributions of the Committee to the efforts of the United Nations to combat racism and all other forms of discrimination based on race, colour, descent or national or ethnic origin,

Reiterating once again the need to intensify the struggle for the elimination of racism and racial discrimination throughout the world, especially its most brutal forms, such as apartheid,

Emphasizing the obligation of all States parties to the Convention to take legislative, judicial and other measures in order to secure full implementation of the provisions of the Convention,

Recalling the urgent appeals made to the States parties by the Secretary-General, the General Assembly, the meetings of States parties to the Convention and the Committee itself to honour their financial obligations under the Convention,

Expressing its appreciation for the efforts of the members of the Committee to explore ways and means to overcome the current financial crisis of the Committee,

Welcoming the decision taken at the Fourteenth Meeting of States Parties to the Convention on 15 January 1992 to amend paragraph 6 of article 8 of the Convention and to add a new paragraph as paragraph 7 of article 8, by which the members of the Committee established under the Convention would henceforth receive emoluments from United Nations resources on such terms and conditions as may be decided by the General Assembly, and aware of the need to consider that decision during its forty-seventh session,

Having considered the report of the Secretary-General on the financial situation of the Committee,

1. *Commends* the Committee on the Elimination of Racial Discrimination for its work with regard to the implementation of the International Convention on the Elimination of All Forms of Racial Discrimination and the Programme of Action for the Second Decade to Combat Racism and Racial Discrimination;

2. *Welcomes* the innovatory procedures adopted by the Committee for reviewing the implementation of the Convention in States whose reports are overdue and for formulating concluding observations on State party reports;

3. *Expresses its profound concern* at the fact that a number of States parties to the Convention still have not fulfilled their financial obligations;

4. *Expresses once again its concern* that such a situation may lead to a further delay in the discharge of the substantive obligations of the Committee under the Convention;

5. *Takes note with appreciation* of the report of the Committee on the work of its forty-first session;

6. *Calls upon* States parties to fulfil their obligations under article 9, paragraph 1, of the Convention, to submit in due time their periodic reports on measures taken to implement the Convention and to pay their outstanding contributions and, if possible, their contributions for 1993 before 1 February 1993, so as to enable the Committee to meet regularly;

7. *Strongly appeals* to all States parties, especially those in arrears, to fulfil their financial obligations under article 8, paragraph 6, of the Convention;

8. *Requests* the Secretary-General to invite those States parties which are in arrears to pay the amounts in arrears, and to report thereon to the General Assembly at its forty-eighth session;

9. *Decides* to consider at its forty-eighth session, under the item entitled "Elimination of racism and racial discrimination", the report of the Secretary-General on the financial situation of the Committee and the report of the Committee.

General Assembly resolution 47/79

16 December 1992   Meeting 89   Adopted without vote

Approved by Third Committee (A/47/658) without vote, 28 October (meeting 20); 32-nation draft (A/C.3/47/L.8); agenda item 91.

Sponsors: Algeria, Australia, Bangladesh, Bosnia and Herzegovina, Bulgaria, Canada, Colombia, Croatia, Cuba, Cyprus, Czechoslovakia, Denmark, Ecuador, Egypt, Finland, Germany, Hungary, Iceland, Mexico, Morocco, New Zealand, Nicaragua, Nigeria, Norway, Pakistan, Poland, Romania, Russian Federation, Slovenia, Sweden, Vanuatu, Venezuela.

Meeting numbers. GA 47th session: 3rd Committee 3-10, 13, 16, 20; plenary 89.

Other aspects of discrimination

Religious freedom

Report of the Special Rapporteur. The Commission on Human Rights had before it a report[27] by Special Rapporteur Angelo Vidal d'Almeida Ribeiro (Portugal) containing information from 25 Governments on their legislative provisions and measures to restrict religious intolerance and discrimination. He discussed allegations of infringements of the rights and freedoms set out in the 1981 Declaration on the Elimination of All Forms of Intolerance and of Discrimination Based on Religion or Belief.[28] He expressed concern at the persistence of the allegations, stating that they ranged from extra-judicial killings of clergy members to the prohibition of specific manifestations relating to a particular religion or belief. He noted, however, continued progress made in the area of religious freedom by countries in Eastern Europe.

The Special Rapporteur urged States that had not done so to ratify the relevant international human rights instruments and recommended that they continue to consider preparing a separate binding international instrument on the elimination of intolerance and discrimination based on religion or belief. He believed that States should adapt legislation to existing international standards, particularly the 1981 Declaration, and make available effective administrative and judicial remedies. He underlined the importance of promoting religious tolerance and understanding by introducing national and international human rights standards in school and university curricula and through the training of teaching staff. In that regard, he noted the important contribution that could be made by advisory services and technical assistance offered by the United Nations. The Special Rapporteur emphasized the significant role of media briefings and information seminars aimed at the broadest possible dissemination of principles set out in the 1981 Declaration.

Human Rights Commission action. As requested by the General Assembly in 1991,[29] the Commission on Human Rights continued in 1992 to consider measures to implement the 1981 Declaration. On 21 February,[30] it urged States to provide adequate constitutional and legal guarantees of freedom of thought, conscience, religion and belief and called on them to encourage understanding, tolerance and respect for freedom of religion or belief and to examine the supervision and training of members of law enforcement bodies, civil servants, educators and other public officials to ensure their respect for different religions and beliefs. It invited the United Nations University (UNU) and other academic and research institutions to undertake programmes and studies on encouraging understanding, tolerance and respect in matters relating to freedom of religion or belief. It considered it desirable to enhance United Nations promotional and public information activities relating to freedom of religion or belief and to ensure that measures were taken to that end in the World Public Information Campaign for Human Rights (see below, under "Advancement of human rights"). The Com-

mission asked the Secretary-General to accord high priority to disseminating the text of the Declaration in all United Nations official languages and in national languages and to make the text available for use by United Nations information centres (UNICs) and other interested bodies. The Commission extended the Special Rapporteur's mandate for three years and called on Governments to cooperate with him. It asked the Secretary-General to provide assistance to enable him to report to the Commission in 1993. The Secretary-General was also asked to report in 1993.

The Commission's decision to extend the mandate of the Special Rapporteur for three years and its request to the Secretary-General to provide all necessary assistance to him was approved by the Economic and Social Council by **decision 1992/226** of 20 July.

GENERAL ASSEMBLY ACTION

On 18 December 1992, the General Assembly, on the recommendation of the Third Committee, adopted **resolution 47/129** without vote.

Elimination of all forms of religious intolerance

The General Assembly,

Recalling that all States have pledged themselves to promote and encourage universal respect for and observance of human rights and fundamental freedoms for all without distinction as to race, sex, language or religion,

Recognizing that those rights derive from the inherent dignity of the human person,

Reaffirming that discrimination against human beings on the grounds of religion or belief constitutes an affront to human dignity and a disavowal of the principles of the Charter of the United Nations,

Reaffirming its resolution 36/55 of 25 November 1981, by which it proclaimed the Declaration on the Elimination of All Forms of Intolerance and of Discrimination Based on Religion or Belief,

Recalling its resolution 46/131 of 17 December 1991, in which it requested the Commission on Human Rights to continue its consideration of measures to implement the Declaration,

Taking note of Commission on Human Rights resolution 1992/17 of 21 February 1992, in which the mandate of the Special Rapporteur appointed to examine incidents and governmental actions in all parts of the world that are incompatible with the provisions of the Declaration and to recommend remedial measures, as appropriate, was extended for three years, and taking note also of Economic and Social Council decision 1992/226 of 20 July 1992,

Recognizing that it is desirable to enhance the promotional and public information activities of the United Nations in matters relating to freedom of religion or belief and that both Governments and non-governmental organizations have an important role to play in this domain,

Emphasizing that non-governmental organizations and religious bodies and groups at every level have an important role to play in the promotion of tolerance and the protection of freedom of religion or belief,

Conscious of the importance of education in ensuring tolerance of religion and belief,

Alarmed that serious instances, including acts of violence, of intolerance and discrimination on the grounds of religion or belief occur in many parts of the world, as evidenced in the report of the Special Rapporteur of the Commission on Human Rights, Mr. Angelo Vidal d'Almeida Ribeiro,

Believing that further efforts are therefore required to promote and protect the right to freedom of thought, conscience, religion and belief and to eliminate all forms of hatred, intolerance and discrimination based on religion or belief;

1. *Reaffirms* that freedom of thought, conscience, religion and belief is a human right derived from the inherent dignity of the human person and guaranteed to all without discrimination;

2. *Urges* States to ensure that their constitutional and legal systems provide adequate guarantees of freedom of thought, conscience, religion and belief, including the provision of effective remedies where there is intolerance or discrimination based on religion or belief;

3. *Recognizes* that legislation alone is not enough to prevent violations of human rights, including the right to freedom of religion or belief;

4. *Urges* all States therefore to take all appropriate measures to combat hatred, intolerance and acts of violence and to encourage understanding, tolerance and respect in matters relating to freedom of religion or belief;

5. *Urges* States to ensure that, in the course of their official duties, members of law enforcement bodies, civil servants, educators and other public officials respect different religions and beliefs and do not discriminate against persons professing other religions or beliefs;

6. *Calls upon* all States to recognize, as provided in the Declaration on the Elimination of All Forms of Intolerance and of Discrimination Based on Religion or Belief, the right of all persons to worship or assemble in connection with a religion or belief, and to establish and maintain places for these purposes;

7. *Also calls upon* all States in accordance with their national legislation to exert utmost efforts to ensure that religious places and shrines are fully respected and protected;

8. *Considers it desirable* to enhance the promotional and public information activities of the United Nations in matters relating to freedom of religion or belief and to ensure that appropriate measures are taken to this end in the World Public Information Campaign for Human Rights;

9. *Invites* the Secretary-General to continue to give high priority to the dissemination of the text of the Declaration, in all the official languages of the United Nations, and to take all appropriate measures to make the text available for use by United Nations information centres and by other interested bodies;

10. *Encourages* the continued efforts on the part of the Special Rapporteur appointed to examine incidents and governmental actions in all parts of the world that are incompatible with the provisions of the Declaration and to recommend remedial measures as appropriate;

11. *Encourages* Governments to give serious consideration to inviting the Special Rapporteur to visit their countries so as to enable him to fulfil his mandate even more effectively;

12. *Recommends* that the promotion and protection of the right to freedom of thought, conscience and religion be given appropriate priority in the work of the United Nations programme of advisory services in the field of human rights, with regard to, *inter alia*, the drafting of basic legal texts in conformity with international instruments on human rights and taking into account the provisions of the Declaration;

13. *Encourages* the Human Rights Committee to give priority to its announced intention to prepare a general comment on article 18 of the International Covenant on Civil and Political Rights, dealing with freedom of thought, conscience and religion;

14. *Welcomes* the efforts of non-governmental organizations to promote the implementation of the Declaration;

15. *Requests* the Secretary-General to invite interested non-governmental organizations to consider what further role they could envisage playing in the implementation of the Declaration and in the dissemination of its text in national and local languages;

16. *Urges* all States to consider disseminating the text of the Declaration in their respective national languages and to facilitate its dissemination in national and local languages;

17. *Requests* the Commission on Human Rights to continue its consideration of measures to implement the Declaration;

18. *Decides* to consider the question of the elimination of all forms of religious intolerance at its forty-eighth session under the item entitled ''Human rights questions''.

General Assembly resolution 47/129

18 December 1992   Meeting 92   Adopted without vote

Approved by Third Committee (A/47/678/Add.2) without vote, 3 December (meeting 56); 55-nation draft (A/C.3/47/L.60), orally revised; agenda item 97 (b).

Sponsors: Albania, Argentina, Australia, Austria, Azerbaijan, Bahamas, Belarus, Belgium, Bulgaria, Canada, Chile, Costa Rica, Côte d'Ivoire, Croatia, Cyprus, Czechoslovakia, Denmark, El Salvador, Fiji, Finland, France, Gambia, Germany, Greece, Guatemala, Hungary, Iceland, Ireland, Italy, Latvia, Liechtenstein, Lithuania, Luxembourg, Malta, Marshall Islands, Micronesia, Morocco, Netherlands, New Zealand, Norway, Peru, Poland, Portugal, Romania, Russian Federation, Samoa, Sierra Leone, Spain, Sweden, Ukraine, United Kingdom, United States, Uruguay, Venezuela, Zimbabwe.

Meeting numbers. GA 47th session: 3rd Committee 47-56; plenary 92.

Indigenous populations

Human Rights Commission action. On 3 March 1992,[31] the Commission recommended to the Economic and Social Council that the Working Group on Indigenous Populations (see below) be authorized to meet for 10 days prior to the 1992 session of the Subcommission on Prevention of Discrimination and Protection of Minorities to intensify efforts to complete a draft declaration on indigenous rights. It asked the Secretary-General to assist the Group and its Chairman-Rapporteur, to transmit the Group's 1991 report[13] to Governments, indigenous peoples' and intergovernmental organizations and NGOs for comments and suggestions, and to ensure that the Group's sessions were provided with interpretation and documentation in English and Spanish. The Commission appealed to Governments, organizations and individuals to consider favourably requests for contributions to the United Nations Voluntary Fund for Indigenous Populations, established by the General Assembly in 1985.[32]

On 20 July, the Economic and Social Council, by **decision 1992/231**, authorized the Group to meet for 10 working days prior to the Subcommission's 1992 session and approved the Commission's request to the Secretary-General to assist the Group.

Working Group activities. At its tenth session (Geneva, 20-31 July), the Working Group on Indigenous Populations[33] continued the first reading of the draft declaration on the rights of indigenous peoples,[34] provision by provision, and began the second reading of draft operative paragraphs 1 to 14. It recommended that the revised text be sent to Governments, intergovernmental and indigenous peoples' organizations and NGOs for their comments.

(For the Group's action on the International Year of the World's Indigenous People, see below.)

Subcommission action. On 27 August 1992, the Subcommission adopted a resolution on the draft declaration on indigenous peoples[35] and another on the relocation of Navajo and Hopi families.[36] It also had before it a report on transnational investments and operations on the lands of indigenous peoples,[37] prepared by the Transnational Corporations and Management Division of the United Nations Department of Economic and Social Development.

Other action. In accordance with a 1990 decision of the Economic and Social Council,[38] the United Nations Technical Conference on Practical Experience in the Realization of Sustainable and Environmentally Sound Self-Development of Indigenous Peoples was held at Santiago, Chile, from 18 to 22 May 1992.[39]

In accordance with a series of working principles that emerged from its discussions, which incorporated many of the concerns and practical experiences of indigenous peoples in achieving sustainable and environmentally sound self-development, the Conference proposed that: national development projects affecting indigenous peoples be preceded by studies of their socio-economic and environmental impact; the United Nations, with the consent of indigenous peoples, take measures to protect their property rights; meetings of United Nations agencies on indigenous peoples include indigenous representation, provide adequate notice and, when possible, be held on indigenous territories; environmentally sound management of resources and ecosystems of indigenous peoples be encouraged through the provision of funds; and mechanisms be developed to identify, prevent and provide sanctions against environmental degradation. It also recommended

that the United Nations consider holding further expert meetings on questions concerning indigenous peoples and the environment, land, resources and culture, and that the Secretary-General give the widest possible distribution to the Conference's report and recommendations.

The United Nations Conference on Environment and Development (UNCED) (see PART THREE, Chapter VIII) made a number of recommendations on recognizing and strengthening the role of indigenous people and their communities.[40]

Economic and social relations between indigenous peoples and States

Human Rights Commission action. On 3 March 1992,[41] the Commission recommended a draft decision on economic and social relations between indigenous peoples and States for adoption by the Economic and Social Council (see below).

ECONOMIC AND SOCIAL COUNCIL ACTION

On 20 July, the Council, by **decision 1992/255**, requested United Nations bodies and specialized agencies to ensure that all technical assistance financed or provided by them was compatible with international instruments and standards applicable to indigenous peoples. It encouraged efforts to promote coordination among United Nations organizations and greater participation of indigenous peoples in planning and implementing projects affecting them. It also encouraged the regional commissions to organize meetings with representative organizations of indigenous peoples in accordance with a 1990 General Assembly resolution.[42]

Protection of property rights

Cultural property

Human Rights Commission action. On 3 March,[43] the Commission recommended to the Economic and Social Council that it endorse the appointment of Erica-Irene A. Daes (Greece) as the Subcommission's Special Rapporteur to prepare and submit in 1993 a study of measures that should be taken by the international community to strengthen respect for the cultural property of indigenous peoples, and ask the Secretary-General to provide her with the assistance required to complete that task.

On 20 July, the Council, by **decision 1992/256**, endorsed the Special Rapporteur's appointment and the request that the Secretary-General provide her with assistance.

Subcommission action. On 27 August,[44] the Subcommission recommended that the Special Rapporteur consider the relationship between indigenous cultural and intellectual property in her study and include recommendations for further research and action on intellectual property.

Intellectual property

In July 1992,[45] the Secretary-General submitted a report to the Subcommission on the extent to which indigenous peoples could utilize existing international standards and mechanisms to protect their intellectual property, drawing attention to gaps or obstacles and to possible measures for addressing them. He stated that the intellectual property of indigenous peoples was divided into three categories (folklore and crafts, biodiversity, and indigenous knowledge) and described protection in force under existing arrangements for each category. He concluded that existing international agreements did not specifically address indigenous concerns and therefore might merit review and amendment.

Study on treaties, agreements and other constructive arrangements

Human Rights Commission action. On 28 February 1992,[46] the Commission endorsed the Subcommission's 1991 requests[13] to Special Rapporteur Miguel Alfonso Martínez (Cuba) to prepare a progress report on treaties, agreements and other constructive arrangements between States and indigenous populations for submission to the Working Group on Indigenous Populations and the Subcommission in 1992 and to the Secretary-General to assist him.

On 20 July, the Economic and Social Council, by **decision 1992/253**, approved the Commission's endorsement of the Subcommission's requests.

Subcommission action. On 27 August 1992,[47] the Subcommission, taking note of the Special Rapporteur's first progress report,[48] regretted that he could not submit it on time to the Working Group and requested him to submit a second progress report to the Group and the Subcommission in 1994.

UN Voluntary Fund for Indigenous Populations

In November 1992,[49] the Secretary-General submitted to the General Assembly a report on the status of the United Nations Voluntary Fund for Indigenous Populations. As at 30 September 1992, contributions totalling $358,704 had been received from 16 Governments. In addition, $18,760 was received from three NGOs. In April, the Board of Trustees of the Fund recommended the awarding of 41 travel and subsistence grants to beneficiaries from 19 countries. The Secretary-General endorsed the Board's recommendation.

On 18 December, the Assembly, by **decision 47/430**, called on Governments, NGOs and representatives of indigenous groups to consider

making contributions to the Fund and to disseminate information about its activities. It also requested the Secretary-General to report in 1994 on the Fund's status.

International Year of the World's Indigenous People (1993)

On 10 December 1992, the International Year of the World's Indigenous People (1993) was launched with the theme "Indigenous people—a new partnership". Preparations for the Year, which was proclaimed by the General Assembly in 1990,[50] were undertaken by the Commission on Human Rights, its Subcommission, the Working Group on Indigenous Populations, the United Nations Development Programme (UNDP), Governments and intergovernmental and indigenous peoples' organizations.

Human Rights Commission action. On 3 March 1992,[51] the Commission recommended that specialized agencies, regional commissions and other United Nations organizations, in considering their contributions to the success of the Year, be guided by how their operational activities could most effectively contribute to solving problems faced by indigenous people and how indigenous people could play an important role in planning, implementing and evaluating projects which might affect them. It asked Member States to inform the Secretary-General of their initiatives and encouraged them to consult indigenous peoples and NGOs working with them. The Commission accepted the task of promoting the programme of activities, annexed to a 1991 Assembly resolution,[52] as a guideline for the Year, and acknowledged the Assembly's request that it convene a meeting after the Year to assess what conclusions could be drawn from the activities.

The Commission acknowledged the appointment of the Under-Secretary-General for Human Rights as the Coordinator of the Year and urged him to solicit the cooperation of other elements of the United Nations, including financial and development institutions. It welcomed his convening of a technical meeting of specialized agencies, regional commissions and other United Nations organizations with representatives of States, organizations of indigenous people and other NGOs (Geneva, 9-11 March 1992)[53] to identify programmes areas; agree on objectives for special projects to be implemented in 1993; consider existing project guidelines and recommend means to include indigenous people in initiating, designing and implementing special projects in 1993; suggest measures to evaluate projects involving indigenous people in 1993 and thereafter; and consider financial provisions needed to implement projects. The Secretary-General was asked to give all necessary assistance to the Coordinator to allow him to carry out his tasks.

The Commission asked the Preparatory Committee for the World Conference on Human Rights (1993) to take into account that the Conference would take place during the Year. It encouraged States in a position to do so to consider means by which they could provide resources to assist United Nations work on the Year and urged them, together with intergovernmental and indigenous peoples' organizations and NGOs, to contribute to the Voluntary Fund for the Year. The Commission proposed to the Assembly that the title of the Year be amended to "1993—The International Year of the World's Indigenous People".

Subcommission action. On 27 August 1992,[54] the Subcommission adopted a resolution on the Year.

Working Group activities. At its July session,[33] the Working Group on Indigenous Populations recommended that, to mark the Year, the United Nations should launch an annual report on the state of the world's indigenous peoples, including statistics and analyses compiled by United Nations bodies and specialized agencies in collaboration with indigenous peoples and their organizations.

UNDP action. In an April report on the Year,[55] the UNDP Administrator described activities relating to indigenous people and proposed future activities that UNDP could support, such as improving living standards, economic and technological development, preserving natural resources and environmental conservation, and cultural revitalization. UNDP would give due consideration to the programme of activities for the Year,[52] continue to participate in meetings to foster coordination among United Nations organizations before and during the Year, and join in efforts to harmonize guidelines concerning activities relevant to indigenous communities.

On 26 May,[56] the UNDP Governing Council asked the Administrator to contribute to the programme of activities for the Year.

GENERAL ASSEMBLY ACTION

On 14 December 1992, the General Assembly adopted **resolution 47/75** without vote.

International Year of the World's Indigenous People, 1993

The General Assembly,

Bearing in mind that one of the purposes of the United Nations, as set forth in the Charter, is the achievement of international cooperation in solving international problems of an economic, social, cultural or humanitarian character, and in promoting and encouraging respect for human rights and for fundamental freedoms for all without discrimination as to race, sex, language or religion,

Recalling its resolution 45/164 of 18 December 1990, in which it proclaimed 1993 as the International Year of the World's Indigenous People, with a view to strengthening international cooperation for the solution of problems faced by indigenous communities in areas such as human rights, the environment, development, education and health,

Recognizing the value and the diversity of the cultures and the forms of social organization of the world's indigenous people,

Welcoming the report of the United Nations Conference on Environment and Development, as well as resolution 1992/45 of 3 March 1992 regarding the International Year of the World's Indigenous People, adopted by the Commission on Human Rights at its forty-eighth session,

Noting the need to conclude the technical meeting provided for in paragraph 8 of General Assembly resolution 46/128 of 17 December 1991 in accordance with the requirements of paragraphs 1 and 2 (*b*) of the same resolution,

1. *Reaffirms* that it proclaimed 1993 as the International Year of the World's Indigenous People, with the theme of "Indigenous people—a new partnership";

2. *Calls upon* the United Nations system and Governments that have not yet done so to develop policies in support of the objectives and the theme of the Year and to strengthen the institutional framework for their implementation;

3. *Urges* the Coordinator for the International Year of the World's Indigenous People to continue to solicit actively the cooperation of specialized agencies, regional commissions, financial and development institutions and other relevant organizations of the United Nations system for the promotion of the programme of activities contained in the annex to General Assembly resolution 46/128;

4. *Requests* the Coordinator to reconvene from within existing resources, in the three working days preceding the eleventh session of the Working Group on Indigenous Populations, the technical meeting provided for in paragraph 8 of resolution 46/128, with a view to concluding its deliberations and finalizing its report;

5. *Stresses* that governmental and intergovernmental activities undertaken within the context of the Year and beyond should take fully into account the development needs of indigenous people and the need for making full use of the contributions that indigenous communities can bring to sustainable national development;

6. *Notes* that there is a continuing need to improve the availability and the means of dissemination of socioeconomic data relating to the development needs of indigenous people and that the Year should contribute to enhancing and to facilitating the coordination capabilities of Member States for collecting and analysing information in that area;

7. *Appeals* to Governments, intergovernmental and non-governmental organizations, as well as indigenous people's organizations, to contribute to the voluntary fund for the Year opened by the Secretary-General;

8. *Recommends* to the Secretary-General that he should give all assistance necessary to the Coordinator to permit him to carry out his tasks;

9. *Recommends* that the Preparatory Committee for the World Conference on Human Rights should continue to consider at its upcoming meeting how issues pertinent to the Year could be addressed within the framework of the Conference;

10. *Stresses* the relevance for the solution of problems faced by indigenous communities of the recommendations made in chapter 26 of Agenda 21, contained in the report of the United Nations Conference on Environment and Development;

11. *Requests* the Commission on Human Rights to ask the Working Group on Indigenous Populations, at its eleventh session, and the Subcommission on Prevention of Discrimination and Protection of Minorities, at its forty-fifth session, to complete their consideration of the draft universal declaration on the rights of indigenous peoples and to submit their report to the Commission at its fiftieth session;

12. *Requests* the Secretary-General to submit a report to the General Assembly at its forty-ninth session on the activities developed and the results achieved within the context of the Year.

General Assembly resolution 47/75

14 December 1992   Meeting 85   Adopted without vote

51-nation draft (A/47/L.33 & Add.1); agenda item 97*(b)*.

Sponsors: Angola, Australia, Bahamas, Belize, Benin, Bolivia, Brazil, Cameroon, Canada, Central African Republic, Chad, Chile, Colombia, Comoros, Costa Rica, Cuba, Cyprus, Denmark, Dominican Republic, Ecuador, Finland, Gambia, Ghana, Greece, Guatemala, Guyana, Honduras, Hungary, Mexico, Morocco, Netherlands, New Zealand, Nicaragua, Niger, Nigeria, Norway, Panama, Peru, Philippines, Russian Federation, Rwanda, Saint Kitts and Nevis, Saint Vincent and the Grenadines, Samoa, Spain, Suriname, Sweden, Tajikistan, Togo, Uruguay, Vanuatu.

Migrant workers

International Convention

As at 31 December 1992, Mexico and Morocco[17] had signed the International Convention on the Protection of the Rights of All Migrant Workers and Members of Their Families, adopted by the General Assembly in 1990.[57]

The Secretary-General reported that, as at 1 August 1992, no ratifications of or accessions to the Convention had been received.[58]

Human Rights Commission action. On 6 March 1992,[59] the Commission urged all States to consider signing and ratifying or acceding to the Convention, and asked United Nations agencies and organizations, intergovernmental organizations and NGOs to disseminate information on it. The Commission asked the Secretary-General to provide all the assistance necessary to promote the Convention through the World Public Information Campaign on Human Rights and the programme of advisory services in the field of human rights (see below, under "Advancement of human rights") and to report on the Convention's status in 1993.

GENERAL ASSEMBLY ACTION

On 16 December 1992, the General Assembly, on the recommendation of the Third Committee, adopted **resolution 47/110** without vote.

International Convention on the Protection of the Rights of All Migrant Workers and Members of Their Families

The General Assembly,

Reaffirming once more the permanent validity of the principles and standards set forth in the basic instruments regarding the international protection of human rights, in particular in the Universal Declaration of Human Rights, the International Covenants on Human Rights, the International Convention on the Elimination of All Forms of Racial Discrimination, the Convention on the Elimination of All Forms of Discrimination against Women and the Convention on the Rights of the Child,

Bearing in mind the principles and standards established within the framework of the International Labour Organisation and the importance of the task carried out in connection with migrant workers and members of their families in other specialized agencies and in various organs of the United Nations,

Reiterating that in spite of the existence of an already established body of principles and standards, there is a need to make further efforts to improve the situation and to ensure the human rights and dignity of all migrant workers and members of their families,

Aware of the situation of migrant workers and members of their families and the marked increase in migratory movements that has occurred, especially in certain parts of the world,

Recalling its resolution 45/158 of 18 December 1990, by which it adopted and opened for signature, ratification and accession the International Convention on the Protection of the Rights of All Migrant Workers and Members of Their Families,

Also recalling that the General Assembly, in its resolution 46/114 of 17 December 1991, requested the Secretary-General to submit to the Assembly at its forty-seventh session a report on the status of the Convention,

1. *Takes note* of the report of the Secretary-General on the status of the International Convention on the Protection of the Rights of All Migrant Workers and Members of Their Families;

2. *Calls upon* all Member States to consider signing and ratifying or acceding to the Convention as a matter of priority, and expresses the hope that it will enter into force at an early date;

3. *Requests* the Secretary-General to provide all facilities and assistance necessary for the promotion of the Convention, through the World Public Information Campaign on Human Rights and the programme of advisory services in the field of human rights;

4. *Invites* the organizations and agencies of the United Nations system and intergovernmental and non-governmental organizations to intensify their efforts with a view to disseminating information on and promoting understanding of the Convention;

5. *Requests* the Secretary-General to submit to the General Assembly at its forty-eighth session a report on the status of the Convention;

6. *Decides* to consider the report of the Secretary-General at its forty-eighth session under the sub-item entitled "Implementation of human rights instruments".

General Assembly resolution 47/110

16 December 1992   Meeting 89   Adopted without vote

Approved by Third Committee (A/47/678/Add.1) without vote, 25 November (meeting 49); 25-nation draft (A/C.3/47/L.41); agenda item 97 *(a)*.

Sponsors: Algeria, Argentina, Colombia, Costa Rica, Croatia, Cuba, Ecuador, France, Greece, Guatemala, Guinea, India, Mali, Mexico, Morocco, Nicaragua, Peru, Portugal, Russian Federation, Rwanda, Sweden, Tunisia, Turkey, Uruguay, Zimbabwe.
Meeting numbers. GA 47th session: 3rd Committee 40, 42-45, 48, 49; plenary 89.

Protection of minorities

Declaration

Human Rights Commission action. On 21 February 1992,[60] the Commission approved the draft declaration on the rights of persons belonging to national or ethnic, religious and linguistic minorities.[61]

In October,[62] the Secretary-General transmitted the text of the draft declaration to the General Assembly.

ECONOMIC AND SOCIAL COUNCIL ACTION

On 20 July, the Economic and Social Council, on the recommendation of its Social Committee, adopted **resolution 1992/4** without vote.

Rights of persons belonging to national or ethnic, religious and linguistic minorities

The Economic and Social Council,

Taking note of Commission on Human Rights resolution 1992/16 of 21 February 1992, in which the Commission approved the text of the draft declaration on the rights of persons belonging to national or ethnic, religious and linguistic minorities,

Aware that persons belonging to minorities may also enjoy under international or domestic law rights other than those set forth in the draft declaration,

Recognizing that there is a continuing need to develop international protection in this area,

Believing that the principles and rights as set forth in the draft declaration involve matters of common interest,

Approves the draft declaration on the rights of persons belonging to national or ethnic, religious and linguistic minorities and recommends it to the General Assembly for adoption and further action.

Economic and Social Council resolution 1992/4

20 July 1992   Meeting 32   Adopted without vote

Approved by Social Committee (E/1992/103) without vote, 15 July (meeting 7); draft by Commission on Human Rights (E/1992/22); agenda item 17.

GENERAL ASSEMBLY ACTION

On 18 December 1992, the General Assembly, on the recommendation of the Third Committee, adopted **resolution 47/135** without vote.

Declaration on the Rights of Persons Belonging to National or Ethnic, Religious and Linguistic Minorities

The General Assembly,

Reaffirming that one of the main purposes of the United Nations, as proclaimed in the Charter of the United Nations, is to achieve international cooperation in promoting and encouraging respect for human rights and for fundamental freedoms for all without distinction as to race, sex, language or religion,

Noting the importance of the even more effective implementation of international human rights instruments with regard to the rights of persons belonging to national or ethnic, religious and linguistic minorities,

Welcoming the increased attention given by human rights treaty bodies to the non-discrimination and protection of minorities,

Aware of the provisions of article 27 of the International Covenant on Civil and Political Rights concerning the rights of persons belonging to ethnic, religious or linguistic minorities,

Considering that the United Nations has an increasingly important role to play regarding the protection of minorities,

Bearing in mind the work done so far within the United Nations system, in particular through the relevant mechanisms of the Commission on Human Rights and the Subcommission on Prevention of Discrimination and Protection of Minorities, in promoting and protecting the rights of persons belonging to national or ethnic, religious and linguistic minorities,

Recognizing the important achievements in this regard in regional, subregional and bilateral frameworks, which can provide a useful source of inspiration for future United Nations activities,

Stressing the need to ensure for all, without discrimination of any kind, full enjoyment and exercise of human rights and fundamental freedoms, and emphasizing the importance of the draft Declaration on the Rights of Persons Belonging to National or Ethnic, Religious and Linguistic Minorities in that regard,

Recalling its resolution 46/115 of 17 December 1991 and taking note of Commission on Human Rights resolution 1992/16 of 21 February 1992, by which the Commission approved the text of the draft declaration on the rights of persons belonging to national or ethnic, religious and linguistic minorities, and Economic and Social Council resolution 1992/4 of 20 July 1992, in which the Council recommended it to the General Assembly for adoption and further action,

Having considered the note by the Secretary-General,

1. *Adopts* the Declaration on the Rights of Persons Belonging to National or Ethnic, Religious and Linguistic Minorities, the text of which is annexed to the present resolution;

2. *Requests* the Secretary-General to ensure the distribution of the Declaration as widely as possible and to include the text of the Declaration in the next edition of *Human Rights: A Compilation of International Instruments*;

3. *Invites* United Nations agencies and organizations and intergovernmental and non-governmental organizations to intensify their efforts with a view to disseminating information on the Declaration and to promoting understanding thereof;

4. *Invites* the relevant organs and bodies of the United Nations, including treaty bodies, as well as representatives of the Commission on Human Rights and the Subcommission on Prevention of Discrimination and Protection of Minorities, to give due regard to the Declaration within their mandates;

5. *Requests* the Secretary-General to consider appropriate ways for the effective promotion of the Declaration and to make proposals thereon;

6. *Also requests* the Secretary-General to report to the General Assembly at its forty-eighth session on the implementation of the present resolution under the item entitled ''Human rights questions''.

ANNEX
Declaration on the Rights of Persons Belonging to National or Ethnic, Religious and Linguistic Minorities

The General Assembly,

Reaffirming that one of the basic aims of the United Nations, as proclaimed in the Charter, is to promote and encourage respect for human rights and for fundamental freedoms for all, without distinction as to race, sex, language or religion,

Reaffirming faith in fundamental human rights, in the dignity and worth of the human person, in the equal rights of men and women and of nations large and small,

Desiring to promote the realization of the principles contained in the Charter, the Universal Declaration of Human Rights, the Convention on the Prevention and Punishment of the Crime of Genocide, the International Convention on the Elimination of All Forms of Racial Discrimination, the International Covenant on Civil and Political Rights, the International Covenant on Economic, Social and Cultural Rights, the Declaration on the Elin ation of All Forms of Intolerance and of Discrimination Based on Religion or Belief, and the Convention on the Rights of the Child, as well as other relevant international instruments that have been adopted at the universal or regional level and those concluded between individual States Members of the United Nations,

Inspired by the provisions of article 27 of the International Covenant on Civil and Political Rights concerning the rights of persons belonging to ethnic, religious or linguistic minorities,

Considering that the promotion and protection of the rights of persons belonging to national or ethnic, religious and linguistic minorities contribute to the political and social stability of States in which they live,

Emphasizing that the constant promotion and realization of the rights of persons belonging to national or ethnic, religious and linguistic minorities, as an integral part of the development of society as a whole and within a democratic framework based on the rule of law, would contribute to the strengthening of friendship and cooperation among peoples and States,

Considering that the United Nations has an important role to play regarding the protection of minorities,

Bearing in mind the work done so far within the United Nations system, in particular by the Commission on Human Rights, the Subcommission on Prevention of Discrimination and Protection of Minorities and the bodies established pursuant to the International Covenants on Human Rights and other relevant international human rights instruments in promoting and protecting the rights of persons belonging to national or ethnic, religious and linguistic minorities,

Taking into account the important work which is done by intergovernmental and non-governmental organizations in protecting minorities and in promoting and protecting the rights of persons belonging to national or ethnic, religious and linguistic minorities,

Recognizing the need to ensure even more effective implementation of international human rights instruments with regard to the rights of persons belonging to national or ethnic, religious and linguistic minorities,

Proclaims this Declaration on the Rights of Persons Belonging to National or Ethnic, Religious and Linguistic Minorities:

Article 1

1. States shall protect the existence and the national or ethnic, cultural, religious and linguistic identity of minorities within their respective territories and shall encourage conditions for the promotion of that identity.

2. States shall adopt appropriate legislative and other measures to achieve those ends.

Article 2

1. Persons belonging to national or ethnic, religious and linguistic minorities (hereinafter referred to as persons belonging to minorities) have the right to enjoy their own culture, to profess and practise their own religion, and to use their own language, in private and in public, freely and without interference or any form of discrimination.

2. Persons belonging to minorities have the right to participate effectively in cultural, religious, social, economic and public life.

3. Persons belonging to minorities have the right to participate effectively in decisions on the national and, where appropriate, regional level concerning the minority to which they belong or the regions in which they live, in a manner not incompatible with national legislation.

4. Persons belonging to minorities have the right to establish and maintain their own associations.

5. Persons belonging to minorities have the right to establish and maintain, without any discrimination, free and peaceful contacts with other members of their group and with persons belonging to other minorities, as well as contacts across frontiers with citizens of other States to whom they are related by national or ethnic, religious or linguistic ties.

Article 3

1. Persons belonging to minorities may exercise their rights, including those set forth in the present Declaration, individually as well as in community with other members of their group, without any discrimination.

2. No disadvantage shall result for any person belonging to a minority as the consequence of the exercise or non-exercise of the rights set forth in the present Declaration.

Article 4

1. States shall take measures where required to ensure that persons belonging to minorities may exercise fully and effectively all their human rights and fundamental freedoms without any discrimination and in full equality before the law.

2. States shall take measures to create favourable conditions to enable persons belonging to minorities to express their characteristics and to develop their culture, language, religion, traditions and customs, except where specific practices are in violation of national law and contrary to international standards.

3. States should take appropriate measures so that, wherever possible, persons belonging to minorities may have adequate opportunities to learn their mother tongue or to have instruction in their mother tongue.

4. States should, where appropriate, take measures in the field of education, in order to encourage knowledge of the history, traditions, language and cul-

ture of the minorities existing within their territory. Persons belonging to minorities should have adequate opportunities to gain knowledge of the society as a whole.

5. States should consider appropriate measures so that persons belonging to minorities may participate fully in the economic progress and development in their country.

Article 5

1. National policies and programmes shall be planned and implemented with due regard for the legitimate interests of persons belonging to minorities.

2. Programmes of cooperation and assistance among States should be planned and implemented with due regard for the legitimate interests of persons belonging to minorities.

Article 6

States should cooperate on questions relating to persons belonging to minorities, *inter alia*, exchanging information and experiences, in order to promote mutual understanding and confidence.

Article 7

States should cooperate in order to promote respect for the rights set forth in the present Declaration.

Article 8

1. Nothing in the present Declaration shall prevent the fulfilment of international obligations of States in relation to persons belonging to minorities. In particular, States shall fulfil in good faith the obligations and commitments they have assumed under international treaties and agreements to which they are parties.

2. The exercise of the rights set forth in the present Declaration shall not prejudice the enjoyment by all persons of universally recognized human rights and fundamental freedoms.

3. Measures taken by States to ensure the effective enjoyment of the rights set forth in the present Declaration shall not *prima facie* be considered contrary to the principle of equality contained in the Universal Declaration of Human Rights.

4. Nothing in the present Declaration may be construed as permitting any activity contrary to the purposes and principles of the United Nations, including sovereign equality, territorial integrity and political independence of States.

Article 9

The specialized agencies and other organizations of the United Nations system shall contribute to the full realization of the rights and principles set forth in the present Declaration, within their respective fields of competence.

General Assembly resolution 47/135

18 December 1992   Meeting 92   Adopted without vote

Approved by Third Committee (A/47/678/Add.2) without vote, 4 December (meeting 58); 37-nation draft (A/C.3/47/L.66); agenda item 97 *(b)*.

Sponsors: Armenia, Australia, Austria, Belarus, Bulgaria, Canada, Cape Verde, Croatia, Czechoslovakia, Denmark, Estonia, Finland, Greece, Guatemala, Hungary, Italy, Latvia, Liechtenstein, Lithuania, Malawi, Morocco, Netherlands, Norway, Poland, Republic of Korea, Republic of Moldova, Romania, Russian Federation, Rwanda, Samoa, Slovenia, Sri Lanka, Sweden, Tajikistan, Ukraine, United States, Uruguay.

Meeting numbers. GA 47th session: 3rd Committee 47-58; plenary 92.

Ethnic cleansing

On 16 December 1992, the General Assembly, on the recommendation of the Third Committee, adopted **resolution 47/80** without vote.

"Ethnic cleansing" and racial hatred

The General Assembly,

Recalling the Charter of the United Nations, the Universal Declaration of Human Rights, the International Covenants on Human Rights and the International Convention on the Elimination of All Forms of Racial Discrimination,

Reaffirming its conviction that any doctrine of superiority based on racial differentiation is scientifically false, morally condemnable, socially unjust and dangerous, and that there is no justification for racial discrimination, in theory or in practice, anywhere,

Reaffirming also its conviction that discrimination between human beings on the grounds of race, colour, religion or ethnic origin is an obstacle to friendly and peaceful relations among nations and is capable of disturbing peace and security among peoples and the harmony of persons living side by side even within the same State,

Convinced that the existence of racial and ethnic barriers is repugnant to the ideals of any human society, and aware of the need to strengthen efforts to eliminate all forms of racial hatred,

Alarmed by the fact that, notwithstanding the efforts of the international community to eradicate them, there are still in many parts of the world manifestations of racial discrimination that are encouraged by a philosophy of racial superiority or hatred,

Deeply alarmed by policies and practices of "ethnic cleansing", which foster hatred and violence, wherever they occur,

Noting the importance of respecting the rights of persons belonging to national or ethnic, religious and linguistic minorities,

Reaffirming its resolution 46/242 of 25 August 1992, in which it states that the abhorrent practice of "ethnic cleansing" constitutes a grave and serious violation of international humanitarian law,

1. *Condemns unreservedly* "ethnic cleansing" and acts of violence arising from racial hatred;

2. *Strongly rejects* policies and ideologies aimed at promoting racial hatred and "ethnic cleansing" in any form;

3. *Reaffirms* that "ethnic cleansing" and racial hatred are totally incompatible with universally recognized human rights and fundamental freedoms;

4. *Reiterates its conviction* that those who commit or order the commission of acts of "ethnic cleansing" are individually responsible and should be brought to justice;

5. *Demands* that all those who commit or order the commission of acts of "ethnic cleansing" put an end to them immediately;

6. *Calls upon* all States to cooperate in eliminating all forms of "ethnic cleansing" and racial hatred.

General Assembly resolution 47/80

16 December 1992   Meeting 89   Adopted without vote

Approved by Third Committee (A/47/658) without vote, 2 November (meeting 25); 57-nation draft (A/C.3/47/L.9/Rev.1), orally revised; agenda item 91.

Sponsors: Afghanistan, Albania, Argentina, Australia, Austria, Belgium, Bosnia and Herzegovina, Brazil, Bulgaria, Canada, Cape Verde, Chile, Colombia, Costa Rica, Croatia, Cyprus, Czechoslovakia, Denmark, Ecuador, El Salvador, Estonia, Finland, France, Germany, Greece, Guatemala, Honduras, Hungary, Iceland, India, Ireland, Italy, Japan, Latvia, Liechtenstein, Lithuania, Luxembourg, Madagascar, Malta, Mexico, Morocco, Netherlands, New Zealand, Nicaragua, Norway, Panama, Paraguay, Peru, Poland, Portugal, Slovenia, Spain, Sweden, Ukraine, United Kingdom, United States, Venezuela.

Meeting numbers. GA 47th session: 3rd Committee 3-10, 13, 16, 20, 25; plenary 89.

Minority problems

Human Rights Commission action. On 3 March 1992,[63] the Commission approved the following requests made by its Subcommission in 1991[64] concerning ways to facilitate the peaceful and constructive solution of problems involving minorities: that the Secretary-General prepare, with the cooperation of the Subcommission's Special Rapporteur, a technical meeting of experts on minorities with a view to its taking place in 1992; that the Special Rapporteur continue consultations with States and submit a progress report on his study on ways to solve problems involving minorities; and that the Secretary-General give the Special Rapporteur all the assistance he might require. On 20 July, the Economic and Social Council, by **decision 1992/254**, endorsed the approval by the Commission of the Subcommission's requests.

On 4 March,[65] the Commission requested the Special Rapporteur, in preparing his study, to pay special attention to the living conditions of the Roma (gypsy) community. It asked States to adopt measures to eliminate discrimination against them and invited States to avail themselves of the advisory services of the Centre for Human Rights for that purpose.

The technical meeting of experts on minorities was postponed until 1993.

Subcommission action. On 27 August 1992,[66] the Subcommission adopted a resolution on facilitating the peaceful and constructive solution of problems involving minorities.

Report of the Special Rapporteur. In July, Special Rapporteur Asbjorn Eide (Norway) submitted his second progress report on national experiences regarding peaceful and constructive solutions of problems involving minorities.[67] In an addendum,[68] he reported on replies to a questionnaire on minorities received as at 15 June 1992 from 33 Governments, 5 specialized agencies and 8 NGOs. A reply from Yugoslavia was submitted separately.[69]

HIV- and AIDS-related discrimination

Human Rights Commission action. On 3 March 1992,[70] the Commission on Human Rights called on States to take steps to ensure the full enjoyment of civil, political, economic, social and cultural rights by people infected with the human immunodeficiency virus (HIV) or with acquired immunodeficiency syndrome (AIDS), their families, those associated with them and people presumed to be at risk of infection, paying particular attention to women, children and other vulnerable groups, in order to prevent discrimination against them. It asked the Human Rights Committee, the Committee on Economic, Social and Cultural Rights and similar bodies to monitor States parties' compliance with their commitments under the relevant human rights instruments regarding the rights of people infected with HIV or AIDS, their families and people with whom they lived, or people presumed to be at risk. It welcomed a 1990 preliminary report[71] and a 1991 progress report[64] of the Subcommission's Special Rapporteur, and endorsed requests made by the Subcommission in 1991 that he submit his final report in 1992 and that the Secretary-General give him any assistance he required.

On 20 July, the Economic and Social Council, by **decision 1992/234**, approved the Commission's endorsement of the Subcommission's requests.

Report of the Special Rapporteur. In July 1992, the Subcommission's Special Rapporteur, Luis Varela Quirós (Costa Rica), submitted a report on discrimination against HIV-infected people or people with AIDS.[72] The report was intended to be a final report but, owing to inadequate support and minimum financial means, it could not be properly completed. The Special Rapporteur described the global AIDS situation, the importance of preventing AIDS-related discrimination, discriminatory practices and legal policy frameworks for protection against discrimination. He provided a synopsis of replies to a questionnaire received from 41 Governments, 2 United Nations specialized agencies, 10 United Nations bodies, 4 intergovernmental organizations and 28 NGOs containing information on the legal and policy framework introduced in response to AIDS. The Special Rapporteur concluded that strategies to prevent AIDS-related discrimination needed to combine education with legal protection against discrimination. He outlined a number of measures for consideration by the Subcommission.

Subcommission action. On 27 August 1992,[73] the Subcommission requested that the Special Rapporteur submit his final report in 1993 and that the Secretary-General assist him.

REFERENCES

[1]YUN 1984, p. 785. [2]YUN 1987, p. 732, GA res. 42/47, annex, 30 Nov. 1987. [3]YUN 1991, p. 530. [4]E/CN.4/1992/39. [5]YUN 1985, p. 836, ESC res. 1985/19, 29 May 1985. [6]YUN 1991, p. 530, ESC res. 1991/2, 29 May 1991. [7]E/1992/66. [8]A/47/432. [9]YUN 1973, p. 524, GA res. 3057(XXVIII), annex, 2 Nov. 1973. [10]E/1992/22 (res. 1992/8). [11]YUN 1965, p. 440, GA res. 2106 A (XX), annex, 21 Dec. 1965. [12]HR/PUB/90/8. [13]YUN 1991, p. 538. [14]E/CN.4/1993/2 (res. 1992/5). [15]E/CN.4/Sub.2/

1992/11. [16]A/47/18. [17]*Multilateral Treaties Deposited with the Secretary-General: Status as at 31 December 1992* (ST/LEG/SER.E/11), Sales No. E.93.V.11. [18]YUN 1969, p. 488. [19]A/47/425. [20]A/47/18 (dec.1 (XXXI)). [21]Ibid. (dec.2 (XXXI)). [22]YUN 1991, p. 533, GA dec. 46/429, 17 Dec. 1991. [23]CERD/SP/45. [24]CERD/SP/44. [25]A/47/481. [26]E/1992/22 (res. 1992/15). [27]E/CN.4/1992/52. [28]YUN 1981, p. 881, GA res. 36/55, 25 Nov. 1981. [29]YUN 1991, p. 536, GA res. 46/131, 17 Dec. 1991. [30]E/1992/22 (res. 1992/17). [31]Ibid. (res. 1992/44). [32]YUN 1985, p. 848, GA res. 40/131, 13 Dec. 1985. [33]E/CN.4/Sub.2/1992/33 & Add.1. [34]E/CN.4/Sub.2/1992/28. [35]E/CN.4/1993/2 (res. 1992/33). [36]Ibid. (res. 1992/36). [37]E/CN.4/Sub.2/1992/54. [38]ESC dec. 1990/238, 25 May 1990. [39]E/CN.4/Sub.2/1992/31 & Add.1. [40]*Report of the United Nations Conference on Environment and Development, Rio de Janeiro, 3-14 June 1992*, vol. I, Sales No. E.93.I.8. [41]E/1992/22 (dec. 1992/113). [42]GA res. 45/97, 14 Dec. 1990. [43]E/1992/22 (dec. 1992/114). [44]E/CN.4/1993/2 (res. 1992/35). [45]E/CN.4/Sub.2/1992/30. [46]E/1992/22 (dec. 1992/111). [47]E/CN.4/1993/2 (dec. 1992/110). [48]E/CN.4/Sub.2/1992/32. [49]A/47/626. [50]GA res. 45/164, 18 Dec. 1990. [51]E/1992/22 (res. 1992/45). [52]YUN 1991, p. 540, GA res. 46/128, annex, 17 Dec. 1991. [53]E/CN.4/1992/AC.4/TM/8. [54]E/CN.4/1993/2 (res. 1992/34). [55]DP/ 1992/61. [56]E/1992/28 (dec. 92/18). [57]GA res. 45/158, annex, 18 Dec. 1990. [58]A/47/429. [59]E/1992/22 (res. 1992/81). [60]Ibid. (res. 1992/16). [61]YUN 1991, p. 542. [62]A/47/501. [63]E/1992/22 (dec. 1992/112). [64]YUN 1991, p. 543. [65]E/1992/22 (res. 1992/65). [66]E/CN.4/1993/2 (res. 1992/37). [67]E/CN.4/Sub.2/ 1992/37. [68]E/CN.4/Sub.2/1992/37/Add.1. [69]E/CN.4/Sub.2/ 1992/37/Add.2. [70]E/1992/22 (res. 1992/56). [71]E/CN.4/Sub.2/ 1990/9. [72]E/CN.4/Sub.2/1992/10. [73]E/CN.4/1993/2 (dec. 1992/108).

Civil and political rights

Covenant on Civil and Political Rights and Optional Protocols

Accessions and ratifications

As at 31 December 1992, the International Covenant on Civil and Political Rights and the Optional Protocol thereto, adopted by the General Assembly in 1966[1] and in force since 1976,[2] had been ratified or acceded to by 115 and 67 States, respectively.[3] Angola, Azerbaijan, Benin, Brazil, Cambodia, Côte d'Ivoire, Croatia, Guatemala, Latvia, Lesotho, Paraguay, Seychelles, Slovenia, Switzerland and the United States became parties to the Covenant in 1992; Angola, Belarus, Benin, Bulgaria, Chile, Cyprus and Seychelles acceded to or ratified the Optional Protocol.

The Second Optional Protocol, aiming at the abolition of the death penalty—adopted by the Assembly in 1989[4] and in force since July 1991[5]—had been ratified or acceded to by 12 States as at 31 December 1992.[3] Germany and Luxembourg ratified it in 1992.

In a report to the Commission on Human Rights,[6] the Secretary-General provided information on the status of the Covenant and the Optional Protocols as at 10 December 1992 (see below, under "Advancement of human rights").

Human Rights Commission action. On 21 February 1992,[7] the Commission on Human Rights appealed to States that had not done so to become parties to the Covenant and Optional Protocols and to consider making the declaration provided for in article 41 of the Covenant. A similar appeal was made in July by the Economic and Social Council in **resolution 1992/11**. The Commission requested the Secretary-General to report in 1993 on the status of the Covenant and its Optional Protocols.

Implementation

Human Rights Committee activities. The Human Rights Committee, established under article 28 of the Covenant, held three sessions in 1992: its forty-fourth in New York from 23 March to 10 April; and its forty-fifth from 13 to 31 July and forty-sixth from 19 October to 6 November, both at Geneva.

At those sessions, the Committee considered reports from 14 States—Algeria, Belarus, Belgium, Burundi, Colombia, Iran, Luxembourg, Mongolia, Peru, Republic of Korea, Senegal, United Republic of Tanzania, Venezuela, Yugoslavia—under article 40 of the Covenant. It adopted views on 21 communications from individuals claiming that their rights under the Covenant had been violated. The cases concerned citizens or residents of Austria, Canada, Ecuador, Finland, France, Hungary, Jamaica, the Netherlands, Panama and Peru. The Committee decided that 22 other such communications were inadmissible.

The Committee adopted and annexed to its report[8] general comments on articles 7 and 10 of the Covenant, which prohibit torture and forced subjection to medical or scientific experimentation and urge humane treatment of prisoners. The comments were intended to assist States parties to fulfil their reporting obligations and promote the Covenant's implementation. In May,[9] the Secretary-General transmitted the general comments to the Economic and Social Council, which, by **decision 1992/263** of 20 July, took note of them.

At its October/November session,[10] the Committee, in view of the situation in the former Yugoslavia, examined special reports submitted by Bosnia and Herzegovina, Croatia and the Federal Republic of Yugoslavia (Serbia and Montenegro). (For details on the human rights situation in the former Yugoslavia, see below, under "Human rights violations".)

State of siege or emergency

Human Rights Commission action. On 28 February 1992,[11] the Commission recommended to the Economic and Social Council a draft decision concerning the work of the Special Rapporteur on human rights and states of emergency (see below). On the same date,[12] it called on States to maintain the right of habeas corpus at all times and under all circumstances, including states of emergency.

On 21 February,[7] the Commission, as did the Council later in the year in **resolution 1992/11**, underlined the necessity for strict observance of the agreed conditions and procedures for derogation under article 4 of the Covenant and the need for States parties to provide full and timely information during states of emergency, so that the justification and appropriateness of measures taken in those circumstances could be assessed.

ECONOMIC AND SOCIAL COUNCIL ACTION

On 20 July, the Economic and Social Council, by **decision 1992/249**, endorsed a 1991 Subcommission request[13] to the Special Rapporteur to continue updating the list of states of emergency and to include in his annual report to the Subcommission and the Commission the completed draft standard provisions on emergency situations. It also endorsed the Subcommission's request that the Secretary-General provide the Special Rapporteur with all the assistance he might require.

Report of the Special Rapporteur. In July, Special Rapporteur Leandro Despouy (Argentina) submitted his fifth annual report containing information on 80 States which, since 1 January 1985, had proclaimed, extended or terminated a state of emergency.[14] Previous reports were issued in 1987,[15] 1988,[16] 1989,[17] and 1991.[13] The Special Rapporteur recommended that the Commission on Human Rights invite countries that made up the former USSR to request advisory services from the Centre for Human Rights. He further recommended that the Commission propose the inclusion in the agenda of the 1993 World Conference on Human Rights (see below, under ''Advancement of human rights'') an item on strengthening protection of human rights during states of emergency.

As requested by the Subcommission on 27 August 1992,[18] the Special Rapporteur revised and updated his fifth report,[19] which the Secretary-General transmitted to the Commission in November.[20]

Self-determination of peoples

By three resolutions adopted in 1992, the Commission on Human Rights reaffirmed the right to self-determination of the people of Afghanistan,[21] Palestine[22] and Western Sahara.[23] A fourth resolution[24] adopted under the item pertained to the use of mercenaries as a means to impede the exercise of the right of peoples to self-determination. In addition, the Commission

adopted a decision on Cambodia,[25] concerning the development by the Centre for Human Rights of a human rights information programme in that country.

With regard to South Africa, the Commission, in a 28 February resolution on the human rights situation there,[26] reaffirmed the international consensus to oppose apartheid, support the peaceful struggle to eradicate apartheid and facilitate the creation of a non-racial, democratic South Africa. In another resolution of the same date,[27] the Commission reaffirmed its support for the eradication of apartheid and the establishment of a democratic South Africa. (For further details on South Africa, see below, under ''Human rights violations''.)

Report of the Secretary-General. In September,[28] the Secretary-General summarized action taken in 1992 by the Commission and the Economic and Social Council on the right of peoples to self-determination. He also summarized a reply received from Cuba in response to his request for information from States for inclusion in his report, prepared in response to two 1991 Assembly resolutions.[29]

GENERAL ASSEMBLY ACTION

In 1992, the General Assembly adopted two resolutions on the right to self-determination, a right it repeatedly reaffirmed for individual Non-Self-Governing Territories (see PART FOUR, Chapter I).

On 16 December, the Assembly, on the recommendation of the Third Committee, adopted **resolution 47/83** without vote.

Universal realization of the right of peoples to self-determination

The General Assembly,

Reaffirming the importance, for the effective guarantee and observance of human rights, of the universal realization of the right of peoples to self-determination enshrined in the Charter of the United Nations and embodied in the International Covenants on Human Rights, as well as in the Declaration on the Granting of Independence to Colonial Countries and Peoples contained in General Assembly resolution 1514(XV) of 14 December 1960,

Welcoming the progressive exercise of the right to self-determination by peoples under colonial, foreign or alien occupation and their emergence into sovereign statehood and independence,

Deeply concerned at the continuation of acts or threats of foreign military intervention and occupation that are threatening to suppress, or have already suppressed, the right to self-determination of an increasing number of sovereign peoples and nations,

Expressing grave concern that, as a consequence of the persistence of such actions, millions of people have been and are being uprooted from their homes as refugees and displaced persons, and emphasizing the urgent need for concerted international action to alleviate their condition,

Recalling the relevant resolutions regarding the violation of the right of peoples to self-determination and other human rights as a result of foreign military intervention, aggression and occupation, adopted by the Commission on Human Rights at its thirty-sixth, thirty-seventh, thirty-eighth, thirty-ninth, fortieth, forty-first, forty-second, forty-third, forty-fourth, forty-fifth, forty-sixth, forty-seventh and forty-eighth sessions,

Reaffirming its resolutions 35/35 B of 14 November 1980, 36/10 of 28 October 1981, 37/42 of 3 December 1982, 38/16 of 22 November 1983, 39/18 of 23 November 1984, 40/24 of 29 November 1985, 41/100 of 4 December 1986, 42/94 of 7 December 1987, 43/105 of 8 December 1988, 44/80 of 8 December 1989, 45/131 of 14 December 1990 and 46/88 of 16 December 1991,

Taking note of the report of the Secretary-General on the right of peoples to self-determination,

1. *Reaffirms* that the universal realization of the right of all peoples, including those under colonial, foreign and alien domination, to self-determination is a fundamental condition for the effective guarantee and observance of human rights and for the preservation and promotion of such rights;

2. *Declares its firm opposition* to acts of foreign military intervention, aggression and occupation, since these have resulted in the suppression of the right of peoples to self-determination and other human rights in certain parts of the world;

3. *Calls upon* those States responsible to cease immediately their military intervention in and occupation of foreign countries and territories and all acts of repression, discrimination, exploitation and maltreatment, particularly the brutal and inhuman methods reportedly employed for the execution of these acts against the peoples concerned;

4. *Deplores* the plight of the millions of refugees and displaced persons who have been uprooted as a result of the aforementioned acts, and reaffirms their right to return to their homes voluntarily in safety and honour;

5. *Requests* the Commission on Human Rights to continue to give special attention to the violation of human rights, especially the right to self-determination, resulting from foreign military intervention, aggression or occupation;

6. *Requests* the Secretary-General to report on this issue to the General Assembly at its forty-eighth session under the item entitled ''Right of peoples to self-determination''.

General Assembly resolution 47/83

16 December 1992   Meeting 89   Adopted without vote

Approved by Third Committee (A/47/659) without vote, 28 October (meeting 20); 34-nation draft (A/C.3/47/L.5); agenda item 92.
Sponsors: Afghanistan, Bahrain, Bosnia and Herzegovina, Botswana, Brunei Darussalam, Cape Verde, Chile, Colombia, Comoros, Costa Rica, Djibouti, Dominican Republic, Ecuador, El Salvador, Guatemala, Iran, Jordan, Kuwait, Malaysia, Mauritania, Morocco, Nicaragua, Oman, Pakistan, Papua New Guinea, Qatar, Samoa, Saudi Arabia, Sierra Leone, Singapore, Sudan, Thailand, Trinidad and Tobago, United Arab Emirates.
Meeting numbers. GA 47th session: 3rd Committee 3-10, 13, 20; plenary 89.

Also on 16 December, on the Third Committee's recommendation, the Assembly adopted **resolution 47/82** by recorded vote.

Importance of the universal realization of the right of peoples to self-determination and of the speedy granting of independence to colonial countries and peoples for the effective guarantee and observance of human rights

The General Assembly,

Reaffirming its faith in the importance of the implementation of the Declaration on the Granting of Independence to Colonial Countries and Peoples contained in its resolution 1514(XV) of 14 December 1960,

Reaffirming also the importance of the universal realization of the right of peoples to self-determination, national sovereignty and territorial integrity and of the speedy granting of independence to colonial countries and peoples as imperatives for the full enjoyment of all human rights,

Reaffirming further the obligation of all Member States to comply with the principles of the Charter of the United Nations and the resolutions of the United Nations regarding the exercise of the right to self-determination by peoples under colonial and foreign domination,

Recalling its resolution 1514(XV) and all relevant resolutions concerning the implementation of the Declaration on the Granting of Independence to Colonial Countries and Peoples,

Considering the urgent need of Namibia for assistance in its efforts to reconstruct and strengthen its fledgling economic and social structures,

Recalling with satisfaction the adoption at Harare on 21 August 1989 of the Declaration of the Ad Hoc Committee of the Organization of African Unity on Southern Africa on the question of South Africa and its subsequent endorsement by the Ninth Conference of Heads of State or Government of Non-Aligned Countries, held at Belgrade from 4 to 7 September 1989, as well as the report of the Monitoring Group of the Ad Hoc Committee of the Organization of African Unity on Southern Africa, and the Declaration on Apartheid and its Destructive Consequences in Southern Africa, adopted by the General Assembly on 14 December 1989,

Welcoming Security Council resolution 765(1992) of 16 July 1992, and Council resolution 772(1992) of 17 August 1992 which, *inter alia*, provides the basis for action by the Secretary-General in South Africa in order to assist the people of South Africa in ending the violence in that country,

Recalling the Abuja Declaration on South Africa, adopted by the Assembly of Heads of State and Government of the Organization of African Unity at its twenty-seventh ordinary session, held at Abuja from 3 to 5 June 1991,

Reaffirming that the system of apartheid imposed on the South African people constitutes a violation of the fundamental rights of that people, a crime against humanity and a threat to regional peace and security,

Deeply concerned that, in spite of the National Peace Accord signed on 14 September 1991, acts of assassination of members and leaders of national liberation movements in South Africa are still continuing,

Recalling its resolution 46/79 A, adopted by consensus on 13 December 1991, in which, *inter alia*, it reaffirmed the need for the full implementation of the provisions of the Declaration on Apartheid and its Destructive Consequences in Southern Africa that were not yet fulfilled,

Noting with concern that, while significant legal and political measures in the right direction have been undertaken by the Government of South Africa, there remain various pieces of security legislation that restrict the possibilities for free and peaceful political activity, and that apartheid remains in place,

Noting also with concern that political trials and the detention of opponents of apartheid continue in South Africa in total disregard of the provisions of the Declaration on Apartheid and its Destructive Consequences in Southern Africa,

Deeply concerned about the current wave of violence in South Africa resulting from the continued existence of apartheid policies, practices and structures as well as from actions of those forces opposed to the democratic transformation of the country,

Gravely concerned that a number of South African patriots remain on death row,

Welcoming the signing of the General Peace Agreement for Mozambique, at Rome on 4 October 1992,[a] which provides for the termination of the armed conflict in that country,

Reaffirming the national unity and territorial integrity of the Comoros,

Recalling the Geneva Declaration on Palestine and the Programme of Action for the Achievement of Palestinian Rights, adopted by the International Conference on the Question of Palestine,

Considering that the continuation of the Israeli oppressive measures and the denial of the inalienable rights of the Palestinian people to self-determination, sovereignty, independence and return to Palestine constitute a serious threat to international peace and security,

Bearing in mind United Nations resolutions related to the question of Palestine and the rights of the Palestinian people,

Deeply concerned and alarmed at the deplorable consequences of Israel's acts of aggression against Lebanon and its practices in and its continuing occupation of parts of southern Lebanon, as well as its refusal to implement the relevant resolutions of the Security Council, in particular resolution 425(1978) of 19 March 1978,

1. *Calls upon* all States to implement fully and faithfully all the relevant resolutions of the United Nations regarding the exercise of the right to self-determination and independence by peoples under colonial and foreign domination;

2. *Reaffirms* the legitimacy of the struggle of peoples for independence, territorial integrity, national unity and liberation from colonial domination, apartheid and foreign occupation, in all its forms and by all available means;

3. *Reaffirms also* the inalienable right of the Palestinian people and all peoples under foreign occupation and colonial domination to self-determination, national independence, territorial integrity, national unity and sovereignty without foreign interference;

4. *Calls upon* those Governments which do not recognize the right to self-determination and independence of all peoples still under colonial domination, alien subjugation and foreign occupation to do so;

5. *Calls upon* Israel to refrain from the constant, deliberate violations of the fundamental rights of the Palestinian people, which constitute an obstacle to the achievement of self-determination and independence by the Palestinian people and the ongoing efforts towards comprehensive peace in the region;

6. *Urges* all States, the specialized agencies and organizations of the United Nations system, as well as other international organizations, to extend their support to the Palestinian people through its sole and legitimate representative, the Palestine Liberation Organization, in its struggle to regain its right to self-determination and independence in accordance with the Charter of the United Nations;

7. *Urgently appeals* to all States, the organizations of the United Nations system and other international organizations to render assistance to Namibia in order to enhance its efforts to promote democracy and economic development;

8. *Reaffirms* its rejection of the so-called "tricameral constitution" of 1983 as null and void, and reiterates that peace in South Africa can be guaranteed only by the establishment of majority rule through the full and free exercise of adult suffrage by all the people in a united and undivided South Africa;

9. *Strongly urges* the Government of South Africa to take additional steps to implement fully the provisions of the Declaration of the Ad Hoc Committee of the Organization of African Unity on Southern Africa on the question of South Africa, and the Declaration on Apartheid and its Destructive Consequences in Southern Africa;

10. *Calls* for an immediate end to violence and calls upon the Government of South Africa to exercise its responsibility to end it through, *inter alia*, strict adherence to the National Peace Accord;

11. *Calls upon* all signatories to the National Peace Accord to manifest their commitment to peace by fully implementing its provisions and calls upon all other parties to contribute to the attainment of its objectives;

12. *Strongly condemns* the establishment and use of armed groups with a view to pitting them against the national liberation movements;

13. *Demands* that the Government of South Africa repeal the security legislation that remains in force, which inhibits free and peaceful political activity;

14. *Requests* the Secretary-General to act speedily to implement Security Council resolution 772(1992) in its entirety, including those parts pertaining to the investigation of criminal conduct and the monitoring of all armed formations in the country;

15. *Demands* the full application of the mandatory arms embargo against South Africa, imposed under Security Council resolution 418(1977) of 4 November 1977, by all countries and more particularly by those countries which maintain military and nuclear cooperation with the Government of South Africa and continue to supply it with related *matériel*;

16. *Expresses its deep concern* about the actions by certain countries whose premature relaxation of existing measures against the South African regime, in flagrant violation of the United Nations consensus declaration, encourages the regime to persist in its oppression of the Black majority with regard to their right to self-determination;

17. *Strongly urges* the international community, pursuant to General Assembly resolution 46/87 of 16 December 1991, to continue to extend maximum assistance

---

[a]S/24635.

to Lesotho to enable it to fulfil its international humanitarian obligations towards refugees;

18. *Pays tribute* to the Government and people of Angola for their noble contribution to the evolving climate of peace in southern Angola;

19. *Demands* that the Government of South Africa pay compensation to Angola for damages caused, in accordance with the relevant decisions and resolutions of the Security Council;

20. *Demands also* that the Government of South Africa pay full and adequate compensation to Botswana for the loss of life and damage to property resulting from the unprovoked and unwarranted military attacks of 14 June 1985, 19 May 1986 and 20 June 1988 on the capital of Botswana;

21. *Calls upon* the international community to extend its generous support to the ongoing efforts aimed at ensuring respect for and the successful implementation of the General Peace Agreement for Mozambique[a] and at assisting the Government of Mozambique in the establishment of lasting peace and democracy and in the promotion of an effective programme of national reconstruction in that country;

22. *Fully supports* the Secretary-General in his efforts to implement the plan for the settlement of the question of Western Sahara by organizing, in cooperation with the Organization of African Unity, a referendum for the self-determination of the people of Western Sahara;

23. *Notes* the contacts between the Government of the Comoros and the Government of France in the search for a just solution to the problem of the integration of the Comorian island of Mayotte into the Comoros, in accordance with the resolutions of the Organization of African Unity and the United Nations on the question;

24. *Strongly condemns* the continued violation of the human rights of the peoples still under colonial domination and alien subjugation;

25. *Calls* for a substantial increase in all forms of assistance given by all States, United Nations organs, the specialized agencies and non-governmental organizations to the victims of racism, racial discrimination and apartheid through anti-apartheid organizations and national liberation movements recognized by the Organization of African Unity;

26. *Reaffirms* that the practice of using mercenaries against sovereign States and national liberation movements constitutes a criminal act, and calls upon the Governments of all countries to enact legislation declaring the recruitment, financing and training of mercenaries in their territories and the transit of mercenaries through their territories to be punishable offences and prohibiting their nationals from serving as mercenaries, and to report on such legislation to the Secretary-General;

27. *Demands* the immediate and unconditional release of all persons detained or imprisoned as a result of their struggle for self-determination and independence, full respect for their fundamental individual rights and compliance with article 5 of the Universal Declaration of Human Rights, under which no one shall be subjected to torture or to cruel, inhuman or degrading treatment;

28. *Expresses its appreciation* for the material and other forms of assistance that peoples under colonial rule continue to receive from Governments, organizations of the United Nations system and other intergovernmental organizations, and calls for a substantial increase in that assistance;

29. *Urges* all States, the specialized agencies and other competent organizations of the United Nations system to do their utmost to ensure the full implementation of the Declaration on the Granting of Independence to Colonial Countries and Peoples and to intensify their efforts to support peoples under colonial, foreign and racist domination in their just struggle for self-determination and independence;

30. *Decides* to consider this question at its forty-eighth session under the item entitled "Right of peoples to self-determination".

General Assembly resolution 47/82

16 December 1992   Meeting 89   107-22-33 (recorded vote)

Approved by Third Committee (A/47/659) by recorded vote (90-22-30), 2 November (meeting 25); draft by Mauritania for African Group (A/C.3/47/L.4), orally revised; agenda item 92.

Meeting numbers. GA 47th session: 3rd Committee 3-10, 13, 20, 25; plenary 89.

Recorded vote in Assembly as follows:

In favour: Afghanistan, Algeria, Angola, Antigua and Barbuda, Armenia, Bahamas, Bahrain, Bangladesh, Barbados, Belize, Benin, Bhutan, Bolivia, Bosnia and Herzegovina, Botswana, Brazil, Brunei Darussalam, Burkina Faso, Burundi, Cameroon, Cape Verde, Chad, Chile, China, Colombia, Comoros, Congo, Côte d'Ivoire, Cuba, Cyprus, Democratic People's Republic of Korea, Djibouti, Ecuador, Egypt, El Salvador, Ethiopia, Fiji, Gabon, Gambia, Ghana, Grenada, Guatemala, Guinea, Guinea-Bissau, Guyana, Haiti, Honduras, India, Indonesia, Iran, Iraq, Jordan, Kenya, Kuwait, Lao People's Democratic Republic, Lebanon, Lesotho, Liberia, Libyan Arab Jamahiriya, Malaysia, Maldives, Mali, Mauritania, Mauritius, Mexico, Mongolia, Morocco, Myanmar, Namibia, Nepal, Nicaragua, Niger, Nigeria, Oman, Pakistan, Papua New Guinea, Peru, Philippines, Qatar, Rwanda, Saint Kitts and Nevis, Saint Lucia, Saint Vincent and the Grenadines, Sao Tome and Principe, Saudi Arabia, Senegal, Seychelles, Sierra Leone, Singapore, Sri Lanka, Sudan, Suriname, Swaziland, Syrian Arab Republic, Tajikistan, Thailand, Togo, Trinidad and Tobago, Tunisia, Uganda, United Arab Emirates, United Republic of Tanzania, Venezuela, Viet Nam, Yemen, Zambia, Zimbabwe.

Against: Argentina, Belgium, Bulgaria, Canada, Czechoslovakia, Denmark, Finland, France, Germany, Hungary, Iceland, Israel, Italy, Luxembourg, Netherlands, Norway, Poland, Romania, Russian Federation, Sweden, United Kingdom, United States.

Abstaining: Albania, Australia, Austria, Azerbaijan, Belarus, Costa Rica, Croatia, Dominican Republic, Estonia, Greece, Ireland, Jamaica, Japan, Kazakhstan, Kyrgyzstan, Latvia, Liechtenstein, Lithuania, Malta, Marshall Islands, Micronesia, New Zealand, Panama, Paraguay, Portugal, Republic of Korea, Republic of Moldova, Samoa, San Marino, Spain, Turkey, Ukraine, Uruguay.

Afghanistan

On 21 February 1992,[21] the Commission requested the Secretary-General and his Personal Representative to continue to facilitate the early realization of a comprehensive political settlement in accordance with the Agreements on the Settlement of the Situation Relating to Afghanistan, concluded at Geneva on 14 April 1988,[30] and a 1991 General Assembly resolution.[31] It called on all parties concerned to work towards a political solution, the cessation of hostilities and the creation of conditions which would enable Afghan refugees to return voluntarily to their homeland in safety and honour. It appealed to States and organizations to continue to extend humanitarian relief assistance to Afghan refugees, in coordination with the United Nations High Commissioner for Refugees (UNHCR), and called on States to provide adequate financial and material resources to the Coordinator for United Nations Humanitarian and Economic Assistance Programmes relating to Afghanistan in order to repatriate and rehabilitate speedily the Afghan refugees and to reconstruct the country economically and socially.

Cambodia

Human Rights Commission action. On 21 February 1992,[25] the Commission welcomed the October 1991 signing in Paris of the Agreement on a Comprehensive Political Settlement of the Cambodia Conflict,[32] under which the Commission was to monitor closely the human rights situation in Cambodia after the end of the transitional period. It encouraged the Centre for Human Rights to develop its human rights information programme throughout Cambodia, in coordination with the United Nations Transitional Authority in Cambodia (UNTAC) (for details on the establishment of UNTAC, see PART TWO, Chapter III). It requested the Secretary-General to inform it in 1993 of the human rights activities carried out by UNTAC and the Centre.

Subcommission action. The Subcommission, on 27 August,[33] asked the Secretary-General to develop and implement, in collaboration with UNTAC, long-term comprehensive programmes of technical assistance and advisory services which would contribute to the enjoyment of human rights and fundamental freedoms in Cambodia. He was to report to the Commission in 1993 on activities undertaken and progress made.

Report of the Secretary-General. In a report to the Commission on the situation in Cambodia,[34] the Secretary-General described the human rights component of UNTAC, which comprised a staff of 10 in Phnom Penh to cover monitoring and investigation and training, education and information. There were also human rights officers in each of the 21 provinces of Cambodia. As at 10 November 1992, the component had received some 300 complaints at its office at Phnom Penh and almost as many from the provinces. They dealt with land disputes, harassment and intimidation, wrongful imprisonment, wrongful death, destruction and seizure of property, cease-fire violations and injuries. A mission from the Centre for Human Rights visited Cambodia from 11 to 17 October to identify further ways to promote respect for human rights and to strengthen cooperation between the Centre and UNTAC.

The Secretary-General concluded that, although there were continuing grounds for serious concern, real progress had been made. The number of political assassinations had declined, political prisoners and prisoners of war had been released and freedom of expression and association had improved. In addition, UNTAC had drawn up and published an electoral law to conduct free and fair elections to a Constituent Assembly for Cambodia, in consultation with the Supreme National Council. He recommended the appointment of a special rapporteur on Cambodia to review and monitor the human rights situation, and the establishment of an operational presence of the Centre to ensure a continuing human rights presence after UNTAC left and to take over the functions of UNTAC's human rights component.

International symposium. An international symposium on human rights in Cambodia (Phnom Penh, 30 November–2 December 1992)[35] took place under the auspices of UNTAC's human rights component to identify ways in which the international community could provide support to human rights institutions and structures in Cambodia and to explore how the United Nations and other international organizations, NGOs and the Cambodian human rights community could work together to safeguard human rights and fundamental freedoms, particularly following the elections and UNTAC's withdrawal from Cambodia.

Palestinians

Human Rights Commission action. By a resolution of 14 February 1992,[22] adopted by a roll-call vote of 31 to 2, with 17 abstentions, the Commission condemned Israel for its continued occupation of the Palestinian territory and called on it to withdraw. It reaffirmed the right of the Palestinians to self-determination and to recover their rights by all means in accordance with the Charter and United Nations resolutions, and affirmed that the *intifadah* of the Palestinian people since 8 December 1987 was legitimate resistance against Israeli military occupation (for details on the *intifadah*, see PART TWO, Chapter V). The Commission reaffirmed its support for the call to convene an international peace conference on the Middle East, with the participation of Security Council permanent members and the parties to the Arab-Israeli conflict, including the Palestine Liberation Organization (PLO). It urged States, United Nations organs, specialized agencies and other international organizations to support and assist the Palestinians through their representative, PLO, and asked the Secretary-General to make available, prior to its 1993 session, information on the implementation of its resolution and to transmit the text to Israel and all other Governments.

Subcommission action. On 26 August,[36] the Subcommission, by a secret ballot of 11 votes to 6, with 6 abstentions, similarly condemned Israel and requested the Secretary-General to provide in 1993 an updated list of reports, studies, statistics and other documents relating to the question of Palestine and other occupied Arab territories, with the texts of relevant United Nations decisions and resolutions, the report of the Special Committee to Investigate Israeli Practices Affecting the Human Rights of the Palestinian People and Other Arabs of the Occupied Territories and all other relevant information.

Western Sahara

On 28 February 1992,[23] the Commission welcomed the 1991 establishment of the United Nations Mission for the Referendum in Western Sahara and the entry into force of a cease-fire on 6 September 1991,[37] accepted by Morocco and the Frente Popular para la Liberación de Saguia el-Hamra y de Río de Oro. It endorsed the call made in 1991 by the Security Council[38] for both parties to cooperate with the Secretary-General in implementing his 1991 plan.[37] The Commission expressed support for the Secretary-General's efforts to organize and supervise, in cooperation with the Organization for African Unity (OAU), a referendum for self-determination.

Mercenaries

Human Rights Commission action. On 21 February,[24] the Commission, reaffirming that the recruitment, use, financing and training of mercenaries should be considered as offences of grave concern, called on all States that had not done so to consider acceding to or ratifying the 1989 International Convention against the Recruitment, Use, Financing and Training of Mercenaries.[39] It decided to extend its Special Rapporteur's mandate for three years to carry out further studies on the use of mercenaries, took note of his 1991 report[40] and requested him to report in 1993.

On 20 July 1992, the Economic and Social Council, by **decision 1992/225**, approved the extension of the Special Rapporteur's mandate and the request that he report in 1993 (see below).

On 28 February,[41] the Commission asked all special rapporteurs and working groups to continue paying particular attention to the adverse effect on the enjoyment of human rights of acts of violence committed by armed groups, regardless of their origin, that spread terror among the population, and by drug traffickers, in their forthcoming reports on the situation of human rights in countries where such acts of violence occurred. It also asked the Secretary-General to continue collecting information on the question from all relevant sources and to make it available to the special rapporteurs and working groups concerned.

Reports of the Special Rapporteur. In response to a 1991 Assembly resolution,[42] the Secretary-General, in September 1992,[43] transmitted a preliminary report containing information on mercenary activities covering January to July 1992, prepared by Special Rapporteur Enrique Bernales Ballesteros (Peru). He noted that the most common form of mercenarism was usually associated with an armed conflict involving the exercise of a people's right to self-determination. In addition, mercenary resources and organized groups were available to undertake mercenary activities having a variety of purposes, such as to reinforce insecure political interests, to assist or impede the actions of opposition groups, and to engage in unlawful actions including terrorist acts, drug- and arms-trafficking operations and paid assassinations.

The number of countries affected by armed conflicts had increased in 1992. The Special Rapporteur specifically discussed mercenary activities in Angola, Liberia, Mozambique, South Africa and the former Yugoslavia. He recommended that the Assembly and other United Nations organs suggest to Member States that they: update their legislation to include provisions defining as an offence the recruitment, use, financing and training of mercenaries, as well as mercenary activities carried out within their territory and the transit of mercenaries through it; prohibit their nationals from serving as mercenaries and regard as aggravating factors the involvement of mercenaries in activities such as trafficking in arms, drugs or illegal currency; and enter into extradition agreements.

In a later report,[44] the Special Rapporteur discussed the use of mercenaries as a means of violating human rights and impeding the exercise of the right of peoples to self-determination. He described his activities during 1992 and correspondence received from Member States concerning mercenary activities. He reported on mercenary activities in Africa and the former Yugoslavia and the consequences for human rights of violent acts committed by armed groups and drug traffickers.

As to the status of the 1989 International Convention against the Recruitment, Use, Financing and Training of Mercenaries,[39] the Special Rapporteur stated that only five States had signed and ratified or acceded to the Convention—Barbados, Maldives, Seychelles, Suriname and Togo; 14 States had signed it—Angola, Belarus, Cameroon, Congo, Germany, Italy, Morocco, Nigeria, Poland, Romania, Ukraine, Uruguay, Yugoslavia and Zaire. In accordance with article 19, the Convention was to enter into force on the thirtieth day following the date of deposit with the Secretary-General of the twenty-second instrument of ratification or accession.

The Special Rapporteur recommended that United Nations organs suggest that Member

States adopt measures to abolish mercenary activity and to prosecute and punish mercenaries. He further recommended that all States be urged to consider ratifying or acceding to the 1989 Convention.

GENERAL ASSEMBLY ACTION

On 16 December 1992, the General Assembly, on the recommendation of the Third Committee, adopted **resolution 47/84** by recorded vote.

Use of mercenaries as a means to violate human rights and to impede the exercise of the right of peoples to self-determination

The General Assembly,

Recalling its resolution 44/34 of 4 December 1989 on the International Convention against the Recruitment, Use, Financing and Training of Mercenaries and its resolutions 45/132 of 14 December 1990 and 46/89 of 16 December 1991 on the use of mercenaries as a means to violate human rights and to impede the exercise of the right of peoples to self-determination,

Reaffirming the purposes and principles enshrined in the Charter of the United Nations concerning the strict observance of the principles of sovereign equality, political independence, territorial integrity of States and self-determination of peoples,

Urging strict respect for the principle of the non-use or threat of the use of force in international relations, as developed in the Declaration on Principles of International Law concerning Friendly Relations and Cooperation among States in accordance with the Charter of the United Nations,

Reaffirming the legitimacy of the struggle of peoples and their liberation movements for their independence, territorial integrity, national unity and liberation from colonial domination, apartheid and foreign intervention and occupation, and that their legitimate struggle can in no way be considered as or equated to mercenary activity,

Convinced that the use of mercenaries is a threat to international peace and security,

Deeply concerned about the menace that the activities of mercenaries represent for all States, particularly African and other developing States,

Profoundly alarmed at the continued international criminal activities of mercenaries in collusion with drug traffickers,

Recognizing that the activities of mercenaries are contrary to the fundamental principles of international law, such as non-interference in the internal affairs of States, territorial integrity and independence, and impede the process of the self-determination of peoples struggling against colonialism, racism and apartheid and all forms of foreign domination,

Recalling all of its relevant resolutions in which, *inter alia*, it condemned any State that permitted or tolerated the recruitment, financing, training, assembly, transit and use of mercenaries with the objective of overthrowing the Governments of States Members of the United Nations, especially those of developing countries, or of fighting against national liberation movements, and recalling also the relevant resolutions of the Security Council, the Economic and Social Council and the Organization of African Unity,

Deeply concerned about the loss of life, the substantial damage to property and the short-term and long-term negative effects on the economy of southern African countries resulting from mercenary aggression,

Convinced that it is necessary to develop international cooperation among States for the prevention, prosecution and punishment of such offences,

Welcoming again the adoption of the International Convention against the Recruitment, Use, Financing and Training of Mercenaries,

1. *Takes note with appreciation* of the report of the Special Rapporteur of the Commission on Human Rights;

2. *Condemns* the continued recruitment, financing, training, assembly, transit and use of mercenaries, as well as all other forms of support to mercenaries, for the purpose of destabilizing and overthrowing the Governments of African States and of other developing States and fighting against the national liberation movements of peoples struggling for the exercise of their right to self-determination;

3. *Reaffirms* that the use of mercenaries and their recruitment, financing and training are offences of grave concern to all States and violate the purposes and principles enshrined in the Charter of the United Nations;

4. *Notes with serious concern* the use by the Government of South Africa of groups of armed mercenaries against national liberation movements;

5. *Denounces* any State that persists in, permits or tolerates the recruitment of mercenaries and provides facilities to them for launching armed aggression against other States;

6. *Urges* all States to take the necessary steps and to exercise the utmost vigilance against the menace posed by the activities of mercenaries and to ensure, by both administrative and legislative measures, that the territory of those States and other territories under their control, as well as their nationals, are not used for the recruitment, assembly, financing, training and transit of mercenaries, or for the planning of activities designed to destabilize or overthrow the Government of any State and to fight the national liberation movements struggling against racism, apartheid, colonial domination and foreign intervention or occupation;

7. *Calls upon* all States to extend humanitarian assistance to victims of situations resulting from the use of mercenaries, as well as from colonial or alien domination or foreign occupation;

8. *Reaffirms* that to use channels of humanitarian and other assistance to finance, train and arm mercenaries is inadmissible;

9. *Calls upon* all States that have not yet done so to consider taking early action to accede to or to ratify the International Convention against the Recruitment, Use, Financing and Training of Mercenaries;

10. *Requests* the Special Rapporteur of the Commission on Human Rights to report to the General Assembly at its forty-eighth session on the use of mercenaries, especially in view of the additional elements highlighted in his report.

General Assembly resolution 47/84

16 December 1992   Meeting 89   118-10-36 (recorded vote)

Approved by Third Committee (A/47/659) by recorded vote (96-10-36), 2 November (meeting 25); 14-nation draft (A/C.3/47/L.7); agenda item 92.

Sponsors: Angola, Colombia, Cuba, Ecuador, Liberia, Mexico, Namibia, Nigeria, Sierra Leone, Uganda, United Republic of Tanzania, Viet Nam, Zambia, Zimbabwe.

Meeting numbers. GA 47th session: 3rd Committee 3-10, 13, 20, 25; plenary 89.

Recorded vote in Assembly as follows:

In favour: Afghanistan, Algeria, Angola, Antigua and Barbuda, Armenia, Bahamas, Bahrain, Bangladesh, Barbados, Belize, Benin, Bhutan, Bolivia, Bosnia and Herzegovina, Botswana, Brazil, Brunei Darussalam, Burkina Faso, Burundi, Cameroon, Cape Verde, Chad, Chile, China, Colombia, Comoros, Congo, Costa Rica, Côte d'Ivoire, Cuba, Cyprus, Democratic People's Republic of Korea, Djibouti, Dominican Republic, Ecuador, Egypt, El Salvador, Ethiopia, Fiji, Gabon, Gambia, Ghana, Grenada, Guatemala, Guinea, Guinea-Bissau, Guyana, Haiti, Honduras, India, Indonesia, Iran, Iraq, Jamaica, Jordan, Kenya, Kuwait, Lao People's Democratic Republic, Lebanon, Lesotho, Liberia, Libyan Arab Jamahiriya, Madagascar, Malaysia, Maldives, Mali, Mauritania, Mauritius, Mexico, Mongolia, Morocco, Myanmar, Namibia, Nepal, Nicaragua, Niger, Nigeria, Oman, Pakistan, Panama, Papua New Guinea, Paraguay, Peru, Philippines, Qatar, Republic of Korea, Republic of Moldova, Rwanda, Saint Kitts and Nevis, Saint Lucia, Saint Vincent and the Grenadines, Sao Tome and Principe, Saudi Arabia, Senegal, Seychelles, Sierra Leone, Singapore, Sri Lanka, Sudan, Suriname, Swaziland, Syrian Arab Republic, Tajikistan, Thailand, Togo, Trinidad and Tobago, Tunisia, Uganda, Ukraine, United Arab Emirates, United Republic of Tanzania, Uruguay, Vanuatu, Venezuela, Viet Nam, Yemen, Zambia, Zimbabwe.

Against: Belgium, Bulgaria, France, Germany, Italy, Luxembourg, Netherlands, Portugal, United Kingdom, United States.

Abstaining: Albania, Argentina, Australia, Austria, Azerbaijan, Belarus, Canada, Croatia, Czechoslovakia, Denmark, Estonia, Finland, Greece, Hungary, Iceland, Ireland, Israel, Japan, Kazakhstan, Kyrgyzstan, Latvia, Liechtenstein, Lithuania, Malta, Marshall Islands, Micronesia, New Zealand, Norway, Poland, Romania, Russian Federation, Samoa, San Marino, Spain, Sweden, Turkey.

Rights of detained persons

Administration of justice

On 28 February 1992,[45] the Commission requested its Subcommission to continue its practice of creating a sessional working group on detention to draw up proposals regarding human rights in the administration of justice, and to formulate proposals to the Secretary-General on the utility and format of his reports prepared in pursuance of a 1974 Subcommission resolution.[46] It invited the new Commission on Crime Prevention and Criminal Justice (see PART THREE, Chapter XII) to explore ways of cooperating with the human rights programme in the administration of justice.

In May,[47] the Secretary-General informed the Subcommission that no information had been received as at 20 May 1992 from States, United Nations organs and specialized agencies in response to his request for information relating to the Subcommission's annual review of developments in the human rights of detainees.

Treatment of prisoners and detainees

A five-member sessional Working Group on Detention, established by the Subcommission on 4 August 1992,[48] met at Geneva on 5 and 6 August.[49] It discussed the annual synopses of material received from Governments, specialized agencies and NGOs and proposed that the Subcommission suspend consideration of the item and mandate the Working Group to consider the best procedures to be followed and formulate concrete proposals for the Secretary-General on the utility

and format of his reports prepared in pursuance of the 1974 Subcommission resolution.[46]

In its discussion of habeas corpus as a nonderogable right and as one of the requirements for the right to a fair trial, the Group's attention was drawn to the third report to the Subcommission on the right to a fair trial (see below),[50] which contained an analysis of sources of international norms relating to amparo or habeas corpus, as well as of any derogations. The Group adopted a proposal to establish and maintain a list of countries that practised the death penalty, distinguishing between: countries that had abolished the death penalty under all circumstances; countries that had abolished it only for crimes committed in normal times, excluding crimes committed during a state of emergency or in time of war; countries that had abolished it de facto, by not carrying out sentences handed down, specifying the date of the last execution; countries that had not yet abolished the death penalty; and countries that had abolished it for persons less than 18 years of age.

In connection with a proposal that the Subcommission prepare a study of the practice of abolitionist countries when presented with an application for extradition for acts that might attract the death penalty in the requesting country, the Group recommended that the Subcommission include the question on its agenda.

The Group noted that, in compliance with a 1991 Subcommission decision,[51] the Secretariat had sent letters to Governments, intergovernmental organizations and NGOs reminding them to submit their views on a study of the privatization of prisons, but few replies had been received. In August,[52] the Secretary-General summarized replies received from three Governments and one NGO on the subject. On 27 August,[53] the Subcommission requested Claire Palley (United Kingdom) to prepare an outline of the possible utility, scope and structure of a special study that might be undertaken on the privatization of prisons, to be submitted to the Working Group and the Subcommission in 1993. It asked the Secretary-General to provide her with all the assistance she might need.

Torture and cruel treatment

Report of the Special Rapporteur. In his seventh report to the Commission on torture,[54] Special Rapporteur Peter H. Kooijmans (Netherlands) said that he continued to receive requests for urgent action or information concerning persons who were allegedly being tortured or about whom fears were expressed that they might be. He brought 64 of those cases to the immediate attention of the respective Governments, appealing to them to ensure humane treatment of the persons concerned while in detention. Details on the contents of those appeals and of government replies were given in the report.

The Special Rapporteur reported on a visit to East Timor and Indonesia from 4 to 16 November 1991, in response to Indonesia's invitation, where he had met with government officials and NGOs concerned with human rights, and visited a prison in the Jakarta area.

The Special Rapporteur recommended concerted and sustained action by Governments and professional and human rights organizations. He also made a number of other recommendations, some of which were taken up by the Commission in February.

Human Rights Commission action. On 28 February 1992,[55] the Commission, commending the Special Rapporteur for his report, stressed his conclusions and recommendations concerning: instituting a system of periodic visits by independent experts to places of detention; guaranteeing to detainees by the judiciary their rights in accordance with international and national standards; declaring illegal incommunicado detention; adopting legal provisions giving a detainee access to legal counsel and the right to initiate promptly after arrest proceedings before a court on the lawfulness of the detention; taking strict measures against members of the medical profession who practised torture; interrogating detainees at official interrogation centres, recording such interrogations and forbidding blindfolding or holding; and establishing at the national level an independent authority to receive complaints about torture or other maltreatment. It endorsed the recommendation that those responsible for acts of torture should be brought to trial and, if found guilty, severely punished. The Commission called on all States to sign and accede to or ratify the 1984 Convention against Torture and Other Cruel, Inhuman or Degrading Treatment or Punishment.[56] It extended the mandate of the Special Rapporteur for three years and asked the Secretary-General to provide all the assistance he might require.

On 20 July 1992, the Economic and Social Council, by **decision 1992/228**, approved the Commission's extension of the Special Rapporteur's mandate and its request to the Secretary-General to provide all necessary assistance.

Convention against torture

As at 31 December 1992, 71 States had ratified or acceded to the Convention against Torture and Other Cruel, Inhuman and Degrading Treatment or Punishment, seven of them (Benin, Cambodia, Cape Verde, Croatia, Latvia, Mauritius, Seychelles) in 1992.[3] The Convention was adopted by the General Assembly in 1984,[56] opened for signature in 1985 and entered into force in 1987.[57] The optional provisions of articles 21

and 22 (under which a party recognized the competence of the Committee against Torture, set up under the Convention, to receive and consider communications to the effect that a party claimed that another was not fulfilling its obligations under the Convention, and to receive communications from or on behalf of individuals claiming to be victims of a violation of the Convention by a State party) also entered into force in 1987; 28 parties had made the required declarations. The Secretary-General reported on the status of the Convention as at 10 December 1992.[58]

On 9 September 1992, the Conference of States Parties to the Convention met to consider amendments to the Convention[59] proposed by Australia, by which members of the Committee against Torture would receive emoluments from United Nations resources on terms and conditions decided by the General Assembly.

The amendments were adopted by the Conference and endorsed by the Assembly on 16 December in **resolution 47/111**.

Human Rights Commission action. On 28 February 1992,[60] the Commission urged all States to become parties to the Convention as a matter of priority; it asked all ratifying or acceding States and those States parties that had not done so to consider making the declaration provided for in articles 21 and 22 and to consider withdrawing their reservations to article 20. It requested the Secretary-General to continue submitting annual reports on the Convention's status and to ensure the provision of appropriate staff and facilities for the effective functioning of the Committee against Torture.

Draft optional protocol

Human Rights Commission action. On 3 March,[61] the Commission decided to establish a working group to elaborate a draft optional protocol to the Convention against Torture and Other Cruel, Inhuman or Degrading Treatment or Punishment, using as a basis for its discussion a 1991 proposal by Costa Rica,[62] and requested it to meet for two weeks prior to the Commission's 1993 session. It asked the Secretary-General to invite Governments, intergovernmental organizations, the Committee against Torture, the Special Rapporteur on the question of torture and NGOs to send comments on the draft optional protocol and its implications, for the working group's consideration. It also asked him to invite international or regional bodies experienced in visiting places of detention to submit their observations to the group and to extend all the necessary facilities to the group for its meeting.

Working group activities. The Working Group on the Draft Optional Protocol to the Convention against Torture and Other Cruel, Inhuman or Degrading Treatment or Punishment (Geneva, 19-30 October 1992) discussed the aims, object and purpose of the optional protocol and carried out an initial examination of the draft.[63]

ECONOMIC AND SOCIAL COUNCIL ACTION

On 20 July 1992, the Economic and Social Council, on the recommendation of its Social Committee, adopted **resolution 1992/6** without vote.

Question of a draft optional protocol to the Convention against Torture and Other Cruel, Inhuman or Degrading Treatment or Punishment

The Economic and Social Council,

Taking note of Commission on Human Rights resolution 1992/43 of 3 March 1992,

1. *Authorizes* the establishment of an open-ended inter-sessional working group in order to elaborate a draft optional protocol to the Convention against Torture and Other Cruel, Inhuman or Degrading Treatment or Punishment, which will use as a basis for its discussion the draft text proposed by the Government of Costa Rica on 22 January 1991, and will meet for a period of two weeks prior to the forty-ninth session of the Commission on Human Rights;

2. *Requests* the Secretary-General to extend all the necessary facilities to the working group to enable it to meet prior to the forty-ninth session of the Commission.

Economic and Social Council resolution 1992/6

20 July 1992   Meeting 32   Adopted without vote

Approved by Social Committee (E/1992/103) without vote, 15 July (meeting 7); draft by Commission on Human Rights (E/1992/22); agenda item 17.

Committee against Torture

The Committee against Torture, established as a monitoring body under the Convention, held its eighth session at Geneva from 27 April to 8 May 1992.[64] It examined reports submitted by Italy, Luxembourg, Romania and Uruguay under article 19 of the Convention.

In three closed meetings devoted to its activities under article 20, the Committee studied confidential information which appeared to contain well-founded indications that torture was systematically practised in a State party to the Convention. Under article 22, the Committee for the first time declared admissible a communication from an individual claiming to be a victim of violations by a State party of rights recognized in the Convention. In addition, the Committee discussed a draft optional protocol to the Convention (see above) and its contribution to the 1993 World Conference on Human Rights. Annexed to the Committee's report was a list of States which had signed, ratified or acceded to the Convention as at 8 May 1992.

The Committee held its ninth session, also at Geneva, from 9 to 20 November 1992, examining reports submitted by Afghanistan, Argentina, Be-

larus, Germany, the Libyan Arab Jamahiriya, Mexico, New Zealand, Norway, Ukraine and the United Kingdom. It was agreed that the Committee would participate in the 1993 World Conference on Human Rights and select a representative in April 1993.

GENERAL ASSEMBLY ACTION

On 16 December 1992, the General Assembly, on the recommendation of the Third Committee, adopted **resolution 47/113** without vote.

Report of the Committee against Torture and status of the Convention against Torture and Other Cruel, Inhuman or Degrading Treatment or Punishment

The General Assembly,

Recalling article 5 of the Universal Declaration of Human Rights and article 7 of the International Covenant on Civil and Political Rights, both of which provide that no one shall be subjected to torture or to cruel, inhuman or degrading treatment or punishment,

Recalling also the Declaration on the Protection of All Persons from Being Subjected to Torture and Other Cruel, Inhuman or Degrading Treatment or Punishment, adopted by the General Assembly in its resolution 3452(XXX) of 9 December 1975 and contained in the annex to that resolution,

Recalling further its resolution 39/46 of 10 December 1984, by which it adopted and opened for signature, ratification and accession the Convention against Torture and Other Cruel, Inhuman or Degrading Treatment or Punishment, contained in the annex to that resolution, and called upon all Governments to consider signing, ratifying and acceding to the Convention as a matter of priority, its subsequent resolutions on the status of the Convention, most recently its resolution 45/142 of 14 December 1990, and its decisions 46/428 and 46/430 of 17 December 1991, as well as the Commission on Human Rights resolutions on the subject, most recently resolution 1992/25 of 28 February 1992,

Taking note of the decision taken at the Conference of States Parties to the Convention, on 9 September 1992,[a] to delete paragraph 7 of article 17 and paragraph 5 of article 18 of the Convention and to insert a new paragraph, as paragraph 4 of article 18, by which the members of the Committee established under the Convention shall receive emoluments from United Nations resources on such terms and conditions as may be decided by the General Assembly,

Mindful of the relevance, for the eradication of torture and other cruel, inhuman or degrading treatment or punishment, of the Code of Conduct for Law Enforcement Officials and of the Principles of Medical Ethics relevant to the role of health personnel, particularly physicians, in the protection of prisoners and detainees against torture and other cruel, inhuman or degrading treatment or punishment,

Recalling the adoption of the Body of Principles for the Protection of All Persons under Any Form of Detention or Imprisonment,

---

[a]CAT/SP/SR.4.

Seriously concerned about the alarming number of reported cases of torture and other cruel, inhuman or degrading treatment or punishment taking place in various parts of the world,

Determined to promote the full implementation of the prohibition, under international and national law, of the practice of torture and other cruel, inhuman or degrading treatment or punishment,

Taking note of the decision of the Commission on Human Rights, in its resolution 1992/32 of 28 February 1992, to extend for three years the mandate of the Special Rapporteur to examine questions relevant to torture,

Noting with appreciation the holding of the first session of the open-ended working group of the Commission on Human Rights elaborating a draft optional protocol to the Convention,

1. *Welcomes* the report of the Committee against Torture;

2. *Notes* the status of submission of reports by States parties to the Convention against Torture and Other Cruel, Inhuman or Degrading Treatment or Punishment;

3. *Emphasizes* the importance of the strictest compliance by States parties with their obligations under the Convention;

4. *Stresses* the importance of strict adherence by States parties to the obligations under the Convention regarding the financing of the Committee against Torture, thus enabling it to carry out in an effective and efficient manner all the functions entrusted to it under the Convention, and urges States parties that have not yet paid their assessed contributions to fulfil their obligations forthwith;

5. *Welcomes* the attention that the Committee against Torture has given to the development of an effective system of reporting on the implementation of the Convention by States parties, and especially its revision of its general guidelines for the submission of reports by States parties, as well as its practice of formulating concluding observations after the consideration of such reports;

6. *Welcomes also* the continuing close contacts and exchange of information, reports and documents between the Committee against Torture and the Special Rapporteur of the Commission on Human Rights on questions relating to torture;

7. *Requests* the Secretary-General to ensure the provision of appropriate staff and facilities for the effective performance of the functions of the Committee against Torture;

8. *Reiterates its request* to all States to become parties to the Convention as a matter of priority;

9. *Invites* all States ratifying or acceding to the Convention and those States parties which have not yet done so to make the declarations provided for in articles 21 and 22 of the Convention, and to consider the possibility of withdrawing their reservations to article 20;

10. *Requests* the Secretary-General to submit to the Commission on Human Rights at its forty-ninth session and to the General Assembly at its forty-ninth session a report on the status of the Convention against Torture and Other Cruel, Inhuman or Degrading Treatment or Punishment;

11. *Decides* to consider the reports of the Secretary-General and the Committee against Torture at its forty-ninth session under the sub-item entitled "Implementation of human rights instruments".

General Assembly resolution 47/113

16 December 1992   Meeting 89   Adopted without vote

Approved by Third Committee (A/47/678/Add.1) without vote, 25 November (meeting 49); 38-nation draft (A/C.3/47/L.44); agenda item 97 *(a)*.

Sponsors: Argentina, Australia, Austria, Belarus, Belgium, Brazil, Bulgaria, Canada, Chile, Costa Rica, Cyprus, Czechoslovakia, Denmark, El Salvador, Finland, France, Germany, Greece, Guinea, Hungary, Ireland, Italy, Liechtenstein, Luxembourg, Mexico, Netherlands, New Zealand, Nicaragua, Norway, Poland, Portugal, Romania, Russian Federation, Spain, Sweden, United Kingdom, Uruguay, Venezuela.

Meeting numbers. GA 47th session: 3rd Committee 40, 42-45, 48, 49; plenary 89.

Fund for victims of torture

On 28 February 1992,[65] the Commission on Human Rights appealed to Governments, organizations and individuals to contribute to the United Nations Voluntary Fund for Victims of Torture, established in 1981.[66] It asked the Secretary-General to submit in 1993 a consolidated report on the Fund's activities, entitled "Ten Years of the United Nations Voluntary Fund for Victims of Torture". The Commission also asked him to assist in making the Fund's humanitarian work better known and to inform it annually of the Fund's operations.

In his annual report to the Assembly on the status of the Fund,[67] the Secretary-General said that, at its eleventh session (Geneva, 22 April–1 May 1992), the Fund's Board of Trustees recommended that 71 new grants be made, of which 46—corresponding to 54 projects and sub-projects and representing an amount of $1,304,800—dealt with continuing support for projects approved in the past; another 16 grants, representing some $198,000, dealt with 15 new projects and sub-projects. An additional $110,000 was recommended for two special projects. The total amount of the grants recommended was $1,600,300 for 1992, compared with $2,238,700 for 1991. The projects recommended by the Board, carried out in some 40 countries and benefiting persons from many others, focused on supporting programmes providing direct medical, psychological, social and other assistance to torture victims and their families. The Board also recommended support for training programmes for health professionals on techniques to treat victims of torture, as well as for meetings of health professionals, in which they could compare their experiences.

The Board again recommended that the 1993 World Conference on Human Rights set aside time to meet as a pledging conference for the Fund. It had submitted that suggestion to the Conference's Preparatory Committee in 1991.[68]

During 1992, the Fund received $1,204,340 from 16 States. Contributions were also received from a number of individuals.

GENERAL ASSEMBLY ACTION

On 16 December 1992, the General Assembly, on the recommendation of the Third Committee, adopted **resolution 47/109** without vote.

United Nations Voluntary Fund for Victims of Torture

The General Assembly,

Recalling article 5 of the Universal Declaration of Human Rights, which states that no one shall be subjected to torture or to cruel, inhuman or degrading treatment or punishment,

Recalling also the Declaration on the Protection of All Persons from Being Subjected to Torture and Other Cruel, Inhuman or Degrading Treatment or Punishment,

Recalling with satisfaction the entry into force on 26 June 1987 of the Convention against Torture and Other Cruel, Inhuman or Degrading Treatment or Punishment,

Recalling its resolution 36/151 of 16 December 1981, in which it noted with deep concern that acts of torture took place in various countries, recognized the need to provide assistance to the victims of torture in a purely humanitarian spirit and established the United Nations Voluntary Fund for Victims of Torture,

Alarmed at the widespread occurrence of torture and other cruel, inhuman or degrading treatment or punishment,

Convinced that the struggle to eliminate torture includes the provision of assistance in a humanitarian spirit to the victims and members of their families,

Taking note of the report of the Secretary-General,

1. *Expresses its gratitude and appreciation* to the Governments, organizations and individuals who have already contributed to the United Nations Voluntary Fund for Victims of Torture;

2. *Calls upon* all Governments, organizations and individuals in a position to do so to respond favourably to requests for initial as well as further contributions to the Fund;

3. *Invites* Governments to make contributions to the Fund, preferably on a regular basis, in order to enable the Fund to provide continuous support to projects that depend on recurrent grants;

4. *Expresses its appreciation* to the Governments that pledged a contribution to the Fund at the 1992 United Nations Pledging Conference for Development Activities;

5. *Requests* the Secretary-General to continue to include the Fund on an annual basis among the programmes for which funds are pledged at the United Nations Pledging Conference for Development Activities;

6. *Expresses its appreciation* to the Board of Trustees of the Fund for the work it has carried out;

7. *Also expresses its appreciation* to the Secretary-General for the support given to the Board of Trustees of the Fund by carrying out its decisions on an increasing number of projects;

8. *Requests* the Secretary-General to make use of all existing possibilities, including the preparation, production and dissemination of information materials, to assist the Board of Trustees of the Fund in its efforts to make the Fund and its humanitarian work better known and in its appeal for contributions.

General Assembly resolution 47/109

16 December 1992   Meeting 89   Adopted without vote

Approved by Third Committee (A/47/678/Add.1) without vote, 25 November (meeting 49); 31-nation draft (A/C.3/47/L.40); agenda item 97 *(a)*.

Sponsors: Argentina, Australia, Austria, Canada, Costa Rica, Czechoslovakia, Denmark, Finland, France, Germany, Greece, Hungary, Iceland, Ireland, Italy, Kenya, Liechtenstein, Luxembourg, Malawi, Malta, Morocco, Netherlands, New Zealand, Nigeria, Norway, Spain, Sri Lanka, Swaziland, Sweden, United Kingdom, United States.

Meeting numbers. GA 47th session: 3rd Committee 40, 42-45, 48, 49; plenary 89.

Detention of juveniles

Report of the Special Rapporteur. In June 1992,[69] Special Rapporteur Mary Concepción Bautista (Philippines) submitted her final report to the Subcommission on the application of international standards concerning the human rights of detained juveniles. The report gave an overview of applicable international standards, among them the 1985 United Nations Standard Minimum Rules for the Administration of Juvenile Justice (The Beijing Rules),[70] the 1989 Convention on the Rights of the Child,[71] the 1990 United Nations Guidelines for the Prevention of Juvenile Delinquency (The Riyadh Guidelines)[72] and the 1990 United Nations Rules for the Protection of Juveniles Deprived of their Liberty.[73] The Special Rapporteur updated information contained in her 1991 report[74] concerning successful efforts to implement international standards, observations relating to practices incompatible with relevant international standards and recommendations concerning measures that should be taken by States and the international community to increase recognition and protection of detained juveniles' rights. Her report was based on information received from five Governments and one NGO; she also took into account other material available to her, particularly the documentation of the Eighth (1990) United Nations Congress on the Prevention of Crime and the Treatment of Offenders.[75]

The Special Rapporteur recommended that countries review their legislation and consider the full application of United Nations rules, guidelines and conventions concerning juvenile justice. She emphasized that juvenile justice should be managed by specially trained personnel and that special care should be devoted to children of migrant families and juveniles suffering from mental illness. She also stressed the importance of rehabilitation programmes.

Note by the Secretary-General. In June,[76] the Secretary-General submitted a note on the feasibility of organizing a meeting of experts, under the auspices of the Centre for Human Rights, the United Nations Children's Fund (UNICEF) and the Crime Prevention and Criminal Justice Branch of the United Nations Centre for Social Development and Humanitarian Affairs, on the application of international standards concerning the human rights of detained juveniles, as proposed by the Subcommission in 1991.[74] He stated that, following consultations with concerned organizations, the Secretariat proposed to hold the meeting in the spring of 1993 at Geneva. Proposed topics for discussion included crime prevention and improved treatment of juvenile offenders, measures to be taken within institutions for juveniles and international action.

Subcommission action. On 27 August 1992,[77] the Subcommission asked the Secretary-General to provide all necessary assistance for the meeting of experts and to report on its results.

Detention without charge or trial

Human Rights Commission action. On 28 February 1992,[78] the Commission asked the Working Group on Arbitrary Detention, created in 1991[74] for a three-year period, to investigate cases of detention imposed arbitrarily or otherwise inconsistently with the international standards set forth in the 1948 Universal Declaration of Human Rights[79] or in relevant international legal instruments. It asked the Group to report in 1993 on its activities and to make suggestions and recommendations to enable it better to carry out its task. It called on the Group to continue to seek information from Governments, intergovernmental organizations, NGOs and individuals concerned or their representatives.

Working Group activities. The Working Group on Arbitrary Detention held three sessions in 1992 (Geneva, 23-27 March, 28 September–2 October, 2-11 December).[80] The activities of the five-member group of independent experts consisted of transmitting letters to the Governments of countries where cases of alleged arbitrary detention were reported to have occurred, asking them to make inquiries and inform the Group of the results within 90 days. The Group sent letters to 24 countries concerning 144 cases of arbitrary detention, to which seven countries replied. In addition, the Group received replies to letters transmitted in 1991.[74] The Group also decided to address 11 urgent-action messages to 10 countries. Most of the cases concerned cases of alleged arbitrary detention which had endangered the health or life of the detainees.

In March, the Group decided that it would consider a number of situations involving questions of principle and adopt decisions thereon, referred to as deliberations. Four deliberations were adopted, relating to house arrest; the Group's methods of work (2); and re-education through labour.

The Group stressed the importance of having timely and comprehensive information and of government efforts to bring laws into line with international human rights instruments. It recommended strengthening habeas corpus and proposed that the Commission on Human Rights recommend to any Government which had been requested to rectify a case of arbitrary detention to report within a four-month period following notification of the decision. Annexed to the report were decisions adopted by the Group concerning communications transmitted in 1991 and 1992.

Hostage-taking

On 28 February,[81] the Commission on Human Rights strongly condemned hostage-taking in all circumstances and demanded the immediate release of all those being held. It appealed for respect for the humanitarian action of the International Committee of the Red Cross (ICRC) and called on States to take preventive and punitive measures and to put an end to cases of abduction and unlawful restraint. It asked the Secretary-General, when a State so requested, to use all available means to obtain the release of hostages.

Detained UN staff members

Report of the Special Rapporteur. In July 1992,[82] the Subcommission's Special Rapporteur Mary Concepción Bautista (Philippines) submitted her final report on the protection of the human rights of United Nations staff members, experts and their families. She made recommendations pertaining to information on detained staff members; United Nations action in such cases; compensation for damage suffered; rehabilitation and indemnification of staff members and their families in case of illness, invalidity or death attributable to arrest, detention or abduction; enhanced security measures; and follow-up of the issue. Annexed to the report were lists of staff members, victims of human rights violations, as at 24 June 1992, and of officials assassinated, executed or killed since 1973, as submitted by the Association for the Security and Independence of International Civil Servants.

Human Rights Commission action. On 28 February,[83] the Commission appealed to Member States to respect and ensure respect for the rights of staff members and others acting under United Nations authority and their families, and urged them, in accordance with the 1988 Body of Principles for the Protection of All Persons under Any Form of Detention or Imprisonment,[84] to provide adequate and prompt information concerning their arrest or detention. It further urged Member States to allow medical teams to investigate the health of detained staff members, experts and their families in order to provide them with medical treatment, and called on them to allow representatives of international organizations to attend hearings. It asked the Secretary-General to continue to ensure that the human rights, privileges and immunities of United Nations staff members, experts and their families were fully respected and to seek compensation for damage suffered, as well as their full reintegration. It also asked him to submit in 1993 an updated report on the situation of United Nations staff members, experts and their families detained, imprisoned, missing or held in a country against their will, including those cases that had been successfully settled since the submission of his last report.[85]

In January 1992,[86] the Secretary-General drew the Commission's attention to his 1991 report on respect for the privileges and immunities of United Nations officials.[87]

Subcommission action. On 27 August,[88] the Subcommission adopted a similar resolution on detained United Nations staff members.

Status of special rapporteurs

In response to a 1991 request of the Commission on Human Rights,[85] the Secretary-General reported in January 1992[89] on measures taken to ensure the protection of special rapporteurs and representatives, members of the Subcommission, independent experts and members of the Secretariat accompanying them on mission.

Extra-legal executions

In January 1992,[90] Special Rapporteur S. Amos Wako (Kenya) submitted to the Commission on Human Rights his tenth report on summary or arbitrary executions, based on information received from Governments, NGOs, groups and individuals. He described urgent appeals and other communications transmitted to Governments, together with any replies or observations received from them, and outlined the legal and analytical framework within which he carried out his mandate. His conclusions focused on death threats, deaths in custody, executions following inadequate trial or judicial procedures and extra-legal executions in situations of internal conflict.

The Special Rapporteur recommended that Governments: ratify international human rights treaties relevant to the protection of the right to life; review national law and practice and provide appropriate training to law enforcement, judicial, correctional and military personnel; investigate allegations of summary or arbitrary execution and ensure prosecution of the responsible parties; take measures to ensure the elimination of unnatural deaths in custody; consider establishing an independent governmental body to promote, defend and protect human rights; cooperate fully with ICRC; and make efforts to eliminate the root causes of violence and intolerance.

The Special Rapporteur urged Governments that had received communications from him to reply promptly and fully and consider participating in an exchange of information or inviting him to undertake a mission to clarify allegations. He suggested that the international community ensure that Governments requiring technical or material assistance to eliminate the causes of summary and arbitrary executions and strengthen national mechanisms to protect human rights were provided with effective assistance. He further suggested that the international community respond rapidly and effectively to situations of internal armed conflict and civil strife, which remained the major cause of such executions, and promote information and awareness campaigns to eliminate the root causes of violence. The Special Rapporteur proposed guidelines concerning the procedures and working arrangements of the Centre for Human Rights and the Special Rapporteur. Annexed to his report was a list of instruments and other standards constituting the legal framework of his mandate.

In April,[91] the Special Rapporteur reported on his 1991 mission to Zaire, at the invitation of the Government, to observe a trial (State v. Koyagialo et al) to establish the facts surrounding events in 1990 at the University of Lubumbashi and responsibility relating thereto in connection with loss of life and threats against the life and physical integrity of persons, as well as material damage to personal and university property.

Human Rights Commission action. On 5 March 1992,[92] the Commission, strongly condemning the large number of extrajudicial, summary or arbitrary executions taking place, appealed to Governments, United Nations bodies, specialized agencies, intergovernmental organizations and NGOs to take action to combat and eliminate them. Noting the impending resignation of the current Special Rapporteur, it asked its Chairman to appoint another for three years to continue to examine situations of extrajudicial, summary or arbitrary executions, paying special attention to executions of children. It requested the Special Rapporteur to continue examining such executions and to respond to information he received, particularly when a summary or arbitrary execution was imminent or threatened or when such an execution had occurred. It asked the Secretary-General to provide assistance to the Special Rapporteur and to consider ways to publicize his work and recommendations. It urged Governments to cooperate with and assist the Special Rapporteur and to take measures to lower the level of violence and needless loss of life during situations of internal violence, disturbances, tensions and public emergency.

On 10 April, the Chairman of the Commission appointed Bacre Waly Ndiaye (Senegal) as Special Rapporteur.

On 20 July, the Economic and Social Council, by **decision 1992/242**, approved the Commission's request to its Chairman to appoint a special rapporteur for three years and to the Secretary-General to provide him with the assistance he required.

On 18 December, on the recommendation of the Third Committee, the General Assembly adopted **resolution 47/136** without vote.

Summary or arbitrary executions

The General Assembly,

Recalling the Universal Declaration of Human Rights, which guarantees the right to life, liberty and security of person,

Having regard to the provisions of the International Covenant on Civil and Political Rights, in which it is stated that every human being has the inherent right to life, that this right shall be protected by law and that no one shall be arbitrarily deprived of his life,

Recalling its resolution 36/22 of 9 November 1981, in which it condemned the practice of summary and arbitrary executions, and its resolutions 37/182 of 17 December 1982, 38/96 of 16 December 1983, 39/110 of 14 December 1984, 40/143 of 13 December 1985, 41/144 of 4 December 1986, 42/141 of 7 December 1987, 43/151 of 8 December 1988, 44/159 of 15 December 1989 and 45/162 of 18 December 1990,

Deeply alarmed at the continued occurrence on a large scale of summary or arbitrary executions, including extra-legal executions,

Recalling Economic and Social Council resolution 1984/50 of 25 May 1984 and the safeguards guaranteeing protection of the rights of those facing the death penalty annexed thereto, which resolution was endorsed by the Seventh United Nations Congress on the Prevention of Crime and the Treatment of Offenders in its resolution 15,

Welcoming the close cooperation established between the Centre for Human Rights and the Crime Prevention and Criminal Justice Branch of the Centre for Social Development and Humanitarian Affairs of the Secretariat and the Committee on Crime Prevention and Control with regard to questions relating to extrajudicial, summary or arbitrary executions,

Convinced of the need for appropriate action to combat and eventually eliminate the abhorrent practice of extrajudicial, summary or arbitrary executions, which represents a flagrant violation of the most fundamental right, the right to life,

1. *Once again strongly condemns* the large number of extrajudicial, summary or arbitrary executions which continue to take place throughout the world;

2. *Demands* that the practice of summary or arbitrary executions be brought to an end;

3. *Appeals urgently* to Governments, United Nations bodies, the specialized agencies, regional intergovernmental organizations and non-governmental organizations to take effective action to combat and eliminate summary or arbitrary executions, including extra-legal executions;

4. *Reaffirms* Economic and Social Council decision 1992/242 of 20 July 1992, in which the Council approved the decision of the Commission on Human Rights to appoint a special rapporteur for three years to consider questions related to summary or arbitrary executions and also approved the Commission's request to the Secretary-General to continue to provide all necessary assistance to the Special Rapporteur;

5. *Urges* all Governments, in particular those that have consistently not responded to communications transmitted to them by the Special Rapporteur, and all others concerned to cooperate with and assist the Special Rapporteur so that he may carry out his mandate effectively;

6. *Requests* the Special Rapporteur, in carrying out his mandate, to respond effectively to information that comes before him, in particular when a summary or ar-

bitrary execution is imminent or threatened, or when such an execution has recently occurred, and, furthermore, to promote exchanges of views between Governments and those who provide reliable information to the Special Rapporteur, where the Special Rapporteur considers that such exchanges of information might be useful;

7. *Welcomes* the recommendations made by the Special Rapporteur in his reports to the Commission on Human Rights at its forty-fourth, forty-fifth, forty-sixth, forty-seventh and forty-eighth sessions with a view to eliminating summary or arbitrary executions;

8. *Encourages* Governments, international organizations and non-governmental organizations to organize training programmes and support projects with a view to training or educating law enforcement officers in human rights issues connected with their work, and appeals to the international community to support endeavours to that end;

9. *Considers* that the Special Rapporteur, in carrying out his mandate, should continue to seek and receive information from Governments, United Nations bodies, specialized agencies, regional intergovernmental organizations and non-governmental organizations in consultative status with the Economic and Social Council, as well as medical and forensic experts;

10. *Requests* the Secretary-General to continue to provide all necessary assistance to the Special Rapporteur so that he may effectively carry out his mandate;

11. *Again requests* the Secretary-General to continue to use his best endeavours in cases where the minimum standard of legal safeguards provided for in articles 6, 14 and 15 of the International Covenant on Civil and Political Rights appears not to have been respected;

12. *Requests* the Commission on Human Rights at its forty-ninth session, on the basis of the report of the Special Rapporteur, to make recommendations concerning appropriate action to combat and eventually eliminate the abhorrent practice of summary or arbitrary executions.

General Assembly resolution 47/136

18 December 1992   Meeting 92   Adopted without vote

Approved by Third Committee (A/47/678/Add.2) without vote, 4 December (meeting 58); 40-nation draft (A/C.3/47/L.67); agenda item 97 *(b)*.

Sponsors: Australia, Austria, Belgium, Benin, Bulgaria, Canada, Chile, Costa Rica, Côte d'Ivoire, Croatia, Cyprus, Czechoslovakia, Denmark, Estonia, Finland, France, Germany, Greece, Hungary, Iceland, Ireland, Italy, Japan, Kenya, Latvia, Lithuania, Luxembourg, Morocco, Netherlands, New Zealand, Norway, Poland, Portugal, Russian Federation, Samoa, Senegal, Spain, Sweden, United Kingdom, United States.

Meeting numbers. GA 47th session: 3rd Committee 47-58; plenary 92.

Disappearance of persons

Human Rights Commission action. On 28 February 1992,[93] the Commission extended for three years the mandate of the Working Group on Enforced or Involuntary Disappearances and asked the Group to submit in 1993 a report on its work and recommendations to help eliminate the practice of enforced or involuntary disappearances. It also asked the Group to draw attention to cases concerning children of disappeared parents. The Commission encouraged Governments concerned to consider inviting the Group to visit their countries and asked the Secretary-General to ensure that the Group was provided all necessary assistance, in particular staff and resources, especially in carrying out missions and holding sessions in countries prepared to receive it.

The Economic and Social Council, on 20 July, by **decision 1992/227**, approved the Commission's decision to extend the Group's mandate for three years and its request to the Secretary-General to ensure that the Group received all necessary assistance. On 30 April, by **decision 1992/220**, the Council had authorized the Group to meet from 18 to 22 May 1992.

Also on 28 February,[94] the Commission, commending Governments that had invited any of the thematic special rapporteurs or the Working Group on Enforced or Involuntary Disappearances to visit their countries, encouraged them to respond expeditiously to requests for information. It invited Governments to study carefully the recommendations addressed to them under thematic procedures and to keep the relevant mechanisms informed on progress made in implementing them. The Commission encouraged thematic special rapporteurs and working groups to follow closely the progress made by Governments in their investigations carried out within their respective mandates. It asked the Secretary-General to issue annually a compilation of general recommendations made by special rapporteurs and working groups and to ensure the availability of resources for an effective implementation of all thematic mandates.

On the same date,[95] the Commission, noting the proposed model autopsy protocol prepared under United Nations auspices,[96] decided that it would be desirable to create a standing team of forensic experts and experts in related areas, to be enrolled on a voluntary basis worldwide, who could be requested by Governments, through the Secretary-General, to assist in exhuming and identifying probable victims of human rights violations or in training local teams for the same purpose. It asked the Secretary-General, with the assistance of the Working Group on Enforced or Involuntary Disappearances, to consult with professional organizations to study the practical and financial viability of such a scheme and to develop workable arrangements for its management. The Commission also asked the Secretary-General to inform it in 1993 of progress made.

Working Group activities. The five-member Working Group on Enforced or Involuntary Disappearances, established in 1980,[97] held three sessions in 1992: its thirty-sixth (New York, 18-22 May) and thirty-seventh and thirty-eighth (Geneva, 31 August-4 September and 25 November-4 December).[98]

During those sessions, the Group held 9 meetings with government representatives and 12 with representatives of human rights organizations, associations of relatives of missing persons and families or witnesses directly concerned with reports of enforced or involuntary disappearances. As a follow-up to a 1991 mission to Sri Lanka,[99] three members of the Group visited the country from 5 to 15 October 1992 at the Government's invitation.[100] They reported that the downward trend of disappearances that had begun in 1991 had continued, with 62 cases reported in 1992 versus 146 in 1991.

In 1992, the Group continued to process a backlog of some 12,000 reports submitted in 1991 and received some 10,000 new reports of disappearances in 36 countries. It transmitted 8,651 newly reported cases to the Governments concerned, of which some 4,000 were received in 1992, while the rest were part of the backlog. It also transmitted to Governments 348 cases under its urgent-action procedure, of which 53 were clarified during the year.

Some 6,000 alleged cases of disappearance occurring in the former Yugoslavia were brought to the Group's attention. The Group stated that, in view of the overwhelming dimensions of the situation, it was urgently seeking the guidance of the Commission on Human Rights on how to approach the matter of the disappeared in the former Yugoslavia. (For details of human rights violations in the former Yugoslavia, see below, under "Human rights violations".)

The Group urged concerned Governments to adopt measures to protect those involved in investigating cases of disappearances and to investigate any act which might affect them. It proposed that the Commission request it to integrate the Declaration on the Protection of All Persons from Enforced Disappearance (see below) into its methods of work and to report on obstacles encountered in implementing the Declaration. It was essential, the Group noted, that legislation and practice provide for an expeditious and easily accessible habeas corpus. The Group reported on its assistance to the Secretary-General in his consultations with professional organizations dealing with forensic science, noting that it had met with organizations in the field of medical or anthropological activities. It drew up a preliminary scheme based on suggestions and comments received from several organizations, which it transmitted to the Secretary-General, together with a recommendation that it continue consultations in 1993. The scheme would involve the maintenance by the Group of a list of organizations with experience in human rights and forensic science; the organizations would designate experts to work on different forensic activities.

Annexed to the Group's report was a summary of replies received from Governments and NGOs on the Group's consideration of impunity; the draft declaration on the protection of all persons from enforced disappearances; and graphs showing the development of disappearances for the period 1973-1991 in countries with more than 50 transmitted cases.

GENERAL ASSEMBLY ACTION

On 18 December, the General Assembly, on the recommendation of the Third Committee, adopted **resolution 47/132** without vote.

Question of enforced or involuntary disappearances

The General Assembly,

Recalling its resolution 33/173 of 20 December 1978 concerning disappeared persons, and its resolution 46/125 of 17 December 1991 on the question of enforced or involuntary disappearances,

Deeply concerned about the persistence of the practice of enforced disappearances in the world,

Expressing its profound emotion at the anguish and sorrow of the families concerned, who are unsure of the fate of their relatives,

Concerned by the growing number of reports concerning harassment, ill-treatment and intimidation of witnesses of disappearances or relatives of persons who have disappeared,

Noting with satisfaction the proclamation of the Declaration on the Protection of All Persons from Enforced Disappearance,

Convinced of the need to continue implementing the provisions of its resolution 33/173 and of the other relevant United Nations resolutions, with a view to finding solutions for cases of disappearances and helping to eliminate enforced disappearances, duly taking into account the provisions of the Declaration,

Bearing in mind Commission on Human Rights resolution 1992/30 of 28 February 1992,

1. *Expresses its appreciation* to the Working Group on Enforced or Involuntary Disappearances for its humanitarian work and thanks those Governments that are cooperating with it;

2. *Welcomes* the decision made by the Commission on Human Rights in its resolution 1992/30 to extend for three years the term of the mandate of the Working Group, as defined in Commission resolution 20(XXXVI) of 29 February 1980, while maintaining the principle of annual reporting, and requests the Working Group to continue to fulfil its mandate in a rigorous and constructive fashion;

3. *Invites* Governments to take appropriate legislative or other steps to prevent and suppress the practice of enforced disappearances and to take action at the national and regional levels and in cooperation with the United Nations to that end;

4. *Appeals* to the Governments concerned, particularly those that have not yet replied to the communications addressed to them by the Working Group, to cooperate fully with it, and in particular to reply more quickly to the requests for information addressed to them so that, while respecting its working methods based on discretion, it may perform its strictly humanitarian role;

5. *Encourages* the Governments concerned seriously to consider inviting the Working Group to visit their countries, thus enabling it to fulfil its mandate even more effectively;

6. *Extends its warm thanks* to those Governments which have cooperated with the Working Group and to those Governments which have invited the Working Group to visit their countries, requests them to give all necessary attention to its recommendations and invites them to inform the Working Group of any follow-up measures taken;

7. *Appeals* to the Governments concerned to take steps to protect the families of persons who have disappeared against any intimidation or ill-treatment of which they may be the target;

8. *Calls upon* all Governments to take steps to ensure that, when a state of emergency is introduced, the protection of human rights is ensured, particularly as regards the prevention of enforced disappearances;

9. *Reminds* all Governments of the need to ensure that their competent authorities conduct prompt and impartial inquiries when there is reason to believe that an enforced disappearance has occurred in territory under their jurisdiction;

10. *Requests* the Working Group, pursuant to its mandate, to take into account the provisions of the Declaration on the Protection of All Persons from Enforced Disappearance;

11. *Also requests* the Working Group to give the necessary attention to cases of children who have disappeared and of children of persons who have disappeared;

12. *Calls upon* the Commission on Human Rights to continue to study this question as a matter of priority and to take any step it may deem necessary to the pursuit of the task of the Working Group and to the follow-up of its recommendations when it considers the report to be submitted by the Working Group to the Commission at its forty-ninth session;

13. *Renews its request* to the Secretary-General to continue to provide the Working Group with all necessary facilities;

14. *Decides* to consider the question of enforced disappearances at its forty-ninth session under the sub-item entitled "Human rights questions, including alternative approaches for improving the effective enjoyment of human rights and fundamental freedoms".

General Assembly resolution 47/132

18 December 1992   Meeting 92   Adopted without vote

Approved by Third Committee (A/47/678/Add.2) without vote, 3 December (meeting 56); 43-nation draft (A/C.3/47/L.63); agenda item 97 *(b)*.

Sponsors: Argentina, Australia, Austria, Belarus, Belgium, Benin, Bulgaria, Canada, Central African Republic, Chile, Costa Rica, Côte d'Ivoire, Cyprus, Denmark, Finland, France, Gabon, Gambia, Greece, Hungary, Ireland, Italy, Luxembourg, Madagascar, Mali, Mauritius, Netherlands, New Zealand, Nicaragua, Norway, Panama, Poland, Portugal, Russian Federation, Rwanda, Samoa, Slovenia, Spain, Sweden, Togo, Ukraine, United Kingdom, Uruguay.

Meeting numbers. GA 47th session: 3rd Committee 47-56; plenary 92.

Draft declaration

Working group action. The Working Group on the Declaration on the Protection of All Persons from Enforced Disappearance, established by the Commission on Human Rights in 1991,[101] having completed consideration of the articles of the draft declaration, met on 29 January 1992 at Geneva to adopt the text of the final draft.[102]

Human Rights Commission action. On 28 February,[103] the Commission approved the draft declaration submitted by the Working Group.[102] It transmitted it to the General Assembly, through the Economic and Social Council, and recommended that, after its adoption by the Assembly, the full text of the declaration be disseminated as widely as possible.

ECONOMIC AND SOCIAL COUNCIL ACTION

On 20 July, the Council, on the recommendation of its Social Committee, adopted **resolution 1992/5** without vote.

Declaration on the protection of all persons from enforced disappearance

The Economic and Social Council,

Recalling Commission on Human Rights decision 1986/106 of 13 March 1986, by which the Commission invited the Subcommission on Prevention of Discrimination and Protection of Minorities to reconsider the question of a declaration against unacknowledged detention of persons,

Recalling also its resolution 1991/27 of 31 May 1991, by which it authorized an open-ended working group of the Commission to consider the draft declaration on the protection of all persons from enforced or involuntary disappearances, prepared by the Subcommission,

Expressing its appreciation to the Commission for finalizing the draft declaration,

1. *Decides* to submit the report of the Working Group on the Declaration on the Protection of All Persons from Enforced Disappearance of the Commission on Human Rights to the General Assembly for consideration, with a view to the adoption by the Assembly, at its forty-seventh session, of the declaration contained in the annex to the reports;

2. *Recommends* that, after adoption by the General Assembly, the full text of the declaration be disseminated as widely as possible.

Economic and Social Council resolution 1992/5

20 July 1992   Meeting 32   Adopted without vote

Approved by Social Committee (E/1992/103) without vote, 15 July (meeting 7); draft by Commission on Human Rights (E/1992/22); agenda item 17.

GENERAL ASSEMBLY ACTION

On 30 September,[104] the Secretary-General transmitted the draft declaration on the protection of all persons from enforced disappearance to the Assembly.

On 18 December, the Assembly, on the recommendation of the Third Committee, adopted **resolution 47/133** without vote.

Declaration on the Protection of All Persons from Enforced Disappearance

The General Assembly,

Considering that, in accordance with the principles proclaimed in the Charter of the United Nations and other international instruments, recognition of the inherent dignity and of the equal and inalienable rights of all members of the human family is the foundation of freedom, justice and peace in the world,

Bearing in mind the obligation of States under the Charter, in particular Article 55, to promote universal respect for, and observance of, human rights and fundamental freedoms,

Deeply concerned that in many countries, often in a persistent manner, enforced disappearances occur, in the sense that persons are arrested, detained or abducted against their will or otherwise deprived of their liberty by officials of different branches or levels of Government, or by organized groups or private individuals acting on behalf of, or with the support, direct or indirect, consent or acquiescence of the Government, followed by a refusal to disclose the fate or whereabouts of the persons concerned or a refusal to acknowledge the deprivation of their liberty, which places such persons outside the protection of the law,

Considering that enforced disappearance undermines the deepest values of any society committed to respect for the rule of law, human rights and fundamental freedoms, and that the systematic practice of such acts is of the nature of a crime against humanity,

Recalling its resolution 33/173 of 20 December 1978, in which it expressed concern about the reports from various parts of the world relating to enforced or involuntary disappearances, as well as about the anguish and sorrow caused by those disappearances, and called upon Governments to hold law enforcement and security forces legally responsible for excesses which might lead to enforced or involuntary disappearances of persons,

Recalling also the protection afforded to victims of armed conflicts by the Geneva Conventions of 12 August 1949 and the Additional Protocols thereto, of 1977,

Having regard in particular to the relevant articles of the Universal Declaration of Human Rights and the International Covenant on Civil and Political Rights, which protect the right to life, the right to liberty and security of the person, the right not to be subjected to torture and the right to recognition as a person before the law,

Having regard also to the Convention against Torture and Other Cruel, Inhuman or Degrading Treatment or Punishment, which provides that States parties shall take effective measures to prevent and punish acts of torture,

Bearing in mind the Code of Conduct for Law Enforcement Officials, the Basic Principles on the Use of Force and Firearms by Law Enforcement Officials, the Declaration of Basic Principles of Justice for Victims of Crime and Abuse of Power and the Standard Minimum Rules for the Treatment of Prisoners,

Affirming that, in order to prevent enforced disappearances, it is necessary to ensure strict compliance with the Body of Principles for the Protection of All Persons under Any Form of Detention or Imprisonment contained in the annex to its resolution 43/173 of 9 December 1988, and with the Principles on the Effective Prevention and Investigation of Extra-legal, Arbitrary and Summary Executions, set forth in the annex to Economic and Social Council resolution 1989/65 of 24 May 1989 and endorsed by the General Assembly in its resolution 44/162 of 15 December 1989,

Bearing in mind that, while the acts which comprise enforced disappearance constitute a violation of the prohibitions found in the aforementioned international instruments, it is none the less important to devise an instrument which characterizes all acts of enforced disappearance of persons as very serious offences and sets forth standards designed to punish and prevent their commission,

Proclaims the present Declaration on the Protection of All Persons from Enforced Disappearance as a body of principles for all States and urges that all efforts be made so that the Declaration becomes generally known and respected:

Article 1

1. Any act of enforced disappearance is an offence to human dignity. It is condemned as a denial of the purposes of the Charter of the United Nations and as a grave and flagrant violation of the human rights and fundamental freedoms proclaimed in the Universal Declaration of Human Rights and reaffirmed and developed in international instruments in this field.

2. Any act of enforced disappearance places the persons subjected thereto outside the protection of the law and inflicts severe suffering on them and their families. It constitutes a violation of the rules of international law guaranteeing, *inter alia*, the right to recognition as a person before the law, the right to liberty and security of the person and the right not to be subjected to torture and other cruel, inhuman or degrading treatment or punishment. It also violates or constitutes a grave threat to the right to life.

Article 2

1. No State shall practise, permit or tolerate enforced disappearances.

2. States shall act at the national and regional levels and in cooperation with the United Nations to contribute by all means to the prevention and eradication of enforced disappearance.

Article 3

Each State shall take effective legislative, administrative, judicial or other measures to prevent and terminate acts of enforced disappearance in any territory under its jurisdiction.

Article 4

1. All acts of enforced disappearance shall be offences under criminal law punishable by appropriate penalties which shall take into account their extreme seriousness.

2. Mitigating circumstances may be established in national legislation for persons who, having participated in enforced disappearances, are instrumental in bringing the victims forward alive or in providing voluntarily information which would contribute to clarifying cases of enforced disappearance.

Article 5

In addition to such criminal penalties as are applicable, enforced disappearances render their perpetrators and the State or State authorities which organize, acquiesce in or tolerate such disappearances liable under civil law, without prejudice to the international responsibility of the State concerned in accordance with the principles of international law.

Article 6

1. No order or instruction of any public authority, civilian, military or other, may be invoked to justify an enforced disappearance. Any person receiving such an order or instruction shall have the right and duty not to obey it.

2. Each State shall ensure that orders or instructions directing, authorizing or encouraging any enforced disappearance are prohibited.

3. Training of law enforcement officials shall emphasize the provisions in paragraphs 1 and 2 of the present article.

Article 7

No circumstances whatsoever, whether a threat of war, a state of war, internal political instability or any other public emergency, may be invoked to justify enforced disappearances.

Article 8

1. No State shall expel, return (*refouler*) or extradite a person to another State where there are substantial grounds to believe that he would be in danger of enforced disappearance.

2. For the purpose of determining whether there are such grounds, the competent authorities shall take into account all relevant considerations including, where applicable, the existence in the State concerned of a consistent pattern of gross, flagrant or mass violations of human rights.

Article 9

1. The right to a prompt and effective judicial remedy as a means of determining the whereabouts or state of health of persons deprived of their liberty and/or identifying the authority ordering or carrying out the deprivation of liberty is required to prevent enforced disappearances under all circumstances, including those referred to in article 7 above.

2. In such proceedings, competent national authorities shall have access to all places where persons deprived of their liberty are being held and to each part of those places, as well as to any place in which there are grounds to believe that such persons may be found.

3. Any other competent authority entitled under the law of the State or by any international legal instrument to which the State is a party may also have access to such places.

Article 10

1. Any person deprived of liberty shall be held in an officially recognized place of detention and, in conformity with national law, be brought before a judicial authority promptly after detention.

2. Accurate information on the detention of such persons and their place or places of detention, including transfers, shall be made promptly available to their family members, their counsel or to any other persons having a legitimate interest in the information unless a wish to the contrary has been manifested by the persons concerned.

3. An official up-to-date register of all persons deprived of their liberty shall be maintained in every place of detention. Additionally, each State shall take steps to maintain similar centralized registers. The information contained in these registers shall be made available to the persons mentioned in the preceding paragraph, to any judicial or other competent and independent national authority and to any other competent authority entitled under the law of the State concerned or any international legal instrument to which a State concerned is a party, seeking to trace the whereabouts of a detained person.

Article 11

All persons deprived of liberty must be released in a manner permitting reliable verification that they have actually been released and, further, have been released in conditions in which their physical integrity and ability fully to exercise their rights are assured.

Article 12

1. Each State shall establish rules under its national law indicating those officials authorized to order deprivation of liberty, establishing the conditions under which such orders may be given, and stipulating penalties for officials who, without legal justification, refuse to provide information on any detention.

2. Each State shall likewise ensure strict supervision, including a clear chain of command, of all law enforcement officials responsible for apprehensions, arrests, detentions, custody, transfers and imprisonment, and of other officials authorized by law to use force and firearms.

Article 13

1. Each State shall ensure that any person having knowledge or a legitimate interest who alleges that a person has been subjected to enforced disappearance has the right to complain to a competent and independent State authority and to have that complaint promptly, thoroughly and impartially investigated by that authority. Whenever there are reasonable grounds to believe that an enforced disappearance has been committed, the State shall promptly refer the matter to that authority for such an investigation, even if there has been no formal complaint. No measure shall be taken to curtail or impede the investigation.

2. Each State shall ensure that the competent authority shall have the necessary powers and resources to conduct the investigation effectively, including powers to compel attendance of witnesses and production of relevant documents and to make immediate on-site visits.

3. Steps shall be taken to ensure that all involved in the investigation, including the complainant, counsel, witnesses and those conducting the investigation, are protected against ill-treatment, intimidation or reprisal.

4. The findings of such an investigation shall be made available upon request to all persons concerned, unless doing so would jeopardize an ongoing criminal investigation.

5. Steps shall be taken to ensure that any ill-treatment, intimidation or reprisal or any other form of interference on the occasion of the lodging of a complaint or during the investigation procedure is appropriately punished.

6. An investigation, in accordance with the procedures described above, should be able to be conducted for as long as the fate of the victim of enforced disappearance remains unclarified.

Article 14

Any person alleged to have perpetrated an act of enforced disappearance in a particular State shall, when the facts disclosed by an official investigation so warrant, be brought before the competent civil authorities of that State for the purpose of prosecution and trial unless he has been extradited to another State wishing to exercise jurisdiction in accordance with the relevant international agreements in force. All States should take any lawful and appropriate action available to them to bring to justice all persons presumed responsible for an act of enforced disappearance, who are found to be within their jurisdiction or under their control

Article 15

The fact that there are grounds to believe that a person has participated in acts of an extremely serious nature such as those referred to in article 4, paragraph 1, above, regardless of the motives, shall be taken into account when the competent authorities of the State decide whether or not to grant asylum.

Article 16

1. Persons alleged to have committed any of the acts referred to in article 4, paragraph 1, above, shall be suspended from any official duties during the investigation referred to in article 13 above.

2. They shall be tried only by the competent ordinary courts in each State, and not by any other special tribunal, in particular military courts.

3. No privileges, immunities or special exemptions shall be admitted in such trials, without prejudice to the provisions contained in the Vienna Convention on Diplomatic Relations.

4. The persons presumed responsible for such acts shall be guaranteed fair treatment in accordance with the relevant provisions of the Universal Declaration of Human Rights and other relevant international agreements in force at all stages of the investigation and eventual prosecution and trial.

Article 17

1. Acts constituting enforced disappearance shall be considered a continuing offence as long as the perpetrators continue to conceal the fate and the whereabouts of persons who have disappeared and these facts remain unclarified.

2. When the remedies provided for in article 2 of the International Covenant on Civil and Political Rights are no longer effective, the statute of limitations relating to acts of enforced disappearance shall be suspended until these remedies are re-established.

3. Statutes of limitations, where they exist, relating to acts of enforced disappearance shall be substantial and commensurate with the extreme seriousness of the offence.

Article 18

1. Persons who have or are alleged to have committed offences referred to in article 4, paragraph 1, above, shall not benefit from any special amnesty law or similar measures that might have the effect of exempting them from any criminal proceedings or sanction.

2. In the exercise of the right of pardon, the extreme seriousness of acts of enforced disappearance shall be taken into account.

Article 19

The victims of acts of enforced disappearance and their family shall obtain redress and shall have the right to adequate compensation, including the means for as complete a rehabilitation as possible. In the event of the death of the victim as a result of an act of enforced disappearance, their dependants shall also be entitled to compensation.

Article 20

1. States shall prevent and suppress the abduction of children of parents subjected to enforced disappearance and of children born during their mother's enforced disappearance, and shall devote their efforts to the search for and identification of such children and to the restitution of the children to their families of origin.

2. Considering the need to protect the best interests of children referred to in the preceding paragraph, there shall be an opportunity, in States which recognize a system of adoption, for a review of the adoption of such children and, in particular, for annulment of any adoption which originated in enforced disappearance. Such adoption should, however, continue to be in force if consent is given, at the time of the review, by the child's closest relatives.

3. The abduction of children of parents subjected to enforced disappearance or of children born during their mother's enforced disappearance, and the act of altering or suppressing documents attesting to their true identity, shall constitute an extremely serious offence, which shall be punished as such.

4. For these purposes, States shall, where appropriate, conclude bilateral and multilateral agreements.

Article 21

The provisions of the present Declaration are without prejudice to the provisions enunciated in the Universal Declaration of Human Rights or in any other international instrument, and shall not be construed as restricting or derogating from any of those provisions.

General Assembly resolution 47/133

18 December 1992   Meeting 92   Adopted without vote

Approved by Third Committee (A/47/678/Add.2) without vote, 3 December (meeting 56); 50-nation draft (A/C.3/47/L.64); agenda item 97 *(b)*.

Sponsors: Argentina, Australia, Austria, Belarus, Belgium, Benin, Bosnia and Herzegovina, Bulgaria, Canada, Central African Republic, Chile, Colombia, Costa Rica, Côte d'Ivoire, Croatia, Cuba, Cyprus, Czechoslovakia, Denmark, Finland, France, Gabon, Gambia, Greece, Hungary, Ireland, Italy, Luxembourg, Madagascar, Mali, Mauritius, Mongolia, Netherlands, New Zealand, Nicaragua, Norway, Panama, Poland, Portugal, Russian Federation, Rwanda, Samoa, Slovenia, Spain, Sweden, Togo, Ukraine, United Kingdom, Uruguay, Venezuela.

Meeting numbers. GA 47th session: 3rd Committee 47-56; plenary 92.

Other aspects of civil and political rights

Slavery

Working Group activities. The Subcommission's five-member Working Group on Contemporary Forms of Slavery, at its seventeenth session (Geneva, 4-13 May 1992),[105] chose as its main theme an evaluation of its activities in 1989,[106] 1990[107] and 1991,[108] during which it discussed the sale of children, child prostitution and child pornography, the exploitation of child labour (see below, under "Other human rights questions") and debt bondage; and the prevention of traffic in persons and the exploitation of the prostitution of others. It reviewed developments in other contemporary forms of slavery, including slavery and the slave trade, slavery-like practices of apartheid and colonialism, child soldiers, and the removal of organs from children for commercial purposes.

Human Rights Commission action. On 3 March 1992,[109] the Commission asked the Secretary-General to invite States parties to the 1926 Slavery Convention, the 1956 Supplementary Convention on the Abolition of Slavery, the Slave Trade, and Institutions and Practices Similar to Slavery,[110] and the 1949 Convention for the Suppression of the Traffic in Persons and of the Exploitation of the Prostitution of Others[111] to submit regular reports to the Subcommission on the situation in their countries. It invited States that had not ratified the relevant Conventions to do so, or to explain in writing why they felt unable to. Intergovernmental organizations, relevant United Nations organizations and NGOs were asked to supply information to the Working Group on Contemporary Forms of Slavery. The Commission encouraged its Subcommission to elaborate recommendations on ways to establish an effective mechanism to implement the slavery Conventions on the basis of a 1989 study by the Secretary-General.[112] He was asked to designate the Centre for Human Rights as the focal point for coordinating United Nations activities to suppress contemporary forms of slavery. It asked the Special Rapporteur on the sale of children to examine ways of cooperating with the Working Group and asked Governments to pursue a policy of information, prevention and rehabilitation of women victims of the exploitation of prostitution and to take appropriate economic and social measures to that effect. The Secretary-General was to report to the Economic and Social Council on steps taken to implement a 1983 Council resolution on suppression of the traffic in persons and of the exploitation of the prostitution of others.[113]

Also on 3 March,[114] the Commission approved a number of requests made by its Subcommission in 1991 pertaining to organizational matters of the Working Group. Those requests were also approved by the Economic and Social Council (see below).

Subcommission action. The Subcommission adopted on 14 August a resolution concerning matters considered by the Working Group.[115]

Report of the Secretary-General. In response to a 1983 request of the Economic and Social Council,[113] the Secretary-General submitted in May 1992 a report summarizing information from seven Governments, one regional commission and three intergovernmental organizations on the suppression of the traffic in persons and of the exploitation of the prostitution of others.[116]

On 20 July, the Council, by **decision 1992/263**, took note of the report.

In July, on the recommendation of its Social Committee, the Council adopted **decision 1992/257** without vote.

Working Group on Contemporary Forms of Slavery

At its 32nd plenary meeting, on 20 July 1992, the Economic and Social Council, taking note of Commission on Human Rights decision 1992/115 of 3 March 1992 and resolution 1991/34 of 29 August 1991 of the Subcommission on Prevention of Discrimination and Protection of Minorities, endorsed the approval by the Commission of the requests of the Subcommission to the Secretary-General: *(a)* to send a representative of the Centre for Human Rights of the Secretariat to participate in a Council of Europe seminar on trafficking in persons and prostitution, at Strasbourg from 25 to 27 September 1991, and to report on the results of this seminar to the Working Group on Contemporary Forms of Slavery at its seventeenth session, *(b)* to reassign to the Working Group a full-time Professional staff member of the Centre for Human Rights to work on issues relating to contemporary forms of slavery, to prepare documentation well in advance, to facilitate the representation at the sessions of the Working Group of the largest possible number of intergovernmental and non-governmental organizations with competence in the fields examined and to report on the measures taken for this purpose to the Commission at its forty-ninth session and the Working Group at its seventeenth session, and *(c)* to examine the possibility of organizing the sessions of the Working Group for eight working days during the month of April or May, in order to avoid overlapping with meetings of other working groups of the Subcommission and the burden this places on the Centre for Human Rights and in view of the impossibility of attendance at simultaneous sessions by representatives of Governments and non-governmental organizations.

Economic and Social Council decision 1992/257

Adopted without vote

Approved by Social Committee (E/1992/103) without vote, 15 July (meeting 7); draft by Commission on Human Rights (E/1992/22); agenda item 17.

Also on 20 July, the Council, on the recommendation of its Social Committee, adopted **resolution 1992/10** without vote.

Suppression of the traffic in persons

The Economic and Social Council,

Recalling Commission on Human Rights resolutions 1982/20 of 10 March 1982, 1988/42 of 8 March 1988, 1989/35 of 6 March 1989, 1990/63 of 7 March 1990, and 1991/58 of 6 March 1991, and taking note of Commission resolutions 1992/47 of 3 March 1992 and 1992/74 of 5 March 1992,

Recalling also its resolutions 1982/20 of 4 May 1982 and 1983/30 of 26 May 1983 on the suppression of the traffic in persons and of the exploitation of the prostitution of others, 1988/34 of 27 May 1988 and 1989/74 of 24 May 1989 on the Working Group on Contemporary Forms of Slavery of the Subcommission on Prevention of Discrimination and Protection of Minorities, and 1990/46 of 25 May 1990 and 1991/35 of 31 May 1991 on the suppression of the traffic in persons,

Considering that the report of the Special Rapporteur of the Economic and Social Council on the suppression of the traffic in persons and of the exploitation of the prostitution of others still constitutes a useful basis for further action,

Having examined the report of the Secretary-General on the implementation of Council resolution 1983/30 on the suppression of the traffic in persons and of the exploitation of the prostitution of others,

Noting that only a few Member States, United Nations organizations and other intergovernmental organizations have submitted information on the steps taken to implement the recommendations contained in Council resolution 1983/30,

Gravely concerned that slavery, the slave trade and slavery-like practices still exist, that there are modern manifestations of those phenomena and that such practices represent some of the gravest violations of human rights,

Convinced that the United Nations Voluntary Trust Fund on Contemporary Forms of Slavery will play an important role in the protection of the human rights of victims of contemporary forms of slavery,

Aware of the complexity of the issue of the suppression of the traffic in persons and the exploitation of the prostitution of others, and the need for further coordination and cooperation to implement the recommendations made by the Special Rapporteur and by various United Nations bodies,

1. *Reminds* States parties to the Slavery Convention of 1926, the Supplementary Convention on the Abolition of Slavery, the Slave Trade and Institutions and Practices Similar to Slavery of 1956, and the Convention for the Suppression of the Traffic in Persons and of the Exploitation of the Prostitution of Others of 1949 that they should submit to the Working Group on Contemporary Forms of Slavery of the Subcommission on Prevention of Discrimination and Protection of Minorities regular reports on the situation in their countries, as provided for under the relevant conventions and under Council decision 16(LVI) of 17 May 1974;

2. *Takes note with appreciation* of the report of the Secretary-General on the implementation of Council resolution 1983/30 on the suppression of the traffic in persons and of the exploitation of the prostitution of others;

3. *Requests* the Secretary-General to submit a further report to the Council, at its substantive session of 1993, on the steps taken to implement the recommendations contained in Council resolution 1983/30 by those Member States, United Nations organizations and other intergovernmental organizations that have not yet submitted such information and to make that report available to the Working Group;

4. *Also requests* the Secretary-General to include in that report information on activities of the supervisory bodies of the International Labour Organisation regarding the implementation of provisions and standards designed to ensure the protection of children and other persons exposed to contemporary forms of slavery;

5. *Further requests* the Secretary-General to include in that report information on any operational activities of the United Nations system that can foster the implementation of standards designed to ensure the protection of children and other persons exposed to contemporary forms of slavery and activities that may be geared to the prevention of violations and alleviation of the plight, or rehabilitation, of victims;

6. *Urges* the Secretary-General to ensure effective servicing of the Working Group and of other activities related to the suppression of contemporary forms of slavery and slavery-like practices, and requests him to report to the Council at its substantive session of 1993 on the steps taken in this regard;

7. *Reiterates its request* to the Secretary-General to designate the Centre for Human Rights of the Secretariat as the focal point for the coordination of activities in the United Nations for the suppression of contemporary forms of slavery;

8. *Urges* the Commission on the Status of Women and the Commission on Crime Prevention and Criminal Justice to collaborate closely with the Centre for Human Rights on the issue of the suppression of contemporary forms of slavery;

9. *Welcomes* the establishment of the United Nations Voluntary Trust Fund on Contemporary Forms of Slavery;

10. *Decides* to consider the question of the suppression of the traffic in persons at its substantive session of 1993 under the item entitled ''Human rights questions''.

Economic and Social Council resolution 1992/10

20 July 1992   Meeting 32   Adopted without vote

Approved by Social Committee (E/1992/103) without vote, 2 July (meeting 5); 13-nation draft (E/1992/C.2/L.2); agenda item 17.

Sponsors: Belgium, Czechoslovakia, Ecuador, France, Gambia, Ireland, Morocco, Netherlands, Nicaragua, Philippines, Romania, Russian Federation, Venezuela.

Draft programme of action to prevent the traffic in persons

On 28 February 1992,[117] the Commission on Human Rights endorsed the views of its Subcommission, expressed in a 1991 resolution,[108] on the desirability of launching a programme of action for the prevention of traffic in persons and the exploitation of the prostitution of others. It decided to transmit the draft programme of action to Governments, specialized agencies, intergovernmental organizations and NGOs and asked the Secretary-General to report in 1993 on the comments received.

UN Voluntary Trust Fund on Contemporary Forms of Slavery

On 3 March,[118] the Commission on Human Rights appealed to Governments, organizations and individuals to respond favourably to requests for contributions to the United Nations Voluntary Trust Fund on Contemporary Forms of Slavery, established by the General Assembly in 1991,[119] and asked the Secretary-General to transmit its appeal to all Governments. It also asked him to appoint a five-person Board of Trustees and to assist the Board in its efforts to make the Fund and its humanitarian work better known.

Freedom of movement

The Secretary-General transmitted to the Commission on Human Rights[120] the 1991 report of the Working Group on a draft declaration on freedom and non-discrimination in respect of the right of everyone to leave any country, including his own, and to return to his country.[121]

Population transfer

On 27 August 1992,[122] the Subcommission, recognizing that population transfer, including the implantation of settlers and settlements, constituted a violation of human rights, entrusted Special Rapporteurs Awn Shawkat Al-Khasawneh (Jordan) and Ribot Hatano (Japan) with preparing a preliminary study, for submission in 1993, on the human rights dimensions of population transfer. It asked Special Rapporteur Asbjorn Eide (Norway), in his next report on possible ways to facilitate the peaceful and constructive solution of problems involving minorities, to address the impact of population transfer on the rights of minorities.

Freedom of speech

Human Rights Commission action. On 28 February,[123] expressing concern at the extensive occurrence of detention of persons exercising their right to freedom of opinion and expression, the Commission appealed to States to ensure respect and support for that right. It also appealed to them to ensure that persons seeking to exercise those rights and freedoms were not discriminated against or harassed, in areas such as employment, housing and social services. It asked the two Special Rapporteurs to submit a final report to the Subcommission, together with conclusions and recommendations. The Commission asked the Secretary-General to provide all the assistance they might require.

Report of the Special Rapporteurs. In July 1992,[124] the Special Rapporteurs, Louis Joinet (France) and Danilo Türk (Yugoslavia), in their final report, discussed general points on the right to freedom of opinion and expression and analysed the relationship between the right to freedom of expression and permissible restrictions. They also considered the question of sanctions against persons exercising their right to freedom of expression, and freedom of opinion and expression in the context of the struggle against racism.

The Special Rapporteurs recommended a discussion of the conditions under which the Subcommission could draw up specific safeguard standards, especially with a view to lessening possible risks to democracy of so-called admissible restrictions, and the introduction of a special procedure to assure the protection of professionals in the field of information. The procedure, they stated, could take the form of the appointment of a special rapporteur or working group of the Commission or a request to the Secretary-General to prepare periodic reports on protecting professionals in that field.

Cooperation with UN human rights bodies

Note by the Secretary-General. In February 1992,[125] the Secretary-General, in response to a 1991 Commission request,[126] provided information on specific cases in which persons had suffered reprisals for availing or attempting to avail themselves of United Nations human rights procedures or had been subjected to intimidation to prevent them from doing so. He also described decisions and measures taken by United Nations policy-making organs in that regard. Annexed to the report were allegations of intimidation and reprisal received and processed by United Nations human rights bodies.

Human Rights Commission action. On 3 March,[127] the Commission urged Governments to refrain from acts of intimidation or reprisal against individuals or groups seeking access to United Nations human rights bodies. It requested representatives of those bodies and treaty bodies monitoring the observance of human rights to help prevent the hampering of access to United Nations human rights procedures and to continue to take urgent steps to prevent the occurrence of intimidation or reprisal. It also requested them to include in their reports a reference to allegations of intimidation or reprisal, as well as an account of action taken by them. It invited the Secretary-General to report in 1993 on the subject.

Amnesty

Report of the Special Rapporteurs. As requested by the Subcommission in 1991,[126] Special Rapporteurs El Hadji Guissé (Senegal) and Louis Joinet (France) submitted a working paper on the practice of impunity for perpetrators of serious human rights violations.[128] They discussed the promotion and protection of human rights through anti-impunity measures and presented an analysis of the legal mechanisms and practices facilitating impunity.

Subcommission action. On 27 August 1992,[129] the Subcommission requested the Special Rapporteurs to draft a study to determine the scale of the phenomenon of impunity for perpetrators of serious human rights violations and to propose measures to combat that practice. It decided to consider the preliminary report in 1993 and asked the Secretary-General to provide the Special Rapporteurs with any assistance they might need.

Independence of the judicial system

Human Rights Commission action. On 28 February 1992,[130] the Commission endorsed the Subcommission's 1991 decision to entrust Louis Joinet (France) with preparing a report on practices and measures which had served to strengthen or weaken the independence of the judiciary and the legal profession.[131] It requested the Secretary-General to provide Mr. Joinet with all the assistance necessary to prepare that report.

By **decision 1992/229** of 20 July, the Economic and Social Council approved the Commission's endorsement and request.

Report of the Special Rapporteur. Special Rapporteur Joinet submitted in June 1992 a report[132] containing information received from 14 States regarding cases of measures and practices that had served to strengthen the safeguards of independence and protection of judges and lawyers. It also examined cases of measures and practices that had weakened those safeguards, based on information from 21 States.

The Special Rapporteur concluded that part of his mandate was to find the best method of assessing interference with the independence of the judiciary and the protection of lawyers. He recommended further testing that method to improve the procedure and submission of his final report in 1994.

Subcommission action. On 28 August,[133] the Subcommission endorsed the Special Rapporteur's recommendation and entrusted him with preparing a report for submission in 1994. He was to elaborate on his 1992 recommendations and to follow up the recommendations in his 1991 report.[126] The Subcommission also asked that his report include information on practices and measures that had served to strengthen or weaken the independence of the judiciary and the legal profession in accordance with United Nations standards and examine ways to enhance cooperation and avoid duplication of work of the Commission on Crime Prevention and Criminal Justice and the Subcommission. It asked the Secretary-General to provide the Special Rapporteur with the necessary assistance to complete that report and to transmit its resolution to Governments, intergovernmental organizations and NGOs, including professional associations of judges and lawyers, requesting them to provide specific information on the subject.

Right to a fair trial

Human Rights Commission action. On 28 February 1992,[134] the Commission, having examined a brief report prepared in 1990 by two Special Rapporteurs[135] and their second (1991) report,[131] endorsed the Subcommission's 1991 request[136] that they continue preparing a study on the right to a fair trial: current recognition and measures to strengthen it. The Commission asked the Secretary-General to provide them with any assistance they might require and to transmit the revised questionnaire annexed to their second report to Governments, specialized agencies and NGOs that had not responded to the earlier questionnaire, as well as to associations of lawyers, and to transmit their responses to the Special Rapporteurs. The Special Rapporteurs were asked to submit a third report to the Subcommission later in the year.

On 20 July, the Economic and Social Council, by **decision 1992/230**, approved the Commission's endorsement of the Subcommission's request and its request to the Secretary-General to assist the Special Rapporteurs.

Report of the Special Rapporteurs. Responding to the Commission's request, the Special Rapporteurs, Stanislav Chernichenko (Russian Federation) and William Treat (United States) submitted in May 1992 their third report on the right to a fair trial: current recognition and measures necessary for its strengthening.[137] They discussed the second report[131] and indicated several revisions to it; identified new sources of international fair trial norms issued since July 1991; and summarized the interpretations of fair trial standards by the European Commission and Court of Human Rights and the Inter-American Commission on and Court of Human Rights. They also summarized information on amparo and habeas corpus and presented a supplemental bibliography of material identified since July 1991. As to the questionnaire on the right to a fair trial, the report summarized replies received as at mid-April 1992 from 27 Governments, 4 specialized agencies, 1 intergovernmental organization and 17 NGOs.

Subcommission action. On 27 August,[138] the Subcommission asked the Special Rapporteurs to submit in 1993 a fourth report analysing national practices regarding the right to a fair trial, including information received in response to the questionnaires. It asked the Secretary-General to transmit the report to Fisseha Yimer (Ethiopia) and invited the latter, an expert, to examine the report with a view to making comments on it at the Subcommission's 1993 session.

REFERENCES

[1]YUN 1966, p. 423, GA res. 2200 A (XXI), annex, 16 Dec. 1966. [2]YUN 1976, p. 609. [3]*Multilateral Treaties Deposited with the Secretary-General: Status as at 31 December 1992* (ST/LEG/SER.E/11), Sales No. E.93.V.11. [4]GA res. 44/128, annex, 15 Dec. 1989. [5]YUN 1991, p. 544. [6]E/CN.4/1993/69. [7]E/1992/22 (res. 1992/14). [8]A/47/40. [9]E/1992/58. [10]A/48/40. [11]E/1992/22 (dec. 1992/107). [12]Ibid. (res. 1992/35). [13]YUN 1991, p. 545. [14]E/CN.4/Sub.2/1992/23. [15]YUN 1987, p. 741. [16]E/CN.4/Sub.2/1988/18/Rev.1. [17]E/CN.4/Sub.2/1989/30/Rev.2. [18]E/CN.4/1993/2 (res. 1992/22). [19]E/CN.4/Sub.2/1992/23/Rev.1. [20]E/CN.4/1993/27. [21]E/1992/22 (res. 1992/5). [22]Ibid. (res. 1992/4). [23]Ibid. (res. 1992/18). [24]Ibid. (res. 1992/6). [25]Ibid. (dec. 1992/102). [26]Ibid. (res. 1992/19). [27]Ibid. (res. 1992/20). [28]A/47/433. [29]YUN 1991, pp. 545 & 546, GA res. 46/87 & 46/88, 16 Dec. 1991. [30]S/19835. [31]YUN 1991,

p. 161, GA res. 46/23, 5 Dec. 1991. [32]Ibid., p. 155. [33]E/CN.4/1993/2 (res. 1992/17). [34]E/CN.4/1993/19. [35]E/CN.4/1993/19/Add.1. [36]E/CN.4/1993/2 (res. 1992/10). [37]YUN 1991, p. 793. [38]Ibid., p. 797, SC res. 725(1991), 31 Dec. 1991. [39]GA res. 44/34, annex, 4 Dec. 1989. [40]YUN 1991, p. 551. [41]E/1992/22 (res. 1992/42). [42]YUN 1991, p. 551, GA res. 46/89, 16 Dec. 1991. [43]A/47/412. [44]E/CN.4/1993/18. [45]E/1992/22 (res. 1992/31). [46]YUN 1974, p. 676. [47]E/CN.4/Sub.2/1992/17. [48]E/CN.4/1993/2 (dec. 1992/101). [49]E/CN.4/Sub.2/1992/22. [50]E/CN.4/Sub.2/1992/24/Add.3. [51]YUN 1991, p. 554. [52]E/CN.4/Sub.2/1992/21. [53]E/CN.4/1993/2 (dec. 1992/107). [54]E/CN.4/1992/17 & Add.1. [55]E/1992/22 (res. 1992/32). [56]YUN 1984, p. 813, GA res. 39/46, annex, 10 Dec. 1984. [57]YUN 1987, p. 755. [58]E/CN.4/1993/21. [59]CAT/SP/13. [60]E/1992/22 (res. 1992/25). [61]Ibid. (res. 1992/43). [62]YUN 1991, p. 555. [63]E/CN.4/1993/28. [64]A/47/44. [65]E/1992/22 (res. 1992/27). [66]YUN 1981, p. 906, GA res, 36/151, 16 Dec. 1981. [67]A/47/662. [68]YUN 1991, p. 556. [69]E/CN.4/Sub.2/1992/20. [70]YUN 1985, p. 747, GA res. 40/33, annex, 29 Nov. 1985. [71]GA res. 44/25, annex, 20 Nov. 1989. [72]GA res. 45/112, annex, 14 Dec. 1990. [73]GA res. 45/113, annex, 14 Dec. 1990. [74]YUN 1991, p. 557. [75]A/CONF.144/28. [76]E/CN.4/Sub/1992/20/Add.1. [77]E/CN.4/1993/2 (res. 1992/25). [78]E/1992/22 (res. 1992/28). [79]YUN 1948-49, p. 535, GA res. 217 A (III), 10 Dec. 1948. [80]E/CN.4/1993/24. [81]E/1992/22 (res. 1992/23). [82]E/CN.4/Sub.2/1992/19. [83]E/1992/22 (res. 1992/26). [84]GA res. 43/173, annex, 9 Dec. 1988. [85]YUN 1991, p. 558. [86]E/CN.4/1992/63. [87]YUN 1991, p. 904. [88]E/CN.4/1993/2 (res. 1992/24). [89]E/CN.4/1992/13. [90]E/CN.4/1992/30 & Corr.1. [91]E/CN.4/1992/30/Add.1. [92]E/1992/22 (res. 1992/72). [93]Ibid. (res. 1992/30). [94]Ibid. (res. 1992/41). [95]Ibid. (res. 1992/24). [96]*Manual on the Effective Prevention and Investigation of Extra-legal, Arbitrary and Summary Executions* (ST/CSDHA/12), Sales No. E.91.IV.1. [97]YUN 1980, p. 843. [98]E/CN.4/1993/25. [99]YUN 1991, p. 560. [100]E/CN.4/1993/25/Add.1. [101]YUN 1991, p. 559. [102]E/CN.4/1992/19/Rev.1. [103]E/1992/22 (res. 1992/29). [104]A/47/434. [105]E/CN.4/Sub.2/1992/34. [106]E/CN.4/Sub.2/1989/39. [107]E/CN.4/Sub.2/1990/44. [108]YUN 1991, p. 561. [109]E/1992/22 (res. 1992/47). [110]YUN 1956, p. 228. [111]YUN 1948-49, p. 613, GA res. 317(IV), annex, 2 Dec. 1949. [112]E/CN.4/Sub.2/1989/37. [113]YUN 1983, p. 918, ESC res. 1983/30, 26 May 1983. [114]E/1992/22 (dec. 1992/115). [115]E/CN.4/1993/2 (res. 1992/2). [116]E/1992/49 & Add.1,2. [117]E/1992/22 (res. 1992/36). [118]Ibid. (res. 1992/46). [119]YUN 1991, p. 563, GA res. 46/122, 17 Dec. 1991. [120]E/CN.4/1992/47. [121]YUN 1991, p. 564. [122]E/CN.4/1993/2 (res. 1992/28). [123]E/1992/22 (res. 1992/22). [124]E/CN.4/Sub.2/1992/9 & Add.1. [125]E/CN.4/1992/29. [126]YUN 1991, p. 565. [127]E/1992/22 (res. 1992/59). [128]E/CN.4/Sub.2/1992/18. [129]E/CN.4/1993/2 (res. 1992/23). [130]E/1992/22 (res. 1992/33). [131]YUN 1991, p. 566. [132]E/CN.4/Sub.2/1992/25 & Add.1. [133]E/CN.4/1993/2 (res. 1992/38). [134]E/1992/22 (res. 1992/34). [135]E/CN.4/Sub.2/1990/34. [136]YUN 1991, p. 567. [137]E/CN.4/Sub.2/1992/24 & Add.1-3. [138]E/CN.4/1993/2 (res. 1992/21).

Economic, social and cultural rights

Human Rights Commission action. On 21 February 1992,[1] the Commission requested the Secretary-General to organize, under the 1992-1993 United Nations human rights programme, an expert seminar to discuss indicators for measuring achievements in realizing economic, social and cultural rights, and to promote coordination between United Nations human rights activities and those of development agencies. It asked the Subcommission's Special Rapporteur Danilo Türk (Yugoslavia), when preparing his next report on problems, policies and progressive measures relating to a more effective realization of economic, social and cultural rights, to take into account comments made in the Commission; it asked that priority be given to identifying practical strategies to promote the rights contained in the International Covenant on Economic, Social and Cultural Rights.[2] It asked the Economic and Social Council to identify ways in which international cooperation and technical assistance would contribute to the effective implementation of the rights recognized in the Covenant. The Commission encouraged States parties to the Covenant to support and cooperate with the Committee on Economic, Social and Cultural Rights and urged them, together with the specialized agencies and NGOs, to contribute actively to the Committee's work (for details of the Committee's action in 1992, see below).

Also on 21 February,[3] the Commission endorsed 1991 requests by its Subcommission[4] to the Special Rapporteur to submit his final report in 1992 (see below) and to the Secretary-General to provide him with any assistance he might need.

The Economic and Social Council, by **decision 1992/248** of 20 July, approved the Commission's endorsement of its Subcommission's requests.

Again on 21 February,[5] by a roll-call vote of 43 to 2, with 7 abstentions, the Commission asked the Subcommission to submit the final report of the Special Rapporteur to the Commission in 1993 and asked Governments and interested intergovernmental and non-governmental organizations to provide him with their comments and information about their experience concerning the impact on the enjoyment of human rights of economic adjustment policies arising from foreign debt.

Report of the Special Rapporteur. Special Rapporteur Danilo Türk submitted to the Subcommission in July 1992 his final report on the realization of economic, social and cultural rights.[6] He had submitted a preliminary report in 1989[7] and progress reports in 1990[8] and 1991.[4]

The final report dealt with the need to strengthen economic, social and cultural rights and the obstacles faced in realizing them. It discussed recent developments in World Bank and International Monetary Fund (IMF) policies regarding poverty reduction and the social aspects of adjustment programmes that were beneficial to the realization of economic, social and cultural rights. The report recommended that the Subcommission: continue to appoint special rapporteurs to study specific aspects of those rights; recommend to the Commission the desirability of appointing special rapporteurs to report on and investigate those rights, with mandates similar to those of thematic rapporteurs; address further recommendations to

the Commission encouraging country rapporteurs to examine the situation of non-compliance by States with respect to economic, social and cultural rights; and encourage the Committee on Economic, Social and Cultural Rights to forward specific recommendations to States parties to the Covenant suggesting legislative and policy changes necessary to bring States' practice into full conformity with the Covenant's provisions. Recommendations also were made for action by the Commission (see below), human rights treaty bodies, the Centre for Human Rights, States, the World Bank, IMF and NGOs.

Subcommission action. On 27 August,[9] the Subcommission endorsed its Special Rapporteur's recommendations and, as proposed by him, requested the Commission to consider appointing thematic rapporteurs dealing with specific economic, social and cultural rights and to forward its views to the Committee on Economic, Social and Cultural Rights as to the feasibility of drafting an optional protocol to the International Covenant. It asked the Secretary-General to ensure the widest possible distribution of the Special Rapporteur's progress reports; prepare policy guidelines on structural adjustment and economic, social and cultural rights; invite the World Bank and IMF to consider organizing an expert seminar on their role in realizing those rights; and inform the Subcommission of progress achieved in implementing the recommendations directed towards the Centre for Human Rights.

Covenant on Economic, Social and Cultural Rights

As at 31 December 1992, the International Covenant on Economic, Social and Cultural Rights, adopted by the General Assembly in 1966[2] and in force since 1976,[10] had been ratified or acceded to by 118 States. Angola, Azerbaijan, Benin, Brazil, Cambodia, Côte d'Ivoire, Croatia, Guinea-Bissau, Latvia, Lesotho, Paraguay, Seychelles, Slovenia and Switzerland became parties to it in 1992.[11]

The Secretary-General provided information on the status of ratifications of or accessions to and signatures of the Covenant as at 10 December 1992[12] (see also below, under "Advancement of human rights").

Implementation of the Covenant

Human Rights Commission action. On 21 February 1992,[13] the Commission appealed to all States that had not become parties to the Covenant to do so. It welcomed the efforts of the Committee on Economic, Social and Cultural Rights in preparing general comments on the provisions of the Covenant and encouraged Governments to publish the Covenant in as many languages as possible and to disseminate it widely. It asked the Secretary-General to report in 1993 on the status of the Covenant.

Committee on Economic, Social and Cultural Rights. The Committee on Economic, Social and Cultural Rights, established in 1985,[14] held its seventh session at Geneva from 23 November to 11 December 1992.[15] Its pre-sessional working group, a five-member group established in 1988[16] to meet for one week prior to each session, met at Geneva from 29 June to 3 July.

Concerning the rights covered by articles 13 to 15 of the Covenant (the rights to education, including compulsory education, and cultural participation), the Committee examined reports from Belarus,[17] Hungary,[18] Norway[19] and Poland.[20]

The Committee considered additional information submitted by Panama on articles 6 to 9 (the right to work and to favourable conditions of work, trade union rights and the right to social security);[21] articles 10 to 12 (covering the protection of the family, mothers and children, and the right to an adequate living standard and to physical and mental health);[22] articles 13 to 15;[23] and supplementary information updating those reports.[24] It also considered additional information submitted in response to its request by France,[25] Jamaica,[26] Jordan,[27] the Netherlands,[28] Panama[29] and the Philippines.[30]

Under articles 1 to 15, the Committee examined a report from Italy.[31]

The Committee's general discussion focused on the right to take part in cultural life as recognized in article 15 of the Covenant.

The Committee expressed strong support for drafting and adopting an optional protocol to the Covenant that would permit the submission of communications pertaining to some or all of the rights recognized in the Covenant. It also discussed the problems of the elderly as they related to the realization of rights recognized in the Covenant. On 7 December, the Committee adopted a draft statement for submission to the 1993 World Conference on Human Rights, the text of which was annexed to its report. Also annexed to its report was the status of submission of reports in accordance with a programme established by the Economic and Social Council.

The Council, by **decision 1992/259** of 20 July, noting the longstanding backlog of States parties' reports awaiting the Committee's consideration, authorized, on an exceptional basis, the holding of an extraordinary additional three-week session of the Committee in the first half of 1993. In addition, the Council, by **decision 1992/261** of the same date, approved the Committee's 1991 initiative[4] to send one or two of its members to ad-

vise the Government of the Dominican Republic regarding efforts to promote full compliance with the Covenant in the case of large-scale evictions, subject to the Dominican Republic accepting the Committee's offer.

Right to development

Report of the Secretary-General. In response to a 1991 General Assembly request,[32] the Secretary-General submitted to the Commission on Human Rights a report[33] on the implementation of the 1986 Declaration on the Right to Development.[34] He discussed some conceptual issues regarding the right to development, described measures taken by Governments, United Nations bodies and specialized agencies to implement that right and made proposals to implement and promote that right further. In October,[35] the Secretary-General transmitted his report to the General Assembly.

Human Rights Commission action. On 21 February 1992,[36] by a roll-call vote of 48 to 1, with 3 abstentions, the Commission asked the Secretary-General to submit concrete proposals on the effective implementation and promotion of the 1986 Declaration. It called on the Preparatory Committee for the 1993 World Conference on Human Rights, in examining the relationship between development and human rights, to take fully into account the Declaration.

GENERAL ASSEMBLY ACTION

On 18 December 1992, the General Assembly, on the recommendation of the Third Committee, adopted **resolution 47/123** without vote.

Right to development

The General Assembly,

Reaffirming the Declaration on the Right to Development, which it proclaimed at its forty-first session,

Recalling its resolutions 45/97 of 14 December 1990 and 46/123 of 17 December 1991, and those of the Commission on Human Rights relating to the right to development, and taking note of Commission resolution 1992/13 of 21 February 1992,

Recalling also the report on the Global Consultation on the Realization of the Right to Development as a Human Right,[a]

Bearing in mind the principles proclaimed in the Rio Declaration on Environment and Development of 14 June 1992,

Reiterating the importance of the right to development for all countries, in particular the developing countries,

Mindful that the Commission on Human Rights entered a new phase in its consideration of this matter, which is directed towards the implementation and further enhancement of the right to development,

---

[a]E/CN.4/1990/9/Rev.1.

Reaffirming the need for an evaluation mechanism so as to ensure the promotion, encouragement and reinforcement of the principles contained in the Declaration on the Right to Development,

Recalling its resolution 45/155 of 18 December 1990, in which it decided, *inter alia*, that one of the objectives of the World Conference on Human Rights to be held in 1993 would be to examine the relationship between development and the enjoyment by everyone of economic, social and cultural rights as well as civil and political rights, recognizing the importance of creating the conditions whereby everyone may enjoy these rights as set out in the International Covenants on Human Rights,

Recalling also that, in order to promote development, equal attention and urgent consideration should be given to the implementation, promotion and protection of civil, political, economic, social and cultural rights,

Having considered the comprehensive report of the Secretary-General prepared pursuant to Commission on Human Rights resolution 1991/15 of 22 February 1991 and General Assembly resolution 46/123,

1. *Reaffirms* the importance of the right to development for all countries, in particular the developing countries;

2. *Takes note with interest* of the comprehensive report of the Secretary-General;

3. *Requests* the Secretary-General to submit to the Commission on Human Rights at its forty-ninth session concrete proposals on the effective implementation and promotion of the Declaration on the Right to Development, taking into account the views expressed on the issue at the forty-eighth session of the Commission as well as any further comments and suggestions that may be submitted on the basis of paragraph 3 of Commission resolution 1992/13;

4. *Reiterates* the need for appropriate ways and means, such as an evaluation mechanism, to ensure the promotion, encouragement and reinforcement of the principles contained in the Declaration;

5. *Requests* the Office of the Under-Secretary-General for Economic and Social Development and the Centre for Human Rights of the Secretariat to continue coordination of the various activities with regard to the implementation of the Declaration;

6. *Urges* all relevant bodies of the United Nations system, particularly the specialized agencies, when planning their programmes of activities, to take due account of the Declaration and to make efforts to contribute to its application;

7. *Also urges* the regional commissions and regional intergovernmental organizations to convene meetings of governmental experts and representative non-governmental and grass-roots organizations for the purpose of seeking agreements for the implementation of the Declaration through international cooperation;

8. *Requests* the Secretary-General to inform the Commission on Human Rights at its forty-ninth session and the General Assembly at its forty-eighth session of the activities of the organizations, programmes and agencies of the United Nations system for the implementation of the Declaration;

9. *Calls upon* the Commission on Human Rights to continue to make proposals to the General Assembly, through the Economic and Social Council, on the future course of action on the question, in particular on

practical measures for the implementation and enhancement of the Declaration, taking into account the conclusions and recommendations of the Global Consultation on the Realization of the Right to Development as a Human Right and replies contained in the report of the Secretary-General prepared in accordance with the relevant decisions of the Commission and the General Assembly;

10. *Calls upon* the World Conference on Human Rights and the Preparatory Committee for the Conference to take fully into account the Declaration in examining the relationship between economic and social development, democracy and the enjoyment of human rights and the indivisibility and interdependency of economic, social, cultural and political rights, and the fact that economic and social progress facilitates the growing trend towards democracy and the promotion and protection of human rights;

11. *Decides* to consider this question at its forty-eighth session under the sub-item entitled "Human rights questions, including alternative approaches for improving the effective enjoyment of human rights and fundamental freedoms".

General Assembly resolution 47/123

18 December 1992   Meeting 92   Adopted without vote

Approved by Third Committee (A/47/678/Add.2) without vote, 3 December (meeting 56); 77-nation draft (A/C.3/47/L.49); agenda item 97 *(b)*.

Sponsors: Afghanistan, Algeria, Argentina, Australia, Austria, Bangladesh, Benin, Bolivia, Brazil, Burkina Faso, Cameroon, Central African Republic, Chad, Chile, China, Colombia, Costa Rica, Côte d'Ivoire, Cuba, Cyprus, Democratic People's Republic of Korea, Dominican Republic, Egypt, Ethiopia, France, Gambia, Ghana, Guatemala, Guinea, Guinea-Bissau, Guyana, India, Indonesia, Iran, Iraq, Jamaica, Jordan, Lao People's Democratic Republic, Lesotho, Libyan Arab Jamahiriya, Madagascar, Malawi, Malaysia, Mali, Mexico, Mongolia, Morocco, Myanmar, Namibia, Nepal, Nicaragua, Niger, Nigeria, Pakistan, Peru, Philippines, Rwanda, Samoa, Senegal, Sierra Leone, Singapore, Sri Lanka, Sudan, Suriname, Swaziland, Thailand, Togo, Tunisia, Uganda, United Republic of Tanzania, Uruguay, Vanuatu, Venezuela, Viet Nam, Yemen, Zambia, Zimbabwe.

Meeting numbers. GA 47th session: 3rd Committee 47-56; plenary 92.

Right to an adequate standard of living

Fraudulent enrichment of State officials

On 3 March 1992,[37] by 49 votes to 0, with 2 abstentions, the Commission decided to keep in mind the question of the fraudulent enrichment of top State officials prejudicial to the public interest, the factors responsible for it and the agents involved when discussing the question of the realization of economic, social and cultural rights. It asked the Secretary-General to bring its decision to the attention of the Commission on Crime Prevention and Criminal Justice.

Extreme poverty

Human Rights Commission action. On 21 February 1992,[38] the Commission called on States, specialized agencies, United Nations bodies and other international organizations to continue to make their views on human rights and extreme poverty known to the Secretary-General, and asked him to disseminate that information as widely as possible. It encouraged the Committee on Economic, Social and Cultural Rights to give greater attention to extreme poverty and exclusion from society, and requested its Subcommission to prepare, as a matter of priority, a study on human rights and extreme poverty for submission in 1993.

Subcommission action. On 27 August,[39] the Subcommission appointed Leandro Despouy (Argentina) as Special Rapporteur on human rights and extreme poverty and asked him to submit a preliminary report in 1993. It also asked him to transmit any useful information on the subject to the 1993 World Conference on Human Rights. The Subcommission requested the Secretary-General to assist the Special Rapporteur and to inform him of the conclusions of any consultations held on human rights and extreme poverty with Governments, specialized agencies, intergovernmental organizations and NGOs.

GENERAL ASSEMBLY ACTION

On 18 December, the General Assembly, on the recommendation of the Third Committee, adopted **resolution 47/134** without vote.

Human rights and extreme poverty

The General Assembly,

Reaffirming the Universal Declaration of Human Rights, the International Covenant on Civil and Political Rights, the International Covenant on Economic, Social and Cultural Rights and other human rights instruments adopted by the United Nations,

Recalling its resolutions 44/148 of 15 December 1989 and 44/212 of 22 December 1989, and other relevant resolutions,

Bearing in mind Commission on Human Rights resolution 1991/14 of 22 February 1991, in which the Commission drew the attention of the General Assembly to the contradiction between the existence of situations of extreme poverty and exclusion from society, which must be overcome, and the duty to guarantee the full enjoyment of human rights,

Recalling its resolution 45/199 of 21 December 1990, in which it proclaimed the Fourth United Nations Development Decade, the main concerns of which are the search for a significant reduction of extreme poverty and the joint responsibility of all countries,

Recognizing that extreme poverty is a violation of human dignity and might, in some situations, constitute a threat to the right to life,

Deeply concerned that extreme poverty continues to spread in all countries of the world, regardless of their economic, social and cultural situation, and seriously affects the most vulnerable and disadvantaged individuals, families and groups, who are thus hindered in the exercise of their human rights and their fundamental freedoms,

Stressing the need for a complete and in-depth study of extreme poverty, based on the experience and the thoughts of the poorest,

Taking note with satisfaction, in that regard, of Commission on Human Rights resolution 1992/11 of 21 February 1992 and resolution 1992/27 of 27 August 1992 of the Subcommission on Prevention of Discrimination and Protection of Minorities, in which the Subcommission designated Mr. Leandro Despouy as Special Rapporteur on this question,

Recognizing that the elimination of widespread poverty and the full enjoyment of economic, social and cultural rights are interrelated goals,

Recognizing also that the grave suffering of the vast majority of human beings who live in conditions of extreme poverty requires the immediate attention of the international community and the adoption of specific measures to eliminate extreme poverty and exclusion from society,

1. *Reaffirms* that extreme poverty and exclusion from society constitute a violation of human dignity and that urgent national and international action is therefore required to eliminate them;

2. *Expresses its satisfaction* that the Commission on Human Rights, in its resolution 1992/11, requested the Subcommission on Prevention of Discrimination and Protection of Minorities to undertake a study of extreme poverty and, in particular, of the following aspects: the effects of extreme poverty on the enjoyment and exercise of all human rights and fundamental freedoms of those experiencing it; the efforts of the poorest to achieve the exercise of those rights and to participate fully in the development of the society in which they live; the conditions in which the poorest may effectively convey their experience and their thoughts and become partners in the realization of human rights; and the means of ensuring a better understanding of the experience and thoughts of the poorest and of the persons working with them;

3. *Again calls upon* States, the specialized agencies, United Nations bodies and other international organizations, including intergovernmental organizations, to give the necessary attention to this problem;

4. *Notes with appreciation* the specific measures taken by the United Nations Children's Fund to mitigate the effects of extreme poverty on children and the efforts of the United Nations Development Programme to give priority to the search for some means of alleviating poverty within the framework of the relevant resolutions;

5. *Decides* to consider this question further at its forty-ninth session under the sub-item entitled ''Human rights questions, including alternative approaches for improving the effective enjoyment of human rights and fundamental freedoms''.

General Assembly resolution 47/134

18 December 1992   Meeting 92   Adopted without vote

Approved by Third Committee (A/47/678/Add.2) without vote, 4 December (meeting 57); 22-nation draft (A/C.3/47/L.65); agenda item 97 *(b)*.

Sponsors: Bahamas, Bolivia, Cameroon, Colombia, Cuba, Dominican Republic, Ecuador, Ethiopia, France, Guinea-Bissau, Mali, Mexico, Morocco, Nigeria, Peru, Philippines, Samoa, Senegal, Spain, Uganda, Uruguay, Venezuela.

Meeting numbers. GA 47th session: 3rd Committee 47-57; plenary 92.

Right to own property

Report of the independent expert. In January 1992,[40] independent expert Luis Valencia Rodríguez (Ecuador) submitted a preliminary report on the means whereby the right of everyone to own property alone as well as in association with others served to foster, strengthen and enhance the exercise of other human rights and fundamental freedoms. He discussed measures taken by United Nations bodies and listed United Nations and regional instruments relating to the right to property. He also noted a number of basic conceptual issues that should be highlighted in the final report.

Human Rights Commission action. The Commission on Human Rights, on 28 February,[41] asked the Secretary-General to assist the independent expert and to transmit his preliminary report to all Member States and interested intergovernmental and non-governmental organizations, requesting them to submit their comments. It would examine the expert's report in 1993.

In July,[42] the Secretary-General informed the General Assembly that, as requested, he had transmitted the preliminary report and asked for comments.

Right to adequate housing

In a June working paper,[43] the Subcommission's expert on the right to adequate housing, Rajindar Sachar (India), identified some of the central issues affecting the realization of that right. He recommended carrying out a longer-term study on the topic.

Subcommission action. On 27 August,[44] the Subcommission appointed Mr. Sachar as Special Rapporteur on promoting the realization of the right to adequate housing and requested him to carry out a two-year study and to submit a progress report in 1993. The Subcommission asked the Secretary-General to request Governments, United Nations bodies, specialized agencies, intergovernmental organizations and NGOs to provide information to the Special Rapporteur. It also asked him to assist the Special Rapporteur in preparing the study.

Forced evictions

On 27 August,[45] the Subcommission recommended a draft resolution on forced evictions to the Commission, by which it would ask the Secretary-General to transmit the text to Governments, United Nations bodies, regional and intergovernmental organizations, NGOs and community-based organizations, soliciting their views and comments. It would also ask him to submit in 1994 an analytical report on forced evictions, based on that information as well as on international law and jurisprudence.

REFERENCES

[1]E/1992/22 (res. 1992/10). [2]YUN 1966, p. 419, GA res. 2200 A (XXI), annex, 16 Dec. 1966. [3]E/1992/22 (dec. 1992/103). [4]YUN 1991, p. 568. [5]E/1992/22 (res. 1992/9). [6]E/CN.4/Sub.2/1992/16. [7]E/CN.4/Sub.2/1989/19. [8]E/CN.4/Sub.2/1990/19. [9]E/CN.4/1993/2 (res. 1992/29). [10]YUN 1976, p. 609. [11]*Multilateral Treaties Deposited with the Secretary-General: Status as at 31 December 1992* (ST/LEG/SER.E/11), Sales No. E.93.V.11. [12]E/CN.4/1993/69. [13]E/1992/22 (res. 1992/14). [14]YUN 1985, p. 878, ESC res. 1985/17, 28 May 1985. [15]E/1993/22. [16]ESC res. 1988/4, 24 May 1988. [17]E/1990/7/Add.5. [18]E/1990/7/Add.10. [19]E/1990/7/Add.7. [20]E/1990/7/Add.9. [21]E/1984/6/Add.19. [22]E/1986/4/Add.22. [23]E/1988/5/Add.9. [24]E/1989/5/Add.5. [25]E/1989/5/Add.1. [26]E/1989/5/Add.4. [27]E/1989/5/Add.6. [28]E/1989/5/Add.2. [29]E/1989/5/Add.8. [30]E/1989/5/Add.7. [31]E/1990/6/Add.2. [32]YUN 1991, p. 569, GA res. 46/123, 17 Dec. 1991. [33]E/CN.4/1992/10. [34]YUN 1986, p. 717, GA res. 41/128, annex, 4 Dec. 1986. [35]A/47/504. [36]E/1992/22 (res. 1992/13). [37]Ibid. (res. 1992/50). [38]Ibid. (res. 1992/11). [39]E/CN.4/1993/2 (res. 1992/27). [40]E/CN.4/1992/9. [41]E/1992/22 (res. 1992/21). [42]A/47/353. [43]E/CN.4/Sub.2/1992/15. [44]E/CN.4/1993/2 (res. 1992/26). [45]Ibid. (res. 1992/14).

Advancement of human rights

On 18 December 1992, the General Assembly, on the recommendation of the Third Committee, adopted **resolution 47/137** by recorded vote.

Alternative approaches and ways and means within the United Nations system for improving the effective enjoyment of human rights and fundamental freedoms

The General Assembly,

Recalling that in the Charter of the United Nations the peoples of the United Nations declared their determination to reaffirm faith in fundamental human rights, in the dignity and worth of the human person and in the equal rights of men and women and of nations large and small and to employ international machinery for the promotion of the economic and social advancement of all peoples,

Recalling also the purposes and principles of the Charter to achieve international cooperation in solving international problems of an economic, social, cultural or humanitarian character and in promoting and encouraging respect for human rights and for fundamental freedoms for all without distinction as to race, sex, language or religion,

Emphasizing the significance and validity of the Universal Declaration of Human Rights and of the International Covenants on Human Rights in promoting respect for and observance of human rights and fundamental freedoms,

Recalling its resolution 32/130 of 16 December 1977, in which it decided that the approach to future work within the United Nations system with respect to human rights questions should take into account the concepts set forth in that resolution,

Noting with concern that many of the principles enunciated in resolution 32/130 have not yet been taken into consideration by the international community with all the necessary dynamism and objectivity,

Emphasizing the special importance of the purposes and principles proclaimed in the Declaration on the Right to Development, contained in the annex to its resolution 41/128 of 4 December 1986,

Recalling its resolutions concerning the right to development, and also its resolution 45/155 of 18 December 1990, in which it decided that one of the objectives of the World Conference on Human Rights to be held in 1993 would be to examine the relation between development and the enjoyment of economic, social and cultural rights as well as civil and political rights, recognizing the importance of creating the conditions whereby everyone may enjoy those rights,

Taking into account the final documents of the Tenth Conference of Heads of State or Government of Non-Aligned Countries, held at Jakarta from 1 to 6 September 1992,

Reiterating that the right to development is an inalienable human right and that equality of development opportunities is a prerogative both of nations and of individuals within nations,

Expressing its particular concern about the progressive worsening of living conditions in the developing world and the negative impact thereof on the full enjoyment of human rights, and especially about the very serious economic situation of the African continent and the disastrous effects of the heavy burden of the external debt for the peoples of Africa, Asia and Latin America,

Reiterating its profound conviction that all human rights and fundamental freedoms are indivisible and interdependent and that equal attention and urgent consideration should be given to the implementation, promotion and protection of civil and political rights and of economic, social and cultural rights,

Deeply convinced that today more than ever, economic and social development and human rights are complementary elements leading to the same goal, that is, the maintenance of peace and justice among nations as the foundation for the ideals of freedom and well-being to which mankind aspires,

Reiterating that cooperation among all nations on the basis of respect for the independence, sovereignty and territorial integrity of each State, including the right of every people to choose freely its own socio-economic and political system, is essential for the promotion of peace and development,

Convinced that the primary aim of such international cooperation must be the achievement by all human beings of a life of freedom and dignity and freedom from want,

Considering that the efforts of the developing countries for their own development should be supported by an increased flow of resources and by the adoption of appropriate and substantive measures for creating an external environment conducive to such development,

1. *Reiterates its request* that the Commission on Human Rights should continue its current work on overall analysis with a view to further promoting and strengthening human rights and fundamental freedoms, including the question of the programme and working methods of the Commission, and on the overall analysis of the alternative approaches and ways and means for improving the effective enjoyment of human rights and fundamental freedoms in accordance with the provisions and ideas set forth in General Assembly resolution 32/130;

2. *Affirms* that a primary aim of international cooperation in the field of human rights is a life of freedom, dignity and peace for all peoples and for every human being, that all human rights and fundamental freedoms are indivisible and interrelated and that the promotion and protection of one category of rights should never exempt or excuse States from promoting and protecting the others;

3. *Reaffirms* that equal attention and urgent consideration should be given to the implementation, promo-

tion and protection of civil and political rights and of economic, social and cultural rights;

4. *Reiterates once again* that the international community should accord, or continue to accord, priority to the search for solutions to mass and flagrant violations of human rights of peoples and individuals affected by situations such as those mentioned in paragraph 1 *(e)* of General Assembly resolution 32/130, paying due attention also to other situations of violations of human rights;

5. *Considers* that the issues mentioned in paragraph 4 above should be approached with due attention in the preparatory work for the World Conference on Human Rights so as to evaluate during the Conference the obstacles to achieving progress in the field of human rights;

6. *Reaffirms* that the right to development is an inalienable human right;

7. *Reaffirms also* that international peace and security are essential elements for achieving full realization of the right to development;

8. *Recognizes* that all human rights and fundamental freedoms are indivisible and interdependent;

9. *Considers it necessary* for all Member States to promote international cooperation on the basis of respect for the independence, sovereignty and territorial integrity of each State, including the right of every people to choose freely its own socio-economic and political system, with a view to solving international economic, social and humanitarian problems;

10. *Urges* all States to cooperate with the Commission on Human Rights in the promotion and protection of human rights and fundamental freedoms;

11. *Reaffirms once again* that, in order to facilitate the full enjoyment of all human rights without diminishing personal dignity, it is necessary to promote the rights to education, work, health and proper nourishment through the adoption of measures at the national level, including those that provide for the right of workers to participate in management, as well as the adoption of measures at the international level, entailing a restructuring of existing international economic relations;

12. *Decides* that the approaches to future work within the United Nations system on human rights matters should take into account the content of the Declaration on the Right to Development and the need for the implementation thereof;

13. *Decides* to consider this question at its forty-eighth session.

General Assembly resolution·47/137

18 December 1992   Meeting 92   115-0-48 (recorded vote)

Approved by Third Committee (A/47/678/Add.2) by recorded vote (102-0-49), 4 December (meeting 58); 27-nation draft (A/C.3/47/L.68); agenda item 97 *(b)*.

Sponsors: Algeria, Angola, Burkina Faso, Central African Republic, Colombia, Cuba, Cyprus, Democratic People's Republic of Korea, Ecuador, Guinea, Guinea-Bissau, India, Iraq, Lao People's Democratic Republic, Lesotho, Libyan Arab Jamahiriya, Mexico, Namibia, Nigeria, Peru, Sierra Leone, Sudan, Uganda, Viet Nam, Yemen, Zambia, Zimbabwe.

Meeting numbers. GA 47th session: 3rd Committee 47-58; plenary 92.

Recorded vote in Assembly as follows:

In favour: Afghanistan, Algeria, Angola, Antigua and Barbuda, Armenia, Bahamas, Bahrain, Bangladesh, Barbados, Belize, Benin, Bhutan, Bolivia, Botswana, Brazil, Brunei Darussalam, Burkina Faso, Burundi, Cameroon, Cape Verde, Central African Republic, Chad, Chile, China, Colombia, Comoros, Congo, Costa Rica, Côte d'Ivoire, Cuba, Cyprus, Democratic People's Republic of Korea, Djibouti, Dominica, Dominican Republic, Ecuador, Egypt, El Salvador, Ethiopia, Gabon, Gambia, Ghana, Grenada, Guatemala, Guinea, Guinea-Bissau, Guyana, Haiti, Honduras, India, Indonesia, Iran, Iraq, Jamaica, Jordan, Kenya, Kuwait, Lao People's Democratic Republic, Lebanon, Lesotho, Liberia, Libyan Arab Jamahiriya, Madagascar, Malawi, Malaysia, Maldives, Mali, Mauritania, Mauritius, Mexico, Mongolia, Morocco, Mozambique, Myanmar, Namibia, Nepal, New Zealand, Nicaragua, Niger, Nigeria, Oman, Pakistan, Papua New Guinea, Paraguay, Peru, Qatar, Republic of Korea, Rwanda, Saint Kitts and Nevis, Saint Lucia, Saint Vincent and the Grenadines, Sao Tome and Principe, Saudi Arabia, Senegal, Seychelles, Sierra Leone, Singapore, Sri Lanka, Sudan, Suriname, Swaziland, Syrian Arab Republic, Thailand, Trinidad and Tobago, Tunisia, Uganda, United Arab Emirates, United Republic of Tanzania, Uruguay, Vanuatu, Venezuela, Viet Nam, Yemen, Zambia, Zimbabwe.

Against: None.

Abstaining: Argentina, Australia, Austria, Azerbaijan, Belarus, Belgium, Bulgaria, Canada, Croatia, Czechoslovakia, Denmark, Estonia, Finland, France, Germany, Greece, Hungary, Iceland, Ireland, Israel, Italy, Japan, Kazakhstan, Latvia, Liechtenstein, Lithuania, Luxembourg, Malta, Marshall Islands, Netherlands, Norway, Panama, Philippines, Poland, Portugal, Republic of Moldova, Romania, Russian Federation, Samoa, Slovenia, Solomon Islands, Spain, Sweden, Togo, Turkey, Ukraine, United Kingdom, United States.

National institutions for human rights protection

On 3 March,[1] the Commission welcomed the principles relating to the status of commissions and their advisory role, as contained in the report of the International Workshop on National Institutions for the Promotion and Protection of Human Rights (Paris, 7-9 October 1991),[2] and decided to rename them the principles relating to the status of national institutions. It further decided to transmit the principles, which were annexed to its resolution, to the General Assembly, through the Economic and Social Council, for adoption. The Commission asked the Secretary-General to publicize the proceedings of the workshop and undertake follow-up activities, transmit the proceedings to the Preparatory Committee for the 1993 World Conference on Human Rights and consider the results of the workshop in preparing a manual on national institutions. It also asked him to begin planning a follow-up international workshop in 1993, following the World Conference on Human Rights, and to submit a report in 1993 on those preparations. It asked the Preparatory Committee of the World Conference to consider ways to promote the principles relating to the status of national institutions.

The Economic and Social Council, by **decision 1992/233** of 20 July, approved the Commission's request that the Secretary-General publicize the proceedings of the 1991 international workshop, undertake follow-up activities, begin planning a follow-up international workshop in 1993, following the World Conference on Human Rights, and submit a report on those preparations to the Commission in 1993. It decided to transmit to the General Assembly for adoption the principles annexed to the Commission's resolution.

By a November note,[3] the Secretary-General transmitted those principles to the General Assembly. On 18 December, the Assembly, by **decision 47/431**, took note of the Secretary-General's note.

UN machinery

Commission on Human Rights

The Commission on Human Rights held its forty-eighth session at Geneva from 27 January to 6 March 1992. At that session, it adopted 83 resolutions and 19 decisions. In addition, the Commission recommended for adoption by the Economic and Social Council 7 draft resolutions and 34 draft decisions. The Commission also held its first special session in 1992 (Geneva, 13 and 14 August) to discuss the dangerous situation in the former Yugoslavia (see below). A second special session on the same matter was held, also at Geneva, on 30 November and 1 December (see below).

The Economic and Social Council, by **decision 1992/264** of 20 July, took note of the Commission's report on its forty-eighth session.[4]

With regard to the organization of its work, the Commission decided to consider a report on the situation of human rights in Guatemala[5] under agenda item 19,[6] request the Economic and Social Council to bring forward its consideration of draft decisions adopted by the Commission at its 1992 session and relating to mandates requiring the Council's approval,[7] and invite a number of experts, special rapporteurs, special representatives and chairman-rapporteurs of working groups to participate in the meetings at which their reports were to be considered.[8]

On 6 March,[9] the Commission expressed its gratitude to the United Nations Under-Secretary-General for Human Rights, Jan Martenson (Sweden), for his services and dedication.

Emergency mechanism of the Commission

On 3 March,[10] the Commission considered that an emergency mechanism of the Commission would enable the United Nations to react appropriately and immediately to acute situations arising from gross human rights violations wherever and whenever they occurred. Recalling a 1990 Economic and Social Council resolution[11] on the enlargement of the Commission and the further promotion of human rights and fundamental freedoms, and bearing in mind the General Assembly's approval in 1991 of the Declaration on Fact-finding by the United Nations in the Field of the Maintenance of International Peace and Security,[12] the Commission took note of a proposal to establish an emergency mechanism of the Commission as outlined in an annex to its resolution and decided to resume consideration of the proposed mechanism in 1993.

Organization of the work of the 1993 session

On 6 March,[13] the Commission recommended that the Economic and Social Council authorize 40 fully serviced additional meetings for the Commission's forty-ninth (1993) session, and requested that the Chairman make every effort to organize the session's work within the time normally allotted, the additional meetings to be utilized only if absolutely necessary.

On 20 July, by **decision 1992/258**, the Council approved the request.

Revised 1993 provisional agenda and rationalization of work

The Commission on Human Rights, on 6 March,[14] recalling its 1991 decision on guidelines for a revised provisional agenda for 1993,[15] stated that the revision of its agenda should be paralleled with a rationalization of its work. The Commission decided to consider the rationalization of its work at the beginning of its 1993 session.

Administrative measures related to mandates

By **decision 1992/221** of 29 May, the Economic and Social Council authorized the Secretariat to take provisional administrative measures related to the mandates adopted by the Commission on Human Rights in 1992 on a temporary basis and until a formal decision on those mandates was taken by the Council.

Subcommission on Prevention of Discrimination and Protection of Minorities

Subcommission session

The Subcommission on Prevention of Discrimination and Protection of Minorities held its forty-fourth session at Geneva from 3 to 28 August 1992.[16] At that session, it adopted 39 resolutions and 12 decisions. In addition, it recommended to the Commission on Human Rights, its parent body, 8 draft resolutions and 13 decisions for adoption.

The Subcommission adopted decisions relating to the composition of its pre-sessional working groups,[17] methods of voting under agenda item 6 (violations of human rights and fundamental freedoms)[18] and its 1993 provisional agenda.[19] It also decided to invite a number of experts and special rapporteurs to participate in the meetings at which their reports were to be considered.[20]

Report of the Subcommission Chairman. In February,[22] the Subcommission's 1991 Chairman, Louis Joinet (France), submitted a report on the implementation of guidelines for the Subcommission provided by the Commission in 1991.[15]

Human Rights Commission action. On 4 March,[22] the Commission, by a roll-call vote of 40 to none with 11 abstentions, endorsed the Subcommission's establishment in 1991,[15] on an exceptional basis, of an inter-sessional Working Group on the rationalization of its work and agenda and asked the Group to make a series of recommendations on a number of points (see below). The Commission invited the Subcommission's 1991 Chairman to consult with the members of the Bureau of the Commission at the end of its 1992 session and the 1992 Chairman to report to the Commission in 1993 on the Subcommission's implementation of the resolution.

On 20 July, the Economic and Social Council, by **decision 1992/238**, approved the Commission's endorsement of the establishment of an inter-sessional Working Group and approved its invitations to the 1991 and 1992 Subcommission Chairmen.

Report of the inter-sessional Working Group. The five-member inter-sessional Working Group on the methods of work of the Subcommission (Geneva, 11-15 May)[23] focused on rationalizing methods of work, restructuring the agenda, coordinating with the Commission and other United Nations human rights bodies, and the independence of experts. The Group adopted a draft decision containing guidelines on the Subcommission's methods of work, which the Subcommission adopted on 26 August.[24] The Group made proposals on restructuring the Subcommission's agenda and on improving coordination with the Commission and other United Nations human rights bodies. It also discussed publicity for the Subcommission's work.

Election of Subcommission members

Between December 1991 and February 1992, the Secretary-General submitted to the Commission the names of candidates and alternates nominated by Governments for election to the Subcommission, along with relevant biographical data.[25] In accordance with a 1986 Economic and Social Council resolution,[26] the Commission elected by secret ballot 13 members (half of the membership) of the Subcommission, and their corresponding alternates, if any, for a period of four years (see APPENDIX III).

Strengthening the Centre for Human Rights

Human Rights Commission action. On 3 March,[27] the Commission on Human Rights recognized that the workload of the Centre for Human Rights had greatly increased while resources had failed to keep pace with the expansion of its responsibilities, as noted in reports of the Secretary-General.[28] It asked the Secretary-General to take into account, when preparing the 1994-1995 budget outline, that adequate resources were projected for human rights, particularly for the Centre, and decided to consider the question again in 1993.

Reports of the Secretary-General. In accordance with a 1991 General Assembly request,[29] the Secretary-General submitted to the Commission, in February, an interim report on developments relating to the activities of the Centre for Human Rights,[30] and, in November, a final report to the General Assembly.[31]

In February, the Secretary-General summarized comments received from three Governments, one intergovernmental organization and four NGOs concerning the Centre's coordinating role.[32]

GENERAL ASSEMBLY ACTION

On 18 December 1992, the General Assembly, on the recommendation of the Third Committee, adopted **resolution 47/127** without vote.

Strengthening of the Centre for Human Rights of the Secretariat

The General Assembly,

Recalling its resolutions 44/135 of 15 December 1989, 45/180 of 21 December 1990 and 46/118 and 46/111 of 17 December 1991,

Bearing in mind Commission on Human Rights resolutions 1989/46 of 6 March 1989, 1990/25 of 27 February 1990, 1991/23 of 5 March 1991 and 1992/53 of 3 March 1992, as well as Economic and Social Council resolutions 1990/47 of 25 May 1990 and 1991/36 of 31 May 1991,

Recalling Commission on Human Rights resolutions 1989/54 of 7 March 1989 and 1991/22 of 5 March 1991 on the coordinating role of the Centre for Human Rights of the Secretariat within the United Nations system,

Considering that the promotion of universal respect for and observance of human rights and fundamental freedoms is one of the basic purposes of the United Nations enshrined in the Charter of the United Nations and an issue of the utmost importance for the Organization,

Bearing in mind that the Secretary-General, in his report on the work of the Organization for 1992, stated that the "Charter of the United Nations places the promotion of human rights as one of our priority objectives along with promoting development and preserving international peace and security", an approach which he also applied in his proposals for the programme budget for the biennium 1994-1995,

Bearing in mind Commission on Human Rights resolution 1992/80 of 5 March 1992 on advisory services and the Voluntary Fund for Technical Cooperation in the Field of Human Rights, and recognizing the growing importance of advisory services for the promotion and strengthening of human rights, as demonstrated by the increasing number of requests from Governments for support and technical assistance in the field of human rights,

Recognizing the important role of the Centre for Human Rights in the promotion, protection and implementation of human rights and the need to provide sufficient human resources to the Centre, particularly in view of the fact that its workload has dramatically increased, while resources have failed to keep pace with the expansion of its responsibilities,

Noting that the difficult financial situation of the Centre during the biennium 1992-1993 has created considera-

ble obstacles in the implementation of the various procedures and mechanisms, negatively influenced the servicing by the Secretariat of the bodies concerned with human rights and impaired the quality and precision of reporting,

Having considered the report of the Secretary-General and his previous reports, and noting that additional posts for the Centre have been authorized by the Secretary-General for an initial period of six months and that some of those posts only replace temporary posts that had been abolished,

Noting that, in spite of recent developments, the disparity between mandates themselves and resources available to carry them out has grown further, as a result of additional mandates given to the Centre by intergovernmental and expert bodies, after the preparation of the proposed programme budget for the biennium 1992-1993 and the adoption of that budget,

Noting also that the Assembly, in section XIX of its resolution 46/185 C of 20 December 1991, requested the Secretary-General, with regard to the recommendation of the Advisory Committee on Administrative and Budgetary Questions on the level of general temporary assistance for section 28 of the programme budget, to ensure that adequate resources were available during the biennium 1992-1993,

Noting further that the Committee for Programme and Coordination, at its thirty-second session, held from 11 to 22 May 1992,[a] reaffirmed its previous recommendations on the strengthening of the programmes and activities of the Centre, in the context of the proposed revisions to the medium-term plan for the period 1992-1997,[b]

Noting that the Advisory Committee on Administrative and Budgetary Questions, in revising estimates for the programme budget for the biennium 1992-1993, took note of the redeployment of five posts to the Centre, which will be used to respond to the mandate established by the Commission on Human Rights at its first special session, held on 13 and 14 August 1992,

1. *Supports* the efforts of the Secretary-General to enhance the role and importance of the Centre for Human Rights of the Secretariat as the coordinating unit within the United Nations system of bodies dealing with the promotion and the protection of human rights;

2. *Takes note* of the statement by the Secretary-General, as reflected in his report concerning the implications of organizational changes in the Secretariat, that he would propose using the remaining vacant posts now available in the Secretariat "in the light of new initiatives and emerging mandates and priorities";[c]

3. *Emphasizes* that, in the review of the programme budget for the biennium 1992-1993, adequate staffing, temporary assistance and other resources should be allocated to the Centre so as to enable it to respond to its increasing workload and its needs in order that it may carry out all the functions assigned to it, including those relating to the preparations for the World Conference on Human Rights and the Conference itself;

4. *Requests* the Secretary-General to ensure that sufficient resources are accorded to the Centre to enable it

---

[a]A/47/16 (Part I).
[b]A/45/6/Rev.1.
[c]A/C.5/47/2 & Corr.1.

to carry out, in full and on time, all the mandates, including the additional ones, resulting from the decisions of intergovernmental and expert bodies;

5. *Also requests* the Secretary-General to submit an interim report to the Commission on Human Rights at its forty-ninth session and a final report to the General Assembly at its forty-eighth session on the developments relating to the activities of the Centre and on the measures taken to implement the present resolution.

General Assembly resolution 47/127

18 December 1992   Meeting 92   Adopted without vote

Approved by Third Committee (A/47/678/Add.2) without vote, 3 December (meeting 56); 90-nation draft (A/C.3/47/L.56); agenda item 97 *(b)*.

Sponsors: Afghanistan, Albania, Argentina, Armenia, Australia, Austria, Bahamas, Belarus, Belgium, Benin, Bolivia, Bulgaria, Cameroon, Canada, Cape Verde, Central African Republic, Chad, Chile, Costa Rica, Côte d'Ivoire, Cyprus, Czechoslovakia, Denmark, Dominican Republic, Ecuador, Egypt, El Salvador, Estonia, Ethiopia, Finland, France, Gambia, Germany, Ghana, Greece, Grenada, Guatemala, Guinea, Guinea-Bissau, Hungary, Iceland, Indonesia, Ireland, Italy, Latvia, Lebanon, Lesotho, Lithuania, Luxembourg, Madagascar, Malta, Marshall Islands, Mauritania, Mauritius, Micronesia, Morocco, Namibia, Nepal, Netherlands, New Zealand, Nicaragua, Niger, Nigeria, Norway, Pakistan, Panama, Peru, Philippines, Poland, Portugal, Republic of Korea, Romania, Russian Federation, Rwanda, Samoa, Senegal, Slovenia, Spain, Suriname, Sweden, Togo, Tunisia, Turkey, Ukraine, United Kingdom, United Republic of Tanzania, United States, Uruguay, Vanuatu, Venezuela.

Meeting numbers. GA 47th session: 3rd Committee 47-56; plenary 92.

Strengthening United Nations action

Human Rights Commission action. On 28 February,[33] the Commission reiterated that all peoples had the right to determine freely their political status and pursue their economic, social and cultural development, and that every State had the duty to respect that right within the provisions of the United Nations Charter (see APPENDIX II), including respect for territorial integrity. It called on Member States to base their activities for the promotion, protection and full realization of human rights and fundamental freedoms, including the development of further international cooperation in that area, on the Charter, the 1966 International Covenants on Human Rights[34] and other relevant international instruments, and to refrain from activities inconsistent with that international legal framework. It underlined the continuing need for accurate, impartial and objective information on political, economic and social situations and events in all countries and asked United Nations human rights bodies and special rapporteurs, special representatives, independent experts and working groups to take into account its resolution in carrying out their respective responsibilities. The Commission regretted that the Secretary-General had not yet submitted recommendations on measures to promote international cooperation in the area of human rights related to ensuring that accurate, impartial and objective information on the political, economic and social situations and developments in all countries was made available to all specialized bodies in the field, as requested by the Commission in 1991.[35] It asked the Secretary-General to submit those recommendations and to make them available to the Prepara-

tory Committee for the 1993 World Conference on Human Rights and to regional conferences, as requested by the General Assembly in 1991.[36]

GENERAL ASSEMBLY ACTION

On 18 December 1992, the General Assembly, on the recommendation of the Third Committee, adopted **resolution 47/131** without vote.

Strengthening of United Nations action in the field of human rights through the promotion of international cooperation and the importance of non-selectivity, impartiality and objectivity

The General Assembly,

Reaffirming its faith in fundamental human rights, in the dignity and worth of the human person and in the equal rights of men and women and of nations large and small, and its determination to promote social progress and better standards of living in greater freedom,

Bearing in mind that one of the purposes of the United Nations is to develop friendly relations among nations based on respect for the principle of equal rights and self-determination of peoples and to take other appropriate measures to strengthen universal peace,

Bearing in mind also that one of the purposes of the United Nations is to achieve international cooperation in solving international problems of an economic, social, cultural or humanitarian character and in promoting and encouraging respect for human rights and fundamental freedoms for all without distinction as to race, sex, language or religion,

Recalling that, in accordance with Article 55 of the Charter of the United Nations, the Organization shall promote universal respect for, and observance of, human rights and fundamental freedoms for all, with a view to the creation of conditions of stability and well-being that are necessary for peaceful and friendly relations among nations, based on respect for the principle of equal rights and self-determination of peoples and that, in accordance with Article 56, all Members pledge themselves to take joint and separate action in cooperation with the Organization for the achievement of the purposes set forth in Article 55,

Reiterating that Member States should continue to act in the human rights field in conformity with the provisions of the Charter,

Desirous of achieving further progress in international cooperation in promoting and encouraging respect for human rights and fundamental freedoms,

Considering that such international cooperation should be based on the principles embodied in international law, especially the Charter, as well as the Universal Declaration of Human Rights, the International Covenants on Human Rights and other relevant instruments,

Deeply convinced that United Nations action in this field should be based not only on a profound understanding of the broad range of problems existing in all societies but also on full respect for the political, economic and social realities of each of them, in strict compliance with the purposes and principles of the Charter and for the basic purpose of promoting and encouraging respect for human rights and fundamental freedoms through international cooperation,

Reaffirming its resolutions 45/163 of 18 December 1990 and 46/129 of 17 December 1991,

Recalling its resolutions 32/130 of 16 December 1977, 37/200 of 18 December 1982, 41/155 of 4 December 1986 and 43/155 of 8 December 1988,

Bearing in mind its resolutions 2131(XX) of 21 December 1965, 2625(XXV) of 24 October 1970 and 36/103 of 9 December 1981,

Taking into account Commission on Human Rights resolution 1992/39 of 28 February 1992,

Taking note of the recommendation made by the Commission on Human Rights in the annex to its resolution 1991/30 of 5 March 1991, that the Preparatory Committee for the World Conference on Human Rights, being guided by a spirit of consensus, should make suggestions aimed at ensuring the universality, objectivity and non-selectivity of the consideration of human rights issues in United Nations human rights forums,

Aware of the fact that the promotion, protection and full exercise of all human rights and fundamental freedoms as legitimate concerns of the world community should be guided by the principles of non-selectivity, impartiality and objectivity and should not be used for political ends,

Affirming the importance of the objectivity, independence and discretion of the special rapporteurs and representatives on thematic issues and countries, as well as of the members of the working groups, in carrying out their mandates,

Underlining the obligation that Governments have to promote and protect human rights and to carry out the responsibilities that they have undertaken under international law, especially the Charter, as well as various international instruments in the field of human rights,

1. *Reiterates* that, by virtue of the principle of equal rights and self-determination of peoples enshrined in the Charter of the United Nations, all peoples have the right freely to determine, without external interference, their political status and to pursue their economic, social and cultural development, and that every State has the duty to respect that right within the provisions of the Charter, including respect for territorial integrity;

2. *Reaffirms* that it is a purpose of the United Nations and the task of all Member States, in cooperation with the Organization, to promote and encourage respect for human rights and fundamental freedoms and to remain vigilant with regard to violations of human rights wherever they occur;

3. *Calls upon* all Member States to base their activities for the protection and promotion of human rights, including the development of further international cooperation in this field, on the Charter, the Universal Declaration of Human Rights, the International Covenant on Economic, Social and Cultural Rights, the International Covenant on Civil and Political Rights and other relevant international instruments, and to refrain from activities that are inconsistent with this international framework;

4. *Considers* that international cooperation in this field should make an effective and practical contribution to the urgent task of preventing mass and flagrant violations of human rights and fundamental freedoms for all and to the strengthening of international peace and security;

5. *Affirms* that the promotion, protection and full realization of all human rights and fundamental free-

doms as legitimate concerns of the world community should be guided by the principles of non-selectivity, impartiality and objectivity, and should not be used for political ends;

6. *Requests* all human rights bodies within the United Nations system, as well as the special rapporteurs and representatives, independent experts and working groups, to take duly into account the content of the present resolution in carrying out their mandates;

7. *Expresses its conviction* that an unbiased and fair approach to human rights issues contributes to the promotion of international cooperation as well as to the effective promotion, protection and realization of human rights and fundamental freedoms;

8. *Underlines*, in this context, the continuing need for impartial and objective information on the political, economic and social situations and events of all countries;

9. *Invites* Member States to consider adopting, as appropriate, within the framework of their respective legal systems and in accordance with their obligations under international law, especially the Charter, and international human rights instruments, the measures that they may deem appropriate to achieve further progress in international cooperation in promoting and encouraging respect for human rights and fundamental freedoms;

10. *Requests* the Commission on Human Rights, at its forty-ninth session, to continue to examine ways and means to strengthen United Nations action in this regard on the basis of the present resolution and of Commission resolution 1992/39;

11. *Invites* the Secretary-General to request from all Member States information and comments on the present resolution for timely transmission to the Preparatory Committee for the World Conference on Human Rights, regional conferences and the World Conference itself for consideration and so that relevant proposals, including ways and means to strengthen United Nations action in this regard, can be formulated;

12. *Requests* the Secretary-General to provide the Preparatory Committee with the documentation relevant to the present resolution;

13. *Decides* to consider this matter at its forty-eighth session under the item entitled "Human rights questions".

General Assembly resolution 47/131

18 December 1992   Meeting 92   Adopted without vote

Approved by Third Committee (A/47/678/Add.2) without vote, 4 December (meeting 59); 11-nation draft (A/C.3/47/L.62), orally revised; agenda item 97 (b).

Sponsors: China, Cuba, Ghana, Lao People's Democratic Republic, Libyan Arab Jamahiriya, Nigeria, Sudan, United Republic of Tanzania, Viet Nam, Zambia, Zimbabwe.

Meeting numbers. GA 47th session: 3rd Committee 47-59; plenary 92.

Rule of law

On 3 March,[37] the Commission on Human Rights, recognizing the need to consider ways by which the United Nations could better contribute to the development and strengthening, by Member States, of the rule of law, requested the Secretary-General of the 1993 World Conference on Human Rights to take its resolution into account in preparing reports for its Preparatory Committee.

1993 World Conference on Human Rights

On 28 February,[38] the Commission called on the Preparatory Committee for the 1993 World Conference on Human Rights to deal with the substantive preparations for the Conference in accordance with a 1990 General Assembly resolution[39] and a 1991 Commission resolution.[40] It encouraged its Chairman, the chairpersons or other designated members of human rights bodies and working groups, as well as special and thematic rapporteurs, to participate in the work of the Preparatory Committee. The Commission welcomed contributions of extrabudgetary resources to meet the costs of representatives from least developed countries and encouraged further contributions to the Voluntary Fund established for that purpose. It also welcomed the willingness of Italy to consider acting as host to the World Conference.

Also on 28 February,[41] the Commission asked the Secretary-General to give priority, under the World Public Information Campaign for Human Rights, to activities aimed at disseminating the objectives of the Conference.

Venue of the Conference

Communications. By a letter of 12 February,[42] Germany withdrew its 1991 invitation to the Secretary-General to hold the 1993 United Nations World Conference on Human Rights at Berlin.[40]

On 31 March, Austria transmitted an invitation to the Secretary-General to hold the Conference at Vienna,[43] and Italy expressed an interest in hosting the Conference at Venice,[44] but requested that the decision be postponed.

Note by the Secretary-General. On 24 April,[45] the Secretary-General transmitted to the General Assembly the text of a draft decision taken by the Preparatory Committee for the World Conference on Human Rights at its second session (see below) concerning the dates and venue of the Conference.

GENERAL ASSEMBLY ACTION

By **decision 46/473** of 6 May 1992, the General Assembly noted with deep satisfaction Austria's decision to invite the 1993 World Conference on Human Rights to meet at Vienna and decided that the Conference would be convened there for two weeks in June 1993.

Subsequently, Austria informed the third session of the Conference's Preparatory Committee that the dates envisaged for the Conference were 14 to 25 June 1993.

Preparatory Committee

The Preparatory Committee for the 1993 World Conference on Human Rights at its second (30 March–10 April 1992)[46] and third sessions (14-18 September),[47] both held at Geneva, elected its officers, adopted its agenda and rules of procedure and discussed its organization of work.

In April, the Committee recommended that the General Assembly ask the Secretary-General to invite specific categories of NGOs to regional meetings for the Conference. It considered a report of the Conference's Secretary-General on the public information programme and information coverage of the Conference and its preparatory process,[48] and urged him to ensure coverage of the regional meetings. The Committee again invited contributions of extrabudgetary resources to provide funds for the participation of representatives of least developed countries in the preparatory meetings and the Conference. The Secretary-General reported on the status of the voluntary fund established for that purpose in April[49] and in September.[50] In September, the Committee had before it a report of the Conference's Secretary-General on that question.[51] The Committee took note of progress achieved in developing a reference guide to United Nations studies and reports on human rights and in updating the publications *United Nations Action in the Field of Human Rights*,[52] *Human Rights: A Compilation of International Instruments*[53] and *Human Rights: Status of International Instruments*.[54] On 14 September, the Committee considered a report of the Secretary-General on the status of the preparation of publications, studies and documentation for the Conference.[55] A report on the status of the fund was also made to the Commission on Human Rights in March.[56]

Pursuant to a 1991 General Assembly request,[57] the Secretary-General submitted to the Committee, in March, a report on progress made on other preparatory meetings related to the Conference[58] that had been organized in response to a 1990 Assembly resolution.[39] In that regard, the Committee asked the Secretary-General, in April, to prepare an analytic compilation of the recommendations of those meetings and of any others; in August, he submitted an initial compilation.[59] In response to a 1991 Assembly request,[57] the Secretary-General submitted a report on studies and documentation for the Conference[60] to the Committee's March/April session, which took note of it.

On 18 September, the Committee adopted its provisional rules of procedure.

GENERAL ASSEMBLY ACTION

On 18 December 1992, on the recommendation of the Third Committee, the General Assembly adopted **resolution 47/122** without vote.

World Conference on Human Rights

The General Assembly,

Mindful of the goal of the United Nations to promote and encourage respect for human rights and fundamental freedoms for all, without distinction as to race, sex, language or religion, as set out in the Charter of the United Nations and the Universal Declaration of Human Rights,

Recognizing that all human rights and fundamental freedoms are indivisible and interrelated and that the promotion and protection of one category of rights should never exempt or excuse States from the promotion and protection of another,

Recalling its resolution 45/155 of 18 December 1990, in which it decided, *inter alia*, to convene at a high level a World Conference on Human Rights in 1993, and its resolution 46/116 of 17 December 1991,

Recalling also Commission on Human Rights resolution 1991/30 of 5 March 1991,

Convinced that the holding of a world conference on human rights could make a significant contribution to the effectiveness of the actions of the United Nations in the promotion and protection of human rights,

Recognizing the urgency of adopting a draft agenda for the World Conference on Human Rights before the final session of the Preparatory Committee for the Conference,

1. *Takes note with appreciation* of the reports of the Preparatory Committee for the World Conference on Human Rights on the work of its second and third sessions;

2. *Expresses its appreciation* to Governments, the bodies and organs of the United Nations system and non-governmental organizations for their contributions to the preparatory process;

3. *Approves* the draft rules of procedure for the World Conference on Human Rights, as recommended by the Preparatory Committee at its second and third sessions, with the exception of rule 15 *(e)*;

4. *Decides* that the distribution of the twenty-nine positions of vice-president of the Conference should be in accordance with the established criteria of the General Assembly based on equitable geographical distribution;

5. *Approves* the recommendation made by the Preparatory Committee at its third session regarding the participation of non-governmental organizations in regional meetings related to the preparatory process;

6. *Also approves* the provisional agenda for the Conference, as annexed to the present resolution, on the understanding that participants can raise issues of interest to them under the appropriate agenda item at the fourth session of the Preparatory Committee and at the Conference for possible inclusion in the final text;

7. *Decides*, in accordance with the decisions adopted by the Preparatory Committee:

   (a) (i) That the Preparatory Committee shall meet for its fourth session at Geneva, for a period of two weeks in April 1993;

   (ii) That the Preparatory Committee shall take up the question of the final outcome of the Conference at its fourth session, taking into consideration, *inter alia*, the preparatory work and conclusions of the regional meetings to be held at Tunis, San José and Bangkok;

   (iii) That the Secretary-General shall give the Conference and the preparatory process thereto the widest possible publicity and ensure full coordination of public information activities in the area of human rights within the United Nations system;

(b) To renew its invitation for contributions of extrabudgetary resources to meet the costs of the participation of representatives of the least developed countries in the preparatory meetings, including regional meetings, and in the Conference itself, and to request the Secretary-General to intensify his efforts in this regard;

8. *Renews its request* to Governments, the specialized agencies, other international organizations, regional organizations and non-governmental organizations concerned with human rights or development to participate actively in the preparatory process and in the Conference itself;

9. *Requests* the Secretary-General to report to the General Assembly at its forty-eighth session on the outcome of the Conference, under the item entitled "Human rights questions".

ANNEX
Provisional agenda for the World Conference on Human Rights

1. Opening of the Conference.
2. Election of the President.
3. Adoption of the rules of procedure.
4. Election of other officers of the Conference.
5. Appointment of the Credentials Committee.
6. Establishment of committees and working groups.
7. Adoption of the agenda.
8. Commemoration of the International Year of the World's Indigenous People.
9. General debate on the progress made in the field of human rights since the adoption of the Universal Declaration of Human Rights and on the identification of obstacles to further progress in this area and ways in which they can be overcome.
10. Consideration of the relationship between development, democracy and the universal enjoyment of all human rights, keeping in view the interrelationship and indivisibility of economic, social, cultural, civil and political rights.
11. Consideration of contemporary trends in and new challenges to the full realization of all human rights of women and men, including those of persons belonging to vulnerable groups.
12. Recommendations for:
    (a) Strengthening international cooperation in the field of human rights in conformity with the Charter of the United Nations and with international human rights instruments;
    (b) Ensuring the universality, objectivity and non-selectivity of the consideration of human rights issues;
    (c) Enhancing the effectiveness of United Nations activities and mechanisms;
    (d) Securing the necessary financial and other resources for United Nations activities in the area of human rights.
13. Adoption of the final documents and report of the Conference.

General Assembly resolution 47/122

18 December 1992   Meeting 92   Adopted without vote

Approved by Third Committee (A/47/678/Add.2) by consensus, 4 December (meeting 57); 134-nation draft (A/C.3/47/L.18/Rev.1); agenda item 97 (b).

Sponsors: Afghanistan, Albania, Angola, Antigua and Barbuda, Argentina, Armenia, Australia, Austria, Azerbaijan, Bahamas, Bangladesh, Barbados, Belarus, Belgium, Belize, Benin, Bhutan, Bolivia, Bosnia and Herzegovina,

Botswana, Brazil, Bulgaria, Burkina Faso, Burundi, Cameroon, Canada, Cape Verde, Central African Republic, Chad, Chile, Comoros, Congo, Costa Rica, Côte d'Ivoire, Croatia, Cyprus, Czechoslovakia, Denmark, Djibouti, Dominican Republic, Egypt, El Salvador, Equatorial Guinea, Estonia, Ethiopia, Finland, France, Gabon, Gambia, Germany, Greece, Grenada, Guatemala, Guinea, Guinea-Bissau, Guyana, Haiti, Honduras, Hungary, Iceland, India, Indonesia, Ireland, Italy, Jamaica, Japan, Jordan, Kazakhstan, Latvia, Lebanon, Lesotho, Liberia, Libyan Arab Jamahiriya, Liechtenstein, Lithuania, Luxembourg, Madagascar, Malawi, Mali, Malta, Marshall Islands, Mauritania, Mauritius, Micronesia, Mongolia, Morocco, Mozambique, Myanmar, Namibia, Netherlands, New Zealand, Nicaragua, Niger, Nigeria, Norway, Panama, Papua New Guinea, Paraguay, Peru, Philippines, Poland, Portugal, Republic of Korea, Republic of Moldova, Romania, Russian Federation, Rwanda, Saint Kitts and Nevis, Samoa, San Marino, Senegal, Sierra Leone, Singapore, Slovenia, Solomon Islands, Spain, Sri Lanka, Sudan, Suriname, Swaziland, Sweden, Thailand, Togo, Trinidad and Tobago, Tunisia, Turkey, Ukraine, United Kingdom, United States, Uruguay, Vanuatu, Venezuela, Yemen, Zaire.

Meeting numbers. GA 47th session: 3rd Committee 47-57; plenary 92.

Public information activities

In a February report to the Commission on Human Rights on the development of public information activities in the human rights field, including the World Public Information Campaign on Human Rights,[61] the Secretary-General described the activities of the Centre for Human Rights and the United Nations Department of Public Information (DPI). He also discussed coordination and cooperation within and outside the United Nations system, human rights observances and national focal points and assessed the Campaign's impact. In a later report,[62] the Secretary-General updated information on public information activities in the human rights field, as requested by the General Assembly in 1990.[63]

The World Public Information Campaign, launched by the Assembly in 1988,[64] sought to increase understanding and awareness of human rights and fundamental freedoms as well as provide education on international human rights machinery and the efforts of the United Nations to promote and protect human rights. Activities within the Campaign focused on preparing and disseminating printed information and reference materials; workshops, seminars and training courses; fellowships and internships; special human rights observances; and coverage and promotion activities.

Human Rights Commission action. On 28 February 1992,[41] the Commission reiterated its request to the Secretary-General to ensure that recent periodic reports of States parties to treaty-monitoring bodies and summary records of discussions of them in the treaty bodies be made available in UNICs of the submitting countries. It encouraged Member States to provide, facilitate and promote publicity for United Nations human rights activities and to accord priority to disseminating in their national and local languages the 1948 Universal Declaration of Human Rights,[65] the 1966 International Covenants on Human Rights[34] and other international instruments. Urging Member States to include in their educational curricula materials relevant to a comprehensive understanding of human rights issues, it encouraged the efforts of the Centre for Human Rights to develop a manual for higher education, in cooperation with the United Nations Educational, Scientific and Cultural Organization. The Commission asked DPI to use fully its available resources in human rights and to produce materials on such issues, and asked the Centre for Human Rights to coordinate the activities of the World Campaign and maintain liaison with Governments, regional and national institutions and individuals in developing and implementing those activities. The Commission asked the Secretary-General to take advantage of NGO collaboration in implementing the World Campaign and to submit a report in 1993 on public information activities.

GENERAL ASSEMBLY ACTION

On 18 December 1992, the General Assembly, on the recommendation of the Third Committee, adopted **resolution 47/128** without vote.

Development of public information activities in the field of human rights

The General Assembly,

Reaffirming that activities to improve public knowledge in the field of human rights are essential to the fulfilment of the purposes of the United Nations set out in Article 1, paragraph 3, of the Charter of the United Nations and that carefully designed programmes of teaching, education and information are essential to the achievement of lasting respect for human rights and fundamental freedoms,

Recalling the relevant resolutions adopted by the General Assembly and the Commission on Human Rights,

Recognizing the catalytic effect of initiatives of the United Nations on national and regional public information activities in the field of human rights,

Recognizing also the valuable role that non-governmental organizations can play in those endeavours,

Taking note of the recommendation of the fourth meeting of persons chairing the human rights treaty bodies to the effect that an expert group from outside the Secretariat should be constituted to undertake a comprehensive review of the existing information programme of the Centre for Human Rights of the Secretariat,

1. *Takes note* of the report of the Secretary-General;

2. *Reaffirms* the need for information materials on human rights to be carefully designed in clear and accessible form, to be tailored to regional and national requirements and circumstances with specific target audiences in mind, and to be effectively disseminated in national and local languages and in sufficient volume to have the desired impact, and for effective use also to be made of the mass media, in particular radio and television and audiovisual technologies, in order to reach wider audiences, priority being given to children, young people and the disadvantaged, including those in isolated areas;

3. *Urges* the Secretariat to take measures to ensure the further production and effective dissemination of human rights information materials, especially those on the basic United Nations human rights instruments and institutions, in national and local languages, in cooperation with regional, national and local organizations, as well as with Governments, making full and effective use of the United Nations information centres;

4. *Reiterates its request* to the Secretary-General to ensure that recent periodic reports of States parties to treaty-monitoring bodies and the summary records of discussions on the reports in the treaty bodies are available in the United Nations information centres of the countries that have submitted them;

5. *Welcomes* the information relative to the situation of documentation on human rights at each United Nations information centre contained in the report of the Secretary-General, and reiterates the need to ensure, within available resources, the collection of basic United Nations information and reference material on human rights and fundamental freedoms at each of those centres and for the centres to disseminate human rights materials in all countries within their designated areas of activity;

6. *Encourages* all Member States to make special efforts, particularly in view of the World Conference on Human Rights to be held in 1993, to provide, facilitate and encourage publicity for the activities of the United Nations in the field of human rights and to accord priority to the dissemination, in their respective national and local languages, of the texts of the Universal Declaration of Human Rights, the International Covenants on Human Rights and major conventions on human rights, as well as information and education on the practical ways in which the rights and freedoms enjoyed under those instruments can be exercised;

7. *Urges* all Member States to include in their educational curricula materials relevant to a comprehensive understanding of human rights issues, and encourages all those responsible for training in law and its enforcement, the armed forces, medicine, diplomacy and other relevant fields to include appropriate human rights components in their programmes;

8. *Notes* the special value, under the advisory services and technical assistance programme, of regional and national training courses and workshops, in cooperation with Governments, regional and national organizations and non-governmental organizations, in promoting practical education and awareness in the field of human rights;

9. *Requests* the Secretary-General to ensure the fullest effective deployment of the skills and resources of all concerned units of the Secretariat and to make available, within existing resources, in particular from the budget of the Department of Public Information of the Secretariat, adequate funding for developing practical and effective human rights information activities;

10. *Calls upon* the Centre for Human Rights of the Secretariat, which has primary responsibility within the United Nations system in the field of human rights, to coordinate the substantive activities of the World Public Information Campaign for Human Rights pursuant to the direction of the General Assembly and the Commission on Human Rights, and to serve as liaison with Governments, regional and national institutions, non-governmental organizations and concerned individuals

in the development and implementation of the activities of the Campaign;

11. *Calls upon* the Department of Public Information, which has primary responsibility for public information activities, to coordinate the public information activities of the Campaign and, in its responsibility as secretariat to the Joint United Nations Information Committee, to promote coordinated system-wide information activities in the field of human rights;

12. *Stresses* the need for close cooperation between the Centre for Human Rights and the Department of Public Information in the implementation of the aims established for the Campaign and the need for the United Nations to harmonize its activities in the field of human rights with those of other organizations, including the International Committee of the Red Cross, with regard to the dissemination of information on international humanitarian law, and the United Nations Educational, Scientific and Cultural Organization with regard to education for human rights;

13. *Requests* the Secretary-General to take advantage, as much as possible, of the collaboration of non-governmental organizations for, *inter alia*, the dissemination of human rights materials, with a view to increasing universal awareness of human rights and fundamental freedoms;

14. *Requests* the Commission on Human Rights, at its forty-ninth session, to consider the recommendation made by the fourth meeting of persons chairing the human rights treaty bodies that an expert group, from outside the Secretariat, should be appointed to review comprehensively the existing information programme of the Centre for Human Rights, with a view to developing a new information strategy that integrates the needs of the various sections within the human rights programme, including treaty bodies;

15. *Requests* the Secretary-General to submit to the General Assembly at its forty-ninth session a comprehensive report on the implementation of the present resolution for consideration under the sub-item entitled "Human rights questions, including alternative approaches for improving the effective enjoyment of human rights and fundamental freedoms".

General Assembly resolution 47/128

18 December 1992   Meeting 92   Adopted without vote

Approved by Third Committee (A/47/678/Add.2) without vote, 3 December (meeting 56); 25-nation draft (A/C.3/47/L.58); agenda item 97 *(b)*

Sponsors: Albania, Argentina, Australia, Belarus, Bosnia and Herzegovina, Chile, Costa Rica, Finland, Germany, Greece, Guatemala, India, Ireland, Italy, Mexico, Morocco, Netherlands, New Zealand, Norway, Romania, Russian Federation, Samoa, Sweden, United Kingdom, Yemen.

Meeting numbers. GA 47th session: 3rd Committee 47-56; plenary 92.

Advisory services

In 1992,[66] under the United Nations programme of advisory services in human rights established in 1955,[67] activities funded by the United Nations regular budget included electoral assistance to Cambodia, Eritrea and Malawi. The following seminars and training courses took place: a training course on free and fair elections and human rights in a democratic society (Luanda, Angola, 31 August–4 September); a technical conference on practical experience in the realization of sustainable and environmentally sound self-development by indigenous peoples (Santiago de Chile, Chile, 18-22 May) (see above, under ''Racial discrimination''); a national training course on the preparation of reports (Tehran, Iran, 2-5 August); a conference on de facto racial discrimination (Pretoria, South Africa, 21-23 October); a training course on international protection of human rights (Lima, Peru, 7-10 April); and a workshop on the situation of human rights in Haiti (New York, 18-20 November). Fellowships were awarded to 32 candidates, and 118 internships were offered to postgraduate students. The advisory services of experts were provided to Guatemala (see below) and the Russian Federation.

Under the Voluntary Fund for Technical Cooperation in the Field of Human Rights, established in 1987,[68] needs assessment missions were carried out in Albania, Benin, Mongolia, Namibia and Sao Tome and Principe, and electoral assistance was provided to Lesotho and Romania. Technical assistance programmes were under way in Colombia, Paraguay and Uruguay. Fellowships were awarded to 10 candidates and an additional 13 under technical assistance projects. Training activities included a training course on implementing human rights standards (Mbabane, Swaziland, 18-22 May); a seminar on human rights (Cotonou, Benin, 2-7 September); a training course on the implementation of human rights instruments and the administration of justice for officials from English-speaking African countries (San Remo, Italy, 9-13 March); a training course on human rights in the administration of criminal justice (Bucharest, Romania, 19-23 October; Tirana, Albania, 2-6 November); a seminar on human rights in the administration of justice (Bucharest, 30 November–4 December); an international symposium on human rights in Cambodia (Phnom Penh, 30 November–2 December) (see above under ''Civil and political rights''); and training courses on teaching human rights in primary and secondary schools (Bucharest, 7-11 December and 14-18 December). The Centre continued its assistance to the African Commission on Human and Peoples' Rights of OAU, the Arab Institute of Human Rights (Tunis, Tunisia), the African Centre for Democracy and Human Rights Studies (Banjul, Gambia) and the Romanian Institute for Human Rights (Bucharest).

The Secretary-General reported that, as at 31 December 1992, the Fund had a negative balance of $549,300. Annexed to the report was an account of the Fund's income and expenditures for the year, its utilization as at 30 November 1992 and project commitments in 1992.

Human Rights Commission action. On 5 March,[69] the Commission, taking note of a report by the Secretary-General on advisory services in the field of human rights during 1991, including the Voluntary Fund for Technical Cooperation in the Field of Human Rights,[70] asked him to provide urgently more human and financial resources to enlarge advisory services; pursue his efforts towards a medium-term plan for advisory services and technical assistance; elaborate comprehensive programmes of advisory services and technical cooperation under the Voluntary Fund; draw the attention of human rights organs and Governments to the possibilities available to provide technical cooperation in the human rights field under the Voluntary Fund; guarantee the transparency of the criteria applied and of the rules of procedure to be followed in carrying out human rights technical cooperation; explore further the possibilities offered by cooperation between the Centre for Human Rights and specialized bodies of the system; bring the need for further technical assistance in the legal field to the attention of the relevant United Nations bodies and specialized agencies; and report to the Commission annually on progress made in implementing the programme of advisory services. It requested its special rapporteurs and representatives, as well as the Working Group on Enforced or Involuntary Disappearances and the Working Group on Arbitrary Detention, to inform Governments of the possibility of availing themselves of the services provided for under the programmes of advisory services and to include in their recommendations proposals for specific projects.

On 4 March,[71] the Commission welcomed the conclusion, on 13 February, of an agreement on technical cooperation between the Centre for Human Rights and the United Nations Fund for Advisory Services and Technical Assistance in the Field of Human Rights, on the one hand, and Albania, on the other. On 3 March,[72] it welcomed the close cooperation between Romania and the Centre in the field of advisory services.

Equatorial Guinea

On 5 March,[73] the Commission on Human Rights, commending Expert Fernando Volio Jiménez (Costa Rica) for his report on the human rights situation in Equatorial Guinea,[74] asked that country to cooperate with a newly appointed expert and the Centre for Human Rights in implementing the emergency plan of action as outlined in the report. It expressed serious concern that, notwithstanding the programme of advisory services offered to the Government, fundamental freedoms were still seriously restricted. It called on Equatorial Guinea to stop using military courts for trying ordinary law offences and to permit the establishment of an independent judiciary; take measures to promote harmonious coexistence of its peoples; free all political prisoners; and take legislative and administrative measures to establish freedom, democracy and the rule of law, as well as to promote and protect human rights and fundamental freedoms. The Commission asked its Chairman to appoint an expert to prepare a study of human rights violations in Equatorial Guinea and asked the Secretary-General to provide all the assistance the expert might need. It asked the expert to report to the Commission in 1993.

The Economic and Social Council, by **decision 1992/247** of 20 July 1992, approved the appointment of such an expert and the Commission's request that the Secretary-General provide assistance.

Guatemala

Human Rights Commission action. Taking note of a report by independent expert Christian Tomuschat (Germany) on the situation of human rights in Guatemala,[5] the Commission on Human Rights, on 5 March,[75] expressed its gratitude to Guatemala for collaborating with the Commission in carrying out its advisory activities and asked the Secretary-General to continue to provide that country and NGOs with advisory services. Urging Guatemala to intensify investigations to identify and bring to justice those responsible for human rights violations, the Commission also requested Guatemala to intensify efforts to ensure that its authorities and security forces fully respected the human rights of the Guatemalan people. It asked the Secretary-General to extend the expert's mandate and asked the expert to report in 1993.

Extension of the expert's mandate was approved by the Economic and Social Council by **decision 1992/246** of 20 July 1992.

Subcommission action. On 27 August,[76] the Subcommission, by a secret ballot of 13 to 4, with 4 abstentions, adopted a resolution on the situation of human rights in Guatemala.

International human rights instruments

On 14 August,[77] the Subcommission, having considered a July note of the Secretary-General relating to communication with Member States concerning the ratification of, or accession to, international human rights instruments and developments in that area since its 1990 session,[78] asked him to renew his invitation to Member States that had not yet replied to previous communications, to submit information on the human rights instruments to which they had not yet become party and to draw their attention to the instruments they had already signed but not ratified. It also asked the Secretary-General to continue holding informal discussions concerning prospects for ratification of human rights instru-

ments, to continue to inform it of his efforts in implementing its resolution and to update the table containing a country-by-country record of developments concerning the ratification of, or accession to, human rights instruments falling under its terms of reference. It requested the Subcommission Chairman to appoint, prior to its 1994 session, one of its members to report on information received under its resolution, to analyse difficulties impeding ratification of, or accession to, human rights instruments and to assess the programme of advisory services in the field of human rights with a view to encouraging universal acceptance of human rights instruments.

Human rights treaty bodies

In 1992, there were seven human rights treaty instruments in force providing for the monitoring of treaty implementation by expert bodies. Those instruments and their respective treaty bodies were the: 1965 International Convention on the Elimination of All Forms of Racial Discrimination[79] (CERD); 1966 International Covenant on Economic, Social and Cultural Rights[34] (Committee on Economic, Social and Cultural Rights); 1966 International Covenant on Civil and Political Rights[34] (Human Rights Committee); 1979 Convention on the Elimination of All Forms of Discrimination against Women[80] (Committee on the Elimination of Discrimination against Women); 1984 Convention against Torture and Other Cruel, Inhuman or Degrading Treatment or Punishment[81] (Committee against Torture); 1989 Convention on the Rights of the Child[82] (Committee on the Rights of the Child); and the 1973 International Convention on the Suppression and Punishment of the Crime of Apartheid[83] (Group of Three).

Human Rights Commission action. On 21 February,[84] the Commission endorsed continuing efforts to streamline, rationalize and improve reporting procedures by treaty bodies and by the Secretary-General. It also endorsed the recommendation made by the third meeting of persons chairing the human rights treaty bodies (Geneva, 1-5 October 1990)[85] to institutionalize the meetings and asked the General Assembly to take action to enable them to be held biennially. It requested the fourth (1992) meeting (Geneva, 12-16 October)[86] to include on its agenda the question of the extent of reservations to human rights instruments. Welcoming the conclusions and recommendations of a 1989 study on possible long-term approaches to enhance the effective operation of existing and prospective bodies established under United Nations human rights instruments,[87] the Commission took note of a January 1992 report of the Secretary-General containing comments of the treaty bodies on the study.[88] The Secretary-

General was asked to consider establishing a committee resource room to gather and facilitate access to various sources of information indispensable for the effective functioning of various treaty bodies and to submit to the Assembly in 1992 a report examining the financial, legal and other implications of providing full funding for the operation of all human rights treaty bodies. He was also asked to expedite the implementation of the 1990 recommendations of the Task Force on Computerization,[89] by asking Member States to contribute voluntarily to cover the cost of the proposed system; prepare an inventory of all international human rights standards-setting activities to facilitate better-informed decision-making; ensure that recent periodic reports of States parties to treaty-monitoring bodies and summary records of committee discussions pertaining to them were made available in the UNICs in the countries submitting the reports; and ensure that the *Manual on Human Rights Reporting*[90] was available in all official languages at the earliest opportunity.

Reports of the Secretary-General. Pursuant to a 1991 General Assembly resolution,[91] the Secretary-General reported in October on the financial and legal implications of fully funding the operation of all human rights treaty bodies.[92]

By a note of 10 November,[86] the Secretary-General transmitted to the Assembly the report of the fourth meeting of persons chairing the human rights treaty bodies convened pursuant to the same 1991 Assembly resolution.

GENERAL ASSEMBLY ACTION

On 16 December 1992, on the recommendation of the Third Committee, the General Assembly adopted **resolution 47/111** without vote.

Effective implementation of international instruments on human rights, including reporting obligations under international instruments on human rights

The General Assembly,

Recalling its resolution 46/111 of 17 December 1991, as well as its other relevant resolutions,

Reaffirming that the effective implementation of United Nations instruments on human rights is of major importance to the efforts of the Organization, pursuant to the Charter of the United Nations and the Universal Declaration of Human Rights, to promote universal respect for and observance of human rights and fundamental freedoms,

Reaffirming its responsibility to ensure the proper functioning of treaty bodies established pursuant to instruments adopted by the General Assembly and, in this connection, also reaffirming the importance of:

(*a*) Ensuring the effective functioning of systems of periodic reporting by States parties to these instruments;

(*b*) Securing sufficient financial resources to overcome existing difficulties with the effective functioning of treaty bodies;

(*c*) Addressing questions of reporting obligations and financial implications whenever elaborating any further instruments on human rights,

Recalling the conclusions and recommendations of the second meeting of persons chairing the human rights treaty bodies, held at Geneva from 10 to 14 October 1988,[a] and the endorsement of the recommendations aimed at streamlining, rationalizing and otherwise improving reporting procedures by the General Assembly in its resolution 46/111 and the Commission on Human Rights in its resolution 1992/15 of 21 February 1992,

Taking particular note of the conclusions and recommendations of the third and fourth meetings of persons chairing the human rights treaty bodies, held at Geneva from 1 to 5 October 1990, and from 12 to 16 October 1992 respectively,

Expressing concern about the increasing backlog of reports on implementation by States parties to United Nations instruments on human rights and about delays in consideration of reports by the treaty bodies,

Taking note of the reports of the Secretary-General on progress achieved in enhancing the effective functioning of the treaty bodies,

Recalling the study[b] on possible long-term approaches to enhancing the effective operation of existing and prospective bodies established under United Nations instruments on human rights, prepared by an independent expert, and aware of the need to update the study,

Welcoming the decision taken at the Fourteenth Meeting of States Parties to the International Convention on the Elimination of All Forms of Racial Discrimination on 15 January 1992 to amend paragraph 6 of article 8 of the Convention and to add a new paragraph, as paragraph 7 of article 8, by which the members of the Committee established under the Convention shall henceforth receive emoluments from United Nations resources on such terms and conditions as may be decided by the General Assembly,

Welcoming also the decision taken at the Conference of the States Parties to the Convention Against Torture and Other Cruel, Inhuman or Degrading Treatment or Punishment, on 9 September 1992, to delete paragraph 7 of article 17 and paragraph 5 of article 18 of the Convention, to insert a new paragraph, as paragraph 4 of article 18, by which the members of the Committee established under the Convention shall receive emoluments from United Nations resources on such terms and conditions as may be decided by the General Assembly, and to recommend that the Assembly take action for the implementation of the proposed amendment at its forty-seventh session,

Welcoming the reports of the Secretary-General examining the financial, legal and other implications of providing full funding for the operation of all human rights treaty bodies,

1. *Endorses* the conclusions and recommendations of the meetings of persons chairing the human rights treaty bodies aimed at streamlining, rationalizing and otherwise improving reporting procedures, and supports the continuing efforts in this connection by the treaty bodies and the Secretary-General within their respective spheres of competence;

---

[a]A/44/98.
[b]A/44/668.

2. *Expresses its satisfaction* with the study by the independent expert on possible long-term approaches to enhancing the effective operation of existing and prospective bodies established under United Nations instruments on human rights, which contains several recommendations on reporting and monitoring procedures, servicing and financing of supervisory bodies and long-term approaches to human rights standard-setting and implementation mechanisms, and which was presented to the Commission on Human Rights for detailed consideration at its forty-sixth session, and, in the light of the conclusions and recommendations contained in the report of the fourth meeting of persons chairing the human rights treaty bodies, requests that the report of the independent expert be updated for submission to the Commission at its fiftieth session and that an interim report be presented to the General Assembly at its forty-eighth session and be made available to the World Conference on Human Rights in June 1993;

3. *Requests* the Secretary-General to give high priority to establishing a computerized database to improve the efficiency and effectiveness of the functioning of the treaty bodies;

4. *Again urges* States parties to make every effort to meet their reporting obligations and to contribute, individually and through meetings of States parties, to identifying and implementing ways of further streamlining and improving reporting procedures as well as enhancing coordination and information flow between the treaty bodies and with relevant United Nations bodies, including specialized agencies;

5. *Welcomes* the emphasis placed by the meetings of persons chairing the human rights treaty bodies and by the Commission on Human Rights on the importance of technical assistance and advisory services and, further to this end:

(a) Endorses the request of the Commission to the Secretary-General to report regularly to it on possible technical assistance projects identified by the treaty bodies;

(b) Invites the treaty bodies to give priority attention to identifying such possibilities in the regular course of their work of reviewing the periodic reports of States parties;

6. *Endorses* the recommendations of the meetings of persons chairing the human rights treaty bodies on the need to ensure financing and adequate staffing resources for the operations of the treaty bodies and, with this in mind:

(a) Reiterates its request to the Secretary-General to provide adequate resources with regard to the various treaty bodies;

(b) Requests the Secretary-General to report on this question to the Commission on Human Rights at its forty-ninth session and to the General Assembly at its forty-eighth session;

7. *Calls upon* all States parties to meet fully and without delay their financial obligations under the relevant instruments on human rights, and requests the Secretary-General to consider ways and means of strengthening collection procedures and making them more effective;

8. *Emphasizes* that any administrative and budgetary measures shall be taken without prejudice to the duty of States parties under United Nations human rights instruments to meet all their current and outstanding financial obligations pursuant to such instruments;

9. *Endorses* the amendments to the International Convention on the Elimination of All Forms of Racial Discrimination and the Convention Against Torture and Other Cruel, Inhuman or Degrading Treatment or Punishment and requests the Secretary-General:

(a) To take the appropriate measures to provide for the financing of the committees established under those conventions from the regular budget of the United Nations, beginning with the budget for the biennium 1994-1995;

(b) To take the necessary measures to ensure that the two committees meet as scheduled until the amendments enter into force;

10. *Requests* the Secretary-General to take the appropriate steps in order to finance the biennial meetings of persons chairing the human rights treaty bodies from the resources available from the regular budget of the United Nations;

11. *Also requests* the Secretary-General, in the light of the views expressed at the forty-ninth session of the Commission on Human Rights and the thirty-seventh session of the Commission on the Status of Women, to submit to the General Assembly at its forty-eighth session a report examining the conclusions and recommendations of the fourth meeting of persons chairing the human rights treaty bodies, held in October 1992;

12. *Decides* to give priority consideration at its forty-eighth session to the conclusions and recommendations of the meetings of persons chairing human rights treaty bodies under the item entitled ''Human rights questions''.

General Assembly resolution 47/111

16 December 1992   Meeting 89   Adopted without vote

Approved by Third Committee (A/47/678/Add.1) without vote, 1 December (meeting 52); 21-nation draft (A/C.3/47/L.42), orally revised; agenda item 97 (a).

Sponsors: Australia, Austria, Belgium, Canada, Chile, Costa Rica, Denmark, Finland, France, Germany, Hungary, Iceland, Italy, Netherlands, New Zealand, Norway, Poland, Portugal, Samoa, Spain, Sweden.

Financial implications. 5th Committee, A/47/789; S-G, A/C.3/47/L.46, A/C.5/47/69.

Meeting numbers. GA 47th session: 3rd Committee 40, 42-45, 48, 49, 52; 5th Committee 45; plenary 89.

Reporting obligations of States parties

Human Rights Commission action. On 21 February,[84] the Commission urged States parties to fulfil their reporting obligations and to contribute to identifying and implementing ways to further streamline and improve reporting procedures.

ECONOMIC AND SOCIAL COUNCIL ACTION

On 20 July 1992, the Economic and Social Council adopted **decision 1992/260**, by which it appealed to the following States, which had been parties to the International Covenant on Economic, Social and Cultural Rights for more than 10 years but had not submitted even an initial report required by the Covenant, to do so as soon as possible: Bolivia, Central African Republic, Egypt, El Salvador, the Gambia, Guinea, Kenya, Lebanon, Mali, Mauritius, Morocco, Saint Vincent and the Grenadines, Solomon Islands, Sri Lanka and Suriname.

International Covenants on Human Rights

Human Rights Commission action. On 21 February,[93] the Commission adopted a resolution on the 1966 International Covenants on Human Rights,[34] which corresponded largely to a resolution adopted by the Economic and Social Council later in the year. The Commission asked the Secretary-General to report in 1993 on the status of the Covenants and on the work of the Committee on Economic, Social and Cultural Rights.

ECONOMIC AND SOCIAL COUNCIL ACTION

On 20 July 1992, the Economic and Social Council adopted **resolution 1992/11** without vote.

International Covenants on Human Rights
The Economic and Social Council,

Bearing in mind its important responsibilities in relation to the coordination of activities to promote the International Covenants on Human Rights,

Mindful that the International Covenants on Human Rights constitute the first all-embracing and legally binding international treaties in the field of human rights and, together with the Universal Declaration of Human Rights, form the core of the International Bill of Human Rights,

Recalling the International Covenant on Economic, Social and Cultural Rights, the International Covenant on Civil and Political Rights and the Optional Protocols to the latter and reaffirming that all human rights and fundamental freedoms are indivisible and interrelated and that the promotion and protection of one category of rights should never exempt or excuse States from the promotion and protection of the other rights,

Noting the entry into force on 11 July 1991 of the Second Optional Protocol to the International Covenant on Civil and Political Rights, aiming at the abolition of the death penalty,

Recognizing the important role of the Human Rights Committee and the Committee on Economic, Social and Cultural Rights in promoting and implementing the International Covenants on Human Rights,

Taking note with appreciation of the report of the Committee on Economic, Social and Cultural Rights on its sixth session, as well as the general and country-specific comments of the Human Rights Committee,

Noting, in this regard, that a number of States Members of the United Nations have yet to become parties to the International Covenants on Human Rights,

Considering that the effective functioning of treaty bodies established in accordance with the relevant provisions of international instruments on human rights plays a fundamental role and hence represents an important continuing concern of the United Nations,

Welcoming the conclusions and recommendations of the meetings of persons chairing the human rights treaty bodies aimed at streamlining, rationalizing and otherwise improving reporting procedures, as well as the continuing efforts in this connection by the treaty bodies and the Secretary-General within their respective spheres of competence,

1. *Reaffirms* the importance of the International Covenants on Human Rights as major parts of the international effort to promote universal respect for and observance of human rights and fundamental freedoms;

2. *Appeals strongly* to all States that have not yet done so to become parties to the International Covenant on Economic, Social and Cultural Rights and the International Covenant on Civil and Political Rights and to consider acceding to the first Optional Protocol to the International Covenant on Civil and Political Rights, as well as to the Second Optional Protocol, aiming at the abolition of the death penalty;

3. *Again invites* the States parties to the International Covenant on Civil and Political Rights to consider making the declaration provided for in article 41 of the Covenant;

4. *Appeals* to States parties to the Covenants that have exercised their sovereign right to make reservations in accordance with relevant rules of international law to consider whether any such reservations should be reviewed;

5. *Invites* the Secretary-General to intensify the systematic efforts to encourage States to become parties to the International Covenants on Human Rights and, through the programme of advisory services in the field of human rights, to provide technical assistance to the States that are not parties to the Covenants, with a view to assisting them in ratifying or acceding to the Covenants;

6. *Emphasizes* the importance of the strictest compliance by States parties with their obligations under the International Covenant on Economic, Social and Cultural Rights, the International Covenant on Civil and Political Rights and, where applicable, the Optional Protocols to the latter;

7. *Stresses* the importance of avoiding the erosion of human rights by derogation and the need for strict observance of all the agreed conditions and procedures for derogation under article 4 of the International Covenant on Civil and Political Rights;

8. *Welcomes* the continuing efforts of the Human Rights Committee to strive for uniform standards in the implementation of the provisions of the International Covenant on Civil and Political Rights and appeals to other bodies dealing with similar questions of human rights to respect those standards as expressed in the general comments of the Human Rights Committee;

9. *Also welcomes* the adoption by the Committee on Economic, Social and Cultural Rights of a general comment at its third, fourth and fifth sessions, and encourages the Committee to continue using that mechanism to develop a fuller appreciation of the obligations of States parties under the International Covenant on Economic, Social and Cultural Rights;

10. *Further welcomes* the fact that the Committee on Economic, Social and Cultural Rights, in its general comment on article 11, paragraph 1, of the Covenant, adopted at its sixth session, dealt with the right to adequate housing;

11. *Invites* States parties to the International Covenant on Economic, Social and Cultural Rights, in conformity with article 2, paragraph 1, of the Covenant, to consider identifying benchmarks to measure achievements in the progressive realization of the rights recognized in the Covenant and, in that context, to pay particular regard to the most vulnerable and disadvantaged groups;

12. *Requests* the Secretary-General to keep the Human Rights Committee and the Committee on Eco-

nomic, Social and Cultural Rights informed of the relevant activities of the General Assembly, the Economic and Social Council, the Commission on Human Rights, the other functional commissions concerned, the Subcommission on Prevention of Discrimination and Protection of Minorities, the other treaty bodies and, as appropriate, the specialized agencies, and also to transmit the annual reports of the Human Rights Committee and the Committee on Economic, Social and Cultural Rights to those bodies;

13. *Encourages* all Governments to publicize the texts of the International Covenant on Economic, Social and Cultural Rights, the International Covenant on Civil and Political Rights and the Optional Protocols to the latter, in all appropriate languages, and to distribute them and make them known as widely as possible in their territories;

14. *Invites* States parties to the Covenants to consider the general comments adopted by the Human Rights Committee and the report of the Committee on Economic, Social and Cultural Rights;

15. *Decides* to transmit the report of the Committee on Economic, Social and Cultural Rights to the General Assembly at its forty-seventh session for consideration under the item entitled "Human rights questions".

Economic and Social Council resolution 1992/11

20 July 1992   Meeting 32   Adopted without vote

Approved by Social Committee (E/1992/103) without vote, 2 July (meeting 5); 27-nation draft (E/1992/C.2/L.3); agenda item 17.
Sponsors: Australia, Austria, Belarus, Benin, Canada, Chile, Colombia, Cyprus, Czechoslovakia, Denmark, Ecuador, El Salvador, Finland, Germany, Hungary, Iceland, Netherlands, Norway, Poland, Portugal, Romania, Russian Federation, Spain, Sweden, Switzerland, United Kingdom, Uruguay.

Universal Declaration of Human Rights

On 18 December 1992, the General Assembly, by **decision 47/429**, asked the Secretary-General to make arrangements to award human rights prizes in 1993, the year marking the forty-fifth anniversary of the 1948 Universal Declaration of Human Rights,[65] as envisaged in a 1966 Assembly resolution.[94]

Electoral processes

Periodic and genuine elections

As requested by the General Assembly in 1991,[95] the Secretary-General in November submitted a report on enhancing the effectiveness of the principle of periodic and genuine elections.[96] The Secretary-General stated that between 1 October 1991 and 16 October 1992, 31 requests had been received from Member States for electoral assistance compared with five such requests at the same time in 1991. Of those requests, 12 related to technical assistance, 8 referred to the sending of observers and 11 involved a combination of the two activities. Annexed to the report was a list of the 31 countries, the nature of their requests and follow-up action taken. The Secretary-General discussed major United Nations missions, including UNTAC (for further details see PART TWO, Chap-

ter III), the United Nations Angola Verification Mission II (see PART TWO, Chapter I) and the United Nations Mission for the Referendum in Western Sahara (see PART FOUR, Chapter I).

In accordance with a 1991 Assembly resolution,[95] the Secretary-General stated that a voluntary fund—the United Nations Trust Fund for Electoral Observation—was established for cases in which the requesting Member State was unable to finance, in whole or in part, the electoral verification mission. In addition, the UNDP Administrator had established a separate Trust Fund for Technical Assistance to Electoral Processes.

In addition to the criteria that should be met before agreeing to requests for electoral verification, as outlined in his 1991 report,[97] the Secretary-General stated that six basic approaches for such involvement could be defined as organization and conduct of elections; supervision; verification; observation; coordination and support of the activities of international observers affiliated with other organizations; and technical assistance.

The Secretary-General summarized additional replies received since his November 1991 report[97] from two Governments and one intergovernmental organization concerning suitable approaches to permit the United Nations to respond to Member States' requests for electoral assistance. Annexed to the report were the recommendations of the United Nations Conference on Coordination of Assistance in the Electoral Field (Ottawa, Canada, 5-8 October 1992).

The addendum to the report contained proposed guidelines, prepared by the Secretariat, for Member States considering the formulation of requests for electoral assistance.

GENERAL ASSEMBLY ACTION

On 18 December 1992, the General Assembly, on the recommendation of the Third Committee, adopted **resolution 47/138** by recorded vote.

Enhancing the effectiveness of the principle of periodic and genuine elections

The General Assembly,

Recalling its resolutions 44/146 of 15 December 1989, 45/150 of 18 December 1990, and especially 46/137 of 17 December 1991, as well as the annex to Commission on Human Rights resolution 1989/51 of 7 March 1989,

Having considered the report of the Secretary-General,

Acknowledging the proposed guidelines on electoral assistance prepared by the Secretariat,

Noting the increase in requests for electoral assistance by Member States,

1. *Takes note with appreciation* of the report of the Secretary-General;

2. *Welcomes* the decision of the Secretary-General to designate a focal point for electoral verification and electoral assistance;

3. *Takes note* of the decision of the Secretary-General to establish the Electoral Assistance Unit within the Secretariat;

4. *Commends* the electoral assistance provided to Member States at their request by the Organization, requests that such assistance continue on a case-by-case basis in accordance with the proposed guidelines on electoral assistance, recognizing that the fundamental responsibility for ensuring free and fair elections lies with Governments, and also requests the Electoral Assistance Unit to inform Member States on a regular basis about the requests received, the responses given to those requests and the nature of the assistance provided;

5. *Welcomes* the establishment by the Secretary-General of the United Nations Trust Fund for Electoral Observation and the establishment by the Administrator of the United Nations Development Programme of a separate fund, the Trust Fund for Technical Assistance to Electoral Processes, and calls upon Member States to consider contributing to the Funds;

6. *Stresses the importance* of coordination by the focal point within the United Nations system, commends the Centre for Human Rights of the Secretariat for the advisory services and technical assistance it provides and the Department of Economic and Social Development of the Secretariat and the United Nations Development Programme for the technical assistance they are providing to requesting Member States, and requests the focal point to continue to collaborate closely with the Centre for Human Rights as well as with the Department of Economic and Social Development and the United Nations Development Programme and inform them of requests presented in the area of electoral assistance;

7. *Requests* the Secretary-General to provide the Electoral Assistance Unit with adequate human and financial resources, under the regular budget of the Organization and within existing resources, to allow it to carry out its regular mandate;

8. *Also requests* the Secretary-General to reinforce the Centre for Human Rights through the redeployment of resources and personnel in order to enable it to answer, in close coordination with the Electoral Assistance Unit, the increasing number of requests from Member States for advisory services in the area of electoral assistance;

9. *Recommends* that the proposed guidelines on electoral assistance be considered as provisional, and requests the Secretary-General to evaluate the guidelines in the light of experience over the next two years;

10. *Requests* the Secretary-General to report to the General Assembly at its forty-eighth session on the implementation of resolution 46/137 and the present resolution, in particular on the status of requests from Member States for electoral assistance and verification, and on the validity of the guidelines in the light of experience;

11. *Decides* that the question of enhancing the effectiveness of the principle of periodic and genuine elections shall be biennialized as of the forty-ninth session of the General Assembly.

General Assembly resolution 47/138

18 December 1992   Meeting 92   141-0-20 (recorded vote)

Approved by Third Committee (A/47/678/Add.2) by recorded vote (129-1-19), 4 December (meeting 58); 44-nation draft (A/C.3/47/L.69); agenda item 97 *(b)*.

Sponsors: Albania, Argentina, Australia, Belgium, Benin, Bulgaria, Canada, Cape Verde, Central African Republic, Chad, Costa Rica, Czechoslovakia, Denmark, El Salvador, Finland, Gambia, Greece, Hungary, Israel, Italy, Lat-

via, Lithuania, Luxembourg, Madagascar, Mali, Malta, Marshall Islands, Nicaragua, Netherlands, Norway, Panama, Poland, Republic of Korea, Republic of Moldova, Romania, Russian Federation, Rwanda, Samoa, Singapore, Tajikistan, Turkey, Ukraine, United Kingdom, United States.

Meeting numbers. GA 47th session: 3rd Committee 47-58; plenary 92.

Recorded vote in Assembly as follows:

In favour: Afghanistan, Algeria, Angola, Antigua and Barbuda, Argentina, Armenia, Australia, Austria, Azerbaijan, Bahamas, Bahrain, Bangladesh, Barbados, Belarus, Belgium, Belize, Benin, Bhutan, Bolivia, Bosnia and Herzegovina, Botswana, Brazil, Bulgaria, Burkina Faso, Burundi, Cameroon, Canada, Cape Verde, Central African Republic, Chad, Chile, Comoros, Congo, Costa Rica, Côte d'Ivoire, Croatia, Cyprus, Czechoslovakia, Denmark, Djibouti, Dominica, Dominican Republic, Ecuador, Egypt, El Salvador, Estonia, Ethiopia, Fiji, Finland, Gabon, Gambia, Germany, Ghana, Greece, Grenada, Guatemala, Guinea, Guinea-Bissau, Guyana, Haiti, Honduras, Hungary, Iceland, India, Indonesia, Ireland, Israel, Italy, Jamaica, Jordan, Kazakhstan, Kenya, Kuwait, Latvia, Lebanon, Lesotho, Liberia, Liechtenstein, Lithuania, Luxembourg, Madagascar, Malawi, Maldives, Mali, Malta, Marshall Islands, Mauritania, Mauritius, Mongolia, Morocco, Mozambique, Nepal, Netherlands, New Zealand, Nicaragua, Niger, Nigeria, Norway, Oman, Pakistan, Panama, Paraguay, Peru, Poland, Portugal, Qatar, Republic of Korea, Republic of Moldova, Romania, Russian Federation, Rwanda, Saint Kitts and Nevis, Saint Lucia, Saint Vincent and the Grenadines, Samoa, Sao Tome and Principe, Senegal, Seychelles, Sierra Leone, Singapore, Slovenia, Solomon Islands, Spain, Sri Lanka, Suriname, Swaziland, Sweden, Thailand, Togo, Trinidad and Tobago, Tunisia, Turkey, Ukraine, United Arab Emirates, United Kingdom, United States, Uruguay, Vanuatu, Venezuela, Yemen, Zambia.

Against: None.

Abstaining: China, Colombia, Cuba, Democratic People's Republic of Korea, France, Iraq, Japan, Lao People's Democratic Republic, Malaysia, Mexico, Myanmar, Namibia, Papua New Guinea, Philippines, Sudan, Syrian Arab Republic, Uganda, United Republic of Tanzania, Viet Nam, Zimbabwe.

Respect for the principles of national sovereignty and non-interference

In response to a 1991 General Assembly request,[98] the Secretary-General in October submitted a report[99] summarizing action taken by the Commission on Human Rights concerning respect for the principles of national sovereignty and non-interference in the internal affairs of States in their electoral processes. He stated that while no specific action had been taken to review the fundamental factors negatively affecting the observance of those principles, a number of resolutions referred to the issue of elections in the context of guaranteeing the free expression of the will of people. They had concerned Afghanistan;[100] Albania;[71] South Africa;[101] and strengthening United Nations action in the field of human rights through the promotion of international cooperation and the importance of non-selectivity, impartiality and objectivity.[33]

GENERAL ASSEMBLY ACTION

By **decision 47/431** of 18 December 1992, the General Assembly, on the recommendation of the Third Committee, took note of the Secretary-General's report.

On the same date, and on the recommendation of the Third Committee, the Assembly adopted **resolution 47/130** by recorded vote.

Respect for the principles of national sovereignty and non-interference in the internal affairs of States in their electoral processes

The General Assembly,

Reaffirming the purposes of the United Nations to develop friendly relations among nations based on respect for the principle of equal rights and self-determination of peoples and to take other appropriate measures to strengthen universal peace,

Recalling its resolution 1514(XV) of 14 December 1960 containing the Declaration on the Granting of Independence to Colonial Countries and Peoples,

Also recalling its resolution 2625(XXV) of 24 October 1970, by which it approved the Declaration on Principles of International Law concerning Friendly Relations and Cooperation among States in accordance with the Charter of the United Nations, contained in the annex to that resolution,

Further recalling the principle enshrined in Article 2, paragraph 7, of the Charter of the United Nations, which establishes that nothing contained in the Charter shall authorize the United Nations to intervene in matters which are essentially within the domestic jurisdiction of any State or shall require the Members to submit such matters to settlement under the Charter,

Reaffirming the legitimacy of the struggle of the oppressed people of South Africa for the elimination of apartheid and for the establishment of a society in which all the people of South Africa as a whole, irrespective of race, colour or creed, will enjoy equal and full political and other rights and participate freely in the determination of their destiny,

Also reaffirming the legitimacy of the struggle of all peoples under colonial and foreign domination, particularly the Palestinian people, for the exercise of their inalienable right to self-determination and national independence, which will enable them to decide freely on their own future,

Recognizing that the principles of national sovereignty and non-interference in the internal affairs of any State should be respected in the holding of elections,

Also recognizing that there is no single political system or single model for electoral processes equally suited to all nations and their peoples, and that political systems and electoral processes are subject to historical, political, cultural and religious factors,

Recalling its resolutions in this regard, in particular resolution 46/130 of 17 December 1991,

1. *Reiterates* that, by virtue of the principle of equal rights and self-determination of peoples enshrined in the Charter of the United Nations, all peoples have the right, freely and without external interference, to determine their political status and to pursue their economic, social and cultural development and that every State has the duty to respect that right in accordance with the provisions of the Charter;

2. *Reaffirms* that it is the concern solely of peoples to determine methods and to establish institutions regarding the electoral process, as well as to determine the ways for its implementation according to their constitution and national legislation;

3. *Also reaffirms* that any activities that attempt, directly or indirectly, to interfere in the free development of national electoral processes, in particular in the developing countries, or that intend to sway the results of such processes, violate the spirit and letter of the principles established in the Charter and in the Declaration on Principles of International Law concerning Friendly Relations and Cooperation among States in accordance with the Charter of the United Nations;

4. *Further reaffirms* that there is no universal need for the United Nations to provide electoral assistance to Member States, except in special circumstances such as cases of decolonization, in the context of regional or international peace processes or at the request of specific sovereign States, by virtue of resolutions adopted by the Security Council or the General Assembly in each case, in strict conformity with the principles of sovereignty and non-interference in the internal affairs of States;

5. *Urges* all States to respect the principle of non-interference in the internal affairs of States and the sovereign right of peoples to determine their political, economic and social system;

6. *Strongly appeals* to all States to refrain from financing or providing, directly or indirectly, any other form of overt or covert support for political parties or groups and from taking actions to undermine the electoral processes in any country;

7. *Condemns* any act of armed aggression or threat or use of force against peoples, their elected Governments or their legitimate leaders;

8. *Reiterates* that only the total eradication of apartheid and the establishment of a non-racial, democratic society based on majority rule, through the full and free exercise of adult suffrage by all the people in a united and non-fragmented South Africa, can lead to a just and lasting solution to the situation in South Africa;

9. *Reaffirms* the legitimacy of the struggle of all peoples under colonial and foreign domination, particularly the Palestinian people, for the exercise of their inalienable right to self-determination and national independence, which will enable them to determine their political, economic and social system, without interference;

10. *Calls upon* the Commission on Human Rights at its forty-ninth session to continue giving priority to the review of the fundamental factors that negatively affect the observance of the principles of national sovereignty and non-interference in the internal affairs of States in their electoral processes and to report to the General Assembly at its forty-eighth session, through the Economic and Social Council;

11. *Requests* the Secretary-General to report to the General Assembly at its forty-eighth session on the implementation of the present resolution under the item entitled "Human rights questions".

General Assembly resolution 47/130

18 December 1992   Meeting 92   99-45-16 (recorded vote)

Approved by Third Committee (A/47/678/Add.2) by recorded vote (82-43-14), 4 December (meeting 57); 9-nation draft (A/C.3/47/L.61); agenda item 97 *(b)*.

Sponsors: China, Cuba, Democratic People's Republic of Korea, Lao People's Democratic Republic, Namibia, Sudan, United Republic of Tanzania, Viet Nam, Zimbabwe.

Meeting numbers. GA 47th session: 3rd Committee 47-57; plenary 92.

Recorded vote in Assembly as follows:

In favour: Afghanistan, Algeria, Angola, Antigua and Barbuda, Bahamas, Bahrain, Bangladesh, Barbados, Belize, Benin, Bhutan, Botswana, Brazil, Brunei Darussalam, Burkina Faso, Burundi, Cameroon, Cape Verde, Central African Republic, Chad, China, Colombia, Côte d'Ivoire, Cuba, Cyprus, Democratic People's Republic of Korea, Djibouti, Dominica, Ecuador, Egypt, Gabon, Gambia, Ghana, Grenada, Guatemala, Guinea, Guinea-Bissau, Guyana, Haiti, India, Indonesia, Iran, Iraq, Jordan, Kenya, Kuwait, Lao People's Democratic Republic, Lebanon, Lesotho, Liberia, Libyan Arab Jamahiriya, Malawi, Malaysia, Maldives, Mali, Mauritania, Mexico, Mongolia, Morocco, Myanmar, Namibia, Nepal, Nicaragua, Niger, Nigeria, Oman, Pakistan, Papua New Guinea, Paraguay, Peru, Qatar, Rwanda, Saint Kitts and Nevis, Saint Lucia, Saint Vincent and the Grenadines, Sao Tome and Principe, Saudi Arabia, Senegal, Seychelles, Sierra Leone, Singapore, Sri Lanka, Sudan, Suriname, Swaziland, Syrian Arab Republic, Thailand, Trinidad and Tobago, Tunisia, Uganda, United Arab Emirates, United Republic of Tanzania, Uruguay, Vanuatu, Venezuela, Viet Nam, Yemen, Zambia, Zimbabwe.

Regional arrangements

Human Rights Commission action. On 3 March,[102] the Commission asked States in areas where regional arrangements in the field of human rights did not exist to consider agreements to establish regional machinery to promote and protect human rights. It welcomed the continued cooperation of the Centre for Human Rights with the Executive Secretary of the Economic and Social Commission for Asia and the Pacific (ESCAP) in establishing a depository centre for United Nations human rights materials at ESCAP headquarters (Bangkok). The Commission asked the Secretary-General, as foreseen in the medium-term plan for 1992-1997, to continue to strengthen exchanges between the United Nations and regional intergovernmental organizations dealing with human rights, and welcomed the continued organization, by the Centre for Human Rights, of national, regional and subregional workshops and training courses for government officials engaged in the administration of justice and in implementing international human rights instruments. It also asked him to submit in 1993 a report on the state of regional arrangements for the promotion of human rights.

Reports of the Secretary-General. As requested by the General Assembly in 1990,[103] the Secretary-General submitted to the Commission in February,[104] and to the Assembly in October,[105] a report describing cooperation to promote and protect human rights between the United Nations and regional bodies and commissions in Africa, the Americas, Asia and the Pacific and Europe.

GENERAL ASSEMBLY ACTION

On 18 December 1992, on the recommendation of the Third Committee, the General Assembly adopted **resolution 47/125** without vote.

Regional arrangements for the promotion and protection of human rights

The General Assembly,

Recalling its resolution 32/127 of 16 December 1977 and all its subsequent resolutions concerning regional arrangements for the promotion and protection of human rights, in particular resolutions 45/167 and 45/168 of 18 December 1990,

Recalling also that, in its resolution 45/167, the General Assembly invited the Secretary-General to submit to the Assembly at its forty-seventh session a report on the state of regional arrangements for the promotion and protection of human rights and to include therein the results of action taken in pursuance of that resolution,

Taking note of Commission on Human Rights resolution 1992/52 of 3 March 1992 on regional arrangements for the promotion and protection of human rights,

Bearing in mind the relevant resolutions of the Commission on Human Rights concerning advisory services in the field of human rights, including its most recent resolution on that subject, 1992/80 of 5 March 1992,

Recalling Commission on Human Rights resolutions 1989/50 of 7 March 1989, 1990/71 of 7 March 1990, 1991/28 of 5 March 1991 and taking note of Commission resolution 1992/40 of 28 February 1992 concerning regional arrangements for the promotion and protection of human rights in the Asian and Pacific region,

Having considered the report of the Secretary-General,

Noting with satisfaction the progress achieved so far in the promotion and protection of human rights at the regional level under the auspices of the United Nations, the specialized agencies and the regional intergovernmental organizations,

Reaffirming that regional arrangements for the promotion and protection of human rights may make a major contribution to the effective enjoyment of human rights and fundamental freedoms and that the exchange of information and experience in this field among the regions, within the United Nations system, may be improved,

Bearing in mind that regional instruments should complement the universally accepted human rights standards and that the persons chairing the human rights treaty bodies noted during their third meeting, held at Geneva from 1 to 5 October 1990, that certain inconsistencies between provisions of international instruments and those of regional instruments might raise difficulties with regard to their implementation,

1. *Takes note* of the report of the Secretary-General;

2. *Welcomes* the continuing cooperation and assistance of the Centre for Human Rights of the Secretariat in the further strengthening of the existing regional arrangements and regional machinery for the promotion and protection of human rights, particularly in regard to advisory services and technical assistance, public information and education, with a view to exchanging any information and experience in the field of human rights;

3. *Welcomes also* in that respect the close cooperation given by the Centre for Human Rights in the organization of regional and subregional training courses or workshops in the field of human rights, including, most recently, those that took place at Barcelona, Brasilia, Cairo, Caracas, Paris, San Remo, Santiago, Teheran, Valetta and Windhoek, aiming at creating greater understanding of the promotion and protection of human rights issues in the regions and at improving procedures and examining the various systems for the promotion and protection of the universally accepted human rights standards;

4. *Stresses* the importance of the programme of advisory services in the field of human rights, and renews its appeal to all Governments to consider making use of the possibilities offered by the United Nations, under this programme, of organizing information and/or training courses at the national level for government personnel on the application of international human rights standards and the experience of relevant international bodies;

5. *Invites* States in areas where regional arrangements in the field of human rights do not yet exist to consider agreements with a view to the establishment within their respective regions of suitable regional machinery for the promotion and protection of human rights;

6. *Requests* the Secretary-General, as foreseen in the medium-term plan for the period 1992-1997, to continue to strengthen exchanges between the United Nations and regional intergovernmental organizations dealing with human rights, and welcomes, in this connection, the fact that the Centre for Human Rights will continue to organize national, regional and subregional workshops and training courses for government officials engaged in the administration of justice and in the implementation of the international human rights instruments and that more countries in all regions of the world are expected to develop forms of cooperation and assistance with the Centre, in keeping with their specific needs;

7. *Invites* the organizers of regional meetings convened in preparation for the World Conference on Human Rights to be held in 1993 to promote further ratification of and accession to United Nations human rights treaties and the implementation of universally accepted human rights standards;

8. *Welcomes* the recommendation of the persons chairing or representing the United Nations human rights treaty bodies concerning a possible meeting, during the World Conference on Human Rights, of the persons chairing or representing the United Nations human rights treaty bodies and those chairing or representing each of the principal regional organizations and institutions in the field of human rights, and requests the Preparatory Committee for the World Conference on Human Rights to consider the holding of such a meeting;

9. *Requests* the Commission on Human Rights to continue to pay special attention to the most appropriate ways of assisting, at their request, countries of the different regions under the programme of advisory services and to make, where necessary, the relevant recommendations;

10. *Requests* the Secretary-General to submit to the General Assembly at its forty-ninth session a report on the state of regional arrangements for the promotion and protection of human rights and to include therein the results of action taken in pursuance of the present resolution;

11. *Decides* to consider this question further at its forty-ninth session.

General Assembly resolution 47/125

18 December 1992   Meeting 92   Adopted without vote

Approved by Third Committee (A/47/678/Add.2) without vote, 3 December (meeting 56); 37-nation draft (A/C.3/47/L.54); agenda item 97 *(b)*.

Sponsors: Argentina, Australia, Austria, Belarus, Belgium, Benin, Brazil, Central African Republic, Chile, Costa Rica, Côte d'Ivoire, Cyprus, Egypt, El Salvador, Gambia, Germany, Guatemala, Honduras, Hungary, Italy, Japan, Malta, Namibia, Netherlands, Nigeria, Norway, Philippines, Romania, Russian Federation, Rwanda, Samoa, Thailand, Togo, Ukraine, Uruguay, Venezuela, Yemen.

Meeting numbers. GA 47th session: 3rd Committee 47-56; plenary 92.

Asia and the Pacific

The General Assembly, in 1990,[106] had welcomed the designation of the ESCAP library as a depository centre for United Nations human rights materials within ESCAP at its Bangkok headquar-

ters. The library's functions included the collection, processing and dissemination of such materials in the Asian and Pacific region.

Human Rights Commission action. On 28 February,[107] the Commission encouraged ESCAP member States and associate members and other parties to use ESCAP's depository centre and asked the Secretary-General to ensure a continuing flow of human rights materials to the library. It encouraged States in the Asian and Pacific region to consider establishing regional arrangements to promote and protect human rights, and asked the Secretary-General to organize a seminar in 1992 to discuss the matter. The Commission appealed to Governments in the region to consider making use of the United Nations to organize, under the programme of advisory services and technical assistance in human rights, information and training courses for government personnel on the application of international human rights standards and the experience of relevant international organs. It requested the Secretary-General to consult the States in the region in the implementation of its resolution, and asked him to submit a report on the progress achieved.

Reports of the Secretary-General. At its 1992 session, the Secretary-General presented to the Commission a progress report on regional arrangements for the promotion and protection of human rights in Asia and the Pacific.[108] He described cooperation between the Centre on Human Rights and ESCAP, and summarized replies received from two specialized agencies and two United Nations bodies containing their suggestions for activities. The Secretary-General also discussed consultations between the United Nations and countries in the region.

In May,[109] the Secretary-General drew to the attention of the General Assembly and the Economic and Social Council his report to the Commission. On 20 July, the Council, by **decision 1992/263**, took note of the Secretary-General's report, as did the Assembly on 18 December by **decision 47/433**.

Responsibility to promote and protect human rights

Working Group activities. The Working Group to draft a declaration on the right and responsibility of individuals, groups and organs of society to promote and protect universally recognized human rights and fundamental freedoms held its seventh session at Geneva from 13 to 24 January and on 18 February.[110] It considered the preamble and chapters I to V with a view to reaching agreement on all matters left outstanding from previous sessions. The Group provisionally adopted a first-reading text but did not finalize several elements of chapters II, III, IV and V of the draft declaration. Annexed to the Group's report were a compilation of all the texts showing the state of the whole draft declaration, a compilation of proposals for a second-reading text and guidelines for a technical review of the draft declaration.

Human Rights Commission action. On 6 March,[111] the Commission requested the Working Group to submit the draft declaration in 1993 and asked the Secretary-General to circulate the group's report to Member States, specialized agencies, intergovernmental organizations and NGOs for their comments on the first-reading text. It also asked the Secretary-General to carry out a technical review of the draft in accordance with the guidelines annexed to the group's report and to distribute the results to Member States, specialized agencies, persons chairing human rights treaty bodies, intergovernmental organizations and NGOs. The Commission decided to continue elaborating the draft declaration at its 1993 session and to make meeting time available to the Working Group prior to and during that session. It recommended a draft resolution to the Economic and Social Council for adoption.

ECONOMIC AND SOCIAL COUNCIL ACTION

On 20 July 1992, the Economic and Social Council, on the recommendation of its Social Committee, adopted **resolution 1992/9** without vote.

Question of a draft declaration on the right and responsibility of individuals, groups and organs of society to promote and protect universally recognized human rights and fundamental freedoms

The Economic and Social Council,

Taking note of Commission on Human Rights resolution 1992/82 of 5 March 1992,

1. *Authorizes* an open-ended working group of the Commission on Human Rights to meet for a period of two weeks prior to the forty-ninth session of the Commission, with a view to completing at that time the second reading of a draft declaration on the right and responsibility of individuals, groups and organs of society to promote and protect universally recognized human rights and fundamental freedoms and to submitting the text to the Commission at its forty-ninth session for adoption;

2. *Requests* the Secretary-General to extend all the necessary facilities to the working group for its meetings.

Economic and Social Council resolution 1992/9

20 July 1992   Meeting 32   Adopted without vote

Approved by Social Committee (E/1992/103) without vote, 15 July (meeting 7); draft by Commission on Human Rights (E/1992/22); agenda item 17.

Internally displaced persons and humanitarian assistance

On 5 March,[112] the Commission on Human Rights, taking note of the Secretary-General's February 1992 analytical report on internally displaced persons,[113] asked him to designate a representative to seek views and information from all Governments on the human rights issues related to such persons, a request approved by the Economic and Social Council on 20 July by **decision 1992/243**. It also encouraged the Secretary-General to seek views and information from specialized agencies, United Nations organs, regional intergovernmental and non-governmental organizations and experts in all regions, as well as from the United Nations Emergency Relief Coordinator, UNHCR, the International Organization for Migration, ICRC and the Ad Hoc Working Group on Early Warning regarding New Flows of Refugees and Displaced Persons. It asked him to submit in 1993 a comprehensive study identifying existing laws and mechanisms to protect internally displaced persons, possible additional measures to strengthen implementation of those laws and mechanisms for addressing protection needs not adequately covered by existing instruments.

Subcommission action. On 26 August 1992,[114] the Subcommission called on all parties involved in the conflict in Somalia to end violations of human rights and humanitarian law and asked UNHCR to ensure adequate protection of and resources for refugees. (For further details on refugees in Somalia, see PART THREE, Chapter XV, and for further details on humanitarian assistance to that country, see PART THREE, Chapter III.)

REFERENCES

[1]E/1992/22 (res. 1992/54). [2]E/CN.4/1992/43 & Add.1,2. [3]A/47/701. [4]E/1992/22. [5]E/CN.4/1992/5. [6]E/1992/22 (dec. 1992/105). [7]Ibid. (dec. 1992/117). [8]Ibid. (dec. 1992/101). [9]Ibid. (dec. 1992/118). [10]Ibid. (res. 1992/55). [11]ESC res. 1990/48, 25 May 1990. [12]YUN 1991, p. 843, GA res. 46/59, 9 Dec. 1991. [13]E/1992/22. (dec. 1992/119). [14]Ibid. (res. 1992/83). [15]YUN 1991, p. 575. [16]E/CN.4/1993/2. [17]Ibid. (dec. 1992/111). [18]Ibid. (dec. 1992/105). [19]Ibid. (dec. 1992/112). [20]Ibid. (dec. 1992/102). [21]E/CN.4/1992/46. [22]E/1992/22 (res. 1992/66). [23]E/CN.4/Sub.2/1992/3 & Add.1. [24]E/CN.4/1993/2 (res. 1992/8). [25]E/CN.4/1992/56 & Corr.1 & Add.1-5. [26]YUN 1986, p. 731, ESC res. 1986/35, 23 May 1986. [27]E/1992/22 (res. 1992/53). [28]E/1990/50, A/45/807. [29]YUN 1991, p. 576, GA res. 46/118, 17 Dec. 1991. [30]E/CN.4/1992/75. [31]A/47/702. [32]E/CN.4/1992/21 & Add.1,2. [33]E/1992/22 (res. 1992/39). [34]YUN 1966, pp. 419 & 423, GA res. 2200 A (XXI), annex, 16 Dec. 1966. [35]YUN 1991, p. 577. [36]Ibid., GA res. 46/129, 17 Dec. 1991. [37]E/1992/22 (res. 1992/51). [38]Ibid. (res. 1992/37). [39]GA res. 45/155, 18 Dec. 1990. [40]YUN 1991, p. 578. [41]E/1992/22 (res. 1992/38.) [42]A/CONF.157/PC/28. [43]A/CONF.157/PC/30. [44]A/CONF. 157/PC/31. [45]A/46/901. [46]A/47/24. [47]A/47/24/Add.1. [48]A/CONF.157/PC/17. [49]A/CONF.157/PC/18/Rev.1. [50]A/CONF.157/PC/45. [51]A/CONF.157/PC/44. [52]*United Nations Action in the Field of Human Rights*, Sales No. E.88.XIV.2. [53]*Human Rights: A Compilation of International Instruments*, Sales No. E.88.XIV.1. [54]*Human Rights: Status of International Instruments*, Sales No. E.87.XIV.2. [55]A/CONF.157/PC/41. [56]E/CN.4/1992/57/Add.1. [57]YUN 1991, p. 579, GA res. 46/116, 17 Dec. 1991. [58]A/CONF.157/PC/22. [59]A/CONF.157/PC/42. [60]A/CONF.157/PC/20. [61]E/CN.4/1992/22. [62]A/47/503. [63]GA res. 45/99, 14 Dec. 1990. [64]GA res. 43/128, 8 Dec.

1988. (65)YUN 1948-49, p. 535, GA res. 217 A (III), 10 Dec. 1948. (66)E/CN.4/1993/61 & Corr.1 & Add.1. (67)YUN 1955, p. 164, GA res. 926(X), 14 Dec. 1955. (68)YUN 1987, p. 790, ESC dec. 1987/147, 29 May 1987. (69)E/1992/22 (res. 1992/80). (70)E/CN.4/1992/49. (71)E/1992/22 (res. 1992/69). (72)Ibid. (res. 1992/64). (73)Ibid. (res. 1992/79). (74)E/CN.4/1992/51. (75)E/1992/22 (res. 1992/78). (76)E/CN.4/1993/2 (res. 1992/18). (77)Ibid. (res. 1992/1). (78)E/CN.4/Sub.2/1992/27 & Corr.1. (79)YUN 1965, p. 440, GA res. 2106 A (XX), annex, 21 Dec. 1965. (80)YUN 1979, p. 895, GA res. 34/180, annex, 18 Dec. 1979. (81)YUN 1984, p. 813, GA res. 39/46, annex, 16 Dec. 1984. (82)GA res. 44/22, 20 Nov. 1989. (83)YUN 1973, p. 103, GA res. 3068(XXVIII), annex, 30 Nov. 1973. (84)E/1992/22 (res. 1992/15). (85)A/45/636. (86)A/47/628. (87)A/44/686. (88)E/CN.4/1992/44. (89)E/CN.4/1990/39. (90)*Manual on Human Rights Reporting*, Sales No. E.91.XIV.1. (91)YUN 1991, p. 583, GA res. 46/111, 17 Dec. 1991. (92)A/47/518. (93)E/1992/22 (res. 1992/14). (94)YUN 1966, p. 457, GA res. 2217 A, 19 Dec. 1966. (95)YUN 1991, p. 588, GA res. 46/137, 17 Dec. 1991. (96)A/47/668 & Corr.1 & Add.1. (97) YUN 1991, p. 587. (98)Ibid., p. 590, GA res. 46/130, 17 Dec. 1991. (99)A/47/479. (100)E/1992/22 (res. 1992/5). (101)Ibid. (res. 1992/19). (102)Ibid. (res. 1992/52). (103)GA res. 45/167, 18 Dec. 1990. (104)E/CN.4/1992/58. (105)A/47/502. (106)GA res. 45/168, 18 Dec. 1990. (107)E/1992/22 (res. 1992/40). (108)E/CN.4/1992/24. (109)A/47/184-E/1992/44. (110)E/CN.4/1992/53 & Corr.1. (111)E/1992/22 (res. 1992/82). (112)Ibid. (res. 1992/73). (113)E/CN.4/1992/23. (114)E/CN.4/1993/2 (res. 1992/11).

Human rights violations

During 1992, situations involving alleged violations of human rights on a large scale in several countries were again examined by the General Assembly, the Economic and Social Council and the Commission on Human Rights, as well as by special bodies and officials appointed to examine some of those situations.

In addition, situations of alleged human rights violations involving the self-determination of peoples (see above, under "Civil and political rights") were discussed with regard to Afghanistan, Cambodia, Western Sahara and the Palestinian people.

Under a procedure established by the Council in 1970 to deal with communications alleging denial or violation of human rights,(1) the Working Group on Communications of the Subcommission on Prevention of Discrimination and Protection of Minorities met from 20 to 31 July 1992. Following its consideration of the Working Group's confidential report, the Subcommission referred to the Commission for consideration certain situations that appeared to reveal a consistent pattern of gross and reliably attested human rights violations. It deferred action on certain communications until 1993 and decided to take no action on communications pending since its 1991 session.(2)

Africa

South Africa

Working Group activities. In 1992, the six-member Ad Hoc Working Group of Experts on Southern Africa, established by the Commission on Human Rights in 1967,(3) submitted to the Commission an interim report(4) and prepared a final report to be submitted to the Commission in 1993.(5)

In its final report, the Group re-examined its mandate and discussed the organization of its work concerning fact-finding missions aimed at gathering testimony from witnesses (Harare, Zimbabwe, 20-24 July, and Gaborone, Botswana, 27-30 July). Subjects of inquiry dealt with by the Group concerned: the right to life; detention and deaths in police custody; capital punishment and executions; administration of justice; political trials; escalating violence resulting in deaths; conditions after the repeal of certain apartheid legislation; return of exiles; constitutional negotiations; the right to education; and children.

The Working Group recommended the implementation of a number of observations contained in a 7 August report of the Secretary-General to the Security Council on the question of South Africa(6) (see PART TWO, Chapter 1) and supported recommendations proposed by the International Labour Organisation (ILO) Fact-finding and Conciliation Commission on Freedom of Association (see below, under "Trade union rights"). It recommended establishing guarantees to secure the safety of witnesses and improving the legal aid system in South Africa. The Group asked the Commission to invite the Government of South Africa to restore confidence in the administration of justice; ensure the independence of the judiciary; prosecute civil servants having committed human rights violations under international human rights instruments; establish a consultative body, including representatives of the black population, to facilitate a dialogue to improve living conditions in rural areas; and facilitate the active participation of all parties concerned in the constitutional negotiations. The Group further asked the Commission to exert pressure on South Africa to grant an unconditional amnesty only to those who had committed acts to combat apartheid; obtain from those who had visited South Africa any relevant information likely to help the Group in fulfilling its mandate; enlist the Secretary-General's support to obtain authorization from the Government for the Group to visit that country in 1993; renew its mandate; and authorize the Group to update its list of civil servants and other South African government officials who had committed acts violating international human rights instruments. It advocated the release of all detained children and the transformation of South Africa's educational system into a non-racial one. Annexed to the report was a list of persons deemed responsible for the crime of apartheid.

Human Rights Commission action. On 28 February,(7) the Commission demanded that the

South African authorities fully respect section 29 of the Prisons Act, prevent the inhuman treatment of children in South Africa and ensure their basic and legitimate freedoms of movement, association and education. It called on the authorities to release all political prisoners; allow an impartial investigation into the alleged complicity by security organs and State-funded organizations in fomenting township violence and harassing legitimate anti-apartheid groups; maintain law and order; repeal the provisions of the Internal Security Act providing for detention without trial; abolish the system of "homelands"; repeal remaining discriminatory laws; accede to the 1966 International Covenants on Human Rights[8] and the International Convention on the Elimination of All Forms of Racial Discrimination;[9] and allow the Ad Hoc Working Group of Experts on Southern Africa to visit South Africa and cooperate with it in appraising human rights developments. It called on the international community to assist the front-line and neighbouring States; increase material and financial assistance to apartheid victims and assist and enhance the role of humanitarian and human rights groups in doing the same; assist UNHCR and other humanitarian organizations in repatriating and reintegrating South African refugees; and observe fully the mandatory arms embargo and the Security Council's 1977 request to monitor effectively the implementation of the arms embargo against South Africa.[10] The Commission called on the Centre for Human Rights to respond to the needs of South Africa during its period of transition, in accordance with a 1991 General Assembly resolution,[11] and asked the Group to report in 1993.

Subcommission action. On 26 August,[12] the Subcommission called on South Africa not to execute persons convicted and sentenced to death for "security", "security-related" or "unrest-related" offences and to bring before the courts any members of the security forces or other government organs or other persons against whom *prima facie* evidence of participation in killing residents in black areas or in murdering political opponents of apartheid existed. It condemned all military collaboration with South Africa, particularly in the nuclear field.

Note by the Secretary-General. By a note of 20 September,[13] the Secretary-General transmitted to the General Assembly a preliminary report on the situation of human rights in South Africa prepared by the Ad Hoc Working Group of Experts on Southern Africa. The report evaluated the principal developments of the human rights situation in South Africa between February and September 1992. The Working Group believed that immediate effect should be given to a number of recommendations contained in the Secretary-

General's 7 August 1992 report to the Security Council.[6] Considering a recommendation by the Secretary-General that the United Nations provide 30 observers to serve in South Africa, the Group recommended that its members be included among the observers. It further recommended transforming the educational system in South Africa to a non-racial one; respect for an agreement between South Africa and UNHCR under a Memorandum of Understanding; according a general amnesty for returning exiles; and incorporating the item on complete abolition of the apartheid system into the draft agenda of the 1993 World Conference on Human Rights. The Group stressed the importance of providing potential witnesses with protection from any form of victimization and recommended the establishment of guarantees to secure the safety of such witnesses with the help of United Nations monitoring.

GENERAL ASSEMBLY ACTION

By **decision 47/431** of 18 December 1992, the General Assembly took note of the Secretary-General's note transmitting the Group's preliminary report on the situation of human rights in South Africa.

1973 Convention against apartheid

As at 31 December 1992, there were 95 parties to the International Convention on the Suppression and Punishment of the Crime of Apartheid,[14] which was adopted by the General Assembly in 1973[15] and entered into force in 1976.[16] In 1992, Croatia, Jordan, Latvia and Slovenia became parties to the Convention. In his annual report to the General Assembly on the status of the Convention,[17] the Secretary-General provided a list of States that had signed, ratified, acceded or succeeded to it as of 1 August.

GENERAL ASSEMBLY ACTION

On 16 December 1992, the General Assembly, on the recommendation of the Third Committee, adopted **resolution 47/81** by recorded vote.

Status of the International Convention on the Suppression and Punishment of the Crime of Apartheid

The General Assembly,

Recalling its resolutions 41/103 of 4 December 1986, 42/56 of 30 November 1987, 43/97 of 8 December 1988, 44/69 of 8 December 1989, 45/90 of 14 December 1990 and 46/84 of 16 December 1991,

Mindful that the International Convention on the Suppression and Punishment of the Crime of Apartheid constitutes an important international treaty in the field of human rights and serves to implement the ideals of the Universal Declaration of Human Rights,

Reaffirming its conviction that apartheid is a crime against humanity and constitutes a total negation of the purposes and principles of the Charter of the United Nations and a gross violation of human rights, seriously threatening international peace and security,

Condemning the abhorrent policy and system of apartheid and the repression it engenders, which continue to aggravate the situation in South Africa,

Emphasizing that the root cause of the conflict in southern Africa is apartheid,

Deeply concerned at the continued collaboration of certain States and transnational corporations with the Government of South Africa, particularly in the military field, as an encouragement of its odious policy of apartheid,

Convinced that universal ratification of or accession to the Convention and the immediate implementation of its provisions will contribute to the eradication of the crime of apartheid,

1. *Takes note* of the report of the Secretary-General on the status of the International Convention on the Suppression and Punishment of the Crime of Apartheid;

2. *Commends* those States parties to the Convention which have submitted their reports under article VII thereof;

3. *Appeals once again* to all States, United Nations organs, the specialized agencies and international and national non-governmental organizations to step up their activities to enhance public awareness by denouncing the crimes committed by the Government of South Africa with a view to promoting further ratification of or accession to the Convention;

4. *Underlines* the importance of the universal ratification of the Convention, which would be an effective contribution to the fulfilment of the ideals of the Universal Declaration of Human Rights and other human rights instruments;

5. *Appeals once again* to those States which have not yet done so to ratify or to accede to the Convention without further delay;

6. *Requests* the Secretary-General to intensify his efforts, through appropriate channels, to disseminate information on the Convention and its implementation with a view to promoting further ratification of or accession to the Convention;

7. *Also requests* the Secretary-General to include in his next annual report under General Assembly resolution 3380(XXX) of 10 November 1975 a special section concerning the implementation of the Convention.

General Assembly resolution 47/81

16 December 1992   Meeting 89   113-2-44 (recorded vote)

Approved by Third Committee (A/47/658) by recorded vote (93-1-42), 2 November (meeting 25); 7-nation draft (A/C.3/47/L.10); agenda item 91.
Sponsors: Angola, Botswana, Mozambique, Namibia, United Republic of Tanzania, Zambia, Zimbabwe.
Meeting numbers. GA 47th session: 3rd Committee 3-10, 13, 16, 20, 25; plenary 89.

Recorded vote in Assembly as follows:

In favour: Afghanistan, Algeria, Angola, Antigua and Barbuda, Armenia, Bahamas, Bahrain, Bangladesh, Barbados, Belarus, Belize, Benin, Bhutan, Bolivia, Bosnia and Herzegovina, Botswana, Brazil, Brunei Darussalam, Burkina Faso, Burundi, Cameroon, Cape Verde, Chad, Chile, China, Colombia, Comoros, Congo, Costa Rica, Côte d'Ivoire, Cuba, Cyprus, Democratic People's Republic of Korea, Djibouti, Dominican Republic, Ecuador, Egypt, El Salvador, Ethiopia, Fiji, Gabon, Gambia, Ghana, Grenada, Guatemala, Guinea, Guinea-Bissau, Guyana, Haiti, Honduras, India, Indonesia, Iran, Iraq, Jamaica, Jordan, Kenya, Kuwait, Lao People's Democratic Republic, Lebanon, Lesotho, Liberia, Libyan Arab Jamahiriya, Madagascar, Malaysia, Maldives, Mali, Mauritania, Mauritius, Mexico, Mongolia, Morocco, Myanmar, Namibia, Nepal, Niger, Nigeria, Oman, Pakistan, Panama, Papua New Guinea, Paraguay, Peru, Philippines, Qatar,

Rwanda, Saint Kitts and Nevis, Saint Lucia, Saint Vincent and the Grenadines, Sao Tome and Principe, Saudi Arabia, Senegal, Sierra Leone, Singapore, Sri Lanka, Sudan, Suriname, Swaziland, Syrian Arab Republic, Tajikistan, Thailand, Togo, Trinidad and Tobago, Tunisia, Uganda, United Arab Emirates, United Republic of Tanzania, Uruguay, Venezuela, Viet Nam, Yemen, Zambia, Zimbabwe.

Against: Latvia, United States.

Abstaining: Albania, Argentina, Australia, Austria, Azerbaijan, Belgium, Bulgaria, Canada, Croatia, Czechoslovakia, Denmark, Estonia, Finland, France, Germany, Greece, Hungary, Iceland, Israel, Italy, Japan, Kazakhstan, Liechtenstein, Lithuania, Luxembourg, Malta, Marshall Islands, Micronesia, Netherlands, New Zealand, Norway, Poland, Portugal, Republic of Korea, Republic of Moldova, Romania, Russian Federation, Samoa, San Marino, Spain, Sweden, Turkey, Ukraine, United Kingdom.

Foreign support of South Africa

Human Rights Commission action. By a resolution of 28 February,[18] adopted by a roll-call vote of 35 to 15, with 3 abstentions, the Commission condemned assistance to South Africa, particularly in the military field. Also condemning the continuing nuclear collaboration of some States, in particular Israel, with South Africa, the Commission urged them to stop supplying it with nuclear equipment and technology. Noting with appreciation measures taken by some States, parliamentarians, institutions, trade unions and NGOs to exert pressure on South Africa, the Commission called on them to maintain their efforts to force South Africa to comply with United Nations resolutions and decisions. It also noted the disinvestment, trade restrictions and other positive measures taken by some countries and transnational corporations and urged them to continue. The Commission called on Governments that had not yet done so to take measures to end economic, financial and technological cooperation with South Africa, to end assistance in the manufacture of arms and military supplies there and to cease nuclear collaboration with South Africa.

It called on Governments to maintain sanctions and all forms of pressure against South Africa until agreement had been reached on drawing up and adopting a new constitution and holding elections. It appealed to the international community to assist the front-line and neighbouring States and to increase its contributions to the victims and opponents of apartheid. The Commission appealed to the international community, specialized agencies and intergovernmental and non-governmental organizations to increase humanitarian and legal assistance to apartheid victims, returning refugees and exiles and released political prisoners.

The Commission asked the Secretary-General to continue to ensure the coordination of activities of the United Nations system in accordance with the 1989 Declaration on Apartheid and its Destructive Consequences in Southern Africa[19] and to continue monitoring its implementation and pursue initiatives leading to the eradication of apartheid. Expressing appreciation to the Subcommission's Special Rapporteur, Ahmed Mohamed Khalifa (Egypt), for his updated 1991 report on the adverse consequences for the enjoyment of human rights of political, military, economic and other forms of assistance given to South Africa,[20] the Commission asked the Secretary-General to give the report the widest dissemination and to issue it as a United Nations publication, and called on Governments to cooperate with the Special Rapporteur.

On 21 February,[21] the Commission, by a roll-call vote of 33 to 14, with 5 abstentions, recommended a draft text to the Economic and Social Council for adoption.

ECONOMIC AND SOCIAL COUNCIL ACTION

On 20 July 1992, the Economic and Social Council, on the recommendation of its Social Committee, adopted **resolution 1992/3** by recorded vote.

Adverse consequences for the enjoyment of human rights of political, military, economic and other forms of assistance given to the racist regime of South Africa

The Economic and Social Council,

Recalling its resolution 1991/26 of 31 May 1991,

Recalling also General Assembly resolutions 39/15 of 23 November 1984, 41/95 of 4 December 1986, 43/92 of 8 December 1988 and 45/84 of 14 December 1990,

1. *Expresses its appreciation* to the Special Rapporteur of the Subcommission on Prevention of Discrimination and Protection of Minorities, Mr. Ahmed Khalifa, for his updated report;

2. *Expresses its thanks* to all Governments and organizations that provided information to the Special Rapporteur;

3. *Invites* the Special Rapporteur:

(a) To continue to update the list of banks, transnational corporations and other organizations assisting the racist regime of South Africa, giving such details regarding enterprises listed as he may consider necessary and appropriate, including explanations of responses, if any, and to submit the updated report to the Commission on Human Rights through the Subcommission;

(b) To use all available material from other United Nations organs, Member States, national liberation movements recognized by the Organization of African Unity, specialized agencies, other intergovernmental and non-governmental organizations and other relevant sources in order to indicate the volume, nature and adverse human consequences of the assistance given to the racist regime of South Africa;

(c) To intensify direct contacts with the Department of Economic and Social Development and the Centre against Apartheid of the Secretariat, with a view to consolidating mutual cooperation in updating his report;

4. *Calls upon* all Governments:

(a) To cooperate with the Special Rapporteur in making the report even more accurate and informative;

(b) To disseminate the updated report and give its contents the widest possible publicity;

5. *Calls upon* all Governments and organizations to maintain sanctions against the regime of South Africa until the total dismantlement of the apartheid system,

in conformity with the Declaration on Apartheid and its Destructive Consequences in Southern Africa, adopted by the General Assembly by its resolution S-16/1 of 14 December 1989 and contained in the annex thereto;

6. *Invites* the Subcommission on Prevention of Discrimination and Protection of Minorities at its forty-fourth session and the Commission on Human Rights at its forty-ninth session to consider the updated report;

7. *Requests* the Secretary-General, in accordance with General Assembly resolution 45/84, to make two economists available to the Special Rapporteur to help him develop his analysis and documentation on specific cases of special importance;

8. *Also requests* the Secretary-General to give the Special Rapporteur all the assistance that he may require in the exercise of his mandate, with a view to intensifying direct contacts with the Department of Economic and Social Development and the Centre against Apartheid and to consolidating mutual cooperation in updating his report;

9. *Further requests* the Secretary-General to bring the updated report of the Special Rapporteur to the attention of Governments whose national financial institutions continue to deal with the regime of South Africa, and to call upon them to provide the Special Rapporteur with any information or comments they may wish to submit on the matter;

10. *Requests* the Secretary-General to contact the Government of South Africa, with a view to enabling the Special Rapporteur to visit South Africa on a special mission for the purpose of the next updating of his report;

11. *Invites* the Secretary-General to continue to give the updated report of the Special Rapporteur the widest possible distribution and publicity as a United Nations publication.

Economic and Social Council resolution 1992/3

20 July 1992   Meeting 32   29-17-3 (recorded vote)

Approved by Social Committee (E/1992/103) by recorded vote (31-16-4), 15 July (meeting 7); draft by Commission on Human Rights (E/1992/22); agenda item 17.

Recorded vote in Council as follows:

In favour: Algeria, Angola, Bahrain, Bangladesh, Benin, Brazil, Burkina Faso, Chile, China, Colombia, Ecuador, Guinea, India, Iran, Jamaica, Kuwait, Madagascar, Malaysia, Mexico, Morocco, Pakistan, Philippines, Rwanda, Somalia, Suriname, Swaziland, Trinidad and Tobago, Yugoslavia, Zaire.

Against: Australia, Austria, Belgium, Bulgaria, Canada, Finland, France, Germany, Italy, Japan, Poland, Romania, Spain, Sweden, Turkey, United Kingdom, United States.

Abstaining: Argentina, Belarus, Russian Federation.

Report of the Special Rapporteur. In June, the Special Rapporteur presented to the Subcommission an updated report[22] with an addendum listing banks, insurance companies, firms and other enterprises giving, directly or indirectly, military, economic and other assistance to South Africa. By a September note and later addendum,[23] the Secretary-General transmitted the Special Rapporteur's report to the General Assembly.

Subcommission action. On 21 August,[24] the Subcommission, expressing its gratitude to the Special Rapporteur, recommended the appointment of a special rapporteur to report on the transition to democracy in South Africa.

On 27 August,[25] it took note of the recommendations of the Pan-African Congress on Democracy and Management of the Transition in Africa (Dakar, Senegal, 25-28 May).

By **decision 47/426** of 16 December 1992, the General Assembly expressed its appreciation to the Special Rapporteur for his contribution to the cause of eliminating apartheid and thanked all Governments and organizations that had supplied him with information.

Also on 16 December, the Assembly, by **decision 47/427**, took note of the Secretary-General's note transmitting the Special Rapporteur's report.

Report of the Ad Hoc Working Group of Experts. The Ad Hoc Working Group of Experts on Southern Africa continued in 1992 to study the situation relating to the right to work and trade union rights and the conditions of black workers. Its findings, as requested by the Economic and Social Council in 1991,[26] were included in its report to the Commission and submitted to the Council separately in April.[27]

By **decision 1992/263** of 20 July 1992, the Council took note of the note by the Secretariat transmitting the report of the Working Group.

Note by the Secretary-General. By a June note,[28] the Secretary-General transmitted to the Economic and Social Council a report of the ILO Fact-finding and Conciliation Commission on Freedom of Association concerning allegations of infringement of trade union rights in South Africa. The Council had referred the allegations to the Commission in May 1991.[26]

The Commission recommended giving priority to enacting legislation extending to agricultural and domestic workers, trade union and collective bargaining rights in common with other workers in South Africa; addressing problems posed by the existence of 11 different sets of labour relations legislation in South Africa's various territories; resolving the outstanding issues in negotiations concerning new legislation to govern labour relations in the public sector; banning by law limits to membership in trade unions or employers' organizations because of race; reforming security or other legislation which had been used to restrict the right of trade unions to freely carry on their activities; bringing to justice those interfering with trade unions and their members and, in particular, for acts of violence against them; and granting free access by unions to workers living and working on employer premises for the purpose of carrying out normal union activities. As South Africa was not an ILO member, the Commission recommended that the Government be invited, through the Council, to submit reports on measures taken to give effect to the Commission's conclusions and

recommendations, and that the Council should transmit such reports to the ILO Director-General, who should in turn provide any advice and comments which the Council might wish to have on them. The Commission recommended that widespread publicity be given to its report in South Africa and that South Africa bring its law and practice into full conformity with the 1948 Freedom of Association and Protection of the Right to Organize Convention (No. 87)[29] and the 1949 Right to Organize and Collective Bargaining Convention (No. 98).[30] As to reforming the industrial court system, the Commission recommended that the ILO Director-General examine favourably any request for assistance from the Government of South Africa.

On 20 July 1992, on the recommendation of its Social Committee, the Economic and Social Council adopted **resolution 1992/12** without vote.

Allegations regarding infringements of trade union rights in South Africa

The Economic and Social Council,

Having considered the report of the Fact-finding and Conciliation Commission on Freedom of Association concerning the Republic of South Africa referred to it by the International Labour Office, pursuant to Council resolution 1991/37 of 31 May 1991,

Taking note with satisfaction of the findings, conclusions and recommendations contained in the report, in particular in paragraph 748, clauses 13, 14 and 15,

1. *Requests* the Secretary-General to invite the Government of South Africa to report, no later than 31 December 1992, on the measures it has taken to give effect to the recommendations contained in the report of the Fact-finding and Conciliation Commission, and thereafter, at yearly intervals until the Economic and Social Council is satisfied that the recommendations have been implemented;

2. *Also requests* the Secretary-General to refer the reports of the Government of South Africa on this matter to the International Labour Office, with the request that the latter transmit to the Council its advice and comments stemming from examination of the reports;

3. *Takes note* of the request of the Government of South Africa that the International Labour Office should provide to it and to labour and management organizations of South Africa technical assistance and advice, in respect of the recasting of that country's labour laws, and invites the International Labour Office to comply with this request and to inform the Council of actions taken in this regard in the context of an annual report to the United Nations.

Economic and Social Council resolution 1992/12

20 July 1992   Meeting 32   Adopted without vote

Approved by Social Committee (E/1992/103) without vote, 15 July (meeting 7); draft by Madagascar for African States (E/1992/C.2/L.4); agenda item 17.

Sudan

On 18 December 1992, the General Assembly, on the recommendation of the Third Committee, adopted **resolution 47/142** by recorded vote.

The situation in the Sudan

The General Assembly,

Guided by the principles embodied in the Charter of the United Nations, the Universal Declaration of Human Rights, the International Covenants on Human Rights, and the International Convention on the Elimination of All Forms of Racial Discrimination,

Reaffirming that all Member States have an obligation to promote and protect human rights and fundamental freedoms and to comply with the obligations laid down in the various instruments in this field,

Taking note of resolution AHG/Res.213 (XXVIII) on the strengthening of cooperation and coordination among African States, adopted by the Assembly of Heads of State and Government of the Organization of African Unity at its twenty-eighth ordinary session, held at Dakar from 29 June to 1 July 1992,[a] and recalling declaration AHG/Decl.1 (XXVI) adopted at the twenty-sixth ordinary session, held at Addis Ababa from 9 to 11 July 1990,[b]

Noting with deep concern reports of grave human rights violations in the Sudan, particularly summary executions, detentions without trial, forced displacement of persons and torture, described in part in the reports submitted to the Commission on Human Rights at its forty-eighth session by the Special Rapporteurs on the question of torture and on extrajudicial, summary or arbitrary executions,[c]

Noting the announcement by the Government of the Sudan of its intention to constitute an independent judicial inquiry commission to investigate the killings of Sudanese nationals employed by foreign government relief organizations,

Deeply concerned that access by the civilian population to humanitarian assistance is being impeded, which poses a threat to human life and an offence to human dignity,

Alarmed by the large number of internally displaced persons and victims of discrimination in the Sudan, including members of minorities who have been forcibly displaced in violation of their human rights and who are in need of relief assistance and of protection,

Alarmed also by the mass exodus of refugees into neighbouring countries, and conscious of the burden that this places on those countries, but expressing its appreciation for the continuing efforts to assist them, thereby easing the burden on host countries,

Emphasizing that it is essential to put an end to the serious deterioration of the human rights situation in the Sudan,

Welcoming the efforts of the United Nations and other humanitarian organizations to provide humanitarian relief to those Sudanese in need,

1. *Expresses its deep concern* at the serious human rights violations in the Sudan, including summary executions, detentions without due process, forced displacement of persons and torture;

2. *Urges* the Government of the Sudan to respect fully human rights, and calls upon all parties to cooperate in order to ensure such respect;

3. *Calls upon* the Government of the Sudan to comply with applicable international human rights instruments, in particular the International Covenants on Human Rights and the International Convention on the Elimination of All Forms of Racial Discrimination, to which the Sudan is a party, and to ensure that all individuals in its territory and subject to its jurisdiction, including members of all religious and ethnic groups, enjoy the rights recognized in those instruments;

4. *Calls upon* all parties to the hostilities to respect fully the applicable provisions of international humanitarian law including article 3 common to the Geneva Conventions of 12 August 1949, and the Additional Protocols thereto, of 1977, to halt the use of weapons against the civilian population and to protect all civilians from violations, including arbitrary detention, ill-treatment, torture and summary execution;

5. *Expresses its appreciation* to the humanitarian organizations for their work in helping displaced persons and drought and conflict victims in the Sudan, and calls upon all parties to protect humanitarian relief workers;

6. *Calls upon* the Special Rapporteur on Summary or Arbitrary Executions to address the killing of Sudanese nationals employed by foreign government relief organizations;

7. *Calls upon* the Government of the Sudan to ensure a full, thorough and prompt investigation of the killings of Sudanese nationals employed by foreign government relief organizations by the independent judicial inquiry commission, to bring to justice those responsible for the killings and to provide just compensation to the families of the victims;

8. *Calls upon* all parties to permit international agencies, humanitarian organizations and donor Governments to deliver humanitarian assistance to the civilian population and to cooperate with the recent initiatives of the Department of Humanitarian Affairs of the Secretariat to deliver humanitarian assistance to all persons in need;

9. *Recommends* that the serious human rights situation in the Sudan be monitored, and invites the Commission on Human Rights at its forty-ninth session to give urgent attention to the situation of human rights in the Sudan;

10. *Decides* to continue its consideration of this question at its forty-eighth session.

---

[a]A/47/558.

[b]A/45/482.

[c]E/CN.4/1992/17, E/CN.4/1992/30 & Corr.1.

General Assembly resolution 47/142

18 December 1992   Meeting 92   104-8-33 (recorded vote)

Approved by Third Committee (A/47/678/Add.2) by recorded vote (102-7-27), 4 December (meeting 58); 29-nation draft (A/C.3/47/L.77); agenda item 97 *(c)*.

Sponsors: Argentina, Armenia, Australia, Belgium, Bulgaria, Canada, Costa Rica, Denmark, Finland, France, Gambia, Germany, Ghana, Greece, Hungary, Iceland, Ireland, Italy, Japan, Luxembourg, Netherlands, Norway, Panama, Portugal, Samoa, Spain, Sweden, United Kingdom, United States.

Meeting numbers. GA 47th session: 3rd Committee 47-58; plenary 92.

Recorded vote in Assembly as follows:

In favour: Algeria, Angola, Argentina, Armenia, Australia, Austria, Azerbaijan, Belarus, Belgium, Benin, Bhutan, Bolivia, Botswana, Brazil, Bulgaria, Burundi, Canada, Cape Verde, Chile, Costa Rica, Croatia, Cyprus, Czechoslovakia, Denmark, Dominican Republic, Ecuador, El Salvador, Estonia, Fiji, Finland, France, Gabon, Gambia, Germany, Ghana, Greece, Guatemala, Guinea, Guinea-Bissau, Honduras, Hungary, Iceland, India, Ireland, Israel,

Italy, Japan, Kazakhstan, Kenya, Kuwait, Latvia, Lesotho, Liberia, Liechten-
stein, Lithuania, Luxembourg, Madagascar, Malawi, Mali, Malta, Marshall
Islands, Mauritius, Mexico, Namibia, Nepal, Netherlands, New Zealand,
Nicaragua, Norway, Panama, Papua New Guinea, Paraguay, Peru, Poland,
Portugal, Republic of Korea, Republic of Moldova, Romania, Russian Fed-
eration, Rwanda, Samoa, Sao Tome and Principe, Saudi Arabia, Sierra
Leone, Singapore, Slovenia, Solomon Islands, Spain, Suriname, Sweden,
Togo, Trinidad and Tobago, Tunisia, Turkey, Uganda, Ukraine, United King-
dom, United Republic of Tanzania, United States, Uruguay, Vanuatu,
Venezuela, Zambia, Zimbabwe.

Against: China, Cuba, Iran, Iraq, Libyan Arab Jamahiriya, Myanmar,
Sudan, Syrian Arab Republic.

Abstaining: Afghanistan, Antigua and Barbuda, Bahamas, Bangladesh,
Barbados, Belize, Brunei Darussalam, Cameroon, Colombia*, Congo, Côte
d'Ivoire, Dominica, Grenada, Guyana, Indonesia, Jamaica, Jordan, Lao People's Democratic Republic, Malaysia, Maldives, Mauritania, Niger, Nigeria, Pakistan, Philippines, Saint Kitts and Nevis, Saint Lucia, Saint Vincent
and the Grenadines, Senegal, Sri Lanka, Swaziland, Thailand, Viet Nam.

*Later advised the Secretariat it had intended to vote in favour.

Before the Third Committee adopted the text,
the United Kingdom, on behalf of the 12 members of the European Community, motioned that
action be taken on the draft on the situation in
the Sudan[31] before taking action on a draft on
the situation of human rights in the Sudan,[32]
sponsored by the Sudan, which would have postponed any action on the former draft until 1993.
The Committee approved the United Kingdom's
motion by a recorded vote of 69 to 13, with 42 abstentions.

The Sudan then motioned that no action be
taken on the draft on the situation in the
Sudan.[31] By a recorded vote of 77 to 12, with 36
abstentions, the Committee rejected that motion.

Asia and the Pacific

Afghanistan

Report of the Special Rapporteur. In Febru-
ary 1992, Special Rapporteur Felix Ermacora
(Austria) presented to the Commission on Human
Rights a report on the human rights situation in
Afghanistan.[33] He had visited Pakistan from 29
December 1991 to 2 January 1992 and Afghanistan
from 2 to 5 January 1992.

The Special Rapporteur stated that since the
submission of his 1991 interim report,[34] hostilities in Afghanistan had diminished. Nevertheless,
fighting between the opposition and Government
forces and among the opposition groups continued to cause casualties.

In response to an appeal made by the Special
Rapporteur, in conformity with a 1991 General Assembly resolution,[35] the President of Afghanistan issued a decree, which entered into force
on 15 January 1992, limiting the number of cases
in which the death penalty might be applied; as
a result, 114 death sentences were commuted. The
number of convicted political prisoners remained
stable at about 2,500. Special courts were abolished and a new judicial system was in place. However, the Special Rapporteur was unable to verify
how it functioned and whether it guaranteed a fair

trial. Detention on remand remained at a critical
stage and continued to be unreasonably long.

The Special Rapporteur described the plight of
some 5 million Afghan refugees living in Iran and
Pakistan and the situation of prisoners of war and
political prisoners.

The Special Rapporteur recommended the incorporation of human rights elements into a political solution, namely: creating conditions for
refugees to exercise their free will to return; calling for the participation by United Nations Member States in demining activities; releasing unconditionally all political prisoners and prisoners of
war; exchanging lists of all prisoners and providing information to their relatives through ICRC;
and ceasing all organized hostilities. He advocated
the following human rights measures, regardless
of when a political solution was arrived at: releasing all former Soviet prisoners; commuting all
death sentences and abolishing the death penalty;
investigating alleged ill-treatment of prisoners; respect for the Standard Minimum Rules for the
Treatment of Prisoners adopted by the first United
Nations Congress on the Prevention of Crime and
the Treatment of Offenders in 1955;[36] allowing
visitation of prisoners by the Special Rapporteur
and ICRC; and establishing a bar association and
training for lawyers.

Human Rights Commission action. On 4
March,[37] the Commission, noting the Special
Rapporteur's report, urged all parties concerned
to increase their efforts to achieve a political solution based on the Secretary-General's 1991 five-
point peace plan,[38] including free and fair elections, the cessation of hostilities and the free return of refugees to their homeland. It also urged
them to respect the accepted humanitarian rules
as set out in the 1949 Geneva Conventions and
their Additional Protocols of 1977,[39] halt the use
of weapons against civilians, protect prisoners from
reprisals and violence, including ill-treatment, torture and summary execution, expedite the exchange of prisoners, transmit to ICRC the names
of all prisoners and grant ICRC unrestricted access
to all parts of the country and the right to visit
all prisoners. The Commission called on States
and parties concerned to release all prisoners of
war detained as a result of the conflict, in particular, the release of former Soviet prisoners of war,
considering that the hostilities in which the former
USSR was involved had legally ended, and asked
that ICRC be given full access to prisoners of war
held by opposition forces. It called on all conflicting parties to investigate the fate of disappeared
persons, apply amnesty decrees equally to foreign
detainees, reduce the period during which
prisoners awaited trial, treat all prisoners in accordance with the Standard Minimum Rules for
the Treatment of Prisoners[36] and apply to all

convicted persons article 14, paragraph 3 *(d)* and paragraph 5 of the International Covenant on Civil and Political Rights.[8] It noted with concern allegations of atrocities committed against Afghan soldiers, civil servants and captured civilians. Expressing concern at reports that the living conditions of refugees, especially those of women and children, were becoming increasingly difficult, the Commission urgently appealed to Member States and humanitarian organizations to promote the implementation of projects envisaged by the Coordinator for United Nations Humanitarian and Economic Assistance Programmes relating to Afghanistan and UNHCR programmes. It also appealed to Member States, humanitarian organizations and all parties concerned to cooperate fully, especially on the subject of mine detection, to facilitate the return of refugees and displaced persons to their homes in safety and dignity. The Commission urged all parties concerned to undertake measures to ensure the safety of personnel of organizations involved in implementing United Nations humanitarian and economic assistance programmes and extend their full cooperation to the Commission and its Special Rapporteur. The Commission extended the Special Rapporteur's mandate and asked him to report to the Assembly in 1992 and the Commission in 1993. The Secretary-General was asked to give him all necessary assistance.

ECONOMIC AND SOCIAL COUNCIL ACTION

On 20 July 1992, the Economic and Social Council, by **decision 1992/240**, approved the Commission's extension of the Special Rapporteur's mandate for one year and its requests that he report to the General Assembly in 1992 and to the Commission in 1993 and that the Secretary-General give him all necessary assistance.

Interim report of the Special Rapporteur. In November, the Secretary-General transmitted to the General Assembly an interim report on the situation of human rights in Afghanistan from March to October 1992,[40] prepared by the Special Rapporteur in accordance with the Commission's request. The Special Rapporteur had visited Pakistan and Afghanistan in September.

Although the period of foreign occupation and communist rule in Afghanistan had ended in April/May 1992, a situation of conflict still prevailed in the country which prevented the effective enjoyment of human rights. During the formation of a transitional Government, different armed groups had entered Kabul (for details on the transition period, see PART TWO, Chapter III). In August 1992, Kabul came under the heaviest rocket attacks during the last 14 years of war. The events in Kabul had resulted in a stream of new

refugees and displaced persons. After the collapse of the former Government, no mass systematic executions were reported, but death sentences had been pronounced and applied in Jalalabad, Kabul and Kandahar.

The Special Rapporteur recommended releasing prisoners of war held by the mujahidin; respect for humanitarian law; issuing a declaration on human rights in emergency situations; respect for the right to life including a speedy demining process; preventing torture; permitting ICRC visits to places of detention; limiting the period of detention on remand or preventive detention to a reasonable length; not discriminating against refugees associated with the former Government and to whom amnesty applied; returning Afghan children remaining in the former Soviet Union to their country; and inviting Afghanistan to accept United Nations monitoring or advisory services in the field of human rights.

Appendices to the report contained the text of the Peshawar Accord (24 April 1992) establishing a structure and timetable for the period of transition and maps identifying the locations of Afghanistan's major ethnic groups.

GENERAL ASSEMBLY ACTION

On 18 December 1992, the General Assembly, on the recommendation of the Third Committee, adopted **resolution 47/141** without vote.

Situation of human rights in Afghanistan
The General Assembly,

Guided by the principles embodied in the Charter of the United Nations, the Universal Declaration of Human Rights, the International Covenants on Human Rights and accepted humanitarian rules, as set out in the Geneva Conventions of 12 August 1949 and the Additional Protocols thereto, of 1977,

Aware of its responsibility to promote and encourage respect for human rights and fundamental freedoms for all and resolved to remain vigilant with regard to violations of human rights wherever they occur,

Reaffirming that all Member States have an obligation to promote and protect human rights and fundamental freedoms and to fulfil the obligations they have freely undertaken under the various international instruments,

Recalling Economic and Social Council resolution 1984/37 of 24 May 1984, in which the Council requested the Chairman of the Commission on Human Rights to appoint a special rapporteur to examine the situation of human rights in Afghanistan, with a view to formulating proposals that could contribute to ensuring full protection of the human rights of the inhabitants of the country before, during and after the withdrawal of all foreign forces,

Recalling also its resolution 46/136 of 17 December 1991 and all its other relevant resolutions, as well as the resolutions of the Commission on Human Rights and the decisions of the Economic and Social Council,

Taking note in particular of Commission on Human Rights resolution 1992/68 of 4 March 1992, in which the Commission decided to extend the mandate of the Special Rapporteur for one year and to request him to report to the General Assembly at its forty-seventh session on the situation of human rights in Afghanistan, and of Economic and Social Council decision 1992/240 of 20 July 1992, in which the Council approved the decision of the Commission,

Noting that, following the demise of the former Afghan Government, a transitional Islamic State of Afghanistan was established on the basis of the Peshawar Accord concluded by resistance parties on 24 April 1992,

Noting with deep concern that in spite of the efforts and initiatives taken by the Government of Afghanistan towards ensuring complete peace and stability, a situation of armed confrontation, which is affecting mainly the civilian population, continues to exist in parts of the territory of Afghanistan, and in particular in Kabul, and much remains to be done for the treatment of prisoners in conformity with the provisions of the Geneva Conventions of 12 August 1949, and the Additional Protocols thereto, of 1977,

Concerned that the prevailing uncertainty in the country over political and legal order may affect the situation of members of ethnic and religious minorities,

Noting with concern reports of violations of rights enshrined in the International Covenant on Civil and Political Rights, such as the right to life, liberty, personal security and freedom of opinion, expression and association,

Concerned that neither the International Committee of the Red Cross nor the Special Rapporteur was able to visit prisoners who were associated with the former Government,

Welcoming the fact that over one million refugees have returned to Afghanistan since April 1992, and hoping that conditions in Afghanistan will allow those still in exile to return as soon as possible,

Aware that peace and security in Afghanistan are prerequisites for the successful repatriation of more than four million refugees, in particular the achievement of a comprehensive political solution and the establishment of a freely and democratically elected government, the end of armed confrontation in Kabul and in some provinces, the clearance of the minefields that have been laid in many parts of the country, the restoration of an effective authority in the whole country and the reconstruction of the economy,

Welcoming the declaration of general amnesty issued by the Islamic State of Afghanistan, which should be applied in a strictly non-discriminatory manner,

Commending the activity carried out by the Office of the United Nations High Commissioner for Refugees and the International Committee of the Red Cross in cooperation with the Afghan authorities, as well as non-governmental organizations, in favour of the people of Afghanistan,

Taking note with appreciation of the report of the Special Rapporteur on the situation of human rights in Afghanistan and of the conclusions and recommendations contained therein,

1. *Welcomes* the cooperation that authorities in Afghanistan have extended to the Special Rapporteur on the situation of human rights in Afghanistan, in view of the circumstances prevailing in the country;

2. *Also welcomes* the cooperation that the authorities in Afghanistan have extended, in particular to the Coordinator for Humanitarian and Economic Assistance Programmes Relating to Afghanistan and to international organizations, such as the specialized agencies, the Office of the United Nations High Commissioner for Refugees and the International Committee of the Red Cross;

3. *Urges* all the Afghan parties to increase their efforts in order to achieve a comprehensive political solution, which is the only way to bring about peace and the full restoration of human rights in Afghanistan, based on the free exercise of the right to self-determination by the people, including free and fair elections, the cessation of armed confrontation and the creation of conditions that will permit the free return, as soon as possible, of the more than four million refugees to their homeland in safety and dignity, whenever they wish, and the full enjoyment of human rights and fundamental freedoms by all Afghans;

4. *Recognizes* that the promotion and protection of human rights should be an essential element in the achievement of a comprehensive solution to the crisis in Afghanistan, and calls upon all Afghan parties to respect human rights;

5. *Urges* all the Afghan parties to respect accepted humanitarian rules as set out in the Geneva Conventions of 12 August 1949, and the Additional Protocols thereto, of 1977, to halt the use of weapons against the civilian population, to protect all prisoners from acts of reprisal and violence, including ill-treatment, torture and summary executions, to transmit to the International Committee of the Red Cross the names of all prisoners, to expedite the exchange of prisoners wherever they may be held and to grant to the Committee unrestricted access to all parts of the country and the right to visit all prisoners in accordance with its established criteria;

6. *Calls upon* all States and parties concerned to make all efforts for the realization of its decision 47/428 of 16 December 1992 entitled "Prisoners of war and persons missing as a result of war in Afghanistan", and calls upon them to make all efforts for the release, as soon as possible, of all prisoners of war as provided for under article 118 of the Geneva Convention relative to the Treatment of Prisoners of War, of 12 August 1949, considering that the hostilities in which the former Soviet Union was involved have legally and effectively ended;

7. *Requests* that the International Committee of the Red Cross be given full access to all prisoners by the warring factions;

8. *Calls upon* the authorities in Afghanistan to investigate thoroughly the fate of those persons who have disappeared, to apply amnesty decrees equally to all detainees, to reduce the period during which prisoners await trial, to treat all prisoners, especially those awaiting trial or those in custody in juvenile rehabilitation centres, in accordance with the Standard Minimum Rules for the Treatment of Prisoners, adopted by the First United Nations Congress on the Prevention of Crime and the Treatment of Offenders, and to apply to all suspected/convicted persons article 14, paragraphs 3 (*d*) and 5 to 7 of the International Covenant on Civil and Political Rights;

9. *Expresses its concern* at reports that the living conditions of refugees, especially those of women and children, are becoming increasingly difficult because of the decline in international humanitarian assistance;

10. *Urgently appeals* to all Member States, humanitarian organizations and all parties concerned to cooperate fully, especially on the subject of mine detection and clearance, in order to facilitate the return of refugees and displaced persons to their homes in safety and dignity;

11. *Also urgently appeals* to all Member States and humanitarian organizations to continue to promote the implementation of the projects envisaged by the Coordinator for Humanitarian and Economic Assistance Programmes Relating to Afghanistan and the programmes of the United Nations High Commissioner for Refugees, especially the pilot projects for the repatriation of refugees;

12. *Urges* all Afghan parties to undertake all necessary measures to ensure the safety of the personnel of humanitarian organizations involved in the implementation of the United Nations humanitarian and economic assistance programmes relating to Afghanistan and the programmes of the United Nations High Commissioner for Refugees;

13. *Urges* the authorities in Afghanistan to extend their full cooperation to the Commission on Human Rights and its Special Rapporteur;

14. *Requests* the Secretary-General to give all necessary assistance to the Special Rapporteur;

15. *Decides* to keep under consideration, during its forty-eighth session, the situation of human rights in Afghanistan in the light of additional elements provided by the Commission on Human Rights and the Economic and Social Council.

General Assembly resolution 47/141

18 December 1992   Meeting 92   Adopted without vote

Approved by Third Committee (A/47/678/Add.2) without vote, 4 December (meeting 58); draft by Chairman (A/C.3/47/L.71); agenda item 97 *(c)*. *Meeting numbers.* GA 47th session: 3rd Committee 47-58; plenary 92.

On 16 December, also on the recommendation of the Third Committee, the Assembly adopted **decision 47/428**, by which it called on Afghanistan and the Russian Federation to negotiate and consult to solve the humanitarian question of prisoners of war and missing persons on both sides, on the basis of a joint statement issued on 14 May. In that statement, they had expressed their readiness to do everything necessary for the earliest and unconditional release of all war prisoners and to seek the whereabouts of missing persons to give them a chance to return to their homes freely. The Governments of the newly independent States concerned and Afghanistan were encouraged to do the same.

Cambodia

The Commission on Human Rights, its Subcommission and the Economic and Social Council expressed concern about the protection of human rights in Cambodia (see above, under ''Civil and political rights'').

East Timor

In an addendum to his report to the Commission on the question of torture,[41] Special Rapporteur Peter H. Kooijmans (Netherlands) discussed his visit to East Timor and Indonesia from 4 to 16 November 1991, in response to Indonesia's invitation, where he had met with Government officials and NGOs concerned with human rights and visited a prison in the Jakarta area.

On 12 November 1991,[42] there had been violent incidents at Dili, East Timor, resulting in loss of life and injuries among civilians. Following those events, the Secretary-General decided to send S. Amos Wako (Kenya) as his personal envoy to report on the incidents.

Subcommission action. By a secret ballot of 13 to 6, with 4 abstentions, on 27 August,[43] the Subcommission invited the Secretary-General to transmit the report of his personal envoy to the Commission on Human Rights and asked him, in preparing his report on the situation in East Timor for the Commission's consideration, to include an analytical compilation of information received from, among others, Governments, intergovernmental organizations and NGOs. It called on Indonesian authorities to honour their commitment to facilitate access to East Timor by humanitarian and human rights organizations.

Iran

Report of the Special Representative. Special Representative Reynaldo Galindo Pohl (El Salvador) in January submitted to the Commission on Human Rights a report on the human rights situation in Iran.[44] He had received information on alleged incidents and cases concerning the right to life; enforced or involuntary disappearances; the right to freedom from torture or cruel, inhuman or degrading treatment or punishment; the administration of justice; freedom of expression, opinion and association and the right to peaceful assembly; political rights; the situation of women and children; the right to leave one's country and to return; freedom of religion; and the Baha'i community. The detailed allegations had been transmitted to Iran to enable it to verify their accuracy; Iran's replies were reflected in the Special Representative's report. He also gave information on his third visit to Iran, which he undertook in December 1991.

The Special Representative concluded that in 1991 Iran had made no real progress towards improved compliance with international human rights instruments. He identified the areas of greatest weakness regarding human rights in Iran as follows: excessive use of the death penalty; lack of guarantees of due process of law; discrimination against citizens because of religious beliefs, specifically the Baha'is; and the absence of independent associations and a climate of legal certainty and guarantees for the expression of literary and artistic thought and creativity. One positive measure was the signing of an agreement to allow ICRC to visit prisons as from January 1992. The Special Representative stated that international monitoring of the situation of human rights and fundamental freedoms in Iran should continue and that Iran should be called on to comply with international human rights standards.

Annexed to the report were lists of names and particulars of persons allegedly executed in Iran as well as information on prisoners.

Note by the Secretary-General. By a July note,[15] the Secretary-General drew the attention of the Subcommission to the Special Representative's report.

Human Rights Commission action. On 4 March,[46] by a roll-call vote of 22 to 12, with 15 abstentions, the Commission, expressing concern at continuing reports of human rights violations in Iran, called on that country to intensify its efforts to investigate and rectify the human rights issues raised by the Special Representative, comply with international instruments on human rights and ensure that all individuals enjoyed the rights recognized in those instruments. It encouraged Iran to continue to cooperate with ICRC and with the Special Representative. The Commission endorsed the Special Representative's view that international monitoring of human rights in Iran should be continued. Deciding to extend the Special Representative's 1984 mandate for another year, the Commission asked him to submit an interim report to the General Assembly in 1992 (see below) and a final report to the Commission in 1993, and asked the Secretary-General to give him all the necessary assistance. Those requests were approved by the Economic and Social Council by **decision 1992/239** of 20 July 1992.

Subcommission action. On 27 August,[47] the Subcommission, by a secret ballot of 18 to 3 with 2 abstentions, asked the Special Representative to include in his 1992 report to the General Assembly (see below) and in his 1993 Commission report information on executions, arrests and measures to suppress political opposition, including the formation of special paramilitary units and any further information on the assassination of Professor Kazem Rajavi, a judge who had tried a case involving the assassination of an Iranian citizen in Germany. The Subcommission asked the Secretary-General to inform it in 1993 of relevant reports by special rapporteurs or bodies, as well as of steps taken by the Assembly and the Commission to prevent human rights violations in Iran.

Interim report of the Special Representative. In November, the Secretary-General transmitted to the General Assembly the Special Representative's interim report on the human rights situation in Iran.[48] The report summarized information he had obtained between January and September 1992 on the right to life; enforced or involuntary disappearances; the right to freedom from torture or cruel, inhuman or degrading treatment or punishment; the administration of justice; freedom of expression, opinion and the press; the situation of women; political rights; the rights to work, education and to own property; freedom of religion and the situation of the Baha'is; and the war on drug traffic. Information was also received on the events of 5 April 1992 relating to an air attack by the Iranian Air Force on the Ashraf military base in Iraqi territory, which belonged to the Iran National Liberation Army of the People's Mujahidin.

The Special Representative noted that excessive application of the death penalty continued and incidents of violence against Iranian citizens living abroad who were members of various opposition organizations were reported. Concerning the investigation of the assassination of Professor Kazem Rajavi, a judge who had tried a case involving the assassination of an Iranian citizen in Germany, a Swiss newspaper, *Le Courrier*, had reported in February that the investigation had confirmed the participation of 13 persons, including a number of Iranian citizens. He stated that there were confirmed cases of persons who had been subjected to torture and allegations of irregularities concerning the administration of justice. In March, Iran had informed ICRC that it must cease its activities and leave the country, which it did on 27 March.

The Special Representative stated that international supervision of the human rights situation should be maintained and that it would be appropriate for the Assembly to call on Iran to continue its cooperation with the Special Representative, to respond to the comments and allegations brought to its attention and to accept another visit by him.

GENERAL ASSEMBLY ACTION

On 18 December 1992, on the recommendation of the Third Committee, the General Assembly adopted **resolution 47/146** by recorded vote.

Situation of human rights in the Islamic Republic of Iran

The General Assembly,

Guided by the principles embodied in the Charter of the United Nations, the Universal Declaration of Human Rights and the International Covenants on Human Rights,

Reaffirming that all Member States have an obligation to promote and protect human rights and fundamental freedoms and to fulfil the obligations they have undertaken under the various international instruments in the field,

Taking note of Commission on Human Rights resolution 1992/67 of 4 March 1992,

Regretting that the Government of the Islamic Republic of Iran, after having allowed the Special Representative of the Commission on Human Rights to pay three visits to that country, has discontinued its cooperation with the Special Representative,

Noting the observation of the Special Representative that international supervision of the situation of human rights in the Islamic Republic of Iran should be maintained,

Noting that the Subcommission on Prevention of Discrimination and Protection of Minorities, in its resolution 1992/15 of 27 August 1992, condemned the continuing grave violations of human rights in the Islamic Republic of Iran,

1. *Takes note with appreciation* of the interim report of the Special Representative of the Commission on Human Rights and the observations contained therein;

2. *Expresses its deep concern* at continuing reports of violations of human rights in the Islamic Republic of Iran;

3. *Expresses its concern* more specifically at the main criticisms of the Special Representative of the human rights situation in the Islamic Republic of Iran, namely, the high number of executions, the practice of torture, the standard of the administration of justice, the absence of guarantees of due legal process, the treatment of the Baha'i community and restrictions of freedom of expression, thought and opinion and of the press;

4. *Expresses its grave concern* at the fact that, contrary to the earlier recommendation of the Special Representative, the application of the death penalty has been excessive;

5. *Regrets* that the Government of the Islamic Republic of Iran has not permitted the Special Representative to visit the country and failed to reply to allegations of human rights violations transmitted to it by the Special Representative in time for the reply to be reflected in the interim report;

6. *Regrets also* that, as the Special Representative concluded, the Islamic Republic of Iran has not given adequate follow-up to many of the recommendations contained in the previous reports;

7. *Calls upon* the Government of the Islamic Republic of Iran to intensify its efforts to investigate and rectify the human rights issues raised by the Special Representative in his observations, in particular as regards the administration of justice and due process of law;

8. *Also calls upon* the Government of the Islamic Republic of Iran to comply with international instruments on human rights, in particular the International Covenant on Civil and Political Rights, to which the Islamic Republic of Iran is a party, and to ensure that all individuals within its territory and subject to its jurisdiction, including religious groups, enjoy the rights recognized in these instruments;

9. *Endorses* the view of the Special Representative that the international monitoring of the human rights situation in the Islamic Republic of Iran should be continued;

10. *Encourages* the Government of the Islamic Republic of Iran to resume cooperation with the Special Representative;

11. *Requests* the Secretary-General to give all necessary assistance to the Special Representative;

12. *Decides* to continue the examination of the situation of human rights in the Islamic Republic of Iran during its forty-eighth session under the item entitled "Human rights questions" in the light of additional elements provided by the Commission on Human Rights and the Economic and Social Council.

General Assembly resolution 47/146

18 December 1992   Meeting 92   86-16-38 (recorded vote)

Approved by Third Committee (A/47/678/Add.2) by recorded vote (83-16-34), 4 December (meeting 59); 23-nation draft (A/C.3/47/L.76), orally revised; agenda item 97 *(c)*.

Sponsors: Australia, Belgium, Canada, Costa Rica, Denmark, Finland, France, Germany, Greece, Iceland, Ireland, Italy, Japan, Liechtenstein, Luxembourg, Netherlands, Norway, Portugal, Samoa, Spain, Sweden, United Kingdom, United States.

Meeting numbers. GA 47th session: 3rd Committee 47-59; plenary 92.

Recorded vote in Assembly as follows:

In favour: Algeria, Antigua and Barbuda, Australia, Austria, Bahamas, Barbados, Belarus, Belgium, Belize, Benin, Bolivia, Botswana, Brazil, Canada, Cape Verde, Chad, Chile, Costa Rica, Croatia, Czechoslovakia, Denmark, Dominica, Dominican Republic, Ecuador, Egypt, El Salvador, Estonia, Fiji, Finland, France, Gambia, Germany, Greece, Grenada, Guatemala, Haiti, Honduras, Hungary, Iceland, Iraq, Ireland, Israel, Italy, Jamaica, Japan, Kenya, Latvia, Liechtenstein, Lithuania, Luxembourg, Malawi, Mali, Malta, Marshall Islands, Mauritius, Mexico, Micronesia, Nepal, Netherlands, New Zealand, Norway, Panama, Papua New Guinea, Paraguay, Peru, Portugal, Russian Federation, Rwanda, Saint Kitts and Nevis, Saint Lucia, Saint Vincent and the Grenadines, Samoa, Sao Tome and Principe, Singapore, Slovenia, Solomon Islands, Spain, Suriname, Swaziland, Sweden, Togo, Trinidad and Tobago, Ukraine, United Kingdom, United States, Venezuela.

Against: Afghanistan, Bangladesh, China, Cuba, Democratic People's Republic of Korea, Indonesia, Iran, Lao People's Democratic Republic, Libyan Arab Jamahiriya, Malaysia, Myanmar, Pakistan, Sri Lanka, Sudan, Syrian Arab Republic, Viet Nam.

Abstaining: Angola, Azerbaijan, Bhutan, Brunei Darussalam, Burkina Faso, Burundi, Cameroon, Colombia, Congo, Côte d'Ivoire, Cyprus, Ethiopia, Gabon, Ghana, Guinea, Guinea-Bissau, Guyana, India, Jordan, Kazakhstan, Lesotho, Liberia, Maldives, Mauritania, Namibia, Niger, Nigeria, Oman, Philippines, Qatar, Republic of Korea, Saudi Arabia, Sierra Leone, Thailand, Turkey, Uganda, United Republic of Tanzania, Zimbabwe.

Iraq

Report of the Special Rapporteur. In February,[49] Special Rapporteur Max van der Stoel (Netherlands) reported on the human rights situation in Iraq, including the plight of refugees. He visited Iraq from 3 to 9 January and travelled to Iran from 13 to 15 January and to Saudi Arabia from 17 to 19 January to hear testimony from Iraqi refugees claiming to be victims and eyewitnesses to human rights violations committed by the Government of Iraq.

Allegations of violations received by the Special Rapporteur involved summary or arbitrary execution; torture and other cruel, inhuman or degrading treatment; enforced or involuntary disappearances; arbitrary arrest and detention; due process and rule of law; freedom of thought, expression and association; access to food and health care; the situation of women and children; and property rights. He also received information on human rights violations in Iraq affecting the Kurdish population, the Assyrian community, the Turkoman minority and the Shiah of southern Iraq. The report contained replies by the Government of Iraq to the Special Rapporteur's enquiries and to the allegations of human rights violations reported by him in 1991.[50]

The Special Rapporteur concluded that there had been massive human rights violations of the gravest nature by Iraq with no indication that steps had been taken to curtail them. The situation demanded an exceptional response, specifically, sending to Iraq a team of human rights monitors who would remain there until the situation had drastically improved. He recommended that Iraq be urged to submit the activities of the security services to transparent legal constraints in order to end arbitrary arrests, torture or extrajudicial execution; set up a commission of inquiry into the fate of tens of thousands of disappeared persons; end the practice of torture; renew negotiations on a food-for-oil formula to enable Iraq to buy food and medical supplies; end the blockade of the Kurdish-controlled area; and restore full religious freedom to the Shiah community. Annexed to the report was a list of NGOs that had provided information, selected official documents of the Government of Iraq allegedly found in Iraqi security offices and a sample list of persons said to have disappeared in Iraqi custody.

In March, Belgium requested that the Special Rapporteur's report be circulated as a Security Council document.[51]

Human Rights Commission action. By a roll-call vote of 35 to 1, with 16 abstentions, the Commission, on 5 March,[52] expressed strong condemnation of massive human rights violations by Iraq, in particular: summary and arbitrary executions; systematic torture; enforced or involuntary disappearances; hostage-taking; suppression of freedom of thought, expression and association; and violations of property rights. It called on Iraq to release persons arbitrarily arrested and detained, including Kuwaitis and nationals of other States, and, as a State party to the International Covenant on Economic, Social and Cultural Rights and the International Covenant on Civil and Political Rights,[8] to abide by its obligations under the Covenants. The Commission urged Iraq to set up an independent commission of inquiry to look into the fate of tens of thousands of disappeared persons. Regretting the failure of Iraq to provide satisfactory replies concerning human rights violations brought to the Special Rapporteur's attention, it called on that country to reply without delay to enable him to formulate recommendations to improve the human rights situation there. It asked the Special Rapporteur, in consultation with the Secretary-General, to develop further his recommendation for an exceptional response and to report thereon to the General Assembly in 1992 (see below). The Commission decided to extend the Special Rapporteur's mandate as contained in a 1991 Commission resolution,[53] asked him to visit again the northern area of Iraq, and to submit an interim report to the Assembly in 1992 and a final report to the Commission in 1993. It asked the Secretary-General to give

him all the assistance he needed and urged Iraq to accord him full cooperation. The decision to extend the Special Rapporteur's mandate and the Commission's requests to him and the Secretary-General were approved by the Economic and Social Council, by **decision 1992/241** of 20 July.

Subcommission action. On 27 August,[54] the Subcommission appealed to the international community and to all Governments, including Iraq, to facilitate the supply of food and medicines to the civilian population of Iraq.

Interim reports of the Special Rapporteur. In August, the Secretary-General transmitted to the General Assembly an interim report by the Special Rapporteur,[55] in which he described grave human rights violations in the marshes of southern Iraq and set forth guidelines for establishing a system of human rights monitoring in that country. Annexed to the report was a letter of 29 July from the Special Rapporteur to the Minister of Foreign Affairs concerning the situation in southern Iraq. Iraq transmitted its response to the interim report by a 5 October letter to the Secretary-General.[56] The subject was also discussed by the Security Council (see PART TWO, Chapter III, for details).

In a later addendum to his interim report,[57] the Special Rapporteur discussed the situation of economic and social rights in Iraq and presented correspondence received from the Government. He recommended that Iraq implement a Memorandum of Understanding signed on 22 October by the Government and the United Nations providing for the presence of United Nations guards in three northern governorates and in Baghdad; remove obstacles, including proclaimed or de facto internal embargos, to the equitable enjoyment of food and medical supplies; accept a United Nations–supervised sale of Iraqi oil; initiate consultations with the tribal peoples of the southern marsh area aimed at securing their economic, social and cultural rights; and accept the deployment of human rights monitors throughout the country, but especially in the southern area.

GENERAL ASSEMBLY ACTION

On 18 December 1992, on the recommendation of the Third Committee, the General Assembly adopted **resolution 47/145** by recorded vote.

Situation of human rights in Iraq

The General Assembly,

Guided by the principles embodied in the Charter of the United Nations, the Universal Declaration of Human Rights and the International Covenants on Human Rights,

Reaffirming that all Member States have an obligation to promote and protect human rights and fundamental freedoms and to fulfil the obligations they have undertaken under the various international instruments in this field,

Mindful that Iraq is a party to the International Covenants on Human Rights and to other human rights instruments,

Recalling its resolution 46/134 of 17 December 1991, in which it expressed its deep concern about the flagrant violations of human rights by the Government of Iraq,

Recalling also Security Council resolution 688(1991) of 5 April 1991, in which the Council demanded an end to the repression of the Iraqi civilian population and insisted that Iraq should cooperate with humanitarian organizations and ensure that the human and political rights of all Iraqi citizens were respected,

Recalling in particular Commission on Human Rights resolution 1991/74 of 6 March 1991, in which the Commission requested its Chairman to appoint a Special Rapporteur to make a thorough study of the violations of human rights by the Government of Iraq, based on all information the Special Rapporteur might deem relevant, including information provided by intergovernmental and non-governmental organizations and any comments and material provided by the Government of Iraq,

Bearing in mind the pertinent resolutions of the Commission on Human Rights condemning the flagrant violations of human rights by the Government of Iraq, including its most recent, resolution 1992/71 of 5 March 1992, in which the Commission decided to extend the mandate of the Special Rapporteur for a further year and requested him in pursuing his mandate to visit again the northern area of Iraq in particular, and to submit an interim report to the General Assembly at its forty-seventh session and a final report to the Commission at its forty-ninth session,

Recalling Security Council resolutions 706(1991) of 15 August 1991, 712(1991) of 19 September 1991 and 778(1992) of 2 October 1992,

Deeply concerned by the massive and grave violations of human rights by the Government of Iraq, such as summary and arbitrary executions, torture and other cruel, inhuman or degrading treatment, enforced or involuntary disappearances, arbitrary arrests and detentions, and lack of due process and the rule of law and of freedom of thought, expression, association and access to food and health care,

Deeply concerned also by the fact that chemical weapons have been used on the Iraqi civilian population, by the forced displacement of hundreds of thousands of Iraqi civilians and by the destruction of Iraqi towns and villages, as well as by the fact that tens of thousands of displaced Kurds had to take refuge in camps and shelters in the north of Iraq,

Deeply concerned further by the current severe and grave violations of human rights by the Government of Iraq against the civilian population in southern Iraq, in particular the Shiah communities in the southern marshes,

Expressing concern in particular that there has been no improvement in the human rights situation in Iraq, and welcoming, therefore, the proposal of the Special Rapporteur for the deployment of a team of human rights monitors in Iraq,

Noting that despite the formal cooperation extended to the Special Rapporteur, the Government of Iraq needs to improve that cooperation, in particular by giving full replies to the inquiries of the Special Rapporteur about acts it is committing that are incompatible with the international human rights instruments that are binding on Iraq,

1. *Takes note with appreciation* of the interim report on the situation of human rights in Iraq submitted by the Special Rapporteur of the Commission on Human Rights and the observations, conclusions and recommendations contained therein;

2. *Expresses its strong condemnation* of the massive violations of human rights of the gravest nature, for which the Government of Iraq is responsible and to which the Special Rapporteur has referred in his recent reports, in particular:

   (*a*)   Summary and arbitrary executions, orchestrated mass executions and burials, extrajudicial killings, including political killings, in particular in the northern region of Iraq, in southern Shiah centres and in the southern marshes;

   (*b*)   The widespread routine practice of systematic torture in its most cruel forms, including the torture of children;

   (*c*)   Enforced or involuntary disappearances, routinely practised arbitrary arrest and detention, including of women and children, and consistent and routine failure to respect due process and the rule of law;

   (*d*)   Suppression of freedom of thought, expression and association, and violations of property rights;

3. *Deplores* the refusal of Iraq to cooperate in the implementation of Security Council resolutions 706(1991) and 712(1991) and its failure to provide the Iraqi population with access to adequate food and health care;

4. *Calls upon* the Government of Iraq to release immediately all persons arbitrarily arrested and detained, including Kuwaitis and nationals of other States;

5. *Calls once again upon* Iraq, as a State party to the International Covenant on Economic, Social and Cultural Rights as well as to the International Covenant on Civil and Political Rights, to abide by its freely undertaken obligations under the Covenants and under other international instruments on human rights, and particularly to respect and ensure the rights of all individuals irrespective of their origin within its territory and subject to its jurisdiction;

6. *Recognizes* the importance of the work of the United Nations in providing humanitarian relief to the people of Iraq, and calls upon Iraq immediately and fully to implement the Memorandum of Understanding signed on 22 October 1992 between the United Nations and the Government of Iraq and to cooperate with the United Nations programmes, including ensuring the safety and security of United Nations personnel and humanitarian workers;

7. *Expresses special alarm* at the repressive policies and practices directed against the Kurds, which continue to have an impact on the lives of the Iraqi people as a whole;

8. *Also expresses special alarm* at the resurgence of grave violations of human rights against Shiah communities, especially in southern Iraq, which is the result of a policy directed against the marsh Arabs in particular;

9. *Further expresses special alarm* at all internal embargoes, which prevent the equitable enjoyment of basic foodstuffs and medical supplies, and calls upon Iraq, which has sole responsibility in this regard, to remove them;

10. _Welcomes_ the proposal of the Special Rapporteur for a system of human rights monitors which would constitute an independent and reliable source of information, and invites the Commission on Human Rights to follow up this proposal at its forty-ninth session;

11. _Urges once more_ the Government of Iraq to set up an independent commission of inquiry to look into the fate of tens of thousands of persons who have disappeared;

12. _Regrets_ the failure of the Government of Iraq to provide satisfactory and convincing replies concerning the violations of human rights brought to the attention of the Special Rapporteur, and calls upon it to reply without delay in a comprehensive and detailed manner;

13. _Urges_, therefore, the Government of Iraq to accord its full cooperation to the Special Rapporteur to enable him to make the appropriate recommendations to improve the human rights situation in Iraq;

14. _Requests_ the Secretary-General to provide the Special Rapporteur with all the assistance necessary to carry out his mandate;

15. _Decides_ to continue its consideration of the situation of human rights in Iraq during its forty-eighth session under the item entitled ''Human rights questions'' in the light of additional elements provided by the Commission on Human Rights and the Economic and Social Council.

General Assembly resolution 47/145

18 December 1992   Meeting 92   126-2-26 (recorded vote)

Approved by Third Committee (A/47/678/Add.2) by recorded vote (110-2-26), 4 December (meeting 59); 33-nation draft (A/C.3/47/L.75); agenda item 97 (c).

Sponsors: Argentina, Australia, Belgium, Bulgaria, Canada, Costa Rica, Czechoslovakia, Denmark, Finland, France, Germany, Greece, Hungary, Iceland, Ireland, Italy, Japan, Kuwait, Latvia, Liechtenstein, Lithuania, Luxembourg, Netherlands, Norway, Panama, Poland, Portugal, Romania, Samoa, Spain, Sweden, United Kingdom, United States.

Meeting numbers. GA 47th session: 3rd Committee 47-59; plenary 92.

Recorded vote in Assembly as follows:

In favour: Afghanistan, Antigua and Barbuda, Argentina, Armenia, Australia, Austria, Azerbaijan, Bahamas, Barbados, Belarus, Belgium, Belize, Benin, Bhutan, Bolivia, Bosnia and Herzegovina, Botswana, Brazil, Bulgaria, Burkina Faso, Burundi, Cameroon, Canada, Cape Verde, Chad, Chile, Colombia, Congo, Costa Rica, Croatia, Cyprus, Czechoslovakia, Denmark, Djibouti, Dominica, Dominican Republic, Ecuador, Egypt, El Salvador, Estonia, Ethiopia, Fiji, Finland, France, Gabon, Gambia, Germany, Ghana, Greece, Grenada, Guatemala, Guinea, Guyana, Haiti, Honduras, Hungary, Iceland, Iran, Ireland, Israel, Italy, Jamaica, Japan, Kazakhstan, Kenya, Kuwait, Latvia, Liechtenstein, Lithuania, Luxembourg, Malawi, Maldives, Mali, Malta, Marshall Islands, Mauritius, Mexico, Micronesia, Mongolia, Nepal, Netherlands, New Zealand, Nicaragua, Niger, Nigeria, Norway, Panama, Papua New Guinea, Paraguay, Peru, Poland, Portugal, Republic of Korea, Republic of Moldova, Romania, Russian Federation, Rwanda, Saint Kitts and Nevis, Saint Lucia, Saint Vincent and the Grenadines, Samoa, Sao Tome and Principe, Saudi Arabia, Senegal, Seychelles, Sierra Leone, Singapore, Slovenia, Solomon Islands, Spain, Suriname, Swaziland, Sweden, Syrian Arab Republic, Thailand, Togo, Trinidad and Tobago, Turkey, Ukraine, United Arab Emirates, United Kingdom, United States, Uruguay, Vanuatu, Venezuela, Zambia.

Against: Iraq, Sudan.

Abstaining: Algeria, Angola, Bangladesh, Brunei Darussalam, China, Côte d'Ivoire, Cuba, Guinea-Bissau, India, Indonesia, Jordan, Lao People's Democratic Republic, Lesotho, Liberia, Libyan Arab Jamahiriya, Malaysia, Mauritania, Morocco, Namibia, Pakistan, Philippines, Sri Lanka, Uganda, United Republic of Tanzania, Viet Nam, Zimbabwe.

Kuwait under Iraqi occupation

Report of the Special Rapporteur. In January, Special Rapporteur Walter Kälin (Switzerland) reported on the human rights situation in Kuwait under Iraqi occupation.[58] Following a description of his mandate and activities and the general

legal framework on which his report was based, he discussed the human rights situation and the corresponding guarantees of international humanitarian law concerning arbitrary arrest, detention and deportation; torture and cruel, inhuman and degrading treatment; the right to life and prohibition of arbitrary and summary execution; disappearances and missing persons; freedom to leave; freedom of religion, expression and assembly; special protection of children and women; and economic, social and cultural rights.

In his recommendations on the fate of missing persons, the Special Rapporteur stated that United Nations organs should urge Iraq to comply with a 1991 General Assembly resolution[59] and provide information on events occurring between 2 August 1990 and 26 February 1991 concerning: persons deported from Kuwait who might still be detained; persons arrested in Kuwait who died during or after that period while in detention and the site of their graves; and executions of persons arrested in Kuwait and carried out in Kuwait or Iraq during or after that period. He recommended that United Nations organs ask Iraq to search for persons still missing and cooperate with international humanitarian organizations in that regard. He also recommended that Kuwait be asked to cooperate with international organizations to identify all remaining unidentified persons killed there. Governments concerned should be urged to allow for the repatriation of persons deported from Kuwait to Iraq to the country of their former residence, and Iraq should be urged to provide compensation for victims of human rights violations committed by the Iraqi occupying forces through a fund established by the Security Council in 1991.[60]

Human Rights Commission action. By a roll-call vote of 47 to 1, with 1 abstention, the Commission, on 3 March,[61] strongly condemned Iraq's failure to treat prisoners of war and detainees in accordance with the internationally recognized principles of humanitarian law and insisted that it refrain from subjecting them to acts of violence, including ill-treatment, torture and summary execution. Expressing deep concern for Kuwaiti and third-country nationals detained and missing in Iraq, it requested Iraq to provide information on those abducted from Kuwait between 2 August 1990 and 26 February 1991 who might still be detained and to free them without delay. It also asked Iraq to provide information on persons arrested in Kuwait within that time period who might have died while in detention, as well as on the location of their graves. It further requested Iraq to search for persons still missing and to cooperate fully with international humanitarian organizations, such as ICRC, in that regard and in their efforts towards an eventual repatriation of

Kuwaiti and third-country nationals detained and missing in Iraq.

Myanmar

Human Rights Commission action. On 3 March,[62] the Commission, expressing concern at the seriousness of the human rights situation in Myanmar and at the fact that political leaders, including Daw Aung San Suu Kyi and other leaders of the National League for Democracy, remained deprived of their liberty, decided to nominate a special rapporteur to establish direct contacts with the Government and people of that country and to report to the General Assembly in 1992 (see below) and to the Commission in 1993. The Economic and Social Council approved that nomination by **decision 1992/235** of 20 July 1992. The Commission urged Myanmar to cooperate fully with the Commission and its special rapporteur and to ensure the special rapporteur's access to any person in Myanmar whom he deemed it appropriate to meet. It asked the Government to ensure that all persons were given the minimum guarantees for a fair trial and called on Myanmar to end the exodus of refugees and to facilitate their early repatriation. The Commission also called on Myanmar to pay attention to prison conditions and allow ICRC to visit prisons there, and urged Myanmar to reopen its universities and other institutions of higher education.

Report of the Special Rapporteur. In November, the Secretary-General transmitted the preliminary report of Special Rapporteur Yozo Yokota (Japan) on the human rights situation in Myanmar.[63] He traced the chronology of events relevant to that situation from 1948 to early 1992.

The Special Rapporteur examined allegations of arbitrary detention; disappearances; torture, cruel, inhuman or degrading treatment; and summary or arbitrary executions. He urged Myanmar to sign and ratify the 1966 Covenants on Civil and Political Rights and Economic, Social and Cultural Rights,[8] and the 1984 Convention against Torture and Other Cruel, Inhuman or Degrading Treatment or Punishment,[64] and encouraged Myanmar to allow an ICRC and UNHCR presence to carry out their humanitarian task. He urged Myanmar to continue its policy of allowing Daw Aung San Suu Kyi to receive visits from her family and to extend that policy to other detainees.

In a later report,[65] the Special Rapporteur described his visit to Myanmar from 7 to 14 December.

GENERAL ASSEMBLY ACTION

On 18 December 1992, the General Assembly, on the recommendation of the Third Committee, adopted **resolution 47/144** without vote.

Situation in Myanmar

The General Assembly,

Recalling its resolution 46/132 of 17 December 1991,

Reaffirming that all Member States have an obligation to promote and protect human rights and fundamental freedoms as stated in the Charter of the United Nations and elaborated in the Universal Declaration of Human Rights, the International Covenants on Human Rights and other applicable human rights instruments,

Aware that, in accordance with the Charter, the Organization promotes and encourages respect for human rights and fundamental freedoms for all and that article 21, paragraph 3, of the Universal Declaration of Human Rights states that "the will of the people shall be the basis of the authority of government",

Taking note of Commission on Human Rights resolution 1992/58 of 3 March 1992, in which the Commission, *inter alia*, decided to nominate a special rapporteur to establish direct contacts with the Government and with the people of Myanmar, including political leaders deprived of their liberty, their families and lawyers, with a view to examining the situation of human rights in Myanmar and following any progress made towards the transfer of power to a civilian government and the drafting of a new constitution, the lifting of restrictions on personal freedoms and the restoration of human rights in Myanmar, and to report to the General Assembly at its forty-seventh session and to the Commission at its forty-ninth session,

Noting the measures taken by the Government of Myanmar, including its accession to the Geneva Conventions of 12 August 1949 for the protection of victims of war, the release of a number of political prisoners, the lifting of the curfew, the revocation of certain martial laws and the reopening of the universities, in response to the concerns expressed by the international community, including the General Assembly and the Commission on Human Rights,

Gravely concerned that the Government of Myanmar still has not implemented its commitments to take all necessary steps towards democracy in the light of the results of the elections held in 1990,

Gravely concerned also at the continued seriousness of the situation of human rights in Myanmar, including reports of torture and arbitrary execution, continued detention of a large number of persons for political reasons, the existence of important restrictions on the exercise of fundamental freedoms and the imposition of oppressive measures directed in particular at ethnic and religious minorities,

Noting that the human rights situation in Myanmar has consequently resulted in massive flows of refugees to neighbouring countries,

Deeply concerned at the continuing problem of large numbers of refugees from Myanmar in neighbouring countries, including the almost 265,000 Myanmar Rohingya refugees in Bangladesh,

1. *Expresses its appreciation* to the Special Rapporteur of the Commission on Human Rights for his preliminary report and the recommendations contained therein;

2. *Calls upon* the Government of Myanmar to extend its full and unreserved cooperation to the Special Rapporteur and to ensure that he has free access to any person in Myanmar whom he deems it appropriate to meet for the conduct of his mandate;

3. *Expresses its grave concern* about the continued seriousness of the human rights situation in Myanmar;

4. *Urges* the Government of Myanmar to take all necessary steps towards the restoration of democracy, fully respecting the will of the people as expressed in the democratic elections held in 1990;

5. *Also urges* the Government of Myanmar to take every appropriate measure to allow all citizens to participate freely in the political process in accordance with the principles of the Universal Declaration of Human Rights and to accelerate the process of transition to democracy, in particular through the transfer of power to the democratically elected representatives;

6. *Further urges* the Government of Myanmar to ensure full respect for human rights and fundamental freedoms and the protection of the rights of persons belonging to ethnic and religious minorities;

7. *Notes* the release of a number of political leaders from detention;

8. *Deeply regrets*, however, that many political leaders are still deprived of their freedom and their fundamental rights;

9. *Calls upon* the Government of Myanmar to release unconditionally the Nobel Peace Laureate Aung San Suu Kyi, who is now in her fourth year of detention without trial, and other political leaders and remaining political prisoners;

10. *Also calls upon* the Government of Myanmar to respect fully the obligations under the Geneva Conventions of 12 August 1949, in particular the obligations under article 3 common to the Conventions and to make use of such services as may be offered by impartial humanitarian bodies;

11. *Requests* the Government of Myanmar to invite the presence of the International Committee of the Red Cross in Myanmar in order for it to carry out its humanitarian tasks;

12. *Calls upon* the Government of Myanmar to create the necessary conditions to ensure an end to the flows of refugees to neighbouring countries and to facilitate their speedy repatriation and to cooperate fully with the relevant United Nations organs on this matter;

13. *Decides* to continue its consideration of this question at its forty-eighth session.

General Assembly resolution 47/144

18 December 1992   Meeting 92   Adopted without vote

Approved by Third Committee (A/47/678/Add.2) without vote, 4 December (meeting 59); 34-nation draft (A/C.3/47/L.74), orally revised; agenda item 97 *(c)*.
Sponsors: Albania, Argentina, Australia, Belgium, Bulgaria, Canada, Chile, Costa Rica, Czechoslovakia, Denmark, Estonia, Finland, France, Germany, Greece, Hungary, Iceland, Ireland, Italy, Latvia, Liechtenstein, Lithuania, Luxembourg, Netherlands, Norway, Panama, Poland, Portugal, Romania, Samoa, Spain, Sweden, United Kingdom, United States.
Meeting numbers. GA 47th session: 3rd Committee 47-59; plenary 92.

Papua New Guinea

Bougainville

Subcommission action. On 27 August,[66] the Subcommission, aware of the continuing allegations of human rights violations relating to the situation on Bougainville, called on Papua New Guinea to restore freedom of movement to the people of Bougainville and asked the Special Rapporteur on the study of treaties, agreements and other constructive arrangements between States and indigenous populations to include in his report the agreements entered into between the indigenous people of Bougainville and Papua New Guinea.

Tibet

Note by the Secretary-General. By a January note,[67] the Secretary-General submitted to the Commission on Human Rights a report on the situation in Tibet containing a reply by China to a note verbale he had sent in December 1991. Annexed to the report were attachments to China's reply and information received from NGOs on human rights violations in Tibet.

Human Rights Commission action. On 4 March 1992,[68] the Commission, by a roll-call vote of 27 to 15, with 10 abstentions, decided to take no decision on a draft concerning the situation in China/Tibet.

Europe and the Mediterranean

Albania

Report of the Secretary-General. In January,[69] the Secretary-General reported on action taken pursuant to a 1991 Commission on Human Rights resolution concerning human rights in Albania,[70] noting that he had requested information from Albania on steps taken to implement the resolution's provisions. Included in the report was a communication from Albania to the Secretary-General describing measures taken in 1991 to guarantee and promote human rights there.

Human Rights Commission action. The Commission, on 4 March 1992,[71] called on Albania to continue to adopt legislative and administrative measures to meet the requirements of relevant international human rights instruments and respect the rights of minorities living there. Welcoming the conclusion, on 13 February, of an agreement on technical cooperation between the Centre for Human Rights and the United Nations Fund for Advisory Services and Technical Assistance in the Field of Human Rights and Albania, it asked the Secretary-General to bring its resolution to Albania's attention, request information regarding its implementation and report to the Commission in 1993.

Cyprus

Report of the Secretary-General. In February,[72] the Secretary-General reported on human rights in Cyprus pursuant to a 1991 Commission decision.[70] The Secretary-General described action taken in 1991 by the Security Council and the Committee on Missing Persons in Cyprus (see PART TWO, Chapter III).

Human Rights Commission action. On 27 February,[73] the Commission postponed until

1993 debate on the question of human rights in Cyprus, on the understanding that action required by previous resolutions would continue to remain operative, including the Commission's request to the Secretary-General to provide a report on their implementation.

Estonia and Latvia

In response to a request by Latvia,[74] the Secretary-General sent a fact-finding mission to that country (27-30 October) to investigate alleged human rights abuses against minorities there. At Latvia's request, the summary report of the fact-finding mission was circulated as an official General Assembly document.[75]

GENERAL ASSEMBLY ACTION

On 16 December 1992, the General Assembly, on the recommendation of the Third Committee, adopted **resolution 47/115** without vote.

Situation of human rights in Estonia and Latvia
The General Assembly,
Guided by the principles embodied in the Charter of the United Nations, the Universal Declaration of Human Rights and the International Covenants on Human Rights,
Reaffirming that all Member States have an obligation to promote and protect human rights and fundamental freedoms for all and to fulfil the obligations they have undertaken under the various international instruments in this field,
Convinced that respect for human rights is an inalienable component of maintaining and promoting good-neighbourly relations between States,
Taking into account the complaint of alleged violations of human rights with respect to the Russian-speaking population in Estonia and Latvia,
Taking note of the conclusions and recommendations made by the United Nations fact-finding mission that visited Riga in October 1992 at the invitation of the Government of Latvia,
1. *Notes with concern* the existence of certain problems that involve large groups of population in Estonia and Latvia;
2. *Welcomes* the cooperation that the Government of Latvia has extended to the United Nations fact-finding mission;
3. *Also welcomes* the invitation of the Government of Estonia to receive a similar United Nations fact-finding mission and its intention to extend to it its cooperation;
4. *Calls upon* the States concerned to intensify their efforts on the bilateral level aimed at resolving concerns with regard to the situation of the Russian-speaking population on the basis of generally accepted norms of international law in the field of human rights;
5. *Requests* the Secretary-General to keep Member States informed of the progress in the field of human rights in Estonia and Latvia and to report thereon to the General Assembly at its forty-eighth session under the item entitled "Situation of human rights in Estonia and Latvia".

General Assembly resolution 47/115
16 December 1992   Meeting 89   Adopted without vote

Approved by Third Committee (A/47/773) without vote, 3 December (meeting 56); draft by Chairman (A/C.3/47/L.52); agenda item 149.
Meeting numbers. GA 47th session: 3rd Committee 47-56; plenary 89.

Romania

Report of the Special Rapporteur. In January,[76] Special Rapporteur Joseph Voyame (Switzerland) outlined the main events relating to the human rights situation in Romania that had occurred since the submission of his previous report in 1991.[70] He described his activities in carrying out his mandate and analysed information compiled in connection with various human rights and fundamental freedoms and their implementation.

The Special Rapporteur concluded that, overall, the human rights situation had continued to improve in Romania. It recently had adopted a modern constitution, which was reproduced in the Special Rapporteur's report. Despite progress made, Romania's minority problem remained a cause for concern, as did the practical application of the new constitutional and legislative rules and the functioning of the justice system.

The Special Rapporteur recommended that the Romanian authorities continue to ensure respect for human rights; pay particular attention to the points raised by him; and consider the possibility of continuing to use the United Nations Fund for Advisory Services and Technical Assistance in the Field of Human Rights.

Human Rights Commission action. The Commission, taking note of the Special Rapporteur's report, incorporated his recommendations into a resolution of 3 March 1992.[77] It asked the Secretary-General to bring the resolution to Romania's attention, ask it to provide information on its implementation and report to the Commission in 1993.

The former Yugoslavia

In 1992, the Commission on Human Rights held two special sessions, both at Geneva (13 and 14 August;[78] 30 November and 1 December[79]), to consider the situation of human rights in the former Yugoslavia. By a 1990 resolution of the Economic and Social Council,[80] the Commission had been authorized to meet exceptionally between its regular sessions, provided that a majority of its States members so agreed.

Human Rights Commission action. On 14 August 1992,[81] the Commission condemned in the strongest terms all human rights violations in the former Yugoslavia, especially in Bosnia and Herzegovina, and called on all parties to end such violations immediately and take steps to ensure full respect for human rights, fundamental freedoms and humanitarian law; cease immediately the human rights violations that had produced refugees and displaced persons and ensure conditions conducive to a safe return to their homes; and fulfil their obligations under the provisions of the 1966 International Covenants on Civil and Political Rights and Economic, Social and Cultural Rights,[8] the 1948 Convention on the Prevention and Punishment of the Crime of Genocide,[82] the 1984 Convention against Torture and Other Cruel, Inhuman or Degrading Treatment or Punishment[64] and the 1965 International Convention on the Elimination of Racial Discrimination.[9] The Commission condemned ethnic cleansing and called on all parties to ensure the protection of the rights of persons belonging to national or ethnic, religious and linguistic minorities.

The Commission demanded that all parties extend full cooperation and protection to UNHCR and other international humanitarian organizations and relief workers assisting refugees and displaced persons. Calling for the release of all persons arbitrarily arrested or detained, it demanded that ICRC be granted access to all camps, prisons and other places of detention and that all parties ensure safety and freedom of movement for ICRC.

The Commission asked its Chairman to appoint a special rapporteur to investigate the human rights situation in the former Yugoslavia, particularly in Bosnia and Herzegovina; visit the area; compile information on possible human rights violations, including war crimes; take into account and seek to complement the efforts being undertaken by the Conference on Security and Cooperation in Europe (a forum of 35 participating States, including Canada and the United States, for the periodic review of the Final Act of the Conference on Security and Cooperation in Europe, adopted in 1975 at Helsinki, Finland, and to facilitate a wider political dialogue in a more united Europe); provide a preliminary report no later than 28 August 1992, including recommendations for ending and preventing such violations; report findings and recommendations to the Commission periodically thereafter until its 1993 session and report to the Assembly in 1992 and to the Commission in 1993. United Nations bodies and specialized agencies, Governments and intergovernmental and non-governmental organizations were asked to assist the special rapporteur, as were the Special Rapporteurs on the question of torture and on summary or arbitrary executions, the Secretary-General's representative on internally displaced persons and the Working Group on Arbitrary Detention. The Commission demanded that all parties cooperate with the special rapporteur in implementing its resolution. The Secretary-General was asked to make the special rapporteur's reports available to the Security Council and to assist him in fulfilling his mandate.

The Economic and Social Council, by **decision 1992/305** of 18 August, endorsed the Commission's resolution.

Annexed to the Commission's resolution was a decision on the situation of human rights in Yugoslavia adopted by the Subcommission on 13 August.[83]

Reports of the Special Rapporteur. By a note of 3 September,[84] the Secretary-General transmitted to the General Assembly and the Security Council the preliminary report on the human rights situation in the former Yugoslavia prepared by Special Rapporteur Tadeusz Mazowiecki (Poland).[85] He had visited the former Yugoslavia, in particular Bosnia and Herzegovina, from 21 to 26 August, and was accompanied by the Chairman of the Working Group on Arbitrary Detention and the Special Rapporteur on extrajudicial, summary or arbitrary executions.

The Special Rapporteur's observations focused on ethnic cleansing directed against Muslims and ethnic Croatians in the territories of Bosnia and Herzegovina and Croatia under the control of ethnic Serbs. He also described the situation of ethnic Serbs in Croatia, which had resulted in the flight of a large number of ethnic Serbs to Serbia and to those parts of Croatia and Bosnia and Herzegovina under their control. The Special Rapporteur had received information on cases of detention, executions, disappearances and other violations such as physical abuse and torture. The causes of human rights violations and the difficulties encountered by humanitarian organizations were discussed.

The Special Rapporteur concluded that mass and grave human rights violations were occurring in Bosnia and Herzegovina and were being perpetrated by all parties to the conflicts. Violence was tolerated and often encouraged by responsible authorities. The situation of detainees and refugees was particularly dramatic, and the indoctrination of a large part of the population encouraged national and religious hatred.

The Special Rapporteur recommended neutralizing the heavy weaponry in Bosnia and Herzegovina; the continued call by the United Nations for an end to ethnic cleansing; increasing the size and expanding the mandate of the United Nations Protection Force; granting ICRC full access to detention camps and centres; reinforcing the efficiency of the information system on the fate of persons forcibly separated from their families; establishing a commission to determine the fate of disappeared persons; setting up an information agency, independent of local authorities, to counteract the dissemination of hatred; creating a commission to assess and further investigate cases warranting prosecution; and concerted international action to improve the fate of victims of human rights violations. Annexed to the report was the programme of the Special Rapporteur's visit and his observations concerning the parties in control of Bosnia and Herzegovina and Croatia.

On 6 November,[86] the Secretary-General transmitted the second report on the human rights situation in the former Yugoslavia[87] based on the Special Rapporteur's visit to the area from 12 to 22 October. Also taking part in that mission were the Special Rapporteurs on extrajudicial, summary or arbitrary executions and on the question of torture, the Chairman of the Working Group on Arbitrary Detention, the Secretary-General's Representative on internally displaced persons and one medical and one forensic expert. The mission included visits to different areas in Bosnia and Herzegovina, Croatia and Serbia, including Kosovo, Vojvodina and Sandjak, and gave special attention to prisons and refugee centres.

The Special Rapporteur noted that since his first visit, widespread and serious human rights violations continued to be committed in Bosnia and Herzegovina and, in certain respects, had intensified. He concluded that the situation required emergency action by the international community with priority being given to protecting the right to life, guarantee for the security of displaced persons, an increase in humanitarian assistance and priority attention to opening humanitarian relief corridors to besieged areas in Bosnia and Herzegovina. He reconfirmed the recommendations made in his preliminary report. Annexed to the report was the programme of the Special Rapporteur's second visit and a statement by the forensic expert concerning several mass graves near Vukovar (Croatia).

The Secretary-General, on 17 November,[88] transmitted the Special Rapporteur's third report on the human rights situation in the former Yugoslavia. His report was based on information received prior to and during his two missions, mainly from credible witnesses or from reliable and impartial sources.

Concerning the human rights situation in Bosnia and Herzegovina, the Special Rapporteur discussed ethnic cleansing and noted that the number of Croat and Muslim refugees fleeing areas of Bosnia and Herzegovina under Serbian control was three to four times greater than the number of Serbian refugees and displaced persons from Bosnia and Herzegovina. Arbitrary executions, terrorist attacks against homes and places of worship and hostage-taking continued there and also in the United Nations Protected Areas (UNPAs) of Croatia (western Slavonia, eastern Slavonia and Krajina). The Serbian authorities in control of certain territories in Bosnia and Herzegovina and in UNPAs were responsible for ethnic cleansing there, as were the Yugoslav National Army and the po-

litical leadership of Serbia. Albanians, Croats, Hungarians, Muslims and other ethnic minorities were discriminated against in the Serbian areas of Kosovo, Vojvodina and Sandjak, and discrimination and human rights violations occurred against the Serbs in territories controlled by the Government of Bosnia and Herzegovina and in territory under the control of Bosnian Croats. Similar abuses occurred in Croatia, particularly against Serbs. The Special Rapporteur observed that there was growing evidence that war crimes had been committed.

The Special Rapporteur recommended investigating war crimes, taking more effective steps to stop ethnic cleansing, establishing security zones in Bosnia and Herzegovina, protecting the right of refugees and displaced persons to return to their homes, opening humanitarian relief corridors and supporting democratically oriented groups. He urged all States, particularly the European ones, in cooperation with ICRC and UNHCR, to offer asylum and temporary refuge to persons at imminent risk of death due to inhumane conditions in detention and transit facilities in northern Bosnia. The Special Rapporteur considered it necessary to have a small number of human rights monitors, under his direction, located in the former Yugoslavia and asked that the necessary arrangements be made.

Report of the Special Rapporteur on extrajudicial, summary or arbitrary executions. In December,[89] the Special Rapporteur on extrajudicial, summary or arbitrary executions, Bacre Waly Ndiaye (Senegal), reported on his participation in two missions to the former Yugoslavia in August and October, when he accompanied the Special Rapporteur on the former Yugoslavia.

He observed that extrajudicial executions were a serious problem in the former Yugoslavia and were used as a method of advancing ethnic cleansing. The shelling of civilian population centres and interference in the delivery of humanitarian relief were also forms of extrajudicial, summary or arbitrary executions.

The Special Rapporteur also visited the former Yugoslavia from 15 to 20 December, where he conducted preliminary investigations into allegations that victims of war crimes were buried in various mass graves, especially in Croatia.[90]

Human Rights Commission action. By a roll-call vote of 45 to 1, with 1 abstention, the Commission on Human Rights, on 1 December,[91] condemned all human rights violations in the former Yugoslavia identified by the Special Rapporteur, as well as the indiscriminate shellings of cities and civilian areas, the systematic terrorization and murder of non-combatants, the destruction of vital services and the besieging of cities and use of military force against civilians and relief operations by all sides, recognizing that the main responsibility lay with Serbian forces. It categorically condemned ethnic cleansing, particularly in Bosnia and Herzegovina, recognizing that the primary responsibility rested with the Serbian leadership in territories under their control in that region, the Yugoslav Army and the political leadership in Serbia. It demanded an immediate end to ethnic cleansing, and particularly that Serbia use its influence with the self-proclaimed Serbian authorities in Bosnia and Herzegovina and Croatia to end that practice and to reverse its effects, re-emphasizing the rights of refugees, displaced persons and other victims of ethnic cleansing to return to their homes and the invalidity of acts made under duress. Expressing grave concern regarding information reported by the Special Rapporteur in his third report[88] on the dangerous situation in the Serbian areas of Kosovo, Sandjak and Vojvodina, the Commission urged all parties in those areas to engage in a meaningful dialogue under the auspices of the International Conference on the Former Yugoslavia (see PART TWO, Chapter IV) and to act with utmost restraint and settle disputes in full observance of human rights and freedoms. The Commission called on the Serbian authorities to refrain from the use of force, stop ethnic cleansing and respect fully the rights of persons belonging to ethnic communities or minorities in order to prevent extending the conflict to other parts of the former Yugoslavia.

Affirming the accountability of States for human rights violations committed by their agents on another State's territory, the Commission condemned such violations relating to detention— including killings, torture and rape—and called on all parties to close immediately all detention centres not authorized by and in compliance with the 1949 Geneva Conventions and to release all detainees. It also called on all parties to end violations of human rights and humanitarian law immediately and to apprehend and punish those guilty of perpetrating or authorizing them, make efforts to account for the missing and consider the extent to which the acts committed in Bosnia and Herzegovina and Croatia constituted genocide, in accordance with the Convention on the Prevention and Punishment of the Crime of Genocide.[82]

The Commission on Human Rights welcomed the establishment of the Commission of Experts to examine information relating to violations of international humanitarian law (see below); encouraged close cooperation between its Special Rapporteur and the Commission; recommended that the Commission be granted the staff and resources to act effectively; and asked the Com-

mission to provide its conclusions to the Secretary-General to allow the Security Council to consider further steps towards bringing those accused to justice. The Commission on Human Rights called on all parties to provide information to the Commission of Experts and urged the Commission, with the assistance of the Centre for Human Rights, to arrange for an urgent investigation of a mass grave near Vukovar and other mass grave sites and places where mass killings were reported to have taken place, and asked the General Assembly to provide the resources to do so.

The Commission welcomed the Special Rapporteur's call to open humanitarian relief corridors and his recommendation to create security zones to protect displaced persons, and asked him to continue his efforts. It called on bodies entrusted with human rights monitoring in the former Yugoslavia to cooperate closely with the Special Rapporteur and the Commission of Experts. It asked the Secretary-General to continue to provide the Security Council with the Special Rapporteur's reports and urged him to ensure the cooperation of all United Nations bodies in implementing its resolution. The General Assembly and the Secretary-General were asked to make available all resources needed by the Special Rapporteur to carry out his mandate and to comply with his request for staff to be based in the former Yugoslavia to enhance effective monitoring of the human rights situation there.

Commission of Experts. In accordance with Security Council **resolution 780(1992)** of 6 October, the Secretary-General, on 14 October,[92] established a Commission of Experts to examine and analyse information submitted on violations of humanitarian law in the former Yugoslavia (see also PART TWO, Chapter IV).

At its first session (New York, 4 and 5 November), the Commission of Experts discussed organizational and procedural questions, dealt with issues related to its mandate and appointed a Rapporteur on issues of law.

The Commission, at its second session (Geneva, 14-16 December), requested Physicians for Human Rights, a United States–based NGO, to investigate a mass grave near Vukovar. A four-member international forensic team, assembled by Physicians for Human Rights, conducted a preliminary site exploration near Vukovar from 17 to 19 December. The forensic team concluded that a mass execution had taken place; the grave contained possibly as many as 200 bodies; the grave site's remote location suggested that the executioners had sought to bury their victims secretly; the grave had not been disturbed since the time of execution or interment; and evidence at the site suggested that the grave most likely contained the remains of Croatians. The conclusions of the forensic team were annexed to the Commission's interim report to the Security Council.[93]

In December, the Commission also adopted its rules of procedure, further discussed its mandate and appointed Rapporteurs on the gathering and analysis of facts and for on-site investigations. It began reviewing numerous reports alleging grave breaches of international humanitarian law received from Governments, intergovernmental organizations and NGOs and other sources.

GENERAL ASSEMBLY ACTION

On 18 December 1992, on the recommendation of the Third Committee, the General Assembly adopted **resolution 47/147** without vote.

Situation of human rights in the territory of the former Yugoslavia

The General Assembly,

Guided by the principles embodied in the Charter of the United Nations, the Universal Declaration of Human Rights, the International Covenants on Human Rights, the International Convention on the Elimination of All Forms of Racial Discrimination, the Convention on the Prevention and Punishment of the Crime of Genocide, the Convention against Torture and Other Cruel, Inhuman or Degrading Treatment or Punishment, and international humanitarian law, including the Geneva Conventions of 12 August 1949 and the Additional Protocols thereto, of 1977,

Deeply concerned about the human tragedy in the territory of the former Yugoslavia, and at the continuing massive and systematic violations of human rights occurring in most of that territory, particularly in the areas of Bosnia and Herzegovina under Serbian control,

Bearing in mind Security Council resolutions 771(1992) of 13 August 1992, 780(1992) of 6 October 1992 and 787(1992) of 16 November 1992, in which, *inter alia*, the Council demanded that all parties and others concerned in the former Yugoslavia should immediately cease and desist from all breaches of international humanitarian law, and pursuant to which the Secretary-General has established a Commission of Experts to examine and analyse information relating to violations of humanitarian law being committed in the territory of the former Yugoslavia,

Recalling its resolution 46/242 of 25 August 1992, in which it demanded an end to the fighting, condemned the massive violations of human rights and international humanitarian law occurring in the territory of the former Yugoslavia, in particular the abhorrent practice of "ethnic cleansing", rejected recognition of the acquisition of territory by force and demanded the safe, unconditional and honourable repatriation of refugees and deportees to their homes,

Bearing in mind its resolution 47/80 of 16 December 1992 in which it condemned unreservedly "ethnic cleansing", and reiterated its conviction that those who committed or ordered the commission of acts of "ethnic cleansing" were individually responsible and should be brought to justice,

Noting that the Commission on Human Rights, at its first special session, devoted to the consideration of the situation of human rights in the former Yugoslavia,

adopted resolution 1992/S-1/1 of 14 August 1992, in which it condemned in the strongest terms all violations of human rights within the territory of the former Yugoslavia, called upon all parties to cease those violations immediately and to take all necessary steps to ensure full respect for human rights and fundamental freedoms and humanitarian law and requested its Chairman to appoint a special rapporteur to investigate the human rights situation in the territory of the former Yugoslavia,

Noting with appreciation the efforts of the Special Rapporteur, as well as those of the Chairman of the Working Group on Arbitrary Detention, the Special Rapporteur on extrajudicial, summary or arbitrary executions, the Special Rapporteur on the question of torture and the Representative of the Secretary-General on internally displaced persons, who accompanied him on one or both of his missions,

Welcoming the decision by the Commission on Human Rights to meet again in special session to consider the reports of the Special Rapporteur,

Encouraging the continuing efforts made in the framework of the International Conference on the Former Yugoslavia to find a peaceful solution to the situation in the former Yugoslavia, including the proposals made by the Co-Chairmen of the Steering Committee of the Conference for a constitution for the Republic of Bosnia and Herzegovina designed to protect human rights on the basis of fundamental human rights instruments,

Welcoming the consideration by the Human Rights Committee of the special reports from the Governments of the Federal Republic of Yugoslavia (Serbia and Montenegro), Croatia and Bosnia and Herzegovina on the human rights situation in those parts of the territory of the former Yugoslavia, with respect to their obligations under the International Covenant on Civil and Political Rights,

Noting with concern the comments adopted by the Human Rights Committee following consideration of those special reports at its meeting held on 6 November 1992,

Welcoming the effort by the Conference on Security and Cooperation in Europe to prevent further human rights violations and its missions dispatched to the territory of the former Yugoslavia, including missions of long duration to Kosovo, Vojvodina and Sandjak, where the human rights situation remains a cause of great concern,

Gravely concerned about the human rights situation in the territory of the former Yugoslavia, and in particular at the continuing, odious practice of "ethnic cleansing", which is the direct cause of the vast majority of human rights violations there and whose principal victims are the Muslim population threatened with virtual extermination,

Alarmed that, although the conflict in Bosnia and Herzegovina is not a religious conflict, it has been characterized by the systematic destruction and profanation of mosques, churches and other places of worship, as well as other sites of cultural heritage, in particular in areas currently or previously under Serbian control,

1. *Commends* the Special Rapporteur for his reports on the situation of human rights in the territory of the former Yugoslavia;

2. *Expresses its grave concern* at the Special Rapporteur's detailed reports of violations of human rights and humanitarian law in Bosnia and Herzegovina, Croatia and the Federal Republic of Yugoslavia (Serbia and Mon-

tenegro) and at his conclusion that most of the territory of the former Yugoslavia, in particular Bosnia and Herzegovina, is the scene of massive and systematic violations of human rights and grave violations of humanitarian law;

3. _Condemns_ in the strongest possible terms the abhorrent practice of ''ethnic cleansing'' and recognizes that the Serbian leadership in territories under its control in Bosnia and Herzegovina, the Yugoslav People's Army and the political leadership of the Republic of Serbia bear primary responsibility for this reprehensible practice, which flagrantly violates the most fundamental principles of human rights;

4. _Condemns also_ the specific violations identified by the Special Rapporteur, most of which are caused by ''ethnic cleansing'', and which include killings, torture, beatings, rape, disappearances, destruction of houses, and other acts or threats of violence aimed at forcing individuals to leave their homes, as well as reports of violations of human rights in connection with detention;

5. _Condemns further_ the indiscriminate shelling of cities and civilian areas, the systematic terrorization and murder of non-combatants, the destruction of vital services, the besieging of cities and the use of military force against civilian populations and relief operations by all sides, recognizing that the main responsibility lies with Serbian forces;

6. _Demands_ that all parties involved in the former Yugoslavia, and especially those most responsible, cease these violations immediately, take appropriate steps to apprehend and punish those who are guilty of perpetrating or authorizing the violations, including those violations in connection with detention, and take all necessary measures to ensure the enjoyment of human rights and fundamental freedoms, in accordance with their obligations under the Geneva Conventions of 12 August 1949, and the Additional Protocols thereto, of 1977, the International Covenants on Human Rights, and other international human rights instruments;

7. _Reaffirms_ that all persons who perpetrate or authorize crimes against humanity and other grave breaches of international humanitarian law are individually responsible for those breaches and that the international community will exert every effort to bring them to justice, and calls upon all parties to provide all pertinent information to the Commission of Experts in accordance with Security Council resolution 780(1992);

8. _Expresses deep concern_ at the number of disappearances and missing persons in the former Yugoslavia, and calls on all parties to make all possible efforts to account for those missing;

9. _Demands_ an immediate end to the practice of ''ethnic cleansing'', and in particular that the Government of the Federal Republic of Yugoslavia (Serbia and Montenegro) use its influence with the self-proclaimed Serbian authorities in Bosnia and Herzegovina and Croatia to bring the practice of ''ethnic cleansing'' to an immediate end and to reverse the effects of that practice;

10. _Reaffirms_ that States are to be held accountable for violations of human rights which their agents commit on the territory of another State;

11. _Expresses its complete support_ for the victims of these violations, reaffirms the right of all persons to return to their homes in safety and dignity, considers invalid all acts made under duress affecting ownership of property and other related questions, and recognizes the right of victims of ''ethnic cleansing'' to receive reparation for their losses;

12. _Condemns_ in particular the violations of human rights and humanitarian law in connection with detention, including killings, torture and the systematic practice of rape, and calls upon all parties in the former Yugoslavia to close immediately all detention centres not in compliance with the Geneva Conventions and to release immediately all persons arbitrarily or illegally detained;

13. _Demands_ that the International Committee of the Red Cross, the Special Rapporteur, the missions of the Conference on Security and Cooperation in Europe and other relevant international humanitarian organizations be granted immediate, unimpeded and continued access to all camps, prisons and other places of detention within the territory of the former Yugoslavia;

14. _Expresses its grave concern_ at the report of the Special Rapporteur on the dangerous situation in Kosovo, Sandjak and Vojvodina, urges all parties there to engage in a meaningful dialogue under the auspices of the International Conference on the Former Yugoslavia, to act with utmost restraint and to settle disputes in full compliance with human rights and fundamental freedoms, and calls upon the Serbian authorities to refrain from the use of force, to stop immediately the practice of ''ethnic cleansing'' and to respect fully the rights of persons belonging to ethnic communities or minorities, in order to prevent the extension of the conflict to other parts of the former Yugoslavia;

15. _Calls upon_ the parties to implement immediately all commitments made in the framework of the International Conference on the Former Yugoslavia and to work together to ensure the success of the Conference, and welcomes in this regard the acceptance by the Government of Bosnia and Herzegovina of the constitutional proposals of the Co-Chairmen of the Steering Committee of the Conference as a basis for negotiations;

16. _Endorses_ the resolution adopted by the Commission on Human Rights at its second special session addressing the reports of the Special Rapporteur, in particular its call for all States to consider the extent to which the acts committed in Bosnia and Herzegovina and in Croatia constitute genocide, in accordance with the Convention on the Prevention and Punishment of the Crime of Genocide;

17. _Calls upon_ all United Nations bodies, including the United Nations Protection Force and the specialized agencies, and invites Governments and informed intergovernmental and non-governmental organizations to cooperate fully with the Special Rapporteur and in particular to provide him on a continuing basis with all relevant and accurate information in their possession on the situation of human rights in the former Yugoslavia;

18. _Urges_ all States, United Nations bodies, including the specialized agencies, the Special Rapporteur and, as appropriate, international humanitarian organizations to make available to the Commission of Experts, pursuant to Security Council resolution 780(1992), substantiated information in their possession or submitted to them relating to the violations of humanitarian law, including grave breaches of the Geneva Conventions, being committed in the territory of the former Yugoslavia;

19. _Urges_ all States and relevant organizations to consider implementation of the recommendations of the Special Rapporteur, and in particular:

(a) Welcomes the call of the Special Rapporteur for the opening of humanitarian relief corridors to prevent the imminent death of tens of thousands of persons in besieged cities;

(b) Welcomes the invitation of the Security Council, in its resolution 787(1992), to the Secretary-General, in consultation with the Office of the United Nations High Commissioner for Refugees and other relevant agencies, to study the possibility of and the requirements for the promotion of safe areas and the recommendation of the Special Rapporteur for the creation of such security zones for the protection of displaced persons, while keeping in mind that the international community must not acquiesce in demographic changes caused by "ethnic cleansing";

(c) Draws the attention of the Commission of Experts established by Security Council resolution 780(1992) to the need for an immediate and urgent investigation by qualified experts of a mass grave near Vukovar and other mass grave sites and places where mass killings are reported to have taken place, and requests the Secretary-General, within the overall budgetary framework of the United Nations, to make available all necessary resources for this undertaking and for the other work of the Commission;

20. *Requests* the Secretary-General to take all necessary steps to ensure the full and effective coordination of all United Nations bodies to implement the present resolution, and calls upon those bodies concerned with the situation in the territory of the former Yugoslavia to coordinate closely with the Special Rapporteur and the Commission of Experts;

21. *Also requests* the Secretary-General, within the overall budgetary framework of the United Nations, to make all necessary resources available for the Special Rapporteur to carry out his mandate and in particular to provide him with a number of staff based in the territories of the former Yugoslavia adequate to ensure effective continuous monitoring of the human rights situation there and coordination with other United Nations bodies involved, including the United Nations Protection Force;

22. *Further requests* the Secretary-General to give all other necessary assistance to the Special Rapporteur to enable him to fulfil his mandate;

23. *Decides* to continue its examination of the situation of human rights in the former Yugoslavia during its forty-eighth session under the item entitled "Human rights questions".

General Assembly resolution 47/147

18 December 1992   Meeting 92   Adopted without vote

Approved by Third Committee (A/47/678/Add.2) without vote, 4 December (meeting 59); 53-nation draft (A/C.3/47/L.79/Rev.1); agenda item 97 *(c)*.

Sponsors: Afghanistan, Albania, Australia, Austria, Belgium, Bulgaria, Canada, Central African Republic, Chile, Colombia, Costa Rica, Croatia, Czechoslovakia, Denmark, Egypt, Finland, France, Gambia, Germany, Greece, Hungary, Iceland, Iran, Ireland, Italy, Japan, Latvia, Liechtenstein, Luxembourg, Madagascar, Malaysia, Morocco, Netherlands, New Zealand, Norway, Pakistan, Panama, Peru, Poland, Portugal, Republic of Moldova, Samoa, Saudi Arabia, Senegal, Slovenia, Spain, Sudan, Sweden, Tunisia, Turkey, United Kingdom, United States, Uruguay.

Meeting numbers. GA 47th session: 3rd Committee 47-59; plenary 92.

Latin America and the Caribbean

Cuba

Report of the Special Representative. In January,[94] Special Representative Rafael Rivas Posada (Colombia) reported on the human rights situation in Cuba. He stated that he had been unable to secure the cooperation of the Government and had based his report on information received from Cubans living outside the country and information that Cuban citizens living in the country had sent abroad. Allegations of human rights abuses dealt with the right to life, the right to physical integrity, disappearances, the right to enter and leave the country, unlawful or arbitrary detention, the right to due process, the right to security, the right to work, religious freedom, freedom of expression and information, and freedom of association. The information supplied to the Special Representative could not be checked against the Cuban authorities' versions, which made it difficult, he stated, to arrive at objective and impartial conclusions.

Human Rights Commission action. By a roll-call vote of 23 to 8, with 21 abstentions, the Commission, on 3 March,[95] commended the Special Representative for his report and noted that it was incomplete because he had been unable to meet with the people or Government of Cuba. It deplored Cuba's decision not to allow the Special Representative to fulfil his mandate and expressed concern that the Government of Cuba, a member of the Commission, had failed to cooperate with the Commission. The Commission regretted the numerous reports of human rights violations described in the report, particularly governmentally organized mob action against human rights activities. It called on Cuba to respect universally recognized human rights standards and fundamental freedoms and to promote their exercise and enjoyment, and to end all such violations, including the detention and imprisonment of those who advocated peaceful change. The Commission asked its Chairman to designate the Special Representative as its special rapporteur to review and report on the human rights situation in Cuba and asked the special rapporteur to report to the Commission in 1993 and to submit an interim report to the General Assembly in 1992. The Commission asked the Special Rapporteur to maintain direct contact with the Government and citizens of Cuba and urged Cuba to cooperate with him.

On 18 March, the Special Representative informed the Centre for Human Rights of his decision not to accept the designation of special rapporteur given to him by the Commission's resolution.

ECONOMIC AND SOCIAL COUNCIL ACTION

In July, the Economic and Social Council, on the recommendation of its Social Committee, adopted **decision 1992/236** by recorded vote.

Situation of human rights in Cuba

At its 32nd plenary meeting, on 20 July 1992, the Economic and Social Council, taking note of Commission on Human Rights resolution 1992/61 of 3 March 1992, approved the Commission's request to its Chairman to designate the Special Representative appointed by the Secretary-General pursuant to Commission resolution 1991/68 of 6 March 1991 as its Special Rapporteur to review and report on the situation of human rights in Cuba, and also approved the Commission's request to the Special Rapporteur to report to the Commission at its forty-ninth session on the results of his endeavours pursuant to Commission resolution 1992/61 and to submit an interim report to the General Assembly at its forty-seventh session.

Economic and Social Council decision 1992/236

20 July 1992   Meeting 32   24-4-23 (recorded vote)

Approved by Social Committee (E/1992/103) by recorded vote (25-4-23), 15 July (meeting 7); draft by Commission on Human Rights (E/1992/22); agenda item 17.

Recorded vote in Council as follows:

In favour: Argentina, Australia, Austria, Belarus, Belgium, Bulgaria, Canada, Chile, Finland, France, Germany, Italy, Japan, Kuwait, Morocco, Poland, Romania, Russian Federation, Spain, Suriname, Sweden, Turkey, United Kingdom, United States.

Against: Angola, China, Iran, Syrian Arab Republic.

Abstaining: Algeria, Bahrain, Bangladesh, Botswana, Brazil, Burkina Faso, Colombia, Ecuador, Guinea, India, Jamaica, Madagascar, Malaysia, Mexico, Pakistan, Peru, Philippines, Rwanda, Somalia, Swaziland, Trinidad and Tobago, Yugoslavia, Zaire.

Report of the Special Rapporteur. By a note of 19 November,[96] the Secretary-General transmitted an interim report on the situation of human rights in Cuba prepared by Special Rapporteur Carl-Johan Groth (Sweden). The Special Rapporteur stated that he had not been able to secure the cooperation of Cuba in carrying out his mandate. Thus, his report was based on meetings with individuals and representatives of organizations and groups concerned with human rights in Cuba operating in New York and Miami (United States). He had travelled to New York (28-30 September) and Madrid (Spain) (13 and 14 October), where he met with Cuban citizens in exile and representatives of human rights organizations.

The Special Rapporteur received information on alleged violations of freedom of opinion, expression and association, the right to leave the country and on alleged conditions in prisons and labour camps.

The Special Rapporteur proposed that Cuba end persecution for reasons related to the freedom of peaceful expression and association; permit legalization of independent groups; respect the guarantees of due process; ensure guarantees in prison; review sentences imposed for political offences and for trying to leave the country unlawfully; and expedite and make more explicit the procedure of applying for a permit to leave the country. Annexed to the report was a note verbale of 27 April from Cuba to the Secretary-General giving its legal interpretation of the resolution adopted by the Commission on Human Rights on

3 March[95] and the legal opinion issued by the United Nations Office of Legal Affairs thereon.

On 18 December, on the recommendation of the Third Committee, the General Assembly adopted **resolution 47/139** by recorded vote.

Situation of human rights in Cuba

The General Assembly,

Reaffirming that all Member States have an obligation to promote and protect human rights and fundamental freedoms as stated in the Charter of the United Nations and elaborated in the Universal Declaration of Human Rights and the International Covenants on Human Rights and other applicable human rights instruments,

Reaffirming that all Member States have an obligation to fulfil the commitments they have freely undertaken under the various international instruments,

Taking particular note of Commission on Human Rights resolution 1992/61 of 3 March 1992, in which the Commission recognized with deep appreciation the efforts of the then Special Representative of the Secretary-General on Cuba,

Noting the appointment of the Special Rapporteur of the Commission on Human Rights on Cuba,

Noting as well concern about ongoing reports of serious violations of human rights in Cuba, as outlined in the interim report on the situation of human rights in Cuba presented to the General Assembly by the Special Rapporteur,

Recalling the failure of the Government of Cuba to cooperate with the Commission on Human Rights with regard to its resolution 1991/68 of 6 March 1991 by refusing to permit the Special Representative to visit Cuba, and noting its response, as cited in appendix I to the interim report of the Special Rapporteur, in which it expresses its decision not to "implement so much as a single comma of resolution 1992/61",

1. *Commends* the Special Rapporteur of the Commission on Human Rights for his interim report on the situation of human rights in Cuba;

2. *Expresses its full support* for the work of the Special Rapporteur;

3. *Calls upon* the Government of Cuba to cooperate fully with the Special Rapporteur by permitting him full and free access so that he may establish contact with the Government and the citizens of Cuba in order to fulfil the mandate entrusted to him;

4. *Regrets profoundly* the numerous uncontested reports of violations of basic human rights and fundamental freedoms that are described in the report of the Special Representative of the Secretary-General and in the interim report of the Special Rapporteur;

5. *Calls upon* the Government of Cuba to adopt measures proposed by the Special Rapporteur to cease the persecution and punishment of citizens for reasons related to freedom of expression and peaceful association, to permit legalization of independent groups, to respect guarantees of due process, to permit access to the prisons by national independent groups and international humanitarian agencies, to review sentences for crimes of a political nature and to cease retaliatory measures towards those seeking permission to leave the country;

6. *Decides* to continue its consideration of this question at its forty-eighth session.

General Assembly resolution 47/139

18 December 1992   Meeting 92   69-18-64 (recorded vote)

Approved by Third Committee (A/47/678/Add.2) by recorded vote (64-17-59), 4 December (meeting 58); 24-nation draft (A/C.3/47/L.70); agenda item 97 *(c)*.

Sponsors: Argentina, Belgium, Bulgaria, Canada, Czechoslovakia, Denmark, Finland, Gambia, Germany, Hungary, Iceland, Ireland, Japan, Latvia, Luxembourg, Netherlands, Norway, Panama, Poland, Portugal, Romania, Sweden, United Kingdom, United States.

Meeting numbers. GA 47th session: 3rd Committee 47-58; plenary 92.

Recorded vote in Assembly as follows:

In favour: Afghanistan, Argentina, Armenia, Australia, Austria, Belgium, Bulgaria, Canada, Cape Verde, Chile, Costa Rica, Croatia, Czechoslovakia, Denmark, Dominica, Dominican Republic, El Salvador, Estonia, Fiji, Finland, France, Gambia, Germany, Greece, Honduras, Hungary, Iceland, Ireland, Israel, Italy, Japan, Kazakhstan, Kenya, Kuwait, Latvia, Liechtenstein, Lithuania, Luxembourg, Malawi, Mali, Malta, Marshall Islands, Mauritius, Morocco, Nepal, Netherlands, New Zealand, Nicaragua, Norway, Panama, Paraguay, Poland, Portugal, Qatar, Republic of Korea, Republic of Moldova, Romania, Russian Federation, Samoa, Saudi Arabia, Singapore, Slovenia, Spain, Sweden, Turkey, Ukraine, United Kingdom, United States, Uruguay.

Against: Angola, China, Cuba, Democratic People's Republic of Korea, Ghana, Iran, Iraq, Lao People's Democratic Republic, Libyan Arab Jamahiriya, Myanmar, Namibia, Sudan, Syrian Arab Republic, Uganda, United Republic of Tanzania, Viet Nam, Zambia, Zimbabwe.

Abstaining: Algeria, Antigua and Barbuda, Azerbaijan, Bahamas, Bangladesh, Barbados, Belarus, Belize, Benin, Bhutan, Bolivia, Botswana, Brazil, Brunei Darussalam, Burkina Faso, Burundi, Cameroon, Central African Republic, Colombia, Congo, Côte d'Ivoire, Cyprus, Ecuador, Egypt, Ethiopia, Gabon, Grenada, Guatemala, Guinea, Guinea-Bissau, Guyana, India, Indonesia, Jamaica, Jordan, Lesotho, Liberia, Madagascar, Malaysia, Maldives, Mauritania, Mexico, Niger, Nigeria, Pakistan, Papua New Guinea, Peru, Philippines, Rwanda, Saint Kitts and Nevis, Saint Lucia, Saint Vincent and the Grenadines, Senegal, Sierra Leone, Solomon Islands, Sri Lanka, Suriname, Swaziland, Thailand, Togo, Trinidad and Tobago, Tunisia, Vanuatu, Venezuela.

On 2 December, Cuba introduced in the Third Committee a draft on cooperation of the Government of Cuba with the Commission on Human Rights in accordance with Economic and Social Council resolutions adopted in 1959[97] and 1971[98] and the Commission's thematic procedures.[99]

By that draft, the Assembly would have considered that the reports on the human rights situation in Cuba showed that the use of procedures envisaged for serious human rights violations should be re-examined. It would have taken note of Cuba's commitment to cooperate with the Commission in accordance with the 1959[97] and 1971[98] Council resolutions and the Commission's procedures and asked the Commission to take account of the resolution in considering the question in 1993. On 3 December, the United States, on behalf of 230 other countries, introduced a draft resolution on the situation of human rights in Cuba.[100] On 4 December, the United States moved that the Committee take action on that draft before taking action on Cuba's draft.[99] The Committee approved that motion by a recorded vote of 59 to 23, with 41 abstentions. Following the adoption of the draft on the situation of human rights in Cuba, Hungary moved that no action be taken on Cuba's draft. The Committee decided not to take action on that draft by a recorded vote of 50 to 25, with 54 abstentions.

El Salvador

Report of the Special Representative. Special Representative José Antonio Pastor Ridruejo (Spain) in January submitted to the Commission his final report on human rights in El Salvador, covering events in 1991.[101] He observed a decrease in the number of human rights violations, but still expressed concern over the situation. Economic, social and cultural rights in El Salvador continued to be adversely affected by the armed conflict, and he noted a lack of progress in the criminal proceedings instituted on many serious human rights violations committed in the past. Politically motivated summary executions and disappearances continued to take place.

The Special Representative reiterated the recommendations he made to El Salvador's constitutional authorities in his report submitted to the Commission in 1991.[102]

Human Rights Commission action. On 3 March,[103] the Commission expressed satisfaction at the agreements set forth in the New York Act of 31 December 1991[104] and the Peace Agreement signed at Mexico City on 16 January 1992 between El Salvador and the Frente Farabundo Martí para la Liberación Nacional[105] whereby the armed conflict was ended and the parties undertook to democratize the country, guarantee unrestricted respect for human rights and help reunify Salvadorian society, and urged both parties to abide by the agreements reached. It also expressed satisfaction at the appointment of the Commission on the Truth, established under the 1991 Mexico Agreements,[106] comprising three persons of acknowledged standing in the human rights field, to investigate serious acts of violence that had occurred since 1980. It welcomed the appointment of the members of the Ad Hoc Commission on the Purification of the Armed Forces and the impending appointment of an attorney-general for the protection of human rights, and endorsed the efforts made by the Secretary-General through the United Nations Observer Mission in El Salvador (ONUSAL).

The Commission encouraged El Salvador to press ahead with its reform of the judiciary, particularly the legal profession; reiterated the need to continue the agrarian reform programme and to carry out other structural reforms permitting the enjoyment of economic, social and cultural rights; and urged the international community to cooperate in El Salvador's reconstruction efforts. It asked the Secretary-General to appoint an independent expert to assist El Salvador in human rights matters, consider the human rights situation there and the effects of the Peace Agreements on the enjoyment of human rights and investigate the manner in which both parties applied the recommendations contained in the Special

Representative's final report and those made by
ONUSAL and the committees established during
the negotiating process. It asked the independent
expert to report to the General Assembly in 1992
and to the Commission in 1993.

By **decision 1992/237** of 20 July, the Economic
and Social Council approved the Commission's
appointment of an independent expert and its request for him to submit a report to the Assembly
in 1992 and to the Commission in 1993.

Subcommission action. On 27 August
1992,[107] the Subcommission offered its full support to the independent expert.

Report of the Independent Expert. By a note
of 13 November,[108] the Secretary-General transmitted the report of Independent Expert Pedro
Nikken (Venezuela) on the human rights situation
in El Salvador, which he visited from 27 September to 4 October.

The Independent Expert stated that the cessation of the armed conflict began as scheduled, and
although it had eliminated an important source
of human rights violations, certain violations persisted. During his visit he was informed of alleged
cases of violations concerning the right to life; enforced or involuntary disappearances; the right to
freedom from torture and other cruel, inhuman
or degrading treatment or punishment; the right
to liberty; the right to due process of law; freedom
of the press; economic, social and cultural rights;
and international humanitarian law. He discussed
the impact of the Peace Agreements on human
rights and the implementation of recommendations made by the Special Representative, ONUSAL
and commissions established in the negotiating
process.

He recommended strengthening the Office of
the National Counsel for the Defence of Human
Rights; setting up and developing the National
Civil Police; guaranteeing the full independence
of judges and lawyers; completing amendments to
the National Council of the Judiciary Act and the
Career Judicial Service Act; a more rapid and
effective functioning of the National Commission
for the Consolidation of Peace, established in
1991;[109] and greater support from the international community for the peace process.

ONUSAL

By a 19 February note, the Secretary-General
transmitted the third report of ONUSAL[110] consisting of the report of the Director of the ONUSAL
Human Rights Division for November and December 1991. In June 1992, he transmitted the
Director's fourth report,[111] covering 1 January to
30 April, which reflected the change in the activities of the ONUSAL Human Rights Division
brought about by the signing of the Peace Agreement on 16 January.[105] In August, the Secretary-

General transmitted the fifth report, covering
ONUSAL activities from 1 May to 30 June.[112]

(For further details concerning the political situation in El Salvador, see PART TWO, Chapter II.)

GENERAL ASSEMBLY ACTION

On 18 December 1992, on the recommendation
of the Third Committee, the General Assembly
adopted **resolution 47/140** without vote.

Situation of human rights and fundamental freedoms in El Salvador

The General Assembly,

Guided by the principles embodied in the Charter of
the United Nations, the Universal Declaration of
Human Rights, the International Covenant on Civil and
Political Rights and the International Covenant on Economic, Social and Cultural Rights,

Convinced that the Peace Agreement reached on 16
January 1992 at Chapultepec, Mexico, between the
Government of El Salvador and the Frente Farabundo
Martí para la Liberación Nacional reflects the country's
profound aspiration for peace and justice, and that scrupulous compliance with the Agreement will not only permit an end to the armed conflict through political means
but also lay the bases for major political, legal, economic
and social changes, which must involve all sectors of the
country in the establishment of a democratic and united
society,

Bearing in mind that the Secretary-General, pursuant
to Commission on Human Rights resolution 1992/62
of 3 March 1992, appointed an independent expert to
provide assistance in human rights matters to the
Government of El Salvador, consider the human rights
situation in the country and the effects of the implementation of the Peace Agreement on the effective enjoyment of human rights and investigate the manner in
which both parties are applying the recommendations
contained in the final report of the Special Representative and those made by the United Nations Observer
Mission in El Salvador and the commissions established
during the negotiating process,

Taking into account the provisional report prepared by
the Independent Expert, as well as the other reports submitted by the Secretary-General and the United Nations
Observer Mission in El Salvador,

Noting with satisfaction that despite the delays and
difficulties that have arisen in the process of implementing the Peace Agreement, both parties have scrupulously
observed the cease-fire and, through the mediation of
the Secretary-General and his representatives, have
adopted agreements which, if implemented within the
new time-limits, will lead to the final cessation of the
armed conflict on 15 December 1992,

Taking into account that after 15 December 1992 the parties will have to fulfil, on the agreed dates, a number
of commitments made in the Peace Agreement which
are necessary for the reunification of Salvadorian society, the stability of the country and the effective enjoyment of human rights,

Bearing in mind that the overall process of implementation of the Peace Agreement requires supervision by
the United Nations Observer Mission in El Salvador

in order to help ensure the scrupulous fulfilment of commitments in accordance with the agreed timetable,

Considering that the Governments of Colombia, Mexico, Spain and Venezuela, which make up the Group of Friends of the Secretary-General, as well as the Government of the United States of America, reiterated on 12 November 1992 their determination to continue to support the work of the Secretary-General until the full and comprehensive implementation of the Peace Agreement is achieved in El Salvador,

Aware that the international community must follow closely and continue to support all efforts to consolidate peace, ensure respect for human rights and undertake the reconstruction of El Salvador,

Bearing in mind that the creation of the Office of the National Counsel for the Defence of Human Rights and of the National Civil Police, as well as the reform of the judicial system, are necessary for putting in place a sound structure for the effective protection of human rights, and that these measures have not proceeded as stipulated in the Peace Agreement,

Considering that a commitment was made to implement the recommendations of the Ad Hoc Commission, the Commission on the Truth and the Human Rights Division of the United Nations Observer Mission in El Salvador,

Observing that the cessation of the armed conflict has itself eliminated an important source of violations of human dignity, but has not been sufficient to prevent the persistence of human rights violations, which, unless punished and eliminated as soon as possible, could cause a recurrence of situations of increased human rights violations since the resources available to civil society with which to combat them are still weak,

1. *Commends* the Independent Expert for his report and the members of the Ad Hoc Commission, the Commission on the Truth and the United Nations Observer Mission in El Salvador for their work in favour of human rights and the consolidation of peace in El Salvador;

2. *Expresses its satisfaction* at the steps taken to implement the vital Peace Agreement reached on 16 January 1992 by the Government of El Salvador and the Frente Farabundo Martí para la Liberación Nacional and at the flexibility shown by both parties in overcoming obstacles and differences and in maintaining the close linkage between the implementation of the various commitments assumed by them, in order to ensure the full and scrupulous implementation of the Agreement;

3. *Welcomes* the fact that the Government of El Salvador and the Frente Farabundo Martí para la Liberación Nacional, on the proposal of the Secretary-General, have agreed to implement the Peace Agreement which will permit the holding, on 15 December 1992, of a national reconciliation ceremony, which should put a final end to the armed conflict, and to step up their commitment to fulfil the remaining agreements in order to guarantee the consolidation of peace;

4. *Urges* the Government of El Salvador and the Frente Farabundo Martí para la Liberación Nacional to fulfil scrupulously all their commitments within the agreed time-limits and, with a heightened sense of responsibility and in a spirit of *détente* and reconciliation, to ensure that as of 15 December 1992 normal living conditions prevail throughout the country, especially in the zones most affected by the armed conflict;

5. *Also urges* all sectors of Salvadorian society to show moderation and act constructively in order to dispel the animosities aroused by the armed conflict and to support the mandate which the President of El Salvador has to carry out in order to achieve the goals of peace, national reconciliation and democratization, in accordance with the Peace Agreement;

6. *Expresses its gratitude* for the effective and timely mediation of the Secretary-General and his representatives, and extends to them its support so that they can continue to take all necessary steps to contribute to the successful implementation of the Peace Agreement;

7. *Welcomes* the fact that the Governments which make up the Group of Friends of the Secretary-General and the Government of the United States of America will continue to support the work of the Secretary-General until the full and comprehensive implementation of the Peace Agreement, which reflects the determination and the desire of the Salvadorian people to live in peace, democracy and prosperity;

8. *Encourages* the Government of El Salvador and the Frente Farabundo Martí para la Liberación Nacional to implement the recommendations of the Ad Hoc Commission, the United Nations Observer Mission in El Salvador and, in due course, the Commission on the Truth;

9. *Endorses* all the recommendations made by the Independent Expert in his report, especially those aimed at strengthening the Office of the National Counsel for the Defence of Human Rights, setting up and developing the National Civil Police in accordance with the model resulting from the Peace Agreement and carrying out the agreed reform of the judicial system;

10. *Reiterates its appeal* to all States to contribute to the consolidation of peace in El Salvador by supporting full compliance with the Peace Agreement and generously financing their implementation and the implementation of the National Reconstruction Plan;

11. *Decides* to keep the situation of human rights in El Salvador under consideration during its forty-eighth session, in the light of the course of events in the country.

General Assembly resolution 47/140

18 December 1992   Meeting 92   Adopted without vote

Approved by Third Committee (A/47/678/Add.2) without vote, 4 December (meeting 58); 25-nation draft (A/C.3/47/L.57); agenda item 97 *(c)*.

Sponsors: Argentina, Belize, Bolivia, Canada, Chile, Colombia, Costa Rica, Cuba, Dominican Republic, Ecuador, El Salvador, France, Guatemala, Honduras, Hungary, Mexico, Nicaragua, Panama, Paraguay, Peru, Samoa, Spain, Sweden, Uruguay, Venezuela.

Meeting numbers. GA 47th session: 3rd Committee 47-58; plenary 92.

Haiti

Report of the Independent Expert. In January, Independent Expert Marco Tulio Bruni Celli (Venezuela) submitted to the Commission a report covering the human rights situation in Haiti during 1991.[113] The Expert visited Haiti from 2 to 6 September 1991 to assess the human rights situation from the beginning of the year and again from 4 to 7 December to evaluate events following the 29 September 1991 *coup d'état* overthrowing President Jean-Bertrand Aristide, elected in December 1990 under that country's first free and democratic elections.

The Expert observed that basic needs had not been fulfilled in Haiti. In terms of income, Haiti ranked below the poorest countries in Asia and Africa. Economic growth was minimal, supply of foodstuffs was scarce, infant mortality was high and enrolment in secondary schools was low. Official figures gave an illiteracy rate of 85 per cent. A worsening unemployment situation had already affected over 30 per cent of the population of working age. In addition to a rise in prices, social services had deteriorated sharply. The judicial system was characterized by the inadequacy and widespread corruption of its various organs.

During 1991, Haiti had had three different Governments, and the human rights situation had varied under each of them. The Expert recommended to the Commission that it condemn the September *coup d'état*, continue to monitor human rights in Haiti, demand Haiti's compliance with the international human rights instruments it had ratified, ask international agencies to assist Haiti in improving its human rights situation and appoint a special rapporteur. He also recommended that the Commission ask Haiti to fulfil its promises to implement the programmes announced to improve the administration of justice and the prison system, modernize civil and criminal legislation, separate the police from the armed forces, investigate crimes violating human rights committed by the authorities, implement Haiti's 1987 Constitution fully and restore the State governed by the rule of law that was overthrown by the *coup d'état*. He recommended that the Centre for Human Rights provide Haiti with a human rights specialist permanently based at the UNDP office at Port-au-Prince.

In a later addendum,[114] the Expert summarized information gathered between 16 November 1991 and 12 February 1992 covering the evolution of the situation in Haiti, the principal human rights violations and the special situation of Haitians who tried to flee the country after the *coup d'état*, known as the boat people.

Human Rights Commission action. On 5 March,[115] the Commission strongly condemned the overthrow of Haiti's constitutionally elected President, the use of violence and military coercion and the subsequent deterioration of the human rights situation. It expressed deep concern over human rights violations committed under the illegal Government set up following the *coup d'état*. Drawing the attention of the international community to the fate of Haitians who were fleeing the country, the Commission asked for support in assisting them. The Commission asked its Chairman to appoint a special rapporteur to prepare a report on the human rights situation in Haiti based especially on information supplied by the Organization of American States (OAS), with a view to submitting an interim report to the General Assembly in 1992 and to the Commission

in 1993. It asked the Secretary-General to assist the special rapporteur. Those requests were approved by the Economic and Social Council by its **decision 1992/245** of 20 July 1992.

Subcommission action. On 27 August,[116] the Subcommission asked all competent international bodies, particularly the United Nations and OAS, to assist the people of Haiti.

Report of the Secretary-General. As requested by the General Assembly in 1991,[117] the Secretary-General, in a November report,[118] provided a brief overview of the situation of human rights and democracy in Haiti one year after the September 1991 *coup d'état* and described the international community's efforts to solve the crisis there. He also summarized replies received from nine Member States on measures taken by them in support of resolutions adopted by OAS in 1991 and welcomed by the Assembly in 1991.[117]

The Assembly, in **resolution 47/20** of 24 November 1992, took note of the Secretary-General's report and strongly condemned the attempted illegal replacement of the constitutional President of Haiti, the use of violence and military coercion and the violation of human rights in the country (see also PART TWO, Chapter II).

Interim report of the Special Rapporteur. By a November note,[119] the Secretary-General transmitted the interim report of Special Rapporteur Marco Tulio Bruni Celli on the human rights situation in Haiti. He had visited Haiti from 18 to 21 August in his capacity as Chairman of the Inter-American Commission on Human Rights. Throughout 1992, Haiti had been governed by de facto Governments, with a change of Government having taken place in May.

The Special Rapporteur had received information alleging incidents of repression and violence and violations of the right to life, liberty and the security of person; the right to protection against arbitrary arrest and detention; the right to protection against torture and cruel, inhuman or degrading treatment or punishment; the right to freedom of opinion and expression; and the right to freedom of assembly and association. In describing the situation of the boat people, the Special Rapporteur noted that as at 8 September 1992, 38,513 Haitians had been intercepted while trying to reach the United States. Between December 1991 and May 1992, United States authorities took the boat people to that country's naval base at Guantánamo Bay (Cuba), where they were interviewed to determine whether they had a plausible claim for asylum. According to information received by the Special Rapporteur, by 8 September, some 31 per cent of Haitian asylum-seekers who had been screened were brought to the United States to pursue further their claims of asylum, except those who were found to be HIV positive, who pursued their claims from Guantánamo. The Special Rapporteur also discussed international negotiations to resolve the political crisis in Haiti.

He concluded that the human rights situation in that country had deteriorated appreciably during 1992. There was virtually no rule of law, the Constitution was not in force and citizens were defenceless in the face of arbitrary action by State agents. Since the 1991 *coup d'état*, power in Haiti rested with the armed forces and, although the international community had made efforts to achieve a political settlement, negotiations were bound to fail unless their terms were endorsed by the military. The Special Rapporteur recommended that the Commission on Human Rights continue to monitor the human rights situation in Haiti; inform the de facto Government that it was not exempt from its obligations to the Haitian people and compliance with all instruments to which Haiti was a State party; and maintain its decision to appoint a special rapporteur and to base permanently one or more human rights specialists at the UNDP office at Port-au-Prince to monitor the human rights situation, encourage the teaching and promotion of human rights and advise the authorities on measures to strengthen institutions for the protection of human rights.

GENERAL ASSEMBLY ACTION

On 18 December 1992, on the recommendation of the Third Committee, the General Assembly adopted **resolution 47/143** without vote.

Human rights in Haiti

The General Assembly,

Recalling its resolutions 46/7 of 11 October 1991 and 46/138 of 17 December 1991,

Guided by the principles embodied in the Charter of the United Nations, the Universal Declaration of Human Rights and the International Covenants on Human Rights,

Aware of its responsibility for the promotion and encouragement of respect for human rights and fundamental freedoms for all, and resolved to keep a close watch on human rights violations wherever they may occur,

Reaffirming that all Member States are required to promote and protect human rights and to comply with the obligations laid down in the various instruments in this field,

Taking note of Commission on Human Rights resolution 1992/77 of 5 March 1992 in which the Commission decided to appoint a special rapporteur with a mandate to prepare a report on the situation of human rights in Haiti based on the information which the special rapporteur deemed relevant, especially information supplied by the Organization of American States, with a view to submitting an interim report to the General Assembly at its forty-seventh session and a report to the Commission on Human Rights at its forty-ninth session,

Deeply concerned about the grave events occurring in Haiti since 29 September 1991, which abruptly and violently interrupted the democratic process in that country and have resulted in the loss of human lives and the violation of human rights,

Concerned also at the mass exodus of Haitian nationals from the country because of the deteriorating political and economic situation since 29 September 1991,

Deeply alarmed by the persistence and worsening of serious violations of human rights, in particular summary and arbitrary executions, forced disappearances, torture and rape, arbitrary arrests and detentions and denial of freedom of expression, assembly and association,

Welcoming the measures taken by the Secretary-General of the United Nations to express support for the Organization of American States, in particular through the participation of his Personal Representative in the mission of the Secretary-General of the Organization of American States that visited Haiti from 18 to 21 August 1992,

1. *Commends* the Special Rapporteur of the Commission on Human Rights, Mr. Marco Tulio Bruni Celli, for his report on the situation of human rights in Haiti and supports the recommendations contained therein;

2. *Once again condemns* the overthrow of the constitutionally elected President, Mr. Jean-Bertrand Aristide, the use of violence and military coercion and the subsequent deterioration of the situation of human rights in Haiti;

3. *Expresses its deep concern* about the substantial worsening of the human rights situation in Haiti during the year 1992 and the resulting increase in violations of the human rights embodied in the International Covenant of Civil and Political Rights, the International Covenant of Economic, Social and Cultural Rights, the American Convention on Human Rights: "Pact of San José, Costa Rica" and other international human rights instruments;

4. *Condemns* the recurrence of the flagrant human rights violations committed under the illegal government that took power following the coup of 29 September 1991, in particular summary executions, arbitrary arrests and detentions, torture, searches without warrant, rape, restrictions on freedom of movement, expression, assembly and association and the repression of popular demonstrations calling for the return of President Jean-Bertrand Aristide;

5. *Calls the attention* of the international community to the fate of the Haitian nationals who are fleeing the country not only, as pointed out by the Special Rapporteur in his report, because of the serious deterioration in economic and social conditions, but also because of indiscriminate political persecution and repression;

6. *Expresses its appreciation* to the Office of the United Nations High Commissioner for Refugees for the work it is doing in favour of the Haitian nationals fleeing the country and invites Member States to continue to give financial and material support to its efforts;

7. *Calls upon* the States Members of the United Nations and of other international organizations to increase their humanitarian assistance to the people of Haiti, to support all efforts to resolve the problems of displaced persons and to encourage the strengthening of institutional coordination among the specialized agencies and between the United Nations and the Organization of American States;

8. *Decides* to keep the situation of human rights and fundamental freedoms in Haiti under review during its forty-eighth session and to consider it further in the light of the information supplied by the Commission on Human Rights and the Economic and Social Council.

General Assembly resolution 47/143

18 December 1992   Meeting 92   Adopted without vote

Approved by Third Committee (A/47/678/Add.2) without vote, 4 December (meeting 59); 47-nation draft (A/C.3/47/L.73); agenda item 97 *(c)*.

Sponsors: Argentina, Bahamas, Barbados, Belgium, Belize, Benin, Bolivia, Brazil, Canada, Chile, Colombia, Costa Rica, Cuba, Denmark, Ecuador, El Salvador, Finland, France, Germany, Greece, Guatemala, Guyana, Haiti, Honduras, Hungary, Ireland, Italy, Jamaica, Japan, Luxembourg, Mexico, Netherlands, Nicaragua, Norway, Panama, Paraguay, Peru, Portugal, Samoa, Spain, Suriname, Sweden, Trinidad and Tobago, United Kingdom, Uruguay, Vanuatu, Venezuela.

Meeting numbers. GA 47th session: 3rd Committee 47-59; plenary 92.

Peru

Subcommission action. On 27 August,[120] the Subcommission expressed its deep concern at the events in Peru since 5 April 1992, when its President dissolved the National Congress, altered the composition of the courts and suspended essential functions of the judiciary, seriously affecting the state of law and the rule of democracy, and noted with deep alarm the growing criminal activities of the terrorist groups *Sendero Luminoso* and *Movimiento Revolucionario Túpac Amaru*. The Subcommission called on Peruvian authorities to strengthen their cooperation with the Inter-American Commission on Human Rights and to reopen dialogue with representative political forces until institutional normalization was restored, human rights fully respected and representative democracy completely re-established.

Communication. On 6 August,[121] Peru transmitted to the Secretary-General an OAS resolution adopted on 24 July condemning terrorist violence in Peru.

Middle East

Lebanon

On 4 March,[122] the Commission, by a roll-call vote of 49 to 1, with 1 abstention, condemned continued Israeli human rights violations in southern Lebanon, manifested by arbitrary detention of civilians, destruction of their homes, confiscation of their property, their expulsion from the occupied area, and bombardment of villages. It called on Israel to end such practices immediately and to implement relevant Security Council resolutions requiring its immediate, total and unconditional withdrawal from all Lebanese territory and respect for Lebanon's sovereignty, independence and territorial integrity. It also called on Israel to comply with the 1949 Geneva Convention relative to the Protection of Civilian Persons in Time of War (fourth Geneva Convention) and to facilitate the humanitarian mission of ICRC and similar organizations. It asked the Secretary-General to bring

the resolution to Israel's attention and to invite Israel to provide information on its implementation. He was asked to report to the General Assembly in 1992 and to the Commission in 1993 on the results of his efforts.

In accordance with the Commission's request, the Secretary-General reported to the Assembly in November[123] that he had asked Israel for information on the implementation of the Commission's resolution and had received no reply.

Territories occupied by Israel

In 1992, the question of human rights violations in the territories occupied by Israel as a result of the 1967 hostilities in the Middle East was again considered by the Commission. Political and other aspects were considered by the General Assembly, its Special Committee to Investigate Israeli Practices Affecting the Human Rights of the Population of the Occupied Territories and other bodies (see PART TWO, Chapter V).

Reports of the Secretary-General. In a report to the Commission,[124] the Secretary-General stated that he had brought the Commission's two resolutions on human rights violations in the Israeli-occupied territories to the attention of Governments, the Special Committee on Israeli practices and the Committee on the Exercise of the Inalienable Rights of the Palestinian People. They had also been transmitted to the specialized agencies, the United Nations Relief and Works Agency for Palestine Refugees in the Near East, international humanitarian organizations and NGOs. Information was also disseminated through United Nations press releases, publications, audiovisual programmes and journalists' encounters on the question of Palestine.

In accordance with a 1991 Commission request,[125] the Secretary-General reported[126] that he had asked Israel for information on the implementation of the Commission's resolution on the situation in occupied Palestine and had received no reply.

In January 1992, the Secretary-General submitted a list of all United Nations reports issued since 8 March 1991 on the situation of the population of the occupied Arab territories.[127]

Human Rights Commission action. By a 14 February 1992 resolution,[128] adopted by a roll-call vote of 30 to 16, with 3 abstentions, the Commission condemned Israel's policies and practices which violated the human rights of the Palestinians in the Israeli-occupied territories. Affirming the right of the Palestinians to resist the Israeli occupation by all means, the Commission called on Israel to desist from all human rights violations in the Palestinian and other occupied Arab territories, to respect the principles of international law and its commitments to the Charter of the United

Nations and to withdraw from the Palestinian territory, including Jerusalem, and other occupied Arab territories in accordance with United Nations and Commission resolutions.

By another resolution, adopted on the same day by a roll-call vote of 31 to 1, with 17 abstentions,[129] the Commission, reaffirming the applicability of the fourth Geneva Convention to the territories, including Jerusalem, strongly condemned Israel for refusing to apply that Convention and for the ill-treatment and torture of Palestinian detainees and prisoners. It also condemned Israel for deporting Palestinians, calling on it to comply with Security Council, General Assembly and Commission resolutions providing for their return to their homeland and to desist from that policy. The Commission asked the Secretary-General to report in 1993 on progress in implementing its resolutions, after bringing them to the attention of Governments, United Nations organs and agencies, intergovernmental and international humanitarian organizations and NGOs.

Also on 14 February,[130] by a roll-call vote of 31 to 1, with 17 abstentions, the Commission strongly condemned Israel for refusing to comply with United Nations resolutions on the Syrian Golan Heights and demanded that Israel rescind its 1981 decision[131] to impose its laws, jurisdiction and administration on the territory, which, the Commission said, was null and void and without international legal effect. Condemning Israel's persistence in changing the physical character, demographic composition, institutional structure and legal status of the Golan Heights, the Commission emphasized that displaced persons must be allowed to return and recover their property. It determined that all Israeli measures that altered the character and legal status of the Syrian Golan were null and void, violated international law and the fourth Geneva Convention and had no legal effect. Strongly condemning Israel for attempting to impose Israeli citizenship and identity cards on Syrians and for its practices of annexation, establishing settlements, confiscating lands, diverting water resources and imposing a boycott on agricultural products, the Commission called on Israel to desist from its settlement designs and policies aimed against academic institutions and from its repressive measures. It again called on Member States not to recognize any of those measures or actions. The Secretary-General was asked to give the resolution wide publicity and to report to the Commission in 1993.

By a fourth resolution, also adopted on 14 February,[132] by a roll-call vote of 45 to none, with 1 abstention, the Commission reaffirmed that the installation of Israeli civilians in the occupied territories was illegal and constituted a violation of the relevant provisions of the fourth Geneva Convention. It urged Israel to abstain from installing settlers, including immigrants, in the occupied territories.

By a decision of 25 February 1992,[133] the Commission decided to postpone to a later year consideration of a draft resolution on the subject recommended by its Subcommission in 1991.[125]

Pursuant to a 1991 Subcommission request,[134] the Secretary-General, in July 1992, provided an updated list of reports, studies, statistics, documents and United Nations decisions and resolutions on Palestine and other occupied Arab territories.[135]

Mass exoduses

Human Rights Commission action. On 3 March,[136] the Commission adopted a resolution inviting Governments and intergovernmental and humanitarian organizations to intensify their cooperation in addressing problems resulting from mass exoduses of refugees and displaced persons (see Chapter XV of this section) and also the causes of such exoduses. It asked Governments to ensure the implementation of relevant international instruments to help avert new exoduses and took note of the Secretary-General's 1991 report on human rights and mass exoduses.[137] Noting that the General Assembly in 1991[138] had encouraged the Secretary-General to implement the recommendations of a 1990 report of the Joint Inspection Unit (JIU) on coordinating activities related to early warning of possible refugee flows,[139] the Commission invited the Secretary-General, intergovernmental agencies and offices and international agencies to implement JIU's recommendations. It asked the Secretary-General to intensify efforts to develop the Secretariat's role in coordinating information-gathering and analysis with international organizations to provide early warning of developing situations requiring his attention and to provide focal points within the United Nations system for policy response, including identification of policy options. He was also asked to make information available to the competent United Nations organs, bearing in mind the JIU recommendations.

The Commission urged the Secretary-General to allocate resources to consolidate the system for undertaking early-warning activities by strengthening coordination among the Secretariat offices concerned, including the office of the United Nations Emergency Relief Coordinator,[140] UNHCR, the Centre for Human Rights and the relevant specialized agencies, in order to ensure that effective action was taken to identify human rights abuses which contributed to mass exoduses. The Commission looked forward to the Secretary-

General's 1992 report to the Assembly on his role in undertaking early-warning activities and on further developments relating to the recommendations contained in a 1986 report of the Group of Governmental Experts on International Cooperation to Avert New Flows of Refugees.[141]

Report of the Secretary-General. In response to a 1991 General Assembly request[138] and the Commission's March resolution,[136] the Secretary-General in October[142] submitted a report on human rights and mass exoduses. He stated that the Emergency Relief Coordinator had assumed his new functions in April 1992 and noted that some progress had been made in computerizing early-warning data-gathering.

Annexed to the report were the views of 10 Governments, 1 specialized agency and 2 NGOs relating to the recommendations contained in a 1986 report of the Group of Governmental Experts on International Cooperation to Avert New Flows of Refugees.[141]

On 18 December 1992, the General Assembly, by **decision 47/431**, took note of the Secretary-General's report.

Genocide

Status of the 1948 Convention

As at 31 December 1992,[14] 108 States had become parties to the 1948 Convention on the Prevention and Punishment of the Crime of Genocide.[82] In 1992, Bosnia and Herzegovina, Croatia, Latvia, Seychelles and Slovenia became parties to the Convention. The Secretary-General reported to the General Assembly on the status of the Convention as at 1 August 1992.[143]

GENERAL ASSEMBLY ACTION

On 16 December, the General Assembly, on the recommendation of the Third Committee, adopted **resolution 47/108** without vote.

> **Status of the Convention on the Prevention and Punishment of the Crime of Genocide**
>
> *The General Assembly,*
>
> *Recalling* its resolutions 40/142 of 13 December 1985, 41/147 of 4 December 1986, 42/133 of 7 December 1987, 43/138 of 8 December 1988, 44/158 of 15 December 1989 and 45/152 of 18 December 1990,
>
> *Recalling also* Commission on Human Rights resolutions 1986/18 of 10 March 1986, 1987/25 of 10 March 1987, 1988/28 of 7 March 1988, 1989/16 of 2 March 1989 and 1990/19 of 23 February 1990,
>
> *Recalling further* its resolution 260 A (III) of 9 December 1948, by which it approved and proposed for signature the Convention on the Prevention and Punishment of the Crime of Genocide annexed thereto,
>
> *Reaffirming once again its conviction* that genocide is a crime that violates the norms of international law and runs counter to the spirit and aims of the United Nations,

> *Recognizing* that crimes of genocide have caused great losses and privations to mankind throughout its history,
>
> *Expressing its conviction* that strict observance of the provisions of the Convention by all countries is necessary for the prevention and punishment of the crime of genocide,
>
> *Taking note* of the report of the Secretary-General,
>
> 1. *Once again strongly condemns* the crime of genocide;
>
> 2. *Reaffirms* the need for international cooperation in order to liberate mankind from such an odious crime;
>
> 3. *Notes with satisfaction* that more than one hundred States have ratified the Convention on the Prevention and Punishment of the Crime of Genocide or have acceded thereto;
>
> 4. *Urges* those States which have not yet done so to become parties to the Convention and to ratify it or accede to it without further delay;
>
> 5. *Invites* the Secretary-General to submit to the General Assembly at its forty-ninth session a report on the status of the Convention.

General Assembly resolution 47/108

16 December 1992   Meeting 89   Adopted without vote

Approved by Third Committee (A/47/678/Add.1) without vote, 25 November (meeting 49); 3-nation draft (A/C.3/47/L.39); agenda item 97 *(a)*.
Sponsors: Belarus, Croatia, Poland.
Meeting numbers. GA 47th session: 3rd Committee 40, 42-45, 48, 49; plenary 89.

Other aspects of human rights violations

Declaration on gross and large-scale human rights violations

On 27 August,[144] the Subcommission, having received a working paper prepared by Stanislav Chernichenko (Russian Federation) on the preparation of a declaration defining gross and large-scale violations of human rights as an international crime,[145] authorized him to submit to the Subcommission a more detailed working paper, including provisions for such a declaration, and to consider the question in 1993.

Restitution for human rights violations

Human Rights Commission action. On 28 February,[146] the Commission endorsed a request made by its Subcommission in 1991[147] concerning the preparation by the Special Rapporteur on the right to restitution, compensation and rehabilitation for victims of gross violations of human rights and fundamental freedoms of a second progress report and its request that the Secretary-General provide the Special Rapporteur with all necessary assistance.

The Economic and Social Council, by **decision 1992/250** of 20 July 1992, approved the Commission's endorsement of its Subcommission's requests.

Report of the Special Rapporteur. In July, the Subcommission's Special Rapporteur, Theo van Boven (Netherlands), submitted a progress report on the right to restitution, compensation and rehabilitation for victims of gross violations of human rights and fundamental freedoms.[148] He reviewed material submitted to the Commission on Human Rights in 1992 and discussed compensation to victims of gross human rights violations resulting from the invasion and occupation of Kuwait by Iraq. The Special Rapporteur also discussed a 1991 report, submitted to the ILO Governing Body by its Commission of Inquiry, on a complaint concerning Romania's observance of the 1958 ILO Convention on Discrimination in respect of employment and occupation,[149] especially a chapter on reparations describing measures taken to remedy the consequences of human rights violations committed by the former regime in Romania and to redress the wrongs suffered. He dealt with the issue of reparation under the European Convention for the Protection of Human Rights and Fundamental Freedoms and expressed some views on the issue of impunity in relation to reparation for victims of gross human rights violations. Annexed to the report were the conclusions of the Maastricht Conference on the Right to Restitution, Compensation and Rehabilitation for Victims of Gross Violations of Human Rights and Fundamental Freedoms (Maastricht, Netherlands, 11-14 March).

Subcommission action. On 27 August,[150] the Subcommission asked the Special Rapporteur to continue his study and to submit in 1993 a final report containing conclusions and recommendations. It asked the Secretary-General to give him all the assistance he might require.

Arms production and trade

On 28 August,[151] the Subcommission, welcoming the General Assembly's adoption in 1991 of a resolution[152] in which it recognized that international arms transfer and production and the illicit arms trade led to human rights violations, recommended that the Commission on Human Rights ask the Secretary-General to prepare an in-depth study on the positive impact on the promotion of human rights, in particular economic, social and cultural rights, of a 10 per cent reduction in world armament expenditure, the savings from which should be allocated to development. It also recommended that the Commission ask the Assembly, through the Economic and Social Council, to consider inviting Member States to approve as soon as possible the elaboration and expansion of the Register of Conventional Arms, established by a 1991 Assembly resolution,[153] to cover national production, small arms and unconventional weapons. (For further details on the Register of Conventional Arms, see PART ONE, Chapter II.)

Civil defence forces

On 3 March 1992,[154] the Commission noted that the formation of civil defence forces appeared to be on the rise, particularly in areas of conflict, and that their actions had in some cases jeopardized the enjoyment of human rights and fundamental freedoms. It requested the Secretary-General to ask Governments and intergovernmental and non-governmental organizations for information on domestic law and civil defence forces and for their comments on the relationship between civil defence forces and human rights. The Commission also asked him to submit in 1993 a report summarizing the information and comments received. It asked the special rapporteurs and working groups concerned to pay attention to the matter of civil defence forces in relation to the protection of human rights and fundamental freedoms.

REFERENCES

[1]YUN 1970, p. 530, ESC res. 1503(XLVIII), 27 May 1970. [2]E/CN.4/1993/2. [3]YUN 1967, p. 509. [4]YUN 1991, p. 593. [5]E/CN.4/1993/14. [6]S/24389. [7]E/1992/22 (res. 1992/19). [8]YUN 1966, p. 419 & 423, GA res. 2200 A (XXI), annex, 16 Dec. 1966. [9]YUN 1965, p. 440, GA res. 2106 A (XX), annex, 21 Dec. 1965. [10]YUN 1977, p. 161, SC res. 418 (1977), 4 Nov. 1977. [11]YUN 1991, p. 111, GA res. 46/79 A, 13 Dec. 1991. [12]E/CN.4/1993/2 (res. 1992/9). [13]A/47/676. [14]*Multilateral Treaties Deposited with the Secretary-General as at 31 December 1992* (ST/LEG/SER.E/11), Sales No. E/93.V.11. [15]YUN 1973, p. 103, GA res. 3068(XXVIII), annex, 30 Nov. 1973. [16]YUN 1976, p. 575. [17]A/47/426. [18]E/1992/22 (res. 1992/20). [19]GA res. S-16/1, 14 Dec. 1989. [20]YUN 1991, p. 597. [21]E/1992/22 (res. 1992/7). [22]E/CN.4/Sub.2/1992/12 & Add.1. [23]A/47/480 & Add.1. [24]E/CN.4/1993/2 (res. 1992/6). [25]Ibid. (res. 1992/30). [26]YUN 1991, p. 597, ESC res. 1991/37, 31 May 1991. [27]E/1992/41. [28]E/1992/70. [29]YUN 1947-48, p. 823. [30]YUN 1948-49, p. 987. [31]A/C.3/47/L.77. [32]A/C.3/47/L.72. [33]E/CN.4/1992/33. [34]YUN 1991, p. 599. [35]Ibid., GA res. 46/136, 17 Dec. 1991. [36]YUN 1955, p. 209. [37]E/1992/22 (res. 1992/68). [38]YUN 1991, p. 161. [39]YUN 1977, p. 706. [40]A/47/656. [41]E/CN.4/1992/17/Add.1. [42]YUN 1991, p. 798. [43]E/CN.4/1993/2 (res. 1992/20). [44]E/CN.4/1992/34. [45]E/CN.4/Sub.2/1992/14. [46]E/1992/22 (res. 1992/67). [47]E/CN.4/1993/2 (res. 1992/15). [48]A/47/617. [49]E/CN.4/1992/31. [50]YUN 1991, p. 603. [51]S/23685 & Add.1. [52]E/1992/22 (res. 1992/71). [53]YUN 1991, p. 602. [54]E/CN.4/1993/2 (dec. 1992/106). [55]A/47/367. [56]A/C.3/47/2. [57]A/47/367/Add.1. [58]E/CN.4/1992/26. [59]YUN 1991, p. 605, GA res. 46/135, 17 Dec. 1991. [60]Ibid., p. 172, SC res. 687(1991), 3 Apr. 1991. [61]E/1992/22 (res. 1992/60). [62]Ibid. (res. 1992/58). [63]A/47/651. [64]YUN 1984, p. 813, GA res. 39/46, annex, 10 Dec. 1984. [65]E/CN.4/1993/37. [66]E/CN.4/1993/2 (res. 1992/19). [67]E/CN.4/1992/37. [68]E/1992/22 (dec. 1992/116). [69]E/CN.4/1992/35. [70]YUN 1991, p. 607. [71]E/1992/22 (res. 1992/69). [72]E/CN.4/1992/25. [73]E/1992/22 (dec. 1992/106). [74]A/47/476. [75]A/47/748. [76]E/CN.4/1992/28 & Add.1. [77]E/1992/22 (res. 1992/64). [78]E/1992/22/Add.1 & Rev.1. [79]E/1992/22/Add.2. [80]ESC res. 1990/48, 25 May 1990. [81]E/1992/22/Add.1/Rev.1 (res. 1992/S-1/1). [82]YUN 1948-49, p. 959, GA res. 260 A (III), annex, 9 Dec. 1948. [83]E/CN.4/1993/2 (dec. 1992/103). [84]A/47/418-S/24516. [85]E/CN.4/1992/S-1/9. [86]A/47/635-S/24766. [87]E/CN.4/1992/S-1/10. [88]A/47/666-S/24809. [89]E/CN.4/1993/46. [90]E/CN.4/1993/50. [91]E/1992/22/Add.2 (res. 1992/S-2/1). [92]S/24657. [93]S/25274. [94]E/CN.4/1992/27 & Corr.1. [95]E/1992/22 (res. 1992/61). [96]A/46/625 & Corr.1. [97]YUN 1959, p. 221, ESC res. 728 F (XXVIII), 30 July 1959. [98]YUN 1971, p. 530, ESC res. 1503(XLVIII), 27 May 1971. [99]A/C.3/47/L.48. [100]A/C.3/47/L.70. [101]E/CN.4/1992/32. [102]YUN 1991, p. 608. [103]E/1992/22 (res. 1992/62). [104]A/46/863-S/23504. [105]A/46/864-S/23501. [106]YUN 1991,

p. 147. ⁽¹⁰⁷⁾E/CN.4/1993/2 (res. 1992/13). ⁽¹⁰⁸⁾A/47/596.
⁽¹⁰⁹⁾YUN 1991, p. 148. ⁽¹¹⁰⁾A/46/876-S/23580. ⁽¹¹¹⁾A/46/935-
S/24066. ⁽¹¹²⁾A/46/955-S/24375. ⁽¹¹³⁾E/CN.4/1992/50.
⁽¹¹⁴⁾E/CN.4/1992/50/Add.1. ⁽¹¹⁵⁾E/1992/22 (res. 1992/77).
⁽¹¹⁶⁾E/CN.4/1993/2 (res. 1992/16). ⁽¹¹⁷⁾YUN 1991, p. 152, GA
res. 46/7, 11 Oct. 1991. ⁽¹¹⁸⁾A/47/599 & Corr.1 & Add.1.
⁽¹¹⁹⁾A/47/621. ⁽¹²⁰⁾E/CN.4/1993/2 (res. 1992/12). ⁽¹²¹⁾A/47/366.
⁽¹²²⁾E/1992/22 (res. 1992/70). ⁽¹²³⁾A/47/630. ⁽¹²⁴⁾E/CN.4/
1992/6. ⁽¹²⁵⁾YUN 1991, p. 612. ⁽¹²⁶⁾E/CN.4/1992/11.
⁽¹²⁷⁾E/CN.4/1992/7. ⁽¹²⁸⁾E/1992/22 (res. 1992/2 A). ⁽¹²⁹⁾Ibid.
(res. 1992/2 B). ⁽¹³⁰⁾Ibid. (res. 1992/1). ⁽¹³¹⁾YUN 1981, p. 308.
⁽¹³²⁾E/1992/22 (res. 1992/3). ⁽¹³³⁾Ibid. (dec. 1992/104).
⁽¹³⁴⁾YUN 1991, p. 550. ⁽¹³⁵⁾E/CN.4/Sub.2/1992/13.
⁽¹³⁶⁾E/1992/22 (res. 1992/63). ⁽¹³⁷⁾YUN 1991, p. 613. ⁽¹³⁸⁾Ibid.,
GA res. 46/127, 17 Dec. 1991. ⁽¹³⁹⁾A/45/649 & Corr.1.
⁽¹⁴⁰⁾YUN 1991, p. 421, GA res. 46/182, 19 Dec. 1991.
⁽¹⁴¹⁾YUN 1986, p. 851. ⁽¹⁴²⁾A/47/552. ⁽¹⁴³⁾A/47/427.
⁽¹⁴⁴⁾E/CN.4/1993/2 (dec. 1992/109). ⁽¹⁴⁵⁾E/CN.4/Sub.2/
1992/51. ⁽¹⁴⁶⁾E/1992/22 (dec. 1992/108). ⁽¹⁴⁷⁾YUN 1991, p. 615.
⁽¹⁴⁸⁾E/CN.4/Sub.2/1992/8. ⁽¹⁴⁹⁾YUN 1958, p. 436.
⁽¹⁵⁰⁾E/CN.4/1993/2 (res. 1992/32). ⁽¹⁵¹⁾Ibid. (res. 1992/39).
⁽¹⁵²⁾YUN 1991, p. 56, GA res. 46/36 H, 6 Dec. 1991.
⁽¹⁵³⁾Ibid., p. 58, GA res. 46/36 L, annex, 9 Dec. 1991.
⁽¹⁵⁴⁾E/1992/22 (res. 1992/57).

Other human rights questions

Additional Protocols I and II to the 1949 Geneva Conventions

In response to a General Assembly request of 1990,⁽¹⁾ the Secretary-General submitted, in July 1992,⁽²⁾ information received from 10 Member States on the status of the two 1977 Protocols Additional to the Geneva Conventions of 12 August 1949 for the protection of war victims.⁽³⁾ As at 2 July 1992, 115 States had ratified or acceded to Protocol I (on protection of victims of international armed conflicts). Seven States—Brazil, Croatia, Kazakhstan, Madagascar, Portugal, Slovenia, Turkmenistan—did so in 1992. All but 12 of the 115 also adhered to Protocol II (on protection of victims of non-international conflicts). Two States—France and the Philippines—adhered only to Protocol II.

Rights of the Child

Convention on the Rights of the Child

Accessions and ratifications

As at 31 December 1992,⁽⁴⁾ there were 127 parties to the Convention on the Rights of the Child, adopted by the General Assembly in 1989⁽⁵⁾ and in force since 2 September 1990. In 1992, 20 States ratified or acceded to the Convention.

The Secretary-General reported on the status of the Convention in January⁽⁶⁾ and again in September 1992.⁽⁷⁾

CRC activities. At its second session (Geneva, 28 September to 9 October),⁽⁸⁾ the Committee on the Rights of the Child (CRC) devoted its general discussion to children in armed conflicts and established a working group to submit final proposals on the subject in 1993. The Committee continued to discuss its participation in the preparatory activities for the 1993 World Conference on Human Rights. It made a number of recommendations concerning the organization of informal regional meetings, sources of information, public information activities, relations with other United Nations and treaty bodies, and the fourth meeting of persons chairing the human rights treaty bodies (see "Advancement of human rights"). The Committee decided to establish a working group to consider the system of information and documentation relevant to its work. Annexed to the report was a list of 123 States which had ratified or acceded to the Convention as at 29 September 1992, together with a list of Committee members, and the submission status of initial reports by States parties due in 1992, 1993 and 1994.

On 20 July 1992, the Economic and Social Council, by **decision 1992/262,** took note of CRC's report on its first (1991) session⁽⁹⁾ and transmitted it to the General Assembly.

The Committee held its first informal regional meeting (Quito, Ecuador, 1-5 June). The meeting, organized by UNICEF with the cooperation of the Centre for Human Rights, discussed various themes, including children's health, nutrition and education, child labour, refugee children and the legislative status of minors.

In accordance with a 1991 General Assembly request,⁽¹⁰⁾ the Fourth Meeting of States parties to the Convention met (New York, 11 November) to determine the duration of CRC meetings as provided for in article 43 of the Convention. By a November 1992 note to the General Assembly,⁽¹¹⁾ the Secretary-General stated that the States parties had approved the 1991 CRC recommendation on the duration of its future meetings, the text of which was annexed to his note and approved by the Assembly in **resolution 47/112.**

Human Rights Commission action. On 5 March 1992,⁽¹²⁾ the Commission called on States that had not done so to sign, ratify or accede to the Convention on the Rights of the Child as a matter of priority and appealed to States parties that had made reservations to review the compatibility of their reservations with article 51 of the Convention and other relevant rules of international law. It asked the Secretary-General to provide facilities and assistance for disseminating information on the Convention and its implementation with a view to promoting further ratification of or accession to it; ensure the provision of staff and facilities for the effective performance of CRC; make the necessary resources available for the Working Group of the Whole of CRC to meet in 1992; and to report on the status of the Convention in 1993. It recommended a draft for adoption by the Economic and Social Council, the text of which follows.

ECONOMIC AND SOCIAL ACTION

On 20 July 1992, the Economic and Social Council, on the recommendation of its Social Committee, adopted **resolution 1992/8** without vote.

Implementation of the Convention on the Rights of the Child

The Economic and Social Council,

Taking note of General Assembly resolution 46/112 of 17 December 1991 and Commission on Human Rights resolution 1992/75 of 5 March 1992,

Concerned about the workload of the Committee on the Rights of the Child and the risk of building up an undesirable backlog in the consideration of reports from States parties,

1. *Notes* that the General Assembly, in its resolution 46/112, supported the organization of the future work of the Committee on the Rights of the Child on the basis of two sessions annually, each for a duration of two or three weeks, and the establishment of a pre-sessional working group for a preliminary review of reports from States parties;

2. *Welcomes* the decision of the General Assembly, in its resolution 46/112, to take appropriate action at its forty-seventh session on the recommendations of the Committee;

3. *Requests* the Secretary-General to make the necessary resources available, within the overall existing budget framework, to enable the Working Group of the Whole of the Committee on the Rights of the Child to meet in 1992 subsequent to the second session of the Committee.

Economic and Social Council resolution 1992/8

20 July 1992   Meeting 32   Adopted without vote

Approved by Social Committee (E/1992/103) without vote, 15 July (meeting 7); draft by Commission on Human Rights (E/1992/22); agenda item 17.

GENERAL ASSEMBLY ACTION

On 16 December 1992, the General Assembly, on the recommendation of the Third Committee, adopted **resolution 47/112** without vote.

Implementation of the Convention on the Rights of the Child

The General Assembly,

Recalling its resolution 44/25 of 20 November 1989, by which it adopted the Convention on the Rights of the Child, continued in the annex to that resolution,

Recalling also its resolution 46/112 of 17 December 1991 and taking note of Commission on Human Rights resolution 1992/75 of 5 March 1992,

Taking note of the report of the Committee on the Rights of the Child on its first session, held at Geneva from 30 September to 18 October 1991, and the meeting of the States parties to the Convention on the Rights of the Child, held in New York on 11 November 1992,

Reaffirming that the rights of children require special protection and call for continuous improvement of the situation of children all over the world, as well as for their development and education in conditions of peace and security,

Profoundly concerned that the situation of children in many parts of the world remains critical as a result of inadequate social and economic conditions, natural disasters, armed conflicts, exploitation, illiteracy, hunger and disability, and convinced that urgent and effective national and international action is called for,

Mindful of the important role of the United Nations Children's Fund and of the United Nations in promoting the well-being of children and their development,

Convinced that the Convention on the Rights of the Child, as a standard-setting accomplishment of the United Nations in the field of human rights, makes a positive contribution to protecting the rights of children and ensuring their well-being,

Recalling the World Declaration on the Survival, Protection and Development of Children and the Plan of Action for Implementing the World Declaration on the Survival, Protection and Development of Children in the 1990s, adopted at the World Summit for Children, held in New York on 29 and 30 September 1990, and stressing the necessity to ensure the follow-up of the Summit at the national and international levels,

Having considered the report of the Secretary-General on the status of the Convention,

Encouraged by the fact that an unprecedented number of States have to date become signatories and parties to the Convention, thereby demonstrating the widespread commitment that exists to strive for the promotion and protection of the rights of the child,

1. *Takes note with appreciation* of the report of the Secretary-General on the status of the Convention on the Rights of the Child;

2. *Recalls with deep satisfaction* the entry into force of the Convention on 2 September 1990 as a major step in international efforts to promote universal respect for and observance of human rights and fundamental freedoms;

3. *Expresses its satisfaction* at the number of States that have signed, ratified or acceded to the Convention since it was opened for signature, ratification and accession on 26 January 1990;

4. *Calls upon* all States that have not done so to sign, ratify or accede to the Convention as a matter of priority;

5. *Requests* the Secretary-General to provide, from within existing resources, all facilities and assistance necessary for the dissemination of information on the Convention and its implementation, with a view to promoting further ratification of or accession to the Convention, as well as the full realization of its principles and provisions;

6. *Emphasizes* the importance of the strict compliance by States parties with their obligations under the Convention;

7. *Appeals* to States parties to the Convention that have made reservations to review the compatibility of their reservations with article 51 of the Convention and other relevant rules of international law;

8. *Recognizes* the important role of the Committee on the Rights of the Child in overseeing the effective implementation of the provisions of the Convention;

9. *Welcomes* the constructive and useful results achieved by the Committee on the Rights of the Child during its first session, including the adoption of the

general guidelines regarding the form and contents of initial reports to be submitted by States parties;

10. *Approves* the recommendation contained in the resolution adopted by consensus at the meeting of the States parties to the Convention on the Rights of the Child on 11 November 1992, in which the States parties reaffirmed the recommendation made by the Committee on the Rights of the Child regarding the organization of the future work of the Committee on the basis of two sessions annually, each of up to three weeks' duration, as may be decided by the Committee in the light of its anticipated workload, and the establishment of a pre-sessional working group that would meet for one week approximately two months in advance of each session for a preliminary review of reports from States parties;

11. *Authorizes* the Secretary-General to implement the recommendation mentioned in paragraph 10 above;

12. *Requests* the Secretary-General to ensure the provision of appropriate staff and facilities, within the overall existing budget framework, for the effective performance of the functions of the Committee on the Rights of the Child;

13. *Requests* bodies and organizations of the United Nations, within the scope of their respective mandates, to intensify their efforts to disseminate information on the Convention, promote understanding of it and assist Governments in its implementation;

14. *Invites* intergovernmental and non-governmental organizations to intensify their efforts with a view to disseminating information on the Convention to adults and children alike and promoting understanding of it;

15. *Requests* the Secretary-General to submit to the General Assembly at its forty-ninth session a report on the status of the Convention;

16. *Decides* to consider the report of the Secretary-General at its forty-ninth session under the item entitled "Human rights questions".

General Assembly resolution 47/112

16 December 1992   Meeting 89   Adopted without vote

Approved by Third Committee (A/47/678/Add.1) without vote, 1 December (meeting 52); 85-nation draft (A/C.3/47/L.43); agenda item 97 *(a)*.

Sponsors: Argentina, Australia, Austria, Bahamas, Bangladesh, Barbados, Belarus, Belgium, Benin, Bolivia, Brazil, Bulgaria, Burkina Faso, Canada, Cape Verde, Central African Republic, China, Colombia, Costa Rica, Côte d'Ivoire, Cuba, Cyprus, Czechoslovakia, Democratic People's Republic of Korea, Denmark, Ecuador, Egypt, El Salvador, Estonia, Ethiopia, Finland, France, Gambia, Germany, Greece, Guatemala, Guinea, Guinea-Bissau, Honduras, Hungary, Iceland, Indonesia, Ireland, Italy, Kenya, Latvia, Lithuania, Luxembourg, Madagascar, Mali, Malta, Mexico, Mongolia, Netherlands, New Zealand, Nicaragua, Niger, Nigeria, Norway, Pakistan, Panama, Peru, Philippines, Poland, Portugal, Romania, Russian Federation, Rwanda, Samoa, Sierra Leone, Spain, Sri Lanka, Sudan, Sweden, Thailand, Tunisia, Turkey, Ukraine, United Kingdom, Uruguay, Venezuela, Viet Nam, Yemen, Zambia, Zimbabwe.

Financial implications. 5th Committee, A/47/789; Secretary-General, A/C.3/47/L.47, A/C.5/47/69.

Meeting numbers. GA 47th session: 3rd Committee 40, 42-45, 48, 49, 52; 5th Committee 45; plenary 89.

Sale of children, child prostitution and pornography

Report of the Special Rapporteur. Special Rapporteur Vitit Muntarbhorn (Thailand) presented his second report in January 1992[13] on the sale of children for, among other things, adoption, labour, prostitution and pornography and organ transplants. He discussed his visits to the

Netherlands in 1991 and Brazil in 1992 to study the situation and recommended a number of preventive measures, among them: a more active role by the private sector and consumers; more effective enforcement of laws to protect children; more collaboration between State and local agencies; establishment of national focal points to coordinate action against the sale of children, child prostitution and child pornography; cooperation between national police forces and Interpol (International Criminal Police Organization) and immigration authorities to curb the traffic in children; and education to create public awareness of the issues. He also made specific recommendations on the sale of children, child prostitution and pornography. Annexed to the report was a questionnaire on the situation of children which the Special Rapporteur sent to a broad range of countries, NGOs and concerned individuals.

Human Rights Commission action. On 5 March,[14] the Commission extended the mandate of its Special Rapporteur for three years and asked him to pay particular attention to areas which were insufficiently documented and to set short- and medium-term priorities in his recommendations. It asked the Secretary-General to assist the Special Rapporteur so that he could submit a report in 1993.

The Economic and Social Council, by **decision 1992/244** of 20 July, approved the Commission's decision to extend the Special Rapporteur's mandate for three years and its request to the Secretary-General to assist him.

Programme of action

On 5 March,[15] the Commission adopted the Programme of Action for the Prevention of the Sale of Children, Child Prostitution and Child Pornography and recommended that all States adopt legislative and administrative measures to carry out the Programme. It urged United Nations bodies and intergovernmental organizations concerned to bear in mind the Programme of Action when designing policies and developing programmes related to children and the family. The Commission also urged NGOs to adopt the Programme of Action and develop activities related to their mandates. It recommended that CRC consider the Programme of Action in studying reports submitted by States parties to the Convention and in all actions carried out under its mandate. It also recommended that the Special Rapporteur on the sale of children bear in mind the Programme of Action when developing activities under his mandate. The Commission asked all States to inform the Subcommission of measures adopted to implement the Programme of Action and their efficacy. It asked the Subcommission to submit a report every two years on implementation of the

Programme of Action by States and asked the Under-Secretary-General on Human Rights to collaborate with the Subcommission in order to fulfil the mandate. Annexed to the Commission's resolution was the Programme of Action.

Child labour

Report of the Secretary-General. The Secretary-General submitted to the Commission an analysis of replies from 14 States, 2 United Nations bodies, 3 specialized agencies and 4 NGOs, on the draft programme of action for the elimination of the exploitation of child labour.[16] The text of the draft programme was annexed to the report.

Human Rights Commission action. On 5 March,[15] the Commission decided to submit to its Subcommission the draft programme of action so that it might amend the draft, taking into account the views of Governments, specialized agencies and intergovernmental and non-governmental organizations. It requested the Subcommission to give the utmost priority to amending the draft programme so that it might be approved by the Commission in 1993. The Commission asked the Special Rapporteur to consider presenting his comments and suggestions to the Working Group on Contemporary Forms of Slavery and asked the Under-Secretary-General for Human Rights to provide the Subcommission with the support needed to fulfil this mandate.

Child soldiers

In June 1992,[17] the Secretary-General updated his 1990 report on the recruitment of children into governmental and non-governmental armed forces.[18] The Secretary-General provided background on the subject and presented information received from 12 Governments, 1 regional commission, 1 specialized agency, 1 intergovernmental organization and 7 NGOs.

Youth and human rights

Human Rights Commission action. On 3 March,[19] the Commission recommended a draft text on human rights and youth for adoption by the Economic and Social Council (see below).

Report of the Special Rapporteur. The Subcommission's Special Rapporteur Dumitru Mazilu (Romania), in his final report on human rights and youth,[20] submitted in June, discussed the increasing violation of young people's human rights. He presented a programme of action to ensure and promote the rights and freedoms of youth, stating that millions of young people continued to be exposed to great harm. There were countries, he said, where the absence of the most elementary rights and freedoms resulted in the arrest, conviction and execution of young people on political grounds. He recom-

mended measures to end violations of young people's fundamental right to life; establish a mechanism to react speedily to threatened or imminent summary or arbitrary executions and enforced or involuntary disappearances; promote a healthier environment through the containment and reduction of disease, famine, war, corruption, criminality and social breakdown; attack every aspect of the illicit drug enterprise; eliminate illiteracy and promote education and vocational training; implement large-scale national employment programmes; and ensure that new technologies enhance the situation of young people.

ECONOMIC AND SOCIAL COUNCIL ACTION

On 20 July, the Economic and Social Council, on the recommendation of its Social Committee, adopted **resolution 1992/7** without vote.

Human rights and youth
The Economic and Social Council,

Taking note of Commission on Human Rights resolution 1992/49 of 3 March 1992 and resolution 1991/20 of 28 August 1991 of the Subcommission on Prevention of Discrimination and Protection of Minorities,

1. *Expresses its appreciation* to the Special Rapporteur of the Subcommission on Prevention of Discrimination and Protection of Minorities, Mr. Dumitru Mazilu, for his progress report;

2. *Expresses its thanks* to all Governments and non-governmental organizations that supplied the Special Rapporteur with relevant information;

3. *Decides* to invite the Special Rapporteur to update his report in the light of the suggestions made at the forty-third session of the Subcommission, giving special attention to the questions of underdevelopment, unemployment, the right to conscientious objection to military service and children in prison throughout the world;

4. *Invites* the Special Rapporteur to consult governmental and non-governmental organizations in order to elaborate further and to complete his work, with a view to submitting his final report to the Subcommission at its forty-fourth session;

5. *Requests* the Secretary-General to continue to gather and supply to the Special Rapporteur information and data relating to his study and to provide him with all the assistance he may need to complete his report, including consultations at the Centre for Human Rights of the Secretariat, in order that he may submit his final report to the Subcommission at its forty-fourth session.

Economic and Social Council resolution 1992/7

20 July 1992   Meeting 32   Adopted without vote

Approved by Social Committee (E/1992/103) without vote, 15 July (meeting 7); draft by Commission on Human Rights (E/1992/22); agenda item 17.

Women

Discrimination

On 14 August,[21] the Subcommission asked the Secretary-General to seek the views of the Committee on the Elimination of Discrimination against Women (CEDAW) on the desirability of obtaining an advisory opinion on the validity and legal effect of reservations to the 1979 Convention on the Elimination of All Forms of Discrimination against Women[22] and to invite them to make further observations on reservations to the Convention. It also asked him to report in 1993 on the results of his consultations. The Subcommission decided to reconsider in 1993 a draft it postponed consideration of in 1991, which recommended to the Commission on Human Rights that it propose that the Economic and Social Council ask the International Court of Justice to give an advisory opinion on the validity and legal effect of reservations to the Convention.

Also on 14 August 1992,[23] the Subcommission recommended that the 1993 World Conference on Human Rights give priority to the question of discrimination affecting women and that information on the equality and empowerment of women, and their access to equality in education, work, health and literacy, be included in States' reports to all human rights monitoring bodies as well as to CEDAW. It asked the Secretary-General to report on implementation of the resolution to the Subcommission at its forty-fifth session.

On 20 July 1992, the Economic and Social Council, by **resolution 1992/20**, invited the Centre for Human Rights and Member States, in preparing for the 1993 World Conference on Human Rights, to use gender-disaggregated data to identify inequalities between women and men.

Traditional practices affecting the health of women and children

On 28 February 1992,[24] the Commission on Human Rights approved its Subcommission's 1991 recommendations concerning traditional practices affecting the health of women and children.[25]

On 20 July 1992, the Economic and Social Council, by **decision 1992/251**, endorsed the Commission's approval of the Subcommission's recommendations.

Human rights and science and technology

In a note of May,[26] the Secretary-General summarized action taken since 1986 by the Commission on Human Rights, its Subcommission and UNU on the use of scientific and technological developments for the promotion and protection of human rights and fundamental freedoms.

On 14 August,[27] the Subcommission decided to consider in 1994 elaborating new human rights standards relating to scientific developments which might affect the mental condition or genetic structure of human beings.

Human rights and the environment

Human Rights Commission action. By a vote of 50 to 1, with 1 abstention, the Commission, on 28 February 1992,[28] endorsed a 1991 Subcommission request[29] that Special Rapporteur Fatma Zohra Ksentini (Algeria) be entrusted with preparing a progress report on human rights and the environment in 1992 and that the Secretary-General be asked to give her all the assistance she might require.

The Economic and Social Council approved those requests by **decision 1992/252** of 20 July.

Report of the Special Rapporteur. In July, the Subcommission's Special Rapporteur submitted a progress report[30] reviewing constitutional, national and regional provisions relating to the environment. The decisions and comments of regional human rights bodies were presented, as were those of United Nations human rights bodies. In a later addendum,[31] the Special Rapporteur highlighted the results of UNCED (Rio de Janiero, Brazil, 3-14 June 1992) (see PART THREE, Chapter VIII) pertaining to human rights and the environment.

Subcommission action. On 27 August,[32] the Subcommission asked its Special Rapporteur to submit a second progress report on human rights and the environment in 1993 and asked the Secretary-General to provide her with all the assistance she might require. It also asked him to invite Governments, United Nations bodies including the specialized agencies, intergovernmental and non-governmental organizations, indigenous peoples' and international human rights organizations to provide the Special Rapporteur with information relating to her report.

Human rights of disabled persons

On 3 March 1992,[33] the Commission on Human Rights asked the Secretary-General to study the technical and financial feasibility of the recommendations made in 1991 by its Special Rapporteur on human rights and disability,[29] with a view to implementing them. It also asked him to ensure better coordination among specialized agencies, United Nations human rights bodies and other organs dealing with the human rights of disabled persons and to ensure that the Special Rapporteur's report was issued as a United Nations publication in all official languages, given the widest possible circulation and transmitted to the Commission for Social Development for consideration. The Economic and Social Council approved those requests by its **decision 1992/232** of 20 July. The Commission further asked the Secretary-General to make available the appropriate computer diskettes to organizations wishing to reproduce the report in Braille, in large print, or on cassette, and to request the United Nations Centre for Social Development and Humanitarian Affairs to continue its efforts to coordinate and supervise the implementation of the 1982 World Programme of Action concerning Disabled Persons[34] and to make available all documentation in Braille and on cassette to organizations wishing to publish it.

Human rights and peace

On 21 August 1992,[35] the Subcommission took note of the recommendations made in a 1991 working paper on the interrelationship between human rights, particularly the right to life and the right to development, and international peace,[29] submitted by Murlidhar Bhandare (India), and asked him to present a further document in 1994.

Trade union rights

On 21 February 1992,[36] the Commission on Human Rights appealed to States to ensure conditions for all persons to exercise freely and fully their trade union rights. It invited States that had not done so to ratify and apply fully the International Covenants on Human Rights,[37] the ILO Freedom of Association and Protection of the Right to Organize Convention (No. 87) and the Right to Organize and Collective Bargaining Convention, 1949 (No. 98),[38] and called on them to involve representative trade union organizations in the processes of popular participation and development.

REFERENCES

[1]GA res. 45/38, 28 Nov. 1990. [2]A/47/324. [3]YUN 1977, p. 706. [4]*Multilateral Treaties Deposited with the Secretary-General: Status as at 31 December 1992* (ST/LEG/SER.E/11), Sales No.E.93.V.II. [5]GA res. 44/25, 20 Nov. 1989. [6]E/CN.4/1992/54. [7]A/47/428. [8]CRC/C/10. [9]A/47/41. [10]YUN 1991, p. 617, GA res. 46/112, 17 Dec. 1991. [11]A/47/667. [12]E/1992/22 (res. 1992/75). [13]E/CN.4/1992/55 & Add.1. [14]E/1992/22 (res. 1992/76). [15]Ibid. (res. 1992/74). [16]E/CN.4/1992/45. [17]E/CN.4/Sub.2/1992/35 & Add.1. [18]E/CN.4/Sub.2/1990/43 & Add.1,2. [19]E/1992/22 (res. 1992/49). [20]E/CN.4/Sub.2/ 1992/36. [21]E/CN.4/1993/2 (res. 1992/3). [22]YUN 1979, p. 895, GA res. 34/180, annex, 18 Dec. 1979. [23]E/CN.4/ 1993/2 (res. 1992/4). [24]E/1992/22 (dec. 1992/109). [25]YUN 1991, p. 619. [26]E/CN.4/Sub.2/1992/26. [27]E/CN.4/1993/2 (dec. 1992/104). [28]E/1992/22 (dec. 1992/110). [29]YUN 1991, p. 627. [30]E/CN.4/Sub.2/1992/7. [31]E/CN.4/Sub.2/1992/ 7/Add.1. [32]E/CN.4/1993/2 (res. 1992/31). [33]E/1992/22 (res. 1992/48). [34]YUN 1982, p. 980. [35]E/CN.4/1993/2 (res. 1992/7). [36]E/1992/22 (res. 1992/12). [37]YUN 1966, pp. 419 & 423, GA res. 2200 A (XXI), annex, 16 Dec. 1966. [38]YUN 1948-49, p. 987.

Chapter XI

Health, food and nutrition

During 1992, the United Nations continued to address health, food and nutrition problems throughout the world.

The World Health Organization (WHO) reported that by late 1992 an estimated 13 million adults were infected with the human immunodeficiency virus (HIV), of which some 2.5 million cases progressed to the acquired immunodeficiency syndrome (AIDS). In addition, some 1 million HIV-infected children, mostly in sub-Saharan Africa, had been born to HIV-infected women, and over half of them developed AIDS or died. In 1992, an updated WHO global strategy for the prevention and control of AIDS was endorsed by the World Health Assembly to meet the new challenges of the pandemic, and the United Nations Development Programme (UNDP) established an HIV and Development Programme to strengthen UNDP efforts to increase global awareness of the threat posed by the disease.

The year marked the conclusion of the United Nations Decade of Disabled Persons (1983-1992). In October, the General Assembly proclaimed 3 December as the International Day of Disabled Persons (resolution 47/3). An expert group meeting to develop a long-term strategy to further the implementation of the 1982 World Programme of Action concerning Disabled Persons drew up a strategy to create a society for all and remove barriers that prevented disabled people from fully participating in the socio-cultural, political and economic development of their countries and societies.

War, civil unrest and drought caused food aid requirements to soar in 1992. The World Food Programme—a joint undertaking of the United Nations and the Food and Agriculture Organization of the United Nations (FAO)—shipped a record 5.2 million tonnes of food, benefiting some 42 million people, including 14.4 million refugees and displaced people.

The international community intensified action on nutritional deficiency diseases during the year. Representatives attending the International Conference on Nutrition, jointly sponsored by FAO and WHO, adopted a World Declaration and Plan of Action for Nutrition in which they declared their determination to eliminate hunger and reduce all forms of malnutrition and made recommendations for action by Governments to improve nutrition.

Health

Primary health care

Strengthening primary health-care services was addressed in 1992 by the United Nations Children's Fund (UNICEF)/WHO Joint Committee on Health Policy and the United Nations Conference on Environment and Development (UNCED) (Rio de Janeiro, Brazil, 3-14 June).

The UNICEF/WHO Joint Committee held a special session (Geneva, 30 and 31 January)[1] to discuss follow-up to the 1990 World Summit for Children and the goals contained in the Summit's World Declaration on the Survival, Protection and Development of Children and its Plan of Action.[2] In that context, the Committee discussed strengthening national health-care capabilities with an emphasis on district health systems, which were intended to decentralize decision-making authority and place it in the hands of local officials with the means to implement action (see PART THREE, Chapter XIV, for specific action concerning children). The Committee considered the district to be the key level of the health delivery system for implementing, monitoring and expanding health services and recommended that priority be given to training and supervision; logistics and supplies; community and health education; community involvement and empowerment; surveillance, information gathering, monitoring and evaluation; and biomedical and operational research. It also recommended that UNICEF and WHO collaborate on, among other things, monitoring water safety and sanitation; combating dracunculiasis (guinea-worm disease), malaria, schistosomiasis and AIDS; research, training and community-based projects on essential drugs; and nutrition. The Committee further recommended that the two organizations work together to strengthen district health systems through a variety of programmes, including the Bamako Initiative (see below). Those recommendations were endorsed in May by the WHO Executive Board[3] and in June by the UNICEF Executive Board.[4] The UNICEF Board also endorsed the Committee's recommendation that WHO and UNICEF assist Governments in providing emergency responses to cholera outbreaks as well as in preparing for, controlling and preventing the spread of the disease.

UNCED action. UNCED, in Agenda 21, a global plan of action for environment and development,[5] made a number of recommendations aimed at protecting and promoting human health. The recommendations dealt with meeting primary health-care needs, particularly in rural areas; controlling communicable diseases; protecting vulnerable groups; meeting the urban health challenge; and reducing health risks from environmental pollution and hazards.

The General Assembly, in **resolution 47/190**, endorsed Agenda 21. (See PART THREE, Chapter VIII, for details on UNCED.)

Bamako Initiative

The 1987 Bamako Initiative,[6] adopted by the African Ministers of Health to improve the quality of primary health care in sub-Saharan Africa through community participation in financing and managing local health services, was evaluated in 1992 on the basis of case-studies conducted in Burundi, Guinea, Kenya, Nigeria and Uganda.[7] At the time, the Initiative was operating in 33 countries. The evaluation, sponsored by the Overseas Development Administration (United Kingdom), the Danish International Development Agency, the Norwegian Agency for International Development and the Swedish International Development Authority, was carried out by the London School of Hygiene and Tropical Medicine, which made recommendations aimed at improving quality of service, affordability, pricing structures and payment mechanisms, cost recovery and community participation. In addition, recommendations were made concerning the need for support for the Initiative as a way of developing primary health care.

In June,[8] the UNICEF Executive Board endorsed those recommendations and called on UNICEF to continue to promote the community-focused approach to health-sector development both within and beyond Africa, in close collaboration with WHO. UNICEF was asked to identify and study other successful examples of community-focused initiatives and to examine the potential for, and risks of, applying the community-focused approach to other sectors. The Board called for the submission in 1994 of a progress report on the implementation of the Initiative.

AIDS prevention and control

In response to a 1991 General Assembly request,[9] the Secretary-General in July 1992 transmitted to the Economic and Social Council and the Assembly a report of the WHO Director-General on the implementation of the WHO global strategy for the prevention and control of AIDS.[10] The Assembly had endorsed the strategy in 1987.[11]

In a later report,[12] the WHO Director-General reported that by late 1992 an estimated 13 million adult men and women were HIV-infected and there had been some 2.5 million cases of adult AIDS. In addition, some 1 million HIV-infected children, mostly in sub-Saharan Africa, had been born to HIV-infected women, and over half of them had developed AIDS or died. WHO projected that by the year 2000 a world total of at least 30 million to 40 million men, women and children would have been infected with HIV since the start of the pandemic.

An updated WHO global strategy for the prevention and control of AIDS was endorsed by the World Health Assembly in 1992.[13] The updated strategy proposed ways of meeting the new challenges of the pandemic, including increased emphasis on health care; more effective treatment for other sexually transmitted diseases; stronger focus on HIV prevention by improving women's health, education and status; a more supportive social environment for prevention programmes; and greater emphasis on the public health dangers of stigmatizing people known to be or suspected of being infected and of discrimination against them. (See PART THREE, Chapter X, for information on discrimination against HIV-infected people or people with AIDS.) The updated strategy was endorsed by the Economic and Social Council and the General Assembly (see below).

The WHO Director-General highlighted the 1992 activities of the WHO global programme on AIDS and those carried out by United Nations organizations and specialized agencies. He discussed coordination mechanisms for HIV/AIDS activities within the United Nations system.

On 7 February, the Economic and Social Council, by **decision 1992/204**, decided that one of the themes of its 1992 coordination segment would be devoted to United Nations policies and activities relating to HIV/AIDS prevention and control and programmes aimed at mitigating its negative socio-economic consequences.

The Secretary-General, in a June report to the Council,[14] discussed the challenges of the evolving HIV/AIDS pandemic as it related to a series of wide-ranging health and socio-economic issues, including preventing the transmission of HIV infection, demographic impact of the disease, effect on vulnerable populations and negative effects on women and their children. He presented the coordination mechanisms that had evolved over the past five years and the policies enacted, and outlined the key principles necessary for improving coordination among the partners of the United Nations system. He also described the prevention and control activities undertaken by the specialized agencies aimed at mitigating negative social and economic effects of the disease.

The Council, by **decision 1992/300** of 31 July, took note of the Secretary-General's report.

UNDP action. In January 1992, UNDP established an HIV and Development Programme to strengthen UNDP efforts to increase global awareness of the threat posed by the epidemic, as well as national capacity to respond to challenges to human development. The Programme was responsible for coordinating and providing policy and programming guidelines for UNDP work in the field. In a report to the UNDP Governing Council,[15] the UNDP Administrator said that the specific UNDP mandates for policy and programme development were to help increase awareness and understanding at global and national levels of the development implications of the epidemic; to support community-based programmes and programmes for women; to strengthen national capacities to develop effective multisectoral HIV strategies; and to minimize the adverse effects of the epidemic.

The Governing Council, on 26 May,[16] took note of the section of the Administrator's report dealing with HIV and development. It asked him to make an assessment of UNDP activities to combat HIV/AIDS and to review the policy framework for the role of UNDP.

Also in May,[17] the Council welcomed the efforts of the United Nations Population Fund (UNFPA) to strengthen its AIDS prevention and control activities (for UNFPA's AIDS-related activities, see PART THREE, Chapter IX).

A memorandum of understanding for implementing a WHO/UNDP alliance to combat HIV/AIDS, signed in July, assigned the two organizations joint responsibility for developing a programme approach at the national and global levels.

UNICEF action. In a February report,[18] the Executive Director of UNICEF recommended that UNICEF intensify and expand its support to HIV/AIDS prevention activities, working in close collaboration with Governments, WHO, bilateral agencies, non-governmental organizations (NGOs) and others. He also recommended that UNICEF-supported programmes should focus on reducing HIV transmission among young people; promoting informed and responsible sexual behaviour; protecting children from sexual exploitation; promoting improved reproductive health of women and youth; expanding the role of NGOs; and supporting creative community-based approaches to provide the support and social services required by AIDS orphans and families affected by HIV/AIDS.

In June,[19] the UNICEF Executive Board took note of the Executive Director's report and asked him to take further steps, in close coordination with specialized agencies, NGOs and donors, to strengthen coordination and accelerate global efforts, including the establishing of and participation in an international AIDS coordination forum. It urged him to give priority to accelerating UNICEF society-focused interventions aimed at promoting mutual fidelity and responsible sexual behaviour, reducing gender disparity, improving the socio-economic status of women and reducing the vulnerability of youth to sexual and other exploitation. He was also requested to strengthen the role of UNICEF in combating HIV/AIDS and to review the UNICEF AIDS programme approach to ensure its consistency with the global AIDS strategy and to make refinements as necessary.

ECONOMIC AND SOCIAL COUNCIL ACTION

On 30 July 1992, the Economic and Social Council, on the recommendation of its Economic Committee, adopted **resolution 1992/33** without vote.

Prevention and control of acquired immunodeficiency syndrome (AIDS)

The Economic and Social Council,

Taking note with appreciation of the report of the Director-General of the World Health Organization on the implementation of the global strategy for the prevention and control of AIDS,

1. *Endorses* the updated global strategy for the prevention and control of AIDS as the global policy framework;

2. *Also endorses* the recommendations of the Management Committee of the World Health Organization Global Programme on AIDS concerning coordination of human immunodeficiency virus (HIV)/AIDS activities at both the global and the country level, and requests all relevant organizations of the United Nations system to collaborate in carrying out those recommendations;[a]

3. *Requests* the relevant agencies of the United Nations system, in elaborating improved country-level coordination mechanisms, to take into account the important role the resident coordinator should play in such mechanisms to ensure effective implementation of the updated global strategy;

4. *Requests* the Secretary-General, in accordance with General Assembly resolution 45/264 of 13 May 1991, to invite the Director-General of the World Health Organization, acting in close collaboration with other appropriate bodies, organs and programmes of the United Nations system, to report, through the Secretary-General, to the Economic and Social Council at its substantive session of 1993 on further developments concerning coordination of HIV/AIDS activities at the global and country levels.

---

[a]WHO document GPA/GMC/92.14.

Economic and Social Council resolution 1992/33

30 July 1992   Meeting 41   Adopted without vote

Approved by Economic Committee (E/1992/109/Add.2) without vote, 28 July (meeting 16); draft by Vice-Chairman (E/1992/C.1/L.21), based on informal consultations on draft by Austria, Norway, Sweden and United States (E/1992/C.1/L.14); agenda item 12 *(k)*.

On 1 December 1992, the General Assembly, on the recommendation of the Second (Economic and Financial) Committee, adopted **resolution 47/40** without vote.

Prevention and control of acquired immunodeficiency syndrome (AIDS)

The General Assembly,

Recalling its resolution 46/203 of 20 December 1991, previous resolutions of the General Assembly and relevant resolutions of other organizations of the United Nations system,

1. *Takes note* of the report of the Director-General of the World Health Organization on the implementation of the global strategy for the prevention and control of acquired immunodeficiency syndrome (AIDS);

2. *Endorses* the action taken by the Economic and Social Council in resolution 1992/33 of 30 July 1992 on prevention and control of AIDS;

3. *Requests* the Secretary-General to invite the Director-General of the World Health Organization, in close collaboration with all other appropriate bodies, organs and programmes of the United Nations system, to report, through the Secretary-General, to the General Assembly at its forty-eighth session, and biennially thereafter, through the Economic and Social Council, on progress in the implementation of the global strategy for the prevention and control of AIDS.

General Assembly resolution 47/40

1 December 1992   Meeting 76   Adopted without vote

Approved by Second Committee (A/47/717) without vote, 25 November (meeting 46); draft by Vice-Chairman (A/C.2/47/L.54), based on informal consultations; agenda item 12.

Meeting numbers. GA 47th session: 2nd Committee 34-37, 46; plenary 76.

Disabled persons

Implementation of the Programme of Action

In response to a 1991 General Assembly request,[20] the Secretary-General submitted a report,[21] in September 1992, on implementation of the 1982 World Programme of Action concerning Disabled Persons[22] and the United Nations Decade of Disabled Persons (1983-1992).[23]

The World Programme provided a policy framework for improving the status of disabled persons, the guiding philosophy of which was a shift away from a charity approach towards integrated social development, reflecting a recognition that the problems of disabled persons could not be solved in isolation from those of the greater society. One of the major achievements of the Decade was increasing the knowledge and understanding of the rights of the disabled through information campaigns directed at politicians, legislators, service providers and disabled persons themselves. In addition, disabled persons, through their organizations, were able to increase their influence, gain respect, achieve greater independence and gain access to community resources.

On the negative side, there were indications that the number of disabled persons had increased during the Decade as a result of disease, famine, malnutrition, poverty, violence and war. The social and economic situation of many countries deteriorated during the period, with the most vulnerable groups, including disabled persons, often being hit the hardest. In addition, the financial resources available were insufficient to carry out the tasks required. Although disabled persons increased their participation in various sectors of society, the goal of full and equal participation was far from being realized. People with visual, auditory and comprehension impairments did not always have access to information, and the mass media continued to use materials based on outdated concepts of disability and terminology that was demeaning to disabled persons. (See PART THREE, Chapter X, for action by the Commission on Human Rights regarding disability.) A major obstacle to implementing the Programme of Action was the absence of national coordinating bodies. In addition, many countries did not have comprehensive disability plans and programmes, and, where they did exist, such programmes remained separate from the country's overall socio-economic development. In the majority of countries, most disabled persons and their families were either not covered by social security or had only limited protection, and in some industrialized countries, income security was often a disincentive, increasing the dependency of disabled persons. There was a scarcity of scientifically developed statistics on disabled persons and a lack of coordination of research being conducted at universities and elsewhere. Financial limitations constituted a major obstacle to implementing the goals of the Programme.

The Secretary-General described national disability-prevention activities, including improved health care, nutrition and immunization; rehabilitation; technical aids and appliances; and equalization of opportunities, including physical accessibility, transportation, education, vocational training and employment. He summarized the activities of the United Nations regional commissions, other United Nations bodies and NGOs and recommended a number of measures for Governments to take to move the disability programme from awareness-raising to action and to implement guidelines and policies developed over the Decade.

Pursuant to a 1991 recommendation of the Economic and Social Council,[24] an expert group meeting to develop a long-term strategy to further the implementation of the Programme of Action was held (Vancouver, Canada, 25-29 April 1992).[25] A number of organizations of disabled persons at the local, national and international levels presented their views and proposals. The experts adopted a strategy reaffirming the validity of the Programme.

The strategy's main objective was to create a society for all and remove barriers that prevented disabled people from participating fully in the socio-cultural, political and economic development of their countries and societies. The strategy was designed to increase the capacity of Member States, United Nations bodies and organizations, and governmental and non-governmental organizations to address adequately the issue of disability and encourage them to develop strategic action plans and establish permanent planning and monitoring mechanisms for implementing the Programme. It was also designed to strengthen the processes that had proved successful and sustainable during the Decade, including integration, involving persons with disabilities and their organizations, effective coordination, developing universal norms and standards, and building new partnerships.

Canada also hosted an International Conference of Ministers Responsible for the Status of Persons with Disabilities (Montreal, 8 and 9 October 1992).

The tenth inter-agency meeting on the United Nations Decade of Disabled Persons (Vienna, 7-10 December 1992)[26] reviewed the major achievements of the Decade and discussed the long-term strategy to the year 2000 and beyond. It welcomed the proclamation of the Asian and Pacific Decade of Disabled Persons (1993-2002) by members of the Economic and Social Commission for Asia and the Pacific. The meeting proposed new terms of reference for future inter-agency meetings, which were annexed to its report. It recommended that the shift from awareness-raising to action should be reflected in joint efforts by the specialized agencies and that emphasis be placed on action in developing countries. It also recommended that an affirmative action plan for the employment of disabled persons within the United Nations system be approved by 1995.

The ad hoc open-ended working group to elaborate standard rules on the equalization of opportunities for disabled persons submitted its final report in November.[27] It recommended a set of draft rules for finalization by the Commission for Social Development in 1993. It also recommended that the Commission consider ways of linking the monitoring of the standard rules, a long-term strategy to the year 2000 and beyond and the World Programme of Action.

GENERAL ASSEMBLY ACTION

On 14 October, the General Assembly adopted **resolution 47/3** without vote.

International Day of Disabled Persons

The General Assembly,

Considering that the United Nations Decade of Disabled Persons has been a period of awareness-raising and of action-oriented measures aimed at the continued improvement of the situation of persons with disabilities and the equalization of opportunities for them,

Aware of the need for more vigorous and broader action and measures at all levels to fulfil the objectives of the Decade and the World Programme of Action concerning Disabled Persons,

Noting the importance of developing and carrying out concrete long-term strategies for full implementation of the World Programme of Action beyond the Decade, with the aim of achieving a society for all by the year 2010,

Welcoming the International Conference of Ministers Responsible for the Status of Persons with Disabilities hosted by the Government of Canada at Montreal, Canada, on 8 and 9 October 1992,

Noting with appreciation the high-level participation in its plenary meetings on 12 and 13 October 1992, marking the conclusion of the Decade,

1. *Invites* all Member States and organizations concerned to intensify their efforts aimed at sustained effective action with a view to improving the situation of persons with disabilities;

2. *Proclaims* 3 December as the International Day of Disabled Persons;

3. *Urges* Governments, as well as national, regional and international organizations, to extend their full cooperation in observing the International Day of Disabled Persons.

General Assembly resolution 47/3

14 October 1992   Meeting 37   Adopted without vote

Draft by President (A/47/L.4); agenda item 93 *(a)*.
Meeting numbers. GA 47th session: plenary 33-37.

UN Voluntary fund

In May 1992,[28] the Secretary-General reviewed the performance of the Voluntary Fund for the United Nations Decade of Disabled Persons from 1980 to 1991. During that period, the Fund provided nearly $3 million in seed-money grants to 161 disability-related projects in Africa, Asia and the Pacific, Latin America and the Caribbean, and western Asia. Global and regional projects accounted for 30 per cent of the total number of projects supported and 37 per cent of the total funds distributed. National capacity-building and institutional development were the main focus of the Fund-assisted activities. Training accounted for 38 per cent of total resources; technical exchange and knowledge, 20 per cent; support to disabled persons' organizations, 19 per cent; data collection and applied research, 13 per cent; and promotional activities, 7.5 per cent. Forty-four Member States provided the majority of the funds.

The Secretary-General believed that the Fund had contributed significantly to the work of the United Nations, and that it should continue under the name United Nations Voluntary Fund on Disability in order to further the international community's goal of achieving a society for all by 2010.[29] He proposed new terms of reference for the Fund, stating that its resources should be used to co-finance field-based technical cooperation activities within the framework of the World Programme of Action. The least developed countries and groups of especially disadvantaged disabled people, including women, the elderly, the hearing-impaired, the mentally disabled and persons with multiple disabilities, would receive special emphasis.

The Economic and Social Council, by **decision 1992/276** of 30 July, recommended that the General Assembly adopt the Secretary-General's recommendations.

GENERAL ASSEMBLY ACTION

On 16 December, the Assembly, on the recommendation of the Third (Social, Humanitarian and Cultural) Committee, adopted **resolution 47/88** without vote.

Towards full integration of persons with disabilities into society: a continuing world programme of action

The General Assembly,

Recalling all its relevant resolutions, including resolutions 37/52 and 37/53 of 3 December 1982 and 46/96 of 16 December 1991, and taking note of Economic and Social Council decision 1992/276 of 30 July 1992 and Commission on Human Rights resolution 1992/48 of 3 March 1992,

Noting the progress achieved during the United Nations Decade of Disabled Persons, including increased awareness and expanded knowledge of disability issues, the increased role played by persons with disabilities and by organizations, and the development of disability legislation,

Aware of the major obstacles to the implementation of the World Programme of Action concerning Disabled Persons, foremost among these being an inadequate allocation of resources,

Mindful of the need for persons with disabilities to be afforded the means to take their place as full-fledged citizens in all fields of society,

Deeply concerned by the increasing numbers of persons with disabilities as a consequence of poverty and disease, wars and civil strife and demographic and environmental factors, including natural disasters and catastrophic accidents,

Acknowledging with appreciation the work of the Centre for Social Development and Humanitarian Affairs of the Secretariat, as the focal point for disability issues within the United Nations system,

Recognizing that the ongoing process of elaborating standard rules on the equalization of opportunities for disabled persons represents one of the important initiatives of the Decade,

Noting the proposed action towards a long-term strategy to implement the World Programme of Action to the year 2000 and beyond, resulting from the meeting of experts held at Vancouver, Canada, in April 1992,

Welcoming the initiative of the Government of Canada in convening the International Conference of Ministers Responsible for the Status of Persons with Disabilities, held at Montreal, Canada, on 8 and 9 October 1992,

Having carefully considered the various reports and statements made during its plenary meetings on 12 and 13 October 1992, devoted to marking the conclusion of the United Nations Decade of Disabled Persons,

Welcoming Economic and Social Council decision 1992/276, in which the Council recommended the continuation of the Voluntary Fund for the United Nations Decade of Disabled Persons under a new name, the United Nations Voluntary Fund on Disability, and under new terms of reference,

Having taken note with appreciation of the report of the Secretary-General concerning the second round of monitoring of the implementation of the World Programme of Action and the United Nations Decade of Disabled Persons,

1. *Reaffirms* the continuing validity and value of the World Programme of Action concerning Disabled Persons, which provides a firm and innovative framework for disability-related issues;

2. *Reiterates* the responsibility of Governments for removing or facilitating the removal of barriers and obstacles to the full integration of persons with disabilities into society, and supports their efforts in developing national policies to reach specific objectives;

3. *Urges* Governments to show their commitment to improving the situation of persons with disabilities, *inter alia*, by:

(*a*) Establishing an appropriate governmental mechanism to be responsible for policy relating to persons with disabilities and overall coordination;

(*b*) Addressing disability issues within integrated social development policies linked to other socio-economic issues and providing preventive and rehabilitative measures and an equalization of opportunities, with the ultimate objective of facilitating the full integration of persons with disabilities into society;

(*c*) Where appropriate, creating new or strengthening existing high-level national coordinating committees or other similar bodies in accordance with the Guidelines for the Establishment and Development of National Coordinating Committees on Disability or Similar Bodies,[a] adopted at Beijing;

(*d*) Supporting the development of organizations of persons with disabilities and using the body of knowledge accumulated by persons with disabilities or their representatives in decision-making processes;

(*e*) Integrating, where possible, disability components into technical assistance and technical cooperation programmes;

4. *Welcomes* the proclamation by the Economic and Social Commission for Asia and the Pacific of the Asian and Pacific Decade of Disabled Persons, 1993-2002;

5. *Also welcomes* the decision of the International Conference of Ministers Responsible for the Status of Persons with Disabilities, held at Montreal, Canada, to establish a Working Group of Ministers and the continuing discussion on the question;

6. *Further welcomes* the initiative of the United States of America to act as host, in cooperation with the United Nations, to an international conference on disability in the autumn of 1993;

7. *Urges* the optimum use of existing United Nations mechanisms and bodies, including regional commissions, specialized agencies, other intergovernmental bodies and non-governmental organizations, especially or-

---

[a]A/C.3/46/4.

ganizations of persons with disabilities, in the planning, coordination, implementation and monitoring of the United Nations programme on disability, in line with the restructuring and streamlining efforts of the United Nations system and in order to make the most cost-effective use of resources;

8. *Requests* the Secretary-General to turn the focus of the United Nations programme on disability from awareness-raising to action, to give higher priority and visibility to disability issues within the work programme of the United Nations system, to provide it, through the use of existing resources, with an adequate allocation of funding to strengthen the leadership role of the United Nations as a catalyst for change, as a standard-setting organization, as a forum for the exchange of views and as a promoter of technical cooperation activities, by:

(a) Integrating disability issues into the policies, programmes and projects of the specialized agencies on a broader scale and with a higher priority;

(b) Concentrating action and assistance in countries and regions that are most needy and paying special attention to especially vulnerable groups;

(c) Considering the creation of a panel of eminent persons, including persons with disabilities, to advise the Secretary-General on disability matters;

(d) Initiating model pilot projects, in partnership with all interested parties, to assist Member States in formulating comprehensive and coherent disability policies and feasible action plans, taking into account diverse socio-cultural factors and varying levels of economic development;

(e) Finalizing the revision of the translation into the official languages of the United Nations of the World Programme of Action, in particular the terms "impairment", "disability", "handicap" and "disabled person";

(f) Reviewing the Human Development Index of the United Nations Development Programme to include an evaluation of the way a society treats its disabled citizens as a factor of the quality of life in that society;

(g) Continuing United Nations inter-agency meetings established as a result of the United Nations Decade of Disabled Persons and focusing such meetings on the implementation of the World Programme of Action;

(h) Asking the Statistical Office of the Secretariat, in close collaboration with the Centre for Social Development and Humanitarian Affairs and the relevant United Nations organizations, to continue its important work of collecting statistical data about disability matters and to publish updated disability statistics;

9. *Urges* the Commission for Social Development to expedite the elaboration of standard rules on the equalization of opportunities for disabled persons;

10. *Encourages* the consideration during major forthcoming events, including the World Conference on Human Rights to be held in 1993, the International Conference on Population and Development to be held in 1994, the International Year of the Family to be observed in 1994, the Fourth World Conference on Women: Action for Equality, Development and Peace, to be held in 1995, and the World Summit for Social Development to be held in 1995, of disability issues relevant to the subject-matter of those events;

11. *Decides* to continue, in response to General Assembly resolution 46/96 and Economic and Social Council decision 1992/276, the United Nations Voluntary Fund on Disability and encourages the Secretary-

General to explore diversified funding arrangements to support and strengthen the Fund involving not only Member States, but also the private sector, with due regard to the need for greater transparency in the management of the Fund;

12. *Appeals* to Member States to highlight the observance of the International Day of Disabled Persons on 3 December every year with a view to furthering the integration into society of persons with disabilities;

13. *Requests* the Secretary-General to report to the General Assembly at its forty-eighth session on the implementation of the present resolution under the item entitled "Social development".

General Assembly resolution 47/88

16 December 1992   Meeting 89   Adopted without vote

Approved by Third Committee (A/47/703) without vote, 2 November (meeting 25); 53-nation draft (A/C.3/47/L.15), orally revised; agenda item 93 (a).
Sponsors: Angola, Australia, Austria, Azerbaijan, Bahamas, Bangladesh, Belarus, Belgium, Burkina Faso, Cameroon, Canada, China, Costa Rica, Côte d'Ivoire, Cyprus, Denmark, Dominican Republic, Egypt, Finland, France, Greece, Guinea, Guinea-Bissau, Iceland, Indonesia, Ireland, Italy, Japan, Kenya, Libyan Arab Jamahiriya, Mali, Malta, Mongolia, Morocco, Namibia, Norway, Pakistan, Panama, Peru, Philippines, Poland, Republic of Korea, Romania, Russian Federation, Spain, Sweden, Thailand, Trinidad and Tobago, Turkey, Ukraine, United Kingdom, Zambia, Zimbabwe.
Meeting numbers. GA 47th session: 3rd Committee 11-18, 22, 25; plenary 33-36, 89.

REFERENCES

(1)E/ICEF/1992/L.18. (2)A/45/625. (3)WHO document EB90/1992/REC/1. (4)E/1992/29 (dec. 1992/29). (5)*Report of the United Nations Conference on Environment and Development, Rio de Janeiro, 3-14 June 1992*, vol. I, Sales No. E.93.I.8. (6)YUN 1987, p. 859. (7)E/ICEF/1992/L.20. (8)E/1992/29 (dec. 1992/22). (9)YUN 1991, p. 633, GA res. 46/203, 20 Dec. 1991. (10)A/47/289-E/1992/68. (11)YUN 1987, p. 645, GA res. 42/8, 26 Oct. 1987. (12)A/48/159-E/1993/59. (13)World Health Assembly document A45/29. (14)E/1992/67. (15)DP/1992/12. (16)E/1992/28 (dec. 92/14). (17)Ibid. (dec. 92/32 A). (18)E/ICEF/1992/L.11. (19)E/1992/29 (dec. 1992/26). (20)YUN 1991, p. 637, GA res. 46/96, 16 Dec. 1991. (21)A/47/415 & Corr.1. (22)YUN 1982, p. 981, GA res. 37/52, 3 Dec. 1982. (23)Ibid., p. 983, GA res. 37/53, 3 Dec. 1982. (24)YUN 1991, p. 636, ESC res. 1991/9, 30 May 1991. (25)E/CN.5/1993/4. (26)ACC/1992/31. (27)E/CN.5/1993/5. (28)A/47/214-E/1992/50. (29)GA res. 45/91, 14 Dec. 1990.

Food and agriculture

World food situation

Despite adequate global food production, modern means of transport and the proliferation of humanitarian relief mechanisms, millions of people in developing regions continued to face the threat of famine, according to a 1992 report of the World Food Council (WFC) on the global state of hunger and malnutrition.[1] While progress in reducing hunger and poverty in some developing regions, especially eastern and southern Asia, was welcomed and encouraged, the deterioration of social and economic conditions in a great many low-income countries had to be viewed with great concern.

The Executive Director of the World Food Programme (WFP) reported that the worst drought in recent history had ruined harvests throughout southern Africa in 1992, threatening more than 18 million people with famine, and warfare and civil unrest continued to devastate other African countries.[2] Emergency needs for nearly 16 million people in the Horn of Africa remained substantial, with conflict continuing to afflict parts of Ethiopia, Somalia and much of southern Sudan.

In Eastern Europe, including the Commonwealth of Independent States, millions of people found it increasingly difficult to gain access to adequate food as a result of economic reforms, and some countries were encountering serious national food shortages. WFC stressed that support to the region must not divert assistance from the developing countries, and expressed confidence that economic progress and a successful transformation of the Eastern European economies would stimulate the world economy and benefit the developing countries by contributing to greater food security.

Emergency food aid was also provided to people affected by conflicts in the Persian Gulf and in the former Yugoslavia, to Afghan refugees in Iran and Pakistan and to victims of natural or man-made disasters in Bangladesh, Cambodia, Haiti and the Philippines. In all, WFP provided a record amount of food—5.2 million tonnes—to approximately 42 million people in 1992.

WFC activities. WFC, the United Nations coordinating body on food issues, held its eighteenth session in 1992 (Nairobi, Kenya, 23-26 June)[3] and made recommendations on the global state of hunger and malnutrition; the need for a new green revolution in Africa; the implications of changes in Eastern Europe and the Commonwealth of Independent States for food security in developing countries; migration and food security; hunger-alleviation targets set out in the Council's 1989 Cairo Declaration,[4] adopted by the General Assembly in the International Development Strategy for the Fourth United Nations Development Decade (1991-2000);[5] a successful conclusion of the multilateral agricultural trade negotiations of the Uruguay Round of the General Agreement on Tariffs and Trade (GATT) aimed at liberalizing agricultural trade based on a 1991 GATT proposal;[6] and the importance of greater political leadership and coordination by a strengthened WFC in the fight against hunger.

WFC welcomed a May 1992 appeal of the Secretary-General to assist the drought-affected countries of southern Africa and expressed satisfaction at the outcome of a pledging conference (Geneva, 1 and 2 June). It called on countries in a position to do so to provide further resources urgently needed to cover the gap between pledges made and the Secretary-General's target of $856

million to meet the most acute emergency needs. It noted the importance of the Special Programme for Sub-Saharan African Countries Affected by Drought and Desertification of the International Fund for Agricultural Development (IFAD). In July, the Economic and Social Council, by **resolution 1992/31**, appealed to the international community to contribute generously to the second phase of the Programme.

In a review of its future role in a changing global economic and social environment, WFC agreed that it had fallen short of achieving the political leadership and coordination role envisioned when it was established after the 1974 World Food Conference.[7] There was a consensus, however, that food and hunger issues must remain at the centre of development efforts. The Council established an Ad Hoc Committee on the Review of WFC (New York, 14 and 15 September 1992)[8] to develop proposals concerning its mandate and role in the future. The Committee considered several options, among them: transferring the Council's mandate and functions elsewhere in the United Nations system (e.g., the Subcommittee on Nutrition of the Administrative Committee on Coordination (ACC), the Economic and Social Council or FAO); and significantly reforming and streamlining WFC. WFC asked the General Assembly to take the Committee's report into account when considering the restructuring of the United Nations intergovernmental machinery.

The Council had before it reports prepared by the World Bank[9] and IFAD[10] on their experiences with hunger- and poverty-alleviation programmes and projects.

The Economic and Social Council, by **decision 1992/207** of 7 February, decided that, during its 1992 substantive session when considering the report of WFC on its eighteenth session, it would not consider new draft proposals except for specific recommendations requiring action by the Council and proposals on coordination-related matters.

ECONOMIC AND SOCIAL COUNCIL ACTION

On 30 July, the Economic and Social Council, on the recommendation of its Economic Committee, adopted **resolution 1992/32** without vote.

Food and agricultural development
The Economic and Social Council,

Having considered the report of the World Food Council on its eighteenth ministerial session, held at Nairobi from 23 to 26 June 1992,

Noting the role of the World Food Council in the fight against hunger,

Expressing concern about the ever-increasing number of people suffering from hunger and situations of famine,

Recognizing the need for the role, functioning and mandate of the World Food Council to be reviewed,

1. *Endorses* the recommendations of the World Food Council at its eighteenth ministerial session;

2. *Welcomes* the decision of the World Food Council to set up an ad hoc committee to make specific proposals concerning the mandate and functions of the World Food Council and options for its future role, for consideration by the General Assembly at its forty-seventh session.

Economic and Social Council resolution 1992/32

30 July 1992   Meeting 41   Adopted without vote

Approved by Economic Committee (E/1992/109/Add.2) without vote, 28 July (meeting 16); draft by Vice-Chairman (E/1992/C.1/L.19), based on informal consultations on draft by Pakistan for Group of 77 (E/1992/C.1/L.13); agenda item 12 *(c)*.

GENERAL ASSEMBLY ACTION

On 18 December 1992, the General Assembly, on the recommendation of the Second Committee, adopted **resolution 47/150** without vote.

Strengthening the United Nations response to world food and hunger problems

The General Assembly,

Taking note of Economic and Social Council resolution 1992/32 of 30 July 1992, and the decisions of the World Food Council at its eighteenth session,

Taking note also of the report of the Ad Hoc Committee on the Review of the World Food Council,

Deeply concerned about the gravity of the world food security situation, in particular the worsening problems of hunger and malnutrition,

Stressing the urgent need for a more effective and better coordinated United Nations response to world food and hunger problems,

Underscoring the increasing importance of intergovernmental policy guidance in this field,

Noting with concern that, despite its efforts, the World Food Council, by its own acknowledgement, has not been able to achieve political leadership and coordination to the extent expected by its founders,

1. *Affirms* the critical importance of establishing the most effective arrangements for the management and coordination of the United Nations response to world food and hunger problems;

2. *Underlines* the need to consider the role of the World Food Council and how its mandate and functions might best be carried out within the wider context of the overall restructuring of the social and economic activities of the United Nations system;

3. *Decides* to address these issues in the context of the discussions on restructuring and revitalization of the United Nations in the economic, social and related fields at the resumed forty-seventh session of the General Assembly, and, in this context, invites the World Food Council to continue its attempts to agree on appropriate measures to be taken and to communicate any agreed conclusions to the Assembly.

General Assembly resolution 47/150

18 December 1992   Meeting 92   Adopted without vote

Approved by Second Committee (A/47/718/Add.3) without vote, 9 December (meeting 49); draft by Vice-Chairman (A/C.2/47/L.76), based on informal consultations on 16-nation draft (A/C.2/47/L.59); agenda item 78 *(b)*.

Meeting numbers. GA 47th session: 2nd Committee 47, 49; plenary 92.

Food aid

CFA activities

In 1992, the Committee on Food Aid Policies and Programmes (CFA), the governing body of WFP, held three sessions at Rome, Italy.

During its second special session (23 and 24 April),[11] Catherine Bertini (United States) took the oath of office as WFP Executive Director. CFA approved WFP financial regulations as amended[12] and one development project, a forestry rehabilitation project in Kenya's semi-arid areas.

At its thirty-third session (25-29 May),[13] CFA approved 15 development projects valued at $245 million and representing 570,000 tonnes of food. Seven of the projects supported the development of human resources, while the other eight focused on productive activities, primarily in rural areas. It also approved five projects, valued at $172 million, providing 325,000 tonnes of food to some 2.5 million refugees and displaced persons. CFA noted the report of the WFP Executive Director covering 1991 activities,[14] which the Economic and Social Council also took note of on 31 July by **decision 1992/301**.

The Committee had before it a report on the WFP cash situation as at April 1992,[15] summarizing the actual movements of cash in 1991 and the projections for 1992 and 1993. The cash balance projected at the end of 1992 and 1993 represented the expenditure for no more than four and three months, respectively. The Deputy Executive Director considered that for a programme of the size and complexity of WFP, only three or four months' availability of cash was a very serious matter. In response to continuing concerns about the WFP cash-flow situation, CFA decided to set up an informal working group to examine all aspects of the long-term financing of its operations and administration.

At its thirty-fourth session (3-6 November),[16] CFA considered an October report by the Executive Director on WFP's cash situation.[17] The informal working group, which met in September, reached agreement on two basic principles, namely, that each WFP activity should pay for itself and that, in a given year or biennium, the cash outflow must not exceed cash inflow. The group made a number of suggestions for action by the secretariat and Governments, which were outlined in the Executive Director's report. The CFA Chairman considered the discussion of the item as an endorsement of the report, subject to the Committee's observations.

CFA approved 11 development projects costing $153 million, representing a food commitment of some 432,000 tonnes, as well as six refugee projects costing $278 million, representing nearly 785,000 tonnes of food to be distributed to some 5.5 million people.

In addition, CFA endorsed a plan for a more extensive and systematic application of WFP assistance to support disaster prevention, preparedness, mitigation and rehabilitation measures in Africa. It also endorsed draft guidelines on the allocation of WFP development assistance, which emphasized providing resources based on need.

WFP activities

WFP, with a total expenditure in 1992 of nearly $1.7 billion, remained the largest source of grant assistance for developing countries in the United Nations system. Of that amount, 65 per cent was for emergency relief, 29 per cent for development projects and the remaining 6 per cent for programme support and administrative costs.

In a report to the UNDP Governing Council on the activities of the United Nations Department of Economic and Social Development (DESD),[18] the Secretary-General stated that it provided technical support to WFP during the year, scrutinizing food-aid projects in low-income, food-deficit and least developed countries. DESD reviewed and dispatched 20 aid projects valued at $272 million in 1992.

Relief activities

In 1992, WFP committed a record amount of emergency food aid—5.2 million tonnes—to meet acute food shortages for some 27.5 million people in 48 countries.

A higher proportion of those receiving emergency food assistance in 1992 were refugees and displaced persons, a result of new working arrangements between WFP and the United Nations High Commissioner for Refugees (UNHCR), which took effect in January 1992, whereby WFP assumed responsibility for all UNHCR-managed refugee feeding operations in developing countries involving more than 1,000 beneficiaries. Thus, refugees and displaced people received more than 60 per cent of all WFP relief food aid in 1992, an increase of some 50 per cent over 1990. WFP committed $874 million to provide 1.9 million tonnes of food to some 14.4 million refugees and displaced people in 23 countries.

The countries of sub-Saharan Africa received nearly 60 per cent of WFP's total food-aid shipments in 1992, nearly 80 per cent of which was for disaster relief. That aid was distributed among 10 million refugees and displaced people in 18 sub-Saharan countries and to 11.4 million victims of drought in 17 countries.

In Somalia, an estimated 1 million people, mostly displaced women and children, were at grave risk of starvation. Because of anarchical conditions in the country that disrupted relief opera-

tions, WFP had to resort to large-scale airlifts to deliver food to those in urgent need until the United Nations Operation in Somalia (UNOSOM) secured access to inland areas and provided armed escorts for food-aid convoys (see PART TWO, Chapter I, for information on UNOSOM).

In the former Yugoslavia, it was estimated that more than 3 million people required emergency food assistance by the end of the year. WFP, under the direction of UNHCR, coordinated and managed the mobilization and delivery of food to Bosnia and Herzegovina, Croatia, Macedonia, Montenegro, Serbia and Slovenia.

In the Persian Gulf region, WFP continued to help people affected by civil turmoil, providing assistance to hundreds of thousands of displaced people and vulnerable groups inside Iraq. Elsewhere in Asia, the security situation in Afghanistan deteriorated in 1992, disrupting the return of millions of refugees from Pakistan and Iran and leading to severe food shortages in many parts of the country. In Cambodia, arrangements for the return of more than 360,000 refugees from camps on the Thai border were delayed because of continuing problems with mine clearance and the upsurge of political unrest; WFP continued to provide relief food to those refugees. Shipments of WFP food for relief activities in Asia in 1992 totalled $108 million.

For the first time in several years, WFP committed emergency food aid—$3.7 million worth—to Latin America and the Caribbean in 1992. Among the groups receiving assistance were Haitians involuntarily returned to their country, Cubans and Ecuadorans hit by floods and Peruvians affected by drought.

Development assistance

WFP development activities were aimed at alleviating poverty in developing countries as a means for the poor to gain self-sufficiency. In 1992, the Programme assisted projects designed to increase food and agricultural production; improve rural infrastructure; create land settlement projects, in which new lands were brought into production; increase food reserves; help vulnerable groups; assist school feeding programmes; and alleviate urban poverty. While development projects continued to form the foundation of WFP operations, the availability of resources for them declined during 1992, largely because budgetary constraints faced by donors caused them to redirect their resources to emergency and refugee food needs. Thus, WFP was obliged for a third consecutive year to ration commodity shipments to ongoing development projects.

In 1992, sub-Saharan Africa received 40 per cent of WFP development resources; Asia and the Pacific, 32 per cent; Latin America and the Caribbean, 18 per cent; and North Africa and the Middle East, 10 per cent. At the end of 1992, WFP was assisting 258 ongoing development projects, which provided an estimated 15 million people with 1.4 million tonnes of food during the year.

Resources

WFP's receipts for 1992 totalled some $1.75 billion, while expenditures amounted to nearly $1.69 billion. Pledges and contributions for the 1991-1992 biennium totalled nearly $3 billion.

Food and agricultural development

Report of the Secretary-General. In response to a 1991 request of the Economic and Social Council,[19] the Secretary-General, in September 1992, submitted a report[20] to the General Assembly on trends in the international market for agricultural and tropical products, developments in the liberalization of international trade in those products and follow-up to the section on agriculture of the International Development Strategy for the Fourth United Nations Development Decade.[5]

Despite a drop in the volume of world food and agricultural production in 1991—the first global decline since 1983—the volume of world agricultural trade had increased faster than in previous years. Much of the expansion in trade was the result of increased imports by countries experiencing production shortfalls, particularly China and the former USSR. Many developing countries continued to depend on the production and export of agricultural products. Agriculture accounted for about 15 per cent of gross domestic product in developing countries overall, compared to about 2 per cent in industrialized countries. A greater dependence on agricultural production in the developing world translated into a high dependence on agricultural exports. For the majority of developing countries, the share of agricultural products in total merchandise exports ranged from 50 to 100 per cent. While developing countries were highly dependent on exports of tropical products, most of them also depended on imports of basic foodstuffs, such as cereals, dairy products, meat and edible oils.

Many developed countries maintained high levels of protection for their agricultural commodity markets, resulting not only in the reduction or elimination of the traditional markets for developing countries, but also in the displacement of those countries on the world market, often as a result of subsidized exports. In contrast, the general policy in developing countries had resulted in discrimination against agriculture. Many of those countries were implementing policy reforms that would change the structure of incentives and liberalize trade in order to bring domestic prices in line with border prices.

WFC activities. At its 1992 session,[3] WFC recommended that a green revolution be launched in the developing world, especially in Africa, to increase significantly yields and production of traditional African crops, such as maize, millet, sorghum, pulses and tubers. Africa did not experience a research and technology breakthrough comparable to Asia's green revolution in the 1960s and early 1970s and remained engulfed in a devastating food crisis. The Council agreed that there was an urgent need for food production breakthroughs based on agricultural research, technology development and application.

UNCED action. Agenda 21, a global plan of action for environment and development, which was adopted by UNCED and endorsed by the General Assembly in **resolution 47/190**, contained a number of recommendations for promoting sustainable agriculture and rural development.[21] The Conference made recommendations on: agricultural policy review, planning and integrated programming, particularly regarding food security and sustainable development; ensuring people's participation and promoting human resource development for sustainable agriculture; improving farm production and farming systems through diversification of farm and non-farm employment and infrastructure development; land-resource planning, information and education for agriculture; land conservation and rehabilitation; water for sustainable food production and sustainable rural development; conservation and sustainable utilization of plant genetic resources for food and sustainable agriculture and of animal genetic resources for sustainable agriculture; integrated pest management and control; sustainable plant nutrition to increase food production; rural energy transition to enhance productivity; and the evaluation of the effects of ultraviolet radiation on plants and animals caused by the depletion of the stratospheric ozone layer. UNCED also made recommendations to strengthen the role of farmers. (See PART THREE, Chapter VIII, for details on UNCED.)

GENERAL ASSEMBLY ACTION

On 18 December 1992, the General Assembly, on the recommendation of the Second Committee, adopted **resolution 47/149** without vote.

Food and agricultural development
The General Assembly,

Reaffirming the importance and continued validity of the Declaration on International Economic Cooperation, in particular the Revitalization of Economic Growth and Development of the Developing Countries, contained in the annex to its resolution S-18/3 of 1 May 1990, the International Development Strategy for the

Fourth United Nations Development Decade, contained in the annex to its resolution 45/199 of 21 December 1990, the Cartagena Commitment, the United Nations New Agenda for the Development of Africa in the 1990s, contained in the annex to its resolution 46/151 of 18 December 1991, the Programme of Action for the Least Developed Countries for the 1990s, and the various consensus agreements and conventions, especially Agenda 21, adopted by the United Nations Conference on Environment and Development,

Reaffirming also its resolution 45/207 of 21 December 1990 on food and agricultural problems and taking note of Economic and Social Council resolution 1992/32 of 30 July 1992,

Reaffirming further that the right to food is a universal human right that should be guaranteed to all people,

Deeply concerned that hunger and malnutrition have been increasing in many areas, particularly in Africa,

Expressing deep concern that the volume of world food and agricultural production fell in 1991, the first global decline since 1983, and that food stocks declined rapidly,

Recognizing the importance of stimulating food production and productivity in developing countries through appropriate policies, taking fully into account Agenda 21, and through the creation of a suitable economic environment, including a more open international trading system, for the development of a viable agricultural sector and improved food security, and, in this context, noting with concern that the Uruguay Round of multilateral trade negotiations have not yet been completed and expressing the hope that they will reach a rapid, balanced and comprehensive conclusion,

1. *Takes note* of the report of the Secretary-General on trends in the international market for agricultural and tropical products, developments in the liberalization of international trade in agricultural and tropical products, and follow-up to the section on agriculture of the International Development Strategy for the Fourth United Nations Development Decade, as well as the conclusions and recommendations of the World Food Council at its eighteenth session;

2. *Affirms* that increasing food production and improving access to food by low-income people in developing countries will significantly contribute to the alleviation of poverty and the elimination of malnutrition and to helping to raise their standard of living;

3. *Stresses* the importance of stimulating food and agricultural production and productivity in developing countries in order to achieve sustainable economic growth and development and, on this basis, to create the conditions for more rapid industrialization and diversification of their economic activities, in particular in the agro-industrial sector;

4. *Calls upon* the international community to consider food and agricultural issues in a comprehensive and multidimensional manner;

5. *Encourages* all relevant organs of the United Nations system dealing with food and agriculture, as well as regional and subregional financial institutions, to improve their cooperation and coordination in the field of food and agricultural development;

6. *Urges* all countries, in particular developed countries, to strengthen their efforts in working towards a more equitable international environment, in particular a fairer, more open and viable international agricultural trading system that will stimulate food production

and productivity in developing countries, and, in this connection, stresses the urgent need for a balanced and successful outcome of the Uruguay Round of multilateral trade negotiations, as well as the need to give effect to the mid-term review agreements, in which it was stated that ways should be developed to take into account the possible negative effects of the reform process on net food-importing developing countries;

7. *Calls upon* the international community to support scientific and technological research and training as well as capacity-building in developing countries in order to promote sustainable agricultural development;

8. *Emphasizes* the urgency of strengthening international cooperation in the transfer of environmentally sound agricultural technology;

9. *Requests* the organs, organizations and bodies of the United Nations system dealing with development to continue their support in providing technical cooperation for agricultural and rural development;

10. *Requests* the international community to continue to assist and support technical cooperation, including technical cooperation among developing countries, in the area of food and agricultural development;

11. *Stresses* the importance of finance for investment and of a favourable economic environment to encourage it, and urges the international community to take further determined action in support of the efforts of developing countries in this regard;

12. *Requests* the Secretary-General, in consultation with relevant organs, organizations and bodies of the United Nations system, to submit to the General Assembly at its forty-ninth session a report on food production, including agro-industrial products, international markets for agricultural and tropical products and the state of global food security, taking into particular account the needs of all developing countries, including net food-importing countries;

13. *Decides* to include in the provisional agenda of its forty-ninth session an item entitled "Food and agricultural development".

General Assembly resolution 47/149

18 December 1992   Meeting 92   Adopted without vote

Approved by Second Committee (A/47/718/Add.3) without vote, 9 December (meeting 49); draft by Vice-Chairman (A/C.2/47/L.77), based on informal consultations on draft by Pakistan for Group of 77 (A/C.2/47/L.57); agenda item 78 (b).

Meeting numbers. GA 47th session: 2nd Committee 47, 49; plenary 92.

REFERENCES

(1)WFC/1992/2. (2)CFA:35/P/4. (3)A/47/19. (4)A/44/19. (5)GA res. 45/199, annex, 21 Dec. 1990. (6)YUN 1991, p. 1016. (7)YUN 1974, p. 501, GA res. 3348(XXIX), 17 Dec. 1974. (8)A/47/19/Add.1. (9)WFC/1992/8. (10)WFC/1992/9. (11)CFA: Special Session 2/6. (12)CFA: Special Session 2/3. (13)CFA:33/17. (14)E/1992/73. (15)CFA:33/8. (16)CFA:34/13. (17)CFA:34/P/6. (18)DP/1993/39/Add.1. (19)YUN 1991, p. 639, ESC res. 1991/53, 26 July 1991. (20)A/47/395. (21)*Report of the United Nations Conference on Environment and Development, Rio de Janeiro, 3-14 June 1992*, vol. I, Sales No. E.93.I.8.

Nutrition

A WFC study on the global state of hunger and malnutrition in 1992[1] reported widespread and severe malnutrition, as well as nutritional deficiency diseases, among refugees and displaced persons receiving international assistance, on a scale unprecedented since the Second World War. In addition, vitamin-A deficiency, which could result in blindness and lesser forms of eye damage, goitre caused by iodine deficiency and iron-deficiency anaemia were endemic in large parts of the developing world. Programmes in various countries to control those deficiencies had shown promise, and it appeared that the international community was preparing to take major steps towards combating micronutrient deficiencies. The subject was addressed in 1992 by the International Conference on Nutrition, organized by FAO and WHO, the ACC Subcommittee on Nutrition and the United Nations University (UNU) (see below). A Micronutrients Secretariat was being established at Canada's International Development Research Centre (Ottawa), with initial funding of $Can 3.5 million provided by the Centre, the Canadian International Development Agency, the World Bank and UNDP.

International Conference on Nutrition

Representatives of 159 States and the European Economic Community, attending the International Conference on Nutrition (Rome, 5-11 December 1992), adopted a World Declaration on Nutrition in which they declared their determination to eliminate hunger and reduce all forms of malnutrition. They expressed concern that about 780 million people in developing countries did not have access to enough food to meet their daily needs and more than 2 billion people, mostly women and children, were deficient in one or more micronutrients, such as iodine, vitamin A and iron. They called on the United Nations to consider declaring an international decade of food and nutrition to emphasize the objectives of the Declaration, giving particular emphasis to the food and nutrition problems of Africa, Asia and Latin America and the Caribbean.

Also adopted was a Plan of Action for Nutrition, which provided guidelines for Governments, acting in partnership with NGOs, the private sector, local communities, families and households and the international community. The Plan's overall objectives were to ensure continued access by all people to sufficient supplies of safe foods for a nutritionally adequate diet; achieve and maintain health and nutritional well-being; achieve environmentally sound and socially sustainable development for improved nutrition and health; and eliminate famines and famine deaths.

Proposed actions for consideration by Governments to improve nutrition included: incorporating nutritional objectives, considerations and components into development policies and programmes; improving household food security; pro-

tecting consumers through improved food quality and safety; preventing and managing infectious diseases; promoting breast-feeding; caring for the socio-economically deprived and nutritionally vulnerable; preventing and controlling specific micronutrient deficiencies; promoting appropriate diets and healthy lifestyles; and assessing, analysing and monitoring nutrition situations.

ACC activities

The nineteenth session of the ACC Subcommittee on Nutrition was held in Rome from 24 to 29 February 1992.[2] The Subcommittee's annual symposium on nutritional issues in food aid (24 and 25 February) discussed public works supported by food aid, supplementary feeding and refugee nutrition. The Subcommittee drew the attention of ACC to statements it approved on nutrition, refugees and displaced persons and on the benefits of preventing growth failure in early childhood.

The Subcommittee also considered iodine, iron and vitamin-A deficiency; a proposal for a micronutrient forum; nutrition and ethics; evaluating nutrition programmes; institutional development; household food security; long-term nutritional effects on development; future nutrition problems; nutritional surveillance; a proposal for an international decade on food and nutrition in Africa; diet and health in Latin America; activities of the International Dietary Energy Consultative Group; food databases, including the International Network of Food Data Systems (INFOODS), the International Food Intake Directory (INFID) and guidelines for rapid assessment procedures (RAP) for supervisors; the use of powdered milk in non-emergency feeding situations; activities of the working group on food aid; a review of country programmes; and reports from participating agencies.

In October, the Subcommittee issued its *Second Report on the World Nutrition Situation*, which described trends in nutrition from 1975 to 1990.

UNU activities

As part of its ongoing INFOODS project, UNU in 1992 installed computer hardware and software for two subregional databases for Asia and the Pacific, and continued work on regional databases in Africa and Latin America. The aim of the INFOODS project was to improve the availability and quality of food composition data worldwide, particularly in developing countries. Efforts were under way to mobilize support to make the UNU Institute for Natural Resources in Africa the headquarters for the INFOODS regional database in Africa and to include in the database information on African plants having both medicinal and economic value.

The joint UNU/UNICEF RAP project continued to disseminate guidelines for using anthropologically based methods to determine the impact of intervention programmes on health-related behaviours. A Chinese edition of RAP guidelines was completed in 1992, adding to the English, French and Spanish editions already available. RAP workshops were held in Argentina, Peru and Turkey, and a new type of RAP, designed primarily for planners, policy makers and administrators rather than researchers, was conducted in Romania for participants from Eastern Europe and the former USSR.

During the year, UNU continued to work closely with the ACC Subcommittee on Nutrition in assembling information on iron deficiency, the most widespread nutrient deficiency in the world. With the support of the World Bank, UNU established a secretariat for the Group for the Control of Iron Deficiency at the University of California, Berkeley (United States). It was to hold subregional meetings to increase awareness of the functional consequences of iron deficiency and promote the development of national plans to control it. Work had also begun on an extensive data bank of persons concerned with iron deficiency in each country.

UNU nutrition-related publications in 1992 included: *Rapid Assessment Methodologies for Planning and Evaluation of Health Related Programmes, Compiling Data for Food Composition Data Bases, INFOODS Food Composition Data Interchange Handbook* and four issues each of the *Food and Nutrition Bulletin* and *Journal of Food Composition and Analysis*. The University awarded five fellowships in the areas of food science and technology (two to the Instituto de Nutrición de Centro-América y Panamá in Guatemala and one to the National Food Research Institute, Japan); nutrition (California Pacific Medical Center, United States); and nutritional immunology (Memorial University of Newfoundland, Canada).

REFERENCES

[1]WFC/1992/2. [2]ACC/1992/5.

Chapter XII

Human resources, social and cultural development

During 1992, the United Nations continued to promote human resources and cultural development and improved crime prevention and criminal justice programmes.

The new United Nations Commission on Crime Prevention and Criminal Justice held its first session in April.

The General Assembly adopted resolutions in December on crime prevention and criminal justice (resolution 47/91), on international cooperation in combating organized crime (47/87), and on the United Nations African Institute for the Prevention of Crime and the Treatment of Offenders (47/89).

The Economic and Social Council adopted resolutions on organized crime (1992/23) and on preparations for the Ninth United Nations Congress on the Prevention of Crime and the Treatment of Offenders in 1995 (1992/24).

The third *Human Development Report* was published by the United Nations Development Programme in 1992. The report focused on the workings of global markets and how they met, or failed to meet, the needs of the world's poorest people.

The Assembly decided to convene a World Summit for Social Development in 1995 (47/92).

Human resources

UNDP activities

Human Development Report

The *Human Development Report 1992*, prepared by the United Nations Development Programme (UNDP), focused on global markets and their impact on the world's poorest people. The report stated that competitive markets were the best guarantee of efficient production and must be open to all people. They required a regulatory framework, supplemented by judicious social policy action and were of little value if they did not serve human development. The report discussed the concept and measurement of human development under the broad headings of: political freedom and human development; the widening gap in global opportunities; global markets, poor nations and poor people; and a new vision for global human development.

The report's main conclusions were that: economic growth did not automatically improve people's lives; rich and poor countries competed in the global market-place as unequal partners; global markets did not operate freely; the world community needed to provide a social safety net for poor nations and poor people; and industrial and developing nations had the opportunity to design a new global compact that would ensure sustainable human development for all.

Global institutions in the twenty-first century, the report suggested, might include a global central bank, a system of progressive income tax, an international trade organization and a strengthened United Nations system that played an increasingly important role in economic and social matters. The latter could be achieved through the creation of a Development Security Council, which would arrive at a consensus on development policy. The report also suggested that: the World Bank should re-establish its role as a sympathetic intermediary between developing countries and global capital markets; the International Monetary Fund should be strengthened to enable it to impose adjustment programmes not only on developing countries but also on industrial nations; and the General Agreement on Tariffs and Trade should have its mandate enlarged to cover most international trade.

UN research and training institutes

UN Institute for Training and Research

UNITAR activities

The United Nations Institute for Training and Research (UNITAR) continued to focus its efforts on training activities. The Acting Executive Director of UNITAR reported[1] that, in spite of staff reductions, the volume of Institute activities had grown. During the period reviewed (1 July 1991 to 30 June 1992), 98 training events involved some 3,847 participants, in courses lasting up to six months. Voluntary contributions to UNITAR's General Fund amounted to $1 million, while special purpose grants totalled $6.7 million.

A major UNITAR innovation was the introduction of a training programme in peace-keeping and peacemaking for United Nations staff members and the diplomatic personnel of permanent missions to the United Nations. Four forums and one training seminar on peace-keeping and peacemaking were held in New York in 1992.

Training programmes also covered environmental and natural resources management, legal aspects of debt management, disaster relief planning and management, economic and social development, and multilateral diplomacy.

Other recent features of UNITAR training programmes included their growing decentralization and increased reliance on inter-agency cooperation. Courses were organized at country or subregional levels in Africa, Asia, Europe and Latin America. They relied as much as possible on existing training centres in the field, and attracted cooperation from institutions both within and outside the United Nations system.

Financial situation and restructuring of UNITAR

The Secretary-General, in response to a 1991 General Assembly resolution,[2] submitted an October report[3] on UNITAR. He discussed interim measures for the Institute and made recommendations with regard to its future.

As at 31 December 1991, UNITAR owed the United Nations more than $10.1 million—a situation which the Secretary-General said could not be allowed to continue. He concluded that the best course of action would be for the United Nations to take over the UNITAR building in New York in exchange for the cancellation of the debt and coverage of UNITAR's 1992 financial obligations. The New York office of UNITAR would be phased out, and a scaled down UNITAR would be transferred to Geneva. In the first phase of this restructuring, the Secretary-General abolished the post of Under-Secretary-General, and appointed the Director of the UNITAR European Office at Geneva as Acting Executive Director.

On 23 December, by **resolution 47/219 A, section XXIV**, the General Assembly authorized the Secretary-General to commit up to $400,000 from 1 January through 28 February 1993 to cover costs related to the security and maintenance of the UNITAR premises, as well as the cost of maintaining the existing New York staff members for whom placement would be sought elsewhere in the United Nations system.

UN University

UNU activities

In 1992,[4] the United Nations University (UNU), an autonomous academic institution within the United Nations system, continued to carry out research, postgraduate training and the dissemination of knowledge focused on five areas: multilateralism, the environment, science and technology, hunger and poverty, and capacity-building.

Several conferences, forums, seminars and workshops were held during the year, including two international conferences to examine issues of governance in future society, held at Meiji Gakuin University (Yokohama, Japan, March), and at Dartmouth College (Hanover, New Hampshire, United States, May). A meeting on the role of the international scholarly community in strengthening multilateral action was held at Geneva in April and a training course in international law and institutions, concentrating on the strengthening of environmental legislation in the South Pacific region, was held in Samoa in November.

A UNU research and training centre, the UNU International Institute for Software Technology, commenced operations in Macau in July.

During the year, 69 UNU fellows completed studies with various academic institutions in different parts of the world and 53 fellows began their training in the areas of multilateralism, environment, science and technology, hunger and poverty. They included 12 fellows in geothermal energy at the National Energy Authority (Iceland); 8 in remote-sensing technology at the Instituto de Pesquisas Espaciais (Brazil); 1 in mountain ecology at the University of Berne (Switzerland); 3 in science and technology policy at the Universidade Estadual de Campinas (Brazil); 9 in biotechnology at various institutions in Argentina, Brazil, Costa Rica, Mexico and Venezuela; 10 in micro-informatics at institutions in Ireland and Macau; 5 in food science and technology and nutrition at Instituto de Nutrición de Centro América y Panamá (Guatemala), the National Food Research Institute (Japan), the California Pacific Medical Centre (United States) and the Memorial University of Newfoundland (Canada); and 5 in economics and quantitative techniques at the Bangladesh Institute of Development Studies.

Among the books published by UNU in 1992 were: *East-West Migration: The Alternatives; Financial Openness and National Autonomy: Opportunities and Constraints; Industrial Pollution in Japan; The Impact of Labour Migration on Households: a Comparative Study in Seven Asian Countries;* and *The Role of Labour-Intensive Sectors in Japanese Industrialization.*

UNU Council

The Council of UNU did not meet as a whole in 1992, although a meeting of its Bureau was held in June. The thirty-ninth session of the Council was scheduled to take place in 1993.

On 7 February 1992, by **decision 1992/208 B**, the Economic and Social Council authorized the Secretary-General to transmit directly to the 1992 General Assembly the UNU Council report on its work in 1991.

On 22 December, the General Assembly, on the recommendation of the Second Committee, adopted without vote **resolution 47/200**.

United Nations University

The General Assembly,

Recalling its resolution 2951(XXVII) of 11 December 1972 on the establishment of the United Nations University,

Recalling also its resolution 45/220 of 21 December 1990 on the United Nations University,

Recognizing the contributions of the University and the relevance of its work to the concerns of the United Nations,

Having considered the report of the Council of the United Nations University on the work of the University in 1991 and the statement made by the Rector of the United Nations University before the Second Committee on 15 October 1992 concerning the activities of the University in 1992 and its plans for the future,

Noting with appreciation the financial and other contributions made by Governments and organizations in support of the University,

Stressing the need to enhance the visibility of the University and its management,

Taking note of decision 4.3.2 adopted on 27 May 1992 by the Executive Board of the United Nations Educational, Scientific and Cultural Organization at its one hundred and thirty-ninth session,

1. *Takes note* of the progress made in the overall activities of the United Nations University within the framework of its second medium-term perspective, for 1990-1995;

2. *Welcomes* the completion of the permanent headquarters building in Tokyo made available to the University by the Government of Japan;

3. *Takes note* of the progress of the work of the World Institute for Development Economics Research of the United Nations University, in Finland, the Institute for New Technologies of the United Nations University, in the Netherlands, and the Programme for Biotechnology in Latin America and the Caribbean, in Venezuela;

4. *Welcomes:*

(a) The establishment of the International Institute for Software Technology of the United Nations University, in Macau, under the joint sponsorship of the Government of China, the Government of Portugal and the Territory of Macau;

(b) The progress made in the negotiations towards the establishment of the research and training centre on governance, state and society, in Spain;

(c) The intention of the Government of Ghana to act as host to the Institute for Natural Resources in Africa;

(d) The initiation of the activities of the Institute of Advanced Studies in Japan;

5. *Stresses* the need, in the light of the institutional development of the University, to maintain and enhance the programming and coordinating role of the University Centre with a view to ensuring the overall coherence, organic integrity and universality of the activities of the University;

6. *Notes* the valuable contributions made by the University to the work of the United Nations, including its input into Agenda 21, adopted by the United Nations Conference on Environment and Development, and encourages the organs, organizations and bodies of the United Nations system to avail themselves of the research capacity and research results of the University, which should come to serve as one of the principal academic institutions of the United Nations through its global network of research and training centres and programmes;

7. *Requests* the University to pursue its efforts:

(a) To enhance its prominence, notably through selection of timely and important research topics, such as the Plan of Action for Academic Initiatives at United Nations Headquarters, launched by the Rector of the United Nations University, intensified coordination and cooperation with other United Nations bodies, wider dissemination of its research results and expanded collaboration with an even wider international academic community of institutions and scholars, particularly in developing countries;

(b) To keep under review the management and administrative functions of the University, particularly with a view to ensuring their efficiency and economy;

(c) To foster its substantive collaboration with other research and training institutes within and outside the United Nations system;

8. *Invites* the Council of the United Nations University:

(a) To intensify its efforts to promote the activities of the University and make them more widely and better known;

(b) To continue to contribute to the effective management of the University, including the administration of its funds;

(c) To study the possibility of reducing the frequency of its meetings, in the interests of efficiency and economy;

9. *Requests* the University to continue its fund-raising efforts vigorously, particularly the effort to increase its Endowment Fund, and appeals to the international community to make voluntary contributions to the University, in particular to its Endowment Fund.

General Assembly resolution 47/200

22 December 1992   Meeting 93   Adopted without vote

Approved by Second Committee (A/47/729) without vote, 7 December (meeting 48); draft by Vice-Chairman (A/C.2/47/L.65), based on informal consultations on 23-nation draft (A/C.2/47/L.43); agenda item 89 *(b)*.

Meeting numbers. GA 47th session: 2nd Committee 3, 15, 41, 42, 44, 47, 48; plenary 93.

REFERENCES

[1]A/47/14. [2]YUN 1991, p. 648, GA res. 46/180, 19 Dec. 1991. [3]A/47/458. [4]E/1993/40.

Social and cultural development

Social aspects of development

World social situation

In response to an Economic and Social Council resolution of 1991,[1] the Secretary-General presented in April[2] a draft framework for the 1993 report on the world social situation.

At the Council's request the draft was reoriented to reflect the intrinsic relationship between economic growth and social development and to analyse in depth the impact of economic problems in the developing countries on the world social situation. The Secretary-General noted that the first chapter of part one of the reoriented report would examine these issues taking into account national and international conditions. Specific social problems including population; hunger, malnutrition and food supplies; housing and sanitation; education and literacy; health; and unemployment and low-productivity employment would be considered in subsequent chapters. Part two would take up such issues as changes in economic and social institutions, challenges to social security policies, and the integration and disintegration of communities.

On 21 April,[3] the Administrative Committee on Coordination (ACC) said it would review the draft report to ensure that it had an integrated interdisciplinary focus.

ECONOMIC AND SOCIAL COUNCIL ACTION

On 30 July, on the recommendation of its Social Committee, the Economic and Social Council adopted without vote **resolution 1992/26.**

World social situation

The Economic and Social Council,

Recalling its resolutions 1989/72 of 24 May 1989 and 1991/4 of 30 May 1991 and taking note of General Assembly resolution 46/95 of 16 December 1991,

Acknowledging the relationship between development, including social development, and the enjoyment by everyone of economic, social and cultural rights, as well as civil and political rights, and recognizing the importance of creating the conditions whereby everyone may enjoy these rights, as set out in the International Covenants on Human Rights,

Noting that in paragraph 4 of its resolution 1991/4 the Secretary-General was requested to reorient the draft framework for the 1993 report on the world social situation so that it was in consonance with the requests set forth in paragraph 4 of its resolution 1989/72, and to submit it to the Council for consideration at its substantive session of 1992,

Bearing in mind the importance of a well-balanced report on the world social situation for increasing international awareness of the efforts being made towards achieving the goals of social progress and better standards of living, established in the Charter of the United Nations, as well as of the obstacles to further progress,

Deeply concerned about the continued worsening of the economic situation in many developing countries, particularly the least developed countries, as evidenced by the significant decline in living conditions, the persistence and increase of widespread poverty in a large number of those countries and the decline of their main social and economic indicators,

Bearing in mind that certain developing countries have been able to achieve some economic and social progress,

Having considered the draft framework for the 1993 report on the world social situation,

1. *Notes* that in the preparation of the draft framework for the 1993 report on the world social situation efforts have been made to reorient it in accordance with the requests of the Council and the General Assembly;

2. *Reaffirms its request* set forth in paragraph 4 of its resolution 1989/72 that, in preparing the next report on the world social situation, the Secretary-General should give high priority to an analysis of the main indicators of social progress and standards of living and make a comprehensive analysis of the main causes and circumstances that explain negative trends in those indicators, and reaffirms that chapters devoted to the study of specific social problems must be related to global economic and social situations, taking into account both national and international conditions;

3. *Requests* the Secretary-General, in preparing the 1993 report, to also take into account the intrinsic relationship between economic growth and social development and to analyse in depth the impact of the economic problems of the developing countries on the world social situation;

4. *Also requests* the Secretary-General to submit to the General Assembly at its forty-eighth session, through the Economic and Social Council, the 1993 report on the world social situation.

Economic and Social Council resolution 1992/26

30 July 1992   Meeting 41   Adopted without vote

Approved by Social Committee (E/1992/106) without vote, 27 July (meeting 20); draft by Pakistan for Group of 77 (E/1992/C.2/L.9), as orally revised; agenda item 19.

Earlier, on 7 February, by **decision 1992/204,** the Council decided that its coordination segment should include the theme of assistance in the eradication of poverty and support to vulnerable groups during the implementation of structural adjustment programmes.

On 31 July, by **decision 1992/30,** the Council took note of the report of the Secretary-General on policies and activities related to assistance in the eradication of poverty and of his report on the prevention and control of human immunodeficiency virus (HIV)/acquired immunodeficiency syndrome (AIDS).

Social development

World summit for social development

The Secretary-General, in response to an Economic and Social Council decision of 1991,[4] submitted a July note[5] on consultations by the Special Representative with Member States on the possibility of convening a world summit for social development. The consultations confirmed that there was widespread support in all regions for convening the summit.

ECONOMIC AND SOCIAL COUNCIL ACTION

On 30 July, the Economic and Social Council, on the recommendation of its Social Committee, adopted without vote **resolution 1992/27**.

Social development

The Economic and Social Council,

Bearing in mind General Assembly resolution 46/139 of 17 December 1991 and Economic and Social Council decision 1991/230 of 30 May 1991,

Welcoming the appointment by the Secretary-General of a Special Representative to assist him in the consultations requested by the Council in decision 1991/230,

Bearing in mind the need to involve the appropriate organs, organizations and programmes of the United Nations system, in particular the Commission for Social Development, in the preparations for the proposed world summit for social development,

Taking note of the statement made by the President of the Economic and Social Council at the conclusion of the high-level segment of the Council, on 8 July 1992, that there was broad support for a summit,

Having considered the report of the Special Representative of the Secretary-General on the results of the consultations carried out in response to the request made by the Council in its decision 1991/230,

1. *Takes note* of the report of the Special Representative of the Secretary-General and the positive results of the consultations on the possibility of convening a world summit for social development;

2. *Expresses its appreciation* to the Secretary-General and the Special Representative for their efforts in carrying out a comprehensive process of consultations on this matter;

3. *Recommends* that the General Assembly convene a world summit for social development, at the level of heads of State or Government, to be held in early 1995;

4. *Also recommends* that the General Assembly, at its forty-seventh session, take action on the proposed summit, including appropriate decisions on the agenda, means of preparation for the summit and other relevant modalities;

5. *Requests* the Secretary-General to carry out consultations on the present resolution and present an oral report to the General Assembly at its forty-seventh session.

Economic and Social Council resolution 1992/27

30 July 1992   Meeting 41   Adopted without vote

Approved by Social Committee (E/1992/106) without vote, 24 July (meeting 19); 118-nation draft (E/1992/C.2/L.10, orally corrected); agenda item 19.

Sponsors: Azerbaijan, Algeria, Angola, Argentina, Australia, Austria, Bahamas, Bangladesh, Barbados, Belarus, Belgium, Benin, Bolivia, Botswana, Brazil, Bulgaria, Burkina Faso, Cameroon, Canada, Cape Verde, Chad, Chile, China, Colombia, Congo, Costa Rica, Côte d'Ivoire, Cuba, Cyprus, Czechoslovakia, Denmark, Ecuador, Egypt, El Salvador, Estonia, Ethiopia, Finland, France, Ghana, Greece, Guatemala, Guinea, Guinea-Bissau, Haiti, Honduras, Hungary, Iceland, India, Indonesia, Iran, Iraq, Ireland, Italy, Jamaica, Japan, Jordan, Kenya, Lebanon, Lesotho, Libyan Arab Jamahiriya, Liechtenstein, Luxembourg, Madagascar, Malawi, Malaysia, Mali, Malta, Mauritania, Mexico, Mongolia, Morocco, Myanmar, Namibia, Nepal, Netherlands, New Zealand, Nicaragua, Niger, Nigeria, Norway, Pakistan, Panama, Papua New Guinea, Paraguay, Peru, Philippines, Poland, Portugal, Republic of Korea, Romania, Rwanda, Saint Lucia, Saint Vincent and the Grenadines, Samoa, Sao Tome and Principe, Senegal, Seychelles, Sierra Leone, Spain, Suriname, Sweden, Togo, Trinidad and Tobago, Tunisia, Turkey, Uganda, Ukraine, United Republic of Tanzania, United Kingdom, United States, Uruguay, Venezuela, Viet Nam, Yemen, Yugoslavia, Zaire, Zambia, Zimbabwe.

GENERAL ASSEMBLY ACTION

On 16 December, following a recommendation of the Third Committee, the General Assembly adopted without vote **resolution 47/92**.

Convening of a world summit for social development

The General Assembly,

Recalling its resolution 46/139 of 17 December 1991 and Economic and Social Council decision 1991/230 of 30 May 1991 and taking note of Council resolution 1992/27 of 30 July 1992,

Having considered the report of the Special Representative of the Secretary-General on the consultations requested by the Economic and Social Council in its decision 1991/230,

Recalling its resolution 45/199 of 21 December 1990, by which it adopted the International Development Strategy for the Fourth United Nations Development Decade, which includes as one of its principal themes the need to strengthen the mutually reinforcing relationship between economic growth and human welfare,

Recalling also its resolution 42/125 of 7 December 1987, by which it endorsed the Guiding Principles for Developmental Social Welfare Policies and Programmes in the Near Future,

Welcoming the support expressed for the convening of a world summit for social development at the Tenth Conference of Heads of State or Government of Non-Aligned Countries, held at Jakarta from 1 to 6 September 1992,

Conscious that increased international cooperation for economic and social development would significantly contribute to the strengthening of international peace and security,

Convinced of the need for the enhancement of the social component of sustainable development to achieve economic growth with social justice,

Reaffirming the right and responsibility of each State to determine freely its own priorities, policies and objectives for social development in accordance with its constitutional and legal systems and social conditions,

Conscious of the need to address ways and means for the elimination of widespread poverty and the full enjoyment of human rights, including civil, political, economic, social and cultural rights, as interrelated goals,

Acknowledging the need for an integrated approach in the fields of social and economic development in the United Nations system in order to deploy more effectively the widespread experience of the system in those areas,

Stressing that poverty, unemployment and social integration are closely interrelated in all societies and have a particularly profound impact on developing countries,

Convinced that a world summit for social development should contribute to efforts by all countries to foster sustainable development and to promote policies against poverty and unemployment in all societies,

1. *Expresses its appreciation* to the Secretary-General and his Special Representative for their efforts in carrying out a comprehensive process of consultations on this matter;

2. *Welcomes with satisfaction* the report of the Special Representative of the Secretary-General concerning the positive outcome of the consultations on the possibility of convening a world summit for social development;

3. *Decides* to convene a World Summit for Social Development at the level of heads of State or Government early in 1995;

4. *Accepts with deep appreciation* the generous offer of the Government of Denmark to act as host to the Summit;

5. *Decides* that the Summit shall have the following objectives:

(*a*) To further the objectives of the Charter of the United Nations, as stated in Article 55, to promote "higher standards of living, full employment, and conditions of economic and social progress and development", and "solutions of international economic, social, health, and related problems", with particular focus on social development aspects;

(*b*) To express a shared world-wide commitment to put the needs of people at the centre of development and of international cooperation as a major priority of international relations;

(*c*) To stimulate international cooperation at the bilateral, regional and multilateral levels, through governmental, private and non-governmental initiatives, in order to assist in the implementation of nationally appropriate, effective and efficient social policies and to formulate strategies which will enable all citizens to be actively engaged in those policies;

(*d*) To formulate strategies on goals, policies and priority actions that could be adopted at the national, regional and international levels to address, in the different development realities, core issues of shared universal concern in the field of social development, giving particular attention to the needs of the least developed countries;

(*e*) To create international awareness of and address the modalities to attain the necessary balance between economic efficiency and social justice in a growth-oriented, equitable and sustainable development environment, in accordance with nationally defined priorities;

(*f*) To address, in creative ways, the interaction between the social function of the State, market responses to social demands and the imperatives of sustainable development;

(*g*) To identify common problems of socially marginalized and disadvantaged groups and promote the integration of those groups into society, highlighting the need for societies to equalize opportunities for all members;

(*h*) To promote programmes to ensure legal protection, foster effective social welfare programmes and enhance education and training for different groups in all societies, including the marginalized and disadvantaged groups;

(*i*) To assist in ensuring a more effective delivery of social services for the more disadvantaged sectors of society;

(*j*) To highlight the need to mobilize resources for social development at the local, national, regional and international levels;

(*k*) To make appropriate recommendations regarding more effective action by the United Nations system in the sphere of social development, in particular, measures and policies for the revitalization of the Commission for Social Development;

6. *Decides*, taking into account the objectives set out in the present resolution, that the core issues affecting all societies to be addressed by the Summit are:

(*a*) The enhancement of social integration, particularly of the more disadvantaged and marginalized groups;

(*b*) Alleviation and reduction of poverty;

(*c*) Expansion of productive employment;

7. *Decides* to establish a Preparatory Committee open to the participation of all States Members of the United Nations and members of the specialized agencies, with the participation of observers in accordance with the established practice of the General Assembly;

8. *Decides also* that the Preparatory Committee shall hold an organizational session for one week in April 1993 and, at the level of personal representatives of the heads of State or Government or other appropriate high-level representatives specifically designated by Governments, three substantive sessions in 1994 of no more than ten working days each, at the Headquarters of the United Nations;

9. *Decides* that the Preparatory Committee, at its organizational session, shall elect, with due regard to equitable geographical representation, a Bureau, of which the host country, Denmark, shall be an ex officio member;

10. *Decides* that the Preparatory Committee shall:

(*a*) Consider reports submitted by the organs, organizations and programmes of the United Nations system on matters relating to the World Summit for Social Development;

(*b*) Draft the provisional agenda of the Summit, in accordance with the provisions of the present resolution;

(*c*) Prepare the draft decisions for the Summit and submit them to the Summit for consideration and adoption;

(*d*) Adopt other appropriate decisions relevant to the successful preparations for, outcome of and follow-up to the Summit;

11. *Requests* the Secretary-General to establish an ad hoc secretariat unit, including personnel of the relevant organizations and programmes of the United Nations system, to assist in the preparatory process and the substantive work of the Preparatory Committee;

12. *Recommends* that the Commission for Social Development give consideration to the agenda of the Summit at its thirty-third session, in 1993, and to the question of holding an extraordinary session dedicated solely to the question of the Summit before the first substantive session of the Preparatory Committee in 1994;

13. *Recommends also* that the Economic and Social Council, at the high-level segment of its substantive session of 1993, consider the theme, "World Summit for Social Development";

14. *Requests* the regional commissions to include in their programme of work for 1993 the question of the World Summit for Social Development, with particular emphasis on the social situation in their respective regions, and to formulate proposals thereon and prepare an integrated report to be submitted to the General Assembly at its forty-eighth session;

15. *Requests* the organs, organizations and programmes of the United Nations system, as well as other intergovernmental organizations, in particular the United Nations Children's Fund, the United Nations Development Programme, the International Labour Organisation, the World Health Organization, the United Nations Educational, Scientific and Cultural Organization, the United Nations Population Fund, the United

Nations Centre for Human Settlements, the International Monetary Fund and the World Bank to contribute fully to the preparations for the Summit;

16. *Recommends* that the Preparatory Committee take full account, as appropriate, of the preparations for and the outcome of the World Conference on Human Rights to be held in 1993 and the International Conference on Population and Development to be held in 1994 and of the preparations for the Fourth World Conference on Women: Action for Equality, Development and Peace, to be held in 1995;

17. *Requests* the non-governmental organizations in consultative status with the Economic and Social Council to contribute in accordance with established practice to the Summit and the preparatory process, as appropriate;

18. *Invites* the Secretary-General to provide the resources required for initiating the preparatory process of the Summit in 1993, including through redeployment;

19. *Also invites* the Secretary-General to establish a trust fund and to mobilize voluntary contributions from public and private sources for the financing of the additional activities required by the preparations for and the holding of the Summit;

20. *Decides* that the resources of the trust fund should be utilized to finance the participation of the least developed countries in the Summit and the preparatory process;

21. *Requests* the Preparatory Committee to report to the General Assembly at its forty-eighth and forty-ninth sessions on the progress of work of the Committee and the preparations for the Summit.

General Assembly resolution 47/92

16 December 1992   Meeting 89   Adopted without vote

Approved by Third Committee (A/47/703/Add.1 & Corr.1) without vote, 9 December (meeting 61); 123-nation draft (A/C.3/47/L.51/Rev.1); agenda item 93 *(a)*.

Sponsors: Afghanistan, Albania, Algeria, Angola, Antigua and Barbuda, Argentina, Australia, Azerbaijan, Bahamas, Bangladesh, Barbados, Belarus, Belize, Benin, Bolivia, Botswana, Brazil, Burkina Faso, Cameroon, Canada, Cape Verde, Central African Republic, Chad, Chile, China, Colombia, Costa Rica, Côte d'Ivoire, Cyprus, Cuba, Democratic People's Republic of Korea, Denmark, Dominican Republic, Ecuador, Egypt, El Salvador, Ethiopia, Fiji, Finland, France, Gambia, Ghana, Greece, Grenada, Guatemala, Guinea, Guinea-Bissau, Guyana, Honduras, Iceland, India, Indonesia, Iran, Iraq, Israel, Italy, Jamaica, Jordan, Kenya, Lebanon, Lesotho, Liberia, Libyan Arab Jamahiriya, Liechtenstein, Luxembourg, Madagascar, Malawi, Malaysia, Mali, Malta, Marshall Islands, Mexico, Micronesia, Mongolia, Morocco, Myanmar, Namibia, Nepal, Netherlands, New Zealand, Nicaragua, Niger, Nigeria, Norway, Pakistan, Panama, Papua New Guinea, Paraguay, Peru, Philippines, Poland, Portugal, Republic of Korea, Romania, Rwanda, Saint Kitts and Nevis, Saint Lucia, San Marino, Sao Tome and Principe, Senegal, Sierra Leone, Slovenia, Spain, Sri Lanka, Sudan, Suriname, Swaziland, Sweden, Thailand, Togo, Trinidad and Tobago, Tunisia, Turkey, Uganda, Ukraine, United Republic of Tanzania, Uruguay, Vanuatu, Venezuela, Viet Nam, Yemen, Zambia, Zimbabwe.

Financial implications. 5th Committee, A/47/788; S-G, A/C.3/47/L.80, A/C.5/47/70.

Meeting numbers. GA 47th session: 3rd Committee 11-18, 22, 23, 25, 30, 41, 54, 56, 59-61; 5th Committee 45; plenary 89.

Evaluation of social development activities

The Secretary-General submitted a progress report to the Committee for Programme and Coordination (CPC) in March[6] on an in-depth evaluation of the social development activities of the United Nations. The report presented an overview of social development activities, their structure and strategies, and reviewed the available information.

It made recommendations on the scope of the final in-depth evaluation, the issues to be addressed and methods of data collection. They were endorsed by CPC at its thirty-second session in May[7].

International year for tolerance

In July,[8] a resolution, adopted by the United Nations Educational, Scientific and Cultural Organization (UNESCO) in 1991, inviting its Director-General to consult with the United Nations on declaring 1995 the United Nations year for tolerance, was transmitted to the Secretary-General in a letter from the UNESCO Director-General.

The Economic and Social Council took note of the letter on 30 July by **decision 1992/267** and conveyed it to the General Assembly.

GENERAL ASSEMBLY ACTION

On 18 December, acting on a recommendation of the Third Committee, the General Assembly adopted without vote **resolution 47/124**.

United Nations year for tolerance

The General Assembly,

Recalling that the Charter of the United Nations affirms in its preamble that to practise tolerance is one of the principles to be applied to attain the ends pursued by the United Nations of preventing war and maintaining peace,

Recalling also that one of the purposes of the United Nations as set forth in the Charter is the achievement of international cooperation in solving international problems of an economic, social, cultural or humanitarian character and in promoting and encouraging respect for human rights and for fundamental freedoms for all without distinction as to race, sex, language or religion,

Mindful of the Universal Declaration of Human Rights and of the International Covenants on Human Rights,

Taking note with appreciation of resolution 5.6 of the General Conference of the United Nations Educational, Scientific and Cultural Organization, concerning the proclamation of 1995 as the United Nations year for tolerance,

Taking note of Economic and Social Council decision 1992/267 of 30 July 1992 and of the note by the Secretary-General,

Bearing in mind its decision 35/424 of 5 December 1980 and Economic and Social Council resolution 1980/67 of 25 July 1980 concerning guidelines for international years and anniversaries,

1. *Welcomes* the initiative of the United Nations Educational, Scientific and Cultural Organization in seeking to have 1995 proclaimed the United Nations year for tolerance;

2. *Requests* the Director-General of the United Nations Educational, Scientific and Cultural Organization to prepare, in cooperation with other interested organizations, his suggestions on the observance of the United Nations year for tolerance and to submit them to the General Assembly at its forty-eighth session, through the Economic and Social Council;

3. *Invites* the Economic and Social Council to consider at its next session the question of proclaiming 1995 the United Nations year for tolerance and to transmit a recommendation to the General Assembly at its forty-eighth session;

4. *Encourages* the United Nations Educational, Scientific and Cultural Organization to prepare, in accordance with General Conference resolution 5.6, a declaration on tolerance;

5. *Decides* to consider the question at its forty-eighth session.

General Assembly resolution 47/124

18 December 1992   Meeting 92   Adopted without vote

Approved by Third Committee (A/47/678/Add.2) without vote, 3 December (meeting 56); 14-nation draft (A/C.3/47/L.53); agenda item 97 *(b)*.

Sponsors: Afghanistan, Albania, Argentina, Austria, Azerbaijan, Chile, Czechoslovakia, Egypt, Indonesia, Morocco, Pakistan, Philippines, Tunisia, Turkey.

Meeting numbers. GA 47the session: 3rd Committee 47-56; plenary 92.

The family

International Year of the Family

The Secretary-General, in response to a 1991 General Assembly resolution,[9] submitted a December report[10] to the Commission for Social Development on the state of preparations for the 1994 International Year of the Family. He reviewed the preparatory process for observance of the Year, reporting that more than 100 countries had initiated actions and that the regional commissions and several bodies and specialized agencies of the United Nations system were also participating.

He stated, however, that several countries had taken little action and the same might be said of several intergovernmental and non-governmental organizations (NGOs), which had a substantive interest in family issues.

As at 20 November 1992, contributions to the Voluntary Fund for the International Year of the Family totalled $1,255,185, of which Governments had contributed $73,055, and organizations and individuals, $1,182,130.

Population growth and changing social conditions

In a November note[11] to the Commission for Social Development, the Secretary-General transmitted a report on the Expert Group Meeting on Social Consequences of Population Growth and Changing Social Conditions, with Particular Emphasis on the Family (Vienna, 21-25 September). The meeting discussed the current situation of the family in the context of: kinship, the community and civil society; national policies affecting families in the context of social and demographic change; and prerequisites for policy-making and implementation.

The meeting concluded, among other things, that demographic, economic, political, organizational and environmental changes frequently exerted serious negative influences on the family. It recommended that the Commission urge Govern-

ments to: give social policies priority on their national agendas; coordinate and harmonize policies affecting the family in order to resolve conflicts and avoid negative side-effects; and evaluate, in the planning of each project, its possible impact on families.

The meeting concluded that the economic well-being of the vast majority of families depended on the health of the national economy and the distribution of national resources. It recommended that the Commission urge Governments to balance macro-level economic policies, especially in countries undergoing structural adjustments, with microlevel policies to enable families to participate constructively in those adjustments through: training and retraining; access to credit for small business enterprises; and the promotion of cooperatives and self-help organizations.

The meeting concluded that, in developing and developed countries, many families were unable to achieve basic economic security, and redistributive public programmes were necessary to fill the gap. It recommended that the Commission urge Governments to: extend contributory and non-contributory programmes of income maintenance to cover the elderly, single-parent families, dependent children, the disabled and the unemployed; ensure that public programmes were equitable in terms of gender, age, ethnicity and other considerations; and carefully target non-contributory assistance and subsidies on families and individuals in need.

Cooperatives

In response to a 1989 General Assembly resolution,[12] the Secretary-General submitted a May report[13] to the Assembly, through the Economic and Social Council, on the status and role of cooperatives in the light of new economic and social trends.

The report was based on 48 replies from governmental agencies or national organizations of cooperatives in 42 countries to a questionnaire from the Secretary-General. It concluded that cooperative enterprises played a key role in the private sector and in agriculture in particular, offering governments a promising economic option when faced with the need for severe structural transformation. Farmers' cooperatives were key institutions in the revitalization of agriculture and the development of rural areas, particularly in Africa, Asia and Latin America and deserved more attention than they had received. It was noted that the global membership of savings and credit cooperatives (credit unions) had grown by more than 8 per cent a year since 1985.

ECONOMIC AND SOCIAL COUNCIL ACTION

On 30 July, the Economic and Social Council, on the recommendation of its Social Committee, adopted without vote **resolution 1992/25**.

The role of cooperatives in the light of new economic and social trends

The Economic and Social Council,

Recalling General Assembly resolution 44/58 of 8 December 1989, particularly paragraph 4, in which the Secretary-General was requested, in consultation with Member States and relevant organizations of the United Nations system, to prepare a report on the status and role of cooperatives in the light of new economic and social trends,

Welcoming the report of the Secretary-General on the status and role of cooperatives in the light of new economic and social trends,

Recognizing the importance of the policy-oriented research being undertaken by the Centre for Social Development and Humanitarian Affairs of the Secretariat concerning the relevance of cooperatives to the achievement of the social policy objectives set forth in the Guiding Principles for Developmental Social Welfare Policies and Programmes in the Near Future, in the execution of which it acts as focal point within the United Nations system,

Bearing in mind that 1995 will mark the centenary of the establishment of the International Cooperative Alliance,

Taking note with satisfaction of the important recommendations contained in the report of the Secretary-General directed towards ensuring the best possible means of dealing with the issue of cooperatives in the light of their broad significance in contributing to the solution of major economic and social problems,

Welcoming the recommendation contained in paragraph 4 *(a)* of the report of the Secretary-General, and bearing in mind the substantial support shown by Governments and by the international cooperative movement for the idea of observing an international day of cooperatives,

Expressing its appreciation to government agencies, national organizations representing cooperatives, specialized agencies and other organizations, especially the Committee for the Promotion and Advancement of Cooperatives, for their valuable contribution,

1. *Takes note with appreciation* of the report of the Secretary-General on the status and role of cooperatives in the light of new economic and social trends;

2. *Recommends* that the General Assembly proclaim an international day of cooperatives to be observed on the first Saturday in July 1995, to mark the centenary of the International Cooperative Alliance, and that it consider the possibility of observing an international day in future years;

3. *Encourages* Governments to consider fully the potential of cooperatives for contributing to the solution of economic, social and environmental problems, in formulating national development strategies;

4. *Encourages* the Centre for Social Development and Humanitarian Affairs of the Secretariat to redouble its efforts of support and coordination in order to achieve the social policy objectives set forth in the Guiding Principles for Developmental Social Welfare Policies and Programmes in the Near Future;

5. *Invites* government agencies, national organizations representing cooperatives, specialized agencies and other organizations, especially the Committee for the Promotion and Advancement of Cooperatives, to maintain and increase their programmes of support to the international cooperative movement, to the extent possible within existing resources;

6. *Also invites,* as it did in its resolution 1668(LII) of 1 June 1972, the specialized agencies that have a substantial interest in cooperatives, especially the United Nations Industrial Development Organization, as well as other organizations, especially the World Bank and the International Fund for Agricultural Development, and other concerned international organizations of cooperatives that are not yet members of the Committee for the Promotion and Advancement of Cooperatives, to become members at an early date in order to ensure its effectiveness by their contribution of appropriate resources;

7. *Recommends* that the General Assembly request the Secretary-General, to the extent possible within existing resources, to maintain and increase the support provided by the United Nations to the programmes and objectives of the international cooperative movement and, in his next report on the status and role of cooperatives in the light of new economic and social trends, to indicate the progress made towards that goal.

Economic and Social Council resolution 1992/25

30 July 1992   Meeting 41   Adopted without vote

Approved by Social Committee (E/1992/106) without vote, 24 July (meeting 19); 21-nation draft (E/1992/C.2/L.7/Rev.1); agenda item 19.
Sponsors: Benin, Bolivia, Canada, Chile, Costa Rica, Côte d'Ivoire, Ecuador, Guatemala, Guinea-Bissau, Honduras, Lebanon, Lesotho, Malawi, Mongolia, Morocco, Nicaragua, Philippines, Poland, Togo, United States, Viet Nam.

GENERAL ASSEMBLY ACTION

On 16 December, the General Assembly, on the recommendation of the Third Committee, adopted without vote **resolution 47/90.**

The role of cooperatives in the light of new economic and social trends

The General Assembly,

Recalling its resolution 44/58 of 8 December 1989, in particular paragraph 4 thereof, and taking note of Economic and Social Council resolution 1992/25 of 30 July 1992,

Welcoming the report of the Secretary-General on the status and role of cooperatives in the light of new economic and social trends,

Recognizing the importance of the policy-oriented research being undertaken by the Centre for Social Development and Humanitarian Affairs of the Secretariat concerning the relevance of cooperatives to the achievement of the social policy objectives set forth in the Guiding Principles for Developmental Social Welfare Policies and Programmes in the Near Future, in the execution of which it acts as a focal point within the United Nations system,

Bearing in mind that 1995 will mark the centenary of the establishment of the International Cooperative Alliance,

Taking note with satisfaction of the important recommendations contained in the report of the Secretary-General directed towards ensuring the best possible means of dealing with the issue of cooperatives in the light of their broad significance in contributing to the solution of major economic and social problems,

Welcoming the recommendation contained in paragraph 4 *(a)* of the report of the Secretary-General, and bearing in mind the substantial support shown by Governments and by the international cooperative movement for the idea of observing an international day of cooperatives,

Expressing its appreciation to government agencies, national organizations representing cooperatives, the specialized agencies and other organizations, especially the Committee for the Promotion and Advancement of Cooperatives, for their valuable contribution,

1. *Takes note with appreciation* of the report of the Secretary-General on the status and role of cooperatives in the light of new economic and social trends;

2. *Proclaims* the first Saturday of July 1995 to be International Day of Cooperatives, marking the centenary of the establishment of the International Cooperative Alliance, and decides to consider the possibility of observing an international day of cooperatives in future years;

3. *Encourages* Governments to consider fully the potential of cooperatives for contributing to the solution of economic, social and environmental problems in formulating national development strategies;

4. *Encourages* the Centre for Social Development and Humanitarian Affairs of the Secretariat to redouble its efforts of support and coordination in order to achieve the social policy objectives set forth in the Guiding Principles for Developmental Social Welfare Policies and Programmes in the Near Future;

5. *Invites* government agencies, national organizations representing cooperatives, the specialized agencies and other organizations, especially the Committee for the Promotion and Advancement of Cooperatives, to maintain and increase their programmes of support to the international cooperative movement, within existing resources;

6. *Also invites*, as the Economic and Social Council already did in its resolution 1668(LII) of 1 June 1972, the specialized agencies that have a substantial interest in cooperatives, especially the United Nations Industrial Development Organization, and other organizations, particularly the World Bank and the International Fund for Agricultural Development, as well as other relevant international organizations of cooperatives that are not yet members of the Committee for the Promotion and Advancement of Cooperatives, to become members at an early date in order to ensure its effectiveness by their contribution of appropriate resources;

7. *Requests* the Secretary-General, within existing resources, to maintain and increase the support provided by the United Nations to the programmes and objectives of the international cooperative movement, and to submit a report to the General Assembly at its forty-ninth session on the status and role of cooperatives in the light of new economic and social trends, indicating in his report the progress made towards that goal.

General Assembly resolution 47/90

16 December 1992   Meeting 89   Adopted without vote

Approved by Third Committee (A/47/703) without vote, 2 November (meeting 25); 33-nation draft (A/C.3/47/L.17); agenda item 93 *(a)*.

Sponsors: Belarus, Benin, Cameroon, Canada, Chile, Costa Rica, Côte d'Ivoire, Dominican Republic, Ecuador, Guatemala, Guinea, Guinea-Bissau, Honduras, Indonesia, Kenya, Lao People's Democratic Republic, Lebanon, Lesotho, Malawi, Micronesia, Mongolia, Morocco, Nepal, Nicaragua, Papua New Guinea, Philippines, Poland, Russian Federation, Rwanda, Togo, United States, Viet Nam, United Republic of Tanzania.

Meeting numbers. GA 47th session: 3rd Committee 11-18, 22, 23, 25; plenary 89.

Institutional machinery

Commission for Social Development

On 28 July, by **decision 1992/266**, the Economic and Social Council decided that the thirty-third session of the Commission for Social Development, which was to have been held at Vienna from 1 to 10 February 1993, would be held from 8 to 17 February 1993.

UN Research Institute for Social Development

The United Nations Research Institute for Social Development (UNRISD), an autonomous institution within the United Nations system, was established to promote research on the social dimensions of development. During 1992 it carried out research on: the environment, sustainable development and social change; the social impact of crisis and adjustment policies; participation and changes in property relations in communist and post-communist societies; ethnic conflict and development; political violence and social movements; refugees, returnees and local society; the socio-economic and political impact of the production, trade and use of illicit narcotic drugs; and patterns of consumption as qualitative indicators of development.

UNRISD held a conference on the Social Dimensions of Environment and Sustainable Development (Valletta, Malta, 22 to 25 April), attended by 80 participants from 31 countries and 18 international and bilateral development agencies. A workshop on political violence and social movements (Geneva, 4-6 May) considered case studies from Colombia, Italy, Lebanon, Northern Ireland, Peru, South Africa, Spain, and Sri Lanka.

The UNRISD Board held its thirtieth session at Geneva on 6 and 7 July.

UNRISD published a number of books, monographs, and discussion papers during the year, as well as its newsletter, *UNRISD News*, in English, French and Spanish.

Crime prevention and criminal justice

Commission on crime prevention and criminal justice

The Commission on Crime Prevention and Criminal Justice, established by the Economic and Social Council in 1992 (see below), held its first session at Vienna from 21 to 30 April.[14]

The Commission considered the implementation of the recommendations of the 1991 Ministerial Meeting on the creation of an effective United Nations Crime Prevention and Criminal Justice programme[15] to strengthen international cooperation in crime prevention and criminal justice and prepare for the Ninth United

Nations Congress on the Prevention of Crime and the Treatment of Offenders in 1995.

The Commission recommended that the Economic and Social Council adopt three draft resolutions on: the implementation of a 1991 Assembly resolution concerning operational activities and coordination in the field of crime prevention and criminal justice;[16] organized crime; and preparations for the Ninth United Nations Congress on the Prevention of Crime and the Treatment of Offenders. (see below)

On 30 July, by **decision 1992/274**, the Economic and Social Council took note of the report of the Commission on its first session and endorsed its adopted resolutions and decisions. The Council also approved the provisional agenda and documentation for the second session of the Commission. On the same date, by **decision 1992/275**, the Council decided that its decision 1992/274, with regard to chapter I, sections A and B, of the report of the Commission, should also apply to section C of that report, containing Commission resolutions calling for action by the Council.

ECONOMIC AND SOCIAL COUNCIL ACTION

On 6 February, the Economic and Social Council adopted **resolution 1992/1** without vote.

Establishment of the Commission on Crime Prevention and Criminal Justice

The Economic and Social Council,

Taking note of General Assembly resolution 46/152 of 18 December 1991 on the creation of an effective United Nations crime prevention and criminal justice programme,

1. *Adopts* the statement of principles and programme of action of the United Nations crime prevention and criminal justice programme, contained in the annex to General Assembly resolution 46/152;

2. *Decides:*

(a) To dissolve the Committee on Crime Prevention and Control;

(b) To establish the Commission on Crime Prevention and Criminal Justice as a functional commission of the Council, in accordance with the statement of principles and programme of action, paragraphs 23 to 26 of which contain the terms of reference of the Commission;

(c) To endorse the role and functions of the United Nations congresses on the prevention of crime and the treatment of offenders, in accordance with the statement of principles and programme of action;

(d) To invite the present members of the Committee on Crime Prevention and Control to participate during the first two days of the inaugural session of the Commission, at the expense of their respective Governments, except in the case of Committee members from least developed countries, in order to facilitate an orderly transition.

Economic and Social Council resolution 1992/1

6 February 1992   Meeting 2   Adopted without vote
Draft by President (E/1992/L.12); agenda item 4.

By **decision 1992/202**, adopted on 7 February, the Council approved the provisional agenda and documentation for the first session of the Commission on Crime Prevention and Criminal Justice.[17] By **decision 1992/201**, of the same date, the Council decided that the Commission's first session would be held at Vienna from 21 to 30 April 1992.

On 3 March, the Commission on Human Rights requested the Secretary-General to bring its resolution on the fraudulent enrichment of State officials to the attention of the Commission on Crime Prevention and Criminal Justice (see PART THREE, Chapter X).

International cooperation

The Secretary General, in a March note,[18] submitted a summary of activities relating to international cooperation in crime prevention and criminal justice.

The note concluded that there was a disparity between the need for practical assistance and technical cooperation activities on the one side, and the availability of resources on the other. Further, the general crime situation, in its most dangerous forms and transnational dimensions, appeared to be deteriorating, thus compounding needs while resources were diminishing. It was of the utmost urgency to reverse that trend.

The addenda to the note of the Secretary-General presented the report of the Ad Hoc Expert Group Meeting on Strategies to Deal with Transnational Crime, Smolenice, Slovak Republic, 27-31 May 1991;[18] and the conclusions and recommendations of the International Seminar on Organized Crime, Suzdal, Russian Federation, 21-25 October 1990;[18] the International Expert Group Meeting for the Elaboration of a Model Treaty on the Transfer of Enforcement of Penal Sanctions, Siracusa, Italy, 3-8 December 1991;[18] and of the Meeting of Experts for the Evaluation of Implementation of United Nations Norms and Guidelines in Crime Prevention and Criminal Justice, Vienna, 14-16 October 1991.[18]

ECONOMIC AND SOCIAL COUNCIL ACTION

On 30 July, the Economic and Social Council, on the recommendation of its Social Committee, adopted **resolution 1992/22** without vote.

Implementation of General Assembly resolution 46/152 concerning operational activities and coordination in the field of crime prevention and criminal justice

The Economic and Social Council,

Recalling its resolution 155 C (VII) of 13 August 1948, by which the United Nations was entrusted with leadership in promoting international cooperation in crime prevention and criminal justice and in making the fullest use of the knowledge and experience of national and international organizations which have an interest and competence in this field,

Recalling also its resolutions 1979/20 of 9 May 1979, 1984/48 of 25 May 1984 and 1990/24 of 24 May 1990, in which it requested the Secretary-General to explore new formulas for providing developing countries with technical cooperation, to develop concrete projects of technical cooperation and to promote education, training and public awareness in the field of crime prevention and criminal justice,

Reaffirming its recommendation, contained in resolution 1990/19 of 24 May 1990, that the international community, working through bilateral or multilateral arrangements, should provide Member States, at their request, with necessary assistance, in order to contribute to the establishment of the infrastructure required for crime prevention and criminal justice,

Recalling its resolutions 1986/11 of 21 May 1986, 1987/53 of 28 May 1987, 1988/44 of 27 May 1988 and 1989/68 of 24 May 1989, on the review of the functioning and programme of work of the United Nations in crime prevention and criminal justice, in which it called for intensified technical cooperation in this field,

Recalling also its resolutions 1989/63 of 24 May 1989 and 1990/21 of 24 May 1990, dealing with United Nations standards and norms in crime prevention and criminal justice,

Recognizing that many States suffer from extreme shortages of human and financial resources, which prevents them from adequately responding to problems related to crime,

Noting with appreciation the efforts made by many States at the bilateral level to provide assistance and know-how in the field of crime prevention and criminal justice,

Acknowledging the need for global efforts commensurate with the magnitude of national and transnational crime,

Bearing in mind that effective international action in crime prevention and criminal justice requires improved coordination of all related activities carried out by United Nations entities,

Recognizing that such improved coordination can only be effected through the continuous and close cooperation of all United Nations entities whose mandates are relevant to crime prevention and criminal justice,

Welcoming with appreciation Commission on Human Rights resolution 1992/31 of 28 February 1992, and emphasizing that all Member States should recognize the fundamental importance of human rights in the daily administration of crime prevention and criminal justice,

Also welcoming with appreciation Commission on Narcotic Drugs resolution 11(XXXV) of 15 April 1992,

Desirous of assisting States in improving their capacity to face the challenge of criminality by fostering new courses of action and enhancing collaborative ties and assistance through mutually supportive partnerships between Member States and the United Nations crime prevention and criminal justice programme, and any regional or subregional United Nations institutes, the establishment of which may be necessary to achieve this goal,

Recalling General Assembly resolution 45/121 of 14 December 1990, in which the Assembly invited Member States to monitor systematically the steps being taken to ensure the coordination of efforts in the planning and implementation of effective and humane measures designed to reduce the social and economic costs of crime and its negative effects on the development process, as well as to continue to explore new avenues for international cooperation in this field,

Recalling also General Assembly resolution 46/152 of 18 December 1991, in which the Assembly emphasized the practical orientation of the United Nations crime prevention and criminal justice programme and decided that it should provide States with practical assistance, such as data collection, information and experience sharing, and training, in order to achieve the goals of preventing crime and of improving the response to it,

Bearing in mind the urgent and specific needs of the least developed countries in the field of training and in the upgrading and development of their human resources,

Convinced of the need to encourage constructive dialogue and collaboration between Governments, intergovernmental and non-governmental organizations and funding agencies, with a view to formulating practical operational plans and policies,

Emphasizing the direct relevance of crime prevention and criminal justice to sustained development, stability, security, democratic change and improved quality of life,

Bearing in mind that many developing countries are faced with a lack of skilled personnel, training opportunities and technological and material know-how and have a keen interest in technical cooperation, advisory services and other types of aid,

Determined to respond to the increasing requests from Governments for technical cooperation and advisory services in crime prevention and criminal justice,

Recognizing that the Secretariat will be called upon to perform new tasks in order to service the annual sessions of the Commission on Crime Prevention and Criminal Justice,

Convinced that operational activities and technical assistance should occupy a prominent place in the United Nations activities in crime prevention and criminal justice, in the light of the recommendations of the Ministerial Meeting on the Creation of an Effective United Nations Crime Prevention and Criminal Justice Programme, held in Paris from 21 to 23 November 1991,

Taking note of the report of the Secretary-General on the implementation of the conclusions and recommendations of the Ministerial Meeting, in pursuance of General Assembly resolution 46/152, the progress report of the Secretary-General on United Nations activities in crime prevention and criminal justice, including detailed information on current programme budget and extrabudgetary activities of the Crime Prevention and Criminal Justice Branch of the Centre for Social Development and Humanitarian Affairs of the Secretariat, the progress report of the Secretary-General on the activities of the United Nations Interregional Crime and Justice Research Institute and the regional institutes for the prevention of crime and the treatment of offenders, the note by the Secretary-General on strengthening existing international cooperation in crime prevention and criminal justice, including technical cooperation in developing countries, with special emphasis on combating organized crime, and the note by the Secretary-General on the proposed revisions to programme 29 of the medium-term plan for the period 1992-1997,

I
Strengthening the operational capacity of the United Nations crime prevention and criminal justice programme, especially operational activities and advisory services

1. *Decides* that, under the guidance of the Commission on Crime Prevention and Criminal Justice, the secretariat of the programme should be responsible for facilitating the planning, coordination and implementation of practical activities in the field of crime prevention and criminal justice, in close collaboration with Governments and interregional and regional institutes, specialized agencies, funding agencies, intergovernmental and non-governmental organizations, the activities of which should be promoted in this field;

2. *Recommends* that the General Assembly at its forty-seventh session take favourable action on the proposals to be submitted by the Secretary-General pursuant to General Assembly resolution 46/152, relating to the strengthening of the programme;

3. *Reaffirms* the request of the General Assembly to the Secretary-General to take the necessary measures to commit the human and financial resources necessary to strengthen the programme as a whole, with emphasis on designing, implementing and monitoring technical cooperation projects at the national, regional and subregional levels, so as to enable it:

(a) To devote greater attention to helping States requesting assistance, including those channelling requests through United Nations peace-keeping operations, to identify their crime prevention and criminal justice needs and address them through technical cooperation, particularly with regard to law reform within their legal systems, including the improvement of legislation and procedures, the elaboration of criminal codes, the improved planning and formulation of national policies concerning crime prevention and criminal justice strategies, the acceleration of human resources development in specialized fields, and to assisting with the practical implementation of United Nations standards, norms and guidelines in crime prevention and criminal justice;

(b) To contribute to the preservation and reinforcement of democracy and justice based on the rule of law, in its field of competence and in collaboration with all the entities of the United Nations system and other appropriate organizations, taking appropriate account of United Nations norms and standards concerning crime prevention, criminal justice, law enforcement and protection of victims, as well as means of conflict resolution and mediation;

(c) To plan, implement and evaluate crime prevention and criminal justice assistance projects and to serve as a facilitating agent and a dynamic operational tool with which to assist countries in preventing crime, promoting security, sustaining national development and enhancing justice and respect for human rights;

(d) To serve as a world-wide training network for developing countries with specific requirements by developing training schemes, including manuals and curricula, by organizing national, regional and cross-sectoral training courses, workshops and seminars on priority issues, tailoring their objectives to the needs of the recipient countries, and by developing fellowship programmes;

(e) To further develop clearing-house facilities in relation to crime prevention and criminal justice issues, including the capacity to match the needs for training with the opportunities available to meet them;

(f) To continue and improve the surveys of crime trends and the operation of criminal justice systems carried out periodically by the United Nations, as a means of obtaining and providing a cross-nationally updated picture of patterns and dynamics of crime in the world, including its transnational forms; to carry out the surveys at two-year intervals, with preparations for the next survey (1990-1992) commencing at the end of 1993, in collaboration with the United Nations Development Programme and, within their competence, in collaboration with interregional, regional and national crime prevention and criminal justice institutes; and to include provisions for the regular publication and dissemination of the surveys, starting with the proposed programme budget for the biennium 1994-1995;

(g) To strengthen the United Nations Criminal Justice Information Network by inviting Governments, interregional and regional organizations, other relevant entities and the private sector to join and support the Network financially and logistically as a viable instrument for the dissemination and exchange of information and the transfer of knowledge for improved criminal justice management and more effective crime prevention;

(h) To promote policy-oriented research and studies on topics of interest to the Commission on Crime Prevention and Criminal Justice, as well as to individual member States or groups of member States;

(i) To determine, in cooperation with Governments and interregional and regional institutes, categories of crime prevention and criminal justice information to be supplied to and exchanged through the United Nations Criminal Justice Information Network, taking into account priorities specified by the Commission, with a view to ensuring more effective functioning of the Network;

(j) To cooperate closely and directly with a variety of national, regional, interregional and international institutions and training agencies and develop a roster of experts in different disciplines with practical experience in the field of crime prevention and criminal justice, as part of the clearing-house function or for such other purposes as the Commission may decide;

(k) To strengthen interregional and regional advisory services in crime prevention and criminal justice, so as to ensure necessary feedback and follow-up action;

(l) To develop and implement the various activities of the programme, in accordance with the priorities recommended by the Commission;

4. *Requests* the Secretary-General, pursuant to the recommendations of the Ministerial Meeting on the Creation of an Effective United Nations Crime Prevention and Criminal Justice Programme, to initiate the necessary consultations for the preparation of a report, to be considered by the Commission at its second session, setting out options and recommendations for the creation of an appropriate mechanism, such as a foundation, to mobilize human, financial and other resources to further technical cooperation.

II
Establishment of a subprogramme on operational activities, planning and overall coordination

1. *Takes note* of the proposed revisions to programme 29 of the medium-term plan for the period 1992-1997, which reflect the programmatic changes resulting from the most recent relevant resolutions of the General Assembly, as well as the conclusions and recommendations of the Ministerial Meeting on the Creation of an Effective United Nations Crime Prevention and Criminal Justice Programme;

2. *Recommends* the establishment, within programme 29 of the medium-term plan, of a subprogramme on operational activities, planning and overall coordination, in response to paragraph 5 of General Assembly resolution 46/152 and the statement of principles and programme of action annexed to the resolution;

3. *Invites* the Committee for Programme and Coordination and the Advisory Committee on Administrative and Budgetary Questions to ensure proper follow-up to the recommendation in paragraph 2 of the present section;

4. *Requests* the Secretary-General to reflect appropriately in the revised estimates to be submitted under section 21 of the programme budget for the biennium 1992-1993 and in subsequent bienniums the changes resulting from the recommendation in paragraph 2 of the present section.

III
Involvement of Member States

1. *Urges* developed countries, as envisaged in General Assembly resolution 46/152, to strengthen their aid programmes and commit themselves to support technical assistance and advisory services in the field of crime prevention and criminal justice in order to enhance the global commitment to improving justice and promoting human rights and the rule of law;

2. *Invites* Member States to establish reliable and effective channels of communication among themselves and with the United Nations crime prevention and criminal justice programme, including the United Nations Interregional Crime and Justice Research Institute, the regional institutes and government-appointed national correspondents in the field of crime prevention and criminal justice, particularly with regard to the facilities available for training, the use of modern techniques to combat crime which are consistent with international human rights standards, the provision of fellowships, study tours and consultancies, and personnel and information exchanges;

3. *Encourages* Governments in need of technical assistance in the field of crime prevention and criminal justice to identify their specific needs and to avail themselves of the services provided by the United Nations crime prevention and criminal justice programme, as well as of those provided bilaterally, access to which should be facilitated by the United Nations Secretariat.

IV
Coordination of activities

1. *Expresses its appreciation* to the Arab Security Studies and Training Centre for acting as host to the annual joint programme coordination meetings of the United Nations crime prevention and criminal justice programme network held in Saudi Arabia;

2. *Notes* that the United Nations Interregional Crime and Justice Research Institute reports to the Economic and Social Council through the Commission on Crime Prevention and Criminal Justice, and invites all other institutes referred to in paragraph 35 of the annex to General Assembly resolution 46/152 to submit, at future sessions of the Commission, statements outlining their programmes of work and the implementation thereof, with a view to assisting the Commission in facilitating the coordination of their activities;

3. *Recommends* that the following activities be undertaken by the Secretary-General:

(a) The promotion of arrangements for various types of exchanges within the programme network, in particular the secondment and exchange of staff;

(b) The collection of information, in particular research results and academic and scientific literature, and dissemination thereof to both professionals and the general public in order to permit the development and evaluation of measures and strategies for crime prevention and criminal justice and the identification of viable policy options for States of different regions;

(c) The development of field-level operations and other forms of direct collaborative activity designed to translate into practical action new policy perspectives, strategies and innovative techniques;

(d) The promotion of closer collaboration and continuing dialogue with Governments on matters of special concern;

(e) The coordination and integration of the activities of the interregional, regional and associate institutes cooperating with the United Nations in the field of crime prevention and criminal justice;

(f) The promotion of collaboration with and among research and training institutions around the world;

(g) The encouragement of Governments to appoint their national correspondents in the field of crime prevention and criminal justice to act as focal points and to foster effective communication and cooperation with the secretariat and other elements of the programme, including the interregional and regional institutes in the field of crime prevention and criminal justice;

(h) The development of criteria and procedures for the creation and affiliation of new United Nations institutes or centres that would be included among those referred to in paragraph 35 of the annex to General Assembly resolution 46/152, for consideration by the Commission at its second session, and the favourable review of requests by groups of States to establish United Nations subregional institutes;

4. *Recognizes* the Commission as the principal policy-making body of the United Nations in the field of crime prevention and criminal justice and requests it to coordinate, as appropriate, relevant activities in this field;

5. *Requests* the Commission on Crime Prevention and Criminal Justice to cooperate closely with the Commission for Social Development, the Commission on Human Rights, the Commission on Narcotic Drugs, the Commission on the Status of Women, other bodies, including the International Law Com-

mission, and the specialized agencies, including the United Nations Educational, Scientific and Cultural Organization, whose activities may have crime prevention and criminal justice aspects, in order to increase the efficiency and effectiveness of United Nations activities in areas of mutual concern and to ensure proper coordination and avoidance of possible duplication;

6. *Requests* the Secretary-General to strengthen cooperation between the Centre for Human Rights and the Centre for Social Development and Humanitarian Affairs of the Secretariat, including, in particular, preparations for the World Conference on Human Rights and coordination of the various technical advisory services provided by both Centres, in order to undertake joint programmes and strengthen existing mechanisms for the protection of human rights in the administration of justice;

7. *Approves* the decision of the Commission on Crime Prevention and Criminal Justice to authorize its secretariat to prepare concrete proposals on how such cooperation can most effectively be realized;

8. *Urges* the Commission to cooperate closely with, and to appropriately utilize the expertise, advocacy and assistance of, intergovernmental and non-governmental organizations in the development and implementation of the programme on crime prevention and criminal justice;

9. *Requests* the Secretary-General to encourage effective cooperation and coordination of relevant activities and to provide to the Commission all the assistance necessary to achieve this goal;

10. *Also requests* the Secretary-General, in order to assist the Commission in the setting of programme priorities:

(a) To conduct a survey of activities carried out in the field of crime prevention and criminal justice within the United Nations system;

(b) To conduct a survey of activities on priority themes identified in section VI, paragraph 1, below, carried out by relevant intergovernmental bodies and non-governmental organizations, including activities at the regional level;

(c) To prepare a report, based on an analysis of the information gathered through the surveys mentioned in subparagraphs (a) and (b), which outlines options relating to the priority themes, with their associated budget implications, for consideration by the Commission at its second session in connection with the development of its programme of work for the period 1992-1996;

11. *Requests* the Secretary-General to provide Governments with the above-mentioned report sixty days in advance of the second session of the Commission.

V

Funding of operational activities

1. *Reaffirms* the crucial role of the Commission on Crime Prevention and Criminal Justice in mobilizing the support of Member States for the United Nations crime prevention and criminal justice programme, as envisaged in paragraph 26 (d) of the annex to General Assembly resolution 46/152;

2. *Recommends* that the General Assembly consider arrangements for funding programme support, taking into account the practices elsewhere in the United Nations system;

3. *Requests* the Secretary-General to assist in mobilizing support for the programme and in undertaking

vigorous fund-raising activities to strengthen particularly the operational capacity of its technical assistance and advisory services:

(a) By broadening the base of the financial support of the programme by approaching Governments, private foundations, intergovernmental and non-governmental organizations, academic institutions and the private sector;

(b) By establishing collaborative relationships with the United Nations Development Programme, the World Bank, other United Nations funding agencies and regional development banks and by exploring innovative partnerships to finance joint technical assistance projects;

(c) By organizing special events that would bring together donor countries, recipient countries and funding agencies, with a view to strengthening the financial base of the United Nations Crime Prevention and Criminal Justice Fund, encouraging voluntary contributions in cash or in kind, and establishing an ongoing dialogue for more effective operational activities.

VI

Priorities

1. *Determines* that the following priority themes should guide the work of the Commission in the development of a detailed programme and the budget allocations for the period 1992-1996:

(a) National and transnational crime, organized crime, economic crime, including money laundering, and the role of criminal law in the protection of the environment;

(b) Crime prevention in urban areas, juvenile and violent criminality;

(c) Efficiency, fairness and improvement in the management and administration of criminal justice and related systems, with due emphasis on the strengthening of national capacities in developing countries for the regular collection, collation, analysis and utilization of data in the development and implementation of appropriate policies;

2. *Recommends* that in the course of the programme budget planning process, allocation should be made for special operational activities and advisory services in situations of urgent need and for programme organization, evaluation and reporting obligations;

3. *Determines* that in the areas noted in paragraph 1 of the present section, the objectives should be:

(a) To concentrate the majority of programme resources on the provision of training, advisory services and technical cooperation in a limited number of areas of recognized need, taking into account the need for technical assistance to developing countries, in order to achieve a synergetic effect, allowing intense and effective use of materials, resources and experience from both regular budgetary resources and voluntary contributions;

(b) In the case of special operational activities and advisory services in situations of urgent need, to offer timely and practical assistance to Governments, upon request, in situations that do not permit a problem to be adopted as a regular priority by the Commission on Crime Prevention and Criminal Justice; in implementing these special operational activities and advisory services, the Secretariat should place major emphasis on serving as a broker and clearing-house, providing advisory services and training to Member States from within existing budgetary resources and through voluntary contributions; the Secretariat should submit to the Commission at its second session a narrative and statistical report on the implementation of these special operational activities and advisory services, together with a statement of expenditure and any appropriate recommendations;

(c) With regard to programme organization, evaluation and reporting obligations, to assist the Commission in reaching agreement on the general goals of the programme and the needs to be met; to ascertain the capacity available to meet those needs; to determine the objectives, specific activities and mechanisms to be used for that purpose; to remain cognizant of pertinent developments and advise the Commission on them, and discharge other reporting responsibilities; and to mobilize support for the programme;

4. *Invites* the Commission to keep its priorities under review and to ensure that the programme developments related to the substantive preparations for the United Nations congresses on the prevention of crime and the treatment of offenders take those priorities into account;

5. *Accords* high priority to the United Nations crime prevention and criminal justice programme, in accordance with General Assembly resolution 46/152, and requests an appropriate share of the overall resources of the United Nations for the programme.

VII
Follow-up

1. *Urges* the Department of Economic and Social Development of the Secretariat, the United Nations Development Programme and other pertinent funding agencies and bodies to give full support to technical assistance projects in crime prevention and criminal justice and to encourage technical cooperation in this field among developed and developing countries;

2. *Decides* that the Commission on Crime Prevention and Criminal Justice shall include in its agenda, beginning with its second session, a standing item on technical assistance, which would deal with the most practical course of action to be followed to render the programme fully operational and enable it to respond to the specific needs of Governments, including financial needs, if possible;

3. *Decides also* that the Commission shall include in its agenda, beginning with its second session, a standing item on existing United Nations standards and norms in the field of crime prevention and criminal justice, which serve as recommendations to Member States, and on, *inter alia*, their use and application;

4. *Requests* the Secretary-General to report to the Economic and Social Council at its substantive session of 1993, through the Commission on Crime Prevention and Criminal Justice, on the progress made in the implementation of the various provisions of the present resolution.

Economic and Social Council resolution 1992/22

30 July 1992   Meeting 41   Adopted without vote

Approved by Social Committee (E/1992/106) without vote, 23 July (meeting 18); draft by Commission on Crime Prevention and Criminal Justice (E/1992/30); agenda item 19.
Financial implications. E/1992/30/Add.1.

On 16 December, the General Assembly, acting on a recommendation of the Third Committee, adopted without vote **resolution 47/91.**

Crime prevention and criminal justice
The General Assembly,

Alarmed by the high costs of crime, particularly in its new and transnational forms, and by the dangers posed to individual and collective security and to the welfare of countries and peoples by the rising incidence of crime,

Emphasizing the need for global efforts commensurate with the magnitude of national and transnational crime, and for strengthened regional and international cooperation to combat crime in all its forms and to improve the effectiveness and efficiency of criminal justice systems,

Bearing in mind the goals of the United Nations in the field of crime prevention and criminal justice, specifically the reduction of criminality, more efficient and effective law enforcement and administration of justice, respect for human rights and the promotion of the highest standards of fairness, humanity and professional conduct,

Recognizing that many States suffer from extreme shortages of human and financial resources, which prevents them from responding adequately to problems related to crime,

Noting with appreciation the efforts made by many States at the bilateral level to provide assistance and know-how in the field of crime prevention and criminal justice,

Bearing in mind that effective international action in crime prevention and criminal justice requires effective cooperation and improved coordination of all related activities carried out at the bilateral and multilateral levels,

Recalling its previous resolutions in which it expressed its concern about the increasing needs of Member States and the capacity of the United Nations crime prevention and criminal justice programme to meet them,

Recalling also the recommendations of the Ministerial Meeting on the Creation of an Effective United Nations Crime Prevention and Criminal Justice Programme, held at Versailles, France, from 21 to 23 November 1991, which were adopted by the General Assembly by its resolution 46/152 of 18 December 1991 on the creation of an effective United Nations crime prevention and criminal justice programme, and which included the statement of principles and programme of action contained in the annex to the resolution,

Taking note of Economic and Social Council resolution 1992/1 of 6 February 1992, by which the Council decided to establish the Commission on Crime Prevention and Criminal Justice,

Mindful of the responsibilities of the Commission, recommended by the Ministerial Meeting and entrusted to it by the General Assembly and the Economic and Social Council in their relevant resolutions,

Recognizing the need for an appropriate Secretariat support structure capable of performing the new functions mandated by the General Assembly in its resolution 46/152 and by the Economic and Social Council in its resolution 1992/22 of 30 July 1992,

Concerned about the disparity between the scope of the required work and the limited resources available, including resources for practical measures, to assist Member States, upon their request, in dealing with their most urgent needs in preventing and combating crime problems,

1. *Welcomes* the establishment of the Commission on Crime Prevention and Criminal Justice and the results of its first session, held at Vienna from 21 to 30 April 1992;

2. *Welcomes with appreciation* Economic and Social Council resolutions 1992/22, 1992/23 and 1992/24 of 30 July 1992;

3. *Takes note* of the reports of the Secretary-General on the measures taken to implement the statement of principles and programme of action of the United Nations crime prevention and criminal justice programme, on the United Nations African Institute for the Prevention of Crime and the Treatment of Offenders and on the strengthening of international cooperation in combating organized crime;

4. *Recognizes* that the United Nations crime prevention and criminal justice programme has a special contribution to make in a world seeking to surmount serious problems of violence and crime;

5. *Recalls* the priority themes established by the Economic and Social Council in its resolution 1992/22 to guide the work of the Commission in the development of a detailed programme and the budget allocations for the period 1992-1996, as follows:

(*a*) National and transnational crime, organized crime, economic crime, including money laundering, and the role of criminal law in the protection of the environment;

(*b*) Crime prevention in urban areas, juvenile and violent criminality;

(*c*) Efficiency, fairness and improvement in the management and administration of criminal justice and related systems, with due emphasis on the strengthening of national capacities in developing countries for the regular collection, collation, analysis and utilization of data in the development and implementation of appropriate policies;

6. *Requests* the Secretary-General to support the operational activities and advisory services of the United Nations crime prevention and criminal justice programme, within existing resources from the regular budget of the Organization commensurate to its high priority and importance, and independently of resources available through voluntary contributions;

7. *Also requests* the Secretary-General to provide from existing resources adequate funds to build and maintain the institutional capacity of the United Nations crime prevention and criminal justice programme to respond to requests of Member States for assistance in this field;

8. *Further requests* the Secretary-General, as a matter of urgency, to take all measures necessary to effect the upgrading of the Crime Prevention and Criminal Justice Branch of the Centre for Social Development and Humanitarian Affairs of the Secretariat into a division, as recommended in and in accordance with resolution 46/152;

9. *Requests* the Secretary-General to take all necessary measures for assisting the Commission in performing its functions as the principal policy-making body in the field of crime prevention and criminal justice and for ensuring the proper coordination of all relevant activities in the field, in particular with the Commission on Human Rights and the Commission on Narcotic Drugs;

10. *Invites* the relevant funding agencies of the United Nations to consider including crime prevention and criminal justice activities in their funding programmes, bearing in mind their established priorities, at a level of priority commensurate to the increasing needs of Member States in the field, and to cooperate closely with the United Nations crime prevention and criminal justice programme in planning and implementing those activities;

11. *Invites* Governments to lend their full support to the United Nations crime prevention and criminal justice programme and to increase their financial contributions to the United Nations Crime Prevention and Criminal Justice Fund.

General Assembly resolution 47/91

16 December 1992　　　Meeting 89　　　Adopted without vote

Approved by Third Committee (A/47/703) without vote, 5 November (meeting 30); 27-nation draft (A/C.3/47/L.19), orally revised; agenda item 93 (*b*).

Sponsors: Australia, Austria, Bahamas, Belarus, Canada, Colombia, Costa Rica, Croatia, Cuba, Egypt, France, Guatemala, Honduras, Hungary, Italy, Mexico, Mongolia, Morocco, Netherlands, Nicaragua, Panama, Peru, Russian Federation, Trinidad and Tobago, Ukraine, Uruguay, Venezuela.

Meeting numbers. GA 47th session: 3rd Committee 11-18, 22, 23, 25, 30; plenary 89.

Organized crime

The Secretary-General, in response to a 1989 General Assembly resolution,[19] submitted a September report[20] to the Assembly on the strengthening of international cooperation in combating organized crime. The report covered the nature and extent of the problem, some recent initiatives, and proposals for follow-up to the Assembly resolution.

The report concluded that, although practically all countries were aware that organized crime posed a threat to their social fabric, full cooperation remained an intention rather than a reality. The most obvious difficulty in this respect was the existence of different legal systems and definitions of crime, accompanied by overly restrictive concepts of sovereignty and jurisdiction.

Money laundering

The Secretary-General submitted a March report[21] to the Commission on Crime Prevention and Criminal Justice on money laundering and associated issues: the need for international cooperation. The report contained an overview of national and international initiatives against money laundering, and a comparative analysis of various approaches to the problem. The report noted that the impact of criminal sanctions alone on criminal organizations was limited and that a more effective alternative could be to follow their money trail. Money-laundering investigations and the confiscation of proceeds from criminal activities undermined the ability of a criminal organization to perform its main task, the production of wealth.

ECONOMIC AND SOCIAL COUNCIL ACTION

On 30 July, the Economic and Social Council, on the recommendation of its Social Committee, adopted without vote **resolution 1992/23**.

Organized crime

The Economic and Social Council,

Alarmed by the rapid growth and geographical extension of organized crime in its various forms, both nationally and internationally,

Concerned about the menace that these developments represent to social stability, economic development, democratic institutions and legitimate business,

Aware that the transnational nature of a large portion of the activities of organized crime requires the intensification of technical and scientific cooperation, as indicated on several occasions by the Committee on Crime Prevention and Control,

Recognizing the importance of initiatives taken in this area by the Committee,

Recalling that the Economic and Social Council, in its resolution 1989/70 of 24 May 1989, called upon Governments, international organizations and interested nongovernmental organizations to cooperate with the Committee in promoting international cooperation in combating organized crime,

Recalling also that the General Assembly, in its resolution 44/71 of 8 December 1989, requested the Committee to consider ways of strengthening international cooperation in combating organized crime and to submit its views, through the Economic and Social Council, to the General Assembly at its forty-seventh session,

Recalling further that the General Assembly, in its resolution 44/72 of 8 December 1989, requested the Eighth United Nations Congress on the Prevention of Crime and the Treatment of Offenders to propose control measures aimed at eradicating the activities of organized crime,

Noting that the Eighth Congress, in its resolution 24, adopted the Guidelines for the prevention and control of organized crime,

Noting also that the General Assembly, in its resolution 45/121 of 14 December 1990, welcomed the instruments and resolutions adopted by the Eighth Congress and invited Governments to be guided by them in the formulation of appropriate legislation and policy directives,

Noting further that the General Assembly, also in its resolution 45/121, endorsed the decision of the Eighth Congress that priority attention should be given to specific practical measures to combat international crime over the forthcoming five-year period,

Noting that the Ad Hoc Expert Group Meeting on Strategies to Deal with Transnational Crime, held at Smolenice, Czechoslovakia, from 27 to 31 May 1991, formulated important recommendations in this area,

Noting also that the International Seminar on Organized Crime, held at Suzdal, Russian Federation, from 21 to 25 October 1991, pursuant to General Assembly resolution 45/123 of 14 December 1990, formulated practical measures against organized crime, aimed at enhancing the struggle against the different manifestations of organized crime,

Reaffirming that priority must be given to the struggle against all activities of organized crime, including money laundering, the infiltration of legitimate business and the corruption of public officials,

1. *Takes note* of the recommendations of the Ad Hoc Expert Group Meeting on Strategies to Deal with Transnational Crime, held at Smolenice, Czechoslovakia, and the practical measures against organized crime, formulated by the International Seminar on Organized Crime, held at Suzdal, Russian Federation, contained in annexes I and II to the present resolution, and offers them for consideration by Governments in their efforts to enhance the struggle against organized crime, both nationally and internationally;

2. *Requests* the Secretary-General to continue the analysis of information on the impact of organized criminal activities upon society at large, including data on the nature, extent, forms and dimensions of organized crime, on legislative measures and the promotion of international cooperation aimed at controlling organized crime, with special emphasis on economic crimes and the laundering of illicit funds, and on judicial practice as regards cases involving organized crime, with a view to keeping the Commission on Crime Prevention and Criminal Justice informed;

3. *Invites* Member States to give favourable consideration to the organization of practice-oriented workshops, research projects and training programmes to deal with specific aspects of organized criminal activities, with a view to exchanging ideas concerning law enforcement methods for control of those activities, which have proved to be both effective and consistent with the concept of respect for human rights.

ANNEX I
Recommendations of the Ad Hoc Expert Group Meeting on Strategies to Deal with Transnational Crime, held at Smolenice, Czechoslovakia, from 27 to 31 May 1991

The following recommendations were drawn up by the Ad Hoc Expert Group Meeting on Strategies to Deal with Transnational Crime for the attention of the Intergovernmental Working Group on the Creation of an Effective International Crime and Justice Programme and the Committee on Crime Prevention and Control, at its twelfth session. They are drawn from the discussions of the substantive agenda items, as well as from the papers presented by experts and the United Nations or United Nations-affiliated institutes for the prevention of crime and the treatment of offenders:

1. The process of studying and combating transnational crime and crimes with transnational aspects should take into account a number of factors, such as the considerable changes in the political, economic and social situation in the world and the extensive development of international business activities, including the creation of common markets and other forms of integration. It should also take into account the vulnerability of national frontiers, the high level

of modern communication, the expansion of the international banking system and resultant simplification of money transfer, the extensive use of computer technology, the universal spread of illegal business in arms and explosives, the growth in the number of enterprises producing and using radioactive and chemical substances and the extensive use of such substances, and the limited geographical reach of national laws and national law enforcement authorities, differences in legal systems, and the limited effect of international procedures for obtaining evidence, apprehension and extradition of offenders.

2. In view of the political and economic changes taking place in many countries, including the newly emerging "market economies", new laws and regulations should be developed to permit anticipation of, and response to, changing situations and emerging economic realities. Exchanges of information on, and experiences with, economic crime and its control by criminal sanctions should be intensified. Due consideration should be given to regulatory mechanisms as essential complements to penal sanctions.

3. In view of the increasing seriousness and gravity of organized crime, terrorism and other transnational crimes, Governments should be encouraged to conclude bilateral and multilateral agreements to carry out or enhance the effectiveness of extradition proceedings and mutual assistance in criminal matters, using as a basis United Nations model treaties and other treaties and agreements concluded at the regional and international levels. The role of regional and subregional intergovernmental organizations in supporting the United Nations in this field would be essential. Appropriate coordination mechanisms should be established and maintained.

4. Countries should consider establishing a national organization with powers to plan and coordinate the domestic criminal justice and crime prevention programme. The composition of this organization should include representatives of the various relevant sectors of Government and the community.

5. Countries should agree to share information and intelligence on non-controversial matters. To facilitate such exchanges, countries should establish national databases with linkage to all other countries. A technical committee should be set up to overview these activities.

6. Countries should study the practices on extradition prevailing in certain regional groups, for example the Council of Europe. This could help to eliminate the difficulties associated with the technical requirements that are the main obstacles to extradition being granted.

7. National and international efforts to achieve more effective strategies to deal with transnational crime should focus on:

(a) Harmonization of legislation and avoidance of conflicts of jurisdiction that may result in serious transnational offenders escaping justice;

(b) Penalization of certain forms of behaviour to eliminate gaps in national legislation;

(c) Cooperation through extradition, mutual assistance, enforcement of foreign judgements, transfer of criminal proceedings, transfer of offenders, including designation of an appropriate coordinating authority to expedite the implementation of treaties;

(d) Integration of the various modalities of international cooperation to provide better and more efficient results;

(e) Reassessment of traditional principles of international cooperation, such as reciprocity, double criminality, specialty, the political offence exception and the non-extradition of nationals and territoriality;

(f) A lessening of the divergence of national conceptions of criminal justice, including substantive law and procedural rules and practices, with due respect for human rights considerations;

(g) The sharing of law enforcement intelligence (information) and the increase of joint activities in inter-State law enforcement collaboration;

(h) The development of effective financial mechanisms to trace the proceeds of illicit activities;

(i) The development of subregional or regional "judicial spaces", with a view to exploring the possibilities for their expansion, in accordance with particular and specific emerging needs;

(j) The inclusion of international and transnational crimes in national legislation, in particular with a view to eliminating safe havens;

(k) The development of the means to prevent, detect and prosecute abuses of power by public officials and other forms of corrupt behaviour;

(l) The development of education and training programmes in international criminal law at the level of legal education, as well as within public agencies;

(m) The development of specialized education and training of judges, prosecutors and law enforcement officials in the areas of transnational crime, money laundering and other economic offences, including corruption, and elaboration of the required training material;

(n) The development of regional centres to increase the availability of specialized library material, documents and research results, with the capacity to provide technical legal advice to countries of the region;

(o) Acceptance of the principle that all countries, regardless of how seriously they are affected by transnational crime, have to collaborate and share information on its nature and extent, to facilitate appropriate policy formulation and planning;

(p) The development of interfaces with existing international and regional networks such as the International Criminal Police Organization (ICPO/Interpol) and other international bodies;

(q) Strengthening of an awareness on the part of Governments and relevant national agencies of the important correlation between socio-economic development and crime control programmes, with appropriate budget and resource allocations, including international aid for crime prevention schemes.

8. Efforts should be pursued to formulate effective strategies for dealing with environmental offences. An assessment of the administrative, civil and criminal laws enforced by different countries should be made in order to identify gaps and propose appropriate remedies. Adequate attention should be given not only to the sanctioning strategies but also to the prevention of environmental abuse and the protection of the environment.

9. Efforts should be made to allow the widest possible distribution of information on stolen art objects so as to prevent their illegal sale, thereby effectively stemming the international traffic in movable cultural property.

10. In order to benefit from both successes achieved and failures, an assessment should be made of the results of cooperation already undertaken to prevent the use of the banking system and financial institutions for money laundering, including successful preventive measures. Initiatives such as the development by the Council of Europe of the Convention on Laundering, Search, Seizure and Confiscation of the Proceeds from Crime, which was opened for signature on 8 November 1990, should be encouraged and efforts should be pursued to develop a multilateral agreement with universal application. The model decree for confiscation is a very practical model, which could prove extremely useful in such an application. A detailed analysis of its provisions is available from the Crime Prevention and Criminal Justice Branch of the Centre for Social Development and Humanitarian Affairs of the Secretariat.

11. Efforts should be made to gather information on corruption and anti-corruption strategies, with a view to assisting Governments in combating corruption and in providing a basis for formulating more effective policies to deal with it. Emphasis should be placed on the formulation of curricula for anti-corruption training courses, benefiting, in particular, developing countries. In addition to research, training and technical assistance in the most advanced methods of corruption control through repression, equal attention should be paid to prevention and education. The efforts of independent commissions against corruption can be useful in devising controls in public administration and in increasing public intolerance for waste and corruption. In its resolution 7, the Eighth United Nations Congress on the Prevention of Crime and the Treatment of Offenders specifically requested the Department of Technical Cooperation for Development of the Secretariat to provide assistance for such outreach, requested the Secretary-General to publish in all the official languages the manual on practical measures against corruption, which had already been prepared, and requested the Crime Prevention and Criminal Justice Branch to develop a draft international code of conduct for public officials for submission to the Ninth Congress on the Prevention of Crime and the Treatment of Offenders.

12. Recognizing that, while bilateral and regional cooperation may provide mechanisms for specific arrangements to prevent or investigate certain types of transnational criminality, they cannot provide a comprehensive solution in matters of cooperation in combating serious forms of organized crime at the international level. Multilateral cooperation should be made more effective, through the United Nations, which has the general mandate and the international constituency necessary to provide countries with guidance and assistance in the prevention and control of transnational crime. This could be pursued in the context of a genuinely international crime and justice programme, which would be capable of responding to the challenges of such crime.

13. United Nations surveys on crime trends should also include information on trends in transnational crime in order to permit an in-depth analysis of its scale, structure and dynamic, and of the extent of its material cost and potential social consequences. In the further development of the United Nations Criminal Justice Information Network, attention should be paid to the setting up of databases on transnational crime.

14. The idea of establishing a world foundation on crime prevention and assistance to victims of transnational crime should be pursued. The proposed foundation could help to identify and mobilize financial resources in support of the implementation of international crime prevention and criminal justice programmes, raise public awareness about crime trends and the rights of victims, develop innovative means of responding to technical assistance needs and provide financial support to victims.

15. The United Nations crime prevention and criminal justice programme should aim at developing the new mechanisms, procedures, conventions and institutions necessary to combat crime with transnational aspects and dimensions and to assist Governments in reducing domestic crime. For example:

(a) This could, in particular, include assistance to countries in:

(i) Gathering information on, and analysing, the incidence of crime and the efficacy of the response to crime;

(ii) Preventing crime and helping victims of crime;

(iii) Enhancing the criminal justice process through improved methods for the investigation of crime and developing pre-trial, trial and appellate review procedures;

(iv) Improving the administration of sentences and the reintegration of offenders into society and the control of recidivism;

(b) On the international level, the mandates should include:

(i)   The drafting of international conventions, declarations and recommendations pertaining to the definition of international offences;

(ii) The enhancement of existing cooperative mechanisms and the development of new ones, including such mechanisms as mutual assistance and extradition;

(iii) The organization of trainee programmes for developing countries;

(iv) The drafting of model penal provisions dealing with selected offences;

(c)   The mandate should further include the development and encouragement of coordinated subregional, regional and international activities from the investigative to the adjudicative stages, including ascertainment of the practicality of establishing subregional and regional penal tribunals with transferred jurisdiction, in order to meet more effectively the problems of particularly severe domestic crime and of crime transcending national frontiers;

(d)   Consideration should also be given to coordination by the United Nations of cooperative arrangements at the bilateral level, including the exchange of crime prevention and criminal justice personnel, such as police officers at different levels, who could in this manner conduct comparative studies in the area of criminal investigations into drug-trafficking and other similar activities. In addition, criminal justice attachés at embassies and consulates could help one another to reach a better understanding of laws and court processes and procedures of their countries. This could be a very useful means of facilitating effective cooperation with respect to transnational crimes involving different countries;

(e)   The United Nations government-appointed national correspondents in the field of crime prevention and criminal justice should become more operational. Ideally, their functions should be coordinated by an office or individual in an agency or institution with responsibilities in the criminal justice systems of the countries; this would permit them to ensure that action was taken when necessary and to respond accurately and with authority to United Nations inquiries;

(f)   Technical cooperation, particularly at the regional and subregional levels, should be intensified through the development of technical assistance projects benefiting developing countries. Special consideration should be given to the strengthening of the operational capacity of the crime prevention and criminal justice programme and its interregional advisory services, to ensure that the most recent developments in modern technology and expertise are placed at the disposal of all Member States. Efforts should also be made to create regional advisers on crime prevention and criminal justice to provide services to the respective regions, in close contact with the regional institutes for the prevention of crime and the treatment of offenders;

(g)   The United Nations crime prevention and criminal justice programme of work should be coordinated with that of ICPO/Interpol and other relevant organizations.

ANNEX II
Practical measures against organized crime, formulated by the International Seminar on Organized Crime, held at Suzdal, Russian Federation, from 21 to 25 October 1991

1.   The International Seminar on Organized Crime, which was attended by leading law enforcement officials and experts from 15 countries, the United Nations Secretariat, the Helsinki Institute for Crime Prevention and Control, affiliated with the United Nations, the International Criminal Police Organization (ICPO/Interpol) and the Office of International Criminal Justice of the University of Illinois at Chicago, United States of America, formulated the following practical measures against organized crime, which are based on a distillation of their considerable experience in its prevention and control. The applicability of these measures depends on particular legal and judicial systems, on the availability of resources and on the specific manifestations of organized crime.

I.   Profile of organized criminal groups

2.   The evolution of organized crime and the forms it takes vary from country to country, although there are common features. The formation of criminal associations is influenced by various social, economic and legal factors. It is, however, possible to single out two basic ways in which organized crime evolves in the majority of countries. These are: involvement in illegal activities (such as property offences, money laundering, drug trafficking, currency violations, intimidation, prostitution, gambling and trafficking in arms and antiquities) and participation in the legal economic sphere (directly or through parasitic means such as extortion). Such participation always tends to use illegal competitive means and can be of greater economic impact than the involvement in entirely illegal activities. In both cases criminal methods are used because the backbone of organized criminal formations is composed of criminal elements.

3.   No uniform definition of organized crime has yet been developed. In essence, however, it is usually understood as being a relatively large group of continuous and controlled criminal entities that carry out crimes for profit and seek to create a system of protection against social control by illegal means such as violence, intimidation, corruption and large-scale theft. A more general description would be "any group of individuals organized for the purpose of profiting by illegal means on a continuing basis".

4.   Organized crime can be divided into many types. One such type is the traditional or the Mafia-style family, where structured hierarchies, internal rules, discipline, codes of behaviour and diversity in illegal activities are common practice. Included in such organizations are the largest and most developed types of criminal groups, involved in a multiplicity of illegal activities. Another type is the profes-

sional. Members of such organizations join together for a certain criminal venture. Such organizations are fluid and not as rigidly structured as those of the traditional type. They are exemplified by entities involved in counterfeiting, car theft, armed robbery, extortion and so forth. The composition of a professional criminal organization may be constantly changing and its members may be involved in a variety of similar criminal enterprises. In addition, there are many organized groups that dominate particular territories, and others that are involved in particular types of crime.

5. There are also organized crime groups divided on the basis of ethnic, cultural and historical ties. These ties link them to their countries of origin, thus forming a major network extending beyond national borders. Exploiting the features of their origins, such as language and customs, they are able to insulate themselves from the actions of law enforcement agencies. Many organized crime groups have significant ethnic or national components and are often commonly referred to by ethnic or national labels. Because of their prevalence and the lack of a practical alternative, these labels are used in the present document, even though such terminology involves oversimplification, risks stereotyping and can be offensive to the vast majority of law-abiding members of that ethnic group or nationality.

6. Identification of these types of organized criminal groups does not necessarily imply rigid borderlines between them. Nearly every organized criminal entity may involve a multiplicity of component features. New forms involving different elements frequently arise. Some countries, for example, have seen the emergence of urban street formations, including juvenile gangs. Organized crime is, indeed, very adaptable; it is often characterized by rapid adaptation of the forms of its activities to the national criminal justice policy and to the protective mechanisms of States. Its leaders are often individuals of great intelligence and extreme cruelty, and are true professionals in crime, making them a particular threat to society.

7. Organized crime produces social, political and economic evils. Among the social evils are the adverse effects of illegal drugs on the behaviour and health of individuals, the growth of violence involving firearms, the fear of crime, manipulation and control of bodies such as labour unions and the increased cost of purchasing goods and services. For example, in one highly developed country, the largest organized crime group has controlled four of that nation's labour unions.

8. The political effects can include infiltration into and influence over political parties and the apparatus of government, including local administrations, and corruption of politicians and state officials. This often leads to a loss of public confidence in the Government and the political process and a breakdown of consensus within society. Many countries report that members of their police forces and armed forces have been corrupted by drug traffickers. Also, assassina-

tions of government officials, judges, mayors and law enforcement officials in certain countries have alarmed public opinion throughout the world.

9. It is not possible to identify accurately or even to estimate all the economic consequences of organized crime. It infiltrates legitimate business, tainting all those with whom it comes into contact, as well as corrupting officials whose services are required to launder illicit profits. In some countries, the profits of organized crime can be compared to those of entire branches of industry; for example, the trade in illegal drugs has been estimated to be the second largest industry in the world, by value of goods. The income of organized crime groups equals the gross national product of many countries.

10. The ability of organized crime to generate a vast supply of capital, to infiltrate legitimate business and to ruin rivals by means of control over prices represents a serious threat to the very future of any society. Legitimate commerce can be undermined by the shadow economy, with all the political and social dangers following that process. The large illicit sums infiltrating the world economy affect a country's balance of payments, the monetary system, bank cooperation, the profitability of private firms and the prices of consumer goods and services.

11. The cooperation between the largest organized criminal entities and the growing internationalization of organized crime may create a system with such economic strength that it poses a threat that many countries would not be able to counteract on their own.

II. Substantive legislation

12. In practically all countries, those engaged in the illegal activities of organized criminal entities are subject to criminal liability in accordance with various laws which establish certain offences, or within the framework of common law in particular categories of crimes. Long experience in organized crime control has led many countries to adopt specific statutes designed to restrict the possibilities for organized crime to flourish. These statutes are both preventive and repressive. Evidence-gathering presents considerable difficulties and there are limits to the application of sanctions and measures against the illegal activities of those involved. Legislation should be kept under review in order to ensure that it is responsive to changing circumstances.

13. It is very important that penal statutes should provide a means of establishing the criminal liability of both the actual perpetrators of a crime and the leaders of criminal entities (who are usually not directly involved in a specific crime). Unless criminal liability of the leadership or membership of criminal entities is established, it will only be possible to prosecute the lower rank of criminals, and not those who control them.

14. The danger and scope of organized crime are considerable. In some countries it may be considered advisable to enact legislation that has a direct impact on the crimes committed by members of organized crime enterprises. Such legislation would be directed not against any specific criminal act but against all

serious crimes committed in a concerted manner by a group of individuals acting together for a common purpose. It may also be considered advisable to enact legislation prohibiting membership in a criminal association. It is advisable to specify in such legislation the elements of the offences committed by organized criminals and the factors that aggravate their seriousness.

15. To counteract effectively the laundering of proceeds of crime it is important that all countries adopt norms for banking and financial institutions and establish criminal liability in order to enable them to comply with the provisions of the United Nations Convention against Illicit Traffic in Narcotic Drugs and Psychotropic Substances, of 1988. Other instruments not limited to drug trafficking, such as regional conventions and model regulations, may also be of value.

16. One approach is to create an obligation to report to competent bodies every financial transaction in excess of an amount stipulated by the legislation, or an obligation to report every suspicious transaction. The establishment of criminal liability in case of failure to abide by such obligations will be of great assistance in combating money laundering. A proper inquiry into particularly suspicious transactions can be initiated on the basis of reports received, and reports can be used by investigators seeking to piece together how a criminal organization handles its flow of money. The reports also can serve the important function of corroborating the testimony of cooperating witnesses and they may bring to the attention of investigators a geographical region that has suddenly shown an increase in sizeable financial transactions (indicating that the area may have become the object of organized crime activities), or a bank where there have been suspicious developments in financial transactions. Appropriate international mechanisms should be developed for the exchange of such information.

17. The success of efforts to combat the laundering of "black money" directly depends on how accessible the activities of financial bodies are to the law enforcement agencies. The problem here is that opening up the activities of the financial bodies of any country to outside scrutiny can affect their competitive position. The activities of organized crime can, however, undermine an entire society. Furthermore, the money derived from organized crime often circulates through the same channels as money concealed from the taxation authorities. In view of this, it is vital for the banks to maintain records of the identity of their clients, and to cooperate with law enforcement agencies whenever there are suspicious deposits or other transactions. It may be necessary to strengthen mechanisms of control over banking operations and even to centralize information of this kind. Governments should encourage banks to take as much responsibility as possible for the controls on criminality.

18. At present, money laundering is considered a crime in some countries only. This gives international organized crime the chance to benefit by using the banking and other services of countries that lack such legislation. All countries should therefore include in their criminal codes a crime of "money laundering", in accordance with the provisions of article 3 of the United Nations Convention against Illicit Traffic in Narcotic Drugs and Psychotropic Substances. Consideration should be given to ensuring that such legislation embraces all proceeds of organized crime.

19. Corruption greatly facilitates the activities of organized criminal groups. In view of this, many countries have enacted special anti-corruption legislation. The fight against organized crime would be greatly assisted if all countries were to follow the anti-corruption recommendations adopted by the Eighth United Nations Congress on the Prevention of Crime and the Treatment of Offenders and make appropriate use of the manual on practical measures against corruption approved at that Congress. It is important that countries take steps to prevent organized crime groups from corrupting individuals and organizations in the economic and financial sectors, particularly in such areas as State contracts and trade services.

20. A crime committed by an organized group may be considered an aggravated one. The criminal codes of many countries define the commission of a crime by an organized group as a qualifying feature.

21. In addition to the traditional sanctions of incarceration or fines that may be imposed upon conviction, consideration should be given to other sanctions designed to deter organized criminality. Some countries use judicially imposed limitations on property, residence, association and daily activities of persons formally adjudged to be criminally dangerous, often taking past convictions into account. The granting of licences and public contracts may be conditional on the absence of criminal connections and proof of good reputation. Individuals and legal entities engaged in economic or financial activities involving great risk to the public, for example deposit-taking institutions or those that deal with toxic waste, should be subject to sufficiently severe and sufficiently enforced regulation to prevent wrongdoing, in particular since penal punishments rarely provide proper compensation for victims. Particular attention must be paid to the deterrence and punishment of misconduct by legal entities, such as multinational and other corporations. Individual executives may frequently be beyond national jurisdiction and personal responsibility may be difficult to establish. Criminal punishment of the entity itself, by fine or by forfeiture of property or legal rights, is used in some jurisdictions against corporate misconduct.

22. Crimes committed for economic gain can be successfully countered by the forfeiture of such gains and of any other assets of the individuals and organization involved. In some legal systems, great

significance is attributed to the freezing, seizure and confiscation of assets related to illegal activity. The need for more effective organized crime control makes it necessary to regard forfeiture as a strategic weapon, an economic method of discouraging organized crime activities and the means of eliminating the financial advantages of such anti-social activities.

23. The procedures for freezing, seizure and confiscation should be broad in their scope and permit the confiscation of a wide range of assets of an offender. The State should be able to eliminate all gain to offenders from their criminal activity. A subsidiary benefit of such action is that law enforcement agencies may be allowed to use confiscated assets or funds to further the activities of the agency. This can be a powerful incentive. International agreements may provide for the sharing of such assets.

24. In dealing with organized crime, it is appropriate to have the following types of assets subject to confiscation: *(a)* any property constituting the proceeds of organized criminal actions and any assets obtained with the help of these proceeds; and *(b)* any property used or intended to be used, in any manner or part, to commit or facilitate the commission of a crime by an organized group, including land, buildings and other private property.

25. Consideration may be given to allowing certain evidentiary rules to be used in the procedures for confiscation of the assets of criminals involved in organized crime. For example, if it is proved that defendants had acquired assets during the time they were committing offences for which they had been convicted, and there is no other likely method by which they could have acquired the assets, then it may be reasonably inferred that the assets are the proceeds of crime. In the drafting of legislation related to such confiscation, whether preventive or repressive, the liberty and property rights of individuals must be protected in accordance with national constitutional principles.

III. Procedural legislation

26. In many countries criminal procedures oblige the court, prosecutor, investigator and police, as appropriate, to carry out investigations within their power whenever there are indications that a crime has been committed. There may, however, be discretionary powers that allow the law enforcement agencies to choose not to investigate a crime or to initiate a prosecution. Where this discretion exists it is often used by investigators when working with informants from criminal circles. Its use requires a high degree of professional responsibility on the part of investigators. Legal systems should be encouraged to recognize the possibility, in some cases, of granting minor criminals immunity from prosecution for their acts, for the purpose of disclosing the leaders of organized criminal groups.

27. The criminal laws of many countries specify the elements that must be established to prove that an offence has been committed. These may include: the act of committing a crime; the defendant's guilt and motives for the crime; any aggravating or extenuating circumstances, including the defendant's record, and the nature and amount of damage inflicted by the crime. Evaluation of the evidence is carried out by the official performing the investigation, the prosecutor, and finally by the court. In practice, there is no difference in the standard of evidence required in respect of crimes committed by organized crime groups against other crimes.

28. Deciding on the verdict must remain a task for the authority exercising judicial powers over serious offences committed by organized crime. In doing so, the principle of the presumption of innocence must be followed.

29. The experience of many countries suggests that it may be advantageous to use information obtained with the help of electronic surveillance, undercover agents, controlled delivery of drugs, the testimony of accomplices and other methods of preliminary investigation as evidence. The acceptability of such methods of preliminary investigation should be limited by strict observance of legal requirements and criminal procedural principles.

30. The use of the testimony of accomplices can be extremely helpful in prosecutions involving organized crime. Careful assessment and use of such testimony can enable the law enforcement process to penetrate the layers of secrecy that are characteristic of criminal organizations and would otherwise protect them from prosecution. Some countries also find it advantageous to enact legislation obliging witnesses to testify truthfully and providing for sanctions if they refuse to do so.

31. The restriction of the liberty of the defendant prior to conviction is frequently allowed by law when there are specified grounds. The main form of such restriction of liberty prior to conviction is pre-trial detention. This can be considered if it is appropriate in view of the seriousness of the case and the possible sentence upon conviction and for other reasons such as the possibility that the defendant will seek to evade justice or has tried to escape, the possibility of concealment of evidence, or the possibility that the defendant will commit further offences or otherwise be a danger to the community.

32. It may be appropriate to have conditional release provisions, so that a defendant who has been accused of an offence could be released upon the payment of a certain sum of money unless the judicial authorities believe that pre-trial detention is necessary. The question whether a criminal may be released on bail should normally be a matter for a judicial or other competent body but the financial resources of an organized criminal often make release inexpedient. The appropriateness of granting conditional release and other benefits in cases of organized criminality must be evaluated with regard

to the criminal record of the accused and the gravity of the accusation.

33. Provisions for the protection of witnesses are of great importance in combating organized crime. It is therefore recommended that national systems of criminal justice pay close attention to provisions, programmes and any legislation aimed at providing for the security of a witness. In particular, they should consider adopting measures for the protection of witnesses that allow for the relocation and change of identity of those witnesses, along with their physical protection if a threat is posed by a defendant and the defendant's associates. This can necessitate making arrangements to provide the witnesses with documents enabling them (and their families) to establish a new identity, with temporary housing, providing for the transportation of household furniture and other personal belongings to a new location, subsistence payments, assisting them in obtaining employment, and providing other necessary services to help the witnesses to lead a full and normal life. In considering the type of protection to be provided, the financial circumstances of a country must be taken into account. In addition, provision should be made for the safe custody of incarcerated witnesses, including separate accommodation. Legislation may also be necessary to deal with the practical problems that can arise in connection with relocated witnesses, such as child custody disputes and crimes committed in the witnesses' new identities.

IV. Law enforcement methods

34. If effective action is to be taken against organized criminal, the law enforcement authorities need to be able to predict and detect organized criminal activity. This requires the systematic collection and analysis of all relevant information from all sources in order to make it possible to produce and use intelligence for both strategic and tactical purposes. The methods employed for the collection and utilization of such information may be authorized and controlled by legislation. Even so, it is important that the technical facilities and techniques that the law enforcement authorities are allowed to use should always be sophisticated enough to enable them to match those employed by organized crime.

35. The production of intelligence requires the collection, collation and analysis of a wide range of information on the persons and organizations suspected of being involved in organized criminal activity, often including information that at first sight is not directly related to organized crime. There may be no rigid borderline between strategic and tactical intelligence but the main aim of tactical intelligence is to help in the planning of particular police operations and to identify the sources for obtaining the evidence that makes it possible to arrest a suspect and to prove guilt. Trained intelligence analysis greatly increases the effective application of law enforcement intelligence. It is important to note that there is often a need to continue the collection of information at all appropriate stages of the legal process. Intelligence should always be collected in such a manner that, even years later, it can be retrieved and used as evidence.

36. Where resources permit, computerized information systems may be of particular benefit in combating organized crime. Computers should be used to store information both on the persons and organizations suspected of being involved in organized criminal activity and on the crimes committed or being planned. Where there are different law enforcement agencies collecting information on organized crime, arrangements need to be made to allow an exchange of information, for example between local and national (or federal) authorities, and between local police forces in different areas. Careful attention must be paid to the compatibility of computerized systems, and the convertibility of manual systems to computerized systems. Creation of a centralized data bank may be appropriate in some countries. This information can be shared internationally on the basis of agreements. Technical assistance in criminal intelligence systems may be of mutual benefit to developing and developed countries.

37. Particular attention should be paid to information from confidential police sources, including prisoners. Further important intelligence will come from other sources, however, including open sources and international liaison. In particular, financial and taxation bodies, when permitted to do so, may be of great assistance in organized crime control, as they frequently find themselves directly in contact with organized groups when these groups seek to use the proceeds of criminal activity. Legislative inquiries and official and public records may also be of value. An essential resource in the effective investigation of organized crime is the capability to collect complicated financial and commercial information and present it in an intelligible manner as evidence. Information concerning forfeitable assets should also be collected, so that such property can be forfeited and made available for police use.

38. The infiltration of organized crime into legal enterprises and any contacts it may make in political circles can create a superficial respectability, facilitate corruption and be used by criminals to hinder investigation of their activities. Therefore, law enforcement agencies, when collecting various data on the criminal activity of a particular person or organization, should try to obtain the most comprehensive intelligence picture possible. Law enforcement agencies should adopt a range of measures, which may include the following:

(a) Developing intelligence, through informants, searches and other techniques, to uncover large-scale organized criminal enterprises;

(b) Determining the factors and conditions that facilitate the development of organized criminal activity;

(c) Providing for centralized collection, storage and analysis of information (including use of criminal organization charts) and for the tactical application of such information;

(d) Ensuring cooperation with law enforcement authorities and other bodies involved, using a multi-agency approach;

(e) Studying the experience of other countries in organized crime control;

(f) Developing, on the basis of the above factors, an integral criminal policy of legislation, allocation of resources and mobilization of public support.

39. To lift the veil of secrecy, conspiracy and fear-induced silence of possible witnesses, as well as to understand how the criminal communities function, who directs their activity, where their illegal income is channelled and so on, it is recommended that law enforcement bodies of all countries collect intelligence and evidence of criminal activities by undercover means. With the right safeguards, secret operations directed against organized crime can be conducted effectively through the use of undercover agents and informants, often in conjunction with the use of technical facilities to intercept and to record conversations the contents of which may facilitate the disclosure of crimes. These techniques may include wire-taps, surveillance by means of closed-circuit systems, night vision equipment etc., as well as video and audio recording of ongoing events. In some jurisdictions, such technical surveillance may be used only if other mechanisms of investigation have failed or there is no reason to think that they will lead to the desired results, or if other mechanisms are deemed to be too dangerous.

40. If extreme care is exercised with regard to the reliability of their testimony, and due account is taken of the gravity of their offence, the cooperating witnesses for the prosecution may be a valuable means of infiltrating organized crime groups. Mitigation of sentence or even dismissal of charges, where possible, can motivate lesser criminals to assist in investigations of organized crime. Incorporation of such procedures into national legislation or recognized practice, together with the protective services previously discussed, may serve to attract such cooperating witnesses.

V.   Organizational structures

41. Organized crime may be investigated by a variety of law enforcement agencies with different jurisdiction. In this connection, it is advisable to ensure that close coordination is maintained between central and peripheral structures and that law enforcement authorities also ensure effective liaison between intelligence and operations. In countries with federal structures, it is essential that effective mechanisms be established to ensure coordination of jurisdiction, intelligence and operations among federal policing agencies and those of other governmental units. Close coordination within and between agencies and units is essential to successful action against organized crime. A clear delineation of jurisdiction among agencies and units can contribute to a harmonious and effective working relationship.

42. When resources permit, it may be very useful to set up one or more specialized units dedicated to the investigation of organized crime, particularly in the areas of corruption, money laundering and illegal drug trafficking. There is a danger, which must be recognized, that exclusive jurisdiction over an area of investigation may create susceptibility to corruption, and appropriate safeguards against this must be developed.

43. Within any individual law enforcement agency, a strictly centralized senior management system that can scrutinize all aspects of investigations and monitor their course is necessary to ensure that all investigations are conducted in accordance with national laws and with proper respect for human rights. It is important for senior management officials to take due account of the necessity of ensuring financial, logistical and moral support.

44. Investigators, and in particular those leading the investigation, should be selected on the basis of their ability, experience, moral qualities and dedication. The importance of basic and in-service training should not be underestimated, for prosecutors and judges as well as for policemen.

45. The relationships between investigative, prosecutorial and judicial functions vary markedly between different legal systems. To combat organized crime successfully, in any system, it is necessary for these three functions to be harmoniously coordinated. Even so, due respect must be accorded to maintaining the proper relationships between the functions.

VI.   International cooperation

46. International experience shows that organized crime has long crossed national borders and is today transnational. The following crimes, in particular, are found most frequently in international dealings: drug trafficking, contraband, counterfeiting of currency, traffic in stolen motor vehicles, money laundering and traffic in minors and arms. It should be noted that aspects of the evolutionary process undergone by society may make powerful criminal organizations even more impenetrable and facilitate the expansion of their illegal activities. Therefore, international cooperation between the law enforcement agencies of all countries is vital for effective organized crime control. Law enforcement operations should pay due respect to the sovereignty of all nations. Such cooperation should be developed on a sound legal basis, created at national, bilateral and multilateral levels. While an international jurisdiction is a remote but possible goal, the easiest mechanism is often bilateral inter-State agreements. Although multilateral agreements require extensive negotiation, they can be of great use, as is the case with the United Nations Convention against Illicit Traffic in Narcotic Drugs and Psychotropic Substances.

47. In addition to cooperation in legal matters, effective international action against organized crime can be promoted through bilateral and multilateral cooperation in training, technical assistance and research, and through the exchange of information, in particular for the benefit of developing countries. The United Nations crime and criminal justice programme provides an appropriate framework for these activities. Effective cooperation is also facilitated by making proper use of the valuable facilities and services provided by the International Criminal Police Organization (ICPO/Interpol), and by various regional and subregional arrangements.

48. Since criminal organizations are very mobile and inventive in their use of the slightest deficiencies in national laws, all States should consider making provision to ensure that their judicial and law enforcement agencies respond adequately to requests for legal assistance from other countries. The main forms of cooperation so far established at the national level include exchange of information on organized crime in general and cooperation in specific operational matters; extradition; the transfer of a witness from one country to another; mutual legal assistance to seize and confiscate the proceeds of illegal activities and other assets; and the provision of training and assistance to other police forces, especially for combating illegal drug trafficking.

VII. Evaluation

49. In order to determine the appropriate level of the law enforcement response, mechanisms to evaluate the gravity of the threat posed by organized crime are needed. The current state of knowledge demonstrates considerable lack of precision in this regard. Some countries have attempted to quantify the financial harm caused by organized crime but these have remained only estimates. More extensive and rigorous research in this area may be of value to legislators and governmental administrators, who have to make appropriate decisions on the allocation of resources to combat organized crime.

50. The prevention and control of organized crime should not remain a matter for the law enforcement authorities alone. It requires broad cooperation with other authorities, the business community, civic organizations and the community as a whole. Mobilization of the public to participate in this work requires educational measures and the responsible cooperation of the mass media to reveal the harm caused by organized crime and its dangers to individuals and to society, and to stimulate public participation in the struggle to defeat it.

Economic and Social Council resolution 1992/23

30 July 1992   Meeting 41   Adopted without vote

Approved by Social Committee (E/1992/106) without vote, 23 July (meeting 18); draft by Commission on crime prevention (E/1992/30); agenda item 19.

On 16 December, the General Assembly, on the recommendation of the Third Committee, adopted without vote **resolution 47/87**.

International cooperation in combating organized crime

The General Assembly,

Alarmed by the rapid growth and geographical extension of organized crime in its various forms, both nationally and internationally, undermining the development process, impairing the quality of life and threatening human rights and fundamental freedoms,

Acknowledging the need for global efforts commensurate with the magnitude of national and transnational crime,

Recalling the responsibility assumed by the United Nations in the field of crime prevention and criminal justice,

Recalling also that the Eighth United Nations Congress on the Prevention of Crime and the Treatment of Offenders adopted resolutions entitled "Organized crime" and "Prevention and control of organized crime",

Recalling further its resolutions 44/71 and 44/72 of 8 December 1989, 45/121 and 45/123 of 14 December 1990, 46/152 of 18 December 1991 and S-17/2 of 23 February 1990 and Economic and Social Council resolutions 1989/70 of 24 May 1989, and taking note of Council resolution 1992/23 of 30 July 1992,

Bearing in mind that the Eighth Congress explored possibilities and ways of strengthening further international cooperation in combating organized crime and adopted the Guidelines for the prevention and control of organized crime, and model treaties relating to this question,

Welcoming with appreciation the results achieved at the Ministerial Meeting on the Creation of an Effective United Nations Crime Prevention and Criminal Justice Programme, held at Versailles, France, from 21 to 23 November 1991,

Acknowledging with appreciation the work done by the Commission on Crime Prevention and Criminal Justice during its first session, held at Vienna from 21 to 30 April 1992,

Noting that the Ad Hoc Expert Group Meeting on Strategies to Deal with Transnational Crime, held at Smolenice, Czechoslovakia, from 27 to 31 May 1991, and the International Seminar on Organized Crime, held at Suzdal, Russian Federation, from 21 to 25 October 1991, formulated important recommendations in this area,

Noting also that the meeting convened by the Resource Committee on Transnational Crime of the International Scientific and Professional Advisory Council for the United Nations crime prevention and criminal justice programme, held at Courmayeur, Italy, from 23 to 28 March 1992, resulted in a proposed outline for an international conference on money laundering and control,

Taking note of Economic and Social Council resolution 1992/24 of 30 July 1992, in which the Council decided that the topic "Action against national and transnational economic, organized and environmental crime: national experiences and international cooperation'' could be included in the provisional agenda of the Ninth United Nations Congress on the Prevention of Crime and the Treatment of Offenders,

Reaffirming that priority must be given to the struggle against all activities of organized crime, including the illicit arms trade and traffic in narcotic drugs, cultural property theft, money laundering, the infiltration of legitimate business and the corruption of public officials,

Emphasizing the role of the United Nations crime prevention and criminal justice programme in that respect,

1. *Urges* Member States to give favourable consideration to the implementation of the Guidelines for the prevention and control of organized crime at both national and international levels;

2. *Invites* Member States, in cooperation with international governmental and non-governmental organizations, to assist in increasing awareness to ensure a broad base of public participation and support for action against organized crime;

3. *Also invites* Member States to make available to the Secretary-General, on request, the provisions of their legislation relating to money laundering, the tracing, seizing and forfeiture of the proceeds of crime and the monitoring of large-scale cash transactions and other measures so that they may be available to Member States desiring to enact or further develop legislation in those fields;

4. *Requests* the Commission on Crime Prevention and Criminal Justice to continue to consider ways of strengthening international cooperation in combating organized crime, taking due account of the opinions of Governments, international organizations and non-governmental organizations expressed at international forums and to submit its views, through the Economic and Social Council, to the General Assembly at its forty-ninth session;

5. *Also requests* the Commission to organize the ongoing review and analysis of the incidence of transnational organized criminal activity and the dissemination of information thereon;

6. *Calls upon* Member States, international organizations and interested non-governmental organizations to cooperate closely with the United Nations in organizing practice-oriented workshops, research projects and training programmes to deal with specific aspects of organized criminal activities.

General Assembly resolution 47/87

16 December 1992   Meeting 89   Adopted without vote

Approved by Third Committee (A/47/703) without vote, 2 November (meeting 25); 23-nation draft (A/C.3/47/L.14), orally revised; agenda item 93 *(b)*.

Sponsors: Albania, Austria, Bahamas, Belarus, Cyprus, France, Germany, Hungary, Israel, Italy, Kazakhstan, Kyrgyzstan, Latvia, Lithuania, Mongolia, Netherlands, Norway, Poland, Russian Federation, Tajikistan, Trinidad and Tobago, Turkey, Turkmenistan.

Meeting numbers. GA 47th session: 3rd Committee 11-18, 22, 23, 25; plenary 89.

Domestic violence

An International Meeting of Experts on Domestic Violence met at Vancouver, Canada, from 22 to 25 March 1992.[22] The Meeting recommended revisions to a draft resource manual on domestic violence, to ensure that it presented globally useful and practical approaches to the problem. The manual had been prepared under the supervision of the Canadian Department of Justice, with the assistance of the Helsinki Institute for Crime Prevention and Control, affiliated with the United Nations, in cooperation with the Crime Prevention and Criminal Justice Branch of the United Nations Secretariat.

The Meeting also made recommendations for the dissemination and implementation of the manual. Twenty-eight experts from 16 countries participated in the Meeting.

UN crime prevention and criminal justice programme

The Secretary-General, pursuant to a 1991 General Assembly resolution,[16] submitted a March report[23] to the Commission on Crime Prevention and Criminal Justice on the conclusions and recommendations of the 1991 Ministerial Meeting on the Creation of an Effective United Nations Crime Prevention and Criminal Justice Programme.[24] The report provided a brief overview of the experience of the former Committee on Crime Prevention and Control, the prospective organization and functioning of the new Commission, the proposed revisions to the medium-term plan for the period 1992-1997, and follow-up to the Ministerial Meeting. The report noted that the continued growth of crime underscored the urgency of incisive action, and its transnational reach demanded a commensurate response. Effective action was needed to confront emerging needs as well as current problems.

Another report on measures taken to implement the 1991 Statement of Principles and Programme of Action of the United Nations crime prevention and criminal justice programme[16] was submitted to the Assembly by the Secretary-General in September.[25] The report considered policy development and programme implementation and the institutional capacity of the new programme.

Crime prevention institutes

The report of the Seventh Joint Programme Co-ordination Meeting of the United Nations Crime Prevention and Criminal Justice Programme Network (Dharan, Saudi Arabia, 7 and 8 January 1992) was submitted to the Commission in April.[26] Attending the meeting were representatives of the United Nations Crime Prevention and Criminal Justice Branch; the United Nations Asia and Far East Institute for the Prevention of Crime and the Treatment of Offenders; the International Centre for Criminal Law Reform and Criminal Justice Policy; the Australian Institute for Criminology; the Arab Security Studies and Training Centre; Rutgers University School of Criminal Justice (United States); the United Nations Latin American

Institute for the Prevention of Crime and the Treatment of Offenders; the Helsinki Institute for Crime Prevention and Control, and the African Regional Institute for the Prevention of Crime and the Treatment of Offenders (UNAFRI).

UNAFRI

The Secretary-General submitted an October report[27] on UNAFRI to the General Assembly, pursuant to a 1991 Assembly request.[28] The report covered the Institute's operations and funding, noting that financial uncertainty had been a major obstacle to its viability. The Secretary-General said that ways had to be found to involve and integrate UNAFRI fully in the operations and work of the United Nations crime prevention and criminal justice programme and its programme network.

GENERAL ASSEMBLY ACTION

On 16 December, the General Assembly, on the recommendation of the Third Committee, adopted by recorded vote **resolution 47/89**.

United Nations African Institute for the Prevention of Crime and the Treatment of Offenders

The General Assembly,

Recalling its resolution 46/153 of 18 December 1991,

Recognizing that criminality is a major concern of all nations and that it calls for a concerted response from the international community aimed at preventing crime, improving the functioning of the criminal justice system and law enforcement, and increasing respect for individual rights,

Conscious of the vital role of regional cooperation in the fight against crime and of the potential contribution of interregional and regional institutes in the prevention of crime and the treatment of offenders,

Recognizing the efforts made thus far by the United Nations African Institute for the Prevention of Crime and the Treatment of Offenders in fulfilling its mandate through, *inter alia*, the organization of training programmes and regional seminars,

Aware of the financial difficulties that the Institute continues to face as a result of the fact that many States of the African region are in the category of the least developed countries and therefore lack the necessary resources with which to support the Institute,

Recognizing the urgent need to promote and intensify international cooperation in crime prevention and criminal justice and the fact that such cooperation can be effective only if it is executed with the direct participation of the receiving States, with due respect for their needs and priorities,

1. *Takes note* of the report of the Secretary-General on the United Nations African Institute for the Prevention of Crime and the Treatment of Offenders;

2. *Expresses its appreciation* to those Governments and intergovernmental organizations that have supported the Institute in the discharge of its responsibilities;

3. *Calls upon* Governments and intergovernmental and non-governmental organizations to intensify financial and other support to the Institute, in order to enable it to fulfil its objectives, particularly in the fields of

training, technical assistance, policy guidance, research and data collection;

4. *Reiterates its request* to the Secretary-General to ensure that sufficient resources are provided to the Institute, within the overall appropriations of the programme budget for the biennium 1992-1993 in support of the Institute, to enable it to carry out, in full and on time, all its mandates;

5. *Requests* the Secretary-General to report on the implementation of the present resolution to the General Assembly at its forty-eighth session.

General Assembly resolution 47/89

16 December 1992   Meeting 89   121-1-45 (recorded vote)

Approved by Third Committee (A/47/703) by recorded vote (97-1-41), 16 November (meeting 41); draft by Mauritania for African Group (A/C.3/47/L.16); agenda item 93 *(b)*.

Financial implications. 5th Committee, A/47/785; S-G, A/C.3/47/L.26, A/C.5/47/54.

Meeting numbers. GA 47th session: 3rd Committee 11-18, 22, 23, 25, 30, 41; 5th Committee 42; plenary 89.

Recorded vote in Assembly as follows:

In favour: Afghanistan, Algeria, Angola, Antigua and Barbuda, Argentina, Bahamas, Bahrain, Bangladesh, Barbados, Belize, Benin, Bhutan, Bolivia, Bosnia and Herzegovina, Botswana, Brazil, Brunei Darussalam, Burkina Faso, Burundi, Cameroon, Cape Verde, Chad, Chile, China, Colombia, Comoros, Congo, Costa Rica, Côte d'Ivoire, Cuba, Cyprus, Democratic People's Republic of Korea, Djibouti, Dominica, Dominican Republic, Ecuador, Egypt, El Salvador, Ethiopia, Fiji, Gabon, Gambia, Ghana, Grenada, Guatemala, Guinea, Guinea-Bissau, Guyana, Haiti, Honduras, India, Indonesia, Iran, Iraq, Jamaica, Jordan, Kenya, Kuwait, Lao People's Democratic Republic, Lebanon, Lesotho, Liberia, Libyan Arab Jamahiriya, Madagascar, Malaysia, Maldives, Mali, Marshall Islands, Mauritania, Mauritius, Mexico, Mongolia, Morocco, Mozambique, Myanmar, Namibia, Nepal, Nicaragua, Niger, Nigeria, Oman, Pakistan, Panama, Papua New Guinea, Paraguay, Peru, Philippines, Qatar, Republic of Korea, Rwanda, Saint Kitts and Nevis, Saint Lucia, Saint Vincent and the Grenadines, Samoa, Sao Tome and Principe, Saudi Arabia, Senegal, Seychelles, Sierra Leone, Singapore, Sri Lanka, Sudan, Suriname, Swaziland, Syrian Arab Republic, Tajikistan, Thailand, Togo, Trinidad and Tobago, Tunisia, Uganda, Ukraine, United Arab Emirates, United Republic of Tanzania, Uruguay, Vanuatu, Venezuela, Viet Nam, Yemen, Zambia, Zimbabwe.

Against: United States.

Abstaining: Albania, Armenia, Australia, Austria, Azerbaijan, Belarus, Belgium, Bulgaria, Canada, Croatia, Czechoslovakia, Denmark, Estonia, Finland, France, Germany, Greece, Hungary, Iceland, Ireland, Israel, Italy, Japan, Kazakhstan, Kyrgyzstan, Latvia, Liechtenstein, Lithuania, Luxembourg, Malta, Micronesia, Netherlands, New Zealand, Norway, Poland, Portugal, Republic of Moldova, Romania, Russian Federation, San Marino, Slovenia, Spain, Sweden, Turkey, United Kingdom.

Preparations for the Ninth (1995) Congress

In a March note[29] to the Commission, the Secretary-General discussed preparations for the Ninth United Nations Congress on the Prevention of Crime and the Treatment of Offenders. The Secretary-General reviewed past congresses, new functions of the Congress, substantive preparations, changes in format, organizational arrangements and rules of procedure. He proposed a number of possible subjects for the Congress, including: crime prevention and justice for the protection of society; the impact of recent transformations on organized, economic and environmental criminality; new forms and transnational dimensions of economic and organized crime and their interfaces; the concept of security and public safety; the exercise of police power and other crime prevention functions; community policing and the maintenance of law and order; science and technology in the service of crime prevention; use of modern technology and management techniques in the administration of justice; and violence prevention and control.

ECONOMIC AND SOCIAL COUNCIL ACTION

On 30 July, the Economic and Social Council, on the recommendation of its Social Committee, adopted without vote **resolution 1992/24**.

Preparations for the Ninth United Nations Congress on the Prevention of Crime and the Treatment of Offenders

The Economic and Social Council,

Considering that, pursuant to General Assembly resolutions 415(V), annex, of 1 December 1950 and 46/152, annex, of 18 December 1991, the Ninth United Nations Congress on the Prevention of Crime and the Treatment of Offenders is to be convened in 1995,

Recognizing the significant contributions of the United Nations congresses on the prevention of crime and the treatment of offenders to the promotion and strengthening of international cooperation in crime prevention and criminal justice,

Bearing in mind the new role of the congresses stipulated in paragraph 29 of the statement of principles and programme of action of the United Nations crime prevention and criminal justice programme, contained in the annex to General Assembly resolution 46/152,

Taking note of the note by the Secretary-General on the preparations for the Ninth Congress,

1. *Decides* that the following topics could be included in the provisional agenda for the Ninth United Nations Congress on the Prevention of Crime and the Treatment of Offenders, as recommended by the Commission on Crime Prevention and Criminal Justice at its first session:

(*a*) International cooperation and practical technical assistance for strengthening the rule of law: promoting the United Nations crime prevention and criminal justice programme;

(*b*) Action against national and transnational economic, organized and environmental crime: national experiences and international cooperation;

(*c*) Criminal justice systems: management and improvement of police, prosecution, courts and corrections;

(*d*) Crime prevention strategies, in particular as related to crimes in urban areas and juvenile and violent criminality, including the question of victims: assessment and new perspectives;

2. *Requests* the Commission at its second session to finalize the provisional agenda for the Ninth Congress and to make its recommendations to the Council, taking into account the following:

(*a*) The Ninth Congress should deal with a limited number of precisely defined substantive topics, which should reflect the urgent needs of the world community;

(*b*) The final selection of those topics should be made in accordance with the priorities set by the Commission;

(*c*) There should be action-oriented research and demonstration workshops related to the topics mentioned in paragraph 1 above, as part of the programme of the Ninth Congress, and ancillary meetings associated with its provisional agenda;

3. *Requests* the Secretary-General to prepare a discussion guide for the consideration of the Commission, which would include proposals for the workshops mentioned in paragraph 2 (*c*) above, in cooperation with the United Nations institutes for the prevention of crime and the treatment of offenders, and invites Member States to be actively involved in that process;

4. *Also requests* the Secretary-General to prepare draft rules of procedure for the Ninth Congress, taking into account:

(*a*) The terms of reference of the United Nations congresses on the prevention of crime and the treatment of offenders, stipulated in the statement of principles and programme of action of the United Nations crime prevention and criminal justice programme;

(*b*) The need for all draft resolutions on the selected topics to be submitted well in advance of the Ninth Congress;

5. *Invites* the regional commissions, the United Nations institutes for the prevention of crime and the treatment of offenders, government-appointed national correspondents in the field of crime prevention and criminal justice, specialized agencies and other entities within the United Nations system, the intergovernmental organizations concerned and relevant non-governmental organizations in consultative status with the Economic and Social Council to become actively involved in the preparations for the Ninth Congress;

6. *Requests* the Secretary-General to facilitate the organization of the following:

(*a*) Ancillary meetings of non-governmental organizations in consultative status with the Council, to be held at the site of the Ninth Congress, to deal with issues relating to substantive items of the provisional agenda for the Ninth Congress, in accordance with existing legislative regulations;

(*b*) Meetings of professional and geographical interest groups to be held at the site of the Ninth Congress;

7. *Also requests* the Secretary-General to provide the United Nations crime prevention and criminal justice programme with the resources necessary to undertake, in an effective and timely manner, within the overall appropriations of the programme budget for the biennium 1992-1993, the preparatory activities for the Ninth Congress, as directed by the Commission, including the organization of regional preparatory meetings, and to ensure adequate resources for the biennium 1994-1995;

8. *Further requests* the Secretary-General to provide resources, as required, in accordance with established United Nations budgetary practice, within the overall appropriations of the programme budget for the biennium 1992-1993, and adequate resources for the biennium 1994-1995, to ensure an appropriate programme of public information relating to the preparations for the Ninth Congress;

9. *Takes note with appreciation* of the offer of the Government of the Islamic Republic of Iran to act as host for the Ninth United Nations Congress on the Prevention of Crime and the Treatment of Offenders.

Economic and Social Council resolution 1992/24

30 July 1992   Meeting 41   Adopted without vote

Approved by Social Committee (E/1992/106) without vote, 23 July (meeting 18); draft by Commission on crime prevention (E/1992/30); agenda item 19.

Financial implications. E/1992/30/Add.1.

UNICRI

In 1992, the United Nations Interregional Crime and Justice Research Institute (UNICRI) continued to work towards the development of improved policies in the field of crime prevention and control. The Rome-based Institute was originally established as the United Nations Social Defence Research Institute (UNSDRI) in 1968.[30] The mandate of UNSDRI was updated and its name changed to UNICRI by a 1989 General Assembly resolution.[31]

The third meeting of the Board of Trustees of UNICRI took place in Rome from 26 to 28 October. In adopting the Institute's work programme, special attention was paid to the priority themes identified by the Commission on Crime Prevention and Criminal Justice at its first session.

REFERENCES

[1]YUN 1991, p. 652, ESC res. 1991/4, 30 May 1991. [2]E/1992/17. [3]ACC/1992/1. [4]YUN 1991, p. 654, ESC dec. 1991/230, 30 May 1991. [5]E/1992/80. [6]E/AC.51/1992/2. [7]A/47/16 (Part I). [8]E/1992/113. [9]YUN 1991, p. 657, GA res. 46/92, 16 Dec. 1991. [10]E/CN.5/1993/3. [11]E/CN.5/1993/6. [12]GA res. 44/58, 8 Dec. 1989. [13]A/47/216-E/1992/43. [14]E/1992/30 & Add.1. [15]YUN 1991, p. 661. [16]Ibid., GA res. 46/152, 18 Dec. 1991. [17]E/CN.15/1992/1 & Corr.1. [18]E/CN.15/1992/4 & Add.1-5. [19]GA res. 44/71, 8 Dec. 1989. [20]A/47/381. [21]E/CN.15/1992/4/Add.5. [22]E/CN.15/1992/CRP.9. [23]E/CN.15/1992/6. [24]YUN 1991, p. 661. [25]A/47/399 & Corr.1. [26]E/CN.15/1992/CRP.5. [27]A/47/379 & Corr.1. [28]YUN 1991, p. 668, GA res. 46/153, 18 Dec. 1991. [29]E/CN.15/1992/5. [30]YUN 1968, p. 509. [31]GA res. 44/72, 8 Dec. 1989.

Chapter XIII

Women

In 1992, a summit held by the wives of heads of State or Government on the economic advancement of rural women (Geneva, 25 and 26 February) declared that Governments, national institutions, non-governmental organizations, the private sector, the United Nations and other donor agencies should allocate greater resources to promote the economic and social advancement of rural women.

The United Nations continued to implement the 1985 Nairobi Forward-looking Strategies for the Advancement of Women, while also preparing for the Fourth World Conference on Women in 1995.

The Commission on the Status of Women held its thirty-sixth session (Vienna, 11-20 March), and recommended seven draft resolutions and two draft decisions to the Economic and Social Council.

The Committee on the Elimination of Discrimination against Women, at its eleventh session (New York, 20-30 January), took up three initial reports and six second periodic reports of States parties to the 1979 Convention on the Elimination of All Forms of Discrimination against Women on the implementation of the Convention. By the end of the year, the Convention had received 96 signatures and 120 ratifications, accessions or successions.

Advancement of women

Implementation of the Nairobi Strategies

The Secretary-General, in accordance with a General Assembly resolution of 1991,[1] submitted a report to the Assembly in September 1992[2] on the implementation of the Nairobi Forward-looking Strategies for the Advancement of Women to the Year 2000, adopted in 1985 by the World Conference to Review and Appraise the Achievements of the United Nations Decade for Women.[3] The Strategies were designed to overcome obstacles to the Decade's goals of equality, development and peace. The report considered cooperation by the organizations of the United Nations system with the Commission on the Status of Women on implementation of the Strategies;

ageing women; the Fourth World Conference on Women in 1995; development; human rights; disabled women; the system-wide medium-term plan for the advancement of women for 1996-2001; an update of the *World Survey on the Role of Women in Development* in 1994; women in the Secretariat; public information regarding the advancement of women; and resources for the programme on the advancement of women.

The report also included an assessment of recent developments relevant to priority themes to be considered by the Commission on the Status of Women at its thirty-seventh session. Among the themes were equality: increased awareness by women of their rights, including legal literacy; development: women in extreme poverty, integration of women's concerns in national development planning; and peace: women and the peace process.

In response to a 1988 Economic and Social Council resolution,[4] the Secretary-General submitted a report[5] to the Commission on the Status of Women at its thirty-sixth session[6] on the monitoring of progress made by the United Nations system in the implementation of the Strategies. The report covered three objectives of the Strategies—equality, development and peace. It dealt with new mandates and programme priorities and significant activities during the biennium 1990-1991.

GENERAL ASSEMBLY ACTION

On 16 December 1992, the General Assembly, on the recommendation of the Third (Social, Humanitarian and Cultural) Committee, adopted without vote **resolution 47/95**.

Implementation of the Nairobi Forward-looking Strategies for the Advancement of Women

The General Assembly,

Recalling all its relevant resolutions, in particular resolution 44/77 of 8 December 1989, in which, *inter alia,* it endorsed and reaffirmed the importance of the Nairobi Forward-looking Strategies for the Advancement of Women for the period up to the year 2000 and set out measures for their immediate implementation and for the overall achievement of the interrelated goals and objectives of the United Nations Decade for Women: Equality, Development and Peace,

Recalling also its resolution 46/98 of 16 December 1991,

Taking into consideration the resolutions adopted by the Economic and Social Council on issues relating to women since the adoption of its resolution 1987/18 of 26 May 1987,

Reaffirming its determination to encourage the full participation of women in economic, social, cultural, civil and political affairs and to promote development, cooperation and international peace,

Conscious of the important and constructive contribution to the improvement of the status of women made by the Commission on the Status of Women, the specialized agencies, the regional commissions and other organizations and bodies of the United Nations system and non-governmental organizations concerned,

Concerned that the resources available to the programme on the advancement of women of the Secretariat are insufficient to ensure adequate support to the Committee on the Elimination of Discrimination against Women and effective implementation of other aspects of the programme, especially the preparations for the Fourth World Conference on Women: Action for Equality, Development and Peace, to be held in 1995,

Welcoming the completion of work on the draft declaration on the elimination of violence against women by the inter-sessional working group of the Commission on the Status of Women,

Recognizing the advancement of women as one of the priorities of the Organization for the biennium 1992-1993,

1. *Takes note* of the report of the Secretary-General;

2. *Reaffirms* paragraph 2 of section I of the recommendations and conclusions arising from the first review and appraisal of the implementation of the Nairobi Forward-looking Strategies for the Advancement of Women, contained in the annex to Economic and Social Council resolution 1990/15 of 24 May 1990, which called for an improved pace in the implementation of the Strategies in the crucial last decade of the twentieth century, since the cost to societies of failing to implement the Strategies would be high in terms of slowed economic and social development, inadequate use of human resources and reduced progress for society as a whole;

3. *Urges* Governments, international organizations and non-governmental organizations to implement the recommendations;

4. *Calls again upon* Member States to give priority to policies and programmes relating to the subtheme "Employment, health and education", in particular to literacy, for self-reliance of women and the mobilization of indigenous resources, as well as to issues relating to the role of women in economic and political decision-making, population, the environment and information;

5. *Reaffirms* the central role of the Commission on the Status of Women in matters related to the advancement of women, and calls upon it to continue promoting the implementation of the Forward-looking Strategies to the year 2000, based on the goals of the United Nations Decade for Women: Equality, Development and Peace and the subtheme "Employment, health and education", and urges all relevant bodies of the United Nations system to cooperate effectively with the Commission in this task;

6. *Requests* the Commission, when considering the priority theme relating to development during its thirty-seventh and subsequent sessions, to ensure its early contribution to the preparatory work of forthcoming major international conferences such as the World Conference on Human Rights, to be held in 1993, the International Conference on Population and Development, to be held in 1994, the Fourth World Conference on Women: Action for Equality, Development and Peace, to be held in 1995, and the World Summit on Social Development, to be held in 1995, and to address the impact of technologies on women;

7. *Also requests* the Commission to give special attention to women in developing countries, particularly in Africa and the least developed countries, who suffer disproportionately from the effects of the global economic crisis and the heavy external debt burden, and to recommend further measures for the equalization of opportunity and for integration of these women into the development process when considering the priority theme relating to development;

8. *Endorses* Economic and Social Council decision 1992/272 of 30 July 1992 concerning the preparations for the Fourth World Conference on Women, in which the Council took note of Commission on the Status of Women resolution 36/8 of 20 March 1992, and expresses its appreciation to the Government of China for its offer to act as host for the Conference, to be held in Beijing from 4 to 15 September 1995;

9. *Requests* the Secretary-General to take into account section A, paragraph 6, of Commission resolution 36/8 when appointing the Secretary-General of the Conference;

10. *Also requests* the Secretary-General to ensure that appropriate staff from the secretariats of the Committee on the Elimination of Discrimination against Women and the Commission on the Status of Women participate in the preparatory process for the World Conference on Human Rights, as well as in the Conference itself, in accordance with General Assembly resolution 40/108 of 13 December 1985;

11. *Recommends* the further development of methods of compilation and data collection in areas of concern identified by the Commission and urges Member States to improve and broaden collection of gender-disaggregated statistical information and make it available to the relevant bodies of the United Nations system with a view to having prepared, in all official languages, as a background document for the Fourth World Conference on Women, an updated edition of *The World's Women 1970-1990: Trends and Statistics*;

12. *Emphasizes*, in the framework of the Forward-looking Strategies, the importance of the total integration of women in the development process, bearing in mind the specific and urgent needs of the developing countries, and calls upon Member States to establish specific targets at each level in order to increase the participation of women in professional, management and decision-making positions in their countries;

13. *Emphasizes once again* the need to give urgent attention to redressing socio-economic inequities at the national and international levels as a necessary step towards the full realization of the goals and objectives of the Forward-looking Strategies;

14. *Urges* the Commission to complete its work on the draft declaration on the elimination of violence against women and to submit it for information to the World Conference on Human Rights;

15. *Strongly urges* that particular attention be given by the relevant United Nations organizations and Governments to the special needs of women with disabilities, to elderly women and also to women in vulnerable situations such as migrant and refugee women and children;

16. *Endorses* the recommendation contained in section B of Commission resolution 36/8 that regional preparatory conferences should include in their agendas the issue of women in public life, as well as the request that the Secretary-General include information on women in public life in the preparation of the priority theme, "Peace: women in international decision-making", for the Commission at its thirty-ninth session, in 1995;

17. *Welcomes* the recommendations on women, environment and development in all programme areas, adopted at the United Nations Conference on Environment and Development, in particular chapter 24 of Agenda 21, entitled "Global action for women towards sustainable and equitable development";

18. *Urges* organs, organizations and bodies of the United Nations to ensure active participation of women in the planning and implementation of programmes for sustainable development, and requests Governments to consider nominating women as representatives to the Commission on Sustainable Development;

19. *Requests* the Secretary-General, in formulating the system-wide medium-term plan for the advancement of women for the period 1996-2001 and in integrating the Forward-looking Strategies into activities mandated by the General Assembly, to pay particular attention to specific sectoral themes that cut across the three objectives, equality, development and peace, and include, in particular, literacy, education, health, population, the impact of technology on the environment and its effect on women and the full participation of women in decision-making, and to continue to assist Governments in strengthening their national machineries for the advancement of women;

20. *Also requests* the Secretary-General to continue updating the *World Survey on the Role of Women in Development*, bearing in mind its importance, placing particular emphasis on the adverse impact of the difficult economic situation affecting the majority of developing countries, particularly on the condition of women, giving special attention to worsening conditions for the incorporation of women into the labour force, as well as the impact of reduced expenditures for social services on women's opportunities for education, health and child care, and to submit a preliminary version of the updated *World Survey on the Role of Women in Development* to the Economic and Social Council, through the Commission, in 1993 and a final version in 1994;

21. *Requests* Governments, when presenting candidatures for vacancies in the Secretariat, in particular at the decision-making level, to give priority to women's candidatures, and requests the Secretary-General in reviewing these candidatures to give special consideration to female candidates from underrepresented and unrepresented developing countries;

22. *Requests* the Secretary-General to invite Governments, organizations of the United Nations system, including the regional commissions and the specialized agencies, and intergovernmental and non-governmental organizations to report periodically to the Economic and Social Council, through the Commission, on activities undertaken at all levels to implement the Forward-looking Strategies;

23. *Also requests* the Secretary-General to continue to provide for the existing weekly radio programmes on women in the regular budget of the United Nations, making adequate provisions for broadcasts in different languages, and to develop the focal point for issues relating to women in the Department of Public Information of the Secretariat, which, in concert with the Centre for Social Development and Humanitarian Affairs of the Secretariat, should provide a more effective public information programme relating to the advancement of women;

24. *Further requests* the Secretary-General to include in his report on the implementation of the Forward-looking Strategies, to be submitted to the General Assembly at its forty-eighth session, an assessment of recent developments that are relevant to the priority themes to be considered at the subsequent session of the Commission and to transmit to the Commission a summary of relevant views expressed by delegations during the debate in the Assembly;

25. *Recommends* that the Commission on the Status of Women, as the preparatory body for the Fourth World Conference on Women, should consider at its next session the relevance of the resolutions drafted at the World Conference to Review and Appraise the Achievements of the United Nations Decade for Women: Equality, Development and Peace, held in 1985, in order to avoid duplication of work, keeping in mind that those resolutions were neither adopted by the Conference nor considered by the General Assembly;

26. *Requests* the Secretary-General to report to the General Assembly at its forty-eighth session on measures taken to implement the present resolution;

27. *Also requests* the Secretary-General to report to the General Assembly at its forty-eighth session on the state of preparation for the Fourth World Conference on Women under the item entitled "Advancement of women";

28. *Decides* to consider the implementation of the Forward-looking Strategies for the period up to the year 2000 at its forty-eighth session under the item entitled "Advancement of women".

General Assembly resolution 47/95

16 December 1992   Meeting 89   Adopted without vote

Approved by Third Committee (A/47/670) without vote, 5 November (meeting 30); draft by Pakistan for Group of 77 (A/C.3/47/L.23), orally revised; agenda item 94.

Meeting numbers. GA 47th session: 3rd Committee 19-26, 28, 30; plenary 89.

Monitoring, review and appraisal

1995 world conference on women

The Secretary-General, responding to a resolution adopted by the Commission on the Status of Women in 1991,[7] submitted a report in January 1992[8] on preparations for the Fourth World Conference on Women: Action for Equality, Development and Peace, to be held in 1995. The report suggested preparatory activities that might be organized at national, regional and interregional levels, and discussed the role of non-governmental organizations (NGOs) in the preparations and the type of public information campaign that would be desirable. It indicated the resources currently allocated for the Conference and additional requirements that might be considered.

By a resolution adopted in March,[9] the Commission on the Status of Women accepted China's offer to host the Conference and decided that it should be held in Beijing from 4 to 15 September 1995. The Commission recommended that the Secretary-General appoint a woman as Secretary-General of the Conference and that Conference staff include persons from developing countries. The Commission also made recommendations on items for inclusion in the Conference agenda, the draft rules of procedure and the Conference preparatory process at national and regional levels.

By **decision 1992/272** of 30 July, the Economic and Social Council took note of the Commission's resolution and endorsed the recommendations contained therein.

Communications on the status of women

On 11 and 12 March 1992, a list of confidential communications on the status of women was distributed to the representative of each State member of the Commission on the Status of Women.[7] On 16 March, the Commission appointed a Working Group on Communications concerning the Status of Women, which held three closed meetings and subsequently submitted its report to the Commission at a closed meeting.

In its report, the Working Group stated that it had received communications from the Division for the Advancement of Women, United Nations Office at Vienna, and the Centre for Human Rights, United Nations Office at Geneva. The Group noted, among the communications received, cases of violence against women by army, security and occupation forces and discrimination against women in their working lives. The Group also proposed ways of improving the communications procedure, including increased publicity for the existing communications mechanism. It noted the importance of concerned Governments replying to communications received.

ECONOMIC AND SOCIAL COUNCIL ACTION

On 30 July 1992, the Economic and Social Council, in accordance with a recommendation of its Social Committee, adopted without vote **resolution 1992/19**.

Communications on the status of women

The Economic and Social Council,

Recalling its resolutions 76(V) of 5 August 1947 and 304 I (XI) of 14 and 17 July 1950, which form the basis for the mandate of the Commission on the Status of Women to receive at each of its regular sessions a list of confidential and non-confidential communications relating to the status of women,

Taking into consideration its resolution 1983/27 of 26 May 1983, in which it reaffirmed the mandate of the Commission to consider confidential and non-confidential communications on the status of women and authorized the Commission to appoint a working group to consider communications, with a view to bringing to the attention of the Commission those communications, including the replies of Governments, which appear to reveal a consistent pattern of reliably attested injustice and discriminatory practices against women,

Reaffirming that discrimination against women is incompatible with human dignity and that women and men should participate on the basis of equality, irrespective of race or creed, in the social, economic and political processes of their countries,

Recalling its resolution 1990/8 of 24 May 1990, in which it requested the Secretary-General to examine, in consultation with Governments, the existing mechanisms for communications on the status of women, in order to ensure that such communications receive effective and appropriately coordinated consideration in view of the role of communications in the work of the Commission, and to report thereon to the Commission at its thirty-fifth session,

Taking note of the report of the Secretary-General on examining existing mechanisms for communications on the status of women, and the various views expressed by Governments,

Taking note also of the conclusion of the Working Group on Communications on the Status of Women, in its report to the Commission at its thirty-fifth session that, while the communications procedure provided a valuable source of information on the effects of discrimination on the lives of women, it should be improved to make it more efficient and useful, and that clear criteria for receiving communications should be given,

1. _Reaffirms_ that the Commission on the Status of Women is empowered to make recommendations to the Economic and Social Council on what action should be taken on emerging trends and patterns of discrimination against women revealed by communications on the status of women;

2. _Requests_ the Secretary-General to publicize widely among international and national organizations, in particular women's groups, the existence and scope of the communication mechanisms of the Commission;

3. _Further requests_ the Secretary-General to support the activities of the Commission with regard to its consideration of communications and to ensure proper coordination of the activities of the Commission in this area and those of the other bodies of the Council, by taking the following action:

   (a) Ensuring that the Division for the Advancement of Women of the Centre for Social Development and Humanitarian Affairs of the Secretariat and the Centre for Human Rights of the Secretariat coordinate closely so that all communications received are sent as soon as possible to the appropriate United Nations bodies and to each concerned Member State, and that the respective offices are informed of the disposition of the communications;

   (b) Encouraging the specialized agencies to provide to the Commission, through the Division for the Advancement of Women, communications or other information in their possession that is relevant to discrimination against women;

   (c) Making available to authors of communications any recommendations by the Commission to the Council on situations brought to the attention of the Commission by the Working Group on Communications on the Status of Women;

4. *Reaffirms* that the consideration by the Commission of the communications shall remain confidential until such time as the Commission may decide to make recommendations to the Council;

5. *Requests* the Commission, in order to avoid duplication of work, to determine whether a trend or pattern of discrimination against women revealed by communications should be brought to the attention of another United Nations body or specialized agency that might be better able to take appropriate action;

6. *Also requests* the Commission to consider, as appropriate, ways of making the existing procedure for receiving and considering communications, including the standard of admissibility, more transparent and efficient, taking into account the report of the Secretary-General on examining mechanisms for communications on the status of women, which was submitted to the Commission at its thirty-fifth session;

7. *Requests* the Secretary-General to ensure that any costs resulting from the activities set out in the present resolution are kept to a minimum and that the activities are carried out within existing resources.

Economic and Social Council resolution 1992/19

30 July 1992   Meeting 40   Adopted without vote

Approved by Social Committee (E/1992/105) without vote, 21 July (meeting 14); draft by Commission on women (E/1992/24); agenda item 18.

System-wide coordination

The sixteenth ad hoc inter-agency meeting on women was held at Vienna on 9 and 10 March 1992.[10] Representatives of 28 organizations and specialized agencies of the United Nations participated. They recommended to the Administrative Committee on Coordination (ACC) that the United Nations report on all activities undertaken in the field of the advancement of women in the quinquennial review and appraisal of the Forward-looking Strategies; that the system-wide monitoring of progress made in implementing the Strategies be linked to the priority themes of equality, development and peace; and that the United Nations system report on activities, progress achieved, lessons learned and obstacles encountered in relation to those themes. Concerning preparations for the Fourth World Conference on Women, the meeting agreed that institutional support for the public information campaign should be strengthened through inter-agency collaboration and that the participation of NGOs in the Conference should be extended beyond those in consultative status with the Economic and Social Council, to include NGOs that had demonstrated their strong commitment to work on women's issues. The meeting also issued a statement on the preparations for the Conference.

Research and Training Institute for the Advancement of Women

The twelfth session of the Board of Trustees of the International Research and Training Institute for the Advancement of Women (INSTRAW) was held at Santo Domingo, Dominican Republic, from 17 to 21 February 1992.[11] The Board reviewed INSTRAW's work during 1991, its training programme, scholarships and internships, its information, documentation and communication facilities and its publication policy. It discussed cooperation with United Nations organizations, research and training institutes and INSTRAW focal points and correspondents. The Board reviewed the work of the Strategic Planning and Finance Committees and decided that their functions should be merged.

The Board noted INSTRAW's continuing activities to improve statistics on the situation of women relative to that of men, including the situations of elderly women and women in the informal sector (see below). The Board stressed INSTRAW's role in the development, evaluation and demonstration of training materials for the inclusion of women in development and recommended that its scholarship and internship programme be extended. The Board stressed the need for continued close collaboration between INSTRAW and the regional commissions and welcomed the trend of increased cooperation among agencies in developing projects for the advancement of women. The Board approved the proposed programme of work and budget of $4,107,906 for 1992-1993.

INSTRAW activities

In 1992,[12] INSTRAW strengthened its collaboration with bodies and entities of the United Nations and governmental, non-governmental and other organizations. It prepared an innovative pre-workshop resource package to strengthen the use of statistical data on women, and tested it at a training workshop on statistics and indicators on women in the Pacific islands (Rarotonga, Cook Islands, 30 November–3 December 1992). INSTRAW also helped to organize a national workshop on statistics and indicators on women in Turkey (Ankara, 21-23 October).

Methods for assessing the value of women's economic contributions, both paid and unpaid, were considered at an interregional workshop on the development of statistics on women's work in the informal sector (Seoul, Republic of Korea, 25-29 May) and at an international meeting on time-use research methodology (Rome, Italy, 15-18 June).

INSTRAW participated in the Summit on the Economic Advancement of Rural Women (see below) and in the twentieth meeting of the ACC Task Force on Rural Development (New York, 22-24 April).

In cooperation with INSTRAW, the United Nations Department of Economic and Social Development and the Economic and Social Commission for Asia and the Pacific organized an interregional workshop applying training modules on women, water supply and sanitation, at Bangkok, Thailand, from 21 to 25 September.

The Institute started work on a long-term research and training programme for women farmers in transitional Eastern European countries. Research was conducted on the situation of women in agriculture in Bulgaria and Hungary. INSTRAW engaged a consultant to attend a workshop on the problems of transforming collective farms into market-oriented units (Godollo, Hungary, 22-26 June), sponsored by the Food and Agriculture Organization of the United Nations and the Economic Commission for Europe.

At the invitation of the Intersecretariat Working Group on National Accounts, INSTRAW participated in an interregional seminar on the revision of the system of national accounts (Aguascalientes, Mexico, 5-9 October).

Two issues of *INSTRAW News* were published —No. 17 (spring) was devoted to women and management and No. 18 (autumn) to the United Nations and women.

Contributions to INSTRAW from Member States during the year amounted to $2,259,392. At the United Nations Pledging Conference for Development Activities held in November, INSTRAW received pledges of contributions totalling $973,971 for 1993.

ECONOMIC AND SOCIAL COUNCIL ACTION

On 30 July, the Economic and Social Council, following the recommendation of its Social Committee, adopted without vote **resolution 1992/21**.

International Research and Training Institute for the Advancement of Women

The Economic and Social Council,

Recalling its resolution 1991/24 of 30 May 1991, in which it took note of the report of the Board of Trustees of the International Research and Training Institute for the Advancement of Women on its eleventh session,

Taking note of General Assembly resolution 46/99 of 16 December 1991, in which the Assembly took note of the report of the International Research and Training Institute for the Advancement of Women on its activities,

Having considered the report of the Board of Trustees of the Institute on its twelfth session,

Reaffirming the specific and unique role of the Institute in the areas of research and training that would lead to the systematic inclusion of women in mainstream development programmes and projects,

1. *Takes note with satisfaction* of the report of the Board of Trustees of the International Research and Training Institute for the Advancement of Women on its twelfth session and the decisions contained therein;

2. *Expresses its appreciation* for the successful implementation of the programmes of the Institute, in particular activities on improving statistics to yield better descriptive data on the situation of women relative to that of men, including elderly women and women in the informal sector; women, the environment and sustainable development; assessing and developing appropriate communication materials on women and development; rural women and credit; and monitoring and evaluation methodologies for programmes and projects on women and development;

3. *Takes note* of the programme budget of the Institute for the biennium 1992-1993, approved by the Board of Trustees at its twelfth session, and notes the commencement of work in the areas of appraisal and evaluation of development strategies and programmes for the maximum impact on women and the long-term research project on methods for the measurement of the value of women's work, including that in the informal sector;

4. *Commends* the sustained efforts made by the Institute to further enhance its linkages with other United Nations organizations, regional commissions, governmental and non-governmental organizations, research institutions and other organizations and groups with similar interests in developing projects for the advancement of women;

5. *Reaffirms* the catalytic and advocatory role of the Institute in facilitating the inclusion of women as partners in development through research, training and information activities on issues affecting women and development;

6. *Recommends*, in view of the increase in research and training being done in the general areas of women and development, that the Institute concentrate on the identification of barriers to improvements in the status of women and the development of tools for the removal of those persistent obstacles to progress;

7. *Calls upon* States and intergovernmental and non-governmental organizations to contribute through voluntary contributions and pledges to the United Nations Trust Fund for the International Research and Training Institute for the Advancement of Women, thus enabling the Institute to continue to respond effectively to its mandate.

Economic and Social Council resolution 1992/21

30 July 1992   Meeting 40   Adopted without vote

Approved by Social Committee (E/1992/105) without vote, 22 July (meeting 15); 30-nation draft (E/1992/C.2/L.6); agenda item 18.

Sponsors: Angola, Argentina, Australia, Bahamas, Bangladesh, Bolivia, Brazil, Chile, Colombia, Costa Rica, Dominican Republic, Ecuador, El Salvador, Guatemala, Honduras, Mexico, Morocco, Netherlands, New Zealand, Nicaragua, Paraguay, Peru, Romania, Spain, Suriname, Tunisia, Turkey, Uruguay, Venezuela, Yugoslavia.

REFERENCES

[1]YUN 1991, p. 673, GA res. 46/98, 16 Dec. 1991. [2]A/47/377. [3]YUN 1985, p. 937. [4]ESC res. 1988/22, 26 May 1988. [5]E/CN.6/1992/2. [6]E/1992/24. [7]YUN 1991, p. 672. [8]E/CN.6/1992/3. [9]E/1992/24 (res. 36/8). [10]ACC/1992/9. [11]E/1992/18. [12]INSTRAW/BT/1993/R.2.

Women and development

The Secretary-General, in accordance with a 1987 Economic and Social Council resolution,[1] submitted a report in January 1992[2] to the Commission on the Status of Women concerning the integration of women in the process of development. The report covered the results of two meetings—a seminar on the integration of women in development (Vienna, 9-11 December 1991) and an expert group meeting on integration of ageing and elderly women into development (Vienna, 7-11 October 1991). According to the report, these two meetings indicated a need to redefine the framework of current approaches to women in development. It noted the need to recognize women's lifetime productivity, including reproductive activities that were essential to the survival and development of society. The seminar discussed the conceptual framework for, and lessons to be drawn from, the women-in-development (WID) concept that looked beyond women's role as mothers. WID activities encouraged the empowerment of women to participate equally with men in all areas of production and economic development. The expert group meeting drew attention to the "economic viability" of older women whose many productive roles contradicted some societies' perception of them as "an economic burden".

The Commission on the Status of Women adopted two resolutions on women and development. In the first,[3] the Commission encouraged Governments, NGOs and other bodies to involve women, including elderly women, in development activities; invited international development agencies to recognize the potential of elderly women as a human resource for development; and called on the Secretary-General to compile a comprehensive annotated bibliography on the status of elderly women worldwide.

In the second resolution,[4] the Commission urged Governments to foster women's full participation in all areas of development; to promote economic development that integrated their needs and concerns; to include gender perspectives in guidelines for policy-making; to foster women's access to income-generating activities; and to identify national targets for women in such areas as education, employment, income, health and public life. It recommended that Governments strengthen national machinery for the advancement of women and that Governments, international donors and NGOs develop gender-oriented research. It appealed to Governments, donor countries, international organizations and financial institutions to support the establishment of cooperative rural banks to assist women, especially those engaged in small- and medium-scale productive activities. It requested Member States to provide technical and managerial training for women in rural and urban areas and called on Governments, donor countries and international organizations to facilitate the access of rural and urban poor women in particular to basic education and health and child-care facilities.

On 30 July, the Economic and Social Council, by **decision 1992/271** on the integration of elderly women into development, took note of the Commission's first resolution.

On 14 February,[5] the Governing Council of the United Nations Development Programme (UNDP) decided to consider the subject of women in development on a biennial basis.

Summit on the Economic Advancement of Rural Women

The Summit on the Economic Advancement of Rural Women was held at Geneva on 25 and 26 February 1992. Prior to the Summit, the eighth session of the United Nations Conference on Trade and Development (Cartagena de Indias, Colombia, 8-25 February)[6] expressed its support for the Summit, commended the group of First Ladies who had organized it and underlined the need to strengthen the productive role of rural women to promote food security, alleviate poverty and accelerate development. The Conference appealed to all Member States and the appropriate organs, organizations and bodies of the United Nations to support the Summit and ensure effective follow-up to its recommendations.

On 30 June,[7] Belgium transmitted to the Secretary-General the text of the Geneva Declaration for Rural Women, adopted at the Summit. The Declaration covered objectives for operational strategies and action programmes, implementation and follow-up. In a preamble, the Summit participants—wives of heads of State or Government from Africa, the Americas, Asia, Europe and Oceania—expressed solidarity with the rural women of the world and their determination to raise awareness of conditions affecting rural women among decision makers, at national, regional and international levels. They declared their commitment to the social and economic advancement of rural families and to sustainable development. They noted that women were the backbone of the agricultural labour force in much of the developing world, producing 35 to 45 per cent of gross domestic product and more than 50 per cent of the developing world's food. Yet, more than half a billion rural women were poor and lacked access to resources and markets. The Summit expressed its determination to mobilize public opinion, political will and resources to raise the status and quality of life of rural women and their families.

The Declaration stated that Governments, national institutions, NGOs and the private sector, and United Nations and other donor agencies should allocate greater resources to promote the economic and social advancement of rural women. Measures should be taken to ensure that women had equity in inheritance, marriage, divorce and child custody. Legal and administrative measures should protect rural women from exploitation in the labour, capital and product markets and assure them of equal pay for equal work. Rural women should be made aware of their rights and the resources, technology, production, social services, market opportunities and credit available to them. Their access to credit and financial services should be improved and facilities for women's education and functional literacy should be strengthened. Rural girls and young women should receive at least primary and secondary education, as well as health and vocational training.

The First Ladies expressed their intention to work together to mobilize political and financial resources for women and to establish procedures for monitoring the implementation of the Declaration. They also resolved to establish, at the global level, a committee of representatives of the wives of heads of State or Government with three members from each continent. The group would meet biennially to review implementation and to support national and regional initiatives for the advancement of rural women.

ECONOMIC AND SOCIAL COUNCIL ACTION

On 31 July, the Economic and Social Council, pursuant to the recommendation of its Economic Committee, adopted without vote **resolution 1992/53**.

Summit on the Economic Advancement of Rural Women

The Economic and Social Council,

Recalling its resolution 1991/64 of 26 July 1991 on the Summit on the Economic Advancement of Rural Women,

Recognizing the critical role of rural women as food producers and architects of household food security,

Noting with deep concern the continuing rise in the number of rural women living in poverty,

Reiterating its commitment to contribute to the improvement of the living conditions of rural women,

Welcoming the organization of the Summit on the Economic Advancement of Rural Women, held at Geneva on 25 and 26 February 1992, with the participation of a large number of First Ladies and high-level delegations,

Expressing its appreciation to the Patron of the Summit, to the core group of First Ladies who launched the initiative to convene the Summit and to the International Fund for Agricultural Development and other institutions that provided support for the Summit,

1. *Welcomes* the adoption by the Summit on the Economic Advancement of Rural Women of the Geneva Declaration for Rural Women;

2. *Urges* all States to work for the achievement of the goals endorsed in the Geneva Declaration;

3. *Urges* all relevant organs, organizations and bodies of the United Nations system to take into account the goals of the Geneva Declaration in carrying out their programmes, and invites the relevant governing bodies to consider specific measures, within their competence, to address the special needs of rural women in the light of the Geneva Declaration.

Economic and Social Council resolution 1992/53

31 July 1992   Meeting 42   Adopted without vote

Approved by Economic Committee (E/1992/109) without vote, 28 July (meeting 16); draft by Vice-Chairman (E/1992/C.1/L.15), based on informal consultations on 40-nation draft (E/1992/C.1/L.5); agenda item 12.

GENERAL ASSEMBLY ACTION

On 22 December, the General Assembly, acting on the recommendation of the Second (Economic and Financial) Committee, adopted without vote **resolution 47/174**.

Summit on the Economic Advancement of Rural Women

The General Assembly,

Recalling Economic and Social Council resolution 1991/64 of 26 July 1991 and taking note of Council resolution 1992/53 of 31 July 1992 on the Summit on the Economic Advancement of Rural Women,

Recognizing the critical role of rural women as food producers and architects of household food security,

Noting with deep concern the continuing rise in the number of rural women living in poverty,

Reaffirming its commitment to helping to improve the living conditions of rural women,

Welcoming the holding of the Summit on the Economic Advancement of Rural Women at Geneva on 25 and 26 February 1992, with the participation of a large number of wives of heads of State or Government and high-level delegations,

Expressing its appreciation to the sponsor of the Summit and the core group of wives of heads of State or Government who launched the initiative to convene the Summit, as well as to the International Fund for Agricultural Development and other institutions that provided support for it,

1. *Welcomes* the adoption by the Summit on the Economic Advancement of Rural Women of the Geneva Declaration for Rural Women;

2. *Urges* all States to work for the achievement of the goals endorsed in the Geneva Declaration;

3. *Urges* all organs, organizations and bodies of the United Nations system to take into account the goals of the Geneva Declaration in carrying out their programmes, and invites the relevant governing bodies to consider, in the light of the Geneva Declaration, the adoption of specific measures, within their respective fields of competence, with a view to meeting the special needs of rural women.

General Assembly resolution 47/174

22 December 1992   Meeting 93   Adopted without vote

Approved by Second Committee (A/47/717/Add.1) without vote, 24 November (meeting 45); 34-nation draft (A/C.2/47/L.39), orally revised; agenda item 12.

Sponsors: Algeria, Angola, Bangladesh, Barbados, Belarus, Belgium, Benin, Colombia, Czechoslovakia, Ecuador, Egypt, Guatemala, Italy, Jamaica, Jordan, Lesotho, Luxembourg, Madagascar, Malaysia, Mali, Mongolia, Morocco, Namibia, Nepal, Nigeria, Peru, Philippines, Senegal, Spain, Sri Lanka, Sudan, Turkey, United Republic of Tanzania, Zaire.
Meeting numbers. GA 47th session: 2nd Committee 3-9, 34-37, 40, 42, 43, 45; plenary 93.

Women, environment and sustainable development

The Secretary-General, in accordance with a 1990 decision of the Economic and Social Council[8] and a 1991 resolution of the General Assembly,[9] submitted to the Commission on the Status of Women in January 1992 a report on women and the environment.[10] The report considered the linkages between the status and role of women and the environment, action by women on behalf of the environment and action to support women and the environment. It also included, in an annex, women's perspectives on the environment: selected conclusions and recommendations of the Global Assembly of Women and the Environment—Partners in Life (Miami, United States, 4-8 November 1991). The report stated that the solution to the environmental crisis was to alleviate the underlying causes, such as the wasteful consumption of natural resources and energy, pollution-producing technologies, poverty and population pressures. It noted that the role of women in society made them significant contributors to environmental protection and that their action at the grass-roots level ranged from efficient household and natural resources management to demonstrations against manufacturing pollution. The report observed that few women, however, had the opportunity, training or financial means to make an impact at higher decision-making levels. The report recommended that women be involved in decisions affecting the distribution and use of land, the allocation of funds, and project design and implementation. It stated that women's approaches, views and priorities should also be included in policy formulation and the design of development programmes, giving weight to the impact of such programmes on the status of women. It was recommended that funding for environmental projects be decentralized and that women be represented at all levels and in all aspects of decision-making. The report also recommended the formulation and enforcement of international laws against the exploitation of the poor, especially women, as cheap labour, and the dumping of hazardous wastes in developing countries.

The Commission on the Status of Women[11] urged that Governments adopt laws, policies and programmes to promote women's participation in the preservation of the environment; that state and local governments, as well as governmental organizations, NGOs and the private sector, involve women in the implementation of environmental protection policies; and that Governments promote the education and professional and leadership training of women in environmental issues. It called for women's participation in managing funds for environmental protection and sustainable development, and urged Governments, NGOs and other social groups to promote changes in production policies and consumption habits, mainly in developed countries. International cooperation was also sought for the development of environmentally sound technologies.

Women and sustainable development

The United Nations Conference on Environment and Development (UNCED) (Rio de Janeiro, Brazil, 3-14 June 1992)[12] adopted the Rio Declaration on Environment and Development, in which it proclaimed that women had a vital role to play in environmental management and development and that their full participation was essential to the achievement of sustainable development (see PART THREE, Chapter VIII).

UNCED also adopted Agenda 21, a chapter of which dealt with global action for women towards sustainable and equitable development. The objectives of this programme area, proposed for Governments, were to implement the Nairobi Foward-looking Strategies for the Advancement of Women,[13] particularly women's participation in national ecosystem management and the control of environmental degradation. The aims were to increase the proportion of women decision makers, planners, technical advisers, managers and extension workers in environment and development fields; to consider developing by the year 2000 a strategy to eliminate all obstacles to women's full participation in sustainable development and in public life; to establish by 1995 mechanisms to assess the implementation and impact of development and environment policies and programmes on women and to ensure their contributions and benefits; to assess, review, revise and implement, where appropriate, curricula and other educational material for the dissemination of gender-relevant knowledge and valuation of women's roles through formal and non-formal education and training institutions; to formulate and implement governmental policies and national guidelines, strategies and plans to achieve equality for women; to implement, as a matter of urgency, measures to ensure the equal right of men and women to decide freely and responsibly the number and spacing of their children and to enable them to exercise that right; and to consider adopting, strengthening and enforcing legislation prohibiting violence against women and to take all necessary measures to eliminate such violence in all its forms.

The Conference identified a number of steps Governments should take in support of those objectives, as well as areas requiring urgent action, activities in the areas of research, data collection and dissemination of information and international and regional cooperation and coordination.

Specifically, the Conference recommended that: the United Nations Development Fund for Women (UNIFEM), in collaboration with the United Nations Children's Fund, should consult with donors to promote programmes and projects that strengthened the participation of women in sustainable development and decision-making; UNDP should establish a women's focal point on development and the environment in the offices of its resident representatives to provide information and exchange experiences in these fields. It was also recommended that the United Nations system, Governments and NGOs involved in the follow-up to the Conference and the implementation of Agenda 21 should ensure that gender considerations were fully integrated into all policies, programmes and activities.

Medium-term plan
for women and development

The Secretary-General, in accordance with a 1989 resolution of the Economic and Social Council,[14] submitted proposals to the Council regarding the framework of the system-wide medium-term plan for the advancement of women for 1996-2001.[15] The focus of the plan would be to eliminate obstacles and achieve the objectives of the Nairobi Forward-looking Strategies for the Advancement of Women.[13] The proposals covered the scope, focus and structure of the system-wide plan, which would comprise seven programmes: elimination of legal and attitudinal forms of discrimination; productive resources, income and employment; human resources development; promotion of peace and conflict resolution; decision-making; improving means of international action; and comprehensive inclusion of women in development.

UN Development Fund for Women

The Consultative Committee on UNIFEM met in New York from 13 to 16 April 1992.

The Committee recommended the following sums for approval:[16] $1 million for African women in crisis, an umbrella project to develop models and strategies for ensuring that refugee, returnee and displaced women were active participants in the search for solutions to their problems; $256,700 for the preparatory phase of an African internship programme, aiming to place 40 to 60 young women annually, for periods of six

months each, in national, regional and international institutions; and $359,000 for the development of new methods for data collection, analysis and use in China which would bring producers and users of statistics into dialogue on gender issues of concern to planners and policy makers.

In a report on the activities of UNIFEM during 1992,[17] the UNDP Administrator stated that, in Africa, a project, operated by UNIFEM in collaboration with the Office of the United Nations High Commissioner for Refugees and various NGOs, was undertaken in Ghana and Côte d'Ivoire to provide support to women refugees from Liberia as well as to local women affected by the influx of refugees. The project offered the women shelter, trauma counselling, health education and training in "portable skills" that could be used to generate income in their current situation and when they returned home.

In conjunction with the African Development Bank, UNIFEM funded a meeting in Côte d'Ivoire in November on mainstreaming gender concerns in African training and research institutes. The meeting brought together trainers working at the grass-roots level with researchers and representatives of institutions in the field of gender training.

Macro/micro linkages, activated in the UNIFEM programme, brought representatives of peasant women from South-East Asia to UNCED. This was the culmination of a process begun in 1991, when national summits on environment and development were held in Bangladesh, India, Nepal and Pakistan. The summits were attended by grass-roots leaders, scientists, politicians, national planners and policy makers. Subsequently, three peasant women leaders attended UNCED and reported back to their constituencies on implementation of environmental agreements.

In Latin America and the Caribbean, UNIFEM called attention to the negative impact on the development process of violence against women. UNIFEM supported networking between women's anti-violence groups; public education programmes involving citizens, police officers, public officials, lawmakers and others; and advocacy work in shelters and women's centres. In August, women from 21 countries of the region gathered in Brazil for a UNIFEM-sponsored conference on women and sexual and domestic violence.

UNIFEM supported a gender-awareness training programme in Venezuela, developed by the Venezuela Association for Alternative Sexual Education (AVESA), for police officers and university security personnel attending battered women in Caracas. Since 1989, more than 450 officers (one fifth of them women) had been sensitized to the issue; an additional 1,000 officers would be trained by AVESA with the Fund's support during the next year.

The Advocacy Facility of UNIFEM became operational in January 1992. Progress was made in the preparation, production, marketing and distribution of papers, training materials, books, newsletters, videos and other women-in-development resource materials.

On 14 February 1992,[5] the UNDP Governing Council decided to consider on a biennial basis the subject of UNIFEM.

On 22 December, by **decision 47/448**, the General Assembly took note of the report of the UNDP Administrator on the 1991 activities of UNIFEM.[18]

REFERENCES

[1]YUN 1987, p. 844, ESC res. 1987/24, 26 May 1987. [2]E/CN.6/1992/8. [3]E/1992/24 (res. 36/4). [4]Ibid. (res. 36/5). [5]E/1992/28 (dec. 92/2). [6]TD/364. [7]A/47/308-E/1992/97. [8]ESC dec. 1990/213, 24 May 1990. [9]YUN 1991, p. 681, GA res. 46/167, 19 Dec. 1991. [10]E/CN.6/1992/9. [11]E/1992/24 (res. 36/6). [12]*Report of the United Nations Conference on Environment and Development, Rio de Janiero, 3-14 June 1992*, vol. I, Sales No. E.93.I.8. [13]YUN 1985, p. 937. [14]ESC res. 1989/105, 27 July 1989. [15]E/1992/6. [16]UNIFEM/CC32/9. [17]DP/1993/41. [18]A/47/340.

Status of women

Commission on the Status of Women

At its thirty-sixth session (Vienna, 11-20 March 1992),[1] the Commission on the Status of Women recommended seven draft resolutions and two draft decisions for adoption by the Economic and Social Council, dealing with improvement of the status of women in the Secretariat (see PART SIX, Chapter II), women and children under apartheid (see PART TWO, Chapter I), Palestinian women, the Convention on the Elimination of All Forms of Discrimination against Women, violence against women, communications on the status of women, and advancement of women and human rights. The draft decisions related to the Commission's 1993 session.

1993 session

On 30 July 1992, by **decision 1992/269**, the Economic and Social Council took note of the Commission's report and approved the provisional agenda and documentation for its thirty-seventh session. On the same date, the Council, by **decision 1992/270**, approved the convening of four additional meetings, to be held simultaneously during the Commission's thirty-seventh session, to consider the preparations for the Fourth World Conference on Women: Action for Equality, Development and Peace.

Women and peace

In response to a 1987 Economic and Social Council resolution,[2] the Secretary-General submitted a report[3] to the Commission on one of its 1992 priority themes—equal participation in efforts to promote international cooperation, peace and disarmament. The report stated that almost no women were involved in decision-making related to peace, international cooperation and disarmament, a reflection of the broader problem of gender inequalities at the national level. The report contended that if women were involved equally in all efforts to promote international cooperation, peace and disarmament, in appropriate numbers, they would make a qualitative difference in the way issues relating to peace were dealt with. It analysed new data on the participation of women in parliaments and Governments worldwide, and identified the factors and conditions that enabled women to participate in public life in sufficient numbers to make a difference.

The report concluded that the low number of women in decision-making positions deprived them of important rights and responsibilities and was not democratic. The slow progress towards equality in participation and decision-making implied a need for new policies and measures by Governments, NGOs and women themselves. United Nations entities should continue their studies of the issue and, in particular, examine the difference women could make in the areas of peace, international cooperation and disarmament.

Women and human rights

On 30 July 1992, the Economic and Social Council, pursuant to the recommendation of its Social Committee, adopted without vote **resolution 1992/20**.

Advancement of women and human rights

The Economic and Social Council,

Recalling General Assembly resolution 45/155 of 18 December 1990, in which it was decided to convene a World Conference on Human Rights in 1993 and to establish a Preparatory Committee for the Conference,

Noting that the General Assembly, in its resolution 46/116 of 17 December 1991, requested concerned United Nations bodies and specialized agencies, among others, to submit recommendations concerning the Conference to the Preparatory Committee,

Taking note of General Assembly resolution 46/98 of 16 December 1991, in particular paragraph 8 thereof,

Bearing in mind its resolution 1990/15 of 24 May 1990, in which it adopted the recommendations and conclusions arising from the first review and appraisal of the implementation of the Nairobi Forward-looking Strategies for the Advancement of Women, contained in the annex to that resolution, and bearing in mind in particular those recommendations and conclusions related to the maintenance of de facto discrimination, which prevents women from achieving effective equality,

Taking into account the fact that the Nairobi Forward-looking Strategies for the Advancement of Women have identified violence against women as one of the major obstacles to the achievement of the objectives of the United Nations Decade for Women: Equality, Development and Peace,

Welcoming general recommendation 19, adopted by the Committee on the Elimination of Discrimination against Women at its eleventh session, and the recommendations of the Expert Group Meeting on Violence against Women, held at Vienna from 11 to 15 November 1991,

Affirming that various forms of violence against women are violations of human rights,

1. *Calls upon* the Preparatory Committee for the World Conference on Human Rights, when preparing the agenda and studies for the World Conference, to take into account the existence of de facto as well as *de jure* discrimination, which continues to impede the full enjoyment by women of their economic, social and cultural rights, as well as their civil and political rights;

2. *Also calls upon* the Preparatory Committee, in preparing for the examination by the Conference of the main obstacles to the implementation of international human rights instruments, to pay adequate attention to the global problem of violence against women;

3. *Invites* the Centre for Human Rights of the Secretariat and Member States, in preparing for the Conference, to make use of gender disaggregated data, which identify situations of inequality between women and men;

4. *Requests* the Secretary-General, in accordance with General Assembly resolution 46/98, to guarantee the participation of the secretariats of the Commission on the Status of Women and the Committee on the Elimination of Discrimination against Women in the preparatory process for the Conference, as well as in the Conference itself;

5. *Requests* the Division for the Advancement of Women of the Centre for Social Development and Humanitarian Affairs, as the secretariat of the Commission, to report to the Commission at its thirty-seventh session on the state of the preparatory process for the Conference and the related activities of the Division, in accordance with General Assembly resolution 46/98;

6. *Requests* the Commission to establish, during its thirty-seventh session, an open-ended working group to consider its contribution to the Conference;

7. *Urges* Member States, when preparing for the Conference at the national level, to consider integrating fully into the scope of the Conference issues related to the rights of women, and to respect the principle of equal participation of women and men in their delegations.

Economic and Social Council resolution 1992/20

30 July 1992   Meeting 40   Adopted without vote

Approved by Social Committee (E/1992/105) without vote, 21 July (meeting 14); draft by Commission on women (E/1992/24); agenda item 18. *Financial implications.* E/1992/24/Add.1.

Also, on 20 July, the Council adopted **decision 1992/251** on traditional practices affecting the health of women and children.

Violence against women

Two reports on violence against women were submitted by the Secretary-General to the Commission.

One of them,[4] prepared in response to a 1990 resolution of the Economic and Social Council,[5] concerned physical violence against detained women and was based on an analysis of information provided by 36 Governments. The report examined legislative, administrative and other measures to prevent violence against detained women that was specific to their sex. Most reporting Governments stated that they did not have any special legal provisions that covered prevention of such violence. However, general legal provisions and rules governing the treatment of prisoners were designed to protect adequately both male and female prisoners from ill-treatment. A number of countries had also adopted sex-specific administrative measures, including some special regulations for female prisoners, and complaint and recourse procedures in cases of irregular conduct or acts of violence by supervising personnel.

The other report,[6] on violence against women in all its forms and the possibilities of preparing an international instrument on the subject, contained the recommendations, summary of discussion and a draft declaration adopted by an expert group meeting on violence against women (Vienna, 11-15 November 1991).

The Committee on the Elimination of Discrimination against Women (CEDAW),[7] in accordance with a 1991 Economic and Social Council decision,[8] considered the question of violence against women and made a number of specific recommendations dealing with the issue.

ECONOMIC AND SOCIAL COUNCIL ACTION

On 30 July, the Economic and Social Council, on the recommendation of its Social Committee, adopted without vote **resolution 1992/18**.

Violence against women in all its forms

The Economic and Social Council,

Recalling its resolution 1991/18 of 30 May 1991, in which it requested that an expert group meeting be held to address the issue of violence against women and to discuss the possibilities of preparing an international instrument on this subject and the elements to be contained therein,

Bearing in mind that the Nairobi Forward-looking Strategies for the Advancement of Women identify violence against women as a major obstacle to the achievement of the objectives of the United Nations Decade for Women: Equality, Development and Peace,

Noting that, in general recommendation 19, adopted by the Committee on the Elimination of Discrimination against Women at its eleventh session, the Committee recognized that gender-based violence was a form of discrimination that seriously inhibited the ability of women to enjoy rights and freedoms on a basis of equality with men,

Noting also the response of the Committee to the report of the Secretary-General on violence against women in all its forms, the annex to which contains the recommendations and a summary of the discussion of the Expert Group Meeting on Violence against Women, held at Vienna from 11 to 15 November 1991,

1. *Calls on* Governments to recognize that the elimination of violence against women is essential to the achievement of equality for women and is a requirement for the full respect of human rights;

2. *Urges* Member States to adopt, strengthen and enforce legislation prohibiting violence against women and to take all appropriate administrative, social and educational measures to protect women from all forms of physical and mental violence, in accordance with its resolution 1991/18;

3. *Calls on* States parties to the Convention on the Elimination of All Forms of Discrimination against Women to take the steps necessary to implement general recommendation 19, adopted by the Committee on the Elimination of Discrimination against Women at its eleventh session;

4. *Takes note* of the report of the Secretary-General on violence against women in all its forms;

5. *Decides* to convene an inter-sessional working group of the Commission on the Status of Women, open to all Member States and observer States, to further develop a draft declaration on violence against women, taking into account the draft declaration contained in the annex to the report of the Secretary-General, and to report to the Commission, at its thirty-seventh session, with a view to recommending a draft declaration to the General Assembly through the Economic and Social Council;

6. *Requests* Governments, international organizations, non-governmental organizations, other relevant bodies and academics to continue to undertake research into the causes of violence against women;

7. *Urges* Governments to address the issue of violence against women at the Fourth World Conference on Women: Action for Equality, Development and Peace, to be held in 1995, as one of the major obstacles to women's advancement.

Economic and Social Council resolution 1992/18

30 July 1992   Meeting 40   Adopted without vote

Approved by Social Committee (E/1992/105) without vote, 21 July (meeting 14); draft by Commission on women (E/1992/24); agenda item 18. *Financial implications.* E/1992/24/Add.1.

Draft declaration on the elimination of violence against women

The Economic and Social Council, by **resolution 1992/18**, decided to convene an inter-sessional working group of the Commission on the Status of Women to develop further a draft declaration on violence against women. Pursuant to that resolution, the Working Group on Violence against Women met at Vienna from 31 August to 4 September[9] to prepare the draft declaration. The Group adopted its report containing the draft declaration for submission to the Commission in 1993, with a view to recommending it to the General Assembly for adoption, through the Council.

Palestinian women

The Economic and Social Council, in a 1991 resolution,[10] had requested the Secretary-General to continue his investigation of the situation of Palestinian women and children and to report to the thirty-sixth session of the Commission. In a note to the Commission,[11] the Secretary-General referred to a statement by Israel emphasizing that the 1991 resolution already contained conclusions concerning the situation, which made an additional investigation unnecessary. Without the means of acquiring the information required by the resolution, the Secretary-General reported that he was not in a position to provide a report.

ECONOMIC AND SOCIAL COUNCIL ACTION

On 30 July, the Economic and Social Council, pursuant to a recommendation of its Social Committee, adopted by recorded vote **resolution 1992/16**.

Situation of and assistance to Palestinian women

The Economic and Social Council,

Having considered the reports of the Secretary-General and the notes by the Secretary-General concerning the situation of Palestinian women living inside and outside the occupied Palestinian territory,

Recalling the Nairobi Forward-looking Strategies for the Advancement of Women, in particular paragraph 260 thereof,

Recalling also its resolutions 1988/25 of 26 May 1988, 1989/34 of 24 May 1989, 1990/11 of 24 May 1990 and 1991/19 of 30 May 1991,

Deeply alarmed by the deteriorating condition of Palestinian women and children in the occupied Palestinian territory, including Jerusalem, as a result of the continued Israeli violation of Palestinian human rights, and oppressive measures, including collective punishments, curfews, demolition of houses, closure of schools and universities, deportation, confiscation of land and settlement activities, which are illegal and contrary to the relevant provisions of the Geneva Convention relevant to the Protection of Civilian Persons in Time of War, of 12 August 1949,

1. *Reaffirms* that the basic improvement of the living conditions of the Palestinian women, their advancement, full equality and self-reliance, can only be achieved by an end to the Israeli occupation and by the attainment of the inalienable rights of the Palestinian people;

2. *Demands* that Israel, the occupying Power, accept the *de jure* applicability of the Geneva Convention relevant to the Protection of Civilian Persons in Time of

War, of 12 August 1949, to the occupied Palestinian territory, including Jerusalem, and to respect the provisions of the Convention;

3. *Also demands* an end to the Israeli violation of human rights in the occupied Palestinian territory, including an immediate halt to the Israeli settlement activities that have harmful effects on Palestinian women and their families;

4. *Calls upon* governmental, non-governmental and intergovernmental organizations, including organizations of the United Nations system, to assist Palestinian women in the occupied Palestinian territory in developing small-scale industry and creating vocational training and legal consultation centres;

5. *Requests* the Commission on the Status of Women to monitor the implementation of the Nairobi Forward-looking Strategies for the Advancement of Women, in particular paragraph 260 concerning assistance to Palestinian women;

6. *Requests* the Secretary-General to continue his efforts in monitoring the implementation of the recommendations contained in the report of the mission of experts to Jordan and the Syrian Arab Republic to investigate the condition of Palestinian women and children in order to improve the condition of Palestinian women and children;

7. *Also requests* the Secretary-General to review the situation of Palestinian women and children in the occupied Palestinian territory and in the refugee camps, and to submit a report to the Commission on the Status of Women at its thirty-seventh session, using all available sources.

Economic and Social Council resolution 1992/16

30 July 1992   Meeting 40   37-1-14 (recorded vote)

Approved by Social Committee (E/1992/105) by recorded vote (36-1-13), 21 July (meeting 14); draft by Commission on women (E/1992/24); agenda item 18.

Recorded vote in Council as follows:

In favour: Algeria, Angola, Australia, Bahrain, Bangladesh, Benin, Botswana, Brazil, Burkina Faso, Chile, China, Colombia, Ecuador, Ethiopia, Finland, Guinea, India, Jamaica, Kuwait, Madagascar, Malaysia, Mexico, Morocco, Pakistan, Peru, Philippines, Rwanda, Somalia, Spain, Suriname, Sweden, Syrian Arab Republic, Togo, Trinidad and Tobago, Turkey, Yugoslavia, Zaire.

Against: United States.

Abstaining: Argentina, Australia, Belarus, Belgium, Bulgaria, Canada, France, Germany, Italy, Japan, Poland, Romania, Russian Federation, United Kingdom.

Women in the informal sector

A report[12] by the Secretariat to CEDAW considered the definition of the informal sector and its possible implications for women. The report noted that international organizations used many definitions according to their objectives and the Statistical Office of the United Nations, in collaboration with INSTRAW, was working to improve statistics by which women's participation and production in the informal sector could be measured. The Statistical Office was preparing a report on the measurement of women's economic activity and other work and was compiling global statistics on women in the informal sector on an experimental basis. The report stated that women in the informal sector were often found in types of employment where they were more likely to be

disadvantaged, dependent and exploited. It was suggested that the progressive integration of segments of the informal sector in the formal economy should provide opportunites for women to overcome institutional and socio-cultural barriers which prevented them from achieving fuller professional careers.

Migrant women workers

On 16 December, the General Assembly, on the recommendation of the Third Committee, adopted without vote **resolution 47/96**.

Violence against migrant women workers

The General Assembly,

Recalling that the Charter of the United Nations reaffirms faith in human rights and fundamental freedoms, in the dignity and worth of the human person and in the equal rights of men and women,

Reaffirming the principles set forth in the Convention on the Elimination of All Forms of Discrimination against Women, adopted by the General Assembly by its resolution 34/180 of 18 December 1979 and contained in the annex to that resolution,

Noting the large numbers of women from developing countries who venture forth to more affluent countries in search of a living for themselves and their families, while acknowledging the primary duty of States to work for conditions that provide employment to their citizens,

Recognizing that poverty, unemployment and other socio-economic situations in their home countries lead people, including women, to seek employment in other countries,

Recognizing also that it is the duty of sending countries to protect and promote the interests of their citizens who seek or receive employment in other countries, to provide them with appropriate training/education, and to apprise them of their rights and obligations in the countries of employment,

Aware of the moral obligation of receiving or host countries to ensure the human rights and fundamental freedoms of all persons within their boundaries, including migrant workers and in particular women migrant workers, who are doubly vulnerable because of their gender and because they are foreigners,

Noting with concern the mounting reports of grave abuses and acts of violence committed against the person of women migrant workers by some of their employers in some host countries,

Stressing that acts of violence directed against women impair or nullify the enjoyment by women of their human rights and fundamental freedoms,

Convinced of the need to eliminate all forms of discrimination against women and to protect them from gender-based violence,

1. *Expresses grave concern* over the plight of migrant women workers who become victims of physical, mental and sexual harassment and abuse;

2. *Calls upon* all countries, particularly the sending and receiving countries, to cooperate with each other in taking appropriate steps to ensure that the rights of women migrant workers are protected;

3.   *Urges* all States to adopt appropriate measures to provide support services to women victims of violence and to provide resources for their physical and psychological rehabilitation;

4.   *Calls upon* relevant bodies and specialized agencies of the United Nations system, intergovernmental organizations and non-governmental organizations to inform the Secretary-General of the extent of the problem and to recommend further measures to implement the purposes of the present resolution;

5.   *Envisages* the inclusion of the subject of violence against women migrant workers in the agenda of the Fourth World Conference on Women: Action for Equality, Development and Peace, to be held in Beijing in 1995;

6.   *Requests* the Secretary-General, in view of the time constraints and pending the completion of a written report, to make a preliminary oral report, through the Commission on the Status of Women and the Economic and Social Council, to the General Assembly at its forty-eighth session, on the implementation of the present resolution under the item entitled "Advancement of women".

General Assembly resolution 47/96

16 December 1992   Meeting 89   Adopted without vote

Approved by Third Committee (A/47/670) without vote, 11 November (meeting 35); 14-nation draft (A/C.3/47/L.24), orally revised; agenda item 94.
Sponsors: Australia, Chile, China, Costa Rica, El Salvador, France, Indonesia, Malaysia, Mexico, Nicaragua, Philippines, Russian Federation, Thailand, Uganda.
Meeting numbers. GA 47th session: 3rd Committee 19-26, 28, 30, 32, 35; plenary 89.

On the same date, the Assembly adopted **resolution 47/110** on the International Convention on the Protection of the Rights of All Migrant Workers and Members of Their Families.

REFERENCES

(1)E/1992/24. (2)YUN 1987, p. 844, ESC res. 1987/24, 26 May 1987. (3)E/CN.6/1992/10. (4)E/CN.6/1992/5. (5)ESC res. 1990/5, 24 May 1990. (6)E/CN.6/1992/4. (7)A/47/38. (8)YUN 1991, p. 685, ESC res. 1991/18, 30 May 1991. (9)E/CN.6/1993/12. (10)YUN 1991, p. 686, ESC res. 1991/19, 30 May 1991. (11)E/CN.6/1992/6. (12)CEDAW/C/1992/6.

Elimination of discrimination against women

Convention on discrimination against women

Established in 1982[1] under the Convention on the Elimination of All Forms of Discrimination against Women,[2] the Committee on the Elimination of Discrimination against Women held its eleventh session in New York from 20 to 30 January 1992.[3]

CEDAW, the treaty-monitoring body for the Convention, considered three initial reports of States parties (Barbados, Ghana, Honduras) and six second periodic reports (China, Czechoslo-

vakia, El Salvador, Spain, Sri Lanka, Venezuela) on legislative, judicial, administrative and other measures they had adopted to give effect to the Convention.

CEDAW concluded that not all the reports adequately reflected the close connection between discrimination against women, gender-based violence, and violations of human rights and fundamental freedoms. It offered general comments on specific articles of the Convention, and, in the light of those comments, recommended, among other things, that: States parties should ensure that laws against family violence and abuse, rape, sexual assault and other gender-based violence gave adequate protection to women; States parties in their reports should include information on sexual harassment and should identify the attitudes, customs and practices that perpetuated violence against women; preventive and punitive measures were necessary to overcome trafficking and sexual exploitation; States parties should ensure that coercion was prevented in regard to fertility and reproduction; and States parties should report on the extent of domestic violence and sexual abuse and on the preventive, punitive and remedial measures that had been taken.

Report of the Secretary-General. The Secretary-General, responding to a 1987 Economic and Social Council resolution,[4] submitted a report[5] to the Commission on the Status of Women on its priority theme—the elimination of *de jure* and de facto discrimination against women. The report considered the extent of discrimination and positive action to correct inequalities. It concluded that in the current context, positive action was not discriminatory but promoted equality, and Governments should make increasing use of it. Positive action programmes should be flexible and selective and some measures should seek to eliminate or counteract prejudicial attitudes towards women. Others should seek to give women access to wider varieties of education, vocational training and employment opportunities, to ensure their access to credit, land and technology, to foster greater sharing of family and social responsibilities between men and women, and to promote women's active participation in economic and political decision-making. In addition, Governments should publicly declare a commitment to provide equal opportunities, especially at the highest levels, identify and evaluate existing inequalities that could be attributed to past discrimination, set targets and, if desirable, quotas, and specify dates by which those targets should be met. They should also consider establishing an institution or appointing an executive to supervise or monitor the positive action effort.

On 30 July, the Economic and Social Council, pursuant to the recommendation of its Social Committee, adopted without vote **resolution 1992/17**.

Convention on the Elimination of All Forms of Discrimination against Women

The Economic and Social Council,

Welcoming the fact that there are now one hundred and twelve States parties to the Convention on the Elimination of All Forms of Discrimination against Women,

Noting the importance of the monitoring function of the Committee on the Elimination of Discrimination against Women, as demonstrated most recently in its general recommendation 19 on violence against women, adopted at its eleventh session,

Recalling its resolution 1991/25 of 30 May 1991 and other relevant resolutions adopted by the General Assembly and the Economic and Social Council relating to support for the Committee,

Concerned that the duration of the annual session of the Committee, which is considerably less than that of other treaty bodies, has prevented the timely consideration by the Committee of many of the reports submitted to it by States parties to the Convention,

Noting with concern that the Convention is the human rights instrument with the most reservations, and welcoming the decision by a number of States parties to withdraw their reservations,

1. *Supports* the request of the Committee on the Elimination of Discrimination against Women for additional meeting time and also supports the proposal that the twelfth session of the Committee should be of three weeks' duration;

2. *Recommends* that three weeks be allocated for each subsequent session until the Committee removes the backlog of reports to be considered;

3. *Strongly supports* general recommendation 19 on violence against women, adopted by the Committee at its eleventh session, and calls on States parties to prepare their reports in accordance with this and other general recommendations of the Committee;

4. *Welcomes* other general recommendations adopted by the Committee at its previous sessions;

5. *Urges* the Secretary-General to continue to widely publicize the decisions and recommendations of the Committee.

Economic and Social Council resolution 1992/17

30 July 1992   Meeting 40   Adopted without vote

Approved by Social Committee (E/1992/105) without vote, 21 July (meeting 14); draft by Commission on women (E/1992/24); agenda item 18. *Financial implications*: E/1992/24/Add.1.

Also on 30 July, by **decision 1992/273**, the Council took note of CEDAW's report on its eleventh session and transmitted it to the General Assembly.

On 16 December, the General Assembly, in accordance with the recommendation of the Third Committee, adopted without vote **resolution 47/94**.

Convention on the Elimination of All Forms of Discrimination against Women

The General Assembly,

Bearing in mind that one of the purposes of the United Nations, as stated in Articles 1 and 55 of the Charter, is to promote universal respect for human rights and fundamental freedoms for all without distinction of any kind, including distinction as to sex,

Affirming that women and men should participate equally in social, economic and political development, should contribute equally to such development and should share equally in improved conditions of life,

Recalling its resolution 34/180 of 18 December 1979, by which it adopted the Convention on the Elimination of All Forms of Discrimination against Women,

Recalling also its previous resolutions on the Convention, and taking note of Economic and Social Council resolution 1992/17 of 30 July 1992,

Taking note of the decisions adopted at the Sixth Meeting of States Parties to the Convention, on 4 February 1992,

Aware of the important contribution that the implementation of the Nairobi Forward-looking Strategies for the Advancement of Women can make to eliminating all forms of discrimination against women and to achieving legal and de facto equality between women and men,

Noting the emphasis placed by the World Conference to Review and Appraise the Achievements of the United Nations Decade for Women: Equality, Development and Peace, on the ratification of and accession to the Convention,

Having considered the reports of the Committee on the Elimination of Discrimination against Women on its tenth and eleventh sessions,

Noting that the Committee agreed, in examining reports, to take due account of the different cultural and socio-economic systems of States parties to the Convention,

Noting also the importance of the monitoring function of the Committee, as demonstrated most recently in its general recommendation No. 19 on violence against women, adopted at its eleventh session,

Concerned about the increased workload of the Committee,

Convinced of the need to adopt measures to enable the Committee to deal in a thorough and timely manner with reports submitted by States parties,

Recalling that, under article 17, paragraph 9, of the Convention, the Secretary-General is required to provide the necessary staff and facilities for the effective performance of the functions of the Committee,

Recalling its resolutions 44/73 of 8 December 1989 and 45/124 of 14 December 1990, in which, *inter alia*, it strongly supported the view of the Committee that the Secretary-General should accord higher priority to strengthening support for the Committee,

Strongly supporting general recommendation No. 19 of the Committee on violence against women, and calling upon States parties to prepare their periodic reports in accordance with this and other general recommendations of the Committee,

Noting with satisfaction that the inter-sessional working group of the Commission on the Status of Women has completed its consideration of the draft declaration on the elimination of violence against women,

Welcoming other general recommendations contained in the reports of the Committee on its tenth and eleventh sessions,

1. *Expresses its satisfaction* with the increasing number of States that have ratified or acceded to the Convention on the Elimination of All Forms of Discrimination against Women, and supports the recommendation of the Committee on the Elimination of Discrimination against Women to draw attention to those reservations which are incompatible with the objective and purpose of the Convention;

2. *Urges* all States that have not yet ratified or acceded to the Convention to do so as soon as possible;

3. *Emphasizes* the importance of the strictest compliance by States parties with their obligations under the Convention;

4. *Takes note* of the report of the Secretary-General on the status of the Convention on the Elimination of All Forms of Discrimination against Women, and requests him to submit annually to the General Assembly a report on the status of the Convention;

5. *Takes note also* of the reports of the Committee on the Elimination of Discrimination against Women on its tenth and eleventh sessions;

6. *Invites* States parties to the Convention to make all possible efforts to submit their initial as well as their second and subsequent periodic reports on the implementation of the Convention, in accordance with article 18 thereof and with the guidelines provided by the Committee, and to cooperate fully with the Committee in the presentation of their reports;

7. *Welcomes* the efforts made by the Committee to rationalize its procedures and expedite the consideration of periodic reports and to develop procedures and guidelines for the consideration of second and subsequent periodic reports, and strongly encourages the Committee to continue those efforts;

8. *Welcomes also*, in accordance with general recommendation No. 11 of the Committee, the initiatives taken to provide regional training courses on the preparation and drafting of reports of States parties for government officials and training and information seminars for States considering acceding to the Convention, and urges the relevant organs and organizations of the United Nations to support such initiatives;

9. *Recognizes* the special relevance of the periodic reports of States parties to the Convention to the efforts of the Commission on the Status of Women to review and appraise the implementation of the Nairobi Forward-looking Strategies for the Advancement of Women in those countries;

10. *Requests* the Secretary-General to continue his efforts to provide secretariat staff, including legal staff members expert in human rights treaty implementation, and technical resources for the effective performance by the Committee of its functions;

11. *Strongly supports* the view of the Committee that the Secretary-General should accord higher priority within existing resources to strengthening technical and substantive support for the Committee, in particular to assist in preparatory research;

12. *Requests* the Secretary-General to continue to provide for, facilitate and encourage, within existing resources, the dissemination of information relating to the Committee, its decisions and recommendations,

the Convention and the concept of legal literacy, taking into account the Committee's own recommendations to that end;

13. *Supports* the request of the Committee for additional meeting time and requests that the twelfth and thirteenth sessions of the Committee should be of three weeks' duration;

14. *Requests* the Secretary-General to ensure adequate support to the Committee, and also requests that sufficient resources from within the existing regular budget be provided for that purpose to enable the Committee to deal in a thorough and timely manner with reports submitted by States parties;

15. *Decides* that, at its forty-ninth session, it will review whether the backlog of the Committee in considering reports has been reduced;

16. *Recommends* that meetings of the Committee should be scheduled, whenever possible, to allow for the timely transmission of the results of its work to the Commission on the Status of Women, for information, in the same year;

17. *Requests* the Secretary-General to submit to the General Assembly at its forty-ninth session a report on the implementation of the present resolution and to make the report available to the Commission on the Status of Women at its thirty-ninth session.

General Assembly resolution 47/94

16 December 1992   Meeting 89   Adopted without vote

Approved by Third Committee (A/47/670) without vote, 5 November (meeting 30); 43-nation draft (A/C.3/47/L.22), orally revised; agenda item 94.
Sponsors: Australia, Austria, Bangladesh, Barbados, Belarus, Canada, Chile, China, Costa Rica, Czechoslovakia, Denmark, Ecuador, Egypt, Estonia, Ethiopia, Finland, France, Germany, Greece, Iceland, Indonesia, Italy, Latvia, Lithuania, Luxembourg, Malawi, Mexico, Netherlands, Nicaragua, Nigeria, Norway, Panama, Poland, Portugal, Romania, Russian Federation, Saint Kitts and Nevis, Samoa, Spain, Sri Lanka, Sweden, Turkey, Ukraine.
Meeting numbers. GA 47th session: 3rd Committee 19-26, 28, 30; plenary 89.

Ratifications, accessions and signatures

As at 31 December 1992,[6] the Convention on the Elimination of All Forms of Discrimination against Women had received 96 signatures and 120 ratifications, accessions or successions. During the year, the Convention was ratified or acceded or succeeded to by Benin, Burundi, Cambodia, Croatia, Jordan, Latvia, Namibia, Samoa, Seychelles and Slovenia.

The Secretary-General submitted to the General Assembly in September 1992[7] his annual report on the status of the Convention, containing information on signatures, ratifications and accessions as at 1 August 1992 and on reservations and withdrawal of reservations from 1 August 1991 to 1 August 1992.

REFERENCES
[1]YUN 1982, p. 1149. [2]YUN 1979, p. 895, GA res. 34/180, annex, 18 Dec. 1979. [3]A/47/38. [4]YUN 1987, p. 844, ESC res. 1987/24, 26 May 1987. [5]E/CN.6/1992/7. [6]*Multilateral Treaties Deposited with the Secretary-General: Status as at 31 December 1992* (ST/LEG/SER.E/11), Sales No. E.93.V.11. [7]A/47/368.

Chapter XIV

Children, youth and ageing persons

In 1992, the United Nations Children's Fund became increasingly involved in emergency situations caused by man and nature or a combination of both. The Fund provided emergency humanitarian assistance to 54 countries in Africa, Asia, Latin America and the Middle East. These emergency situations took place against a backdrop of some 35,000 largely preventable child deaths in the developing world each day from causes associated with poverty, malnutrition and diseases.

The problems affecting the health and well-being of youth were also widespread in developed and developing countries. More than 1.5 billion people—about one third of the world's population—were aged between 10 and 24 and many of the dramatic forces that were shaping the world were impacting negatively on them.

In October, the Assembly held four special meetings devoted to a conference on the ageing at which it adopted a Proclamation on Ageing and designated the year 1999 as the International Year of Older Persons.

Children

UN Children's Fund

During 1992,[1] the United Nations Children's Fund (UNICEF) cooperated in programmes in more than 130 countries, the majority of which were in Africa (44), followed by Latin America and the Caribbean (35), Asia (34) and the Middle East and North Africa (14). Programme expenditures totalled $744 million, of which $228 million (31 per cent) was spent on child health; $167 million (22 per cent) on emergency operations; $108 million (15 per cent) on planning programme advocacy and support; $84 million (11 per cent) on water supply and sanitation; $72 million (10 per cent) on education; $32 million (4 per cent) on nutrition and household food security; and $53 million (7 per cent) on other programme areas.

Major emergency operations were carried out in Afghanistan, Angola, Haiti, Iraq, Liberia, Mozambique, Somalia, the Sudan and the former Yugoslavia.[2] UNICEF provided emergency assistance to more than 40 countries affected by natural disasters and health emergencies, including floods in Ecuador, Lebanon and Pakistan; a volcanic eruption in the Philippines; earthquakes in Egypt, Indonesia and Turkey; cholera outbreaks in El Salvador and Peru; and an outbreak of cerebrospinal meningitis in Cameroon. Drought continued to affect 13 countries in Africa, putting 22 million people at risk of starvation and disease. Countries such as Bangladesh, Côte d'Ivoire, Djibouti, Ethiopia, Guinea, Kenya, Mauritania and Sierra Leone were affected by influxes of refugees from conflicts in neighbouring countries. UNICEF also provided emergency support for children and women in many of the successor States of the former USSR and for returnees and displaced persons in Sri Lanka.

The UNICEF Executive Board[3] held its regular session in New York from 15 to 26 June 1992 and elected officers for the period 1 August 1992 to 31 July 1993. The Programme Committee convened from 15 to 23 and on 26 June, while the Committee on Administration and Finance met on 22, 23 and 26 June.

On 31 July, by **decision 1992/301**, the Economic and Social Council took note of an extract from the report of the Board on its 1992 session.

Programme policy decisions

The Executive Board approved a number of recommendations by its Programme Committee for programme cooperation in Africa, the Americas and the Caribbean, Asia, and the Middle East and North Africa (see below).[4] It requested the Executive Director to ensure that national capacity-building was a component in all relevant UNICEF programmes,[5] and requested him to include in his annual report to the Board, from 1993 onwards, a section on measures taken to strengthen national capacities. It decided that representatives of Board member countries should visit the field for a better insight into UNICEF's activities.[6]

Having reviewed the medium-term plan for 1992-1995,[7] the Board[8] reaffirmed the priority of the country programming process in all UNICEF field activities and reconfirmed that situation analysis should be broad and holistic, providing the basis for UNICEF advocacy on behalf of children. It also endorsed the programme objectives contained in the medium-term plan. The Board[9] approved the medium-term plan as a framework of projections for 1992-1995, including the preparation of up to $400 million in programme expenditures from general resources to be submitted to the Board in 1993.

Follow-up to 1990 World Summit for Children

After reviewing the Executive Director's report on the follow-up to the 1990 World Summit for Children,[10] the Executive Board[11] welcomed initiatives taken by States to expedite national programmes of action (NPAs) and invited those that had not initiated or completed their NPAs to do so.

The Secretary-General, pursuant to a 1990 General Assembly resolution,[12] submitted a June 1992 report[13] to the Assembly, providing information on action by the international community in response to the World Summit. The report covered, among other things, NPAs, regional developments, the 1989 Convention on the Rights of the Child,[14] education and literacy, health, nutrition, water and sanitation, children in especially difficult circumstances, urban children, women and the girl child, and responses of the United Nations system and non-governmental organizations (NGOs).

The report noted that, although follow-up had been substantial, much remained to be done and donor countries still needed to demonstrate their commitment to "human priorities". United Nations agencies and international financial institutions also needed to report their plans for World Summit follow-up to their respective governing bodies, in keeping with the Summit's Plan of Action. As of 31 May, only the World Health Organization (WHO) and the United Nations Educational, Scientific and Cultural Organization (UNESCO) had done so.

On 31 July 1992, the Economic and Social Council adopted **decision 1992/301**, taking note of the report of the Secretary-General on the World Summit. On 22 December, by **decision 47/447**, the General Assembly also took note of the Secretary-General's report, and asked him to submit an updated report in 1993.

Convention on the Rights of the Child

The Committee on the Rights of the Child submitted a June 1992 report[15] to the General Assembly, providing an overview of its activities related to provisional rules of procedure, methods of work, cooperation with specialized agencies, UNICEF and other United Nations organs, and its future meetings.

The Committee held its second session at Geneva from 28 September to 9 October,[16] adopting a report which provided an overview of its activities and the provisional agenda for its third session to be held in 1993. The States parties to the Convention on the Rights of the Child held their second meeting (New York, 11 November),[17] and discussed future meetings and their duration.

On 16 December 1992, the General Assembly adopted **resolution 47/112** on implementation of the Convention. As at 31 December, the number of parties to the Convention stood at 127 and a total of 133 States had signed it.

Universal Children's Day

The Executive Board[18] invited all States to observe Universal Children's Day each year, on 20 November or on a day they considered appropriate, with special emphasis on the promotion of the Convention on the Rights of the Child.

GENERAL ASSEMBLY ACTION

On 18 December 1992, the General Assembly, on the recommendation of the Third (Social, Humanitarian and Cultural) Committee, adopted **resolution 47/126** without vote.

Plight of street children

The General Assembly,

Recalling the Convention on the Rights of the Child as a major contribution to the protection of the rights of all children,

Recalling also the World Declaration on the Survival, Protection and Development of Children and the Plan of Action for Implementing the World Declaration on the Survival, Protection and Development of Children in the 1990s, adopted at the World Summit for Children on 30 September 1990, the World Declaration on Education for All adopted by the World Conference on Education for All on 9 March 1990 and chapter 25 of Agenda 21 adopted at the United Nations Conference on Environment and Development, on 14 June 1992,

Reaffirming that children are a particularly vulnerable section of society whose rights require special protection and that children living under especially difficult circumstances, such as street children, deserve special attention, protection and assistance from their families and communities and as part of national efforts and international cooperation,

Profoundly concerned that the killing of street children and violence against them threaten the most fundamental right of all, the right to life,

Recognizing that all children have the right to health, shelter and education, to an adequate standard of living and to freedom from violence and harassment,

Deeply concerned about the growing number of street children worldwide and the squalid conditions in which these children are often forced to live,

Recognizing the responsibility of Governments to investigate all cases of offences against children and to punish offenders,

Recognizing also that legislation *per se* is not enough to prevent violation of human rights, including those of street children, and that Governments should implement their laws and complement legislative measures with effective action, *inter alia*, in the fields of law enforcement and the administration of justice,

Welcoming the efforts made by countries to address the question of street children,

Welcoming also the publicity given to, and the increased awareness of, the plight of street children, and the achievements of non-governmental organizations in promoting the rights of these children and in providing practical assistance to improve their situation, and expressing its appreciation for their continued efforts,

Welcoming further the valuable work of the United Nations Children's Fund and its National Committees in reducing the suffering of street children,

Noting with appreciation the important work carried out in this field by the United Nations, in particular the Committee on the Rights of the Child, the Special Rapporteur of the Commission on Human Rights on the sale of children, child prostitution and child pornography and the United Nations International Drug Control Programme,

Bearing in mind the diverse causes of the emergence and marginalization of street children, including poverty, rural-to-urban migration, unemployment, broken families, intolerance and exploitation, and that such causes are often aggravated and their solution made more difficult by serious socio-economic difficulties,

Reaffirming the importance of international cooperation for improving the living conditions of children in every country,

Recognizing that the prevention and solution of certain aspects of this phenomenon could also be facilitated in the context of economic and social development,

1. *Expresses grave concern* at the growing number of incidents worldwide and at reports of street children being involved in and affected by serious crime, drug abuse, violence and prostitution;

2. *Urges* Governments to continue actively to seek comprehensive solutions to tackle the problems of street children and to take measures to restore their full participation in society and to provide, *inter alia*, adequate nutrition, shelter, health care and education;

3. *Strongly urges* Governments to respect fundamental human rights, particularly the right to life, and to take urgent measures to prevent the killing of street children and to combat violence and torture against street children;

4. *Emphasizes* that strict compliance with the provisions of the Convention on the Rights of the Child constitutes a significant step towards solving the problems of street children;

5. *Calls upon* all States that have not done so to become parties to the Convention as a matter of priority;

6. *Calls upon* the international community to support, through effective international cooperation, the efforts of States to improve the situation of street children, and encourages States parties to the Convention on the Rights of the Child, in preparing their reports to the Committee on the Rights of the Child, to bear this problem in mind and to consider requesting, or indicating their need for, technical advice and assistance for initiatives aimed at improving the situation of street children, in accordance with article 45 of the Convention;

7. *Invites* the Committee on the Rights of the Child to consider the possibility of a general comment on street children;

8. *Recommends* that the Committee on the Rights of the Child and other relevant treaty-monitoring bodies bear this growing problem in mind when examining reports from States parties;

9. *Invites* Governments, United Nations bodies and organizations and intergovernmental and non-governmental organizations to cooperate among themselves and to ensure greater awareness and more effective action to solve the problem of street children by, among other measures, supporting development projects that can have a positive impact on the situation of street children;

10. *Calls upon* special rapporteurs, special representatives and working groups of the Commission on Human Rights and of the Subcommission on the Prevention of Discrimination and Protection of Minorities, within their mandates, to pay particular attention to the plight of street children;

11. *Invites* the Commission on Human Rights to examine this problem at its forty-ninth session;

12. *Decides* to consider the question further at its forty-eighth session under the item entitled "Human rights questions".

General Assembly resolution 47/126

18 December 1992   Meeting 92   Adopted without vote

Approved by Third Committee (A/47/678/Add.2) without vote, 4 December (meeting 59); 62-nation draft (A/C.3/47/L.55), orally revised; agenda item 97 *(b)*.

Sponsors: Armenia, Australia, Austria, Belarus, Belgium, Benin, Brazil, Cameroon, Canada, Cape Verde, Central African Republic, Colombia, Costa Rica, Côte d'Ivoire, Cyprus, Denmark, Dominican Republic, Ecuador, Finland, France, Gabon, Gambia, Germany, Ghana, Greece, Guatemala, Guinea, Guinea-Bissau, Haiti, Honduras, Iceland, Ireland, Italy, Jamaica, Lesotho, Liechtenstein, Luxembourg, Madagascar, Malawi, Mali, Marshall Islands, Mexico, Mongolia, Morocco, Netherlands, Nicaragua, Niger, Norway, Peru, Philippines, Portugal, Russian Federation, Rwanda, Senegal, Sierra Leone, Spain, Sweden, Turkey, Ukraine, United Kingdom, United Republic of Tanzania, Uruguay.

Meeting numbers. GA 47th session: 3rd Committee 47-59; plenary 92.

Maurice Pate Memorial Award

In 1992, the Maurice Pate Award, established in 1966[19] to commemorate the first Executive Director of UNICEF, was presented to the Bangladesh Rural Advancement Committee to honour its outstanding service to the poor and most vulnerable populations, children and women. The $25,000 award recognized the Committee's innovative ideas in providing basic education, especially to girls, and health care.[20]

UNICEF programmes by region

Africa

Programme expenditures in Africa increased to $284 million in 1992, which represented 38 per cent of total UNICEF programme expenditures.

Africa remained the region of highest priority to UNICEF. Twenty-two countries were affected by emergencies, including military and civil strife, deteriorating economic conditions and environmental degradation leading to drought, massive population displacement, famine and death. Infant and under-five mortality rates remained at 108 and 180 deaths per 1,000 live births, respectively, and African women had the second highest maternal mortality rate in the world, with an average of 626 deaths per 100,000 live births, resulting in more than 140,000 deaths each year.

The main UNICEF response to Africa's needs was through its country programmes which focused on child survival and development and strengthened national capacities to plan, implement, monitor and evaluate programmes for children and women. To counter widespread and recurrent emergencies in Africa, UNICEF rapidly adapted its regular programmes to emergencies as they arose, and incorporated rehabilitation in relief measures.

In the area of child survival, UNICEF placed priority on the reduction of immunizable diseases and diarrhoea using Bamako Initiative activities to help involve the community in the management and financing of health services (see PART THREE, Chapter XI). UNICEF water supply and sanitation activities also addressed hygiene education and community maintenance of water supply systems.

In November, the Organization of African Unity sponsored an International Conference on Assistance to African Children (Dakar, Senegal), outlining the commitments of African countries and donors to meet a series of mid-decade health goals for children and recommend the establishment of a continental follow-up mechanism. The UNICEF Executive Board[21] called on UNICEF, in collaboration with other United Nations agencies, to continue providing emergency assistance to African refugee women and children. It urged the donor community to increase its development cooperation in Africa and encouraged other United Nations agencies, NGOs and multilateral financial institutions to help African countries achieve the goals of the World Summit for Children.

On 30 July 1992, the Economic and Social Council adopted **resolution 1992/15** on women and children under apartheid, demanding the immediate release of political prisoners and appealing to all countries and United Nations bodies to increase their support for education, health, vocational training and employment opportunities for women and children living under apartheid.

Americas and the Caribbean

In 1992, UNICEF programme expenditures in the Americas and the Caribbean amounted to $68 million, or 9 per cent of total programme expenditures.

The countries of the region managed in general terms to survive the most acute manifestations of the crisis of the 1980s but it was estimated that by the end of the century, the region's case-load of 195 million poor inhabitants would grow by 4-6 million.

Children, more than any other group, suffered the impact of poverty. Six million children under five years of age were moderately malnourished and one million were severely malnourished. The regional death toll of under five-year-olds was 900,000. Social services remained inadequate for many of the survivors. Some 88 million people were without safe drinking-water, about 139 million did not have basic sanitation services and an estimated 12 million children did not attend school. Twenty-two countries had, however, completed NPAs and regional health ministers had agreed on the need to consolidate targets for universal child immunization. Social mobilization, information and communication continued to rank high among the components of UNICEF assistance.

The Executive Board[22] decided to: consider the question of financial support to the Special Adjustment Facility for Latin America and the Caribbean (SAFLAC); request Latin American and Caribbean Governments to assure the implementation and continuity of projects under SAFLAC; and take up the renewal or expansion of SAFLAC at its next regular session, in 1993.

Asia

UNICEF programme expenditures in Asia totalled $250 million in 1992, or 34 per cent of total expenditures. An analysis of major new trends in UNICEF programmes found that development strategies had not yet made sufficient inroads on the poverty causing malnutrition, disease and neglect among millions of children and women in the region; it reflected on the unique challenge of providing support to countries across the spectrum of socio-economic development. At one end of the spectrum were countries undergoing major structural reforms. In these countries, the indicators for children and women pointed to substantial needs in all sectors. At the other end were countries enjoying robust economic growth and remarkable progress in social services—countries which nevertheless faced the risks of rapidly expanding populations living under marginal circumstances, the negative impact of acquired immune deficiency syndrome (AIDS), and growing numbers of children in difficult circumstances.

In response to situations of varied scope and dimension, UNICEF helped Governments to maintain and expand the reach of social services while also addressing issues of equal access for communities that were poor or exploited.

Commitments to the World Summit Declaration and Plan of Action continued to be pursued through advocacy, policy dialogue, planning and additional resource mobilization. In China, Indonesia, the Philippines, Thailand and Viet Nam, NPAs were an integral part of national development plans, but in low-income countries such as Cambodia, the Lao People's Democratic Republic, Mongolia, Viet Nam and the least developed island countries of the Pacific, there was a need for substantial international support to implement NPAs.

The East Asia and Pacific Regional Office, in cooperation with China and the UNICEF office at Beijing, organized a second regional consultation on the Convention on the Rights of the Child (Beijing, 4-6 August), while in South Asia, UNICEF helped to form small, high-level professional groups to agree on strategies and policy goals for child development. Seven countries in South Asia were implementing NPAs.

Middle East and North Africa

In 1992, UNICEF programme expenditure in the Middle East and North Africa amounted to $95 million, which represented 13 per cent of total programme expenditures.

The Middle East and North Africa region was prone to violence and conflict, and man-made emergencies left many children in Djibouti, Iraq, Lebanon, the Sudan, and the West Bank and Gaza in difficult circumstances. UNICEF country programmes in Iraq and the Sudan, in particular, combined emergency operations with normal development activities.

UNICEF-supported work aimed at addressing the psycho-social effects of armed conflict on children in Iraq and Kuwait and a series of regional consultations resulted in a two-year programme to: produce guidebooks for teachers, health and other community outreach workers; create training modules for psychologists; and produce case materials on conflict-induced trauma in children.

Regional activities also focused on the eradication of poliomyelitis, the expansion of measles coverage, the immunization of women with tetanus toxoid and the promotion of safe motherhood. Outbreaks of poliomyelitis occurred in countries with strong prevention programmes and there was concern about slippage in diarrhoeal disease programmes as well. Studies showed a drop in the use of oral rehydration therapy in some countries and the failure to expand its use in others.

Central and Eastern Europe

The Executive Board[23] recognized the need to enhance temporarily the role of UNICEF in Central and Eastern Europe, the Baltic States and the Commonwealth of Independent States, and called for UNICEF activities in the areas of advocacy, technical assistance, training and programme support. It decided that funding for advocacy and policy work would include an additional $1 million for 1992 and $2 million per year for 1993-1994. It authorized the Executive Director to provide on a temporary basis, under exceptional circumstances, technical assistance to non-qualifying countries from supplementary funds.

UNICEF programmes by sector

Immunization

During 1992, immunization coverage was sustained and improved in a majority of countries. Most countries of Asia and the Middle East and North Africa began to implement plans for the eradication of polio and neonatal tetanus and the control of measles. Some countries, mostly in sub-Saharan Africa, were unable to sustain the high levels of immunization coverage achieved in 1990, however, for reasons that included civil unrest, drought and a lack of infrastructure. During 1992, vaccine prices also rose an average of 23 per cent and UNICEF negotiated with suppliers to moderate their increases.

The Children's Vaccine Initiative, which was organized by WHO, UNICEF, the United Nations Development Programme, the World Bank and the Rockefeller Foundation in 1991 to develop new and improved vaccines, began work on a more heat-stable polio vaccine and a single-dose vaccine for tetanus.

Meanwhile, UNICEF supported national efforts to strengthen surveillance systems and the reporting of polio, measles and neonatal tetanus. Many countries had already begun to map the incidence of polio and neonatal tetanus to identify high-risk areas where immunization coverage was low.

The Executive Board[24] requested UNICEF to continue to collaborate with other parties in support of the Children's Vaccine Initiative and approved $3 million in additional funds for 1992-1993. It also requested the Executive Director to provide a progress report on the Initiative in 1993.

Control of diarrhoeal diseases

Although the global use of oral rehydration therapy (ORT) had increased from 17 to 38 per cent since 1985, 3 million children still died each year from dehydration caused by diarrhoea and a revitalized programme was needed at global and country levels.

During 1992, with the collaborative support of WHO and UNICEF, local personnel were trained in improved case-management and a series of country-based reviews looked at national plans, goals and targets, as well as the production and availability of oral rehydration salts.

Global and national data indicated that countries must address diarrhoeal disease control with greater specificity and Morocco provided an example of intensified national effort. The King of Morocco declared that deaths due to diarrhoea would be reduced to a minimum within two years and a revised communication strategy focused on family-level decision-making, the social marketing of oral rehydration salts, and the training of health personnel.

Regional meetings of African, Latin American and Asian Governments also identified the control of diarrhoeal diseases as a major area for renewed action.

Acute respiratory infections

Acute respiratory infections, primarily pneumonia, caused the deaths of more than 3.5 million children under five years of age every year.

More than 65 countries in 1992 had plans of action to control acute respiratory infections that included training for medical and paramedical workers and communication activities to improve the response to, and treatment of, pneumonia.

In Latin America, a consultative group was being formed to provide intercountry support for various activities, including surveys, epidemiology, training and communication. In several Asian countries, an integrated package of services was provided for child survival, with a distinct component on acute respiratory infections.

The Executive Board[25] endorsed actions to: support national control programmes and activities; build on existing structures; establish national policies and plans of action; improve the sustainability of control programmes; involve community health workers in the diagnosis and treatment of pneumonia; and ensure the full involvement of mothers and communities in these efforts. The Board decided that UNICEF would continue to offer training and supervision in the standard case-management of acute respiratory infections, provide drugs, develop sound communication strategies, provide technology for the diagnosis and treatment of pneumonia, and try to prevent pneumonia by ensuring access to immunization and by promoting breast-feeding, good nutrition and a healthy environment.

Nutrition

In many countries, there had been slow but significant declines in malnutrition as measured by the numbers of underweight children. The prevalence of protein-energy malnutrition in recent years had fallen in Brazil, China, Egypt, India, Indonesia, Kenya, Thailand, Venezuela and Zimbabwe, while the situation had remained static in countries such as Bangladesh, Colombia, the Philippines and Rwanda, and deteriorated in several African countries. Wars and domestic conflicts caused famine in Angola, Ethiopia, Liberia, Mozambique, Somalia and the Sudan, while severe drought affected household food security and nutrition in most countries of eastern and south-ern Africa. Global data indicated that 100 million of the world's 184 million malnourished children lived in South Asia.

UNICEF continued to promote its nutrition strategy throughout the developing world in 1992 although the rapid development of a coherent strategy at the national level was constrained by factors such as: a lack of national consensus on the nature of the nutrition problem; continued marginalization of the problem by Governments, agencies and universities; a lack of recognition of the important role of sectoral policies for nutrition related to agriculture, health, education, water supply and sanitation; and an inadequate understanding of the key role women can play in improving nutrition.

In the UNICEF medium-term plan for 1992-1995, four strategies were selected to help countries achieve nutrition goals. They were: control of the three major forms of micronutrient malnutrition (iron, iodine and vitamin-A deficiencies); protection, promotion and support of breast-feeding and improved child feeding practices; community participation and empowerment through improved assessment, analysis and capacity to design sustainable actions; and improved national nutrition policies emphasizing dialogue, advocacy, training and the use of information systems.

Breast-feeding

During 1992, 90 developing countries encouraged their hospitals to become "baby-friendly" by providing optimum support for breast-feeding. In more than half of those countries, a total of 767 hospitals were committed to achieving, or had already achieved, "baby-friendly" status. UNICEF found that there was a universal need for retraining health workers to support breast-feeding and, in response to national demand for support, the Fund recruited a full time lactation management specialist to be based at headquarters. UNICEF and WHO enhanced the training curricula for health care professionals and special regional training meetings were held in Central America, North America, South-East Asia, West Africa and China.

The availability of artificial feeding products and utensils within health-care facilities was found to be an obstacle to breast-feeding in many countries; in 1991,[26] the UNICEF Executive Board had called on manufacturers and distributors of breast-milk substitutes to end the distribution of free, low-cost supplies by the end of 1992. The International Association of Infant Food Manufacturers promised that its 29 members would stop providing free and lost-cost supplies to maternity wards in developing countries, provided that Governments prohibited the practice by all manufacturers. The Association later extended its promise to include Eastern Europe and the republics of the former USSR.

Basic education

Of all the major goals for children in the 1990s, none was more critical than basic education. After the World Conference on Education for All in 1990, some international donors committed additional resources for education but bilateral donors were slow to respond and those countries in sub-Saharan Africa, Latin America and the Middle East that had lagged in the area still had not developed feasible strategies for achieving universal primary education within the decade.

The UNICEF Executive Board,[27] noting the report of the third meeting of the UNESCO/UNICEF Joint Committee on Education (Paris, 6-7 May 1992): urged the UNESCO and UNICEF secretariats to appeal to member countries to give education the highest priority; called on heads of Government to assume personal leadership in the achievement of basic education goals for the year 2000; endorsed the analysis and dissemination of key innovations in basic education; and also endorsed the monitoring of progress towards education for all at country levels.

Children in especially difficult circumstances

Armed conflicts in many parts of the world in 1992 continued to put large numbers of children in grave and unusual danger.

Increasingly, the rehabilitation of children suffering from psycho-social stress in particular was incorporated into emergency programmes. UNICEF assisted programmes for psycho-social rehabilitation in 13 countries, including Croatia, Iraq and Liberia, and methods were developed to extend assistance through schools, health care systems, community organizations and mass media.

UNICEF also continued to assist the early detection and community-based rehabilitation of physically disabled children in many countries affected by armed conflict, but its capacity to respond was limited in comparison with the size of the problem.

Continuing studies of child abuse and neglect in industrialized countries indicated that the problems were much more widespread than previously realized; however, they were hardly acknowledged as problems in most developing countries. Few countries had programmes to monitor, respond to or prevent them. However, the increased membership of developing countries in the International Society for Prevention of Child Abuse and Neglect indicated a growing interest in the issue, and the increasing attention of WHO and the International Paediatric Association had helped to mobilize the medical community.

Child prostitution, particularly as it related to tourism in South-East Asia and Latin America, and trafficking in children in South Asia, were the subject of regional meetings in 1992. Several regional NGO networks were being organized to combat the problem and UNICEF assisted their efforts through the Campaign to End Child Prostitution in Asian Tourism, the International Catholic Child Bureau, and the International Abolitionist Federation. A number of local NGOs developed education programmes to prevent children being sold or lured into prostitution, and others helped young prostitutes to obtain medical, educational and other services, as well as to protect their rights.

Street children remained one of the largest categories of children in especially difficult circumstances and the killing of street children in Brazil and other Latin American countries drew increased attention to their plight.

UNICEF finances

In 1992, UNICEF income totalled $938 million, $131 million more than in 1991. Income by source included: $688 million from Government contributions, $135 million from non-governmental sources, $95 million from greeting card and related operations, and $19 million from the United Nations system.

Expenditures totalled $922 million, $170 million more than in 1991. Of the total, $836 million was for programme expenditures and $86 million for administrative expenditures.

Budget appropriations

At its 1992 session, the UNICEF Executive Board approved[28] a total of $419,915,000 for general resources funding and a total of $565,356,000 for supplementary funding for programme cooperation. For each region, the respective amounts were: Africa, $178,275,000 and $192,384,000; the Americas and the Caribbean, $65,060,000 and $99,059,000; Asia, $154,201,000 and $238,888,000; and the Middle East and North Africa, $22,379,000 and $35,025,000.

The Board, in a decision regarding the use of global funds,[29] adopted resolutions on the general resources and supplementary funds programme budget estimates for 1992-1993, as well as the supplementary funds programme plan estimates for 1994-1995.

Further, the Board[30] approved the medium-term plan as a framework of projections for 1992-1995, including the preparation of up to $400 million in programme expenditures from general resources to be submitted to the Board in 1993.

In another action, the Board[31] approved, on an interim basis, the recommendations of the Executive Director regarding UNICEF recovery policy, and requested him to review all elements of the structure and adequacy of the recovery policy, taking into account the views of delegations.

The Board[32] also noted the financial report and statements for the biennium ended 31 December 1991 and approved recommendations on the structure and format of budget documents.[33]

Organizational questions

The Executive Board[34] noted a report on the composition of all international Professional core staff and international project staff by title, grade, duty station and nationality. It deferred until 1993 a decision on whether to proceed with a review of administrative and management structure at UNICEF headquarters.[35]

Basic cooperation agreement

A report on the standard Basic Cooperation Agreement between UNICEF and Governments was submitted to the March 1992 organizational session of the UNICEF Executive Board.[36]

The Executive Director presented to the Board for its consideration the text of the standard Basic Cooperation Agreement[37] which had been revised in the light of observations made by delegations at the 1991 regular Board session.

The Board took note[38] of the Agreement, and requested the secretariat to continue discussions with concerned Governments.

Greeting Card Operation

During its 1991-92 season,[1] the Greeting Card Operation (GCO) contributed $82.2 million to UNICEF general resources, $5.6 million more than in the previous year. The total number of cards sold was estimated at 150 million.

The Executive Board[39] approved the greeting card and related operations work plan and proposed budget for 1992. It also noted the GCO financial report and accounts for the 1990 season for the year ended 30 April 1991 and the GCO provisional report for the 1991 season (covering 1 May 1991–30 April 1992).[40]

REFERENCES

[1]E/ICEF/1993/2 (Part II). [2]E/ICEF/1993/11. [3]E/1992/29. [4]Ibid. (dec. 1992/15). [5]Ibid. (dec. 1992/23). [6]Ibid. (dec. 1992/32). [7]E/ICEF/1992/3. [8]E/1992/29 (dec. 1992/12). [9]Ibid. (dec. 1992/33). [10]E/ICEF/1992/12. [11]E/1992/29 (dec. 1992/13). [12]GA res. 45/217, 21 Dec. 1990. [13]A/47/264-E/1992/71. [14]GA res. 44/25, annex, 20 Nov. 1989. [15]A/47/41. [16]CRC/C/10. [17]CRC/SP/SR.4. [18]E/1992/29 (dec. 1992/10). [19]YUN 1966, p. 385. [20]E/1992/29 (dec. 1992/1). [21]Ibid. (dec. 1992/21). [22]Ibid. (dec. 1992/18). [23]Ibid. (dec. 1992/19). [24]Ibid. (dec. 1992/17). [25]Ibid. (dec. 1992/27). [26]YUN 1991, p. 693. [27]E/1992/29 (dec. 1992/30). [28]Ibid. (dec. 1992/15). [29]Ibid. (dec. 1992/16). [30]Ibid. (dec. 1992/33). [31]Ibid. (dec. 1992/37). [32]Ibid. (dec. 1992/34). [33]Ibid. (dec. 1992/36). [34]Ibid. (dec. 1992/38). [35]Ibid. (dec. 1992/39). [36]E/ICEF/1992/L.1 & Add.1-3 & Corr.1. [37]E/ICEF/1992/L.2 & Corr.1,2. [38]E/1992/29 (dec. 1992/6). [39]Ibid. (dec. 1992/40). [40]Ibid. (dec. 1992/41).

Youth

The Secretary-General, in response to a 1990 General Assembly resolution,[1] submitted a report in July 1992[2] on policies and programmes involving youth. The report provided an overview of the situation of youth, highlighting critical issues, and analysed the implementation of guidelines[3] for further planning and follow-up in the area of youth. It also discussed channels of communication between the United Nations and youth and youth organizations and preparations for the tenth anniversary in 1995 of the International Youth Year (IYY).[3]

The report stated that in recent years unemployment and underemployment had worsened among youth in many developing and developed countries. In the countries of the Organisation for Economic Cooperation and Development, the rate of youth unemployment was 13 per cent and rising. The least developed countries were worst hit by this problem, which was compounded by stagnant economies, illiteracy and lack of skills. Problems affecting the health and well-being of adolescents, including nutrition, sexually transmitted diseases, alcohol consumption, drug abuse, smoking, early marriages, teenage pregnancy and induced abortion, were widespread and the rising incidence of juvenile delinquency in many countries was precipitated by socio-economic problems. Illiteracy among rural young people in several developing countries remained high.

Analysing implementation of the guidelines, the report stated that the existing global distribution of opportunities and the external debt of many developing countries had caused the retrenchment of youth programmes and policies. Policy implementation for youth had also suffered from a lack of integrated planning and a narrow concept of development that favoured economic dimensions over social needs.

The report observed that the anniversary of IYY would offer an opportunity for active and continued advocacy on behalf of youth and that the United Nations Centre for Social Development and Humanitarian Affairs had begun to prepare for its observance.

On 20 July 1992, the Economic and Social Council adopted **resolution 1992/7** on human rights and youth.

GENERAL ASSEMBLY ACTION

On 16 December, on the recommendation of the Third Committee, the General Assembly adopted **resolution 47/85** without vote.

Policies and programmes involving youth

The General Assembly,

Recalling its resolutions 32/135 of 16 December 1977 and 36/17 of 9 November 1981, by which it adopted guidelines for the improvement of the channels of communication between the United Nations and youth and youth organizations, and its other relevant resolutions,

Recalling also resolution 40/14 entitled "International Youth Year: Participation, Development, Peace", adopted on 18 November 1985 by the General Assembly acting as the United Nations World Conference for the International Youth Year, by which the guidelines for further planning and suitable follow-up in the field of youth were endorsed, and its other relevant resolutions,

Recalling further its resolution 45/103 of 14 December 1990, in which it decided to devote a plenary meeting at its fiftieth session to youth questions,

Noting that the year 1995 will mark the fiftieth anniversary of the Charter of the United Nations and the tenth anniversary of the International Youth Year,

Recognizing that, in implementing the guidelines, priority should be given to the enjoyment by youth of human rights, including the right to education and to work, and to the resolution of other urgent problems faced by young people in the present-day world, such as hunger, drug abuse, diseases, including acquired immunodeficiency syndrome (AIDS), and the deterioration of the environment,

Recalling the Convention on the Rights of the Child, which entered into force on 2 September 1990, the World Declaration on the Survival, Protection and Development of Children and the Plan of Action for Implementing the World Declaration on the Survival, Protection and Development of Children in the 1990s, adopted by the World Summit for Children on 30 September 1990,

Noting the holding of the Youth Forum of the United Nations System, at Vienna from 27 to 29 May 1991,

Noting also the fifth anniversary of the youth employment programme HOPE '87, and welcoming with appreciation its increasing activities and close collaboration with the United Nations, in particular the Centre for Social Development and Humanitarian Affairs of the Secretariat and the United Nations Educational, Scientific and Cultural Organization, and with the Council of Europe in bringing about employment opportunities for young people, especially in developing countries,

Taking note of the proposals of the ad hoc open-ended working group established by the Commission for Social Development to elaborate standard rules on the equalization of opportunities for disabled persons, in accordance with Economic and Social Council resolution 1990/26 of 24 May 1990, with regard to achieving the equitability of young persons with disabilities, made at its second session, held at Vienna from 11 to 15 May 1992,

1. *Calls upon* all States, all United Nations bodies, in particular the Economic and Social Council through the Commission for Social Development, the specialized agencies and the intergovernmental and non-governmental organizations concerned, in particular youth organizations, to continue to exert all possible efforts for the implementation of the guidelines for further planning and suitable follow-up in the field of youth;

2. *Requests* the Secretary-General to continue to promote and monitor, by using the Centre for Social Development and Humanitarian Affairs of the Secretariat as a focal point, the inclusion of youth-related projects and activities in the programmes of United Nations bodies and specialized agencies, specifically on such themes as communication, health, malnutrition, poverty, housing, culture, youth employment, illiteracy, juvenile delinquency, education, leisure-time activities, drug abuse and the environment;

3. *Calls upon* Member States to enable young people to obtain a modern education on such subjects as environmental and human rights issues;

4. *Calls once again upon* the United Nations Postal Administration to produce commemorative United Nations stamps in 1995 to mark the tenth anniversary of the International Youth Year;

5. *Emphasizes* the need for a review and appraisal of the progress achieved and the obstacles encountered in the implementation of the guidelines and, on the basis of the evaluation, for preparation of a world youth programme of action to the year 2000 and beyond, with a target orientation and within a specific time-frame;

6. *Invites* all Member States to consider preparing a national plan of action or a national calendar of events, for 1993-1995, based on an analytical national evaluation of the situation and needs of youth;

7. *Calls once again upon* Member States, United Nations bodies, the specialized agencies and other governmental and intergovernmental organizations to implement fully the guidelines for the improvement of the channels of communication between the United Nations and youth and youth organizations, adopted by the General Assembly in its resolutions 32/135 and 36/17;

8. *Invites* the regional commissions, as appropriate, together with regional youth and youth-serving organizations, to undertake a comprehensive review of the progress achieved and the obstacles encountered in the regions since 1985 and to propose draft regional youth programmes of action to the year 2000 and beyond;

9. *Requests* the Secretary-General to continue the preparation of a draft world youth programme of action to the year 2000 and beyond in accordance with proposals to be submitted by Member States, the United Nations and non-governmental youth organizations and in consultation with the specialized agencies and other organizations of the United Nations system and the relevant intergovernmental and non-governmental organizations, and to report thereon to the General Assembly at its forty-ninth session;

10. *Calls upon* youth mechanisms that have been set up by youth and youth organizations at the national, regional and international levels to continue to act as channels of communication between the United Nations system and youth and youth organizations and, especially, to contribute to the preparations for the tenth anniversary of the International Youth Year and to the formulation of a world youth programme of action to the year 2000 and beyond;

11. *Again invites* Governments, whenever possible, to include youth representatives in their national delega-

tions to the General Assembly and other relevant United Nations meetings, thus enhancing and strengthening the channels of communication through the discussion of youth-related issues, with a view to finding solutions to the problems confronting youth in the contemporary world;

12. *Invites* Governments and intergovernmental and non-governmental organizations to contribute to the United Nations Youth Fund, in order to enable it to continue its mandated role and to contribute effectively to the needs of developing countries in the field of youth;

13. *Decides* to consider the question of policies and programmes involving youth under the item entitled "Social development" at its forty-ninth session on the basis of a report of the Secretary-General on the implementation of the present resolution.

General Assembly resolution 47/85

16 December 1992   Meeting 89   Adopted without vote

Approved by Third Committee (A/47/703) without vote, 2 November (meeting 25); 18-nation draft (A/C.3/47/L.11); agenda item 93 *(a)*.

Sponsors: Austria, Belarus, Burkina Faso, Cape Verde, Chad, Czechoslovakia, Egypt, Guinea, Guinea-Bissau, Honduras, Malawi, Malta, Morocco, Netherlands, Romania, Russian Federation, Togo, United Republic of Tanzania.

Meeting numbers. GA 47th session: 3rd Committee 11-18, 22, 23, 25; plenary 89.

REFERENCES

[1]GA res. 45/103, 14 Dec. 1990. [2]A/47/349. [3]YUN 1985, p. 978.

Ageing persons

Two reports on ageing—implementation of the International Plan of Action[1] and global targets for the year 2001[2]—were submitted by the Secretary-General to the General Assembly during 1992.

In September, in accordance with Assembly resolutions adopted in 1991,[3] the Secretary-General presented the report on implementing the 1982 International Plan of Action on Ageing.[4] The report was before the Assembly at four special meetings of the plenary (15-16 October) devoted to a conference on ageing. The Conference examined the impact of ageing on national life, infrastructure and spending and focused on future strategies and a Proclamation on Ageing was adopted (see below). The Conference was preceded by a non-governmental forum in observance of the International Day for the Elderly, 1 October. The report concluded that the next decade would usher in what it called the age of ageing, during which the world's population would emerge with an elderly population of 10 per cent, projected to increase to 20 per cent and more in subsequent decades. Adjustment of social and economic infrastructures was expected to lag in many places, posing a challenge to individual countries and the international community.

Also in September, pursuant to General Assembly resolutions of 1991,[3] as well as an Assembly resolution of 1990,[5] the Secretary-General presented the report on global targets that gave special attention to practical strategies. The report proposed eight targets for the year 2001, with enabling steps for each one. The target strategies were to: support countries in setting national targets on ageing; generate support for integrating ageing into development plans and programmes; generate support for community-based programmes of care and participation of older persons; improve cross-national research on ageing; include an item on ageing in international events and meetings; establish a global network of senior volunteers for social and economic development; and facilitate closer cooperation among NGOs and intergovernmental organizations on ageing. A guide for setting national targets was included.

GENERAL ASSEMBLY ACTION

On 16 October, the General Assembly adopted **resolution 47/5** without vote.

Proclamation on Ageing

The General Assembly,

Having convened an international conference on ageing on 15 and 16 October 1992 on the occasion of the tenth anniversary of the adoption of the International Plan of Action on Ageing,

Adopts the Proclamation on Ageing, annexed to the present resolution.

ANNEX
Proclamation on Ageing

The General Assembly,

Noting the unprecedented ageing of populations taking place throughout the world,

Conscious that the ageing of the world's population represents an unparalleled, but urgent, policy and programme challenge to Governments, non-governmental organizations and private groups to ensure that the needs of the aged and their human resource potential are adequately addressed,

Conscious also that population ageing in developing regions is proceeding much more rapidly than it occurred in the developed world,

Aware that a revolutionary change in the demographic structure of societies requires a fundamental change in the way in which societies organize their affairs,

Optimistic that the coming decade will see an increase in partnerships, practical initiatives and resources devoted to ageing,

Welcoming the increasing contributions of older persons to economic, social and cultural development,

Welcoming also broad participation in the United Nations programme on ageing,

Recognizing that ageing is a life-long process and that preparation for old age must begin in childhood and continue throughout the life cycle,

Recognizing also that older persons are entitled to aspire to and attain the highest possible level of health,

Recognizing further that with increasing age some individuals will need comprehensive community and family care,

Reaffirming the International Plan of Action on Ageing, which it endorsed in its resolution 37/51 of 3 December 1982, and the United Nations Principles for Older Persons, annexed to its resolution 46/91 of 16 December 1991,

Noting the many United Nations activities that address ageing in the context of development, human rights, population, employment, education, health, housing, family, disability and the advancement of women,

Having considered the challenges inherent in implementing the Plan of Action,

Recognizing the need for a practical strategy on ageing for the decade 1992-2001,

1. *Urges* the international community:

(a) To promote the implementation of the International Plan of Action on Ageing;

(b) To disseminate widely the United Nations Principles for Older Persons;

(c) To support the practical strategies for reaching the global targets on ageing for the year 2001;

(d) To support the continuing efforts of the Secretariat to clarify policy options by improving data collection, research, training, technical cooperation and information exchange on ageing;

(e) To ensure that the ageing of populations is adequately addressed in the regular programmes of competent United Nations organizations and bodies, and that adequate resources are assigned through redeployment;

(f) To support broad and practical partnerships within the United Nations programme on ageing, including partnerships between Governments, specialized agencies and United Nations bodies, non-governmental organizations and the private sector;

(g) To strengthen the Trust Fund for Ageing as a means of supporting developing countries in adjusting to the ageing of their populations;

(h) To encourage donor and recipient countries to include older persons in their development programmes;

(i) To highlight ageing at major forthcoming events, including, in the near future, events in the areas of human rights, the family, population, the advancement of women, crime prevention, youth and the proposed world summit for social development;

(j) To encourage the press and the media to play a central role in the creation of awareness of population ageing and related issues, including the celebration of the International Day for the Elderly on 1 October and the dissemination of the United Nations Principles for Older Persons;

(k) To promote intraregional and interregional cooperation and exchange of resources for programmes and projects on ageing, including those for life-long healthy ageing, income generation and new forms of productive ageing;

(l) To provide the immense human and material resources now urgently needed for adjustments to humanity's coming of age, which can be understood as a demographic phenomenon, but also as a social, economic and cultural one of great promise;

2. *Also urges* the support of national initiatives on ageing in the context of national cultures and conditions, so that:

(a) Appropriate national policies and programmes for the elderly are considered as part of overall development strategies;

(b) Policies which enhance the role of Government, the voluntary sector and private groups are expanded and supported;

(c) Governmental and non-governmental organizations collaborate in the development of primary health care, health promotion and self-help programmes for the elderly;

(d) Older persons are viewed as contributors to their societies and not as a burden;

(e) The entire population is engaged in preparing for the later stages of life;

(f) Old and young generations cooperate in creating a balance between tradition and innovation in economic, social and cultural development;

(g) Policies and programmes are developed which respond to the special characteristics, needs and abilities of older women;

(h) Older women are given adequate support for their largely unrecognized contributions to the economy and the well-being of society;

(i) Older men are encouraged to develop social, cultural and emotional capabilities which they may have been prevented from developing during breadwinning years;

(j) Community awareness and participation is encouraged in the formulation and implementation of programmes and projects with the involvement of older persons;

(k) Families are supported in providing care and all family members are encouraged to cooperate in caregiving;

(l) Local authorities cooperate with older persons, businesses, civic associations and others in exploring new ways of maintaining age integration in family and community;

(m) Decision makers and researchers cooperate in undertaking action-oriented studies;

(n) Policy makers focus attention and resources on tangible opportunities rather than on desirable but unobtainable goals;

(o) International cooperation is expanded to the extent feasible in the context of the strategies for reaching the global targets on ageing for the year 2001;

3. *Decides* to observe the year 1999 as the International Year of Older Persons, supported by the regular programme budget for the biennium 1998-1999 and by voluntary contributions, in recognition of humanity's demographic coming of age and the promise it holds for maturing attitudes and capabilities in social, economic, cultural and spiritual undertakings, not least for global peace and development in the next century.

General Assembly resolution 47/5

16 October 1992   Meeting 42   Adopted without vote

33-nation draft (A/47/L.5/Rev.1 & Add.1), orally revised; agenda item 93 *(a)*.

Sponsors: Angola, Argentina, Azerbaijan, Bahamas, Cameroon, Chile, China, Costa Rica, Côte d'Ivoire, Cuba, Dominican Republic, Ecuador, Gambia, Grenada, Guatemala, Guinea, Guinea-Bissau, Guyana, Haiti, Honduras, India, Jamaica, Mali, Malta, Mongolia, Morocco, Paraguay, Senegal, Suriname, Togo, Turkey, Uruguay, Viet Nam.

Meeting numbers. GA 47th session: plenary 39-42.

On 16 December, on the recommendation of the Third Committee, the General Assembly adopted **resolution 47/86** without vote.

Implementation of the International Plan of Action on Ageing: integration of older persons in development

The General Assembly,

Mindful of the challenges the ageing of populations poses to all countries,

Noting with appreciation the activities of the global information campaign for the tenth anniversary of the adoption of the International Plan of Action on Ageing and the many observances of the International Day for the Elderly,

Noting with satisfaction the active participation of Member States, specialized agencies, United Nations bodies, non-governmental organizations, older persons and experts in developing a practical strategy on ageing in the form of a set of targets on ageing for the year 2001,

Welcoming the convening of the XVth International Congress of Gerontology at Budapest, from 4 to 9 July 1993,

Welcoming with appreciation the participation of older persons in development programmes and projects,

Aware of the plight of older persons, particularly those in developing countries and those in difficult circumstances,

Aware also of the heavy obligations on families that provide care to older persons and the need for comprehensive community care programmes,

Aware further of the increasing concern of development agencies for securing the human and financial resources needed for adjusting policies and programmes to population ageing,

1. *Takes note with appreciation* of the reports of the Secretary-General on the global targets on ageing for the year 2001: a practical strategy and on the implementation of the International Plan of Action on Ageing;

2. *Adopts* the global targets on ageing for the year 2001 as a practical strategy on ageing, and urges Member States to support that strategy and to consult the guide for setting national targets on ageing;

3. *Invites* the Centre for Social Development and Humanitarian Affairs of the Secretariat, as the lead and coordinating agency for the global targets, to update the target strategies periodically on the basis of achievements and new opportunities and to refine indicators for measuring progress in cooperation with the International Institute on Ageing in Malta and others;

4. *Invites* the regional commissions to assist Member States in their regions in setting regional targets on ageing for the year 2001, bearing in mind the global targets and the diverse national needs in their regions;

5. *Invites* the specialized agencies and United Nations bodies to examine technical, organizational and financial means of strengthening the inter-agency consultative process, including the biennial meetings on ageing, and to suggest measures for the consideration of the Administrative Committee on Coordination;

6. *Calls upon* the Secretary-General to give all possible support, in the form of both regular and extrabudgetary resources, to the Ageing Unit of the Centre, to enable it to fulfil its mandate as lead agency for the action programme on ageing for 1992 and beyond;

7. *Welcomes* the support of the United Nations Population Fund, the Government of Sweden and two non-governmental organizations for the research project of the Centre entitled "Developmental Implications of Demographic Change: Global Population Ageing" and invites continuing support for this project as the basis of a global research component at the Centre;

8. *Invites* Member States to second national experts and junior professional officers to the Ageing Unit of the Centre to support selected target strategies;

9. *Requests* the Commission for Social Development to convene an ad hoc informal working group at its thirty-third session for the third review and appraisal of the International Plan of Action on Ageing and for proposing measures in support of setting national targets on ageing in the decade ahead;

10. *Invites* interested Member States and organizations to support the Centre in establishing and maintaining a data bank on ageing policies and programmes so that the data gathered in the quadrennial reviews can be systematized and made available to Member States and others on a continuing basis;

11. *Acknowledges with appreciation* the major contribution of the Department of Public Information of the Secretariat to the global information campaign, and requests it to continue its work on ageing during the coming decade;

12. *Also acknowledges with appreciation* the initiative, expertise and dedication of the non-governmental community, and invites the Centre to explore the feasibility of establishing a non-governmental advisory committee, funded by voluntary contributions, to assist the Secretariat in promoting the United Nations Principles for Older Persons and in implementing the Plan of Action and the target strategies;

13. *Commends* the International Institute on Ageing on its training programme and related activities, and invites national, regional and international organizations to cooperate closely with the Institute;

14. *Urges* the United Nations, Member States and non-governmental organizations to support the African Society of Gerontology in developing and implementing a regional programme of activities on ageing;

15. *Invites* interested Member States and others to explore the feasibility of establishing a training institute on ageing for Latin America and the Caribbean;

16. *Also invites* Member States generously to support the United Nations Trust Fund for Ageing in order to enable it to continue serving as an operational tool of the United Nations programme on ageing;

17. *Invites* Member States, corporations and foundations to support the Banyan Fund Association: A World Fund for Ageing;

18. *Urges* the United Nations Development Programme and other development agencies to include a component on ageing in their regular programmes;

19. *Requests* the Secretary-General to report to the General Assembly at its forty-eighth session on the implementation of the present resolution under the item entitled "Social development".

General Assembly resolution 47/86

16 December 1992   Meeting 89   Adopted without vote

Approved by Third Committee (A/47/703) without vote, 2 November (meeting 25); 30-nation draft (A/C.3/47/L.13); agenda item 93 (a).

Sponsors: Angola, Argentina, Austria, Bahamas, Cameroon, Chile, Costa Rica, Côte d'Ivoire, Dominica, Dominican Republic, Ecuador, El Salvador, Guatemala, Guinea, Guinea-Bissau, Guyana, Honduras, Jamaica, Mali, Malta, Mongolia, Morocco, Nicaragua, Panama, Paraguay, Senegal, Sudan, Suriname, Togo, Trinidad and Tobago.

Meeting numbers. GA 47th session: 3rd Committee 11-18, 22, 23, 25; plenary 89.

REFERENCES

(1)A/47/369. (2)A/47/339. (3)YUN 1991, pp. 698 & 700, GA res. 46/91 & 46/94, 16 Dec. 1991. (4)YUN 1982, p. 1184. (5) GA res. 45/106, 14 Dec. 1990.

Chapter XV

Refugees and displaced persons

During 1992, the world's refugee population increased by almost 2 million, to 18.9 million. In the post–cold war era, resurgent nationalism, together with the economic and social consequences of the collapse of the old world order, had led to a multiplication of conflicts, many of which also resulted from ethnic, tribal or religious tensions.

The Office of the United Nations High Commissioner for Refugees (UNHCR) undertook to strengthen its emergency preparedness and response capacity, and to couple it with political initiatives to promote the safe and voluntary return of refugees to their countries of origin.

In October, the UNHCR Executive Committee considered international protection of refugees; the refugee situation in Afghanistan, Africa, Cambodia and Yugoslavia; the follow-up to the International Conference on Central American Refugees; and refugee women and children.

The Nansen Medal for 1992—presented since 1954 in honour of Fridtjof Nansen, the first League of Nations High Commissioner for Refugees—was awarded to Dr. Richard von Weizsäcker, President of Germany, for his stand against all forms of intolerance and xenophobia and his support for refugees.

Programme and finances of UNHCR

Programme policy

Executive Committee action. At its forty-third session (Geneva, 5-9 October 1992), the Executive Committee of the UNHCR Programme[1] expressed concern about the inadequacy of international protection for various groups of refugees and noted the scale and complexity of the refugee problem, the risk of new refugee situations developing, and the challenges posed to refugee protection by the constantly changing global political, social and economic climate. The Executive Committee deplored ethnic and other forms of intolerance as a major cause of forced migratory movement, and expressed its concern regarding xenophobia in segments of the population in a number of countries receiving refugees and asylum-seekers.

Deploring the tragic events in the former Yugoslavia, which had resulted in the displacement of more than 3 million persons, the Executive Committee urged all Governments and parties concerned to contribute generously to the United Nations Consolidated Inter-Agency Programme of Action and Appeal for Former Yugoslavia, which had been issued on 4 September 1992.

The Committee noted the precarious situation of many refugee women, whose physical safety was often endangered and who did not always have access to basic necessities. It encouraged UNHCR to take further measures to enhance the protection of refugee women and children and welcomed the appointment of a Senior Coordinator for Refugee Children.

The Executive Committee requested the High Commissioner to seek expanded cooperation with other international bodies, such as the United Nations Development Programme (UNDP), the United Nations Children's Fund (UNICEF), the World Food Programme (WFP), the Food and Agriculture Organization of the United Nations (FAO), the United Nations Environment Programme, the United Nations Centre for Human Rights, the International Organization for Migration and the International Committee of the Red Cross (ICRC), to expand awareness of the link between refugees and human rights, as well as development and environmental issues.

ECONOMIC AND SOCIAL COUNCIL ACTION

On 31 July 1992, by **decision 1992/304**, the Economic and Social Council took note of the High Commissioner's report for 1991/92.[2]

GENERAL ASSEMBLY ACTION

On 16 December 1992, the General Assembly, on the recommendation of the Third (Social, Humanitarian and Cultural) Committee, adopted without vote **resolution 47/105**.

Office of the United Nations High Commissioner for Refugees

The General Assembly,

Having considered the report of the United Nations High Commissioner for Refugees on the activities of her Office, as well as the report of the Executive Committee of the Programme of the United Nations High Commissioner on the work of its forty-third session, and taking note of the statement made by the High Commissioner on 10 November 1992,

Recalling its resolution 46/106 of 16 December 1991,

Reaffirming the purely humanitarian and non-political character of the activities of the Office of the High Commissioner, as well as the fundamental importance of the international protection function of the High Commissioner and the need for States to cooperate with the High Commissioner in the exercise of this primary and essential responsibility,

Noting with satisfaction that one hundred and fourteen States are now parties to the 1951 Convention and/or the 1967 Protocol relating to the Status of Refugees,

Welcoming the valuable support extended by Governments to the High Commissioner in carrying out her humanitarian tasks,

Noting with concern that the number of refugees and displaced persons of concern to the High Commissioner, as well as of other persons to whom her Office is asked to extend assistance and protection, has continued to increase and that their protection continues to be seriously jeopardized in many situations as a result of non-admission, expulsion, *refoulement* and unjustified detention, as well as other threats to their physical security, dignity and well-being, and lack of respect for fundamental freedoms and human rights,

Commending the continued efforts of the High Commissioner to improve the situation of refugee women and children, who represent the majority of refugee populations and who, in many cases, are exposed to a variety of difficult situations affecting their physical and legal protection, as well as their psychological and material well-being,

Emphasizing the need for States to assist the High Commissioner in her efforts to find durable and timely solutions to the problems of refugees based on new approaches that take into account the current size and characteristics of these problems and are built on respect for fundamental freedoms and human rights and internationally agreed protection principles and concerns,

Welcoming the commitment of the High Commissioner, bearing in mind her mandate and responsibilities, to explore and undertake activities aimed at preventing conditions that give rise to refugee outflows, as well as to strengthen emergency preparedness and response mechanisms and the concerted pursuit of voluntary repatriation,

Commending those States, particularly the least developed among them, which, despite severe economic and development challenges of their own, continue to admit large numbers of refugees and displaced persons of concern to the High Commissioner into their territories, and emphasizing the need to share the burden of these States to the maximum extent possible through international assistance, including development-oriented assistance, and through promotion of durable solutions,

Commending the High Commissioner and her staff for the dedicated manner in which they discharge their responsibilities, and paying special tribute to those staff members who have lost their lives in the course of their duties,

1. *Strongly reaffirms* the fundamental nature of the function of the Office of the United Nations High Commissioner for Refugees to provide international protection and the need for States to cooperate fully with the Office in fulfilling this function, in particular by acceding to and fully and effectively implementing the relevant international and regional refugee instruments;

2. *Recognizes* the increasing magnitude and complexity of present refugee problems, the risk of further refugee outflows in certain countries or regions and the challenges confronting refugee protection;

3. *Emphasizes* the need to keep issues related to refugees, displaced persons, asylum-seekers and other migratory flows firmly on the international political agenda, especially the question of solution-oriented approaches to deal with such contemporary problems and their causes;

4. *Calls upon* all States to refrain from taking measures that jeopardize the institution of asylum, in particular by returning or expelling refugees contrary to the fundamental prohibitions against these practices, and urges States to ensure fair and efficient determination procedures for asylum-seekers and to continue to give humane treatment and to grant asylum to refugees;

5. *Expresses deep concern* regarding persistent problems in some countries or regions, which seriously jeopardize the security or well-being of refugees, including incidents of *refoulement*, expulsion, physical attacks and detention under unacceptable conditions, and calls upon States to take all measures necessary to ensure respect for the principles of refugee protection as well as humane treatment of asylum-seekers in accordance with internationally recognized human rights norms;

6. *Acknowledges with appreciation* the progress made in the implementation of the Guidelines on the Protection of Refugee Women and calls upon States, the High Commissioner and other parties concerned to cooperate in eliminating all forms of discrimination, sexual exploitation and violence against female refugees and asylum-seekers and in promoting their active involvement in decisions affecting their lives and communities;

7. *Welcomes* the appointment of a Senior Coordinator for Refugee Children, and reiterates the importance of promoting measures to ensure the protection and well-being of refugee children, in particular unaccompanied minors, in coordination with States and other international, intergovernmental and non-governmental organizations;

8. *Welcomes also* the proposal of the High Commissioner to appoint an environmental coordinator responsible for developing guidelines and taking other measures for incorporating environmental considerations into the programmes of the Office of the High Commissioner, especially in the least developed countries, in view of the impact on the environment of the large numbers of refugees and displaced persons of concern to the High Commissioner;

9. *Reaffirms* the importance of attaining durable solutions to refugee problems, including voluntary repatriation, integration in the country of asylum and resettlement in third countries, as appropriate, and urges all States and relevant organizations to support the High Commissioner in her efforts to search for durable solutions to the problem of refugees and displaced persons, primarily through the preferred solution of voluntary repatriation;

10. *Underlines strongly* State responsibility, particularly as it relates to the countries of origin, including addressing root causes, facilitating voluntary repatriation of refugees and the return, in accordance with international practice, of their nationals who are not refugees;

11. *Notes* the significant organized voluntary repatriation movements that have taken place in 1992, and calls

upon all States and relevant organizations to support the High Commissioner in continuing and further reinforcing her efforts to promote conditions conducive to voluntary return in safety and dignity;

12. *Urges* the High Commissioner to continue her efforts to involve international, national and intergovernmental development agencies, as well as non-governmental agencies, in the planning phases for voluntary repatriation, so as to ensure that basic reintegration assistance is complemented by broader development initiatives focused on the areas of return;

13. *Supports* the strengthened efforts by the High Commissioner to explore protection and assistance strategies that aim at preventing conditions that give rise to refugee outflows and at addressing their root causes, and urges her to pursue such efforts, bearing in mind fundamental protection principles and her mandate, in close coordination with the Governments concerned and within an inter-agency, intergovernmental and non-governmental framework as appropriate;

14. *Welcomes*, in this context, efforts by the High Commissioner, on the basis of specific requests from the Secretary-General or the competent principal organs of the United Nations and with the consent of the concerned State, to undertake activities in favour of internally displaced persons, taking into account the complementarities of the mandates and expertise of other relevant organizations;

15. *Recognizes* the importance of the promotion of refugee law as an element of emergency preparedness, as well as to facilitate prevention of and solutions to refugee problems, and calls upon the High Commissioner to continue to strengthen the training and promotion activities of her Office;

16. *Strongly deplores* ethnic and other forms of intolerance as one of the major causes of forced migratory movements, and urges States to take all necessary steps to ensure respect for human rights, especially the rights of persons belonging to minorities;

17. *Notes* the relationship between situations giving rise to refugee flows and lack of respect for human rights, and encourages the High Commissioner to continue her efforts to increase cooperation with the Commission on Human Rights, the Centre for Human Rights of the Secretariat and relevant organizations;

18. *Expresses concern* regarding xenophobia and racist attitudes in segments of the population in a number of countries receiving refugees and asylum-seekers, which expose them to considerable danger, and, therefore, calls upon States and the Office of the High Commissioner to continue to work actively to promote broader understanding throughout national communities of the plight of refugees and asylum-seekers;

19. *Welcomes* the progress made by the High Commissioner in her efforts to enhance the capacity of her Office to respond to emergencies, and encourages her to continue to work closely with the Under-Secretary-General for Humanitarian Affairs, as well as with United Nations organizations and governmental, intergovernmental or non-governmental bodies, to assure a coordinated and effective response to complex, humanitarian emergency situations;

20. *Expresses deep concern* at conditions, in a number of countries or regions, which seriously endanger the delivery of humanitarian assistance and the security of the staff of the High Commissioner and other relief workers, deplores the recent loss of lives among the staff involved in humanitarian operations, and calls upon States to take all necessary measures to ensure the safe and timely access for humanitarian assistance and the security of international and local staff undertaking humanitarian work in their countries;

21. *Expresses deep appreciation* for the generous humanitarian response of receiving countries, in particular those developing countries that, despite limited resources, continue to admit large numbers of refugees;

22. *Urges* the international community, including non-governmental organizations, in accordance with the principle of international solidarity and in the spirit of burden-sharing, to continue to assist the countries referred to in paragraph 21 and the High Commissioner in order to enable them to cope with the additional burden that the care of refugees and asylum-seekers represents;

23. *Calls upon* all Governments and other donors to contribute to the programmes of the High Commissioner and, taking into account the need to achieve greater burden-sharing among donors, to assist the High Commissioner in securing additional and timely income from traditional governmental sources, other Governments and the private sector in order to ensure that the needs of refugees, returnees and displaced persons of concern to the High Commissioner are met.

General Assembly resolution 47/105

16 December 1992   Meeting 89   Adopted without vote

Approved by Third Committee (A/47/715) without vote, 18 November (meeting 43); 66-nation draft (A/C.3/47/L.36), orally revised; agenda item 96.

Sponsors: Afghanistan, Albania, Argentina, Australia, Austria, Azerbaijan, Belgium, Belize, Bulgaria, Burundi, Cameroon, Canada, Chile, Costa Rica, Côte d'Ivoire, Croatia, Cyprus, Czechoslovakia, Denmark, Egypt, El Salvador, Ethiopia, Finland, France, Germany, Ghana, Greece, Guatemala, Guinea-Bissau, Haiti, Hungary, Iceland, Ireland, Israel, Italy, Japan, Luxembourg, Mauritius, Morocco, Mozambique, Namibia, Netherlands, New Zealand, Nicaragua, Nigeria, Norway, Pakistan, Panama, Philippines, Poland, Portugal, Republic of Korea, Romania, Russian Federation, Rwanda, Samoa, Spain, Sudan, Sweden, Togo, Turkey, United Kingdom, United Republic of Tanzania, United States, Uruguay, Venezuela.

Meeting numbers. GA 47th session: 3rd Committee 34-39, 41-43; plenary 89.

Continuation of UNHCR

In accordance with a 1987 General Assembly resolution,[(3)] the Assembly reviewed the arrangements for UNHCR to determine whether the Office should continue beyond 31 December 1993.

On 16 December 1992, the Assembly, on the recommendation of the Third Committee, adopted without vote **resolution 47/104**.

Continuation of the Office of the United Nations High Commissioner for Refugees

The General Assembly,

Recalling its resolution 42/108 of 7 December 1987, in which it decided to review, not later than at its forty-seventh session, the arrangements for the Office of the United Nations High Commissioner for Refugees with a view to determining whether the Office should be continued beyond 31 December 1993,

Recognizing the need for concerted international action on behalf of the increasing numbers of refugees and displaced persons of concern to the High Commissioner,

Considering the outstanding work that has been performed by the Office of the High Commissioner in providing international protection and material assistance to refugees and displaced persons as well as in promoting permanent solutions to their problems,

Noting with deep appreciation the effective manner in which the Office of the High Commissioner has been dealing with various essential humanitarian tasks entrusted to it,

1. *Decides* to continue the Office of the United Nations High Commissioner for Refugees for a further period of five years from 1 January 1994;

2. *Decides also* to review, not later than at its fifty-second session, the arrangements for the Office of the High Commissioner with a view to determining whether the Office should be continued beyond 31 December 1998.

General Assembly resolution 47/104

16 December 1992   Meeting 89   Adopted without vote

Approved by Third Committee (A/47/715) without vote, 18 November (meeting 43); 65-nation draft (A/C.3/47/L.34); agenda item 96.

Sponsors: Afghanistan, Argentina, Australia, Austria, Azerbaijan, Bangladesh, Belgium, Belize, Bulgaria, Canada, Chile, China, Costa Rica, Côte d'Ivoire, Croatia, Cyprus, Czechoslovakia, Denmark, Djibouti, El Salvador, Egypt, Ethiopia, Finland, France, Germany, Greece, Guatemala, Guinea, Guinea-Bissau, Haiti, Honduras, Hungary, Iceland, Ireland, Israel, Italy, Japan, Liechtenstein, Luxembourg, Malaysia, Mauritius, Morocco, Namibia, Netherlands, New Zealand, Nicaragua, Nigeria, Norway, Panama, Philippines, Poland, Portugal, Romania, Rwanda, Samoa, Spain, Sudan, Sweden, Thailand, Turkey, United Kingdom, United Republic of Tanzania, United States, Venezuela, Uruguay.

Meeting numbers. GA 47th session: 3rd Committee 34-39, 41-43; plenary 89.

Financial and administrative questions

UNHCR total voluntary funds expenditure in 1992 amounted to $1,071.9 million. In addition, the United Nations regular budget contribution to UNHCR amounted to $21.2 million. In terms of activities and related expenditure, 1992 was a record year in UNHCR's history, exceeding 1991 expenditure by 24 per cent. In 1992, expenditures under General Programmes amounted to $382.1 million. Expenditures under Special Programmes totalled $689.8 million, with about 45 per cent of that amount relating to UNHCR's activities in the former Yugoslavia. Other important expenditures concerned Indo-Chinese refugees, Afghan and Cambodian repatriation programmes and special emergency programmes in the Horn of Africa. Special appeals were made in 1992 for repatriation (Angola, Cambodia, the Comprehensive Plan of Action for Indo-Chinese Refugees, Eritrea, Sri Lanka) while others were made for emergencies (Bangladesh, the former Yugoslavia). UNHCR also appealed for funds in cooperation with the United Nations. In 1992, it contributed to consolidated inter-agency appeals issued by the United Nations Department of Humanitarian Affairs and the Secretary-General for Afghanistan, Armenia, Azerbaijan, Cambodia, the Horn of Africa, the drought emergency in southern Africa and the former Yugoslavia (for details on the activities of the United Nations Department of Humanitarian Affairs, see PART THREE, Chapter III).

The Executive Committee in 1991 had approved a budgetary target for General Programmes amounting to $373.1 million for 1992.[4] Projected needs for Special Programmes at that time amounted to $568.1 million, bringing total needs for 1992 to an estimated $941.2 million. An increase in the General Programmes target for 1992 from $373.1 million to $386.4 million, mainly to cover newly identified needs in Africa in addition to measures under the Emergency Fund, was approved by a special session of the Executive Committee on 26 June.[5] Projections made in December 1991 for Special Programmes activities were updated during the first half of 1992 in response to developments in the former Yugoslavia and to meet the needs of the repatriation programme for Afghan refugees.

In October,[1] the Executive Committee approved the country and area programmes and the overall allocations for the 1993 General Programmes, amounting to $378.2 million, including $20 million for the Emergency Fund.

On 17 December,[6] the Executive Committee approved a 1993 General Programmes target of $413.6 million (including $25 million for the Emergency Fund, $20 million for a General Allocation for Voluntary Repatriation and a Programme Reserve of $33.5 million). Projections for 1993 under Special Programmes amounted to $959.7 million, of which $447.6 million was budgeted for the former Yugoslavia.

Accounts

1991 accounts

The audited financial statements on funds administered by UNHCR for the year ended 31 December 1991 showed a total expenditure of $863 million and total income of $952 million.[7]

In October,[1] the Executive Committee noted the observations of the Board of Auditors relating to management issues, especially those dealing with financial management and control systems, and urged UNHCR to enhance its internal control procedures and those of its operational partners.

In December, the General Assembly, in **resolution 47/211**, accepted the financial report of the Board of Auditors and a summary of its principal findings, conclusions and recommendations for remedial action[8] and approved the Board's recommendations and conclusions together with the comments contained in the report of the Advisory Committee on Administrative and Budgetary Questions.[9]

Subcommittee on Administrative and Financial Matters

The Executive Committee's Subcommittee on Administrative and Financial Matters in 1992

(Geneva, 2 October)[10] considered a broad range of issues, including an update on UNHCR programmes and funding; refugee women and children; UNHCR's emergency response capacity; voluntary repatriation; evaluation activities; refugee statistics; the environment; and the status of women in UNHCR.

REFERENCES

[1]A/47/12/Add.1. [2]A/47/12. [3]YUN 1987, p. 879, GA res. 42/108, 7 Dec. 1987. [4]YUN 1991, p. 705. [5]A/AC.96/791. [6]A/AC.96/806. [7]A/47/5/Add.5. [8]A/47/315. [9]A/47/500. [10]A/AC.96/803.

Refugee assistance and protection

Assistance

During 1992,[1] UNHCR continued to implement the High Commissioner's three-pronged strategy of prevention, preparedness and solutions, as the global refugee situation again deteriorated. While responding to refugee situations in countries of asylum, it also sought to prevent and contain refugee movements. UNHCR began to provide assistance not only to refugees, returnees and displaced persons, but also, in the case of the former Yugoslavia, to people directly threatened by expulsion or ethnic cleansing.

UNHCR was confronted with emergency situations in many parts of the world. It actively pursued durable solutions for refugees, especially through voluntary repatriation, while seeking to interest Governments, development agencies and financial institutions in improving infrastructure in areas of return devastated by war.

The UNHCR Emergency Fund was used frequently in response to emerging refugee situations. It was used in 1992 to assist Somali refugees in Yemen ($3.8 million) and Kenya ($2.5 million), Bhutanese refugees in Nepal ($3.4 million), Sierra Leonean refugees in Liberia ($2.5 million), Mozambican refugees in Zimbabwe ($1.5 million), as well as refugees and displaced persons from Armenia and Azerbaijan ($1.5 million). Total expenditure from the Emergency Fund in 1992 amounted to $19.2 million. In December,[2] the Executive Committee approved an increase, effective 1 January 1993, raising the ceiling of the Fund from $20 million to $25 million, and increasing the amount available for a single emergency in a given year from $6 million to $8 million. Emergency assistance programmes that were funded from special appeals included: the former Yugoslavia, to assist those uprooted by the ongoing conflict ($294.4 million); Bangladesh, to assist a new influx of Rohingya refugees from Myanmar ($18.4 million); and Iraq, for assistance to the Kurdish population in the north of the country ($17.7 million).

Following the emergency phase of a refugee operation, the basic needs of the refugees were met through care and maintenance assistance. During 1992, such assistance amounted to $214.7 million under General Programmes and $91.3 million under Special Programmes. In Africa, care and maintenance programmes continued in Kenya ($59 million), Ethiopia ($29 million), Malawi ($27.4 million) and Guinea ($16.3 million). The situation in the Horn of Africa required large-scale care and maintenance assistance, which was mostly provided in Kenya for Somali refugees. A significant cross-border operation inside Somalia aimed to avert further influxes of refugees into Kenya. Substantial care and maintenance programmes were also implemented in Côte d'Ivoire, the Sudan and Zimbabwe. Elsewhere, care and maintenance assistance continued for Vietnamese in South-East Asian camps and Hong Kong. The largest programmes were in Hong Kong ($17.1 million) and Thailand ($16.4 million). During 1992, however, new arrivals of Vietnamese asylum-seekers virtually ceased. In addition, major programmes were carried out in South-West Asia, particularly in Pakistan where a sizeable Afghan refugee population remained ($24.1 million). In Latin America, the only significant care and maintenance programme was in Mexico for Guatemalan refugees ($3.1 million), pending their voluntary repatriation.

UNHCR also continued its efforts to provide durable solutions to refugees through local integration and resettlement in addition to voluntary repatriation. In 1992, expenditures to promote durable solutions under both General and Special Programmes amounted to some $319 million.

An estimated 2.4 million refugees returned to their homes during the year. Among the most significant repatriation movements were 360,000 persons to Cambodia, principally from Thailand, and 1,274,016 from Pakistan to Afghanistan. Another 250,000 Afghans returned from Iran. About 1.5 million Mozambican refugees were also being prepared for repatriation. Expenditures on voluntary repatriation under both General and Special Programmes totalled $229 million.

UNHCR supported the local settlement of refugees within host countries, obligating some $76 million under General and Special Programmes. Assistance included the promotion of agricultural and non-agricultural activities, improvements in infrastructure, and skills training in Côte d'Ivoire, Guinea and Senegal. Organized rural settlements were supported in China, Ethiopia, Mexico, Uganda, Zaire and Zambia.

Resettlement was sought for some 42,300 persons in 1992 and, of that number, UNHCR registered 34,510 departures. The main focus for resettlement activity was the Middle East, where UNHCR sought to resettle some 30,000 Iraqi refugees from Saudi Arabia. About 7,200 of them were accepted for resettlement, including almost 3,000 in Iran. More than 5,600 Iraqis and Iranians were resettled from Turkey. In addition to these two operations, some 2,300 refugees from the Middle East and South-West Asia were also resettled. An emergency operation started on 1 October 1992 for Bosnian former detainees whose release was secured by ICRC and who were transferred to Croatia. By the end of the year, about 5,100 had been registered by UNHCR.

In Africa, resettlement efforts remained focused on countries in the Horn of Africa. A total of 6,010 African refugees departed for resettlement during the year.

In South-East Asia, a total of 19,516 refugees from seven countries were resettled during 1992. Global expenditures on resettlement were estimated at $15 million.

In 1992, expenditures on UNHCR assistance activities in Africa totalled $284 million; in the Americas, $50 million; in Asia and Oceania, $175 million; in Europe, $337 million; and in South-West Asia, North Africa and the Middle East, $159 million.

Refugee aid and development

During 1992, UNHCR and the African Development Bank (AfDB) undertook project identification missions in Malawi, Mozambique and the Sudan. UNHCR contributed to the AfDB-financed south-east rangeland rehabilitation project in Ethiopia, and the UNHCR/International Fund for Agricultural Development (IFAD) South Khorasan rangeland rehabilitation and a refugee income-generating project in Iran was being implemented on a reduced scale. An income-generating project for refugee areas in Pakistan continued with a major emphasis on training relevant to repatriation.

Joint UNDP/UNHCR missions to prepare repatriation and reintegration programmes were undertaken in Cambodia and Mozambique.

In October,[3] the UNHCR Executive Committee urged the High Commissioner to involve international, national, intergovernmental and non-governmental agencies in the planning phases of voluntary repatriation.

Assistance to refugees in Africa

In Africa, millions of people had been uprooted from their homes because of civil and ethnic conflict, human rights abuses, drought, and the famine and suffering that accompanied those events. Some had fled to neighbouring African countries, which hosted about 6 million refugees—a third of the world's total refugee population. In 1992, it was estimated that an additional 15 million people had become internally displaced persons in Africa, an almost fourfold increase on the figure for 1980.

Conflicts in a number of countries, coupled with severe drought in southern Africa, once again resulted in major population movements. There were large influxes from Mozambique into Malawi (77,000) and Zimbabwe (39,261), and the continuing conflict in Liberia drove refugees from that country into Côte d'Ivoire (15,000) and Guinea (20,000). Kenya faced a major emergency with the arrival of refugees from Ethiopia (58,000), Somalia (189,000) and the Sudan (21,800). Sudanese refugees also entered northern Uganda (15,000) and the Central African Republic (17,700). In October, Uganda also received 6,000 refugees from north-eastern Rwanda, followed in December by 15,000 refugees from eastern Zaire. Another emergency in December brought Togolese refugees into Benin (180,000) and Ghana (100,000).

The disintegration of government authority and law and order in Somalia left UNHCR with the task of caring for almost 1 million Somali refugees in neighbouring countries.

Despite ongoing crises in the Horn of Africa, some progress was made towards solutions. Discussions continued with Eritrean authorities about UNHCR involvement in the repatriation of Eritrean refugees from the Sudan, and, in Mozambique, the consolidation of the peace process opened the way to repatriation of 1.5 million refugees, the largest such organized movement in UNHCR history.

Events elsewhere were not as positive. The peace process suffered a set-back in Angola, to which some 95,000 persons had already returned, and peace efforts continued to be frustrated in Liberia, Rwanda, southern Sudan and Togo. Landmines and other unexploded ordnance threatened returnees and local populations in Angola, Mozambique and north-west Somalia, where UNHCR was obliged to support mine clearance activities, although not on the scale necessary to ensure the safety of access routes and areas of return.

UNHCR implemented a new cross-mandate and cross-border approach to the delivery of assistance to needy persons living in the same community—an approach that had been adopted in Ethiopia's eastern, southern and Ogaden regions. Under the cross-mandate approach, mixed populations comprising refugees, returnees, internally displaced persons, demobilized soldiers and civilians affected by war and drought received basic food rations, agricultural seeds and veterinary drugs. They also benefited from improved water supplies, rehabilitated schools, and expanded medical clinics. Cross-mandate activities were implemented collectively by the United Nations, non-governmental organizations (NGOs), Government bodies and donors.

The cross-border approach, which was implemented along the borders of Djibouti, Ethiopia, Kenya, Somalia and the Sudan, was aimed at creating conditions for the voluntary repatriation of refugees and the safe return of internally displaced persons. Some 120 Quick Impact Projects to meet the special needs of returnees in Somalia were launched from Kenya. They covered water, health, agriculture, livestock and infrastructural development needs. The major constraint on this initiative was the lack of security in the region. Efforts were made by the United Nations Operation in Somalia and the United Nations Task Force to improve border security.

In 1992, the Department of Humanitarian Affairs, UNHCR, FAO, UNDP, UNICEF, WFP and the World Health Organization made efforts to coordinate humanitarian relief with ICRC and NGOs, particularly in the context of the Special Emergency Programme for the Horn of Africa and Drought Emergency Operations in Southern Africa.

Total expenditures in Africa amounted to $284.4 million, of which $187 million was spent under General Programmes and $97.4 million under Special Programmes.

Report of the Secretary-General. In response to a General Assembly request of 1991,[4] the Secretary-General presented a report describing action taken by the United Nations system and nine Member States to assist refugees, returnees and displaced persons in Africa.[5]

GENERAL ASSEMBLY ACTION

On 16 December 1992, the General Assembly, on the recommendation of the Third Committee, adopted **resolution 47/107** without vote.

Assistance to refugees, returnees and displaced persons in Africa

The General Assembly,

Recalling its resolution 46/108 of 16 December 1991,

Having considered the report of the Secretary-General and that of the United Nations High Commissioner for Refugees,

Bearing in mind that most of the affected countries are least developed countries,

Convinced of the necessity to strengthen the capacity within the United Nations system for the implementation and overall coordination of relief programmes for refugees, returnees and displaced persons,

Welcoming the prospects for voluntary repatriation and durable solutions across the continent,

Recognizing the need for States to create conditions conducive to the prevention of flows of refugees and displaced persons and to voluntary repatriation,

Bearing in mind that the majority of refugees and displaced persons are women and children,

Noting with appreciation the commitment of the countries concerned to do their utmost to facilitate the provision of assistance to the affected populations and to take the necessary measures in this regard,

Realizing the importance of assisting the host countries, in particular those countries that have been hosting refugees for a longer time, to remedy environmental deterioration and the negative impact on public services and the development process,

Recognizing the mandate of the High Commissioner to protect and assist refugees and returnees and the catalytic role she plays, together with the international community and development agencies, in addressing the broader issues of development relating to refugees, returnees and displaced persons,

Bearing in mind the necessity of facilitating the work of humanitarian organizations, in particular the supply of food, medicine and health care to refugees, returnees and displaced persons, deploring acts of aggression against personnel of humanitarian organizations, particularly those that have led to the loss of life, and stressing the need to guarantee the safety of the personnel of those organizations,

Deeply concerned about the critical humanitarian situation in African countries, in particular in the Horn of Africa, caused by drought, conflict and population movements,

Welcoming regional efforts to resolve refugees problems, such as the Declaration adopted at the Summit of the Heads of State and Government of the countries of the Horn of Africa, held at Addis Ababa on 8 and 9 April 1992,[a]

Taking into account the revised appeal of the Secretary-General for the Special Emergency Programme for the Horn of Africa,

Deeply concerned by the massive presence of refugees and externally displaced persons in Djibouti, which represents more than 20 per cent of the total population of the country, and by their uninterrupted influx due to the tragic situation in Somalia,

Deeply concerned also by the serious consequences of the presence of refugees and externally displaced persons for the already difficult economic and social situation in Djibouti, which is suffering from prolonged drought and the negative impact of the critical situation in the Horn of Africa,

Recognizing that more than half of the refugees and externally displaced persons in Djibouti are located in Djibouti City in most serious difficulties and without direct international assistance, exerting an intolerable pressure on the limited resources of the country and the social infrastructure and causing, in particular, serious problems of security,

Also recognizing the need for cooperation between the Government of Djibouti and the High Commissioner and relevant organizations to find alternative solutions for the problem of refugees in Djibouti City and to be able to mobilize the necessary external assistance to meet their specific needs,

Aware that the refugee population in the refugee camps throughout Djibouti is in a precarious situation, facing the threat of famine, malnutrition and disease, and that it needs adequate external assistance for the provision

---

[a]A/47/182.

of foodstuff, medical assistance and the necessary infrastructure for shelter,

Deeply concerned about the massive presence of refugees, voluntary returnees, displaced persons and demobilized soldiers in Ethiopia and the enormous burden that this has placed on the infrastructure and meagre resources of the country,

Deeply concerned also about the grave consequences that this has entailed for Ethiopia's capability to grapple with the effects of the prolonged drought and rebuild the economy of the country,

Aware of the heavy burden placed on the Government of Ethiopia and of the need for immediate and adequate assistance to refugees, voluntary returnees, displaced persons, demobilized soldiers and victims of natural disasters,

Deeply concerned about the burden that has been placed on the Government and people of Kenya because of the continuing influx of refugees from neighbouring countries that have been stricken by strife and famine,

Recognizing the great contribution and sacrifices that the Government of Kenya has made and continues to make in dealing with this situation while facing deteriorating conditions caused by the impact of the long drought that has affected its own population,

Emphasizing the importance and necessity of continuing assistance to the refugees and displaced persons in Kenya, estimated at over half a million, until such time as this situation changes,

Deeply concerned about the tragic impact that the civil war in Somalia continues to have on the lives of its people, affecting four to five million people who are either refugees in neighbouring countries or internally displaced and are in need of urgent humanitarian assistance,

Aware that the voluntary repatriation of large numbers of Somali refugees in neighbouring countries and elsewhere, as well as the return of internally displaced persons to their homes of origin, would require a planned and integrated international assistance programme designed to cover their basic needs, ensure adequate reception arrangements and facilitate their smooth integration into their respective communities,

Convinced that it is necessary that humanitarian assistance to Somali refugees, returnees and displaced persons be mobilized urgently and delivered without delay in view of the deteriorating situation of the displaced persons and returnees and the mounting pressure the refugees continue to place on the host countries,

Recognizing that the Sudan has been hosting large numbers of refugees over an extended period of time,

Aware of the economic difficulties facing the Government of the Sudan, and the need for adequate assistance for the refugees and displaced persons in the Sudan and the rehabilitation of the areas in which they are located,

Encouraging the Government of the Sudan and the Office of the High Commissioner for Refugees for the efforts they have undertaken towards voluntary repatriation of large numbers of refugees to their homelands,

Deeply concerned about the plight of Sudanese refugee children, particularly the problem of unaccompanied minors, and emphasizing the need for their protection, well-being and reunification with their families,

Considering that the repatriation and reintegration of returnees and the relocation of displaced persons are hindered by natural disasters and that the process poses serious humanitarian, social and economic problems to the Government of Chad,

Cognizant of the appeal to Member States and intergovernmental and non-governmental organizations to continue to provide the necessary assistance to the Government of Chad to alleviate its problems and improve its abilities to implement the programme of repatriation, reintegration and relocation of voluntary returnees and displaced persons,

Noting with appreciation the continuing mediatory efforts of the Economic Community of West African States to find a peaceful solution to the Liberian crisis, and the important decision incorporated in both the Yamoussoukro IV Accord of 29 October 1991 and the Final Communiqué of the Authority of Heads of State and Government of the Economic Community of West African States of 29 July 1992 aimed at a final settlement of the conflict,

Bearing in mind the findings and recommendations contained in the report of the Secretary-General on emergency humanitarian assistance to Liberian refugees, returnees and displaced persons, particularly the need to continue emergency relief operations since the security situation is not yet propitious for the conduct of large-scale voluntary repatriation,

Taking into account the special emergency appeal for displaced persons in Liberia made by the Special Coordinator for Emergency Relief Operations in Liberia,

Deeply concerned about the influx of internally displaced persons, returnees and refugees to Monrovia and the enormous burden this has placed on the infrastructure and fragile economy of the country,

Also deeply concerned that, despite the efforts made to provide the necessary material and financial assistance for the refugees, returnees and displaced persons, the situation still remains precarious and has serious implications for the long-term national development of Liberia, as well as for those West African countries hosting Liberian refugees,

Recognizing the heavy burden placed on the people and Government of Malawi and the sacrifices they are making in caring for the refugees, given the country's limited social services and infrastructure, and the need for adequate international assistance to Malawi to enable it to continue its efforts to provide assistance to the refugees,

Gravely concerned about the continuing serious social, economic and environmental impact of the massive presence of refugees, as well as its far-reaching consequences for the long-term development process and environmental effects,

Bearing in mind the findings and recommendations of the 1991 inter-agency mission to Malawi, particularly on the need to strengthen the country's socio-economic infrastructure in order to enable it to provide for the immediate humanitarian relief requirements of the refugees and on the long-term national development needs of the country,

Convinced that, because of the serious economic situation and, in particular, because of the devastating drought in southern Africa, there is an urgent need for the international community to extend maximum and concerted assistance to southern African countries sheltering refugees, returnees and displaced persons,

Welcoming with appreciation the activities of the High Commissioner for the voluntary repatriation and reintegration of South African returnees, and hoping that the obstacles to the return of all refugees and exiles in conditions of safety and dignity will be removed without delay,

Recognizing the need to integrate refugee-related development projects in local and national development plans,

1. *Takes note* of the reports of the Secretary-General and that of the United Nations High Commissioner for Refugees;

2. *Commends* the Governments concerned for their sacrifices, for providing assistance to refugees, returnees and displaced persons and their efforts to promote voluntary repatriation and other measures taken in order to find appropriate and lasting solutions;

3. *Expresses deep concern* at the serious and far-reaching consequences of the presence of large numbers of refugees and displaced persons in the countries concerned and the implications for their long-term socio-economic development;

4. *Expresses its appreciation* to the Secretary-General, the High Commissioner, the specialized agencies of the United Nations, the International Committee of the Red Cross, donor countries and intergovernmental and non-governmental organizations for their assistance in mitigating the plight of the large number of refugees, returnees and displaced persons;

5. *Expresses the hope* that additional resources will be made available for general refugee programmes to keep pace with refugee needs;

6. *Appeals* to Member States, international organizations and non-governmental organizations to provide adequate and sufficient financial, material and technical assistance for relief and rehabilitation programmes for the large number of refugees, voluntary returnees and displaced persons and victims of natural disasters;

7. *Requests* all Governments and intergovernmental and non-governmental organizations to pay particular attention to the special needs of refugee women and children;

8. *Calls upon* the Secretary-General, the High Commissioner, the Department of Humanitarian Affairs of the Secretariat and United Nations humanitarian agencies to continue their efforts to mobilize humanitarian assistance for the relief, repatriation, rehabilitation and resettlement of refugees, returnees and displaced persons, including those refugees in urban areas;

9. *Requests* the Secretary-General to continue his efforts to mobilize adequate financial and material assistance for the full implementation of ongoing projects in rural and urban areas affected by the presence of refugees, returnees and displaced persons;

10. *Requests* the High Commissioner to continue her efforts with the appropriate United Nations agencies and intergovernmental, governmental and non-governmental organizations in order to consolidate and increase essential services to refugees, returnees and displaced persons;

11. *Requests* the Secretary-General to submit a comprehensive and consolidated report on the situation of refugees, returnees and displaced persons in Africa to the General Assembly at its forty-eighth session, under the item entitled "Report of the United Nations High Commissioner for Refugees, questions relating to refugees, returnees and displaced persons and humanitarian questions", and an oral report to the Economic and Social Council at its substantive session of 1993.

General Assembly resolution 47/107

16 December 1992   Meeting 89   Adopted without vote

Approved by Third Committee (A/47/715) without vote, 18 November (meeting 43); 66-nation draft (A/C.3/47/L.38), orally revised; agenda item 96.

Sponsors: Afghanistan, Angola, Austria, Azerbaijan, Bangladesh, Belgium, Benin, Botswana, Burkina Faso, Burundi, Cameroon, Canada, Central African Republic, Chad, Chile, China, Côte d'Ivoire, Croatia, Cuba, Cyprus, Denmark, Djibouti, Dominican Republic, Egypt, Ethiopia, Finland, France, Germany, Ghana, Greece, Guatemala, Guinea, Guinea-Bissau, Haiti, Honduras, Iceland, India, Italy, Japan, Kenya, Lesotho, Liberia, Libyan Arab Jamahiriya, Luxembourg, Madagascar, Malaysia, Malawi, Mali, Morocco, Netherlands, New Zealand, Nigeria, Norway, Philippines, Republic of Korea, Rwanda, Samoa, Sierra Leone, Singapore, Sudan, Sweden, Togo, Turkey, Uganda, United Kingdom, Zambia.

Meeting numbers. GA 47th session: 3rd Committee 34-39, 41-43; plenary 89.

The Americas and the Caribbean

During 1992, progress towards durable solutions for refugees was accompanied by a risk of new movements of asylum-seekers in the Americas and the Caribbean. The situation regarding Haitian asylum-seekers remained a major concern for UNHCR.

Repatriation and local integration continued to be supported, especially in the Central American region through follow-up to the 1989 International Conference on Central American Refugees (CIREFCA).[6] In Central America, the international community continued to support the attainment of lasting solutions for refugees, returnees and displaced persons, pledging $82.7 million at the Second International Meeting of the CIREFCA Follow-up Committee (San Salvador, El Salvador, 7-8 April 1992). The Committee decided to extend the CIREFCA Concerted Plan of Action to May 1994 (for more details, see below).

Progress made on peace in El Salvador in January 1992 stimulated the repatriation of 3,204 Salvadorian refugees during the year. In other developments, 2,319 returnees arrived in Guatemala, where UNHCR established field offices at Nenton, Barillas, Cantabal and Betel; and 4,492 Surinamese were voluntarily repatriated from Guyana.

Elsewhere in Latin America, 1,292 refugees were repatriated from various countries to Chile.

Since the 1991 military coup in Haiti,[7] some 48,000 Haitians had fled the country in search of asylum. Direct arrivals of Haitian boat people were recorded during 1992 in Cuba (2,451), the Bahamas (1,404), the Dominican Republic (735), Jamaica (142) and Panama (22). The United States continued its policy of interdiction and by May 1992 had transferred to its naval base at Guantanamo Bay, Cuba, a total of 41,019 Haitians. Of that number, 11,617 were screened in by the United States Immigration and Naturalization Service. Owing to the continuing large-scale influx, the United States began implementing a policy of summary return of all Haitians interdicted on the high seas.

During 1992, total expenditures in the Americas and the Caribbean amounted to $50 million, of which $24 million was spent under General Programmes and $26 million under Special Programmes.

Follow-up to the International Conference on Central American Refugees

In August 1992,[8] the Secretary-General reported that significant progress had been made in the Central American peace process and that support for CIREFCA's objectives had continued (for further details on the Central American peace process, see PART TWO, Chapter II). In describing the contribution of the CIREFCA Concerted Plan of Action,[6] he stated that returnees currently outnumbered refugees in the region and that new CIREFCA initiatives had been designed to address the special needs of women and returnee communities. The First Regional Forum on the Gender Approach to Work with Refugee, Returnee and Displaced Central American Women (Guatemala City, February 1992) aimed at drawing attention to the special protection and assistance needs of uprooted women by including a gender focus in CIREFCA project planning and execution. Quick Impact Projects were being implemented through UNHCR in Nicaragua on behalf of returnee communities and similar projects were being initiated in Belize and Guatemala.

The Second International Meeting of the CIREFCA Follow-up Committee (San Salvador, 7-8 April 1992) adopted a Declaration[9] deciding to extend the process until May 1994 and stressed that during that period attention should be given to sustained support for peace and democracy in the region and to the design of a resource mobilization strategy. The Declaration requested the continued support of the United Nations system through UNHCR, UNDP and the CIREFCA Joint Support Unit, stressing the need for coordination with the other agencies and closer consultation with donors and NGOs. At the meeting, a total of $82.67 million was announced by donors, of which $51.55 million was earmarked for CIREFCA projects and $31.12 million for other initiatives within the framework of CIREFCA. The UNHCR component, covering announcements to both General and Special Programmes, totalled $11.8 million.

In October,[3] the UNHCR Executive Committee expressed support for proposed new inter-agency arrangements by UNHCR and UNDP for technical support and follow-up of CIREFCA which conferred the lead agency role on UNDP.

GENERAL ASSEMBLY ACTION

On 16 December 1992, the General Assembly, on the recommendation of the Third Committee, adopted **resolution 47/103** without vote.

International Conference on Central American Refugees

The General Assembly,

Recalling its resolutions 42/1 of 7 October 1987, 42/110 of 7 December 1987, 42/204 of 11 December 1987, 42/231 of 12 May 1988, 43/118 of 8 December 1988, 44/139 of 15 December 1989, 45/141 of 14 December 1990 and 46/107 of 16 December 1991,

Recalling that the International Conference on Central American Refugees is related to the initiative of the Central American Presidents expressed in the procedures for the establishment of a firm and lasting peace in Central America concluded at the Esquipulas II summit meeting in August 1987, as indicated in the San Salvador communiqué on the Central American refugees, of 9 September 1988,

Recognizing the importance and validity of the Declaration and the Concerted Plan of Action in favour of Central American Refugees, Returnees and Displaced Persons, adopted at the International Conference on Central American Refugees held at Guatemala City from 29 to 31 May 1989 and the Declaration of the First International Meeting of the Follow-Up Committee of the Conference, especially the framework contained in the Concerted Plan of Action,

Noting with satisfaction the concerted efforts being made by the Central American countries, Belize and Mexico to find lasting solutions to the problems of the refugees, returnees and displaced persons in implementing the aims and objectives of the Concerted Plan of Action as an integral part of efforts to achieve a stable and lasting peace and democratization of the region,

Welcoming the peace agreements achieved in the peace process in El Salvador, whereby efforts are being made to consult with all national sectors, the peace dialogue in Guatemala and the progress being made in Nicaragua in the implementation of its national reconciliation policy and in assistance to the uprooted populations, which continues to encourage movements of voluntary repatriation and settlement of internally displaced persons,

Recognizing the substantial support that, *inter alia*, the Secretary-General, the Office of the United Nations High Commissioner for Refugees, the United Nations Development Programme, the donor community and national and international non-governmental organizations have given the Conference since its inception,

Taking note of the Declaration of the Second International Meeting of the Follow-Up Committee of the Conference, held at San Salvador on 7 and 8 April 1992,

Convinced that peace, liberty, development and democracy are essential in order to solve the problems of uprooted populations in the region,

1. *Takes note* of the reports submitted by the Secretary-General and the United Nations High Commissioner for Refugees and of the second status report on the implementation of the Concerted Plan of Action of the International Conference on Central American Refugees;

2. *Welcomes with satisfaction* the outcome of the meetings of the Follow-Up Committee of the International Conference on Central American Refugees, held at San José on 2 and 3 April 1991, at San Pedro Sula, Honduras, from 17 to 19 June 1991, at Tegucigalpa on 13 and 14 August 1991, at Managua on 25 and 26 October 1991, at San Salvador on 7 and 8 April 1992 and at Managua on 29 September and 28 October 1992;

3. *Urges* the Central American countries, Belize and Mexico to continue to implement and follow up the programmes benefiting refugees, returnees and displaced persons in accordance with their national development plans;

4. *Reaffirms its conviction* that the voluntary repatriation of refugees and the return of displaced persons to their countries or communities of origin is one of the most positive signs of the progress of peace in the region;

5. *Expresses its conviction* that the processes of return to and reintegration in the countries and communities of origin should take place in conditions of dignity and security and with the necessary guarantees to ensure that the affected populations are included in the respective national development plans;

6. *Requests* the Secretary-General, the Office of the United Nations High Commissioner for Refugees, the United Nations Development Programme and other organs of the United Nations system to continue their support for and involvement in the planning, implementation, evaluation and follow-up of the programmes generated through the Conference process;

7. *Supports* the Governments of the Central American countries, Belize and Mexico in urgently seeking more precise details about the support to be provided by the United Nations Development Programme in the immediate future, once the emergency stage has been completed, with the assistance of the United Nations High Commissioner for Refugees, and once the transition towards a process of sustained development of the target populations has been initiated, within the framework of the Conference;

8. *Welcomes with satisfaction* the progress made in the implementation of the Development Programme for Displaced Persons, Refugees and Repatriated Persons, and urges the Central American countries to continue their determined support to ensure that the Programme achieves its aims;

9. *Appeals* to the international community, particularly to the donor community, to continue and to strengthen their support for the Conference and to continue complying with the financing offered so as to be able effectively to achieve the goals and objectives of the Concerted Plan of Action, and to consolidate the progress made thus far in humanitarian assistance to refugees and repatriated and displaced persons of the region;

10. *Supports* the special attention that the Central American countries, Belize and Mexico are giving to the particular needs of refugee, repatriated and displaced women and children and to the measures being adopted to protect and improve the environment and to preserve ethnic and cultural values;

11. *Resolves* to give its full support to the Declaration of the Second International Meeting of the Follow-Up Committee of the International Conference on Central American Refugees, held at San Salvador on 7 and 8 April 1992 and the communiqués of the meetings of the Follow-up Committee held at Managua on 29 September and 28 October 1992;

12. *Supports* the initiative of the Governments of the countries of Central America, Belize and Mexico to extend the duration of the Conference process until May 1994, in the light of the new needs that have emerged following the changes in the region;

13. *Requests* the Secretary-General to submit to the General Assembly at its forty-eighth session a report on the implementation of the present resolution.

General Assembly resolution 47/103

16 December 1992   Meeting 89   Adopted without vote

Approved by Third Committee (A/47/715) without vote, 18 November (meeting 43); 31-nation draft (A/C.3/47/L.27); agenda item 96.
Sponsors: Argentina, Belgium, Belize, Bolivia, Chile, Colombia, Costa Rica, Côte d'Ivoire, Croatia, Cuba, Egypt, El Salvador, Finland, France, Germany, Guatemala, Haiti, Honduras, Italy, Jamaica, Mexico, Morocco, Nicaragua, Nigeria, Norway, Panama, Spain, Suriname, Sweden, Uruguay, Venezuela.
Meeting numbers. GA 47th session: 3rd Committee 34-39, 41-43; plenary 89.

East and South Asia and Oceania

Significant steps were taken in 1992 to implement the Comprehensive Plan of Action for Indo-Chinese Refugees (CPA), adopted at the 1989 International Conference on Indo-Chinese Refugees,[10] and the Orderly Departure Programme (ODP) for Vietnamese refugees. Slow but steady progress was also recorded in repatriating refugees from Thailand to the Lao People's Democratic Republic.

During the year, UNHCR was confronted with new refugee problems in South Asia. An influx of Myanmar refugees into Bangladesh, which began in 1991, continued until the summer of 1992. By September, there were 250,877 Myanmar refugees in 20 camps mainly in Cox's Bazaar, a district of Bangladesh. An agreement signed by Bangladesh and Myanmar in April 1992 prepared the way for the voluntary repatriation of the refugees.

A major influx of ethnic Nepalese from Bhutan into Nepal continued, with 65,938 arriving at six camps in south-eastern Nepal during the year. Their needs were addressed with the help of international and local NGOs. Repatriation of the Bhutanese was discussed separately between UNHCR and Bhutan and Nepal.

Since mid-1992, events in Afghanistan had produced a new influx of refugees into India, most of them Hindus or Sikhs. At year's end the number of Afghans in India totalled 11,002. In the course of the year, 28,971 Sri Lankan refugees returned from India and were received at reception centres assisted by UNHCR, but repatriation was suspended in late October 1992 due to problems in securing sea transport.

From 1980 to the end of 1992, a total of 14,723 Lao refugees and asylum-seekers, mainly from Thailand and China, were repatriated to the Lao People's Democratic Republic under UNHCR auspices. More than half were repatriated during 1991 and 1992. At the end of 1992, some 41,000 Lao refugees remained in Thailand and about 2,000 in China. Each person repatriated under UNHCR auspices received a cash grant equivalent to $80 in the country of asylum, followed by $40 and an 18-month rice ration upon arrival in the Lao People's Democratic Republic.

The Secretary-General launched a Consolidated Appeal for the Cambodia Repatriation Operation on 15 March as preparations were made for the repatriation of some 330,000 Cambodian refugees and displaced persons.

The repatriation of Cambodians, carried out within the framework of the Paris Peace accords of 23 October 1991,[11] began on 30 March 1992. On that date, UNHCR closed the last of seven camps for Cambodians in Thailand. By mid-year over 70,000 Cambodians had returned from Thailand.

The UNHCR Executive Committee[3] welcomed progress made at the Fifth Tripartite Thai/Lao/UNHCR Meeting (Rayong, Thailand, 13-14 July 1992) on the repatriation of Lao refugees and asylum-seekers and called on the international community to ensure that all the financial needs of the Cambodian repatriation operation were met.

Under the CPA, a total of 55 Vietnamese asylum-seekers arrived by boat in Hong Kong and in countries of South-East Asia in 1992, compared with 22,422 in 1991. Many factors contributed to the decrease, including developments in Viet Nam, a mass information campaign, and a reduction in cash assistance to asylum-seekers. A total of 16,952 Vietnamese were repatriated voluntarily in 1992 and 9,644 were resettled.

During 1992, expenditures in East and South Asia and Oceania amounted to $175 million, of which $50 million was spent under General Programmes and $125 million under Special Programmes.

Europe

During 1992, refugee and asylum issues continued to be a major concern for European States. By the end of the year, the United Nations was assisting 3,055,000 refugees, displaced persons, and others affected by the war in the former Yugoslavia. A humanitarian airlift to Sarajevo began on 3 July 1992, carrying a daily average of 200 metric tons of food and medical supplies. The operation was interrupted several times due to security incidents. On 29 July, UNHCR convened in Geneva a high-level international meeting on aid to victims of the conflict. It endorsed a Comprehensive Response to the Humanitarian Crisis in the former Yugoslavia, as proposed by the High Commissioner, including respect for human rights and humanitarian law; humanitarian access; preventive and temporary protection; material assistance; special needs; and return and rehabilitation. Implementation was reviewed at follow-up meetings held at Geneva on 4 September, 9 October and 4 December. European countries, responding to UNHCR's appeal to admit persons fleeing the conflict, guaranteed temporary protection to more than 600,000 persons. UNHCR estab-

lished more than 20 offices in the former Yugoslavia, employing some 600 international and local staff. UNHCR expenditures in 1992 for the former Yugoslavia totalled $297 million.

The magnitude and complexity of the United Nations humanitarian operation in the former Yugoslavia increased dramatically, as reflected by a series of appeals, each with a larger target population and a correspondingly greater appeal total. The first appeal, issued on 3 December 1991, set a target of $24.3 million (for all United Nations agencies), with the number of planned beneficiaries specified at 500,000. By 8 April 1992 the target had risen to $37.5 million and the number of beneficiaries was 650,000. One month later, on 19 May, a revised appeal was issued for $174.5 million, for 1,000,000 beneficiaries. The 4 September appeal set a target of $561.7 million, for 2,780,000 beneficiaries, and the 4 December appeal was issued for 3,055,000 planned beneficiaries with a target of $642.5 million. (For details on the situation in the former Yugoslavia, see PART TWO, Chapter IV.)

In Western Europe, the estimated number of asylum-seekers in 1992 was almost 700,000, compared to 545,000 in 1991. Governments in the region introduced legislation and measures to streamline status determination procedures, and distinguish at an early stage between founded and unfounded applications for asylum. Difficulties in managing the great influx of asylum-seekers in 1992 were aggravated by increasing manifestations of xenophobia and racism, including attacks on reception centres.

UNHCR further established representation in Central and Eastern European States, including the Commonwealth of Independent States, focusing its activities on protection, refugee law promotion and institution-building, with some limited assistance programmes. UNHCR assisted the most destitute asylum-seekers in Moscow through a care and maintenance project. Responding to requests from the Governments of Armenia and Azerbaijan, UNHCR initiated six-month relief projects in each of those States.

During 1992, UNHCR's expenditures in Europe amounted to $337 million, of which $25 million was spent under General Programmes and $312.2 under Special Programmes.

South-West Asia, North Africa and the Middle East

Despite continued civil strife in Afghanistan, some 1.5 million Afghan refugees were voluntarily repatriated from neighbouring countries during 1992 with an expenditure of $48.6 million. UNHCR's programme for returnees within Afghanistan focused on limited emergency rehabilitation related to the need for shelter and irrigation, mainly through food-for-work projects. The withdrawal of most international staff from the country due to unstable conditions prevented the United Nations from addressing reconstruction needs. The situation was aggravated by the internal displacement of hundreds of thousands of persons who fled Kabul during the last quarter of the year.

In December 1992, Afghanistan also became a country of asylum, with an influx of some 50,000 refugees from civil war in Tajikistan. UNHCR provided them with basic emergency assistance. About 500,000 additional persons were displaced inside Tajikistan.

A total of 1,274,000 Afghans in Pakistan benefited from a repatriation scheme under which UNHCR offered a cash grant and wheat provided by WFP. With large-scale repatriation, the number of Afghan refugees in Pakistan declined, and UNHCR closed or merged 157 camp administration units, leaving 190 units at year's end. However, even as Afghans returned home in large numbers, Pakistan received some 80,000 new Afghan refugees from fighting in and around Kabul after a change of regime in April 1992.

In Iran, UNHCR helped Afghan refugees to return home through a network of in-country transit centres, border-exit stations and organized internal transport. Although some 400,000 persons were estimated to have returned to Afghanistan from Iran in 1992, about 2.5 million remained in Iran.

The Executive Committee[3] welcomed the voluntary repatriation to Afghanistan of more than 1 million refugees from Iran and Pakistan during 1992, but noted that humanitarian assistance had been constrained by inadequate funding. Addressing the situation of refugees, returnees and displaced persons in Africa, the Committee noted that internal conflicts, insecurity and the disintegration of institutions continued to cause massive displacements, and called on the High Commissioner to continue her initiatives to deal with the root causes of the problem.

By the end of 1992, over 90 per cent of the Iraqi refugees in the western provinces of Iran had returned to Iraq. While 65,000 Kurdish refugees still residing in Iran continued to return to Iraq in small numbers, prospects for the repatriation of 30,000 Iraqi Shiites residing in Iran were remote. In Iraq, UNHCR focused on the needs of returnee villages, many of which had been razed during fighting. Of the 4,000 villages believed to have been destroyed, UNHCR helped to reconstruct about 1,200, and NGOs, 562. After completing a winterization programme, including the supply of adequate shelter, UNHCR phased out its activities in northern Iraq in June 1992.

The Persian Gulf conflict generated new groups of Iraqi refugees in Kuwait, Saudi Arabia and the Syrian Arab Republic. In Kuwait, some 8,000 Iraqis obtained resident permits during the year, while UNHCR continued to cooperate with the Government to find durable solutions for more than 60,000 stateless persons. About 28,000 Iraqis were being accommodated at the Rafha camp in Saudi Arabia. A further 2,100 refugees arrived in the Syrian Arab Republic from northern Iraq during 1992, while some 5,700 persons remained in El Hol refugee camp in El Hassake district.

In Yemen, the number of Somali refugees increased to nearly 51,800, located at an emergency camp in Aden. Construction of a more durable UNHCR camp was under way, however, in the Abyan governorate, 50 kilometres from Aden. Some 250 Ethiopian refugees either repatriated under UNHCR auspices or spontaneously moved to other countries in the region.

The number of refugees in the Libyan Arab Jamahiriya continued to grow, with new arrivals from Ethiopia (Eritrea), Liberia, Nigeria, Somalia and the Sudan. The influx of 19,500 Malian refugees to Mauritania brought the total number receiving assistance at Bassikounou, Aghor and Fassala to 38,000. In southern Algeria, about 50,000 refugees from Mali and Niger received assistance.

During 1992, total expenditures in South-West Asia, North Africa and the Middle East amounted to $159 million, of which $61 million was spent under General Programmes and $98 million under Special Programmes.

Refugee protection

The right to seek and to enjoy asylum, and the corresponding principle of non-refoulement, remained the cornerstone of UNHCR's efforts to ensure that the persons needing international protection received it.

The scale and complexity of population displacements, however, had in some cases placed serious strains on the international system for the protection of refugees, endangering asylum at times. During 1992, UNHCR recognized the need to develop new, complementary protection strategies. They included support for conditions in countries of origin that would allow the safe return of refugees, and efforts to prevent or attenuate conditions that might force people to flee.

An August 1992 note by the High Commissioner on international protection[13] was presented to the UNHCR Executive Committee, summarizing the main protection challenges for UNHCR's activities as reflected in the findings and recommended approaches of a UNHCR Working Group on International Protection. The note discussed, among other matters, UNHCR's activities and competence; new approaches to asylum, prevention and other activities in the country of origin; and solutions with emphasis on voluntary repatriation and concerted regional arrangements.

The Executive Committee reaffirmed the primary importance of the principles of non-refoulement and asylum as basic to refugee protection. It renewed its expressions of concern regarding problems jeopardizing the security of refugees, including numerous incidents of refoulement, expulsion, physical attacks, and detention under unacceptable conditions. It noted that UNHCR's broad humanitarian expertise provided a basis for the exploration of new options in the areas of asylum, prevention and solutions, and in that connection, supported efforts by the High Commissioner to explore further approaches to conditions that gave rise to refugee situations.

The UNHCR Centre for Documentation on Refugees (CDR) houses information relating to those in flight through asylum and resettlement. In 1992, CDR developed its services, publications and databases and responded to more than 1,400 requests for information.

On the publication side, CDR entered its tenth year with the quarterly *Refugee Abstracts*, and collaboration continued on the *International Journal of Refugee Law*, published by Oxford University Press. The movement of the CDR literature and legal databases to the UNHCR Local Area Network was initiated and the Government of Canada made possible the addition of continuously updated country databases.

The Subcommittee of the Whole on International Protection[12] of the UNHCR Executive Committee (Geneva, 1 October 1992) discussed the work of the Subcommittee's inter-sessional meetings held for the first time in 1992 (Geneva, 23 January and 13 and 14 April). The meetings covered issues including the protection of refugee women and refugee law promotion, dissemination and training.

International instruments

As at 31 December 1992, the 1951 Convention relating to the Status of Refugees[14] had been acceded or succeeded to by 112 States as a result of the 1992 accessions by Albania, Cambodia, Honduras and the Republic of Korea and successions by Croatia and Slovenia. The 1967 Protocol[15] to the Convention had 113 States parties as a result of the 1992 accessions and successions by the same States.[16]

Other intergovernmental legal instruments of benefit to refugees included the 1969 Organization of African Unity Convention governing the Specific Aspects of Refugee Problems in Africa, the 1957 Agreement relating to Refugee Seamen and its 1973 Protocol, the 1959 European Agreement on the Abolition of Visas to Refugees, the 1980 European Agreement on Transfer of Responsibility for Refugees, and the 1969 American Convention on Human Rights, Pact of San José, Costa Rica.

As at 31 December 1992, there were 38 States parties to the 1954 Convention relating to the Status of Stateless Persons[17] and 16 States parties to the 1961 Convention on the Reduction of Statelessness.[18]

REFERENCES

[1]A/47/12. [2]A/AC.96/806. [3]A/47/12/Add.1. [4]YUN 1991, p. 710, GA res. 46/108, 16 Dec. 1991. [5]A/47/529 & Corr.1. [6]A/44/527 & Corr.1,2. [7]YUN 1991, p. 151. [8]A/47/364. [9]CIREFCA/CS/92/11. [10]A/44/523. [11]YUN 1991, p. 155. [12]A/AC.96/802. [13]A/AC.96/799. [14]YUN 1951, p. 520. [15]YUN 1967, p. 769. [16]*Multilateral Treaties Deposited with the Secretary-General: Status as at 31 December 1992* (ST/LEG/SER.E/11), Sales No. E.93.V.11. [17]YUN 1954, p. 416. [18]YUN 1961, p. 533.

Chapter XVI

Drugs of abuse

Drug abuse and illicit trafficking, accompanied by violence and corruption, remained a serious problem worldwide during 1992. National and international drug control measures that Governments had agreed upon in international conventions and resolutions had not yet yielded to universally visible results and their validity continued to be questioned. In its annual report, the International Narcotics Control Board (INCB) stated, however, that it was not convinced that valid alternatives to present policies had been found that would meaningfully reverse the situation. The Board felt that world-wide efforts to combat drug abuse and trafficking would have to be continuous, balanced and applied in an internationally concerted manner for further results to be achieved. Drug abuse was closely linked to political, social and economic problems and progress in these areas would undoubtedly help to solve the problem. Positive experiences in the fight against drugs were reported in a number of countries, and INCB suggested that those experiences be carefully examined to determine whether they could be duplicated elsewhere. INCB continued to supervise the implementation of drug control treaties as well as the comprehensive survey of the world-wide drug control situation.

The United Nations International Drug Control Programme (UNDCP) provided leadership and coordination for all United Nations activities against drug abuse and trafficking. The Commission on Narcotic Drugs reviewed all United Nations drug control programmes and activities, provided broad policy guidelines and made recommendations to the Economic and Social Council. During the year, the General Assembly passed six resolutions dealing with international drug control.

Drug abuse and international control

UN International Drug Control Programme

United Nations efforts to combat drug abuse and illicit trafficking were coordinated under the leadership of the United Nations International Drug Control Programme, established in 1991.[1] In its first year, the Programme was able to expand its activities, intensify its contact with Governments, define its priorities and objectives and, given the various mandates entrusted to it, consult extensively with organizations within and outside the United Nations system. The first annual report of the Programme's Executive Director to the Commission on Narcotic Drugs[2] noted that the objective of UNDCP as the coordinating point for comprehensive drug control was for all multilateral and bilateral initiatives to be supportive of an agreed strategy, with UNDCP acting as the international custodian and a source of inspiration. Important developments in the Programme related to its activities in the areas of money-laundering and the control of chemical precursors. It was also able to expand its capacity to analyse the drug problem in all its dimensions and help Governments define comprehensive national strategies and plans for drug control. UNDCP also undertook a pioneering initiative in 1991: the development of a "debt-for-drugs" swap concept.

The annual report detailed the Programme's policy framework, including its integrated approach, coordination measures, technical cooperation, plans and subregional strategies. It also described its programme activities to: strengthen the licit drug control system; prevent and reduce illicit demand for drugs; treat and rehabilitate drug users; eliminate the supply of narcotic drugs and psychotropic substances from illicit sources; and suppress illicit traffic.

In an addendum to the report,[3] the Executive Director outlined the elements of a strategy whereby UNDCP would work in partnership with all countries to prevent and control drug production, trafficking and abuse by increasing awareness of the problem; strengthening national and international drug abuse control; enhancing north-south and south-south cooperation; reconstructing the social and economic fabric of communities disrupted by drug abuse problems; promoting new community partnerships; identifying new directions and concepts through international multidisciplinary discussions; and improving the capacity of countries to prevent drug abuse by applying state-of-the-art techniques to public education. The strategy identified activities for UNDCP in support of these goals.

The role and work of UNDCP was also discussed by the Secretary-General, pursuant to a General Assembly request,[4] in an October report[5] outlining the coordination of drug control activities within the United Nations system between July and December 1991.

Budget and administration

The Advisory Committee on Administrative and Budgetary Questions (ACABQ)[6] considered the administrative and programme costs of UNDCP for the biennium 1992-1993, as well as a note by UNDCP on its programme of future work and priorities.[7] ACABQ was of the opinion that for UNDCP's budget cycle to synchronize with the rest of the United Nations, the Commission on Narcotic Drugs should approve its budget and the administrative and programme support costs in odd-numbered years and prior to the start of the United Nations financial period. ACABQ suggested that every effort should be made to provide it with revised budget estimates for 1992-1993 and proposed estimates for 1994-1995, and that the UNDCP budget should be fully synchronized with the rest of the United Nations system by the 1996-1997 biennium at the latest.

The proposed budget estimate for the 1992-1993 biennium was $168 million, of which $82 million was identified for 1992 and $86 million for 1993 to cover ongoing country and regional projects, new projects, global projects and contingency and field operations support. The Committee also recommended eight new temporary posts, pending the review of UNDCP's administrative structure, and that future budget submissions include detailed information on estimates, sources and components of income.

The Secretariat submitted a note in November,[8] in response to a 1991 General Assembly request,[9] on the administrative and financial arrangements for the UNDCP programme budget for 1992-1993. The Assembly had invited the Secretary-General to consider ways to streamline the proposed structure of UNDCP, and to submit a report at its forty-seventh session. The Secretariat's note indicated that the structure of UNDCP could not be separated from its financial and personnel arrangements, which were still under review. In addition, the ongoing restructuring exercise of the United Nations might have implications for the structure of its office at Vienna. Consequently, it was proposed that the requested report be submitted to the General Assembly at its forty-eighth session.

By **resolution 47/219 A, section XXII,** of 23 December 1992, the General Assembly took note of the note by the Secretariat on the administrative and financial arrangements regarding the Programme.

Action by the Commission on Narcotic Drugs. On 14 April,[10] the Commission requested the Executive Director of UNDCP to examine the feasibility of mechanisms to evaluate operational activities relating to narcotic drugs and psychotropic substances in each region and to advise the Commission on existing and possible new activities. On the same date, the Commission approved the budget estimates for 1992 and 1993.

On 15 April,[11] the Commission endorsed comments and recommendations contained in the ACABQ report on the proposed administrative and programme support costs of UNDCP and approved, as a temporary procedure, a calendar for budget submissions which stipulated, *inter alia*, that in the second year of the biennium 1992-1993, the Programme would submit revised budget estimates based on known expenditures and programme performance and delivery during the first year, and projections for the first year of the 1994-1995 biennium.

It also decided that, to assist the Commission in its administrative and budgetary functions, UNDCP should submit documentation outlining general criteria for the use of resources, programme goals and objectives, budgeted operational activities, and trust funds created from voluntary contributions for specific purposes. The Commission decided to convene informal consultations in the fourth quarter of 1992, to discuss revised budget estimates for 1993 to ensure the active involvement of Member States and facilitate approval of the estimates at the Commission's thirty-sixth session. It also decided to review the budget format and methodology at its thirty-seventh session.

GENERAL ASSEMBLY ACTION

On 16 December 1992, on the recommendation of the Third (Social, Humanitarian and Cultural) Committee, the General Assembly adopted **resolution 47/101** without vote.

United Nations International Drug Control Programme

The General Assembly,

Recalling its resolution 46/104 of 16 December 1991, in which it requested that the restructuring process of the United Nations International Drug Control Programme be completed as soon as possible so that the Programme could fulfil its mandate with enhanced effectiveness and efficiency,

Recalling also the Political Declaration and the Global Programme of Action adopted at its seventeenth special session on 23 February 1990,

Emphasizing that the problem of drug abuse and illicit trafficking has to be considered within the broader economic and social context,

Reaffirming the importance of the role of the United Nations International Drug Control Programme as the main focus for concerted international action for drug abuse control,

Underlining the role of the Commission on Narcotic Drugs as the principal United Nations policy-making body on drug control issues, and endorsing paragraph 1 *(c)* of Economic and Social Council resolution 1991/38 of 21 June 1991,

Recognizing that international cooperation against illicit trafficking should be pursued in full conformity with the principles enshrined in the Charter of the United Nations and the principles of international law,

Noting that in the consideration of the programme budget proposals submitted by the Secretary-General for the biennium 1992-1993 full account should be taken of the measures proposed pursuant to resolution 45/179 of 21 December 1990 and Commission on Narcotic Drugs resolution 13(XXXV), adopted at its thirty-fifth session,

Commending the United Nations International Drug Control Programme for the activities undertaken so far in the performance of the functions entrusted to it,

Considering the need for an evaluation of the problems, achievements and challenges related to drug control programmes, with a view to strengthening international cooperation,

1. *Takes note* of the report of the Secretary-General on the measures taken to implement resolution 46/104, and welcomes the drug control efforts of the United Nations International Drug Control Programme to date;

2. *Reaffirms* Economic and Social Council resolution 1991/38, which calls on the Commission on Narcotic Drugs to give policy guidance to the United Nations International Drug Control Programme and to monitor its activities;

3. *Urges* the United Nations International Drug Control Programme to give special emphasis to the implementation of those issues from the Global Programme of Action identified as priorities by the Commission on Narcotic Drugs in its resolution 2(XXXIV), adopted at its thirty-fourth session;

4. *Stresses* the importance of the smooth functioning of the United Nations International Drug Control Programme for the achievement of the best possible results in the implementation of its mandate;

5. *Calls upon* the Secretary-General to take, as a matter of urgency, all necessary measures to complete the organizational and administrative structure of the United Nations International Drug Control Programme, in accordance with the relevant General Assembly resolutions;

6. *Requests* the Executive Director of the United Nations International Drug Control Programme, in accordance with the authority delegated to him by the Secretary-General, to coordinate and provide effective leadership for all United Nations drug control activities in order to ensure coherence of actions within the Programme as well as coordination, complementarity and non-duplication of such activities across the United Nations system, and in this context actively to seek cooperation and support for a global approach from other international organizations, non-governmental organizations, bilateral programmes and national institutions;

7. *Strongly urges* all Governments to provide the fullest possible financial and political support to the United Nations International Drug Control Programme, in particular by increasing the voluntary contributions to the Programme, with a view to expanding and strengthening its operational activities and technical cooperation, in particular with developing countries;

8. *Requests* the Secretary-General to report to the General Assembly at its forty-eighth session on measures taken to implement the present resolution.

General Assembly resolution 47/101

16 December 1992   Meeting 89   Adopted without vote

Approved by Third Committee (A/47/710) without vote, 18 November (meeting 43); 53-nation draft (A/C.3/47/L.32); agenda item 95.

Sponsors: Australia, Bahamas, Belgium, Belize, Bolivia, Canada, Chile, Colombia, Costa Rica, Côte d'Ivoire, Cuba, Denmark, Ecuador, Egypt, El Salvador, Finland, France, Germany, Greece, Guatemala, Honduras, Hungary, Ireland, Italy, Jamaica, Japan, Luxembourg, Malaysia, Mexico, Morocco, Myanmar, Netherlands, New Zealand, Nicaragua, Nigeria, Norway, Peru, Philippines, Portugal, Republic of Korea, Russian Federation, Samoa, Singapore, Spain, Suriname, Sweden, Thailand, Turkey, United Kingdom, United States, Uruguay, Vanuatu, Venezuela.

Meeting numbers. GA 47th session: 3rd Committee 27-29, 31-33, 41, 43; plenary 89.

Illicit traffic

Drug law enforcement

A Secretariat report in March presented the results of a study, requested by the Commission on Narcotic Drugs, on the nature, frequency and duration of meetings of the Heads of National Drug Law Enforcement Agencies (HONLEA), which also covered, because of its similar nature, the Subcommission on Illicit Drug Traffic and Related Matters in the Near and Middle East.[12] The study made proposals for strengthening the capacity of these two subsidiary bodies of the Commission to combat drug abuse and illicit trafficking. These proposals covered: the terms of reference and organization of meetings, membership, frequency and duration of meetings, sources of funding, training programmes, reports on illicit traffic and the performance of Commission functions. It was recommended, among other things, that: the Commission should decide that whenever HONLEA meetings take place in a region where other drug law enforcement meetings occur, the regional HONLEA should be convened every other year and UNDCP should participate in the other regional meeting during those years when the regional HONLEA did not meet; the Commission should clarify the criteria for membership in each subsidiary body and review its observer list; the subsidiary bodies should monitor the implementation of UNDCP drug law enforcement training programmes at the regional level and make recommendations for enhancing them; subsidiary bodies should report regularly to the Commission on current trends in illicit traffic in the respective regions; the Commission should consider ways of using its subsidiary bodies to monitor implementation of the Global Programme of Action on international cooperation against illicit production, supply, demand, trafficking and distribution of narcotic drugs and psychotropic substances.[13]

Action by the Commission on Narcotic Drugs. The Commission on Narcotic Drugs considered the Secretariat report and, in particular, the recommendation relating to the frequency of meetings of HONLEA. The Commission was also informed that the International Criminal Police Organization (Interpol) and UNDCP had agreed to rotate their meetings, on a trial basis over a period of two years, among the regions of Africa, Europe, and Latin America and the Caribbean, and had taken initiatives to coordinate regional drug law enforcement meetings. The Customs Cooperation Council (CCC) stressed the need to involve customs officials in all drug law enforcement meetings held at the regional level, whether convened by UNDCP or Interpol.

The Commission agreed that the frequency of meetings of HONLEA should be determined on a regional basis, taking into account country needs and the meetings of other bodies. It also agreed, in view of new trends in illicit traffic in Eastern Europe, that the meeting of HONLEA, Europe, should focus on enhanced cooperation in drug law enforcement between States in Eastern and Western Europe. There was also a consensus that meetings of HONLEA should remain focused on drug law enforcement.

On 15 April,[14] the Commission approved recommendations for the organization of work of its subsidiary bodies, and decided that the fifth meeting of HONLEA, Latin America and the Caribbean, should be held in Mexico.

On the same date, the Commission also decided,[15] pursuant to an invitation and date determined by the Government of Iran, to convene a ministerial-level conference of the Subcommission on Illicit Drug Traffic and Related Matters in the Near and Middle East, in consultation with UNDCP, and approved a provisional agenda for the proposed conference.

ECONOMIC AND SOCIAL COUNCIL ACTION

On 30 July, the Economic and Social Council, on the recommendation of its Social Committee, adopted **resolution 1992/28** without vote.

Improvement of the functioning of the subsidiary bodies of the Commission on Narcotic Drugs

The Economic and Social Council,

Taking note of the report of the Executive Director of the United Nations International Drug Control Programme on the nature, frequency and duration of the meetings of heads of national drug law enforcement agencies, requested by the Commission on Narcotic Drugs at its thirty-fourth session, and the comments of the Commission on the report at its thirty-fifth session,

Welcoming the possibility of more active participation of the Customs Cooperation Council and the International Criminal Police Organization in the meetings of subsidiary bodies of the Commission on Narcotic Drugs,

Aware of the ongoing examination of possible ways of scheduling various regional meetings related to drug law enforcement of United Nations bodies and other intergovernmental organizations so as to increase cooperation between those bodies and organizations and to avoid duplication of effort and overlapping,

1. *Decides* to approve the application by Iraq for membership in the Subcommission on Illicit Drug Traffic and Related Matters in the Near and Middle East;

2. *Endorses* in principle that, for the regional meetings of heads of national drug law enforcement agencies, membership should be based on membership in the respective regional commissions;

3. *Reiterates* that observer status in all subsidiary bodies of the Commission on Narcotic Drugs is open to all States requesting such status;

4. *Decides* that in future the Subcommission on Illicit Drug Traffic and Related Matters in the Near and Middle East shall, in principle, meet annually for a period of five days in one of the countries covered by the region of the Subcommission;

5. *Confirms* that the Meeting of Heads of National Drug Law Enforcement Agencies, African Region, the Meeting of Heads of National Drug Law Enforcement Agencies, Asia and the Pacific Region, and the Meeting of Heads of National Drug Law Enforcement Agencies, Latin American and Caribbean Region, shall each continue to be held annually in a country of their respective regions;

6. *Decides* that the Second Meeting of Heads of National Drug Law Enforcement Agencies, European Region, shall convene in 1993 at the United Nations Office at Vienna;

7. *Invites* the Second Meeting of Heads of National Drug Law Enforcement Agencies, European Region, to review its schedule of future meetings, taking into account regional meetings organized by the International Criminal Police Organization;

8. *Invites* the Executive Director of the United Nations International Drug Control Programme to continue to explore possible means of rationalizing the schedule of regional meetings related to drug law enforcement so as to avoid duplication of effort and possibly free resources that could be used for other meetings;

9. *Requests* the Commission on Narcotic Drugs to examine further, on a regular basis, the functioning of its subsidiary bodies.

Economic and Social Council resolution 1992/28

30 July 1992   Meeting 41   Adopted without vote

Approved by Social Committee (E/1992/107) without vote, 27 July (meeting 21); draft by Commission on Narcotic Drugs (E/1992/25); agenda item 20.

By **decision 1992/211** of 7 February, the Economic and Social Council decided to cancel the meeting of the Subcommission on Illicit Drug Traffic and Related Matters in the Near and Middle East of the Commission on Narcotic Drugs, which was scheduled to be held at Vienna on 24 and 25 February 1992.

Implementation of the UN Convention against Illicit Traffic

In response to a 1990 request of the General Assembly,[16] the Secretary-General submitted a report[17] in September on the implementation of the 1988 United Nations Convention against Illicit Traffic in Narcotic Drugs and Psychotropic

Substances.[18] He reported that there had been extensive legislative activity to implement the Convention. Implementation laws and regulations of 34 States not yet parties to the Convention, but implementing various provisions thereof, were given to the Secretary-General and published by UNDCP. A number of other States made progress in amending laws and administrative arrangements in line with the provisions of the Convention.

UNDCP provided comprehensive legal assistance to more than 40 States in Africa, Asia and the Pacific, Europe, and Latin America and the Caribbean to adjust national laws, policies and infrastructures to implement the requirements and objectives of all the international drug control conventions, particularly the 1988 Convention, and to train judges, prosecutors and investigators to apply the new laws. Assistance was provided through regional workshops which helped States identify and overcome limitations in their legal capacity to implement fully all international drug control conventions. Model legislation was also being developed by UNDCP to accelerate more widespread and uniform implementation while promoting maximum international cooperation. A package of model texts for use in all main legal systems was expected to be completed early in 1993.

In related action, UNDCP reported a trend towards the ratification and implementation of the 1961 Single Convention on Narcotic Drugs,[19] as amended by the 1972 Protocol,[20] and the 1971 Convention on Psychotropic Substances.[21]

Action by the Commission on Narcotic Drugs. On 15 April,[22] the Commission called upon all States that had not already done so to adopt legislative measures to facilitate mutual legal assistance and establish internal mechanisms for the timely transfer of evidence in investigations, prosecutions and judicial proceedings connected with illicit drug trafficking and related offences. It also urged the international community to conclude bilateral or multilateral agreements or arrangements for expeditiously processing requests for legal assistance, and requested the Executive Director of UNDCP to include, in the five-year plan for the implementation of the Global Programme of Action, legal cooperation and, in particular, assistance related to illicit drug trafficking and related offences.

On the same date,[23] the Commission noted that the control of money-laundering was an essential element in the struggle against illicit traffic in narcotic drugs and invited Member States to bring their legislation into conformity with the 1988 Convention, taking into account the recommendations of the Financial Action Task Force, (established in 1989 by the Group of Seven major industrialized countries and the President of the Commission of the European Communities at the fifteenth annual economic summit) and those contained in the Global Programme of Action. The Commission also invited Member States to consider contributing forfeited property or proceeds to the UNDCP Fund to help it fulfil its mandate. UNDCP was invited to continue developing programmes of technical cooperation that included assistance in drafting or revising legislation, training for investigative and financial personnel, the development of intercountry collaboration and the provision of advice on strategies and techniques.

Also on 15 April,[24] the Commission noted the work of CCC with respect to cooperation between customs administrations and international traders and carriers, to combat, *inter alia*, illicit traffic in narcotic drugs and psychotropic substances. It called upon all parties to the 1988 Convention that had not already done so to implement fully the provisions of article 17, entitled ''Illicit traffic by sea'', and encouraged those States not parties to the 1988 Convention to adopt, to the extent possible, the provisions, or equivalent measures, against illicit traffic by sea. The Commission also recommended that UNDCP, in developing its regional programmes, should recognize the importance of technical assistance to States, especially for the development and maintenance of databases or other records of vessels in their registries, and invited States to establish procedural and cooperative measures of the kind developed by CCC to ensure that commercial forms of transport were not used in the commission of drug offences. The Commission also urged States to consider bilateral and regional arrangements to enhance the framework provided in article 17 for cooperation in maritime drug law enforcement.

Also on 15 April,[25] the Commission welcomed the establishment of the Commission on Crime Prevention and Criminal Justice as a functional commission of the Economic and Social Council. The Commission on Narcotic Drugs decided to cooperate actively with this new Commission as well as with the Commission for Social Development, the Commission on Transnational Corporations and other intergovernmental bodies to increase the effectiveness of United Nations activities in areas of mutual concern. It requested the Executive Director of UNDCP to suggest ways in which cooperation could be most effectively realized.[26]

GENERAL ASSEMBLY ACTION

On 16 December 1992, on the recommendation of the Third Committee, the General Assembly adopted **resolution 47/97** without vote.

Implementation of the United Nations Convention against Illicit Traffic in Narcotic Drugs and Psychotropic Substances

The General Assembly,

Recalling its resolution 45/146 of 18 December 1990 and other relevant resolutions,

Reaffirming the importance of the United Nations Convention against Illicit Traffic in Narcotic Drugs and Psychotropic Substances of 1988 for improving international cooperation in that field and further strengthening the existing international instruments for the control of narcotic drugs and psychotropic substances, namely, the Single Convention on Narcotic Drugs of 1961, and that Convention as amended by the 1972 Protocol, and the Convention on Psychotropic Substances of 1971,

Reaffirming also the Political Declaration and the Global Programme of Action adopted at its seventeenth special session on 23 February 1990,

Bearing in mind that the United Nations Convention against Illicit Traffic in Narcotic Drugs and Psychotropic Substances entered into force on 11 November 1990 and that, so far, sixty-three States have ratified or adhered to that Convention,

Commending the work done by the Secretariat to disseminate the text of the Convention in the official languages of the United Nations, thereby helping to make its provisions more widely known,

1. *Takes note* of the report of the Secretary-General submitted pursuant to resolution 45/146;

2. *Urges* States that have not yet done so to ratify or accede to the Convention as soon as possible, in order to make its provisions more universally effective;

3. *Also urges* States to establish the necessary legislative and administrative measures so that their internal juridical regulations may be compatible with the spirit and the scope of the Convention;

4. *Invites* States, to the extent that they are able to do so, to apply provisionally the measures set forth in the Convention, pending its entry into force for each of them;

5. *Once again urges* all States that have not yet done so to ratify or accede to the Single Convention on Narcotic Drugs of 1961, and that Convention as amended by the 1972 Protocol, and the Convention on Psychotropic Substances of 1971;

6. *Requests* the United Nations International Drug Control Programme to continue to provide legal assistance to Member States that request it in the adjustment of their national laws, policies and infrastructures to implement the international drug control conventions, as well as in the training of personnel responsible for applying the new laws;

7. *Expresses its satisfaction* at the programme of regional legal workshops initiated by the United Nations International Drug Control Programme to assist States in identifying limitations in their legal capacity to implement the relevant international conventions fully and in developing appropriate measures and arrangements to overcome such limitations;

8. *Once again requests* the Secretary-General, within existing resources and drawing, in particular, on funds available to the Department of Public Information of the Secretariat, to promote and support public information activities relating to the Convention;

9. *Requests* the Secretary-General to report to the General Assembly at its forty-ninth session on the implementation of the present resolution.

General Assembly resolution 47/97

16 December 1992   Meeting 89   Adopted without vote

Approved by Third Committee (A/47/710) without vote, 18 November (meeting 43);

60-nation draft (A/C.3/47/L.28); agenda item 95.

Sponsors: Bahamas, Bangladesh, Barbados, Belgium, Belize, Bolivia, Brazil, Bulgaria, Canada, Chile, China, Colombia, Costa Rica, Côte d'Ivoire, Cuba, Cyprus, Denmark, Dominican Republic, Ecuador, Finland, France, Germany, Ghana, Greece, Guatemala, Guinea, Guinea-Bissau, Haiti, Honduras, Hungary, India, Indonesia, Ireland, Italy, Jamaica, Japan, Luxembourg, Madagascar, Mexico, Morocco, Myanmar, Netherlands, Nicaragua, Nigeria, Norway, Pakistan, Peru, Philippines, Portugal, Russian Federation, Senegal, Spain, Suriname, Sweden, Turkey, United Kingdom, United States, Uruguay, Venezuela, Zambia.

Meeting numbers. GA 47th session: 3rd Committee 27-29, 31-33, 41, 43; plenary 89.

Economic and social consequences of illicit drug trafficking

In compliance with a 1991 General Assembly request,[4] the Commission on Narcotic Drugs considered a note by the Executive Director of UNDCP commenting on the recommendations of the Intergovernmental Expert Group to study the economic and social consequences of illicit traffic in drugs, and action envisaged or already taken by UNDCP along lines traced by the Expert Group.[27] He noted that the Expert Group had concentrated on the availability of reliable data for determining the economic and social consequences of illicit drug trafficking and possible measures to address the issue of money-laundering, and had urged the United Nations to develop a comprehensive, unified information system for that purpose. UNDCP felt the Expert Group had underestimated the difficulty and complexity of that task. UNDCP estimated that the development of a comprehensive data system would take years and would first require a detailed cost proposal.

It was noted that the International Drug Abuse Assessment System (IDAAS) was being implemented and its list of country profiles was growing. UNDCP had also undertaken, in January 1992, a project to improve its illicit traffic data and improve cooperation with Interpol and CCC. Progress was also being made on the development of a data system related to precursors. A major worldwide research project on the "socio-economic and political impact of production, trade and use of illicit narcotic drugs" was under way, jointly sponsored by the United Nations Research Institute for Social Development (UNRISD) and the United Nations University.

On the question of money-laundering, UNDCP had agreed to collaborate with the Financial Action Task Force on a programme of technical assistance emphasizing advisory services and training, supplemented by assistance to prepare or adapt legislation.

In his report on UNDCP,[2] the Executive Director described the development of a "debt-for-drugs" initiative based on the "debt-for-development" concept (see below).

The Secretary-General, in his report on narcotic drugs,[17] informed the General Assembly of the conclusions of the Commission on Narcotic Drugs on steps taken with regard to the economic and social consequences of illicit trafficking in narcotic drugs and psychotropic substances.

Action by the Commission on Narcotic Drugs. The Commission acknowledged difficulties related to data collection and expressed interest in having an estimate of the practical and resource implications of a "truly global effort" to construct a database.

On 15 April,[28] the Commission noted the pioneering initiative of UNDCP in developing the concept of debt swaps for alternative development. Under this initiative, part of the official bilateral debt of heavily indebted countries, in agreement with their creditors, could be set aside in local currency to be used specifically for alternative development activities. The Commission recommended that the Executive Director submit a progress report to the thirty-sixth session.

Implementation of the Global Programme of Action

The Secretary-General continued to monitor implementation of the Global Programme of Action.[13] In compliance with a 1991 General Assembly request,[29] his October report on narcotic drugs[5] discussed efforts by UNDCP, other agencies of the United Nations system and Governments to implement the Global Programme.

Activities of UNDCP concentrated on the servicing of drug control bodies, strengthening of the international system to control licit narcotic drugs and psychotropic substances, prevention and reduction of illicit demand for such substances, treatment and rehabilitation, the elimination of illicit drug supplies and the suppression of illicit drug traffic. Multisectoral activities were undertaken in Africa, Asia and the Pacific, Latin America and the Caribbean, the Middle East and the Balkans.

Within the United Nations, the Department of Public Information produced 47 radio programmes on various drug control themes, and produced and distributed a television programme—"UN in Action"—on drug rehabilitation in Thailand, to television networks around the world. One 27-minute video, entitled "High Hopes", was produced in English, French and Spanish. Under the crime prevention and criminal justice programme of the Centre for Social Development and Humanitarian Affairs, two expert group meetings were convened in October 1991 (Suzdal, Russian Federation, and Bratislava,

Czechoslovakia) on issues related to drug control, including money-laundering, tracing and forfeiture of illegal proceeds, monitoring of large-scale transactions, sentencing of drug offenders, and law enforcement intelligence gathering and exchange.

The United Nations Development Programme, as mandated by its Governing Council, was applying the principle of sustainable human development to its drug control priorities and advocacy. It was also collaborating in a four-country joint programming initiative in drug abuse control.

The 1992-1997 medium-term plan of the Economic Commission for Latin America and the Caribbean (ECLAC) was revised to include action in the area of drug control as part of the regular work programme for the 1994-1995 biennium. A project initiated in 1989 to reduce illicit drug demand in Grenada was completed. The Economic and Social Commission for Western Asia (ESCWA) initiated a study of the nature and extent of drug abuse among youth in countries of the ESCWA region and of drug abuse intervention services for youth. A study was also designed on economic and social approaches to the eradication of hashish and opium production and consumption in Lebanon.

UNRISD and the United Nations University were conducting the second phase of a research programme on the socio-economic and political impact of production, trade and use of illicit narcotic drugs. A handbook and two discussion papers from the first phase were published and, in the second phase, 2 out of 10 ongoing country studies were completed.

The United Nations Interregional Crime and Justice Research Institute (UNICRI) collaborated with the United Nations Educational, Scientific and Cultural Organization (UNESCO) on a drug abuse education and prevention project for high-school students in Malta. UNICRI also prepared educational videotapes to help young people resist pressure to use drugs. It organized two training seminars on prevention and training methodology for health and social workers, and prepared a two-volume handbook on training techniques for the prevention of drug abuse and related phenomena. The Drug Abuse Comprehensive Centre, which began operations in the autumn of 1991, published and distributed the first four issues of its bulletin.

The International Labour Organisation (ILO) continued to expand its programmes on vocational rehabilitation and the social reintegration of recovering addicts in the community and on drug prevention and assistance in the workplace. During the year, ILO was involved in six projects related to drug abuse in the workplace and four projects related to the training of personnel working with drug addicts.

The Remote Sensing Centre in the Research and Technology Development Division of the Food and Agriculture Organization of the United Nations (FAO) was involved in a project aimed at refining satellite imagery technology and ground verification procedures for the detection of poppy cultivation.

Drug control–related activities were also carried out by UNESCO, the International Civil Aviation Organization, the World Health Organization, the World Bank, the International Monetary Fund, the International Fund for Agricultural Development, the United Nations Industrial Development Organization and the General Agreement on Tariffs and Trade.

The Secretary-General also reported on the efforts of Governments to implement the Global Programme of Action. A number of States amended their penal codes to provide for more stringent drug trafficking penalties, and new legislative texts relating to the 1988 Convention were transmitted to the Secretary-General by several States. Governments in all geographical areas reported the implementation of programmes for the treatment, rehabilitation and social reintegration of drug abusers, and positive results were reported from the establishment of bilateral and multilateral agreements.

The Executive Director of UNDCP submitted an April report on the five-year plan developed by UNDCP to implement the Global Programme of Action.[30] The report proposed global action related to prevention and reduction of drug abuse, treatment and rehabilitation of addicts, control of narcotic drugs and psychotropic substances, suppression of illicit trafficking and money-laundering issues, and strengthening of judicial and legal systems. The report also described master plans for implementing national and regional drug control strategies and the United Nations Decade against Drug Abuse, which was proclaimed as part of the Global Programme of Action.

The Commission on Narcotic Drugs agreed that the five-year plan should not overlap with the United Nations System-Wide Action Plan on Drug Abuse Control, which outlined activities and strategies for implementation by the various United Nations entities involved in drug abuse control.

United Nations Decade against Drug Abuse

The General Assembly, at its seventeenth special session in 1990, proclaimed 1991-2000 as the United Nations Decade against Drug Abuse, devoted to implementation of the Global Programme of Action. In the five-year plan to implement the Programme, specific activities were outlined for UNDCP under the general theme ''A global response to a global challenge'', by which

UNDCP would encourage application of the recommendations of the Comprehensive Multidisciplinary Outline of Future Activities in Drug Abuse Control, adopted by the 1987 International Conference on Drug Abuse and Illicit Trafficking,[31] and support implementation of the United Nations System-Wide Action Plan on Drug Abuse Control of 1990,[32] aimed at fulfilling all existing mandates of the United Nations system and related intergovernmental decisions. Information was also being requested from Governments for the compilation of a master directory of national focal points to facilitate the exchange of information. The directory would be supplemented by lists of focal points in relevant intergovernmental organizations and specialized agencies.

In addition, UNDCP would undertake specific activities related to Global Programme targets and priorities established by the Commission on Narcotic Drugs. It was also proposed that: a world conference be organized for non-governmental organizations in 1993; the Decade include a strong public information component with close collaboration with the mass media; and well-known individuals become special ambassadors for the Decade.

Action by the Commission on Narcotic Drugs. On 15 April,[33] the Commission invited all Governments, specialized agencies and intergovernmental and non-governmental organizations to cooperate with and support UNDCP in coordinating and implementing the United Nations Decade against Drug Abuse. It considered that the Decade, having been proclaimed by the General Assembly as a response to the global challenge of drug abuse, should, where possible, be financed from the regular budget of the United Nations. Member States were invited to make voluntary contributions to strengthen the impact and effectiveness of the Decade.

GENERAL ASSEMBLY ACTION

On 16 December, the General Assembly, on the recommendation of the Third Committee, adopted **resolution 47/102** without vote.

International action to combat drug abuse and illicit trafficking

The General Assembly,

Gravely concerned that the illicit demand for, production of and traffic in narcotic drugs and psychotropic substances continue to threaten seriously the socio-economic and political systems and the stability, national security and sovereignty of an increasing number of States,

Reaffirming the principle of shared responsibility of the international community in combating drug abuse and illicit trafficking,

Reaffirming also that the Declaration and the Comprehensive Multidisciplinary Outline of Future Activities in Drug Abuse Control, adopted by the International Conference on Drug Abuse and Illicit Trafficking, the Political Declaration and the Global Programme of Action adopted by the General Assembly at its seventeenth special session and the Declaration adopted by the World Ministerial Summit to Reduce the Demand for Drugs and to Combat the Cocaine Threat, held in London from 9 to 11 April 1990, together with the international drug control treaties, provide a comprehensive framework for international cooperation in drug control,

Recognizing the efforts of the United Nations International Drug Control Programme to implement its mandates within this comprehensive framework,

Noting with satisfaction the efforts of the Commission on Narcotic Drugs to improve the effectiveness of the regional meetings of heads of national drug law enforcement agencies and of the Subcommission on Illicit Traffic and Related Matters in the Near and Middle East in addressing specific drug law enforcement problems of the various regions,

Emphasizing the need for an analysis of transit routes used by drug traffickers, which are constantly changing and expanding to include a growing number of countries and regions in all parts of the world, particularly those that are vulnerable to illicit transit traffic on account, *inter alia*, of their geographical location,

Alarmed by the growing connection between drug trafficking and terrorism in various parts of the world,

Recognizing the efforts of countries that produce narcotic drugs for scientific, medicinal and therapeutic uses to prevent the channelling of such substances to illicit markets and to maintain production at a level consistent with licit demand,

Reiterating its condemnation of criminal activities that involve children in the use, production and illicit distribution of narcotic drugs and psychotropic substances, and emphasizing the need for the United Nations International Drug Control Programme and other competent agencies to give high priority to measures designed to address this problem,

Noting the increasing number of States acceding to or ratifying the international drug control treaties, including those that have become States parties to the United Nations Convention against Illicit Traffic in Narcotic Drugs and Psychotropic Substances of 1988,

Reaffirming that all efforts to combat problems related to the consumption, production and manufacture of and traffic in narcotic drugs and psychotropic substances and the flow of money related to these activities should be accompanied by effective measures to promote the economic and social development of affected States,

Recalling its resolution 46/103 of 16 December 1991, in which it reiterated its invitation to the Commission on Narcotic Drugs to consider, at its thirty-fifth session, the recommendations of the Intergovernmental Expert Group to Study the Economic and Social Consequences of Illicit Traffic in Drugs, together with the comments of the Executive Director of the United Nations International Drug Control Programme, with a view to recommending appropriate follow-up activity,

Noting also the action taken by the Commission on Narcotic Drugs on this issue, including its decision to study the issue again at its thirty-seventh session,

I

International action to combat drug abuse and illicit trafficking

1. *Takes note* of the reports of the Secretary-General;

2. *Reiterates its condemnation* of the crime of drug trafficking in all its forms, and urges continued and effective international action to combat it, in keeping with the principle of shared responsibility and with full respect for national sovereignty, territorial integrity and the cultural identity of States;

3. *Welcomes* the initiatives of the United Nations International Drug Control Programme to implement its mandates within the framework of the international drug control treaties, the Comprehensive Multidisciplinary Outline of Future Activities in Drug Abuse Control, the Global Programme of Action and relevant consensus documents;

4. *Supports* the focus on national and regional strategies for drug abuse control, particularly the master-plan approach, and urges that the United Nations International Drug Control Programme to keep in mind that these should be complemented with effective interregional strategies;

5. *Notes with appreciation* the activities of the United Nations International Drug Control Programme to promote and monitor the United Nations Decade against Drug Abuse, 1991-2000, under the theme "A global response to a global challenge", including the successful launching by the Programme of the goodwill ambassadors initiative, and invites Governments to cooperate with the Programme in further developing this initiative;

6. *Takes note* of the recommendation that Governments should establish national focal points or coordinating mechanisms for the Decade;

7. *Recommends* that Governments cooperate fully with the Coordinator for the Decade to enhance and facilitate the report of the Commission on Narcotic Drugs on progress made in attaining the objectives of the Decade, to be submitted to the General Assembly, through the Economic and Social Council;

8. *Requests* the United Nations International Drug Control Programme, in cooperation with relevant agencies, including the United Nations Children's Fund, to study the involvement of children in drug-related criminal activities and the abuse of narcotic drugs and psychotropic substances by children, with a view to recommending measures that may be taken to address this problem;

9. *Welcomes* the trend towards ratification and implementation of the Single Convention on Narcotic Drugs of 1961, that Convention as amended by the 1972 Protocol, the Convention on Psychotropic Substances of 1971 and the United Nations Convention against Illicit Traffic in Narcotic Drugs and Psychotropic Substances of 1988;

10. *Requests* the United Nations International Drug Control Programme to include in its report to the Commission on Narcotic Drugs on the implementation of the United Nations Convention against Drug Abuse and Illicit Trafficking of 1988 a section on experience gained to date in implementing the Convention, which should contain recommendations and strategies for its further implementation;

11. *Recommends* that the United Nations International Drug Control Programme invite the cooperation of the Crime Prevention and Criminal Justice Branch of the Centre for Social Development and Humanitarian Affairs of the Secretariat in its activities to counter drug-related criminality, including money-laundering, to ensure complementarity of their efforts and to avoid duplication;

12. *Encourages* all countries to take action to prevent the illicit arms trade by which weapons are provided to drug traffickers;

13. *Expresses its satisfaction* with the efforts of the Commission on Narcotic Drugs to improve the functioning and impact of the meetings of heads of national drug law enforcement agencies and with its decision that the heads of national drug law enforcement agencies of Africa, Asia, Latin America and the Caribbean and the Subcommission on Illicit Trafficking and related Matters in the Near and Middle East should continue to meet annually;

14. *Requests* the United Nations International Drug Control Programme in its report on illicit traffic in drugs to analyse world-wide trends in illicit traffic and transit in narcotic drugs and psychotropic substances, including methods and routes used, and to recommend ways and means for improving the capacity of States along those routes to deal with all aspects of the drug problem;

15. *Emphasizes* the connection between the illicit production and supply of, demand for, sale of and traffic and transit in narcotic drugs and psychotropic substances and the economic, social and cultural conditions of the countries affected and that solutions to these problems must take into account the differences and diversity of the problem in each country;

16. *Calls upon* the international community to provide increased international economic and technical cooperation to Governments, at their request, in support of programmes for the substitution of illicit crops by means of integrated rural development and alternative development programmes that respect fully the jurisdiction and sovereignty of countries and the cultural traditions of peoples;

17. *Takes note* of the initiative of the United Nations International Drug Control Programme to study the concept of swapping debt for alternative development in the area of international drug abuse control and the decision of the Commission on Narcotic Drugs to consider this matter at its thirty-sixth session on the basis of the report of the Executive Director of the Programme;

18. *Encourages* Governments to nominate experts for the roster to be maintained by the United Nations International Drug Control Programme, to ensure that the Programme may draw from the widest pool of expertise and experience in implementing its policies and programmes;

19. *Stresses* the need for effective action to prevent the diversion for illicit purposes of precursors and other chemicals, materials and equipment frequently used in the illicit manufacture of narcotic drugs and psychotropic substances;

20. *Commends* the International Narcotics Control Board for its valuable work in monitoring production and distribution of narcotic drugs and psychotropic substances so as to limit their use to medical and scientific purposes, and for the effective manner in which it has implemented its additional responsibilities under article 12 of the United Nations Convention against Illicit Traffic in Narcotic Drugs and Psychotropic Substances concerning the control of precursors and essential chemicals;

21. *Takes note* of the conclusions of the Commission on Narcotic Drugs at its thirty-fifth session on the economic and social consequences of illicit trafficking;

22. *Expresses its satisfaction* with efforts being made by the United Nations International Drug Control Programme and other United Nations bodies to obtain reliable data on drug abuse and illicit trafficking, including the development of the International Drug Abuse Assessment System, the project to determine possible improvements to the international system for the collection of data on illicit traffic and money-laundering, as well as the programme of technical cooperation with developing countries in collaboration with the Financial Action Task Force, and requests the United Nations International Drug Control Programme to report to the Commission on Narcotic Drugs at its thirty-sixth session on the progress being made in these areas;

23. *Notes with satisfaction* that the United Nations Social Defence Research Institute will complete its world-wide research study on the economic and social consequences of drug abuse and illicit trafficking in 1993;

24. *Recommends* to the Commission on Narcotic Drugs that, when it studies the report of the Executive Director of the United Nations International Drug Control Programme on the economic and social consequences of drug abuse and illicit trafficking at its thirty-seventh session, to consider including this issue as an item on its agenda;

25. *Appeals* to States and the international donor community to increase voluntary contributions to the Fund of the United Nations International Drug Control Programme to enable it to expand its programmes further;

II

Implementation of the Global Programme of Action against illicit production, supply, demand, trafficking and distribution of narcotic drugs and psychotropic substances

1. *Takes note* of the report of the Secretary-General concerning the implementation of the Global Programme of Action;

2. *Reaffirms its commitment* to implementing the mandates contained in the Global Programme of Action and the Comprehensive Multidisciplinary Outline of Future Activities in Drug Abuse Control;

3. *Notes with satisfaction* the framework established by the Commission on Narcotic Drugs to monitor implementation of the Global Programme of Action;

4. *Calls upon* States to take all possible steps to promote and implement individually and in cooperation with other States the mandates and recommendations contained in the Global Programme of Action, with a view to translating the Programme into practical action to the widest possible extent at the national, regional and international levels;

5. *Calls upon* the United Nations and its relevant bodies, the specialized agencies, other relevant intergovernmental organizations and non-governmental organizations to extend their cooperation and assistance to States in the promotion and implementation of the Global Programme of Action;

6. *Requests* the Secretary-General to report to the General Assembly at its forty-eighth session on the implementation of the present resolution under the item entitled ''International drug control''.

General Assembly resolution 47/102

16 December 1992   Meeting 89   Adopted without vote

Approved by Third Committee (A/47/710) without vote, 18 November (meeting 43); 54-nation draft (A/C.3/47/L.33), orally revised; agenda item 95.
Sponsors: Antigua and Barbuda, Austria, Azerbaijan, Bahamas, Bangladesh, Barbados, Belize, Benin, Bolivia, Cameroon, Chile, Colombia, Costa Rica, Côte d'Ivoire, Cuba, Cyprus, Dominican Republic, Ecuador, El Salvador, France, Ghana, Greece, Grenada, Guatemala, Guinea, Guinea-Bissau, Haiti, Honduras, India, Italy, Jamaica, Madagascar, Malaysia, Mexico, Morocco, Myanmar, Nicaragua, Nigeria, Pakistan, Panama, Paraguay, Peru, Philippines, Republic of Korea, Saint Kitts and Nevis, Senegal, Spain, Suriname, Trinidad and Tobago, Uganda, Ukraine, Uruguay, Vanuatu, Venezuela.
Meeting numbers. GA 47th session: 3rd Committee 27-29, 31-33, 41, 43; plenary 89.

Also on 16 December, the General Assembly adopted **resolution 47/99** without vote.

Examination of the status of international cooperation against the illicit production, sale, demand, traffic and distribution of narcotic drugs and psychotropic substances

The General Assembly,

Deeply concerned that the illicit production, trafficking and abuse of narcotic drugs and psychotropic substances are increasing every day, and that these illicit activities are claiming a growing number of victims,

Considering that, despite the continued and vigorous fight that is being waged by countries at the local, regional, bilateral and multilateral levels and some encouraging developments, the global situation with respect to drug abuse and illicit trafficking continues to worsen,

Convinced that, given the magnitude and global nature of the drug problem, international cooperation in conformity with the international drug control treaties, the Global Programme of Action adopted at its seventeenth special session, the Comprehensive Multidisciplinary Outline of Future Activities in Drug Abuse Control adopted by the International Conference on Drug Abuse and Illicit Trafficking and other relevant consensus documents is fundamental to confronting this scourge,

Acknowledging that there are obvious links, under certain circumstances, between poverty and the increase in the illicit production and trafficking of narcotic drugs and psychotropic substances and that policies of alternative economic development can make a contribution in addressing this problem,

Acknowledging the responsibility of Governments in alleviating poverty, reducing the dependency of their citizens on narcotics and narcotics production and enforcing legal measures against narcotics,

Reaffirming its resolutions 45/147 of 18 December 1990 and 46/101 of 16 December 1991 concerning respect for the principles enshrined in the Charter of the United Nations and international law, which are indispensable to establishing a basis for international cooperation in the war against drug abuse and illicit trafficking,

Reaffirming also the importance of the role of the United Nations International Drug Control Programme as the main focus for concerted international action for drug abuse control,

Reaffirming further the multifaceted nature of the problem and the principle of shared responsibility for drug abuse control contained in the Declaration adopted by the International Conference on Drug Abuse and Illicit Trafficking,

Convinced of the necessity of further strengthening international cooperation and redoubling efforts to broaden the areas appropriate for this cooperation, taking into account experience gained and the need to renew commitment and establish goals to guide the decisions aimed at eradicating this scourge,

Calling attention to the growing connection between terrorist groups and drug traffickers,

Bearing in mind the commitment made in the Political Declaration adopted at its seventeenth special session to keep under constant review the activities set out in the Global Programme of Action,

1. *Decides* to hold four plenary meetings, at a high level at its forty-eighth session, to examine urgently the status of international cooperation against the illicit production, sale, demand, traffic in and distribution of narcotic drugs and psychotropic substances, with a view to:

(a) Evaluating the implementation by Member States of the Global Programme of Action and making recommendations on improving cooperation in the field of drug abuse control, taking into account the priority given to this issue by the international community;

(b) Identifying those policies on which there has not been satisfactory progress in order to expand and increase the effectiveness of this cooperation and to establish measurable goals and renew commitments;

(c) Promoting the universal ratification of or accession to the international drug control treaties, particularly the United Nations Convention against Illicit Traffic in Narcotic Drugs and Psychotropic Substances of 1988;

(d) Encouraging the adoption and implementation of legislative and administrative measures necessary to ensure that national judicial systems are compatible with the spirit and the intent of the treaties and to encourage States that are not yet parties, to the extent they are able, to apply provisionally the provisions of the treaties;

(e) Encouraging the pursuit of trade liberalization measures which will enhance the trading opportunities of all countries affected by the illicit production of narcotic drugs and psychotropic substances;

(f) Considering ways to strengthen and enhance international cooperation in programmes of alternative rural development;

(g) Strengthening international cooperation to eradicate the growing and dangerous links between terrorist groups, drug traffickers and their paramilitary gangs, which have resorted to all types of violence, thus endangering the constitutional order of States and violating basic human rights;

2. *Requests* the Secretary-General to take the necessary steps to implement the present resolution;

3. *Also requests* the Secretary-General to present, at the next regular session of the Commission on Narcotic Drugs, an evaluative report containing recommendations on measures to be taken with regard to paragraph 1 of the present resolution;

4. *Requests* the Commission on Narcotic Drugs to submit, through the Economic and Social Council, its comments regarding the report of the Secretary-General to the General Assembly at the high-level plenary meetings of its forty-eighth session.

General Assembly resolution 47/99

16 December 1992   Meeting 89   Adopted without vote

Approved by Third Committee (A/47/710) without vote, 18 November (meeting 43); 31-nation draft (A/C.3/47/L.30), orally revised; agenda item 95.

Sponsors: Austria, Bahamas, Bolivia, Cameroon, Chile, Colombia, Costa Rica, Cuba, Ecuador, Egypt, El Salvador, France, Guatemala, Honduras, Italy, Mexico, Morocco, Myanmar, Nicaragua, Panama, Peru, Philippines, Russian Federation, Spain, Suriname, Sweden, Turkey, Ukraine, United Kingdom, Uruguay, Venezuela.

Meeting numbers. GA 47th session: 3rd Committee 27-29, 31-33, 41, 43; plenary 89.

Implementation of the System-Wide Action Plan

The Ad Hoc Inter-Agency Meeting on Coordination in Matters of International Drug Abuse Control (Vienna, 16 April)[34] considered the review of the United Nations System-Wide Action Plan on Drug Abuse Control, as requested by the General Assembly.[35] The review, conducted by UNDCP, took account of structural and functional changes resulting from the establishment of UNDCP; deficiencies noted in the original version of the Plan; resolutions and decisions of the General Assembly, the Economic and Social Council and the Commission on Narcotic Drugs during the previous two years; revisions outlined in the report of the Secretary-General and integrated into the Plan; the objectives of the Global Programme of Action; and the need to add a chapter on intersectoral activities. To make the Plan a more dynamic, action-oriented document, participants recommended that the five-year plan be used; that activities be grouped under subheadings; and that a system be developed for more inter-agency consultations.

In September,[36] the Ad Hoc Inter-Agency Meeting considered modifications to the document, including the incorporation of a new chapter VI, ''Multisectoral activities'', into the draft. The meeting agreed that the revised draft should be finalized by UNDCP for submission to the Commission on Narcotic Drugs at its thirty-sixth session.

GENERAL ASSEMBLY ACTION

On 16 December, on the recommendation of the Third Committee, the General Assembly adopted **resolution 47/100** without vote.

Implementation of the United Nations System-Wide Action Plan on Drug Abuse Control and the Global Programme of Action against illicit production, supply, demand, trafficking and distribution of narcotic drugs and psychotropic substances: action by agencies of the United Nations system

The General Assembly,

Recalling its resolutions 44/16 of 1 November 1989, 44/141 of 15 December 1989, 45/148 of 18 December 1990, 45/179 of 21 December 1990 and 46/102 of 16 December 1991,

Fully aware that the international community is confronted with the dramatic problem of drug abuse and the illicit cultivation, production, demand, processing, distribution and trafficking of narcotic drugs and psychotropic substances and that States need to work at the international level as well as individually to deal with this scourge, which has a strong potential to undermine development, economic and political stability and democratic institutions,

Stressing the important role of the United Nations, its relevant bodies and the specialized agencies in supporting concerted action in the fight against drug abuse at the national, regional and international levels,

Recalling that in its resolution 44/141 it requested the Secretary-General, in his capacity as Chairman of the Administrative Committee on Coordination, to coordinate at the inter-agency level the development of a United Nations system-wide action plan on drug abuse control and that the Secretary-General submitted to the Economic and Social Council at its second regular session of 1990 a report on the United Nations System-Wide Action Plan on Drug Abuse Control as an instrument to facilitate coordination, complementarity and non-duplication in drug control activities within the United Nations system,

Affirming the proposals as laid out in the System-Wide Action Plan, and recognizing that further efforts are needed to implement and update it,

Recalling that in its resolution 44/141 it also requested the Administrative Committee on Coordination to make the necessary adjustments to the System-Wide Action Plan annually and requested that the executive heads of United Nations bodies report annually on the progress made in implementing the Action Plan and that the Administrative Committee on Coordination include the information in its annual report, so as to enable the Committee for Programme and Coordination and the Economic and Social Council to consider it, within their respective mandates, and to make appropriate recommendations to the General Assembly,

Expressing concern that there has been limited progress by the agencies of the United Nations system in incorporating within their programmes and activities action aimed at dealing with drug-related problems in the manner envisioned in the System-Wide Action Plan,

Recalling and emphasizing the continuing importance of the Political Declaration and Global Programme of Action adopted at its seventeenth special session on 23 February 1990,

Emphasizing the continuing importance and validity of the Declaration and the Comprehensive Multidisciplinary Outline of Future Activities in Drug Abuse Control, as adopted by the International Conference on Drug Abuse and Illicit Trafficking, and the Declaration adopted at the World Ministerial Summit to Reduce the Demand for Drugs and to Combat the Cocaine Threat, held in London from 9 to 11 April 1990,

1. *Reaffirms* the commitment expressed in the Global Programme of Action and the Comprehensive Multidisciplinary Outline of Future Activities in Drug Abuse Control, and calls upon States to take all possible steps to promote and implement, individually and in cooperation with other States, the mandates and recommendations contained in the Global Programme of Action, with a view to translating the Programme into practical action to the widest possible extent at the national, regional and international levels;

2.   _Calls upon_ all relevant United Nations agencies, particularly those associated with the United Nations System-Wide Action Plan on Drug Abuse Control, to establish agency-specific implementation plans to incorporate fully into their programmes all the mandates and activities contained in the System-Wide Action Plan, and to submit a report to the Secretary-General by 1 March 1993 on progress made in establishing such agency-specific plans, for inclusion in an annex to the System-Wide Action Plan;

3.   _Calls upon_ the governing bodies of all United Nations agencies associated with the System-Wide Action Plan to facilitate its implementation by designating an agenda item under which the Action Plan may be considered at their next regular meeting;

4.   _Reaffirms_ the role of the Executive Director of the United Nations International Drug Control Programme to coordinate and provide effective leadership for all United Nations drug control activities, in order to ensure coherence of actions within the Programme as well as coordination, complementarity and non-duplication of such activities across the United Nations system;

5.   _Requests_ the Administrative Committee on Coordination to give due attention in its work to the coordination of drug control activities and, under the direction of the Executive Director of the United Nations International Drug Control Programme, to update the System-Wide Action Plan for the consideration of the Economic and Social Council at its substantive session of 1993 and of the General Assembly at its forty-eighth session, keeping in mind the need to revise and update the Action Plan as necessary, _inter alia_, by:

(a)   The addition of an annex containing agency-specific implementing plans, as noted in paragraph 2 above;

(b)   The inclusion of a reference to the important role of the international financial institutions, as noted in chapter II of the Comprehensive Multidisciplinary Outline of Future Activities in Drug Abuse Control, and the ability of such institutions to promote economic stability and undermine the drug industry;

6.   _Also requests_ the Administrative Committee on Coordination to review and update, as necessary, the System-Wide Action Plan on a biennial basis, taking into account the need to simplify and streamline its presentation;

7.   _Requests_ the Commission on Narcotic Drugs, and in particular the United Nations International Drug Control Programme, to promote and continuously monitor the implementation of the Global Programme of Action, giving special attention to the System-Wide Action Plan;

8.   _Requests_ the Secretary-General to report annually to the General Assembly on activities undertaken by the United Nations International Drug Control Programme and Governments relating to the implementation of the Global Programme of Action.

General Assembly resolution 47/100

16 December 1992   Meeting 89   Adopted without vote

Approved by Third Committee (A/47/710) without vote, 18 November (meeting 43);

33-nation draft (A/C.3/47/L.31); agenda item 95.

Sponsors: Australia, Bahamas, Belgium, Bulgaria, Cameroon, Canada, Côte d'Ivoire, Czechoslovakia, Egypt, Finland, Germany, Guatemala, Guinea-Bissau, Iceland, Italy, Luxembourg, Mexico, Morocco, Myanmar, Netherlands, New Zealand, Norway, Pakistan, Peru, Philippines, Romania, Samoa, Singapore, Sweden, Thailand, Turkey, United Kingdom, United States.

Meeting numbers. GA 47th session: 3rd Committee 27-29, 31-33, 41, 43; plenary 89.

UN Charter and international law

In his September report on narcotic drugs,[17] the Secretary-General, in responding to a General Assembly request,[37] referred to the guiding principles of the United Nations in the fight against drugs as recalled in the Political Declaration and the Global Programme of Action,[13] namely: the sovereignty of States; shared responsibility in combating drug abuse and illicit trafficking; non-interference in the internal affairs of States; and the strengthening of cooperation under mutually agreed conditions through bilateral, regional and multilateral mechanisms. Explicit guarantees of these principles were incorporated in the four main international drug control treaties.

GENERAL ASSEMBLY ACTION

On 16 December, the General Assembly, on the recommendation of the Third Committee, adopted **resolution 47/98** without vote.

Respect for the principles enshrined in the Charter of the United Nations and international law in the fight against drug abuse and illicit trafficking

The General Assembly,

Recalling its resolution 46/101 of 16 December 1991,

Conscious that the adoption of the Political Declaration and the Global Programme of Action at its seventeenth special session, devoted to the question of international cooperation against illicit production, supply, demand, trafficking and distribution of narcotic drugs and psychotropic substances, was an important step in the harmonization of the efforts of all to combat this scourge of mankind,

Reaffirming the purpose of the United Nations to develop friendly relations among nations based on respect for the principle of equal rights and self-determination of peoples, and to take other appropriate measures to strengthen universal peace,

Convinced that the intensification of international cooperation and concerted action among States is the fundamental basis for confronting the problem of drug abuse and illicit trafficking,

Recognizing that the international fight against illicit trafficking should be pursued in full conformity with the principles enshrined in the Charter of the United Nations, and the principles of international law, particularly respect for the sovereignty and territorial integrity of States, non-interference in the internal affairs of States, and non-use of force or the threat of force in international relations,

1.   _Reaffirms_ that the fight against drug abuse and illicit trafficking should continue to be based on strict respect for the principles enshrined in the Charter of the United Nations and international law, particularly respect for the sovereignty and territorial integrity of States and non-use of force or the threat of force in international relations;

2.   _Calls upon_ all States to intensify their actions to promote effective cooperation in the efforts to combat drug abuse and illicit trafficking, so as to contribute to a climate conducive to achieving this end, and to refrain from using the issue for political purposes;

3. *Reaffirms* that the international fight against drug trafficking should not in any way justify violation of the principles enshrined in the Charter and international law, particularly the right of all peoples freely to determine, without external interference, their political status and to pursue their economic, social and cultural development, and that every State has the duty to respect this right in accordance with the provisions of the Charter;

4. *Invites* the Secretary-General, in preparing the report to be submitted to the General Assembly at its forty-eighth session, and the Executive Director of the United Nations International Drug Control Programme, to continue to give due consideration to the principles set out in the present resolution;

5. *Decides* to consider at its forty-eighth session the question of respect for the principles enshrined in the Charter of the United Nations and international law in the fight against drug abuse and illicit trafficking under the item entitled "International drug control".

General Assembly resolution 47/98

16 December 1992   Meeting 89   Adopted without vote

Approved by Third Committee (A/47/710) without vote, 18 November (meeting 43); 11-nation draft (A/C.3/47/L.29), orally revised; agenda item 95.
Sponsors: Bolivia, Chile, Colombia, Cuba, Ecuador, Guatemala, Mexico, Myanmar, Peru, Philippines, Vanuatu.
Meeting numbers. GA 47th session: 3rd Committee 27-29, 31-33, 41, 43; plenary 89.

Supply and demand

Demand reduction

UNDCP carried out a number of prevention and demand reduction projects during 1991. In Africa, preventive education was a specific element of law enforcement projects in Egypt, Ghana, Kenya, Mauritius, Nigeria, Senegal and the United Republic of Tanzania. Governments in eastern and southern Africa planned the establishment of a drug abuse monitoring system which would, among other things, facilitate prompt responses to new developments. In Latin America, demand reduction programmes were carried out in eight countries, with many activities concentrating on school-age children. Projects in Bolivian and Colombian cities were aimed especially at "street children" and included recreation, counselling, education and vocational training activities. In the Caribbean, prevention programmes were operating in the Bahamas, Belize, the Dominican Republic, Grenada, Guyana, Jamaica, the Netherlands Antilles, Saint Lucia, and Trinidad and Tobago. A project to produce model prevention materials for use in schools in the eastern Caribbean was completed in collaboration with UNESCO.

In South-East Asia, many highland development projects in Thailand incorporated prevention activities. In Myanmar, the third phase of UNDCP assistance for the period 1986-1991 ended, and a new demand reduction project for Malaysia was to begin in 1992. Several preventive education programmes were designed for the countries of South-West Asia in 1991. A UNDCP mission designed a five-year comprehensive preventive education programme for Bangladesh, Pakistan's integrated drug demand reduction programme was extended to 1994, and Sri Lanka's second three-year project was to begin in 1992. A drug information and reference programme was developed for Afghanistan, and coverage of the drug awareness campaign for Afghan refugees in camps in Peshawar, Pakistan, was widened to include extensive training for teachers, religious leaders and community workers.

UNDCP also assisted national drug testing laboratories with demand reduction activities and supported special courses organized by the International Council on Alcohol and Addictions to upgrade the qualifications of some 170 professionals from 24 countries working in the field of demand reduction.

International drug abuse assessment system

UNDCP continued to develop the International Drug Abuse Assessment System (IDAAS) and its database, which had been expanded through the computerization of information submitted over the previous six years by nations replying to part B (Drug Abuse) of the annual reports questionnaire. A March report[38] on measures to control and reduce illicit demand analysed global reporting patterns and trends related to drug abuse and gave an overview of them by region. The report reflected data on the workings of international drug control treaties, submitted to the Secretary-General in 1991 by 81 countries and territories. Annexes presented data on the reporting pattern, by year, and on the annual prevalence, daily abuse and registered abusers of cannabis, cocaine and heroin. The report also analysed the reporting capacity of Governments and noted that only 34 Governments had responded every year for the previous eight years to part B of the questionnaire and that even they were not always in a position to furnish the information requested.

A March Secretariat report[39] supplemented a 1991 report[40] providing responses to a 1990 questionnaire on progress in the implementation of the first seven targets of the 1987 Comprehensive Multidisciplinary Outline.[31] Of the replies received, 44 were from Governments, three from intergovernmental organizations and nine from non-governmental organizations. The report found that 39 of the 44 countries reporting had adopted measures to assess drug abuse or collect data, but still needed financial support and human-resource training to help overcome organizational and methodological problems. Activities in the area of preventive education were targetted at specific groups and actively pursued by nearly all States in the five regions. States also reported on activities to prevent drug abuse in the workplace, mostly by creating awareness among employers through workshops, conferences or the distribution of information. Most countries were involved in some form of prevention through local community organizations, professional associations, religious groups and international action groups. Leisure-time activities were a major topic in Europe, and most countries in the Americas and in Asia and the Pacific had implemented them, but very few countries in Africa focused on them. The media were considered highly influential, as reflected in the number and wide variety of activities that involved the media in drug control initiatives.

The Secretariat also reported[12] that, based on information available, a data sheet on intergovernmental organizations had been developed for UNDCP inventory, and some 200 non-governmental organizations active in the field of drug and substance abuse issues had also been identified. The process of tabulating and updating information on each of them had started, drawing on data collected from responses to the UNDCP questionnaire on the implementation of the first seven targets of the Comprehensive Multidisciplinary Outline. These inventories would be used by UNDCP to improve collaboration, avoid duplication of effort, broaden the information base for the Secretary-General's annual report to the Assembly, and facilitate world-wide dissemination of information on demand reduction activities at the national or regional levels.

Control of illicit supply

Action by the Commission on Narcotic Drugs. On 15 April,[41] the Commission asked UNDCP to consider assisting States, at their request, to evaluate and control the production of both natural narcotic drugs and psychotropic substances. It also asked UNDCP to assist in the application of appropriate modern technologies to evaluate, control, and eradicate illicit crop production and assess the possibility of crop substitution or development alternatives.

Also on 15 April,[42] the Commission considered the impact on indigenous peoples and ecosystems of deforestation and other activities to prepare land for illicit drug crops. It urged the Executive Director of UNDCP to convey to the United Nations Conference on Environment and Development (Rio de Janeiro, Brazil, 3-14 June) the importance of analysing the link between illicit drug production and environmental damage and to report, with the help of the United Nations Environment Programme, to the Commission at its thirty-sixth session.

Narcotic raw material for licit use

In 1992, INCB continued to monitor the demand for and supply of opiates for medical and scientific needs. It stated that the world consumption of opiates had stabilized at 200 tonnes in morphine equivalent per year, of which codeine accounted for 160 tonnes. Of the principal opiates, consumption increased only for dihydrocodeine and morphine, reaching 18 and 11 tonnes respectively in 1991, the latest year for which complete statistical information was available. The consumption of ethylmorphine and pholcodine decreased, while the use of codeine and opium-based preparations appeared to stabilize.

Recognizing the need for a balance between supply and demand, INCB requested the Governments concerned to avoid overproduction and, in April, the Board organized an informal meeting between the main opiate producers and importers. In collaboration with the World Health Organization, the Board continued to review Governments' methods for estimating medical needs for opiates.

ECONOMIC AND SOCIAL COUNCIL ACTION

On 30 July, the Economic and Social Council adopted **resolution 1992/30** without vote.

Demand for and supply of opiates for medical and scientific needs

The Economic and Social Council,

Recalling its resolutions 1979/8 of 9 May 1979, 1980/20 of 30 April 1980, 1981/8 of 6 May 1981; 1982/12 of 30 April 1982, 1983/3 of 24 May 1983, 1984/21 of 24 May 1984, 1985/16 of 28 May 1985, 1986/9 of 21 May 1986, 1987/31 of 26 May 1987, 1988/10 of 25 May 1988, 1989/15 of 22 May 1989, 1990/31 of 24 May 1990 and 1991/43 of 21 June 1991,

Emphasizing once again that achieving a balance between the licit supply of opiates and the legitimate demand for opiates for medical and scientific purposes constitutes an important aspect of the international strategy and policy of drug abuse control and that resolving the problem of excess stocks of opiate raw materials is an essential step in that direction,

Noting the fundamental need for international cooperation and solidarity in overcoming the problem of excess stocks, which has been imposing heavy financial and other burdens on the traditional supplier countries,

Having noted the valuable recommendations made by the International Narcotics Control Board in its special reports on the demand for and supply of opiates for medical and scientific needs,

Having considered the report of the International Narcotics Control Board for 1991, in particular paragraphs 81 to 88 on the demand for and supply of opiates for medical and scientific needs,

1. *Urges* all Governments to continue to give serious consideration to ways to bring about rapid improvement in solving the problem of excess stocks of opiate raw materials held by the traditional supplier countries;

2. *Requests* all Governments to take measures to implement Council resolutions on the demand for and supply of opiates for medical and scientific needs, particularly in the light of the cautionary note contained in
paragraph 82 of the report of the International Narcotics
Control Board for 1991 to the effect that, starting in
1992, projected figures show that world production of
opiate raw materials may cease to be below global consumption of opiates;

3. *Commends* the International Narcotics Control
Board for its efforts to monitor the implementation of
the recommendations contained in its special report for
1989 on the demand for and supply of opiates for medical and scientific needs, prepared in conjunction with
the World Health Organization;

4. *Encourages* the International Narcotics Control
Board to continue its informal discussions with the main
producers of raw materials for opiates and the main importers about the supply and demand question during
sessions of the Commission;

5. *Requests* the Secretary-General to transmit the
present resolution to all Governments for consideration
and implementation.

Economic and Social Council resolution 1992/30

30 July 1992   Meeting 41   Adopted without vote

Approved by Social Committee (E/1992/107) without vote, 27 July (meeting 21); draft by Commission on Narcotic Drugs (E/1992/25); agenda
item 20.

Diversion of chemicals
for illicit drug production

INCB informed the Commission in February of
steps to implement article 12 of the 1988 Convention to prevent the diversion of precursors into illicit traffic and to assess substances for possible inclusion in the Convention Tables.[43] It noted that
the Chemical Action Task Force (CATF), established in 1990 by the Group of Seven major industrialized countries, had recommended that 10
additional substances frequently used in the
manufacture of narcotic drugs and psychotropic
substances be placed under international control
and that Governments take steps to prevent their
diversion. The Task Force recommended, among
other things: vigilance on the part of commercial
operators; administrative surveillance; registra-
tion/authorization of commercial exporters; and
import and export authorization.

CATF had also recommended that INCB publish
detailed information on global trading patterns for
those chemicals recommended for control, together
with directories of competent administrative and
enforcement authorities. A Conference on Chemical
Control Operations, organized by the United States,
Interpol and INCB in September 1991, recommended, *inter alia*, the creation of a standard system by which Governments could decide the
legitimacy of precursor imports and exports. Consideration was given to the establishment of an electronic communication network linking the secretariat
of INCB with Interpol, CCC and the Commission
of the European Communities.

Action by the Commission on Narcotic Drugs.
On 9 April,[44] the Commission decided that
N-acetylanthranilic acid, isosafrole, 3,4-methylene-
dioxyphenyl-2-propanone, piperonal and safrole
should be included in Table I of the Convention,
and that hydrochloric acid, excluding its salts, methyl
ethyl ketone (also referred to as 2-Butanone or
MEK), potassium permanganate, sulphuric acid, excluding its salts, and toluene should be included
in Table II.

ECONOMIC AND SOCIAL COUNCIL ACTION

On 30 July, the Economic and Social Council
adopted **resolution 1992/29** without vote.

**Measures to prevent the diversion of precursor and
essential chemicals to the illicit manufacture of
narcotic drugs and psychotropic substances**

The Economic and Social Council,

Concerned about the diversion of precursor and essential chemicals from commercial channels to the illicit
manufacture of heroin, cocaine and other narcotic drugs
and psychotropic substances,

Recalling the provisions of articles 3 and 12 of the United
Nations Convention against Illicit Traffic in Narcotic Drugs
and Psychotropic Substances of 1988 and Tables I and
II of that Convention,

Noting the constructive work of the Chemical Action
Task Force established by the heads of State of Government of the Group of Seven major industrialized countries and the President of the Commission of the European Communities at the sixteenth annual economic
summit, held at Houston, United States of America, in
July 1990, in developing effective procedures to prevent
the diversion of precursor and essential chemicals,

Taking note of the recommendations contained in the final
report of the Chemical Action Task Force, in particular
those on international and domestic trade in substances
subject to international control, together with the practical measures for preventing chemical diversion and for
developing international cooperation between the competent administrative and law enforcement authorities,

Taking note also of the decision by the Commission on
Narcotic Drugs at its thirty-fifth session to add five substances to Table I and five substances to Table II of the
1988 Convention,

Welcoming the outcome of the Conference on Chemical Control Operations convened at Lyon, France, in September 1991 by the Government of the United States of
America, in association with the International Narcotics
Control Board, the Customs Cooperation Council and
the International Criminal Police Organization [see
E/CN.7/1992/2, para. 17], and the work that was done
subsequently on the establishment of mechanisms for sharing information between the databases of those organizations and the establishment of procedures to verify the
authenticity of applications for export authorizations,

Recognizing the importance of close collaboration between Governments and the chemical industry in preventing chemical diversion,

1. *Invites* all Governments which have not already done so to establish effective legislative, procedural and cooperative measures to implement article 12 of the United Nations Convention against Illicit Traffic in Narcotic Drugs and Psychotropic Substances of 1988;

2. *Underlines* the importance of applying suitable regulatory measures, in accordance with the provisions of article 18 of the 1988 Convention, to every stage of the receipt, storage, handling, processing and delivery of precursor and essential chemicals in free ports and free trade zones and in other sensitive areas such as bonded warehouses;

3. *Invites* the Secretary-General to develop suitable model texts for the implementation of articles 3 and 12 of the 1988 Convention, taking into account work already undertaken by organizations and bodies such as the European Economic Community, the Organization of American States and the Chemical Action Task Force;

4. *Invites* all chemical-manufacturing States to monitor routinely the export trade in precursor and essential chemicals in a way that will enable them to identify changes in export patterns that suggest the diversion of such chemicals into illicit channels;

5. *Invites* States in which precursor and essential chemicals are manufactured and States in regions in which narcotic drugs and psychotropic substances are illicitly manufactured to establish close cooperation in order to prevent the diversion of precursor and essential chemicals into illicit channels and, if necessary, on a regional basis, to consider the establishment of bilateral agreements or arrangements where appropriate;

6. *Urges* States that export chemicals essential to the illicit production of heroin and cocaine, namely acetic anhydride, acetone, ethyl ether, hydrochloric acid, methyl ethyl ketone (MEK), potassium permanganate, sulphuric acid and toluene, to establish suitable mechanisms to detect and prevent their diversion and illicit trafficking and, where there is a risk of diversion of or illicit trafficking in those substances, to ensure that:

(*a*) Exporters of those essential chemicals are identified;

(*b*) Exporters of those essential chemicals are required to keep detailed records of all export transactions, including details of ultimate consignees, and to make these available for inspection by the competent authorities;

(*c*) An export authorization is required in respect of any consignments of commercial quantities of those essential chemicals to any State that has been identified as being concerned about the illicit manufacture of heroin or cocaine on its territory or as sensitive as regards the possible diversion of essential chemicals, taking into account the relevant reports of the International Narcotics Control Board, the Customs Cooperation Council and the International Criminal Police Organization;

(*d*) Applicants for export authorizations are required to provide full details of ultimate consignees and transport arrangements;

(*e*) The competent authorities, in considering applications for export authorizations, take reasonable steps to verify the legitimacy of transactions, in consultation, where appropriate, with their counterparts in importing countries;

7. *Recommends* that, if permitted by the basic principles of their legal systems, States should strengthen law enforcement cooperation by applying the technique of controlled delivery at the international level in appropriate circumstances to suspect consignments of precursor and essential chemicals;

8. *Requests* the United Nations International Drug Control Programme, in preparing assistance programmes for law enforcement and other agencies in States and regions in which drugs are illicitly manufactured, to give priority to providing resources for improving communications, equipment and training in preventing chemical diversion;

9. *Invites* the Programme and national laboratories to consider how they might assist in developing reliable field and laboratory testing methods to be used by national law enforcement agencies and laboratories in identifying scheduled chemicals;

10. *Invites* Member States to consider how to fund the production and distribution of the field testing kit developed by the laboratory of the Programme;

11. *Invites* the International Narcotics Control Board to consider, in consultation with Governments, the feasibility of compiling and making available to Governments information on the global pattern of trade in scheduled chemicals, bearing in mind the resource implications of such a requirement and the need to protect information of a commercially sensitive nature;

12. *Also invites* the Board to publish and maintain a directory containing the following information:

(*a*) The names, addresses and telephone and telefacsimile numbers of the administrative and law enforcement authorities responsible for regulating or enforcing national controls over precursor and essential chemicals;

(*b*) A summary of the regulatory controls that apply in each State, especially with regard to the importation and exportation of substances listed in Tables I and II of the Convention;

13. *Requests* the General Assembly to allocate adequate resources from within the existing level of resources of the regular budget of the United Nations to enable the Board and the Programme to discharge their functions under the present resolution and article 12 of the Convention;

14. *Commends* the Customs Cooperation Council for its work in establishing a discrete tariff code in the Customs Nomenclature for each of the substances specified in Tables I and II of the Convention;

15. *Invites* the Customs Cooperation Council to establish a discrete tariff code for any new substance commonly used in the manufacture of narcotic drugs and psychotropic substances, the monitoring of which the Board might consider to be justified;

16. *Invites* Governments to establish close cooperation with the chemical industry with a view to identifying suspicious transactions of precursor and essential chemicals and, where appropriate, to encourage the industry to establish codes of conduct to complement and enhance compliance with regulatory requirements;

17. *Requests* the Secretary-General to transmit the present resolution to all Governments for consideration and implementation.

Economic and Social Council resolution 1992/29

30 July 1992   Meeting 41   Adopted without vote

Approved by Social Committee (E/1992/107) without vote, 27 July (meeting 21); draft by Commission on Narcotic Drugs (E/1992/25); agenda item 20.

Follow-up action

INCB urged Governments to establish practical mechanisms and procedures to prevent illicit diversion before considering further additions to the Tables. The Board also considered that any future modification of the scope of control would need to be supported by sufficient data on the licit and illicit movements of the substances in question.

Diversion of psychotropic drugs for illicit use

INCB reported that close cooperation with Governments had enabled it to thwart attempts to divert psychotropic substances in Schedule II of the 1971 Convention, mainly methaqualone, fenetylline and secobarbital from licit sources. The Board noted that more than 70 Governments were applying additional control measures for most of the substances in Schedules III and IV, but that some parties to the 1971 Convention had failed for several years to control substances on the Schedules, allowing traffickers to exploit the international control system, particularly in the case of pemoline. In 1991 and 1992, traffickers had manufactured pemoline tablets in India from bulk shipments out of Europe, and the Board noted that this activity had been facilitated by the fact that pemoline was not under national control in India. After the Board's intervention, however, India updated its list of controlled psychotropic substances in October to include pemoline.

Regional issues

Africa

The drug abuse and illicit trafficking situation in Africa continued to deteriorate and the Board warned that if effective action were not taken soon the drug problem would escalate, compounding misery, violence, corruption and instability in the region. Although many African countries had demonstrated their willingness to fight the drug menace, they lacked the necessary resources and needed support to put effective drug control programmes and strategies in place. There were no reliable drug abuse assessments or estimates for the region, but epidemiological studies, with the financial support of UNDCP, were planned.

Cannabis continued to be the most abused drug in Africa and was the focus of a UNDCP mission to Morocco in 1992 to discuss national and international drug control. Cannabis continued to be widely cultivated throughout the region. Several countries reported an increase in cocaine abuse, and the abuse of stimulants remained a major problem in many countries. In general, non-adherence to the 1971 Convention, loopholes in import controls, inadequate pharmaceutical control services, and corruption contributed to the spread of large quantities of psychotropic substances for which there was no medical need, and illicit traffic in pemoline reached enormous proportions. The Board also noted an increase in traffic in khat (*Catha edulis*), a stimulant drug that was not under international control and was cultivated mainly in Ethiopia, Kenya and Yemen. The International Conference on Drug Abuse Control in East and South Africa, held at Arusha, United Republic of Tanzania, in January, recommended that khat cultivation, use and trade be under national and international control. The Board observed that there were few drug demand reduction programmes in Africa.

The fifth meeting of HONLEA, Africa, was held at Abuja, Nigeria, from 18 to 22 May 1992.

Asia

East and South-East Asia. Cooperation in drug control between neighbouring countries in the region was supported by UNDCP. Bilateral agreements were signed by China, the Lao People's Democratic Republic, Myanmar and Thailand, and the first regional Ministerial Conference on the fight against drug abuse was held at Bangkok in March 1992. The region continued to be a major supplier of illicit heroin, with Bangkok the main centre for trafficking by sea and air. Cannabis remained one of the most abused and trafficked substances in the region, with the principal producer countries being the Lao People's Democratic Republic, the Philippines and Thailand. Several countries, including Japan, the Philippines and Thailand, were concerned about an increase in abuse and illicit traffic in stimulants, particularly methamphetamine. Increased drug trafficking through China from across its southern border created addiction problems in parts of the country, and the National Narcotics Control Commission was coordinating the fight against illicit cultivation, trafficking and abuse. There were indications that Singapore had become a major centre for money-laundering, and legislation to curb this was under consideration. The Board noted that economic changes in Viet Nam, and proximity to the producer countries of the Golden Triangle, would undoubtedly make the country a target for traffickers as a source of illicit drugs, a transit country and a potential market.

South Asia. The spread of intravenous heroin abuse in north-eastern India remained a major concern. Intravenous drug abuse had been followed by a sharp increase in HIV infection in the States of Manipur and Nagaland and the territory of Mizovam. At least 50 per cent of the heroin abusers in Manipur had been found to be HIV-positive. The Government of Bangladesh was finalizing an amendment to the 1990 Narcotics Control Act that would incorporate provisions of the 1988 Convention and the 1990 South Asian Association for Regional Cooperation Convention with respect to the forfeiture of assets, controlled delivery, extradition and international cooperation. Licit cultivation of cannabis in Bangladesh was stopped in 1990 and there have been no reports of illicit opium cultivation, but it appeared that Bangladesh was being used increasingly as a transit country for illicit drugs. A UNDCP assistance programme for Bangladesh was expected to start in 1993.

Heroin destined for Europe continued to be smuggled across the India-Pakistan border and, with UNDCP assistance, India expected to conduct a complete review of its drug abuse situation. In Nepal, heroin smuggled through India was the most abused drug. Cannabis and cannabis resin were also abused, and the illicit use of psychotropic substances was on the rise. In Sri Lanka, the drug abuse situation among the young continued to worsen and the cultivation of cannabis was increasing.

The seventeenth meeting of HONLEA, Asia and the Pacific, was held at Bangkok from 23 to 27 November 1992.

Europe

There was an urgent need for the newly independent States of the former USSR and of Yugoslavia to be integrated into the system of international drug control treaties. Although drug abuse in those States had not reached the levels of Western Europe, recent changes in those countries could affect the drug abuse and illicit trafficking situation in Europe as a whole. The INCB invited Western European countries to help the former socialist countries of the region to create or strengthen drug control administrations.

In Western Europe, with the expected entry into force on 1 January 1993 of the Single European Act, which envisaged the free movement of persons, goods, services and capital, the Board called for the strengthening of control measures within and outside the European Economic Community (EEC). The Board noted with satisfaction directives for monitoring the trade in precursors, the prevention of money-laundering and the establishment of a customs information system. Drug control and cooperation among countries were further strengthened by the establishment of the European Monitoring Centre on Drugs and Drug Addiction and initiatives of the Pompidou Group of the Council of Europe and the Nordic Committee on Narcotic Drugs. A cooperation group

of officials responsible for controls in eastern Mediterranean ports was also created. Cannabis continued to be the principal drug of abuse in Europe, although attention was shifting to heroin and cocaine in several countries. LSD abuse seemed to be reappearing in some countries.

In the Commonwealth of Independent States (CIS), it was difficult to get a clear view of the extent of drug abuse, but there was evidence that cannabis and cannabis resin were abused in most States. Following a fact-finding mission in April, UNDCP assisted several CIS members to draft new laws and regulations, but international assistance was needed to establish national drug control administrations. Most newly independent States lacked customs services and there were no controls at the new borders.

Near and Middle East

Although the abuse of cannabis and cannabis resin was widespread, heroin and opium abuse constituted the main drug problem in the region. Equally disturbing was the illicit cultivation of cannabis and poppies, the illicit production of cannabis resin and opium, the clandestine manufacture of morphine and heroin, and the illicit traffic in cannabis resin and heroin through the Islamic Republic of Iran and Turkey to Western Europe via the Balkan route. Many countries were seriously affected by the illicit traffic in psychotropic substances. Small-scale surveys in refugee camps in Pakistan indicated that heroin addiction among Afghan refugees had reached alarming proportions among women as well as men.

The twenty-ninth session of the Subcommission on Illicit Drug Traffic and Related Matters in the Near and Middle East, including the Ministerial-level Conference at that session, was held in Iran from 24 to 28 October.

North America

In Canada, cannabis products remained the most easily available and abused drugs, although recent surveys indicated a decline in their abuse. The availability and abuse of cocaine remained high and the use of crack was spreading from larger to smaller cities and towns across the country. The diversion of licit pharmaceuticals was also a significant problem. In April, the Canadian Government announced that it was extending its national drug strategy for an additional five years with increased funding.

Mexico continued to be a major producer of cannabis and, to some extent, opium poppies. In the first nine months of 1992, law enforcement officers eradicated more than 8,000 hectares of poppies—47 per cent more than in 1991. Cannabis and heroin ("black tar") were smuggled across the border into the United States, and a considerable amount of cocaine continued to pass through Mexico. The Mexican Government was drafting legislation that would include measures against money-laundering and the control of precursors and chemicals used in the manufacture of illicit drugs. National studies and surveys showed that, with the exception of cocaine, drug abuse had not increased significantly during the previous five years.

In the United States, drug abuse and trafficking remained a great concern. According to surveys, the number of drug abusers continued to decline, but at a slower pace than in previous years. The number of cannabis users declined, but there was a marked increase in the potency of cannabis on the illicit market. Heroin abuse remained at about the 1988 level, but the abuse of cocaine increased, reversing a downward trend. The abuse of crack stabilized, having fallen by as much as 50 per cent since 1989. A major national trafficking ring, based in Los Angeles, was broken in January 1992. The success of the National Air Interdiction Strategy in the United States forced traffickers to use more complex modes of smuggling, including concealment in commercial maritime cargoes.

Latin America and the Caribbean

Major drug law enforcement efforts in South and Central America and the Caribbean resulted in the reduction of illicit coca bush cultivation; the seizure of large quantities of cocaine; and greater difficulties for traffickers engaged in money-laundering and illicit trafficking in precursors. The countries of the Andean subregion strengthened bilateral cooperation in law enforcement and were developing ways to replace the coca economy with legal economic activities. Traffickers found it more difficult to find alternative routes and secure environments in which to operate. Argentina, Bolivia, Brazil, Chile, Paraguay and Uruguay established the Conference of the Operational Forces of the Southern Cone for the exchange of information and for joint operations.

Most countries introduced mechanisms to prevent the diversion of precursors and chemicals to illicit cocaine manufacture, and a number took legal and administrative steps to prevent money-laundering. In February, Bolivia, Colombia, Ecuador, Mexico, Peru, the United States and Venezuela participated in a drug summit in San Antonio, United States, as a follow-up to a 1990 drug summit in Cartagena, Colombia. The San Antonio summit reflected their commitment to work together through drug law enforcement and the administration of justice, economic and financial efforts, drug abuse prevention and demand reduction. Virtually all countries in the region were being used more frequently for the

storage and transshipment of illicit drugs and chemicals used for illicit cocaine manufacture.

Cocaine abuse in the region was increasing and drug abuse among street children reached alarming proportions. Illicit poppy cultivation was creating new problems in several countries. The waters of Caribbean island States continued to be used as a significant transshipment route for drugs destined for North America and Europe, and the abuse of cocaine, mainly in the form of crack, had been reported in almost all of the Caribbean countries. The Government of the Bahamas believed that tough legislation, together with strict monitoring of the banking system, had been successful in preventing money-laundering.

The fifth meeting of HONLEA, Latin America and the Caribbean, was held at Acapulco, Mexico, from 28 September to 2 October 1992.

Action by the Commission on Narcotic Drugs. On 15 April,[46] the Commission associated itself with the spirit of the Declaration of San Antonio,[47] signed on 27 February 1992, and encouraged States, separately or in groups, to create mechanisms for joint action. It also invited more States to associate themselves with the Declaration.

Oceania

Law enforcement agencies continued to have difficulty securing the isolated coastal areas between Australia and the island countries of the South Pacific against maritime drug trafficking. It appeared that several of the island countries were being used as stepping-stones to move illicit drugs into Australia.

Cannabis remained the most available drug of abuse in Australia, but amphetamine abuse was also widespread. A national drug abuse campaign, launched in 1985, was evaluated in 1988 and in 1991 and appeared to be achieving its objectives. Its main focus was on women and young people. In June, the Australian Government and INCB hosted the region's first international training seminar for drug control officials.

Large-scale illicit cultivation of cannabis continued in New Zealand and increased in Papua New Guinea, where it was used primarily by young people. Large quantities of cannabis were being grown in Papua New Guinea and transshipped to Australia and other countries.

Conventions

INCB reported that, as of 1 November 1992, the number of parties to the 1961 Single Convention on Narcotic Drugs,[19] in its original or amended form, increased to 135. Of that number, 110 were parties to the Convention as amended by the 1972 Protocol.[20] Since the Board's 1991 report,

Seychelles and Slovenia had become parties to the 1961 Convention and to that Convention as amended. In addition, Burkina Faso, which was already a party to the 1961 Convention, became a party to the Convention in its amended form. The Board was concerned that, 30 years after the Convention's entry into force, 52 States were not parties to it in either its original or amended form. A number of countries did not have comprehensive and up-to-date regulations that conformed to international drug control conventions.

The Board reported that late submissions of statistics and annual estimates of narcotic drugs to the Secretariat by several countries had delayed the detailed analysis necessary for prompt action and control. The Board urged Governments to fulfil their obligations in that regard.

The Board also reported that, as of 1 November 1992, there were 109 parties to the 1971 Convention on Psychotropic Substances,[21] including Ireland, the Seychelles and Slovenia, which became parties in 1992. The Board was concerned by the late submission of reports by several parties whose control of the licit movement of psychotropic substances was affected by budgetary constraints. It expressed hope that the Governments concerned would be able to make the necessary budgetary allocations to ensure the full implementation of their obligations under the Convention, including timely compliance with reporting duties.

The 1988 United Nations Convention against Illicit Traffic in Narcotic Drugs and Psychotropic Substances[18] entered into force on 11 November 1990. As of 1 November 1992, 67 States and EEC had become parties to it. The Board urged all States which had not done so to become parties to the Convention. It also invited all States, even before the Convention became formally binding on them, to provisionally apply its measures to ensure its universal application.

Organizational questions

Commission on Narcotic Drugs

The Commission on Narcotic Drugs held its thirty-fifth session at Vienna from 6 to 15 April 1992.[48] It considered a Secretariat note on its programme of future work and priorities,[7] which examined its new mandates and the provisional agenda for its thirty-sixth session. The Commission also considered the revision of the medium-term plan for the period 1992-1997, programme 28: International Drug Control.[49] The revisions reflected programmatic changes resulting from re-

cent mandates and from the new organizational structure following the creation of UNDCP.

On 30 July, the Economic and Social Council, by **decision 1992/279**, took note of the report of the Commission on Narcotic Drugs on its thirty-fifth session and, by **decision 1992/277**, approved the provisional agenda and documentation for the thirty-sixth session.

Action by the Commission on Narcotic Drugs. On 14 April,[50] the Commission considered that its work programme should allow time for a substantive exchange of views on recent developments in the illicit drug situation and their effects on activities of UNDCP. It decided that, starting with its thirty-sixth session, under the agenda item "General debate", there would be sub-items covering general statements, and substantive debate and conclusions leading to the adoption of a text that reflected the main concerns, appraisals and orientations of the Commission with regard to drug abuse issues and the activities of the UNDCP.

International Narcotics Control Board

INCB held its fifty-first session from 6 to 10 January; its fifty-second session from 4 to 15 May; and its fifty-third session from 9 to 26 November, at Vienna.

By **decision 1992/278** of 30 July, the Economic and Social Council took note of the Board's 1991 report.[51]

REFERENCES

[1]YUN 1991, p. 721. [2]E/CN.7/1992/7. [3]E/CN.7/1992/7/Add.1. [4]YUN 1991, p. 724, GA res. 46/103, 16 Dec. 1991. [5]A/47/471. [6]E/CN.7/1992/12/Add.3. [7]E/CN.7/1992/12. [8]A/C.5/47/44. [9]YUN 1991, p. 870, GA res. 46/185C, 20 Dec. 1991. [10]E/1992/25 (res. 10(XXXV)). [11]Ibid. (res. 13(XXXV)). [12]E/CN.7/1992/4. [13]GA res. S-17/2, 23 Feb. 1990. [14]E/1992/25 (dec.3(XXXV)). [15]Ibid. (dec. 1(XXXV)). [16]GA res. 45/146, 18 Dec. 1990. [17]A/47/378. [18]*United Nations Convention against Illicit Traffic in Narcotic Drugs and Psychotropic Substances* (E/CONF.82/15 & Corr.1,2.), Sales No. 91.XI.6. [19]YUN 1961, p. 382. [20]YUN 1972, p. 397. [21]YUN 1971, p. 380. [22]E/1992/25 (res. 4(XXXV)). [23]Ibid. (res. 1(XXXV)). [24]Ibid. (res. 8(XXXV)). [25]Ibid. (res. 11(XXXV)). [26]YUN 1991, p. 661, GA res. 46/152, 18 Dec. 1991. [27]E/CN.7/1992/11. [28]E/1992/25 (res. 2(XXXV)). [29]YUN 1991, p. 727, GA res. 46/102. [30]E/CN.7/1992/10 & Corr.1. [31]YUN 1987, p. 901. [32]E/1990/39 & Corr.1,2 & Add.1. [33]E/1992/25 (res. 7(XXXV)). [34]ACC/1992/17. [35]GA res. 45/179, 21 Dec. 1990. [36]ACC/1992/26. [37]YUN 1991, p. 728, GA res. 46/101, 16 Dec. 1991. [38]E/CN.7/1992/8. [39]E/CN.7/1992/9. [40]E/1991/24. [41]E/1992/25 (res. 5(XXXV)). [42]Ibid. (res. 3(XXXV)). [43]E/CN.7/1992/2. [44]E/1992/25 (dec. 4(XXXV)). [45]Ibid. (dec. 5(XXXV)). [46]Ibid. (res. 6(XXXV)). [47]A/47/210. [48]E/1992/25. [49]E/CN.7/1992/12/Add.2/Rev.1. [50]E/1992/25 (res. 9(XXXV)). [51]*Report of the International Narcotics Control Board for 1991* (E/INCB/1991/1), Sales No. E.91.XI.4.

Chapter XVII

Statistics

During 1992, the United Nations continued its statistical work programme, including the improvement of statistical methodology; the collection, compilation and dissemination of international statistical data; support for technical cooperation activities and the promotion of coordination in international statistical work. The Statistics Division of the United Nations Secretariat—part of the newly created Department of Economic and Social Development (DESD)—assumed the functions of the former Statistical Office.

In anticipation of an increased demand for environment statistics and indicators in the wake of the 1992 United Nations Conference on Environment and Development, the Statistical Division proposed the establishment of a new branch for environment and energy statistics.

The Secretary-General issued a number of reports on statistical issues and activities for consideration by the twenty-seventh session of the Statistical Commission, to be held in 1993. The Commission, which meets biennially, did not meet in 1992.

UN statistical bodies

Working Group on International Statistical Programmes and Coordination

The Working Group on International Statistical Programmes and Coordination of the Statistical Commission held its fifteenth session in New York from 29 June to 1 July 1992.[1] The Working Group made a number of recommendations to the Statistical Commission on strengthening international statistical cooperation and improving the functioning of the international statistical system. It also reviewed progress on the revision of the System of National Accounts (SNA). Recommendations related to the cycle and organization of the Statistical Commission, its Working Group and the Subcommittee on Statistical Activities of the Administrative Committee on Coordination (ACC), and coordination among those bodies. Other recommendations dealt with the integration of work programmes, standards, a system of monitoring, and reducing duplication in data collection and processing. The Working Group also reviewed and discussed publications, called for an inventory to be made of the gaps and weaknesses in the international statistical system, and discussed the need for an orderly approach to changes

in data collection, including the development of a 10-year plan for methodological work adjustments of nationally supplied statistical data. Aspects of technical cooperation were also addressed.

The Working Group was informed of the status of revisions to SNA being carried out by the Inter-Secretariat Working Group on National Accounts (ISWGNA). ISWGNA's participating organizations were the United Nations Statistical Division, the International Monetary Fund (IMF), the World Bank, the Organisation for Economic Cooperation and Development (OECD), the Statistical Office of the Commission of the European Economic Community (EEC) (EUROSTAT) and the United Nations regional commissions. The revised SNA would be presented to the Statistical Commission in 1993.

By **decision 1992/210** of 7 February 1992, the Economic and Social Council decided that the Working Group would meet in June/July 1992 instead of in the second half of 1993.

ACC Subcommittee

The ACC Subcommittee on Statistical Activities held its twenty-sixth session in 1992 (Geneva, 6-10 April).[2] The Subcommittee identified four matters to be brought to the attention of ACC: the review of the structure and operation of the Global Statistical System, being carried out by the Statistical Commissions's Working Group on International Statistical Programmes and Coordination; action taken to improve coordination and cooperation in statistical matters with countries in transition; the initiatives taken on coordination in strategies for statistical development in Africa as reflected in the Strategy for the Implementation of the Addis Ababa Plan of Action for Statistical Development in Africa in the 1990s (see PART TWO, Chapter VI); and plans of the United Nations Development Programme (UNDP) to improve collaboration with members of the Subcommittee on the statistical aspects of UNDP's *Human Development Report*.

The Subcommittee endorsed a draft policy position for consideration by the Statistical Commission on policies in international organizations concerning adjusting nationally supplied data and making estimates for non-reported data. It reviewed the statistical implications of the single market of EEC; revision of SNA; implications for technical cooperation in statistics of changes in UNDP and United Nations Population Fund (UNFPA) policies relating to project execution and agency support costs and the UNFPA Technical Support Services System. The Subcommittee also considered the International Comparison Programme, procedures for adopting joint international statistical standards among two or more organizations, international trade statistics, environment statistics, monitoring achievements of social goals, the base year for international statistics, and preparations for the 1993 session of the Statistical Commission.

The Subcommittee recommended that its next session be held from 7 to 11 June 1993 at Rome, Italy.

Economic statistics

National accounts and balances

ISWGNA completed a report in December[3] on the revision of SNA, which played a major role in macroeconomic description, analysis and policy-making at both the national and international levels. The report included an overview of the revised SNA and described the review process. It showed how the process had initiated parallel revisions of related statistical standards and would result in the development of SNA handbooks containing information on the System, its implementation and special applications. The report summarized the activities of ISWGNA and the Expert Group on SNA coordination (EGC) during 1991-1992.

The sixth meeting of EGC (Aguascalientes, Mexico, 2, 3 and 10 October 1992) discussed the revision of SNA and related technical issues. Participants in an interregional seminar on the revision of SNA (Aguascalientes, 5-9 October) contributed comments on a number of issues, including the process for possible future refinements to SNA.

ISWGNA held a meeting (Paris, 14-16 December), following which it prepared a report[4] reflecting decisions taken at that meeting that affected the second draft of the revised SNA. Those decisions responded to issues brought to ISWGNA's attention through the broad distribution of the revised draft, including comments from statistical offices and other experts, comments from the interregional seminar on the revision of SNA and comments from the sixth meeting of EGC. Major substantive issues dealt with financial intermediation service charges indirectly measured, imputed rent on government buildings, monetary gold, market/non-market output, mineral exploration, consumer subsidies, formal/informal activities and environmental accounting. Technical points addressed included time of recording taxes on in-

come, net worth of quasi-corporations, privately funded pension schemes, the output of non-life insurance and of autonomous pension funds and the time of recording gross fixed capital formation in large equipment.

Price statistics

In a December report,[5] the Secretary-General reviewed progress in phase VI of the International Comparison Programme (ICP), which compared real product and purchasing power in order to assess the relative economic development of countries and other related international comparison issues. Under phase V of ICP, with 1985 as the reference year, published results were available for all six individually conducted regional comparisons. The processing of the world results, covering 63 countries with reference year 1985, was being carried out by EUROSTAT. The processing had generated world results for 53 categories of final expenditure on gross domestic product.

Regarding progress in phase VI, three country groups, OECD, EUROSTAT and ICP Group II (Eastern Europe), had conducted comparisons with reference year 1990. In the developing regions, due mainly to insufficient financial support, a late start implementing phase VI did not permit comparisons to be conducted for 1990. Consequently, the phase VI global comparison would have a later reference year.

The *Handbook of the International Comparison Programme*[6] was issued in English in November.

Industrial statistics

An October report[7] by the Secretary-General presented an overview of preparatory work relating to the 1993 World Programme of Industrial Statistics at the national and international levels. The report provided a review of current national practices in industrial statistics with respect to the scope and frequency of inquiries covering the industrial sector; summarized stated national intentions regarding participation in the 1993 World Programme; and linked current national statistical programmes planning to take part. The Programme was to encourage the orderly development of national inquiries into the structure and activity of the industrial sector, and to obtain benchmark data. Fifty-six countries had indicated they would participate.

The report discussed two documents being prepared in connection with the 1993 World Programme: a technical report on national strategies for measuring industrial structure and growth and a guide for the conversion from revision 2 to revision 3 of the International Standard Industrial Classification of All Economic Activities (ISIC) in the compilation and reporting of industrial data.

The role of technical cooperation in industrial statistics in promoting national participation in the Programme was also discussed, including background information, a review of the current situation, and proposals and resources for the Programme.

Environment statistics

The Secretary-General, in a June report,[8] reviewed the ongoing methodological work in environment statistics, and described draft reports on selected topics prepared in the context of the Intergovernmental Working Group on the Advancement of Environment Statistics. The Working Group met twice in 1992 (Arusha, United Republic of Tanzania, 17-21 February, and Wiesbaden, Germany, 14-18 December). The report addressed progress made in environmental accounting, in particular the SNA draft handbook of integrated environmental and economic accounting; reviewed progress made in developing and establishing regional and national programmes of environment statistics, and in the programme of work of the United Nations Statistical Division. The Division proposed creating a new branch for environment and energy statistics in anticipation of the increased demand for environmental statistics and indicators following the United Nations Conference on Environment and Development (UNCED) (see PART THREE, Chapter VIII).

UNCED[9] proposed the establishment of national systems of integrated environmental and economic accounting (IEEA) in all countries, which would play an integral part in national development decision-making. The Conference requested the Statistical Division to make available to all Member States the methodologies contained in the *SNA Handbook on Integrated Environmental and Economic Accounting*, once completed, and to coordinate training of national technical staff for the establishment, adaptation and development of national IEEAs. DESD, of which the Statistical Division was a part, was requested to support the use of sustainable development indicators in national economic and social planning to ensure the integration of IEEAs. The Department was further asked to promote improved environmental, economic and social data collection.

The second meeting of the Intersecretariat Working Group on Environmental Data was convened at Geneva on 21 May under the auspices of the Economic Commission for Europe (ECE). It was decided that work on the survey to compile information on international environmental databases, carried out by EUROSTAT, should continue.

The Working Group on International Statistical Programmes and Coordination[1] requested the Statistical Division to convene a task force on environment statistics. To that end, the Division circulated a questionnaire to explore the planned involvement of international organizations in the areas of environmental statistics and accounting.

International trade and transport statistics

In the area of of trade statistics, work continued on methodological development and publications consequent to the publication of the *Commodity Indexes for the Standard International Trade Classification, Revision 3*.

New projects included research on technical problems related to the rebasing of trade index numbers to a new base year and on possible improvements in the country coverage of samples used in estimating both the regional/world unit value indexes of total imports and manufactured goods exports and of the export price index for machinery and transport equipment.

In the area of international seaborne trade statistics, collection of limited statistical data on goods loaded and unloaded in seaborne trade continued, based on questionnaires sent to countries. The Division also entered into an arrangement with a private firm to make the firm's seaborne trade data available to the United Nations and other selected organizations.

In July,[10] the Secretary-General and the General Agreement on Tariffs and Trade (GATT) presented their views on the future relationship between the Standard International Trade Classification and the Harmonized Commodity Description and Coding System.

Service statistics

In a report on work carried out by national and international agencies in the field of service statistics,[11] the Secretary-General reviewed developments in methodology, application of international classifications and technical cooperation. It considered experience with the use of the International Standard Industrial Classification of all Economic Activities, Revision 3, and the provisional Central Product Classification; summarized national practices in price and volume measures for financial intermediation, business services, education and health services, and public administration; and described progress made in discussions of proposed international guidelines on price and volume measures for services.

The report also summarized the work of the Voorburg Group on Service Statistics,[12] a cooperative effort by volunteer statistical agencies to address problems associated with data gaps and conceptual issues. At its seventh meeting (Washington, D.C., 19-23 October), the Voorburg Group emphasized the importance of constructing and implementing a model survey to broaden the Group's experience with issues concerning measurement, classification and data collection.

In addition, the report included information on the methodological work of ECE, EUROSTAT, GATT, IMF, OECD, the United Nations Conference on Trade and Development and the Statistical Division to advance service statistics in member countries and described their future plans.

Social and demographic statistics

Population and housing censuses

In December, the Secretary-General reported on progress achieved in the 1990 World Population and Housing Census Programme,[13] stating that, as at 1 April 1992, 194 out of 232 countries or areas had carried out or planned to have a population and/or housing census during the period 1985-1994. Some of the 1990 round's achievements included an overall improvement in many phases of census-taking, particularly in regard to data processing, owing to the widespread adoption of microcomputers by developing countries. There had also been an increase in the number of housing censuses carried out by countries, mostly in conjunction with population censuses. Preparations for the World Population and Housing Census Programme were discussed.

Civil registration and vital statistics

In 1992,[14] as part of the International Programme for Accelerating the Improvement of Vital Statistics and Civil Registration Systems, missions were carried out by representatives of the Statistical Division to the Economic and Social Commission for Western Asia (ESCWA) and the Economic Commission for Africa (ECA) to coordinate efforts and make technical and administrative arrangements for a possible workshop in each region in 1993. Provisional agendas, lists of technical papers to be presented for discussion and their potential authors, and budgets were drawn up, and countries were identified as potential participants.

The Division also issued guidelines for a review and assessment of national civil registration and vital statistics systems in Arabic and French to assist participating countries to prepare their country reports for the workshops.

In the area of methodology, the Division undertook a study on national procedures in more than 100 countries or areas for recording vital events on a daily basis and reporting them to the agency or agencies that compiled continuous vital statistics. The study was a supplement to the *Handbook of Vital Statistics Systems and Methods*, which dealt with issues of layout and content, numbering, filing, storage, retrieval and presentation of records.

Special population groups

Work on special population groups focused on children, persons with disabilities and elderly persons, and involved the development of concepts, definitions and classifications; data-collection strategies and international database development; training manuals and handbooks; and technical cooperation, including training workshops and advisory services.[13]

In 1992, the Statistical Division, in collaboration with the United Nations Educational, Scientific and Cultural Organization and Thailand, conducted an Interregional Workshop on Developmental Delay and Disability among Children Living in Especially Difficult Circumstances (Bangkok, 9-13 September).

With respect to people with disabilities, the International Disability Statistical Database (DISTAT, version 2) was being prepared for dissemination. DISTAT contained national disability statistics from censuses, household surveys and administrative registries, and presented data on 12 major socio-economic and demographic topics concerning disability. The Statistical Division, in cooperation with Statistics Canada, organized an International Workshop on Development and Dissemination of Statistics on Persons with Disabilities (Ottawa, 13-16 October). The workshop considered national work and the need for international recommendations on disability statistics. It also considered the concerns of producers of disability statistics, regarding the quality of disability data and the need for comparability. With funds from the Swedish International Development Authority, the Division was preparing an efficient and standardized data collection procedure for national and international monitoring and evaluation of World Health Organization (WHO) community-based rehabilitation programmes. It was collaborating with WHO in revising the International Classification of Impairments, Disabilities and Handicaps.

Statistics on women

During 1991-1992,[13] the Statistical Division concentrated on preparing and disseminating version 2 of the Women's Indicators and Statistics Database (WISTAT). WISTAT provided internationally available gender-based statistics in a single, comprehensive, well-documented source, covering 178 countries and areas of the world.

The Commission on the Status of Women (see PART THREE, Chapter XIII), at its 1992 session,[15] recommended that preparations for the Fourth World Conference on Women (1995) should include assembling information and gender-disaggregated statistics for elaborating national reports on the situation of women. Documentation for the Conference should include an updated version of *The World's Women, 1970-1990: Trends and Statistics*.

National Household
Survey Capability Programme

A report by the Secretary-General and the World Bank[16] reviewed progress in implementing the National Household Survey Capability Programme (NHSCP), the Living Standards Measurement Study (LSMS) and the Social Dimensions of Adjustment Programme (SDA). Five countries (Burkina Faso, Cayman Islands, Guinea, Guyana, Seychelles) joined NHSCP during 1992, bringing to 50 the total number of countries participating.

The review of LSMS and SDA highlighted implementation as well as methodological issues. It underlined the measures taken to build up national capabilities to collect, process and analyse statistical information.

In another report,[17] the Secretary-General and the World Bank addressed the differences and similarities between the three programmes in objectives, characteristics and methodology. It stated that collaboration between NHSCP and LSMS/SDA at the country level was the best strategy to assist countries to address their data requirements for general and specific programmes.

Other statistical activities

Technical cooperation

A summary of technical cooperation programmes in statistics of organizations of the United Nations system and several multilateral organizations during 1989-1992 was presented in a November report[18] by the Secretary-General. The report reviewed the impact of a 1989 General Assembly resolution on operational activities for development[19] and of new agency support cost arrangements on the provision of technical cooperation in statistics. It contained information on the technical cooperation programmes of the United Nations system, and information supplied by EEC and the International Statistics Institute was summarized.

The main objective of the United Nations technical assistance programme (DESD and the regional commissions) was to assist developing countries to strengthen and extend national services and capabilities to collect, process, disseminate and use a broad range of development-related statistics. The programme's expenditures on statistical projects in 1992 totalled some $23.6 million, down from $30.6 million in 1991.

The Secretary-General also reported in December[20] on a programme to monitor the achievement of social goals in the 1990s. The programme was being developed by the United Nations Children's Fund, UNFPA, UNDP and the Statistical Division. The report gave the conclusions of pilot studies carried out in five countries (Ecuador, Kenya, Mali, Mexico, Philippines) and described post–pilot study developments. It also proposed elements of a Statistical Division work programme on monitoring social-goal attainment.

Programme questions

In an overall review of the statistical activities of the United Nations system and other international organizations for the period January 1990 to December 1991, and up to November 1992 for the Statistical Division,[21] the Secretary-General provided information on major achievements, new activities, and activities cancelled or modified significantly.

The Secretary-General also provided updated information on the future activities in statistics of the organizations of the United Nations system and of several international organizations outside the system.[22]

REFERENCES

[1]E/CN.3/1993/21. [2]ACC/1992/16. [3]E/CN.3/1993/4. [4]E/CN.3/1993/4/Add.1,2. [5]E/CN.3/1993/11. [6]*Handbook of the International Comparison Programme,* Sales No. E.92.XVII.1. [7]E/CN.3/1993/9. [8]E/CN.3/1993/13. [9]*Report of the United Nations Conference on Environment and Development, Rio de Janeiro, 3-14 June 1992,* vol. I, Sales No. E.93.I.8. [10]E/CN.3/1993/15/Add.1. [11]E/CN.3/1993/10. [12]YUN 1991, p. 745. [13]E/CN.3/1993/12. [14]E/CN.3/1993/24. [15]E/1992/24. [16]E/CN.3/1993/18. [17]E/CN.3/1993/19. [18]E/CN.3/1993/17. [19]GA res. 44/211, 22 Dec. 1989. [20]E/CN.3/1993/20. [21]E/CN.3/1993/22. [22]E/CN.3/1993/23.

Chapter XVIII

Institutional arrangements

During 1992, the restructuring of the Economic and Social Council and its subsidiary bodies continued. Following the adoption in April of General Assembly resolution 46/235, which had as its goal the enhancement of the effectiveness and efficiency of the United Nations in the economic, social and related fields, the Council established three new subsidiary bodies and approved the work programmes for their first sessions. The Council's work at its 1992 substantive session was conducted in accordance with newly established guidelines.

Upon consideration of a review of the conditions necessary for the effective functioning of the Non-Governmental Organizations Unit, the Council requested the Secretary-General to consider increasing the Unit's resources.

The Administrative Committee on Coordination and the Committee for Programme and Coordination continued efforts to harmonize system-wide work programmes and activities.

Restructuring questions

In 1990, the General Assembly, by a resolution on the restructuring and revitalization of the United Nations in the economic and social fields,[1] had stressed the need for more effective and efficient functioning of the United Nations intergovernmental machinery in order for it to be more responsive to the needs of enhancing international economic cooperation and promoting the development of developing countries. The Assembly had also endorsed a 1990 Economic and Social Council resolution[2] by which the Council President was given a mandate to undertake broad consultations with Member States on the matter.

In 1991, the Assembly had adopted certain measures on the restructuring and revitalization of the Council,[3] and in April 1992, it adopted further measures.

GENERAL ASSEMBLY ACTION (April)

On 13 April, the General Assembly, at its resumed forty-sixth session, adopted without vote **resolution 46/235**.

Restructuring and revitalization of the United Nations in the economic, social and related fields

The General Assembly,

Reaffirming its resolutions 45/177 of 19 December 1990 and 45/264 of 13 May 1991 on the restructuring and revitalization of the United Nations in the economic, social and related fields,

1. *Adopts* the text contained in the annex to the present resolution;

2. *Requests* the Secretary-General to implement the proposed restructuring measures as contained in the annex to the present resolution and to report to the General Assembly at its forty-seventh session on the action he has taken.

ANNEX
Background

1. At its resumed forty-fifth session, the General Assembly, in the annex to its resolution 45/264 of 13 May 1991, agreed that a review of the functioning of the subsidiary bodies of the Economic and Social Council and of the General Assembly should take place during the forty-sixth session of the Assembly. In the same resolution, the Assembly underlined the objectives of the overall exercise as being the enhancement of the effective and efficient functioning of the intergovernmental machinery of the United Nations system in the economic, social and related fields in order to be more responsive to the needs of enhancing international economic cooperation and promoting the development of the developing countries.

2. The review at the forty-sixth session of the General Assembly of the subsidiary bodies of the Economic and Social Council and the General Assembly should be carried out with the objective of possible restructuring and revitalization, and the review of their reporting responsibilities and procedures should be carried out with a view to avoiding duplication, where possible. The review should be on the basis of the criteria listed in paragraph 6 (3) of the annex to resolution 45/264.

Framework

3. Some consideration has been given to the restructuring and revitalization of the subsidiary machinery in the social and related fields in the United Nations. Similar attention should be given to the restructuring and revitalization of the subsidiary machinery of the economic sector of the United Nations, with a view to its strengthening.

4. In accordance with the basic principles and guidelines for the restructuring and revitalization of the United Nations in the economic, social and related fields outlined in resolution 45/264, the following common understanding should guide the entire exercise of the restructuring and revitalization of the subsidiary bodies, with the aim of adopting measures to sustain and

strengthen the quality and impact of the output of these bodies:

(a) The issues of which the subsidiary bodies are seized are of vital importance to Member States, especially for the development of developing countries;

(b) The ability of the United Nations system to deal more effectively with such vital issues should help to enhance its relevance and credibility in the economic, social and related fields;

(c) Activities in pursuance of these issues must be implemented in an effective and efficient manner in order to enhance international economic cooperation and to promote, in particular, the development of developing countries;

(d) Subsidiary bodies should provide the General Assembly and the Economic and Social Council, as principal organs of the United Nations responsible for system-wide policies in the economic, social and related fields, with high-quality advice on relevant issues, through analysis and appropriate policy recommendations or options, in order to enable them to guide future work in the United Nations, develop common policies and agree on appropriate actions;

(e) The composition of each subsidiary body that does not have universal participation must be determined with due regard to equitable geographical representation. Members will be eligible for re-election;

(f) In cases where Governments or government-nominated experts are elected to subsidiary bodies, the experts should possess the necessary qualifications and professional or scientific knowledge. Travel and/or daily subsistence allowance to cover the participation of experts shall be financed from the regular budget in accordance with established rules;

(g) No single or uniform approach to restructuring and revitalization is applicable to all subsidiary bodies. Each body must be reviewed on its own merits through an open and thorough process.

Reporting procedures for subsidiary bodies

5. The Economic and Social Council should provide guidance to and follow up the work of its subsidiary bodies whose reports should contain clear and cogent recommendations and proposals to facilitate their consideration by a revitalized Economic and Social Council in a substantive and integrated manner.

Subsidiary bodies identified for restructuring and revitalization

6. *Regional commissions*

The regional commissions should be enabled fully to play their role under the authority of the General Assembly and the Economic and Social Council. Their effectiveness should be strengthened. The regional commissions, particularly those located in developing countries, should also be strengthened in terms of their activities and participation in operational activities of the United Nations system, bearing in mind the overall objectives of the restructuring and the revitalization process and taking into account paragraph 3 *(h)* of the annex to General Assembly resolution 45/264. In this context, the regional commissions are requested to provide recommendations for consideration by the General Assembly at its forty-seventh session.

7. *Other subsidiary bodies:*

(a) *Intergovernmental Committee on Science and Technology for Development*

(i) Name: Commission on Science and Technology for Development (New York)

The Intergovernmental Committee on Science and Technology for Development and its subsidiary body, the Advisory Committee on Science and Technology for Development, will be transformed into a functional commission of the Economic and Social Council.

Such functional commission should examine at its first session the question of funding arrangements and the modalities for the convening of ad hoc panels/workshops which will meet intersessionally to examine specific issues of science and technology for development within the framework of General Assembly resolutions 34/218 of 19 December 1979 and 41/183 of 8 December 1986. In this connection, the Commission could consider the practice of the Advisory Committee on Science and Technology for Development.

(ii) Membership and participation: fifty-three members elected by the Economic and Social Council for a term of four years. Travel expenses shall be paid by the United Nations for one representative of each of the Member States participating in the Commission.

(iii) Primary programme objective: as stipulated in General Assembly resolutions 34/218 and 41/183.

(iv) Nature of output and reporting procedure: report to the Economic and Social Council with policy options and recommendations.

(v) Frequency and duration of meetings: the Commission will meet once every two years for two weeks.

(vi) Secretariat support: the Department of Economic and Social Development will serve the Commission and Member States, in particular developing countries, effectively.

(b) *Committee on Natural Resources*

(i) Name: Committee on Natural Resources (New York)

(ii) Membership and participation: twenty-four government-nominated experts from different Member States, who possess the necessary qualifications and professional or scientific knowledge, who will act in their personal capacities, elected by the Economic and Social Council for a four-year term. Travel expenses and daily subsistence allowance shall be paid by the United Nations for each member of the Committee.

The Committee will have two working groups, one on minerals, and one on water resources.

(iii) Primary programme objective: current mandate of the Committee on Natural Resources pertaining to minerals and water resources.

The mandate of the Committee on Natural Resources in respect of energy will be assumed by the Committee on New and Renewable Sources of Energy and on Energy for Development (see (c) below).

(iv) Nature of output and reporting procedure: report to the Economic and Social Council with policy options and recommendations.

(v) Frequency and duration of meetings: the Committee will meet once every two years for two weeks.

(vi) Secretariat support: the Department of Economic and Social Development and any other relevant existing entities of the Secretariat.

(c) *Committee on the Development and Utilization of New and Renewable Sources of Energy*

(i) Name: Committee on New and Renewable Sources of Energy and on Energy for Development (New York)

(ii) Membership and participation: twenty-four government-nominated experts from different Member States, who possess the necessary qualifications and professional or scientific knowledge, who will act in their personal capacities, elected by the Economic and Social Council for a four-year term. Travel expenses and daily subsistence allowance shall be paid by the United Nations for each member of the Committee.

(iii) Primary programme objective: the Committee will retain the current mandate of the Committee on the Development and Utilization of New and Renewable Sources of Energy, including the consideration of its relation to environment and development.

In addition, it will take over the present mandate of the Committee on Natural Resources pertaining to energy, as defined in Economic and Social Council resolution 1535(XLIX) of 27 July 1970.

(iv) Nature of output and reporting procedure: report to the Economic and Social Council with policy options and recommendations.

(v) Frequency and duration of meetings: once every two years for two weeks.

(vi) Secretariat support: the existing arrangements for servicing the Committee on the Development and Utilization of New and Renewable Sources of Energy may be strengthened through consolidation, in accordance with paragraph 6 (4) of the annex to General Assembly resolution 45/264, to provide adequate technical support to the Committee on New and Renewable Sources of Energy and on Energy for Development.

Future work

8. The specific regional allocation of seats for each of the bodies mentioned above should be decided upon at the next organizational session of the Economic and Social Council, in accordance with paragraph 4 *(e)* above.

Review

9. Any relevant institutional changes and recommendations by the eighth session of the United Nations Conference on Trade and Development and the United Nations Conference on Environment and Development regarding, in particular, the Committee on Natural Resources and the Committee on New and Renewable Sources of Energy and on Energy for Development shall be considered at the forty-seventh session of the General Assembly.

10. A review of the implementation of the present exercise, including the consideration of further steps, is to be undertaken during the forty-eighth session of the General Assembly, in accordance with resolution 45/264.

General Assembly resolution 46/235

13 April 1992   Meeting 84   Adopted without vote

Draft by President (A/46/L.57/Rev.1), based on informal consultations on draft by Peru (A/46/L.57); agenda item 137.
Financial implications. 5th Committee, A/46/898/Rev.1; S-G, A/C.5/46/83.
Meeting numbers. GA 46th session: 5th Committee 63; plenary 38, 84.

By **decision 47/438** of 22 December, the Assembly, acting on the recommendation of the Second (Economic and Financial) Committee, deferred until 1993 consideration of a draft resolution[4] on implementation of section II (on the Economic and Social Council) of the annex to a 1977 Assembly resolution on the restructuring of the economic and social sectors of the United Nations system.[5]

Report of the Secretary-General (October). The Secretary-General, in response to the April 1992 Assembly resolution (see above), submitted an October report[6] on the implementation of the result of the restructuring and revitalizing process in the economic, social and related fields. The report also included information on recommendations that had not been implemented as scheduled.

Among the measures adopted for restructuring and revitalizing the Council were: the holding of an organizational session, not to exceed four days, to determine the Council's annual agenda and related organizational matters; the holding of a substantive session of the Council, which would include the high-level (see below), coordination (see below), operational activities, and committee segments; a restructuring of the subsidiary machinery; recommendations on the role of the regional commissions; and streamlining of Secretariat operations. Recommendations received from the five regional commissions on strengthening their role were annexed to the report (for details, see PART TWO, Chapter VI).

Revitalization of the Economic and Social Council

In June 1992, the Secretary-General submitted a report on the revitalization of the Economic and Social Council,[7] in which he reviewed the implementation of relevant Council resolutions and decisions adopted since 1988. Those resolutions and decisions related to the reorganization of the annual general discussion; in-depth consideration of major policy themes; monitoring of implementation of overall strategies, policies and priorities established by the General Assembly and the Council; the Council's role with regard to operational activities for development; the Council's responsibilities for coordinating the activities of the specialized agencies, United Nations organs and organizations in the economic, social and related fields; recommendations and steps taken to improve working methods and organization of work;

the consolidation of similar issues under a single agenda item; the calendar of conferences; documentation; election of the Bureau of the Council; preparations for the organizational session; and Secretariat support.

On 31 July 1992, by **decision 1992/303**, the Council took note of the Secretary-General's report.

Establishment of new subsidiary bodies

In April 1992, in accordance with the General Assembly's earlier resolutions on restructuring (see above), the Economic and Social Council established a functional Commission on Science and Technology for Development, an expert Committee on Natural Resources, replacing the Council's standing Committee of the same name, and a Committee on New and Renewable Sources of Energy and on Energy for Development. In July, the Council reaffirmed the mandates of the new subsidiary bodies and approved the draft provisional agendas and programmes of work for their first sessions.

ECONOMIC AND SOCIAL COUNCIL ACTION (April)

At its resumed organizational session, the Economic and Social Council adopted without vote **decision 1992/218**.

Establishment of new subsidiary bodies of the Economic and Social Council

At its 7th plenary meeting, on 30 April 1992, the Economic and Social Council, recalling General Assembly resolution 46/235 of 13 April 1992 on the restructuring and revitalization of the United Nations in the economic, social and related fields, decided:

(*a*) To abolish its Committee on Natural Resources;

(*b*) To establish a functional Commission on Science and Technology for Development, a Committee on Natural Resources and a Committee on New and Renewable Sources of Energy and on Energy for Development, in accordance with General Assembly resolution 46/235;

(*c*) To request the Secretary-General to submit, for approval by the Council at its substantive session of 1992, the consolidated mandates of the new subsidiary bodies, in accordance with the provisions of General Assembly resolution 46/235;

(*d*) To hold elections for the membership of the bodies mentioned above at its substantive session of 1992, as an exceptional measure;

(*e*) To request the Secretary-General to submit to the Council, at its substantive session of 1992, a draft provisional agenda for the Commission on Science and Technology for Development and recommendations for the programme of work of the Committee on Natural Resources;

(*f*) That the Commission on Science and Technology for Development should hold its first session from 12 to 23 April 1993 and that the Committee on Natural Resources should hold its first session from 22 March to 2 April 1993.

Economic and Social Council decision 1992/218

30 April 1992   Meeting 7   Adopted without vote

Draft by Vice-President (E/1992/L.18), orally revised and orally amended by United Kingdom; agenda item 2.

(See Appendix III for the regional allocations of seats in the three new subsidiary bodies of the Council.)

Note of the Secretary-General (June). In June,[8] the Secretary-General submitted for consideration by the Economic and Social Council a note containing the proposed consolidated mandates of the new subsidiary bodies of the Council. It also contained the draft provisional agendas and documentation for the first sessions of the Commission on Science and Technology for Development and of the Committee on New and Renewable Sources of Energy and on Energy for Development and recommendations for the programme of work of the Committee on Natural Resources.

ECONOMIC AND SOCIAL COUNCIL ACTION (July)

On 31 July, Economic and Social Council adopted without vote **resolution 1992/62**.

Establishment of new subsidiary bodies of the Economic and Social Council

The Economic and Social Council,

Reaffirming General Assembly resolution 46/235 of 13 April 1992,

Reaffirming also its decision 1992/218 of 30 April 1992,

Taking note of the note by the Secretary-General on the proposed consolidated mandates of the new subsidiary bodies of the Council,

Bearing in mind that these new subsidiary bodies will contribute to the efforts of the international community towards sustainable development,

1. *Reaffirms* the mandates of the new subsidiary bodies, namely, the Commission on Science and Technology for Development, the Committee on Natural Resources and the Committee on New and Renewable Sources of Energy and on Energy for Development, as set forth in the relevant resolutions of the Economic and Social Council and the General Assembly, including General Assembly resolution 46/235;

2. *Approves* the draft provisional agendas and programmes of work for the first sessions of the new subsidiary bodies, as contained in the note by the Secretary-General;

3. *Requests* those bodies to make recommendations, at their first sessions, about their future work programmes, taking into account their respective mandates and the follow-up of the relevant provisions of Agenda 21 as may be approved by the General Assembly at its forty-seventh session;

4. *Invites* the General Assembly, in accordance with paragraph 9 of the annex to its resolution 46/235, to consider, at its forty-seventh session, any relevant institutional changes and recommendations made by the United Nations Conference on Trade and Development at its eighth session and by the United Nations Conference on Environment and Development regarding, in particular, the Committee on Natural Resources and the

Committee on New and Renewable Sources of Energy and on Energy for Development.

Economic and Social Council resolution 1992/62

31 July 1992   Meeting 42   Adopted without vote

Draft by Vice-President (E/1992/L.40), based on informal consultations on draft by Pakistan for Group of 77 (E/1992/L.32); agenda item 21.

REFERENCES

[1]GA res. 45/177, 19 Dec. 1990. [2]ESC res. 1990/69, 27 July 1990. [3]YUN 1991, p. 749, GA res. 45/264, 13 May 1991. [4]A/C.2/47/L.2. [5]YUN 1977, p. 438, GA res. 32/197, 20 Dec. 1977. [6]A/47/534. [7]E/1992/86. [8]E/1992/76.

Economic and Social Council

1992 sessions

Agendas

On 6 February, the Economic and Social Council adopted a five-item agenda for its organizational session,[1] on 29 April a three-item agenda[2] and on 28 May a two-item agenda for its resumed organizational session.[3]

On 7 February, by **decision 1992/205**, the Council approved the provisional agenda for its 1992 substantive session, including the high-level, operational activities and coordination segments. It also adopted the agenda of items for consideration by its Economic and Social Committees.

On 29 June, by **decision 1992/223**, the Council adopted the agenda for its 1992 substantive session and approved the organization of work.[4] On 30 June, it decided to consider under agenda item 2 on the adoption of the agenda and other organizational matters, the question of post-United Nations Conference on Environment and Development (UNCED) institutional arrangements, as requested in a 25 June letter to the Secretary-General from the United States.[5] On 6 July, it adopted the agenda and proposals for the organization of work for the high-level segment of its session.[4]

(For agenda lists, see APPENDIX IV.)

Resumption of organizational session

On 30 April, the Economic and Social Council adopted **decision 1992/219** without vote.

Resumption of the organizational session for 1992 of the Economic and Social Council

1. At its 7th plenary meeting, on 30 April 1992, the Economic and Social Council, in the spirit of the restructuring and revitalization of the United Nations in the economic, social and related fields, as provided for in General Assembly resolutions 45/264 of 13 May 1991 and 46/235 of 13 April 1992, and in response to the request of the Commission on Human Rights contained in Commission decision 1992/117 of 5 March 1992, decided, as an exceptional measure and without prejudice to the content of Assembly resolution 45/264, to

resume its organizational session on 28 and 29 May 1992 to assure the continued, timely and efficient functioning of its subsidiary bodies.

2. The Council, at its resumed organizational session, would consider and decide on provisional administrative measures related to the mandates adopted by the Commission on Human Rights at its forty-eighth session, which would apply on a temporary basis until the Council had taken a formal decision on those mandates at its substantive session of 1992, it being understood that the provisional administrative measures should not be construed or interpreted as a confirmation of the mandates and that the mandates could not be confirmed before the Council held a substantive discussion on them.

3. The Council stressed that that decision had been taken on the clear understanding that it responded to the requirements of an exceptional situation resulting from the reorganization of its work. It was thus understood that the decision should by no means constitute a precedent and that it was the intention of the Council to ensure that, in the future, administrative arrangements for the implementation of activities related to Council mandates had to be initiated after, and on the basis of, substantive consideration and express approval of each specific mandate by the Council. It was agreed that the need for strictly observing that practice would be of paramount concern in the organization of all future work of the Council and of its subsidiary bodies, in accordance with General Assembly resolution 45/264.

4. Provisional administrative arrangements decided upon by the Council at its resumed organizational session to facilitate the activities of special rapporteurs/representatives and working groups would be automatically terminated if their corresponding mandates were not confirmed by the Council at its substantive session of 1992.

5. The Council, at its resumed organizational session, would consider and decide on the regional allocation of seats in the three subsidiary bodies which the General Assembly in its resolution 46/235 had requested it to establish, namely, the Commission on Science and Technology for Development, the Committee on Natural Resources and the Committee on New and Renewable Sources of Energy and on Energy for Development.

6. The Council decided that nothing contained in the present decision was to be considered in any way to prejudge or determine the substantive discussion of human rights, including the question of mandates, to be held at the substantive session of 1992 of the Council.

7. The Council also decided to consider, at its resumed organizational session, subjects that merited urgent consideration, referred to it by its other subsidiary bodies.

Economic and Social Council decision 1992/219

Adopted without vote

Draft by Vice-President (E/1992/L.19), orally revised; agenda item 2.

Substantive session

Work programme

ECONOMIC AND SOCIAL COUNCIL ACTION

In April, the Council adopted **decision 1992/217** without vote.

Programme of work for the substantive session of 1992 of the Economic and Social Council

I

Programme of work of the Council

At its 7th plenary meeting, on 30 April 1992, the Economic and Social Council, having reviewed the preparations for its substantive session of 1992, decided that, as an exceptional measure and without prejudice to the content of General Assembly resolution 45/264 of 13 May 1991, the programme of work for the substantive session should be as follows:

29 June	Opening of the session and adoption of the agenda
30 June-2 July	Committee segment (Economic and Social Committees)
6-8 July	High-level segment
9-10 and 13-14 July	Coordination segment
15-17 July	Operational activities segment Committee segment (Social Committee)
20-24 and 27-28 July	Committee segment (Economic and Social Committees)
29-30 July	Plenary meetings
31 July	Conclusion of the work of the Council

II

High-level segment of the Economic and Social Council

The Economic and Social Council decided that:

(*a*) The meeting of 6 July would be reserved for statements by Ministers and other high-level representatives;

(*b*) The one-day policy dialogue with executive heads of multilateral financial and trade institutions of the United Nations system would take place on 7 July and executive heads would be requested to circulate their statements beforehand;

(*c*) Heads of delegation would be requested to make no more than three interventions of no longer than five minutes each during the three-day period, and would be requested to circulate their main statements beforehand. A press conference or briefing session with the media would be organized for heads of delegation who desire it;

(*d*) The high-level segment would take place in the Economic and Social Council Chamber, which was a suitable venue for round-table discussions and dialogue among the participants. Throughout the segment, the President of the Council would be expected to take a leading role in stimulating interaction among the participants, summarizing the discussions as they progressed and initiating the successive stages of the dialogue.

III

Coordination segment of the Economic and Social Council

The Economic and Social Council, recalling its decision 1992/204 of 7 February 1992 on the coordination segment of the Council of 1992, decided that:

(*a*) The Bureau, with the assistance of the Secretariat, would identify a number of executive heads of specialized agencies and other bodies of the United Nations

system who would be specifically invited to take part in the discussion of the two themes to be considered under the segment. The President of the Council would then address a personal invitation to the executive heads concerned;

(*b*) Executive heads would be requested to have their statements circulated beforehand;

(*c*) The segment would begin with précis presentations of the statements of the executive heads most concerned with the subject-matter; their remarks would focus on the theme at hand;

(*d*) Executive heads would be encouraged to identify coordination problems in the course of their interventions, including problems created by a lack of adequate coordination within Governments at the national level;

(*e*) Without prejudice to the rights of all States to participate in the discussion, the regional and interest groups represented at the Council would be encouraged to select from among their number "discussion leaders" to undertake the necessary research work on the themes under discussion;

(*f*) The segment would conclude with recommendations to the organizations of the United Nations system related to the two themes under discussion.

Economic and Social Council decision 1992/217

Adopted without vote

Draft by Acting President (E/1992/L.17), based on informal consultations; agenda item 2.

Segments of substantive session

In 1991,[6] the General Assembly had decided that the substantive session of the Council should contain a high-level segment of four days open to all Member States, with ministerial participation, devoted to the consideration of major economic and/or social policy themes. It should further include a segment on coordination of the activities of United Nations agencies, organizations and bodies. Also included should be an operational activities segment of two to three days, focusing in particular on follow-up of policy recommendations and decisions of the Assembly and coordination of operational activities on a system-wide basis; and a committee segment devoted to consideration of specific economic, social and related issues in two separate committees to consider and take decisions on reports of subsidiary bodies of the Council.

In 1992, the operational activities segment did not result in policy recommendations and the experience of the committee segment suggested strongly, according to the Secretary-General in his October report[7] on restructuring and revitalizing the United Nations in the economic, social and related fields (see above), that further consideration needed to be given to the agenda before the Council's Economic and Social Committees as well as to their methods of work.

High-level segment

The Economic and Social Council, by **decision 1992/203** of 7 February 1992, decided that the high-level segment of its substantive session should be devoted to the consideration of the following major theme: ''Enhancing international cooperation for development: the role of the United Nations system''; that, without prejudice to the provisions of the 1991 General Assembly resolution on the restructuring and revitalization of the United Nations in the economic, social and related fields,[6] the duration of the high-level segment with ministerial participation should be one to three days; and to invite the Secretary-General to provide his views and recommendations on the selected theme. By **decision 1992/205** of the same date, the Council approved the provisional agenda for the high-level segment of 1992.

On 6 July, by **decision 1992/223**, the Council adopted the agenda and proposals for the organization of work for the high-level segment.

In his October report on restructuring and revitalizing the United Nations in the economic, social and related fields,[7] the Secretary-General stated that the Council's first experiment with holding a high-level segment had been successful, but in order to enhance its value, it might be necessary to devote less time to formal statements and more time to debate. Statements should be circulated in advance and it would seem best to continue to limit the segment to one theme. A consensus emerged that the subject of the role of the United Nations system in enhancing economic cooperation for development needed to be pursued (see PART THREE Chapter I); an Ad Hoc Open-Ended Working Group was established to continue deliberations on the matter.

Coordination segment

On 7 February, by **decision 1992/204**, the Economic and Social Council decided that its coordination segment in 1992 should be devoted to coordinating the policies and activities of the specialized agencies and other United Nations bodies related to the following themes—assistance in the eradication of poverty and support to vulnerable groups, and prevention and control of human immunodeficiency virus/acquired immunodeficiency syndrome (HIV/AIDS) and programmes addressed to the mitigation of its negative socio-economic consequences—and decided to request the President of the Council and other members of the Bureau to finalize arrangements for the coordination segment on the basis of consultations with members of the Council.

In accordance with the 1991 Assembly resolution on restructuring and revitalizing the United Nations,[6] the Secretary-General presented to the Council in 1992 a report on each of the two themes[8] selected for the Council's 1992 coordination segment. Although the Council did not adopt formal recommendations as a result of its discussions on the segment, the President on his own authority made statements on both themes which contained recommendations in a number of areas to be forwarded to the governing bodies of the organizations of the United Nations system for review. As the President's statements did not reflect a formal conclusion of the Council, the Secretary-General said in his October report on restructuring and revitalization of the United Nations in the economic, social and related fields,[7] the outcome of the coordination segment was not as authoritative as it might have otherwise been.

Report for 1992

The work of the Economic and Social Council at its organizational, resumed organizational and substantive sessions in 1992 was summarized in its report to the General Assembly.[9]

On 18 December, on the recommendation of the Third (Social, Humanitarian and Cultural) Committee, the Assembly adopted **decision 47/433**, by which it took note of chapters I, V (sections B, C, E, F and H), VII and IX of the Council's report. On 23 December, the Assembly adopted two decisions by which it took note of the chapters of the report as follows: chapters I, V (sections B to D) and IX, on the recommendation of the Fifth (Administrative and Budgetary) Committee (**decision 47/461**), and chapters I, V (sections C and G), VIII and IX (**decision 47/462**).

Cooperation with other organizations

Non-governmental organizations

NGO Unit

Report of the Secretary-General (June). In response to a 1991 General Assembly request,[10] the Secretary-General submitted a June 1992 report to the Economic and Social Council,[11] in which he reviewed the conditions necessary for the effective functioning of the Non-Governmental Organizations (NGO) Unit of the United Nations Department of Economic and Social Development. The Unit acted as substantive secretariat of the Committee on NGOs and of related meetings. It also assisted the Committee and the Council in implementing the 1968 Council resolution on arrangements for consultations with NGOs[12] and acted as the focal point within the Secretariat for providing advice and information to Secretariat officials, the United Nations system, Member States and outside users, with regard to NGOs. In 1991, the Committee on NGOs had strongly recommended an urgent review of the grave situation with regard to the staff resources of the Unit in view of the ever-expanding volume of documentation and the constant increase in the number of NGOs in consultative status with the Council, which resulted in extended demands on the Unit.[13]

In his report, the Secretary-General examined the functions of the Unit, its increased workload and existing staff resources. He suggested that a discussion of the matter by the Council would be useful in defining the means for ensuring the Unit's effective functioning.

ECONOMIC AND SOCIAL COUNCIL ACTION

On 30 July 1992, the Economic and Social Council adopted without vote **resolution 1992/39**.

Review of the conditions necessary for the effective functioning of the Non-Governmental Organizations Unit of the Department of Economic and Social Development

The Economic and Social Council,

Having regard to Article 71 of the Charter of the United Nations which provides that the Economic and Social Council may make suitable arrangements for consultation with non-governmental organizations which are concerned with matters within its competence,

Recalling General Assembly decision 46/431 of 17 December 1991,

Bearing in mind Economic and Social Council resolution 1296(XLIV) of 23 May 1968 containing arrangements for consultation with non-governmental organizations, paragraph 43 of which provides that the Secretariat should be so organized as to enable it to carry out the duties assigned to it concerning the consultative arrangements,

Considering the unique role played by the Non-Governmental Organizations Unit of the Department of Economic and Social Development of the Secretariat as the focal point for cooperation between the United Nations and the non-governmental organizations in consultative status with the Economic and Social Council,

Considering also the increasing importance of the role and activities of the non-governmental organizations in consultative status, particularly with regard to United Nations conferences and their related preparatory activities,

Having considered the report of the Secretary-General on the review of the conditions necessary for the effective functioning of the Non-Governmental Organizations Unit prepared in pursuance of General Assembly decision 46/431,

1. *Takes note with appreciation* of the report of the Secretary-General;

2. *Notes with concern* that, as documented in the report of the Secretary-General, the workload of the Non-Governmental Organizations Unit of the Department of Economic and Social Development of the Secretariat has consistently increased over the years, while resources have remained at the same level since 1947, when the Unit was established;

3. *Invites* the Secretary-General to respond to the needs of the Non-Governmental Organizations Unit and

to adopt appropriate measures, to the extent possible within existing resources during the biennium 1992-1993, to address the problems posed by the situation, in particular relating to the resources required for the Unit to carry out its functions effectively;

4. *Also invites* the Secretary-General to submit to the General Assembly at its forty-seventh session a brief report on actions taken in 1992 and those planned for 1993 as short-term solutions to improve the situation of the Non-Governmental Organizations Unit;

5. *Requests* the Secretary-General to consider, to the extent possible within existing resources, increasing the human and financial resources of the Non-Governmental Organizations Unit in order to enable it to fulfil its mandate under Economic and Social Council resolution 1296(XLIV) within the framework of the proposed programme budget for the biennium 1994-1995;

6. *Also requests* the Secretary-General to submit a report on the implementation of the present resolution to the Economic and Social Council at its substantive session of 1993, through the Committee on Non-Governmental Organizations.

Economic and Social Council resolution 1992/39

30 July 1992   Meeting 41   Adopted without vote

29-nation draft (E/1992/L.30), orally amended; agenda item 2.

Sponsors: Belgium, Bulgaria, Burundi, Chile, Costa Rica, Cuba, Cyprus, Denmark, Ethiopia, Finland, France, Greece, Hungary, Iceland, Iraq, Ireland, Japan, Lesotho, Libyan Arab Jamahiriya, Morocco, Netherlands, Nicaragua, Norway, Oman, Philippines, Russian Federation, Sudan, Sweden, Tunisia.

Report of the Secretary-General (November). In response to the Council's July resolution, the Secretary-General submitted a November report to the General Assembly on the functioning of the NGO Unit.[14] He said he had given careful consideration to the request to respond to the Unit's needs and adopt measures during the biennium 1992-1993 to address its problems. He had decided to allocate to the Unit, through redeployment of existing resources, one Professional post at the P-2 level and one General Service post, thus augmenting its resources by 33 per cent. With those additional resources, the Unit should be able to cope with its responsibilities more effectively in the future.

By **decision 47/433** of 18 December 1992, the Assembly took note of the Secretary-General's report.

Request from NGOs for hearings

The Committee on NGOs met in New York on 25 June 1992 to hear requests from NGOs in consultative status, category I, to address the Economic and Social Council or its sessional committees in connection with items on the Council's agenda. The Committee recommended that 14 NGOs be heard.[15] The Council approved their requests on 29 June, by **decision 1992/223**.

Intergovernmental organizations

Regional Organization for Protection of the Marine Environment

On 22 July, the Economic and Social Council, by **decision 1992/265** on the participation of intergovernmental organizations in its work, decided that the Regional Organization for the Protection of the Marine Environment might participate on a continuing basis, without the right to vote, in Council deliberations on questions within the scope of its activities.

Other organizational matters

Amendments to rules of procedure

On 7 February, the Economic and Social Council adopted **resolution 1992/2** without vote.

Amendments to the rules of procedure of the Economic and Social Council

The Economic and Social Council

Adopts the following amendments to the rules of procedure of the Council:

(*a*) Replace rule 1 by the following text:

"Organizational and substantive sessions
"Rule 1

"The Council shall normally hold an organizational session and one substantive session each year."

(*b*) Replace rule 2 by the following text:

"Dates of convening and adjournment
"Rule 2

"Subject to rule 3, and following a meeting early in the year for the purpose of electing the President and the Bureau, the organizational session shall be convened on the first Tuesday in February and resumed at the end of April. The substantive session shall take place between May and July and shall be adjourned at least six weeks before the opening of the regular session of the General Assembly."

(*c*) Replace rule 9, paragraphs 1 and 4, by the following text:

"Drawing up of the provisional agenda
"Rule 9

"1. The Secretary-General shall draw up the provisional agenda for each session of the Council. He shall submit to the Council:

"(*a*) The provisional agenda for the organizational session at least three weeks in advance of the opening of that session;

"(*b*) The provisional agenda for the substantive session at the organizational session.

"4. The agenda for the organizational session shall include the consideration of the provisional agenda for the substantive session of the Council."

Economic and Social Council resolution 1992/2

7 February 1992   Meeting 3   Adopted without vote

Draft by President (E/1992/L.11); agenda item 2.

Election of the Bureau

On 29 April, by **decision 1992/215**, the Economic and Social Council deferred consideration of the item on the election of its Bureau until its substantive session. On 29 June, the Council elected Poland Council President to replace Yugoslavia which had been elected President on 27 January but had resigned.

Calendar of meetings

On 7 February, by **decision 1992/214**, the Economic and Social Council, taking note of a provision of a 1991 General Assembly resolution on the pattern of conferences,[16] granted authority to its Bureau to approve inter-sessional departures from its approved calendar of conferences and meetings in respect of its subsidiary bodies when the Council was not in session and after consultation with the Committee on Conferences.

Summary records

On 30 July, by **decision 1992/288**, the Economic and Social Council decided to discontinue, from 1993, summary records for its sessional committees, the regional commissions and the following other subsidiary bodies: Commission for Social Development; Commission on the Status of Women; Commission on Narcotic Drugs; Commission on Science and Technology for Development; Commission on Crime Prevention and Criminal Justice; Committee on NGOs; Committee on Natural Resources; Committee for Programme and Coordination; Commission on Transnational Corporations; and Committee on New and Renewable Sources of Energy and on Energy for Development.

1993 work programme

By **decision 1992/209** of 7 February, the Economic and Social Council took note of a list of questions for inclusion in its programme of work for 1993: major policy themes (environment and development, population, development and socio-economic indicators) and items for the substantive session, including programme and coordination questions; operational activities for development; regional cooperation; development and international economic cooperation; special economic, humanitarian and disaster relief assistance; the International Decade for Natural Disaster Reduction (1990-2000); NGOs; human rights; advancement of women; social development; the world social situation; and narcotic drugs.

REFERENCES

[1]E/1992/2 & Add.1. [2]E/1992/36. [3]E/1992/56. [4]E/1992/100. [5]E/1992/90. [6]YUN 1991, p. 749, GA res. 45/264, 13 May 1991. [7]A/47/534. [8]E/1992/47, E/1992/67. [9]A/47/3/Rev.1. [10]YUN 1991, p. 772, GA dec. 46/431, 17 Dec. 1991.

(11)E/1992/63. (12)YUN 1968, p. 647, ESC res.1296 (XLIV), 23 May 1968. (13)YUN 1991, p. 763. (14)A/C.3/47/13. (15)E/1992/89. (16)YUN 1991, p. 915, GA res. 46/190, 20 Dec. 1991.

Coordination in the UN system

ACC activities

In 1992, the Administrative Committee on Coordination (ACC) reviewed its methods of work and functioning in the context of the new challenges which the 1990s posed for international cooperation and the need to strengthen policy coordination at both national and international levels.[1] It agreed on a number of guidelines. The Secretary-General would submit for discussion by ACC any programme or proposal of a general or system-wide nature and would keep the Economic and Social Council and specialized agencies fully apprised of the outcome of consultations held with the agencies concerned. Members of ACC would carry out the necessary consultations within the ACC framework when launching, on their own initiative, an operation requiring contributions by its members. They would convey to their deliberative organs major initiatives within the United Nations system of particular relevance to their organizations. ACC also agreed on measures to improve its working procedures.

ACC further extensively discussed follow-up to UNCED, held in June 1992, with particular focus on Agenda 21 (see PART THREE, Chapter VIII). It established a Task Force on Environment and Development, under the chairmanship of the Director-General of the Food and Agricultural Organization of the United Nations, to prepare proposals for follow-up. On the Task Force's recommendation, ACC decided to establish an Inter-Agency Committee on Sustainable Development to identify major policy issues relating to UNCED follow-up. The Inter-Agency Committee was to hold its first meeting in 1993.

With the assistance of its Consultative Committee on Substantive Questions (Operational Activities) (CCSQ/OPS), ACC focused on improving the effectiveness of operational activities for development (see PART THREE, Chapter II), with emphasis on field coordination.

Among other issues discussed by ACC were the implications for the United Nations system of the economic and social changes in Eastern and Central Europe and the Russian Federation. An Inter-Agency Task Force on the New Independent States was established in early 1992.

During the year, ACC held two regular sessions (Geneva, 8-10 April, New York, 20-21 October). Its principal subsidiary bodies met as follows:

Organizational Committee (New York, 10-13 February, Geneva, 25-27 March, 7 and 10 April, New York, 16 and 17 July, 14-16 and 21 and 22 October); CCSQ (Programme Matters) (PROG) (Geneva, 9-11 March); Consultative Committee on Administrative Questions (CCAQ) (Financial and Budgetary Questions) (FB) (Geneva, 9-13 March, New York, 31 August-4 September); CCAQ (Personnel and General Administrative Questions (PER) (Geneva, 9-11 March, London, 6-10 July); Joint Meeting of CCSQ (PROG) and CCAQ (FB) (Geneva, 11 March); CCSQ (OPS) (Geneva, 16-19 March; New York, 22-25 September).

Bodies on specific subjects met as follows:

Inter-Agency Group on New and Renewable Sources of Energy, eleventh session (New York, 3 and 4 February); Subcommittee on Nutrition, nineteenth session (Rome, 24-29 February); ACC Task Force on Long-term Development Objectives, twenty-first session (Geneva, 3-6 March); second Ad Hoc Inter-Agency Meeting on the International Year of the Family (Vienna, 5 and 6 March); sixteenth Ad Hoc Inter-Agency Meeting on Women (Vienna, 9 and 10 March); Subcommittee on Statistical Activities, twenty-sixth session (Geneva, 6-10 April); Ad Hoc Inter-Agency Meeting on Coordination in Matters of International Drug Abuse Control (Vienna, 16 April, 14-16 September); ACC Task Force on Rural Development, twentieth meeting (New York, 22-24 April); Ad Hoc Inter-Agency Working Group on Demographic Estimates and Projections, seventeenth session (Rome, 23-25 June); second Inter-Agency Consultation on the Follow-up to the Programme of Action for the Least Developed Countries for the 1990s (Geneva, 25 and 26 June); ACC Ad Hoc Task Force for the International Conference on Population and Development, 1994 (New York, 6 July 1992); Joint United Nations Information Committee, eighteenth session (Rome, 7-9 July); Ad Hoc Inter-Agency Meeting on Outer Space Activities (Paris, 5-7 October); ACC Intersecretariat Group for Water Resources, thirteenth session (New York, 7-9 October); ACC Task Force on Science and Technology for Development, thirteenth session (30 November-2 December); and tenth Inter-Agency Meeting on the United Nations Decade of Disabled Persons (Vienna, 7-10 December).

Report for 1991

The ACC annual overview report for 1991[2] was considered on 11 and 12 May 1992 by the Committee for Programme and Coordination (CPC),[3] which welcomed ACC's intention to review its role and functioning, including the functioning of its subsidiary machinery, and stressed the importance of field-level coordination and of the need to improve inter-agency coordination further. Emphasizing that the purpose of ACC's annual overview report was to enable both Member States and ACC to identify and overcome system-wide coordination problems, CPC said a more analytical and forward-looking report was necessary. It also regretted the late issuance of some ACC documentation.

CPC activities

During 1992, CPC met in New York for an organizational meeting on 10 April, for its thirty-second session from 11 to 22 May and for its resumed thirty-second session from 31 August to 18 September.[3]

The Committee reviewed its work programme and suggestions on the timing and duration of its session. It considered the programme performance of the United Nations for the biennium 1990-1991; proposed revisions to the medium-term plan for 1992-1997; coordination questions; and reports of the Joint Inspection Unit.

It also considered questions related to the programme budget for the biennium 1992-1993; an outline of the proposed programme budget for 1994-1995; and the methodology for preparing the programme budget (see PART SIX, Chapter I).

ECONOMIC AND SOCIAL COUNCIL ACTION

On 31 July, by **decision 1992/302**, the Economic and Social Council took note of the report of CPC on the first part of its thirty-second session[3] and endorsed its recommendations. It also took note of the annual overview report of ACC for 1991[2] and of the report of the Chairmen of CPC and ACC on the twenty-sixth series of Joint Meetings of the two Committees held in October 1991.[4]

GENERAL ASSEMBLY ACTION

By **resolution 47/214, section IV**, the General Assembly emphasized the need for enhanced coor-

dination in the United Nations system; endorsed CPC's recommendations on the annual overview report of ACC for 1991; and took note of CPC's decision to propose to ACC that the twenty-seventh series of the Joint Meetings of CPC and ACC, tentatively scheduled for 1993, discuss the results of UNCED and their implications for the United Nations system.

By **decision 47/458**, the Assembly decided that CPC should meet for one week in May 1993 and for three weeks in August/September 1993.

REFERENCES

[1]E/1993/81. [2]E/1992/11 & Add.1,2. [3]A/47/16. [4]YUN 1991, p. 763.

Other institutional questions

Work programmes of the Second and Third Committees of the General Assembly

The General Assembly, on 18 December 1992, by **decision 47/432**, approved the organization of work of the Third Committee and its draft biennial programme of work for 1993-1994. On 22 December 1992, by **decision 47/440**, the Assembly decided to defer further consideration of the draft biennial programme of work for the Second (Economic and Financial) Committee for 1993-1994.

PART FOUR

Trusteeship and decolonization

Chapter I

Questions relating to decolonization

During 1992, the United Nations continued its efforts to eliminate colonialism in all its forms and manifestations. The General Assembly's Special Committee on the Situation with regard to the Implementation of the Declaration on the Granting of Independence to Colonial Countries and Peoples (the Committee on colonial countries) held its session in New York (5 February–1 June and 20 July–7 August), at which it considered various aspects of the implementation of the 1960 Declaration on the Granting of Independence to Colonial Countries and Peoples. The Committee examined decolonization in general as well as individual Non-Self-Governing Territories.

1960 Declaration on colonial countries

The United Nations, in 1992, reaffirmed the 1960 Declaration on the Granting of Independence to Colonial Countries and Peoples[1] as the basis for the decolonization process.

Plan of Action for the Decade for the Eradication of Colonialism

In accordance with the Plan of Action adopted by the General Assembly in 1991[2] for the Decade for the Eradication of Colonialism (1990-2000), which the Assembly had declared in 1988,[3] the Committee on colonial countries organized a seminar in the Caribbean region to review the special development needs of island territories (St. George's, Grenada, 17-19 June 1992). The seminar was attended by representatives from the Non-Self-Governing Territories (NSGTs) of Bermuda, British Virgin Islands, Montserrat, Turks and Caicos Islands and United States Virgin Islands and focused on a broad range of economic and social conditions, including: problems of small, structurally open economies; food production; tourism development; development of offshore financial centres; drug trafficking and money laundering; development of financial management expertise; industrial development; human resources development; environmental issues; disaster preparedness and relief; the role of specialized agencies, international and regional organizations in economic and social development;

and the provision of technical assistance. It also considered regional cooperation concerning the preservation and protection of marine resources from over-exploitation; sea and air transport; higher education; research and development; and regional pooling arrangements for sharing special skills and expertise. On 19 June, the seminar adopted a final document summarizing its discussions and recommendations which was contained in the Committee's report on the seminar.[4] The seminar's guidelines and rules of procedure were contained in a separate report to the Committee on colonial countries.[5]

On 4 August,[6] the Working Group of the Committee on colonial countries decided to recommend to the Committee that the conclusions and recommendations of the seminar be taken into account in considering the situation in the Caribbean Territories. Noting that the Plan of Action for the Decade provided for the holding of seminars in the Caribbean and Pacific regions alternately, the Working Group decided to recommend that the Committee organize a seminar in the Pacific region in 1993 to consider issues relating to the Trust and Non-Self-Governing Territories. The Working Group further decided to recommend that the Committee invite United Nations organs, agencies and institutions to inform the Secretary-General of actions taken in implementing a 1991 Assembly resolution relating to the Plan of Action.[2] The Committee on colonial countries approved those recommendations without objection.[7]

Committee on colonial countries

The Committee on colonial countries held its 1992 session in two parts, with a total of 14 meetings from 5 February to 1 June and from 20 July to 7 August in New York,[7] at which it considered aspects of the implementation of the 1960 Declaration. It considered the reports of its Working Group,[6] a report of an open-ended Working Group on improving the efficiency of the Committee's work[8] and five reports of the newly merged Subcommittee on Small Territories, Petitions, Information and Assistance (formerly the Subcommittee on Small Territories and the Subcommittee on Petitions, Information and Assistance) on the dissemination of information on decolonization,[9] examination of petitions,[10] Pitcairn,[11] St. Helena,[12] and 10 other small Territories.[13]

In February,[14] the United States informed the General Assembly that it had decided to suspend its cooperation with the Special Committee, claiming that it had focused on an outmoded agenda instead of new approaches aimed at addressing the specific needs of the few remaining NSGTs.

Implementation of the Declaration

GENERAL ASSEMBLY ACTION

On 25 November 1992, the General Assembly adopted **resolution 47/23** by recorded vote.

Implementation of the Declaration on the Granting of Independence to Colonial Countries and Peoples

The General Assembly,

Having examined the report of the Special Committee on the Situation with regard to the Implementation of the Declaration on the Granting of Independence to Colonial Countries and Peoples,

Recalling its resolution 1514(XV) of 14 December 1960, containing the Declaration on the Granting of Independence to Colonial Countries and Peoples, and all its previous resolutions concerning the implementation of the Declaration, most recently resolution 46/71 of 11 December 1991, as well as the relevant resolutions of the Security Council,

Recognizing that the eradication of colonialism is one of the priorities of the Organization for the decade that began in 1990,

Deeply conscious of the need to take, speedily, measures to eliminate the last vestiges of colonialism by the year 2000, as called for in its resolution 43/47 of 22 November 1988,

Reiterating its conviction of the need for the elimination of colonialism, as well as of the need for the total eradication of racial discrimination, apartheid and violations of basic human rights,

Conscious that the success of national liberation struggles and the resultant international situation have provided the international community with a unique opportunity to make a decisive contribution towards the elimination of colonialism in all its forms and manifestations,

Noting with satisfaction the achievements of the Special Committee in contributing to the effective and complete implementation of the Declaration and other relevant resolutions of the United Nations on decolonization,

Stressing the importance of the participation of the administering Powers in the work of the Special Committee,

Noting also with satisfaction the cooperation and active participation of some administering Powers in the work of the Special Committee, as well as their continued readiness to receive United Nations visiting missions in the Territories under their administration,

Noting with concern the negative impact which the non-participation of certain administering Powers has had on the work of the Special Committee, depriving it of an important source of information on the Territories under their administration,

Aware of the pressing need of newly independent and emerging States for assistance from the United Nations and its system of organizations in the economic, social and other fields,

Aware also of the pressing need of the remaining Non-Self-Governing Territories, including particularly the small island Territories, for economic, social and other assistance from the United Nations and the organizations within its system,

1. *Reaffirms* its resolution 1514(XV) and all other resolutions on decolonization, including its resolution 43/47 in which it declared the decade that began in 1990 as the International Decade for the Eradication of Colonialism, and calls upon the administering Powers, in accordance with those resolutions, to take all necessary steps to enable the peoples of the Territories concerned to exercise fully as soon as possible their right to self-determination and independence;

2. *Affirms once again* that the continuation of colonialism in any form or manifestation—including racism, apartheid and economic exploitation, as well as policies and practices to suppress legitimate national liberation movements—is incompatible with the Charter of the United Nations, the Universal Declaration of Human Rights and the Declaration on the Granting of Independence to Colonial Countries and Peoples and poses a threat to international peace and security;

3. *Reaffirms its determination* to continue to take all steps necessary to bring about the complete and speedy eradication of colonialism and the faithful and strict observance by all States of the relevant provisions of the Charter, the Declaration on the Granting of Independence to Colonial Countries and Peoples and the Universal Declaration of Human Rights;

4. *Affirms once again* its support for the struggle of the peoples under colonial rule to exercise their right to self-determination and independence;

5. *Approves* the report of the Special Committee on the Situation with regard to the Implementation of the Declaration on the Granting of Independence to Colonial Countries and Peoples covering its work during 1992, including the programme of work envisaged for 1993;

6. *Calls upon* all States, in particular the administering Powers, as well as the specialized agencies and other organizations of the United Nations system, to give effect within their respective spheres of competence to the recommendations of the Special Committee for the speedy implementation of the Declaration and other relevant resolutions of the United Nations;

7. *Condemns* the activities of those foreign economic and other interests which impede the implementation of the Declaration as well as the elimination of colonialism, apartheid and racial discrimination;

8. *Calls upon* the administering Powers to ensure that no activity of foreign economic and other interests in the Non-Self-Governing Territories under their administration hinders the peoples of those Territories from exercising their right to self-determination and independence;

9. *Strongly condemns* any nuclear collaboration with the Government of South Africa and calls upon any States that are so involved to cease all such collaboration forthwith;

10. *Calls upon* the administering Powers to terminate military activities in the Territories under their administration and to eliminate military bases there in compliance with the relevant resolutions of the General Assembly and urges them not to involve those Territories in any offensive acts or interference against other States;

11. *Urges* all States, directly and through their action in the specialized agencies and other organizations of the United Nations system, to provide moral and material assistance to the peoples of colonial Territories and requests that the administering Powers, in consultation with the Governments of the Territories under their administration, take steps to enlist and make effective use of all possible assistance, on both a bilateral and a multilateral basis, in the strengthening of the economies of those Territories;

12. *Requests* the Special Committee to continue to seek suitable means for the immediate and full implementation of the Declaration and to carry out those actions approved by the General Assembly regarding the International Decade for the Eradication of Colonialism in all Territories that have not yet attained independence and, in particular:

(a) To formulate specific proposals for the elimination of the remaining manifestations of colonialism and to report thereon to the General Assembly at its forty-eighth session;

(b) To make concrete suggestions which could assist the Security Council in considering appropriate measures under the Charter with regard to developments in colonial Territories that are likely to threaten international peace and security;

(c) To continue to examine the compliance of Member States with resolution 1514(XV) and other relevant resolutions on decolonization;

(d) To continue to pay special attention to the small Territories, in particular through the dispatch of regular visiting missions, and to recommend to the General Assembly the most suitable steps to be taken to enable the populations of those Territories to exercise their right to self-determination and independence;

(e) To take all necessary steps to enlist world-wide support among Governments, as well as national and international organizations, for the achievement of the objectives of the Declaration and the implementation of the relevant resolutions of the United Nations;

13. *Also calls upon* the administering Powers to continue to cooperate with the Special Committee in the discharge of its mandate and to receive visiting missions to the Territories to secure first-hand information and ascertain the wishes and aspirations of their inhabitants;

14. *Further calls upon* the administering Powers that have not participated in the work of the Special Committee to do so at its 1993 session;

15. *Requests* the Secretary-General, the specialized agencies and other organizations of the United Nations system to provide economic, social and other assistance to the Non-Self-Governing Territories and to continue to do so, as appropriate, after they exercise their right to self-determination and independence;

16. *Requests* the Secretary-General to provide the Special Committee with the facilities and services required for the implementation of the present resolution, as well as of the other resolutions and decisions on decolonization adopted by the General Assembly and the Special Committee.

General Assembly resolution 47/23

25 November 1992   Meeting 72   127-2-22 (recorded vote)

16-nation draft (A/47/L.17 & Add.1); agenda item 18.
Sponsors: Algeria, Barbados, Cuba, Grenada, India, Libyan Arab Jamahiriya, Marshall Islands, Micronesia, Namibia, Papua New Guinea, Sierra Leone, Solomon Islands, Tunisia, United Republic of Tanzania, Vanuatu, Zimbabwe.

Financial implications. 5th Committee, A/47/711; S-G, A/C.5/47/48.
Meeting numbers. GA 47th session: 5th Committee 31; plenary 61, 72.

Recorded vote in Assembly as follows:

In favour: Afghanistan, Albania, Algeria, Angola, Antigua and Barbuda, Argentina, Australia, Austria, Bahamas, Bahrain, Bangladesh, Barbados, Belize, Benin, Bolivia, Bosnia and Herzegovina, Botswana, Brazil, Brunei Darussalam, Burkina Faso, Cameroon, Central African Republic, Chad, Chile, China, Colombia, Costa Rica, Côte d'Ivoire, Cuba, Cyprus, Democratic People's Republic of Korea, Denmark, Djibouti, Ecuador, Egypt, El Salvador, Ethiopia, Fiji, Gabon, Ghana, Greece, Grenada, Guatemala, Guinea, Guinea-Bissau, Guyana, Haiti, Iceland, India, Indonesia, Iran, Iraq, Ireland, Jamaica, Japan, Kenya, Kuwait, Lao People's Democratic Republic, Latvia, Lebanon, Libyan Arab Jamahiriya, Liechtenstein, Lithuania, Madagascar, Malaysia, Maldives, Mali, Malta, Marshall Islands, Mauritania, Mauritius, Mexico, Micronesia, Mongolia, Morocco, Mozambique, Myanmar, Namibia, Nepal, New Zealand, Nicaragua, Niger, Nigeria, Norway, Oman, Pakistan, Panama, Papua New Guinea, Paraguay, Peru, Philippines, Poland, Portugal, Qatar, Republic of Korea, Rwanda, Saint Kitts and Nevis, Saint Lucia, Saint Vincent and the Grenadines, Samoa, Sao Tome and Principe, Saudi Arabia, Senegal, Seychelles, Sierra Leone, Singapore, Spain, Sri Lanka, Sudan, Suriname, Swaziland, Sweden, Syrian Arab Republic, Thailand, Togo, Trinidad and Tobago, Tunisia, Uganda, United Arab Emirates, United Republic of Tanzania, Uruguay, Vanuatu, Venezuela, Viet Nam, Yemen, Zambia, Zimbabwe.

Against: United Kingdom, United States.

Abstaining: Belarus, Belgium, Bulgaria, Canada, Czechoslovakia, Estonia, Finland, France, Germany, Hungary, Israel, Italy, Kazakhstan, Lesotho, Luxembourg, Netherlands, Republic of Moldova, Romania, Russian Federation, Slovenia, Turkey, Ukraine.

Implementation by international organizations

Reports of the Secretary-General. In response to a General Assembly request of 1991,[15] the Secretary-General submitted a June report with a later addendum[16] containing summaries of information submitted by five specialized agencies on action taken to implement the Declaration.

In November,[17] the Secretary-General submitted a report on cooperation and coordination of specialized agencies and international institutions associated with the United Nations in their assistance to NSGTs, as requested by the Assembly in 1991.[18] He discussed their participation in the Assembly's Fourth (Decolonization) Committee, cooperation and coordination among them and action taken by the Governing Council of the United Nations Development Programme (UNDP). The Secretary-General noted that the UNDP Governing Council, on 14 February 1992, had approved the extension of the first country programme for Anguilla[19] and on 26 May had approved the second country programme for Anguilla, the third country programmes for Montserrat and Tokelau and the fifth multi-island programme for countries of the Eastern Caribbean, including Anguilla, the British Virgin Islands and Montserrat.[20] On the same date, the Council noted extensions of the second country programmes for the British Virgin Islands, the Cayman Islands and the Turks and Caicos Islands and of the intercountry programme for Latin America and the Caribbean. The Secretary-General's report contained tables presenting an overview of the assistance extended in 1991 by the specialized agencies and international institutions associated with the United Nations to non-Member countries, including NSGTs, as well as UNDP indicative planning figures from 1972 to

1996 for NSGTs in Asia and the Pacific and Latin America and the Caribbean.

Report of the Acting President of the Economic and Social Council. In a June report,[21] the Acting President of the Economic and Social Council presented an overview of continuing consultations with the Chairman of the Committee on colonial countries and the Chairman of the Special Committee against Apartheid on the implementation of the Declaration by the United Nations system. While drawing attention to the extremely fragile economies of the small island Territories, the Acting President appealed to the specialized agencies and other organizations concerned to expand and increase their assistance programmes to all Trust and Non-Self-Governing Territories. Consultations between the Chairman of the Special Committee against Apartheid and the Acting President focused on recent developments in South Africa and action taken by the international community. The Chairman said that strengthened assistance to disadvantaged segments of the society was crucial in preparing South Africans to fully participate in rebuilding their country. The Chairman and the Acting President considered that a large trained cadre of black South Africans would play a critical role in facilitating a smooth transition to a post-apartheid society.

In July,[22] the Chairman of the Committee on colonial countries stated that his consultations with the Acting President on the topic were set out in the June report.[21]

ECONOMIC AND SOCIAL COUNCIL ACTION

On 31 July 1992, the Economic and Social Council adopted **resolution 1992/59** by recorded vote.

Implementation of the Declaration on the Granting of Independence to Colonial Countries and Peoples by the specialized agencies and the international institutions associated with the United Nations

The Economic and Social Council,

Having examined the report of the Secretary-General and the report of the Acting President of the Economic and Social Council on consultations held with the Chairman of the Special Committee on the Situation with regard to the Implementation of the Declaration on the Granting of Independence to Colonial Countries and Peoples and the Chairman of the Special Committee against Apartheid,

Having heard the statement made by the Chairman of the Special Committee on the Situation with regard to the Implementation of the Declaration on the Granting of Independence to Colonial Countries and Peoples,

Recalling General Assembly resolution 1514(XV) of 14 December 1960, containing the Declaration on the Granting of Independence to Colonial Countries and Peoples, and all other resolutions adopted by United Nations bodies on the subject, including in particular Economic and Social Council resolution 1991/68 of 26 July 1991,

Reaffirming the responsibility of the specialized agencies and other organizations of the United Nations system to take all effective measures, within their respective spheres of competence, to assist in the full and speedy implementation of the Declaration and other relevant resolutions of the United Nations bodies,

Recalling also General Assembly resolution S-16/1 of 14 December 1989, containing the Declaration on Apartheid and its Destructive Consequences in Southern Africa,

Recognizing that permanent peace and stability in southern Africa can only be achieved when the system of apartheid in South Africa has been eradicated and South Africa has been transformed into a united, democratic and non-racial country, and reiterating, therefore, that all the necessary measures should be adopted at the present time to bring a speedy end to the apartheid system in the interest of all the people of southern Africa, the African continent and the world at large,

Deeply concerned that the objectives of the Charter of the United Nations and the Declaration on the Granting of Independence to Colonial Countries and Peoples have not been fully achieved,

Bearing in mind the extremely fragile economies of the Non-Self-Governing small island Territories and their vulnerability to natural disasters, such as hurricanes and cyclones, and recalling relevant General Assembly resolutions,

Also bearing in mind the conclusions and recommendations of the Meeting of Governmental Experts of Island Developing Countries and Donor Countries and Organizations, held in New York from 25 to 29 June 1990,[a]

Recalling General Assembly resolution 46/70 of 11 December 1991 on cooperation and coordination of specialized agencies and the international institutions associated with the United Nations in their assistance to Non-Self-Governing Territories,

Noting with appreciation that assistance has continued to be extended to refugees from southern Africa through the Office of the United Nations High Commissioner for Refugees,

1. *Takes note* of the report of the Acting President of the Economic and Social Council, and endorses the observations and suggestions contained therein;

2. *Also takes note* of the report of the Secretary-General;

3. *Reaffirms* that the recognition by the General Assembly, the Security Council and other United Nations organs of the legitimacy of the aspiration of colonial peoples to exercise their right to self-determination and independence entails, as a corollary, the extension by the organizations of the United Nations system of all the necessary moral and material assistance to those peoples;

4. *Expresses its appreciation* to those specialized agencies and other organizations of the United Nations system that have continued to cooperate in varying forms and degrees with the United Nations and the regional organizations concerned in the implementation of the Declaration on the Granting of Independence to Colonial Countries and Peoples and other relevant resolutions of United Nations bodies, and urges all the spe-

---

[a]A/CONF.147/5-TD/B/AC.46/4.

cialized agencies and other organizations of the United Nations system to contribute to the full and speedy implementation of the relevant provisions of those resolutions;

5. *Recommends* that all States intensify their efforts in the specialized agencies and other organizations of the United Nations to ensure the full and effective implementation of the Declaration and other related resolutions of the United Nations system;

6. *Requests* the specialized agencies and the international institutions associated with the United Nations to strengthen existing measures of support and formulate additional programmes of assistance to the remaining Trust and Non-Self-Governing Territories within the framework of their respective mandates;

7. *Requests* the specialized agencies and other organizations of the United Nations system, as well as international and regional organizations, to take appropriate measures within their spheres of competence in order to accelerate progress in the economic and social sectors of those Territories;

8. *Also requests* the specialized agencies and other organizations of the United Nations system, in formulating their assistance programmes, to take due account of the text entitled ''Challenges and opportunities: a strategic framework'', which was adopted unanimously by the Meeting of Governmental Experts of Island Developing Countries and Donor Countries and Organizations;

9. *Welcomes* the continued initiative exercised by the United Nations Development Programme in maintaining close liaison among the specialized agencies and other organizations of the United Nations system and in coordinating the activities of the specialized agencies in extending effective assistance to the peoples of colonial Territories, and calls upon the specialized agencies and other organizations of the United Nations system, as a matter of urgency, to contribute generously to the relief, rehabilitation and reconstruction efforts in the Non-Self-Governing Territories affected by natural disasters;

10. *Urges* the administering Powers concerned to facilitate the participation of the representatives of the Governments of Trust and Non-Self-Governing Territories at the relevant meetings and conferences of the agencies and organizations so that the Territories may draw the maximum benefits from the related activities of the specialized agencies and other organizations of the United Nations system;

11. *Urges* the governing bodies of those specialized agencies and other organizations of the United Nations system that have not already done so to include in the agenda of their regular sessions a separate item on the progress made and action to be taken by their organizations in the implementation of the Declaration and other relevant resolutions of United Nations bodies;

12. *Urges* the executive heads of the specialized agencies and other organizations of the United Nations system to formulate, with the active cooperation of the regional organizations concerned, concrete proposals for the full implementation of the relevant United Nations resolutions and to submit the proposals as a matter of priority to their governing and legislative organs;

13. *Urges* the specialized agencies and other organizations of the United Nations system to adhere to the Programme of Action contained in the Declaration on

Apartheid and its Destructive Consequences in Southern Africa, in particular with regard to increased support for the opponents of apartheid, the use of concerted and effective measures aimed at applying pressure to ensure a speedy end to apartheid and ensuring the non-relaxation of existing measures to encourage the South African regime to eradicate apartheid until there is clear evidence of profound and irreversible changes;

14. *Stresses*, in the context of the Declaration on Apartheid and its Destructive Consequences in Southern Africa, the need for the specialized agencies and other organizations of the United Nations system to render all possible assistance to the front-line and neighbouring States to enable them to rebuild their economies, which have been adversely affected by South Africa's acts of aggression and destabilization, to withstand any further such acts and to continue to support the people of South Africa;

15. *Draws the attention* of the Special Committee on the Situation with regard to the Implementation of the Declaration on the Granting of Independence to Colonial Countries and Peoples to the present resolution and to the discussion held on the subject at the substantive session of 1992 of the Economic and Social Council;

16. *Requests* the President of the Economic and Social Council to continue to maintain close contact on these matters with the Chairman of the Special Committee on the Situation with regard to the Implementation of the Declaration on the Granting of Independence to Colonial Countries and Peoples and to report thereon to the Council;

17. *Also requests* the President of the Council to maintain contact with the Chairman of the Special Committee against Apartheid, which is the focal point for the international campaign against apartheid, and to report thereon to the Council as appropriate;

18. *Requests* the Secretary-General to follow the implementation of the present resolution, with particular attention to coordination and integration arrangements for maximizing the efficiency of the assistance activities undertaken by various organizations of the United Nations system, and to report thereon to the Council at its substantive session of 1993;

19. *Decides* to keep these questions under continuous review.

Economic and Social Council resolution 1992/59

31 July 1992   Meeting 42   35-11-8 (recorded vote)

17-nation draft (E/1992/L.38), orally revised; agenda item 6 *(b)*.

Sponsors: Algeria, Angola, Benin, Congo, Fiji, Guinea, Iran, Jamaica, Malaysia, Namibia, Papua New Guinea, Somalia, Suriname, Trinidad and Tobago, Tunisia, Uganda, Zambia.

Recorded vote in Council as follows:

In favour: Algeria, Angola, Bahrain, Bangladesh, Benin, Botswana, Brazil, Burkina Faso, Chile, China, Colombia, Ecuador, Ethiopia, Guinea, India, Iran, Jamaica, Kuwait, Madagascar, Malaysia, Mexico, Morocco, Pakistan, Peru, Philippines, Rwanda, Somalia, Suriname, Swaziland, Syrian Arab Republic, Togo, Trinidad and Tobago, Turkey, Yugoslavia, Zaire.

Against: Austria, Belgium, Bulgaria, France, Germany, Italy, Japan, Poland, Romania, United Kingdom, United States.

Abstaining: Argentina, Australia, Belarus, Canada, Finland, Russian Federation, Spain, Sweden.

GENERAL ASSEMBLY ACTION

On 16 November 1992, on the recommendation of the Fourth Committee, the General Assembly adopted **resolution 47/16** by recorded vote.

Implementation of the Declaration on the Granting of Independence to Colonial Countries and Peoples by the specialized agencies and the international institutions associated with the United Nations

The General Assembly,

Having considered the item entitled "Implementation of the Declaration on the Granting of Independence to Colonial Countries and Peoples by the specialized agencies and the international institutions associated with the United Nations",

Having considered the reports submitted on the question by the Secretary-General and the Chairman of the Special Committee on the Situation with regard to the Implementation of the Declaration on the Granting of Independence to Colonial Countries and Peoples,

Having examined the chapter of the report of the Special Committee on the Situation with regard to the Implementation of the Declaration on the Granting of Independence to Colonial Countries and Peoples relating to the question,

Recalling its resolution 1514(XV) of 14 December 1960, containing the Declaration on the Granting of Independence to Colonial Countries and Peoples, and resolution 1541(XV) of 15 December 1960, as well as all its other resolutions on this subject, including, in particular, resolution 46/181 of 19 December 1991, endorsing the Plan of Action for the International Decade for the Eradication of Colonialism,

Recalling also its resolution S-16/1 of 14 December 1989, the annex to which contains the Declaration on Apartheid and its Destructive Consequences in Southern Africa,

Bearing in mind the relevant provisions of the final documents of the successive Conferences of Heads of State or Government of Non-Aligned Countries and of the resolutions adopted by the Assembly of Heads of State and Government of the Organization of African Unity,

Deeply concerned that the objectives of the Charter of the United Nations and the Declaration on the Granting of Independence to Colonial Countries and Peoples have not been fully achieved,

Recognizing that permanent peace and stability in southern Africa can only be achieved when the system of apartheid in South Africa has been eradicated and South Africa has been transformed into a united, democratic and nonracial country, and reiterating therefore that all the necessary measures should be adopted at the present time to bring a speedy end to the apartheid system in the interest of all the people of southern Africa, the African continent and the world at large,

Noting that the large majority of the remaining colonial Territories are small island Territories,

Recalling its resolution 43/189 of 20 December 1988, concerning specific measures in favour of island developing countries,

Bearing in mind the conclusions and recommendations of the Meeting of Governmental Experts of Island Developing Countries and Donor Countries and Organizations held in New York from 25 to 29 June 1990,

Recalling relevant resolutions of the Caribbean Development and Cooperation Committee concerning the access of colonial Territories to programmes of the United Nations system,

Noting the assistance extended thus far to colonial Territories by certain specialized agencies and other organizations of the United Nations system, in particular the United Nations Development Programme, and considering that such assistance should be expanded further, commensurate with the pressing needs of the peoples concerned for external assistance,

Stressing the importance of securing necessary resources for funding expanded assistance programmes for the peoples concerned and the need to enlist the support of all major funding institutions within the United Nations system in that regard,

Noting with serious concern the continuing effects of the acts of aggression and destabilization that have been committed by South Africa against neighbouring independent African States,

Reaffirming the responsibility of the specialized agencies and other organizations of the United Nations system to take all the necessary measures, within their respective spheres of competence, to ensure the full implementation, without further delay, of General Assembly resolution 1514(XV) and other relevant resolutions of the United Nations, particularly those relating to the extension of assistance to the peoples of the colonial Territories,

Expressing its appreciation to the Organization of African Unity, the South Pacific Forum and the Caribbean Community, as well as other regional organizations, for the continued cooperation and assistance they have extended to the specialized agencies and other organizations of the United Nations system in this regard,

Concerned by the fact that not all Member States have adhered to the measures provided for in the Programme of Action contained in the Declaration on Apartheid and its Destructive Consequences in Southern Africa and have thus continued or re-established relations with South Africa in a number of fields,

Bearing in mind the importance of the activities of nongovernmental organizations aimed at putting an end to the assistance that is still being rendered to South Africa by some specialized agencies,

Expressing its conviction that closer contacts and consultations between and among the specialized agencies and other organizations of the United Nations system and regional organizations help to facilitate the effective formulation of assistance programmes to the peoples concerned,

Mindful of the imperative need to keep under continuous review the activities of the specialized agencies and other organizations of the United Nations system in the implementation of the various United Nations decisions relating to decolonization,

Bearing in mind the extremely fragile economies of the small island Territories and their vulnerability to natural disasters, such as hurricanes and cyclones, and recalling relevant resolutions of the General Assembly,

Recalling its resolution 46/70 of 11 December 1991 on cooperation and coordination of the specialized agencies and the international institutions associated with the United Nations in their assistance to Non-Self-Governing Territories,

1. *Approves* the chapter of the report of the Special Committee on the Situation with regard to the Implementation of the Declaration on the Granting of Independence to Colonial Countries and Peoples relating to the question;

2. *Takes note* of the report of the Chairman of the Special Committee on the Situation with regard to the Im-

plementation of the Declaration on the Granting of Independence to Colonial Countries and Peoples on his consultations with the Acting President of the Economic and Social Council, and endorses the observations and suggestions arising therefrom;

3. *Recommends* that all States intensify their efforts in the specialized agencies and other organizations of the United Nations system to ensure the full and effective implementation of the Declaration on the Granting of Independence to Colonial Countries and Peoples and other relevant resolutions of the United Nations;

4. *Reaffirms* that the specialized agencies and other organizations and institutions of the United Nations system should continue to be guided by the relevant resolutions of the United Nations in their efforts to contribute to the full implementation, without further delay, of the Declaration on the Granting of Independence to Colonial Countries and Peoples and all other relevant General Assembly resolutions;

5. *Reaffirms also* that the recognition by the General Assembly, the Security Council and other United Nations organs of the legitimacy of the aspiration of colonial peoples to exercise their right to self-determination and independence entails, as a corollary, the extension of all necessary moral and material assistance to those peoples and their national liberation movements by the specialized agencies and other organizations of the United Nations system;

6. *Expresses its appreciation* to those specialized agencies and other organizations of the United Nations system that have continued to cooperate with the United Nations and the regional and subregional organizations in the implementation of General Assembly resolution 1514(XV) and other relevant resolutions of the United Nations, and urges all the specialized agencies and other organizations of the United Nations system to accelerate the full and speedy implementation of the relevant provisions of those resolutions;

7. *Requests* the specialized agencies and other organizations of the United Nations system, as well as international and regional organizations, to examine and review conditions in each Territory so as to take appropriate measures to accelerate progress in the economic and social sectors of the Territories;

8. *Requests* all specialized agencies and other organizations of the United Nations system to strengthen measures of support and formulate adequate programmes of assistance to the peoples of colonial Territories, bearing in mind that such assistance should not only meet their immediate needs but also create conditions for development after they have exercised their right to self-determination and independence;

9. *Also requests* the specialized agencies and other organizations of the United Nations system to provide, through an inter-agency framework, the assistance necessary to small island Territories to alleviate the adverse conditions arising from the interplay of factors relating mainly to their size and geographical location;

10. *Further requests* the specialized agencies and other organizations of the United Nations system, in formulating their assistance programmes, to take due account of the conclusions and recommendations, entitled "Challenges and opportunities: a strategic framework", of the Meeting of Governmental Experts of Island Developing Countries and Donor Countries and Organizations held in New York in June 1990;

11. *Once again requests* the specialized agencies and other organizations of the United Nations system to continue to provide all humanitarian, material and moral assistance to Namibia and all newly independent and emerging States so as to enable them to consolidate their political independence and achieve genuine economic independence;

12. *Urges* the executive heads of the specialized agencies and other organizations of the United Nations system, in cooperation with the regional and other organizations where appropriate, to submit to their governing and legislative organs concrete proposals for the full implementation of the relevant United Nations decisions, particularly specific programmes of assistance to the peoples of the colonial Territories and their national liberation movements;

13. *Recommends* that the executive heads of the World Bank and the International Monetary Fund draw the attention of their governing bodies to the present resolution and consider introducing flexible procedures to prepare specific programmes for the peoples of the Non-Self-Governing Territories;

14. *Urges* the specialized agencies and other organizations of the United Nations system that have not already done so to include in the agenda of the regular meetings of their governing bodies a separate item on the progress they have made in the implementation of General Assembly resolution 1514(XV) and other relevant resolutions of the United Nations;

15. *Welcomes* the continued initiative exercised by the United Nations Development Programme in maintaining close liaison among the specialized agencies and other organizations of the United Nations system and in coordinating the activities of the agencies in extending effective assistance to the peoples of the Non-Self-Governing Territories, and calls upon the specialized agencies and other organizations of the United Nations system, as a matter of urgency, to contribute generously to the relief, rehabilitation and reconstruction efforts in those Non-Self-Governing Territories affected by natural disasters;

16. *Urges* the administering Powers concerned to facilitate the participation of the representatives of the Governments of Trust and Non-Self-Governing Territories in the relevant meetings and conferences of the agencies and organizations so that the Territories may draw the maximum benefits from the related activities of the specialized agencies and other organizations of the United Nations system;

17. *Urges* the specialized agencies and other organizations of the United Nations system to adhere to the Programme of Action contained in the Declaration on Apartheid and its Destructive Consequences in Southern Africa, in particular with regard to increased support for the opponents of apartheid, the use of concerted and effective measures aimed at applying pressure to ensure a speedy end to apartheid, and ensuring the non-relaxation of existing measures to encourage the South African regime to eradicate apartheid until there is clear evidence of profound and irreversible changes;

18. *Stresses*, in the context of the Declaration on Apartheid and its Destructive Consequences in Southern Africa, the need for the specialized agencies and other organizations of the United Nations system to render all possible assistance to the front-line and neighbouring States to enable them to rebuild their econo-

mies, which have been adversely affected by acts of aggression and destabilization by South Africa, to withstand any further such acts and to continue to support the people of South Africa;

19. *Invites* the specialized agencies and other organizations of the United Nations system to cooperate with the Action for Resisting Invasion, Colonialism and Apartheid Fund established by the Eighth Conference of Heads of State or Government of Non-Aligned Countries, held at Harare from 1 to 6 September 1986, with the common objective of providing emergency assistance to the front-line States and national liberation movements struggling against the apartheid regime, and in other measures taken by the Movement of Non-Aligned Countries and the Organization of African Unity;

20. *Urges* all States, especially those that have economic, financial or other links to South Africa, to adhere fully to the Programme of Action contained in the Declaration on Apartheid and its Destructive Consequences in Southern Africa until the establishment of a united, democratic and non-racial South Africa;

21. *Recommends* that all Governments intensify their efforts in the specialized agencies and other organizations of the United Nations system of which they are members to ensure the full and effective implementation of General Assembly resolution 1514(XV) and other relevant resolutions of the United Nations and, in that connection, accord priority to the question of providing assistance on an emergency basis to the peoples of the Non-Self-Governing Territories;

22. *Requests* the Secretary-General to continue to assist the specialized agencies and other organizations of the United Nations system in working out appropriate measures for implementing the relevant resolutions of the United Nations and to prepare for submission to the relevant bodies, with the assistance of those agencies and organizations, a report on the action taken in implementation of the relevant resolutions, including the present resolution, since the circulation of his previous report;

23. *Commends* the Economic and Social Council for its debate and its resolution 1992/59 of 31 July 1992 on this issue and requests it to continue, as appropriate, to consider, in consultation with the Special Committee on the Situation with regard to the Implementation of the Declaration on the Granting of Independence to Colonial Countries and Peoples, appropriate measures for coordination of the policies and activities of the specialized agencies and other organizations of the United Nations system in implementing the relevant resolutions of the General Assembly;

24. *Requests* the specialized agencies to report periodically to the Secretary-General on the implementation of the present resolution;

25. *Requests* the Secretary-General to transmit the present resolution to the governing bodies of the appropriate specialized agencies and international institutions associated with the United Nations so that those bodies take the necessary measures to implement the resolution, and also requests the Secretary-General to report to the General Assembly at its forty-eighth session on the implementation of the present resolution;

26. *Requests* the Special Committee to continue to examine the question and to report thereon to the General Assembly at its forty-eighth session.

General Assembly resolution 47/16

16 November 1992   Meeting 61   100-30-19 (recorded vote)

Approved by Fourth Committee (A/47/646) by recorded vote (93-27-13), 3 November (meeting 8); draft by Committee on colonial countries (A/47/23); agenda items 12 & 100.
Meeting numbers. GA 47th session: 4th Committee 2-8; plenary 61.

Recorded vote in Assembly as follows:

In favour: Afghanistan, Algeria, Angola, Bahamas, Bahrain, Bangladesh, Barbados, Belize, Benin, Bolivia, Botswana, Brazil, Brunei Darussalam, Burkina Faso, Burundi, Cameroon, Cape Verde, Chile, China, Colombia, Costa Rica, Cuba, Cyprus, Democratic People's Republic of Korea, Djibouti, Dominica, Ecuador, Egypt, El Salvador, Equatorial Guinea, Ethiopia, Fiji, Gambia, Ghana, Grenada, Guatemala, Guinea, Guinea-Bissau, Guyana, Haiti, Honduras, India, Indonesia, Iran, Iraq, Jamaica, Jordan, Kenya, Kuwait, Lao People's Democratic Republic, Lebanon, Lesotho, Liberia, Libyan Arab Jamahiriya, Malaysia, Maldives, Mali, Mauritania, Mexico, Mongolia, Morocco, Myanmar, Namibia, Nepal, Nicaragua, Niger, Nigeria, Oman, Pakistan, Papua New Guinea, Peru, Philippines, Qatar, Rwanda, Saint Lucia, Saint Vincent and the Grenadines, Sao Tome and Principe, Saudi Arabia, Senegal, Seychelles, Sierra Leone, Singapore, Sri Lanka, Sudan, Suriname, Swaziland, Syrian Arab Republic, Thailand, Togo, Trinidad and Tobago, Tunisia, Uganda, United Arab Emirates, United Republic of Tanzania, Vanuatu, Venezuela, Viet Nam, Yemen, Zambia, Zimbabwe.

Against: Australia, Austria, Belgium, Bulgaria, Canada, Czechoslovakia, Denmark, Estonia, Finland, France, Germany, Hungary, Iceland, Israel, Italy, Latvia, Liechtenstein, Lithuania, Luxembourg, Netherlands, Norway, Poland, Portugal, Republic of Moldova, Romania, Russian Federation, Slovenia, Sweden, United Kingdom, United States.

Abstaining: Argentina, Belarus, Congo, Côte d'Ivoire, Greece, Ireland, Japan, Malta, Marshall Islands, Micronesia, New Zealand, Panama, Paraguay, Republic of Korea, Samoa, Spain, Turkey, Ukraine, Uruguay.

On 25 November, the Assembly adopted **resolution 47/22** without vote.

Cooperation and coordination of the specialized agencies and the international institutions associated with the United Nations in their assistance to Non-Self-Governing Territories

The General Assembly,

Recalling its resolution 46/70 of 11 December 1991,

Having considered the report of the Secretary-General on cooperation and coordination of the specialized agencies and the international institutions associated with the United Nations in their assistance to Non-Self-Governing Territories,

Aware that, in addition to general problems facing developing countries, the remaining Non-Self-Governing Territories, many of which are small island Territories, also suffer handicaps arising from the interplay of such factors as their size, remoteness, geographical dispersion, vulnerability to natural disasters, lack of natural resources, shortage of administrative personnel and migration, particularly of personnel with high-level skills,

Recalling resolution 24(XI) of 22 November 1988, on the Programme of Assistance to Small Island Developing Countries, adopted by the Caribbean Development and Cooperation Committee at its eleventh session, in which the Committee directed its secretariat to continue to examine the access of the non-independent Caribbean countries to programmes and activities of the United Nations system with the aim of identifying areas within that system which could provide technical and other assistance to those countries in the furtherance of their development process, and other resolutions of the Committee,

Mindful of the growing importance that the General Assembly attaches to the contributions of the specialized agencies and the international institutions to the economic and social development of Non-Self-Governing Territories, and the role being played by the United Nations Development Programme and the specialized agencies in that regard,

Taking note of the report of the Secretary-General on the specific problems and needs of island developing countries,[a]

Noting that several of the Non-Self-Governing Territories in the Caribbean may reach net contributor status during the fifth programming cycle of the United Nations Development Programme (1992-1996) under the current criteria for the allocation of Programme-funded country programmes,

Recalling also the plan of action contained in Agenda 21,[b] adopted by the United Nations Conference on Environment and Development,

1. *Takes note with satisfaction* of the report of the Secretary-General;

2. *Welcomes* the contributions being made to Non-Self-Governing Territories by the specialized agencies and the international institutions associated with the United Nations and urges them to intensify their assistance to those Territories;

3. *Takes note* of the recommendation contained in the report of the Secretary-General on the specific problems and needs of island developing countries, prepared by the secretariat of the United Nations Conference on Trade and Development, regarding the establishment of a family of indicators of vulnerability of island developing countries;

4. *Recommends* that the specialized agencies and the international institutions consider the question of the cooperation and coordination of assistance to Non-Self-Governing Territories within the context of the Administrative Committee on Coordination and its subsidiary bodies;

5. *Welcomes* the statements made by the representatives of the United Nations Educational, Scientific and Cultural Organization, the Food and Agriculture Organization of the United Nations and the United Nations Development Programme,[c] and invites other specialized agencies and the international institutions associated with the United Nations to participate in future debates of the General Assembly on the remaining Non-Self-Governing Territories, with a view to apprising the Assembly of their development programmes in those Territories and thereby facilitating more informed comments on their work;

6. *Requests* the Secretary-General to report to the General Assembly at its forty-eighth session on the implementation of the present resolution;

7. *Decides* to keep this question under review.

---

[a]A/47/414 & Add.1.

[b]*Report of the United Nations Conference on Environment and Development, Rio de Janeiro, 3-14 June 1992*, vol. I, Sales No. E.93.I.8.

[c]A/C.4/47/SR.3 & 5.

General Assembly resolution 47/22

25 November 1992   Meeting 72   Adopted without vote

10-nation draft (A/47/L.16/Rev.1); agenda item 18.

Sponsors: Barbados, Belize, Grenada, Guyana, Jamaica, Papua New Guinea, Saint Lucia, Saint Vincent and the Grenadines, Trinidad and Tobago, Vanuatu.

Meeting numbers. GA 47th session: plenary 61, 72.

Foreign interests impeding implementation of the Declaration

In 1992,[7] the Committee on colonial countries considered foreign economic and other interests which impeded implementation of the 1960 Declaration. It had before it working papers prepared by the Secretariat on economic conditions and foreign activities in Anguilla,[23] Bermuda,[24] the Cayman Islands,[25] Montserrat,[26] the Turks and Caicos Islands[27] and the United States Virgin Islands.[28]

The Committee drafted a resolution on the activities of foreign interests which it recommended to the General Assembly for adoption.

GENERAL ASSEMBLY ACTION

On 16 November 1992, the General Assembly, on the recommendation of the Fourth Committee, adopted **resolution 47/15** by recorded vote.

Activities of those foreign economic and other interests which impede the implementation of the Declaration on the Granting of Independence to Colonial Countries and Peoples in Territories under colonial domination and efforts to eliminate colonialism, apartheid and racial discrimination in southern Africa

The General Assembly,

Having considered the item entitled "Activities of those foreign economic and other interests which impede the implementation of the Declaration on the Granting of Independence to Colonial Countries and Peoples in Territories under colonial domination and efforts to eliminate colonialism, apartheid and racial discrimination in southern Africa",

Having examined the chapter of the report of the Special Committee on the Situation with regard to the Implementation of the Declaration on the Granting of Independence to Colonial Countries and Peoples relating to the question,

Recalling its resolution 1514(XV) of 14 December 1960, containing the Declaration on the Granting of Independence to Colonial Countries and Peoples, as well as all its other resolutions on this subject, including, in particular, resolution 46/181 of 19 December 1991, endorsing the Plan of Action for the International Decade for the Eradication of Colonialism,

Reaffirming the solemn obligation of the administering Powers under the Charter of the United Nations to promote the political, economic, social and educational advancement of the inhabitants of the Territories under their administration and to protect the human and natural resources of those Territories against abuses,

Reaffirming also that those economic and other activities which impede the implementation of the Declaration on the Granting of Independence to Colonial Countries and Peoples and obstruct efforts aimed at the elimination of colonialism, apartheid and racial discrimination in South Africa and in colonial Territories are in direct violation of the rights of the inhabitants and of the principles of the Charter and all relevant resolutions of the United Nations,

Seriously concerned about the activities of those foreign economic, financial and other interests which continue to exploit the natural resources that are the heritage of the indigenous populations of the colonial and Non-Self-Governing Territories in the Caribbean, the Pacific and other regions, as well as their human resources, to the detriment of their interests, thus depriving them of their right to control the resources of their Territories and impeding the realization by those peoples of their legitimate aspirations for self-determination and independence,

Bearing in mind the relevant provisions of the final documents of the successive Conferences of Heads of State or Government of Non-Aligned Countries and of the resolutions adopted by the Assembly of Heads of State and Government of the Organization of African Unity,

Gravely concerned that certain countries, transnational corporations and international financial institutions have continued their economic relations with South Africa,

Recognizing the crucial and decisive role that the imposition of international sanctions has played in applying the necessary pressure on the South African regime to undertake significant measures towards the eradication of apartheid,

1. *Approves* the chapter of the report of the Special Committee on the Situation with regard to the Implementation of the Declaration on the Granting of Independence to Colonial Countries and Peoples relating to the question;

2. *Reaffirms* the inalienable right of the peoples of colonial and Non-Self-Governing Territories to self-determination and independence and to the enjoyment of the natural resources of their Territories, as well as their right to dispose of those resources in their best interests;

3. *Reiterates* that any administering or occupying Power that deprives the colonial peoples of the exercise of their legitimate rights over their natural resources or subordinates the rights and interests of those peoples to foreign economic and financial interests violates the solemn obligations it has assumed under the Charter of the United Nations;

4. *Reaffirms* its concern over the activities of those foreign economic, financial and other interests which continue to exploit the natural resources that are the heritage of the indigenous populations of the colonial and Non-Self-Governing Territories in the Caribbean, the Pacific and other regions, as well as their human resources, to the detriment of their interests, thus depriving them of their right to control the resources of their Territories and impeding the realization by those peoples of their legitimate aspirations for self-determination and independence;

5. *Condemns* the activities of those foreign economic and other interests in the colonial Territories which impede the implementation of the Declaration on the Granting of Independence to Colonial Countries and Peoples, contained in General Assembly resolution 1514(XV), and the efforts to eliminate colonialism, apartheid and racial discrimination;

6. *Strongly condemns* the collaboration with the South African regime by certain countries as well as transnational corporations that continue to make new investments in South Africa and supply the racist regime with armaments, nuclear technology and all other materials that are likely to buttress it and thus aggravate the threat to peace in the region;

7. *Calls upon* all States to maintain the existing measures against the apartheid regime as specified in the Declaration on Apartheid and its Destructive Consequences in Southern Africa, annexed to General Assembly resolution S-16/1 of 14 December 1989;

8. *Calls once again upon* all Governments that have not yet done so to take, in accordance with the relevant provisions of General Assembly resolution 2621(XXV) of 12 October 1970, legislative, administrative or other measures in respect of their nationals and the bodies corporate under their jurisdiction that own and operate enterprises in colonial Territories that are detrimental to the interests of the inhabitants of those Territories, in order to put an end to such enterprises and to prevent new investments that run counter to the interests of the inhabitants of those Territories;

9. *Calls upon* those oil-producing and oil-exporting countries that have not yet done so to take effective measures against the oil companies concerned so as to terminate the supply of crude oil and petroleum products to the racist regime of South Africa;

10. *Reiterates* that the exploitation and plundering of the marine and other natural resources of colonial and Non-Self-Governing Territories by foreign economic interests, in violation of the relevant resolutions of the United Nations, are a grave threat to the integrity and prosperity of those Territories;

11. *Invites* all Governments and organizations of the United Nations system to take all possible measures to ensure that the permanent sovereignty of the peoples of colonial and Non-Self-Governing Territories over their natural resources is fully respected and safeguarded;

12. *Urges* the administering Powers concerned to take effective measures to safeguard and guarantee the inalienable right of the peoples of the colonial and Non-Self-Governing Territories to their natural resources and to establish and maintain control over the future development of those resources, and requests the administering Powers to take all necessary steps to protect the property rights of the peoples of those Territories;

13. *Calls upon* the administering Powers concerned to ensure that no discriminatory and unjust wage systems or working conditions prevail in the Territories under their administration and to apply in each Territory a uniform system of wages to all the inhabitants without any discrimination;

14. *Requests* the Secretary-General to continue, through all means at his disposal, to inform world public opinion of those activities of foreign economic and other interests which impede the implementation of the Declaration on the Granting of Independence to Colonial Countries and Peoples;

15. *Appeals* to mass media, trade unions and non-governmental organizations, as well as individuals, to continue their efforts for the full implementation of the Declaration on the Granting of Independence to Colonial Countries and Peoples and in the struggle against apartheid and the mobilization of international public opinion against the policy pursued by the South African apartheid regime and to oppose the relaxation of existing measures against the regime, in order to accelerate the process of constitutional change with the aim of establishing a united, democratic and non-racial South Africa;

16. *Decides* to continue to monitor closely the situation in the colonial and Non-Self-Governing Territories so as to ensure that all economic activities in those Territories are aimed at strengthening and diversifying their economies in the interest of the indigenous peoples and at promoting the economic and financial viability of those Territories, in order to facilitate and accelerate the

exercise by the peoples of those Territories of their right to self-determination and independence;

17.   *Requests* the Special Committee on the Situation with regard to the Implementation of the Declaration on the Granting of Independence to Colonial Countries and Peoples to continue to examine this question and to report thereon to the General Assembly at its forty-eighth session.

General Assembly resolution 47/15

16 November 1992   Meeting 61   95-34-12 (recorded vote)

Approved by Fourth Committee (A/47/645) by recorded vote (89-32-8), 3 November (meeting 8); draft by Committee on colonial countries (A/47/23); agenda item 99.

Meeting numbers. GA 47th session: 4th Committee 2-8; plenary 61.

Recorded vote in Assembly as follows:

In favour: Afghanistan, Algeria, Angola, Bahamas, Bahrain, Bangladesh, Barbados, Belize, Benin, Bolivia, Botswana, Brazil, Brunei Darussalam, Burkina Faso, Burundi, Cameroon, Cape Verde, Chile, China, Colombia, Costa Rica, Cuba, Cyprus, Democratic People's Republic of Korea, Djibouti, Dominica, Ecuador, Egypt, El Salvador, Equatorial Guinea, Ethiopia, Fiji, Gambia, Ghana, Guatemala, Guinea, Guinea-Bissau, Guyana, Haiti, Honduras, India, Indonesia, Iran, Iraq, Jamaica, Jordan, Kenya, Kuwait, Lao People's Democratic Republic, Lebanon, Liberia, Libyan Arab Jamahiriya, Malaysia, Maldives, Mali, Mauritania, Mexico, Mongolia, Myanmar, Namibia, Nepal, Nicaragua, Niger, Nigeria, Oman, Pakistan, Papua New Guinea, Peru, Philippines, Qatar, Rwanda, Saint Lucia, Saint Vincent and the Grenadines, Sao Tome and Principe, Saudi Arabia, Senegal, Seychelles, Sierra Leone, Singapore, Sri Lanka, Suriname, Syrian Arab Republic, Thailand, Togo, Trinidad and Tobago, Tunisia, Uganda, United Arab Emirates, United Republic of Tanzania, Vanuatu, Venezuela, Viet Nam, Yemen, Zambia, Zimbabwe.

Against: Australia, Austria, Belgium, Bulgaria, Canada, Czechoslovakia, Denmark, Finland, France, Germany, Greece, Hungary, Iceland, Ireland, Israel, Italy, Japan, Liechtenstein, Luxembourg, Malta, Netherlands, New Zealand, Norway, Poland, Portugal, Republic of Moldova, Romania, Russian Federation, Slovenia, Spain, Sweden, Turkey, United Kingdom, United States.

Abstaining: Argentina, Belarus, Congo, Croatia, Marshall Islands, Micronesia, Panama, Paraguay, Republic of Korea, Samoa, Ukraine, Uruguay.

Military activities in colonial countries

In 1992, the Committee on colonial countries again considered military activities by colonial Powers in Territories under their administration which might impede the implementation of the 1960 Declaration. It had before it working papers prepared by the Secretariat on military activities and arrangements in Bermuda,[29] Guam[30] and the United States Virgin Islands.[31]

The Committee drafted a decision on military activities in colonial countries[32] which it recommended to the General Assembly for adoption.

On 21 August,[33] the Chairman of the Committee transmitted to the Security Council the text of that decision,[32] drawing particular attention to paragraph 7, which urged the Council to consider, as a matter of urgency, the report of the Security Council Committee established in 1977[34] and to adopt further measures to widen the scope of another 1977 Council resolution[35] to make it more effective and comprehensive. The Committee further called for scrupulous observance of a 1984 Council resolution[36] in which the Council enjoined Member States from importing armaments from South Africa.

On 16 November 1992, the General Assembly, on the recommendation of the Fourth Committee, adopted **decision 47/409** by recorded vote.

Military activities and arrangements by colonial Powers in Territories under their administration which might be impeding the implementation of the Declaration on the Granting of Independence to Colonial Countries and Peoples

At its 61st plenary meeting, on 16 November 1992, the General Assembly, on the recommendation of the Fourth Committee, adopted the following text:

''1.   The General Assembly, having considered the chapter of the report of the Special Committee on the Situation with regard to the Implementation of the Declaration on the Granting of Independence to Colonial Countries and Peoples relating to an item on the agenda of the Special Committee entitled 'Military activities and arrangements by colonial Powers in Territories under their administration which might be impeding the implementation of the Declaration on the Granting of Independence to Colonial Countries and Peoples' and recalling its resolution 1514(XV) of 14 December 1960 and all other resolutions and decisions of the United Nations relating to military activities in colonial and Non-Self-Governing Territories, reaffirms its strong conviction that military bases and installations in the Territories concerned could constitute an obstacle to the exercise by the people of those Territories of their right to self-determination and reiterates its strong views that existing bases and installations, which are impeding the implementation of the Declaration, should be withdrawn and that no further entrenchment should be condoned.

''2.   Aware of the presence of such bases and installations in some of those Territories, the General Assembly urges the administering Powers concerned to continue to take all necessary measures not to involve those Territories in any offensive acts or interference against other States, and to comply fully with the purposes and principles of the Charter of the United Nations.

''3.   The General Assembly reiterates its condemnation of all those military activities and arrangements by colonial Powers in Territories under their administration that might run counter to the rights and interests of the colonial peoples concerned, especially their right to self-determination and independence. The Assembly once again calls upon the colonial Powers concerned to terminate such activities and to eliminate such military bases in compliance with the relevant resolutions of the Assembly.

''4.   The General Assembly reiterates that the colonial Territories and areas adjacent thereto should not be used for nuclear testing, dumping of nuclear wastes or deployment of nuclear and other weapons of mass destruction.

''5.   The General Assembly welcomes the important changes taking place in South Africa aimed at facilitating the commencement of substantive constitutional negotiations. The Assembly notes that, these developments notwithstanding, apartheid remains firmly entrenched and that as a result there is a continuing threat to the peace and security of the region.

"6. The General Assembly notes with grave concern revelations of covert funding and collusion by the South African regime with certain political organizations and reports of the involvement of its security forces in perpetrating acts of violence.

"7. The General Assembly condemns the continued military, nuclear and intelligence collaboration between South Africa and certain countries, which constitutes a violation of the military embargo imposed against South Africa by the Security Council in its resolution 418(1977) of 4 November 1977, and which poses a threat to international peace and security. The Assembly urges the Council to consider, as a matter of urgency, the report of the Security Council Committee established under its resolution 421(1977) of 9 December 1977 and to adopt further measures to widen the scope of Council resolution 418(1977) in order to make it more effective and comprehensive. The Assembly calls for an immediate end to all forms of such collaboration. The Assembly further calls for the scrupulous observance of resolution 558(1984) of 13 December 1984, in which the Council enjoined Member States to refrain from importing armaments from South Africa.

"8. The General Assembly considers that the acquisition of nuclear-weapon capability by the South African regime, with its infamous record of violence and aggression, constitutes a further effort on its part to terrorize and intimidate independent States in the region into submission. The Assembly condemns the continuing support to the South African regime in the military and other fields. In this context, the Assembly expresses its concern at the grave consequences for international peace and security of the collaboration between the apartheid system in South Africa and certain Western Powers and other countries in the military and nuclear fields. It calls upon the States concerned to end all such collaboration and, in particular, to halt the supply to the apartheid system of equipment, technology, materials and training enabling the regime to increase its capability to manufacture nuclear weapons.

"9. The General Assembly strongly condemns the continuing collaboration of certain countries with the racist regime in the military and nuclear fields and expresses its conviction that such collaboration is in contravention of the arms embargo imposed against South Africa under Security Council resolution 418(1977) and undermines international solidarity against the apartheid regime. The Assembly thus calls for the termination forthwith of all such collaboration.

"10. The General Assembly is particularly mindful in that regard of the Declaration on South Africa, adopted by the Assembly of Heads of State and Government of the Organization of African Unity at its twenty-seventh ordinary session, held at Abuja, Nigeria, from 3 to 5 June 1991,[a] the report of the Tenth Conference of Ministers for Foreign Affairs of Non-Aligned Countries, held at Accra from 2 to 7 September 1991,[b] and the Communiqué adopted by the Heads of Government of the countries of the Commonwealth at their meeting held at Harare from 16 to 22 October 1991.[c]

"11. The General Assembly urges all Governments, the specialized agencies and other intergovernmental organizations to provide increased material assistance to the thousands of refugees who have been forced by the oppressive policies of the apartheid regime in South Africa to flee into the neighbouring States and for the purpose of resettlement of those who are returning.

"12. The General Assembly deplores the continued alienation of land in colonial Territories, particularly in the small island Territories of the Pacific and Caribbean regions, for military installations. The large-scale utilization of the local resources for this purpose could adversely affect the economic development of the Territories concerned.

"13. The General Assembly requests the Secretary-General to continue, through all means at his disposal, to inform world public opinion of the facts concerning the military activities and arrangements in colonial Territories which are impeding the implementation of the Declaration on the Granting of Independence to Colonial Countries and Peoples, contained in Assembly resolution 1514(XV).

"14. The General Assembly requests the Special Committee on the Situation with regard to the Implementation of the Declaration on the Granting of Independence to Colonial Countries and Peoples to continue to examine this question and to report thereon to the Assembly at its forty-eighth session.''

---

[a]A/46/390.

[b]A/46/726-S/23265.

[c]A/46/708.

General Assembly decision 47/409

98-39-10 (recorded vote)

Approved by Fourth Committee (A/47/645) by recorded vote (90-33-7), 3 November (meeting 8); draft by Committee on colonial countries (A/47/23); agenda item 99.

Meeting numbers. GA 47th session: 4th Committee 2-8; plenary 61.

Recorded vote in Assembly as follows:

In favour: Afghanistan, Algeria, Angola, Bahamas, Bahrain, Bangladesh, Barbados, Belize, Benin, Bolivia, Botswana, Brazil, Brunei Darussalam, Burkina Faso, Burundi, Cameroon, Cape Verde, Chile, China, Colombia, Costa Rica, Cuba, Cyprus, Democratic People's Republic of Korea, Djibouti, Dominica, Ecuador, Egypt, El Salvador, Equatorial Guinea, Ethiopia, Fiji, Gambia, Ghana, Guatemala, Guinea, Guinea-Bissau, Guyana, Haiti, Honduras, India, Indonesia, Iran, Iraq, Jamaica, Jordan, Kenya, Kuwait, Lao People's Democratic Republic, Lebanon, Liberia, Libyan Arab Jamahiriya, Madagascar, Malaysia, Maldives, Mali, Mauritania, Mexico, Mongolia, Myanmar, Namibia, Nepal, Nicaragua, Niger, Nigeria, Oman, Pakistan, Papua New Guinea, Peru, Philippines, Qatar, Rwanda, Saint Lucia, Saint Vincent and the Grenadines, Sao Tome and Principe, Saudi Arabia, Senegal, Seychelles, Sierra Leone, Singapore, Sri Lanka, Sudan, Suriname, Swaziland, Syrian Arab Republic, Thailand, Togo, Trinidad and Tobago, Tunisia, Uganda, United Arab Emirates, United Republic of Tanzania, Vanuatu, Venezuela, Viet Nam, Yemen, Zambia, Zimbabwe.

Against: Australia, Austria, Belgium, Bulgaria, Canada, Croatia, Czechoslovakia, Denmark, Estonia, Finland, France, Germany, Greece, Hungary, Iceland, Ireland, Israel, Italy, Japan, Latvia, Liechtenstein, Lithuania, Luxembourg, Malta, Netherlands, New Zealand, Norway, Poland, Portugal, Republic of Moldova, Romania, Russian Federation, Slovenia, Spain, Sweden, Turkey, Ukraine, United Kingdom, United States.

Abstaining: Argentina, Belarus, Congo, Marshall Islands, Micronesia, Panama, Paraguay, Republic of Korea, Samoa, Uruguay.

Information dissemination

The Committee on colonial countries, acting on the recommendation of its Subcommittee on Small Territories, Petitions, Information and Assistance,[(9)] adopted recommendations for the dissemination of information on decolonization. It requested the United Nations Department of Public Information (DPI) to intensify its publicity on decolonization; disseminate this information more widely; and produce new visual material on problems of decolonization. The Committee also requested DPI to provide it with reports from United Nations information centres about the dissemination of information on decolonization and appealed to the mass media to also support the peoples of colonial countries by addressing decolonization issues. The Committee also called on DPI, in cooperation with the United Nations Department of Political Affairs, to increase its speaking engagements at universities and to intensify their cooperation with non-governmental organizations.

GENERAL ASSEMBLY ACTION

On 25 November, the General Assembly adopted **resolution 47/24** by recorded vote.

Dissemination of information on decolonization

The General Assembly,

Having examined the chapter of the report of the Special Committee on the Situation with regard to the Implementation of the Declaration on the Granting of Independence to Colonial Countries and Peoples relating to the dissemination of information on decolonization and publicity for the work of the United Nations in the field of decolonization,

Recalling its resolution 1514(XV) of 14 December 1960, containing the Declaration on the Granting of Independence to Colonial Countries and Peoples, and other resolutions and decisions of the United Nations concerning the dissemination of information on decolonization, in particular General Assembly resolution 46/72 of 11 December 1991,

Reiterating the importance of publicity as an instrument for furthering the aims of the Declaration and mindful of the role of world public opinion in effectively assisting the peoples of the colonial Territories to achieve self-determination and independence,

Noting that while censorship laws have been repealed, existing legislation and other measures still curtail the freedom of the press in South Africa,

Aware of the importance of non-governmental organizations in the dissemination of information on decolonization,

1. *Approves* the chapter of the report of the Special Committee on the Situation with regard to the Implementation of the Declaration on the Granting of Independence to Colonial Countries and Peoples relating to the dissemination of information on decolonization and publicity for the work of the United Nations in the field of decolonization;

2. *Considers it important* for the United Nations to continue to play an active role in the process of decolonization and to intensify its efforts to ensure the widest possible dissemination of information on decolonization, with a view to further mobilizing international public opinion in support of complete decolonization by the year 2000;

3. *Requests* the Secretary-General, taking into account the suggestions of the Special Committee, to continue to take concrete measures through all the media at his disposal, including publications, radio and television, to give widespread and continuous publicity to the work of the United Nations in the field of decolonization and, *inter alia*:

(a) To continue, in consultation with the Special Committee, to collect, prepare and disseminate basic material, studies and articles relating to the problems of decolonization and, in particular, to continue to publish the periodical *Objective: Justice* and other publications, special articles and studies, including the *Decolonization* series, and to increase the information on all the Territories under consideration by the Special Committee, selecting appropriate material for wider dissemination by reprints in various languages;

(b) To seek the full cooperation of the administering Powers in the discharge of the tasks referred to above;

(c) To intensify the decolonization-oriented activities of all United Nations information centres;

(d) To maintain a working relationship with the Organization of African Unity and appropriate regional and intergovernmental organizations, particularly in the Pacific and Caribbean regions, by holding periodic consultations and exchanging information;

(e) To solicit, in consultation with United Nations information centres, assistance in the dissemination of information on decolonization from non-governmental organizations;

(f) To continue to produce comprehensive press releases for all meetings of the Special Committee and its subsidiary bodies;

(g) To ensure that the necessary facilities and services to that end are made available;

(h) To report to the Special Committee on measures taken in the implementation of the present resolution;

4. *Requests* all States, in particular the administering Powers, as well as the specialized agencies and other organizations of the United Nations system and non-governmental organizations with a special interest in decolonization, to undertake or intensify, in cooperation with the Secretary-General and within their respective spheres of competence, the large-scale dissemination of information referred to in paragraph 2 above;

5. *Requests* the Special Committee to follow the implementation of the present resolution and to report thereon to the General Assembly at its forty-eighth session.

General Assembly resolution 47/24

25 November 1992   Meeting 72   132-2-17 (recorded vote)

16-nation draft (A/47/L.18 & Add.1); agenda item 18.

Sponsors: Algeria, Barbados, Cuba, Grenada, India, Libyan Arab Jamahiriya, Madagascar, Marshall Islands, Micronesia, Namibia, Papua New Guinea, Sierra Leone, Solomon Islands, Tunisia, United Republic of Tanzania, Vanuatu, Zimbabwe.

Financial implications. 5th Committee, A/47/711; S-G, A/C.5/47/48.

Meeting numbers. GA 47th session: 5th Committee 31; plenary 61, 72.

Recorded vote in Assembly as follows:

In favour: Afghanistan, Albania, Algeria, Angola, Antigua and Barbuda, Argentina, Australia, Austria, Bahamas, Bahrain, Bangladesh, Barbados, Belarus, Belize, Benin, Bolivia, Bosnia and Herzegovina, Botswana, Brazil, Brunei Darussalam, Burkina Faso, Cameroon, Central African Republic, Chad, Chile, China, Colombia, Costa Rica, Côte d'Ivoire, Cuba, Cyprus, Democratic People's Republic of Korea, Denmark, Djibouti, Ecuador, Egypt, El Salvador, Ethiopia, Fiji, Gabon, Ghana, Greece, Grenada, Guatemala, Guinea, Guinea-Bissau, Guyana, Haiti, Honduras, Iceland, India, Indonesia, Iran, Iraq, Ireland, Jamaica, Japan, Kazakhstan, Kenya, Kuwait, Lao People's Democratic Republic, Latvia, Lebanon, Lesotho, Libyan Arab Jamahiriya, Liechtenstein, Lithuania, Madagascar, Malaysia, Maldives, Mali, Malta, Marshall Islands, Mauritania, Mauritius, Mexico, Micronesia, Mongolia, Morocco, Mozambique, Myanmar, Namibia, Nepal, New Zealand, Nicaragua, Niger, Nigeria, Norway, Oman, Pakistan, Panama, Papua New Guinea, Paraguay, Peru, Philippines, Portugal, Qatar, Republic of Korea, Russian Federation, Rwanda, Saint Kitts and Nevis, Saint Lucia, Saint Vincent and the Grenadines, Samoa, Sao Tome and Principe, Saudi Arabia, Senegal, Seychelles, Sierra Leone, Singapore, Spain, Sri

Lanka, Sudan, Suriname, Sweden, Syrian Arab Republic, Thailand, Togo, Trinidad and Tobago, Tunisia, Turkey, Uganda, Ukraine, United Arab Emirates, United Republic of Tanzania, Uruguay, Vanuatu, Venezuela, Viet Nam, Yemen, Zambia, Zimbabwe.
Against: United Kingdom, United States.
Abstaining: Belgium, Bulgaria, Canada, Czechoslovakia, Estonia, Finland, France, Germany, Hungary, Israel, Italy, Luxembourg, Netherlands, Poland, Republic of Moldova, Romania, Slovenia.

Puerto Rico

In 1992, the Committee on colonial countries endorsed the recommendation made by the open-ended Working Group[8] that the Committee defer until 1993 consideration of its decision of 15 August 1991[37] by which it deplored the fact that the United States Congress had not adopted a legal framework for holding a referendum to enable the people of Puerto Rico to determine their political future. The Committee also endorsed the Group's suggestion that requests for hearings be given due consideration by the Committee. Accordingly, the Committee, during its July session, heard 19 representatives of organizations from Puerto Rico.

In July,[38] the Committee's Rapporteur drew attention to related reports prepared in 1982,[39] 1984,[40] 1985,[41] 1986,[42] 1987,[43] 1988,[44] 1989,[45] 1990[46] and 1991,[47] as well as a study prepared by him in 1985.[41]

New Caledonia

During its consideration of New Caledonia, the Committee on colonial countries had before it a working paper prepared by the Secretariat[48] on recent political and economic developments. It recalled that under the provisions of the 1988 Matignon Agreement,[49] a self-determination referendum would be held in 1998 following a 10-year period of development aimed at effecting more equitable economic distribution between the indigenous Melanesians, known as Kanaks, who comprised about 45 per cent of the population, and persons of European origin, mainly French.

The Committee to Monitor the Matignon Agreement, at its third meeting (Paris, 17 and 18 October 1991), agreed that progress was being made in economic and social areas but stressed the need for France to increase its efforts to bring about more equitable economic distribution and provide education and training that would enable Kanaks to participate equally in the economy and Government of the Territory. As to political developments, the review of electoral rolls and preparation of voter lists was continuing with the help of magistrates from France.

The paper noted that for many years the majority of Kanaks had been dependent for their livelihood on subsistence agriculture because the mining sector and most land suitable for commercial agriculture were controlled by inhabitants of European origin. As called for by the Matignon Agreement, a large proportion of government de-velopment funds were being channelled to areas inhabited by Kanak majorities. Development projects included the construction of roads, schools, colleges, medical centres, hotels and housing as well as electrification and the laying of telephone lines and water distribution systems. Under land redistribution projects, from 1988 to 1991, 62,500 hectares of land were redistributed, of which 75 per cent went to Kanaks.

GENERAL ASSEMBLY ACTION

On 25 November 1992, the General Assembly, on the recommendation of the Fourth Committee, adopted **resolution 47/26** without vote.

Question of New Caledonia

The General Assembly,

Having considered the question of New Caledonia,

Having examined the chapter of the report of the Special Committee on the Situation with regard to the Implementation of the Declaration on the Granting of Independence to Colonial Countries and Peoples relating to New Caledonia,

Reaffirming the right of peoples to self-determination as enshrined in the Charter of the United Nations,

Recalling its resolutions 1514(XV) of 14 December 1960 and 1541(XV) of 15 December 1960,

Noting the importance of the positive measures being pursued in New Caledonia by the French authorities, in cooperation with all sectors of the population, to promote political, economic and social development in the Territory, including measures in the area of environmental protection and action with respect to drug abuse and trafficking, in order to provide a framework for its peaceful progress to self-determination,

Noting also, in this context, the importance of equitable economic and social development, as well as continued dialogue among the parties involved in New Caledonia in the preparation of the act of self-determination of New Caledonia,

1. *Approves* the section of the report of the Special Committee on the Situation with regard to the Implementation of the Declaration on the Granting of Independence to Colonial Countries and Peoples relating to New Caledonia;

2. *Urges* all the parties involved, in the interest of all the people of New Caledonia, to maintain their dialogue in a spirit of harmony;

3. *Invites* all the parties involved to continue promoting a framework for the peaceful progress of the Territory towards an act of self-determination in which all options are open and which would safeguard the rights of all New Caledonians;

4. *Welcomes* measures taken recently and those anticipated to strengthen and diversify the New Caledonian economy in all fields;

5. *Also welcomes* the call by the Committee to Monitor the Matignon Agreement, at its meeting held in Paris on 17 and 18 October 1991, for greater progress in housing, employment, training, education and health care in New Caledonia;

6. *Commends* the decision to establish a Melanesian cultural centre as a contribution to preserving the indigenous culture of New Caledonia;

7. *Takes note* of the recent positive initiatives aimed at protecting New Caledonia's natural environment, notably the "Zoneco" operation designed to map and evaluate marine resources within the economic zone of New Caledonia;

8. *Acknowledges* the close links between New Caledonia and the peoples of the South Pacific and the positive actions being taken by the French authorities to facilitate the further development of those links, including the development of closer relations with the member countries of the South Pacific Forum;

9. *Requests* the Special Committee to continue the examination of this question at its next session and to report thereon to the General Assembly at its forty-eighth session.

General Assembly resolution 47/26

25 November 1992   Meeting 72   Adopted without vote

Approved by Fourth Committee (A/47/648) without objection, 3 November (meeting 8); draft by Committee on colonial countries (A/47/23); agenda item 18.

Meeting numbers. GA 47th session: 4th Committee 2-8; plenary 72.

REFERENCES

(1)YUN 1960, p. 49, GA res. 1514(XV), 14 Dec. 1960. (2)YUN 1991, p. 777, GA res. 46/181, 19 Dec. 1991. (3)GA res. 43/47, 22 Nov. 1988. (4)A/AC.109/1114. (5)A/AC.109/1107. (6)A/AC.109/L.1791 & Corr.1. (7)A/47/23. (8)A/AC.109/L.1776. (9)A/AC.109/L.1780. (10)A/AC.109/L.1782. (11)A/AC.109/L.1777. (12)A/AC.109/L.1778. (13)A/AC.109/L.1779. (14)A/47/86. (15)YUN 1991, p. 782, GA res. 46/65, 11 Dec. 1991. (16)A/47/281 & Add.1. (17)A/47/649. (18)YUN 1991, p. 784, GA res. 46/70, 11 Dec. 1991. (19)E/1992/28 (dec. 92/10). (20)Ibid. (dec. 92/25). (21)E/1992/85. (22)A/AC.109/L.1785. (23)A/AC.109/1119. (24)A/AC.109/1104. (25)A/AC.109/1117. (26)A/AC.109/1118. (27)A/AC.109/1124. (28)A/AC.109/1123. (29)A/AC.109/1103. (30)A/AC.109/1113. (31)A/AC.109/1110. (32)A/AC.109/1136. (33)S/24471. (34)YUN 1977, p. 162, SC res. 421(1977), 9 Dec. 1977. (35)Ibid., p. 161, SC res. 418(1977), 4 Nov. 1977. (36)YUN 1984, p. 143, SC res. 558(1984), 13 Dec. 1984. (37)YUN 1991, p. 790. (38)A/AC.109/L.1788. (39)YUN 1982, p. 1276. (40)A/AC.109/L.1519. (41)YUN 1985, p. 1081. (42)A/AC.109/L.1598. (43)YUN 1987, p. 972. (44)A/AC.109/L.1676. (45)A/AC.109/L.1703. (46)A/AC.109/L.1746. (47)YUN 1991, p. 789. (48)A/AC.109/1120. (49)A/AC.109/964.

Other general questions

Scholarships

The Secretary-General, in accordance with a General Assembly request of 1991,(1) reported in September 1992(2) on offers made by Member States of study and training facilities for inhabitants of NSGTs. Five Member States informed the Secretary-General of scholarships offered to inhabitants of NSGTs during the 1991-1992 or 1992-1993 academic year. Australia had granted awards to 15 students from New Caledonia to attend Australian institutions of higher education; Barbados had awarded a total of 14 scholarships to nationals from NSGTs of the Caribbean; Cyprus offered one scholarship at the Cyprus Forestry College; New Zealand had granted study awards to 7 students

from New Caledonia and to 13 from Tokelau; and the United Kingdom had offered a total of 159 scholarships to students from British dependent Territories.

Between 1 October 1991 and 30 September 1992, the Secretariat had received requests from 42 students for information on the availability of scholarships. None were inhabitants of NSGTs.

GENERAL ASSEMBLY ACTION

On 16 November 1992, the General Assembly, on the recommendation of the Fourth Committee, adopted **resolution 47/17** without vote.

Offers by Member States of study and training facilities for inhabitants of Non-Self-Governing Territories

The General Assembly,

Recalling its resolution 46/66 of 11 December 1991,

Having examined the report of the Secretary-General on offers by Member States of study and training facilities for inhabitants of Non-Self-Governing Territories, prepared pursuant to General Assembly resolution 845(IX) of 22 November 1954,

Conscious of the importance of promoting the educational advancement of the inhabitants of Non-Self-Governing Territories,

Strongly convinced that the continuation and expansion of offers of scholarships is essential in order to meet the increasing need of students from Non-Self-Governing Territories for educational and training assistance, and considering that students in those Territories should be encouraged to avail themselves of such offers,

1. *Takes note* of the report of the Secretary-General;

2. *Expresses its appreciation* to those Member States that have made scholarships available to the inhabitants of Non-Self-Governing Territories;

3. *Invites* all States to make or continue to make generous offers of study and training facilities to the inhabitants of those Territories that have not yet attained self-government or independence and, wherever possible, to provide travel funds to prospective students;

4. *Urges* the administering Powers to take effective measures to ensure the widespread and continuous dissemination in the Territories under their administration of information relating to offers of study and training facilities made by States and to provide all the necessary facilities to enable students to avail themselves of such offers;

5. *Requests* the Secretary-General to report to the General Assembly at its forty-eighth session on the implementation of the present resolution;

6. *Draws the attention* of the Special Committee on the Situation with regard to the Implementation of the Declaration on the Granting of Independence to Colonial Countries and Peoples to the present resolution.

General Assembly resolution 47/17

16 November 1992   Meeting 61   Adopted without vote

Approved by Fourth Committee (A/47/647) without objection, 3 November (meeting 8); 47-nation draft (A/C.4/47/L.4); agenda item 101.

Sponsors: Algeria, Antigua and Barbuda, Argentina, Australia, Barbados, Belize, Benin, Brazil, Bulgaria, Burkina Faso, Burundi, China, Costa Rica, Cuba, Cyprus, El Salvador, Fiji, Guatemala, Guinea, Guyana, Honduras, Indonesia, Iran, Jamaica, Madagascar, Malaysia, Mali, New Zealand, Nicaragua, Nigeria, Pakistan, Panama, Papua New Guinea, Philippines, Saint Lucia,

Information to the United Nations

States responsible for the administration of NSGTs continued to inform the Secretary-General about the Territories' economic, social and educational conditions under the terms of Article 73 *e* of the United Nations Charter (see APPENDIX II). In reports to the Committee[3] and the General Assembly,[4] the Secretary-General listed the date of receipt of the information provided by the administering States and the period covered by their reports. In 1992, he stated that he had received information with respect to the following NSGTs:

New Zealand: Tokelau
United Kingdom: Bermuda, British Virgin Islands, Cayman Islands, Gibraltar, St. Helena
United States: American Samoa, Guam, United States Virgin Islands

GENERAL ASSEMBLY ACTION

On 16 November 1992, the General Assembly, on the recommendation of the Fourth Committee, adopted **resolution 47/14** by recorded vote.

Information from Non-Self-Governing Territories transmitted under Article 73 of the Charter of the United Nations

The General Assembly,

Having examined the chapter of the report of the Special Committee on the Situation with regard to the Implementation of the Declaration on the Granting of Independence to Colonial Countries and Peoples relating to the information from Non-Self-Governing Territories transmitted under Article 73 *e* of the Charter of the United Nations and the action taken by the Special Committee in respect of that information,

Having also examined the report of the Secretary-General on the question,

Recalling its resolution 1970(XVIII) of 16 December 1963, in which it requested the Special Committee to study the information transmitted to the Secretary-General in accordance with Article 73 *e* of the Charter and to take such information fully into account in examining the situation with regard to the implementation of the Declaration on the Granting of Independence to Colonial Countries and Peoples, contained in General Assembly resolution 1514(XV) of 14 December 1960,

Recalling also its resolution 46/63 of 11 December 1991, in which it requested the Special Committee to continue to discharge the functions entrusted to it under resolution 1970(XVIII),

Stressing the importance of timely transmission by the administering Powers of adequate information under Article 73 *e* of the Charter, in particular in relation to the preparation by the Secretariat of the working papers on the Territories concerned,

1. *Approves* the chapter of the report of the Special Committee on the Situation with regard to the Implementation of the Declaration on the Granting of Independence to Colonial Countries and Peoples relating to the information from Non-Self-Governing Territories

transmitted under Article 73 *e* of the Charter of the United Nations;

2. *Reaffirms* that, in the absence of a decision by the General Assembly itself that a Non-Self-Governing Territory has attained a full measure of self-government in terms of Chapter XI of the Charter, the administering Power concerned should continue to transmit information under Article 73 *e* of the Charter with respect to that Territory;

3. *Requests* the administering Powers concerned to transmit or continue to transmit to the Secretary-General the information prescribed in Article 73 *e* of the Charter, as well as the fullest possible information on political and constitutional developments in the Territories concerned, within a maximum period of six months following the expiration of the administrative year in those Territories;

4. *Requests* the Secretary-General to continue to ensure that adequate information is drawn from all available published sources in connection with the preparation of the working papers relating to the Territories concerned;

5. *Requests* the Special Committee to continue to discharge the functions entrusted to it under General Assembly resolution 1970(XVIII), in accordance with established procedures, and to report thereon to the Assembly at its forty-eighth session.

General Assembly resolution 47/14

16 November 1992   Meeting 61   142-0-3 (recorded vote)

Approved by Fourth Committee (A/47/644) by recorded vote (129-0-3), 3 November (meeting 8); draft by Committee on colonial countries (A/47/23); agenda item 98.
Meeting numbers. GA 47th session: 4th Committee 2-8; plenary 61.
Recorded vote in Assembly as follows:

In favour: Afghanistan, Algeria, Angola, Argentina, Australia, Austria, Bahamas, Bahrain, Bangladesh, Barbados, Belarus, Belgium, Belize, Benin, Bolivia, Botswana, Brazil, Brunei Darussalam, Bulgaria, Burkina Faso, Burundi, Cameroon, Canada, Cape Verde, Chile, China, Colombia, Congo, Costa Rica, Côte d'Ivoire, Croatia, Cuba, Cyprus, Czechoslovakia, Democratic People's Republic of Korea, Denmark, Djibouti, Dominica, Ecuador, Egypt, El Salvador, Ethiopia, Fiji, Finland, Germany, Ghana, Greece, Grenada, Guatemala, Guinea, Guinea-Bissau, Guyana, Haiti, Honduras, Hungary, Iceland, India, Indonesia, Iran, Iraq, Ireland, Israel, Italy, Jamaica, Japan, Jordan, Kenya, Kuwait, Lao People's Democratic Republic, Lebanon, Lesotho, Liberia, Libyan Arab Jamahiriya, Liechtenstein, Luxembourg, Madagascar, Malaysia, Maldives, Mali, Malta, Marshall Islands, Mauritania, Mexico, Micronesia, Mongolia, Morocco, Myanmar, Namibia, Nepal, Netherlands, New Zealand, Nicaragua, Niger, Nigeria, Norway, Oman, Pakistan, Panama, Papua New Guinea, Paraguay, Peru, Philippines, Poland, Portugal, Qatar, Republic of Korea, Republic of Moldova, Romania, Russian Federation, Rwanda, Saint Lucia, Saint Vincent and the Grenadines, Samoa, Sao Tome and Principe, Saudi Arabia, Senegal, Seychelles, Sierra Leone, Singapore, Slovenia, Spain, Sri Lanka, Suriname, Swaziland, Sweden, Syrian Arab Republic, Thailand, Togo, Trinidad and Tobago, Tunisia, Turkey, Uganda, Ukraine, United Arab Emirates, United Republic of Tanzania, Uruguay, Vanuatu, Venezuela, Viet Nam, Yemen, Zambia, Zimbabwe.
Against: None.
Abstaining: France, United Kingdom, United States.

Visiting missions

The Chairman of the Committee on colonial countries, as requested by the Committee in 1991,[5] held consultations with representatives of the administering Powers on the question of sending visiting missions to NSGTs. The Chairman reported in July 1992[6] that he had also informed the Powers of progress in the reforms that the Committee had initiated to improve its efficiency and methods of work. One administering Power indicated that the possibility of a further visiting mission to the Territory under its administration was under review by the leaders of that Territory. Another stated that missions should be studied on a case-by-case basis to determine their objectives and assess whether they would be productive. The United Kingdom stated that it saw no case for missions by the Committee on colonial countries to its dependent Territories.

On 28 July,[7] the Committee adopted a resolution on the question of sending missions to Territories, stressing the need to dispatch periodic visiting missions to facilitate full implementation of the 1960 Declaration,[8] calling on the administering Powers to continue to cooperate by receiving United Nations missions in the Territories under their administration and to participate in the work of the Committee, and requesting its Chairman to continue consultations with those Powers and to report to the Committee thereon.

REFERENCES

[1]YUN 1991, p. 791, GA res. 46/66, 11 Dec. 1991. [2]A/47/486. [3]A/AC.109/1121. [4]A/47/473. [5]YUN 1991, p. 793. [6]A/AC.109/L.1783. [7]A/AC.109/1131. [8]YUN 1960, p. 49, GA res. 1514(XV), 14 Dec. 1960.

Other colonial Territories

East Timor

During its consideration of East Timor, the Committee on colonial countries heard statements by Portugal as the administering Power, Indonesia and 23 petitioners.

The Committee had before it a July working paper[1] prepared by the Secretariat reviewing political developments, the human rights situation, economic and social conditions and other developments. It also outlined United Nations consideration of the question.

Regarding the comprehensive settlement of the question of East Timor, it was noted that the Secretary-General had been in contact with the parties concerned with a view to reactivating a dialogue that could lead to a settlement. The Governments of Indonesia and Portugal had presented proposals and views on a dialogue to the Secretary-General, who continued his efforts to obtain an agreement on the modalities and format of such talks.

Acting on the proposal of its Chairman, the Committee decided without objection to continue consideration of the item at its next session, subject to any directives by the General Assembly.

By **decision 47/402** of 18 September 1992, the General Assembly, on the recommendation of the General Committee, deferred consideration of the item on East Timor to its forty-eighth (1993) session.

Falkland Islands (Malvinas)

The Committee on colonial countries again considered the question of the Falkland Islands (Malvinas) in 1992. The United Kingdom, the administering Power concerned, did not participate in the consideration of the item. The Committee acceded to a request from Argentina to participate. It had before it a July working paper,[2] prepared by the Secretariat, which described political developments and economic, social and educational conditions in the islands and also discussed consideration of the question by the United Nations and the Organization of American States.[3] In September 1991,[4] Argentina and the United Kingdom had signed an agreement revising the terms of the Madrid Agreement of 1990, which dealt with the Interim Reciprocal Information and Consultation System as it applied to military vessels.[5]

By a vote of 20 to 0 with 3 abstentions, the Committee adopted a resolution on the question on 29 July[6] that requested Argentina and the United Kingdom to consolidate the current process of dialogue and cooperation by resuming negotiations to find a peaceful solution to the sovereignty dispute relating to the islands; reiterated its firm support for the mission of good offices of the Secretary-General in assisting the parties; and decided to keep the issue under review.

On 10 November 1992, the General Assembly, by **decision 47/408**, decided to defer consideration of the question of the Falkland Islands (Malvinas) and to include it in the provisional agenda of its forty-eighth (1993) session.

Western Sahara

Security Council consideration. As requested by the Security Council in 1991,[7] the Secretary-General, in February 1992, submitted a further report on the United Nations Mission for the Referendum in Western Sahara (MINURSO).[8] The report described the military aspects of MINURSO and all other aspects of the operation, including developments since his last report to the Council in December 1991.[9] The Secretary-General noted that the referendum for self-determination of the people of Western Sahara should have taken place in January 1992. However, it had not been possible to proceed with the original timetable, in view of continuing problems and differences of interpretation by Morocco and the Frente Popular para la Liberación de Saguia el-Hamra y de Río de Oro (Frente POLISARIO) regarding the implementation of the Secretary-General's settlement plan,[10] approved by the Council in April 1991.[11] He proposed a three-month target period for resolving all outstanding issues blocking the plan's implementation, after which he would report further to the Security Council, not later than the end of May 1992. If by that date no agreement had been reached on implementing the existing plan, he said it would be necessary to consider alternative courses of action and possibly adopt a new approach. Meanwhile, the Secretary-General recommended that the current level of MINURSO activity be maintained and that the mandate of its military elements continue to be restricted to verifying the cease-fire and cessation of hostilities in the areas defined in September 1991.[12]

On 25 March 1992,[13] the President of the Security Council informed the Secretary-General that the members of the Council had taken note of his February report on MINURSO and reiterated their support for his efforts and the efforts to be made by the Secretary-General's Special Representative for Western Sahara to accelerate the implementation of the settlement plan.

In May,[14] the Secretary-General submitted to the Council a further report on the situation in Western Sahara in which he addressed the current status of the plan in its military and other aspects. The Secretary-General stated that the role of the MINURSO military unit was essentially limited to monitoring and verifying the cease-fire into which Morocco and the Frente POLISARIO had entered. He said the Special Representative had toured the mission area and neighbouring countries from 19 to 30 April 1992, meeting with the King of Morocco, the Secretary-General of the Frente POLISARIO and the Heads of State of Algeria and Mauritania. Based on his initial contacts with the parties, the Special Representative concluded that their respective positions remained far apart and that their differences had continued to present serious obstacles to the implementation of the settlement plan. At the same time, he was encouraged to find that both parties remained committed to the plan as a framework for a solution to the Western Sahara conflict. Algeria and Mauritania promised him their full support and cooperation to overcome existing obstacles and facilitate the execution of the plan.

The Secretary-General also stated that regardless of the progress of the current talks, he remained convinced of the need to maintain the military strength of MINURSO in Western Sahara to adequately monitor the cease-fire. He recom-

mended that the Council extend MINURSO's mandate until the end of August. He hoped that by then substantial progress would have been made to prepare the ground for a referendum. If by that time, however, the peace process remained deadlocked, despite the efforts of the Special Representative, the Security Council might wish to consider a different approach.

The President of the Security Council, in June,[15] informed the Secretary-General that the Council members welcomed the fact that the two parties had agreed to engage in discussions with the Special Representative, with a view to reactivating the settlement plan. They reaffirmed their support for the efforts which the Secretary-General and his Special Representative were making and asked him to submit a further progress report on implementation of the plan. The members of the Council shared the Secretary-General's views on the need to maintain the presence of MINURSO personnel in Western Sahara to monitor the cease-fire.

As requested, the Secretary-General submitted a further progress report on the situation on 20 August 1992.[16] He reported that the Special Representative had had talks with both parties beginning in mid-June, meeting separately with them at Geneva, in the mission area and finally in New York, where the talks concluded on 2 July. The talks had focused on safeguards to protect the political, economic, social and other rights and liberties of the losing side in the referendum, whatever the outcome. The talks were expected to create a climate of mutual trust and confidence in which obstacles to the referendum, such as the criteria for eligibility to vote, could be overcome. Both parties agreed to engage in a new round of talks with the Special Representative, this time devoted to the interpretation of the criteria for eligibility to vote as contained in a 1991 report of the Secretary-General.[9] Morocco had accepted those criteria, despite reservations on provisions which it found to be unnecessarily restrictive. However, the Frente POLISARIO had rejected those criteria on the grounds that they would unduly enlarge the electoral body beyond the voters included in the 1974 census. Nevertheless, the Frente POLISARIO had gradually reassessed its position in the light of the Special Representative's efforts to relaunch the settlement plan. Without prejudice to its position on the criteria, the POLISARIO Front agreed to support the efforts of the Special Representative to ensure that both parties arrived at the same interpretation of all criteria. The Secretary-General stated that he intended to submit a further report to the Council before the end of September, focusing on the results of the next round of talks by his Special Representative and the parties, which were due to begin on 24 August. He proposed maintaining the existing deployment and staffing of MINURSO.

On 31 August,[17] the President of the Security Council stated that the Council members hoped both parties would cooperate fully with the Secretary-General and the Special Representative in their efforts to achieve speedy progress in implementing the plan and strongly urged the parties to make extraordinary efforts to ensure the plan's success. The Council members looked forward to receiving a further progress report before the end of September.

The Secretary-General, on 2 October,[18] reported to the Council that talks concerning the interpretation of the criteria for eligibility to vote, held from 25 August to 25 September, were inconclusive, and that he had agreed with a proposal by the Special Representative to hold further consultations to clarify unresolved questions. In addition, there were plans to try to determine with the parties whether a meeting of tribal chiefs could help resolve the problems impeding implementation of the settlement plan. The Secretary-General proposed postponing his report to the Council pending the close of these consultations. Replying to the Secretary-General, the Council, on 8 October,[19] welcomed the plan to explore with the parties a meeting of tribal chiefs and emphasized the urgency of the pending questions being settled. It awaited a further progress report from the Secretary-General.

On 22 December,[20] the Secretary-General informed the Council that it was not possible to hold a consultative meeting of tribal chiefs due to discrepancies regarding the notion of tribal chiefs. In addition, despite the efforts of the Special Representative, agreements among all concerned on the major aspects of the settlement plan had not been reached. The Secretary-General stated that he felt obliged to take concrete steps towards holding the referendum and would set forth the necessary steps to do so in January 1993.

Consideration by the Committee on colonial countries. The Committee heard the views of one representative of the Frente POLISARIO and considered a working paper prepared by the Secretariat containing information on developments in Western Sahara.[21] The paper discussed General Assembly consideration of the question in 1991, activities of the Secretary-General's good offices and political and other developments from August 1991 to July 1992.

General Assembly consideration. The Assembly's Fourth Committee heard statements by four petitioners on behalf of the Frente POLISARIO, the Western Sahara Awareness Project, the Sahara Fund and Brown University (Providence, United States).[22]

As requested by the General Assembly in 1991,[23] the Secretary-General reported in October 1992[24] on the situation in Western Sahara and described the activities he had taken from 24 October 1991 to 2 October 1992 towards a settlement.

GENERAL ASSEMBLY ACTION

On 25 November 1992, the General Assembly, on the recommendation of the Fourth Committee, adopted **resolution 47/25** without vote.

Question of Western Sahara

The General Assembly,

Having considered the question of Western Sahara,

Reaffirming the inalienable right of all peoples to self-determination and independence, in accordance with the principles set forth in the Charter of the United Nations and in General Assembly resolution 1514(XV) of 14 December 1960, containing the Declaration on the Granting of Independence to Colonial Countries and Peoples,

Recalling its resolution 46/67 of 11 December 1991,

Recalling also the agreement in principle given on 30 August 1988 by the Kingdom of Morocco and the Frente Popular para la Liberación de Saguia el-Hamra y de Río de Oro to the proposals of the Secretary-General of the United Nations and the current Chairman of the Assembly of Heads of State and Government of the Organization of African Unity in the context of their joint mission of good offices,

Recalling further Security Council resolutions 621(1988) of 20 September 1988, 658(1990) of 27 June 1990, 690(1991) of 29 April 1991, and 725(1991) of 31 December 1991, relating to the question of Western Sahara,

Recalling with satisfaction the entry into force of the cease-fire in Western Sahara on 6 September 1991, in accordance with the proposal of the Secretary-General accepted by the two parties,

Noting with satisfaction the appointment on 23 March 1992 of Mr. Sahabzada Yaqub-Khan as Special Representative of the Secretary-General for Western Sahara,

Taking note with satisfaction of the section on Western Sahara in the Final Document of the Tenth Conference of Heads of State or Government of Non-Aligned Countries, held at Jakarta from 1 to 6 September 1992,[a]

Having examined the relevant chapter of the report of the Special Committee on the Situation with regard to the Implementation of the Declaration on the Granting of Independence to Colonial Countries and Peoples,

Having also examined the report of the Secretary-General,

1. *Takes note with appreciation* of the report of the Secretary-General;

2. *Pays tribute* to the Secretary-General for his action with a view to settling the question of Western Sahara by the implementation of the settlement plan;

3. *Reiterates its support* for further efforts of the Secretary-General for the organization and supervision by the United Nations, in cooperation with the Organization of African Unity, of a referendum for self-determination of the people of Western Sahara, in conformity with resolutions 658(1990) and 690(1991) by which the Security Council adopted the settlement plan for Western Sahara;

---

[a]A/47/675-S/24816.

4.   *Endorses* the contents of the letter dated 31 August 1992 from the President of the Security Council to the Secretary-General in which the members of the Council informed the Secretary-General that they shared his views on the necessity of the two parties scrupulously abiding by the cease-fire and abstaining from any provocative behaviour endangering the settlement plan, and expressed their hope that both parties would extend their full cooperation to the Secretary-General and the Special Representative in their efforts to achieve speedy progress in the implementation of the plan and would make extraordinary efforts to ensure the success of the plan;

5.   *Requests* the Special Committee on the Situation with regard to the Implementation of the Declaration on the Granting of Independence to Colonial Countries and Peoples to continue to consider the situation in Western Sahara, bearing in mind the ongoing referendum process, and to report thereon to the General Assembly at its forty-eighth session;

6.   *Invites* the Secretary-General to submit to the General Assembly at its forty-eighth session a report on the implementation of the present resolution.

General Assembly resolution 47/25

25 November 1992   Meeting 72   Adopted without vote

Approved by Fourth Committee (A/47/648) without vote, 3 November (meeting 8); draft by Chairman (A/C.4/47/L.2); agenda item 18.
Meeting numbers. GA 47th session: 4th Committee 2-8; plenary 72.

Financing of MINURSO

GENERAL ASSEMBLY ACTION

On 14 September 1992, the General Assembly adopted **decision 46/481** by which it included in the draft agenda of its forty-seventh (1992) session the item entitled "Financing of the United Nations Mission for the Referendum in Western Sahara".

Report of the Secretary-General. In December,[25] the Secretary-General submitted a report on financing MINURSO in which he discussed the status of assessed contributions, voluntary contributions, the financial performance report on MINURSO from 17 May 1991 to 30 November 1992 and cost estimates for the period from 1 December 1992 to 30 November 1993. Annexed to the report were statistical tables.

GENERAL ASSEMBLY ACTION

On 22 December 1992, the General Assembly adopted **decision 47/451 A**, by which it authorized the Secretary-General to enter into commitments up to the amount of $7.1 million gross ($6.8 million net) for the maintenance of MINURSO for the period ending 28 February 1993 and that the amount be provided from the unencumbered balance of the appropriation provided for the Mission. It deferred the question of financing the Mission until its resumed forty-seventh session.

Other Territories

The Committee on colonial countries also dealt with the following 13 island Territories and had before

it working papers prepared by the Secretariat describing constitutional and political developments and economic and social conditions in them: American Samoa,[26] Anguilla,[27] Bermuda,[28] British Virgin Islands,[29] Cayman Islands,[30] Guam,[31] Montserrat,[32] Pitcairn,[33] St. Helena,[34] Tokelau,[35] Trust Territory of the Pacific Islands (see Chapter II of this section), Turks and Caicos Islands[36] and United States Virgin Islands.[37] It also considered a working paper on Gibraltar.[38]

The Committee allocated the item to its Subcommittee on Small Territories[39] for preliminary consideration and subsequently took up the item between 1 June and 29 July. It adopted a consolidated draft resolution, the first part of which dealt with decolonization in general and the second with 10 specific Territories, and two draft decisions, one on Pitcairn and the other on St. Helena, as recommendations to the General Assembly.

GENERAL ASSEMBLY ACTION

On 25 November, the General Assembly, on the recommendation of the Fourth Committee, adopted **resolutions 47/27 A and B** without vote.

Questions of American Samoa, Anguilla, Bermuda, the British Virgin Islands, the Cayman Islands, Guam, Montserrat, Tokelau, the Turks and Caicos Islands and the United States Virgin Islands

A
General

The General Assembly,

Having considered the questions of American Samoa, Anguilla, Bermuda, the British Virgin Islands, the Cayman Islands, Guam, Montserrat, Tokelau, the Turks and Caicos Islands and the United States Virgin Islands,

Having examined the relevant chapter of the report of the Special Committee on the Situation with regard to the Implementation of the Declaration on the Granting of Independence to Colonial Countries and Peoples,

Recalling its resolution 1514(XV) of 14 December 1960, containing the Declaration on the Granting of Independence to Colonial Countries and Peoples, and all resolutions and decisions of the United Nations relating to those Territories, including, in particular, those resolutions adopted by the General Assembly at its forty-sixth session on the individual Territories covered by the present resolution,

Recalling also its resolution 1541(XV) of 15 December 1960, containing the principles which should guide Member States in determining whether or not an obligation exists to transmit the information called for under Article 73 *e* of the Charter of the United Nations,

Conscious of the need to ensure the full and speedy implementation of the Declaration in respect of those Territories, in view of the target set by the United Nations to eradicate colonialism by the year 2000,

Aware of the special circumstances of the geographical location and economic conditions of each Territory, and bearing in mind the necessity of promoting economic stability and diversifying and strengthening further the economies of the respective Territories as a matter of priority,

Conscious of the particular vulnerability of the small Territories to natural disasters and environmental degradation,

Mindful that United Nations visiting missions provide a means of ascertaining the situation in the small Territories, and considering that the possibility of sending further visiting missions to those Territories at an appropriate time and in consultation with the administering Powers should be kept under review,

Noting with appreciation the contribution to the development of some Territories by specialized agencies and other organizations of the United Nations system, in particular the United Nations Development Programme, as well as regional institutions such as the Caribbean Development Bank,

Bearing in mind the fragile economy of the small Territories and their vulnerability to natural disasters and environmental degradation, and recalling General Assembly resolutions and the recommendations of the Meeting of Governmental Experts of Island Developing Countries and Donor Countries and Organizations, held in New York from 25 to 29 June 1990,[a]

Recalling the conclusions and recommendations of the United Nations regional seminars on decolonization held in 1990 in observance of the thirtieth anniversary of the Declaration on the Granting of Independence to Colonial Countries and Peoples, as well as the position taken by the territorial Governments contained in the reports of the seminars,[b]

1. *Approves* the chapter of the report of the Special Committee on the Situation with regard to the Implementation of the Declaration on the Granting of Independence to Colonial Countries and Peoples relating to American Samoa, Anguilla, Bermuda, the British Virgin Islands, the Cayman Islands, Guam, Montserrat, Tokelau, the Turks and Caicos Islands and the United States Virgin Islands;

2. *Reaffirms* the inalienable right of the people of those Territories to self-determination and independence in conformity with the Charter of the United Nations and General Assembly resolution 1514(XV), containing the Declaration on the Granting of Independence to Colonial Countries and Peoples;

3. *Reaffirms also* that it is ultimately for the people of those Territories themselves to determine freely their future political status in accordance with the relevant provisions of the Charter, the Declaration and the relevant resolutions of the General Assembly and, in that connection, calls upon the administering Powers, in cooperation with the territorial Governments, to facilitate programmes of political education in the Territories in order to foster an awareness among the people of the possibilities open to them in the exercise of their right to self-determination, in conformity with the legitimate political status options clearly defined in General Assembly resolution 1541(XV);

4. *Reiterates* that it is the responsibility of the administering Powers to create such conditions in the Territories as will enable their people to exercise freely and without interference their inalienable right to self-determination and independence;

5. *Reiterates the view* that such factors as territorial size, geographical location, size of population and limited nat-

ural resources should in no way serve as a pretext to delay the speedy exercise by the peoples of those Territories of their inalienable right to self-determination;

6. *Reaffirms* the responsibility of the administering Powers under the Charter to promote the economic and social development and to preserve the cultural identity of those Territories, and recommends that priority should continue to be given, in consultation with the territorial Governments concerned, to the strengthening and diversification of their respective economies;

7. *Urges* the administering Powers, in cooperation with the territorial Governments concerned, to take or continue to take effective measures to safeguard and guarantee the inalienable right of the peoples of those Territories to own, develop or dispose of the natural resources of those Territories, including marine resources, and to establish and maintain control over the future development of those resources;

8. *Also urges* the administering Powers to take all necessary measures to protect and conserve the environment of the Territories under their administration against any environmental degradation, and requests the specialized agencies concerned to continue to monitor environmental conditions in those Territories;

9. *Calls upon* the administering Powers to continue to take all necessary measures, in cooperation with the respective territorial Governments, to counter problems related to drug trafficking;

10. *Urges* the administering Powers to foster or continue to foster close relations between the Territories and other island communities in their respective regions, and to promote cooperation between the respective territorial Governments and regional institutions, as well as the specialized agencies and other organizations of the United Nations system;

11. *Also urges* the administering Powers to cooperate or continue to cooperate with the Special Committee in its work by providing timely and up-to-date information for each Territory under their administration, in accordance with Article 73 *e* of the Charter, and by facilitating the dispatch of visiting missions to the Territories to secure first-hand information thereon and to ascertain the wishes and aspirations of the inhabitants;

12. *Appeals* to the administering Powers to continue or to resume their participation in future meetings and activities of the Special Committee and to ensure the participation in the work of the Special Committee of representatives of the Non-Self-Governing Territories;

13. *Urges* Member States to contribute to the efforts of the United Nations to achieve the eradication of colonialism by the year 2000, and calls upon them to continue to give their full support to the action of the Special Committee towards the attainment of that objective;

14. *Invites* the specialized agencies and other organizations of the United Nations system to initiate or to continue to take all necessary measures to accelerate progress in the social and economic life of the Territories;

15. *Requests* the specialized agencies and other organizations of the United Nations system, in formulating their assistance programmes, to take due account of the text entitled "Challenges and opportunities: a strate-

---

[a]A/CONF.147/5-TD/B/AC.46/4.
[b]A/AC.109/1040 & Corr.1. and A/AC.109/1043.

gic framework'', which was adopted unanimously by the Meeting of Governmental Experts of Island Developing Countries and Donor Countries and Organizations;

16. *Requests* the Special Committee to continue the examination of the question of the small Territories and to recommend to the General Assembly the most suitable steps to be taken to enable the populations of those Territories to exercise their right to self-determination and independence, and to report thereon to the Assembly at its forty-eighth session.

B
Individual Territories

I. *American Samoa*

The General Assembly,

Referring to resolution A above,

Having heard the statement of the representative of the United States of America as the administering Power,[c]

Noting the establishment of a new Political Status and Constitutional Review Commission by the Governor and the *Fono*, the legislature of the Territory,

Noting the need to diversify and develop the economy of the Territory through the expansion of the existing small and service-oriented industries as well as through the development of commercial fishing and the tourism industry,

Noting also the devastation caused by hurricane Val in December 1991 and the recovery efforts of the territorial Government in conjunction with the administering Power and the international community,

Recalling the dispatch in 1981 of a United Nations visiting mission to the Territory,

1. *Welcomes* the establishment of a new Political Status and Constitutional Review Commission created under executive order by the Governor in August 1992;

2. *Calls upon* the administering Power, in cooperation with the territorial Government, to continue to promote the economic and social development of the Territory in order to reduce its heavy economic and financial dependence on the United States of America;

3. *Urges* the administering Power to continue to support measures by the territorial Government aimed at promoting the diversification of the economy and the development of the existing industries, particularly commercial fishing and tourism;

4. *Calls upon* the administering Power to continue to provide the Territory with the necessary assistance, through a number of its agencies, to reconstruct the many public facilities and thousands of family dwellings destroyed or heavily damaged by hurricane Val;

5. *Notes* that a period of eleven years has elapsed since a United Nations mission visited the Territory.

II. *Anguilla*

The General Assembly,

Referring to resolution A above,

Having heard the statement of the representative of the United Kingdom of Great Britain and Northern Ireland, as the administering Power,[d]

Aware of the desire of the people of Anguilla for a higher level of self-government,

Taking note of the statement by the administering Power that it would help the people of Anguilla to become independent when and if that was their constitutionally expressed wish,

Noting the reaction of the political leaders to the abolishment of the death penalty by the administering Power and the statement of the Chief Minister on this question,

Noting the admission of the Territory as an observer in the Organization of Eastern Caribbean States in 1991,

Noting that the unemployment rate in the Territory fell from 27 per cent in 1984 to 1.1 per cent in 1989, that salaries and allowances in the public sector have risen substantially since 1984 and that the number of posts has increased by 34 per cent since 1985,

Aware of the inability of Anguilla's educational system to alleviate the problem of scarcity of skilled national personnel, particularly in the fields of economic management and tourism, and that educational reform is of paramount importance to the achievement of the long-term economic goals of the Territory,

Noting further that the Government's Public Sector Investment Programme for 1991-1995, estimated at 35 million United States dollars, is expected to be financed by external donors through grants and concessional loans,

Taking into account the main development objectives established by the Territory's Executive Council, namely, the improved management of the economy through a more efficient public sector, the strategic development of human resources through the reform of the educational and training systems and the development of integrated policies of physical infrastructural improvements, as well as the preservation of the natural environment,

Recognizing the contribution of the marine resources of Anguilla to its local economy,

Recalling the dispatch in 1984 of a United Nations visiting mission to the Territory,

1. *Takes note* of the statement of the Chief Minister that the Government of Anguilla has no intention of moving towards independence during its current term of office;

2. *Notes with concern* that the administering Power continues to deny further delegation of competence over the special areas of responsibility of the Governor to ministers of the territorial Government prior to setting a time-frame for independence;

3. *Calls upon* the administering Power to consult with, and take into account the wishes of, the Government and the people of Anguilla prior to taking any decision likely to impact on their livelihood;

4. *Welcomes* the admission of the Territory as an observer in the Organization of Eastern Caribbean States, and requests the administering Power to facilitate the Territory's participation in other regional and/or international organizations;

5. *Commends* the territorial Government for the virtual full-employment situation prevailing in the Territory, and for the increases in the salaries and number of posts in the public sector over the past years;

6. *Notes with concern* the incapacity of Anguilla's educational system to supply the Territory's labour market with skilled managers, particularly in the areas of economic management and tourism;

7. *Calls upon* the administering Power, as well as other Member States and international organizations, to af-

[c]A/C.4/47/SR.7.

[d]A/C.4/47/SR.4.

ford or continue to afford the Government of Anguilla training possibilities for its staff in that respect;

8. *Invites* the international donor community to contribute generously to the Government's Public Sector Investment Programme for 1991-1995 and to grant the Territory all possible assistance to enable it to reach the main development objectives established by the Executive Council of the Territory;

9. *Welcomes* the measures taken by the territorial Government to protect and conserve marine resources and to control the activities of foreign fishermen operating illegally in the area;

10. *Calls upon* the administering Power to provide the Territory with the necessary assistance to mitigate the adverse effects of hurricane Hugo and to facilitate the provision of additional assistance and funds from international organizations and specialized agencies to the Territory;

11. *Notes* that a period of eight years has elapsed since a United Nations mission visited the Territory and calls upon the administering Power to facilitate the dispatch of a further visiting mission to Anguilla.

III. *Bermuda*

The General Assembly,

Referring to resolution A above,

Having heard the statement of the representative of the United Kingdom of Great Britain and Northern Ireland, as the administering Power,[d]

Noting with satisfaction the programme of Economic Stability and Responsible Management undertaken by the Government and the steps taken to offset a decline in revenue from tourism,

Noting a marked increase in unemployment in the Territory,

Noting with concern an increase in the illegal drug trade in the Territory,

Reaffirming its strong conviction that the presence of military bases and installations in the Territory could, in certain circumstances, constitute an obstacle to the implementation of the Declaration on the Granting of Independence to Colonial Countries and Peoples,

Noting that the Territory has never been visited by a United Nations visiting mission,

1. *Expresses the view* that it is ultimately for the people of Bermuda to decide their own future;

2. *Requests* the administering Power to assist the territorial Government in the implementation of its programme of Economic Stability and Responsible Management with a view to reducing the impact of the recession on the economy of the Territory and the unprecedented increase in unemployment;

3. *Calls upon* the administering Power to continue to take all necessary measures, in cooperation with the territorial Government, to counter problems related to drug trafficking;

4. *Also calls upon* the administering Power to ensure that the presence of military bases and installations in the Territory would not constitute an obstacle to the implementation of the Declaration on the Granting of Independence to Colonial Countries and Peoples nor hinder the population of the Territory from exercising its right to self-determination and independence in conformity with the purposes and principles of the Charter of the United Nations;

5. *Further calls upon* the administering Power to facilitate the dispatch of a United Nations visiting mission to the Territory.

IV. *British Virgin Islands*

The General Assembly,

Referring to resolution A above,

Having heard the statement of the representative of the United Kingdom of Great Britain and Northern Ireland, as the administering Power,[d]

Noting the participation of the Territory as an associate member in some regional and international organizations,

Noting also the application of the Territory for membership in the Food and Agriculture Organization of the United Nations,

Taking into account that, according to the annual report of the Caribbean Development Bank for 1990, there has been sustained growth in the economy of the Territory, and noting the measures taken by the territorial Government to develop the agricultural and industrial sectors,

Noting that the Territory might graduate to net-contributor status in the fifth programming cycle of the United Nations Development Programme, thereby requiring the Territory to contribute to the financing of its projects,

Noting also that the Caribbean Development Bank has reported that the scarcity of skilled manpower is the single most important constraint to the realization of the full development potential of the economy of the Territory,

Noting further that the United Nations Children's Fund is considering the continuation beyond 1992 of its five-year Multi-island Programme, which has funded educational projects in the British Virgin Islands,

Recognizing the measures being taken by the territorial Government to prevent drug trafficking and money laundering,

1. *Welcomes* the admission of the British Virgin Islands as an associate member of the Caribbean Community;

2. *Reiterates its call* upon the administering Power to facilitate the admission of the Territory to associate membership in the Food and Agriculture Organization of the United Nations, as well as its participation in other regional and international organizations;

3. *Calls upon* the administering Power to provide the Territory with the necessary assistance to mitigate the adverse effects of hurricane Hugo and to facilitate the provision of additional assistance and funds to the Territory from international organizations and specialized agencies;

4. *Welcomes* the efforts by the territorial Government to raise the quality of the labour force and to meet the trained labour requirements of the public service through its development plan for education;

5. *Calls upon* the United Nations Development Programme to continue its technical assistance to the British Virgin Islands, bearing in mind the vulnerability of the Territory to external economic factors and the scarcity of skilled workers in the Territory;

6. *Expresses its satisfaction* at the consideration being given by the United Nations Children's Fund to the continuation of its five-year Multi-island Programme aimed at improving education, health and social services in the Territory;

7.   *Urges* the regional and international financial institutions, as well as the specialized agencies and other organizations of the United Nations system, to assist the Government of the British Virgin Islands in identifying its medium- and long-term needs and to increase their participation in the full recovery of the Territory;

8.   *Notes with satisfaction* the measures being taken by the territorial Government to prevent drug trafficking and money laundering, and urges the administering Power to continue its assistance to the Territory in those endeavours;

9.   *Notes with regret* that a period of sixteen years has elapsed since a United Nations mission visited the Territory and appeals to the administering Power to facilitate the dispatch of such a mission.

V.   *Cayman Islands*

The General Assembly,

Referring to resolution A above,

Having heard the statement of the representative of the United Kingdom of Great Britain and Northern Ireland, as the administering Power,[d]

Noting the completion of the constitutional review exercise in the Cayman Islands, as well as the established timetable for the bringing into force of the amended Constitution,

Aware that the general election in the Territory is scheduled for November 1992,

Noting the measures being taken by the territorial Government to promote agricultural production with a view to reducing the heavy dependence of the Territory on imported provisions,

Expressing its concern that property and land continue to be owned and developed largely by foreign investors,

Noting that an increased proportion of the labour force of the Territory consists of expatriates and that there is a need for the training of nationals in the technical, vocational, managerial and professional fields,

Noting also the action taken by the territorial Government to implement its localization programme to promote increased participation of the local population in the decision-making process in the Cayman Islands,

Noting further the policy of the territorial Government to control the growth and to upgrade the efficiency of the public service,

Noting with concern the vulnerability of the Territory to drug trafficking and related activities,

Noting with satisfaction the efforts of the territorial Government, the Governments of other countries of the region, and the United Kingdom of Great Britain and Northern Ireland, as the administering Power, to prevent and repress illicit activities such as money laundering, funds smuggling, false invoicing and other related frauds, as well as the use of and trafficking in illegal drugs,

Recalling the dispatch in 1977 of a United Nations visiting mission to the Territory,

1.   *Requests* the administering Power to expedite the bringing into force of the amended Constitution, in close cooperation with the territorial Government and in conformity with the wishes and aspirations of the Caymanian population, with a view to enabling the people of the Cayman Islands to exercise their inalienable right to self-determination;

2.   *Notes with satisfaction* that the general election in the Territory is scheduled for November 1992 and re-

quests the administering Power, in close cooperation with the territorial Government, to continue the efforts aimed at ensuring that a free and fair general election is conducted in the Cayman Islands;

3.   *Calls upon* the administering Power, in consultation with the territorial Government, to continue to promote the agricultural development of the Cayman Islands with a view to reducing the dependence of the Territory on imported food supplies;

4.   *Urges* the administering Power, in consultation with the territorial Government, to continue to facilitate the expansion of the current programme of securing employment for the local population, in particular at the decision-making level;

5.   *Requests* the administering Power, in consultation with the territorial Government, to provide the assistance necessary to enhance the efficiency of the public service;

6.   *Calls upon* the administering Power to continue to take all necessary measures, in cooperation with the territorial Government, to counter problems related to money laundering, funds smuggling and other related crimes, as well as drug trafficking;

7.   *Notes with regret* that a period of fifteen years has elapsed since a United Nations mission visited the Territory, and appeals to the administering Power to facilitate the dispatch of such a mission.

VI.   *Guam*

The General Assembly,

Referring to resolution A above,

Having heard the statement of the representative of the United States of America, as the administering Power,[c]

Recalling that the second round of negotiations between the Government of the United States of America and the Government of Guam aimed at transferring land and facilities at the Naval Air Station, Agana, opened in July 1991,

Aware that large tracts of land in the Territory continue to be reserved for the use of the Department of Defense of the administering Power,

Cognizant that the administering Power has undertaken a programme of transferring surplus federal land to the Government of Guam,

Cognizant also of the potential for diversifying and developing the economy of Guam through commercial fishing and agriculture,

Mindful of discussions between the Guam Commission on Self-Determination and the executive branch of the administering Power on the draft Guam Commonwealth Act, which were recently concluded and will lead to consideration of the measure by the legislative branch of the administering Power,

Recalling that, in referendums held in Guam in 1987, a draft Commonwealth Act was endorsed by the people of Guam that, upon expeditious enactment by the Congress of the United States of America, would reaffirm the right of the people of Guam to draft their own constitution and to govern themselves,

Recalling the dispatch in 1979 of a United Nations visiting mission to the Territory,

1.   *Calls upon* the administering Power to continue to ensure that the presence of military bases and installations in the Territory should not constitute an obstacle to the implementation of the Declaration on the Granting of Independence to Colonial Countries and Peoples nor hinder the population of the Territory from exer-

cising its right to self-determination, including independence, in conformity with the purposes and principles of the Charter of the United Nations;

2. *Also calls upon* the administering Power, in cooperation with the territorial Government, to continue to expedite the transfer of land to the people of the Territory and to take the necessary steps to safeguard their property rights;

3. *Notes* that discussions held since 1990 between the Government of the United States of America and the Guam Commission on Self-Determination have resulted in qualified agreements on the provisions of the Guam Commonwealth Act, including agreements to disagree on several substantive portions of the Guam proposal, which are to be forwarded to the Congress of the United States for consideration;

4. *Urges* the administering Power to continue to support appropriate measures by the territorial Government aimed at promoting growth in commercial fishing and agriculture;

5. *Reiterates its request* to the administering Power that it continue to recognize and respect the cultural and ethnic identity of the Chamorro people, the indigenous inhabitants of Guam;

6. *Notes* that a period of thirteen years has elapsed since a United Nations mission visited the Territory.

VII. *Montserrat*

The General Assembly,

Referring to resolution A above,

Having heard the statement of the representative of the United Kingdom of Great Britain and Northern Ireland, as the administering Power,[d]

Recalling the devastation caused by hurricane Hugo in September 1989 and the recovery efforts of the territorial Government in conjunction with the administering Power and the international community,

Taking into account the membership of Montserrat in regional and international bodies and the outstanding request of the Territory for readmission to associate membership in the United Nations Educational, Scientific and Cultural Organization,

Noting the general elections held in Montserrat on 8 October 1991 and the election of a new Chief Minister,

Noting also that it is the policy of the territorial Government, while considering that independence is inevitable, to pursue a gradual approach to preparing the people of Montserrat for independence,

Noting further that, according to the Eastern Caribbean Central Bank, the economy of the Territory has continued its recovery,

Taking note of the statement of the Chief Minister at the Fifteenth Annual Miami Conference on the Caribbean, held at Miami from 2 to 6 December 1991, that the offshore financial services industry requires little or no natural resources and could make a substantial contribution to small island countries,

Noting the policy of the territorial Government to replace expatriates with suitably trained and qualified nationals,

Noting also that planned developments in the Territory aimed at enhancing the island's attractiveness as a tourist destination may impact negatively on the environment, in the absence of effective natural resource management,

Recalling that the last United Nations visiting mission to the Territory took place in 1982,

1. *Urges* the administering Power to continue to intensify and expand its programme of aid in order to accelerate the development of the economic and social infrastructure of the Territory;

2. *Reiterates its call* upon the administering Power, in cooperation with the territorial Government, to take, as a matter of urgency, the necessary steps to facilitate the readmission of Montserrat as an associate member of the United Nations Educational, Scientific and Cultural Organization;

3. *Urges* the specialized agencies and other organizations of the United Nations system, as well as regional and other multilateral financial institutions, to continue to expand their assistance to the Territory in the strengthening, development and diversification of the economy of Montserrat in accordance with its medium- and long-term development plans, as well as in alleviating the devastation caused by hurricane Hugo;

4. *Requests* the administering Power to continue to facilitate the assistance of the specialized agencies and other organizations of the United Nations system, as well as regional and multilateral financial institutions, to the Government of Montserrat;

5. *Calls upon* the administering Power, in cooperation with the territorial Government, to assist the Territory in its efforts to implement an ecotourism strategy aimed at developing its natural resources in a manner consistent with environmental considerations;

6. *Notes with satisfaction* the measures being taken by the territorial Government, in cooperation with the administering Power, to restore the Territory's offshore financial services industry;

7. *Urges* the administering Power to continue its assistance to the Territory in the prevention of drug trafficking and money laundering;

8. *Also urges* the administering Power, in cooperation with the territorial Government, to provide the necessary assistance for the training of local personnel in the skills essential to the development of the Territory and to encourage skilled workers to remain in the Territory;

9. *Notes with regret* that a period of ten years has elapsed since a United Nations mission visited the Territory and calls upon the administering Power to facilitate the dispatch of a visiting mission to Montserrat.

VIII. *Tokelau*

The General Assembly,

Referring to resolution A above,

Having heard the statement of the representative of New Zealand, the administering Power,[e]

Noting the continuing devolution of power to the local authority, the General *Fono* (Council), and mindful that the cultural heritage and traditions of the people of Tokelau should be taken fully into account in the evolution of the political institutions of Tokelau,

Noting also the endeavours of Tokelau to develop its marine and other resources and its efforts to diversify the income-earning ability of its population,

Noting further the concern of the people of the Territory regarding the serious consequences of changes in climatic patterns on the future of Tokelau,

Welcoming the information that Tokelau, while wishing to preserve the benefits of its current relationship

---

[c]A/C.4/47/SR.6.

with New Zealand, is exploring ways of achieving greater political and administrative autonomy,

Noting with appreciation the assistance extended to Tokelau by the administering Power, other Member States and international organizations, in particular the United Nations Development Programme, and its preparation of a third country programme for Tokelau for the period 1992-1996,

1. *Encourages* the Government of New Zealand, the administering Power, to continue to respect fully the wishes of the people of Tokelau in carrying out the political and economic development of the Territory in such a way as to preserve their social, cultural and traditional heritage;

2. *Calls upon* the administering Power, in consultation with the General *Fono* (Council), to continue to expand its development assistance to Tokelau in order to promote the economic and social development of the Territory;

3. *Notes* that the plan to transfer the Office for Tokelau Affairs from Apia to Tokelau is being pursued within the context of the exploration of ways of achieving greater political and administrative autonomy, and invites the administering Power to continue to provide maximum assistance in this regard;

4. *Invites* all governmental and non-governmental organizations, financial institutions, Member States and organizations of the United Nations system to grant or to continue to grant Tokelau special emergency economic assistance to mitigate the effects of cyclonic storms and to enable the Territory to meet its medium- and long-term reconstruction and rehabilitation requirements and address the issues of changes in climatic patterns.

IX. *Turks and Caicos Islands*

The General Assembly,

Referring to resolution A above,

Having heard the statement of the representative of the United Kingdom of Great Britain and Northern Ireland, as the administering Power,[d]

Noting the territorial Government's plan to reform the public service to enhance its efficiency,

Noting also the administrative steps taken by the territorial Government to implement its policy of localization of employment,

Noting further the Government's expressed need for 11.5 million United States dollars per year in development assistance to achieve its stated goal of economic independence by the year 1996,

Noting the Government's efforts to set up a Turks and Caicos development corporation,

Noting further that the agricultural sector is small and limited to subsistence farming for the local market and that 90 per cent of the food consumed in the Territory is imported,

Concerned at the continued decline of fisheries and marine production in relative terms in the past year,

Noting the Chief Minister's attendance at the Twelfth Meeting of the Conference of Heads of Government of the Caribbean Community, held at Basseterre, Saint Kitts and Nevis, from 2 to 4 July 1991,

1. *Calls upon* the territorial Government to promote alternative employment opportunities for those civil servants whose employment would be terminated as a result of the public service reform and the planned reduction of employees in the service;

2. *Also calls upon* the territorial Government to ensure that the employment of expatriates in the Territory's labour force is not prejudicial to the recruitment of suitably qualified and available islanders;

3. *Calls upon* the specialized agencies and other institutions of the United Nations system to explore concrete ways of assisting the Turks and Caicos Government to reach its stated goal of achieving economic independence by 1996;

4. *Urges* the administering Power to study favourably, in cooperation with the territorial Government, the needs of the Territory in this respect with a view to meeting those needs;

5. *Invites* international financial institutions and donor organizations, including the European Investment Bank and the Commonwealth Development Corporation, to provide the Territory with the necessary assistance for the setting up and/or operation of the Turks and Caicos Development Corporation;

6. *Urges* the administering Power and the relevant regional and international organizations to assist the territorial Government in increasing the efficiency of the agricultural and fisheries sectors;

7. *Also urges* the administering Power and the relevant regional and international organizations to support the efforts of the territorial Government to address the problem of environmental pollution and degradation;

8. *Notes* the admission of the Turks and Caicos Islands as an associate member of the Caribbean Community and invites other regional and international organizations to consider granting the Territory a similar status should the territorial Government so request;

9. *Notes with regret* that a period of twelve years has elapsed since a United Nations mission visited the Territory and appeals to the administering Power to facilitate the dispatch of such a mission.

X. *United States Virgin Islands*

The General Assembly,

Referring to resolution A above,

Having heard the statement of the representative of the United States of America, as the administering Power,[c]

Having heard the statement of the representative of the Government of the United States Virgin Islands,[d]

Noting that legislation has been approved in the Virgin Islands Senate and signed into law by the Governor of the Territory to conduct a referendum on political status in 1993,

Noting also that the extension to ninety days of the residency requirement for voting has not addressed the concerns of the representatives of the territorial Government and those of the Commission on Status and Federal Relations regarding eligibility to participate in a referendum on self-determination,

Noting further that legislation has been proposed in the United States Congress to transfer Water Island to the Territory at the end of 1992, and that the issue remains under consideration,

Noting the position of the judicial authorities of the United States of America regarding the issue of the West Indian Company's title and rights to the reclamation and development of the submerged land at Long Bay in the Charlotte Amalie Harbour,

Noting also the continuing interest of the territorial Government in seeking associate membership in the Organization of Eastern Caribbean States and observer status in the Caribbean Community, and its inability, for financial reasons, to participate in the Food and Agriculture Organization of the United Nations and the World Health Organization,

Noting further the expressed concerns of the Virgin Islands Government and people of the Territory over the vacancy of the District Court judgeship and their wish for the appointment of Virgin Islanders to other top posts in the judicial system,

Recalling the dispatch in 1977 of a United Nations visiting mission to the Territory and the outstanding request by the territorial Government for a United Nations mission to the Territory to observe the referendum process,

1. *Requests* the administering Power to provide the fullest cooperation and assistance to the territorial Government and the Commission on Status and Federal Relations in their review of the residency requirement for those eligible to participate in a genuine exercise of the right to self-determination in the United States Virgin Islands;

2. *Invites* the administering Power, as a matter of urgency, to facilitate the termination of Federal ownership of Water Island at the end of 1992;

3. *Notes* that a nominee has been named for a district court judgeship and that the district court judge on Saint Croix is a Virgin Islander;

4. *Reiterates its request* to the administering Power to facilitate as appropriate the participation of the Territory in the Organization of Eastern Caribbean States and the Caribbean Community, as well as in various international and regional organizations, including the Caribbean Group for Cooperation in Economic Development of the World Bank, in accordance with the policy of the administering Power and the terms of reference of such organizations;

5. *Calls upon* the administering Power to respond favourably to the request of the territorial Government for the dispatch of a United Nations visiting and observer mission to the Territory.

General Assembly resolution 47/27 A and B

25 November 1992   Meeting 72   Adopted without vote

Approved by Fourth Committee (A/47/648) without objection, 5 November (meeting 9); draft by Committee on colonial countries (A/47/23), as amended by United States (A/C.4/47/L.6, A/C.4/47/L.7, A/C.4/47/L.8); agenda item 18.
Meeting numbers. GA 47th session: 4th Committee 2-9; plenary 72.

Gibraltar

On 25 November, the General Assembly, on the recommendation of the Fourth Committee, adopted **decision 47/411** without vote.

Question of Gibraltar

At its 72nd plenary meeting, on 25 November 1992, the General Assembly, on the recommendation of the Fourth Committee, adopted the following text as representing the consensus of the members of the Assembly:

"The General Assembly, recalling its decision 46/420 of 11 December 1991 and recalling at the same time that the statement agreed to by the Governments of Spain and the United Kingdom of Great Britain and Northern Ireland at Brussels on 27 November 1984 stipulates, *inter alia,* the following:

'The establishment of a negotiating process aimed at overcoming all the differences between them over Gibraltar and at promoting cooperation on a mutually beneficial basis on economic, cultural, touristic, aviation, military and environmental matters. Both sides accept that the issues of sovereignty will be discussed in that process. The British Government will fully maintain its commitment to honour the wishes of the people of Gibraltar as set out in the preamble of the 1969 Constitution',

takes note of the fact that, as part of this process, the Ministers for Foreign Affairs have held annual meetings alternately in each capital, and urges both Governments to continue their negotiations with the object of reaching a definitive solution to the problem of Gibraltar in the light of relevant resolutions of the General Assembly and in the spirit of the Charter of the United Nations."

General Assembly decision 47/411

Adopted without vote

Approved by Fourth Committee (A/47/648) without objection, 3 November (meeting 8); draft consensus (A/C.4/47/L.3); agenda item 18.
Meeting numbers. GA 47th session: 4th Committee 2-8; plenary 72.

Pitcairn

The Subcommittee on Small Territories, Petitions, Information and Assistance noted with regret that the United Kingdom, the administering Power concerned, did not participate in its deliberations on Pitcairn and appealed to the United Kingdom to reconsider its position and resume its participation in the Committee on colonial countries.[40]

GENERAL ASSEMBLY ACTION

On 25 November 1992, the General Assembly, on the recommendation of the Fourth Committee, adopted **decision 47/412** without vote.

Question of Pitcairn

At its 72nd plenary meeting, on 25 November 1992, the General Assembly, on the recommendation of the Fourth Committee, adopted the following text as representing the consensus of the members of the Assembly:

"The General Assembly, having examined the situation in Pitcairn, reaffirms the inalienable right of the people of Pitcairn to self-determination in conformity with the Declaration on the Granting of Independence to Colonial Countries and Peoples, contained in Assembly resolution 1514(XV) of 14 December 1960, which fully applies to the Territory. The Assembly further reaffirms the responsibility of the administering Power to promote the economic and social development of the Territory. The Assembly urges the administering Power to continue to respect the very individual lifestyle that the people of the Territory have chosen and to preserve, promote and protect it. The Assembly requests the Special Committee on the situation with regard to the Implementation of the Declaration on the Granting of Independence to Colonial Countries and Peoples to continue to examine the question of Pitcairn at its next session and to report thereon to the Assembly at its forty-eighth session."

General Assembly decision 47/412

Adopted without vote

Approved by Fourth Committee (A/47/648) without objection, 3 November
(meeting 8); draft by Committee on colonial countries (A/47/23); agenda
item 18.
Meeting numbers. GA 47th session: 4th Committee 2-8; plenary 72.

St. Helena

The Subcommittee on Small Territories, Petitions, Information and Assistance noted with regret that the United Kingdom, the administering Power concerned, did not participate in its deliberations on St. Helena and appealed to the United Kingdom to reconsider its position and resume its participation in the Committee on colonial countries.[41]

GENERAL ASSEMBLY ACTION

On 25 November 1992, the General Assembly, on the recommendation of the Fourth Committee, adopted **decision 47/413** by recorded vote.

Question of St. Helena

At its 72nd plenary meeting, on 25 November 1992, the General Assembly, on the recommendation of the Fourth Committee, adopted the following text:

"1. The General Assembly, having examined the question of St. Helena, reaffirms the inalienable right of the people of St. Helena to self-determination and independence in conformity with the Declaration on the Granting of Independence to Colonial Countries and Peoples, contained in Assembly resolution 1514(XV) of 14 December 1960. The Assembly urges the administering Power, in consultation with the Legislative Council and other representatives of the people of St. Helena, to continue to take all necessary steps to ensure the speedy implementation of the Declaration in respect of the Territory and, in that connection, reaffirms the importance of promoting an awareness among the people of St. Helena of the possibilities open to them in the exercise of their right to self-determination.

"2. The General Assembly reaffirms the responsibility of the administering Power to promote the economic and social development of the Territory and calls upon the administering Power to continue, in cooperation with the territorial Government, to strengthen the economy, to encourage local initiative and enterprise and to increase its assistance to diversification programmes with the aim of improving the general welfare of the community, including the employment situation of the Territory.

"3. The General Assembly urges the administering Power, in cooperation with the territorial Government, to continue to take effective measures to safeguard and guarantee the inalienable right of the people of St. Helena to own and dispose of the natural resources of the Territory, including marine resources, and to establish and maintain control over the future development of those resources.

"4. The General Assembly reaffirms that continued development assistance from the administering Power, together with any assistance that the international community might be able to provide, constitutes an important means of developing the economic potential of the Territory and of enhancing the capacity of its people to realize fully the goals set forth in the relevant pro-

visions of the Charter of the United Nations. The Assembly, in that connection, welcomes the assistance rendered by the United Nations Development Programme and invites other organizations of the United Nations system to assist in the development of the Territory.

"5. The continued presence of military facilities in the Territory prompts the General Assembly, on the basis of previous United Nations resolutions and decisions concerning military bases and installations in colonial and Non-Self-Governing Territories, to urge the administering Power to take measures to avoid the involvement of the Territory in offensive acts or interference against neighbouring States.

"6. The General Assembly considers that the possibility of dispatching a United Nations visiting mission to St. Helena at an appropriate time should be kept under review, and requests the Special Committee on the situation with regard to the Implementation of the Declaration on the Granting of Independence to Colonial Countries and Peoples to continue to examine the question of St. Helena at its next session and to report thereon to the Assembly at its forty-eighth session.''

General Assembly decision 47/413

104-2-43 (recorded vote)

Approved by Fourth Committee (A/47/648) by recorded vote (96-2-34), 3
November (meeting 8); draft by Committee on colonial countries
(A/47/23); agenda item 18.
Meeting numbers. GA 47th session: 4th Committee 2-8; plenary 72.

Recorded vote in Assembly as follows:

In favour: Algeria, Angola, Antigua and Barbuda, Argentina, Bahamas, Bahrain, Bangladesh, Barbados, Belize, Benin, Bolivia, Botswana, Brazil, Brunei Darussalam, Burkina Faso, Cape Verde, Chad, Chile, China, Colombia, Congo, Costa Rica, Côte d'Ivoire, Cuba, Cyprus, Democratic People's Republic of Korea, Djibouti, Ecuador, Egypt, El Salvador, Equatorial Guinea, Ethiopia, Fiji, Gabon, Ghana, Grenada, Guatemala, Guinea, Guinea-Bissau, Guyana, Haiti, Honduras, India, Indonesia, Iran, Jamaica, Kazakhstan, Kenya, Kuwait, Lao People's Democratic Republic, Lebanon, Lesotho, Libyan Arab Jamahiriya, Madagascar, Malaysia, Maldives, Mali, Mauritania, Mauritius, Mexico, Micronesia, Mongolia, Morocco, Mozambique, Myanmar, Nepal, Nicaragua, Niger, Nigeria, Oman, Pakistan, Papua New Guinea, Paraguay, Peru, Philippines, Qatar, Republic of Korea, Russian Federation, Rwanda, Saint Kitts and Nevis, Saint Lucia, Saint Vincent and the Grenadines, Sao Tome and Principe, Saudi Arabia, Senegal, Sierra Leone, Singapore, Sudan, Suriname, Syrian Arab Republic, Thailand, Togo, Trinidad and Tobago, Tunisia, Uganda, United Arab Emirates, United Republic of Tanzania, Uruguay, Vanuatu, Venezuela, Viet Nam, Yemen, Zambia, Zimbabwe.

Against: United Kingdom, United States.

Abstaining: Australia, Austria, Belarus, Belgium, Bosnia and Herzegovina, Bulgaria, Cameroon, Canada, Czechoslovakia, Denmark, Estonia, Finland, France, Germany, Greece, Hungary, Iceland, Ireland, Israel, Italy, Japan, Latvia, Liechtenstein, Lithuania, Luxembourg, Malta, Marshall Islands, Namibia, Netherlands, New Zealand, Norway, Panama, Poland, Portugal, Republic of Moldova, Romania, Samoa, San Marino, Slovenia, Spain, Sweden, Turkey, Ukraine.

REFERENCES

[1]A/AC.109/1115. [2]A/AC.109/1122 & Corr.1. [3]A/47/319. [4]A/46/596-S/23164. [5]A/45/136-S/21159. [6]A/47/23 (A/AC.109/1132). [7]YUN 1991, p. 797, SC res. 725(1991), 31 Dec. 1991. [8]S/23662. [9]YUN 1991, p. 797. [10]Ibid., p. 793. [11]Ibid., p. 794, SC res. 690(1991), 29 Apr. 1991. [12]Ibid., p. 796. [13]S/23755. [14]S/24040. [15]S/24059. [16]S/24464. [17]S/24504. [18]S/24644. [19]S/24645. [20]S/25008. [21]A/AC.109/1125. [22]A/C.4/47/SR.4. [23]YUN 1991, p. 796, GA res. 46/67, 11 Dec. 1991. [24]A/47/506. [25]A/47/743. [26]A/AC.109/1108. [27]A/AC.109/1106. [28]A/AC.109/1102. [29]A/AC.109/1100. [30]A/AC.109/1097. [31]A/AC.109/1111. [32]A/AC.109/1101. [33]A/AC.109/1098. [34]A/AC.109/1105. [35]A/AC.109/1112. [36]A/AC.109/1099. [37]A/AC.109/1109. [38]A/AC.109/1116. [39]A/AC.109/L.1779. [40]A/AC.109/L.1777. [41]A/AC.109/L.1778.

Chapter II

International Trusteeship System

The Trusteeship Council continued during 1992 to supervise, on behalf of the Security Council, the one Trust Territory remaining under the International Trusteeship System—Palau, Trust Territory of the Pacific Islands, a strategic territory administered by the United States.

The Trusteeship Council, composed of five members—China, France, Russian Federation, United Kingdom, United States—held its fifty-ninth regular session in 1992.

Trust Territory of the Pacific Islands

In 1992, Palau was the last remaining entity of the Trust Territory of the Pacific Islands still under the 1947 Trusteeship Agreement,[1] which had designated the United States as the Administering Authority of the Territory. The Security Council, in December 1990,[2] had determined that, in view of the entry into force of new status agreements between the United States and the other three entities of the Trust Territory—the Marshall Islands, the Federated States of Micronesia and the Northern Mariana Islands[3]—the objectives of the Trusteeship Agreement had been fully attained, and that the applicability of the Agreement to them had terminated.

Palau, located in the Western Caroline Islands, is composed of several islands with a total land area of 492 square kilometres. The estimated 1992 population was 16,386, two thirds of which lived in the capital, consisting of Koror and several adjacent islands.

In a working paper submitted to the Trusteeship Council in May 1992,[4] the Secretariat described conditions in the Trust Territory, covering political, economic, social and educational developments.

Political status of Palau

A proposed Compact of Free Association between Palau and the United States would recognize Palau as fully self-governing, while the United States would remain responsible for its defence. However, because the Compact would conflict with the non-nuclear provisions of Palau's Constitution, local courts ruled that it would need to be approved by 75 per cent of the voters—the same margin required for a constitutional amendment. In none of the seven plebiscites (February 1983,[5] September 1984,[6] February and December 1986,[7] June and August 1987[8] and February 1990[9]) was the required 75 per cent vote obtained.

Constitutional and political developments

In 1992, Palau held talks with the United States on possible modifications to the Compact of Free Association. Palau had written to the Administering Authority in October 1991 recommending three modifications: separation of the nuclear provision from the Compact for discussion at a later stage, thereby allowing the Compact to be approved by a simple majority vote; reassessment by the United States of its operating rights and military land requirements; and reduction of the term of the Compact from 50 years to 15.[6]

The United States responded that it was unable to accept the first proposal since the nuclear clause, in its view, was an integral part of the Compact. In response to the two other proposals, the United States reiterated its belief that a military presence in Palau was highly unlikely to be required in future, but promised full prior consultations with Palau to address defence issues. It further noted that if the duration of the Compact were shortened, then the trust fund for long-term development would have to be proportionately reduced, and that new funding for the Compact would require offering reductions elsewhere in the United States budget under the 1990 Budget Enforcement Act, to which there would be strong domestic opposition. The United States concluded by noting three possibilities for Palau's future political status—the existing Compact, independence and a renegotiated, modified Compact—and by recording its full support for the current Compact.

On 14 April, representatives of 3,300 petitioners presented to the President and leaders of the Palau National Congress (*Olbiil Era Kelulau*) a petition to amend Palau's Constitution to allow passage of the Compact of Free Association, including the section allowing the United States to operate nuclear-powered vessels in Palau's waters, with a simple majority. The petitioners requested a vote within 90 days following the presentation of their petition. The President scheduled a vote on 13 July, which the Supreme Court then enjoined. The National Congress subsequently enacted legislation calling for a vote on the amendment on 4 November, the same time as Palau's general election. On that date, Palauan voters approved the amendment.[10]

Consideration by the Committee on colonial countries. The General Assembly's Special Committee on the Situation with regard to the Implementation of the Declaration on the Granting of Independence to Colonial Countries and Peoples (Committee on colonial countries)[11] on 1 June decided to defer consideration of the Trust Territory of the Pacific Islands to its 1993 session since discussions were under way between the Administering Authority and the Trust Territory to find a solution to the future political status of the Territory. That decision was based on a recommendation of an open-ended Working Group, established in 1992 to make recommendations on improving the efficiency of the Committee's work.[12]

General Assembly consideration. On 6 October, the Chairman of the General Assembly's Fourth (Decolonization) Committee suggested that the Committee take note of the recommendation of the Committee on colonial countries to defer consideration of the Trust Territory until 1993. The Committee decided to do so.[13]

Visiting mission

In accordance with a 1991 Trusteeship Council resolution,[14] a visiting mission was dispatched to Palau in March 1992.

Report of the Visiting Mission. The Council's 1992 Visiting Mission[6] was composed of four Council members—one representative each from China, France, the Russian Federation and the United Kingdom—and two representatives of countries of the region that were not Council members—the Federated States of Micronesia and Papua New Guinea. The visit began on 25 March at Koror, Palau, and lasted until 1 April. The Mission held meetings concerning political, economic and social development with Palauan officials.

The Mission expressed the hope that the impasse concerning the future political status of Palau could be resolved speedily so that the Security Council and Trusteeship Council could proceed to terminate Palau's trusteeship status.

The 1990 Order by the United States Secretary of the Interior (Secretary's Order 3142)[15] defining the responsibilities of the Administering Authority and the Trust Territory, established the presence of a representative of the Assistant Secretary of the Interior in Koror to carry out liaison between the two parties, and provided for Palau, with the assistance of the United Nations Development Programme (UNDP), to develop a master national development plan to be the framework for its future economic development. The Order contained a number of fiscal measures restricting Palau's ability to borrow money from outside sources or to enter into business agreements with foreign partners. The Mis-

sion noted that Palauans viewed the Order as a major impediment to economic and social development and charged that it hindered their ability to manage the national and state budgets.

The Administering Authority, asked by the Mission to clarify the issue, replied that the Order had been intended in part to ensure that appropriations would be made only when funds were available and that they would be used for the purpose for which they were earmarked. The United States pointed out that a number of lawsuits had been filed by creditors of Palau seeking to put a lien on the financial assistance it provided to the Territory.

The Mission was left with three main impressions regarding the Order: it was in Palau's own interest, as a potential borrower of external funds for development, that its financial affairs should be in order and past borrowings repaid; there might be either a misunderstanding of parts of the Order or insufficiently close day-to-day consultations on their precise implications; and the Mission did not doubt that the Administering Authority needed to fulfil its responsibilities for Palau's foreign relations and its financial standing. The Mission's view was that it was important, nevertheless, to prepare for the day when Palau's political status was resolved and to ensure its ability immediately to assume its responsibilities.

The Mission also examined issues relating to health care, law and order, educational development, land claims and disputes, illegal fishing by foreigners in Palau's waters and the environment.

Trusteeship Council consideration. In May,[16] the Secretary-General forwarded to the Security Council and the Trusteeship Council a report by the United States on the administration of the Trust Territory for the year ending 30 September 1991.

The Council held its fifty-ninth regular session in New York from 26 May to 2 June and on 21 December.[17]

On 2 June, the Council adopted the conclusions and recommendations prepared by its Drafting Committee (China, France, Russian Federation, United Kingdom). Taking note of a 1986 Trusteeship Council resolution[18] and a 1990 Security Council resolution[2] on the Trust Territory, the Trusteeship Council expressed hope that the people of Palau would soon be able to exercise freely their right to self-determination and that it would be possible to terminate the Trusteeship Agreement.

It also expressed the hope that progress would continue to be made in economic and social development, and noted the assurances by the Administering Authority that it would continue to do what it could to assist the people of the Territory to attain greater self-sufficiency through responsible economic development. The Council noted Palau's concern regarding the implementation of Secretary's Order 3142, and hoped that the need for the Order would be diminished. It noted with satisfaction the Administering Authority's assurances that it would continue to fulfil its responsibilities under the Charter of the United Nations and the Trusteeship Agreement, and further noted that the United States had no plans to establish military bases in Palau.

The Council heard one petitioner on various issues concerning conditions in and the future status of the Trust Territory and took note of three written communications.

On 21 December, the Council adopted its report to the Security Council, which also covered its twenty-first (1991) special session.

TRUSTEESHIP COUNCIL ACTION

On 29 May 1992, the Trusteeship Council adopted **resolution 2195(LIX)** without vote.

Report of the United Nations Visiting Mission to Palau, Trust Territory of the Pacific Islands, 1992
The Trusteeship Council,
Having examined at its fifty-ninth session the report of the United Nations Visiting Mission to Palau, Trust Territory of the Pacific Islands, 1992,
Having heard the statements made by its members concerning the report,
1. *Approves* the report of the Visiting Mission;
2. *Expresses its appreciation* of the work accomplished by the Visiting Mission on its behalf;
3. *Decides* that it will continue to take the recommendations, conclusions and observations of the report of the Visiting Mission into account in future examination of matters relating to the Trust Territory;
4. *Invites* the Administering Authority to take into account the recommendations and conclusions of the Visiting Mission as well as the comments made thereon by the members of the Trusteeship Council.

Trusteeship Council resolution 2195(LIX)

29 May 1992   Meeting 1694   Adopted without vote

4-nation draft (T/L.1282), orally revised; agenda item 5.
Sponsors: China, France, Russian Federation, United Kingdom.

REFERENCES
[1]YUN 1946-47, p. 398. [2]SC res. 683(1990), 22 Dec. 1990. [3]YUN 1986, p. 917. [4]T/L.1281. [5]YUN 1983, p. 1034. [6]T/1964. [7]YUN 1986, p. 920. [8]YUN 1987, p. 978. [9]YUN 1991, p. 810. [10]T/L.1284. [11]A/47/23. [12]A/AC.109/L.1776. [13]A/C.4/47/SR.2. [14]YUN 1991, p. 812, TC res. 2194(S-XXI), 19 Dec. 1991. [15]YUN 1991, p. 810. [16]S/23871 (T/1962). [17]S/25261 & Corr.1. [18]YUN 1986, p. 918, TC res. 2183(LIII), 28 May 1986.

Other aspects of the International Trusteeship System

Fellowships and scholarships

Under a scholarship programme launched by the General Assembly in 1952,[1] 11 Member States had in past years made scholarships available for students from Trust Territories: Czechoslovakia, Hungary, Indonesia, Italy, Mexico, Pakistan, Philippines, Poland, Tunisia, the former USSR and Yugoslavia. In a report to the Trusteeship Council covering the period from 2 May 1991 to 15 May 1992,[2] the Secretary-General stated that he had requested up-to-date information on scholarships for students from the Trust Territory of the Pacific Islands, but had received no response. On 27 May,[3] the Council took note of the report.

Information dissemination

The United Nations Department of Public Information (DPI) in 1992 continued to disseminate information on the United Nations and the International Trusteeship System in the Trust Territory of the Pacific Islands. Those activities were described in a report of the Secretary-General covering the period from 1 May 1991 to 30 April 1992.[4] The information, including printed materials and audio and video programmes, were aimed at enlightening the people about their right to self-determination. DPI during the year mailed 97 questionnaires to recipients of United Nations information in the Territory soliciting feedback.[5] The Secretary-General reported that response to a similar mailing in 1991 had been poor.

The representatives of China and the United Kingdom to the Trusteeship Council voiced concern over the failure to elicit a large return of responses to the DPI questionnaire and over DPI's efforts to improve its distribution of information in the Territory. The Russian Federation expressed similar views.[3]

On 27 May, the Council took note of the Secretary-General's report.

Cooperation with the Committee on colonial countries

At its 1992 session, the Trusteeship Council considered the attainment of self-government or independence by the Trust Territory together with cooperation with the Committee on colonial countries.[3]

During the discussion, Papua New Guinea said it interpreted the General Assembly's 1988 declaration of the International Decade for the Eradication of Colonialism (1990-2000)[6] and its plan of action[7] to include Palau, giving added reason for cooperation among United Nations organs dealing with those issues. (For further details on the Decade, see Chapter I of this section.) It suggested that the Chairman of the Committee on colonial countries should be requested to address the Council. The Russian Federation expressed hope that cooperation would continue between the two bodies.

On 2 June,[3] the Trusteeship Council drew the Security Council's attention to its conclusions and recommendations concerning the attainment of self-government or independence by the Trust Territory and to the statements made by the Council's members on those questions.

Cooperation with CERD and the
Decade against racial discrimination

In 1992, the Trusteeship Council considered the question of cooperation with the Committee on the Elimination of Racial Discrimination (CERD) together with the Second Decade to Combat Racism and Racial Discrimination (see also PART THREE, Chapter X). During the debate, the Russian Federation expressed regret that the Council had not yet demonstrated good will regarding cooperation with other bodies, and said cooperation with CERD should have been established. On 28 May,[3] the Council took note of that statement.

REFERENCES

[1]YUN 1951, p. 788, GA res. 557(VI), 18 Jan. 1952. [2]T/1965. [3]S/25261 & Corr.1. [4]T/1966. [5]T/1972. [6]GA res. 43/47, 22 Nov. 1988. [7]YUN 1991, p. 777.

PART FIVE

Legal questions

Chapter I

International Court of Justice

In 1992, the International Court of Justice (ICJ) continued its deliberations on 10 contentious cases. Three new disputes were referred to the Court, and two cases were removed from its list. The Court delivered two Judgments and 12 Orders.

Bulgaria, Madagascar and Hungary deposited with the Secretary-General, in June, July and October, respectively, a declaration recognizing as compulsory the jurisdiction of the Court, as contemplated by Article 36 of the Statute of the Court.

In a statement read on his behalf at the United Nations Conference on Environment and Development (Rio de Janeiro, Brazil, 3-14 June), the President of the Court drew attention to the role of ICJ in relation to the environment and sustainable development. On 21 October, he addressed the General Assembly on the work of the Court.

Judicial work of the Court

In 1992, the President made two Orders recording the discontinuance of proceedings in the cases concerning *Passage through the Great Belt (Finland v. Denmark)* and *Border and Transborder Armed Actions (Nicaragua v. Honduras)*, directing their removal from the Court's list. The Court also made an Order on the Libyan Arab Jamahiriya's request for an indication of provisional measures in each of the cases concerning *Questions of Interpretation and Application of the 1971 Montreal Convention arising from the Aerial Incident at Lockerbie (Libyan Arab Jamahiriya v. United Kingdom)* and *(Libyan Arab Jamahiriya v. United States of America)*. It gave a Judgment on the preliminary objections filed by Australia in the case concerning *Certain Phosphate Lands in Nauru (Nauru v. Australia)*. A Chamber of the Court delivered its Judgment in the case concerning the *Land, Island and Maritime Frontier Dispute (El Salvador/Honduras: Nicaragua intervening)*, and the Court and its President made several Orders on the conduct of proceedings in pending cases.

In a dispute concerning the projected diversion of the Danube, Hungary presented to ICJ an Application against the Czech and Slovak Federal Republic, inviting the latter to accept the Court's jurisdiction. In accordance with Article 38 of the Rules of Court, the Application was transmitted to the Government of that Federal Republic for its consent.

The 1992 activities of ICJ were described in two reports to the General Assembly, covering the periods 1 August 1991 to 31 July 1992[1] and 1 August 1992 to 31 July 1993.[2] By **decision 47/405** of 21 October 1992, the Assembly took note of the 1991/92 report.

Border and transborder armed actions (Nicaragua v. Honduras)

The proceedings instituted by Nicaragua against Honduras alleging border and transborder armed actions had been before the Court since 1986.[3] The time-limits for the written proceedings were fixed in April 1989. An Order in August extended the time-limit for Nicaragua and reserved the question of extending that for Honduras. Nicaragua filed its Memorial within the prescribed time-limit. In December 1989, both Parties transmitted to the Court the text of an agreement for an extra-judicial settlement of the dispute and requesting postponement of the date for fixing the time-limit for the Honduran Counter-Memorial until June 1990. It was so decided by a Court Order of December 1989. The Parties subsequently informed the President of the Court that, for the time being, they did not desire a new time-limit for the Counter-Memorial to be fixed. The President so advised the Court.

On 11 May 1992, Nicaragua informed the Court that because the Parties had reached an out-of-court agreement aimed at good-neighbourly relations it had decided to renounce all further right of action based on the case and did not wish to go on with the proceedings. Within the time-limit (25 May 1992) fixed by the President of the Court, Honduras, by a letter of 14 May, advised the Court that it did not oppose discontinuance of the proceedings. Consequently, the Court, on 27 May, made an Order[4] recording the discontinuance of the proceedings and directing the removal of the case from the Court's list.

Maritime delimitation in the area between Greenland and Jan Mayen (Denmark v. Norway)

Denmark, in 1988, had instituted proceedings against Norway, requesting the Court to decide where a single line of delimitation should be drawn between Denmark's and Norway's fishing zones and continental shelf areas in the waters between the east coast of Greenland and the Norwegian island of Jan Mayen.

Taking into account an agreement between the Parties that there should be a Reply and a Rejoinder to a 1989 Memorial of Denmark and a 1990 Counter-Memorial of Norway, the President of the Court, by a June 1990 Order, fixed 1 February and 1 October 1991 as the time-limits for, respectively, the Reply of Denmark and the Rejoinder of Norway. Both were filed within those time-limits. The Court fixed 11 January 1993 as the date for the opening of hearings in the case.

Aerial incident of 3 July 1988 (Iran v. United States)

Iran, in 1989, had instituted proceedings against the United States, referring to the destruction of an Iranian aircraft on 3 July 1988 and the killing of its 290 passengers and crew by missiles launched in Iranian airspace from the United States guided-missile cruiser USS *Vincennes*. The time-limits for written proceedings, fixed in a December 1989 Court Order, were extended by an Order in June 1990. The Memorial of Iran was filed within the prescribed time-limit.

In March 1991, within the time-limit fixed for its Counter-Memorial, the United States filed certain preliminary objections to the Court's jurisdiction. By an April Order,[5] the Court fixed 9 December as the time-limit within which Iran might present a written statement of its observations and submissions on those objections. As requested by Iran, and after the views of the United States had been ascertained, the President of the Court, by Orders of 18 December 1991[5] and 5 June 1992,[6] extended that time-limit to 9 June and 9 September 1992, respectively. Iran's written statement was filed within the prescribed time-limit.

Certain phosphate lands in Nauru (Nauru v. Australia)

In 1989, Nauru had instituted proceedings against Australia in a dispute concerning the rehabilitation of certain phosphate lands mined under Australian administration before Nauruan independence.

As fixed by the Court in July 1989, the time-limits for written proceedings were 20 April 1990 for Nauru and 21 January 1991 for Australia. Within those time-limits Nauru filed its Memorial, while Australia filed certain preliminary objections to the Court's jurisdiction and on the admissibility of the case. Within the time-limit of 19 July 1991, fixed by an Order of the previous February,[5] Nauru filed its observations and submissions on those objections.

Hearings on the issues of jurisdiction and admissibility were held in November 1991. On 26 June 1992, at a public sitting, the Court delivered a Judgment on the Preliminary Objections,[7] the operative paragraph of which read as follows:

The Court,

(1) (a) *rejects*, unanimously, the preliminary objection based on the reservation made by Australia in its declaration of acceptance of the compulsory jurisdiction of the Court;

(b) *rejects*, by twelve votes to one, the preliminary objection based on the alleged waiver by Nauru, prior to accession to independence, of all claims concerning the rehabilitation of the phosphate lands worked out prior to 1 July 1967;

In favour: President Sir Robert Jennings; Judges Lachs, Ago, Schwebel, Bedjaoui, Ni, Evensen, Tarassov, Guillaume, Shahabuddeen, Aguilar Mawdsley, Ranjeva;

Against: Vice-President Oda;

(c) *rejects*, by twelve votes to one, the preliminary objection based on the termination of the Trusteeship over Nauru by the United Nations;

In favour: President Sir Robert Jennings; Judges Lachs, Ago, Schwebel, Bedjaoui, Ni, Evensen, Tarassov, Guillaume, Shahabuddeen, Aguilar Mawdsley, Ranjeva;

Against: Vice-President Oda;

(d) *rejects*, by twelve votes to one, the preliminary objection based on the effect of the passage of time on the admissibility of Nauru's Application;

In favour: President Sir Robert Jennings; Judges Lachs, Ago, Schwebel, Bedjaoui, Ni, Evensen, Tarassov, Guillaume, Shahabuddeen, Aguilar Mawdsley, Ranjeva;

Against: Vice-President Oda;

(e) *rejects*, by twelve votes to one, the preliminary objection based on Nauru's alleged lack of good faith;

In favour: President Sir Robert Jennings; Judges Lachs, Ago, Schwebel, Bedjaoui, Ni, Evensen, Tarassov, Guillaume, Shahabuddeen, Aguilar Mawdsley, Ranjeva;

Against: Vice-President Oda;

(f) *rejects*, by nine votes to four, the preliminary objection based on the fact that New Zealand and the United Kingdom are not parties to the proceedings;

In favour: Judges Lachs, Bedjaoui, Ni, Evensen, Tarassov, Guillaume, Shahabuddeen, Aguilar Mawdsley, Ranjeva;

Against: President Sir Robert Jennings; Vice-President Oda; Judges Ago, Schwebel;

(g) *upholds*, unanimously, the preliminary objection based on the claim concerning the overseas assets of the British Phosphate Commissioners being a new one;

(2) *finds*, by nine votes to four, that, on the basis of Article 36, paragraph 2, of the Statute of the Court, it has jurisdiction to entertain the Application filed by the Republic of Nauru on 19 May 1989 and that the said Application is admissible;

In favour: Judges Lachs, Bedjaoui, Ni, Evensen, Tarassov, Guillaume, Shahabuddeen, Aguilar Mawdsley, Ranjeva;

Against: President Sir Robert Jennings; Vice-President Oda; Judges Ago, Schwebel;

(3) *finds*, unanimously, that the claim concerning the overseas assets of the British Phosphate Commissioners, made by Nauru in its Memorial of 20 April 1990, is inadmissible.

Judge Shahabuddeen appended a separate opinion to the Judgment. President Sir Robert Jennings, Vice-President Oda and Judges Ago and Schwebel appended dissenting opinions.

By an Order of 29 June 1992,[8] the President of the Court, having ascertained the views of the Parties, fixed 29 March 1993 as the time-limit for the Australian Counter-Memorial.

Territorial dispute
(Libyan Arab Jamahiriya/Chad)

In this case, before the Court since 1990, each Party had duly filed a Memorial in 1991 within the prescribed time-limit. Within the further time-limit of 27 March 1992, fixed by the President of the Court in an August 1991 Order,[9] each Party filed a Counter-Memorial. By an Order of 14 April 1992,[10] the Court decided to authorize the presentation by each Party of a Reply within the same time-limit, and fixed 14 September 1992 as that time-limit. Both Replies were filed accordingly.

The Libyan Arab Jamahiriya chose José Sette-Camara to sit as Judge ad hoc in the case. Chad had chosen Judge ad hoc Abi-Saab in 1990.

East Timor (Portugal v. Australia)

In 1991,[9] Portugal had instituted proceedings against Australia in a dispute concerning certain activities of Australia with respect to East Timor. Portugal claimed that Australia, by negotiating with Indonesia an agreement signed on 11 December 1989 relating to the exploration and exploitation of the continental shelf in the area of the Timor Gap, had caused legal and moral damage to the people of East Timor and Portugal, which would become material if the exploitation of hydrocarbon resources began there.

In a May 1991 Order,[9] the President of the Court fixed 18 November 1991 as the time-limit for the filing of a Memorial by Portugal and 1 June 1992 for a Counter-Memorial by Australia. Both were filed within the prescribed time-limits. By an Order of 19 June 1992,[11] the Court fixed 1 December 1992 as the time-limit for the filing of a Reply by Portugal and 1 June 1993 for a Rejoinder by Australia. The Reply by Portugal was filed within the prescribed time-limit.

Portugal chose António de Arruda Ferrer-Correia and Australia chose Sir Ninian Stephen, to sit as Judges ad hoc in the case.

Maritime delimitation (Guinea-Bissau v. Senegal)

When proceedings were instituted against Senegal in this case in 1991, proceedings were still in progress in a case instituted by Guinea-Bissau against Senegal in 1989 concerning the *Arbitral Award of 31 July 1989 (Guinea-Bissau v. Senegal)*.[5]

Guinea-Bissau claimed that the result of the Arbitration was not such as to make possible a definitive delimitation of all the maritime areas over which the Parties had rights, and asked the Court to adjudge and declare what should be the line delimiting all the maritime territories appertaining respectively to Guinea-Bissau and Senegal.

However, as was made clear in the Application instituting the new case, the question of the Court's jurisdiction to entertain it would appear in a different light according to the Court's decision in the first case, on the validity of the Award of 31 July 1989. Accordingly, with the agreement of the Parties, no action was taken to fix time-limits for the pleadings in the new case, pending the Court's decision in the first case. Following the 1991 Judgment in the case concerning the *Arbitral Award of 31 July 1989 (Guinea-Bissau v. Senegal)*,[5] the President of the Court met with the two Parties in February 1992. They asked that no time-limit be fixed for the initial pleadings of the case, pending the outcome of negotiations on the question of maritime delimitation. The negotiations were to continue for six-months, after which, if they had not been successful, a further meeting would be held with the President. As no indications were received from the Parties as to the state of their negotiations, the President on 6 October, met with the agents of the parties who stated that some progress had been made toward an agreement. The President agreed to their request to allow a further period of three months, with a possible further extension of three months, to continue the negotiations.

Passage through the
Great Belt (Finland v. Denmark)

Finland had instituted proceedings against Denmark in 1991 in a dispute concerning the passage of oil rigs through the Great Belt (Store Baelt—one of the three straits linking the Baltic to the Kattegat and then to the North Sea).[9] The Court had by a July 1991 Order[12] fixed 30 December 1991 as the time-limit for the filing of a Memorial by Finland and 1 June 1992 for a Counter-Memorial by Denmark. Both were filed within the prescribed time-limits.

In September, Finland notified the Court that it had discontinued the case as the dispute had been settled through negotiations. Subsequently, Denmark stated that it had no objections to the discontinuance. On 10 September 1992, the President of the Court made an Order[13] placing the discontinuance on record and removing the case from the Court's list.

Maritime delimitation and territorial questions between Qatar and Bahrain (Qatar v. Bahrain)

Qatar had instituted proceedings in 1991 against Bahrain in respect of disputes relating to sovereignty over the Hawar islands, sovereign rights over the shoals of Dibal and Qit'at Jaradah and the delimitation of the maritime areas of the two States.[12]

In August 1991, Bahrain contested the basis of jurisdiction invoked by Qatar. By an October 1991 Order,[12] the President of the Court decided that written proceedings should first be addressed to the questions of the jurisdiction of the Court to entertain the dispute and of the admissibility of the Application. He fixed 10 February 1992 as the time-limit for the filing of a Memorial by Qatar and 11 June 1992 for a Counter-Memorial by Bahrain. Both were filed within the prescribed time-limits.

By an Order of 26 June 1992,[14] the Court directed that a Reply and a Rejoinder be filed, and fixed 28 September 1992 as the time-limit for the Reply of Qatar and 29 December 1992 for the Rejoinder of Bahrain. Both were filed within the prescribed time-limits.

Qatar chose José Maria Ruda, and Bahrain chose Nicolas Valticos, to sit as Judges ad hoc in the case.

Questions of interpretation and application of the 1971 Montreal Convention arising from the aerial incident at Lockerbie (Libyan Arab Jamahiriya v. United Kingdom) and (Libyan Arab Jamahiriya v. United States)

On 3 March 1992, the Libyan Arab Jamahiriya filed in the Registry of the Court two separate Applications instituting proceedings against the United Kingdom and the United States in respect of a dispute over the interpretation and application of the 1971 Montreal Convention for the Suppression of Unlawful Acts Against the Safety of Civil Aviation,[15] which arose from its alleged involvement in the crash of Pan Am flight 103 over Lockerbie, Scotland, on 21 December 1988.

In the applications, the Libyan Arab Jamahiriya referred to the charging and indictment of two of its nationals by the Lord Advocate of Scotland and by a United States Grand Jury, respectively, with having caused a bomb to be placed aboard Pan Am flight 103. The bomb subsequently exploded, causing the aircraft to crash, killing all persons aboard. The Libyan Arab Jamahiriya pointed out that the alleged acts constituted an offence within the meaning of Article 1 of the 1991 Montreal Convention, which it claimed was the only appropriate Convention in force between the Parties. The Libyan Arab Jamahiriya claimed that it had fully complied with its own obligations under that instrument, Article 5 of which required a State to establish its own jurisdiction over alleged offenders present in its territory in the event of their non-extradition. As there was no extradition treaty between the Libyan Arab Jamahiriya and the other parties, the Libyan Arab Jamahiriya was obliged under the Convention to submit the case to its authorities for prosecution.

The Libyan Arab Jamahiriya contended that the United Kingdom and the United States were in breach of the Montreal Convention through rejection of its efforts to resolve the matter within the framework of international law, including the Convention itself, in that they were placing pressure on it to surrender the two Libyan nationals for trial. According to the Applications, it had not been possible to settle by negotiation the disputes that had thus arisen, nor had the parties been able to agree upon the organization of an arbitration to hear the matter. The Libyan Arab Jamahiriya therefore submitted the disputes to the Court on the basis of Article 14, paragraph 1, of the Montreal Convention.

The Libyan Arab Jamahiriya requested the Court to adjudge and declare that the Libyan Arab Jamahiriya had complied fully with all of its obligations under the Convention and that the United Kingdom and the United States had breached, and were continuing to breach, the Convention and were under a legal obligation to cease and desist from such breaches and from the use of force or threats against the Libyan Arab Jamahiriya.

The Libyan Arab Jamahiriya also made two separate requests to the Court to indicate provisional measures to enjoin the United Kingdom and United States from taking any action to coerce or compel it to surrender the accused individuals to any jurisdiction outside of the Jamahiriya, and to ensure that no steps were taken to prejudice its rights with respect to legal proceedings that were the subject of the Jamahiriya's Applications.

The Libyan Arab Jamahiriya chose Ahmed S. El-Kosheri to sit as Judge ad hoc in both cases.

At five public sittings held on 26, 27 and 28 March, both Parties in each of the two cases presented oral arguments on the request for the indication of provisional measures. By two Orders of 14 April 1992,[16],[17] the Court found, by 11 votes to 5, that the circumstances of the case were not such as to require the exercise of its power to indicate provisional measures. Acting President Oda and Judge Ni each appended a declaration to the Order of the Court; Judges Evensen, Tarassov, Guillaume and Aguilar Mawdsley appended a joint declaration. Judges Lachs and Shahabuddeen appended separate opinions, and Judges Bedjaoui, Weeramantry, Ranjeva, Ajibola and Judge ad hoc El-Kosheri appended dissenting opinions to the Orders.

By Orders of 19 June 1992,[18],[19] the Court fixed 20 December 1993 as the time-limit for the filing of a Memorial by the Libyan Arab Jamahiriya and 20 June 1995 for Counter-Memorials by the United Kingdom and United States, respectively.

Oil platforms (Iran v. United States)

On 2 November 1992, Iran filed in the Registry of the Court an Application instituting proceedings against the United States regarding a dispute in which Iran alleged that the destruction of three offshore oil production complexes owned and operated by the National Iranian Oil Company by several United States warships on 19 October 1987 and 18 April 1988, constituted a breach of international law and the 1955 Iran/United States Treaty of Amity, Economic Relations and Consular Rights. Iran requested the Court to rule on the matter.

By an Order of 4 December 1992,[20] the President of the Court fixed 31 May 1993 as the time-limit for the filing of a Memorial by Iran and 30 November 1993 for a Counter-Memorial by the United States.

Land, island and maritime frontier dispute (El Salvador/Honduras: Nicaragua intervening)

El Salvador and Honduras had, in 1986,[21] submitted a frontier dispute to the Court which had acceded to their request for a Special Chamber to deal with the case. Both Parties duly filed their Memorials in 1988. By Orders of January and December 1989, the Court had extended time-limits for the filing of Counter-Memorials and Replies, which were subsequently filed within the prescribed time-limits.

In November 1989, Nicaragua addressed an Application to the Court for permission to intervene in the case, its object being the protection of the legal rights of Nicaragua in the Gulf of Fonseca and adjacent maritime areas. Permission was granted by a September 1990 Judgment of the Chamber. The written statement by Nicaragua and the written observations thereon by the two Parties were filed in 1990 and 1991,[12] respectively, within the time-limits fixed in a September 1990 Order of the Chamber.

Having heard oral arguments in the case between 15 April and 14 June 1991, the Chamber, at a public sitting of 11 September 1992, delivered its Judgment,[22] the operative paragraphs of which read as follows:

425. For the reasons set out in the present Judgment, in particular paragraphs 68 to 103 thereof,

The Chamber,

Unanimously,

Decides that the boundary line between the Republic of El Salvador and the Republic of Honduras in the first sector of their common frontier not described in Article 16 of the General Treaty of Peace signed by the Parties on 30 October 1980, is as follows:

From the international tripoint known as El Trifinio on the summit of the Cerro Montecristo (point A on Map No. I annexed;[a] coordinates: 14°25'10'' N, 89°21'20'' W), the boundary runs in a generally easterly direction along the watershed between the rivers Frío or Sesecapa and Del Rosario as far as the junction of this watershed with the watershed of the basin of the *quebrada* de Pomola (point B on Map No. I annexed; coordinates: 14°25'05'' N, 89°20'41'' W); thereafter in a north-easterly direction along the watershed of the basin of the *quebrada* de Pomola until the junction of this watershed with the watershed between the *quebrada* de Cipresales and the *quebrada* del Cedrón, Peña Dorada and Pomola proper (point C on Map No. I annexed; coordinates: 14°25'09'' N, 89°20'30'' W); from that point, along the last-named watershed as far as the intersection of the centre-lines of the *quebradas* of Cipresales and Pomola (point D on Map No. I annexed; coordinates: 14°24'42'' N, 89°18'19'' W); thereafter, downstream along the centre-line of the *quebrada* de Pomola, until the point on that centre-line which is closest to the boundary marker of Pomola at El Talquezalar; and from that point in a straight line as far as that marker (point E on Map No. I annexed; coordinates: 14°24'51'' N, 89°17'54'' W); from there in a straight line in a south-easterly direction to the boundary marker of the Cerro Piedra Menuda (point F on Map No. I annexed; coordinates: 14°24'02'' N, 89°16'40'' W), and thence in a straight line to the boundary marker of the Cerro Zapotal (point G on Map No. I annexed; coordinates: 14°23'26'' N, 89°14'43'' W); for the purposes of illustration, the line is indicated on Map No. I annexed.

426. For the reasons set out in the present Judgment, in particular paragraphs 104 to 127 thereof,

The Chamber,

Unanimously,

Decides that the boundary line between the Republic of El Salvador and the Republic of Honduras in the second sector of their common frontier not described in Article 16 of the General Treaty of Peace signed by the Parties on 30 October 1980, is as follows:

From the Peña de Cayaguanca (point A on Map No. II annexed; coordinates: 14°21'54'' N, 89°10'11'' W), the boundary runs in a straight line somewhat south of east to the Loma de Los Encinos (point B on Map No. II annexed; coordinates: 14°21'08'' N, 89°08'54'' W), and from there in a straight line to the hill known as El Burro or Piedra Rajada (point C on Map No. II annexed; coordinates: 14°22'46'' N, 89°07'32'' W); from there the boundary runs in a straight line to the head of the *quebrada* Copantillo, and follows the middle of the *quebrada* Copantillo downstream to its confluence with the river Sumpul (point D on Map No. II annexed; coordinates: 14°24'12'' N, 89°06'07'' W), and then follows the middle of the river Sumpul downstream to its confluence with the *quebrada* Chiquita or Oscura (point E on Map No. II annexed; coordinates: 14°20'25'' N, 89°04'57'' W); for the purposes of illustration, the line is indicated on Map No. II annexed.

427. For the reasons set out in the present Judgment, in particular paragraphs 128 to 185 thereof,

---

[a]For maps referred to hereafter, see *Land, Island and Maritime Frontier Dispute (El Salvador/Honduras: Nicaragua intervening), Judgment of 11 September 1992,* I.C.J. Sales No. 626.

The Chamber,
Unanimously,
Decides that the boundary line between the Republic of El Salvador and the Republic of Honduras in the third sector of their common frontier not described in Article 16 of the General Treaty of Peace signed by the Parties on 30 October 1980, is as follows:

From the Pacacio boundary marker (point A on Map No. III annexed; coordinates: 14°06'28'' N, 88°49'18'' W) along the rio Pacacio upstream to a point (point B on Map No. III annexed; coordinates: 14°06'38'' N, 88°48'47'' W), west of the Cerro Tecolate or Los Tecolates; from there up the *quebrada* to the crest of the Cerro Tecolate or Los Tecolates (point C on Map No. III annexed; coordinates: 14°06'33'' N, 88°48'18'' W), and along the watershed of this hill as far as a ridge approximately 1 kilometre to the north-east (point D on Map No. III annexed; coordinates: 14°06'48'' N, 88°47'52'' W); from there in an easterly direction to the neighbouring hill above the source of the Torrente La Puerta (point E on Map No. III annexed; coordinates: 14°06'48'' N, 88°47'31'' W) and down that stream to where it meets the river Gualsinga (point F on Map No. III annexed; coordinates: 14°06'19'' N, 88°47'01'' W); from there the boundary runs along the middle of the river Gualsinga downstream to its confluence with the river Sazalapa (point G on Map No. III annexed; coordinates: 14°06'12'' N, 88°46'58'' W), and thence upstream along the middle of the river Sazalapa to the confluence of the *quebrada* Llano Negro with that river (point H on Map No. III annexed; coordinates: 14°07'11'' N, 88°44'21'' W); from there south-eastwards to the top of the hill (point I on Map No. III annexed; coordinates: 14°07'01'' N, 88°44'07'' W), and thence south-eastwards to the crest of the hill marked on the map as a spot height of 1,017 metres (point J on Map No. III annexed; coordinates: 14°06'45'' N, 88°43'45'' W); from there the boundary, inclining still more to the south, runs through the triangulation point known as La Cañada (point K on Map No. III annexed; coordinates: 14°06'00'' N, 88°43'52'' W) to the ridge joining the hills indicated on the map as Cerro El Caracol and Cerro El Sapo (through point L on Map No. III annexed; coordinates: 14°05'23'' N, 88°43'47'' W) and from there to the feature marked on the map as the Portillo El Chupa Miel (point M on Map No. III annexed; coordinates: 14°04'35'' N, 88°44'10'' W); from there, following the ridge, to the Cerro El Cajete (point N on Map No. III annexed; coordinates: 14°03'55'' N, 88°44'20'' W), and thence to the point where the present-day road from Arcatao to Nombre de Jesús passes between the Cerro El Ocotillo and the Cerro Lagunetas (point O on Map No. III annexed; coordinates: 14°03'18'' N, 88°44'16'' W); from there south-eastwards to the crest of a hill marked on the map as a spot height of 848 metres (point P on Map No. III annexed; coordinates: 14°02'58'' N, 88°43'56'' W); from there slightly south of eastwards to a *quebrada* and down the bed of the *quebrada* to its junction with the Gualcuquín river (point Q on Map No. III annexed; coordinates: 14°02'42'' N, 88°42'34'' W); the boundary then follows the middle of the Gualcuquín river downstream to the Poza del Cajon (point R on Map No. III annexed; coor-

dinates: 14°01'28'' N, 88°41'10'' W); for purposes of illustration, this line is shown on Map No. III annexed.

428. For the reasons set out in the present Judgment, in particular paragraphs 186 to 267 thereof,
The Chamber,
By four votes to one,
Decides that the boundary line between the Republic of El Salvador and the Republic of Honduras in the fourth sector of their common frontier not described in Article 16 of the General Treaty of Peace signed by the Parties on 30 October 1980, is as follows:

From the source of the Orilla stream (point A on Map No. IV annexed; coordinates: 13°53'46'' N, 88°20'36'' W) the boundary runs through the pass of El Jobo to the source of the Cueva Hedionda stream (point B on Map No. IV annexed; coordinates: 13°53'39'' N, 88°20'20'' W), and thence down the middle of that stream to its confluence with the river Las Cañas (point C on Map No. IV annexed; coordinates: 13°53'19'' N, 88°19'00'' W), and thence following the middle of the river upstream as far as a point (point D on Map No. IV annexed; coordinates: 13°56'14'' N, 88°15'33'' W) near the settlement of Las Piletas; from there eastwards over a col indicated as point E on Map No. IV annexed (coordinates: 13°56'19'' N, 88°14'12'' W), to a hill indicated as point F on Map No. IV annexed (coordinates: 13°56'11'' N, 88°13'40'' W), and then north-eastwards to a point on the river Negro or Pichigual (marked G on Map No. IV annexed; coordinates: 13°57'12'' N, 88°13'11'' W); downstream along the middle of the river Negro or Pichigual to its confluence with the river Negro-Quiagara (point H on Map No. IV annexed; coordinates: 13°59'37'' N, 88°14'18'' W); then upstream along the middle of the river Negro-Quiagara as far as the Las Pilas boundary marker (point I on Map No. IV annexed; coordinates: 14°00'02'' N, 88°06'29'' W), and from there in a straight line to the Malpaso de Similatón (point J on Map No. IV annexed; coordinates: 13°59'28'' N, 88°04'22'' W); for the purposes of illustration, the line is indicated on Map No. IV annexed.

In favour: Judge Sette-Camara, President of the Chamber; President Sir Robert Jennings; Vice-President Oda; Judge ad hoc Torres Bernárdez;
Against: Judge ad hoc Valticos.

429. For the reasons set out in the present Judgment, in particular paragraphs 268 to 305 thereof,
The Chamber,
Unanimously,
Decides that the boundary line between the Republic of El Salvador and the Republic of Honduras in the fifth sector of their common frontier not described in Article 16 of the General Treaty of Peace signed by the Parties on 30 October 1980, is as follows:

From the confluence with the river Torola of the stream identified in the General Treaty of Peace as the *quebrada* de Mansupucagua (point A on Map No. V annexed; coordinates: 13°53'59'' N, 87°54'30'' W) the boundary runs upstream along the middle of the river Torola as far as its confluence with a stream known as the *quebrada* del Arenal or *quebrada* de Aceituno (point B on Map No. V annexed; coordinates: 13°53'50'' N, 87°50'40'' W); thence up the course of that stream as far as a point at or near its source (point C on Map No. V annexed; coordinates: 13°54'30'' N, 87°50'20'' W), and thence in a straight line somewhat north of east to a hill some 1,100 metres high (point D on Map No. V annexed; coordinates: 13°55'03'' N, 87°49'50'' W); thence in a straight line to a hill near the river Unire (point E on Map No. V annexed; coordinates: 13°55'16'' N, 87°48'20'' W), and thence to the nearest point on the river Unire; downstream along the middle of that river to the point known as the Paso de Unire (point F on Map No. V annexed; coordinates: 13°52'07'' N, 87°46'01'' W); for the purposes of illustration, the line is indicated on Map No. V annexed.

430. For the reasons set out in the present Judgment, in particular paragraphs 306 to 322 thereof,
The Chamber,
Unanimously,
Decides that the boundary line between the Republic of El Salvador and the Republic of Honduras in the sixth sector of their common frontier not described in Article 16 of the General Treaty of Peace signed by the Parties on 30 October 1980, is as follows:

From the point on the river Goascorán known as Los Amates (point A on Map No. VI annexed; coordinates: 13°26'28'' N, 87°43'25'' W), the boundary follows the course of the river downstream, in the middle of the bed, to the point where it emerges in the waters of the Bahía La Unión, Gulf of Fonseca, passing to the north-west of the Islas Ramaditas, the coordinates of the end-point in the bay being 13°24'26'' N, 87°49'05'' W; for the purposes of illustration, the line is indicated on Map No. VI annexed.

431. For the reasons set out in the present Judgment, in particular paragraphs 323 to 368 thereof,
The Chamber,
1. By four votes to one,
Decides that the Parties, by requesting the Chamber, in Article 2, paragraph 2, of the Special Agreement of 24 May 1986, ''to determine the legal situation of the islands . . .'', have conferred upon the Chamber jurisdiction to determine, as between the Parties, the legal situation of all the islands of the Gulf of Fonseca; but that such jurisdiction should only be exercised in respect of those islands which have been shown to be the subject of a dispute;
In favour: Judge Sette-Camara, President of the Chamber; President Sir Robert Jennings; Vice-President Oda; Judge ad hoc Valticos;
Against: Judge ad hoc Torres Bernárdez.
2. *Decides* that the islands shown to be in dispute between the Parties are:
(i) by four votes to one, El Tigre;
In favour: Judge Sette-Camara, President of the Chamber; President Sir Robert Jennings; Vice-President Oda; Judge ad hoc Valticos;
Against: Judge ad hoc Torres Bernárdez;
(ii) unanimously, Meanguera and Meanguerita.
3. Unanimously,
Decides that the island of El Tigre is part of the sovereign territory of the Republic of Honduras.
4. Unanimously,
Decides that the island of Meanguera is part of the sovereign territory of the Republic of El Salvador.
5. By four votes to one,
Decides that the island of Meanguerita is part of the sovereign territory of the Republic of El Salvador;

In favour: Judge Sette-Camara, President of the Chamber; President Sir Robert Jennings; Vice-President Oda; Judge ad hoc Valticos;
Against: Judge ad hoc Torres Bernárdez.
432. For the reasons set out in the present Judgment, in particular paragraphs 369 to 420 thereof,
The Chamber,
1. By four votes to one,
Decides that the legal situation of the waters of the Gulf of Fonseca is as follows: the Gulf of Fonseca is an historic bay the waters whereof, having previously to 1821 been under the single control of Spain, and from 1821 to 1839 of the Federal Republic of Central America, were thereafter succeeded to and held in sovereignty by the Republic of El Salvador, the Republic of Honduras, and the Republic of Nicaragua, jointly, and continue to be so held, as defined in the present Judgment, but excluding a belt, as at present established, extending 3 miles (1 marine league) from the littoral of each of the three States, such belt being under the exclusive sovereignty of the coastal State, and subject to the delimitation between Honduras and Nicaragua effected in June 1900, and to the existing rights of innocent passage through the 3-mile belt and the waters held in sovereignty jointly; the waters at the central portion of the closing line of the Gulf, that is to say, between a point on that line 3 miles (1 marine league) from Punta Amapala and a point on that line 3 miles (1 marine league) from Punta Cosigüina, are subject to the joint entitlement of all three States of the Gulf unless and until a delimitation of the relevant maritime area be effected;
In favour: Judge Sette-Camara, President of the Chamber; President Sir Robert Jennings; Judge ad hoc Valticos; Judge ad hoc Torres Bernárdez;
Against: Vice-President Oda.
2. By four votes to one,
Decides that the Parties, by requesting the Chamber, in Article 2, paragraph 2, of the Special Agreement of 24 May 1986, ''to determine the legal situation of the . . . maritime spaces'', have not conferred upon the Chamber jurisdiction to effect any delimitation of those maritime spaces, whether within or outside the Gulf;
In favour: Judge Sette-Camara, President of the Chamber; President Sir Robert Jennings; Vice-President Oda; Judge ad hoc Valticos;
Against: Judge ad hoc Torres Bernárdez.
3. By four votes to one,
Decides that the legal situation of the waters outside the Gulf is that, the Gulf of Fonseca being an historic bay with three coastal States, the closing line of the Gulf constitutes the baseline of the territorial sea; the territorial sea, continental shelf and exclusive economic zone of El Salvador and those of Nicaragua off the coasts of those two States are also to be measured outwards from a section of the closing line extending 3 miles (1 marine league) along that line from Punta Amapala (in El Salvador) and 3 miles (1 marine league) from Punta Cosigüina (in Nicaragua) respectively; but entitlement to territorial sea, continental shelf and exclusive economic zone seaward of the central portion of the closing line appertains to the three States of the Gulf, El Salvador, Honduras and Nicaragua; and that any delimitation of the relevant maritime areas is to be effected by agreement on the basis of international law.

In favour: Judge Sette-Camara, President of the Chamber; President Sir Robert Jennings; Judge ad hoc Valticos; Judge ad hoc Torres Bernárdez;
Against: Vice-President Oda.

Vice-President Oda appended a declaration to the Judgment. Judges ad hoc Valticos and Torres Bernárdez appended separate opinions. Vice-President Oda appended a dissenting opinion.

Other questions

Role of the Court

In a June report on preventive diplomacy, peacemaking and peace-keeping,[23] prepared pursuant to a statement adopted by the first summit meeting of the Security Council at the level of heads of State and Government on 31 January 1992,[24] the Secretary-General proposed steps to reinforce the role of ICJ. He recommended that all Member States accept the general jurisdiction of the Court under Article 36 of its Statute (see APPENDIX II), without any reservation, before the end of the United Nations Decade of International Law (1990-1999), declared by the General Assembly in 1989,[25] and that they agree to a comprehensive list of matters for submission to ICJ and withdraw their reservations to its jurisdiction in the dispute settlement clauses of multilateral treaties. The Secretary-General also recommended that when submission of a dispute to the full court was not practical, the Chambers jurisdiction should be used. He called on States to support the Trust Fund established to assist countries unable to afford the cost involved in bringing a dispute to the Court and urged such countries to take advantage of the Fund (see below).

The Court took note of the Secretary-General's report.

Trust Fund to Assist States in the Settlement of Disputes

In October 1992,[26] the Secretary-General reported on the activities of the Secretary-General's Trust Fund to Assist States in the Settlement of Disputes through ICJ, established in 1989 under the Financial Regulations and Rules of the United Nations to provide a practical means of overcoming financial obstacles to the judicial settlement of legal disputes by offering limited financial assistance to States to encourage them to reach a solution of their disputes through ICJ. The Secretary-General reported that in 1991 the Fund awarded limited amounts of money to two developing countries to defray expenses in their disputes. He stated that 34 States had contributed $583,705 to the Fund since its creation. Annexed to the report was the Fund's terms of references, guidelines and rules.

On 21 October, the General Assembly took note of the Secretary-General's report by **decision 47/406**.

Request for an advisory opinion

In July, the Ibero-American Summit of Heads of State and Government (Madrid, Spain, 23-24 July 1992)[27] decided to ask the General Assembly to request an advisory opinion from ICJ on the conformity with international law of certain acts involving the extraterritorial exercise of the coercive power of a State and the subsequent exercise of its criminal jurisdiction, and called for the item to be included in the Assembly's 1992 agenda.

On 23 November, by **decision 47/402**, the Assembly, acting on a request from Argentina, Bolivia, Brazil, Chile, Colombia, Costa Rica, Cuba, Dominican Republic, Ecuador, El Salvador, Guatemala, Honduras, Mexico, Nicaragua, Panama, Paraguay, Peru, Portugal, Spain, Uruguay and Venezuela,[28] included the item in its 1992 agenda and allocated it to its Sixth (Legal) Committee. On 25 November, on the recommendation of the Sixth Committee,[29] the Assembly decided to continue consideration of the item and include it in the provisional agenda of its 1993 session (**decision 47/416**).

REFERENCES

[1]A/47/4. [2]A/48/4. [3]YUN 1986, p. 983. [4]*Border and Transborder Armed Actions (Nicaragua v. Honduras), Order of 27 May 1992*, I.C.J. Sales No. 610. [5]YUN 1991, p. 818. [6]*Aerial Incident of 3 July 1988 (Islamic Republic of Iran v. United States of America), Order of 5 June 1992*, I.C.J. Sales No. 611. [7]*Certain Phosphate Lands in Nauru (Nauru v. Australia), Preliminary Objections, Judgment of 26 June 1992*, I.C.J. Sales No. 616. [8]*Ibid., Order of 29 June 1992*, I.C.J. Sales No. 617. [9]YUN 1991, p. 819. [10]*Territorial Dispute (Libyan Arab Jamahiriya/Chad), Order of 14 April 1992*, I.C.J. Sales No. 609. [11]*East Timor (Portugal v. Australia), Order of 19 June 1992*, I.C.J. Sales No. 612. [12]YUN 1991, p. 820. [13]*Passage through the Great Belt (Finland v. Denmark), Order of 10 September 1992*, I.C.J. Sales No. 625. [14]*Maritime Delimitation and Territorial Questions between Qatar and Bahrain (Qatar v. Bahrain), Order of 26 June 1992*, I.C.J. Sales No. 615. [15]YUN 1971, p. 739. [16]*Questions of Interpretation and Application of the 1971 Montreal Convention arising from the Aerial Incident at Lockerbie (Libyan Arab Jamahiriya v. United Kingdom), Provisional Measures, Order of 14 April 1992*, I.C.J. Sales No. 607. [17]*Ibid. (Libyan Arab Jamahiriya v. United States of America), Provisional Measures, Order of 14 April 1992*, I.C.J. Sales No. 608. [18]*Ibid. (Libyan Arab Jamahiriya v. United Kingdom), Order of 19 June 1992*, I.C.J. Sales No. 613. [19]*Ibid. (Libyan Arab Jamahiriya v. United States of America), Order of 19 June 1992*, I.C.J. Sales No. 614. [20]*Oil Platforms (Islamic Republic of Iran v. United States of America), Order of 4 December 1992*, I.C.J. Sales No. 628. [21]YUN 1986, p. 984. [22]*Land, Island and Maritime Frontier Dispute (El Salvador/Honduras: Nicaragua intervening), Judgment of 11 September 1992*, I.C.J. Sales No. 626. [23]A/47/277-S/24111. [24]S/23500. [25]GA res. 44/23. 17 Nov. 1989. [26]A/47/444. [27]A/47/356-S/24367. [28]A/47/249 & Add.1. [29]A/47/713.

PUBLICATION

International Court of Justice Yearbook 1991-1992, No. 46, I.C.J. Sales No. 630.

Chapter II

Legal aspects of international political relations

In 1992, the General Assembly, its Sixth (Legal) Committee and the International Law Commission continued to consider legal aspects of international political and state relations.

The International Law Commission took up the question of an international criminal jurisdiction in the context of the draft Code of Crimes against the Peace and Security of Mankind. It further considered State responsibility and international liability for injurious consequences arising out of acts not prohibited by international law. The Assembly, in November, requested the Commission to elaborate a draft statute for an international criminal court as a matter of priority beginning in 1993 (resolution 47/33).

Also in November, the Assembly urged States to ensure compliance with the existing international law applicable to the protection of the environment in times of armed conflict, to incorporate the relevant legal provisions into their military manuals and to ensure their effective dissemination (47/37). It appealed to all States parties to the 1949 Geneva Conventions that had not yet done so to consider becoming parties to the additional Protocols I and II (47/30). Alarmed by repeated acts of violence against diplomatic and consular representatives, as well as against representatives to international intergovernmental organizations and officials of such organizations, the Assembly urged States to enforce the international law governing diplomatic and consular relations and to ensure the protection, security and safety of such personnel (47/31). In other action, it urged States, in applying the 1963 Vienna Convention on Consular Relations and corresponding provisions of other agreements, to accord full facilities to consular officers in the performance of their functions (47/36).

International Law Commission

The International Law Commission (ILC), at its forty-fourth session (Geneva, 4 May–24 July 1992),[1] continued work on the progressive development and codification of international law. The Commission held 42 public meetings; in addition, its newly appointed Drafting Committee held 27 meetings, the Enlarged Bureau of the Commission, 3, and the Bureau's Planning Group, 11.

In 1992, ILC considered an international criminal jurisdiction in the context of the draft Code of Crimes against the Peace and Security of Mankind, State responsibility for wrongful acts and international liability for injurious consequences arising out of acts not prohibited by international law.

The Commission did not take up proceedings in 1992 on sets of draft articles provisionally adopted by ILC in 1991 on the law of non-navigational uses of international watercourses[2] and on the draft Code of Crimes against the Peace and Security of Mankind,[3] pending receipt of comments and observations thereon, which the General Assembly in 1991[4] had urged Governments to submit by 1 January 1993. The Commission decided not to pursue further, during the current term of office of its members, the second part of the topic "Relations between States and international organizations", unless the Assembly decided otherwise. The Assembly endorsed that decision in resolution 47/33. ILC continued in 1992 to cooperate with the Asian-African Legal Consultative Committee, the European Committee on Legal Cooperation and the Inter-American Juridical Committee.

In accordance with an Assembly request (**resolution 47/33**), the Secretariat prepared for ILC's attention a topical summary of the Assembly's Sixth (Legal) Committee discussion in 1992[5] on ILC's report for that year.

The twenty-eighth session of the International Law Seminar—for postgraduate students and young professors or government officials dealing with international law—was held during the ILC session (Geneva, 1-19 June), with 4 United Nations Institute for Training and Research (UNITAR) fellows and 21 other participants, of different nationalities and mostly from developing countries. The participants attended ILC meetings and lectures. Austria, Denmark, Finland, France, Hungary, Jamaica, Morocco, Sweden, Switzerland and the United Kingdom had made voluntary financial contributions, thus making it possible to award 15 full fellowships and 1 partial fellowship. Since the first seminar in 1964, fellowships had been awarded to 324 of the 619 participants representing 147 nationalities.

International criminal jurisdiction

In accordance with a General Assembly resolution of 1991,[4] ILC considered in 1992[1] the question of an international criminal jurisdiction in the context of the draft Code of Crimes against the Peace and Security of Mankind. The draft Code, originally prepared by ILC in 1954,[6] defined offences which were crimes under international law and for which the responsible individual was to be punished.

The Commission had before it the tenth report[7] on the draft Code, submitted by its Special Rapporteur on the topic, Doudou Thiam (Senegal), which covered certain objections to the possible establishment of an international criminal jurisdiction and presented prospective draft provisions dealing with the law to be applied by the court, the jurisdiction of the court *ratione materiae*, complaints before the court, proceedings relating to compensation for injury, handing over the alleged offender to the court and the double-hearing principle.

Following examination of the Special Rapporteur's report, the Commission set up, on 19 May, a Working Group which proposed establishing an international criminal court by a statute in the form of a treaty agreed to by States parties, which, at least in the first phase of its operations, should exercise jurisdiction over only private persons as distinct from States. It proposed that the court's jurisdiction be limited to international crimes defined in specified international treaties, including but not limited to the crimes defined in the draft Code of Crimes against the Peace and Security of Mankind, and that a State should be able to become a party to the statute without becoming a party to the Code. Other proposals dealt with the court's structure and other mechanisms. The Working Group recommended that the Commission endorse its proposals as set out in its report, which was annexed to ILC's report on its 1992 session.

On 17 July, the Commission accepted the Working Group's proposals as a basis for future work and concluded that through the Special Rapporteur's ninth[3] and tenth[7] reports and the Working Group's report it had concluded its task of analysing the establishment of an international criminal court or other criminal trial mechanism, entrusted to it by the Assembly in 1989.[8] It further concluded that a structure such as that suggested by the Working Group could be workable and that further work on the issue required a renewed mandate from the Assembly.

State responsibility for wrongful acts

In 1992, ILC considered State responsibility for wrongful acts on the basis of the third[9] and fourth[10] reports by its Special Rapporteur on the topic, Gaetano Arangio-Ruiz (Italy), which dealt

with countermeasures—consequences of an intentionally wrongful act—and contained draft articles on countermeasures by an injured State (article 11), conditions of resort to countermeasures (article 12), proportionality (article 13) and prohibited countermeasures (article 14), as well as a possible new article on the question of a plurality of injured States (article 5 *bis*). The Commission referred the articles to its Drafting Committtee.

The Drafting Committee, in a July report,[11] set forth draft articles it had adopted on first reading which were contained in the Special Rapporteur's preliminary[12] and second[13] reports of 1988 and 1990, respectively. Those articles related to cessation of wrongful conduct (article 6), reparation (article 6 *bis*), restitution in kind (article 7), compensation (article 8), satisfaction (article 10), and assurances and guarantees of non-repetition (article 10 *bis*) of Chapter Two (Legal consequences deriving for an international delict) of Part Two of the draft articles. The Committee also adopted on first reading a new paragraph 2 to be included in article 1. In line with its policy of not adopting articles not accompanied by commentaries, ILC took note of the July report and decided to defer action on it until its next session.

International liability

Draft articles on international liability for injurious consequences arising out of acts not prohibited by international law continued to be considered by ILC in 1992 on the basis of the eighth report[14] of its Special Rapporteur on the subject, Julio Barboza (Argentina). The Special Rapporteur briefly reviewed the status and purpose of the articles proposed so far and indicated that, apart from the first nine articles then before the Drafting Committee, the other articles that had been proposed were merely exploratory, except for article 10 on the principle of non-discrimination, a principle which was generally supported by the Commission. He presented a more extensive examination of the development of the principle of prevention and proposed nine articles thereto dealing with preventive measures (article 1), notification and information (article 2), national security and industrial secrets (article 3), prior consultation on activities with harmful effects (article 4), alternatives to an activity with harmful effects (article 5), activities involving risk: consultations on a regime (article 6), initiative by the affected State (article 7), settlement of disputes (article 8) and factors involved in a balance of interest (article 9). The Special Rapporteur made further proposals on some of the terms used in article 2, such as the concepts of risk and harm.

Due to uncertainties among members of the Commission, ILC on 16 June established a Working Group to examine general matters relating to the scope, the approach to be taken and the possible direction of future work on the topic. On the basis of the Working Group's recommendations, ILC adopted a decision requesting the Special Rapporteur to examine further the issue of prevention only in respect of activities having a risk or causing transboundary harm and to propose a revised set of draft articles to that effect.

GENERAL ASSEMBLY ACTION

On 25 November 1992, the General Assembly, on the recommendation of the Sixth Committee, adopted **resolution 47/33** without vote.

Report of the International Law Commission on the work of its forty-fourth session

The General Assembly,

Having considered the report of the International Law Commission on the work of its forty-fourth session,

Emphasizing the need for the progressive development of international law and its codification in order to make it a more effective means of implementing the purposes and principles set forth in the Charter of the United Nations and in the Declaration on Principles of International Law concerning Friendly Relations and Cooperation among States in accordance with the Charter of the United Nations and to give increased importance to its role in relations among States,

Recognizing the importance of referring legal and drafting questions to the Sixth Committee, including topics that might be submitted to the International Law Commission, and of enabling the Sixth Committee and the Commission further to enhance their contribution to the progressive development of international law and its codification,

Recalling the need to keep under review those topics of international law which, given their new or renewed interest for the international community, may be suitable for the progressive development and codification of international law and therefore may be included in the future programme of work of the International Law Commission,

Recognizing the role of the International Law Commission in the fulfilment of the objectives of the United Nations Decade of International Law,

Taking note with appreciation of the sections of the report of the International Law Commission concerning the question of the possible establishment of an international criminal jurisdiction and noting the debate in the Sixth Committee pertaining to this question,

Considering that experience has demonstrated the usefulness of structuring the debate on the report of the International Law Commission in the Sixth Committee in such a manner that conditions are provided for concentrated attention on each of the main topics dealt with in the report, and that this process is facilitated when the Commission indicates specific issues on which expressions of views by Governments are of particular interest for the continuation of its work,

1. *Takes note* of the report of the International Law Commission on the work of its forty-fourth session;

2. *Expresses its appreciation* to the International Law Commission for the work accomplished at that session;

3. *Recommends* that, taking into account the comments of Governments, whether in writing or expressed orally in debates in the General Assembly, the International Law Commission should continue its work on the topics in its current programme;

4. *Takes note with appreciation* of chapter II of the report of the International Law Commission, entitled "Draft Code of Crimes against the Peace and Security of Mankind", which was devoted to the question of the possible establishment of an international criminal jurisdiction;

5. *Invites* States to submit to the Secretary-General, if possible before the forty-fifth session of the International Law Commission, written comments on the report of the Working Group on the question of an international criminal jurisdiction;

6. *Requests* the International Law Commission to continue its work on this question by undertaking the project for the elaboration of a draft statute for an international criminal court as a matter of priority as from its next session, beginning with an examination of the issues identified in the report of the Working Group and in the debate in the Sixth Committee with a view to drafting a statute on the basis of the report of the Working Group, taking into account the views expressed during the debate in the Sixth Committee as well as any written comments received from States, and to submit a progress report to the General Assembly at its forty-eighth session;

7. *Endorses* the decision of the International Law Commission not to pursue further, during the present term of office of its members, the consideration of the second part of the topic "Relations between States and international organizations";

8. *Expresses its appreciation* for the efforts of the International Law Commission to improve its procedures and methods of work;

9. *Requests* the International Law Commission:

(a) To consider thoroughly:

(i) The planning of its activities and programme for the term of office of its members, bearing in mind the desirability of achieving as much progress as possible in the preparation of draft articles on specific topics;

(ii) Its methods of work in all their aspects, bearing in mind that the staggering of the consideration of some topics might contribute, *inter alia*, to a more effective consideration of its report in the Sixth Committee;

(b) To continue to pay special attention to indicating in its annual report, for each topic, those specific issues on which expressions of views by Governments, either in the Sixth Committee or in written form, would be of particular interest for the continuation of its work;

10. *Takes note* of the comments of the International Law Commission on the question of the duration of its session, as presented in paragraph 377 of its report, and expresses the view that the requirements of the work for the progressive development of international law and its codification and the magnitude and complexity of the subjects on the agenda of the Commission make it desirable that the usual duration of its sessions be maintained;

11. *Reaffirms* its previous decisions concerning the role of the Codification Division of the Office of Legal Affairs of the Secretariat and those concerning the summary records and other documentation of the International Law Commission;

12. *Again draws the attention* of Governments to the importance, for the International Law Commission, of having their views on the draft articles on the law of the non-navigational uses of international watercourses and on the draft Code of Crimes against the Peace and Security of Mankind, adopted on first reading by the Commission, and urges them to present in writing their comments and observations by 1 January 1993, as requested by the Commission;

13. *Once again expresses the wish* that seminars will continue to be held in conjunction with the sessions of the International Law Commission and that an increasing number of participants from developing countries will be given the opportunity to attend those seminars, appeals to States that can do so to make the voluntary contributions that are urgently needed for the holding of the seminars, and expresses the hope that every effort will continue to be made by the Secretary-General, within existing resources, to provide the seminars with adequate services, including interpretation, as required;

14. *Requests* the Secretary-General to forward to the International Law Commission, for its attention, the records of the debate on the report of the Commission at the forty-seventh session of the General Assembly, together with such written statements as delegations may circulate in conjunction with their oral statements, and to prepare and distribute a topical summary of the debate;

15. *Recommends* the continuation of efforts to improve the ways in which the report of the International Law Commission is considered in the Sixth Committee, with a view to providing effective guidance for the Commission in its work;

16. *Also recommends* that the debate on the report of the International Law Commission at the forty-eighth session of the General Assembly commence on 25 October 1993.

General Assembly resolution 47/33

25 November 1992   Meeting 73   Adopted without vote

Approved by Sixth Committee (A/47/584) without vote, 16 November (meeting 35); draft by Chairman (A/C.6/47/L.14); agenda item 129.
Meeting numbers. GA 47th session: 6th Committee 20-30, 35; plenary 73.

REFERENCES
[1]A/47/10. [2]YUN 1991, p. 825. [3]Ibid., p. 823. [4]Ibid., p. 848, GA res. 46/54, 9 Dec. 1991. [5]A/CN.4/446. [6]YUN 1954, p. 408. [7]A/CN.4/442. [8]GA res. 44/39, 4 Dec. 1989. [9]YUN 1991, p. 831. [10]A/CN.4/444 & Add.1 & Add.1/Corr.1 & Add.2,3. [11]A/CN.4/L.472. [12]A/CN.4/416 & Corr.1,2 & Add.1 & Add.1/Corr.1. [13]A/CN.4/425 & Corr.1 & Add.1 & Add.1/Corr.1. [14]A/CN.4/443 & Corr.1,2.

International State relations and international law

Prevention of terrorism

Terrorism in all its aspects remained a concern of the United Nations in 1992.

Acting on allegations of involvement by nationals of the Libyan Arab Jamahiriya in two aerial incidents (see PART ONE, Chapter I)—the crash in December 1988 of Pan American flight 103 over Lockerbie, Scotland, and the attack in September 1989 on Union de transports aériens flight 772 over the Ténéré desert in the Niger—the Security Council, in January, urged the Libyan Arab Jamahiriya to respond to requests by France, the United Kingdom and the United States in connection with those incidents (**resolution 731(1992)**). In March, the Council imposed an air and arms embargo against the Libyan Arab Jamahiriya (**resolution 748(1992)**).

Protection of the environment in times of armed conflict

Report of the Secretary-General. As requested by the General Assembly in 1991,[1] the Secretary-General in July[2] presented information received by the International Committee of the Red Cross (ICRC) on the protection of the environment in times of armed conflict. ICRC reviewed the existing law on the subject and described related work carried out under its auspices. In 1992, ICRC convened a meeting of experts (Geneva, 27-29 April) to define the content of existing law, identify problems in its implementation and any gaps it might have and determine what action needed to be taken. The experts concluded that there was a general interest in preserving the environment and encouraged ICRC to carry on its work to clarify and, where necessary, develop rules to protect the natural environment in times of armed conflict. ICRC decided to continue to consult experts in order to study specific and unresolved matters and to set up a programme of further activities. In particular, it was ready to work on preparing a handbook of model guidelines for military manuals.

Other action. The Second Review Conference of the Parties to the Convention on the Prohibition of Military or Any Other Hostile Use of Environmental Modification Techniques (Geneva, 14-18 September),[3] adopted by the Assembly in 1976[4] and in force since 1978,[5] (see PART ONE, Chapter II), declared that all research and development on environmental modification techniques as well as their use should be dedicated solely to peaceful ends. It noted that the Assembly's Sixth Committee and the experts' meetings of ICRC would address the laws of armed conflict as they pertained to the environment and expressed support for those efforts.

The United Nations Conference on Environment and Development (Rio de Janeiro, Brazil, 3-14 June)[6] proclaimed that warfare was inherently destructive of sustainable development and that States should therefore respect international law providing protection for the environment in times of armed conflict and cooperate further in its development (see PART THREE, Chapter VIII).

On 25 November 1992, on the recommendation of the Sixth Committee, the General Assembly adopted **resolution 47/37** without vote.

Protection of the environment in times of armed conflict

The General Assembly,

Recognizing that the use of certain means and methods of warfare may have dire effects on the environment,

Recognizing also the importance of the provisions of international law applicable to the protection of the environment in times of armed conflict and, in particular, both the rules of universal applicability laid down in the Hague Convention respecting the Laws and Customs of War on Land, of 18 October 1907, with the Regulations annexed thereto, and the Geneva Convention relative to the Protection of Civilian Persons in Time of War, of 12 August 1949, and the applicable rules of the Protocol Additional to the Geneva Conventions of 12 August 1949, and relating to the Protection of Victims of International Armed Conflicts (Protocol I), of 1977, and of the Convention on the Prohibition of Military or Any Other Hostile Use of Environmental Modification Techniques, of 1976,

Expressing its deep concern about environmental damage and depletion of natural resources, including the destruction of hundreds of oil-well heads and the release and waste of crude oil into the sea, during recent conflicts,

Noting that existing provisions of international law prohibit such acts,

Stressing that destruction of the environment, not justified by military necessity and carried out wantonly, is clearly contrary to existing international law,

Concerned that the provisions of international law prohibiting such acts may not be widely disseminated and applied,

Noting the work on environmental protection carried out within the United Nations system and at meetings and symposia on the subject,

Taking note of the Final Declaration of the Second Review Conference of the Parties to the Convention on the Prohibition of Military or Any Other Hostile Use of Environmental Modification Techniques,

Taking note also of the Rio Declaration on Environment and Development, adopted at the United Nations Conference on Environment and Development at Rio de Janeiro on 14 June 1992, in particular its principle 24 thereof, and other relevant decisions of the Conference,

Expressing its appreciation for the report of the Secretary-General submitted pursuant to General Assembly decision 46/417 of 9 December 1991,

Welcoming the activities of the International Committee of the Red Cross in this field, including plans to continue its consultation of experts with an enlarged basis of participation and its readiness to prepare a handbook of model guidelines for military manuals,

1. *Urges* States to take all measures to ensure compliance with the existing international law applicable to the protection of the environment in times of armed conflict;

2. *Appeals* to all States that have not yet done so to consider becoming parties to the relevant international conventions;

3. *Urges* States to take steps to incorporate the provisions of international law applicable to the protection of the environment into their military manuals and to ensure that they are effectively disseminated;

4. *Requests* the Secretary-General to invite the International Committee of the Red Cross to report on activities undertaken by the Committee and other relevant bodies with regard to the protection of the environment in times of armed conflict, and to submit to the General Assembly at its forty-eighth session, under the item entitled ''United Nations Decade of International Law'', a report on activities reported by the Committee.

General Assembly resolution 47/37

25 November 1992   Meeting 73   Adopted without vote

Approved by Sixth Committee (A/47/591) without vote, 23 October (meeting 19); 31-nation draft (A/C.6/47/L.2/Rev.1); agenda item 136.

Sponsors: Armenia, Australia, Austria, Bangladesh, Belgium, Benin, Bulgaria, Chile, Croatia, Cyprus, Czechoslovakia, Denmark, Finland, Greece, Hungary, Ireland, Jordan, Lebanon, Morocco, Netherlands, New Zealand, Norway, Philippines, Poland, Republic of Korea, Romania, Russian Federation, Sweden, United Kingdom, United States, Yemen.

Meeting numbers. GA 47th session: 6th Committee 8, 9, 19; plenary 73.

Additional Protocols I and II to the 1949 Geneva Conventions

As requested by the General Assembly in 1990,[7] the Secretary-General in July[8] submitted information received from 10 Member States on the status of the two 1977 Protocols Additional to the 1949 Geneva Conventions for the protection of war victims.[9] As at 2 July 1992, 115 States had ratified or acceded to Protocol I (on protection of victims of international armed conflicts). Seven States —Brazil, Croatia, Kazakhstan, Madagascar, Portugal, Slovenia and Turkmenistan—did so in 1992. All of these parties—except 12—also adhered to Protocol II (on protection of victims of non-international conflicts). Two States—France and the Philippines— adhered only to Protocol II. By 31 December, Bosnia and Herzegovina, Egypt, Kyrgyzstan and Zimbabwe had also become parties to the two Protocols.

On 25 November 1992, on the recommendation of the Sixth Committee, the General Assembly adopted **resolution 47/30** without vote.

Status of the Protocols Additional to the Geneva Conventions of 1949 and relating to the protection of victims of armed conflicts

The General Assembly,

Recalling its resolutions 32/44 of 8 December 1977, 34/51 of 23 November 1979, 37/116 of 16 December 1982, 39/77 of 13 December 1984, 41/72 of 3 December 1986, 43/161 of 9 December 1988 and 45/38 of 28 November 1990,

Having considered the report of the Secretary-General on the status of the Protocols Additional to the Geneva Conventions of 1949 and relating to the protection of victims of armed conflicts,

Convinced of the continuing value of established humanitarian rules relating to armed conflicts and the need to respect and ensure respect for these rules in all circumstances within the scope of the relevant international instruments, pending the earliest possible termination of such conflicts,

Noting with satisfaction that, pursuant to article 90 of Additional Protocol I, the International Fact-Finding Commission has become operational,

Stressing the need for consolidating and implementing the existing body of international humanitarian law and for the universal acceptance of such law,

Mindful of the role of the International Committee of the Red Cross in offering protection to the victims of armed conflicts,

Noting with appreciation the continuing efforts of the International Committee of the Red Cross to promote and to disseminate knowledge of the two additional Protocols,

1. *Appreciates* the virtually universal acceptance of the Geneva Conventions of 1949 and the increasingly wide acceptance of the two additional Protocols of 1977;

2. *Notes*, however, the fact that, in comparison with the Geneva Conventions, the number of States parties to the two additional Protocols is still limited;

3. *Appeals* to all States parties to the Geneva Conventions of 1949 that have not yet done so to consider becoming parties also to the additional Protocols at the earliest possible date;

4. *Calls upon* all States which are already parties to Protocol I, or those States not parties, on becoming parties to Protocol I, to consider making the declaration provided for under article 90 of that Protocol;

5. *Requests* the Secretary-General to submit to the General Assembly at its forty-ninth session a report on the status of the additional Protocols based on information received from Member States;

6. *Decides* to include in the provisional agenda of its forty-ninth session the item entitled "Status of the Protocols Additional to the Geneva Conventions of 1949 and relating to the protection of victims of armed conflicts".

General Assembly resolution 47/30

25 November 1992   Meeting 73   Adopted without vote

Approved by Sixth Committee (A/47/581) without vote, 8 October (meeting 11); 23-nation draft (A/C.6/47/L.3); agenda item 126.

Sponsors: Algeria, Australia, Austria, Bangladesh, Belarus, Belgium, Canada, Chile, Czechoslovakia, Denmark, Egypt, Finland, Germany, Iceland, Latvia, Netherlands, New Zealand, Norway, Romania, Russian Federation, Spain, Sweden, Ukraine.

Meeting numbers. GA 47th session: 6th Committee 6, 11; plenary 73.

Jurisdictional immunities of States and their property

Report of the Secretary-General. In response to a 1991 General Assembly resolution,[10] the Secretary-General in August[11] presented comments received from 19 Governments on draft articles on jurisdictional immunities of States and their property, which were adopted on second reading by ILC in 1991.[12]

Working Group report. By a 1991 resolution,[10] the Assembly decided to establish, in 1992, an open-ended Working Group of the Sixth Committee to examine issues relating to the draft articles on jurisdictional immunities of States and their property and to explore the convening of an international conference, to be held in 1994 or later, to conclude a convention on the topic. The Working Group held 10 meetings between 25 September and 6 November, during which it discussed the main issues concerning the draft articles, identified by its Chairman as follows: the definitions contained in article 2 on use of terms, particularly the definitions of "State" and "commercial transaction"; the question of State immunity from measures of constraint in connection with proceedings before a court (part IV of the draft); and cases in which State immunity could not be invoked as provided for in part III of the draft. A summary of views exchanged on the draft articles was annexed to the Working Group's report,[13] as was a proposal on the settlement of disputes. The Group explored ways of reconciling the divergent views expressed during the first phase of the proceedings. The Chairman made proposals on the draft articles, and, although none of them elicited general support and several gave rise to objections or reservations, the Working Group felt that they deserved serious consideration to determine whether they could pave the way towards compromise solutions.

GENERAL ASSEMBLY ACTION

On 25 November, the General Assembly, on the recommendation of the Sixth Committee, adopted **decision 47/414**, whereby it took note of the report of the Working Group[13] and decided to reestablish it in 1993 to continue its consideration of issues of substance arising out of the draft articles on jurisdictional immunities in order to facilitate the successful conclusion of a convention through the promotion of general agreement. It decided to include the item in the provisional agenda of its forty-eighth (1993) session.

REFERENCES

(1)YUN 1991, p. 33, GA dec. 46/417, 9 Dec. 1991. (2)A/47/328. (3)ENMOD/CONF.II/12. (4)YUN 1976, p. 45, GA res. 31/72, annex, 10 Dec. 1976. (5)YUN 1978, p. 964. (6)*Report of the United Nations Conference on Environment and Development, Rio de Janeiro, 3-14 June 1992*, vol. I (Sales No. E.93.I.8). (7)GA res. 45/38, 28 Nov. 1990. (8)A/47/324. (9)YUN 1977, p. 706. (10)YUN 1991, p. 830, GA res. 46/55, 9 Dec. 1991. (11)A/47/326 & Add.1-5. (12)YUN 1991, p. 830. (13)A/C.6/47/L.10.

Diplomatic relations

Protection of diplomats

As at 31 December 1992[1], the number of parties to the various international instruments relating to the protection of diplomats and diplomatic and consular relations was as follows: 165 States were parties to the 1961 Vienna Convention on Diplomatic Relations,[2] with Croatia and Slovenia succeeding and Azerbaijan, Grenada, Latvia, Lithuania, Namibia, Suriname and Uzbekistan acceding in 1992; 46 States were parties to the Optional Protocol concerning the acquisition of nationality,[3] with Suriname and Switzerland acceding in 1992; and 59 States were parties to the Optional Protocol concerning the compulsory settlement of disputes,[3] with Slovenia succeeding and Suriname acceding during the year.

The 1963 Vienna Convention on Consular Relations[4] had 144 parties, with Croatia and Slovenia succeeding and Azerbaijan, Bahrain, Barbados, Grenada, Latvia, Lithuania, Namibia, Uzbekistan and Viet Nam acceding in 1992; 36 States were parties to the Optional Protocol concerning the acquisition of nationality,[5] with Switzerland acceding; and 44 States were parties to the Optional Protocol concerning the compulsory settlement of disputes.[5]

The 1973 Convention on the Prevention and Punishment of Crimes against Internationally Protected Persons, including Diplomatic Agents,[6] had 83 States parties, with Croatia and Slovenia having succeeded and Cameroon and Latvia having acceded in 1992.

Report of the Secretary-General. In response to General Assembly requests of 1987[7] and 1990,[8] the Secretary-General, in January 1992, requested States to submit information on serious violations of the protection, security and safety of diplomatic and consular missions and representatives, and on action taken to bring offenders to justice. In August, the Secretary-General submitted to the Assembly a report, with later addenda,[9] containing an analytical summary and the texts of the information received. A total of 82 new cases of violations, as well as additional information on previous cases, were reported by States during the period 1 October 1991 to 18 September 1992. No views were received with respect to enhancing diplomatic protection.

GENERAL ASSEMBLY ACTION

On 25 November 1992, on the recommendation of the Sixth Committee, the General Assembly adopted **resolution 47/31** without vote.

Consideration of effective measures to enhance the protection, security and safety of diplomatic and consular missions and representatives

The General Assembly,

Having considered the report of the Secretary-General,

Conscious of the need to develop and strengthen friendly relations and cooperation among States,

Convinced that respect for the principles and rules of international law governing diplomatic and consular relations is a basic prerequisite for the normal conduct of relations among States and for the fulfilment of the purposes and principles of the Charter of the United Nations,

Alarmed by the repeated acts of violence against diplomatic and consular representatives, as well as against representatives to international intergovernmental organizations and officials of such organizations, which endanger or take innocent lives and seriously impede the normal work of such representatives and officials,

Concerned at the failure to respect the inviolability of diplomatic and consular missions and representatives,

Concerned also at the abuse of diplomatic or consular privileges and immunities, particularly if acts of violence are involved,

Emphasizing the duty of States to take all appropriate measures as required by international law, including measures of a preventive nature, and to bring offenders to justice,

Welcoming measures already taken by States to this end in conformity with their international obligations,

Convinced that the role of the United Nations, which includes the reporting procedures established under General Assembly resolution 35/168 of 15 December 1980 and further elaborated in later Assembly resolutions, is important in promoting efforts to enhance the protection, security and safety of diplomatic and consular missions and representatives,

1. *Takes note* of the report of the Secretary-General;

2. *Strongly condemns* acts of violence against diplomatic and consular missions and representatives, as well as against missions and representatives to international intergovernmental organizations and officials of such organizations, and emphasizes that such acts can never be justified;

3. *Urges* States to observe, implement and enforce the principles and rules of international law governing diplomatic and consular relations and, in particular, to ensure, in conformity with their international obligations, the protection, security and safety of the missions, representatives and officials mentioned in paragraph 2 above officially present in territories under their jurisdiction, including practical measures to prohibit in their territories illegal activities of persons, groups and organizations that encourage, instigate, organize or engage in the perpetration of acts against the security and safety of such missions, representatives and officials;

4. *Also urges* States to take all necessary measures at the national and international levels to prevent any acts of violence against the missions, representatives and officials mentioned in paragraph 2 above and to bring offenders to justice;

5. *Recommends* that States should cooperate closely through, *inter alia*, contacts between the diplomatic and consular missions and the receiving State, with regard to practical measures designed to enhance the protection, security and safety of diplomatic and consular missions and representatives and with regard to the exchange of information on the circumstances of all serious violations thereof;

6. *Calls upon* States that have not yet done so to consider becoming parties to the instruments relevant to the protection, security and safety of diplomatic and consular missions and representatives;

7. *Also calls upon* States, in cases where a dispute arises in connection with a violation of their international obligations concerning the protection of the missions or the security of the representatives and officials mentioned in paragraph 2 above, to make use of the means for peaceful settlement of disputes, includ-

ing the good offices of the Secretary-General, and requests the Secretary-General, when he deems it appropriate, to offer his good offices to the States directly concerned;

8. *Requests* all States to report to the Secretary-General in accordance with paragraph 9 of resolution 42/154 of 7 December 1987;

9. *Requests* the Secretary-General to issue a report on the item, in accordance with paragraph 12 of resolution 42/154, containing also an analytical summary of the reports received under paragraph 8 above, on an annual basis, as well as to proceed with his other tasks pursuant to the same resolution;

10. *Decides* to include in the provisional agenda of its forty-ninth session the item entitled "Consideration of effective measures to enhance the protection, security and safety of diplomatic and consular missions and representatives".

General Assembly resolution 47/31

25 November 1992   Meeting 73   Adopted without vote

Approved by Sixth Committee (A/47/582) without vote, 23 October (meeting 19); 24-nation draft (A/C.6/47/L.6); agenda item 127.
Sponsors: Argentina, Australia, Austria, Belarus, Botswana, Bulgaria, Canada, Chile, Czechoslovakia, Denmark, Finland, Germany, Hungary, Iceland, Japan, Netherlands, Norway, Philippines, Romania, Russian Federation, Sweden, Turkey, Ukraine, Uruguay.
Meeting numbers. GA 47th session: 6th Committee 10, 11, 19; plenary 73.

Consular relations

Pursuant to a 1991 General Assembly resolution,[10] the Secretary-General in July submitted a report, with a later addendum,[11] containing the views of six States on a 1990 proposal,[12] submitted by Austria and Czechoslovakia, concerning the elaboration of an additional protocol on consular functions to the 1963 Vienna Convention on Consular Relations.[4]

As requested by the Assembly in 1991,[10] the Sixth Committee held informal consultations to examine the proposal on the additional protocol at eight meetings convened between 22 September and 29 October 1992.[13]

GENERAL ASSEMBLY ACTION

On 25 November 1992, the General Assembly, on the recommendation of the Sixth Committee, adopted **resolution 47/36** without vote.

Additional protocol on consular functions to the Vienna Convention on Consular Relations

The General Assembly,

Recalling its resolutions 45/47 of 28 November 1990 and 46/61 of 9 December 1991,

Having considered the report of the Secretary-General containing the replies received from Member States and other States parties to the Vienna Convention on Consular Relations concerning an additional protocol on consular functions to that Convention,

1. *Notes with appreciation* the valuable work done during its forty-fifth, forty-sixth and forty-seventh sessions on the basis of the proposal concerning the elaboration of an additional protocol on consular functions to the Vienna Convention on Consular Relations;

2. *Urges* States, in applying the Vienna Convention on Consular Relations and corresponding provisions of other agreements, to accord full facilities to consular officers in the performance of their functions;

3. *Takes note* of the report of the Sixth Committee on the matter.

General Assembly resolution 47/36

25 November 1992   Meeting 73   Adopted without vote

Approved by Sixth Committee (A/47/590) without vote, 10 November (meeting 32); draft by Vice-Chairman (A/C.6/47/L.9); agenda item 135.
Meeting numbers. GA 47th session: 6th Committee 2, 26, 32; plenary 73.

Status of the diplomatic courier and bag

As requested by the General Assembly in 1991,[14] the Sixth Committee continued, at eight meetings held between 22 September and 6 November 1992, informal consultations to study the draft articles on the status of the diplomatic courier and the diplomatic bag not accompanied by diplomatic courier and the draft optional protocols thereto,[15] on which ILC had completed a second reading in 1989.[16] The Committee also examined how to deal further with the draft instruments, with a view to facilitating a decision.

GENERAL ASSEMBLY ACTION

On 25 November 1992, the General Assembly, on the recommendation of the Sixth Committee, adopted **decision 47/415**, by which it decided to include in the provisional agenda of its fiftieth (1995) session the item entitled "Consideration of draft articles on the status of the diplomatic courier and the diplomatic bag not accompanied by diplomatic courier and of the draft optional protocols thereto".

REFERENCES

[1]*Multilateral Treaties Deposited with the Secretary-General: Status as at 31 December 1992* (ST/LEG/SER.E/11), Sales No. E.93.V.11. [2]YUN 1961, p. 512. [3]Ibid., p. 516. [4]YUN 1963, p. 510. [5]Ibid., p. 512. [6]YUN 1973, p. 775, GA res. 3166(XXVIII), annex, 14 Dec. 1973. [7]YUN 1987, p. 1068, GA res. 42/154, 7 Dec. 1987. [8]GA res. 45/39, 28 Nov. 1990. [9]A/47/325 & Add.1,2. [10]YUN 1991, p. 828, GA res. 46/61, 9 Dec. 1991. [11]A/47/327 & Add.1. [12]A/45/141. [13]A/C.6/47/L.7. [14]YUN 1991, p. 829, GA res. 46/57, 9 Dec. 1991. [15]A/47/587. [16]A/44/10.

Treaties and agreements

Treaties involving international organizations

The 1986 Vienna Convention on the Law of Treaties between States and International Organizations or between International Organizations[1] was ratified in 1992 by Belgium and Greece.[2] As at 31 December, 18 States had ratified or acceded to the Convention, which had not yet entered into force.

Registration and publication
of treaties by the United Nations

During 1992, some 1076 international agreements and 230 subsequent actions were received by the Secretariat for registration or filing and recording. In addition, there were 505 registrations of formalities concerning agreements for which the Secretary-General performs depositary functions.

The texts of international agreements registered or filed and recorded are published in the United Nations *Treaty Series* in the original languages, with translations into English and French where necessary. In 1992, the following volumes of the *Treaty Series* covering treaties registered or filed in 1978, 1980, 1981, 1982, 1983, 1984, 1985 and 1986 were issued:

1099, 1100, 1168, 1179, 1204, 1223, 1245, 1248, 1252, 1258, 1259, 1261, 1263, 1276, 1281, 1283, 1287, 1290, 1302, 1305, 1306, 1309, 1310, 1311, 1312, 1313, 1314, 1319, 1320, 1321, 1322, 1330, 1331, 1332, 1335, 1336, 1339, 1340, 1341, 1343, 1344, 1345, 1346, 1347, 1348, 1350, 1351, 1352, 1355, 1357, 1359, 1360, 1365, 1369, 1371, 1372, 1382, 1383, 1384/85, 1391, 1420.

Multilateral treaties

New multilateral treaties
concluded under United Nations auspices

The following treaties, concluded under United Nations auspices, were deposited with the Secretary-General during 1992:[2]

Agreement establishing the Fund for the Development of the Indigenous Peoples of Latin America and the Caribbean, concluded at Madrid, Spain, on 24 July 1992
International Sugar Agreement, 1992, concluded at Geneva on 20 March 1992
Convention on the Protection and Use of Transboundary Watercourses and International Lakes, concluded at Helsinki, Finland, on 17 March 1992
Convention on the Transboundary Effects of Industrial Accidents, concluded at Helsinki on 17 March 1992
United Nations Framework Convention on Climate Change, concluded at New York on 9 May 1992
Convention on Biological Diversity, opened for signature at Rio de Janeiro, Brazil, on 5 June 1992
Agreement on the Conservation of Small Cetaceans of the Baltic and North Seas, opened for signature at New York on 17 March 1992
Amendment to the Montreal Protocol on Substances that Deplete the Ozone Layer, adopted at the Fourth Meeting of the Parties at Copenhagen, Denmark, on 25 November 1992
Amendment to article 8 of the International Convention on the Elimination of All Forms of Racial Discrimination, 1966, adopted on 15 January 1992 at the twenty-second meeting of the Fourteenth Meeting of the States Parties to the Convention
Amendments to articles 17 (7) and 18 (5) of the Convention against Torture and Other Cruel, Inhumane or Degrading Treatment or Punishment, adopted by the Conference of the States Parties on 9 September 1992

Multilateral treaties
deposited with the Secretary-General

The number of multilateral treaties for which the Secretary-General performed depositary functions stood at 432 at the end of 1992. During the year, 408 signatures were affixed to treaties for which he performed depositary functions and 782 instruments of ratification, accession, acceptance and approval or notification were transmitted to him. In addition, he received 200 communications from States expressing observations or declarations and reservations made at the time of signature, ratification or accession.

The following multilateral treaties in respect of which the Secretary-General acts as depositary came into force during 1992:[2]

United Nations Convention on the Carriage of Goods by Sea, 1978, concluded at Hamburg, Germany, on 31 March 1978
Third extension, under Resolution No. 355, adopted by the International Coffee Council on 27 September 1991, of the *International Coffee Agreement, 1983*, adopted by the International Coffee Council on 16 September 1982, as further extended
International Coffee Agreement, 1983, adopted by the International Coffee Council on 16 September 1982, as further extended under Resolution No. 355 of 27 September 1991
Terms of Reference of the International Copper Study Group, adopted on 24 February 1989 by the United Nations Conference on Copper, 1988
Amendment to the Montreal Protocol on Substances that Deplete the Ozone Layer, adopted at the Second Meeting of the Parties at London on 29 June 1990
Basel Convention on the Control of Transboundary Movements of Hazardous Wastes and their Disposal, concluded at Basel, Switzerland, on 22 March 1989
Regulation No. 89: Uniform Provisions concerning the approval of:
    I. Vehicles with regard to limitation of their maximum speed;
    II. Vehicles with regard to the installation of a speed limitation device (SLD) of an approved type;
    III. Speed limitation devices (SLD)
Regulation No. 90: Uniform provisions concerning the approval of replacement brake lining assemblies for power-driven vehicles and their trailers

REFERENCES

[1]YUN 1986, p. 1006. [2]*Multilateral Treaties Deposited with the Secretary-General: Status as at 31 December 1992* (ST/LEG/SER.E/11), Sales No. E.93.V.11.

Chapter III

Law of the sea

The year 1992 marked the tenth anniversary of the adoption of the United Nations Convention on the Law of the Sea. Since its adoption, its impact on State practice worldwide showed a remarkable convergence of acceptance of its concepts, principles and basic provisions, given the fact that it had not yet entered into force.

The United Nations system was undertaking a number of initiatives to promote universal acceptance of the Convention, to facilitate the actions required following its eventual entry into force and to ensure that international cooperation in ocean affairs evolved in a coherent manner.

In December, the General Assembly adopted resolution 47/65 containing a call on States that had not done so to consider ratifying or acceding to the Convention to allow the effective entry into force of the new legal regime for the uses of the sea and its resources.

UN Convention on the Law of the Sea

Signatures and ratifications

The number of ratifications of or accessions to the United Nations Convention on the Law of the Sea increased to 53 during 1992 (51 ratifications, 2 accessions) with the receipt of instruments of ratification by Costa Rica and Uruguay.[1] The Convention, which was adopted by the Third United Nations Conference on the Law of the Sea in 1982,[2] would enter into force 12 months following receipt of the sixtieth instrument of ratification or accession.

The signatories to the Convention numbered 159 when the period for its signature closed in 1984.[3] Owing to the merger in 1990 of Democratic Yemen and Yemen (both of which were signatories) into one State, as well as to the accession of the German Democratic Republic (a signatory) to the Federal Republic of Germany (a non-signatory), that number became 157 as from 31 December 1991.[4]

Developments relating to the Convention

Pursuant to a 1991 resolution of the General Assembly,[5] the Secretary-General in 1992 submitted to it two reports on the law of the sea.

The first report, dated 5 November,[6] reviewed progress made in implementing the legal regime embodied in the United Nations Convention on the Law of the Sea since its adoption in 1982 to its tenth anniversary in 1992. Material for the report and a book to commemorate the anniversary was drawn from contributions presented by 17 experts representing all the regions of the world who met in New York from 27 to 29 January. The report gave an overview of the current status of the Convention; its impact on State practice with respect to 13 key subjects covering the major maritime zones or areas defined by the Convention, the rights of land-locked States, environmental protection and marine scientific research; and global, regional and subregional cooperation based on the Convention.

The report observed a striking degree of convergence of practice towards accepting the Convention's concepts, principles and basic provisions as they related to the territorial sea, the regime of straits used for international navigation, the archipelagic waters, the exclusive economic zone and the protection and preservation of the marine environment. Progress had been slow or lacking, however, in such areas as the new criteria for defining the continental shelf, access to resources in the exclusive economic zones of other States, control of certain types of pollution, the transfer of technology and the right of transit for land-locked States. The international regime for the development of mineral resources of the deep seabed remained unaccepted by the industrialized States. In addition, the introduction of the 200-mile exclusive economic zone resulted in increased fishing activities on the high seas by distant-water-fishing States. This in turn led to new problems, such as large-scale pelagic drift-net fishing of stocks straddling the 200-mile limit (see PART THREE, Chapter VIII). Those exceptions notwithstanding, the overall assessment was that the Convention, even before entering into force, had already played a significant role in maintaining international stability and promoting peaceful relations among States in respect of the uses of the seas and oceans.

The second report, dated 24 November,[7] summarized developments in 1992 relating to the Convention. Part One reviewed the status of the Convention, its impact on State practice and national policy, dispute settlement, criminal law enforcement, the main trends in cooperation on ocean affairs, marine environmental law and policy, conservation and management of living marine resources, marine scientific research and the work of the Preparatory Commission for the International Seabed Authority and for the International Tribunal for the Law of the Sea. Part Two outlined the activities of the Secretariat's Division for Ocean Affairs and the Law of the Sea (see below).

States continued to adopt or modify legislation in accordance with the provisions of the Convention relating to the outer limits of the various maritime zones and to the passage of ships through territorial seas or straits used for international navigation. By the end of 1992, the number of States claiming a 12-mile territorial sea, measured from baselines, had increased from 113 to 114, those claiming a 24-mile contiguous zone had increased from 33 to 38 and those claiming a 200-mile exclusive economic zone had increased from 82 to 86; 42 States based their continental shelf on a depth of 200 metres or on the exploitability criterion, whereas 21 established theirs to the outer edge of the continental margin or to 200 miles. In addition, 16 States had claimed archipelagic status, although not all had specified archipelagic baselines. Of note was the continued interest of the Russian Federation in developing the northern sea route (from the Novaya Zemlya Straits to the Bering Strait) as a viable north-east passage for international shipping, for which non-discriminatory rules applicable to domestic and foreign shipping had been promulgated to ensure safe navigation and prevent pollution.

In view of the political and economic changes that had taken place in the 10 years since the adoption of the Convention, the Secretary-General had taken the initiative of convening informal consultations aimed at achieving universal participation in the Convention. In the course of those consultations, which began in 1990, nine items relating to the regime for deep-seabed mining as contained in the Convention were identified as problem areas, particularly for industrialized States: costs to States parties, the Enterprise (see below), decision-making, the review conference, technology transfer, production limitation, the compensation fund, the financial terms of contracts and environmental considerations. The last item, no longer considered controversial in 1992, was removed from the list.

Disputes over maritime delimitation continued to be settled by negotiation, interim solutions, arbitration and the International Court of Justice (ICJ). Examples of negotiated settlement included the agreements delimiting the continental shelf between Belgium and the United Kingdom and between France and the United Kingdom. As an interim measure, the use of provisional lines, adopted for the purposes of the 1987 Treaty on Fisheries (concluded by certain central Pacific island States, Australia, New Zealand and the United States), was encouraged in the 1992 Niue Treaty on Cooperation in Fisheries Surveillance and Law Enforcement in the South Pacific Region (see below). A dispute between Canada and France over the waters surrounding St. Pierre et Miquelon was settled by the International Arbitral Tribunal, which rendered its award on 10 June 1992 delimiting a single maritime boundary, as requested by the parties. The decision created for France a zone of 3,607 square miles extending 12 miles to the east of the islands, 24 miles to the west and 200 miles to the south in a narrow corridor 10.5 miles wide.

Pending with ICJ were several delimitation cases, including the 1991 application of Guinea-Bissau for the delimitation of "the whole of the maritime territories" of Guinea-Bissau and Senegal.[8] In September 1992, ICJ delivered its Judgment on the land, island and maritime frontier dispute between El Salvador and Honduras, with Nicaragua intervening. It decided that the Gulf of Fonseca was a historic bay held in sovereignty jointly by the three countries, but excluding the existing three-mile belt held under the exclusive sovereignty of each. The Bay, including the three-mile belt, continued to be subject to the right of innocent passage. The waters at the central portion of the Gulf's closing line were subject to the joint entitlement of all three States unless and until a delimitation was effected. As to the waters outside the Gulf, the closing line would constitute the baseline; all three States were entitled to territorial sea, continental shelf and exclusive economic zone. Also in September 1992, the 1991 case concerning "passage through the Great Belt" (Finland v. Denmark),[9] a dispute over the passage of oil rigs through the Belt that generated considerable debate on the regime for international straits and on the definition of ships, was removed from the ICJ list. (For details on the ICJ cases, see PART FIVE, Chapter I.)

Of the nine coastal States in South-East Asia, seven claimed an exclusive economic zone. However, since the entire region is geologically one single continental shelf (the Sundra Shelf), there were several potential conflict areas: the Spratly Islands (Nansha) in the South China Sea, the Gulf of Tonkin, the Gulf of Thailand, the Celebes Sea, the Natuna Islands, the Straits of Malacca and the Timor Sea. The complex situation surrounding the Spratly Islands—China, Taiwan and Viet Nam claimed sovereignty over the whole archipelago, while Brunei Darussalam, Malaysia and the Philippines claimed various atolls lying within their exclusive economic zones—was brought to the fore following China's adoption of legislation in February designating the islands as Chinese territory and the subsequent award of an offshore exploration contract in an area also claimed by Viet Nam.

Various informal meetings held on the issue of managing conflicts in the region highlighted the value of intraregional consultations as the most viable means of resolving threats to regional peace. Such meetings paved the way for the adoption by the Association of South-East Asian Nations (ASEAN) of the Declaration on the South China Sea (Manila, Philippines, 22 July),[10] calling on the six parties to the Spratly Islands dispute—three of them ASEAN members—to apply the principles of the 1976 Treaty of Amity and Cooperation in South-East Asia (see PART ONE, Chapter II) as the basis for establishing a code of international conduct over the South China Sea.

In the area of criminal law enforcement, commitments by Governments to promote regional cooperation on the control of drug traffic by sea were contained in such 1992 documents as the Declaration of San Antonio (27 February), the South Pacific Forum Communiqué (9 July) and the Declaration of the South China Sea, by which the ASEAN members had resolved to collaborate on anti-piracy operations and in the campaign against drug trafficking.

The year saw a number of new international agreements, rules, standards and policy instruments that served to complement the Convention on the Law of the Sea with respect to the protection and sustainable development of the marine and coastal environment and its resources. Among them were two major global conventions: the Framework Convention on Climate Change and the Convention on Biological Diversity. A prominent development was the adoption by the United Nations Conference on Environment and Development (UNCED) of Agenda 21, which included a chapter on the protection of the oceans and development of their living resources that was applauded for being detailed and comprehensive, for including forward-looking initiatives and for supporting and building on the Convention on the Law of the Sea. (For details on these conventions and Agenda 21 see PART THREE, Chapter VIII.)

Three new regional conventions were agreed upon in 1992: the Convention on the Protection of the Black Sea against Pollution, with three protocols and four resolutions, signed by Bulgaria, Georgia, Romania, the Russian Federation, Turkey and Ukraine (Bucharest, Romania, 21 April); the Convention on the Protection of the Marine Environment of the Baltic Sea Area (Helsinki, Finland, 9 April) to replace a similar convention of 1974; and the Convention for the Protection of the Marine Environment of the North-East Atlantic, adopted by 14 European countries and the European Economic Community (September), to replace the 1972 Convention for the Prevention of Marine Pollution by Dumping from Ships and Aircraft (Oslo Dumping Convention) and the 1974

Paris Convention for the Prevention of Marine Pollution from Land-based Sources.

Recent revelations of nuclear dumping and other munitions disposal in European waters, as well as by the growing number of decommissioned nuclear submarines, underscored the need for an international convention on nuclear safety. This was affirmed by the International Atomic Energy Agency (IAEA) (Vienna, 22-26 February) and by the Conference on Security and Cooperation in Europe (Helsinki, 9 and 10 July).

The rapid response of the international community to conservation issues relating to marine living resources was evident at the global and regional levels. The Food and Agriculture Organization of the United Nations (FAO) stressed that the most important issue was the growing demand for fish in a situation where major fisheries were over-fished. Increasingly complex challenges demanded that fisheries management encompass biological, ecological, economic and social aspects; command a higher political and financial priority in many developing countries; and deal with issues as matters for regional or subregional cooperation. In this connection, the Secretary-General's recommendations on cooperation in fisheries in Africa had wide application (see PART TWO, Chapter VI). The International Conference on Responsible Fishing (Cancun, Mexico, 6-8 May) emphasized the need for fishing to develop within a comprehensive and balanced system (see PART THREE, Chapter VIII).

Regarding regional agreements, Canada, Japan, the Russian Federation and the United States signed the Convention for the Conservation of Anadromous Stocks in the North Pacific Ocean (Moscow, 11 February). That Convention, prohibiting directed fishing for anadromous fish, was of interest because of possible precedents for the definition of "directed fishing" (fishing targeted at a particular species or stock of fish), "incidental taking" (catching, taking or harvesting a species or stock of fish while conducting directed fishing for another species or stock) and "ecologically related species" (living marine resources associated with anadromous stocks found in the Convention area, including but not restricted to both predators and prey), and the relationship among the three.

The twenty-third South Pacific Forum (Honiara, Solomon Islands, 8 and 9 July),[11] by its final communiqué, underlined the importance of cooperation in and coordination of maritime surveillance for the enforcement of fisheries regulations. The adoption of the Niue Treaty on Cooperation in Fisheries Surveillance and Law Enforcement in the South Pacific Region illustrated the determination of the Pacific island States to expand such cooperation. Based on article 73 of the Convention on the Law of the Sea, the Treaty addressed cooperation in implementing harmonized minimum terms and conditions of access, information exchange, surveillance, prosecutions and penalty enforcement.

The FAO Technical Consultation on High Seas Fishing (Rome, 7-15 September) agreed on the need for accurate statistical reporting on fisheries in all waters, particularly on the high seas, for monitoring and evaluating catches and as an essential instrument for research and management.

As to marine scientific research, chapter 17 of UNCED's Agenda 21 was unique in that it contained a separate programme area to deal directly with the scientific uncertainties and challenges for international cooperation in marine sciences and services. The sponsoring bodies of the Group of Experts on the Scientific Aspects of Marine Pollution (the United Nations, UNEP, IAEA, FAO, UNESCO, WHO, WMO, IMO) were considering how best to pursue the work of assessing the state of marine and coastal environments both globally and regionally.

Vandalism and theft of expensive equipment deployed in international waters for climate study purposes underscored persistent questions regarding the legal status of ocean-data acquisition systems, whether drifting or moored, surface or subsurface instrumentation. According to the Executive Council of the Intergovernmental Oceanographic Commission (a body with functional autonomy within the United Nations Educational, Scientific and Cultural Organization), the Convention on the Law of the Sea would be insufficient for developing the proposed Global Ocean Observing System, given its heavy dependence on automated equipment.

(For General Assembly action with regard to the Convention, see **resolution 47/65** below.)

Preparatory Commission

During 1992, the Preparatory Commission for the International Seabed Authority and for the International Tribunal for the Law of the Sea held its tenth session at Kingston, Jamaica (24 February–13 March), and a meeting in New York (10–21 August).[7] Among the matters considered were the implementation of resolution II on the registration of pioneer investors in deep-seabed mining, adopted by the Third United Nations Conference on the Law of the Sea in 1982,[12] and preparation of draft agreements, rules, regulations and procedures.[13]

The General Committee, acting on behalf of the Preparatory Commission as the executive organ for the implementation of resolution II, adopted an Understanding on the Fulfilment of Obligations by the Registered Pioneer Investor for each of two pioneer investors registered in 1991:[14] the China Ocean Mineral Resources Research and Development Association and its certifying State—China—on 12 March; and the Interoceanmetal Joint Organization and its certifying States—Bulgaria, Cuba, Czechoslovakia, Poland and the Russian Federation—on 18 August.

The General Committee approved the recommendations of the Group of Technical Experts, which met in New York between 18 and 20 February to review documents submitted jointly by three registered pioneer investors—France, Japan and the Russian Federation—on the preparatory work concerning the exploration of reserved areas in the central region of the north-east Pacific, consisting of six sectors that constituted a total area of 71,570 square kilometres, including the area of 52,300 square kilometres contributed by the pioneer investors. The Group's recommendations specified details for the implementation of stage I of the exploration plan, which was ready to be undertaken.

The General Committee considered and took note of the periodic reports submitted by the certifying States of the first group of pioneer investors (France, India, Japan, Russian Federation). It took note of the report of the Training Panel on its third meeting, approved its recommendations and designated the six candidates recommended for the training programmes offered by France and Japan. It also took note of a communication on the training programmes offered by India and the Russian Federation.

Concerning preparation of the draft rules of procedure for the organs of the International Seabed Authority, the Plenary of the Preparatory Commission completed its consideration of the draft Agreement between the International Seabed Authority and the Government of Jamaica regarding the Headquarters of the International Seabed Authority; the draft Protocol on the Privileges and Immunities of the International Seabed Authority; and the draft Agreement concerning the Relationship between the United Nations and the International Seabed Authority.

The Preparatory Commission decided to hold its eleventh session at Kingston, Jamaica, from 22 March to 2 April 1993.

Special Commissions

The Preparatory Commission's four Special Commissions[7] continued to work in accordance with their respective mandates.

Developing land-based producer States

Special Commission 1 completed work on the three "hard-core" issues entrusted to it: criteria for identifying developing land-based producer States likely to be or actually affected by seabed production; assistance for such States, including the establishment of a compensation fund; and the effects of subsidized seabed mining. The 17 provisional conclusions and their annexes, forming the basis of recommendations to the Authority, were reviewed by the Chairman's negotiating group. Having examined the background paper on projection of demand, supply and price of metals contained in polymetallic nodules, Special Commission 1 completed consideration of all items on its work programme.

The Enterprise

Special Commission 2 continued preparations for the early entry into operation of the Enterprise—the operational arm of the Authority—which was to begin functioning upon the Convention's entry into force.

The Special Commission focused on working papers and documents on the structure and organization of the Enterprise, as provided for by the Convention on the Law of the Sea, on suggestions to facilitate discussion on transitional arrangements, on joint venture as an operational option at the initial stage of operation and on the Preparatory Commission's training programme. It agreed on the contents of its draft final report.

The Special Commission also considered the draft final report of its Advisory Group on Assumptions, which concluded that there was a need for continuity in its work and suggested that its successors should concentrate, *inter alia*, on periodic analysis of world markets and metal prices and their trends and forecasts, collection of information on and evaluation of technological developments, and assessment of the state of knowledge of deep-sea environments and possible impacts of mining activities.

Seabed mining code

Special Commission 3, charged with preparing the rules, regulations and procedures for the exploration and exploitation of the deep seabed (the seabed mining code), completed consideration of the draft regulations on accounting principles and procedures relating to the financial terms of contracts between the Authority and its contractors, as well as those on labour, health and safety standards. It thus concluded the final examination of all parts of the draft code. In August, the Special Commission began consideration of its draft final report.

International Tribunal

Special Commission 4, charged with the practical arrangements for the establishment of the International Tribunal for the Law of the Sea, completed its review of the revised draft Headquarters Agreement between the International Tribunal for the Law of the Sea and the Federal Republic of Germany. It adopted the draft Protocol on the Privileges and Immunities of the International Tribunal. It also decided to survey its draft final report, including pending issues, at its eleventh (1993) session.

GENERAL ASSEMBLY ACTION

On 11 December 1992, the General Assembly adopted **resolution 47/65** by recorded vote.

Law of the sea

The General Assembly,

Recalling its previous resolutions, including resolution 46/78 of 12 December 1991, on the law of the sea,

Recognizing that, as stated in the third preambular paragraph of the United Nations Convention on the Law of the Sea, the problems of ocean space are closely interrelated and need to be considered as a whole,

Convinced that it is important to safeguard the unified character of the Convention and related resolutions adopted therewith and to apply them in a manner consistent with that character and with their object and purpose,

Emphasizing the need for States to ensure consistent application of the Convention, as well as the need for harmonization of national legislation with the provisions of the Convention,

Considering that, in its resolution 2749(XXV) of 17 December 1970, it proclaimed that the seabed and ocean floor, and the subsoil thereof, beyond the limits of national jurisdiction (hereinafter referred to as "the Area"), as well as the resources of the Area, are the common heritage of mankind,

Recalling that the Convention provides the regime to be applied to the Area and its resources,

Recalling with satisfaction the expressions of willingness to explore all possibilities of addressing issues of concern to some States in order to secure universal participation in the Convention,

Recognizing the need for cooperation in the early and effective implementation by the Preparatory Commission of resolution II of the Third United Nations Conference on the Law of the Sea,

Noting with satisfaction the progress made in the Preparatory Commission since its inception, including the registration of six pioneer investors and the designation by the Preparatory Commission of reserved areas for the International Seabed Authority from the application areas submitted by the pioneer investors pursuant to resolution II, bearing in mind that such registration entails both rights and obligations for pioneer investors,

Noting the increasing needs of countries, especially developing countries, for information, advice and assistance in the implementation of the Convention and in their developmental process for the full realization of the benefits of the comprehensive legal regime established by the Convention,

Concerned that the developing countries are as yet unable to take effective measures for the full realization of these benefits owing to the lack of resources and of the necessary scientific and technological capabilities,

Recognizing the need to enhance and supplement the efforts of States and competent international organizations aimed at enabling developing countries to acquire such capabilities,

Recognizing also that the Convention encompasses all uses and resources of the sea and that all related activities within the United Nations system need to be implemented in a manner consistent with it,

Deeply concerned at the current state of the marine environment,

Mindful of the importance of the Convention for the protection of the marine environment,

Noting with concern the use of fishing methods and practices, including those aimed at evading regulations and controls, which can have an adverse impact on the conservation and management of living marine resources,

Considering the need for effective and balanced conservation and management of living marine resources, giving full effect to the relevant provisions in the Convention,

Taking note of activities carried out in 1992 under programme 10 (Law of the sea and ocean affairs) in the medium-term plan for the period 1992-1997, taking into account the restructuring of the Secretariat of the Organization, and of the report of the Secretary-General, prepared pursuant to paragraph 23 of General Assembly resolution 46/78,

Noting with satisfaction the special report of the Secretary-General prepared pursuant to paragraph 22 of General Assembly resolution 46/78, on the progress made in the implementation of the comprehensive legal regime embodied in the United Nations Convention on the Law of the Sea, in the light of the tenth anniversary in 1992 of its adoption,

1. *Recalls* the historic significance of the United Nations Convention on the Law of the Sea, especially on the occasion of the tenth anniversary in 1992 of its adoption, as an important contribution to the maintenance of peace, justice and progress for all peoples of the world;

2. *Expresses its satisfaction* at the increasing and overwhelming support for the Convention, as evidenced, *inter alia*, by the one hundred and fifty-nine signatures and fifty-three of the sixty ratifications or accessions required for entry into force of the Convention;

3. *Invites* all States to make renewed efforts to facilitate universal participation in the Convention;

4. *Notes with appreciation* the initiative of the Secretary-General to promote dialogue aimed at addressing issues of concern to some States in order to achieve universal participation in the Convention;

5. *Recognizes* that political and economic changes, including particularly a growing reliance on market principles, underscore the need to re-evaluate, in the light of the issues of concern to some States, matters in the regime to be applied to the Area and its resources, and that a productive dialogue on such issues involving all interested parties would facilitate the prospect of universal participation in the Convention, for the benefit of mankind as a whole;

6. *Calls upon* all States that have not done so to consider ratifying or acceding to the Convention at the earliest possible date to allow the effective entry into force of the new legal regime for the uses of the sea and its resources and calls upon all States to take appropriate steps to promote universal participation in the Convention, including through dialogue aimed at addressing the issues of concern to some States;

7. *Calls upon* all States to safeguard the unified character of the Convention and related resolutions adopted therewith and to apply them in a manner consistent with that character and with their object and purpose;

8. *Also calls upon* States to observe the provisions of the Convention when enacting their national legislation;

9. *Notes* the progress being made by the Preparatory Commission for the International Seabed Authority and for the International Tribunal for the Law of the Sea in all areas of its work;

10. *Recalls* the Understanding on the Fulfilment of Obligations by the Registered Pioneer Investors and their Certifying States adopted by the Preparatory Commission on 30 August 1990, as well as the understandings adopted on 12 March 1992 and 18 August 1992;

11. *Expresses its appreciation* to the Secretary-General for his efforts in support of the Convention and for the effective execution of programme 10 (Law of the sea and ocean affairs) in the medium-term plan for the period 1992-1997, and requests him, in the execution of programme 10, to continue to provide an effective response to the increased needs of States for assistance in the implementation of the Convention;

12. *Also expresses its appreciation* to the Secretary-General for the report prepared pursuant to paragraph 23 of General Assembly resolution 46/78 and requests him to carry out the activities outlined therein, as well as those aimed at the strengthening of the legal regime of the sea, special emphasis being placed on the work of the Preparatory Commission, including the implementation of resolution II of the Third United Nations Conference on the Law of the Sea;

13. *Welcomes* regional efforts being undertaken by developing countries to integrate the ocean sector in national development plans and programmes through the process of international cooperation and assistance, in particular the initiatives mentioned in the report of the Secretary-General;

14. *Calls upon* the Secretary-General to continue to assist States in the implementation of the Convention and in the development of a consistent and uniform approach to the legal regime thereunder, as well as in their national, subregional and regional efforts towards the full realization of the benefits therefrom, and invites the organs and organizations of the United Nations system to cooperate and lend assistance in these endeavours;

15. *Urges* interested Member States, in particular States with advanced marine capabilities, to review relevant policies and programmes in the context of the integration of the marine sector in national development strategies, and to explore prospects for intensifying cooperation with developing countries, including those of regions active in this field;

16. *Requests* the competent international organizations, the United Nations Development Programme, the World Bank and other multilateral funding agencies, in accordance with their respective policies, to intensify financial, technological, organizational and managerial assistance to the developing countries in their efforts to realize the benefits of the comprehensive legal regime established by the Convention and to strengthen cooperation among themselves and with donor States in the provision of such assistance;

17. *Also requests* the Secretary-General to keep under review, in cooperation with States and the competent

international organizations, the measures being undertaken and any necessary follow-up action, in order to facilitate the realization by States of the benefits of the comprehensive legal regime established by the Convention and to report thereon periodically to the General Assembly;

18. *Approves* the decision of the Preparatory Commission to hold its eleventh regular session at Kingston from 22 March to 2 April 1993 and to hold, as appropriate, a summer meeting in New York in 1993;

19. *Recognizes* that the protection of the marine environment will be significantly enhanced by the implementation of applicable provisions of the Convention;

20. *Reiterates its call* to States and other members of the international community to strengthen their cooperation and to take measures with a view to giving full effect to the provisions in the Convention on the conservation and management of living marine resources, including the prevention of fishing methods and practices which can have an adverse impact on the conservation and management of living marine resources and, in particular, to comply with bilateral and regional measures applicable to them aimed at effective monitoring and enforcement;

21. *Requests* the Secretary-General to report to the General Assembly at its forty-eighth session on developments pertaining to the Convention and all related activities and on the implementation of the present resolution;

22. *Decides* to include in the provisional agenda of its forty-eighth session the item entitled "Law of the sea".

General Assembly resolution 47/65

11 December 1992   Meeting 84   135-1-9 (recorded vote)

44-nation draft (A/47/L.28 & Add.1), orally amended; agenda item 32.

Sponsors: Australia, Barbados, Brazil, Cameroon, Canada, Cape Verde, Chile, Comoros, Costa Rica, Cyprus, Denmark, Djibouti, Fiji, Grenada, Guinea-Bissau, Guyana, Iceland, Indonesia, Ireland, Jamaica, Lesotho, Madagascar, Malta, Mauritania, Mexico, Micronesia, Myanmar, Namibia, New Zealand, Norway, Philippines, Portugal, Saint Lucia, Samoa, Senegal, Sierra Leone, Singapore, Solomon Islands, Sri Lanka, Sweden, Thailand, Trinidad and Tobago, Ukraine, Uruguay.

Meeting numbers: GA 47th session: plenary 83, 84.

Recorded vote in Assembly as follows:

In favour: Algeria, Angola, Antigua and Barbuda, Argentina, Australia, Austria, Bahamas, Bahrain, Bangladesh, Barbados, Belarus, Belgium, Benin, Bhutan, Bolivia, Botswana, Brazil, Brunei Darussalam, Bulgaria, Burkina Faso, Cameroon, Canada, Cape Verde, Central African Republic, Chad, Chile, China, Colombia, Congo, Costa Rica, Côte d'Ivoire, Croatia, Cuba, Cyprus, Czechoslovakia, Denmark, Djibouti, Dominica, Dominican Republic, Egypt, El Salvador, Estonia, Ethiopia, Fiji, Finland, France, Gabon, Ghana, Greece, Guinea, Guinea-Bissau, Guyana, Haiti, Hungary, Iceland, India, Indonesia, Iran, Iraq, Ireland, Italy, Jamaica, Japan, Kenya, Kuwait, Lao People's Democratic Republic, Latvia, Lesotho, Libyan Arab Jamahiriya, Liechtenstein, Lithuania, Luxembourg, Madagascar, Malaysia, Maldives, Mali, Malta, Mauritania, Mauritius, Mexico, Micronesia, Mongolia, Morocco, Myanmar, Namibia, Nepal, Netherlands, New Zealand, Nicaragua, Niger, Nigeria, Norway, Oman, Pakistan, Paraguay, Philippines, Poland, Portugal, Qatar, Republic of Korea, Republic of Moldova, Romania, Russian Federation, Rwanda, Saint Kitts and Nevis, Saint Lucia, Saint Vincent and the Grenadines, Samoa, Sao Tome and Principe, Saudi Arabia, Senegal, Seychelles, Sierra Leone, Singapore, Slovenia, Solomon Islands, Spain, Sri Lanka, Sudan, Suriname, Swaziland, Sweden, Syrian Arab Republic, Thailand, Togo, Trinidad and Tobago, Tunisia, Ukraine, United Arab Emirates, United Republic of Tanzania, Uruguay, Vanuatu, Viet Nam, Yemen, Zimbabwe.

Against: Turkey.

Abstaining: Azerbaijan, Ecuador, Germany, Israel, Panama, Peru, United Kingdom, United States, Venezuela.

Also on 22 December, the Assembly, in **resolution 47/192**, reaffirmed that the work and results

of a conference on straddling and highly migratory fish stocks, to be convened in 1993, should be fully consistent with the provisions of the United Nations Convention on the Law of the Sea, in particular the rights and obligations of coastal States and States fishing on the high seas, and that States should give full effect to the high seas fisheries provisions of the Convention with regard to fisheries populations whose ranges lay both within and beyond exclusive economic zones (straddling fish stocks) and highly migratory fish stocks.

Division for Ocean Affairs and the Law of the Sea

Under a new organizational arrangement in the United Nations Secretariat, the Office for Ocean Affairs and the Law of the Sea was integrated, effective 1 March 1992, with the Office of Legal Affairs as its Division for Ocean Affairs and the Law of the Sea.[7] The programme on the law of the sea and ocean affairs, including its subprogramme on structure and priorities, as set out under programme 10 of the medium-term plan for 1992-1997,[15] remained unchanged.

During 1992, the Division continued to provide direct assistance, on request, to Member States and intergovernmental organizations. It assisted the members of the Indian Ocean Marine Affairs Cooperation process (comprising the African and Asian States bordering the Indian Ocean) and its secretariat, and assisted in preparations for the eighth meeting of its Standing Committee (Colombo, Sri Lanka, 26-30 October). At the request of Côte d'Ivoire, the Division organized an interministerial meeting there (Abidjan, 30 September–3 October) that adopted a programme recommending an integrated marine policy aimed at the better use of that country's national resources and marine environment. The Division contributed two papers on conflict resolution and possible cooperation in marine affairs to the seventh International Conference on Peace and Security in Southern Africa (Arusha, United Republic of Tanzania, 20-24 July).

As to policy formulation, planning and management relating to coastal areas and exclusive economic zones, the Division cooperated in organizing an International Conference on Ocean Management in Global Change (Genoa, Italy, 22-26 June), which emphasized the relationship between resource development and environmental protection, with particular attention to the results of UNCED. It also provided technical advice to the Marine Institute, Newfoundland, Canada, for the design and implementation of a simulation exercise in sea-use planning.

The Division contributed special papers and studies on issues related to the Convention on the

Law of the Sea for conferences, seminars and workshops, such as the sixteenth annual seminar, titled "National Energy Policy and the Oceans", organized by the Center for Ocean Law and Policy (Key Largo, United States, 9-11 January) and the twelfth Training Programme on Management and Conservation of Marine Resources within the Exclusive Economic Zone, organized by the International Ocean Institute (Halifax, Canada, 27 and 28 July).

Other activities included the further development of the computerized Law of the Sea Information System, composed of a group of databases, each containing information on different aspects of the law of the sea; the extensive revision of the Country Marine Profile Database and the National Marine Legislation Database in the light of recent changes in the United Nations membership; expansion of the holdings and services of the Law of the Sea Library through acquisitions of the latest publications and the continued updating of the Library Bibliographic Information System, a computerized database of the Library's holdings, which was being expanded to include the library holdings of the Kingston Office of the Law of the Sea; and publication of two issues of the *Law of the Sea Bulletin*[16] in English, French and Spanish.

The Division maintained close cooperation with other Secretariat units, as well as with agencies and other bodies within the United Nations system, in matters relating to sea law and other marine affairs.

The Hamilton Shirley Amerasinghe Fellowship on the Law of the Sea—established in 1981[17] and presented annually in honour of the first President of the Third United Nations Conference on the Law of the Sea—was awarded to Igor Vio, assistant lecturer on the law of the sea, University of Rijeka, Croatia.

REFERENCES

[1]*Multilateral Treaties Deposited with the Secretary-General: Status as at 31 December 1992* (ST/LEG/SER.E/11), Sales No. E.93.V.11. [2]YUN 1982, p. 178. [3]YUN 1984, p. 108. [4]*Multilateral Treaties Deposited with the Secretary-General: Status as at 31 December 1991* (ST/LEG/SER.E/10), Sales No. E.92.V.4. [5]YUN 1991, p. 838, GA res. 46/78, 12 Dec. 1991. [6]A/47/512. [7]A/47/623. [8]YUN 1991, p. 819. [9]Ibid. [10]A/47/357. [11]A/47/391. [12]YUN 1982, p. 216. [13]LOS/PCN/L.102. [14]YUN 1991, p. 835. [15]A/45/6/Rev.1. [16]*Law of the Sea Bulletin*, No. 20, March; No. 21, Aug. 1992. [17]YUN 1981, p. 139.

OTHER PUBLICATIONS

The Law of the Sea: A Select Bibliography—1991 (LOS/LIB/7), Sales No. E.92.V.6. *The Law of the Sea: Exclusive Economic Zone—Legislative History of Articles 56, 58 and 59 of the United Nations Convention on the Law of the Sea*, Sales No. E.92.V.8. *The Law of the Sea: The Regime for the High-Seas Fisheries—Status and Prospects*, Sales No. E.92.V.12. *The Law of the Sea: Current Developments in State Practice*, Sales No. E.92.V.13. *The Law of the Sea: Straits Used for International Navigation—Legislative History of Part III of the United Nations Convention on the Law of the Sea*, Sales No. E.92.V.14.

Chapter IV

Other legal questions

In 1992, the United Nations continued to work on various aspects of international law and international economic law.

The Secretary-General noted that the first summit meeting of the Security Council at the level of Heads of State and Government, in January 1992, represented an unprecedented recommitment, at the highest political level, to the purposes and principles of the Charter. He noted in his report "An Agenda for Peace" that preventive diplomacy, peacemaking, peace-keeping and post-conflict peace-building offered a coherent contribution towards securing peace in the spirit of the Charter. It was time, he stated, to move towards the realization of the Organization's vast potential and bring new life to the Charter.

The General Assembly, in November, requested the Special Committee on the Charter of the United Nations and on the Strengthening of the Role of the Organization to give priority, in 1993, to the question of the maintenance of international peace and security in all its aspects in order to strengthen the role of the United Nations and to continue its work on the peaceful settlement of disputes between States (resolution 47/38). The Assembly expressed hope that the host country of the United Nations Headquarters, the United States, would continue to take all measures necessary to prevent interference with the functions of permanent missions to the United Nations and welcomed a recent lifting of travel restrictions by the host country on mission personnel and United Nations Secretariat staff members of certain nationalities. It urged the host country to continue to abide by its obligations to the United Nations and the missions accredited to it (resolution 47/35). Also in November, the Assembly adopted the programme of activities for the second term (1993-1994) of the United Nations Decade of International Law (1990-1999) (resolution 47/32).

Legal aspects of international economic law continued to be considered during the year by the United Nations Commission on International Trade Law (UNCITRAL) and by the Sixth (Legal) Committee of the General Assembly. The Assembly took note of the Commission's adoption, in 1992, of the Model Law on International Credit Transfers and of the Legal Guide on International Countertrade Transactions. It noted with satisfaction the entry into force on 1 November 1992 of the 1978 United Nations Convention on the Carriage of Goods by Sea (Hamburg Rules) and requested the Secretary-General to increase efforts to promote wider adherence to the Convention (resolution 47/34).

International organizations and international law

Strengthening the role of the United Nations

The Secretary-General, in his annual report to the General Assembly on the work of the Organization (see p. 3), said that the first summit meeting of the Security Council at the level of Heads of State and Government represented the start of a new phase in the history of the Organization. He said that with the end of the bipolar era, States saw the United Nations once again as an international instrument capable of maintaining international peace and security, of advancing justice and human rights, and of "achieving social progress and better standards of life in larger freedom". Never before had the United Nations been so action-oriented, actively engaged and widely expected to respond to needs both immediate and pervasive.

The Secretary-General noted that the Security Council's workload, compared with that of the cold-war period, had increased dramatically to the point where it was administering 12 peace-keeping operations in various regions, with nearly 40,000 military personnel at an estimated cost of some $3,000 million in the current 12-month period. The responsibilities of the Secretariat had also expanded in terms of diplomatic missions of fact-finding, representation and good offices undertaken on the Secretary-General's behalf. He noted that available resources had not paralleled the rapid expansion of these activities and he had therefore initiated a restructuring of the Secretariat to make the most effective use of resources through the rationalization and streamlining of structures and procedures, together with managerial improvements.

To enable the Secretariat to respond swiftly and efficiently to the mandates of the Security Council and the General Assembly concerning the maintenance of international peace and security, the Secretary-General stated that his aim was to enhance its capacity for good offices, preventive diplomacy, peacemaking, research and analysis and early warning, as well as to strengthen its planning and managerial capability in peace-keeping. A primary objective was a more effective Organization-wide distribution of responsibilities and a balance between functions performed at Headquarters and those carried out by the regional commissions and other United Nations organs and programmes. He firmly believed that the focus of the United Nations must remain in the field, where economic, social and political decisions took effect.

The Secretary-General said that the Organization's responsibilities and commitments in the political and security areas should not be pursued at the expense of responsibilities for development. It was essential that they be carried out in an integrated, mutually supportive way. In his June report, "An Agenda for Peace",[1] the Secretary-General recommended that the Security Council invite a reinvigorated and restructured Economic and Social Council to provide reports, in accordance with Article 65 of the Charter, on those social and economic developments that might threaten international peace and security. He said that the United Nations must foster, through peace-building, the process of democratization in situations characterized by long-standing conflicts, both within and among nations. He said he was committed to reforming the Organization to ensure that each of its organs fulfilled its capabilities as envisioned in the Charter. The pace of reform, he stressed, must increase if the United Nations was to stay ahead of history.

Special Committee on the Charter

The Special Committee on the Charter of the United Nations and on the Strengthening of the Role of the Organization[2] (New York, 3-21 February 1992) continued to discuss proposals for the maintenance of international peace and security, together with its examination of the peaceful settlement of disputes between States, as requested by the General Assembly in 1991.[3]

Concerning the maintenance of international peace and security, the Committee had before it two working papers submitted by the Russian Federation. One proposed new issues for consideration by the Committee,[4] and the other contained a draft declaration on improved cooperation between the United Nations and regional organizations.[5] The Committee also examined: a working paper submitted by 41 States on provisions of the United Nations Charter related to assistance to third States affected by the application of sanctions under Chapter VII of the Charter;[6] a 1991 proposal by the Libyan Arab Jamahiriya dealing

with enhancing the effectiveness of the Security Council in regard to the maintenance of international peace and security;[7] and a working paper submitted by Cuba on strengthening the role of the United Nations in the maintenance of international peace and security.

In considering the peaceful settlement of disputes between States, the Committee discussed a draft text submitted by Guatemala in 1990 proposing conciliation rules for the United Nations.[8] The Committee completed a first reading of the draft rules which dealt with their application; the initiation of conciliation proceedings; cases in which more than one State had the same interest; the number of conciliators; the appointment of conciliators; rules applicable to conciliation by a sole conciliator; rules applicable to conciliation by commission; and rules applicable to all conciliation proceedings conducted in accordance with the rules. Guatemala offered to submit, at a later stage, a revised draft of its proposal taking into consideration the comments made on the articles at the Special Committee's 1992 session.

Report of the Secretary-General. In his June report, "An Agenda for Peace",[1] the Secretary-General addressed various issues relating to the Charter and to strengthening the role of the Organization, *inter alia*, in the context of the maintenance of international peace and security and the peaceful settlement of disputes between States.

Egypt chaired the informal open-ended Working Group on the report. It was stressed that the Group's mandate did not conflict with that of the Special Committee and that every effort would be made to avoid conflict between them.

GENERAL ASSEMBLY ACTION

On 25 November 1992, the General Assembly, on the recommendation of the Sixth (Legal) Committee, adopted **resolution 47/38** without vote.

Report of the Special Committee on the Charter of the United Nations and on the Strengthening of the Role of the Organization

The General Assembly,

Recalling its resolution 3499(XXX) of 15 December 1975, by which it established the Special Committee on the Charter of the United Nations and on the Strengthening of the Role of the Organization, and its relevant resolutions adopted at subsequent sessions,

Bearing in mind the reports of the Secretary-General on the work of the Organization submitted to the General Assembly at its thirty-seventh, thirty-ninth, fortieth, forty-first, forty-second, forty-third, forty-fourth, forty-fifth, forty-sixth and forty-seventh sessions, as well as the views and comments expressed on them by Member States,

Noting the recommendations relevant to the work of the Special Committee contained in the report of the Secretary-General entitled "An Agenda for Peace", in the light of the debate within the United Nations, particularly within the General Assembly,

Having considered the report of the Special Committee on the work of its session held in 1992,

Mindful of the desirability of further work being done by the Special Committee in the fields of the maintenance of international peace and security and the peaceful settlement of disputes between States,

Bearing in mind various proposals presented to the General Assembly at its forty-seventh session aimed at strengthening the role of the Organization and enhancing its effectiveness,

1. *Takes note* of the report of the Special Committee on the Charter of the United Nations and on the Strengthening of the Role of the Organization;

2. *Decides* that the Special Committee will hold its next session from 1 to 19 March 1993;

3. *Requests* the Special Committee, at its session in 1993, in accordance with the provisions of paragraph 4 below:

(*a*) To accord priority to the question of the maintenance of international peace and security in all its aspects in order to strengthen the role of the United Nations and, in this context:

(i) To continue its consideration of the proposal on the enhancement of cooperation between the United Nations and regional organizations;

(ii) To continue its consideration of the proposal on the implementation of the provisions of the Charter of the United Nations related to assistance to third States affected by the application of sanctions under Chapter VII of the Charter;

(iii) To consider other specific proposals relating to the maintenance of international peace and security already submitted to the Special Committee or which might be submitted to the Special Committee at its session in 1993;

(*b*) To continue its work on the question of the peaceful settlement of disputes between States and, in this context:

(i) To consider the proposal on United Nations rules for the conciliation of disputes between States;

(ii) To consider other specific proposals relating to the question of the peaceful settlement of disputes between States already under consideration in the Special Committee or those that might be submitted to the Special Committee at its session in 1993;

(*c*) To consider various proposals with the aim of strengthening the role of the Organization and enhancing its effectiveness;

4. *Also requests* the Special Committee to be mindful of the importance of reaching general agreement whenever that has significance for the outcome of its work;

5. *Decides* that the Special Committee shall accept the participation of observers of Member States in its meetings, including those of its working group, and also decides that the Special Committee shall be authorized to invite other States or intergovernmental organizations to participate in the debate in plenary meetings of the Special Committee on specific items where it considers that such participation would assist in its work;

6. *Requests* the Special Committee to submit a report on its work to the General Assembly at its forty-eighth session;

7. *Decides* to include in the provisional agenda of its forty-eighth session the item entitled "Report of the Special Committee on the Charter of the United Nations and on the Strengthening of the Role of the Organization".

General Assembly resolution 47/38

25 November 1992   Meeting 73   Adopted without vote

Approved by Sixth Committee (A/47/588) without vote, 19 November (meeting 37); 33-nation draft (A/C.6/47/L.15); agenda item 133.

Sponsors: Argentina, Belgium, Brazil, Canada, Chile, Colombia, Cyprus, Czechoslovakia, Ecuador, Egypt, El Salvador, Finland, Germany, Guatemala, Guinea, Hungary, Indonesia, Italy, Japan, Malaysia, Mexico, Morocco, New Zealand, Nigeria, Oman, Philippines, Republic of Moldova, Romania, Sierra Leone, Spain, Tunisia, Uruguay, Venezuela.

Meeting numbers. GA 47th session: 6th Committee 12-18, 37; plenary 73.

Host country relations

Pursuant to a General Assembly request of 1991,[9] the Committee on Relations with the Host Country in 1992 continued to consider various aspects of relations between the United Nations diplomatic community and the United States, its host country. At four meetings between 22 April and 27 October, the Committee considered: host country travel regulations; entry visas issued by the host country; the acceleration of immigration and customs procedures under issues arising in connection with the implementation of the 1947 Headquarters Agreement between the United Nations and the United States;[10] the responsibilities of permanent missions to the United Nations and their personnel, in relation to financial indebtedness in particular; and matters related to insurance, education and health. Summaries of the Committee's deliberations were contained in its 1992 report to the Assembly.[11] The Working Group on Indebtedness, established in 1991,[12] met on 12 March and 9 June.

At the end of 1991, travel restrictions imposed on United Nations staff members of Vietnamese nationality and their dependents were lifted. On 24 April 1992, all travel restrictions on members of the permanent missions of Belarus and Ukraine, as well as on United Nations staff members of those nationalities, were removed by the host country. Effective 13 July, all restrictions on travel to closed areas in the United States to which Russian Federation mission personnel and their dependents were subject were abolished. In September, all travel restrictions on members of the permanent mission of Georgia and Georgian nationals who were Secretariat staff members were also removed. Additionally, the United States lifted the numerical ceilings imposed on staff levels of the permanent missions of Belarus, the Russian Federation and Ukraine.

Iraq urged the host country to remove the freeze on its liquid assets in the United States to enable its mission to pay staff salaries and rents. The Libyan Arab Jamahiriya stated that its officials continued to have difficulties obtaining United States entry visas when coming to New York to participate in United Nations meetings. The United States observed that the permanent mission of the

Libyan Arab Jamahiriya had not provided documentation on any discriminatory delay in the issuance of visas and the United States was ready to respond in writing should such documentation be furnished. The Libyan Arab Jamahiriya further informed the Committee that the United States had reduced its mission personnel in New York by 25 per cent. In reply, the United States noted that the reduction of personnel was in compliance with Security Council resolution 748(1992) (see PART ONE, Chapter I). Cuba alleged that 13 new incidents of provocation and harassment had taken place against its permanent mission and staff. In response, the United States stated that there was no hostility and observed a difference of opinion about what constituted democratic process and freedom of speech. The United Republic of Tanzania expressed concern in the Committee over insurance arrangements in the host country governing motor vehicles for missions and their personnel, which it termed onerous.

The problem of indebtedness was seen by the host country as a priority issue. It was noted that when a diplomat, a diplomatic mission or a staff member of the Secretariat failed to pay just debts, this reflected poorly on the entire United Nations community. In the view of the United States, a failure to satisfy debts could give rise to the expulsion of members of a mission on the grounds of abuse of residence.

In April, the United States introduced to the Committee the newly appointed New York City Commissioner for the United Nations and Consular Corps, Nadine B. Hack, who succeeded Paul O'Dwyer.

Among the recommendations and conclusions approved on 27 October, the Committee anticipated that the host country would continue to take all measures necessary to prevent interference with the functioning of missions; expressed hope that remaining travel restrictions would be removed by the host country as soon as possible; and reminded missions and their personnel of their financial obligations, while expressing strong support for the continued efforts of the Working Group on Indebtedness to find a solution to this problem.

GENERAL ASSEMBLY ACTION

On 25 November, the General Assembly, on the recommendation of the Sixth Committee, adopted **resolution 47/35** without vote.

Report of the Committee on Relations with the Host Country

The General Assembly,

Having considered the report of the Committee on Relations with the Host Country,

Recalling Article 105 of the Charter of the United Nations, the Convention on the Privileges and Immunities of the United Nations and the Agreement between the United Nations and the United States of America regarding the Headquarters of the United Nations and the responsibilities of the host country,

Recognizing that effective measures should continue to be taken by the competent authorities of the host country, in particular to prevent any acts violating the security of missions and the safety of their personnel,

Noting the spirit of cooperation and mutual understanding which has guided the deliberations of the Committee on issues affecting the United Nations community and the host country,

Welcoming the increased interest shown by Member States in participating in the work of the Committee,

1. *Endorses* the recommendations and conclusions of the Committee on Relations with the Host Country contained in paragraph 55 of its report;

2. *Considers* that the maintenance of appropriate conditions for the normal work of the delegations and the missions accredited to the United Nations is in the interests of the United Nations and all Member States, and expresses the hope that the host country will continue to take all measures necessary to prevent any interference with the functioning of missions;

3. *Expresses its appreciation* for the efforts made by the host country and hopes that outstanding problems raised at the meetings of the Committee will be duly resolved in a spirit of cooperation and in accordance with international law;

4. *Welcomes* the recent lifting of travel controls by the host country with regard to certain missions and staff members of the Secretariat of certain nationalities, and urges the host country to continue to abide by its obligations to the United Nations and the missions accredited to it;

5. *Notes* the establishment by the Committee of a working group to consider problems of financial indebtedness and stresses the importance of efforts undertaken in this regard;

6. *Stresses* the importance of a positive perception of the work of the United Nations, and urges that efforts be continued to build up public awareness by explaining, through all available means, the importance of the role played by the United Nations and the missions accredited to it in the strengthening of international peace and security;

7. *Requests* the Secretary-General to remain actively engaged in all aspects of the relations of the United Nations with the host country;

8. *Requests* the Committee to continue its work, in conformity with General Assembly resolution 2819(XXVI) of 15 December 1971;

9. *Decides* to include in the provisional agenda of its forty-eighth session the item entitled "Report of the Committee on Relations with the Host Country".

General Assembly resolution 47/35

25 November 1992   Meeting 73   Adopted without vote

Approved by Sixth Committee (A/47/589) without vote, 16 November (meeting 35); 8-nation draft (A/C.6/47/L.13); agenda item 134.

Sponsors: Belarus, Bulgaria, Canada, Costa Rica, Côte d'Ivoire, Cyprus, Russian Federation, Spain.

Meeting numbers. GA 47th session: 6th Committee 33, 35; plenary 73.

United Nations Decade of International Law

The General Assembly in 1989[13] had declared the United Nations Decade of International Law

(1990-1999) to promote acceptance of and respect for the principles of international law; promote means for the peaceful settlement of disputes between States, including resort to, and full respect for, the International Court of Justice (ICJ); encourage the progressive development of international law and its codification; and encourage its teaching, study, dissemination and wider appreciation. The Assembly had adopted the programme of activities for the first term of the Decade (1990-1992) in 1990.[14]

Report of the Secretary-General. Pursuant to a General Assembly resolution of 1991,[15] the Secretary-General submitted, in August 1992, a report with a later addendum[16] summarizing replies received from States and international organizations on steps taken to implement the programme of activities for the first term of the Decade (1990-1992), and views on possible activities for the second term (1993-1994). The report described new activities of various United Nations bodies related to the progressive development of international law and its codification.

Sixth Committee action. The Sixth Committee's Working Group on the Decade, established in 1990 pursuant to an Assembly resolution of 1989[13] with a view to preparing recommendations on the programme for the activities for the Decade, held 14 meetings between 28 September and 6 November 1992. The Working Group discussed the implementation of the programme of activities for the first term (1990-1992) of the Decade and the Secretary-General's report. Annexed to the report of the Working Group[17] was the programme of activities for the second term (1993-1994), which the Assembly adopted by **resolution 47/32.**

GENERAL ASSEMBLY ACTION

On 25 November 1992, the General Assembly, on the recommendation of the Sixth Committee, adopted **resolution 47/32** without vote.

United Nations Decade of International Law

The General Assembly,

Recalling its resolution 44/23 of 17 November 1989 by which it declared the period 1990-1999 the United Nations Decade of International Law,

Recalling also that the main purposes of the Decade, according to resolution 44/23, should be, *inter alia*:

(a) To promote acceptance of and respect for the principles of international law;

(b) To promote means and methods for the peaceful settlement of disputes between States, including resort to and full respect for the International Court of Justice;

(c) To encourage the progressive development of international law and its codification;

(d) To encourage the teaching, study, dissemination and wider appreciation of international law,

Recalling further its resolution 45/40 of 28 November 1990, to which was annexed the programme for the activities to be commenced during the first term (1990-1992) of the United Nations Decade of International Law,

Expressing its appreciation for the report of the Secretary-General, submitted pursuant to resolution 46/53 of 9 December 1991,

Recalling that the Sixth Committee established at the forty-fifth session the Working Group on the United Nations Decade of International Law with a view to preparing generally acceptable recommendations on the programme of activities for the Decade,

Noting that the Sixth Committee reconvened the Working Group at the forty-sixth and the forty-seventh sessions to continue its work in accordance with resolutions 45/40 and 46/53,

Having considered the report of the Working Group submitted to the Sixth Committee,

1. *Expresses its appreciation* to the Sixth Committee for the elaboration, within the framework of its Working Group on the United Nations Decade of International Law, of the programme for the activities to be commenced during the second term (1993-1994) of the Decade, and requests the Working Group to continue its work at the forty-eighth session in accordance with its mandate and methods of work;

2. *Also expresses its appreciation* to States and international organizations and institutions that have undertaken activities in implementation of the programme for the first term (1990-1992) of the Decade, including sponsoring conferences on various subjects of international law;

3. *Adopts* the programme for the activities to be commenced during the second term (1993-1994) of the Decade as an integral part of the present resolution, to which it is annexed;

4. *Invites* all States and international organizations and institutions referred to in the programme to undertake the relevant activities outlined therein and, as appropriate, to submit to the Secretary-General interim or final reports for transmission to the General Assembly at its forty-eighth session or, at the latest, its forty-ninth session;

5. *Requests* the Secretary-General to submit, on the basis of such information, a report to the General Assembly at its forty-eighth session on the implementation of the programme;

6. *Also requests* the Secretary-General to supplement his report, as appropriate, with new information on the activities of the United Nations relevant to the progressive development of international law and its codification and to submit it to the General Assembly on an annual basis;

7. *Further requests* the Secretary-General to submit to the General Assembly at its forty-eighth session a report containing the plan referred to in section V, paragraph 3, of the programme for the second term of the Decade;

8. *Encourages* States to disseminate at the national level, as appropriate, information contained in the report of the Secretary-General;

9. *Appeals* to States, international organizations and non-governmental organizations working in the field of international law and to the private sector to make finan-

cial contributions or contributions in kind for the purpose of facilitating the implementation of the programme;

10. *Requests* the Secretary-General to bring to the attention of States and international organizations and institutions working in the field of international law the programme annexed to the present resolution;

11. *Decides* to include in the provisional agenda of its forty-eighth session the item entitled "United Nations Decade of International Law".

ANNEX
Programme for the activities for the second term (1993-1994) of the United Nations Decade of International Law

I. Promotion of the acceptance of and respect for the principles of international law

1. The General Assembly, bearing in mind that maintenance of international peace and security is the underlying condition for the success of the implementation of the programme for the United Nations Decade of International Law, calls upon States to act in accordance with international law, and particularly the Charter of the United Nations, and encourages States and international organizations to promote the acceptance of and respect for the principles of international law.

2. States are invited to consider, if they have not yet done so, becoming parties to existing multilateral treaties, in particular those relevant to the progressive development of international law and its codification. International organizations under whose auspices such treaties are concluded are invited to indicate whether they publish periodic reports on the status of ratifications of and accessions to multilateral treaties, and if they do not, to indicate whether in their view such a process would be useful. Consideration should be given to the question of treaties which have not achieved wider participation or entered into force after a considerable lapse of time and the circumstances causing the situation.

3. States and international organizations are encouraged to provide assistance and technical advice to States, in particular to developing countries, to facilitate their participation in the process of multilateral treaty-making, including their adherence to and implementation of multilateral treaties, in accordance with their national legal systems.

4. States are encouraged to report to the Secretary-General on ways and means provided for in the multilateral treaties to which they are parties, regarding the implementation of such treaties. International organizations are similarly encouraged to report to the Secretary-General on ways and means provided for by the multilateral treaties concluded under their auspices, regarding the implementation of such treaties. The Secretary-General is requested to prepare a report on the basis of this information and to submit it to the General Assembly.

II. Promotion of means and methods for the peaceful settlement of disputes between States, including resort to and full respect for the International Court of Justice

1. States, the United Nations system of organizations and regional organizations, including the Asian-African Legal Consultative Committee, as well as the International Law Association, the Institute of International Law, the Hispano-Luso-American Institute of International Law and other international institutions working in the field of international law, and national societies of international law, are invited to study the means and methods for the peaceful settlement of disputes between States, including resort to and full respect for the International Court of Justice, and to present suggestions for the promotion thereof to the Sixth Committee.

2. Taking into account the suggestions mentioned in paragraph 1 of the present section and with due regard to the recommendations contained in the report of the Secretary-General entitled "An Agenda for Peace", the Sixth Committee should consider, where appropriate, on the basis of a report of the Special Committee on the Charter of the United Nations and on the Strengthening of the Role of the Organization, or of the Working Group on the United Nations Decade of International Law, the following questions:

(a) Strengthening the use of means and methods for the peaceful settlement of disputes, with particular attention to the role to be played by the United Nations, as well as methods for early identification and prevention of disputes and their containment;

(b) Procedures for the peaceful settlement of disputes arising in specific areas of international law;

(c) Ways and means of encouraging greater recognition of the role of the International Court of Justice and its wider use in the peaceful settlement of disputes;

(d) Enhancement of cooperation of regional organizations with the United Nations system of organizations in respect of the peaceful settlement of disputes;

(e) Wider use of the Permanent Court of Arbitration.

III. Encouragement of the progressive development of international law and its codification

1. International organizations, including the United Nations system of organizations and regional organizations, are invited to submit to the Secretary-General of the United Nations summary information regarding the programme and results of their work relevant to the progressive development of international law and its codification, including their suggestions for future work in their specialized field, with an indication of the appropriate forum to undertake such work. Similarly, the Secretary-General is requested to prepare a report on the relevent activities of the United Nations, including those of the International Law Commission. Such information should be presented in a report by the Secretary-General to the Sixth Committee.

2. On the basis of the information mentioned in paragraph 1 of the present section, States are invited to submit suggestions for consideration by the Sixth Committee and, as appropriate, recommendations. In particular, efforts should be made to identify areas of international law which might be ripe for progressive development or codification.

3. The Sixth Committee should study, taking into account General Assembly resolution 684(VII) of 6 November 1952, its coordinating role with respect, *inter alia*, to the drafting of provisions of a legal nature and the consistent use of legal terminology in international instruments adopted by the General Assembly. States are invited to present proposals in this regard to the Sixth Committee.

4. The Special Committee on the Charter of the United Nations and on the Strengthening of the Role of the Organization should continue to study possible measures to strengthen the United Nations system for the maintenance of international peace and security. In that context, the Special Committee should take note of the Secretary-General's report entitled "An Agenda for Peace" in the light of the debate within the United Nations, particularly within the General Assembly.

IV. Encouragement of the teaching, study, dissemination and wider appreciation of international law

1. The Advisory Committee on the United Nations Programme of Assistance in the Teaching, Study, Dissemination and Wider Appreciation of International Law should, in the context of the Decade, continue to formulate, as appropriate and in a timely manner, relevant guidelines for the Programme's activities and report to the Sixth Committee on the activities carried out under the Programme in accordance with such guidelines. Special emphasis should be given to supporting academic and professional institutions already carrying out research and education in international law, as well as to encouraging the establishment of such institutions where they might not exist, particularly in the developing countries. States and other public or private bodies are encouraged to contribute to the strengthening of the Programme.

2. States should encourage their educational institutions to introduce courses in international law for students studying law, political science, social sciences and other relevant disciplines; they should study the possibility of introducing topics of international law in the curricula of schools at the primary and secondary levels. Cooperation between institutions at the university level amongst developing countries, on the one hand, and their cooperation with those of developed countries on the other, should be encouraged.

3. States should consider convening conferences of experts at the national and regional levels in order to study the question of preparing model curricula and materials for courses in international law, training of teachers in international law, preparation of textbooks on international law and the use of modern technology to facilitate the teaching of and research in international law.

4. States, the United Nations system of organizations and regional organizations should consider organizing seminars, symposia, training courses, lectures and meetings and undertaking studies on various aspects of international law.

5. States are encouraged to organize special training in international law for legal professionals, including judges, and personnel of ministries of foreign affairs and other relevant ministries as well as military personnel. The United Nations Institute for Training and Research, the United Nations Educational, Scientific and Cultural Organization, the Hague Academy of International Law, regional organizations and the International Committee of the Red Cross are invited to continue cooperating in this respect with States.

6. Cooperation among developing countries, as well as between developed and developing countries, in particular among those persons who are involved in the practice of international law, for exchanging experience and for mutual assistance in the field of international

law, including assistance in providing textbooks and manuals of international law, is encouraged.

7. In order to make better known the practice of international law, States and international and regional organizations should endeavour to publish, if they have not done so, summaries, repertories or yearbooks of their practice.

8. States and international organizations should encourage the publication of important international legal instruments and studies by highly qualified publicists, bearing in mind the possibility of assistance from private sources.

9. Other international courts and tribunals, including the European Court of Human Rights and the Inter-American Court of Human Rights, are invited to disseminate more widely their judgements and advisory opinions, and to consider preparing thematic or analytical summaries thereof.

10. International organizations are requested to publish treaties concluded under their auspices, if they have not yet done so. Timely publication of the United Nations *Treaty Series* is encouraged and efforts directed towards adopting an electronic form of publication should be continued. Timely publication of the *United Nations Juridical Yearbook* is also encouraged.

V. Procedures and organizational aspects

1. The Sixth Committee, working primarily through its Working Group on the United Nations Decade of International Law and with the assistance of the Secretariat, will be the coordinating body of the programme for the Decade. The question of the use of an intra-sessional, inter-sessional or existing body to carry out specific activities of the programme may be considered by the General Assembly.

2. The Sixth Committee is requested to continue to prepare the programme of activities for the Decade.

3. The Secretariat, on the basis of informal consultations with the members of the Sixth Committee, should draw up a preliminary operational plan for a possible United Nations congress on public international law, based on the proposal that the congress should be held in 1994 or 1995, and within existing resources and assisted by voluntary contributions, and submit it to the Sixth Committee for consideration by general agreement at the forty-eighth session of the General Assembly.

4. All organizations and institutions referred to and invited to submit reports to the Secretary-General under sections I to IV above are requested to submit interim or final reports preferably at the forty-eighth session but not later than the forty-ninth session of the General Assembly.

5. States are encouraged to establish, as necessary, national, subregional and regional committees which may assist in the implementation of the programme for the Decade. Non-governmental organizations are encouraged to promote the purposes of the Decade within the fields of their activities, as appropriate.

6. It is recognized that, within the existing overall level of appropriations, adequate financing for the implementation of the programme for the Decade is necessary and should be provided. Voluntary contributions from Governments, international organizations and other sources, including the private sector, would be useful and are strongly encouraged. To this end, the establishment of a trust fund to be administered by the Secretary-General might be considered by the General Assembly.

General Assembly resolution 47/32

25 November 1992   Meeting 73   Adopted without vote

Approved by Sixth Committee (A/47/583) without vote, 19 November (meeting 37); 64-nation draft (A/C.6/47/L.16); agenda item 128.

Sponsors: Algeria, Argentina, Australia, Austria, Belarus, Belgium, Bulgaria, Bolivia, Brazil, Cameroon, Canada, Chile, Colombia, Costa Rica, Cyprus, Czechoslovakia, Denmark, Ecuador, Egypt, Ethiopia, Finland, France, Germany, Ghana, Greece, Guatemala, Guinea, Hungary, India, Indonesia, Iran, Ireland, Italy, Japan, Jordan, Madagascar, Malaysia, Malta, Mauritania, Mexico, Mongolia, Morocco, Netherlands, New Zealand, Nigeria, Norway, Pakistan, Poland, Republic of Korea, Republic of Moldova, Romania, Russian Federation, Senegal, Singapore, Spain, Sweden, Thailand, Trinidad and Tobago, Tunisia, Ukraine, United Kingdom, United Republic of Tanzania, Uruguay, Viet Nam.

Meeting numbers. GA 47th session: 6th Committee 34-37; plenary 73.

Observer status of national liberation movements

In accordance with a General Assembly resolution of 1990,[18] the Secretary-General submitted, in July 1992,[19] a report containing replies from five Governments on the implementation of that resolution, concerning the observer status of national liberation movements recognized by the Organization of African Unity and/or by the League of Arab States.

GENERAL ASSEMBLY ACTION

On 25 November 1992, the General Assembly, on the recommendation of the Sixth Committee, adopted **resolution 47/29** by recorded vote.

Observer status of national liberation movements recognized by the Organization of African Unity and/or by the League of Arab States

The General Assembly,

Recalling its resolutions 35/167 of 15 December 1980, 37/104 of 16 December 1982, 39/76 of 13 December 1984, 41/71 of 3 December 1986, 43/160 B of 9 December 1988 and 45/37 of 28 November 1990,

Recalling also its resolutions 3237(XXIX) of 22 November 1974 and 3280(XXIX) of 10 December 1974,

Taking note of the report of the Secretary-General,

Bearing in mind the resolution of the United Nations Conference on the Representation of States in Their Relations with International Organizations relating to the observer status of national liberation movements recognized by the Organization of African Unity and/or by the League of Arab States,

Noting that the Vienna Convention on the Representation of States in Their Relations with International Organizations of a Universal Character, of 14 March 1975, regulates only the representation of States in their relations with international organizations,

Taking into account the current practice of inviting the above-mentioned national liberation movements to participate as observers in the sessions of the General Assembly, specialized agencies and other organizations of the United Nations system and in the work of the conferences held under the auspices of such international organizations,

Convinced that the participation of the national liberation movements referred to above in the work of international organizations helps to strengthen international peace and cooperation,

Desirous of ensuring the effective participation of the above-mentioned national liberation movements as observers in the work of international organizations and of regulating, to that end, their status and the facilities, privileges and immunities necessary for the performance of their functions,

Noting that many States have recognized those national liberation movements and have granted them facilities, privileges and immunities in their countries,

1. *Calls upon* all States that have not done so, in particular those which are host to international organizations or to conferences convened by, or held under the auspices of, international organizations of a universal character, to consider as soon as possible the question of ratifying, or acceding to, the Vienna Convention on the Representation of States in Their Relations with International Organizations of a Universal Character;

2. *Urges* the States concerned to accord to the delegations of the national liberation movements recognized by the Organization of African Unity and/or by the League of Arab States and accorded observer status by international organizations, the facilities, privileges and immunities necessary for the performance of their functions, in accordance with the provisions of the Vienna Convention on the Representation of States in Their Relations with International Organizations of a Universal Character;

3. *Requests* the Secretary-General to report to the General Assembly at its forty-ninth session on the implementation of the present resolution.

General Assembly resolution 47/29

25 November 1992   Meeting 73   100-9-34 (recorded vote)

Approved by Sixth Committee (A/47/580) by recorded vote (61-9-28), 23 October (meeting 19), 11-nation draft (A/C.6/47/L.5); agenda item 125.

Sponsors: Cameroon, Cuba, Egypt, Ghana, Libyan Arab Jamahiriya, Mozambique, Namibia, Nigeria, Senegal, United Republic of Tanzania, Zimbabwe.

Meeting numbers. GA 47th session: 6th Committee 7, 19; plenary 73.

Recorded vote in Assembly as follows:

In favour: Afghanistan, Algeria, Angola, Antigua and Barbuda, Armenia, Bahamas, Bahrain, Barbados, Belize, Benin, Bolivia, Botswana, Brazil, Brunei Darussalam, Burkina Faso, Cameroon, Central African Republic, Chad, Chile, China, Colombia, Congo, Côte d'Ivoire, Cuba, Cyprus, Democratic People's Republic of Korea, Djibouti, Ecuador, Egypt, El Salvador, Ethiopia, Gabon, Gambia, Ghana, Grenada, Guatemala, Guinea, Guinea-Bissau, Haiti, Honduras, India, Indonesia, Iran, Iraq, Jordan, Kenya, Kuwait, Lebanon, Lesotho, Liberia, Libyan Arab Jamahiriya, Madagascar, Malawi, Malaysia, Maldives, Mali, Mauritania, Mexico, Morocco, Mozambique, Myanmar, Namibia, Nepal, Nicaragua, Niger, Nigeria, Oman, Pakistan, Panama, Papua New Guinea, Paraguay, Peru, Philippines, Qatar, Rwanda, Saint Vincent and the Grenadines, Sao Tome and Principe, Saudi Arabia, Senegal, Seychelles, Sierra Leone, Singapore, Sri Lanka, Sudan, Suriname, Swaziland, Syrian Arab Republic, Thailand, Togo, Trinidad and Tobago, Tunisia, Uganda, United Arab Emirates, United Republic of Tanzania, Uruguay, Venezuela, Viet Nam, Yemen, Zambia, Zimbabwe.

Against: Belgium, France, Germany, Israel, Italy, Luxembourg, Netherlands, United Kingdom, United States.

Abstaining: Argentina, Australia, Austria, Azerbaijan, Bulgaria, Canada, Costa Rica, Czechoslovakia, Denmark, Estonia, Finland, Greece, Hungary, Iceland, Ireland, Japan, Latvia, Liechtenstein, Lithuania, Malta, Marshall Islands, Micronesia, New Zealand, Norway, Poland, Portugal, Republic of Korea, Romania, Russian Federation, San Marino, Spain, Sweden, Turkey, Ukraine.

Asian-African Legal Consultative Committee

Pursuant to a General Assembly request of 1990,[20] the Secretary-General submitted, in August 1992, a report[21] on cooperation between the United Nations and the Asian-African Legal Consultative Committee (AALCC), an organization which the Assembly had invited to participate in its sessions and work in the capacity of a permanent observer in 1980.[22]

The report reviewed the activities of the Committee in the context of a 1987 programme of cooperation in the following areas: cooperative framework; representation at meetings and conferences; role of the United Nations and the United Nations Decade of International Law; promoting wider use of ICJ; measures designed to further the work of the Sixth Committee; measures to promote ratification and implementation of the United Nations Convention on the Law of the Sea;[23] international economic cooperation for development; refugees; zones of peace and international cooperation; and illicit traffic in narcotic drugs. The Committee also dealt with criteria for the distinction between terrorism and the struggle for liberation and the deportation of Palestinians as a violation of international law, particularly the 1949 Geneva Conventions.

GENERAL ASSEMBLY ACTION

On 21 October 1992, the General Assembly adopted **resolution 47/6** without vote.

Cooperation between the United Nations and the Asian-African Legal Consultative Committee

The General Assembly,

Recalling its resolutions 36/38 of 18 November 1981, 37/8 of 29 October 1982, 38/37 of 5 December 1983, 39/47 of 10 December 1984, 40/60 of 9 December 1985, 41/5 of 17 October 1986, 43/1 of 17 October 1988 and 45/4 of 16 October 1990,

Having considered the report of the Secretary-General on cooperation between the United Nations and the Asian-African Legal Consultative Committee,

Having heard the statement made on 21 October 1992 by the Secretary-General of the Asian-African Legal Consultative Committee on the steps taken by the Consultative Committee to ensure continuing, close and effective cooperation between the two organizations,[a]

1. *Takes note with appreciation* of the report of the Secretary-General;

2. *Notes with satisfaction* the continuing efforts of the Asian-African Legal Consultative Committee towards strengthening the role of the United Nations and its various organs, including the International Court of Justice, through programmes and initiatives undertaken by the Consultative Committee;

3. *Notes with satisfaction* the commendable progress achieved towards enhancing cooperation between the United Nations and the Consultative Committee in wider areas;

4. *Notes with appreciation* the decision of the Consultative Committee to participate actively in the programmes of the United Nations Decade of International Law;

5. *Requests* the Secretary-General to submit to the General Assembly at its forty-ninth session a report on cooperation between the United Nations and the Consultative Committee;

6. *Decides* to include in the provisional agenda of its forty-ninth session the item entitled "Cooperation between the United Nations and the Asian-African Legal Consultative Committee".

[a]A/47/PV.43.

General Assembly resolution 47/6

21 October 1992   Meeting 43   Adopted without vote

21-nation draft (A/47/L.3 & Add.1); agenda item 20.

Sponsors: Australia, China, Cyprus, Egypt, Guinea-Bissau, India, Indonesia, Iran, Iraq, Japan, Kenya, Mongolia, Namibia, Nepal, New Zealand, Nigeria, Pakistan, Philippines, Sri Lanka, Syrian Arab Republic, United Republic of Tanzania.

REFERENCES

[1]A/47/277-S/24111. [2]A/47/33. [3]YUN 1991, p. 842, GA res. 46/58, 9 Dec. 1991. [4]A/AC.182/L.65 & Corr.1. [5]A/AC/182/L.72. [6]A/AC./182/L.73/Rev.1. [7]YUN 1991, p. 842. [8]A/45/742. [9]YUN 1991, p. 845, GA res. 46/60, 9 Dec. 1991. [10]YUN 1947-48, p. 199, GA res. 169(II), 31 Oct. 1947. [11]A/47/26. [12]YUN 1991, p. 845. [13]GA res. 44/23, 17 Nov. 1989. [14]GA res. 45/40, annex, 28 Nov. 1990. [15]YUN 1991, p. 846, GA res. 46/53, 9 Dec. 1991. [16]A/47/384 & Add.1. [17]A/C.6/47/L.12. [18]GA res. 45/37, 28 Nov. 1990. [19]A/47/323. [20]GA res. 45/4, 16 Oct. 1990. [21]A/47/385. [22]YUN 1980, p. 469, GA res. 35/2, 13 Oct. 1980. [23]YUN 1982, p. 178.

International economic law

In 1992, legal aspects of international economic law continued to be considered by the United Nations Commission on International Trade Law (UNCITRAL) and by the Sixth Committee of the General Assembly.

International trade law

Report of UNCITRAL

At its twenty-fifth session (New York, 4-22 May 1992), UNCITRAL adopted a draft Model Law on International Credit Transfers, which was annexed to its report on the session,[1] and a Legal Guide on International Countertrade Transactions. The Commission also examined international countertrade; legal problems of electronic data interchange; procurement; guarantees and stand-by letters of credit; Interpretation of Commercial Terms, (INCOTERMS) 1990; case law on UNCITRAL texts (CLOUT); coordination of work; status of conventions; training and assistance; and relevant General Assembly resolutions. In addition, in accordance with a Secretariat proposal of 1991,[2] the Commission organized, in the context of the United Nations Decade of International Law (1990-1999) (see above), the UNCITRAL Congress on International Trade Law under the theme of uniform commercial law in the twenty-first century (New York, 18-22 May 1992). The Congress dealt with the process and value of unification of commercial law; sale of goods; supply of services;

payments; credits and banking; electronic data interchange; transport; dispute settlement; and the future role of UNCITRAL. The Commission noted the publication of a bibliography[3] of recent writings related to its work.

As in previous years, UNCITRAL's annual report was forwarded to the United Nations Conference on Trade and Development for comments.

Report of the Secretary-General. In response to a General Assembly request of 1991,[4] the Secretary-General reported, in September 1992,[5] on providing travel assistance to least developed countries (LDC)s that were Commission members to enable them to attend UNCITRAL meetings and working groups, and on the feasibility of UNCITRAL holding consecutive meetings of its working groups to lessen travel expenses. The Secretary-General drew attention to discussion on the rationalization of UNCITRAL's work during its 1992 session,[1] wherein it was observed that holding consecutive working group meetings was impracticable. It was noted that because of the nature of the work assigned to each working group, delegations were usually composed of different experts. It was further noted that if working groups met consecutively, experts might be away from their duty stations for too long. In addition, States might be encouraged to retain experts already present for a particular working group meeting for a subsequent meeting, even though they might not have the appropriate expertise.

UNCITRAL was in general agreement with efforts to find ways of assisting developing countries, and LDCs in particular, and expressed the view that assistance would have to be considered in the context of the overall budget. It was noted that recommendations on the subject might require consideration by the Fifth (Administrative and Budgetary) Committee.

Referring to the Secretary-General's report, the Sixth Committee Chairman suggested in October[6] that the Fifth Committee consider the matter of granting travel assistance to least developed and other developing countries and take a substantive decision on it.

GENERAL ASSEMBLY ACTION

On 23 December, the General Assembly, on the recommendation of the Fifth Committee, adopted without vote **resolution 47/219 A, section XXX**.

Granting of travel assistance to least developed and other developing countries that are memebers of the United Nations Commission on International Trade Law

[*The General Assembly . . .*]

Decides to defer consideration of this question until resumed forty-seventh session of the General Assembly.

General Assembly resolution 47/219 A, section XXX
23 December 1992   Meeting 94   Adopted without vote

Approved by Fifth Committee (A/47/835) without vote, 20 December (meeting 51); draft based on informal consultations on reports of the Secretary-General (A/46/349, A/47/454, A/C.5/47/CRP.1); agenda item 104.
Meeting numbers. GA 47th session: 5th Committee 28 and 51; plenary 94.

Unification of trade law

International credit transfers

In considering the draft Model Law on International Credit Transfers in 1992, the Commission had before it a Secretariat note[7] containing suggestions for the final review of its text. The most important problems identified by the Secretariat related to the various time-periods during which the receiving bank must perform a certain number of actions.

By a decision of 15 May, the Commission, after considering the text of the draft Model Law, adopted the UNCITRAL Model Law on International Credit Transfers, as annexed to its 1992 report.[1] By that decision, UNCITRAL requested the Secretary-General to transmit the text of the Model Law, together with the *travaux préparatoires* from its twenty-fourth[2] and twenty-fifth sessions,[1] to Governments and other interested bodies, and recommended that all States give due consideration to the Model Law when enacting or revising their laws, given the need for uniformity of the law applicable to international credit transfers.

International countertrade

In 1992, the Commission had before it draft material for the Legal Guide on International Countertrade Transactions, including a covering report and draft chapters dealing with: the origin and purpose of the guide; the scope and terminology of the guide; contracting approach; countertrade commitment; general remarks on drafting; type, quality and quantity of goods; pricing of goods; participation of third parties; payment; restrictions on resale of goods; liquidated damages and penalty clauses; security for performance; failure to complete countertrade transaction; choice of law; settlement of disputes; draft illustrative provisions and chapter summaries.[8]

On 12 May, the Commission adopted the UNCITRAL Legal Guide on International Countertrade Transactions; invited the General Assembly to recommend the use of the Legal Guide for international countertrade transactions and requested the Secretary-General to take effective measures for its widespread distribution and promotion. The Secretariat was requested to edit the text and to publish it expeditiously. UNCITRAL decided that the publication containing the Legal Guide should include an invitation to readers to send their comments to the Secretariat.

Electronic data interchange

UNCITRAL had before it in 1992 a report[9] of the Working Group on International Payments—which had been renamed the Working Group on Electronic Data Exchange—on the work of its twenty-fourth (1992) session. The report contained recommendations for future work by the Commission with respect to the legal issues of electronic data interchange (EDI). The report suggested that any related future work by UNCITRAL should be aimed at the increased use of EDI.

The Working Group recommended that the Commission prepare legal norms and rules on the use of EDI in international trade that were sufficiently detailed to provide practical guidance to EDI users as well as to national legislators and regulatory authorities.

UNCITRAL endorsed the Working Group's recommendations and entrusted it with preparing legal rules on EDI. It decided that the Secretariat should: continue to monitor legal developments in other organizations such as the Economic Commission for Europe, the European Communities and the International Chamber of Commerce; facilitate the exchange of relevant documents between the Commission and those organizations; and report to the Commission and its relevant Working Groups on the work accomplished within those organizations.

Procurement

The Commission considered the 1991 reports of the Working Group on the New International Economic Order[10] as they pertained to draft articles 28-35 and 1-27 of the Model Law on Procurement.

UNCITRAL accepted the Working Group's recommendation that priority be given to preparing a commentary to guide legislatures preparing legislation based on the Model Law, but that this should not delay the completion of the Model Law. The Commission also noted that the draft commentary would be prepared by the Secretariat and that a small and informal ad hoc working party of the Working Group would be convened to review it.

Noting that the preparation of a Model Law on procurement was urgently needed, given that an increasing number of States were considering reforming their procurement laws, the Commission requested the Working Group to proceed with its work expeditiously so that it could consider the draft Model Law at its 1993 session.

At its fifteenth (1992) session (New York, 22 June–2 July), the Working Group adopted 41 draft articles of the Model Law on Procurement, which were annexed to its report.[11]

Guarantees and stand-by letters of credit

The Commission considered the reports of its Working Group on International Contract Practices at its sixteenth[12] (1991) and seventeenth[13] (1992) sessions, during which it examined draft articles 1 to 13 and 14 to 27 of a uniform law on international guarantee letters, respectively. The Commission noted that the Working Group had requested the Secretariat to prepare a revised draft of articles 1 to 27. It further noted that, when discussing the appropriateness of including provisions on conflicts of law and jurisdiction in the uniform law, the Working Group had requested the Secretariat to consult with the Hague Conference on Private International Law on possible methods of cooperation. UNCITRAL asked the Working Group to continue to carry out its task expeditiously.

INCOTERMS 1990

UNCITRAL agreed that INCOTERMS 1990 had succeeded in providing a modern set of international rules for interpreting the most commonly used terms in international trade. It noted with appreciation that the new method of presenting INCOTERMS 1990 facilitated their reading and understanding. Several delegations reported that IN-COTERMS 1990 was already widely used in their countries. On 12 May, the Commission commended the use of INCOTERMS 1990 in international sales transactions.

Coordination of work

The Commission had before it a note by the Secretariat on assistance by multilateral organizations and bilateral aid agencies in modernizing commercial laws in developing countries.[14] It was noted that assistance was typically provided in the form of experts and funding for projects and that those activities concentrated on: investment laws; intellectual property law; maritime legislation; and laws and regulations in areas such as taxation, insurance, customs, procurement and export and import trade.

The note recommended that the Commission ask the Secretariat to continue to monitor the work of the multilateral organizations and bilateral aid agencies and recommend to those that had not provided assistance to consider doing so. In addition, UNCITRAL might urge greater cooperation and consultation between it and the organizations and aid agencies when executing projects to modernize commmercial law in developing countries.

Training and assistance

The Commission had before it a note by the Secretariat[15] describing UNCITRAL's continued cooperation and participation in seminars and symposia on international trade law. In 1992, a seminar on international commercial arbitration (Mexico City, 20 and 21 February), jointly organized by the Mexican Ministry of External Relations and the secretariat of the Commission, presented lectures on various legal texts by four experts from Mexico, a consultant and a member of UNCITRAL.

GENERAL ASSEMBLY ACTION

On 25 November, the General Assembly, on the recommendation of the Sixth Committee, adopted **resolution 47/34** without vote.

Report of the United Nations Commission on International Trade Law on the work of its twenty-fifth session

The General Assembly,

Recalling its resolution 2205(XXI) of 17 December 1966, by which it created the United Nations Commission on International Trade Law with a mandate to further the progressive harmonization and unification of the law of international trade and in that respect to bear in mind the interests of all peoples, in particular those of developing countries, in the extensive development of international trade,

Reaffirming its conviction that the progressive harmonization and unification of international trade law, in reducing or removing legal obstacles to the flow of international trade, especially those affecting the developing countries, would significantly contribute to universal economic cooperation among all States on a basis of equality, equity and common interest and to the elimination of discrimination in international trade and, thereby, to the well-being of all peoples,

Stressing the value of participation by States at all levels of economic development and from different legal systems in the process of harmonizing and unifying international trade law,

Having considered the report of the United Nations Commission on International Trade Law on the work of its twenty-fifth session,

Mindful of the valuable contribution to be rendered by the United Nations Commission on International Trade Law within the framework of the United Nations Decade of International Law, particularly as regards the dissemination of international trade law,

Concerned about the relatively low incidence of expert representation from developing countries at sessions of the Commission and particularly of its working groups during recent years, due in part to inadequate resources to finance the travel of such experts,

1. *Takes note with appreciation* of the report of the United Nations Commission on International Trade Law on the work of its twenty-fifth session;

2. *Takes note with particular satisfaction* of the completion and adoption by the Commission of the Model Law on International Credit Transfers;

3. *Recommends* that, in view of the current need for uniformity of the law applicable to international credit transfers, all States give due consideration to the enactment of legislation based on the Model Law;

4. *Takes note with particular satisfaction* of the completion and adoption by the Commission of the Legal Guide on International Countertrade Transactions;

5. *Recommends* the use of the Legal Guide to parties involved in international countertrade transactions;

6. *Recommends also* that all efforts be made to ensure that the Legal Guide becomes generally known and available;

7. *Notes with satisfaction* the entry into force on 1 November 1992 of the United Nations Convention on the Carriage of Goods by Sea, 1978 (Hamburg Rules), and requests the Secretary-General to make increased efforts to promote wider adherence to the Convention;

8. *Reaffirms* the mandate of the Commission, as the core legal body within the United Nations system in the field of international trade law, to coordinate legal activities in this field in order to avoid duplication of effort and to promote efficiency, consistency and coherence in the unification and harmonization of international trade law and, in this connection, recommends that the Commission, through its secretariat, continue to maintain close cooperation with the other international organs and organizations, including regional organizations, active in the field of international trade law;

9. *Reaffirms* the importance, in particular for developing countries, of the work of the Commission concerned with training and assistance in the field of international trade law and the desirability for it to sponsor seminars and symposia to provide such training and assistance, and, in this connection:

(a) Expresses its appreciation to the Commission for organizing two seminars on international trade law, the first held at Suva, from 21 to 25 October 1991, and the second at Mexico City, on 20 and 21 February 1992, and to the Governments whose contributions enabled the seminars to take place;

(b) Invites Governments, the relevant United Nations organs, organizations, institutions and individuals to make voluntary contributions to the trust fund for the United Nations Commission on International Trade Law symposia and, where appropriate, to the financing of special projects, and otherwise to assist the secretariat of the Commission in financing and organizing seminars and symposia, in particular in developing countries, and in the award of fellowships to candidates from developing countries to enable them to participate in such seminars and symposia;

10. *Expresses its appreciation* to the Commission for organizing, as a contribution to the activities of the United Nations Decade of International Law, a Congress under the theme "Uniform commercial law in the twenty-first century", held in New York from 18 to 22 May 1992, during the last week of the twenty-fifth session of the Commission, which provided a useful assessment of the progress made to date in the unification and harmonization of international trade law and will assist the Commission and other organizations involved in the unification and harmonization of international trade law in laying out the course of their future work;

11. *Repeats its invitation* to those States that have not yet done so to consider signing, ratifying or acceding to the conventions elaborated under the auspices of the Commission;

12. *Requests* the Fifth Committee, in order to ensure full participation by all Member States, to continue to consider granting travel assistance, within existing resources, to the least developed countries that are members of the Commission, as well as, on an exceptional

basis, to other developing countries that are members of the Commission at their request, in consultation with the Secretary-General, to enable them to participate in the sessions of the Commission and its working groups;

13. *Recommends* that the Commission pay special attention to the rationalization of the organization of its work and consider all possibilities for rationalization, in particular the holding of consecutive meetings of its working groups;

14. *Requests* the Secretary-General to submit a report on the implementation of paragraphs 12 and 13 above to the General Assembly at its forty-eighth session.

General Assembly resolution 47/34

25 November 1992   Meeting 73   Adopted without vote

Approved by Sixth Committee (A/47/586) without vote, 19 November (meeting 37); 32-nation draft (A/C.6/47/L.4/Rev.1); agenda item 131.
Sponsors: Argentina, Austria, Belarus, Brazil, Chile, Colombia, Cyprus, Czechoslovakia, Denmark, Egypt, Finland, France, Germany, Greece, Guinea, Hungary, India, Indonesia, Italy, Kenya, Mexico, Morocco, Myanmar, Nigeria, Norway, Poland, Spain, Sweden, Thailand, Turkey, Russian Federation, Uruguay.
Meeting numbers. GA 47th session: 6th Committee 3-5, 9, 37; plenary 73.

REFERENCES

[1]A/47/17. [2]YUN 1991, p. 852. [3]A/CN.9/369. [4]YUN 1991, p. 853, GA res. 46/56 B, 9 Dec. 1991. [5]A/47/454. [6]A/C.6/47/4. [7]A/CN.9/367. [8]A/CN.9/362 & Add.1-17. [9]A/CN.9/360. [10]YUN 1991, p. 854. [11]A/CN.9/371. [12]A/CN.9/358. [13]A/CN.9/361. [14]A/CN.9/364. [15]A/CN.9/363.

PART SIX

Administrative and budgetary questions

Chapter I

United Nations financing and programming

In 1992, the United Nations continued to operate under difficult financial conditions brought about by the non-payment of assessed contributions by a number of Member States. The problem was exacerbated further by the rapidly rising number of peace-keeping activities throughout the world.

The General Assembly took action towards improving the ability of the Organization to finance its peace-keeping activities more effectively, by authorizing the establishment of a Peace-keeping Reserve Fund, at a level of $150 million (resolution 47/217). It called on the Fifth (Administrative and Budgetary) Committee to examine the current placement of Member States in the groups for the apportionment of peace-keeping expenses, with a view to establishing standard criteria for all future operations (47/218). The Assembly also considered proposals by the Secretary-General to stabilize the financing of peace-keeping operations, as outlined in "An Agenda for Peace" (see PART ONE, Chapter I).

The Assembly increased appropriations to the 1992-1993 approved programme budget to $2.5 billion. Total budget appropriations for 1993 alone were $1.3 billion. Original income estimates for the biennium were also revised upwards to $471 million (47/220 A and B).

The Committee on Contributions made recommendations regarding the assessed contributions of 18 new Member States, which the Assembly subsequently adopted (decision 47/456).

The Assembly accepted the financial reports and audited financial statements for the period ended 31 December 1991 for the United Nations and eight development and humanitarian assistance programmes, as well as the audit opinions of the Board of Auditors (47/211). By the same resolution, the Assembly requested the Secretary-General to prepare separate financial reports and statements for peace-keeping operations for submission in 1993.

United Nations financing

Financial situation

The precarious financial condition of the United Nations, brought on by the non-payment of dues

by a number of Member States, was the subject of several reports of the Secretary-General in 1992. The problem had become worse due to the rising quantity and growing complexity of tasks in the areas of peace-keeping and conflict resolution. If Member States did not promptly provide the resources needed for those expanded responsibilities, it might not be possible to maintain the Organization's operations, the Secretary General said in May.[1]

The level of outstanding contributions, both to the regular budget and to peace-keeping operations, continued to rise dramatically throughout 1992. As at 30 April, unpaid contributions totalled $1,898.7 million, virtually double the amount outstanding six months before. That figure comprised $1,093.4 million due to the regular budget, of which $416 million was outstanding for 1991 and prior years, and $805.3 million for peace-keeping.

At the end of April 1992, just 34.7 per cent of the 1992 regular budget assessments had been paid, with only 39 Member States having fully paid their assessment for 1992 and prior years. Sixty-five Members had made no payment at all and 74 owed more than their current year's assessment. A total of 124 Member States had failed to meet the statutory financial obligation under the Charter to pay their assessed contributions to the regular budget in full and on time.

On average, only 36.3 per cent of the first assessment for newly established peace-keeping operations was paid at the end of the operations' first three months, and only 56.8 per cent was paid after six months. As a result, short-term loans between certain peace-keeping accounts continued to be necessary in 1992 to cover daily operational requirements. However, such short-term borrowing mechanisms were inadequate, in the face of the cash required, particularly for the operations in Cambodia and the former Yugoslavia.

By mid-July,[2] only 52 Member States had paid in full their dues to the regular budget, and unpaid assessed contributions totalled $908.5 million. Outstanding contributions to peace-keeping operations amounted to $844.4 million. Considering regular budget and peace-keeping operations together, for both receipts and disbursements, a deficit of about $55 million was projected for November, to reach $81 million by the end of December. At that time, the Secretary-General said, it would not be possible to effect short-term loans from peace-keeping operations to the regular budget and, without an immediate inflow of cash, the Organization would have to cease operations.

In October,[3] the Secretary-General reported that the pattern of contribution collection had continued to fluctuate widely from month to month, requiring him to borrow again from peace-keeping funds to provide for the Organization's daily operations in August and September. At the time of the report, it was estimated that, given anticipated payments in October, November and December totalling some $308 million, the United Nations would end the year with a deficit of $12 million in its regular budget. An improvement in collections in the first six months of 1992 had been more than offset by poor collections in the third quarter, resulting in a much worse than average collection pattern as at 30 September.

With three months left in 1992, unpaid contributions to the regular budget stood at a cumulative total of $826.3 million for the current and prior years, equalling 80 per cent of the 1992 regular budget. In the previous year at that same time, total contributions outstanding had represented 75 per cent of the 1991 assessment. More Member States actually paid their dues to the regular budget in 1992 than in 1991 or 1990; however, non-payment by the third major contributor in 1992 had served to widen the margin of total uncollected funds beyond that of the prior year.

As at 31 December 1992, $500,607,665 was outstanding to the regular budget, of which $403,859,879 was due for 1992 and $96,747,786 for past years.[4] Outstanding contributions to peace-keeping operations totalled approximately $664.3 million.

At the end of the year, there were nine such operations financed from assessed contributions: the United Nations Disengagement Observer Force (UNDOF), the United Nations Interim Force in Lebanon (UNIFIL), the United Nations Angola Verification Mission, the United Nations Iraq-Kuwait Observation Mission (UNIKOM), the United Nations Mission for the Referendum in Western Sahara (MINURSO), the United Nations Observer Mission in El Salvador (ONUSAL), the United Nations Transitional Authority in Cambodia (UNTAC), the United Nations Protection Force (UNPROFOR) and the United Nations Operation in Somalia (UNOSOM). Of the three recently completed operations, the United Nations Iran-Iraq Military Observer Group (UNIIMOG) and the United Nations Observer Group in Central America (ONUCA) still had outstanding contributions due to their accounts, totalling $13.8 million, while the account of the United Nations Transition Assistance Group (UNTAG) showed a surplus for 1992 of some $6.6 million (for further financing of UNTAG, see below). Not included was the

United Nations Peace-keeping Force in Cyprus (UNFICYP), which was financed from voluntary contributions.

In his October report,[3] the Secretary-General stressed that an immediate and continuing cash inflow was needed for the Organization to survive; if it could not collect its debts, it would be unable to pay its creditors. The United Nations was obliged to pay back any balances of appropriations remaining at the end of a financial period, but in recent years, the General Assembly had suspended such obligations on a number of occasions and allowed the withholding of payments to Member States totalling some $350 million. A further $75 million could become available in residual balances of UNTAG and UNIIMOG, although some of that had been proposed for transfer to a peace-keeping reserve fund. About $200 million was due to troop-contributing countries, and there were other routine balances due to creditors, in all funds, which were expected to total between $150 million and $200 million by year-end. If outstanding assessed contributions were to be paid in full, the Organization could pay all those debts and have enough left to replenish its Working Capital Fund.

The persistent financial difficulties were becoming politically incongruous—as both the regular and peace-keeping budgets were adopted by the consensus of Member States—as well as increasingly damaging to the implementation of mandated programmes, since severe monetary concerns had taken on an inordinately important role in the choice of activities and priorities. Should the Assembly choose to revise the basic membership principles and financial regulations derived from the relevant Articles of the Charter, the Secretariat would assist Member States to the best of its ability. Until then, full and timely payment by all Members of their assessed contributions was the only solution.

The proposals made by the Secretary-General in November 1991[5] to alleviate the financial situation of the Organization were reviewed in an annex to his October 1992 report. They included charging interest on assessed contributions not paid on time; suspending certain financial regulations to permit retention of budgetary surpluses; increasing the Working Capital Fund to $250 million and endorsing the principle that the Fund's level should be about 25 per cent of the annual regular budget; establishing a temporary peace-keeping reserve fund at a level of $50 million (see below); and authorizing the Secretary-General to borrow commercially, should other sources of cash be inadequate.

Other proposals included the creation of a humanitarian emergency fund in the order of $50 million, which was implemented in the form of the creation of a Central Emergency Revolving Fund that became operational in May 1992 (see PART THREE, Chapter III), and the establishment of a United Nations Peace Endowment Fund, with an initial target of $1 billion. In "An Agenda for Peace" (see PART ONE, Chapter I), the Secretary-General further proposed the establishment of a revolving peace-keeping reserve fund.

Responding to these proposals, the Advisory Committee on Administrative and Budgetary Questions (ACABQ) said the establishment of a revolving peace-keeping reserve fund would have to be considered in the light of the proposals to increase the Working Capital Fund and the possible establishment of a reserve for peace-keeping operations.[6] Moreover, it pointed out that the proposal was not in conformity with the financial regulations and budgetary process. With regard to the reporting of outstanding contributions in lump sums—comprising both regular budget and peace-keeping funds—ACABQ felt that it concealed year-to-year changes in the amounts of contributions received, as well as the amounts in arrears relative to the outstanding contributions in the current year; thus, the method failed to reflect clearly the financial situation. ACABQ recommended that future submissions should report the balance due as at 1 January of the current year, in addition to the balance due as at the date of reporting, separately for the regular budget and for assessed peace-keeping operations.

GENERAL ASSEMBLY ACTION

By **decision 46/476** of 14 September 1992, at its resumed forty-sixth session, the General Assembly, decided to include in the draft agenda of its forty-seventh session the item on the current financial crisis of the United Nations.

On 23 December, the Assembly, on the recommendation of the Fifth Committee, adopted **resolution 47/215** without vote.

Improving the financial situation of the United Nations

The General Assembly,

Recalling the purposes and principles of the Charter of the United Nations and, in particular, Article 17, paragraph 1, which states that the General Assembly shall consider and approve the budget of the Organization, and Article 17, paragraph 2, which stipulates that the expenses of the Organization shall be borne by the Members as apportioned by the Assembly,

Recalling also the Financial Regulations and Rules of the United Nations and particularly regulation 5.4, according to which contributions and advances shall be considered as due and payable in full within thirty days of the receipt of the communication of the Secretary-General,

Expressing its appreciation to those Member States that pay their assessed contributions in full and on time,

Recognizing that while the level of outstanding contributions to the regular budget and peace-keeping oper-

ations has remained significant in 1992, there has been progress in the pattern of payments by Member States, notably for peace-keeping operations,

Recalling its resolution 41/213 of 19 December 1986 on the review of the efficiency of the administrative and financial functioning of the United Nations and its resolutions 45/236 A and B of 21 December 1990 on the current financial crisis and financial emergency of the United Nations,

1. *Takes note* of the reports of the Secretary-General on the financial situation and on possible measures to address the financial problems of the Organization submitted to the General Assembly at its forty-sixth and forty-seventh sessions;

2. *Also takes note* of the related observations and recommendations of the Advisory Committee on Administrative and Budgetary Questions;

3. *Expresses its appreciation* for the provision of information on the financial situation of the Organization on a regular basis, and requests the Secretary-General to continue providing such information as often as necessary, through specific reports and through reports on the status of contributions, and to include in those reports information on arrears and outstanding contributions in relation to assessments, on the cash flow situation of the Organization and on any possible additional elements which would enable Member States to be fully apprised of the various aspects of the financing of United Nations activities, including consolidated information on a biannual basis on the amounts owed to each troop-contributing country based on existing data;

4. *Urges* the Secretary-General to increase his efforts in encouraging Member States to meet their financial obligations towards the Organization with regard to all outstanding assessed contributions to the regular budget and all peace-keeping operations, as requested in resolutions 45/236 A and B, and to reflect the results in the reports mentioned in paragraph 3 above;

5. *Expresses its concern* that the financial situation of the Organization has remained uncertain and precarious during the year 1992 and that late payments or nonpayments of assessed contributions to the regular budget and peace-keeping accounts over the years by a majority of Member States have resulted in the depletion of reserves and cash flow problems;

6. *Regrets* that the Organization has to operate with large arrears and unpaid contributions, and notes with concern that ad hoc measures had to be adopted during 1992, including borrowing from peace-keeping funds and delays in reimbursement to troop contributors, in addition to the previous suspension on a number of occasions of the Financial Regulations requiring the surrendering to Member States of remaining balances of appropriations;

7. *Reaffirms* that all Member States have the obligation to pay their assessed contributions in full and on time;

8. *Notes* that if all outstanding assessed contributions were to be paid in full, the Organization could reimburse Member States and replenish its reserves;

9. *Requests* the Secretary-General to undertake a study of the United Nations financial and budgetary practices, drawing upon the experiences of other organizations within the system, particularly the calendar for the consideration and adoption of the programme budget and the timing of issuance of assessments, with a view to facilitating timely and full payments by Member States;

10. *Invites* the Secretary-General to make proposals for possible systems of incentives for implementation on or before 1 January 1995, taking into account proposals made by Member States during the forty-seventh session, in order to encourage Member States to pay all their assessments in full and on time, and to report thereon to the General Assembly at its forty-eighth session, and in this connection requests the Secretary-General to consider proposing revisions to the relevant Financial Regulations and Rules;

11. *Requests* the Secretary-General to report to the General Assembly at its forty-eighth session on the contingency measures taken to face cash shortages in the Organization;

12. *Takes note* of the proposal of the Secretary-General for an increase in the level of the Working Capital Fund and the observations of the Advisory Committee in this regard and decides to revert to this matter, if necessary, at the forty-eighth session;

13. *Emphasizes* the need to continue to ensure overall efficient and prudent management by the Secretary-General of all the resources of the Organization entrusted by Member States for the implementation of all its mandates and, in particular, stresses the need to ensure full accountability and responsibility in the management and use of these resources;

14. *Notes with concern* that the lack of cash reserves and the cash flow problems have a negative impact on the capacity of the Secretariat to manage the Organization;

15. *Requests* the Secretary-General to take steps to strengthen, *inter alia*, through the application of the integrated management information system, the central management of all cash resources available within the Organization, including optimizing the use of available cash, taking into account resources earmarked for discharging unliquidated obligations and those appropriated for implementing multi-year projects under the General Fund;

16. *Decides* to consider in the future the agenda items entitled "Current financial crisis of the United Nations" and "Financial emergency of the United Nations" under one agenda item entitled "Improving the financial situation of the United Nations";

17. *Invites* the Secretary-General to submit a report on the financial situation of the Organization no later than 15 November 1993;

18. *Also decides* to consider the financial situation of the Organization as and when required.

General Assembly resolution 47/215

23 December 1992   Meeting 94   Adopted without vote

Approved by Fifth Committee (A/47/816) without vote, 20 December (meeting 51); draft by Sweden (A/C.5/47/L.25); agenda items 106 & 107.
Meeting numbers. GA 47th session: 5th Committee 4-10, 51; plenary 94.

Establishment of a Peace-keeping Reserve Fund

In a November 1991 report on the financial situation of the Organization,[(5)] as well as in "An Agenda for Peace", the Secretary-General proposed establishing a temporary Peace-keeping Reserve Fund, at a level of $50 million, to meet initial expenses of peace-keeping operations pending receipt of assessed contributions. The General Assembly, in December, established such a Fund at a level of $150 million, as a cash-flow mechanism to ensure the Organization's rapid response to the needs of peace-keeping operations.

GENERAL ASSEMBLY ACTION

The General Assembly, on the recommendation of the Fifth Committee, adopted **resolution 47/217** without vote on 23 December 1992.

Establishment of a Peace-keeping Reserve Fund

The General Assembly,

Having considered with appreciation the report of the Secretary-General entitled "An Agenda for Peace",

Having considered with appreciation also the reports of the Secretary-General, including his report on the work of the Organization, and of the Advisory Committee on Administrative and Budgetary Questions,

Noting that the Organization is confronted with increasing demands and challenges in the area of peace-keeping operations,

Recognizing the unpredictable nature of peace-keeping operations and the consequent necessity of giving the Secretary-General adequate resources to respond in a timely manner to a crisis,

Recognizing also that it is essential to provide peace-keeping operations, especially in their start-up phases, with the necessary financial resources to enable the timely, full and effective implementation of their mandates,

Decides:

(*a*) To establish under the authority of the Secretary-General effective 1 January 1993 a Peace-keeping Reserve Fund as a cash flow mechanism to ensure the rapid response of the Organization to the needs of peace-keeping operations;

(*b*) To authorize the Secretary-General to advance from the Fund such sums as may be necessary to finance:

(i) Unforeseen and extraordinary expenses relating to peace-keeping operations within the commitment authority established by the General Assembly;

(ii) Budgetary appropriations, including start-up costs, approved by the General Assembly for new, expanded or renewed peace-keeping operations pending the collection of assessed contributions;

(*c*) That the advances authorized in accordance with subparagraph (*b*) above shall be reimbursed as soon as receipts from contributions are available for these purposes;

(*d*) That the level of the Fund shall be 150 million United States dollars;

(*e*) That Member States' shares of the Fund shall remain fixed and shall be calculated on the basis of the ad hoc apportionment as set out in General Assembly resolution 45/247 of 21 December 1990;

(*f*) That the Fund shall be financed as follows:

(i) By the transfer of the balance for the excess of income over expenditures in the special accounts for the United Nations Transition Assistance Group and the United Nations Iran-Iraq Military Observer Group after the credits to Member States have been applied in accordance with General Assembly resolutions 45/265 of 17 May 1991, 47/206 and 47/207 of 22 December 1992, based on the latest rates of apportionment applied for the Transition Assistance Group and the Military Observer Group;

(ii) By the transfer of whatever portion of the amount of 154,881,112 dollars retained in the General Fund pursuant to General Assembly resolution 42/216 A of 21 December 1987 is needed for each Member State to reach its fixed share of the Peace-keeping Reserve Fund based on the ad hoc apportionment set out in General Assembly resolution 45/247;

(g) That States which become Members of the United Nations following the date of the adoption of the present resolution and which do not have a claim to a share in the Fund shall contribute to the Fund in accordance with the scale of apportionment for peace-keeping operations in effect on the date of their first assessment for United Nations peace-keeping operations;

(h) That all outstanding contributions to the United Nations Transition Assistance Group and/or the United Nations Iran-Iraq Military Observer Group at the date of the final liquidation of these accounts shall be transferred as receivable assets to the Fund;

(i) (i) That the sum referred to in subparagraph *(f)* (i) above shall become credits available to Member States that have paid their assessed contributions in full to the United Nations Transition Assistance Group and/or the United Nations Iran-Iraq Military Observer Group upon the liquidation of the Fund;

(i i) That the sum referred to in subparagraph *(f)* (ii) above shall reduce the credits available to Member States in the General Fund by the amounts transferred to the Peace-keeping Reserve Fund and shall become credits to Member States which have no unpaid assessed contributions to the regular budget for the biennium 1986-1987, upon the liquidation of the Peace-keeping Reserve Fund;

(j) To address the issue of the imputation of interest income earned in the Fund at the earliest opportunity during its forty-seventh session;

(k) That the Fund shall be administered in accordance with the Financial Regulations and Rules of the United Nations, without prejudice to the funding of the activities of the regular budget;

(l) To request the Secretary-General to report on actions taken to implement the present resolution at the earliest opportunity during its forty-seventh session.

General Assembly resolution 47/217

23 December 1992   Meeting 94   Adopted without vote

Approved by Fifth Committee (A/47/832) without vote, 19 December (meeting 50); draft by Canada (A/C.5/47/L.8), based on informal consultations; agenda item 124.
Meeting numbers. GA 47th session: 5th Committee 4-10, 34, 42, 45, 50; plenary 94.

Financing of peace-keeping operations

At its resumed forty-sixth session, on 14 September 1992, the General Assembly, by **decision 46/480**, included in the draft agenda of its forty-seventh session an item on administrative and budgetary aspects of the financing of the United Nations peace-keeping operations.

Apportionment of costs

In September 1992, the Secretary-General reported on the composition of the existing groups of Member States for the apportionment of the costs of peace-keeping operations financed through assessed contributions.[7] The report was submitted in response to General Assembly **resolution 46/240** of 22 May 1992 (see PART TWO, Chapter II), which, as well as defining the ad hoc arrangement for the financing of ONUSAL, requested the Secretary-General to prepare a report on anomalies in the allocation of countries to the four groups created to define the amount of payments assessed for peace-keeping operations. First specified in 1973[8] and again in March 1989,[9] the groups were subsequently adjusted by the Assembly in December 1989[10] and in 1991.[11]

The original four groups consisted of the States which were: (1) permanent members of the Security Council; (2) specifically named economically developed Member States not permanent members of the Council; (3) economically less developed Member States; and (4) economically less developed Member States that were specifically named. The methodology used to establish those groups was aimed at producing the following results: Member States in the fourth group would pay 10 per cent of their assessment rates established for the regular budget; those in the third group would pay 20 per cent; the second group would pay 100 per cent and the first group would pay 100 per cent plus the amounts not otherwise apportioned. Within each group, according to the terms of the 1973 resolution, the amount appropriated was to be distributed among the respective group members on the basis of the relative weight of each group member's regular rate of assessment in relation to the total rate for the group. Since 1989, the composition of the groups had changed due to a number of transfers among the groups by various countries and the increase in the number of Member States. The resulting composition of the groups, along with the current assessment rates, were reflected in an annex to the Secretary-General's report.

In addressing anomalies in the allocation of countries to the four groups, the Secretary-General said the Assembly might consider automatically allocating least developed countries (LDCs) to the fourth group. It might also consider allocating to that group LDCs only. Currently, 14 Member States were included which were not in that category. Another suggestion was to establish a fifth group for LDCs alone. More generally, the issue could perhaps be addressed by increasing the number of groups. The per capita income of countries was suggested as a criterion for determining and eliminating such anomalies.

By a letter of 14 September to the Secretary-General, transmitted to the Fifth Committee in October,[12] Czechoslovakia requested that it be moved from the second group, which it had occupied since 1973, to the third. It said its economic situation had undergone a number of negative changes. Currently, it was passing through the first stage of its economic reform, amidst a disintegrating market of the former Council for Mutual Economic Assistance. Its national income per capita had fallen to $1,794 in 1991, from $2,435 in 1990.

Reimbursement of troop-contributing States

In a December 1992 report, the Secretary-General reviewed the rates of reimbursement to troop-contributing States,[13] pursuant to a 1987 General Assembly request.[14] The standard rates, initially established in 1974,[15] had been revised several times, most recently in 1991.[16]

Under current rates, $988 was paid per person per month for salary and allowances of all ranks. Supplementary pay for specialists was $291 per person per month; specialists comprised 25 per cent of logistics contingents and 10 per cent of other contingents. A usage factor of $65 was given for personal clothing, gear and equipment for all ranks, and $5 was allowed for personal weaponry, including ammunition, for all ranks, per person per month. Those rates became applicable to UNDOF, UNIFIL and UNIKOM on 1 July 1991. They were also applied to the newly established peace-keeping operations since their inception, namely MINURSO, UNTAC, UNPROFOR, UNOSOM and the United Nations Advance Mission in Cambodia.

The initial introduction of standard rates of reimbursement established the amounts payable, on an equal basis, to Governments for their troops that served in peace-keeping forces. In formulating the rates, three points were considered: troops serving side-by-side should be reimbursed on the same basis for identical services; no Government should receive a higher reimbursement than its actual cost; and some Governments would not be fully reimbursed based on any standard cost-reimbursement formula, but should receive at least that which was paid as actual overseas allowance.

As the current standard rates of reimbursement did not fully compensate all Governments for their troop costs, the overflow was absorbed by the respective troop-contributing States themselves, through what was referred to as the absorption factor.

The current review utilized information based on military salary scales in effect as of December 1991. Information was requested by the Secretary-General from 57 Member States, of which 17 were providing troops to peace-keeping operations and 40 were providing military observers only. Of the 20 States that replied, 11 were providing troops in December 1991, with the standard rates of reimbursement being applicable to 9.

It was found that the average cost for pay and allowances in December 1991 ranged from $797 to $9,845 per person per month, with an overall average of $4,559 and a median of $4,217. The comparable overall average cost from a 1989 survey was $2,297 and the median cost, $2,356. The distribution in 1991 indicated a range of absorption factors, borne by the troop-contributing Governments in respect of pay and allowances, from a high of 89.2 per cent to a low of -33.1 per cent, with an overall average of 63.3 per cent and a median of 74.8 per cent.

The Secretary-General noted that although the overall average absorption factor had risen to 63.3 per cent in 1991, up from 49.3 per cent in 1988 (after eliminating the highest and lowest absorption factors), no clear-cut conclusion could be drawn since the composition and ranking of troop-contributing States for both years were not the same. Regarding the consideration that the reimbursement rates should at least cover the actual overseas allowance paid by States to their troops, it was pointed out that three of the nine States were not being fully reimbursed for such allowance. The overall average monthly overseas allowance (excluding salary) paid by troop-contributing States to their troops amounted to $865, while the average United Nations reimbursement for troop costs (including basic pay and supplementary allowance for a limited number of specialists) was $1,048.

Support account for peace-keeping operations

In a November 1992 report,[17] the Secretary-General discussed the support account for peace-keeping operations, established effective 1 January 1990. The operation of the account became effective on 1 May 1990 by incorporating the resources relating to the overload posts that were funded from the separate budgets of the five peace-keeping operations financed, at that time, outside the scope of the United Nations regular budget, namely, UNDOF, UNFICYP, UNIFIL, UNIIMOG and ONUCA. The account was intended to meet the needs at Headquarters for the support of ongoing peace-keeping operations, as well as some of the additional workload associated with the pre-implementation phase of prospective ones. It was envisaged that additional posts would be provided from the account to meet the increased workload created by new peace-keeping operations.

Income credited to the account from its inception until 31 December 1992 totalled $25,125,392, as at 30 September 1992, while expenditures were estimated at $22,664,739 (including projected expenditure of $2,778,900 for the period from 1 October to 31 December 1992), leaving an unencumbered balance of $2,460,653.

Resources from the account were provided to the Departments of Peace-keeping Operations and Administration and Management, the Executive Office of the Secretary-General and the Office of Legal Affairs, in order to cope with the increased number of good offices, peace-making and peace-keeping activities. However, as all requests for new posts and temporary assistance required ACABQ approval, they were often granted some time after their submission. Consequently, the staff shortage was most critical during periods of intensive activity; i.e., when new peace-keeping operations were being established. Therefore, the Secretary-General proposed that the General Assembly allow him, through the Controller, to authorize the use of temporary assistance when there was a demonstrated need, and to report on it to ACABQ within two months of authorization.

The Secretary-General also recommended that common service costs connected with posts financed from the account, which were currently charged to the regular budget, be charged to the support account as of January 1994. In addition, he suggested maintaining the current funding arrangements for the support account through the provision in each of the budgets of the peace-keeping operations of an amount equal to 8.5 per cent of the cost of the civilian component of the missions.

ACABQ, in December,[18] reported that it had had difficulty in assessing the appropriateness of the current funding arrangements in the absence of detailed information on the criteria for establishing posts or providing temporary assistance, and noted a need for more transparency in the use of posts and temporary assistance financed from the account. It expressed the view that the application of an across-the-board percentage did not reflect the varied requirements of different peace-keeping operations and that the current rate of 8.5 per cent of the civilian component of each operation in the mission area was high.

With regard to the common service costs attributable to the posts financed from the support account, which would have resulted in an additional amount of $1,138,400, currently absorbed by the regular budget, being charged to the account, ACABQ concurred with the Secretary-General that those costs be charged to the support account. It recommended, however, that this be effective 1 January 1993, rather than 1 January 1994.

The Advisory Committee also questioned the use of resources from the support account for the increased number of good offices of the Secretary-General, peacemaking and other related activities which, it said, appeared to relate to core functions under international peace and security. The account should not be seen as a reserve fund to fi-nance new posts as requested; rather, it was a mechanism for distributing the costs of overload posts among peace-keeping operations. In view of those observations, it was time to consider alternative arrangements for the support of peace-keeping operations. The Secretary-General was requested to submit proposals to the Advisory Committee at its spring 1993 session, indicating how such arrangements could operate.

Financing of UNFICYP

In a December report to the Security Council[19] on the financing of UNFICYP, the Secretary-General reiterated the Secretariat's prediction that unless financing was assured by assessed contributions, it would prove impossible to maintain the Force. Since agreement did not exist in the Council for a decision on a change in UNFICYP financing, he was pursuing consultations on restructuring the Force, which were welcomed by the Council in **resolution 796(1992)**. (For details, see PART TWO, Chapter III; for financing of other peace-keeping operations, see respective chapters.)

GENERAL ASSEMBLY ACTION

On 23 December 1992, on the recommendation of the Fifth Committee, the General Assembly adopted **resolution 47/218** without vote.

Administrative and budgetary aspects of the financing of the United Nations peace-keeping operations

The General Assembly,

Having considered the report of the Secretary-General on the composition of the existing groups of Member States for the apportionment of the costs of peace-keeping operations financed through assessed contributions,

Also having considered the note by the Secretary-General transmitting a communication from Czechoslovakia to the Fifth Committee,

Bearing in mind the special responsibilities of the States permanent members of the Security Council in the financing of peace-keeping operations, as indicated in General Assembly resolution 1874(S-IV) of 27 June 1963, entitled "General principles to serve as guidelines for the sharing of the costs of future peace-keeping operations involving heavy expenditures",

Recalling its resolution 3101(XXVIII) of 11 December 1973, in which the composition of groups for the assessment of contributions to the United Nations Emergency Force is set out, and its subsequent resolutions relating to the composition of groups, the latest of which is resolution 47/41 of 1 December 1992 on the financing of the United Nations Operation in Somalia,

Also recalling its previous decisions regarding the fact that, in order to meet the expenditures caused by peacekeeping operations, a different procedure is required from the one applied to meet expenditures of the regular budget of the United Nations,

Taking into account the facts that the economically more developed countries are in a position to make relatively larger contributions and that the economically less developed countries have a relatively limited capacity to contribute towards such operations,

Reaffirming that the financing of peace-keeping operations is the collective responsibility of all Member States, in accordance with Article 17, paragraph 2, of the Charter of the United Nations,

I

Recalling paragraph 6 of its resolution 46/233 of 19 March 1992 on the financing of the United Nations Protection Force,

1. *Decides,* as an ad hoc arrangement, in respect of the apportionment of the appropriations referred to in General Assembly resolutions 46/233 of 19 March 1992, 46/222 B and 46/240 of 22 May 1992, 46/195 B of 31 July 1992 and 47/41 of 1 December 1992, that:

(a) San Marino shall be included in the group of Member States set out in paragraph 3 *(b)* of Assembly resolution 43/232 of 1 March 1989 and that its contributions to the financing of peace-keeping operations shall be calculated in accordance with the provisions of the relevant resolutions to be adopted by the Assembly regarding the scale of assessments;

(b) Armenia, Azerbaijan, Bosnia and Herzegovina, Croatia, Georgia, Kazakhstan, Kyrgyzstan, the Republic of Moldova, Slovenia, Tajikistan, Turkmenistan and Uzbekistan shall be included in the group of Member States set out in paragraph 3 *(c)* of General Assembly resolution 43/232, that their contributions to the financing of peace-keeping operations shall be calculated in accordance with the provisions of the relevant resolutions to be adopted by the Assembly regarding the scale of assessments, and that the assessment rate of the Russian Federation shall be based on its relevant regular budget assessment rates;

2. *Takes note* of the fact that Czechoslovakia will cease to exist as at 31 December 1992;

II

Recognizing that the composition of groups for the apportionment of peace-keeping expenses presently applied constitutes an ad hoc arrangement,

Noting that the report of the Secretary-General on the composition of the existing groups of Member States for the apportionment of the costs of peace-keeping operations financed through assessed contributions has not addressed all the aspects in the allocation of countries to the four groups as set out in the relevant General Assembly resolutions for the financing of peace-keeping operations,

Requests the Chairman of the Fifth Committee to call together an open-ended working group of the Fifth Committee during the forty-seventh session of the General Assembly to examine the placement of Member States in the groups for the apportionment of peace-keeping expenses, with the objective of establishing standard criteria, in order to ensure that that placement is applied in a consistent manner which could be used to allocate Member States to the groups for all future peace-keeping operations, and to report thereon to the General Assembly at its forty-eighth session;

III

Recalling its resolutions 44/192 A to C of 21 December 1989 and 45/258 of 3 May 1991,

Having considered the report of the Secretary-General on the support account for peace-keeping operations and the related report of the Advisory Committee on Administrative and Budgetary Questions,

Also having considered the report of the Secretary-General on the review of the rates of reimbursement to the Governments of troop-contributing States,

Reaffirming the need to continue to improve the administrative and financial management of peace-keeping operations,

1. *Takes note* of the report of the Secretary-General on the support account for peace-keeping operations, and concurs with the observations and recommendations contained in the related report of the Advisory Committee on Administrative and Budgetary Questions;

2. *Also takes note* of the report of the Secretary-General on the review of the rates of reimbursement to the Governments of troop-contributing States, and requests the Secretary-General to keep this matter under review and to report thereon to the General Assembly at its forty-eighth session;

3. *Encourages* those Member States which have not yet responded to the questionnaire sent out by the Secretary-General requesting information on military salary scales in effect as at December 1991 to do so as rapidly as possible;

4. *Notes with concern* that, in consequence of the shortfall of financial contributions, troop-contributing States are not being reimbursed to the full extent of the established rates for some operations;

5. *Reaffirms its request* that the Secretary-General, to the extent possible, make payment of arrears due to current and former troop-contributing States;

6. *Invites* the Secretary-General, as chief administrative officer, to continue the strengthening and reform of the Secretariat units dealing with peace-keeping operations, so that they can deal effectively and efficiently with the planning, launching, ongoing management and termination of those operations;

7. *Reiterates its call* upon all Member States to pay their assessed contributions in full and on time, and encourages those States which can do so to make voluntary contributions acceptable to the Secretary-General;

8. *Notes* that the reports requested of the Secretary-General on the reserve stock of commonly used equipment and supply items and the use of civilians in peace-keeping operations, in paragraph 13 of General Assembly resolution 45/258, have not been submitted, and requests that these reports be submitted to the Assembly at its forty-eighth session;

9. *Also notes* that the report requested of the Secretary-General in paragraph 14 of General Assembly resolution 45/258 on a review of the present practices and approaches regarding the calculation of expenditures incurred by the United Nations in the conduct of peace-keeping operations, including the financial arrangements of the Organization with Governments in respect of such calculations, has not yet been submitted, and requests that this report be submitted to the Assembly at its forty-eighth session;

10. *Decides* to include in the provisional agenda of its forty-eighth session the item entitled "Administrative and budgetary aspects of the financing of the United Nations peace-keeping operations";

IV

Taking note of the report of the Secretary-General on the United Nations Operation in Cyprus and the decision of the Security Council as contained in its resolution 796(1992) of 14 December 1992,

Noting the appeal of the Secretary-General to all Member States to make voluntary contributions to the Special Account for the United Nations Peace-keeping Force in Cyprus,

Invites all States Members of the United Nations to respond positively to the appeal of the Secretary-General for voluntary contributions to the United Nations Peace-keeping Force in Cyprus.

General Assembly resolution 47/218

23 December 1992   Meeting 94   Adopted without vote

Approved by Fifth Committee (A/47/832) without vote, 21 December (meeting 52); draft by Canada (A/C.5/47/L.19) based on informal consultations, orally revised; agenda item 124.
Meeting numbers. GA 47th session: 5th Committee 4-10, 34, 42, 45, 50, 52; plenary 94.

Financing of UNTAG

On 14 September, the General Assembly, by **decision 46/479**, included the financing of UNTAG, established under a 1978 Security Council resolution to ensure the independence of Namibia,[20] in the draft agenda of its forty-seventh session.

According to an October 1992 report of the Secretary-General on the status of UNTAG's finances,[21] total cumulative income of UNTAG as at 30 September amounted to $415,898,456. Portions of UNTAG property retained by the United Nations, with a residual value of $14,505,309, were utilized in other peace-keeping operations, for which $12,719,989 had been credited as miscellanous income to the UNTAG Special Account as at 30 September. The estimated operating costs of UNTAG were reduced to $366,388,371 as at the same date. The unutilized balance in the Account amounted to $44,544,408.

The Secretary-General recommended that from that balance, $2,006,977—representing the unencumbered balance of appropriations ($1,952,629) and additional voluntary contributions in cash ($54,348)—be credited to Member States, and that the $42,537,431 remaining in the Special Account—consisting of interest ($33,832,418) and additional miscellaneous income ($11,023,949), with outstanding contributions amounting to $2,318,936—be retained until a decision was taken by the Assembly on the proposed peace-keeping reserve fund.

The Secretary-General further recommended that the shortfall of $3,351,395 for funding the repatriation of some 45,000 Namibians by the United Nations High Commissioner for Refugees (UNHCR) be charged to the Special Account.

ACABQ in December[22] endorsed those recommendations, with the exception of reimbursement to UNHCR for the repatriation of Namibians, as representatives of the Secretary-General had informed the Committee that the UNHCR deficit had been covered by voluntary contributions from two Member States.

GENERAL ASSEMBLY ACTION

On 22 December 1992, the General Assembly, on the recommendation of the Fifth Committee, adopted **resolution 47/207** without vote.

Financing of the United Nations Transition Assistance Group

The General Assembly,

Having considered the reports of the Secretary-General on the financing of the United Nations Transition Assistance Group, the report of the Board of Auditors on the audit of the Special Account for the United Nations Transition Assistance Group and the related report of the Advisory Committee on Administrative and Budgetary Questions,

Bearing in mind Security Council resolution 435(1978) of 29 September 1978, by which the Council established the United Nations Transition Assistance Group for a period of up to twelve months, as well as Council resolutions 629(1989) of 16 January 1989 and 632(1989) of 16 February 1989,

Recalling its resolution 43/232 of 1 March 1989 on the financing of the Group and its subsequent resolutions thereon, the latest of which was resolution 45/265 of 17 May 1991,

Reaffirming that the costs of the Group are expenses of the Organization to be borne by Member States in accordance with Article 17, paragraph 2, of the Charter of the United Nations,

Recalling its previous decision regarding the fact that, in order to meet the expenditures caused by the Group, a different procedure is required from the one applied to meet expenditures of the regular budget of the United Nations,

Taking into account the fact that the economically more developed countries are in a position to make relatively larger contributions and that the economically less developed countries have a relatively limited capacity to contribute towards such an operation,

Bearing in mind the special responsibilities of the States permanent members of the Security Council, as indicated in General Assembly resolution 1874(S-IV) of 27 June 1963, in the financing of the Group,

Noting with appreciation that voluntary contributions in cash and in kind have been made to the Group,

1. *Endorses* the observations and recommendations contained in the report of the Advisory Committee on Administrative and Budgetary Questions;

2. *Urges* all Member States to make every possible effort to ensure payment of their assessed contributions to the United Nations Transition Assistance Group in full;

3. *Takes note with appreciation* of the financing by two Member States through voluntary contributions of the shortfall of the Office of the United Nations High Commissioner for Refugees for the repatriation of Namibians, and decides that the corresponding amount in the Special Account for the United Nations Transition Assistance Group shall be transferred to the Peace-keeping Reserve Fund;

4. *Decides* that 2,006,977 United States dollars, representing the unencumbered balance of appropriations (1,952,629 dollars) and the additional voluntary contributions in cash (54,348 dollars), in the Special Account shall be credited to Member States;

5. *Decides also* to transfer any additional amount remaining in the Special Account after liquidation of obligations owed to Member States to the Peace-keeping Reserve Fund.

General Assembly resolution 47/207

22 December 1992   Meeting 93   Adopted without vote

Approved by Fifth Committee (A/47/822) without vote, 19 December (meeting 50); draft by Kenya (A/C.5/47/L.14); agenda item 118.
Meeting numbers. GA 47th session: 5th Committee 46, 50; plenary 93.

Efficiency review

In July,[23] the Secretary-General presented to the Fifth Committee a report on the financial implications of the restructuring of the Secretariat of the Organization, pursuant to a 1991 General Assembly resolution[24] and **resolution 46/232** of 2 March 1992. The Committee considered the report under the agenda item on the review of the efficiency of the administrative and financial functioning of the United Nations, in conjunction with the programme budget for the 1992-1993 biennium (see below).

Revised estimates for 27 sections of the programme budget for the biennium were submitted to the General Assembly as the result of the restructuring effort begun in February 1992 by the Secretary-General. The restructuring involved changes in the organizational structure at Headquarters, the abolition of a number of high-level posts and the redistribution of Professional and General Service posts (for further details, see PART SIX, Chapter II). The programme of activities adopted by the Assembly for the 1992-1993 budget were not directly affected by this restructuring.

The restructured and consolidated entities involved 25 of the 41 sections of the programme budget and represented $1,148,633,900, or 48.1 per cent, of the regular budget for 1992-1993. The revised estimates related only to the offices and departments affected by the first phase of restructuring.

Annexed to the report were tables showing the composition of new budget sections; revised estimates and revised staffing tables by section; and a breakdown of the redeployments of posts.

The Secretary-General requested the Assembly to approve transfers between budget sections of the 1992-1993 programme budget, and estimated the net reduction from those transfers and from the savings generated by the abolition of high-level posts at $4,307,500.

The Committee for Programme and Coordination (CPC), in the report on its 1992 session,[25] recommended that the Assembly endorse the proposed reduction in the number of high-level posts. It expressed regret at the lack of information on the programmatic aspects of the revised estimates and recommended that such information be provided to the Assembly.

In August,[26] the Secretary-General reported on the prototype of a new budget format, in accordance with a 1991 resolution,[27] by which the Assembly had endorsed recommendations of CPC calling for a restructured format to provide more information on the programmatic content of the budget, greater transparency to Member States, optimum use of resources and more flexibility. To that end, a seminar was held (Mohonk, United States, 22-28 April) to review the methodology used in preparing the programme budget. It was attended by 26 participants, all current and past members of CPC and ACABQ. The Secretary-General's report reflected the outcome of the seminar and made a number of proposals for the new format, as well as a prototype of a section of the proposed programme budget.

Commenting in October on the Secretary-General's revised estimates resulting from restructuring,[28] ACABQ said its consideration of the report had been hampered in large part by the lack of information therein, especially regarding the Secretary-General's statement that programme activities were not directly affected, as well as lack of information about the analysis preceding the restructuring process. It was essential, the Advisory Committee said, that such reports contain the necessary clarification and justification to enable the Assembly to determine the impact of the restructuring exercise on the effective and efficient use of resources.

In December,[29] ACABQ commented on the prototype of the new budget format. It welcomed the changes, which it believed would greatly simplify the budget document; it intended to comment on them in greater detail when examining the proposed programme budget for 1994-1995.

GENERAL ASSEMBLY ACTION

On 23 December 1992, the General Assembly, on the recommendation of the Fifth Committee, adopted **resolution 47/212 A** without vote.

Review of the efficiency of the administrative and financial functioning of the United Nations and programme budget for the biennium 1992-1993

The General Assembly,

Recalling its resolutions 41/213 of 19 December 1986, 42/211 of 21 December 1987, 43/213 of 21 December 1988, 44/200 A to C of 21 December 1989 and 45/254 A to C of 21 December 1990 on the review of the efficiency of the administrative and financial functioning of the United Nations,

Reaffirming its resolution 46/232 of 2 March 1992 on the revitalization of the Secretariat,

Recalling its resolutions 46/185 A to C of 20 December 1991 on questions relating to the proposed programme budget for the biennium 1992-1993 and 46/186 A to C of 20 December 1991 on the programme budget for the biennium 1992-1993,

Having considered the documents submitted under the items on the review of the efficiency of the administrative and financial functioning of the United Nations and on the programme budget for the biennium 1992-1993,

Also having considered the relevant parts of the report of the Committee for Programme and Coordination on the work of its thirty-second session and the reports of the Advisory Committee on Administrative and Budgetary Questions,

I

1. *Reaffirms* that the search for efficiency initiated through resolution 41/213 is a continuing process;

2. *Notes* that workload standards and other management techniques which are of crucial importance to the determination of the resources required for the fulfilment of mandates in the various domains of activity of the Organization remain unutilized;

3. *Reiterates its request* to the Secretary-General to develop such standards and to use them to the extent possible for his preparation of the proposed programme budget for the biennium 1994-1995, as well as for the submission of statements of programme budget implications, revised estimates and other documents related to the use of resources of the Organization;

4. *Emphasizes* that the presentation of extrabudgetary resources in the programme budget, in relation to posts, priorities and other aspects of the functioning of the Organization, needs to be further improved, and, in particular, that it is necessary to present in the programme budget data on the actual amount of extrabudgetary resources received and utilized during the previous period, as well as to improve the quality of the forecasts for such resources;

II

1. *Stresses* that the restructuring of the Secretariat should be in conformity with the objectives and guidelines/principles set out in its resolution 46/232 and in close consultation with Member States and relevant intergovernmental bodies;

2. *Reaffirms* the role of the General Assembly with regard to the structure of the Secretariat, including the creation, suppression and redeployment of posts financed from the regular budget of the Organization, and requests the Secretary-General to provide the Assembly with comprehensive information on all decisions involving established and temporary high-level posts, including equivalent positions financed from the regular budget and extrabudgetary resources;

3. *Takes note* of the relevant parts of the report of the Committee for Programme and Coordination;

4. *Concurs* with relevant comments and observations of the Advisory Committee on Administrative and Budgetary Questions;

5. *Regrets* that the report of the Secretary-General on revised estimates does not include information on the programmatic aspects and implications of the restructuring as requested in resolution 46/232;

6. *Requests* the Secretary-General to provide the Committee for Programme and Coordination and other concerned intergovernmental bodies with all relevant information which will enable them to identify and analyse the programmatic aspects and consequences of the restructuring of the Secretariat in the areas of their competence and invites them to submit their comments and recommendations to the General Assembly at its forty-eighth session;

7. *Takes note* of the current revised estimates arising from the initial phase of the restructuring of the Secretariat, including the proposals for transfers of resources among sections, on the understanding that, pending the work of the relevant intergovernmental bodies, the Secretary-General will submit to the General Assembly, through the Advisory Committee, early in 1993 revised estimates of the programme budget for the biennium 1992-1993;

8. *Requests* the Secretary-General to submit in these revised estimates all the revisions in the programme budget for the biennium 1992-1993 associated with the restructuring process as well as the programmatic aspects and justifications of the restructuring of the Secretariat requested in resolution 46/232;

9. *Decides*, with regard to the recommendation of the Committee for Programme and Coordination contained in paragraph 261 of its report, to consider early in 1993 the proposed reduction of high-level posts contained in the current revised estimates, and requests the Secretary-General to submit to the General Assembly, in the context of the revised estimates referred to in paragraph 8 above, his proposals for the number and distribution of high-level posts in the Secretariat for the remaining part of the 1992-1993 biennium;

III

1. *Endorses* the proposed new budget format and the related conclusions and recommendations of the Committee for Programme and Coordination and the Advisory Committee on Administrative and Budgetary Questions, and invites the Secretary-General to continue improving the presentation of the programme budget, notably in terms of facilitating a comparison of appropriations and actual level of expenditure by object;

2. *Regrets* that the note by the Secretary-General on procedures and norms for changes in the staffing table does not contain proposals for improving the current methods and processes;

3. *Requests* the Secretary-General to improve the presentation and justification of the changes in the staffing table of the Organization that he may propose in the context of the proposed programme budget for the biennium 1994-1995;

4. *Also requests* the Secretary-General to submit to the General Assembly at its forty-eighth session a report on all issues related to the creation, suppression, reclassification and redeployment of posts;

5. *Further requests* the Secretary-General to submit an analytical report on all aspects of the restructuring of the Secretariat, including its effects on programme delivery, to the General Assembly at its forty-eighth session, in the context of the implementation of resolutions 41/213, 44/211, 43/213, 44/200 A to C, 46/232 and the present resolution.

General Assembly resolution 47/212 A

23 December 1992   Meeting 94   Adopted without vote

Approved by Fifth Committee (A/47/830) without vote, 20 December (meeting 51); draft by Vice-Chairman (A/C.5/47/L.17) based on informal consultations, orally corrected; agenda item 103.
Meeting numbers. GA 47th session: 5th Committee 14-17, 19-21, 40, 44, 45, 51; plenary 94.

REFERENCES

[1]A/46/600/Add.2. [2]A/46/600/Add.3. [3]A/C.5/47/13.
[4]ST/ADM/SER.B/395. [5]YUN 1991, p. 860. [6]A/47/565.
[7]A/47/484. [8]YUN 1973, p. 222, GA res. 3101(XXVIII), 11
Dec. 1973. [9]GA res. 43/232, 1 Mar. 1989. [10]GA
res. 44/192 B, 21 Dec. 1989. [11]YUN 1991, p. 129, GA
res. 45/269, 27 Aug. 1991; ibid., p. 159, GA res. 46/198 A, 20
Dec. 1991. [12]A/C.5/47/22. [13]A/47/776. [14]YUN 1987,
p. 295, GA res. 42/224, 21 Dec. 1987. [15]YUN 1974, p. 105,
GA res. 3239(XXIX), 29 Nov. 1974. [16]YUN 1991, p. 862,
GA res. 45/258, 3 May 1991. [17]A/47/655 & Corr.1.
[18]A/47/757. [19]S/24917 & Add.1. [20]YUN 1978, p. 915, SC
res. 435(1978), 29 Sep. 1978. [21]A/47/555 & Corr.1.
[22]A/47/756. [23]A/C.5/47/2 & Corr.1. [24]YUN 1991, p. 876,
GA res. 46/185 B, sect. IV, 20 Dec. 1991. [25]A/47/16 (Part II).
[26]A/C.5/47/3. [27]YUN 1991, p. 877, GA res. 46/185 B, sect.
VIII, 20 Dec. 1991. [28]A/47/7/Add.1. [29]A/47/7/Add.9.

UN budget

Budget for 1992-1993

Appropriations

In December, the General Assembly adopted revisions to the 1992-1993 programme budget approved in 1991,[1] increasing it by $78,804,300 to a total of $2,468,039,200. In approving the increase, the Assembly followed the recommendations of the Fifth Committee on revised estimates submitted by the Secretary-General, as well as on programme budget implications adopted by the Assembly under items considered by other Main Committees or in respect of items dealt with in plenary meetings.

The largest increases were for the following activities: $27.9 million under staff assessment; political affairs, $13.9 million; common support services, $13.1 million; human rights and humanitarian affairs, $8.7 million; international cooperation for development, $7.7 million; capital expenditures, $3.3 million; public information and special expenses, $2.6 million each; and international justice and law, $2.1 million. Reductions of $2.5 million were made in the budget section covering regional cooperation for development, and $0.6 million under overall policy-making, direction and coordination.

In his first performance report on the programme budget for 1992-1993,[2] submitted to the Fifth Committee in December, the Secretary-General said that an increase in net requirements of $38,691,800, or 2 per cent, was needed over the originally approved amount of $1,940,021,600. The increase reflected the actual experience in 1992 regarding salary costs, inflation and rates of exchange; projections for 1993 in terms of inflation and on the basis of the recommendations of the International Civil Service Commission (ICSC) (see PART SIX,

Chapter II) to the Assembly at its 1992 session; additional provisions in connection with the implementation of decisions of policy-making organs which could not be deferred to the 1994-1995 biennium; and the net effect of transfers between sections due to the restructuring of the Secretariat.

With regard to the impact of the first phase of the restructuring of the Organization, the report was written under the assumption that the Assembly would approve the transfers between sections proposed by the Secretary-General in his revised estimates[3] (see above), but would postpone action on the question of high-level posts addressed therein. Those transfers were proposed in connection with the establishment of five new budget sections corresponding to five newly created or expanded departments. The proposed redeployment of resources to those new sections represented 75 per cent of the biennial appropriations released under 14 of the initial budget sections following their discontinuation as of 30 June 1992. That operation required a comparatively small increase of $134,500, reflecting transfers of posts between duty stations.

The report detailed the impact of decisions of policy-making organs; other changes, including unforeseen and extraordinary expenses; changes in the operational rates of exchange and rates of inflation; and adjustments to standard costs.

In a 19 December note,[4] the Secretariat informed the Fifth Committee that an additional amount of $121,300 was required as a result of the recosting of requests for additional resources contained in statements of programme budget implications and revised estimates presented to the Committee at its current session. The recosting took place to bring the amounts approved by the Committee into line with the operational rates of exchange, inflation assumptions and other adjustments reflected in the first performance report adopted by the Fifth Committee after taking account of the related recommendations of ACABQ.

GENERAL ASSEMBLY ACTION

On 23 December 1992, the General Assembly, on the recommendation of the Fifth Committee, adopted **resolution 47/220 A** without vote.

**Revised budget appropriations for
the biennium 1992-1993**

The General Assembly

Resolves that, for the biennium 1992-1993, the amount of 2,389,234,900 United States dollars appropriated by its resolution 46/186 A of 20 December 1991 shall be increased by 78,804,300 dollars as follows:

Section	Amount approved by resolution 46/186 A	Increase or (decrease)	Revised appropriation
	(United States dollars)		
PART I. Overall policy-making, direction and coordination			
1. Overall policy-making, direction and coordination	35,256,900	(635,200)	34,621,700
Total, PART I	35,256,900	(635,200)	34,621,700
PART II. Political affairs			
2. Peace-keeping operations and special missions	96,225,000	12,863,400	109,088,400
3. Political and Security Council affairs	15,796,000	(11,794,800)	4,001,200
4. Political and General Assembly affairs and Secretariat services	12,411,600	(9,149,900)	3,261,700
5. Disarmament	13,108,800	(8,531,300)	4,577,500
6. Special political questions, regional cooperation, trusteeship and decolonization	9,365,100	(6,513,600)	2,851,500
7. Elimination of apartheid	8,234,900	(6,104,000)	2,130,900
37. Department of Political Affairs	—	43,085,300	43,085,300
Total, PART II	155,141,400	13,855,100	168,996,500
PART III. International justice and law			
8. International Court of Justice	17,484,000	1,001,000	18,485,000
9. Legal activities	21,698,300	(16,355,700)	5,342,600
10. Law of the sea and ocean affairs	9,032,800	(6,719,900)	2,312,900
38. Legal activities	—	24,155,600	24,155,600
Total, PART III	48,215,100	2,081,000	50,296,100
PART IV. International cooperation for development			
11. Development and international economic cooperation	18,933,000	(4,433,900)	14,499,100
12. Regular programme of technical cooperation	40,679,800	(533,600)	40,146,200
13. Department of International Economic and Social Affairs	54,691,200	(40,953,600)	13,737,600
14. Department of Technical Cooperation for Development	27,394,600	(20,608,300)	6,786,300
15. United Nations Conference on Trade and Development	90,040,700	2,473,300	92,514,000
16. International Trade Centre	17,916,200	573,600	18,489,800
17. United Nations Environment Programme	12,743,600	88,500	12,832,100
18. Centre for Science and Technology for Development	4,824,900	(3,422,200)	1,402,700
19. United Nations Centre for Human Settlements (Habitat)	11,405,700	624,200	12,029,900
20. United Nations Centre on Transnational Corporations	12,740,900	(8,992,600)	3,748,300
21. Social development and humanitarian affairs	13,798,300	902,000	14,700,300
22. International drug control	13,499,700	(115,900)	13,383,800
39. Department of Economic and Social Development	—	82,116,600	82,116,600
Total, PART IV	318,668,600	7,718,100	326,386,700
PART V. Regional cooperation for development			
23. Economic Commission for Africa	74,547,000	(2,497,700)	72,049,300
24. Economic and Social Commission for Asia and the Pacific	51,605,000	3,696,900	55,301,900
25. Economic Commission for Europe	41,124,400	1,385,400	42,509,800
26. Economic Commission for Latin America and the Caribbean	67,371,000	(20,300)	67,350,700
27. Economic and Social Commission for Western Asia	50,381,500	(5,047,600)	45,333,900
Total, PART V	285,028,900	(2,483,300)	282,545,600
PART VI. Human rights and humanitarian affairs			
28. Human rights	23,297,200	1,710,300	25,007,500
29. Protection of and assistance to refugees	60,771,100	2,840,600	63,611,700
30. Disaster relief operations	7,770,000	(5,759,400)	2,010,600
40. Department of Humanitarian Affairs	—	9,870,700	9,870,700
Total, PART VI	91,838,300	8,662,200	100,500,500
PART VII. Public information			
31. Public information	100,371,000	2,635,000	103,006,000
Total, PART VII	100,371,000	2,635,000	103,006,000
PART VIII. Common support services			
32. Conference services	421,556,200	(315,114,800)	106,441,400
33. Administration and management	418,473,600	(315,363,400)	103,110,200
41. Administration and management	—	643,588,100	643,588,100
Total, PART VIII	840,029,800	13,109,900	853,139,700
PART IX. Special expenses			
34. Special expenses	45,035,000	2,626,700	47,661,700
Total, PART IX	45,035,000	2,626,700	47,661,700
PART X. Capital expenditures			
35. Construction, alteration, improvement and major maintenance	95,512,700	3,337,500	98,850,200
Total, PART X	95,512,700	3,337,500	98,850,200

Section	Amount approved by resolution 46/186 A	Increase or (decrease)	Revised appropriation
	(United States dollars)		
PART XI. *Staff assessment*			
36. Staff assessment	374,137,200	27,897,300	402,034,500
Total, PART XI	374,137,200	27,897,300	402,034,500
GRAND TOTAL	2,389,234,900	78,804,300	2,468,039,200

General Assembly resolution 47/220 A

23 December 1992   Meeting 94   Adopted without vote

Approved by Fifth Committee (A/47/835) without vote, 22 December (meeting 53); draft contained in report of Committee (A/C.5/47/L.20); agenda item 104.

Meeting numbers. GA 47th session: 5th Committee 14-17, 19, 20, 23, 28, 29, 31, 32, 35, 37-40, 42-45, 47, 49-53; plenary 94.

On the same date, the Assembly adopted without vote **resolution 47/219 A, section XXVI**, also on the recommendation of the Fifth Committee.

First performance report on the programme budget for the biennium 1992-1993

[*The General Assembly* . . .]

1. *Takes note* of the report of the Secretary-General;

2. *Approves* the revised requirements submitted by the Secretary-General in his report;

3. *Requests* the Secretary-General to take steps to improve the budget performance report to make its presentation more timely and more transparent;

4. *Urges* the International Civil Service Commission to review the rates of staff assessment during 1993;

. . .

General Assembly resolution 47/219 A, section XXVI

23 December 1992   Meeting 94   Adopted without vote

Approved by Fifth Committee (A/47/835) without vote, 19 December (meeting 50); oral proposal by Chairman; agenda item 104.

Meeting numbers. GA 47th session: 5th Committee 47, 50; plenary 94.

Also on 23 December, the Assembly adopted without vote **resolution 47/219 A, section XXIX**, again on the Fifth Committee's recommendation.

Recosting of decisions of the Fifth Committee concerning statements of programme budget implications and revised estimates

[*The General Assembly* . . .]

Approves an increase of 121,300 dollars under the expenditure sections and 18,500 dollars under income section 1 of the programme budget for the biennium 1992-1993;

. . .

General Assembly resolution 47/219 A, section XXIX

23 December 1992   Meeting 94   Adopted without vote

Approved by Fifth Committee (A/47/835) without vote, 20 December (meeting 51); oral proposal by Chairman; agenda item 104.

Financing 1993 appropriations

The General Assembly specified in December 1992 that for 1993, total budget appropriations were $1,273,421,750; i.e., one half of the total funds approved for the 1992-1993 biennium, plus an additional $78,804,300 approved under **resolution 47/220 A** for the revised 1992-1993 appropriations.

GENERAL ASSEMBLY ACTION

The General Assembly, on 23 December 1992, on the recommendation of the Fifth Committee, adopted without vote **resolution 47/220 C**.

Financing of appropriations for the year 1993

The General Assembly

Resolves that for the year 1993:

1. Budget appropriations in a total amount of 1,273,421,750 United States dollars, consisting of 1,194,617,450 dollars, being half of the appropriations initially approved for the biennium 1992-1993 by General Assembly resolution 46/186 A of 20 December 1991, plus 78,804,300 dollars, being the increase in the appropriations approved during the forty-seventh session by resolution A above, shall be financed in accordance with regulations 5.1 and 5.2 of the Financial Regulations of the United Nations, as follows:

(*a*) 40,176,315 dollars, consisting of:

(i) An amount of 28,368,850 dollars, which is the net of 34,643,650 dollars, being half of the estimated income approved for the biennium 1992-1993 by its resolution 46/186 B of 20 December 1991 other than staff assessment income, offset by an amount of 6,274,800 dollars, being the decrease in estimated income other than staff assessment income approved by resolution B above;

(ii) 11,807,465 dollars, being the balance of the surplus account as at 31 December 1991;

(*b*) 1,233,245,435 dollars, being the assessment on Member States in accordance with General Assembly resolution 46/221 A of 20 December 1991 and decision 47/456 of 23 December 1992 on the scale of assessments for the years 1992, 1993 and 1994;

2. There shall be set off against the assessment on Member States in accordance with the provisions of General Assembly resolution 973(X) of 15 December 1955, their respective share in the Tax Equalization Fund in the total amount of 218,040,900 dollars, consisting of:

(*a*) 189,963,000 dollars, being half of the estimated staff assessment income approved by resolution 46/186 B;

(*b*) Plus 28,077,900 dollars, being the estimated increase in income from staff assessment approved by the Assembly in its resolution B above.

General Assembly resolution 47/220 C

23 December 1992   Meeting 94   Adopted without vote

Approved by Fifth Committee (A/47/835) without vote, 22 December (meeting 53); draft contained in report of Committee (A/C.5/47/L.20); agenda item 104.

Meeting numbers. GA 47th session: 5th Committee 14-17, 19, 20, 23, 28, 29, 31, 32, 35, 37-40, 42-45, 47, 49-53; plenary 94.

1992-1993 income sources

In December, the General Assembly approved an increase of $21,803,100 in estimated income for 1992-1993, raising the total to $471,016,400. The increase resulted from an additional $28,077,900 in staff assessment, partly offset by a reduction of $3,149,600 in general income (reimbursement for services provided to specialized agencies, income from rental of premises, contributions from non-member States, and television and related services) and a $3,125,200 reduction in income from services to the public.

GENERAL ASSEMBLY ACTION

On 23 December 1992, the General Assembly, on the recommendation of the Fifth Committee, adopted without vote **resolution 47/220 B**.

Revised income estimates for the biennium 1992-1993

The General Assembly

Resolves that, for the biennium 1992-1993, the estimates of income of 449,213,300 United States dollars approved by its resolution 46/186 B of 20 December 1991 shall be increased by 21,803,100 dollars as follows:

Income Section	Amount approved by resolution 46/186 B	Increase or (decrease)	Revised estimates
	(United States dollars)		
1. Income from staff assessment	379,926,000	28,077,900	408,003,900
Total, INCOME SECTION 1	379,926,000	28,077,900	408,003,900
2. General income	62,444,800	(3,149,600)	59,295,200
3. Revenue-producing activities	6,842,500	(3,125,200)	3,717,300
Total, INCOME SECTIONS 2 AND 3	69,287,300	(6,274,800)	63,012,500
GRAND TOTAL	449,213,300	21,803,100	471,016,400

General Assembly resolution 47/220 B

23 December 1992   Meeting 94   Adopted without vote

Approved by Fifth Committee (A/47/835) without vote, 22 December (meeting 53); draft contained in report of Committee (A/C.5/47/L.20), agenda item 104.

Meeting numbers. GA 47th session: 5th Committee 14-17, 19, 20, 23, 28, 29, 31, 32, 35, 37-40, 42-45, 47, 49-53; plenary 94.

Questions related to the 1992-1993 programme budget

The General Assembly in December adopted an omnibus resolution (47/219 A) on a number of questions related to the 1992-1993 programme budget. (Several of those questions are discussed in PART SIX, Chapters II and III.)

Report of ACABQ

During 1992, ACABQ met in three special sessions (New York, 10-14 February; 9-13 March; 6-17 July) and in regular session (New York, 7 April–22 May; The Hague, Netherlands, 26 and 27 May; Copenhagen, Denmark, 28 and 29 May; Geneva, 1-12 June).[5]

The Advisory Committee met with the Administrator of the United Nations Development Programme (UNDP) and submitted to the UNDP Governing Council at its May 1992 session a report dealing with revised budget estimates for 1992-1993; a report on the Commonwealth of Independent States and the Baltic States; and trust funds established by the Administrator in 1991.

In May, ACABQ met with the Executive Director of the United Nations Children's Fund (UNICEF) to submit a report dealing with the proposed format of future global funds programme budgets; criteria for core versus project posts; budget format for country programme recommendations; revisions to the budget format for the administrative and programme support budget; structure and format of income projections and of the financial medium-term plan; review of the UNICEF job classification system; recovery of costs for prorated project posts and incremental field overheads on supplementary-funded programmes and report on headquarters office accommodation.

At a meeting with representatives of the Executive Director of the United Nations Population Fund (UNFPA), the Advisory Committee concurred with a request to transfer credits among programmes.

ACABQ also met with the Acting Executive Director of the United Nations Institute for Training and Research (UNITAR) to consider the 1992 budget proposals for the Institute. It noted that an advance of some $2 million from the United Nations had been included in those proposals. Upon being informed that the United Nations had been paying costs which UNITAR could not meet from voluntary contributions, the Advisory Committee expressed its concern to the Secretary-General about the legislative basis for such financing. It requested the Secretary-General to have UNITAR submit a revised budget and to submit on a priority basis a report on the Institute's future role in United Nations training programmes.

ACABQ considered the administrative and programme support costs of the United Nations International Drug Control Programme for the first time for the 1992-1993 biennium. It also considered a proposal from UNHCR that it avail itself of office space offered by Switzerland.

During its sessions in New York, the Advisory Committee examined a number of reports related to peace-keeping matters. At its April/May session, it dealt with questions related to the regular budget and to other issues, including administrative and budgetary coordination and a coordinated interagency procurement system.

On 23 December, by **resolution 47/219 A, section I**, the General Assembly, on the recommendation of the Fifth Committee, took note with appreciation of ACABQ's first report.

UN Institute for Disarmament Research

By a 12 October note,[6] the Secretary-General transmitted to the Fifth Committee a recommendation by the Board of Trustees of the United Nations Institute for Disarmament Research (UNIDIR) for a subvention of $220,000 from the United Nations regular budget.

In 1991,[7] the General Assembly had approved a subvention of $440,000 to cover the Institute's 1992-1993 budget, of which $220,000 had been earmarked for each year of the biennium. The request was made in accordance with an ACABQ recommendation that, notwithstanding the inclusion of that amount in the 1992-1993 programme budget, a formal request for a subvention for 1993 would have to be made to the General Assembly.

Included in the recommendation was a status report on the financial situation of the Institute, pursuant to a 1989 Assembly request.[8] At the start of 1992, $357,100 was available. Income for the year was estimated at $857,300, including $573,500 from voluntary contributions and the $220,000 subvention from the United Nations regular budget, while estimated expenditures amounted to $1,091,900, including $38,900 for programme support costs.

The Fifth Committee Chairman proposed that the Committee approve the recommendation for a $220,000 subvention on the understanding that the level of support costs charged to UNIDIR would be kept under review. No additional appropriations would be required under the 1992-1993 programme budget.

On 23 December, by **resolution 47/219 A, section III**, the General Assembly, on the recommendation of the Fifth Committee, took note of the Secretary-General's note and decided to keep under review the level of support costs charged to UNIDIR.

Revised estimates resulting from Economic and Social Council decisions

Additional requirements resulting from resolutions and decisions adopted by the Economic and Social Council at its 1992 session totalled $2,158,900 for 1992-1993 and $5,132,800 for 1994-1995. The requirements covered both substantive ($3,183,700) and conference-servicing ($4,108,000) costs. Accordingly, revised estimates were submitted to the Fifth Committee by the Secretary-General in an October 1992 report.[9] Additional requirements for activities not provided for in the 1992-1993 programme budget were estimated at $292,500. ACABQ in November[10] stated that it had no objection to those additional requirements.

In December,[11] the Secretary-General sought approval of a further $71,300 for expenditures in connection with the Fourth World Conference on Women (1995).

Pursuant to a Fifth Committee recommendation, the General Assembly, on 23 December 1992, adopted **resolution 47/219 A, section IV**, without vote.

Revised estimates resulting from resolutions and decisions of the Economic and Social Council at its substantive session of 1992

[*The General Assembly* . . .]

1. *Approves* the revised estimates submitted by the Secretary-General in his report of an additional amount of 292,500 United States dollars under sections 21, 23, 24 and 26 to 28 of the programme budget for the biennium 1992-1993;

2. *Also approves* the additional revised estimates of 71,300 dollars under section 21 submitted by the addendum to his report, on the understanding that the Secretary-General will consider possible redeployment in the context of his revised estimates to be submitted to the General Assembly early next year;

. . .

General Assembly resolution 47/219 A, section IV

23 December 1992   Meeting 94   Adopted without vote

Approved by Fifth Committee (A/47/835) without vote, 25 November (meeting 32) and 15 December (meeting 45); oral proposal by Chairman; agenda item 104.

Meeting numbers. GA 47th session: 5th Committee 32, 45; plenary 94.

ESCAP

In an October report,[12] the Secretary-General requested additional net appropriations of $95,000 for the Economic and Social Commission for Asia and the Pacific (ESCAP) under the regular 1992-1993 budget to cover the costs of consultant services and travel. ACABQ in November[13] saw no need for authorizing an additional $95,000, considering that the restructuring of ESCAP was in process and it was difficult to project any overexpenditure at the present time, and taking into account both the low implementation level under consultancy and the extrabudgetary resources of $37.2 million available to the Commission for 1992-1993.

The General Assembly, on 23 December 1992, adopted without vote **resolution 47/219 A, section VIII**, on the recommendation of the Fifth Committee.

Revised estimates under section 24 (Economic and Social Commission for Asia and the Pacific)

[*The General Assembly* . . .]

1. *Takes note* of the revised estimates submitted by the Secretary-General in his report to appropriate an additional amount of 95,000 dollars under this section and the recommendations of the Advisory Committee on Administrative and Budgetary Questions;

2. *Recommends* that such additional appropriations as may be necessary should be indicated by the Secretary-General in his final performance report on the programme budget for the biennium 1992-1993 under this section;

. . .

General Assembly resolution 47/219 A, section VIII
23 December 1992   Meeting 94   Adopted without vote
Approved by Fifth Committee (A/47/835) without vote, 7 December (meeting 37); oral proposal by Chairman; agenda item 104.

Crime prevention and criminal justice

According to a November report of the Secretary-General,[14] the activities proposed under the newly established United Nations crime prevention and criminal justice programme[15] represented a significant expansion of international cooperation in that area, which would call for additional resources. Should the Crime Prevention and Criminal Justice Branch, which was part of the Division for Social Development of the Centre for Social Development and Humanitarian Affairs, become a separate Division, it would remain part of the Centre and would be headed by a Director at the D-2 level.

Additional requirements were projected for staff resources, consultant services, travel and computer equipment, as well as in conjunction with preparations for the Ninth United Nations Congress on the Prevention of Crime and the Treatment of Offenders (1995). All additional costs were to be absorbed from within overall appropriations.

In November,[13] ACABQ agreed to the overall proposals of the Secretary-General. It trusted, however, that any proposed redeployment of posts for 1993 would be submitted to it for approval, in accordance with the Financial Regulations and Rules of the Organization.

GENERAL ASSEMBLY ACTION

On 23 December 1992, on the Fifth Committee's recommendation, the General Assembly adopted **resolution 47/219 A, section IX**, without vote.

Revised estimates under section 21D (Crime prevention and criminal justice)

[*The General Assembly . . .*]

1. *Takes note* of the revised estimates submitted by the Secretary-General in his report and the recommendations of the Advisory Committee on Administrative and Budgetary Questions;

2. *Endorses* the proposals of the Secretary-General to finance the additional requirements for the expansion of the crime prevention and criminal justice programme from within the overall appropriations of sections 21, 23 to 26 and 33 of the programme budget for the biennium 1992-1993;

. . .

General Assembly resolution 47/219 A, section IX
23 December 1992   Meeting 94   Adopted without vote
Approved by Fifth Committee (A/47/835) without vote, 7 December (meeting 37); oral proposal by Chairman; agenda item 104.

ESCWA

In a November report,[16] the Secretary-General projected savings of approximately $5.6 million at the end of the 1992-1993 biennium due to temporary relocation of the Economic and Social Commission for Western Asia headquarters from Baghdad, Iraq, to Amman, Jordan, in August 1991.

However, in view of projected additional commitments in relation, *inter alia*, to late charges for costs incurred at Baghdad, and bearing in mind a possible relocation at the end of the biennium, he proposed that the approved appropriation of $50,381,500 be maintained.

ACABQ, also in November,[11] voiced no objections to the Secretary-General's proposal.

GENERAL ASSEMBLY ACTION

The General Assembly, on 23 December 1992, acting on the recommendation of the Fifth Committee, adopted without vote **resolution 47/219 A, section X**.

Revised estimates under section 27 (Economic and Social Commission for Western Asia)

[*The General Assembly . . .*]

1. *Takes note* of the revised estimates submitted by the Secretary-General in his report and the recommendations of the Advisory Committee on Administrative and Budgetary Questions;

2. *Endorses* the proposals of the Secretary-General to reflect the projected savings of 5.6 million dollars for the biennium 1992-1993 in the first performance report on the programme budget for the biennium and to maintain the appropriation approved by the General Assembly under this section (50,381,500 dollars) at the present time, taking into account the projected additional commitments in relation to late charges for costs incurred at Baghdad and the possibility of a relocation of the headquarters of the Economic and Social Commission for Western Asia towards the end of the current biennium;

. . .

General Assembly resolution 47/219 A, section X
23 December 1992   Meeting 94   Adopted without vote
Approved by Fifth Committee (A/47/835) without vote, 7 December (meeting 37); oral proposal by Chairman; agenda item 104.

African Institute for Economic Development and MULPOCs

In a November 1992 report,[17] the Secretary-General dealt with the financial situation of the African Institute for Economic Development and Planning (IDEP) (Dakar, Senegal), established in 1962 by the Conference of Ministers of Economic

Planning and Development of the Economic Commission for Africa (ECA). Because of a persistent decline in contributions and the complete withdrawal of assistance by UNDP for funding Professional posts, IDEP had come to rely on grants from the United Nations regular budget. Despite IDEP's efforts to reorient its programmes and enlarge its resource base, its financial situation remained fragile, and United Nations assistance would most likely be required for the foreseeable future.

In the proposed programme budget for 1992-1993, the Secretary-General recommended the establishment of five new Professional posts in order to strengthen the capacity of ECA's Multinational Programming and Operational Centres (MULPOCs) in promoting subregional economic cooperation and integration in Africa. Since the outcome of the review of ECA in the context of the ongoing restructuring of offices away from Headquarters was not yet known, it was not possible to submit final proposals regarding additional resources and modifications of administrative and reporting arrangements. For those reasons, the Secretary-General proposed to report on the issue in 1993, in the context of the 1994-1995 proposed programme budget.

ACABQ, in a statement before the Fifth Committee, recalled its comments on the subject contained in its October report[18] on the audited financial statements and reports of the Board of Auditors, where it had stated that it would be necessary to clarify further the role of the ECA secretariat and MULPOCs in programme formulation and implementation, and that every effort should be made to avoid duplication of activities and to clarify further the role of supervising the MULPOCs. The Advisory Committee requested that ECA undertake the necessary corrective measures to resolve those problems and to take into account the findings of the Board of Auditors of deficiencies in the MULPOCs, which it said were due in part to the lack of adequate supervision.

The General Assembly, in **resolution 47/219 A, section XII**, endorsed the Secretary-General's proposals and the observations of ACABQ.

Human rights

In December,[19] the Secretary-General submitted a request to the General Assembly for additional appropriations of $1,650,400 for the section of the 1992-1993 programme budget covering human rights. That amount consisted of $760,000 for the expanding work programme of the Centre for Human Rights, including special rapporteurs, and $890,400 for the Special Rapporteur on the situation of human rights in the territory of the former Yugoslavia, appointed in August 1992.

In an oral report before the Fifth Committee in October, the Chairman of ACABQ said the Ad-

visory Committee was not convinced that adequate justification had been made in terms of workload for the redeployment of 16 Professional posts to the Centre, with the exception of the 5 posts to assist the Special Rapporteur to investigate the situation in the former Yugoslavia. He recommended a comprehensive review of the transfer of posts, and further recommended that the Secretary-General's request for an additional $760,000 not be approved, and that it should be justified in the context of the budget performance report. ACABQ did, however, recommend the approval of $890,000 to support the work of the Special Rapporteur.

GENERAL ASSEMBLY ACTION

On 23 December 1992, pursuant to a Fifth Committee recommendation, the General Assembly adopted **resolution 47/219 A, section XVI**, without vote.

Revised estimates under section 28 (Human rights)

[*The General Assembly . . .*]

1. *Takes note* of the revised estimates submitted by the Secretary-General in his report and the recommendations of the Advisory Committee on Administrative and Budgetary Questions;

2. *Endorses* the proposal of the Secretary-General, on the understanding that, with regard to his request for 760,000 dollars, he would implement, within the overall level of the revised appropriation for the biennium 1992-1993, the other activities of the Centre for Human Rights, for which he has requested additional resources and would report to the General Assembly in the final performance report on the programme budget for the biennium 1992-1993;

. . .

General Assembly resolution 47/219 A, section XVI

23 December 1992   Meeting 94   Adopted without vote

Approved by Fifth Committee (A/47/835) without vote, 19 December (meeting 50); oral proposal by Chairman; agenda item 104.

Meeting numbers. GA 47th session: 5th Committee 45, 50; plenary 94.

Commission of experts on violations of international law in the former Yugoslavia

In December,[20] the Secretary-General requested that an additional amount of $681,900 be appropriated to cover the 1992-1993 programme budget costs for the newly established Commission of Experts on violations of international law committed in the former Yugoslavia, established by the Security Council in 1992 (see PART TWO, Chapter IV). The Secretary-General believed that those requirements should be treated outside the procedure related to the contingency fund.

On a full-cost basis, requirements for the Commission were estimated at $1,238,700 for 1992-1993, which were to be met as far as possible through existing resources. The Secretary-General pointed out that the estimate of $681,900 did not anticipate requirements that might arise from decisions the Commission might take at its meeting to be held from 14 to 18 December 1992 or at subsequent meetings on investigations in the former Yugoslavia, such as the examination of mass grave sites or other activities pursuant to requests made by other bodies such as the Commission on Human Rights.

In an oral report to the Fifth Committee in December, the Chairman of ACABQ concurred with the Secretary-General's proposal. However, bearing in mind the small amount required in respect of data-processing services, rental and maintenance of office equipment, supplies and office automation equipment, he recommended that the Assembly decrease the additional appropriation by $35,200, to $646,700.

By **resolution 47/219 A, section XVII**, adopted on 23 December on the Fifth Committee's recommendation, the General Assembly took note of the revised estimates submitted by the Secretary-General and the recommendations of ACABQ. It approved an additional appropriation of $646,700 on the understanding that the requirements would be treated outside the contingency fund.

Committee for Programme and Coordination

CPC/ACC joint meetings

Programme budget implications arising from the report of CPC on its 1992 session (see PART THREE, Chapter XVIII) were submitted to the General Assembly by the Secretary-General in October[21] and December.[22] The December statement projected requirements of an additional $135,000 under the 1992-1993 programme budget if the twenty-seventh series of Joint Meetings of CPC and the Administrative Committee on Coordination (ACC) were to be held at Rome in 1993. Those funds were to be used to reimburse the Food and Agriculture Organization of the United Nations (FAO) for conference-servicing costs.

In an oral statement before the Fifth Committee in December, ACABQ recommended that the Secretariat make every effort to persuade FAO not to seek such reimbursement, since ACC would be meeting at Rome at the invitation of FAO. The Advisory Committee noted that there would be no reimbursement of travel costs for the joint meetings in 1993 since the respective appropriation had been used up in 1992. The Chairman of CPC informed the Fifth Committee that he had sent a letter on behalf of the Committee to the Secretary-General stating that CPC members would prefer the next joint meetings to be held in New York.

By **resolution 47/219 A, section XX**, adopted on the recommendation of the Fifth Committee,

the General Assembly took note of the information provided by the Secretary-General and the observations made by CPC and ACABQ. The Assembly recommended that the next series of joint meetings take place in New York.

Travel expenses

By **decision 47/458** of 23 December 1992, the General Assembly decided that CPC should meet for its 1993 session for one week in May and for three weeks in August/September.

In a December statement,[23] the Secretary-General indicated additional requirements of $86,400 under the 1992-1993 budget to cover travel expenses of representatives to the second part of CPC's 1993 session.

In an oral statement before the Fifth Committee, ACABQ concurred with those estimates.

The General Assembly, by **resolution 47/219 A, section XXV**, adopted on the recommendation of the Fifth Committee, took note of the statement of programme budget implications on the subject and approved an additional appropriation of $86,400 under section 1 (Overall policy-making, direction and coordination) of the programme budget for 1992-1993.

Contingency fund

The contingency fund was established under a 1986 General Assembly resolution[24] to accommodate additional expenditures for each biennium derived from mandates not provided for in the budget or from revised estimates. For 1992-1993, the fund level was set at $19 million, or 0.75 per cent of the overall programme budget,[25] revised in 1991 to $18 million.[26]

The Fifth Committee, in 1992, approved revised estimates in the amount of $3,529,400, to be appropriated to 11 budget sections, which left the fund with a balance of $11,707,700. The Secretary-General, in a December consolidated statement of programme budget implications and revised estimates falling under the guidelines for the fund,[27] proposed that the Committee request the Assembly to take note of that balance. ACABQ, in an oral report to the Fifth Committee, recommended acceptance of the proposals in the Secretary-General's report. However, it noted that not included in the balance was an amount of $5.3 million, which represented cost estimates of some programme budget implications which the Committee had decided to refer to the resumed forty-seventh session of the Assembly in 1993 and which related mainly to institutional arrangements for the United Nations Conference on Environment and Development (UNCED) and Department of Public Information offices.

By **resolution 47/219 A, section XXVIII**, the General Assembly, on the recommendation of the

Fifth Committee, noted that a balance of $11,753,700 dollars remained in the contingency fund.

1990-1991 programme budget

Final appropriations

In 1991, the General Assembly had approved final appropriations for 1990-1991 in a total net amount of $1,767,318,300.[28] In addition, the Assembly had provided that up to $13,867,100 net might be committed in respect of the regular budget for the biennium with the prior concurrence of ACABQ, a mechanism intended to enable the Advisory Committee to determine the actual level of commitments after review of any additional information justifying such a commitment.

In February 1992, the Secretary-General submitted a report on programme budget performance for 1990-1991,[29] covering overall policy-making, direction and coordination; political and Security Council affairs and peace-keeping activities; economic, social and humanitarian activities; international justice and law; public information; common support services; special expenses; staff assessment; capital expenditures; and income sections.

In the Secretary-General's December report on final appropriations for 1990-1991 on an *ex post facto* basis,[30] he indicated that he had sought the concurrence of the Advisory Committee to enter into commitments of $11,971,200 net over the amount approved by the Assembly, that raised final expenditures to $1,779,289,500 which included some $55.8 million in unliquidated obligations. It was anticipated that a reduction of $3 million in unliquidated obligations would leave a net amount of $8,971,200 to be appropriated and assessed to Member States in 1993. Within that amount there were several items, totalling $1.5 million, where it was already known that delivery of goods or services under the terms of the contracts would not be made before the end of the year. The Secretary-General therefore requested that, on an exceptional basis, the period stipulated in financial regulation 4.3, i.e., 31 December 1992, be extended to 31 December 1993 in respect of unliquidated obligations in the amount of $1.5 million.

ACABQ, in an oral report to the Fifth Committee in December, recommended that those unliquidated obligations be cancelled and reobligated to the 1992-1993 programme budget. The Advisory Committee did not believe that sufficient effort had been made to deal with the question of unliquidated obligations and, accordingly, also recommended that the balance of $7,471,000 not be approved for appropriation and assessment to Member States for 1990-1991, and that a final determination of the level of additional appropria-

tions, on an *ex post facto* basis if necessary, be reviewed at the resumed forty-seventh session of the Assembly in 1993.

On 22 December 1992, by **decision 47/453**, the General Assembly accepted the recommendations of ACABQ with regard to unliquidated obligations and decided to revert to the question of final appropriations for 1990-1991 at its resumed forty-seventh session.

1994-1995 proposed programme budget

A proposed programme budget outline for the 1994-1995 biennium, with total appropriations estimated at $2,410 million, was submitted by the Secretary-General in August 1992,[31] in accordance with a 1986 General Assembly resolution.[24] The proposed outline related to a biennium which would reflect fully the effects of the restructuring of the Secretariat during 1992 (see above). It also reflected changes in the preparation of the programme budget proposed by the Secretary-General to the Assembly at its current session, as had been requested in 1991.[32] The calculation rested on a comparison at current rates between projected estimates for 1994-1995 and a resource base represented by the projected level of the current budget as at the end of the 1992 Assembly session.

The preliminary estimate of resources of $2,410 million given by the Secretary-General represented a growth rate of 0.2 percent over the anticipated revised appropriation for the 1992-1993 budget, estimated at $2,406 million, or $16.8 million above the initial appropriation. The 1994-1995 estimate was $20.8 million, or 0.9 per cent, higher than the initial appropriation for 1992-1993 approved by the Assembly in 1991.[1]

The actual resource growth for 1994-1995, projected at $4 million, was the net result of additional requirements estimated at $152.4 million; discontinuation of non-recurrent provisions, totalling $153 million, included in the anticipated revised appropriation for 1992-1993; and technical adjustments, i.e., a $4.6 million provision for the delayed impact of 1992-1993 growth. No significant changes in staffing levels were projected for 1994-1995, and no provision was made in the preliminary estimates for inflation or currency fluctuations.

With regard to priorities, increases in the share of resources were allocated to four areas: overall policy-making, direction and coordination; political affairs; international cooperation for development; and human rights and humanitarian affairs. More precise priorities among programmes and types of activity were to be presented in the proposed programme budget for 1994-1995.

The Secretary-General recommended that the level of the contingency fund be maintained at 0.75 per cent, the same percentage as for the two preceding bienniums. Following consideration of the Secretary-General's report, CPC[33] recommended that the priorities of the outline be considered further by the Assembly in light of broad trends as derived from the mandates of the legislative organs, as well as the views expressed by Member States, as requested in two 1990 Assembly resolutions.[34]

In a December 1992 report,[35] ACABQ recommended a reduction of $23.6 million, lowering the preliminary estimates to $2,386.4 million, then adjusted them upward to $2,702.7 million, after recosting them at revised 1992-1993 and at 1994-1995 rates.

ACABQ's lower preliminary estimates resulted mainly from its recommendation that additional requirements of $28 million for preventive diplomacy and peace-making missions not be included in the 1994-1995 outline. The Advisory Committee believed that by their very nature, those activities were generally unpredictable and that the Assembly, in its 1991 resolution on unforeseen and extraordinary expenses,[36] had adequately provided for any unexpected activity.

GENERAL ASSEMBLY ACTION

On 23 December 1992, on the recommendation of the Fifth Committee, the General Assembly adopted without vote **resolution 47/213**.

Proposed programme budget outline for the biennium 1994-1995

The General Assembly,

Recalling its resolution 41/213 of 19 December 1986, by which, *inter-89-alia*, it requested the Secretary-General to submit in off-budget years an outline of the programme budget for the following biennium,

Recalling also its resolution 43/214 of 21 December 1988 on the proposed programme budget outline for the biennium 1990-1991 and use and operation of the contingency fund and its resolution 45/255 of 21 December 1990 on the proposed programme budget outline for the biennium 1992-1993,

Having considered the report of the Secretary-General, and the relevant parts of the report of the Committee for Programme and Coordination and of the report of the Advisory Committee on Administrative and Budgetary Questions,

1. *Reaffirms* that the proposed programme budget outline shall contain, in accordance with the provisions of annex I to resolution 41/213, an indication of *(a)* a preliminary estimate of resources to accommodate the proposed programme of activities during the biennium; *(b)* priorities reflecting general trends of a broad sectoral nature; *(c)* real growth, positive or negative, compared with the previous budget; and *(d)* the size of the contingency fund expressed as a percentage of the overall level of resources;

2. *Reaffirms also* that the outline should provide a greater level of predictability of resources required for the following biennium, promote a greater involvement of Member States in the budgetary process and thereby facilitate the broadest possible agreement on the programme budget;

3. *Notes* that the proposed programme budget outline for the biennium 1994-1995 takes into account the budgetary aspects of the restructuring of the Secretariat;

4. *Approves* the methodological changes reflected in the report of the Secretary-General and recognizes that further improvements in the preparation and presentation of the outline may be required;

5. *Endorses* the conclusions and recommendations of the Committee for Programme and Coordination and the Advisory Committee on Administrative and Budgetary Questions, subject to the provisions of paragraphs 6 to 11 below;

6. *Invites* the Secretary-General to prepare the proposed programme budget for the biennium 1994-1995 on the basis of the total preliminary estimate provided by the Advisory Committee of 2,386,400,000 United States dollars at the initial 1992-1993 rates, to be adjusted at revised 1992-1993 rates;

7. *Reaffirms* the need for a comprehensive and satisfactory solution to the problem of controlling the effects of inflation and currency fluctuation on the budget of the United Nations;

8. *Decides* that the contingency fund of the programme budget for the biennium 1994-1995 shall be established at the level of 0.75 per cent of the preliminary estimate of resources for the biennium 1994-1995, to be recosted at 1994-1995 rates;

9. *Recalls*, in this regard, that a review of the level and use and operation of the contingency fund, a well as the procedures for the provision of statements of programme budget implications, shall be undertaken by the General Assembly at its forty-eighth session;

10. *Takes note* of the proposals contained in paragraphs 10 to 12 of the report of the Secretary-General, paragraph 223 of the report of the Committee for Programme and Coordination and the views expressed by Member States on priorities, and requests the Secretary-General, when preparing the proposed programme budget for the biennium 1994-1995, to give particular attention to them and to the priorities contained in the introduction to the medium-term plan for the period 1992-1997 and endorsed by the General Assembly in its resolutions 45/253 and 45/255 of 21 December 1990;

11. *Requests* the Secretary-General to submit the proposed programme budget for the biennium 1994-1995 in accordance with the present resolution and all resolutions and decisions of the General Assembly pertinent to the new budgetary process.

General Assembly resolution 47/213

23 December 1992   Meeting 94   Adopted without vote

Approved by Fifth Committee (A/47/830) without vote, 20 December (meeting 51); draft by Vice-Chairman (A/C.5/47/L.24), based on informal consultations; agenda item 103.

Meeting numbers. GA 47th session: 5th Committee 14-17, 19-21, 40, 44, 45, 51; plenary 94.

REFERENCES

[1]YUN 1991 p. 867, GA res. 46/186 A, 20 Dec. 1991.
[2]A/C.5/47/47 & Corr.1. [3]A/C.5/47/2 & Corr.1.
[4]A/C.5/47/86. [5]A/47/7. [6]A/C.5/47/19. [7]YUN 1991, p. 871,
GA res. 46/185 C, sect. V, 20 Dec. 1991. [8]GA res. 44/201 B,
sect. IV, 21 Dec. 1989. [9]A/C.5/47/21. [10]A/47/7/Add.4.
[11]A/C.5/47/21/Add.1. [12]A/C.5/47/29. [13]A/47/7/Add.7.
[14]A/C.5/47/40. [15]YUN 1991, p. 661, GA res. 46/152, 18
Dec. 1991. [16]A/C.5/47/41. [17]A/C.5/47/53. [18]A/47/500.
[19]A/C.5/47/71. [20]A/C.5/47/68. [21]A/47/16/Add.1.
[22]A/47/16/Add.2. [23]A/C.5/47/84. [24]YUN 1986, p. 1024,
GA res. 41/213, 19 Dec. 1986. [25]GA res. 45/255, 21
Dec. 1990. [26]YUN 1991, p. 875, GA res. 46/185 B IX, 20
Dec. 1991. [27]A/C.5/47/85. [28]YUN 1991, p. 865, GA
res. 46/184 C, 20 Dec. 1991. [29]A/C.5/46/46/Add.1.
[30]A/C.5/47/77 & Add.1. [31]A/47/358. [32]YUN 1991, p. 877,
GA res. 46/185 B VIII, 20 Dec. 1991. [33]A/47/16 (Part II).
[34]GA res. 45/253 & 45/255, 21 Dec. 1990. [35]A/47/7/Add.9.
[36]YUN 1991, p. 869, GA res. 46/187, 20 Dec. 1991.

Contributions

Scale of assessments

The Committee on Contributions, at its fifty-second session (New York, 15 June–2 July 1992),[1] made recommendations on the amount 18 new Member States were to be assessed for contributions to the regular budget of the United Nations.

Of those, Estonia,[2] Latvia[3] and Lithuania,[4] which had joined the Organization in 1991, were recommended to be assessed 0.07, 0.13 and 0.15 per cent, respectively, for the 1992, 1993 and 1994 regular budgets. Twelve Member States admitted to the Organization in 1992 (see PART TWO, Chapter IV) received assessment recommendations for 1993 and 1994: Armenia (0.13 per cent), Azerbaijan (0.22 per cent), Bosnia and Herzegovina (0.04 per cent), Croatia (0.13 per cent), Kazakhstan (0.35 per cent), Kyrgyzstan (0.06 per cent), Republic of Moldova (0.15 per cent), San Marino (0.01 per cent), Slovenia (0.09 per cent) Tajikistan (0.05 per cent), Turkmenistan (0.06 per cent) and Uzbekistan (0.26 per cent). Of those 12, the eight that had been members of the former USSR and San Marino were recommended to pay nine twelfths of their suggested rates for 1992, while the three that had been republics of the former Yugoslavia were recommended to pay seven twelfths for 1992.

In considering the rates for the 15 successor States to the former USSR, the Committee adopted a uniform approach. It dealt with them on the basis of 10.90 per cent, representing the combined rates of Belarus, Ukraine and the former USSR, adopted by the Assembly in 1991[5] and national income and population statistics. Included in the consideration was Georgia, owing to its 6 May 1992 application for United Nations membership[6] and its relationship with the former USSR. Georgia was subsequently granted United Nations membership by General Assembly **resolution 46/241** of 31 July. Its rate of assessment was recommended to be set at 0.21 per cent for 1993 and 1994. For 1992, its proportional rate was to equal the number of calendar months of full membership multiplied by one twelfth of 0.21 per cent, and its actual assessments were to be deducted from those of the Russian Federation for that year.

The rates for Bosnia and Herzegovina, Croatia and Slovenia were based on similar calculations that took into account the 0.42 per cent rate adopted by the Assembly for the former Socialist Federal Republic of Yugoslavia. For Belarus, the Russian Federation and Ukraine, recommendations for assessment in 1993-1994 were 0.48, 6.71, and 1.87 per cent, respectively. For 1992, the Committee said Belarus and Ukraine should be assessed at the rates adopted for them by the Assembly in 1991,[5] i.e., 0.31 and 1.18 per cent, respectively.

In making its recommendations for each of the above Member States, the Committee considered national income and population data available from the Statistical Division of the United Nations. In addition, it contacted separately eight States of the former USSR as well as the three new Member States that had been part of the former Yugoslavia to request relevant national income and population statistics. Responses of varying completeness were received from three Member States.

Scale methodology

The Committee on Contributions, at its 1992 session, prepared illustrative scales of assessment as requested by the Assembly in 1991.[7] In doing so, it analysed the following elements: use of uniform exchange rates; debt-adjusted income; the low per capita income allowance formula; and a method for phasing out the scheme of limits. The Committee also examined possible improvements of the methodology for future scales, including adjustments to national and per capita income; the application of price-adjusted exchange rates (PARE) used for countries that demonstrated extremely large discrepancies between exchange rate movements over time and changes in domestic prices; and alternative methodologies. Exploration of alternative approaches had been requested by the Assembly, also in 1991.[8]. They included: division of the budget into parts, one according to capacity to pay and the other(s) according to other criteria; incorporation of an element of weighted voting; division of the membership into groups for determining contributions; equal-share apportionment; and relating costs to benefits derived by Member States from the Organization.

On 23 December 1992, on the recommendation of the Fifth Committee, the General Assembly, adopted **decision 47/456** by recorded vote.

Scale of assessments for the apportionment of the expenses of the United Nations

The General Assembly, on the recommendation of the Fifth Committee, decides to adopt the recommendations of the Committee on Contributions with respect to the rates of assessment of Member States contained in paragraphs 51 to 64 of the report of the Committee on Contributions; paragraph 1 of General Assembly resolution 46/221 A of 20 December 1991 is amended accordingly.

General Assembly decision 47/456

23 December 1992   Meeting 94   104-16-34 (recorded vote)

Approved by Fifth Committee (A/47/833) by recorded vote (62-15-19), 21 December (meeting 52); draft by Barbados (A/C.5/47/L.29); agenda item 111.
Meeting numbers. GA 47th session: 5th Committee 17-20, 23-27, 36-38, 44, 45, 52; plenary 94.

Recorded vote in Assembly as follows:

In favour: Afghanistan, Albania, Angola, Argentina, Australia, Bahrain, Bangladesh, Barbados, Belgium, Benin, Bolivia, Botswana, Brazil, Brunei Darussalam, Burkina Faso, Burundi, Cameroon, Cape Verde, Chad, Chile, China, Colombia, Congo, Costa Rica, Côte d'Ivoire, Cuba, Djibouti, Dominican Republic, Ecuador, Egypt, El Salvador, Ethiopia, Gabon, Gambia, Germany, Ghana, Greece, Guinea, Haiti, Honduras, India, Indonesia, Iran, Iraq, Ireland, Italy, Japan, Jordan, Kenya, Kuwait, Kyrgyzstan, Lebanon, Lesotho, Liberia, Libyan Arab Jamahiriya, Luxembourg, Malawi, Malaysia, Mauritania, Mexico, Morocco, Myanmar, Namibia, Nepal, Netherlands, Nicaragua, Niger, Nigeria, Oman, Pakistan, Panama, Paraguay, Peru, Philippines, Portugal, Qatar, Russian Federation, Rwanda, Sao Tome and Principe, Saudi Arabia, Senegal, Singapore, Spain, Sri Lanka, Sudan, Suriname, Syrian Arab Republic, Tajikistan, Thailand, Togo, Tunisia, Turkmenistan, Uganda, United Arab Emirates, United Kingdom, United Republic of Tanzania, United States, Uruguay, Vanuatu, Venezuela, Yemen, Zaire, Zambia, Zimbabwe.

Against: Armenia, Azerbaijan, Belarus, Canada, Denmark, Estonia, Finland, Iceland, Latvia, Lithuania, New Zealand, Norway, Republic of Moldova, Sweden, Turkey, Ukraine.

Abstaining: Algeria, Antigua and Barbuda, Austria, Bahamas, Belize, Bhutan, Bulgaria, Cyprus, Czechoslovakia, Dominica, Fiji, France, Grenada, Guinea-Bissau, Guyana, Hungary, Israel, Jamaica, Kazakhstan, Liechtenstein, Madagascar, Maldives, Mali, Marshall Islands, Micronesia, Poland, Republic of Korea, Romania, Saint Lucia, Samoa, Sierra Leone, Slovenia, Solomon Islands, Trinidad and Tobago.

The Legal Counsel, speaking before the Fifth Committee, said the treatment of Belarus and Ukraine as new Member States for the purposes of assessment was neither consistent with the 1991 Assembly resolution on the scale of assessments,[3] nor with rule 160 of the Assembly's rules of procedure.

Budget contributions in 1992

Of the $1,476,855,541 in contributions payable to the United Nations regular budget as at 1 January 1992, $976,247,876 had been collected from Member States by 31 December, leaving $500,607,665 outstanding.[9] Of the total, $1,037,471,596 was due for 1992 alone, while $439,383,945 was outstanding from previous years. In addition, non-member States owed $3,835,466 for their share of United Nations activities in which they participated. Of that amount —which comprised $3,453,448 for 1992 and $382,018 from past years— $377,066 was outstanding as at 31 December 1992.

On 4 February,[10] the Secretary-General informed the President of the General Assembly that 20 Member States—Benin, Cambodia, the Central African Republic, Chad, the Dominican Republic, El Salvador, Equatorial Guinea, the Gambia, Guatemala, Haiti, Kenya, Liberia, Mali, Mauritania, Nicaragua, the Niger, Panama, Sao Tome and Principe, Sierra Leone and South Africa—were over two years in arrears in the payment of their budget contributions. By four more letters, dated 13 April,[11] 18 June,[12] and 24[13] and 25 August,[14] the Secretary-General stated that the necessary payments had been made by Benin, El Salvador, Guatemala, Mauritania, Nicaragua and Panama. By a letter of 15 September,[15] the Secretary-General stated that at that time, 12 Member States were in arrears— Cambodia, the Central African Republic, Chad, the Dominican Republic, Equatorial Guinea, the Gambia, Haiti, Liberia, the Niger, Sao Tome and Principe, Sierra Leone and South Africa. In subsequent letters, of 18,[16] 22[17] and 24 September,[18] 2 October[19] and 16[20] and 30 November,[21] he said the necessary payments had been made by the Central African Republic, Chad, the Dominican Republic, Equatorial Guinea, the Gambia, Haiti, Liberia, the Niger, Sao Tome and Principe and Sierra Leone. As a result, those 16 Members had reduced their arrears below the amount required under Article 19 of the Charter, thus regaining voting privileges in the Assembly.

REFERENCES

[1]A/47/11. [2]YUN 1991, p. 97, GA res. 46/4, 17 Sep. 1991. [3]Ibid., GA res. 46/5, 17 Sep. 1991. [4]Ibid., p. 98, GA res. 46/6, 17 Sep. 1991. [5]Ibid., p. 879, GA res. 46/221 A, 20 Dec. 1991. [6]A/46/938-S/24116. [7]YUN 1991, p. 881, GA res. 46/221 B, 20 Dec. 1991. [8]Ibid., p. 883, GA res. 46/221 D, 20 Dec. 1991. [9]ST/ADM/SER.B/395. [10]A/46/868. [11]A/46/868/Add.1. [12]A/46/868/Add.2. [13]A/46/868/Add.3. [14]A/46/868/Add.4. [15]A/47/442. [16]A/47/442/Add.1. [17]A/47/442/Add.2. [18]A/47/442/Add.3. [19]A/47/442/Add.4. [20]A/47/442/Add.5. [21]A/47/442/Add.6.

Accounts and auditing

In 1992, the General Assembly accepted the accounts and financial statements for the year or biennium ended 31 December 1991 for the United Nations and eight development and humanitarian programmes, along with conclusions and recommendations of the Board of Auditors and the comments of ACABQ.

The findings and recommendations of the Board were transmitted by its Chairman to the Assembly on 30 June, three months after having received the accounts from the Secretary-General, who in August submitted a summary of the principal findings of the Board.[1]

Financial reports and audited statements were submitted on the United Nations,[2] including the International Trade Centre (ITC)[3] and the United Nations University;[4] UNDP;[5] UNICEF;[6] the United Nations Relief and Works Agency for Palestine Refugees in the Near East;[7] UNITAR;[8] voluntary funds administered by UNHCR;[9] the United Nations Environment Programme;[10] UNFPA;[11] and the United Nations Habitat and Human Settlements Foundation.[12]

For the 1990-1991 biennium, the Board decided to carry out horizontal studies in three main areas, namely: expendable and non-expendable property; internal audit; and trust funds. Therefore, in addition to the regular coverage of specific areas, the three Board members examined simultaneously the three main areas in most of the organizations under the Board's responsibility; this helped identify commonality of issues throughout the system.

Three of the 10 reports received qualified audit opinions from the Board: the United Nations, UNDP and UNFPA. Also, the Board issued a qualified audit opinion on compliance with the financial regulations and legislative authority of the transactions of UNITAR.

Regarding the United Nations, the Board said the statement fairly portrayed its financial position, subject to the ultimate resolution of unpaid assessed contributions from Member States totalling over $1 billion as at 31 December 1991. The UNDP report received a qualified opinion, due in part to insufficient audit evidence regarding executing agencies at the time the accounts were finalized. Also, as at the end of April 1992, out of a total of 1,358 nationally executed projects, only 21 had sent in the necessary certified reports. The qualified opinion of UNFPA was based on the fact that the Board was not in a position to comment on the fairness of 14.6 per cent of total expenditure because of a lack of adequate audit evidence.

ACABQ submitted its comments on the financial reports and audited financial statements and on the Board of Auditors' reports in October.[13] The Advisory Committee exchanged views with members of the Audit Operations Committee on the format and content of audit reports. In that connection, the Advisory Committee was informed of the Board's intention to review the format of its report. ACABQ said the Board should continue to be fully responsible for deciding the format and content of its report and cautioned against giving the Board too many instructions in that regard.

On the related question of presentation, the Advisory Committee believed that the Board's suggestion to include the liquidity position of each agency and programme in future financial reports and accounts would streamline the audit reports.

Also in October, pursuant to a 1991 Assembly resolution,[14] the Secretary-General submitted a report on measures to facilitate reporting by staff members of inappropriate uses of the Organization's resources, internal controls relating to the payment of allowances and benefits and efforts to recover outstanding excess income tax reimbursements;[15] and another on the administrative system of ITC.[16]

On 23 December 1992, the General Assembly, on the recommendation of the Fifth Committee, adopted without vote **resolution 47/211**.

Financial reports and audited financial statements, and reports of the Board of Auditors

The General Assembly,

Having considered the financial reports and audited financial statements for the period ended 31 December 1991 of the United Nations, including the International Trade Centre and the United Nations University, the United Nations Development Programme, the United Nations Children's Fund, the United Nations Relief and Works Agency for Palestine Refugees in the Near East, the United Nations Institute for Training and Research, the voluntary funds administered by the United Nations High Commissioner for Refugees, the Fund of the United Nations Environment Programme, the United Nations Population Fund, and the United Nations Habitat and Human Settlements Foundation, the reports and audit opinions of the Board of Auditors, the concise summary of principal findings, conclusions and recommendations for remedial action of the Board of Auditors, and the report of the Advisory Committee on Administrative and Budgetary Questions,

Taking note of the report of the Secretary-General on measures to facilitate reporting by staff members of inappropriate uses of the resources of the Organization, internal controls relating to the payment of allowances and benefits, and efforts to recover outstanding excess income tax reimbursements and the report of the Secretary-General on the administrative system of the International Trade Centre, prepared in response to General Assembly resolution 46/183 of 20 December 1991,

Noting the steps taken by executive heads and governing bodies of the United Nations organizations and programmes to give appropriate consideration and attention to the recommendations in earlier audit reports, as commented upon by the Board of Auditors in annexes to its current reports,

Stressing the importance of efficient resource management in all United Nations organizations and programmes,

Concerned about the cases of deficiencies in programme and financial management and inappropriate or fraudulent use of resources reported by the Board of Auditors, and other such alleged cases,

Recognizing that the Board of Auditors conducts its reviews in a comprehensive manner, as stipulated in regulation 12.5 of the Financial Regulations of the United Nations,

1. *Accepts* the financial reports and audited financial statements and the audit opinions and reports of the Board of Auditors regarding the aforementioned organizations;

2. *Also accepts* the concise summary of principal findings, conclusions and recommendations for remedial action of the Board of Auditors;

3. *Notes with concern* that the Board of Auditors issued qualified audit opinions on the financial statements of the United Nations, the United Nations Development Programme and the United Nations Population Fund, and that it also issued a qualified audit opinion on compliance with the financial regulations and legislative authority of the transactions of the United Nations Institute for Training and Research;

4. *Approves* all the recommendations and conclusions of the Board of Auditors and the comments thereon contained in the report of the Advisory Committee on Administrative and Budgetary Questions;

5. *Requests* the Secretary-General to submit to the Board of Auditors in a separate document financial reports and financial statements for peace-keeping operations and then to submit the reports and statements together with the recommendations of the Board thereon, to the General Assembly, without precluding the presentation of consolidated financial statements of the United Nations;

6. *Requests* the Board of Auditors to expand its audit coverage of all peace-keeping operations without reducing the coverage of regular budget and extrabudgetary activities, and decides that any additional costs shall be charged to the peace-keeping budgets concerned;

7. *Recalls* the importance for the Board of Auditors to provide the Secretary-General and the executive heads of United Nations organizations and programmes with an adequate opportunity to comment on its findings, in accordance with the relevant financial regulations and rules, before the Board arrives at its final conclusions and recommendations;

8. *Also recalls* its resolution 46/183, and in that connection invites the Board of Auditors to continue to include in its report separate sections that contain a summary of recommendations for corrective action to be taken by the United Nations organizations and programmes concerned, with an indication of relative urgency;

9. *Takes note with concern* of the findings of the Board of Auditors, and requests the Secretary-General and the executive heads of United Nations organizations and programmes:

(a) To strengthen budgetary control in order to avoid over-expenditure of approved budgets or allotments;

(b) To make purchasing policy on the acquisition of goods and services more cost-effective and transparent, *inter alia*, by reducing the number of exceptions to competitive bidding and ensuring that the reasons for such exceptions are recorded in writing;

(c) To give priority attention to compliance with the recommendations of the Board of Auditors on the hiring, granting of remuneration and performance evaluation of experts, consultants and personnel engaged on a short-term basis;

(d) To install a more effective system of managing and controlling the granting of allowances and benefits to staff members;

(e) To tighten control over the inventory of non-expendable property in all locations, including peace-keeping operations;

and to report on these matters to the General Assembly at its forty-eighth session;

10. *Reaffirms* the importance of timetables for compliance with recommendations of the Board of Auditors approved by the General Assembly, and requests the Secretary-General and the executive heads of United Nations organizations and programmes to submit to the General Assembly at its forty-eighth session, through the Advisory Committee at its spring session in 1993 and through the appropriate intergovernmental bodies, an action-oriented report outlining steps to be taken in response to the recommendations of the Board, including timetables for their implementation;

11. *Notes with appreciation* the action taken by the United Nations Development Programme to develop an internal mechanism to follow up on the recommendations of the Board of Auditors;

12. *Requests* the Secretary-General and the executive heads of United Nations organizations and programmes to ensure that all existing financial and staff regulations and rules are strictly complied with, including those relating to internal control over expenditure and those which assign staff members personal responsibility and accountability in their performance, and to report to the General Assembly at its forty-ninth session on measures taken to strengthen internal controls in those areas where weaknesses have been identified;

13. *Requests* the Secretary-General to make proposals to the General Assembly at its forty-seventh session on:

(a) Establishing legal and effective mechanisms to recover misappropriated funds, as recommended by the Advisory Committee on Administrative and Budgetary Questions in paragraph 53 of its report;

(b) Seeking criminal prosecution of those who have committed fraud against the Organization;

14. *Encourages* the Secretary-General and the executive heads of United Nations organizations and programmes to take urgent steps to strengthen the independence and effectiveness of the internal audit function, to strengthen measures to ensure an adequate response to internal audit findings and to report thereon to the General Assembly;

15. *Requests* the Board of Auditors to evaluate the extent of compliance with their recommendations, to report thereon to the General Assembly at its forty-ninth session through the Advisory Committee, which shall recommend such measures as it deems appropriate to ensure implementation of those recommendations, and to draw attention to any of those recommendations that have not yet been implemented;

16. *Welcomes* the identification by the Board of Auditors of areas of horizontal study across the organizations audited, and endorses the intention of the Board to continue this practice in future audits;

17. *Invites* the Board of Auditors, in the context of regulation 12.5 of the Financial Regulations of the United Nations, to report at its discretion on the efficient and effective utilization of trust funds under the control of the Secretary-General;

18. *Also invites* the Board of Auditors, in its concise summary of principal findings, conclusions and recommendations, to report in a consolidated fashion on major deficiencies in programme and financial management

and cases of inappropriate or fraudulent use of resources together with the measures taken by United Nations organizations in this regard;

19. *Endorses* the efforts of the Panel of External Auditors to ensure that common auditing standards for the United Nations system are consistent with those of recognized international auditing bodies;

20. *Urges* the Secretary-General and the executive heads of United Nations organizations and programmes to accelerate their efforts to develop common accounting standards for the organizations of the United Nations system and to take these standards into account in the preparation of their financial statements for the period ending 31 December 1993;

21. *Requests* the Secretary-General and the executive heads of United Nations organizations and programmes to ensure that future presentations of liquidity position should be made in the context of common accounting standards;

22. *Notes with concern* that the opinion of the Board of Auditors on the financial statements of the United Nations is subject to the ultimate resolution of unpaid assessed contributions from Member States;

23. *Calls the attention* of the Secretary-General to the implications that the findings of the Board of Auditors about the management of the Organization may have for the image of the United Nations.

General Assembly resolution 47/211

23 December 1992   Meeting 94   Adopted without vote

Approved by Fifth Committee (A/47/827) without vote, 19 December (meeting 50); draft by Rapporteur (A/C.5/47/L.23), based on informal consultations; agenda item 102.
Meeting numbers. GA 47th session: 5th Committee 5, 6, 8, 10-13, 22, 50; plenary 94.

On the same date, the Assembly adopted **decision 47/454** without vote.

Financial reports and audited financial statements, and reports of the Board of Auditors

At its 94th plenary meeting, on 23 December 1992, the General Assembly, on the recommendation of the Fifth Committee:

(a)   Requested the Secretary-General to review the operation and effectiveness of each of the specialized administrative and budgetary support units of the Secretariat, including the Management Advisory Service, the Central Evaluation Unit, the Central Monitoring Unit and the Internal Audit Division, with a view to strengthening their efficiency, and to submit a report thereon with recommendations to the General Assembly at its forty-eighth session through the Advisory Committee on Administrative and Budgetary Questions;

(b)   Decided, without prejudice to its existing relevant resolutions, to consider the roles and coverage of the subsidiary bodies responsible for coordination, administrative questions and budgetary matters, including the Advisory Committee on Administrative and Budgetary Questions, the Board of Auditors, the Joint Inspection Unit and the Committee for Programme and Coordination, with a view to improving the effectiveness of their oversight and coordination mechanisms, and requested the Secretary-General to provide relevant background material together with his views and those of the bodies concerned to the General Assembly as soon as possible, but not later than at its forty-ninth session.

General Assembly decision 47/454

                                                      Adopted without vote

Approved by Fifth Committee (A/47/827) without vote, 19 December (meeting 50); draft by Rapporteur (A/C.5/47/L.27), based on informal consultations; agenda item 102.
Meeting numbers. GA 47th session: 5th Committee 5, 6, 8, 10-13, 22, 50; plenary 94.

REFERENCES

[1]A/47/315. [2]A/47/5, vol. I & Corr.1. [3]A/47/5, vol. II. [4]A/47/5, vol. III. [5]A/47/5/Add.1. [6]A/47/5/Add.2. [7]A/47/5/Add.3. [8]A/47/5/Add.4 & Corr.1. [9]A/47/5/Add.5. [10]A/47/5/Add.6. [11]A/47/5/Add.7. [12]A/47/5/Add.8 & Corr.1. [13]A/47/500. [14]YUN 1991, p. 884, GA res. 46/183, 20 Dec. 1991. [15]A/47/510. [16]A/47/460.

United Nations programmes

Programme planning

Medium-term plan 1992-1997

The medium-term plan for 1992-1997, adopted by the General Assembly in 1990[1] and revised in 1991,[2] was the principal policy directive of the United Nations and served as the framework for the formulation of the biennial programme budgets. It covered the entire range of United Nations activities, both global and regional, describing them in major programmes or chapters covering a broad sectoral area, which themselves were broken down into programmes and subprogrammes. The activities were designed to be carried out by various organizations within the United Nations system—the Secretariat, the regional commissions and United Nations agencies. In August 1992,[3] the Secretary-General proposed revisions to the plan and submitted them to CPC at its 1992 session as well as to ACABQ. The Assembly adopted the proposed revisions to 40 programmes, as amended by the Second Committee,[4] CPC and the Committee on Conferences, with additional conclusions annexed to its **resolution 47/214** on programme planning (see below).

CPC reviewed 37 of the proposed revisions to the plan.[5] It noted that to a considerable extent, the revisions incorporated the outcome of UNCED (see PART THREE, Chapter VIII), of the eighth session of the United Nations Conference on Trade and Development (UNCTAD) (see PART THREE, Chapter IV) and of the first phase of the restructuring of the Organization. It recommended approval of the revisions, on the understanding that further modifications would be made to relevant programmes to take into account decisions made by the Assembly, *inter alia*, on the follow-up of the above-mentioned activities. The Committee also commented separately on the individual revisions proposed to each programme of the plan. With regard to the format of the plan, CPC considered that every effort should be made to maintain the prominent place of the plan as a policy directive. It recommended that a prototype of a possible new format of the plan be presented to it in 1993.

The Committee on Conferences made suggestions and endorsed the proposed revisions to the medium-term plan regarding common support services and conference and library services.[6]

Commenting on the proposed revisions before the Fifth Committee in December, ACABQ noted that the reasons for the proposed revisions were not clearly stated, but it had been informed that it was mainly due to the need to take into account the effect of the restructuring of the Secretariat. The Advisory Committee reiterated its 1990 comments[7] on various aspects of the medium-term plan, its role, quality, content and preparation, including recommendations on such issues as the presentation of substantive and support programmes, the role of intergovernmental bodies in examining the proposed programmes and revisions thereto, and the effect of evaluation on the quality of the plan, which were endorsed by the Assembly that same year.[1]

ACABQ shared the view of many delegations that the time had come for a thorough assessment of the plan and the planning process in the United Nations. It welcomed CPC's proposal that an ad hoc technical seminar of experts be convened on programme planning, to assist in drafting the protoype of a possible new format of the medium-term plan.

By a November 1992 note,[4] the Fifth Committee Chairman presented the views of the General Assembly and its Main Committees on the relevant portions of the proposed medium-term plan.

1990-1991 programme performance

In April 1992,[8] the Secretary-General submitted a report on programme performance of the United Nations for the biennium 1990-1991, which measured performance by comparing the number of final outputs programmed with the number of those implemented. Of the 7,011 programmed outputs, 6,237 were to be implemented under the 1990-1991 programme budget, and an additional 774 were carried over from previous bienniums. Of those, 5,417—or 77 per cent—were actually implemented during 1990-1991. By category of output, the rate of implementation was as follows: servicing of meetings, 83 per cent; reports, 82 per cent; public information, 77 per cent; publications, 70 per cent; and others—comprising activities which did not fall in the standard categories of outputs mentioned, such as organization of hearings, investigations, studies and consultations, ad hoc meetings, briefings of official visitors and other

forms of assistance, responses to government inquiries, including legal opinions, conduct of legal proceedings, etc.—88 per cent.

The overall rate of implementation by the 25 major programmes of the medium-term plan for 1984-1989, extended to 1991, ranged from 65 and 68 per cent in the major programmes of transnational corporations and international trade and development finance, respectively, to 85 per cent and over in major programmes on political and Security Council affairs activities, disaster relief, public information, human settlements, marine affairs and protection and assistance to refugees. As in previous bienniums, the overall implementation rate was considerably affected by the actual delivery of publications, given their weight in the total number of programmed outputs. Similarly, the servicing of meetings and preparation of reports to intergovernmental bodies, the implementation of which was left to the discretion of the Secretariat, weighed heavily in the performance of some major programmes.

Of the total programmed outputs, 10 per cent (703 outputs) were postponed and 13 per cent (891 outputs) were terminated. The postponed outputs were mainly publications (77 per cent). More than half of the terminated outputs were concentrated in UNCTAD, ITC, UNCTAD/the General Agreement on Tariffs and Trade and the regional commissions. The termination of outputs reflected to a large extent the response to political changes and other unforeseen developments.

In addition to the 5,417 outputs implemented, 477 were added to the 1990-1991 programme budget during the biennium, either by intergovernmental bodies or at the initiative of the Secretariat.

While the number of programmed outputs for 1990-1991 was substantially lower than that programmed in 1988-1989, the overall implementation level was higher (77 compared to 74 per cent), mainly on account of a lower percentage of terminations (13 against 15 per cent).

With regard to resource utilization, a total of 60,300 work-months, in terms of Professional staff and consultant services, were reported available to programme managers for the production of 7,011 outputs; of those total work-months, an estimated 17,200 Professional work months, or 28 per cent, were funded from extrabudgetary resources.

Programme performance by each section of the programme budget for 1990-1991 was contained in an addendum to the Secretary-General's report.[9]

Considering the 1990-1991 programme performance report, CPC[5] noted that it did not yet reflect the improvements proposed by the Secretary-General in 1991.[10] It stressed that future reports should balance the current quantitative approach with an analysis that would provide more useful information on implementation of the various activities in the programme budget and on departures from programmed commitments. It agreed that while the counting of outputs implemented against those programmed continued to have a role to play, such statistics were of limited value in providing an overall assessment of programme budget implementation. The Committee noted that global rates of implementation could be misleading when all outputs were treated equally; it expressed the view that only through a differentiation between the diverse activities would the comparison of implementation rates become meaningful. Noting the low implementation rate for publications (70 per cent), it reiterated the need to review the Organization's publication policies.

The Committee stressed the need for a closer link between programme performance and budget performance reports. In that connection, it recalled its recommendations concerning the establishment of a system of accountability, endorsed by the Assembly in 1991.[2]

Programme evaluation

An assessment of the activities exercised in programme evaluation and proposals for strengthening the role of evaluation were contained in an April 1992 report of the Secretary-General.[11] The report covered evaluation activities for 1984-1991, including resources for evaluation.

The report found that the percentage of subprogrammes evaluated was low for most of the organizational entities and that self-evaluation was not yet widely accepted as a useful management tool. Only a small number of organizational entities submitted reports on self-evaluation to their governing bodies, and there were significant differences in the degree of interest shown in in-depth evaluation by intergovernmental and expert bodies.

According to the report, coordination of evaluation with auditing and other disciplines was necessary in order to enhance effectiveness and avoid omissions, and there was a need for balance between internal management-oriented and traditional external evaluations.

The report offered recommendations with regard to self-evaluation, in-depth evaluations, including a timetable for them, resources for evaluation, coordination of activities aiming at improving organizational performance and action requiring the attention of specialized governing bodies.

CPC[5] recommended that the General Assembly, when examining those recommendations, take into account the following: proposals for strengthening evaluation capacity, as suggested in the re-

port, would be reviewed on a case-by-case basis, taking into account CPC's report on the work of its 1990 session[12] and the Secretary-General's restructuring plan for the Secretariat (see above); arrangements for requesting comments from relevant specialized governing bodies on evaluation reports, as well as CPC's conclusions and recommendations, would be adopted on a case-by-case basis.

In general, the Committee concluded that the methodology for self-evaluation and training in programme evaluation needed to be improved and that some central standard-setting was required. Findings from self-evaluation should be reported by programme managers to their respective governing bodies, and reports on the results of self-evaluations should be placed on the agendas of the specialized governing bodies. The mode of transmission to special intergovernmental bodies of in-depth evaluation reports, together with the relevant recommendations of CPC, should be improved.

Accountability of programme managers

In connection with the consideration of the programme budget, CPC, at its 1992 session,[5] recognized the need for direct responsibility of programme managers in the implementation of mandated programmes. It emphasized that responsibility and accountability were essential for progress in implementation of the programme budget, and recalled its 1991 recommendations on the establishment of a system of accountability,[13] which were endorsed by the General Assembly.[2] Such a system, the Committee said in 1991, would provide for a closer linkage between programme performance and budget performance.

On 23 December 1992, the General Assembly, on the recommendation of the Fifth Committee, adopted **resolution 47/214** without vote.

Programme planning

The General Assembly,

Recalling its resolutions 37/234 of December 1982, 41/213 of 19 December 1986, 42/211 of 21 December 1987, 43/219 of 21 December 1988, 44/194 of 21 December 1989, 45/253 of 21 December 1990 and 46/189 of 20 December 1991,

Having examined the proposed revisions to the medium-term plan for the period 1992-1997,

Having considered the note by the Chairman of the Fifth Committee reporting on the review of the proposed revisions to the medium-term plan for the period 1992-1997 by the other Main Committees of the General Assembly,

Having also considered the report of the Committee for Programme and Coordination on the work of its thirty-second session, the report of the Committee on Conferences and the oral report of the Advisory Committee on Administrative and Budgetary Questions,

Having further considered the reports of the Secretary-General on the programme performance of the United Nations for the biennium 1990-1991 and on the assessment of evaluation activities and proposals for strengthening the role of evaluation;

I
Medium-term plan for the period 1992-1997

1. *Adopts* the Secretary-General's proposed revisions to the medium-term plan for the period 1992-1997, as amended by the recommendations of the Second Committee, the Committee for Programme and Coordination and the Committee on Conferences, and the additional conclusions contained in the annex to the present resolution;

2. *Takes note* of the views of the other Main Committees of the General Assembly and the observations made by the Advisory Committee on Administrative and Budgetary Questions;

3. *Reaffirms* that the medium-term plan is the principal policy directive of the United Nations and shall serve as the framework for the formulation of the biennial programme budgets;

4. *Emphasizes* the importance of the contribution of the sectoral, regional and central intergovernmental bodies, in particular the Main Committees of the General Assembly, in reviewing and improving the quality of the plan and its revisions;

5. *Regrets* that there are still considerable practical problems which limit the availability of such contributions;

6. *Calls upon* intergovernmental bodies to take appropriate measures to ensure their active participation in the review of the medium-term plan and its revisions;

7. *Endorses* the recommendation of the Committee for Programme and Coordination that a prototype of a possible new format of the medium-term plan should be presented to the Committee at its thirty-third session;

8. *Endorses also* the recommendation of the Committee for Programme and Coordination that an ad hoc technical seminar of experts should be convened in the field of programme planning of the United Nations, without additional cost to the Organization, to assist the Secretariat in the drafting of the prototype of the new format of the medium-term plan;

9. *Decides* that the prototype, as recommended by the Committee for Programme and Coordination, should take into account the relevant conclusions of the seminar on the prototype of a new budget document and address, in particular, issues concerning the manageability of the drafting and revision process, including the questions of preparation and submission of documentation and the review of programme planning documents by subsidiary intergovernmental machinery;

10. *Expresses its concern* at the negative impact of late issuance of documentation on the in-depth review of the revisions to the medium-term plan and endorses the related recommendations of the Committee for Programme and Coordination as contained in its report on the work of its thirty-second session;

11. *Recommends* that, within the framework of the review of the format and structure of the medium-term plan, the seminar give particular attention to ensuring the timeliness of the provision of documentation;

II
Programme performance report

1. *Takes note* of the report of the Secretary-General on the programme performance of the United Nations for the biennium 1990-1991;

2. *Endorses* the conclusions and recommendations of the Committee for Programme and Coordination on the report of the Secretary-General on the programme performance of the United Nations for the biennium 1990-1991;

3. *Requests* the Secretary-General to reflect the improvements proposed in his report to the General Assembly at its forty-sixth session in his report on the programme performance of the United Nations for the biennium 1992-1993;

III
Programme evaluation in the United Nations

1. *Takes note* of the report of the Secretary-General on the assessment of evaluation activities and proposals for strengthening the role of evaluation;

2. *Endorses* the conclusions and recommendations of the Committee for Programme and Coordination at its thirty-second session on this question and urges the Secretary-General to improve the methodology for self-evaluation;

IV
Coordination

1. *Emphasizes* the need for enhanced coordination in the United Nations system and welcomes the intention of the Secretary-General, as Chairman of the Administrative Committee on Coordination, to assign a high priority to coordination and to work with the executive heads of the organizations of the system to develop new approaches for collaboration with the purpose of improving the effectiveness and efficiency of coordination;

2. *Endorses* the conclusions and recommendations made by the Committee for Programme and Coordination at its thirty-second session on the annual overview report of the Administrative Committee on Coordination for 1991;

3. *Endorses also* the recommendations made by the Committee for Programme and Coordination at its thirty-second session on the report of the Secretary-General on the System-wide Plan of Action for African Economic Recovery and Development and invites the Secretary-General:

(*a*) To launch, at the earliest possible time, the System-wide Plan of Action for African Economic Recovery and Development and the United Nations New Agenda for the Development of Africa in the 1990s;

(*b*) To call upon all the relevant executive heads of the United Nations agencies and bodies to accord high priority to the implementation of the Plan and to use it as a guideline for their activities related to African development;

4. *Takes note* of the preparation of the system-wide medium-term plan for the advancement of women for the period 1996-2001 and the amendments proposed to the plan by the Committee for Programme and Coordination;

5. *Takes note also* of the decision of the Committee for Programme and Coordination to propose to the Administrative Committee on Coordination that at the twenty-seventh series of their joint meetings, the Committee for Programme and Coordination and the Administrative Committee on Coordination should discuss

the results of the United Nations Conference on Environment and Development and their implications for
the United Nations system;

V

Other matters

1. *Recalls* its resolutions 46/185 B and 46/189 of 20
December 1991, by which it endorsed the recommendation of the Committee for Programme and Coordination at its thirty-first session to establish a system of
responsibility and accountability of programme
managers of the United Nations;

2. *Endorses* the recommendations of the Committee
for Programme and Coordination in its report and invites the Secretary-General to report to the General Assembly at its forty-eighth session on the establishment
of such a system.

ANNEX

Conclusions on revisions to the major programmes,
programmes and subprogrammes of the
medium-term plan for the period 1992-1997

*Programme 1.   Good offices and peacemaking, peace-keeping,
research and the collection of information*

The General Assembly endorses the recommendations of the Committee for Programme and Coordination contained in paragraphs 30 and 31 of its report and
invites the Secretary-General to take into account the
decisions of the Assembly on preventive diplomacy and
related matters in the implementation of this programme.

In the fourth line of new paragraph 1.21 *(b)* and in
the second line of new paragraph 1.21 *(i)*, insert international *before* peace and security

Programme 2.   Political and Security Council affairs

Retain the title "Political and Security Council affairs" for the programme.

*Programme 4.   Special political questions, trusteeship and
decolonization*

*Subprogramme 4:   Enhancing the effectiveness of the principle
of periodic and genuine elections*

For the text of new paragraph 4.37, substitute:

4.37. The legislative mandate of the subprogramme is provided by the General Assembly
in its resolution 46/137 of 17 December 1991 and
its implementation will be carried out in the context of Assembly resolutions 47/130 and 47/138 of
18 December 1992 and in full coordination with programme 35, Promotion and protection of human
rights.

At the end of new paragraph 4.39 *delete* and provide development assistance.

Programme 6.   Elimination of apartheid

In new paragraph 6.2, *delete* consensus
In new paragraph 6.36 *(a)*, *for* the consensus *read* related

Programme 7.   Disarmament

Not applicable to English.

Programme 13.   Trade and development

Paragraph 13.30 should read:

13.30. Subprogrammes 1 to 5, 7 to 9 and 11 are
designated high priority.

Subprogramme 1:   International competition and trade policies
Paragraph 13.34 (c)

At the end of the paragraph *delete* ensuring
transparency and defining consultation procedures

Paragraph 13.35 (d)

For the existing text, substitute:

(d) Enhancing knowledge of restrictive business practices and encouraging the elimination
of those practices which adversely affect international trade, particularly that of developing countries and the economic development of those
countries;

Subprogramme 2:   Commodities

Paragraph 13.41 (d)

In the first line *after* diversification *insert* and
crop substitution

Paragraph 13.41 (g)

For the existing text, substitute:

(g) Review developments, undertake analysis and provide information and support to technical cooperation in the field of commodities and
sustainable development;

Subprogramme 3:   Development finance and debt

Paragraph 13.45 (g)

In the second line, *after* debt *insert* management
and

Subprogramme 4:   Investment and technology

Paragraph 13.49 (b)

At the beginning of the paragraph, *for* formulation and adoption of *read* Analysis and advice on

Paragraph 13.50 (h)

For the existing text, substitute:

(h) Consider whether there is the convergence
of views of Governments on a code of conduct on
the transfer of technology necessary to reach
agreement on all outstanding issues. If there is
convergence of views, contribute to further work
on the code;

Add a paragraph 13.50 *(j)* reading:

(j) Analyse challenges and opportunities for
transfer of technology to and from countries undergoing transition processes to a market
economy.

Subprogramme 5:   Poverty alleviation

Paragraph 13.53 (b)

At the end of the paragraph, *after* poverty *insert*
and the participation of the poor and vulnerable
groups in development

Paragraph 13.53 (d)

The second line should read:

social development programmes, particularly
in developing countries, especially in the

*Subprogramme 6:   Economic cooperation among developing
countries*

Paragraph 13.62 (a)

For both among developed and developing *read*
among developing

*Subprogramme 7:   Global interdependence: the international
trading, monetary and financial
systems; international implications of
macroeconomic policies*

Paragraph 13.66 (b)

In the first line, *for* study *read* consider.

Paragraph 13.67 (b)

for the existing text, substitute:

(b) Study trends in the international trading, monetary and financial systems with a view to identifying the coherence of these systems and alternative responses required to ensure good macroeconomic management at the global level and adequate coordination and surveillance of national policies;

Subprogramme 8:   Enlarged economic spaces, regional integration processes and systematic issues of international trade

Paragraphs 13.70 (c) and (d)

For the existing text, substitute:

(c) To contribute to the promotion of regional and subregional economic integration, particularly among developing countries, as a complementary means of strengthening the trade liberalization process in order to facilitate, in a timely way, the smooth and equitable integration of all countries into the international trading system.

Subprogramme 9:   Privatization, entrepreneurship and competitiveness

Paragraph 13.77 (a)

In the second line, *delete* appropriate

Paragraph 13.78 (c)

In the second line, *for* and *read* and/or

Add a paragraph 13.78 (j) reading:

(j) Provide support for the presentation of national programmes and plans for privatization.

Subprogramme 10:   Domestic reforms and resource mobilization

Paragraph 13.80

At the end of the first line, *delete* developing

Paragraph 13.82 (a)

The paragraph should read:

(a) To help to identify, taking into account the diversity of country situations, the scope and nature of domestic economic reforms needed; the costs and benefits of alternative policy approaches and options; and measures and mechanisms for effective mobilization of domestic financial resources;

Paragraph 13.82 (b)

For generation of additional finance for sustainable development *read* of increasing the availability of development finance

Subprogramme 11:   Environment and sustainable development

Paragraph 13.88 (a)

In the second line, *for* coexistence *read* coherence and complementarity

Paragraph 13.88 (c)

In the first line, *after* developing countries with *insert* new and

Subprogramme 12:   Data management

Paragraph 13.96 (d)

In the first line, *for* assistance to developing countries *read* assistance, particularly to developing countries,

Programme 14.   Trade expansion, export promotion and service sector development

Paragraph 14.13 should read:

14.13. Subprogrammes 1, 3 and 4 are accorded high priority.

Subprogramme 1:   Structural adjustment and trading opportunities

Paragraph 14.16 (f)

In the seventh line, *before* increase *insert* the encouragement of preference-giving countries to consider an

Paragraph 14.16 (g)

For in Central and Eastern Europe *read* in transition

Paragraph 14.17 (g)

In the third line, *for* of Central and Eastern Europe *read* in transition

Paragraph 14.18 (j)

In the first line, *after* increasing *insert*, where possible,

Paragraph 14.18 (k)

For of Central and Eastern Europe *read* in transition

Subprogramme 3:   Trade efficiency

Paragraph 14.30 (i)

For the existing text, substitute:

(i) Undertake research and development of new automatic data-processing systems such as ASYCUDA for use at the country level;

Subprogramme 4:   Service development

Paragraph 14.33 (b)

In the first line, *after* examine *insert* ways of overcoming

Paragraph 14.34 (b)

The paragraph should read:

(b) Elaborating policies aimed at strengthening the service sector in the developing countries, including issues relating to production and export capacity, and increasing their participation in wolrd trade in this sector;

Paragraph 14.34 (g)

At the beginning of the paragraph, *insert* Elaborating policies aimed at

Paragraph 14.35 (a)

The paragraph should read:

(a) Analyse specific ways to allow an increasing participation of developing countries in trade in services; to overcome difficulties they face in their export of services and to improve the functioning of service markets, including through analysis of relevant restrictive business practices;

Subprogramme 5:   Shipping, ports and multimodal transport

Paragraph 14.37

For the existing text, substitute:

14.37. Most of world trade is carried on ocean transport and many developing countries have put priority on participating in this sector. Given the growing interdependence among the service sectors, their efforts to develop competitive shipping sectors may be facilitated by increasing their capacity to cope with rapidly changing structural and technological developments in improving the efficiency of their maritime and multimodal transport and related services and infrastructure facilities.

Paragraph 14.41 (a)

In the third line, *after* countries *insert* , in particular,

Paragraph 14.41 (c)

For in the fields of shipping, ports and multimodal transport, *read* in the development of competitive shipping, ports and multimodal transport services,

Paragraph 14.41 (e)

The first two lines should read:

To promote the development of port services, in particular through heightened awareness of technological improvements and measures which may enhance the

Paragraph 14.41 (g)

In the second line, *after* with a view *insert*, *inter alia*,

Paragraph 14.42 (a)

For the existing text, substitute:

(a) Preparing comparative analyses of national shipping policies, including such strategies and options as privatization, commercialization or possible elimination of State shipping companies, and their impact on the establishment of a national institutional environment aimed at fostering competitive shipping services, fleet development, service quality and increased trade, and reducing the technological gap;

Paragraph 14.42 (c)

For the existing text, substitute:

(c) Promoting a balance of interests between users and providers of shipping services, with particular regard to encouraging regular consultations among them;

Paragraph 14.42 (d)

In the fourth line, *for* application *read* by increasing awareness

In the fifth line, *for* transport *read* shipping

Paragraph 14.42 (f)

For the existing text, substitute:

(f) Monitoring structural changes in multimodal transport supply services, including multimodal sea/air services; promoting the use of international multimodal transport operations and the development of transport technologies, including the application of the agreed modal rules for container tariffs as well as UNCTAD/ICC standard form and modal provisions for multimodal transport documents and the use of transport-related information technologies such as EDI and the Advance Cargo Information System (ACIS);

Paragraph 14.42 (g)

For the existing text, substitute:

(g) Encouraging a better understanding of the utilization of the latest techniques and developments in multimodal transport and physical dis-

tribution management and disseminating such knowledge to countries in need thereof;

Paragraph 14.42 (h)

Insert a new subparagraph *(h)* reading:

(h) Elaborating reference documents setting up the basic concepts of multimodal transport and major issues to be dealt with in a market-oriented implementation process in order to achieve a stronger awareness of these issues;

Renumber former paragraphs 14.42 *(h)* to *(j)* as paragraphs 14.42 *(i)* to *(k)*.

Add a paragraph 14.42 *(l)* reading:

(l) Increasing knowledge of laws and regulations related to maritime and multimodal standards for the purpose, *inter alia*, of adapting them to modern shipping, ports and multimodal transport market conditions, with a view to promoting the competitiveness and economic development of countries, in particular developing countries; and providing assistance to Governments, on request, in the formulation of national legislation, including advice on the application of international conventions adopted within UNCTAD.

Paragraph 14.43

For the existing text, substitute:

14.43. In the light of the above-outlined framework, the UNCTAD secretariat will:

(a) Undertake research and prepare comparative analyses of national shipping policies and their impact on fleet development and the quality of shipping services, and of structural, technological and institutional changes in trade and transport and their impact on ports and multimodal transport operations;

(b) Study strategies and options aimed at fostering competitive shipping services, as well as possibilities of economic cooperation among developing countries in the fields of shipping, ports and multimodal transport, and monitor developments in transport technology;

(c) Enhance the exchange and dissemination of relevant information in these fields and increase the knowledge of laws and regulations responding to the requirements of modern international transport conditions;

(d) Assist Governments in implementing the main findings of the above-mentioned studies and reports through the development and support of technical cooperation projects.

Delete paragraphs 14.44 to 14.46 and renumber subsequent paragraphs accordingly.

Subprogramme 6: Insurance

Paragraph 14.53 (a) (v)

In the first line, *after* authorities *insert* in developing countries

Paragraph 14.53 (d) (ii)

In the second line, *after* supervisory capacity *insert* in developing countries

*Programme 15.   Least developed, land-locked and island developing
countries, and special programmes*

In the last but three lines of paragraph 15.3, *delete* and

In the last line of paragraph 15.3, *after* Action *add* and that the UNCTAD Intergovernmental Group on the Least Developed Countries will hold a mid-term review in 1995

Programme 23.   Transnational corporations

Paragraph 23.13

In the third sentence, *for* While the original objectives of the code are still valid, *read* On the other hand,

Paragraph 23.15 (a),

In the first line, *for* through the adoption of a code of conduct *read* through the adoption of appropriate international arrangements

Programme 28.   International drug control

Delete the designation of high priority for sub-programme 2 recommended by the Committee for Programme and Coordination in paragraph 155 (c) of its report.

Programme 38.   Public information

In new paragraphs 38.3, 38.7 (h) and 38.17 (m), *insert* international *before* peace and security

General Assembly resolution 47/214

23 December 1992   Meeting 94   Adopted without vote

Approved by Fifth Committee (A/47/828) without vote, 19 December (meeting 50); draft by Chairman (A/C.5/47/L.18) based on informal consultations; agenda item 105.
Meeting numbers. GA 47th session: 5th Committee 13-17, 19, 20, 24, 28-31, 36, 50; plenary 94.

Joint Inspection Unit

In its report presented to the General Assembly's 1992 session, the Joint Inspection Unit (JIU) gave an overview of its activities between 1 July 1991 and 30 June 1992.[14] The work programme of the Unit for 1992 was transmitted to the General Assembly by a March note of the Secretary-General.[15] The work programme covered a series of studies on management, programme and policy issues, as well as development cooperation.

In June,[16] the Secretary-General reported on measures taken by participating organizations to enhance consideration of JIU reports by the respective governing bodies, in accordance with a 1990 General Assembly request.[17] The United Nations Secretariat and all United Nations subsidiary bodies and programmes that had their own governing bodies had designated focal points for their relations with JIU. The mechanism for ensuring a thorough consideration of JIU reports by the governing bodies of the participating organizations consisted of the following components: the governing bodies annually considered an agenda item on JIU or, in case of some specialized agencies, a similar sub-item within an agenda item on relations with the United Nations and other international organizations; in most cases, prior to submission to a governing body, JIU reports were reviewed by relevant subordinate committees; JIU reports were presented to a governing body in conjunction with the comments of an executive head

and ACC; and a responsible Inspector introduced the report and was present during its consideration.

In August,[18] the Secretary-General submitted a report on implementation of recommendations contained in two JIU reports—a 1989 report on a review of the use of equipment provided to technical cooperation projects in developing countries[19] and a report submitted in 1990 evaluating the programme on joint studies on Latin American economic integration.[20]

In its report,[14] JIU summarized its recent reports on the growing overlap between the remuneration of staff at the lower Professional levels and a broad range of General Service staff (see PART SIX, Chapter II); an assessment of the technical cooperation programme of the International Civil Aviation Organization and the annual deficits of its Administrative and Operational Services Cost Fund; advantages and disadvantages of the post classification system; United Nations system cooperation with multilateral financial institutions; the second report on the cost benefits of office accommodation for the Economic Commission for Latin America and the Caribbean (ECLAC) at Port-of-Spain, Trinidad and Tobago (see PART TWO, Chapter VI); a revised round-table process used to assist the LDCs in raising additional funds for technical cooperation; and a note on the contingency margin of the United Nations Industrial Development Organization budget.

JIU also made observations concerning its recommendations and the short- and long-term impact of its work. During the period covered by the report, the Unit continued to maintain contact with the various management and financial entities having similar responsibilities, in particular, ACABQ; ICSC; CPC; the Inter-Agency Meeting on Language Arrangements, Documentation and Publications; and the management, evaluation and audit services of secretariats.

JIU's relations with ACABQ were advanced through joint discussions (Geneva, 8 and 11 June), convened in accordance with a 1991 Assembly decision[21] by which the Advisory Committee was requested to examine the functioning of the Unit and to submit in 1992 recommendations for enhancing its productivity and performance.

Accordingly, ACABQ in December submitted its observations and recommendations on JIU.[22] After discussions with the Inspectors and participating agencies, the Advisory Committee concluded that the problem of enhancing JIU's productivity could be addressed without modifying the basic principles underlying the Unit's existence and functioning. Noting that closer adherence to JIU's statute would result in better functioning, ACABQ grouped its recommendations along the basic areas covered by the articles of the statute, namely: selection and appointment of Inspectors; functions and responsibilities of Inspectors; mode of operation; conditions of service; and administrative, budgetary and financial arrangements.

GENERAL ASSEMBLY ACTION

The General Assembly, on 22 December 1992, adopted without vote **resolution 47/201**, on the recommendation of the Fifth Committee.

Joint Inspection Unit

The General Assembly,

Recalling its decision 46/446 of 20 December 1991 and its relevant resolutions, in particular resolution 45/237 of 21 December 1990,

Having considered the reports of the Joint Inspection Unit on its activities during the periods 1 July 1990 to 30 June 1991 and 1 July 1991 to 30 June 1992, the work programmes of the Unit for the same periods and the reports of the Secretary-General on the implementation of the recommendations of the Unit,

Having considered also the report of the Advisory Committee on Administrative and Budgetary Questions on the Joint Inspection Unit, submitted in accordance with decision 46/446,

1. *Takes note* of the reports of the Joint Inspection Unit for the periods 1990-1991 and 1991-1992, its work programmes for the same periods and the reports of the Secretary-General on the implementation of the recommendations of the Unit;

2. *Takes note also* of the report of the Advisory Committee on Administrative and Budgetary Questions on the Joint Inspection Unit;

3. *Invites* the Joint Inspection Unit, in drawing up its work programme for 1993 and its preliminary work programme for 1994-1995, to make proposals to reflect the recommendations of the Advisory Committee on Administrative and Budgetary Questions and to submit the work programme to the General Assembly as soon as possible;

4. *Decides*, in accordance with its resolution 46/220 of 20 December 1991, to resume consideration of the reports of the Joint Inspection Unit and that of the Advisory Committee on Administrative and Budgetary Questions at its forty-eighth session.

General Assembly resolution 47/201

22 December 1992   Meeting 93   Adopted without vote

Approved by Fifth Committee (A/47/818) without objection, 19 December (meeting 50); draft by Ghana (A/C.5/47/L.10); agenda item 109.

Meeting numbers. GA 47th session: 5th Committee 37, 42, 43, 50; plenary 93.

On 23 December, by **decision 47/460**, the Assembly took note of a 1990 report of JIU on extra-budgetary resources of the United Nations.[23]

REFERENCES

[1]GA res. 45/253, 21 Dec. 1990. [2]YUN 1991, p. 887, GA res. 46/189, 20 Dec. 1991. [3]A/47/6. [4]A/C.5/47/46 & Add.1,2. [5]A/47/16 & Add.1,2. [6]A/47/32 & Add.1. [7]A/45/617. [8]A/47/159. [9]A/47/159/Add.1. [10]YUN 1991, p. 886. [11]A/47/116. [12]A/45/16. [13]A/46/16. [14]A/47/34. [15]A/47/119. [16]A/47/276. [17]GA res. 45/237, 21 Dec. 1990. [18]A/47/373. [19]E/1989/7. [20]A/45/77-E/1990/10. [21]YUN 1991, p. 890, GA dec. 46/446, 20 Dec. 1991. [22]A/47/755.[23]

Administrative and budgetary coordination

In November[1] and December 1992,[2] ACC submitted the first two in a series of statistical reports on the budgetary and financial situation of organizations of the United Nations system, as requested by ACABQ.

On 30 September,[3] the Secretary-General submitted a report on accounting standards for common application in the United Nations system, for which the General Assembly had requested the hiring of a consultant in 1991.[4] He stated that ACC's Consultative Committee on Administrative Questions (Financial and Budgetary) Working Party on Accounting Standards, open to accounting specialists from all United Nations organizations, at its first (4-6 December 1991) and second (25-27 May 1992) meetings, had drafted and developed further a large number of core provisions for inclusion in the common standards. The Consultative Committee, at its September 1992 session, requested the Panel of External Auditors to examine the draft at its 1992 session in November so that its comments could be taken into consideration at the Working Party's third meeting, scheduled for 1 to 3 December.

On 22 December, the General Assembly, by **decision 47/449**, took note of the two statistical reports and the Secretary-General's report. It requested the Secretary-General, as Chairman of ACC, to continue submitting the Committee's statistical reports on a biennial basis. It also requested him and the executive heads of United Nations programmes and organizations to complete the draft of common accounting standards, with the Secretary-General reporting on the matter in 1993.

By **decision 47/455** of 23 December 1992, the General Assembly approved the biennial work programme of the Fifth Committee for 1993-1994.

REFERENCES

[1]A/47/593 & Corr.1. [2]A/47/746. [3]A/47/443. [4]YUN 1991, p. 890, GA dec. 46/445, 20 Dec. 1991.

Chapter II

United Nations officials

In 1992, the Secretary-General began restructuring the Secretariat, with the creation of new departments, redeployment of posts and a redistribution of resources among various sections of the programme budget for the remaining part of the biennium 1992-1993.

Efforts continued to improve staff distribution with regard to nationality and the status of women in the Secretariat. The General Assembly, by resolution 47/93, urged the Secretary-General to overcome obstacles to improving the status of women in the Secretariat, to accord greater priority to the recruitment and promotion of women, and to increase the number of women from developing countries.

The International Civil Service Commission made several recommendations to the Assembly, including changes in the methodology for conducting salary surveys of the General Service and related categories. The Assembly acted on those recommendations in resolution 47/216.

The number of fatalities among United Nations personnel, including those engaged in peace-keeping operations, was on the rise, a fact which the Assembly strongly deplored. It requested continued efforts to ensure respect for the privileges and immunities of United Nations officials (47/28).

Restructuring of the Secretariat

The Secretary-General, in a February 1992 note,[1] announced a number of changes related to the restructuring of the United Nations Secretariat, with effect from 1 March.[2] He stated that the changes in the departments and top echelon of the Secretariat were intended to consolidate and streamline the Organization's activities into well-defined functional categories.

The main aspects of the restructuring included the establishment of a Department of Political Affairs headed by two Under-Secretaries-General (USGs) with clearly defined geographical responsibilities and functions. The new Department would incorporate the activities of the former Office for Political and General Assembly Affairs and Secretariat Services; Office for Research and the Collection of Information; Department of Political and Security Council Affairs; Department for

Special Political Questions, Regional Cooperation, Decolonization and Trusteeship; and the Department of Disarmament Affairs.

Also established was a Department of Peace-Keeping Operations, incorporating the former Office of Special Political Affairs. The Department would be headed by a USG and reinforced by an Assistant Secretary-General (ASG).

Various units were incorporated in the Department of Economic and Social Development, headed by a USG. Those units were the Office of the Director-General for Development and International Economic Cooperation; Department of International Economic and Social Affairs; Department of Technical Cooperation for Development; Centre for Science and Technology for Development; and the United Nations Centre on Transnational Corporations.

The Department of Humanitarian Affairs was established under a USG. It would draw on the resources of the Office of the United Nations Disaster Relief Coordinator and would consolidate existing offices dealing with complex emergencies. The secretariat of the International Decade for Natural Disaster Reduction would become an integral part of the Department. The USG would work closely with United Nations organizations and entities, as well as with the International Committee of the Red Cross, the League of Red Cross and Red Crescent Societies, the International Organization for Migration and relevant non-governmental organizations. At the country level, the USG would maintain close contact with, and provide leadership to, United Nations resident coordinators on matters relating to humanitarian assistance. He would also assume responsibility for all emergency relief activities currently being undertaken by the Secretariat.

The Department of Administration and Management would include the former Department of Conference Services. The Office of Legal Affairs would incorporate the Office of Ocean Affairs and the Law of the Sea.

The Secretary-General stated that those changes represented the first phase of restructuring. The regrouping and consolidation of departments entailed a reduction in the number of high-level posts in the Secretariat.

In a December note,[3] the Secretary-General announced the establishment of three new departments, headed by USGs, as part of the next phase of restructuring. They were: the Department for Policy Coordination and Sustainable Development, which would provide support for central coordinating and policy-making functions vested in the Economic and Social Council and its subsidiary bodies, including the new Commission on Sustainable Development; the Department for Economic and Social Information and Policy Analysis, which would focus on the compilation and dissemination of economic and social statistics, the analysis of long-term trends, the elaboration of projections, and the assessment of economic and social policies; and the Department for Development Support and Management Services, which would serve as a focal point for providing management services for technical cooperation and act as an executing agency in selected cross-sectoral areas.

He also announced his intention to eliminate four ASG posts in the Department of Administration and Management and to propose the redeployment of a number of high-level posts from administrative to substantive areas.

GENERAL ASSEMBLY ACTION

On 2 March, at its resumed forty-sixth session, the General Assembly adopted without vote **resolution 46/232**.

Revitalization of the United Nations Secretariat

The General Assembly,

Reaffirming the purposes and principles of the Charter of the United Nations,

Mindful of the vital role of the United Nations in the maintenance of international peace and security and in the promotion of international cooperation and development,

Recalling its resolutions on the reform and revitalization of the United Nations,

1. _Approves_ the launching by the Secretary-General of a further process of restructuring and streamlining of the Secretariat, in the exercise of his responsibilities as Chief Administrative Officer of the United Nations, in the framework of the Charter of the United Nations and the relevant resolutions of the General Assembly;

2. _Takes note_ of positive actions undertaken by the Secretary-General as set out in his document of 21 February 1992 as a first phase of that process;

3. _Decides_ that the restructuring of the Secretariat is a vital part of the reform and revitalization of the United Nations and should be aimed at:

(_a_) Enhancing the capacity of the United Nations in the maintenance of international peace and security and in the area of economic and social development, which is of vital concern to the membership as a whole and in particular to the developing countries;

(_b_) Ensuring effective implementation of the objectives of the Charter and of the mandates entrusted by the policy-making organs, taking into account the medium-term plan for the period 1992-1997 adopted by the General Assembly;

(_c_) Ensuring transparency in recruitment procedures and practices, including those for senior posts;

(_d_) Ensuring that the highest standards of efficiency, competence and integrity are the paramount considerations in the recruitment and performance of international civil servants;

(_e_) Ensuring a more effective application of the principle that the recruitment of staff should be on as wide a geographical basis as possible and that, as a general rule, no national of a Member State should succeed a national of that State in a senior post and there should be no monopoly on senior posts by nationals of any State or group of States;

(_f_) Improving the representation and the status of women in the Secretariat, in particular its higher echelons;

(_g_) Ensuring the exclusively international character of the staff as set out in the relevant Articles of the Charter and the Staff Rules and Regulations of the United Nations;

(_h_) Rationalizing the structure of the Secretariat by dividing its major activities along functional lines in a way that would group them into a limited number of consolidated departments to enable more efficient supervision and control by the Secretary-General and to avoid duplication and enhance the coordination and streamlining of the activities in each sector;

4. _Calls upon_ Member States to provide the conditions for the effective functioning of the Organization, in particular through the fulfilment of their financial obligations as set out in the Charter;

5. _Requests_ the Secretary-General to submit to the General Assembly at the earliest opportunity a report on the programmatic impact as well as the financial implications of organizational changes involved in his initiatives and the progress attained in accordance with the present resolution.

General Assembly resolution 46/232

2 March 1992   Meeting 82   Adopted without vote

Draft by President (A/46/L.67); agenda item 105.

In **resolution 47/212** of 23 December, the Assembly stressed that the restructuring of the Secretariat should be in conformity with the objectives and guidelines set out in its March resolution and in close consultation with Member States and relevant intergovernmental bodies. It reaffirmed its role with regard to the Secretariat's structure, including the creation, suppression and redeployment of posts financed from the United Nations regular budget, and requested the Secretary-General to provide the Assembly with comprehensive information on all decisions involving established and temporary high-level posts. It decided to consider in 1993 the proposed reduction of high-level posts contained in revised estimates of the programme budget for the biennium 1992-1993, and requested the Secretary-General to submit his proposals for the number and distribution of high-level posts in the Secretariat for the remaining part of the biennium 1992-1993.

REFERENCES

(1)A/46/882. (2)ST/SGB/248. (3)A/47/753.

International Civil Service Commission

The International Civil Service Commission (ICSC) held two sessions in 1992, its thirty-fifth from 10 to 27 March in New York and its thirty-sixth from 13 July to 7 August in London. The Commission examined issues that derived from General Assembly decisions and resolutions as well as from its own statute. A summary of its deliberations, recommendations and decisions was provided in its eighteenth annual report,[1] on which the General Assembly acted in **resolution 47/216**. The total financial implications of the Commission's 1992 decisions and recommendations relevant to the United Nations common system were approximately $10 million for 1993.

GENERAL ASSEMBLY ACTION

On 23 December, the General Assembly, on the recommendation of the Fifth (Administrative and Budgetary) Committee, adopted without vote **resolution 47/216**.

United Nations common system: report of the International Civil Service Commission
The General Assembly,
Having considered the eighteenth annual report of the International Civil Service Commission and other related reports,
Reaffirming its commitment to a single unified United Nations common system of conditions of service,

I
A. *Role and functioning of the International Civil Service Commission*
Reaffirming that, under article 9 of its statute, the International Civil Service Commission, in the exercise of its functions, shall be guided by the principle set out in the agreements between the United Nations and the other organizations, which aims at the development of a single unified international civil service through the application of common personnel standards, methods and arrangements,
Recalling its request to the Commission to assess the impact on the United Nations common system of resolution No. 1024 of the Administrative Council of the International Telecommunication Union with respect to the payment of the special post allowance,
Recalling also its request to the Commission to propose measures to be undertaken by all organizations of the common system to enforce and enhance respect for, and adherence to, the common system of salaries, allowances and conditions of service,
Noting with regret that a further payment of the special post allowance was made to the staff of the International Telecommunication Union in spite of the views expressed by the General Assembly in section II of its resolution 46/191 of 20 December 1991 against such action,
1. *Reaffirms* the central role of the General Assembly with regard to the elaboration of the conditions of service for the United Nations common system as a whole and that of the International Civil Service Commission as the independent technical body responsible

to the Assembly for the regulation and coordination of the conditions of service of the common system;
2. *Notes with satisfaction* the efforts made by the Commission to enhance its contacts with the governing bodies, executive heads and staff of organizations of the common system in order to strengthen the cohesiveness and unity of the system and, in this context, to emphasize its advantages;
3. *Endorses* the views of the Commission concerning the impact on the common system of resolution No. 1024 of the Administrative Council of the International Telecommunication Union with respect to the payment of the special post allowance;
4. *Urges* the governing bodies and the executive heads of all organizations to ensure that the Commission is invited in its own right to be represented at meetings where proposals pertaining to salaries, allowances, benefits and other conditions of employment are to be discussed;
5. *Notes* that the Commission will study in 1993 the issues of accelerated language increments and working hours;

B. *Staff participation in the work of the Commission*
Reaffirming that article 28, paragraph 2, of the statute of the International Civil Service Commission, elaborated in its rules of procedure, provides staff representatives with the right, collectively or separately, to present facts and views on any matter within the competence of the Commission and that staff representatives may attend meetings and may address the Commission on matters on its agenda,
Recalling section II, paragraph 2, of its resolution 45/241 of 21 December 1990, by which it expressed satisfaction with the establishment of a more active dialogue between the Commission and representatives of the organizations and staff, and section I, paragraph 5, of resolution 46/191 A, by which it took note with appreciation of the improvements that have taken place in the functioning of the Commission,
Regrets the suspension of the participation of the staff bodies in the work of the International Civil Service Commission and urges the resumption of the dialogue between the Commission and the staff bodies, which is of fundamental importance for the achievement of the goals of the common system;

C. *Biennialization of the programme of work of the Fifth Committee*
Welcoming the adaptations that the International Civil Service Commission is making to its work programme in the light of the biennialization of the work of the Fifth Committee,
Taking note of the conclusions reached in respect of the current work schedule of the Commission as contained in paragraph 29 of its report,
Concurs with the arrangements proposed for dealing exceptionally with the base/floor salary scale on an annual basis and other urgent salary matters on a timely basis as set forth in paragraph 28 of the report of the International Civil Service Commission;

II
Conditions of service of the
Professional and higher categories

A. *Margin considerations*
Recalling its decision that the Noblemaire principle should continue to serve as the basis for the determina-

tion of conditions of service of the United Nations common system for staff in the Professional and higher categories,

Recalling also that it had endorsed the methodological approach, as outlined in paragraph 173 *(d)* of volume II of the fifteenth annual report of the International Civil Service Commission, for the calculation of the net remuneration margin,

Recalling further section IV, paragraph 1, of resolution 46/191 A, by which it decided, without prejudice to previous decisions on the averaging of the margin around the mid-point over a five-year period, that any post adjustment increase in New York which might become due until 1994 might be implemented to the extent that it was compatible with the upper limit of the margin and that, in this regard, it endorsed the procedure proposed for the management of the post adjustment system within the current margin range as contained in paragraph 109 *(b)* of volume I of the seventeenth annual report of the Commission,

1. *Takes note* of the conclusions of the International Civil Service Commission as contained in chapter IV, Section A, of its eighteenth annual report regarding the evolution of the margin and its management over the five-year period 1990-1994;

2. *Takes note also* of the study by the Commission of the methodology for determining the cost-of-living differential between New York and Washington, D.C., in the context of net remuneration margin calculations;

3. *Requests* the Commission to take into account the views expressed by Member States on the completion of the above mentioned study and to submit a report on the application of the methodology to the General Assembly;

B. *Base/floor salary scale*

Recalling section I.H, paragraph 1, of its resolution 44/198 of 21 December 1989, by which it approved the establishment of a floor net salary scale by reference to the corresponding base net salary levels of officials in comparable positions serving at the base city of the comparator civil service,

Approves, with effect from 1 March 1993, the revised scale of gross and net salaries for staff in the Professional and higher categories contained in annex I to the present resolution and the consequential amendment to the Staff Regulations of the United Nations as reflected in annex II to the present resolution, and takes note of the views expressed by Member States in this regard, and its linkage with the mobility and hardship matrix referred to in section V of the present resolution;

C. *Comparator*

Recalling section VI, paragraph 1, of its resolution 46/191 A, by which it endorsed the conclusions of the International Civil Service Commission in respect of a methodology for conducting checks to determine the highest-paid civil service, as contained in annex V to volume I of its seventeenth annual report,

Recalling also that, by section VI, paragraph 2, of its resolution 46/191 A, it invited the Commission to analyse the potential consequences of the Federal Employees Pay Comparability Act of 1990 on the pay levels of the current comparator, the United States federal civil service, providing in the analysis full details of all the special pay systems which have been introduced by the com-

parator civil service, and to report thereon to the General Assembly at its forty-ninth session,

Noting that the comparisons with other major international organizations outside the United Nations common system carried out by the Commission in response to a request from the Administrative Committee on Coordination had indicated that the remuneration levels at those organizations were higher than those of the common system,

Reiterates its request to the International Civil Service Commission to complete phase I of its study leading to the identification of the highest-paying civil service, and to report thereon to the General Assembly at its forty-ninth session, and in this context invites the Commission also to study all aspects of the application of the Noblemaire principle with a view to ensuring the competitiveness of the United Nations common system;

D. *Rental subsidy scheme*

Recalling its request to the International Civil Service Commission to examine experience gained with the functioning of the current rental subsidy scheme at headquarters duty stations as contained in section III, paragraph 5, of its resolution 45/241,

1. *Concurs* with the conclusions of the International Civil Service Commission as contained in paragraph 130 of its report;

2. *Requests* the Commission to ensure that the modalities for implementation of the rental subsidy scheme are conveyed to the organizations of the United Nations common system;

E. *Special occupational rates*

Mindful of its resolutions 46/191 A and B of 20 December 1991 and 31 July 1992, by which it acknowledged that the United Nations common system and the International Civil Service Commission should be responsive to the special needs and concerns of the participating organizations, while emphasizing that such needs and concerns should be addressed within the common system,

Taking note of the views of the Commission concerning the introduction of special occupational rates within the common system, as set out under paragraphs 172 to 175 and 177 of its report and of the views expressed by Member States in the Fifth Committee,

Stressing that special occupational rates should be introduced only in exceptional cases of proven recruitment and retention difficulties, as determined by the Commission in close cooperation with the organizations concerned,

1. *Endorses* in principle, the approach outlined by the International Civil Service Commission in paragraph 177 of its report for the introduction of the special occupational rates in the United Nations common system, and requests the Commission to submit recommendations for the consideration of the General Assembly at its forty-eighth session;

2. *Emphasizes* that special occupational rates should be subject to the provisions of paragraph 174 of the report of the Commission and should be specific to individual posts where there are demonstrable recruitment and retention problems and should be time limited;

3. *Requests* the Commission to consider the feasibility and effects of including the special occupational rates in the calculation of the margin and to report thereon to the General Assembly at its forty-ninth session;

F. *Dependency allowances*

Recalling section I.G, paragraph 4, of its resolution 44/198, by which it requested the International Civil Service Commission to reconsider the methodology for the determination of dependency allowances in the light of the tax practices of the comparator,

Noting the Commission's review of this matter, as contained in paragraphs 178 to 193 of its report,

1. *Approves*, with effect from 1 January 1993, an increase of 21 per cent in the children's allowance and an increase of 50 per cent in the secondary dependant's allowance, and the recommendations of the International Civil Service Commission in respect of eligibility criteria and the maintenance of the local-currency entitlement system;

2. *Notes* that the Commission will review the level of dependency allowances every two years, in order to ensure, *inter alia*, that all relevant changes in tax and social legislation have been taken into consideration;

G. *Conditions of service of assistant secretaries-general and under-secretaries-general and structure of the salary scale*

Recalling section V of its resolution 45/241, by which it requested the International Civil Service Commission to reconsider, in a comprehensive manner, the remuneration of staff of the organizations of the United Nations common system at the assistant secretary-general, under-secretary-general and equivalent levels,

Recalling also the recommendations of the Commission as contained in paragraph 173 of volume I of its seventeenth annual report and repeated in paragraph 207 of its eighteenth annual report,

Recalling further section VII of its resolution 46/191 A, by which it deferred a decision on the recommendations of the Commission until its forty-seventh session,

Recalling that, in section IX, paragraph 3, of its resolution 46/191 A, it requested the Commission to include in its work programme a review of the differences between United Nations and United States net remuneration at individual grade levels and to report to it at the earliest opportunity,

Mindful of the proposals of the Secretary-General in respect of the conditions of service of under-secretaries-general and assistant secretaries-general and the reports of the Secretary-General on representation allowances for this category of staff in the United Nations,

Taking note of the views expressed on this question by the Advisory Committee on Administrative and Budgetary Questions,

Taking into account the comments of Member States in the Fifth Committee,

Taking note also of the recommendation of the Administrative Committee on Coordination to the Commission concerning the levels of remuneration of staff at the D-1 and D-2 levels and the conclusions of the Commission as contained in paragraph 176 of its report,

1. *Requests* the International Civil Service Commission, in close cooperation with the organizations, to develop appropriate guidelines for the administration of the revised housing arrangements for eligible officials outlined in paragraph 173 *(c)* of its seventeenth annual report, taking into account the views expressed by Member States;

2. *Decides* to revert to the consideration of the conditions of service, including the question of representation allowances, of assistant secretaries-general and under-secretaries-general and equivalent levels at the earliest possible opportunity;

3. *Invites* the Commission to continue to keep under review the structure of the salary scale at all levels of the Professional and higher categories, taking into account, *inter alia*, the overall level of the margin as established by the General Assembly and the imbalance between the margin levels for different Professional grade levels, and to report thereon to the Assembly at its forty-ninth session;

III
General Service salary survey methodology

Recalling section XIII, paragraph 4, of its resolution 45/241 and section X of its resolution 46/191 A, by which, *inter alia*, it requested the International Civil Service Commission to report on its review of the methodology for the conduct of salary surveys of the General Service and related categories at headquarters duty stations,

Taking note of the conclusions of the Commission on the matter as contained in chapter V of its report,

Recalling also its request to the Secretary-General, in section XIII, paragraph 3, of its resolution 45/241, to submit to it at its forty-seventh session a report on procedures whereby the Secretary-General and other executive heads could take measures regarding salary scales of the General Service category at variance with recommendations of the Commission only after consultations with appropriate intergovernmental bodies and the Commission,

1. *Endorses* the reaffirmation by the International Civil Service Commission of the Flemming principle as enunciated at its fifteenth session as the basis for the determination of conditions of service of the General Service and related categories;

2. *Takes note* of the decisions of the Commission in respect of the refinements and modifications to the methodology as contained in paragraph 231 of its report, and the procedures for their introduction as outlined in paragraph 232 of its report, on the understanding that such modifications will be taken into account beginning with the salary survey being carried out in Paris;

3. *Calls upon* all organizations to ensure that interim adjustments to salaries are not resumed until the recommendations from the Commission based on the comprehensive General Service salary survey are acted upon by the organizations;

4. *Regrets* that it has not so far received the report on procedures to be taken in the event that the implementation of a General Service salary survey is at variance with the recommendations of the Commission, welcomes the intention of the Secretary-General to implement resolution 45/241, and requests the Secretary-General to provide the report no later than the forty-ninth session of the Assembly;

IV
Education grant

Recalling section III.B, paragraph 2, of its resolution 43/226 of 21 December 1988, by which it approved as an interim measure the recommendations of the International Civil Service Commission for the management of the reimbursement of expenses under the education grant on the basis of different currency areas,

1. *Endorses* the revised methodology for the determination of the education grant as contained in annex VII to the report of the International Civil Service Commission;

2. *Approves* increases in the maximum reimbursement levels in five currency areas, as recommended by the Commission in paragraph 252 of its report;

3. *Requests* the Commission to report to the General Assembly at its fifty-first session on the operation of the education grant on the basis of the revised methodology, taking into account the views of Member States on this matter;

V
Mobility and hardship scheme
Recalling section I.E of its resolution 44/198, by which it introduced a mobility and hardship allowance with effect from 1 July 1990 and requested the International Civil Service Commission to report to the General Assembly at its forty-seventh session on the operation of the allowance and the assignment grant,

Recalling also section V, paragraph 1, of its resolution 46/191 A, by which it requested the Commission to include in its report on the operation of the mobility and hardship allowance a cost-benefit analysis of the operation of that allowance as well as an assessment of the personnel management benefits,

1. *Takes note* of the conclusions of the International Civil Service Commission in respect of the operation of the mobility and hardship scheme as contained in chapter VII of its report;

2. *Concurs* that the existing parameters of the mobility and hardship scheme be maintained;

3. *Takes note also* of the intention of the Commission to review the operation of the scheme after more experience has been gained in its operation;

4. *Requests* the Commission to include the following elements in its forthcoming review:

(*a*) The adjustment procedure which links the mobility and hardship matrix to revisions of the base/floor salary;

(*b*) The percentage levels attributed to the matrix also in comparison with those applicable in the comparator civil service and in particular those pertaining to the H and A categories;

(*c*) An analysis of the extent to which each of the component parts that make up the matrix meets the needs of the organizations;

(*d*) A precise quantification of the cost savings; and to report thereon to the General Assembly at its fifty-first session;

VI
Status of women in the United Nations system
Recalling section XI of its resolution 45/241, by which it invited the International Civil Service Commission, working together with the organizations of the United Nations common system and with the staff representatives, to examine specific and practical steps to translate into action earlier recommendations and requests relating to the status of women in the United Nations system,

Appreciating the work done by the Commission's Working Group on the Status of Women in the United Nations system, as outlined in chapter VIII of the report of the Commission,

1. *Urges* the organizations of the United Nations common system to introduce a coherent plan for improving the status of women in each organization in the course of 1993 with full respect for their basic instruments and taking into account the recommendations of the International Civil Service Commission, and in this context to give attention not only to the representation, promotion and career progression of women but also to work/family-related issues, spouse employment and the creation of an organizational climate conducive to the equal participation of men and women in the work of the organizations;

2. *Requests* the Commission to continue to report on a regular basis both on the extent of implementation of previous recommendations in this area and on new initiatives proposed or introduced by the organizations to enhance the status of women in the common system;

VII
Personnel policy considerations
Recalling its requests in section XII, paragraph 1, of its resolution 45/241 and in section VIII of resolution 46/191 A that, as a matter of priority, the International Civil Service Commission resume active consideration of the substantive areas covered under articles 13 and 14 of its statute and, notably, review merit systems and performance appraisal in the common system,

Noting, inter alia, the inclusion of studies on performance appraisal and the recognition of merit in the work programme of the Commission for 1993 and 1994,

Urges the International Civil Service Commission, as a complement to studies being undertaken in the remuneration area, to give equal attention in its work programme to measures designed to promote sound personnel management in the international public service, including recruitment forecasting, human resources planning, performance management and staff development and training.

[See following page for Annex I.]

ANNEX II
Amendments to the Staff Regulations of the United Nations

Regulation 3.3
Replace the second table in paragraph (*b*) (i) by the following table:

Total assessable payments (US dollars)	Staff assessment rates used in conjuction with gross base salaries	
	Staff member with a dependent spouse or a dependent child	Staff member with neither a dependent spouse nor a dependent child
First $15,000 per year	13.0	17.1
Next $5,000 per year	31.0	34.2
Next $5,000 per year	34.0	38.4
Next $5,000 per year	37.0	41.7
Next $5,000 per year	39.0	43.7
Next $10,000 per year	41.0	45.8
Next $10,000 per year	43.0	48.1
Next $10,000 per year	45.0	50.2
Next $15,000 per year	46.0	50.8
Next $20,000 per year	47.0	52.2
Remaining assessable payments	48.0	56.4

ANNEX I
SALARY SCALE FOR THE PROFESSIONAL AND HIGHER CATEGORIES
showing annual gross salaries and net equivalents after application of staff assessment*
(US dollars)
(Effective 1 March 1993)

Level	Steps														
	I	II	III	IV	V	VI	VII	VIII	IX	X	XI	XII	XIII	XIV	XV
Under-Secretary-General															
USG Gross	148,296														
Net D	86,914														
Net S	78,122														
Assistant Secretary-General															
ASG Gross	134,454														
Net D	79,716														
Net S	72,087														
Director															
D-2 Gross	109,444	111,946	114,448	116,948	119,450	121,952									
Net D	66,711	68,012	69,313	70,613	71,914	73,215									
Net S	61,183	62,273	63,364	64,454	65,545	66,636									
Principal Officer															
D-1 Gross	96,315	98,417	100,529	102,667	104,810	106,952	109,094	111,237	113,377						
Net D	59,847	60,961	62,075	63,187	64,301	65,415	66,529	67,643	68,756						
Net S	55,304	56,308	57,296	58,228	59,162	60,096	61,030	61,964	62,897						
Senior Officer															
P-5 Gross	84,528	86,430	88,332	90,234	92,136	94,036	95,938	97,840	99,740	101,673	103,612	105,548	107,487		
Net D	53,600	54,608	55,616	56,624	57,632	58,639	59,647	60,655	61,662	62,670	63,678	64,685	65,693		
Net S	49,669	50,579	51,488	52,397	53,306	54,214	55,123	56,033	56,941	57,794	58,640	59,484	60,329		
First Officer															
P-4 Gross	69,020	70,843	72,661	74,480	76,302	78,120	79,941	81,794	83,649	85,502	87,355	89,213	91,066	92,921	94,775
Net D	45,271	46,255	47,237	48,219	49,203	50,185	51,168	52,151	53,134	54,116	55,098	56,083	57,065	58,048	59,031
Net S	42,103	43,000	43,894	44,789	45,686	46,580	47,476	48,363	49,249	50,135	51,021	51,909	52,795	53,681	54,567
Second Officer															
P-3 Gross	55,753	57,431	59,111	60,787	62,467	64,145	65,839	67,550	69,259	70,970	72,680	74,389	76,098	77,807	79,519
Net D	38,014	38,937	39,861	40,783	41,707	42,630	43,553	44,477	45,400	46,324	47,247	48,170	49,093	50,016	50,940
Net S	35,520	36,356	37,192	38,027	38,864	39,699	40,538	41,380	42,220	43,062	43,904	44,744	45,585	46,426	47,268
Associate Officer															
P-2 Gross	44,351	45,779	47,226	48,675	50,123	51,572	53,021	54,468	55,953	57,453	58,953	60,456			
Net D	31,517	32,344	33,169	33,995	34,820	35,646	36,472	37,297	38,124	38,949	39,774	40,601			
Net S	29,603	30,359	31,110	31,862	32,614	33,366	34,118	34,869	35,620	36,367	37,114	37,862			
Assistant Officer															
P-1 Gross	33,277	34,580	35,910	37,256	38,600	39,944	41,292	42,636	43,980	45,337					
Net D	24,949	25,744	26,537	27,331	28,124	28,917	29,712	30,505	31,298	32,092					
Net S	23,565	24,299	25,028	25,758	26,486	27,215	27,945	28,674	29,402	30,130					

D = Rate applicable to staff members with a dependent spouse or child.
S = Rate applicable to staff members with no dependent spouse or child.
*This scale represents the result of a consolidation of 6.9 multiplier points of post adjustment into net base salary. There will be consequential adjustments in the post adjustment indices and multipliers at all duty stations effective 1 March 1993. Thereafter, changes in post adjustment classifications will be effected on the basis of the movements of the newly consolidated post adjustment indices.

General Assembly resolution 47/216

23 December 1992   Meeting 94   Adopted without vote

Approved by Fifth Committee (A/47/831) without vote, 19 December (meeting 50); draft by Committee Chairman (A/C.5/47/L.7), following informal consultations; agenda item 113.
Meeting numbers; GA 47th session: 5th Committee 23, 27, 29, 31, 35, 50; plenary 94.

REFERENCE
[1]A/47/30 & Corr.1.

Personnel management

In 1991,[1] the General Assembly had decided to retain on the agenda of its resumed forty-sixth session in 1992 the item on personnel questions. On 14 September 1992, by **decision 46/477**, the Assembly included the item in the draft agenda of its forty-seventh session.

On 23 December, by **decision 47/457 A**, the Assembly deferred consideration of the composition of the Secretariat and other personnel questions to its resumed forty-seventh session.

In February, the Secretary-General suspended external recruitment for posts in the Professional category until further notice; exceptions to the suspension were to be limited to an absolute minimum.

In an August report, the Secretary-General stated[2] that competitive examinations had been conducted to fill entry-level posts at the P-3 level, in response to a 1990 General Assembly request.[3] The first P-3 level examinations were conducted on an experimental basis in four Member States in 1991: Czechoslovakia, Hungary, Italy and Japan. Ninety-two candidates took the examinations; two received offers of appointment in the administration area and two in the economics area. In 1992, a second round of P-3 level examinations was held in Finland, Germany, Japan, Russian Federation and the United States. Eighty-three candidates took the examinations in economics, public information, statistics, social affairs and demography. They were subsequently to undergo oral examination and interviews.

In September,[4] the Secretary-General submitted a report on 13 posts formerly attached to the subprogramme on trade among countries having different economic and social systems of the United Nations Conference on Trade and Development. He proposed that the posts be extended temporarily through 1993. A final decision on the posts would be taken in the context of a review of the programme budget proposals for 1994-1995.

In October,[5] the Secretary-General transmitted for consideration by the Fifth Committee the views of the staff unions and associations of the United Nations Secretariat, covering security and independence of the international civil service, staff management relations and the restructuring of the Secretariat, career development and training, status of women in the Secretariat, and administration of justice.

Staff composition

In October 1992,[6] the Secretary-General presented his annual report to the General Assembly on the composition of the United Nations Secretariat—by nationality, gender and type of appointment—for the period 1 July 1991 to 30 June 1992. The total number of staff of the United Nations Secretariat as at 30 June 1992 was 13,883, of whom 9,084 were paid from the regular budget and 4,779 from extrabudgetary sources.

Staff in the Professional category and above numbered 3,945; staff in the General Service and related categories numbered 9,017; and project personnel numbered 921.

As at 30 June, there were 29 unrepresented Member States, including 19 newly admitted States and 21 underrepresented Member States. Changes in the representation of Member States resulted not only from the appointments and separations from service of staff, but also from the adjustments of the desirable ranges resulting from an increase or decrease in the number of posts subject to geographical distribution, changes in the number of Member States, variations in the assessed contribution of individual States or in their population, as well as from changes in the status of some staff members.

During the reporting period, 50 women were appointed to posts subject to geographical distribution, representing 39.1 per cent of the 128 appointments made, compared with 57, or 33.5 per cent, during the previous period. As at 30 June, the number of women in posts subject to geographical distribution was 797, or 30.6 per cent.

On 23 December, by **decision 47/457 A**, the General Assembly, on the recommendation of the Fifth Committee, deferred consideration of subitems *(a)*, composition of the Secretariat, and *(c)*, other personnel questions, of agenda item 112 (Personnel questions) to its resumed session, on the understanding that a working paper prepared by the Committee's Vice-Chairman would constitute a basis for further negotiations on the issue.

Status of women in the Secretariat

During 1992, the Secretary-General submitted two reports on improving the status of women in the United Nations Secretariat.

In a March report to the Commission on the Status of Women,[7] submitted in response to a 1991 General Assembly resolution,[8] he provided a statistical update and an evaluation of the status of women in the Secretariat, described institutional arrangements for implementing the action programme for improving that status and summarized the recommendations of the Steering Committee for the Improvement of the Status of Women in the Secretariat.

In higher-level posts (D-1 level and above), women numbered 32, or 8.6 per cent of the total of 372 staff members at those levels as at the end of June 1991. By 31 December 1991, the number of women in posts D-1 and above rose to 35, or 9.3 per cent of the total of 375 posts at those levels. The goal for the number of women occupying higher-level posts was 25 per cent by 1995.

During 1991, the number of women promoted was 45, or 33.6 per cent, as compared with 89 men.

The Steering Committee recommended, with regard to assignment and promotion, that in departments with less than 35 per cent women overall and in those with less than 25 per cent women at levels P-5 and above, qualified women candidates be given priority for promotion and recruitment. To improve the career prospects for secretaries, the Committee recommended that the Secretary-General either promote staff members to the next grade or restructure the occupation, or combine both approaches. Responding to a recommendation of the Committee, the Office of Human Resources Management (OHRM) was developing procedures to deal with sexual harassment in the Secretariat; three working groups, chaired by the Director of Staff Management, were drafting documents on those procedures.

In an October report on the status of women in the Secretariat,[9] presented in response to a 1991 Assembly request,[8] the Secretary-General described the situation as at 30 June 1992, developments between July 1991 and June 1992, and obstacles to the advancement of women in the Secretariat. An action programme developed to cover the period ending in 1995 was described. The strategy for the programme included the coordination of recruitment, placement and promotion in relation to the filling of vacancies for levels P-3 to D-1, the setting of departmental targets for the following three years and a career development system.

ICSC, in its 1992 report,[10] endorsed the recommendations of its Working Group on the Status of Women in the United Nations system. The recommendations concerned overall strategy/policy, targets for representation, career progression, the General Service category, the Professional category and above, work/family-related issues, child-care, spouse employment, leave arrangements, organizational climate, and monitoring and accountability.

ECONOMIC AND SOCIAL COUNCIL ACTION

On 30 July, the Economic and Social Council, on the recommendation of its Social Committee, adopted without vote **resolution 1992/14**.

Improvement of the status of women in the Secretariat

The Economic and Social Council,

Recalling Articles 8 and 101 of the Charter of the United Nations, and recalling also the Nairobi Forward-looking Strategies for the Advancement of Women, in particular paragraphs 79, 306, 315, 356 and 358, in which importance is attached to the appointment of women in the Secretariat at senior decision-making and managerial levels,

Recalling also the relevant resolutions and decisions of the General Assembly, the Economic and Social Council and other bodies that have been adopted since Assembly resolution 2715(XXV) of 15 December 1970, in which the question of the employment of women in the Professional category was first addressed,

Noting with concern that the goal of a 30 per cent participation rate of women in posts subject to geographical distribution by the end of 1990 had not been achieved by the end of 1991,

Bearing in mind the goal of achieving by 1995 an overall participation rate of women of 35 per cent of all posts subject to geographical distribution, set by the General Assembly in resolutions 45/125 of 14 December 1990 and 45/239 C of 21 December 1990, and a participation rate of women in posts at the D-1 level and above, set by the Assembly in resolution 45/239 C, of 25 per cent of the total within the overall participation rate of 35 per cent of posts subject to geographical distribution,

Also bearing in mind that a visible commitment of the Secretary-General is essential to the achievement of the targets set by the General Assembly of an overall participation rate of 35 per cent, and, at the D-1 level and above, of 25 per cent by 1995,

Welcoming the progress report of the Secretary-General concerning the comprehensive study of the barriers to the advancement of women and elements of the action programme for the advancement of women in the Secretariat for the period 1991-1995,

1. *Strongly urges* the Secretary-General to increase the number of women in posts subject to geographical distribution, particularly in senior policy-level and decision-making posts, in order to achieve an overall participation rate of 35 per cent by 1995, and a goal of 25 per cent of the total within the overall participation rate of 35 per cent in posts at the D-1 level and above, taking into consideration the need to increase the representation of women from countries with a low representation or no representation of women, especially the developing countries;

2. *Urges* the Secretary-General to appoint women to senior policy-level and decision-making posts in his next appointments, and to achieve the targets set for the Secretariat by 1995;

3. *Also urges* the Secretary-General to ensure that achievement of these goals will not be impeded by the temporary suspension of regular recruitment imposed in the context of the current restructuring;

4. *Calls upon* all Member States to contribute fully to increasing the participation rate of women in the Professional category and above throughout the United Nations system by, *inter alia*, nominating more women candidates, especially for senior policy-level and decision-making posts, encouraging women to apply for vacant posts and creating national rosters of women candidates to be shared with the Secretariat and the executive bodies of the specialized agencies and related organizations, taking into consideration the need to increase the representation of women from countries with a low representation or no representation of women, especially the developing countries;

5. *Recommends* that all organizations of the United Nations system accord priority to increasing the numbers of women in Professional and senior policy-level and decision-making posts to achieve the same targets set for the Secretariat by 1995;

6. *Welcomes* the decision of the Secretary-General to regularize the post of Focal Point in the Office of the Assistant Secretary-General for Human Resources Management of the Secretariat, as well as the establishment of an additional General Service post to assist the official serving as the Focal Point;

7. *Requests* the Secretary-General to ensure that the findings of the comprehensive study of the barriers to the advancement of women and a full action programme for the advancement of women in the Secretariat for the period 1991-1995 are submitted to the General Assembly at its forty-seventh session;

8. *Also requests* the Secretary-General to ensure that his annual report on the status of women in the Secretariat includes strategies and modalities for implementing the action programme and the relevant mandates adopted by the General Assembly and the Economic and Social Council, and to submit the report to the Commission on the Status of Women at its thirty-

seventh session and to the General Assembly at its forty-seventh session, as well as to those bodies that have administrative, budgetary and personnel responsibilities for the improvement of the status of women in the Secretariat.

Economic and Social resolution 1992/14

30 July 1992   Meeting 40   Adopted without vote

Approved by Social Committee (E/1992/105) without vote, 21 July (meeting 14); draft by Commission on Women (E/1992/24); agenda item 18.

GENERAL ASSEMBLY ACTION

On 16 December, the General Assembly, on the recommendation of the Third (Social, Humanitarian and Cultural) Committee, adopted without vote **resolution 47/93**.

Improvement of the status of women in the Secretariat

The General Assembly,

Recalling Articles 1 and 101 of the Charter of the United Nations,

Recalling also Article 8 of the Charter, which provides that the United Nations shall place no restrictions on the eligibility of men and women to participate in any capacity and under conditions of equality in its principal and subsidiary organs,

Recalling further the relevant paragraphs of the Nairobi Forward-looking Strategies for the Advancement of Women, especially paragraphs 79, 315, 356 and 358,

Recalling its resolution 2715(XXV) of 15 December 1970, in which it first addressed the question of the employment of women in the Professional category, and all relevant resolutions that have continued to focus on this area since then,

Noting with concern that the goal of a 30 per cent participation rate of women in posts subject to geographical distribution by the end of 1990 was not achieved,

Recalling the goal set in its resolutions 45/125 of 14 December 1990, 45/239 C of 21 December 1990 and 46/100 of 16 December 1991 of a 35 per cent overall participation rate of women in posts subject to geographical distribution by 1995,

Recalling also the goal set in resolution 45/239 C of a 25 per cent participation rate of women in posts at the D-1 level and above by 1995,

Deeply concerned that there are now no women at the under-secretary-general level and only one at the assistant secretary-general level in the Secretariat,

Bearing in mind that a visible commitment by the Secretary-General, especially during the continuing restructuring phase, is essential to the achievement of the targets set by the General Assembly,

Welcoming the evaluation and analysis of the main obstacles to the improvement of the status of women in the Secretariat as contained in the report of the Secretary-General,

Welcoming also the action programme outlined in the report of the Secretary-General, designed to overcome the obstacles to the improvement of the status of women in the Secretariat,

1.   *Urges* the Secretary-General to implement the action programme outlined in his report, designed to overcome the obstacles to the improvement of the status of women in the Secretariat, noting that his visible commitment is essential to the achievement of the targets set by the General Assembly;

2.   *Also urges* the Secretary-General, in accordance with the Charter of the United Nations, to accord greater priority to the recruitment and promotion of women in posts subject to geographical distribution, particularly in senior policy-level and decision-making posts, in order to achieve the goals set in resolutions 45/125, 45/239 C and 46/100 of an overall participation rate of 35 per cent by 1995 and 25 per cent in posts at the D-1 level and above by 1995;

3.   *Further urges* the Secretary-General to use the opportunity offered by the United Nations reorganization process and the establishment of the Commission on Sustainable Development to promote more women into senior-level positions;

4.   *Urges* the Secretary-General to increase the number of women employed in the Secretariat from developing countries and other countries that have a low representation of women;

5.   *Strongly encourages* Member States to support the efforts of the United Nations and the specialized agencies to increase the percentage of women in Professional posts, especially at the D-1 level and above, by identifying and submitting more women candidates, encouraging women to apply for vacant posts and creating national rosters of women candidates to be shared with the Secretariat, specialized agencies and regional commissions;

6.   *Requests* the Secretary-General, within existing resources, to ensure that adequate machinery, with the authority of enforcement and the responsibility of accountability, including a senior-level official devoted to the implementation of the action programme and the recommendations in the report on the improvement of the status of women in the Secretariat, is maintained and strengthened during the course of the programme for the period 1991-1995;

7.   *Also requests* the Secretary-General to ensure that a progress report is given to the Commission on the Status of Women at its thirty-seventh session, and to the General Assembly at its forty-eighth session.

General Assembly resolution 47/93

16 December 1992   Meeting 89   Adopted without vote

Approved by Third Committee (A/47/670) without vote, 5 November (meeting 30); 82-nation draft (A/C.3/47/L.21); agenda item 94.

Sponsors: Afghanistan, Albania, Angola, Australia, Austria, Bahamas, Bangladesh, Barbados, Belarus, Belize, Benin, Botswana, Burkina Faso, Burundi, Cameroon, Canada, Cape Verde, Central African Republic, Chad, Chile, Costa Rica, Côte d'Ivoire, Cyprus, Czechoslovakia, Denmark, Djibouti, Dominican Republic, Ecuador, El Salvador, Estonia, Finland, Greece, Grenada, Guinea, Guinea-Bissau, Haiti, Honduras, Iceland, Indonesia, Ireland, Italy, Jamaica, Kenya, Latvia, Lesotho, Libyan Arab Jamahiriya, Liechtenstein, Lithuania, Malawi, Malaysia, Mali, Mexico, Mongolia, Morocco, Myanmar, Nepal, Netherlands, New Zealand, Nicaragua, Niger, Nigeria, Norway, Pakistan, Panama, Peru, Philippines, Poland, Republic of Korea, Romania, Saint Kitts and Nevis, Samoa, Senegal, Singapore, Sweden, Thailand, Togo, Turkey, Ukraine, United States, Uruguay, Venezuela, Zimbabwe.

Meeting numbers: GA 47th session: 3rd Committee 19-26, 28, 30; plenary 89.

Staffing tables and workload standards

In August 1992,[11] the Secretary-General submitted a note on procedures and norms for the creation, suppression, reclassification, conversion and redeployment of posts, in response to a 1991 General Assembly request.[12] By its 1991 resolution, the Assembly had endorsed the recommendation of the Committee for Programme and Coordination (CPC) that simpler, more transparent and more rational procedures and norms be developed.

The Secretary-General's note summarized current procedures for changes in the Organization's staffing table and suggested improvements. Proposals for such changes were normally formulated in the context of preparing the biennial programme budget; they reflected the outcome of consultations between departments and Secretariat officials responsible for reviewing budget proposals.

Decisions about creating new posts and redeploying or reclassifying existing posts were based on recommendations by the Compensation and Classification Service of OHRM. Posts were classified on the basis of standards promulgated by ICSC and approved by the Assembly.

According to the report, the application of those procedures had produced uneven results. Changes in the staffing table should be based on agreed workload standards, full and comparable information on the workload for each department and effective application of the classification process. However, workload analysis had only been applied to language services in the Office of Conference Services. There were constraints to extending the analysis to other areas, such as the amount of research required, complex methodology and the need for a data collection system. However, the Secretariat would continue to study methodology, formulation and application of workload standards, which should be viewed as a long-term process.

In December, the Secretary-General presented a report[13] on the elaboration of unified workload standards for conference-servicing staff in the United Nations common system (see next chapter).

Post classification system

The Secretary-General transmitted to the General Assembly in April 1992 a Joint Inspection Unit (JIU) report on advantages and disadvantages of the post classification system.[14] The report, which had been requested by the United Nations Educational, Scientific and Cultural Organization, gave the background to the post classification system, described its implementation and concluded that it was a useful management tool.

The report recommended that the capacity of personnel services be reinforced; that training courses for classifiers and programme managers be organized regularly; that automated processes for classification be considered; that the filling of posts, except for certain key positions, be left to programme managers; that the staff at large be

informed about the concept of classification; that the reclassification of posts be done by well-trained specialists; that an appeals mechanism be set up; that a study be carried out on attracting qualified staff at P-1 and P-2 entry level; that a more dynamic approach to attracting qualified staff be pursued; and that the possibility of introducing personal promotion and linked grades be studied.

Linked grades would permit staff, when being recruited, to have a notion for a possible career, that is, one entry grade in which the incumbent would stay for a probationary period, and then the formal grade of the post, as classified, given on certain conditions.

The Secretary-General submitted his comments on the JIU report in June[15] and the comments of member organizations of the Administrative Committee on Coordination (ACC) in December.[16]

Career development

Responding to a 1990 General Assembly request,[17] the Secretary-General submitted an August 1992 report on career development at the United Nations.[18] The report explained the concept and scope of a career scheme; highlighted the integrated nature of the scheme's components; emphasized the role of career development in creating an atmosphere conducive to high staff morale; and outlined an implementation plan.

The report stated that the Secretariat had adopted a long-term approach to establishing a career development system, which reflected the intention of the Secretary-General to adjust, phase by phase, the structure and *modus operandi* of the Secretariat to the new era the world was entering. The Secretariat had embarked on a multi-year implementation plan, including the conducting of pilot projects. A progress report would be submitted to the Assembly in 1994.

Training

The Secretary-General, in response to a 1990 General Assembly request,[17] submitted an October 1992 report[19] covering training programmes in the Secretariat, evaluation of training, strengthening inter-agency cooperation with regard to training efforts, and budgetary arrangements.

The report stated that the Secretariat had concentrated most of its training resources in the following priority areas: developing a comprehensive management development plan; offering mission-oriented training for specific peace-keeping and peacemaking operations; upgrading professional knowledge and skills in substantive areas; improving the staff's capability to use technological innovations; providing orientation programmes for newly recruited or promoted staff members; and enhancing the linguistic and communication capabilities of United Nations staff. Efforts to strengthen inter-agency cooperation were made through the Subcommittee on Training of the Consultative Committee on Administrative Questions of ACC; areas in which training efforts could be shared included crisis management, security questions and human rights issues.

While a centralized budgetary process made it possible for all offices to formulate a biennial training plan, it also revealed a serious gap between training requirements and resource availability. Currently, the United Nations devoted only 0.29 per cent of its staff costs to occupational and management training, while comparable entities within the system spent as much as 2 per cent.

The report concluded that training was increasingly important to ensure that staff in political areas developed skills in preventive diplomacy and that staff in the economic and social sectors had strong, substantive, up-to-date expertise. Training should also ensure that a cadre of well-trained, capable staff was developed to provide effective and efficient administration and management.

Staff rules and regulations

In November 1992,[20] the Secretary-General resubmitted an amendment to the Staff Regulations of the United Nations concerning an education grant for staff members serving outside their recognized home country. The amendment, which had been submitted first in 1991[21] without the General Assembly's taking action on it, was intended to delete any references to actual amounts, so as to obviate the need to present an amendment to the Staff Regulations whenever there was a revision to those amounts.

Also in November 1992, the Secretary-General submitted his annual report[22] containing the texts of provisional amendments to the Staff Rules. The changes, applicable to all staff except technical cooperation project personnel and staff specifically engaged for conferences and other short-term services, concerned the application of the Secretary-General's discretion to evaluate the eligibility for permanent appointments of staff members on fixed-term appointments and to waive, totally or partially, the requirement of probationary service; the deletion from a number of rules of references to regular appointments, which were no longer used in the United Nations system; temporary and permanent appointments; the incorporation of agree-

ments reached between organizations of the common system and at staff-management coordination meetings; and staff specifically recruited for service with technical cooperation projects.

In December, the Secretary-General proposed an amendment to paragraph 5 of annex I to the Regulations concerning personnel specifically engaged for short-term missions.[23] He also proposed an amendment to regulation 3.4(a) concerning dependent children's and secondary dependants' allowances.[24]

Staff representation

Cost of staff representation activities

In response to a 1991 General Assembly request,[25] the Secretary-General submitted a November 1992 report[26] reviewing the nature and level of regular budget funding of Staff Union activities. The report identified the mandates for those activities and described the administrative facilities provided to staff representatives to enable them to carry out their functions.

The report noted that while the Staff Rules provided for both staff-management and staff representation activities, only staff-management activities were budgeted, in the form of travel to the Staff-Management Coordinating Committee. In the 1990-1991 biennium, the amount appropriated for travel totalled $232,900; the resources appropriated for 1992-1993 amounted to $204,500. To decrease expenditures for that item, measures were taken to limit the venues of those meetings to New York and Geneva.

On 23 December 1992, by **decision 47/460 A**, the Assembly deferred consideration of the Secretary-General's report until 1993.

Level of secretaries of intergovernmental organs

Responding to a 1991 General Assembly resolution,[27] the Secretariat submitted an October 1992 note[28] on the level of secretaries of intergovernmental policy-making organs, describing the types of committee secretaries, their functions and levels. The latter were influenced by a variety of factors, including scope of responsibilities, placement of posts within the organizational structure of the Secretariat, and mandates of the committees. The note stated that, subject to any decision the Assembly might take in 1992, the situation would be reviewed in the context of the preparation of the 1994-1995 programme budget.

On 23 December, by **resolution 47/219 A, section VII**, the Assembly took note of the Secretariat's note and asked the Secretary-General to review the situation in the context of preparing the programme budget for 1994-1995.

Privileges and immunities

In response to a 1990 General Assembly request,[(29)] the Secretary-General, on behalf of and with the approval of ACC, submitted an October 1992 report[(30)] on respect for the privileges and immunities of officials of the United Nations and the specialized agencies and related organizations.

During the period 1 July 1991 to 30 June 1992, which was marked by complex developments requiring peace-keeping and humanitarian missions, often in areas of military confrontation, there were 11 fatalities among staff members of different organizations. The number of new cases of arrest and detention of officials was less than in the previous reporting period due to a decline in the numbers of arrested staff members of the United Nations Relief and Works Agency for Palestine Refugees in the Near East (UNRWA). Of 66 UNRWA staff members arrested during the reporting period, 49 were subsequently released without charge or trial.

The report also discussed restrictions on official and private travel of officials of the United Nations by host countries. On 23 December 1991, the Secretary-General had received from the United States a note verbale stating that United Nations staff members who were nationals of Viet Nam and their dependents could enjoy unrestricted travel in the United States; however, they would still be required to notify the Department of State of any intended non-official travel, specifically recreational travel.

On 24 April 1992, the United States informed the Secretary-General that, effective immediately, staff members from Belarus and Ukraine would no longer be required to request permission for private recreational travel. Similarly, there would be no restrictions for travel in the United States for staff members from Armenia, Azerbaijan, Estonia, Kazakhstan, Kyrgyzstan, Latvia, Lithuania, Republic of Moldova, Tajikistan, Turkmenistan and Uzbekistan. On 7 August, the United States said that staff members from the Russian Federation would no longer be required to request such approval; they would have to file a streamlined travel notification form with the United States Mission.

An inter-agency meeting (Geneva, 12-15 May) discussed approaches and procedures to ensure the best possible security arrangements for United Nations staff. The meeting stressed the need to apply a uniform security regime to all United Nations system staff and recommended that, in addition to existing measures, the United Nations Security

Coordinator should determine in which countries it was desirable to appoint area coordinators.

On 25 November, on the recommendation of the Fifth Committee, the General Assembly adopted without vote **resolution 47/28**.

Respect for the privileges and immunities of officials of the United Nations and the specialized agencies and related organizations

The General Assembly,

Recalling that, under Article 105 of the Charter of the United Nations, all officials of the Organization shall enjoy in the territory of each of its Member States such privileges and immunities as are necessary for the independent exercise of their functions in connection with the Organization,

Also recalling that, under Article 100 of the Charter, each Member of the United Nations undertakes to respect the exclusively international character of the responsibilities of the Secretary-General and the staff and not to seek to influence them in the discharge of their responsibilities,

Further recalling the Convention on the Privileges and Immunities of the United Nations, the Convention on the Privileges and Immunities of the Specialized Agencies, the Agreement on the Privileges and Immunities of the International Atomic Energy Agency and the United Nations Development Programme Standard Basic Assistance Agreements,

Stressing that respect for the privileges and immunities of officials of the United Nations and the specialized agencies is becoming even more imperative owing to the growing number of assignments entrusted to the organizations of the United Nations system by Member States,

Recalling its resolution 76(I) of 7 December 1946, in which it approved the granting of the privileges and immunities referred to in articles V and VII of the Convention on the Privileges and Immunities of the United Nations to all members of the staff of the United Nations, with the exception of those who are recruited locally and are assigned to hourly rates,

Also recalling its resolution 43/173 of 9 December 1988, to which is annexed the Body of Principles for the Protection of All Persons under Any Form of Detention or Imprisonment, including the principle that all persons under arrest or detention shall be provided whenever necessary with medical care and treatment,

Reiterating the obligation of all officials of the Organization in the conduct of their duties to observe fully both the laws and regulations of Member States and their duties and responsibilities to the Organization,

Mindful of the responsibilities of the Secretary-General to safeguard the functional immunity of all United Nations officials,

Mindful also of the importance in this respect of the provision by Member States of adequate and immediate information concerning the arrest and detention of staff members and, more particularly, their granting of access to them,

Bearing in mind the considerations of the Secretary-General to guarantee appropriate standards of justice and due process to United Nations officials,

1. *Takes note with grave concern* of the report submitted by the Secretary-General on behalf of the members of the Administrative Committee on Coordination, and of the developments indicated therein;

2. *Strongly deplores* the unprecedented and still increasing number of fatalities which have occurred among United Nations personnel, including those engaged in peace-keeping operations;

3. *Deplores* the continuing existence of cases where the functioning, safety and well-being of officials have been placed in jeopardy;

4. *Condemns and deplores* the disregard for Article 105 of the Charter of the United Nations displayed by some Member States;

5. *Reaffirms* in its entirety its resolution 45/240 of 21 December 1990;

6. *Reiterates* the importance of providing access of United Nations medical teams to detained staff, and requests Member States to facilitate medical care deemed necessary by such teams;

7. *Requests* the Secretary-General to take all necessary measures to ensure the safety of United Nations personnel, as well as those engaged in peace-keeping and humanitarian operations;

8. *Reminds* host countries of their responsibility for the safety of peace-keeping and all United Nations personnel on their territory;

9. *Strongly affirms* that disregard for the privileges and immunities of officials has always constituted one of the main obstacles to the implementation of the missions and programmes assigned to the organizations of the United Nations system by Member States;

10. *Requests* the Secretary-General and Member States to continue their efforts to ensure respect for the privileges and immunities of officials, and requests the Secretary-General to continue to submit, on behalf of the Administrative Committee on Coordination, reports thereon to the General Assembly.

General Assembly resolution 47/28

25 November 1992   Meeting 72   Adopted without vote

Approved by Fifth Committee (A/47/708) without vote, 18 November (meeting 28); draft submitted by Chairman (A/C.5/47/L.2) following informal consultations; agenda item 112 (*b*).
Meeting numbers. GA 47th session: 5th Committee 13, 15-17, 19-22, 25, 28; plenary 72.

In related action, the Assembly adopted **resolution 47/72** on the protection of United Nations peace-keeping personnel.

REFERENCES

(1)YUN 1991, p. 904, GA dec. 46/468, 20 Dec. 1991. (2)A/C.5/47/5. (3)GA res. 45/239, 21 Dec. 1990. (4)A/C.5/47/7. (5)A/C.5/47/20 & Corr.1. (6)A/47/416. (7)E/CN.6/1992/11. (8)YUN 1991, p. 893, GA res. 46/100, 16 Dec. 1991. (9)A/47/508. (10)A/47/30 & Corr.1. (11)A/C.5/47/4. (12)YUN 1991, p. 894, GA res. 46/185 B, sect. II, 20 Dec. 1991. (13)A/C.5/47/67. (14)A/47/168. (15)A/47/168/Add.1. (16)A/47/168/Add.2. (17)GA res. 45/239 A, 21 Dec. 1991. (18)A/C.5/47/6. (19)A/C.5/47/9. (20)A/C.5/47/42. (21)YUN 1991, p. 896. (22)A/C.5/47/43. (23)A/C.5/47/42/Add.1. (24)A/C.5/47/42/Add.2. (25)YUN 1991, p. 896, GA res. 46/185 B, sect. X, 20 Dec. 1991. (26)A/C.5/47/59. (27)YUN 1991, p. 870, GA res. 46/145 C, 20 Dec. 1991. (28)A/C.5/47/28. (29)GA res. 45/240, 21 Dec. 1990. (30)A/C.5/47/14.

Staff costs

In its 1992 report,[1] ICSC continued to advise the General Assembly on staff salaries and allowances and made recommendations regarding pensionable remuneration and pension entitlements. The Commission continued to monitor the net remuneration margin between officials in comparable positions of the United States Federal Civil Service and the United Nations system. The application of the margin calculation methodology endorsed by the Assembly in 1989[2] resulted in a margin for the 1992 calendar year of 117.6, while the average margin for 1990-1992 was 117.8. The Commission reported to the Assembly that no action was necessary at the current stage in the management of the margin over the five-year period 1990-1994.

ICSC recommended that the current base/floor salary scale be increased by 6.9 per cent through consolidation of post adjustment classes, with effect from 1 March 1993, and, as an exception to the Assembly's 1991 resolution on the biennialization of the work of the Fifth Committee,[3] that the item be considered on an annual basis. The Commission noted that the financial implication of the salary scale increase for the 10 months of 1993 would be $3,564,000.

Having reviewed the methodology for measuring the cost-of-living differential between New York and Washington, D.C., used in net remuneration margin calculations, the Commission concluded that it was deficient and recommended an alternative methodology.

The Commission also reviewed the operation of the rent subsidy scheme at headquarters duty stations for the period 1983-1991. It recommended maintaining the scheme in its present form. In other action, the Commission invited the Assembly to endorse the introduction of special occupational rates in the common system as a means of addressing recruitment and retention problems for some specialized technical fields. On the basis of a review of the methodology for determining children's and secondary dependants' allowances for the Professional and higher categories, it recommended that, with effect from 1 January 1993, the children's allowance be increased by 21 per cent and the secondary dependants' allowance by 50 per cent, and that the level of dependency allowances be reviewed every two years. The Commission noted that the financial implications of those recommendations amounted to $3.1 million per annum for the common system.

The Secretary-General submitted, in accordance with a 1980 General Assembly resolution,[4] comments on the ICSC report by the Federation of International Civil Servants' Associations[5] and by the Coordinating Committee for Independent Staff Unions and Associations of the United Nations System.[6]

The General Assembly acted on ICSC's recommendations in **resolution 47/216**.

Emoluments of top-echelon officials

Honoraria

In 1991,[7] the Secretary-General had proposed a 25 per cent increase in the rates of honoraria payable to members of organs and subsidiary organs of the United Nations in cases that the General Assembly had already authorized on an exceptional basis, namely, the International Law Commission, the International Narcotics Control Board, the United Nations Administrative Tribunal, the Human Rights Committee, the Committee on the Elimination of Discrimination against Women and the Committee on the Rights of the Child. The Assembly had deferred consideration of the issue.[8]

In November 1992, the Secretary-General, in response to a 1991 Assembly request,[9] submitted a comprehensive study of the question of honoraria payable to members of organs and subsidiary organs of the United Nations.[10] He reviewed the level of honoraria paid and proposed that the new rates, if approved by the Assembly, would also apply to the Committee on the Protection of the Rights of All Migrant Workers and Members of Their Families once the 1990 Convention on the Protection of the Rights of all Migrant Workers and Members of Their Families[11] entered into force. He also reviewed the workload of the committees and commissions concerned and indicated that, should the Assembly approve the proposed 25 per cent increase, additional appropriations of $86,600 would be required in 1993. Also, should the Assembly decide to defray the costs of airfare for spouses of overseas members of the Advisory Committee on Administrative and Budgetary Questions (ACABQ) effective 1 January 1993, an additional appropriation of $46,000 would be required in the 1992-1993 programme budget.

ACABQ, in December 1992,[12] did not object to the Secretary-General's proposal but noted that there was little evidence to suggest that questions such as whether there might be other bodies within the system eligible for payment of honoraria, or the implications of introducing uniformity into the conditions for the payment of honoraria, had been dealt with.

GENERAL ASSEMBLY ACTION

On 23 December, the General Assembly, on the recommendation of the Fifth Committee, adopted without vote **resolution 47/219 A, section XV**.

Comprehensive study of the question of honoraria payable to members of organs and subsidiary organs of the United Nations
[*The General Assembly. . .*]

1. *Decides* to postpone to its resumed forty-seventh session the review of the whole question of honoraria;

2. *Authorizes* the Secretary-General, pending the results of the review, to take appropriate measures on an exceptional basis and with the concurrence of the Advisory Committee on Administrative and Budgetary Questions with regard to paragraph 55 of his report, within the overall framework of the current pertinent resolutions and decisions, recommends that he reflect the measures he takes in the final performance report on the programme budget for the biennium 1992-1993, and decides to revert to this matter again at its forty-eighth session;

. . .

General Assembly resolution 47/219 A, section XV
23 December 1992   Meeting 94   Adopted without vote

Approved by Fifth Committee (A/47/835/Add.1) without vote, 20 December (meeting 51); agenda item 104.
Meeting numbers. GA 47th session: 5th Committee 43, 51; plenary 94.

Representation allowance

In 1991, the General Assembly had deferred consideration of proposals by the Secretary-General for an increase in representation allowance for USGs and ASGs.[13]

In an October 1992 report,[14] the Secretary-General updated his previous proposal and included an overview of the origins and policies with respect to official hospitality. The report stated that, since 1991, the net remuneration of USGs and ASGs had increased in dollar terms owing to changes in the post adjustment classification of different duty stations. The new period for the staggered increases in the level of the allowance would be 1993-1996 instead of 1992-1996, and the amounts would be established at 60 per cent of one month's net remuneration in 1993, 70 per cent in 1994, 80 per cent in 1995 and 100 per cent starting in 1996.

The Secretary-General also considered hospitality allotments for official functions, the current rates for which had been in effect since January 1984. They were being reviewed by the Office of Programme Planning, Budget and Finance.

ACABQ[15] recommended that consideration of the representation allowance be deferred until the restructuring process of the Secretariat was completed.

On 23 December, by **resolution 47/219 A, section XI**, the Assembly took note of the Secretary-General's 1991 reports, recommended that consideration of the question be deferred and that a further review be undertaken in the light of future decisions on restructuring of the Secretariat.

Remuneration of JIU members

In two 1991 reports,[16] the Secretary-General had proposed that the new level of remuneration for inspectors of JIU be established at the top step of the Director (D-2) level of the salary scale for staff in the Professional and higher categories, with a consequent amendment of article 14 of the Statute of JIU, which would require approval by the General Assembly and acceptance by the organizations of the United Nations system. Should the Assembly approve the proposal, with effect from 1 January 1992, the financial implications related to the difference in net remuneration between step IV and step VI of the D-2 level would amount to $51,600 a year for 1992 and 1993.

On 23 December 1992, by **decision 47/460 A**, the General Assembly deferred consideration of the reports.

Salaries and allowances

Staff assessment

By **decision 47/459** of 23 December 1992, taken on the recommendation of the Fifth Committee, the General Assembly requested the Secretary-General to review all aspects of the question of staff assessment as they affected the budgets of United Nations organizations and programmes, taking into account the views of ICSC and the experience of other organizations of the system, as well as established principles and practices, including the principle of ensuring equality of pay and benefits for all staff members, and to present proposals, through ICSC, in 1993.

Special post allowance

In 1991,[17] the General Assembly had deplored the decision of the International Telecommunication Union (ITU), in applying its staff regulation 3.8 *(b)*, to grant a special post allowance to headquarters staff of the Professional and higher categories, contrary to the norms of the common system. The Assembly had requested ICSC to assess the impact of that decision on the common system and to propose measures to enhance respect for and adherence to the common system of salaries, allowances and conditions of service by all governing bodies. Also in 1991,[18] the Assembly had requested ICSC and the United Nations Joint Staff Pension Board to examine the basis for ITU's decision and its implications for the common system.

ICSC, at its 1992 session,[1] reiterated its regret concerning ITU's unilateral action, which should not constitute a precedent. It urged organizations, when confronting problems pertaining to issues falling under the Commission's mandate, to consult with it in a timely manner. ICSC decided to undertake a study of organizations' staff rules and regulations and recommended that the Assembly make it mandatory for all organizations to invite the Commission to be represented at meetings where proposals pertaining to salaries, allowances, benefits and other conditions of employment were being discussed.

The Secretary-General, in a July note,[19] transmitted correspondence from ITU including a 1992 resolution of its Administrative Council accepting the view of ICSC and the Assembly that its action with regard to special post allowances was incompatible with the common system. The Council resolved that any further application of staff regulation 3.8 *(b)* must be in strict conformity with the wording of that regulation and fully in line with the common system, and that a consultative group be established to study staff issues. It recommend to the Council specific actions, in conformity with the common system.

GENERAL ASSEMBLY ACTION

On 31 July, at its resumed forty-sixth session, the General Assembly, on the recommendation of the Fifth Committee, adopted without vote **resolution 46/191 B**.

United Nations common system

The General Assembly,

Recalling its resolutions 45/268 of 28 June 1991 and, in particular, 46/191 A of 20 December 1991,

Emphasizing the importance of, and benefits derived from, maintaining a coherent and unified United Nations common system,

Acknowledging that the United Nations common system should be responsive to the special needs and concerns of the participating organizations, while emphasizing that such needs and concerns should be addressed within the common system,

Emphasizing the obligation of all organizations of the United Nations common system to consult and cooperate fully with the International Civil Service Commission and the United Nations Joint Staff Pension Board on matters relating to conditions of service and pensions,

Noting that the Administrative Council of the International Telecommunication Union recognized, in its resolution No. 1024 of 8 July 1992, that the action taken by the Union in regard to a special post allowance was incompatible with the common system,

Considering that the adoption of Administrative Council resolution No. 1024 does not prohibit further payment of the special post allowance,

Recognizing that such payment is in contravention of staff regulation 3.8 *(b)* of the International Telecommunication Union as well as the accepted norms of United Nations common system,

Noting with deep concern that prior consultation with the International Civil Service Commission by the International Telecommunication Union as called for in General Assembly resolution 46/191 A, section II, paragraph 7, had not taken place,

1. *Strongly deplores* the decision of the Secretary-General of the International Telecommunication Union to make payment of the special post allowance to headquarters Professional staff in the circumstances described in paragraphs 33 to 35 of the report of the International Civil Service Commission;

2. *Determines* that such payment is in contravention of General Assembly resolution 46/191 A;

3. *Regrets* that the Administrative Council of the International Telecommunication Union did not explicitly exclude further payment of the special post allowance;

4. *Reiterates* its endorsement of the view of the International Civil Service Commission that the action taken by the International Telecommunication Union in regard to special post allowances is incompatible with the common system;

5. *Calls upon* executive heads and governing bodies of the United Nations common system to respect fully the decisions taken by the General Assembly, on the recommendations of the International Civil Service Commission and the United Nations Joint Staff Pension Board, concerning the conditions of service of the staff, and points out that failure to do so on the part of any organization could prejudice its claim to enjoy the benefits of participation in the common system;

6. *Stresses* that the action of the International Telecommunication Union should in no way be invoked as a precedent by other organizations or by the Union itself;

7. *Calls again upon* the organizations of the United Nations common system to refrain from seeking to establish for their staff, whether by provisions in their staff regulations or by other means, additional entitlements and benefits;

8. *Requests* the executive heads of the participating organizations to consult the International Civil Service Commission and the United Nations Joint Staff Pension Board prior to the submission of proposals relating to staff conditions of service to their respective governing bodies, in order to avoid action inconsistent with the statute of the Commission and the Regulations of the United Nations Joint Staff Pension Fund as accepted by the organizations;

9. *Requests* the International Civil Service Commission, at its current session, to assess the impact on the common system of resolution No. 1024 of the Administrative Council of the International Telecommunication Union with respect to the payment of the special post allowance, the interpretation of staff rules and the convening of the tripartite consultative group outside the rules of procedure of the Commission, and to recommend in its report to the General Assembly at its forty-seventh session appropriate measures to be taken by the Assembly;

10. *Also requests* the International Civil Service Commission, at its current session, to propose measures to be undertaken by all organizations of the United Nations common system to enforce and enhance respect for, and adherence to, the common system of salaries, allowances and conditions of service, and to report thereon to the General Assembly at its forty-seventh session, as well as on its consideration of the question of the improvement of the responsiveness of the common system to the concerns and needs of the different organizations;

11. *Calls upon* the Economic and Social Council, at its substantive session of 1993, to review and, where appropriate, strengthen the applicable sections of the relationship agreements between the United Nations and member organizations of the United Nations common system, in particular article VIII of the Agreement between the United Nations and the International Telecommunication Union, in order to enhance comparability and further adherence to the goals and objectives of the common system;

12. *Requests* the International Telecommunication Union to ensure that any consultative meeting convened pursuant to Administrative Council resolution No. 1024 proceeds with the clear awareness that the General Assembly is the authority for determining conformity with the United Nations common system.

General Assembly resolution 46/191 B

31 July 1992   Meeting 88   Adopted without vote

Approved by Fifth Committee (A/46/808/Add.1) without vote, 30 July (meeting 67); draft by Committee Chairman, orally revised (A/C.5/46/L.27); agenda item 116.
Meeting numbers. GA 46th session: 66-67; plenary 88.

General Service salary survey

In response to a 1990 General Assembly request[20] for a report to be submitted in 1992 on the review of the methodology for the conduct of salary surveys of the General Service and related categories at headquarters duty stations, ICSC in March 1992 established a formal Working Group to review data provided by an informal working group and to report to the Commission on the Flemming principle the modalities for its application and the survey methodology. At its July/August session,[1] ICSC received the report of the Working Group, which conveyed views on the Flemming principle, as well as on the four stages of the survey methodology, namely: the preparation, data-collection, data-analysis and decision phases, including construction of the salary scale.

The Commission took a number of decisions relating to the different phases of the methodology for surveys of the best prevailing conditions at headquarters duty stations. It decided that changes in methodology as a result of its decisions should be incorporated in a revised methodology, and instructed its secretariat to reorder and present for adoption in 1993 a revised methodology. Until that time, any survey preparations should be conducted on the basis of the current methodology, as modified by decisions taken at the current session.

ICSC also agreed on arrangements to review in 1993 the general methodology for surveys of the best prevailing conditions at non-headquarters duty stations.

Grade overlap

For more than a decade, there had been an overlap in the salaries of the senior General Service and junior Professional staff categories in the United Nations system, according to a JIU report transmitted by the Secretary-General to the General Assembly in April 1992.[21]

The cause of the overlap lay primarily in the different methodologies used to set and adjust the levels of remuneration. While salaries of Professionals were based on the Noblemaire principle, which compared the salaries of international civil servants with the highest paid civil service of a Member State, salaries of General Service staff were determined on the basis of the best prevailing rates of the local area. The application of those methodologies led to anomalies. It was recognized that the salaries of the United States civil service, the comparator under the Noblemaire principle, were some 28 per cent behind the private sector and that steps were being taken by the United States to rectify the situation over time.

The report noted that the salary overlap was being viewed with increasing concern. In Geneva, for example, the overlap had reached more than three levels in terms of net remuneration and four levels in terms of pensionable remuneration. Such levels of overlap were incompatible with sound management principles and made it impossible to pursue a realistic career development path from the General Service to the Professional category.

JIU also examined the possibility of a one-grade structure as a possible solution to salary overlap. However, there had been continuous resistance to that idea, echoed by the Salary Review Committees in 1956 and 1972, the General Assembly and ICSC. Any action to change the two-grade structure would require well-founded research and a new formula other than the Noblemaire principle which could be applied fairly to the system worldwide.

The report noted with satisfaction a 1990 General Assembly request[20] that ICSC consider the relativities between the terms and conditions of staff in the Professional and higher categories and those in other categories.

Commenting on the JIU report,[22] the Secretary-General noted that salary overlap was by and large limited to headquarters duty stations; that the overlap between senior General Service and junior Professional posts might be more indicative of the overlap found in the labour market between senior clerical and junior management positions rather than functional overlap; and that the JIU report assumed that ICSC would recommend measures to correct the distortions in the current salary system.

In December,[23] the Secretary-General transmitted to the Assembly the comments of member organizations of ACC on the JIU report, which emphasized that the problem should be urgently studied by ICSC with a view to developing recommendations for corrective action.

In July,[24] the Secretary-General transmitted correspondence from ITU containing two resolutions adopted by ITU's Administrative Council on the conditions of employment of staff in the General Service and Professional and higher categories. In December,[25] at the request of the Director-General of the Food and Agriculture Organization of the United Nations (FAO), the Secretary-General transmitted to the Assembly an FAO Council resolution on remuneration and conditions of service of staff.

Pensions

During 1992, the number of participants in the United Nations Joint Staff Pension Fund increased from 60,183 to 61,968. On 31 December, there were 33,923 periodic benefits in award: 11,264 retirement benefits, 6,093 early retirement benefits, 5,598 deferred retirement benefits, 4,592 widows' and widowers' benefits, 5,679 children's benefits, 642 disability benefits and 55 secondary benefits. In the course of the year, 3,635 lump-sum withdrawal and other settlements were paid.

During the same period, the principal of the Fund increased from $9,304,981,285 to $10,246,849,744.

The investment income of the Fund during the year amounted to $899,878,894, comprising $532,179,470 in interest and dividends, $354,646,665 in net profit on sales of investments, and $13,052,759 in other income. After deduction of investment management costs amounting to $12,884,664, net investment income was $886,994,230.

The Fund was administered by the 33-member United Nations Joint Staff Pension Board, which held its forty-fourth session at Montreal, Canada, from 25 June to 3 July 1992.[26]

The major items dealt with by the Board were: the comprehensive review of the pensionable remuneration and consequent pensions of staff in the General Service and related categories, which the General Assembly had requested in 1990;[27] amendments to the Regulations of the Fund governing the pensionable remuneration and pensions of ungraded officials as requested by the Assembly in 1991;[28] additional studies of possible changes in the pension adjustment system, requested by the Assembly in the same resolution; implications for the work of the Board of the biennialization of the work of the Fifth Committee;[29] methodology and actuarial assumptions to be used in the next actuarial valuation of the Fund; a proposed agreement between the Fund and the Inter-American Development Bank on the transfer of pension rights; and matters related to the interpretation and application of the three transfer agreements between the Fund and the former USSR, the Byelorussian SSR and the Ukrainian SSR.

The Board also examined the management of the Fund's investments, financial statements and schedules for the year ending 31 December 1991, and a progress report on administrative and operational changes in the Fund secretariat.

In accordance with rule 4 of the Fund's Regulations, the Board appointed a Standing Committee to act on its behalf when it was not in session.

ACABQ submitted its comments on the Board's report in October.[30]

Pension Fund investments

The market value of the assets of the Fund as at 31 March 1992 was $10,111 million, an increase of $772 million, or 8.3 per cent over the previous year and $771 million above the book value. The total investment return for the year ended 31 March 1992 was 7.6 per cent, which, after adjusting for inflation, represented a "real" rate of return of 4.3 per cent.

The Fund remained one of the most diversified pension funds in the world. Investments were held in 38 different currencies and 47 countries; 55 per cent of the assets were exposed to currencies other than the United States dollar, which was the Fund's unit of account. Of the Fund's investments, 65 per cent were in markets outside the United States.

Equities constituted 47 per cent of the assets as at 31 March 1992, an increase from 39 per cent for the previous year; 45 per cent of those were in United States equities and 55 per cent in other equity markets. The bond proportion declined to 37 per cent from 39 per cent, and the breakdown between United States dollar–denominated bonds and other currency bonds was 38 and 62 per cent, respectively. Investments in real estate–related securities amounted to 9 per cent of the portfolio, compared with 10 per cent a year earlier. Short-term investments and reserves, that is, cash and fixed income investments with maturity dates of less than one year, decreased to 7 per cent from 12 per cent a year earlier.

In order to preserve the Fund's principal, the defensive policy adopted in the mid-1980s was continued but slightly changed. It consisted of increasing holdings in selected equities which appeared undervalued and with potential for future appreciation.

As at 30 June 1992, the book value of development-related investments increased by 7.1 per cent over the previous year, from $1,453.2 million to $1,537.6 million. Investments in development institutions amounted to $1,050 million compared with $1,137.2 million a year earlier, a decrease of 7.7 per cent; direct investments in specific developing countries increased by 63.6 per cent to $487.6 million from $298 million. The Fund's direct investments and those through regional development institutions in Africa increased by 32.1 per cent to $191.2 million from $144.7 million; Latin America decreased by 14.4 per cent to $270.8 million from $316.3 million, and Asia increased by 46.8 per cent to $583 million

from $397.1 million. The combined development-related assets as at 30 June 1992 represented 16 per cent of the total book value of the Fund.

The Joint Staff Pension Board[26] indicated its concern that outstanding tax claims were having an adverse impact on the Fund's investment returns and requested that detailed information be provided to the General Assembly on the results of negotiations with certain countries regarding tax exemptions for the Fund's investments and on action taken or contemplated when efforts to obtain recognition of tax-exempt status did not succeed. The Board was concerned about investment "opportunity losses" arising from delays in reimbursements of taxes withheld at source by countries which had accepted the tax-exempt status of the Fund and it agreed to advise the Assembly of such delays.

In a September report on the Fund's investments,[31] the Secretary-General noted that, considering the world-wide slowdown in economic growth, the volatility of financial markets, and fluctuations of exchange rates, the investment return of 7.6 per cent for the year ended 31 March 1992, when measured in United States dollars, was satisfactory. The defensive strategy of taking profits where appropriate and increasing investments in those markets and instruments that performed better contributed to the Fund's satisfactory performance. He considered the policy of diversification and careful selection of investment instruments, including consistent investigation of opportunities in developing countries, to be the best way to achieve the goal of preserving the Fund's principal and enhancing its investment return over the medium and long term. He would continue to discharge his fiduciary responsibilities through investment decisions that adhered to the principles of sound investment management and met the requirements of safety, profitability, liquidity and convertibility.

UN common system and pension system

By an October 1992 note,[32] the Secretary-General transmitted to the General Assembly a statement adopted by ACC in 1992 which emphasized the importance of making the conditions of service of the United Nations common system competitive. ACC believed that early action was needed to avoid individual attempts to remedy the most glaring deficiencies, with the attendant risk to the cohesion of the common system.

Accordingly, ACC requested the Assembly to endorse ICSC's recommendations with regard to base/floor salary scale, mobility and hardship allowances, education grant and dependency allowances; to invite ICSC to pursue its examination of the competitiveness of the common system and, in particular, that of the staff in the Professional and higher categories; and to note ACC's concern that in considering the salary and pension methodologies for the General Service category, any modifications should be technically sound and not result in an erosion of current conditions. It urged that ICSC's recommendations pertaining to the methodology for determining pensionable remuneration be deferred until the results of using the new recommended salary survey methodology were known, and requested the Assembly to consider positively ICSC's recommendations for an increase of between 7 and 11 per cent in the remuneration at the ASG and USG levels, as well as ACC's recommendations to ICSC for increases of 3 and 5 per cent at the levels of D-1 and D-2, respectively.

GENERAL ASSEMBLY ACTION

On 22 December, the General Assembly, on the recommendation of the Fifth Committee, adopted **resolution 47/203** without vote.

United Nations pension system

The General Assembly,

Recalling its resolutions 46/192 and 46/220 of 20 December 1991,

Having considered the report of the United Nations Joint Staff Pension Board for 1992 to the General Assembly and to the member organizations of the United Nations Joint Staff Pension Fund, chapter III of the report of the International Civil Service Commission, the report of the Secretary-General on the investments of the Fund, and the related report of the Advisory Committee on Administrative and Budgetary Questions,

I

Implications for the United Nations Joint Staff Pension Board of the biennialization of the work programme of the Fifth Committee

Bearing in mind its resolution 46/220 on the biennialization of the programme of work of the Fifth Committee,

1. *Takes note* of the decision of the United Nations Joint Staff Pension Board to reschedule the next actuarial valuation of the United Nations Joint Staff Pension Fund to be as of 31 December 1993, instead of as of 31 December 1992, with subsequent valuations being carried out every two years;

2. *Takes note also* of the additional responsibilities delegated by the Board to its Standing Committee to be carried out in odd-numbered years, as set out in paragraph 14 of the report of the Board;

3. *Takes note further* of the observations of the Board on the rescheduling of the dates for the next comprehensive review of the pensionable remuneration and consequent pensions of staff in the Professional and higher categories, and of the review of the maximum number of years of creditable contributory service in the Fund;

II

Actuarial matters

1. *Takes note* of the observations of the United Nations Joint Staff Pension Board in section III.B of its report on the methodology and assumptions to be used in the actuarial valuation of the United Nations Joint Staff Pension Fund as at 31 December 1993;

2. *Requests* the Board to consider the form in which it presents the results of actuarial valuations, taking into account the views of the Committee of Actuaries and the Board of Auditors;

3. *Takes note* of the observations of the Board in section III.B of its report on matters related to the application of the transfer agreements between the Fund and the former Union of Soviet Socialist Republics, Ukrainian Soviet Socialist Republic and Byelorussian Soviet Socialist Republic;

4. *Concurs* in the agreement with the Inter-American Development Bank, approved by the Board under article 13 of the Regulations of the Fund, with a view to securing the continuity of pension rights between the Bank and the Fund, as set out in annex IV to the report of the Board;

III

Pensionable remuneration and consequent pensions of staff in the General Service and related categories

Recalling that in section III of its resolution 45/242 of 21 December 1990, the General Assembly requested the International Civil Service Commission, in full cooperation with the United Nations Joint Staff Pension Board, to submit recommendations to the General Assembly at its forty-sixth session, in respect of the comprehensive review of the methodology for determining the pensionable remuneration and consequent pensions of staff in the General Service and related categories,

Also recalling section II of its resolution 46/192,

Further recalling its concurrence with the observation of the Advisory Committee on Administrative and Budgetary Questions that the Commission and the Board should aim to eliminate current anomalies in the system without creating new ones,

Recognizing that the Statute of the Commission and the Regulations of the United Nations Joint Staff Pension Fund define the complementary and essential roles of the Commission and the Board in reviewing issues related to pensionable remuneration and consequent pensions, which are indispensable components of the conditions of service in the United Nations common system, and that pensionable remuneration has a decisive impact on the levels of contributions to be paid into the Fund by member organizations and by participants,

Noting that, based on a pilot study of six locations, the Commission and the Board had concluded that the approach of determining pensionable remuneration and/or pensions by reference to the local practices of employers used in General Service salary surveys should not be pursued further,

Also noting that

(a) The Commission and the Board had concluded that the methodology for determining General Service pensionable remuneration should relate the pensionable remuneration to the net base salaries received while in service,

(b) Regrettably, the Board had not been able to achieve agreement on the modalities for applying such an approach, as reflected in the table in paragraph 76 of the report of the Board and in annex VIII to the report, containing respectively, the positions of the three groups in the Board, together with the proposal of the Chairman of the Board, and the statements of the three groups on the Chairman's proposal,

(c) The Commission, in paragraphs 99 and 100 of its report, had reached conclusions on certain aspects of the methodology, indicated its intention to consider other outstanding aspects in 1993 and concluded that the implementation date for the revised methodology should be 1 January 1994,

Reiterating that the future work of the Board and the Commission should focus on the elimination or significant reduction of the "income inversion anomaly", as described and discussed in paragraphs 73 and 74 of the report of the Board, and in paragraphs 88 to 92 of the report of the Commission,

Reiterating also its appreciation of the complexities and the importance of the issues involved for all parties concerned,

Taking note of the fact that the Board has not yet had an opportunity to consider the conclusions of the Commission, in paragraphs 99 and 100 of the report of the Commission, on certain aspects of the methodology, in the light of the views of the Commission contained in paragraphs 88 to 98 of its report,

1. *Endorses* the conclusions of the United Nations Joint Staff Pension Board and the International Civil Service Commission that the methodology for determining the pensionable remuneration of staff in the General Service and related categories should relate the levels of pensionable remuneration and consequent pensions to salaries while in service;

2. *Endorses also* the approach in paragraph 1 above for future work on the various aspects of the matter, as reflected in the proposal of the Chairman of the Board in paragraphs 76 and 77 of the report of the Board, and in the conclusions and recommendations of the Commission in its report;

3. *Endorses further* the conclusions reached by the Commission on those aspects of the methodology discussed in its report;

4. *Requests* the Commission, in close cooperation with the Board, as appropriate, to finalize the comprehensive review in 1993, and to submit recommendations on all aspects of the methodology to determine pensionable remuneration and consequent pensions, including the effective date of implementation and transitional measures to protect acquired rights, to the General Assembly at its forty-eighth session;

5. *Also requests* the Commission to recommend consequential amendments to the staff regulations of the member organizations and the Board to consider amendments to the Regulations of the United Nations Joint Staff Pension Fund, which may be required in order to implement the revised methodology, in their respective reports to the General Assembly at its forty-eighth session;

IV
Pensionable remuneration and pensions of ungraded officials

Recalling section III, paragraph 9, of its resolution 46/192, in which it requested the International Civil Service Commission to recommend guidelines for determining the pension arrangements for ungraded officials who do not become participants in the United Nations Joint Staff Pension Fund so as to ensure system-wide comparability, as well as appropriate monitoring procedures, and to submit recommendations thereon to the General Assembly at its forty-seventh session and to the governing bodies of the other organizations of the United Nations common system,

Also recalling that, in paragraph 7 the same resolution, the General Assembly requested the United Nations Joint Staff Pension Board to consider amendments to the Regulations of the Fund to incorporate provisions governing the pensionable remuneration of ungraded officials and to extend the provisions placing a limit on the highest levels of pensions to cover all participants in the Fund, including ungraded officials,

1. *Decides* to convey to the governing bodies of the other member organizations of the United Nations Joint Staff Pension Fund its view that their ungraded officials should become participants in the Fund so as to ensure system-wide comparability and that, if a governing body decides to make arrangements outside the Fund, only the option currently available in the International Civil Aviation Organization, as described in paragraph 64 of the report of the International Civil Service Commission, would be appropriate;

2. *Concurs* with the decision of the United Nations Joint Staff Pension Board to defer, until its next regular session, in 1994, consideration of an amendment to article 54 of the Regulations of the Fund to incorporate provisions governing the pensionable remuneration of ungraded officials, in order to allow time for the governing bodies of all member organizations of the Fund to take up the matters referred to them by the General Assembly in section III, paragraphs 5 and 6, of its resolution 46/192;

3. *Approves*, with effect from 1 April 1993, an amendment to article 28 *(d)* of the Regulations of the Fund, as set out in annex I to the present resolution, to extend the ceiling on pensions to ungraded officials, as well as to other participants who are not currently covered by article 28 *(d)* of the Regulations but whose pensionable remuneration is greater than that at the D-2 level, top step, in the scale of pensionable remuneration appended to article 54 of the Regulations;

V
Changes in the pension adjustment system

Recalling section IV, paragraph 31 of its resolution 46/192, in which it approved the longer-term modification of the pension adjustment system that the United Nations Joint Staff Pension Board had recommended in 1991,

1. *Takes note* of the observations of the Board on the additional studies related to that modification, including, in particular, a change in the "120 per cent cap" provision, reviews of the special index for pensioners, the applicability to staff in the General Service and related categories of the longer-term modification of the pension adjustment system, as well as of the observations on the intention of the Board to make recommendations on these matters to the General Assembly at its forty-ninth session, in 1994;

2. *Reiterates* its request in section IV, paragraph 6, of its resolution 46/192 that the Board continue to consider economy measures, including, in particular, a change of the "120 per cent cap" provision under the two-track pension adjustment system;

3. *Approves*, effective 1 April 1993, modification of the schedule for the special adjustment of small pensions under section E of the pension adjustment system, as recommended by the Board in paragraph 104 of its report, and the consequential changes in the pension adjustment system, as set out in annex II to the present resolution;

VI
Other matters

1. *Concurs* with the decisions of the United Nations Joint Staff Pension Board, set out in paragraphs 124 and 125 of its report, to consider again, at its next regular session, in 1994, amendments to article 54 of the Regulations of the United Nations Joint Staff Pension Fund to incorporate therein provisions governing the longevity/merit steps granted by some organizations to their staff, as well as a definition of the pensionable remuneration of staff in the United Nations Field Service category;

2. *Takes note* of the other matters dealt with in the report of the Board;

VII
Investments of the United Nations Joint Staff Pension Fund

1. *Takes note* of the report of the Secretary-General on the investments of the United Nations Joint Staff Pension Fund and welcomes, in particular, the commitment to global investment as indicated in paragraph 46 of the report of the Board and takes into account the comments of the Advisory Committee on Administrative and Budgetary Questions in paragraph 23 of its report to the General Assembly at its forty-sixth session;

2. *Reiterates* its request to Member States that do not now grant tax exemptions for the investments of the Fund to make every possible effort to permit such exemptions as soon as possible.

ANNEX I
Amendment to the Regulations of the United Nations Joint Staff Pension Fund

Article 28
Retirement benefit

Replace paragraph *(d)* by the following:

"*(d)*   (i)   However, except as provided in (ii) below, the benefit otherwise payable at the standard annual rate in accordance with the applicable provisions of *(b)* or *(c)* above to a participant at a level above D-2, top step, of the scale of pensionable remuneration appended to article 54, shall not exceed, as at the time of the participant's separation, the greater of:

"(A)   60 per cent of his pensionable remuneration on the date of separation; or

"(B)   The maximum benefit payable under the same provisions of *(b)* or *(c)* above to a participant at the level D-2 (top step for the preceding five years of the scale of pensionable remuneration appended to article 54, as adjusted), with 35 years of contributory service, separating on the same date as the participant;

"(ii)   However, for a participant separating at the level of Under-Secretary-General, Assistant Secretary-General or their equivalent level to whom the provisions of (i) above are applicable, the benefit payable shall not be less than the benefit that would have been payable to him at the standard annual rate if he had separated from service on 31 March 1986; for participants separating at other levels above D-2, top step, in the scale of pensionable remuneration appended to article 54, to whom the provisions of (i) above are applicable, the benefit payable shall not be less than the benefit that would have been payable to the participant at the standard annual rate if he/she had separated from service on 31 March 1993; for participants who entered or re-entered the Fund at an ungraded level before 1 April 1993, the provisions of (i) above shall not be applicable."

ANNEX II
Changes in the pension adjustment system

E.   Special adjustments for small pensions
Replace paragraph 7 by the following:
"7.   Whenever the standard annual rate of a retirement or disability benefit under the Fund's Regulations, before any commutation, is less than the highest dollar amount in the applicable table below, the benefit shall be subject to a special adjustment as follows:

"Annual amount of pension (US dollars)	Special adjustment (Percentage)
"Separations before 1 April 1993	
$4 000	0
3 800	3
3 600	7
3 400	12
3 200	17
3 000	22
2 800	28
2 600	34
2 400	40
2 200 or less	46
"Separations on or after 1 April 1993	
$6 500	0
6 250	3
6 000	6
5 750	9
5 500	12
5 250	15
5 000	18
4 750	21
4 500	25
4 250	28
4 000	31
3 750	34
3 500	37
3 250	40
3 000	43
2 750 or less	46

General Assembly resolution 47/203

22 December 1992   Meeting 93   Adopted without vote

Approved by Fifth Committee (A/47/807) without vote, 17 December (meeting 47); draft by Hungary, following informal consultations (A/C.5/47/L.6); agenda item 114.
Meeting numbers. GA 47th session: 5th Committee 23, 27, 29, 31, 35-47; plenary 93.

REFERENCES

[1]A/47/30 & Corr.1. [2]GA res. 44/198, 21 Dec. 1989. [3]YUN 1991, p. 888, GA res. 46/220, 20 Dec. 1991. [4]YUN 1980, p. 1196, GA. res. 35/213, 17 Dec. 1980. [5]A/C.5/47/38. [6]A/C.5/47/36. [7]YUN 1991, p. 905. [8]Ibid., GA res. 46/185 A, sect. V, 20 Dec. 1991. [9]Ibid., p. 917, GA res. 46/185 B, sect. VII, 20 Dec. 1991. [10]A/C.5/47/45. [11]GA res. 45/158, annex, 18 Dec. 1990. [12]A/47/7/Add.10. [13]YUN 1991, p. 905, GA res. 46/185 A, sect. VI, 20 Dec. 1991. [14]A/C.5/47/39. [15]A/47/7/Add.6. [16]YUN 1991, p. 905 & A/C.5/46/17. [17]YUN 1991, p. 900, GA res. 46/191 A, 20 Dec. 1991. [18]Ibid., p. 911, GA res. 45/268, 28 June 1991. [19]A/C.5/46/85. [20]GA res. 45/241, 21 Dec. 1990. [21]A/47/140. [22]A/47/140/Add.1. [23]A/47/140/Add.2. [24]A/C.5/46/85. [25]A/C.5/47/66. [26]A/47/9. [27]GA res. 45/242, 21 Dec. 1990. [28]YUN 1991, p. 907, GA res. 46/192, 20 Dec. 1991. [29]Ibid., p. 888, GA res. 46/220, 20 Dec. 1991. [30]A/47/578. [31]A/C.5/47/8. [32]A/C.5/47/25.

Travel

Standards of accommodation for air travel

Responding to a 1991 General Assembly request,[1] the Secretary-General submitted an October 1992 report[2] on standards of accommodation for air travel covering the period from 1 July 1991 to 30 June 1992. With regard to delegation travel, 31 journeys in first class air accommodation for one representative of each Member State designated as a least developed country (LDC) attending regular, special or emergency sessions of the General Assembly were paid for at a cost of $146,287. With regard to exceptions to the standards of accommodation of staff and others travelling on behalf of the Organization, which the Secretary-General was authorized to make on a case-by-case basis, 112 cases of first class travel and 55 cases of business class travel were authorized at a total additional cost of $199,675, compared with $106,600 for the previous reporting period. That significant increase in exceptions was attributable to the category of "eminent persons", for which in 1991-1992 there were 78 trips costing $91,071, compared with 34 trips costing $34,093 for 1990-1991.

ACABQ recommended that future reports of the Secretary-General on the issue should include information on the source of funding (regular budget, trust funds or the United Nations Development Programme) for the additional cost attributable to the granting of exceptions.[3]

On 23 December, by **decision 47/460 A**, the General Assembly deferred consideration of the issue.

Review of travel and related entitlements

In a November 1992 report,[4] submitted in response to a 1991 General Assembly request,[1] the Secretary-General reviewed travel and related entitlements for members of organs and subsidiary organs and staff members of the United Nations. The report noted that the question of travel entitlements was being reviewed in the ACC subsidiary structure. Also, it had proved more difficult than expected to prepare reliable cost estimates relating to proposals under consideration for the travel of Secretariat staff. It was, therefore, considered advisable to postpone the submission of recommendations relating to staff travel to the 1993 Assembly session. Consequently, the major part of the review dealt with the travel of members of United Nations organs and subsidiary bodies.

The report examined the legislative history of such travel, the current provisions for it, and the provisions in other United Nations organizations. It also analysed inconsistencies in current provisions and noted that travel entitlements for members of organs and subsidiary bodies differed considerably from one organization to another and from those of the United Nations. Therefore, it would not be possible in the near future to achieve uniformity and consistency by adapting the provisions of the United Nations to those of the specialized agencies and related organizations.

The Secretary-General said that the Assembly might decide to limit the payment of travel expenses for representatives in subsidiary organs of the Assembly and the Economic and Social Council to those from LDCs. With regard to the issues of exceptional payment of travel and subsistence expenses to representatives of Member States in CPC, he proposed a number of alternatives. He also proposed that the Assembly examine its past decisions on travel entitlements for representatives in functional commissions of the Council nominated directly by their Governments; provide clarification regarding the travel entitlements for members of the Commission on Crime and Criminal Justice; and address the issue of exceptional travel assistance to representatives from LDCs and other developing countries.

On 23 December, by **decision 47/460 A**, the Assembly deferred consideration of the report.

REFERENCES

[1]YUN 1991, p. 913, GA dec. 46/450, 20 Dec. 1991. [2]A/C.5/47/17. [3]A/47/7/Add.5. [4]A/C.5/47/61.

Administration of justice

In its annual note to the General Assembly,[1] the United Nations Administrative Tribunal reported that it had rendered 43 judgements during the year in cases brought by staff members against the Secretary-General or the executive heads of other United Nations organizations to resolve disputes involving terms of appointment and related rules and regulations.

The Tribunal met in annual plenary session in New York on 19 November 1992 and held two panel sessions (Geneva, 1 June–2 July; New York, 19 October–20 November).

REFERENCE

[1]A/INF/47/7.

Chapter III

Other administrative and management questions

In 1992, the Committee on Conferences considered ways to improve the utilization of conference-servicing within the United Nations system. It recommended measures to control and limit documentation, and reviewed the functioning of the Office of Conference Services to ensure the most efficient and cost-effective management. The Committee reviewed requests for changes to the 1992 approved calendar and examined the draft revised calender for 1993, which was subsequently approved by the General Assembly in December. Action was also taken by the Assembly on a number of issues related to conference-servicing.

The Assembly, in the context of the 1992-1993 programme budget, reviewed the status of the construction of conference facilities at Bangkok, Thailand, and Addis Ababa, Ethiopia; initiatives to enhance the technological infrastructure of the United Nations; and administrative and budgetary arrangements for the United Nations Scientific Committee on the Effects of Atomic Radiation, the United Nations Institute for Training and Research, and the International Computing Centre. The Economic and Social Council examined ways to improve the access of Member States to the United Nations Information System and a study on the harmonization and improvement of the system.

Conferences and meetings

In 1992, the Committee on Conferences examined requests for additions and changes to the approved calendar of conferences for 1992.[1] It also examined the draft revised calendar of conferences and meetings for 1993.

The Committee discussed a number of issues related to the calendar, including measures to improve the utilization of conference-servicing resources, the organization of work, and the coordination of all organizational aspects of conference servicing. It also dealt with the need to control the amount of documentation. The Committee reviewed the United Nations publications policy, the workings of the Office of Conference Services, the 1992-1997 medium-term plan, and the organization of work of the Committee on Conferences.

Other matters dealt with in the Committee's September report[2] included the feasibility of installing an appropriate signalling system at meetings where time-limits were set for speeches.

The Committee held an organizational session on 17 March and a substantive session from 24 to 28 August.

Mandate of the Committee on Conferences

During the year, the Committee continued its main task of presenting to the Assembly, through the Fifth (Administrative and Budgetary) Committee, a draft calendar of conferences and meetings for the following year or biennium. It also recommended measures to promote the efficiency of the Secretariat in terms of the planning and servicing of meetings and conferences, the provision of documentation, and the efficiency with which intergovernmental bodies utilized the conference-servicing resources available to them, tasks that had been extended to the Committee by the Assembly in 1988.[3]

Calendar of meetings

Calendar for 1992

At its organizational session in March 1992, the Committee on Conferences agreed that proposed changes to the calendar that did not have programme budget implications could be dealt with by the Secretariat in consultation with the Bureau of the Committee. A number of such proposals were made in 1992.

The Committee approved a two-day extension of the fifth session of the Intergovernmental Negotiating Committee for a Framework Convention on Climate Change, on the understanding that the change would not give rise to administrative or programme budget implications.

In April, the secretariat of the Economic and Social Council informed the Committee that the twenty-eighth session of the Committee for Development Planning (CDP), originally scheduled for New York from 20 to 24 April, would be held in Kuwait City from 18 to 22 April, following Kuwait's offer to host the session. No objection was raised by the Committee, on the further understanding that CDP would waive interpretation and other services for the meeting, which would be conducted in English, and that the Office of Conference Services would not assume any responsibility for the manner and level of servicing of the proposed session.

In April, the Committee was informed of the decision of the International Civil Service Commission (ICSC) to hold its thirty-sixth session at the headquarters of the International Maritime Organization (IMO) in London, in accordance with a 1985 General Assembly resolution[4], and of the request that the session be extended by one week. The Committee raised no objections provided the additional costs were met from within the 1992-1993 programme budget.

Also in April, the Committee approved a one-day extension of the meeting of the Commission on Transnational Corporations, originally scheduled to end 15 April, on the understanding that it be serviced from within existing resources.

In May, the Committee approved a request to schedule a resumed session of the Advisory Committee on Administrative and Budgetary Questions (ACABQ) in New York from 6 July for up to two weeks, on the understanding that the costs involved in servicing the session would be met from within the overall appropriations for conference servicing.

A request to schedule a reconvened session of the technical meeting for the International Year of the World's Indigenous People at Geneva from 3 to 5 August, following the session of the Working Group on Indigenous Populations, was also approved, provided it caused no administrative difficulties for the Office of Conference Services and that the costs of servicing the meetings would be met from within overall appropriations for conference servicing.

In June, the Committee approved a request to schedule the sixth session of the Intergovernmental Negotiating Committee for a Framework Convention on Climate Change from 19 to 23 October at Geneva, on the understanding that any additional costs would be met from within the appropriations of the 1992-1993 programme budget.

The Committee received a request in July from the Centre for Human Rights to schedule a one-day conference of the States parties to the Convention against Torture and other Cruel, Inhuman or Degrading Treatment or Punishment, in New York during the second week of September, to consider and vote on a proposed amendment to the Convention. The request was granted, provided the conference-servicing costs involved would be met from within the overall appropriations for conference services and would not give rise to programme budget implications.

Also in July, the Committee approved a two-day meeting of the World Food Council (WFC) Ad Hoc Committee on the Review of the Council, in New York on 14 and 15 September, on the understanding that additional servicing costs would be met from the overall appropriations for conference services and that travel costs and related expenses would be also met from overall appropriations for that purpose.

Draft revised calendar 1993

From 25 to 27 August, the Committee on Conferences reviewed the draft revised calendar of conferences and meetings for 1993. It also considered a consolidated statement of scheduled special conferences for 1993[5] and considered a review of meeting and documentation requirements of the United Nations Development Programme (UNDP) and the United Nations Children's Fund (UNICEF). The Secretariat reported orally on possible alternative scheduling arrangements for the Economic and Social Council.

During the discussion, the Committee noted the overlap of some meetings, particularly the World Conference on Human Rights and the United Nations Commission on International Trade Law, meeting concurrently at Vienna, and the Commission on Human Rights at Geneva, which overlapped with the organizational session of the Economic and Social Council in New York.

The Committee recommended that the General Assembly adopt the draft revised calendar for 1993 as amended and authorize the Committee to make any necessary adjustments arising from actions taken by the Assembly. It also recommended that the Assembly request all subsidiary bodies to seek the technical advice of the Office of Conference Services on the availability of conference-servicing facilities and resources prior to adjusting the dates and periodicity of future sessions, and that the Executive Board of UNICEF and the Governing Council of UNDP continue to evaluate and reduce, where possible, their meeting and documentation requirements.

The Committee requested the Secretariat to present to the 1992 session of the General Assembly a statement of programme budget implications on the proposed restructuring of the intergovernmental machinery of the United Nations Conference on Trade and Development (UNCTAD).

The Committee Chairman was requested to suggest to all organs that they examine a comprehensive list of the reports being requested in draft decisions prior to the end of each regular session, so as to reduce the number and volume of separate reports.

ECONOMIC AND SOCIAL COUNCIL ACTION

By **decision 1992/214** of 7 February 1992, the Economic and Social Council, following an invitation by the General Assembly in 1991,[1] granted authority to its Bureau to approve intersessional departures from its calendar of conferences and meetings in respect of its subsidiary bodies when the Council was not in session and after consulting with the Committee on Conferences.

GENERAL ASSEMBLY ACTION

On 22 December 1992, on the recommendation of the Fifth Committee, the General Assembly adopted **resolution 47/202 A** without vote.

The General Assembly,

Having considered the report of the Committee on Conferences,

Recalling its relevant resolutions, including resolutions 43/222 B of 21 December 1988 and 46/190 of 20 December 1991,

1. *Approves* the draft revised calendar of conferences and meetings of the United Nations for 1993 as submitted and amended by the Committee on Conferences;

2. *Authorizes* the Committee on Conferences to make adjustments in the calendar of conferences and meetings for 1993 that may become necessary as a result of action and decisions taken by the General Assembly at its forty-seventh session;

3. *Urges* all subsidiary bodies of the General Assembly and of the Economic and Social Council to seek the technical advice of the Office of Conference Services on the availability of conference-servicing facilities and resources in the process of the determination and adjustment of the dates and periodicity of their sessions in order to enhance planning and optimize utilization of conference-servicing resources;

4. *Urges* all United Nations organs to utilize conference-servicing resources allocated to them in the most efficient and cost-effective manner and to maximize the accuracy with which they forecast the number of fully serviced meetings;

5. *Requests* the Secretariat to bring the relevant General Assembly resolutions and guidelines on the use of conference-servicing resources, and information on the notional costs per hour of meeting time, to the attention of all organs;

6. *Urges* all subsidiary bodies of the General Assembly and of the Economic and Social Council to comply with the request of the General Assembly contained in paragraph 11 of its resolution 46/190 to undertake informal consultations on a regular basis for the purpose of improving the utilization of their conference-servicing resources;

7. *Renews its request* contained in paragraph 12 of its resolution 46/190 to the Chairmen of those subsidiary bodies to report the results of the consultations mentioned in paragraph 6 above to the Chairman of the Committee on Conferences, and requests the Committee on Conferences to carry out a comprehensive analysis of replies received;

8. *Urges* the subsidiary bodies of the General Assembly and of the Economic and Social Council, in the context of the required consultations mentioned in paragraph 6 above, to evaluate and report on the measures taken, including the convening of meetings in a timely manner, rationalizing their meeting requirements, improving the scheduling of informal consultations, the possibility of biennializing agenda items, and monitoring the timely issuance and availability of documentation;

9. *Invites* the Executive Board of the United Nations Children's Fund and the Governing Council of the United Nations Development Programme to continue to evaluate their meeting and documentation requirements, with a view to rationalizing them, and to report on progress made thereon to the General Assembly at its forty-eighth session, through the Committee on Conferences;

10. *Endorses* the decision of the Committee on Conferences to request its Chairman to consult on its behalf with the Chairmen of organs concerned, where the utilization factor is lower than the established benchmark figure for the last three years, and requests the Committee on Conferences to report the results of the consultations to the General Assembly at its forty-eighth session;

11. *Decides* that the consultations should be held with a view to making appropriate recommendations in order to achieve the optimum utilization of conference-servicing resources and rationalizing the duration and frequency of conference-servicing time allocated, taking into account the high costs of conference servicing and the demands placed upon the Organization;

12. *Welcomes* the decision of the Committee on Conferences to incorporate availability and compliance indices on pre-session documentation into the experimental methodology on the utilization of conference-servicing resources;

13. *Requests* the Secretary-General to provide the Committee on Conferences with, in addition to the utilization rate, qualitative indicators and information about the way conference time is used in order to enable the Committee to make recommendations on conference time allocated to different bodies;

14. *Requests* the Committee on Conferences to finalize its analysis of the experimental methodology on the utilization of conference-servicing resources, to report on its conclusions and to submit its recommendations, as appropriate, including a revision of the benchmark figure requested in paragraph 15 of General Assembly resolution 46/190, to the Assembly at its forty-eighth session;

15. *Demands* that all subsidiary organs of the General Assembly comply with the provisions of section I, paragraph 7, of its resolution 40/243 of 18 December 1985;

16. *Reaffirms* that the Committee on Conferences and the Secretary-General should take account, in drawing up the calendar of conferences and meetings, of the principles contained in section I, paragraph 10, of resolution 40/243;

17. *Reaffirms also* that United Nations bodies may hold sessions away from their established headquarters when a Government issuing an invitation for a session to be held within its territory has agreed to defray the actual additional costs directly or indirectly involved, after consultation with the Secretary-General as to their nature and possible extent;

18. *Requests* the Secretary-General to submit a revised consolidated statement of scheduled special conferences convened under United Nations auspices towards the end of each of its sessions.

General Assembly resolution 47/202 A

22 December 1992   Meeting 93   Adopted without vote

Approved by Fifth Committee (A/47/806) without vote, 17 December (meeting 47); draft by Bangladesh (A/C.5/47/L.11), based on informal consultations; agenda item 110.

Meeting numbers. GA 47th session: 5th Committee 4, 5, 8-11, 47; plenary 93.

Conference and meeting services

The Secretary-General, pursuant to a 1991 General Assembly resolution,[1] submitted a July 1992 report on the review of the Office of Conference Services.[6] The review concentrated on the Office of Conference Services at United Nations Headquarters. In summarizing the findings, the Secretary-General stated that the Office's working methods were generally efficient and effective, but there was room for improvement in some areas. The problems encountered resulted from external factors, including an increased demand for meetings; the concentration of conferences and meetings at certain times of the year; a significant number of meetings cancelled or convened at short notice; late submission of documents for processing; and the submission of incomplete or illegible documents.

The review covered the planning of meetings; interpretation services; verbatim reporting and précis writing; document processing, including editing, translations, text processing and reproduction; publications; library and information services; and technological innovations. The review indicated that steps were being taken towards improving the organizational structure of the Office. The Secretary-General reported that steps had also been taken towards implementation of many of the measures arising from the review, including the establishment of a meetings planning database, the cross-exchange of language staff, the issuance of verbatim records in final form only, the establishment of a separate organizational unit for contractual translations within the Translation Division, the introduction of new formats and typesetting for United Nations documents, improved costing and planning in publishing, and improved documents storage in the library. He recommended, as a means of improving the scheduling of meetings, that the precise requirements of a body and the schedule of its meetings be determined well in advance; that the entitlements of bodies with a utilization factor below the benchmark standard be reviewed by the Committee on Conferences; and that the Office be given sufficient notice of changes in requirements for language services.

The Secretary-General also recommended that a cost-benefit analysis of state-of-the-art teleconferencing be carried out and that intergovernmental bodies be encouraged to discuss the drafting of reports or resolutions in informal sessions for which summary or verbatim records would not be required.

None of the recommendations proposed by the Secretary-General carried financial implications for the 1992-1993 biennium.

In its discussion of the report on 25 and 26 August 1992,[2] the Committee on Conferences noted the recommendations but stated that their cost-benefit aspects of applying new technologies in conference servicing should be addressed further. It requested the Secretariat to continue to monitor developments affecting the performance of the Office of Conference Services by: helping the Committee to fulfil its mandate; identifying constraints to the six-week rule for availability of presession documentation; ensuring adequate interdepartmental cooperation and capitalizing on the features of the Document Records, Information and Tracking System for the timely submission of documents; forecasting meeting requirements and necessary support services; analysing the utilization worldwide of conference-servicing capacity; ensuring system-wide coordination of conference services; and by conducting a cost-benefit analysis of video-conferencing.

ACABQ noted in October[7] that the report of the Secretary-General had referred to productivity gains from technological innovations and trusted that more information would be provided in the proposed programme budget for 1994-1995.

GENERAL ASSEMBLY ACTION

On 22 December 1992, the General Assembly, on the recommendation of the Fifth Committee, adopted **resolution 47/202 C** without vote.

The General Assembly,

Taking note of the report of the Secretary-General on the review of the Office of Conference Services submitted in accordance with resolution 46/190 of 20 December 1991, which was considered by the Committee on Conferences to be a good description of the existing problems facing the Office but which lacked far-reaching proposals,

Reaffirming that the provision of appropriate, high-quality conference services to the United Nations is an essential element in the efficient functioning of the Organization,

Concurring with the conclusion of the Committee on Conferences that the ultimate aim for all organizational aspects of conference servicing would be to develop further a system of global planning and coordination—in order to ensure the most cost-effective management of the meeting and documentation resources—while maintaining the requisite high quality of services,

1. *Requests* the Secretary-General, in the context of the review of the Office of Conference Services, to continue to monitor various factors affecting the performance of the Office, taking into account paragraph 100 of the report of the Committee on Conferences and the views expressed by Member States in the Fifth Committee, and to provide recommendations thereon to the General Assembly at its forty-ninth session through the Committee on Conferences and the Advisory Committee on Administrative and Budgetary Questions;

2. *Also requests* the Secretary-General:

(a) To submit to the General Assembly at its forty-ninth session, through the Committee on Conferences and the Advisory Committee on Administrative and Budgetary Questions, in the context of the review mentioned in paragraph 1 above, a comprehensive review taking into account the reports of external consultants and all the recommendations of the Management Advisory Service, including the cost/benefit aspects of new technologies and the financial implications of the recommendations;

(b) To undertake a follow-up to the review of the Office of Conference Services by the Management Advisory Service and to submit a report thereon to the General Assembly at its forty-ninth session;

(c) To submit, if necessary, recommendations on possible restructuring of the Office of Conference Services to the General Assembly at its forty-eighth session through the Committee on Conferences and the Advisory Committee on Administrative and Budgetary Questions;

3. *Urges* the Committee on Conferences to continue to explore ways and means for a more effective implementation of its terms of reference as set out in resolution 43/222 B of 21 December 1988 and the relevant recommendations contained in the report of the Group of High-Level Intergovernmental Experts to Review the Efficiency of the Administrative and Financial Functioning of the United Nations, as approved by the General Assembly in its resolution 41/213 of 19 December 1986, with a view to ensuring the optimum utilization of conference-servicing resources, via, *inter alia*, minimizing wastage and the rationalization of meeting programmes and documentation requirements.

General Assembly resolution 47/202 C

22 December 1992   Meeting 93   Adopted without vote

Approved by Fifth Committee (A/47/806) without vote, 17 December (meeting 47); draft by Bangladesh (A/C.5/47/L.11), based on informal consultations; agenda item 110.
Meeting numbers. GA 47th session: 5th Committee 4, 5, 8-11, 47; plenary 93.

Language services

GENERAL ASSEMBLY ACTION

On 22 December 1992, the General Assembly, on the recommendation of the Fifth Committee, adopted **resolution 47/202 D** without vote.

The General Assembly,

Recalling all its previous resolutions on the use of languages in the United Nations,

Also recalling its resolution 42/207 C of 11 December 1987 on the equal treatment of all official languages of the United Nations,

Renews its request to the Secretary-General to take the necessary measures to ensure the provision of conference services as specified in its relevant resolutions and with due respect for the equal treatment of all official languages of the United Nations.

General Assembly resolution 47/202 D

22 December 1992   Meeting 93   Adopted without vote

Approved by Fifth Committee (A/47/806) without vote, 17 December (meeting 47); draft by Bangladesh (A/C.5/47/L.11), based on informal consultations; agenda item 110.
Meeting numbers. GA 47th session: 5th Committee 4, 5, 8-11, 47; plenary 93.

Electronic signalling system

In June 1992,[8] the Secretary-General reported on the feasibility of installing an electronic signalling system at a number of the Organization's headquarters locations to monitor the length of speeches when time-limits were in effect. The feasibility of installing such a system, including technical specifications, was considered for New York, Geneva, Vienna, Santiago, Nairobi, Addis Ababa, Bangkok and the Economic and Social Commission for Western Asia (ESCWA). The Secretary-General also reviewed the experiences of other United Nations organizations with signalling devices and identified three possible systems. The first, involving an installation at each microphone position, was considered to be prohibitively expensive. The second, a permanently installed wall-mounted device would cost about $186,450 for 60 units. And the third, would involve portable units, which could be deployed wherever and whenever necessary at a total cost of $62,520 for 20 units. The Secretary-General recommended the portable system and in November, the Committee on Conferences, reporting on the programme budget implications,[9] stated that 29 portable signalling devices would be required for the conference centres in New York, Geneva, Vienna, Nairobi, Addis Ababa, Santiago, Bangkok and ESCWA at a total cost of $88,100, to be absorbed under appropriations for the 1992-1993 programme budget.

Speaking before the Fifth Committee, the Chairman of ACABQ said that in the Advisory Committee's view, the General Assembly should first decide whether there should be time-limits on speeches and statements and whether that decision would be consistently enforced; otherwise, the installation of a signalling system would be a waste of money. The Advisory Committee had been informed that there was such a device in the General Assembly Hall for enforcing time-limits, but it was hardly ever used.

The Assembly, by **resolution 47/219 A, section XXI**, adopted on the recommendation of the Fifth Committee, endorsed ACABQ's comments and recommendations.

Workload standards
for conference-servicing staff

The Secretary-General submitted in December, pursuant to a 1990 General Assembly request,[10] a report on the elaboration of unified workload standards for conference-servicing staff within the United Nations system.[12] The report set out the findings and recommendations of the Inter-Agency Meeting on Language Arrangements, Documentation and Publications (IAMLADP), which had been mandated by the Organizational Committee of the Administrative Committee on Coordination (ACC) to gather data on the workload standards of the specialized agencies. Information submitted by the participating organizations related to interpreters, translators, revisers, précis-writers, text processors, verbatim reporters and reproduction staff.

At its 1991 session, IAMLADP found that the standards applied in most organizations for both regular staff and freelance interpreters, were virtually the same, and that this was also the case for précis-writers. Verbatim reporting was used only at the United Nations and the Food and Agriculture Organization of the United Nations (FAO), and their requirements were also virtually identical.

There was, however, a lack of consistency in the standards applied by the different organizations to translations and text processing which led IAMLADP to recommend that uniform standards be applied throughout the United Nations system. To that end, a Working Group met at the United Nations office at Geneva and devised a set of possible standards to cover translation, précis-writing and text processing.

At the 1992 session of IAMLADP, participating organizations agreed to a variable scale for translators and revisers and proposed standards for précis-writers. They also accepted a range of figures proposed by the Working Group for translators and text processors, on the understanding that each organization would have flexibility in applying the standards as circumstances required.

IAMLADP agreed that it was not practical to establish a common standard for the printing of documents, because of the diverse work requirements of the different organizations.

The General Assembly, by **decision 47/460 A** of 23 December, deferred until its 1993 session consideration of the Secretary-General's report.

REFERENCES

[1]YUN 1991, p. 915, GA res. 46/190, 20 Dec. 1991. [2]A/47/32. [3]GA res. 43/222 B, 21 Dec. 1988. [4]YUN 1985, p. 1256, GA res. 40/243, 18 Dec. 1985. [5]A/C.5/47/1. [6]A/47/336. [7]A/47/7/Add.1. [8]A/47/287. [9]A/C.5/47/23. [10]GA res. 45/248 A, 21 Dec. 1990. [11]A/C.5/47/67.

Documents and publications

Documentation control and limitation

In June 1992,[1] the Secretary-General published an updated version of a document setting forth policies laid down by the General Assembly regarding the control and limitation of documentation, as requested by the Assembly in 1969.[2] The note, enumerating policy decisions adopted by the Assembly over the years, most recently in 1991,[3] was distributed to all Member States.

Most of the decisions applied to documentation for the Assembly and its subsidiary bodies. The Assembly had also invited United Nations organs, particularly the Economic and Social Council and its subsidiary bodies, to apply the same policies to their documentation. Those organs had in general accepted the policies laid down by the Assembly with further instructions as their particular circumstances required.

The note summarized specific Assembly recommendations to limit and control general documents, meeting records, statements, reports and studies, annexes and supplements of the Official Records, documentation for treaty bodies and special conferences, statements of programme budget implications and notes. Annexes to the note outlined current meeting record entitlements and gave revised guidelines for the format and contents of reports of the subsidiary organs of the General Assembly.

In August, the Committee on Conferences[4] reviewed a report by the Secretariat containing statistics on communications from Member States circulated as United Nations documents for 1991, as well as a monthly breakdown of the total number of communications circulated from 1988 to May 1992.[5]

The Committee renewed the appeal to Member States to exercise restraint in their requests for the circulation of communications and recommended that the Assembly appeal to Member States to submit requests for the circulation of communications in the most appropriate, brief, complete, concise and timely manner possible.

Regarding the reports of subsidiary organs to the Assembly, the Committee, on 24 and 26 August, considered a Secretariat study[6] that indicated that there had been no recent improvement in compliance with an Assembly request that written records of meetings be limited to 32 pages.

The Committee recommended that the Assembly request the Secretariat to bring the relevant Assembly resolutions and rules and regulations on control and limitation of documentation to the attention of all organs at the start of sessions, and that Member States exercise restraint in requesting documentation and in the submission of their reports. It also recommended that the Assembly urge those subsidiary organs that had not been able to comply with the 32-page limit to continue attempts to reduce the length of future reports without compromising quality or mandated obligations. The Committee requested the Secretariat to prepare a model for final reports and to work with the United Nations Institute for Training and

Research (UNITAR) to incorporate the preferred format for reports and documentation costs into existing training programmes for new delegates and Secretariat officials.

Also in August, the Committee considered information on the number of meetings with summary records in New York, Geneva and Vienna from 1988-1991. Over the years, the Assembly had decided which subsidiary and governing bodies should receive summary records. The Secretariat reported that technological innovations had increased the capacity of the Verbatim Reporting Section and proposed issuing verbatim records of the Security Council and the Assembly in final form, on the understanding that consolidated corrigenda would be issued at appropriate intervals.

The Committee also discussed a general failure to comply with the six-week rule for the issuance of pre-session documentation. It recommended that the Assembly urge subsidiary organs to review their agendas and help remedy the situation.

GENERAL ASSEMBLY ACTION

On 22 December, the General Assembly, on the recommendation of the Fifth Committee, adopted **resolution 47/202 B** without vote.

The General Assembly,

Recalling its resolutions on the control and limitation of documentation, including resolutions 33/56 of 14 December 1978, 36/117 B of 10 December 1981, 37/14 C of 16 November 1982 and 45/238 B of 21 December 1990,

Recognizing the sovereign right of Member States to request circulation of communications as official documents,

Emphasizing the importance of timely availability of pre-session documentation,

Noting that summary records for some bodies entitled to such records have been discontinued for some time,

Taking into account annex VI, section III, to the rules of procedure of the General Assembly,

Noting with concern that some United Nations bodies may not be able to consider agenda items for which pre-session documents are submitted after those sessions have begun,

1. *Renews its appeal* to Member States to exercise restraint in their requests for circulation of communications and to submit their communications in the most appropriate, brief, complete and concise form possible and in a timely manner;

2. *Requests* Member States to exercise restraint in requesting documentation and in the submission of their reports;

3. *Encourages* those subsidiary organs that comply with the desirable thirty-two-page limit to continue that welcome practice;

4. *Urges* those subsidiary organs that have been unable to comply with the desirable thirty-two-page limit, in particular those provided with summary records, to make efforts to reduce the length of future reports;

5. *Encourages* those bodies that receive summary records and whose reports exceed the thirty-two-page limit to consider relinquishing their entitlement to summary records;

6. *Urges* those bodies that receive summary records to consider relinquishing their entitlement when drafting is being undertaken in formal session and duly recorded in the report;

7. *Urges* the Secretary-General to take necessary measures to ensure that pre-session documents for meetings are distributed no less than six weeks before the meetings in all official languages, unless there is a specific decision by the body concerned regarding the timing of issuance of pre-session documentation;

8. *Urges* the substantive departments of the Secretariat to comply with the rule which requires them to submit pre-session documents to the Office of Conference Services at least ten weeks before the beginning of sessions, in order to permit processing in time in all official languages;

9. *Requests* the Secretary-General, in the context of the measures mentioned in paragraphs 7 and 8 above, to review all of the factors involved in the timely issuance of pre-session documentation, including the quality and timeliness of submission to the Office of Conference Services, and to report thereon to the General Assembly at its forty-ninth session through the Committee on Conferences;

10. *Requests* the Secretariat to bring to the attention of all organs and the substantive offices concerned the relevant General Assembly resolutions, rules and regulations on control and limitation of documentation, including the guidelines for drafting reports contained in General Assembly resolution 37/14 C and information on the notional cost per page of documentation;

11. *Requests* the Secretary-General to review current mailing lists with the aim of pruning and updating them and eliminating waste;

12. *Urges* subsidiary organs to review their agendas with a view to enabling the Secretariat to comply with the six-week rule, *inter alia*, through combining agenda items and limiting requests for pre-session documentation, and requests the Secretary-General to inform the subsidiary organs of this appeal and to report orally to the Committee on Conferences on the measures taken to this effect;

13. *Appeals* to intergovernmental bodies to make active use of the report on the state of preparation of pre-session documentation when reviewing the organizational arrangements for substantive sessions;

14. *Welcomes* the decision of the Committee on Conferences to review the criteria for, status of and guidelines on the provision of written meeting records, and requests the Committee, taking into account the costs of conference servicing, to report thereon to the General Assembly at its forty-eighth session with concrete recommendations;

15. *Requests* the Secretary-General to provide summary records in a timely manner, particularly for the meetings of the Main Committees of the General Assembly, and in this regard urges him to improve the overall efficiency of conference services within existing resources;

16. *Decides* that, at its forty-ninth session, there shall be a comprehensive review of, *inter alia*, the need for and usefulness and timely issuance of verbatim and sum-

mary records, on the basis of a report by the Secretary-General through the Committee on Conferences and the Advisory Committee on Administrative and Budgetary Questions;

17. *Requests* the Secretariat to issue the verbatim records of the plenary meetings of the General Assembly in final form only, on the understanding that those records would be issued promptly and that consolidated corrigenda would be issued at appropriate intervals;

18. *Also requests* the Secretariat to pursue the possibility of issuing the verbatim records of the Security Council in a similar manner, on the understanding that these records would be issued as promptly as the provisional ones are issued at present.

General Assembly resolution 47/202 B

22 December 1992   Meeting 93   Adopted without vote

Approved by Fifth Committee (A/47/806) without vote, 17 December (meeting 47); draft by Bangladesh (A/C.5/47/L.11), based on informal consultations; agenda item 110.

Meeting numbers. GA 47th session: 5th Committee 4, 5, 8-11, 47; plenary 93.

Publications policy

In August,[4] the Committee on Conferences reviewed a provisional outline of a report of the Secretary-General on the overall publications policy of the Organization, which was being prepared for the 1993 session of the General Assembly, as requested in 1991.[7]

The Committee stressed that the report should be analytical in nature, presenting a critical assessment of publications policies and practices, identifying possible duplications or contradictions between instructions, and elaborating on current or proposed controls that could assist evaluation of the extent to which publications met their objectives.

Organization of editorial services

During 1992, in the process of restructuring the United Nations, editorial units at Headquarters were grouped along functional lines. An October note of the Secretariat[8] briefly outlined those changes; however, the question of whether it would be advantageous to consolidate editorial services under the Office of Conference Services would be examined further in the context of ongoing reviews of the Secretariat structure and the Organizations's overall publications policy.

On 23 December, by **decision 47/460 A**, the General Assembly took note of the Secretariat note.

REFERENCES

[1]A/INF/47/1. [2]YUN 1969, p. 830, GA res. 2538(XIV), 11 Dec. 1969. [3]YUN 1991, p. 920. [4]A/47/32. [5]A/AC.172/148. [6]A/AC.172/149. [7]YUN 1991, p. 921, GA res. 46/185 B, sect. VI, 20 Dec. 1991. [8]A/C.5/47/12.

UN premises

Addis Ababa and Bangkok conference facilities

The annual progress report of the Secretary-General on the construction of additional conference facilities at Addis Ababa and Bangkok was submitted to the Fifth Committee in October 1992.[1] The report summarized the development of the two projects, approved in 1984,[2] and outlined the current status of construction and revised projections for their completion.

The Secretary-General reported that the pace of construction at Addis Adaba had improved substantially, but the project was only 13 per cent complete as of 1 September 1992, representing a delay of about six to seven months. Problems related to transportation and the availability of materials and labour continued to affect project timetables and cost estimates and the contractor had assumed a *force majeure* extension of 57 days and submitted a revised project timetable showing the completion of construction in December 1994. It was expected that the delays, the *force majeure* situation and other factors would affect the total original project cost of $107,576,900; however, it was anticipated that those factors could be absorbed within the present project budget.

The conference facilities at Bangkok were expected to be completed in November/December 1992, and commissioned in January/March 1993. Regarding damages brought by the United Nations against the contractor for failure to complete the project on time and the counter-suit by the contractor against the Organization, a comprehensive agreement was reached by the two parties. It was expected that the total project cost would not exceed the authorized $48,540,000.

Commenting on the Secretary-General's report,[3] ACABQ noted that the contractor in Addis Ababa had submitted a claim on 28 April for approximately $600,000 to cover the cost of the 57-day *force majeure* period and a second claim for approximately $14 million. He had also requested a 244-day extension of the completion deadline. The Advisory Committee shared the view of the Secretariat that the second claim, representing 20 per cent of the base contract total, was very high. ACABQ trusted that any settlement regarding those claims would be absorbed within the approved budget, and requested that it receive a progress report on the Addis Ababa project in 1993.

On 23 December, by **resolution 47/219 A, section II**, the General Assembly, on the Fifth Committee's recommendation, took note of the Secretary-General's report and concurred with ACABQ's recommendations and requests.

Reimbursement of office accommodation costs

The Secretary-General presented in December 1991 a report to the Fifth Committee on the issue of reimbursement to the regular budget of the cost of accommodation for posts related to extra-budgetary activities,[4] as requested by the Assembly in 1989.[5] The report was not considered by the General Assembly at its 1991 session and was therefore resubmitted in 1992. According to the report, the regular budget of the United Nations bore a large portion of the cost of accommodation for staff charged against extrabudgetary resources. In the absence of a definitive policy on this matter, it had proved difficult to obtain reimbursement for those costs.

One suggestion to improve the current reimbursement system was that all specialized agencies be charged a proportionate share of operating expenses and common service costs in addition to rent.

ACABQ, in December 1992,[6] said the report was incomplete and requested an updated and thorough analysis, which it would consider with the proposed programme budget for 1994-1995.

By **decision 47/460** of 23 December, the General Assembly took note of the Secretary-General's report.

REFERENCES

[1]A/C.5/47/11. [2]YUN 1984, pp. 620 & 628, GA res. 39/236, sect. III & XI, 18 Dec. 1984. [3]A/47/7/Add.2. [4]A/C.5/46/56. [5]GA res. 44/201 B, 21 Dec. 1989. [6]A/47/7/Add.9.

Information systems and computers

Technological innovations

During 1992, efforts continued to upgrade the technological infrastructure of the United Nations in the areas of desktop and larger computers and in communications technology to enhance connectivity among major duty stations.

According to the second annual report of the Secretary-General on the status of technological innovations in the United Nations,[1] presented in October 1992 in response to a 1991 General Assembly request,[2] the total number of personal computers at Headquarters had increased 23 per cent from 2,800 in 1991 to 3,450 in 1992. At offices away from Headquarters, the number had increased 127 per cent, from 2,470 in 1991 to 5,600 in 1992. The capacity to share information among users was increased through local area networks (LANs). The number of LAN servers increased by 61 per cent from 28 in 1991 to 45, supporting 830 personal computers. At other duty stations, the number of LAN servers increased by 135 per cent to 80, with the total number of personal computers connected to LANs up by 251 per cent from 700 to 2,460.

A more powerful LAN server—the UNIX—was being acquired to house large organizational databases, such as the integrated management information system (IMIS) and the optical disk system.

Establishing a comprehensive, global network system for the Organization remained a high priority. In the 1992-1993 biennium, the first phase of the installation of wiring for LANs, capable of carrying both voice and high-speed data traffic, was undertaken. The entire project was expected to be completed by the end of 1995 at a cost of $6 million. Efforts were also being made to modernize local communications systems at other duty stations.

The upgrading of the Organization's telecommunications network from analog to digital technology continued, with the provision of additional voice channel capacity between New York and Bangkok. Upgrades between New York and Nairobi and Addis Ababa through the deployment of digital Earth stations were also under way and the existing network of Earth stations used to support peace-keeping operations was gradually being retrofitted for digital operation. In addition, the United Nations was undertaking a comprehensive replacement and modernization of telephone systems at its offices in Addis Ababa, Bangkok, Geneva, Nairobi and Vienna.

The Organization also planned to replace existing data network facilities with packet switching equipment. Several other new technological applications were in the process of being installed during 1992, including IMIS, scheduled to become partly operational early in 1993 and the optical disk document storage and retrieval system.

Other applications discussed in the report included the United Nations standard word processing package; electronic mail; connection to Internet, a network of non-commercial organizations; and specialized applications developed by individual departments.

Telecommunications support for peace-keeping operations remained a major focus. Rapid-deployment communications kits were used for work in remote areas and the Field Operations Division was engaged in strategic planning for the use of new technologies for headquarters operations as well as for established and upcoming missions.

ACABQ submitted its comments on the report in December, together with comments on the optical disk project.[3]

Optical disk project

In November 1992,[4] the Secretary-General presented a progress report on the optical disk storage and retrieval system, as requested by the General Assembly in 1991.[2] At that time, the Assembly also approved phase II of the project for 1992-1993, subject to a performance report in 1992. The system uses international standards for storing, retrieving and transmitting text and image documents. In January, the optical disk storage equipment, UNIX servers and software, purchased as a part of phase I of the optical disk storage and retrieval project, were installed in Geneva and New York and the customized software was installed in June. The system was being integrated with the United Nations Bibliographic Information System (UNBIS) and the Document Recording, Information and Tracking System (DRITS). It was also expected that permanent missions of Member States at Geneva and New York would be linked to the system through the integrated services digital networks (ISDN) during the first quarter of 1993.

The Secretary-General proposed a revised distribution of the $1,564,500 already budgeted for phase II of the project among its various components. He also proposed that priority be given to establishing the system database during the remainder of the current biennium.

During phase III of the project, projected to cost $5.1 million and scheduled for 1994-1995, more resources would be devoted to extending system access within the Secretariat to translators, revisers, editors, reference and terminology and library staff in New York and Geneva.

Expected benefits from the completed system included reduced need for document storage; reduced print runs for parliamentary documents; improved efficiency through elimination of the need to prepare separate diskettes for various user departments; simplification of document archiving; and elimination of the need for missions to keep reference units for United Nations documents.

In December,[3] ACABQ agreed to the Secretary-General's proposed revised distribution of funds to cover phase II of the project.

On 23 December, by **resolution 47/219 A, section XIII**, adopted on the recommendation of the Fifth Committee, the General Assembly took note of the Secretary-General's report and endorsed ACABQ's recommendations.

Integrated management information system

The fourth progress report on the IMIS project was submitted to the Fifth Committee by the Secretary-General in October 1992.[5] The project, approved by the General Assembly in 1988,[6] was to develop an integrated system for the processing of and reporting on administrative actions at all major duty stations, to replace numerous independent systems.

Originally, the project was to be implemented over a three-and-one-half year period at a cost not to exceed $28 million. The report outlined a revised implementation strategy for IMIS, which at Headquarters was planned to occur in five releases, between the beginning of 1993 and January 1994. Upon completion, the installation of the entire system would be undertaken at other offices, at Addis Ababa, Ethiopia; Amman, Jordan; Bangkok, Thailand; Geneva; Nairobi, Kenya; Santiago, Chile; Vienna, Mexico City and Port-of-Spain, Trinidad. The report discussed the construction of the system, the installation of local area networks, the training of technical staff and users, and work-flow studies. It also presented the conclusions of independent experts, who evaluated the project, in accordance with a 1991 Assembly request,[2] and detailed the anticipated benefits to be derived from the System.

The total reassessed cost of the project through mid-1994, the expected completion date, was $41,332,900. The regular budget share of the project (65.1 per cent) would amount to $26,907,700, of which $19,579,200 had already been appropriated.

An appropriation for the regular budget share of the remaining costs of the project would be requested in the context of the proposed programme budget for 1994-1995, not including additional requirements for general temporary assistance amounting to $747,900 in 1993 and $808,800 for 1994-1995. In addition, hardware and software maintenance costs were estimated at approximately $750,000 per year (or 15 per cent of their estimated purchase cost). These costs were not included in the total estimate of $41.3 million for developing the project. The combined estimate for hardware and software amounted to $6.2 million.

ACABQ, in December,[3] noted that estimated expenditures for 1989-1993 totalled $22,167,500, against regular budget appropriations amounting to $19,579,200, leaving a shortfall in 1993 of $2,588,300. The Secretary-General therefore requested the Assembly to reconsider its proposed programme budget for 1992-1993 and restore $2,588,000 out of a reduction approved in 1991. The Advisory Committee believed that implementation of IMIS should proceed as outlined by the Secretary-General but it recommended that the Assembly defer action on the request to restore the shortfall.

The General Assembly, by **resolution 47/219 A, section XIV**, adopted on 23 December on the recommendation of the Fifth Committee, took note of the Secretary-General's report and endorsed ACABQ's recommendations.

UN informatics systems

In June 1992, the Secretary-General submitted a report[7] to the Economic and Social Council on international cooperation in the field of informatics, pursuant to a 1991 Council resolution,[8] which had recommended more effective use of the existing coordinating mechanisms for informatics within the United Nations system.

The report provided information on the current and planned activities of the United Nations and its agencies in this field as well as arrangements for cooperation and coordination with other organizations of the system.

The report found that informatics projects fell under two main groupings; those that were global and mainly directed to the headquarters functions of United Nations agencies, but were also available to other agencies and governmental offices; and technical cooperation projects that were implemented at the national or regional level and designed to reinforce national capacities to manage specific substantive programmes. It noted, however, that there was no general framework for overall coordination and applications in developing countries. The report recommended that the new Department of Economic and Social Development consider developing a framework to identify problems that could be addressed through cooperation among United Nations bodies for the benefit of developing countries; and propose projects and programme activities at national and regional levels to foster the use of modern informatics technology for economic and social development.

In another June report,[9] the Secretary-General presented the results of a study, requested by the Council in 1991,[10] outlining means of giving Member States, particularly developing countries, economical and unhindered access to United Nations databases, information systems and services. The report summarized the results of a questionnaire that was submitted to the missions of all Member States in New York and Geneva to determine their technological infrastructure, and described the status of the most-requested databases and database activities of the regional commissions. It also discussed the need for user-friendly access to data, a continuous flow of information to Member States, training and policy coordination, and the need to expand on-line services beyond the United Nations system.

The report cited a one-time cost of $226,000 and a recurring cost of $32,000 directly attributable to database activities, which could be absorbed within existing budget resources for 1994-1995. The Secretary-General noted that phase one to provide easy access to systems and services had begun. In phase two, longer-term components, such as the acquisition of the gateway computer and the provision of a continuous computer literacy training programme, would require additional resources.

ECONOMIC AND SOCIAL COUNCIL ACTION

On 31 July, the Economic and Social Council adopted **resolution 1992/60** without vote.

The need to harmonize and improve United Nations informatics systems for optimal utilization and accessibility by all States

The Economic and Social Council,

Recalling its resolution 1991/70 of 26 July 1991,

Taking note with appreciation of the report prepared by the Secretary-General analysing the causes of the present situation with respect to United Nations informatics systems, and of the outline of solutions presented in that report,

1. *Stresses* the priority that it attaches to easy, economical, uncomplicated and unhindered access for States Members of the United Nations and for observers to the growing computerized databases and information systems and services of the United Nations;

2. *Reiterates* the urgent need for representatives of States to be closely consulted and actively associated with the respective executive and governing bodies of the concerned United Nations institutions, such as the International Computing Centre and the Advisory Committee for the Coordination of Information Systems, dealing with informatics within the United Nations system, so that the specific needs of States as internal end-users can be given due priority;

3. *Calls* for the urgent implementation of measures, if necessary in a phased programme, in order to achieve the objective of easy, economical, uncomplicated and unhindered access for all Member States and observers, in particular through their permanent missions, to United Nations computerized databases and information systems and services;

4. *Requests* that the initial phases of this action programme be implemented from within existing resources and in full consultation with the representatives of States;

5. *Requests* the Secretary-General to report on the follow-up action taken on the present resolution to the Economic and Social Council at its substantive session of 1993;

6. *Calls on* Member States to pursue similar action in the governing bodies of the specialized agencies within which they are represented.

Economic and Social Council resolution 1992/60

31 July 1992   Meeting 42   Adopted without vote

25-nation draft (E/1992/L.37), orally revised; agenda item 6 *(c)*.

Sponsors: Argentina, Australia, Austria, China, Colombia, Egypt, Finland, Hungary, Israel, Lebanon, Malaysia, Mexico, Morocco, Myanmar, Norway, Pakistan, Philippines, Poland, Republic of Korea, Romania, Russian Federation, Sri Lanka, Sweden, Switzerland, Turkey.

International Computing Centre

The 1993 budget estimates for the International Computing Centre (ICC) were submitted by the Secretary-General in October 1992.[11] The Centre, established in 1971, provided a comprehensive range of data and text processing and related telecommunications services to those organizations of the United Nations system wishing to use them. Its 1993 budget estimate was $13,789,700, compared with $13,053,600 in 1992. Those organizations expected to use the Centre in 1993 included: the United Nations, the World Health Organization, UNDP, UNICEF, the International Labour Organisation, the World Meteorological Organization , the United Nations Research Institute for Social Development, the United Nations Environment Programme, the General Agreement on Tariffs and Trade, the World Intellectual Property Organization, the United Nations Educational, Scientific and Cultural Organization, the International Trade Centre, the Office of the United Nations High Commissioner for Refugees, the World Food Programme, the World Bank, the International Fund for Agricultural Development, the United Nations Industrial Development Organization, the International Monetary Fund, FAO, and the International Atomic Energy Agency (IAEA).

The estimated cost to the United Nations for its use of the Centre in 1993 was $2,924,300. The ICC Management Committee agreed that its Director should recommend to the Consultative Committee on Administrative Questions (Financial and Budgetary Questions) a biennial budget for ICC.

On 23 December, by **resolution 47/219 A, section V**, adopted on the recommendation of the Fifth Committee, the General Assembly approved the 1993 budget estimates of ICC, amounting to $13,789,700, as proposed in the report of the Secretary-General.

REFERENCES

[1]A/C.5/47/18. [2]YUN 1991 p. 924, GA res. 46/185 B, 20 Dec. 1991. [3]A/47/7/Add.8. [4]A/C.5/47/18/Add.1. [5]A/C.5/47/27. [6]GA res. 43/217, 21 Dec. 1988. [7]E/1992/55. [8]YUN 1991, p. 484 ESC res. 1991/71, 26 July 1991. [9]E/1992/78. [10]YUN 1991, p. 925, ESC res. 1991/70, 26 July 1991. [11]A/C.5/47/24.

Other administrative and budgetary arrangements

UNSCEAR

The results of a study on possible alternative arrangements for the secretariat of the United Nations Scientific Committee on the Effects of Atomic Radiation (UNSCEAR), including its merger with IAEA, were addressed in an October 1992 report of the Secretary-General,[1] as requested by the Assembly in 1991.[2] UNSCEAR was located in the United Nations Office at Vienna and was served by a small secretariat. Its mandate was to review

published reports and technical documents submitted by Member States of the Organization, the specialized agencies and IAEA on the sources and effects of ionizing radiation, and to evaluate the global exposure of man and assess the risk of harmful effects.

The proposal for a possible merger with IAEA was prompted by the location of both bodies at Vienna and their concern with atomic radiation. The Secretary-General was of the view that, because of the differing mandates, a merger of the UNSCEAR secretariat with IAEA would compromise the independent standing of UNSCEAR and he recommended that its present organizational location and administrative support be maintained.

ACABQ[3] recommended that other alternatives for the organizational location of and administrative support arrangements for the UNSCEAR secretariat be explored. (For information on the 1992 session of UNSCEAR, see PART ONE, Chapter IV.)

The General Assembly, by **resolution 47/219 A, section VI**, adopted on 23 December on the recommendation of the Fifth Committee, took note of the report of the Secretary-General and requested him to explore possible alternatives for the organizational location of and administrative support arrangements for the secretariat of UNSCEAR.

UNITAR

In October 1992, the Secretary-General, as requested by the General Assembly in 1991,[4] submitted a report on the United Nations Institute for Training and Research (UNITAR)[5] in which he proposed that the United Nations take over UNITAR's building in New York in exchange for cancelling its debt to the United Nations which, as of 30 June 1992, stood at $10,970,800, and for coverage of UNITAR's 1992 financial obligations (see PART THREE, Chapter XII).

The Secretary-General, in December,[6] stated that the total additional appropriations required under the programme budget for 1992-1993, covering the cancellation of UNITAR's debt, its financial obligations in 1992, the annual cost for building maintenance and security, repairs and improvements, and transitional arrangements from 1 January to 30 June 1993, was $15,989,000.

The Fifth Committee, in considering the programme budget for 1992-1993, recommended that, in order to provide the minimal transitional requirements for UNITAR until the Assembly could consider this matter at its resumed forty-seventh session, the Assembly authorize the Secretary-General to commit funds, not to exceed $400,000, with the concurrence of ACABQ, for the period

1 January through 28 February 1993, with advances from the Working Capital Fund, to cover all building security and maintenance costs and to maintain the existing number of staff members at UNITAR's New York office for whom placement was to be sought elsewhere within the United Nations system.

GENERAL ASSEMBLY ACTION

On 23 December, on the recommendation of the Fifth Committee, the General Assembly adopted **resolution 47/219 A, section XXIV,** without vote.

United Nations Institute for Training and Research
[*The General Assembly . . .*]

Decides, in order to provide for the minimal transitional requirements for the United Nations Institute for Training and Research until the General Assembly can consider this matter at its resumed forty-seventh session, to authorize the Secretary-General to commit funds, not to exceed 400,000 dollars, for the period 1 January through 28 February 1993, by advances from the Working Capital Fund, to cover all costs related to the provision of security and maintenance of the premises of the Institute, as well as the costs of maintaining the existing number of staff members of the New York office of the Institute for whom placement is to be sought elsewhere within the United Nations system, in accordance with General Assembly resolution 42/197 of 11 December 1987;

. . .

General Assembly resolution 47/219 A, section XXIV

23 December 1992   Meeting 94   Adopted without vote

Approved by Fifth Committee (A/47/835) without vote, 19 December (meeting 50); oral proposal by Chairman; agenda item 104.
Meeting numbers. GA 47th session: 5th Committee 50; plenary 94.

The General Assembly, on 22 December, decided to defer consideration of a draft resolution on UNITAR,[7] originating in the Second (Economic and Financial) Committee, until its resumed forty-seventh session.

REFERENCES

[1]A/C.5/47/26. [2]YUN 1991, p. 872, GA res. 46/185 C, 20 Dec. 1991. [3]A/47/7/Add.3. [4]YUN 1991, p. 648, GA res. 46/180, 19 Dec. 1991. [5]A/47/458. [6]A/C.5/47/82. [7]A/C.2/47/L.91.

UN Postal Administration

In 1992, the gross revenue of the United Nations Postal Administration (UNPA) from its sale of philatelic items both at Headquarters and at overseas offices totalled more than $15 million. Revenue from the sale of stamps for philatelic purposes was retained by the United Nations. Under the terms of an agreement between the Organization and the United States, revenue from the sale of United States dollar-denominated stamps used for postage from Headquarters was reimbursed to the United States Postal Service. Similarly, postal agreements between the United Nations and the Governments of Switzerland and Austria required that revenue derived from the sale of Swiss franc-denominated stamps and Austrian schilling-denominated stamps for postage be reimbursed to the Swiss and Austrian postal authorities, respectively.

During the year, UNPA released six commemorative stamp issues, six definitive stamps, two souvenir cards, nine maximum cards, three pictorial postcards and two airletters.

The first set of six commemorative stamps, entitled ''World Heritage—UNESCO'', was released on 24 January to honour UNESCO's efforts to protect world heritage sites.

On 13 March, commemorative stamps were also issued on the theme ''Clean Oceans'', and on 22 May, a third issue, entitled ''Earth Summit'' was released to commemorate the United Nations Conference on Environment and Development, held in Rio de Janeiro, Brazil, from 3 to 14 June 1992.

Stamps were issued on 4 September to commemorate International Space Year—Mission to Planet Earth, and on 2 October on the theme ''Science and Technology for Development''.

The fourth set of stamps in the Human Rights Series was issued on 20 November, illustrating articles 19 to 24 of the Universal Declaration of Human Rights.[1]

REFERENCE
[1]YUN 1948-49, p. 535, GA res. 217 A (III), 10 Dec. 1948.

PART SEVEN

Intergovernmental organizations related to the United Nations

Chapter I

International Atomic Energy Agency (IAEA)

In 1992, the International Atomic Energy Agency (IAEA) continued to foster peaceful uses of nuclear energy and the exchange of scientific and technical information, to establish and administer safeguards, to provide technical assistance to its member States and to establish health and safety standards.

In September, a review conference of the 1987 Convention on the Physical Protection of Nuclear Material,[a] convened by the Director General as depositary, affirmed that the Convention provided a sound basis for the physical protection of nuclear material during international transport and was acceptable in its current form.

Under the auspices of IAEA, an agreement on the International Thermonuclear Experimental Reactor Engineering Design Activities (ITER-EDA) was signed (Washington, D.C., 21 July 1992) by the four ITER parties—the European Atomic Energy Community, Japan, the Russian Federation and the United States.

IAEA carried out inspections in the Democratic People's Republic of Korea, Iraq and South Africa.

The thirty-sixth session of the IAEA General Conference (Vienna, 21-25 September 1992) adopted resolutions relating to measures to strengthen international cooperation in nuclear safety and radiological protection; South Africa's nuclear capabilities; Iraq's non-compliance with its safeguards obligations; IAEA safeguards in the Middle East; strengthening safeguards; practical use of food irradiation in developing countries; and a plan to produce potable water economically.

Estonia and Slovenia became members of IAEA, bringing the number of member States to 114 at the end of 1992. (See Annex I for complete membership.)

Nuclear safety and radiation protection

In 1992, IAEA's work under the programme on safety and nuclear installations continued to shift from establishing standards of safety to providing for their application. It also focused on the safety of nuclear powerplants in Eastern Europe and the successor States of the former USSR.

A new safety series report, updating a publication on the 1986 accident at the Chernobyl nuclear powerplant in Ukraine, reviewed earlier conclusions about the causes of the accident and found

that the design of the reactor's control rods and safety systems and deficiencies in the regulation and management of safety played a greater role than was previously acknowledged.

During 1992, there were five Operational Safety Review Team missions to nuclear powerplants, four follow-up visits and two technical exchange visits. In addition, 18 Assessment of Safety Significant Events Team missions were carried out and an International Regulatory Review Team visited Romania to advise and assist in strengthening and enhancing its nuclear regulatory body.

The International Nuclear Event Scale (INES) was used in many countries to rate nuclear incidents. A related information system was made operational, through which INES national officers in 50 member States were provided with timely information. In 1992, information on 72 nuclear events was communicated through the continuously operational system. A test period began for the use of INES in non-reactor facilities.

IAEA continued to implement an extra-budgetary programme of assistance to Eastern Europe and the successor States of the former USSR. In the area of nuclear plant safety assessment, Agency efforts helped to achieve a consensus on the technical safety issues for first-generation pressurized-water reactors.

Several site/seismic safety reviews carried out in 1992 were follow-up activities of recommendations made in missions to sites in 1990 (Kozloduy, Bulgaria; Bohunice, Czechoslovakia; Muria, Indonesia; Chashma, Pakistan). New reviews involved a plant currently shut down (the Armenia nuclear powerplant) and one in operation (Krsko, Slovenia).

IAEA conducted Integrated Safety Assessment of Research Reactors (INSARR) reviews in 1992 in Peru, Portugal and Turkey. INSARR teams visited research reactors in Argentina, Peru, Romania, Slovenia and Turkey to review safety standards and measures.

The radiation protection programme focused on developing international basic safety standards for protection against ionizing radiation and the safety of radiation sources. The 1992 IAEA General Conference approved a proposal for education and

---

[a]YUN 1987, p. 1187.

training in radiation protection and nuclear safety and asked IAEA to implement it. Support was given to the United Nations International Cooperation Project for Chernobyl through a joint project with the Food and Agriculture Organization of the United Nations (FAO) on the use of caesium binders for reducing radiocaesium contamination of the milk and meat of grazing animals. IAEA Radiation Protection Advisory Teams visited Albania, Poland and the United Arab Emirates. A project to provide radiation protection services to 16 African member States showed that 11 of them had enforced radiation protection legislation and 4 had at least an advanced draft ready to be promulgated. The IAEA Emergency Response Unit was maintained in a fully operational state 24 hours a day.

Nuclear power

Assistance to IAEA developing member States for nuclear power programme planning and development included support to China, for nuclear power economics and development plans; Peru, for energy and power assessment programmes; and Romania, for energy demand forecasting and electricity expansion planning. Czechoslovakia received assistance, with support from Spain, for the preliminary evaluation of bids for the next nuclear powerplant to be ordered. A case-study on the feasibility of small and medium power reactors in Egypt was completed, and support continued to be provided to the National Atomic Energy Agency of Indonesia in training personnel to conduct a feasibility study for its first nuclear powerplant.

At the end of 1992, the Power Reactor Information System (PRIS) database included information on the status and operating experience of some 423 nuclear powerplants. There were 64 users in 26 countries and 3 international organizations. A subset of the databank, MicroPRIS, was distributed to 147 users in 50 member States and 7 international organizations.

In the area of nuclear fusion, activities focused on lifetime predictions for fusion materials.

Nuclear fuel cycle

Uranium production outside the centrally planned economies declined further in 1992, by about 4,500 tonnes to 23,500 tonnes, due to continuing unfavourable market conditions. Nine countries produced 95 per cent of the total and eight countries contributed the remaining 5 per cent. The resulting production was covered by material held in stock and inventories in China and the former USSR.

In the area of reactor-fuel technology and performance, technical committee meetings were held on fuel failure (Dimitrovgrad, Russian Federa-

tion); the behaviour of core materials and fission-product release in accident conditions in light water reactors (Cadarache, France); fission-gas release and fuel-rod chemistry related to extended burn-up (Ontario, Canada); and in-core instrumentation and *in situ* measurements (Petten, Netherlands).

Missions to Hungary and Ukraine advised on the management of spent fuel from nuclear power reactors.

Radioactive waste management

In 1992, IAEA's radioactive waste management programme focused on: developing and implementing its Radioactive Waste Safety Standards programme; strengthening the waste-management infrastructure in countries where waste arose from the use of radioactive materials; and collecting and distributing technical information on handling, processing and disposing of radioactive waste generated from nuclear applications. Other areas emphasized strengthening the capabilities of member States in: technical and regulatory aspects of decommissioning nuclear facilities (including research reactors and uranium mining and milling plants); assessing the radiological and environmental impacts of waste disposal; and quality assurance methods for waste packages and disposal systems.

Under the radioactive waste management advisory programme, two regular missions and one fact-finding mission were carried out. Assistance was provided to member States in the form of fact-finding missions to assess the safety of uranium mine-mill tailing sites and the effectiveness of waste-management infrastructures. Training courses were organized on a systems approach to radioactive waste management (Czechoslovakia and Egypt); management of spent radiation sources (Brazil); ageing, decommissioning and major refurbishment of research reactors (Thailand); and marine radioactivity studies (Mexico). A symposium on the geological disposal of spent-fuel, high-level and alpha-bearing wastes was organized jointly with the Commission of the European Communities and the Nuclear Energy Agency of the Organisation for Economic Cooperation and Development.

IAEA initiated with Norway and the Russian Federation a programme to investigate and assess the consequences of dumping radioactive wastes in the Arctic seas and to consider the feasibility of possible remedial actions. The programme had the support of the parties to the Convention on the Prevention of Marine Pollution by Dumping of Wastes and Other Matter (London Convention 1972, formerly known as the London Dumping Convention).

Food and agriculture

Under a joint IAEA/FAO programme, member States were assisted in using nuclear techniques in their agricultural research and development to improve food production, reduce food losses and protect the environment. In keeping with worldwide trends, greater emphasis was placed on nuclear biotechnology tools and environmental problems. IAEA sought to contribute to increasing and sustaining soil fertility and crop production by focusing on identifying and selecting genotypes of crops that were capable of growing and producing well in soils low in plant nutrients, in saline and acidic soils and under drought conditions. A wheat genotype was discovered in Morocco with both high yield and high water-use efficiency.

A project on the genetic improvement of basic food crops in Africa emphasized the domestication of local plant species as sources of food. The first phase of a regional project on cereal improvement in Latin America found that, through intensive training, expert services and a research network, it was possible to integrate modern mutation techniques into plant-breeding practices on a large scale.

Support was provided for national animal production and veterinary institutes in the use of radioimmunoassay, enzyme-immunoassay and deoxyribonucleic acid probes to improve the sustainability of livestock production systems through better feeding, reproductive management, and diagnosis and control of animal diseases. Strides were made towards eradicating rinderpest in Africa, so that in 1992 the disease occurred in only two countries.

The sterile insect technique programme in the Libyan Arab Jamihiriya eradicated the screwworm fly from North Africa (see PART THREE, Chapter III). Also in North Africa, the Maghrebmeb project evaluated the feasibility of medfly eradication from Algeria, the Libyan Arab Jamahiriya, Morocco and Tunisia, where it caused losses of $90 million annually. Other species of fruit fly were the targets of activities in Pakistan, the Philippines and Thailand. Further progress was achieved in combating tsetse flies in Zanzibar, United Republic of Tanzania.

In 1992, an action plan was developed for utilizing food irradiation in developing countries. In France, Indonesia and the United States, three additional food irradiators became available for processing food and other products, bringing the total number of such facilities to 53. Support was given to Bangladesh, Ghana and Viet Nam to build demonstration irradiators for treating food and sterilizing medical supplies.

Human health

The programme on human health addressed issues where nuclear techniques were especially efficient and cost-effective in the prevention, diagnosis, prognosis and treatment of diseases, or in the analysis of health problems related to the environment, such as pollution and the availability of nutrients. In collaboration with the World Health Organization (WHO), it emphasized techniques suitable for the study and management of communicable diseases, nutritional problems, and cancer, heart and brain diseases, all of which were of special significance to developing countries. Projects in 1992 continued to focus on strengthening indigenous skills and capabilities not only in methodology, but also in reagent production and in maintenance, repair and upgrading of medical nuclear instruments.

The IAEA/WHO Secondary Standard Dosimetry Laboratory Network included 65 laboratories and 6 national organizations in 52 member States, as well as 14 affiliated members. Services continued in the areas of dose intercomparison and assurance, and support for technology transfer.

Nutritional and health-related environmental studies focused on micronutrient nutrition projects, research on environmental pollution using nuclear and isotope techniques and services to international pollution-monitoring programmes.

Physical and earth sciences

IAEA continued to promote the exchange of information on physical and earth sciences and to assist countries with the application of nuclear techniques in experimental physics, analytical and radiation chemistry, non-destructive testing, radiation processing, industrial process control, geology, mining and hydrology.

Some 4,000 scientists participated in the activities of the International Centre for Theoretical Physics (Trieste, Italy) and in the programme for training at Italian laboratories. Over 56 per cent of the scientists came from developing countries.

The industry and earth sciences programme focused on nuclear methods to monitor and control environmental pollution; assessment and transfer of radiation technology; assessment and transfer of nucleonic control systems and radiotracer applications in the mineral industry; assessment of water resources, emphasizing arid and semi-arid regions; evaluation of the contamination risk for water resources and of processes of contaminant transport in water bodies; exploration of geothermal areas, emphasizing high enthalpy fluids; and studies of sediment transport–related problems.

Environmental protection

The IAEA Marine Environment Laboratory (Monaco) continued its collaboration with the United Nations Environment Programme (UNEP) and the Intergovernmental Oceanographic Commission of the United Nations Educational, Scientific and Cultural Organization (UNESCO) to provide comprehensive technical support for the assessment of global and regional marine pollution. An IAEA/UNEP/UNESCO Memorandum of Understanding was signed to set out strategies for tripartite coordinated planning and implementation of activities on marine pollution by the Laboratory.

During the year, there was an increasing demand for the services of the Laboratory. It participated in an assessment of the consequences of past disposals of high-activity-reactor components in the marginal seas of the Arctic Ocean. Besides waste-disposal impact assessment, the Laboratory's programme included analytical quality control services, in-house and field training, capacity-building, radioactivity monitoring, radiological assessment, marine modelling, database provision, emergency response planning and the application of nuclear and isotopic techniques to the marine sciences, including assessment of post-war pollution in the Persian Gulf, contributions to understanding the global carbon cycle and commencement of a Black Sea pollution tracer study. In addition, the Laboratory participated in an extensive experimental survey of nuclear and non-nuclear contamination along the Danube River basin.

IAEA laboratories (Seibersdorf, Austria) participated in many environmental activities of the Agency. The chemistry unit continued to assist in the World Meteorological Organization's Background Air Pollution Monitoring Network by acting as a sample collection, data acquisition and distribution centre.

Technical cooperation

During 1992, a total of 1,094 projects were operational under IAEA's technical cooperation programme for the transfer of nuclear technologies in medicine, agriculture, industry and other fields, of which 193 were completed. Activities included the provision of training to more than 2,150 scientists, the assignment of some 2,250 experts and lecturers, and the completion of 37 training courses. Total new resources available for technical cooperation amounted to $40.3 million as against $49.1 million in 1991, reflecting a sharp drop in the exchange rate of non-convertible currencies. The Technical Assistance and Cooperation Fund accounted for 82.9 per cent of those resources, with extrabudgetary funds accounting for 12.4 per cent, assistance in kind for 3.2 per cent, and the United Nations Development Programme for 1.5 per cent. The programme placed continuing emphasis on radiation protection and safety-related activities, which accounted for 21.9 per cent of all disbursements, followed by 19.8 per cent for activities related to physical and chemical sciences and 18.3 per cent for those concerning food and agriculture. Human health accounted for 14.5 per cent of all disbursements, followed by industry and earth sciences with 13 per cent.

Agency safeguards responsibilities

During 1992, IAEA carried out eight inspections in Iraq, bringing the total number of inspections to 16 since May 1991, and implemented the essential elements of the plan for the destruction, removal or rendering harmless of the items indicated in a 1991 Security Council resolution.[b] Inspections also were carried out in the Democratic People's Republic of Korea and South Africa. (For details of IAEA activities in the Democratic People's Republic of Korea and Iraq, see PART TWO, Chapter III.)

At the end of December 1992, 188 safeguards agreements were in force with 110 States (and with Taiwan). In 1992, safeguards agreements pursuant to the 1968 Treaty on the Non-Proliferation of Nuclear Weapons[c] (NPT) entered into force with the Democratic People's Republic of Korea, Lithuania, Malawi, Saint Vincent and the Grenadines, the Syrian Arab Republic and Trinidad and Tobago. The remaning two nuclear-weapon States—China and France—acceded to NPT, as did Azerbaijan, Estonia, Latvia, Myanmar, Namibia, the Niger, Slovenia and Uzbekistan, bringing the total number of States parties to 156.

During 1992, safeguards were applied in 44 States under agreements pursuant to NPT or to NPT and the 1967 Treaty for the Prohibition of Nuclear Weapons in Latin America and the Caribbean (Treaty of Tlatelolco), in one State under an agreement pursuant to the Treaty of Tlatelolco, and in 10 States under bi- or trilateral agreements; at the end of 1992, safeguards in 1 of those 10 States were being applied pursuant to NPT. Preliminary visits were made in one State with which a safeguards agreement pursuant to NPT entered into force late in the year. Safeguards activities pursuant to NPT in Iraq continued and IAEA applied safeguards to nuclear installations in Taiwan.

As at 31 December 1992, safeguards agreements were in force with 94 States pursuant to NPT. For 55 non-nuclear-weapon States party to NPT, there was still no safeguards agreement in force in accordance with the Treaty. As far as IAEA was aware, only three of those States had significant nuclear activities.

NPT safeguards agreements had been concluded with all 11 signatories of the South Pacific Nuclear Free Zone Treaty (Rarotonga Treaty). Safeguards were applied in one of those States.

---

[b]YUN 1991, p. 172, SC res. 687(1991), 3 Apr. 1991.
[c]YUN 1968, p. 17, GA res. 2373(XXII), annex, 12 June 1968.

Twenty of the 24 States party to the Treaty of Tlatelolco had concluded agreements with IAEA pursuant to that Treaty, and 17 of those agreements were in force. Safeguards agreements pursuant to Additional Protocol I of the Treaty of Tlatelolco were in force with two States with territories in the zone of application of the Treaty, and a similar agreement with a third such State was approved by the Board of Governors.

Nuclear information

The International Nuclear Information System (INIS), with 81 States and 17 international organizations participating, had a bibliographic database on nuclear literature totalling 1,628,962 records by year's end.

The INIS Clearing-house distributed about 490,000 microfiches, representing over 24 million printed pages of non-conventional literature documents, plus about 1.6 million printed pages of *INIS Atomindex*, which was available on microfiche.

Secretariat

At the end of 1992, the IAEA secretariat staff totalled 2,135, with 798 in the Professional and higher categories and 1,337 in the General Service category. Among the 596 staff members in posts subject to geographical distribution, 80 nationalities were represented.

Budget

The regular budget for 1992 amounted to $206,217,000, of which $197,656,000 was to be financed by member States on the basis of the 1992 scale of assessment; $5,021,000 from income from reimbursable work for others; and $3,540,000 from other miscellaneous income. However, because of a shortfall in expected receipts, steps were taken to reduce the budget by 13 per cent to $179,865,400. Actual expenditures from the regular budget amounted to $178,659,358; the authority to spend an amount of $16,229,600 was reserved for deferred programme activities to be carried out in 1993 if arrears of contributions were received in time. Together with the actual expenditures, this resulted in an unused budget of $11,328,042.

The target for voluntary contributions to the Technical Assistance and Cooperation Fund in 1992 was established at $52.5 million, of which $37.6 million was pledged by member States.

NOTE: For further information, see *The Annual Report for 1992*, published by IAEA.

Annex I.   MEMBERSHIP OF THE INTERNATIONAL ATOMIC ENERGY AGENCY
          (As at 31 December 1992)

Afghanistan, Albania, Algeria, Argentina, Australia, Austria, Bangladesh, Belarus, Belgium, Bolivia, Brazil, Bulgaria, Cambodia, Cameroon, Canada, Chile, China, Colombia, Costa Rica, Côte d'Ivoire, Cuba, Cyprus, Czechoslovakia, Democratic People's Republic of Korea, Denmark, Dominican Republic, Ecuador, Egypt, El Salvador, Estonia, Ethiopia, Finland, France, Gabon, Germany, Ghana, Greece, Guatemala, Haiti, Holy See, Hungary, Iceland, India, Indonesia, Iran, Iraq, Ireland, Israel, Italy, Jamaica, Japan, Jordan, Kenya, Kuwait, Lebanon, Liberia, Libyan Arab Jamahiriya, Liechtenstein, Luxembourg, Madagascar, Malaysia, Mali, Mauritius, Mexico, Monaco, Mongolia, Morocco, Myanmar, Namibia, Netherlands, New Zealand, Nicaragua, Niger, Nigeria, Norway, Pakistan, Panama, Paraguay, Peru, Philippines, Poland, Portugal, Qatar, Republic of Korea, Romania, Russian Federation, Saudi Arabia, Senegal, Sierra Leone, Singapore, Slovenia, South Africa, Spain, Sri Lanka, Sudan, Sweden, Switzerland, Syrian Arab Republic, Thailand, Tunisia, Turkey, Uganda, Ukraine, United Arab Emirates, United Kingdom, United Republic of Tanzania, United States, Uruguay, Venezuela, Viet Nam, Yugoslavia,* Zaire, Zambia, Zimbabwe.

*Following Security Council and General Assembly actions (see PART ONE, Chapter IV), the IAEA General Conference, on 24 September 1992, decided that Yugoslavia (Serbia and Montenegro) could not continue automatically the membership of the former Yugoslavia and that, therefore, it should apply for membership and should not take any further part in the work of the Board and the General Conference.

Annex II.   OFFICERS AND OFFICES OF THE INTERNATIONAL ATOMIC ENERGY AGENCY

BOARD OF GOVERNORS
(For the period October 1992–September 1993)

OFFICERS
Chairman: Ramtane Lamamra (Algeria).
Vice-Chairmen: Mihai Balanescu (Romania), Ramón Perez Simarro (Spain).

MEMBERS
Algeria, Argentina, Australia, Brazil, Bulgaria, Canada, Chile, China, Ecuador, Egypt, Finland, Germany, Greece, Hungary, India, Japan, Libyan Arab Jamahiriya, Malaysia, Mexico, Nigeria, Norway, Pakistan, Paraguay, Romania, Republic of Korea, Russian Federation, Saudi Arabia, Spain, Sweden, Syrian Arab Republic, United Kingdom, United States, Viet Nam, Zaire.

SENIOR SECRETARIAT OFFICERS

Director General: Hans Blix.
Special Assistants to the Director General: Nina Alonso, John Tilemann, Pierre Villaros.
Secretary, Secretariat of the Policy-making Organs: Muttusamy Sanmuganathan.

Deputy Director General for Safeguards: Bruno Pellaud.
Deputy Director General for Nuclear Energy and Safety: Boris Semenov.
Deputy Director General for Administration: David B. Waller.
Deputy Director General for Technical Cooperation: Jihui Qian.
Deputy Director General for Research and Isotopes: Sueo Machi.

HEADQUARTERS AND OTHER OFFICES

HEADQUARTERS
International Atomic Energy Agency
Wagramerstrasse 5
(P.O. Box 100, Vienna International Centre)
A-1400 Vienna, Austria
  Cable address: INATOM VIENNA
  Telephone: (43) (1) 23600
  Telex: 1-12645 ATOM A
  Facsimile: (43) (1) 234564

LIAISON OFFICE
International Atomic Energy Agency
  Liaison Office at the United Nations
United Nations Headquarters, Room DC1-1155
New York, N.Y. 10017, United States
  Telephone: (1) (212) 963-6010, 6011, 6012
  Telex: 42 05 44 UNH
  Facsimile: (1) (212) 751-4117

The Agency also maintained offices at Geneva; Tokyo; and Toronto, Canada.

Chapter II

International Labour Organisation (ILO)

In 1992, the International Labour Organisation (ILO) continued activities in its six major programme areas: promotion of policies to create employment and satisfy basic human needs; development of human resources; improvement of working and living conditions and environment; promotion of social security; strengthening of industrial relations and tripartite (government/employer/worker) cooperation; and the advancement of human rights in the social and labour fields. The main instruments of action continued to be standard-setting, technical cooperation activities, research and publishing.

Azerbaijan, Croatia, Estonia, Kyrgyzstan, the Republic of Moldova, Slovenia and Uzbekistan joined ILO, and Viet Nam resumed its membership, bringing its total membership to 160. (See Annex I for complete membership.)

Meetings

The seventy-ninth session of the International Labour Conference (Geneva, 3-23 June 1992) was attended by some 2,000 delegates and advisers from 151 countries. The Conference had before it the annual report of the ILO Governing Body, the report of the Director-General concerning democratization and ILO, and the twenty-eighth special report on the effect of apartheid on labour and employment in South Africa.

The Conference adopted a new Convention and Recommendation on the protection of workers' claims in the event of the insolvency of their employer. It held a first discussion on the prevention of industrial disasters with a view to adopting standards in 1993.

A general discussion focused on ways of making fullest use of human resources in countries grappling with economic crisis and structural adjustment. A special sitting discussed the Director-General's report on the situation of workers of the occupied Arab territories.

A tripartite Conference committee again examined the application of ILO Conventions and Recommendations by member States (Geneva, 12-25 March) and reviewed the application of ILO standards on minimum wages.

Delegates from 33 countries met in the Thirteenth Conference of American States Members of ILO (Caracas, Venezuela, 30 September–7 October). The Conference discussed economic restructuring and the role of social security in the restructuring process. It adopted conclusions on ILO technical cooperation and international labour standards and a resolution on democratization.

Among industrial meetings held during the year were: the twelfth session of the Inland Transport Committee (Geneva, 22-30 January) dealing with social and legal protection of transport workers; the Fourth Tripartite Technical Meeting for the Leather and Footwear Industry (Geneva, 12-20 February) covering employment competitiveness issues; the twelfth session of the Iron and Steel Committee (Geneva, 1-9 April) dealing with training; a Tripartite Meeting on Conditions of Employment and Work of Performers (Geneva, 5-13 May); a Tripartite Meeting on Social and Labour Issues in the Pulp and Paper Industry (Geneva, 20-28 October); and the twelfth session of the Building, Civil Engineering and Public Works Committee (Geneva, 2-10 December) focusing on skill requirements and training.

Other meetings included a Meeting of Experts on Labour Statistics (Geneva, 28 January–6 February); a Meeting of Experts on Safety in the Use of Chemicals at Work (Geneva, 24 March–1 April); the eleventh session of the Joint ILO/WHO Committee on Occupational Health (Geneva, 27-29 April); and a Tripartite Advisory Meeting on Environment and the World of Work (Geneva, 2-4 November).

International standards

During 1992, ILO activities concerning Conventions and Recommendations consisted of standard-setting and supervision of standards.

Standard-setting

In 1992, the International Labour Conference adopted the Protection of Workers' Claims (Employer's Insolvency) Convention (No. 173) and Recommendation (No. 180).

The Social Security (Seafarers) Convention (Revised), 1987 (No. 165), entered into force on 2 July 1992, having received the requisite number of ratifications (Hungary on 13 December 1989 and Spain on 2 July 1991).

During the year, 154 ratifications of ILO Conventions by 24 member States were registered, bringing the total number of ratifications as at 31 December 1992 to 5,716. There were also 13 denunciations, including one of the Night Work (Women) Convention, 1919, by Argentina, and four of the Fee-Charging Employment Agencies Convention (Revised), 1949 (No. 96), by Côte d'Ivoire, Finland, Germany and Sweden.

Supervision of standards

The Committee of Experts on the Application of Conventions and Recommendations met in March to carry out its supervisory functions regarding compliance by member States with their obligations under the ILO Constitution and international labour standards. The Committee examined 2,351 reports by countries on their compliance with ratified Conventions and made 1,707 comments on them. It was able to note 50 instances in 1992 in which Governments had changed their law and practice to come into closer conformity with ratified Conventions, following the Committee's earlier comments. It also noted more than 200 instances in which employers' or workers' organizations exercised their right to make observations on Governments' reports.

The Committee also carried out a general survey of the application by member States of selected international labour standards, whether or not they had been ratified by all countries. The 1992 survey dealt with the application of the Minimum Wage-Fixing Machinery Convention (No. 26) and Recommendation (No. 30), 1928; the Minimum Wage-Fixing Machinery (Agriculture) Convention (No. 99) and Recommendation (No. 89), 1951; and the Minimum Wage-Fixing Convention (No. 131) and Recommendation (No. 135), 1970.

The Governing Body's Committee on Freedom of Association, which examined complaints of violations of freedom of association received from employers' and workers' organizations, met three times during 1992. The Committee dealt mostly with complaints alleging violations of trade union rights. A Fact-finding and Conciliation Commission on Freedom of Association completed its examination of a complaint by the Congress of South African Trade Unions against South Africa. Its report was transmitted to the Economic and Social Council of the United Nations.

A number of special procedures were pursued during 1992 to examine complaints and representations under various articles of the ILO Constitution. Complaints under article 26 were examined concerning the application of ratified Conventions by Côte d'Ivoire and Sweden, and representations under article 24 were examined concerning Venezuela and Yugoslavia (Serbia and Montengro).

Employment and development

Active labour market policies

The active labour market policies programme assisted member States to formulate and implement labour market policies to improve access to employment and incomes and the functioning of the labour market. It also assisted in preventing the marginalization and impoverishment of vulnerable groups, and to stimulate labour productivity in order to create favourable conditions for economic growth and income with employment security.

Tripartite meetings were held in Moscow and St. Petersburg on labour market policies, trends and challenges posed by the market-oriented reforms being implemented in the Russian Federation, especially the employment impact of enterprise restructuring. A regional seminar on labour market information and analysis was held at Montreal, Canada, for officials from eight African countries. Technical advice on labour market issues was provided to trade union officers from several Asian and African countries.

Technical cooperation projects on labour market information and analysis were in operation in the Gambia, Indonesia, Kenya, Turkey and Zimbabwe. Similar projects were completed in Nigeria and Zambia. New projects were started in Angola, Cape Verde, Ghana, Guinea-Bissau, Mozambique and Sao Tome and Principe. Projects aimed at assisting countries in transition to a market economy were operational in Czechoslovakia and in five successor States of the former USSR. Technical advisory missions on labour market policy analysis and information visited eight countries.

Working environment

The International Programme for the Improvement of Working Conditions and Environment continued to assist countries in promoting occupational safety and health and improving general working conditions.

A regional project in Asia for improving safety and health practices and strengthening advisory, training and information activities was extended to 21 countries. In Africa, a regional project on occupational safety and health training and information assisted 19 countries. Workshops and seminars were held in Africa and in Asia and the Pacific on the safe use of chemicals at work and on preventing major hazards. Twenty-one extra-budgetary projects were conducted in 14 countries, and consultancies, fellowships and assistance to seminars were provided in 18 developing countries. Technical cooperation activities were also aimed at improving working conditions and productivity in small and medium-sized enterprises and at preventing and reducing alcohol and drug problems in the workplace.

The protection of working children and the gradual elimination of child labour were also of concern to ILO. The International Programme on the Elimination of Child Labour was launched with the support of Germany. More than 80 projects with government institutions, trade unions, employers' organizations and non-governmental organizations were being implemented in six countries.

A code of practice and a training manual on safety and health in the use of chemicals at work and guides on protection from non-ionizing radiation were prepared. Issues of the *Conditions of Work Digest* were published on sexual harassment and on preventing stress at work.

Field activities

In 1992, total expenditure on operational activities from all sources of funds stood at nearly $164 million (approximately 3.7 per cent less than the previous year). As in the past, the United Nations Development Programme remained the largest single source of external funding, providing about $76 million, which represented close to 46.4 per cent of overall ILO expenditure on operational activities.

Trust funds and multi-bilateral sources provided close to $65 million, representing some 40 per cent of overall expenditure. The ILO regular budget provided close to $14 million, representing 8.4 per cent, and the United Nations Population Fund some $9.1 million, representing 5.6 per cent.

The three leading programmes in terms of annual expenditure were the employment and development programme ($46.2 million), comprising primarily projects in support of rural development, migration and population and employment strategies; the enterprise and cooperative development programme ($43.6 million); and the programme on vocational training systems, rehabilitation and training policies ($26 million). Other significant technical programmes focused on industrial relations and labour administration ($7.9 million), working conditions and environment ($6.8 million), and sectoral activities ($9.2 million), of which more than half were activities in support of the hotel and tourism sector. There was also a significant growth in expenditure on programmes concerned with the promotion of social security, which rose to $4.2 million from $3 million in 1991. ILO devoted $1.6 million and $8.3 million, respectively, for activities in support of employers' and workers' organizations. Africa remained in the forefront of ILO operational activities ($76 mil-

lion, representing 46.6 per cent of the total expenditure), followed by Asia and the Pacific ($40.1 million) and the Americas ($23.2 million).

Educational activities

In 1992, in addition to focusing on the vocational training needs of the disadvantaged, ILO paid particular attention to the reform of training policies and systems in the context of structural adjustment and economic transition. Emphasis was placed on increasing the responsiveness of training systems to changes in the demand for labour and on the role of training in mitigating the social costs of adjustment. It provided advisory services in the formulation of coherent policies and programmes to support national skills development efforts. In the context of the growth of nationally executed technical cooperation activities, it provided training and advisory services to member States on planning and managing technical assistance. Research activities undertaken by ILO regional centres were coordinated with the analytical work undertaken by ILO headquarters units; ILO also participated in organizations, such as the Donors to African Education group, which aimed at achieving greater coherence and coordination among donors supporting education and training assistance to developing countries.

The activities of ILO's International Institute for Labour Studies were guided in 1992 by a new core theme on the interaction between labour institutions and the changing economic, social and technological environment. Two new programmes were established—labour institutions and economic development and labour institutions and new industrial organization.

The programme on economic development started work on the conceptual and statistical characteristics of labour institutions to develop a typology of development patterns reflecting both labour institutions and macroeconomic policies and outcomes. It launched a series of eight seminars on labour institutions and economic transformation. The programme also promoted capacity-building in labour market research in Africa through networks and training.

The programme on labour institutions and new industrial organization examined new forms of production and industrial organization and explored their relationships with labour institutions. It concentrated on the implications for labour of the changing geography of production and explored the prospects of endogenous development and social dialogue and labour standards, at local and regional levels. Two conferences studied inter-enterprise networks, labour and labour institutions and the social implications of lean production (a Japanese model of work and production organization).

The twenty-seventh annual international internship course on active labour policy development was attended by participants from 17 countries, who were introduced to the objectives, structure and programmes of ILO and to major labour and social policy issues. A regional internship course on economic reform and labour policy in Central and Eastern Europe was designed to enhance the capacity of middle-level officials from that region to develop and manage labour policy in the context of economic and social transition.

Two social policy forums were held in 1992. The first—on work, culture and religion—examined the influence of religious ethics in shaping attitudes towards work and economic growth. The second—on social dialogue and industrial relations in Latin America—examined the relationship between social dialogue, political participation and economic and social change.

Secretariat

As at 31 December 1992, the total number of full-time staff under permanent, fixed-term and short-term appointments at ILO headquarters and elsewhere was 3,263. Of these, 1,330 were in the Professional and higher categories and 1,933 were in the General Service or Maintenance categories. Of the Professional staff, 580 were assigned to technical cooperation projects.

Budget

The International Labour Conference in June 1991 adopted a budget of $405.69 million for the 1992-1993 biennium, which, at the exchange rate of 1.55 Swiss francs to the United States dollar, amounted to 628,819,500 Swiss francs.

NOTE: For further information on ILO, see *Report of the Director-General, Activities of the ILO, 1992.*

Annex I. MEMBERSHIP OF THE INTERNATIONAL LABOUR ORGANISATION
(As at 31 December 1992)

Afghanistan, Albania, Algeria, Angola, Antigua and Barbuda, Argentina, Australia, Austria, Azerbaijan, Bahamas, Bahrain, Bangladesh, Barbados, Belarus, Belgium, Belize, Benin, Bolivia, Botswana, Brazil, Bulgaria, Burkina Faso, Burundi, Cambodia, Cameroon, Canada, Cape Verde, Central African Republic, Chad, Chile, China, Colombia, Comoros, Congo, Costa Rica, Côte d'Ivoire, Croatia, Cuba, Cyprus, Czechoslovakia, Denmark, Djibouti, Dominica, Dominican Republic, Ecuador, Egypt, El Salvador, Equatorial Guinea, Estonia, Ethiopia, Fiji, Finland, France, Gabon, Germany, Ghana, Greece, Grenada, Guatemala, Guinea, Guinea-Bissau, Guyana, Haiti, Honduras, Hungary, Iceland, India, Indonesia, Iran, Iraq, Ireland, Israel, Italy, Jamaica, Japan, Jordan, Kenya, Kuwait, Kyrgyzstan, Lao People's Democratic Republic, Latvia, Lebanon, Lesotho, Liberia, Libyan Arab Jamahiriya, Lithuania, Luxembourg, Madagascar, Malawi, Malaysia, Mali, Malta, Mauritania, Mauritius, Mexico, Mongolia, Morocco, Mozambique, Myanmar, Namibia, Nepal, Netherlands, New Zealand, Nicaragua, Niger, Nigeria, Norway, Pakistan, Panama, Papua New Guinea, Paraguay, Peru, Philippines, Poland, Portugal, Qatar, Republic of Korea, Republic of Moldova, Romania, Russian Federation, Rwanda, Saint Lucia, San Marino, Sao Tome and Principe, Saudi Arabia, Senegal, Seychelles, Sierra Leone, Singapore, Slovenia, Solomon Islands, Somalia, Spain, Sri Lanka, Sudan, Suriname, Swaziland, Sweden, Switzerland, Syrian Arab Republic, Thailand, Togo, Trinidad and Tobago, Tunisia, Turkey, Uganda, Ukraine, United Arab Emirates, United Kingdom, United Republic of Tanzania, United States, Uruguay, Uzbekistan, Venezuela, Viet Nam, Yemen, Yugoslavia, Zaire, Zambia, Zimbabwe.

Annex II. OFFICERS AND OFFICES OF THE INTERNATIONAL LABOUR ORGANISATION
(As at 31 December 1992)

MEMBERSHIP OF THE GOVERNING BODY OF THE INTERNATIONAL LABOUR OFFICE

Chairman: Marcelo Vargas Campos (Mexico), Government Group.
Vice-Chairmen: Jean-Jacques Oechslin (France), Employers' Group; Shirley
Carr (Canada), Workers' Group.

REGULAR MEMBERS

Government members
Australia, Bangladesh, Belarus, Belgium, Brazil,* Bulgaria, Cameroon, Canada, China,* Costa Rica, France,* Germany,* India,* Italy,* Japan,* Lesotho, Madagascar, Mexico, Morocco, Nigeria, Philippines, Russian Federation,* Togo, United Arab Emirates, United Kingdom,* United States,* Uruguay, Venezuela.

Employers' members
M. Eurnekian (Argentina), A. Gazarin (Egypt), C. Hak (Netherlands), A. Katz (United States), A. M. Mackie (United Kingdom), F. Moukoko Kingue (Cameroon), M. Nasr (Lebanon), J.-J. Oechslin (France), T. D. Owuor (Kenya), A. Periquet (Philippines), J. de Regil Gomez (Mexico), A. Tabani (Pakistan), R. Thüsing (Germany), H. Tsujino (Japan).

Workers' members
W. Brett (United Kingdom), S. Carr (Canada), El-Sayed Rashed (Egypt), U. Engelen-Kefer (Germany), M. Ferguson (Australia), V. G. Gopal (India), C. Gray (United States), M. Kebe (Guinea), I. E. Klochkov (Russian Federation), Y. Maruyama (Mexico), K. Tapiola (Finland).

DEPUTY MEMBERS

Government deputy members
Argentina, Bolivia, Central African Republic, Congo, Czechoslovakia, Denmark, Honduras, Indonesia, Ireland, Kenya, Malawi, Malta, New Zealand, Niger, Pakistan, Peru, Romania, Tunisia.

Employers' deputy members
A. Al-Jassem (Kuwait), D. Chanaiwa (Zimbabwe), G. Hultin (Finland), J. M. Lacasa Aso (Spain), C. McVeigh (Canada), A. Muyumbu (Burundi), B. M. Noakes (Australia), G. C. Okogwu (Nigeria), M. A. Ould Sidi Mohamed (Mauritania), J. Santos Neves (Brazil), L. Sasso-Mazzufferi (Italy), O. Touré (Mali), H. G. Villalobos (Venezuela), D. Yankana (Guyana).

Workers' deputy members
K. Ahmed (Pakistan), M. Blondel (France), M. Bonmati Portillo (Spain), M. Bustos (Chile), A. Chirwa (Zambia), B. Karambe (Mali), N. Kombo (Zaire), D. T. Mendoza (Philippines), M. P. Sundaram (Sri Lanka), E. Tchinde (Togo), L. Trotman (Barbados), R. Vanni (Italy), T. Wojcik (Poland), M. Zeidan (Lebanon).

---

*Member holding a non-elective seat as a State of chief industrial importance.

SENIOR OFFICIALS OF THE INTERNATIONAL LABOUR OFFICE

Director-General: Michel Hansenne.
Deputy Directors-General: David Taylor, Heribert Maier, Mary Chinery-Hesse.
Assistant Directors-General: M. Abdel-Rahman, Jorge Capriate d'Auro, Vladi-lan Morozov, Tadashi Nakamura, Renquan Yu, Anees Ahmad, Shukri Dajani.

Director of the International Centre for Advanced Technical and Vocational Training: Jean-François Trémeaud.
Director of the International Institute for Labour Studies: Padmanabh Gopinath.

HEADQUARTERS, LIAISON AND OTHER OFFICES

HEADQUARTERS

International Labour Office
4 Route des Morillons
CH-1211 Geneva 22, Switzerland
  Cable address: INTERLAB GENEVE
  Telephone: (41) (22) 799-6111
  Telex: 415647 ILO CH
  Facsimile: (41) (22) 798-8686

LIAISON OFFICE

International Labour Organisation Liaison
  Office with the United Nations
820 Second Avenue, 18th floor
New York, N.Y. 10017, United States

ILO also maintained regional offices at Abidjan, Côte d'Ivoire; Bangkok, Thailand; Geneva; and Lima, Peru; as well as other liaison offices with the European Community at Brussels, Belgium, and ECLAC at Santiago, Chile.

Chapter III

Food and Agriculture Organization of the United Nations (FAO)

The 49-member Council of the Food and Agriculture Organization of the United Nations (FAO), the organization's governing body, held its one hundred and second session in 1992 (Rome, Italy, 9-20 November). The Council urged that food aid deliveries to developing countries not be reduced as a result of the significant assistance requirements of some countries of Eastern Europe and the successor States of the USSR. It emphasized the increasing role played by FAO in providing policy advice to member States in the areas of food security and nutrition, structural adjustment and economic transformation, trade, sustainable development and environmental resource management, as related to agriculture, fisheries and forestry. It requested FAO to assist member States in their efforts to implement the principles of the United Nations Conference on Environment and Development (see PART THREE, Chapter VIII) to achieve sustainable development. It urged the countries and groups of countries involved in the General Agreement on Tariffs and Trade (see PART SEVEN, Chapter XVIII) negotiations to bridge their remaining differences in order to reach a successful conclusion.

During 1992, FAO held five regional conferences—in Africa, Asia and the Pacific, Europe, Latin America and the Caribbean, and the Near East—to assess problems in agriculture, forestry, fisheries and rural development unique to those regions and to review its work within each region.

The Conference for Africa (Accra, Ghana, 20-24 July), attended by representatives of 35 nations, called for FAO's assistance in responding to the effects, particularly on food security, of structural adjustment programmes. It expressed grave concern about the worsening of rural poverty and urged developed countries to intensify assistance. It adopted the Accra Declaration on a Sound Environment for Sustainable Development in Africa, appealing for a mobilization of resources to enable Africa to feed its people.

At the Conference for Asia and the Pacific (New Delhi, India, 10-14 February), representatives of 27 nations discussed measures to alleviate rural poverty, arrest land degradation, intensify pest control and develop agro-processing industries in a region where more than 400 million people remained undernourished, and stressed the importance of vocational education and skill development, especially for women.

The Conference for Europe (Prague, Czechoslovakia, 24-28 August), at which 28 nations and the European Economic Community (EEC) were represented, discussed the food and agricultural situation in Europe, FAO's medium-term plan in the European region, 1994-1999, and alternative uses of marginal land and set-aside farmland in Europe. The Conference called on FAO to help Eastern European countries formulate agricultural policies and establish sustainable production structures and modern distribution systems.

The Conference for Latin America and the Caribbean (Montevideo, Uruguay, 28 September-2 October), attended by representatives of 25 nations, stressed the importance of improved food quality and safety systems for all countries of a region plagued by increasing malnutrition and a persistent cholera epidemic. It recommended the creation of information exchange networks, such as the FAO-sponsored Technical Cooperation Network on Plant Biotechnology, to help develop sustainable production alternatives.

At the Conference for the Near East (Tehran, Iran, 17-21 May), representatives of 23 nations requested FAO assistance in water management, including the formulation of national water policies, the monitoring of water quality, agricultural extension services and information systems for water use. It also discussed requests for FAO assistance in controlling animal diseases such as foot-and-mouth disease, rinderpest, brucellosis and para sites.

As at 31 December 1992, FAO membership remained at 161 and 1 associate member. (See Annex I for complete membership.)

World food situation

In 1992, the world food supply increased, reversing the sharp fall that had occurred in the previous year. Gains resulted mainly from increased cereal production in developed countries, leading to a general decline in cereal prices. Regional food problems continued, however, with acute food shortages affecting Ethiopia, Kenya, Somalia, the Sudan and other African countries, as well as Bosnia and Herzegovina and several central Asian successor States of the USSR. Deteriorating terms of trade and world recession, both of which reduced the import capacity of poor countries, exacerbated their problem of maintaining adequate food supplies.

Production of staple foods increased during 1992 by 2.5 per cent over 1991, largely because favourable weather conditions and policy initiatives, particularly in the United States, resulted in an increase in cereal output. The global cereal harvest was about 1 per cent below the record 1990 level of 1,972 million tonnes. World output in 1992 was estimated at some 1,952 million tonnes. Wheat production rose by 21 million tonnes to 567 million tonnes, and coarse grains increased by 48 million to 861 million tonnes. Rice (paddy) production came to a record 524 million tonnes, an increase of 7 million tonnes over the previous year. For roots and tubers, the second most important group of staple foods, production rose slightly, by 1 million tonnes, to 143 million tonnes. The world output of pulses was estimated to have fallen by more than 5 per cent to 55.1 million tonnes. World milk production was estimated to have declined by 1 per cent.

The International Conference on Nutrition (Rome, 5-11 December), co-sponsored by FAO and the World Health Organization, was attended by nearly 1,400 delegates from more than 160 countries and 144 non-governmental organizations. The Conference addressed eight nutritional issues: preventing micronutrient deficiencies; preventing and managing infectious diseases; improving household food security; promoting healthy diets and lifestyles; enhancing the capacity for care; improving food quality and safety; assessing, analysing and monitoring nutrition situations; and incorporating nutrition objectives in development policy. It adopted a World Declaration and Plan of Action on Nutrition, which provided guidelines for Governments and contained recommendations on policies, programmes and activities (for further information, see PART THREE, Chapter XI).

Activities in 1992

Food emergencies and rehabilitation

Severe food shortages affected many African countries during the review period. Famine still threatened Ethiopia, which was dependent on an estimated 1 million tonnes of food aid. In Somalia, drought and civil war placed half the population at risk from famine. Kenya faced a critical food situation; 679,000 people were in need of aid.

In Asia, severe food shortages affected Afghanistan, Cambodia and the Lao People's Democratic Republic. In Europe, the food situation was unstable in the former Yugoslavia, where cereal and food crop supplies were sharply reduced; there was danger of starvation in Bosnia and Herzegovina, and emergency assistance was needed in Albania, Armenia and Romania.

The Near East and North Africa was the second largest food-aid recipient for the second consecutive year, with Iraq, Jordan and Lebanon being particularly vulnerable. In Latin America and the Caribbean, food production failed to keep pace with population growth, with serious food shortages being reported in Haiti and Peru.

Total shipments of cereal food aid during the 1991/92 marketing year came to 13.52 million tonnes, an increase of about 1.5 million tonnes from the previous year. Of that total, some 10.57 million tonnes were provided to low-income food-deficit countries.

Pledges to the International Emergency Food Reserve (IEFR) in 1992 reached a record level of 1,202,400 tonnes of food commodities, compared to 703,000 tonnes in 1991. Further pledges, totalling 948,448 tonnes, were made to the World Food Programme to supply food for protracted operations assisting refugees and displaced persons. A special interim cash fund, the Immediate Response Account, was established during the year within IEFR to facilitate the purchase and delivery of food in response to sudden emergencies. A minimum annual target of $30 million was set.

In 1992, an upsurge of the African migratory locust was reported in Madagascar, creating a potential for widespread destruction. The FAO Emergency Centre for Locust Operations was reactivated, and it coordinated assistance from France, Germany, the United Kingdom and the United States to fight the outbreak.

In North Africa, the Libyan Arab Jamahiriya announced the eradication of the screw-worm, confirming the success of a campaign mobilized by FAO and the Screw-worm Emergency Centre for North Africa (see PART THREE, Chapter III).

FAO intensified its monitoring of global food security via satellite surveillance and early warning networks. It set up the Regional Early Warning System for Food Security in Southern Africa, which reduced the effects of the drought, and began testing the Direct Information Access Network for Africa—a satellite communications system providing early warning of food crises caused by drought and natural disasters. The Global Information and Early Warning System expanded its membership to 104 with the admission of Cuba, Estonia, Hungary, Mongolia and Viet Nam. The System intensified its monitoring of the monsoon in south-western Asia and of crop growing conditions in Africa, Eastern Europe and the successor States of the USSR.

Field programmes

FAO provided technical advice and support through its field programmes in all areas of food and agriculture, fisheries, forestry and rural development. In 1992, 2,157 field projects were under way at an expenditure of $336.6 million. They were funded through trust funds provided by donor countries and other international funding sources ($164.3 million), the United Nations Development Programme (UNDP) ($136.2 million) and the technical cooperation programme from FAO's regular budget ($36.1 million).

During the year, international financing institutions approved some $1,587 million in funding for 43 agricultural and rural development projects, prepared with the assistance of FAO's Investment Centre. Total investments in those projects, including contributions from recipient Governments, amounted to $2,224 million.

Rural development

In 1992, FAO strengthened implementation of the Plan of Action on People's Participation, which was approved by the FAO Conference in 1991. Under the plan, poor farmers were encouraged to form informal groups of 8 to 15 people, organized around income-generating activities that the groups themselves identified, such as land reclamation, introduction of small-scale agricultural processing technology in sesame oil extraction or introduction of pigeon peas and other drought-resistant crops. FAO was executing nearly 200 participatory rural development projects in 40 countries in 1992.

There was also increased focus on promoting the Plan of Action for the Integration of Women in Development (WID), which called for equal rights and opportunities for rural women by improving access to land, credit, extension services, rural organizations and improved technology. During the year, FAO assisted in the creation of three new government units responsible for WID, in the Central African Republic, Egypt and Guatemala.

The Agricultural Services Division continued to support farming system analysis, which assessed all the factors affecting farming households from crop and livestock production to quality of the environment. Land evaluation and soil conservation were given particular emphasis. FAO developed software showing the environmental aspects of a wide range of agricultural projects in various types of agro-ecological zones. It also completed a digitized version of the FAO/United Nations Educational, Scientific and Cultural Organization Soil Map of the World, which was to be used together with a global database of crop environmental requirements being developed to identify suitable crop and tree species for cultivation in any part of the world.

Water resources, whether for drinking-water supply, sanitation, irrigation, livestock supply or aquaculture, were a major concern. FAO played a central role in the International Conference on Water and the Environment (Dublin, Ireland, 26-31 January) and was appointed the lead agency for the working group dealing with water for sustainable food production, drinking-water supply and sanitation in the rural context.

FAO also supported farmers in agricultural engineering and farm mechanization, post-harvest systems, agro-industries, biotechnology and marketing. Agricultural credit was improved for rural financial institutions and cooperatives with the *Microbanker* software system, which helped lower service costs of rural savings and loan operations. By the end of 1992, the software was being used in more than 160 installations in Indonesia, Nepal, the Philippines, Sri Lanka and Thailand.

In addition, FAO developed a computerized system for food and agricultural policy analysis and planning to constitute the new version of its Computerized System for Agricultural and Population Planning Assistance and Training.

Crops

During the year, FAO completed a world-wide directory of 8,000 plant-breeding, crop genetic resources and seed firms. Work also began on a list of crop varieties, aimed at creating a world register of local, improved or hybrid varieties of agricultural crops, agro-forestry species and horticultural crops, excluding ornamentals. Cereal breeding and improvement programmes ranged from work on tropical fruit and cassava to maize and rice. Advances were made in hybrid rice research and technologies, including an induced new mutation (Hezu 8), which was released in China. A recently developed technique for transplanting maize proved highly successful in Viet Nam, and the area planted with the crop had increased from 50,000 hectares from 1983 to 1986 to 250,000 hectares in 1990.

In 1992, the FAO Fertilizer Programme operated in 27 countries, and conducted trials and demonstrations on fertilizer techniques in small-scale farms. To make the Programme more effective, FAO implemented broad-context appraisals and upgrading of results from projects in the Gambia, Guinea-Bissau, Madagascar, Nicaragua, Sri Lanka and Zaire. The studies provided a comprehensive analysis of the situation in each country to assist in formulating long-term policy. They examined soil fertility management in the context of sustainable agricultural development. With funding from EEC, a regional project was launched to check the spread of the large grain borer, an insect pest that attacked stored maize and dried cassava. The pest had threatened self-sufficiency in maize and cassava in an increasing number of African countries since the late 1970s, and had severely damaged the region's grain trade.

FAO promoted the application of integrated pest management (IPM) as a key element in many crop programmes. The aim of the IPM project was to reduce reliance on pesticides by encouraging farmers to use biological control methods and natural predators, such as spiders and wasps, to avert pests. The IPM principles, initially applied to rice in South-East Asia, were currently being used on cotton, vegetables, citrus and wheat throughout the developing world.

Livestock

In 1992, FAO supported a wide range of livestock-related activities, from feeding systems and meat and dairy production to animal health and the conservation and management of animal genetic resources.

Livestock disease continued to be a major threat to rural incomes and food security. FAO helped strengthen veterinary health in developing countries with work in diagnosis, disease control, vaccine production, immunization and information programmes. In particular, it supported the large-scale immunization of cattle against ticks and tick-borne diseases in eastern, central and southern Africa and ongoing regional campaigns against rinderpest in Africa, Asia and the Near East. Control policies against African animal trypanosomiasis—a highly contagious disease transmitted by the tsetse fly—were revised to decrease large-scale spraying of insecticide.

Sustainable feeding systems and resources received increasing attention. A project in China fed cattle on agricultural residues—straw treated with urea and supplemented with cotton-seed cake. The urea made the crop residues digestible, providing an alternative to grain-based livestock production and reducing the pollution from traditional straw-burning.

Animal genetic diversity was diminishing rapidly, and FAO focused efforts on conserving those resources. In the developing world in particular, the diversity of livestock breeds had been undermined by reliance on a few breeds imported from the developed world, selected for maximum productivity under conditions that often did not exist in tropical climates and developing countries. To help counter that trend, FAO began preparations to launch a special action programme to stem the rapid extinction of livestock and poultry breeds that had been domesticated and bred over thousands of years. The programme was launched following an expert consultation on the management of global animal genetic resources. Among other activities, it explored the establishment of a world centre for domestic animal diversity, based at FAO, to coordinate the global effort to identify, document, characterize, improve and conserve the diversity remaining within each of the 30 or so animal species that contributed substantially to food and agriculture.

An FAO/United Nations Environment Programme project began compiling a data bank on domestic livestock in 1992, entering data on 3,000 breeds.

Fisheries

FAO took part in the International Conference on Responsible Fishing (Cancun, Mexico, 6-8 May), which recommended that FAO draft an international code of conduct for responsible fishing to ensure equitable and sustainable fishery development. Many of the FAO activities in fisheries focused on support for small-scale, artisanal fishery development, including aquaculture and inland fisheries. The Aquaculture for Local Community Development Programme helped rural populations to improve their living standards through the practice of aquaculture. The extension of fish farming in Zambia was one of 12 projects under FAO's regional fisheries and aquaculture programme.

FAO provided information and training needed by fish-exporting developing countries to increase their access to international markets. In particular, it provided training and helped set up the national control systems needed to meet more stringent health and sanitary requirements imposed in recent years by major importers, such as EEC, Japan and the United States. FAO also assisted efforts to improve income and employment opportunities in the fishing industry in Eastern Europe. Almost 800 people attended nine seminars organized to help the industry adapt to the new economic situation and find suitable business and joint venture partners to enable them to sell their products on the international market.

Forestry

In 1992, FAO's various forestry activities, from forestry development and management to technology and research, focused on environmental issues.

More than one third of the 90 countries in Africa, Asia, and Latin America and the Caribbean completed national forest action plans as part of an international effort to combat deforestation and degradation of forest resources through the Tropical Forests Action Programme (TFAP). FAO was the coordinating agency for TFAP, which involved 86 countries by the end of 1992 and was co-sponsored by UNDP, the World Bank and FAO.

The TFAP approach emphasized collaboration of different sectors, such as agriculture and forestry, as well as broad-based popular participation. In Viet Nam, FAO held its first training course in participatory rural appraisal, aimed at adapting projects in forestry conservation and development to focus on farmers' needs. In Guatemala, more than 100 Mayan women and 120 other people from forestry cooperatives participated in training courses for forestry development and conservation. In Cameroon, agro-forestry schemes within the TFAP framework continued, with the creation of tree plantations and the introduction of mixed farming systems.

FAO completed its Forest Resources Assessment 1990 Project, which analysed existing survey data of 90 tropical countries to assess the forest cover area for 1990 and the extent of deforestation from 1981 to 1990. The findings showed that during that period approximately 154 million hectares had been deforested.

FAO provided support to a number of national programmes to identify, conserve, collect, evaluate, exchange and improve forest genetic resources. Through contributions to institutes in Brazil, Indonesia and Peru, FAO supported the establishment and management of pilot on-site conservation areas. Contracts were also made with India, Myanmar, Pakistan and Thailand to search for and collect seeds of neem, a multi-purpose tree native to Asia, which was also widely grown in West Africa and parts of Latin America and the Caribbean. It also helped establish national tree-seed centres in a number of countries in the Sahelian zone of Africa.

Nuclear techniques

During the year, the joint FAO/International Atomic Energy Agency (IAEA) Division of Nuclear Techniques in Food and Agriculture conducted research on a variety of topics in animal disease diagnosis, food irradiation, plant improvement and nitrogen fixation.

The Division had become leader in the development of the sterile insect technique (SIT), a revolutionary system based on the use of ionizing radiation to sterilize mass numbers of male insects raised in captivity. When the sterile males mated with wild females, no offspring were produced. SIT was used to eliminate the new world screwworm from North Africa (see PART THREE, Chapter III).

Researchers used nuclear radiation to induce new mutant cereal varieties. An FAO/IAEA Coordinated Research Programme resulted in many mutants in doubled haploid lines. The doubled haploid technique resulted in much quicker recovery of useful mutants and significantly sped up breeding programmes. The programme also resulted in a new mutant strain of importance for hybrid rice in China. Gamma radiation was used with *in vitro* culture to induce male sterility in rice together with better flower structure for outcrossing. Production of hybrids required that plants of one of the strains to be crossed be prevented from pollinating themselves. In addition, advances were made in transferring technology to developing countries. The first phase of an FAO/IAEA regional project on cereal improvement in Latin America was completed. A training programme, expert services and a research network helped introduce modern mutation techniques to plant breeding in the region on a large scale.

Information

During 1992, a total of 220 major publications were produced by FAO, and more than 3 million pieces were distributed. Grass-roots publications, training manuals, film strips and radio, television and video programmes were produced. Publications were issued in Arabic, Chinese, English, French and Spanish. To reach small farmers and extension workers not using the official United Nations languages, FAO encouraged the adaptation, translation and distribution of its publications in local languages.

FAO compiled and coordinated international databases on agriculture, forestry, fisheries and nutrition, including the International Information System for the Agricultural Sciences and Technology and the Current Agricultural Research Information System. The second edition of AGROVOC, a thesaurus which allowed retrieval of information in English, French and Spanish on agricultural sciences, forestry and fisheries, used by libraries and information and documentation centres around the world, was published in 1992.

Nutrition

FAO continued to help countries improve nutrition, promote healthy diets and ensure access to safe food. It participated in efforts to combat the cholera epidemic in Latin America in 1992 through a variety of food safety and control projects designed to reduce the risk of transmission through food and water. The epidemic, which began in 1991, had caused more than 6,500 deaths.

To improve the safety of street foods and foods for export, FAO collaborated with authorities in Belize, Bolivia, Chile, Colombia, Mexico and English-speaking Caribbean countries to strengthen their food control systems. It provided technical assistance to a subregional project to strengthen food control systems in Costa Rica, El Salvador, Guatemala, Honduras, Nicaragua and Panama.

FAO was also active in proposing strategies to combat diseases caused by deficiencies in vitamin A, iron and iodine. Three multi-media workshops were conducted as part of the FAO Nutrition Communications Support Project in the Sahel, involving Burkina Faso, Chad, Mali, Mauritania and the Niger.

There was concern in 1992 over the deteriorating food situation in Eastern Europe. FAO assisted Bulgaria, Czechoslovakia and Hungary in restructuring their food control administrations, updating food laws and regulations and training staff in food control and inspection techniques. It held a workshop on the reorientation of cooperative structures in Central and Eastern Europe, gathering 20 participants from nine countries to identify possible reforms.

On 16 October, more than 130 nations observed World Food Day, established in 1981, which in 1992 was dedicated to the theme of food and nutrition.

Secretariat

At the end of 1992, the number of staff employed at FAO headquarters was 3,213, of whom 1,204 were in the Professional and higher categories. Field project personnel and those in regional and country offices numbered 2,923: 976 in the Professional category and 1,741 in the General Services category. Of the 272 Associate Professional officers working with FAO, 66 were at FAO headquarters and 206 were in the field or in regional or country offices.

Budget

The FAO Council reported in 1992 on progress made in implementing the 1992-1993 programme budget, amounting to $645.6 million, approved by the FAO Conference in 1991. The Council recalled the Conference's explicit understanding that approval by consensus of the 1992-1993 programme budget was based on a specific commitment from the United States to pay current assessments and arrears. Accordingly, the Council expressed satisfaction with the steps taken by the United States to fulfil that commitment in 1992.

NOTE: For further information on FAO, see *FAO Annual Review: A Summary of the Organization's Activities During 1992*, issued by FAO.

Annex I.   MEMBERSHIP OF THE FOOD AND AGRICULTURE ORGANIZATION

(As at 31 December 1992)

Afghanistan, Albania, Algeria, Angola, Antigua and Barbuda, Argentina, Australia, Austria, Bahamas, Bahrain, Bangladesh, Barbados, Belgium, Belize, Benin, Bhutan, Bolivia, Botswana, Brazil, Bulgaria, Burkina Faso, Burundi, Cambodia, Cameroon, Canada, Cape Verde, Central African Republic, Chad, Chile, China, Colombia, Comoros, Congo, Cook Islands, Costa Rica, Côte d'Ivoire, Cuba, Cyprus, Czechoslovakia, Democratic People's Republic of Korea, Denmark, Djibouti, Dominica, Dominican Republic, Ecuador, Egypt, El Salvador, Equatorial Guinea, Estonia, Ethiopia, European Economic Community, Fiji, Finland, France, Gabon, Gambia, Germany, Ghana, Greece, Grenada, Guatemala, Guinea, Guinea-Bissau, Guyana, Haiti, Honduras, Hungary, Iceland, India, Indonesia, Iran, Iraq, Ireland, Israel, Italy, Jamaica, Japan, Jordan, Kenya, Kuwait, Lao People's Democratic Republic, Latvia, Lebanon, Lesotho, Liberia, Libyan Arab Jamahiriya, Lithuania, Luxembourg, Madagascar, Malawi, Malaysia, Maldives, Mali, Malta, Mauritania, Mauritius, Mexico, Mongolia, Morocco, Mozambique, Myanmar, Namibia, Nepal, Netherlands, New Zealand, Nicaragua, Niger, Nigeria, Norway, Oman, Pakistan, Panama, Papua New Guinea, Paraguay, Peru, Philippines, Poland, Portugal, Qatar, Republic of Korea, Romania, Rwanda, Saint Kitts and Nevis, Saint Lucia, Saint Vincent and the Grenadines, Samoa, Sao Tome and Principe, Saudi Arabia, Senegal, Seychelles, Sierra Leone, Solomon Islands, Somalia, Spain, Sri Lanka, Sudan, Suriname, Swaziland, Sweden, Switzerland, Syrian Arab Republic, Thailand, Togo, Tonga, Trinidad and Tobago, Tunisia, Turkey, Uganda, United Arab Emirates, United Kingdom, United Republic of Tanzania, United States, Uruguay, Vanuatu, Venezuela, Viet Nam, Yemen, Yugoslavia,* Zaire, Zambia, Zimbabwe; *Associate member:* Puerto Rico.

*Following Security Council and General Assembly action (see PART ONE, Chapter IV), the FAO Council, at its one hundred and second session, decided that thenceforth Yugoslavia (Serbia and Montenegro) should not participate in the work of the Council or its subsidiary bodies.

Annex II.   MEMBERS OF THE COUNCIL OF THE FOOD AND AGRICULTURE ORGANIZATION

(As at 31 December 1992)

Independent Chairman: Antoine Saintraint.
Angola, Argentina, Australia, Bangladesh, Belgium, Brazil, Canada, Cape Verde, Chile, China, Colombia, Congo, Costa Rica, Côte d'Ivoire, Cuba, Cyprus, Czechoslovakia, Egypt, France, Germany, Hungary, India, Indonesia, Iran, Italy, Japan, Kenya, Lebanon, Libyan Arab Jamahiriya, Madagascar, Mexico, Nigeria, Pakistan, Philippines, Republic of Korea, Rwanda, Saudi Arabia, Spain, Sudan, Sweden, Thailand, Trinidad and Tobago, Tunisia, United Kingdom, United Republic of Tanzania, United States, Venezuela, Zaire, Zambia.

Annex III.   OFFICERS AND OFFICES OF THE FOOD AND AGRICULTURE ORGANIZATION

SENIOR OFFICERS

Director-General: Edouard Saouma.
Deputy Director-General: H. W. Hjort.
Deputy Director-General, Office of Programme, Budget and Evaluation: V. J. Shah.
Director, Office of Internal Audit, Inspection and Management Control: G. Peter Wilson.
Special Adviser to the Director-General/Assistant Director-General for Environment and Sustainable Development: P. J. Mahler.

Assistant Director-General, Administration and Finance Department: K. Mehboob.
Assistant Director-Gener al, Agriculture Department: H. de Haen.
Assistant Director-General, Development Department: André G. Regnier.
Assistant Director-General, Economic and Social Policy Department: F. B. Zenny (Officer-in-Charge).
Assistant Director-General, Fisheries Department: W. Krone.
Assistant Director-General, Forestry Department: C. H. Murray.

Assistant Director-General, Department of General Affairs and Information:
M. Alessi.
Assistant Director-General and Regional Representative for Africa:
R. T. N'Daw.
Assistant Director-General and Regional Representative for Asia and the
Pacific: A. Z. M. Obaidullah Khan.

Regional Representative for Europe: M. Zjalic.
Assistant Director-General and Regional Representative for Latin America
and the Caribbean: R. Moreno.
Assistant Director-General and Regional Representative for the Near East:
Atif Yehya Bukhari.

HEADQUARTERS AND OTHER OFFICES

HEADQUARTERS
Food and Agriculture Organization
Viale delle Terme di Caracalla
00100 Rome, Italy
  Cable address: FOODAGRI ROME
  Telephone: (39) (6) 52251
  Telex: 610181 FAO I
  Facsimile: (39) (6) 5225-3152

LIAISON OFFICE
Food and Agriculture Organization Liaison
  Office with the United Nations
1 United Nations Plaza, Room 1125
New York, N.Y. 10017, United States
  Cable Address: FOODAGRI NEWYORK
  Telephone: (1) (212) 963-6036
  Facsimile: (1) (212) 888-6188

FAO also maintained liaison offices in Washington, D.C., and at Geneva, and regional offices at Accra, Ghana; Bangkok, Thailand; Cairo, Egypt; and Santiago, Chile.

Chapter IV

United Nations Educational, Scientific and Cultural Organization (UNESCO)

During 1992, the United Nations Educational, Scientific and Cultural Organization (UNESCO) continued to promote cooperation among nations through its education, science and technology, social and human sciences, culture and communications, information and informatics activities.

In 1992, UNESCO's membership increased to 171 with the admission of Armenia, Azerbaijan, Croatia, Georgia, Kazakhstan, Kyrgyzstan, Republic of Moldova, and Slovenia. (See Annex I for complete membership.)

Education

UNESCO's major education activities focused on basic education, the renewal of educational systems and educational advancement and policy. Special priority was given to the Education for All (EFA) programmes—a follow-up to the World Conference on EFA held at Jomtien, Thailand, in 1990. Under those programmes, UNESCO assisted member States in diagnosing basic learning needs, setting national EFA objectives and devising effective strategies to move towards EFA. The Steering Committee of the International Consultative Forum on EFA met at Geneva (14-19 September) to monitor progress since the 1990 World Conference. The meeting was held in conjunction with the International Conference on Education.

The UNESCO Institute for Education, the International Institute for Educational Planning and the International Bureau of Education contributed to the follow-up of the EFA Conference by launching projects and comparative studies and organizing regional forums, training courses and programmes.

The first of a series of regional seminars on policy, planning and organization of education for children and young people with special needs was held at Gaborone, Botswana (3-6 August). At the request of Mozambique, UNESCO drew up an emergency plan to educate demobilized child soldiers and war victims. It also facilitated access to education for refugees and displaced persons in Angola, Croatia and Slovenia. A mission to Somalia assessed the feasibility of establishing educational activities at various levels within the framework of other humanitarian initiatives.

UNESCO contributed to improving the quality, relevance and efficiency of higher education through strengthening regional centres and assisting member States to reform their national systems, as well as by disseminating topical and comparative studies and monographs on national systems and by training 140 university administrators.

An initiative launched in 1991 to foster inter-university cooperation (UNITWIN) and the UNESCO Chairs scheme helped establish a number of chairs at various universities. During the year, 200 requests were made to join the scheme and 18 new networks and 53 chairs were set up.

UNESCO prepared two draft standard-setting instruments concerning the Universal Convention and the Recommendation on the Recognition of Studies and Qualifications in Higher Education, which were revised by a meeting of governmental experts (Paris, 29-30 October). UNESCO also convened an international congress on academic mobility and recognition of studies (Paris, 2-5 November) and sponsored the International Conference on Academic Freedom and University Autonomy (Sinaia, Romania, 5-7 May).

Health education programmes continued in 1992, in cooperation with the World Health Organization. An agreement was signed in July 1992 with the Commission of the European Communities to develop an information network in preventive education against drug abuse. With regard to education for the prevention of acquired immunodeficiency syndrome (AIDS), UNESCO took part in the Eighth International Conference on AIDS (Amsterdam, Netherlands, 18-24 July) and the Maghreb Conference on AIDS (Marrakech, Morocco, 19-23 May).

Natural sciences

UNESCO elaborated strategies for the management of science and technology systems in different regions of the world during 1992. To that end, a number of conferences, research seminars, training programmes and workshops were organized.

Three hundred scientists met at UNESCO headquarters for an international conference on "Cancer, AIDS and Society: Integrating Science, Medical Practice and Health Policy" (Paris, 23-26 March).

Under the "Diversitas" programme, UNESCO continued work to establish an international network to take inventory of and to monitor biological diversity. In collaboration with the International Union of Biological Sciences and the Scientific Committee on Problems of the Environment, it launched a 10-year project (BIO-D) to increase understanding of biodiversity. It also launched the second phase of the Regional Programme for Biotechnology in Latin America and the Caribbean. The first regional programme on the human genome was launched in Latin America and served as the basis for several international training courses. UNESCO also organized the first North-South Genome Conference (Caxambu, Brazil, 12-15 May), which discussed perspectives for molecular genetics and biology in developing countries.

In collaboration with the International Council of Scientific Unions and the Third World Academy of Sciences, UNESCO established an International Network for the Availability of Scientific Publications to facilitate and improve the access of scientists from developing countries and from Eastern and Central Europe to scientific and technical literature.

An international centre for bioethical studies, established at the initiative of UNESCO, the Council of Europe, the Commission of the European Communities and other international organizations, was inaugurated at Trieste, Italy, on 6 March. The third UNESCO Science and Culture Forum, "Towards eco-ethics: alternative visions of culture, science, technology and nature", was held (Belém, Brazil, 6-10 April).

A number of regional activities were conducted by UNESCO's Intergovernmental Oceanographic Commission (IOC). In collaboration with other United Nations bodies, IOC was involved in the United Nations Inter-Agency Plan for the Persian Gulf. Its activities included the collection by marine researchers of an information base to assess conditions in the Gulf. A steering committee meeting to put forward the plans for an expanded interdisciplinary, multidisciplinary programme in the eastern Mediterranean took place at UNESCO headquarters (Paris, 22 and 23 January 1992). The second Marine Debris Workshop (Merida, Mexico, 17-19 August) focused on the long-term consequences of marine debris pollution and elaborated an action plan for the wider Caribbean. Following tidal waves in September 1992, IOC sponsored a reconnaissance mission to Nicaragua which formulated recommendations for protective measures to be taken against similar disasters in the future.

UNESCO organized a scientific symposium (Paris, 3 and 4 July) on the variability of interdependence of time and space scales in various hydrological processes. This was followed by the tenth session of the Intergovernmental Council of the International Hydrological Programmes (Paris, 6-11 July).

The International Geological Correlation Programme continued to foster international collaboration in the earth sciences through 56 research projects in 22 countries. The geology for development project focused on applied regional geological studies, training related to environmentally sound and sustainable socio-economic development and the transfer of new technologies, such as computerized information handling and remote sensing analysis, to developing countries. Several activities were conducted in connection with the International Decade for Natural Disaster Reduction, aimed at strengthening hazard-monitoring network systems and post-disaster investigations.

An inter-agency meeting (Paris, 5-7 October) on outer space in the service of development, organized as part of International Space Year (see PART ONE, Chapter III), discussed the practical applications of space technology, such as communications, meteorology, navigation and disaster management.

Within the frame of a project on transformation of science and technology management systems in the Central and Eastern European countries during their transition to a market economy, UNESCO organized a conference on the organizational structures of science in transition (Venice, Italy, 27-29 April).

Social and human sciences

In 1992, UNESCO continued to promote the social sciences as academic disciplines, primarily by strengthening regional and global networks of specialized institutions that fostered research, training and information exchange.

It completed a feasibility study on the establishment of an intergovernmental programme in the social sciences and, in cooperation with the International Social Science Council, organized a consultation (Paris, 18-20 March) of representatives of social science organizations to discuss the current state of international social science cooperation.

UNESCO assisted the International Council of Women to organize a conference on changing families in changing societies (Brussels, Belgium, 8-10 February). It also launched a pilot training project in social policies and legislation for family and child promotion, conceived as preparatory activities for the International Year of the Family (1994). An international symposium on the educational function of the family and cultural change to identify ways to strengthen family and school collaboration took place at UNESCO headquarters (Paris, 12 and 13 March).

Other activities organized or supported by UNESCO included a forum on women as creators and transmitters of culture in the Mediterranean region (Valencia, Spain, November); an international seminar focusing on the sex trade and human rights (Brussels, 6 March); a summer university for women on feminism: international experience and solidarity (Samaia, Romania, 29 June–5 July); a seminar on social change, demographic trends, family structure and gender relations in Muslim societies—with special reference to Central Asia (London, 5-10 July); and an expert meeting on human rights and human rights education in the process of transition to democracy (Prague, Czechoslovakia, 2-6 November).

Under activities related to the promotion of human rights, a second enlarged edition of the *World Directory of Human Rights Training and Research Institutions* was published in 1992. As part of a special project on UNESCO's contribution to the elmination of apartheid, an international workshop on culture and educational policies in a post-apartheid South Africa was held (Abidjan, Côte d'Ivoire, 16-19 June).

UNESCO awarded several prizes in 1992, including the UNESCO Prize for Peace Education, awarded to Mother Teresa of Calcutta, India, and the UNESCO Prize for Human Rights Teaching, awarded to the Arab Institute for Human Rights (Tunis, Tunisia). The 1992 Félix Houphouët-Boigny Prize for Peace Research was awarded to the South African leaders Nelson Mandela and Frederik W. de Klerk.

In December, the United Nations General Assembly welcomed the 1991 proposal of the UNESCO General Conference to proclaim 1995 as the United Nations Year for Tolerance and encouraged it to prepare a declaration on tolerance (see PART THREE, Chapter XII).

Culture

In 1992, UNESCO's main cultural activities were devoted to safeguarding the cultural heritage, preservation of and respect for cultural identities and diversity and promotion of all creative and intellectual expression. Those activities took place in the context of the World Decade for Cultural Development (1988-1997), which was proclaimed by the General Assembly in 1986.[a] During the year, the focus was on culture and environment in honour of the United Nations Conference on Environment and Development (see PART THREE, Chapter VIII). A number of regional and subregional consultations of national committees for the Decade were organized.

The UNESCO Director-General, responding to a 1991 General Conference request,[b] established the World Commission on Culture and Develop-

ment to prepare proposals for both urgent and long-term action to meet cultural needs in the context of deivelopment. A regional seminar on the cultural dimension of development (Abidjan, 2-7 November), organized jointly by UNESCO, the World Bank, the United Nations Children's Fund and the African Development Bank, discussed concepts of decision-making, participation and integration—inseparable from cultural models.

UNESCO undertook a study on ways to strengthen the application of the 1954 Hague Convention for the Protection of Cultural Property in the Event of Armed Conflict and carried out training activities to promote wider application of the 1970 Convention on the Means of Prohibiting and Preventing the Illicit Import, Export and Transfer of Ownership of Cultural Property.

UNESCO continued to coordinate operations to preserve and enhance the site of Angkor Wat in Cambodia and to cooperate with the organizations in charge of safeguarding the old city of Dubrovnik in Croatia. UNESCO's World Heritage Centre was established in May. The sixteenth session of the World Heritage Committee (Santa Fe, United States, 7-14 December) placed 20 additional sites on the World Heritage list and seven sites on the list of World Heritage in Danger. The Committee also reviewed the state of preservation of 51 sites and commended the results of the permanent monitoring mission, which inspected 38 sites in Latin America, the Caribbean and Portuguese-speaking Africa.

The first International Congress on Cultural and Scientific Cooperation in Central Asia (Shiraz, Iran, 14-18 November) studied a proposal for the establishment of an International Institute of Central Asian Studies.

A symposium on the role and challenge of copyright on the eve of the twenty-first century was held at UNESCO headquarters (Paris, 16-18 November) on the occasion of the fortieth anniversary of the Universal Copyright Convention.

Communication

UNESCO's communication programme continued to support the development of free, independent and pluralistic media in the public and private sectors.

At its thirteenth session (Paris, 17-24 February), the Intergovernmental Council of the International Programme for the Development of Communication (IPDC) decided, to give priority to the issues of freedom of the press and the pluralism and independence of the media. It also approved 38

[a]YUN 1986, p. 624, GA res. 41/187, 8 Dec. 1986.
[b]YUN 1991, p. 949.

projects. Arrangements were made to implement UNESCO's Recovery Plan, adopted by the Summit of African Heads of State (Dakar, Senegal, 22-26 June), which sought to develop the Pan-African News Agency.

As a follow-up to the Seminar on Promoting Independent and Pluralistic Asian Media (Alma Ata, Kazakhstan, 5-9 October), eight projects were identified for consideration by the IPDC Council. Following a workshop of heads of Asian press institutes (Kathmandu, Nepal, 17-19 November), initiatives were taken to create new press institutes in Cambodia, Fiji and Mongolia through regional twinning arrangements.

The Intergovernmental Council for the General Information Programme (Paris, 16-19 November) defined the main missions of its long-term strategy, namely safeguarding the memory of the world; information for education and learning; information for human development; and information for environmental management. In that context, an international programme entitled "Memory of the World" was initiated to preserve and restore rare library and archival materials. Under the programme, pilot projects were launched in Czechoslovakia, Yemen, and several countries in Latin America and the Caribbean.

In the field of informatics, implementation began on 18 projects totalling $1.8 million, which were approved by the Bureau of the Intergovernmental Informatics Programme (IIP) at its sixth session (Dakar, 25-27 February). The Intergovernmental Committee for IIP (Paris, 1-4 December) focused on the priorities of training, the role of computer networks as a means of fostering regional and international cooperation, software development and research and development.

The Regional Informatics Networks for Africa to link major African institutions engaged in the collection, processing and dissemination of scientific and technical data was launched (Dakar, 27-29 February).

UNESCO provided technical assistance to Mauritius and Zambia under the project on national education statistical information systems for planning and management in sub-Saharan Africa. Four regional case-studies were completed on the needs, availability, concepts, definitions and classifications in science and technology statistics, covering 14 countries, and training seminars on education statistics were organized in the Congo, Costa Rica, Malawi, Philippines, Rwanda and the United Arab Emirates. It also published a methodological report on literacy assessment and its implications for statistical measures.

Secretariat

As at 31 December 1992, UNESCO had a full-time staff of 2,544, comprising 956 in the Professional or higher categories, drawn from 137 nationalities, and 1,588 in the General Service.

Budget

The General Conference of UNESCO, at its 1991 session, approved a budget of $444,704,000 for the 1992-1993 biennium. The level of the Working Capital Fund was fixed at $17,200,000 and the total assessment on member States (after deducting miscellaneous income) was $432,216,000.

Annex I.   MEMBERSHIP OF THE UNITED NATIONS
EDUCATIONAL, SCIENTIFIC AND CULTURAL ORGANIZATION
(As at 31 December 1992)

Afghanistan, Albania, Algeria, Angola, Antigua and Barbuda, Argentina, Armenia, Australia, Austria, Azerbaijan, Bahamas, Bahrain, Bangladesh, Barbados, Belarus, Belgium, Belize, Benin, Bhutan, Bolivia, Botswana, Brazil, Bulgaria, Burkina Faso, Burundi, Cambodia, Cameroon, Canada, Cape Verde, Central African Republic, Chad, Chile, China, Colombia, Comoros, Congo, Cook Islands, Costa Rica, Côte d'Ivoire, Croatia, Cuba, Cyprus, Czechoslovakia, Democratic People's Republic of Korea, Denmark, Djibouti, Dominica, Dominican Republic, Ecuador, Egypt, El Salvador, Equatorial Guinea, Estonia, Ethiopia, Fiji, Finland, France, Gabon, Gambia, Georgia, Germany, Ghana, Greece, Grenada, Guatemala, Guinea, Guinea-Bissau, Guyana, Haiti, Honduras, Hungary, Iceland, India, Indonesia, Iran, Iraq, Ireland, Israel, Italy, Jamaica, Japan, Jordan, Kazakhstan, Kenya, Kiribati, Kuwait, Kyrgyzstan, Lao People's Democratic Republic, Latvia, Lebanon, Lesotho, Liberia, Libyan Arab Jamahiriya, Lithuania, Luxembourg, Madagascar, Malawi, Malaysia, Maldives, Mali, Malta, Mauritania, Mauritius, Mexico, Monaco, Mongolia, Morocco, Mozambique, Myanmar, Namibia, Nepal, Netherlands, New Zealand, Nicaragua, Niger, Nigeria, Norway, Oman, Pakistan, Panama, Papua New Guinea, Paraguay, Peru, Philippines, Poland, Portugal, Qatar, Republic of Korea, Republic of Moldova, Romania, Russian Federation, Rwanda, Saint Kitts and Nevis, Saint Lucia, Saint Vincent and the Grenadines, Samoa, San Marino, Sao Tome and Principe, Saudi Arabia, Senegal, Seychelles, Sierra Leone, Slovenia, Somalia, Spain, Sri Lanka, Sudan, Suriname, Swaziland, Sweden, Switzerland, Syrian Arab Republic, Thailand, Togo, Tonga, Trinidad and Tobago, Tunisia, Turkey, Tuvalu, Uganda, Ukraine, United Arab Emirates, United Republic of Tanzania, Uruguay, Venezuela, Viet Nam, Yemen, Yugoslavia, Zaire, Zambia, Zimbabwe.

Associate members
Aruba, British Virgin Islands, Netherlands Antilles.

Annex II. OFFICERS AND OFFICES OF THE UNITED NATIONS EDUCATIONAL, SCIENTIFIC AND CULTURAL ORGANIZATION
(As at 31 December 1992)

MEMBERS OF THE EXECUTIVE BOARD

Chairman: Marie Bernard-Meunier (Canada).

Vice-Chairmen: Musa Hassan (Oman), Alexei D. Joukov (Russian Federation), Kurt Müller (Germany), Ana Isabel Prera Flores (Guatemala), Teng Teng (China), G. W. Ladepon Thomas (Gambia).

Members: Abdul Amir Al-Anbari (Iraq), Jean-Pierre Angremy (France), Immanuel K. Bavu (United Republic of Tanzania), Mongi Chemli (Tunisia), Alvaro Costa-Franco (Brazil), Ingrid Eide (Norway), Tom Erdimi (Chad), Ali Mohamed Fakhro (Bahrain), Maria Luisa Ferro Ribeiro (Cape Verde), Tae-Hyuk Hahm (Republic of Korea), Talat S. Halman (Turkey), Dan Haulica (Romania), Attiya Inayatullah (Pakistan), Michelangelo Jacobucci (Italy), Barry O. Jones (Australia), Balla Keita (Côte d'Ivoire), Natarajan Krishnan (India), Torben Krogh (Denmark), Anatoly Lobanok (Belarus), Wataru Miyakawa (Japan), Mouhoussine Nacro (Burkina Faso), Gilles Nageon de Lestang (Seychelles), Rex Nettleford (Jamaica), Gloria Pachón de Galán (Colombia), Punisa A. Pavlovic (Yugoslavia),* Lourdes R. Quisumbing (Philippines), Abdelatif Rahal (Algeria), Guy Rajaonson (Madagascar), Luc Rukingama (Burundi), Zaïnoul Abidine Sanoussi (Guinea), Ahmed Saleh Sayyad (Yemen), José Augusto Seabra (Portugal), Mwindaace N. Siamwiza (Zambia), Johannes Sizoo (Netherlands), Ahmed Fathi Sorour (Egypt), Thérèse E. Striggner Scott (Ghana), Jerry Emaus Tetaga (Papua New Guinea), Thomas Tlou (Botswana), Alfredo Traversoni (Uruguay), Carlos Tunnermann Bernheim (Nicaragua), Alvaro Umana Quesada (Costa Rica), Adul Wichiencharoen (Thailand), Jorge Cayetano Zain Asis (Argentina), Ernesto Zedillo Ponce de Leon (Mexico).

*On 12 October 1992, the UNESCO Executive Board decided that the member of the Board elected following nomination by the Government of the former Yugoslavia should not participate in its work.

PRINCIPAL OFFICERS OF THE SECRETARIAT

Director-General: Federico Mayor.
Deputy Directors-General: Eduardo Portella, Chaman-Lal Sharma.

Assistant Directors-General: Thomas Keller, Khamliène Nhouyvanisvong *(acting)*, Colin Power, Adnan Badran, Francine Fournier, Henri Lopes, Henrikas Iouchkiavitchious.

HEADQUARTERS AND OTHER OFFICE

HEADQUARTERS
UNESCO House
7 place de Fontenoy
75700 Paris, France
Cable address: UNESCO PARIS
Telephone: (33) (1) 45-68-10-00
Telex: 204461
Facsimile: (33) (1) 45-67-16-90

NEW YORK OFFICE
United Nations Educational, Scientific and Cultural Organization
2 United Nations Plaza, Room 900
New York, N.Y., 10017, United States
Cable address: UNESCORG NEWYORK
Telephone: (1) (212) 963-5995
Facsimile: (1) (212) 355-5627

Chapter V

World Health Organization (WHO)

The World Health Assembly, the governing body of the World Health Organization (WHO), at its forty-fifth annual session (Geneva, 4-14 May 1992), reviewed a second evaluation of implementation of the global strategy for health for all by the year 2000 and adopted resolutions on: strengthening nursing and midwifery; disability prevention and rehabilitation; immunization and vaccine quality; health and environment; and national strategies for overcoming micronutrient malnutrition. The Assembly urged member States to improve the health of the most vulnerable population groups, analyse the health impact of development projects, and ensure that health protection was an integral part of sustainable development policies. It endorsed an updated and expanded global strategy for combating the acquired immunodeficiency syndrome (AIDS), as well as guidelines for implementing the WHO Certification Scheme on the Quality of Pharmaceutical Products moving in International Commerce. Technical discussions focused on women, health and development and the Assembly requested the WHO Director-General to establish a global commission on women's health.

Within the framework of United Nations relief efforts, WHO undertook 24 projects to rehabilitate the health sector in Afghanistan and provided medical support for the repatriation of Cambodian refugees by the United Nations High Commissioner for Refugees. Emergency humanitarian aid was provided to Djibouti, Eritrea, Ethiopia, Somalia and the Sudan, and emergency health kits were supplied to a number of countries affected by natural disasters, including Albania, Bangladesh, Egypt, Kyrgyzstan, Madagascar, Pakistan, the Philippines, Rwanda and Yemen.

During 1992, the membership of WHO increased to 182, with the admission of Armenia, Azerbaijan, Bosnia and Herzegovina, Croatia, Georgia, Kazakhstan, Kyrgyzstan, Republic of Moldova, Slovenia, Tajikistan, Turkmenistan and Uzbekistan. Puerto Rico became an associate member in May and Ukraine notified the Organization that it had reactivated its membership (see Annex I for complete membership).

Health system infrastructure

Health systems development and research

Advisory services were provided to member States for the development of health information systems, as part of a WHO initiative to intensify cooperation with countries and peoples in greatest need. Missions were organized for Bangladesh, Cambodia, Guinea-Bissau and Maldives. By the end of 1992, WHO had intensified its cooperation with 25 countries and new partnerships were formed with bilateral and multilateral development agencies in Bolivia, Chad, Ethiopia, Lao People's Democratic Republic, Mozambique, Viet Nam and Zambia.

WHO organized a five-country workshop on health information support at the district level (Togo); a regional workshop on strengthening national epidemiological capacity (Pakistan); a ten-country workshop on surveillance of childhood diseases (Cameroon); a national workshop on cholera surveillance (Zambia); and two meetings on aspects of health systems research (Cairo, Egypt, June; Damascus, Syrian Arab Republic, October). A third interregional workshop for senior research managers (Cuernavaca, Mexico, July) focused on promoting networks of lead institutions in health systems research and an international conference on economics and health (Geneva, 24-26 June) discussed the relationship between macroeconomics and the health sector in countries in greatest need.

WHO continued to provide legislative information to its members through the quarterly *International Digest of Health Legislation* and on an ad hoc basis. An international legislative information network was initiated in cooperation with other agencies and an international meeting was held on the subject (Washington, D.C., December). Consultant services were provided to 10 countries during the year.

Other activities in 1992 included an international computer-based training course on use of the tenth revision of the International Classification of Diseases (Southampton, United Kingdom, April); a meeting to plan a revision of the international classification of impairments, disabilities and handicaps (Zoetermeer, Netherlands, March); and advisory services on establishing an emergency monitoring system in Yugoslavia.

Primary health care systems

Research and development support to improve district health systems management continued in Indonesia, Zambia and Zimbabwe. Initiatives for strengthening district health systems in Ghana led to a revision of its national health policy and strategy. The strengthening of informational support for district health management was the subject of an African regional consultation (Lomé, Togo, September). Joint activities with the United Nations Development Programme (UNDP) to develop district health system infrastructure in six Western Pacific countries were completed in 1992.

Intercountry seminars on health economics and cost analysis for French-speaking countries were held in Algeria and Senegal with the support of the Economic Development Institute of the World Bank. Technical support was provided to the first international seminar on economic evaluation of maternal and child health programmes (Paris, June) and to a regional seminar on financing of the health sector in a crisis situation (Havana, Cuba, March). Regional training initiatives were supported at Chulalongkorn University (Thailand) and the National Institute of Public Health (Algeria). A meeting on the future of health care financing (Kiel, Germany, November) considered ways of coping with increasing demand for health services in the face of limited resources. A seminar on hospital cooperation in Europe (Strasbourg, France, November), convened jointly with the European Community, formulated responses to changes in Central and Eastern Europe. WHO prepared a document on contemporary standards for the organization of health care to assist national and district-level decision-makers in analysing their hospital services.

Human resources for health

Further progress was made in designing computerized tools for more flexible planning in human resources development. Meetings reviewed the existing planning methodology (Bangkok, Thailand, March) and studied the conceptual framework for a projection planning model (York, United Kingdom, June). Development work continued on issues related to the "skills mix", productivity and workload of health personnel, and "the public/private mix of human resources" was the subject of a consultation (Bangkok, Thailand, June/July). Workshops were conducted with a revised WHO manual on human resource management (Colombo, Sri Lanka, May; Kathmandu, Nepal, September).

Among activities in nursing were an intercountry workshop on leadership and management issues (Mbabane, Swaziland, April) for Lesotho, Namibia, Swaziland and Zambia, and a third meeting of Government chief nurses (Bucharest, Romania, October), which underlined a priority commitment to Central and Eastern Europe. A global multidisciplinary advisory group on the role of nursing and midwifery held its first meeting in November/December and produced recommendations to ensure an adequate contribution by nurses and midwives to the achievement of health goals.

A study group in October recommended that educational institutions develop new alliances with professional associations, authorities and the community, conduct service-oriented research, and adapt their programmes accordingly. Workshops to revise physician training programmes in Africa were held in the Congo, Ethiopia, Ghana, Zambia and Zimbabwe, and the first issue of the newsletter *Changing medical education and medical practice* was published during the year. The first regional meeting on continuing education programmes for health personnel was held in Tunis, Tunisia, in June.

The health learning materials programme continued to expand and supported more than 35 countries in 1992. Meetings were held to plan future strategies and collaboration between country projects (Harare, Zimbabwe, April) and to examine project evaluation and planning in South-East Asian countries (Colombo, August).

Public information and education for health

During the year, WHO prepared information materials such as press releases, features and press kits, quarterly radio programmes and video newsreels; arranged four television co-productions; and supported the production of a film on health by Nigerian television.

Audiovisual support was provided for technical programmes dealing with environmental health; cardiovascular, tobacco-related and other life-style diseases; AIDS; malaria; onchocerciasis; mental health; and human reproduction. Information campaigns were organized for major international conferences and other events. World Health Day (7 April) had the theme "Heartbeat—the rhythm of health". World No-Tobacco Day (31 May) was devoted to smoke-free workplaces, and World AIDS Day (1 December) focused on community involvement.

Comprehensive school health education was the subject of an intercountry consultation for nine countries in South-East Asia (Colombo, October). A research project on the health behaviour of school-age children was launched in the United Republic of Tanzania and in Zimbabwe in collaboration with the University of Bergen (Norway). The aim was to design strategies for health education and promote healthy life-styles. A meeting of the WHO/United Nations Educational, Scientific and Cultural Organization/United Nations Children's Fund (UNICEF) working group for increased cooperation in an integrated approach to school health education was held in conjunction with the Eighth International Conference on AIDS (Amsterdam, Netherlands, July), while an interagency meeting in November discussed communication and advocacy strategies to ensure the support of health policy-makers. WHO revised a training manual for community health workers on human relations, communications and community organization, based on training programmes in Kenya and Sierra Leone. The first international symposium on health education was held in China in October in collaboration with the Shanghai Health Education Institute.

Health science and technology

Health protection and promotion

The WHO Advisory Committee on Health Research (Geneva, September/October) recommended further study in the areas of nursing and women's health, global developments relating to cancer and injuries, and the strengthening of research capability in Central and Eastern Europe and in Africa.

WHO collaborated with the Food and Agriculture Organization of the United Nations (FAO) in convening the International Conference on Nutrition (Rome, Italy, 5-11 December). The Conference sought ways to eliminate hunger and malnutrition world-wide. Meetings to promote the iodization of salt were held in Africa, Europe and the Western Pacific, in collaboration with UNICEF and the International Council for the Control of Iodine Deficiency Disorders, and a consultation was held on supplementation methods for populations severely deficient in vitamin A. A joint WHO/UNICEF strategy was developed to prevent iron deficiency anaemia in pregnancy and an African data bank on iodine and vitamin A deficiency was established. In 1992, the global breast-feeding data bank, established in 1986, contained information from more than 1,500 surveys or studies carried out in some 150 countries and territories. Activities dealing with food safety centred on food export difficulties faced by WHO members as a result of the cholera epidemic. Recommendations to control the disease were provided by a technical consultation on food safety and the food trade (Buenos Aires, Argentina, April).

Activities in the area of oral health care included a demonstration study of non-invasive and inexpensive oral care procedures in Thailand; a project providing special curative and preventive oral health care in zones contaminated by the 1986 nuclear accident at Chernobyl in Ukraine; an international action network on oro-facial mutilations and noma (*cancrum oris*), dealing with severe and destructive oral diseases and conditions as well as oral manifestations of the human immunodeficiency virus (HIV); and feasibility studies and demonstration projects on the use of milk as a vehicle for fluorides in Bulgaria, Chile, Italy, the Russian Federation and the United Kingdom. An

intercountry centre for oral health was opened in Belarus, in addition to those operating in Nigeria, the Syrian Arab Republic and Thailand.

Two epidemiological studies were under way in accident prevention, one dealing with falls among the elderly, and the other with burns. The Second International Safe Communities Conference (Glasgow, Scotland, September) assessed a project on community safety under implementation in Argentina, Australia, Canada, Denmark, France, Sweden, Thailand, the United Kingdom and the United States and decided to extend its scope to include the prevention of violence. In 1992, WHO took part in the Eighth World Conference on Tobacco or Health (Buenos Aires, March-April); the International Symposium on Public Health Surveillance (Atlanta, United States, April); and the First International Conference on Women and Smoking (Newcastle, Northern Ireland, October). Missions were fielded on tobacco control policies in Bangladesh; legislation and other control measures in India; planning for tobacco control in Nepal; and regulatory measures in Thailand.

Health of specific population groups

In 1992, a workplan was drawn up outlining a new strategy and activities for 1992-1993 in the area of maternal health and safe motherhood. It focused on technical support for planning, implementing and evaluating national safe motherhood programmes. WHO continued to monitor infant and young-child feeding and nutrition and implementation of the International Code of Marketing of Breast-milk Substitutes.

In connection with the Twentieth International Congress of Pediatrics (Rio de Janeiro, Brazil, September), the International Pediatric Association, WHO and UNICEF convened a joint workshop on health, nutrition and the quality of maternal care. Under the auspices of the three organizations, workshops were conducted in China, India and Nigeria to prepare national strategies and approaches for maternal and child care and family planning in the 1990s.

Trials of a once-a-month injectable contraceptive, developed with WHO support, were completed in Mexico and continued in Chile, Indonesia, Jamaica, Thailand and Tunisia. WHO also continued long-term studies and comparative trials of intrauterine devices and produced a special feature on the global status of reproductive health under the Special Programme of Research, Development and Research Training in Human Reproduction on the occasion of its twentieth anniversary.

WHO and the International Labour Organisation (ILO) convened an international symposium on the prevention and control of work-related diseases (Linz, Austria, October). Planning was undertaken for medical surveillance of workers exposed to mineral dusts inducing pneumoconiosis; methods and quality assurance in evaluating exposure to fibres and airborne contaminants; and biological monitoring to assess the risk from exposure to chemicals.

A study on dementias among the elderly was carried out in Canada, Chile, Malta, Nigeria, Spain and the United States, and a cross-national study on osteoporosis was initiated in Barbados, Brazil, China, Hong Kong, Hungary, Iceland and Nigeria. A project on successful ageing was planned for Costa Rica, Indonesia, Israel, Italy, Jamaica, Thailand and Zimbabwe. WHO received external support in determining the needs for long-term and home care for the rapidly growing elderly population in the developing world.

Protection and promotion of mental health

Methods were developed, with the support of the World Bank, to assess cost-effectiveness in mental health programmes, and information systems were established to support them at the national level. National workshops were organized in some 40 countries to share information about programme development. Three meetings were held as part of a new WHO study aimed at producing an instrument for assessing changes in the quality of life after health care interventions.

A major international review of laws concerning the promotion of mental health and support to the mentally ill, covering 45 countries in all regions, was started with funding from the United States National Institute of Mental Health. Several studies were completed on differential diagnosis of different types of dementia; clinical and pharmacokinetic factors in predicting the efficacy of lithium prophylaxis for manic depressive disorders; the epidemiology of cognitive impairment and dementia; and psychological problems in general health care. Work continued on preventing and treating neurological disorders, including a project to improve the treatment of epilepsy and a meeting on diagnostic criteria for acute onset of flaccid paralysis (Geneva, July).

WHO made a feasibility study of a system for reporting trends in drug and alcohol abuse and its health consequences; promoted a revised abuse trends linkage alerting system; established a network of centres in 17 countries to assess the global impact of cocaine and study national patterns of its use; and issued a report on simple treatment interventions for alcohol-related problems and their usefulness in primary health care settings.

Environmental health

In response to a 1992 World Health Assembly resolution, WHO drafted a new global strategy for health and environment, based on a report of its Commission on Health and Environment, entitled *Our Planet, our Health* and the outcome of the United Nations Conference on Environment and Development (Rio de Janeiro, June).

During 1992, national monitoring of funding, operations and maintenance costs related to water supply and sanitation coverage was supported under a five-year WHO/UNICEF programme. The programme, launched in 1991, was operational in some 70 countries. Subregional workshops on this subject were held in the Caribbean (Kingston, Jamaica, March) southern Africa (Mbabane, Swaziland, June) and West Africa (Cotonou, Benin, September). Assistance was provided in preparing national action plans on hygiene education and environmental health, and the development of teaching materials, school curricula and training courses. Training workshops were organized for national specialists in water resources development in Zimbabwe and for agricultural extension programmes in Honduras. WHO supported cholera control in Africa and Latin America by providing technical and material services for strengthening water quality assessment and the operation of water and sanitation facilities.

The WHO Director-General established a WHO/ILO/United Nations Environment Programme (UNEP) International Programme on Chemical Safety in 1992, as the nucleus for international cooperation on the environmentally sound management of chemicals.

Diagnostic, therapeutic and rehabilitative technology

Several training workshops, using WHO handbooks, were held to improve surgical and anaesthetic services at district hospitals in developing countries. Meetings were held on the integration of basic surgery into primary health care (Irbid, Jordan, November); the strengthening of public health laboratories (New Delhi, India, November); and on standardization and quality assessment in Latin American laboratories (Guatemala City, Guatemala, November). WHO provided support through the Global Programme on AIDS for the preparation of learning materials on the appropriate use of blood and other aspects of blood safety; upgraded its database on blood transfusion services; and established regional training centres in Amman (Jordan) and Tunis (Tunisia).

A draft manual on diagnostic ultrasound was produced in 1992, as well as ten examples of the most common radiographs, for use in training programmes and as a simple quality assurance tool. A survey was also made of mammographic equipment in the Eastern Mediterranean and support was provided to Romania for the reorganization of its radiation medicine services. The WHO Expert Committee on Specifications for Pharmaceutical Preparations approved a revision of key WHO guidelines on good manufacturing practices for pharmaceutical products, and the Expert Committee on Biological Standardization adopted revised requirements for the production and quality control of blood products, reflecting policy issues related to blood donation and the latest information on testing for HIV and hepatitis viruses.

WHO co-sponsored the International Symposium on Traditional Medicine (Toyama, Japan, August), which reviewed current research and the place of traditional medicine in health systems.

By year's end, 113 WHO members had adopted essential drug lists, and 66 had essential drugs programmes in operation.

At intercountry workshops on rehabilitation (Harare, Zimbabwe, July; Dakar, Senegal, October), participants outlined measures for strengthening rehabilitation in Africa, including the formulation of national policies on disability, the integration of community-based rehabilitation into primary health care, the strengthening of the referral system and the provision of aids and appliances. Guidelines for the care of children with cerebral palsy were prepared in 1992, as was an action plan for the emergency rehabilitation of war victims in the former Yugoslavia. The latter emphasized physical trauma, prosthetics, training and logistic support.

Disease prevention and control

By 1992, WHO had provided funds for national AIDS programmes in 153 countries and at year's end 126 medium-term plans for national AIDS programmes had been finalized. At its meetings in April and September, the Steering Committee on Social and Behavioural Research endorsed research activities related to the individual, household, community and societal response to HIV/AIDS; personal and social factors of sexual behaviour; women's role in sexual negotiation and the potential impact of the female condom; social and behavioural issues in vaccine trials; and synthesis of studies on knowledge, attitudes, beliefs and practices in partner relations. Another meeting in May considered 15 interventions aimed at encouraging people to change risky sexual behaviour and discussed factors contributing to the success of such interventions. A meeting on AIDS drug and vaccine supply in July, held under the sponsorship of WHO and UNDP, reviewed the first year of collaboration with major research-based pharmaceutical companies and the International Federation of Pharmaceutical Manufacturers Associations (Geneva).

In May, the World Health Assembly endorsed an updated global AIDS strategy, with the principal objectives of preventing HIV infection, reducing the personal and social impact of HIV infection, and mobilizing and unifying national and international efforts against AIDS. Also in May, WHO and UNICEF co-sponsored a meeting of experts on HIV transmission through breast-feeding.

WHO continued its activities for the prevention, early detection and treatment of cancer. National policies, technical guidelines and an international network of experts and institutes on cancer pain relief and palliative care were further strengthened. Projects on visual and physical examination for cancer of the cervix, breast and oral cavity at primary care level were initiated in India and Sri Lanka, and local training in radiotherapy and oncology continued in Sri Lanka and Zimbabwe.

In November, a scientific group recommended further research on the role of alcohol, physical activity, sex hormones, psychosocial, economic, metabolic and haemostatic factors in cardiovascular diseases. Under a project for multinational monitoring of trends and determinants in cardiovascular diseases, the first trend analysis for risk factor data was carried out together with a first cross-sectional comparison of morbidity data for coronary events and stroke. A joint WHO/United States Institute of Medicine meeting (Washington, D.C., October) established priorities for the prevention and control of cardiovascular diseases and developed a plan of action focusing on health statistics and epidemiology as well as prevention and case management, with particular attention to developing countries.

In 1992, for the first time, there were no recorded cases of poliomyelitis in the Western Hemisphere—a dramatic illustration of effective immunization coverage. Globally, it was estimated that, compared with pre-immunization levels, cases of the disease had fallen by 81 per cent. Measles incidence and mortality dropped by 66 and 88 per cent, respectively, and neonatal tetanus mortality by 54 per cent. The Children's Vaccine Initiative, launched at the end of 1991 with its secretariat at WHO, was pursued in partnership by WHO, UNICEF, UNDP, the World Bank and the Rockefeller Foundation (New York). Its goals included the development of new vaccines, improvements in the quality of vaccines produced in developing countries, and steps to ensure that vaccines reached all children in viable forms.

The world malaria situation deteriorated during 1992, with over 1 million people dying from the disease and more than 100 million falling ill. A Ministerial Conference on Malaria (Amsterdam, October) endorsed a global malaria control strategy drafted at interregional meetings in Brazzaville (Congo), New Delhi (India) and Brasilia (Brazil) in April. WHO also prepared a global action plan for malaria control for the period 1993-2000, with the objective of reducing mortality from the disease by at least 20 per cent in all WHO regions and in at least 75 per cent of endemic countries.

By September 1992, the total number of registered leprosy patients had fallen to 2.84 million, a 7.8 per cent decrease during the year and a decline of 47 per cent since 1985 when multidrug therapy was introduced. Courses on leprosy programme management were organized in Brazil, India, Indonesia, and the Philippines, in 21 African countries, and in 10 countries of the Eastern Mediterranean. Other WHO activities in the area of tropical diseases focused on the eradication of dracunculiasis, the control of schistosomiasis, onchocerciasis, lymphatic filariasis, African trypanosomiasis and the prevention of leishmaniasis.

Research in diarrhoeal diseases focused on improving infant and child nutrition, vitamin A supplementation and personal and domestic hygiene, as well as vaccine testing. A multicentre study was carried out in six countries to test a standard protocol for managing persistent diarrhoea, and investigations continued on the efficacy of oral rehydration fluids and antibiotics and the use of antidiarrheal drugs. WHO continued to coordinate activities on cholera control and to cooperate with countries affected by the disease, especially in Latin America. It produced guidelines and materials on travel precautions, food safety and cholera vaccination.

By the end of the year, 64 countries had implemented a programme for the control of acute respiratory infections and in March, interventions to prevent pneumonia in children were reviewed. Research continued on the case-management of pneumonia in malnourished children; clinical predictors of severe pneumonia; comparative methods of oxygen delivery; the clinical relevance of *in vitro* cotrimoxazole resistance; and the identification of simpler and cheaper antibiotic regimes for pneumonia in children.

A set of comprehensive training modules for district management of tuberculosis was completed in 1992. A global training workshop was conducted in September, followed by a national training course (Arusha, United Republic of Tanzania, November). Research was started on diagnosis, drug development and monitoring of HIV-associated tuberculosis in Uganda and the United Republic of Tanzania; chemotherapy for HIV-infected patients in the Dominican Republic and Haiti; and preventive chemotherapy in Brazil, Uganda and Zambia.

Workshops on the prevention and control of human and canine rabies for countries in West Africa (Kaduna, Nigeria, April) and southern Africa (Lusaka, Zambia, June) facilitated technical cooperation and the elaboration of national control programmes. At a consultation in July, specific safety requirements were established for a candidate oral vaccine for rabies.

WHO was also active in the prevention of diabetes mellitus blindness and deafness; the control of various species of intestinal helminths and protozoa; and vaccine research and development.

Secretariat

As at 31 December 1992, the total number of full-time staff employed by WHO stood at 4,659 on permanent and fixed-term contracts. Of these, 1,584 staff members, drawn from 140 nationalities, were in the Professional and higher categories, and 3,075 were in the General Service category. Of the total number, 48 were in posts financed by UNDP, UNEP, the United Nations Fund for Drug Abuse Control and the United Nations Population Fund.

Budget

The forty-fourth (1991) World Health Assembly approved an effective working budget of $734,936,000 for the 1992-1993 biennium.

Annex I.   MEMBERS OF THE WORLD HEALTH ORGANIZATION
(As at 31 December 1992)

Afghanistan, Albania, Algeria, Angola, Antigua and Barbuda, Argentina, Armenia, Australia, Austria, Azerbaijan, Bahamas, Bahrain, Bangladesh, Barbados, Belarus, Belgium, Belize, Benin, Bhutan, Bolivia, Bosnia and Herzegovina, Botswana, Brazil, Brunei Darussalam, Bulgaria, Burkina Faso, Burundi, Cambodia, Cameroon, Canada, Cape Verde, Central African Republic, Chad, Chile, China, Colombia, Comoros, Congo, Cook Islands, Costa Rica, Côte d'Ivoire, Croatia, Cuba, Cyprus, Czechoslovakia, Democratic People's Republic of Korea, Denmark, Djibouti, Dominica, Dominican Republic, Ecuador, Egypt, El Salvador, Equatorial Guinea, Ethiopia, Fiji, Finland, France, Gabon, Gambia, Georgia, Germany, Ghana, Greece, Grenada, Guatemala, Guinea, Guinea-Bissau, Guyana, Haiti, Honduras, Hungary, Iceland, India, Indonesia, Iran, Iraq, Ireland, Israel, Italy, Jamaica, Japan, Jordan, Kazakhstan, Kenya, Kiribati, Kuwait, Kyrgyzstan, Lao People's Democratic Republic, Latvia, Lebanon, Lesotho, Liberia, Libyan Arab Jamahiriya, Lithuania, Luxembourg, Madagascar, Malawi, Malaysia, Maldives, Mali, Malta, Marshall Islands, Mauritania, Mauritius, Mexico, Micronesia, Monaco, Mongolia, Morocco, Mozambique, Myanmar, Namibia, Nepal, Netherlands, New Zealand, Nicaragua, Niger, Nigeria, Norway, Oman, Pakistan, Panama, Papua New Guinea, Paraguay, Peru, Philippines, Poland, Portugal, Qatar, Republic of Moldova, Romania, Russian Federation, Rwanda, Saint Kitts and Nevis, Saint Lucia, Saint Vincent and the Grenadines, Samoa, San Marino, Sao Tome and Principe, Saudi Arabia, Senegal, Seychelles, Sierra Leone, Singapore, Slovenia, Solomon Islands, Somalia, South Africa, Spain, Sri Lanka, Sudan, Suriname, Swaziland, Sweden, Switzerland, Syrian Arab Republic, Tajikistan, Thailand, Togo, Tonga, Trinidad and Tobago, Tunisia, Turkey, Turkmenistan, Uganda, Ukraine, United Arab Emirates, United Kingdom, United Republic of Tanzania, United States, Uruguay, Uzbekistan, Vanuatu, Venezuela, Viet Nam, Yemen, Yugoslavia, Zaire, Zambia, Zimbabwe.

Associate members
Puerto Rico, Tokelau.

Annex II.   OFFICERS AND OFFICES OF THE WORLD HEALTH ORGANIZATION
(As at 31 December 1992)

OFFICERS OF THE FORTY-FIFTH WORLD HEALTH ASSEMBLY

President: A. Al-Badi (United Arab Emirates).
Vice-Presidents: M. Maiorescu (Romania), J. Eckstein (Trinidad and Tobago), Dr. M. Adhyatma (Indonesia), Dr. N. Ngendabanyikwa (Burundi), Pham Song (Viet Nam).
Chairman, Committee A: Dr. Catherine L. Mead (Australia).
Chairman, Committee B: Dr. A.-S. Yoosuf (Maldives).

*MEMBERS OF THE EXECUTIVE BOARD**

Chairman: O. Ransome-Kuti (Nigeria).
Vice-Chairmen: Dr. P. Caba-Martín (Spain), J. M. Borgoño (Chile), Dr. A. R. I. Khairy (Sudan).
Rapporteurs: Dr. A.-S. Yoosuf (Maldives), Dr. L. C. Sarr (Senegal).

Members were designated by: Afghanistan, Bahamas, Bolivia, Bulgaria, Chile, China, Colombia, Democratic People's Republic of Korea, Denmark, France, Greece, Iraq, Maldives, Myanmar, Niger, Nigeria, Philippines, Russian Federation, Rwanda, Sao Tome and Principe, Senegal, Seychelles, Sierra Leone, Spain, Sudan, Tunisia, United States, Uruguay, Yemen, Yugoslavia.

*The Board consists of 31 persons designated by member States elected by the World Health Assembly.

SENIOR OFFICERS OF THE SECRETARIAT

Director-General: Dr. Hiroshi Nakajima.
Deputy Director-General: Dr. Mohammed L. Abdelmoumène.
Assistant Directors-General: Denis G. Aitken, Dr. Ralph H. Henderson, Dr. Hu Ching-Li, Dr. Jean-Paul Jardel, Dr. Nikolai P. Napalkov.
Director, Regional Office for Africa: Dr. Gottlieb L. Monekosso.

Director, Regional Office for the Americas (Pan American Sanitary Bureau): Dr. Carlyle Guerra de Macedo.
Director, Regional Office for South-East Asia: Dr. U Ko Ko.
Director, Regional Office for Europe: Dr. Jo Eirik Asvall.
Director, Regional Office for the Eastern Mediterranean: Dr. Hussein A. Gezairy.
Director, Regional Office for the Western Pacific: Dr. Sang Tae Han.

HEADQUARTERS AND OTHER OFFICES

HEADQUARTERS
World Health Organization
20 Avenue Appia
CH 1211 Geneva 27, Switzerland
  Cable address: UNISANTE GENEVA
  Telephone: (41) (22) 791-21-11
  Telex: 415416
  Facsimile: (41) (22) 791-07-46

WHO OFFICE AT THE UNITED NATIONS
2 United Nations Plaza
New York, NY 10017, United States
  Cable address: UNSANTE NEW YORK
  Telephone: (1) (212) 963-6001
  Telex: 234292
  Facsimile: (1) (212) 223-2920

WHO also maintained regional offices at Alexandria, Egypt; Brazzaville, Congo; Copenhagen, Denmark; Manila, Philippines; New Delhi, India; and Washington, D.C.

Chapter VI

International Bank for
Reconstruction and Development (World Bank)

During the fiscal year 1992 (1 July 1991 to 30 June 1992), the International Bank for Reconstruction and Development (World Bank) and its affiliate, the International Development Association (IDA), continued to provide economic assistance to developing countries. The Bank's strategies for reducing poverty, promoting private-sector development and contributing to the global effort to safeguard the environment shaped its activities in fiscal 1992.

The dissolution of the former USSR into 15 independent, sovereign States and progress towards peace in several of the Bank's regions led to a sharp expansion in the demand for its services. With special funding approved by its Executive Board, the Bank undertook activities to help ease the transition by the successor States of the former USSR to market-oriented economies.

Commitments by the Bank during fiscal 1992 totalled $24,933 million as follows: $15,156 million for loans made by the Bank; $6,550 million for IDA credits; and $3,227 million for gross investments made by the Bank's second affiliate, the International Finance Corporation.

As at 31 December 1992, 172 States were members of the World Bank. New members in 1992 were Armenia, Azerbaijan, Belarus, Estonia, Georgia, Kazakhstan, Kyrgyzstan, Latvia, Lithuania, the Marshall Islands, the Republic of Moldova, the Russian Federation, Switzerland, Turkmenistan, Ukraine and Uzbekistan. (See Annex I for complete membership.)

Lending operations

In the fiscal year ending 30 June 1992, the World Bank made 112 loans to 43 countries amounting to $15,156 million, a decrease of $1,236 million from fiscal 1991. This brought the cumulative total of loan commitments made by the Bank since its inception in 1946 to $218,210 million.

Agriculture and rural development

Continuing its commitment to agriculture and rural development, the Bank made 25 loans to 17 countries totalling $2,525.7 million during fiscal 1992. Mexico received $600 million, of which $400 million provided funding for a project under the Government's irrigation and drainage investment programme. Of the three loans to Indonesia to-

talling $418.7 million, $225 million was to ensure the efficiency and sustainability of existing irrigation infrastructure through support for operations and maintenance, cost recovery and strengthening of operations and maintenance-related institutions, as well as for improved management and allocation of water. Brazil received $372 million, of which $205 million was to implement an improved strategy for natural resources management, conservation and development in the State of Mato Grosso. Venezuela received $300 million to support increased efficiency in the agricultural sector and to achieve sustainable growth and exports through the restructuring of an incentive system, expanding public investments in agricultural infrastructure and services, increasing the availability of credit and strengthening the sector's institutions.

Development finance companies

The Bank made six loans totalling $802 million in fiscal 1992 to assist development finance companies in five countries. A loan of $400 million to Peru supported the country's medium-term programme of macroeconomic stabilization and structural reforms, particularly in the financial sector. Côte d'Ivoire received $225 million, of which $150 million assisted the country's financial sector reform programme by stabilizing the financial system and restoring to health the country's system of financial intermediation. A loan of $100 million to Colombia aimed at improving the financial situation and operational efficiency of the Instituto de Fomento Industrial, the country's largest public development bank and holding company, and supporting the withdrawal of the public sector from productive sector activities.

Education

Sixteen loans amounting to $1,299.6 million were made to 12 countries for education projects during fiscal 1992. Of $439 million extended to Mexico, $250 million was for implementing a primary education project in four states with the highest incidence of poverty and the lowest education indicators. A loan of $170 million was granted to Chile to enhance the efficiency, quality and equity of primary education in urban and rural areas and to expand and upgrade the coverage and quality of pre-school education. Indonesia received $143.1 million, of which $69.5 million provided vocational and income-generating skills to some 400,000 disadvantaged beneficiaries from impoverished areas. Côte d'Ivoire was granted $125 million for its human resources development programme.

Energy

Twenty-one energy projects—in oil, gas, coal and power—were assisted in 16 countries during fiscal 1992 at a cost of $2,828.9 million. China received $900 million, of which $380 million funded the construction of a dam and an underground power house and provided generating units to help eliminate power shortages in Sichuan Province. Of the $765 million extended to India, $350 million helped increase the power supply in Maharashtra State and provide capacity-building assistance to the state electricity board to improve its operational efficiency and strengthen its finances and managerial autonomy. A loan of $423.6 million was granted to Indonesia to construct three coal-fired units which would expand the generating capacity of the State electricity corporation in Java.

Industry

In fiscal 1992, loans for the industrial sector totalling $382.7 million were granted to two countries. Peru received $300 million to assist the Government's medium-term programme of trade policy reform, while China received $82.7 million to support the cement industry through a regional cement production and distribution scheme that included modern large-scale cement production facilities.

Non-project

The Bank granted non-project loans totalling $1,970 million to eight countries. Romania received $400 million to support its programme of structural reforms, designed to transform the command-driven economy to a market-oriented system. A loan of $300 million was made to Peru to assist its Government's medium-term programme of macroeconomic stabilization and broad-based structural reforms. Morocco received $275 million to support the last phase of its stabilization and adjustment programme, designed to achieve a sustainable increase in the rate of economic growth in order to ensure employment opportunities and acceptable living standards.

Population, health and nutrition

The Bank made three loans in fiscal 1992 amounting to $307 million for population, health and nutrition projects. Romania received $150 mil-

lion to rehabilitate and upgrade its primary health care delivery system. A loan of $130 million was granted to Poland to assist its health sector reform plan by strengthening health promotion programmes, supporting the first steps in sectoral restructuring by shifting the focus from institutional to primary care, strengthening sectoral institutional capacity and ensuring sustainability of services by controlling costs. Chile received $27 million to support the development and testing of critical policy reforms in the health sector and the rehabilitation of hospitals in the metropolitan Santiago area.

Public sector management

Two loans totalling $525 million were granted for public sector management in fiscal 1992. Argentina received $325 million to support its public sector reform programme, which sought to reduce the negative effects of chronic macroeconomic instability that had occurred during the past decade. A loan of $200 million was made to Hungary to assist its enterprise reform programme, which was aimed at accelerating sharply the privatization and restructuring of the State enterprise sector as well as improving State enterprise governance.

Small-scale enterprises

In fiscal 1992, a single loan of $60 million was granted for small-scale enterprises to Poland to provide financing for efficient investment in private enterprises, particularly in small and medium-sized firms.

Technical assistance

Five loans for technical assistance totalling $69.4 million were granted in fiscal 1992. A loan of $20 million to Argentina aimed at strengthening the country's tax administration, by financing consulting services, training, office refurbishing, equipment and software required by a newly established General Tax Directorate. A loan of $17.2 million was granted to Chile to strengthen key government institutions responsible for national policy-making and to increase the effectiveness of financial management institutions through the provision of consultant services, equipment and training. Indonesia was extended a loan of $12 million to assist in the implementation of a five-year development programme of the newly established Environmental Impact Management Agency. El Salvador received $11 million for assistance in developing its energy policy and improving the efficiency of the energy sector through institutional and legal reform.

Telecommunications

In fiscal 1992, a single loan of $375 million for telecommunications was granted to Indonesia to enhance sector performance by promoting a regulatory regime conducive to competition in providing telecommunications services and to meet growing demand for services through the rehabilitation of existing facilities, the installation of switching equipment for the local cable network and the installation and upgrading of fibre-optic-transmission and microwave-transmission facilities to improve long-distance service.

Transportation

The Bank made 10 loans to 9 countries in fiscal 1992 for transportation projects, totalling $1,618.7 million. China received $550 million, of which $330 million supported a railway project that would introduce, on a system-wide basis, advanced technology, equipment and materials for track rehabilitation and maintenance. A $266 million loan to Colombia aimed to upgrade 10 per cent of the national road network, reduce vehicle-operating costs and improve access to markets. Indonesia received $215 million to improve the quality of the road network in 73 districts of nine provinces and enhance the capability of government agencies in charge of district roads.

Urban development

The Bank made seven loans in fiscal 1992 amounting to $994 million for urban development projects. Mexico received $450 million to expand the supply of finance for low-cost housing to be built by private developers and remove regulatory barriers to housing, thus helping to lower housing costs and encourage commercial banks to increase lending for housing. Poland received $200 million to support the Government's steps to move from a heavily subsidized, centrally controlled mode of housing production to a more efficient, market-based system of supply through private initiative. In Brazil, a $126 million loan helped to create the foundations for the policy changes required to achieve sustainable, integrated multimodal transport in the São Paulo metropolitan region.

Water supply and sanitation

The Bank made six loans totalling $534 million in fiscal 1992 for water supply and sanitation. Brazil received $250 million to finance a time-slice of the six-year investment programme of the state water companies of Bahia, Mato Grosso do Sul and Santa Catarina to provide water-supply and sewerage services in those states. Credits totalling $110 million were extended to Lesotho to enable it to export water to the industrial heartland of South Africa under a 30-year scheme involving the

construction of facilities to permit water transfers. A loan of $57 million was granted to Iran to rehabilitate and upgrade dikes along the southern shore of Lake Hirmand.

Economic Development Institute

Fiscal 1992 marked the mid-point of the Economic Development Institute's (EDI) five-year plan (1990-1994). The plan aimed to help countries improve the quality of their macroeconomic management, the efficiency of their public sector management and the effectiveness of their poverty-reduction efforts.

Of the 117 training programmes organized by EDI, 14 of them dealt with agriculture; 29 with development and management; 26 with finance and industry; 17 with human resources; 19 with infrastructure; and 12 with macroeconomics.

During fiscal 1992, about one third of EDI's training programmes were targeted towards sub-Saharan Africa. The number of activities carried out in and for the countries of Central and Eastern Europe rose sharply in response to the demand accompanying their transition from command to market economies. In addition, EDI implemented eight activities in the former USSR that were financed by the Bank's Technical Cooperation Agreement.

EDI dealt with several new demands on its services in fiscal 1992, foremost among them the need for training in the successor States of the former USSR. In addition, a number of other countries either joined the Bank during the year or sought to reactivate their borrowing activities; a demand for EDI to provide training in project analysis re-emerged; EDI introduced training programmes in such areas as women in development, the role of non-governmental organizations, poverty reduction, the environment and civil service reform; and the growing number of countries engaged in structural reform increased the demand for training government officials involved in formulating and managing programmes.

During the fiscal year, EDI initiated a systematic evaluation of its institution-building efforts that focused on targeting, selectivity, longer-term sustainability of assistance, and building an adequate internal information system in partner institutions.

Co-financing

The volume of co-financing anticipated in support of Bank-assisted operations approved in fiscal 1992 was approximately $13,266 million. Roughly 52 per cent of all Bank-assisted projects and programmes attracted some form of co-financing. The largest source of co-financing in fiscal 1992 continued to be official bilateral and multilateral development institutions, which together accounted for $8,872 million, or 67 per cent of total co-financing.

In addition to co-financing, the donor community provided substantial support to the Bank during the year through trust funds and other arrangements that, directly or indirectly, benefited recipient countries.

Other major co-financing activities carried out in fiscal 1992 included those under the Special Programme of Assistance (SPA) for debt-distressed, low-income countries in sub-Saharan Africa, which was in its second phase, covering the period 1991 to 1993. Under the second phase, 17 bilateral and multilateral donors had pledged $7.3 billion in quick-disbursing assistance in support of adjustment programmes in 26 countries. As at 31 December 1992, SPA donors had allocated some $5.3 billion, or nearly 80 per cent of the $7.3 billion pledged for co-financing and coordinated financing.

Financing activities

In fiscal 1992, the Bank raised $11,788.7 million through medium- and long-term borrowings in 11 currencies and currency units, made up of $4,008 million in United States dollars, $3,619 million in Japanese yen, $479 million in deutsche mark, $465.1 million in Swiss francs and $3,218 million in European currency units, French francs, Hong Kong dollars, Italian lire, Portuguese escudos, Spanish pesetas and Swedish kronor.

After $3,200 million of currency swaps and a notional par volume of $3,700 million of interest-rate swaps, all of the year's borrowings were fixed-rate liabilities denominated in United States dollars, Japanese yen, deutsche mark and Swiss francs.

During the fiscal year, the Bank refinanced $5,400 million of short-term borrowings that had been outstanding at the end of fiscal 1991. As at 30 June 1992, short-term borrowings outstanding were $5,400 million equivalent, comprising $2,600 million from official sources through the Bank's central bank facility, $2,800 million from market borrowings in United States dollars and $25 million equivalent in short-term Swiss franc borrowings.

Capitalization

Effective 30 June 1987,[a] the Bank's capital stock was expressed in the special drawing right (SDR) introduced by the International Monetary Fund as it was valued in terms of United States dollars immediately before the introduction of the basket method (the value based on a basket of 16 major currencies) of valuing the SDR on 1 July 1974 (SDR 1 = $US 1.20635).

The total subscribed capital of the Bank as at 30 June 1992 was $152,200 million, or 83 per cent of authorized capital of $184,050 million. The permissible increase of net disbursements was $67,600 million, or 40 per cent of the Bank's lending limit. In April 1992, the Bank's Board of Governors approved an increase in authorized capital of 77,159 shares ($9,300 million) to accommodate the membership of the 15 successor States of the former USSR.

Secretariat

As at 30 June 1992, the staff of the World Bank numbered 6,046, of whom 3,893 were staff in the Professional or higher categories, drawn from 117 nationalities (see also Annex II).

Income, expenditures and reserves

The Bank's gross revenues, generated primarily from loans and investments, totalled $9,674 million in fiscal 1992, a decline of $49 million from fiscal 1991. Net income was $1,645 million, an increase of $445 million over the previous fiscal year's figure of $1,200 million. Expenses were down by $495 million to $7,965 million, of which administrative costs amounted to $615 million, up by $41 million from fiscal 1991.

On 30 June, reserves amounted to $11,200 million and the reserves-to-loan ratio stood at 11.5 per cent, excluding prefunding of interest waivers.

NOTE: For further details regarding the Bank's activities, see *The World Bank: Annual Report 1992.*

[a]YUN 1987, p. 1234.

Annex I.   MEMBERSHIP OF THE WORLD BANK
(As at 31 December 1992)

Afghanistan, Albania, Algeria, Angola, Antigua and Barbuda, Argentina, Armenia, Australia, Austria, Azerbaijan, Bahamas, Bahrain, Bangladesh, Barbados, Belarus, Belgium, Belize, Benin, Bhutan, Bolivia, Botswana, Brazil, Bulgaria, Burkina Faso, Burundi, Cambodia, Cameroon, Canada, Cape Verde, Central African Republic, Chad, Chile, China, Colombia, Comoros, Congo, Costa Rica, Côte d'Ivoire, Cyprus, Czechoslovakia, Denmark, Djibouti, Dominica, Dominican Republic, Ecuador, Egypt, El Salvador, Equatorial Guinea, Estonia, Ethiopia, Fiji, Finland, France, Gabon, Gambia, Georgia, Germany, Ghana, Greece, Grenada, Guatemala, Guinea, Guinea-Bissau, Guyana, Haiti, Honduras, Hungary, Iceland, India, Indonesia, Iran, Iraq, Ireland, Israel, Italy, Jamaica, Japan, Jordan, Kazakhstan, Kenya, Kiribati, Kuwait, Kyrgyzstan, Lao People's Democratic Republic, Latvia, Lebanon, Lesotho, Liberia, Libyan Arab Jamahiriya, Lithuania, Luxembourg, Madagascar, Malawi, Malaysia, Maldives, Mali, Malta, Marshall Islands, Mauritania, Mauritius, Mexico, Mongolia, Morocco, Mozambique, Myanmar, Namibia, Nepal, Netherlands, New Zealand, Nicaragua, Niger, Nigeria, Norway, Oman, Pakistan, Panama, Papua New Guinea, Paraguay, Peru, Philippines, Poland, Portugal, Qatar, Republic of Korea, Republic of Moldova, Romania, Russian Federation, Rwanda, Saint Kitts and Nevis, Saint Lucia, Saint Vincent and the Grenadines, Samoa, Sao Tome and Principe, Saudi Arabia, Senegal, Seychelles, Sierra

Leone, Singapore, Solomon Islands, Somalia, South Africa, Spain, Sri Lanka, Sudan, Suriname, Swaziland, Sweden, Switzerland, Syrian Arab Republic, Thailand, Togo, Tonga, Trinidad and Tobago, Tunisia, Turkey, Turkmenistan, Uganda, Ukraine, United Arab Emirates, United Kingdom, United Republic of Tanzania, United States, Uruguay, Uzbekistan, Vanuatu, Venezuela, Viet Nam, Yemen, Yugoslavia, Zaire, Zambia, Zimbabwe.

Annex II. EXECUTIVE DIRECTORS AND ALTERNATES PRINCIPAL OFFICERS AND OFFICES OF THE WORLD BANK

(As at 30 June 1992)

EXECUTIVE DIRECTORS AND ALTERNATES

Appointed Director	*Appointed Alternate*	*Casting the vote of*
E. Patrick Coady	Mark M. Collins, Jr.	United States
Yasuyuki Kawahara	Kiyoshi Kodera	Japan
Fritz Fischer	Harald Rehm	Germany
Jean-Pierre Landau	Phillippe de Fontaine Vive	France
David Peretz	Robert Graham-Harrison	United Kingdom
Elected Director	*Elected Alternate*	*Casting the vote of*
Bernard Snoy (Belgium)	Walter Rill (Austria)	Austria, Belgium, Czechoslovakia, Hungary, Luxembourg, Turkey
Rosario Bonavoglia (Italy)	Fernando S. Carneiro (Portugal)	Greece, Italy, Malta, Poland, Portugal
Frank Potter (Canada)	Hubert Dean (Bahamas)	Antigua and Barbuda, Bahamas, Barbados, Belize, Canada, Dominica, Grenada, Guyana, Ireland, Jamaica, Saint Kitts and Nevis, Saint Lucia, Saint Vincent and the Grenadines
J.S. Baijal (India)	M.A. Syed (Bangladesh)	Bangladesh, Bhutan, India, Sri Lanka
Moisés Naim (Venezuela)	Gabriel Castellanos (Guatemala)	Costa Rica, El Salvador, Guatemala, Honduras, Mexico, Nicaragua, Panama, Spain, Venezuela
Eveline Herfkens (Netherlands)	Boris Skapin (Yugoslavia)	Bulgaria, Cyprus, Israel, Netherlands, Romania, Yugoslavia
Einar Magnussen (Norway)	Jorunn Maehlum (Norway)	Denmark, Finland, Iceland, Norway, Sweden
Ernest Leung (Philippines)	Paulo C. Ximenes-Ferreira (Brazil)	Brazil, Colombia, Dominican Republic, Ecuador, Haiti, Philippines, Suriname, Trinidad and Tobago
John H. Cosgrove (Australia)	A. John Wilson (New Zealand)	Australia, Kiribati, New Zealand, Papua New Guinea, Republic of Korea, Samoa, Solomon Islands, Vanuatu.
Wang Liansheng (China)	Jin Liqun (China)	China
Aris Othman (Malaysia)	Aung Pe (Myanmar)	Fiji, Indonesia, Lao People's Democratic Republic, Malaysia, Myanmar, Nepal, Singapore, Thailand, Tonga, Viet Nam
Mohamed Benhocine (Algeria)	Salem Mohamed Omeish (Libyan Arab Jamahiriya)	Afghanistan, Algeria, Ghana, Iran, Libyan Arab Jamahiriya, Morocco, Tunisia
Fawzi Hamad Al-Sultan (Kuwait)	Mohamed W. Hosny (Egypt)	Bahrain, Egypt, Jordan, Kuwait, Lebanon, Maldives, Oman, Pakistan, Qatar, Syrian Arab Republic, United Arab Emirates, Yemen
Jabez A. Langley (Gambia)	O.K. Matambo (Botswana)	Angola, Botswana, Burundi, Ethiopia, Gambia, Guinea, Kenya, Lesotho, Liberia, Malawi, Mozambique, Namibia, Nigeria, Seychelles, Sierra Leone, Sudan, Swaziland, Uganda, United Republic of Tanzania, Zambia, Zimbabwe
Ibrahim A. Al-Assaf (Saudi Arabia)	Ahmed M. Al-Ghannam (Saudi Arabia)	Saudi Arabia
Félix Alberto Camarasa (Argentina)	Nicolás Flaño (Chile)	Argentina, Bolivia, Chile, Paraguay, Peru, Uruguay
Jean-Pierre Le Bouder (Central African Republic)	Ali Bourhane (Comoros)	Benin, Burkina Faso, Cameroon, Cape Verde, Central African Republic, Chad, Comoros, Congo, Côte d'Ivoire, Djibouti, Equatorial Guinea, Gabon, Guinea-Bissau, Madagascar, Mali, Mauritania, Mauritius, Niger, Rwanda, São Tome and Principe, Senegal, Somalia, Togo, Zaire

PRINCIPAL OFFICERS*

President: Lewis T. Preston.
Vice President and Special Adviser: Willi Wapenhans.
Managing Director: Attila Karaosmanoglu.
Managing Director: Sven Sandstrom.
Managing Director: Ernest Stern.
Vice President and Controller: Stephen D. Eccles.
Vice President, Financial Policy and Risk Management: Johannes F. Linn.
Vice President and Treasurer: Jessica P. Einhorn.
Vice President, Latin America and the Caribbean Regional Office: S. Shahid Husain.
Vice President, Africa Regional Office: Edward V.K. Jaycox.
Vice President, East Asia and Pacific Regional Office: Guatam S. Kaji.
Vice President, Middle East and North Africa Regional Office: Caio Koch-Weser

Vice President, Europe and Central Asia Regional Office: Wilfried P. Thalwitz.
Vice President, South Asia Regional Office: D. Joseph Wood.
Vice President, Co-financing and Financial Advisory Services: Koji Kashiwaya.
Vice President, Development Economics and Chief Economist: Lawrence H. Summers.
Vice President, Sector and Operations Policy: Visvanathan Rajagopalan.
Director-General, Operations Evaluation: Yves Rovani.
Vice President and General Counsel: Ibrahim F. I. Shihata.
Vice President and Secretary: Timothy T. Thahane.
Vice President Personnel and Administration Bilsel Alisbah

*The World Bank and IDA had the same officers and staff..

HEADQUARTERS AND OTHER OFFICES

HEADQUARTERS
The World Bank
1818 H Street, N.W.
Washington, D.C. 20433, United States
Cable address: INTBAFRAD WASHINGTONDC
Telephone: (1) (202) 477-1234
Telex: FTCCQ 82987
    RCA 248423 WORLDBANK
    WUI 64145 WORLDBANK
    TRT 197688 WORLDBANK
Facsimile: (1) (202) 477-6391

NEW YORK OFFICE.
The World Bank Mission to the United Nations.
809 UN Plaza, Suite 900.
New York, N.Y. 10017, United States.
Cable address: INTBAFRAD NEWYORK
Telephone: (1) (212) 963-6008
Facsimile: (1) (212) 697-7020

The Bank also maintained major regional offices at Abidjan, Côte d'Ivoire; Bangkok, Thailand; Geneva; Nairobi, Kenya; Paris; and Tokyo.

Chapter VII

International Finance Corporation (IFC)

The International Finance Corporation (IFC), established in 1956 as an affiliate of the International Bank for Reconstruction and Development (World Bank), is a multilateral development institution that furthers economic growth in developing member countries by promoting private sector investment. It provides direct loans and equity financing without government guarantees to private companies in developing countries. IFC also mobilizes additional financing in international capital markets and provides an array of advisory services to businesses and Governments on issues related to private investment.

During the 1992 fiscal year (1 July 1991 to 30 June 1992), Albania, Bulgaria, Equatorial Guinea, the Lao People's Democratic Republic and Switzerland joined IFC, bringing its membership to 146 countries. (See Annex I for complete membership.)

Demand for IFC's finance and advisory services intensified as countries throughout the developing world persevered with free-market reforms. IFC's project financing approvals for the fiscal year ending 30 June 1992 totalled $3,300 million. Of that amount, $1,800 million was for IFC's own account and the balance, a record $1,500 million, was used in loan syndications and underwriting of securities issues and investment funds. IFC provided financing for 167 projects with total project costs of $12,000 million in 51 countries in Africa, Asia, Europe, Latin America and the Middle East. Projects financed by IFC were in a broad range of sectors, including financial services, tourism, mining, power, oil and gas exploration, agribusiness and general manufacturing.

The more than $1,800 million of IFC financing approved for the Corporation's own account included $1,200 million in loans, $375 million in equity and $251 million in guarantees, swaps and stand-by arrangements. All IFC's loans were made at market rates of interest and carried maturities of 4 to 15 years. The $375 million in equity and quasi-equity financing set a new volume record for IFC and represented a 21 per cent share of the financing approved for IFC's own account. This increasing percentage of IFC equity investments was consistent with the Corporation's efforts to reduce reliance on debt financing by businesses in developing countries.

In May, the Corporation's Board of Governors approved a $1,000 million increase in the Corpo-

ration's authorized capital, thus raising it to $2,300 million. The increase was intended to enable IFC to increase new investment approvals in all regions by 10 per cent a year until 1998, bringing annual approvals to about $4,000 million by the end of the decade.

On 18 June 1992, the IFC Board of Directors recommended a $150 million selective capital increase to accommodate the membership of the successor States of the former USSR. Of that amount, $132 million would be allocated to the new members, and the balance would be available to accommodate future requests for shares.

IFC strengthened its commitment to support only those projects which were environmentally responsible. A study on investing in the environment highlighted the potential growth in private sector investment opportunities in environmental goods and services and summarized the findings of nine separate analyses which identified specific environmental market opportunities in Chile, Hungary, Indonesia, Malaysia, Mexico, Pakistan, Poland, Thailand and Turkey.

Regional projects

In fiscal 1992, IFC approved 167 projects located in 51 countries. Some 47 per cent of IFC's financing approvals were for projects in member countries which had per capita incomes of $830 or less per year.

Sub-Saharan Africa

IFC approved 50 projects in 20 countries in sub-Saharan Africa in fiscal 1992. As at 30 June, its committed portfolio included loans and investments for 152 companies in 33 countries.

Several large energy, mining and infrastructure projects were approved, the largest of which was a $305 million expansion of Ashanti Goldfields Corporation (Ghana) to increase its gold production. For a $123 million project to increase oil production in Cameroon, IFC approved a $30 million quasi-equity investment for its own account and a $30 million loan syndication. In Mali, IFC approved equity and quasi-equity financing of $23 million for a mining investor with a foreign private sponsor. In infrastructure, the Corporation approved a $33 million loan, including $17 million for its own account and a syndicated loan of $16 million, to help finance the construction of a

204-kilometre extension of a pipeline that would connect Harare, Zimbabwe, with the port of Beira, Mozambique.

In the financial sector, the Corporation approved several innovative projects, including investments in Ghana's first leasing company, Kenya's first financial services company and Nigeria's first discount house. It also approved agency credit lines for the Mauritius Commercial Bank and the First Merchant Bank of Zimbabwe and participated in a rights issue by the Development Finance Company of Uganda. In Botswana, IFC approved a multi-year guarantee facility on behalf of a local leasing company.

IFC provided technical assistance and advisory services in Africa during the year, including advice to small-scale entrepreneurs, technical assistance to Governments in connection with capital market development and advice on privatization and foreign direct investment. The Foreign Investment Advisory Service (FIAS) completed assignments relating to a general diagnosis of investment policy issues in Angola, Benin, Burkina Faso, Mali and Mozambique; preparation of new investment legislation in Equatorial Guinea, Malawi and Namibia; formulation of foreign investment promotion strategy in Madagascar; and an assessment of prospects for backward linkages between foreign and local firms in Kenya.

Through its African Enterprise Fund (AEF), IFC directly financed smaller companies. In fiscal 1992, total financing of $14 million was approved—$12 million in loans and $2 million in equity and quasi-equity investments—for 22 small projects in 11 countries. The AEF projects spanned a broad spectrum of sectors, including agriculture and agro-processing, small-scale manufacturing, quarrying and printing.

Asia

In fiscal 1992, IFC approved 34 projects in 9 countries in Asia. As at 30 June, the Corporation's committed portfolio included loans and investments for 178 companies in 12 countries in the region.

Investments in East Asia continued to be diversified, with the largest loans and equity investments approved for projects in the petroleum-refining and chemicals and petrochemicals sectors. In the Philippines, IFC approved a $35 million loan and a syndicated loan of $85 million to modernize a refinery. A loan syndication of $95 million was arranged by IFC for a corporation in Indonesia that was building a greenfield petrochemicals plant in Merak (West Java). IFC also approved a loan of $30 million and quasi-equity financing of $10 million for its own account for the project.

In fiscal 1992, IFC also emphasized financing for labour-intensive, export-oriented industries, aimed at creating more jobs in populous countries such as China and Indonesia. In Indonesia, IFC helped finance a $208 million programme of investments by a holding company in affiliates in export-oriented light manufacturing industries, which was expected to lead to substantial employment and foreign exchange gains.

Special attention continued to be paid to the Philippines, which was trying to stabilize its economy while stimulating economic growth. IFC provided financing for large projects with substantial amounts of foreign investment and helped restructure and strengthen domestic industries, such as a diversified food-processing company modernizing its flour mills and sugar plants. In addition to a quasi-equity investment of over $15 million and assistance with financial restructuring, IFC would help the mostly family-owned company to go public.

IFC's investment operations in India and Pakistan emphasized energy-related projects (gas development, power) and manufacturing projects. In fiscal 1992, it approved $20 million to expand a producer of natural gas in Pakistan, making energy the sector with the largest share of IFC's committed portfolio in the country. In South Asia, IFC approved over $60 million in financing for three manufacturing projects in industrial subsectors—steel and engineering products.

Regarding capital market development, IFC provided financing to financial institutions in South-East Asia offering sophisticated products such as big-ticket leasing, high-quality investment banking services and regional venture capital funds. During fiscal 1992, IFC helped Thailand to restructure the operations of the Bank of Asia, a privately owned commercial bank, and invested in its equity. Other projects approved included a factoring company in Indonesia, two guarantee facilities in Malaysia and a leasing company in Thailand.

In South Asia, IFC's programmes emphasized institution-building to broaden the range of financial services available to the private sector. In fiscal 1992, IFC helped restructure one of the first all-Pakistan stock brokerage firms.

IFC's technical assistance and advisory services in Asia in fiscal 1992 included advice to small-scale entrepreneurs, technical assistance in connection with capital market development and advice to Governments on attracting foreign investment. FIAS carried out diagnostic studies of the foreign investment climate in China, Pakistan and Samoa; studied investment policies in the Lao People's Democratic Republic and Malaysia; and reviewed the institutional framework for investment in the Philippines. It completed studies in the Philippines and Thailand to identify policy issues in connection with backward linkages between foreign and domestic companies.

Europe

In fiscal 1992, IFC approved 23 projects in 5 countries in Europe. As at 30 June, IFC's committed portfolio included loans and investments to 93 companies in 7 countries. IFC approved its first projects in Czechoslovakia and Romania during the fiscal year.

Projects approved in Czechoslovakia included a joint venture between a United States company and a domestic carbon-black manufacturer; the privatization, expansion and modernization of a large cement producer, a joint venture with a Belgian company; and a joint venture between a German bank and Czechoslovakia's first privatized commercial bank.

IFC approved financing for several infrastructure projects in Central and Eastern Europe, including a $6 million loan and $730,000 quasi-equity investment for a joint venture in Romania between a Romanian and a French company to produce telecommunications equipment; a $15 million loan for a cellular telephone project in Hungary; and a $10 million equity participation in a regional project (Czechoslovakia, Hungary, Poland) for distribution of liquefied petroleum gas.

In Turkey, IFC approved syndicated loans for the country's largest producer of bed linens and home textiles and for the the country's largest privately owned conglomerate. It also approved financing totalling $75 million for Turkey's first large-scale private sector mining company.

IFC technical assistance and advisory services in Europe during fiscal 1992 included advice to small-scale enterprises, technical assistance with capital market development and advice on privatization, corporate restructuring and foreign direct investment. FIAS organized a round-table on the impact of corporate tax structures on foreign direct investment in Bulgaria, Czechoslovakia, Hungary, Poland and Romania. Assistance was also provided to Belarus and the Russian Federation, under the World Bank Technical Assistance Trust Fund, to help their Governments frame laws and organize institutions to attract foreign investment. FIAS sent a mission to Ukraine to identify possible advisory projects and carried out general diagnostic studies in Estonia, Latvia and Lithuania.

Latin America and the Caribbean

In fiscal 1992, IFC approved 45 projects in 13 countries in Latin America and the Caribbean; as at 30 June, its committed portfolio included loans and investments for 231 companies in 22 countries.

During the fiscal year, IFC introduced more medium-sized Mexican companies to international markets through loan syndications, such as one that operated 37 hotels. In addition, IFC mobilized funds in the international markets for several companies, by underwriting and planning securities issues, yielding a $72 million equity offering by the hotel group and a $100 million Eurobond offering by Mexico's second largest cement producer. IFC also approved a project in which it would co-lead/manage a $208 million international revenue bond offering for the Mexico City-Toluca Toll Road. The development of new financial instruments for Mexican companies was an important element of the Corporation's strategy. A $40 million risk-management line extended to Banco Nacional de Mexico, Mexico's largest commercial bank, would allow the bank to provide its clients with collars, currency and interest rate swaps and swaptions, hedging instruments for which demand in Mexico had been growing as substantial foreign exchange inflows resumed.

In Argentina, IFC helped to finance the privatization of a railroad company and approved some $233 million in financing, including loan syndications of $138 million, for oil and gas projects. Loans and equity investments were approved for three companies that were developing oilfields acquired from YPF, the State-owned gas company.

In Colombia, IFC emphasized projects in natural resource–based industries, approving loans for a natural gas pipeline and an oil pipeline. The Corporation approved a currency-hedging facility to enable a banana trading company to manage currency mismatches between its future transportation costs and its revenues while allowing it to benefit from a potential improvement in foreign exchange rates.

In Venezuela, IFC supported large greenfield ventures that took advantage of the country's low-cost natural gas and abundant hydroelectricity and minerals. For a $340 million project to build a methanol plant, IFC approved an equity investment of $7 million and a loan of $134 million, including a syndication of $100 million.

In Brazil, IFC helped a polyvinyl chloride producer complete a $235 million financial restructuring by providing a counter-guarantee of up to $75 million on the company's five-year international floating-rate note issue. IFC also invested in and helped place a $43 million country fund for Brazil.

In Peru, IFC approved an equity investment and credit line for a leasing company that was expanding its operations to provide lease financing to small and medium-sized private companies.

In addition, IFC provided technical assistance and advisory services in the region by advising small and medium-sized enterprises and assisting Governments with capital market development. It provided advice on corporate restructuring and privatization and on foreign direct investment. FIAS completed projects in the Bahamas, Honduras and Venezuela.

Middle East and North Africa

In fiscal 1992, IFC approved 15 projects in 4 countries in the Middle East and North Africa; as at 30 June, IFC's committed portfolio included loans and investments for 46 companies in 7 countries. The volume of financing approved by the Corporation for projects in the fiscal year more than doubled over fiscal 1991, reflecting an improving economic environment in the region.

In Egypt, IFC agreed to arrange a second currency swap for a rebar producer, enabling the company to hedge a substantial portion of its currency exposure resulting from mismatches in its revenues and obligations. It also approved $9 million in financing for a new resort hotel on the Red Sea and approved loan and equity financing for the first company in the Middle East to produce tropicalized refrigerator compressors. In the energy sector, IFC approved an additional equity investment of $13 million in the development of an oilfield in the Western Desert.

IFC supported Morocco's financial sector reforms by arranging syndicated credit lines with 10 international banks for 4 Moroccan commercial banks. It also helped finance a lead and zinc mine in Tunisia, the country's first private-sector mining venture, and approved a $10 million loan for its first project in Algeria, a joint venture between Algerian and foreign investors that would produce liquid helium for export to Europe.

IFC offered technical assistance and advisory services in the region, including advice to Govern-

ments on capital market development, privatization and foreign direct investment. FIAS completed projects in Tunisia and Yemen and conducted a project identification mission in Algeria.

Financial operations

For fiscal 1992, IFC net income was $180 million, representing a return of 7.5 per cent on the Corporation's net worth. Income from IFC's loan portfolio decreased slightly from the previous fiscal year, while income from the equity portfolio increased. Capital gains from sales of equity investments reached $113 million, the same as in fiscal 1991. Service fee income increased by 28 per cent, from $25 million in fiscal 1991 to $32 million in fiscal 1992.

Capital and retained earnings

During fiscal 1992, member countries paid in capital of $107 million. As at 30 June 1992, total paid-in capital reached $1,300 million and retained earnings came to $1,100 million, bringing IFC net worth to $2,400 million.

Secretariat

As at 30 June 1992, IFC's regular staff numbered 732, drawn from 91 countries.

NOTE: For further details on IFC activities, see *International Finance Corporation 1992 Annual Report*, published by IFC.

Annex I.   MEMBERSHIP OF THE INTERNATIONAL FINANCE CORPORATION
           (As at 30 June 1992)

Afghanistan, Albania, Algeria, Angola, Antigua and Barbuda, Argentina, Australia, Austria, Bahamas, Bangladesh, Barbados, Belgium, Belize, Benin, Bolivia, Botswana, Brazil, Bulgaria, Burkino Faso, Burundi, Cameroon, Canada, Cape Verde, Central African Republic, Chile, China, Colombia, Congo, Costa Rica, Côte d'Ivoire, Cyprus, Czechoslovakia, Denmark, Djibouti, Dominica, Dominican Republic, Ecuador, Egypt, El Salvador, Equatorial Guinea, Ethiopia, Fiji, Finland, France, Gabon, Gambia, Germany, Ghana, Greece, Grenada, Guatemala, Guinea, Guinea-Bissau, Guyana, Haiti, Honduras, Hungary, Iceland, India, Indonesia, Iran, Iraq, Ireland, Israel, Italy, Jamaica, Japan, Jordan, Kenya, Kiribati, Kuwait, Lao People's Democratic Republic, Lebanon, Lesotho, Liberia, Libyan Arab Jamahiriya, Luxembourg, Madagascar, Malawi, Malaysia, Maldives, Mali, Mauritania, Mauritius, Mexico, Mongolia, Morocco, Mozambique, Myanmar, Namibia, Nepal, Netherlands, New Zealand, Nicaragua, Niger, Nigeria, Norway, Oman, Pakistan, Panama, Papua New Guinea, Paraguay, Peru, Philippines, Poland, Portugal, Republic of Korea, Romania, Rwanda, Saint Lucia, Samoa, Saudi Arabia, Senegal, Seychelles, Sierra Leone, Singapore, Solomon Islands, Somalia, South Africa, Spain, Sri Lanka, Sudan, Swaziland, Sweden, Switzerland, Syrian Arab Republic, Thailand, Togo, Tonga, Trinidad and Tobago, Tunisia, Turkey, Uganda, United Arab Emirates, United Kingdom, United Republic of Tanzania, United States, Uruguay, Vanuatu, Venezuela, Viet Nam, Yemen, Yugoslavia, Zaire, Zambia, Zimbabwe.

Annex II.   EXECUTIVE DIRECTORS AND ALTERNATES, OFFICERS AND OFFICES
            OF THE INTERNATIONAL FINANCE CORPORATION
            (As at 30 June 1992)

Appointed Director	*Appointed Alternate*	*Casting the vote of*
E. Patrick Coady	Mark M. Collins, Jr.	United States
Yasuyuki Kawahara	Kiyoshi Kodera	Japan
Fritz Fischer	Harald Rehm	Germany
Jean-Pierre Landau	Phillippe de Fontaine Vive	France
David Peretz	Robert Graham-Harrison	United Kingdom

Elected Director	*Elected Alternate*	*Casting the vote of*
Bernard Snoy (Belgium)	Walter Rill (Austria)	Austria, Belgium, Czechoslovakia, Hungary, Luxembourg, Turkey
Rosario Bonavoglia (Italy)	Fernando S. Carneiro (Portugal)	Greece, Italy, Poland, Portugal
J.S. Baijal (India)	M.A. Syed (Bangladesh)	Bangladesh, India, Sri Lanka
Moises Naim (Venezuela)	Gabriel Castellanos (Guatemala)	Costa Rica, El Salvador, Guatemala, Honduras, Mexico, Nicaragua, Panama, Spain, Venezuela
Frank Potter (Canada)	Hubert Dean (Bahamas)	Antigua and Barbuda, Bahamas, Barbados, Belize, Canada, Dominica, Grenada, Guyana, Ireland, Jamaica, Saint Lucia
Einar Magnussen (Norway)	Jorunn Maehlum (Norway)	Denmark, Finland, Iceland, Norway, Sweden
Eveline Herfkens (Netherlands)	Boris Skapin (Yugoslavia)	Bulgaria, Cyprus, Israel, Netherlands, Romania, Yugoslavia
John H. Cosgrove (Australia)	A. John Wilson (New Zealand)	Australia, Kiribati, New Zealand, Papua New Guinea, Republic of Korea, Samoa, Solomon Islands, Vanuatu
Ernest Leung (Philippines)	Paulo C. Ximenes-Ferreira (Brazil)	Brazil, Colombia, Dominican Republic, Ecuador, Haiti, Philippines, Trinidad and Tobago
Aris Othman (Malaysia)	Aung Pe (Myanmar)	Fiji, Indonesia, Lao People's Democratic Republic, Malaysia, Myanmar, Nepal, Singapore, Thailand, Tonga, Viet Nam
Felix Alberto Camarasa (Argentina)	Nicolás Flaño (Chile)	Argentina, Bolivia, Chile, Paraguay, Peru, Uruguay
Fawzi Hamad Al-Sultan (Kuwait)	Mohamed W. Hosny (Egypt)	Egypt, Jordan, Kuwait, Lebanon, Maldives, Oman, Pakistan, Syrian Arab Republic, United Arab Emirates, Yemen
Jabez A. Langley (Gambia)	O. K. Matambo (Botswana)	Angola, Botswana, Burundi, Ethiopia, Gambia, Guinea, Kenya, Lesotho, Liberia, Malawi, Mozambique, Namibia, Nigeria, Seychelles, Sierra Leone, Sudan, Swaziland, Uganda, United Republic of Tanzania, Zambia, Zimbabwe
Jean-Pierre Le Bouder (Central African Republic)	Ali Bourhane (Comoros)	Benin, Burkina Faso, Cameroon, Cape Verde, Central African Republic, Congo, Côte d'Ivoire, Djibouti, Equatorial Guinea, Gabon, Guinea-Bissau, Madagascar, Mali, Mauritania, Mauritius, Niger, Rwanda, Senegal, Somalia, Togo, Zaire
Mohamed Benhocine (Algeria)	Salem Mohamed Omeish (Libyan Arab Jamahiriya)	Afghanistan, Algeria, Ghana, Iran, Libyan Arab Jamahiriya, Morocco, Tunisia
Ibrahim A. Al-Assaf (Saudi Arabia)	Ahmed M. Al-Ghannam (Saudi Arabia)	Saudi Arabia
Wang Liansheng (China)	Jin Liqun (China)	China

PRINCIPAL OFFICERS

President: Lewis T. Preston.*
Executive Vice President: William S. Ryrie.
Vice President, Capital Markets: Daniel F. Adams.
Vice President, Corporate Business Development: Makarand V. Dehejia.
Vice President, Finance and Planning: Richard H. Frank.
Vice Presidents, Operations: Wilfried E. Kaffenberger, Jemal-ud-din Kassum.
Vice President and General Counsel: José E. Camacho.
Secretary: Timothy T. Thahane.*

Director, Asia Department: Pho Ba Quan.
Director, Central Asia, Middle East and North Africa Department: André G. Hovaguimian.
Director, Europe Department: Edward A. Nassim.
Director, Latin America and the Caribbean Department: Helmut Paul.
Director, Sub-Saharan Africa Department: Irving Kuczynski.

Director, Agribusiness Department: Karl Voltaire.
Director, Central Capital Markets Department: Farida Khambata.
Director, Chemicals, Petrochemicals and Fertilizers Department: Jean-Philippe F. Halphen.
Director, Corporate Finance Services Department: Philippe Liétard.
Director, Infrastructure Department: Everett J. Santos.
Director, Oil, Gas, and Mining Department: M. Azam K. Alizai.
Director, Controller's and Budgeting Department: R. Michael Barth.
Director, Corporate Planning Department: Nissim Ezekiel.
Director, Economics Department and Chief Economic Adviser: Guy Pierre Pfeffermann.
Director, Personnel and Administration: Christopher Bam.
Director, Technical and Environment Department: Andreas M. Raczynski.
Director, Treasury and Financial Policy Department: Robert D. Graffam.

*Held the same position in the World Bank.

HEADQUARTERS AND OTHER OFFICE

HEADQUARTERS
International Finance Corporation
1850 I Street, N.W.
Washington, D.C. 20433, United States
  Cable address: CORINTFIN WASHINGTONDC
  Telephone: (1) (202) 477-1234
  Telex: FTCC 82987, RCA 248423, WU 64145
  Facsimile: (1) (202) 477-6391

NEW YORK OFFICE
International Finance Corporation
809 UN Plaza, Suite 900
New York, N.Y. 10017, United States
  Cable address: CORINTFIN NEWYORK
  Telephone: (1) (212) 963-6008
  Facsimile: (1) (212) 697-7020

Chapter VIII

International Development Association (IDA)

The International Development Association (IDA) was established in 1960 as an affiliate of the International Bank for Reconstruction and Development (World Bank) to provide assistance for the same purposes as the Bank, but primarily to poorer developing countries and on easier terms. Though legally and financially distinct from the Bank, IDA shares the same staff.

The funds used by IDA—called credits to distinguish them from World Bank loans—come mostly as subscriptions in convertible currencies from members, general replenishments from its more industrialized and developed members and transfers from the Bank's net earnings. Credits are made only to Governments, have 10-year grace periods and 35- or 40-year maturities and are interest-free.

During the fiscal year 1992 (1 July 1991 to 30 June 1992), IDA continued to promote economic development, concentrating on countries with annual per capita gross national product of $610 or less (in 1990 dollars). IDA's 110 approved credits in the amount of $6,549.7 million were distributed among 49 countries and an African regional project in fiscal 1992.

For the most part, IDA funds for lending were provided by its Part I (industrialized) member countries and several Part II (developing) countries under a series of replenishment agreements. Fiscal 1992 was the second year of the ninth replenishment of IDA resources (IDA-9), which provided funds to finance commitments to IDA borrowers in fiscal years 1991-1993. IDA's commitment authority for the fiscal year amounted to some 4,760 million special drawing rights (SDRs) and was derived mainly from the receipt of formal notifications to contribute and from the release of the second tranche of donors' contributions to IDA-9. During the year, formal notifications to participate in IDA-9 were received from Belgium, Czechoslovakia, Italy, Netherlands and the Russian Federation, as well as an additional contribution of $25 million from Kuwait, thus increasing IDA's commitment authority during the year by SDR 397 million. Commitment authority also increased by SDR 3,310 million when IDA received a substantial portion of the United States' second installment to IDA-9. Other sources of commitment authority for fiscal 1992 included the transfer from the World Bank's fiscal 1991 income of some SDR 260 million as well

as funds available from future reflows amounting to about SDR 795 million.

Negotiations on a tenth replenishment of IDA's resources (IDA-10) to provide funds to cover credit commitments in fiscal years 1994-1996 were launched with a meeting of IDA deputies in January 1992 in Paris and at a subsequent meeting in April in Washington, D.C.

During 1992, membership of IDA rose to 147, with the admission of Kazakhstan, Kyrgyzstan, Latvia, Portugal, the Russian Federation, Switzerland and Uzbekistan. (See Annex I for complete membership.)

Lending operations (credits)

By 30 June 1992, IDA had made cumulative commitments totalling $71,065 million. In fiscal year 1992, commitments amounted to $6,549.7 million, of which $3,235.2 million went to 31 countries in Africa and the Africa region; $1,640.8 million to five countries in South Asia; $1,069.6 million to five countries in East Asia; $405 million to five countries in Latin America and the Caribbean; $158 million to two countries in the Middle East and North Africa; and $41.1 million to one country in Europe. India was the largest borrower, with six credits totalling $1,023.5 million, followed by China with eight ($948.6 million).

Agriculture and rural development

In fiscal 1992, IDA granted 29 credits totalling $1,368.4 million for agriculture and rural development projects in 25 countries. China received $287 million, of which $162 million supported a project in Guangdon province to increase fish production from the South China Sea, develop aquaculture facilities and boost production of fruits and sugar cane. Of the three credits provided to India totalling $243 million, $124 million was used to finance forestry and environmentally beneficial investment to assist some 800,000 households, comprising forest dwellers, tribal persons and smallholder farms. A $150 million credit went to Zimbabwe to assist the Government's drought-relief and recovery programme by providing agriculture inputs, rehabilitating the water supply system, providing critical inputs for the transport of goods needed for relief and recovery and upgrading the public works programme through which drought relief was distributed. Ghana received two credits totalling $110.4 million, of which $80 million supported government reforms in the agricultural sector involving the liberalization of agricultural pricing, marketing and input supply. A credit of $29.2 million was granted to Pakistan to strengthen the country's environmental protection institutions and initiate a series of related operations, studies and pilot activities.

Development finance companies

IDA extended five credits valued at $223.3 million to assist development finance companies in five countries during fiscal 1992. Ghana received $100 million to support the second phase of its financial sector adjustment, which was expected to result in a broader-based and more diversified financial sector with a stronger, more efficient, and responsive banking system. Of $75 million received by Côte d'Ivoire, $50 million supported the country's multifaceted financial sector reform programme, through an operation which was designed to stabilize the financial system and restore to health the country's system of financial intermediation. Bangladesh received $28.4 million, of which $25.5 million provided a line of credit to selected financial intermediaries for term lending to privately controlled firms, thus furthering the liberalization of the financial system.

Education

Eleven credits totalling $584.1 million were granted to 10 countries in fiscal 1992 for education projects. Kenya received two credits totalling $155 million, of which $100 million supported the Government's education reform programme which sought to limit the demands of the education sector on the public budget. A $130 million credit to China assisted governments of six provinces in initiating institutional and policy reforms to improve the management of education and its quality and efficiency within a newly decentralized framework. In Pakistan, $115 million helped improve access and participation, especially for girls, in middle schools in the Punjab province's rural and urban slum areas.

Energy

In fiscal 1992, seven countries received $228 million for energy-related projects. Of $82.1 million received by Honduras, $50.6 million supported the Government's energy sector reform programme, which included measures to make the national power company a financially viable entity and develop the country's oil and gas potential by the private sector. Nepal received a credit of $65 million to increase the supply capacity of the Nepal Electricity Authority by improving technical and operational efficiency and upgrading existing generating capacity. Malawi received $55 million for the con-

struction of a hydroelectric scheme and rehabilitation of existing power stations. A credit of $50 million was granted to Sri Lanka to rehabilitate the remaining 53 power-distribution systems that were still operated by local authorities. The systems were to be taken over by the Ceylon Electricity Board in the next few years.

Industry

IDA granted three credits for industrial projects totalling $406 million in fiscal 1992. A $200 million credit to the United Republic of Tanzania supported the Government's financial sector reform programme, the objective of which was to create a system based on market-oriented principles. A $200 million credit to Zambia supported the next stages of the country's structural adjustment programme, which focused on market liberalization and civil service reform, together with new initiatives in private sector development, privatization and parastatal reform. Mali received $6 million to develop the mining industry. Mines of all sizes would be financed with both foreign and local capital.

Non-project credits

Twenty countries received credits in the amount of $1,460.1 million to finance non-project areas in fiscal 1992. A credit of $250 million went to India to support the initial phase of the Government's programme of macroeconomic stabilization and structural reform. Mozambique received $180 million to help enhance private sector–based growth, redeploy budgetary expenditures towards key social sectors and smallholder agriculture and provide support for drought relief. Bangladesh received $150 million to implement a programme of fiscal reforms designed to increase public investment and savings. A $150 million credit was extended to Ethiopia for a multisectoral operation, which would include improvements in public health and education and increase employment opportunities generated through reconstruction works. Nicaragua received $110 million for its structural adjustment programme designed to downsize and restructure the public sector, improve resource allocation and mobilization and reform incentive systems.

Population, health and nutrition

IDA granted 13 credits totalling $654.7 million to assist population, health and nutrition projects in 11 countries. India received a total of $377.5 million, of which $214.5 million helped to finance the cost of expanding and enhancing of the Government's national maternal and child health programme and of introducing a safe motherhood initiative. A credit of $129.6 million to China supported national programmes to control tuberculosis and schistosomiasis in selected provinces. With a credit of $31 million to Kenya, the Kenyatta National Hospital, the national referral hospital that also served the Nairobi area, was rehabilitated and its clinical and administrative efficiency improved.

Public sector management

Credits amounting to $76.7 million to improve public sector management were granted to four countries. Uganda received $65.6 million to enhance the role of private enterprises by reducing the size of the public enterprise sector through privatization and by facilitating access to term finance. Guinea received $7.3 million to help the Government formulate and implement the next stage of its Public Enterprise Rationalization and Privatization Programme, which emphasized public enterprise privatization and strengthening of key institutions involved in programme implementation.

Technical assistance

Twelve IDA credits totalling $127 million provided for technical assistance in fiscal 1992. Bangladesh received $25 million to prepare investment projects and for investments related to IDA's lending programme. Of $21.2 million received by the United Republic of Tanzania, $11.2 million financed an urban sector engineering project to strengthen the institutional and financial capacities of the country's urban councils and prepare the groundwork for subsequent investment projects in urban infrastructure. Burkina Faso received $15 million to reinforce major public institutions charged with economic and sector management. A $15 million credit was extended to Côte d'Ivoire to provide general institutional support to government entities in charge of the country's privatization programme.

Telecommunications

An IDA credit of $55 million was extended to Nepal during fiscal 1992 to provide telecommunications equipment and technical assistance for institutional building.

Transportation

During fiscal 1992, eight credits totalling $490.8 million were granted to eight countries for transportation projects. India received $153 million to modernize key sections of the national highway network and to promote the use of improved road engineering and construction standards, network management and contract management. A credit of $80 million to Bolivia contributed to upgrading about one third of the country's maintainable road network, thus reducing both a large backlog of maintenance and vehicle operating costs. Mozambique was granted $74.3 million to develop the institutional capacity in the Ministry of Construction and Water and the Ministry of Transport and Commu-

nications needed to plan and supervise road rehabilitation and maintenance and improve small coastal ports serving priority districts. Burkina Faso received $66 million to assist in rehabilitating and maintaining essential transport infrastructure and improving sectoral efficiency. Ghana received $55 million to finance a portion of the Government's 1992-1999 feeder roads programme. A $37.7 million credit to Angola financed economic and financial-feasibility studies, as well as basic engineering studies and environment assessments, for the rehabilitation and maintenance of key transport and urban systems.

Urban development

Eight countries received credits totalling $382.6 million for urban development in fiscal 1992. Of $160 million received by China, $100 million went to a project to improve Tianjin's urban infrastructure and environment. Uganda received $71.2 million to finance short- and medium-term reconstruction of essential economic and social infrastructure in the north to restore the region's economic productivity and begin the process of reducing the historical disparity between the northern and southern areas of the country. Angola received $45.6 million to rehabilitate its water and sewer networks, provide clean water and affordably priced latrines and rehabilitate storm-drainage and solid-waste management systems for the twin cities of Lobito and Benguela.

Water supply and sewerage

IDA granted credits to six countries totalling $377.4 million for water supply and sewerage. Of $190 million granted to China, $110 million helped to increase coverage of water supply in six underdeveloped island provinces and autonomous regions. The increased coverage was to be complemented by sanitation services, health and hygiene education, technical assistance and training. Nigeria received $101 million to improve the quantity and reliability of the water supply in the more important towns and settlements of the Katsina and Kaduna States. The National Water Conservation and Pipeline Corporation in Kenya was assisted with a credit of $43.2 million to carry out a preparatory project to improve and extend the water supply and wastewater disposal systems in Mombasa and other locations in the coastal region. Burundi received $32.7 million to improve public health and living conditions through the construction of rural water-supply systems in 9 of the country's 15 provinces.

Secretariat

The principal officers, staff, headquarters and other offices of IDA are the same as those of the World Bank (see PART SEVEN, Chapter VI).

Annex I. MEMBERS OF THE INTERNATIONAL DEVELOPMENT ASSOCIATION
          (As at 31 December 1992)

Part I members*

Australia, Austria, Belgium, Canada, Denmark, Finland, France, Germany, Iceland, Ireland, Italy, Japan, Kuwait, Luxembourg, Netherlands, New Zealand, Norway, Russian Federation, South Africa, Sweden, Switzerland, United Arab Emirates, United Kingdom, United States.

Part II members*

Afghanistan, Albania, Algeria, Angola, Argentina, Bangladesh, Belize, Benin, Bhutan, Bolivia, Botswana, Brazil, Burkina Faso, Burundi, Cambodia, Cameroon, Cape Verde, Central African Republic, Chad, Chile, China, Colombia, Comoros, Congo, Costa Rica, Côte d'Ivoire, Cyprus, Czechoslovakia, Djibouti, Dominica, Dominican Republic, Ecuador, Egypt, El Salvador, Equatorial Guinea, Ethiopia, Fiji, Gabon, Gambia, Ghana, Greece, Grenada, Guatemala, Guinea, Guinea-Bissau, Guyana, Haiti, Honduras, Hungary, India, Indonesia, Iran, Iraq, Israel, Jordan, Kazakhstan, Kenya, Kiribati, Kyrgyzstan, Lao People's Democratic Republic, Latvia, Lebanon, Lesotho, Liberia, Libyan Arab Jamahiriya, Madagascar, Malawi, Malaysia, Maldives, Mali, Mauritania, Mauritius, Mexico, Mongolia, Morocco, Mozambique, Myanmar, Nepal, Nicaragua, Niger, Nigeria, Oman, Pakistan, Panama, Papua New Guinea, Paraguay, Peru, Philippines, Poland, Portugal, Republic of Korea, Rwanda, Saint Kitts and Nevis, Saint Lucia, Saint Vincent and the Grenadines, Samoa, Sao Tome and Principe, Saudi Arabia, Senegal, Sierra Leone, Solomon Islands, Somalia, Spain, Sri Lanka, Sudan, Swaziland, Syrian Arab Republic, Thailand, Togo, Tonga, Trinidad and Tobago, Tunisia, Turkey, Uganda, United Republic of Tanzania, Uzbekistan, Vanuatu, Viet Nam, Yemen, Yugoslavia, Zaire, Zambia, Zimbabwe.

*Members of IDA are classified in two parts on the basis of the level of their contributions and voting power.

Annex II. EXECUTIVE DIRECTORS AND ALTERNATES AND OFFICES OF
           THE INTERNATIONAL DEVELOPMENT ASSOCIATION
           (As at 30 June 1992)

Appointed Director	*Appointed Alternate*	*Casting the vote of*
E. Patrick Coady	Mark M. Collins, Jr.	United States
Yasuyuki Kawahara	Kiyoshi Kodera	Japan
Fritz Fischer	Harald Rehm	Germany
Jean-Pierre Landau	Phillippe de Fontaine Vive	France
David Peretz	Robert Graham-Harrison	United Kingdom

Elected Director	*Elected Alternate*	*Casting the vote of*
Bernard Snoy (Belgium)	Walter Rill (Austria)	Austria, Belgium, Czechoslovakia, Hungary, Luxembourg, Turkey
Rosario Bonavoglia (Italy)	Fernando S. Carneiro (Portugal)	Greece, Italy, Poland
Frank Potter (Canada)	Hubert Dean (Bahamas)	Belize, Canada, Dominica, Grenada, Guyana, Ireland, Saint Kitts and Nevis, Saint Lucia, Saint Vincent and the Grenadines
J.S. Baijal (India)	M.A. Syed (Bangladesh)	Bangladesh, Bhutan, India, Sri Lanka
Moisés Naim (Venezuela)	Gabriel Castellanos (Guatemala)	Costa Rica, El Salvador, Guatemala, Honduras, Mexico, Nicaragua, Panama, Spain
Eveline Herfkens (Netherlands)	Boris Skapin (Yugoslavia)	Cyprus, Israel, Netherlands, Yugoslavia
Einar Magnussen (Norway)	Jorunn Maehlum (Norway)	Denmark, Finland, Iceland, Norway, Sweden
Ernest Leung (Philippines)	Paulo C. Ximenes-Ferreira (Brazil)	Brazil, Colombia, Dominican Republic, Ecuador, Haiti, Philippines, Trinidad and Tobago
John H. Cosgrove (Australia)	A. John Wilson (New Zealand)	Australia, Kiribati, New Zealand, Papua New Guinea, Republic of Korea, Samoa, Solomon Islands, Vanuatu,
Wang Liansheng (China)	Jin Liqun (China)	China
Aris Othman (Malaysia)	Aung Pe (Myanmar)	Fiji, Indonesia, Lao People's Democratic Republic, Malaysia, Myanmar, Nepal, Thailand, Tonga, Viet Nam
Mohamed Benhocine (Algeria)	Salem Mohamed Omeish (Libyan Arab Jamahiriya)	Afghanistan, Algeria, Ghana, Iran, Libyan Arab Jamahiriya, Morocco, Tunisia
Fawzi Hamad Al-Sultan (Kuwait)	Mohamed W. Hosny (Egypt)	Egypt, Jordan, Kuwait, Lebanon, Maldives, Oman, Pakistan, Syrian Arab Republic, United Arab Emirates, Yemen
Jabez A. Langley (Gambia)	O. K. Matambo (Botswana)	Angola, Botswana, Burundi, Ethiopia, Gambia, Guinea, Kenya, Lesotho, Liberia, Malawai, Mozambique, Nigeria, Sierra Leone, Sudan, Swaziland, Uganda, United Republic of Tanzania, Zambia, Zimbabwe
Ibrahim A. Al-Assaf (Saudi Arabia)	Ahmed M. Al-Ghannam (Saudi Arabia)	Saudi Arabia
Félix Alberto Camarasa (Argentina)	Nicolás Flaño (Chile)	Argentina, Bolivia, Chile, Paraguay, Peru.
Jean-Pierre Le Bouder (Central African Republic)	Ali Bourhane (Comoros)	Benin, Burkina Faso, Cameroon, Cape Verde, Central African Republic, Chad, Comoros, Congo, Côte d'Ivoire, Djibouti, Equatorial Guinea, Gabon, Guinea-Bissau, Madagascar, Mali, Mauritania, Mauritius, Niger, Rwanda, Sao Tome and Principe, Senegal, Somalia, Togo, Zaire

NOTE: Cambodia, Iraq and South Africa did not participate in the 1990 regular election of Executive Officers. Albania, Mongolia, the Russian Federation and Switzerland became members after the election.

HEADQUARTERS AND OTHER OFFICES

HEADQUARTERS
International Development Association
1818 H Street, N.W.
Washington, D.C. 20433, United States
  Cable address: INDEVAS WASHINGTONDC
  Telephone: (1) (202) 477-1234
  Telex: FTCCQ 82987 INDEVAS
      RCA 248423 INDEVAS
      WUI 64145 INDEVAS
      TRT 197688 INDEVAS
Facsimile: (1) (202) 477-6391

NEW YORK OFFICE
International Development Association
809 United Nations Plaza (9th Floor)
New York, N.Y. 10017, United States
  Cable address: INDEVAS NEWYORK
  Telephone: (1) (212) 963-6008
  Facsimile: (1) (212) 308-5320

IDA also maintained offices at Geneva, Paris and Tokyo.

Chapter IX

International Monetary Fund (IMF)

During 1992, the International Monetary Fund (IMF) increased its assistance to the formerly centrally planned economies in transition to market-based systems and focused on initiatives to improve prospects for the world economy.

IMF provided the machinery for, and promoted, international monetary cooperation through surveillance of the exchange-rate policies of its member States. Surveillance was carried out through consultations analysing the economic and financial conditions of IMF members and regular discussions on the world economic outlook.

IMF operates on a fiscal year; fiscal year 1992 covered the period from 1 May 1991 to 30 April 1992.

As at 31 December 1992, IMF membership stood at 175, with the admission of Armenia, Azerbaijan, Belarus, Croatia, Estonia, Georgia, Kazakhstan, Kyrgyzstan, Latvia, Lithuania, the Marshall Islands, the Republic of Moldova, the Russian Federation, San Marino, Slovenia, Switzerland, the former Yugoslav Republic of Macedonia, Turkmenistan, Ukraine and Uzbekistan. (See Annex I for complete membership.)

IMF facilities and policies

The Fund's financial support assisted member States to regain a viable balance of payments combined with economic growth and exchange-rate stability. The facilities and policies through which it provided such support differed, depending on the nature of the macroeconomic and structural problems to be addressed and the terms and degree of conditionality attached to them.

Stand-by arrangements, typically covering periods of one to two years, focused on specific macroeconomic policies, such as exchange-rate and interest-rate policies, aimed at overcoming balance-of-payments difficulties. Extended arrangements, which supported medium-term programmes generally running for three years, were available to overcome more intractable balance-of-payments difficulties, attributable to structural as well as macroeconomic problems.

IMF's enlarged access policy was used to increase the resources available under stand-by or extended arrangements for programmes needing substantial Fund support. It was financed with ordinary resources and resources borrowed for that purpose, the combination of which was determined according to IMF policy. Access to the Fund's general resources under the enlarged access policy had been subject to annual limits of 90 or 110 per cent of quota, three-year limits of 270 or 330 per cent of quota and cumulative limits of 400 or 440 per cent of quota. Once borrowed resources were fully used, ordinary resources were substituted to meet commitments. The substitution was applicable until 30 September 1992. In November, the Ninth General Review of Quotas took effect, increasing the amount of IMF quotas to 144.8 billion special drawing rights (SDRs) from SDR 97.4 billion.

The structural adjustment facility (SAF), launched in 1986,[a] provided balance-of-payments assistance on concessional terms to support medium-term macroeconomic adjustment and structural reform in low-income countries facing protracted balance-of-payments problems. The enhanced structural adjustment facility (ESAF), established in 1987[b] and operational since 1988—similar in objective, conditions for eligibility and programme features to SAF, but differing in scope and strength of structural policies, terms of access levels, monitoring procedures and sources of funding—was extended by the Executive Board for a fourth year, to November 1993, its cut-off date. The Board agreed to examine options and modalities for a possible successor facility.

The compensatory and contingency financing facility (CCFF) provided resources to members to cover temporary export shortfalls and excesses in cereal import costs arising from events beyond their control, and helped with IMF arrangements to maintain the momentum of reforms in the face of adverse external shocks, such as declines in export prices or increases in import prices and fluctuations in interest rates.

Under the buffer stock financing facility, IMF provided resources to help finance members' contributions to approved buffer stocks of commodities.

Financial assistance

In 1992, much of IMF's financial support went to its new members, the previously centrally

---

[a]YUN 1986, p. 1159.
[b]YUN 1987, p. 1252.

planned economies of Eastern Europe and the successor States of the former USSR, to establish effective monetary arrangements and integrate them into the international monetary system. IMF approved a first credit-tranche arrangement for the Russian Federation and stand-by arrangements for Estonia and Latvia.

The number of IMF arrangements in effect increased by one over 1991 to 51 at the end of 1992, with total commitments of SDR 29.8 billion. As at 31 December 1992, there were 22 stand-by arrangements (Albania, Barbados, Brazil, Bulgaria, Czechoslovakia, Dominican Republic, Egypt, El Salvador, Estonia, Gabon, Guatemala, India, Jordan, Latvia, Lithuania, Morocco, Nicaragua, Panama, Philippines, Romania, Russian Federation, Uruguay); 7 extended arrangements (Argentina, Hungary, Jamaica, Mexico, Poland, Venezuela, Zimbabwe); 4 SAF arrangements (Burkina Faso, Comoros, Ethiopia, Rwanda); and 18 ESAF arrangements (Bangladesh, Bolivia, Burundi, Guinea, Guyana, Honduras, Kenya, Lesotho, Malawi, Mali, Mauritania, Mozambique, Nepal, Sri Lanka, Togo, Uganda, United Republic of Tanzania, Zimbabwe). In April 1992, 11 low-income developing countries were added to the list of countries eligible to make purchases under ESAF (Albania, Angola, Côte d'Ivoire, Dominican Republic, Egypt, Honduras, Mongolia, Nicaragua, Nigeria, Philippines, Zimbabwe).

Total IMF disbursements to its members declined to SDR 5.3 billion in 1992 from SDR 8.2 billion in 1991. Disbursements under the General Resources Account declined to SDR 4.8 billion in 1992 from SDR 7.4 billion in the previous year. Disbursements under stand-by arrangements rose to SDR 3.1 billion in 1992 from SDR 2.6 billion in 1991, whereas disbursements under extended arrangements declined to SDR 0.9 billion from SDR 1.9 billion. Disbursements under CCFF also declined, to SDR 0.6 billion from SDR 3 billion in 1991, when many countries drew on the facility in the wake of oil price increases resulting from events in the Persian Gulf. Under SAF, disbursements declined to SDR 20 million in 1992 from SDR 149.9 million the year before, and those under ESAF declined to SDR 524.3 million from SDR 633 million. Repurchases under the General Resources Account decreased in 1992, to SDR 4.2 billion from SDR 4.7 billion in 1991.

In response to a rising number of countries seeking IMF support and increased demand for its resources, the Board of Governors authorized a 50 per cent increase in the size of quotas under the Ninth General Review of Quotas, which took effect in November 1992, bringing the total of IMF quotas to SDR 144.8 billion.

Liquidity

As at 30 April 1992, the Fund's adjusted and uncommitted usable resources totalled SDR 20.9 billion, compared with SDR 23.8 billion the previous fiscal year. The decline resulted from the exclusion of two currencies from the operational budget and the excess of purchases (drawings) over repurchases (repayments) during 1991/92.

IMF's liquid liabilities declined to SDR 25.6 billion as at 30 April 1992 from SDR 26.2 billion a year earlier, representing reserve tranche positions of SDR 21.9 billion and loan claims on the Fund of SDR 3.7 billion, a decline of SDR 0.6 billion. The ratio of the Fund's adjusted and uncommitted usable resources to its liquid liabilities—the liquidity ratio—declined by 12 per cent over the course of 1991/92 to 81.6 per cent, owing largely to the high level of new commitments, including commitments of ordinary resources to be substituted for borrowed resources.

SDR activity

Total transfers of SDRs during fiscal 1992 declined to SDR 13.4 billion from SDR 14.8 billion in fiscal 1991, representing decreases in transfers among participants and prescribed holders (SDR 5.8 billion); transfers from participants to the General Resources Account (SDR 3.8 billion); and transfers from the General Resources Account to participants and prescribed holders (SDR 3.8 billion). SDRs used in operations involving SAF, ESAF, Trust Fund loans and the Supplementary Financing Facility Subsidy Account amounted to SDR 149 million in fiscal 1992.

Policy on arrears

Overdue financial obligations to IMF continued to be a serious concern in fiscal 1992, although their increase and the rate of growth were the lowest since fiscal 1982. Total overdue obligations rose from SDR 3.4 billion at the end of fiscal 1991 to SDR 3.5 billion at the end of fiscal 1992, almost all of which was due from members in arrears to IMF by six months or more; the number of such members increased from 9 to 10. As at 30 April 1992, eight members were ineligible to use IMF general resources; one member, previously declared ineligibile, cleared its overdue obligations and regained eligibility.

IMF continued to implement a strengthened cooperative strategy to resolve members' arrears problems. The strategy involved increased efforts to ensure that all members using IMF resources were able to meet their obligations when they fell due and remedial and deterrent measures, including a tightening of the timing of procedures for dealing with members in arrears. Under IMF's rights-accumulation programme, established in

1990, members could obtain future financing from the Fund once they cleared their arrears. By April 1992, the Executive Board had endorsed rights-accumulation programmes for three member States. Moreover, with the entry into force on 11 November 1992 of the Third Amendment of IMF's Articles of Agreement, the Executive Board, by a 70 per cent majority of the total voting power, was empowered to suspend the voting rights and certain related rights of a member that had been declared ineligible to use IMF's resources and which persisted in its failure to settle its outstanding obligations.

Technical assistance and training

Demand for IMF's technical assistance services increased sharply in 1992, with requests from countries making the transition from centrally planned to market economies, notably members in Eastern Europe and the successor States of the former USSR. Technical assistance programmes in those countries focused on establishing central banks and banking systems; regulatory systems; fiscal institutions, such as tax administration and tax policies, budgetary practices and social security schemes; and statistical databases. Programmes were also set up in many previously non-market developing countries, such as Algeria, Angola, Benin, Cape Verde, the Lao People's Democratic Republic, Mongolia, Mozambique and Viet Nam.

The Fund's technical assistance was provided through advisory visits, formal training and advice extended in the course of other staff contacts with authorities of member States. Assistance focused on improving macroeconomic management through training economic policy officials, enhancing the quality of economic statistical data, helping to reform tax systems and tax administration, and developing and improving the operations of central banking and financial systems.

Resources for IMF's technical assistance services were supplemented through a 1989 agreement, under which the Fund served as an executing agency for United Nations Development Programme assistance, and a special technical assistance account set up in March 1990 and funded by Japan.

The IMF Institute provided training to officials of member States through courses and seminars at IMF headquarters and abroad. During fiscal 1992, the Institute held 15 courses and 3 seminars at headquarters, including one course specifically directed at centrally planned economies in transition. The Institute conducted 19 courses and 4 seminars overseas for government officials, of which 10 courses provided training in the former USSR and Eastern Europe.

In September 1992, IMF, together with five other international institutions, established the Joint Vienna Institute to assist officials and private-sector managers from former centrally planned economies. Through December 1992, the Institute offered 14 courses, including a seminar on public expenditure policies in transition economies. In August, a technical assistance secretariat was set up in IMF to advise management on all aspects of technical assistance and to provide a focal point to coordinate such assistance.

IMF–World Bank collaboration

IMF recognized that balance-of-payments problems arose not only from a temporary lack of liquidity and inadequate financial and budgetary policies, but also from long-standing contradictions in the structure of members' economies. Broadening its focus to include structural reform resulted in considerable convergence in the efforts of IMF and the World Bank and led them to rely more on each other's special expertise.

IMF continued to collaborate closely with the Bank by coordinating both policy advice and financial assistance. During fiscal 1992, collaboration intensified with the provision of advice to the successor States of the former USSR.

IMF and the Bank were both concerned with economic issues and worked at broadening and strengthening the economies of their members. However, IMF was primarily a cooperative institution that sought to maintain an orderly system of payments and receipts between countries.

Secretariat

As at 31 December 1992, the total full-time staff of IMF—including permanent, fixed-term and temporary employees—was 2,167, drawn from 121 nationalities.

NOTE: For details of IMF activities in 1992, see _International Monetary Fund, Annual Report of the Executive Board for the Financial Year Ended April 30, 1992,_ and _Annual Report of the Executive Board for the Financial Year Ended April 30, 1993,_ published by IMF.

Annex I.   MEMBERSHIP OF THE INTERNATIONAL MONETARY FUND
   (As at 31 December 1992)

Afghanistan, Albania, Algeria, Angola, Antigua and Barbuda, Argentina, Armenia, Australia, Austria, Azerbaijan, Bahamas, Bahrain, Bangladesh, Barbados, Belarus, Belgium, Belize, Benin, Bhutan, Bolivia, Botswana, Brazil, Bulgaria, Burkina Faso, Burundi, Cambodia, Cameroon, Canada, Cape Verde, Central African Republic, Chad, Chile, China, Colombia, Comoros, Congo, Costa Rica, Côte d'Ivoire, Croatia, Cyprus, Czechoslovakia, Denmark, Djibouti, Dominica, Dominican Republic, Ecuador, Egypt, El Salvador, Equatorial Guinea, Estonia,

Ethiopia, Fiji, Finland, France, Gabon, Gambia, Georgia, Germany, Ghana, Greece, Grenada, Guatemala, Guinea, Guinea-Bissau, Guyana, Haiti, Honduras, Hungary, Iceland, India, Indonesia, Iran, Iraq, Ireland, Israel, Italy, Jamaica, Japan, Jordan, Kazakhstan, Kenya, Kiribati, Kuwait, Kyrgyzstan, Lao People's Democratic Republic, Latvia, Lebanon, Lesotho, Liberia, Libyan Arab Jamahiriya, Lithuania, Luxembourg, Madagascar, Malawi, Malaysia, Maldives, Mali, Malta, Marshall Islands, Mauritania, Mauritius, Mexico, Mongolia, Morocco, Mozambique, Myanmar, Namibia, Nepal, Netherlands, New Zealand, Nicaragua, Niger, Nigeria, Norway, Oman, Pakistan, Panama, Papua New Guinea, Paraguay, Peru, Philippines, Poland, Portugal, Qatar, Republic of Korea, Republic of Moldova, Romania, Russian Federation, Rwanda, Saint Kitts and Nevis, Saint Lucia, Saint Vincent and the Grenadines, San Marino, Samoa, Sao Tome and Principe, Saudi Arabia, Senegal, Seychelles, Sierra Leone, Singapore, Slovenia, Solomon Islands, Somalia, South Africa, Spain, Sri Lanka, Sudan, Suriname, Swaziland, Sweden, Switzerland, Syrian Arab Republic, Thailand, the former Yugoslav Republic of Macedonia, Togo, Tonga, Trinidad and Tobago, Tunisia, Turkey, Turkmenistan, Uganda, Ukraine, United Arab Emirates, United Kingdom, United Republic of Tanzania, United States, Uruguay, Uzbekistan, Vanuatu, Venezuela, Viet Nam, Yemen, Zaire, Zambia, Zimbabwe.

NOTE: On 14 December 1992, IMF determined that the former Yugoslavia had ceased to exist and therefore ceased to be a member of the Fund. The Fund decided that Bosnia and Herzegovina, Croatia, Slovenia, the former Yugoslav Republic of Macedonia and Yugoslavia (Serbia and Montenegro) were the successors to the assets and liabilities of the former Yugoslavia, and, subject to specified conditions, could succeed its membership in the Fund.

Annex II. EXECUTIVE DIRECTORS AND ALTERNATES, OFFICERS AND OFFICES OF THE INTERNATIONAL MONETARY FUND
(As at 31 December 1992)

Appointed Director	*Appointed Alternate*	*Casting the vote of*
Thomas C. Dawson II	Quincy M. Krosby	United States
Stefan Schoenberg	Bernd Esdar	Germany
Jean-Pierre Landau	Isabelle Martel	France
Hiroo Fukui	Naoki Tabata	Japan
David Peretz	John Dorrington	United Kingdom

Elected Director	*Elected Alternate*	*Casting the votes of*
Jacques de Groote (Belgium)	Johann Prader (Austria)	Austria, Belarus, Belgium, Czechoslovakia, Hungary, Kazakhstan, Luxembourg, Turkey
Godert A. Posthumus (Netherlands)	Oleh Havrylyshyn (Ukraine)	Armenia, Bulgaria, Cyprus, Georgia, Israel, Netherlands, Republic of Moldova, Romania, Ukraine
Roberto Marino (Mexico)	Gerver Torres (Venezuela)	Costa Rica, El Salvador, Guatemala, Honduras, Mexico, Nicaragua, Spain, Venezuela
Giulio Lanciotti (Italy)	Ioannis Papadakis (Greece)	Albania, Greece, Italy, Malta, Portugal, San Marino
Douglas E. Smee (Canada)	Garrett F. Murphy (Ireland)	Antigua and Barbuda, Bahamas, Barbados, Belize, Canada, Dominica, Grenada, Ireland, Jamaica, Saint Kitts and Nevis, Saint Lucia, Saint Vincent and the Grenadines
Ingimundur Fridriksson (Iceland)	Jon A. Solheim (Norway)	Denmark, Estonia, Finland, Iceland, Latvia, Lithuania, Norway, Sweden
E. A. Evans (Australia)	Amando M. Tetangco, Jr. (Philippines)	Australia, Kiribati, Marshall Islands, Mongolia, New Zealand, Papua New Guinea, Philippines, Republic of Korea, Samoa, Seychelles, Solomon Islands, Vanuatu
A. Shakour Shaalan (Egypt)	Yacoob Yousef Mohammed (Bahrain)	Bahrain, Egypt, Iraq, Jordan, Kuwait, Lebanon, Libyan Arab Jamahiriya, Maldives, Oman, Qatar, Syrian Arab Republic, United Arab Emirates, Yemen
Muhammad Al-Jasser (Saudi Arabia)	Abdulrahman A. Al-Tuwaijri (Saudi Arabia)	Saudi Arabia
L. J. Mwananshiku (Zambia)	Barnabas S. Dlamini (Swaziland)	Angola, Botswana, Burundi, Ethiopia, Gambia, Kenya, Lesotho, Liberia, Malawi, Mozambique, Namibia, Nigeria, Sierra Leone, Sudan, Swaziland, Uganda, United Republic of Tanzania, Zambia, Zimbabwe
Konstantin G. Kagalovsky (Russian Federation)	Aleksei V. Mozhin (Russian Federation)	Russian Federation
G. K. Arora (India)	L. Eustace N. Fernando (Sri Lanka)	Bangladesh, Bhutan, India, Sri Lanka
Daniel Kaeser (Switzerland)	Krzysztof Link (Poland)	Azerbaijan, Kyrgyzstan, Poland, Switzerland, Turkmenistan, Uzbekistan
Alexandre Kafka (Brazil)	Juan Carlos Jaramillo (Colombia)	Brazil, Colombia, Dominican Republic, Ecuador, Guyana, Haiti, Panama, Suriname, Trinidad and Tobago
Abbas Mirakhor (Iran)	Omar Kabbaj (Morocco)	Afghanistan, Algeria, Ghana, Iran, Morocco, Pakistan, Tunisia
J. E. Ismael (Indonesia)	Kleo-Thong Hetrakul (Thailand)	Fiji, Indonesia, Lao People's Democratic Republic, Malaysia, Myanmar, Nepal, Singapore, Thailand, Tonga, Viet Nam
Che Peiqin (China)	Wei Benhua (China)	China

A. Guillermo Zoccali (Argentina)

Corentino V. Santos (Cape Verde)

Manuel Estela (Peru)

Yves-Marie T. Koissy (Côte d'Ivoire)

Argentina, Bolivia, Chile, Paraguay, Peru, Uruguay

Benin, Burkina Faso, Cameroon, Cape Verde, Central African Republic, Chad, Comoros, Congo, Côte d'Ivoire, Djibouti, Equatorial Guinea, Gabon, Guinea, Guinea-Bissau, Madagascar, Mali, Mauritania, Mauritius, Niger, Rwanda, Sao Tome and Principe, Senegal, Togo, Zaire

SENIOR OFFICERS

Managing Director: Michel Camdessus.
Deputy Managing Director: Richard D. Erb.
Economic Counsellor: Michael Mussa.
Counsellor: Sterie T. Beza.
Counsellor: Leo Van Houtven.
Counsellor: Mamoudou Touré.
Director, Administration Department: Graeme F. Rea.
Director, African Department: Mamoudou Touré.
Director, Central Asia Department: Hubert Neiss.
Director, European I Department: Massimo Russo.
Director, European II Department: John Odling-Smee.
Director, External Relations Department: Shailendra J. Anjaria.
Director, Fiscal Affairs Department: Vito Tanzi.
Director, IMF Institute: Patrick B. de Fontenay.
General Counsel, Legal Department: François P. Gianviti.
Director, Middle Eastern Department: Paul Chabrier.

Director, Monetary and Exchange Affairs Department: J. B. Zulu.
Director, Policy Development and Review Department: John T. Boorman.
Director, Research Department: Michael Mussa.
Secretary, Secretary's Department: Leo Van Houtven.
Director, South-East Asia and Pacific Department: Kunio Saito.
Director, Statistics Department: John B. McLenaghan.
Treasurer, Treasurer's Department: David Williams.
Director, Western Hemisphere Department: Sterie T. Beza.
Director, Bureau of Computing Services: Warren N. Minami.
Director, Bureau of Language Services: Patrick Delannoy.
Acting Director, Office in Europe (Paris): Joaquin Ferrán.
Director and Special Trade Representative, Office in Geneva: Helen B. Junz.
Director, Office of Budget and Planning: Lindsay A. Wolfe.
Acting Director, Office of Internal Audit and Review: Alain Coune.

HEADQUARTERS AND OTHER OFFICES

HEADQUARTERS
International Monetary Fund
700 19th Street N.W.
Washington, D.C. 20431, United States
  Cable address: INTERFUND WASHINGTONDC
  Telephone: (1) (202) 623-7000
  Telex: (RCA) 248331 IMF UR, (MCI) 64111 IMF UW,
      (TRT) 197677 FUND UT
  Facsimile: (1) (202) 623-4661

  IMF also maintained offices at Geneva and in Paris.

IMF OFFICE, UNITED NATIONS, NEW YORK
International Monetary Fund
1 United Nations Plaza, Room 1140
New York, N.Y. 10017, United States
  Cable address: INTERFUND NEW YORK
  Telephone: (1) (212) 963-6009
  Facsimile: (1) (212) 319-9040

Chapter X

International Civil Aviation Organization (ICAO)

The International Civil Aviation Organization (ICAO) facilitates the safety and efficiency of civil air transport. Its objectives were set forth in annexes to the Convention on International Civil Aviation (Chicago, United States, 1944) which prescribe standards, recommended practices and procedures for facilitating civil aviation operations.

In 1992, scheduled traffic of the world's airlines increased to some 245 billion tonne-kilometres, indicating a recovery from the first-ever annual decline recorded in 1991. The airlines carried about 1.17 billion passengers and 17 million tonnes of freight. In 1992, the passenger load factor on total scheduled services (domestic and international) remained unchanged at 66 per cent, whereas the weight load factor decreased slightly from 59 to 58 per cent. Air freight rose by 5 per cent to 61.2 billion tonne-kilometres, and airmail traffic increased by 2 per cent. Overall passenger/freight/mail tonne-kilometres were up by 6 per cent and international tonne-kilometres by 11 per cent.

The ICAO Assembly, which meets triennially, held its twenty-ninth session (Montreal, Canada, 29 September–8 October 1992). It elected a new Council, reviewed the organization's activities during the previous three years, and adopted 34 resolutions dealing with budgetary matters, navigation surveillance and air traffic management systems, environmental protection, implementation of the 1991 Convention on the Marking of Plastic Explosives for the Purpose of Detection,[a] technical cooperation, the role of ICAO in preventing substance abuse in the workplace, and smoking restrictions on international flights. The Assembly endorsed a programme of activities to mark the fiftieth anniversary of ICAO in December 1994.

The ICAO Council held three regular sessions. In December, at the request of Japan, the Republic of Korea, the Russian Federation and the United States, the Council decided to complete the investigation which ICAO had initiated in 1983 regarding the shooting down of Korean Air Lines flight KAL-007 on 31 August 1983.

In 1992, membership of ICAO rose to 174 with the admission of Armenia, Azerbaijan, Croatia, Estonia, Kazakhstan, Latvia, Lithuania, the Republic of Moldova, Slovenia, Ukraine and Uzbekistan. (See Annex I for complete membership.)

Activities in 1992

Air navigation

ICAO's main efforts in air navigation continued to focus on updating and implementing its specifications and regional plans. The specifications consisted of International Standards and Recommended Practices contained in 18 technical annexes to the Chicago Convention and Procedures for Air Navigation Services. To promote their uniform application, ICAO made available guidance material consisting of new and revised technical manuals and circulars. Regional plans covered air navigation facilities and services required for international air navigation in the nine ICAO regions. ICAO's efforts in this area were supplemented by experts who advised States on the installation of new facilities and services and the operation of existing ones.

Seven air navigation meetings covering a wide range of subjects recommended changes to ICAO specifications. The Limited North Atlantic Regional Air Navigation Meeting (Cascais, Portugal, 3-18 November) was the first regional meeting held since the Council's adoption of a new ICAO system concept for communications, navigation, surveillance/air traffic management (CNS/ATM). The new technologies employed by CNS/ATM were to replace current air-traffic control methods over a 10- to 15-year period, and the meeting took a number of decisions governing that transition to a modern space-age environment. A second draft plan for the transition to CNS/ATM systems was produced by the third meeting of the Special Committee for the Monitoring and Coordination of Development and Transition Planning for the Future Air Navigation System (Montreal, 30 March–15 April 1992).

Project areas that received special attention during the year included accident investigation and prevention, aerodromes, airport and airspace congestion, bird strikes to aircraft, audiovisual training aids, aviation medicine, environmental matters, aircraft airworthiness, flight safety and human factors, security in aircraft design, meteorology, personnel licensing and training, rules of the air and air traffic services, search and rescue, and units of measurement.

[a]YUN 1991, p 982.

Air transport

ICAO continued its programmes of regulatory and economic studies, economic research, analysis and forecasting, air carrier tariffs, collection and publication of air transport statistics, airport and route facility management and the promotion of international air transport.

A World-wide Air Transport Colloquium (Montreal, 6-10 April) explored the future of international air transport regulation. A Facilitation Area Meeting (Nairobi, Kenya, 17-21 February) discussed a wide range of facilitation problems in Africa. The Statistics Panel (Montreal, 9-13 March) reviewed progress in implementing recommendations of the eighth (1989) session of the Statistics Division and provided advice on a number of substantive issues. The Technical Advisory Group on Machine-Readable Travel Documents (Montreal, 4-8 May) developed generic specifications for official identity documents for travel purposes, as well as a smaller size visa as an alternative to the full size machine-readable visa. The Pacific Area Traffic Forecasting Group (Bangkok, Thailand, 6-16 April) developed traffic forecasts for the Asia and Pacific region to assist in air navigation systems planning. Workshops were held during the year on forecasting and economic planning (Bangkok, March/April; Nairobi, May); airport and route facility management (Aruba, July; Cairo, Egypt, December); and statistics (Nairobi, May).

ICAO continued to cooperate closely with other international organizations, including the International Air Transport Association, the Airports Association Council International, the Customs Cooperation Council, the World Tourism Organization, the International Organization for Standardization, the International Maritime Organization and the Universal Postal Union. It also continued to provide secretariat services to three independent regional civil aviation bodies—the African Civil Aviation Commission, the European Civil Aviation Conference and the Latin American Civil Aviation Commission.

ICAO maintained its responsibilities for the administration of the Danish and Icelandic Joint Financing Agreements, to which 22 Governments were contracting parties in 1992. The two agreements, which were signed in 1956 and amended in 1982, concerned air navigation services for Greenland and the Faeroe Islands and in Iceland. The protocols of amendment were accepted by all 22 Governments parties to the Agreements.

Legal matters

The Legal Committee, at its twenty-eighth session (Montreal, 11-22 May), considered institutional and legal aspects of future air navigation systems and legal aspects of global air-ground communications. The ICAO Assembly in 1992 had adopted a resolution on the legal aspects of global air-ground communications.

In November, the ICAO Council approved the general work programme of the Legal Committee, including: consideration, with regard to global navigation satellite systems, of the establishment of a legal framework; action to expedite ratification of Montreal Protocols Nos. 3 and 4 of the Warsaw System; study of the instruments of the Warsaw System; liability rules which might be applicable to air traffic services providers as well as to other potentially liable parties; liability of air traffic control agencies; and the 1982 United Nations Convention on the Law of the Sea;[b] and the implications, if any, for the application of the Chicago Convention, its annexes and other international air-law instruments.

The following conventions and protocols on international air law concluded under ICAO auspices were ratified or adhered to by the additional member States listed below in 1992:

Convention on the International Recognition of Rights in Aircraft (Geneva, 1948)
Oman

Convention, Supplementary to the Warsaw Convention, for the Unification of Certain Rules Relating to International Carriage by Air Performed by a Person other than the Contracting Carrier (Guadalajara, 1961)
Burkina Faso

Convention on Offences and Certain other Acts Committed on Board Aircraft (Tokyo, 1963)
Djibouti, Slovenia

Convention for the Suppression of Unlawful Seizure of Aircraft (The Hague, 1970)
Comoros, Djibouti, Malta, Slovenia

Convention for the Suppression of Unlawful Acts against the Safety of Civil Aviation (Montreal, 1971)
Comoros, Djibouti, Malta, Slovenia

Protocol to Amend the Convention for Damage Caused by Foreign Aircraft to Third Parties on the Surface Signed at Rome on 7 October 1952 (Montreal, 1988)
Burkina Faso

Protocol for the Suppression of Unlawful Acts of Violence at Airports Serving International Civil Aviation, Supplementary to the Convention for the Suppression of Unlawful Acts against the Safety of Civil Aviation, done at Montreal on 23 September 1971 (Montreal, 1988)
Argentina, Fiji, Iraq, Ireland, Jordan, Malta, Oman, Slovenia

Convention on the Marking of Plastic Explosives for the Purpose of Detection (Montreal, 1991) (not in force)
Mexico, Norway, United Arab Emirates

[b]YUN 1982, p. 181.

Technical cooperation

During 1992, ICAO's technical cooperation programmes were financed by the United Nations Development Programme (UNDP), trust funds and the associate experts programme. Total 1992 expenditures for all technical cooperation programmes amounted to $44.3 million, compared with $45.8 million in 1991.

ICAO had resident missions in 48 countries during all or part of the year and gave assistance to 79 others in the form of fellowships and experts assigned to intercountry or subcontractual arrangements. It engaged 401 experts from 50 countries during all or part of 1992, of whom 280 were on assignment under UNDP and 121 on trust fund projects (including six under the associate experts programme). There were 136 experts in the field at the end of 1992. A total of 741 fellowships were awarded during the year, of which 703 were implemented.

Equipment purchases and subcontracts continued to represent a substantial portion of the technical cooperation programme. In addition to UNDP and trust fund projects, 66 Governments or organizations were registered with ICAO under its Civil Aviation Purchasing Services at the end of 1992. The total for equipment and subcontracts committed during 1992 was an aggregate of $13.73 million, compared with $9.81 million in 1991.

The following were recipients of UNDP country projects executed by ICAO.

Africa: Benin, Botswana, Burkina Faso, Burundi, Cameroon, Central African Republic, Chad, Ethiopia, Gambia, Guinea, Kenya, Lesotho, Malawi, Mali, Mauritania, Mauritius, Mozambique, Namibia, Niger, Nigeria, Rwanda, Sao Tome and Principe, Seychelles, Sierra Leone, Swaziland, Togo, Uganda, United Republic of Tanzania, Zaire, Zambia, Zimbabwe.

Americas: Argentina, Bahamas, Brazil, Chile, Dominican Republic, Ecuador, El Salvador, Honduras, Panama, Peru, Suriname, Uruguay.

Arab States: Egypt, Jordan, Kuwait, Lebanon, Oman, Saudi Arabia, Somalia, Sudan, United Arab Emirates, Yemen.

Asia/Pacific: Bangladesh, Bhutan, Cambodia, China, Democratic People's Republic of Korea, India, Indonesia, Lao People's Democratic Republic, Maldives, Micronesia, Mongolia, Myanmar, Nepal, Pakistan, Philippines, Republic of Korea, Sri Lanka, Tonga, Viet Nam.

Europe: Portugal, Romania, Turkey.

Also, UNDP intercountry and interregional projects were executed by ICAO in Africa, the Americas, the Arab States, and Asia and the Pacific.

Trust fund projects were executed by ICAO in Angola, Argentina, Bolivia, Brunei Darussalam, Côte d'Ivoire, Cyprus, Fiji, Guinea-Bissau, Indonesia, Jordan, Lebanon, Lesotho, the Libyan Arab Jamahiriya, Papua New Guinea, Peru, Sao Tome and Principe, Saudi Arabia, Sierra Leone, Singapore, Trinidad and Tobago, Venezuela, Viet Nam, Yemen and Zambia.

Secretariat

As at 31 December 1992, the total number of staff members employed in the ICAO secretariat stood at 762: 303 in the Professional and higher categories, drawn from 81 nationalities, and 459 in the General Service and related categories. Of the total, 194 persons were employed in regional offices (see Annex II for ICAO officers).

Budget

Appropriations for the 1992 financial year, including amounts carried over from previous years, totalled $48,073,000.

NOTE: For further details on ICAO, see *Annual Report of the Council—1992.*

Annex I. MEMBERSHIP OF THE INTERNATIONAL CIVIL AVIATION ORGANIZATION
(As at 31 December 1992)

Afghanistan, Albania, Algeria, Angola, Antigua and Barbuda, Argentina, Armenia, Australia, Austria, Azerbaijan, Bahamas, Bahrain, Bangladesh, Barbados, Belgium, Belize, Benin, Bhutan, Bolivia, Botswana, Brazil, Brunei Darussalam, Bulgaria, Burkina Faso, Burundi, Cambodia, Cameroon, Canada, Cape Verde, Central African Republic, Chad, Chile, China, Colombia, Comoros, Congo, Cook Islands, Costa Rica, Côte d'Ivoire, Croatia, Cuba, Cyprus, Czechoslovakia, Democratic People's Republic of Korea, Denmark, Djibouti, Dominican Republic, Ecuador, Egypt, El Salvador, Equatorial Guinea, Estonia, Ethiopia, Fiji, Finland, France, Gabon, Gambia, Germany, Ghana, Greece, Grenada, Guatemala, Guinea, Guinea-Bissau, Guyana, Haiti, Honduras, Hungary, Iceland, India, Indonesia, Iran, Iraq, Ireland, Israel, Italy, Jamaica, Japan, Jordan, Kazakhstan, Kenya, Kiribati, Kuwait, Lao People's Democratic Republic, Latvia, Lebanon, Lesotho, Liberia, Libyan Arab Jamahiriya, Lithuania, Luxembourg, Madagascar, Malawi, Malaysia, Maldives, Mali, Malta, Marshall Islands, Mauritania, Mauritius, Mexico, Micronesia, Monaco, Mongolia, Morocco, Mozambique, Myanmar, Namibia, Nauru, Nepal, Netherlands, New Zealand, Nicaragua, Niger, Nigeria, Norway, Oman, Pakistan, Panama, Papua New Guinea, Paraguay, Peru, Philippines, Poland, Portugal, Qatar, Republic of Korea, Republic of Moldova, Romania, Russian Federation, Rwanda, Saint Lucia, Saint Vincent and the Grenadines, San Marino, Sao Tome and Principe, Saudi Arabia, Senegal, Seychelles, Sierra Leone, Singapore, Slovenia, Solomon Islands, Somalia, South Africa, Spain, Sri Lanka, Sudan, Suriname, Swaziland, Sweden, Switzerland, Syrian Arab Republic, Thailand, Togo, Tonga, Trinidad and Tobago, Tunisia, Turkey, Uganda, Ukraine, United Arab Emirates, United Kingdom, United Republic of Tanzania, United States, Uruguay, Uzbekistan, Vanuatu, Venezuela, Viet Nam, Yemen, Yugoslavia,* Zaire, Zambia, Zimbabwe.

*Following Security Council and General Assembly action (see PART ONE, Chapter IV), the ICAO Assembly, on 25 September 1992, decided that Yugoslavia (Serbia and Montenegro) could not continue automatically the membership of the former Yugoslavia and that, therefore, it should apply for membership.

Annex II.   OFFICERS AND OFFICES OF THE INTERNATIONAL CIVIL AVIATION ORGANIZATION
(As at 31 December 1992)

ICAO COUNCIL

OFFICERS

President: Assad Kotaite (Lebanon).
First Vice-President: D. O. Eniojukan (Nigeria).
Second Vice-President: R. F. Cardoso (Argentina).
Third Vice-President: A. Kundycki (Belgium).
Secretary: Philippe Rochat (Switzerland).

MEMBERS

Argentina, Australia, Belgium, Brazil, Cameroon, Canada, China, Colombia, Czechoslovakia, Ecuador, Egypt, France, Germany, Iceland, India, Indonesia, Italy, Japan, Kenya, Lebanon, Mexico, Morocco, Nicaragua, Nigeria, Pakistan, Russian Federation, Saudi Arabia, Senegal, Spain, Trinidad and Tobago, United Kingdom, United Republic of Tanzania, United States.

PRINCIPAL OFFICERS OF THE SECRETARIAT

Secretary-General: Philippe Rochat.
Director, Bureau of Administration and Services: M. Pereyra.
Director, Air Transport Bureau: V. D. Zubkov.
Director, Air Navigation Bureau: W. Fromme.

Acting Director, Technical Cooperation Bureau: K. K. Wilde.
Director, Legal Bureau: M. Pourcelet.
Chief, External Relations Office: E. Faller.
Chief, Public Information Office: Hutton G. Archer.

HEADQUARTERS AND OTHER OFFICES

HEADQUARTERS
International Civil Aviation Organization
1000 Sherbrooke Street West, Suite 400
Montreal, Quebec, Canada H3A 2R2
   Cable address: ICAO MONTREAL
   Telephone: (1) (514) 285-8219
   Telex: 05-24513
   Facsimile: (1) (514) 288-4772

ICAO also maintained regional offices in Bangkok, Thailand; Cairo, Egypt; Dakar, Senegal; Lima, Peru; Mexico City; Nairobi, Kenya; and Neuilly-sur-Seine, France.

Chapter XI

Universal Postal Union (UPU)

The Universal Postal Union (UPU), established in 1874 at Berne, Switzerland, serves to exchange postal services among nations. It promotes the organization and improvement of postal services and development of international collaboration in this area. At the request of its members, it participates in various forms of postal technical assistance.

In 1992, UPU membership rose to 177, with the admission of Armenia, Croatia, Estonia, Kazakhstan, Latvia, Lithuania, Namibia, the Republic of Moldova and Slovenia. (See Annex I for complete membership.)

Activities of UPU organs

Universal Postal Congress

The Universal Postal Congress, the supreme legislative authority of UPU composed of all member States, normally meets every five years. The most recent Congress, the twentieth, took place at Washington, D.C., in 1989, and the twenty-first was scheduled to meet at Seoul, Republic of Korea, in 1994.

The work of the Congress consists mainly of examining and revising the acts of the Union based on proposals submitted by member States, the Executive Council or the Consultative Council for Postal Studies (CCPS), and of making administrative arrangements for UPU activities. The acts in force since 1 January 1991 were those of the 1989 Congress.

Executive Council

At its 1992 session (Berne, 22 April–13 May), the Executive Council—which carries out the work of UPU between Congresses—considered administrative matters and examined studies concerning international mail referred to it by the 1989 Congress.

The Council held a general discussion on postal administration profitability and reviewed the following issues: customs treatment of postal items; marking of goods that should not be exposed to radiographic control or opened; use of a symbol for literature for blind persons; express mail service (EMS); philatelic activities; pricing and remuneration of letter post; air conveyance and quality control; postal financial services; technical cooperation; and a number of items concerning parcel post, including land and sea rates and transit of parcels.

An extraordinary high-level meeting (Berne, 14 and 15 May), attended by senior postal officials representing 78 countries, discussed trends regarding the role, structure and operation of postal services, as well as the mission, structure and functioning of UPU.

Consultative Council for Postal Studies

The annual session of CCPS (Berne, 12-23 October) considered progress achieved in implementing the Washington General Action Plan, adopted at the 1989 Congress to serve as a master plan for the bodies of the Union and for postal administrations during 1990-1994.

During 1992, symposia were held on new product development, EMS, postal technology research and development, and human resources. The work of the Electronic Transmission Standards Group, aimed at establishing a world-wide postal electronic data interchange (EDI) system adapted to postal operational needs and accessible to all UPU members, focused on the distribution of an EDI business plan, creation of an EDI unit at UPU headquarters, development of standard-setting procedures, preparation of a message development guide, and consideration of legal issues concerning EDI.

Postal security matters continued to be dealt with by the Postal Security Action Group, which focused on establishing a postal security network. The *Airport Mail Security and Operations Manual*, adopted by CCPS, was to serve as a guide for postal administrations and airlines, as well as airport authorities. In 1992, the Executive Council made monitoring aviation/mail security-related issues a permanent UPU activity.

Activities of the Postal Development Action Group centred on promoting financial assistance for postal development and incorporating postal needs into national economic planning.

A new edition of the *Multilingual Vocabulary of the International Postal Service* was issued in 1992, and supplements were being developed on marketing of postal services and postal information technology and telematics.

International Bureau

Under the general supervision of the Executive Council, the International Bureau—the UPU secretariat—serves the postal administrations of member States as an organ for liaison, information and consultation.

During 1992, the Bureau collected, coordinated, published and disseminated international postal service information and, at the request of postal administrations, conducted inquiries and acted as a clearing-house for settling certain accounts between them. It continued its programme of studying the operation of the international postal network and monitoring the quality of international mail circulation, and carried out six service-quality tests, two for EMS and four for ordinary mail. A *Compendium of Delivery Standards* containing information from some 40 postal administrations was distributed in January and the Market Analysis Information System was launched. The Bureau fielded 11 missions to 29 countries to examine the state of regional postal services.

As at 31 December 1992, the number of permanent and temporary staff members employed by the UPU secretariat was 146, of whom 58 were in the Professional and higher categories (drawn from 42 countries) and 88 in the General Service category. Also, as French remained the sole official UPU language, 15 officials were employed in the Arabic, English, Portuguese, Russian and Spanish translation services.

Technical cooperation

In 1992, technical cooperation provided by UPU was financed for the most part by the United Nations Development Programme (UNDP), with UNDP/UPU project expenditures amounting to $2.2 million. Assistance was also provided through the UPU Special Fund (voluntary contributions in cash and kind from member States) and the regular budget for a total of $1.6 million. Multi-year projects financed by UPU and in execution numbered 37; 52 experts and consultants undertook missions during the year and 230 fellowships were awarded.

In addition, bilateral and multilateral assistance was provided to national postal administrations and under special programmes in such areas as the Transport and Communications Decades for Asia and the Pacific and in Africa; technical cooperation among developing countries; the action programme for the least developed countries; and cooperation in combating the illicit transmission of narcotics by post, including the third seminar for training postal employees in drug-detection techniques (Rufisque, Senegal, 18-21 March). Fellowships and training courses were also offered by several countries.

The six UPU regional advisers appointed in 1991 (two in Africa, one in Latin America and the Caribbean, two in Asia and the Pacific and one in the Arab countries) conducted programming and follow-up missions in 60 countries in support of governmental authorities and UNDP resident representatives. Thirty-seven technical assistance country projects were proposed, revised or approved for financing. UNDP also approved a project on management of telecommunications and postal services in Europe and a sectoral support project for a number of African, Arab, Asian, Latin American and European countries.

Budget

Under UPU's self-financing system, contributions are payable in advance by member States based on the following year's budget. At its 1991 session, the Executive Council approved the 1992 budget of 27,622,265 Swiss francs, to be financed by contributions from member States. In 1992, the Council approved the 1993 budget at a total of SwF 29,087,690, also to be financed by member States.

NOTE: For details of UPU activities, see *Report on the Work of the Union, 1992*, published by UPU.

Annex I.   MEMBERSHIP OF THE UNIVERSAL POSTAL UNION

(As at 31 December 1992)

Afghanistan, Albania, Algeria, Angola, Argentina, Armenia, Australia, Austria, Bahamas, Bahrain, Bangladesh, Barbados, Belarus, Belgium, Belize, Benin, Bhutan, Bolivia, Botswana, Brazil, Brunei Darussalam, Bulgaria, Burkina Faso, Burundi, Cambodia, Cameroon, Canada, Cape Verde, Central African Republic, Chad, Chile, China, Colombia, Comoros, Congo, Costa Rica, Côte d'Ivoire, Croatia, Cuba, Cyprus, Czechoslovakia, Democratic People's Republic of Korea, Denmark, Djibouti, Dominica, Dominican Republic, Ecuador, Egypt, El Salvador, Equatorial Guinea, Estonia, Ethiopia, Fiji, Finland, France, Gabon, Gambia, Germany, Ghana, Greece, Grenada, Guatemala, Guinea, Guinea-Bissau, Guyana, Haiti, Honduras, Hungary, Iceland, India, Indonesia, Iran, Iraq, Ireland, Israel, Italy, Jamaica, Japan, Jordan, Kazakhstan, Kenya, Kiribati, Kuwait, Lao People's Democratic Republic, Latvia, Lebanon, Lesotho, Liberia, Libyan Arab Jamahiriya, Liechtenstein, Lithuania, Luxembourg, Madagascar, Malawi, Malaysia, Maldives, Mali, Malta, Mauritania, Mauritius, Mexico, Monaco, Mongolia, Morocco, Mozambique, Myanmar, Namibia, Nauru, Nepal, Netherlands, Netherlands Antilles and Aruba, New Zealand, Nicaragua, Niger, Nigeria, Norway, Oman, Pakistan, Panama, Papua New Guinea, Paraguay, Peru, Philippines, Poland, Portugal, Qatar, Republic of Korea, Republic of Moldova, Romania, Russian Federation, Rwanda, Saint Kitts and Nevis, Saint Lucia, Saint Vincent and the Grenadines, Samoa, San Marino, Sao Tome and Principe, Saudi Arabia, Senegal, Seychelles, Sierra Leone, Singapore, Slovenia, Solomon Islands, Somalia, Spain, Sri Lanka, Sudan, Suriname, Swaziland, Sweden, Switzerland, Syrian Arab Republic, Thailand, Togo, Tonga, Trinidad and Tobago, Tunisia, Turkey, Tuvalu, Uganda, Ukraine, United Arab Emirates, United Kingdom, United Kingdom Overseas Territories, United Republic of Tanzania, United States, Uruguay, Vanuatu, Vatican City State, Venezuela, Viet Nam, Yemen, Yugoslavia, Zaire, Zambia, Zimbabwe.

Annex II.   ORGANS, OFFICERS AND OFFICE OF THE UNIVERSAL POSTAL UNION
(As at 31 December 1992)

EXECUTIVE COUNCIL
(Elected to hold office until the twenty-first (1994) Universal Postal Congress)

Chairman: United States.
Vice-Chairmen: Cameroon, China, Hungary, Italy.
Secretary-General: Adwaldo Cardoso Botto de Barros, Director-General of the International Bureau.

Members: Argentina, Australia, Bahamas, Belgium, Benin, Brazil, Cameroon, Canada, China, Colombia, Costa Rica, Cuba, Ethiopia, Germany, Hungary, Indonesia, Italy, Japan, Kenya, Kuwait, Lebanon, Mongolia, Morocco, New Zealand, Nigeria, Pakistan, Poland, Republic of Korea, Sweden, Switzerland, Togo, Tunisia, United Arab Emirates, United Kingdom, United Republic of Tanzania, United States, Venezuela, Yugoslavia, Zambia, Zimbabwe.

CONSULTATIVE COUNCIL FOR POSTAL STUDIES
(Elected to hold office until the twenty-first (1994) Universal Postal Congress)

Chairman: Russian Federation.
Vice-Chairman: Canada.
Secretary-General: Adwaldo Cardoso Botto de Barros, Director-General of the International Bureau.

Members: Algeria, Argentina, Australia, Austria, Belgium, Brazil, Canada, China, Cuba, Denmark, Egypt, France, Germany, Greece, India, Indonesia, Iraq, Ireland, Italy, Japan, Jordan, Kenya, Mexico, Morocco, Netherlands, New Zealand, Pakistan, Russian Federation, Saudi Arabia, Spain, Switzerland, Thailand, Tunisia, United Kingdom, United States.

INTERNATIONAL BUREAU

SENIOR OFFICERS
Director-General: Adwaldo Cardoso Botto de Barros.
Deputy Director-General: Jaime Ascandoni.
Assistant Directors-General: El Mostafa Gharbi, Musarapakkam S. Raman, Moussibahou Mazou.

HEADQUARTERS
Universal Postal Union
Weltpoststrasse 4
Berne, Switzerland
  Postal address: Union postale universelle
                     Case postale
                     3000 Berne 15, Switzerland
  Cable address: UPU BERNE
  Telephone: (41) (31) 350-3111
  Telex: 912761 UPU CH
  Facsimile: (41) (31) 43 22 10

Chapter XII

International Telecommunication Union (ITU)

In 1992, the Administrative Council of the International Telecommunication Union (ITU), at its forty-seventh session (Geneva, 21 June–9 July; 20 December), reviewed financial and administrative matters and provisionally approved a cooperation agreement between ITU and the United Nations Educational, Scientific and Cultural Organization The Council decided to convene a World Radiocommunication Conference in 1993 at Geneva.

The additional Plenipotentiary Conference (Geneva, 7-22 December) revised the Constitution and Convention adopted at the 1989 Plenipotentiary Conference, providing for a new ITU structure, as reflected in the following basic instruments: the Plenipotentiary Conference, the Council, world conferences on international telecommunications, the radiocommunication sector, the telecommunication standardization sector, the telecommunication development sector and the General Secretariat. It decided to implement the new structure and working methods provisionally as from 1 March 1993, pending the entry into force of the Constitution and Convention on 1 July 1994. As a result of the restructuring, the International Radio Consultative Committee (CCIR), the International Telegraph and Telephone Consultative Committee (CCITT) and the International Frequency Registration Board (IFRB) would cease to exist.

In 1992, ITU membership rose to 174 with the admission of Armenia, Azerbaijan, Bosnia and Herzegovina, Croatia, Estonia, the Republic of Moldova, Slovenia and Uzbekistan. (See Annex I for complete membership.)

World Administrative Radio Conference

The World Administrative Radio Conference for dealing with frequency allocations in certain parts of the spectrum (WARC-92) (Málaga-Torremolinos, Spain, 3 February–3 March) adopted a partial revision of the radio regulations and appendices thereto and revised resolutions and recommendations of previous WARCs. It adopted new resolutions and recommendations, dealing with, *inter alia*, the implementation of changes in frequency allocations between 5,900 and 19,020 kilohertz; assistance to developing countries to facilitate the implementation of changes in frequency band allocations necessitating the transfer of existing assignments; establishment of stand-

ards for operating low-orbit satellite systems; allocation of frequencies to the fixed-satellite service in the band 13.75 to 14 gigahertz; implementation of future public land mobile telecommunication systems; further work by CCIR concerning the broadcasting-satellite service (sound); terrestrial VHF (very high frequency) digital sound broadcasting; studies of the maximum permitted levels of spurious emissions; and multiservice satellite networks using the geostationary-satellite orbit.

International consultative committees

During 1992, CCIR study group meetings made progress on recommendations dealing with spectrum management techniques; fixed-satellite service; radiowave propagation in non-ionized and ionized media; science services; mobile, radio-determination, amateur and related satellite services; fixed service; broadcasting service (sound and television); and television transmission. In June, CCIR's Ad Hoc Group for Strategic Review and Planning considered the adaptation and continuity of the work of study groups under the new ITU radiocommunication sector and the CCIR questions to be studied by the radiocommunication sector, the standardization sector, or jointly. CCIR held an information meeting (Acapulco, Mexico, April) and convened an information seminar on administrative and operational regulatory matters for Estonia, Latvia and Lithuania (July).

CCITT completed its last year of the 1989-1992 study period, with study groups focusing on network operation; transmission performance of telephone networks and terminals; tariff and accounting principles; protection against electromagnetic effects; switching and signalling; data communications networks; terminals for telematics services; telegraph networks and telegraph terminal equipment; languages for telecommunications applications; data transmission over the telephone network; and maintenance.

At the end of 1992, 225 private companies and 37 international organizations were registered participants in CCITT.

International Frequency Registration Board

Major activities of IFRB during 1992 included follow-up action on decisions of: WARC-88 on the use of the geostationary-satellite orbit and on the planning of space services utilizing it; and the second (1989) session of the Regional Administrative Radio Conference for the planning of VHF/UHF (very high frequency/ultra high frequency) television broadcasting in the African broadcasting area and neighbouring countries. IFRB actively prepared for and participated in WARC-92. Other activities included examination and recording in the Master International Frequency Register of 72,595 frequency assignment notices received from member countries. At the end of 1992, the Register contained particulars of 1,158,643 assignments representing 5,467,616 records. IFRB studied 28 requests for special assistance for terrestrial and space radiocommunication services, and completed 26 requests for frequency selection for stations in the fixed service. It considered 37 cases of harmful interference and issued two summaries of monitoring information.

The fifteenth regular IFRB seminar on frequency management (Geneva, 5-9 October) focused on space radiocommunications and organized a special session on international satellite organizations. IFRB conducted national seminars on space matters, including regulatory and technical aspects, in Iran (20-27 November), the Republic of Korea (12-15 May) and Thailand (15-17 July), and provided technical assistance to two multilateral planning meetings (Geneva, 1-5 June and 12-16 October) for the coordination of frequency assignments to the ARABSAT-2A and ARABSAT-2B satellite networks.

Technical cooperation

In 1992, under various ITU technical cooperation programmes in developing countries, 318 experts were recruited and 1,313 fellowships were awarded. Equipment delivered during the year was valued at $4.5 million, and funds from a variety of sources were allocated to 167 projects.

In Africa, the ITU Telecommunication Development Bureau (BDT) granted technical assistance to: Benin, to purchase teaching material; Burundi, for telecommunication training; Cape Verde, for training telecommunication staff; the Congo, for telecommunication development; Lesotho, to prepare a telecommunication master plan and improve frequency management; Mauritania, to computerize frequency management; and the United Republic of Tanzania, to study the development of national broadcasting development. The second Conference of African Ministers of Telecommunications (Abidjan, Côte d'Ivoire, 25-27 May) adopted a convention and an operational agreement setting up a regional African satellite communication organization with headquarters at Abidjan. BDT convened the first African information and telecommunication policy study group

(Nairobi, Kenya). A seminar was organized for French-speaking countries (Cotonou, Benin) to train 34 national coordinators on the use of the BDT planning guide related to the development of maritime radiocommunications. A similar workshop was organized for Portugese-speaking countries (Bissau, Guinea-Bissau). Two regional meetings discussed new human resources development and management strategies and training approaches (Dakar, Senegal, May; Conakry, Guinea, October).

Projects in the Americas, mostly financed by trust funds, provided assistance to Bolivia, to apply computer techniques to frequency management; Brazil, to research and develop the design of telecommunication equipment and modernize its telecommunication system; Colombia, to implement an advanced training programme; Costa Rica, to develop a community centre system and a telecommunications software development centre; the Dominican Republic, for regulatory aspects; El Salvador, to strengthen organizations; Honduras, to improve institutional management; Mexico, to study the possibilities of developing telecommunication, micro-electronics and computer industries; Nicaragua, to strengthen its Posts and Telecommunications Institute; Panama, to review and improve national telecommunication legislation and define a new tariff structure; Paraguay, to prepare a first model plan for developing a telecommunications master plan; and Peru, to design, construct and install a digital telephone exchange. The American Regional Telecommunication Development Conference (Acapulco, 31 March–4 April) took decisions on establishing a regional telecommunication policy mechanism, a regional programme for rural areas and low-income strata and a special programme to develop telecommunications in the Caribbean; creating a favourable climate for investments; improving spectrum utilization and human resources development and management; and the full interconnectivity of networks. The Conference adopted the Acapulco Declaration containing goals to be achieved by the countries of the region, bearing in mind the role of telecommunications in socioeconomic development.

In Asia and the Pacific, ITU focused on introducing new technologies, modernizing services and computer-aided management techniques. Activities included workshops on digital-switching hardware maintenance and frequency management; courses on telecommunications software application and maintenance, computer networking and office automation; and technical training and advisory assistance in sound and television broadcasting, hosted by the Asia Pacific Broadcasting Union. Projects to strengthen national telecommunication technical and administrative services, funded primarily through the United Nations Development Programme (UNDP), were being implemented in Afghanistan, to prepare a telecommunication rehabilitation plan; Bhutan, to provide expertise and fellowship training; the Democratic People's Republic of Korea, to assist in digital switching and optical-fibre transmission; India, to refurbish stored material and introduce optical-disc storage facilities; Iran, to train local engineers in rural telecommunications; the Lao People's Democratic Republic, to expand and manage the telecommunication network, facilitate equipment procurement and manage a training subcontract with the Telephone Organization of Thailand; Nepal, for quality assurance; Sri Lanka, for telecommunication management development and developing national capabilities to carry out regulatory functions; and Viet Nam, for telecommuncations development and a multi-agency project for a typhoon-proof pilot radio trunk system for essential telecommunication and rehabilitation of outside plant equipment. Assistance in developing human resources for telecommunications was provided to Bhutan, India, Indonesia and Pakistan. At the regional level, seven seminars were held on telecommunication management topics.

Support to develop regional telecommunication in the Arab States was provided mainly under the Modern Arab Telecommunication Development (MODARABTEL) project financed by UNDP. ITU also provided support to strengthen national technical and administrative services through UNDP-financed projects in the Libyan Arab Jamahiriya, to improve telecommunication maintenance and operations and prepare a master plan for telecommunication development; Saudi Arabia, for frequency management and international relations, as well as satellite communications and high-power broadcasting; the Sudan, to prepare a draft telecommunication development plan; and Yemen, to install a radio frequency-monitoring system, inspection services and medium-wave radio coverage. Assistance in developing human resources for telecommunications included training projects in Algeria, Djibouti, Lebanon and Morocco. The Regional Telecommunication Development Conference for the Arab States (Cairo, Egypt, 25-29 October) considered issues concerning policy and investment, network harmonization, and human resources development and management,

Activities carried out by the ITU Focal Point for Europe and the Commonwealth of Independent States, nominated as from 1 October 1992, included projects for strengthening national technical and administrative services in Czechoslovakia and Poland with UNDP preparatory assistance funding. A World Bank–financed project on human resources management and development was launched in Hungary, and a project document was elaborated for implementing new business-oriented telecommunication services in Central and Eastern Europe.

Other technical cooperation activities focused on technology-based training (TBT) in Colombia, Costa Rica, Fiji, India, Jordan and Uruguay, and regional TBT workshops for the Arab States (Jordan) and South Pacific islands (Fiji). Activities under the special programme for the least developed countries (LDCs) included a workshop on telecommunications management for Asian and Pacific LDCs (Singapore, November); a mission to the Lao People's Democratic Republic on outside plant maintenance; and a study on the review of tariff situations in LDCs and the need for a new approach.

Secretariat

As at 31 December 1992, 729 officials (excluding staff on short-term contracts and project personnel) were employed by ITU either at its headquarters or in the field. Of these, nine were elected officials, 581 had permanent contracts and 139 had fixed-term contracts; 71 nationalities were represented in posts subject to geographical distribution.

Budget

The adjusted budget for 1992 totalled SwF 139,908,500 or $97,158,680 (based on an exchange rate as at 31 December 1992 of $US 1.00 = SwF 1.44). The actual income, however, amounted to SwF 142,340,288 ($98,847,422), which was equal to regular budget expenditures for the year. In addition, SwF 6,988,500 ($4,853,125) was programmed for technical cooperation special accounts, and SwF 7,714,700 ($5,357,430) for the supplementary publications budget.

In 1992, the Administrative Council adopted a budget for 1993 totalling SwF 146,226,000, including SwF 132,610,000 for the regular budget, SwF 5,101,000 for the technical cooperation special accounts and SwF 8,515,000 for the supplementary publications budget.

NOTE: For further information on ITU activities, see *Report on the Activities of the International Telecommunication Union in 1992*, published by ITU.

Annex I.   MEMBERSHIP OF THE INTERNATIONAL TELECOMMUNICATION UNION
(As at 31 December 1992)

Afghanistan, Albania, Algeria, Angola, Antigua and Barbuda, Argentina, Armenia, Australia, Austria, Azerbaijan, Bahamas, Bahrain, Bangladesh, Barbados, Belarus, Belgium, Belize, Benin, Bhutan, Bolivia, Bosnia and Herzegovina, Botswana, Brazil, Brunei Darussalam, Bulgaria, Burkina Faso, Burundi, Cambodia, Cameroon, Canada, Cape Verde, Central African Republic, Chad, Chile, China, Colombia, Comoros, Congo, Costa Rica, Côte d'Ivoire, Croatia, Cuba, Cyprus, Czechoslovakia, Democratic People's Republic of Korea, Denmark, Djibouti, Dominican Republic, Ecuador, Egypt, El Salvador, Equatorial Guinea, Estonia, Ethiopia, Fiji, Finland, France, Gabon, Gambia, Germany, Ghana, Greece, Grenada, Guatemala, Guinea, Guinea-Bissau, Guyana, Haiti, Honduras, Hungary, Iceland, India, Indonesia, Iran, Iraq, Ireland, Israel, Italy, Jamaica, Japan, Jordan, Kenya, Kiribati, Kuwait, Lao People's Democratic Republic, Latvia, Lebanon, Lesotho, Liberia, Libyan Arab Jamahiriya, Liechtenstein, Lithuania, Luxembourg, Madagascar, Malawi, Malaysia, Maldives, Mali, Malta, Mauritania, Mauritius, Mexico, Monaco, Mongolia, Morocco, Mozambique, Myanmar, Namibia, Nauru, Nepal, Netherlands, New Zealand, Nicaragua, Niger, Nigeria, Norway, Oman, Pakistan, Panama, Papua New Guinea, Paraguay, Peru, Philippines, Poland, Portugal, Qatar, Republic of Korea, Republic of Moldova, Romania, Russian Federation, Rwanda, Saint Vincent and the Grenadines, Samoa, San Marino, Sao Tome and Principe, Saudi Arabia, Senegal, Sierra Leone, Singapore, Slovenia, Solomon Islands, Somalia, South Africa, Spain, Sri Lanka, Sudan, Suriname, Swaziland, Sweden, Switzerland, Syrian Arab Republic, Thailand, Togo, Tonga, Trinidad and Tobago, Tunisia, Turkey, Uganda, Ukraine, United Arab Emirates, United Kingdom, United Republic of Tanzania, United States, Uruguay, Uzbekistan, Vanuatu, Vatican City State, Venezuela, Viet Nam, Yemen, Yugoslavia, Zaire, Zambia, Zimbabwe.

ANNEX II. OFFICERS AND OFFICE OF THE INTERNATIONAL TELECOMMUNCATION UNION

ADMINISTRATIVE COUNCIL, INTERNATIONAL FREQUENCY REGISTRATION BOARD AND PRINCIPAL OFFICERS

PRINCIPAL OFFICERS OF THE UNION
Secretary-General: Pekka Tarjanne (Finland).
Deputy Secretary-General: Jean Jipguep (Cameroon).

ITU ADMINISTRATIVE COUNCIL
Algeria, Argentina, Australia, Benin, Brazil, Bulgaria, Burkina Faso, Cameroon, Canada, Cape Verde, China, Colombia, Cuba, Czechoslovakia, Egypt, France, Germany, Greece, India, Indonesia, Italy, Jamaica, Japan, Kenya, Kuwait, Malaysia, Mali, Mexico, Morocco, Nigeria, Pakistan, Philippines, Republic of Korea, Romania, Russian Federation, Saudi Arabia, Senegal, Spain, Sweden, Switzerland, Thailand, United Republic of Tanzania, United States.

INTERNATIONAL FREQUENCY REGISTRATION BOARD
Chairman: William H. Bellchambers (United Kingdom).
Vice-Chairman: M. Miura (Japan).
Members: Gary C. Brooks (Canada), Mohamed Harbi (Algeria), Vladimir V. Koslov (Russian Federation).

OFFICERS OF THE INTERNATIONAL CONSULTATIVE COMMITTEES
Director, International Radio Consultative Committee (CCIR):Richard C. Kirby (United States).
Director, International Telegraph and Telephone Consultative Committee (CCITT): Theodor Irmer (Germany).

HEADQUARTERS
International Telecommunication Union
Place des Nations
CH-1211 Geneva 20, Switzerland
Cable address: ITU GENEVE
Telephone: (41) (22) 730-5111
Telex: 421000 UIT CH
Facsimile: (41) (22) 733-7256 (Group 2/3)
E-Mail addresses: X.400   C = CH, A = ARCOM,
                              P = ITU, S = ITUMAIL
                      Internet: itumail @ itu.ch

Chapter XIII

World Meteorological Organization (WMO)

In 1992, the World Meteorological Organization (WMO) continued to implement its activities in accordance with the programmes and budget for the period 1992-1995, adopted in 1991 by the World Meteorological Congress, which meets at least once every four years.

The 36-member Executive Council meets annually to supervise the implementation of programmes and regulations. At its forty-fourth session (Geneva, 22 June–4 July 1992), the Council agreed that in the fourth WMO long-term plan (1996-2005) priority should be given to meteorological and hydrological activities in support of sustainable development, the implementation of the Framework Convention on Climate Change, signed in 1992, and a future international convention on desertification.

WMO's involvement in sectoral areas of sustainable development, identified by the United Nations Conference on Environment and Development (UNCED) (see PART THREE, Chapter VIII), related mainly to protection of the atmosphere, oceans and freshwater resources, and combating drought and desertification.

During the year, six new States—Armenia, Croatia, Estonia, Latvia, Lithuania and Slovenia—acceded to the WMO Convention, bringing WMO membership to 161 States and 5 Territories as at 31 December 1992. (See Annex I for complete membership.)

World Weather Watch

The World Weather Watch (WWW), the basic programme of WMO, continued to provide in 1992 global observational data and processed information required by members for operational and research purposes. Its essential elements were the Global Observing System (GOS), whereby observational data were obtained; the Global Telecommunication System, which offered telecommunication facilities for the rapid collection, exchange and distribution of observational data and processed information; and the Global Data-Processing System, which provided for the processing, storage and retrieval of observational data and made available processed information. The Commission for Basic Systems, which had responsibility for the planning, organization and development of WWW, reviewed each of those elements and implementation support activities at its tenth session (Geneva, 2-13 November).

World Weather Watch implementation

The Joint Scientific and Technical Committee Task Group on Atmospheric Processes (Geneva, 29 September–2 October) met to consider the interaction between GOS and the Global Climate Observing System (GCOS), established in 1991 by the WMO Congress. The Group recognized the need to improve the observational accuracy, representativeness and coverage of GCOS and recommended the establishment of a global baseline reference network of 100 to 150 stations with high-quality surface and upper-air observations.

In 1992, changes and improvements were introduced to the GOS space-based component. Several countries set up satellite-based telecommunication systems at the national or multinational level, and the plan for a new regional meteorological telecommunication network in North and Central America entered its implementation phase. The Commission for Basic Systems recommended that five new Regional Specialized Meteorological Centres (RSMCs) be designated: four on transport model products for environmental emergency response (Bracknell, England; Montreal, Canada; Toulouse, France; Washington, D.C.); and one on tropical cyclones in the Indian Ocean (Saint Denis, Réunion). It expanded WWW data-management activities to incorporate requirements of other WMO-related programmes such as GCOS, and agreed on guidelines for computer projects for automating key WWW facilities. The Commission examined the final report on the implementation of phase I of the operational WWW systems evaluation in Africa.

The Aircraft-to-Satellite Data Relay (ASDAR) programme continued to grow during the year. At the end of 1992, eight of the original 13 systems were in use, and a contract had been placed for the delivery of an additional 10 units in 1993. Efforts were also being made to place ASDAR systems on aircraft of developing countries. The coordinating group for the Composite Observing System for the North Atlantic held its third session (Geneva, 25-27 August). Among other activities were expert meetings on code matters and emergency response data formats (Geneva, 15-19 June) and on the implementation and operation of satellite-based telecommunications systems (Miami, Florida, United States, 13-25 October).

Instruments and methods of observation

During the year, WMO provided forums for technology transfer and exchange of experience between developing and developed countries in meteorological instrumentation and methods of observation. A technical conference on instruments and methods of observation (Vienna, May) considered issues related to systems and facilities, upper-air measurements, intercomparisons and performance tests, automation of visual observations, calibration procedures and facilities, and accuracy of measurements.

Tropical cyclones

The Economic and Social Commission for Asia and the Pacific (ESCAP)/WMO Typhoon Committee and the WMO/ESCAP Panel on Tropical Cyclones for the Bay of Bengal and the Arabian Sea, at their first joint session (Pattaya, Thailand, 18-27 February), decided to cooperate in methods and technical procedures to improve the accuracy of forecasts, timeliness of warnings, and disaster prevention and preparedness procedures. An interregional seminar on tropical cyclone forecasting and research (Nanjing, China, 27 October–7 November) dealt with techniques in forecasting cyclone motion and intensity and research initiatives arising from a 1990 experiment on typhoon recurvature and unusual movement in the western North Pacific. A technical coordination meeting on operational forecasting and dissemination of results by RSMCs (Tokyo, 16-21 December) focused on improving cooperation and coordination among the Tropical Cyclone Programme regional bodies.

Other activities included a regional workshop on hurricane forecasting and warning (Miami, 6-17 April), the fourteenth session of the Hurricane Committee for North and Central America (Belize City, Belize, 28 April-5 May); the fourth session of the Tropical Cyclone Committee for the South Pacific and South-East Indian Ocean (Nouméa, New Caledonia, 6-12 October), and the twenty-fifth session of the ESCAP/WMO Typhoon Committee (Zhuhai, China, 8-14 December).

Environmental emergencies

In the context of the International Decade for Natural Disaster Reduction (1990-1999), which was proclaimed by the General Assembly in 1989[a] (see PART THREE, Chapter III), WMO organized in June 1992 an expert mission to Kenya, Madagascar, Mauritius, Réunion and Seychelles to assist in implementing a project on enhancing meteorological observational and telecommunication networks to improve data handling and processing as well as monitoring and forecasting of tropical cyclones. In March, a meeting of experts and representatives of international organizations developed plans to implement a comprehensive risk assessment project through a series of pilot projects in developing countries. WMO was also involved in the System for Technology Exchange for Natural Disasters.

In 1992, timely warnings issued by national meteorological services and RSMCs helped reduce the loss of life from Hurricane Andrew in the Bahamas and southern parts of the United States as well as from typhoons and cyclone activity in the South Pacific, western North Pacific and Indian Oceans.

World Climate Programme

The World Climate Programme (WCP) consisted of the World Climate Data and Monitoring Programme (WCDMP), the World Climate Applications and Services Programme (WCASP), the World Climate Impact Assessment and Response Strategies Programme (WCIRP) and the World Climate Research Programme (WCRP). The WCP Coordinating Committee, at its first session (Geneva, 4 and 5 May), reviewed the WCP coordination mechanisms, discussed the relationship between WCP and related activities and programmes, and made recommendations concerning preparations for and the programme of a 1993 intergovernmental meeting on WCP. Activities of WCP were also reviewed at the second session of the Advisory Committee on Climate Applications and Data (Geneva, 16 and 17 November).

At the end of the year, climate computing (CLICOM) systems were operational in 104 countries, and funds were secured for CLICOM projects in 10 others. New CLICOM software was released in 1992. Activities under the climate system monitoring (CSM) project included publication of the monthly *CSM Bulletin* and *The Global Climate System*, a biennial review covering late 1988 to May 1991.

Activities within WCASP focused on promoting sustainable development using climate as a resource, as well as on food production and water-resource management in cooperation with the Agricultural and the Hydrology and Water Resources Programmes. The regional WMO/United Nations Development Programme (UNDP) project on meteorological information for development of renewable energy, involving many Eastern European and some Mediterranean countries, was successfully concluded, and a plan of action was proposed to follow up on the experience gained. Other areas of WMO involvement related to climate and tourism, urban climatology, and the Climate Applications Referral System as a component complementary to CLICOM.

[a]GA res. 44/236, 22 Dec. 1989.

Main activities under WCIRP, for which the United Nations Environment Programme (UNEP) was responsible, related to greenhouse gases and climate change, methodology of climate impact assessment, coordination of activities in studies of climate impacts and related response strategies, and monitoring climate change and impacts. Support was provided to the Intergovernmental Panel on Climate Change, special monitoring programmes and country studies on methodologies for compiling inventories of sources and sinks of greenhouse gases and on the cost of greenhouse gas abatement.

WCRP, undertaken jointly by WMO and the International Council of Scientific Unions (ICSU), organized a range of research activities directed at understanding the basic physical processes determining the Earth's climate, including interactions between the different components of the climate system. The Baseline Surface Radiation Network was being implemented to provide precise and frequent measurements of short- and long-wave surface radiation fluxes at selected sites in contrasting climatic zones. A workshop on global observations, analyses and simulation of precipitation (Washington, D.C., 27-30 October) was held under the global precipitation climatology project.

The tropical ocean and global atmosphere programme achieved significant skill in predicting transient climate anomalies linked to El Niño/Southern Oscillation phenomena up to one year in advance. Its associated coupled ocean-atmosphere response experiment began collecting atmospheric and oceanic observations in the western Pacific warm pool region for a four-month intensive observing period. The atmospheric model intercomparison project continued in 1992, and a study of stratospheric processes and their role in climate was launched. Meetings held under WCRP included the fourth session of the Scientific Steering Group for the global energy and water cycle experiment (Tokyo, 27-31 January); the first session of its Cloud System Study Science Panel (Reading, England, 14 and 15 December); the thirteenth session of the Joint Scientific Committee for WCRP (Victoria, Canada, 23-28 March); and meetings of steering groups on global climate modelling (Hamburg, Germany, 14-16 September) and on an arctic climate system study (Seattle, Washington, United States, 2-6 November).

Atmospheric research and environment

The Atmospheric Research and Environment Programme (AREP), aimed at coordinating and fostering research on the structure and composition of the atmosphere, physics of weather processes and weather forecasting, had four major components: the Global Atmosphere Watch (GAW), and programmes on weather prediction research, tropical meteorology research, and the physics and chemistry of clouds and weather modification research.

In the context of GAW, the Background Air Pollution Monitoring Network (BAPMoN) was expanded with the addition of two new and one improved regional station in Egypt, Iran and Pakistan. Agreements were also signed to establish global stations in Algeria, Argentina, Brazil, China and Indonesia. A WMO/UNEP consultation on BAPMoN operations was held (Toronto, Canada, 14-17 December). Background air pollution was also the subject of an international meeting on geophysics and the environment (Rome, Italy, 16-18 June), while the possible atmospheric impact of the Kuwait oil fires was assessed at a WMO meeting of experts (Geneva, 25-29 May).

Ozone-related activities were intensified and included a meeting of experts on ozone measurements by Brewer Instruments (1-6 June), an international workshop on total ozone data re-evaluation (8-10 June) (both at Charlottesville, Virginia, United States), and a meeting on a study of ozone-climate-chemistry interaction (Oslo, Norway, 19-21 August). The European Arctic stratospheric ozone experiment, completed in March, was repeated for the winter 1992/93.

The CAS Group of Rapporteurs on Tropical Meteorology Research (first session, Monterey, California, United States, 21-26 September) redefined existing projects of the tropical meteorology research programme and discussed future strategies. It accorded high priority to the ICSU/WMO demonstration project on tropical cyclone disasters. A symposium on such disasters (Beijing, China, 12-16 October) recommended the development of an automatic aircraft system, at an estimated cost of $1 million, as a cost-effective way of acquiring operational data. A regional workshop (Kuala Lumpur, Malaysia, 5-10 October) focused on the Asian winter monsoon and the use of numerical weather-prediction products.

In the field of physics and chemistry of clouds and weather modification research, an updated WMO statement on the status of weather modification and revised guidelines for advice and assistance related to the planning of weather modification activities were approved by the WMO Executive Council. The *1990 Register of National Weather Modification Projects* was published; meetings included a third international cloud-modelling workshop and a workshop on cloud microphysics and application to global change (Toronto, 10-14 August), and the Eleventh International Cloud Physics Conference (Montreal, Canada, 17-21 August).

Applications of meteorology

Agricultural meteorology

Issues relating to desertification and drought received particular attention at a workshop on the interrelationship between the Global Environment Facility and desertification, land degradation and deforestation (Nairobi, Kenya, October). Among other workshops and seminars organized were a symposium/workshop on meteorology and plant protection, which demonstrated the use of meteorological data in crop protection activities (Asunción, Paraguay, 1-10 April); a workshop on the dissemination of agrometeorological information by rural or national mass media, which developed a broadcasting plan (Bamako, Mali, 18-22 May); a workshop on using the interactive statistics package adapted for agrometeorological information (Bujumbura, Burundi, 7-20 October); and several national seminars on the application of meteorological data and information for effective planning and management of water resources.

Aeronautical meteorology

The WMO Technical Conference on Tropical Aeronautical Meteorology (Geneva, 5-9 October) discussed issues relating to the tropics and subtropics, including numerical weather prediction, satellite and radar imagery interpretation, hazards and applications to aviation, national aeronautical meteorological practices and training issues. Under the World Area Forecast System, plans were being finalized at its centres in London and Washington, D.C., to uplift products to a satellite-based dissemination system for global coverage. A pilot project was also initiated in North and Central America on the feasibility of combining the satellite communication systems of WMO and the International Civil Aviation Organization. Working groups at Geneva discussed the provision of meteorological information required before and after flight (13-17 July) and advanced techniques applied to aeronautical meteorology (12-14 October).

Marine meteorology

The first joint meeting of the WMO Bureau and officers of the Intergovernmental Oceanographic Commission (Geneva, 19 June) established a working group to develop proposals on enhanced regional cooperation, improved coordination between the two organizations and possible joint follow-up action to UNCED. The Working Group on Basic Marine Meteorological Services designed a new globally coordinated WMO marine broadcast system covering all ocean areas with either full maritime forecasts and warnings or an interim urgent warning service where coastal earth stations were not available. The system would operate parallel to the traditional marine broadcast system until 1999. An operational quality-control system, using freely drifting ocean data buoys to improve the quality of meteorological and oceanographic data from remote ocean areas, was also implemented experimentally in 1992. The Integrated Global Ocean Services System task team on quality control for automated systems completed an intensive study in the accuracy of the fall-rate equation and prepared a scientific paper on possible errors in the assumed fall rate of certain expendable bathythermographs.

Workshops were held on ocean climate data (Washington, D.C., 21-24 February); the Global Maritime Distress and Safety System, introduced in 1992 by the International Maritime Organization (Geneva, 18-22 May) (see PART SEVEN, Chapter XIV); and low-cost drifting buoys (Paris, 13 October).

Public weather services

Three broad projects were identified in the field of public weather services, dealing with formulation and content of forecasts and warnings; presentation and dissemination techniques, public understanding, public information and education; and exchange and coordination of hazardous weather information among neighbouring countries.

Hydrology and water resources

The Hydrology and Water Resources Programme continued to assist and support the activities of bodies responsible for operational hydrology. The main event in 1992 was the International Conference on Water and the Environment (Dublin, Ireland, 26-31 January), which adopted the Dublin Statement on Water and Sustainable Development that called for fundamental new approaches to the assessment, development and management of freshwater resources and established guiding principles for action (see also PART THREE, Chapter VI).

In 1992, four hydrology projects came to fruition in Albania, Algeria, Bangladesh and Papua New Guinea. WMO developed 20 national and six regional projects designed to assist hydrological services facing difficulties, particularly in Africa. In the context of consultations on the application of management overview of flood forecasting systems in South-East Asia (Kuala Lumpur, 28 and 29 February), 12 countries designated 27 flood-forecasting systems for evaluation. The collection of river-flow data was reviewed at a workshop on the Global Runoff Data Centre (Koblenz, Germany, 15-17 June) and at a workshop on projects within WCP (Geneva, 9-13 November). The commercialization of meteorological and hydrological services was considered by a working group (Geneva, 26-30 October).

WMO also co-sponsored the International Conference on Interaction of Computational Methods and Measurements in Hydraulics and Hydrology (Budapest, Hungary, 25-29 May); international symposia on erosion and sediment transport monitoring programmes in river basins (Oslo, 24-28 August), on torrential rain and floods (Huangshan, China, 5-9 October) and on snow and glacier hydrology (Kathmandu, Nepal, 16-20 November); a symposium on progress in scientific hydrology and water resources management using remote sensing (Washington, D.C., 28 August–5 September); and an international conference and symposia on managing water resources during global change (Reno, Nevada, United States, 1-5 November).

Education and training

Three education and training meetings sponsored by WMO were held during 1992: a course on training methodology and programme design for instructors (Turin, Italy, 7-25 September); the second session of the Coordinating Committee of the Standing Conference of Heads of Training Institutions of National Meteorological Services (Geneva, 19-23 October); and a training seminar for national instructors from the Americas (San José, Costa Rica, 16-27 November).

Under funds from various sources administered by WMO in 1992, a total of 78 long-term and 140 short-term fellowships were awarded. During the year, 197 persons participated in 14 training events organized by WMO in 13 countries. WMO also co-sponsored or jointly supported 23 training events organized by members or national institutions. The Regional Meteorological Training Centres maintained routine training programmes for meteorological and operational hydrological personnel. The WMO Training Library continued to strengthen and expand its holdings, mainly in audiovisual training aids and computer-assisted learning materials, to meet the increasing needs of WMO members. The Library made available 197 videos and 18 slide sets in response to requests from members, training institutions, WMO/UNDP projects and others.

Technical cooperation

In 1992, assistance was provided to 125 WMO member States at a value of $24.8 million, financed from UNDP (48.3 per cent), the WMO Voluntary Cooperation Programme (VCP) (25 per cent), trust funds (23.4 per cent) and WMO's regular budget (3.3 per cent). A total of 176 expert missions were fielded during the year. Under VCP, 16 projects were completed and 57 new projects were approved; as at 31 December 1992, 101 projects were being implemented in 67 countries. An additional 85 VCP training projects were approved, covering 29 long-term and 56 short-term fellowships. The estimated value of equipment, services and fellowships provided to WMO members in 1992 amounted to $5.7 million; assistance in the amount of some $0.8 million was also extended to 80 countries under the regular budget.

Secretariat

As at 31 December 1992, the total number of full-time staff employed by WMO (excluding 26 professionals on technical assistance projects) on permanent and fixed-term contracts stood at 293. Of these, 134 were in the Professional and higher categories (drawn from 56 nationalities) and 159 in the General Service and related categories.

Budget

The year 1992 was the first year of the eleventh financial period (1992-1995), for which the 1991 WMO Congress had established a maximum expenditure of 236,100,000 Swiss francs (SwF). Of the assessed contributions totalling SwF 56,005,000 for the year, SwF 14,333,539 remained unpaid; total unpaid contributions due from members stood at SwF 25,530,251.

The approved regular budget for the 1992-1993 biennium was SwF 112,010,000. The accumulated cash deficit for that biennium was expected to reach SwF 7.4 million. In addition to regular budget expenditure, there were extrabudgetary activities in respect of technical cooperation projects. WMO also administered several trust funds and special accounts financed by various members and international organizations.

NOTE: For further details on WMO's activities see *World Meteorological Organization Annual Report, 1992* published by the agency.

Annex I.   MEMBERSHIP OF THE WORLD METEOROLOGICAL ORGANIZATION
            (As at 31 December 1992)

Afghanistan, Albania, Algeria, Angola, Antigua and Barbuda, Argentina, Armenia, Australia, Austria, Bahamas, Bahrain, Bangladesh, Barbados, Belarus, Belgium, Belize, Benin, Bolivia, Botswana, Brazil, Brunei Darussalam, Bulgaria, Burkina Faso, Burundi, Cambodia, Cameroon, Canada, Cape Verde, Central African Republic, Chad, Chile, China, Colombia, Comoros, Congo, Costa Rica, Côte d'Ivoire, Croatia, Cuba, Cyprus, Czechoslovakia, Democratic People's Republic of Korea, Denmark, Djibouti, Dominica, Dominican Republic, Ecuador, Egypt, El Salvador, Estonia, Ethiopia, Fiji, Finland, France, Gabon, Gambia, Germany, Ghana, Greece, Guatemala, Guinea, Guinea-Bissau, Guyana, Haiti, Honduras, Hungary, Iceland, India, Indonesia, Iran, Iraq, Ireland, Israel, Italy, Jamaica, Japan, Jordan, Kenya, Kuwait,

Lao People's Democratic Republic, Latvia, Lebanon, Lesotho, Liberia, Libyan Arab Jamahiriya, Lithuania, Luxembourg, Madagascar, Malawi, Malaysia, Maldives, Mali, Malta, Mauritania, Mauritius, Mexico, Mongolia, Morocco, Mozambique, Myanmar, Namibia, Nepal, Netherlands, New Zealand, Nicaragua, Niger, Nigeria, Norway, Oman, Pakistan, Panama, Papua New Guinea, Paraguay, Peru, Philippines, Poland, Portugal, Qatar, Republic of Korea, Romania, Russian Federation, Rwanda, Saint Lucia, Sao Tome and Principe, Saudi Arabia, Senegal, Seychelles, Sierra Leone, Singapore, Slovenia, Solomon Islands, Somalia, South Africa,* Spain, Sri Lanka, Sudan, Suriname, Swaziland, Sweden, Switzerland, Syrian Arab Republic, Thailand, Togo, Trinidad and Tobago, Tunisia, Turkey, Uganda, Ukraine, United Arab Emirates, United Kingdom, United Republic of Tanzania, United States, Uruguay, Vanuatu, Venezuela, Viet Nam, Yemen, Yugoslavia, Zaire, Zambia, Zimbabwe.

*Suspended by the Seventh (1975) Congress from exercising the rights and privileges of a member.

Territories

British Caribbean Territories, French Polynesia, Hong Kong, Netherlands Antilles, New Caledonia.

Annex II.   OFFICERS AND OFFICE OF THE WORLD METEOROLOGICAL ORGANIZATION

MEMBERS OF THE WMO EXECUTIVE COUNCIL

President: Zou Jingmeng (China).
First Vice-President: J. W. Zillman (Australia).
Second Vice-President: S. Alaimo (Argentina).
Third Vice-President: A. Lebeau (France).

Members: M. E. Abdalla (Sudan), J. A. Adejokun (Nigeria), A. A. Algain (Saudi Arabia), M. Bautista Pérez (Spain), W. Castro Wrede (Paraguay), A. Cissoko (Côte d'Ivoire), A. J. Dania (Netherlands Antilles), E. Dowdeswell (Canada), E. Ekoko-Etoumann (Cameroon), G. Faraco (Italy) *(acting)*, H. M. Fijnaut (Netherlands), E. W. Friday (United States), J. Hunt (United Kingdom) *(acting)*, N. Kawas (Honduras), R. L. Kintanar (Philippines), J. Marques (Brazil), B. Mlenga (Malawi), T. Mohr (Germany) *(acting)*, E. A. Mukolwe (Kenya), L. Ndorimana (Burundi) *(acting)*, T. Nitta (Japan) *(acting)*, N. Sen Roy (India) *(acting)*, H. Trabelsi (Tunisia), J. Zielinski (Poland), Yu. F. Zubov (Russian Federation) *(acting)*.

NOTE: The Executive Council is composed of four elected officers, the six Presidents of the regional associations (see below), who are *ex-officio* members, and 26 elected members. Members serve in their personal capacities, not as representatives of Governments. As at 31 December 1992, one seat in the Executive Council was vacant.

SENIOR MEMBERS OF THE WMO SECRETARIAT

Secretary-General: G. O. P. Obasi.
Deputy Secretary-General: D. N. Axford.
Assistant Secretary-General: A. S. Zaitsev.
Director, World Weather Watch Department: J Rasmussen.
Director, Basic Systems: D. C. Schiessl.
Director, World Climate Programme Department: V. Boldirev.
Director, Joint Planning Staff for the World Climate Research Programme: P. Morel.
Director, Joint Planning Staff for the Global Climate Observing System: T. W. Spence.
Director, Atmospheric Research and Environment Programme Department: F. Delsol.
Director, Hydrology and Water Resources Department: J. Rodda.

Director, Technical Cooperation Department: R. A. de Guzman.
Director, Education and Training Department: G. Necco.
Director, Administration Department: J. K. Murithi.
Director, Languages, Publications and Conferences Department: A. W. Kabakibo.
Regional Director for Africa: W. Degefu.
Regional Director for Asia and the South-West Pacific: T. Y. Ho.
Regional Director for the Americas: G. Lizano.
Special Assistant to the Secretary-General: S. Chacowry.
Secretary, Intergovernmental Panel on Climate Change: N. Sundararaman.
Acting Director, Intergovernmental Negotiating Committee for a Framework Convention on Climate Change: J. L. Breslin.

PRESIDENTS OF REGIONAL ASSOCIATIONS AND TECHNICAL COMMISSIONS

REGIONAL ASSOCIATIONS

I.   Africa: K. Konaré (Mali).
II.   Asia: H. A. Taravat (Iran).
III.   South America: G. S. Palacios Aguirre (Chile) *(acting)*.
IV.   North and Central America: C. E. Berridge (British Caribbean Territories).
V.   South-West Pacific: P. Lo Su Siew (Singapore).
VI.   Europe: A. Grammeltvedt (Norway).

TECHNICAL COMMISSIONS

Aeronautical Meteorology: C. H. Sprinkle (United States).
Agricultural Meteorology: C. J. Stigter (Netherlands).
Atmospheric Sciences: D. J. Gauntlett (Australia).
Basic Systems: A. A. Vasiliev (Russian Federation).
Climatology: W. J. Maunder (New Zealand).
Hydrology: O. Starosolszky (Hungary).
Instruments and Methods of Observation: J. Kruus (Canada).
Marine Meteorology: R. J. Shearman (United Kingdom).

HEADQUARTERS

World Meteorological Organization
41, Avenue Giuseppe-Motta
(Case postale No. 2300)
CH-1211, Geneva 2, Switzerland
Cable address: METEOMOND GENEVA
Telephone: (41) (22) 730-81-11
Telex: 414199 OMM CH
Facsimile: (41) (22) 734-23-26

Chapter XIV

International Maritime Organization (IMO)

In 1992, several legal instruments adopted under the auspices of the International Maritime Organization (IMO) entered into force. The Convention for the Suppression of Unlawful Acts against the Safety of Maritime Navigation and a Protocol for the Suppression of Unlawful Acts against the Safety of the Fixed Platforms Located on the Continental Shelf, adopted in 1988, entered into force on 1 March. Amendments to the International Convention for the Prevention of Pollution from Ships, 1973, as modified by the 1978 Protocol (MARPOL 73/78) entered into force, as did amendments to the International Convention for the Safety of Life at Sea, 1974 (SOLAS Convention).

During 1992, IMO membership rose to 137 with the acceptance of the IMO Convention by Croatia and Estonia. There were also two associate members (Hong Kong and Macau). (See Annex I for complete membership.)

Activities in 1992

In September, the International Maritime Prize for 1991 was presented to Dr. Chandrika Prasad Srivastava (India), who served as IMO Secretary-General from 1974 to 1989. The Prize is awarded annually to the individual or organization judged to have done the most to further the aims of IMO.

The theme for World Maritime Day, which was celebrated at IMO headquarters on 17 September, was "Marine environment and development: the IMO role".

World Maritime University

In 1992, a new class of 99 students was enrolled at the World Maritime University, Malmö, Sweden, six of them from countries that had not previously sent students to the University, bringing the total number of countries that had done so to 115. The University was established in 1983 under the auspices of IMO to provide advanced training for personnel, mainly from developing countries, in maritime administration, technical management of shipping companies and maritime education. The University had prepared some 800 students to take up important posts in shipping and related industries since its inception.

Prevention of pollution

In March, the Marine Environment Protection Committee, acting on the conclusions of a study

on the design and construction of new and existing tankers, approved amendments to annex I of MARPOL 73/78, adding two regulations to the annex concerning pollution by oil, including operational and accidental pollution. The amendments were expected to enter into force on 6 July 1993, under MARPOL's tacit acceptance procedure. The Committee also adopted guidelines to develop shipboard oil pollution emergency plans, intended to assist in implementing relevant amendments to annex I.

Amendments making Antarctica a special area under MARPOL's annexes I (pollution by oil) and V (pollution by garbage) entered into force on 17 March. The annexes banned the discharge of oil and the dumping of certain wastes into special areas—seas especially vulnerable to pollution, usually almost enclosed by land or environmentally sensitive. MARPOL's annex III (pollution by harmful substances carried in packaged form, including freight containers, portable tanks or road and rail tank wagons) entered into force on 1 July. Further amendments to the annex, adopted by the Marine Environment Protection Committee in October, were to take effect on 28 February 1994. Also in October, the Committee adopted amendments to two codes dealing with the carriage of chemicals by sea, the International Code for the Construction and Equipment of Ships Carrying Dangerous Chemicals in Bulk (IBC), which was mandatory under MARPOL 73/78 and the 1974 SOLAS Convention, and the voluntary Code for the Construction and Equipment of Ships Carrying Dangerous Chemicals in Bulk (BCH). In 1992, the only MARPOL annex not yet in force was annex IV (pollution by sewage).

Meeting at IMO headquarters (9-13 November), the contracting parties to the 1972 Convention on the Prevention of Marine Pollution by Dumping of Wastes and Other Matter (the London Convention as of November 1992, formerly the London Dumping Convention) agreed to begin procedures to amend the Convention and identified 13 core issues as a basis for preparations for an amendments conference scheduled for 1994. As a follow-up to the 1992 United Nations Conference on Environment and Development, the meeting considered the long-term strategy for the Convention and adopted a resolution banning the incineration of noxious liquid wastes at sea from 31 December 1992.

Oil spill compensation

A conference held at IMO headquarters (November) adopted protocols to the 1969 International Convention on Civil Liability for Oil Pollution Damage[a] and the 1971 International Convention on the Establishment of an International Fund for Compensation for Oil Pollution Damage,[b] raising the limit of compensation available to victims of oil spills from 54 million pounds sterling for each incident to some 122 million pounds. The new protocols were to replace those adopted in 1984[c] and amend the entry into force provisions. In the case of the 1969 Convention, the protocol was to enter into force 12 months after being accepted by ten states, including four with not less than 1 million units of gross tanker tonnage. The Fund protocol was to enter into force after being accepted by eight states which had imported 450 million tons of what was termed contributing oil during the previous year. The conference called on Governments only to ratify the 1992 protocols and proposed the establishment of an international oil pollution compensation fund, 1992, similar to the 1971 Fund. It adopted resolutions on certificates of insurance issued in connection with the new protocols and on the interim cap on contributions payable by oil receivers in any given State.

Ship security and safety of life at sea

The Global Maritime Distress and Safety System (GMDSS), which was adopted in 1988 at a conference convened by IMO of contracting Governments to the 1974 SOLAS Convention, entered into force on 1 February 1992. GMDSS, a ship-to-shore, shore-to-ship and ship-to-ship system, incorporating technological advances such as satellite communications, was to be phased in between 1992 and 1999. It was designed to overcome the shortcomings of the existing system—a combination of radiotelephony and Morse radiotelegraphy—and utilized such features as emergency position-indicating radio beacons, digital selective calling, survival craft radar transponders and enhanced group calling. Two other groups of amendments to the 1974 SOLAS Convention also entered into force on 1 February. One group, adopted in 1989, dealt with ships' construction and with fire protection, detection and extinction, while the other group, adopted in 1990, included important changes to the way of calculating the subdivision and stability of dry cargo ships of 100 metres or more in length built after 1 February 1992. Other amendments affected the International Gas Carrier Code (IGC), the IBC Code and the International Code for the Construction and Equipment of Ships Carrying Liquefied Gases in Bulk.

In April, the Maritime Safety Committee modified the amendments to the 1974 SOLAS Convention, which had entered into force on 29 April 1990, concerning the stability of roll-on/roll-off (ro-ro) passenger ships after damage, such as a grounding or a collision. The new measures were to be introduced over an 11-year period beginning on 1 October 1994.

In December, the Committee adopted further amendments to the SOLAS Convention dealing with construction requirements for new tankers and fire safety standards for new passenger ships built on or after 1 October 1994, the date on which the amendments were expected to enter into force under the Convention's tacit acceptance provisions.

The Committee amended the IGC Code and chapters of the IBC Code relating to cargo-tank venting and gas-freeing arrangements, summary of minimum requirements and the list of chemicals exempt from the Code. The BCH Code, optional under the Convention, was also amended. The changes were expected to enter into force on 1 July 1994.

A number of draft amendments to the 1972 International Regulations for Preventing Collisions at Sea,[d] including changes to regulations dealing with high-speed craft and signals for trawlers, were approved by the Maritime Safety Committee for submission to the IMO Assembly in 1993. The Committee also adopted amendments to the 1972 International Convention for Safe Containers,[d] relating to test loads and applied forces and the content of the Safety Approval Plate. They were to enter into force 12 months after being accepted by two-thirds of the contracting parties. The Committee agreed to undertake by 1996 a complete review of the 1978 International Convention on Standards of Training, Certification and Watchkeeping for Seafarers (STCW)[e] and to consider introducing provisions for port State control of operational requirements into the SOLAS and STCW Conventions. A draft protocol to ensure the enactment of the 1977 Torremolinos International Convention for the Safety of Fishing Vessels was completed by an IMO working group (Reykjavik, Iceland, June) for adoption in 1993.

Unlawful acts at sea

During 1992, IMO considered matters related to piracy and armed robbery at sea, maritime fraud and barratry, the use of cargo oil as fuel, unlawful acts against passengers and crews, drug trafficking, and drug and alcohol abuse by seafarers.

[a]YUN 1969, p. 940.
[b]YUN 1971, p. 756.
[c]YUN 1984, p. 1275.
[d]YUN 1972, p. 813.
[e]YUN 1978, p. 1161.

On 1 March, the 1988 Convention for the Suppression of Unlawful Acts against the Safety of Maritime Navigation, and a protocol extending the Convention's provisions to unlawful acts against fixed platforms located on the continental shelf, entered into force. The Convention included provisions for the absolute and unconditional application of the principle either to punish or to extradite persons who committed or who were alleged to have committed offences specified in the Convention.

The Maritime Safety Committee approved guidelines concerning drug and alcohol abuse programmes, which were intended to help assist in establishing screening programmes.

In response to increasing reports of incidents of piracy, especially along the West African coast and in South-East Asia, IMO considered organizing regional seminars to elaborate joint plans of action for combating piracy and armed robbery, and established a working group to examine the problem in the Strait of Malacca, specify necessary navigation techniques and recommend appropriate safety precautions and enforcement arrangements.

Secretariat

As at 31 December 1992, the IMO secretariat employed 297 full-time staff members at headquarters (excluding those on technical assistance projects). Of these, 115 were in the Professional and higher categories and 182 were in the General Service and related categories. There were 11 Professional and 16 General Service staff employed on technical assistance projects. IMO also employed 2 national officers.

Annex I.   MEMBERSHIP OF THE INTERNATIONAL MARITIME ORGANIZATION

   (As at 31 December 1992)

Algeria, Angola, Antigua and Barbuda, Argentina, Australia, Austria, Bahamas, Bahrain, Bangladesh, Barbados, Belgium, Belize, Benin, Bolivia, Brazil, Brunei Darussalam, Bulgaria, Cambodia, Cameroon, Canada, Cape Verde, Chile, China, Colombia, Congo, Costa Rica, Côte d'Ivoire, Croatia, Cuba, Cyprus, Czechoslovakia, Democratic People's Republic of Korea, Denmark, Djibouti, Dominica, Dominican Republic, Ecuador, Egypt, El Salvador, Equatorial Guinea, Estonia, Ethiopia, Fiji, Finland, France, Gabon, Gambia, Germany, Ghana, Greece, Guatemala, Guinea, Guinea-Bissau, Guyana, Haiti, Honduras, Hungary, Iceland, India, Indonesia, Iran, Iraq, Ireland, Israel, Italy, Jamaica, Japan, Jordan, Kenya, Kuwait, Lebanon, Liberia, Libyan Arab Jamahiriya, Luxembourg, Madagascar, Malawi, Malaysia, Maldives, Malta, Mauritania, Mauritius, Mexico, Monaco, Morocco, Mozambique, Myanmar, Nepal, Netherlands, New Zealand, Nicaragua, Nigeria, Norway, Oman, Pakistan, Panama, Papua New Guinea, Peru, Philippines, Poland, Portugal, Qatar, Republic of Korea, Romania, Russian Federation, Saint Lucia, Saint Vincent and the Grenadines, Sao Tome and Principe, Saudi Arabia, Senegal, Seychelles, Sierra Leone, Singapore, Solomon Islands, Somalia, Spain, Sri Lanka, Sudan, Suriname, Sweden, Switzerland, Syrian Arab Republic, Thailand, Togo, Trinidad and Tobago, Tunisia, Turkey, United Arab Emirates, United Kingdom, United Republic of Tanzania, United States, Uruguay, Vanuatu, Venezuela, Viet Nam, Yemen, Yugoslavia, Zaire

Associate members

Hong Kong, Macau

Annex II.   OFFICERS AND OFFICE OF THE INTERNATIONAL MARITIME ORGANIZATION

   (As at 31 December 1992)

IMO COUNCIL AND MARITIME SAFETY COMMITTEE

IMO COUNCIL
Chairman: M.M.S.Tighilt (Algeria).
Members: Algeria, Argentina, Australia, Bahamas, Brazil, Canada, China, Cyprus, Egypt, France, Germany, Greece, India, Indonesia, Iran, Italy, Japan, Mexico, Morocco, Netherlands, Nigeria, Norway, Pakistan, Panama, Philippines, Republic of Korea, Russian Federation, Saudi Arabia, Spain, Sweden, United Kingdom, United States.

MARITIME SAFETY COMMITTEE
Chairman: T. Funder (Denmark).
Membership in the Maritime Safety Committee is open to all IMO member States.

OFFICER AND OFFICE

PRINCIPAL OFFICER OF IMO SECRETARIAT
Secretary-General: W.A. O'Neil.

HEADQUARTERS
International Maritime Organization
4 Albert Embankment
London SE1 7SR, England
   Cable address: INTERMAR LONDON, SE1
   Telephone: (44) (71) 735-7611
   Telex: 23588
   Facsimile: (44) (71) 587-3210

Chapter XV

World Intellectual Property Organization (WIPO)

In 1992, the World Intellectual Property Organization (WIPO) marked the twenty-fifth year of its establishment. WIPO's General Assembly, its governing bodies and the Unions administered by it held their twenty-third series of meetings at Geneva (21-29 September).

The number of States parties to the Paris Convention for the Protection of Industrial Property rose to 106 with the accession of Croatia, Slovenia and Ukraine, and States parties to the Berne Convention for the Protection of Literary and Artistic Works increased to 95 with the accession of China, Croatia, the Gambia, Paraguay and Slovenia. Croatia, Slovenia and Ukraine became parties to the Madrid Agreement Concerning the International Registration of Marks, bringing the number of contracting States to 32. The Democratic People's Republic of Korea and Romania became members of the Hague Agreement Concerning the International Deposit of Industrial Designs, bringing the number of States parties to 21. The number of parties to the Nice Agreement Concerning the International Classification of Goods and Services for the Purpose of the Registration of Marks rose to 35 with the addition of Croatia and Slovenia, which also became members of the Locarno Agreement Establishing an International Classification for Industrial Designs, bringing that instrument's membership to 18. The number of States parties to the Patent Cooperation Treaty (PCT) rose to 54 with the accession of Ireland, New Zealand, the Niger, Portugal and Ukraine to the PCT Union. Argentina and Australia acceded to the International Convention for the Protection of Producers of Phonograms Against Unauthorized Duplication of Their Phonograms, bringing the number of States parties to 37. The Convention Relating to the Distribution of Programme-Carrying Signals Transmitted by Satellite had 15 States parties at the end of 1992 with the accession of Slovenia. With the accession of Argentina to the Treaty on the International Registration of Audiovisual Works, its membership was brought to six.

The 17 treaties in the two main fields of intellectual property administered by WIPO in 1992 were as follows, listed in order of the year of adoption:

Industrial property: Paris Convention for the Protection of Industrial Property; Madrid Agreement for the Repression of False or Deceptive Indications of Source on Goods; Madrid Agreement Concerning the International Registration of Marks; the Hague Agreement Concerning the International Deposit of Industrial Designs; Nice Agreement Concerning the International Classification of Goods and Services for the Purpose of the Registration of Marks; Lisbon Agreement for the Protection of Appellations of Origin and their International Registration; Locarno Agreement Establishing an International Classification for Industrial Designs; PCT; Strasbourg Agreement Concerning the International Patent Classification; Budapest Treaty on the International Recognition of the Deposit of Microorganisms for the Purposes of Patent Procedure; Nairobi Treaty on the Protection of the Olympic Symbol; Vienna Agreement Establishing an International Classification of the Figurative Elements of Marks.

Copyright and neighbouring rights: Berne Convention for the Protection of Literary and Artistic Works; Rome Convention for the Protection of Performers, Producers of Phonograms and Broadcasting Organizations; Geneva Convention for the Protection of Producers of Phonograms Against Unauthorized Duplication of Their Phonograms; Brussels Convention Relating to the Distribution of Programme-Carrying Signals Transmitted by Satellite; Treaty on the International Registration of Audiovisual Works.

During 1992, the membership of WIPO increased to 135 with the accession of Albania, Croatia, Lithuania and Slovenia. (See Annex I for complete membership.)

Activities in 1992

Development cooperation

Although extrabudgetary funds from the United Nations Development Programme declined in 1992, WIPO was able to respond to training demands from developing countries and to provide professional skills for the administration and use of the intellectual property system. Training was given to government officials and personnel from the technical, legal, industrial and commercial sectors in the form of courses, study visits, workshops, seminars, training attachments abroad and on-the-job training by international experts.

About 95 courses, workshops and seminars were given at the global, national, regional and sub-regional levels. They provided basic knowledge of industrial property or copyright, or specialized information in such areas as: the computerization of industrial property office administration, the use of computerized patent information databases, legal and economic aspects of industrial property, the administration of the collection and distribution of copyright royalties, and the promotion of technological inventiveness. Thirty-seven study visits were organized for officials of developing countries. In all, 33 developing countries, 19 industrialized countries and 9 intergovernmental organizations hosted meetings and visits or organized them jointly with WIPO for more than 5,000 participants.

WIPO continued to emphasize assistance to developing countries for the improvement of legislation. It prepared draft laws and regulations dealing with intellectual property or commented on drafts prepared by Governments. Some 85 countries received such assistance.

Some 140 missions to 60 developing countries were undertaken by WIPO officials and consultants. They advised government authorities on the upgrading of administrative procedures, computerization, patent information services and the setting up of organizations for the collective administration of rights under copyright law. WIPO's state-of-the-art search service for developing countries provided some 460 search reports and copies of 2,100 patent documents to 28 Governments and institutions.

In March, WIPO jointly sponsored with Senegal the Conference of Ministers in Charge of Copyright in West Africa on the Eradication of the Piracy of Musical, Literary and Artistic Works (Dakar, Senegal). The Conference adopted the Dakar Appeal, calling on States to combat piracy through national measures, international cooperation and accession to international treaties dealing with copyright and neighbouring rights. Fourteen states were represented.

In September, a ministerial meeting of Central American countries (San Salvador, El Salvador) adopted a joint declaration on the intention of Central American countries to accede to the Paris Convention for the Protection of Industrial Property. Costa Rica, El Salvador, Guatemala, Honduras, Nicaragua and Panama participated.

Setting of norms and standards

In February, the second session of the Committee of Experts on a Possible Protocol to the Berne Convention examined a memorandum prepared by WIPO's International Bureau on questions concerning the Protocol. Discussions dealt with general questions, including rights related to works in computer systems, reprographic reproduction by libraries, archives and educational establishments, private reproduction for personal use, non-voluntary licences for sound recording, public display, rental and public lending, importation and broadcasting. The Committee also discussed the definition of the notion of "public" in respect of certain qualified acts and term of protection. In September, the Assembly of the Berne Union decided on the continuation of the Committee and on the creation of another Committee of Experts on a Possible Instrument on the Protection of the Rights of Performers and Producers of Phonograms.

In June, the first session of the Committee of Experts on a WIPO Model Law on the Protection of Producers of Sound Recordings considered a draft Model Law prepared by the International Bureau. The Committee recommended that the Model Law also cover the rights of performers, which was approved in September by the Assembly of the Berne Union.

The Committee of Experts on the Settlement of Intellectual Property Disputes between States held its fourth session in July.

The Committee of Experts on the Harmonization of Laws for the Protection of Marks held its third and fourth sessions in June and November, respectively. It considered the draft of the Treaty on the Simplification of Administrative Procedures Concerning Marks, prepared by the International Bureau. The Preparatory Working Group of the Committee of Experts of the Nice Union held its twelfth session in November.

International registration activities

Patent Cooperation Treaty (PCT). In 1992, the International Bureau received 25,917 copies of international applications, 16.5 per cent more than in 1991. The average number of PCT contracting States designated per international application was 25.5. International applications thus replaced some 661,000 national applications. Amendments to the PCT Regulations, adopted in 1991, entered into force on 1 July 1992 and the new and improved Computer-Assisted System for the Processing of International Applications became operational in July 1992.

In March, a meeting of the International Searching and International Preliminary Examining Authorities under PCT adopted modifications to the PCT Search Guidelines and the PCT Preliminary Examination Guidelines.

In September, the Assembly of the PCT Union adopted a number of amendments to PCT regulations relating to China's anticipated accession to PCT.

Madrid Agreement. In 1992, the International Bureau received a combined total of 21,143 international trade-mark registrations and renewals, an increase of 1.7 per cent over 1991. There were 15,702 international registrations, 1.6 per cent fewer than in 1991. As the average number of countries covered by each international registration was 9.1, the international registrations in 1992 had the equivalent effect of some 143,000 national registrations. There were 5,441 renewals in 1992, an increase of 12.6 per cent over 1991.

In September, the Assembly of the Madrid Union adopted a new rule related to international registrations in successor States. The rule was to become applicable by 1 January 1993 to the Czech Republic, Croatia, Kazakhstan, Slovakia, Slovenia and Ukraine. The archival sub-system of the Marks Information Optically Stored system became fully operational in 1992.

Hague Agreement. In 1992, the number of industrial design deposits, renewals and prolongations received by the International Bureau totalled 4,783, an increase of 9.6 per cent over 1991.

In April, the second session of the Committee of Experts on the Development of the Hague Agreement Concerning the International Deposit of Industrial Designs discussed a draft Treaty on the International Registration of Industrial Designs aimed at improving the current registration system and encouraging new States to accede to the Agreement.

Countries in transition to market economies

During the year, a special unit in the International Bureau offered its cooperation to the following countries in transition to market economies: Albania, Armenia, Azerbaijan, Belarus, Bosnia and Herzegovina, Bulgaria, Croatia, Czechoslovakia, Estonia, Georgia, Hungary, Kazakhstan, Kyrgyzstan, Latvia, Lithuania, Poland, Republic of Moldova, Romania, Russian Federation, Slovenia, Tajikistan, Turkmenistan, Ukraine and Uzbekistan. WIPO invited officials of those countries for discussions at its Geneva headquarters and organized study visits by them to various countries. The International Bureau also helped them to prepare legislation on aspects of intellectual property. The special unit was established in 1991.

Secretariat

As at 1 January 1992, WIPO employed 402 staff members. Of these, 126 were in the Professional and higher categories, drawn from 55 countries, and 276 were in the General Service category. In addition, 90 WIPO consultants undertook technical assistance missions.

Budget

WIPO's principle income was derived from ordinary and special contributions from member States and from international registration services (primarily under PCT and the Madrid Agreement). Contributions were paid on the basis of a class-and-unit system by members of the Paris, Berne, International Patent Classification, Nice, Locarno and Vienna Unions and by WIPO member States not belonging to any of the Unions. Income in 1992 amounted to $75.9 million; expenditures totalled $61.4 million, of which $36.5 million was staff costs.

NOTE: For further information on the agency, see *Governing Bodies of WIPO and the Unions Administered by WIPO*, published by WIPO.

Annex I. MEMBERSHIP OF THE WORLD INTELLECTUAL PROPERTY ORGANIZATION AND UNIONS ADMINISTERED BY WIPO
(As at 31 December 1992)

Albania, Algeria, Angola, Argentina, Australia, Austria, Bahamas, Bangladesh, Barbados, Belarus, Belgium, Benin, Brazil, Bulgaria, Burkina Faso, Burundi, Cameroon, Canada, Central African Republic, Chad, Chile, China, Colombia, Congo, Costa Rica, Côte d'Ivoire, Croatia, Cuba, Cyprus, Czechoslovakia, Democratic People's Republic of Korea, Denmark, Dominican Republic, Ecuador, Egypt, El Salvador, Fiji, Finland, France, Gabon, Gambia, Germany, Ghana, Greece, Guatemala, Guinea, Guinea-Bissau, Haiti, Holy See, Honduras, Hungary, Iceland, India, Indonesia, Iran, Iraq, Ireland, Israel, Italy, Jamaica, Japan, Jordan, Kenya, Lebanon, Lesotho, Liberia, Libyan Arab Jamahiriya, Liechtenstein, Lithuania, Luxembourg, Madagascar, Malawi, Malaysia, Mali, Malta, Mauritania, Mauritius, Mexico, Monaco, Mongolia, Morocco, Namibia, Netherlands, New Zealand, Nicaragua, Niger, Nigeria, Norway, Pakistan, Panama, Paraguay, Peru, Philippines, Poland, Portugal, Qatar, Republic of Korea, Romania, Russian Federation, Rwanda, San Marino, Saudi Arabia, Senegal, Sierra Leone, Singapore, Slovenia, Somalia, South Africa, Spain, Sri Lanka, Sudan, Suriname, Swaziland, Sweden, Switzerland, Syrian Arab Republic, Thailand, Togo, Trinidad and Tobago, Tunisia, Turkey, Uganda, Ukraine, United Arab Emirates, United Kingdom, United Republic of Tanzania, United States, Uruguay, Venezuela, Viet Nam, Yemen, Yugoslavia,* Zaire, Zambia, Zimbabwe.

*See next page for footnote.

Annex II. OFFICERS AND OFFICES OF THE WORLD INTELLECTUAL PROPERTY ORGANIZATION
(As at 31 December 1992)

GENERAL ASSEMBLY

OFFICERS
Chairman: Abdelhamid Semichi (Algeria).
Vice-Chairmen: Wieslaw Kotarba (Poland), Roland Grossenbacher (Switzerland).

MEMBERS
Algeria, Argentina, Australia, Austria, Bahamas, Bangladesh, Barbados, Belgium, Benin, Brazil, Bulgaria, Burkina Faso, Burundi, Cameroon, Canada, Central African Republic, Chad, Chile, China, Colombia, Congo, Costa Rica, Côte d'Ivoire, Croatia, Cuba, Cyprus, Czechoslovakia, Democratic People's Republic of Korea, Denmark, Ecuador, Egypt, Fiji, Finland, France, Gabon, Germany, Ghana, Greece, Guinea, Guinea-Bissau, Haiti, Holy See, Honduras, Hungary, Iceland, India, Indonesia, Iraq, Ireland, Israel, Italy, Japan, Jordan, Kenya, Lebanon, Lesotho, Liberia, Libyan Arab Jamahiriya, Liechtenstein, Luxembourg, Madagascar, Malawi, Malaysia, Mali, Malta, Mauritania, Mauritius, Mexico, Monaco, Mongolia, Morocco, Netherlands, New Zealand, Niger, Norway, Pakistan, Peru, Philippines, Poland, Portugal, Republic of Korea, Romania, Russian Federation, Rwanda, San Marino, Senegal, Slovenia, South Africa, Spain, Sri Lanka, Sudan, Suriname, Swaziland, Sweden, Switzerland, Thailand, Togo, Trinidad and Tobago, Tunisia, Turkey, Uganda, United Kingdom, United Republic of Tanzania, United States, Uruguay, Venezuela, Viet Nam, Yugoslavia,* Zaire, Zambia, Zimbabwe.

COORDINATION COMMITTEE

OFFICERS
Chairman: Mounir Zahran (Egypt).
Vice-Chairmen: Jean-Claude Combaldieu (France), Vitaly P. Rassokhin (Russian Federation).

MEMBERS
Algeria, Argentina, Australia, Austria, Belgium, Brazil, Bulgaria, Burkina Faso, Cameroon, Canada, Chile, China, Colombia, Côte d'Ivoire, Cuba, Czechoslovakia, Democratic People's Republic of Korea, Denmark, Egypt, France, Germany, Ghana, Hungary, India, Ireland, Italy, Japan, Kenya, Lebanon, Libyan Arab Jamahiriya, Mexico, Namibia, Netherlands, Nicaragua, Norway, Pakistan, Panama, Poland, Portugal, Republic of Korea, Russian Federation, Senegal, Singapore, Spain, Sri Lanka, Switzerland, Syrian Arab Republic, United Kingdom, United States, Uruguay, Venezuela, Yugoslavia.*

*Following Security Council and General Assembly actions (see PART ONE, Chapter IV), the Governing Bodies of WIPO and the Unions administered by it, during their twenty-third series of meetings (Geneva, 21-29 September), decided that Yugoslavia (Serbia and Montenegro) should not participate in any meetings of WIPO's Governing Bodies.

INTERNATIONAL BUREAU

Director-General: Arpad Bogsch.
Deputy Directors-General: Shahid Alikhan, François Curchod.
Assistant Director-General and Legal Counsel: Gust Ledakis.
Directors, Office of the Director-General: Francis Gurry, Geoffrey Yu.
Director, Copyright and Public Information Department: Mihály Ficsor.
Director, Developing Countries (Copyright) Division: Carlos Fernández Ballesteros.
Director, Industrial Property Division: Ludwig Baeumer.
Director, Developing Countries (Industrial Property) Division: James Quashie-Idun.
Director, Patent Cooperation Treaty Administration Division: Daniel Bouchez.
Director, Patent Cooperation Treaty Legal Division: Busso Bartels.

Director-Advisors: Paul Claus, Wang Zhengfa.
Director, Industrial Property Information Division: Akihiro Nakamura.
Director, International Classifications Division: Bo Hansson.
Directors, Development Cooperation and External Relations Bureaux: Ibrahima Thiam (Africa), Kamil Idris (Arab Countries), Narendra Kumar Sabharwal (Asia and the Pacific), Ernesto Rubio (Latin America and the Caribbean).
Director, Bureau for Relations with International Organizations: Khamis Suedi.
Controller and Director, Budget and Finance Division: Thomas A.J. Keefer.
Director, General Administrative Services: Gust Ledakis.
Director, Computerization Division: Phillip Higham.
Director, Languages Division: Bernard Dondenne.
Director, Personnel Division: Bruno Machado.

HEADQUARTERS AND OTHER OFFICE

HEADQUARTERS
World Intellectual Property Organization
34 chemin des Colombettes
1211 Geneva 20, Switzerland
Cable address; WIPO Geneva or OMPI Genève
Telephone: (41) (22) 730-91-11
Telex: 412 912 OMPI CH
Facsimile: (41) (22) 733-5428

WIPO OFFICE AT THE UNITED NATIONS
2 United Nations Plaza, Room 560
New York, N.Y. 10017, USA
Telephone: (1) (212) 963-6813
Telex: 420544 UNH UI
Facsimile: (1) (212) 963-4801

Chapter XVI

International Fund for Agricultural Development (IFAD)

The International Fund for Agricultural Development (IFAD) continued to provide concessional assistance for financing agricultural projects in developing countries. The Fund's objectives were to increase food production, reduce malnutrition and alleviate rural poverty. It continued to concentrate on low-income, food-deficit countries which received most of IFAD's lending and on providing the poorest farmers with the necessary production means and institutional support. Particular emphasis was given to restoring the agricultural capacity of sub-Saharan African countries, as well as to the issues of women in development, cooperation with non-governmental organizations and the environment.

Membership of IFAD rose to 147 with the admission of Albania and Cambodia. Of the current member countries, 22 were in Category I (developed countries), 12 in Category II (oil-exporting developing countries) and 113 in Category III (other developing countries). (See Annex I for full membership.)

The fifteenth session of the Governing Council of IFAD (Rome, 21-23 January 1992) adopted a budget for 1992 of $53.2 million plus a contingency of $0.9 million. It approved by acclamation the applications for non-original membership by Albania and Cambodia in Category III. The Council considered a report on the Special Programme for Sub-Saharan African Countries Affected by Drought and Desertification (SPA) and reiterated its appeal to all members to contribute generously to the Programme's second phase (see below). It also endorsed IFAD's Strategies for the Economic Advancement of Rural Women and requested that guidelines for action under the Strategies be further developed.

The Council established a consultation on the fourth replenishment of the Fund's resources, consisting of all member States from Categories I and II and 12 members from Category III. The consultation held four meetings during 1992 and agreed, subject to agreement between Categories I and II in respect of burden-sharing, that $600 million would be an appropriate target for the fourth replenishment covering the period 1994-1996.

The IFAD Executive Board held three regular sessions in 1992 (April, September and December), approving 27 loans for 25 projects, including one loan under SPA and two from both the Regular Programme and SPA resources, and four technical assistance grants. At each session, the Board reviewed a number of operational matters, including IFAD's experimental procedure for design and development of grant programmes for agricultural research and training and the evolving approach to environmentally sustainable rural poverty alleviation.

In financial matters, the Board reviewed reports on the management of IFAD's Investment Portfolio and approved a transfer of $5 million to the General Reserve for 1992, bringing the Reserve's total amount to $85 million.

The Board approved a programme of work at a level of special drawing rights (SDRs) 245 million for loans, grants and project-related activities and services to member States under the Regular Programme in 1993, and endorsed a budget of $54.9 million, plus a contingency of $0.65 million. It also approved the programme of work and estimated administrative expenditures of SPA for 1993 of SDR 56.1 million and $6.35 million respectively, including a contingency of $75,000.

Resources

Member States pledged $567.4 million in the third replenishment of resources for a period of two and a half years with effect from January 1990. By the end of 1992, members' contributions over the 15 years of IFAD's operations totalled $3.16 billion.

Contributions to the first phase of SPA, initiated in 1986 with a target of $300 million, totalled $288.25 million as at 31 December 1992. Contributions received towards the second and final phase of SPA (SPA-II), initiated in 1992, amounted to $26 million at year's end.

Activities in 1992

The 27 new loans for 25 projects approved by IFAD in 1992 totalled SDR 229.1 million ($320.8 million), including three loans for SDR 9.2 million ($12.8 million) financed from SPA resources. An allocation of SDR 7.1 million ($9.9 million) for 42 technical assistance grants included four grants amounting to SDR 0.7 million ($1.1 million) from SPA. Total financial assistance provided in 1992 amounted to SDR 236.2 million ($330.8 million), compared to SDR 204.9 million ($280.9 million) in 1991.

Twenty-four projects approved were IFAD-initiated, with 66 per cent of them attracting cofinancing from other donors. External cofinancing mobilized during the year amounted to $82.5 million, or 25 per cent of total project costs.

During the year, nine projects for eight countries of the African region were approved for a total of SDR 58 million ($81.6 million) under the Regular and Special Programmes combined. Projects under the Regular Programme dealt with agricultural services in the Gambia; smallholder development in Guinea; improved flood recession farming in Mauritania; agricultural and community development in Nigeria; intensified land use management in Rwanda; village organization and management in Senegal; and cotton production in Uganda. Three projects approved under SPA were for protected area management in Mauritania, agricultural development in Sierra Leone and irrigation rehabilitation in the Sudan.

The eight projects approved for eight countries in Asia, involving SDR 80.5 million ($112.1 million), emphasized protecting agricultural and natural resources and developing sustainable farming systems in Bhutan; low-lying land development in China; tree crop development in Indonesia; extension services to increase agricultural production in Iran among poor smallholders, particularly women; raising the living standard of smallholders, livestock owners, the landless and poor rural women in Pakistan; communal irrigation in the Philippines; long-term development in Samoa; and poverty alleviation and the provision of resource management and institutional support to small farmers in Sri Lanka.

The four projects for Latin America and the Caribbean received loans of SDR 44.2 million ($62.1 million), aimed at rural development in Ecuador and in Mexico; rehabilitation of war-torn areas in El Salvador; and establishing a peasant development fund in Paraguay.

For the Near East and North Africa, four projects amounting to SDR 46.9 million ($64.9 million) were approved to assist smallholders and other poor settlers in Egypt's reclaimed Newlands; smallholder livestock rehabilitation in Lebanon; irrigation in the Sudan; and agricultural development in the Syrian Arab Republic.

The Fund continued its special programming and strategy missions, nine of which were undertaken in 1992 to Costa Rica, Côte d'Ivoire, Guyana, Jamaica, Mexico, Sri Lanka, Syrian Arab Republic, United Republic of Tanzania and Zambia. Pre-strategy missions were conducted in Cambodia and Rwanda. The missions focused on issues relating to poverty alleviation and IFAD's role in improving national economic performance. They recommended strategies involving diversification of production towards higher value crops; elimination of large productivity gaps; improved management of the forestry and livestock sectors; increased labour productivity; and support for smallholder farmers and livestock owners, landless farmers, wage labourers and populations in the hinterlands.

In 1992, three seminars on project implementation were held in the Latin America and Caribbean region (San Pedro Sula, Honduras, 14-17 September; Sucre, Bolivia, 9-13 November; Barbados, 16-19 November). The Summit on the Economic Advancement of Rural Women, organized by the Fund at Geneva in February, adopted the Geneva Declaration on Rural Women. Following the Summit, representatives of the International Steering Committee on the subject held their first meeting (Rome, 13 and 14 October). (For details, see PART THREE, Chapter XIII.) A book entitled _The State of World Rural Poverty_ was completed and published in 1992, representing the most recent and comprehensive study on the subject.

Secretariat

In December 1992, the IFAD secretariat totalled 258 staff, of whom 106 were in the Professional and higher categories—drawn from 49 nationalities—and 152 in the General Service category.

Income and expenditure

Total revenue under the Regular Programme for 1992 was $137.9 million, consisting of $101.3 million from investment income, including gains of $3.6 million resulting from active portfolio management, and $36.7 million from interest and service charges on loans. Total operational and administrative expenses for the year amounted to $48.9 million (including an exchange gain on operations of $0.17 million), compared with a budget, before contingency, of $52.4 million. The excess of revenue over expenses for the year was $89 million.

Total revenue under SPA for 1992 was $13.3 million, consisting of $12.6 million of investment income, including gains of $0.5 million from active portfolio management, and $0.7 million from interest and service charges on loans. Total expenses for the year amounted to $3.1 million, compared with a budget, before contingency, of $5.2 million. The excess of revenue for the year was $10.2 million.

NOTE: For further details on IFAD activities in 1992, see _Annual Report 1992_, published by the Fund.

Annex I. MEMBERS OF THE INTERNATIONAL FUND FOR AGRICULTURAL DEVELOPMENT
(As at 31 December 1992)

Category I members
Australia, Austria, Belgium, Canada, Denmark, Finland, France, Germany, Greece, Ireland, Italy, Japan, Luxembourg, Netherlands, New Zealand, Norway, Portugal, Spain, Sweden, Switzerland, United Kingdom, United States

Category II members
Algeria, Gabon, Indonesia, Iran, Iraq, Kuwait, Libyan Arab Jamahiriya, Nigeria, Qatar, Saudi Arabia, United Arab Emirates, Venezuela

Category III members
Afghanistan, Albania, Angola, Antigua and Barbuda, Argentina, Bangladesh, Barbados, Belize, Benin, Bhutan, Bolivia, Botswana, Brazil, Burkina Faso, Burundi, Cambodia, Cameroon, Cape Verde, Central African Republic, Chad, Chile, China, Colombia, Comoros, Congo, Costa Rica, Côte d'Ivoire, Cuba, Cyprus, Democratic People's Republic of Korea, Djibouti, Dominica, Dominican Republic, Ecuador, Egypt, El Salvador, Equatorial Guinea, Ethiopia, Fiji, Gambia, Ghana, Grenada, Guatemala, Guinea, Guinea-Bissau, Guyana, Haiti, Honduras, India, Israel, Jamaica, Jordan, Kenya, Lao People's Democratic Republic, Lebanon, Lesotho, Liberia, Madagascar, Malawi, Malaysia, Maldives, Mali, Malta, Mauritania, Mauritius, Mexico, Morocco, Mozambique, Myanmar, Namibia, Nepal, Nicaragua, Niger, Oman, Pakistan, Panama, Papua New Guinea, Paraguay, Peru, Philippines, Republic of Korea, Romania, Rwanda, Saint Kitts and Nevis, Saint Lucia, Saint Vincent and the Grenadines, Samoa, Sao Tome and Principe, Senegal, Seychelles, Sierra Leone, Solomon Islands, Somalia, Sri Lanka, Sudan, Suriname, Swaziland, Syrian Arab Republic, Thailand, Togo, Tonga, Trinidad and Tobago, Tunisia, Turkey, Uganda, United Republic of Tanzania, Uruguay, Viet Nam, Yemen, Yugoslavia,* Zaire, Zambia, Zimbabwe

*Following Security Council and General Assembly action (see PART ONE, Chapter IV), the IFAD Executive Board, during its forty-seventh session (1-4 December 1992), decided that Yugoslavia (Serbia and Montenegro) could not continue automatically the membership of the former Yugoslavia and that, therefore, it should apply for membership. In the meantime, Yugoslavia was not to participate in the work of the governing bodies of IFAD.

Annex II. OFFICERS AND OFFICES OF THE INTERNATIONAL FUND FOR AGRICULTURAL DEVELOPMENT
(As at 31 December 1992)

EXECUTIVE BOARD

Chairman: Idriss Jazairy.

MEMBERS
Category I: Germany, Italy, Japan, Netherlands, Norway, United States.
Alternates: Canada, France, Luxembourg, Sweden, United Kingdom.
Category II: Algeria, Indonesia, Kuwait, Nigeria, Saudi Arabia, Venezuela.

Alternates: Gabon, Iran, Iraq, Libyan Arab Jamahiriya, Qatar, United, Arab Emirates.
Category III: Argentina, Brazil, Côte d'Ivoire, Lesotho, Pakistan, Thailand.
Alternates: Ethiopia, India, Mexico, Panama, Senegal, Turkey.

SENIOR SECRETARIAT OFFICERS

President: Idriss Jazairy.
Chef de Cabinet: Isa Babaa.
Internal Auditor: Jean Pierre Matras.
Vice-President: Donald S. Brown.
Controller: Vernon Jorssen.
Treasurer: Tor Myrvang.

Chief, Personnel Services: Alan Prien.
Manager, Management Information System: Massimo Aureli.
Assistant President, Project Management Department: Moise Mensah.
Officer-in-Charge, Economic and Planning Department: Donald S. Browr
Assistant President, General Affairs Department: Abdou Ciss.
Director, Legal Services: Mohammed Nawaz.

HEADQUARTERS AND OTHER OFFICE

HEADQUARTERS
International Fund for Agricultural Development
Via del Serafico 107
00142 Rome, Italy
 Cable address: IFAD ROME
 Telephone: (39) (6) 54591
 Telex: 620330
 Facsimile: 5043463

LIAISON OFFICE
International Fund for Agricultural Development
1889 F Street, N.W.
Washington, D.C. 20006, United States
 Telephone: (1) (202) 289-3812

Chapter XVII

United Nations Industrial Development Organization (UNIDO)

In 1992, the United Nations Industrial Development Organization (UNIDO) continued its activities in the areas of industrial operations, strategies and promotion. Its special programmes, calling for multidisciplinary or interdepartmental approaches, supported industrial growth and restructuring and included the Industrial Development Decade for Africa, assistance to least developed countries, industrial cooperation among developing countries, integration of women in industrial development, cooperation with industrial enterprises and non-governmental organizations, environment and private sector development. The Industrial Development Board reviewed the Organization's overall activities at its ninth and tenth regular sessions held in May and November, respectively. Financial concerns dominated its deliberations, with member States owing the Organization $98.8 million in assessed contributions as of the end of April.

The Board stressed the need for UNIDO to focus its technical cooperation activities on its areas of particular expertise, emphasizing the importance of coordination, complementarity, systematic monitoring and evaluation. The Programme and Budget Committee held its eighth session during June and July.

As at 31 December 1992, 160 States were members of UNIDO, with Armenia, Bosnia and Herzegovina, Croatia, Georgia and Slovenia having joined during the year. Australia renewed its membership as of 1 January, but on 3 December, Canada gave notice of its intention to withdraw its membership, effective 31 December 1993. (See Annex I for complete membership.)

Policy issues

In 1992, UNIDO took steps towards structural reform, the implementation of its role in the successor arrangements of the United Nations Development Programme (UNDP), which were decided upon in 1991,[a] the improvement of programme and project quality and the development of new programme initiatives. Those efforts were only partially successful, however, due to factors largely beyond the Secretariat's influence. The Organization took the initiative early in the year to train all operational and administrative staff at headquarters in the workings of the new regime in support of programmes and projects funded by UNDP.

Industrial strategies and operations

A total of 1,745 technical assistance projects valued at $135.6 million were implemented or under implementation in 1992. Asia and the Pacific received 28.5 per cent; Africa, 34.3 per cent; the Arab States (including the African Arab States), 11.6 per cent; Latin America and the Caribbean, 8.4 per cent; and Europe, 3.9 per cent. Interregional and global projects accounted for 22.5 per cent.

Emphasis was placed on the application of environment-friendly technologies in all technical cooperation projects.

Implementation of industrial operations

Agro-based industries. Technical cooperation expenditures in 1992 under the heading of agro-based industries amounted to $10.3 million. Some 38 per cent of the total was financed by UNDP and 153 projects were implemented or under implementation.

Projects related to agro-based industries continued to focus on the development and adaptation of technologies to suit the needs of small- and medium-scale industries with priority given to the modernization, rehabilitation and sizing of private-sector facilities to improve profitability.

Chemical industries. Expenditures for technical cooperation in the chemical industry sector totalled $28.5 million, with 38 per cent being financed from UNDP resources. A total of 284 projects were either implemented or under implementation.

The UNIDO Chemical Industries Branch devoted increasing attention to environmental considerations, including the location of chemical plants and the introduction of cleaner technologies; increased plant and operator safety in the pesticide and fertilizer industries; waste management; waste recycling and utilization of wastes and by-products in the plastics, paper, building materials and pharmaceutical industries; and the maintenance of biodiversity through the systematic cultivation of medicinal plants. Special emphasis was given to the rehabilitation of the small-scale industry sector as well as to industries in Central and Eastern Europe.

[a]YUN 1991, p. 382.

Metallurgical industries. Technical cooperation expenditures in metallurgical industries amounted to $6 million, with 70 per cent financed from UNDP resources. Ninety-nine projects were implemented or under implementation. They focused mainly on the introduction and dissemination of cleaner production technologies, economy in energy, increased environmental management techniques at the individual plant level and cooperation at the regional level.

Engineering industries. Expenditures for engineering industry projects amounted to $16.7 million. About 70 per cent of the funds came from UNDP, with special trust-fund arrangements and resources from the Industrial Development Fund representing an increased portion. A total of 179 projects were implemented or under implementation in such areas as computer applications to industrial design; manufacturing; maintenance and automation; electronic components and equipment; medical equipment; telecommunications equipment and systems; environmental monitoring and control equipment; industrial process control and automation equipment and systems; and high-precision components.

Industrial strategies and policies. Under this subprogramme, 97 projects were implemented or under implementation. Technical cooperation expenditures totalled $6.4 million, of which about 64 per cent was financed from UNDP resources.

Activities concentrated on the industrial restructuring process driven by increasing global competition and technological and political changes. Emphasis was placed on the formulation and implementation of strategies and policies for industrial restructuring; enhancement of the productive capacity of industrial subsectors; and the development of information systems. Special attention was given to developments in Eastern Europe and environmental policies there.

Institutional infrastructure. Expenditures in the area of institutional infrastructure totalled $14.4 million. About 83 per cent came from UNDP resources and 223 projects were implemented or under implementation.

This subprogramme addressed the pressing needs of developing countries and countries in transition from centrally planned to market economies. Technical cooperation continued to be consolidated in the areas of small- and medium-scale industries and institutional support for industrial development.

Industrial management and rehabilitation. Technical cooperation expenditures in this sector amounted to $5.6 million, with some 60 per cent coming from UNDP resources. A total of 60 projects were implemented or under implementation.

The management and rehabilitation programme continued to place emphasis on assistance in the commercialization of industry, increasing direct assistance to the private sector, and the transfer of commercially oriented management technologies and systems. New ground was broken in the management programme with the inclusion of computer-aided process planning.

Industrial human resource development. Expenditures for fellowship and other training components in all technical cooperation projects implemented by UNIDO in 1992 amounted to $16.4 million, compared with $17.6 million in 1991. Of that total, $11.3 million was spent on fellowships and study tours and $5.1 million on group training activities and meetings. A total of 103 projects were implemented.

To enhance human resource development in developing countries, increased attention was paid to the identification and clarification of training needs, the formulation of policies and strategies for human resource development and the development of effective training systems to execute industrial development programmes and projects at the sectoral, subsectoral and enterprise levels. Special efforts were made to strengthen the linkage between human resource development and the transfer of advanced technologies and to create awareness of the environmental aspects of industrial development.

Industrial promotion

Industrial promotion activities focused on reinforcing links in the areas of industrial investment, consultations and industrial technology development and promotion.

Industrial investment programme. Activities of the Industrial Investment Division aimed primarily at assisting cooperation between sponsors of industrial investment projects in developing countries and their partners and advising developing countries on ways of identifying investment opportunities. Steps were taken to streamline the Division's operations and improve internal coordination.

The value of investment projects successfully concluded by UNIDO rose to $1,473 million in 1992, with the Industrial Cooperation Centres in Beijing and Moscow promoting projects valued $197 million and $24.1 million, respectively. Of the 194 projects concluded, 41 totalling $15.6 million were in Africa; 41 valued at $672 million were in the Arab countries, Europe and the Mediterranean; 60 amounting to $473 million were in Asia and the Pacific; and 52 costing $178 million were in Latin America and the Caribbean.

System of Consultations. The UNIDO System of Consultations, a mechanism for achieving the goals of the 1975 Lima Declaration and Plan of Action on Industrial Development and Cooperation,[b] principally to restructure world industry and increase the share of developing countries in world production, held two consultations during 1992: the Regional Consultation on the Restructuring of the Capital Goods Industry in Latin America and the Caribbean (Caracas, Venezuela, 9-12 November) and the Regional Consultation on the Petrochemical Industry in the Arab Countries (Innsbruck, Austria, 22-25 June). As a follow-up to earlier consultations, a workshop on quality and hygiene regulations in the fisheries industries took place (Shetland Islands, United Kingdom, 6-10 July). A meeting was held (Singapore, 25-30 October) on cooperation between specialists from African and Asian fisheries to address problems relating to post-harvest technology and infrastructure in the fisheries sector. Other activities included a seminar on total quality management in the iron and steel industry (Buenos Aires, Argentina, 24-27 August); a workshop on the industrial utilization of medicinal and aromatic plants (Milan, Italy, 24-27 March); and a round-table discussion on the restructuring of small- and medium-scale enterprises with special focus on African/Asian cooperation (New Delhi, India, 29 September–2 October).

Industrial technology development and promotion. Under the newly created Technology Development and Promotion Division, a feasibility study on the establishment of an industrial technology and market information network for Sri Lanka was successfully completed. Operational frameworks were established in Brazil and Colombia to integrate their computerized information systems into the Latin America and Caribbean network. Progress was also made in the development of a world-wide referral system. A workshop on advanced information technology applications and network integration held at Odessa, Ukraine, resulted in a regional project for the development of a Euro-Asian network to exchange technology and market information. Technology market fairs were held in Zimbabwe (September) and India (November) to give entrepreneurs from over 30 countries direct access to alternative technologies from both industrialized and developing countries in manufacturing and agro-based industries.

The Biotechnology and Genetic Engineering Unit continued to be involved in the establishment and programmes of the International Centre for Genetic Engineering and Biotechnology, which expanded its training programmes in 1992. UNIDO organized workshops on technology transfer negotiation and contracting at Brno, Czechoslovakia, in March; at Zanzibar, United Republic of Tanzania, in September; and at Kathmandu, Nepal, in November.

Area programmes

The Area Programme Division developed, implemented and monitored operational programmes at the country, subregional and regional levels. Project approvals from UNDP indicative planning figures, cost-sharing, cash counterpart and special measures in 1992 amounted to $9.6 million. The UNDP Governing Council, at its thirty-ninth session in 1992, approved a list of 59 technical support services (TSS-1) at the programme level with a global ceiling of $4.9 million for implementation by UNIDO in the biennium 1992-1993. Twenty-six TSS-1 projects commenced activities in 1992. During the year, 150 country programme reviews and five regional programme reviews were undertaken, 916 project ideas and concepts were identified and 407 projects were further developed.

Second Industrial Development Decade for Africa (1993-2002)

The Second Industrial Development Decade for Africa (IDDA) was proclaimed by the General Assembly in 1989.[c] Its programme, adopted by the Tenth Conference of African Ministers of Industry and the Fourth General Conference of UNIDO in 1991,[d] consisted of 50 national and four subregional programmes. By **resolution 47/177** of 22 December 1992, the Assembly adopted the programme for the Second IDDA, adjusted the programme to cover the years 1993-2002, urged the UNIDO Director-General to integrate the relevant provisions of Agenda 21—formulated by the United Nations Conference on Environment and Development (UNCED) (Rio de Janeiro, Brazil, 3-14 June)—in the implementation of the Second Decade, and to undertake a mid-term evaluation of the programme in 1998.

Under technical cooperation activities, an allotment of $1,446,200 for 1992 was fully programmed. Eighteen projects totalling $2,687,220 were approved. They consisted of six national projects valued at $768,485 and 12 regional projects costed at $1,918,735. They reflected the priorities of national and subregional programmes for the Second IDDA. As at 31 December 1992, $549,000 worth of projects had been implemented. An amount of $4.75 million, budgeted for supplementary activities for the 1992-1993 biennium, was entirely programmed, and an allotment of $2 million for 1992 was allocated to the technical cooperation component of the Decade. More than $606,000 worth of short-term advisory services were provided, mainly to least developed African countries, and as at 31 December 1992, $814,135 worth of supplementary activities had been implemented.

[b]YUN 1975, p. 473.
[c]GA res. 44/237, 22 Dec. 1989.
[d]YUN 1991, p. 1012.

Assistance to LDCs

Responding to the 1990 Paris Declaration and Programme of Action for the Least Developed Countries (LDCs)[e] and the 1991 UNIDO industrial action programme for LDCs, a concerted effort was made in 1992 to programme and utilize available funds allocated to LDCs according to the priorities set out in the UNIDO programme of action. A seed programme to promote traditional wood industries in Central and West African LDCs was being implemented, and a support programme to mobilize financial resources for industrial development in Asian LDCs was approved. Other programmes submitted for approval addressed the mobilization of financial resources for industrial development, environmental rehabilitation and small-scale and micro-industries. Projects on food production, privatization and technology transfer were approved from the IDDA supplementary activities budget.

New approvals for LDCs amounted to $14.4 million for 100 projects. Delivery reached a level of $23.7 million.

Industrial cooperation among developing countries

Efforts to improve industrial cooperation among developing countries in the framework of the UNIDO-wide programme in the 1990s were centred on updating the information referral system technical cooperation among developing countries (TCDC) database. Information was collected within the Organization and more than 200 institutions were contacted for updated information on their training programmes and expert services.

Activities with regional and subregional groupings focused on the development of industrial cooperation in the Arab Maghreb Union in textiles and leather, agro-industries, agricultural machinery, pharmaceuticals, electronics and informatics, and in the Gulf Cooperation Council in small- and medium-scale industries. Under the regional cooperation programme for the Industrial Recovery of Latin America and the Caribbean, work continued on the promotion of TCDC potentials in industrial subcontracting, automation of the capital goods industry, and computerized maintenance management in the iron and steel industry.

Workshops were held on enterprise-to-enterprise cooperation meetings on machine tools (New Delhi, India); man-made fibre technology (Beijing, China); and the metalworking industry (Bandung, Indonesia).

Integration of women in industrial development

The implementation of the 1990-1995 UNIDO programme for the integration of women in in-

dustrial development concentrated on measures to ensure the consideration of women in programme and project design and implementation, and on the design and implementation of projects directed specifically towards women's needs. This approach was applied to technical cooperation programmes and projects as well as to research and studies. Projects targeting women focused on the development of female entrepreneurship and the access of women to environmentally sound technologies. Projects were formulated to introduce the UNIDO training programme for women entrepreneurs in the food-processing industry in the Gambia, the United Republic of Tanzania, and countries of Central America. A proposal was formulated for the establishment of a women's unit within the Entrepreneurial Centre of the Jamaican Promotion Corporation together with a programme to promote the entrepreneurial and managerial skills of women in China's township industries.

Environment

To develop UNIDO's response to Agenda 21 and define the Organization's role in its implementation, the Director-General set up an Organization-wide Task Force on Environment, updated UNIDO's environmental programme, delineated the Organization's potential response in terms of sustainable development, and defined the Organization's position for consideration by the Administrative Committee on Coordination (ACC). The discussions by ACC led to the creation of the Inter-Agency Committee on Sustainable Development, a coordinating body under the aegis of ACC. UNIDO became the fourth executing agency for the Interim Multilateral Fund for the Implementation of the 1987 Montreal Protocol on Substances that Deplete the Ozone Layer.[f]

The Environment Coordination Unit fulfilled a vital function in coordinating UNIDO environment-related activities, including implementation of its environment programme, recommendations from the UNIDO Conference on Ecologically Sustainable Industrial Development and follow-up to UNCED. In July, the Unit was assigned as secretariat to the newly created UNIDO Task Force on the Environment.

Secretariat

As at 31 December 1992, UNIDO had 1,343 staff members, of whom 437 were in the Professional and higher categories and 922 in the General Service and related categories. Of 718 women staff members, 104 were Professionals and 614 were in

---

[e]GA res. 45/206, 21 Dec. 1990
[f]YUN 1987, p. 686.

other grades. Women were in 24.4 per cent of posts subject to geographical distribution in 1992 as against 21.5 per cent in 1991. UNIDO was represented in developing countries by 40 UNIDO Country Directors who worked with UNDP Resident Coordinators.

Technical cooperation

Technical cooperation for the benefit of developing countries continued to be the main UNIDO activity, with the net value of project approvals totalling $113.6 million compared with $130.4 million in 1991. Of that amount, $100.7 million was for non-UNDP funded activities. Total technical cooperation delivery totalled $135.6 million, a decrease of 8 per cent compared with 1991.

Budget

At its fourth session in 1991, the General Conference approved the regular budget for the biennium 1992-1993 at the level of $181,013,400, to be financed from assessed contributions of member States, in both dollars and Austrian schillings. On the basis of an exchange rate of $1.00 = AS 12.90, member States were assessed $179,262,600, consisting of $19,718,900 plus the equivalent in dollars of AS 2,058,116,310. For the Regular Programme of Technical Cooperation—including IDDA—the General Conference had appropriated $10,755,700 for the biennium and allocated $8.6 million to be used as seed money to mobilize additional financial resources for technical assistance and investment needs in the context of the Second IDDA.

In 1992, both the regular budget and the operational budgets were affected by income shortfalls. The Programme and Budget Committee requested the Director-General to take the necessary measures to balance the operational budget as soon as possible while preserving the capacity of the organization for technical cooperation delivery.

NOTE: For futher information on UNIDO, see *Annual Report of UNIDO 1992*, published by UNIDO.

Annex I.   MEMBERSHIP OF THE UNITED NATIONS INDUSTRIAL DEVELOPMENT ORGANIZATION
(As at 31 December 1992)

Afghanistan, Albania, Algeria, Angola, Argentina, Armenia, Australia, Austria, Bahamas, Bahrain, Bangladesh, Barbados, Belarus, Belgium, Belize, Benin, Bhutan, Bolivia, Bosnia and Herzegovina, Botswana, Brazil, Bulgaria, Burkina Faso, Burundi, Cameroon, Canada, Cape Verde, Central African Republic, Chad, Chile, China, Colombia, Comoros, Congo, Costa Rica, Côte d'Ivoire, Croatia, Cuba, Cyprus, Czechoslovakia, Democratic People's Republic of Korea, Denmark, Djibouti, Dominica, Dominican Republic, Ecuador, Egypt, El Salvador, Equatorial Guinea, Ethiopia, Fiji, Finland, France, Gabon, Gambia, Georgia, Germany, Ghana, Greece, Grenada, Guatemala, Guinea, Guinea-Bissau, Guyana, Haiti, Honduras, Hungary, India, Indonesia, Iran, Iraq, Ireland, Israel, Italy, Jamaica, Japan, Jordan, Kenya, Kuwait, Lao People's Democratic Republic, Lebanon, Lesotho, Liberia, Libyan Arab Jamahiriya, Lithuania, Luxembourg, Madagascar, Malawi, Malaysia, Maldives, Mali, Malta, Mauritania, Mauritius, Mexico, Mongolia, Morocco, Mozambique, Myanmar, Namibia, Nepal, Netherlands, New Zealand, Nicaragua, Niger, Nigeria, Norway, Oman, Pakistan, Panama, Papua New Guinea, Paraguay, Peru, Philippines, Poland, Portugal, Qatar, Republic of Korea, Romania, Russian Federation, Rwanda, Saint Kitts and Nevis, Saint Lucia, Saint Vincent and the Grenadines, Sao Tome and Principe, Saudi Arabia, Senegal, Seychelles, Sierra Leone, Slovenia, Somalia, Spain, Sri Lanka, Sudan, Suriname, Swaziland, Sweden, Switzerland, Syrian Arab Republic, Thailand, Togo, Tonga, Trinidad and Tobago, Tunisia, Turkey, Uganda, Ukraine, United Arab Emirates, United Kingdom, United Republic of Tanzania, United States, Uruguay, Vanuatu, Venezuela, Viet Nam, Yemen, Yugoslavia, Zaire, Zambia, Zimbabwe.

Annex II.   OFFICERS AND OFFICES OF THE UNITED NATIONS
INDUSTRIAL DEVELOPMENT ORGANIZATION
(As at 31 December 1992)

INDUSTRIAL DEVELOPMENT BOARD

OFFICERS
President: Péter Balázs (Hungary).
Vice-Presidents: Gerald Clark (United Kingdom), Ali Khalid El-Hussein (Sudan), Thereza Maria Machado Quintella (Brazil).
Rapporteur: Morteza Damanpak Jami (Iran).

MEMBERS
Austria, Belarus, Belgium, Bolivia, Brazil, Cameroon, Chile, China, Costa Rica, Cuba, Czechoslovakia, Egypt, Ethiopia, Finland, France, Germany, Ghana, Greece, Guinea, Hungary, India, Indonesia, Iran, Iraq, Italy, Japan, Kuwait, Mexico, Morocco, Netherlands, Nigeria, Norway, Pakistan, Peru, Republic of Korea, Romania, Russian Federation, Saudi Arabia, Senegal, Spain, Sudan, Switzerland, Syrian Arab Republic, Thailand, Trinidad and Tobago, Tunisia, Turkey, Uganda, United Kingdom, United States, Venezuela, Zaire, Zimbabwe.

PROGRAMME AND BUDGET COMMITTEE

OFFICERS
Chairman: Gerald Clark (United Kingdom).
Vice-Chairmen: Simeon Adewale Adekanye (Nigeria), Jasim Youssouf Jamal (Qatar), Marek Wejtko (Poland).
Rapporteur: Santiago Quijano-Caballero (Colombia).

MEMBERS
Algeria, Austria, Brazil, Bulgaria, China, Colombia, Cuba, Egypt, France, Germany, India, Italy, Japan, Kenya, Malawi, Mexico, Netherlands, Nigeria, Philippines, Poland, Qatar, Russian Federation, Rwanda, Sweden, United Kingdom, United States, Yugoslavia.

HEADQUARTERS AND OTHER OFFICES

HEADQUARTERS
United Nations Industrial Development Organization
Vienna International Centre
P.O. Box 300
A-1400 Vienna, Austria
   Cable address: UNIDO Vienna
   Telephone: (43) (1) 211310
   Telex: 135612
   Facsimile: (43) (1) 232156

LIAISON OFFICE
UNIDO Liaison Office
1 United Nations Plaza, Room 1110
New York, N.Y. 10017, United States
   Telephone: (1) (212) 963-6882

UNIDO also maintained an office at Geneva.

Chapter XVIII

Interim Commission for the International Trade Organization (ICITO) and the General Agreement on Tariffs and Trade (GATT)

During 1992, the General Agreement on Tariffs and Trade (GATT) continued to serve as a multilateral instrument with the principal objective of liberalizing international trade to facilitate economic growth and development. It provided agreed rules for international trade and served as a forum in which countries could discuss trade problems and negotiate the reduction of various restrictive and distortive measures. GATT focused significantly on promoting economic growth of the developing countries, particularly the least-developed among them.

The United Nations Conference on Trade and Employment (Havana, Cuba, November 1947–March 1948) drew up a charter for an International Trade Organization (ITO) and established an Interim Commission for the International Trade Organization (ICITO). The charter of ITO was never accepted, but the Conference's Preparatory Committee members negotiated tariffs among themselves and drew up GATT, which entered into force on 1 January 1948. Since then, ICITO has served as the GATT secretariat.

The most authoritative body of GATT was the Session of Contracting Parties, which, in 1992, held its forty-eighth session (Geneva, 2 and 3 December).

In 1992, the number of Contracting Parties to GATT rose to 105 with the addition of Mozambique and Namibia. (See Annex I for complete membership.)

Multilateral trade negotiations

Uruguay Round

The Uruguay Round of Multilateral Trade Negotiations, launched in September 1986,[a] was originally scheduled to conclude by 1990 but continued through December 1991, when the Trade Negotiations Committee tabled the Draft Final Act of the Uruguay Round.[b] The text set out some 28 specific agreements representing the potential results of the Uruguay Round in all areas except those relating to market access for goods and initial commitments in services. However, no single element could be considered as agreed until agreement was reached on the entire package.

In January 1992, the Trade Negotiations Committee agreed to continue to work on the basis of a global approach and established a four-track negotiating strategy. Track 1 dealt with market-access negotiations at the bilateral and multilateral levels, including specific commitments on internal support and export competition in agriculture; Track 2 was concerned with initial national commitments in the services area; Track 3 focused on detailed examination of all draft agreements to ensure legal conformity and internal consistency; and Track 4 examined possible adjustments to the Draft Final Act in certain specific areas.

In April, the Chairman of the Committee drew attention to a widespread perception that the Round was losing momentum, which was reflected in the reports by the chairmen of the negotiations on Tracks 1 and 2. In addition, major differences between the European Community (EC) and the United States made a meaningful or definitive Track 4 exercise unlikely.

Although the delays in the Round and the number of informally proposed amendments to the Draft Final Act were of concern at the Committee's December meeting, there was an overwhelming view that negotiating continuity and urgency were essential if the Round was to be concluded early in 1993. Several sets of intensive bilateral and multilateral market-access negotiations during 1992 resulted in the tabling of comprehensive draft tariff schedules and nine non-comprehensive schedules by 38 participants representing 49 countries. Six rounds of bilateral services negotiations took place, resulting in the tabling of 54 initial commitment lists on services, covering 67 countries. A number of technical issues relating to the General Agreement on Trade in Services text in the Draft Final Act were largely resolved through informal consultations, while the Air Transport and Telecommunications annexes were developed further.

Implementation of the Tokyo Round agreements

The agreements of the Tokyo Round (1973-1979), the seventh round of multilateral trade

[a]YUN 1986, p. 1211.
[b]YUN 1991, p. 1016.

negotiations, had concluded with a major package of tariff concessions, a series of new agreements on non-tariff measures (NTMs) and an improved legal framework for GATT. Various committees established at the conclusion of the Tokyo Round continued to supervise tariff schedules, administer the new agreements and provide a forum for discussing related issues.

Reports received by the Committee on Anti-Dumping Practices covering the period from 1 July 1991 to 30 June 1992 indicated that among the 25 parties to the Agreement on Anti-Dumping Practices, 76 investigations had been initiated by Australia, 62 by the United States, 25 by Mexico, 23 by EC, 16 by Canada, 13 by New Zealand, 9 by Brazil, 5 by India, 4 by Austria, 3 by Japan and 1 by Sweden. Dumped products were defined as those sold to an importer at a price lower than that charged by the producer in his domestic market.

Four of the 24 signatories to the Subsidies Agreement notified the Committee on Subsidies and Countervailing Measures that they had initiated countervailing duty investigations during the same period: the United States had initiated 15; Australia, 8; Brazil, 8; and Chile, 5. Two dispute-settlement panels were established in 1992 to examine United States measures affecting the export of pure and alloy magnesium from Canada and Australia's countervailing duties on imports of glacé cherries from France and Italy. Two panel reports were adopted in 1992—both from the United States—on Canadian countervailing duties on grain corn and the definition of "industry" concerning wine and grape products.

In January, negotiations to improve, broaden and expand the Agreement on Government Procurement led to acceptance of a draft by an informal working group. Later in the year, a consensus was reached that decision-making in dispute cases would be dealt with by the Dispute-Settlement Body negotiated in the Uruguay Round draft package. As to dispute settlement, the Committee in May adopted the panel report on the procurement by Norway of toll collection equipment for the city of Trondheim.

In 1992, Australia accepted the Agreement on Technical Barriers to Trade, bringing the total number of signatories to 38. In April and October, the Committee on Technical Barriers to Trade dealt with the implementation and administration of the Agreement and conducted its annual review. The Committee on Customs Valuation examined national legislation of Argentina, Cyprus, EC, India, Malawi and Romania related to the implementation and administration of the Customs Valuation Agreement. Of the 27 signatories to the Agreement on Import Licensing Procedures, 12 brought their national information up to date by replying to a GATT questionnaire on the subject.

The Committee on Trade in Civil Aircraft examined the text of a bilateral agreement on subsidies in the large civil aircraft sector presented by EC and the United States.

Other GATT activities

Regular session of Contracting Parties

The Contracting Parties, at their forty-eighth regular session, discussed trade and environment, new initiatives for the GATT Council of Representatives, disputes in the steel sector and follow-up action concerning several dispute panel reports.

Council of Representatives

In 1992, the Council of Representatives, GATT's highest body between sessions of the Contracting Parties, oversaw trade and environment activities, monitored the implementation of panel reports and conducted trade policy reviews of individual GATT members.

Trade and development

The Committee on Trade and Development continued to review, discuss and negotiate trade issues of interest to developing countries. It reviewed the implementation of part IV of the General Agreement, dealing with special treatment for developing countries, and of the enabling clause, an agreement resulting from the Tokyo Round providing for differential and more favourable treatment of developing countries in various areas of trade policy. With regard to the enabling clause, the Committee reviewed the participation of developing countries, including least developed countries (LDCs), in the multilateral trading system. The review covered recent developments in trade among developing countries and with industrial nations; external developments having a bearing on trade and the economic situation of developing countries; and developments in trade policies of developing and industrial countries as well as in relevant GATT bodies.

Trade and environment

GATT contributed to the United Nations Conference on Environment and Development (UNCED) (Rio de Janiero, Brazil, 3-14 June 1992) and participated in the follow-up action to that Conference (see PART THREE, Chapter VIII).

In December, the forty-eighth session of the Contracting Parties adopted a work programme for follow-up action to UNCED, under which the Committee on Trade and Development would deal with matters relating to the promotion of sustainable development through trade liberalization; the Group on Environmental Measures and International Trade would focus on issues related to making trade and environmental policies mutually supportive; and the Council of Representatives would be responsible for inter-institutional and other external relations questions. The Contracting Parties recalled the Council's decision of July 1991 to extend the mandate of the Working Group on Domestically Prohibited Goods for a period of three months from the date of the Group's next meeting in the context of UNCED follow-up action.

Textile arrangement

In December, the Textiles Committee decided to maintain in force the Multifibre Arrangement (MFA), as extended by a 1986 Protocol, for an additional period of 12 months from 1 January to 31 December 1993, since the Uruguay Round had not been completed. MFA had governed much of the world's trade in textiles and clothing since 1974 and had 42 members at the end of the year.

Technical cooperation

During 1992, the GATT secretariat's Technical Cooperation Division assisted developing countries by providing data on trade flows, tariff and non-tariff measures, trade and tariff data for specific products, background information and factual notes on various issues in negotiations. Between November 1991 and the end of 1992, it organized 16 country missions and seminars in Africa, Asia, Eastern Europe and Latin America. Special attention was given to the technical assistance requirements of LDCs.

Training programme

From the programme's inception in 1955 to the end of 1992, a total of 1,269 officials from 116 countries and 10 regional organizations had attended GATT trade policy courses.

To facilitate the integration of Central and Eastern European countries into the multilateral trading system, the GATT secretariat held a nine-week Special Trade Policy Course (Geneva, May) attended by officials from Albania, Belarus, Bulgaria, Czechoslovakia, Estonia, Hungary, Latvia, Lithuania, Poland, Romania, the Russian Federation and Ukraine.

International Trade Centre

The International Trade Centre (ITC), established by GATT in 1964 and jointly operated with the United Nations Conference on Trade and Development since 1968, implemented various technical cooperation activities with GATT, and GATT officials lectured in a number of ITC training events. ITC also organized two trade promotion sessions as part of the regular programme for GATT trade policy courses in 1992. Activities receiving special attention in 1992 were export business development, promoting trade in environmentally sound products, and the integration of women into trade-development and trade-promotion activities. ITC was also involved in the development and promotion of a variety of commodities. GATT and the United Nations contributed equally to the ITC budget, which totalled $18.8 million in 1992. The Centre's technical cooperation activities with developing countries in trade promotion amounted to $34.5 million, with some 105 national, 63 regional and 101 interregional projects under implementation in 1992.

Secretariat

As at 31 December 1992, the GATT secretariat employed 410 staff members (including temporary posts connected with the Uruguay Round negotiations)—168 in the Professional and higher categories and 242 in the General Service category.

Budget

Member countries of GATT contributed to the budget in accordance with a scale assessed on the basis of each country's share in the total trade of the Contracting Parties and associated Governments. The total budget for 1992 was 85,973,327 Swiss francs, or approximately $59.7 million. (The United Nations rate of exchange as at 31 December 1992 was SwF 1.44 = $US 1.)

NOTE: For further information on GATT, see *GATT Activities 1992: An Annual Review of the Work of the GATT*, published by GATT.

Annex I.   CONTRACTING PARTIES TO THE GENERAL AGREEMENT ON TARIFFS AND TRADE

(As at 31 December 1992)

Antigua and Barbuda, Argentina, Australia, Austria, Bangladesh, Barbados, Belgium, Belize, Benin, Bolivia, Botswana, Brazil, Burkino Faso, Burundi, Cameroon, Canada, Central African Republic, Chad, Chile, Colombia, Congo, Costa Rica, Côte d'Ivoire, Cuba, Cyprus, Czechoslovakia, Denmark, Dominican Republic, Egypt, El Salvador, Finland, France, Gabon, Gambia, Germany, Ghana, Greece, Guatemala, Guyana, Haiti, Hong Kong, Hungary, Iceland, India, Indonesia, Ireland, Israel, Italy, Jamaica, Japan, Kenya, Kuwait, Lesotho, Luxembourg, Macau, Madagascar, Malawi, Malaysia, Maldives, Malta, Mauritania, Mauritius, Mexico, Morocco, Mozambique, Myanmar, Namibia, Netherlands, New Zealand, Nicaragua, Niger, Nigeria, Norway, Pakistan, Peru, Philippines, Poland, Portugal, Republic of Korea, Romania, Rwanda, Senegal, Sierra Leone, Singapore, South Africa, Spain, Sri Lanka, Suriname, Sweden, Switzerland, Thailand, Togo, Trinidad and Tobago, Tunisia, Turkey, Uganda, United Kingdom, United Republic of Tanzania, United States, Uruguay, Venezuela, Yugoslavia,* Zaire, Zambia, Zimbabwe.

*On 19 June 1992, the GATT Council of Representatives agreed that the former Yugoslavia should refrain from participating in the Council until it further considered the issue.

Annex II.   OFFICERS AND OFFICE OF THE GENERAL AGREEMENT ON TARIFFS AND TRADE
(As at 31 December 1992)

OFFICERS

OFFICERS OF THE CONTRACTING PARTIES*
Chairman of the Contracting Parties: B. K. Zutshi (India).
Vice-Chairmen of the Contracting Parties: Alastair Bisley (New Zealand), Jakob Esper Larsen (Denmark), Jesús Seade (Mexico).
Chairman of the Council of Representatives: András Szepesi (Hungary).
Chairman of the Committee on Trade and Development: Mohammed Zahran (Egypt).

SENIOR OFFICERS OF THE SECRETARIAT
Director-General: Arthur Dunkel.
Deputy Director-General: Charles R. Carlisle.
Assistant Directors-General: Kenneth Broadbridge, Arif Hussain.

SENIOR OFFICER OF THE
INTERNATIONAL TRADE CENTRE UNCTAD/GATT
Officer-in-Charge: Raju Makil.

*Elected at the December 1992 session of the Contracting Parties to hold office until the end of the next session.

HEADQUARTERS

GATT Secretariat
Centre William Rappard
154, rue de Lausanne
1211 Geneva 21, Switzerland

Cable address: GATT GENEVA

Telephone: (41) (22) 739-51-11

Telex: 412 324 GATT CH

Facsimile: (41) (22) 731-42-06

Appendices

Appendix I

Roster of the United Nations

(As at 31 December 1992)

MEMBER	DATE OF ADMISSION	MEMBER	DATE OF ADMISSION	MEMBER	DATE OF ADMISSION
Afghanistan	19 Nov. 1946	Fiji	13 Oct. 1970	Myanmar	19 Apr. 1948
Albania	14 Dec. 1955	Finland	14 Dec. 1955	Namibia	23 Apr. 1990
Algeria	8 Oct. 1962	France	24 Oct. 1945	Nepal	14 Dec. 1955
Angola	1 Dec. 1976	Gabon	20 Sep. 1960	Netherlands	10 Dec. 1945
Antigua and Barbuda	11 Nov. 1981	Gambia	21 Sep. 1965	New Zealand	24 Oct. 1945
Argentina	24 Oct. 1945	Georgia	31 July 1992	Nicaragua	24 Oct. 1945
Armenia	2 Mar. 1992	Germany[2]	18 Sep. 1973	Niger	20 Sep. 1960
Australia	1 Nov. 1945	Ghana	8 Mar. 1957	Nigeria	7 Oct. 1960
Austria	14 Dec. 1955	Greece	25 Oct. 1945	Norway	27 Nov. 1945
Azerbaijan	2 Mar. 1992	Grenada	17 Sep. 1974	Oman	7 Oct. 1971
Bahamas	18 Sep. 1973	Guatemala	21 Nov. 1945	Pakistan	30 Sep. 1947
Bahrain	21 Sep. 1971	Guinea	12 Dec. 1958	Panama	13 Nov. 1945
Bangladesh	17 Sep. 1974	Guinea-Bissau	17 Sep. 1974	Papua New Guinea	10 Oct. 1975
Barbados	9 Dec. 1966	Guyana	20 Sep. 1966	Paraguay	24 Oct. 1945
Belarus	24 Oct. 1945	Haiti	24 Oct. 1945	Peru	31 Oct. 1945
Belgium	27 Dec. 1945	Honduras	17 Dec. 1945	Philippines	24 Oct. 1945
Belize	25 Sep. 1981	Hungary	14 Dec. 1955	Poland	24 Oct. 1945
Benin	20 Sep. 1960	Iceland	19 Nov. 1946	Portugal	14 Dec. 1955
Bhutan	21 Sep. 1971	India	30 Oct. 1945	Qatar	21 Sep. 1971
Bolivia	14 Nov. 1945	Indonesia[3]	28 Sep. 1950	Republic of Korea	17 Sep. 1991
Bosnia and Herzegovina	22 May 1992	Iran (Islamic Republic of)	24 Oct. 1945	Republic of Moldova	2 Mar. 1992
Botswana	17 Oct. 1966	Iraq	21 Dec. 1945	Romania	14 Dec. 1955
Brazil	24 Oct. 1945	Ireland	14 Dec. 1955	Russian Federation[5]	24 Oct. 1945
Brunei Darussalam	21 Sep. 1984	Israel	11 May 1949	Rwanda	18 Sep. 1962
Bulgaria	14 Dec. 1955	Italy	14 Dec. 1955	Saint Kitts and Nevis	23 Sep. 1983
Burkina Faso	20 Sep. 1960	Jamaica	18 Sep. 1962	Saint Lucia	18 Sep. 1979
Burundi	18 Sep. 1962	Japan	18 Dec. 1956	Saint Vincent and the Grenadines	16 Sep. 1980
Cambodia	14 Dec. 1955	Jordan	14 Dec. 1955	Samoa	15 Dec. 1976
Cameroon	20 Sep. 1960	Kazakhstan	2 Mar. 1992	San Marino	2 Mar. 1992
Canada	9 Nov. 1945	Kenya	16 Dec. 1963	Sao Tome and Principe	16 Sep. 1975
Cape Verde	16 Sep. 1975	Kuwait	14 May 1963	Saudi Arabia	24 Oct. 1945
Central African Republic	20 Sep. 1960	Kyrgyzstan	2 Mar. 1992	Senegal	28 Sep. 1960
Chad	20 Sep. 1960	Lao People's Democratic Republic	14 Dec. 1955	Seychelles	21 Sep. 1976
Chile	24 Oct. 1945	Latvia	17 Sep. 1991	Sierra Leone	27 Sep. 1961
China	24 Oct. 1945	Lebanon	24 Oct. 1945	Singapore[4]	21 Sep. 1965
Colombia	5 Nov. 1945	Lesotho	17 Oct. 1966	Slovenia	22 May 1992
Comoros	12 Nov. 1975	Liberia	2 Nov. 1945	Solomon Islands	19 Sep. 1978
Congo	20 Sep. 1960	Libyan Arab Jamahiriya	14 Dec. 1955	Somalia	20 Sep. 1960
Costa Rica	2 Nov. 1945	Liechtenstein	18 Sep. 1990	South Africa	7 Nov. 1945
Côte d'Ivoire	20 Sep. 1960	Lithuania	17 Sep. 1991	Spain	14 Dec. 1955
Croatia	22 May 1992	Luxembourg	24 Oct. 1945	Sri Lanka	14 Dec. 1955
Cuba	24 Oct. 1945	Madagascar	20 Sep. 1960	Sudan	12 Nov. 1956
Cyprus	20 Sep. 1960	Malawi	1 Dec. 1964	Suriname	4 Dec. 1975
Czech and Slovak Federal Republic	24 Oct. 1945	Malaysia[4]	17 Sep. 1957	Swaziland	24 Sep. 1968
Democratic People's Republic of Korea	17 Sep. 1991	Maldives	21 Sep. 1965	Sweden	19 Nov. 1946
Denmark	24 Oct. 1945	Mali	28 Sep. 1960	Syrian Arab Republic[1]	24 Oct. 1945
Djibouti	20 Sep. 1977	Malta	1 Dec. 1964	Tajikistan	2 Mar. 1992
Dominica	18 Dec. 1978	Marshall Islands	17 Sep. 1991	Thailand	16 Dec. 1946
Dominican Republic	24 Oct. 1945	Mauritania	27 Oct. 1961	Togo	20 Sep. 1960
Ecuador	21 Dec. 1945	Mauritius	24 Apr. 1968	Trinidad and Tobago	18 Sep. 1962
Egypt[1]	24 Oct. 1945	Mexico	7 Nov. 1945	Tunisia	12 Nov. 1956
El Salvador	24 Oct. 1945	Micronesia (Federated States of)	17 Sep. 1991	Turkey	24 Oct. 1945
Equatorial Guinea	12 Nov. 1968	Mongolia	27 Oct. 1961	Turkmenistan	2 Mar. 1992
Estonia	17 Sep. 1991	Morocco	12 Nov. 1956	Uganda	25 Oct. 1962
Ethiopia	13 Nov. 1945	Mozambique	16 Sep. 1975	Ukraine	24 Oct. 1945

MEMBER	DATE OF ADMISSION	MEMBER	DATE OF ADMISSION	MEMBER	DATE OF ADMISSION
United Arab Emirates	9 Dec. 1971	United States		Viet Nam	20 Sep. 1977
United Kingdom of		of America	24 Oct. 1945	Yemen[7]	30 Sep. 1947
Great Britain and		Uruguay	18 Dec. 1945	Yugoslavia	24 Oct. 1945
Northern Ireland	24 Oct. 1945	Uzbekistan	2 Mar. 1992	Zaire	20 Sep. 1960
United Republic		Vanuatu	15 Sep. 1981	Zambia	1 Dec. 1964
of Tanzania[6]	14 Dec. 1961	Venezuela	15 Nov. 1945	Zimbabwe	25 Aug. 1980

[1]Egypt and Syria, both of which became Members of the United Nations on 24 October 1945, joined together—following a plebiscite held in those countries on 21 February 1958—to form the United Arab Republic. On 13 October 1961, Syria, having resumed its status as an independent State, also resumed its separate membership in the United Nations; it changed its name to the Syrian Arab Republic on 14 September 1971. The United Arab Republic continued as a Member of the United Nations and reverted to the name of Egypt on 2 September 1971.

[2]Through accession of the German Democratic Republic to the Federal Republic of Germany on 3 October 1990, the two German States (both of which became United Nations Members on 18 September 1973) united to form one sovereign State. As from that date, the Federal Republic of Germany has acted in the United Nations under the designation Germany.

[3]On 20 January 1965, Indonesia informed the Secretary-General that it had decided to withdraw from the United Nations. By a telegram of 19 September 1966, it notified the Secretary-General of its decision to resume participation in the activities of the United Nations. On 28 September 1966, the General Assembly took note of that decision and the President invited the representatives of Indonesia to take their seats in the Assembly.

[4]On 16 September 1963, Sabah (North Borneo), Sarawak and Singapore joined with the Federation of Malaya (which became a United Nations Member on 17 September 1957) to form Malaysia. On 9 August 1965, Singapore became an independent State and on 21 September 1965 it became a Member of the United Nations.

[5]The Union of Soviet Socialist Republics was an original Member of the United Nations from 24 October 1945. On 24 December 1991, the President of the Russian Federation informed the Secretary-General that the membership of the USSR in all United Nations organs was being continued by the Russian Federation.

[6]Tanganyika was admitted to the United Nations on 14 December 1961, and Zanzibar, on 16 December 1963. Following ratification, on 26 April 1964, of the Articles of Union between Tanganyika and Zanzibar, the two States became represented as a single Member: the United Republic of Tanganyika and Zanzibar; it changed its name to the United Republic of Tanzania on 1 November 1964.

[7]Yemen was admitted to the United Nations on 30 September 1947 and Democratic Yemen on 14 December 1967. On 22 May 1990, the two countries merged and have since been represented as one Member.

Appendix II

Charter of the United Nations and Statute of the International Court of Justice

Charter of the United Nations

NOTE: The Charter of the United Nations was signed on 26 June 1945, in San Francisco, at the conclusion of the United Nations Conference on International Organization, and came into force on 24 October 1945. The Statute of the International Court of Justice is an integral part of the Charter.

Amendments to Articles 23, 27 and 61 of the Charter were adopted by the General Assembly on 17 December 1963 and came into force on 31 August 1965. A further amendment to Article 61 was adopted by the General Assembly on 20 December 1971, and came into force on 24 September 1973. An amendment to Article 109, adopted by the General Assembly on 20 December 1965, came into force on 12 June 1968.

The amendment to Article 23 enlarges the membership of the Security Council from 11 to 15. The amended Article 27 provides that decisions of the Security Council on procedural matters shall be made by an affirmative vote of nine members (formerly seven) and on all other matters by an affirmative vote of nine members (formerly seven), including the concurring votes of the five permanent members of the Security Council.

The amendment to Article 61, which entered into force on 31 August 1965, enlarged the membership of the Economic and Social Council from 18 to 27. The subsequent amendment to that Article, which entered into force on 24 September 1973, further increased the membership of the Council from 27 to 54.

The amendment to Article 109, which relates to the first paragraph of that Article, provides that a General Conference of Member States for the purpose of reviewing the Charter may be held at a date and place to be fixed by a two-thirds vote of the members of the General Assembly and by a vote of any nine members (formerly seven) of the Security Council. Paragraph 3 of Article 109, which deals with the consideration of a possible review conference during the tenth regular session of the General Assembly, has been retained in its original form in its reference to a "vote of any seven members of the Security Council", the paragraph having been acted upon in 1955 by the General Assembly, at its tenth regular session, and by the Security Council.

WE THE PEOPLES
OF THE UNITED NATIONS
DETERMINED
to save succeeding generations from the scourge of war, which twice in our lifetime has brought untold sorrow to mankind, and
to reaffirm faith in fundamental human rights, in the dignity and worth of the human person, in the equal rights of men and women and of nations large and small, and
to establish conditions under which justice and respect for the obligations arising from treaties and other sources of international law can be maintained, and
to promote social progress and better standards of life in larger freedom,

AND FOR THESE ENDS
to practice tolerance and live together in peace with one another as good neighbours, and
to unite our strength to maintain international peace and security, and
to ensure, by the acceptance of principles and the institution of methods, that armed force shall not be used, save in the common interest, and
to employ international machinery for the promotion of the economic and social advancement of all peoples,

HAVE RESOLVED TO
COMBINE OUR EFFORTS TO
ACCOMPLISH THESE AIMS
Accordingly, our respective Governments, through representatives assembled in the city of San Francisco, who have exhibited their full powers found to be in good and due form, have agreed to the present Charter of the United Nations and do hereby establish an international organization to be known as the United Nations.

Chapter I
PURPOSES AND PRINCIPLES

Article 1
The Purposes of the United Nations are:
1. To maintain international peace and security, and to that end: to take effective collective measures for the prevention and removal of threats to the peace, and for the suppression of acts of aggression or other breaches of the peace, and to bring about by peaceful means, and in conformity with the principles of justice and international law, adjustment or settlement of international disputes or situations which might lead to a breach of the peace;
2. To develop friendly relations among nations based on respect for the principle of equal rights and self-determination of peoples, and to take other appropriate measures to strengthen universal peace;
3. To achieve international co-operation in solving international problems of an economic, social, cultural, or humanitarian character, and in promoting and encouraging respect for human rights and for fundamental freedoms for all without distinction as to race, sex, language, or religion; and
4. To be a centre for harmonizing the actions of nations in the attainment of these common ends.

Article 2
The Organization and its Members, in pursuit of the Purposes stated in Article 1, shall act in accordance with the following Principles.
1. The Organization is based on the principle of the sovereign equality of all its Members.
2. All Members, in order to ensure to all of them the rights and benefits resulting from membership, shall fulfil in good faith the obligations assumed by them in accordance with the present Charter.

3. All Members shall settle their international disputes by peaceful means in such a manner that international peace and security, and justice, are not endangered.

4. All Members shall refrain in their international relations from the threat or use of force against the territorial integrity or political independence of any state, or in any other manner inconsistent with the Purposes of the United Nations.

5. All Members shall give the United Nations every assistance in any action it takes in accordance with the present Charter, and shall refrain from giving assistance to any state against which the United Nations is taking preventive or enforcement action.

6. The Organization shall ensure that states which are not Members of the United Nations act in accordance with these Principles so far as may be necessary for the maintenance of international peace and security.

7. Nothing contained in the present Charter shall authorize the United Nations to intervene in matters which are essentially within the domestic jurisdiction of any state or shall require the Members to submit such matters to settlement under the present Charter; but this principle shall not prejudice the application of enforcement measures under Chapter VII.

Chapter II
MEMBERSHIP

Article 3

The original Members of the United Nations shall be the states which, having participated in the United Nations Conference on International Organization at San Francisco, or having previously signed the Declaration by United Nations of 1 January 1942, sign the present Charter and ratify it in accordance with Article 110.

Article 4

1. Membership in the United Nations is open to all other peace-loving states which accept the obligations contained in the present Charter and, in the judgment of the Organization, are able and willing to carry out these obligations.

2. The admission of any such state to membership in the United Nations will be effected by a decision of the General Assembly upon the recommendation of the Security Council.

Article 5

A Member of the United Nations against which preventive or enforcement action has been taken by the Security Council may be suspended from the exercise of the rights and privileges of membership by the General Assembly upon the recommendation of the Security Council. The exercise of these rights and privileges may be restored by the Security Council.

Article 6

A Member of the United Nations which has persistently violated the Principles contained in the present Charter may be expelled from the Organization by the General Assembly upon the recommendation of the Security Council.

Chapter III
ORGANS

Article 7

1. There are established as the principal organs of the United Nations: a General Assembly, a Security Council, an Economic and Social Council, a Trusteeship Council, an International Court of Justice, and a Secretariat.

2. Such subsidiary organs as may be found necessary may be established in accordance with the present Charter.

Article 8

The United Nations shall place no restrictions on the eligibility of men and women to participate in any capacity and under conditions of equality in its principal and subsidiary organs.

Chapter IV
THE GENERAL ASSEMBLY

Composition

Article 9

1. The General Assembly shall consist of all the Members of the United Nations.

2. Each Member shall have not more than five representatives in the General Assembly.

Functions and powers

Article 10

The General Assembly may discuss any questions or any matters within the scope of the present Charter or relating to the powers and functions of any organs provided for in the present Charter, and, except as provided in Article 12, may make recommendations to the Members of the United Nations or to the Security Council or to both on any such questions or matters.

Article 11

1. The General Assembly may consider the general principles of co-operation in the maintenance of international peace and security, including the principles governing disarmament and the regulation of armaments, and may make recommendations with regard to such principles to the Members or to the Security Council or to both.

2. The General Assembly may discuss any questions relating to the maintenance of international peace and security brought before it by any Member of the United Nations, or by the Security Council, or by a state which is not a Member of the United Nations in accordance with Article 35, paragraph 2, and, except as provided in Article 12, may make recommendations with regard to any such questions to the state or states concerned or to the Security Council or to both. Any such question on which action is necessary shall be referred to the Security Council by the General Assembly either before or after discussion.

3. The General Assembly may call the attention of the Security Council to situations which are likely to endanger international peace and security.

4. The powers of the General Assembly set forth in this Article shall not limit the general scope of Article 10.

Article 12

1. While the Security Council is exercising in respect of any dispute or situation the functions assigned to it in the present Charter, the General Assembly shall not make any recommendation with regard to that dispute or situation unless the Security Council so requests.

2. The Secretary-General, with the consent of the Security Council, shall notify the General Assembly at each session of any matters relative to the maintenance of international peace and security which are being dealt with by the Security Council and shall similarly notify the General Assembly, or the Members of the United Nations if the General Assembly is not in session, immediately the Security Council ceases to deal with such matters.

Article 13

1. The General Assembly shall initiate studies and make recommendations for the purpose of:
   a. promoting international co-operation in the political field and encouraging the progressive development of international law and its codification;
   b. promoting international co-operation in the economic, social, cultural, educational, and health fields, and assisting in the realization of human rights and fundamental freedoms for all without distinction as to race, sex, language, or religion.

2. The further responsibilities, functions and powers of the General Assembly with respect to matters mentioned in paragraph 1(b) above are set forth in Chapters IX and X.

Article 14

Subject to the provisions of Article 12, the General Assembly may recommend measures for the peaceful adjustment of any situation, regardless of origin, which it deems likely to impair the general welfare or friendly relations among nations, including situations resulting from a violation of the provisions of the present Charter setting forth the Purposes and Principles of the United Nations.

Article 15

1. The General Assembly shall receive and consider annual and special reports from the Security Council; these reports shall include an account of the measures that the Security Council has decided upon or taken to maintain international peace and security.

2. The General Assembly shall receive and consider reports from the other organs of the United Nations.

Article 16

The General Assembly shall perform such functions with respect to the international trusteeship system as are assigned to it under Chapters XII and XIII, including the approval of the trusteeship agreements for areas not designated as strategic.

Article 17

1. The General Assembly shall consider and approve the budget of the Organization.

2. The expenses of the Organization shall be borne by the Members as apportioned by the General Assembly.

3. The General Assembly shall consider and approve any financial and budgetary arrangements with specialized agencies referred to in Article 57 and shall examine the administrative budgets of such specialized agencies with a view to making recommendations to the agencies concerned.

Voting

Article 18

1. Each member of the General Assembly shall have one vote.

2. Decisions of the General Assembly on important questions shall be made by a two-thirds majority of the members present and voting. These questions shall include: recommendations with respect to the maintenance of international peace and security, the election of the non-permanent members of the Security Council, the election of the members of the Economic and Social Council, the election of members of the Trusteeship Council in accordance with paragraph 1(c) of Article 86, the admission of new Members to the United Nations, the suspension of the rights and privileges of membership, the expulsion of Members, questions relating to the operation of the trusteeship system, and budgetary questions.

3. Decisions on other questions, including the determination of additional categories of questions to be decided by a two-thirds majority, shall be made by a majority of the members present and voting.

Article 19

A Member of the United Nations which is in arrears in the payment of its financial contributions to the Organization shall have no vote in the General Assembly if the amount of its arrears equals or exceeds the amount of the contributions due from it for the preceding two full years. The General Assembly may, nevertheless, permit such a Member to vote if it is satisfied that the failure to pay is due to conditions beyond the control of the Member.

Procedure

Article 20

The General Assembly shall meet in regular annual sessions and in such special sessions as occasion may require. Special sessions shall be convoked by the Secretary-General at the request of the Security Council or of a majority of the Members of the United Nations.

Article 21

The General Assembly shall adopt its own rules of procedure. It shall elect its President for each session.

Article 22

The General Assembly may establish such subsidiary organs as it deems necessary for the performance of its functions.

Chapter V
THE SECURITY COUNCIL

Composition

Article 23[1]

1. The Security Council shall consist of fifteen Members of the United Nations. The Republic of China, France, the Union of Soviet Socialist Republics, the United Kingdom of Great Britain and Northern Ireland, and the United States of America shall be permanent members of the Security Council. The General Assembly shall elect ten other Members of the United Nations to be non-permanent members of the Security Council, due regard being specially paid, in the first instance to the contribution of Members of the United Nations to the maintenance of international peace and security and to the other purposes of the Organization, and also to equitable geographical distribution.

2. The non-permanent members of the Security Council shall be elected for a term of two years. In the first election of the non-permanent members after the increase of the membership of the Security Council from eleven to fifteen, two of the four additional members shall be chosen for a term of one year. A retiring member shall not be eligible for immediate re-election.

3. Each member of the Security Council shall have one representative.

Functions and powers

Article 24

1. In order to ensure prompt and effective action by the United Nations, its Members confer on the Security Council primary responsibility for the maintenance of international peace and security, and agree that in carrying out its duties under this responsibility the Security Council acts on their behalf.

2. In discharging these duties the Security Council shall act in accordance with the Purposes and Principles of the United Nations. The specific powers granted to the Security Council for the discharge of these duties are laid down in Chapters VI, VII, VIII, and XII.

3. The Security Council shall submit annual and, when necessary, special reports to the General Assembly for its consideration.

Article 25

The Members of the United Nations agree to accept and carry out the decisions of the Security Council in accordance with the present Charter.

Article 26

In order to promote the establishment and maintenance of international peace and security with the least diversion for armaments of the world's human and economic resources, the Security Council shall be responsible for formulating, with the

---

[1]Amended text of Article 23, which came into force on 31 August 1965. (The text of Article 23 before it was amended read as follows:

1. The Security Council shall consist of eleven Members of the United Nations. The Republic of China, France, the Union of Soviet Socialist Republics, the United Kingdom of Great Britain and Northern Ireland, and the United States of America shall be permanent members of the Security Council. The General Assembly shall elect six other Members of the United Nations to be non-permanent members of the Security Council, due regard being specially paid, in the first instance to the contribution of Members of the United Nations to the maintenance of international peace and security and to the other purposes of the Organization, and also to equitable geographical distribution.

2. The non-permanent members of the Security Council shall be elected for a term of two years. In the first election of non-permanent members, however, three shall be chosen for a term of one year. A retiring member shall not be eligible for immediate re-election.

3. Each member of the Security Council shall have one representative.)

assistance of the Military Staff Committee referred to in Article 47, plans to be submitted to the Members of the United Nations for the establishment of a system for the regulation of armaments.

Voting

Article 27 [2]

1. Each member of the Security Council shall have one vote.
2. Decisions of the Security Council on procedural matters shall be made by an affirmative vote of nine members.
3. Decisions of the Security Council on all other matters shall be made by an affirmative vote of nine members including the concurring votes of the permanent members; provided that, in decisions under Chapter VI, and under paragraph 3 of Article 52, a party to a dispute shall abstain from voting.

Procedure

Article 28

1. The Security Council shall be so organized as to be able to function continuously. Each member of the Security Council shall for this purpose be represented at all times at the seat of the Organization.
2. The Security Council shall hold periodic meetings at which each of its members may, if it so desires, be represented by a member of the government or by some other specially designated representative.
3. The Security Council may hold meetings at such places other than the seat of the Organization as in its judgment will best facilitate its work.

Article 29

The Security Council may establish such subsidiary organs as it deems necessary for the performance of its functions.

Article 30

The Security Council shall adopt its own rules of procedure, including the method of selecting its President.

Article 31

Any Member of the United Nations which is not a member of the Security Council may participate, without vote, in the discussion of any question brought before the Security Council whenever the latter considers that the interests of that Member are specially affected.

Article 32

Any Member of the United Nations which is not a member of the Security Council or any state which is not a Member of the United Nations, if it is a party to a dispute under consideration by the Security Council, shall be invited to participate, without vote, in the discussion relating to the dispute. The Security Council shall lay down such conditions as it deems just for the participation of a state which is not a Member of the United Nations.

Chapter VI
PACIFIC SETTLEMENT OF DISPUTES

Article 33

1. The parties to any dispute, the continuance of which is likely to endanger the maintenance of international peace and security, shall, first of all, seek a solution by negotiation, enquiry, mediation, conciliation, arbitration, judicial settlement, resort to regional agencies or arrangements, or other peaceful means of their own choice.
2. The Security Council shall, when it deems necessary, call upon the parties to settle their dispute by such means.

Article 34

The Security Council may investigate any dispute or any situation which might lead to international friction or give rise to a dispute, in order to determine whether the continuance of the dispute or situation is likely to endanger the maintenance of international peace and security.

Article 35

1. Any Member of the United Nations may bring any dispute, or any situation of the nature referred to in Article 34, to the attention of the Security Council or of the General Assembly.
2. A state which is not a Member of the United Nations may bring to the attention of the Security Council or of the General Assembly any dispute to which it is a party if it accepts in advance, for the purposes of the dispute, the obligations of pacific settlement provided in the present Charter.
3. The proceedings of the General Assembly in respect of matters brought to its attention under this Article will be subject to the provisions of Articles 11 and 12.

Article 36

1. The Security Council may, at any stage of a dispute of the nature referred to in Article 33 or of a situation of like nature, recommend appropriate procedures or methods of adjustment.
2. The Security Council should take into consideration any procedures for the settlement of the dispute which have already been adopted by the parties.
3. In making recommendations under this Article the Security Council should also take into consideration that legal disputes should as a general rule be referred by the parties to the International Court of Justice in accordance with the provisions of the Statute of the Court.

Article 37

1. Should the parties to a dispute of the nature referred to in Article 33 fail to settle it by the means indicated in that Article, they shall refer it to the Security Council.
2. If the Security Council deems that the continuance of the dispute is in fact likely to endanger the maintenance of international peace and security, it shall decide whether to take action under Article 36 or to recommend such terms of settlement as it may consider appropriate.

Article 38

Without prejudice to the provisions of Articles 33 to 37, the Security Council may, if all the parties to any dispute so request, make recommendations to the parties with a view to a pacific settlement of the dispute.

Chapter VII
ACTION WITH RESPECT TO THREATS TO THE PEACE, BREACHES OF THE PEACE, AND ACTS OF AGGRESSION

Article 39

The Security Council shall determine the existence of any threat to the peace, breach of the peace, or act of aggression and shall make recommendations, or decide what measures shall be taken in accordance with Articles 41 and 42, to maintain or restore international peace and security.

Article 40

In order to prevent an aggravation of the situation, the Security Council may, before making the recommendations or deciding upon the measures provided for in Article 39, call upon the parties concerned to comply with such provisional measures as it deems necessary or desirable. Such provisional measures shall be without prejudice to the rights, claims, or position of the parties concerned. The Security Council shall duly take account of failure to comply with such provisional measures.

---

[2]Amended text of Article 27, which came into force on 31 August 1965. (The text of Article 27 before it was amended read as follows:
  1. Each member of the Security Council shall have one vote.
  2. Decisions of the Security Council on procedural matters shall be made by an affirmative vote of seven members.
  3. Decisions of the Security Council on all other matters shall be made by an affirmative vote of seven members including the concurring votes of the permanent members; provided that, in decisions under Chapter VI, and under paragraph 3 of Article 52, a party to a dispute shall abstain from voting.)

Article 41

The Security Council may decide what measures not involving the use of armed force are to be employed to give effect to its decisions, and it may call upon the Members of the United Nations to apply such measures. These may include complete or partial interruption of economic relations and of rail, sea, air, postal, telegraphic, radio, and other means of communication, and the severance of diplomatic relations.

Article 42

Should the Security Council consider that measures provided for in Article 41 would be inadequate or have proved to be inadequate, it may take such action by air, sea, or land forces as may be necessary to maintain or restore international peace and security. Such action may include demonstrations, blockade, and other operations by air, sea, or land forces of Members of the United Nations.

Article 43

1.   All Members of the United Nations, in order to contribute to the maintenance of international peace and security, undertake to make available to the Security Council, on its call and in accordance with a special agreement or agreements, armed forces, assistance, and facilities, including rights of passage, necessary for the purpose of maintaining international peace and security.

2.   Such agreement or agreements shall govern the numbers and types of forces, their degree of readiness and general location, and the nature of the facilities and assistance to be provided.

3.   The agreement or agreements shall be negotiated as soon as possible on the initiative of the Security Council. They shall be concluded between the Security Council and Members or between the Security Council and groups of Members and shall be subject to ratification by the signatory states in accordance with their respective constitutional processes.

Article 44

When the Security Council has decided to use force it shall, before calling upon a Member not represented on it to provide armed forces in fulfilment of the obligations assumed under Article 43, invite that Member, if the Member so desires, to participate in the decisions of the Security Council concerning the employment of contingents of that Member's armed forces.

Article 45

In order to enable the United Nations to take urgent military measures, Members shall hold immediately available national air-force contingents for combined international enforcement action. The strength and degree of readiness of these contingents and plans for their combined action shall be determined, within the limits laid down in the special agreement or agreements referred to in Article 43, by the Security Council with the assistance of the Military Staff Committee.

Article 46

Plans for the application of armed force shall be made by the Security Council with the assistance of the Military Staff Committee.

Article 47

1.   There shall be established a Military Staff Committee to advise and assist the Security Council on all questions relating to the Security Council's military requirements for the maintenance of international peace and security, the employment and command of forces placed at its disposal, the regulation of armaments, and possible disarmament.

2.   The Military Staff Committee shall consist of the Chiefs of Staff of the permanent members of the Security Council or their representatives. Any Member of the United Nations not permanently represented on the Committee shall be invited by the Committee to be associated with it when the efficient discharge of the Committee's responsibilities requires the participation of that Member in its work.

3.   The Military Staff Committee shall be responsible under the Security Council for the strategic direction of any armed forces placed at the disposal of the Security Council. Questions relating to the command of such forces shall be worked out subsequently.

4.   The Military Staff Committee, with the authorization of the Security Council and after consultation with appropriate regional agencies, may establish regional sub-committees.

Article 48

1.   The action required to carry out the decisions of the Security Council for the maintenance of international peace and security shall be taken by all the Members of the United Nations or by some of them, as the Security Council may determine.

2.   Such decisions shall be carried out by the Members of the United Nations directly and through their action in the appropriate international agencies of which they are members.

Article 49

The Members of the United Nations shall join in affording mutual assistance in carrying out the measures decided upon by the Security Council.

Article 50

If preventive or enforcement measures against any state are taken by the Security Council, any other state, whether a Member of the United Nations or not, which finds itself confronted with special economic problems arising from the carrying out of those measures shall have the right to consult the Security Council with regard to a solution of those problems.

Article 51

Nothing in the present Charter shall impair the inherent right of individual or collective self-defence if an armed attack occurs against a Member of the United Nations, until the Security Council has taken measures necessary to maintain international peace and security. Measures taken by Members in the exercise of this right of self-defence shall be immediately reported to the Security Council and shall not in any way affect the authority and responsibility of the Security Council under the present Charter to take at any time such action as it deems necessary in order to maintain or restore international peace and security.

Chapter VIII
REGIONAL ARRANGEMENTS

Article 52

1.   Nothing in the present Charter precludes the existence of regional arrangements or agencies for dealing with such matters relating to the maintenance of international peace and security as are appropriate for regional action, provided that such arrangements or agencies and their activities are consistent with the Purposes and Principles of the United Nations.

2.   The Members of the United Nations entering into such arrangements or constituting such agencies shall make every effort to achieve pacific settlement of local disputes through such regional arrangements or by such regional agencies before referring them to the Security Council.

3.   The Security Council shall encourage the development of pacific settlement of local disputes through such regional arrangements or by such regional agencies either on the initiative of the states concerned or by reference from the Security Council.

4.   This Article in no way impairs the application of Articles 34 and 35.

Article 53

1.   The Security Council shall, where appropriate, utilize such regional arrangements or agencies for enforcement action under its authority. But no enforcement action shall be taken under regional arrangements or by regional agencies without the authorization of the Security Council, with the exception of measures against any enemy state, as defined in paragraph 2 of this Article, provided for pursuant to Article 107 or in regional arrangements directed against renewal of aggressive policy on the part of any such state, until such time as the Organization may, on request of the Governments concerned, be charged with the responsibility for preventing further aggression by such a state.

2. The term enemy state as used in paragraph 1 of this Article applies to any state which during the Second World War has been an enemy of any signatory of the present Charter.

Article 54
The Security Council shall at all times be kept fully informed of activities undertaken or in contemplation under regional arrangements or by regional agencies for the maintenance of international peace and security.

Chapter IX
INTERNATIONAL ECONOMIC AND SOCIAL CO-OPERATION

Article 55
With a view to the creation of conditions of stability and well-being which are necessary for peaceful and friendly relations among nations based on respect for the principle of equal rights and self-determination of peoples, the United Nations shall promote:
a. higher standards of living, full employment, and conditions of economic and social progress and development;
b. solutions of international economic, social, health, and related problems; and international cultural and educational co-operation; and
c. universal respect for, and observance of, human rights and fundamental freedoms for all without distinction as to race, sex, language, or religion.

Article 56
All Members pledge themselves to take joint and separate action in co-operation with the Organization for the achievement of the purposes set forth in Article 55.

Article 57
1. The various specialized agencies, established by intergovernmental agreement and having wide international responsibilities, as defined in their basic instruments, in economic, social, cultural, educational, health, and related fields, shall be brought into relationship with the United Nations in accordance with the provisions of Article 63.
2. Such agencies thus brought into relationship with the United Nations are hereinafter referred to as specialized agencies.

Article 58
The Organization shall make recommendations for the co-ordination of the policies and activities of the specialized agencies.

Article 59
The Organization shall, where appropriate, initiate negotiations among the states concerned for the creation of any new specialized agencies required for the accomplishment of the purposes set forth in Article 55.

Article 60
Responsibility for the discharge of the functions of the Organization set forth in this Chapter shall be vested in the General Assembly and, under the authority of the General Assembly, in the Economic and Social Council, which shall have for this purpose the powers set forth in Chapter X.

Chapter X
THE ECONOMIC AND SOCIAL COUNCIL

Composition

Article 61 [3]
1. The Economic and Social Council shall consist of fifty-four Members of the United Nations elected by the General Assembly.
2. Subject to the provisions of paragraph 3, eighteen members of the Economic and Social Council shall be elected each year for a term of three years. A retiring member shall be eligible for immediate re-election.
3. At the first election after the increase in the membership of the Economic and Social Council from twenty-seven to fifty-

four members, in addition to the members elected in place of the nine members whose term of office expires at the end of that year, twenty-seven additional members shall be elected. Of these twenty-seven additional members, the term of office of nine members so elected shall expire at the end of one year, and of nine other members at the end of two years, in accordance with arrangements made by the General Assembly.
4. Each member of the Economic and Social Council shall have one representative.

Functions and powers

Article 62
1. The Economic and Social Council may make or initiate studies and reports with respect to international economic, social, cultural, educational, health, and related matters and may make recommendations with respect to any such matters to the General Assembly, to the Members of the United Nations, and to the specialized agencies concerned.
2. It may make recommendations for the purpose of promoting respect for, and observance of, human rights and fundamental freedoms for all.
3. It may prepare draft conventions for submission to the General Assembly, with respect to matters falling within its competence.
4. It may call, in accordance with the rules prescribed by the United Nations, international conferences on matters falling within its competence.

Article 63
1. The Economic and Social Council may enter into agreements with any of the agencies referred to in Article 57, defining the terms on which the agency concerned shall be brought into relationship with the United Nations. Such agreements shall be subject to approval by the General Assembly.
2. It may co-ordinate the activities of the specialized agencies through consultation with and recommendations to such agencies and through recommendations to the General Assembly and to the Members of the United Nations.

Article 64
1. The Economic and Social Council may take appropriate steps to obtain regular reports from the specialized agencies. It may make arrangements with the Members of the United Nations and with the specialized agencies to obtain reports on the steps taken to give effect to its own recommendations and to recommendations on matters falling within its competence made by the General Assembly.
2. It may communicate its observations on these reports to the General Assembly.

Article 65
The Economic and Social Council may furnish information to the Security Council and shall assist the Security Council upon its request.

Article 66
1. The Economic and Social Council shall perform such functions as fall within its competence in connexion with the carrying out of the recommendations of the General Assembly.

---

[3]Amended text of Article 61, which came into force on 24 September 1973. (The text of Article 61 as previously amended on 31 August 1965 read as follows:
1. The Economic and Social Council shall consist of twenty-seven Members of the United Nations elected by the General Assembly.
2. Subject to the provisions of paragraph 3, nine members of the Economic and Social Council shall be elected each year for a term of three years. A retiring member shall be eligible for immediate re-election.
3. At the first election after the increase in the membership of the Economic and Social Council from eighteen to twenty-seven members, in addition to the members elected in place of the six members whose term of office expires at the end of that year, nine additional members shall be elected. Of these nine additional members, the term of office of three members so elected shall expire at the end of one year, and of three other members at the end of two years, in accordance with arrangements made by the General Assembly.
4. Each member of the Economic and Social Council shall have one representative.)

2. It may, with the approval of the General Assembly, perform services at the request of Members of the United Nations and at the request of specialized agencies.

3. It shall perform such other functions as are specified elsewhere in the present Charter or as may be assigned to it by the General Assembly.

Voting

Article 67

1. Each member of the Economic and Social Council shall have one vote.

2. Decisions of the Economic and Social Council shall be made by a majority of the members present and voting.

Procedure

Article 68

The Economic and Social Council shall set up commissions in economic and social fields and for the promotion of human rights, and such other commissions as may be required for the performance of its functions.

Article 69

The Economic and Social Council shall invite any Member of the United Nations to participate, without vote, in its deliberations on any matter of particular concern to that Member.

Article 70

The Economic and Social Council may make arrangements for representatives of the specialized agencies to participate, without vote, in its deliberations and in those of the commissions established by it, and for its representatives to participate in the deliberations of the specialized agencies.

Article 71

The Economic and Social Council may make suitable arrangements for consultation with non-governmental organizations which are concerned with matters within its competence. Such arrangements may be made with international organizations and, where appropriate, with national organizations after consultation with the Member of the United Nations concerned.

Article 72

1. The Economic and Social Council shall adopt its own rules of procedure, including the method of selecting its President.

2. The Economic and Social Council shall meet as required in accordance with its rules, which shall include provision for the convening of meetings on the request of a majority of its members.

Chapter XI
DECLARATION REGARDING
NON-SELF-GOVERNING TERRITORIES

Article 73

Members of the United Nations which have or assume responsibilities for the administration of territories whose peoples have not yet attained a full measure of self-government recognize the principle that the interests of the inhabitants of these territories are paramount, and accept as a sacred trust the obligation to promote to the utmost, within the system of international peace and security established by the present Charter, the well-being of the inhabitants of these territories, and, to this end:

a. to ensure, with due respect for the culture of the peoples concerned, their political, economic, social, and educational advancement, their just treatment, and their protection against abuses;

b. to develop self-government, to take due account of the political aspirations of the peoples, and to assist them in the progressive development of their free political institutions, according to the particular circumstances of each territory and its peoples and their varying stages of advancement;

c. to further international peace and security;

d. to promote constructive measures of development, to encourage research, and to co-operate with one another and,

when and where appropriate, with specialized international bodies with a view to the practical achievement of the social, economic, and scientific purposes set forth in this Article; and

e. to transmit regularly to the Secretary-General for information purposes, subject to such limitation as security and constitutional considerations may require, statistical and other information of a technical nature relating to economic, social, and educational conditions in the territories for which they are respectively responsible other than those territories to which Chapters XII and XIII apply.

Article 74

Members of the United Nations also agree that their policy in respect of the territories to which this Chapter applies, no less than in respect of their metropolitan areas, must be based on the general principle of good-neighbourliness, due account being taken of the interests and well-being of the rest of the world, in social, economic, and commercial matters.

Chapter XII
INTERNATIONAL TRUSTEESHIP SYSTEM

Article 75

The United Nations shall establish under its authority an international trusteeship system for the administration and supervision of such territories as may be placed thereunder by subsequent individual agreements. These territories are hereinafter referred to as trust territories.

Article 76

The basic objectives of the trusteeship system, in accordance with the Purposes of the United Nations laid down in Article 1 of the present Charter, shall be:

a. to further international peace and security;

b. to promote the political, economic, social, and educational advancement of the inhabitants of the trust territories, and their progressive development towards self-government or independence as may be appropriate to the particular circumstances of each territory and its peoples and the freely expressed wishes of the peoples concerned, and as may be provided by the terms of each trusteeship agreement;

c. to encourage respect for human rights and for fundamental freedoms for all without distinction as to race, sex, language, or religion, and to encourage recognition of the interdependence of the peoples of the world; and

d. to ensure equal treatment in social, economic, and commercial matters for all Members of the United Nations and their nationals, and also equal treatment for the latter in the administration of justice, without prejudice to the attainment of the foregoing objectives and subject to the provisions of Article 80.

Article 77

1. The trusteeship system shall apply to such territories in the following categories as may be placed thereunder by means of trusteeship agreements:

a. territories now held under mandate;

b. territories which may be detached from enemy states as a result of the Second World War; and

c. territories voluntarily placed under the system by states responsible for their administration.

2. It will be a matter for subsequent agreement as to which territories in the foregoing categories will be brought under the trusteeship system and upon what terms.

Article 78

The trusteeship system shall not apply to territories which have become Members of the United Nations, relationship among which shall be based on respect for the principle of sovereign equality.

Article 79

The terms of trusteeship for each territory to be placed under the trusteeship system, including any alteration or amendment, shall be agreed upon by the states directly concerned, including the mandatory power in the case of territories held under mandate by a Member of the United Nations, and shall be approved as provided for in Articles 83 and 85.

Article 80

1. Except as may be agreed upon in individual trusteeship agreements, made under Articles 77, 79, and 81, placing each territory under the trusteeship system, and until such agreements have been concluded, nothing in this Chapter shall be construed in or of itself to alter in any manner the rights whatsoever of any states or any peoples or the terms of existing international instruments to which Members of the United Nations may respectively be parties.

2. Paragraph 1 of this Article shall not be interpreted as giving grounds for delay or postponement of the negotiation and conclusion of agreements for placing mandated and other territories under the trusteeship system as provided for in Article 77.

Article 81

The trusteeship agreement shall in each case include the terms under which the trust territory will be administered and designate the authority which will exercise the administration of the trust territory. Such authority, hereinafter called the administering authority, may be one or more states or the Organization itself.

Article 82

There may be designated, in any trusteeship agreement, a strategic area or areas which may include part or all of the trust territory to which the agreement applies, without prejudice to any special agreement or agreements made under Article 43.

Article 83

1. All functions of the United Nations relating to strategic areas, including the approval of the terms of the trusteeship agreements and of their alteration or amendments, shall be exercised by the Security Council.

2. The basic objectives set forth in Article 76 shall be applicable to the people of each strategic area.

3. The Security Council shall, subject to the provisions of the trusteeship agreements and without prejudice to security considerations, avail itself of the assistance of the Trusteeship Council to perform those functions of the United Nations under the trusteeship system relating to political, economic, social, and educational matters in the strategic areas.

Article 84

It shall be the duty of the administering authority to ensure that the trust territory shall play its part in the maintenance of international peace and security. To this end the administering authority may make use of volunteer forces, facilities, and assistance from the trust territory in carrying out the obligations towards the Security Council undertaken in this regard by the administering authority, as well as for local defence and the maintenance of law and order within the trust territory.

Article 85

1. The functions of the United Nations with regard to trusteeship agreements for all areas not designated as strategic, including the approval of the terms of the trusteeship agreements and of their alteration or amendment, shall be exercised by the General Assembly.

2. The Trusteeship Council, operating under the authority of the General Assembly, shall assist the General Assembly in carrying out these functions.

Chapter XIII
THE TRUSTEESHIP COUNCIL

Composition

Article 86

1. The Trusteeship Council shall consist of the following Members of the United Nations:

a. those Members administering trust territories;
b. such of those Members mentioned by name in Article 23 as are not administering trust territories; and
c. as many other Members elected for three-year terms by the General Assembly as may be necessary to ensure that the total number of members of the Trusteeship Council is equally divided between those Members of the United Nations which administer trust territories and those which do not.

2. Each member of the Trusteeship Council shall designate one specially qualified person to represent it therein.

Functions and powers

Article 87

The General Assembly and, under its authority, the Trusteeship Council, in carrying out their functions, may:
a. consider reports submitted by the administering authority;
b. accept petitions and examine them in consultation with the administering authority;
c. provide for periodic visits to the respective trust territories at times agreed upon with the administering authority; and
d. take these and other actions in conformity with the terms of the trusteeship agreements.

Article 88

The Trusteeship Council shall formulate a questionnaire on the political, economic, social, and educational advancement of the inhabitants of each trust territory, and the administering authority for each trust territory within the competence of the General Assembly shall make an annual report to the General Assembly upon the basis of such questionnaire.

Voting

Article 89

1. Each member of the Trusteeship Council shall have one vote.

2. Decisions of the Trusteeship Council shall be made by a majority of the members present and voting.

Procedure

Article 90

1. The Trusteeship Council shall adopt its own rules of procedure, including the method of selecting its President.

2. The Trusteeship Council shall meet as required in accordance with its rules, which shall include provision for the convening of meetings on the request of a majority of its members.

Article 91

The Trusteeship Council shall, when appropriate, avail itself of the assistance of the Economic and Social Council and of the specialized agencies in regard to matters with which they are respectively concerned.

Chapter XIV
THE INTERNATIONAL COURT OF JUSTICE

Article 92

The International Court of Justice shall be the principal judicial organ of the United Nations. It shall function in accordance with the annexed Statute, which is based upon the Statute of the Permanent Court of International Justice and forms an integral part of the present Charter.

Article 93

1. All Members of the United Nations are *ipso facto* parties to the Statute of the International Court of Justice.

2. A state which is not a Member of the United Nations may become a party to the Statute of the International Court of Justice on conditions to be determined in each case by the General Assembly upon the recommendation of the Security Council.

Article 94

1. Each Member of the United Nations undertakes to comply with the decision of the International Court of Justice in any case to which it is a party.

2. If any party to a case fails to perform the obligations incumbent upon it under a judgment rendered by the Court, the other party may have recourse to the Security Council, which may, if it deems necessary, make recommendations or decide upon measures to be taken to give effect to the judgment.

Article 95

Nothing in the present Charter shall prevent Members of the United Nations from entrusting the solution of their differences to other tribunals by virtue of agreements already in existence or which may be concluded in the future.

Article 96

1. The General Assembly or the Security Council may request the International Court of Justice to give an advisory opinion on any legal question.

2. Other organs of the United Nations and specialized agencies, which may at any time be so authorized by the General Assembly, may also request advisory opinions of the Court on legal questions arising within the scope of their activities.

Chapter XV
THE SECRETARIAT

Article 97

The Secretariat shall comprise a Secretary-General and such staff as the Organization may require. The Secretary-General shall be appointed by the General Assembly upon the recommendation of the Security Council. He shall be the chief administrative officer of the Organization.

Article 98

The Secretary-General shall act in that capacity in all meetings of the General Assembly, of the Security Council, of the Economic and Social Council, and of the Trusteeship Council, and shall perform such other functions as are entrusted to him by these organs. The Secretary-General shall make an annual report to the General Assembly on the work of the Organization.

Article 99

The Secretary-General may bring to the attention of the Security Council any matter which in his opinion may threaten the maintenance of international peace and security.

Article 100

1. In the performance of their duties the Secretary-General and the staff shall not seek or receive instructions from any government or from any other authority external to the Organization. They shall refrain from any action which might reflect on their position as international officials responsible only to the Organization.

2. Each Member of the United Nations undertakes to respect the exclusively international character of the responsibilities of the Secretary-General and the staff and not to seek to influence them in the discharge of their responsibilities.

Article 101

1. The staff shall be appointed by the Secretary-General under regulations established by the General Assembly.

2. Appropriate staffs shall be permanently assigned to the Economic and Social Council, the Trusteeship Council, and, as required, to other organs of the United Nations. These staffs shall form a part of the Secretariat.

3. The paramount consideration in the employment of the staff and in the determination of the conditions of service shall be the necessity of securing the highest standards of efficiency, competence, and integrity. Due regard shall be paid to the importance of recruiting the staff on as wide a geographical basis as possible.

Chapter XVI
MISCELLANEOUS PROVISIONS

Article 102

1. Every treaty and every international agreement entered into by any Member of the United Nations after the present Charter comes into force shall as soon as possible be registered with the Secretariat and published by it.

2. No party to any such treaty or international agreement which has not been registered in accordance with the provisions of paragraph 1 of this Article may invoke that treaty or agreement before any organ of the United Nations.

Article 103

In the event of a conflict between the obligations of the Members of the United Nations under the present Charter and their obligations under any other international agreement, their obligations under the present Charter shall prevail.

Article 104

The Organization shall enjoy in the territory of each of its Members such legal capacity as may be necessary for the exercise of its functions and the fulfilment of its purposes.

Article 105

1. The Organization shall enjoy in the territory of each of its Members such privileges and immunities as are necessary for the fulfilment of its purposes.

2. Representatives of the Members of the United Nations and officials of the Organization shall similarly enjoy such privileges and immunities as are necessary for the independent exercise of their functions in connexion with the Organization.

3. The General Assembly may make recommendations with a view to determining the details of the application of paragraphs 1 and 2 of this Article or may propose conventions to the Members of the United Nations for this purpose.

Chapter XVII
TRANSITIONAL SECURITY ARRANGEMENTS

Article 106

Pending the coming into force of such special agreements referred to in Article 43 as in the opinion of the Security Council enable it to begin the exercise of its responsibilities under Article 42, the parties to the Four-Nation Declaration, signed at Moscow, 30 October 1943, and France, shall, in accordance with the provisions of paragraph 5 of that Declaration, consult with one another and as occasion requires with other Members of the United Nations with a view to such joint action on behalf of the Organization as may be necessary for the purpose of maintaining international peace and security.

Article 107

Nothing in the present Charter shall invalidate or preclude action, in relation to any state which during the Second World War has been an enemy of any signatory to the present Charter, taken or authorized as a result of that war by the Governments having responsibility for such action.

Chapter XVIII
AMENDMENTS

Article 108

Amendments to the present Charter shall come into force for all Members of the United Nations when they have been adopted by a vote of two thirds of the members of the General Assembly and ratified in accordance with their respective constitutional processes by two thirds of the Members of the United Nations, including all the permanent members of the Security Council.

Article 109 [4]

1.   A General Conference of the Members of the United Nations for the purpose of reviewing the present Charter may be held at a date and place to be fixed by a two-thirds vote of the members of the General Assembly and by a vote of any nine members of the Security Council. Each Member of the United Nations shall have one vote in the conference.

2.   Any alteration of the present Charter recommended by a two-thirds vote of the conference shall take effect when ratified in accordance with their respective constitutional processes by two thirds of the Members of the United Nations including all the permanent members of the Security Council.

3.   If such a conference has not been held before the tenth annual session of the General Assembly following the coming into force of the present Charter, the proposal to call such a conference shall be placed on the agenda of that session of the General Assembly, and the conference shall be held if so decided by a majority vote of the members of the General Assembly and by a vote of any seven members of the Security Council.

Chapter XIX
RATIFICATION AND SIGNATURE

Article 110

1.   The present Charter shall be ratified by the signatory states in accordance with their respective constitutional processes.

2.   The ratifications shall be deposited with the Government of the United States of America, which shall notify all the signatory states of each deposit as well as the Secretary-General of the Organization when he has been appointed.

3.   The present Charter shall come into force upon the deposit of ratifications by the Republic of China, France, the Union of Soviet Socialist Republics, the United Kingdom of Great Britain and Northern Ireland, and the United States of America, and by a majority of the other signatory states. A protocol of the ratifications deposited shall thereupon be drawn up by the Government of the United States

of America which shall communicate copies thereof to all the signatory states.

4.   The states signatory to the present Charter which ratify it after it has come into force will become original Members of the United Nations on the date of the deposit of their respective ratifications.

Article 111

The present Charter, of which the Chinese, French, Russian, English, and Spanish texts are equally authentic, shall remain deposited in the archives of the Government of the United States of America. Duly certified copies thereof shall be transmitted by that Government to the Governments of the other signatory states.

IN FAITH WHEREOF the representatives of the Governments of the United Nations have signed the present Charter.

DONE at the city of San Francisco the twenty-sixth day of June, one thousand nine hundred and forty-five.

---

[4]Amended text of Article 109, which came into force on 12 June 1968. (The text of Article 109 before it was amended read as follows:

1.   A General Conference of the Members of the United Nations for the purpose of reviewing the present Charter may be held at a date and place to be fixed by a two-thirds vote of the members of the General Assembly and by a vote of any seven members of the Security Council. Each Member of the United Nations shall have one vote in the conference.

2.   Any alteration of the present Charter shall take effect when ratified in accordance with their respective constitutional processes by two thirds of the Members of the United Nations including all the permanent members of the Security Council.

3.   If such a conference has not been held before the tenth annual session of the General Assembly following the coming into force of the present Charter, the proposal to call such a conference shall be placed on the agenda of that session of the General Assembly, and the conference shall be held if so decided by a majority vote of the members of the General Assembly and by a vote of any seven members of the Security Council.)

Statute of the International Court of Justice

Article 1

THE INTERNATIONAL COURT OF JUSTICE established by the Charter of the United Nations as the principal judicial organ of the United Nations shall be constituted and shall function in accordance with the provisions of the present Statute.

Chapter I
ORGANIZATION OF THE COURT

Article 2

The Court shall be composed of a body of independent judges, elected regardless of their nationality from among persons of high moral character, who possess the qualifications required in their respective countries for appointment to the highest judicial offices, or are jurisconsults of recognized competence in international law.

Article 3

1.   The Court shall consist of fifteen members, no two of whom may be nationals of the same state.

2.   A person who for the purposes of membership in the Court could be regarded as a national of more than one state shall be deemed to be a national of the one in which he ordinarily exercises civil and political rights.

Article 4

1.   The members of the Court shall be elected by the General Assembly and by the Security Council from a list of persons nominated by the national groups in the Permanent Court of Arbitration, in accordance with the following provisions.

2.   In the case of Members of the United Nations not represented in the Permanent Court of Arbitration, candidates shall be nominated by national groups appointed for this purpose by their governments under the same conditions as those prescribed for mem-

bers of the Permanent Court of Arbitration by Article 44 of the Convention of The Hague of 1907 for the pacific settlement of international disputes.

3.   The conditions under which a state which is a party to the present Statute but is not a Member of the United Nations may participate in electing the members of the Court shall, in the absence of a special agreement, be laid down by the General Assembly upon recommendation of the Security Council.

Article 5

1.   At least three months before the date of the election, the Secretary-General of the United Nations shall address a written request to the members of the Permanent Court of Arbitration belonging to the states which are parties to the present Statute, and to the members of the national groups appointed under Article 4, paragraph 2, inviting them to undertake, within a given time, by national groups, the nomination of persons in a position to accept the duties of a member of the Court.

2.   No group may nominate more than four persons, not more than two of whom shall be of their own nationality. In no case may the number of candidates nominated by a group be more than double the number of seats to be filled.

Article 6

Before making these nominations, each national group is recommended to consult its highest court of justice, its legal faculties and schools of law, and its national academies and national sections of international academies devoted to the study of law.

Article 7

1.   The Secretary-General shall prepare a list in alphabetical order of all the persons thus nominated. Save as provided in Article 12, paragraph 2, these shall be the only persons eligible.

2. The Secretary-General shall submit this list to the General Assembly and to the Security Council.

Article 8
The General Assembly and the Security Council shall proceed independently of one another to elect the members of the Court.

Article 9
At every election, the electors shall bear in mind not only that the persons to be elected should individually possess the qualifications required, but also that in the body as a whole the representation of the main forms of civilization and of the principal legal systems of the world should be assured.

Article 10
1. Those candidates who obtain an absolute majority of votes in the General Assembly and in the Security Council shall be considered as elected.

2. Any vote of the Security Council, whether for the election of judges or for the appointment of members of the conference envisaged in Article 12, shall be taken without any distinction between permanent and non-permanent members of the Security Council.

3. In the event of more than one national of the same state obtaining an absolute majority of the votes both of the General Assembly and of the Security Council, the eldest of these only shall be considered as elected.

Article 11
If, after the first meeting held for the purpose of the election, one or more seats remain to be filled, a second and, if necessary, a third meeting shall take place.

Article 12
1. If, after the third meeting, one or more seats still remain unfilled, a joint conference consisting of six members, three appointed by the General Assembly and three by the Security Council, may be formed at any time at the request of either the General Assembly or the Security Council, for the purpose of choosing by the vote of an absolute majority one name for each seat still vacant, to submit to the General Assembly and the Security Council for their respective acceptance.

2. If the joint conference is unanimously agreed upon any person who fulfils the required conditions, he may be included in its list, even though he was not included in the list of nominations referred to in Article 7.

3. If the joint conference is satisfied that it will not be successful in procuring an election, those members of the Court who have already been elected shall, within a period to be fixed by the Security Council, proceed to fill the vacant seats by selection from among those candidates who have obtained votes either in the General Assembly or in the Security Council.

4. In the event of an equality of votes among the judges, the eldest judge shall have a casting vote.

Article 13
1. The members of the Court shall be elected for nine years and may be re-elected; provided, however, that of the judges elected at the first election, the terms of five judges shall expire at the end of three years and the terms of five more judges shall expire at the end of six years.

2. The judges whose terms are to expire at the end of the above-mentioned initial periods of three and six years shall be chosen by lot to be drawn by the Secretary-General immediately after the first election has been completed.

3. The members of the Court shall continue to discharge their duties until their places have been filled. Though replaced, they shall finish any cases which they may have begun.

4. In the case of the resignation of a member of the Court, the resignation shall be addressed to the President of the Court for transmission to the Secretary-General. This last notification makes the place vacant.

Article 14
Vacancies shall be filled by the same method as that laid down for the first election, subject to the following provision: the Secretary-General shall, within one month of the occurrence of the vacancy, proceed to issue the invitations provided for in Article 5, and the date of the election shall be fixed by the Security Council.

Article 15
A member of the Court elected to replace a member whose term of office has not expired shall hold office for the remainder of his predecessor's term.

Article 16
1. No member of the Court may exercise any political or administrative function, or engage in any other occupation of a professional nature.

2. Any doubt on this point shall be settled by the decision of the Court.

Article 17
1. No member of the Court may act as agent, counsel, or advocate in any case.

2. No member may participate in the decision of any case in which he has previously taken part as agent, counsel, or advocate for one of the parties, or as a member of a national or international court, or of a commission of enquiry, or in any other capacity.

3. Any doubt on this point shall be settled by the decision of the Court.

Article 18
1. No member of the Court can be dismissed unless, in the unanimous opinion of the other members, he has ceased to fulfil the required conditions.

2. Formal notification thereof shall be made to the Secretary-General by the Registrar.

3. This notification makes the place vacant.

Article 19
The members of the Court, when engaged on the business of the Court, shall enjoy diplomatic privileges and immunities.

Article 20
Every member of the Court shall, before taking up his duties, make a solemn declaration in open court that he will exercise his powers impartially and conscientiously.

Article 21
1. The Court shall elect its President and Vice-President for three years; they may be re-elected.

2. The Court shall appoint its Registrar and may provide for the appointment of such other officers as may be necessary.

Article 22
1. The seat of the Court shall be established at The Hague. This, however, shall not prevent the Court from sitting and exercising its functions elsewhere whenever the Court considers it desirable.

2. The President and the Registrar shall reside at the seat of the Court.

Article 23
1. The Court shall remain permanently in session, except during the judicial vacations, the dates and duration of which shall be fixed by the Court.

2. Members of the Court are entitled to periodic leave, the dates and duration of which shall be fixed by the Court, having in mind the distance between The Hague and the home of each judge.

3. Members of the Court shall be bound, unless they are on leave or prevented from attending by illness or other serious reasons duly explained to the President, to hold themselves permanently at the disposal of the Court.

Article 24
1. If, for some special reason, a member of the Court considers that he should not take part in the decision of a particular case, he shall so inform the President.

2. If the President considers that for some special reason one of the members of the Court should not sit in a particular case, he shall give him notice accordingly.

3. If in any such case the member of the Court and the President disagree, the matter shall be settled by the decision of the Court.

Article 25

1. The full Court shall sit except when it is expressly provided otherwise in the present Statute.

2. Subject to the condition that the number of judges available to constitute the Court is not thereby reduced below eleven, the Rules of the Court may provide for allowing one or more judges, according to circumstances and in rotation, to be dispensed from sitting.

3. A quorum of nine judges shall suffice to constitute the Court.

Article 26

1. The Court may from time to time form one or more chambers, composed of three or more judges as the Court may determine, for dealing with particular categories of cases; for example, labour cases and cases relating to transit and communications.

2. The Court may at any time form a chamber for dealing with a particular case. The number of judges to constitute such a chamber shall be determined by the Court with the approval of the parties.

3. Cases shall be heard and determined by the chambers provided for in this Article if the parties so request.

Article 27

A judgment given by any of the chambers provided for in Articles 26 and 29 shall be considered as rendered by the Court.

Article 28

The chambers provided for in Articles 26 and 29 may, with the consent of the parties, sit and exercise their functions elsewhere than at The Hague.

Article 29

With a view to the speedy dispatch of business, the Court shall form annually a chamber composed of five judges which, at the request of the parties, may hear and determine cases by summary procedure. In addition, two judges shall be selected for the purpose of replacing judges who find it impossible to sit.

Article 30

1. The Court shall frame rules for carrying out its functions. In particular, it shall lay down rules of procedure.

2. The Rules of the Court may provide for assessors to sit with the Court or with any of its chambers, without the right to vote.

Article 31

1. Judges of the nationality of each of the parties shall retain their right to sit in the case before the Court.

2. If the Court includes upon the Bench a judge of the nationality of one of the parties, any other party may choose a person to sit as judge. Such person shall be chosen preferably from among those persons who have been nominated as candidates as provided in Articles 4 and 5.

3. If the Court includes upon the Bench no judge of the nationality of the parties, each of these parties may proceed to choose a judge as provided in paragraph 2 of this Article.

4. The provisions of this Article shall apply to the case of Articles 26 and 29. In such cases, the President shall request one or, if necessary, two of the members of the Court forming the chamber to give place to the members of the Court of the nationality of the parties concerned, and, failing such, or if they are unable to be present, to the judges specially chosen by the parties.

5. Should there be several parties in the same interest, they shall, for the purpose of the preceding provisions, be reckoned as one party only. Any doubt upon this point shall be settled by the decision of the Court.

6. Judges chosen as laid down in paragraphs 2, 3 and 4 of this Article shall fulfil the conditions required by Articles 2, 17 (paragraph 2), 20, and 24 of the present Statute. They shall take part in the decision on terms of complete equality with their colleagues.

Article 32

1. Each member of the Court shall receive an annual salary.

2. The President shall receive a special annual allowance.

3. The Vice-President shall receive a special allowance for every day on which he acts as President.

4. The judges chosen under Article 31, other than members of the Court, shall receive compensation for each day on which they exercise their functions.

5. These salaries, allowances, and compensation shall be fixed by the General Assembly. They may not be decreased during the term of office.

6. The salary of the Registrar shall be fixed by the General Assembly on the proposal of the Court.

7. Regulations made by the General Assembly shall fix the conditions under which retirement pensions may be given to members of the Court and to the Registrar, and the conditions under which members of the Court and the Registrar shall have their travelling expenses refunded.

8. The above salaries, allowances, and compensation shall be free of all taxation.

Article 33

The expenses of the Court shall be borne by the United Nations in such a manner as shall be decided by the General Assembly.

Chapter II
COMPETENCE OF THE COURT

Article 34

1. Only states may be parties in cases before the Court.

2. The Court, subject to and in conformity with its Rules, may request of public international organizations information relevant to cases before it, and shall receive such information presented by such organizations on their own initiative.

3. Whenever the construction of the constituent instrument of a public international organization or of an international convention adopted thereunder is in question in a case before the Court, the Registrar shall so notify the public international organization concerned and shall communicate to it copies of all the written proceedings.

Article 35

1. The Court shall be open to the states parties to the present Statute.

2. The conditions under which the Court shall be open to other states shall, subject to the special provisions contained in treaties in force, be laid down by the Security Council, but in no case shall such conditions place the parties in a position of inequality before the Court.

3. When a state which is not a Member of the United Nations is a party to a case, the Court shall fix the amount which that party is to contribute towards the expenses of the Court. This provision shall not apply if such state is bearing a share of the expenses of the Court.

Article 36

1. The jurisdiction of the Court comprises all cases which the parties refer to it and all matters specially provided for in the Charter of the United Nations or in treaties and conventions in force.

2. The states parties to the present Statute may at any time declare that they recognize as compulsory *ipso facto* and without special agreement, in relation to any other state accepting the same obligation, the jurisdiction of the Court in all legal disputes concerning:

a. the interpretation of a treaty;

b. any question of international law;

c. the existence of any fact which, if established, would constitute a breach of an international obligation;

d. the nature or extent of the reparation to be made for the breach of an international obligation.

3. The declarations referred to above may be made unconditionally or on condition of reciprocity on the part of several or certain states, or for a certain time.

4. Such declarations shall be deposited with the Secretary-General of the United Nations, who shall transmit copies thereof to the parties to the Statute and to the Registrar of the Court.

5. Declarations made under Article 36 of the Statute of the Permanent Court of International Justice and which are still in force shall be deemed, as between the parties to the present Statute, to be acceptances of the compulsory jurisdiction of the International Court of Justice for the period which they still have to run and in accordance with their terms.

6. In the event of a dispute as to whether the Court has jurisdiction, the matter shall be settled by the decision of the Court.

Article 37

Whenever a treaty or convention in force provides for reference of a matter to a tribunal to have been instituted by the League of Nations, or to the Permanent Court of International Justice, the matter shall, as between the parties to the present Statute, be referred to the International Court of Justice.

Article 38

1. The Court, whose function is to decide in accordance with international law such disputes as are submitted to it, shall apply:

a. international conventions, whether general or particular, establishing rules expressly recognized by the contesting states;

b. international custom, as evidence of a general practice accepted as law;

c. the general principles of law recognized by civilized nations;

d. subject to the provisions of Article 59, judicial decisions and the teachings of the most highly qualified publicists of the various nations, as subsidiary means for the determination of rules of law.

2. This provision shall not prejudice the power of the Court to decide a case *ex aequo et bono*, if the parties agree thereto.

Chapter III
PROCEDURE

Article 39

1. The official languages of the Court shall be French and English. If the parties agree that the case shall be conducted in French, the judgment shall be delivered in French. If the parties agree that the case shall be conducted in English, the judgment shall be delivered in English.

2. In the absence of an agreement as to which language shall be employed, each party may, in the pleadings, use the language which it prefers; the decision of the Court shall be given in French and English. In this case the Court shall at the same time determine which of the two texts shall be considered as authoritative.

3. The Court shall, at the request of any party, authorize a language other than French or English to be used by that party.

Article 40

1. Cases are brought before the Court, as the case may be, either by the notification of the special agreement or by a written application addressed to the Registrar. In either case the subject of the dispute and the parties shall be indicated.

2. The Registrar shall forthwith communicate the application to all concerned.

3. He shall also notify the Members of the United Nations through the Secretary-General, and also any other states entitled to appear before the Court.

Article 41

1. The Court shall have the power to indicate, if it considers that circumstances so require, any provisional measures which ought to be taken to preserve the respective rights of either party.

2. Pending the final decision, notice of the measures suggested shall forthwith be given to the parties and to the Security Council.

Article 42

1. The parties shall be represented by agents.

2. They may have the assistance of counsel or advocates before the Court.

3. The agents, counsel, and advocates of parties before the Court shall enjoy the privileges and immunities necessary to the independent exercise of their duties.

Article 43

1. The procedure shall consist of two parts: written and oral.

2. The written proceedings shall consist of the communication to the Court and to the parties of memorials, counter-memorials and, if necessary, replies; also all papers and documents in support.

3. These communications shall be made through the Registrar, in the order and within the time fixed by the Court.

4. A certified copy of every document produced by one party shall be communicated to the other party.

5. The oral proceedings shall consist of the hearing by the Court of witnesses, experts, agents, counsel, and advocates.

Article 44

1. For the service of all notices upon persons other than the agents, counsel, and advocates, the Court shall apply direct to the government of the state upon whose territory the notice has to be served.

2. The same provision shall apply whenever steps are to be taken to procure evidence on the spot.

Article 45

The hearing shall be under the control of the President or, if he is unable to preside, of the Vice-President; if neither is able to preside, the senior judge present shall preside.

Article 46

The hearing in Court shall be public, unless the Court shall decide otherwise, or unless the parties demand that the public be not admitted.

Article 47

1. Minutes shall be made at each hearing and signed by the Registrar and the President.

2. These minutes alone shall be authentic.

Article 48

The Court shall make orders for the conduct of the case, shall decide the form and time in which each party must conclude its arguments, and make all arrangements connected with the taking of evidence.

Article 49

The Court may, even before the hearing begins, call upon the agents to produce any document or to supply any explanations. Formal note shall be taken of any refusal.

Article 50

The Court may, at any time, entrust any individual, body, bureau, commission, or other organization that it may select, with the task of carrying out an enquiry or giving an expert opinion.

Article 51

During the hearing any relevant questions are to be put to the witnesses and experts under the conditions laid down by the Court in the rules of procedure referred to in Article 30.

Article 52

After the Court has received the proofs and evidence within the time specified for the purpose, it may refuse to accept any further oral or written evidence that one party may desire to present unless the other side consents.

Article 53

1. Whenever one of the parties does not appear before the Court, or fails to defend its case, the other party may call upon the Court to decide in favour of its claim.

2. The Court must, before doing so, satisfy itself, not only that it has jurisdiction in accordance with Articles 36 and 37, but also that the claim is well founded in fact and law.

Article 54

1. When, subject to the control of the Court, the agents, counsel, and advocates have completed their presentation of the case, the President shall declare the hearing closed.
2. The Court shall withdraw to consider the judgment.
3. The deliberations of the Court shall take place in private and remain secret.

Article 55

1. All questions shall be decided by a majority of the judges present.
2. In the event of an equality of votes, the President or the judge who acts in his place shall have a casting vote.

Article 56

1. The judgment shall state the reasons on which it is based.
2. It shall contain the names of the judges who have taken part in the decision.

Article 57

If the judgment does not represent in whole or in part the unanimous opinion of the judges, any judge shall be entitled to deliver a separate opinion.

Article 58

The judgment shall be signed by the President and by the Registrar. It shall be read in open court, due notice having been given to the agents.

Article 59

The decision of the Court has no binding force except between the parties and in respect of that particular case.

Article 60

The judgment is final and without appeal. In the event of dispute as to the meaning or scope of the judgment, the Court shall construe it upon the request of any party.

Article 61

1. An application for revision of a judgment may be made only when it is based upon the discovery of some fact of such a nature as to be a decisive factor, which fact was, when the judgment was given, unknown to the Court and also to the party claiming revision, always provided that such ignorance was not due to negligence.
2. The proceedings for revision shall be opened by a judgment of the Court expressly recording the existence of the new fact, recognizing that it has such a character as to lay the case open to revision, and declaring the application admissible on this ground.
3. The Court may require previous compliance with the terms of the judgment before it admits proceedings in revision.
4. The application for revision must be made at latest within six months of the discovery of the new fact.
5. No application for revision may be made after the lapse of ten years from the date of the judgment.

Article 62

1. Should a state consider that it has an interest of a legal nature which may be affected by the decision in the case, it may submit a request to the Court to be permitted to intervene.
2. It shall be for the Court to decide upon this request.

Article 63

1. Whenever the construction of a convention to which states other than those concerned in the case are parties is in question, the Registrar shall notify all such states forthwith.
2. Every state so notified has the right to intervene in the proceedings; but if it uses this right, the construction given by the judgment will be equally binding upon it.

Article 64

Unless otherwise decided by the Court, each party shall bear its own costs.

Chapter IV
ADVISORY OPINIONS

Article 65

1. The Court may give an advisory opinion on any legal question at the request of whatever body may be authorized by or in accordance with the Charter of the United Nations to make such a request.
2. Questions upon which the advisory opinion of the Court is asked shall be laid before the Court by means of a written request containing an exact statement of the question upon which an opinion is required, and accompanied by all documents likely to throw light upon the question.

Article 66

1. The Registrar shall forthwith give notice of the request for an advisory opinion to all states entitled to appear before the Court.
2. The Registrar shall also, by means of a special and direct communication, notify any state entitled to appear before the Court or international organization considered by the Court, or, should it not be sitting, by the President, as likely to be able to furnish information on the question, that the Court will be prepared to receive, within a time limit to be fixed by the President, written statements, or to hear, at a public sitting to be held for the purpose, oral statements relating to the question.
3. Should any such state entitled to appear before the Court have failed to receive the special communication referred to in paragraph 2 of this Article, such state may express a desire to submit a written statement or to be heard; and the Court will decide.
4. States and organizations having presented written or oral statements or both shall be permitted to comment on the statements made by other states or organizations in the form, to the extent, and within the time limits which the Court, or, should it not be sitting, the President, shall decide in each particular case. Accordingly, the Registrar shall in due time communicate any such written statements to states and organizations having submitted similar statements.

Article 67

The Court shall deliver its advisory opinions in open court, notice having been given to the Secretary-General and to the representatives of Members of the United Nations, of other states and of international organizations immediately concerned.

Article 68

In the exercise of its advisory functions the Court shall further be guided by the provisions of the present Statute which apply in contentious cases to the extent to which it recognizes them to be applicable.

Chapter V
AMENDMENT

Article 69

Amendments to the present Statute shall be effected by the same procedure as is provided by the Charter of the United Nations for amendments to that Charter, subject however to any provisions which the General Assembly upon recommendation of the Security Council may adopt concerning the participation of states which are parties to the present Statute but are not Members of the United Nations.

Article 70

The Court shall have power to propose such amendments to the present Statute as it may deem necessary, through written communications to the Secretary-General, for consideration in conformity with the provisions of Article 69.

Appendix III

Structure of the United Nations

General Assembly

The General Assembly is composed of all the Members of the United Nations.

SESSIONS
Resumed forty-sixth session: 4 and 14 February, 2 and 19 March, 13 April, 6 and 22 May, 29 and 31 July, 24 and 25 August and 14 September 1992.
Forty-seventh session: 15 September–23 December 1992 (suspended).

OFFICERS
Resumed forty-sixth session
President: Samir S. Shihabi (Saudi Arabia).
Vice-Presidents: Australia, Belize, Botswana, China, Ecuador, France, Guinea, Honduras, Italy, Malaysia, Myanmar, Oman, Qatar, Russian Federation, Togo, Tunisia, Ukraine, United Kingdom, United Republic of Tanzania, United States, Zaire.

Forty-seventh session
President: Stoyan Ganev (Bulgaria).[a]
Vice-Presidents:[b] Afghanistan, Belize, Benin, Cape Verde, China, Comoros, France, Gabon, Ireland, Kuwait, Lesotho, Libyan Arab Jamahiriya, Nicaragua, Philippines, Russian Federation, Sri Lanka, Suriname, Turkey, United Kingdom, United States, Yemen.

[a]Elected on 15 September 1992 (dec. 47/302).
[b]Elected on 15 September 1992 (dec. 47/304).

The Assembly has four types of committees: (1) Main Committees; (2) procedural committees; (3) standing committees; (4) subsidiary and ad hoc bodies. In addition, it convenes conferences to deal with specific subjects.

Main Committees
Seven Main Committees have been established as follows:

Political and Security Committee (disarmament and related international security questions) (First Committee)
Special Political Committee
Economic and Financial Committee (Second Committee)
Social, Humanitarian and Cultural Committee (Third Committee)
Trusteeship Committee (including Non-Self-Governing Territories) (Fourth Committee)
Administrative and Budgetary Committee (Fifth Committee)
Legal Committee (Sixth Committee)

The General Assembly may constitute other committees, on which all Members of the United Nations have the right to be represented.

OFFICERS OF THE MAIN COMMITTEES

Resumed forty-sixth session

Fifth Committee[a]
Chairman: Ali Sunni Muntasser (Libyan Arab Jamahiriya).
Vice-Chairmen: Norma Goicochea Estenoz (Cuba), Kees Spaans (Netherlands).
Rapporteur: Mahmoud Barimani (Iran).

[a]The only Main Committee to meet at the resumed session.

Forty-seventh session[a]

[a]Chairmen elected by the Main Committees; announced by the Assembly President on 15 September 1992 (dec. 47/303).

First Committee
Chairman: Nabil A. Elaraby (Egypt).
Vice-Chairmen: Pasi Patokallio (Finland), Dae Won Suh (Republic of Korea).
Rapporteur: Jerzy Zaleski (Poland).

Special Political Committee
Chairman: Hamadi Khouini (Tunisia).
Vice-Chairmen: Abdullah Mohamed Alsaidi (Yemen), Moises Fuentes-Ibañez (Bolivia).
Rapporteur: Yuriy Shevchenko (Ukraine).

Second Committee
Chairman: Ramiro Piriz-Ballon (Uruguay).
Vice-Chairmen: Maymouna Diop (Senegal), Jose Lino B. Guerrero (Philippines).
Rapporteur: Walter Balzan (Malta).

Third Committee
Chairman: Florian Krenkel (Austria).
Vice-Chairmen: Andras Dekany (Hungary), Momodou K. Jallow (Gambia).
Rapporteur: Vitavas Srivihok (Thailand).

Fourth Committee
Chairman: Guillermo A. Melendez-Barahona (El Salvador).
Vice-Chairmen: James L. Kember (New Zealand), Ulli Mwabulukutu (United Republic of Tanzania).
Rapporteur: Khalid Mohammad Al-Baker (Qatar).

Fifth Committee
Chairman: Marian-George Dinu (Romania).
Vice-Chairmen: Maria Rotheiser (Austria), El Hassane Zahid (Morocco).
Rapporteur: Jorge Osella (Argentina).

Sixth Committee
Chairman: Javad Zarif (Iran).
Vice-Chairmen: Maria del Lujan Flores (Uruguay), Peter Tomka (Czechoslovakia).
Rapporteur: Wael Ahmed Kamal Aboulmagd (Egypt).

Procedural committees

General Committee
The General Committee consists of the President of the General Assembly, as Chairman, the 21 Vice-Presidents and the Chairmen of the seven Main Committees.

Credentials Committee
The Credentials Committee consists of nine members appointed by the General Assembly on the proposal of the President.

Forty-seventh session
Argentina, Barbados, Burundi, China, Kenya, New Zealand, Papua New Guinea, Russian Federation, United States.[a]

[a]Appointed on 15 and 18 September 1992 (dec. 47/301).

Standing committees

The two standing committees consist of experts appointed in their individual capacity for three-year terms.

Advisory Committee on Administrative and Budgetary Questions

Members:

To serve until 31 December 1992: Carlos Casap (Bolivia); Yogesh Kumar Gupta (India);[a] Tadanori Inomata (Japan); Wolfgang Münch (Germany); Irmeli Mustonen (Finland); Yang Hushan (China).

To serve until 31 December 1993: Leonid E. Bidny (Russian Federation); Even Fontaine-Ortiz (Cuba); Richard Kinchen (United Kingdom); M'hand Ladjouzi (Algeria); Linda S. Shenwick (United States).

To serve until 31 December 1994: Ahmad Fathi Al-Masri (Syrian Arab Republic); Kwaku Dua Dankwa (Ghana); Zoran Lazarevic (Yugoslavia); Ernest Besley Maycock (Barbados); C. S. M. Mselle, *Chairman* (United Republic of Tanzania).

[a]Resigned in August 1992; Ranjit Rae (India) was appointed on 24 September (dec. 47/305 A) to fill the resultant vacancy.

On 23 December 1992 (dec. 47/305 B), the General Assembly appointed the following six members for a three-year term beginning on 1 January 1993 to fill the vacancies occurring on 31 December 1992: Gérard Biraud (France), Jorge José Duhalt (Mexico), Tadanori Inomata (Japan), Wolfgang Münch (Germany), Ranjit Rae (India), Yu Mengjia (China).

Committee on Contributions

Members:

To serve until 31 December 1992: Bagbeni Adeito Nzengeya (Zaire); Sergio Chapparo Ruíz (Chile); Peter Gregg (Australia); Atilio Norberto Molteni, *Vice-Chairman* (Argentina); Mohamed Mahmoud Ould Cheikh El Ghaouth (Mauritania); Dimitri Rallis (Greece).

To serve until 31 December 1993: Amjad Ali, *Chairman* (Pakistan); Henrik Amneus (Sweden); Yuri A. Chulkov (Russian Federation); Jorge José Duhalt (Mexico);[a] Ugo Sessi (Italy); Wang Liansheng (China).

To serve until 31 December 1994: Kenshiroh Akimoto (Japan); David Etuket (Uganda); John D. Fox (United States); Ion Gorita (Romania); Imre Karbuczky (Hungary); Vanu Gopala Menon (Singapore).

[a]Resigned effective 31 December 1992; Atilio Norberto Molteni (Argentina) was appointed on 23 December (dec. 47/313) for a one-year term beginning on 1 January 1993 to fill the resultant vacancy.

On 23 December 1992 (dec. 47/313), the General Assembly appointed the following six members for a three-year term beginning on 1 January 1993 to fill the vacancies occurring on 31 December 1992: Tarak Ben Hamida (Tunisia), Sergio Chapparo Ruíz (Chile), Norma Goicochea Estenoz (Cuba), Peter Gregg (Australia), Mohamed Mahmoud Ould Cheikh El Ghaouth (Mauritania), Dimitri Rallis (Greece).

Subsidiary and ad hoc bodies

The following subsidiary and ad hoc bodies were functioning in 1992, or were established during the General Assembly's resumed forty-sixth session or forty-seventh session. (For other related bodies, see p. 1222.)

Ad Hoc Committee on the Indian Ocean

The 44-member Ad Hoc Committee on the Indian Ocean, continuing the preparatory work for the Conference on the Indian Ocean (to be convened as soon as possible, at Colombo, Sri Lanka), met at United Nations Headquarters from 18 to 22 May 1992.

Members: Australia, Bangladesh, Bulgaria, Canada, China, Djibouti, Egypt, Ethiopia, Germany, Greece, India, Indonesia *(Vice-Chairman)*, Iran, Iraq, Italy, Japan, Kenya, Liberia, Madagascar *(Rapporteur)*, Malaysia, Maldives, Mauritius, Mozambique *(Vice-Chairman)*, Netherlands, Norway, Oman, Pakistan, Panama, Poland, Romania, Russian Federation, Seychelles, Singapore, Somalia, Sri Lanka *(Chairman)*, Sudan, Thailand, Uganda, United Arab Emirates, United Republic of Tanzania, Yemen, Yugoslavia, Zambia, Zimbabwe.

Sweden, a major maritime user of the Indian Ocean, participates as an observer.

Advisory Committee on the United Nations Educational and Training Programme for Southern Africa

Members: Belarus, Canada, Denmark, India, Japan, Liberia, Nigeria, Norway *(Chairman)*, United Republic of Tanzania, United States, Venezuela, Zaire, Zambia *(Vice-Chairman)*.

Advisory Committee on the United Nations Programme of Assistance in the Teaching, Study, Dissemination and Wider Appreciation of International Law

The Advisory Committee on the United Nations Programme of Assistance in the Teaching, Study, Dissemination and Wider Appreciation of International Law did not meet in 1992.

Members (until 31 December 1995): Bangladesh, Colombia, Cuba, Cyprus, Ethiopia, France, Germany, Ghana, India, Iran, Italy, Kenya, Malaysia, Mexico, Netherlands, Nigeria, Romania, Russian Federation, Sudan, Trinidad and Tobago, Ukraine, United Kingdom, United Republic of Tanzania, United States, Uruguay.

Board of Auditors

The Board of Auditors consists of three members appointed by the General Assembly for three-year terms.

Members:

To serve until 30 June 1993: Chairman of the Commission on Audit of the Philippines.

To serve until 30 June 1994: Auditor-General of Ghana.

To serve until 30 June 1995: Comptroller and Auditor-General of the United Kingdom.

On 23 December 1992 (dec. 47/314), the General Assembly appointed the Comptroller and Auditor-General of India for a three-year term beginning on 1 July 1993.

Committee for the United Nations Population Award

The Committee for the United Nations Population Award is composed of: *(a)* 10 representatives of United Nations Member States elected by the Economic and Social Council for a three-year period, with due regard for equitable geographical representation and the need to include Member States that had made contributions for the Award; *(b)* the Secretary-General and the UNFPA Executive Director, to serve *ex officio;* and *(c)* five individuals eminent for their significant contributions to population-related activities, selected by the Committee, to serve as honorary members in an advisory capacity for a renewable three-year term.

The Committee met at United Nations Headquarters on 21 January and 5 February 1992.

Members (until 31 December 1994): Belarus, Burundi, Cameroon, Ecuador, El Salvador, India, Japan, Mexico *(Chairman)*, Netherlands, Rwanda.

Ex-officio members: The Secretary-General and the UNFPA Executive Director.

Honorary members (until 31 December 1994):[a] Takeo Fukuda, F. Bradford Morse.

[a]Three seats were vacant in 1992.

Committee of Trustees of the United Nations Trust Fund for South Africa

Members: Chile, Morocco, Nigeria *(Vice-Chairman)*, Pakistan, Sweden *(Chairman)*.

Committee on Applications for Review of Administrative Tribunal Judgements

The Committee on Applications for Review of Administrative Tribunal Judgements held its thirty-ninth session at United Nations Headquarters on 30 March and 1, 2 and 9 April 1992.

Members (until 14 September 1992) (based on the composition of the General Committee at the General Assembly's forty-sixth session): Australia, Belize, Botswana, China, Ecuador, France, Guinea, Honduras, Ireland, Italy, Libyan Arab Jamahiriya, Malaysia, Mozambique *(Chairman)*, Myanmar, Oman, Poland, Qatar, Russian Federation, Saint Lucia, Saudi Arabia, Thailand, Togo, Tunisia, Ukraine, United Arab Emirates, United Kingdom *(Rapporteur)*, United Republic of Tanzania, United States, Zaire.

Members (from 15 September 1992) (based on the composition of the General Committee at the General Assembly's forty-seventh session): Afghanistan, Austria, Belize, Benin, Bulgaria, Cape Verde, China, Comoros, Egypt, El Salvador, France, Gabon, Iran, Ireland, Kuwait, Lesotho, Libyan Arab Jamahiriya, Nicaragua, Philippines, Romania, Russian Federation, Sri Lanka, Suriname, Tunisia, Turkey, United Kingdom, United States, Uruguay, Yemen.

Committee on Conferences

The Committee on Conferences consists of 21 Member States appointed by the President of the General Assembly according to a specific pattern of equitable geographical distribution, to serve for a three-year term.

Members:
To serve until 31 December 1992: Austria, Iraq, Liberia, Mexico, Pakistan, Uganda, United States.
To serve until 31 December 1993: Chile, Cyprus, France, Gabon, Japan, Kenya, Russian Federation.
To serve until 31 December 1994: Honduras *(Vice-Chairman)*, Hungary *(Chairman)*, Iran *(Vice-Chairman)*, Jamaica, Mozambique, Senegal *(Rapporteur)*, Turkey *(Vice-Chairman)*.

On 22 December 1992 (dec. 47/311 A), the General Assembly took note of the appointment by its President of the following members for a three-year term beginning on 1 January 1993 to fill five of the seven vacancies occurring on 31 December 1992: Austria, Fiji, Grenada, Jordan, United States. No further appointments were made in 1992 to fill the remaining seats, allocated to two members from African States.

Committee on Information

The 79-member Committee on Information held its fourteenth session at United Nations Headquarters from 30 March to 16 April 1992.

Members: Algeria *(Rapporteur)*, Argentina *(Chairman)*, Bangladesh, Belarus, Belgium, Benin, Brazil, Bulgaria, Burkina Faso, Burundi, Chile, China, Colombia, Congo, Costa Rica, Côte d'Ivoire, Cuba, Cyprus, Czechoslovakia, Denmark, Ecuador, Egypt, El Salvador, Ethiopia, Finland, France, Germany, Ghana, Greece, Guatemala, Guinea, Guyana, Hungary, India, Indonesia, Iran, Ireland, Italy, Jamaica, Japan, Jordan, Kenya, Lebanon, Malta, Mexico, Mongolia, Morocco, Nepal, Netherlands *(Vice-Chairman)*, Niger, Nigeria, Pakistan *(Vice-Chairman)*, Peru, Philippines, Poland *(Vice-Chairman)*, Portugal, Romania, Russian Federation, Singapore, Somalia, Spain, Sri Lanka, Sudan, Syrian Arab Republic, Togo, Trinidad and Tobago, Tunisia, Turkey, Ukraine, United Kingdom, United Republic of Tanzania, United States, Uruguay, Venezuela, Viet Nam, Yemen, Yugoslavia, Zaire, Zimbabwe.

On 14 December 1992 (dec. 47/424), the General Assembly increased the membership of the Committee from 79 to 81 and appointed the Republic of Korea and Senegal as members.

Committee on Relations with the Host Country

Members: Bulgaria *(Vice-Chairman)*, Canada *(Vice-Chairman)*, China, Costa Rica *(Rapporteur)*, Côte d'Ivoire *(Vice-Chairman)*, Cyprus *(Chairman)*, France, Honduras, Iraq, Mali, Russian Federation, Senegal, Spain, United Kingdom, United States (host country).

Committee on the Development and Utilization of New and Renewable Sources of Energy

The Committee on the Development and Utilization of New and Renewable Sources of Energy, open to the participation of all States as full members, held its sixth (final) session at United Nations Headquarters from 3 to 14 February 1992.

Chairman: Venezuela.
Vice-Chairman: Germany.
Rapporteur: Ukraine.

On 30 April 1992, the Economic and Social Council established a Committee on New and Renewable Sources of Energy and on Energy for Development, which is to retain the mandate of the above Committee and take over the current mandate of the Committee on Natural Resources pertaining to energy (see below, under "Economic and Social Council").

Committee on the Exercise of the Inalienable Rights of the Palestinian People

Members: Afghanistan *(Vice-Chairman)*, Belarus, Cuba *(Vice-Chairman)*, Cyprus, Guinea, Guyana, Hungary, India, Indonesia, Lao People's Democratic Republic, Madagascar, Malaysia, Mali, Malta *(Rapporteur)*, Nigeria, Pakistan, Romania, Senegal *(Chairman)*, Sierra Leone, Tunisia, Turkey, Ukraine, Yugoslavia.

Committee on the Peaceful Uses of Outer Space

The 53-member Committee on the Peaceful Uses of Outer Space held its thirty-fifth session at United Nations Headquarters from 15 to 26 June 1992.

Members: Albania, Argentina, Australia, Austria *(Chairman)*, Belgium, Benin, Brazil *(Rapporteur)*, Bulgaria, Burkina Faso, Cameroon, Canada, Chad, Chile, China, Colombia, Czechoslovakia, Ecuador, Egypt, France, Germany, Hungary, India, Indonesia, Iran, Iraq, Italy, Japan, Kenya, Lebanon, Mexico, Mongolia, Morocco, Netherlands, Niger, Nigeria, Pakistan, Philippines, Poland, Portugal, Romania *(Vice-Chairman)*, Russian Federation, Sierra Leone, Sudan, Sweden, Syrian Arab Republic, Turkey, Ukraine, United Kingdom, United States, Uruguay, Venezuela, Viet Nam, Yugoslavia.

Disarmament Commission

The Disarmament Commission, composed of all the Members of the United Nations, met at United Nations Headquarters between 20 April and 11 May 1992.

Chairman: Hungary.
Vice-Chairmen: Brazil, Cameroon, Egypt, Finland, Malaysia, Nepal, Romania, Uruguay.
Rapporteur: Netherlands.

High-level Committee on the Review of Technical Cooperation among Developing Countries

The High-level Committee on the Review of Technical Cooperation among Developing Countries, composed of all States participating in UNDP, did not meet in 1992.

Intergovernmental Committee on Science and Technology for Development

On 13 April 1992, the General Assembly decided to transform the Intergovernmental Committee on Science and Technology for Development and its subsidiary body, the Advisory Committee on Science and Technology for Development, into a functional commission of the Economic and Social Council (see below).

Intergovernmental Group to Monitor the Supply and Shipping of Oil and Petroleum Products to South Africa

The Intergovernmental Group to Monitor the Supply and Shipping of Oil and Petroleum Products to South Africa is composed of 10 Member States appointed by the Assembly President, in consultation with the regional groups and the Chairman of the Special Committee against Apartheid, on the basis of equitable geographical distribution and ensuring representation of oil-exporting and -shipping States.

Members: Algeria, Cuba, Indonesia, Kuwait *(Vice-Chairman)*, New Zealand, Nicaragua, Nigeria, Norway *(Rapporteur)*, Ukraine, United Republic of Tanzania *(Chairman)*.

Intergovernmental Negotiating Committee for a Framework Convention on Climate Change

The Intergovernmental Negotiating Committee for a Framework Convention on Climate Change, open to all States Members of the United Nations or members of the specialized agencies, held two sessions in 1992: the first and second parts of its fifth at United Nations Headquarters from 18 to 28 February and from 30 April to 9 May; and its sixth at Geneva from 7 to 10 December.

Chairman: France.
Vice-Chairmen: Algeria, Argentina, India.
Vice-Chairman/Rapporteur: Romania.

Intergovernmental Negotiating Committee for the Elaboration of an International Convention to Combat Desertification in Those Countries Experiencing Serious Drought and/or Desertification, Particularly in Africa

On 22 December 1992, the General Assembly established an Intergovernmental Negotiating Committee for the elaboration of an international convention to combat desertification in those countries experiencing serious drought and/or desertification, particularly in Africa, open to all States Members of the United Nations or members of the specialized agencies.

The Committee did not meet in 1992.

International Civil Service Commission

The International Civil Service Commission consists of 15 members who serve in their personal capacity as individuals of recognized competence in public administration or related fields, particularly in personnel management. They are appointed by the General Assembly, with due regard for equitable geographical distribution, for four-year terms.

The Commission held two sessions in 1992: its thirty-fifth at United Nations Headquarters from 10 to 27 March, and its thirty-sixth in London from 13 July to 7 August.

Members:
To serve until 31 December 1992: Amjad Ali (Pakistan); Francesca Yetunde Emanuel (Nigeria); Valery Fiodorovich Keniaykin (Russian Federation);[a] Omar Sirry (Egypt); M. A. Vellodi (India).
To serve until 31 December 1993: Mario Bettati (France);[b] Lucretia Myers (United States);[b] Antônio Fonseca Pimentel (Brazil); Alexis Stephanou (Greece); Ku Tashiro (Japan).
To serve until 31 December 1994: Mohsen Bel Hadj Amor, *Chairman* (Tunisia); Turkia Daddah (Mauritania); André Xavier Pirson (Belgium); Jaroslav Riha (Czechoslovakia); Carlos S. Vegega, *Vice-Chairman* (Argentina).

[a]Appointed on 2 March 1992 (dec. 46/323 B) to fill the vacancy created by the resignation of Anatoly M. Dryukov (Russian Federation).
[b]Appointed on 14 February 1992 (dec. 46/323 A) to fill the vacancies created by the resignation of Michel Jean Bardoux (France) and Claudia Cooley (United States), respectively.

On 23 December 1992 (dec. 47/317), the General Assembly appointed the following for a four-year term beginning on 1 January 1993 to fill the vacancies occurring on 31 December 1992:

Humayun Kabir (Bangladesh), Valery Fiodorovich Keniaykin (Russian Federation), Ernest Rusita (Uganda), Missoum Sbih (Algeria), Mario Yango (Philippines).

ADVISORY COMMITTEE ON POST ADJUSTMENT QUESTIONS

The Advisory Committee on Post Adjustment Questions consists of six members, of whom five are chosen from the geographical regions of Africa, Asia, Latin America, Eastern Europe, and Western Europe and other States; and one, from ICSC, who serves *ex officio* as Chairman. Members are appointed by the ICSC Chairman to serve for four-year terms.

The Advisory Committee did not meet in 1992.

International Law Commission

The International Law Commission consists of 34 persons of recognized competence in international law, elected by the General Assembly to serve in their individual capacity for a five-year term. Vacancies occurring within the five-year period are filled by the Commission.

The Commission held its forty-fourth session at Geneva from 4 May to 24 July 1992.

Members (until 31 December 1996): Husain M. Al-Baharna (Bahrain); Awn S. Al-Khasawneh (Jordan); Gaetano Arangio-Ruiz (Italy); Julio Barboza (Argentina); Mohamed Bennouna (Morocco); Derek William Bowett (United Kingdom); Carlos Calero Rodrigues, *First Vice-Chairman* (Brazil); James R. Crawford (Australia); John De Saram (Sri Lanka); Gudmundur Eiriksson (Iceland); Salifou Fomba (Mali); Mehmet Guney (Turkey); Kamil E. Idris (Sudan); Andreas J. Jacovides, *Second Vice-Chairman* (Cyprus); Peter C. R. Kabatsi (Uganda); Abdul G. Koroma (Sierra Leone); Mochtar Kusuma-Atmadja (Indonesia); Ahmed Mahiou (Algeria); Vaclav Mikulka (Czechoslovakia); Guillaume Pambou-Tchivounda (Gabon); Alain Pellet (France); Pemmaraju Sreenivasa Rao (India); Edilbert Razafindralambo, *Rapporteur* (Madagascar); Patrick Lipton Robinson (Jamaica); Robert B. Rosenstock (United States); Shi Jiuyong (China); Alberto Szekely (Mexico); Doudou Thiam (Senegal); Christian Tomuschat, *Chairman* (Germany); Edmundo Vargas Carreño (Chile); Vladlen Vereshetin (Russian Federation); Francisco Villagran Kramer (Guatemala); Chusei Yamada (Japan); Alexander Yankov (Bulgaria).

Investments Committee

The Investments Committee consists of nine members appointed by the Secretary-General, after consultation with the United Nations Joint Staff Pension Board and ACABQ, subject to confirmation by the General Assembly. Members serve for three-year terms.

Members:
To serve until 31 December 1992: Yves Oltramare (Switzerland); Emmanuel Noi Omaboe (Ghana); Juergen Reimnitz (Germany).
To serve until 31 December 1993: Jean Guyot, *Chairman* (France); Francine J. Bovich (United States); Michiya Matsukawa (Japan).
To serve until 31 December 1994: Ahmed Abdullatif (Saudi Arabia); Aloysio de Andrade Faria (Brazil); Stanislaw Raczkowski (Poland).

On 23 December 1992 (dec. 47/315), the General Assembly confirmed the appointment by the Secretary-General of Yves Oltramare (Switzerland), Emmanuel Noi Omaboe (Ghana) and Juergen Reimnitz (Germany) as members for a three-year term beginning on 1 January 1993 to fill the vacancies occurring on 31 December 1992.

Joint Advisory Group on the International Trade Centre UNCTAD/GATT

The Joint Advisory Group was established in accordance with an agreement between UNCTAD and GATT with effect from 1 January 1968, the date on which their joint sponsorship of the International Trade Centre commenced.

Participation in the Group is open to all States members of UNCTAD and to all contracting parties to GATT.

The Group held its twenty-fifth session at Geneva on 26 and 27 November 1992.

Chairman: Finland.
Vice-Chairman: El Salvador.
Rapporteur: United Republic of Tanzania.

Joint Inspection Unit

The Joint Inspection Unit consists of not more than 11 Inspectors appointed by the General Assembly from candidates nominated by Member States following appropriate consultations, including consultations with the President of the Economic and Social Council and with the Chairman of ACC. The Inspectors, chosen for their special experience in national or international administrative and financial matters, with due regard for equitable geographical distribution and reasonable rotation, serve in their personal capacity for five-year terms.

Members:
To serve until 31 December 1992: Adib Daoudy, *Chairman* (Syrian Arab Republic); Mohamed Salah Eldin Ibrahim (Egypt); Boris P. Prokofiev (Russian Federation); Siegfried Schumm (Germany); Norman Williams (Panama).[a]
To serve until 31 December 1993: Raúl Quijano (Argentina).
To serve until 31 December 1994: Kahono Martohadinegoro (Indonesia).
To serve until 31 December 1995: Andrzej Abraszewski (Poland); Erica-Irene A. Daes, *Vice-Chairman* (Greece); Richard Vognild Hennes (United States); Kabongo Tunsala (Zaire).

[a]Died on 10 March 1992.

On 14 September 1992 (dec. 46/314 B), the General Assembly appointed the following for a five-year term beginning on 1 January 1993 to fill the vacancies occurring on 31 December 1992: Fatih Bouayad-Agha (Algeria), Homero Luis Hernández Sánchez (Dominican Republic), Boris Petrovitch Krasulin (Russian Federation), Francesco Mezzalama (Italy), Khalil Issa Othman (Jordan).

Office of the United Nations High Commissioner for Refugees (UNHCR)

The United Nations High Commissioner for Refugees reports to the General Assembly through the Economic and Social Council.

EXECUTIVE COMMITTEE OF THE HIGH COMMISSIONER'S PROGRAMME

The Executive Committee held its forty-third session at Geneva from 5 to 9 October 1992.

Members: Algeria, Argentina *(Chairman)*, Australia, Austria, Belgium, Brazil, Canada, China, Colombia, Denmark, Ethiopia,[a] Finland, France, Germany, Greece, Holy See, Hungary,[a] Iran, Israel, Italy, Japan, Lebanon, Lesotho, Madagascar, Morocco, Namibia, Netherlands *(Vice-Chairman)*, Nicaragua, Nigeria, Norway, Pakistan, Philippines, Somalia, Sudan *(Rapporteur)*, Sweden, Switzerland, Thailand, Tunisia, Turkey, Uganda, United Kingdom, United Republic of Tanzania, United States, Venezuela, Yugoslavia, Zaire.

[a]Elected by the Economic and Social Council on 29 April 1992 (dec. 1992/216), pursuant to a 1991 General Assembly decision to increase the membership from 44 to 46 (YUN 1991, p. 706, GA res. 46/105, 16 Dec. 1991).

United Nations High Commissioner for Refugees: Sadako Ogata.
Deputy High Commissioner: Martin Douglas Stafford.

Panel of External Auditors

The Panel of External Auditors consists of the members of the United Nations Board of Auditors and the appointed external auditors of the specialized agencies and IAEA.

Preparatory Committee for the Fiftieth Anniversary of the United Nations

On 13 April 1992 (dec. 46/472), the General Assembly established a Preparatory Committee for the Fiftieth Anniversary of the United Nations, consisting of the members of the General Committee and open to the participation of all Member States.

The Committee met at United Nations Headquarters on 22 October and 30 November 1992.

Chairman: Australia.
Vice-Chairmen: Botswana, Chile, Finland, Malaysia, Mauritania, Oman, Poland.
Rapporteur: Jamaica.

Preparatory Committee for the Global Conference on the Sustainable Development of Small Island Developing States

On 22 December 1992, the General Assembly established a Preparatory Committee for the Global Conference on the Sustainable Development of Small Island Developing States (scheduled for 1994), open to all invited to participate in the 1992 United Nations Conference on Environment and Development.[1]

The Committee did not meet in 1992.

Preparatory Committee for the United Nations Conference on Environment and Development

The Preparatory Committee for the United Nations Conference on Environment and Development (held in June 1992), open to all States Members of the United Nations or members of the specialized agencies, held its fourth (final) session at United Nations Headquarters from 2 March to 3 April 1992.

Chairman: Singapore.
Vice-Chairmen: Argentina, Australia, Bangladesh, Barbados, Belarus, Brazil *(ex officio)*, China, Colombia, Costa Rica, Djibouti, Egypt, France, Germany, India, Indonesia, Italy, Jamaica, Japan, Kenya, Kuwait, Malaysia, Mauritania, Mexico, Mozambique, Norway, Pakistan, Papua New Guinea, Peru, Poland, Russian Federation, Senegal, Togo, Tunisia, Uganda, United Kingdom, United States, Venezuela, Yugoslavia, Zaire, Zambia.
Rapporteur: Algeria.

Preparatory Committee for the United Nations Conference on Human Settlements (Habitat II)

On 22 December 1992, the General Assembly established a Preparatory Committee for the United Nations Conference on Human Settlements (Habitat II) (scheduled for 1996), open to all States Members of the United Nations or members of the specialized agencies.

The Committee did not meet in 1992.

Preparatory Committee for the World Conference on Human Rights

The Preparatory Committee for the World Conference on Human Rights (scheduled for 1993), open to all States Members of the United Nations or members of the specialized agencies, held two sessions in 1992, at Geneva: its second from 30 March to 10 April, and its third from 14 to 18 September.

Chairman: Morocco.
Vice-Chairmen: India (third session), Ireland, Philippines (second session), Venezuela.
Rapporteur: Poland.

Preparatory Committee for the World Summit for Social Development

On 16 December 1992, the General Assembly established a Preparatory Committee for the World Summit for Social Devel-

[1]YUN 1991, p. 489, GA res. 46/168, 19 Dec. 1991.

opment (scheduled for 1995), open to all States Members of the United Nations or members of the specialized agencies.

The Committee did not meet in 1992.

Scientific and Technical Committee on the International Decade for Natural Disaster Reduction

The Scientific and Technical Committee on the International Decade for Natural Disaster Reduction, composed of 25 scientific and technical experts appointed by the Secretary-General in consultation with their Governments, met at Geneva from 16 to 20 March 1992.

Members: Alexandra Amagka-Mensah (Ghana); Anand S. Arya (India); F. Barberi (Italy); Mohammed Benblidia (Algeria); Driss Ben Sari (Morocco); G. Arthur Brown (Jamaica); James Bruce, *Chairman* (Canada); C. Candanedo (Panama); Princess Chulaborn (Thailand); U. G. Cordani (Brazil); Alberto Giesecke (Peru); Y. A. Izrael (Russian Federation); Vit Karnik (Czechoslovakia); Elizabeth Kassaye (Ethiopia); Vaino Kelha (Finland); Takeo Kinoshita (Japan); Roman L. Kintanar (Philippines); M. Lechat (Belgium); Philippe Masure (France); Thomas Odhiambo (Kenya); Dallas Peck (United States); E. Plate (Germany); Aura Elena Rodrigues Marrero (Venezuela); Marilo Ruiz de Elvira (Spain); Xie Li-Li (China).

Special Committee against Apartheid

Members: Algeria, Ghana, Guinea, Haiti, India *(Rapporteur)*, Indonesia, Malaysia, Nepal *(Vice-Chairman)*, Nigeria *(Chairman)*, Peru, Philippines, Somalia, Sudan, Syrian Arab Republic, Trinidad and Tobago *(Vice-Chairman)*, Ukraine *(Vice-Chairman)*, Zimbabwe.

SUBCOMMITTEE ON DEVELOPMENTS IN SOUTH AFRICA

Members: Algeria, Haiti, India, Indonesia, Malaysia, Peru, Trinidad and Tobago, Ukraine, Zimbabwe *(Chairman)*.

SUBCOMMITTEE ON THE IMPLEMENTATION OF UNITED NATIONS RESOLUTIONS ON SOUTH AFRICA

Members: Ghana *(Chairman)*, Guinea, Nepal, Nigeria, Philippines, Somalia, Sudan, Syrian Arab Republic.

Special Committee on Peace-keeping Operations

In 1992, the 34-member Special Committee on Peace-keeping Operations met at United Nations Headquarters from 24 to 30 April, on 1 June and on 17 and 25 August.

Members: Afghanistan, Algeria, Argentina *(Vice-Chairman)*, Australia, Austria, Canada *(Vice-Chairman)*, China, Denmark, Egypt *(Rapporteur)*, El Salvador, Ethiopia, France, Germany, Guatemala, Hungary, India, Iraq, Italy, Japan *(Vice-Chairman)*, Mauritania, Mexico, Netherlands, Nigeria *(Chairman)*, Pakistan, Poland *(Vice-Chairman)*, Romania, Russian Federation, Sierra Leone, Spain, Thailand, United Kingdom, United States, Venezuela, Yugoslavia.

Special Committee on the Charter of the United Nations and on the Strengthening of the Role of the Organization

The 47-member Special Committee on the Charter of the United Nations and on the Strengthening of the Role of the Organization met at United Nations Headquarters from 3 to 21 February 1992.

Members: Algeria, Argentina *(Vice-Chairman)*, Barbados, Belgium, Brazil, China, Colombia, Congo, Cyprus, Czechoslovakia *(Chairman)*, Ecuador, Egypt, El Salvador, Finland, France, Germany, Ghana, Greece, Guyana, Hungary, India, Indonesia, Iran *(Vice-Chairman)*, Iraq, Italy, Japan, Kenya *(Vice-Chairman)*, Liberia, Mexico, Nepal, New Zealand, Nigeria, Pakistan, Philippines, Poland, Romania, Russian Federation, Rwanda, Sierra Leone, Spain, Tunisia, Turkey *(Rapporteur)*, United Kingdom, United States, Venezuela, Yugoslavia, Zambia.

Special Committee on the Situation with regard to the Implementation of the Declaration on the Granting of Independence to Colonial Countries and Peoples

Members: Afghanistan, Bulgaria, Chile, China, Congo, Côte d'Ivoire, Cuba *(Vice-Chairman)*, Czechoslovakia *(Vice-Chairman)*, Ethiopia, Fiji, India, Indonesia, Iran, Iraq, Mali, Papua New Guinea *(Chairman)*, Russian Federation, Sierra Leone *(Vice-Chairman)*, Syrian Arab Republic *(Rapporteur)*, Trinidad and Tobago, Tunisia, United Republic of Tanzania, Venezuela, Yugoslavia.

On 22 December 1992 (dec. 47/312 A), the General Assembly took note of the nomination by its President of Grenada as a member of the Special Committee.

SUBCOMMITTEE ON SMALL TERRITORIES, PETITIONS, INFORMATION AND ASSISTANCE[a]

The Subcommittee is composed of all the members of the Committee.

Chairman: Tunisia.
Rapporteur: Iran.

[a]Formerly the Subcommittee on Small Territories and the Subcommittee on Petitions, Information and Assistance.

Special Committee to Investigate Israeli Practices Affecting the Human Rights of the Palestinian People and Other Arabs of the Occupied Territories

Members: Senegal, Sri Lanka *(Chairman)*, Yugoslavia.

Special Committee to Select the Winners of the United Nations Human Rights Prize

The Special Committee to Select the Winners of the United Nations Human Rights Prize was established pursuant to a 1966 General Assembly resolution[2] recommending that a prize or prizes in the field of human rights be awarded not more often than at five-year intervals. Prizes were awarded for the fourth time on 10 December 1988.

Members: The Presidents of the General Assembly and the Economic and Social Council, and the Chairmen of the Commission on Human Rights, the Commission on the Status of Women and the Subcommission on Prevention of Discrimination and Protection of Minorities.

United Nations Administrative Tribunal

Members:
To serve until 31 December 1992: Jerome Ackerman, *President* (United States); Arnold Wilfred Geoffrey Kean, *First Vice-President (until 1 June)* (United Kingdom).
To serve until 31 December 1993: Luis de Posadas Montero, *Second Vice-President* (Uruguay); Ioan Voicu (Romania).
To serve until 31 December 1994: Balanda Mikuin Leliel (Zaire); Samarendranath Sen, *First Vice-President (from 1 June)* (India); Hubert Thierry (France).

On 23 December 1992 (dec. 47/316), the General Assembly appointed Jerome Ackerman (United States) and Francis R. Spain (Ireland) for a three-year term beginning on 1 January 1993 to fill the vacancies occurring on 31 December 1992.

United Nations Capital Development Fund

The United Nations Capital Development Fund was set up as an organ of the General Assembly to function as an autonomous organization within the United Nations framework. The chief executive officer of the Fund, the Managing Director, exercises his functions under the general direction of the Executive Board, which reports to the Assembly through the Economic and Social Council.

---

[2]YUN 1966, p. 458, GA res. 2217 A (XXI), annex, 19 Dec. 1966.

EXECUTIVE BOARD

The UNDP Governing Council acts as the Executive Board of the Fund and the UNDP Administrator as its Managing Director; UNDP provides the Fund with, among other things, all headquarters administrative support services.

Managing Director: William H. Draper III (UNDP Administrator).

United Nations Commission on International Trade Law (UNCITRAL)

The United Nations Commission on International Trade Law consists of 36 members elected by the General Assembly, in accordance with a formula providing equitable geographical representation and adequate representation of the principal economic and legal systems of the world. Members serve for six-year terms.

The Commission held its twenty-fifth session at Vienna from 4 to 22 May 1992.

Members:

To serve until the day preceding the Commission's regular annual session in 1995: Bulgaria, Cameroon, Canada, China, Costa Rica, Denmark, Egypt *(Vice-Chairman)*, France, Germany, Japan, Mexico *(Chairman)*, Morocco, Nigeria, Russian Federation, Singapore, Togo, United Kingdom.

To serve until the day preceding the Commission's regular annual session in 1998: Argentina, Austria *(Rapporteur)*, Chile, Czechoslovakia, Ecuador, Hungary, India, Iran *(Vice-Chairman)*, Italy, Kenya, Poland *(Vice-Chairman)*, Saudi Arabia, Spain, Sudan, Thailand, Uganda, United Republic of Tanzania, United States, Uruguay.

United Nations Conciliation Commission for Palestine

Members: France, Turkey, United States.

United Nations Conference on Trade and Development (UNCTAD)

Members of UNCTAD are Members of the United Nations or members of the specialized agencies or of IAEA.

The Conference held its eighth session at Cartagena de Indias, Colombia, from 8 to 25 February 1992.

Following are the States members of UNCTAD:

Part A. Afghanistan, Algeria, Angola, Bahrain, Bangladesh, Benin, Bhutan, Botswana, Brunei Darussalam, Burkina Faso, Burma, Burundi, Cameroon, Cape Verde, Central African Republic, Chad, China, Comoros, Congo, Côte d'Ivoire, Democratic Kampuchea, Democratic People's Republic of Korea, Djibouti, Egypt, Equatorial Guinea, Ethiopia, Fiji, Gabon, Gambia, Ghana, Guinea, Guinea-Bissau, India, Indonesia, Iran, Iraq, Israel, Jordan, Kenya, Kuwait, Lao People's Democratic Republic, Lebanon, Lesotho, Liberia, Libyan Arab Jamahiriya, Madagascar, Malawi, Malaysia, Maldives, Mali, Mauritania, Mauritius, Mongolia, Morocco, Mozambique, Namibia, Nepal, Niger, Nigeria, Oman, Pakistan, Papua New Guinea, Philippines, Qatar, Republic of Korea, Rwanda, Samoa, Sao Tome and Principe, Saudi Arabia, Senegal, Seychelles, Sierra Leone, Singapore, Solomon Islands, Somalia, South Africa, Sri Lanka, Sudan, Swaziland, Syrian Arab Republic, Thailand, Togo, Tonga, Tunisia, Uganda, United Arab Emirates, United Republic of Tanzania, Vanuatu, Viet Nam, Yemen, Yugoslavia, Zaire, Zambia, Zimbabwe.

Part B. Australia, Austria, Belgium, Canada, Cyprus, Denmark, Finland, France, Germany, Greece, Holy See, Iceland, Ireland, Italy, Japan, Liechtenstein, Luxembourg, Malta, Monaco, Netherlands, New Zealand, Norway, Portugal, San Marino, Spain, Sweden, Switzerland, Turkey, United Kingdom, United States.

Part C. Antigua and Barbuda, Argentina, Bahamas, Barbados, Belize, Bolivia, Brazil, Chile, Colombia, Costa Rica, Cuba, Dominica, Dominican Republic, Ecuador, El Salvador, Grenada, Guatemala, Guyana, Haiti, Honduras, Jamaica, Mexico, Nicaragua, Panama, Paraguay, Peru, Saint Kitts and Nevis, Saint Lucia, Saint Vincent and the Grenadines, Suriname, Trinidad and Tobago, Uruguay, Venezuela.

Part D. Albania, Belarus, Bulgaria, Czechoslovakia, Hungary, Poland, Romania, Russian Federation, Ukraine.

New members in 1991 and 1992. Armenia,[a] Azerbaijan,[a] Bosnia and Herzegovina,[b] Croatia,[b] Estonia, Georgia,[c] Kazakhstan,[a] Kyrgyzstan,[a] Latvia, Lithuania, Marshall Islands, Micronesia, Republic of Moldova,[a] Slovenia,[b] Tajikistan,[a] Turkmenistan,[a] Uzbekistan.[a]

[a]Became a Member of the United Nations and, *ipso facto*, of UNCTAD on 2 March 1992.
[b]Became a Member of the United Nations and, *ipso facto*, of UNCTAD on 22 May 1992.
[c]Became a Member of the United Nations and, *ipso facto*, of UNCTAD on 31 July 1992.

President: Colombia.
Vice-Presidents: Brazil, Bulgaria, Chile, China, Cuba, Czechoslovakia, Democratic People's Republic of Korea, Egypt, Ethiopia, Indonesia, Iran, Italy, Jamaica, Japan, Jordan, Morocco, Namibia, Netherlands, Nigeria, Norway, Oman, Pakistan, Peru, Poland, Portugal, Russian Federation, Spain, Switzerland, Uganda, United States, Venezuela, Zambia.
Rapporteur: Philippines.

TRADE AND DEVELOPMENT BOARD

The Trade and Development Board is a permanent organ of UNCTAD. It reports to UNCTAD as well as annually to the General Assembly through the Economic and Social Council.

BOARD MEMBERS AND SESSIONS

The membership of the Board is open to all UNCTAD members. Those wishing to become members of the Board communicate their intention to the Secretary-General of UNCTAD for transmittal to the Board President, who announces the membership on the basis of such notifications.

The Board held the following sessions in 1992, at Geneva: the second part of its seventeenth special session from 15 to 24 January, the second part of its thirty-eighth session from 21 April to 7 May, its first (pre-sessional) executive session on 21 September, and the first part of its thirty-ninth session from 28 September to 14 October.

Members: Afghanistan, Albania,[a] Algeria, Angola, Argentina, Armenia,[b] Australia, Austria, Bahrain, Bangladesh, Barbados, Belarus, Belgium, Benin, Bhutan, Bolivia, Brazil, Bulgaria, Burkina Faso, Burundi, Cameroon, Canada, Central African Republic, Chad, Chile, China, Colombia, Congo, Costa Rica, Côte d'Ivoire, Cuba, Cyprus, Czechoslovakia, Democratic People's Republic of Korea, Denmark, Dominica, Dominican Republic, Ecuador, Egypt, El Salvador, Equatorial Guinea,[b] Ethiopia, Finland, France, Gabon, Georgia,[c] Germany, Ghana, Greece, Grenada, Guatemala, Guinea, Guyana, Haiti, Honduras, Hungary, India, Indonesia, Iran, Iraq, Ireland, Israel, Italy, Jamaica, Japan, Jordan, Kenya, Kuwait, Lebanon, Liberia, Libyan Arab Jamahiriya, Liechtenstein, Luxembourg, Madagascar, Malaysia, Mali, Malta, Mauritania, Mauritius, Mexico, Mongolia, Morocco, Myanmar, Namibia, Nepal, Netherlands, New Zealand, Nicaragua, Nigeria, Norway, Oman, Pakistan, Panama, Papua New Guinea, Paraguay, Peru, Philippines, Poland, Portugal, Qatar, Republic of Korea, Romania, Russian Federation, Sao Tome and Principe, Saudi Arabia, Senegal, Sierra Leone, Singapore, Somalia, Spain, Sri Lanka, Sudan, Suriname, Sweden, Switzerland, Syrian Arab Republic, Thailand, Togo, Trinidad and Tobago, Tunisia, Turkey, Uganda, Ukraine, United Arab Emirates, United Kingdom, United Republic of Tanzania, United States, Uruguay, Venezuela, Viet Nam, Yemen, Yugoslavia, Zaire, Zambia, Zimbabwe.

[a]Became a member on 7 May 1992.
[b]Became a member on 21 September 1992.
[c]Became a member on 29 September 1992.

OFFICERS (BUREAU) OF THE BOARD

Seventeenth special session (second part), thirty-eighth session (second part) and first (pre-sessional) executive session
President: Kenya (seventeenth special and thirty-eighth sessions), Jordan (first executive session) (acting).
Vice-Presidents: Algeria, Czechoslovakia, Indonesia, Ireland (thirty-eighth and first executive sessions), Italy (seventeenth special session), Jamaica, Jordan, Netherlands (thirty-eighth session), Portugal (seventeenth special and first executive sessions), Russian Federation, Sweden, United States.
Rapporteur: Ecuador (seventeenth special and thirty-eighth sessions), Venezuela (first executive session).

Thirty-ninth session (first part)
President: Turkey.
Vice-Presidents: Bolivia, Democratic People's Republic of Korea, Honduras, Japan, Mauritius, Morocco, Poland, Russian Federation, United Kingdom, United States.
Rapporteur: Nepal.

SUBSIDIARY ORGANS OF THE TRADE AND DEVELOPMENT BOARD

The main committees of the Board are open to the participation of all interested UNCTAD members, on the understanding that those wishing to attend a particular session of one or more of the committees communicate their intention to the Secretary-General of UNCTAD during the preceding regular session of the Board. On the basis of such notifications, the Board determines the membership of the main committees.

On the recommendation of UNCTAD at its eighth session, the Board, on 7 May 1992, adopted the terms of reference of four new standing committees: Standing Committee on Commodities, Standing Committee on Developing Services Sectors: Fostering Competitive Services Sectors in Developing Countries, Standing Committee on Economic Cooperation among Developing Countries and Standing Committee on Poverty Alleviation. The existing main committees were suspended (Committee on Commodities, Committee on Economic Cooperation among Developing Countries, Committee on Invisibles and Financing related to Trade, Committee on Manufactures, Committee on Shipping, Committee on Transfer of Technology), with the exception of the Special Committee on Preferences and the Intergovernmental Group of Experts on Restrictive Business Practices.

INTERGOVERNMENTAL GROUP OF EXPERTS ON RESTRICTIVE BUSINESS PRACTICES

The Intergovernmental Group of Experts on Restrictive Business Practices held its eleventh session at Geneva from 23 to 27 November 1992.

Members: Algeria, Argentina *(Vice-Chairman)*, Austria, Bangladesh, Belgium, Brazil, Bulgaria, Canada *(Rapporteur)*, Chile, China, Colombia, Cuba, Czechoslovakia *(Vice-Chairman)*, Democratic People's Republic of Korea, Egypt, El Salvador, Ethiopia, Finland, France, Germany, Ghana, Greece, Hungary, India *(Vice-Chairman)*, Indonesia, Ireland, Italy, Jamaica, Japan, Kenya, Lebanon, Libyan Arab Jamahiriya, Malaysia, Mauritius, Mexico, Morocco, Nepal, Netherlands, Nigeria, Norway, Pakistan, Peru, Philippines *(Chairman)*, Poland, Portugal, Qatar, Republic of Korea, Romania, Russian Federation, Saudi Arabia, Senegal, Sri Lanka, Sweden, Switzerland, Syrian Arab Republic, Thailand, United Kingdom *(Vice-Chairman)*, United Republic of Tanzania, United States, Venezuela, Viet Nam, Zambia, Zimbabwe *(Vice-Chairman)*.

SPECIAL COMMITTEE ON PREFERENCES

The Special Committee on Preferences, which is open to the participation of all UNCTAD members, held its nineteenth session at Geneva from 18 to 22 May 1992.

Chairman: Germany.
Vice-Chairmen: Chile, India, Japan, Morocco.
Rapporteur: Colombia.

STANDING COMMITTEE ON COMMODITIES

The Standing Committee on Commodities held its first session at Geneva from 19 to 23 October 1992.

Members: Afghanistan, Algeria, Argentina, Armenia, Australia, Austria, Bangladesh, Belgium, Bolivia, Brazil, Bulgaria, Canada, China, Colombia, Côte d'Ivoire, Cuba *(Vice-Chairman)*, Czechoslovakia, Democratic People's Republic of Korea, Denmark, Ecuador, Egypt, El Salvador, Equatorial Guinea, Ethiopia, Finland, France, Germany, Ghana, Greece, Honduras, Hungary, India, Indonesia, Iran, Iraq, Ireland, Israel, Italy, Jamaica, Japan, Jordan, Kenya, Lebanon, Libyan Arab Jamahiriya, Madagascar, Malaysia, Mali, Mexico, Morocco, Myanmar, Nepal, Netherlands, New Zealand, Nigeria *(Vice-Chairman)*, Norway, Pakistan, Panama, Paraguay, Peru, Philippines *(Rapporteur)*, Poland, Portugal, Republic of Korea, Romania, Russian Federation *(Vice-Chairman)*, Saudi Arabia, Senegal, Singapore, Spain, Sri Lanka, Sudan *(Chairman)*, Sweden, Switzerland, Thailand, Togo, Trinidad and Tobago, Tunisia, Turkey, United Kingdom *(Vice-Chairman)*, United Republic of Tanzania, United States *(Vice-Chairman)*, Uruguay, Venezuela, Viet Nam, Yugoslavia, Zambia, Zimbabwe.

STANDING COMMITTEE ON DEVELOPING SERVICES SECTORS: FOSTERING COMPETITIVE SERVICES SECTORS IN DEVELOPING COUNTRIES

The Standing Committee on Developing Services Sectors: Fostering Competitive Services Sectors in Developing Countries held its first session at Geneva from 26 to 30 October 1992.

Members: Afghanistan, Algeria, Argentina, Armenia, Australia, Austria, Bangladesh, Belgium, Bolivia, Brazil, Bulgaria, Cameroon, Chile, China, Colombia, Costa Rica, Côte d'Ivoire, Croatia, Cuba *(Rapporteur)*, Cyprus, Czechoslovakia, Democratic People's Republic of Korea, Denmark, Egypt, El Salvador, Ethiopia, Finland, France, Germany, Ghana, Greece, Honduras, Hungary, India *(Vice-Chairman)*, Indonesia, Iran, Iraq, Ireland, Israel, Italy, Jamaica, Japan *(Vice-Chairman)*, Jordan, Kenya, Lebanon, Lesotho, Liberia, Libyan Arab Jamahiriya, Malaysia *(Chairman)*, Mali, Mauritius, Mexico, Mongolia, Morocco, Myanmar, Nepal, Netherlands, New Zealand, Niger, Nigeria, Norway, Pakistan, Paraguay, Peru, Philippines, Poland, Republic of Korea, Romania, Russian Federation *(Vice-Chairman)*, Saudi Arabia, Senegal, Seychelles, Spain, Sri Lanka, Sudan, Sweden, Switzerland, Thailand, Trinidad and Tobago, Tunisia *(Vice-Chairman)*, Turkey, United Kingdom *(Vice-Chairman)*, United Republic of Tanzania, United States, Uruguay, Venezuela, Viet Nam, Yugoslavia, Zambia, Zimbabwe.

STANDING COMMITTEE ON DEVELOPING SERVICES SECTORS: FOSTERING COMPETITIVE SERVICES SECTORS IN DEVELOPING COUNTRIES--SHIPPING

The Standing Committee on Developing Services Sectors: Fostering Competitive Services Sectors in Developing Countries—Shipping held its first session at Geneva from 2 to 6 November 1992.

Members: Afghanistan, Algeria, Argentina, Armenia, Australia, Austria, Bangladesh, Belgium, Bolivia, Brazil, Bulgaria, Cameroon, Canada, Chile, China, Colombia, Costa Rica, Côte d'Ivoire, Croatia, Cuba, Cyprus, Czechoslovakia, Democratic People's Republic of Korea, Denmark, Egypt *(Chairman)*, El Salvador, Ethiopia, Finland, France, Germany, Ghana, Greece *(Vice-Chairman)*, Honduras, Hungary, India *(Vice-Chairman)*, Indonesia, Iran, Iraq, Ireland, Israel, Italy, Jamaica, Japan *(Rapporteur)*, Jordan, Kenya, Lebanon, Lesotho, Liberia, Libyan Arab Jamahiriya, Madagascar, Malaysia, Mali, Mauritius, Mexico, Mongolia, Morocco, Myanmar, Nepal, Netherlands, New Zealand, Niger, Nigeria *(Vice-Chairman)*, Norway, Pakistan, Paraguay, Peru *(Vice-Chairman)*, Philippines, Poland, Republic of Korea, Romania, Russian Federation *(Vice-Chairman)*, Saudi Arabia, Senegal, Seychelles, Spain, Sri Lanka, Sudan, Sweden,

Switzerland, Thailand, Trinidad and Tobago, Tunisia, Turkey, United Kingdom, United Republic of Tanzania, United States, Uruguay, Venezuela, Viet Nam, Yugoslavia, Zambia, Zimbabwe.

STANDING COMMITTEE ON ECONOMIC COOPERATION AMONG DEVELOPING COUNTRIES

The Standing Committee on Economic Cooperation among Developing Countries did not meet in 1992.

Members: Afghanistan, Algeria, Argentina, Armenia, Austria, Bangladesh, Bolivia, Brazil, China, Colombia, Côte d'Ivoire, Cuba, Democratic People's Republic of Korea, Denmark, Egypt, El Salvador, Ethiopia, France, Georgia, Germany, Ghana, Greece, Honduras, India, Indonesia, Iran, Iraq, Israel, Jamaica, Japan, Jordan, Kenya, Lebanon, Libyan Arab Jamahiriya, Madagascar, Malaysia, Mali, Mauritius, Mexico, Mongolia, Morocco, Myanmar, Nepal, Netherlands, Niger, Nigeria, Norway, Pakistan, Panama, Peru, Philippines, Republic of Korea, Romania, Russian Federation, Saudi Arabia, Senegal, Spain, Sri Lanka, Sudan, Sweden, Switzerland, Syrian Arab Republic, Thailand, Togo, Trinidad and Tobago, Tunisia, Turkey, United Kingdom, United Republic of Tanzania, United States, Uruguay, Venezuela, Viet Nam, Yugoslavia, Zambia, Zimbabwe.

STANDING COMMITTEE ON POVERTY ALLEVIATION

The Standing Committee on Poverty Alleviation did not meet in 1992.

Members: Afghanistan, Algeria, Argentina, Armenia, Australia, Austria, Bangladesh, Belgium, Bolivia, Brazil, Cameroon, Canada, Chile, China, Colombia, Côte d'Ivoire, Cuba, Czechoslovakia, Democratic People's Republic of Korea, Denmark, Dominican Republic, Egypt, El Salvador, Ethiopia, Finland, France, Germany, Ghana, Greece, Honduras, India, Indonesia, Iran, Iraq, Ireland, Israel, Italy, Jamaica, Japan, Jordan, Kenya, Lebanon, Libyan Arab Jamahiriya, Madagascar, Malaysia, Mali, Mexico, Morocco, Myanmar, Nepal, Netherlands, Nigeria, Norway, Pakistan, Panama, Paraguay, Peru, Philippines, Poland, Portugal, Republic of Korea, Romania, Russian Federation, Saudi Arabia, Senegal, Spain, Sri Lanka, Sudan, Sweden, Switzerland, Thailand, Togo, Tunisia, Turkey, United Kingdom, United States, Uruguay, Viet Nam, Yugoslavia, Zambia, Zimbabwe.

United Nations Development Fund for Women (UNIFEM)

The United Nations Development Fund for Women is a separate entity in autonomous association with UNDP. The Director of the Fund, appointed by the UNDP Administrator, conducts all matters related to its mandate and the Administrator is accountable for its management and operations.

CONSULTATIVE COMMITTEE

The Consultative Committee on UNIFEM to advise the UNDP Administrator on all policy matters affecting the Fund's activities is composed of five Member States designated by the General Assembly President with due regard for the financing of the Fund from voluntary contributions and to equitable geographical distribution. Each State member of the Committee serves for a three-year term and designates a person with expertise in development cooperation activities, including those benefiting women.

The Committee held its thirty-first session at United Nations Headquarters from 13 to 16 April 1992.

Members (until 31 December 1994): Bahamas *(Chairman)*, Denmark, Indonesia, Poland,[a] Uganda.

[a]Appointed by the President of the forty-sixth session of the General Assembly, as communicated to the Secretary-General on 14 April 1992; on 22 May (dec. 46/311 C), the Assembly took note of the appointment.

Director of UNIFEM: Sharon Capeling-Alakija.

United Nations Environment Programme (UNEP)

GOVERNING COUNCIL

The Governing Council of UNEP consists of 58 members elected by the General Assembly according to a specific pattern of equitable geographical representation.

The Governing Council, which reports to the Assembly through the Economic and Social Council, held its third special session at Nairobi, Kenya, from 3 to 5 February 1992.

Members:
To serve until 31 December 1993: Argentina, Austria, Barbados, Brazil, Burundi, China, France, Gabon, Gambia, Germany, Indonesia *(Vice-President)*, Japan, Kuwait, Lesotho, Mauritius, New Zealand, Norway, Peru, Philippines, Russian Federation, Spain, Thailand, Tunisia, Ukraine, United States, Venezuela, Yugoslavia, Zaire, Zimbabwe *(Rapporteur)*.
To serve until 31 December 1995: Australia, Bangladesh, Bhutan, Botswana, Cameroon, Chile, Colombia, Congo, Côte d'Ivoire, Czechoslovakia *(Vice-President)*, Denmark, Guyana *(Vice-President)*, India, Iran, Italy, Kenya, Malaysia, Mexico, Netherlands *(President)*, Nigeria, Pakistan, Poland, Portugal, Romania, Rwanda, Senegal, Sri Lanka, United Kingdom, Uruguay.

Executive Director of UNEP: Mostafa Kamal Tolba.
Deputy Executive Director: William H. Mansfield III (until 30 April), Anthony T. Brough (from 1 May).

On 8 December 1992 (dec. 47/310), the General Assembly elected Elizabeth Dowdeswell as Executive Director for a four-year term beginning on 1 January 1993.

United Nations Institute for Disarmament Research (UNIDIR)

BOARD OF TRUSTEES

The Secretary-General's Advisory Board on Disarmament Matters, composed in 1992 of 15 eminent persons selected on the basis of their personal expertise and taking into account the principle of equitable geographical representation, functions as the Board of Trustees of UNIDIR; the Director of UNIDIR reports to the General Assembly and is an *ex-officio* member of the Advisory Board when it acts as the Board of Trustees.

Members: Ednan T. Agaev (Russian Federation); A. Bolaji Akinyemi (Nigeria); Martin Chungong Ayafor (Cameroon); Marcos Castrioto de Azambuja (Brazil); Léon Bouvier (France); J. Soedjati Djiwandono (Indonesia); Mitsuro Donowaki (Japan); Muchkund Dubey (India); Josef Holik (Germany); Juraj Kralik (Czechoslovakia); Bjorn Inge Kristvik, *Chairman* (Norway); Li Changhe (China); Joseph S. Nye, Jr. (United States); John Simpson (United Kingdom); Klaus Törnudd (Finland).

Director of UNIDIR: Jayantha Dhanapala (until 26 June), Serge Sur (from 27 June until 31 October, a.i.), Sverre Lodgaard (from 1 November).

United Nations Institute for Training and Research (UNITAR)

The Executive Director of UNITAR, in consultation with the Board of Trustees of the Institute, reports through the Secretary-General to the General Assembly and, as appropriate, to the Economic and Social Council and other United Nations bodies.

BOARD OF TRUSTEES

The Board of Trustees of UNITAR is composed of: *(a)* not less than 11 and not more than 30 members, which may include one or more officials of the United Nations Secretariat, appointed on a broad geographical basis by the Secretary-General, in consultation with the Presidents of the General Assembly and the Economic and Social Council; and *(b)* four *ex-officio* members.

The Board held its thirtieth session at United Nations Headquarters from 31 August to 3 September 1992.

Members:

To serve until 31 December 1992: G. Arthur Brown (Jamaica); Jaime de Piniés (Secretariat); J. Isawa Elaigwu (Nigeria); Lucio Garcia del Solar (Argentina); Jean-Pierre Keusch, *Vice-Chairman* (Switzerland); Kiyoaki Kikuchi (Japan); Slobodan Kotevski (Yugoslavia); Eduard V. Kudryavtsev (Russian Federation); Jacques Leprette (France); Jamsheed K. A. Marker (Pakistan); Missoum Sbih, *Chairman* (Algeria); Leticia Ramos Shahani (Philippines); Mohamed Ahmed Sherif (Libyan Arab Jamahiriya).

Ex-officio members: The Secretary-General, the President of the General Assembly, the President of the Economic and Social Council and the Executive Director of UNITAR.

Executive Director of UNITAR: Michel Doo Kingué (until 28 February), Marcel Boisard (acting) (from 1 March).

United Nations Joint Staff Pension Board

The United Nations Joint Staff Pension Board is composed of 33 members, as follows:

Twelve appointed by the United Nations Staff Pension Committee (four from members elected by the General Assembly, four from those appointed by the Secretary-General, four from those elected by participants);

Twenty-one appointed by staff pension committees of other member organizations of the United Nations Joint Staff Pension Fund (seven from those chosen by the bodies corresponding to the General Assembly, seven from those appointed by the chief administrative officers, seven from those chosen by the participants).

The Board held its forty-fourth session at Montreal, Canada, from 25 June to 3 July 1992.

Members:
United Nations
  Representing the General Assembly: Members: J. J. Duhalt (Mexico); T. Inomata, *Second Vice-Chairman* (Japan); M. G. Okeyo (Kenya); S. Shearouse (United States). Alternates: M. F. Belhaj (Tunisia); L. E. Bidny (Russian Federation); R. Kinchen (United Kingdom); R. Rae (India).
  Representing the Secretary-General: Members: A. Ciss (Senegal); J. R. Foran (Canada); A. Miller (Australia); A. Duque (Colombia). Alternates: D. Bull (United Kingdom); A. Barabanov (Russian Federation).
  Representing the Participants: Members: B. Hillis (Canada); S. Johnston (United States); V. Baeza (Chile); N. Watanaphanich (Thailand). Alternate: N. Kakar (India).
Food and Agriculture Organization of the United Nations
  Representing the Governing Body: Member: C. Bonaparte (Haiti).
  Representing the Executive Head: Member: G. Zorn (United States). Alternate: A. T. Slater (United States).
  Representing the Participants: Member: A. Marcucci, *First Vice-Chairman* (Italy). Alternate: M. Arrigo (Italy).
World Health Organization
  Representing the Governing Body: Member: Sir John Reid (United Kingdom).
  Representing the Executive Head: Member: D. G. Aitken, *Chairman* (United Kingdom). Alternate: A. Asamoah (Ghana).
  Representing the Participants: Member: M. A. Dam (United States). Alternate: M. Melloni (France).
International Labour Organisation
  Representing the Governing Body: Member: Y. Chotard (France). Alternate: W. M. Yoffee (United States).
  Representing the Executive Head: Member: S. C. Cornwell (United States). Alternate: A. Castro Gutiérrez (Nicaragua).
United Nations Educational, Scientific and Cultural Organization
  Representing the Governing Body: Member: G. V. Rao (India).
  Representing the Participants: Member: A. McLurg (United Kingdom).
United Nations Industrial Development Organization
  Representing the Governing Body: Member: E. Zador (Hungary).
  Representing the Executive Head: Member: U. Peer (Austria).

International Civil Aviation Organization
  Representing the Executive Head: Member: D. J. Goossen, *Rapporteur* (Netherlands).
  Representing the Participants: Member: C. Gallagher-Croxen (Canada). Alternate: L. Mortimer (United Kingdom).
International Atomic Energy Agency
  Representing the Participants: Member: W. Scherzer (Austria).
International Telecommunication Union
  Representing the Participants: Member: H. Eckert (France). Alternate: V. Paratian (Mauritius).
International Maritime Organization
  Representing the Participants: Member: D. Bertaud (France). Alternate: M. Tun (Myanmar).
Interim Commission for the International Trade Organization/General Agreement on Tariffs and Trade
  Representing the Governing Body: Member: J. Clarke (United Kingdom).
World Meteorological Organization
  Representing the Executive Head: Member: M. Mlaki (United Republic of Tanzania).
World Intellectual Property Organization
  Representing the Executive Head: Member: B. Machado (France).
International Fund for Agricultural Development
  Representing the Governing Body: Member: M. Deregibus (Argentina).

STANDING COMMITTEE OF THE PENSION BOARD

In 1992, the Standing Committee met in New York from 26 to 28 February and at Montreal from 25 June to 3 July.

Members (elected at the Board's forty-fourth session):
United Nations (Group I)
  Representing the General Assembly: Members: T. Inomata, M. F. Belhaj. Alternates: R. Rae, S. Shearouse.
  Representing the Secretary-General: Members: A. Ciss, A. Miller. Alternates: A. Duque, D. Bull.
  Representing the Participants: Members: B. Hillis, S. Johnston. Alternates: V. Baeza, N. Watanaphanich.
Specialized agencies (Group II)
  Representing the Governing Body: Member: C. Bonaparte (FAO).
  Representing the Executive Head: Member: D. G. Aitken (WHO). Alternate: A. Asamoah (WHO).
  Representing the Participants: Member: M. Dam (WHO). Alternate: A. Marcucci (FAO).
Specialized agencies (Group III)
  Representing the Governing Body: Member: W. M. Yoffee (ILO). Alternate: Y. Chotard (ILO).
  Representing the Executive Head: Member: D. Daly (UNESCO). Alternate: C. Kerlouegan (UNESCO).
Specialized agencies (Group IV)
  Representing the Executive Head: Member: D. Goethel (IAEA). Alternate: U. Peer (UNIDO).
  Representing the Participants: Member: H. Eckert (ITU). Alternate: C. Gallagher-Croxen (ICAO).
Specialized agencies (Group V)
  Representing the Governing Body: Member: R. G. Lewis (IMO). Alternate: J. Clarke (ICITO/GATT).
  Representing the Participants: Member: S. Mbele-Mbong (WMO). Alternate: V. Yossifov (WIPO).

COMMITTEE OF ACTUARIES

The Committee of Actuaries consists of five members, each representing one of the five geographical regions of the United Nations.

Members: A. O. Ogunshola (Nigeria), *Region I* (African States); K. Takeuchi (Japan), *Region II* (Asian States); E. M. Chetyrkin (Russian Federation), *Region III* (Eastern European States); H. Perez Montas (Dominican Republic), *Region IV* (Latin American States); L. J. Martin (United Kingdom), *Region V* (Western European and other States).

United Nations Population Fund (UNFPA)

The United Nations Population Fund, a subsidiary organ of the General Assembly, plays a leading role in the United Nations system in promoting population programmes and assists developing countries at their request in dealing with their population problems. It operates under the overall policy guidance of the Economic and Social Council and under the financial and administrative policy guidance of the Governing Council of UNDP.

Executive Director: Dr. Nafis I. Sadik.
Deputy Executive Director (Policy and Administration): Katsuhide Kitatani.
Deputy Executive Director (Programme): Joseph Van Arendonk.

United Nations Relief and Works Agency for Palestine Refugees in the Near East (UNRWA)

ADVISORY COMMISSION OF UNRWA

The Advisory Commission of UNRWA met at Vienna on 10 September 1992.

Members: Belgium, Egypt, France, Japan, Jordan, Lebanon, Syrian Arab Republic, Turkey *(Chairman)*, United Kingdom, United States.

WORKING GROUP ON THE FINANCING OF UNRWA

Members: France, Ghana, Japan, Lebanon, Norway *(Rapporteur)*, Trinidad and Tobago, Turkey *(Chairman)*, United Kingdom, United States.

Commissioner-General of UNRWA: Ilter Türkmen.
Deputy Commissioner-General: William L. Eagleton.

United Nations Scientific Committee on the Effects of Atomic Radiation

The 21-member United Nations Scientific Committee on the Effects of Atomic Radiation held its forty-first session at Vienna from 15 to 19 June 1992.

Members: Argentina, Australia, Belgium *(Chairman)*, Brazil, Canada *(Vice-Chairman)*, China, Czechoslovakia, Egypt, France, Germany, India, Indonesia, Japan, Mexico, Peru *(Rapporteur)*, Poland, Russian Federation, Sudan, Sweden, United Kingdom, United States.

United Nations Staff Pension Committee

The United Nations Staff Pension Committee consists of four members and four alternates elected by the General Assembly, four members and two alternates appointed by the Secretary-General, and four members and two alternates elected by the participants in the United Nations Joint Staff Pension Fund. The term of office of the elected members is three years, or until the election of their successors.

Members:
Elected by Assembly (to serve until 31 December 1994): *Members:* Jorge Duhalt (Mexico), Tadanori Inomata (Japan), Michael G. Okeyo (Kenya), Susan Shearouse (United States). *Alternates:* Mohamed Ferid Belhaj (Tunisia), Leonid E. Bidny (Russian Federation), Richard Kinchen (United Kingdom), Ranjit Rae (India).
Appointed by Secretary-General (to serve until further notice): *Members:* Abdou Ciss, Armando Duque, J. Richard Foran, Maryan Baquerot, Anthony J. Miller. *Alternates:* Alexander Barabanov, Dulcie Bull.
Elected by Participants (to serve until 31 December 1992): *Members:* Bruce C. Hillis, Susanna H. Johnston, Gualtiero Fulcheri, Viviana Baeza. *Alternates:* Naowalak Watanaphanich, Narinder Kakar.

United Nations Trust Committee for the United Nations Fund for Namibia

Members: Australia, Finland, India, Nigeria, Romania, Senegal, Turkey, Venezuela *(Vice-Chairman/Rapporteur)*, Yugoslavia, Zambia *(Chairman)*.

United Nations University

COUNCIL OF THE UNITED NATIONS UNIVERSITY

The Council of the United Nations University, the governing board of the University, reports annually to the General Assembly, to the Economic and Social Council and to the UNESCO Executive Board through the Secretary-General and the UNESCO Director-General. It consists of: *(a)* 24 members appointed jointly by the Secretary-General and the Director-General of UNESCO, in consultation with the agencies and programmes concerned including UNITAR, who serve in their personal capacity for six-year terms; *(b)* the Secretary-General, the Director-General of UNESCO and the Executive Director of UNITAR, who are *ex-officio* members; and *(c)* the Rector of the University, who is normally appointed for a five-year term.

The Council did not meet in 1992.

Members:
To serve until 2 May 1995: Claude Frejacques (France), Sippanondha Ketudat (Thailand), Felipe E. MacGregor (Peru), Lucille Mair (Jamaica), Abdel Salam Majali (Jordan), Lydia Makhubu (Swaziland), Vladlen A. Martynov (Russian Federation), Fatima Mernissi (Morocco), Rafael Portaencasa (Spain), Mihaly Simai (Hungary), Raimo Vayrynen (Finland), Josephine Guidy-Wandja (Côte d'Ivoire), Wang Shaoqi (China).
To serve until 2 May 1998: Vladimir Dlouhy (Czechoslovakia), Hideo Kagami (Japan), Sang Soo Lee (Republic of Korea), Madina Ly-Tall (Mali), Lucien F. Michaud (Canada), A. P. Mitra (India), Jacob L. Ngu (Cameroon), Luis Manuel Peñalver (Venezuela), Victor Rabinowitch (United States), Edson Machado de Sousa (Brazil), Frances Stewart (United Kingdom), J. A. van Ginkel (Netherlands).
Ex-officio members: The Secretary-General, the Director-General of UNESCO and the Executive Director of UNITAR.

Rector of the United Nations University: Heitor Gurgulino de Souza.

The Council maintained four standing committees during 1992: Committee on Finance and Budget; Committee on Institutional and Programmatic Development; Committee on Statutes, Rules and Guidelines; Committee on the Report of the Council.

United Nations Voluntary Fund for Indigenous Populations

BOARD OF TRUSTEES

The Board of Trustees to advise the Secretary-General in his administration of the United Nations Voluntary Fund for Indigenous Populations consists of five members with relevant experience in issues affecting indigenous populations, appointed in their personal capacity by the Secretary-General for a three-year term. At least one member is a representative of a widely recognized organization of indigenous people.

The Board held its fifth session at Geneva from 27 April to 2 May 1992.

Members: Leif Dunfjeld (Norway); Alioune Séné (Senegal); Hiwi Tauroa (New Zealand); Danilo Turk (Yugoslavia); Augusto Willemsen-Díaz, *Chairman* (Guatemala).

United Nations Voluntary Fund for Victims of Torture

BOARD OF TRUSTEES

The Board of Trustees to advise the Secretary-General in his administration of the United Nations Voluntary Fund for Victims of Torture consists of five members with wide experience in the field of human rights, appointed in their personal capacity by the Secretary-General with due regard for equitable geographical distribution and in consultation with their Governments.

The Board held its eleventh session at Geneva from 22 April to 1 May 1992.

Members: Elizabeth Odio Benito (Costa Rica); Ribot Hatano (Japan); Ivan Tosevski (Yugoslavia); Amos Wako (Kenya); Jaap Walkate, *Chairman* (Netherlands).

United Nations Voluntary Trust Fund on Contemporary Forms of Slavery

The United Nations Voluntary Trust Fund on Contemporary Forms of Slavery provides financial assistance to representatives of non-governmental organizations dealing with the matter to participate in the deliberations of the Working Group on Contemporary Forms of Slavery of the Subcommission on Prevention of Discrimination and Protection of Minorities, and extends humanitarian, legal and financial aid to individuals whose human rights have been severely violated as a result of contemporary forms of slavery.

BOARD OF TRUSTEES

The Board of Trustees to advise the Secretary-General in his administration of the Fund consists of five persons with relevant experience in the field of human rights and contemporary forms of slavery in particular, appointed in their personal capacity by the Secretary-General for a three-year renewable term, in consultation with the Chairman of the Subcommission and with due regard to equitable geographical distribution.

Members:[a]
To serve until 31 December 1995: Swami Agnivesh (India), Michel Bonnet (France), Tatiana Matveeva (Russian Federation), Cheikh Saad-Bouh Kamara (Mauritania), Eugenia Zamora Chavarria (Uruguay).

[a]Appointed on 16 November 1992 for a three-year term beginning on 1 January 1993.

World Food Council

The World Food Council, at the ministerial or plenipotentiary level, functions as an organ of the United Nations and reports to the General Assembly through the Economic and Social Council. It consists of 36 members nominated by the Economic and Social Council and elected by the Assembly according to a specific pattern of equitable geographical distribution. Members serve for three-year terms.

The Council held its eighteenth session at Nairobi, Kenya, from 23 to 26 June 1992.

Members:
To serve until 31 December 1992: Argentina, Burundi, Denmark, Egypt, France, Hungary, Iran *(President)*, Italy, Japan, Peru, Rwanda, Yemen.
To serve until 31 December 1993: Bangladesh, Bulgaria, Canada, China, Colombia, Gambia, Kenya *(Vice-President)*, Lesotho, Mexico *(Vice-President)*, Nepal, Turkey *(Vice-President)*, United States.
To serve until 31 December 1994: Albania, Australia, Central African Republic, Germany, Guatemala, Honduras, Indonesia, Nicaragua, Russian Federation *(Vice-President)*, Swaziland, Thailand, Uganda.

Executive Director: Gerald Ion Trant (until 30 June 1992).

On 29 April 1992 (dec. 1992/216), the Economic and Social Council nominated the following States for election by the General Assembly for a three-year term beginning on 1 January 1993 to fill 11 of the 12 vacancies occurring on 31 December 1992: Ecuador, France, Guinea-Bissau, Hungary, Iran, Italy, Japan, Nigeria, Norway, Peru, Tunisia. The Assembly elected them on 21 October (dec. 47/306 A). No further elections were held in 1992 to fill the remaining seat, allocated to a member from Asian States.

Conference

United Nations Conference on Environment and Development

The United Nations Conference on Environment and Development was held at Rio de Janeiro, Brazil, from 3 to 14 June 1992. Participating were the following 176 States and Territories and the European Economic Community:

Afghanistan, Albania, Algeria, Angola, Antigua and Barbuda, Argentina, Armenia, Australia, Austria, Azerbaijan, Bahamas, Bahrain, Bangladesh, Barbados, Belarus, Belgium, Belize, Benin, Bhutan, Bolivia, Botswana, Brazil, Brunei Darussalam, Bulgaria, Burkina Faso, Burundi, Cambodia, Cameroon, Canada, Cape Verde, Central African Republic, Chad, Chile, China, Colombia, Comoros, Congo, Cook Islands, Costa Rica, Côte d'Ivoire, Croatia, Cuba, Cyprus, Czechoslovakia, Democratic People's Republic of Korea, Denmark, Djibouti, Dominica, Ecuador, Egypt, El Salvador, Equatorial Guinea, Estonia, Ethiopia, Fiji, Finland, France, Gabon, Gambia, Germany, Ghana, Greece, Grenada, Guatemala, Guinea, Guinea-Bissau, Guyana, Haiti, Holy See, Honduras, Hungary, Iceland, India, Indonesia, Iran, Iraq, Ireland, Israel, Italy, Jamaica, Japan, Jordan, Kazakhstan, Kenya, Kiribati, Kuwait, Lao People's Democratic Republic, Latvia, Lebanon, Lesotho, Liberia, Libyan Arab Jamahiriya, Liechtenstein, Lithuania, Luxembourg, Madagascar, Malaysia, Maldives, Mali, Malta, Marshall Islands, Mauritania, Mauritius, Mexico, Micronesia, Monaco, Mongolia, Morocco, Mozambique, Myanmar, Namibia, Nauru, Nepal, Netherlands, New Zealand, Nicaragua, Niger, Nigeria, Norway, Oman, Pakistan, Panama, Papua New Guinea, Paraguay, Peru, Philippines, Poland, Portugal, Qatar, Republic of Korea, Republic of Moldova, Romania, Russian Federation, Rwanda, Saint Kitts and Nevis, Saint Lucia, Saint Vincent and the Grenadines, Samoa, San Marino, Sao Tome and Principe, Saudi Arabia, Senegal, Seychelles, Sierra Leone, Singapore, Slovenia, Solomon Islands, Spain, Sri Lanka, Sudan, Suriname, Swaziland, Sweden, Switzerland, Syrian Arab Republic, Thailand, Togo, Trinidad and Tobago, Tunisia, Turkey, Tuvalu, Uganda, Ukraine, United Arab Emirates, United Kingdom, United Republic of Tanzania, United States, Uruguay, Vanuatu, Venezuela, Viet Nam, Yemen, Yugoslavia, Zaire, Zambia, Zimbabwe.

President: Brazil.
Vice-Presidents: Argentina, Barbados, Benin, Canada, China, Costa Rica, Finland, France, Gabon, Germany, Guinea-Bissau, India, Indonesia, Iran, Jamaica, Kenya, Malaysia, Maldives, Mauritania, Mexico, Mozambique, Nigeria, Peru, Poland, Republic of Korea, Romania, Russian Federation, Senegal, Switzerland, Tunisia, Ukraine, United Kingdom, United Republic of Tanzania, United States, Vanuatu, Venezuela, Zaire, Zimbabwe.
Rapporteur-General: Algeria.

Security Council

The Security Council consists of 15 Member States of the United Nations, in accordance with the provisions of Article 23 of the United Nations Charter as amended in 1965.

MEMBERS

Permanent members: China, France, Russian Federation, United Kingdom, United States.

Non-permanent members: Austria, Belgium, Cape Verde, Ecuador, Hungary, India, Japan, Morocco, Venezuela, Zimbabwe.

On 27 October 1992 (dec. 47/308), the General Assembly elected Brazil, Djibouti, New Zealand, Pakistan and Spain for a two-year term beginning on 1 January 1993, to replace Austria, Belgium, Ecuador, India and Zimbabwe, whose terms of office were to expire on 31 December 1992.

PRESIDENTS

The presidency of the Council rotates monthly, according to the English alphabetical listing of its member States. The following served as Presidents during 1992:

Month	Member	Representative
January	United Kingdom	Sir David Hannay
		John Major
February	United States	Thomas R. Pickering
March	Venezuela	Diego Arria
April	Zimbabwe	Simbarashe Simbanenduku Mumbengegwi
		Stanislaus Garikai Chigwedere
May	Austria	Peter Hohenfellner
June	Belgium	Paul Noterdaeme
July	Cape Verde	José Luis Jesus
August	China	Li Daoyu
September	Ecuador	José Ayala Lasso
October	France	Jean-Bernard Mérimée
November	Hungary	André Erdos
December	India	Chinmaya Rajaninath Gharekhan

Military Staff Committee

The Military Staff Committee consists of the chiefs of staff of the permanent members of the Security Council or their representatives. It meets fortnightly.

Standing committees

Each of the three standing committees of the Security Council is composed of representatives of all Council members:

Committee of Experts (to examine the provisional rules of procedure of the Council and any other matters entrusted to it by the Council)
Committee on the Admission of New Members
Committee on Council Meetings Away from Headquarters

Peace-keeping operations and special missions

United Nations Truce Supervision Organization (UNTSO)

Chief of Staff: Major-General Hans Christensen (until 24 October), Major-General Krishna Narayan Singh Thapa (from 25 October).

United Nations Military Observer Group in India and Pakistan (UNMOGIP)

Chief Military Observer: Brigadier-General Jeremiah Enright (until 20 June), Brigadier-General Ricardo Jorge Galarza-Chans (from 21 June).

United Nations Peace-keeping Force in Cyprus (UNFICYP)

Special Representative of the Secretary-General in Cyprus: Oscar Hector Camilión.
Force Commander: Major-General Clive Milner (until 7 April), Major-General Michael F. Minehane (from 8 April).

United Nations Disengagement Observer Force (UNDOF)
Force Commander: Major-General Roman Misztal.

United Nations Interim Force in Lebanon (UNIFIL)
Force Commander: Lieutenant-General Lars-Eric Wahlgren.

United Nations Observer Group in Central America (ONUCA)

The mandate of ONUCA was terminated by the Security Council with effect from 17 January 1992.

Chief Military Observer: Brigadier-General Víctor Suanzes Pardo.

United Nations Iraq-Kuwait Observation Mission (UNIKOM)
Chief Military Observer: Major-General Günther G. Greindl (until 10 July), Major-General Timothy K. Dibuama (from 12 July).

United Nations Angola Verification Mission (UNAVEM II)
Special Representative of the Secretary-General: Margaret Joan Anstee.
Chief Military Observer: Major-General Edward Ushie Unimna.

United Nations Mission for the Referendum in Western Sahara (MINURSO)
Special Representative of the Secretary-General: Johannes J. Manz (until 31 March), Sahabzada Yaqub-Khan (from 1 April).
Force Commander: Major-General Armand Roy (until 24 April), Brigadier-General Luis Block Urban (from 24 April to 30 September, a.i.), Colonel André Van Baelen (from 1 October, a.i.).

United Nations Observer Mission in El Salvador (ONUSAL)

On 14 January 1992, the Security Council enlarged the mandate of ONUSAL to include the verification of the implementation of the Peace Agreement for El Salvador, signed on 16 January.

Special Delegate of the Secretary-General: Iqbal Syed Riza.
Chief Military Observer: Brigadier-General Víctor Suanzes Pardo (from 18 January).

United Nations Advance Mission in Cambodia (UNAMIC)

The work of UNAMIC was assumed by UNTAC on 15 March 1992 (see below).

Chief Liaison Officer: A. H. S. Ataul Karim.
Senior Military Liaison Officer: Brigadier-General Michel Loridon.

United Nations Protection Force (UNPROFOR)

On 21 February 1992, the Security Council established a United Nations Protection Force, for an initial period of 12 months, to create the conditions of peace and security required for the negotiation of an overall settlement of the Yugoslav crisis.

Personal Envoy of the Secretary-General: Cyrus R. Vance.
Force Commander: Lieutenant-General Satish Nambiar.

United Nations Transitional Authority in Cambodia (UNTAC)

On 28 February 1992, the Security Council established a United Nations Transitional Authority in Cambodia, for a period not to exceed 18 months, to contribute to the restoration and maintenance of peace and the holding of free elections. Into UNTAC was subsumed the work of UNAMIC.

Special Representative of the Secretary-General: Yasushi Akashi.
Force Commander: Lieutenant-General John M. Sanderson.

United Nations Operation in Somalia (UNOSOM)

On 24 April 1992, the Security Council established a United Nations Operation in Somalia to facilitate an immediate cessation of hostilities and the maintenance of a cease-fire, to promote a political settlement and to provide urgent humanitarian assistance.

Special Representative of the Secretary-General: Mohammed Sahnoun.
Chief Military Observer: Brigadier-General Imtíaz Shaheen.

United Nations Operation in Mozambique (ONUMOZ)

On 16 December 1992, the Security Council established a United Nations Operation in Mozambique, until 31 October 1993, to facilitate the implementation of the peace agreement, to monitor and verify the cease-fire and the electoral process and to coordinate all humanitarian assistance.

Special Representative of the Secretary-General: Aldo Ajello (from 13 October, a.i.)

Economic and Social Council

The Economic and Social Council consists of 54 Member States of the United Nations, elected by the General Assembly, each for a three-year term, in accordance with the provisions of Article 61 of the United Nations Charter as amended in 1965 and 1973.

MEMBERS

To serve until 31 December 1992: Algeria, Bahrain, Bulgaria, Burkina Faso, Canada, China, Ecuador, Finland, Iran, Jamaica, Mexico, Pakistan, Romania, Russian Federation, Rwanda, Sweden, United Kingdom, Zaire.

To serve until 31 December 1993: Argentina, Austria, Botswana, Chile, France, Germany, Guinea, Japan, Malaysia, Morocco, Peru, Somalia, Spain, Syrian Arab Republic, Trinidad and Tobago, Togo, Turkey, Yugoslavia.

To serve until 31 December 1994: Angola, Australia, Bangladesh, Belarus, Belgium, Benin, Brazil, Colombia, Ethiopia, India, Italy, Kuwait, Madagascar, Philippines, Poland, Suriname, Swaziland, United States.

On 28 October 1992 (dec. 47/309), the General Assembly elected the following for a three-year term beginning on 1 January 1993 to fill the vacancies occurring on 31 December 1992: Bahamas, Bhutan, Canada, China, Cuba, Denmark, Gabon, Libyan Arab Jamahiriya, Mexico, Nigeria, Norway, Republic of Korea, Romania, Russian Federation, Sri Lanka, Ukraine, United Kingdom, Zaire.

SESSIONS

Organizational session for 1992: United Nations Headquarters, 27 January and 6 and 7 February.

Resumed organizational session for 1992: United Nations Headquarters, 29 and 30 April and 28 and 29 May.

Substantive session of 1992: United Nations Headquarters, 29 June–31 July and 18 August (high-level segment, 6-9 July).

OFFICERS

President: Darko Silovik (Yugoslavia) (organizational session), Robert Mroziewicz (Poland) (substantive session).

Vice-Presidents: Ahmed Amaziane (Morocco), José Lino Guerrero (Philippines), Juan Somavía (Chile), Vieri Traxler (Italy).

Subsidiary and other related organs

SUBSIDIARY ORGANS

In addition to two regular sessional committees, the Economic and Social Council may, at each session, set up other committees or working groups, of the whole or of limited membership, and refer to them any items on the agenda for study and report.

Other subsidiary organs reporting to the Council consist of functional commissions, regional commissions, standing committees, expert bodies and ad hoc bodies.

The inter-agency Administrative Committee on Coordination also reports to the Council.

Sessional bodies

SESSIONAL COMMITTEES

Each of the sessional committees of the Economic and Social Council consists of the 54 members of the Council.

Economic Committee. Chairman: Juan Somavía (Chile). *Vice-Chairmen:* Mohamed Mudzakir Sinon (Malaysia), Selim Yenel (Turkey).

Social Committee. Chairman: Vieri Traxler (Italy). *Vice-Chairmen:* Ileka Atoki (Zaire), Luis Fernando Jaramillo (Colombia).

Functional commissions

Commission for Social Development

The Commission for Social Development consists of 32 members, elected for four-year terms by the Economic and Social

Council according to a specific pattern of equitable geographical distribution.

The Commission did not meet in 1992.

Members:

To serve until 31 December 1992: Burundi, Cameroon, Chile, China, Ecuador, Finland, Malta, Philippines, Poland, Spain.

To serve until 31 December 1994: Argentina, Austria, Cyprus, Dominican Republic, Ghana, Guinea, Iran, Madagascar, Nigeria, Sweden, Ukraine.

To serve until 31 December 1995: Belarus, Côte d'Ivoire, France, Germany, Haiti, Indonesia, Mexico, Pakistan, Russian Federation, Sudan, United States.

On 29 April 1992 (dec. 1992/216), the Economic and Social Council elected the following for a four-year term beginning on 1 January 1993 to fill the vacancies occurring on 31 December 1992: Bolivia, Cameroon, Chile, China, Denmark, Malta, Netherlands, Philippines, Yugoslavia, Zimbabwe.

Commission on Crime Prevention and Criminal Justice

On 6 February 1992, the Economic and Social Council established the Commission on Crime Prevention and Criminal Justice as a functional commission of the Council, in accordance with the statement of principles and programme of action of the United Nations crime prevention and criminal justice programme.[3]

The Commission consists of 40 Member States, elected by the Council for three-year terms, except that the terms of half of the first-elected members, chosen by lot, were to expire after two years. The geographical distribution of the seats is: African States (12), Asian States (9), Latin American and Caribbean States (8), Western European and other States (7), Eastern European States (4).

The Commission held its first session at Vienna from 21 to 30 April 1992.

Members:[a]

To serve until 31 December 1993: Austria, Burkina Faso, Costa Rica, Cuba, Dominican Republic, Finland, Gabon, Germany, Guinea-Bissau, Hungary, Japan, Libyan Arab Jamahiriya, Malawi, Malaysia *(Vice-Chairman)*, Russian Federation, Saudi Arabia, Sri Lanka, Tunisia, Uganda, Zaire.

To serve until 31 December 1994: Australia *(Vice-Chairman)*, Bolivia *(Vice-Chairman)*, Bulgaria, China, France, Ghana, Indonesia, Iran, Italy, Madagascar, Nicaragua, Nigeria *(Chairman)*, Paraguay, Peru, Philippines, Poland *(Rapporteur)*, Republic of Korea, Sierra Leone, Uruguay, United States.

[a]Elected on 6 February 1992 (dec. 1992/200).

Commission on Human Rights

The Commission on Human Rights consists of 53 members, elected for three-year terms by the Economic and Social Council according to a specific pattern of equitable geographical distribution.

In 1992, the Commission held the following sessions, at Geneva: its forty-eighth session from 27 January to 6 March, its first special session on 13 and 14 August and its second special session on 30 November and 1 December.

Members:

To serve until 31 December 1992: Brazil, France, Ghana, Hungary *(Chairman)*, Iraq, Italy, Madagascar, Mexico, Pakistan, Philippines, Senegal, Somalia, United States, Yugoslavia.

To serve until 31 December 1993: Argentina, Australia *(Vice-Chairman)*, Austria, Burundi, China, Czechoslovakia, Gambia,

---

[3]YUN 1991, p. 662, GA res. 46/152, annex, 18 Dec. 1991.

Germany, Indonesia, Japan, Mauritania, Peru, Portugal, Venezuela, Zambia.

To serve until 31 December 1994: Angola, Bangladesh, Barbados, Bulgaria, Canada, Chile, Colombia *(Rapporteur)*, Costa Rica, Cuba, Cyprus, Gabon, India, Iran *(Vice-Chairman)*, Kenya, Lesotho, Libyan Arab Jamahiriya, Netherlands, Nigeria, Russian Federation, Sri Lanka, Syrian Arab Republic, Tunisia *(Vice-Chairman)*, United Kingdom, Uruguay.

On 29 April 1992 (dec. 1992/224), the Economic and Social Council elected the following for a three-year term beginning on 1 January 1993 to fill the vacancies occurring on 31 December 1992: Brazil, Finland, France, Guinea-Bissau, Malaysia, Mauritius, Mexico, Pakistan, Poland, Republic of Korea, Romania, Sudan, Togo, United States.

SUBCOMMISSION ON PREVENTION OF
DISCRIMINATION AND PROTECTION OF MINORITIES

The Subcommission consists of 26 members elected by the Commission on Human Rights from candidates nominated by Member States of the United Nations, in accordance with a scheme to ensure equitable geographical distribution. Members serve in their individual capacity as experts, each for a four-year term.

The Subcommission held its forty-fourth session at Geneva from 3 to 28 August 1992.

Members:

To serve until February 1994: Awn Shawkat Al-Khasawneh (Jordan); Judith Sefi Attah (Nigeria); Stanislav V. Chernichenko, *Vice-Chairman* (Russian Federation); Erica-Irene A. Daes (Greece); Leandro Despouy (Argentina); El Hadji Guissé (Senegal); Claude Heller (Mexico); Louis Joinet (France); Fatma Zohra Ksentini, *Vice-Chairman* (Algeria); Claire Palley (United Kingdom); Gilberto Bergne Saboia (Brazil); Rajindar Sachar, *Vice-Chairman* (India); Tian Jin (China).

To serve until February 1996:[a] Miguel Alfonso Martínez, *Chairman* (Cuba); Marc Bossuyt, *Rapporteur* (Belgium); Volodymyr Boutkevitch (Ukraine); Linda Chavez (United States); Asbjorn Eide (Norway); Clemencia Forero Ucros (Colombia); Ribot Hatano (Japan); Ahmed Mohamed Khalifa (Egypt); Ioan Maxim (Romania); Muksum-Ul-Hakim (Bangladesh); Said Naceur Ramadhane (Tunisia); Halima Embarek Warzazi (Morocco); Fisseha Yimer (Ethiopia).

[a]Elected on 6 March 1992.

Commission on Narcotic Drugs

The Commission on Narcotic Drugs consists of 53 members, elected for four-year terms by the Economic and Social Council from among the Members of the United Nations and members of the specialized agencies and the parties to the Single Convention on Narcotic Drugs, 1961, with due regard for the adequate representation of *(a)* countries which are important producers of opium or coca leaves, *(b)* countries which are important in the manufacture of narcotic drugs, and *(c)* countries in which drug addiction or the illicit traffic in narcotic drugs constitutes an important problem, as well as taking into account the principle of equitable geographical distribution.

The Commission held its thirty-fifth session at Vienna from 6 to 15 April 1992.

Members:

To serve until 31 December 1993: Australia, Bahamas, Belgium, Bulgaria, China, Colombia, Ecuador, Gambia, Ghana, Hungary, Indonesia, Japan, Libyan Arab Jamahiriya, Malaysia, Mexico *(Chairman)*, Russian Federation, Senegal, Spain, Sweden, United Kingdom.

To serve until 31 December 1995: Bolivia, Canada, Chile,[a] Czechoslovakia[a] *(Vice-Chairman)*, Egypt,[a] France, Gabon, Germany, India *(Vice-Chairman)*, Iran,[a] Italy, Jamaica,[a] Lesotho, Madagascar, Morocco,[a] Netherlands, Nicaragua,[a] Nigeria[a] *(Vice-Chairman)*, Norway, Pakistan, Peru, Philippines,[a] Poland,

Republic of Korea, Switzerland,[a] Syrian Arab Republic,[a] Thailand, Tunisia,[a] Turkey *(Rapporteur)*, United States, Uruguay,[a] Venezuela, Yugoslavia.

[a]Elected on 6 February 1992 (dec. 1992/200) in accordance with the Council's 1991 decision to increase the membership from 40 to 53 (YUN 1991, p. 739, ESC res. 1991/49, 21 June 1991).

Commission on Science and Technology for Development

On 30 April 1992 (dec. 1992/218), the Economic and Social Council established a Commission on Science and Technology for Development, to consist of 53 members elected by the Council for four-year terms. On 29 May (dec. 1992/222), the Council decided on the following regional allocation of seats: African States (13), Asian States (11), Latin American and Caribbean States (10), Eastern European States (6), Western European and other States (13).

On 30 July (dec. 1992/268), the Council elected the following 36 States for a term beginning on 1 January 1993: Antigua and Barbuda, Austria, Belarus, Belgium, Bolivia, Brazil, Bulgaria, Chile, China, Colombia, Costa Rica, Egypt, Ethiopia, Germany, Guatemala, India, Jamaica, Japan, Jordan, Kuwait, Libyan Arab Jamahiriya, Marshall Islands, Mexico, Morocco, Netherlands, Pakistan, Philippines, Romania, Russian Federation, Saudi Arabia, Spain, Uganda, Ukraine, United Kingdom, United States, Uruguay. No further elections were held in 1992 to fill the remaining seats, allocated to eight members from African States, two from Asian States, one from Eastern European States and six from Western European and other States.

Commission on the Status of Women

The Commission on the Status of Women consists of 45 members, elected for four-year terms by the Economic and Social Council according to a specific pattern of equitable geographical distribution. In 1992, it also acted as the preparatory body for the Fourth World Conference on Women: Action for Equality, Development and Peace (scheduled for Beijing, China, 4-15 September 1995).

The Commission held its thirty-sixth session at Vienna from 11 to 20 March 1992.

Members:

To serve until 31 December 1992: Austria, Brazil, Canada, Colombia, France, Japan, Morocco, Poland *(Rapporteur)*, Sudan, Thailand, United Republic of Tanzania.

To serve until 31 December 1993: Bahamas, Cyprus, Ecuador, Egypt *(Chairman)*, Ghana, India, Indonesia *(Vice-Chairman)*, Iran, Jamaica, Malaysia, Nigeria, Uganda, Zimbabwe.

To serve until 31 December 1994: Bangladesh, Bulgaria, Côte d'Ivoire, Italy, Mexico *(Vice-Chairman)*, Netherlands *(Vice-Chairman)*, Philippines, Russian Federation, Rwanda, United States, Zaire.

To serve until 31 December 1995: Chile, China, Czechoslovakia, Finland, Madagascar, Pakistan, Peru, Spain, Venezuela, Zambia.

On 29 April 1992 (dec. 1992/216), the Economic and Social Council elected the following for a four-year term beginning on 1 January 1993 to fill the vacancies occurring on 31 December 1992: Algeria, Australia, Austria, Belarus, Colombia, Cuba, France, Guinea-Bissau, Japan, Sudan, Thailand.

Population Commission

The Population Commission consists of 27 members elected for four-year terms by the Economic and Social Council according to a specific pattern of equitable geographical distribution. The Commission did not meet in 1992.

Members:

To serve until 31 December 1992: Bangladesh, Belgium, Brazil, Colombia, Egypt, Germany, Turkey, Uganda, Ukraine.

To serve until 31 December 1993: Botswana, China, Iran, Mexico, Panama, Russian Federation, United Kingdom, United States, Zambia.

To serve until 31 December 1995: France, Honduras, Japan, Madagascar, Netherlands, Pakistan, Poland, Rwanda, Sudan.

On 29 April and 30 July 1992 (dec. 1992/216 and 1992/268), the Economic and Social Council elected the following for a four-year term beginning on 1 January 1993 to fill the vacancies occurring on 31 December 1992: Bangladesh, Belgium, Cameroon, Canada, Colombia, Germany, Hungary, Nicaragua, United Republic of Tanzania.

Statistical Commission

The Statistical Commission consists of 24 members elected for four-year terms by the Economic and Social Council according to a specific pattern of equitable geographical distribution.

The Commission did not meet in 1992.

Members:
To serve until 31 December 1992: Brazil, Canada, Hungary, Iran, Japan, Mexico, Norway, United Kingdom.
To serve until 31 December 1993: Argentina, France, Germany, Kenya, Netherlands, Russian Federation, Togo, Zambia.
To serve until 31 December 1995: China, Czechoslovakia, Ghana, Jamaica, Morocco, Pakistan, Poland, United States.

On 29 April 1992 (dec. 1992/216), the Economic and Social Council elected the following for a four-year term beginning on 1 January 1993 to fill the vacancies occurring on 31 December 1992: Australia, Brazil, India, Japan, Mexico, Sweden, Ukraine, United Kingdom.

Regional commissions

Economic and Social Commission for Asia and the Pacific (ESCAP)

The Economic and Social Commission for Asia and the Pacific held its forty-eighth session at Beijing, China, from 14 to 23 April 1992.

Members: Afghanistan, Australia, Azerbaijan,[a] Bangladesh *(Vice-Chairman)*, Bhutan, Brunei Darussalam *(Vice-Chairman)*, Cambodia, China *(Chairman)*, Democratic People's Republic of Korea,[b] Fiji *(Vice-Chairman)*, France, India *(Vice-Chairman)*, Indonesia *(Vice-Chairman)*, Iran *(Vice-Chairman)*, Japan *(Vice-Chairman)*, Kazakhstan,[a] Kiribati *(Vice-Chairman)*, Kyrgyzstan,[a] Lao People's Democratic Republic *(Vice-Chairman)*, Malaysia *(Vice-Chairman)*, Maldives, Marshall Islands,[b] Micronesia,[b] Mongolia *(Vice-Chairman)*, Myanmar *(Vice-Chairman)*, Nauru, Nepal *(Vice-Chairman)*, Netherlands, New Zealand, Pakistan *(Vice-Chairman)*, Papua New Guinea, Philippines, Republic of Korea *(Vice-Chairman)*, Russian Federation, Samoa, Singapore *(Vice-Chairman)*, Solomon Islands *(Rapporteur)*, Sri Lanka, Tajikistan,[a] Thailand, Tonga *(Vice-Chairman)*, Turkmenistan,[a] Tuvalu, United Kingdom, United States, Uzbekistan,[a] Vanuatu *(Vice-Chairman)*, Viet Nam *(Vice-Chairman)*.
Associate members: American Samoa, Cook Islands, French Polynesia,[c] Guam, Hong Kong, Macau, New Caledonia,[c] Niue, Northern Mariana Islands, Palau.

[a]Became a member on 31 July 1992.
[b]Became a member in April 1992.
[c]Became an associate member in April 1992.

Switzerland, not a Member of the United Nations, participates in a consultative capacity in the work of the Commission.

Economic and Social Commission for Western Asia (ESCWA)

The Economic and Social Commission for Western Asia held its sixteenth session at Amman, Jordan, from 30 August to 3 September 1992.

Members: Bahrain, Egypt, Iraq, Jordan *(Chairman)*, Kuwait, Lebanon, Oman *(Rapporteur)*, Palestine, Qatar, Saudi Arabia, Syrian Arab Republic *(Vice-Chairman)*, United Arab Emirates, Yemen *(Vice-Chairman)*.

Economic Commission for Africa (ECA)

The Economic Commission for Africa meets in annual session at the ministerial level known as the Conference of Ministers.

The Commission held its twenty-seventh session (eighteenth meeting of the Conference of Ministers) at Addis Ababa, Ethiopia, from 20 to 23 April 1992.

Members: Algeria *(Second Vice-Chairman)*, Angola, Benin, Botswana, Burkina Faso, Burundi, Cameroon *(First Vice-Chairman)*, Cape Verde, Central African Republic, Chad, Comoros, Congo, Côte d'Ivoire, Djibouti, Egypt, Equatorial Guinea, Ethiopia, Gabon, Gambia, Ghana, Guinea, Guinea-Bissau, Kenya, Lesotho *(Rapporteur)*, Liberia, Libyan Arab Jamahiriya, Madagascar, Malawi, Mali, Mauritania, Mauritius, Morocco, Mozambique, Namibia, Niger, Nigeria, Rwanda, Sao Tome and Principe, Senegal *(Chairman)*, Seychelles, Sierra Leone, Somalia, South Africa,[a] Sudan, Swaziland, Togo, Tunisia, Uganda, United Republic of Tanzania, Zaire, Zambia, Zimbabwe.

[a]On 30 July 1963, the Economic and Social Council decided that South Africa should not take part in the work of ECA until conditions for constructive cooperation had been restored by a change in South Africa's racial policy (YUN 1963, p. 274, ESC res. 974 D IV (XXXVI)).

Switzerland, not a Member of the United Nations, participates in a consultative capacity in the work of the Commission.

Economic Commission for Europe (ECE)

The Economic Commission for Europe held its forty-seventh session at Geneva from 7 to 15 April 1992.

Members: Albania, Austria, Belarus, Belgium, Bosnia and Herzegovina,[a] Bulgaria, Canada, Croatia,[a] Cyprus, Czechoslovakia, Denmark, Estonia,[b] Finland, France, Germany, Greece, Hungary, Iceland, Ireland, Israel, Italy, Latvia,[b] Liechtenstein, Lithuania,[b] Luxembourg, Malta, Netherlands, Norway, Poland, Portugal, Republic of Moldova,[c] Romania, Russian Federation, San Marino,[c] Slovenia,[a] Spain, Sweden, Switzerland *(Vice-Chairman)*, Turkey, Ukraine *(Chairman)*, United Kingdom, United States, Yugoslavia.

[a]Became a member on 22 May 1992.
[b]Became a member on 17 September 1991.
[c]Became a member on 2 March 1992.

The Holy See, which is not a Member of the United Nations, participates in a consultative capacity in the work of the Commission.

Economic Commission for Latin America and the Caribbean (ECLAC)

The Economic Commission for Latin America and the Caribbean held its twenty-fourth session at Santiago, Chile, from 8 to 15 April 1992.

Members: Antigua and Barbuda, Argentina, Bahamas, Barbados, Belize, Bolivia, Brazil, Canada, Chile *(Chairman)*, Colombia, Costa Rica *(Rapporteur)*, Cuba *(Third Vice-Chairman)*, Dominica, Dominican Republic, Ecuador *(First Vice-Chairman)*, El Salvador, France, Grenada, Guatemala, Guyana, Haiti, Honduras, Italy, Jamaica, Mexico, Netherlands, Nicaragua, Panama, Paraguay, Peru, Portugal, Saint Kitts and Nevis, Saint Lucia, Saint Vincent and the Grenadines, Spain *(Second Vice-Chairman)*, Suriname, Trinidad and Tobago, United Kingdom, United States, Uruguay, Venezuela.
Associate members: Aruba, British Virgin Islands, Montserrat, Netherlands Antilles, Puerto Rico, United States Virgin Islands.

The Holy See and Switzerland, which are not Members of the United Nations, participate in a consultative capacity in the work of the Commission.

Standing committees

Commission on Human Settlements

The Commission on Human Settlements consists of 58 members elected by the Economic and Social Council for four-year terms according to a specific pattern of equitable geographical distribution; it reports to the General Assembly through the Council.

The Commission did not meet in 1992.

Members:
To serve until 31 December 1992: Bolivia, Canada, China, France, Guatemala, Hungary, Indonesia, Iraq, Italy, Lesotho, Malawi, Netherlands, Paraguay, Somalia, Swaziland, Sweden, Syrian Arab Republic, Tunisia, Yugoslavia.
To serve until 31 December 1994: Antigua and Barbuda, Bangladesh, Brazil, Cameroon, Chile, Colombia, Egypt, Finland, Iran, Japan, Nigeria, Pakistan, Romania, Russian Federation, Sierra Leone, Turkey, Uganda, United Kingdom, United States, Zimbabwe.
To serve until 31 December 1995: Austria, Barbados, Belarus, Botswana, Bulgaria, Germany, Ghana, Greece, Haiti, India, Jordan, Kenya, Malaysia, Mexico, Norway, Philippines, Sri Lanka, Sudan, United Republic of Tanzania.

On 29 April and 30 July 1992 (dec. 1992/216 and 1992/268), the Economic and Social Council elected the following for a four-year term beginning on 1 January 1993 to fill 16 of the 19 vacancies occurring on 31 December 1992: Bahamas, Canada, China, France, Hungary, Indonesia, Italy, Libyan Arab Jamahiriya, Malawi, Netherlands, Papua New Guinea, Somalia, Sweden, United Arab Emirates, Venezuela. No further elections were held in 1992 to fill the remaining seats, allocated to two members from African States and one from Eastern European States.

Commission on Transnational Corporations

The Commission on Transnational Corporations consists of 48 members, elected from all States for three-year terms by the Economic and Social Council according to a specific pattern of geographical distribution.

The Commission held its eighteenth session at United Nations Headquarters from 23 to 25 January and from 8 to 16 April 1992.

Members:
To serve until 31 December 1992: Argentina, China, Czechoslovakia, Egypt, France, Germany, Iran, Japan, Peru, Philippines, Romania, Sierra Leone, Switzerland, Tunisia, Uruguay, Zimbabwe.
To serve until 31 December 1993:[a] Bahamas,[b] Bangladesh *(Chairman)*, Belgium, Bulgaria, Burundi, Chile, Colombia, Ghana, India, Iraq, Italy, Kenya, Poland *(Rapporteur)*, Republic of Korea, Zambia *(Vice-Chairman)*.
To serve until 31 December 1994: Congo, Costa Rica, Gabon, Guatemala, Indonesia, Jamaica *(Vice-Chairman)*, Mexico, Netherlands, Pakistan, Russian Federation, Sudan, Swaziland, Sweden, Thailand, United Kingdom, United States.
Expert advisers (served through the eighteenth session): José Maria Basagoiti (Mexico), Antonio Colombo (Italy), Chakufwa Chihana (Malawi), Sidney Dell (United Kingdom), Peter Frerk (Germany), Gosta Karlsson (Sweden), Samuel Esson Kwesi Jonah (Ghana), Lawrence McQuade (United States), Karl-Erik Onnesjo (Sweden), Sylvia Ostry (Canada), Rudolph Oswald (United States), Oscar Schachter (United States), Manmohan Singh (India), Oswaldo Sunkel (Chile), Wang Linsheng (China), Nikolai G. Zaitsev (Russian Federation).

[a] One seat allocated to a member from Western European and other States remained unfilled in 1992.
[b] Elected on 29 April 1992 (dec. 1992/216).

On 13 April 1992, the Commission selected the following expert advisers to serve until the end of the twentieth (1994) session: Peter Hansen (Denmark), Ivan Ivanov (Russian Federation). It authorized the Director of the Transnational Corporations and Management Division, in consultation with the Chairman of the Commission, to fill the other vacant posts.

On 29 April (dec. 1992/216), the Economic and Social Council elected the following for a three-year term beginning on 1 January 1993 to fill 14 of the 16 vacancies occurring on 31 December 1992: Algeria, Argentina, Belarus, Benin, China, France, Germany, Japan, Peru, Romania, Switzerland, Tunisia, Uruguay, Zimbabwe. No further elections were held in 1992 to fill the remaining seats, allocated to two members from Asian States.

Committee for Programme and Coordination

The Committee for Programme and Coordination is the main subsidiary organ of the Economic and Social Council and of the General Assembly for planning, programming and coordination and reports directly to both. It consists of 34 members nominated by the Council and elected by the Assembly for three-year terms according to a specific pattern of equitable geographical distribution.

During 1992, the Committee held, at United Nations Headquarters, an organizational meeting on 10 April, and its thirty-second session from 11 to 22 May and from 31 August to 18 September.

Members:
To serve until 31 December 1992: Algeria, Argentina, Cameroon, China, Japan *(Vice-Chairman)*, Morocco, Sri Lanka.
To serve until 31 December 1993: Brazil, Bulgaria, Burundi, Chile, Colombia, Congo, Germany, India, Indonesia, Iraq, Italy, Netherlands *(Chairman)*, Nigeria, Norway, Pakistan, Poland *(Vice-Chairman)*, Trinidad and Tobago, Uganda *(Vice-Chairman)*, Ukraine, United Kingdom.
To serve until 31 December 1994: Bahamas *(Rapporteur)*, France, Ghana, Russian Federation, United States, Uruguay, Zambia.

On 29 April 1992 (dec. 1992/216), the Economic and Social Council nominated the following seven Member States for a three-year term beginning on 1 January 1993 to fill the vacancies occurring on 31 December 1992: China, Egypt, Japan, Kenya, Nicaragua, Republic of Korea, Togo. They were elected by the Assembly on 21 October (dec. 47/307).

Committee on Natural Resources

On 30 April 1992 (dec. 1992/218), the Economic and Social Council abolished its standing Committee on Natural Resources and established an expert Committee on Natural Resources (see below).

Committee on Non-Governmental Organizations

The Committee on Non-Governmental Organizations consists of 19 members elected by the Economic and Social Council for a four-year term according to a specific pattern of equitable geographical representation.

The Committee met at United Nations Headquarters on 25 June 1992.

Members (until 31 December 1994): Bulgaria *(Rapporteur)*, Burundi, Chile, Costa Rica, Cuba, Cyprus, Ethiopia, France, Greece, Iraq, Ireland, Lesotho, Libyan Arab Jamahiriya, Nicaragua, Oman, Philippines *(Vice-Chairman)*, Russian Federation, Sudan, Sweden *(Chairman)*.

Expert bodies

Ad Hoc Group of Experts on International Cooperation in Tax Matters

The membership of the Ad Hoc Group of Experts on International Cooperation in Tax Matters—to consist of 25 members, from 15 developing and 10 developed countries, appointed by the Secretary-General to serve in their individual capacity—remained at 24 in 1992, with one member from a developing country still to be appointed.

The Ad Hoc Group, which normally meets biennially, did not meet in 1992.

Members:[a] Julius Olasoji Akinmola (Nigeria), E. Bunders (Netherlands), Mohamed Chkounda (Morocco), Imad El-ish (Syrian Arab Republic), Mordecai S. Feinberg (United States), D. José Ramón Fernández-Pérez (Spain), Antonio H. Figueroa (Argentina), Mayer Gabay (Israel), Hugo Hanisch-Ovalle (Chile), Jose Rodolfo Hülse (Brazil), Nemi Chand Jain (India), Daniel Lüthi (Switzerland), Reksoprajitno Mansury (Indonesia), Thomas Menck (Germany), Canute R. Miller (Jamaica), Naoti Oka (Japan), Alfred Philipp (Austria), Alain Ruellan (France), Aaron Schwartzman (Mexico), J. B. Shepherd (United Kingdom), Rainer Söderholm (Finland), Mohammed Taraq (Pakistan), André Titty (Cameroon).

[a]The seat held by an expert from Egypt was vacant in 1992.

Committee for Development Planning

The Committee for Development Planning is composed of 24 experts representing different planning systems. They are appointed by the Economic and Social Council, on nomination by the Secretary-General, to serve in their personal capacity for a term of three years.

The Committee held its twenty-eighth session at Kuwait City from 18 to 22 April 1992.

Members (until 31 December 1992): Abdlatif Y. Al-Hamad, *Chairman* (Kuwait); Gerassimos D. Arsenis (Greece); Edmar Bacha, *Vice-Chairman* (Brazil); Prithvi Nath Dhar (India); Karel Dyba (Czechoslovakia); Just Faaland, *Vice-Chairman* (Norway); Ricardo Ffrench-Davis (Chile); Tchabouré Aymé Gogue (Togo); Keith Broadwell Griffin, *Rapporteur* (United Kingdom); Patrick Guillaumont (France); Ryokichi Hirono (Japan); Helen Hughes (Australia); Nicolai N. Liventsev (Russian Federation); Solita C. Monsod (Philippines); Henry Nau (United States); Maureen O'Neil (Canada); T. Ademola Oyejide, *Vice-Chairman* (Nigeria); Pu Shan (China); Akilagpa Sawyerr (Ghana); Udo Ernst Simonis (Germany); George Suranyi (Hungary); Mahbub ul Haq (Pakistan); Miguel Urrutia (Colombia); Ferdinand Van Dam (Netherlands).

Committee of Experts on the Transport of Dangerous Goods

The Committee of Experts on the Transport of Dangerous Goods is composed of experts from countries interested in the international transport of dangerous goods. The experts are made available by their Governments at the request of the Secretary-General. The membership, to be increased to 15 in accordance with a 1975 resolution of the Economic and Social Council,[4] was 14 in 1992.

The Committee held its seventh session at Geneva from 7 to 16 December 1992.

Members: Canada, China, France, Germany, India, Italy, Japan, Netherlands, Norway, Poland, Russian Federation, Sweden, United Kingdom, United States.

Committee on Crime Prevention and Control

The Committee on Crime Prevention and Control was dissolved by the Economic and Social Council on 6 February 1992, when it established the Commission on Crime Prevention and Criminal Justice (see above).

Committee on Economic, Social and Cultural Rights

The Committee on Economic, Social and Cultural Rights consists of 18 experts serving in their personal capacity, elected by the Economic and Social Council from among persons nominated by States parties to the International Covenant on Economic, Social and Cultural Rights. The experts have recognized competence in the field of human rights, with due consideration given to equitable geographical distribution and to the representation of different forms of social and legal systems. Members serve for four-year terms.

The Committee held its seventh session at Geneva from 23 November to 11 December 1992.

Members:
To serve until 31 December 1992: Juan Alvarez Vita (Peru); Mohamed Lamine Fofana (Guinea); María de los Angeles Jiménez Butragueño (Spain); Samba Cor Konate (Senegal); Vassil Mrachkov, *Rapporteur* (Bulgaria); Wladyslaw Neneman (Poland); Kenneth Osborne Rattray, *Vice-Chairman* (Jamaica); Mikis Demetriou Sparsis (Cyprus); Philippe Texier (France).
To serve until 31 December 1994: Philip Alston, *Chairman* (Australia); Abdel Halim Badawi (Egypt); Virginia Bonoan-Dandan, *Vice-Chairman* (Philippines); Luvsandanzangiin Ider (Mongolia); Valeri I. Kouznetsov (Russian Federation); Jaime Alberto Marchan Romero (Ecuador); Alexandre Muterahejuru, *Vice-Chairman* (Rwanda); Bruno Simma (Germany); Javier Wimer Zambrano (Mexico).

On 29 and 30 April 1992 (dec. 1992/216), the Economic and Social Council elected the following for a four-year term beginning on 1 January 1993 to fill the vacancies occurring on 31 December 1992: Madoe Virginie Ahodikope (Togo), Juan Alvarez Vita (Peru), Dumitru Ceausu (Romania), Abdessatar Grissa (Tunisia), María de los Angeles Jiménez Butragueño (Spain), Kenneth Osborne Rattray (Jamaica), Chikako Taya (Japan), Philippe Texier (France), Margerita Vysokajova (Czechoslovakia).

Committee on Natural Resources

On 30 April 1992 (dec. 1992/218), the Economic and Social Council established a Committee on Natural Resources, to consist of 24 government-nominated experts from different Member States, who possess the necessary qualifications and professional or scientific knowledge, who act in their personal capacity, elected by the Council for four-year terms. On 29 May (dec. 1992/222), the Council decided on the following regional allocation of seats: African States (6), Asian States (5), Latin American and Caribbean States (4), Eastern European States (3), Western European and other States (6).

On 30 and 31 July (dec. 1992/268), the Council elected the following 14 experts for a term beginning on 1 January 1993: Regis Percy Arslanian (Brazil), Denis A. Davis (Canada), Vladislav M. Dolgopolov (Russian Federation), Malin Falkenmark (Sweden), Ugo Farinelli (Italy), Patricio Jerez (Nicaragua), José Manuel Mejía Angel (Colombia), Lukabu Khabouji N'Zaji (Zaire), Hendrik Martinus Oudshoorn (Netherlands), Neculai Pavlovschi (Romania), Karlheinz Rieck (Germany), R. W. Roye Rutland (Australia), Aldo Truccio (Argentina), Zhang Hai-Lun (China). No further elections were held in 1992 to fill the remaining seats, allocated to five members from African States, four from Asian States and one from Eastern European States.

Committee on New and Renewable Sources of Energy and on Energy for Development

On 30 April 1992 (dec. 1992/218), the Economic and Social Council established a Committee on New and Renewable Sources of Energy and on Energy for Development, to consist of 24 government-nominated experts from different Member States, who possess the necessary qualifications and professional or scientific knowledge, who act in their personal capacity, elected by the Council for four-year terms. On 29 May (dec. 1992/222), the Council decided on the following regional allocation of seats: African States (6), Asian States (5), Latin American and Caribbean States (4), Eastern European States (3), Western European and other States (6).

On 30 and 31 July (dec. 1992/268), the Council elected the following 20 experts for a term beginning on 1 January 1993: Marcelino K. Actouka (Micronesia), Mohammad Al Ramadhan

---

[4]YUN 1975, p. 734, ESC res. 1973(LIX), 30 July 1975.

(Kuwait), Mohammed Salem Sarur Al-Sabban (Saudi Arabia), Messaoud Boumaour (Algeria), José Luis Bozzo (Uruguay), Bernard Devin (France), Ronaldo Costa Filho (Brazil), Paul-Georg Gutermuth (Germany), Wolfgang Hein (Austria), Christian Atoki Ileka (Zaire), Thomas B. Johansson (Sweden), Virgil Musatescu (Romania), Alexander A. Penchev (Bulgaria), Giovanni Carlo Pinchera (Italy), Juan Camilo Restrepo Salazar (Colombia), Zoilo Rodas Rodas (Paraguay), E. V. R. Sastry (India), Wilhelmus C. Turkenburg (Netherlands), Dmitri B. Volfberg (Russian Federation), Zhang Guocheng (China). No further elections were held in 1992 to fill the remaining seats, allocated to four members from African States.

Intergovernmental Working Group of Experts on International Standards of Accounting and Reporting

The Intergovernmental Working Group of Experts on International Standards of Accounting and Reporting, which reports to the Commission on Transnational Corporations, consists of 34 members, elected for three-year terms by the Economic and Social Council according to a specific pattern of equitable geographical distribution. Each State elected appoints an expert with appropriate experience in accounting and reporting.

The Group held its tenth session at United Nations Headquarters from 5 to 13 March 1992.

Members:

To serve until 31 December 1993:[a] Brazil *(Rapporteur)*, China, Egypt, France, Gabon, Kenya, Mauritius, Mexico, Morocco *(Vice-Chairman)*, Panama,[b] Russian Federation, Spain, Sweden *(Vice-Chairman)*, Switzerland, Thailand, Turkey.

To serve until 31 December 1994: Bulgaria, Chile, Costa Rica, Cyprus, Germany, Hungary *(Chairman)*, India *(Vice-Chairman)*, Italy, Jordan, Malawi, Netherlands, Nigeria, Pakistan, Sudan, Swaziland, United Kingdom, Uruguay.[c]

[a]One seat allocated to a member from Asian States remained unfilled in 1992.
[b]Elected on 30 July 1992 (dec. 1992/268).
[c]Elected on 29 April 1992 (dec. 1992/216).

United Nations Group of Experts on Geographical Names

The United Nations Group of Experts on Geographical Names represents various geographical/linguistic divisions, of which there were 21 in 1992, as follows: Africa Central; Africa East; Africa South; Africa West; Arabic; Asia East (other than China); Asia South-East and Pacific South-West; Asia South-West (other than Arabic); Baltic; Celtic; China; Dutch- and German-speaking; East Central and South-East Europe; East Mediterranean (other than Arabic); Eastern Europe, Northern and Central Asia; India; Latin America; Norden; Romano-Hellenic; United Kingdom; United States of America/Canada.

The Group of Experts held its sixteenth session at United Nations Headquarters on 24 August and 4 September 1992.

Chairman: South Africa.
Vice-Chairman: Canada.
Rapporteur: United States.

Ad hoc body

Population Commission acting as the Preparatory Committee for the International Conference on Population and Development

The Population Commission acting as the Preparatory Committee for the International Conference on Population and Development (scheduled for Cairo, Egypt, 5-13 September 1994), open to the participation of all States, did not meet in 1992.

Administrative Committee on Co-ordination

The Administrative Committee on Co-ordination held two sessions in 1992: the first at Geneva from 8 to 10 April, and the second at United Nations Headquarters on 20 and 21 October.

The membership of ACC, under the chairmanship of the Secretary-General of the United Nations, includes the executive heads of ILO, FAO, UNESCO, ICAO, WHO, the World Bank, IMF, UPU, ITU, WMO, IMO, WIPO, IFAD, UNIDO, IAEA and the secretariat of the Contracting Parties to GATT.

ACC also invites to take part in the work of its sessions senior officers of the United Nations and the executive heads of UNCTAD, UNDP, UNEP, UNFPA, UNHCR, UNICEF, UNITAR, UNRWA, WFP and the United Nations International Drug Control Programme.

ACC has established subsidiary bodies on organizational, administrative and substantive questions.

Other related bodies

International Research and Training Institute for the Advancement of Women (INSTRAW)

The International Research and Training Institute for the Advancement of Women, a body of the United Nations financed through voluntary contributions, functions under the authority of a Board of Trustees.

BOARD OF TRUSTEES

The Board of Trustees is composed of 11 members serving in their individual capacity, appointed by the Economic and Social Council on the nomination of States; and *ex-officio* members. Members serve for three-year terms, with a maximum of two terms.

The Board, which reports periodically to the Council and where appropriate to the General Assembly, held its twelfth session at Santo Domingo, Dominican Republic, from 17 to 21 February 1992.

Members (until 30 June 1992):
To serve until 30 June 1992: Penelope Ruth Fenwick (New Zealand); Victoria N. Okobi (Nigeria); Virginia Olivo de Celli, *President* (Venezuela).
To serve until 30 June 1993: Gertrude Ibengwe Mongella (United Republic of Tanzania); Amara Pongsapich, *Rapporteur* (Thailand); Pilar Escario Rodriguez-Spiteri, *Vice-President* (Spain).
To serve until 30 June 1994: Fatima Benslimane Hassat (Morocco); Gule Afruz Mahbub (Bangladesh); D. Gail Saunders (Bahamas); Renata Siemienska-Zochowska (Poland); Kristin Tornes (Norway).

On 29 April 1992 (dec. 1992/216), the Economic and Social Council appointed the following for a three-year term beginning on 1 July 1992 to fill the vacancies occurring on 30 June: Ihsan Abdalla Algabshawi (Sudan), Aida González Martínez (Mexico), Els Postel-Coster (Netherlands).

Members (from 1 July 1992):
To serve until 30 June 1993: Gertrude Ibengwe Mongella (United Republic of Tanzania), Amara Pongsapich (Thailand), Pilar Escario Rodriguez-Spiteri (Spain).
To serve until 30 June 1994: Fatima Benslimane Hassat (Morocco), Gule Afruz Mahbub (Bangladesh), D. Gail Saunders (Bahamas), Renata Siemienska-Zochowska (Poland), Kristin Tornes (Norway).
To serve until 30 June 1995: Ihsan Abdalla Algabshawi (Sudan), Aida González Martínez (Mexico), Els Postel-Coster (Netherlands).
Ex-officio members: The Director of the Institute, and a representative of the Secretary-General, each of the regional commissions and the Institute's host country (Dominican Republic).

Director of the Institute: Margaret Shields.

United Nations Children's Fund (UNICEF)

EXECUTIVE BOARD

The UNICEF Executive Board, which reports to the Economic and Social Council and, as appropriate, to the General Assembly, consists of 41 members elected by the Council from Member States of the United Nations or members of the specialized agencies or of IAEA, for three-year terms.

In 1992, the Board held, at United Nations Headquarters, an organizational session on 24 and 25 March, its regular session from 15 to 26 June and (with its composition as at 1 August) an organizational session on 26 June.

Members (until 31 July 1992):
To serve until 31 July 1992: Barbados, Canada, China, Finland, Germany, Netherlands, Peru, Poland, Thailand, Zimbabwe.
To serve until 31 July 1993: Czechoslovakia *(Second Vice-Chairman)*, Denmark *(First Vice-Chairman)*, India *(Chairman)*, Indonesia, Liberia, Sierra Leone, Spain, Sri Lanka, Switzerland, Uruguay.
To serve until 31 July 1994: Angola, Australia, Brazil, Central African Republic, Congo, Ethiopia, France, Italy, Jamaica, Japan, Nicaragua *(Fourth Vice-Chairman)*, Norway, Pakistan, Republic of Korea, Russian Federation, Senegal *(Third Vice-Chairman)*, United Kingdom, United Republic of Tanzania, United States, Yemen, Yugoslavia.

On 29 April 1992 (dec. 1992/216), the Economic and Social Council elected the following for a three-year term beginning on 1 August 1992 to fill the vacancies occurring on 31 July: Bulgaria, Canada, China, Colombia, Costa Rica, Germany, Mozambique, Netherlands, Nepal, Sweden.

Members (from 1 August 1992):
To serve until 31 July 1993: Czechoslovakia *(Second Vice-Chairman)*, Denmark, India, Indonesia, Liberia, Sierra Leone, Spain, Sri Lanka, Switzerland, Uruguay.
To serve until 31 July 1994: Angola, Australia, Brazil, Central African Republic, Congo, Ethiopia, France, Italy, Jamaica *(Fourth Vice-Chairman)*, Japan, Nicaragua, Norway, Pakistan, Republic of Korea, Russian Federation, Senegal *(First Vice-Chairman)*, United Kingdom, United Republic of Tanzania, United States, Yemen, Yugoslavia.
To serve until 31 July 1995: Bulgaria, Canada *(Chairman)*, China, Colombia, Costa Rica, Germany, Mozambique, Netherlands, Nepal *(Third Vice-Chairman)*, Sweden.

Executive Director of UNICEF: James P. Grant.

United Nations Development Programme (UNDP)

GOVERNING COUNCIL

The Governing Council of UNDP, which reports to the Economic and Social Council and through it to the General Assembly, consists of 48 members, elected by the Council from Member States of the United Nations or members of the specialized agencies or of IAEA. Twenty-seven seats are allocated to developing countries and 21 to economically more advanced countries; members serve three-year terms.

In 1992, the Governing Council held an organizational session and a special session at United Nations Headquarters from 10 to 14 February and its thirty-ninth session at Geneva from 4 to 26 May.

Members:
To serve until the day preceding the February 1993 organizational session: Bulgaria, Denmark, Djibouti, Germany, Guyana, India, Malaysia, Mauritania, Netherlands, Nigeria, Poland, Portugal, Sri Lanka, Switzerland, Uruguay, Venezuela.
To serve until the day preceding the February 1994 organizational session: Algeria, Austria, China, Cuba, Finland *(President)*, Ghana, Indonesia, Italy, Japan, Kuwait, Nicaragua *(Vice-President)*, Russian Federation, Saint Lucia, United Kingdom, United States, Zimbabwe.
To serve until the day preceding the February 1995 organizational session: Belgium, Bolivia, Cameroon, Canada, Congo *(Vice-President)*, Fiji *(Vice-President)*, France, Gambia, Lesotho, New Zealand, Norway, Pakistan, Romania *(Vice-President)*, Somalia, Spain, Yemen.

On 29 April 1992 (dec. 1992/216), the Economic and Social Council elected the following for a three-year term beginning on the first day of the February 1993 organizational session to fill the vacancies occurring the preceding day: Benin, Côte d'Ivoire, Czechoslovakia, Ecuador, Germany, India, Iran, Jamaica, Netherlands, Peru, Poland, Portugal, Republic of Korea, Sudan, Sweden, Switzerland.

Administrator of UNDP: William H. Draper III.
Associate Administrator: Luis Maria Gomez.

United Nations Research Institute for Social Development (UNRISD)

BOARD OF DIRECTORS

The Board of Directors of UNRISD reports to the Economic and Social Council through the Commission for Social Development. The Board consists of:

The Chairman, appointed by the Secretary-General: Keith Griffin (United Kingdom);
Ten members, nominated by the Commission for Social Development and confirmed by the Economic and Social Council (to serve until 30 June 1993): Lars Anell (Sweden), Ingrid Eide (Norway), Tatyana Koryagina (Russian Federation), Maureen O'Neil (Canada), Akilagpa Sawyerr (Ghana); (to serve until 30 June 1995): Fahima Charaf-Eddine (Lebanon), Georgina Dufoix (France), Kinhide Mushakoji (Japan), Guillermo O'Donnell (Argentina), Rehman Sobhan (Bangladesh);
Nine other members, as follows: a representative of the Secretary-General, a representative of the United Nations Office at Vienna/Centre for Social Development and Humanitarian Affairs, the Director of the Latin American Institute for Economic and Social Planning, the Director of the Asian and Pacific Development Institute, the Director of the African Institute for Economic Development and Planning, the Executive Secretary of ESCWA, the Director of UNRISD *(ex officio)*, and the representatives of two of the following specialized agencies, appointed in rotation: ILO, FAO, UNESCO, WHO.

Director of the Institute: Dharam Ghai.

World Food Programme

COMMITTEE ON FOOD AID POLICIES AND PROGRAMMES

The Committee on Food Aid Policies and Programmes, the governing body of WFP, reports annually to the Economic and Social Council, the FAO Council and the World Food Council. It consists of 42 members (27 from developing countries and 15 from more economically developed ones), of which 21 are elected by the Economic and Social Council and 21 by the FAO Council, from Member States of the United Nations or from members of FAO. Members serve for three-year terms.

The Committee held three sessions during 1992, at Rome, Italy: its second special session on 23 and 24 April, its thirty-third session from 25 to 29 May, and its thirty-fourth session from 3 to 6 November.

J. Glistrup (Denmark) was Chairman at the special session.

Members:
To serve until 31 December 1992:
Elected by Economic and Social Council: Algeria,[a] Dominican Republic,[a] Finland, Hungary, India, Italy, Sudan.
Elected by FAO Council: Australia, Bangladesh *(Second Vice-Chairman)*, Burkina Faso, Canada *(First Vice-Chairman)*, Guinea, Sri Lanka, United States.
To serve until 31 December 1993:
Elected by Economic and Social Council: Belgium, Egypt, El Salvador,[a] Indonesia,[a] Japan, Pakistan, Sweden.
Elected by FAO Council: Argentina, Brazil, Burundi, China, Netherlands *(Rapporteur, thirty-fourth session)*, Saudi Arabia, United Republic of Tanzania.

To serve until 31 December 1994:
   Elected by Economic and Social Council: Colombia, Cuba, Ethiopia,[a] Ghana, Norway, Syrian Arab Republic,[a] United Kingdom *(Rapporteur, special session).*
   Elected by FAO Council: Angola, Cameroon *(Rapporteur, thirty-third session),* Democratic People's Republic of Korea, France, Germany, Mexico *(Chairman, regular sessions),* Romania.

[a]Elected on 6 February 1992 (dec. 1992/200).

On 29 April and 31 July 1992 (dec. 1992/216 and 1992/268), the Economic and Social Council elected Denmark, the Dominican Republic, Hungary, India, Italy, the Niger and Nigeria and, on 16 November, the FAO Council elected Australia, Bangladesh, Burkina Faso, Canada, Senegal, Sri Lanka and the United States, all for a three-year term beginning on 1 January 1993 to fill the vacancies occurring on 31 December 1992.

Executive Director of WFP: James Charles Ingram (until 4 April), Catherine Bertini (from 5 April).
Deputy Executive Director: Salahuddin Ahmed.

Conference

Sixth United Nations Conference on the Standardization of Geographical Names

The Sixth United Nations Conference on the Standardization of Geographical Names was held at United Nations Headquarters from 25 August to 3 September 1992. Participating were the following 68 States:

Antigua and Barbuda, Argentina, Australia, Austria, Azerbaijan, Bahrain, Botswana, Brazil, Brunei Darussalam, Cameroon, Canada, China, Cyprus, Czechoslovakia, Democratic People's Republic of Korea, Denmark, Egypt, El Salvador, Estonia, Finland, France, Germany, Greece, Guinea, Holy See, Hungary, Indonesia, Iran, Ireland, Israel, Italy, Jamaica, Japan, Jordan, Libyan Arab Jamahiriya, Lithuania, Luxembourg, Malaysia, Maldives, Marshall Islands, Morocco, Namibia, Netherlands, New Zealand, Norway, Oman, Pakistan, Peru, Portugal, Qatar, Republic of Korea, Russian Federation, Saudi Arabia, Slovenia, South Africa, Spain, Sri Lanka, Sweden, Switzerland, Thailand, Turkey, Turkmenistan, Ukraine, United Kingdom, United States, Venezuela, Yemen, Zimbabwe.

Trusteeship Council

Article 86 of the United Nations Charter lays down that the Trusteeship Council shall consist of the following:

Members of the United Nations administering Trust Territories;
Permanent members of the Security Council which do not administer Trust Territories;
As many other members elected for a three-year term by the General Assembly as will ensure that the membership of the Council is equally divided between United Nations Members which administer Trust Territories and those which do not.[a]

[a]During 1992, only one Member of the United Nations was an administering member of the Trusteeship Council, while four permanent members of the Security Council continued as non-administering members.

MEMBERS
Member administering a Trust Territory: United States.
Non-administering members: China, France, Russian Federation, United Kingdom.

SESSION
Fifty-ninth session: United Nations Headquarters, 26 May–2 June and 21 December 1992.

OFFICERS
President: Jean Félix-Paganon (France).
Vice-President: Thomas L. Richardson (United Kingdom).

International Court of Justice

Judges of the Court

The International Court of Justice consists of 15 Judges elected for nine-year terms by the General Assembly and the Security Council.

The following were the Judges of the Court serving in 1991, listed in the order of precedence:

Judge	Country of nationality	End of term[a]
Sir Robert Y. Jennings, *President*	United Kingdom	2000
Shigeru Oda, *Vice-President*	Japan	1994
Manfred Lachs	Poland	1994
Roberto Ago	Italy	1997
Stephen M. Schwebel	United States	1997
Mohammed Bedjaoui	Algeria	1997
Ni Zhengyu	China	1994
Jens Evensen	Norway	1994
Nikolai K. Tarassov	Russian Federation	1997
Gilbert Guillaume	France	2000
Mohamed Shahabuddeen	Guyana	1997
Andrés Aguilar Mawdsley	Venezuela	2000

Judge	Country of nationality	End of term[a]
Christopher G. Weeramantry	Sri Lanka	2000
Raymond Ranjeva	Madagascar	2000
Bola A. Ajibola	Nigeria	1994

[a]Term expires on 5 February of the year indicated.

Registrar: Eduardo Valencia-Ospina.
Deputy Registrar: Bernard Noble.

Chamber formed in the case concerning the *Land, Island and Maritime Frontier Dispute (El Salvador/Honduras)*

Members: José Sette Câmara *(President),* Sir Robert Y. Jennings, Shigeru Oda.
Ad hoc members: Nicolas Valticos, Santiago Torres Bernárdez.

Chamber of Summary Procedure

Members: Sir Robert Y. Jennings *(ex officio),* Shigeru Oda *(ex officio),* Stephen M. Schwebel, Ni Zhengyu, Jens Evensen.
Substitute members: Nikolai K. Tarassov, Andrés Aguilar Mawdsley.

Parties to the Court's Statute

All Members of the United Nations are *ipso facto* parties to the Statute of the International Court of Justice. Also parties to it are the following non-members: Nauru, Switzerland.

States accepting the compulsory jurisdiction of the Court

Declarations made by the following States, a number with reservations, accepting the Court's compulsory jurisdiction (or made under the Statute of the Permanent Court of International Justice and deemed to be an acceptance of the jurisdiction of the International Court) were in force at the end of 1992:

Australia, Austria, Barbados, Belgium, Botswana, Bulgaria,[a] Cambodia, Canada, Colombia, Costa Rica, Cyprus, Denmark, Dominican Republic, Egypt, El Salvador, Estonia, Finland, Gambia, Guinea-Bissau, Haiti, Honduras, India, Japan, Kenya, Liberia, Liechtenstein, Luxembourg, Madagascar,[a] Malawi, Malta, Mauritius, Mexico, Nauru, Netherlands, New Zealand, Nicaragua, Nigeria, Norway, Pakistan, Panama, Philippines, Poland, Portugal, Senegal, Somalia, Spain, Sudan, Suriname, Swaziland, Sweden, Switzerland, Togo, Uganda, United Kingdom, Uruguay, Zaire.

[a]Declaration deposited with the Secretary-General on 24 June and 2 July 1992, respectively.

United Nations organs and specialized and related agencies authorized to request advisory opinions from the Court

Authorized by the United Nations Charter to request opinions on any legal question: General Assembly, Security Council.

Authorized by the General Assembly in accordance with the Charter to request opinions on legal questions arising within the scope of their activities: Economic and Social Council, Trusteeship Council, Interim Committee of the General Assembly, Committee on Applications for Review of Administrative Tribunal Judgements, ILO, FAO, UNESCO, ICAO, WHO, World Bank, IFC, IDA, IMF, ITU, WMO, IMO, WIPO, IFAD, UNIDO, IAEA.

Committees of the Court

BUDGETARY AND ADMINISTRATIVE COMMITTEE

Members: Sir Robert Y. Jennings *(ex officio)*, Shigeru Oda *(ex officio)*, Stephen M. Schwebel, Mohammed Bedjaoui, Nikolai K. Tarassov, Gilbert Guillaume, Mohamed Shahabuddeen.

COMMITTEE ON RELATIONS

Members: Mohammed Bedjaoui, Ni Zhengyu, Andrés Aguilar Mawdsley.

LIBRARY COMMITTEE

Members: Roberto Ago, Christopher G. Weeramantry, Raymond Ranjeva.

RULES COMMITTEE

Members: Manfred Lachs, Roberto Ago, Mohammed Bedjaoui, Ni Zhengyu, Jens Evensen, Nikolai K. Tarassov.

Other United Nations–related bodies

The following bodies are not subsidiary to any principal organ of the United Nations but were established by an international treaty instrument or arrangement sponsored by the United Nations and are thus related to the Organization and its work. These bodies, often referred to as "treaty organs", are serviced by the United Nations Secretariat and may be financed in part or wholly from the Organization's regular budget, as authorized by the General Assembly, to which most of them report annually.

Commission against Apartheid in Sports

The Commission against Apartheid in Sports was established under the International Convention against Apartheid in Sports.[5] It consists of 15 members elected for four-year terms by the States parties to the Convention to serve in their personal capacity, with due regard for equitable geographical distribution and representation of the principal legal systems, particular attention being paid to participation of persons having experience in sports administration.

The Commission, which reports annually to the General Assembly through the Secretary-General, held its third session at United Nations Headquarters from 28 to 30 October 1992.

Members:
To serve until 2 March 1993: Tesfay Fichala (Ethiopia); Raul González Rodriguez (Mexico); Lionel A. Hurst (Antigua and Barbuda); Sedfrey Ordoñez (Philippines); Allan Rae (Jamaica); Boris Topor	nin (Russian Federation).
To serve until 24 June 1995: Gbedevi Zikpi Aguigah (Togo); Abdul Karim Al-Ethawy (Iraq); James Victor Gbeho, *Vice-Chairman* (Ghana); Joseph Lagu (Sudan); Francis Malambugi (United Republic of Tanzania); Ernest Besley Maycock, *Chairman* (Barbados); Vladimir Platonov (Ukraine); Jai Pratap Rana, *Rapporteur* (Nepal); Zoumana Traoré (Burkina Faso).

Committee against Torture

The Committee against Torture was established under the Convention against Torture and Other Cruel, Inhuman or Degrading Treatment or Punishment.[6] It consists of 10 experts elected for four-year terms by the States parties to the Convention to serve in their personal capacity, with due regard for equitable geographical distribution and for the usefulness of the participation of some persons having legal experience.

In 1992, the Committee, which reports annually to the General Assembly, held, at Geneva, its eighth session from 27 April to 8 May and its ninth session from 9 to 20 November.

Members:
To serve until 31 December 1993: Alexis Dipanda Mouelle, *Vice-Chairman* (Cameroon); Yuri A. Khitrin (Russian Federation); Dimitar Nikolov Mikhailov, *Vice-Chairman* (Bulgaria); Bent Sorensen (Denmark); Joseph Voyame, *Chairman* (Switzerland).
To serve until 31 December 1995: Hassib Ben Ammar (Tunisia); Peter Thomas Burns, *Rapporteur* (Canada); Fawzi El Ibrashi (Egypt); Ricardo Gil Lavedra, *Vice-Chairman* (Argentina); Hugo Lorenzo (Uruguay).

Committee on the Elimination of Discrimination against Women

The Committee on the Elimination of Discrimination against Women was established under the Convention on the Elimination of All Forms of Discrimination against Women.[7] It consists of 23 experts elected for four-year terms by the States parties to the Convention to serve in their personal capacity, with due regard for equitable geographical distribution and for representation of the different forms of civilization and principal legal systems.

The Committee, which reports annually to the General Assembly through the Economic and Social Council, held its eleventh session at United Nations Headquarters from 20 to 30 January 1992.

---

[5]YUN 1985, p. 166, GA res. 40/64 G, annex, 10 Dec. 1985.
[6]YUN 1984, p. 815, GA res. 39/46, annex, article 17, 10 Dec. 1984.
[7]YUN 1979, p. 898, GA res. 34/180, annex, article 17, 18 Dec. 1979.

Members:
To serve until 15 April 1992: Ana Maria Alfonsín de Fasan, *Vice-Chairman* (Argentina); Désirée P. Bernard (Guyana); Carlota Bustelo García del Real (Spain); Elizabeth Evatt (Australia); Grethe Fenger-Möller (Denmark); Aida González Martínez (Mexico); Chryssanthi Laiou-Antoniou, *Rapporteur* (Greece); Edith Oeser (Germany); Hanna Beate Schöpp-Schilling (Germany); Kongit Sinegiorgis (Ethiopia); Kissem Walla-Tchangai (Togo).
To serve until 15 April 1994: Charlotte Abaka (Ghana); Ryoko Akamatsu, *Vice-Chairman* (Japan); Emna Aouij (Tunisia); Dora Gladys Nancy Bravo Nuñez de Ramsey (Ecuador); Ivanka Corti (Italy); Norma Monica Forde (Barbados); Zagorka Ilic, *Vice-Chairman* (Yugoslavia); Tatiana Nikolaeva (Russian Federation); Teresita Quintos-Deles (Philippines); Lin Shangzhen (China); Mervat Tallawy, *Chairman* (Egypt); Rose N. Ukeje (Nigeria).

On 4 February, the States parties elected the following for a four-year term beginning on 16 April 1992 to fill the vacancies occurring on 15 April: Gul Aykor (Turkey), Carlota Bustelo García del Real (Spain), Silvia Rose Cartwright (New Zealand), Evangelina García-Prince (Venezuela), Liliana Gurdulich de Correa (Argentina), Salma Khan (Bangladesh), Pirkko Anneli Mäkinen (Finland), Elsa Victoria Muñoz Gómez (Colombia), Ahoua Ouedraogo (Burkina Faso), Hanna Beate Schöpp-Schilling (Germany), Kongit Sinegiorgis (Ethiopia).

Committee on the Elimination of Racial Discrimination

The Committee on the Elimination of Racial Discrimination was established under the International Convention on the Elimination of All Forms of Racial Discrimination.[8] It consists of 18 experts elected for four-year terms by the States parties to the Convention to serve in their personal capacity, with due regard for equitable geographical distribution and for representation of the different forms of civilization and principal legal systems.

The Committee, which reports annually to the General Assembly through the Secretary-General, held its forty-first session at Geneva from 3 to 14 August 1992.

Members:
To serve until 19 January 1994: Mahmoud Aboul-Nasr (Egypt); Hamzat Ahmadu, *Vice-Chairman* (Nigeria); Michael Parker Banton, *Rapporteur* (United Kingdom); Régis de Gouttes (France); George O. Lamptey (Ghana); Carlos Lechuga Hevia (Cuba); Agha Shahi (Pakistan); Michael E. Sherifis (Cyprus); Rüdiger Wolfrum (Germany).
To serve until 19 January 1996:[a] Theodoor van Boven (Netherlands); Ion Diaconu, *Vice-Chairman* (Romania); Eduardo Ferrero Costa (Peru); Ivan Garvalov (Bulgaria); Yuri A. Rechetov (Russian Federation); Shanti Sadiq Ali, *Vice-Chairman* (India); Song Shuhua (China); Luis Valencia Rodriguez, *Chairman* (Ecuador); Mario Jorge Yutzis (Argentina).

[a]Elected on 15 January 1992.

Committee on the Rights of the Child

The Committee on the Rights of the Child was established under the Convention on the Rights of the Child.[9] It consists of 10 experts elected for four-year terms by the States parties to the Convention to serve in their personal capacity, with due regard for equitable geographical distribution and for representation of the principal legal systems.

The Committee, which reports biennially to the General Assembly through the Economic and Social Council, held its second session at Geneva from 28 September to 9 October 1992.

Members:
To serve until 28 February 1993: Hoda Badran, *Chairman* (Egypt); Flora C. Eufemio, *Vice-Chairman* (Philippines); Antônio Carlos Gomes da Costa (Brazil);[a] Swithun Tachiona Mombeshora (Zimbabwe); Marta Santos País, *Rapporteur* (Portugal).

To serve until 28 February 1995: Luis A. Bambaren Gastelumendi, *Vice-Chairman* (Peru); Akila Belembaogo (Burkina Faso); Thomas Hammarberg (Sweden); Youri Kolosov, *Vice-Chairman* (Russian Federation); Sandra Prunella Mason (Barbados).

[a]Appointed in 1992 to fill the vacancy created by the resignation of Maria de Fatima Borges de Omena (Brazil) on 1 October 1991.

Conference on Disarmament

The Conference on Disarmament, the multilateral negotiating forum on disarmament, reports annually to the General Assembly and is serviced by the United Nations Secretariat. It had 39 members in 1992.

The Conference met at Geneva from 21 January to 27 March, from 11 May to 26 June and from 20 July to 3 September 1992.

Members: Algeria, Argentina, Australia, Belgium, Brazil, Bulgaria, Canada, China, Cuba, Czechoslovakia, Egypt, Ethiopia, France, Germany, Hungary, India, Indonesia, Iran, Italy, Japan, Kenya, Mexico, Mongolia, Morocco, Myanmar, Netherlands, Nigeria, Pakistan, Peru, Poland, Romania, Russian Federation, Sri Lanka, Sweden, United Kingdom, United States, Venezuela, Yugoslavia, Zaire.

The presidency, which rotates in English alphabetical order among the members, was held by the following in 1992: Yugoslavia, Zaire, Algeria, Argentina, Australia, Belgium, the last also for the recess until the 1993 session.

Human Rights Committee

The Human Rights Committee was established under the International Covenant on Civil and Political Rights.[10] It consists of 18 experts elected by the States parties to the Covenant to serve in their personal capacity for four-year terms.

In 1992, the Committee, which reports annually to the General Assembly through the Economic and Social Council, held three sessions: its forty-fourth at United Nations Headquarters from 23 March to 10 April, its forty-fifth at Geneva from 13 to 31 July and its forty-sixth at Geneva from 19 October to 6 November.

Members:
To serve until 31 December 1992: Francisco José Aguilar Urbina, *Vice-Chairman* (Costa Rica); Janos Fodor (Hungary); Rosalyn Higgins (United Kingdom); Rajsoomer Lallah (Mauritius); Andreas V. Mavrommatis (Cyprus); Rein A. Mullerson (Russian Federation); Fausto Pocar, *Chairman* (Italy); Alejandro Serrano Caldera (Nicaragua); S. Amos Wako (Kenya).
To serve until 31 December 1994: Nisuke Ando, *Rapporteur* (Japan); Christine Chanet (France); Vojin Dimitrijevic, *Vice-Chairman* (Yugoslavia); Omran El-Shafei, *Vice-Chairman* (Egypt); Kurt Herndl (Austria); Birame Ndiaye (Senegal); Julio Prado Vallejo (Ecuador); Waleed Sadi (Jordan); Bertil Wennergren (Sweden).

On 10 September 1992, the States parties elected the following for a four-year term beginning on 1 January 1993 to fill the vacancies occurring on 31 December 1992: Francisco José Aguilar Urbina (Costa Rica), Marco Tulio Bruni Celli (Venezuela), Elizabeth Evatt (Australia), Janos Fodor (Hungary), Laurel Francis (Jamaica), Rosalyn Higgins (United Kingdom), Rajsoomer Lallah (Mauritius), Andreas V. Mavrommatis (Cyprus), Fausto Pocar (Italy).

International Narcotics Control Board (INCB)

The International Narcotics Control Board, established under the Single Convention on Narcotic Drugs, 1961, as amended by the 1972 Protocol, consists of 13 members, elected by the Eco-

---

[8]YUN 1965, p. 443, GA res. 2106 A (XX), annex, article 8, 21 Dec. 1965.
[9]GA res. 44/25, annex, 20 Nov. 1989.
[10]YUN 1966, p. 427, GA res. 2200 A (XXI), annex, part IV, 16 Dec. 1966.

nomic and Social Council for five-year terms, three from candidates nominated by WHO and 10 from candidates nominated by Members of the United Nations and parties to the Single Convention.

The Board held three sessions in 1992, at Vienna: its fifty-first from 6 to 10 January, its fifty-second from 4 to 15 May and its fifty-third from 9 to 26 November.

Members:

To serve until 1 March 1995: Dr. Cai Zhi-ji, *Second Vice-President* (China);[a] Huáscar Cajías Kauffmann (Bolivia); Mohsen Kchouk, *First Vice-President* (Tunisia); Mohamed Mansour, *Rapporteur* (Egypt); Maruthi Vasudev Narayan Rao (India); Oskar Schröder, *President* (Germany).

To serve until 1 March 1997: Sirad Atmodjo (Indonesia);[a] Abdol-Hamid Ghodse (Iran);[a] Gottfried Machata (Austria); Bunsom Martin (Thailand); Herbert S. Okun (United States); Manuel Quijano (Mexico); Sahibzada Raoof Ali Khan (Pakistan).

[a]Elected from candidates nominated by WHO.

Preparatory Commission for the International Seabed Authority and for the International Tribunal for the Law of the Sea

The Preparatory Commission for the International Seabed Authority and for the International Tribunal for the Law of the Sea was established by the Third United Nations Conference on the Law of the Sea. It consists of States, self-governing associated States, territories enjoying full internal self-government and international organizations which have signed or acceded to the United Nations Convention on the Law of the Sea. As at 31 December 1992, the Commission had 159 members.

In 1992, the Commission held the first part of its tenth session at Kingston, Jamaica, from 24 February to 13 March and the second part at United Nations Headquarters from 10 to 21 August.

Members: Afghanistan, Algeria *(Vice-Chairman)*, Angola, Antigua and Barbuda, Argentina, Australia, Austria, Bahamas, Bahrain, Bangladesh, Barbados, Belarus, Belgium, Belize, Benin, Bhutan, Bolivia, Botswana, Brazil *(Vice-Chairman)*, Brunei Darussalam, Bulgaria, Burkina Faso, Burundi, Cambodia, Cameroon *(Vice-Chairman)*, Canada, Cape Verde *(Chairman)*, Central African Republic, Chad, Chile *(Vice-Chairman)*, China *(Vice-Chairman)*, Colombia, Comoros, Congo, Cook Islands, Costa Rica, Côte d'Ivoire, Cuba, Cyprus, Czechoslovakia, Democratic People's Republic of Korea, Denmark, Djibouti, Dominica, Dominican Republic, Egypt, El Salvador, Equatorial Guinea, Ethiopia, European Economic Community, Fiji, Finland, France *(Vice-Chairman)*, Gabon, Gambia, Ghana, Greece, Grenada, Guatemala, Guinea, Guinea-Bissau, Guyana, Haiti, Honduras, Hungary, Iceland, India *(Vice-Chairman)*, Indonesia, Iran, Iraq *(Vice-Chairman)*, Ireland, Italy, Jamaica *(Rapporteur-General)*, Japan *(Vice-Chairman)*, Kenya, Kuwait, Lao People's Democratic Republic, Lebanon, Lesotho, Liberia *(Vice-Chairman)*, Libyan Arab Jamahiriya, Liechtenstein, Luxembourg, Madagascar, Malawi, Malaysia, Maldives, Mali, Malta, Marshall Islands, Mauritania, Mauritius, Mexico, Micronesia, Monaco, Mongolia, Morocco, Mozambique, Myanmar, Namibia, Nauru, Nepal, Netherlands *(Vice-Chairman)*, New Zealand, Nicaragua, Niger, Nigeria *(Vice-Chairman)*, Niue, Norway, Oman, Pakistan, Panama, Papua New Guinea, Paraguay, Philippines, Poland, Portugal, Qatar, Republic of Korea, Romania, Russian Federation *(Vice-Chairman)*, Rwanda, Saint Kitts and Nevis, Saint Lucia, Saint Vincent and the Grenadines, Samoa, Sao Tome and Principe, Saudi Arabia, Senegal, Seychelles, Sierra Leone, Singapore, Solomon Islands, Somalia, South Africa, Spain, Sri Lanka *(Vice-Chairman)*, Sudan, Suriname, Swaziland, Sweden, Switzerland, Thailand, Togo, Trinidad and Tobago, Tunisia, Tuvalu, Uganda, Ukraine, United Arab Emirates, United Republic of Tanzania, Uruguay, Vanuatu, Viet Nam, Yemen, Yugoslavia, Zaire, Zambia, Zimbabwe.

Principal members of the United Nations Secretariat

(as at 31 December 1992)

Secretariat

The Secretary-General: Boutros Boutros-Ghali

Executive Office of the Secretary-General

Under-Secretary-General, Senior Adviser to the Secretary-General: Virendra Dayal
Under-Secretary-General, Special Representative of the Secretary-General for Public Affairs: Joseph V. Reed
Assistant Secretary-General, Chief of Staff: Jean-Claude Aimé
Assistant Secretary-General, Chief of Protocol: Aly I. Teymour
Assistant Secretary-General, Senior Political Adviser: Alvaro de Soto

Office of Legal Affairs

Under-Secretary-General, Legal Counsel: Carl-August Fleischhauer

Department of Political Affairs

Under-Secretaries-General: James O. C. Jonah, Vladimir F. Petrovsky
Assistant Secretary-General: Benon V. Sevan

Department of Peace-keeping Operations

Under-Secretary-General: Marrack I. Goulding
Assistant Secretary-General: Kofi Annan

Department of Economic and Social Devlopment

Under-Secretary-General: Ji Chaozhu

Assistant Secretary-General for Development Research and Policy Analysis: P. Göran Ohlin

Economic and Social Commission for Asia and the Pacific

Under-Secretary-General, Executive Secretary: Rafeeuddin Ahmed

Economic and Social Commission for Western Asia

Under-Secretary-General, Executive Secretary: Tayseer Abdel Jaber

Economic Commission for Africa

Under-Secretary-General, Executive Secretary: Layashi Yaker

Economic Commission for Europe

Under-Secretary-General, Executive Secretary: Gerald Hinteregger

Economic Commission for Latin America and the Caribbean

Under-Secretary-General, Executive Secretary: Gert Rosenthal

United Nations Centre for Human Settlements

Under-Secretary-General, Executive Director: Arcot Ramachandran
Assistant Secretary-General, Deputy Administrator, United Nations Habitat and Human Settlements Foundation: Sumihiro Kuyama

Department of Humanitarian Affairs

Under-Secretary-General, Emergency Relief Coordinator: Jan K. Eliasson

Department of Administration and Management
Under-Secretary-General: Dick Thornburgh

OFFICE OF GENERAL SERVICES
Assistant Secretary-General: J. Richard Foran

OFFICE OF CONFERENCE SERVICES
Assistant Secretary-General: Françoise Cestac

Department of Public Information
Under-Secretary-General: Eugeniusz Wyzner

United Nations Office at Geneva
Under-Secretary-General, Director-General of the United Nations Office at Geneva: Antoine Blanca
Assistant Secretary-General, Personal Representative of the Secretary-General: Sotirios G. Mousouris

Centre for Human Rights
Under-Secretary-General: Antoine Blanca

United Nations Office at Vienna
Under-Secretary-General, Director-General of the United Nations Office at Vienna: Giorgio Giacomelli

Centre for Social Development and Humanitarian Affairs
Under-Secretary-General, Head: Margaret Joan Anstee

International Court of Justice Registry
Assistant Secretary-General, Registrar: Eduardo Valencia-Ospina

Secretariats of subsidiary organs, special representatives and other related bodies

International Trade Centre UNCTAD/GATT
Assistant Secretary-General, Executive Director: Goran M. Engblom

Office of the Personal Representative of the Secretary-General for the controversy between Guyana and Venezuela
Under-Secretary-General, Personal Representative: Alister McIntyre

Office of the Special Representative of the Secretary-General for the Promotion of the United Nations Decade of Disabled Persons
Assistant Secretary-General, Special Representative: Hans Hoegh

Office of the Special Representative of the Secretary-General to the Middle East
Under-Secretary-General, Special Representative: Edouard Brunner

Office of the United Nations Disaster Relief Coordinator
Under-Secretary-General, Disaster Relief Coordinator: M'Hamed Essaafi

Office of the United Nations High Commissioner for Refugees
Under-Secretary-General, High Commissioner: Sadako Ogata
Assistant Secretary-General, Deputy High Commissioner: Martin Douglas Stafford

United Nations Angola Verification Mission
Under-Secretary-General, Special Representative of the Secretary-General: Margaret Joan Anstee
Assistant Secretary-General, Chief Military Observer: Major-General Edward Ushie Unimna

United Nations Assistance for the Reconstruction and Development of Lebanon
Coordinator: Christer Elfverson

United Nations Children's Fund
Under-Secretary-General, Executive Director: James P. Grant
Assistant Secretary-General, Deputy Executive Director, Programmes: Richard Jolly

United Nations Compensation Commission
Assistant Secretary-General, Executive Secretary: Carlos Alzamora Traverso

Department for Policy Coordination and Sustainable Development
Under-Secretary-General: Nitin Desai

United Nations Conference on Population and Development
Assistant Secretary-General, Secretary-General of the Conference: Dr. Nafis I. Sadik

United Nations Conference on Trade and Development
Under-Secretary-General, Secretary-General of the Conference: Kenneth K. S. Dadzie (extension of appointment for one year (until 31 March 1993) confirmed by the General Assembly on 2 March 1992 **(decision 46/316 B)**)
Assistant Secretary-General, Deputy Secretary-General of the Conference: Yves Berthelot

United Nations Development Programme
Administrator: William H. Draper III
Associate Administrator: Luis Maria Gomez
Assistant Administrator and Director, Bureau for Finance and Administration: Toshiyuki Niwa
Assistant Administrator and Director, Bureau for Resources and Special Activities: Aldo Ajello
Assistant Administrator and Director, Bureau for Programme Policy and Evaluation: Gustav Edgren
Assistant Administrator and Director, Office for Project Services: Daan Willem Everts
Executive Director, United Nations Population Fund: Dr. Nafis I. Sadik
Deputy Executive Director, United Nations Population Fund, Policy and Administration: Katsuhide Kitatani
Deputy Executive Director, United Nations Population Fund, Programme: Joseph Van Arendonk
Assistant Administrator and Regional Director, Regional Bureau for Africa: Pierre-Claver Damiba
Assistant Administrator and Regional Director, Regional Bureau for Arab States and Europe: Ali Ahmed Attiga
Assistant Administrator and Regional Director, Regional Bureau for Asia and the Pacific: Krishan Singh
Assistant Administrator and Regional Director, Regional Bureau for Latin America and the Caribbean: Fernando Zumbado

United Nations Disengagement Observer Force
Assistant Secretary-General, Force Commander: Major-General Roman Misztal

United Nations Environment Programme
Under-Secretary-General, Executive Director: Mostafa Kamal Tolba
Assistant Secretary-General, Deputy Executive Director: Anthony T. Brough

United Nations Fund for Drug Abuse Control
Assistant Secretary-General, Executive Director: Giuseppe di Gennaro

United Nations Institute for Training and Research
Acting Executive Director: Marcel Boisard

United Nations Interim Force in Lebanon
Assistant Secretary-General, Force Commander: Major-General Lars-Eric Wahlgren

United Nations International Drug Control Programme

Under-Secretary-General, Executive Director: Giorgio Giacomelli

United Nations Iraq-Kuwait Observation Mission

Assistant Secretary-General, Chief Military Observer: Major-General Timothy K. Dibuama

United Nations Military Observer Group in India and Pakistan

Chief Military Observer: Brigadier-General Ricardo Jorge Galarza-Chans

**United Nations Mission for the Organization
of a Referendum in Western Sahara**

Under Secretary-General, Special Representative of the Secretary-General: Sahabzada Yaqub-Khan

United Nations Observer Mission in El Salvador

Assistant Secretary-General, Special Delegate of the Secretary-General: Iqbal Syed Riza

United Nations Operation in Somalia

Under-Secretary-General, Special Adviser to the Secretary-General: Ismat T. Kittani

United Nations Peace-keeping Force in Cyprus

Under-Secretary-General, Special Representative of the Secretary-General: Oscar Hector Camilión
Assistant Secretary-General, Force Commander: Major-General Michael F. Minehane

United Nations Protection Force

Assistant Secretary-General, Force Commander: Lieutenant-General Satish Nambiar

**United Nations Relief and Works Agency for Palestine
Refugees in the Near East**

Under-Secretary-General, Commissioner-General: Ilter Türkmen
Assistant Secretary-General, Deputy Commissioner-General: William L. Eagleton

United Nations Transitional Authority in Cambodia

Under-Secretary-General, Special Representative of the Secretary-General: Yasushi Akashi
Assistant Secretary-General, Deputy Special Representative: Behrooz Sadry
Assistant Secretary-General, Force Commander: Lieutenant-General John M. Sanderson

United Nations Truce Supervision Organization

Assistant Secretary-General, Chief of Staff: Krishna Narayan Singh Thapa

United Nations University

Under-Secretary-General, Rector: Heitor Gurgulino de Souza
Assistant Secretary-General, Director, World Institute for Development Economics Research: Lalith R. U. Jayawardena

World Food Council

Assistant Secretary-General, Executive Director: Gerald Ion Trant

---

On 31 December 1992, the total number of staff of the United Nations holding permanent, probationary and fixed-term appointments with service or expected service of a year or more was 14,212. Of these, 4,929 were in the Professional and higher categories and 9,283 were in the General Service, Manual Worker and Field Service categories. Of the same total, 12,859 were regular staff serving at Headquarters or other established offices and 1,353 were assigned as project personnel to technical cooperation projects. In addition, at the end of December 1992, UNRWA had some 19,608 local area staff, including temporary assistance.

Appendix IV

Agendas of United Nations principal organs in 1992

This appendix lists the items on the agendas of the General Assembly, the Security Council, the Economic and Social Council and the Trusteeship Council during 1992. For the Assembly and the Economic and Social Council, the column headed "Allocation" indicates the assignment of each item to plenary meetings or committees.

Agenda item titles have been shortened by omitting mention of reports, if any, following the subject of the item. Where the subject-matter of an item is not apparent from its title, the subject is identified in square brackets; this is not part of the title.

General Assembly

Agenda items considered at the resumed forty-sixth session
(4 February–14 September 1992)

Item No.	*Title*	*Allocation*
2.	Minute of silent prayer or meditation.	Plenary
8.	Adoption of the agenda and organization of work.	Plenary
18.	Appointments to fill vacancies in subsidiary organs and other appointments:	
	(g) Appointment of members of the Joint Inspection Unit;	Plenary
	(h) Appointment of the members of the Consultative Committee on the United Nations Development Fund for Women;	Plenary
	(j) Confirmation of the appointment of the Secretary-General of the United Nations Conference on Trade and Development;	Plenary
	(k) Appointment of members of the International Civil Service Commission.[1]	5th
20.	Admission of new Members to the United Nations.	Plenary
31.	The situation in Central America: threats to international peace and security and peace initiatives.	Plenary
33.	Question of Palestine.	Plenary
35.	The situation in the Middle East.	Plenary
37.	Policies of apartheid of the Government of South Africa.	Plenary
42.	Armed Israeli aggression against the Iraqi nuclear installations and its grave consequences for the established international system concerning the peaceful uses of nuclear energy, the non-proliferation of nuclear weapons and international peace and security.	Plenary
45.	Question of Cyprus.	2
46.	Consequences of the Iraqi occupation of and aggression against Kuwait.	Plenary
78.	United Nations Conference on Environment and Development.	3
84.	Special economic and disaster relief assistance.	3
98.	Human rights questions:	
	(b) Human rights questions, including alternative approaches for improving the effective enjoyment of human rights and fundamental freedoms.	4
105.	Review of the efficiency of the administrative and financial functioning of the United Nations.	Plenary
107.	Proposed programme budget for the biennium 1992-1993.	5
109.	Current financial crisis of the United Nations.	5
110.	Financial emergency of the United Nations.	5
114.	Scale of assessments for the apportionment of the expenses of the United Nations.	5
115.	Personnel questions.	5
116.	United Nations common system.	5th
119.	Financing of the United Nations Iran-Iraq Military Observer Group.	5
120.	Financing of the United Nations Angola Verification Mission.	5th
121.	Financing of the United Nations Transition Assistance Group.	5
123.	Administrative and budgetary aspects of the financing of the United Nations peace-keeping operations.	5

---

[1]Sub-item added at the resumed session.
[2]Not allocated; consideration deferred to the forty-seventh session.
[3]Allocated to the Second Committee at the first part of the session in 1991 but considered only in plenary meeting at the resumed session.
[4]Allocated to the Third Committee at the first part of the session in 1991 but considered only in plenary meeting at the resumed session.
[5]Allocated to the Fifth Committee at the first part of the session in 1991 but considered only in plenary meeting at the resumed session.

Item No.	Title	Allocation
137.	Restructuring and revitalization of the United Nations in the economic, social and related fields.	Plenary
138.	Financing of the United Nations Mission for the Referendum in Western Sahara.	5
139.	Financing of the United Nations Observer Mission in El Salvador.	5th
144.	Revitalization of the work of the General Assembly.	Plenary
145.	The situation of democracy and human rights in Haiti.	Plenary
146.	Financing of the United Nations Advance Mission in Cambodia.	5th
147.	Commemoration of the fiftieth anniversary of the United Nations in 1995.	Plenary
148.	Financing of the United Nations Transitional Authority in Cambodia.[6]	5th
149.	Financing of the United Nations Protection Force.[6]	5th
150.	The situation in Bosnia and Herzegovina.[6]	Plenary

Agenda of the forty-seventh session
(first part, 15 September–23 December 1992)

Item No.	Title	Allocation
1.	Opening of the session by the Chairman of the delegation of Saudi Arabia.	Plenary
2.	Minute of silent prayer or meditation.	Plenary
3.	Credentials of representatives to the forty-seventh session of the General Assembly:	
	(a) Appointment of the members of the Credentials Committee;	Plenary
	(b) Report of the Credentials Committee.	Plenary
4.	Election of the President of the General Assembly.	Plenary
5.	Election of the officers of the Main Committees.	Plenary
6.	Election of the Vice-Presidents of the General Assembly.	Plenary
7.	Notification by the Secretary-General under Article 12, paragraph 2, of the Charter of the United Nations.	Plenary
8.	Adoption of the agenda and organization of work.	Plenary
9.	General debate.	Plenary
10.	Report of the Secretary-General on the work of the Organization.	Plenary
11.	Report of the Security Council.	Plenary
12.	Report of the Economic and Social Council.	Plenary, 2nd, 3rd, 4th, 5th
13.	Report of the International Court of Justice.	Plenary
14.	Report of the International Atomic Energy Agency.	Plenary
15.	Elections to fill vacancies in principal organs:	
	(a) Election of five non-permanent members of the Security Council;	Plenary
	(b) Election of eighteen members of the Economic and Social Council.	Plenary
16.	Elections to fill vacancies in subsidiary organs and other elections:	
	(a) Election of twelve members of the World Food Council;	Plenary
	(b) Election of seven members of the Committee for Programme and Coordination;	Plenary
	(c) Election of the Executive Director of the United Nations Environment Programme.	Plenary
17.	Appointments to fill vacancies in subsidiary organs and other appointments:	
	(a) Appointment of members of the Advisory Committee on Administrative and Budgetary Questions;	5th
	(b) Appointment of members of the Committee on Contributions;	5th
	(c) Appointment of a member of the Board of Auditors;	5th
	(d) Confirmation of the appointment of members of the Investments Committee;	5th
	(e) Appointment of members of the United Nations Administrative Tribunal;	5th
	(f) Appointment of members of the International Civil Service Commission;	5th
	(g) Appointment of members of the Committee on Conferences;	Plenary
	(h) Appointment of a member of the Joint Inspection Unit;	Plenary
	(i) Confirmation of the appointment of the Secretary-General of the United Nations Conference on Trade and Development.	Plenary
18.	Implementation of the Declaration on the Granting of Independence to Colonial Countries and Peoples.	Plenary, 4th[7]

---

[6]Item added at the resumed session.

[7]Chapters of the report of the Special Committee on the Situation with regard to the Implementation of the Declaration on the Granting of Independence to Colonial Countries and Peoples relating to specific Territories.

Item No.	Title	Allocation
19.	Admission of new Members to the United Nations.	Plenary
20.	Cooperation between the United Nations and the Asian-African Legal Consultative Committee.	Plenary
21.	Cooperation between the United Nations and the Organization of American States.	Plenary
22.	The situation of democracy and human rights in Haiti.	Plenary
23.	Question of the Comorian island of Mayotte.	Plenary
24.	Cooperation between the United Nations and the Latin American Economic System.	Plenary
25.	Cooperation between the United Nations and the Organization of the Islamic Conference.	Plenary
26.	Zone of peace and cooperation of the South Atlantic.	Plenary
27.	Cooperation between the United Nations and the Organization of African Unity.	Plenary
28.	The situation in Afghanistan and its implications for international peace and security.	Plenary
29.	Cooperation between the United Nations and the League of Arab States.	Plenary
30.	Question of Palestine.	Plenary
31.	Revitalization of the work of the General Assembly.	Plenary
32.	Law of the sea.	Plenary
33.	Policies of apartheid of the Government of South Africa.	Plenary, SPC[8]
34.	United Nations Educational and Training Programme for Southern Africa.	Plenary
35.	The situation in the Middle East.	Plenary
36.	The situation in Central America: procedures for the establishment of a firm and lasting peace and progress in fashioning a region of peace, freedom, democracy and development.	Plenary
37.	Strengthening of the coordination of humanitarian emergency assistance of the United Nations.	Plenary
38.	Question of the Falkland Islands (Malvinas).	Plenary, 4th[8]
39.	Necessity of ending the economic, commercial and financial embargo imposed by the United States of America against Cuba.	Plenary
40.	Question of equitable representation on and increase in the membership of the Security Council.	Plenary
41.	Declaration of the Assembly of Heads of State and Government of the Organization of African Unity on the aerial and naval military attack against the Socialist People's Libyan Arab Jamahiriya by the present United States Administration in April 1986.	Plenary
42.	Armed Israeli aggression against the Iraqi nuclear installations and its grave consequences for the established international system concerning the peaceful uses of nuclear energy, the non-proliferation of nuclear weapons and international peace and security.	Plenary
43.	Launching of global negotiations on international economic cooperation for development.	Plenary
44.	Implementation of the resolutions of the United Nations.	Plenary
45.	Question of Cyprus.	9
46.	Consequences of the Iraqi occupation of and aggression against Kuwait.	Plenary
47.	Restructuring and revitalization of the United Nations in the economic, social and related fields.	Plenary
48.	Commemoration of the fiftieth anniversary of the United Nations in 1995.	Plenary
49.	Reduction of military budgets.	1st
50.	Scientific and technological developments and their impact on international security.	1st
51.	Science and technology for disarmament.	1st
52.	Verification in all its aspects, including the role of the United Nations in the field of verification.	1st
53.	Amendment of the Treaty Banning Nuclear Weapon Tests in the Atmosphere, in Outer Space and under Water.	1st
54.	Comprehensive nuclear-test-ban treaty.	1st
55.	Establishment of a nuclear-weapon-free zone in the region of the Middle East.	1st
56.	Establishment of a nuclear-weapon-free zone in South Asia.	1st
57.	Conclusion of effective international arrangements to assure non-nuclear-weapon States against the use or threat of use of nuclear weapons.	1st
58.	Prevention of an arms race in outer space.	1st
59.	Implementation of the Declaration on the Denuclearization of Africa.	1st
60.	Chemical and bacteriological (biological) weapons.	1st
61.	General and complete disarmament:	
	(a) Notification of nuclear tests;	1st
	(b) Further measures in the field of disarmament for the prevention of an arms race on the seabed and the ocean floor and in the subsoil thereof;	1st
	(c) Conventional disarmament;	1st

[8]Hearings of organizations and individuals having an interest in the question.
[9]On 18 September 1992, the General Assembly adopted the General Committee's recommendation that the item be allocated at an appropriate time during the session.

Item No.	Title	Allocation
	(d) Nuclear disarmament;	1st
	(e) Defensive security concepts and policies;	1st
	(f) Relationship between disarmament and development;	1st
	(g) Prohibition of the production of fissionable material for weapons purposes;	1st
	(h) Prohibition of the development, production, stockpiling and use of radiological weapons;	1st
	(i) International arms transfers;	1st
	(j) Regional disarmament;	1st
	(k) Prohibition of the dumping of radioactive wastes;	1st
	(l) Transparency in armaments;	1st
	(m) Conventional disarmament on a regional scale;	1st
	(n) Treaty on the Non-Proliferation of Nuclear Weapons: 1995 Conference and its Preparatory Committee.	1st
62.	Review and implementation of the Concluding Document of the Twelfth Special Session of the General Assembly:	
	(a) World Disarmament Campaign;	1st
	(b) Regional confidence-building measures;	1st
	(c) Nuclear-arms freeze;	1st
	(d) Convention on the Prohibition of the Use of Nuclear Weapons;	1st
	(e) United Nations disarmament fellowship, training and advisory services programme;	1st
	(f) United Nations Regional Centre for Peace and Disarmament in Africa, United Nations Regional Centre for Peace and Disarmament in Asia and the Pacific and United Nations Regional Centre for Peace, Disarmament and Development in Latin America and the Caribbean.	1st
63.	Review of the implementation of the recommendations and decisions adopted by the General Assembly at its tenth special session:	
	(a) Report of the Disarmament Commission;	1st
	(b) Report of the Conference on Disarmament;	1st
	(c) Status of multilateral disarmament agreements;	1st
	(d) Advisory Board on Disarmament Matters;	1st
	(e) United Nations Institute for Disarmament Research;	1st
	(f) Disarmament Week;	1st
	(g) Implementation of the guidelines for appropriate types of confidence-building measures;	1st
	(h) Comprehensive programme of disarmament;	1st
	(i) Transfer of high technology with military applications.	1st
64.	Israeli nuclear armament.	1st
65.	Convention on Prohibitions or Restrictions on the Use of Certain Conventional Weapons Which May Be Deemed to Be Excessively Injurious or to Have Indiscriminate Effects.	1st
66.	Question of Antarctica.	1st
67.	Strengthening of security and cooperation in the Mediterranean region.	1st
68.	Implementation of the Declaration of the Indian Ocean as a Zone of Peace.	1st
69.	Review of the implementation of the Declaration on the Strengthening of International Security.	1st
70.	Science and peace.	SPC
71.	Effects of atomic radiation.	SPC
72.	International cooperation in the peaceful uses of outer space.	SPC
73.	United Nations Relief and Works Agency for Palestine Refugees in the Near East.	SPC
74.	Report of the Special Committee to Investigate Israeli Practices Affecting the Human Rights of the Palestinian People and Other Arabs of the Occupied Territories.	SPC
75.	Comprehensive review of the whole question of peace-keeping operations in all their aspects.	SPC
76.	Questions relating to information.	SPC
77.	Question of the composition of the relevant organs of the United Nations.	SPC
78.	Development and international economic cooperation:	
	(a) Trade and development;	2nd
	(b) Food and agricultural development;	2nd
	(c) New and renewable sources of energy;	2nd
	(d) Development of the energy resources of developing countries;	2nd
	(e) International cooperation to mitigate the environmental consequences on Kuwait and other countries in the region resulting from the situation between Iraq and Kuwait.	2nd
79.	Report of the United Nations Conference on Environment and Development.	2nd[10]
80.	Protection of global climate for present and future generations of mankind.	2nd
81.	International cooperation for the eradication of poverty in developing countries.	2nd
82.	External debt crisis and development.	2nd

---

[10]The General Assembly decided that the debate on the item would be held in plenary meeting, on the understanding that action would be taken in the Second Committee.

Item No.	Title	Allocation
83.	Operational activities for development:	
	(a) Operational activities of the United Nations system;	2nd
	(b) United Nations Development Programme;	2nd
	(c) United Nations Population Fund;	2nd
	(d) United Nations Children's Fund;	2nd
	(e) World Food Programme.	2nd
84.	International cooperation for economic growth and development:	
	(a) Implementation of the commitments and policies agreed upon in the Declaration on International Economic Cooperation, in particular the Revitalization of the Economic Growth and Development of the Developing Countries;	2nd
	(b) Implementation of the International Development Strategy for the Fourth United Nations Development Decade.	2nd
85.	Industrial development cooperation and the diversification and modernization of productive activities in developing countries.	2nd
86.	International conference on the financing of development.	2nd
87.	Special economic and disaster relief assistance:	
	(a) Office of the United Nations Disaster Relief Coordinator;	2nd
	(b) Special programmes of economic assistance.	2nd
88.	International assistance for the economic rehabilitation of Angola.	2nd
89.	Training and research:	
	(a) United Nations Institute for Training and Research;	2nd
	(b) United Nations University.	2nd
90.	Strengthening of international cooperation and coordination of efforts to study, mitigate and minimize the consequences of the Chernobyl disaster.	2nd
91.	Elimination of racism and racial discrimination.	3rd
92.	Right of peoples to self-determination.	3rd
93.	Social development:	
	(a) Questions relating to the world social situation and to youth, ageing, disabled persons and the family;	3rd
	(b) Crime prevention and criminal justice.	3rd
94.	Advancement of women.	3rd
95.	Narcotic drugs.	3rd
96.	Report of the United Nations High Commissioner for Refugees, questions relating to refugees, returnees and displaced persons and humanitarian questions:	
	(a) Report of the United Nations High Commissioner for Refugees;	3rd
	(b) Questions relating to refugees, returnees and displaced persons;	3rd
	(c) Humanitarian questions.	3rd
97.	Human rights questions:	
	(a) Implementation of human rights instruments;	3rd
	(b) Human rights questions, including alternative approaches for improving the effective enjoyment of human rights and fundamental freedoms;	3rd
	(c) Human rights situations and reports of special rapporteurs and representatives.	3rd
98.	Information from Non-Self-Governing Territories transmitted under Article 73 *e* of the Charter of the United Nations.	4th
99.	Activities of those foreign economic and other interests which impede the implementation of the Declaration on the Granting of Independence to Colonial Countries and Peoples in Territories under colonial domination and efforts to eliminate colonialism, apartheid and racial discrimination in southern Africa.	4th
100.	Implementation of the Declaration on the Granting of Independence to Colonial Countries and Peoples by the specialized agencies and the international institutions associated with the United Nations.	4th
101.	Offers by Member States of study and training facilities for inhabitants of Non-Self-Governing Territories.	4th
102.	Financial reports and audited financial statements, and reports of the Board of Auditors:	
	(a) United Nations;	5th
	(b) United Nations Development Programme;	5th
	(c) United Nations Children's Fund;	5th
	(d) United Nations Relief and Works Agency for Palestine Refugees in the Near East;	5th
	(e) United Nations Institute for Training and Research;	5th
	(f) Voluntary funds administered by the United Nations High Commissioner for Refugees;	5th
	(g) Fund of the United Nations Environment Programme;	5th
	(h) United Nations Population Fund;	5th
	(i) United Nations Habitat and Human Settlements Foundation.	5th
103.	Review of the efficiency of the administrative and financial functioning of the United Nations.	5th
104.	Programme budget for the biennium 1992-1993.	5th
105.	Programme planning.	5th
106.	Current financial crisis of the United Nations.	5th

Item No.	Title	Allocation
107.	Financial emergency of the United Nations.	5th
108.	Administrative and budgetary coordination of the United Nations with the specialized agencies and the International Atomic Energy Agency.	5th
109.	Joint Inspection Unit.	5th
110.	Pattern of conferences.	5th
111.	Scale of assessments for the apportionment of the expenses of the United Nations.	5th
112.	Personnel questions:	
	(a) Composition of the Secretariat;	5th
	(b) Respect for the privileges and immunities of officials of the United Nations and the specialized agencies and related organizations;	5th
	(c) Other personnel questions.	5th
113.	United Nations common system.	5th
114.	United Nations pension system.	5th
115.	Financing of the United Nations peace-keeping forces in the Middle East:	
	(a) United Nations Disengagement Observer Force;	5th
	(b) United Nations Interim Force in Lebanon.	5th
116.	Financing of the United Nations Iran-Iraq Military Observer Group.	5th
117.	Financing of the United Nations Angola Verification Mission.	5th
118.	Financing of the United Nations Transition Assistance Group.	5th
119.	Financing of the United Nations Observer Group in Central America.	5th
120.	Financing of the activities arising from Security Council resolution 687(1991):	
	(a) United Nations Iraq-Kuwait Observation Mission;	5th
	(b) Other activities.	5th
121.	Financing of the United Nations Mission for the Referendum in Western Sahara.	5th
122.	Financing of the United Nations Observer Mission in El Salvador.	5th
123.	Financing of the United Nations Transitional Authority in Cambodia.	5th
124.	Administrative and budgetary aspects of the financing of the United Nations peace-keeping operations.	5th
125.	Observer status of national liberation movements recognized by the Organization of African Unity and/or by the League of Arab States.	6th
126.	Status of the Protocols Additional to the Geneva Conventions of 1949 and relating to the protection of victims of armed conflicts.	6th
127.	Consideration of effective measures to enhance the protection, security and safety of diplomatic and consular missions and representatives.	6th
128.	United Nations Decade of International Law.	6th
129.	Report of the International Law Commission on the work of its forty-fourth session.	6th
130.	Convention on jurisdictional immunities of States and their property.	6th
131.	Report of the United Nations Commission on International Trade Law on the work of its twenty-fifth session.	6th
132.	Consideration of the draft articles on the status of the diplomatic courier and the diplomatic bag not accompanied by diplomatic courier and of the draft optional protocols thereto.	6th
133.	Report of the Special Committee on the Charter of the United Nations and on the Strengthening of the Role of the Organization.	6th
134.	Report of the Committee on Relations with the Host Country.	6th
135.	Additional protocol on consular functions to the Vienna Convention on Consular Relations.	6th
136.	Protection of the environment in times of armed conflict.	6th
137.	Financing of the United Nations Protection Force.	5th
138.	Observer status for the International Organization for Migration in the General Assembly.	Plenary
139.	Complete withdrawal of foreign military forces from the territories of the Baltic States.	Plenary
140.	Coordination of the activities of the United Nations and the Conference on Security and Cooperation in Europe.	Plenary
141.	Emergency international assistance for the reconstruction of war-stricken Afghanistan.	Plenary[11]
142.	Consolidation of the regime established by the Treaty for the Prohibition of Nuclear Weapons in Latin America and the Caribbean.	1st
143.	The situation in Bosnia and Herzegovina.	Plenary
144.	International cooperation and assistance to alleviate the consequences of war in Croatia and to facilitate its recovery.	2nd
145.	Financing of the United Nations Operation in Somalia.	5th
146.	Emergency assistance to Pakistan.	Plenary

[11]Originally allocated to the Second Committee; allocation changed on 20 November 1992.

Item No.	Title	Allocation
147.	Programme budget for the biennium 1990-1991.	5th
148.	Emergency assistance to the Philippines.	Plenary
149.	The situation of human rights in Estonia and Latvia.	3rd
150.	International assistance for the rehabilitation and reconstruction of Nicaragua: aftermath of the war and natural disasters.	Plenary
151.	Requests for an advisory opinion from the International Court of Justice.	6th
152.	Convening of an international conference on Somalia.	Plenary

Security Council

Agenda items considered during 1992

Item No.[12]

Title

1. The situation in the occupied Arab territories.

2. Oral report of the Secretary-General pursuant to his report of 5 January 1992 (situation in Yugoslavia).

3. Further report of the Secretary-General pursuant to Security Council resolution 721(1991) (situation in Yugoslavia).

4. The situation in Cambodia.

5. Central America: efforts towards peace.

6. Admission of new Members.

7. Letters dated 20 and 23 December 1991 (France, United Kingdom and United States v. Libyan Arab Jamahiriya, in connection with legal procedures related to the attacks against Pan Am flight 103 and UTA flight 772).

8. Letter dated 20 January 1992 from the Chargé d'affaires a.i. of the Permanent Mission of Somalia to the United Nations addressed to the President of the Security Council (situation in Somalia).

9. The situation in the Middle East.

10. The responsibility of the Security Council in the maintenance of international peace and security.

11. The situation between Iraq and Kuwait.

12. *(a)* The situation between Iraq and Kuwait. *(b)* Letter dated 2 April 1991 from the Permanent Representative of Turkey to the United Nations addressed to the President of the Security Council; letter dated 4 April 1991 from the Chargé d'affaires a.i. of the Permanent Mission of France to the United Nations addressed to the President of the Security Council; letter dated 5 March 1992 from the Chargé d'affaires a.i. of the Permanent Mission of Belgium to the United Nations addressed to the President of the Security Council.

13. The situation in Somalia.

14. Further report of the Secretary-General on the United Nations Angola Verification Mission (UNAVEM II).

15. *(a)* Letters dated 20 and 23 December 1991. *(b)* Report by the Secretary-General pursuant to paragraph 4 of Security Council resolution 731(1992). *(c)* Further report by the Secretary-General pursuant to paragraph 4 of Security Council resolution 731(1992) (France, United Kingdom and United States v. Libyan Arab Jamahiriya, in connection with legal procedures related to the attacks against Pan Am flight 103 and UTA flight 772).

16. Letter dated 2 April 1992 from the Permanent Representative of Venezuela to the United Nations addressed to the President of the Security Council (Venezuela v. Libyan Arab Jamahiriya, in connection with attacks on and destruction of Venezuelan Embassy in Tripoli).

17. Report of the Secretary-General pursuant to Security Council resolution 743(1992) (situation in Yugoslavia).

18. The situation in Cyprus.

19. Letter dated 23 April 1992 from the Chargé d'affaires a.i. of the Permanent Mission of Austria to the United Nations addressed to the President of the Security Council; letter dated 24 April 1992 from the Permanent Representative of France to the United Nations addressed to the President of the Security Council (situation in Bosnia and Herzegovina).

20. The situation in Liberia.

21. The situation relating to Nagorno-Karabakh.

22. Further report of the Secretary-General pursuant to Security Council resolution 749(1992) (United Nations Protection Force).

23. Letter dated 27 April 1992 from the Permanent Representative of Cuba to the United Nations addressed to the President of the Security Council (Cuba v. United States).

24. Report of the Secretary-General pursuant to Security Council resolution 752(1992); letter dated 26 May 1992 from the Permanent Representative of Canada to the United Nations addressed to the President of the Security Council; letter dated 27 May 1992 from the Minister for Foreign Affairs of Bosnia and Herzegovina addressed to the President of the Security Council (situation in Bosnia and Herzegovina).

25. Report of the Secretary-General pursuant to Security Council resolution 757(1992) (situation in Bosnia and Herzegovina).

26. Report of the Secretary-General pursuant to paragraph 15 of Security Council resolution 757(1992) and paragraph 10 of Security Council resolution 758(1992) (situation in Bosnia and Herzegovina).

27. Oral reports by the Secretary-General on 26 and 29 June 1992 pursuant to resolution 758(1992) (situation in Bosnia and Herzegovina).

---

[12]Numbers indicate the order in which items were taken up in 1992.

Item
No. 12   *Title*

28. Further report of the Secretary-General pursuant to Security Council resolution 752(1992) (situation in Bosnia and Herzegovina).

29. An agenda for peace: preventive diplomacy, peacemaking and peace-keeping.

30. Further report of the Secretary-General pursuant to Security Council resolutions 757(1992), 758(1992) and 761(1992) (situation in Bosnia and Herzegovina).

31. The question of South Africa.

32. Letter dated 11 July 1992 from the Minister for Foreign Affairs of Croatia addressed to the President of the Security Council; letter dated 12 July 1992 from the Minister for Foreign Affairs of Croatia addressed to the President of the Security Council; letter dated 13 July 1992 from the Permanent Representative of Bosnia and Herzegovina to the United Nations addressed to the President of the Security Council; letter dated 13 July 1992 from the Chargé d'affaires a.i. of the Permanent Mission of Slovenia to the United Nations addressed to the President of the Security Council; letter dated 17 July 1992 from the Permanent Representatives of Belgium, France and the United Kingdom of Great Britain and Northern Ireland to the United Nations addressed to the President of the Security Council (situation in Bosnia and Herzegovina).

33. Report of the Secretary-General on the situation in Bosnia and Herzegovina.

34. Letter dated 4 August 1992 from the Chargé d'affaires a.i. of the United States Mission to the United Nations addressed to the President of the Security Council; letter dated 4 August 1992 from the Permanent Representative of Venezuela to the United Nations addressed to the President of the Security Council (situation in Bosnia and Herzegovina).

35. Report of the Secretary-General pursuant to Security Council resolution 762(1992) (situation in Bosnia and Herzegovina).

36. Letter dated 7 August 1992 from the Chargé d'affaires a.i. of the Permanent Mission of Belgium to the United Nations addressed to the President of the Security Council; letter dated 7 August 1992 from the Chargé d'affaires a.i. of the Permanent Mission of France to the United Nations addressed to the President of the Security Council; letter dated 7 August 1992 from the Permanent Representative of the United Kingdom of Great Britain and Northern Ireland to the United Nations addressed to the President of the Security Council; letter dated 7 August 1992 from the Chargé d'affaires a.i. of the United States Mission to the United Nations addressed to the President of the Security Council (human rights situation in Iraq).

37. Letter dated 10 August 1992 from the Permanent Representative of Bosnia and Herzegovina to the United Nations addressed to the President of the Security Council; letter dated 10 August 1992 from the Chargé d'affaires a.i. of the Permanent Mission of Turkey to the United Nations addressed to the President of the Security Council; letter dated 10 August 1992 from the Chargé d'affaires a.i. of the Permanent Mission of the Islamic Republic of Iran to the United Nations addressed to the President of the Security Council; letter dated 10 August 1992 from the Permanent Representative of Malaysia to the United Nations addressed to the President of the Security Council; letter dated 11 August 1992 from the Permanent Representative of Senegal to the United Nations addressed to the President of the Security Council; letter dated 11 August 1992 from the Chargé d'affaires a.i. of the Permanent Mission of Saudi Arabia to the United Nations addressed to the President of the Security Council; letter dated 10 August 1992 from the Chargé d'affaires a.i. of the Permanent Mission of Kuwait to the United Nations addressed to the President of the Security Council; letter dated 11 August 1992 from the Permanent Representative of Pakistan to the United Nations addressed to the President of the Security Council; letter dated 12 August 1992 from the Permanent Representative of Egypt to the United Nations addressed to the President of the Security Council; letter dated 13 August 1992 from the Permanent Representative of the United Arab Emirates to the United Nations addressed to the President of the Security Council; letter dated 13 August 1992 from the Permanent Representative of Bahrain to the United Nations addressed to the President of the Security Council; letter dated 13 August 1992 from the Permanent Representative of the Comoros to the United Nations addressed to the President of the Security Council; letter dated 13 August 1992 from the Permanent Representative of Qatar to the United Nations addressed to the President of the Security Council (situation in Bosnia and Herzegovina).

38. Letter dated 28 August 1992 from the Secretary-General addressed to the President of the Security Council (situation in Bosnia and Herzegovina).

39. Letter dated 24 August 1992 from the Secretary-General addressed to the President of the Security Council (human rights situation in Iraq).

40. The situation in Bosnia and Herzegovina.

41. Draft resolution contained in document S/24570 (membership of Yugoslavia in the United Nations).

42. Further report of the Secretary-General pursuant to Security Council resolutions 743(1992) and 762(1992) (situation in Bosnia and Herzegovina).

43. Letter dated 10 August 1992 from the Permanent Representative of Bosnia and Herzegovina to the United Nations addressed to the President of the Security Council; letter dated 10 August 1992 from the Chargé d'affaires a.i. of the Permanent Mission of Turkey to the United Nations addressed to the President of the Security Council; letter dated 10 August 1992 from the Chargé d'affaires a.i. of the Permanent Mission of the Islamic Republic of Iran to the United Nations addressed to the President of the Security Council; letter dated 10 August 1992 from the Permanent Representative of Malaysia to the United Nations addressed to the President of the Security Council; letter dated 11 August 1992 from the Permanent Representative of Senegal to the United Nations addressed to the President of the Security Council; letter dated 11 August 1992 from the Chargé d'affaires a.i. of the Permanent Mission of Saudi Arabia to the United Nations addressed to the President of the Security Council; letter dated 10 August 1992 from the Chargé d'affaires a.i. of the Permanent Mission of Kuwait to the United Nations addressed to the President of the Security Council; letter dated 11 August 1992 from the Permanent Representative of Pakistan to the United Nations addressed to the President of the Security Council; letter dated 12 August 1992 from the Permanent Representative of Egypt to the United Nations addressed to the President of the Security Council; letter dated 13 August 1992 from the Permanent Representative of the United Arab Emirates to the United Nations addressed to the President of the Security Council; letter dated 13 August 1992 from the Permanent Representative of Bahrain to the United Nations addressed to the President of the Security Council; letter dated 13 August 1992 from the Permanent Representative of the Comoros to the United Nations addressed to the President of the Security Council; letter dated 13 August 1992 from the Permanent Representative of Qatar to the United Nations addressed to the President of the Security Council; letter dated 5 October 1992 from the representatives of Egypt, the Islamic Republic of Iran, Pakistan, Saudi Arabia, Senegal and Turkey addressed to the President of the Security Council (situation in Bosnia and Herzegovina).

*Item
No.*[12]　　　　　　　　　　　　　　　　　　*Title*

44. Oral report of the Secretary-General on the United Nations Angola Verification Mission (UNAVEM II).
45. The situation in Georgia.
46. The situation in Mozambique.
47. Letter dated 27 October 1992 from the Secretary-General addressed to the President of the Security Council (situation in Angola).
48. Letter dated 29 October 1992 from the Secretary-General addressed to the President of the Security Council (situation in Angola).
49. The situation in Tajikistan.
50. *(a)* The situation between Iraq and Kuwait. *(b)* Letter dated 2 April 1991 from the Permanent Representative of Turkey to the United Nations addressed to the President of the Security Council; letter dated 4 April 1991 from the Chargé d'affaires a.i. of the Permanent Mission of France to the United Nations addressed to the President of the Security Council; letter dated 5 March 1992 from the Chargé d'affaires a.i. of the Permanent Mission of Belgium to the United Nations addressed to the President of the Security Council; letter dated 3 August 1992 from the Chargé d'affaires a.i. of the Permanent Mission of Belgium to the United Nations addressed to the President of the Security Council; letter dated 19 November 1992 from the Permanent Representative of Belgium to the United Nations addressed to the President of the Security Council.
51. Report of the Secretary-General on the former Yugoslav Republic of Macedonia.
52. Letter dated 18 December 1992 from the Secretary-General addressed to the President of the Security Council (situation in Angola).

Economic and Social Council
Agenda of the organizational session for 1992
(27 January and 6 and 7 February 1992)

Item No.	*Title*	*Allocation*
1.	Election of the Bureau.	Plenary
2.	Adoption of the agenda and other organizational matters.	Plenary
3.	Basic programme of work of the Council.	Plenary
4.	Establishment of a commission on crime prevention and criminal justice.	Plenary
5.	Elections and appointments to subsidiary bodies of the Council, and confirmation of representatives on the functional commissions.	Plenary

Agenda of the resumed organizational session for 1992
(29 and 30 April 1992)

Item No.	*Title*	*Allocation*
1.	Election of the Bureau.	Plenary
2.	Adoption of the agenda and other organizational matters.	Plenary
3.	Elections and nominations.	Plenary

Agenda of the reconvened resumed organizational session for 1992
(28 and 29 May 1992)

Item No.	*Title*	*Allocation*
1.	Adoption of the agenda and other organizational matters.	Plenary
2.	Human rights questions.	Plenary

Agenda of the substantive session of 1992
(29 June–31 July and 18 August 1992)

Item No.	*Title*	*Allocation*
High-level segment (6-9 July)		
1.	Adoption of the agenda.	Plenary
2.	Enhancing international cooperation for development: the role of the United Nations system.	Plenary

Item No.	Title	Allocation

3. Policy dialogue and discussion on important developments in the world economy and international economic cooperation with heads of multilateral financial and trade institutions of the United Nations system. — Plenary

4. Conclusion of the high-level segment with the presentation of a summary by the President. — Plenary

Other segments

1. Election of the Bureau. — Plenary

2. Adoption of the agenda and other organizational matters. — Plenary

3. Coordination of the policies and activities of the specialized agencies and other bodies of the United Nations system related to the following themes:
   (a) Assistance in the eradication of poverty and support to vulnerable groups, including assistance during the implementation of structural adjustment programmes; — Plenary
   (b) Prevention and control of HIV/AIDS and programmes addressed to the mitigation of its negative socio-economic consequences. — Plenary

4. Operational activities for development. — Plenary

5. Technical cooperation among developing countries as a modality in the formulation, preparation, execution and evaluation of the projects implemented by the specialized agencies and other bodies of the United Nations system in the economic, social and related fields. — Plenary

6. Coordination questions:
   (a) Reports of the coordination bodies; — Plenary
   (b) Implementation of the Declaration on the Granting of Independence to Colonial Countries and Peoples by the specialized agencies and the international institutions associated with the United Nations; — Plenary
   (c) International cooperation in the field of informatics. — Plenary

7. Revitalization of the Economic and Social Council. — Plenary

8. Programme and related questions. — Plenary

9. Special economic, humanitarian and disaster relief assistance:
   (a) Special programmes of economic assistance; — Plenary
   (b) Humanitarian assistance; — Plenary
   (c) Disaster relief coordination. — Plenary

10. Report of the United Nations High Commissioner for Refugees. — Plenary

11. Regional cooperation. — Economic

12. Development and international economic cooperation:
    (a) Implementation of the International Development Strategy for the Fourth United Nations Development Decade; — Economic
    (b) Trade and development; — Economic
    (c) Food and agricultural development; — Economic
    (d) International cooperation in tax matters; — Economic
    (e) Transnational corporations; — Economic
    (f) International Conference on Population and Development; — Economic
    (g) Development and utilization of new and renewable sources of energy; — Economic
    (h) Development of the energy resources of developing countries; — Economic
    (i) International cooperation to mitigate the environmental consequences for Kuwait and other countries in the region resulting from the situation between Iraq and Kuwait; — Economic
    (j) Consumer protection; — Economic
    (k) Prevention and control of acquired immune deficiency syndrome (AIDS). — Economic

13. Permanent sovereignty over national resources in the occupied Palestinian and other Arab territories. — Economic

14. Strengthening of international cooperation and coordination of efforts to study, mitigate and minimize the consequences of the Chernobyl disaster. — Economic

15. Public administration and finance. — Economic

16. Implementation of the Programme of Action for the Second Decade to Combat Racism and Racial Discrimination. — Social

17. Human rights questions. — Social

18. Advancement of women. — Social

19. Social development questions:
    (a) Crime prevention and criminal justice; — Social
    (b) Social development. — Social

20. Narcotic drugs. — Social

21. Establishment of new subsidiary bodies of the Council. — Plenary

22. Elections. — Plenary

Trusteeship Council
Agenda of the fifty-ninth session
(26 May–2 June and 21 December 1992)

Item No.   *Title*

1. Adoption of the agenda.

2. Report of the Secretary-General on credentials.

3. Election of the President and the Vice-President.

4. Examination of the annual report of the Administering Authority for the year ended 30 September 1991: Trust Territory of the Pacific Islands.

5. Report of the United Nations Visiting Mission to Palau, Trust Territory of the Pacific Islands, March 1992.

6. Examination of petitions.

7. Offers by Member States of study and training facilities for inhabitants of Trust Territories.

8. Dissemination of information on the United Nations and the International Trusteeship System in Trust Territories.

9. Cooperation with the Committee on the Elimination of Racial Discrimination.

10. Second Decade to Combat Racism and Racial Discrimination.

11. Attainment of self-government or independence by the Trust Territories and the situation in Trust Territories with regard to the implementation of the Declaration on the Granting of Independence to Colonial Countries and Peoples.

12. Cooperation with the Special Committee on the Situation with regard to the Implementation of the Declaration on the Granting of Independence to Colonial Countries and Peoples.

13. Adoption of the report of the Trusteeship Council to the Security Council.

Appendix V

United Nations Information Centres and Services

(As at January 1993)

ACCRA. United Nations Information Centre
Gamel Abdul Nassar/Liberia Roads
(P.O. Box 2339)
Accra, Ghana
   Serving: Ghana, Sierra Leone

ADDIS ABABA. United Nations Information
   Service, Economic Commission for Africa
Africa Hall
(P.O. Box 3001)
Addis Ababa, Ethiopia
   Serving: Ethiopia

ALGIERS. United Nations Information Centre
19 Avenue Chahid El Ouali, Mustapha Sayed
(Boîte Postale 823, Alger-Gare, Algeria)
Algiers, Algeria
   Serving: Algeria

ANKARA. United Nations Information Centre
197 Ataturk Bulvari
(P.K. 407)
Ankara, Turkey
   Serving: Turkey

ANTANANARIVO. United Nations Information
   Centre
22 Rue Rainitovo, Antasahavola
(Boîte Postale 1348)
Antananarivo, Madagascar
   Serving: Madagascar

ASUNCION. United Nations Information
   Centre
Casilla de Correo 1107
Asunción, Paraguay
   Serving: Paraguay

ATHENS. United Nations Information Centre
36 Amalia Avenue
GR-10558 Athens, Greece
   Serving: Cyprus, Greece, Israel

BAGHDAD (relocated to Amman). United
   Nations Information Service, Economic and
   Social Commission for Western Asia
P.O. Box 927115
Amman, Jordan
   Serving: Iraq

BANGKOK. United Nations Information Serv-
   ice, Economic and Social Commission for
   Asia and the Pacific
United Nations Building
Rajdamnern Avenue
Bangkok 10200, Thailand
   Serving: Cambodia, Hong Kong, Lao
   People's Democratic Republic, Malaysia,
   Singapore, Thailand, Viet Nam

BEIRUT. United Nations Information Centre
Apt. No. 1, Fakhoury Building
Montée Bain Militaire, Ardati Street
(P.O. Box 4656)
Beirut, Lebanon
   Serving: Jordan, Kuwait, Lebanon,
   Syrian Arab Republic

BRAZZAVILLE. United Nations Information
   Centre
Avenue Foch, Case Ortf 15
(P.O. Box 13210)
Brazzaville, Congo
   Serving: Congo

BRUSSELS. United Nations Information Centre
Avenue de Broqueville 40
1200 Brussels, Belgium
   Serving: Belgium, Luxembourg,
   Netherlands; liaison with EEC

BUCHAREST. United Nations Information
   Centre
16 Aurel Vlaicu
(P.O. Box 1-701)
Bucharest, Romania
   Serving: Romania

BUENOS AIRES. United Nations Information Centre
Junín 1940 (1er piso)
1113 Buenos Aires, Argentina
   Serving: Argentina, Uruguay

BUJUMBURA. United Nations Information
   Centre
117 Avenue de la Poste
(Boîte Postale 2160)
Bujumbura, Burundi
   Serving: Burundi

CAIRO. United Nations Information Centre
1 Osiris Street
Tagher Building (Garden City)
(Boîte Postale 262)
Cairo, Egypt
   Serving: Egypt, Saudi Arabia, Yemen

COLOMBO. United Nations Information Centre
202-204 Bauddhaloka Mawatha
(P.O. Box 1505, Colombo)
Colombo 7, Sri Lanka
   Serving: Sri Lanka

COPENHAGEN. United Nations Information
   Centre
37 H.C. Andersens Boulevard
DK-1553 Copenhagen V, Denmark
   Serving: Denmark, Finland, Iceland,
   Norway, Sweden

DAKAR. United Nations Information
   Centre
72 Boulevard de la République
(Boîte Postale 154)
Dakar, Senegal
   Serving: Cape Verde, Côte d'Ivoire,
   Gambia, Guinea, Guinea-Bissau, Maurita-
   nia, Senegal

DAR ES SALAAM. United Nations Information
   Centre
Samora Machel Avenue
Matasalamat Building (1st floor)
(P.O. Box 9224)
Dar es Salaam, United Republic of Tanzania
   Serving: United Republic of Tanzania

DHAKA. United Nations Information Centre
House 25, Road 11
Dhanmandi
(G.P.O. Box 3658, Dhaka 1000)
Dhaka 1209, Bangladesh
   Serving: Bangladesh

GENEVA. United Nations Information Service,
   United Nations Office at Geneva
Palais des Nations
1211 Geneva 10, Switzerland
   Serving: Bulgaria, Poland, Switzerland

HARARE. United Nations Information
   Centre
Dolphin House (ground floor)
123 L. Takawira Street/Union Avenue
(P.O. Box 4408)
Harare, Zimbabwe
   Serving: Zimbabwe

ISLAMABAD. United Nations Information
   Centre
House No. 26
88th Street, Ramna 6/3
(P.O. Box 1107)
Islamabad, Pakistan
   Serving: Pakistan

JAKARTA. United Nations Information Centre
Gedung Dewan Pers (5th floor)
32-34 Jalan Kebon Sirih
Jakarta, Indonesia
   Serving: Indonesia

KABUL. United Nations Information Centre
Shah Mahmoud Ghazi Watt
(P.O. Box 5)
Kabul, Afghanistan
   Serving: Afghanistan

KATHMANDU. United Nations Information Centre
Pulchowk, Patan
(P.O. Box 107, Pulchowk)
Kathmandu, Nepal
Serving: Nepal

KHARTOUM. United Nations Information Centre
United Nations Compound
University Avenue
(P.O. Box 1992)
Khartoum, Sudan
Serving: Somalia, Sudan

KINSHASA. United Nations Information Centre
Bâtiment Deuxième République
Boulevard du 30 Juin
(Boîte Postale 7248)
Kinshasa, Zaire
Serving: Zaire

LAGOS. United Nations Information Centre
17 Kingsway Road, Ikoyi
(P.O. Box 1068)
Lagos, Nigeria
Serving: Nigeria

LA PAZ. United Nations Information Centre
Av. Mariscal
Santa Cruz No. 1350
(Apartado Postal 9072)
La Paz, Bolivia
Serving: Bolivia

LIMA. United Nations Information Centre
320/326 Genera Jacinto Lara
San Isidro
(P.O. Box 14-0199)
Lima, Peru
Serving: Peru

LISBON. United Nations Information Centre
Rua Latino Coelho, 1
Ed. Aviz, Bloco A-1, 10º
1000 Lisbon, Portugal
Serving: Portugal

LOME. United Nations Information Centre
107 Boulevard du 13 Janvier
(Boîte Postale 911)
Lomé, Togo
Serving: Benin, Togo

LONDON. United Nations Information Centre
20 Buckingham Gate
London SW1E 6LB, England
Serving: Ireland, United Kingdom

LUSAKA. United Nations Information Centre
P.O. Box 32905
Lusaka 10101, Zambia
Serving: Botswana, Malawi, Swaziland, Zambia

MADRID. United Nations Information Centre
Avenida General Perón, 32-1
(P.O. Box 3400, 28080 Madrid)
28020 Madrid, Spain
Serving: Spain

MANAGUA. United Nations Information Centre
De Plaza España
2 Cuadras Abajo, Bolonia
(P.O. Box 3260)
Managua, Nicaragua
Serving: Nicaragua

MANAMA. United Nations Information Centre
House No. 131, Road 2803
Segaya 328
(P.O. Box 26004)
Manama, Bahrain
Serving: Bahrain, Qatar, United Arab Emirates

MANILA. United Nations Information Centre
NEDA Building
106 Amorsolo Street
Legaspi Village, Makati
(P.O. Box 7285 (DAPO), 1300 Domestic Road, Pasay City)
Metro Manila, Philippines
Serving: Papua New Guinea, Philippines, Solomon Islands

MASERU. United Nations Information Centre
Corner Kingsway and Hilton Hill Road opposite Sanlam Centre
(P.O. Box 301, Maseru 100)
Maseru, Lesotho
Serving: Lesotho

MEXICO CITY. United Nations Information Centre
Presidente Masaryk 29 (7º piso)
11570 México, D.F., Mexico
Serving: Cuba, Dominican Republic, Mexico

MOSCOW. United Nations Information Centre
4/16 Ulitsa Lunacharskogo
Moscow 121002, Russian Federation
Serving: Belarus, Russian Federation, Ukraine

NAIROBI. United Nations Information Centre
United Nations Office
Gigiri
(P.O. Box 34135)
Nairobi, Kenya
Serving: Kenya, Seychelles, Uganda

NEW DELHI. United Nations Information Centre
55 Lodi Estate
New Delhi 110003, India
Serving: Bhutan, India

OUAGADOUGOU. United Nations Information Centre
218 Rue de la Gare
Secteur No. 3
(Boîte Postale 135)
Ouagadougou 01, Burkina Faso
Serving: Burkina Faso, Chad, Mali, Niger

PANAMA CITY. United Nations Information Centre
Urbanización Obarrio
Calle 54 y Avenida Tercera Sur, Casa No. 17
(P.O. Box 6-9083 El Dorado)
Panama City, Panama
Serving: Panama

PARIS. United Nations Information Centre
1 Rue Miollis
75732, Paris Cedex 15, France
Serving: France

PORT OF SPAIN. United Nations Information Centre
2nd floor, Bretton Hall
16 Victoria Avenue
(P.O. Box 130)
Port of Spain, Trinidad
Serving: Antigua and Barbuda, Bahamas, Barbados, Belize, Dominica, Grenada, Guyana, Jamaica, Netherlands Antilles, Saint Kitts and Nevis, Saint Lucia, Saint Vincent and the Grenadines, Suriname, Trinidad and Tobago

PRAGUE. United Nations Information Centre
Panska 5
11000 Prague 1, Czech Republic
Serving: Czech Republic, Slovakia

RABAT. United Nations Information Centre
Angle Charia Ibnouzaid et Zankat Roundanat, No. 6
(Boîte Postale 601)
Rabat, Morocco
Serving: Morocco

RIO DE JANEIRO. United Nations Information Centre
Palácio Itamaraty
Ave. Marechal Floriano 196
20080 Rio de Janeiro, RJ, Brazil
Serving: Brazil

ROME. United Nations Information Centre
Palazzetto Venezia
Piazza San Marco 50
00186 Rome, Italy
Serving: Holy See, Italy, Malta

SAN SALVADOR. United Nations Information Centre
Edificio Escalón (2º piso)
Paseo General Escalón y 87 Avenida Norte
Colonia Escalón
(Apartado Postal 2157)
San Salvador, El Salvador
Serving: El Salvador

SANTA FE DE BOGOTA. United Nations Information Centre
Calle 100 No. 8A-55, Of. 815
(Apartado Aéreo 058964)
Santa Fé de Bogotá 2, Colombia
Serving: Colombia, Ecuador, Venezuela

SANTIAGO. United Nations Information Service, Economic Commission for Latin America and the Caribbean
Edificio Naciones Unidas
Avenida Dag Hammarskjöld
(Avenida Dag Hammarskjöld s/n, Casilla 179-D)
Santiago, Chile
Serving: Chile

SYDNEY. United Nations Information Centre
Suite 1, 125 York Street
(P.O. Box 4045, Sydney N.S.W. 2001)
Sydney N.S.W. 2000, Australia
Serving: Australia, Fiji, Kiribati, Nauru, New Zealand, Samoa, Tonga, Tuvalu, Vanuatu

TEHRAN. United Nations Information Centre
185 Ghaem Magham Farahani Avenue
(P.O. Box 15875-4557, Tehran)
Tehran, 15868 Iran
Serving: Iran

TOKYO. United Nations Information Centre
Shin Aoyama Building Nishikan (22nd floor)
1-1 Minami Aoyama 1-chome, Minato-ku
Tokyo 107, Japan
Serving: Japan, Trust Territory of the Pacific Islands

TRIPOLI. United Nations Information Centre
Muzzafar Al Aftas Street
Hay El-Andalous (2)
(P.O. Box 286)
Tripoli, Libyan Arab Jamahiriya
Serving: Libyan Arab Jamahiriya

TUNIS. United Nations Information Centre
61 Boulevard Bab-Benat
(Boîte Postale 863)
Tunis, Tunisia
Serving: Tunisia

VIENNA. United Nations Information Service, United Nations Office at Vienna
Vienna International Centre
Wagramer Strasse 5
(P.O. Box 500, A-1400 Vienna)
A-1220 Vienna, Austria
Serving: Austria, Germany, Hungary

WASHINGTON, D.C. United Nations Information Centre
1889 F Street, N.W.
Washington, D.C. 20006, United States
Serving: United States

YANGON. United Nations Information Centre
6 Natmauk Road
(P.O. Box 230)
Yangon, Myanmar
Serving: Myanmar

YAOUNDE. United Nations Information Centre
Immeuble Kamden, Rue Joseph Clère
(Boîte Postale 836)
Yaoundé, Cameroon
Serving: Cameroon, Central African Republic, Gabon

Indexes

Using the subject index

The index contains two types of entries:

Subject terms, including geographical names, are in most cases based on the subject descriptors used in the United Nations Bibliographical Information System (UNBIS), published in the *UNBIS Thesaurus* (United Nations Publication: Sales No. E.85.I.20). In order to minimize subentries, the index lists broad and narrow terms in their separate alphabetical positions; for example, ''human rights'', ''racial discrimination'' and ''right to development''. Subjects pertaining to the United Nations or the system as a whole, such as ''contributions (UN)'', ''finances (UN)'' and ''staff (UN/UN system)'', are indexed separately, with cross-references under ''United Nations''.

Names of organizations and subsidiary bodies, conferences, United Nations Secretariat departments and offices, programmes, and special decades and observances are indexed under their key word: Apartheid, Spec. Ct. against; Development Decade, 4th UN; Law of the Sea, 3rd UN Cf. on the; Maritime Day, World; Technical Cooperation for Development, Department of. Names of specialized agencies and of non–United Nations organizations are alphabetized under the first word of their title: Inter-American Cs. on Human Rights; World Meteorological Organization.

Bodies/subjects/topics are listed only when substantive information is given.

In addition to the abbreviations listed on p. xv, the subject index uses the following:

ASG	Assistant Secretary-General
CD	Conference on Disarmament
cf(s).	conference(s)
cl(s).	council(s)
cs(s).	commission(s)
ct(s).	committee(s)
DC	Disarmament Commission
DG	Director-General
LOS	Law of the Sea
mtg(s).	meeting(s)
sess.	session
SCPDPM	Subcommission on Prevention of Discrimination and Protection of Minorities of the Commission on Human Rights
spec.	special
UNCLS	United Nations Conference on the Law of the Sea
UNJSPB	United Nations Joint Staff Pension Board
USG	Under-Secretary-General

Subject index

Page numbers in bold-face type indicate resolutions and decisions

Abuse Trends Linkage Alerting System (WHO), see under drugs of abuse

Accounting and Reporting, Intergovernmental Working Group of Experts on International Standards of (TNCs Cs.): 10th sess., 645, **652** (SG/ESC); members/officers, 1219

accounts/auditing (UN) (1990), 1041-42, **1042-44**, **1044** (ACABQ/Auditors' Board/GA/SG); see also organizational entries

acquired immunodeficiency syndrome (AIDS)
cases reported, 818, 819 (WHO); WHO projections, 819
HIV and Development Programme, establishment, 562, 818, 820 (UNDP) & human rights and dignity, 725 (Human Rights Cs./ESC/SCPDPM Spec. Rapporteur)
prevention/control, 697 (UNFPA), 819-21 (ESC, 819, **820**; GA, **821**; SG, 819-20; WHO, 819); WHO Global Strategy, 819, 1116; WHO/UNICEF Joint Ct., 819
transmission through breast-feeding, expert mtg., 1120 (WHO/UNICEF)
UNDP programmes, 551 (Africa/Asia)
vaccine/drug supply, mtg. on, 1120 (WHO/UNDP)
see also children; women; and youth

Ad Hoc Committee . . . for specific ct., see key word(s) of title

Administration and Finance, UN Programme in Public: 10th Mtg. of Experts on, 541, 542 (SG/ESC);

Administration and Management, Department of (Secretariat), 1053; USG, 1225

administrative and budgetary questions, 1019-52, 1053-76; coordination, 1051 (SG/GA); see also budgets (UN); financial situation (UN); staff (UN)

Administrative and Budgetary Questions, Advisory Ct. on (ACABQ), 1040; sess./report, 1033 (GA)

administrative and management questions (UN/UN system), 1077-89; see also conferences/mtgs. (UN); documentation (UN); Secretariat (UN); staff (UN/UN system); and under United Nations main heading

Administrative Ct. on Coordination, see Coordination, Administrative Ct. on (ACC)

Administrative Questions (Financial and Budgetary), ACC Consultative Ct. on: Working Party on Accounting Standards, 944, 1052

Administrative Tribunal, UN: judgements, 1076; members/officers, 1206

Administrative Tribunal Judgements, Ct. on Applications for Review of (GA): members/officers, 1203

aeronautical meteorology, 1159 (WMO)
Aeronautics and Astronautics, American Institute of: joint COSPAR/IAF symposium on space technology, 113

Afghanistan: asylum-seekers, 904; drug use & refugees, 924; food aid, 827 (WFP); economic trends, 480; refugee situation, 784, 785, 902 (Spec. Rapporteur/Human Rights Cs./UNHCR); & self-determination, 730-31 (Human Rights Cs.); rehabilitation, 560 (UNDP)

Afghanistan, UN Office for the Coordination of Humanitarian and Economic Assistance Relating to, 597

Afghanistan situation, 262-65 (communications, 264; SG, 263, 264-65; SC, 263, 265)
humanitarian/economic assistance, **597, 598** (UNHCR/WFP/SG/GA), Operation Salam, 597
human rights situation, 784-87 (Spec. Rapporteur, 784, 785; Cs., 784-85; GA, **785-87**, 787); Spec. Rapporteur, mandate renewed, 785
political/military events: 1988 Geneva Agreements, 264; proposed Afghan gathering on transition period, 262-63, 264 (SG Representative/SG); resignation of President/transfer of power (Peshawar Agreement), 264; renewed fighting, cease-fire/amnesty appeal, 264, 265 (SG/SC), 597; safety of UN/diplomatic personnel/missions, 264, 265 (SG/SC)

Afghanistan and Pakistan, Office of the Secretary-General in: headquarters/Military Advisory Unit, 265

Africa, 126 (DPI), 151-217, 650 (TNCs/ECA Joint Unit), 652 (TNCs Centre), 459-77 (ECA), 559-60 (UNDP), 1100 (ILO), 1147 (IFC), 1147 (ICAO), 1152 (ITU), 1170 (IFAD)
accounting, training/education, 645
agriculture: production, 463-64 (ECA)
AIDS/HIV health crisis, 464, 475 (ECA)
children in, 882-83 (UNICEF); Bamako Initiative, 883; cf. on, 475
debt, 126 (DPI), 463 (ECA/SG); outstanding, 463
denuclearization of, Declaration on, 88, **88-89** (GA); proposed convention or treaty on, 88, **89** (expert mtg./GA); see also South Africa: nuclear capability
development policy/advisory services, 465-66 (ECA); & research, proposed foundation/forum, 465
diseases, increase in, 464 (ECA)
drug abuse/control, 919 (UNDCP), 923 (UNDCP/HONLEA)
economic trends, 462-64 (ECA), 540 (1992 World Survey/Trade and Development Report); subregional performance, 464
energy planning/management, 472

environment/development, 474-75 (ECA); & African Programme, Common Position on, 460, 474
fisheries cooperation, 473-74, **474** (SG/ECA/ESC)
food/agriculture, 472-73 (ECA); 825 (WFP); 827 (CFA), 828 (WFC), 1104, 1105 (FAO)
hazardous wastes: Bamako Convention on import ban/transboundary control, **103** (GA)
human resources development, 475 (ECA)
human settlements, 476 (ECA)
industrial development, 467-70 (ECA/IDDA); see also Africa, 2nd Industrial Development Decade for
information/documentation (PADIS), 664; publications, 466; ECA Working Group on Information Systems, establishment, 664
international trade/development finance, 467; trends, 464
least developed countries in, 464, 465 (ECA); Cf. of Ministers of, 460; industrialization proposals, 468
locust/grasshopper infestation, 1105 (FAO)
media development: IPDC projects, 124 (UNESCO); 1991 Windhoek Declaration, implementation, 123-24 (UNESCO/DPI), 124 (IPDC)
natural resources development: marine, 472; mineral/water, 472
Multinational Programming and Operational Centres (MULPOCs): strengthening, 460, **462** (ECA/ESC)
population, 475-76 (ECA)
public administration/finance, 466-67 (ECA); Spec. Action Programme for, 467 (ECA/UNDP)
refugee assistance, 897-98, **898-900** (SG/GA); expenditures, 898; 1969 OAU Convention, 905; population in, 465 (ECA), 897; see also country names; regional entries
science/technology, 471-72; Intergovernmental Experts Ct., 669
social trends, 464-65
space applications, 112 (UN Programme/ESA)
statistical development, 465-66 (ECA); Addis Ababa Action Plan for, Implementation Strategy, 465, 927 (ACC); Coordinating Ct. on, 466; publications, 664
toxic wastes: 1991 Bamako Convention banning, 674 (Agenda 21)
transport/communications, 470-71 (ECA); see also Africa, 2nd Transport and Communications Decade; Gibraltar, Strait of

women in crisis, UNIFEM programmes, 872; in development, 476-77 (ECA)

see also country names and organizational, regional and subject entries

Africa, Declaration on the Denuclearization of (1964): implementation, 88, **88-89** (GA); see also South Africa: nuclear capability

Africa, Economic Cs. for (ECA), 459-77; Cf. of Ministers (18th mtg.), 459-60; Executive Secretary, 1224; Multidisciplinary Regional Advisory Group, establishment, 460; medium-term plan, 1992-1997, revised, 477 (CPC/GA/ Technical Ct.); members/officers, 1216; Multinational Programming and Operational Centres (MULPOCs), strengthening, 460, **462** (Technical Ct./ESC); role/functions of, 457, **458-59** (ESC); 27th sess., **459**; 1993 sess., venue, 477 (ESC); strengthening, 460-61, **461-62**; Technical Preparatory Ct. of the Whole, 460; work programme, 1992-1993, update, 460

Africa, FAO Cf. for: Accra Declaration, 1104

Africa, Heads of State or Government of the countries of the Horn of: Declaration/Action Programme, 588

Africa, Horn of: Spec. Emergency Programme for, 588-89; Consolidated Inter-Agency Appeal for, 588; UNDP action, 588-89; see also Djibouti; Ethiopia; Kenya; Somalia; Sudan

Africa, International Cf. on Accountancy Development in (1st), 645

Africa, 1980 Lagos Plan of Action for the Implementation of the Monrovia Strategy for the Economic Development of (OAU), 460 (ECA)

Africa, 2nd Industrial Development Decade for (1991-2000): implementation, 468, **468-69**, **469-70** (ECA/ESC/GA), 1174 (UNIDO)

Africa, 2nd Transport and Communications Decade in (1991-2000), 470-71, **471** (ESC), 1174 (UNIDO)

Africa, UN Regional Centre for Peace and Disarmament in, 105 (SG/GA)

Africa in the 1990s, UN New Agenda for the Development of, 460; implementation, 126, **127** (DPI/GA), 460, 575-77 (TDB, 575; UNCTAD VIII, 575-76; UNDP, 576-77); & IDDA II, **469** (ESC), 215 (OAU); SG High-level Panel, 575; System-wide Plan of Action, 577, (SG/CPC)

Africa Recovery, 126, **127** (DPI/GA)

Africa Region: Mtg. of Heads of National Drug Law Enforcement Agencies (HONLEA): 5th mtg., **909**, 923

African Alternative Framework to Structural Adjustment Programmes for Socioeconomic Recovery and Transformation (1989): implementation, 460, (ECA); & agriculture, 472

African Centre of Meteorological Applications for Development, 475; budget approval, 461

African Charter for Popular Participation in Development and Transformation (1990), 460 (ECA)

African Children, International Cf. on Assistance to (OAU), 883 (UNICEF)

African Development Bank; & ECA, 460; mtgs., 467; refugee aid, 897; training/research, women, 872

African Economic Community (OAU): Abuja Treaty (1991), ratification, 460, 465, 467 (ECA)

African Institute for Economic Development and Planning, 461, **462**

African Institute for the Prevention of Crime and the Treatment of Offenders (UNAFRI), 860, **860-61** (SG/GA); amendments to statutes, 461

African Ministers of Telecommunications, Spec. Cf. of, 470, 1153

African National Congress of South Africa (ANC): advisory services, investment, 652-53 (TNCs Centre); funding, New York office, **154** (GA); & CODESA, 155-56; & Peace Accord, 156-57; UNCED, 670

African Planners, Statisticians and Demographers, Joint Cf.: 7th sess., 465

African Population Cf., 3rd: Declaration, adoption/recommendations, 476, 694

African Population and Self-Reliant Development: 1984 Kilimanjaro Action Plan, 476

African Railways, Union of: Assembly/Symposium, 470 (ECA)

African Society of Gerontology, **893**

African States Bordering the Atlantic Ocean, 1992 Ministerial Cf. on Cooperation in Fisheries among the: Action Programme/Regional Convention, 473, **474** (SG/ESC); 1993 sess., **474** (ESC)

African Training and Research Centre for Women, 477

Ageing, International Action Plan (1982): implementation, 889, **889-90** (SG/GA); 10th anniversary, Proclamation, 889 (SG/GA); global targets for the year 2001, 889, **889-90** (SG/GA)

Ageing, International Institute on (Valletta): training, **891** (GA)

ageing persons, 489 (ESCAP), 889-91; Day for, 889, **890** (GA); & health, 1119 (WHO); integration of in development, **891-92** (GA); statistics, 930; strategy (1991-2001), 889, **890**; 1999 proclaimed International Year for, **890**; UN principles for, **890**; UN Trust Fund for, **890** (GA); & world population, percentage of, 889

agrarian reform and rural development, see under rural development

agreements, see subject entries; treaties

agricultural commodities, see names of individual commodities

agricultural development, see FAO; IFAD; regional entries; rural development

Agricultural Statistics in Europe, Study Group on Food and, 500 (ECE)

agriculture, 463-64 (ECA), 500, (ECE) 517 (ESCWA); meteorology applications, 1159 (WMO); nuclear techniques in, 660; see also entries under food

Agriculture, Ct. on (ECE), 500

agro-industries, 1172 (UNIDO)

agrometeorology remote-sensing uses, training, 113 (UN/ESA)

AIDS, see acquired immunodeficiency syndrome (AIDS)

AIDS, 8th International Cf. on, 1111, 1117 (WHO)

AIDS, Maghreb Cf. on, 1111

AIDS, WHO/UNDP Global Alliance to Combat, 819-20, **820**, **821** (SG/UNDP/ UNICEF/ESC/GA), 1116, 1120 (WHO)

AIDS Day, World, 1117

air navigation, regional plans/mtgs., 1145; see also civil aviation

Air Navigation Services, Procedures for, 1145

air pollution, long-range transmission, 501-502 (ECE); see also names of pollutant

Air Pollution, ECE Convention on Long-range Transboundary (1979)/Protocols, 501-502; Executive Body/Working Group on Strategies, mandate amended, 501

Air Pollution Monitoring Network, Background (BAPMoN), 1096 (IAEA/WMO); expansion, 1158; & Global Atmosphere Watch, 1158 (WMO)

air transport: colloquium on regulation, 1146; joint finance agreements (Denmark/Iceland), 1146; see also civil aviation

Air Transportation Association, International (IATA), 1146

Albania, admission to IFAD: 1169, IFC, 1129, WIPO, 1165; & human rights, 767 (UN/Human Rights Centre), 794 (SG/Cs.); UNDP projects, 561; see also Macedonia

Alcohol and Addiction, International Cl. on: UNDCP courses, 919

Algeria, 1132 (IFC); refugees in, 904 (UNHCR); see also Western Sahara

Amerasinghe (Hamilton Shirley) Fellowship on Law of the Sea, see under law of the sea

American Regional Telecommunication Development Cf.: Acapulco Declaration, 1153 (ITU)

American Samoa, 964, **966** (Colonial Countries Ct./GA); information to UN, 960

American States, Members of ILO, 13th Cf., 1099

Americas, 218-39; civil aviation, 1147 (ICAO); telecommunications, 1153 (ITU); UNICEF programmes, 883; see also Andean Pact subregion and country, organizational and subject entries

Amnesty International: report on Palestinian detainees, 431

Andean region: drug control cooperation, 925

Angola, 21-22 (SG), 178-86; elections in, 178; Spec. Relief Programme-II, 589 (SG); Peace Accords (1991): implementation, **51** (GA), 178 (SC Cs.); resumed fighting/cease-fire, 178; resumed talks, 185, 186; rehabilitation assistance, international, 589, **589-590** (SG/GA); SG Spec. Representative appointed, 178; urban development credit, 1137 (IDA)

Angola Verification Mission, UN (UNAVEM), 178-79, **179** (SG/SC); Chief of, appointed, 178, 1213, 1225; enlargement, 179, **179** (SG/SC), 184, 185; extensions, 181, **183** (SG/SC), 184, **184** (SG/SC); financing,

186-88 (ACABQ, 186; GA, **186-87**, 188; SG, 186, 187-88); SG Spec. Representative, 1213, 1225

Anguilla, 964, **966-67** (Colonial Countries Ct./GA)

animals, see livestock

Antarctic Treaty (1959), 130-33; 1991 Madrid Protocol to, 130, **132** (SG/GA); secretariat, proposed, 130; 16th Consultative Mtg. (1991), 130, **131-32** (SG/GA); & South Africa participation, 131, 132, 133 (GA/SG); States parties, 130; 30th anniversary of entry into force, 130

Antarctica, question of, 130-33; conventions on, 130; environmental issues, 130, 131, **132** (SG/GA), 133 (SG/UNEP/UNCED); & MARPOL 73/78, 1162 (IMO); mining/prospecting ban, 130, **132** (Madrid Protocol/GA); nature reserve, proposed, **132**; scientific/logistic cooperation in, 130, **132** (SG/GA)

Anti-Dumping Practices, Ct. on, 1179; see also international trade

apartheid, 151-68
    aid to victims of, 780 (Human Rights Cs.)
    Boipatong massacre, 154 (SG), 155, 157, **159** (SC)
    dismantling: negotiations, CODESA process, 154-56, 160, 162; & UN Observers, deployment, 161, 164; violence, 156-64 (GA, 162, **162-64**; Goldstone Cs., 157, 158, 160, **163**; SC, 158, **158-59**, 159, **160-61**; SG, 159-60, 161-62)
    general aspects, 151-54 (Apartheid Ct., 152-53; GA, **153-54**; SG, 154) & homelands, 159; reincorporation, 155, 156, 779 (group of experts); see also Bophuthatswana; Ciskei; KwaZulu
    information dissemination, DPI action, 126, **127** (SG/GA)
    labour/employment under, 28th spec. report, 1093 (ILO)
    political prisoners/exiles, 162, 165 (SG); 1991 Pretoria Minute, 165
    refugee repatriation, & UNHCR Memorandum of Understanding, 779 (SG)
    social/economic consequences, 166-67 (Apartheid Ct.); & future UN role, Windhoek Seminar, 152, **153** (Apartheid Ct./UN Centre/GA)
    in sports, Olympics participation, 167, **167-68**, 168 (Cs./GA)
    women & children under, 165, **165-66** (SG/ESC), 883 (ESC)
    see also racial discrimination/racism; South Africa; southern Africa

Apartheid, 1973 International Convention on the Suppression and Punishment of the Crime of, 779, **779-80** (SG/GA)

Apartheid, Spec. Ct. against, 153-54; spec. projects, **154** (GA); members/officers, 1206; Subcts. on Developments in/Implementation of UN resolutions on South Africa, 1206 (members/chairmen)

Apartheid, UN Centre against, 152

Apartheid and its Destructive Consequences in Southern Africa: 1989 Declaration, 152, 153, **153**, 154, **164**

(Apartheid Ct./GA/SG), 780, **781** (Human Rights Cs./ESC)

Apartheid in Sports, Cs. against, 167; members/officers, 1222

Apartheid in Sports, International Convention against (1985): signatories/accessions, 167

aquaculture (fish farming), 473 (ECA), 1107 (FAO); see also fisheries

Arab Gulf Programme for UN Development Organizations (AGFUND): & status of women, 698 (UNFPA)

Arab-Israeli conflict, see Lebanon; Middle East situation; Palestine question

Arab Maghreb Union (Algeria, Libyan Arab Jamahiriya, Mauritania, Morocco, Tunisia): 1989 Treaty, 49; industrial cooperation, 1175 (UNIDO)

Arab States, 1147 (ICAO); Regional Bureau for (UNDP), 1225; technical cooperation, 561 (UNDP); telecommunications, 1154 (ITU); UNFPA programmes, 699; see also ESCWA; Middle East; western Asia and country names

Arab States, League of: cooperation with UN, 142, **142-44**; & Libya aerial incident, 52; participation in SC, 53; & Iran-United Arab Emirates, 275

Arbitrary Detention, Working Group on, 863

arbitrary executions, see detained persons: extra-legal executions

Argentina, 1131 (IFC); World Bank loans, 1124; see also Falkland Islands (Malvinas)

arid/semi-arid lands, see desertification; drought control; regional and country names

Armenia, admission to: ICAO, 1145, IMF, 1140, ITU, 1152, UN, **134** (SC/GA), UNESCO, 1115, UNIDO, 1172, UPU, 1149, WHO, 1117, World Bank, 1123; contribution to UNIFIL, **415**, to UNDOF, **419**; see also Nagorno-Karabakh

arms race: in outer space, prevention of 97-98, **98-100** (CD/GA), **121**, (GA); ballistic missiles, bilateral negotiations on ban, 98; see also disarmament; nuclear disarmament

Arms Race in Outer Space, Ad Hoc Ct. on the Prevention of, 97, **99** (CD/GA)

arts: conventions, 1165 (WIPO); performers, working conditions, 1099 (ILO)

Asia, 1100 (ILO), 1130 (IFC); 1170 (IFAD); & children, 883-84 (UNICEF); disarmament issues 72-74; drug abuse/traffic, 923-24 (HONLEA); economic trends, 540 (World Survey/Trade and Development Report); food aid (WFP); humanitarian/economic assistance, 597-600; media development, 124 (IPDC); & Palestine question, symposium, 400; scientific reporting in, 665; see also East Asia; South Asia; South-East Asia; western Asia

Asia and the Pacific, 560-61 (UNDP), 477-93 (ESCAP), 650 (TNCs-ESCAP Joint Unit); & AIDS, 481, 560 (UNDP); civil aviation, 1147 (ICAO); consumer protection, 485; desertification control, 686; disabled persons, 478, 490; & drugs, 481, 923-24 (HONLEA); economic trends, 479-81; energy, 488; environment, 491-92; human resources, 489-

90; human rights depositary library, 776; human settlements, 491; industrial development, 486-87; information network, 482; international trade/finance, 484-85; LDCs in, 483; marine affairs, 487; media training, 124 (IPDC); natural disasters, 492; natural resources, 487-88; population, 478, 490-91, 699; regional cooperation: Beijing Declaration, 477, Ct. for, 482; remote sensing, 488-89; rural development, 488; science/technology, 488; social development, 489; social trends, 481-82; space communication, 113; statistics, 492; technical cooperation, 484; telecommunications, 1153-54; tourism, 486; & TNCs, 485 (TNCs/ESCAP Joint Unit); transport/communications, 485-86; women, 491; see also country names, regional and subject entries

Asia and the Pacific, Desertification Control Research and Training Network for, 686

Asia and the Pacific, Economic and Social Cs. for (ESCAP), 477-79; Executive Secretary, 1224; 48th sess., 477; 49th sess., venue, 493; members/associates, 484, 492-93 (ESC), 1216; restructuring, 478, 479 (GA/ESC); subsidiary/related bodies, reorganization, 478; technical cooperation, 484

Asia and the Pacific, FAO Cf. for, 1104

Asia and the Pacific, Inter-agency Ct. on Environment and Development in, 492 (ESCAP)

Asia and the Pacific, Mtg. of Ministers of Industry and Technology: Regional Strategy and Action Plan, 486; Tehran Declaration on Strengthening Regional Cooperation, 486, 487; & Seoul Action Plan (1992-2001), 486

Asia and the Pacific, Ministerial Cf. on Environment and Development (1990), 491-92

Asia and the Pacific, Statistical Institute for, 492

Asia and the Pacific, Transport and Communications Decade for (1985-1994): implementation/mid-term review, 486 (SG/ESC); & ESCWA, 486 (SG); phase II (1992-1996), 486 (SG)

Asia and the Pacific, UN Regional Centre for Peace and Disarmament in, 105 (SG/GA)

Asia and the Pacific Region, Mtg. of Heads of National Drug Law Enforcement Agencies (HONLEA): 17th mtg., **909**, 924

Asia-Pacific, 1994 International Trade Fair, 478, 485

Asia Pacific Broadcasting Union, 1153

Asian-African Legal Consultative Ct.: cooperation with UN, 1011-12, **1012**

Asian and Pacific Centre for Transfer of Technology (ESCAP), 488

Asian and Pacific Decade of Disabled Persons (1993-2002): proclamation, 478, 490 (ESC), 822, **823** (inter-agency mtg./GA)

Asian and Pacific Development Centre: projects/funding, 487

Asian and Pacific Ministerial Cf. on Social Welfare and Social Development, 4th (1991): Strategy implementation, 489 (expert group mtgs./Inter-Agency Task Force); 1996 Cf. on, preparations, 489

Asian and Pacific Ministerial Cf. on Women and Development (1994): preparations, 491

Asian and Pacific Population Cf., 4th: Bali Declaration, 478, 490-91, 694; Preparatory Ct., 3rd sess., 491

Asian Development Bank, 485

Asian International Silk Fair, 485

Asian Offshore Areas, Ct. for Coordination of Joint Prospecting for Mineral Resources in, 487

Association of South-East Asian Nations, see South-East Asian Nations, Association of (ASEAN)

Astronautical Federation, International: communications symposium with COSPAR, 110, **120** (COPUOS/GA); & ISY, 110; & space applications, 116

astronomy, 110, **120** (COPUOS/GA)

Atlantic Ocean, see South Atlantic

atmosphere, 1158 (WMO); research/environment, 1158; see also air pollution; climate; nuclear weapon tests in; ozone layer; weather

Atmospheric Research and Environment Programme (WMO): components/activities, 1158

Atmospheric Processes, Joint Scientific and Technical Ct. Task Group on: mtg., 1156

Atmospheric Sciences, WMO Cs. for, 1158

atomic energy, see nuclear energy

Atomic Radiation, UN Scientific Ct. on the Effects of, see Radiation, UN Scientific Ct. on the Effects of Atomic (UNSCEAR)

auditing, see accounts/auditing (UN)

Auditors, Board of: members, 1202

Auditors, Panel of External, 1052; members, 1205

Australia: economic trends, 480, 481; renewal, UNIDO membership, 1172; see also East Timor; Nauru

Austria: microwave technology, 112; postal agreement with UN, 1089; UNDOF observer, 416; & UNFICYP, status of troops for, 270, 271

aviation, see air transport; civil aviation

Azania, Pan-Africanist Congress of, see Pan-Africanist Congress of Azania

Azerbaijan, admission to: ESCAP, 484, ICAO, 1145, ILO, 1099, IMF, 1140, ITU, 1152, UN, **136** (SC/GA), UNESCO, 1111, WHO, 1116, World Bank, 1123; contribution to UNIFIL, **415**, to UNDOF **419**; see also Nagorno-Karabakh

Bacteriological (Biological) and Toxin Weapons, 1971 Convention on the Prohibition of the Development, Production and Stockpiling of, and on Their Destruction: parties to, 63; 3rd Review Cf./Final Document (1991), 78; & verification, Ad Hoc Group of Governmental Experts on, 78

Bahrain: see Qatar, disputes with

Baltic States, withdrawal of foreign forces, 387, **387-88** (CSCE/GA); see also country names

Baltic Sea Area, Convention on the Protection of the Marine Environment of the, 998

Bangladesh: development non-project credits, 1136 (IDA); drug traffic/control, 924; economic trends, 480 (1992 Survey); human development, 560 (UNDP); refugees in, 902 (UNHCR)

"bantustanization," see under South Africa, situation in: homelands

Belarus, admission to: IMF, 1140, World Bank, 1123

Benin: spec. economic assistance to, 577, **578** (UNDP/Round-table Ct./GA)

Bermuda, 964, **967** (Colonial Countries Ct./GA); information to UN, 960

Berne Convention, see Literary and Artistic Works, Berne Convention for the Protection of

Berne Union, 1166

Bhutan: economic trends, 480; refugee repatriation, 902; UNDP project, 560

biological diversity, 673 (Agenda 21), 1112 (UNESCO)

Biological Diversity, Convention on, **675**, 683-84 (GA/Negotiating Ct.); Intergovernmental Negotiating Ct., 684; signatures/ratifications, 683; & LOS Convention, 998

bioethical studies/forum, 1112 (UNESCO)

biological weapons, see bacteriological weapons; chemical weapons

biotechnology, 488 (ESCAP), 499 (ECE), 1174 (UNIDO); see also genetic engineering

birth control, see contraceptives; family planning

Black Sea: pollution protection, 1992 Convention (protocols/resolutions), 998

Bolivia: gold exploration, 654 (UNRFNRE); transportation credit, 1137 (IDA)

Bophuthatswana: & South Africa, 156, 159

Bosnia and Herzegovina, admission to: ITU, 1152, UN, **137** (SC/GA), UNIDO, 1172, WHO, 1116; contribution to UNIFIL, **415**, to UNDOF, **419**

Bosnia and Herzegovina, political/military developments, 344-81
    armed forces in, withdrawal status, 354-56 (SG)
    cease-fire agreement, 347, 348 (SC/SG), 349 (SG), 358; London agreement, 362-63, 363, **364** (SC/SG)
    constitutional arrangements, 345, 348, 348-49, **350** (SG/SC/International Cf.), 358 (SG), **362**; draft constitution, 374, **375** (SG/SC); resumption of talks, 363; Geneva talks, 381
    human rights violations: ethnic cleansing/prisoners, 348 (SG), 364 (SC), 365, **365** (UNPROFOR/SC), 364-69 (GA, **366-68**, 368-69); Human Rights Cs./ESC, 366; SC, 364-65, **365**), 370, **370-71**, 378 (SC); Cs. of Experts, establishment, **371**, 371, **376** (SC/SG); Spec. Rapporteur, appointment/reports, 366, 371 (Human

Rights Cs./SG), 374; of women, rape/detention, EC delegation, **378**, 378 (SC)
    humanitarian aid, 347, 349, **350-51** (SG/SC), 369-70, **370** (SG/SC); basic principles, Geneva mtg./agreement, 351, **354**; delivery of supplies/airport security, **351**, 356-57, **357** (SG/SC), 358, 359, **359-60**, 360-61 (SG/SC); ban on military flights/monitoring, **371-72**, 372 (Working Group/SC); 372-73, **373-74**, 374 (UNPROFOR/SG/SC); coordination, **365**; UNPROFOR-Sarajevo agreement, 153, 361, **362**; imposition of sanctions, 351-52, **352-54** (SG/SC), 356, **359**, **376** (SG/SC), 381-83 (Security Cl. Ct.)
    peace-keeping operation, feasibility, 346-47, 348-50, **350-51** (SG/SC); Goulding mission, 348-49; UNPROFOR Military Observers, 347, 349, 350 (SG); Sarajevo Sector: activities, update, 376-77, 377-78 (SG/SC); attacks on/casualties, 162, **369** (SC); Mixed Military Cs., **375**, 377 (SC/SG)
    see also Yugoslavia situation

Brazil, 1131 (IFC): & street children, 886; & remote sensing, 112; UNIFEM cf. on violence, 872; World Bank loans, 1123, 1125

breast-feeding: & artificial feeding products, 885 (UNICEF/WHO); promotion of, 1118 (WHO/UNICEF); see also under children

Breast Milk Substitutes, International Code of Marketing of, 1118 (WHO)

British Virgin Islands, 964, **967-68** (Colonial Countries Ct./GA); information to UN, 959

budget (UN), (1990-1991) 1038
    appropriations, final, 1038 (ACABQ/SG/GA)
    unliquidated balances, 1038 (SG/GA)

budget (UN), (1992-1993) 1030-37
    appropriations, revised, 1030, **1030-32**; financing for, 1028, **1028** (GA)
    first performance report on, **1032** (GA)
    contingency fund, 1035, 1037-38 (ACABQ/GA)
    income sources, estimates, 1033, **1033** (GA)
    questions related to, 1033-38
    see also contributions (UN); financial situation (UN); programmes (UN)

budget (UN), (1994-1995) proposed: outline, 1038-39, **1039** (SG/ACABQ/GA)

Buenos Aires Plan of Action for Promoting and Implementing TCDC, see under Technical Cooperation among Developing Countries (TCDC)

building materials, see construction/building materials

Bulgaria, admission to IFC, 1129

Burkina Faso: mining, 655 (DESD), 472 (ECA); technical assistance credit, 1137 (IDA); transportation credit, 1137 (IDA); UNDP project, 560

Burundi: water supply credit, 1137 (IDA)

Cambodia: admission to IFAD, 1169; & human rights in, 731, 787 (Cs./SCPDPM/ SG/UNTAC symposium); natural resources, export moratorium, 259 (SC); rejoins Mekong Basin Coordination Ct., 487

Cambodia, Ministerial Cf. on the Reconstruction and Rehabilitation of, 560 (UNDP), 256, 259 (SC); Declarations on Peace Process, 253, 253 (SC), on guidelines for assistance, 253 (SC); participants, 252; pledges, 252

Cambodia, 1991 International Cf. on, 240

Cambodia, UN Advance Mission in (UNAMIC): financing, 242, 242-43 (SG/ACABQ/GA); 248-49, 249-50 (SG/ACABQ/GA); liaison officers, 1213; mine-clearance programme, 241, 241-42 (SG/SC); troop strength/appointment, Spec. Representative, 242 (SG/SC)

Cambodia, UN Transitional Authority in (UNTAC), 250-62; establishment/ deployment, 241; implementation plan, 243-47, 246, 247 (SG/SC); Commander/Deputy, 246-47 (SG/SC), 1213, 1226; components, 244-45, 731 (human rights); financing, 247, 247-48, 248-49, 249-50, 259-60, 260-61 (SG/ACABQ/GA); operations, 250-59 (SC, 251-52, 253, 255-56, 258-59, 259; SG, 250-51, 252-53, 256-58); SG Spec. Representative/Deputy, 1226; & SNC, 243, 250; structure/personnel, 245-46 (SG/survey missions); safety of, 256, 257, 259, 261-62, 262 (SC/SG); troop contributing nations, 247 (list)

Cambodia Peace Process, Declaration on the, 253, 253 (SC)

Cambodia situation, 19-20 (SG), 241-62
cease-fire developments/implementation, 250-51, 251-53, 253, 256 (SG/SC)
civil administration, arrangements for, 244-45, 251, 253, 254 (SC/SG)
elections, constitutional assembly, 244, 246, 250 (UNTAC/SC/SG), 254, 255, 258 (SG/SC), & head of State, 254, 257 (SG); & voter registration, 255, 257
& human rights, 244, 254 (SG), 260, 787
military deployment, 244, 252 (SG); border checkpoints (Laos, Thailand, Viet Nam), 250, 251, 254, 255, 257 (SG/SC); mine-clearing operations, 241, 241-42 (UNAMIC/SC), 251, 254
Paris Agreements (1991), implementation, 241, 243, 245, 251, 256 (SG/SC); tripartite consultations, 256-57
reconstruction/rehabilitation, 245, 250, 251, 253, 255 (SG/SC/ UNICEF); Coordinator for, 245 (SG); SG appeal, 251; & SNC Technical Advisory Ct., 255; Tokyo Cf. on, 252, 255, 259 (SG/SC)
refugees/displaced persons, 243, 903; SG Consolidated Appeal, 903; & UNHCR, 245, 250; WFP aid, 827

Supreme National Cl. (SNC): accession to human rights conventions, 250; chairman/members, 241, 243; mtgs., 258; sole legal authority, 243, 252; Technical Advisory Ct. established, 250

Canada: drug abuse/control, 924; troop contributions, UNFICYP, 270, 271; UNDOF observer, 416; & UNIDO withdrawal, 1172

cancer, 1120 (WHO)

cannabis, 923, 924, 925

Capital Development Fund, UN, see Development Fund, UN Capital

carbon dioxide emissions: & energy use, 659-61 (SG); & nuclear power, 660

cardiovascular diseases, 1120 (WHO)

Carribean Community (CARICOM): & human settlements, 707 (UNCHS)

Carribean Community, 13th Mtg. of the Cf. of Heads of Government of the, 147

Caribbean Cl. for Science and Technology, 512

Caribbean Development and Cooperation Ct. (CDCC), 512-13

Caribbean region: & non-independent countries in, 513; & North American Free Trade Agreement, 512; political questions, 232-38; tourism, 512; UNICEF programmes, 883; see also Eastern Caribbean States, Organization of; ECLAC; and country names and organizational entries

Cartagena Commitment, see Trade and Development, UN Cf. on (8th sess.)

cartography, 661-62 (DESD/US); see also country names

Cayman Islands, 964, 968 (Colonial Countries Ct./GA); information to UN, 960

Central Africa: confidence-building/arms limitation, 72, 72-73 (SG/GA); Standing Advisory Ct. on Security Questions in, establishment, 72; Mineral Resources Development Centre, 472 (ECA); Ministerial mtg., 72

Central African Republic: spec. economic assistance, 577, 578 (UNDP/GA); water supply project, 656

Central African States: & arms limitation, 72, 72 (SG/GA); Economic Community of, 72; Standing Advisory Ct. established/mtg. 72, 72

Central America: food/agriculture, 511, 513; peace/security issues, 218-32; refugee repatriation, 900, 901; & TCDC, 512; & trade with Mexico, 511; & WIPO Paris Convention, 1163; see also Americas; Caribbean region; country names; subject entries

Central America, Action Ct. for the Economic and Social Development of, 514

Central America, UN Observer Group in (ONUCA), 218, 221; Chief Observer, 1213; financing, 221 (SG); transfer, equipment/personnel to ONUSAL, 221 (SG); termination, 221, 221 (SG/SC), 1213

Central America situation, 218-32
economic cooperation/assistance, 218, 219, 220 (Managua Agenda/GA); & EEC/Group of 24, 218, 220; & Panama, 220 (GA)

declared region of peace/freedom, Managua summit: Managua Agenda, 218, 218-21 (SC); National Reconciliation Ceremony, 220 (GA)
Esquipulas II Agreement (1987), implementation, 219
Security Cs., 1990 Agreement: mandate renewed, 218, 220 (Managua Agenda/GA)
see also country names

Central America, Partnership for Democracy and Development in (Group of 24), 220

Central America, 1988 Special Plan of Economic Cooperation for/Action Plan, 220

Central American Integration System: implementation of Tegucigalpa Protocol, Preparatory Cs. established, 218, 219 (Managua Agenda/GA)

Central American Peace Process, Personal Representative of the Secretary-General for the, 222

Central American Refugees, 1989 International Cf. on: Concerted Plan of Action, implementation, 901, 901 (SG/GA); Follow-up Ct., 2nd International Mtg.: Declaration, 901, 901-902 (SG/GA); interagency arrangements, 901 (UNDP/ UNHCR/GA); quick impact projects, 901

Central American Women, First Regional Forum on the Gender Approach to Work with Refugee, Returnee and Displaced, 901 (SG)

Central Europe, see Europe, Central/Eastern

cereals, see grains

Chad: dispute with Libya, 981 (ICJ); spec. economic assistance, 579, 579 (SG/UNHCR/FAO/WFP/GA); see also Lake Chad basin

Charter of the UN, 1187-96 (text)

Charter of the UN, Spec. Ct. on the, and on the Strengthening of the Role of the Organization, 1005, 1005-1006 (SG/GA); members/officers, 1206

Chemical Action Task Force, 921 (Group of 7)

Chemical Control Operations, 1991 Cf. on: recommendations, 921

chemical industry, 497 (ECE); Directory, producers/products, 497; technical cooperation, 1173 (UNIDO); see also fertilizer industry; pesticides; petrochemical industry; pharmaceutical industry

Chemical Industry, Working Party on the (ECE): 2nd sess., 497

chemical weapons: alleged use, missions, 65 (SG); bilateral consultations/agreements, 64-65 (Russian Federation/US); convention banning, 35, 65 (SC summit), 65-66; export controls/equipment, 64; regional seminar, 65; see also bacteriological (biological) weapons

Chemical Weapons, Ad Hoc Ct. on, 64

Chemical Weapons, Convention on the Prohibition of the Development, Production, Stockpiling and Use of, and on Their Destruction, 64, 65-66, 66 (Preparatory Ct./GA); annexes on Chemicals, on Verification, on Confidentiality, 224-25; signature, 224, 225 (GA)

Chemical Weapons, Organization for the Prohibition of (The Hague): establishment/composition, 65; Preparatory Cs. for, 65, 66 chemicals: illicit diversion of, 921, **921-22** (Cs./ESC); see also pesticides; toxic substances

Chernobyl nuclear accident: aftermath, 608-609, **610** (SG/ESC/GA); UNICEF aid, 609; radiation, UN/FAO Cooperation Project, 1094; report update, 1093 (IAEA)

Chicago Convention, see Civil Aviation, 1944 International Convention on

Child, Ct. on the Rights of the (CRC), 812; lst sess./2nd sess., 812, **813**, 881 (ESC); members/officers, 1223

Child, 1989 Convention on Rights of the: implementation, 812-14 (CRC, 812; Cs., 812-13; ESC, **813**; GA, **813-14**), 881; States parties, 2nd mtg., 881; status, 881 (GA)

Child Abuse and Neglect, International Society for Prevention of, 886

Child Labour, International Programme on the Elimination of, 1101 (ILO)

children, 880-87; abuse/neglect, 886; & AIDS, 810, 811 (UNICEF/WHO); breast-feeding, 885; diarrhoeal diseases/ cholera, 884-85; & drugs, **914**; education, 886; hunger/malnutrition, deaths from, 885; immunization, 884; labour exploitation, draft action programme, 815 (SG/Cs.); prostitution/exploitation/sale, 747, 814-15; respiratory infections, 885, 886 (UNICEF); soldiers, 815 (SG); street children, **881-82** (GA), 925 (drug abuse); see also apartheid; primary health care; and regional and country entries

Children, Child Prostitution and Child Pornography, Programme of Action for the Prevention of the Sale of, 814-15 (Human Rights Cs.)

Children, 1990 World Summit on: Declaration on Protection, Survival and Development/Action Plan: follow-up, 881 (SG/ESC/GA), 908 (UNICEF/WHO Ct.)

Children's Day, observance, 881 (UNICEF Board)

Children's Fund, UN (UNICEF), 880-87 administration/management structure, review deferred, 887
budget appropriations, 886-87
Executive Director, 1220, 1225; Deputy, 1225
Greeting Card Operation, 887
income/expenditures, 886
Joint Ct. with UNESCO, 886
Maurice Pate Memorial Award (1992), 882
programme policy, 880-81; medium-term plan (1992-1995), 880-81
programmes, by region, 882-84; by sector, 884-86

Children's Fund, UN: Executive Board, 880, 1219-20; Administration & Finance Ct., 880; members/officers, 880, 1220; Programme Ct., 880

Children's Vaccine Initiative (WHO/ UNICEF/UNDP/World Bank), 884; funding, 883

Chile: education, 1123; health/technical assistance, 1124 (World Bank)

China: coal utilization/hydropower, 658 (DESD); & drug traffic, 923; economic trends, 525 (CDP), 479 (1992 Survey); energy/industry, 1123 (World Bank); IDA

credits, 1135, 1136, 1137; mineral exploration, 654 (UNRFNRE); & peacekeeping operation, 413 (UNIFIL), 418 (UNDOF); refugees in, 902; & space applications, 112; trade, 481; transportation, 1125 (World Bank); see also Tibet

cholera epidemic, 818-19 (UNICEF/WHO); 1108 (FAO), 1119

chlorofluorocarbons, see ozone layer

Ciskei, 156; & ANC marchers (Bisho), 158

civil and political rights, 726-52; state of siege/emergency, 726-27 (Human Rights Cs./ESC/Spec. Rapporteur); see also under human rights and relevant subject entries

Civil and Political Rights, 1966 International Covenant/Optional Protocols: accessions/ratifications, 726 (SG/Human Rights Cs./ESC); implementation, 726 (Human Rights Ct./ESC); 2nd Optional Protocol (1989) on death penalty, 726; see also Human Rights, International Covenants on

civil aviation, 1145-47; accident investigations, 1145 (ICAO); air navigation, conventions/protocols, status, 1146 (list); navigation, 1145; Plastic Explosives, Convention on Marking, 1145, 1146; Purchasing Service, status, 1147; Statistics Panel, 1146; technical cooperation, 1146-47 (ICAO/UNDP); trade in, 1179 (GATT); transport, 1146; world traffic/air freight, 1145

Civil Aviation, 1971 Convention for the Suppression of Unlawful Acts against the Safety of: ratifications, 1146 (list)

Civil Aviation, 1944 International Convention on (Chicago Convention), 1145

Civilian Persons in Time of War, Convention on Protection of (4th Geneva Convention), see under Geneva Conventions

climate: applications, 1157; computing systems, 1157; & greenhouse effect, remote sensing, 116, 1158; research, 1158 (ICSU/WMO); see also air pollution

Climate Change, Intergovernmental Negotiating Ct. for a Framework Convention on, **675** (GA), 681-82, **682-83** (GA); members/officers, 1204

Climate Change, Framework Convention on (opened for signature), 681-82, **682-83**, 683 (Negotiating Ct./SG/GA); parties to, lst sess., preparations, 682, **683**; signatures/ratifications, 681; voluntary funds, 682; & LOS Convention, 998 (SG)

Climate Observing System, Global, 1156

Climate Programme, World, 1156-57; publications, 1157

coal, 499 (ECE); & air emissions, 660 (SG); clean technologies, mtgs., 668 (DESD); consumption, 657 (SG); degasification techniques, 659 (DESD); feasibility study, 659 (DESD); utilization expansion/improvement, 658 (DESD)

coarse roots/tubers, production, 1105

cocaine abuse/traffic, 924; "crack", 924; see also under regional entries

Cocoa Agreement, International (1986): 1992 UN Cf. on, 625

Colombia, 1131 (IFC); development finance, 1123; transportation, 1125 (World Bank); radio centre, 124 (IPDC)

colonial countries, 945-72

& foreign interests in, 953, **953-55** (Colonial Countries Ct./GA)
information dissemination, 956-57, **957-58** (Colonial Countries Ct./GA)
military activities in, 955, **955-56** (Colonial Countries Ct./GA)
see also Trusteeship System, International; Non-Self-Governing Territories; self-determination of peoples; and names of territories

Colonial Countries and Peoples, 1960 Declaration on the Granting of Independence to: implementation, **946-47** (Colonial Countries Ct./GA); by international organizations, 947-48, 948, **948-49**, **950-52**, **952-53** (SG/ESC/GA)

Colonial Countries and Peoples, Spec. Ct. on the Situation with regard to the Implementation of the Declaration on the Granting of Independence to, 945-46; cooperation suspended (US), 946; members/officers, 1206; Subct. on Small Territories, Petitions, Information and Assistance (formerly Subcts. on Small Territories & on Petitions, Information, Assistance), 1206 (members/ officers)

Colonialism, International Decade for the Eradication of (1990-2000): Action Plan, seminar, 125, **127**, 945 (DPI/GA)

Committee . . . for specific ct., see key word(s) of title

commodities, 622-27 (World Survey/Trade and Development Report/UNCTAD VIII); coding system, 929; compensatory mechanisms, 624 (EEC/IMF); & diversification, 624 (UNCED/UNCTAD VIII); outlook/trends, 624, **626-27** (UNCTAD SG/GA); see also metals; minerals; and individual commodities

Commodities, Ct. on: suspended, 1208

Commodities, Common Fund for, 625; 1980 Agreement Establishing: signatures/ratification, 625 (UNCTAD VIII); withdrawal (Australia), 625

Commodities, Standing Ct. on (TDB): establishment/lst mtg., 624-25; members, 1208; subsidiary organs, 625

Commodity Description and Coding System, Harmonized, 929 (SG/GATT)

Commonwealth Group of Experts on the Impact of Global Economic and Political Change on the Development Process; see Development Process, Commonwealth Group of Experts on the Impact of Global Economic and Political Change

Commonwealth of Independent States: drug abuse in, 924; economic trends, 494-95, 540; energy/environment, 658 (DESD); telecommunications, 1153 (ITU); UN/UNDP offices, 126, **126** (ESC/SG/GA), 561-62; UNICEF projects, 884; US travel ban lifted, 1006; see also Central/Eastern Europe and country names

Communication, International Programme for the Development of (IPDC), 124, **125**, 1113 (UNESCO); Intergovernmental Cl., 13th sess./projects, 124, 1113-14 (UNESCO); see also mass communication; public information; and country and regional entries

communications satellites; see satellites and under regional entries

Comorian island of Mayotte, 188, **188-89** (SG/OAU/GA)

Comoros, 188

Compensation Cs., UN: & Iraq, 277; Executive Secretary, 1225

Conference Services, Office of: restructuring, 1053; USG, 1225

Conferences, Ct. on: mandate, 1077; members/officers, 1203; sess., 1077

conferences/meetings (UN), 1077-82
calendar of: (1992), 1077-78; (1993) (revised), 1078-79, **1079-80** (Ct. on Cfs./ESC/GA)
services, 1080, **1080-81** (SG/ACABQ/GA); language, **1081** (GA); electronic signalling, 1081 (SG/ACABQ/GA); staff workload standards, 1081-82 (SG/interagency mtg./GA)
see also geographic and subject entries and names of cfs.

Congo: mineral exploration, 654 (UNRFNRE)

conservation, animals/plants, ECE Code of Practice for, 501; Birds and Mammals, Indicative Lists of, 501

construction/building materials: energy efficiency in, 706 (UNCHS); ILO Ct. on, 1187

Consular Relations, 1963 Vienna Convention/Optional Protocols: States parties, 993; additional protocol on functions, 994, **994** (SG/GA)

consumer protection, 1985 guidelines: implementation, 485 (ESCAP), 629 (SG/DESD/ESC)

continental shelf, 997

Contraceptive Requirements and Logistics Management Needs, Global Initiative on (UNFPA), 697

contraceptives, 697 (UNFPA), 1118 (WHO)

Contract Practices, International Working Group on (UNCITRAL), 1047

Contract Practices in Industry, ECE International Working Party on, 497

contributions (UN): scale of assessments, 1039-40, **1041**, 1041 (Contributions Ct./GA); & new members, 1040; 1992 contributions, 1041 (SG)

Contributions, Ct. on, 1040

conventional weapons, see under disarmament

Conventional Weapons Which May Be Deemed to Be Excessively Injurious or to Have Indiscriminate Effects, 1981 Convention on Prohibitions or Restrictions on the Use of Certain/Protocols: status, 63

conventions, see multilateral treaties; treaties; and under subject entries

cooperatives, 839-41; International Day for (1995), proclaimed, **841** (GA); Ct. for promotion/advancement, **840, 841**

Coordination, Administrative Ct. on (ACC), 6-7 (SG), 941; bodies on specific subjects, 941; Joint Mtgs. with CPC, 942 (GA); members, 1219; overview report (1991), 941 (CPC); subsidiary bodies, 941, 1219

Coordination, Ct. for Programme and (CPC), 942 (ESC/GA); Joint Mtgs. with ACC, 1037 (SG/ACABQ/GA); travel expenses, 1037; members/officers, 1217; 32nd sess., 942

coordination in UN system, 941-42 (ACC/CPC); see also Economic and Social Cl.; Joint Inspection Unit (JIU); programmes (UN)

Copper Study Group, International, 626

copyright/neighbouring rights, 1165 (WIPO); see also industrial property; intellectual property

Costa Rica: space science workshop, 113; see also Central America situation

Côte d'Ivoire: development finance, 1123, 1136 (World Bank/IDA); education loan, 1124 (World Bank); marine resources development, 1002 (Ocean Affairs Division); privatization credit, 1137 (IDA)

"crack", see cocaine

Crime, 1991 International Seminar on Organized: practical measures, 852-59

Crime, 1991 Ad Hoc Expert Group Mtg. on Strategies to Deal with Transnational, 849-52

Crime and Justice Research Institute, UN Interregional, 862, 912

Crime and the Treatment of Offenders, 9th UN Congress on the Prevention of (1995): preparations, 861, **861-62** (SG/ESC)

Crime Prevention and Control, Ct. on: dissolution, **1211** (ESC), 1218; overview report, 860 (SG); see also Crime Prevention and Criminal Justice, Cs. on

crime prevention and criminal justice, 841-62; domestic violence, expert mtg., 860; drug control, 912 (expert group mtgs.); institutes for, 860; international cooperation, 842. **842-47, 847-48**; money laundering, 848 (SG), 910, 911-12 (Narcotics Cs./UNDCP); organized crime, 848-49, **849-59, 859** (SG/ESC/ GA); UN programme, 860; see also prisoners/detainees; summary or arbitrary executions; terrorism; torture

Crime Prevention and Criminal Justice, Cs. on (ESC), 841-42, 910 (Narcotics Cs.); agenda/documentation, 842 (ESC); establishment, **842** (ESC); lst sess./report, 1211 (ESC); members/officers, 1214

Crime Prevention and Criminal Justice, UN Programme, 860 (SG); Statement of Principles/Action Programme, 860

Crime Prevention and Criminal Justice Branch (CSDHA): & UNDCP, **915** (GA)

Crime Prevention and Criminal Justice Programme, 1991 Ministerial Mtg. on the Creation of an Effective UN: follow-up, 860 (SG); officers, 1053

Crimes against Internationally Protected Persons, including Diplomatic Agents, 1973 Convention on the Prevention and Punishment of: States parties, 993

Criminal Police Organization, International (Interpol), 909, 911

Croatia, political/military developments in, 327-44
air corridor, establishment, 335 (ICAO/SG)
cease-fire implementation, Croatia-JNA accord, 329 (SG); on-site assessment, 330 (USG/SG); violations, 329, **329-30**, 330; military liaison group, 329, **329** (SG/SC), 330-31, **331** (SG/SC)
international assistance, 591-92, **592** (GA)

& Peruca Dam, UNPROFOR inspection/control, 342, **343** (SC/SG)

pink zones, monitoring, 328 (UNPROFOR/ECMM), 336 (SG), 337-39, **339** (SG/SC), 343 (SG); Joint Cs. establishment, 338, **339** (SG/SC), 340 (SG), 342 (SG), **343** (SC/SG)

Prevlaka Peninsula, withdrawal of JNA forces, 328, 343, **343** (SG/SC); & UNPROFOR military presence, 340 (SG)

refugees/displaced persons, 332, 343 (SG/UNHCR/UNPROFOR), 344 (SG)

UN Protected Areas (UNPAs): demilitarization, 328, 332, 335 (UNPROFOR/SG), **339**, 339, 340, 342, **343** (SC/SG); entry of civilians/immigration/customs functions, 340, 341-42 (SG/ UNPROFOR); division into sectors, 332; humanitarian aid requests, 340 (SG); incidents in, 341 (SG); USG mission, 133 (SG), 344 (SG)
see also Yugoslavia situation

Croatia, admission to: ICAO, 1145, ILO, 1099, ITU, 1152, UN, **136, 137** (SC/GA), 326, UNESCO, 1111, UNIDO, 1172, UPU, 1149, World Bank, 1123, WHO, 1116, WIPO, 1165, WMO, 1156; contribution to UNIFIL, **415**, to UNDOF, **419**

crops: breeding/genetic resources, 1095 (IAEA); FAO directory on, 1106; integrated pest management, 1106-1107 (FAO); see also names of individual crops

Cuba: human rights situation, 801, **802**, **802-803**, 803 (Spec. Rapporteur/Cs./ ESC/GA); & US: alleged terrorist activities, 232-33, 233 (SC); & embargo against, 234, **234-35** (communications/GA)

Cultural and Scientific Cooperation, International Congress, 1113

Cultural Development, World Decade for (1988-1997), 1113 (UNESCO)

cultural property: protection/restoration, 1113 (UNESCO); in armed conflict, 1954 Hague convention, 1113; conventions, 1113; & copyright, 1113; World Heritage list, sites, 1113; list of endangered sites, 1113; see also under world heritage

Cultural Property, 1970 Convention on the Means of Prohibiting and Preventing the Illicit Import, Export and Transfer of Ownership of: implementation, 1113

Culture and Development, World Cs. on, establishment, 1113

Customs Cooperation Council: & drug law enforcement, 909, 910, 911, **922** (Narcotics Cs./ESC)

cyclones, see tropical cyclones; typhoons

Cyprus, Ct. on Missing Persons in, 794

Cyprus, UN Peace-keeping Force in (UNFICYP), 270-72; command/change of, 270, 1213, 1226; financing/Spec. Account deficit, 271, 272, **272** (SC/SG/GA), 1025, **1025-27** (SG/GA); humanitarian assistance, 270; mandate extended, 270, **270-71** (SG/SC), 271, **271-72** (SG/SC); military personnel, reductions, 270, 271; observation posts,

status, 270, 271; restructuring, proposed, 270, **271**, **272** (SG/SC)
Cyprus question, 17 (SG), 265-72; framework agreement, proximity talks on set of ideas, 266-69 (SC, **266-67**, **267**, **268**; SG, 266, 267, 267-68; SG good offices mission, 276); confidence-building measures, 268-69 (SG/SC); de-militarization proposal, 266 (communications); demographic structure, 266 (communication); human rights situation, 266, 794-95 (SG/Cs.); SG good offices mission, 266, **271** (SC); SG Spec. Envoy, 1226; SG Spec. Representative in, 266, 1213, 1226
Czechoslovakia: dissolution, 138; see also Danube River; data processing, electronic; and under regional and subject entries

Dangerous Goods, Ct. of Experts on the Transport of, see Transport of Dangerous Goods, Ct. of Experts on
Danube River, projected diversion: Hungary-Czechoslovakia dispute, 979 (ICJ)
debt crisis, 635-38, **637-38** (World Survey/Trade and Development Report/UNCTAD VIII/UNCED/GA); information dissemination, **127** (DPI/GA); see also under developing countries; development finance; export earnings; and country names
decolonization, see colonial countries
Democratic Kampuchea, Party of, see Cambodia situation
Democratic People's Republic of Korea: economic trends, 479; technology assessment, 650; see also Korean situation
demographic trends, 1113 (UNESCO); see also population; and under regional entries
Denmark: & Iceland, 1146; troop contributions, UNFICYP, 270, 271; see also Faeroe Islands; Finland; Greenland
denuclearization, see disarmament; nuclear-free zones; regional entries
Desertification, Intergovernmental Negotiating Group, established, **687** (GA)
Desertification, 1977 Plan of Action to Combat: implementation, 685-86 (UNEP/Agenda 21/SG); see also under Sub-Saharan African Countries; Sudano-Sahelian region
desertification, 673 (Agenda 21), 685-88; (SG, 685-86; UNDP/UNEP, 686); convention on, proposed, **686-88** (GA); information/publications, 686 (UNEP); & space applications, 111; see also country names and regional entries
Desertification, Intergovernmental Negotiating Ct. for the Elaboration of an International Convention to Combat, 1204
detained persons: administration of justice, 734 (Human Rights Cs./SG); extra-legal executions, 740, **741** (Spec. Rapporteur/Cs./ESC/GA); juveniles, 738-39 (Spec. Rapporteur/SG/SCPDPM); without trial, 739 (Human Rights Cs./working group); see also death penalty; hostage-taking; prisoners/detainees; treatment of; torture and other cruel treatment

Detention, Working Group on (SCPDPM), 734
developing countries, 542-49; economic growth, 525-26, 540-41 (CDP); economic stabilization programmes, 540 (CDP); energy demand, 657; & globalization, UN symposium on, **653** (ESC); industrial cooperation, 534-35, **535** (SG/UNIDO/GA), 1175 (UNIDO); mass communication, 123-24 (SG/UNESCO/IPDC); remote sensing, 113 (COPUOS); & technological capacity, 664 (UNCTAD VIII); trade, 1179 (GATT); see also debt crisis; ECDC; least developed countries; TCDC
Developing Countries, Group of Experts on Island: mtg., 545, **546** (UNCTAD/GA)
developing countries, island: specific measures for, 545-46, **546-47** (SG/expert group/GA); & small islands, sustainable development, 546, 675 (UNCED/GA); global cf., proposed, 525, **547-49**, 673 (Agenda 21); see also under Pacific region
developing countries, land-locked, 483 (ESCAP)
Developing Countries, Standing Ct. on Developing Service Sectors: Fostering Competitive Service Sectors in: members/officers, 1208
Developing Island States, Global Cf. on Sustainable Development of Small, 525, **547-49** (GA); Preparatory Ct., establishment/chairman/sess., **548-49** (GA), 1205
development, 9-11, 23-24 (SG), 525-39
finance, 633-35; companies, 1123 (World Bank), 1136 (IDA)
planning, 540-41 (CDP/ESC)
private sector in: & entrepreneurship, 532 (1992 World Economic Survey/UNDP), 532-33 (DESD); privatization & economic restructuring, 533-34 (ESC, **533**; GA, **533-34**; UNCTAD Cartegena Commitment/Ad Hoc Working Group, 533); Spec. Programme Resources, allocation for, 532 (UNDP)
public administration, 541-42 (SG/ESC/expert mtg.)
science for sustainable, 665 (UNCED/Agenda 21)
see also cultural development; rural development; social development; women in development; and under disarmament; environment and regional entries
Development, Department for Policy Coordination and Sustainable: Executive Secretary, 1225
Development, Department of Technical Cooperation for, see Technical Cooperation for Development, Department of (DTCD)
Development, Division for the Private Sector in (UNDP), 532
development, operational activities, 14 (SG), 550-70
country/intercountry programmes (UNDP): mid-term reviews, 559; (UNDP Cl.); by region, 559-62; global/interregional, 562-63; new recipients, 565
financing of: contributions/UN Pledging Cf., 557; expenditures, 556

strengthening of, 550 (ESC)
triennial policy review, 550-52, **552-56** (SG/GA);
see also technical cooperation; TCDC; and country, organizational, and subject entries
development, right to, 753, **753-54** (SG/GA); 1986 Declaration, implementation, 753, **754** (Human Rights Cs./GA); 1990 Global Consultation, **753**
development and international economic cooperation, 13 (SG), 525-49
coordination, 525-26, 526 (CDP)
& economic growth, 530 (ESC/Commonwealth Experts)
& economies in transition, integration, 528-29, **529-30** (SG/GA); impact, **530** (GA)
financing, 624-25 (SG/expert mtg./ESC); companies for, 1123 (World Bank), 1136 (IDA); & environment, 634 (UNCTAD VIII); proposed cf. on, 634-35 (SG/GA)
global negotiations, deferred, 528 (GA)
1990 Declaration on, implementation, 530-31, **532** (SG/GA)
UN role: ESC high-level segment on, 526-28, **528** (SG/GA), 938 (ESC); Ad Hoc Open-Ended Working Group, establishment, 527-28, 938 & world economic trends, 526 (ESC/World Economic Survey); & research finding, 526
see also industrial development; poverty, eradication of; and under regional entries
development assistance, official (ODA), 543 (UNCTAD); growth prospects, 541 (CDP); see also debt crisis; UNDP; technical cooperation
Development Decade, 4th UN (1991-2000): International Development Strategy, 531, **531-32** (SG/ESC/GA); priority areas, 531
Development Forum, 127, **127** (DPI/JUNIC/GA)
Development Fund, UN Capital (UNCDF), 565, 574; Executive Board/Managing Director, 1207
Development Institute, Economic (World Bank), see Economic Development Institute
Development Objectives, Task Force on Long-Term (ACC): mtg., 536
Development Planning, Ct. for (CDP); members/officers, 1218; 28th sess., 540
Development Process, Commonwealth Group of Experts on the Impact of Global Economic and Political Change on the: ESC/Commonwealth exchange of views on, 1991 report, 530
Development Programme, UN (UNDP), 557-70
audit reports, 567 (ACABQ/Board of Auditors/Cl.)
budgets: revised (1992-1993), 566-67 (ACABQ/UNDP Cl.); budget (1994-1995), 567 (Cl./Administrator)
& cooperation with DTCD/DESD, 571
coordination in UN, 570 (Cl.)
financial situation: annual review, 566 (Administrator/Cl.)
financial regulations, 568

Governing Cl., 558, 1220; members, 1220; 39th/spec. sess., 558; Standing Ct. for Programme Matters, 558, 564 (field visits)
headquarters location, proposal, 570
management services, status, 567-68 (Administrator/Cl.)
net contributor status, 569
programme planning/management, 563; evaluation/field visits, 564; 4th cycle, (1987-1991), 564, 565; 5th cycle, (1992-1996), 564; national execution, 563-64
Spec. Representative, Jerusalem, 405
Spec. Programme Resources, 568 (Administrator/Cl.)
structure: Bureaux, administrators/directors, 1225
support costs, 568-69 (Administrator/Cl.)
staff matters: senior management structure, 569-70 (Administrator/Cl.)
trust funds under, 568

diabetes, 1121 (WHO)

diarrhoeal diseases, 884-85 (UNICEF), 1121 (WHO)

Dietary Energy Consultative Group, International, 830 (ACC)

diplomacy: & Agenda for Peace, 35-36 (SG); & fact-finding missions, 38 (SC/GA); resources for, 41; GA role in, 41 (GA)

diplomatic relations, 993-94; diplomatic bags/couriers, draft articles/protocols, 994 (ICJ/GA); protection of diplomats, 993, 993-94 (SG/GA); conventions/protocols, States parties, 993; see also consular relations, Vienna Convention; Crimes against Internationally Protected Persons, Convention on; host country relations (UN/United States); hostage-taking/abductions

Diplomatic Relations, 1961 Vienna Convention on/Optional Protocols: accessions/States parties, 993

direct broadcast satellites, see communication satellites

Disabilities, International Cf. of Ministers Responsible for the Status of Persons with, 822, **823** (GA)

Disability, International Congress and Exhibition on, 125

disabled persons, 475 (ECA), 490 (ESCAP), 521 (ESCWA), 821-24
1993 cf. on, **823** (GA)
coordination, **823-24** (GA); 10th inter-agency mtg., 822, **824**
employment in UN system, action plan, 822 (inter-agency mtg.)
equal opportunity for, draft rules, 822, **824** (working group/GA)
human rights of, 825-26 (Cs./ESC)
national coordinating cts., 821 (SG); Beijing guidelines, **823** (GA)
statistics, 930; CSDHA/Statistical Office, collection/update, **824** (GA)

Disabled Persons, International Day for, **822**, **824** (GA)

Disabled Persons, UN Decade of (1983-1992), World Action Programme

achievements/obstacles, 821 (SG)
long-term strategy beyond year 2000, 821-22, **822**, **823** (inter-agency mtg./GA/SG); expert mtg., 821
prevention of disabilities, activities, 821 (SG)
regional, 821 (SG); see also regional and subject entries
SG Spec. Representative, 1225
Voluntary Fund for, continuation as UN Voluntary Fund on Disability, 822-23, **824** (SG/GA)

disappearance, 741-42, **743** (Cs./Working Group/GA); declaration on the protection of all persons from enforced, 743-47

Disappearance, Declaration on the Protection of All Persons from Enforced, 743-44, **744-47**, (Working Group/Human Rights Cs./ESC/GA)

Disappearances, Working Group on Enforced or Involuntary, 742-43, **743** (GA); mandate extended, 742 (ESC)

disarmament, 59-110; 1st SC summit, 34-35, 62-63
agreements: multilateral, parties to, 63 (list); ratification/implementation, 34-35 (SC summit)
& confidence-building measures, **40** (GA); transparency: Conventional Arms Register, 75, **75-76** (CD/SG/GA); guidelines for, 77, **77** (SG/GA); information on military matters, 76, **76-77** (DC/GA)
conventional weapons: 1980 convention, 96-97; international transfers, 94 (SG/GA); SC summit, 35; & science/technology, 91-95, **95-96** (DC/SG), **96** (GA); & regional approach, 96 (SG/GA); Register of, 75
& development, 100, **100** (SG/GA); 1990 task force/international mtgs., 100
economic aspects: investment, 100-110 (UNIDIR/GA); military budgets, reductions, 101 (SG/GA)
& environment: Convention on Hostile Use, 1st Review Cf., 101; 2nd Review Cf., 101, **101-102** (Preparatory Ct./GA); States parties, 101; protection in armed conflict, 102 (GA); see also radioactive waste
fellowships/training/advisory services, UN programme, 109, **109** (SG/GA)
military budgets, reduction of, 101 (SG/GA)
Open Skies, Treaty on, 78; parties to, 63
publications, 63
regional approach to, 70-72 (DC/SG 70; GA, **70-71**, **71-72**); Centres for peace and, 105, **106** (SG/GA); see also Africa; Asia; Europe; South-East Asia
studies/research, 108, **108-109** (SG/GA); defensive security concepts, 108, **108** (group of experts/GA)
verification, 78, **78-79** (SG/expert group/GA)
weapons/systems of mass destruction, 35 (SC summit)

see also arms race; bacteriological (biological) weapons; chemical weapons; nuclear disarmament; nuclear-weapon-free zones; nuclear weapons; outer space: arms race; radiological weapons; zones of peace

Disarmament, Cf. on, 62, **62** (GA); mtgs./membership increase, proposed, 62; members/presidency, 1223

Disarmament and Development, International Cf. on Relationship between (1987): implementation, 100, **100** (SG/GA)

Disarmament Campaign, World (1982), 103-104, **104-105** (SG/GA); financing, 104, **104-105** (GA); 9th UN Pledging Cf., 104; name change, 103-104; see under Disarmament Information Programme, UN

Disarmament Cs., 60-61, **61** (GA); Ct. of the Whole/working groups, establishment, 60, **61** (GA); members/officers, 1203

Disarmament Information Programme, UN (World Disarmament Campaign), 103-104, **104** (GA); Voluntary Trust Fund for, 104

Disarmament Matters, Advisory Board on, 104, 106-107; as UNIDIR Board of Trustees, 107

Disarmament Research, UN Institute for (UNIDIR), 107, **107-108** (SG/GA); budget, 107; Advisory Board/Trustees, 1209 (members/Director)

Disarmament Week, 106, **106** (SG/GA)

Disarmament Yearbook, UN, 63

Disaster Management Training Programme (DHA-UNDP), 603; expansion, 584

Disaster Reduction, International Decade for Natural (1990-1999), 1157 (WMO); & Department of Humanitarian Affairs, 584; Scientific/Technical Ct. on, 1206

Disaster Relief Coordinator, Office of the UN (UNDRO): report, 584 (SG/GA)

disasters, 492 (ESCAP), 603-610; emergency humanitarian assistance, coordination, 584-86 (DHA/SG, 584; GA, **585-86**; UNDP, 584; Central Emergency Revolving Fund, 584; central registers/directories, 584; consolidated appeals, 585; food aid, 825 (WFC); inter-agency consultations, 585 (Inter-Agency Working Group); USG, 1225; see also cyclones; drought-stricken areas; earthquakes; floods; typhoons; volcanic eruptions; and country names and regional entries

discrimination, 715-26; see also indigenous populations; migrant workers; minorities; nazism/fascism; racial discrimination; religious freedom; and under human rights

Discrimination and Protection of Minorities, Subcs. on Prevention of (SCPDPM), 759 (Human Rights Cs./ESC); elections, 759; members/officers, 1215; restructuring, 759 (Working Group/Human Rights Cs.)

Discrimination Based on Religious Belief, 1981 Declaration on Elimination of All Forms of Intolerance and, see Religious Belief, Declaration on Elimination of All Forms of Intolerance and Discrimination Based on diseases: diagnostic/therapeutic technology, 1119-20; international classification, 1116; prevention/control, 1120-21 (WHO); see also immunization; names of diseases; tropical diseases

Disengagement Observer Force, UN, see UN Disengagement Observer Force (UNDOF)

displaced persons, see refugees/displaced persons; Palestine refugees

disputes, peaceful settlement of, 39 (GA); Trust Fund for, 986 (SG/GA); see also under international relations; States

Djibouti: spec. economic assistance, 579-80, 580 (SG/UNDP/UNCDF/GA); refugees influx, 579

documentation (UN): limitation/control, 1082-83, 1083-84 (SG/Ct. on Cfs./GA); see also publications (UN)

Documentation and Information System, Pan-African, see Pan-African Documentation and Information System (PADIS)

Dosimetry Laboratory Network, IAEA/WHO Secondary Standard, 1095

dracunculiasis (guinea-worm disease), 818 (UNICEF/WHO Ct.); eradication, 1121 (WHO)

drift-net fishing, 689 (SG/GA); see also fisheries/fishing

drinking-water supply/sanitation, 1106 (FAO)

Drought and Development, Intergovernmental Authority on (IGADD): ECA advisory services, 475; & UNSO, 605

Drought Control in the Sahel, Permanent Inter-State Ct. on, see Sahel, Permanent Inter-State Ct. on Drought Control

drought-stricken areas, 603-605, 825 (SG/WFC); see also Africa; desertification; Sahel; southern Africa; sub-Saharan Africa; Sudano-Sahelian region and country names

Drug Abuse, UN Decade against (1991-2000), 913, 914 (UNDCP/Cs./GA)

Drug Abuse and Illicit Trafficking, International Cf. on (1987): Comprehensive Multidisciplinary Outline of Future Activities, 913, 914, 918 (GA), 919-20

Drug Abuse Assessment System, International, 911, 919-20

Drug Abuse Comprehensive Centre, 912

Drug Abuse Control, Ad Hoc Inter-Agency Mtg. on Coordination in Matters of International, 917; proposed modifications, 917

Drug Abuse Control, UN Fund for: Executive Director, 1225

Drug Abuse Control, UN System-Wide Action Plan on: implementation, 917, 917-18 (Inter-Agency Mtg./GA)

Drug Control Programme, UN International (UNDCP), 906-907, 907-908 (Executive Director/SG/GA); budget/administration, 907 (ACABQ/GA/Narcotic Drugs Cs.); Executive Director, 1226

Drug Law Enforcement Agencies, Mtgs. of Heads of National (HONLEA): frequency of mtgs./functions, 908-909, 909, 915 (Cs./ESC/GA); see also names of regional agencies

Drug Traffic and Related Matters in Near and Middle East, Subcs. on Illicit, see Near and Middle East, Subcs. on Illicit Drug Traffic and Related Matters

drugs of abuse, 906-26
conventions, 914 (GA), 925-26; see also names of conventions
control of: & diversion of chemicals, 915, 921, 921-23 (GA/INCB/ESC); illicit supply, 920 (Cs.)
coordination, 906, 908 (SG/GA)
crops, illicit: detection, 913 (FAO Centre); & substitution, 915, 920 (GA)
demand reduction, 919-20
economic/social consequences, 911-12, 915 (Cs./Expert Group/GA)
Global Action Programme/Declaration (1990); implementation, 911 (GA), 912-13, 915-16 (SG/Cs./GA/UNDCP); 1993 high-level mtgs., 916 (GA); by UN system, 912-13
illicit traffic: international action to combat, 912-13, 913-15 (SG/UNDCP/GA), & status of, review, 916-17 (GA); 1988 Convention, implementation, 909-10, 910-11 (Narcotics Cs./GA); regional mtgs., 908-909, 910 (Cs./GA); by sea, 910 (Narcotics Cs.); UNSDRI study, 915 (GA)
& law enforcement, 908-909; San Antonio summit/Declaration, follow-up to 1990 summit, 925
& international law/UN Charter, 918, 918 (SG/GA)
licit use: supply/demand: 920, 920-21 (INCB/ESC); annual consumption, 920
vocational rehabilitation, 912-13 (ILO)
see also chemicals; narcotic drugs; psychotropic substances; and names of individual substances and regional entries

Drugs, Intergovernmental Expert Group to Study the Economic and Social Consequences of Illicit Traffic in, 911

earthquakes, see disasters; Nicaragua

East Africa, see Djibouti; Ethiopia; Kenya; Somalia; Sudan; Uganda

East Asia, see country names

East Timor, 961 (Colonial Countries Ct.); GA consideration deferred, 961; human rights situation, 787 (Spec. Rapporteur/SCPDPM); oil exploration in, Australia-Portugal dispute, 966, 981 (ICJ)

Eastern and Southern Africa: Mineral Resources Development Centre, 472 (ECA)

Eastern and Southern African States, Preferential Trade Area of: Trade Fair, 467

Eastern Caribbean States, Organization of (Caribbean Community), 504

Eastern Europe, see Europe, Central/Eastern

East-West relations: evolution in, economic impact, 528-29, 529, 530 (World Survey/SG/GA)

economic, social and cultural rights, 751-58; general aspects, 751-52 (Human Rights/Spec. Rapporteur/SCPDPM); reports backlog, 753; see also development, right to; and under human rights

Economic, Social and Cultural Rights, Ct. on, 753; members/officers, 1218

Economic, Social and Cultural Rights, International Covenant on (1966), accessions/ratifications, 752 (SG); implementation, 748-53 (Ct. on/ESC); see also Human Rights, International Covenants on

economic, social and related fields of the UN, restructuring/revitalization: ESC high-level segment on, 526-28 (GA, 528, 528; SG, 527); ad hoc working group established, 527-28; see also individual UN bodies

Economic and Social Cs. for Asia and the Pacific, see Asia and the Pacific, Economic and Social Cs. for (ESCAP)

Economic and Social Cs. for Western Asia, see Western Asia, Economic and Social Cs. for (ESCWA)

Economic and Social Cl. (ESC), 12-13 (SG), 1214-21
ad hoc/related bodies, 1219-21
agendas (1992), 936, 1235-36 (list)
Bureau elections, 940 (ESC)
calendar of cfs./mtgs., 940 (ESC)
expert bodies, 1217-19
functional css., 1214-16
& intergovernmental organizations, 940 (ESC)
members/officers, 1214
regional css., 1216-17; see also ECA; ECE; ECLAC; ESCAP; ESCWA
report (1992), 1214
restructuring: high-level segment, 12-13 (SG), 526-28; measures for, 932, 932-34, 934 (GA/SG)
revitalization, 934-35 (ESC)
rules of procedure, amendments, 940 (ESC)
sess.: organizational, resumption, 936 (ESC); segments, substantive, 937-38 (SG), high-level, 938 (ESC/SG), coordination, 938 (ESC/SG)
standing css., 1217
subsidiary organs/sessional cts., 1214
summary records, discontinuance, 940 (ESC)
work programme (1993), 940 (ESC)

Economic and Social Development, UN Department of (DESD), 655, 1053 (SG); NGO Unit, 938-39, 939 (SG/ESC)

Economic and Social Planning, Latin American Institute for, see Latin American Institute for Economic and Social Planning

economic assistance, spec. programmes, see country names; development assistance; humanitarian assistance & disaster relief

Economic Assistance, Council for Mutual, dismantled, 622

Economic Community of the Great Lakes Countries (Africa), 465 (ECA)

economic cooperation, see development and international economic cooperation; and country names and regional and subject entries

Economic Cooperation in Europe, Cf. on (1990): Bonn Document, 493

economic cooperation among developing countries (ECDC), 621 (UNCTAD); see also country names; regional and organizational entries and TCDC

Economic Cooperation among Developing Countries, Standing Ct. on (TDB): establishment, 621; members, 1209

Economic Cooperation and Development, Organisation for (OECD): & environmental issues, 501; & ECA, 462; & ODA, 633 (Development Assistance Ct.); transparency/trade preferences, 618

Economic Cs. for Africa, see Africa, Economic Cs. for (ECA)

Economic Cs. for Europe, see Europe, Economic Cs. for (ECE)

Economic Cs. for Latin America and the Caribbean, see Latin America and the Caribbean, Economic Cs. for (ECLAC)

economic development, see developing countries

Economic Development Institute (World Bank), 1117, 1125

economic relations, international: & development policy, 525-49; & TNCs, 649 (SG)

Economic summits: 18th: debt crisis, 636, resources transfer, 632, 636; 14th, Toronto: & debt crisis, 636

economic surveys/trends, 539-40; Africa, 462-63; Asia and the Pacific, 476; Europe, summary, 494; see also Trade and Development Report, 1992; World Economic Survey 1992

economic zones, see exclusive economic zones

ecosystems, 673 (Agenda 21), 685-89; inland waters, eutrophication, 501 (ECE); see also desertification; marine environment; ozone layer; and under regional and organizational entries

Ecuador: communication policies, 124 (IPDC); space applications, Cotopaxi ground station, 112-13

education, 1101-1102 (ILO), 1111 (UNESCO), 1123-24 (World Bank), 1135 (IDA); UNESCO-WHO cooperation, 1111; see also human resources; illiteracy; vocational training; and regional and subject entries

Education, World Cf. on, for All (1990), 886; follow-up, 1111 (UNESCO)

Educational, Scientific and Cultural Organization, United Nations, see United Nations Educational, Scientific and Cultural Organization (UNESCO)

Egypt, 1132 (IFC); economic trends, 516 (ESCWA); external debt, 463; IPDC project, 124; see also Middle East

El Salvador, 1124 (World Bank); & human rights in, 803, **804-805** (Spec. Representative/Cs./Independent Expert/GA); Independent Expert appointed, 804 (ESC/SCPDPM); refugee repatriation, 900; see also Honduras

El Salvador, UN Observer Mission in (ONUSAL): Chief Observer, 1213; composition, 225-26; financing, 224, **224-25** (SG/ACABQ/GA), 230, **230** (SG/GA); human rights component, 223, 804; mandate enlargement/extensions, 223, **224**, 228, **228**, **229** (SC/SG); ONUCA Chief named to, 224; SG Spec. Delegate, 1213, 1226

El Salvador situation, 22 (SG), 222-31 armed conflict in: cease-fire, 226-28 (SG/ONUSAL); Peace Agreement/Declaration, 222, 222-23 (SC/SG); formal conclusion, 230; negotiations leading to, 222; provisions & implementation, 226-31 (SG/SC)

Cs. on Truth: establishment/members/secretariat, 231

National Cs. for the Consolidation of Peace, 230; & ONUSAL, 226 (SG)

reconstruction/development, 601-602, **602**; & UNDP assistance, 231 (inter-agency mission), 601-602

see also Central America situation

elderly persons, see ageing persons

electric power, 644 (ECE): consumption trends, 657 (SG); feasibility study, 658 (DESD); & nuclear power, 660 (IAEA)

Electronic Data Interchange for Administration, Commerce and Transport, UN: streamlining/expansion, 497; see also trade facilitation

electronic data processing, see under subject entries

emergency relief/assistance, see humanitarian assistance & disaster relief; and country names

employment: apartheid effects, 1099; & development, market policies, 1100 (ILO); international standards on setting/supervision, 1099-1100 (ILO Cf./Ct. of Experts); workers' claims, convention on employer insolvency, 1100 (ILO); see also labour; social security; working conditions; and country names and subject entries

energy, 472 (ECA), 488 (ESCAP), 499 (ECE), 508 (ECLAC), 520 (ESCWA), 1124 (World Bank), 1136 (IDA); coordination issues, 655 (ACC/SG); consumption trends, 657 (SG); resources development, 657 (UNCED); technical cooperation, 657-58, **658**, 658 (DESD/ESC/GA); use and air emissions, 659-60 (SG/GA); see also nuclear energy and under names of fuels

Energy, Ct. on (ECE), 499; working parties, 499

Energy, Ct. on Development and Utilization of New and Renewable Sources of: members, 1203; 6th sess., 658-59; for name change, see following entry

Energy for Development, Ct. on New and Renewable Sources of Energy and on: establishment, 654, 659 (GA/ESC); experts, members of, 1218-19; & Ct. on Natural Resources, 654, 659

Energy, Inter-Agency Group on New and Renewable Sources of (ACC), 659

Energy, Intergovernmental Group of Experts on New and Renewable Sources of: report, 659

energy, new and renewable sources of (non-conventional), 658 (DESD), 658-59

coordination in UN, 659 (Inter-Agency Group)

international centres, proposed: feasibility survey, 658 (Ct. on)

Nairobi Action Programme (1981): implementation, 658

see also coal; gas; electricity; geothermal energy; nuclear energy; solar power

Energy Efficiency 2000 Project: follow-up, 472 (ECA), 488 (ESCAP), 499 (Steering Ct.)

engineering industries, 497-98 (ECE), 1173 (UNIDO); privatization, workshops, 497

Engineering Industries and Automation, Working Party on (ECE), 12th sess., 497

environment, 474-75 (ECA), 491-92 (ESCAP), 501-502 (ECE), 509-10 (ECLAC), 521 (ESCWA), 670-92, 1158 (WMO), 1175 (UNIDO)

in armed conflict, protection of, 692, 990-91, **991** (SG/UNCED/GA); see also Iraq-Kuwait situation

emergencies, 1157 (WMO); UN Centre for, **679**

information dissemination, 127 (JUNIC)

international conventions/protocols, 501 (ECE), 681-84; see also names of individual conventions & international trade, 1179 (GATT Group on)

state of (1972-1992), report, 684-85 (UNEP Cl.)

statistics, 929 (SG/Statistical Division); proposed task force, 929

& sustainable development, 681 (SG/UNEP/ESC/UNCTAD); Cs. on, **676-78** (GA); & Department for Policy Coordination, establishment, 676 (SG); Inter-Agency Ct. for (ACC), establishment, 681

& technology, risks/opportunities, 668 (expert mtg.)

see also air pollution; climate; ecosystems; energy; marine environment; oil pollution; nuclear accidents; radioactive waste management; water resources; and under chemicals and regional entries

Environment and Development, Inter-Agency Task Force: establishment, 680

Environment and Development, UN Cf. on (UNCED), 11-12 (SG), 670-81, **675** (GA); Agenda 21, 672-74; Declaration, 670, 670-72 (text); Non-binding Statement of Principles, 674; officers/participants, 670, 675 (GA), 1212, 1225

follow-up: financing, 674; & institutional arrangements: Cs. on Sustainable Development, 674, 676, **676-80** (SG/GA); & capacity-building (Capacity 21), 680, **680** (UNDP/JIU/GA); coordination, 680-81 (ACC Inter-Agency Task Force/Inter-Agency Ct.); High-level Advisory Board/Secretariat, **679-80** (GA)

preparations, 647-48 (TNCs Cs.), 675-76, 698 (UNFPA); energy resources, 657; information system (proposed), 126, **129** (SG/GA), 676 (DPI); & JUNIC, 127; & water resources, 656

Preparatory Ct.: 4th sess., 675 (UNEP/ESC/GA); information programme, 676 (SG/DPI); UNCTAD, 676; members/officers, 1205

Environment Day, World, 670

Environment Fund (UNEP), 689-90 (UNEP Cl.)

Environmental Assistance, UN Centre for Urgent: establishment (UNEP), 676

Environmental Impact Assessment in a Transboundary Context, Convention on/Protocol (organic compounds): signatures/ratifications, 501

Environment Programme, UN (UNEP), 12 (SG), 689-92
  finances, 689-90; 1990-1991 accounts, 690
  Global Environment Facility (World Bank/UNDP/UNEP), 684
  Governing Cl., members/officers, 1209; 3rd spec. sess., 676, 1209
  Executive Director, election, 689, 1209; Deputies, 1209, 1225
  trust funds, 690

Environment Statistics, Intergovernmental Working Group on the Advancement of: mtgs./report, 929

Environmental Modification Techniques, Convention on the Prohibition of Military or Any Other Hostile Use of: parties to/accessions, 63 (list), 101; 2nd Review Cf., 990, **991**; see also under disarmament and the environment

Environmental Protection, 1991 Madrid Protocol on, see under Antarctic Treaty 1959

Equatorial Guinea: admission to IFC, 1129; gold-mining, 472 (ECA); human rights in, 767-68 (Human Rights Cs./Expert/ESC)

Eritrea: international referendum, 189-90, **190-91** (SG/GA); 1991 Cf. on, 189; returnees, 897 (UNHCR); spec. emergency programme, 588

Eritrea, UN Observer Mission to Verify the Referendum in (UNOVER), 190

Estonia, admission to: ECE, 493, IAEA, 1093, ICAO, 1145, ILO, 1099, IMF, 1140, ITU, 1152, UPU, 1149, World Bank, 1123, WMO, 1156; human rights violations, 795

Ethiopia, 17 (SG); refugees/returnees, 897, 898 (UNHCR); non-project credit, 1136 (IDA); small-scale milling, training, 655 (DESD); see also Eritrea

Europe, 561 (UNDP), 493-503 (ECE), 650 (TNCs Centre-ECE Joint Unit), 699 (UNFPA); agriculture, 500; drug control, 919; economic cooperation, 1990 Bonn Cf., 493; economic trends, 494-95, 501; energy, 499; environment, 501-502; human settlements, 502; industry, 497-98; international trade, 496-97; & Palestine question, symposium, 400; refugees in, 903; refugees, conventions on, 905; science/techology, 499-500; security & cooperation in, 74-75, 77-78; standardization, 502; statistics, 502-503; telecommunications, 1154 (ITU); transport, 498-99; see also country names; ECE

Europe, Central/Eastern, 10 (SG), 650 (TNCs Centre-ECE Joint Unit/expert group), 868 (INSTRAW), 1131 (IFC); ac-

counting standards, 645 (intergovernmental expert group); economic integration, 528-29, **529-30** (World Survey/SG/GA), 540 (Trade and Development Report); economic trends, 494-95, 501 (ECE), 525 (CDP); energy issues, 658 (DESD); food situation, 825 (WFP), 1109 (FAO); remote sensing, 4th UN training course, 113; technology needs, 666 (UNCTAD); & UNICEF, 884; UN/ECE Trust Fund, 496; Western aid, 640-41, **641** (UNDP/ESC); see also country names, organizational and subject entries

Europe, Cf. on Security and Cooperation in (CSCE): cooperation with UN, 146, **146** (CSCE/GA); Final Act (1975), **146** (GA); Cl. of Ministers for Foreign Affairs, 2nd Mtg.: Declaration, 67; 1990 Charter of Paris, 493; Helsinki summit: Helsinki Document, **50**, 74, **75** (GA), 146, 493; Forum for Security Cooperation, establishment, 74, **75** (GA); & Yugoslavia, 327

Europe, Charter of Paris for a New (1990), **146**, 493

Europe, Economic Cs. for (ECE), 493-503; budget/secretariat, 494; Executive Secretary, 1224; membership, 493, 639, 1216; restructuring, 493; sess. (47th), 493; strengthening role of, 494; work programmes, 494

Europe, FAO Cf. on, 1104

Europe, Treaty on Conventional Armed Forces in (1990): Extraordinary Cf. of States Parties to, signature, 74, **75** (CSCE/GA); ratifications/entry into force, 74; Concluding Act on Personnel Strength, 74

European Bank for Reconstruction and Development, 494

European Communities, Cs. for: at UN Cf. on Geographical Names, 662

European Community (EC): & Eastern Europe, bilateral trade pacts, 496; & Libya aerial incident, 54; Edinburgh summit, 494; UNDP projects, 561-62; UNICEF role in, 496; & Yugoslavia, 138, 327, 328

European Community Monitoring Mission (ECMM), 328; attack on helicopter, 329, 329-30, **330** (SC)

European Economic Community (EEC), 540 (Trade and Development Report); & Central America, 218, **220** (Managua Agenda/GA); Declaration on Maghreb, 49, **50**; & Cuba, 234; & GSP, 618 (TDB Ct.); Statistical Division (Eurostat), 927, 929

European Region, 2nd Mtg. (1993) of Heads of National Drug Law Enforcement Agencies, 909, **909** (GA)

European Space Agency (ESA), see Space Agency, European

European Statisticians, Cf. of: Bureau of, cooperation with Eurostat/OECD, 503; 40th sess., 502-503

Exclusive Economic Zone, 12th Training Programme on Management and Conservation of Marine Resources within, 1003

exclusive economic zones, 997 (SG), 1002, 1003 (Ocean Affairs Division); & straddling fish stocks, 688; see also continental shelf; fisheries

extra-legal executions, see under human rights

Faeroe Islands: Danish-Icelandic air navigation agreement, 1146

Falkland Islands (Malvinas), 961 (Colonial Countries Ct./GA); consideration deferred, 961 (GA)

families, 839; well-being, 693 (Population Cs.), 1112 (UNESCO)

Family, International Year of the (1994): status, 839 (SG); 1112

family planning, 693 (Population Cs.), 696, 697 (UNFPA); & health, 696 (UNFPA)

Far East Region, Meetings of Heads of National Drug Law Enforcement Agencies (HONLEA), see Asia and the Pacific Region

Federated States of Micronesia, see Micronesia, Federated States of

fellowships, 571 (DESD/ILO); space applications, 112, **121** (UN Programme/GA); see also regional and subject entries

fertility, see human reproduction

Fertilizer Programme, FAO, 1106

fertilizers, 1106 (FAO); nuclear techniques, 660 (IAEA)

Fiji: economic trends, 480; troop contribution, UNIFIL, 410

financial situation (UN), 8-9 (SG), 1019-21, **1021-22** (SG/ACABQ/GA); efficiency review, restructuring implications, 1028, **1028-29** (SG/CPC/ACABQ/GA); see also budget (UN); contributions (UN); peace-keeping, financing

Finland: dispute with Denmark (Great Belt Strait), 981-82 (ICJ); troop contributions, UNDOF, 416, UNFICYP, 270, 271, UNIFIL, 410

fisheries/fishing, 473 (SG/GA/ESC), 506 (ECLAC), 1107 (FAO); & anadromous stocks, convention on, 998; drift-net fishing, **689** (SG/GA), 996 (SG); in high seas, 996 (SG), 999 (FAO), **1002** (GA); management/conservation, 998; regional agreements, 998-99; straddling/migratory stocks, 688 (Agenda 21), 1993 cf. on, **688-89**, **1002** (GA)

Fisheries Management and Development, World Conference on: Strategy for, implementation, 473, **688** (GA)

Fishing, FAO Technical Consultation on High Seas, 999

Fishing, International Cf. on Responsible, 688, 998, 1107

Fishing Vessels, Torremolinos International Convention for the Safety of (1977): draft protocol, 1163 (IMO working group)

fissionable materials, prohibition of production, see under nuclear weapons

floods, see disasters; country names

food, 826-29; emergencies, 1105 (IEFR); nuclear techniques, 1095 (IAEA), 1108 (FAO/IAEA),; see also agriculture; commodities; grains; hunger and malnutrition; nutrition; and names of food products and the following entries food aid, 826-28 (CFA, 826-27; WFP, 827); development assistance, 827-28; emergency relief, 826, 1105 (IAEA)

Food Aid Policies and Programmes, Ct. on (CFA): members/chairman, 1220-23; 2nd spec./33rd/34th sess., 826; projects, 826-27; see also Food Programme, World (WFP)

food and agriculture, 472-73 (ECA), 510-11 (ECLAC), 519-20 (ESCWA), 824-25, **825-26**, **826** (WFC/ESC/GA), 1095 (IAEA), 1104-1109; development, 828-29 (SG/WFC/UNCED, 828; **828-29**); environmental aspects, 828, **829** (UNCED/GA), 1107 (FAO/UNEP); 1989 Cairo Declaration, 825; shortages/security, warning, 1105; & Uruguay Round, 825; world situation, 824-25, 1104-1105; see also hunger; nutrition; regional entries

Food and Agriculture, Global Information and Early Warning System in (FAO), 1105

Food and Agriculture, Joint FAO/IAEA Division on Nuclear Techniques in, 1108

Food and Agriculture Organization of the UN (FAO), 1104-10;

Food Cf., World (1974), 825

Food Council, World (WFC), 825; Executive Director, 1212, 1226; members/officers, 1212; 18th sess., 825, 1212; future role, Ad Hoc Review Ct., 825, **826** (ESC/GA)

Food Data Systems, International Network of, 830 (ACC/UNU)

Food Day, World: observation, 1109

Food Intake Directory, International, 830

Food Programme, World (WFP), 827-28, 1219-20; contributions/pledges/expenditures, 828; Executive Director/Deputy, 1221; finances, 826 (CFA); governing body (CFA), 826-27; report, 1991 activities, 826 (ESC/CFA)

Food Reserve, International Emergency, 1105; Immediate Response Account, 1105

foreign direct investment: IFC advisory service, 1130; & TNCs, 648 (SG); research, 651 (TNCs Centre); see also development: & privatization; investment

Forest Economies and Statistics, Joint FAO/ECE working party, 500

Forest Technology, Management and Training, Joint FAO/ECE/ILO Ct., 500

Forests, Non-legally Binding Authoritative Statement of Principles for a Global Consensus on the Management, Conservation and Sustainable Development of All Types of, 674, **675** (UNCED/GA)

forests/forest products, 500 (ECE), 1107-1108 (FAO); 1990 FAO/ECE resource assessment 500, 1108; & radiation contamination, 500; Statement of Principles (UNCED), 674; see also tropical forests

fossil fuels: world consumption (annual), 659 (SG); see also names of fuels

France: troop contribution, UNIFIL, 410; see also Comorian island of Mayotte

francophone countries: accounting standards, 645; health economics seminar, 1117 (WHO); UNEP workshop, 686

front-line States (Angola; Botswana; Mozambique; United Republic of Tanzania; Zambia; Zimbabwe): spec. assistance to, 580, **581** (SG/GA)

gas, see natural gas

Gas, Ct. on (ECE), 499

Gaza Strip: citrus-processing/irrigation projects, 405 (UNDP); refugees in, 440; situation in, 421, 429, 432 (communications); see also Palestinians; assistance to; territories occupied by Israel

General Agreement on Tariffs and Trade (GATT), 1178-82; see also multilateral trade negotiations

General Assembly (GA), 140-41, 1201-12
5th Ct., work programme, 1052 (GA)
Main Cts./officers, 1201
Procedural Cts. (Credentials/General): officers, 1201-1202
2nd Ct., biennial work programme (1993-1994), 942 (GA)
Standing Cts. (ACABQ/Contributions): members, 1202
subsidiary/ad hoc/related bodies, 1202-12
3rd Ct., biennial work programme (1993-1994), 942 (GA)

General Assembly (46th sess., resumed), 140; agenda, 141, 1227-28; dates/officers, 1201

General Assembly (47th sess.): agenda, 142 (General Ct./GA), 1228-33 (list); dates/officers, 1201; organization, 141; representatives' credentials, 140-41; subsidiary organs, mtgs., 141

General Assembly (48th sess., 1993): provisional agenda, 142

generalized system of preferences (GSP), see under international trade

Genetic Engineering and Biotechnology, International Centre for, 1174 (UNIDO)

Geneva Conventions (1949): Additional Protocols I, II (1977), 821 (SG); & Golan Heights, **416** (GA); & Israel, 420 (communication), 422, **423** (SC/SG/GA), 424, **425** (Israeli Practices Ct./GA), 427, **427** (SG/GA); & Palestine, 400, 401 (Ct. on Palestinian rights), 420, 421 (communications); Protocols I & II, status, 991, **991-92**; see also under territories occupied by Israel: 4th Geneva Convention

Geneva Protocol for the Prohibition of the Use in War of Asphyxiating, Poisonous or Other Gases, and of Bacteriological Methods of Warfare (1925), see under bacteriological (biological) weapons; chemical weapons

Genocide, 1948 Convention on the Prevention and Punishment of the Crime of: status, 819, **819** (SG/GA)

Genome Cf., North-South, 1112

geographical names, cfs. on standardization of: Third (1977), Fifth (1987), Seventh (1997), 662

Geographical Names, 6th UN Cf. on the Standardization of: observers/participants/organization, 662, 1221; resolutions, 662

Geographical Names, UN Group of Experts on: members/officers, 1219; 16th sess., 662, 1219; statute approved, 662

Geological Correlation Programme, International, 1112 (UNESCO)

geological sciences: & remote sensing applications, 4th UN training course, 113

Georgia, admission to: IMF, 1140, UN, **137-38**, **138** (SC/GA), UNESCO, 1111, UNIDO, 1172, WHO, 1116, World Bank, 1123; armed conflict in, 391-94 (communications, 393-94; SC, 391, 392-93; SG missions, 391-92, 393); contribution to UNIFIL, **415**, to UNDOF, **419**

Geosphere-Biosphere Programme (CO-SPAR), 115, 116, **120** (COPUOS/GA)

geostationary orbit: legal aspects, 119, **120** (COPUOS/GA); technical aspects, 112, **120** (COPUOS/GA); & ITU, 1153

geothermal energy, 658 (DESD), 1095 (IAEA); UNRFNRE projects, 654

Germany: economic trends, 615 (Trade and Development Report)

Ghana, 1129, 1130 (IFC), 1135-35, 1136, 1137 (IDA); TNCs investment registry, 650; UNIFIL troop contribution, 410

Gibraltar, 964, **971** (Colonial Countries Ct./GA); information to UN, 960

Gibraltar, Strait of: Europe-Africa link, 471, **471** (ECE/ESC)

global economic negotiations, see under development and international economic co-operation

Global Information and Early Warning System in Food and Agriculture, see Food and Agriculture, Global Information and Early Warning System in (FAO)

Global Observing System, see under Weather Watch, World

Golan Heights (Syrian), 415, **415-16** (Israeli Practices Ct./GA); annexation, 1991 Knesset decision, 415, **416** (Israeli Practices Ct./GA); & cease-fire implementation, 416, 417, **418** (UNDOF/SG/SC); legal status, 420, 434-35 (Israeli Practices Ct./SG, 434; GA, **434-35**); Human Rights Cs., 435; school closings in, **425** (GA); see also UN Disengagement Observer Force (UNDOF); territories occupied by Israel

gold: exploration/development, 654 (UNRFNRE), 655 (DESD)

grains: world output/stocks, 1105

Greece: see Cyprus

Greenland: Denmark-Iceland air agreement, 1146 (ICAO); Denmark-Norway dispute, maritime delimitation, 979-80 (ICJ)

Grenada: drug abuse in, 912

Group of 77: 16th annual mtg.: Declaration on ESC high-level mtg., **530** (GA); information network established (Cameroon), 466; international trade/finance, 467; outer space proposals, 119; & Palestinian aid, 407;

Guam, 964, **968-69** (Colonial Countries Ct./GA); information to UN, 960

Guatemala: gold deposits development, 654 (UNRFNRE); 1990/1991 agreements, implementation, 231-32, 232 (SG/GA); & human rights in, 231 (SG), 768 (Human Rights Cs./SCPDPM Expert/ESC); refugee repatriation, 900; see also under Central America situation

Guinea: iron deposits, 472 (ECA); management credit, 1137 (IDA)

Guinea-Bissau: maritime boundary dispute with Senegal, 981, 997 (ICJ); water supply project, 656

Gulf Cooperation Cl.: economic trends, 516 (ESCWA); industrial cooperation, 1175 (UNIDO); Supreme Cl. of, 13th sess., 147

Guyana: dispute with Venezuela, SG Representative, 1225

Habitat, see under Human Settlements, UN Centre for (Habitat)

Habitat and Human Settlements Foundation, UN, see Human Settlements Foundation, UN Habitat and

Hague Agreement on Industrial Design, see Industrial Designs, Hague Agreement Concerning the International Deposit of

Haiti: asylum-seekers, 900; economy, 236, 806; GA credentials, 238 (SG); humanitarian aid, 236 (OAS), 594 (SG/GA); inter-agency ct., draft plan, 236, **237** (SG/GA), 603; human rights situation, 235, **237** (SG/GA), 805-808 (Expert, 805-806; Cs./SCPDPM/SG, 806; Spec. Rapporteur, 806-807; GA, **807-808**); refugees from, 235 (SG)

Haiti, political developments: 1991 coup in, 17 (SG), 235-38 (communications, 235; GA, 236, **236-37**; SG, 235-36, 237-38), 805 (Independent Expert); OAS resolutions/missions, 235-36; trade embargo, 235, 236; Washington Protocols/ Florida Declaration, 236; SG Spec. Envoy, appointment/activities, 237-38

hazardous wastes: ban on, Bamako Convention, **103** (GA), 674; protection against, review, 685 (ESC); transboundary movements, Basel Convention, 674, 685; see also radioactive wastes; toxic chemicals

Hazardous Wastes, Global Convention on the Control of Transboundary Movements of (1989 Basel Convention): ratifications/accessions, 685

health, 818-24, 1095 (IAEA), 1116-21 (WHO), 1136-37 (IDA); development/research infrastructure, 1116 (WHO), 1124 (World Bank); diagnostic/therapeutic technology, 1119-20 (WHO/IAEA); environmental, 819 (UNCED), 1119; human resources, 1117; legislation digest, 1116; occupational (ILO/WHO/Joint Ct.), 1099, 1118-19; promotion/care, 1118; public information/education, 1117-18; of specific populations, 1118-19; see also ageing persons; AIDS; children; disabled persons; diseases; mental health; nutrition; primary health care, and regional entries

Health Day, World, 1117

Health for All by the Year 2000, Global Strategy: 2nd evaluation, 1116

Health Policy, UNICEF/WHO Joint Ct. on: spec. sess., 818-19

heroin: abuse/traffic, 923, 924; chemicals diversion, **922** (ESC)

highways, see road transport/roads

Holy See: consultative status in ECE, 1216, in ECLAC, 1217; observer, UN Cf. on Geographical Names, 662

Honduras: energy credit, 1136 (IDA); maritime frontier dispute with El Salvador, 231 (SG), 983-86 (ICJ); gold/silver exploration, 654; see also Central America situation; Nicaragua

Hong Kong: asylum seekers, 903; economic trends, 479

Horn of Africa, see Africa, Horn of

Host Country, Ct. on Relations with the, 1006, **1007** (GA); members/officers, 1203; Working Group on Indebtedness, 1006

host country relations (UN/US), 1006-1007, **1007** (Ct./GA); 1947 US/UN Headquarters Agreement, 1006, **1007** (GA); indebtedness issue, 1007; travel restrictions lifted, 1006-1007

hostage-taking/abductions, 739 (Human Rights Cs.); 1988 Body of Principles, 739; see also terrorism, international; and under staff (UN/UN system)

Household Survey Capability Programme, National, 931 (SG/World Bank)

housing, 706 (UNCHS); census, 1990 Programme, 931 (SG/World Bank); forced evictions, 756 (SCPDPM); right to, 756 (SCPDPM); see also human settlements; shelter; urban development/planning

human immunodeficiency virus (HIV), 818, 819; see also acquired immunodeficiency syndrome (AIDS)

Human Reproduction, Spec. Programme of Research, Development and Research Training in (WHO), 1118

human resources development, 489-90 (ESCAP), 832-34; report, 832 (UNDP); training programmes, 832-33 (UNITAR/ UNU)

Human Resources Development in the ESCAP Region: Jakarta Action Plan (1988), implementation, 478, 489-90

Human Resources Development, Network of National Focal Points for: establishment, 489 (ESCAP)

human rights, 14-15 (SG), 709-817
  advancement within UN, **756-58** (GA); national institutions for, 758 (Cs./ESC/SG/GA); International Workshop, 758; & UN machinery, 758-62; see also names of bodies and promotion/protection below
  advisory services, 766-67 (Cs.); Voluntary Fund, 767 (SG/Cs.); see also under Equatorial Guinea; Guatemala
  amnesty, 750 (SCPDPM/Spec. Rapporteurs)
  elections, periodic/genuine, 772, **772-73** (SG/GA); Trust Fund for, **773** (GA)
  & the environment, 816 (Cs./ESC/ Spec. Rapporteur/SCPDPM)
  & fair trial, right to, 750-51 (Cs./ESC/ Spec. Rapporteur/SCPDPM)
  freedom of movement, draft declaration, 749 (Working Group/SG); & population transfers, 749 (SCPDPM)
  freedom of speech, 749-50 (Cs./Spec. Rapporteurs); & human rights bodies, 740 (SG/Cs.)
  internally displaced persons, 777 (Cs./SG/ESC/SCPDPM)

international instruments: implementation, 768-71 (Cs./GA); reporting obligations, 770-71, **771-72** (Cs./ESC); treaty bodies, 768-69, **769-70** (Cs./SG/GA); see also Human Rights, International Covenants on; Human Rights, Universal Declaration of
  judicial system, independence of, 750 (Cs./Spec. Rapporteur/SCPDPM)
  living standard, right to adequate: & extreme poverty, 754-55, **755** (Cs./SCPDPM/GA); & fraudulent enrichment, 754 (Cs.)
  national sovereignty/non-interference, 773, **773-75** (SG/GA)
  promotion/protection: individual/group responsibility in, draft declaration, 776-77, **777** (Working Group/ Cs./ESC); regional arrangements, 775, **775-76** (Cs./SG/GA); & use of science/technology for, 824 (SG/SCPDPM)
  property, right to own, 755-56 (experts/Cs.)
  public information, 765, **765-67** (SG/Cs./GA); & World Campaign, 765
  rule of law, 762 (Cs.)
  & trade union rights, 817
  & UN action, strengthening, 761, **761-62** (Cs./GA)
  see also apartheid; civil and political rights; development, right to; economic/social/cultural rights; racism and racial discrimination; self-determination; and under country names and subject entries

Human Rights, 1969 American Convention on, 905

Human Rights, Centre for, 747; USG, 1225; strengthening, 759-60, **760-61** (Cs./SG/GA)

Human Rights, Cs. on, 758-59; emergency mechanism, 758; mandates, provisional measures, 759 (ESC); members/officers, 1214-15; 1993 revised agenda, 759; work organization, 758-59 (ESC); see also Discrimination and Protection of Minorities, Subcs. on Prevention of

Human Rights, Inter-American Court for, 231

Human Rights, Inter-American Institute for, 231

Human Rights, International Covenants on, 765, 771, **771-72** (Cs./GA); 778 (group of experts); see also names of covenants

Human Rights, Universal Declaration of, 739, 765, 772

Human Rights, World Cf. on (1993): preparations, 125, 127, **127** (DPI/SG/JUNIC/ GA), 720 (Cs.), 763, **763-64** (Cs./GA); Preparatory Ct., 763, 1205 (members/officers); dates/venue, 763 (communications/SG/GA)

Human Rights, World Public Information Campaign (1989), 716, **717** (Human Rights Cs./GA); & migrant workers, 721, **721** (Cs./GA)

Human Rights Ct., 726; members/officers, 1223; sess. (44th, 45th, 46th), 1223

Human Rights Prize, Spec. Ct. to Select the Winners of the UN: members, 1206 human rights violations, 778-811; & arms transfers, 811 (SCPDPM); civil defence forces, 811 (Cs.); gross/large-scale, draft declaration, 810; mass exoduses, 812-13 (Cs./SG/GA); restitution for, 810-11 (Cs./ESC/Rapporteur); see also civil & political rights; criminal justice; disappearance of persons; genocide; and country names

human settlements, 476 (ECA), 491 (ESCAP), 502 (ECE), 511 (ECLAC), 521 (ESCWA), 702-708; coordination in UN system, 706-707; & environment, 705-706 (UNCHS/UNCED); financial resources, 705; indigenous construction, 706; land management, 705; national strategies, 705; production, 705; technical cooperation, 704-705; & women, role of, 707; see also construction/building materials; housing; shelter; urban planning/cities; water and sanitation

Human Settlements, Ct. on (ECE), 502

Human Settlements, Cs. on: members, 1217

Human Settlements, Mtg. on Governmental-Non-governmental Cooperation in the Field of, 707

Human Settlements, UN Cf. on (1976), 702

Human Settlements, UN Cf. on (Habitat II, 1996): preparations, 702, **702-704** (SG/GA); Preparatory Ct., establishment, **704** (GA); members, 1205

Human Settlements, UN Centre for (Habitat), 704-706; Executive Director/Deputy Administrator, 1223; financing, 707; work programme/subprogrammes, 705-706

Human Settlements and Development, Cf. of Global Parliamentarians on: Declaration, 707

Human Settlements Foundation, UN Habitat and, 708

Humanitarian Affairs, Centre for Social Development and: USG, 1225

Humanitarian Affairs, Department of (DHA): coordinator, 584, 1224; establishment, 584-85; offices/staff, 584; Registers/Directories, 584; & UNDRO, 1053

humanitarian assistance and disaster relief, 22-23 (SG), 584-610; coordination, 584-85, 585-86; delivery, facilitation of, 586-87 (SG); see also disasters; peacekeeping operations; refugees; UNDRO; and regional and country entries

humanitarian order, new international, 587, **587-88** (SG/GA)

Hungary: privatization loan, 1124 (World Bank); see also Danube River

hunger and malnutrition: world situation, 824, 825 (WFC/World Bank/IFAD), 829-30 (WFC); see also nutrition; and entries under food

Hydrological Programme, International: Intergovernmental Cl. sess., 1112 (UNESCO/WMO)

hydrology, 1159-60; & remote sensing use in, UN/ESA training course, 113; projects, 1159; see also water resources

Hydrology and Water Resources Programme (WMO), 866

hydropower: DESD projects, 659; 1991 symposium, report, 659

Ibero-American and Caribbean television network, 124 (IPDC)

Ibero-American Summit of Heads of State and Government: request for ICJ advisory opinion, 986 (GA)

Iceland: air agreements (Faeroe Islands/Greenland) with Denmark, 1146 (ICAO)

immunization, 1120 (WHO); Vaccine Initiative, 1120; see also under children; and country names and regional entries

India: agricultural development, 1135 (IDA); drug abuse, 923-24; energy loans, 1124 (World Bank); health, 1136 (IDA); non-project, 1136 (IDA); refugees in, 902 (UNHCR); transportation, 1137 (IDA)

India and Pakistan, UN Military Observer Group in (UNMOGIP), 1213

Indian Ocean, Ad Hoc Ct. on the, 93; members/chairman, 1202

Indian Ocean, as zone of peace: Declaration, implementation, 93, **93-94** (Ad Hoc Ct./GA); proposed UN Cf. on, 93 (Ad Hoc Ct.)

Indian Ocean Marine Affairs Cooperation Cf., 1002 (Ocean Affairs Division); Standing Ct., 8th mtg., 1002

Indigenous People, International Year of the World's (1993): preparations, 125 (DPI), 719-20, **720-21** (Human Rights Cs./SCPDPM/UNDP/GA); Coordinator appointed (USG for Human Rights), 719

indigenous populations: draft declaration on rights, 717-19 (Human Rights Cs./ESC/Working Group/SCPDPM); economic/social issues, 718 (ESC); environment/development, UN Technical Cf./UNCED, 718; property: cultural/intellectual, 718-19 (Cs./SCPDPM/SG); study on agreements with States, 719 (Cs./ESC/SCPDPM); Voluntary Fund: status, 719 (SG/GA), Board of Trustees, 1211 (members/officers/sess.)

Indigenous Populations, Working Group on (SCPDPM), 718

Indo-China: refugees, Comprehensive Plan of Action on, 902 (UNHCR); see also country names; Cambodia situation; South-East Asia

Indo-Chinese Refugees, 1989 Cf. on, 902

Indonesia: World Bank loans, 1123, 1124, 1125; see also East Timor; Papua New Guinea

Industrial Accidents, ECE Convention on the Transboundary Effects of: signatories, 501; Mtg. of Signatories/Working Party on Water Problems, 501

Industrial Designs, Hague Agreement concerning the International Deposit of: 1165, 1167; proposed draft treaty, 1167 (Experts Ct.)

industrial development, 467-70 (ECA), 486-87 (ESCAP), 497-98 (ECE), 506-507 (ECLAC), 517, 520 (ESCWA), 1172-75 (UNIDO)
Consultations, System of, 1173-74; see also specific industries
human resources development, 928
institutional infrastructure, technical cooperation, 1173
investment programme, 1173
management/rehabilitation, 1173
small/medium-scale enterprises, 1124

(World Bank); promotion of, 649 (TNCs Centre)
statistics, 1993 World Programme, preparations, 928-29 (SG)
strategies/operations, 1172, 1173
technical cooperation, 1176
technology development/promotion, 1174
women in, 1174
see also Africa, 2nd Industrial Development Decade for; developing countries; technology, transfer of; women in development; and names of specific industries and regional entries

Industrial Development Decade for Africa, see Africa, 2nd Industrial Development Decade for

Industrial Development Organization, United Nations (UNIDO), 1172-77

industrial property: assistance to countries in transition, 1167 (WIPO); conventions/agreements (WIPO), 1165 (list); designs, deposit, 1167; see also marks; patents; trade marks

Industrial Property, 1883 Paris Convention for the Protection of: 1165, 1166

industry, 1124 (World Bank), 1136 (IDA); & accidents, prevention of, 1099 (ILO); consultations system, 1173-74 (UNIDO); & women, role in, 1175 (UNIDO); see also agro-industries; chemical industries; engineering industries; metallurgical industries

informatics, 663-64 (SG), 1114 (UNESCO)

Informatics Programme, Intergovernmental: Bureau, 5th sess., 1114

information, 123-29; see also mass communication; new world information and communication order; public information; regional entries and the following entries

Information, Ct. on, 123, **127** (GA); members/officers, 1203; membership increase, 123, **1203**; role of, consolidation, **127**

Information, Department of Public, see Public Information, Department of

Information Centres/Services, UN (UNICs), 126, **128** (DPI/GA), 1238-40 (list)

Information Ct., Joint UN (JUNIC): 18th sess., 123 (SG), 126-27

information systems, 1097 (IAEA), 1108 (FAO); ocean affairs, 1003; science/technology, 663-64; see also UN: information/computers; and names of systems

Information Systems, Advisory Ct. for the Coordination of, 664

inland transport, see railway transport; road transport

Inland Transport Ct. (ILO): 12th sess., 1099

inland waters, see under rivers; water resources

intellectual property, 1165-67 (WIPO); assistance to countries in transition, 1167; conventions/agreements, 1165 (list); standard setting, expert cts., 1166; technical cooperation, 1165-66; see also copyright/neighbouring rights; industrial property; patents; trade marks

Intellectual Property Disputes between States, Ct. of Experts on the Settlement of: 4th sess., 1166

Inter-American Development Bank: & ECLAC, 507

intergovernmental organizations, 1093-1181; see also names of organizations and specialized agencies

International Atomic Energy Agency (IAEA), 1093-98

International Bank for Reconstruction and Development (IBRD/World Bank), 1123-28

International Civil Aviation Organization (ICAO), 1145-48

international civil service, 7-8 (SG), 1055, **1055-58** (GA); staff assessments, **1058** (table); salary scale, professional categories, **1059** (table)

International Civil Service Cs., 1055, **1055-58** (GA); members/officers, 1204

International Contract Practices, Working Group on, see Contract Practices, Working Group on International (UNCITRAL)

International Ct. of the Red Cross, see Red Cross, International Ct. of the (ICRC)

International Court of Justice (ICJ), 6-7 (SG), 979-86

  advisory opinions, request for, 986;
    organs authorized to request, 1222
  Chamber of Summary Procedure,
    members, 1221
  cts., 1222
  compulsory jurisdiction, States ac-
    cepting, 979, 1222
  dispute settlement, Trust Fund for,
    986 (SG/GA)
  judges, 1222 (list)
  judicial work of, 979-86, 1221; see
    also country names
  publications, 986
  Registrar/Deputy, 1221, 1225
  reports, 979 (GA)
  role of in environment and develop-
    ment, 979; in peace-keeping, 986
    (SG)
  Statute, 1196-1200 (text); parties to,
    1222

International Development Association (IDA), 1135-39

International Development Strategy, see under Development Decade, 4th UN

International Economic Cooperation, 1990 Declaration on, see Development of the Developing Countries, 1990 Declaration on International Economic Cooperation, in particular the Revitalization of Economic Growth and

international economic law, 1012-15; see also international trade law; new international economic order

International Emergency Food Reserve, see Food Reserve, International Emergency (IEFR)

international finance, 630-39, 1129-32; see also debt problems; development finance; IMF; international monetary and financial affairs; international trade; investment; taxation

International Finance Corporation (IFC), 1129-34

International Fund for Agricultural Development (IFAD), 1169-71

International Labour Organisation (ILO), 1099-1103

international law: fellowships, 987; & international relations, 987-95; publications, 996; see also Asian-African Legal Consultative Ct.; diplomatic relations; Inter-American Juridical Ct.; international economic law; international trade law; law of the sea; outer space; treaties; watercourses, international; and under States

International Law, Advisory Ct. on the UN Programme of Assistance in the Teaching, Study, Dissemination and Wider Appreciation of: members, 1202

International Law, Hague Cf. on Private, 1014

International Law, UN Decade for (1990-1999), 986, 1007-1008, **1008-1009**, **1009-1011** (Annex) (SG/GA); working group (6th Ct.), 1008

International Law Cs. (ILC), 987, **989-90** (GA); Drafting Ct./Bureau, 987; members/officers, 1204; sess. (44th), 987, 1204

International Law Seminar: 27th sess., participants, 987

International Maritime Organization (IMO), 1162-64

international monetary and financial affairs, 1140-42 (IMF); net resources transfer, 631-32, **632-33** (World Survey/Munich Summit); see also debt problems; development finance; economic summits; international trade; taxation; trade-related finance

International Monetary Fund (IMF), 1140-44

international organizations, 1011; colonial countries Declaration, 947-52; see also intergovernmental organizations; international economic law; non-governmental organizations; specialized agencies; and under treaties

International Payments, Working Group on: renamed, 1014; see UNCITRAL

international relations: legal aspects, 987-96; see also diplomatic relations; disputes, peaceful settlement of; mercenaries; peace and security, international; terrorism; treaties; and under States

International Telecommunication Union (ITU), 1152-55

international trade, 467 (ECA), 484-85 (ESCAP), 496-97 (ECE), 507-508 (ECLAC), 518, 519 (ESCWA), 615-30 (Trade and Development Report/economic surveys/UNCTAD VIII/Uruguay Round), 1178-80 (GATT)

  anti-dumping practices, investiga-
    tions, 1179 (Anti-Dumping Ct.)
  dispute settlement, 1179 (Tokyo
    Round)
  environmental issues, 628-29
    (UNCTAD VIII/UNCED), 1179-80
    (GATT)
  facilitation: UN/EDIFACT, 497,
    620-22
  & IMF facilities, 1140
  institutional arrangements, strength-
    ening, 617, **617** (SG/GA)
  preferences, generalized system of
    (GSP), 618 (TDB Spec. Ct.); &
    LDCs, 619 (Paris Declaration); &
    non-tariff measures, 1179; rules of

  origin, 619 (UNCTAD); & technical
    cooperation, 618-19 (UNCTAD/
    UNDP); & UNCTAD VIII, 619
  promotion, 619-20 (ITC/JAG); global
    trust fund, 620
  protectionism/structural adjustment,
    transparency mechanisms, 617-18
    (TDB/UNCTAD VIII); structural ad-
    justment facility, 1140 (IMF)
  restrictive business practices, 622
    (intergovernmental experts
    group/UNCTAD VIII); handbook,
    622; Set of Agreed Principles, 622
  services, 629-30 (UNCTAD VIII); TDB
    Standing Ct. on, established, 629
  subsidies code/countervailing duties,
    investigations, 1179 (GATT)
  technical barriers to, 1179 (GATT)
  trends, 620 (World Survey/Trade and
    Development Report)
  see also agriculture; commodities;
    GATT; multilateral trade negotia-
    tions; new international economic
    order; and under trade

International Trade Centre (UNCTAD/GATT), 619-20 (JAG); budget, 1180; Executive Director, 1225; financial report, Board of Auditors, **620** (GA); technical cooperation, 1180; see also under GATT

International Trade Centre, Joint Advisory Group on the (JAG), 620; members/officers, 1205

international trade law, 1012-16; Convention, **1015** (GA); coordination, 1014; countertrade, legal guide on, 1013, **1015** (UNCITRAL/GA); credit transfers, Model Law, 1013, **1015** (UNCITRAL/GA); electronic data, 1014 (working group); guarantee letters, 1014 (UNCITRAL); procurement, 1014 (working group); publication, 1016; seminars, 1014-15 (SG); trade terms, rules for, 1014 (UNCITRAL); training, 1014-15, **1015** (SG/GA); see also under new international economic order

International Trade Law, UN Cs. on (UNCITRAL), 1012-13, **1015-16** (GA); & LDC members, travel aid for, 1013 (SG/GA); members/officers, 1207; Working Groups: on Electronic Data Exchange (formerly International Payments), on International Contract Practices, on New International Economic Order, 1014

International Trade Law, UNCITRAL Congress, 1012-13, **1015** (GA)

International Trade Procedures, Working Party on Facilitation of (ECE), 497

international treaties and agreements, see under treaties

International Trusteeship System, see Trusteeship System, International

international watercourses, see watercourses, international

Inter-Parliamentary Cf., 87th, 147

Interpol, see Criminal Police Organization, International (Interpol)

investment: advisory service, 1129, 1132 (IFC); & financial flows, 638-39 (Ad Hoc Working Group); foreign direct, 631 (UNCTAD VIII), 648-49 (TNCs Cs./SG); promotion, 1174 (UNIDO); see also regional entries; technology transfer

Investments Ct.: members/officers, 1204

Iran: food aid, 825, 827 (WFC/WFP); human rights in, 787-88, **1080-81** (Spec. Representative/SG/Cs./SCPDPM/ GA); nuclear programme & Israel, 274-75 (IAEA/SG); refugees in, 904 (UNHCR); & US: aerial incident, 980 (ICJ), oil platforms, 983 (ICJ); World Bank loan, 1125; see also Afghanistan; United Arab Emirates

Iran-Iraq conflict: cease-fire violations, 272-73 (communications); prisoner release/repatriation, 273

Iran-Iraq Military Observer Group, UN (UNIIMOG): liquidation/assets, 273-74 **274** (GA/ACABQ/SG/GA)

Iraq, 561 (UNDP); food aid, 825, 827 (WFP/WFC); & human rights, 789-90, **790-91** (Cs./SCPDPM/Spec. Rapporteur/GA); humanitarian aid, Inter-Agency Programme-Memorandum of Understanding, extended, 280, 295 (SG/communication), 321-23 (SC, 322, 323; SG, 322-23), 599 (DHA); & IAEA safeguards, non-compliance, 276; nuclear installations, Israeli attacks, GA consideration deferred, 408; refugee returnees, 904 (UNHCR); & SDR arrears, 277, 279 (IMF); & terrorism, 276, 282, 292 (SG/communication/SC)

Iraq, UN Inter-Agency Humanitarian Programme for, 599

Iraq-Kuwait Boundary Demarcation Cs., 277, 279 (SG), 297; costs, reimbursement, 277 (SG); 6th sess., 298

Iraq-Kuwait Observation Mission, UN (UNIKOM), 298-99, 299-300 (SG); Chief Military Observers, 1213, 1226; composition, 300; financing, 300, **300-301** (SG/ACABQ/GA); mandate extended, 299, 300 (SG/SC)

Iraq-Kuwait situation: 275-325
   boundary demarcation, 297-98 (communications, 297, 298; SC, 297-98, **298**)
   cease-fire compliance, 275-97
   environmental consequences, 324; inter-agency action plan, 690-92 (ESC/UNEP, 691; GA, **691-92**; SG, 690-91); SG Spec. Representative, 691
   human rights violations, Kurds/other minorities, 279-80 (SG), 323-24, 324-25 (Spec. Rapporteur/SC)
   humanitarian assistance: Executive Delegate, 321; financing, 282 (SC), 319-23 (communication, 319-20; SC, 319, **320-21**, 321)
   Kuwaiti property, return of, 279 (SG/UN Coordinator), 282, 292 (SC); 317 (SG)
   monitoring/verification, 314-17 (SG, 315-16; IAEA, 316-17), 660 (IAEA DG)
   on-site inspections: IAEA, 288-89, 301-305; IAEA reports, 305; Spec. Cs.; 287-88; spec. missions (Jan.), 306, 306-307 (SG/SC), (Feb.), 307-308, 308-309 (Executive Chairman/SC, (July), 312-13, 313-14 (communications); reports (June), 309-11, 311 (SC), (Dec.), 311-12, 312 (SC)

refugees/displaced persons, 904 (UNHCR)
   repatriation issues, 282 (SC), 318-19; Geneva mtg./protocol, 318
   sanctions, 277 (SG); guidelines, implementation, 318 (Sanctions Ct./SC); reports, 318
   Spec. Cs., 287-88; financing, 306; missions, 306-309, 312-13; offices/privileges/immunities, 305; reports, 309-12
   UN Compensation Cs./Fund: Governing Cl., 317-18; headquarters/report/mtgs., 317

Ireland: troop contributions, UNFICYP, 270, UNIFIL, 410

Iron and Steel Ct. (ILO): 12th sess., 1099

Iron Deficiency, Group for the Control of: UNU secretariat established, 831

Iron Ore, Intergovernmental Group of Experts on: lst sess., 625, 626

Islamic Cf., Organization of: & Afghanistan, 264; Cf. of Foreign Ministers, 6th extraordinary sess., 147; cooperation with UN, 144-45, **145-46** (SG/GA); education/training, working group, 144; participation in SC, 54; sectoral mtg., 145, **423**; & Yugoslavia, 327

island developing countries, see developing countries, island

Israel: & nuclear armament 91, **91-92** (IAEA/GA); see also Golan Heights; Iraq; Lebanon situation; Middle East situation; Palestine question; territories occupied by Israel; and under South Africa

Israel-Syria Mixed Armistice Cs.: & UNTSO, 416

Italy, troop contribution, UNIFIL, 410

Jamaica: marble quarries, task force, 655 (DESD)

Japan: economic trends, 525 (CDP), 677; investment, 481; trade, 615

Jerusalem, status of, 403, **403-404**, 436 (SG/GA); Medical Hospice, closing, **425** (GA)

Jerusalem, University of (Al Quds), proposed, see under Palestine refugees: education/training

Joint Inspection Unit (JIU), 1051-52, **1052** (SG/GA); members, 1205; see also subject entries

Joint Staff Pension Board, UN, see Pension Board, UN Joint Staff

Jordan: economic trends, 516 (ESCWA); Palestine refugees in, 440, 441; UNRWA schools in, 440; see also Jerusalem, status of; Middle East situation

journalists/broadcasters: DPI annual training programme, participants, 126; training/safety, 124, **125**, 125 (UNESCO/GA)

judicial system, independence of, see under human rights

juveniles, detention of, 738-39 (Spec. Rapporteur/SG/SCPDPM)

Kampuchea, see Cambodia situation

Kazakhstan, admission to: ESCAP, 484, ICAO, 1145, IDA, 1135, IMF, 1140, UN, **133**, 133-34 (SC/GA), UNESCO, 1111,

UPU, 1149, WHO, 1104, World Bank, 1123; contribution to UNDOF, **419**, to UNIFIL, **415**

Kenya: drought relief/refugee aid, Consolidated Appeal for, 588; education credit, 1136 (IDA); food situation, 1105 (FAO); forestry project, 826 (CFA); health credit, 1137 (IDA); water supply credit, 1137 (IDA)

khat: Cf. on control of, 923

Khmer People's National Liberation Front, see Cambodia situation

Korea, Democratic People's Republic of, see Democratic People's Republic of Korea

Korea, Republic of, see Republic of Korea

Korean question: Armistice Agreement (1953), violations, 241; denuclearization, proposed, 27, 241; Military Armistice Ct., 240; military training exercises ("Team Spirit"), 240; 1991 reconciliation accord, 240-41; UN Command report, 240-41, ROK representative, 240; war remains, return of, 240

Kuwait: economic trends, 516; human rights & Iraq occupation, 792-93 (Spec. Rapporteur/Cs.); refugees in, 442, 904; see also Iraq-Kuwait situation; Western Asia

KwaZulu, 156

Kyrgyzstan, admission to: ESCAP, 484, IDA, 1135, ILO, 1099, IMF, 1140, UN, **134** (SC/GA), UNESCO, 1111, WHO, 1104, World Bank, 1123; troop contribution to UNIFIL, **415**; UNDOF observer, **419**

labour, 1099-1102; conventions in force/ratified/denounced, 1099-1100; social policy, 1102 (ILO); statistics, experts' mtg., 1099 (ILO); see also apartheid; employment; industry; ILO; trade unions; technical/vocational training; working conditions

Labour Studies, International Institute for (ILO), 1101-1102

Lagos Plan of Action, see Africa, 1980 Lagos Plan of Action for the Implementation of the Monrovia Strategy

Lake Chad basin (Cameroon, Chad, Niger, Nigeria): water resources development, 656 (DESD)

land-locked developing countries, see developing countries, land-locked

land management, 686 (UNEP); see also soil management

Lao People's Democratic Republic: admission to IFC, 1129; asylum-seekers, 902; 5th Tripartite Thai/Lao/UNHCR Mtg., 903; economic trends, 480; mining projects, 654 (DESD); radio services, 124 (IPDC); UNDP project, 560; see also Mekong River Basin Ct.

Latin America: cholera epidemic, 1108 (FAO); economic trends, 525-26 (CDP), 540 (World Economic Survey); UNICEF programme, 885; see also ECLAC; and country names, organizational and subject entries

Latin America, Agency for the Prohibition of Nuclear Weapons in: General Cf. (12th sess.), **24** (GA)

Latin America and the Caribbean, 562 (UNDP), 650-51 (TNCs Centre-ECLAC Joint Unit), 503-15 (ECLAC), 1131 (IFC), 1170 (IFAD); debt, 505; drug control/traffic, 919, 925; economic trends, 503-504; energy, 508; environment, 509-10, 513; family issues, 509; food/agriculture, 510-11; food aid, 827 (WFP); human settlements, 510; industrial cooperation, 506-507, 1175 (UNIDO); information systems, 506, 513; international trade/finance, 507-508; media development/training, 124 (IPDC); natural resources/energy, 508; population, 510, 699 (UNFPA); refugee situation, 900-902 (UNHCR/IOM); social development, 508-509; space applications, 112, 113; statistics, 511; technical cooperation, 511-12; & TNCs, 511; transport, 508; UNIFEM projects, 872; see also country names; organizational and subject entries

Latin America and the Caribbean, Cf. of Ministers and Heads of Planning of, 506; Regional Planning Cl., recommendations, 506

Latin America and the Caribbean, Economic Cs. for (ECLAC), 503-506, 515; Ct. of High-level Government Experts, 18th sess., 506; development policy 505-506; Executive Secretary, 1224; members/associates, 1216-17; Port of Spain office, 515 (JIU/SG/ESC); 24th sess., 503; 25th sess., venue, 515; subregional activities, 512-13; technical cooperation, 511-12; women, integration of, 509

Latin America and the Caribbean, FAO Cf. for, 1093

Latin America and the Caribbean, Housing and Urban Development Sector in: Regional Mtg. of High-level Authorities/Santiago Declaration, 510

Latin America and the Caribbean, Mtg. of Government Experts on Population and Development in, 510

Latin America and the Caribbean, Mtg. of the Heads of National Drug Law Enforcement Agencies (HONLEA): frequency of mtgs., 908-909, **909** (Cs./ESC); 4th mtg., 925

Latin American and the Caribbean, National Information Networks and Systems for Development in, 505

Latin America and the Caribbean, Regional Cf. on the Integration of Women into the Economic and Social Development of: presiding officers, mtgs. of, 509

Latin America and the Caribbean, Regional Bureau (UNDP): Director, 1225

Latin America and the Caribbean, Spec. Adjustment Facility for: & UNICEF projects, 883

Latin America and the Caribbean, 3rd Regional Cf. on Poverty in, 508

Latin America and the Caribbean, 1967 Treaty for the Prohibition of Nuclear Weapons in (Treaty of Tlatelolco): Additional Protocol I, French ratification, 68,

90 (GA); parties to 63, 68; amendments, consolidating regime established by, 89, **89-90** (CD/GA)

Latin America and the Caribbean, UN Centre for Peace, Disarmament and Development in, 105 (SG/GA)

Latin American and Caribbean Forum on Intellectual Property Policies, 514

Latin American and Caribbean Institute for Economic and Social Planning, 503, 506; & SELA, 506

Latin American Centre for Economic and Social Documentation, 505

Latin American Demographic Centre, 503, 510

Latin American Economic System (SELA), cooperation with UN, 513-14, **514-15** (SG/GA); Action Ct. for Social Development, 514; intellectual property, 514; & ozone layer protocol, 514; Simon Bolivar Programme, 514

Latin American Integration Association, 507, 512

Latin American Mining Organization, 508

Latin American Railways Association, 508

Latin American Regional Mining Information and Documentation System: phase 2 implementation, 508

Latvia, admission to: ICAO, 1145, IDA, 1135, IMF, 1140, UPU, 1149, WMO, 1156, World Bank, 1123; human rights violations, 795, **795** (GA); representatives' credentials, 141

law of the sea, 996-1003
 Amerasinghe Fellowship: award, 1003
 criminal law enforcement, regional cooperation, 998 (SG)
 dispute settlement, 997 (SG/ICJ)
 information/database systems/libraries, 1003
 medium-term plan (1992-1997), **1001**, 1002 (GA)
 publications, 1003 (list)
 see also exclusive economic zones; fishing/fisheries; marine affairs; ocean affairs; sea; sea-bed; and country names and regional entries

Law of the Sea, International Tribunal for, 999, **1001** (Spec. Css./GA); draft headquarters agreement, 1000; draft Protoçol on Privileges/Immunities, 1000 (Spec. Cs.); see also Sea-Bed Authority, International Preparatory Cs. for

Law of the Sea, Office for Ocean Affairs and the Law of the, see Ocean Affairs and the Law of the Sea, Division for

Law of the Sea, Preparatory Cs. for the International Seabed Authority and for the International Tribunal for the: sess./members, 1224

Law of the Sea, 3rd UN Cf. on the (1982), 999, **1001** (Preparatory Cs./GA)

Law of the Sea, UN Convention on the (1982): developments relating to, 996-99, **1001-1002** (SG/GA); implementation, 996, **1001** (SG/GA); parties, 996; ratifications/signatures, 996, **1001** (SG/GA); 10th anniversary, 996, **1001** (experts' mtg./GA); & universal acceptance, 997, **1001** (SG/GA)

Law of the Sea Bulletin, 1003

Law of the Sea Information System, 1003

League of Arab States, see Arab States, League of

League of Red Cross Societies, see Red Cross Societies, League of

least developed countries (LDCs), 483 (ESCAP), 542-45; applying criteria for identifying, 542 (CDP); designation as, 542 (list); mineral resources, seminar, 487; publication, 549; & science/technology, 664-65 (high-level experts), 666 (UNCTAD VIII); telecommunications, 1154 (ITU); see also country names and regional entries

Least Developed Countries, 2nd UN Cf., (1990): Action Programme, implementation, 483 (ESCAP), 542-45 (ACC, 544; SG, 542-43; UNCTAD, 543; UNDP/UNCED, 544); 1175 (UNIDO); & ODA targets, 483 (ESCAP); 2nd annual review, 544, **545** (TDB/GA)

leather/footwear industry, ILO mtg., 1099

Lebanon: economy, 408; hashish/opium production in, 912; & human rights violations, 817 (Cs./SG); reconstruction/development, 599-600, **600**, **600** (SG/ESC/GA); refugees in, 440; UNICEF/UNDP activities, 600; UNRWA emergency programmes in, 442; World Bank assessment mission, 599-600

Lebanon, UN Assistance for Reconstruction and Development of, 599-601; UNDP Resident Coordinator, 599, 1225

Lebanon, UN Interim Force in (UNIFIL), 410-15; casualties, 410, 411, 412 (SG); Commander/appointment of new, 410, 1225; composition, 410, 412 (SG); deployment, 410-11 (SG); financing, 413-15 (ACABQ, 414; GA, **414-15**; SG, 413-14); mandate, extensions, 411, **411-12**, 412 (SG/SC), 413, **413** (SG/SC); Observer Group Lebanon, 410; Suspense Account, 414, ACABQ (SG); transfer of authority, 410-11, 412 (SC/SG); troop strength/civilian staff, 410

Lebanon situation, 395, 408-15 (communications, 410; SC, 409-10, SG, 410-11, 412-13); Hezbollah, 409, 412; hostages, status, 408 (SG spec. envoy); humanitarian aid, 411; Israel Defense Forces/South Lebanon Army, 408-409, 411, 412-13; 1989 Taif Agreement, 412, 413 (SC)

Legal Affairs, Office of (Secretariat): USG, 1224; Codification Division, role of, **989-90** (GA); absorbs Office of Ocean Affairs, 1053

legal questions, 979-1016

leprosy, 1121 (WHO)

Lesotho: water supply, 1125 (World Bank)

liberation movements, see national liberation movements

Liberia: conflict in, 17 (SG), 191-93, 192, **192-93** (SC/SG); & ECOWAS monitoring force/peace plan, 191-92; emergency rehabilitation assistance, 590-91, **591** (SG/UNSCOL/GA); food needs/health/education, 590 (WFP/UNICEF/WHO); 1990 ECOWAS Peace Plan, implementation, **51** (GA), **591**; refugees/displaced persons, 192, 590; SG Spec. Representative named, 192, 193; UN Spec. Coordinator for Emergency Relief Operations in (UNSCOL), 590

Libyan Arab Jamahiriya: aerial incidents: Pan Am flight 103 (1988), 17 (SG), 52, 57, 982 (ICJ); incident, Venezuela Embassy, Tripoli, 57-58 (SC); refugees in, 904 (UNHCR); see also Chad

life sciences, 110, 115, **120** (COPUOS/GA), 1111-12 (UNESCO)

Literary and Artistic Works, Berne Convention for the Protection of (WIPO), 1165; proposed Protocol/draft treaty, 1166 (expert cts.)

Lithuania, admission to: ICAO, 1145, IMF, 1140, WIPO, 1165, WMO, 1156, World Bank, 1123

livestock: data bank, compilation, 1107 (FAO/UNEP); diseases, 1095 (IAEA), 1104, 1107 (FAO); genetic diversity, 1107 (FAO); see also names of diseases

Living Standards Measurement Study: review, 931 (SG/World Bank)

Locust Operations, Emergency Centre for (FAO): reactivated, 1105; see also Africa: locust infestation

Macedonia, 386, **387** (SC/SG/GA); admission to: IMF, 1140, World Bank, 1123; & Albania, 386

Madagascar: cyclone/drought assistance, 577-78, **578** (SG/GA); locust upsurge, 1105 (FAO)

Madrid Agreement concerning the International Registration of marks: see marks, Madrid Agreement concerning the International Registration of

Madrid Protocol on Environmental Protection (1991), see Antarctica, question of: mining/prospecting ban

Maghreb countries: & Europe, EEC declaration 49; see also Arab Maghreb Union

malaria, 1120-21 (WHO)

Malawi: energy, 1136 (IDA); refugees, 897

Malaysia: economic trends, 480

Maldives: economic trends, 479, 480

Mali: mining cooperatives, 655 (DESD), 1136 (IDA)

malnutrition/undernutrition, see famine; hunger; nutrition

Malta: drug education project, 912

Malvinas, see Falkland Islands (Malvinas)

Manufactures, Ct. on (TDB): suspended, 1208

Mariana Islands, see Northern Mariana Islands

marijuana, see cannabis

marine affairs, 487 (ESCAP), 508 (ECLAC), 673 (Agenda 21), **1002** (GA), 1112 (UNESCO); ecosystems, 688-89; living resources, conservation, 996, **1001** (SG/GA); pollution, assessment, 1096 (IAEA/UNEP/IOC); protection, 1096-97; regional conventions, 998; see also drift-net fishing; exclusive economic zones; fisheries/fishing; oceans; oil pollution; ships

Marine Environment, Regional Organization for the Protection of, 690; participation in ESC, 940 (ESC)

Marine Environment Laboratory (Monaco), 1095-96 (IAEA)

Marine Environment of the North-East Atlantic, Convention for the Protection of (1992): replaces Oslo Dumping/Land-based Sources Convention, 998 (SG)

Marine Pollution by Dumping from Ships and Aircraft, Convention for the Prevention of (Oslo Dumping Convention), see Marine Environment of the North-East Atlantic, Convention for the Protection of the (1992)

Marine Pollution by Dumping of Wastes and Other Matter, 1972 Convention on the Prevention of (London Dumping Convention/London Convention): 1994 cf. on amendments, preparations, 1162; & liquid wastes, 1162; & radioactive wastes, 1094

Marine Pollution from Land-based Sources, 1974 Paris Convention for the Prevention of, see Marine Environment of the North-East Atlantic, Convention for the Protection of

maritime issues: delimitation, 997 (SG/ICJ); IMO conventions, 1162, 1163, 1164 (ITU); pollution prevention, 1162-63; unlawful acts, 1163-64; training, 1162 (IMO); see also continental shelf; exclusive economic zones; multimodal transport; oceans; ports; sea; seafarers; shipping

Maritime Day, World (IMO), 1162

Maritime Distress and Safety System, Global (1988): in force, 1163

maritime law, see under law of the sea; maritime boundaries, delimitation; shipping; ships

Maritime Navigation, 1988 Convention for the Suppression of Unlawful Acts against the Safety of Protocol: 1164 (IMO)

Maritime Prize, International (IMO): 1162

maritime transport, 639-40; technical assistance/training, 640 (UNCTAD)

Maritime University, World (IMO), 1162

marks: conventions/agreements, 892 (list); information system, 1167; see also trade marks

Madrid Agreement concerning the International Registration of, 894-95, 1165

MARPOL 73/78, Protocol, see under Ships, International Convention for the Prevention of Pollution from

Marshall Islands, admission to: IMF, 1140, World Bank, 1123; Trusteeship Agreement (1990), termination, 765

mass communication, 123-25 (GA, **124-25**; UNESCO/IPDC, 123-24), 1113-14 (UNESCO); 1991 Windhoek seminar, 124; see also communication; new world information and communication order; public information

mass exoduses, see under human rights violations

maternal health care, 696; Safe Motherhood Initiative, 696 (UNFPA); see also family planning

Mauritania: electric power project, 559-60 (UNDP); refugees in, 904 (UNHCR); see also Western Sahara

Mauritius, 1114 (UNESCO)

Mayotte, see Comorian island of Mayotte

Mediterranean, Inter-Parliamentary Cf. on Security and Cooperation in the, 49, **50** (GA)

Mediterranean Countries, 2nd Ministerial Mtg. of the Western (1991), **50** (GA)

Mediterranean region: CSCE seminar, **50** (GA); drug control cooperation, 924; economic cooperation, **50-51** (ECE/GA); environment action programme/assistance, 501 (ECE); & Maghreb, 49, **50** (EEC/GA); pollution, 1112 (UNESCO); security/cooperation in, 49, **50-51** (SG/GA); in 1991 Helsinki Document, **50** (GA); & women, status of, 1113 (UNESCO); see also Arab Maghreb Union and country names

Mekong River Basin development: Interim Ct. for Coordination, 487-88 (ESCAP); contributions, 488; members, 487-88

Members (UN), see under United Nations

mental health: promotion/protection of, 1119 (WHO)

mercenaries: recruitment/use of, 732-33, **733-34** (Human Rights Cs./Spec. Rapporteur/GA)

Mercenaries, 1989 International Convention against the Recruitment, Use, Financing and Training of: status, 731, **733** (Spec. Rapporteur/GA)

metallurgical industries: technical cooperation, 1173 (UNIDO)

metals: UNRFNRE projects, 654; see also names of metals

meteorology: agricultural/aeronautical/marine applications, 1159; education/training, 867 (WMO); remote sensing uses, 114, 116; see also climate; environmental pollution; hydrology; weather; WMO

Mexico, 1131 (IFC); & Central America, 513; drug control, 924-25; World Bank loans, 1123, 1125

Micronesia, Federated States of: member, Palau Visiting Mission, 974; Trusteeship Agreement, termination, 973

micronutrients, see under nutrition

Middle East: nuclear-free zone, proposed, 90, **90-91**; refugee expenditures, 904 (UNHCR); UNICEF programmes, 882; see also Arab States; ESCWA; western Asia

Middle East situation, 17 (SG), 395-455
general aspects, 395-96 (SG/GA); 1991 resolutions, implementation, 396 (SG); multilateral negotiations, Madrid (1991)/Washington (1992), 396, **397**; UN participation, 396
information dissemination, 126, **127** (SG/GA)
international cf., proposed, 396-99 (communications, 397; GA, **397-98**, 398-99; SG, 396-97), 400 (Ct. on Palestinian rights)
SG Spec. Representative to, 396 (SG), 1225
see also Golan Heights; Lebanon, situation in; Palestine question; territories occupied by Israel; and country names

migrant workers, see women, violence against

Migrant Workers and Members of Their Families, 1990 International Convention on the Protection of the Rights of All: accessions/ratifications, 721; implementation, 721, **721** (Human Rights Cs./GA)

Migration, Intergovernmental Ct. for, 475 (ECA)

Migration, International Organization for (IOM), 650; observer status for, 146, **147** (Governing Cl./ GA) mineral resources, 472 (ECA), 487 (ESCAP), 655 (DESD); exploration, 654 (UNRFNRE); & environment, 655; see also metals; mining; seabed; and country names; regional entries

Mineral Resources Development Centre, Central African, see under Central Africa

Mineral Resources Development Centre, Eastern and Southern African, see under Eastern and Southern African Mineral Resources Development Centre

mining, 655; ban on (Antarctica), **132** (GA); base metals market, 462; & foreign investment, 654 (UNRFNRE), 655 (DESD seminar); see also metals; seabed mining

Mining Sector, Interregional Seminar on Foreign Investment and Joint Ventures in the, 576 (DESD)

minorities, protection of, 722-24; & ethnic cleansing, **724-25** (GA); problems, 725 (Human Rights Cs./SCPDPM)

Minorities, Declaration on the Rights of Persons Belonging to National or Ethnic, Religious and Linguistic, 722, **722-24** (Cs./ESC/GA)

missing persons, see disappearance of persons and under Cyprus

Moldova, Republic of, admission to: ICAO, 1145, ILO, 1099, IMF, 1140, ITU, 1152, UN, **135** (SC/GA), UNESCO, 1111, UPU, 1149, WHO, 1116, World Bank, 1123; contribution to UNIFIL, **415**, to UNDOF, **419**; violence in, 18 (SG)

Mongolia: economic trends, 479 (1992 Survey)

Monrovia Strategy for the Economic Development of Africa, Lagos Plan of Action for Implementation of, see Africa, Lagos Plan of Action for the Implementation of the Monrovia Strategy for the Economic Development of

monsoon, monitoring, 1105

Montreal Protocol on Ozone Layer, see Ozone Layer, Montreal Protocol on Substances that Deplete the

Montserrat, 964, **969** (Colonial Countries Ct./GA)

Moon and Other Celestial Bodies, 1979 Agreement Governing Activities of States on the, parties to, 63

Morocco, 1132 (IFC); cannabis usage, control, 923 (UNDCP); diarrhoeal disease, control, 884-85 (UNICEF); non-project loan, 1124 (World Bank); see also Gibraltar, Strait of: Europe-Africa link; Western Sahara

mountain ecosystems, 673 (UNCED Agenda 21)

Mozambique: admission to GATT, 1178; coal degasification techniques, 655 (DESD); displaced persons, 592; emergency/rehabilitation programmes, 591-92, **592** (SG/SADC/GA); food/health aid, 592 (WFP/UNICEF/WHO); IDA credits, 1136, 1137

Mozambique situation, 193-98; cease-fire talks, 18 (SG), 193; chemical weapons, alleged use, SG mission, 198; General Peace Agreement, 193-98 (SC, **195**, 195-96; SG, 195); UN Operation in Mozambique (ONUMOZ), deployment, 196-97, **197-98** (SG/GA), 1213 (SG Representative)

Multifibre Arrangement (Textiles, Arrangement regarding International Trade in), 618, 1180

multilateral trade: strengthening international organizations in, 617, **617** (SG/GA); proposed organization for, 617

multilateral trade negotiations, 1178-80 (GATT)

Tokyo Round (7th): Agreement on environment, 628; implementation, 1178-79

Uruguay Round (8th), 616-17 (UNCTAD VIII), 1178; & environment, 628; multilateral organization, proposed, 617; negotiations, 616; services, 1178; global approach strategy, 1178 (Trade Negotiations Ct.)

see also entries under international trade; trade

multilateral treaties: concluded under UN auspices, 995 (list); deposited with SG, 995 (list); see also subject entries and under treaties

multimodal transport, 498 (ECE), 639-40 (group of experts); see also shipping; ships

Multinational Programming and Operational Centres (MULPOCS), see under ECA

Myanmar: economic trends, 480; human rights in, 793, **793-94** (Cs./Spec. Rapporteur/GA); refugees from, 902; UNDP programme, 559

Nagorno-Karabakh, 388-90; communications, 389-90; SC, 389, 389-90, 390; chemical weapons, alleged use, 390-91

Nairobi Forward-looking Strategies for the Advancement of Women, see under women, advancement of

Namibia, 1130 (IFC); admission to: GATT, 1178, UPU, 1149; broadcast training, 124 (UNESCO); scholarships, 176; UN Transition Assistance Group (UNTAG), liquidation costs, 1027, **1027-28** (SG/GA)

Namibia, UN Trust Ct. for the UN Fund for: members/officers, 1211

narcotic drugs: conventions/treaties, 925-26; licit use, raw materials for, 920, **921** (INCB/ESC); see also drugs of abuse; psychotropic substances

Narcotic Drugs, Cs. on, 926 (ESC); members/officers, 1215; work programme, 925; subsidiary bodies, 908-909, **909**

Narcotic Drugs, Single Convention (1961)/Protocol (1972): implementation, 910, **911** (UNDCP/GA); States parties, 925

Narcotic Drugs and Psychotropic Substances, 1988 UN Convention against Illicit Traffic in: implementation, 909-10, **910-11** (Cs./GA); ratifications, **914**, **916** (GA); States parties, 926

Narcotics Control Board, International (INCB), 906, **926** (ESC); members/officers, 1223

National Accounts, UN System of: coordination, 928; revisions, 927, 928; interregional seminars, 928 (expert group); 2nd draft, 928

National Accounts, Inter-Secretariat Working Group on: participants, 927; report/mtgs., 928

national liberation movements: observer status, 1011, **1011** (SG/GA); see also names of movements

natural disasters, see disasters

natural gas: consumption trends, 657 (SG); feasibility study, 658 (DESD)

natural resources, 472 (ECA), 487-88 (ESCAP), 508 (ECLAC), 520 (ESCWA), 654-58; coordination in UN, 655-57; exploration, 113 (FAO/COPUOS), 654 (UNRFNRE); UNU Institute for (Africa) & INFOODS, 830; see also energy resources; marine resources; metals; minerals; remote sensing; water resources; and under sea-bed

Natural Resources, Ct. on (ESC): reorganization, 654-55 (GA/ESC), 1218; 1993 draft agenda/work programme, 655 (ESC); experts, 1218

Natural Resources Exploration, UN Revolving Fund for (UNRFNRE), 654; contributions/expenditures/replenishments, 654

natural sciences, 1111-12 (UNESCO)

Nauru: phosphate lands, dispute with Australia, 980-81 (ICJ)

Near East, 1170 (IFAD); drug control, 924; see also Middle East

Near East, FAO Cf. for, 1104

Near and Middle East, Subcs. on Illicit Drug Traffic and Related Matters in the: 909 (ESC); 28th sess./Ministerial mtg., 924; mtgs., frequency, 908, **909** (ESC); members/officers

neighbouring rights, see copyright/neighbouring rights

Nepal: drug abuse, 924; economic trends, 480; energy credit, 1136 (IDA); refugee returnees, 902 (UNHCR); technology transfer, information system, 650 (TNCs Centre); telecommunications credit, 1137 (IDA); troop contribution, UNIFIL, 410

New Caledonia, 958, **958-59** (Colonial Countries Ct./GA); Matignon Agreement on, Ct. to Monitor, 958

new international economic order: Procurement, Model Law, draft articles, 1014 (working group)

New International Economic Order, Working Group on the (UNCITRAL): 15th sess., 1014

New Zealand: economic trends, 480; NSGT information to UN, 960

Nicaragua: IDA non-project credit, 1136

Nicaragua situation, 232 (GA); border incidents, dispute with Honduras, 232, 979 (ICJ); earthquake/tidal wave, 607, **607** (SG/GA), 1112 (UNESCO); & El Salvador/Honduras dispute, intervention; volcano eruption, 606, **606-607** (GA); see also Central America situation

Nigeria: water supply credit, 1136 (IDA)

Non-Aligned Countries, Coordinating Bureau of the Movement of: Ministerial Mtg., 147

Non-Aligned Countries, News Agencies Pool of: & DPI, 125, **128** (DPI/GA)

Non-Aligned Countries, 10th Cf. of Heads of State or Government, 147; & chemical weapons, **66** (GA); & Mediterranean security, 49, **50** (GA); & SC membership, 140 non-conventional energy sources, see geothermal energy; nuclear energy; solar energy; and under energy, new and renewable sources of

non-governmental organizations (NGOs)
  & child prostitution, 886
  & drug abuse, 920; proposed world cf. on, 911
  & ESC, consultative status with, 939
  & Habitat II role, 702 (SG)
  & Lebanon, 411
  & Palestine question, symposium, 400
  & regional conflicts, cf. on, 125 (DPI)
  & Somalia, 202, 206, **207** (SG/SC)
  see also intergovernmental organizations

Non-Governmental Organizations, Ct. on, 938-39; members/officers, 1217; NGO Unit/DESD, 938-39, **939** (SG/ESC/GA); request for hearings, 939

Non-Governmental Liaison Services: work programme/funding, 126-27 (JUNIC)

non-nuclear-weapon States: & IAEA safeguards, 1096; strengthening security of, proposed international arrangements, 68, **68-70** (CD/Ad Hoc Ct./GA)

non-project sector: IDA credits, 1136; World Bank loans, 1124

non-proliferation, nuclear, 67-70; & arms transfers/non-production of plutonium/uranium (communications); & SC summit, 35; see also nuclear-weapon-free zones; zones of peace; and under regional accords

Non-Proliferation of Nuclear Weapons, 1968 Treaty on the (NPT): accessions, 67; parties, 63; preparations for 5th Review Cf. (1995), 67, **67-68** (GA); regional accords, 68; safeguards agreements, 35 (SC summit), 1096-97

Non-Self-Governing Territories (NSGTs), 959-61; information to UN, 960, **960** (GA); scholarships, 959, **959-60** (SG/GA); visiting missions, 960-61 (Colonial Countries Ct.); see also colonial countries; self-determination of peoples; and names of territories

non-tariff measures, see under GATT; international trade; UNCTAD; Uruguay Round

North Africa: agriculture, 463 (ECA), 907 (IFAD); refugees, expenditures, 904 (UNHCR); screw-worm eradication programme, suspension/costs, 608 (FAO/ESC/IFAD); UNICEF programme, 884; water resources, 295

North Africa: Screw-Worm Emergency Centre, 1105

North America: drug abuse/trafficking, 924-25; economic trends, 525 (CDP); & Palestine question, symposia, 400

North American Free Trade Area, 540

North-East Asia: arms limitation issues, 73; see also Democratic People's Republic of Korea, Republic of Korea

North Pacific Ocean, Convention on the Conservation of Anadromous Stocks in, 998

Northern Mariana Islands: Trusteeship Agreement, termination, 973

Norway: troop contribution, UNIFIL, 410

nuclear disarmament, 79-94
  arms freeze, **81-82** (GA)

bilateral negotiations (Russian Federation/US), 79-80, **80-81** (GA)
  fissionable material for, prohibition of production, **82** (GA)
  & international peace & security, 81 (DC/CD); & arms race cessation, 82 (CD)
  use of nuclear arms, draft convention prohibiting, **83** (GA)
  see also non-nuclear-weapons States; non-proliferation, nuclear; peace and security, international; zones of peace

Nuclear Energy Agency (OECD), 1094

Nuclear Events Scale, International, 1093

Nuclear Material, 1987 Convention on Physical Protection of: Cf., 1093

nuclear non-proliferation, see non-proliferation, nuclear

nuclear power, 1093-94 (IAEA)
  fuel cycle, technology/performance, 1094
  Information System, International Nuclear, 1097
  peaceful uses, 660, **660-61** (IAEA); food/health, 1095; medicine, 1095
  power plants, safety, 1093-94; attacks against, preventing, 87 (CD); incidents assessment, 1093; review teams/information system, 1093; see also Chernobyl nuclear accident; radiation; radioactive waste
  safeguards agreements, 660, **661** (IAEA/GA), 1096-97
  reactors, safety assessment, 1093 (IAEA)
  see also outer space: nuclear power sources in

nuclear-weapon-free zones, see Africa, denuclearization; Indian Ocean; Korea; Latin America and the Caribbean; Middle East; seabed; South Asia; South Atlantic; South Pacific; zones of peace

nuclear-weapon tests: comprehensive ban, expert study, 84; 1992 explosions, 84-85; Ad Hoc Ct. on, proposed re-establishment, 243, **244** (CD/GA); proposed comprehensive treaty on, **85-86** (GA); see also seismic events

Nuclear Weapon Tests in the Atmosphere, in Outer Space and Under Water, 1963 Treaty Banning (partial test-ban Treaty): 1991 Amendment Cf., follow-up, 86, **86-87**, 87 (GA); parties to, 63

nuclear weapons, see non-nuclear-weapon States; Non-Proliferation Treaty; Seabed Treaty; South Africa: nuclear capability

Nuclear Weapons, 1968 Treaty on the Non-Proliferation of, see Non-Proliferation of Nuclear Weapons, Treaty on

Nuclear Weapons in Latin America, Agency for the Prohibition of, see Latin America, Agency for the Prohibition of Nuclear Weapons in

Nuclear Weapons in Latin America, Treaty for the Prohibition of (Treaty of Tlatelolco, 1967), see Latin America, Treaty for the Prohibition of Nuclear Weapons in

nutrition, 829-31, 1108-1109 (FAO); assessment procedures, guidelines for rapid, 830, 831; deficiency diseases

(vitamin A/iron), 829-30, 831 (UNU), 885 (UNICEF), 1108; international cf., 830; & micronutrients, 830; publications, 831; regional databases, 830 (UNU)

Nutrition, ACC Subct. on: 19th sess., 830

Nutrition, FAO/WHO International Cf. on: World Declaration/Action Plan, 830, 1105

occupational safety and health, see working conditions

ocean affairs, 1002-1003 (Division for), 1159; conflict/cooperation in, 1002; data acquisition equipment, legal status, 999 (IOC); pollution, 1096 (IAEA/WMO); remote sensing training, 113 (UNESCO/COPUOS); resources development, in Agenda 21, 998; see also air pollution; law of the sea; marine affairs; sea; seabed

Ocean Affairs and the Law of the Sea, Division for, 1002

Ocean Management in Global Change, International Cf. on, 1002

Ocean Observing System, Global: legal status, 999 (IOC)

Ocean Services System, Integrated Global (WMO/IOC), 1159

Oceania: drug traffic, 925; refugees, UNHCR expenditures, 903

Oceanographic Cs., Intergovernmental (IOC), 1159 (WMO); Executive Cl., 999; regional activities, 1112 (UNESCO)

oil: consumption trends, 657 (SG); exploration, 652 (TNCs Centre); & Persian Gulf crisis, 518 (ESCWA); pollution, 690; compensation fund, 1163; production, 517 (ESCWA); see also OPEC

Oil Pollution Damage, International Convention on Civil Liability for (1969): IMO cf. on Protocol to, 1163

Oil Pollution Damage, International Convention on Establishment of an International Fund for Compensation for (1971): IMO cf. on Protocol to, 1163

olive oil: 1986 International Agreement extended, 625; 1993 UN cf. on, 625

Olympic Games, participation of South Africa, 167

Oman: economic trends, 516 (ESCWA)

onchocerciasis, 1121 (WHO)

operational safety review team (OSART), see under IAEA

Organisation for Economic Cooperation and Development, see Economic Cooperation and Development, Organisation for (OECD)

Organization of African Unity (OAU): cooperation with UN, 214-15, **215-17** (SG/GA); 1991 Declaration on South Africa, **956** (GA); UN/OAU mtg. on new joint action, 215

Organization of American States (OAS): & Central America, 238, **239** (GA/SG); cooperation with UN: consultations on 1993 agreement, 238, **238-39** (SG/GA); & Haiti crisis, 235-36, **237-39** (SG/GA)

Organization of the Islamic Cf., see Islamic Cf., Organization of

Organization of Petroleum Exporting Countries, see Petroleum Exporting Countries, Organization of (OPEC)

outer space, peaceful uses of, 110-22
  applications, UN programme: im-
    plementation, 110, 112-13, **121**
    (space expert/GA); IAF report, 116;
    reports/studies, 111; symposium,
    113, 1112 (UNESCO)
  bilateral cooperation (Russian Federa-
    tion/US), 98
  communications, 113-14, **120**; stud-
    ies, 111; symposium (proposed),
    120-21 (COPUOS/GA); UN work-
    shop, 113
  coordination in UN, 115, **120**
  definition/delimitation, 116, **120** (CO-
    PUOS/GA)
  environmental aspects, 110, 114-15,
    115, **120**, **121** (COPUOS/GA); see
    also geosphere-biosphere pro-
    gramme; space debris
  fellowship programme 112, **121** (CO-
    PUOS/GA)
  information service, 112, **121** (UN
    Programme/GA)
  international cooperation in, 110, 119,
    119-22 (COPUOS/GA)
  microgravity, effects on human phys-
    iology, 115 (COPUOS); see also life
    sciences
  legal aspects, 116-19, **120** (CO-
    PUOS/GA)
  nuclear power sources in, 114; draft
    principles, 116, **116-19**, **120** (CO-
    PUOS/GA); see also space debris
  regional activities/missions, 112
    (Secretariat), 112-13 (UN pro-
    gramme/space expert); see also
    country and regional entries
  science/technology aspects, 110-16,
    120-21 (COPUOS/GA)
  technology, 110 (COPUOS Subct./
    ISY), 111, **121** (Secretariat/GA);
    spin-off benefits, 115, **122** (CO-
    PUOS/GA)
  & telecommunications, ITU report,
    114
  treaties/conventions status, **120** (GA),
    122; States parties, 63
  see also arms race; astronomy; geo-
    stationary orbit; planetary explora-
    tion; remote sensing; spacecraft;
    and entries under space

Outer Space, Ad Hoc Inter-Agency Mtg.:
  consideration of 1991 report, 115

Outer Space, Convention on Registration
  of Objects Launched into: status, 122

Outer Space, Ct. on the Peaceful Uses of
  (COPUOS), 110, **120** (GA); spec. com-
  memorative mtg., 110; members/
  officers, 1203
  Legal Subct. (31st sess.), 116, **120**
    (GA)
  Scientific and Technical Subct. (29th
    sess.), 110, **120-21** (GA); Cts. of
    the Whole on UNISPACE, 111, on
    Nuclear Power Sources, 114

Outer Space, including the Moon and
  Other Celestial Bodies, Treaty on Principles Governing the Activities of States
  in the Exploration and Use of (1967),
  258; parties to, 63 (list); & nuclear
  power sources, **116**, **118**, **119** (GA)

Outer Space, Principles Relevant to the
  Use of Nuclear Power Sources in: adop-
  tion, 114 (working group), 116, **116** (CO-
  PUOS/GA)

Outer Space, 2nd UN Cf. on the Exploration and Peaceful Uses of (UNISPACE-
  82): implementation, 110-12, **121** (CO-
  PUOS/SG/GA); evaluation, 110, 111, **121**
  (Working Group on/GA); 1995 cf., proposed, 111, **121** (COPUOS/GA)

Outer Space, Working Group on International Cooperation in the Peaceful Uses
  of (GA SPC): & UNISPACE budget, 112

ozone layer, 1158 (WMO); depleting substances: proposed phase-out/amend-
  ments regulating, 684; & Global Atmosphere Watch, 1158 (WMO); & remote
  sensing, 116

Ozone Layer, 1987 Montreal Protocol on
  Substances that Deplete the Ozone
  Layer: in force, 684; implementation,
  1175 (UNIDO); multilateral assistance
  fund, amendments, 684; London
  Amendment, 684; States parties, 684

Pacific Operations Centre, ESCAP, 483

Pacific region: & child rights, regional consultation, 884 (China/UNICEF); development, women in, 867-68 (INSTRAW/
  ESCAP); island countries, spec. problems, 483-84; Trust Fund established,
  481-82; see also South Pacific; and
  country names

Pakistan: agriculture/energy credits, 1136
  (IDA); floods, emergency aid, 606, **606**
  (GA); 825, 827 (WFC/WFP); human development project, 560 (UNDP); refugees in, 904 (UNHCR); see also Afghanistan situation; India and Pakistan,
  UN Military Observer Group in

Palau (Western Caroline Islands):
  area/population, 973; Compact of Free
  Association, status, 973; constitutional/
  political developments, 973-74 (TC/Co-
  lonial Countries Ct./GA); hearing/peti-
  tions, 975; Visiting Mission, 974-75,
  975 (TC)

Palestine, UN Conciliation Cs. for, **401**,
  451, **452** (GA); members, 1207

Palestine Liberation Organization (PLO):
  participation in Middle East peace cf.,
  398 (GA), in SC, 421, in UN Cf. on Geographical Names, 662

Palestine question, 399-408
  general aspects, 400-402 (communi-
    cations, 399-400; GA, **401-402**,
    402, 402; Palestinian rights Ct.,
    400-401)
  information dissemination, 126, **127**
    (SG/GA), 402-403, **403** (DPI/Pales-
    tinian rights Ct./GA); publications,
    651-52
  regional symposia/seminars, 400 (Pal-
    estinian rights Ct.)
  see also Jerusalem, status of; Leba-
    non situation; Middle East situa-
    tion; territories occupied by Israel

Palestine refugees/displaced persons,
  440-55
  assistance, 440-43, **442-43**
    (UNRWA/GA)

displaced persons, humanitarian as-
    sistance, 446, **446** (UNRWA/GA);
    returnees, situation, 445-46
  education/training: protection of
    schools/institutions, 448, **448-49**
    (SG/Commissioner-General/GA);
    schools/training centres, 440-41
    (Commissioner-General); scholar-
    ships, 450, **450-51** (SG/GA);
    University of Jerusalem (Al Quds),
    proposed, 449, **450-51**
  food aid, 447, **447-48** (SG/GA)
  health programmes, 441 (UNRWA/
    UNICEF/WHO); HIV/AIDS projects,
    441
  number registered, 440
  property rights, 451, **452** (SG/Concili-
    ation Cs./GA)
  protection, 452-53, **453-54**
    (SG/Commissioner-General/GA)
  removal/resettlement, 454, **455**
    (SG/GA)
  repatriation, 446, **446-47** (SG/GA)
  & women/children, 441 (UNRWA)
  see also territories occupied by Israel

Palestine Refugees in the Near East, UN
  Relief and Works Agency for (UNRWA),
  440-45
  accounts (1991), 444 (Board of Audi-
    tors/ACABQ/GA)
  Advisory Cs.: members/Chairman,
    1211
  Commissioner-General/Deputy, 1211,
    1226
  compensation claims, 445 (SG/GA)
  financing, 443, 443-44 (Commission-
    er-General/Working Group)
  headquarters, location of, **442** (GA)
  staff: arrests/detentions, 444-45
  Working Group on the Financing of,
    443-44, **444** (GA); members, 1211
  Palestinian People, Ct. on the Exer-
    cise of the Inalienable Rights of
    the (Ct. on Palestinian rights), 395,
    400-401, **401** (GA); mem-
    bers/officers, 1203

Palestinian People, International Day of
  Solidarity with: observance, **402** (GA)

Palestinian People and Other Arabs, Spec.
  Ct. to Investigate Israeli Practices Affecting, 415, 423-24, **425** (GA); mem-
  bers/chairman, 1206

Palestinian Rights, Division for (Secretariat), 399, 400, **402** (Palestinian rights
  Ct./GA); proposed database, 403

Palestinians: assistance to, 404-407 (ESC,
  406; GA, **406-407**; SG, 404-406);
  agricultural sector (FAO/UNDP mission),
  406-407; development projects, 405
  (ESCWA); children, (UNICEF/UNRWA),
  404; employment/training, 405 (ILO);
  economic development project/expert
  mtgs., 407 (UNCTAD Spec. Unit); field
  missions, 405 (UNDP/FAO/ESCWA);
  food aid, 405 (WFP); human settlements, 404 (UNCHS); maternal
  health/family planning, 405 (UNFPA);
  marketing centres, proposed, 407
  (UNCTAD/ITC); self-determination, 731-
  32 (Human Rights Cs./SCPDPM);
  UNCTAD activities, 407, 407-408; &
  UNDP, 404-405; & UNIDO, 406; see
  also Palestine refugees; territories occupied by Israel; women, status of

Pan-African Documentation and Information System, **461**, 466 (ESC/ECA)

Pan-African News Agency, 124 (UNESCO)

Pan-Africanist Congress of Azania (PAC): & CODESA negotiations, 155, 156; funding, New York office, **154** (GA); at UNCED, 670

Papua New Guinea: armed incident & Solomon Islands, 262 (SC); economic trends, 480; human rights violations, 794 (SCPDPM); member, Palau Visiting Mission, 974

Paris Convention for the Protection of Industrial Property, see Industrial Property, Paris Convention for the Protection of

Patent Cooperation Treaty, 1165, 893

patents, 1166 (WIPO); agreements/conventions, 1165 (list); see also copyright/neighbouring rights; industrial property; marks; trademarks

peace: in post-conflict situation, 35, 36, 1005 (SG); & human rights, 826 (SCPDPM) & science, consideration deferred, 43 (GA); UNESCO prizes, 1113; see also zones of peace

Peace, An Agenda for: Preventive Diplomacy, Peacemaking and Peacekeeping, 35-41 (GA, **38-41**; SC, 37-38; SG, 35-36), **39-41** (text), 44 (Spec. Ct. on Peace-Keeping); working group, **47** (GA)

Peace, International Year of (1986): follow-up, 43 (GA)

Peace, University for: & DPI, **128** (GA)

peace and security, international, 33-58
Draft Code of Crimes against, **990** (GA)
maintenance of, **41-42**, 42 (GA); ICJ role, 36, 41 (SG/GA); SC Summit, 33-35 (SC); Agenda for Peace, 35-41 (GA, **38-41**; SC, 37-38; SG 35-36); early warning/information, **39-40** (GA)
regional aspects, 36 (SG), 49-52; see also Mediterranean region; South Atlantic Zone of Peace
strengthening of: implementation of 1970 Declaration, 42, **42-43** (SG/GA); UN role in, 1004-1006 (GA, **1005-1006**; SG, 1004-1005; Spec. Ct., 1005)
see also diplomacy; disarmament; and regional entries

Peace and Security, 1991 Declaration on Fact-finding by the UN in the Field of Maintenance of International: 38, **40** (SC/GA), **47** (GA), 125 (DPI)

Peace and Security of Mankind, Code of Crimes against the: draft articles, 988, **989** (ILC Working Group/Spec. Rapporteur/GA)

peace-keeping operations (UN), 5, 19 (SG), 36 (SG); & civilian police, proposed Senior Police Officer, **46** (GA); comprehensive review, 44, **44-48** (GA); contributions, **45** (GA); financing/administration, 36, 37-38 (SG/SC), 38 (SC Summit), **45-46**, 48 (GA), 1023-25 (SG), 1026 (reimbursement); & humanitarian assistance, **40-41** (GA); number deployed, 44; organization/effectiveness, 44, **46** (Spec. Ct./GA); personnel, protection, 48-49 (GA, **48-49**); SC, 48; SG, 48), 1066; publication, 47 (GA); radio pro-

gramme, 125 (DPI); reserve fund established, **45**, 48 (GA); training, fellowship programme, 44, **46** (Spec. Ct./SG/GA); see also Cambodia, UN Transitional Authority (UNTAC); Cyprus, UN Peacekeeping Force in (UNFICYP); Disengagement Observer Force, UN (UNDOF); Lebanon, UN Interim Force in (UNIFIL); Somalia, UN Operation in; Truce Supervision Organization, UN (UNTSO); UN Protection Force (UNPROFOR) (Yugoslavia)

Peace-keeping Operations, Department of, 44 (Spec. Ct.), 1053 (SG), 1224

Peace-keeping Operations, Spec. Ct. on, 44, **45** (GA); members, 1206; spec. sess., report on Agenda for Peace, 37 (SC Summit), 44, **48** (GA)

Peace-keeping Reserve Fund: establishment, 1022, **1022-23** (Agenda for Peace/GA)

Pension Board, UN Joint Staff (UNJSPB): 44th sess., 1070-71, 1210; (ACABQ): members, 1210; Ct. of Actuaries, 1210-11 (members); Standing Ct. appointed, 1071, 1210 (members)

Pension Ct., UN Staff, members, 1211

Pension Fund, UN Joint Staff (UNJSPF), 1070-71 (ACABQ); amendments to regulations, **1074** (GA); investments, 1071, **1074** (GA); participants, 1068

pensions (UN system), 1070-72, **1072-75** (ACC/GA); adjustments, changes, **1073-74** (GA); pensionable remuneration, **1072-73** (GA)

Persian Gulf region: economic situation, 540 (World Economic Survey); food aid, 825, 827 (WFC/WFP); hostilities, economic impact, 531 (SG); imports, 615; recovery programme, Gulf Task Force, establishment/proposals, 598-99 (UNDP); oil disaster, 1096 (IAEA); see also country names; Iran-Iraq conflict; Iraq-Kuwait situation; western Asia

Peru, 1124 (World Bank), 1131 (IFC); human rights in, 817 (SCPDPM/OAS)

pesticides, 1107 (FAO); & biological control of pests, 1107

Petroleum Exporting Countries, Organization of (OPEC): & African members, 462; production, post Gulf-crisis, 517

Philippines: 1130 (IFC); mineral exploration, 654 (UNRFNRE); human development, 560 (UNDP); volcanic eruption (Mount Pinatubo)/typhoons, 607-608, **608** (GA)

phonogram conventions (WIPO): protection of performers/producers of (Rome Convention) parties to, 1165

physical sciences, 1096 (IAEA)

Physics, International Centre for Theoretical, 1096 (IAEA)

Pitcairn, 964, **971-72** (Colonial Countries Ct./GA)

planetary exploration, 115, **120** (COPUOS/GA)

Planetary Society/UN/ESA workshop, 2nd, 113

Poland: troop contribution, UNDOF, 416, UNIFIL, 410; UN Information component, **128** (GA); World Bank loans, 1124, 1125

poliomyelitis, 884 (UNICEF); 1120 (WHO)

Political Affairs, Department of: establishment/components, 1053 (SG), 1224

Political and General Assembly Affairs and Secretariat Services, Office for: restructured, 1053

Political and SC Affairs, Department of: restructured, 1053

Political Questions, Office for Spec.: restructured, 1053

pollution, prevention of, see under environmental, regional and subject entries

population, 475-76 (ECA), 490-91 (ESCAP), 511 (ECLAC), 521 (ESCWA), 693-701 (UNFPA)
award, 701
communication/education/information, 697
coordination, 698
country/intercountry programmes, 699
data collection, 697-98
& development, 1994 Cf. on, 693-95
programme planning/evaluation, 699-772 (UNFPA); allocation, 698; Programme Review & Strategy Development, 700 (missions)
publications, 694, 698
technical cooperation (DESD), 701 (SG)
world growth, 693
see also demographic activities; family planning; fertility; maternal health care; and regional and subject entries

Population, UN Fund for (UNFPA), 696-701; finances, 700-701 (ACABQ/UNDP); Executive Director/Deputies, 1211; report, 696-98, 698 (UNDP/ESC); work programmes, 699 (UNDP Cl./Executive Director)

Population and Development, Global Programme of Training in (UNFPA), 698

Population and Development, International Cf. on: Cf. SG, 1225; preparations, 127 (DPI), 693-96 (Cf. SG, 693-94; ESC, **695**; GA, **695-96**); expert group mtgs., 694; funding, 694; Preparatory Ct., 693; regional activities, 694

Population and Housing Census Programme, World (1990), 930

Population Award, Ct. for the UN: members/chairman, 1202

Population Cs. (ESC), 693; members/officers, 1215-16; as Preparatory Ct., 1994 Cf., 693; 27th (1993) sess., 693

Population Division (Secretariat), 693

ports, 640 (Ad Hoc Expert Group/UNCTAD)

Portugal: admission to IDA, 1135; see also Africa; Angola; East Timor

Post Adjustment Questions, Advisory Ct. on, 1204

Postal Administration, UN, see UN Postal Administration (UNPA)

postal services, international, 1148-49 (UPU/UNDP)

poverty, eradication of: coordination, 535-36 (ESC/SG); international cooperation for, 535-38 (GA, **537-38**; UNCTAD VIII, 536-38); international day for, **538** (GA); Standing Ct. established, 536

Poverty Alleviation, Standing Ct. on: establishment/mandate, 536-37, **538** (TDB/GA); members, 1209

Preferences, Spec. Ct. on (TDB), 618; member/officers, 1208

premises (UN): cf. facilities, 1084 (SG/ACABQ/GA); reimbursement, accommodation costs, 1085, (SG/ACABQ/GA)

primary health care, 482 (ESCAP), 818-19 (UNICEF/WHO/UNCED/GA), 1116-17 (WHO); Bamako Initiative (1987): implementation, 818, 1102 (UNICEF/WHO)

prisoners and detainees, see detained persons; torture and other cruel treatment

prisoners of war, treatment of, see under Geneva Conventions

privileges and immunities, see under staff (UN)

Programme and Coordination, Ct. for, see Coordination, Ct. for Programme and

programmes (UN), 1044-46, **1046-51** (GA) accountability of managers, 1046, **1048** (CPC/GA)
coordination, **1047-48** (GA)
medium-term plan, 1044-45, **1047** (SG/CPC/ACABQ/GA)
1990-1991 programme budget: performance, 1045-46, **1047** (SG/CPC/GA)
1984-1991 programmes: evaluation, 1046, **1047** (SG/CPC/GA)
see also coordination in UN system; Joint Inspection Unit (JIU); subject entries

prostitution: suppression of traffic/exploitation of, 747, **748-49** (SG/GA); draft action programme to prevent, 749; see also under children

protectionism, see under international trade

psychotropic substances: diversion for illicit use, 923

Psychotropic Substances, 1971 Convention, 910; States parties, 926

public accounting, see accounts (UN)

public administration and finance, 541-42 (SG/ESC)

Public Administration and Finance, UN Programme in; 10th Mtg. of Experts (1991), 541

public information (UN system), 125-29 (DPI, 125-26; GA, **403-407**); co-ordination in UN system, 126-27 (JUNIC); & news agencies, 125, **128** (DPI/GA); UN publications, 126, **127-28** (DPI/GA); UN/UNDP interim offices, 126; **126** (SG/GA); see also mass communication; new world information and communication order

Public Information, Department of (DPI), 125-26; computerized telecommunications system, 126; USG, 1225; see also Information Centres (UN)

public sector management: IDA credits, 1137; World Bank loans, 1124

publications/printing policy (UN): **1084**, (SG/Ct. on Cf.); editorial services, 1084 (GA); see also documentation (UN)

Puerto Rico, 958 (Rapporteur/Colonial Countries Ct.)

Qatar: aquifer project, 561 (UNDP); maritime/territorial disputes with Bahrain, 981-82 (ICJ)

rabies, 1121 (WHO)

racial discrimination/racism, 709-15; proposed 3rd decade on, 709- 710, **710**, **712** (SG/Human Rights Cs./ESC/GA); see also apartheid; discrimination; human rights; and relevant subject entries

Racial Discrimination, Ct. on the Elimination of (CERD): cooperation with TC, 976; finances, 714, **715** (SG/GA); members/officers, 1223; 41st sess., 714, **1007** (GA), 1223

Racial Discrimination, 1965 International Convention on the Elimination of All Forms of: accessions/ratifications, 713, **713** (Human Rights Cs./GA); implementation, 714-15, **715** (CERD); States parties, 14th mtg./reports, 714; dissemination, global study on extent, 710 (Cs.)

Racial Discrimination, 2nd Decade for Action to Combat Racism and (1983-1993): Action Programme, implementation, 709-13 (Ct. on/Human Rights Cs./SCPDPM), 710; ESC, **710-11**; GA, **711-13**; Trust Fund for, status, 709, **713** (SG/Human Rights Cs./GA)

Radiation, UN Scientific Ct. on the Effects of Atomic (UNSCEAR), 129, **130**; members/officers, 1211

radiation effects, 129, **129-30** (GA/UNSCEAR); protection, safety standards, 1093-94; see also Chernobyl nuclear accident

Radiation Protection Advisory Team (IAEA): missions, 1094

radio broadcasting, 1152-53 (ITU); frequency allocation, 1153 (ITU); see also telecommunications

Radio Cf., World Administrative, 1152-53 (ITU)

Radiocommunication Cf., World (1993), 1152 (ITU)

Radio Consultative Ct., International, 1152; review/planning, Ad Hoc Group on, 1152

radioactive wastes, 674 (Agenda 21), 1094 (IAEA); dumping of, 102, **102-103** (CD Ad Hoc Ct./GA), 530 (IAEA draft guidelines); IAEA code on transboundary movement, 103 (GA); see also marine environment; oceans

radiological weapons: convention prohibiting, draft articles, 87, **87-88**, 102, **102** (Ad Hoc Ct./CD/GA)

Radiological Weapons, Ad Hoc Ct. on, 87, 102

railways, 470 (ECA), 485 (ESCAP), 498 (ECE), 508 (ECLAC); see also under transport

Red Cross, International Ct. of the (ICRC): & Afghanistan, 265; & Cyprus, 270; & humanitarian assistance, 585; Iraq-Kuwait situation, 276-77; & Lebanon, 411; & occupied territories, 424, **426** (GA); & Palestine detainees, 424, 432; & Somalia, 206, **207**; & UNDOF, 417 (SG)

refugees/displaced persons, 892-905
assistance, UNHCR programmes, 896-904; Emergency Fund, 896; & development, 897; see also country names; regional entries
cooperation with UN organizations, 892
emergency food aid, 826-27 (CFA), 827 (WFP)

international agreements, status, 905
Nansen Medal, (1992) award, 892
programme policy, 892 (UNHCR Executive Ct./ESC/GA), **892-94**
protection, **893**, 904-905 (GA/UNHCR); documentation on/publications, 905; international instruments, status, 905
returnees/resettlements, 896-97 (UNHCR)
total: world, 892
women/children: protection guidelines, women, 892, **893**, 905 (Executive Ct./GA); coordinator for children, appointed, 892, **893** (GA)
see also human rights violations: mass exoduses; Palestine refugees; and country names; regional entries

Refugees, 1951 Convention relating to Status of: accessions/successions, 905, **893**; 1967 Protocol, status, **893**, 905

Refugees, Executive Ct. of the UNHCR Programme, 892, 1205 (members); Administrative and Financial Matters, Subct. on, 895-96; International Protection, Subct. of the Whole on, 905; 43rd sess., 892, 1205

Refugees, Office of the UN High Commissioner for (UNHCR), 892; accounts, 895 (ACABQ/Auditors' Board/GA); continuation, 894, **894-95** (GA); finances, 895 (Executive Ct.); Working Group on International Protection, 904

Refugees, UN High Commissioner/Deputy, 1205, 1225

Refugees and Displaced Persons, ACC Ad Hoc Working Group on Early Warning of New Flows of, 585

Refugees in the Near East, UN Relief and Works Agency for Palestine, see Palestine Refugees in the Near East, UN Relief and Works Agency for (UNRWA)

regional css., 1216-17; cooperation among, strengthening role of, 13 (SG), 456-59; environment/development, 459 (SG/GA), **679** (GA); & Joint Units with TNCs Centre, 650-51, 652, **653** (Cs./ESC); space cooperation, 112; see also names of css. and regional entries

Regional Economic Cooperation, Ct. for, 482; Steering Group, 482

Religious Belief, Declaration on the Elimination of All Forms of Intolerance and Discrimination Based on: 1981 Declaration, implementation, 715-16, **716-17** (Spec. Rapporteur/Human Rights Cs./GA)

remote sensing, 112 (UN Programme/ESA), 113-14, **120** (COPUOS/GA), 488-89 (ESCAP); FAO/UNESCO activities, 113; technology transfer, seminar, 668 (DESD); training/fellowships, 113, 472 (ECA), 488-89 (ESCAP); US/UN international cf., 113

Remote Sensing, International Society for Photogrammetry and, 110, 113; seminar, 661, 668

Republic of Korea: 1983 airliner attack, ICAO investigation, 1145; economic trends, 479; & IAEA safeguards, 73; space communications, workshop, 113; see also Korean question

respiratory infections, acute, 885 (UNICEF), 1121 (WHO)

Restrictive Business Practices, Intergovernmental Group of Experts on (UNCTAD): 11th sess., 622; members/officers, 1208

Restrictive Business Practices, Set of Multilaterally Agreed Equitable Principles and Rules for the Control of, 622 (Intergovernmental Group); see also under international trade

rice production, 1105; pest management, 1107 (FAO)

right to development, see development, right to

rights of the child, see child, rights of the

rinderpest eradication, 1095 (IAEA), 1107 (FAO)

Rio Declaration, see Environment and Development, UN Cf. on

Road Safety Week, 498

road transport/roads, 470 (ECA), 485 (ESCAP), 498 (ECE); safety, 471 (ECA); North-South Motorway, 498 (ECE); Trans-African Highways, Bureau, draft statutes, 470 (ECA)

Romania: association agreement with ECE, 495; human rights in, 795 (Spec. Rapporteur/Cs.); human rights advisory service, 767 (UN/Human Rights Centre); IPDC project, 124; non-project/health loans, 1124 (World Bank); privatization strategy, 561 (UNDP)

Rubber Agreement, 1987 International Natural: working group on renegotiation, 620 (Rubber Cl.)

rural development, 488 (ESCAP), 538-39, 539 (ACC/UNCTAD/ESC/FAO), 673 (Agenda 21), 1106 (FAO), 1123 (World Bank), 1135-36 (IDA); & agrarian reform, 3rd FAO report, 539 (ESC); human resources/poverty alleviation, 539 (FAO); natural resources, space applications, 111; see also agricultural development

Rural Development, ACC Task Force on, 538-39

Rural Development, 1979 World Cf. on Agrarian Reform and: Action Plan implementation, 539

Rural Development, Plan of Action for People's Participation in, 1106 (FAO Cf.)

Rural Development and Agriculture, Plan of Action for Integration of Women into, 1106

Rural Women, Strategies for the Economic Advancement of (IFAD), 1169

Russian Federation, admission to: IDA, 1135, IMF, 1140, World Bank, 1123; economy, 540 (World Survey), 1100 (ILO); trade liberalization, 479; UNDP projects, 561; see also Commonwealth of Independent States

Sahel: desertification, 605 (UNSO); mineral resources, Undugu Group, 472 (ECA); nutrition project, 1109 (FAO); tree seed centres, 1108 (FAO); see also Sudano-Sahelian region

Sahel, Permanent Inter-State Ct. on Drought Control in the (CILSS); & UNSO 596

St. Helena, 964, **972** (UNDP/GA); information to UN, 960

Samoa: cyclone damage, 605, **605** (UNDP/GA); economic trends, 480

sanitation, 1125 (World Bank), see also drinking-water

San Marino, admission to: IMF, 1140, UN, **136, 136** (SC/GA), World Bank, 1123; contribution to UNIFIL, **415**, to UNDOF, **419**

satellites: communication technology workshop, 113 (UN Applications Programme); see also communication satellites; geostationary orbit; remote sensing

Saudi Arabia: economic trends, 516 (ESCWA); refugees in, 904

schistosomiasis: control of, 1121 (WHO)

scholarships, see country, regional entries and subject entries

science, see life sciences; natural sciences; physical sciences; social sciences; and under the following entries

science and technology, 471-72 (ECA), 488 (ESCAP), 499 (ECE), 663-69
  assessment, 668
  coordination, 668-69 (ACC)
  endogenous capacities, strengthening, 668 (DESD); High-level Mtg./Cartagena Commitment, 664 (UNCTAD); Rio Declaration, 665
  financial resources, mobilization, 665
  information, cooperation/harmonization: ACC advisory services, 664; global network, proposed, 663-64, (SG/ESC)
  institutional arrangements, 668; see also names of bodies
  national focal points, registry of, 668 (DESD)
  1979 Vienna Programme of Action: implementation, 663 (SG/CPC/DESD)
  see also human rights; outer space; technology transfer; and regional and subject entries

Science and Technology for Development, ACC Task Force on, 664

Science and Technology for Development, Advisory Ct. on, 665; incorporated into Cs. on, 668, 1204

Science and Technology for Development, Centre for, incorporation into DESD Division, 663, 668

Science and Technology for Development, Cs. (ESC): replaces Intergovernmental Ct. on and Advisory Ct., 663, 668 (GA/ESC), 1204; members, 1215

Science and Technology for Development, Mtg. of High-level Experts on, 664-65

Science and Technology for Development, UN Fund for, 665; operational activities, 665-66

Science, Technology, Energy, Environment and Natural Resources, Division of (DESD), 668

Scientific Unions, International Cl. for: publications network, 1112

screw-worm infestation, FAO Emergency Centre, 1105; see also North Africa

sea: archipelagic claims, 997 (SG); liquid waste incineration ban, 1162 (IMO); nuclear dumping, 998; safe containers, 1972 convention amendments, 1163; safety of life/property at, conventions, 1163 (IMO); seafarers, convention on training, 1163

(IMO); unlawful acts, 1163-64 (IMO); see also marine affairs; maritime affairs; oceans; oil pollution; regional seas; territorial seas

Sea, International Convention for the Safety of Life at (1974 SOLAS Convention): amendments, 1163 (IMO)

Sea, International Regulations for Preventing Collisions at Sea (1972): draft amendments, 1163 (IMO)

sea, law of the, see law of the sea

Sea, UN Convention on the Carriage of Goods by Sea, 1978 (Hamburg Rules): in force, **1015** (GA)

Sea, UN Convention on the Law of the, see Law of the Sea, UN Convention on the

seabed
  developing land-based producers, 999-1000 (Spec. Cs. 1)
  mining code, draft regulations, 1000 (Spec. Cs. 3)
  transitional arrangements/price trends/forecasts, 1000 (Cs. 2/Assumptions Advisory Group)
  pioneer investors: exploration, reserved areas, 999 (General Ct./technical experts); obligations, Understanding on, 999, **1001** (Preparatory Cs./GA); training programmes, 999 (Training Panel/General Ct.)

Seabed and the Ocean Floor and in the Subsoil Thereof, 1971 Treaty on the Prohibition of the Emplacement of Nuclear Weapons and Other Weapons of Mass Destruction on the: parties to, 63 (list)

Seabed Authority, International, 996-97 (SG), 1000, **1001** (Spec. Cs. 4/GA); Cts. (Credentials/General), 1228 (officers); Enterprise (operational arm), transitional arrangements, 1000; headquarters agreement/privileges and immunities/UN relations, 1000 (Preparatory Cs.)

Seabed Authority, International: Preparatory Cs. for, 999-1000, **1001** (GA); sess./mtgs., 999, **1002** (GA); Spec. Css. on land-based producers (Cs. 1), 999-1000, on Enterprise (Spec. Cs. 2), 1000, on mining code (Spec. Cs. 3), 1000, on International Tribunal (Spec. Cs. 4), 1000

Seafarers, 1978 International Convention on Standards of Training, Certification and Watchkeeping for, 1163

Secretariat (UN): composition/principal members, 1224-26; restructuring, 5-7 (SG), 1053-54, **1054**, (SG/GA); staff/breakdown, 1226; see also administrative and management questions; pensions (UN system); regional css.; staff (UN/UN system); and names of departments and offices under key word

Secretary-General (UN): annual report (1992), 3-23; Executive Office, 1224; see also under multilateral treaties and subject entries

Security and Cooperation in Europe, Cf. on, see Europe, Cf. on Security and Cooperation in (CSCE)

Security Cl., 4-5 (SG), 140
  agenda, 140 (GA/SG), 1233-35 (list)
  cts., 1213
  members, 1212; equitable representation and increase in, 140, **140** (GA)

peace-keeping operations/special missions, 1213

presidents, 1213 (list)

Seismic Events, Ad Hoc Group of Experts to Consider International Cooperative Measures to Detect and Identify, 84, **85-86** (GA)

self-determination of peoples, 727, **727-28, 728-30** (SG/GA); see also country names and regional entries

Serbia, see Yugoslavia situation

shelter, see housing; human settlements

Shelter to the Year 2000, Global Strategy for (1988): implementation, **703** (GA), 705 (UNCHS)

shipping, 634; safety, 1163 (IMO); unlawful acts against, 1163-64 (IMO); see also maritime transport; multimodal transport; ports

Shipping, Ct. on (TDB): suspended, 634, 1208

Shipping, Standing Ct. on Developing Service Sectors: Fostering Competitive Service Sectors in Developing Countries, members/officers, 1208-1209

ships: oil pollution from, 1162; safe containers, convention, 1163 (IMO); tanker design study, 1162; see also sea, safety of life at

Ships, International Convention for Prevention of Pollution from (MARPOL 73/78), 1162

Singapore: & drug money laundering in, 923; economic trends, 480, 481 (1992 Survey)

slavery/slavery-like practices: conventions, 747; 1983 resolution, implementation, 747, **748** (SG/ESC); see also children; prostitution

Slavery, UN Trust Fund on Contemporary Forms of, 749; Board members, 1212;

Slavery, Working Group on Contemporary Forms of (SCPDPM), 747, **748** (ESC)

Slovenia, admission to: IAEA, 1093, ICAO, 1145, ILO, 1099, IMF, 1140, ITU, 1152, UN, **137**, 326, UNESCO, 1111, UNIDO, 1172, UPU, 1149, WHO, 1116, WIPO, 1165, WMO, 1156, World Bank, 1123; independence declaration, 326; contribution to UNIFIL, **415**, to UNDOF, **419**; see also Yugoslavia situation

small/medium-scale enterprises, see under industrial development

smoking, 1118 (WHO); World No Tobacco Day, 1117

social development, 13-14 (SG), 475 (ECA), 489 (ESCAP), 508-509 (ECLAC), 518, 521 (ESCWA), 835-41

  changing conditions: effects of population growth, 839 (expert mtg.)

  cooperatives, status/role, 839, **839-40, 840-41** (SG/ESC/GA)

  training/research, 832-33 (UNITAR/UNU)

  UN activities, evaluation, 838 (SG/CPC)

  world situation, draft framework, 834-35, **835** (SG/ACC/ESC)

  see also crime prevention/criminal justice; families; Tolerance, International Year for

Social Development, Cs. for: 841 (ESC); members, 1214

Social Development, UN Research Institute for (UNRISD), 841; Board of Directors/Chairman, 1220; Director, 1220; publication, 841

Social Development, World Summit for (1995), 835-36, **836-38** (SG/GA); consultations on holding, 835, **836** (Spec. Representative/ESC); Preparatory Ct. for, 1206

Social Development and Humanitarian Affairs, UN Centre for, 1225

Social Development Strategy for the ESCAP Region Towards the Year 2000 and Beyond, 478

social sciences, 1112-13 (UNESCO)

Social Security (Seafarers), 1987 Convention (revised): in force, 1099

social statistics, 930-31; spec. groups, 931

Social Welfare Policies and Programmes in the Near Future, Guiding Principles for Developmental (1987), **840** (ESC)

soil management, FAO/UNESCO Soil Map of the World, 1106; see also desertification; land management

solar energy: DESD missions, 658; & environment, 659 (SG)

Solomon Islands: economic trends, 480; see also Papua New Guinea

Somalia, 206 (WFP/UNICEF), 827 (WFP), 1105; displaced persons/returnees, 897, **899** (GA); emergency assistance (UNDP), 593; refugee flows, 202, 777 (SCPDPM); starvation/malnutrition, 199, 827 (WFP); see also drought-stricken areas

Somalia, situation in, 21 (SG), 198-214, 593-95

  hostilities/cease-fire, 198-99, **199-200**, 200-201 (SC/SG), 203-204, **205-206**, 206 (SG/SC), 208-209, **209-10** (SG/SC); Operation Restore Hope/Unified Task Force, 210-11 (SG); SG Spec. Representative, 199, 203, 204

  humanitarian aid, 201-202, **202-203**, 206-207, **207**, 207-208 (SG/SC); inter-agency plan, 202, 206, 593 (SG/SC); Action Programme, 213, 593-94, **594-95** (SG/GA), 827; operational zones, proposed establishment, 204, **205**, **207** (SG/SC); UN Coordinator, 201, 202, 584

  international cf. on, proposed, 213-14, **214** (GA)

  UN security force/observers, deployment, 584

Somalia, UN Operation in (UNOSOM), 207; Commander, 1226; composition/Chief Military Observer, 211, 1213; establishment, 202, **204** (SG/SC); financing, 211-12, **212-13** (ACABQ/SG/GA); SG Spec. Adviser, 1226; SG Spec. Representative, 1213; strengthening, 211 (SG), 827

South Africa, African National Congress of, see African National Congress of South Africa (ANC)

South Africa, Day of Solidarity with the Struggle of Women in: observance, 152 (Apartheid Ct.)

South Africa, Intergovernmental Group to Monitor the Supply and Shipping of Oil and Petroleum Products to, 169-70, **170** (GA); members/officers, 1204

South Africa, International Day of Solidarity with the Struggling People of, 152

South Africa, relations with, 168-74

  arms embargo: implementation, 171, **172** (Apartheid Ct./GA)

  foreign support for, 780-81, **781**, 781-82 (Human Rights Cs./ESC/Spec. Rapporteur/SCPDPM)

  & neighbouring States, 168; see also country names; front-line States

  & Israel, 123, **173-74** (Apartheid Ct./GA); trade, 173

  military/nuclear collaboration, 171-72, **172-73** (Apartheid Ct./GA), 780 (Human Rights Cs.)

  nuclear capability: accession to NPT, 172; & IAEA safeguards agreement, 172, **172** (IAEA/GA)

  oil embargo, 169-70, **170-71**, (Intergovernmental Group/GA)

  TNCs in, 171 (SG/ESC); SG reports, 646, **646-47** (Cs./ESC)

  trade/finance, 168-69

  see also Antarctica; apartheid; country names

South Africa, situation in, 18 (SG)

  aid programmes, inter-agency cooperation, 174-77

  children, treatment, 778 (Ad Hoc Expert Group)

  human rights violations, 778-82 (Ad Hoc Group/Human Rights Cs./SCPDPM/SG/GA); effects of foreign support, 779-82 (Cs., 780-81; ESC, **781**; GA/SG, 782; Spec. Rapporteur, 781; SCPDPM, 781-82)

  media in post-apartheid South Africa, 123-24 (UNESCO)

  National Peace Accord (1991): implementation, 153 (Apartheid Ct.), 160 (SG), **161** (SC), 161-62, **163** (SG/GA)

  returnees, 165 (UNHCR)

  & trade union rights, 782, **782** (Ad Hoc Working Group/SG/GA); & ILO Conciliation Cs., 782

  see also apartheid; colonial countries; Namibia; self-determination

South Africa, Convention for a Democratic (CODESA), 123-24 (UNESCO); CODESA II (2nd sess.), 154-55, 156, 160

South Africa, UN Military Observers in (UNOMSA): Chief/headquarters, 164; appropriation, for, 164, **164-65** (SG/GA); deployment, 161, 164

South Africa, UN Trust Fund for, 174-75, **175**, 175 (SG/GA); Trustees Ct., 174, 175, 1203 (members/officers)

South African Political Prisoners, International Day of Solidarity: observance, 152

South African Trade Unions, Congress of: & CODESA, 155; & economic policy options, 167

South Africans, Follow-up Cf. on International Educational Assistance to Disadvantaged, 176, **177** (GA)

South Asia, 1130 (IFC); child development, 884 (UNICEF); desertification/drought, 685, **686** (SG/ESC); drug abuse/traffic, 924 (UNDCP); media education projects, 124 (IPDC); nuclear-free zone, proposed, 92, **92-93** (SG/GA); refugee assistance, 902 (UNHCR); see also country names and organizational entries

South Asian Association for Regional Cooperation: 1990 convention, 924

South Atlantic zone of peace/cooperation, 51, **51-52** (SG/GA); & Tlatelolco Treaty, **51** (GA)

South-East Asia
  drug abuse/traffic, 923 (UNDCP)
  piracy/drug trafficking, declarations against, 1164 (IMO), 998
  refugees: assistance, 902-903 (UNHCR); total in, 897 (UNHCR)
  UNIFEM programmes, 872
  see also Cambodia situation; Mekong River development; and country and organizational names

South-East Asia, 1976 Treaty of Amity and Cooperation in, **73-74** (GA), 998; accessions, **73**

South-East Asian Nations, Association of (ASEAN): economic trends/trade, 480, 481; 4th summit mtg., 147; Declaration, **73-74** (GA); South China Sea Declaration on Spratly Islands dispute, 998; 25th Ministerial Mtg., 147; see also country names

South Pacific: cyclones/typhoons in, assistance, 605, **605-606** (UNDP/GA); fisheries cooperation, 997, 998

South Pacific Forum: communique, 998

South Pacific Nuclear-Free-Zone Treaty (Treaty of Rarotonga): & IAEA safeguards agreements, 1096; parties to, 63, 68

South-West Asia: & drugs, 919 (UNDPC); refugees, 903-904 (UNHCR): see also country names

southern Africa: drought in, 603-604 (DHA/SADC), 559 (UNDP); education/training, 175-76; Pledging Cf., 603; refugee situation, 897; water resources development, 656 (DESD); see also apartheid and country names

Southern Africa, Ad Hoc Working Group of Experts on, interim report, 778, 779 (Human Rights Cs./SG); see also South Africa: human rights in

Southern Africa, 7th International Cf. on Peace and Security in, 1002

Southern Africa, 1989 Declaration on Apartheid and its Destructive Consequences in, see Apartheid and its Destructive Consequences in Southern Africa, 1989 Declaration

Southern Africa, UN Educational and Training Programme for, 175-76, **176-77** (SG/GA); Advisory Ct., 176, 1202 (members/officers); Cf. on disadvantaged, 176, **177** (GA); contributions/pledges, 176

Southern African Development Community (SADC), 168-69; treaty establishing, **580** (GA); & front-line States, 580

Southern African Development Coordination Conference: replaced by SADC, 168

space, see outer space and following entries

Space Agency, European (ESA): ISY contribution, 111; space transportation programme, 114

Space Applications Programme (UN), 112-13, **120** (UN expert/GA); finances, 112, 113, **121** (UN expert/GA); reports/studies on, 111

Space Cf. of the Americas, 2nd (1993), 113, **121** (GA)

space objects/spacecraft: launchings, information/Convention, status, 122; debris, collisions with, 114-15, **121** (COPUOS/GA)

Space Research, Ct. on (COSPAR) 110; remote sensing workshop, 113

space transportation, 114, **120** (COPUOS/GA)

Space Year, International: 110-11, **121** (COPUOS/GA)

Spain, see Gibraltar, Strait of

Special Ct., see under key word(s) of title

special economic, humanitarian and disaster relief assistance, see country names and regional and subject entries

specialized agencies, 1093-1181; see also intergovernmental organizations; names of agencies

Sri Lanka: drug abuse, 924; energy credit, 1136 (IDA); refugee returnees, 902 (UNHCR)

staff (UN/UN system), 1053-66
  arrests/detentions, 739-40; status of spec. rapporteurs/experts, 740 (SG)
  career development, 1063 (SG); training, 1063-64 (SG)
  composition: geographic distribution, 1060 (SG/GA); status of women, 1054, **1060-61**, **1061-62** (SG/ESC/GA)
  justice, system of administration, 1076
  personnel management, **1059-60** (GA/SG)
  post classification system, 1063 (JIU/SG)
  privileges/immunities, 1053, 1065, **1065-66**, 1066 (SG/inter-agency mtg./GA)
  representation (staff), costs of, **1064** (SG/GA)
  rules/regulations, amendments, 1064 (SG)
  salaries/allowances, 1066-67, **1068** (ICSC/GA); spec. post allowance, 1068, **1068-69** (ICSC/SG/GA); general services, survey, 1069 (ICSC); grade overlap, 1069-70 (JIU/SG)
  secretaries of intergovernmental organs, level, 1064-65 (SG/GA)
  staffing tables/workload standards, 1062-63 (SG)
  top echelon officials, emoluments: honoraria, 1067, **1067** (SG/ACABQ/GA); representation allowance, **1067** (SG/ACABQ/GA); remuneration, JIU members, 1067-68 (SG/GA)
  total, Secretariat, 1060 (SG)

travel arrangements, 1075 (SG/ACABQ/GA); review of, 1075 (SG/GA)
  see also Administrative Tribunal, UN; International Civil Service Cs.; pensions (UN system); privileges and immunities (UN system)

Stateless Persons, 1954 Convention relating to, 905

States: disputes between, draft rules on, 1005, **1006** (Spec. Ct./GA); jurisdictional immunity, draft articles, 992 (working group/GA); liability, 989-90 (ILC/Spec. Rapporteur); relations with international organizations, 987, **989** (ILC/GA); responsibility (in wrongful acts), 988 (Spec. Rapporteur/ILC); see also diplomatic relations; disputes, peaceful settlement of; international relations; treaties

States, Representation of, in Their Relations with International Organizations of a Universal Character, 1975 Vienna Convention, **1011** (GA)

Statistical Activities, Subct. on (ACC), 927-28; & UNDP, 927

Statistical Cs. (ESC): members/officers, 1216; 27th sess. (1993), 1172 (SG)

Statistical Division (DESD), 932 (SG); assumes functions of Statistical Office, 927; vital statistics, missions, 930

Statistical Programmes and Coordination, Working Group on International: 15th sess., 927

Statistical System, Global: review, structure/operation, 927 (ACC)

statistics, 465-66 (ECA), 492 (ESCAP), 502-503 (ECE), 511 (ECLAC), 521-22 (ESCWA), 927-31; coordination in UN system, 927-28 (working group/ACC); economic, 928-30; international classifications, 929 (SG/GATT); living standards, 931 (SG/World Bank); prices (International Comparison Programme) 928; programme questions, 932 (SG); publications, 930, 932; & service sector, 929-30 (SG); social/demographic, 930-32; technical cooperation, 931 (SG); vital statistics (Handbook/International) Programme, 930; see also organizational, regional and subject entries

steel industries, 498 (ECE); restructuring techniques, 498; statistics, 498

Strategic Offensive Arms, Treaty on the Reduction and Limitation of, 59, **79** 79-80; Protocol, 80

student refugees, see under southern Africa

sub-Saharan Africa: 1129-30 (IFC); AIDS/HIV cases, 819; development assistance, 827 (WFP); economic growth, 526 (CDP); food aid, 827 (WFP); population assistance, 699 (UNFPA); see also primary health care, Bamako Initiative; and country names

Sub-Saharan African Countries Affected by Drought and Desertification, Spec. Programme for (IFAD): phase 2, 686 (ESC), 604 (OAU), **604**, (ESC/GA), 1169, 1126 (World Bank); SG appeal, 825 (WFC)

Subsidies and Countervailing Measures, Ct. on (GATT), 1179; see also under international trade

Sudan: emergency aid, 595-96, **596-97** (SG/GA); & human rights in, **783**, 784 (GA); refugees, 596 (FAO/WFP); see also Ethiopia

Sudan, Operation Lifeline, UN emergency programme, 595, **596** (GA)

Sudano-Sahelian Office, UN (UNSO): goals, redefinition, 604-605 (UNCED)

Sudano-Sahelian region, 604-605 (UNSO/SG/GA); desertification control, 605; 1977 Action Plan, implementation, 685 (UNEP)

Sugar Agreement, 1987 International: expiration/extension, 625 (UN Sugar Cf.); signatures/ratifications, 625

summary executions, see human rights: extra-legal executions

sulphur dioxide emissions: & energy use, 659-60 (SG)

Sweden: troop contributions, UNFICYP, 270, UNIFIL, 410; & space applications, 113

Switzerland, admission to: IDA, 1135; IFC, 1129; IMF, 1140; World Bank, 1123; consultative status in: ECA/ESCAP, 1216, in ECLAC, 1217; postal agreement with UN, 1089; & UNIFIL, 414 (SG)

Syrian Arab Republic: economic trends, 516; refugees in, 904, see also Disengagement Observer Force, UN; Golan Heights

Taiwan: economic trends, 481

Tajikistan, admission to: ESCAP, 484, UN, **134** (SC/GA), WHO, 1116; contribution to UNIFIL, **415**, to UNDOF, **419**; fighting in, 394 (SG mission/SC)

Tanzania, United Republic of, see United Republic of Tanzania

Tax Matters, Ad Hoc Group of Experts on International Cooperation in, **639** (ESC); members, 1217-18

technical cooperation, 511-12 (ECLAC), 557-63 (UNDP), 570-72 (DESD), 651-52 (TNCs), 1096 (IAEA), 1124 (World Bank), 1137 (IDA), 1142 (IMF), 1146-47 (ICAO), 1150 (UPU), 1153-54 (ITU), 1160 (WMO), 1165-66 (WIPO), 1176 (UNIDO), 1180 (GATT); see also development, operational activities; development assistance; Development Programme, UN; and under specific economic and social headings

technical cooperation among developing countries (TCDC), 512 (ECLAC), 572-74, **573-74** (UNDP/DESD/SG/ESC)

Buenos Aires Action Plan (1978): implementation, 512 (ECLAC), 572-73 (SG)

focal points, strengthening, 572, 573; 5th TCDC Focal Point Mtg., 572

Information Referral System (INRES), 573, **573** (ESC)

intercountry/regional workshops, 572

UNDP Spec. Unit for: & DESD, 572

see also economic cooperation among developing countries; subject entries

Technical Cooperation among Developing Countries, High-level Ct. on the Review of; members/officers, 1203

Technical Cooperation Division (GATT), 1803

technology: assessment, 668; economic growth through & TNCs, 648 (SG); pilot incubator scheme, 665; see also biotechnology

Technology, Ct. on Transfer of (UNCTAD), 666; suspended, 1208

Technology, International Institute for Software (UNU), 834

Technology Assessment System, Advanced: DESD activities, 668; publications, 668

technology transfer, 488 (ESCAP), 666-67 (UNCTAD); draft code of conduct, 667, **667** (UNCTAD/GA); in energy resources, 659; environmental issues, Agenda 21, 667 (UNCED); & intellectual property rights, 666 (UNCTAD VIII); & investment, 666; & TNCs, 648-49

Technology Transfer, Ad Hoc Working Group on Interrelationship between Investment and (TDB), 666-67

telecommunications, 1152-54 (ITU), 1125 (World Bank), 1135 (IDA), 1153 (ITU); see also regional entries; satellites

territorial seas: & LOS Convention, 997 (SG)

territories occupied by Israel, 420-40

general aspects, 420-27 (communications, 420-21; GA, **422-23**, **424-26**; Human Rights Cs., 426; Israeli practices ct., 423-24; SC, 421-22; SG, 422, 424)

& educational institutions, 433, **433-34** (Israeli practices ct./SG/GA)

expulsions/deportations, 427-31 (communications, 429, 430; GA, **431**; Israeli practices ct., 427-28; SC, 428, **428**, 428-29, 429, **429-30**, 430; SG, 430-31)

& 4th Geneva Convention, applicability, 426-27, **427** (Israeli practices ct./SG/GA)

housing, & effects of immigration, 437 (SG)

human rights in, **425**, 426 (GA/Human Rights Cs.), 437 (SG), 808-809 (SG/Cs.)

land/water practices, 420 (ESC/GA), 437-38 (SG)

living conditions, 423-24 (Israeli practices ct.)

prisoners/detainees, treatment of, 424, **425**, **426**, 431-33 (communications, 432; GA, **432-33**; Israeli practices ct., 431-32)

settlements policy, 435-37 (GA, **436-37**; Human Rights Cs./SG, 437; Israeli practices ct., 435-36; SG, 436); economic/social repercussions, 437-40 (ESC, **438-39**; GA, **439-40**; SG, 437-38)

uprising (intifadah), escalation, 400 (Ct. on Palestinian rights), 421, 423 (communication/Israeli practices ct.); & UNRWA emergency operations, 441, 442

worker safety in, 1099 (ILO)

see also Gaza Strip; Golan Heights; Jerusalem, status of; Lebanon situation; West Bank; and under Palestinian people; women, status of

terrorism, international: prevention, 990; & DPI, **127** (GA); 1991 Convention on Plastic Explosives, 1145, 1146 (ICAO); see also hostage-taking; Libyan Arab Jamahiriya

textiles: arrangements, 1180 (GATT)

Textiles, Arrangement regarding International Trade in, see Multifibre Arrangement (MFA)

Textiles Ct. (GATT), 1180

Thailand: economic trends, 264; refugees in, 902 (UNHCR); primary commodities, TNCs role in trade of, 650 (TNCs Centre-ESCAP Joint Unit); TNCs investment project, 650; see also Cambodia situation; Lao People's Democratic Republic

Tibet: human rights situation, 794 (SG/Cs.)

Timber Ct. (ECE), 500

tin: mtgs./publication, 626

Tin, International Study Group, 626

tobacco and health, 1118 (WHO); World No-Tobacco Day, 1117

Tokelau, 964, **969-70** (GA/Colonial Countries Ct.); information to UN, 960

Tokyo Round, see multilateral trade negotiations

Tolerance, International Year for (1995), proposed, 838, **838-39** (UNESCO/ESC), 1113 (UNESCO)

Tonga: economic trends, 480

Torture, Ct. against: members, emoluments for, 735, **736** (GA), officers/members, 1222; 9th sess./report, **736-37** (GA)

torture and cruel treatment, 734-37 (Spec. Rapporteur/Human Rights Cs./ESC); convention against/draft protocol, 735-36; Victims of, UN Voluntary Fund for, 737, **737-38** (Cs./GA), 1211-12 (Board of Trustees/sess.); see also prisoners/detainees

Torture and Other Cruel, Inhuman or Degrading Treatment or Punishment, 1984 Convention on: accessions/ratifications, 735 (SG/GA); amendments, 735; Articles 21, 22 (optional provisions), 735, **737** (Human Rights Cs./GA); compliance, 432; draft optional protocol, 735-36, **736** (Human Rights Cs./Working Group/ESC)

tourism, 486 (ESCAP); & child prostitution, 886

Tourism Organization, World (WTO): & ICAO, 1146

toxic chemicals: list, 673-74, 685 (SG); see also under air pollution; chemicals; hazardous wastes; pesticides

trade: facilitation, 620-21; services in, 1178 (GATT); statistics, 929 (SG/GATT); see also international trade; multilateral trade negotiations

Trade, Ct. on Development of (ECE): 41st sess., 496; ECE/UNCTAD/ITC intersecretariat task force, 496

Trade, Ct. on Invisibles and Financing Related to: suspended, 1208

Trade and Development, Ct. on (GATT), 1179

Trade and Development, UN Cf. on (UNCTAD), 611-43; finances, 642 (Working Party/SG/GA); intergovernmental structure, 641; medium-term plan/programme budget (working party), 642; SG/ASG, 1225; structure, 1207-1209; technical cooperation, 642-43; work methods, 641

Trade and Development, UN Cf. on (UNCTAD VIII), 11 (SG), 611-15; Declaration/Final Document, 612-13, **613-615** (GA); follow-up, 613; pre-cf. activities, 611-12 (TDB/ministerial mtgs.)

Trade and Development Board (TDB/UN-CTAD), 611, 641-42, 1207-1209; members, 1207-1208; officers/sess., 1208; subsidiary organs, 1208-1209; institutional matters, 613; see also Commodities, Ct. on; Commodities, Permanent Subct. on; Developing Countries, Ct. on Economic Cooperation among; Manufactures, Ct. on; Preferences, Spec. Ct. on; Shipping, Ct. on; Shipping Legislation, Working Group on; Technology, Ct. on Transfer of; Trade, Ct. on Invisibles and Finance Related to; Tungsten, Ct. on

Trade and Development Report (1992), 540, 615, 616, 623

Trade Centre, International, see International Trade Centre

Trade Efficiency, Ad Hoc Working Group on (TDB): establishment, 621

trade law, see international trade law

trademarks, registration, 1167 (WIPO)

trade preferences, see generalized system of preferences; global system of trade preferences (proposed); Preferences, Spec. Ct. on

trade restrictions, see international trade; protectionism; restrictive business practices

trade unions, rights of, 826 (Human Rights Cs.); ILO Conventions, 826, 1100; see also under South Africa, situation in

Trading Opportunities, Ad Hoc Working Group on Expansion of (TDB): establishment, 622

training and research, 832-33 (UNITAR/UNU); 843 (UNRISD); 1160 (WMO); shipping, 640; trade, 1179 (GATT); see also education; fellowships; human resources; vocational training; and under disarmament

Training and Research, UN Institute for (UNITAR), 832-33; Board of Trustees, sess., 1209-1210; members/Executive Director (Acting), 1210; finances & restructuring, 833, 1088-89, **1089** (SG/GA)

TRAINMAR, 640

transboundary air pollution, see air pollution

transfer of technology, see technology transfer

transnational corporations (TNCs), 485 (ESCAP), 511 (ECLAC), 644-53
accounting and reporting practices, 645, **652** (Intergovernmental Group/Cs./ESC)
bilateral/regional/international arrangements, 645, 649 (SG)
code of conduct (draft), 644-45 (Cs./SG/GA), 649 (SG); consultations, new round, 644
& economic relations: reports, 648-49 (Cs./ESC/SG)

environmental issues: contributions to UNCED, 647-48; corporate reporting on, 645, 647 (Intergovernmental Expert Group/SG)
information system, 649-50
publications, 649, 651, 653
research, 650-51
technical co-operation, 651-52, **652-53** (SG/ESC); financing, 652 (UN/UNDP/Trust Fund)
see also under apartheid; colonial countries; development: private sector in; South Africa; technology transfer; and regional entries

Transnational Corporations, Cs. on, 646-49; agenda/documentation (19th sess.), 646 (ESC); members/officers, 1217; 18th sess., 646 (ESC); Triad members (EC/Japan/US), 649 (SG); report, 651

Transnational Corporations, UN Centre on, 649-53; financing/TrustFund, 652; regional css., joint units with, 650; successor to, see following entry

Transnational Corporations and Management Division, 532-33, 649, **649** (ESC)

Transport, Working Party on Combined (ECE), 498

Transport Charter, European, 498

Transport Ct., Inland (ECE): 54th sess., 498

transport/communications, 470-71 (ECA), 485-86 (ESCAP), 498-99 (ECE), 520 (ESCWA), 1125 (World Bank), 1137 (IDA); conventions, 498; 1991 Pan-European Cf., 498 (ECE); statistics, 929; see also Africa, Transport and Communications Decade; air transport; Asia and Pacific, Transport and Communications Decade; inland transport; maritime transport; multimodal transport; ports; railways; roads; shipping; space transportation

Transport, UN Electronic Data Interchange for Administration, Commerce and, see under trade

transport of dangerous goods: regulations update, 498 (ECE)

Transport of Dangerous Goods, Ct. of Experts on: 7th sess./members, 1218

treaties/agreements, 995-96; publications, 996; registration/publication, 995; see also multilateral treaties and under subject entries

Treaties between States and International Organizations or between International Organizations, 1986 Vienna Convention on the Law of, 995

Treaty Series (UN), 995

Trinidad and Tobago: map surveys, 661 (DESD)

tropical cyclones, 1157 (WMO/ESCAP)

Tropical Cyclone Ct., 1157 (WMO/ESCAP)

Tropical Forests Action Programme (FAO), 1107-1108

tropical diseases, 1121 (WHO)

Truce Supervision Organization, UN, see UN Truce Supervision Organization (UNTSO)

Trust Territory of the Pacific Islands, see Palau

trusteeship and decolonization, 8 (SG) 945-76; see also names of territories; Non-Self-Governing Territories and entries following colonial countries

Trusteeship, Office for Spec. Political Questions, Regional Cooperation, Decolonization and, see Political Affairs, Department of

Trusteeship Cl. (TC): 59th sess., 973, 974; agenda, 973, 1237 (list); & CERD, 976; & Colonial Countries Ct., 975-76; members, 973, 1221; officers, 1221; report, 1991 spec. sess., 975

Trusteeship System, International, 973-76; fellowships/scholarships, 975 (SG/TC); information dissemination, 975 (SG/TC); 1947 Trusteeship Agreement, 973

trypanosomiasis: control, 1107 (FAO), 1121 (WHO)

tuberculosis, 1121 (WHO)

tungsten: project proposals, Industry Association/China, 626

Tungsten, Ct. on (TDB), 625, 626

Tunisia, 1132 (IFC)

Turkey, 1131 (IFC); see also Cyprus question

Turkmenistan, admission to: ESCAP, 484, IMF, 1140, UN, **135**, 135-36 (SC/GA), WHO, 1116, World Bank, 1123; contribution to UNIFIL, **415** (GA), to UNDOF, **419** (GA)

Turks and Caicos Islands, 964, **970-71** (Colonial Countries Ct./GA)

Typhoon Ct. (ESCAP/WMO), 1157

Uganda: mapping & remote sensing, 661 (DESD); management/urban development credits, 1137 (IDA)

Ukraine, admission to: ICAO, 1145; IMF, 1140; World Bank, 1123; rejoins WHO, 1116

Union of Soviet Socialist Republics (USSR): dissolution of, 528 (World Survey), 531 (SG); see also Commonwealth of Independent States; Russian Federation

United Arab Emirates: meteorology services, 561 (UNDP); & Iran occupation of Persian Gulf islands, 275 (SC/GA)

United Kingdom: economic trends, 540 (Trade and Development Report); NSGT information to UN, 960; troop contributions, UNFICYP, 270, 271; see also Falkland Islands (Malvinas); Gibraltar; Hong Kong; Libyan Arab Jamahiriya

United Nations
anniversary, commemoration of 50th (1995): preparations, 127 (JUNIC), 142 (GA)
annual report on work of (SG), 3-23 (GA)
Charter, 1187-96 (text)
cooperation with other organizations, 142-47
Headquarters: total staff, 1060; see also premises (UN)
information systems/computer use: access to informatics system, 1087, **1087** (SG/ESC); optical disk project, 1086 (SG/ACABQ/GA); technological innovations, 1085 (SG/ACABQ); International Computing Centre, 1087-88, (SG/GA)
institutional machinery, 140-42
members: admissions, 4 (SG), 123, 133-40; roster/dates of admission, 1185-86
offices: Geneva, 1225, Vienna, 1225
organs/subsidiary bodies: agendas (principal organs), 1227-37 (lists)
related bodies (treaty organs), 1222-24

strengthening role of, 1004-1006 (GA, **1005-1006**; SG, 1004-1005; Spec. Ct., 1005)

structure, 1201-26

see also accounts; administration and management; budget (UN); conferences/meetings; contributions; coordination in UN system; documentation; financial situation; host country relations; information centres/services; pensions; privileges and immunities (UN); premises (UN); programme planning (UN); and under principal organs

United Nations . . . for specific bodies see key word(s) of title

United Nations, Yearbook of the, see Yearbook of the United Nations

United Nations, Preparatory Ct. for the 50th Anniversary of: members/officers, 1205

UN Chronicle, 126, **127** (DPI/SG)

United Nations Disengagement Observer Force (UNDOF), 416-20; Commander, 417, 1213, 1225; composition, 415-16; financing, 418, **418-20** (SG/ACABQ/GA); mandate renewed, 417, **417**, **418** (SG/SC); Suspense Account, 418, **419** (SG/GA)

United Nations Educational, Scientific and Cultural Organization (UNESCO), 1111-15

United Nations Postal Administration: agreements with governments/commemorative stamps, 1089

United Nations Preparatory Ct. for the 50th Anniversary of the: mtgs., authorization, 141 (GA); activities, 142 (GA)

United Nations Transition Assistance Group (UNTAG), see Namibia

UN Truce Supervision Organization (UNTSO): strength/composition, 399; Chief of Staff, 1213, 1226; & Observer Groups, 400, 410 (Lebanon); & UNDOF/Israel-Syria Mixed Armistice Cs., 416

United Nations University (UNU), 833, **834** (ESC); Council, 833, 1211 (members); headquarters (Tokyo), completion, **834**; publications, 833; Rector, 1211, 1226; Standing Cts., 1211

United Republic of Tanzania: gold exploration, 654 (UNRFNRE); IDA credits, 1136, 1137

United States: drug abuse/trafficking, 925; economic trends, 540 (Trade and Development Report); NSGT information to UN, 960; postal agreement with UN, 1089; see also Iran; Libyan Arab Jamahiriya; Nicaragua; Puerto Rico

United States Virgin Islands, 964, **970-71**, 976-77 (Colonial Countries Ct./GA); information to UN, 960

Universal Declaration of Human Rights, see Human Rights, Universal Declaration of

Universal Postal Union (UPU), 1148-51

uranium: production, 1094

urban development, 491 (ESCAP), 1125 (World Bank), 1137 (IDA); & regional research, 706 (UNCHS)

Uruguay Round, see under multilateral trade negotiations

Uzbekistan, admission to: ESCAP, 484, ICAO, 1145, IFC, 1135, ILO, 1099, IMF, 1140, ITU, 1152, UN, **135**, (SC/GA), WHO, 1116, World Bank, 1123; contribution to UNIFIL, **415**, to UNDOF, **419**

Vanuatu: economic aid, 581-82, **582** (SG/GA); economic trends, 480

Vatican, see Holy See

Venezuela: 1123 (World Bank), 1131 (IFC); UNIFEM project, 872; see also Guyana

Viet Nam: admission to ILO resumed, 1099; asylum-seekers/returnees, 903 (UNHCR); & drug trafficking, 923; economic trends, 480; energy sector, 658 (DESD/World Bank); Orderly Departure Programme (UNHCR), 902; see also China-Viet Nam dispute; Cambodia situation

vocational training, 1101 (ILO)

Volunteers, UN (UNV), 571-72 (UNDP Cl.); Domestic Development Services (DDS), 572; Spec. Voluntary Fund, contributions, 572

Water, World Day for, 654, 656, **657** (GA)

Water and the Environment, International Cf. on: statement, 656 (ACC/UNCED), & FAO, 1106; WMO, 1159

water resources, 472 (ECA), 487 (ESCAP); 655-57, 1106 (FAO), 1160 (WMO); coordination, 656 (ACC Group); environmental aspects, 673; technical cooperation/seminars, 655-56 (DESD/UNCDF/UNDP); & women, 656; see also drinking water and sanitation; hydrology; rivers

Water Resources, Intersecretariat Group for (ACC), 656

watercourses, non-navigational uses of international, **990** (GA)

Watercourses and International Lakes, Convention on the Protection and Use of Transboundary: adoption, 501 (ECE Advisers)

Weapons Which May Be Deemed to Be Excessively Injurious or to Have Indiscriminate Effects, Convention on Prohibitions or Restrictions on the Use of Certain Conventional/Protocol (1981): parties to, 63, 96 (SG); status, 96-97, **97** (GA)

weather: instruments/observation, 1157; public services, 1159; see also air pollution; climate; meteorology; tropical cyclones

Weather Watch, World, 1156-57

welfare, see social welfare

West Africa, 665 (UNFSTD); economy, 464 (ECA); small-scale industries, 468 (ECA); see also country names and organizational entries

West African States, Economic Community of, see Liberia

West Bank: industrial sector, 406 (UNIDO); irrigation project, 405 (UNDP); see also Palestinians, aid to; territories occupied by Israel: economic/social repercussions

Western Asia, 515-22 (ESCWA): agriculture, 517; development planning/finance, 519; drug abuse, 912; economic

trends, 516-17; environment, 521; food/agriculture, 519-20; industrial development, 517-18, 520; natural resources/energy, 520; oil/natural gas, 517; political and security issues, 272-325; population/human settlements, 521; reconstruction/rehabilitation, 405, 516; science/technology, 520; social development, 518-19; statistics, 521-22; studies, 651 (ESCWA/TNCs Joint Unit); technical cooperation, 522; trade, 518, 519; transport/communications, 520; women, status, 521; see also country names

Western Asia, Economic and Social Cs. for (ESCWA), 515-22; Executive Secretary, 1224; headquarters offers, 522; medium-term plan, amended, 519; members, 1216; Persian Gulf crisis, impact, 515, 519; programme budget (1992-1993), 519; secretariat, 405, 519; 16th sess., 515, 1216; Technical Ct., 519; 7th sess., 522

Western Asia, Reconstruction and Rehabilitation Decade for (1994-2003), declared, 405, 516 (ESCWA)

Western Sahara, 18-19 (SG), 961-63, **963-64** (SC/SG/Colonial Countries Ct./GA); self-determination, 730 (Human Rights Cs.); referendum, UN Mission for, 962, 964 (SG/GA), 1213, 1226 (SG Representative); Commanders, 1213

Windhoek Declaration (1991): implementation, 124 (UNESCO/IPDC)

Women: Action for Equality, Development and Peace, 4th World Cf. on (1995): preparations, 863, 865 (SG); Cf. SG, **864**, 866 (GA/Cs.); venue/dates, **864**, 866 (GA/Cs./ESC)

women: advancement of, 863-68

information dissemination, 125, **127** (DPI/GA); publication, 125

medium-term plan (1996-2000), **865** (GA)

Nairobi Strategies, implementation, 863, **863-65** (GA/SG); monitoring/coordination, 863, 867 (SG/inter-agency mtg.); Review Cf., 863, **865** (SG)

regional activities, 867-68 (INSTRAW)

in public life, **865** (GA)

in politics, seminar on: Seoul Statement on Empowering, 491

research/training, 867, 868, **868** (IN-STRAW/ESC)

statistics on, strengthening use of, **864**, 867, 876 (GA/IN-STRAW/Statistical Office)

status in Secretariat, 1060-61, **1062** (SG/ICSC/ESC/GA); Steering Ct. on, 1060

see also under regional and subject entries

Women, Ad Hoc Inter-Agency Mtg. on: 15th sess., 867

Women, Cs. on the Status of (36th sess.), 873 (ESC); agenda/additional mtgs., 37th sess., 873; Working Group on Communications, establishment/report, 866, **866** (ESC); members/officers, 1215

Women, Ct. on the Elimination of Discrimination against (CEDAW): 11th sess., 877, 878 (ESC); members/officers, 1222

Women, 1979 Convention on the Elimination of All Forms of Discrimination against: implementation, 877-79 (CEDAW/SG, 877; ESC, **878**, 878-79); ratifications/accessions/signatures, 863, 879 (SG)

Women, Division for the Advancement of, 125, 866, **866** (ESC)

Women, International Research and Training Institute for the Advancement of (INSTRAW), 867-68, **868** (ESC); Director, 1219; members, 1219

women, status of, 698 (UNFPA), 873-77
disabled, 823 (SG), **864** (GA)
discrimination against, 825 (SCPDPM/ESC), 877 (CEDAW/SG); convention on, 877-79
elderly, **864**, 867 (GA/INSTRAW); in development, 869 (SG/CS); 1991 seminar/expert mtg., 869 (SG)
& HIV/AIDS, 819, 820 (WHO/UNICEF)
& human rights, **873-74** (ESC)
in informal sector, **868**, 876 (ESC/Statistical Office/INSTRAW)
Palestinian women, 875, **875-76** (SG/ESC)
& peace, 873 (SG)
regional activities, 867-68 (INSTRAW), 872 (UNIFEM)
statistics, 930 (Statistical Division/Cs. on Women)
traditional practices & health of, 825 (Cs./ESC), 874 (ESC)
violence against, 875, **874-75** (SG/CEDAW/ESC); draft declaration, working group mtg., **864**, **875** (GA/ESC); expert group mtg., 874 (SG); against migrant workers, 876, **876-77** (GA)
see also under apartheid; staff (UN)

Women, UN Development Fund for (UNIFEM), 872, 872-73 (Consultative Ct./UNDP); Advocacy Ct., 873; UNDP consideration, 873; Consultative Ct., mtg./report, 872, 873 (UNDP/GA); Consultative Ct./Director/members, 1209

women and development, 476-77 (ECA), 491 (ESCAP), 509 (ECLAC), 521 (ESCWA), 869 (CS/ESC/SG)
& environment, 871; & sustainable development, role on, **865** (GA), 871-72
industrial development, 930 (UNIDO)
medium-term plan for 1996-2001, 872 (SG)
& population: UNFPA strategy, 698

& rural women, 867 (ACC Task Force); Summit on economic advancement of, 867, 869 (UNCTAD); Declaration, 869-70, **870**, **870-71** (ESC/GA)
UNDP consideration, biennial, 869
World Survey on the Role of in: update, 863, **864**, **865** (SG/GA)
see also regional and subject entries

working conditions, 1100-1101; occupational safety/health, 1100, 1101; training manual/code of practice, 1101; see also child labour; employment

Working Conditions and Environment, International Programme for the Improvement of (ILO): implementation, 1100

World Bank system, see International Bank for Reconstruction and Development; International Development Association; International Finance Corporation

World Bank Economic Development Institute, see Economic Development Institute (World Bank)

World Climate Programme, see Climate Programme, World (WCP)

World Disarmament Campaign, see Disarmament Campaign, World

World Economic Survey, 526 (ESC); integration of economies in transition, 528-29; & international trade patterns, 615; see also subject entries

world economic situation, 525-26 (CDP/ESC), 539-40 (World Economic Survey), 540 (Trade and Development Report)

World Health Organization (WHO), 1116-22

World Heritage Ct., 16th sess., 1113

World Heritage Centre, establishment, 1113

World Intellectual Property Organization (WIPO), 1165-68

World Meteorological Organization (WMO), 1156-61

World Weather Watch (WMO), see Weather Watch, World (WWW)

Yearbook of the United Nations, 126, **127** (SG/GA)

Yemen: economic assistance to, 582-83, **583**, **583** (SG/ESC/GA); economic trends, 516; unification, 516; refugees in, 583, 904 (UNHCR); returnees, 584 (SG)

youth, 489 (ESCAP), 697 (UNFPA), 887-89
action programme to year 2000, proposed, 887, **888** (SG/GA)
& AIDS prevention/control, 820 (UNICEF)
& communication channels, guidelines for improving, 887, **888** (SG/GA)

disabled, ad hoc working group, **888** (GA)
health, 697 (UNFPA), 887
& human rights, 824, **824** (Cs./Spec. Rapporteur/ESC)
illiteracy/unemployment, 887 (SG)
see also juvenile justice

Youth Forum of the UN System, **888** (GA)

Youth Year, International (1985): follow-up, 887 (SG); 10th anniversary observation, preparations, 887, **888** (SG/GA); commemorative stamps, **888**

Yugoslavia, Federal Republic of (Serbia and Montenegro): creation of, 138; & UN membership, 138-40 (communications, 138; GA, **139**, 139-40; SC, **138**, 138-39); UNDP project, 559

Yugoslavia situation, 20-21 (SG), 327-32
emergency food aid, 825, 827 (WFP/UNHCR)
humanitarian aid, 327 (International Cf.), 337; consolidated appeal, 601
human rights violations, 795-801 (Cs., 795-96, 796-98; Spec. Rapporteur, 796-97; Expert Cs., 798-99; GA, **799-801**); International Cf. on, 327 (SG), 374, **375**, **376**, 379 (SG/SC); Co-Chairmen, 327; participation in SC mtg., 374; structure/participants, 327
peace-keeping operation, UN Protection Force (UNPROFOR), 326, 327-28; Commander/Deputy/senior aides, 333-34, 1213, 1225; composition, 332 (SG); deployment, 330, 332, 334, **334**, **337**; financing, 383-86 (ACABQ, 385; GA, 383, **384-85**, **385-86**; SG, 383-84, 385); mandate broadened, 357, **357** (SG/SC); SG Personal Envoy, 1213
refugees/displaced persons, 895 (UNHCR); UN Inter-Agency Programme/Appeal, 892
SC Ct. on, 381-83
SG Personal Envoy: missions, 328-29 (SG), 342, 1213
weapons embargo, **330**, 331 (SG); sanctions, 381-83 (SC Ct.)

Zaire: refugee resettlement, 896 (UNHCR)

Zambia, 1114 (UNESCO); fish farming, 1107 (FAO); industry credit, 1136 (IDA); refugee resettlement, 896 (UNHCR)

Zimbabwe: drought relief programme, 1135 (IDA)

zones of peace, see under Arctic region; Indian Ocean; nuclear-weapon-free zones; South Atlantic

Index of resolutions and decisions

Numbers in italics indicate that the text is summarized rather than reprinted in full. (For dates of sessions, refer to Appendix III.)

General Assembly

Forty-sixth session

Resolution No.	Page
46/191	
Res. B	1068
46/195	
Res. B	186
46/198	
Res. B	242
46/222	
Res. A	247
Res. B	249
46/223	135
46/224	133
46/225	134
46/226	135
46/227	134
46/228	134
46/229	135
46/230	136
46/231	136
46/232	1054
46/233	384
46/234	605
46/235	932
46/236	137
46/237	137
46/238	137
46/239	606
46/240	224
46/241	138
46/242	366

Decision No.	Page
46/311	
Dec. C	1209
46/314	
Dec. B	1205
46/316	
Dec. B	1225
46/323	
Dec. A	1204
Dec. B	1204
46/402	
Dec. B	141
Dec. C	141
Dec. D	141
46/468	675
46/469	675
46/470	675
46/471	675
47/472	142, 1205
46/473	763
46/474	141, 265
46/475	142
46/476	142, 1021
46/477	1059
46/478	273
46/479	1027
46/480	1023
46/481	964

Forty-seventh session

Resolution No.	Page
47/1	139
47/2	606
47/3	822
47/4	147
47/5	889
47/6	1012
47/7	608
47/8	660
47/9	188
47/10	146
47/11	238
47/12	142
47/13	514
47/14	960
47/15	953
47/16	950
47/17	959
47/18	145
47/19	234
47/20	
Res. A	236
47/21	387
47/22	952
47/23	946
47/24	957
47/25	963
47/26	958
47/27	
Res. A	964
Res. B	966
47/28	1065
47/29	1011
47/30	991
47/31	993
47/32	1008
47/33	989
47/34	1015
47/35	1007
47/36	994
47/37	991
47/38	1005
47/39	66
47/40	821
47/41	
Res. A	212
47/42	592
47/43	95
47/44	96
47/45	79
47/46	86
47/47	85
47/48	90
47/49	92
47/50	68
47/51	98
47/52	
Res. A	67
Res. B	88
Res. C	82
Res. D	102
Res. E	101
Res. F	100
Res. G	70
Res. H	108
Res. I	74
Res. J	71
Res. K	80
Res. L	75

Resolution No.	Page
47/53	
Res. A	109
Res. B	73
Res. C	83
Res. D	104
Res. E	81
Res. F	72
47/54	
Res. A	61
Res. B	76
Res. C	106
Res. D	77
Res. E	62
Res. F	107
47/55	91
47/56	97
47/57	131
47/58	50
47/59	93
47/60	
Res. A	42
Res. B	41
47/61	89
47/62	140
47/63	
Res. A	415
Res. B	403
47/64	
Res. A	401
Res. B	402
Res. C	403
Res. D	397
Res. E	422
47/65	1000
47/66	129
47/67	119
47/68	116
47/69	
Res. A	442
Res. B	444
Res. C	446
Res. D	450
Res. E	455
Res. F	447
Res. G	446
Res. H	452
Res. I	453
Res. J	449
Res. K	448
47/70	
Res. A	425
Res. B	427
Res. C	436
Res. D	432
Res. E	431
Res. F	434
Res. G	433
47/71	45
47/72	48
47/73	
Res. A	124
Res. B	127
47/74	51
47/75	720
47/76	88
47/77	711
47/78	713
47/79	715

Resolution No.	Page
47/80	724
47/81	779
47/82	728
47/83	727
47/84	733
47/85	888
47/86	891
47/87	858
47/88	823
47/89	860
47/90	840
47/91	847
47/92	836
47/93	1062
47/94	878
47/95	863
47/96	876
47/97	911
47/98	918
47/99	916
47/100	917
47/101	907
47/102	913
47/103	901
47/104	894
47/105	892
47/106	587
47/107	898
47/108	810
47/109	738
47/110	721
47/111	769
47/112	813
47/113	736
47/114	190
47/115	795
47/116	
Res. A	162
Res. B	153
Res. C	175
Res. D	170
Res. E	172
Res. F	173
Res. G	167
47/117	176
47/118	218
47/119	598
47/120	38
47/121	379
47/122	763
47/123	753
47/124	838
47/125	775
47/126	881
47/127	760
47/128	765
47/129	716
47/130	773
47/131	761
47/132	743
47/133	744
47/134	755
47/135	722
47/136	741
47/137	756
47/138	772
47/139	802
47/140	804
47/141	785

GENERAL ASSEMBLY, 47th SESSION *(cont.)*

Resolution No.	Page
47/142	783
47/143	807
47/144	793
47/145	790
47/146	788
47/147	799
47/148	215
47/149	828
47/150	826
47/151	691
47/152	531
47/153	535
47/154	591
47/155	600
47/156	579
47/157	580
47/158	602
47/159	578
47/160	594
47/161	582
47/162	596
47/163	581
47/164	589
47/165	610
47/166	601
47/167	214
47/168	585
47/169	607
47/170	406
47/171	533
47/172	439
47/173	544
47/174	870
47/175	530
47/176	695
47/177	469
47/178	632
47/179	583
47/180	702
47/181	528
47/182	667
47/183	613
47/184	617
47/185	626
47/186	546
47/187	529
47/188	686
47/189	547
47/190	675
47/191	676
47/192	688
47/193	657
47/194	680
47/195	682
47/196	538
47/197	537
47/198	637
47/199	552
47/200	834
47/201	1052
47/202	
Res. A	1079
Res. B	1083
Res. C	1080
Res. D	1081
47/203	1072
47/204	419
47/205	414
47/206	274
47/207	1027
47/208	300

Resolution No.	Page
47/209	260
47/210	385
47/211	1042
47/212	
Res. A	1028
47/213	1039
47/214	1046
47/215	1021
47/216	1055
47/217	1022
47/218	1025
47/219	
Res. A	
Section I	1033
Section II	1084
Section III	1034
Section IV	1034
Section V	1088
Section VI	1088
Section VII	1064
Section VIII	1034
Section IX	1035
Section X	1035
Section XI	1067
Section XII	1036
Section XIII	1086
Section XIV	1086
Section XV	1067
Section XVI	1036
Section XVII	1037
Section XVIII	126
Section XIX	164
Section XX	1037
Section XXI	1081
Section XXII	907
Section XXIII	112
Section XXIV	1089
Section XXV	1037
Section XXVI	1032
Section XXVII	642
Section XXVIII	1037
Section XXIX	1032
Section XXX	1013
47/220	
Res. A	1030
Res. B	1033
Res. C	1032

Decision No.	Page
47/301	1201
47/302	1201
47/303	1201
47/304	1201
47/305	
Dec. A	1202
Dec. B	1202
47/306	
Dec. A	1212
47/307	1217
47/308	1212
47/309	1214
47/310	1209
47/311	
Dec. A	1203
47/312	
Dec. A	1206
47/313	1202
47/314	1202
47/315	1204
47/316	1206
47/317	1204
47/401	141

Decision No.	Page
47/402	142, 265, 961, 986
47/403	
Dec. A	141
Dec. B	141
Dec. C	141
47/404	140
47/405	979
47/406	986
47/407	3
47/408	142, 961
47/409	955
47/410	162
47/411	971
47/412	971
47/413	972
47/414	992
47/415	994
47/416	986
47/417	142
47/418	101
47/419	94
47/420	96
47/421	105
47/422	60
47/423	43, 142
47/424	123, 1203
47/425	142
47/426	782
47/427	782
47/428	787
47/429	772
47/430	719
47/431	758, 773, 779, 810
47/432	942
47/433	776, 938, 939
47/434	659
47/435	658
47/436	635
47/437	584
47/438	934
47/439	645, 685, 701
47/440	942
47/441	528
47/442	635
47/443	689
47/444	459, 473, 530, 605, 660, 676, 681, 688
47/445	407
47/446	683
47/447	881
47/448	873
47/449	1052
47/450	
Dec. A	188
47/451	
Dec. A	964
47/452	230
47/453	1038
47/454	1044
47/455	1052
47/456	1041
47/457	
Dec. A	1059, 1060
47/458	942, 1037
47/459	1068

Decision No.	Page
47/460	
Dec. A	1052, 1064, 1068, 1075, 1082, 1084
47/461	938
47/462	938
47/463	142
47/464	408
47/465	528
47/466	142
47/467	142, 265

Security Council

Resolution No.	Page
726(1992)	428
727(1992)	330
728(1992)	241
729(1992)	223
730(1992)	221
731(1992)	53
732(1992)	133
733(1992)	199
734(1992)	411
735(1992)	134
736(1992)	134
737(1992)	135
738(1992)	134
739(1992)	135
740(1992)	331
741(1992)	135
742(1992)	136
743(1992)	333
744(1992)	136
745(1992)	246
746(1992)	201
747(1992)	179
748(1992)	55
749(1992)	334
750(1992)	266
751(1992)	202
752(1992)	350
753(1992)	136
754(1992)	137
755(1992)	137
756(1992)	417
757(1992)	352
758(1992)	357
759(1992)	270
760(1992)	359
761(1992)	359
762(1992)	339
763(1992)	137
764(1992)	362
765(1992)	158
766(1992)	253
767(1992)	205
768(1992)	413
769(1992)	341
770(1992)	365
771(1992)	366
772(1992)	160
773(1992)	298
774(1992)	268
775(1992)	207
776(1992)	370
777(1992)	138
778(1992)	320
779(1992)	343
780(1992)	370
781(1992)	371
782(1992)	195

SECURITY COUNCIL (cont.)

Resolution No.	Page
783(1992)	255
784(1992)	228
785(1992)	183
786(1992)	373
787(1992)	375
788(1992)	192
789(1992)	269
790(1992)	418
791(1992)	229
792(1992)	258
793(1992)	184
794(1992)	209
795(1992)	386
796(1992)	271
797(1992)	197
798(1992)	378
799(1992)	429

Economic and Social Council

Organizational session, 1992

Resolution No.	Page
1992/1	842
1992/2	940

Decision No.	Page
1992/200	1214, 1215
1992/201	842
1992/202	842
1992/203	526, 938
1992/204	535, 819, 835, 938
1992/205	572, 936, 938
1992/206	456
1992/207	659, 825
1992/208	
Dec. A	642
Dec. B	833
Dec. C	698
1992/209	940
1992/210	927
1992/211	909
1992/212	515
1992/213	459
1992/214	940, 1078

Resumed organizational session, 1992

Decision No.	Page
1992/215	940
1992/216	1205, 1212,

Resolution No.	Page
	1214, 1215, 1216, 1217, 1218, 1219, 1220, 1221
1992/217	937
1992/218	935
1992/219	936
1992/220	742
1992/221	759
1992/222	1218

Substantive session, 1992

Resolution No.	Page
1992/3	781
1992/4	722
1992/5	744
1992/6	736
1992/7	815
1992/8	813
1992/9	777
1992/10	748
1992/11	771
1992/12	782
1992/13	710
1992/14	1061
1992/15	165
1992/16	875
1992/17	878
1992/18	874
1992/19	866
1992/20	873
1992/21	868
1992/22	842
1992/23	849
1992/24	861
1992/25	840
1992/26	835
1992/27	836
1992/28	909
1992/29	921
1992/30	920
1992/31	604
1992/32	825
1992/33	820
1992/34	646
1992/35	652
1992/36	533
1992/37	695
1992/38	609
1992/39	939
1992/40	496
1992/41	573
1992/42	600
1992/43	458
1992/44	468
1992/45	471
1992/46	492
1992/47	492

Resolution No.	Page
1992/48	492
1992/49	492
1992/50	492
1992/51	461
1992/52	458
1992/53	870
1992/54	474
1992/55	686
1992/56	658
1992/57	438
1992/58	406
1992/59	948
1992/60	1087
1992/61	583
1992/62	935

Decision No.	Page
1992/223	936, 938, 939
1992/224	515, 1215
1992/225	732
1992/226	716
1992/227	742
1992/228	735
1992/229	750
1992/230	751
1992/231	718
1992/232	816
1992/233	758
1992/234	725
1992/235	793
1992/236	802
1992/237	804
1992/238	759
1992/239	788
1992/240	785
1992/241	790
1992/242	740
1992/243	777
1992/244	814
1992/245	806
1992/246	768
1992/247	768
1992/248	752
1992/249	727
1992/250	810
1992/251	816, 874
1992/252	681, 816
1992/253	719
1992/254	725
1992/255	718
1992/256	718
1992/257	748
1992/258	759
1992/259	753
1992/260	770
1992/261	753
1992/262	812
1992/263	726, 747, 776, 782

Decision No.	Page
1992/264	758
1992/265	940
1992/266	841
1992/267	838
1992/268	1216, 1217, 1218, 1219, 1221
1992/269	873
1992/270	873
1992/271	869
1992/272	866
1992/273	878
1992/274	842
1992/275	842
1992/276	823
1992/277	926
1992/278	926
1992/279	926
1992/280	539
1992/281	639
1992/282	646
1992/283	646
1992/284	629
1992/285	691
1992/286	609
1992/287	542
1992/288	940
1992/289	490
1992/290	479
1992/291	515
1992/292	477
1992/293	468
1992/294	471
1992/295	459, 468, 486, 494, 515
1992/296	526, 541, 676, 681, 685
1992/297	531
1992/298	642
1992/299	659
1992/300	536, 820, 835
1992/301	550, 558, 826, 880, 881
1992/302	942
1992/303	935
1992/304	892
1992/305	796

Trusteeship Council

Fifty-ninth session

Resolution No.	Page
2195 (LIX)	975

How to obtain volumes of the *Yearbook*

The 1985 to 1987, 1991 and 1992 volumes of the *Yearbook of the United Nations* are sold and distributed in the United States, Canada and Mexico by Kluwer Academic Publishers, 101 Philip Drive, Norwell, Massachusetts 02061; in all other countries by Kluwer Academic Publishers Group, P.O. Box 322, 3300 AH Dordrecht, Netherlands.

Other recent volumes of the *Yearbook* may be obtained in many bookstores throughout the world and also from United Nations Publications, Sales Section, Room DC2-853, United Nations, New York, N.Y. 10017, or from United Nations Publications, Palais des Nations, Office C-115, 1211 Geneva 10, Switzerland.

Older editions are available in microfiche.

Yearbook of the United Nations, 1991
Vol. 45, Sales No. E.92.I.1 $115.

Yearbook of the United Nations, 1983
Vol. 37. Sales No. E.86.I.1 $85.

Yearbook of the United Nations, 1987
Vol. 41. Sales No. E.91.I.1 $105.

Yearbook of the United Nations, 1982
Vol. 36. Sales No. E.85.I.1 $75.

Yearbook of the United Nations, 1986
Vol. 40. Sales No. E.90.I.1 $95.

Yearbook of the United Nations, 1981
Vol. 35. Sales No. E.84.I.1 $75.

Yearbook of the United Nations, 1985
Vol. 39. Sales No. E.88.I.1 $95.

Yearbook of the United Nations, 1980
Vol. 34. Sales No. E.83.I.1 $72.

Yearbook of the United Nations, 1984
Vol. 38. Sales No. E.87.I.1 $90.

Yearbook of the United Nations, 1979
Vol. 33. Sales No. E.82.I.1 $72.

Yearbook of the United Nations, 1978
Vol. 32. Sales No. E.80.I.1 $60.

The Yearbook *in microfiche*

Yearbook Volumes 1-39 (1946-1985) are now available in microfiche. Individual volumes are also available, and prices can be obtained by contacting the following: United Nations Publications, Sales Section, Room DC2-853, United Nations, New York, N.Y. 10017, or United Nations Publications, Palais des Nations, Office C-115, 1211 Geneva 10, Switzerland.

NOTES

NOTES

NOTES

T